Footprint

Caribbean Islands

The travel guide

Handbook 2002

Sarah Cameron

*A good holiday is one spent among
people whose notions of time
are vaguer than yours.*

JB Priestley

Caribbean Islands Handbook 2002
Thirteenth edition
© Footprint Handbooks Ltd 2001

Published by Footprint Handbooks
6 Riverside Court
Lower Bristol Road
Bath BA2 3DZ. England
T +44 (0)1225 469141
F +44 (0)1225 469461
Email discover@footprintbooks.com
Web www.footprintbooks.com

ISBN 1 900949 89 X
ISSN 0967-4748
CIP DATA: A catalogue record for this
book is available from the British Library

Distributed in the USA by
Publishers Group West

Neither the black and white nor
coloured maps are intended to have
any political significance.

Credits

Series editors
Patrick Dawson and Rachel Fielding

Editorial
Editor: Sarah Thorowgood
Maps: Sarah Sorensen

Production
Typesetting: Jo Morgan and
Leona Bailey
Maps: Robert Lunn, Claire Benison and
Angus Dawson
Colour maps: Kevin Feeney
Cover: Camilla Ford

Design
Mytton Williams

Photography
Front cover: Liza Berry
Back cover: James Davis Travel
Photography
Inside colour section: BBC Natural
History Unit Picture Library, gettyone
Stone, James Davis Travel Photography,
Robert Harding Picture Library,
Travel Ink

Print
Manufactured in Italy by LEGOPRINT

Every effort has been made to ensure
that the facts in this Handbook are
accurate. However, travellers should still
obtain advice from consulates, airlines
etc about current travel and visa
requirements before travelling. The
authors and publishers cannot accept
responsibility for any loss, injury or
inconvenience however caused.

Contents

Left: the rounded shapes of limestone mogotes in the Valle de Vinales, Pinar del Rio province, Cuba.

4

Right: it's a dog's life – siesta time at Treasure Beach, Jamaica.

Highlights

Beach Babylon   The Caribbean Sea entices and lures visitors, with its warm blue or turquoise waters, sandy beaches and coral reefs, and despite the fact that the islands offer a huge and wide-ranging variety of other attractions besides the obvious beach holiday, this is undeniably a good reason for coming here, so here, without further ado, is a basic guide to getting the right beach. As a general rule, the low-lying coral islands have the best beaches, with miles of white sand and good swimming. A reef offshore usually provides calm seas and great snorkelling and diving. Away from the beach, however, the landscape is flat, covered with scrub, cactus and maybe pine trees. These islands include the Bahamas, The Turks and Caicos, Anegada in the British Virgin Islands, Anguilla, St Martin, Aruba, Bonaire and Curaçao and the islands off the Venezuelan coast. The volcanic or mountainous islands have beaches, but these are usually fairly narrow and can be black or grey sand or even shingle. On the other hand, they can be stunningly beautiful, with steep, forested hills tumbling into the sea, horse shoe shaped bays with picturesque headlands and palm trees providing shade on the shore. The Windward Islands are typical of this scenery: Dominica, Martinique, St Lucia, St Vincent and Grenada. The larger islands in the Greater Antilles: Cuba, Hispaniola (Haiti and the Dominican Republic), Jamaica and Puerto Rico are big enough to have everything. You just need to decide which end of the island you want to be, or how long it will take you to see it all. Wherever you are, remember that the Atlantic coast will be more rugged and have rougher seas than the Caribbean coast. There are few Atlantic beaches on the eastern islands where it is safe to swim, although they can be fascinating to beachcomb for flotsam and jetsam from Africa.

A drop in the ocean   Watersports are available everywhere and hotels provide a wide variety of toys for entertainment on the water. Places like Cabarete in the Dominican Republic, Aruba, Bonaire and the Virgin Islands have the best winds for windsurfing and excellent equipment and instruction. Sailing is also another very good excuse for coming to the Caribbean and all islands have craft of varying sizes, from hobie cats and dinghies to large liveaboard yachts for charter. Two of the best places for sailing are the Virgin Islands and the Grenadines, where there are pretty clusters of small islands for you to anchor safely around and take advantage of the bars and restaurants dotted among the bays. Regattas and races are organized by local yacht clubs throughout the year in all islands, great if you want to participate or just spectate. Scuba diving and snorkelling, popular everywhere, are sometimes too popular if you are on a boat with dozens of other people. Marine parks have been established in many islands keen to protect their underwater charms, but the best places are usually the more remote where there are not so many tourists anyway. Try Bonaire, Tobago, Saba, Dominica, Grand Turk, Little Cayman or the Isla de la Juventud off Cuba, where there are reefs, walls and drop-offs to trenches many miles deep, the coral is in good condition and there is plenty of marine life. Small, intimate lodges cater to divers' needs and are cheerful and relaxed places to stay. Seasonal whale watching is becoming a big tourist attraction and is contributing to the conservation of these tremendous marine mammals. The Dominican Republic has boat excursions to see the hump backed whales during the breeding season, the Turks Passage off Grand Turk is a good place to see them on their migration and boats with sonar tracking equipment take visitors out off the coast of Dominica and St Lucia. Wild dolphins are easy to see, playing in the wake of a ferry or leaping alongside the bow of a yacht and provide far more of a thrill in their natural habitat.

Outward bound   'Not all of the people want to sunbathe or play in the water all of the time' and, despite being relatively small, the Caribbean islands have loads in the way of land-based sports. Hiking is rewarding in places like Dominica, Grenada and Jamaica in the mountains and rainforests. For those who want to cover larger distances than their legs can manage, horseriding can be arranged in the Dominican Republic, Cuba and many of the smaller islands. For the ascent of

Left: how to get across the water as fast as possible; gommier racing in Martinique is just one of the many and varied boat races held around the Caribbean. **Below**: fishing at Courland Bay, Tobago, a shared task benefiting the whole community and a social occasion in itself. **Bottom right**: harbour front buildings in Willemstad, Curaçao, have been painted in pastel colours ever since 1817 when an eccentric governor blamed his headaches on the glare of white houses. **Bottom left**: Río Chavón, Dominican Republic, meanders through a gorge from the eastern mountains to the south coast.

Next page: music and dance – the life blood of the Cuban people in particular, but then rhythm flows in the veins of anyone from the Caribbean.

Pico Duarte in the Dominican Republic, the highest mountain in the Caribbean, mules are on hand to carry your provisions but can easily be adapted to take you if you tire. Cycling is a great way to get around Cuba, while off-road and downhill mountain biking is brilliant in the Dominican Republic. Birdwatching is superb in Trinidad and increasingly popular in Bonaire, Cuba and elsewhere. There are endemic species on most islands, but many are endangered or rare. Other sporting activities include tennis and golf, which can be played at many of the larger hotels. Some of the best golf courses have been built by world famous designers on islands like Jamaica, Grand Bahama and the Dominican Republic. For some people, of course, their only reason for going to the Caribbean is to watch cricket in the former English islands, although baseball in the Hispanic islands commands equally enthusiastic support. Get tickets for a match and find out what makes the local people jump for joy or drown in despair. Either way it will be a noisy affair with much audience participation.

A cultural mix Colonial architecture varies according to whether the islands were once Spanish, English, French or Dutch, but the most impressive colonial cities today are Havana, Santo Domingo and San Juan, all once part of the Spanish Empire. Willemstad in Curaçao is a charming example of Dutch architecture in the tropics, remnants of Danish building can be seen in St Croix, while the French islands retain the gingerbread style with intricate fretwork, and elegant plantation houses adorn the former British islands. Cultural life in the Caribbean is varied, depending on the tastes of former European colonial rulers and the customs of other immigrants such as Africans, East Indians and Chinese. Very little indigenous influence remains and the tribes living on the islands at the time of Columbus' arrival were soon eradicated, only a handful surviving into the 19th century. Society in Cuba has been described as being like an ajiaco, a soup made of leftovers with several different meats and vegetables, and this hotch potch of races is true of all the islands. However, culture throughout the region is overwhelmingly influenced by the African traditions brought to the islands by thousands of slaves from hundreds of tribes. Their religions have been adapted and preserved, particularly in Haiti (voodoo) and Cuba (santería), where African gods are worshipped in parallel with Catholicism, but Protestantism is also strong, with gospel singing heard loud and clear in the Anglophone islands. Caribbean literature, developed by free men and women in the 20th century after abolition of slavery, is often concerned with displacement, either through loss of the African homeland, or loss of island life by migrants to North America and Europe in search of jobs and prosperity.

Rhythm & rum But it is rhythm which makes the greatest impact on a visitor. Caribbean music and dance are cultural exports of tremendous worldwide importance, whether reggae, calypso, rumba, zouk, salsa, merengue or any number of other styles. Discos offer a selection of any or all of these for an international audience, but to hear what local people are keen on, take a bus. The driver will have his favourite style thumping from the speakers of his tap tap in Haiti, jitney in the Bahamas or taxi in Trinidad. Jamaica is synonymous with reggae, the Dominican Republic with merengue and Trinidad with calypso, seek out a local dance hall or jump up in the streets to get the latest vibe. In the Anglophone islands you will be hard pushed to avoid a steel band, serenading the latest tourist wedding, churning out old favourites like Yellow Bird, or hammering out the latest Carnival hits. Wherever you go there will be some sensuous dance style for the intrepid to learn and the faint hearted to tap their feet to while sipping their rum. For serious aficionados, there are festivals dedicated to music, such as the St Lucia Jazz Festival or the Festival de Música Latina in Santo Domingo, which bring artists from all over the region. Carnival is the best way for a visitor to experience local talent and while all the islands have their own vibrant celebrations, carnival in Trinidad is second to none. The colours, heat, sweat, noise, exertion and sleep deprivation merge in a haze of rum and beer as you are swept along with the crowd. Love it or leave it, if this doesn't appeal, you can always go to the opera in Barbados or the ballet in Cuba.

Left: the massive fortress of La Citadelle, 900m high in northern Haiti, is the most spectacular historical site in the region, built by 20,000 labourers to deter a French invasion. *Below*: the Virgin Islands are perfect for sailing, with dozens of harbours and safe anchorages like this one in St Thomas.

Above: Les Saintes, off Guadeloupe, are among the least spoilt destinations in the French Antilles, a string of little islands with excellent beaches. *Left*: smiling faces waiting for the school bus outside a rum shop in Roxborough, Tobago.

Wet and wild

Previous page: there are several species of whale around the Caribbean, including pilot, sperm, orcas and Bryde's but the one you are most likely to see is the acrobatic humpback whale (Megaptera novaeangliae), a thrilling sight if you are lucky enough to see one breaching. **Right**: Southern stingrays (Dasyatis americana) congregate in large numbers on a sand bar on Grand Cayman where the water ranges from only knee deep to about 4 m. Around 250 are believed to come to Stingray City to find the free meal of squid.

Centre: a queen angel fish (Holacanthus ciliariaris), just one of the many colourful fish you can find on the reefs of the Caribbean. **Above**: a Nassau grouper (Epinephelus striatus) with an obliging goby (Gobiosoma genie) giving it the full valet service, including teeth cleaning and removal of parasites and any diseased scales or skin. **Right**: sponges and other invertebrates are found in the Caribbean, including the yellow tube sponge and the pink vase sponge (Niphates digitalis), pictured here, on the reefs and walls, while deeper you can see the rope sponges and, most dramatic, the giant barrel sponge.

Left: the manatee (trichechus manatus latirostrisis), or sea cow, is extremely rare and protected now everywhere. Once thought by sailors to be mermaids, they are actually a distant relative of the elephant and are the largest vegetarians living in the sea. Living in mangroves and muddy lagoons, their bubbles and a ripple on the surface of the water is all you are likely to see of them.

Centre: bottlenose dolphins, give untold pleasure as they play in the wake of boats. But their popularity has led to many being incarcerated in dolphinariums for the amusement of tourists. Often caught in the wild and separated from their pods they are kept alive on imported frozen fish and antibiotics. **Above**: a spotted moray eel (Gymnothorax moringa), night-time predator on the reef who has fallen foul of the greatest predator of them all: man. A fishing hook, which may be the death of him, protrudes from his mouth. **Left**: clad in chain mail, a dive master feeds sharks for the amusement of divers. Wild, free animals they may be, but daily handouts lead to an unnatural concentration of a single predator species.

Essentials

2

Essentials

Planning your trip

Holiday companies and travel agents tend to market the Caribbean as a homogenous tropical destination, but in reality each island has its own personality and what suits one person will not suit another. You have a choice between English, Spanish, French, American and Dutch islands, so language might be a consideration. Some islands are more difficult to get to than others. How much time do you want to spend travelling to your destination? Do you want to stay in one place or indulge in a spot of island-hopping? Do you like company and organized activities or would you prefer an exclusive hotel and deserted beach? Do you want to take it easy and relax or are you an active person who needs to face challenges?

Island hopping

Transport links between islands are OK if you want to fly everywhere, but after several hours in an aeroplane getting to the Caribbean from Europe, South or North America, you may prefer to travel by sea, which is cheaper but takes longer and can be either fascinating or unpleasant if you suffer from seasickness in rough weather. The best international ferry links are in the **Windward Islands** and down to **Trinidad** and **Venezuela**. The Windward Lines link Venezuela (Isla Margarita or the mainland) with Trinidad, St Vincent, Barbados and St Lucia. This is a great way to see several islands with very different characters, but you need a relaxed attitude to timetables and plenty of leeway in your travel plans. The length of time spent in port depends on the amount of cargo to be loaded and unloaded, while any repairs can mean a lost week, but the boat is comfortable and we have received few complaints so far. In fact most of our readers enthuse about their journey and revel in the experience of arriving at a shipping port instead of an airport without being categorised as a cruise ship passenger. You must check they are running, however, as the ship was out of commission for most of 2001. There is also a ferry between Dominica, St Lucia and the French islands of Martinique and Guadeloupe, well used by local shoppers as well as tourists, which offers you the chance of combining the nature tourism of Dominica and the beach resorts of St Lucia with the flavours of France in the Caribbean. You can travel from St Vincent down through the Grenadines to Grenada by mail boat, fishing boat and hovercraft, a cheaper alternative to chartering a yacht and doing it yourself, and certainly more sociable. A car ferry links the **Dominican Republic** with **Puerto Rico** and there are ferries between the **US** and **British Virgin Islands** letting you visit a number of islands without having the work of sailing your own yacht. Sint Maarten/Saint-Martin is a useful hub for transatlantic flights from where ferries go out to Anguilla, St-Barts and Saba like spokes of a wheel, allowing you to sample English, French and Dutch islands. A few days on each island would be plenty, as they are small and compact, but each has its own individual style.

Resorts or hideaways

The popularity of the Caribbean islands has led to some areas being developed for mass tourism, while others concentrate on a niche market and a few rely on their exclusivity to attract a wealthy clientèle. Some of the larger islands manage to combine all three elements. Jamaica, for instance, appeals to the mass all-inclusive market with large resorts (*Sandals*, *Superclubs* etc) built along the north coast, yet there is room for a few luxury hideaways such as Island Outpost's *Strawberry Hill*, once a fruit plantation, overlooking Kingston Bay. The most famous patch of Caribbean hedonism is probably Richard Branson's private Virgin Island; a stay on his Balinese-style Necker Island will cost you from US$14,000 a day and guests have included Diana, Princess of Wales, Robert de Niro, Steven Spielberg and Oprah Winfrey. Less ostentatious, but the height of luxury and privacy, nonetheless, is Petit St Vincent, PSV, in the Grenadines, owned by Hazen Richardson. Staff outnumber guests two to one, but you need never see anyone at all; just hoist a flag for room service if you don't want to join others in the restaurant and bar. There are of course many other desirable getaway places, from *Small Hope Bay Lodge* on Andros in the Bahamas, *Parrot Cay Resort* on Parrot Cay in the Turks and Caicos Islands, *Biras Creek* on Virgin Gorda in the BVI, *Coco Point Lodge* on Barbuda, any of the plantation inns on St Kitts and Nevis, *Cap Juluca* or *Malliouhana Hotel* on Anguilla, *Ladera Resort* on St Lucia, *Cotton House* on Mustique and the very elegant *Glitter Bay* and others in Barbados. All these hideaways cost an arm and a leg, space is at a

Essentials

premium in the Caribbean and you have to pay for the privilege of being isolated with comfort and style.

There are, however, some exceptions and it is still possible to find a reasonably priced hotel away from the hordes. Try the northeast coast of Trinidad around Grand Riviere, where you can have a beach front room at the *Mount Plaisir Estate Hotel* and stroll along the sand where the turtles come ashore to nest. The *Southern Cross Club* on Little Cayman on a sandy beach opposite Owen Island, offers peace and quiet in abundance, with diving if you want some gentle activity. Another dive resort with the most delightful hammocks for après-diving, is *María La Gorda* in Cuba, miles from anywhere, wonderful warm, clear water in a sheltered bay, its only drawback being the boring food. In the Grenadines there are many guest houses and small hotels in secluded locations, usually with a sea view, which won't break the bank. Try the hospitality of the *Caribbee* on Carriacou, or the multilingual care and attention of *The Old Fort* on Bequia. For the adventurous, Haiti offers undisturbed beaches away from Port-au-Prince, with few tourists nowadays. Head out to the southwest to beautiful Anse du Clerc, near the old town of Jérémie, where there is a seven room beach hotel and not much else besides. For US$40 per person per night you can have an excellent dinner, bed and breakfast in perfect tranquillity.

At the other end of the scale, huge resorts dominate in Nassau, Grand Bahama, Aruba, Jamaica, Varadero in Cuba, parts of the Dominican Republic and Puerto Rico, Antigua, Sint Maarten and Grand Cayman. These islands can be crowded, and although you can get away from other holiday makers you will have to make a determined effort. Anyone staying at the 2,355-room *Atlantis*, on Paradise Island, Bahamas, the 720-room *Renaissance Jamaica Grande Resort* in Ocho Rios, Jamaica, or the massive 5-star hotel *Bávaro Beach Resort* in the Dominican Republic is unlikely to want to venture outside and explore. All-inclusives are hugely popular but are to be avoided if you want to get to know the people and the island you are visiting.

In general, you will not find a remote hideaway on islands like Antigua and Sint Maarten, which receive transatlantic charter flights. However, they are useful jumping off points for smaller islands. If you have a tight budget, it is worth investigating where cheap flights go to from your country and then finding out which islands can be easily reached from there. For example, there are often cheap charter flights to Antigua, Sint Maarten or St Lucia from Europe, which connect with *Liat* flights to the British Virgin Islands and all the Leeward and Windward Islands. Connections are good between France and Guadeloupe and Martinique, which could combine with a visit to Les Saintes and Dominica. There are lots of flights from the USA to Nassau and Freeport in the Bahamas, allowing island hopping to the Family Islands, and to Puerto Rico, which again has lots of links with nearly all the other Caribbean Islands. Only Cuba has rather poor inter-island links, both by air and by sea, but then there is enough to keep you busy on such a large island for you not to need to combine it with anywhere else.

Before you travel

Getting in

Documents
Individual island entry requirements are given in the relevant chapters under 'Essentials'
North Americans, British and Commonwealth citizens in some cases need only show proof of identity, but it is always best to carry a **passport**. Immigration authorities are not keen on driver's licences or voter registration cards, even if technically they are adequate forms of identification. If intending to visit Puerto Rico or the US Virgin Islands, or making connections through Miami or another US gateway, a **visa** for the United States will not be necessary if your home country and the airline on which you are travelling are part of the US Visa Waiver Program. A US consulate will supply all relevant details. An **onward ticket** is a common prerequisite for entry (see below). Australians and New Zealanders should note that many islands impose strict entry laws on holders of the above passports. Satisfying visa and other requirements, if not done at home, can take at least a day, usually involve expense, and passport photographs will be needed: be prepared.

On all forms, refer to yourself as a 'visitor' rather than a 'tourist'. If asked where you are staying and you have not booked in advance, say any hotel (they do not usually check), but do not say you are going to camp and do not say that you are going to arrange accommodation later.

Onward ticket

Many islands insist that visitors have an air ticket to their home country before being allowed to enter; for non-US citizens travelling to the Caribbean from the USA, this means a ticket from the USA to their home country, not a ticket back to the USA. Tickets to other countries will not suffice. This becomes a problem if you are not going home for 12 months since airline tickets become void after a year. Some airlines sell tickets on the six to 12 month extended payment plan; these can be credited when you have left the islands with restrictive entry requirements. Even if you propose to take some boat trips between islands, we recommend that you purchase flights in advance and refund those that have not been used later.

Passport

You should always carry your passport in a safe place about your person, or if not going far, leave it in the hotel safe. If staying in a place for several weeks, it is worth while registering at your embassy or consulate. Then, if your passport is stolen or lost, the process of replacing it is quicker. Keeping photocopies of essential documents, and some additional passport-sized photographs, is also a good idea.

Money

Cost of visiting

The following tips on economizing were sent by Steve Wilson and Debra Holton of San Francisco: look out for bunk rentals on boats (see below, page 29); happy hours in bars often have free food; couples sharing costs can often take advantage of Ladies' Night in a bar or nightclub, which either permits free entry or cheap drinks

The Caribbean is not a cheap area to visit. Transport is expensive (unless you are staying in one place and using only buses), but if you book your flights in advance, taking advantage of whatever air pass or stopovers are suitable, that expenditure at least will be out of the way.

Accommodation is generally expensive, too, even at the lower end of the market. There is no shortage of luxury resorts and beach hotels throughout the upper price ranges. In a number of instances you can book all-inclusive packages which are often good value and let you know in advance almost exactly what your expenditure will be. However, you will not see much of your chosen island outside your enclave and organized excursions can be costly. To find cheaper accommodation you need mobility, probably a hired car. One option is renting a self-catering apartment, villa or house, the range of which is also vast, and here the advantage is that a group of people can share the cost (not so economical for single travellers).

Since on a number of islands resort-type hotels form the majority, turning up at a cheaper place may not always yield a room because competition is great. The term 'guest house' is usually applied to places at the lower end of the market; they tend, but by no means in all cases, to be basic. Note also that, if booking ahead, tourist office lists may not include the cheapest establishments, so you may have to reserve a room, then look around. This is probably what you will have to do in any event, time permitting, to find the best value. In the main, tourist offices publish accurate, up-to-date lists of accommodation, which are a great help for making preliminary bookings. Remember that the Dominican Republic and Cuba

Essentials

WATERFORD

Essentials

Exchange rates (July 2001)

Source:
www.oanda.com

See also Comparative
cost of living table,
page 26

Country	Currency	Abbreviation	Exchange RATE/US$
Anguilla	East Caribbean dollar	EC$	2.70
Antigua & Barbuda	East Caribbean dollar	EC$	2.70
Aruba	Aruban florin	Afl	1.79
Bahamas	Bahamian dollar	B$	1.00
Barbados	Barbados dollar	B$	1.99
Bonaire	Netherlands Antillies (NA) guilder	Naf	1.78
British Virgin Islands	US dollar	US$	1.00
Cayman Islands	Cayman dollar	CI$	1.22
Cuba	Cuban peso	$	1.00
		Market rate	21.00
Curaçao	NA guilder	Naf	1.78
Dominica	East Caribbean dollar	EC$	2.70
Dominican Rep	Dominican peso	RD$	16.20
Grenada	East Caribbean dollar	EC$	2.70
Guadeloupe	French franc	F	7.66
Haiti	Gourde		24.35
Jamaica	Jamaican dollar	J$	45.45
Martinique	French franc	F	7.66
Montserrat	East Caribbean dollar	EC$	2.70
Puerto Rico	US dollar	US$	1.00
Saba	NA guilder	Naf	1.78
St Barthélémy	French franc	F	7.66
St Kitts & Nevis	East Caribbean dollar	EC$	2.70
St Lucia	East Caribbean dollar	EC$	2.70
St Martin	French franc	F	7.66
St Vincent & the Grenadines	East Caribbean dollar	EC$	2.70
Sint Eustatius	NA guilder	Naf	1.78
Sint Maarten	NA guilder	Naf	1.78
Trinidad & Tobago	Trinidad dollar	TT$	6.18
Turks & Caicos	US dollar	US$	1.00
US Virgin Islands	US dollar	US$	1.00
Venezuela	Bolivar	Bs	717.36

have the most hotel rooms in the Caribbean, so there is no real problem in finding a space there. The most popular form of accommodation for independent travellers in Cuba is to stay with a registered family in their home, a *casa particular*. Food and lodging with families is far better value and much more rewarding than staying in a hotel, although it is not possible in the beach resorts of Varadero of Guardalavaca. Some islands, such as Puerto Rico or the French Antilles, have well organized camp sites, but on many camping is actually prohibited.

Currency In general, the US dollar is the best currency to take, in cash or travellers' cheques. The latter are the most convenient and, if you follow the issuer's instructions, can be replaced if lost or stolen. On the most frequently visited holiday islands, eurocurrencies can be exchanged without difficulty but at a poor rate and US dollars are preferred. In some places, the US dollar is accepted alongside local currency (but make sure in which currency prices are being quoted). In others, only the local currency is accepted. On the French islands dollars are accepted, but the franc is the preferred currency. Credit cards are widely used. Remember to keep your money, credit cards, etc, safely on your person, or in a hotel safe. If your guesthouse has no safe in which to store money, passport, tickets, etc, try local banks.

Airline websites

Although useful for gaining information about flights, as yet you are unlikely to get the best price from airline websites, so use them for advice only.

ACES www.acescolombia.com
AeroCaribe www.aerocaribe.com
Aeropostal www.aeropostal.com
Air Canada www.aircanada.ca
Air France www.airfrance.com or
   www.airfrance.fr
Air Jamaica www.airjamaica.com
ALM www.airalm.com
American Airlines www.aa.com
American Eagle www3.aa.com
AOM www.aom-minerve.fr
Aserca www.asercaairlines.com
Avianca www.avianca.com.co
Bahamas Air www.bahamasair.com
British Airways www.british-airways.com
BWIA www.bwee.com
Canadian Airlines www.cdnair.ca
Caribbean Star Airlines
   www.caribbeanstar.com
Cayman Airways www.caymanairways.com

Condor www.condor.de
Continental Airlines
   www.continental.com
Copa www.copaair.com
Cubana www.cubana.cu
Delta www.delta-air.com
Hapag Lloyd www.wlf.de or
   www.hapag-lloyd.de
Iberia www.iberia.com
KLM www.klm.com
Lacsa www.grupotaca.com
Lan Chile www.lanchile.com
Liat www.liatairline.com
LTU www.ltu.com
Lynx Air www.lynxair.com
Martinair www.martinair.de
Northwest Airlines www.nwa.com
Sky King www.skyking.tc
TAP www.tap-airportugal.pt
TWA www.twa.com
United Airlines www.ual.com

If you want to read horror stories from fellow travellers about their airline experiences, try www.traveldesk.com

Essentials

Getting there

Air

In addition to the scheduled flights listed, there are a great many charter flights from Europe and North America. For details on both types of service, you are advised to consult a good travel agent. An agent will also be able to tell you if you qualify for any student or senior citizen discount on offer. From the USA, Puerto Rico and Antigua are the only islands to which student fares are available; it is worth checking these out since it may be cheaper to take a student flight then continue to your destination rather than flying direct to the island of your choice. If buying tickets routed through the USA, check that US taxes are included in the price. At certain times of the year, *Air France* and *AOM* have flights at very advantageous prices from several southern French cities and Paris to Guadeloupe and Martinique; travellers from France, Switzerland and southern Germany should be able to use them. *Air France* flights can also be combined with *Liat* air passes.

Airlines
See individual islands for major airlines flying to each island

Airlines will only allow a certain weight of luggage without a surcharge; this is normally 30 kg for first class and 20 kg for business and economy classes, but these limits may not be strictly enforced if the plane is not going to be full. *JMC Airways* (year round charter from the UK) allows 40 kg, which is very popular with travellers visiting friends and relatives in the Caribbean. Weight limits for inter-island flights are often much lower; it is best to enquire beforehand.

Baggage allowance

In Switzerland, *Globetrotter Travel Service*, Rennweg, 8001 Zürich, has been recommended for arranging cheap flights to the region. In the UK, *The Caribbean Experience* (ATOL 5149), 70 Pembroke Road, Kensington, London, W8 6NX, T020-76024021, F020-76036101, www.

Specialist operators

caribbean-ex.co.uk, specialize in the Eastern Caribbean, booking accommodation or flights for independent travellers, or package deals. *Exodus Travels*, 9 Weir Road, London, SW12 0LT, T020-87723822, www.exodus.co.uk

International Student Identity Card (ISIC) If you are in full-time education you will be entitled to an ISIC, which is distributed by student travel offices and travel agencies in 77 countries. The ISIC gives you special prices on all forms of transport (air, sea, rail, etc), and access to a variety of other concessions and services. If you need to find the location of your nearest ISIC office contact: The ISIC Association, Box 15857, 1001 NJ Amsterdam, Holland T+45-33939303.

Sea

Cruise lines & cargo ships The most popular way of visiting the Caribbean by ship is on a cruise liner, as the figures given in the economy sections below attest. There are also sailing cruisers (eg the Windjammer and Star Clipper fleets) which allow flexible itineraries for cruising between the islands: very spectacular when under sail. *Windjammer Barefoot Cruises*, which operates five tall-masted ships (*Flying Cloud*, British Virgin Islands; *Legacy*, US and British Virgin Islands; *Mandalay*, Leeward and Windward Islands; *Polynesia*, French West Indies; *Yankee Clipper*, Grenadines) and a supply ship (*Amazing Grace*, see below), can be contacted direct at PO Box 190120, Miami Beach, Florida 33119-0120, USA, T305-6726453, F305-6741219, www.windjammer.com

For cargo ships which carry passengers, it is best to enquire in your own country. In general, it is very difficult to secure a passage on a cargo ship from Europe to the Caribbean without making full arrangements in advance. Round trips are easier to organize than one-way passages, although some companies are now offering a flight home. Fares range from about US$70-130 per person per day, cheaper than a passenger cruise, but without the continuous entertainment. Full details on this type of travel are available in the UK from *Strand*

Voyages, Charing Cross Shopping Concourse, The Strand, London WC2N 4HZ, T020-78366363, F020-74970078; *Cargo Ship Voyages Ltd*, Hemley, Woodbridge, Suffolk, IP12 4QF, T/F01473-736265. In Switzerland, *Wagner Frachtshiffreisen*, Stadlerstrasse 48, CH-8404, Winterthur, T052-2421442, F2421487. In the USA, contact *Freighter World Cruises*, 180 South Lake Av, Suite 3335, Pasadena, CA 91101, T800-5317774, 626-4493106, F4499573, www. freighterworld.com, or *Travltips Cruise and Freighter Association*, 163-07 Depot Road, PO Box 580218, Flushing, NY 11358, T800-8728584, 718-0302400, F718-9392047, www. travltips.com Other websites worth checking are www.freighter-cruises.com, www.navigator.com, www.atwtraveler.com/frei-fac.htm, http://members@aol.com/CruiseAZ/freighters. htm *Reed Travel Group*, Dunstable, Bedfordshire, LU5 4HB, UK, T0582-600111, publishes the *ABC Passenger Shipping Guide*, a monthly list of companies offering freighter transport for passengers.

From Europe: *Strand Voyages* can also advise on the **Compagnie Générale Maritime's** three sailings a month from Dunkerque or Le Havre to Fort-de-France and Pointe-à-Pitre, 23 days' voyage. CGM's *Cap Blanco* (on charter to Furness Withy) calls at Kingston, Jamaica, on its sailings from Felixstowe, via various North European ports, to the west coast of South America. CGM's *Caravelle* sails from Rotterdam to Ponce (Puerto Rico), Port of Spain (Trinidad), Willemstad (Curaçao), Aruba, Puerto Cabello (Venezuela), Santa Marta (Colombia), Cartagena (Colombia), Puerto Limón (Costa Rica), Kingston (Jamaica), and sometimes unscheduled ports. **Safmarine's** *Author*, on a 42-day round trip, sails Felixstowe, Rotterdam, Le Havre, Ponce (Puerto Rico), Port-of-Spain, La Guaira and Puerto Cabello (Venezuela), Willemstad, Oranjestad, Cartagena (Colombia), Puerto Limón (Costa Rica), Santa Marta (Colombia), Kingston (Jamaica), Rotterdam, Hamburg, Felixstowe. The **Horn Line** has regular sailings on the following route: Hamburg, Le Havre, Fort-de-France, Pointe-à-Pitre, Willemstad, Cartagena (Colombia), Chiriquí Grande (Panama), Moín (Costa Rica), Antwerp, Hamburg. From Felixstowe, **Projex Line's** *EWL West Indies* sails to Paramaribo, Georgetown, Port of Spain, La Guaira and Puerto Cabello (Venezuela), Willemstad, Oranjestad, Cartagena and Santa Marta, Bremen, Rotterdam to Felixstowe, 44-day round trip. **Fyffes** banana boats carry passengers from Portsmouth and Flushing direct to Paramaribo, Suriname, and occasionally to Georgetown. From Livorno, a German consortium sails via Valencia (Spain) to San Juan (Puerto Rico), Cartagena (Colombia), Panama Canal, Guayaquil (Ecuador), Panama Canal, Cartagena, Santa Marta, San Juan, Livorno, 35-day round trip. A German consortium sails Hamburg, Bilbao, San Juan, Río Haina (Dominican Republic), Veracruz or Tampico, La Guaira, Río Haina, San Juan, Bilbao, Antwerp, Hamburg on a 55-day round trip. There is a 45-day round-trip sailed by a German consortium from Liverpool, via Hamburg, Rotterdam and Bilbao, to Havana, Tampico and Veracruz, then back to Liverpool. Another German consortium makes a seven-day round trip Río Haina, San Juan, Puerto Cabello, Port-of-Spain, Río Haina.

From the USA: *Ivaran Lines'* container ship, *Americana*, carries 80 passengers in luxury accommodation: New Orleans to Houston, Altamira and Veracruz in Mexico, Puerto Limón, Cartagena, Puerto Cabello, La Guaira, San Juan, Río Haina, New Orleans, 21 days round trip. The *Sven Oltmann* makes an 11-14 day round trip Port Everglades (Florida), Fernandina Beach, back to Port

Essentials

Comparative cost of living, US$

Country	Coke in a bar	Beer/rum in a bar	Burger & chips
Antigua	1.10-2.00	2.25-3.00	3.00-7.50
Bahamas	2.50-3.00	4.00	8.00
Bonaire	1.50	2.00	4.00
Cuba	1.00	1.00	2.50
Dominica	0.50	0.60-1.20	4.50
Grenada	1.00	2.00-3.00	5.00-8.00
Guadeloupe	1.50	1.50	3.60-4.30
Jamaica	1.20	3.50	6.00
Martinique	1.75	2.10	4.75
Montserrat	1.00-1.50	1.25-3.00	3.00-6.00
St Croix	1.80	2.50	7.50
St Kitts & Nevis	0.65-1.00	0.90-1.50	2.60-3.70
St Thomas	2.25	3.00	7.50
St Vincent & the Grenadines	0.40-0.75	1.15-2.00	3.00-9.50
Trinidad & Tobago	0.50-1.00	1.00-2.00	2.50-3.50
Turks & Caicos	1.50-3.00	2.50-5.00	7.50-9.50

Everglades, then Oranjestad, La Guaira and Puerto Cabello (Venezuela), Port Everglades. The supply ship, MV *Amazing Grace*, sails every month from West Palm Beach, picking up southbound passengers in Freeport, Bahamas and visiting lots of islands as it meets up with the *Windjammer* tall ships, delivering monthly supplies, before turning round in Trinidad after two weeks and stopping at different ports from the southbound trip.

Yacht crewing For those with 1,000 miles offshore sailing experience, a cheap way to get to the Caribbean is crewing on a yacht being delivered from Europe or the USA to the region.

Where to stay

See inside front cover for hotel price guide and guide to abbreviations used in listings

Your budget is likely to be the key determining factor in where you stay, but this will stretch further in some islands than others. The key we use in the hotel price guide on the inside front cover is for the price of a double room (rack rate) and takes no account of the facilities offered. In some places a hotel in category **B** will be clean and simple, but in others it will represent the height of luxury. In many islands there are no hotels at all in the **F** category and those in **E** will be hard to find. Camping is not a viable option in general and on some islands it is forbidden, while youth hostels are non-existent. The cheapest accommodation can be found in guest houses, small, privately-run establishments which sometimes offer breakfast but do not rely on a full restaurant service. Many of these are not registered with the local tourist office and therefore difficult to find until you get there. They may be perfectly adequate if you are not very demanding, or they may be flea pits. You will soon find out why they have been left off the list.

Cheap places to stay can be found in Cuba, where families are allowed to rent spare rooms to foreigners. In Havana they cost around US$25-30, but elsewhere they are about US$15-20. Cheap meals can also be negotiated with the families, currently the best way of feeding yourself in Cuba. In Jamaica there are places costing less than US$20 but they are not to be recommended, the **E** range is more possible and **D** will be comfortable. Haiti is surprisingly expensive with most of the guest houses charging rates in our **B-C** range unless you get right off the beaten track. The Dominican Republic, on the other hand, has a far greater range and

Daily special in a local restaurant/ café	Local bus fare	Average salary/ month for Govt. Worker	Average rent/ month on 1-2 bed-room apartment
7.50-15.00	1.00		
8.00-10.00	1.00	1,625	700-800
6.50	2.00	2,500	350-500
5.00-7.00	0.01	20	
3.75-9.25	1.10		
8.00	0.60		
6.50	1.00	715	285-360
8.00	0.25-0.45	750	330-500
7.00-8.50	0.90	750	285-500
3.50-7.00	0.75		
9.00	0.75-1.00	2,550	600
5.60-7.50	0.75	925	600-1,000
9.00	0.75-1.00	2,550	600
2.75-7.75	0.50	350	150
3.00-4.00	0.60	700	150-1,850
12.00	1.00	1,125	750-1,000

E-F hotels can be found in fairly decent areas, although not beachfront properties. In the eastern Caribbean cheap places can be found in the **D-E** ranges in the capital cities, from where you can use public transport to get out to beaches and places of interest, but you will have to pay more if you want to be on the beach. Further south, Trinidad & Tobago have lots of good value places to stay, either in town or close to the beach, while Margarita is also relatively cheap.

It is usually best to reserve one or two nights at a mid-price hotel for when you arrive and then ask around for cheaper accommodation if that is what you want. The longer you stay the better deal you will get, so negotiation is recommended. Remember also that high season runs from mid December to mid-April and everything is more expensive then as well as being more heavily booked. The best deals can be found in – you guessed it – hurricane season.

We assume that most of our readers are not particularly interested in the all-inclusive resorts, although we include details of a few, partly to alert you if they predominate, such as in Ocho Rios in Jamaica or Playa Dorada in the Dominican Republic. We also include the super-luxury hotels to whet your appetite for the day you win the lottery, although we realise that few of you will be able to afford Richard Branson's Necker Island at US$14,000 a day. Some, however, are within range for a special occasion, such as a honeymoon and it can be nice to know they are there. Our **LL** range is therefore very broad, taking in everything from US$200 a night and up to the stars.

Getting around

Air

The most extensive links between islands are by air, either with the scheduled flights on the regional and international carriers, or by chartered plane. If you are in a group, or family, the latter option may not cost very much more than a scheduled flight. It often has the advantage of linking the charter direct to your incoming or homeward flight.

Air passes

The regional carriers with most routes in the Caribbean are LIAT (with its headquarters in Antigua), BWIA (based in Trinidad) and ALM (of the Netherlands Antilles)

LIAT LIAT has two passes called *Explorer tickets*: the *LIAT Explorer* costs US$279, valid for 21 days, maximum three stops between San Juan, Puerto Rico and Trinidad; the *LIAT Super Explorer* costs US$475 for a 30-day ticket, allowing unlimited stop overs in 23 destinations between San Juan and Caracas and Georgetown as well (do not overload your itinerary, a lot of time can be spent waiting at airports for flights). LIAT also operates an *Eastern Caribbean* airpass in which each flight costs US$85, valid for 21 days; minimum three stop overs, maximum six. These tickets may only be issued in conjunction with an international flight to a Caribbean gateway, the itinerary must be settled in advance, with no changes permitted, and no child discounts. A specialist travel agency may be able to book a return ticket with stopovers cheaper than the airpass, so it is worth enquiring. The Eastern Caribbean airpass is only sold in Europe (including the UK and Eire), while the *Explorer* is sold worldwide except for the Caribbean area and Venezuela, and the *Super Explorer* is sold worldwide except Venezuela. In the USA, contact a specialist travel agent. LIAT's telephone number on Antigua is (268) 462 0700, or 462 2682 for fax.

For those who fly regularly within the Caribbean, LIAT runs a frequent flyer club, organized in Antigua. Try to book LIAT flights as far in advance as possible; planes are not large and fill up quickly. A golden rule when flying with LIAT: just because you are *not* booked on a flight it does not mean you will not get on (be patient and sweet-talking); just because you *are* booked on a flight it does not mean you will get on (never be last in the queue). Note also that LIAT is in financial difficulties and travel companies are warning clients that there can be no refunds once a ticket is issued, some also charge a booking fee.

For information on LIAT airpasses contact *The Caribbean Experience* (ATOL 5149), 70 Pembroke Road, Kensington, London W8 6NX, T020-76024021, F020-76036101, www.caribbean-ex.co.uk, who specialize in the Eastern Caribbean.

Note that one-way tickets are hard to organize if you have not booked all your flights in advance. For instance if your trans-Atlantic flight is to Barbados and back from Guadeloupe, Liat will not let you buy (in Barbados) a ticket to St Lucia and will force you to buy the portion from St Lucia to Guadeloupe even if you are intending to take the ferry. Refunds are predictably hard to obtain as processing is done in Antigua.

BWIA BWIA's intra-Caribbean unlimited mileage fare is US$399 which allows 4 stopovers; no destination may be visited more than once, except for making a connection and the entire journey must be fixed at the time of payment (changes are subject to a US$20 surcharge); dates may be left open. This airpass is valid for 30 days, no refunds are given for unused sectors. It may not be used between 19 December and 6 January. BWIA also has a frequent flyer scheme for accumulating air miles.

American Airlines American Airlines includes its Caribbean destinations in its Visit USA air pass (minimum three, maximum 10 coupons). This is available to transatlantic passengers using American, British Airways, Virgin Atlantic or any non-US carrier.

Sea

Departure tax is payable on leaving every island; make sure you know what this is in advance so you do not get caught out

Island-hopping by boats with scheduled services is fairly limited. Boat services are more common between dependent islands, eg St Vincent and the Grenadines, Trinidad and Tobago. Again, full details are given in the relevant sections below. *The Windward Lines*, used to run a weekly passenger and cargo ferry service: St Lucia-Barbados-St Vincent-Trinidad-Güiria or Isla Margarita-Trinidad-St Vincent-Barbados-St Lucia, an excellent way of seeing the southern Caribbean, however, this service was suspended at time of going to press and the company is unsure when, or if, the service will resume. Cabins are available. Their local agents for ticket sales are: **Barbados** *Windward Agencies Ltd*, Brighton Warehouse Complex, Brighton, T246 4257402, F246 4257399, windward@sjds.net; **St Lucia** *Mendes Shipping*, Valco Street, Cadet Street, Castries, T758-4521364, F758-4531654, mendesshipslu@candw.lc; **St Vincent** *Perry's Customs & Shipping*, Sharpe St, Kingstown, T784-4572920, F784-4562619, dhlsvg@caribsurf.com; **Trinidad** *Global Steamship Agencies*, Mariners Club, Wrightson Road, Port of Spain, T868-6242279, F868-6275091, globalship@carib-link.net;

Venezuela *Acosta Asociados SA*, Calle Bolívar, Guiria, Estado Sucre, T58(0)94 820058, F58(0)94 81112, grupoacosta@cantv.net There are also good connections by sea in the French Antilles and with their neighbours, Dominica and St Lucia. *L'Express des Iles* has a daily car ferry service between Fort-de-France and Pointe-à-Pitre and a high speed catamaran passenger ferry service five days a week between Martinique, Guadeloupe, Dominica and St Lucia. Two days a week it also goes to Les Saintes. There are family rates, child, youth and senior citizen discounts and package deals. Remember that port taxes must be added for all destinations: US$2.60 from St Lucia or Dominica, US$3.50 from Pointe-à-Pitre to Dominica and US$7.25 from Pointe-à-Pitre to St Lucia, US$8.15 from Fort-de-France to Dominica or St Lucia (www.whitchurch.com/express.htm or www.martinique.org/transportation.htm).

Irregular passenger services on cargo boats (with basic accommodation, usually a hammock on deck, no meals supplied), schooners, crewing or hitching on yachts can only be discovered by asking around when you are in port. Crewing on yachts is not difficult in winter (in the hurricane season yachtsmen stay away). If you are looking for a job on a yacht, or trying to hitch a ride, it will be easier to make contact if you are living at the yacht harbour. Boat owners often advertise bunks for rent, which is a very cheap form of accommodation (US$10-30); ask around, or look on the bulletin boards. If arriving by sea, make sure you are aware of the island's entry requirements before setting out.

Road

Buses are cheap, but services tend not to be very convenient, they often involve a night away **Bus** from the point of departure, even on small islands. This is because buses start in outlying towns in the early morning and return from the capital in the afternoon. Another limiting factor to public transport is a shortage of funds for spare parts, so buses may be scarce and crowded. Many smaller islands do not even have a bus service.

Taxis are plentiful, but generally not cheap. Some islands, eg Trinidad, have route taxis, which **Taxi** are inexpensive and travel only on set routes. On many islands, taxi fares are set by the tourist office or government.

Renting a car gives the greatest flexibility, but is also hardest on the pocket. You can expect to **Car hire** pay more than in the USA or Europe. A number of islands require drivers to take out a temporary, or visitor driver's licence (these are mentioned in the text), but some places will not issue a licence to those over 70 without a medical certificate. The minimum age for rental is usually 25. In small places, renting a motorcycle, scooter or bicycle is a good idea.

Keeping in touch

In the majority of cases, **English** is widely spoken and understood (although you may have **Language** difficulty understanding some of the local dialects). In the French Antilles and Haiti, **French** is the main language. However, in these last, and on English islands which at one time belonged to France, **Créole** is spoken. The population is bilingual, so on English islands the English-speaking traveller will have no problems with communication and on the French islands, knowledge of French is of great benefit. The Netherlands Antilles speak **Dutch**, English and **Papiamento**. English and **Spanish** are both spoken on Puerto Rico. The principal language in the Dominican Republic, Cuba and the Venezuelan islands is Spanish. If visiting non-English islands, a basic knowledge of the main language is a great advantage. Language courses in Spanish, plus volunteer programmes and travel advice, are run in Puerto Rico and the Dominican Republic by *AmeriSpan Unlimited*, PO Box 40007, Philadelphia, PA 19106-0007, USA, T215-7511100, (800-8796640 in USA and Canada), F215-7511986. Other language courses are available with other companies in those islands and the universities run good programmes in Cuba.

Essentials

Post There are Post Offices in all the main towns but you can often buy stamps in hotels. Islands like Montserrat, the Cayman Islands and Nevis pride themselves on their philatelic issues, which are collectors' items. Postal service is not very efficient and for sending packages or parcels a courier service is recommended for speed and security.

Telephone, fax & internet
See inside front cover for a list of the phone codes for all the islands

Many airport lounges and phone companies in the region have *AT&T's* USA Direct phones by which the USA and Canada may be called using a charge card (which bills your home phone account), or by calling collect. The service is not available to Europe, but the *BT* chargecard, for example, can be used on many of the islands (check with your phone company). Public card phones have been introduced by *Cable and Wireless* on those islands where it operates. This company offers discounts on evening rates for IDD calls from cardphones: 1800-2300 15%, 2300-0500 40%. Discounts do not apply to credit card calls (1-800-877-8000). Phone cards usually come in several denominations, with a tax added on, and can be useful for local and international calls, particularly as you then avoid the extra charges made by hotels on phone calls. Communicating by fax is a convenient way of sending messages home. Places with public fax machines may receive messages as well as send. A few countries have cybercafés and the number is expanding all the time. Many hotels have business centres with terminals which can be used by their guests and are often open to the public. Often the local telephone office will have a terminal you can use to send emails, but don't rely on it actually working.

Food and drink

As you might expect of islands, there is a wide variety of seafood on offer which is fresh and tasty and served in a multitude of ways. Fish of all sorts, lobster and conch are commonly available and are usually better quality than local meat. Beef and lamb are often imported from the USA or Argentina, but goat, pork and chicken are produced locally. There is no dairy industry to speak of, so cheeses are also usually imported. There is, however, a riot of tropical fruit and vegetables and a visit to a local market will give you the opportunity to see unusual and often unidentifiable objects as well as more familiar items found in supermarkets in Europe and North America but with ten times the flavour. The best bananas in the world are grown in the Caribbean on small farms using the minimum of chemicals, if not organic. They are cheap and incredibly sweet and unlike anything you can buy at home. Many of the wonderful tropical fruits you will come across in juices or in ice cream. Don't miss the rich flavours of the soursop, the guava or the sapodilla. Mangoes in season drip off the trees and those that don't end up on your breakfast plate can be found squashed in abundance all over the roads. Avocado trees also provide a surplus of fruit and you will be doing everyone a favour if you eat as many as possible. Avocados have been around since the days of the Arawaks, who also cultivated cassava and cocoa, but many vegetables have their origins in the slave trade, brought over to provide a starchy diet for the slaves. The breadfruit, a common staple rich in carbohydrates and vitamins A, B and C, was brought from the South Seas in 1793 by Captain Bligh, perhaps more famous for the mutiny on the *Bounty*. The slaves were needed for work in the sugar plantations and sugar cane is still grown on some islands today, often ending up as rum, see box opposite.

Restaurants range from gourmet to cafés but they will all make the most of local ingredients. If you are economizing, find a local place and choose the daily special, which will give you a chance to try the typical food of the island, usually in generous portions. See our Comparative cost of living table, page 26, for what you might expect to pay on each island. Fast food is also available, but you will be better off going to a local place serving chicken and chips or burgers, rather than the international chains, which do not exist on many islands in any case. Trinidad has some of the best food around, drawing on the cultures of its many immigrants: Indian, African, Chinese, Syrian, etc, and fast food there is almost an art form. The *roti*, a thin chapatti wrap filled with spicy or curried meat, fish or vegetables is hugely popular as a lunch time or midnight takeaway meal and its success has led to its spread to many other islands. Each island has its own specialities and these are described in the following chapters.

Top rum cocktails - author's addictions

There is nothing better at the end of a busy day than finding a pleasant spot overlooking the sea with a rum in your hand to watch the sunset and look out for the green flash. The theory is that the more rum you drink, the more likely you are to see this flash of green on the horizon as the sun goes down.

There are hundreds of different rums in the Caribbean, each island producing the best, of course. The main producers are Jamaica, Cuba, Barbados, Guyana, Martinique and the Dominican Republic, but other islands such as Grenada also produce excellent brands. The Bacardí family, the most important firm in Cuba for 100 years, no longer distils rum in Cuba, having moved to Puerto Rico and worldwide after the Revolution. Generally, the younger, light rums are used in cocktails and aged, dark rums are drunk on the rocks or treated as you might a single malt whisky. Cocktails first became popular after the development of ice-making in the USA in 1870, but boomed in the 1920s partly because of prohibition in the USA and the influx of visitors to Cuba, the Bahamas and other islands, escaping stringent regulations. People have been drowning their rum in cola ever since the Americans brought bottled drinks in to Cuba during the war against Spain at the end of the 19th century, hence the name, **Cuba Libre**. *You can in fact adapt any cocktail recipe to substitute other spirits and incorporate rum. It makes an excellent* **Bloody Mary***, the spicier the better.*

One of the nicest and most refreshing cocktails is a **Daiquirí***, invented in Santiago de Cuba in 1898 by an engineer in the Daiquirí mines. The natural version combines 1½ tablespoons of sugar, the juice of half a lime, some drops of maraschino liqueur, 1½ oz light dry rum and a lot of shaved ice, all mixed in a blender and then served piled high in a*

wide, chilled champagne glass with a straw. You can also have fruit versions, with strawberry, banana, peach or pineapple, using fruit or fruit liqueur.

Another Cuban favourite, drinkable at any time of the day or night, is the **Mojito***, once popular with Ernest Hemingway and his friends in Havana. Put half a tablespoon of sugar, the juice of half a lime and some lightly crushed mint leaves in a tall glass. Stir and mix well, then add some soda water, ice cubes, 1½ oz light dry rum and top up with soda water to taste. Garnish with mint leaves and serve with a straw.*

Everybody has heard of the old favourite, **Piña Colada***, which can be found on all the islands and is probably the most popular of the fruit-based cocktails, ideal by the side of the pool. Combine and blend coconut liqueur, pineapple juice, light dry rum and shaved ice, then serve with a straw in a glass, a pineapple or a coconut.*

Many Caribbean hotels offer you a welcome cocktail when you stagger out of the taxi, jet-lagged from your transatlantic flight. This is often an over-sweet, watered-down punch, with a poor quality rum and sickly fruit juice. You are more likely to find something palatable in the bar, but it always depends on which blend of juice the barman favours. In Grenada, **rum punch** *is improved enormously with the addition of nutmeg sprinkled on top. The standard recipe for a rum punch is: 'one of sour, two of sweet, three of strong and four of weak'. If you measure that in fluid ounces, it comes out as 1 oz of lime juice, 2 oz of syrup (equal amounts of sugar and water, boiled for a few minutes), 3 oz of rum and 4 oz of water, fruit juices, ginger ale, or whatever takes your fancy. You could add ice and a dash of Angostura Bitters from Trinidad, or nutmeg from Grenada, garnished with a slice of lime. Delicious.*

Essentials

Festivals

Every island celebrates Carnival in some form or other, mostly as a pre-lenten event, but several countries schedule it for later in the year, partly to spread out the revelries. The biggest and best Carnival is in Trinidad, famous for its music and parades with lavish costumes and more spontaneity than its rival in Rio. For a full description and how to take part, see page 925.

Essentials

Caribbean festivals at a glance

	Jan	Feb	Mar	Easter	April
Aruba	🎉	🎭	🎉		
Anguilla			🎵 🏆		
Antigua					⛵
Bahamas					
Barbados		🎉 ⛵	🎭	🎉	
Bonaire		🎭			
British Virgin Islands			⛵ ⛵	🎉	
Carriacou		🎭		🎉	
Cayman Islands					🎭
Cuba	🎉				⛵
Curaçao	⛵	🎭	🐟	🎉	⛵
Dominica		🎭			⛵
Dominican Republic		🎭			
Grenada	🐟 ⛵ 🏆	🎉		⛵	
Guadeloupe		🎭			
Haiti	🎉	🎭			
Isla de Margarita		🎭		🎉	
Jamaica					🎭
Martinique	⛵/🎉	🎭	⛵		⛵
Montserrat			🎉	🎉	🎉
Nevis					
Puerto Rico			⛵		🎭
Saba					
Sint Maarten		⛵			🎭 🎉
St Eustatius					🎉
St Kitts					
St Lucia		🎭 🎉			
St Vincent & the Grenadines			🐟	⛵	
Bequia				⛵	
Union Island				🏆	
St-Barthélémy		🎭			
St-Martin		🎭 ⛵			
Tobago		🎭 🐟		🎉	
Trinidad		🎭 🎉			
Turks & Caicos					
Grand Turk					
Providenciales					
South Caicos					
North Caicos					
Middle Caicos					
USVI St Thomas			⛵		🎭
St John					
St Croix	⛵	🏆	🎉 🏆		

🎭 Carnival (usually means pre-Lenten)   🎉 Festival   🎵 Music and arts festival

/ = two types of event combined; without / = two separate events fall within same month. is given.

Essentials

May	Jun	Jul	Aug	Sep	Oct	Nov	Dec

🐟 Angling tournament ⛵ Regatta 🏄 Windsurf races 🏆 Other sports

Where an event begins in one month and ends in another, the month of commencement

See Festivals, Watersports, Culture and Public holidays sections.

The common theme of all the carnivals is the masquerade, where masked and elaborately costumed dancers 'rush' through the streets, usually in the early hours of the morning on 'J'ouvert', Carnival Monday. Their disguises can be traced back to legends from Africa and colonial times and vary from country to country depending on their own histories. In the Dominican Republic they dress up as devils, piglets or bulls, with battles between rival factions, while in Carriacou, in the Grenadines, they celebrate Shakespeare Mas, where masked characters from Shakespeare's plays recite long speeches until they forget their lines and are beaten over the head by their rivals.

Even if you are not around for Carnival, you are sure to catch some other festivity. Each town celebrates its patron saint's day, often with a street party incorporating traditional food and drink, music and dance. There are several music festivals throughout the year, jazz being particularly popular in the eastern Caribbean, although Barbados stands out for offering an opera season. Regattas and all sorts of sailing activities inevitably end in parties and associated events in which visitors are welcome to participate. Our table of events, Caribbean festivals at a glance, gives a broad sweep of what you might expect on any island in any month, but is far from comprehensive as new festivities are always popping up.

Sports

Information on sport is given under each island, but for those visiting the former British colonies, British dependencies and even the US Virgin Islands, an understanding of **cricket** is an advantage. It is more than a national game, having become a symbol of achievement and a unifying factor. Spectating at a match is entertaining both for the cricket itself and for the conversation that arises. **Baseball** and **basketball** serve much the same function in the Dominican Republic, Cuba and Puerto Rico, and if you are interested in the game, or just want to watch the crowd, it is worth finding out in advance about when the season is.

Watersports

See individual islands for detailed information

The crystal clear waters of the sunny Caribbean combined with the constant northeast trade winds make the islands a paradise for watersports enthusiasts. The great increase in tourism in the area has brought a corresponding development in watersports and every conceivable watersport is now available. Some of the best islands to head for are Barbados, Jamaica, Antigua, Martinique, the Bahamas, Cayman Islands, Puerto Rico and the Virgin Islands. On these islands you can find hobie-cats and sunfishes for rent, windsurfing, water skiing, glass-bottomed boats plying the reefs, charter yachts and booze cruises, scuba diving, snorkelling and deep sea fishing. Prices for such watersports vary from island to island and often increase by about 30% in the peak tourist season (December to April). It is worth knowing that prices can often be reduced for regular or long term rentals and that bargaining with individual beach operators is definitely worth trying.

Swimming   If all you want is sea and sand, these abound on nearly every island. The coral islands have the white postcard-perfect beaches and some of the islands of the Grenadines are nothing more than this. Swimming is safe on almost all Caribbean coasts, but do be careful on the exposed Atlantic coasts in the east where waves are big at times and currents rip. Swimming in the Atlantic can be dangerous and in some places it is actually forbidden.

Water-skiing   This is almost always available in developed resort areas and beginners are looked after well. If you are a serious water skier it may be worth bringing your own slalom ski as many boats only cater for beginners.

Surfing   Good breaks for surfing and boogey-boarding can be found on the north shores of Puerto Rico, the Dominican Republic, Tobago and in Barbados. In both Puerto Rico and Barbados, custom-made surfboards can be bought and several competitions are organized every year. There are several good surf spots in Puerto Rico and the most consistent break in Barbados is

Cricket in the Caribbean

Test matches in the Caribbean are played, to date, in five countries: Jamaica, Barbados, Guyana, Trinidad and Antigua. Other first-class and one-day matches may be played in some of the smaller islands, part of either the Windward Islands or Leeward Islands teams, such as Grenada, Dominica, St Lucia, St Vincent, St Kitts and Nevis or Anguilla. The six first class teams are: Jamaica, Trinidad and Tobago, Barbados, Guyana, Windward Islands and Leeward Islands. Antigua is hoping to play separately from the Leeward Islands at some time in the future.

Large numbers of visitors go to the Caribbean to watch international matches. Book accommodation well in advance, particularly in Antigua. Note that it frequently rains in Guyana and that Barbados is expensive.

Huge and more relaxed entertainment can also be enjoyed by going to inter-island matches. Currently the one-day competition is being played before Christmas; it has suffered a lot of disruption from rain and this might not be the best time to go. The four-day competition, currently called the BUSTA Cup, runs from January to March. Unless West Indies are on tour at the time all the international players are required to play in the competition, so it is high standard.

Information about international matches can be obtained in the UK from the Test and County Cricket Board, Lord's Cricket Ground, St

John's Wood, London NW8 8QN, T020-74321200. However, finding out about the first class matches between the islands is difficult. First ring the International Cricket Council (ICC), also at Lord's Cricket Ground (the Clock Tower) in London, T020-72661818, F020-72661777 (no resources for email queries). They may give you the address and number of the West Indies Cricket Board which is based in Antigua. This is of little use, however, because the board does not answer letters and their number does not accept international calls! The best ploy is to ask someone at the ICC if they can help. (Don't ring up when a test match is being played.) They may give you the number of one of the local organizations, eg the Trinidad and Tobago or Windward Islands Board, or may even be prepared to ring themselves. If all else fails, a hotel or other organization in the Caribbean may be able to find out for you.

It is a lot of trouble but well worth it!

Some useful websites for news, scores and statistics:

www.caribinfo.com
www.caribbeansports.com
www.candw.cricket.bb/ (schedule for the Cable & Wireless Test Series, toll free West Indies ticket line 1-800-744-GAME)
www.caribcentral.com/cricket.htm
www.cricket.org

---

at Bathsheba. In the Dominican Republic and Tobago, the sport is less developed. Waves tend to be bigger and more consistent in winter.

Sportfishing is excellent in many of the islands of the North Caribbean. Almost every variety of deep-sea game fish: marlin, swordfish, tuna, mackerel and dorado abound in the waters. Over 50 world record catches have been made off the Bahamas alone. In the reefs and shallows there are big barracuda, tarpon and bonefish. There are areas for all methods of fishing: surf fishing, bottom fishing or trolling. Spearfishing, however, is banned in many islands. Although most fish seem to run between November and March, there is really no off-season in most islands and a good local captain will always know where to find the best fishing grounds.

Fishing
Fishermen should beware of eating large predators (eg grand barracuda) and other fish which accumulate the ciguatera toxin as a result of eating coral-browsing smaller fish

Fishing is very well organized in such islands as the Bahamas where Bimini, lying close to the Gulf Stream, is devoted entirely to game fishing. Exciting game fishing is also available very close to the shore off Puerto Rico, especially in the area which has become known to the enthusiasts as Blue Marlin Alley. Fishing is also very good off the Cayman Islands, Jamaica and the US Virgin Islands. Hemingway made fishing off Cuba famous and it remains an exciting sport there. In many islands there are annual fishing tournaments open to all, such as the International Fishing Tournament held in April in the Caymans. Deep-sea fishing boats can be chartered for a half or full day and some are available on a weekly basis. Anglers can also pay individually on split charters. When arranging a charter, be careful to clarify all details in advance.

Sailing
See individual islands for detailed information

Exploring the Caribbean by boat has never been easier. New marinas and local communities near popular anchorages are catering to the increasing number of yachts which have made the Caribbean their home. The Caribbean islanders have coined the name 'yachties' to refer to those people who live and travel on their own boats as contrasted with those who visit the islands on their vacations on chartered boats, cruise ships or landbased resorts. While this information is directed toward the yachties, bareboat charterers will also find it useful.

From Europe to the Caribbean For boats crossing the Atlantic along the trade wind route, Barbados is the first landfall. Boats have the option of going on to Venezuela and Central America or through the Windward Islands of Grenada, St Vincent and the Grenadines. The Atlantic Rally for Cruisers offers support and entertainment for any sailors contemplating an Atlantic crossing. Departure is from Gran Canaria at the end of November and the yachts arrive in St Lucia to a warm welcome for Christmas.

From the USA to the Caribbean The two routes from the USA to the Caribbean are (a) from New England or Norfolk directly to the US Virgin Islands with the possibility of a stop in Bermuda or (b) island-hopping from Florida through the Bahamas across the 'Thornless Path' to windward described by Bruce Van Sant in his book *Passages South*. The Caribbean 1500 Rally organizes cruisers wishing to travel in a group to the Caribbean and depart from Newport, Rhode Island or Norfolk, Virginia, in late October arriving in St Thomas in the US Virgin Islands.

Ports of entry Arrive during weekday working hours to avoid overtime fees. Have the sun at your back to navigate through reefs, sand bars or other water hazards even if it means a midnight or late afternoon departure and an overnight sail. When making windward passages, overnight trips often mean lighter winds and seas.

Customs and immigration Yachties cross many countries and have to deal with more officials and procedures than tourists aboard cruise ships or travelling to resorts. No matter how many guidebooks are available, there will be at least one country with a change in procedures. Be careful to clear immigration on arrival as there are heavy fines for failing to do so. Plan to pay fees and to fill out paperwork in all countries. Occasionally, there are no fees; however, most countries have airport departure taxes and most have realized that these fees are another source of income. Different fees are often charged for charter boats and cruisers on their own boats who may wish to stay for a longer period of time.

Q Flag and courtesy flags Fly your 'Q' or quarantine flag until paperwork is completed. The captain should take ship's papers, passports and a list of the places you wish to stop and visit as in some countries you must be given specific clearance to stop and anchor. All crew should remain aboard until they have received clearance from the port authorities. Even though many of the islands are still a part of the British Commonwealth, they prefer to see their country's courtesy flag flown. (And fly it the right side up!)

Liveaboard community anchorages are found with a good, well protected anchorage, provisions, water, laundry available in Marsh Harbour in the Abacos, Georgetown in the Exumas, Luperón, Samaná and Puerto Plata in the Dominican Republic, Boquerón in Puerto Rico, Phillipsburg in Sint Maarten, Bequia in the Grenadines, Secret Harbour and Prickly Bay in Grenada, Chaguaramas in Trinidad, Porlamar, Margarita and Puerto la Cruz in Venezuela. Cruisers Net in Puerto la Cruz, Venezuela VHF 72 0745, during hurricane season in Porlamar, Margarita VHF 72 0800. Radio nets provide information about social activities, including ladies lunches and especially Carnival activities in Trinidad, that might be of interest to tourists with extra time as well as cruisers.

Yacht charters Charter fleets operate from the US and British Virgin Islands, in the Abacos in the Bahamas, Antigua, Sint Maarten/St-Martin, Martinique, Guadeloupe, St Lucia, St Vincent and Grenada. One way charters can often be arranged for an additional fee. Yachts can be chartered on a daily or term basis, either bareboat or with skipper and crew. Skippered day charters are now found in almost any area where there are landbased tourists.

Marinas Dry dock facilities for long term boat storage are found in the Turks and Caicos, Puerto Rico, the Virgin Islands, St Martin, St Lucia, St Vincent, Antigua, Grenada, Trinidad and Venezuela. Marinas with slips of different types (slips, stern-to, pilings) are found in the majority of the islands and new ones are opening frequently. Most marinas will hold mail addressed to yachts for pickup.

Hitching rides Hitching and working on yachts is another way to see the islands for the adventurous person with time on his/her hands. Many yachts charter in the Caribbean in winter and go north to the USA or Mediterranean for the charter season there. Other yachts are cruisers passing on their way around the world. Yachties are friendly people and if you ask in the right places, frequent the yachtie bars and put up a few notices, crew positions can often be found. Bulletin boards are found in Georgetown (Bahamas), Turtle Cove Marina (Turks and Caicos), Great Bay and Bobby's Marina in the Lagoon (Sint Maarten), Fort-de-France, Trois-Ilets and Le Marin (Martinique), Rodney Bay and Marigot Bay (St Lucia), English Harbour (Antigua), Admiralty Bay (Bequia) and Anchorage (Union Island) in the Grenadines, Secret Harbour and Spice Island Marina (Grenada), Porlamar (Margarita), any of the marinas in El Morro complex in Puerto la Cruz (Venezuela) where foreign yachties hang out, and any marina or yacht club in Chaguaramas in Trinidad. If you want to crew, check you have all necessary visas and documentation and confirm with the skipper that your paperwork is in order. Puerto Rico and the US Virgin Islands require visas for boat travellers as though you were travelling to the USA. To visit the USA from the Caribbean by yacht, many yachts leave Trinidad after Carnival in late February; boat deliveries back to the USA are also possible.

Weather Information SSB US weather broadcasts, US Ham net (east coast of USA & Bahamas), in the Caribbean, David on SV *Mystine* is on SSB kHz 6224 at 0800, with weather summaries covering the Dominican Republic, Puerto Rico, Virgin Islands, Leewards and Windwards, Trinidad and Tobago, northern Venezuela, central Caribbean basin, Colombia and Honduras. In case of marine advisory, he will come up on 6224 at 1815 with updates. Cruisers are invited to call in their location and current information. Alex from SV *Albatross* operates a morning 'chat net' on 5104 from 0700-0800 out of Venezuela. He reads weather forecasts from earlier hamnet reports. Caribbean weather is found on SSB 4003, 0815-0830 and 8104 0830-0900 Caribbean time and has been handled by volunteers since 1996; however, it is anticipated that David Jones, author of *A Concise Guide to Caribbean Weather* will take over the net in the near future from the British Virgin Islands. Yachts crossing the Atlantic use Herb from *Southbound II* 1600-1700, 12359. Weather information is critical before making long passages or during hurricane season (June-November). This is also the rainy season as tropical waves cross over the Caribbean bringing rain and squalls.

VHF Nets In those areas where there are a substantial number of liveaboard sailors, VHF nets seem to spring up with volunteers taking turns providing weather information, arrivals and departures, information about services and announcements about local activities, sharing taxis or tours; guests returning home often offer to take mail back to the USA or Europe. Email is becoming a popular means of communication. Local access can be obtained by boats staying in a marina.

Fishing permits, park rules The Caribbean islands are becoming more ecoconscious. They are interested in preserving their natural resources and beauty and have established parks, marine preserves or national trust foundations. Some have mooring buoys, no-anchoring or anchoring limitations. Most prohibit taking of coral or live creatures in shells; many prohibit taking of shells. Don't anchor in areas where coral may be growing. Don't dispose of rubbish

Hurricane Season

See also box,
page 62

June too soon
July stand by
August it must
September remember
October all over
If only! In recent years there have been several late storms and the 'October all over' proved a myth. There was little hurricane activity in the region from the 1950s until the late 1980s. Many of the islands were not affected by hurricanes and residents thought little of them. Homes were not built to withstand severe storms. In 1989 this all started to change when several violent storms roared through the islands and Hurricane Hugo did untold damage in the US Virgin Islands. The next few years were relatively quiet but 1995 struck with a bang (three names were 'retired' in deference to the dead and injured) and was the start of a five-year cycle that has gone down in history as the most active stretch on record for hurricanes: 41 developed with 20 major ones (Category 3 at 111 mph or more). 1996 brought nine hurricanes; 1997 gave the islands a breather with only three. 1998 was another active season with 10, one of which did much damage. On 25 September 1998 there were a record four hurricanes at the same time. 1999 brought eight hurricanes, five of which were Category 4 (130mph or over) and two came late in the season, in October and November.

In the daily weather forecasts, a **tropical depression** is an organized system of clouds and thunderstorms with a defined circulation and maximum sustained winds of 38 mph (33 knots) or less; a **tropical storm** is an organized system of strong thunderstorms with a defined circulation and maximum sustained winds of 39 to 73 mph (34 –63 knots); a **hurricane** is an intense tropical weather system with a well-defined circulation and maximum sustained winds of 74 mph (64 knots) or more.

A hurricane develops in warm waters and air, which is why the tropics are known for hurricanes. Powered by heat from the sea they are steered by the easterly trade winds and the temperate westerly winds, as well as their own ferocious energy. In the Atlantic, these storms form off the African coast and move west, developing as they come into warmer water. Around the core, winds grow to great velocity, generating violent seas. The process by which a disturbance forms and strengthens into a hurricane depends on at least three conditions: warm water, moisture and wind pattern near the ocean surface that spirals air inward. Bands of thunderstorms form and allow the air to warm further and rise higher into the atmosphere. If the winds at these higher levels are light, the structure remains intact and allows for further strengthening. If the winds are strong, they will shear off the top and stop the development. If the system develops, a definite eye is formed around which the most violent activity takes place; this is known as the eyewall. The center of the eye is relatively calm. When the eye passes over land those on the ground are often misled that the hurricane is over; some even abandon safe shelter, not aware that as the eye passes the other side of the eyewall will produce violent winds and the other half of the hurricane. At the top of the eyewall (around 50,000 ft), most of the air is propelled outward, increasing the air's upward motion. Some of the air however, moves inward and sinks into the eye and creates a cloud-free area.

The word 'hurricane' is derived from the Amerindian 'Hurakan', both the Carib god of evil and also one of the Maya creator gods who blew his breath across the chaotic water and brought forth dry land. In the North Atlantic, Gulf of Mexico, Caribbean and the Eastern Pacific they are called hurricanes, in Australia, cyclones or 'willy

in enclosed anchorages. **Rubbish** is a problem on many of the smaller islands; don't give rubbish to boat boys as they often just take the money and throw the waste into the water. Try to dispose of edible waste at sea while travelling between islands in deep water; take paper, cans and bottles ashore to the town dump or a marina where they have waste disposal facilities.

Scuba diving   Do not assume you can dive wherever you like even if you have all your own tanks and equipment. Several islands require divers to go with a local dive group and it is best

Essentials

willy', and in the Philippines, 'baguio'. In the Western North Pacific tropical cyclones of hurricane force are called typhoons. The first time hurricanes were named was by an Australian forecaster in the early 1900s who called them after political figures he disliked. During World War II US Army forecasters named storms after their girlfriends and wives. Between 1950-52 they were given phonetic names (able, baker, charlie). In 1953 the Weather Bureau started giving them female names again. Today individual names (male and female) are chosen by the National Hurricane Center in Miami and submitted to the World Meteorology Organization in Geneva, Switzerland. If approved these become the official names for the upcoming hurricane season. As a system develops and becomes a tropical depression (TD), it is assigned a name in alphabetical order from the official list.

There is very good information before hurricanes hit any land, thanks to accurate weather data gathered by the Hurricane Hunters from Keesler Airforce Base in the USA. During the storm season they operate out of St Croix in the US Virgin Islands, where they are closer to storms. This elite group of men and women actually fly through the eye of a hurricane in C130 airplanes gathering critical information on the wind speeds and directions and other data. This is sent to the Miami Hurricane Center where a forecast is made and sent to all islands in the potential path so they can prepare for the storm. Most of the island governments are now well prepared to cope with hurricanes and have disaster relief teams in place, while many of the island resorts, especially the larger ones, have their own generators and water supplies.

While a hurricane can certainly pose a threat to life, in most cases if precautions are taken the risks are reduced. Some of the main hazards are storm surge, heavy winds and rains. There is usually disruption of services such as communications, internal transport and airline services. The tourist may be left stranded while the roads and power lines are cleared and airline service is renewed. Communications home may be impossible for some days. Ideally, if a hurricane is approaching, it is better for the tourist to evacuate the island. During the hurricane, which is usually 6-36 hours, you have to be shut up inside a closed area, often with little ventilation or light, which can be stressful. Some tourists think a hurricane will be "fun" and want to remain on island to see the storm. This is short sighted and foolish. If you do remain you should register with your local consulate or embassy. You should also be prepared to be inconvenienced in the ways already mentioned and even to help out in the clearing up afterwards.

When there is potentially violent weather approaching, the local government met office issues advisories:

A tropical storm watch is an announcement to be on alert for a storm (winds of 39- 73 mph) which may pose threats to coastal areas within 36 hours.

A tropical storm warning is issued if the storm is expected within 24 hours.

A hurricane watch is given if hurricane conditions could be coming in 36 hours.

A hurricane warning is issued if the hurricane is expected within 24 hours.

One of the best internet sites for information and data from reporters on the islands during an actual hurricane is Storm 2001 **www.gopbi.com/weather/storm**

The Web site of the Hurricane Hunters is **www.hurricanehunters.com** (virtual reality flight with them into the eye of a hurricane on this site).

Miami National Hurricane Center **www.nhc.noaa.gov/**

to contact a local dive shop for advice. Many dive operators have special rates and packages for yachtie divers and will pick you up from your yacht.

Weapons Some countries want weapons and ammunition checked in ashore until you are ready to depart. Others will let you keep them locked on board and others don't really ask questions. Make sure clearance papers have the correct serial numbers and ammunition counts to avoid confusion when it comes to picking up the weapons that were checked ashore. Some areas even consider spearguns weapons and require them to be turned in until you leave.

Regattas or special activities Sailboat races of all types are held throughout the Caribbean during the entire year. Spectator boats may go out to watch the races, there may be crew-sign-up lists for those who would like to sail and best of all, there are usually parties and other activities on shore. Most regattas have various different types of classes, even including liveaboard classes.

Guidebooks cover most areas of the Caribbean and are updated periodically. Julius Wilensky's guides have good sketch charts that are still useful even if not updated. *Yachtsman's Guide to the Bahamas and Turks and Caicos*, *Cruising Guide to Abaco*, Steve Dodge; *Cruising Guide to the Abacos* (2nd edition) Julius Wilensky; *Yachtsman's Guide to the Virgin Islands*, *Southern Waterway Guide* (covers Bahamas and Turks & Caicos), *Passages South*, Bruce Van Sant; *Guide to the Leeward Islands*, Chris Doyle; *VIP Cruising Guide* (Sint Maarten area), *Guide to the Windward Islands*, Chris Doyle; *Guide to Venezuela, Trinidad & Tobago*, Chris Doyle; *Guide to Trinidad and Tobago*, Chris Doyle; *Guide to Venezuela*, Chris Doyle; *Donald Street's Guides to the Caribbean* (Volumes I, II, III, IV). There are several 'yachting newspapers' that are distributed free around the Caribbean that have things to do, reports on regattas, tourist and sailing events: *Nautical Scene* (St Thomas to Venezuela), *The Compass* (Bequia and southern Caribbean), *All at Sea* (northern Caribbean), *The Boca* (Trinidad and Tobago) and *Mar y Tierra* (Venezuela).

Scuba diving

See individual islands for detailed information

The numbers of scuba divers has increased dramatically in recent years and the Caribbean is a scuba diver's paradise, for there is a conglomeration of islands surrounded by living reefs providing different types of diving to suit everyone's dreams. Unfortunately, as a result, some of the islands have turned into a 'diving circus', particularly in some of the more developed northern Caribbean islands where 30 or 40 divers are herded onto large dive boats and dropped on somewhat packaged dive sites where 'tame' fish come for handouts. However, other islands in the region are still virginal in the diving sense, which can lead to an exciting undersea adventure. On the more remote islands be aware that facilities are not often available and that the diving can be more difficult and basic.

Cayman Islands These are among the most developed for scuba diving and there is a fine organization of over 20 dive operations, including liveaboard boats. *The Aggressor Fleet*, PO Drawer K, Morgan City, LA 70881-000K, T504-3852416, F504-3840817 or (USA & Canada) 800-3482628, www.aggressor.com There is also a well run decompression facility on Grand Cayman, which is an added safety factor. The Caymans are very conservation minded and it is a criminal offence to take ANY form of marine life while scuba diving. In fact, it is illegal on Cayman Brac, the smaller sister island, even to wear gloves while scuba diving. This helps ensure that divers will not hold or damage the delicate coral formations and other marine life.

British Virgin Islands With some 50 coral islands, these islands are well worth a mention as the diving is exciting and varied. Both liveaboard and land-based operations are available with well developed facilities for divers. Popular diving sites include the wreck of the *HMS Rhone*, a 310-ft British mail ship sunk in 1867 in a hurricane. She was the site for the Hollywood movie *The Deep*. Other interesting sites include Turtle Cave in Brewers Bay which offers a spiral arch divers can swim through beginning at a depth of 45 ft and winding up to 15 ft. Many sites lie in the string of islands to the south between Tortola and the island of Virgin Gorda. To the north lies Mosquito Island, the site of The Cousteau Society's Project Ocean Search. Hosted annually by Jean-Michel Cousteau, the expedition gives a small number of participants the chance to find out what it is like to be on a Cousteau expedition (*The Cousteau Society*, 870 Greenbrier Circle, Suite 402, Chesapeake, Virginia 23320, T1-800-4414395, www.cousteausociety.org).

Saba, a tiny Dutch island, only five miles long, is truly one of the most protected places for divers. The entire reef surrounding the island was established as a marine park in 1987 and this conservation effort has led to an abundance of 'tame' fish. Saba diving is known for several deep pinnacles including Third Encounter, Twilight Zone and Shark Shoal. For the less adventurous and experienced, sites like Diamond Rock and Tent Reef offer the thrill of seeing large French Angels swimming up to you. The sport has been developing with both land-based and liveaboard diving boat facilities available, as well as a recompression chamber facility.

Dominica 'The Nature Island', or 'The Water Island', is a lush, mountainous island with rugged topside and underwater terrain. It is diving for the adventurous and not for the diver who wants it easy although there are a few beginner sites. This is one of few islands left where black coral abounds along the wall drop-offs starting at 60 ft. For the more experienced the Atlantic east coast offers some spectacular wall dives.

Turks and Caicos Islands They consist of over 40 lovely sand islands and cays and are located on the Turks Island Passage, a 22-mile channel which is 7,000 ft deep connecting the Atlantic Ocean and the Caribbean Sea. This contributes to the abundance of marine life and large pelagic fish seen in these waters and spectacular wall diving in the channel. The islands are surrounded by coral reefs that cover over 200 square miles. Visibility is usually 100 ft or more and marine life plentiful. A wild Atlantic bottle nosed dolphin, JoJo, occasionally interacts with swimmers, snorkellers, divers and boaters and has actually been made a national treasure of the TCI. There is also a dolphin rehabilitation project, *Into the Blue*, in Providenciales, which has so far released three dolphins from UK zoos, but they have no contact now with people. The strong attitude towards conservation is reinforced by **Protection of Reefs and Islands from Degradation and Exploitation (PRIDE)**, based at the Sea Island Centre, a commercial conch farm. PRIDE is a US-based foundation which has helped in numerous conservation projects. There are several dive shops on Providenciales and Grand Turk, mostly catering for small groups of divers, and there are three or four liveaboard boats in the islands' waters at any one time.

St Vincent and the Grenadines Lying in the South Eastern Caribbean these islands offer pristine diving, although facilities are limited. Grenada and tiny sister island of Carriacou offer limited diving facilities, as does Bequia, although nearby St Vincent is more developed for scuba diving.

Tobago An unspoiled destination well worth visiting. This small island is close to the South American coast and large marine life is encouraged by the flow of plankton-rich water from the continent's rivers. Manta ray are especially attracted by the plankton and at Speyside (also called Manta City) where currents meet they are seen on nearly every dive. Most diving is along the west and north coast.

Barbados Among the more developed islands in the Caribbean though the surrounding reef life is not as unspoiled as on some of the less developed islands. However, there are some thriving reefs and within the last few years the island has become known as a wreck diving destination. Five shipwrecks have been intentionally sunk as diving sites, offering interesting underwater photography. In addition, the island is the base for the regional organization, **The Eastern Caribbean Safe Diving Association**. This association helps to maintain a decompression facility for the Leeward and Windward islands and is attempting to establish minimum safe operating standards for dive shops, initially in the East Caribbean and eventually, regionally. For more information write ECSDA, Box 86 WRD, Welches Post Office, Barbados.

Bonaire Just off the South American coast Bonaire has long been known as a 'hot spot' for diving, and is one of the few islands (like the Caymans) which has devoted itself to scuba diving. A far-sighted government established a marine park way back in 1979 when conservation was not even being discussed by most diving destinations. Neighbouring Curaçao has now joined her in this reputation, with an expansion of diving facilities and exciting diving sites. Aruba is not likely to equal her sister islands as she lacks the reefs which surround Bonaire and Curaçao, although diving is available. Bonaire, being very experienced in offering diving, has a wide selection of about a dozen dive operations, including photo and marine life education facilities. Diving sites are also varied with reef, wreck and wall dives. In fact, the Marine Park Guide for Bonaire lists over 50 dive sites. The town pier, right off the capital, has long been a favourite night dive and the pilings are covered in soft sponges and invertebrate life.

Curaçao Offers the reef diving of Bonaire and a couple of wreck dives of interest. The freighter, *Superior Producer* (rather deep at 100 ft) is intact and has a variety of growth including beautiful orange tubastera sponges.

Aruba While the reefs may not be as prolific as her sister islands, there is an interesting wreck site, with which few other sites around the island compare in marine life. The *Antilla*, a 400 ft German ship, is in 70 ft (and less) of water. Her massive hull has provided a home for an amazing variety and size of fish life and night dives are truly a thrill. More wrecks are being sunk to create an artificial reef.

Most Caribbean destinations offer some form of scuba diving, although not all operations are **safety** minded. While scuba diving is exciting and thrilling, it can also be dangerous, particularly for beginners who are not aware of what to look for in a safe diving operation. Proper instruction from a recognized scuba instructor is a must. Not all diving shops in the Caribbean adhere to the recommended safety standards, so it is important to ensure the level of training an instructor has and request to see certificates of instructor training if they are not displayed.

Good **health** is a must, but the myth that one needs to be a super man or super woman is not true. Important health aspects are healthy lungs, sinus and the ability to equalize your ears (by gently blowing air into the eustachian tube while blocking your nose). A medical exam by a physician trained in hyperbaric (diving) medicine is recommended and required by many instructors. A good basic swimming ability is necessary, although you do not need to be an Olympic swimmer. For female divers, smaller, lighter scuba tanks are available at some dive shops which makes the cumbersome, heavy gear easier to handle.

Most scuba training organizations offer several types of diving **courses**. A 'resort course' provides diving instruction in a condensed version (about three hours) with a minimum of academic knowledge, one confined water session (usually in a swimming pool) and one scuba dive. This type of course is done by many tourists who do not have the time to do a full certification course, which requires written exams, classroom lectures, several confined water sessions and several scuba dives. For the serious diver, however, a full certification course should be taken.

Windsurfing

For operators & associations, see individual islands

Whether you are an accomplished windsurfer or merely wishing to give it a try, the Caribbean offers warm clear water, trade winds and a wealth of locations to choose from. Throughout the Caribbean there are hundreds of pristine windsurfing locations, many undeveloped. Bring your own gear and have an adventure, or sail with the many schools across the islands. The strongest, steadiest winds are in June and July when the trade winds are at their most constant. Winter brings either howling winds or flat calm and is unpredictable. In summer the gentle breezes provide good learning conditions. Each island has different winds and conditions, there is something for everyone, even if you just want to sit on the beach and watch.

Antigua Steady winds and good locations, at present there is only one dedicated school, although hotels often have learner boards. Best wind November-February, June-July.

Aruba Well known as a centre for great windsurfing, flat waist deep water on the leeward side with strong wind make this an ideal location for learners and advanced windsurfers, the perfect family windsurf vacation. Best wind May-July.

Barbados Sun, sand, wind and waves make Barbados one of the favourite locations for many pro windsurfers on the World Tour. For those not willing to try the waves, flat water can be found at Oistins Bay. Best wind and wave conditions December-January and June.

Bequia Bequia is a beautiful island, but though the wind blows and the sun shines, there is only one windsurf school run by Basil, a Bequian with a big smile. Good location for learners or advanced sailors with flat water and wave sailing, well off the beaten track. Best winds November-February, June-July.

Bonaire Good winds and locations for all levels of sailors from flat water to gentle waves. Best winds December-August.

British Virgin Islands The centre for windsurf cruising, with over 50 small islands scattered within 40 miles and steady trades, the islands are perfect for flat water cruising and blasting. Already a popular yachting centre, the two sports fuse with international events such as the Hi Ho (hook in and hold on), a week long windsurf race and yacht cruise. Good sailing for all levels. Best winds December-January, June-July.

Grand Cayman Famous for its diving, Grand Cayman also offers good windsurfing, the east end is popular for beginners to advanced and everything in between, flat water on the inside and bump and jump further out. Best wind November-March.

Dominican Republic Voted by many top sailors as one of the most exciting places to sail in the Caribbean, Cabarete, on the north coast, offers everything a windsurfer could want: flat water for beginners and great wavesailing on the outside with thermally affected winds that mean you can take the morning off. Lots of schools and hotels on the strip of beach and some of the best gear in the Caribbean. Best wind January-March and June-August.

Grenadines Great location with no facilities, take your own gear and hire a yacht out of Grenada or St Vincent, or visit Basil at Bequia (see above) the only rental centre in the area.

Nevis A windsurfer's paradise waiting to be discovered, good flat water and wavesailing, definitely no crowds, the island is small enough to offer all conditions for every skill level. Best wind December-January, June-July.

Puerto Rico Great wave sailing spot, the Caribbean's answer to Maui. The location is The Shacks at Isabela on the northwest point of the island. Thermal winds make this a winter spot for the committed wave sailor, gentler sailing is offered in the San Juan area and in the summer. Best waves and wind December-April, slalom July-September.

St Barts Small exclusive island with some good windsurf spots for beginners and advanced, and it is quiet. Best wind December-February.

St Croix A great sailing spot and often overlooked, the guys here are good wave sailors and slalom racers as the island boasts all conditions at many locations. Best wind January-February and July.

St Lucia A beautiful destination for any visitor and for the windsurfer it offers uncrowded sailing and plenty to do on no wind days. Bring your own gear if you are an advanced sailor, although there is limited good gear to rent at Windsurf Cas-en-Bas. Best winds December-June.

St Martin Orient Bay (Baie Orientale) has good winds and plenty of facilities. St Martin offers good learning and advanced slalom sailing. Best winds December-January and July.

St Thomas Everything you expect from a Caribbean windsurf vacation, with shopping malls. St Thomas boasts a lively local windsurfing community, flat water and lots of races and events to attend. Best wind December-January and July, join the fun at the Caribbean Team Boardsailing Championships in July.

Trinidad & Tobago In the prime trade wind zone, Tobago's Pigeon Point is the place to go, unexplored and beautiful with some excellent sailing spots. You will probably need to take your own gear. Best wind December-May.

Turks & Caicos Flat turquoise waters and steady winds make this an ideal learner and intermediate destination, perfect for a family diving and windsurf vacation. Best winds February-March intermediate, October-November for beginners.

Walking

The Caribbean provides ideal conditions for medium-distance walking in the tropics. Small islands avoid the very high temperatures which are common in India, Africa, or the South American mainland. Distances are manageable; a hard day's walk will take you from coast to coast on the smaller islands, and a few days is enough for a complete circuit. The scenery is varied: peasant farms with fruit trees, rain forests, and high mountains. Mountain streams and waterfalls which would be ice-cold in temperate countries are perfect for bathing. The sea is never far away. Nor are road transport, comfortable accommodation, rum shops and restaurants. Nevertheless, the illusion of remoteness can sometimes be complete. And much of the nastier *mainland* wildlife can't swim, so there are no large carnivores and few poisonous snakes on the islands.

See individual islands for further details

Good large scale maps (1:25,000 or 1:50,000) are available for all the British Commonwealth islands. These can be obtained from the local Lands and Surveys department on each island; and usually from **Stanfords**, 12/14 Long Acre, London WC2E 9LP (T020-78361321, F020-78360189), sales@stanfords.co.uk, or **The Map Shop**, 15 High Street, Upton-upon-Severn,

Maps

Worcestershire, WR8 0HJ (T01684-593146), www.themapshop.co.uk The Ordnance Survey (Romsey Road, Southampton, UK, T01703-792763, F01703-792404) publishes a series of colourful world maps including some holiday destinations. They contain comprehensive tourist information ranging from hotels and beaches to climbing and climate. Each map is produced in association with the country concerned. Relevant titles so far are: Barbados, St Lucia, Cayman Islands, British Virgin Islands, St Vincent, Dominica. There are also good large scale Serie Bleu maps of Guadeloupe and Martinique (1:25,000, seven maps of Guadeloupe, No 4601G-4607G) issued by the Institut Géographique National, Paris, which include all hiking trails. Footpath information on maps is not always reliable, however.

Hints

A small, collapsible umbrella may be useful and can also provide protection against the sun

Clothing Lightweight cotton clothing, with a wide brimmed hat to keep off the sun. Shorts are more comfortable, but can leave the legs exposed to sunburn or sharp razor grasses; ditto short sleeved shirts. It is best to carry short and long, and change en route as appropriate. Wear a shirt with a collar to avoid sunburn on the back of your neck. Rain comes in intense bursts. Raincoats are not particularly comfortable. A better technique is to strip down to light clothes and dry off when the rain stops. There are many new fabrics on the market which are designed to wick away moisture from your body, keeping you cool, while drying rapidly if you are caught in a downpour. In the rainy season leather footwear is of little use as it will be permanently wet and muddy. Use trainers instead and be prepared to discard them at the end of your trip.

Timing An early start is ideal, preferably just before sunrise. This will give several hours walking before the sun becomes too hot. Public transport starts running surprisingly early in most places.

Water Carry a large thermos. This can keep water ice-cold through a full day. Refilling from mountain streams is generally safe if purification tablets are used, but be careful of streams *below* villages especially in islands like St Lucia and Martinique where there is some bilharzia, and of springs in cultivated areas where generously applied pesticides may have leached into the groundwater.

Sunburn Remember that the angle of the sun in the sky is what counts, not the temperature. So you may get burnt at midday even if you feel cool, but are unlikely to have trouble before 1000 or after 1500. Forearms can get burnt, and so can the back of your legs if you are walking away from the sun. It is a good idea to walk west in the morning and east in the afternoon to avoid strong sun on the face.

Snakes The only islands where these are a worry are Trinidad, St Lucia, and Martinique. Trinidad has several dangerous species, and also has African killer bees. All three islands have the venomous Fer de Lance. This snake, however, is usually frightened off by approaching footsteps, so snakebites are rare, but they can be fatal. The Fer de Lance prefers bush country in dry coastal areas. Ask and accept local advice on where to go, and stick to well marked trails. Some other islands have boa constrictors, which can bite but are not poisonous. In Trinidad, beware of the coral snake; visitors with children should take care because the snake looks like a colourful bracelet coiled on the ground. Snakes are also found in the interior jungles of the Guianas; walk with a guide. Most snakes will only attack in the breeding season if they feel the nest is threatened. Large centipedes (sometimes found in dry coastal areas) can also give a very nasty bite.

Marijuana farmers In remote mountain areas in most islands these people are likely to assume that outsiders have come either to steal the crop or as police spies. On most islands they are armed, and on some they set trap guns for the unwary. Again, the best way to avoid them is to keep to well marked trails, and accept local advice about where to go. In some places, however, they assume you are a customer. One hiker was stopped by a farmer on his descent from a volcano. Although the machete was alarming, in fact he offered to sell him ganja. When the goods were politely declined, he offered to sell him guns instead.

Jamaica Spectacular scenery especially in the Blue Mountains and in the Cockpit country. Marijuana growers are a real problem in the remote areas, but the main trails in the Blue Mountains are safe. *Jamaica Camping and Hiking Association* and Ministry of Tourism have a useful *Hikers Guide to the Blue Mountains*.

Dominican Republic Home to the two highest peaks in the Caribbean (Pico Duarte and Pico La Pelona) in addition to many smaller mountains, it is being discovered as one of the great places for hiking. For information contact the Dirección Nacional de Parques, Av Máximo Gómez, Santo Domingo, Apartado Postal 2487.

Haiti Another story altogether. Walking is the normal means of transport in rural areas, so there are masses of well-trodden trails, but it is better to walk with a group. Maps are rudimentary and small scale. Few people speak French in remote areas – try to pick up some Créole. Make sure you carry basic supplies, particularly water. Hiring a guide should be no problem.

Guadeloupe Network of waymarked trails on the mountainous half (Basse Terre) in the Parc Naturel and up La Soufrière. Contact the *Organisation des Guides de Montagne de la Caraïbe* (Maison Forestière, 97120 Matouba, T590-800579) for a guide and/or the booklet *Promenades et Randonnées*.

Martinique The *Parc Naturel Régional* (9 Boulevard Géneral-de-Gaulle, T596-731930) organizes group hikes, usually on Sundays, and publishes a useful *Guide des Sentiers Pedestres à la Martinique*. Good trails on Mont Pelée and along the north coast.

Dominica Probably has the best unspoiled mountain scenery in the Caribbean. Some of the long distance trails are hard to follow, though. Guides readily available. Try the path via Laudat to the Boiling Lake.

St Lucia Very well marked east-west trail through Quillesse forest reserve. Other walks organized by the Forestry Department. Also a good trail up Gros Piton. See St Lucia chapter for details.

St Vincent Spectacular but sometimes difficult trail across the Soufrière volcano from Orange Hill to Richmond. Guide advisable. North coast trail past Falls of Baleine is spectacular, but hard to follow. Marijuana growers.

Grenada Very accessible mountain and rainforest scenery. Good network of signposted trails linking Grand Etang, Concord waterfall, and other points. The mountains to the southeast of the Grand Étang Forest Reserve are less well marked and you may need a local guide, but the walking is spectacular with marvellous views.

Barbados Very safe and pleasant walking, especially on the east coast, but little really wild scenery. *Barbados National Trust* (T246-4262421/4369033) organizes regular hikes.

Trinidad Some fine scenery, but marijuana growers are a problem, particularly in the Northern Range and you are advised always to walk in a group. Well marked trails are safe. Those at the Asa Wright Nature Centre are recommended (T868-6674655, F6670493). Trinidad Field Naturalists Club (PO Box 642, Port of Spain, T868-6248017, evenings only) organizes long distance hikes, and visits to caves etc.

Tobago Safe and pleasant walking; distances are not too great. The scenery is varied: hills, woodland and unspoilt beaches.

For groups organizing a serious hiking/camping expedition in the Caribbean, contact the *Duke of Edinburgh's Award Scheme*, Bridge House, Cavans Lane, Bridgetown, Barbados (T246-4369763). They may be able to provide advice and to supply the address of a local organization on most islands with expedition experience.

Cycling

You can rent bikes on almost every island and because of the mountainous terrain and cool breezes, it is quite a comfortable way to get around and visit Caribbean villages. There has even been a Caribbean cup bike race, with bike clubs from each island travelling to different islands for the competition. Some of the islands have mountains as high as 3,000 m towering above the ocean, making the Caribbean one of the most exciting new mountain bike destinations in the world.

Essentials

Cyclist's Caribbean comments

Having just returned to Canada after cycling in the eastern Caribbean for four months and not seeing ONE other cyclist, I am not sure if we are pioneers, lucky or just plain stupid! Our travels took us through Trinidad, Tobago, Grenada, Carriacou, St Vincent and the Grenadines (including Bequia, Union Island, Mayreau, Tobago Cays and Palm Island), Barbados, St Lucia, Martinique, Dominica, Montserrat and Antigua. My overall feeling is that there is some exceptional cycling for a strong rider. Apart from on Barbados and Antigua there are plenty of hills and some fantastic scenery. However, away from the main tourist areas on each island, the tourist infrastructure is not well developed and the potential for crime is high. There are substantial social problems stemming from poverty and drug abuse. There were only a few times we felt truly uneasy but it made us realize how vulnerable we really were in relatively remote areas on bicycles. It is definitely not a trip for a lone female. Most locals seemed genuinely friendly and interested in our chosen mode of transport, but in many countries there is that small percentage of the population who openly display their dislike of the white tourist.

Antigua   Has good bike shops, eg *Cycle Krazy*, and great single track, in addition to a local bike club. However the roads are generally flat, traffic moderately heavy and cycling is not as interesting as on some other islands.

Barbados   Mountain biking on back country roads with bike rental available. The east coast is best but elsewhere there is constant heavy traffic. Rush hour starts at 1600 everywhere.

Cuba   Mountain bike tour companies, good terrain. Charity sponsored tours frequently organized. The west is the more popular part for touring, with gentle hills and plenty of places to stop. The centre can be flat and boring with miles of sugar cane or cattle lands. The Sierra Maestra in the east is demanding and very hot. Distances are huge, always start early and take a long lunch break. Roads are good and empty but poorly signed. Get to your destination before dark as street lighting is poor to non-existent.

Dominica   A new attraction, with bike rental and tours offered by *Nature Island Dive*. Roads are good for cycling, traffic is generally light with the exception of the stretch between Layou and Roseau. Canefield to Pont Casse is very steep, twisty and challenging. This is one of the most enjoyable islands to cycle due to the friendliness of the people, there are plenty of natural sites to visit and the coastal roads are quite easy even with gear (ie not so steep).

Dominican Republic   Coined as the mountain bike mecca of the Caribbean, has a bicycle club with over 300 members with both mountain bike and road bike races held monthly. Bike shops throughout the island. *Iguana Mama* for tours. The north coast, the Cordillera Septentional and the slopes of the Cordillera Central are great places for scenery and challenging cycling. Exhilarating downhills.

Grenada   Bike rental available. Parts (but no repairs) at *Ace Hardware*. Accommodation is strategically placed for cycling round the island. The cycle between Sauteurs and Victoria is a peaceful ride with spectacular views. The ride through the Grand Etang is rewarding but difficult, 5-6 hours with some steep hills but the beauty of the forest reserve and the small friendly communities are well worth it. **Carriacou** has great cycling. Many of the roads are in very poor repair giving it the semblance of off road cycling. Traffic is light. Potential for lots of flat tyres in the dry season when the trail is overgrown with cactii.

Jamaica   Bike rental and tour operators offering trips, excellent terrain, mountains, coastal routes, rolling hills. However, beware fast drivers on hairpin bends.

Martinique   Do not attempt to cycle from the airport to either Fort-de-France or Trois-Ilets as the only route is via the main highway, four lanes each way with fast, heavy traffic and the shoulder is narrow to non-existent.

Montserrat   The east coast is scenic with only light traffic to the former airport, which is the furthermost point you can travel. Immigration is strict and you have to leave a deposit to take bicycles in for a day trip from Antigua.

Puerto Rico   Bike touring companies and rentals throughout the island, excellent terrain.

St Croix Cycling tours of the forest or beach are offered by *St Croix Bikes & Tours*, while *VI Cycling* organize weekly rides and races.

St Kitts Bike rental and tours available.

St Martin *Frogs Legs* is a good bike shop in town, the owner David will take you out on great rides.

St Lucia The best way to cycle the island is anti-clockwise. This will ensure long but gradual uphills and steep, fast downhills. Be extremely careful between Dennery and Castries. This is a drug growing area and the locals are not particularly friendly. Those that are friendly will warn you not to stop. Castries to Soufriere is enjoyable with a fairly demanding but scenic section through the rainforest. Has the potential be to quite wet! Soufriere to Vieux Fort is another good ride and not so hard physically.

St Vincent & the Grenadines *Sailors* is a good cycle shop in Kingstown, also offering tours. The cycle between Layou and Richmond is a strenuous four hours one way, an absolutely spectacular ride, not to be missed, but expect long, steep hills and lots of them. The northern part of St Vincent is notorious for being a drug producing area, travel with caution. **Bequia** has really enjoyable cycling, lots of hills but not too steep and not a lot of traffic, great views and beaches scattered over the island.

Tobago Repairs and parts at *Numero Uno* in Carnbee, who can put you in touch with local riders for run road riding. Mountain bike needed for the trail between L'Anse Fourni and Charlotteville.

Trinidad *Geronimos* is an excellent bike shop owned by a retired professional cyclist.

Health

Staying healthy in the Caribbean is straightforward. With the following advice and precautions you should keep as healthy as you do at home and most travellers experience no problems at all beyond an upset stomach. Obviously this in part depends on how you are travelling: the beach tourist who stays in good hotels is much less at risk than the backpacker who slings his hammock in the back of beyond. Most of the islands have a tropical climate but this does not mean that tropical diseases as such are a great problem or even the main problem for visitors. Should you fall ill, remember that throughout the islands there are well qualified doctors who speak good English (or French or Spanish). Medical practices may vary from those you are used to but there is likely to be better experience in dealing with locally occurring diseases. Most of the better hotels have a doctor on standby; ask at reception.

Before travelling

Take out medical insurance. Make sure it covers all eventualities especially evacuation to your home country by a medically equipped plane, if necessary. You should have a dental check up, obtain a spare glasses prescription, a spare oral contraceptive prescription (or enough pills to last) and, if you suffer from a chronic illness (such as diabetes, high blood pressure, ear or sinus troubles, cardio-pulmonary disease or a nervous disorder) arrange for a check-up with your doctor, who can at the same time provide you with a letter explaining the details of your disability in English or, if necessary, French or Spanish. Check the current practice in countries you are visiting for malaria prophylaxis (prevention) if you are going to the Dominican Republic or Haiti.

Children More preparation is probably necessary for babies and children than for an adult and perhaps a little more care should be taken when travelling to remote areas where health services are primitive. This is because children can become more rapidly ill than adults (on the other hand they often recover more quickly). Diarrhoea and vomiting are the most common problems, so take the usual precautions, but more intensively. Breastfeeding is best and most convenient for babies, but powdered milk is generally available and so are baby foods. Papaya, bananas and avocados are all nutritious and can be cleanly prepared. The treatment of diarrhoea is the same as for adults, except that it should start earlier and be continued with more persistence. Children get dehydrated very quickly in hot countries and can become drowsy and unco-operative unless cajoled to drink water or juice plus salts. Upper respiratory infections, such as colds, catarrh and middle ear infections are also common and if your child suffers from these normally take some antibiotics against the possibility. Outer ear infections after swimming are also common and antibiotic eardrops will help. 'Wet wipes' are always useful and sometimes difficult to find in the Caribbean, as in some places such as Cuba, are disposable nappies.

What to take   There is little control on the sale of drugs and medicines in some of the Caribbean. You may be able to buy any and every drug in pharmacies without a prescription. Be wary of this because pharmacists can be poorly trained and might sell you drugs that are unsuitable, dangerous or old. Many drugs and medicines are manufactured under licence from American or European companies, so the trade names may be familiar to you. This means you do not have to carry a whole chest of medicines with you (except in Cuba, where there are shortages) but remember that the shelf life of some items, especially vaccines and antibiotics, is markedly reduced in hot conditions. Buy your supplies at the better outlets where there are refrigerators, even though more expensive and check the expiry date of all preparations you buy. Immigration officials occasionally confiscate scheduled drugs (Lomotil is an example) if they are not accompanied by a doctor's prescription.

Self-medication may be forced on you by circumstances so the following text does include the names of drugs and medicines which you may find useful in an emergency or in out-of-the-way places and you may like to take some of the following items with you from home: sunglasses designed for intense sunlight; earplugs for sleeping on aeroplanes and in noisy hotels; suntan cream with high protection factor; insect repellent containing DET for preference; mosquito net lightweight permethrin-impregnated for choice; tablets for travel sickness; tampons can be expensive in some countries; condoms; contraceptives; water sterilizing tablets; antimalarials; anti-infective cream eg Cetrimide; dusting powder for feet etc containing fungicide; antacid tablets for indigestion; sachets of rehydration salts plus anti-diarrhoea preparations; painkillers such as paracetamol or aspirin; antibiotics for diarrhoea etc; a simple first aid kit; small pack containing a few sterile syringes and needles and disposable gloves. The risk of catching hepatitis etc from a dirty needle used for injection is now negligible in the Caribbean but some may be reassured by carrying their own supplies, available from camping shops and often at airports.

Vaccination &   Smallpox vaccination is no longer required anywhere in the world. Neither is yellow fever
immunization   vaccination unless you are going to or are coming from South America. The cholera epidemic in South and Central America has not spread to any of the Caribbean islands but they are all on the alert for the possibility. Although cholera vaccination is largely ineffective, immigration officers may ask for proof of such vaccination if coming from a country where the epidemic has occurred.

Typhoid   A disease spread by the insanitary preparation of food. A number of new vaccines against this condition are now available; the older TAB and monovalent typhoid vaccines are being phased out. The newer, eg Typhim Vi, cause fewer side effects, but are more expensive. For those who do not like injections, there are now oral vaccines. **Poliomyelitis**   Despite its decline in the world this remains a serious disease if caught and is easy to protect against. There are live oral vaccines and in some countries injected vaccines. Whichever one you choose it is a good idea to have a booster every three to five years if visiting developing countries regularly. **Tetanus**   One dose should be given with a booster at six weeks and another at six months and 10 yearly boosters thereafter are recommended. Children should already be properly protected against diphtheria, poliomyelitis and pertussis (whooping cough), measles and HIB, all of which can be more serious infections in the Caribbean than at home. Measles, mumps and rubella vaccine is also given to children throughout the world, but those teenage girls who have not had rubella (German measles) should be tested and vaccinated. Hepatitis B vaccination for babies is now routine in some countries. Consult your doctor for advice on tuberculosis innoculation: the disease is still present on some of the

Islands – BVI, Grenada, Guadeloupe, Haiti and Martinique. **Infectious Hepatitis** Less of a problem for travellers than it used to be because of the development of two extremely effective vaccines against the A and B form of the disease. It remains common, however, in some of the islands. A combined hepatitis A and B vaccine is now licensed – one jab covers both diseases. **Other vaccinations** Might be considered in the case of epidemics, eg meningitis. There is an effective vaccination against rabies which should be considered by all travellers, especially those going through remote areas or if there is a particular occupational risk, eg for zoologists or veterinarians.

Further information on health risks abroad, vaccinations etc, may be available from a local **Further** travel clinic. If you wish to take specific drugs with you such as antibiotics these are best **information** prescribed by your own doctor. Bear in mind that not all doctors can be experts on the health problems of remote countries. More detailed or more up-to-date information than local doctors can provide are available from various sources. In the UK there are hospital departments specializing in tropical diseases in London, Liverpool, Birmingham and Glasgow and the Malaria Reference Laboratory at the *London School of Hygiene and Tropical Medicine* provides free advice about malaria, T0891-600350. In the USA the local Public Health Services can give such information and information is available centrally from the Centres for Disease Control (CDC) in Atlanta, T404-3324559.

There are in addition computerized databases which can be accessed for destination-specific up-to-the-minute information. In the UK there is *MASTA* (Medical Advisory Service to Travellers Abroad) T020-76314408, Tx8953473, F020-74365389 and *Travax* (Glasgow, telephone 0141 946 7120 extension 247). Other information on medical problems overseas can be obtained from the book by Richard Dawood (Editor) – *Travellers' Health, How to Stay Healthy Abroad*, Oxford University Press 1992 £7.99 (new edition imminent). We strongly recommend the revised and updated edition, especially to the intrepid traveller heading for the more out of the way places. General advice is also available in the UK in 'Health Information for Overseas Travel' published by the Department of Health and available from HMSO and 'International Travel and Health' published by WHO Handbooks on First Aid are produced by the British & American Red Cross and by St John's Ambulance (UK).

On the road

If a trip to the Caribbean crosses time zones then jetlag can be a problem where your body's biological clock gets out of synchrony with the real time at your destination. The main symptoms are tiredness and sleepiness at inconvenient times and, conversely, a tendency to wake up in the middle of the night feeling like you want your breakfast. Most find that the problem is worse when flying in an easterly direction. The best way to get over jetlag is probably to try to force yourself into the new time zone as strictly as possible which may involve, on a westward flight, trying to stay awake until your normal bedtime and on an eastward flight forgetting that you have lost some sleep on the way out and going to bed relatively early but near your normal time the evening after you arrive. The symptoms of jetlag may be helped by keeping up your fluid intake on the journey, but not with alcohol. The hormone melatonin seems to reduce the symptoms of jetlag but is not presently licensed in most of Europe although can be obtained from health food stores in the USA.

On long-haul flights it is also important to stretch your legs at least every hour to prevent slowing of the circulation and the possible development of blood clots. Drinking plenty of non-alcoholic fluids will also help.

If travelling by boat then sea sickness can be a problem – dealt with in the usual way by taking anti-motion sickness pills.

The thought of catching a stomach bug worries visitors to the Caribbean but there have been **Intestinal** great improvements in food hygiene and most such infections are preventable. Travellers' **upsets** diarrhoea and vomiting is due, most of the time, to food poisoning, usually passed on by the insanitary habits of food handlers. As a general rule the cleaner your surroundings and the smarter the restaurant, the less likely you are to suffer.

Essentials

Foods to avoid Uncooked, undercooked, partially cooked or reheated meat, fish, eggs. Raw vegetables and salads, especially when they have been left out and exposed to flies. Stick to fresh food that has been cooked from raw just before eating and make sure you peel fruit yourself. Wash and dry your hands before eating – disposable wet-wipe tissues are useful for this. Shellfish eaten raw are risky and at certain times of the year some fish and shellfish concentrate toxins from their environment and cause various kinds of food poisoning. The local authorities notify the public not to eat these foods. Do not ignore the warning. Heat treated milk (UHT) pasteurized or sterilized is becoming more available in the Caribbean as is pasteurized cheese. On the whole matured or processed cheeses are safer than the fresh varieties. Fresh unpasteurized milk from whatever animal can be a source of food poisoning germs, tuberculosis and brucellosis. This applies equally to ice cream, yoghurt and cheese made from unpasteurized milk, so avoid these homemade products – the factory made ones are probably safer.

Water Tap water is rarely safe outside the major cities, especially in the rainy season and stream water, if you are in the countryside, is often contaminated by communities living surprisingly high in the mountains. Filtered or bottled water is usually available and safe, although you must make sure that somebody is not filling such bottles from the tap and hammering on a new crown cap. If your hotel has a central hot water supply this water is safe to drink after cooling. Ice for drinks should be made from boiled water, but rarely is so stand your glass on the ice cubes, rather than putting them in the drink. The better hotels have water purifying systems.

Travellers' This is usually caused by eating food which has been contaminated by food poisoning germs.
diarrhoea Drinking water is rarely the culprit. Sea water or river water is more likely to be contaminated by sewage and so swimming can also be a cause. Infection with various organisms can give rise to travellers' diarrhoea. They may be viruses, bacteria, eg Escherichia coli (probably the most common cause worldwide), protozoal (such as amoebas and giardia) salmonella and cholera. The diarrhoea may come on suddenly or rather slowly. It may or may not be accompanied by vomiting or by severe abdominal pain and the passage of blood or mucus when it is called dysentery.

How do you know which type you have caught and how to treat it? If you can time the onset of the diarrhoea to the minute ('acute') then it is probably due to a virus or a bacterium and/or the onset of dysentery. The treatment in addition to rehydration is Ciprofloxacin 500 mg every 12 hours; the drug is now widely available and there are many similar ones. If the diarrhoea comes on slowly or intermittently ('sub-acute') then it is more likely to be protozoal, ie caused by an amoeba or giardia. Antibiotics such as Ciprofloxacin will have little effect. These cases are best treated by a doctor as is any outbreak of diarrhoea continuing for more than three days. Sometimes blood is passed in amoebic dysentery and for this you should certainly seek medical help. If this is not available then the best treatment is probably Tinidazole (Fasigyn) one tablet four times a day for three days. If there are severe stomach cramps, the following drugs may help but are not very useful in the management of acute diarrhoea: Loperamide (Imodium) and Diphenoxylate with Atropine (Lomotil). They should not be given to children.

Any kind of diarrhoea, whether or not accompanied by vomiting, responds well to the replacement of water and salts, taken as frequent small sips, of some kind of rehydration solution. There are proprietary preparations consisting of sachets of powder which you dissolve in boiled water or you can make your own by adding half a teaspoonful of salt (3.5 grammes) and four tablespoonsful of sugar (40 grammes) to a litre of boiled water.

Thus the linchpins of treatment for diarrhoea are rest, fluid and salt replacement, antibiotics such as Ciprofloxacin for the bacterial types and special diagnostic tests and medical treatment for the amoeba and giardia infections. Salmonella infections and cholera, although rare, can be devastating diseases and it would be wise to get to a hospital as soon as possible if these were suspected.

Fasting, peculiar diets and the consumption of large quantities of yoghurt have not been found useful in calming travellers' diarrhoea or in rehabilitating inflamed bowels. Oral rehydration has on the other hand, especially in children, been a life saving technique and should always be practised, whatever other treatment you use. As there is some evidence that alcohol and milk might prolong diarrhoea they should be avoided during and immediately after an attack.

Diarrhoea occurring day after day for long periods of time (chronic diarrhoea) is notoriously resistent to amateur attempts at treatment and again warrants proper diagnostic tests.

There are ways of preventing travellers' diarrhoea for short periods of time by taking antibiotics, but this is not a foolproof technique and should not be used other than in exceptional circumstances. Doxycycline is possibly the best drug. Some preventatives such as Enterovioform can have serious side effects if taken for long periods.

Paradoxically constipation is also common, probably induced by dietary change, inadequate fluid intake in hot places and long bus journeys. Simple laxatives are useful in the short-term and bulky foods such as maize, beans and plenty of fruit are also useful.

Heat & cold

Full acclimatization to high temperatures takes about two weeks. During this period it is normal to feel a bit apathetic, especially if the relative humidity is high. Drink plenty of water (up to 15 litres a day are required when working physically hard in the tropics) use salt on your food and avoid extreme exertion. Tepid showers are more cooling than hot or cold ones. Large hats do not cool you down, but do prevent sunburn. Remember that, especially in the highlands, there can be a large and sudden drop in temperature between sun and shade and between night and day, so dress accordingly. Warm jackets or woollens are essential after dark at high altitude. Loose cotton is still the best material when the weather is hot.

Insects

These are mostly more of a nuisance than a serious hazard and if you try, you can prevent yourself entirely from being bitten. Some, such as mosquitoes are, of course, carriers of potentially serious diseases, so it is sensible to avoid being bitten as much as possible. Sleep off the ground and use a mosquito net or some kind of insecticide. Preparations containing pyrethrum or synthetic pyrethroids are safe. They are available as aerosols or pumps and the best way to use these is to spray the room thoroughly in all areas (follow the instructions rather than the insects) and then shut the door for a while, re-entering when the smell has dispersed. Mosquito coils release insecticide as they burn slowly. They are widely available and useful out of doors. Tablets of insecticide which are placed on a heated mat, and plugged into a wall socket are probably the most effective. They fill the room with insecticidal fumes in the same way as aerosols or coils.

You can also use insect repellents, most of which are effective against a wide range of pests. The most common and effective is diethyl metatoluamide (DET). DET liquid is best for arms and face (care around eyes and with spectacles – DET dissolves plastic). Aerosol spray is good for clothes and ankles and liquid DET can be dissolved in water and used to impregnate cotton clothes and mosquito nets. Some repellents now contain DET and permethrin insecticide. Impregnated wrist and ankle bands can also be useful.

If you are bitten or stung, itching may be relieved by cool baths, antihistamine tablets (care with alcohol or driving) or mild corticosteroid creams, eg hydrocortisone (great care, never use if any hint of infection). Careful scratching of all your bites once a day can be surprisingly effective. Calamine lotion and cream have limited effectiveness and antihistamine creams are not recommended – they can cause allergies themselves.

Bites which become infected should be treated with a local antiseptic or antibiotic cream, such as Cetrimide as should any infected sores or scratches.

When living rough, skin infestations with body lice (crabs) and scabies are easy to pick up. Use whatever local commercial preparation is recommended for lice and scabies. Crotamiton cream (Eurax) alleviates itching and also kills a number of skin parasites. Malathion lotion 5% (Prioderm) kills lice effectively, but avoid the use of the toxic agricultural preparation of Malathion.

Ticks

Usually attach themselves to the lower parts of the body, often after walking in areas where cattle have grazed. They take a while to attach themselves strongly, but swell up as they start to suck blood. The important thing is to remove them gently, so that they do not leave their head parts in your skin because this can cause a nasty allergic reaction some days later. Do not use petrol, vaseline, lighted cigarettes etc. to remove the tick, but, with a pair of tweezers remove the beast gently by gripping it at the attached (head) end and rock it out in very much the same way that a tooth is extracted. Certain tropical flies which lay their eggs under the skin of sheep and cattle also occasionally do the same thing to humans with the unpleasant result that a maggot grows under the skin and pops up as a boil or pimple. The best way to remove these is to cover the boil with oil, vaseline or nail varnish so as to stop the maggot breathing, then to squeeze it out gently the next day.

Sunburn The burning power of the tropical sun, especially at altitude, is phenomenal. Always wear a wide brimmed hat and use some form of suncream lotion on untanned skin. Normal temperate zone suntan lotions (protection factor up to seven) are not much good; you need to use the types designed specifically for the tropics or for mountaineers or skiers with protection factors up to 15 or above. These may be available in all the islands. Glare from the sun can cause conjunctivitis, so wear sunglasses, especially on tropical beaches, where high protection factor sunscreen should also be used.

AIDS In the Caribbean AIDS is increasing and is not wholly confined to high risk sections of the population, ie homosexual men, intravenous drug users and children of infected mothers. Heterosexual transmission is now the dominant mode and so the main risk to travellers is from casual sex. The same precautions should be taken as with any sexually transmitted disease. The AIDS virus (HIV) can be passed by unsterilized needles which have been previously used to inject an HIV positive patient, but the risk of this is negligible. It would, however, be sensible to check that needles have been properly sterilized or disposable needles have been used. If you wish to take your own disposable needles be prepared to explain what they are for. The risk of receiving a blood transfusion with blood infected with the HIV virus is greater than from dirty needles because of the amount of fluid exchanged. Supplies of blood for transfusion should now be screened for HIV in all reputable hospitals, so again the risk is very small indeed. Catching the AIDS virus does not always produce an illness in itself (although it may do). The only way to be sure if you feel you have been put at risk is to have a blood test for HIV antibodies on your return to a place where there are reliable laboratory facilities. The test does not become positive for some weeks.

Malaria In the West Indies, malaria is confined to the island of Hispaniola, being more prevalent in Haiti than the Dominican Republic. It remains a serious disease and you are advised to protect yourself against mosquito bites as above, and to take prophylactic (preventive) drugs. Start taking the tablets a few days before exposure and continue to take six weeks after leaving the malaria zone. Remember to give drugs to babies and children also. The subject of malaria prevention is becoming more complex as the malaria parasite becomes immune to some of the older drugs. However, at the present time Chloroquine should give sufficient protection. You can catch malaria even when taking these drugs, though it is unlikely. If you do develop symptoms (high fever, shivering, headaches), seek medical advice immediately. If this is not possible and the likelihood of malaria is high the treatment is Chloroquine, a single dose of four tablets (600 milligrammes) followed by two tablets (300 milligrammes) in six hours and 300 milligrammes each day following. Pregnant women are particularly prone to malaria and should stick to Proguanil for prophylaxis. The risk of malaria is obviously greater the further you move from cities and into rural areas with primitive facilities and standing water.

Infectious Hepatitis (Jaundice) The main symptoms are pains in the stomach, lack of appetite, lassitude and yellowness of the eyes and skin. Medically speaking there are two main types. The less serious, but more common is hepatitis A for which the best protection is the careful preparation of food, the avoidance of contaminated drinking water and scrupulous attention to toilet hygiene. The other, more serious, version is hepatitis B which is acquired usually as a sexually transmitted disease or by blood transfusion. It can less commonly be transmitted by injections with unclean needles and possibly by insect bites. The symptoms are the same as for hepatitis A. The incubation period is much longer (up to six months compared with six weeks) and there are more likely to be complications.

Hepatitis A can be protected against with gamma globulin. It should be obtained from a reputable source and is certainly useful for travellers who intend to live rough. You should have a shot before leaving and have it repeated every six months. The dose of gamma globulin depends on the concentration of the particular preparation used, so the manufacturers advice should be taken. The injection should be given as close as possible to your departure and as the dose depends on the likely time you are to spend in potentially affected areas. Again follow the manufacturer's instructions. Gamma globulin has really been superseded now by a proper vaccination against hepatitis A (Havrix), which gives immunity lasting up to 10 years. After that boosters are required. Havrix monodose is now widely available as is junior Havrix. The vaccination has negligible side effects and is extremely effective. Gamma globulin injection can be a bit painful, but it is cheaper than Havrix and may be more available in some places.

Hepatitis B can be effectively prevented by a specific vaccine (Engerix) – three shots over six months before travelling. If you have had jaundice in the past it would be worthwhile having a blood test to see if you are immune to either of these two types, because this might obviate the necessity and cost of vaccination or gamma globulin. There are other kinds of viral hepatitis (C, E, etc) which are very similar to A and B, but vaccines are not available as yet.

Snake bite

This is a very rare event indeed for travellers. If you are unlucky (or careless) enough to be bitten by a venomous snake, spider, scorpion or sea creature, try to identify the creature, but do not put yourself in further danger. Snake bites in particular are very frightening, but in fact rarely poisonous – even venomous snakes bite without injecting venom. What you might expect if bitten are: fright, swelling, pain and bruising around the bite and soreness of the regional lymph glands, perhaps nausea, vomiting and a fever. Signs of serious poisoning would be the following symptoms: numbness and tingling of the face, muscular spasms, convulsions, shortness of breath and bleeding. Victims should be got to a hospital or a doctor without delay. Commercial snake bite and scorpion kits are available, but usually only useful for the specific type of snake or scorpion for which they are designed. Most serum has to be given intravenously so it is not much good equipping yourself with it unless you are used to making injections into veins. It is best to rely on local practice in these cases, because the particular creatures will be known about locally and appropriate treatment can be given.

Treatment Reassure and comfort the victim frequently. Immobilize the limb by a bandage or a splint or by getting the person to lay still. Do not slash the bite area and try to suck out the poison because this sort of heroism does more harm than good. If you know how to use a tourniquet in these circumstances, you will not need this advice. If you are not experienced, do not apply a tourniquet.

Precautions Avoid walking in snake territory in bare feet or sandals – wear proper shoes or boots. If you encounter a snake stay put until it slithers away, and do not investigate a wounded snake. Spiders and scorpions may be found in the more basic hotels. If stung, rest and take plenty of fluids and call a doctor. The best precaution is to keep beds away from the walls and look inside your shoes and under the toilet seat every morning.

Certain tropical sea fish when trodden upon inject venom into bathers' feet. This can be exceptionally painful. Wear plastic shoes when you go bathing if such creatures are reported. The pain can be relieved by immersing the foot in extremely hot water for as long as the pain persists.

Other afflictions

Prickly heat A very common intensely itchy rash is avoided by frequent washing and by wearing loose clothing. Cured by allowing skin to dry off through use of powder and spending two nights in an air-conditioned hotel! **Athletes foot** This and other fungal skin infections are best treated with Tolnaftate or Clotrimazole. **Dengue Fever** This is increasing worldwide including in South and Central American countries and the Caribbean. It can be completely prevented by avoiding mosquito bites in the same way as malaria. No vaccine is available. Dengue is an unpleasant and painful disease, presenting with a high temperature and body pains, but at least visitors are spared the more serious forms (haemorrhagic types) which are more of a problem for local people who have been exposed to the disease more than once. There is no specific treatment for dengue – just pain killers and rest. **Typhus** Can still occur carried by ticks but is exceptionally rare in the Caribbean. There is usually a reaction at the site of the bite and a fever. Seek medical advice. **Intestinal worms** These are common and the more serious ones such as hookworm can be contracted from walking barefoot on infested earth or beaches. Some cause an itchy rash on the feet 'cutaneous larva migrans'. **Leptospirosis** Various forms of leptospirosis occur throughout the Caribbean, transmitted by a bacterium which is excreted in rodent urine. Fresh water and moist soil harbour the organisms which enter the body through cuts and scratches. If you suffer from any form of prolonged fever consult a doctor.

When you return home Remember to take your antimalarial tablets for six weeks after leaving the malarial area. If you have had attacks of diarrhoea it is worth having a stool specimen tested in case you have picked up amoebas. If you have been living rough, blood tests may be worthwhile to detect worms and other parasites. If you have been exposed to bilharzia (schistosomiasis) by swimming in lakes etc check by means of a blood test when you get home, but leave it for six weeks because the test is slow to become positive. Report any untoward symptoms to your doctor and tell the doctor exactly where you have been and, if you know, what the likelihood of disease is to which you were exposed.

Responsible travel

Travel to the furthest corners of the globe is now commonplace and the mass movement of people for leisure and business is a major source of foreign exchange and economic development in many parts of the Caribbean. In many areas it is the most significant economic activity.

The benefits of international travel are self-evident for both hosts and travellers: employment; increased understanding of different cultures; business and leisure opportunities. At the same time there is clearly a downside to the industry. Where visitor pressure is high and/or poorly regulated, adverse impacts to society and the natural environment may be apparent. Paradoxically, this is as true in undeveloped and pristine areas (where culture and the natural environment are less 'prepared' for even small numbers of visitors) as in major resort destinations.

The travel industry is growing rapidly and increasingly the impacts of this supposedly 'smokeless' industry are becoming apparent. These impacts can seem remote and unrelated to an individual trip or holiday (for example air travel is clearly implicated in global warming and damage to the ozone layer, resort location and construction can destroy natural habitats and restrict traditional rights and activities), but individual choice and awareness can make a difference in many instances, and collectively, travellers are having a significant effect in shaping a more responsible and sustainable industry.

In an attempt to promote awareness of and credibility for responsible tourism, organizations such as *Green Globe* (UK), T44-020-79308333, greenglobe@compuserve.com and the *Centre for Environmentally Sustainable Tourism (CERT)* (UK), T44-1268-795772, now offer advice on destinations and sites that have achieved certain commitments to conservation and sustainable development. Generally these are larger mainstream destinations and resorts, but they are still a useful guide and increasingly aim to provide information on smaller operations.

Of course travel can have beneficial impacts and this is something to which every traveller can contribute. Many national parks are part funded by receipts from visitors. Similarly, travellers can promote patronage and protection of important archaeological sites and heritage through their interest and contributions via entrance and performance fees. They can also support small-scale enterprises by staying in locally run hotels and hostels, eating in local restaurants and by purchasing local goods, supplies and arts and crafts.

Since the early 1990s there has been a phenomenal growth in tourism that promotes and supports the conservation of natural environments and is also fair and equitable to local communities. This 'ecotourism' segment is probably the fastest growing sector of the travel

A few ideas

Where possible choose a destination, tour operator or hotel with a proven ethical and environmental commitment; if in doubt, ask. Spend money on locally produced (rather than imported) goods and services and use common sense when bargaining, your few dollars saved may be a week's salary to someone else.
Use water and electricity carefully, travellers may receive preferential supply while the needs of local communities are overlooked. Learn about local etiquette and culture, consider local norms of behaviour and dress appropriately for local cultures and

situations.
Protect wildlife and other natural resources: don't buy souvenirs or goods made from wildlife unless they are clearly sustainably produced and are not protected under CITES legislation (CITES controls trade in endangered species).
Always ask before taking photographs or videos of people.
Consider staying in local accommodation rather than foreign owned hotels, the economic benefits for host communities are far greater and there are far greater opportunities to learn about local culture.

Essentials

industry and provides a vast and growing range of destinations and activities in the Caribbean. While the authenticity of some ecotourism operators claims need to be interpreted with care, there is clearly both a huge demand for this type of activity and also significant opportunities to support worthwhile conservation and social development initiatives.

Organizations such as **Conservation International**, T1-202-4295660, www.ecotour. org, **The Eco-Tourism Society**, T1-802-4472121, http://ecotourism.org *Planeta*, www2.planeta. com/mader and **Tourism Concern**, (UK) T020-77533330, www.gn.apc.org/ tourism-concern, have begun to develop and/or promote ecotourism projects and destinations, and their websites are an excellent source of information and details for sites and initiatives throughout Latin America and the Caribbean. Additionally, organizations such as **Earthwatch**, (UK) T1-865-311601, www.earthwatch.org and **Discovery International**, (UK) T020-72299881, www.discoveryinitiatives.com, offer opportunities to participate directly in scientific research and development projects throughout the region.

The Caribbean offers unique and unforgettable experiences – often based on the natural environment, cultural heritage and local society. These are the reasons many of us choose to travel and why many more will want to do so in the future. Shouldn't we provide an opportunity for future travellers and hosts to enjoy the quality of experience and interaction that we take for granted?

Further reading

By no means all the writers of history, fiction, poetry and other topics will be found below. There is no room to talk of the many authors who have been inspired by aspects of the Caribbean for their fiction such as Robert Louis Stevenson, Graham Greene, Ernest Hemingway, Gabriel García Márquez. Nor have travel writers, such as Patrick Leigh Fermor, *The Traveller's Tree*, Quentin Crewe, *Touch the Happy Isles*, Trollope, *Travels in the West Indies and the Spanish Main*, Alec Waugh, *The Sugar Isles*, James Pope-Hennessy, *West Indian Summer*, among others. This list is not exhaustive, concentrating mainly on books in English, published (or readily available) in the UK. For any favourites omitted, we apologize.

Other books have been suggested in culture, tourist information & other sections. See individual islands & page 43 for maps

Of the histories of the region, **James Ferguson**, *A Traveller's History of the Caribbean*, (1998), The Windrush Press. Concise and easy to dip in to. More academic is **J H Parry, P M Sherlock and Anthony Maingot**, *A Short History of The West Indies*, (1987) Macmillan. Very accessible. Also **Eric Williams**, *From Columbus to Castro: The History of the Caribbean 1492-1969*, (1970) Harper and Row.

History

Surfing the Caribbean

Nearly all the tourist offices have their own websites and are also linked to:
Caribbean Tourism Organization www.caribtourism.com

Each country has its own pages on the CTO website and it is a good place to start a general search for information.

The following is a list of general sites for each country, a combination of official tourist office and private sector sites:
Anguilla www.anguilla-vacation.com
http://net.ai
Antigua www.interknowledge.com/antigua-barbuda
Aruba www.aruba.com
Bahamas www.bahamas.com
www.bahama-out-islands.com
www.bahamasvg.com
Barbados www.barbados.org
Bonaire www.InfoBonaire.com
British Virgin Islands www.b-v-i.com
www.bviwelcome.com
www.ultimatebvi.com
www.britishvirginislands.com
Cayman Islands www.caymanislands.ky
Cuba www.dtcuba.com
Curaçao www.curacao-tourism.com
Dominica www.dominica.dm
Dominican Republic www.hispaniola.com
www.dominicana.com.do
www.domrep-hotels.com.do
Grenada www.grenada.org
www.travelgrenada.com
www.grenadines.net
Guadeloupe
www.antilles-info-tourism.com/guadeloupe
Haiti www.haititourisme.com

Jamaica www.jamaicatravel.com
www.jamaicans.com
Martinique http://martinique.org
Montserrat www.visitmontserrat.com
Puerto Rico www.prtourism.com
www.travelandsports.com
www.culebra.org
www.vieques-island.com
www.viequespr.net
Saba www.turq.com/saba
St-Barthélémy www.st.barths.com
www.saint-barths.com
St Kitts and Nevis www.stkitts-nevis.com
www.nevisweb.kn
www.nevis1.com
St Lucia www.stlucia.org
St-Martin www.st-martin.org
www.destination.st-martin.com
St Vincent and the Grenadines
http://stvincentandgrenadines.com
www.vincy.com
www.svgtourism.com
www.grenadines.net
Sint Eustatius www.turq.com/statia
Sint Maarten www.st-maarten.com
Trinidad and Tobago www.visittnt.com
Turks and Caicos Islands
www.turksandcaicostourism.com
www.tcimall.tc
US Virgin Islands www.usvi.net
Venezuelan Islands www.chevere.com
www.infoguia.net

Useful general websites and search engines for the Caribbean include:
www.caribbean-on-line.com
www.turq.com
www.caribseek.com
www.caribsurf.com

Geography   James Ferguson, *Far from Paradise, An Introduction to Caribbean Development*, (1990) Latin American Bureau. An introductory book. For an introduction to the geography of the Caribbean, **Mark Wilson**, *The Caribbean Environment*, (1989) Oxford University Press. Prepared for the Caribbean Examinations Council, a fascinating text book.

Field guides   The number of good books on Caribbean wildlife is slowly increasing. Look out for the following: P Bacon, *Flora and Fauna of the Caribbean*, Key Caribbean Publications, PO Box 21, Port of Spain, Trinidad. **J Bond**, *Birds of the West Indies*, Collins. **C C Chaplin**, *Fishwatchers Guide to West Atlantic Coral Reefs*, Horowood Books. Some printed on plastic paper for use underwater. I Greenberg, *Guide to Corals and Fishes of Florida, the Bahamas and the Caribbean*, Seahawk Press. **P Honeychurch**, *Caribbean Wild Plants and their Uses*, Macmillan. **Raffaele et al**, *A Guide to the Birds of the West Indies*, (1998) Princeton University Press. Thorough and rather heavy.

Macmillan also produce short field guides on *The Flowers of the Caribbean, The Fishes of the Caribbean, Fishes of the Caribbean Reefs, Marine Life of the Caribbean, Butterflies and Other Insects of the Caribbean*; and the *Ephemeral Isles, a Natural History of the Bahamas*.

A recent study of tourism in the Caribbean and its impact on the economies and people is **Economics** Polly Pattullo's, *Last Resort, The Cost of Tourism in the Caribbean*, (1996) Cassell and Latin American Bureau. An economic study is **Clive Y Thomas**, *The Poor and the Powerless, Economic Policy and Change in the Caribbean*, (1988) Latin American Bureau.

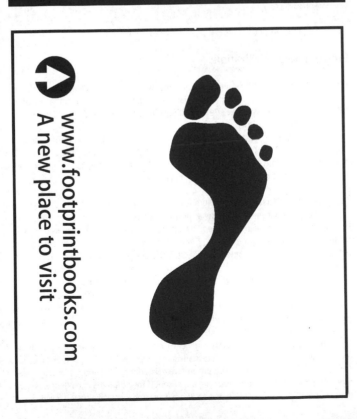

Literature   For an introduction to Caribbean writers and writers on the Caribbean, with extracts from numerous literary works, **James Ferguson**, *Traveller's Literary Companion to the Caribbean*, with chapters on Cuba and Puerto Rico by Jason Wilson, (1997) In Print. Highly recommended. The work of a great many English-speaking poets is collected in *The Penguin Book of Caribbean Verse in English*, edited by **Paula Burnett** (1986) see also *Hinterland: Caribbean Poetry From the West Indies and Britain*, edited by **E A Markham**— (1990) Bloodaxe, and *West Indian Poetry*, edited by **Kenneth Ramchand and Cecil Gray** (1989) Longman Caribbean. For a French verse anthology, see *La Poésie Antillaise*, collected by **Maryse Condé** (1977) Fernand Nathan. There are a number of prose anthologies of stories in English, eg *The Oxford Book of Caribbean Short Stories*, **Stewart Brown and John Wickham** (1999), *Stories from the Caribbean*, introduced by **Andrew Salkey** (1972) Paul Elek, or *West Indian Narrative: an Introductory Anthology*, **Kenneth Ramchand** (1966) Nelson. Heinemann's Caribbean Writers series publishes works of fiction by well-established and new writers. The *Story of English*, by **Robert McCrumb**, **William Cran** and **Robert MacNeil** (1986) Faber and Faber/BBC, has an interesting section on the development of the English language in the Caribbean.

Caribbean Insight, published weekly by the Caribbean Council for Europe (Suite 18, Westminster Palace Gardens, 1-7 Artillery Row, London SW1P 1RR, T020-77991521, insight@caribbean-council.com) is an informative online newsletter covering the entire region. Finally, a generally excellent series of Caribbean books is published by Macmillan Caribbean; this includes island guides, natural histories, books on food and drink, sports and pirates, and wall maps (for a full catalogue, write to Macmillan Caribbean, Houndmills, Basingstoke, Hampshire, RG21 2XS, England). An excellent source of maps is *Stanfords* at 12-14 Long Acre, London WC2, T020-78361321, F020-78360189, www.standfords.co.uk

Background

Pre-columbian civilizations

Today's visitors to the Caribbean find an arc of islands whose culture has been determined by its immigrants: colonists, slaves, indentured labourers, from Europe, Africa and the East. It is easy to forget that there was a well developed Amerindian society which was obliterated by Europeans in the 16th century.

The recorded history of the Caribbean islands begins with the arrival of Christopher Columbus' fleet in 1492. Our knowledge of the native peoples who inhabited the islands before and at the time of his arrival is largely derived from the accounts of contemporary Spanish writers and from archaeological examinations.

Tribes   The Amerindians encountered by Columbus in the Greater Antilles had no overall tribal name but organized themselves in a series of villages or local chief doms, each of which had its own tribal name. The name now used, 'Arawak', was not in use then. The term was used by the Indians of the Guianas, a group of whom had spread into Trinidad, but their territory was not explored until nearly another century later. The use of the generic term 'Arawak' to describe the Indians Columbus encountered, arose because of linguistic similarities with the Arawaks of the mainland. It is therefore surmised that migration took place many centuries before Columbus' arrival, but that the two groups were not in contact at that time. The time of the latest migration from the mainland, and consequently the existence of the island Arawaks, is in dispute, with some academics tracing it to about the time of Christ (the arrival of the Saladoids) and others to 1000 AD (the Ostionoids).

The inhabitants of the Bahamas were generally referred to as Lucayans, and those of the Greater Antilles as Tainos, but there were many sub-groupings. The inhabitants of the Lesser Antilles were, however, referred to as Carib and were described to Columbus as an aggressive tribe which sacrificed and sometimes ate the prisoners they captured in battle. It was from them that the Caribbean gets its name and from which the word cannibal is derived.

The earliest known inhabitants of the region, the 'Siboneys', migrated from Florida (some say Mexico) and spread throughout the Bahamas and the major islands. Most archaeological evidence of their settlements has been found near the shore, along bays or streams, where they lived in small groups. The largest discovered settlement has been one of 100 inhabitants in Cuba. They were hunters and gatherers, living on fish and other seafood, small rodents, iguanas, snakes and birds. They gathered roots and wild fruits, such as guava, guanabana and mamey, but did not cultivate plants. They worked with primitive tools made out of stone, shell, bone or wood, for hammering, chipping or scraping, but had no knowledge of pottery. The Siboneys were eventually absorbed by the advance of the Arawaks migrating from the south, who had made more technological advances in agriculture, arts and crafts.

The people now known as Arawaks migrated from the Guianas to Trinidad and on through the island arc to Cuba. Their population expanded because of the natural fertility of the islands and the abundance of fruit and seafood, helped by their agricultural skills in cultivating and improving wild plants and their excellent boat-building and fishing techniques. They were healthy, tall, good looking and lived to a ripe old age. It is estimated that up to eight million may have lived on the island of Hispaniola alone, but there was always plenty of food for all.

Society

Their society was essentially communal and organized around families. The smaller islands were particularly egalitarian, but in the larger ones, where village communities of extended families numbered up to 500 people, there was an incipient class structure. Typically, each village had a headman, called a 'cacique', whose duty it was to represent the village when dealing with other tribes, to settle family disputes and organize defence. However, he had no powers of coercion and was often little more than a nominal head. The position was largely hereditary, with the eldest son of the eldest sister having rights of succession, but women could and did become caciques. In the larger communities, there was some delegation of responsibility to the senior men, but economic activities were usually organized along family lines, and their power was limited.

The division of labour was usually based on age and sex. The men would clear and prepare the land for agriculture and be responsible for defence of the village, while women cultivated the crops and were the major food producers, also making items such as mats, baskets, bowls and fishing nets. Women were in charge of raising the children, especially the girls, while the men taught the boys traditional customs, skills and rites.

Food & farming

The Tainos hunted for some of their food, but fishing was more important and most of their settlements were close to the sea. Fish and shellfish were their main sources of protein and they had many different ways of catching them – from hands, baskets or nets to poisoning, shooting or line fishing. Cassava was a staple food, which they had successfully learned to leach of its poisonous juice. They also grew yams, maize, cotton, arrowroot, peanuts, beans, cocoa and spices, rotating their crops to prevent soil erosion. It is documented that in Jamaica they had three harvests of maize annually, using maize and cassava to make bread, cakes and beer.

Cotton was used to make clothing and hammocks (never before seen by Europeans), while the calabash tree was used to make ropes and cords, baskets and roofing. Plants were used for medicinal and spiritual purposes, and cosmetics such as face and body paint. Also important, both to the Arawaks and later to the Europeans, was the cultivation of tobacco, as a drug and as a means of exchange.

Arts & crafts

They had no writing, no beasts of burden, no wheeled vehicles and no hard metals, although they did have some alluvial gold for personal ornament. The abundance of food allowed them time to develop their arts and crafts and they were skilled in woodwork and pottery. They had polished stone tools, but also carved shell implements for manioc preparation or as fish hooks. Coral manioc graters have also been found. Their boatbuilding techniques were noted by Columbus, who marvelled at their canoes of up to 75 ft in length, carrying up to 50 people, made of a single tree trunk in one piece. It took two months to fell a tree by gradually burning and chipping it down, and many more to make the canoe.

Religion The Arawaks had three main deities, evidence of which have been found in stone and conch carvings in many of the Lesser Antilles as well as the well populated Greater Antilles, although their relative importance varied according to the island. The principal male god was Yocahú, yoca being the word for cassava and hú meaning 'giver of'. It is believed that the Indians associated this deity's power to provide cassava with the mystery of the volcanoes, for all the carvings, the earliest out of shells and the later ones of stone, are conical. The Yocahú cult was wiped out in the Lesser Antilles by the invading Caribs, and in the Greater Antilles by the Spaniards, but it is thought to have existed from about 200AD.

The main female deity was a fertility goddess, often referred to as 'Atabeyra', but she is thought to have had several names relating to her other roles as goddess of the moon, mother of the sea, the tides and the springs, and the goddess of childbirth. In carvings she is usually depicted as a squatting figure with her hands up to her chin, sometimes in the act of giving birth.

A third deity is a dog god, named Opiyel-Guaobiran, meaning 'the dog deity who takes care of the souls of the immediately deceased and is the son of the spirit of darkness'. Again, carvings of a dog's head or whole body have been found of shell or stone, which were often used to induce narcotic trances. Many of the carvings have holes and Y-shaped passages which would have been put to the nose to snuff narcotics and induce a religious trance in the shaman or priest, who could then ascertain the status of a departed soul for a recently bereaved relative.

Sport One custom which aroused interest in the Spaniards was the ball game, not only for the sport and its ceremonial features, but because the ball was made of rubber and bounced, a phenomenon which had not previously been seen in Europe. Catholicism soon eradicated the game, but archaeological remains have been found in several islands, notably in Puerto Rico, but also in Hispaniola. Excavations in the Greater Antilles have revealed earth embankments and rows of elongated upright stones surrounding plazas or courts, pavements and stone balls. These are called *bateyes, juegos de indios, juegos de bola, cercados* or *corrales de indios*. Batey was the aboriginal name for the ball game, the rubber ball itself and also the court where it was played. The word is still used to designate the cleared area in front of houses in the country.

The ball game had religious and ceremonial significance but it was a sport and bets and wagers were important. It was played by two teams of up to 20 or 30 players, who had to keep the ball in the air by means of their hips, shoulders, heads, elbows and other parts of their body, but never with their hands. The aim was to bounce the ball in this manner to the opposing team until it hit the ground. Men and women played, but not usually in mixed sex games. Great athleticism was required and it is clear that the players practised hard to perfect their skill, several, smaller practice courts having been built in larger settlements. The game was sometimes played before the village made an important decision, and the prize could be a sacrificial victim, usually a prisoner, granted to the victor.

Invaders In 1492 Arawaks inhabited all the greater islands of the Caribbean, but in Puerto Rico they were being invaded by the Caribs who had pushed north through the Lesser Antilles, stealing their women and enslaving or killing the men. The Caribs had also originated in South America, from around the Orinoco delta. In their migration north through the Caribbean islands they proved to be fierce warriors and their raids on the Arawak settlements were feared. Many of their women were captured Arawaks, and it was they who cultivated the land and performed the domestic chores. Polygamy was common, encouraged by the surplus of women resulting from the raids, and the Arawak female influence on Carib culture was strong.

Despite rumours of cannibalism reported to Columbus by frightened Arawaks, there appears to be no direct evidence of the practice, although the Spaniards took it seriously enough to use it as an excuse to justify taking slaves. After some unfortunate encounters, colonizers left the Caribs alone for many years. The Arawaks, on the other hand, were soon wiped out by disease, cruelty and murder. The Spanish invaders exacted tribute and forced labour while allowing their herds of cattle and pigs to destroy the Indians' unfenced fields and clearings. Transportation to the mines resulted in shifts in the native population which could not be fed from the surrounding areas and starvation became common. Lack of labour in the Greater Antilles led to slave raids on the Lucayans in the Bahamas, but they also died or committed collective suicide. They felt that their gods had deserted them and there was nowhere for them to retreat or escape. Today there are no full-blooded Arawaks and only some 2,000 Caribs are left on Dominica (there has been no continuity of Carib language or religious belief on Dominica). The 500 years since Columbus' arrival have served to obliterate practically all the evidence of the indigenous civilization.

Flora and fauna

For many travellers, a trip to the Caribbean offers a first glimpse of the tropics, complete with luxuriant vegetation and exotic wildlife. Images of untouched beaches and rainforest form a major selling point of many travel brochures. In fact there is very little 'untouched' wilderness left and what visitors see is an environment that has been affected by the activities of man. Forestry, agriculture, fisheries and increasingly tourism have all helped to mould the modern landscape and natural heritage of the Caribbean. However, there is still much of interest to see, and it is true to say that small islands can combine a variety of habitats within a limited area. On many islands, it is possible to move between the coastal reefs and beaches through thorn scrub and plantation into rainforest within a matter of miles. Increasingly, the complexity and fragility of island ecosystems is being appreciated and fortunately most countries have recognized the value of balancing development and the protection of the natural environment and have begun to develop national parks and protected areas programmes. Many islands also have active conservation societies or national wildlife trusts (see page 54).

Over long periods of time, islands tend to develop their own unique flora and fauna. These endemic species add to the interest of wildlife and natural history tours. The St Lucia parrot and Dominica's sisserou have become a regular part of the tour circuit of these islands, and have undoubtedly benefited from the interest that tourists have shown in their plight. Details of National Parks and wildlife are included under the specific island chapter headings (Fauna and Flora). This section provides a broad overview of the range of animals, plants and habitats that are to be found in the region.

Mammals Mammals are not particularly good colonizers of small islands and this has resulted in a general scarcity of species in the Caribbean. Many of the more commonly seen species (mongoose, agouti, opossum, and some of the monkeys) were introduced by man. Bats are the one exception to this rule and most islands have several native species. Mongoose were introduced to many islands to control snakes, they have also preyed on many birds, reptiles and other animals and have had a devastating effect on native fauna.

Of the monkeys, the green monkeys of Barbados, Grenada and St Kitts and Nevis were introduced from West Africa in the 17th century. Similarly, rhesus monkeys have been introduced to Desecheo Island off Puerto Rico. The red howler monkeys on Trinidad are native to the island as are several other mammals including the brocket deer, squirrel and armadillo. These species have managed to colonize from nearby Venezuela.

Sailors may encounter marine mammals including dolphin, porpoise and whales. Between November and December hump back whales migrate through the Turks and Caicos Passage on their way to the Silver Banks breeding grounds off the Dominican Republic. The ungainly manatee, or sea cow, can still be seen in some coastal areas in the Greater Antilles (especially Jamaica, Cuba – Zapata Peninsula – and Puerto Rico) although it is becoming increasingly uncommon.

Birds It is the birds perhaps more than any other group of animals that excite the most interest from visitors to the region. Many islands have their own endemic species such as the Grenada dove, yellow-billed parrot and 24 other species in Jamaica and Guadeloupe woodpecker. The islands also act as important stepping stones in the migration of many birds through the Americas. As a result, the region is highly regarded by ornithologists and there are several important nature reserves.

Essentials

 Disasters

*If you live in the Caribbean you become accustomed to insurance companies taking a dim view of your prospects for a safe and untroubled life. **Hurricanes** are the most frequent sources of disaster, not only for the winds which can uproot trees, rip roofs from buildings and tear down power lines and telephone cables, but also for the rain, which often brings flooding and mudslides. Every year hurricanes rip through a selection of islands causing material damage to a greater or lesser degree. Although early warning systems have succeeded in cutting deaths to a minimum, damage to housing and infrastructure is usually costly. Some of the worst in recent years include Gilbert (8-20 Sep 1988), one of the strongest ever which tore through Jamaica, Hugo (10-25 Sep 1989), which damaged Montserrat (95% of houses were ruined), Puerto Rico and the Virgin Islands with winds of 140mph, and Andrew, (16-28 Aug 1992), which charged through the Bahamas before hitting the USA, causing damage of over US$25 billion. In 1994, Tropical Storm Debbie dumped 26 inches of rain in seven hours on St Lucia, causing flooding and mudslides which wiped out much of the banana crop, while at the same time Guadeloupe was declared a disaster area because of drought. In 1995, two hurricanes in quick succession, Luis and Marilyn, wreaked havoc in the Leeward Islands, while in November 1999, Lenny took everyone by surprise by attacking from the Caribbean rather than the Atlantic, bringing strong winds and flooding and taking away normally protected beaches and buildings. Hurricanes, however, are not the only problem. Since records began with colonization, earthquakes and volcanoes have also produced massive disasters in the region.*

*2002, the year of this edition of the Caribbean Islands Handbook, marks the centenary of major eruptions of the **volcanoes** in St Vincent and in Martinique. On 6 May 1902, the Soufrière on St Vincent erupted, killing nearly 2,000 people and ruining farming in the area (see page 847). Activity continued until the end of March the following year, when the volcano returned to its slumbers. It awakened again in 1979, but the dangers were taken seriously and action was taken to prevent loss of life. Far worse than the St Vincent explosion was the*

Trinidad and Tobago demonstrate the influence of the nearby South American mainland. While they have no endemic species they still support at least 433 species and the Asa Wright Centre is regarded as one of the premier bird watching sites in the world. At the other end of the Caribbean, Inagua (Bahamas) is the site of the world's largest flamingo colony at Lake Windsor. There is also an important flamingo colony on Bonaire in the southern Caribbean.

Many of the endemic species have become rare as a result of man's activities. Habitat destruction, introduction of new species (especially the mongoose) and hunting for food and the international pet trade have all had an effect. Parrots in particular have suffered as a result of these activities. Fortunately, measures are now being undertaken to protect the birds and their habitats on many islands (eg Bahamas, Jamaica, Dominica, Puerto Rico and St Lucia).

Reptiles   Lizards and geckos are common on virtually all the islands in the region and may even be seen on very small offshore islets. There are also a number of species of snakes, iguanas and turtles scattered throughout the region. Many are restricted to one island and Jamaica has at least 27 island endemics including several species of galliwasp. The vast majority of reptiles found in the region are completely harmless to man although there are strong superstitions about the geckos (*mabouya*) and of course the snakes. For example, the skin and fat of boa constrictors (*tête chien*) are used for bush remedies on some of the Windward Islands.

The fer de lance snake (St Lucia, Martinique and also South America), deserves to be treated with extreme caution; although the bite is not usually lethal, hospitalization is required. It is found in isolated areas of dry scrubland and river valley. The best protection is to wear long trousers and stout boots and to avoid walking in these areas at night. Local advice should be sought if in doubt.

Iguanas are still found on many islands although they have declined as a result of hunting throughout the region. Although of fearsome appearance, they are herbivorous and spend eruption on Martinique when Mt Pelée burst into life on 8 May 1902 (see page 741). The pyroclastic flow swallowed up the chic and cultured city of St-Pierre, killing nearly 30,000 and leaving only one survivor, an inmate in the prison cells. More recently, the Soufrière Hills volcano in Montserrat began erupting in July 1995 and within two years the southern part of the island was covered in ash and lava and uninhabitable (see box, page 654). On 25 June 1997 the worst explosion yet trapped people who had returned to their homes and land to tend their crops and animals, killing 20. Although the volcano is still being monitored closely, activity has lessened and it seems to be starting to slumber again. The chain of dormant or active volcanoes runs down the eastern Caribbean all the way from Mt Liamuiga in St Kitts to the mud volcanoes of Trinidad. The volcano in the region which has erupted most frequently has in fact done the least damage. Kick 'em Jenny is an underwater volcano found in 1939, 8km north of Grenada. Since that date it is known to have erupted eleven times, and who knows how many times before then.

The islands are in a seismically active area and have had a number of nasty **earthquakes**. According to some, the 'sinful' town of Port Royal in Jamaica, known for its pirates and prostitutes, got its just rewards on 7 June 1692 when it was hit by an earthquake which destroyed 90% of the town. Some 5,000 inhabitants were killed as the town slid into the sea, or perished in a subsequent fever epidemic (see page 291). Jamaica has had several earthquakes, one of which was in our centenary year of 1902, but most recently in 1993, when 5.3 on the Richter scale was recorded. In 1843 a massive earthquake struck the eastern Caribbean, affecting islands all down the chain from St Kitts to Dominica. The disaster was worst in Guadeloupe, where 5,000 people were killed and most buildings collapsed in Point-à-Pitre, but there were also 30 dead in Antigua, where much of English Harbour sank, and a handful of deaths on Montserrat and Dominica. The most recent earthquakes to have caused material damage to housing and other buildings were felt in the southern Caribbean, particularly Trinidad and Tobago, in April and July 1997.

much of their time in trees and low scrub feeding on leaves and trying to avoid man.

Marine turtles including the loggerhead, leatherback, hawksbill and green turtles are found throughout Caribbean waters and on the coasts of the Guianas and they may occasionally be seen by divers and snorkellers. Females come ashore on isolated sandy beaches between the months of May and August to lay eggs. There may be opportunities for assisting natural history and wildlife societies (St Lucia Naturalists Society, Fish and Wildlife Dept in the US Virgin Islands) in their turtle watches, to record numbers and locations of nests and to protect the turtles from poachers. There is a large commercial breeding programme for green turtles in the Cayman Islands. Freshwater turtles are also found on some islands including Jamaica and Cat Island (Bahamas). Caiman have been introduced to Puerto Rico and are also found on Cuba and the Dominican Republic.

Many species of reptile are now protected in the region (especially the marine turtles and iguana) and reserves have been specifically established to protect them. For example, the Maria Islands Nature Reserve on St Lucia is home to the St Lucia ground lizard and grass snake. The latter is possibly the rarest snake in the world with an estimated population of 150 individuals.

Frogs and toads are common in a variety of shapes and colours. There are generally more **Amphibians** species on the larger islands (Greater Antilles and Trinidad; there are also many in the Guianas). The Cuban pygmy frog is described as the world's smallest frog, while at the other end of the scale, the mountain chicken of Dominica and Montserrat is probably the largest frog in the region. Its name relates to its supposed flavour. The call of the piping frogs (eleutherodactylus spp) is often mistaken for a bird and these small animals are common throughout the Lesser Antilles, becoming especially vocal at night and after rain. The largest and most visible amphibian is probably the marine toad which has been introduced to islands throughout the region in an attempt to control insects and other invertebrate pests. The male toads use flat exposed areas from which to display, often roads. Unfortunately, they have not evolved to deal with the car yet and as a result many are killed.

Invertebrates This group includes the insects, molluscs, spiders and a host of other animals that have no backbones. For first time travellers to the tropics, the huge range of invertebrates can seem daunting and it is estimated that there are at least 290 species of butterfly in the Caribbean. No one knows how many species of beetles, bugs or mollusc there are.

Of the butterflies, the swallowtails are perhaps the most spectacular, with several species being found in the Greater Antilles (especially Cuba). However the other islands also have large colourful butterflies including the monarch and flambeau which are present throughout the region. Another insect of note is the hercules beetle, reportedly the world's second largest beetle with a large horn that protrudes from its thorax, occasionally found in rainforest in the Lesser Antilles.

Land and freshwater crabs inhabit a range of environments from the rainforest (eg bromeliad crab from Jamaica) to the dry coastal areas (many species of hermit crab). Tarantula spiders are also fairly common, although they are nocturnal and rarely seen. Their bite is painful but, in most of the species found in the region, no worse than a bee sting. Of far more concern are the large centipedes (up to 15cm long) that can inflict a nasty and painful bite with their pincers. They are mostly restricted to the dry coastal areas and are most active at night. Black widow spiders are also present on some of the islands in the Greater Antilles. Fortunately they are rarely encountered by the traveller.

Environments

Beaches, coral reef, sea cliffs A diving or snorkelling trip over a tropical reef allows a first hand experience of this habitat's diversity of wildlife. There are a number of good field guides to reef fish and animals and some are even printed on waterproof paper. Alternatively, glass bottomed boats sail over some sites (Buccoo Reef, Tobago), and there are underwater trails which identify types of corals and marine habitats.

Amongst the commonest fish are the grunts, butterfly, soldier, squirrel and angel fish. Tiny damsel fish are very territorial and may even attempt to nip swimmers who venture too close to their territories (more surprising than painful).

There are over fifty species of hard coral (the form that builds reefs) with a variety of sizes and colours. Amongst the most dramatic are the stagshorn and elkhorn corals which are found on the more exposed outer reefs. Brain coral forms massive round structures up to 2 m high and pillar coral forms columns that may also reach 2 m in height. Soft corals, which include black corals, sea fans and gorgonians, colonize the surface of the hard coral adding colour and variety. Associated with these structures is a host of animals and plants. Spiny lobsters may be seen lurking in holes and crevices along with other crustaceans and reef fish. The patches of sand between outcrops of coral provide suitable habitat for conch and other shellfish. Some islands now restrict the collection and sale of corals (especially black corals) and there are also legal restrictions on the sale of black corals under CITES. Overfishing has affected conch and lobster in places and there are reports of them being taken from the sea too small.

The delights of swimming on a coral reef need to be tempered by a few words of caution. Many people assume the water will be seething with sharks, however these animals are fairly uncommon in nearshore waters and the species most likely to be encountered is the nurse shark, which is harmless unless provoked or cornered. Other fish to keep an eye open for include the scorpion fish with its poisonous dorsal spines; it frequently lies stationary on coral reefs onto which the incautious can blunder. Finally moray eels may be encountered, a fearsome looking fish, but harmless unless provoked at which point they can inflict serious bites. Of far more concern should be the variety of stinging invertebrates that are found on coral reefs. The most obvious is fire coral which comes in a range of shapes and sizes but is recognizable by the white tips to its branches. In addition, many corals have sharp edges and branches that can graze and cut. Another common group of stinging invertebrates are the fire worms which have white bristles along the sides of their bodies. As with the fire coral, these can inflict a painful sting if handled or brushed against. Large black sea urchins are also common on some reefs and their spines can penetrate unprotected skin very easily. The best advice when observing coral reefs and their wildlife is to look, not touch.

Other coastal habitats that may have interesting wildlife include beaches and sea cliffs. Some islands, especially those in the southern part of the Caribbean, have spectacular cliffs and offshore islets. These are home to large flocks of sea birds including the piratical frigate bird which chases smaller birds, forcing them to disgorge their catch; another notable species is the tropic bird with its streamer like tail feathers. The cliffs may also provide dry sandy soils for the large range of Caribbean cacti, including prickly pear (*opuntia sp*) and the Turks head cactus.

Wetlands include a wide range of fresh and brackish water habitats such as rivers, marsh and mangroves. They are important for many species of bird, as well as fish. Unfortunately they are also home to an array of biting insects, including mosquitos which are unpleasant and a serious problem where malaria or dengue are present. **Rivers, swamps, mangroves**

Important coastal wetlands include the Baie de Fort de France (Martinique), the Cabrits Swamp (Dominica), Caroni and Nariva Swamps (Trinidad), Negril and Black Morass (Jamaica). These sites all support large flocks of migratory and resident birds including waders, herons, egrets and ducks. In addition, some of the mangroves in the Greater Antilles also provide habitats for manatee, and the Negril and Black Morass has a population of American crocodiles. Large freshwater lakes are less common although Grenada, Dominica and St Vincent all have volcanic crater lakes and these are used by migratory waders and ducks as well as kingfishers.

There is little if any primary rainforest left in the Caribbean Islands, although there may be small patches in Guadeloupe. Nevertheless, many of the islands still have large areas of good secondary forest which has only suffered from a limited amount of selective felling for commercially valuable wood (eg gommier, balata and blue mahoe). **Thorn scrub, plantations, rainforest**

Martinique has some of the largest tracts of forest left in the Caribbean (eg rainforest at Piton du Carbet, cloud forest on Mt Pelée, dry woodland in the south). Many other islands also have accessible forest, although you should always use a local guide if venturing off the beaten track.

The Caribbean rainforests are not as diverse as those on the South and Central American mainland, however they still support a very large number of plant species many of which are endemic (Jamaica has over 3,000 species of which 800 are endemic). The orchids and bromeliads are particularly impressive in many forests and it is not unusual to see trees festooned with both these groups. The wildlife of the rainforest includes both native and introduced species, although they are often difficult to see in the rather shady conditions. Agouti, boa constrictor, monkeys and opossum may be seen, but it is the bird life that is most evident. Hummingbirds, vireos, thrashers, todies and others are all found along with parrots, which are perhaps the group most associated with this habitat. Early morning and evening provide the best times for birdwatching.

Plantations of commercial timber (blue mahoe, Caribbean pine, teak, mahogany and others) have been established in many places. These reduce pressure on natural forest and help protect watersheds and soil. They are also valuable for wildlife and some species have adapted to them with alacrity.

Closer to the coasts, dry scrub woodland often predominates. The trees may lose their leaves during the dry season. One of the most recognizable of the trees in this woodland is the turpentine tree, also known as the tourist tree because of its red peeling bark! Bush medicines and herbal remedies are still used in the countryside although less so than previously. Leaves and bark can be seen for sale in markets.

Whale and dolphin watching

Whale and dolphin watching, long popular around North America, is starting to take off in the Caribbean too. There are three main attractions. The **humpback** whales, the acrobatic whale-watchers' favourite, who come to the Caribbean during the winter to mate, raise their calves and sing. The **sperm** whales are resident in various spots around the Caribbean but are easiest to see along the west coast of Dominica. Spotted and other **dolphin** species travel in large herds and are resident around many of the reefs, mangrove forests and offshore fishing banks. It is possible to see whales and dolphins from land and on some regular ferries, and even on air flights between the islands, but the best way to encounter them close-up is on boat tours. Some of these are general marine nature or even birding tours that include whales and dolphins. Others are specialized tours offered by diving, sportfishing or new eco-tourism ventures. Following is a guide to the best of whale and dolphin watching in the waters covered by this book.

Bahamas Tours to meet and sometimes swim with Atlantic spotted and bottlenose dolphins are offered mainly May to September, though some are almost year round. The tours leave either from East Florida ports, North Bimini, or from West End, on Grand Bahama Island. Cost starts at about US$1,500 for a week on the 62 ft catamaran *Stenella* and various other boats. Some trips last 10 days. Tour operators include *Wild Dolphin Project*, PO Box 8436, Jupiter, FL 33468 USA, T407-5755660 or *Oceanic Society Expeditions*, Fort Mason Center, Building E, San Francisco, CA 94123 USA, T415-4411106. Others include: *Windward Adventures*, PO Box 1713, Dania, FL 33004-1713, USA T/F954-9222351; *Dream Team*, PO Box 12714, Lake Park, FL 33403, USA, T888-2778181, F561-8407946; *Calusa Coast Outfitters Educational Tours*, PO Box 55, Fort Myers Beach, FL33932 T941-4185941, F941-9481991, www.calusacoast.com; *Sea Fever Diving Cruises Inc*, PO Box 39-8276, Miami Beach, FL 33239, T305-8613603, F305-8613625, www.seafever.com; *Discover the World Ltd*, 29 Nork Way, Banstead, Surrey SM7 1PB, UK, T01737-218800, 016977-48361/56, F01737-362341; *Wild Oceans/Wild Wings*, International House, Bank Road, Kingswood, Bristol BS15 8LX, UK, T0117-9848040, F0117-9610200. Various excellent wildlife and dolphin tours, led by scientist Diane Claridge, are offered on Abaco by *Bahamas Naturalist Expeditions* (BNE), Marsh Harbour, Great Abaco, Bahamas, T242-3674505. Extended whale-watching trips with researchers and a chance to help on whale surveys to determine the abundance and distribution of large whales in the Bahamas are offered by *Earthwatch*, 680 Mount Auburn Street, PO Box 403, Watertown, MA 02272 USA, T617-9268200.

Turks & Caicos Islands Humpbacks can be found offshore late January-early April with bottlenose and other dolphins sometimes seen close to shore. Contact *Blue Water Divers*, Grand Turk, T649-9462432; *Sea Eye Diving*, T649-9461407, F649-9461408; *Oasis Divers*, T/F649-9461128, www.oasisdivers.com

Puerto Rico Humpback whales and dolphins can be seen from land and occasional tours, particularly out of Rincón on the west coast of the island. Best lookouts are Aguadilla and from an old lighthouse near Punta Higuera, outside Rincón.

Dominican Republic The most popular and well-established whale watching in the Caribbean is found here. The industry is centred on humpback whales, but pilot whales and spotted dolphins can also be seen in Samaná Bay, and bottlenose, spinner, and spotted dolphins, Bryde's and other whales on Silver Bank. The season for both locales is January through March with whale watching tours in Samaná Bay 15 January-15 March. In recent years, more than 32,000 people a year have gone whale watching in the 20,000 sq km marine sanctuary, most of them to Samaná Bay where the trips last two to four hours. The trips to Silver Bank are more educational and are usually arranged by specialist groups. In Samaná Bay, *Whale Samaná* is the oldest tour operator in the region and highly rated. There are about 40 registered boats; some specialize in speed, some in mass tourism and some in education and information. You will get a better view of the whales from a big boat, the smaller ones can get dwarfed by the waves. For more information there is a general Samaná website, www. samana.org.do The national parks whale watch co-ordinator in Samaná can be contacted at T809-5382042, dnpballenas@yahoo,com Contact: Kim Beddall, *Whale Samaná*, Victoria Marine, PO Box 53-2, Samaná, Dominican Republic, T/F809-5382494, Kim.Beddall@usa.net Miguel Bezi, another operator, has five boats of different sizes. Contact: *Transporte Marítimo Minadiel*, Samaná Bay, Dominican Republic, T809-5382556, F5382098. For tours to see humpbacks on Silver Bank, some 50 miles (33 km) north of Puerto Plata, contact: *Oceanic Society Expeditions*, Fort Mason Center, Bldg E, San Francisco, CA 94123-1394 USA,

T415-4411106, F415-4743395, www.oceanic-society.org; *Wild Oceans*, International House, Bank Road, Kingswood, Bristol BS15 8LX, England, T0117-9848040, F0117-9610200, www. wildwings.co.uk; and *Bottom Time Adventures*, PO Box 11919, Ft Lauderdale, FL 33339-1919, USA, T831-8840122, F8840125.

For whale watching from land from January to March, but especially in February, try Cabo Francés Viejo, east along the coast from Puerto Plata, near Cabrera, as well as Punta Balandra light and Cabo Samaná (near Samaná). At Cueva de Agua there is a volunteer land-based whale watching project.

US Virgin Islands and **British Virgin Islands** They have periodic trips to see the 60-100 humpback whales that winter north of the islands. There are also spinner and other dolphins to be seen. The season is January through March. For a full-day catamaran sail contact Grethelyn Piper, *Environmental Association of St Thomas and St John* (EAST), PO Box 12379, St Thomas, USVI 00801, T340-7761976. In the BVI, humpback whale listening tours are offered from 30 December to 15 April on a 13-ft motor cruiser or a 30-ft sloop close to shore. The whales are rarely seen and never close-up, but their sounds fill the boat. Excellent tapes and CDs of whale songs are also sold. Departure is from Brewers Bay Campground, Tortola. Contact: Paul Knapp, Jr, PO Box 185, Road Town, Tortola, British Virgin Islands, T284-4943463.

St Kitts-Nevis From the island of Nevis, trips to see bottlenose dolphins and sometimes humpback whales can be arranged through dive boat operator Ellis Chaderton. Contact: *Scuba Safaris Ltd*, Qualie Beach, Nevis, T869-469 9518, F869-4699619.

Guadeloupe There are year-round half-day tours to see sperm and pilot whales and spotted dolphins offered by Caroline and Renato Rinaldi of *Association Evasion Tropicale*. Naturalists on board talk to passengers and collect scientific data. The whale watch runs from the dive centre Les Heures Saines in Malendure, about 4 km north of Bouillant on Basse-Terre. Contact: *Evasion Tropicale*, Courbaril, 971125 Bouillante, Guadeloupe, T590-571944, or *Les Heures Saines*, Rocher de Malendure, 97132 Pigeon, Guadeloupe, T590-988663, F590-987776.

Dominica Eight to 12 resident sperm whales delight visitors almost year-round. You can also see spinner and spotted dolphins, pilot whales, false killer whales, and pygmy sperm whales. Occasional sightings are made of bottlenose, Risso's and Fraser's dolphins, orcas, dwarf sperm whales and melon-headed whales. The tours are run out of the *Anchorage Hotel*. Hydrophones are used to find and listen to the whales. The tours are three to four hours. *Anchorage Hotel & Dive Centre*, PO Box 34, Roseau, Dominica, T 767-4482638, F767-4485680. Tours are also offered by a well-equipped diving operator, Derek Perryman, next to the *Anchorage* at the *Castle Comfort Lodge* near Roseau. *Dive Dominica Ltd*, PO Box 2253, Roseau, Dominica, T767-4482188, F767-4486088. For land-based whale watching of sperm whales and others, Scotts Head, at the southwest tip of Dominica, overlooking Martinique Passage, is good most of the year.

St Lucia Sperm whales and various dolphins can be seen and on occasions humpback and pilot whales, Bryde's whales and orcas. The St Lucia Whale and Dolphin Watching Association is helping to organize and field enquiries for tours and to make sure that the whale watching is conducted with appropriate regulations. Contact *St Lucia Whale and Dolphin Watching Association*, c/o PO Box 1114, Castries, St Lucia, T758-452456, F758-452117, www.geocities.com/slwdwa The 60-ft *Free Willy* offers 3-hr morning trips all year round, but November to June is best when sperm whales and sometimes humpbacks are seen. Contact: *Captain Mike's Sport Fishing*, Pleasure Cruises and Whale Watching, PO Box GM617, Sunny Acres, St Lucia, T758-4527044/4501216, F758-4524845, www.captmikes.com Trips can also be arranged through *The Soufriere Water Taxi Association*, Bay St, Soufriere, St Lucia, T758-4597239.

St Vincent Off the west coast, large herds of spinner and spotted dolphins are seen regularly. Sometimes bottlenose dolphins and pilot whales are also found and, sporadically, sperm and humpback whales. Tours go aboard the 36-ft sloop, *Sea Breeze*, or on a 28-ft power boat. Snorkelling and a trip to Baleine Falls can also be included. Almost year-round but avoid windy weather months of mid-December to mid-February. Best April to September when there is an 80% success rate. Trips depart from Calliaqua Lagoon on Indian Bay, southeast of Kingstown and Arnos Vale Airport. Cost for tours is US$30-40. Contact: Hal

Daize, *Sea Breeze Tours/Guesthouse*, Arnos Vale Post Office, St Vincent, T784-4584969.

Petit Nevis   Off Bequia, nine miles (15 km) south of St Vincent is the site of the old whaling station, once the hub of Caribbean whaling in this century. Access will require making arrangements locally.

Grenada   From St George's Marina, Mosden Cumberbatch offers year-round whale watching from his reliable 44 ft sloop or 19-ft power boat. He takes people off the south coast and to the Grenada Bank where humpbacks are often sighted from January through March, as well as up the coast to meet various dolphins and sometimes pilot whales, US$60 includes lunch and snorkelling. Contact: *First Impressions Ltd*, c/o Blue Lagoon Real Estate Corporation, PO Box 446, St George's, Grenada, T/F473-4403678.

Conservation   By watching whales and dolphins in the Caribbean, you can actually contribute to saving them. Many dolphins are still killed, mainly by fishermen, for food or fish bait. As well, pilot whales and even rare beaked whales are commonly harpooned, particularly in the eastern Caribbean. Almost every winter, over the past few years, two humpbacks have been killed off Bequia, nearly always a precious mother and calf. Mother and calf humpbacks have very high site fidelity on the mating and calving grounds and local whalers are effectively removing what could be a healthy whale watch industry. Whale and dolphin watching provides local people with another way to look at these intriguing animals – as well as a potentially more sustainable source of income.

Your support of whale watching may have the biggest impact in countries of the eastern Caribbean: Dominica, Grenada, St Lucia, and St Vincent and the Grenadines. Over the past few years, Japan has contributed to the development of these nations, by helping to build airports and adding fish docks and piers. In exchange, Japan has counted on the support of these four governments, all members of the International Whaling Commission (IWC), in its attempt to re-open commercial whaling. You can help conservation here by simply saying you enjoy seeing whales and dolphins in local waters. However, when referring to dolphins, use the word 'porpoises'. In most parts of the Caribbean, the word 'dolphin' means the dolphin fish. Best to specify that it is the mammal and not the fish that you want to see. And if you see whales and dolphins being killed at sea, express your views to local and national tourism outlets of the country concerned.

For more information contact the *Whale and Dolphin Conservation Society*, Alexander House, James Street West, Bath, BA1 2BT, UK, www.wdcs.org

The Bahamas

3

The Bahamas

Hundreds of flat, sandy islands, specks of green set in ever changing hues of aquamarine – these are the Bahamas. Cruise ships bring customers for casinos and shopping malls in Freeport and Nassau, but elsewhere the islands are quiet, often deserted, places to chill out. There are fabulous opportunities for all watersports in crystal clear water and hotels have a variety of water toys. Reefs and walls offer spectacular diving while the islands are world famous for bonefishing and deep sea fishing adventures, sailing, snorkelling and anything else you can think of. Formerly a haven for pirates, smugglers and bootleggers, the islands' proximity to the USA has shaped their development. The main tourist areas are Paradise Island and Cable Beach, on New Providence, and Freeport and Port Lucaya, on Grand Bahama, where huge resorts attract mass tourism. Most cruise ships come in to Nassau, the capital, on New Providence, and its main shopping street can be packed when several ships are in port. The other islands, known as the 'Family Islands', or 'Out Islands', are largely unspoilt and include Bimini, the Berry Islands, Abaco, Eleuthera (these two are particularly attractive), the Exumas, Andros, Cat Island, Long Island, San Salvador, Rum Cay, Inagua, Acklins and Crooked Island.

Essentials

Before you travel

Documents   All visitors to the Bahamas must have a **passport** valid for at least six months and a return ticket. US visitors may use a driver's licence instead of a passport. Visitors who stay for less than eight months should be in possession of a birth or naturalization certificate. Visitors from EU member countries and South Africa do not require a **visa** for stays of up to three months. Citizens of Russia, Czech Republic, Hungary, Poland, Ukraine and Slovakia may stay one month without a visa. Visas are not required by nationals of Commonwealth countries, South Korea, Israel and Japan (length of permitted stay varies between three and eight months), nor by most Latin American nationals if staying no longer than 14 days. Colombians without a US visa need a Bahamian visa. Nationals of Haiti and communist countries need a visa. You will need a certificate of vaccination against yellow fever if you are coming from an infected area. To enter the Bahamas for business purposes the permission of the Immigration Department, Nassau, must be obtained. Apply in writing to: Director of Immigration, Immigration Department, PO Box N3002, Nassau. No expatriate can be employed in a post for which a suitably qualified Bahamian is available, nor can a permit be considered if the prospective employee is in the country, having come in as a visitor.

Money   **Banks**   There are several hundred banks licensed to do banking or trust business in the Bahamas. Some of the largest commercial banks are *Royal Bank of Canada* at Nassau, the airport, Abaco, Andros (Fresh Creek), Bimini, Grand Bahama, Harbour Island, Long Island, Lyford Cay, and Spanish Wells; *Lloyds Bank* (Bahamas); *Barclays Bank Plc*, at Nassau, Grand Bahama, Eleuthera, Abaco; *Scotiabank*, at Nassau, Abaco, Grand Bahama, Exuma, Long Island; *Canadian Imperial Bank of Commerce* also at Nassau, Grand Bahama, Andros (Nicholl's Town), Abaco; *Bank of the Bahamas Ltd,* Nassau, Grand Bahama, Andros and Inagua; *Citibank*.

Currency   The unit of currency is the Bahamian Dollar (B$) which is at par with the US dollar. Both currencies are accepted everywhere. There is no restriction on foreign currency taken in or out; Bahamian currency may be exported up to B$70 per person. Notes of B$ 100, 50, 20, 10, 5, 3, 1 and 50c; coins of B$5, 2, 1, 50c, 25c, 15c, 10c, 5c and 1c.

Credit cards   All major credit cards are accepted on New Providence and Grand Bahama. Not all the hotels and restaurants on the Family Islands take credit cards, although most take American Express, Mastercard and Visa.

Climate   The sunshine and warm seas attract visitors throughout the year but winter, from December
Jun-Nov is the official   to April, is the high season. Temperatures are around 68°F. Summer temperatures average
hurricane season   86°F. Humidity is fairly high, particularly in the summer. The rainy season is May to October, when the showers are usually short but heavy. The weather can be pleasant in the winter season although cold fronts from the North American continent can bring strong north winds, heavy rain and surprisingly low temperatures. The summer months are hot, humid and often windless, with frequent thunderstorms. In August 1992 Hurricane Andrew hit the Bahamas, making over 1,200 homeless, killing four people and causing damage of over US$250 mn. North Eleuthera was badly damaged. In October 1996 Hurricane Lili destroyed houses and crops and cut power lines in Exuma, Long Island and other islands after passing over Cuba. In June 1997 unprecedented rainfall and a spring tide caused flooding in New Providence while a tornado struck Hope Town, damaging boats and power supplies. In August 1999 the islands were again hit, by Hurricane Floyd. Businesses soon get back to normal, however, and there is usually little evidence of storm damage by the time the tourist high season is in full swing.

Getting there

Most flights to the Bahamas originate in the USA, see Transport Air, pages 90 and 101 for details of airlines and flights to Nassau and Freeport. Connecting flights by *Bahamasair* go out from Nassau like spokes of a wheel to the Family Islands although many airlines now fly direct from Florida to the Family Islands.

There are several commuter airlines serving some of the **Family Islands** direct from airports in Florida including *Gulfstream International Airlines* (in Miami T305-8711200, F305-8713540), *Island Express* (T3673597, in USA 954-3590380, F954-3592752), *Walkers International* (T954-3591405, F954-3591414), *US Air Express* (T800-6221015), *Chalk's International* (T800-4242557), (Miami T305-3718628, Bimini T3473024, Nassau T3632845), *Air Sunshine* (T800-4358900), *Continental, American Eagle, Lynx Air* and *Pan Am Airbridge.* Also in Miami, *Bahamasair*, T305-5931910, 800-2224262. Tickets can be booked through computer systems but are normally purchased on the spot at the airport, routing and timing subject to last minute alteration depending on demand. For details of services to each island, see individual Ins and outs sections. *LB Limited* (T3523389) has charter flights to Freeport from Florida with some flights timed so that gamblers can do a day-trip to the casino. Other charter airlines including *Cleare Air* (T3770341, F3770342), *Congo Air* (T3778329, F3777413, Fort Lauderdale T305-4565611, F305-9850855) and *Island Air Charters* (T305-3599942, 800-4449904). Private pilots should ask the tourist office for the Air Navigation Chart or contact the Private Pilot Briefing Centre, T800-3277678 in the USA.

Ports of entry (Own flag) **Abaco**: Walker's Cay, Green Turtle Cay, Marsh Harbour, Sandy Point. **Andros**: Morgan's Bluff, Fresh Creek, Mangrove Cay, Congo Town. **Berry Islands**: Great Harbour Cay, Chub Cay. **Bimini**: Alice Town, Cat Cay, Gun Cay. **Eleuthera**: Harbour Island, Hatchet Bay, Governor's Harbour, Rock Sound. **Exuma**: George Town. **Grand Bahama**: West End, Freeport Harbour, Port Lucaya, Lucaya Marina, Xanadu Marina. **Inagua**: Matthew Town. **Long Island**: Stella Maris. **New Providence**: Nassau (any yacht basin). **Ragged Island**: Duncan Town. **San Salvador**: Cockburn Town.

Boat documents Complete duplicate copies of Maritime Declaration of Health, Inwards Report for Pleasure Vehicles and crew/passengers lists required. The vessel will be issued with a one-year cruising permit, US$10. During regular working hours, the only charge is for transportation for the clearing officer. Individuals will be given 60 days clearance with extensions obtained at a port of entry. A boat with a cruising permit may import parts duty-free.

Radio communications Morning ham net 0745-0845 7268; Nassau and George Town have VHF net. Exuma Markets in George Town will accept and hold faxes and mail for visiting boats. Marinas also hold mail, be sure the name of the vessel is clearly marked.

Touching down

Airlines *American Airlines,* T1800-4337300. *Air Canada,* T3278411. *Bahamasair,* T3773223 in Nassau, T3528341 in Freeport, 800-2224262 in the USA. *Delta Airlines/Comair,* T3771043, 800-2211212. *Gulfstream International,* T3528532. *Air Jamaica,* T800-5235585. *AOM,* T3777035. *Chalk's International,* T3632845. *Condor,* T800-5246975. *Continental,* T800-2310856. *United,* T3524511. See above for charter airlines.

Departure tax Airport and security tax is US$15 from Nassau and US$18 from Freeport except for children under the age of three. US immigration and customs formalities for those going to the USA are carried out at Nassau airport. Harbour departure tax is US$15.

Local tourist offices *The Bahamas Ministry of Tourism*, Market Plaza, Bay Street, Nassau, Bahamas, T3227500, F3255835, www.bahamas.com There are representatives of the

Touching down

Business hours Banks: in Nassau, Monday-Thursday 0930-1500, Friday 0930-1700; in Freeport, Monday-Friday 0900-1300 and Friday 1500-1700. **Shops:** 0900-1700 Monday-Saturday. **Government offices:** 0900-1730 Monday-Friday.
Emergency numbers on New Providence Police: T3224444. Ambulance: T3222221. Hospital: T3222861. **Med Evac:** T3222881. BASRA: T3223877. The Police have offices at East Bay T3221275, Paradise Island T3633160, Cable Beach T3278800 and downtown T3223114.
Official time Bahamas time is five hours behind GMT, except in summer when Eastern Daylight Time (GMT –4 hours) is adopted.

Voltage 120 volt/60 cycles.
Safety Nassau is less dangerous than Kingston or Port of Spain. However visitors should be extremely careful, particularly at night or when venturing off the beaten track. Do not be lulled into a false sense of security. Vigilance is also advised in Freeport. Never leave screen doors open at night, there have been a number of armed robberies and sexual assaults where intruders have just walked in through screen doors left open.
Tipping The usual tip is 15%, including for taxi drivers. Hotels and restaurants include a service charge on the bill, sometimes a flat rate per day, or a percentage.

Bahamas Tourist Office on Abaco, Eleuthera, Exuma and throughout the USA. **Maps** The Lands and Surveys Department on East Bay Street, Nassau, PO Box 592, has an excellent stock of maps, including a marine chart of the whole archipelago for US$10 and 1:25,000 maps covering most of the islands for US$1 per sheet (several sheets per island). These are also available from Fairey Surveys, Maidenhead, Berks, UK. A good, up-to-date street map of New Providence is available from most Bahamian bookstores for US$2.95.

Religion There are about 20 denominations represented in the Bahamas, of which those with the largest congregations are the Baptists, Roman Catholics and Anglicans. There are synagogues in Nassau and Freeport and a Mosque in Nassau. The Tourist Office publishes a leaflet called *Bahamas Places of Worship*, with a full list of addresses and services.

Where to stay

Accommodation ranges from luxury hotels and resorts with every conceivable facility, to modest guest houses or self-catering apartments and villas. Some of the larger properties have T800 reservations numbers in the USA and Canada. You will often get a cheaper package if you book from abroad. These packages often include restaurants, tours, day trips and airfare and are cheap enough for you to discard the bits you do not want. In restaurants, visitors on a package can pay 25-50% less than locals.

Getting around

Air *Bahamasair* operates scheduled flights between Nassau and the Family Islands. Charter flights and excursions available through them and several private companies, see Prestel for details. Seaplanes fly to those islands which have no landing strip. Inter-island travel is difficult given that nearly all flights originate in Nassau. To fly from Abaco to Eleuthera with Bahamasair, for example, you have to change planes in Nassau, often with a wait of several hours and thus waste a day. Each island has developed direct transport links with the USA rather than with each other. *Bahamasair* now has a scheme for multiple island destinations (*Discover the Bahamas*) from Miami, Orlando or Nassau, based on the number of flights you want to take, valid 21 days, for example from Miami, four flights US$180; from Orlando eight flights US$380; from Nassau six flights US$125.

Road Visitors are permitted to drive on a valid foreign licence or International Permit for up to three months. Beyond that they need a local licence issued by the Road Traffic Department in

Tourist offices overseas

Canada 1255 Phillips Sq, Montreal,
T514-8616797; 121 Bloor Street E, Toronto,
T416-3634441.
France 60 rue Saint Lazare, 75009 Paris,
T1-45-266262, F-1-48-740605.
Germany Leipziger Strasse 67d, D 60487,
Frankfurt am Main, T069-9708340,
F069-97083434, info-line T01030-813118.
Italy, Via Cusani 7, 20121, Milano,
T02-72022526, Toll free 02-1-678-77225,
F02-72023123.
Japan 4-9-17 Akasaka, Minato-Ku, Tokyo,
T813-4706162.
Sweden Gumshornsgatan 7, S-11460
Stockholm, T8-6632850, F8-6605780.
UK 3 The Billings, Walnut Tree Close, Guildford,
Surrey, T01483-448900, F01483-571846.
USA 150 East 52nd Street, 28th floor N, NY
10022, T212-7582777; also in other major US
cities.

**The Bahama Out Islands Promotion
Board offices:**
Germany, Am Schleifweg 16, D-55128 Mainz,
T0049-613199330, F0049-61319931
www.bahama-out-islands.com **USA**, 1100
Lee Wagener Boulevard, Suite 204, Fort
Lauderdale, FLB3315, T305-3598099,
800-6884752, F305-3598098.
**The Nassau/Paradise Island Promotion
Board:**
USA, T800-3279019, in the **UK** at Suite 31,
Parkway House, Sheen Lane, East Sheen,
London, SW14 8LS, T020-88785569,
F020-88787854, in **Canada** T800-6673777.
The Bahamas Reservation Service:
UK 79 Dean Street, London W1V 6HY,
T020-74349915, F020-7346460
sales@bahamasreservations.co.uk
Bahamasair is at the same address,
T020-74378766, F020-77346460.

Nassau. Traffic keeps left, although most cars are left-hand drive. Strict speed limits: Nassau and Freeport 35 miles per hour; elsewhere 45 mph. The roads are in good condition but are congested in town; drivers pay scant attention to the laws.

On many of the Family Islands bicycles and mopeds are appropriate. These can be hired in Nassau, Freeport and in many other places through hotels; helmets should be worn. Approximate rates: bicycles US$10 per day, US$40 per week; mopeds: US$30-45 per day. Scooters and light motorcycles can also be hired. Helmets are mandatory. Remember, though, that rates for car and bike hire tend to vary according to season. Minimum age for hiring in Exuma is 25 years.

Ferries A high-speed 177-passenger a/c catamaran ferry, the *Bo Hengy*, makes daily 3-hr **Sea** crossings from Nassau/Paradise Island (Potter's Cay dock at the foot of the Paradise Island bridge) to Eleuthera (Governor's Harbour), Harbour Island and Spanish Wells, www.bahamasferries.com US$100 return (US$60 for children), or US$149 (US$89 for children) for a 'day away' to Harbour Island, which includes a walking historical tour, lunch and cabana privileges, beach towels included, on the pink sand beach. Reported efficient, always on time, excellent value and has virtually replaced Bahamasair as the best way of getting to Eleuthera. A colourful way of travelling between the islands is on the **mail boats**, which also carry passengers and merchandise. They leave from Potter's Cay Dock, just below the Paradise Island Bridge in Nassau, and Woodes Rogers Walk; their drawback is that they are slow and accommodation on board is very basic, but they do go everywhere, usually once a week. The Bahamas Family Islands Association has a helpful brochure listing fares (US$20-50) and schedules, but do not expect the boats to leave according to the timetable. For the latest information listen to the radio on ZNS, which lists the daily schedule with last minute changes broadcast at lunchtime, or ask for information at the Dock Master's office on Potter's Cay, T3931064.

We give here the name of the boat, its destination and travel time: *Bahamas Daybreak III*, to North Eleuthera, Spanish Wells, Harbour Island, Bluff, 5½ hours; *Captain Moxey*, to South Andros, Kemp's Bay, Long Bay Cays, Bluff, 7½ hours; *Central Andros Express*, to Fresh Creek, Staniard Creek, Blanket Sound, Bowne Sound, 3½ hours; *Sea Hauler*, to Cat Island, Bluff, Smith's Bay, 10 hours; *North Cat Island Special*, to North Cat Island, Arthur's Town, Bennet's Harbour, 14 hours; *Maxine*, to San Salvador, United Estates, Rum Cay, 18 hours; *Grand Master, Seahauler,*

Lady Roslyn, Captain Moxey, to Exuma, George Town, Mt Thompson, 14 hours; *Abilin*, to Long Island, Clarence Town, 18 hours; *Champion II*, to Abaco, Sandy Point, Bullock Harbour, Moore Island, 11 hours; *Lisa J II*, to North Andros, Nichol's Town, Mastic Point, Lowe Sound, five hours; *Lady Francis*, to Exuma Cays, Staniel Cay, Black Point, Farmer's Cay, Barraterre; *Deborah K*, Abaco, Marsh Harbour, Hope Town, Treasure Cay, Green Turtle Cay, Coopers Town, 12 hours; *Mangrove Cay Express* to Mangrove Cay, Lisbon Creek, 5½ hours; *Lady Gloria* to Mangrove Cay, Behring Point, Cargill Creek, five hours; *Current Pride* to Current Island, Upper and Lower Bogue, Eleuthera, five hours; *Emmette and Cephas* to Ragged Island, 21 hours; *Bahamas Daybreak III*, to Rock Sound, Davis Harbour, South Eleuthera, seven hours; *Nay Dean*, to North Long Island, Salt Pond, Deadman's Cay, Stella Maris, 14 hours; *Marcella III*, to Grand Bahama, Freeport, High Rock, Eight Mile Rock, West End, 12 hours; *Windward Express*, to Crooked Island, Acklins, Mayaguana, Inagua; *Spanish Rose*, to Spanish Wells, 5½ hours; *Eleuthera Express*, to Rock Sound, five hours; *Challenger*, to North Andros; *Lady Margo*, also to North Andros; *Eleuthera Express*, Spanish Wells, Harbour Island, five hours; *Bimini Mack*, to Bimini, Cat Cay, 12 hours.

Yacht charter   A pleasant way of seeing the islands is to charter your own yacht and several companies offer boats with or without crews. **Abaco Bahamas Charters** (ABC) is based in Hope Town. **Bahamas Yachting Service** (BYS) is based in Marsh Harbour, Abaco, T305-4678644 or toll free 800-3272276 in North America, prices start from about US$50 per person per day. **Moorings** bases its bareboat charters at Marsh Harbour and has crewed yacht charters in George Town, Exuma. Contact the Bahamas Reservation Service for the Bahamas Marina Guide, marina reservations, known as 'book-a-slip', with details of over 50 marinas in the Bahamas and confirmation of boat slip reservations down as far as Grand Turk. Most resort islands have boats to rent.

Keeping in touch

Post   Main post office is at East Hill Street, Nassau. Letters to North America and the Caribbean US$0.65, to Europe, Central and South America US$0.70; to Africa, Asia and Australia US$0.80. All postcards US$0.50. Air mail to Europe takes 4-8 days, surface mail takes a couple of months. There is no door to door mail delivery in the Bahamas, everything goes to a PO Box. Parcels must be opened at the Post Office with customs officials present. Stamp collectors can contact the Bahamas Philatelic Bureau at East Hill Street, PO Box N8302, Nassau, for current mint stamps and first day covers.

Telephone   There is a public telephone and cable open 24 hours in the *Batelco* office on East Street, near
IDD code: 242   the BITCO building in Nassau. *Batelco* also provides internet services and several internet cafés can be found in the downtown areas of Nassau, Freeport and other urban centres. International calls can be made and faxes sent/received from here; also Prince George Dock, Shirley Street, Blue Hill Road, Mall at Marathon, Golden Gates and Fox Hill (0700-2000). *Batelco*'s mailing address is PO Box N3048, Nassau (T3234911). Grand Bahama, New Providence and most of the other islands have automatic internal telephone systems. Direct dialling is available from New Providence and most of the other islands all over the world. International calls are expensive: US$5 per minute to the UK through the operator, US$2.50 to the Caribbean. Using direct distance dialling it costs US$0.90 to the USA, US$1.15 to Canada, US$0.25 to Barbados, Panama, the Cayman Islands, Jamaica and Puerto Rico, US$2.75 to France, Germany, Italy, Mexico, the UK and Switzerland. Pay phones can be used to contact USA Direct (1-800-2822881) for more economical rates than *Batelco*. Credit card facilities. Phone cards are now quite widely available in denominations of US$5, US$10 and US$20. A call to the UK with a phone card is US$4 per minute. Not all phones take cards. Facilities are available at most Batelco offices in Nassau and Freeport, Nassau and Freeport airports and several of the Family Islands. Videoconferencing facilities at Batelco's offices in the Mall at Marathon, Nassau and in Freeport. Cellular service is available for most islands. Check with *Batelco* to see if they have reciprocal agreements with your cellular company, otherwise sign up for a roaming agreement.

Newspapers There are three daily newspapers: the *Nassau Guardian*, *The Tribune* and the **Media**
Bahama Journal. There are lots of tourist magazines, for example *What's On, Dining and Entertainment Guide, Nassau, Cable Beach, Paradise Island*; *What-To-Do, Freeport Lucaya*; *Getaway, Bahamas Out Islands*; *The Cruising Guide to Abaco, Bahamas* (annual); *Abaco Life*.
Radio The local commercial radio stations are ZNS1, owned by the Government and covering all the Bahamas, ZNS2 and ZNS3 covering New Providence and the North Bahamas. There are also Radio Abaco, Cool 96 (Freeport), More FM (Nassau and Grand Bahama) and Love 97 (Nassau). The local commercial television station is ZNS TV 13. Transmissions from Florida can be picked up and satellite reception is common.

The People-to-People programme is a recommended way to meet local Bahamians. Fill in a **People-to-**
form from the Ministry of Tourism giving age, occupation and interests and you will be **People**
matched with a Bahamian. Each experience is different but it might lead to a meal in a Bahamian home, a tour of out of the way places or a trip to church. They also hold a tea party at Government House in January to August on the last Friday of each month and can arrange weddings. T3265371, F3280945 in Nassau or 3528044, F3522714 in Freeport, or ask at your hotel. The programme is also available in Eleuthera (T3322142, F3322480), Abaco (T3673067, F3673068), San Salvador, Exuma (T3362430, F3662431) and Bimini. There is also now an extension to the programme to include Cuba, so that you can stay with local families in Nassau and Havana.

Food and drink

Conch is the staple diet of many Bahamians. It is considered an aphrodisiac and a source of *Conch, crab, grouper,*
virility, especially the small end part of the conch which is bitten off and eaten from the live *snapper, dolphin (not*
conch for maximum effect. Conch is prepared in a variety of ways; conch fritters and cracked *the Flipper variety) &*
conch are both coated in batter and fried, while conch salad is made from raw, shredded *other seafood are on*
conch, onion, lime, lettuce and tomatoes. It can be bought daily from vendors who let you *all the menus*
choose your conch from their truck and will 'jewk' it from the shell and prepare it for you in salad. Although delicious, conch has been linked to major outbreaks of food poisoning, so treat with caution. Bahamian cuisine is tasty, if a little predictable. The standard fare at most parties/cookouts is peas'n'rice, barbecue ribs and chicken wings, conch salad or fritters, potato salad, coleslaw and macaroni. Bahamian potato salad and macaroni are far richer than their English/Italian counterparts. The Bahamas have some good fruit: sapodilla, mango, breadfruit, sugar apple and pawpaw. Try soursop ice cream, coconut tarts and sugar bananas, which have an apple flavour. Guava duff is a popular sweet, a bit like jam roly poly pudding topped with guava sauce (often flavoured with rum). Tap water can be salty; Bahamians drink bottled water, bought at the supermarket. The local beer brewed in Nassau, Kalik, is worth trying, it has won several international prizes. The local rum is Bacardi; the Anejo variety is OK. Bahama Mammas, Yellowbirds and Island Woman are all popular rum-based cocktails. Many bars have their own special cocktails.

Shopping

For those who want to pick up a bargain, prices of crystal, china and jewellery are cheaper than in the USA. You can find designer clothes and other goods from all over the world at the International Bazaar in Freeport. Local products including straw items, Androsia batik printed silk and cotton, shell jewellery and wood carvings. Bargaining is expected in the markets. Duty-free shopping was introduced on 11 categories of goods on 1 January 1992; the Bahamas Duty-Free Promotion Board was formed to monitor the system and ensure that merchants participating in the scheme sell authentic goods.

Sport

Annual fishing permits: US$20 per boat for hook and line. Lobster season from 1 August to 31 **Fishing**
March. Conch must have fully formed lip to be taken. Hawaiian slings are permitted but

spearfishing is not. Within Bahamas National Parks you may not fish, take lobster, conch, coral or shells, etc. Fishing is good all year with peak times for bonefish in March to April, permit March to August, snapper Spring to Summer, barracuda June to August, blue marlin March to July, white marlin March to June, sailfish March to June, broadbill swordfish May to September, Allison tuna March to May, blackfin tuna May to July, bluefin tuna April to June. The best flats for reef fishing are found off Andros, the Abacos, Eleuthera, the Exumas, Grand Bahama and San Salvador. The best big game fishing is off Bimini, also good off Cat Island, Chub Cay, Nassau, the Abacos and many other islands. Contact the tourist office for lists of operators, fishing lodges and prices.

Scuba diving In addition to the land-based dive operators mentioned in the text for each island, there are several liveaboard boats which cruise the Bahamas and offer less crowded and unspoilt sites: *Blackbeard's Cruises*, contact Bruce Purdy, PO Box 66-1091, *Miami Springs*, FL 33266, T800-3279600, 305-8881226, F305-8844214, sales@blackbeard-cruises.com; *Nekton Diving Cruises*, contact Lynn A Oetzman, 520 SE 32nd Street, Fort Lauderdale, FL 33316, T954-4639324, F954-4638938; the first Bahamian owned and operated boat, *MV Ballymena*, *Out Island Voyages*, contact James or Marilynn Nottage, PO Box N-7775, Nassau, T242-3940951, F3940948; *Sea Fever Diving Cruises*, PO Box 398276, Miami Beach, FL 33239, T305-8613603, www.seafever.com, *Sea Dragon*, contact Dan Doyle, Sue Ford, 717SW Coconut Drive, Fort Lauderdale, FL 33315, T954-5220161. All the above are BDA members. There are hyperbaric chambers in Freeport, Lyford Cay and Andros. All dive operators should carry oxygen and a first aid kit. Diving can be enjoyed all year round although the waters are cooler in the winter months: about 76°F in the northern Bahamas. In the summer the water temperature rises to about 84°F throughout the island chain. Possession of spearguns is illegal.

Holidays and festivals

Public holidays
See individual island listings for local festivals

New Year's Day, Good Friday, Easter Monday (very busy at the airport), Whit Monday, Labour Day (first Friday in June, a parade is organized by the trade unions), Independence Day (10 July), Emancipation Day (first Monday in August), Discovery Day (12 October), Christmas Day, Boxing Day.

Further reading

Out-island Doctor by **Evans Cottman** (Hodder and Stoughton) gives a picture of the 1940s; an interesting comparison can be made with *Cocaine Wars* by **Paul Eddy** et al (Bantam), a fascinating study of the 1980s. *Talkin' Bahamian*, by **Patricia Glinton Meicholas**, is a charming collection of tongue-in-cheek definitions of popular Bahamian sayings, complete with cartoon illustrations. *The Bahamas Handbook*, Dupuch Publications, is an annual publication for residents and visitors with detailed information on government, the economy, finance, history, investment and tourism. *Nassau Memories* by **Deby Nash** (Travel Memories Press) illustrated by Elyse Wasile, contains titbits of history and culture of Nassau and Paradise Island, with commentary and signature dishes from over 20 restaurants. For a history of Paradise Island, read *Paradise Island Story*, by **Paul Albury** (Macmillan Caribbean).

New Providence

Population: 212,432
2000 census
Colour map 2, grid B2

New Providence is in the centre of the Bahamas archipelago and despite being one of the smallest major islands is home for two thirds of the population. The centre of Nassau has some fine historic buildings and there are some good beaches, but most of the island is covered by sprawling suburbia, scrubby woodland or swamp. Paradise Island, just off the north coast, is 826 acres of tourist resort. Once known as Hog Island, because it reminded Governor Nicholas Trott of his pig farm in Bermuda, it was developed as a resort in the 1950s by Huntington Hartford. The name was changed after a bridge was built to connect the island with Nassau and the first casino licence was granted.

Ins and outs

Getting there
See transport, page 90, for further information

Nassau International Airport (NAS), is about 14 miles from Nassau. Taxi to Cable Beach US$12, to Nassau US$17-20 and to Paradise Island US$20-25. Third and subsequent extra passengers should be charged US$3, but drivers sometimes try to charge everyone a separate full fare, which is illegal. Make sure meter is turned on and used. There is no public bus service to or from the airport, though some hotels have buses. For the return journey there is a bus from Nassau to Clifton (US$1.50); it leaves on the hour from Bay and Frederick Sts (Western Transportation Company) and will drop you 1½ miles from the airport, not recommended option. Left luggage space is available in lockers outside the doors mid-way between the domestic and international ends of the terminal, they take 4 US quarter coins.

Getting around

Buses called 'jitneys', are mostly a/c and good value at US$1, carrying from 9-44 people and going all over New Providence Island between 0630 and 2000. Have the exact fare, by law the driver keeps the change. If you want to see some of the island catch any bus in town and it will bring you back about an hour later. They can be crowded but service is regular. To cross to Paradise Island from Woodes Rogers Walk take the Paradise Express boat for US$2, it leaves when full and stops at several docks on Paradise Island. A small rental **car** can cost US$70 a day or US$400-450 a week. Prices depend on the model and features. **Bicycles** can be hired for US$10 per day with US$10 deposit. Traffic for such a small island is busy and roads are not well maintained. Take care.

Diving and marine life

Dive sites

Wrecks have been planted by film crews off the southwest corner of New Providence, which attract scuba divers eager to see the underwater scenes of James Bond films (the James Bond wreck was damaged by Hurricane Andrew and the front part collapsed, but it is still being dived), or Walt Disney's *20,000 Leagues Under the Sea* was filmed. Just off Paradise Island there is a series of caves and a 19th-century wreck, there is a Blue Hole 10 miles east of Nassau, while to the west of New Providence there are dramatic walls and drops leading to the mile-deep 'Tongue of the Ocean'. Marine conservation is not as highly developed as in some of the other Bahamian islands where dive tourism is promoted, although there are 50 permanent moorings and seven dive operations, all offering PADI certification courses and trips to wrecks, reefs and walls, as well as other activities. Shark feeding and swimming with dolphins are two popular dives. The former involves sitting on the ocean floor and watching a dive master, clad in chain mail or other protective gear, feed several large sharks. Critics claim that more sharks are attracted to the dive site than is natural and are becoming dependent upon daily handouts.

New Providence

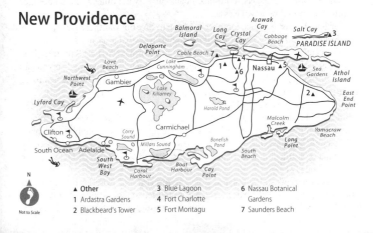

▲ Other
1 Ardastra Gardens
2 Blackbeard's Tower
3 Blue Lagoon
4 Fort Charlotte
5 Fort Montagu
6 Nassau Botanical Gardens
7 Saunders Beach

The Bahamas

The Bahamas

★ A Foot in the door

- **Conch** fritters, conch salad, cracked conch - no man should resist the chewy aphrodisiac.
- Ogle the monstrous 2,355-room Atlantis resort on Paradise Island with its massive casino, freeform pool and aquarium.
- Visit during **Junkanoo** or at least see the museum where the costumes, cow bells and other carnival gear is displayed.
- Take the Fast Ferry catamaran to **Harbour Island**, with stops at **Spanish Wells** and **Governor's Harbour**, and spend time on the pink sand beach - so good you may end up staying the night.
- Witness the sunset at **Compass Point**. Nothing beats the huge orange ball descending from the skies past the water line - enough to make anyone sigh over their sundowner.

Dive centres On the south coast, Stuart Cove's *Dive South Ocean* is particularly recommended (T3624171, F3625227), but the others include *Bahama Divers Ltd* (T3935644/1466, F3936078, www.bahamadivers.com, East Bay Street, in the Nassau Yacht Haven Marina), *Dive, Dive, Dive Ltd* (T3621143/1401, F3621994, Coral Harbour, Nitrox certification available), *Diver's Haven* (T3933285, F3933695, East Bay Street), *Nassau Scuba Centre* (T3621964/1379, F3621198, Coral Harbour) and *Sunskiff Divers Ltd* (T/F3621979, Coral Harbour, speciality diving). The cost of a two-tank scuba dive with all equipment and transport included is about US$70. A learn-to-dive package costs much the same and enables you to dive with the same company throughout your stay on the island. Snorkelling trips for non-divers are US$25-35. Shark dives cost US$75 or more; you can see silky sharks, bull sharks and reef sharks. Stuart Cove's *Dive South Ocean* also offers a Shark Awareness certification course for US$210.

Beaches and watersports

Beaches are best near the hotels where the seaweed is cleaned off. The nicest ones are **Love Beach** (west), **South Ocean Beach** (the sea here is very shallow) and beaches on the small islands off New Providence. One of the best and longest beaches is **Lyford Cay**, which is behind barriers in an exclusive housing area for the rich and famous in the west, but not impossible to enter with enough confidence. It is unwise to go to a beach where you might be on your own. Watersports include **waterskiing** (no tuition), **parasailing**, **windsurfing** and **snorkelling**. Some of the larger hotels offer full facilities to guests and non-guests. For those who prefer a less active encounter with the sea, glass-bottomed boats leave several times a day from Prince George Wharf in downtown Nassau.

Hartley's Undersea Walk, for those not keen to dive but wanting to see coral reefs up close, at 0930 and 1330, US$40 (T3938234, www.bahamasnet.com/hartleys). Check in at the houseboat, *Full Circle*, at Nassau Yacht Haven, East Bay Street. You walk down a 12 ft ladder wearing a helmet into which air is pumped so you can breath normally. The *Seaworld Explorer* is a semi-submarine which descends 10-15 ft and is reached by a shuttle boat which leaves from Captain Nemo's dock. Two trips daily except Sunday and Wednesday of 1½ hours, 1100 and 1500, US$33 adults, US$19 children under 12, T3238426, 3562548. Stuart Cove's (see above) offers a 40-minute underwater trip in a sub (scenic underwater bubble), which is a submersible scooter with a clear dome allowing a 180° view of the undersea world. No scuba or snorkelling experience is necessary, just US$89, which includes pilot guides, T3624171.

For **island cruises**, the Calypso Blue Lagoon trip and Rose Island excursions aboard large MVs with three decks are recommended (daily at 1000 except Wednesday, T3633577, US$35 for the day with lunch, although it is unlikely to be as good as in the brochure pictures, no complimentary snorkelling equipment). The *Swim With The Dolphins Experience* is at Blue Lagoon, Salt Cay, reached by tender from several cruise ships or on a day excursion with Calypso 1 and 11, reservations required, T3631003, www.dolphinswims.com You get a 15-minute lecture on the dolphins, then you wade or swim with the dolphins; a full-day trip including lunch, drinks, beach, equipment, is US$75 or US$145. *Flying Cloud* catamaran cruises depart from Paradise Island West Dock for sunset, half-day, dinner or Sunday cruises for US$35-50 including snorkelling gear and transport from hotels (T3931957). *Sea Island Adventure* also do boat trips to Rose Island with lunch, snorkelling etc (T3253910, 3282581, www.bahamasnet.com/seaisland), while *Yellow Bird* (250 passengers) and *Tropic Bird* (170 passengers) catamarans cater to cruise ships with three-hour cruises. *Top Sail Yacht Charters* (T3930820) have three boats and offer an all-day cruise from *British Colonial Hilton Hotel* dock 0945, Paradise Island ferry dock 1015, arriving Rose Island 1200, depart 1400, snorkelling included, US$49, private charters from US$370.

Powerboat Adventures go further in a high-speed boat; day trip departing from Captain Nemo's dock 0900, with lavish picnic to the Exuma Cays for US$159, including seeing iguanas on Allan's Cay, a nature trail walk and drift snorkelling (T3261936, 3275385, Monday-Friday 0800-2000). *Out Island Safaris* (seaplane and boat, Captain Paul Harding, T3932522/1179) also offers day trips to other islands, for example Harbour Island, the Exumas, Hope Town, with scuba, snorkelling and lunch. A captained boat for **fishing** trips is US$300 for four hours or US$600 for a day for up to six people (T3632335, Captain Jesse Pinder, or T3228148, F3264140, Captain Mike Russell of Chubasco Charters, or T3934144, 3632003, Captain Philip Pinder, excellent), or arranged through hotel tour desks for US$60 per person for a half day.

The most popular and well developed sport on dry land is probably **golf**. There are four world class courses on New Providence: *Cable Beach Golf Course* (T3278617), *South Ocean Golf Club* (T3624391), *Ocean Club Golf Course* on Paradise Island (T3633000) and the private *Lyford Cay Golf Course*. Green fees vary and hotel guests can get package deals or discounts.

Other sports

There are over 100 **tennis** courts in the Nassau/Cable Beach/Paradise Island area and many of them are lit for night-time play until 2200 (with an extra charge). Most of the larger hotels have tennis courts, usually free for guests. *The Racquets Club*, on Independence Drive (T3231854) has **squash** courts at about US$7 per hour. Very popular with Bahamians, it has European-sized courts. *The Radisson Resort Sports Centre* charges US$6 an hour for guests, US$10 for others, and has racquet-ball, squash and tennis available. Smarter, but the squash courts are smaller, being converted racquet-ball courts.

You can go **horse riding** for US$45 an hour, including transport, along the beach at *Happy Trails*, Coral Harbour (T3621820).

Cricket is played every Saturday and Sunday during the cricket season (5 March to 27 November) at Haynes Oval, West Bay Street, Nassau. Matches begin at 1200. For further details contact Sydney Deveaux of the Bahamas Cricket Association, T3221875.

Gambling at *Paradise Island and Crystal Palace* casinos, 1000-0400. Enquire about lessons free of charge. It is fascinating to see the massed ranks of flashing fruit machines and the many games tables. Bahamians and permanent residents are not allowed to gamble in the casinos.

Nassau

Nassau is the capital of the Bahamas. It looks comfortably old-fashioned with its white and pink houses: by-laws forbid skyscrapers. Bay Street is the main shopping street, which is packed with cruise ship visitors seeking duty-free bargains during the day, but deserted at night. Parliament Square is typical of the colonial architecture with the

Houses of Assembly, the old Colonial Secretary's Office and the Supreme Court clustered around a statue of Queen Victoria.

Sights On the north side of the Parliament Square, government buildings overlook the bust of Sir Milo B Butler, the first Bahamian Governor-General. To the right, 25-minute surrey rides can be taken through the town. ■ *US$10 per person (horses rest 1300-1500 May-Oct, 1300-1400 Nov-Apr).* Walking up Parliament Street you pass the Cenotaph on the left and the *Parliament Inn*, built in the 1930s, on the right. The octagonal pink building bordering on Shirley Street is the **Public Library**, built in 1798, which was once used as a prison. Inside you can climb stairs and look out from the balcony, but unfortunately the old dungeons below are no longer open to the public. ■ *T3224907. Mon-Thu 1000-2000, Fri 1000-1700, Sat 1000-1600.* Opposite the library is the site of the *Royal Victoria Hotel*, the first hotel in the Bahamas, built in 1859-61, which closed in 1971. It was built by the Government to accommodate the influx of visitors during the American Civil War, but sold in 1898, after when it changed hands several times. There is not much to see and it looks like a park with some lovely tall trees providing shade, while much of it is used as a car park.

On Elizabeth Avenue on the corner with Shirley Street is the **Bahamas Historical Society**, which organizes monthly talks and houses a small museum. There is a collection of old pictures, historical documents, a few old household items and things brought up from the sea, not all of which are well labelled; it is an old-fashioned display with little information. ■ *Mon-Fri 1000-1600, Sat 1000-1200, closed Thu, T3224231.* Nearby is the **Queen's Staircase**. The 65 steps (102 ft climb) at the end of a gorge (thought to have been cut out of the limestone by slaves in 1790, the canyon is now lined with palm trees and there is an attractive waterfall alongside the steps) lead to the ruined **Fort Fincastle**. Ignore men offering information on the history of the area unless you want to pay for it. They are very persistent. The fort itself was built in 1789 in the shape of a ship's bow. The Water Tower beside the fort was declared a water landmark in 1993. Take the lift (US$0.50) or the stairs to the top to see the shape of the fort. This is the highest point on the island (216 ft above sea level)

Nassau

■ **Sleeping**
1 British Colonial Hilton
2 Buena Vista
3 Club Land'Or & Blue Lagoon Restaurant
4 Dillet's
5 Diplomat Inn
6 El Greco
7 Graycliff
8 Holiday Inn Junkanoo Beach

and gives some lovely views of the island. There is another guide at the top who also expects a tip. The area is heavily visited by cruise ship tours and there are many souvenir stalls.

Government House in traditional Bahamian pink (built 1801) is pretty. Gregory's Arch is an overpass to Government House. On alternate Saturday mornings at 1000, the Royal Bahamian Police Force Band plays in front of the **Christopher Columbus Statue** at the top of the flight of stairs. **Balcony House** on Market Street is the oldest wooden residence in Nassau, built in the 18th century. ■ *T3262568. Mon, Wed, Fri, 1000-1600, closed 1300-1400, donations required.* On West Hill Street is a plaque set in the rock which claims the site as being that of the oldest church in Nassau. Further along the street you pass several old houses including the Postern Gate on the left and the Sisters of Charity Convent on the right. Turning down the steps to Queen Street you pass by some of the oldest and prettiest houses in Nassau (no 16 is said to be 200 years old). The **St Francis Xavier Catholic Cathedral** is on West Street and down the hill is the quaint **Greek Orthodox Church** in blue and white. **Christ Church Cathedral** (built 1837) stands on the corner of George's Street and immediately to the south is **Lex House**, thought to have housed the Spanish Garrison in 1782-83.

Vendue House on Bay Street, close to the *British Colonial Hilton Hotel*, was the site of slave auctions, and has now been restored (with a grant from Bacardi to commemorate 1492) and converted into the **Pompey Museum**. It has drawings, artefacts and documents relating to slavery and emancipation in the Bahamas. The collection is limited but well displayed and interesting. Upstairs there is a permanent art exhibition of paintings by Mr Amos Ferguson, who uses house paints. ■ *Mon-Fri 1000-1630, Sat 1000-1300, adults US$1, children under 12, US$0.50.* The renowned **Straw Market** has the offices of the Ministry of Tourism above it. Almost all the straw work is imported from East Asia and is no longer native (better prices upstairs); they also sell carvings, jewellery and T-shirts. Bargain with the saleswomen but do not expect to get more than 15% off the originally stated price. Running behind the market is the enormous **Wellcome Centre** (formerly **Prince**

● **Eating**

9 Ocean Spray
10 Towne

1 Bahamian Kitchen
2 Brussels Brasserie
3 Café Matisse

The Bahamas

George Wharf) which can take up to 11 big cruise ships at once (peak time Saturday). A multi-million dollar renovation programme has been completed and it now has brightly painted and covered seating areas, a hair braiding area and sidewalk stalls where vendors have wares similar to the main straw market on Bay Street, just a few hundred yards away. Enlargement of the terminal allows the mega-cruise ships to come to Nassau. The **Junkanoo Museum** on the waterfront, also renovated, shows the colourful costumes used in the parades. Highly recommended, this is a good chance to see the workmanship up close. ■ *0900-1700 daily, closed on holidays, US$2 for adults, US$0.50 children, T3562731.* Guided **walking tours** of old Nassau start from Rawson Square, daily at 1000 and 1400, US$2, contact the Tourist Information Centre, T3269772.

Around the island

Go west along Bay Street, past Nassau Street and continue to the Road Traffic Centre where you turn left to **Fort Charlotte**, built in 1787-89 out of limestone. It has a dry moat and battlements. The fort was manned during the Napoleonic Wars but never saw action. The soldiers left some interesting graffiti. Look down on the cricket field, the guns (not original cannon), Arawak Cay and the west end of Paradise Island. Guides will fill you in on the history for a small tip or just wander at leisure. The guides have Ministry of Tourism name badges and are not as pushy as at Fort Fincastle.

Arawak Cay, along West Bay St, opposite the cricket pitch, is now the site of the annual Junkanoo in June at the weekends. It is also home to the Arawak Cay Fish Fry, where, from 0900-2300 every day, you can sample fried fish and conch salad, freshly prepared at a collection of some 20 wooden frame eateries painted in bright Junkanoo colours. Initially a small entrepreneurial effort by a few out of work fishermen, it has slowly won the approval of the Ministry of Tourism. The buildings have expanded their menus to include salads and other hot and cold seafood dishes, while some have added a second storey, with balconies providing great views of the neighbourhood. Locals play dominoes or checkers, or you can catch the sports news on TV. Live bands perform on the patios during the weekend evenings.

Crystal Cay Marine Park and Observatory is on a 16-acre island, reached by a bridge from the manmade Arawak Cay (made when the harbour was dredged to allow cruise ships in), which is in turn reached by a bridge. Highlights include descending the observatory tower to view the sea below (lots of fish and masses of lobsters), wandering through the excellent indoor exhibits of reef ecology, watching sting ray and sharks feed and selecting your own oyster with a pearl inside. The only drawback is the small size of the pools housing turtles, rays and sharks. A snorkelling trail has been added, US$12 for hire of mask, snorkel and fins, and mandatory life jacket. It is open 0930-1600, off a small beach overlooking Arawak Cay, where there are plenty of rest rooms and sun beds. Allow half a day for a visit. There is a restaurant, gift shops and also stands with sea biscuits and sand dollars for sale. ■ *T3281036. 0900-1800, US$16 adults, US$11 children, annual membership US$21 adults, US$15 children, under 4s free. A US$3 bus runs from Cable Beach, a US$3 boat goes from Woodes Rodgers dock (daily except Thu, 1015, 1230, 1530, return 1200, 1500, 1700), or a US$3 bus from Paradise Island.*

Going up Chippingham Road you come to the **Nassau Botanic Gardens** where there are 18 acres of tropical plants. ■ *Mon-Fri, 0800-1600, Sat-Sun 0900-1600, adults US$1, children US$0.50.* Also **The Ardastra Gardens and Zoo**. Trained, parading flamingos march just after 1100, 1400, and 1600, but can be a disappointment. There are also parrots and some other animals, but not really enough to warrant the term zoo. ■ *T3235806. 0900-1700, last admission 1630, adults US$7.50, children US$3.75.*

Going west along the coast, Saunders Beach is bordered by casuarina trees and Brown's Point looks across to the *Nassau Marriott Resort and Crystal Casino* (and

Radisson Resort) at **Cable Beach**, which at night is a multi-coloured sight when the dayglo lights are switched on. Leaving Cable Beach you soon come to Delaporte Point (once a slave village) and Sandy Port residential areas. Further on are some local bars (*Nesbits* is very popular in the evenings) where you can buy drinks and native conch salad before you get to some limestone caves. There is an inscription commemorating the first visit by the British Royal Family in 1841. Just beyond is **Conference Corner** where Macmillan, Kennedy and Diefenbaker planted trees in 1962. At this point Blake Road leads to the airport while West Bay Street continues past Orange Hill Beach and Gambier Village, another slave village. *Travellers Rest*, a bar and restaurant, overlooks the sea, and is very pleasant to watch the sunset (excellent daiquiris and minced lobster). **Love Beach** further on the right is probably one of the best beaches on New Providence. Park on the side of the road and walk down between the apartments, you can not see the beach from the road. *Compass Point Beach Club* is on this stretch of coast. You can walk along the beach at the trendy *Club*, and across the street are the Compass Point Recording Studios, both of which are Chris Blackwell properties, brightening up the oldest community on New Providence Island. The Rolling Stones, Backstreet Boys, Lenny Kravitz and hundreds of other famous artists have recorded here and their music is played at the hotel.

Continuing as far west as you can go you reach **Lyford Cay**, a private residential area for the rich, protected by barriers. Turn left at the roundabout for Clifton, a stretch of rocky coast now being developed for a power station and industry. In 2000 **Clifton** was the site of some controversy when a US$400 mn tourism project was proposed for a 600-acre beachfront location. Environmentalists and locals campaigned against the planned digging of canals for boats because it would remove sand, destroy the habitat of turtles, and three endangered bird species, and threaten two Lucayan Indian villages and the remains of a walled slave plantation. The luxury gated estate would also restrict public access to the beach. The road then leads to South West Bay where you can turn off to visit the *Clarion Hotel* and beachfront (a good stop for a swim and a drink) before returning east. After two miles there is a signpost to **Adelaide Village**. This settlement is one of the oldest, founded when illegal slave traders were intercepted by the British Navy in the 19th century and the human cargo was taken to the Bahamas. The traditional houses are brightly painted, the beach is quite good, though the water is shallow, and the bars prepare fresh fish or conch salad. Continue east on Adelaide Road and you come to the Coral Harbour roundabout. To the right, the Bahamas Defence Force has its base. Coral Harbour was designed as a second Lyford Cay, exclusive, with security barriers, but when it was built in the 1960s there was considerable local opposition to it becoming a select ghetto. The development company went bankrupt leaving it incomplete. The shell of the hotel still stands and the area is now an upper middle class subdivision. At the roundabout you can turn off for the airport or join Carmichael Road and you will pass the Bacardi Company, open weekdays until 1600. At the end of Carmichael Road turn left to go along Blue Hill Road and join Independence Drive at the roundabout (with the cock on top). Here on the north side is the Town Centre Shopping Mall. In this area you will see many examples of the Government's low-cost housing. Rows of rectangular houses have been painted and adapted by their owners to make each one individual. Notice also that cemeteries are built on hills, where you can dig down 6 ft and not hit water; elsewhere water is too close to the surface.

Continue east on Independence until you come to traffic lights with another mall. At Marathon Mall turn right on to Prince Charles Drive and follow this to the sea. Turn left and you will be on Eastern Road, which hugs the coast and has many impressive homes overlooking the sea. **Blackbeard's Tower**, an old lookout point, is now closed. **Fort Montagu** (and beach), constructed in 1741, is famous for having been captured briefly by Americans during the Revolution. It is a rather smelly area where conch and fish are sold. If you turn left into Shirley Street and immediately left again into Village Road, you will come to **The Retreat** (opposite Queen's College), the headquarters of the Bahamas National Trust and an 11-acre botanical park.

■ *Guided tours (20 min) US$2, Tue-Thu at 1150*. Members of the BNT (PO Box N4105) are entitled to discounts at several tourist destinations locally (for example Crystal Cay, Power Boat Adventures, Ardastra Gardens) and free admission to National Trust properties worldwide. The BNT was set up in 1959. It publishes a quartely newsletter, *Currents*.

Returning to East Bay Street you will pass the *Club Waterloo* and the *Nassau Yacht Club* before reaching the toll bridge which crosses over to **Paradise Island**. A new bridge was opened at the end of 1998 and traffic now crosses over to Paradise Island on the new bridge (US$1 per car), returning to Nassau via the old bridge. Alternatively there is a water taxi, US$3, to the Calypso Dock on Paradise Island. Stop at the **Versailles Gardens and Cloisters** on the way to the Ocean Club golf course. The gardens with various statues were allowed to fall into disrepair for a while, but have been restored. The Augustinian cloisters were brought in pieces from France and date back to the 14th century. The gazebo looking across to Nassau is a favourite spot for weddings. The *Atlantis Resort* with its aquarium and waterscapes is worth a visit; you could spend half a day walking the pathways among turtle habitats, the predator pool and the aquarium (see the huge jewfish), including one with a glass tunnel where sharks swim all round you (all for free). Paradise had some lovely stretches of beach on the north side, but most of the island has now been gobbled up by *Atlantis* construction crews adding condos on one side of the island and more hotel rooms on the other. Unless you are an *Atlantis* hotel guest, you'll look long and hard before finding a stretch of accessible beach.

Potters Cay, next to the old Paradise Island toll bridge, has the main fish and produce market. Try freshly made conch salad or scorched conch, very spicy and fresh.

Essentials

Sleeping

You can usually pick up a cheaper package deal in the USA than by arranging a hotel on arrival

The two main resort areas on New Providence are **Cable Beach**, which stretches 3 miles west of Nassau along the north coast, and **Paradise Island**, 5 mins across Nassau harbour. The benefit of staying at Cable Beach is that the jitney service into town is very easy to use, while from Paradise Island you need a taxi. Other hotels are in the town and suburbs. There is a great variety of accommodation, ranging from small guest houses, offering only rooms, to luxury hotels and sprawling resorts. *Small Treasures* are a collection of small hotels which have been inspected by the Ministry of Tourism, T800-3279019 for directory and comments, T800-5233782 for reservations. Prices vary according to the season. Standards at hotels are good, helped by the privatization of state hotels, greater competition and huge refurbishment programmes, but even so, service is slow at reception desks. Watch out for tax (8-10%), resort levies (10%), fuel surcharges and compulsory maid gratuities which are added to the basic price quoted. Up to date rates available at the Tourist Information Centres in Nassau, or write to the Tourist Offices listed on page 75.

Nassau The most expensive hotel is **LL-AL** *Graycliff*, West Hill, PO Box N-10246, T3222796, F3266110. 14 large rooms in an 18th-century mansion, some suites, some balconies, Olympic sized swimming pool, jacuzzi, sauna, elegant gourmet restaurant boasting the largest wine cellar in the Caribbean, cigars a speciality, produced by Graycliff Cigar Co using Cuban cigar rollers. The largest hotel is **L-AL** *British Colonial Hilton Hotel* conveniently located at the beginning of Bay St, PO Box N-7148, T3223301, F3222286. Built in 1923 on site of Fort Nassau, the cannon outside were found when the foundations were dug, being restored to its former glory, small beach, complimentary non-motorized watersports, view of cruise ships. **L** *Holiday Inn Junkanoo Beach Hotel*, opposite the Western Esplanade, 5-min walk from town centre, PO Box SS-19055, T3560000, F3231408. Good value, small but nicely appointed dining room.

On West Bay St close to the junction with Nassau St, are middle range hotels along the road overlooking Long Walk Beach. **A-B** *Dillet's*, Dunmore Av and Strachan St, PO Box N-204, Chippingham, T3251133, F3257183. 7 a/c suites, non-smoking, some have cooking facilities, includes continental breakfast, bicycles for hire, parking, internet café, Pop Pop Studios, a fine arts gallery, won the 2001 *Cacique Award* for best small hotel in the Bahamas. **A-B** *Towne Hotel*, 40 George St, PO Box N-4808, T3228452, F3281512. **A-C** *El Greco*, PO Box N4187, West Bay and Augusta Sts, T3251121, F3251124. Pool, restaurant, 26 rooms. **B-C** *Ocean Spray*, PO Box N-3035, T3228032, F3255731. 28 rooms, restaurant. Guest houses include **D** *Mignon* 12 Market St, PO Box N-786, T/F3224771. 6 rooms. **D** *Diplomat Inn*, Delancey St on top of the hill, PO Box N-4, T3252688, F3562138. Budget hotel in a less salubrious area. **E** *Olive's* on Blue Hill Rd, PO Box GT-2130, T3235298.

Cable Beach **LL** *Breezes*, PO Box CB13049, T3275356, F3275155. A SuperClubs resort for singles and couples over 16, 392 rooms and suites expanding to 492, a/c, TV, phone, pool, games room, fitness centre, outdoor sports and watersports. **LL-L** *Nassau Beach Hotel*, PO Box N-7756, T3277711, F3278829. 408 rooms, lots of restaurants, 2 pools, free tennis and non-motorized watersports, *King & Knights* native show club. Next door is the sister resort, **LL-AL** *Nassau Marriott Resort and the Crystal Palace Casino*, PO Box N-8306, T3276200, F3276459. Suites up to US$25,000 per night. This huge landmark hotel is usually lit up in dayglo orange, yellow, purple and magenta at night and contains shops, bars, 12 restaurants and a casino the size of a football pitch, Rainforest Theatre with *Magical Voyage* dinner show. **LL-L** *Radisson Cable Beach Casino and Golf Resort*, next door, adjacent to the casino, PO Box N-4914, T3276000, F3376987. 2 wings extend from central lobby area (from where you can see the beach), curving around lagoons and pools, long walk to some rooms down dark corridors, lots of packages, children's activities, all facilities. Further along the beach **LL** *Sandals Royal Bahamian Resort and Spa*, PO Box CB-13005, T3276400, F3272009. Couples only, 406 rooms, all-inclusive, minimum 2 nights, lots of sports, every luxury, 3 pools, spa, further pool on private island, 8 gourmet restaurants.

West of Cable Beach Close to the airport: **LL-L** *Compass Point Beach Club*, on Love Beach, PO Box CB-13842, West Bay St, Nassau, T3274500, F3273299, www.islandlife.com 18 rooms in wooden cabanas, cottages on stilts or huts, all brightly painted in multi colours, wild orange, green and purple, fan, TV, CD, radio, bathrobes, mini bar, kitchens, pool, diving, part of Chris Blackwell's Island Outpost chain, background music all on his recording label. Most popular small property on the island drawing a big crowd to its restaurant, gorgeous waterfront patio for lunch and dinner at sunset. **AL-B** *Orange Hill Beach Inn*, PO Box N-8583, T3277157, F3275186, www.orangehill.com 32 rooms, pool, near beach, restaurant, bar, balconies, popular with divers, packages available, long term rates on request.

Paradise Island Sun International Hotels owns the huge **LL-L** *Atlantis*, PO Box N-4777, T3633000, F3633524. The feature of the new 2,355-room resort is the 14-acre waterscape and free form pool area with aquarium, 30,000 sq ft casino, 18-hole golf course, tennis courts, lots of restaurants including *Lagoon Bar and Grill* reached by underwater glass walkway with fish swimming all round you, a waterslide actually takes you via a perspex tunnel through the shark tank, lots of package deals available, including golf, air fares. Expansion and construction continues. Other large hotels include **LL-L** *Sheraton Grand Resort*, PO Box SS-6307, T3632011, F3633900, www.sheratongrand.com Refurbished 2000, 340 rooms, tennis, pool. **LL** *Club Mediterranée*, PO Box N-7137, T3632640, F3633496, www.clubmed.com 310 rooms, children from 12 years, large tennis centre with 20 courts, watersports. **LL** *Ocean Club*, T3636000, 800-3213000. Renovated and expanded in 2000 with new rooms and suites, work also being done to renew the beautiful Versailles gardens and Augustinian cloister in the grounds, fitness and tennis centre, former Paradise Island Golf Club redesigned by Tom Weiskopf as the new Ocean Club Golf Course, clubhouse and spa. Along Cabbage Beach, Smugglers Beach and other coastal strips by the golf course are the *Ocean Club Estates*, with 110 properties available. **B-C** *The Pink House*, PO Box SS-19157, T3633363, F3773383, pinkhouse@batelnet.bs Includes breakfast, a very small 4-roomed smart hotel in the grounds of the *Club Med*. **LL** *Club Land'Or*, T3632400, F3633403. Good suites and time share hotel, with good restaurant, shares *Atlantis* facilities. **LL-AL** *Paradise Harbour Club and Marina*, T800-7424276, phc@bahamas.net.bs 23 apartments and rooms, specializes in watersports for active guests. At the opposite end of the spectrum the **B** *Yoga Retreat*, PO

The Bahamas

Box N-7550, T3632902, F3633783. 40 rooms, very strict, no onions, not allowed to skip meditation, guests cook and wash up.

Crystal Cay   LL-L *Villas on Crystal Cay*, PO Box N-7797, T3281036, F3233202. Built in a row along rocky coastline but very private and enclosed, renovated in 1999, each of the 22 suites has small pool, bed sitting room, small kitchenette/dining area, large bathroom, luxury furnishings, leafy surroundings, unlimited access to the marine park.

South coast   LL-A *Clarion South Ocean Beach Resort*, PO Box N-8191 (Adelaide Rd) South Ocean, T3624391, F3624810. Set in 195 acres, with the main hotel attractively situated in the middle of the 18-hole, PGA-rated, par 72, 6,707yd golf course, ocean front rooms with jacuzzi in a separate section between main hotel and sea convenient for dive shop, several restaurants and bars, nightclub, 2 pools, exercise room, games, jogging trail, watersports, tennis.

Eating

A 15% gratuity will be added to every food & drink bill although service can be very slow & poor

Lunch is always cheaper than dinner and can be taken until 1700. The large hotels often offer free snack buffets during happy hours. Most hotels have expensive and formal restaurants but they also have good value buffets (US$12-20): *Portofino* in the *British Colonial Hilton*, downtown, sounds Italian but actually serves excellent buffets and à la carte selections, European and Bahamian cuisine, quiet ambiance.

Over US$60   For a special meal visitors are often encouraged to go to *Graycliff*, West Hill St. In a colonial mansion (also a hotel, see above), but service and food are not always up to the prices charged. *Blue Lagoon* in *Club Land'Or* for fish. Recommended (over US$50 per person). Also expensive but good are *Ocean Club* on Paradise Island and *Buena Vista*, on Delancey St, T322-2811/4039. Reservations required, men wear jackets, popular with business people, pianist, also 10-12 guest rooms. *Chez Willie*, West Bay Street. Serves fine Bahamian and French cuisine, management and executive chef trained at the 5-star *Graycliff*, just down the road. **US$41-60**   *Café Matisse*, Bank Lane, off Parliament Square. Classy, specializes in home made pasta and real Italian pizza, Impressionist art on the walls and classical music in the background, courtyard for outdoor dining. *Vesuvio's* on West Bay St. Good Italian restaurant. *East Villa* on East Bay St, T393-3377/3385. Chinese restaurant. *Compass Point*, see 'Sleeping', above, open air dining room overlooks sea, great for sunset watching, music on Island Record label, laid-back island atmosphere but service first class, menu selections, whether appetisers or main course, are gourmet and worth taking your time to savour. **US$21-40**   *Capriccio* on Cable Beach, tiny Italian eatery with home made pasta and equally authentic Greek salads. *Blue Marlin*, T3632660. One of only 2 restaurants on Paradise Island not owned by a hotel, lunch and dinner, steel band most nights, cheaper than hotels. For al fresco dining try *Passin' Jacks* or the *Poop Deck* on East Bay, *Traveller's Rest* near Gambier Village (always enjoyable). *Brussels Brasserie*, Frederick St, near Straw Market. Small non-descript room, but serving authentic Belgian cuisine in a Belgian bistro atmosphere, Belgian chocolate desserts, Belgian beer, home made breads, recommended for lunch. **US$11-20**   *Café Johnny Canoe*, Cable Beach, T3273373. Decorated entirely in the vibrant rainbow colours of Junkanoo (named after Johnny Canoe, see Festivals below), walls plastered with sepia photographs of early Nassau, most evenings a small group of Junkanooers parade through the restaurant in full regalia, playing goatskin drums, whistles and other traditional instruments. Food good too, excellent boiled fish and Johnny cake, sumptuous conch chowder. *Coconuts* (indoors) and *Le Shack* (same place but outside), East Bay St between Paradise Bridge and Nassau backing onto the harbour, T3252148. Where you can get exotic cocktails, Bahamian food and hamburgers. Cheap, cheerful and Bahamian are *The Shoal*, on Nassau St, and *Briteleys.Blue Lagoon* on Paradise Island has music, a trio. **Less than US$10**   Opposite the Central Bank, through arch down Market St is *Palm Tree*, which has very good native cooking and does takeaway. *The Bahamian Kitchen*, Trinity Plaza, opposite the Central Bank. No frills, neighbourhood restaurant specializing in the stick-to-the-ribs meals Bahamian mothers make, run by Mena Wallace.

The Joker's Wild Comedy Club, T3633000. Mostly US comedians and entertainers perform Tue-Sat. The *King and Knights* at *Nassau Beach Hotel* has a good native show, with steel drums etc. Native shows generally do not mean native to the Bahamas, but borrow from the culture of Trinidad and Jamaica with Junkanoo added. *Blue Marlin*, a restaurant/bar and nightclub on Paradise Island, offers a native revue similar to that at *King and Knights*, every night except Mon, starts 2115, lasts about 1½ hrs. *Club 601*, Bay Street. Live bands every evening, decor reminiscent of *Studio 54* (minus the glitter ball), it has the best Bahamian live music in town. Live bands can be heard at the *Waterloo*, East Bay (where you can bungee jump from 40 ft over the indoor swimming pool). Several restaurants have live music, see above. *We Place*, Thompson Av, US$4, is full of Bahamians and very lively at weekends. *Bahama Boom Beach Club*, down town on Elizabeth Av, T3257733. New dance nightclub, combination of techno pop and Caribbean. *The Zoo*, West Bay St. Tue-Sat, 2 restaurants, dancing areas, state of the art private lounges, theme bar, multi-faceted club caters for wide clientèle, from young parties to the sophisticated executive. Discos can be found in most of the larger hotels. Dinner cruises in the harbour on the *Majestic Lady*, Bay St, T3222606. Nightly for US$35pp. The *Dundas Centre for the Performing Arts*, Mackey St, T3222728. Regularly has shows and plays by local groups.

Junkanoo is a loud and boisterous national festivity loosely derived from African customs, celebrated on New Providence at 0300 on *26 Dec* and *1 Jan* (see more page 89) and, since 1999, in *Jun*. Every weekend in Jun there is live entertainment by Bahamian recording artists, dancers and performance artists, at an outdoor bandstand by the Arawak Cay Fish Fry. Festivities also include storytelling sessions and poetry readings on a porch patio, demonstrations of Junkanoo costume making and cowbell creations. An instant hit with locals and visitors alike, it has enlivened an otherwise quiet month. While the exact origins of Junkanoo are unknown, it is thought to have its roots in slave celebrations on their only days off in the year, at Christmas. John Canoe is said to have been a popular slave leader. Wild costumed rushers dance in Bay Street until dawn beating cowbells, heated goat skin drums and shak-shaks, and blowing whistles. As in Carnival in many countries, local businesses sponsor groups who spend the whole year making their costumes. There is a Junkanoo Museum at the Welcome Centre, by the cruise ships, where previous years' costumes are stored. Small Junkanoo displays can be seen on certain days in many of the large hotels. Parades with a military spirit and fireworks celebrate **Independence Day** on *10 Jul*.

Shops are open 0900-1700, Mon to Sat, but some close at 1200 on Thu. As there is no sales tax and many items are duty free, buying imported goods can save you about 20-50%, but shop around. The *English Shops* have Irish linen and gifts from England. Look in the *Perfume Shop* for French perfume. Try *John Bull* for watches and cameras. For unusual gifts look in *Seagrapes Too* and *Androsia of Cable Beach*, both in the Radisson Mall, which joins the *Radisson* and the Casino. *Marlborough Antiques*, West Bay, *Coin of the Realm*, Charlotte St, or *Best of the Bahamas*, east of the square. There are also international names like *The Body Shop*, *Benetton*, *Gucci* and *Colombian Emeralds* all in Nassau. In general, however, buy everything you could possibly need before you arrive as regular import duties are high. Most of the smarter, tourist-oriented shops are on (or just off) Bay St. For everyday shopping most people use suburban centres, of which the most convenient is in the Mackey St-Madeira St area. *Super Value* supermarkets have good variety of breads and salad bar (sold by the pound). The main fish and produce market is on Potters Cay (see above). Other fresh fish markets are Montague Foreshore, next to the Sailing Club and on West Bay St, opposite Fort Charlotte and at the entrance to Crystal Cay. The best book shop is *Logos Bookstore*, at the East Bay Shopping Centre, just past the Paradise Island Bridge, good selection and good quality. Also reasonable is the book department of the *Island Shop* on Bay St, but most cater for 'holiday reading'. Service in shops is often poor, be prepared to wait. Film developing at the *Island Colour Lab* in the Island shop, opposite the Straw Market, on Bay St or *Mr Photo* chain on the Market Range off Bay St.

Nightlife
Some clubs have a cover charge or a 2-drink minimum

Festivals

Shopping

The Bahamas

Transport   **Air From the USA**: from Albany(*US Air*), Atlanta (*Delta*), Boston (*Delta*), Buffalo (*US Air*), Burlington (*US Air*), Charlotte (*US Air*), Cincinnati (*Comair*), Columbus (*US Air*), Fort Lauderdale (*American Eagle, Continental Connection/Gulfstream International, Bahamasair, Chalks* to Paradise Island), Key West (*Continental Connection/Gulfstream*), Miami (*Continental Connection/Gulfstream, American Eagle, Bahamasair, Chalks* to Paradise Island), New York (*TWA, Continental, Delta, US Air*), Orlando (*Delta Connection, Comair, Continental Connection/Gulfstream, American Eagle, Bahamasair*), Philadelphia (*US Air*), Raleigh/Durham (*Comair*), Richmond, Virginia (*US Air*), Rochester, New York (*US Air*), St Louis (*Delta Connection*), Savannah (*Delta*), Tallahassee (*Gulfstream*), Tampa/St Petersburg (*Gulfstream/Continental Connection*), Washington DC (*Delta*), West Palm Beach (*Gulfstream/ Continental Connection*). **From Canada**: *Air Canada* flies from Montréal and Toronto. **From Europe**: *British Airways* have four flights a week from London (Gatwick); *AOM French Airlines* fly twice a week from Paris and Condor have charters from Germany. **From the Caribbean**: *Bahamasair* connects Providenciales with Nassau, *British Airways* flies from Grand Cayman on its way back to London but it is difficult to get on this flight unless you are going all the way to London, *AOM* from Havana, *Air Jamaica* from Montego Bay.

Local Bus: most buses run on one-way circular routes, which can be confusing. Route 10 goes out to Cable Beach along the coast road (leaving from beside *British Colonial Hilton Hotel*), route 16 goes along Eastern Rd to Fox Hill and Western Transportation buses go to the *Clarion* from Queen St (US$1.75). A bus runs between hotels and the golf course on Paradise Island (blue and white striped bus, US$0.50, 30-min intervals between 0800-0130) but no buses go over the bridge. **Car hire**: *Avis* (T3266380 or 3777121 at airport, avis@batelnet.bs); *Hertz* (T3778684); *Dollar* (T3778300) and *Budget* (T3777406) have offices at the airport and at other locations but local firms can be cheaper. *Orange Creek Rent-a-Car* has Suzuki runabouts for US$39 (T3234967). Large cash deposits can be required if you have no credit card. Scooters can be hired,*Gibson's Scooter Rentals*, T3252963, US$30-45. Helmets are provided and it is mandatory that you wear them. **Taxi**: taxis are abundant but expensive. The rates are government-controlled and are for two people. Zoned taxi fares: airport to Cable Beach, US$14, airport to downtown, US$20, airport to Paradise Island, US$24 (not including US$1 bridge toll), Cable Beach to downtown, US$10. You will be charged US$3 extra for additional passengers and for more than two pieces of luggage. To avoid overcharging, agree a price beforehand, or check that the meter is used. Taxi drivers in Nassau may "take you for a ride" otherwise. Taxis can be hired by the hour, US$20 per hour for up to 5 passengers, larger taxis for seven or more cost US$23 per hour. Tipping is not necessary but 15% is normally expected. For a limousine service, *Romeo's Executive Limousine Service* is highly recommended. Run by Bahamahost guide, Romeo Farrington, who has a white stretch limo and a fleet of lovely Bentleys, used for official visitors, special occasions or just sightseeing tours in style, T3276400, PO Box GT-2280. For radio-dispatched taxis T3235111 or 3234555.

Anchorage   At West Bay at west end of island is protected in most weather and you can stop there if it is too late to enter Nassau. Cruise ships, commercial shipping and yachts make Nassau harbour very busy. All vessels must check in and out with Harbour Control, VHF 16, when entering or leaving harbour. There is a VHF net for cruising boats. Anchorage in Nassau is limited and holding is poor. Theft and other security problems make it preferable to take a slip in one of the many marinas: West Bay, Lyford Cay Club and Marina, Great Harbour Cay Marina, East Bay Yacht Basin, Nassau Yacht Haven, Nassau Harbour Club Hotel & Marina, Paradise Harbour Club and Marina. If you need to clear customs, enter with quarantine flag raised and contact marina; customs and immigration staff will come to your vessel.

Directory   **Banks** See page 72. **Communications** See page 76. **Embassies & consulates** *British High Commission*, Bitco Building, East Street, T3257471. *Canada*, T3932123. *US* Embassy, Mosmar Building, Queen Street, PO Box N-8197, T3221181. Honorary consulates: *Denmark* and *Norway*, T3221340, F3288779. *France*, T3265061. *Germany*, T3228032 (office), T3243780 (residence). *Israel*, T3224130. *Japan*, T3228560. *The Netherlands*, T3235275. *Spain*, T3621271. *Sweden*, T3277944. *Switzerland*, T3221412. There is a *Haitian* Embassy, East and Bay Sts, T3260325. Consulate of the *Dominican*

Republic, T3255521. **Tour companies & travel agents** *Majestic Tours*, PO Box N-1401, Hillside Manor, Cumberland St, T3222606, F3261995. One of the main agents for trips to Cuba, although *Havanatur*, T3947195, F3945196, is better. *Happy Tours* (T3224011) arrange day trips to 'deserted' islands or cays, although the Blue Lagoon trip (see page 80) is probably better value. Many organized excursions offer the visitor an easy way of getting about but you can sometimes do the same thing by yourself for a lot less. As well as drives to places of interest, tours include visits to beaches on the Family Islands and trips aboard a catamaran with stops for swimming and sunbathing. **Tourist office** In the straw market, extremely helpful. Ask for the monthly *What's On* (www.whatsonbahamas.com) and the *Tourist News*. Another, *Best-Buys*, is also in your hotel or at the airport. There is also an information booth in Rawson Square (T3269772) and at the airport which will help you find accommodation. A Ministry of Tourism hotline for urgent assistance or complaints is T3256694, Mon-Sat 0900-1700, T3256694, Sun and holidays 0900-1300. The tourist office has a list of churches (and church services).

Grand Bahama

The nearest to the USA, this is where the most spectacular development has taken place. Nearly all the hotels are in Freeport/Lucaya, where golf and gambling are major attractions. The Freeport/Lucaya area is isolated from the rest of the island and most tourists never venture into the settlements. There is a marked division between the wealthy, Americanized and manicured tourist area and the rest of the island which looks like a Family Island, is less developed, almost forgotten, has a laid-back atmosphere and pot holes in the roads.

*Population: 46,954
2000 census
Colour map 2, grid A2*

The Bahamas

Ins and outs

For flights and ferries to Freeport see 'Transport', below. Taxis are available at the airport; expect to share, they leave when full and they are big. To Port Lucaya it costs US$10.50 for two people, tip at your discretion. Establish the fare before you set off.

Getting there

Getting to see most of Grand Bahama without a car is difficult. Cars can be rented at the airport or in Freeport on a daily basis (US$75 for a compact car, plus optional insurance of about US$12 a day), as can jeeps (US$60 per day), mopeds (US$20 per day) and bicycles. Public buses run from Freeport to Lucaya (US$0.75) and less frequently from Freeport to High Rock, Eight Mile Rock (US$1), Holmes Rock (US$2), West End (US$3) and East End. Check for timetable details. Buses are smaller than those in Nassau, carrying a maximum of about 20 people. There are routed stops with pink and white bus shelters in Freeport/Lucaya, but usually drivers will stop wherever you shout "bus stop coming up". Buses do not generally leave the bazaar or centre until full. Many hotels have a complimentary bus service for guests to the beach or in to Freeport. Taxi fares are fixed and cabs are metered but expect additional charges for extra passengers and more than two pieces of luggage.

Getting around
See 'Transport', page 101, for further details

Be careful of wild dogs. If out walking or jogging carry a stick. If bothered, local people stoop as if to pick up a stone. This gives some breathing space

Grand Bahama

The Bahamas

★ A Foot in the door

- **Kayak** the north coast through the quiet, undisturbed mangroves with Mrs Moultrie.
- Lunch at Tony Macaroni's **Roast Conch Stand** on Taino Beach, where he roasts delicious conch and fish in a barbeque pit made from half an oil drum while you recline in his plastic chairs, the surf lapping your heels drinking a cool beer.
- Rent a **dune buggy** and explore the beaches in the remote east end of the island away from the crowds.
- Head for McLean's Town and the conch cracking competition on **Discovery Day**, 12 October.
- Dance the night away at the open air **Count Basie Square** in Port Lucaya, with live local entertainment, great view of the marina and lots of gift shops and eateries around the square.

History

Thanks to a freshwater table under the island it has no water problem. The pinewoods which this natural irrigation supports were, indirectly, the beginning of the present prosperity. Early in the 1940s, an American millionaire financier, Wallace Groves, bought a small timber company and developed it into an enterprise employing 2,000 people. In 1955, the Bahamas Government entered into an agreement with him as president of the Grand Bahama Port Authority Ltd, granting to the specific area, called **Freeport**, owned by the Port Authority, certain rights and privileges which apply to that area only and to no other section of the Colony. Most important, the area was to be free of taxes and with certain concessions on several imported goods. In return, Groves would pay for government services within the area, promote industry and dredge a deepwater harbour. By 1961 a large cement works was under construction and the harbour housed a thriving ship bunkering terminal. Seeing the potential for a tourist industry, Groves made a further agreement with the Government in 1960. He formed the Grand Bahama Development Company and purchased a large area of land which was to become **Lucaya**. He also built a luxury hotel and casino, the first of its kind in the Bahamas.

So successful was this that the population of the island grew from 9,500 in 1963 to 35,250 in 1967. In the same period, the total investment rose from US$150 mn to US$577 mn and the tonnage of cargo handled increased 10 times to 1.25 mn tonnes. In 1969, however, the Government decided to introduce controls on the expansion of Freeport, and the vertiginous growth process slowed down. However, construction and sustained activity at the container port have begun affecting the fresh water table as well as the coral reefs and blue holes around the island.

Flora and fauna

Watch out for poison wood which is found in the bush and pine copses around beaches: it causes a very unpleasant rash over the body

Grand Bahama is mostly covered in scrub or Caribbean pines. The Royal and Cabbage palms found on the island have been imported, the former coming originally from Cuba. In the north there are marsh and mangrove swamps. Much of the coast supports the attractive sea-grape tree and it is not unusual to see children collecting grapes from the trees. Common flowers and trees are the yellow elder, the national flower of the Bahamas, the lignum vitae, the national tree, hibiscus, bougainvillea, oleander, poinciana and poinsettia. Common fruit trees include avocado, lime, grapefruit, mango and custard apple. There is not a great deal of wildlife on Grand Bahama, although you may see racoons, snakes, lizards and frogs. Birds include pelicans, herons, egrets, owls, woodpeckers, magpies, humming birds (mostly Cuban Emeralds), the rare olive-capped warbler, cranes and ospreys.

Diving and marine life

The paucity of wildlife on land is compensated by the richness of the marine life offshore. Rays often spring from the water in pairs, but be careful not to stand on them when snorkelling as they have a powerful whiplash sting. The spotted eagle rays are particularly beautiful when seen from above. Sea horses and moray eels are also common along the coral reef. It is illegal to break off coral or harvest starfish and there are fines for offenders. Shell collectors will find sand dollars and sea biscuits on the beaches. Conch usually has to be dived for but the beaches are often littered with empty shells.

Scuba diving is popular, with attractions such as **Treasure Reef**, where more than US$1 mn in sunken treasure was discovered in 1962, and **Theo's Wreck**, a deliberately sunk steel hulled freighter. The Underwater Explorers Society (UNEXSO) in Port Lucaya (T3731244, F3738956, PO Box F-42433, in the USA T954-3519889, F3519740) has a deep training tank and recompression chamber, and offers PADI, SSI and NAUI certification courses. This is a huge operation with a staff of 80, including 16 instructors and eight boats taking 10-30 divers. Snorkelling trips are US$15 including equipment. They rent underwater photographic equipment, film processing is available daily and video tapes of your dive or dolphin encounter are sold. The Dolphin Experience is a popular programme, usually booked well in advance. You take a boat from the UNEXSO dock to Sanctuary Bay, about 25 minutes, where large pens have been put in the lagoon to house the captive bottlenose dolphins. After a lecture on dolphins you can get into the water with them to touch them. Sessions at 1000, 1100 and 1400. You can also dive with the dolphins. Two dolphins are released from the pens, follow the dive boat out to the ocean, where they swim with the divers and return home afterwards.

UNEXSO

Other dive operators include Xanadu Undersea Adventures at the *Xanadu Hotel* (T3523811, F3524731), which offers certification courses (PADI, SSI, NAUI) and resort courses. Both UNEXSO and Xanadu offer shark dives. They take it in turns to dive the same site, so the sharks are fed nearly every day with frozen fish from Canada, just like the dolphins. The fish is free of parasites, but not their natural diet. *Caribbean Divers* are at *Bell Channel Inn*, across from Port Lucaya Marina, T3739111-2; *Sun Odyssey Divers*, T3734014. There is also the *Deep Water Cay Club* at East End, with no certification courses available. The *Deep Water Cay Club* is primarily a bone fishing lodge. Their boats fish over 200 square miles of flats and creeks. Accommodation is in cottages and cabins, there is a restaurant and private air strip, PO Box F-40039, T3533073, F3533095)

Dive centres

For the non-diver, there is a 1 ½ hr snorkelling cruise run by Paradise Water Sports, T3522887. You snorkel over the coral reefs and then over *Winky's* 40ft wreck, US$25 adults, US$18 children, equipment included.

Beaches and watersports

Generally, beaches can be classed as tourist or local, the former having sports and refreshment facilities as well as security and regular cleaning. The more remote beaches, on the other hand, are usually completely empty, unspoiled by commercialism and very peaceful, their only drawback being that there is often considerable domestic waste and rubbish washed ashore, probably emanating from the garbage collection ships on their way to Florida.

The island has several natural advantages over others in the group. It has miles of south-facing beaches sheltered from northerly winds and enjoys the full benefit of the Gulf Stream

Do exercise caution on the beaches as crime is common and most beaches have a security guard because of the high incidence of robbery and assault. Walking on beaches at night is definitely not a good idea and there is not necessarily safety in numbers. Also theft from parked cars is common so do not leave valuables in your car. Fortune Beach and the National Park Beach are both areas in which to be careful. Topless sunbathing is frowned upon by the Bahamians and skinny dipping is against the law.

Coral Beach is popular with windsurfers, cleaned regularly and has a small bar. Beach facilities are for hotel residents only and this policy is sporadically enforced with vigour. **Xanadu Beach** serves the *Bahamia and Xanadu Hotels* and various watersports are available through Paradise Watersports (T3522887), including jet skis, water-skiing, paddle boats, catamarans, snorkelling equipment (there is a good reef here within easy reach), fishing and parasailing. Use of jet skis and boats is limited to a cordoned area. Hair braiding is done on the beach by local children who have fixed prices according to the number of plaits and length of hair. Watch out for scalp burn afterwards. There is a straw market and a bar which has very loud live music on Sunday. Drinks or conch salad can be bought more cheaply if you walk just beyond the boundary fence where locals bring ice boxes of cold sodas. The *Glass Bottom Boat* operates from Xanadu Marina, tickets on sale on the beach. Make sure the sea is calm, it can be very rough outside the marina and then water visibility is poor and most passengers get seasick.

The **Lucayan Beach** area includes the beaches for the big resort hotels which are clean, with bar and sports facilities. Windsurfers, hobie cats, Boston whalers, snorkelling equipment, water skis and wave runners can all be hired here. At nearby Port Lucaya, Reef Tours operate the *Mermaid Kitty*, a glass bottomed boat which sails several times a day. They also have two-hour snorkelling trips, US$15 per person. Various booze cruises depart daily as well as a trimaran sunset trip.

On the road to West End past Eight Mile Rock are two good beaches for shelling, **Bootle Bay** and **Shell Bay**. At West End, the beach is rather small. There are good coral heads here, close enough to wade to.

One of the nicest beaches on the island with attractive palms and a few broken down old umbrellas is **Taino Beach**, which is over a mile long and has an excellent stretch of coral for snorkelling very close to the shore. The *Taino Beach Resort* on the first part of the beach has expensive condominiums which can be rented on a short term basis. The *Club Viva Fortuna Beach Resort* has been built with Italian investment in this area. **Fortune Beach** is sometimes used for tourist beach parties which are noisy and to be avoided. The renovated *Running Mon Marina and Resort*, T3526834, runningmon@batelnet.bs, is pristine and pretty. Austrian chef, Franz Seyser, prepares gourmet meals for the circular upstairs dining room and there is live music at the white grand piano in the centre of the room. The main attraction of the beach is the restaurant *Bahama Bay*. The beach is a bit rocky especially at low tide. Take care in this area, it is best to park near the restaurant as there have been many cars broken into in the rather lonely car park further along. The walk from William's Town along the beach is very pleasant, the vegetation being lush, mostly mangrove, sea grapes and tall grasses along the shore. The beach is used by Pinetree Riding Stables and occasionally local churches hold services here. Other beaches on the island include **Smith's Point** and **Mathers Town** just outside Freeport. Here you will find two popular bars: *Club Caribe* (Mathers Town) and the *White Wave Club* (Smith's Point).

Peterson's Cay is the archetypal one tree desert island and because of this can be crowded. Some tour companies run day trips to snorkel and eat lunch here. You can hire a boat to get there from Port Lucaya, the approach is a bit tricky because of the reef. Directly opposite is **Barbary Beach**, pleasant and backed by a wide pine copse (good for hanging hammocks). An old church here called the Hermitage was built in 1901 by an ex-trappist monk,

Of the less commercial beaches, **Gold Rock Beach** is probably the most beautiful on the island, about 20 miles east of Freeport and part of the Bahamas National Trust. *En route* to it you cross the Grand Lucayan Waterway, a canal built in the 1960s when development was booming. Barely used today, the canal bisects the island and the abandoned building sites are a reminder of what Freeport could have become had the planned development taken place. Once past the canal turn right and further along this road is a deserted, never-used film studio. If you take the left turn before the studio you come to a signposted road for the crossing to **Water Cay**. It is not always easy to get a boat across. If you take the left turn but carry on, the road becomes overgrown and pot holed, and the area is littered with small planes shot down by drug enforcement officers or abandoned by drug traffickers. Fat Albert, a barrage balloon full of radar equipment is supposed to have put a stop to aircraft landing on the road undetected. Another detour before reaching Gold Rock is to take the first turning after the film studio to Old Free Town, where there are blue holes and Mermaid's Lair, an opening to an underwater cave system. Further inland is a sink hole, the Owl Hole. Back on the road, turn off when you see the sign for the **Lucayan National Park**. There is a car park and a map. The 50-acre park was set up by workers from Operation Raleigh and a subsequent expedition laid the foundations (but nothing more) for a visitors centre. A Lucayan village and burial ground have been found here. The park contains the largest charted underwater cave system in the world. You can see two caves and climb to a lookout point. As well as bromeliads and orchids there are hundreds of bats in the first cave in the breeding season; also a rare water centipede found only in these waters. Across the road from the caves is a 1,000-yd board walk through mangrove swamp which leads to Gold Rock Beach. The beach is best seen at low tide as the sea goes out a long way and there is not much room to sit when the tide is in. The beach stretches for over a mile and is usually deserted. There are dunes and a large rock sticks out of the water giving the beach its name. It is excellent for shell collecting, but horseflies are very persistent so bring insect repellent. The picnic area is often too strewn with rubbish to be pleasant. Occasionally the area is cleaned.

Another wide, beautiful beach is **Pelican Point**, at the east end of the island, backed by Royal Palms and a very pretty and colourful village. There are fishing boats on the beach and it is not uncommon to see people gutting or cooking fish here. Pelicans can be seen flopping by. Roads out to the East End are poor and in places four-wheel drive is preferable.

Kayaking can be done with Kayak Nature Tours run by Mrs Moultrie from Hawksbill Creek, Queen's Cove, along north shore through mangrove creeks or Gold Rock Creek in the National Park, US$75 for all-day trip including lunch and transport; 16ft kayaks, single or double, no experience necessary, minimum age 10, T3732485.

There is no shortage of **golf** courses on Grand Bahama. The *Country Club at the Bahamia* has two heavily wooded, well conditioned, PGA championship courses, the 6,679yd Emerald and the 6,750yd Ruby, with 162 bunkers between them (also tennis courts and a six-mile jogging trail). The length of each hole is changed daily by moving the holes on the putting green. Reservations for starting times are essential and in peak season, winter, times are often booked a month in advance, T3526721, ext 4600. Carts are mandatory. The *Fortune Hills Golf and Country Club* is a 3,458yd, 9-hole scenic par 36 course with the longest par 5 (530 yards) in the Bahamas (T3732222). A challenging third hole (par 4) requires a difficult second shot over water. Friday night outdoor fish fry. The *Our Lucaya Reef Golf and Country Club* is a brand new 18-hole course designed by the Robert Trent Jones II Group and opened in 2000, T3731333. Thirteen of the holes are bordered by water. It is also home to the newly-opened *Butch Harmon School of Golf*. Butch Harmon has been described as the hottest teacher in golf by *Sports Illustrated*, and golf greats such as Tiger Woods and Greg Norman are often at the course getting lessons too. You can play **tennis** at the large resort hotels, courts often open to non-guests. The Grand Bahama Tennis and Squash Club (T3734567), behind the Freeport High School Auditorium on East Sunrise Highway, has courts available from 0930-2400 but you have to be a member.

Horse riding is available at Pinetree Stables (T3733600, PO Box F-2915), US$65 for 2-hour trail and beach ride with guide (20 horses, rider's weight limit 200 pounds), lessons can also be arranged with BHS and AIRA instructor (no credit cards). There is a **Rugby** and **Hockey** Club (Pioneers Way), which organizes various social events.

Other sports

The YMCA next to the Rugby Club can give information about watching local **basketball** and **softball** matches. **Volleyball** is a popular sport and many beaches and residential street corners have nets. There is a Super-Cross **Motor Cycle** dash in the autumn. **Aerobics** classes are available at most of the major hotels. There are several **jogging** routes but watch out for dogs. The Conchman Triathlon (swim/cycle/jog) is held in November. The GB5000 road race is in February, a 5 km flat race from *Bahamia Country Club*, with a one-mile fun run/walk and a run for children. Contact the Grand Bahama Island Promotion Board, T3528356, for information and registration. UNEXSO organizes a conch diving competition for locals at Port Lucaya.

Freeport

Freeporters have a reputation of being less friendly than other Bahamians, but this is often blamed on the design of the town and the lack of community spirit. Avenues are large and buildings are spaced far apart, there are few corner shops or neighbourhood bars and it is hard to go anywhere without a car. In downtown Freeport there are a few small shopping malls. If you take East Mall Drive out of town towards the airport you will pass the Rand Memorial Hospital and the excellent **Wallace Groves Library**. On the other side of the road is a bright pink pseudo classical building which is the Grand Bahama Port Authority Building. East Mall Drive connects with the Ranfurly Circle (named after 1950s British Colonial Governor) and the **International Bazaar**, a 10-acre integrated shopping complex on East Mall and West Sunrise Highway, with streets built in various assorted national styles with international merchandise and food. There is also a straw market and an Arts and Crafts Village behind it. ■ *Both open Mon-Sat 0900-1600, some stores on Sun.* To the rear of the International Bazaar, the other side of the street from *Colombian Emeralds International* and the Straw Market, is a perfume factory in a replica of an old Bahamian mansion, which you can tour briefly and even mix your own perfume. ■ *T3529391, F3529040, orders in USA 1-800-6289033, PO Box F-770, Freeport, open Mon-Fri,*

Freeport/Lucaya

N

Not to scale

■ **Sleeping**
1 Bahamia
2 Club Viva Fortuna
3 New Victoria Inn

4 Ocean Reef Yacht
   Club & Resort
5 Our Lucaya

6 Port Lucaya Resort
   & Yacht Club
7 Royal Islander

8 Royal Palm
9 Running Mon
   Marina & Resort

1000-1730. Just over a mile east of Ranfurly Circle you come to another roundabout. Turn right to get to the Lucaya area, where there is the **Port Lucaya** shopping and entertainment complex and a number of hotels, casino, marinas with lots of construction going on in 2000. At the Market place there is another straw and crafts market, open daily. UNEXSO is based here. In the evenings live music is played at the bandstand by the waterwalk.

Around the island

The **Hydroflora Gardens** on East Beach Drive, five minutes' drive from Ranfurly Circle, contain four acres of tropical plants grown hydroponically. Although the garden is on pure oolite rock, growth of up to 5 ft a year is achieved by this method. ■ *T3526052. Mon-Sat 0900-1730, US$1 or US$2 guided tour.*

Parrot Jungle's Garden of Groves is a 12-acre botanical garden of flowers, birds, pools and waterfalls. The centrepiece is a stone replica of the original church built for the loggers on Pine Ridge, and is a popular place for weddings. A children's petting zoo has pygmy goats and pot-bellied pigs and a jerk pit and picnic area has been added to give a family appeal. ■ *0900-1600 except Wed. Closed holidays. US$7.95. T3524045 for up to date information. Gardens located on Magellan Drive, 8 miles out of Freeport.*

The **Rand Nature Centre**, East Settlers Way, opposite the Catholic High School, two miles out of town, is a 100-acre forest with a few flamingos, hummingbirds and the rare olive capped warbler. Great birdwatching. Highly recommended for its explanation of the ecology of a Bahamian forest. Run by the Bahamas National Trust since 1992, work is being done on more educational programmes, more trail development and an improved self-guided tour. A replica of a Lucayan village is under construction. ■ *Mon-Fri 0900-1600, guided tours 1000 and 1400, US$5 (children US$3), T3525438, randnature@batelnet.bs, PO Box F-3441, Freeport. Special birdwatching walks are offered on the first Saturday of each month at 0700, 1½ hours, US$5 unless you are a BNT member, bring binoculars and field guide.*

Excursions from Freeport

The Bahamas

To High Rock, McLean's Town, Barbary Beach & Lucayan National Park

● Eating
10 Xanadu Resort & Marina
1 Bahama Bay
2 Phoenix
3 Pier One
4 Stoned Crab
5 Tony Macaroni's

West of Freeport   **Eight Mile Rock** (eight miles from Freeport) is the name given to eight miles of rock stretching east and west of Hawksbill Creek. The name refers to the town west of the creek. The Rock, as locals call it, has a strong sense of community not found in Freeport. The coastal road is prettier than the road directly through EMR although if you pass through the town you can see the original wooden clapboard dwellings raised off the ground, some with verandas where the inhabitants sit chillin' and rapping. Local bar, *The Ritz*, very friendly, see further page 100. Sample Mr Wildgoose's tequila. Along the coastal road is a boiling hole and the Catholic church in Hepburn Town with walls shaped like praying hands. East of Hawksbill Creek are the settlement areas of Pinders Point, Lewis Yard and Hunters. Off Pinders Point is a boiling hole called the Chimney, which causes a vortex. Below is a large cave system but you need to go with a very experienced cave diver to see it.

West End, 21 miles from Freeport, was supposedly the first settlement on Grand Bahama. It enjoyed prosperity as a haven for rum-runners during the American prohibition era. The coastal road is pleasant with local fishermen hooking conch from their boats on one side and bars, shops and houses in pastel shades on the other. At the most westerly point is new *Old Bahama Bay Hotel*, and marina, www.oldbahamabay.com built on the site of the *Jack Tar Hotel Village*, brainchild of Sir Billy Butlin, which was closed in 1990.

East of Freeport   Driving east from Freeport, you can see evidence of the aborted development plans, with many half-built plots, now mostly covered by bush, and roads which lead to nowhere. Fifteen miles east of Freeport, towards High Rock, is the 42-acre **Lucaya National Park**, with about 250 plant species, caves, plus a path through a mangrove swamp, built in March 1985 by volunteers from 'Operation Raleigh'. Continuing east you get to High Rock (20 miles) (*Ezekiel Pinder's Restaurant* has an ocean view – almost) and Pelican Point (10 miles further), excellent deserted beach. The road on to **McLean's Town** (see page 101 for details of the festival) and East End is poor, but passable. From McLean's Town you can get a boat across to Sweetings or Deep Water Cay. Neither has vehicular traffic. There is the *Traveller's Rest Bar* on Sweetings Cay. *Deep Water Cay Club* was established in 1958 and now has seven ocean front cottages and two 2-bedroomed houses for rent with packages for fishermen, T800-6884752, 954-3599488, Bahamabone@aol.com *East End Adventures* run four-wheel drive tours to Sweetings Cay and Lightbourne's Cay via the Lucaya National Park and McLean's Town, ■ *US$110 per person, US$50 for children under 12, including lunch. Also Blue Hole Shark Safari, US$85 for adults, US$35 for children. T3736662, 3526222 (after hrs), eastendsafari@hotmail.com*

Essentials

Sleeping   Price lists can be obtained from the tourist office in the Bazaar or in Lucaya. There has been
See also note   considerable development over the last few years with many of the large resorts sold,
on page 86   merged or rebuilt. Still in limbo is the former *Bahamas Princess Resort and Casino*, comprising the *Princess Tower* and the *Princess Country Club,* which were known in 2000 as the *Resorts at Bahamia* but are up for sale again.

Self-catering apartments are available at many resorts. To stay with a Bahamian family, write to the Grand Bahama Island Promotion Board, Freeport, see page 96 (tourist offices), and for details of the People-To-People Program me, see page 77 .

Port Lucaya **LL-AL** *The Our Lucaya*, Royal Palm Way, across the street from Port Lucaya Market Place, T3731333, F3738804, www.ourlucaya.com A merger and rebuilding of 3 hotels has created this huge 1,350-room resort with 7 ½ acres of private white sand beach, 2 swimming pools with water slides and waterfalls, spa, gym, full service conference centre, 15 restaurants and lounges, casino, lots of packages. **LL-AL** *Royal Palm*, Port Lucaya Marina Village, at the intersection of East Mall Drive and East Settler's Way, PO Box F-42654, Port Lucaya, T3739550, F3739551. 48 rooms, superior and deluxe all with balconies, a/c, phone,

TV, pool, hot tub, restaurant, bar. **LL-A** *Port Lucaya Resort and Yacht Club*, PO Box F-42452, T3736618, F3736652, www.portlucaya.com/resort Pool, jacuzzi, bars, restaurant, on reclaimed land jutting out into harbour, rooms and 1-2 bedroom suites, slips for 50 boats of 40-125 ft surround the resort, the adjoining marina caters for all sizes of yachts including a luxury, private dock, all services and facilities, for information on dockage call Jack Chester, T3739090, F3735884.

West along the coast LL-A *Xanadu Beach Resort and Marina*, PO Box F-42438, T3526782, F3525799, Xanadu@batelnet.bs Where Howard Hughes, the recluse, used to live on the top floors, there is a small study/library dedicated to him on the ground floor of the tower, which has a ring of apartments on top. Alongside is a lower rise block of rooms and restaurants, small pool, bar, 3 tennis courts with pro, dive shop and watersports centre on site, nice beach, 67 slips in marina. **AL** *Royal Islander Hotel*, on East Mall Drive opposite the International Bazaar, T3516000, F3513546. 100 rooms. **LL** *Ocean Reef Yacht Club & Resort*, T3734662, F3738261, geltex@batelnet.bs 63 waterfront suites. **A** *Running Mon Marina & Resort*, T3526834, F3526835, runningmon@batelnet.bs 32 waterfront rooms, meeting room. Less expensive hotels are **B** *The New Victoria Inn* off Midshipman Rd at the intersection with West Beach Drive, PO Box F-41261, T3733040, F3733874, 40 rooms, 2-bedroom suite, pool, transport to beach, shops, casino and **A-B** *Castaways* next to the Bazaar off the Ranfurly Circle, PO Box F-42629, T3526682, F3525087. 130 rooms on 4 floors, poolside or noisy roadside, TV, a/c, phone, small bathroom, courtesy transport to beach, avoid overpriced excursions, but none can be recommended for service.

Fortuna Beach LL-L *Club Viva Fortuna* , on 26 acres on south side of island, 4 miles east of Port Lucaya, PO Box F-42398, T3734000, F3735555, www.vivaresorts.com All-inclusive, 276 rooms with garden or ocean view, a/c, phone, cable TV, 2 big beds, lots of sports on land and in water.

The hotels have several expensive restaurants which serve native/international cuisine. Buffet brunches on Sunday are recommended, you can eat as much as you like at some of the major hotels (US$20 including as much champagne as you can drink). Many restaurants, particularly those in hotels, do Early Bird Specials from 1730-1830. Although some restaurants are efficient and friendly, be prepared for indifferent service and long waits in many. A cheap alternative is to go to one of the many cook outs, usually of a high standard. Often the proceeds go to a good cause, such as someone's hospital bills. Taino Beach hosts cook outs but best to look in local press for details.

Eating
Restaurants open & close with alarming speed, check the local newspapers for new ones or special offers

US$41-60 *Pier One*, at Freeport Harbour, where they feed the sharks around 2100, and *The Stoned Crab* on Taino Beach where West Beach Drive meets the sea, are both expensive, romantic, with good waterfront views. *The Ferry House*, at the edge of Port Lucaya Market Place, T3731595. Superb gourmet dishes, 4 freshly made types of bread with every meal, flickering candles on linen tablecloths, lovely view of the bay, expensive but worth every penny. The *Ruby Swiss Restaurant* on West Sunrise (seafood) is expensive but service is good. **US$21-40** *Bahama Bay* on Fortune Beach, friendly, reasonably priced menu, mosquitoes and no see'ums can be troublesome if you eat outside. *The Buccaneer Club* at Deadman's Reef has a courtesy bus (call 349 3794) but if you use it you will be presented with a higher priced menu on arrival, about 40-mins' drive from Freeport, Wed night specials, closed in Oct, interesting guest signature book. *Luciano's* in Port Lucaya, good, book a table outside to see fireworks over the square on Sat evenings at 2030-2100, noisy music though. *Fat Man's Nephew* in Port Lucaya, T3738520. Reasonably priced, good view of bandstand, open 1200-2400 except Tue 1700-2400 and Sun 1700-2300. (*Fat Man* in Pinder's Point used to be popular but the owner, Fat Man, was gunned down by an armed robber.) **US$11-20** *The Traveller's Rest*, Williams Town. Good cheap breakfasts, Johnny Cake and soused fish are popular. *The Outriggers* at Smith's Point, just outside Lucaya at the far end of Taino Beach, T3734811. Distinctly Bahamian flavour, phone to check menu, fish fry outdoors on Wed night. Nearby at Smith's Point is *Mama Flo's*, similar, even more popular for fish fry on Wed when there is lots of loud music and barbecues. *Silvano's* on Ranfurly Circus, along the entrance to the International Bazaar, at the intersection of West Sunrise Highway and East Mall Drive, serves Italian. *Islander's Roost*, opposite International Bazaar, by *Silvano's*, open-air dining patio, live entertainment, variety of Bahamian and American dishes, mascot Bella the parrot oversees all. For oriental dishes there are at least 3 Chinese restaurants in the International Bazaar, the one at the entrance is not recommended. The *Phoenix* (*Silver Sands Hotel*) serves kebabs and curries and has an unusual bar. *Kristi's* in the Bain Building, West Atlantic Drive, Downtown, T3523149. Takeaway or eat in, open Mon-Sat 0800-1600. *Tony Macaroni's Roast Conch Stand*, Taino Beach, just west of *The Stoned Crab*. An open air stall under a tiny thatched roof, Anthony (Macaroni) Hanna prepares roast conch, fish and some- times crayfish, served in aluminium foil pouches with fresh raisin buns, cooked in a barbeque pit made from a half 55-gallon drum, relax on one of his plastic lawn chairs at the water's edge with food and a cold beer. **Less than US$10** *The Back Home Native Hut*, Sergeant Major Drive, pea soup, Bahamian cooking.

Nightlife **Bars** There are many in Freeport, most have a Happy Hour between 1700-1900, and most of the restaurants mentioned above have bars. The *Pub on the Mall, Britannia Pub* and the *Winston Churchill* are all English style pubs. The *Winston Churchill*, T3528866, serves pizzas, fish 'n' chips, sells draught Courage and hosts the Gong Show on Wed (starts around 2330, open 1100-0200). *Shenanigan's* in Port Lucaya with an English-style pub menu is in a very pleasant location overlooking the waterfront and band stand where live calypso music is played most nights. *The Prop Club* sports bar & grill across the street at *The Our Lucaya* has an ocean front setting, big screen TV, beachfront activities and a native show. For cheaper drinks in a less touristy environment, *Outriggers, Surfside* and *The Traveller's Rest* are recommended. *The Ritz* in Eight Mile Rock has a number of hammocks outside which overlook the sea (rubbish spoils the view), there has been some night-time violence at the bar, better to go during the day. *The Ruby Swiss* on East Sunrise Highway, lively 0100-0400 when casino workers gather there after their shift ends. *The Bahama Mama* in the east corner of the Port Lucaya complex is one of the most popular bars, attracting local, expatriate and tourist customers giving it a lively, cosmopolitan atmosphere, interesting music, busy from 2300 onwards.

Shows Most hotels have native shows. The *Yellow Bird Club* close to the International Bazaar, T3522325. Limbo, drums, fire dancing and a glass eater. The casino show at the *Bahamia* is good, with a large cast, well-choreographed, bright and lively. The huge casino has 20,000 sq ft of gaming space. At the *Bahamia Country Club* there is *Goombaya*, a dinner and island music review, culminating in a Junkanoo rush-out. At the *Yellowbird Show Club* in the International Bazaar, the *Yellowbird Island Review* features fire and limbo dancers. The *Bahamian Native Cultural Show* is held at the Port Lucaya Market Place, at Count Basie Square, with dancing, live bands and fire eating. *Club Amnesia*, T3522899, has Bahamian and Las Vegas revues three nights a week, a magic act and island review, *Sensation*, live Caribbean bands at the weekend, and is often the nightclub of choice for visiting entertain- ers who want a smaller venue with more intimate contact with guests.

Discos At most of the large hotels, with two drinks in entrance fee. If you want to know which disco is flavour of the month, ask the croupiers at the casino as they closely monitor the nightlife. *Goombay Land* behind *The Party Palace* has roller skating and go-karts, very popular with local youth, entrance US$5.

Festivals **Junkanoo** is held on *1 Jan* in Freeport. Beginning from the Ranfurly Circle, dancing outside *Bahamia Hotel* 0400 onwards with drums, cowbells, whistles, brass instruments and fog- horns. Scrap gangs, impromptu groups, join in with the rushin'. Much smaller than Nassau's but worth seeing. Go to Ranfurly Circle early to see the participants flame heating their goat skin drums to stretch them. On *10 Jul*, **Independence Day**, a Junkanoo parade is held at 0400 in West End and also on the first Mon in *Aug*, which is a holiday to commemorate the emancipation of the slaves. Many of the hotels include a small Junkanoo as part of their native show.

On **Discovery Day**, *12 Oct*, a fair is held at McLean's Town, including a conch-cracking competition started by a British couple in the 1940s. The aim is to see who can remove the most conch from their shell in 10 mins. The women's competition has many machete-wielding experts who bring a lot of partisan support. There is also a swimming race to a nearby islet and back, which attracts a lot of local competition. The plaiting of the Maypole is an interesting Caribbean version of the English tradition, with children dancing round the pole to the beat of Reggae songs. Although much of the road to McLean's Town has been paved, the road is very poor in parts. Minibuses run regularly from Ranfurly Circle (US$2). If you rent a car it is sometimes difficult to park. Look out for details of local fairs in the Freeport News and at the Ranfurly Circle.

Shopping

Many items are tax exempt in the bonded area of Freeport/Lucaya and bargains include perfume, linens, sweaters, china, cameras, emeralds, watches, leather goods and alcoholic drinks. The two main shopping areas are the International Bazaar and Port Lucaya. The **International Bazaar** is off Ranfurly Circle. Built in 1967, the 10-acre complex was designed by a film special effects expert, with shops designed in national styles and selling corresponding food and goods, although the overall effect is very American. The entrance is a giant Torri gate, the Japanese symbol of welcome. **Port Lucaya** was the brainchild of Count Basie, who used to live on Grand Bahama. The atmosphere is usually friendly and there is live music most evenings. There are many different shops to buy souvenirs as well as a straw market. The Rastafarian Shop has some interesting souvenirs and there is a Bahamian Arts and Crafts stall in the centre of the complex, one row back from the central bandstand. In downtown Freeport there are a few small shopping malls.

A Vendors Committee has been set up for hair braiders, conch sellers and peddlers, to control and regulate their operation and prevent complaints of hassling by tourists. A photo identification card is to be worn by all vendors and they will generally wear Androsia batik tops. They must have a permit and to have completed a Bahamahost programme. Hair braiding is US$2-3 per braid.

Transport

Air From the USA: *Airtran Airways* from Atlanta and Chicago, *TWA* from New York (La Guardia), *American Eagle*, *Gulfstream International* and *Bahamasair* from Miami. *LB Limited* from Baltimore, Cincinnati, Cleveland, Fort Lauderdale, Hartford, Pittsburgh, Raleigh/Durham, Richmond and West Palm Beach; *Gulfstream/Continental Connection* from Fort Lauderdale, Jacksonville, Key West, Miami, Orlando, Tampa and West Palm Beach. *Grand Bahama Vacations* flies two weekly non-stop jets from 10 US cities including Pittsburgh and Memphis, and daily from Fort Lauderdale. **From the Caribbean:** *Aerocaribbean* flies twice a week from Havana.

Sea From the USA: *Sea Jets* have two 250-passenger jet foils from Palm Beach twice daily, Thu-Mon, 1½ hours, US$99 return (US$49 for children under 16), plus arrival and departure tax of US$25. The *Discovery Cruise Line* has a daily round trip between Fort Lauderdale and Freeport, US$109 plus taxes. **From Nassau**: The mailboat, *M/V Marcella III*, sails from Nassau on Wed 1600, returns Fri 1700, 12 hours.

Car hire *Five Wheels Car Hire*, T3527001; *Hertz*, T3522977; *Dollar Rent A Car*, T3529325 at the airport, T3739139 at Lucaya. *Bahama Buggies*, T3528750, dune buggy rentals at low rates, free pick up and drop off. Check the telephone yellow pages for many more. Rates are US$49-119 for 24 hrs, with unlimited mileage. **Taxi** From the Harbour to the International Bazaar cost US$10 and to Port Lucaya US$14, for 2 people, tip at your discretion. Be sure to establish the fare in advance especially when there are people going to different destinations. Report any problems to the Ministry of Tourism. A strict rotation system is used and **buses** are not allowed into the harbour area.

Directory

Banks See beginning of the chapter page 72. **Communications** See page 76. **Tourist office** In Freeport, Bazaar, Port Lucaya Market Place, as well as in any large hotel. The Tourist Information Centres in Freeport/Lucaya can give a brochure listing all licensed hotels in the Bahamas and their rates. *The Grand Bahama Island Promotion Board* can be contacted through PO Box F-40251, Freeport, T3528044, F3527840, or in Florida, PO Box 22857, Fort Lauderdale, FL33335, T800-4483386. Port Lucaya Market Place information, T3738446, Marina information, T3739090, www.portlucaya.com

The Family Islands

The Family Islands, often called the Out Islands, are very different in atmosphere from New Providence and Grand Bahama. The larger islands are up to 100 miles long, but have only a few thousand inhabitants. Sea and sky come in every possible shade of blue, there are wild cliffs and miles of white sand beaches. Inland, pine forests grow in the northern islands, dry woodland in the central islands and sparse scrub vegetation in the southern islands. Red-coloured salt ponds were once the basis of a thriving salt industry on the south islands, but the land offered few other economic possibilities, though one other product was Cascarilla bark, used to flavour Vermouth and Campari. Thousands of yachts visit the islands, mainly during the winter season. The sea is clean and clear and ideal for swimming, snorkelling and scuba diving. Most of the islands have relatively few tourists, although Eleuthera and one or two others have big, resort-type hotels with marinas and sports facilities.

Ins & outs

Getting there Most islands have at least one *Bahamasair* flight a day and at least one mailboat a week. If you are travelling in a group, a small charter plane may be much more convenient and only a little more expensive. Some islands also have a direct flight from Miami or another Florida airport; this cuts out the need for an unreliable, time-consuming connection in Nassau.

Getting around Travel is restricted to one main road per island, usually called the Queen's Highway. Car, jeep or bike rental is generally available; there are taxis and water taxis but no bus service.

Abaco

Population: 13,174
2000 census
Colour map 2, grid A2

The Abaco islands, a chain of islands and cays within the Family Islands, are covered in pine forests, stretching in a curve for 130 miles. It is the second largest land mass in the Bahamas after Andros. The main centre on Abaco is Marsh Harbour, which is the third largest town in the Bahamas. Its name reflects the swampy nature of much of Greater Abaco. The scrub and swamp give the island a rather desolate appearance, but like many islands, life revolves around the offshore cays and the coastal settlements. The area south of Marsh Harbour owes its development and particularly its roads to lumber companies. There are miles and miles of pine forests, secondary growth after the heavy logging earlier this century. Nobody lives south of Sandy Point although there is a lighthouse at Hole in the Wall. Roads are better in the north, where they are mostly paved, while in the south they are dirt. Resorts are small and the atmosphere is casual and friendly even in the most luxurious hotels.

Ins and outs

Getting there There are airstrips at Marsh Harbour (MHH), Treasure Cay (TCB) and Walker's Cay (WKR). American (T800-4337300), Island Express (T3673597). Several airlines fly to Marsh Harbour and/or Treasure Cay from Fort Lauderdale, Key West, Miami, Orlando, Tampa and West Palm Beach in Florida. *Bahamasair* provides domestic air services to Nassau, Freeport and on to other islands. Walker's Cay is served by Pan Am Air Bridge from Fort Lauderdale. Look out for package deals to the various resorts with Bahamasair. Charter planes including *Abaco Air*,

T3672266, 3672205, PO Box 492, Marsh Harbour, VHF 74; *Cherokee Air*, T3672089, 3672613, 3672530, PO Box 485, Marsh Harbour; *Zig Zag Airplane Charter*, T3672889, Marsh Harbour.

A **taxi** from Marsh Harbour airport to the ferry dock costs US$12 for two; from Treasure Cay airport to the ferry for Green Turtle Cay US$3 per person, minimum US$5. Unmetered taxis charge US$1.50 per mile. **Car rental** can be arranged in Marsh Harbour or Treasure Cay with a number of companies: *H & L Car Rental* (Marsh Harbour, T3672840); *Wilmac Rent-a-Car* (Marsh Harbour Airport, T3674314); *Carl's Car Rentals* (Marsh Harbour Airport, T3672493, Visa/MC accepted); *Cornish Car Rental* (Treasure Cay, T3658623); *McKenzies Car Rental* (Treasure Cay, T3658849/3652249).

Getting around
Several inter-island ferries transport residents and visitors from one settlement or cay to another. For ferry information see transport, page 111

History

The Taino name for Abaco was Lucayoneque, although the first Spanish reference to it was Habacoa, a name also used for Andros. The Spanish did not settle, but by 1550

The Bahamas

Abaco Islands

National Parks
1 Fowl Cay, Bahamas National Trust Preserve
2 Pelican Cays Land & Sea Park

0 km 5
0 miles 5

N

they had kidnapped all the Indian inhabitants for slavery elsewhere and the islands remained uninhabited for 200 years, despite a brief French attempt at settlement in 1625 and visits by pirates and fishermen. In 1783 over 600 loyalists left New York for Abaco, settling first at Carleton (north of Treasure Cay beach but no longer visible) and then moving to Marsh Harbour. Other groups settled further south but all found it hard to make a living on the small pockets of soil and of the 2,000 who arrived in the 1780s, only about 400 (half white and half black) were left in 1790.

Wrecking was a profitable pastime and Abaco was ideally placed on a busy shipping route to take advantage of its reefs and sand banks. Sponge, pineapple, sisal, sugar and lumber were later developed but never became big business. Wrecking also declined after the construction of lighthouses. The lighthouse on Elbow Cay at Hope Town was built in 1863, after the wreck in 1862 of the *USS Adirondack*, despite sabotage attempts by local people. By 1900 Hope Town was the largest town in the Abacos, with a population of 1,200 engaged in fishing, sponging, shipping and boat building. The boats made in Abaco were renowned for their design and the builders became famous for their construction skills. Boats, though made of fibreglass, are still made on Man-O-War Cay today.

The inhabitants of Abaco continued to live barely at subsistence levels until after the Second World War, when the Owens-Illinois Corporation revived the lumber business, built roads and introduced cars. An airport was built at Marsh Harbour and banks arrived. When the pulpwood operation ended in the 1960s sugar replaced it but was short lived. Nowadays the major agribusiness is citrus from two huge farms which export their crop to Florida. Abaco has developed its tourist industry slowly and effectively and has a high employment rate. The population increased by nearly a third during the 1990s.

Flora and fauna

Like other northern Family Islands, Abaco is mostly covered by secondary growth stands of Caribbean pine, interspersed with hammocks or coppices of hardwoods such as mahogany and wild coffee. The Bahama parrot, extinct on all other islands bar Inagua, survives in these coppices, 42 breeding pairs have been counted. A captive breeding programme is now in progress and fledglings will be released back into these areas. In the wild, the parrots nest around Hole in the Wall and the area is to be made a reservation for them. A herd of wild horses roams the citrus groves and pine forests in the north. They are a hardy breed of work horses descended from those used in the sawmills which closed in the 1920s and 1930s.

Diving and marine life

Dive sites Many areas are now officially protected and fish life is abundant, green turtles and porpoises numerous in and around harbour areas. Fishing is strictly controlled in reef areas although the coral still shows signs of previous damage by bleaching and careless sailors. Three of the best reefs for diving or snorkelling are **Sandy Cay Reef** (part of Pelican Cay Park), **Johnny's Cay Reef** and **Fowl Cay Reef** at each of which there are several dive sites and a few permanent moorings for small boats. Don't miss **Pelican Cay Land and Sea Park**, which is an underwater wildlife sanctuary, fishing or spear fishing allowed and **Fowl Cay Bahamas National Trust Preserve** with similar restrictions. If you like exploring wrecks, the 110-year old *USS Adirondack* with her rusting cannon is worth a visit. If it is windy or the sea rough there is unlikely to be any diving because of poor visibility in the shallow waters. Inland you can dive into Devil's Hole.

For offshore **snorkelling**, *Captain Nick's Tours*, from the *Jib Room* marina and restaurant, runs trips out to local reefs and beauty spots, including Pelican Cay. Snorkel gear is available for hire. For **dolphin-watching** and other nature tours, Diane Claridge, T3674545. Marsh Harbour lacks good beaches, but **Mermaid's**

Revolution Abaco style

The 1967 elections resulted in a victory for Lynden Pindling's party the Progressive Liberal Party (PLP), which represented the black majority of the Bahamas. Abaco, which was 50% white, voted for the opposition.

In the early 1970s some Abaco residents formed the Greater Abaco Council which was opposed to Bahamian independence. When independence became a reality in 1973, the Abaco Independence Movement tried to assert Abaco's independence from the rest of the Bahamas. This breakaway movement by white residents caused the islanders to split into two camps and there were bitter conflicts.

According to local storytellers, there was going to be a revolution, but there was confusion over whether it was planned for Wednesday or Thursday, then some men went fishing and, well ....

Support for the main opposition party, the Free National Movement (FNM), remained strong in Abaco. In 1992, and again in 1997, it was elected to government and its Prime Minister, Hubert Ingraham, lives near Coopers Town.

Cove on the road to the Point is a pretty little beach with excellent snorkelling. The best beach on Great Abaco is probably that at **Treasure Cay**, there is a large, sandy bay backed by casuarina trees and a friendly beach bar. On the cays there are lots of sandy beaches, many of which are best reached by boat. Boat rental, *Rich's Boat Rentals*, across from the fish house, Marsh Harbour, T3672742; *Blue Wave Boat Rentals*, at Harbour View Marina between *Tiki Hut* and *Mangoes*, T3673910; *The Moorings*, at the *Conch Inn Marina*, T3674000; *Pier One Boat Rentals*, at the *Jib Room*, Marsh Harbour Marina, T3672700 and *Sea Horse Boat Rentals*, at *Abaco Beach Resort*, T3672513.

Dive centres Specialist dive operations include: *Dive Abaco* at Marsh Harbour (*Conch Inn Marina*, T3672787, VHF 16, F3674779, dives in the morning, one boat, two instructors but often only one member of staff per dive; *Abaco Beach Resort Dive Centre*, T3674646, offers day trips, reef dives, wrecks, snorkelling; *Divers Down* at Treasure Cay (T3658465, F3658508, one tank US$50, two tanks US$70, snorkelling US$30); *Brendal's Dive Shop* at Green Turtle Cay, who can offer introductory courses, wreck, catacomb and cavern dives, and a wide variety of facilities, T/F3654411; *Green Turtle Divers*, T3654271, is a PADI International Resort member and a NAUI Dream Resort, with a wide range of offerings, from PADI Bubble makers for children to blue hole diving for experts, Mark Knowles runs the facility and his pet nurse shark, Bandit, is a featured attraction; *Dave's Dive Shop*, Hope Town, T3660029, is a fully equipped dive shop with dive gear and boat rentals, and guided snorkelling and scuba; *Froggies Out Island Adventure*, next to the Post Office, Hope Town, T3656494, PADI dive instructor, all day scuba and snorkel trips to Fowl Cay and Sandy Cay.

Sailing Life revolves around the sea and Abaco is sometimes called the 'sailing capital of the world', with good marina facilities at the 150-slip *Treasure Cay Hotel Resort & Marina*, one of the largest tourist resorts in the Family Islands, the *Conch Inn Resort and Marina* (a 75-slip marina can accommodate boats up to 140ft), the Boat Harbour Marina by the *Great Abaco Beach Hotel* (160 slips, boat hire, services, showers, laundromat, will hold mail, T3672736, VHF 16) and the *Green Turtle Yacht Club and Marina*. Winter (December-March) can be harsh with strong cold fronts and gale-force northerly winds making sailing and other watersports uncomfortable. Spring and summer are better. Most yachts prefer to winter further south in the Exumas and return to the Abacos later in the year. Marsh Harbour Regatta is 22 June to 4 July. Marsh Harbour is the starting place/drop off for many sailing charter companies. Charters can be arranged by the day or week, through numerous agencies (such as Sun Sail at Marsh Harbour, ABC at Hope Town or JIC Boat Rentals and Charter at Treasure Cay, T3672507), or more cheaply by private arrangement with

The Bahamas

boat owners. Ask at local marinas such as the *Jib Room*. Fishing charters can also be arranged.

Other sports   You can play tennis at *Bluff House, Great Abaco Beach Hotel, Green Turtle Club* or *Walker's Cay Hotel and Marina. Treasure Cay Beach Hotel and Villas,* has a 6,972yd, 18-hole championship golf course (T3672570) and tennis.

Marsh Harbour

Population 6,000, the third largest town in the Bahamas after Nassau and Freeport   The town straggles along the flat south shore of a good and busy yachting harbour. It has the major airport about three miles from the town and is the commercial centre of Abaco. As you drive in from the airport you pass government offices, supermarkets and lots of churches and liquor stores. The town has a large white population, but at the 1990 census 40% were found to be Haitian, most of whom lived in the districts of Pigeon Pea and The Mud and worked as domestic servants in the white suburbs. Many Haitians have since been repatriated, but others have put down roots, raised families and now have resident status. Shops are varied and well stocked and international banks are represented. The only traffic lights on the island are outside Barclays. Batelco is a yellow building off Queen Elizabeth Drive. The Tourist Office is nearby. The main food stores are *Golden Harvest; A&A Food Store* (T3674521), *Boat Harbour Mini Market* (T3674711), *Roderick's Convenience Store* (T3673237) and *Wilson's Quick Trip* (T3672653). The Bahamas Family Market on Front Street sells mainly fruit and vegetables grown on Abaco.

Around the island

The roads are better in the northern half of the island and it is easy to drive the 26 miles to **Treasure Cay**, a self-contained resort approached by a long drive through the grounds, past the golf course. There is a nice beach here, ranked by *National Geographic* in 2000 as one of the top ten in the world, and lots of watersports available at the marina. The main road continues past Treasure Cay airport and several small communities, where most of the workers for *Treasure Cay* live, to **Coopers Town**. Twenty miles from Treasure Cay, it has lots of little painted wooden houses and an air of bustling importance. It is the seat of the commissioner for North Abaco and about 900 people live here. The Prime Minister, Hubert Ingraham, was raised here, but now lives in Nassau. In 1993-94 a new health clinic was built, the biggest on the island with doctors, dentists and nurses working there. There is no harbour but along the waterfront are wooden jetties where fishermen clean their catch, leaving piles of conch shells. Offshore on Powell Cay (uninhabited), there are some lovely beaches, good shelling and the *Shipwreck Bar and Grill*. The paved road carries on another 15 miles to Crown Haven, the end of the island.

South of Marsh Harbour it is 56 miles to **Sandy Point**, through citrus groves, or you can fork left to Hole in the Wall, the area where parrots breed. On the way you can visit Spencer Bight and the abandoned Wilson City, a company town founded in 1906 by the Bahamas Timber Company but closed in 1916. In its heyday there was a saw mill and dock facilities and it boasted electricity and an ice plant, both rarities at that time. At **Little Harbour** you find the highest point in Abaco, which is 120 ft. Little Harbour is a small, pretty and protected anchorage, famed for the Johnston family's artwork in bronze, ceramics and jewellery. Their work is on display in two galleries. ■ *1030-1200, 1400-1500 or by appointment, closed Sun.* Pete Johnston also has *Pete's Pub*, where there are moorings and you can eat at the open-air bar on the beach (hot dogs, hamburgers, lobster). There is a nice walk to the old lighthouse and snorkelling is good over the small reef at the east entrance to the harbour. There are caves where the Johnstons lived when they first came to Little Harbour. If you go on Independence Day, 10 July, there is a free for all on the beach, everyone chips in, roast wild pig a feature.

The name Elbow Cay is rarely used, people refer to the settlement as **Hope Town**, the main town. It is marked by a striped lighthouse from the top of which you can get lovely views. Built by the British Imperial Lighthouse Service in 1863, it is one of the last hand-powered Kerosene-fuelled beacons still in use. ■ *Mon-Fri 1000-1600.* **Hope Town** is very picturesque, set around a charming harbour, cluttered with jetties and brightly painted wooden houses. Cars are not allowed along the narrow streets edged by white picket fences and saltbox cottages. Visit the Wyannie Malone Historical Museum which has a collection of old furniture, genealogies and memorabilia from the town. The museum is staffed by volunteers. If it is not open, call Peggy Thompson at *Hope Town Hideaways*. The town's jail is no longer used as such, but is filled with visitor's brochures. There are several places to eat and drink in the town, there are grocery stores, bakeries and gift shops. **White Sound**, southwest of the town, has a couple of resorts. A lovely beach runs along the ocean side of the island and **Tahiti Beach** is at the extreme end in the southwest. Bicycles can be hired but it is a rough ride down to the south. Dave's Boat Rentals, T3660029, VHF 16, next to Hope Town Lower Ferry Dock, rents Boston Whalers or larger boats, which are an easier way of getting around. Dave also rents diving gear and tanks. Hopetown marina has fuel, moorings, dockage.

Man-O-War Cay

This cay is a boat building and repair centre with New England Loyalist origins, where, until recently, blacks were not allowed to stay overnight. Nearly everyone on the island can trace their family back to Pappy Ben and Mammy Nellie, a young couple who settled there in the 1820s. There are two boatyards now, Edwin's Boat Yard, which specializes in boat repair and building fibreglass outboard boats, and Albury Brothers Boat Building, which makes smaller, fibreglass runabouts. Albury's Ferry is based here. It is very pretty, with a good beach on the east side and snorkelling at the north point. The Marina offers full services, T3656008, VHF 16, and a gift shop. There are a couple of small places to eat, but they really cater for the takeaway trade, and a couple of grocery stores. No alcohol is sold on the island, you have to go to Marsh Harbour for that. The CIBC bank is open Thursday only. There are no cars, people use golf carts and scooters. Sundays are graveyard quiet.

Great Guana Cay

The population of Great Guana Cay is about 100. There are a few shops, including a grocery and a liquor store, and most services are available. A wide, sandy beach extends nearly the length of the ocean side of the island, about 5½ miles, although the north end has been developed for use of Treasure Cay visitors. For snorkellers there is a reef just off the beach at High Rocks, southeast of Guana Harbour.

Green Turtle Cay

The picturesque and quaint village of **New Plymouth** can be reached from Treasure Cay airport by a short taxi ride (US$3 per person, minimum US$5) and then a ferry from Treasure Cay Dock (US$8, children 2-11yr, US$4, one-way, to Black Sound, White Sound, Bluff Cay or Coco Bay, ferry is three times a day, timed to meet planes, but can be chartered any time, VHF 16). The **Albert Lowe Museum** chronicles the British settlers who came in the 18th century and their shipbuilding skills. The **Memorial Sculpture Garden** is also worth a visit. The island has some lovely beaches, ideal for shelling, and boats are easily rented for exploring other cays. On New Year's Day, the inhabitants celebrate the capture of Bunce, a legendary figure said to have lived in Abaco's pine forests.

Spanish Cay

Spanish Cay is a private 185-acre island off Cooper's Town which has recently been developed as a resort. There is a 5,000 ft runway and a full-service marina with a dive shop, *Spanish Cay Diving*. Transport on the island is by golf cart or walking. **LL-L** *Spanish Cay Inn and Marina* has five villas and seven apartments, a restaurant and store overlook the marina, another restaurant is at the tip of one of the five beaches, tennis, snorkelling, diving and fishing available, T3650083, F3650466, PO Box 882,

Cooper's Town, reservations essential. The cay can be reached from Abaco at Coopers Town, where the resort's ferry will pick you up from the government dock.

's Cay Walker's Cay was named after Judge Thomas Walker, who was banished to the island in the 18th century. It is the furthest north of all the Abaco cays and is dominated by the **L-AL** *Walker's Cay Hotel and Marina*, which offers sailors and fishermen lots of facilities and hosts several fishing tournaments. Yachtsmen approaching Abaco from the north clear customs and immigration here. There are restaurants, bars, tennis and two pools for when you are on land, 62 rooms, four suites and four villas. Enquire about package deals with airfares from Fort Lauderdale if you do not want to tour other cays, T3525252, F3523301, or write to 700 SW 34 Street, Ft Lauderdale, FL 33315. You can visit the fish farm on Walker's Cay, the Aqua Life Mariculture Project, the largest in the world breeding tropical fish.

Essentials

Sleeping: Marsh Harbour LL-AL *Abaco Towns By the Sea*, PO Box 20486, T3672227, F3673927,
Abaco canam@bigsky.net 2-bedroom villas, timeshare resort, short walk to water, convenient for restaurants, tennis. **L** *Abaco Beach Resort*, 52 rooms and 6 villas, 2 pools, tennis, beach, attached to *Boat Harbour Marina*, T3672158, F3672819, PO Box AB-20511. With 180 slips, nice location, comfortable rooms. **A** *Conch Inn Hotel and Marina*, PO Box AB-20469, T3674000, F3674004. 9 rooms, full marina facilities, pool, restaurant, dockside bar and cable TV, well located and a yachtie meeting place. **LL-L** *Pelican Beach Villas*, PO Box AB-20304, T3673600, F912-4376223, pelican@g-net.net 5 villas, 2 bedroom, 2 bath, fully equipped, a/c, phone, on beach, need car to get to shops, boat dock, hammocks. **AL-A** *Lofty Fig*, PO Box AB-20437, T/F3672681. 6 villas, nice looking, opposite water, near *Conch Inn*. **B** *Ambassador Motel*, PO Box AB-20484, T3672022, F3672113. Cheaper but not well located. **A** *D's Guest House*, T/F3673980. 5 mins from airport, weekly rates cheaper, cable TV, pool, designed for couples.

Casuarina Point (18 miles south of Marsh Harbour) **LL-AL** *Different of Abaco*, VHF 16, PO Box AB-20092, T3662150, F3278152, www.oii.net/different A bonefishing lodge and home of Great Abaco Bone Fishing Club, in a nature park with flamingos, iguanas and donkeys, 8 rooms, 15 huts, 8 bonefishing boats, good restaurant open from 0900.

Sandy Point B *Oeisha's Motel*, T3664139, F3664283, and **C** *Pete and Gay's Guest House* T3664119, F3664007, which cater to an increasing number of bonefishermen using local fishermen as guides, very casual, all doors left unlocked.

Treasure Cay, a peninsula 26 miles north of Marsh Harbour, **LL-A** *Treasure Cay Hotel*, PO Box AB-22183, T3658535, F3658847, info@treasurecay.com 96 rooms, 7 villas, there are also 600 homes owned by non-residents, 18-hole golf course, tennis, fishing, watersports on site, marina, restaurants, bars, shops, bank, doctor, pleasant resort, lovely beach close by, a 54-room hotel and 12 acres which were once part of the resort have been sold for redevelopment to Sandals. **LL** *Banyan Beach Club*, Treasure Cay, T3654181, www.banyanbeach.com. 2-3 bedroom luxury beachfront condos.

Wood Cay, off Little Abaco, **B** *Tangelo Hotel*, PO Box 830, T3652222, F3652200. 12 rooms, TV, a/c, fans, restaurant, bar, taxi from Treasure Cay airport will cost US$50 for 2 people, but if you call the hotel in advance they will provide a bus for US$10 for 2 people.

Eating: Marsh Harbour There are several restaurants within walking distance of each other, look
Abaco out for special menus and happy hours on different days. *Mangoes* restaurant and marina, T3672366. Patio bar from 1130, lunch 1130-1430, dinner 1830-2100, good food, about US$25 for dinner. *Wally's*, nearby, other side of road, T3672074. Good Bahamian food, popular happy hour, Wed 1600-1800, open lunch Mon 1130-1400, Tue-Sat 1130-1500, dinner Mon by reservation only, Sat 1800-2100, bar daily except Sun 1100-1700, music, boutique. The *Jib Room* at Marsh Harbour Marina on north side of harbour, PO Box AB 20518, T3672700, F3672033. Very long walk, coffee and croissants from 0830, lunch daily 1130-1500, daily special activities for dinner, huge ribs on Wed US$12 recommended, happy hour Thu 1830-1930 all drinks US$1, closed Tue. *Sapodilly's*, T3673498, VHF 19. Waterfront,

deli, beer and wine, picnic baskets, provisioning, breakfast and lunch from 0830 Mon-Sat, 0930 Sun. *Angler's Restaurant*, Boat Harbour Marina, T3672158. Serves breakfast, lunch, dinner, with a lovely view of the harbour. *George 'Sho Bo' Wilmore* makes fresh conch salad before your eyes, adjacent to the Harbour View Marina. *Kool Scoops Ice Cream Parlour*, Stratton Drive, T3673880, also serves sandwiches. *Mavis Country Restaurant*, Don McKay Blvd, T3672002. Specializes in Bahamian and Jamaican dishes. **Casaurina Point** *Nettie's Different of Abaco*, south of Marsh Harbour, T3662150. Interesting and unusual lunch and dinner prepared in traditional Bahamian style.

Treasure Cay There are several restaurants and bars here. *Island Boil*, a yellow wooden shack near Treasure Cay ferry serves Bahamian dishes, fish for breakfast, cheap, used by locals, tourists, air arrivals. **Coopers Town**, *M & M,* restaurant and disco serves local dishes with peas 'n' rice. A converted van, *Mac's Rolling Kitchen*, goes out to Treasure Cay and nearby settlements for lunches. *Conch Crawl*, T3650423. A shack and pier, the fresh conch salad is made in front of you, fish fries and barbecues on different nights, sit inside or outside; there are lots of jetties along this stretch of coast, all with piles of conch shells underneath.

Elbow Cay

Elbow Cay

Cook's Cove
Anna Cay
Eagle Rock
Parrot Cays
Light House
Hope Town Harbour
Wyannie Malone Museum
Cemetery
Atlantic Ocean
White Sound
Aunt Pats Bay
Tahiti Beach

0 metres 500
0 yards 500

■ **Sleeping**
1 Club Soleil Resort & Hope Town Hideaways
2 Hope Town Harbour Lodge
3 Abaco Inn
4 Sea Spray Villas & Marinas

● **Eating**
1 Captain Jack's Bar
2 Harbour's Edge Restaurant

Sleeping & eating: Elbow Cay

L-AL *Hope Town Harbour Lodge*, T3660095, F3660286, www.hopetownlodge.com Bar and pool the Atlantic side of the hill overlooking beach, lunch by pool, no pre-booking in restaurant, rooms with harbour view in main hotel, or with ocean view, lovely location, friendly. *Hope Town Villas*, T3660030, F3660377, htvillas@batelnet. bs Run by Michael Myers, clapboard cottages, overlooking lighthouse, or nearer the beach, US$950-1,500 per week, fully equipped. On the other side of the water, reached by boat, is **AL** *Club Soleil Resort*, T3660003, F3660254. Restaurant on waterfront, good menu, fish, chicken, champagne Sun brunch, always full, reservations needed, try their drink Tropical Shock, 6 rooms, bright, cheerful, TV, VCR, a/c, fridge, all overlook harbour, balcony, German and Dutch also spoken, own boat for deep sea fishing. A walkway connects with **LL-L** *Hope Town Hideaways and Marina*, T3660224, F3660434, www.hopetown.com An attractive cluster of 4 villas, run by Chris and Peggy Thompson, very friendly, lovely location but you have to go everywhere by boat, each villa has 2 master bedrooms, full kitchen/diner, a/c, fans, TV, music centre, telephone, videos, games, beautifully decorated, small pool, manmade beach and infants' sand play area, rental boats US$75-95 per day, cheaper for longer, 12 large slips, power and water, no restaurant but local cooks can be contracted if you do not want to go next door. On White Sound, **AL** *Abaco Inn* overlooks the calm water and also the ocean, T3660133, F3660113. There is a dirt road from Hope Town, or you can hire a boat or charter a ferry, small rooms harbour side or ocean side, wonderful view, a/c, fan, hammocks, restaurant and pool overlook ocean, bar overlooks harbour, nude bathing area, snorkelling gear and bicycles free for guests, small children not encouraged, no evening entertainment, owned by John Goodloe, usually full. *Seaspray Resort and Marina*, also on White Sound, T3660065, F3660383, www.seasprayresort.com Boats for hire, 1-2 bedroom villas US$910-1,235 per week, have spacious living area, full kitchen, small bedrooms, a/c, minimum 3-nights, run by Monty and Ruth Albury, Monty's mother runs a bakery and will cook Bahamian meals if required, pool, windsurfing, sunfish, motorboats US$65-95 per day, snorkelling, sailing and fishing trips, freshwater pool, games room with pool table, quiet, villas spread out, free Hope Town shuttle. There are several bars and restaurants: *Captain Jack's*, T3660247. Tables on its own jetty, lovely views across the water to the mangroves, breakfast 0830-1030, lunch and dinner 1100-2100, happy hour 1700-1830. *Harbour's Edge*, T3660087. Bar open from 1000, free transport for dinner, good food, open-air or indoors, Sat night live band, weather permitting, pool table, satellite TV, bicycle rental US$8 per day, friendly, happy hour 1700-1800, VHF 16, closed around Oct for 6 weeks.

Sleeping:
Man-O-War
Cay
L *Schooner's Landing Resort*, T3656072, F3656285. 2-bedroom condos on the beach, a/c, tennis, minimum 3 nights' stay, manageress Brenda Sawyer can arrange sailing, diving, snorkelling, fishing, boat rentals etc. Contact Bill and Sherry Albury for rental cottages, US$450-650 per week, T3656009.

Sleeping
& eating:
Great Guana
Cay
LL-AL *Guana Beach Resort and Marina*, PO Box AB-20474, T3655133, F3655134, guanabeach@guanabeach.com Small, informal, 11 rooms, 8 suites, in villas, own beach off the harbour cove and 5 mins' walk from ocean beach, pool, docks and marina offering full service and yacht management programme. The restaurant is open 0730-1000 for indoor or outdoor dining. Guests are picked up by boat from *Conch Inn*, Marsh Harbour, at 0930 and 1600 or by arrangement. **L-AL** *Guana Seaside Village*, T3655106, F3655146, guanaseaside@oii.net 4 villas, fully equipped, pool, beach, restaurant, diving. **L-AL** *Dolphin Beach Resort*, T/F3655137, www.dolphinbeachresort.com 4 rooms, 3 cottages, breakfast included, pool, beach, kitchenette. *Mermaid Café*, at *Dolphin Beach Resort*, T3655137. Serves breakfast, lunch, dinner, adjoining Potcakes Boutique. *Coco Paradise* , T3655197. Overlooking gorgeous beach, complimentary transport from the main dock, offers selections like garlic shrimp, scampi, coconut shrimp, crab meat quiche, free coffee.

Sleeping
& eating:
Green Turtle
Cay
In the village the only place to stay is the **L-A** *New Plymouth Inn*, T3654161, F3654138. A restored colonial building with 9 rooms, pool, restaurant and bar, good food, Bahamian dishes, cocktails 1830, dinner 1945, also breakfast, lunch and Sun brunch. Further east along the coast, are **LL-L** *Linton's Beach and Harbour Cottages*, PO Box 158601, T3654003, F365-4002/4261. 1-2 bedrooms, on the ocean, fans. Overlooking White Sound and beautifully sheltered is **LL-AL** *Green Turtle Club and Marina*, PO Box AB-22792, T3654271, F3654272, www.greenturtleclub. com Deluxe accommodation with diveshop

Green Turtle Cay

0 km   1
0 miles   1

■ **Sleeping**
1 Green Turtle Club & Marina
2 Bluff House Club
3 Linton Cottages
4 Roosters Rest
5 New Plymouth Inn

▲ **Other**
1 Albert Lowe
   Museum & Post Office

and all watersports, 32 rooms and cottages, in yellow wooden villas, beautifully furnished in hardwoods, clean, fresh, the beach at Coco Bay is a 5-min walk, lots of repeat guests, Brendal's Dive Shop on site does scuba, snorkelling, island excursions, and bicycle rentals, T3654411, VHF 16, there is also a gym, boat rental, bone fishing and deep sea fishing, PO Box 462, New Plymouth. **LL-A** *Bluff House Club & Marina*, T3654200, F3654248, www.bluffhouse.com A marvellous view of the sea, fully renovated and remodelled after 1999 hurricane damage, pool, tennis, Boston whalers and sailboats US$50-80 per day, bicycles, relaxed atmosphere, 23 rooms in 3 rustic, painted villas on small beach, suites and cottages 1-3 bedrooms, 6 high seasons, lots of repeat business, great food and view at new beach bar and deck overlooking ocean, reservations needed for candlelit dinners at excellent restaurant up the hill, no locks, no TV. Boat rides to New Plymouth 3 mornings a week and for Sat night dance. Day trips to other cays with Lincoln Jones, barbecued lobster on the beach for lunch. Fishing and diving arranged. 20-min walk to Coco Bay, a 3-mile beach. Popular with honeymooners, a secluded and friendly resort. **LL-L** *Coco Bay Cottages*, PO Box AB-22795, T3655464, F3655465, cocobay@oii.net 4 cottages, each with 2 bedrooms, comfortably furnished, in 5 acres of beach front property, fruit trees, snorkelling equipment available. **AL** *Treehouse By The Sea*, T/F3654258, www.oii.net/treehouse 3 cottages, minimum 3 nights, beach nearby, solitude, relaxation. To rent cottages sleeping up to 8 people/cottage, phone Sid's Grocery Store in New Plymouth, but take mosquito repellent in summer and autumn. *Miss Emily's Blue Bee Bar*, T3654181, is worth a visit, located in the centre of the settlement, next to the netball pitch, it is bursting with memorabilia of previous famous and infamous customers and serves unforgettable and very strong cocktails. *Laura's Kitchen*, near the ferry dock, open 1100-1500, 1830-2100, T3654287, VHF 16. *Rooster's Restaurant & Pub*, T3654066, on the outskirts, painted red, is a bar, restaurant and club, Gully's Roosters play there 2-3 nights a week, going to other clubs on other nights. Nearby, on Black Sound, the Alton Lowe art gallery is open to the public.

Guy Fawkes Day is celebrated on *5 Nov* with parades through the streets led by the Guy to a big bonfire in the evening (no fireworks). **Festivals**

Boat *Albury's Ferry Service* (T3656010, F3656487, www.oii.net/AlburysFerry) runs from Sandy Crossing, 2 miles east of Marsh Harbour to Hope Town and Man-O-War Cay, US$8 single, US$12 day return. Separate boats leave each cay at 0800 and 1330, returning from the mainland at 1030 and 1600. Albury's boats can also be chartered to these 2 cays and to other islands. For 5 or more, a charter to Hope Town or Man-O-War works out at US$10 per person each way, to Guana Cay for 6 or more US$12 per person, or US$70 for 1-5 pax. All day excursions to Treasure Cay, Guana Cay, Hope Town, Man-O-War, Little Harbour and Green Turtle Cay. Green Turtle Cay (see above) is reached from the ferry dock at Treasure Cay, US$8 per person, you can be dropped off wherever you are staying. Great Guana Cay can be reached by ferry, US$8 per person, or the *Guana Beach Resort* boat from *Conch Inn*, Marsh Harbour. The *Spanish Cay Inn* ferry picks up guests from Coopers Town. **Transport**

Tourist office *Ministry of Tourism*, Abaco Tourist Office, PO Box AB 0464, Marsh Harbour, Abaco, T3673067, F3673068. Most businesses in the Abacos can be found at www.oii.net, which runs a noticeboard service and helpful forums. **Directory**

Andros

Andros is the largest island in the Bahamas, at 2,300sq miles, with pine and mahogany forests, creeks and prolific birdlife. According to Indian legend, the forests house the 'chickcharnie', a mythical, three-fingered, three-toed, red-eyed creature who hangs upside down and can cause good or bad luck. It is also blamed when tools or other things go missing. In fact, a large, three-toed, burrowing owl of this description did inhabit the forests until the early 16th century when it became extinct. More recent legend has it that the pirate, Sir Henry Morgan, lit a beacon on the top of Morgan's Bluff, the highest

Population: 7,615
2000 census
Colour map 2, grid B2

The Bahamas

Andros & Berry Islands

The Bahamas

Great Stirrup Cay
Great Harbour Cay
BERRY ISLANDS
Hoffman's Cay
Bonds Cay
Chub Cay
Whale Cay

Joulter Cays
Morgan's Bluff
Red Bays
Low Sound
Nicholl's Town
Conch Sound
San Andros
Mastic Point

NEW PROVIDENCE

Owen's Town
Stafford Creek
Staniard Creek
Small Hope
Rising Point
Hard Bargain
Coakley Town (Fresh Creek)
Andros Town

WILLIAMS ISLAND

Bowen Sound
Man of War Sound
Cargill Creek
Behring Point

Northern Bight
Big Wood Cay
Moxey Town
Bight
Mangrove Cay
Yellow Cay
Drigg's Hill
Congo Town
Middle Bight
The Bluff
South Bight
Kemp's Bay
Red Shank Point
Deep Creek
Muddy Point
Little Creek
Mars Bay

Leaf Cay
Water Cays
Ratman Cay

N
Not to scale

*point on the island at 67ft. This lured passing ships on to the treacherous reef close by.
Sir Henry and his pirates then ransacked the ships and hid their treasure in the caves
below. The Spanish called the island La Isla del Espíritu Santo, but its present name is
said to come from the British commander Sir Edmund Andros.*

Ins & outs

Bahamasair has daily flights to all four from Nassau. *Small Hope Bay Lodge* runs its own charter flights from Fort Lauderdale to Fresh Creek/Andros Town, US$220 per person round trip, minimum 2 people, children under 12 half price, 1 hr, T305-3598240, F305-3598241 or phone the Lodge on Andros. Airports are at Fresh Creek/Andros Town (ASD), Mangrove Cay (MAY) (both central), San Andros (SAQ) and Congo Town/South Andros (TZN).

Getting there
*See transport,
page 116, for
further details*

There are two separate islands, North and South Andros, with the central regions (middle bights) accessible by boat from either direction. No roads connect the different parts and unless you have a boat you have to fly between them. Cars and scooters can be rented.

Getting around

The Bahamas

Flora and fauna

Andros has an extensive creek system which is largely unexplored. In South Andros the 40-square-mile area beyond the half mile long ridge is also uninhabited and rarely visited. The large pine forests and mangrove swamps are home to a variety of birds and animals. In the south there are wild bird reserves which allow hunting in the season (September-March). Sightings of the Bahamian parrot have been reported in South Andros, while rare terns and whistling tree ducks, roseatte spoonbills and numerous different herons have been seen in the north and central areas. Green Cay, one of the many small islands off Andros (20 miles east of Deep Creek) has the world's second largest population of white crowned pigeons. These pigeons are prey to hunters from September to March each year. The west side of Andros is undeveloped and other than Red Bays in the northwest corner there are no settlements on this side, making it ideal for wildlife; large rock iguanas up to 6 ft long and hundreds of flamingos live here. During May to August the Andros land crabs migrate from the pine forests to the sea. These enormous crabs are to be found everywhere during this time. Many are caught and exported to Nassau.

Diving and marine life

Visitors mostly come for the unspoiled beaches, the diving on pristine reefs in 80°F water with excellent visibility and extraordinary bonefishing. Development has been concentrated on the east coast facing one of the world's largest underwater reefs. This huge barrier reef, the second largest in the Western Hemisphere, plunges 6,000 ft to the Tongue of the Ocean, an exciting drop-off dive. **Wreck** dive sites include the *Lady Gloria*, an old mailboat sunk recently off Morgan's Bluff, and the *Potomac*, a steel-hulled barge which sank just after the war and is now home to many huge, friendly grouper and parrot fish, as well as some impressive barracuda. Andros has 197 **blue holes**, of these 50 are oceanic, the rest inland. Formed by water erosion then flooded at the end of the last ice-age, the oceanic holes actually connect to the intricate inland underwater cave system. As tide rushes in and out ideal feeding grounds are created and consequently the oceanic blue holes harbour prolific and diverse marine life and are excellent dive sites at slack tide. The inland blue holes can be very deep (up to 350 ft) and contain a lens of freshwater 40-100ft deep floating on seawater, which is beautiful to swim in. **Charlie's blue hole**, near Nicholl's Town is clearly signposted as is **Church's blue hole**, just north of Fresh Creek. Marine life in the inland blue holes is limited, though the rare crustacean *Remepedidia* and the blind cave fish *Lucifuga* have been found. Earthwatch is currently conducting a detailed study on the mosquito fish, one of the few colonists of

Dive sites
The underwater cave system on Andros is considered to have some of the world's longest, deepest & most stunning caves

the blue holes on North Andros. On South Andros two popular blue holes are the **Giant Doughnut** near Deep Creek, south of Kemps Bay, and Inland Blue Hole **Lissy** near the Bluff, South Andros. Legends abound about blue holes, serpents known as *Luska*, originally a part of Seminole Indian legends are thought to drag unsuspecting swimmers and fishermen below. Caution should be exercised at some of the holes as they are extremely deep. A 1991 expedition discovered remains of a Lucayan burial site in one of the blue holes of South Andros. Intact Lucayan skulls were recovered, as well as femurs and hip bones.

Dive centres *Small Hope Bay Lodge* is the place to go for diving, just north of Fresh Creek and a short boat journey from the barrier reef, wrecks, caves and an ocean blue hole. A well-run operation with several decades of experience in Andros, they cater for beginners as well as specialty divers and have an excellent safety record. Most guests are on all-inclusive packages, otherwise diving is US$45 for a single tank dive, US$10 for a second tank, US$50 night dive, US$5 snorkelling boat trip. Specialty diving is tailored to individual requirements. This dive operation is one of the more conservation-minded in the Bahamas. There are also daily snorkel trips to the reef and snorkel trails from the shore. Dive Propulsion Vehicles are available for wall riding (scuba) or reef riding (snorkel). Liveaboard dive boats also cruise around Andros and Stuart Cove's Dive South Ocean occasionally come over from Nassau and dive in Andros waters. For ecological tours *Forfar Field Station*, at Blanket Sound north of Fresh Creek, runs guided diving, snorkelling and inland excursions, mainly for high school students or college groups from the USA, T3682014, F3682015 for details. Accommodation sometimes available.

Fishing *Small Hope Bay Lodge* also does **bonefishing** (US$325 per day boat and guide for
All sportfishing is two people or US$380-480 per day reef fishing for up to four), but the best place for
catch & release serious fishermen and women is the **Cargill Creek** area, where there are lots of guides. You can stay at *Grassy Camp* further south, or do a one-day Grassy Cay trip for US$800 (maximum five people). There is also *Andros Island Bonefish Club* (known locally as Rupert's Place) where deep sea fishing can be arranged.

The usual weight of bonefish is 5-7 pounds but on most days you will find fish of 12 pounds and over. There are around 100 square miles of flats in the north and middle bights which are fished by Cargill Creek resorts. Most are fished infrequently and you see hardly anyone else. The west side of the island can also be fished, depending on the weather and tide, but it will cost an extra US$50 per day for fuel as it is 1½ hours from Cargill Creek. You can still see traditional Bahamian wooden sailboats here, made by local craftsman Ronald Young, although nowadays he makes mostly fishing boats. On Christmas Day, Columbus' Discovery Day and Easter Monday sailboat races, featuring locally made Bahamian sloops, are held at Lowe Sound, Nicholl's Town and sometimes Conch Sound. Ask locals for details. Regattas also combine cook-outs, local music and dancing. On Independence Day there is a sailboats race in the Regatta.

Beaches and watersports

In the north, **Nicholl's Town** has the best beach. A wide, golden beach runs the length of the north coast, almost to Morgan's Bluff. It is ideal for swimming and excellent snorkelling spots are to be found directly off the beach. **Lowe Sound**, **Conch Sound** and **Mastic Point** all have good beaches. A very pleasant, 2½-mile walk from Nicholl's Town to Morgan's Bluff along a leafy overgrown road (in fact the first road built on the island) leads to the caves at Morgan's Bluff and offers beautiful views of this part of the coast. Further south near Fresh Creek is **Staniard Creek** where there is an attractive palm-fringed beach with white sand and pleasant settlement close by. Sand bars, exposed at the mouth of Staniard Creek at low tide, are excellent shelling spots. **Somerset beach** is just south of Fresh Creek, signposted from the main highway. It is a spectacular spot, especially at low tide and another excellent shelling beach. At **Victoria Point** in central Andros there is a graveyard right on the water's edge. In some parts of Andros on Easter Monday at 0200-0600 there is a candlelight vigil by gravesites at which Easter hymns are sung. The east side of Mangrove Cay has spectacular beaches all lined with coconut groves. In South Andros along the 28-mile stretch from Mars Bay to Drigg's Hill are beautiful palm-lined beaches with occasional picturesque settlements.

Around the island

The main settlements in the north are **Nicholl's Town, Lowe Sound, Conch Sound, Red Bays, Mastic Point** and **Fresh Creek** (previously known as Andros Town and Coakley Town). **Mangrove Cay** is in central Andros, while in the south are **Congo Town, Deep Creek** and the late Prime Minister Sir Lynden Pindling's constituency at **Kemp's Bay**.

Near Fresh Creek, you can visit the Androsia clothing factory which makes batik fabrics in tropical colours and watch the whole process from the wax painting to the drying of the dyed cloth. Ask in the shop for a factory tour. Henry Wallace is a rastafarian wood carver, usually to be found chipping away to the beat of reggae music. He is also the curator of a small museum of the island's culture and history, near the mailboat dock in Fresh Creek (the old health clinic buildings), worth a visit. South of Fresh Creek is the Atlantic Underwater Testing and Evaluation Center (Autec), a joint venture between the USA and the UK for underwater testing of weapons and consequently top secret.

Nicholl's Town has a lively Junkanoo on Boxing Day (very early morning) and New Year's Eve, and Goombay Festival on every Thursday in July and August from 1900 onwards on Seaview Square. There are many government administration buildings, schools, clinic, Batelco office, in what is a straggling, spread-out town with no apparent centre. **Conch Sound** is very close, almost an extension of Nicholl's Town; between the two are shops, a bakery, auditorium, laundry and disco. At **Morgan's Bluff** you can visit the caves where pirates were rumoured to have hidden their treasure. Both the Bluff and the caves are signposted; the caves are in fact quite small and rather a disappointment. The area nowadays is more important for the docks, from where water is barged to Nassau. The mailboat comes in at the old harbour.

Red Bays (population under 200) is the only settlement on the west coast of the island and is about five minutes' drive from Red Bays beach, where there are a few small motor boats moored but nothing else. Long isolated and reached only by boat it is now connected by a good paved road cutting across the wild interior of the island. Originally a Seminole Indian settlement many of the people have distinctly Indian features and a true out island lifestyle. The village welcomes visitors. Contact Rev Bertram A Newton for his history of Red Bays. Locally caught sponges and hand made baskets can all be bought very cheaply. The straw work here is excellent. Mrs Marshall is the local bush granny and community celebrity. Usually found weaving in the centre of the village she will show how baskets are made, and explain local culture, politics and bush medicine to visitors. Mr Russell always has plenty of sponges for sale (and illegally caught turtle and iguanas, don't buy these) and also works as a bonefishing guide. There is only one telephone in Red Bays, T3292369 and leave a message for the person you want to contact.

Essentials

A-B *Green Windows Inn*, PO Box 23076, T3292194, F3292016. 5 mins' walk to beach, pool, 12 rooms, bar, restaurant. **B** *Conch Sound Resort Inn*, Conch Sound, Nicholl's Town, T3292060. 6 rooms, restaurant, bar. Staniard Creek is a settlement of small, mostly single storey houses with a clinic and school, reached by rutted road across swamp (turn off main road by

Sleeping
Listed from north to south

The Bahamas

Batelco). **B-C** *Beneby's Bayside Motel*, south Mastic Point, T3293035. Waterside motel with ice cream parlour attached. **B-C** *Quality Inn*, T3686217. Also known as *Dicky's Place*, owned by Richard Riley, remote, small, jetty, on creek short way from sea, cheaper rooms in main house, or better rooms in new annex, food and drinks available, fishing. **L** *Small Hope Bay Lodge*, between Staniard Creek and Fresh Creek, T3682014, F3682015, Box CB11 817, Nassau, or PO Box 21667, Ft Lauderdale, Fl 33335-1667, T305-3598240, F3598241, www.SmallHope.com The nicest place to stay and highly recommended, having won the Ministry of Tourism's coveted Cacique Award in 2000 and 2001 for best small business. It specializes in diving and fishing but still good if only one partner dives/fishes, informal, cabin accommodation among trees right on seafront, all inclusive with 3 hearty meals, drinks, taxes, service and scuba lesson, child and teen discounts, rustic but comfortable, good beds and lots of towels, fans, no phones, TV or a/c, sailboat, windsurfers, hot tub, bicycles, books, games, children's toys, birdwatching, yoga, run by Birch family since 1960s, very friendly, staff and guests mingle at meals and after dinner, excellent service. In Fresh Creek, **B** *Chickcharnie's Hotel*, T3682025. Overlooks harbour, lovely view, 75ft dock, restaurant, bar, foodstore, rooms with shared bath and fan, or with bath and a/c, or new rooms with view, Bahamian decor. **AL** *Andros Lighthouse Yacht Club and Marina*, T3682305-8, F3682300. The other side of the creek, government owned, up for sale, appalling service, unfriendly and usually empty but otherwise lovely location on waterfront, attractive buildings with luxury yachts moored at dock, big, tiled rooms, a/c, cool, TV, fridge, phones, bar, restaurant, tennis, bicycles, pool, ping pong, 12 rooms, 2 villas, 18 boat slips with fuel available.

Around Behring Point and Cargill Creek the lodges offer fishing and nothing else, all guests are expected to be anglers: **L** *Andros Island Bonefishing Club* (*Rupert's Place*), T368-5167/5200, F3685235, www.bahamas.com/hotels/abone Owned by Rupert Leadon, 12 rooms with 2 double beds, a/c, some with fan and fridge, includes meals, 4-night package with fishing US$960 per person double occupancy, 2-3 months reservation needed, 80-90% repeat guests, comfortable but not luxurious, friendly, most fishermen go out by 0730, return 1600, shower, cocktails, supper 1900, bed by 2100. **LL** *Cargill Creek Fishing Lodge*, next door, PO Box N-1882, Cargill Creek, T3685129, F3685046. 7 double rooms, 4 singles, 3 cottages with 2 bedrooms (sleep 4), TV, pool, 10% discount for Autec employees, boats and guides for fishing. **LL-AL** *Tranquillity Hill Bone Fish Lodge*, T/F3684132. All-inclusive, 9 rooms, bar, restaurant, TV. On Mangrove Cay, **AL-B** *Mangrove Cay Inn*, T3690069, F3690014. 8 rooms, restaurant, fishing. **AL-A** *Seascape Inn*, PO Box 023824, T/F3690342, www.seascapeinn.com. 5 rooms, fishing, diving, restaurant, breakfast included, transfer to hotel included. **AL** per person *Moxey's Bonefishing Lodge*, Little Harbour, T/F3690023. All-inclusive, 10 rooms, diving. On the border of Congo Town and Long Bay, **L-A** *Emerald Palms-By-The-Sea*, PO Box N-9520, T3692661, F3692667. Modern with balconies facing the sea, swimming pool, tennis court and boats for charter.

Eating   Andros has an exportable surplus of crabs, so crab dishes are very popular. May to Jul is the crab season. Try baked Andros crab, which uses the crab's own fat to cook it in, also Vetol's crab'n'rice and stewed crab cooked with conch. Andros is relatively undeveloped and some restaurants may need advance warning. For a cheap meal look out for cook outs.

Rupert's Fish Camp, Cargill Creek, very good local game fish, candlelit veranda overlooks sea. *Seaview Restaurant and Bar* at the *Andros Island Bone Fishing Club* is nearby. **Dig Dig's** is an excellent restaurant at Cargill Creek, on side of main road, T3685097 for reservations in evening. 1 hr notice enough at lunchtime. The *Small Hope Bay Lodge* serves large, filling meals, well cooked. *Chickcharnie Hotel* in Fresh Creek. **Nicholl's Town** *Rolle's* takeaway serves best local food on island, cracked conch, chicken etc; *Rumours* restaurant, T3292398. Bar and disco, Fri, Sat, 2100-0300. **Kemps Bay**, *Dudley's Pink Pussy Cat Club* has a rake'n'scrape band and traditional stepping dancing with Rosita on saw and Ben on drums.

Transport   **Car hire**   In Kemps Bay *Mr Rahming* rents cars and also provides a charter service to any of the Family Islands (T3691608). At San Andros airport *Cecil Gaitor* has cars for hire. *Small Hope Bay Lodge* will organize car hire for US$65-75 per day. It is often possible to hire cars for the day from private individuals, ask locally, taxi drivers have details. Most settlements are linked by paved roads with plenty of potholes to keep you awake. **Taxis** are available. A taxi from the airport at Fresh Creek to *Small Hope Bay Lodge* is US$20 (fare usually included in all-inclusive package), to Cargill Creek US$37. **Boat** Boats can dock at Mastic Point (north), Fresh Creek (central) and Congo Town (south). For mailboat schedules and fares see ferries in the Essentials section at the front of the chapter.

Berry Islands

There are thirty Berry Islands, all of which offer wonderful opportunities for divers and snorkellers. Most are the private homes of the wealthy or inhabited only by wildlife.

Population: 707
Colour map 2, grid A2

Great Harbour Cay (GHC) and Chub Cay (CCZ) have airports served by Island Express from Fort Lauderdale (T954-3590380). *Southern Pride Aviation/Bimini Island Air* fly daily to Chub Cay from Fort Lauderdale's Executive Airport. Other carriers include *Island Air Charters*, T954-3599942, and *Pan Am Air Bridge*, T800-4242557.

Ins & outs

Bullock's Harbour in **Great Harbour Cay** is the main settlement in the area, Great Harbour Cay is the largest cay in the Berry chain at just two miles across. First settled by ex-slaves in 1836, the cay proved difficult to farm. **LL-A** *The Great Harbour Cay Club* is here, with 28 rooms and villas, T954-9219084, F954-9211044. There are facilities for yachts and a nine-hole golf course. Cruise ships drop anchor off Great Sturrup Cay and passengers can spend the day on the deserted beach there.

Around the islands

The only other spot in the Berry Islands which caters for tourists is **Chub Cay**, which has been extensively rebuilt since Hurricane Andrew in 1992. The **LL-L** *Chub Cay Club* (PO Box 661067, Miami Springs, FL 33266, www.chubcay.com, T3251490, F3225199), has rooms and villas, its own airstrip, tennis courts, restaurant, 96-slip marina and extensive dive facilities offered by Chub Cay Undersea Adventures T4623400, F4624100, www.chubcaydive. com Chub Cay is a port of entry and has a surge-proof harbour. There is a US$25 charge to use the marina docks to clear customs and immigration unless you take a slip. It is a good place to stop and clean off the salt after a hard crossing. There is a deep water canyon at Chub Cay where you can find a variety of colourful reef fish and open water marine life. Schools of up to 300 Nassau groupers have been seen. Staghorn coral can be seen in the shallow waters near Mamma Rhoda Rock. Less natural, but still fascinating is the submarine deliberately sunk in 90 ft of water off Bond Cay, named after James himself.

Many of the cays do not welcome uninvited guests. Interesting wildlife can be found on Frozen Cay and Alder Cay. Terns and pelicans can be seen here and although they are privately owned, sailors may anchor here to observe the birds. Hoffman's Cay, now deserted, was originally home to a thriving farming settlement. Ruins of houses, a church and a graveyard still stand. Paths also lead to a deep blue hole. A golden beach runs along the length of the east coast of the island. On Little Whale Cay, Wallace Groves, the founder of Freeport, has his own home and airstrip.

Bimini

Once thought to be the site of the lost city of Atlantis, the Bimini chain of islands, only 50 miles from Florida, is divided into North and South Bimini and a series of cays. There are more bars than shops on Bimini and service is minimal. It is not a glamorous resort, although there are plenty of luxury yachts moored there. The big attraction on Bimini is the deep sea fishing, which has drawn sportsmen to its waters for generations. The theme of big game fishing is reflected in the bars and restaurants, which also have Hemingway associations.

Population: 1,601
2000 census
Colour map 2, grid A1

The Bahamas

Chalk's

Chalk's seaplanes are a popular and exciting feature of travelling to Bimini and conjure up a certain nostalgia for pre-war adventure travel. Founded in 1919 by Arthur B 'Pappy' Chalk on the docks of the Royal Palm Hotel in Miami, the company is now the largest seaplane airline in the world. Famous passengers in the 1930s included Ernest Hemingway, who travelled frequently to Bimini along with many other Americans escaping Prohibition, and the Cuban dictator, Gerardo Machado, who fled a coup in 1933 in a chartered Chalk's plane. His occupation on the manifest was listed as 'retired'.

Ins & outs   **Getting there**   Chalk's Ocean Airways flies daily from Fort Lauderdale, Miami and Nassau into the harbour(T800-4242557, in Alice Town T3473024, in Bailey Town T3473131). For mailboat details see Essentials sections at the beginning of the chapter. Bimini is the port of entry for most boats coming from Florida. **Getting around**   There is no car rental. People use golf carts and boats to get around.

Background   Ernest Hemingway lived on Bimini in 1931-37 at Blue Marlin Cottage and his novel *Islands in the Stream* was based on Bimini. A display of Hemingway memorabilia can be seen at Compleat Angler Hotel and Museum. On South Bimini is the legendary site of the Fountain of Youth, sought by Ponce de León in 1512. The pool known as the Healing Hole on North Bimini is claimed to have some beneficial effects. In 1994, a Spanish treasure ship, believed to be the *Santiago El Grande*, which sank in 1766 while heading for Spain laden with gold, silver and emeralds, was discovered off the southern tip of Bimini.

Diving &   Bimini is famous for **big game fishing**. Fishing is excellent all year round although 7
marine life   May to 15 June is the tuna season (blue fin), June and July are best for blue marlin, winter and spring for white marlin. Blue marlin are the favourite target, averaging between 150 lbs and 500 lbs, but which can exceed 1,000 lbs. The South Biminis, Cat Cay and Gun Cay are the places to catch billfish and bluefin. There are lots of fishing tournaments and the Ministry of Tourism promotes over 40 annually, including the Bacardi Billfish Tournament, the Bimini Benefit Tournament, the Bahamas Championship Tournament and the Bahamas Billfish Championship series. *The Bimini Big Game Fishing Club* caters for most fishermen's needs and can arrange fishing trips with guides. It has 180 slips, charter/boat rental, all supplies and a large walk-in freezer for daily catches. Fishing can also be arranged through the *Compleat Angler Hotel*, Brown's Marina or Weech's Bimini Dock.

Scuba diving is recommended, particularly over the Bimini Wall with its black coral trees, or at the lovely reefs off Victory Cay. *Bimini Undersea*, run by Bill and Nowdla Keefe, has a comprehensive list of facilities and can also offer **dolphin excursions**, **sailing**, **sea kayaking**, **fishing** and **tennis**, T3473089, F3473079, in the USA T305-6535572, info@biminiundersea.com

Around the   **Alice Town** is the capital of Bimini although most people live in **Bailey Town** to the
island   north along the King's Highway. Alice Town has a lot of bars and a straw market, and little else. Heading north from Alice Town you come to *The Anchorage*, a restaurant on the highest point on the island with good views of the sea. The beach in either direction is excellent with white sand and good surfing waves. Above the beach is a pathway which passes the picturesque Methodist Church (1858) and leads to Bailey Town.

The airplane wrecks at the edge of the airfield at **Alice Town** on North Bimini are mostly the results of unsuccessful drugs running attempts en route from Colombia to Miami. Bimini has been claimed as an important success in the fight against drug running to the US mainland; **Gun Cay** has become the centre for drug interdiction operations and is full of US DEA personnel. Bimini suffered flood damage caused by Hurricane Andrew in 1992 but soon recovered.

The Bahamas

Cat Cay, to the south, was hit by Hurricane Andrew in August 1992, with winds of 180 mph, gusting to 250 mph. Damage to island property was estimated at US$100mn. First developed in 1932 it had a golf course, 68 houses for the rich and their staff, and lots of expensive yachts. The private club here accepts transient yachts except on big holiday weekends when members converge. There is a marina fee for customs and immigration.

Sleeping & eating

LL-L *Bimini Big Game Fishing Club* (T3473391, F3473392, www.bimini-big-game-club.com, PO Box 699, Alice Town), owned by Bacardi, this is the main hotel (rooms, suites and cottages) and social centre (beware the Beastwhacker, a cocktail of champagne and Bacardi rum) and has swimming pool and tennis courts as well as a marina with charter boats and all facilities for deep sea fishing or bonefishing. **LL-A** *Bimini Blue Water*, PO Box 601, T3473166, F3473293. Rooms, 3-bedroomed cottage, suites also include Hemingway's Marlin Cottage, private beach, swimming pool and 32-slip marina. **A-B** *Compleat Angler Hotel*, PO Box 601, T3473122, F3473293. In town, popular bar. **LL-AL** *All My Children Hotel*, T3473334, F3473333. Owned by Glen Rolle, 33 rooms, bar, restaurant (see below). **L-A** *Sea Crest Hotel & Marina*, PO Box 654, Alice Town, T3473071, F3473495. Managed by Alfred Sweeting.

Nightlife

After dark activities consist of drinking and dancing. *The Red Lion Pub*, T3473259, is recommended for its seafood, as is *Captain Bob Smith's*, T3473260, and *The Big Game Restaurant* on the sea front in Alice Town. The *Calypsonians* play weekly at *The Compleat Angler*, worth seeing, and *Glen Rolle and the Surgeons* provide musical entertainment at *All My Children Hotel*.

Cat Island

Cat Island

Named after Arthur Catt, a British pirate who was in league with Henry Morgan and Edward Teach (Blackbeard), Cat Island boasts Lucayan Indian caves near Port Howe, as well as the usual underwater sites of interest and beauty. Fifty miles long, it was once called San Salvador, and is a contender for the site of Columbus' first landfall. It has rolling hills and the highest point in the Bahamas, Mount Alvernia, 206 ft above sea level. The island is a centre for the practice of Obeah, a Bahamian voodoo incorporating both bush medicine and witchcraft, which is indicated by bottles and other small objects hanging from the branches of the trees.

Population: 1,548
2000 census
Colour map 2, grid B4

Ins & outs

Getting there *Bahamasair* has flights to Arthur's Town (ATC) from Nassau 3 times a week. There is also an airport at New Bight which is more convenient for most hotels but there are no scheduled services. Some hotels have their own airstrips. For details see mailboats page 75 at the beginning of this chapter. **Getting around** Transport is difficult in the north as there are no taxis or buses and few cars for hitching lifts.

Flora & fauna

Uninhabited **Conception Island** and its adjoining reefs, between Cat Island and

Long Island, is a land and sea park visited by migrating birds and nesting turtles, protected by the Bahamas National Trust. Many great and little blue herons can be seen at Hawksnest Creek bird sanctuary. In inland ponds it is possible to find the Cat Island turtle (*pseudyms felis*). Unfortunately, the turtles are a source of very rich meat and their numbers have recently dwindled. Near the settlements of Gaitors and Stephenson you can visit large caves full of bats. There are more bat caves south of Gaitors, near Stephenson. Farming is mostly subsistence, using slash and burn to grow crops such as red corn, guinea corn, cassava, okra, peas, beans, sugarcane, watermelons, pineapples, coconuts and bananas. Pot hole farming uses small amounts of soil in deep limestone holes to cultivate plants like the banana tree.

Around the island
Most development has taken place in the south

New Bight is the capital and shares an impressive bay with the quaint Old Bight, the site of an early 19th-century attempt to establish a cotton plantation. You can see the ruins of Pigeon Bay Cottage, an old plantation house just outside Old Bight. New Bight has a few shops. The annual regatta is held here in August. Above the village you can climb **Mount Alvernia** and visit Father Jerome's Hermitage. The **Stations of the Cross** are carved along a winding path leading to the Hermitage, built by Father Jerome, an Anglican priest who converted to Roman Catholicism and designed several churches on Cat Island and Long Island. Fernandez Bay, three miles north of New Bight and home to *The Fernandez Bay Village Resort*, has one of the island's best beaches, a secluded cove with excellent sands. On the most southerly tip of the island are two beaches with facilities: *The Cutlass Bay Club* (tennis, water-skiing) has its own airstrip and a good restaurant. World famous **bonefishing** flats are within wading distance of the beach. Close by along the crumbling cliff tops are the impressive ruins of the **Richman Hill plantation**, with ruins of slave quarters, an overseer's house and a plantation house. The original plantation stretched from the ocean to the inland lake. Another interesting ruin is Colonel Andrew Deveaux' mansion at **Port Howe**. Granted land on Cat Island for delivering Nassau from the Spanish, he set up a briefly prosperous cotton plantation here. Early settlers in Port Howe lured ships on to the rocks in order to loot their cargoes. Today Port Howe is famous for its coconuts and pineapples, while the bread, cooked in Dutch or Rock wood-fuelled ovens, is said to be the Bahamas' tastiest. The *Greenwood Dive Centre* at The Greenwood Beach Resort, Port Howe offers **scuba diving** and **snorkelling**. Run by Waldemar Illing, the hotel attracts German and other European visitors (T/F3423053). There are two boats taking 4-20 passengers on diving or snorkelling trips, but diving can also be done from the shore. Yachting facilities and activities are found at Hawks Nest Marina.

The main settlement in the north of the island is **Arthur's Town**, but other than an airstrip there is not much else; there are no restaurants and only one shop which does not sell much. Local people rely on the weekly mailboat from Nassau for groceries. There are bars but none serves food. Two miles inland is a small lake surrounded by mangrove thickets. Islanders refer to it as a blue hole and tell stories of its supernatural inhabitants. The beaches in the north are excellent. Northside Beach, reached by dirt road, stretches for 20 miles but has no facilities at all and has the ubiquitous debris. Orange Creek is an attractive inlet three miles north of Arthur's Town. Along the nearby shores are the 'white sand farms' with small scale farming of beets, potatoes and carrots.

Sleeping

LL-L *Fernandez Bay Village*, New Bight, T3423043, F3423051, www.fernandezbayvillage. com 1-2 bedroomed cottages, kitchens in larger ones, built of stone and tile, garden showers, fans, private terrace, meal plans available, most watersports available, diving arranged, snorkelling, fishing, sailing, paddle tennis, volley ball, waterskiing, boat rental with or without captain, canoes and kayaks complimentary, bicycles, beach bar, restaurant, hammocks, relaxed, unpretentious, flights can be arranged, US$100 per person one way from Nassau. **LL** *Cutlass Bay Club*, Port Howe, T3423085, F3425048. All-inclusive, 3 nights minimum, pool, beach, in USA, PO Box 273767, Tampa, FL33688, F813-2690556. **AL-B** *Greenwood Beach*

Resort, at Port Howe, T3423053, F3425053, www.hotelgreenwoodinn.com German-run, good snorkelling, scuba diving from the beach, pool, satellite TV, bicycles, fishing, car and scooter rental. **LL** *Hawks Nest Resort & Marina*, T3427050, half board, 10 rooms. **LL-AL** *Pigeon Cay Beach Club*, T3544116, F3544161. Reservations T800-6884752, 5 cottages, 4 day minimum, reduced rates for longer stays. **AL** *The Bridge Inn*, New Bight, T3423013, F3423041. With disco, reasonable accommodation, good food, bar, fishing. **B** *Orange Creek Inn*, T3544110, F3544042. 3 mins from airport, free transport, 16 rooms with kitchenettes, laundromat, store. **B** *Sea Spray Hotel*, Orange Creek, T3544116. 15 rooms.

The Bahamas' biggest goat farm is near New Bight. Goat meat is used in a local dish called 'souce stew', cooked with potatoes, onions and a lemon lookalike fruit called souce. The restaurant at the *Fernandez Bay Resort* is elegant and expensive. *Greenwood Inn* has Bahamian and European menu. *Blue Bird*, open air restaurant in New Bight, T3423095. Dinner from US$16, access by boat. *Pilot Harbour* on waterfront at Old Bight, T3424066, VHF 16, Bahamian specials, cocktails. **Bars in Arthur's Town**: *Miss Nelly's* (pool table), the *Hard Rock Oasis Restaurant and Bar* (T3427050) and *Mr Pratt's Bar* (dominoes). Also *Lovers' Boulevard Disco and Satellite Lounge* (T3542207) is popular and has a good local band playing Rake'n'Scrape.

Eating

The Bahamas

Crooked Island, Long Cay and Acklins

Crooked Island, Long Cay and Acklins comprise Crooked Island District, stretching three sides round the Bight of Acklins and bordered by 45 miles of treacherous barrier reef. At Crooked Island Passage, coral reefs can be found in very shallow water, falling sharply in walls housing sponges of every shape and colour. Although at 92 square miles, Crooked Island is larger than New Providence the population is sparce and still declining because of emigration.

Crooked Island population: 341 Acklins population: 423 2000 census Colour map 2, grid C5

Crooked Island and Acklins

Ins & outs   **Getting there**   The main airport (Crooked Island – CRI) is at Major Cay; Acklins has an airport at Spring Point (AXP). *Bahamasair* has two flights a week from Nassau, one goes to Major Cay first, the other lands first at Spring Point. The *Windward Express* mailboat docks at the harbour in Landrail Point once a week, see page 75. **Getting around**   The two islands are linked by a ferry, which runs twice a day between Lovely Bay and Richmond.

Crooked Island   Once as many as 40 plantations thrived here, but as in other islands, the crops failed because of poor soil and the industry declined. Nowadays, two valuable exports from the Crooked Island and Acklins District are aloe vera for use in skin preparations and the cascarilla bark which is sold to Italy for the production of Campari. Remains of the plantation era can be seen in Marine Farm and at Hope Great House in the north of the island. **Bird Rock Lighthouse** in the north is said to be the site of one of Columbus' original anchor spots on his first voyage. Close by is **Pittstown** where you can see the Bahamas' first General Post Office built in the era of William Pitt. It is now the restaurant of the hotel **A** *Pittstown Point Landings* (14 rooms in cottages, T3362507, www.pittstownpointlandings.com), which has its own airstrip, beaches, fishing, snorkelling, windsurfing and diving facilities. **Gun Bluff**, near the hotel was thought to have been a pirate's lookout, cannons have been found close by. In the surrounding area many North Americans have winter residences. Two miles away is **Landrail Point**, the main centre of the island, which has *Landrail Point* (T3444233, 12 rooms, simply furnished, neighbourly atmosphere, home cooking, inexpensive, a restaurant and store). The people here are Seventh Day Adventists so no pork or alcohol is sold and everything closes on Saturday. *Mrs Gibson's Lunch Room* is recommended for its freshly baked bread and simple Bahamian dishes.

Further south at **Cabbage Hill B-C** *Crooked Island Beach Inn* and the 6-room *Cabbage Hill* (both at T3442321, F3442502 at Batelco, fishing available), the former is near the beach and airport, owned by Rev Ezekiel Thompson, who is the Bahamasair representative. The capital of Crooked Island is **Colonel Hill**. There is a restaurant/baker's/guesthouse here run by Mrs Deleveaux, called *Sunny Lea*. Rooms have a good view of Major Cay Harbour. Close to the sheltered lagoon near Major Cay is a large cave; bromeliads can be seen at its entrance.

Acklins   Acklins is a few miles from Crooked Island and a ferry operates between the two
Atwood Bay is   islands, docking at **Lovely Bay** twice a day. The island is 192 square miles and was
recommended as one   named La Isabella by Columbus before being known as Acklins Cay and then just
of the Family Islands'   Acklins. Archaeological evidence points to a large Indian community once existing
most beautiful   between Jamaica Cay and Delectable Bay (possibly the largest in the Bahamas).
curved bays

The main settlement on Acklins is **Spring Point**, which has an airport. The *Airport Inn* run by Curtis Hanna is a popular meeting place, with rooms to rent and a restaurant/bar. **B** *Nae's Guest House*, T3443089, run by Mrs Naomi Hanna, five rooms, restaurant, beach. At nearby **Pompey Bay** it is still possible to see rock walls which were plantation demarcation boundaries. Pompey was once prosperous and busy; today most of the town is deserted and a tall church on the coast is abandoned. There is also a guesthouse at Pinefield run by the Williams family.

Long Cay   To the south of Acklins is a group of uninhabited cays sometimes referred to as the **Mira Por Vos Cays**. The most southerly is called **Castle Island** and is distinguished easily from afar by its tall battery operated lighthouse. There is a large seabird population here. South, North Guana and Fish Cay are all noted as havens for wildlife. **Long Cay** is the largest of the cays in this area and is inhabited. Long Cay was once known as Fortune Island and enjoyed great prosperity in the 19th century as a clearing house for ships between Europe and the Americas. The advent of the steamship made the use of Long Cay port redundant. Today you can see reminders of its former prosperity in the large unused Catholic church, various civic buildings and the relics of a railway system. On the south end of this island there is a large nesting ground for the West Indian flamingo.

Eleuthera

Eleuthera is 110 miles long but thin, two miles at its widest and only the width of a car at its narrowest. It has lovely pink sand beaches, particularly on the Atlantic side, coves and cliffs. This was the first permanent settlement in the Bahamas when Eleutheran Adventurers came from Bermuda and American colonial loyalists fled the mainland during the American Revolution. Their descendants still live here, living in houses painted in pastel colours. The first black settlers were slaves and free Africans from Bermuda.

Population: 8,114
2000 census
Colour map 2, grid B3

Getting there There are airports at **Governor's Harbour** (GHB) (8 miles from the town, US$20 taxi fare for 2 people), **North Eleuthera** (ELH) and **Rock Sound** (RSD). *Bahamasair* have scheduled flights daily from Nassau to all three. Governor's Harbour and North Eleuthera are served also by *Gulfstream International* in conjunction with *Continental Connection*, *Island Express*, *US Airways Express*, *Air Sunshine*, *Twin Air*, *Sandpiper Air*, *Bel Air Transport* and *American Eagle* from Fort Lauderdale, Miami, Key West and/or Orlando. Four mailboats and a very efficient ferry from Nassau call at Eleuthera. See page 75. The harbour master or shopkeepers will also tell you about mailboat sailings. **Getting around** The main road which runs down the backbone of the island is called the Queen's Highway and makes exploring by car easy and direct. Car hire from all 3 airports and in town costs about US$60 per day, *ASA Rent-A-Car Service* (T3322575); *Hilton Johnson* (near Hatchet Bay, T3320241); also *Ethel Knowles* at *Ethel's Cottages*, at Tarpum Bay. You can also hire mopeds. There are some public buses.

Ins and outs

Eleuthera is visited by many migrant birds. At **Hatchet Bay**, a few miles south of the Glass Window, there are ring necked pheasants. The Schooner and Kinley Cays in the **Bight of Eleuthera** are uninhabited but have large populations of white crowned pigeons. On **Finlay Cay** there are also sooty terns and noddy terns. The cays are

Flora & fauna

The Bahamas

Eleuthera

protected by the Wild Bird Act. Local indigenous flowers include yellow elder, poincianas and hibiscus. Lizards, chicken snakes and feral goats and pigs are common. North of Hatchet Bay you can visit a bat cave where there are thousands of roosting leaf-nosed bats.

Diving & marine life

Dive sites The **Plateau** became an underwater national park in 1993. It is a pretty site with mini walls, ledges, fissures and lots of fish in an area about ¾ mile by ½ mile. The usual regulations apply, with no fish feeding, no reef touching, no collecting and no spear fishing. The Plateau is about a mile from the Glass Window, seven miles from Harbour Island. If you like exciting diving, try riding the **Current Cut** on the incoming tide, which propels you between islands at a speed of about seven knots. Surfing is also good here. A 300-year old shipwreck at **Yankee Channel** lies in only 10 ft of water, while on the shallow, sharp reefs to the north called the **Devil's Backbone**, there is the wreck of a train where a barge once sank with its cargo on its way to Cuba, and a 19th-century passenger steamship. Four miles south of Royal Island is an old freighter, sunk by fire while loaded with a cargo of bat guano, now used as a landmark by sailors. The guano is an excellent fish food and the wreck is home to enormous fish, with Angel fish weighing up to 15 lbs and parrot fish of 20-30 lbs. A remarkable dive or snorkel site. Unfortunately, illegal bleach used by craw fishermen has spoiled many west side reefs.

Dive centres Diving and other watersports can be arranged with *Romora Bay Club* (T3332323, T/F3332500, PO Box 146, Harbour Island), where the dive operation is run by Jeff Fox and his diving dog. There is one boat taking out groups of 12-14 divers for single tank dives only, US$28 including tank and weights, resort course US$55-65, full PADI certification available. Individual specialized trips can be arranged. If the wind is north-northeast there is no diving.

Beaches & watersports

Beaches There are excellent beaches on the east side of southern Eleuthera. The west coast, however, is a little rocky. Many of the easterly beaches are backed by coconut palms or rocky cliffs with cedars. Three miles north of Alice Town in North Eleuthera there is a bushy and bumpy road off the main road which leads to **Surfers Beach**. It has the best surfing waves in the Bahamas and is frequently visited by surfing enthusiasts. **Harbour Island** has a beautiful pink sand beach which is said to be one of the most photographed beaches in the world. **Lighthouse Beach** at Cape Eleuthera has three miles of good beach.

Sailing Sailing boats are recommended to use a local pilot along the notoriously dangerous stretch of coast between Harbour Island and Spanish Wells. Valentine's Yacht Club, Harbour Island, has a 50-slip marina taking boats of up to 140ft and offering full services but no charter yachts. A regatta held to celebrate Discovery Day in November results in Valentine's bursting at the seams. Also on Harbour Island is the *Harbour Island Club and Marina* with 32 slips for 50-60 ft boats. Full service facilities are gradually coming on stream, contact Roger Ironside for details (T/F3332427, VHF 16, PO Box 43). At Spanish Wells there is the *Spanish Wells Yacht Haven* (T3334255, VHF 16), with 30 slips, and several boatyards for repairs. On the west side of Eleuthera, *Marine Services* of Eleuthera (T/F3350186, VHF 16), with 20 slips, and *Hatchet Bay Yacht Club* are at Hatchet Bay. The grassy bottom at Hatchet Bay makes anchoring difficult, so it is best to take a mooring or dock. Round Cape Eleuthera is *Davis Harbour Marina*, with 40 slips (T3134-6303/6101, VHF 16). This is also the centre for the deep sea and bonefishing charter companies. *Cape Eleuthera Marina* has docks, sometimes with water and electricity and rubbish collection, which yachts may use for a nominal fee. Redevelopment of the resort has been rumoured for years but nothing has happened yet. Harbour Island, Hatchet Bay, Governor's Harbour, Rock Sound and Cape Eleuthera are all ports of entry.

In 1999 Hurricane Floyd hit the island, causing extensive damage. Some resorts stayed closed for the winter season, some went out of business, while others soon reopened. Many homes were destroyed and they took longer than the resorts to be repaired. On Harbour Island some homes were badly damaged. The southern part of the island was hardest hit economically. To a visitor now, however, there is little evidence of the hurricane.

Around the island

Just north of Gregory Town is the **Glass Window Bridge**, where you can compare the blue Atlantic Ocean with the greenish water of the Caribbean on the other side, separated by a strip of rock just wide enough to drive a car across. Nearby are two small farming communities, Upper and Lower Bogue. **The Bogue** was once known as 'the bog' because of its marshy ground. During the hurricane in 1965 the sea flooded the land and now there are saltwater pools where you can find barracuda, grouper and snapper which were washed there by the tide. Also in the north is **The Cave**, which contains some impressive stalagmites and stalactites and the **Preacher's Cave**, where the Adventurers took shelter. The latter is reached by a rough unpaved track about 10 miles north of North Eleuthera; there is a pulpit carved out of rock from when the cave became a place of worship. **Rock Sound Water Hole Park** is an ocean or blue hole well stocked with grouper and yellowtail, while the walls are encrusted with flat oysters. Swimming is dangerous. Fishing is restricted.

Gregory Town is the main settlement in the north of the island. Pineapples here take 18 months to grow, making them sweeter than plants grown in six months with the help of commercial chemicals. All the farms are small and there are no large plantations. There is a beach with good surfing. It is 20 minutes drive from the airport. Locally-made stained glass can be seen and bought at the Simba studio gallery and shop.

Home of pineapple rum where a pineapple festival is held annually in Jun/Jul

Governor's Harbour is one of the oldest settlements in the Bahamas with several interesting colonial period houses. The harbour is picturesque and is linked by a causeway to Cupid's Cay, the original settlement. A new cruise ship pier was built in 1991 but is unusable as no deep water channel was dredged. On 10 November a Guy Festival celebrates Guy Fawkes Day and parades are held, culminating in an evening bonfire. Tourism used to be dominated here by *Club Med Eleuthera*, on the Atlantic beachfront.

In the south, **Windermere Island**, linked to the mainland by a small bridge, was an exclusive resort popular with the British Royal Family. The resort is closed now but opulent holiday homes remain. **Tarpum Bay** is the home of MacMillan-Hughes' Art Gallery and Castle. It used to be a big pineapple centre and there are many examples of wooden colonial houses in good repair.

Further south is **Rock Sound**, the largest settlement on the island with a population of about 1,100. It was first known as New Portsmouth and then Wreck Sound. Rock Sound is surrounded by limey, bush covered hills. It has a large modern shopping centre, three churches and many bars.

A few farming villages exist in the extreme south with more stretches of beach and fishing. One such is **Bannerman Town**, once known as the Pearl of the South. In the 1930s it was a prosperous sponge fishing centre with 20 or more sponging schooners anchored off the west shore. Today the settlement is like a ghost town with large churches in ruins and few people. Those who have stayed eke out a living by farming goats and pineapples and catching land crabs to send to Nassau. At the most southerly point of the island, **Cape Eleuthera** and **Point Eleuthera** are sometimes likened to the opposite points on the tail of a fish. On Cape Eleuthera there is a lighthouse which was repaired by the Raleigh Expedition in 1988. At one time the keeper, Captain Finby, was also the local obeah man. Legend has it that he slept with a ghost called the White Lady, who visited him nightly. Lighthouse Beach is three miles long. At Eleuthera Point there is a good cliff top view of Cat Island and Little San Salvador. Be careful as the edges are badly eroded. From here you can also see nesting stacks of fairy terns, shark and barracuda channels and the spectacular blues, greens,

The Bahamas

yellows, reds and browns of fringing reefs. A lone tarpon known as Tommy cruises off this beach often in less than 4 ft of water.

Spanish Wells
Population: 1,524
2000 census
See page 75 for the
ferry from Nassau

On St George's Cay, an island off the north of Eleuthera (a short ferry ride), Spanish Wells gets its name from the use of the cay by Spanish ships as a water supply. One and three quarter miles long and half a mile wide, until the hurricane disaster of 1992 it was reputed to have the highest per capita income of the Bahamas islands, with the wealth coming from 300 years of fishing the spiny Bahamian lobster, or crayfish (known locally as bugs), as well as tourism. Most of the boats were wrecked by the storm and the fishermen lost their livelihoods, but they were back in business less than a year later. The population are descended from the original settlers, the Eleutheran Adventurers from Bermuda and the British Loyalists from the mainland, and are all white. Old Town has well-preserved architecture, while the newer, western part reveals the wealth derived from the main industry. The Spanish Wells Museum in a restored wooden house with shutters has exhibits of the island's history and culture. ■ *1000-1200, 1300-1500, Mon-Sat. To get to Spanish Wells from North Eleuthera airport, take a Pinders Taxi to the ferry dock, then ferry to the island (US$10).*

A number of local fishermen can be hired as fishing guides off nearby **Russell** and **Royal Islands** (inhabited by a group of Haitians), payment by negotiation. Royal Island was once developed as a sheep farm by an estranged English dignitary. The old house still stands and paths weave through the overgrown grounds and gardens. Visitors can hire bicycles, but there are no cars.

Harbour Island
Population: 1,631
2000 census
See page 75 for the
ferry from Nassau

This is the most desirable place to stay in North Eleuthera. From the airport it is a quick taxi ride, US$3 per person, to the dock and from there water taxis wait to take passengers on a 10-minute ride to the island (US$4 per person one-way or US$8 for only one person). Taxis from the harbour to most resorts cost US$3 per person. **Dunmore Town**, named after Lord Dunmore, Governor 1786-1797, is a mixture of pastel coloured cottages, white picket fences and a number of small hotels and restaurants. It was the capital of the Bahamas for a time and once an important shipyard and sugar refining centre. Rum making was particularly popular during Prohibition. The three mile pink sand beach is popular. Bicycles can be rented at the dock. Fishing trips are easily arranged (US$85 per half day). Reggie does taxi tours of the island for day trippers and he and his wife Jena run a regular taxi service, recommended, T3332116. Access by yacht should be done with a hired local guide as you have to pass by a reef called the Devil's Backbone and the trip appears to take the yacht almost on the beach.

Essentials

Sleeping
All the major hotels
close in the autumn
for some weeks so
plan ahead if
visiting Sep-Nov

Gregory Town B *Cambridge Villas*, in Gregory Town, PO Box GT-1548, T3355080, F3355308. Run by Mr and Mrs Harcourt Cambridge, painted yellow, 21 rooms of different sizes, pool, transport to Golden Key beach for swimming or elsewhere for surfing, bar/restaurant, music some nights, rental cars available. **AL-A** *The Cove Eleuthera*, also known as *Pineapple Cove*, PO Box GT-1548, T3355142, F3355338, www.thecoveeleuthera.com Rooms in scattered cottages on headland with rocky cove one side, sandy cove the other. Triples available, children under 12 free, large airy dining room, rather spartan but relaxed, small pool, tennis, snorkelling, sea kayaks, volley ball, badminton, hammocks, is just outside the town within walking distance.

Hatchet Bay, L-AL *Rainbow Inn*, PO Box EL 25053, T/F3350924, www.Rainbowinn.com A/c rooms with fan, deck, kitchenette, or 2-3-bedroomed villa, tennis, swimming pool and a good restaurant, rocky outlook, good snorkelling, caves, fantastic view, Rainbow beach 1 mile, two beaches just other side of hill, bicycles for guests, live entertainment Wed evenings in nautical bar, popular, run by Ken Keene, friendly host, closed mid-Sep to mid-Nov. Nearby is *Hilton & Elsie Island House*, T3356241, 3320241. 1-2 bedroom apartments US$500-700 per week, rental car US$200 per week, on hill, great view of island, Rainbow beach close or walk 1 mile to Eden beach on other side if rough, good kitchens, ideal for families, food stores in nearby Hatchet Bay or Rainbow Bay, Hilton is a taxi driver and does car rentals.

Governor's Harbour and the south *Club Med Eleuthera*, www.clubmed.com, due to reopen late 2001 after extensive renovations. North of the town near North Palmetto Point on the ocean beach is **L-AL** *Unique Village*, PO Box 187, T3322288, F3321838. Rooms, apartments or 2-bedroom villas, restaurant, bar, satellite TV, children under 18 free in summer, under 12 in winter, all with seaviews. **A-B** *Laughing Bird Apartments*, PO Box EL-25076, T3322012, F3322358, ddavies@grouper. batelnet.bs Efficiency units and a guesthouse for 1-4 people, in town, overlooking the beach, owned and managed by nurse Jean Davies and her British architect husband Dan. **A** *Buccaneer Club*, T3322000, F3322888. Formerly a farmhouse, converted to 5 modern double rooms, pool. **AL-A** *Duck Inn Cottages*, T/F3322160. Rooms or full house sleeps 8, 2-night minimum. **Tarpum Bay: B-C** *Hilton's Haven* near beach and Rock Sound airport, T3344231, F3344020. Owned and managed by nurse Mary Hilton, bicycles, car rental, bar/restaurant with Bahamian specials. **L-A** *Cartwrights Ocean View*, T3344215. Room or cottage with full kitchen, run by Iris Cartwright. **B** *Ethel's Cottages*, on the waterfront, PO Box 27, T3344233. Families welcomed, Mrs Ethel Knowles also rents out cars. **Rock Sound: B** *Edwina's Place*, PO Box 30, T3342094, F3342280. Run by Edwina Burrows, modest accommodation but good. **AL-A** *Palmetto Shores Vacation Villas*, at South Palmetto Point, 12 miles south of the airport, PO Box EL25131, T/F3321305. 1-3 bedroom villas, a/c, snorkelling gear, watersports, rental cars or scooters.

Spanish Wells AL-B *Spanish Wells Yacht Haven*, PO Box EL-27427, T3334255, F3334649. 5 rooms, pool, beach.

Harbour Island L-A *Romora Bay Club*, PO Box 146, T3332325, F3332500. Wide variety of units scattered around the property, all decorated differently, dive packages available with dive shop on site, sailing, tennis, fishing available, day trips for couples with picnic hamper to deserted Jacob or Man Island, bicycles, bar, restaurant on hill top, one sitting for dinner. **LL** *Dunmore Beach Club*, PO Box EL-27122, T3332200, F3332429. Very expensive, 12 rooms, tennis, fishing, scuba equipment, a hideaway hotel. **LL-A** *The Landing*, PO Box 190, T3332707, F3332650. Run by former Miss Bahamas, Brenda Berry and her daughter Tracey, 6 rooms in colonial wooden house, balcony overlooking sea, Australian chef serves varied international menu. **LL-AL** *Coral Sands Hotel*, T3332320, F3332368, www.coralsands. com Right on the beach with 14 acres stretching over the hill to Dunmore Town, concrete block painted blue and yellow, cottages in gardens, 23 rooms and 8 suites, beach bar, restaurant, twice weekly evening entertainment, tennis lit for night play, watersports, games room, library. **AL-A** *Valentine's Yacht Club and Inn*, PO Box 1, T3332080, F3332135, T800-3235655. In town, has rooms which get heavily booked during regatta, pool side or garden side, pool, jacuzzi, tennis, 2 restaurants and all the facilities of the marina and dive shop, friendly. On the other side of the island overlooking the pink sand beach, there are several lovely places to stay. **LL-L** *Runaway Hill*, PO Box EL 27031, PO Box EL 27031, T3332150, F3332420. Built as a private home in the 1940s, now extended, lovely bar, restaurant, pool and deck all overlooking the sea, 10 luxury rooms, all different in size and character, casual but smart, men wear jackets for candlelit dinner. **LL** *Ocean View Club*, PO Box 134, T3332276, F3332459. Only open for winter season, split level overlooking sea, 10 rooms, those upstairs are larger, lovely old furniture, designer decorated, lower rooms smaller, children under 12 half price, meals US$60 per person, large chessmen on patio. **LL-L** *Pink Sands*, PO Box 87, T3332030, F3332060. A Chris Blackwell hotel, high luxury 26 1, 2 and 3 bedroom cottages, a/c, fans, stereo and CD player, tennis, on the beach, lovely location, although the US$70pp dinner is overrated and overpriced.

The Bahamas

Eating

Pineapple upside down pudding is a common dish

The pineapples on Eleuthera are said to be the world's sweetest. In Gregory Town they produce a pineapple rum called 'Gregory Town Special' which is highly recommended. Other local dishes include Cape Eleuthera's conch chowder, which is a substantial meal, the best is from Mary Cambridge in Gregory Town, hulled bonavas (a type of bean which tastes like split pea soup) or hulled corn soup with dumplings of rice. This is eaten traditionally after a special church service on Good Friday. On New Year's Eve traditional fare includes Benny Cake, pig's feet or mutton souse, or cassava/potato bread. In many of the smaller settlements such as James Cistern, outdoor or Dutch ovens are still used to bake bread.

Most of the resorts have their own restaurants. Others which have been recommended are *Cambridge Villas*, in Gregory Town, good seafood, fairly expensive. In Governor's Harbour there are plenty of Bahamian places to eat, fairly smart are *Buccaneer* (open Mon-Sat, no credit cards, T3322500, on New Bond St on top of hill) and *Sunset Inn* (on water, open daily from 0800, pool table, satellite TV, juke box). *Lady Blanche's Lifesaver Restaurant* in Upper Bogue serves the best cracked conch in the area, run by hospitable family, prices reasonable; for very cheap, tasty food try a takeaway meal of barbecue ribs or chicken for less than US$5 at roadside stands in James Cistern. *Blue Room* (T3322736) is a restaurant/bar/disco, as is *Ronnie's* in Cubid's Cay, free transport to yacht or hotel at night. *Big Sally's Disco*, just north of Rock Sound, cocktails, bar snacks, dancing. *Cush's Place* (between Gregory Town and Hatchet Bay) does cookouts Sat and Sun afternoons with music and dancing, US$10; Lida Scavella in Hatchet Bay does cheap food, her pastries are recommended; a popular bar in the Palmetto Point area is *Mate and Jenny's Pizza*, T3322504, try conch pizza, good cocktails. In Rock Sound, *Edwina Burrows'* restaurant is highly recommended, good food reasonably priced, popular barbecue dishes. *Sammy's Place*, T3342121. Another recommended restaurant and bar, open daily 0800-2200. Several bars in Wemyss Bight and Green Castle sell spirits in half pint glasses very cheaply; recommended in Deep Creek are *Bab's Place* and *Mr Pratt's Bar*. *The Waterfront Bar* in Rock Sound is cheap, no food, while *The Ponderosa* and *The Dark Side* are bars and cheap fast food restaurants. In Harbour Island, *The Landing* , serves a blend of sumptuous gourmet and nouvelle cuisine in a delightful setting, get a patio table facing the dock and catch the sunset on the water at dinner. A nice place to eat is *Harbour Lounge*, T3332031. In an old wooden building overlooking the ferry dock with a bar and indoor or outdoor dining, good food but not cheap, bar food all day and late, Sun brunch in high season. *Arthur's Bakery* does lunch and breakfast as well as being a bakery. *Miss Mae's Tearoom* is principally a gift shop selling prints, textiles etc but you can get salads and other food in the courtyard at lunchtime. There is an ice cream parlour and also a 2-bedroom apartment to rent upstairs, US$750 per week, contact through *Ocean View Club*. *Ma Rubie's* restaurant at *Tingum Village*, PO Box 61, T/F3332161. Good for native food but is particularly noted for its cheeseburgers, apparently among the world's top 10, there are also 12 rooms **B** and a 3-bedroom, 2-bath cottage **L**, under 12s free, 3 mins from beach.

Directory

Tourist office *Ministry of Tourism*, Eleuthera Tourist Office, Governors Harbour, Eleuthera, T3322142, F3322480.

The Exumas

*Population: 3,575
2000 census
Colour map 2, grid B3*

The chain of 365 Exuma cays and islands stretches for 90 miles although the majority of the inhabitants live on Great Exuma and Little Exuma at the south end. Great Exuma is long and narrow, covered with scrub and dry woodland. The soil is pitifully thin but there are aromatic shrubs, curly-tailed lizards and songbirds and a few wild peacocks. Around the villages are a few patches of what the Lands and Surveys map accurately calls 'casual cultivation'. The main industry is tourism, based on yachting and a few hundred winter visitors who own houses on the island.

Ins & outs

Getting there There is an international airport at Moss Town with an 8,000ft runway, 2 miles from George Town, and another airport at George Town with an 8,000ft runway but closed to commercial traffic. Confusingly the **Exuma International Airport** at Moss Town carries the (GGT) George Town code. *American Eagle* flies daily from Miami in high season, 5 times a week in summer. *Bahamasair* flies from Fort Lauderdale, Nassau and Stella Maris, Long Island. *Air Sunshine* flies from Fort Lauderdale and Sarasota/Bradenton, Florida, 4 times a week. *Lynx Air* also fly non-stop from Fort Lauderdale. Mr Harry Nixon runs a charter service, *Nixon Aviation* (PO Box 3, Airport, George Town, T3362104). For flight information to Staniel Cay, Capt Dennis Rotolo, *Executive Air Travel*, T2246002, F9795103. For details on mailboat sailings see page 75.

Getting around **Taxis** are expensive but plentiful. The fare from the airport to George Town is US$22. **Hitching** is easy. **Cars** can be rented at the airport and from George Town, ask at *Peace and Plenty Hotel*. **Buses** run between Rolleville and George Town. Christine Rolle runs *Island Tours* from George Town, leaving at 1000 and 1400, including a native lunch, visits to various settlements and to Gloria, the 'shark lady,' on Little Exuma, who catches sharks and sells the teeth as souvenirs. **Bicycles** can be rented from *Two Turtles* shop or several hotels. The island of Barreterre (pronounced Barra Terry) can be reached from Great Exuma by a bridge. There is a **ferry** to Stocking Island from Great Exuma and another to Lee Stocking Island from Barreterre, but otherwise the cays are difficult to visit unless you have a boat or small plane.

The islands were virtually uninhabited until after the American Revolution, when **History** Loyalists from the south colonies were given land and brought their slaves to grow cotton. During the late 18th century the British Crown granted Denys Rolle, an Englishman, 7,000 acres of land and he set up cotton plantations at Rolletown, Rolleville, Mt Thompson, Steventon and Ramsey. Following the emancipation of

The Exumas

The Bahamas

the slaves and poor cotton harvests because of the exhaustion of the soil, it was believed that Rolle's son gave away his lands to his former slaves, who were also called Rolle as was customary at the time. However, no deeds have been found confirming transfer of title and longstanding squatter's rights provide an adequate title to the land for many. Today, half the population bears the surname Rolle and two of the largest settlements are Rolleville and Rolletown.

The Exuma cays are in general isolated communities which are difficult to get to (the exception being Staniel Cay). Their inaccessibility has attracted undesirable attention; Norman's Cay was for some time the drug smuggling centre of Carlos Lehder, the Colombian drug baron deported from the Bahamas in 1982 and now in prison in the USA. In 1993 the cay was confiscated by the Government and put up for sale. Recent attempts to control drug smuggling include mooring Fat Albert, an airship full of radar equipment, over Great Exuma, and low flying helicopters also monitor activity.

In 1994 the government approved a US$90mn residential and resort development covering 518 acres on Exuma. A US$35mn hotel was to be built in the first phase and there would eventually be a marina, golf course and casino as well. In 1997 it was again announced that a 200-room hotel, casino, marina and golf course would be built, but at a cost of US$70mn.

Diving & marine life

At Stocking Island is the oldest evidence of life on earth

Dive sites The Exuma Cays begin at Sail Rocks about 35 miles from Nassau. On the northerly Allen Cays can be seen the protected Rock Iguanas which grow up to 2 ft long and are known as Bahamian Dragons, but they are extremely tame. Much of the Exuma chain is encompassed in the **Exuma Cays Land and Sea Park**, an area of some 176 square miles set up by the Bahamas National Trust to conserve all underwater life and for boating, diving and observation of wildlife. Moorings (US$15 per two nights) have been placed in the main area of the park and anchoring is not allowed. There is a warden's residence on Waderick Wells Cay. The park stretches between Wax Cay and Conch Cut, 22 miles away and offers more delights for underwater explorers, with beautiful coral and limestone reefs, blue holes and shipwrecks. *Sampson Cay Club and Marina*, south of Waderick Wells, offers a 500ft dock and 30 full-service slips. Get in touch with marine biologist, Johnny Dye (*Exuma Dive*) for information on a stromatolite reef on the east (Atlantic) shore of **Stocking Island**. This is a growing reef of layered limestone, a living fossil and the oldest evidence of life on earth. Worth visiting are the underwater valley at **Ocean Rock**, the huge caves filled with black coral called the **Iron Curtain**, or **Thunderball Grotto** at Staniel Cay, where part of the James Bond film and the Disney film *Splash*, were made. Watch out for dangerous currents; you can snorkel here at slack tide, in a giant fishbowl with sunlight shining in through a hole.

Dive centres Individual and package diving can be arranged with *Exuma Dive Centre and Watersports* in Georgetown, PO Box EX-29238, T3362390, F3362391, www.bahamasvg.com/exumadive. Dive trips start at US$60 and three-hour snorkelling trips at US$35, with rental equipment available, maximum six divers on board. Instruction from resort course to advanced scuba on offer with NAUI, IDEA, IANTD and PADI instructors and dive masters. Scooters can be rented for US$35 per day and 17-ft boats for use in the harbour, US$80 per day.

Beaches & watersports

Stocking Island is a long thin island about a mile from the mainland at Elizabeth Harbour, George Town. Its shape and position provide a natural protection for the harbour. It has good beaches and a burger bar and is famous for its **Mysterious Cave**, but this can only be reached by divers. A boat leaves the *Peace and Plenty Hotel* in George Town at 1000 and 1300, roundtrip US$8, free for guests, or boats can be hired from Exuma Dive Centre and Watersports in George Town to visit the reefs off Stocking Island. **The Three Sisters Rocks** which rise out of the water some 100 ft from the shore, are situated between two very good beaches: Jimmy Hill, which is a long empty beach good for swimming, and the beautiful bay of Ocean Bight. Other recommended beaches are the **Tropic of Cancer Beach**, 15 miles east of George Town, **Cocoplum Beach**, 20 miles north of George Town and **Jollie Hall Beach**, two miles west of George Town (no land access).

The **Visiting Yachts Regatta** is held in early March and on the fourth Thursday in April the Family Island Regatta is held at George Town when working boats compete for the title of 'Best in the Bahamas'. During August there is a series of smaller regattas at Black Point, Barreterre and Rolleville.

For details of **sportfishing**, contact Bob Hyde, Director of Sportfishing at Staniel Cay's *Peace and Plenty, the Bonefish Lodge*, T3455556, who runs a bonefishing school and trains flyfishing guides; there are certified guides and three areas to fish. In October the Bonefish Bonanza Tournament is held at *Peace and Plenty Hotel*, George Town. In November a second Bonefish Bonanza Tournament is held at the *Peace and Plenty*.

There are several **marinas** in the Exumas. Exuma Docking Service, 52 slips, usual services, bar, fuel, showers etc, T3362578, VHF 16; Happy People Marina, Staniel Cay, six slips, 6ft depth, showers, laundry, grocery, restaurant, T3552008; Staniel Cay Yacht Club, four slips, all services, tackle and bait, hotel, repairs, T3552024, VHF 16; Highborne Cay, fuel, electricity, supplies, restaurant, bar, VHF 16; Sampson Cay Colony, 30 slips, 7ft depth, all services, charters and boat rentals, hotel, wet and dry storage, T3552034, VHF 16.

Great Exuma

The main town on Great Exuma is **George Town**, a pleasant little town built on a strip of land between a round lake and the sea. A narrow channel allows small boats to use the lake as a harbour but yachts moor offshore, often several hundred at a time in the peak winter months. The large and beautiful bay is called **Elizabeth Harbour** and is yet another contender for the site of Columbus' harbour that could "hold all the ships in Christendom." The main building is the Government Administration Building, pseudo colonial, pink and modelled on Nassau's Government House. Opposite is a large tree under which women plait straw and sell their wares. There are several pretty buildings, St Andrew's Church (Anglican), blue and white on the top of a little hill and the *Peace and Plenty Hotel* in an old cotton warehouse which was formerly the site of a slave market. There is a good range of shops and the supermarket is well stocked. The Sandpiper shop has an interesting array of clothes and souvenirs.

To the south of George Town is **Rolletown**, a small village on a hill overlooking the sea. Many old houses are painted in bright blues, yellows and pinks. There is a small cemetery in which are buried settlers from the 18th century in three family tombs: husband, wife and small child of the Mackay family. **The Ferry** is a small settlement by the beautiful strait which separates Great and Little Exuma, but there is a bridge there now, not a ferry.

North of George Town there is a thin scatter of expatriate holiday houses and a few shops along the Queen's Highway. East of the road are several fine beaches, including **Hoopers Bay** and **Tar Bay**. The airport turning is north of George Town. Small villages are Moss Town, Mount Thompson, Steventon and Rolleville. Moss Town was once an important sponging centre. Close by you can see The Hermitage, brick tombs dating back to just after the American War of Independence, not to be confused with the Hermitage or Cotton House close to Williams Town on Little Exuma. Mt Thompson was once the farming centre of Exuma and is important for its onion packing house. Some of the cottages in **Rolleville**, 16 miles northwest of George Town, were originally slave quarters. The town overlooks a harbour and was the base of a group of rebellious slaves who attempted to escape and thereafter refused to work except in the mornings, until emancipation. Unfortunately, quite a large area of North Exuma is disfigured by roads which were laid out as part of a huge speculative land development scheme in the 1960s. Almost all the lots are still empty, but **Cocoplum Beach** and the coastal scenery are unspoilt. At the north end

The Bahamas

of the island is a bridge to Barreterre, with more fine scenery and places to eat lunch. At **Lee Stocking Island**, just offshore, the Caribbean Marine Research Centre is involved in research into the tilapia, a freshwater fish brought from Africa which can grow in saltwater. This can be visited by prior appointment.

Little Exuma

On Good Friday a tree near the fort is said to give off a substance the colour of blood

A bridge leads to Little Exuma, which is 12 miles long and one mile wide. An attractive cove is Pretty Molly Bay, next to the abandoned *Sand Dollar Hotel*. A mermaid story is based on Pretty Molly, a slave girl who sat on the rocks at night and gazed by the light of the moon towards Africa. Near Forbes Hill is the 'fort', built in 1892 and said to be haunted. **Williams Town** is the most southerly of the settlements on Exuma. Salt used to be made in the lagoon. Perched on the cliff top here is a tall white obelisk which not only guided passing ships safely in the 19th century, but was an advertisement that salt and freshwater could be picked up here. The Cotton House, near Williams Town, is the only plantation owner's house still standing in the Exumas. It is at the end of a driveway marked by a pair of trees, but is tiny, not grand. Slave quarters can be seen close by.

The Cays

Staniel Cay has excellent beaches with a half mile of sand dunes on the ocean side of the cay and good watersports facilities. *Staniel Cay Yacht Club* and *Happy People Marina* have dockage, water and restaurants, but beware of bad weather. On Staniel Cay during Bahamian Independence Day weekend on 10 July, there is a bonefishing festival, entrance fee US$20. The Staniel Cay Yacht Club provides free food in the evening and a rake'n'scrape band plays traditional music. The morning before the contest there is a sailing regatta for working Bahamian sailboats. A Bahamian sailboat regatta is held on New Year's Day. The Royal Entertainers Lounge serves food and drinks.

Farmer's Cay to the south of Staniel Cay has a lively annual festival called The Farmer's Cay First Friday in February Festival at which there are races, dancing games and the Bahamas' only Hermit Crab Race. *Farmer's Cay Yacht Club and Marina* has dockage, moorings and a restaurant. *Ocean Cabin* restaurant has a mooring for diners. Further south on **Darby Island** is an old mansion which is probably the remains of a large coconut plantation.

Off Staniel Cay on the edge of the Tongue of the Ocean is **Green Cay**, home to the world's second largest population of white crowned pigeons.

Sleeping

LL-AL *Coconut Cove*, PO Box EX 29299, T3362659, F3362658. A mile west of George Town. Newest hotel, 9 beach or garden rooms, one suite, about 20% less in summer, diving/honeymoon/pilots packages available, a/c and fans, minibar, beach towels and robes provided, dirty beach reported with lots of mosquitoes, transport to town and to Stocking Island costs extra, boat rentals, pool, popular Mon barbecue. **AL-B** *Two Turtles Inn*, T3362545, F3362528. 200 yds from harbour in George Town, 12 rooms, rooms large enough for 4, a/c, TV, some have kitchenettes, barbecue on Fri nights. **AL** *Club Peace and Plenty*, PO Box 29055, T3362551/2, F3362093, www.peaceandplenty.com Dive, fishing, photography, honeymoon packages available, 300 yds from harbour, the pink building was once the slave market and sponge warehouse, 35 rooms/suites, a/c, all rooms have balcony overlooking harbour, entertainment some evenings, pool, sailboats, bicycles, restaurant, bar. The hotel also has a *Bonefish Lodge*, PO Box 29173, T3455556. 8 rooms in a timber building close to the fishing grounds overlooking blue hole, 10 miles east of *Peace and Plenty*, restaurant/bar, games room, all fishing facilities, certified guides. **L-AL** *Regatta Point*, PO Box 29173, T3362206. On a point just outside George Town, private beach, 5 apartments and 1 house for 2-4 people, kitchens, bicycles, sunfish, dock, run by Nancy Bottomlea. **LL** *Hotel Higgins Landing*, PO Box EX-29146, T3362460, F3570008, www.higginslanding.com The only hotel on Stocking Island, 5 luxury rooms with antique furniture, 3 nights minimum, all-inclusive, complimentary kayaks, sailboats, snorkelling gear, also rental boats, diving, fishing, award-winning eco-resort. **A-B** *The Palms At Three Sisters Beach Resort*, Mount Thompson, PO Box EX 29215, T3584040, F3584043, 800-2532711. 12 rooms, on beach, tennis, satellite TV, live music Fri, Sat nights, restaurant. **C** *Marshall's Guesthouse*, PO Box 29027, T3362328, F3362081. John Marshall (grocery shop in George Town) has apartments to rent by week/month.

Staniel Cay LL-A *Staniel Cay Yacht Club*, T3552024, F3552044, www.stanielcay.com Own private airstrip, accommodation in waterfront cottages sleep 2-7, packages available, including all meals and use of Boston whalers and golf carts, beach, marina, scuba diving gear available. *Staniel Cay Yacht Club* restaurant is open to non-guests if prior notice is given, VHF 16, breakfast 0800, lunch 1300, dinner 1900 one sitting, box lunches available.

The main hotels in George Town have good restaurants, *Peace and Plenty* (dance with local band Sat nights), and *Two Turtles* (barbecue Fri nights, very lively and good value but take your own cutlery if you want to cut up your steak, plastic only provided, happy hour 1700-2300, US$1.50 for spirit and mixer, frequented by visitors and ex-pats). For sandwiches and light meals, *Ruth's Deli*, in George Town, T3362596. Open Mon-Sat 0900-1700, no credit cards. *Marshall's Restaurant*, George Town. Small, homely, good home made bread. *Eddy's Edgewater*, T3362050. Specializes in Bahamian food, fried conch is recommended, open Mon-Sat 0730-2300, no credit cards. *Sam's Place*, T3362579, at dock. Run by Mr Sam Gray, manager of the marina, open daily from 0730 (expensive). *La Shante*, Forbes Hill, T3454136. Good, open daily 1000-0200, happy hour Sun 1800-1900, 3 a/c rooms to rent, guided bonefishing. *Silver Dollar*, George Town, T3362939. Traditional Bahamian cooking, no credit cards. *Central Highway Inn*, T3457014. On the road 6 miles northwest of George Town, Bahamian specialities. *Rodriguez Neighbourhood Bar/Restaurant & Lounge*, at Harts, a settlement 13 miles outside George Town. Largest nightclub on Exuma, on waterfront, live band Fri, disco Sat, Sun, famous for its conch fritters. Others doing mainly peas'n'rice type dishes are *Iva Bowes* and *Three Sisters* in Mount Thompson, *Kermit Rolle's*, in Rolleville is by appointment only but he also has a good restaurant opposite the airport building, *Kermit's Airport Lounge*, T3450002, VHF 16. For breakfast, lunch or dinner, takeaway service; and *Fisherman's Inn*, Barreterre, very good. Discos at *Paramount Club* (Moss Town), *Oasis* (Queen's Highway near Mt Thompson), *Flamingo Bay* (George Town).

Eating

Tourist office *Ministry of Tourism*, Exuma Tourist Office, Cousins Building, Queens Highway, George Town, Exuma, T3362430, F3662431.

Directory

Inagua

Inagua (Great and Little) is the most southerly of the Bahamas Islands and the third largest. Little Inagua is uninhabited now, but the 49-square mile island is reputed to hide the treasure of Henri Christophe, one-time ruler of Haiti. On a clear day, Great Inagua is visible from both Cuba and Haiti.

Population: 1,046
2000 census
Colour map 2, grid C5

Inagua

Land & Sea Park
LITTLE INAGUA
Old Refuge
Carmicheal Point
Ocean Bight
Alfred Sound
GREAT INAGUA
Man of War Bay
Bahamas National Trust Park
Doghead Point
Lake Rosa
Matthew Town
Sandy Point

N

0 km 10
0 miles 10

Getting there The airport (IGA) is 2 miles from town, its runway resurfaced in 2000 at a cost of US$1 mn. *Bahamasair* have 3 scheduled flights a week from Nassau. *Air Sunshine* flies 4 times a week from Fort Lauderdale and from Sarasota/ Bradenton, Florida. The mailboat takes 2 days from Nassau, see page 75. Mosquitoes can be a problem at some times of the year, avoid May. **Getting around** A **taxi** from the airport to Matthew Town costs about US$4. There are taxis but no buses. Mr Harry Ingraham runs a fleet of three **tour buses** called *Great Inagua Tours*, rates negotiable. Most roads are paved, except for those leading into the interior. Taxis cannot be used for

Ins & outs

The Bahamas

birdwatching tours because of the state of the roads. If you want to see the island properly you will need transport, particularly if you travel to the north side of the island. Local people are very friendly and helpful and will organize sightseeing/wildlife trips. See transport, page 135, for more details.

Flora & fauna The southeast side of the island is rocky and because of the effects of the sea and wind, the trees do not grow more than a foot tall. Further inland trees have a better chance of maturing. Many cactii are found in this rocky part of Inagua, in particular the dildo cactus and the woolly-nipple. On Little Inagua, although it is largely over-grown, it is possible to see some of the only natural palms in the Bahamas. The whole of Little Inagua is a Land and Sea Park and is a Bird Sanctuary.

Inagua has a restricted access national park which is home to a wide range of birds including the world's largest flamingo colony on Lake Rosa (sometimes called Lake Windsor), a 12-mile stretch of marshy wildlife sanctuary. Almost half of Great Inagua is included in the 287-square-mile park. Visitors should contact the Bahamas National Trust in Nassau (PO Box N-4105, T3931317). A basic but comfortable camp has been established on the west side, 23 long miles by jeep from Matthew Town. National Trust wardens will accompany you on tours of the area and it is possible to view the flamingos close up. At certain times of the year they cannot be approached. Jimmy Nixon, one of the original wardens, is recommended as a guide. Early spring is the breeding season when large numbers of flamingos congregate on the lake. At the Union Creek camp on the northwest side of the island is a breeding and research area for Green and Hawksbill turtles, called Turtle Sound. It is ideal for observing sea turtles at close quarters. On the east side of the island are mangrove swamps which are the nesting grounds for many birds including cormorants, pelicans and the rare reddish egret. Here you can also see the white tailed tropic bird and inland, the Bahamas parrot, the most northerly species of parrot in the world.

Beaches & sports
Apart from the rocky SE side of the island, Inagua has many deserted & unspoiled beaches

Beaches that are used by locals include **Cartwright's beach**, with bar/restaurant, within easy reach of Matthew Town, **Farquharson's Beach** and **Matthew Town Beach**, which is pleasant and conveniently located. **Man of War Bay** has a lovely beach with some shade.

It is possible to play **tennis** and **basketball** in Matthew Town, but the most popular pastime is **hunting**. You can arrange to go on a wild boar hunt with Herman Bowe (known as the Crocodile Dundee of the Bahamas, who prefers to hunt barefoot) or Jimmy Nixon (the excellent National Trust guide). On Emancipation Day (1 August) and other holidays, wild boar is roasted on the beach and there are wild donkey races. Rodeos take place on an ad hoc basis.

Around the island Vegetation is sparse because of low rainfall, the buffeting trade winds and lack of freshwater, but this has granted ideal conditions for salt production leading to a development and prosperity not enjoyed by any of the surrounding islands. It is thought that the name Inagua comes from the Spanish *lleno* (full) and *agua* (water): *henagua*. This was apparently the name of the island when the first salt farmers settled there. In 1803 records show only one inhabitant, but the success of the salt industry meant that by 1871 the population had risen to 1,120. Although trade barriers in the USA caused the decline of the salt trade in Inagua for many years, the industry was revitalized in the 1930s with the establishment of the Morton Salt Company, which now utilizes 12,000 acres. Morton Bahamas Ltd installed a power plant which supplies electricity to all homes in **Matthew Town**. Inagua has the best telecommunications system in the Family Islands and nearly everyone has a telephone. For a while the island supported a cotton plantation; although a shortlived enterprise, wild cotton can still be found growing on Inagua today. Outside Matthew Town you can still see the ruins of the cotton mill and the narrow plantation roads, as well as the ruins of a prison from the days when the community was large enough to need one. The highest points on the island are Salt Pond Hill at 102 ft and East Hill at 132 ft.

There are several guesthouses in Matthew Town. The **C** *Main House*, T3391267, F3391265. 6 **Sleeping**
rooms. **B-C** *Walkine's*, T3391612. 5 rooms, satellite TV, fishing. *Crystal Beach View Hotel* ,
T3391550. *Pour More Hotel* , T3391659.

Eating out is cheaper than Nassau or Grand Bahama. For a typical Bahamian meal of maca- **Eating**
roni, coleslaw, ribs or chicken and potato salad, expect to pay US$6-7. Local dishes include
roast wild boar, baked box fish, crab meat 'n rice and roast pigeon and duck. A popular local
drink is gin and coconut, which is made with fresh coconuts on special occasions. *Topps Restaurant and Bar*, run by the Palacious brothers is recommended for its seafood dishes, fresh
boiled fish is served for breakfast. Nightlife revolves around the local bars, which periodically
have live music and dancing.

Car hire   Jeeps for hire from Mr Burrows at Matthew Town Service Station, rates negotiable **Transport**
but expect to pay at least US$40 per day. To get out to the camps arrange transport with the
warden in Matthew Town (about US$10). To arrange fishing expeditions or trips around the
island contact the local repair man, Cecil Fawkes (nicknamed the old Red Fox), whose boat is
called *The Foxy Lady*, or Mr Cartwright. There is no set rate, prices are negotiated. There is a
marina and boats can moor here and refuel.

Banks   Matthew Town has a *Bank of the Bahamas Ltd* (open 0930-1430 Mon-Thu, 1030-1830 Fri) **Directory**
and 6 churches. Credit cards are not generally accepted, take plenty of cash with you.

Long Island

Long Island lies southeast of Little Exuma and is 57 miles long and four miles across at its   Population: 2,945
widest. Columbus made a stop here and changed its name from the Arawak name Yuma   2000 census
*to Fernandina, after Ferdinand, the King of Spain. The island has a variety of communi-
ties from different ethnic backgrounds, from Europe, Africa and North America.*

Getting there   There are 2 airports, **Stella Maris** (SML) and **Deadman's Cay** (LGI). *Island*   **Ins & outs**
Express flies several times a week from Fort Lauderdale to Stella Maris, while *Bahamasair*
flies there from Deadman's Cay, George Town, Fort Lauderdale (via Exuma) and Nassau.
Deadman's Cay only receives Bahamasair flights from Nassau and Stella Maris. **Getting
around Taxis** are available and **private
cars** often negotiate to carry passengers too.
Taxis are generally expensive. If you are
going to Stella Maris it is better to get a flight
to the airport there if possible, (Deadman's
Cay to Stella Maris is a 2 hrs' drive) from
where it is only 20 mins, US$3 per person, to
the resort. The main road connecting all the
main settlements on the island is the
Queen's Highway. Avoid night driving.

Long Island

Cape Santa Maria
Seymour
Hog ⚓ Glentons
Cay ⚓ Stella Maris
Millerton ✈ *Atlantic*
O'Neil's
Simms *Ocean*
Bain's
Whitehouse
Indian Head Point ⚓ Salt Pond
Sandy Cay Pinder's
Gray's
Deadman's Cay
Sandy
Cay Mangrove Bush
Clarence
Town
Dunmore
N
Diamond Roads
Berry's
Gordon's
0 km   10
0 miles   10
Cape Verde

The *Stella Maris Marina* is the only   **Diving &**
full-service marina in the area and is a   **marine life**
port of entry. There are 12 slips and all
facilities including repairs, VHF 16, and
facilities for diving, snorkelling, reef,
bone and deep sea fishing and boat
charters, T3382050. Dive instruction
(PADI, SSI) is in English or German.
This was where shark dives started; reef
sharks wait for the boat anchor to be
dropped and the divers to be lined up
against the reef before their feeding

The Bahamas

frenzy begins. At Clarence Town dock you can get fuel, water, ice and supplies. At Harding's Supplies Center on Salt Pond you can also find showers and a laundry. There are safe anchorages at Cape Santa Maria, Salt Pond and Little Harbour. Cape Santa Maria has lovely beaches, caves and bays but do not anchor there if there is a strong north or west wind. A lagoon just beyond the west end of the cape can accommodate boats of 60 ft with depths of 6 ft. Diving and snorkelling are also good in this area and the Cape Santa Maria Fishing Club operates from here. On the east coast, good anchorages are at Clarence Town (groceries and other supplies) and Little Harbour (no facilities). The annual **Long Island Regatta** at Salt Pond is held in May. Locals compete for best seaman award, the fastest boat and the best kept boat over five years old. The Regatta is popular and accompanied by authentic Bahamian food and traditional rake'n'scrape music.

Around the island Most islanders live on the west side where the hills and dunes offer some protection from the sea. There are paths and dirt tracks to the east side, mostly used by fishermen. Villages to the south are rather neglected. The landscape is diverse, with tall white cliffs at Cape Santa Maria with caves below, old salt pans near Clarence Town, dense bush over much of the island and scattered areas of cactii. It has a rocky coastline on one side and lovely beaches and crystal clear water on the other, with the usual friendly fish and lots of convenient wrecks. One, a German freighter sunk in 1917, lies in 25ft of water only 200 yds from the beach at Guana Cay, south of Salt Pond. Beaches in the south are good but rather hard to get to. Long Island is a major producer of vegetables and cattle and is known for its pot-hole farming which gives hearty supplies of tomatoes, bananas and onions. The *Stella Maris Resort Club* in the north is the biggest employer, but there are not enough jobs and most young people leave to work in Nassau or Grand Bahama. Hog Cay, Long Island, is home to 380 West Indian Whistling Ducks, the most endangered duck in North America and one of the two rarest ducks in the Western Hemisphere.

The main settlements are **Deadman's Cay** and **Clarence Town** further south. Most tourists stay at **Stella Maris**, which is supposed to have the best yachting marina in the southern Bahamas. From a lookout tower here it is possible to see right across the island and to see the nearby ruins of the Adderly Plantation House. The town of **Simms** is the home of some of the best straw work in the Bahamas, made by Ivy Simms and her workers. The mailboat calls here and there is a high school, magistrate's court and Commissioner's office. The settlement of Clarence Town in the south half of the island is very pretty and boasts two white, twin-spired churches built on opposite hilltops by Father Jerome (see under Cat Island). St Paul's is the Anglican church and St Peter's the Catholic. Both are still in use today. There are many caves to explore and ruins of old plantation houses: Adderly's near Stella Maris and the remains of a cotton gin and plantation gate posts at Dunmore. At Glenton's, north of Stella Maris, archaeologists have found the remains of an Arawak village, and at Hamilton, south of Deadman's Cay, caves have been discovered with Arawak drawings and carvings.

Sleeping The **LL-AL** *Stella Maris Resort Club*, PO Box LI-33105, T3382051, F3382052, www.stella marisresort.com It has 47 rooms, suites, 1-4-bedroom villas. A shopping centre has a bank and post office. There are 3 pools and 8 beaches along with tennis, volley ball, table tennis, bicycles, diving, windsurfing (guests free) and water-skiing (US$25). Bicycles are free for guests; cars and scooters can be rented. Full service marina, free daily snorkelling and land excursions. Glass bottom boat trips can be taken for US$20. Cave parties, Rum Punch party and other weekly entertainment. 25 different diving areas offer a lot of variety for the experienced or the beginner and there is a shark reef with shark feeding. Fishing trips can be arranged: during Nov and Dec huge shoals of grouper make fishing easy in the waters around Long Island. Bone fishing US$200 per day. The blue hole close to the harbour at Clarence Town is good for line fishing. **LL-L** *Cape Santa Maria Beach Resort* on the island's north point, PO Box LI-30117, T3385273, F3386013, www.obmg.com Full board, closed mid-Sep to mid-Nov, taxi from Stella Maris airport about US$20, arguably the best beach hotel on the island, new restaurant with great ocean view added in 1999. There are a few private guesthouses but these are unregistered. Ask around, we have heard of places to stay at Hardings, Clarence Town, Hamilton, Deadman's Cay and Simms, about **C**.

Two island dishes to try are wild hog with onion and spices and grouper roe with liver. **Eating** *Thompson's Bay Inn* has a good restaurant but reservations essential. *The Blue Chip Restaurant and Bar* in Simms is recommended. *The Harbour Bar and Restaurant* at Clarence Town has Bahamian dishes. *Sabrina's*, at Burnt Ground Village, is by appointment only, cheap and simple, occasional disco. In Hard Bargain in the south, the *Forget Me Not Club* has a popular bar and restaurant. In Mangrove Bush the Knowles family run the hillside tavern and bar. They also sell fresh fish at *Summer Seafood* close by.

Mayaguana

Mayaguana (an Arawak name), located 50 miles east of Acklins and 60 miles north of Inagua, is the least developed and most isolated of the Family Islands although there are now three Bahamasair flights a week (Monday, Wednesday and Friday) from Nassau, via Inagua. The main settlement is **Abraham's Bay**, a small town with a few shops and one bar/restaurant run by the Brown family who also own the guesthouse (Batelco T3393065). There are two other settlements, **Betsy Bay** and **Pirate's Well**, which are both very isolated. Several people will rent you a room in their homes for US$30-60; freshwater and food can sometimes be hard to come by, young coconuts are recommended if short of water. Take mosquito repellent. Most people earn their living from fishing or farming and many leave for Nassau and Freeport to look for work. In 1993 the Government approved a tourist development by a Californian group in East Mayaguana. About half of the 50,000-acre project will be a botanical garden and park. If it is implemented it will provide employment but no doubt change the island considerably.

The island is on a direct route to the Caribbean and as such is sometimes visited by yachtsmen, although it is not a port of entry. There is a very large reef around the northwest side of the island and excellent diving, although a liveaboard dive boat is necessary. 20 miles from Mayaguana are the Plana and Samana Cays, notable for their interesting wildlife, where you can see the Bahama hutia, thought to be extinct until the mid-1960s. A cross between a rat and a rabbit, this rodent's flesh is said to be similar to pork.

*Population: 262
2000 census
Colour map 2, grid C6*

Rum Cay

Some 35 miles south of San Salvador, this small island is approximately 20 miles square. First known as Mamana by the Lucayan Indians, the cay was later renamed

Mayaguana

Santa María de la Concepción by Columbus. Spanish explorers once found a lone rum keg washed up on a shore and changed the name again to Rum Cay. In the north there is an interesting cave which has Lucayan drawings and carvings. Various artefacts from the Arawak period have been found by farmers in the fertile soil which the Indians enriched with bat guano. In common with other islands, Rum Cay has experienced a series of booms and busts. Pineapple, salt and sisal have all been important industries, but competition and natural disasters, such as the 1926 hurricane, have all taken their toll and today tourism is the main source of employment. Plantation boundaries known as 'margins' can be seen all over the island, which date from the beginning of the 19th century when Loyalists settled here. Only a few dozen people live on the island. Nearly everybody lives in **Port Nelson** where cottages can be rented. Settlements such as Port Boyd, Black Rock and Gin Hill are now deserted and overgrown.

This former pirates' haven is surrounded by deep reefs and drop-offs. There is staghorn coral at Summer Point Reef and good diving at Pinder's Point. At the Grand Canyon, huge 60ft coral walls almost reach the surface. Summer Point Marina has dockage, moorings, bar and restaurant. There is a small guesthouse available from Constable Ted Bain. The Last Chance Yacht Supply has groceries. Batelco office for phone calls closes at lunchtime. Yachts wait here before sailing to Mayaguana or the Turks and Caicos Islands, or before returning to Georgetown and points north.

San Salvador

Population: San Salvador and Rum Cay 1,028 2000 census Colour map 2, grid B5

San Salvador is famous for being the probable site of Columbus' first landing in the New World in 1492. Nowadays it is also noted for its reefs, beautiful bays, creeks and lakes. Fishing, diving and sailing are all popular. There are shallow reefs, walls, corals and several wrecks to interest scuba divers and underwater life here is said to be some of the most spectacular in the Bahamas. The entire east coastline, with the exception of the creek areas, is uninhabited and has fine beaches of white sand. East of Dixon Lighthouse past the sand dunes is East Beach, a mile-long stretch of excellent sands. The island is about 12 miles long and six miles wide with a network of inland lakes (with names like Granny Lake and Old Granny Lake) which were once the main transport routes.

Ins & outs **Getting there** There are daily scheduled Bahamasair flights from Nassau to San Salvador (ZSA). Bahamasair also has 3 flights a week from Miami and Air Sunshine flies from Fort Lauderdale. For details of mailboat sailings see Ferries section in Essentials at the beginning of this chapter. **Getting around** If you avoid the bush and water it is perfectly feasible to walk around San Salvador. The Queen's Highway encircles the island and there are no other main roads. You can hire cars, enquire in Cockburn Town. Mopeds are not available. There is a bus tour which visits the main points of interest, ask at Riding Rock Inn.

Background Known as Guanahani by the original Lucayan inhabitants, this island claims to be the first place that Columbus landed after crossing the Atlantic in search of the East Indies. Four sites vie for recognition as the first landing place and celebrations marked the quincentennial anniversary in 1992. One of the sites where Columbus may have come ashore is **Long Bay**. There is a bronze monument under the sea where he was supposed to have anchored and a white cross on the shore where he was said to have landed. Close by is the **Mexican Monument** commemorating the handing over of the Olympic flame to the New World for the 1968 Olympics in Mexico. At **Crab Cay** in the east is the Chicago Herald Monument, erected in 1892 to commemorate the 400th anniversary of Columbus' landing.

Flora & fauna At **Pigeon Creek** in the southeast there is a large lagoon, edged by mangroves, which is a nursery for many different kinds of large fish, including sharks. White Cay and

Green Cay, off Graham's Harbour, are designated land and sea parks. **White Cay** has tall white cliffs on one side where there are large numbers of Brown Boobies. They are docile and you can get very close (once making them easy prey for hunters). **Green Cay** also has a large bird population. **Manhead Cay** off the northeast is home to a rare species of iguana over 1ft in length. There are large rock formations on the north side of the cay, access is possible from the south but is not easy, involving a climb up a rocky hill. Frigate birds can sometimes be seen here. Some subsistence farming using old slash and burn methods is still done on San Salvador.

The wall to the south and west of the island is very impressive, dropping from only 12 m to thousands of metres deep. *Club Med Columbus Isle* offers scuba diving. *Riding Rock Inn* has a full range of watersports activities on offer, an eight slip marina and daily scuba excursions. There are facilities for taking and developing underwater colour photographs (T3312631, F3312020). On Discovery Day, 12 October, there is a dinghies race.

French Bay is a popular beach with excellent shelling and snorkelling. There are large reefs of elk and staghorn coral in less than 50 ft of water, some of which are exposed at low tide. Overlooking French Bay are the ruins of **Watling's Castle**, now better known as the Sandy Point Estate. Going south following the Queen's Highway along the bay you come to the **Government Dock** and further on Sandy Point. Both spots are recommended for their privacy and good reefs for scuba divers and snorkellers.

San Salvador

The Bahamas

Around the island For a good view, climb the lookout tower east of the airport on Mount Kerr, at 140ft the highest point on the island. Until the 1920s San Salvador was known as Watling's Island after the legendary pirate John Watling, who was said to have built Watling's Castle on French Bay in the 17th century. Archaeologists have now proven that the ruins are the remains of a loyalist plantation. You can see the stone ruins including the master's house, slave quarters and a whipping post. Access to the ruins is via the hill to the west of the Queen's Highway near the bay.

In the 1950s and 1960s, the US military leased land from the British Crown and built a submarine tracking station at **Graham's Harbour** in the north. Roads, an airport, a Pan American Base and a US Coast Guard Station were also built. The withdrawal of the military in the late 1960s led to unemployment and emigration. The building at Graham's Harbour is now occupied by the Bahamian Field Station, a geological and historical research institute. Further development took place under the Columbus Landing Development Project, which built houses, condominiums, roads and a golf course around Sandy Point. In the 1990s, *Club Med* built a resort near Cockburn Town, known as *Columbus Isle*, which has provided some jobs. In 1995, *Club Med* was granted a casino licence, the first ever to be awarded to any of the Family Islands. The largest settlement is **Cockburn** in the northwest.

North of Cockburn on the Queen's Highway is the small settlement of **Victoria Hill** where the New World Museum is owned by the local historian Ruth Wolper. There are interesting Lucayan artefacts, most of which came from the remains of an Indian settlement at Palmetto Grove, named after the silver top palmettos found there. **Dixon Hill Lighthouse**, which was built in Birmingham in the 19th century and rebuilt in 1930 is on the northeast coast, still on the Queen's Highway. Mrs Hanna, the keeper, gives tours of the lighthouse, which is run by candle power and clockwork and is one of the few remaining hand operated lighthouses. South of the lighthouse and past East Beach you get to Crab Cay and the Chicago Herald Monument.

Sleeping **L-AL** per person *Club Med Columbus Isle*, PO Box N-7525 Nassau, T3312000, F3312458, www.clubmed.com One of the nicer *Club Med* resorts, comfortable, well integrated into surroundings, usual facilities and more, 286 rooms, a/c, TV, phone, mini-fridge, no children under 12, casino approved, tennis, horse riding, sailing, massage, fishing and diving at extra cost. **L-AL** *Riding Rock Inn Resort and Marina*, north of Cockburn Town, T3312631, F3312020, www.ridingrock.com 30 rooms, 6 villas, swimming pool and a restaurant overlooking the bay, tennis, beach, diving, bicycles to rent, island tours, weekly charter flights from Fort Lauderdale, write to 1170 Lee Wagner Blvd 103, Fort Lauderdale, FL 33315 for details, T800-2721492, F305-3598254.

Eating *Riding Rock Inn* is considered expensive at US$30, but it has a rake'n'scrape band once a week featuring Bernie the Band Leader (also Bernie the airport manager). *Dixie Hotel and Restaurant*, Dixon Hill and *Ocean Cabin*, Cockburn Town, are both reasonable. *Harlem Square Rip Club* is recommended, friendly, Fri night disco. The local dish is crab'n'rice, made from the plentiful land crabs found on the island, average cost US$5-7.

Background

History

The first inhabitants were probably the Siboneys, fishermen who migrated from Florida and the Yucatán. The Indians Columbus found in the southern Bahamas were Arawaks, practising a culture called Tainan. They called themselves Lukku-cairi, island people, and became known as Lucayans. They were primitive farmers and fishermen, but produced the best cotton known to the Arawaks. The island of Guanahani is generally credited with Columbus' first landfall in the New

World on 12 October 1492. Columbus called Guanahani San Salvador but it was not until 1926 that the Bahamas Parliament officially renamed Watling Island, an island which best fitted his rather vague description, as San Salvador. Columbus visited Rum Cay, which he named Santa María de la Concepción, Long Island, which he called Fernandina, and several other islands and cays, but finding no gold he set off for brighter horizons. The lack of mineral deposits meant that the islands held little interest for the Spanish and there is no evidence of permanent settlement. However, the development of Hispaniola and Cuba led to shortages of labour on those islands and to the depopulation of the Bahamas as the Lucayans were captured and carried off as slaves. By 1520 about 20,000 had been captured for use in the plantations, mines or pearl fisheries in the Spanish colonies and the Bahamas were uninhabited. The islands and cays became feared by navigators and many ships were wrecked there, including a whole fleet of 17 Spanish ships off Abaco in 1595.

It was after founding their first colonies in Virginia that the English realized the strategic importance of the Bahamas, and in 1629 the islands received their first constitution as part of the Carolinas. In fact, the first settlers came from Bermuda with the aim of founding a colony free from the religious and constitutional troubles of Charles I's England. Then William Sayle, who had been Governor of Bermuda, published in London in 1647 *A Broadside Advertising Eleuthera and the Bahama Islands*. As a result of this publicity, a company of Eleutherian Adventurers was formed and a party of about 70 settlers and 28 slaves, led by Sayle himself, set out for Eleuthera. Their ship was wrecked on the reefs. The party managed to land but most of the stores were lost and the settlers barely managed to survive by trading ambergris.

From this time on, the life of the Bahamas was largely influenced by their proximity to the North American mainland and their place on the sea routes. Piracy, buccaneering and the slave trade were features of the next two centuries. Pirates began to make the Bahamas their base after 1691 when they were thrown out of Tortuga. Conditions there were perfect, with creeks, shallows, headlands, rocks and reefs for hiding or making surprise attacks. By 1715 there were about 1,000 pirates active in the Bahamas, of whom the most notorious was Blackbeard, who wore his beard in plaits and was renowned for his cruelty. The colony was very poor and survived on the fortunes of shipping, both legal and illicit. In 1739 during the War of Jenkins' Ear, privateering brought a boom in trading activity but peace returned the islands to poverty. A revival of trade during the Seven Years' War was welcomed but peace once more brought depression to Nassau. When not involved in piracy or privateering, many of the inhabitants lived off wrecks, and great was their enthusiasm when whole fleets were destroyed.

A new form of piracy began after the abolition of the British slave trade, when illegal slave traders used the Bahamas as a base to supply the southern states of the mainland. This was followed during the 1861-65 American Civil War by the advent of blockade runners, shipowners and adventurers drawn by the prospect of vast profits. New, fast ships were developed which were unable to carry large cargoes and needed to find a safe, neutral port within two or three days' steaming. Nassau was again ideal, and the port prospered, the harbour and shops being packed with merchandise. The captains and pilots of the blockade running ships became as famous as their pirate predecessors. The end of the war provoked a severe and prolonged recession, with the cotton warehouses lying empty for 50 years. The inhabitants turned again to wrecking but even this livelihood was denied them when lighthouses and beacons were introduced, leaving few stretches of dangerous waters.

In 1919, with the advent of Prohibition in the United States, Nassau became a bootleggers' paradise, but with the repeal of Prohibition, this source of wealth dried up and the islands had little to fall back on. The Thirties, a time of severe depression, ended in disaster in 1939 when disease killed off the sponges which had provided some means of livelihood. Once again, it was war which brought prosperity back. This time, however, foundations were laid for more stable conditions in the future and the two bases of prosperity, tourism and offshore finance, became firmly

The Bahamas

established. Nevertheless, the Bahamas' location and the enormous difficulty in policing thousands of square miles of ocean has attracted both drug trafficking and the laundering of the resulting profits. About 11% of the cocaine entering the USA has been officially estimated to pass through the Bahamas. The Bahamas Government, in full co-operation with the US anti-narcotics agencies, has stepped up efforts to eradicate the trade.

For three centuries the merchant class elite of Nassau, known as the 'Bay Street Boys', influenced government and prevented universal adult suffrage until 1961. In the 1967 elections, an administration supported by the black majority came to power, led by Lynden (later Sir Lynden) Pindling, of the Progressive Liberal Party (PLP), who retained power until 1992. In the first half of the 1980s allegations were made that he was involved in the drugs trade, but they were never conclusively proven. This and subsequent scandals led to the resignation or removal of a number of public officials, and contributed, together with economic decline, to the growing distrust and unpopularity of the Government.

General elections were held in August 1992 and a landslide victory was won by the Free National Movement (FNM), led by Hubert Ingraham. Mr Ingraham, a former PLP minister, had been dismissed from his post as Housing Minister after he supported a move for the resignation of Sir Lynden in 1984. Subsequently expelled from the party, he was elected as an Independent in 1987, joining the FNM in 1990. The new Prime Minister promised an improved climate for investment and tourism and an end to political patronage. A series of inquiries were held into the finances of state corporations including Bahamasair, and the Hotel Corporation, where corruption and misuse of public funds were alleged.

Legal challenges delayed the inquiry into the Bahamas Hotel Corporation, but the Commission resumed its hearings in January 1997. Sir Lynden Pindling returned to the islands after cancer treatment in the USA to face questions about deposits of US$3.9mn in his bank accounts in 1978-93. The Commission found that Sir Lynden acted improperly in accepting loans from businessmen and in dealing with a transaction involving the *Emerald Palms* hotel in his constituency. The report cited 'gross mismanagement' of the corporation and major projects leading to an accumulated loss of US$46mn which was written off in 1991. No action was taken against Sir Lynden. Two former cabinet members were found to have accepted illegal payments during their terms as chairman of Bahamasair; Philip Bethel and Darrell Rolle both stood down from their seats in the House of Assembly at the 1997 elections.

A general election was called on 14 March 1997, six months early. The number of seats in the House of Assembly was reduced from 49 to 40 because of new boundaries designed to give a more equitable distribution of voters per constituency. The FNM won a resounding victory with 57.6 of the vote and 34 seats. The turn out was high, at 91.7 of the electorate. The Bahamian Freedom Alliance's eight candidates and 11 independents failed to win any seats and the PLP won only six, despite gaining nearly 42 of the vote. After the elections Perry Christie became leader of the opposition PLP when Sir Lynden Pindling resigned. The new government announced legislation to establish a stock exchange, improve regulation of the insurance industry and management of pension funds and increase the role of the Bahamas Development Bank. A by-election for Sir Lynden Pindling's South Andros seat was held in September 1997 and won by the FNM candidate who had failed to unseat Sir Lynden at the general elections. Sir Lynden lost his battle with cancer and died on 26 August 2000.

Geography

The Bahamas is a coral archipelago consisting of some 700 low-lying islands, and over 2,000 cays (pronounced "keys"). The highest hills, on Cat Island, are less than 400 ft and most islands have a maximum height of 100 ft. The total area of the islands is about 5,400 square miles, roughly the same as Jamaica. The whole archipelago extends for about 600 miles southeast from the Mantanilla shoal off the coast of Florida to 50 miles north of Haiti. Some of the smaller cays are privately owned but most of them are uninhabited. The islands are made up of limestone over 5,000 m deep, most of it Oolite, laid down for more than 150 million years on a gradually sinking sea bed. New material accumulated constantly and the seas of the Bahamas Platform remained remarkably shallow, often only a few metres deep. From the air, the different shades of turquoise, ultramarine and blue in these shallow waters are spectacular. On land, the soil is thin and infertile except for a few pockets of fertile soil. In many places, bare limestone rock is exposed at the surface while much land is swampy, impenetrable and uninhabitable. There are many large cave systems, including the impressive blue holes, formed when sea levels were lower and since flooded. There are no rivers or streams on any of the islands, but there is some fresh-water, found close to the surface but resting on underlying saltwater. If wells are drilled too deep, they produce brackish or saltwater. Andros has a surplus of fresh-water, which is barged to Nassau. Most people drink bottled water. Desalination plants are being built.

About 15 island areas have been developed. They have a total population of about 287,000; about two thirds live in New Providence and 16% in Grand Bahama. The weather can be pleasant in the winter season although cold fronts from the North American continent can bring strong north winds, heavy rain and surprisingly low temperatures. The summer months are hot, humid and often windless, with frequent thunderstorms. In August 1992 Hurricane Andrew hit the Bahamas, making over 1,200 homeless, killing four people and causing damage of over US$250mn. North Eleuthera was badly damaged. In October 1996 Hurricane Lili destroyed houses and crops and cut power lines in Exuma, Long Island and other islands after passing over Cuba. In June 1997 unprecedented rainfall and a spring tide caused flooding in New Providence while a tornado struck Hope Town, damaging boats and power supplies. In 1999 Hurricane Floyd hit Abaco, Cat Island and Eleuthera before heading for Grand Bahama and Florida. Wind speeds of 100 mph were recorded on Nassau, where coastal areas were flooded and power cut off, but on Eleuthera winds reached 155 mph and about 25% of houses were damaged. Businesses soon got back to nor-mal, however, and there is little evidence of storm damage now.

Government

The Bahamas became independent, within the Commonwealth, in July 1973. The new Constitution provided for a Governor General to represent the British monarch who is head of state, a nominated 16-member Senate and an elected 49-member, now 40-member House of Assembly, with a parliamentary life of a maximum of five years. The Free National Movement (FNM) holds 35 seats while the Progressive Liberal Party (PLP) holds four. A new party, the Coalition for Democratic Reform, has one seat, held by a former PLP member who resigned from the party in 1999. Sir Orville Turnquest, former Attorney General and Minister of Foreign Affairs, was appointed Governor General at the end of 1994.

Economy

The economy of the Bahamas is based on tourism, financial services and shipping registration. Visitors are attracted throughout the year and since 1986, total arrivals have exceeded three million a year, mostly from the USA, of whom over half are cruise ship passengers or day trippers. Also, since 1986, annual total visitor expendi-ture has exceeded US$1,100 mn. Stopover tourists spend an average of US$794 per head while cruise ship passengers average US$60-70. In 1990 and 1991 the Gulf war and US recession took their toll on the Bahamian tourist industry with many airlines and hotels shedding staff and fiscal problems becoming more acute. Average hotel occupancy fell to 62 in 1990, 57 in 1993 and 62 in 1994, as US stopover visitors (82 of the total) declined. Room rates fell as over capacity in the hotel industry became critical. By 1994 prospects for the industry were improving, with a 5% increase in North American stopover visitors. In 1996, combined stopover and cruise visitors increased to 3.4 mn, a rise of 5.5% over 1995 and the first rise since 1992 but by 1998 the total was down to 3.3 million again. The sale of most of the state-run hotels to private investors improved quality and revenue. In 1997 there were 13,398 hotel rooms in the Bahamas, with up to 5,000 more planned by 2002. Expansion and new construction works led to a temporary decline in visitor arrivals as many rooms were out of action, but by 2000 marketing efforts were keeping pace with new rooms opening and average room rates were US$132 per night.

Agriculture is much less important than tourism, contributing only 2.9% of gdp. A third of farmers are women, the average age is 59, and half of all farm labourers are Haitian. Emphasis is on fruit farming, taking advantage of the lack of frost and competing with the Florida citrus growers. Economic activity is principally restricted to the two main islands although on the Family Islands tourist facilities are being developed and agriculture extended.

Some steps have been taken to encourage light industries, notably salt, pharmaceuticals, rum and beer production, and substantial investment has taken place in the free-trade zone of Freeport, Grand Bahama. The financial sector, with its banks, insurance companies and finance companies, has developed since the 1920s, but since the mid-1980s has suffered from competition from other offshore centres such as the Cayman Islands and Barbados and from pressure from US bank regulators to reduce secrecy. In 2000 the Bahamas was among several countries to be blacklisted by the financial action task force, but within months the Government had instituted laws dealing with bank secrecy and anti-money laundering. Eleven laws were passed by the end of the year, in an effort to be more compliant and compatible with other offshore jurisdictions. The Bahamas shipping registry is the fifth largest in the world.

Cuba

146

Cuba

Cuba's charms are as varied as they are fascinating. Most people spend some time relaxing and enjoying the sun and sand on Cuba's extensive beaches, but there is so much more to do. Go before Castro dies and see one of the last bastions of Communism and a culture which has denied itself the influences of the USA for so long. Visit the Spanish colonial cities, where the architecture is being beautifully preserved, go hiking or cycling in the countryside and see rural life in Cuba, take a ride in one of those famous fifties cars, go birdwatching or scuba diving, the list is endless. No one will leave the island without being affected by the pulsating rhythms of the music and dance, the racial mixture which has produced such creativity and exuberance in the arts and entertainment, without being diverted into advertising bill boards and neon lights. And of course, you haven't lived until you've learned to dance the rumba.

A Foot in the door

- Go private, stay with a Cuban family, eat at a **paladar** for a taste of the real Cuba.
- Work your way through your barman's list of **cocktails**: mojito, daiquirí, zombie, cubanito, or even a Cuba Libre.
- Seek out the **Casa de la Trova** in any city for the best of traditional Cuban music.
- Pay homage to **Che Guevara** at his mausoleum in Santa Clara.
- Go back in time with a stroll through the cobbled streets of **Trinidad**.
- For the ultimate party, hit **Santiago at Carnival** time in July.

Essentials

Before you travel

Documents   Visitors from the majority of countries need only a **passport**, **return ticket** and 30-day **tourist card** to enter Cuba, as long as they are going solely for tourist purposes. Tourist cards may be obtained from Cuban embassies, consulates, airlines, or approved travel agents (price in the UK £15 from the consulate, or from travel agents, some other countries US$15 or Can$15). To get a tourist card at a consulate you have to fill in an application form, photocopy the main pages of your passport (valid for more than six months after departure from Cuba), submit confirmation of your accommodation booking and your return or onward flight

Cuba

♦ National parks & reserves	5 Parque Nacional La Mensura Pilotos
1 Parque Nacional Alejandro de Humboldt	6 Parque Nacional Pico Cristal
2 Parque Nacional Turquino	7 Parque Nacional Caguanes
3 Parque Nacional Desembarque de Granma	8 Parque Nacional Viñales
4 Parque Nacional La Bayamesa	9 Parque Nacional Punta Francés, Punta Pedernales

ticket. Immigration in Havana airport will only give you 30 days on your tourist card, but you can get it extended for a further 30 days at Immigration in Miramar (see below) and some other towns. You have first to buy stamps (US$25) at the bank on Calle 42 esq 29, Miramar. Expect a long queue and a longer lunch break.

Nationals of countries without visa-free agreement with Cuba, journalists, students and those visiting on other business must check what visa requirements pertain and, if relevant, apply for an **official/business visa**. For this you must submit two application forms, two passport photos, your passport and a letter from the Cuban organization or company which has invited you. A business visa is issued for one entry into Cuba and can take at least 10 days to process.

There is also a **family visa**, for those who are visiting relatives, valid for one entry into Cuba. You have to fill in an application form naming the relative who has invited you (in duplicate), submit your passport (which must be valid for six months after your departure from Cuba) and pay a fee of £45.

The **US** government does not normally permit its citizens to visit Cuba. US citizens should have a US licence to engage in any transactions related to travel to Cuba, but tourist or business travel are not licensable, even through a third country such as Mexico or Canada. For further information on entry to Cuba from the US and customs requirements, US travellers should contact the *Cuban Interests Section*, an office of the Cuban government, at 2630 16th St NW, Washington DC 20009, T202-7978518. They could also contact *Marazul Tours*, New York, T212-5829570, or Miami, T305-2328157, (information also from *Havanatur*, C 2 No 17 Miramar, Havana, T332121/2318). The Cuban Interests Section in Washington DC will process applications for visas. Visas can take several weeks to be granted, and are apparently difficult

Cuba

•••••••••• Motorway under construction

Archipiélago Jardín del Rey

Cayo Coco

Caibarién

7♦

Majagua

Atlantic Ocean

Ciego de Ávila

Zaza Dam

14♦

Júcaro

Florida

Santa Lucía

Camagüey

Nuevitas

Guáimaro

Puerto Padre

Guardalavaca

Holguín

Moa

Las Tunas

Mayarí

Amancio

15

♦5 ♦6

1

Baracoa

12♦

Santa Cruz del Sur

Manzanillo

Bayamo

Guantánamo

Archipiélago Jardines de la Reina

Niquero

Sierra Maestra

Playa Sevilla

16♦

♦20

US Naval base

♦3

Pilón

4♦

Santiago de Cuba

Baconao

Cuban embassies overseas

Australia *Consulate: 18 Manwaring Ave, Maroubra NSW, 2035, T61-2-93114611, F931155112*

Austria *Himmelhofgasse 40 A-C, A-1130, Vienna, T43-1-8778198/8778159, F8777703*

Canada *388 Main Street, Ottawa, Ontario, K11E3, T1-613-5630141/ 5630326/5630136/ 5630209*

Denmark *See Sweden*

France *16 Rue de Presles 75015, Paris, T33-1-45675535, F45658092*

Germany *Kennedyallee 22-24, Bad Godesberg 53175, Bonn, T49-228-3090, F309244*

Italy *Via Licinia No 7, 00153, Rome, T39-06-5742347/5755984, F5745445*

Malaysia *20 Lengkongan Uthant, Kuala Lumpur, T03-4516808.*

Netherlands *Mauritskade 49, 2514 HG The Hague, T31-70-3606061, F3647586*

Norway *See Sweden*

Portugal *Rua Pero Da Covilha No 14, Restelo, 1400, Lisbon, T351-1-3015318, F3011895*

South Africa *45 Mackenzie St, Brooklyn 0181, Pretoria, PO Box 11605, Hatfield 0028, T27-12-3462215, F3462216*

Spain *Paseo de La Habana No 194 entre Calle de la Macarena y Rodríguez, Pinilla, 28036, Madrid, T34-91-3592500, F3596145*

Sweden *Karlavagen 49, 11449 Stockholm, T46-8-6630850, F6611418*

Switzerland *Gesellsschaftsstrasse 8, CP 5275, 30112, Berne, T41-31-3022111/ 3029830 (Tourist Office), F3022111*

UK *167 High Holborn, London WC1 6PA, T020-72402488/8367886, F78362602*

to obtain for US citizens other than businessmen, guests of the Cuban Government or Embassy officials. Many travellers conceal their tracks by going via Mexico, the Bahamas, or Canada, when only the tourist card is stamped, not the passport. The Cuban Consulate in Mexico City refuses to issue visas unless you have pre-arranged accommodation and book through a travel agent; even then, only tourist cards are available, US$20. In Mérida or at Cancún airport, a travel agent will arrange your documents so you do not need to go to a consulate.

Visitors travelling on a visa must go in person to the Immigration Office for registration the day after arrival. The office is on the corner of C 22 and Av 3, Miramar. When you register you will be given an exit permit. Travellers coming from or going through infected areas must have certificates of vaccination against **cholera** and **yellow fever**. The Cuban authorities do not insist on stamping your passport in and out but they often do so. They will stamp your tourist card instead if you ask.

Customs Personal baggage and articles for personal use are allowed in free of duty; so are one carton of cigarettes and two bottles of alcoholic drinks. Visitors importing new goods worth between US$100 and US$1,000 will be charged 100% duty, subject to a limit of two items a year. No duty is payable on goods valued at under US$100. You may take in up to 10kg of medicine. It is prohibited to bring in fresh fruit and vegetables, which will be confiscated if found. On departure you may take out tobacco worth US$1,000 with a receipt, or only 50 cigars without a receipt, up to six bottles of rum and personal jewellery. To take out works of art you must have permission from the Registro Nacional de Bienes Culturales de la Dirección de Patrimonio del Ministerio de Cultura.

Money **Currency** The monetary unit is the **peso Cubano**. The official exchange rate is US$1=1 peso. There are notes for 3, 5, 10 and 20 pesos, and coins for 5, 20 and 40 centavos and 1 peso. You must have a supply of 5 centavo coins if you want to use the local town buses (20 or 40 centavos) or pay phones (very few work). The 20 centavo coin is called a *peseta*. In 1995 the government introduced a new freely 'convertible peso' on a par with the US dollar, with a new set of notes and coins. It is fully exchangeable with authorized hard currencies circulating in the economy. Remember to spend or exchange any *pesos convertibles* before you leave the country as they are worthless outside Cuba.

Exchange As a result of currency reforms the black/street exchange rate fell from 130 pesos Cubanos = US$1 in May 1994 to 20 pesos = US$1 in May 1997 and it has stayed at around that level since then. Official Casas de Cambio (CADECA) rates fluctuate between 19-23 pesos to the dollar and there is now virtually no black market. The 'peso convertible' is equal to the dollar and can be used freely in the country. Cubans are allowed to hold US$ and to have a bank account. There will be very little opportunity for you to spend pesos Cubanos unless you are self-catering or travelling off the beaten track. Food in the markets (*agromercados*), at street stalls, on trains, books, popular cigarettes, but not in every shop, can be bought in pesos. You will need pesos for the toilet, rural trains, trucks, food at roadside cafeterías during a journey and drinks and snacks for a bus or train journey. Away from tourist hotels, in smaller towns there are very few dollar facilities and you will need pesos for everything. Visitors on pre-paid package tours need not acquire any pesos at all. Bring US$ in small denominations for spending money. US dollars are the only currency accepted in all tourist establishments. **Travellers' cheques** expressed in US or Canadian dollars or sterling are valid in Cuba. Travellers' cheques issued on US bank paper are not accepted so it is best to take Thomas Cook or Visa. Commission ranges from 2-4%. Don't enter the place or date when signing cheques, or they may be refused. There are **banks** and CADECAS (exchange houses) for changing money legally. Non-dollar currencies can be changed into dollars. Commission charges vary widely between banks and can be different from one town to the next, or even on different days of the week. Visitors have difficulties using torn or tatty US dollar notes.

Banks & money changers are listed in individual town directories

Credit cards The following credit cards are acceptable in most places: *Visa, MasterCard, Access, Diners, Banamex* (Mexican) and *Carnet*. No US credit cards are accepted so a Visa card issued in the USA will not be accepted. *American Express*, no matter where issued, is unacceptable. A master list of stolen and rogue cards is kept at the *Habana Libre* and any transaction over US$50 must be checked there; this can take up to three hours. You can obtain cash advances with a credit card at branches of the *Banco Financiero Internacional* and several other banks, but it is best to bring plenty of cash as there will often be no other way of paying for what you need. For Visa or MasterCard problems go to Av 23 entre L y M, Vedado, or phone the credit card centre on T344444, F334001. If you get really stuck and need money sent urgently to Cuba, you can get money transferred from any major commercial bank abroad direct to Asistur (see page 155) immediately for a 10% commission.

Many restaurants are often reluctant to take credit cards

The high season is mid-December to mid-April, when there are more dry days, more sunshine and less humidity. Hurricanes and tropical storms begin in August and can go on until the end of November. In the last few years there have been several storms which have caused flooding and damage. There are also variations in climate: it is hotter and drier in Santiago than in Havana, and wetter and cooler in the mountains than in the lowlands. Northeast trade winds temper the heat, but summer shade temperatures can rise to 33°C (91°F) in Havana, and higher elsewhere. In winter, day temperatures drop to 20°C (68°F) and there are a few cold days, 8°-10°C (45°-50°F), with a north wind. Average rainfall is from 860mm in Oriente to 1,730mm in Havana; it falls mostly in the summer and autumn, but there can be torrential rains at any time. Walking is uncomfortable in summer but most offices, hotels, leading restaurants and cinemas are air-conditioned.

Climate

July is a good time to visit Santiago if you want to catch the **carnival**, although **New Year** is also lively with parades and street parties (Havana's **carnival** is in *February*, but it is not such an exciting affair). New Year is celebrated everywhere as the anniversary of the **Revolution**, so you can expect speeches as well as parties. Throughout the year there are lots of excuses for music and dancing in the street, washed down with quantities of rum and local food. Some towns even do it weekly, called a **Noche Cubana**.

Festivals

Bring all medicines you might need as they can be difficult to find. Even painkillers are in very short supply. Many other things are scarce or unobtainable in Cuba, so take in everything you are likely to need other than food: razor blades; medicines and pills; heavy duty insect

What to take

Cuba

repellent; strong sun protection and after-sun preparations; toilet paper; tampons; disposable nappies; materials; photographic supplies; torch and batteries.

Finding out more

Travel agents **UK** Agents who sell holidays in Cuba include: *Regent Holidays*, 15 John St, Bristol BS1 2HR, T0117-9211711, F0117-9254866, ABTA and AITO members, holding ATOL and IATA Licences; *Trips Worldwide*, 9 Byron Pl, Clifton, Bristol BS8 1JT, T0117-9872626, F0117-9872627, enquires@trips.demon.co.uk, ATOL, member of IATA, specialists in holidays to help you get off the beaten track; *South American Experience Ltd*, 47 Causton St, Pimlico, London SW1P 4AT, T020-79765511, F020-79766908, IATA, ATOL; *Progressive Tours*, 12 Porchester Pl, Marble Arch, London W2 2BS, T020-72621676, F020-77246941, ABTA, ATOL, IATA; *Scuba en Cuba*, 7 Maybank Gardens, Pinner, Middlesex HA5 2JW, www.scuba_en_cuba.com, T01895- 624100, F01895-624377; *Interchange*, Interchange House, 27 Stafford Rd, Croydon, Surrey CR0 4NG, T020-86813612, F020-87600031; *Journey Latin America*, 12-13 Heathfield Terrace, Chiswick, London W4 4JE, T020-87478315, F020-87421312, www.journeylatinamerica.co.uk; *Regal Diving*, T01353-778950, F01353-777897; *Travelcoast Captivating Cuba*, T0870-8870123, F0870-8870128, www.captivating_cuba.co.uk; *Cubanacan UK Ltd*, Skylines, Unit 49, Limeharbour Docklands, London E14 9TS, T020-75377909, F020-75377747; *The Holiday Place*, T020-74310670, F020-74313657; *Havanatour UK Ltd*, 3 Wyllyotts Pl, Potters Bar, Hertfordshire EN6 2JD, T01707-646463, F01707-663139, havanatour@compuserve. com Check with these agents for special deals combined with jazz or film festivals. **Eire** Cubatur agent is *Cubatravel*, T016-713422, F016-798006. See page 149 under *Marazul Tours* with regard to documents. **Germany** *Danza Y Movimiento Travel*, T+49-4035716163, www.dym.de/events/ Specialists in music and dance tours in Cuba.

Mexico Many agencies in the Yucatán peninsula offer packages which are very good value and popular with travellers wanting to avoid Mexico City. There are several daily flights from Cancún. Aerocaribe charges US$274 return to Havana, Mexicana US$265, Aviacsa US$208 and Cubana US$175. Flights are heavily booked. A recommended agency is *Viñales Tours*, in Mexico City at Oaxaca 80, Col Roma, T525-2089900, F2083704, www.spin.com.mx/vinales; in Guadalajara at Avenida Adolfo López Mateos Norte 1038-9, Plaza Florencia, T523-8172860, F8172983, vinales@infosel.net.mx; in Cancún at Av Coba 5, local A6, Plaza América, Super Manzana 4, T529-8840326, F8840396, adiel@cancun.rce.com.mex; and in Havana at Av 3 B 9207 entre 92 y 94, Miramar, T331051/5, F331054, vintours@ceniai.inf.cu

Canada *World of Vacations* has package tours to Varadero, Santiago de Cuba, Holguín, Cayo Coco, Cayo Guillermo all year round from Toronto, or Nov-Apr from Vancouver, Calgary, Edmonton and Halifax with connecting flights from other cities. *Signature Vacations* offers similar deals from the same cities, as does the popular *Air Transat Holidays*. *Fiesta West* has tours and packages from the western part of Canada Nov-Apr and the same or expanded destinations from Toronto and the Maritimes all year round. *Sunquest* and *Alba Tours* are also big tour operators with similar arrangements. All of these companies offer flights if you want them, for mostly one or two weeks. For longer stays, independent travel needs to be arranged with an agent who is familiar with this procedure, such as *Cubana* or charter airlines, for example *Canada 3000*, *Air Transat*. Some of these companies use Cubanacán to offer eco-tours. *Friendship Tours*, run by Joyce Holmes, 12883-98th Ave, Surrey, BC, V3T 1B1, T1604-5814065, F5810785, friendship@home.com, offer tours in conjunction with conferences in Cuba, bird watching or other eco-tours, beach retreats or May Day tours with farm or factory visits. For more details, www.members.home.com/friendship

USA *AdventureCuba.com*, 4492 Camino de la Plaza, San Diego, California 92173, T310-8424148, www.adventurecuba.com a full service online travel agency. The site contains over 80 pages of useful information on hotels, transportation as well as travel tips and practical advice. *Cuban Adventures*, call toll free from US/Canada T1-877-2822386, specialist tours (cigar, scuba, culture/music etc), www.cubanadventures.com

Cuban tourist offices overseas

Argentina, T541-3267810, 541-3267995, F541-3263325, oturcuar@tournet.com.ar

Belgium, Robert Jones Straat 77, Brussels 18, T32-2-3430022

Canada, 440 Blvd René Levesque, Suite 1402, Montréal, Quebec H2Z 1V7, T1-514-8758004/5, F8758006, mintur@generation.net

55 Queen Street E, Suite 705, Toronto, M5C 1R5, T1-416-3620700/2, F3626799, cuba.tbtor@simpatico.ca

China, T86-10-65322129, F65322017, menendez@public.bta.net.cn

France, 280 Bd aspail, 75014 Paris, T33-14-5389010, F5389930, ot.cuba@wanadoo.fr

Germany, Frankfurt, T49-69-288322/3, F296664, gocuba@compuserve.com

Italy, Via General Fara 30, Terzo Plano, 20124 Milan, T39-2-66981463, F6690042, ufficioturisticodicuba@interbusiness.it

Mexico, T52-5-2555897, 2507974, F2555866, otcumex@mail.internet.com.mex

Russia, T/F7-095-2430383

Spain, Paseo de la Habana No 28 iro derecha, 28036 Madrid, T34-91-4113097, F5645804, otcuba@octocuba.esp.com

Switzerland, Gesellschastsstrasse 8, 3012 Berne, Case Postale 52725, T/F41-31-3022111

UK, 154 Shaftesbury Avenue, London WC2H 8JT, T020-72406655, F778369265, cubatouristboard.london@virgin.net

Bahamas, *Havanatur* in Nassau, T242-3947195, F3945196, sells package tours and charter flights to Havana or Holguín (see page 153). In Havana C 2 17 entre 1 y 3, Miramar, T247413. A package includes the tourist card, hotel, breakfast, transfers and city tour of Havana, prices start at US$239 for return flight plus two nights at *Hotel Inglaterra*. You can use these two nights at the beginning and end of your visit, and travel on your own in between.

Getting there

Air *Cubana* and a number of international airlines have **scheduled** flights to Havana from Amsterdam, Barcelona, Bogotá, Buenos Aires, Cancún, Caracas, Córdoba, Curaçao, Fort-de-France, Frankfurt, Freeport, Guatemala City, Kingston (Jamaica), Las Palmas, Lima, London, Madrid, Managua, Mendoza, Mérida, Mexico City, Milan, Montego Bay, Monterrey, Montevideo, Montréal, Moscow, Munich, Nassau, Oaxaca, Panama City, Paris, Pointe-à-Pitre, Quito, Rome, San José, San Salvador, Santiago (Chile), Santo Domingo, São Paulo, Shannon, Toronto, Tuxtla Gutierrez, Veracruz and Villahermosa. International scheduled flights also go to Camagüey, Cayo Largo, Ciego de Avila, Holguín, Santiago and Varadero There are **charters** from London, Frankfurt, Brussels, Toronto, Vancouver, Montréal, Quebec, Halifax, Buenos Aires, Cancún, and between Santiago de Cuba and Montego Bay, Jamaica. There are also regular charters between Cayo Largo and Grand Cayman and occasional charters between Providenciales, Turks and Caicos Islands and Santiago de Cuba. The Cuban air charter line *AeroCaribbean* has an arrangement with *Bahamasair* for a (nearly) daily service Miami-Nassau-Havana, changing planes in Nassau; the Cuban tourist agency *Amistur* organizes the service. This route is probably the cheapest and quickest from the USA (see page 152). *ABC* charters have direct flights Miami-Havana. *Havanatur* has eight weekly charter flights, five to Cancún and three to Nassau. At certain times of the year there are special offers available from Europe; enquire at specialist agents. There are also many combinations of flights involving Cuba and Mexico, Venezuela, Colombia and the Dominican Republic; again ask a specialist agent. *AeroCaribbean* flies from Port-au-Prince, Haiti, to Santiago and Havana on Thursdays, US$100 one-way to Santiago if paid for 14 days in advance, otherwise US$200. The cheapest flight from Santo Domingo to Santiago is US$150.

Touching down

Airport information **On arrival** Immigration can be very slow if you come off a busy Iberia DC10 flight but speedy off smaller *Cubana* aircraft. At Havana airport there are taxi dispatchers who can get you in a taxi or minibus for US$18, although *Panataxi* charges around US$12 and a *Víazul* bus

Touching down

Hours of business Government offices: 0830-1230 and 1330-1730 Monday to Friday. Some offices open on Saturday morning. **Banks:** 0830-1200, 1330-1500 Monday to Friday. **Shops:** 0830-1800 Monday to Saturday, 0900-1400 Sunday. Hotel tourist (hard currency) shops generally open 1000-1800 or 1900.

Official time Eastern Standard Time, five hours behind GMT; Daylight Saving Time, four hours behind GMT.

Voltage 110 Volts, 3 phase 60 cycles, AC. Plugs are usually of the American type.

Weights and measures The metric system is compulsory, but exists side by side with American and old Spanish systems.

Public Holidays Liberation Day (1 January), Labour Day (1 May), Revolution Day (26 July and the day either side), Beginning of War of Independence (10 October) and Christmas Day (25 December).

Other **festive days** which are not public holidays are 28 January (birth of José Martí 1853), 24 February (anniversary of renewal of War of Independence, 1895), 8 March (International Women's Day), 13 March (anniversary of 1957 attack on presidential palace in Havana by a group of young revolutionaries), 19 April (anniversary of defeat of mercenaries at Bay of Pigs, 1961), 30 July (martyrs of the Revolution day), 8 October (death of Che Guevara, 1967), 28 October (death of Camilo Cienfuegos, 1959), 27 November (death by firing squad of eight medical students by Spanish colonial government, 1871), 7 December (death of Antonio Maceo in battle in 1896).

transfer will be about US$4. **NB** remember to reconfirm your onward or return flight as soon as you arrive in Cuba and certainly 48 hours before departure, otherwise you will lose your reservation. Cuba has several airports classified as international, but only Havana is of any size. Havana now has three terminals, the third and newest one being for international flights, with exchange facilities, snack bars, shops etc.

On departure It is advisable to book your flight out of Cuba before actually going there, as arranging it there can be time-consuming. The airport departure tax is US$20 at Havana and Varadero airports, US$15 at other international airports. The seating in the Havana departure lounge is uncomfortable. The restaurant is OK for sandwiches or full meals, which will be welcome after your three-hour check-in and this will be your last chance to hear a live Cuban band while eating. The selection of shops is limited but there is lots of rum, coffee, a few books and magazines on sale. The selection of cigars is poor and overpriced. The Cubita coffee, on the other hand, is marginally cheaper than in the dollar shops in town.

Tourist information **Internet** www.dtcuba.com has lots of details and addresses of hotels, tour companies, car hire etc. They also have a weekly newsletter, Boletín Semanal DTC News, listmaster@dtcuba.com www.cubaweb.cu, has sections on news, travel, politics, business, internet and technology, health, science, art and culture, festivals and events. There is also a section, Cocoweb, where they will answer your questions by email, extremely useful and recommended.

Local tours Several state-owned tour companies offer day trips or excursion packages including accommodation to many parts of the island, as well as tours of colonial and modern Havana. Guides speak Spanish, English, French, Italian or German; the tours are generally recommended as well-organized and good value. Actual departure depends on a minimum number of passengers (usually 6).

Tour companies Rumbos, O 108 entre 1 y 3, Miramar, Havana, T249626-8, F247167, director@rumvia.rumb.cma.net, organize excursions and run bars and cafés. Horizontes, 23 156 entre N y O, Vedado, Havana, T662004, 662160, F333161, www.horizontes.cu Their hotels tend to be on the outskirts of towns and the chain provides activities for 'eco' tourists and hunters. Fly-drive tours can be arranged. Cubanacán Recreación y Ocio (for fishing, hunting), Dirección Comercial, T336868, 330345, F336986, gerente@cubasol.cha.cyt.cu Cubanacán

Agencia de Viajes, T337952, 330607, www.cubanacan.cu In Santiago, T356156, or for Recreación y Ocío T39317. *Sol y Son*, 23 64, La Rampa, Vedado, T333271, 335159, F333385, solyson@ceniai.inf.cu The travel company of *Cubana* airlines. (Also has offices in some hotels.) *Cubamar Viajes*, Paseo 306 entre 13 y 15, Vedado, T662523-4, F333111, www.cubamar.cubaweb.cu Some camping resorts, student groups. *Gaviota Tours*, Hotels *Kohly* and *El Bosque* in Havana, T244781, 294528, 247683, F249470, gavitour@gavitur. gav.cma.net. Also Guardalavaca, Varadero, and in Topes de Collantes near Trinidad. Tours of the Oriente have been recommended, they include two nights in *Hotel Porto Santo*, Baracoa. *Havanatur*, Edif Sierra Maestra, Av 1 entre 0 y 2, Miramar, T247541, 241549, F242074, 242877, recommended for independent travellers who want tailor-made but reasonably priced tours. *Islazul*, Malecón y G, Vedado, T325152, 320571, F333458, 324410, cmazul@Teda.get. cma.net *Cuba Deportes*, C 29 710 entre 7 y 9, Miramar, T240945, F241914. Arrange all-inclusive sporting holidays and are the people to contact if you want to participate in a sporting event, eg a cycle race.

Agencies specializing in **marinas** and **diving**, including packages with accommodation and transfers, are: *Cubamar* (see above); *Ecotur*, 98 y Av 5, Playa, T/F290230; *Gaviota* (see above), Av del Puerto 102, Edif La Marina, La Habana Vieja, T339780-1, 666777, F332780, 330742, gaviota@nwgaviot.gav.cma.net; *Horizontes* (see above); *Marlin*, 184 123, Reparto Flores, Playa, T336675, 339436, F337020; *Marsub*, B 310 esq 15, Vedado, T333055, 334638, F333481; *Puertosol*, Edif Focsa, 17 y M, Vedado, T334705-8, F334703.

Travel assistance *Asistur, in Hotel Casa del Científico*, Paseo del Prado 254, entre Animas y Trocadero, Habana Vieja, for 24-hour service T338527, F338088, cellular Asis 2747, linked to overseas insurance companies, can help with emergency hospital treatment, robbery, direct transfer of funds to Cuba etc. Also office in *Hotel Casa Granda*, Santiago.

Cuba had a reputation for prostitution before the Revolution and after a gap of some decades it has resurfaced. Behind every girl there is a pimp. In 2001 a German tourist was murdered by a pimp in Santiago for not paying the girl US$20 for sex. Despite government crackdowns and increased penalties, everything is available for both sexes if you know where to look. Be warned, you are likely to be fleeced. The age of consent is 18 in Cuba, so if you are introduced to a young girl you are in danger of being led into a blackmail trap. Hotels are not allowed to let Cubans enter the premises in the company of foreigners, so sexual encounters now often take place in *casas particulares*, private homes where there is little security and lots of risk. If you or your travelling companion are dark skinned, you may suffer from the exclusion policy in hotels as officials will assume he/she is Cuban until proved otherwise. If you are a man out alone at night in Havana you will find the market very active and you will be tugged at frequently, mostly by females, but around *Coppelia* the prostitutes are mostly males.

Sex tourism

Cubans who offer their services (whether sexual or otherwise) in return for dollars are known as jineteros, or jineteras ('jockeys', because they 'ride on the back' of the tourists)

In general the Cuban people are very hospitable. The island is generally safer than many of its Caribbean and Latin neighbours, but certain precautions should be taken. Visitors should never lose sight of their luggage or leave valuables in hotel rooms (most hotels have safes). Do not leave your things on the beach when going swimming. Guard your camera closely. Pickpocketing and purse-snatching on buses is quite common in Havana and Santiago. Also beware of bag-snatching by passing cyclists. In the capital, street lighting is poor so care is needed when walking or cycling the city at night. Some people recommend walking in the middle of the street. Old Havana is now much safer, with police on nearly every street corner. If you are in Santiago for the carnival do not wear any jewellery and leave your watch and other valuables behind. The police are very helpful and thorough when investigating theft, ask for a stamped statement for insurance purposes.

Safety

Where to stay

Casas particulares

Despite the pitfalls, this is currently the most popular form of accommodation for individual travellers and we have received hundreds of recommendations, not all of which we have space to include in this book

Tourists to Cuba often stay in rooms or apartments in private houses, known as *casas particulares*. You pay in US dollars for both accommodation and food, but prices are considerably less than in hotels while the service is much more friendly and the food infinitely better quality and more plentiful. It is an ideal way of getting to know the people of Cuba, even if they don't all speak your language. A taxation system for this form of 'self-employment' was introduced in 1997 so that it is now legal. However, the casas must be registered to pay taxes for whatever services they offer. All *casas particulares* should have a yellow registration book you have to sign, and a sticker on their door of a blue triangle on a white background, if they are legal. An unlicensed casa owner will face a huge dollar fine if caught, which is quite likely given the neighbourhood watch system. Taxes and licences are high at US$60-200 per room per month, depending on the region, plus 10% of earnings to be paid at the end of each year, so profit margins are tight. To offer food, Cubans have to buy a licence, US$30 per month, although many do not. They have to pay a further tax if they want to put up a sign outside the house and if they rent out a garage, etc. Private homes vary considerably and can be extremely comfortable or very basic. Because of shortages things often don't work, there may be cold water only, once a day, and the lights often go off. A torch is useful. The families may offer you cheap transport too. Remember that rates can often be bargained down if you go direct to the owners, negotiate a package of bed, breakfast and evening meal, or stay for several nights. The owners pay US$5 per night per room for each client brought to them by a tout (who does not pay taxes), which will inevitably end up on your bill, so avoid being taken to a house by anyone. If you are given a business card for a casa by someone selling bus tickets or a taxi driver, they will get their commission if you end up staying at that casa. We have even heard of disreputable operators who pretend to be a member of the family so that they can get their cut.

Getting around

Air

Return fare is twice the single fare

There are **Cubana de Aviación** services from Havana to most of the main towns: Camagüey, Holguín , Trinidad, Baracoa, Guantánamo, Manzanillo, Moa, Nueva Gerona/Isla de Juventud, Bayamo, Ciego de Avila, Las Tunas, Santiago, Cayo Largo, Cayo Coco, Varadero, all have airports. Santa Clara and some places with airstrips are reached by Aerotaxi. Tourists must pay air fares in US$; Havana to Santiago costs US$100 one way; it is advisable to prebook flights at home as demand is very heavy, although you can get interprovincial flights from hotel tour desks if you are on a package deal. It is difficult to book flights from one city to another when you are not at the point of departure, except from Havana; the computers are not able to cope. Airports are usually a long way from the towns, so extra transport costs will be necessary. Delays are common. *Cubana* flights are very cold, take warm clothes and possibly some food for a long flight. Aerotaxi flights can also be cold, they are flying buses and you often get wooden bench seating in an old Soviet aircraft. Although theoretically possible to get a scheduled flight as listed above, it is often only possible for tourists to travel on excursions: day trips or packages with flights, accommodation, meals and sightseeing.

Bicycle

For people who really want to explore the country in depth and independently, cycling around is excellent, although you are advised to bring your own bike and all spare parts. *Iberia* and *Cubana* airlines both accept bicycles as normal luggage as long as you do not take more than 20 kg, but some charters, such as *Martinair*, charge extra. A good quality bicycle is essential if you are going to spend many hours in the saddle, although that does not mean it has to be very sophisticated. We have heard from cyclists who have toured Cuba without gears, although they did have plenty of muscle. Most of Cuba is flat, the road network is good and there is little traffic. In cities there are *parqueos bicicletas*, where you can store your bike while walking around. Cycling can get very hot, so you are advised to do long distances early in the morning.

For organized cycling tours of Cuba contact **Blazing Saddles**, in the UK, T020-84240483, saddles100@aol.com; **Bike Tours**, in the UK, T01225-480130, F01225-480132; **Fietsvakan** *tiewinkel*, Spoorlaan 19, 3445 AE Woerden, Holland, T31-3480-21844, F31-3480-23839. You may also be able to join a group of Cuban bikers (mostly English speaking) through the **Club Nacional de Cicloturismo** (National Bike Club), Gran Caribe, Transnico Internacional, Lonja del Comercio Oficina 6d, La Habana Vieja, T969193, F669908, trans@mail.infocom.etecsa.cu. They run tours of 1-28 days in all parts of the country, some with political themes.

Bus

The urban bus fare throughout Cuba is 20 centavos for camellos & 40 centavos for all others; it helps to have the exact fare

Local The local word for bus is *guagua*. In Havana there are huge double jointed buses pulled by a truck, called *camellos* (camels) because of their shape, also irreverently known as 'Saturday night at the cinema' because they are full of 'sex, crime and alcohol'. In the rush hours they are filled to more than capacity, making it hard to get off if you have managed to get on. Buses are running but fuel shortages limit services. Urban tickets can only be bought in pesos Cubanos.

Long distance For bus transport to other provinces from Havana there is a dollar ticket office in the Terminal de Omnibus Nacional, Boyeros y 19 de Mayo (third left via 19 de Mayo entrance), T703397, open daily 0700-2100, very helpful staff. You don't have to book in advance but it might be wiser to do so. There may be cancellations. The best service is *Víazul* (Viajes Azul), at Av 26 entre Av Zoológico y Ulloa, Nuevo Vedado, T811413/811108/815652, F666092, www.viazul.cu open 0900-2300, with long distance buses and minibuses. You have to pay in dollars and you will travel with other foreigners, not Cubans, but it is an efficient and comfortable service. The terminal is a long way from the centre and not near any hotels, so you have to get a taxi. On some routes their buses pass the terminal on Boyeros and you can join them there. If you are coming in to Havana from Varadero you can be dropped off in Old Havana, more convenient than continuing to the terminal. In 2001 they had the following routes: Havana-Santiago via Jagüey, Santa Clara, Sancti Spíritus, Ciego de Avila, Camagüey, Las Tunas, Holguín and Bayamo; Havana-Varadero via Matanzas and Varadero airport; Havana-Viñales via Pinar del Río; Havana-Trinidad via Jagüey and Cienfuegos; Varadero-Trinidad via Cárdenas, Coliseo, Jovellanos, Jagüey, Santa Clara and Sancti Spíritus; and Trinidad-Santiago via Sancti Spíritus, Jatibonico, Ciego de Avila, Florida, Camagüey, Sibanicú, Guáimaro, Las Tunas, Holguín, Bayamo and Palma Soriano. There is a weight limit for luggage of 20 kg on all long distance bus journeys and the bus-hoverfoil to Isla de la Juventud.

Car

Shortage of fuel & decline in public transport has meant Cubans have taken to organized hitching

Car hire Through state rental companies at the International Airport and most large hotels, www.dtcuba.com/esp/transporte_tierra.asp Minimum US$40 a day (or US$50 for air conditioning) with limited mileage of 100 km a day, and US$8-20 a day optional insurance, or US$50-88 per day unlimited mileage; cheaper rates over seven days. Visa, Mastercard, Eurocard, Banamex, JCB and Carnet accepted for the rental, or cash or traveller's cheques paid in advance, guarantee of US$200-250 required; you must also present your passport and home driving licence. In practice, you may find car hire rates prohibitively expensive when small cars are 'unavailable' and a four-door sedan at US$93, unlimited km, insurance included, is your only option. Staff have been reported as 'unhelpful' in finding what you want. It pays to shop around, even between offices of the same company. Cubans are not allowed to hire cars (although they may drive them), so even if you have organized a local driver you will have to show a foreign driving licence. If you want to drive from Havana to Santiago and return by air, try *Havanautos.* They will charge at least US$80 to return the car to Havana, but most companies will not even consider it. Fly and drive packages can be booked from abroad through *Cubacar*, part of the Grupo Cubanacán, who have a wide range of jeeps and cars all over the country and can even arrange a driver (pmando@cubacar.cha.cyt.cu). Most vehicles are Japanese or Korean makes, Suzuki jeeps can be hired for six to 12 hours in beach areas, US$11-22, plus US$8 insurance, extra hours US$5. Watch out for theft of the radio and spare tyre; you will have to pay about US$350 if stolen unless you take out the costly extra insurance. **Moped** rental at resorts is around US$8-10 per hour, cheaper for longer, US$25-30 per day, US$80 per week.

Taxi

See also page 183

There are three types of taxi: tourist taxis, Cuban taxis and private taxis (*particulares*). **Dollar tourist taxis** can be hired for driving around; you pay for the distance, not for waiting time. On short routes, fares are metered. From the airport to Havana (depending on destination) costs US$12-18 with *Panataxi*, to Playas del Este US$30, to Varadero US$90; Cuban taxis, or *colectivos*, also operate on fixed routes and pick you up only if you know where to stand for certain destinations. Travelling on them is an adventure and a complicated cultural experience. Cubans are not allowed to carry foreigners in their vehicles, but they do; private taxis, *particulares*, are considerably cheaper than other taxis, for example airport to Havana centre US$8-12, from Santiago to the airport US$5. A *particular* who pays his tax will usually display a 'taxi' sign, which can be a hand-written piece of board, but have a private registration plate. Some have meters, in others you have to negotiate a price in either pesos or dollars, although as a foreigner you will be urged to pay in dollars. If not metered, 10 km should cost around US$5. For long distances you can negotiate with official taxis as well as *particulares*, and the price should be around US$10 per hour. As a general rule, the cost will depend on the quality of your Spanish and how well you know the area.

Train

Travel between provinces is usually booked solid several days or weeks in advance. If you are on a short trip you may do better to go by Viazul bus or on a package tour with excursions

Although delays and breakdowns must be expected. Be at the station at least one hour before the scheduled departure time. Fares are reasonable but have to be paid for in dollars, which will usually entitle you to a waiting area, seat reservation and to board the train before the big rush starts. There is a dollar ticket office in every station. Alternatively, the tourist desks in some of the larger hotels sell train tickets to foreigners, in dollars. Long distance trains allow only seated passengers, they are spacious and comfortable, but extremely cold unless the air conditioning is broken, so take warm clothes and a blanket (if you can). A torch is useful for the toilet. All carriages are smoking areas. Bicycles can be carried as an express item only and often cost more than the fare for a person (see Cycling, page 156). There is no food service except on the *especial*, when a trolley passes through once with sandwiches and juice, followed later by coffee (pay in pesos). Sometimes there are additional sandwiches and drinks for sale at a bar (dollars only), but it is advisable to take food with you. If you are 15-16 hours late you will be glad you took snacks and drinks. So will your fellow passengers.

Keeping in touch

Telephone

IDD code: 53

Most hotels have facilities for international calls and faxes which you can use even if you are not staying there. Phone cards are now used elsewhere and can be quite economical. Cuba does not have a reputation for good communications; it can take time to get a line and email is rare, but things are gradually improving with help from foreign telecommunications companies. The downside is that numbers and codes are frequently changing.

Local telephone calls can be made from public telephones for five centavos. To phone abroad on a phone with international dialling facility, dial 119 followed by the country and regional codes and number. Many hotels and airports have telephone offices where international calls can be made at high prices. Look for the *Telecorreos* or *Etecsa* signs. No 'collect' calls allowed and only cash accepted. Collect calls to some places, are possible from private Cuban telephones. In a few top class hotels you can direct dial foreign countries from your room. Phonecards are in use at Etecsa callboxes, in different denominations from US$10-50, much cheaper for phoning abroad, for example US$2 per minute to USA and Canada, US$2.60 per minute to Central America and the Caribbean, US$3.40 to South America, US$4 to Europe and US$4.40 to the rest of the world. Mobile phones are commonly used in Cuba.

Internet

Cybercafés for internet access by the public do not exist yet. There is a public service in the Capitol building in Havana, see below, and the Post Office under the Ministerio de Comunicaciones, opposite the bus terminal at Plaza de la Revolución has internet facilities. The *Golden Tulip Plaza Central* has a business centre from where you can send emails and faxes, as well as make phone calls. The other large hotels: *Nacional, Habana Libre*, etc also offer business facilities. Outside Havana, ask in telecommunications offices, the major towns often have computers you can use for a few dollars, and in Santiago, *DHL* offer email access.

Newspapers *Granma*, mornings except Sunday and Monday; *Trabajadores*, Trade Union **Media** weekly; *Tribuna* and *Juventud Rebelde*, also only weekly. *Opciones* is a weekly national and international trade paper. *Granma* has a weekly edition, *Granma International*, published in Spanish, English, French and Portuguese, and a monthly selected German edition; all have versions on the Internet, www.granma.cu. Main offices: Av Gen Suárez y Territorial, Plaza de la Revolución, La Habana 6, T816265, F335176, in UK 928 Bourges Blvd, Peterborough PE1 2AN. Foreign magazines and newspapers are sometimes on sale at the telex centre in *Habana Libre* and in the *Riviera* (also telex centre, open 0800-2000). The previous day's paper is available during the week. Weekend editions on sale Tuesday.

Television There are two national channels: Cubavisión and Tele Rebelde, which broadcast morning and evening. The Sun Channel can be seen at hotels and broadcasts a special programme for tourists 24 hours a day. Some of the upmarket hotels also have satellite TV. The most watched programme is the Colombian telenovela, *Café con la aroma de mujer*, about a love triangle between Sebastián, his wife Lucía and his mistress, Gaviota.

Spanish, with local variants in pronunciation and vocabulary. English, German, Italian and **Language** French are spoken by those in the tourist industry. There are **language courses** available at the universities of Havana, Cienfuegos and Santiago. They generally start on the first Monday of the month and you study 20 hours a week, Monday-Friday 0900-1300. There are different levels of study and Cuban cultural courses are also available. At Havana, latest prices are US$250 for two weeks, US$650 full board. In Santiago, university accommodation is available for US$21 per person per day, including breakfast and evening meal. In Havana, contact Damaris Valdez, T335842, 704667; in Santiago, Enrique Vallejo, T43186. Information also from Eddy González, Mercado SA, 13 951 esq 8, Vedado, T333893, F333028.

Food and drink

Hotels tend to serve buffet meals which can get tedious after a while, but breakfast is usually **Food** good and plentiful and you can stock up for the day. The best meals at reasonable prices are *Food is not Cuba's* to be had in the private restaurants, known as *paladares*, where you can get items paid for in *strong point, although* dollars which are not available to Cubans on their ration cards. *Paladares* are licensed and *the supply of fresh* taxed and limited to 12 chairs, as well as having employment restrictions. Some very good *food has improved* family-run businesses have been set up, offering a three-course meal in Havana for US$10-15 per person, half that outside the capital, excellent value. They are not allowed to have lobster or shrimp on the menu as these are reserved for the dollar hotels and the export market. However, if you ask, there are often items available which are not on the menu. Many families who rent out rooms also provide food in plentiful proportions. Breakfast, including eggs, is around US$3, while dinner costs about US$6-8. This is generally of excellent quality with the advantage that they will cook whatever you want and is particularly recommended for vegetarians as well as those on a tight budget. Remember, however, that it is not always strictly legal as many families provide meals without paying the required tax. State-owned 'dollar' restaurants are recognizable by the credit card stickers on the door, where meals are about US$15-25, paid only in US dollars.

The **national dish** is *congrís* (rice mixed with black beans), roast pork and yuca (cassava) or fried plantain. Pork is traditionally eaten for the New Year celebrations, so before then all the pigs which have been fattened up on people's balconies or smallholdings are on the move (in various forms) in the backs of trucks, cars and bicycles, to be sold privately or at the markets. Salads in restaurants are mixed vegetables which are slightly pickled and not to everyone's taste. For **vegetarians** the choice is very limited, normally only cheese sandwiches, spaghetti, pizzas, salads, bananas and omelettes. Even beans (and *congris*) are usually cooked with meat or in meat fat. If you are staying at a *casa particular* licensed to serve food, or eating in a *paladar*, they will usually prepare meatless meals for you with advance warning. Always ask for beans to be cooked in vegetable oil.

Cuba

Drink **Rum** is the national drink and all cocktails are rum-based. There are several brand names and
each has a variety of ages, so you have plenty of choice. The locally grown **coffee** is good,
although hotels often manage to make it undrinkable in the mornings. The most widely
available **beer** throughout the island is *Cristal*, made by Cervecería Mayabe, in Holguín. From
the same brewery is *Mayabe*, also popular. *Hatuey*, made in Havana, is reckoned by some to be
the best of Cuba's many beers, named after an Indian chief ruling when the Spanish arrived. It
is becoming more widely available after a lengthy patent battle. *Bucanero*, from Holguín, is
easily bought in the east of the island.

Cuba now also produces **wines** under the *Soroa* label, grown and produced in Pinar del
Río and sold for about US$3.15 in shops. There is also a more expensive and better range sold
for about US$8, including Cabernet Sauvignon, Chardonnay, Tempranillo and other grapes,
produced with the help of a Spanish company in a joint venture.

Tobacco Tobacco is of course excellent, but remember that all the best leaves go into cigar making
rather than cigarettes. Make sure you buy the best to take home and don't get tricked into
buying fakes, you may not get them through customs. Buying cigars on the street is not legal,
they are often not genuine, and may be confiscated at customs if you cannot produce an
official receipt of purchase.

Flora and fauna

When the Spanish arrived at the end of the 15th century more than 90% of Cuba was covered
with forest. However, clearance for cattle raising and sugar cane reduced this proportion: 75%
of the land is now savannah or plains, 18% mountains and 4% swamps. A reforestation
programme aims to increase Cuba's forests to 27% of the total area. Besides semi-deciduous
woodland, vegetation types include rainforest, coastal and upland scrub, distinctive
limestone vegetation found in the Sierra de los Organos and similar areas, savannah
vegetation found on nutrient-deficient white silica sands, pine forests, xerophytic coastal
limestone woodland, mangroves and other coastal wetlands.

Cuba is characterized by extraordinarily high rates of biodiversity and endemism,
particularly in four regions: the Montañas de Moa-Nipe-Sagua-Baracoa, which have the
greatest diversity in all the Caribbean and are among the highest in the world, and 30% of the
endemic species on the island; Parque Nacional Sierra de los Organos, the Reserva de la
Biósfera Sierra del Rosario and the Reserva Ecológica del Macizo de Guamuhaya.

There are over 7,000 plant species in Cuba, which around 3,000 are endemic. 950 plant
species are endangered, rare, or have become extinct in the last 350 years. Oddities in the plant
world include the **Pinguicola lignicola**, the world's only carniverous epiphytic plant; the **cork
palm** (*Microcycas colocoma*), an endemic living fossil which is a threatened species; and the
Solandra grandiflora, one of the world's largest flowers, 10 cm across at the calyx and 30 cm
at the corolla. There are around 100 different palm trees in Cuba, of which 90 are endemic. The
Royal palm is the national tree and can be seen throughout the island. Cubans use the small,
purple fruits to feed pigs, as they are oily and nutritious. There is one tiny orchid, *Pleurothallis
shaferi*, which is only 1 cm, with leaves measuring 5 mm and flowers of only 2 mm.

Animal life is also varied, with nearly 14,000 species of fauna, of which 10 % could be on
the verge of extinction. There are no native large mammals but some genera and families
have diversified into a large number of distinct island species. These include mammals such
as the **hutia**, **bats** and the protected **manatee** with more than 20 breeding groups, mostly
in the Ciénaga de Zapata and north of Villa Clara. Reptiles range from three types of
crocodiles including the **Cuban crocodile** now found only in the Ciénaga de Zapata (there is
a farm on the Zapata Peninsula) to iguanas to tiny salamanders. Cuba claims the smallest of a
number of animals, for example the **Cuban pygmy frog**, 12 mm long, the **almiquí**, a
shrew-like insectivore, the world's smallest mammal, the **butterfly** or **moth bat** and the **bee
hummingbird**, 63 mm long, called locally the *zunzuncito*. The latter is an endangered
species, like the **carpintero real woodpecker**, the **cariara** or **caracara**, the **pygmy owl**, the
Cuban green parrot and the *fermina*, or **Zapata wren**. Less attractively, there is also a **dwarf
scorpion**, *alacrán*, 10 mm long.

The best place for birdwatching on the island is the Zapata Peninsula, where 170 species of Cuban birds have been recorded, including the majority of endemic species. In winter migratory waterbirds, swallows and others visit the marshes. The national bird is the forest-dwelling **Cuban trogon**, the *tocororo*, partly because of its blue head, white chest and red underbelly, the colours of the Cuban flag.

Protected areas cover 30% of Cuba including its marine platform. There are 14 national parks and four UNESCO biosphere reserves: **Guanahacabibes** in the extreme western tip of the island; the **Sierra del Rosario**, 60 km west of Havana; **Baconao** in the east and **Cuchillas del Toa**. However, not all legally established conservation areas have any infrastructure, personnel or administration in place.

Sport

Trekking, **hiking, rafting** and **bird watching** are elements of adventure or nature travel which are still in their infancy in Cuba but are sure to be heavily promoted in the near future. The island's plentiful fauna and flora, its mountains, cays and wetlands, and its expanding system of national parks and other protected areas, are perfect for getting close to nature. Hunting lodges still attract those who enjoy blasting ducks out of the sky and sport fishing is available in many marinas, but in the last few years the emphasis has been on looking and not touching, as in bird watching and scuba diving. The state travel agencies are opening specialist operations for organized tours, with expert staff on hand to advise on biology, botany or forestry (see page 154). However, often facilities are limited and many sports are simply unavailable. Traditionally, tourists have been expected to spend their time on the beach, with sightseeing excursions to colonial cities and night time forays into bars and clubs.

Cycling
An integral part of local culture with an estimated 2 million bicycles in Cuba

Cuba has an extensive network of tarmac and concrete roads, covering nearly 17,600 km. This impressive infrastructure means that the vast majority of the country is accessible to the cyclist, and there are some dramatic roads to climb and descend. There is total freedom of movement and the rewards can be immense. However, many of the roads are in a poor condition, particularly in the rural areas. See page 156.

Diving

Cuba's marine environment is pristine compared with many Caribbean islands, where there has often been overharvesting and overdevelopment of the dive industry. The majority of coral reefs are alive and healthy and teeming with assorted marine life. The government has established a marine park around the **Isla de la Juventud** and much marine life is protected around the entire island, including turtles, the manatee and coral. There are three main marine platforms, the **Archipiélago del Rey** (Sabana-Camagüey), the **Archipiélago de la Reina** and the **Archipiélago de los Canarreos**. The first one has the greatest diversity of marine species and is being explored and classified with the aim of making it a protected zone. There are believed to be some 900 species of fish, 1,400 species of molluscs, 60 species of coral, 1,100 species of crustaceans, 67 species of sharks and rays and four types of marine turtles around the island, as well as the manatee. The main dive areas are Isla de la Juventud, Varadero, Faro de Luna, María La Gorda, Santa Lucía and Santiago de Cuba.

Fishing
Equipment can be hired, but serious fishermen will prefer to bring their own & large quantities of insect repellent

Cuba has been a fisherman's dream for many decades, not only for its deep sea fishing, popularized by Ernest Hemingway, but also for its freshwater fishing in the many lakes and reservoirs spread around the island. **Freshwater fishing** is mostly for the largemouth bass (*trucha*), which grow to a great size in the Cuban lakes. *Horizontes* is the travel company to contact for accommodation and fishing packages, which can be arranged all year round. The main places are Maspotón, in Pinar del Río, where you can fish in La Juventud reservoir or in the mouth of the Río Los Palacios or Río Carraguao; Laguna del Tesoro in the Ciénaga de Zapata, where there is a wide variety of fish; Presa Alacranes in Villa Clara province, which is the second largest reservoir in the country; Presa Zaza, in Sancti Spíritus, the largest artificial lake in Cuba, where the record catch of *trucha* is 16.5 lbs; Lago La Redonda, near Morón in Ciego de Avila province, where the clear waters hold such a concentration of fish that a group of US fishermen were able to catch 5,078 *trucha* in five days. **Deep sea fishing** can be organized at most marinas around the island, although most of the tournaments and the best facilities are at the Marina Hemingway, just west of Havana. The waters are home to a variety of beaked fish: marlin, swordfish, tarpon, sawfish, yellowfin tuna, dorado, wahoo, shark and a host of others are all caught here. Varadero is a good point from which to go fishing and take advantage of the Gulf Stream which flows between Key West in Florida and Cuba, but records have been broken all along the northern coast in the cays of the Archipiélago de Sabana and the Archipiélago de Camagüey. There is also good fishing off the south coast around the Isla de la Juventud and Cayo Largo. **Bonefishing** is best done off the south coast in the Archipiélago de los Jardines de la Reina, or off Cayo Largo.

Sailing   There are 18 marinas around the country offering moorings, boat rental and a variety of services. Diving and fishing are on offer at many. The largest is the Marina Hemingway in Havana, see page 185. For technical specifications, see www.dtcuba.com/esp/naturaleza_marinas.asp. Marinas are owned by Cubanacán Náutica (formerly Marlin Marinas), Puertosol and Gaviota. Not many 'yachties' (people who live and travel on their own boats) visit the island because of the political difficulties between Cuba and the USA. The US administration forbids any vessel, such as a cruise ship, cargo ship or humble yacht from calling at a US port if it has stopped in Cuba. This effectively prohibits anyone sailing from the US eastern seaboard calling in at a Cuban port on their way south through the Caribbean islands, or vice versa. It is better to rent a bareboat yacht from a Cuban marina and sail around the island, rather than include it in a Caribbean itinerary. It would be worthwhile to invest in *The Cruising Guide to Cuba*, by Simon Charles (Cruising Guide Publications, 1017, Dunedin, FL 34697-1017, USA, T813-7335322, F813-7348179) before embarking.

Walking
A good pair of hiking books are essential

The three main mountain ranges are excellent for hill walking in a wide range of tropical vegetation, where many national parks are being established and trails demarcated. The highest peaks are in the **Sierra Maestra** in the east, where there are also many historical landmarks associated with the Wars of Independence and the Revolution. Unfortunately you are not currently allowed to walk in much of this area without permission and it is not clear from whom permission should be obtained. A three day walk used to be possible which would take you from Alto del Naranjo up the island's highest peak, Pico Turquino, and down to the Caribbean coast at Las Cuevas, giving you fantastic views of the mountains and the coastline. The **Sierra del Escambray**, in the centre of the island, is conveniently located just north of the best preserved colonial city, Trinidad, and there are some lovely walks in the hills, along trails beside rivers, waterfalls and caves. The mountains of the west of the island, the **Sierra del Rosario** and the **Sierra de los Organos**, have some of the most unusual geological features, notably the large number of caves and the limestone *mogotes*, straight sided, flat topped hills rising from the midst of tobacco fields and looking almost Chinese, particularly in the early morning mist. Good large scale maps are non-existent and you are advised to take a guide when embarking on long walks.

Health

Local health facilities are listed in individual town directories
See also main Health section page 47

Cuba has a high quality national health service and is one of the healthiest countries in Latin America and the Caribbean. Medical service is no longer free for foreign visitors in Havana, Santiago de Cuba and Varadero, where there are international clinics that charge in dollars (credit cards accepted). Visitors requiring medical attention will be sent to them. Emergencies are handled on an ad hoc basis. Check with your national health service or health insurance on coverage in Cuba and take a copy of your insurance policy with you. Remember you cannot dial any toll-free numbers abroad so make sure you have a contact number. Charges are generally lower than those in Western countries. According to latest reports, visitors are still treated free of charge in other parts of the country, with the exception of tourist enclaves with on-site medical services.

The most common affliction of travellers to any country is probably diarrhoea and the same is true of Cuba. Tap water is safe in most areas of the country, but bottled water is widely available if you prefer. Doctors will advise you to get hepatitis A and typhoid inoculations. Always carry toilet paper with you, it is not often available in public toilets and even some hotels do not have it.

The climate is hot; Cuba is a tropical country and protection against the sun will be needed. Take a high factor sun screen, apply it regularly and stay out of the midday sun. Children need to be particularly well protected and wear a hat. The breeze at the beach is deceptive, you may not feel hot, but the sun will burn very quickly. Between May and October, the risk of sunburn is high, sun blocks are recommended when walking around the city as well as on the beach. In the cooler months, limit beach sessions to two hours.

Havana

Of all the capital cities in the Caribbean, Havana has the reputation for being the most splendid and sumptuous. Before the Revolution, its casinos and nightlife attracted the megastars of the day in much the same way as Beirut and Shanghai, and remarkably little has changed (architecturally) since then. There have been no tacky modernizations, partly because of lack of finance and materials. Low level street lighting, relatively few cars (and many of those antiques), no (real) estate agents or Wendyburgers, no neon and very little advertising (except for political slogans), all give the city plenty of scope for nostalgia. Restoration works in the old part of the city are revealing the glories of the past, although most of the city is fighting a losing battle against the sea air – many of the finest buildings along the sea front are crumbling.

Havana is not a modern city in the materialist sense and is no good for people for whom shopping and eating well are the central leisure activities. It is, however, probably the finest example of a Spanish colonial city in the Americas. Many of its palaces were converted into museums after the Revolution and more work has been done (with millions of dollars of foreign aid and investment) since the old city was declared a UNESCO World Heritage Site in 1982. Away from the old city, there is some stunning modern architecture from the first half of the 20th century.

Colour map 1, grid A2
Population: 2,204,300

Cuba

Ins and outs

The **José Martí international airport** is 18 km from Havana. The most expensive **taxis** are *Turistaxi*, while the cheapest are *Panataxi*. Fares range from US$15-20, but US$18 is commonly asked to the old city. On the way back to the airport it is possible to arrange a private taxi, which may work out cheaper, if you negotiate with the driver. To get to the airport by bus, it is difficult with luggage, and it will take forever, but *Víazul* operates a transfer service from some hotels for US$4 or the M2 *camello* runs from the park two blocks west of Parque Fraternidad on Av Simón Bolívar to within walking distance of terminal 3 for only 20 centavos. The main **bus** terminal is very near the Plaza de la Revolución in Vedado, central and convenient for accommodation. *Víazul* dollar buses stop much further out and a taxi will be arranged for you by the company. The **train** station is at the southern end of the old city, within walking distance of any of the hotels there or in Centro Habana, although if you arrive at night, take a taxi.

Getting there

Buses involve complicated queuing procedures and a lot of pushing and shoving. A dollar bus, *Vaivén*, runs on a huge circular route and allows you to get on and off as often as you like. **Bicitaxi**, bicycle taxi, rates negotiable but generally only a fraction of what you would pay a normal taxi. Havana is very spread out along the coast. Those with really good walking boots can cover much of the city on foot, but the average visitor will be content with one district at a time, eg Old Havana one day, Vedado the next, and still feel well exercised.

Getting around
See transport, page 182, for further details

The centre is divided into five sections, three of which are of most interest to visitors, **Old Havana** (Habana Vieja), **Central Havana** (Centro) and **Vedado**. The oldest part of the city, around the **Plaza de Armas**, is quite near the docks. Here are the former **Palace of the**

Orientation

Captains-General, the temple of **El Templete**, and **Castillo de La Real Fuerza**, the oldest of all the forts. From Plaza de Armas run two narrow and picturesque streets, Calles Obispo and O'Reilly (there are several old-fashioned pharmacies on Obispo with traditional glass and ceramic medicine jars and decorative perfume bottles on display in shops that gleam with polished wood and mirrors). These two streets go west to the heart of the city to **Parque Central**, with its laurels, poincianas, almonds, palms, shrubs and gorgeous flowers. To the southwest rises the golden dome of the **Capitol**. From the northwest corner of Parque Central a wide, tree-shaded avenue with a central walkway (where small boys wizz up and down on homemade skateboards and other vehicles), the **Paseo del Prado**, runs to the fortress of **La Punta**. At its north sea-side end is the **Malecón**, a splendid highway along the coast to the west residential district of Vedado. The sea crashing along the seawall here is a spectacular sight when the wind blows from the north. On calmer days, fishermen lean over the parapet, lovers sit in the shade of the small pillars, and joggers sweat along the pavement. On the other side of the six-lane road, buildings which from a distance look stout and grand, with arcaded pavements, balconies, mouldings and large entrances, are salt-eroded, faded and sadly decrepit inside. Restoration is progressing slowly, but the sea is destroying old and new alike and creating a mammoth renovation task.

Further west, Calle San Lázaro leads directly from the monument to **General Antonio Maceo** on the Malecón to the magnificent central stairway of **Havana University**. A monument to **Julio Antonio Mella**, founder of the Cuban Communist Party, stands across from the stairway. Further out, past **El Príncipe** castle, is **Plaza de la Revolución**, with the impressive monument to **José Martí** at its centre. The large buildings surrounding the square were mostly built in the 1950s and house the principal government ministries. The long grey building behind the monument is the former Justice Ministry (1958), now the headquarters of the Central Committee of the Communist Party, where Fidel Castro has his office. The Plaza is the scene of massive parades (May Day) and speeches marking important events. It was completely transformed for an open air mass held by the Pope in January 1998 with huge religious paintings suspended over the surrounding buildings.

From near the fortress of **La Punta** a tunnel runs east under the mouth of the harbour; it emerges in the rocky ground between the **Castillo del Morro** and the fort of **La Cabaña**, some 550 m away, and a 5 km highway connects with the Havana-Matanzas road.

Havana orientation

Old Havana (La Habana Vieja)

Built between 1589 and 1630, with a 20 m moat, but much altered. It stands on a bold **Castillo del**
headland, with the best view of Havana and is illuminated at night. It was one of the **Morro**
major fortifications built to protect the natural harbour and the assembly of Spain's
silver fleets from pirate attack. The flash of its lighthouse, built in 1844, is visible 30
km out to sea. It now serves as a museum with a good exhibition of Cuban history
since the arrival of Columbus. On the harbour side, down by the water, is the **Battery of the 12 Apostles**, each gun being named after an Apostle. Every Saturday at
around 1000-1100 there is a display of AfroCuban dancing and music. ■ *0830-2030
(museum, 1000-1800). US$1 for the parque, US$3 for the Castillo, US$2 for photo-
graphs and US$2 for the lighthouse. Access to the Castillo del Morro is from any bus
going through the tunnel (20 or 40 centavos), board at San Lázaro and Av del Puerto
and get off at the stop after tunnel, cross the road and climb following the path to the left.
Alternatively take a taxi, or a 20-min walk from the Fortaleza de la Cabaña.*

Fronting the harbour is a high wall; the ditch on the landward side, 12 m deep, has a **Fortaleza de**
drawbridge to the main entrance. Inside are **Los Fosos de los Laureles** where politi- **la Cabaña**
cal prisoners were shot during the Cuban fight for independence. Every night the
cannons are fired in an historical ceremony recalling the closing of the city walls in
the 17th century to protect it from pirates; this starts at 2045 so that the walls are
closed at 2100. There are two museums here, one about Che Guevara and another
about fortresses with pictures and models, some old weapons and a replica of a large
catapult and battering ram. ■ *Open 0830-2200, US$3, extra charge for camera or
video. Access as for Castillo del Morro or via Casablanca.*
    The **National Observatory** and the station for trains to Matanzas are on the same
side of the Channel as the forts, at **Casablanca**. This charming town is also the site of
a statue of a very human Jesus Christ, erected during the Batista dictatorship as a
pacifying exercise. Go up a steep, twisting flight of stone steps, starting on the other
side of the plaza in front of the landing stage, and you can walk from the statue to the
Fortaleza (10 minutes) and then on to the Castillo del Morro. ■ *Left-hand ferry
queue next to the Customs House, opposite Calle Santa Clara, 10 centavos.*

Built at the end of the 16th century, a squat building with 250cm thick walls. ■ *Open* **Castillo de**
daily. Free. Opposite the fortress, across the Malecón, is the **monument to Máximo** **la Punta**
Gómez, the independence leader.

Cuba's oldest building and the second oldest fort in the New World. Built in 1558 **Castillo de la**
after the city had been sacked by buccaneers and rebuilt in 1582. It is a low, long **Real Fuerza**
building at the end of O'Reilly entre Av del Puerto y Tacón, with a picturesque tower
from which there is a grand view. Inside the castle is a museum with armour and
Cuban ceramic art dating from the 1940s onwards. ■ *Open daily, 0800-1900, US$2,
T615010. Art exhibitions downstairs. Shop upstairs.* There are two other old forts in
Havana: **Atarés**, finished in 1763, on a hill overlooking the southwest end of the har-
bour; and **El Príncipe**, on a hill at the far end of Av Independencia (Av Rancho
Boyeros), built 1774-94, now the city gaol. Amazing views of Havana.

Construction of a church on this site was begun by Jesuit missionaries at the beginning of **Cathedral**
the 18th century. After the Jesuits were expelled in 1767, the church was converted into a
cathedral. On either side of the Spanish colonial baroque façade are bell towers, the left
one (west) being half as wide as the right (east), which has a grand view. The church is
officially dedicated to the Virgin of the Immaculate Conception, but is better known as
the church of Havana's patron saint, San Cristóbal, and as the Columbus cathedral. The
bones of Christopher Columbus were sent to this cathedral when Santo Domingo was
ceded by Spain to France in 1795; they now lie in Santo Domingo (Dominican Republic). ■ *Mon-Tue, Thu-Sat 0930-1230, Sun 0830-1230, Mass at 1030.*

Central & Old Havana

Cuba

Cuba

Plaza de Armas The statue in the centre is of Carlos Manuel de Céspedes. In the northeast corner of the square is the church of **El Templete**; a column in front of it marks the spot where the first mass was said in 1519 under a ceiba tree. A sapling of the same tree, blown down by a hurricane in 1753, was planted on the same spot, and under its branches the supposed bones of Columbus reposed in state before being taken to the cathedral. This tree was cut down in 1828, the present tree planted, and the Doric temple opened. There are paintings by Vermay, a pupil of David, inside. On the north side of the Plaza is the **Palacio del Segundo Cabo**, the former private residence of the Captains General, now housing the Feria Cubana del Libro. Its patio is worth a look. On the east side is the small luxury hotel, the *Santa Isabel*, and on the south side the modern **Museo Nacional de Historia Natural**. Outside in the Plaza de Armas there is a small **book market** daily except Monday. On the west side of Plaza de Armas is the former **Palace of the Captains General**, built in 1780, a charming example of colonial architecture. The Spanish Governors and the Presidents lived here until 1917, when it became the City Hall. It is now the **Museo de la Ciudad**, the Historical Museum of the city of Havana. There are no explanations, even in Spanish. Nineteenth-century furnishings illustrate the wealth of the Spanish colonial community. The building was the site of the signing of the 1899 treaty between Spain and the USA. The arcaded and balconied patio is well worth a visit. The courtyard contains royal palms, the Cuban national tree. An extension to the museum is the **Casa de la Plata**, a silverware collection on Obispo entre Mercaderes y Oficios, fine pieces, jewellery and old frescoes on the upper floor, free with ticket to Museo de la Ciudad. The former **Supreme Court** on the north side of the Plaza is another colonial building, with a large patio. ■ *Open daily 0930-1830, camera fee US$3, T615001, 639981. It is possible to buy a combined one-day ticket which allows access to several museums.*

The church & convent of San Francisco Built in 1608 and reconstructed in 1730, this is a massive, sombre edifice suggesting defence, rather than worship. The three-storey tower was both a landmark for returning voyagers and a look-out for pirates. The Basílica Menor de San Francisco de Asís is now a concert hall and the convent is a museum containing religious pieces. Restoration work is still going on. Most of the treasures, however, were removed by the government and some are in museums. ■ *Daily 0900-1900, US$2, photos US$2, video US$10, guide US$1, bell tower with stunning views of the city and port an extra US$1.* The Corinthian white marble building on Calle Oficios, south of the post office was the legislative building before the Capitol was built.

The Convento de Santa Clara Founded in 1644 by nuns from Cartagena in Colombia, it was in use as a convent until 1919, when the nuns sold the building. Restoration began in 1982, and is still continuing. The convent occupies four small blocks in Old Havana, bounded by Calles Habana, Sol, Cuba and Luz, and originally there were three cloisters and an orchard. You can see the cloisters, the nuns' cemetery and their cells. The first cloister has been carefully preserved; the ground floor is a grand porticoed stone gallery surrounding a large patio packed with vegetation, in it are the city's first slaughterhouse, first public fountain and public baths. The Sailor's House in the second cloister, reputedly built by a sailor for his love-lorn daughter, is now a *Residencia Académica* for student groups (and independent travellers if room). The convent is topped by an extensive tiled roof with a stone turret next to the church choir. ■ *Mon-Fri 0900-1500, US$2 for guided tour in Spanish or French, entrance on Cuba.*

La Merced Construction of this church began in 1755, and was still incomplete in 1792, when work stopped. Building was completed late in the 19th century. It has an unremarkable exterior and a redecorated lavish interior.

Parque Fraternidad The park has been landscaped to show off the **Capitol**, north of it, to the best effect. At its centre is a ceiba tree growing in soil provided by each of the American republics. Also in the park is a famous statue of the Indian woman who first welcomed the Spaniards: La Noble Habana, sculpted in 1837. From the southwest corner the handsome Avenida Allende runs due west to the high hill, on which stands **El Príncipe Castle** (now the city gaol). The **Quinta de los Molinos**, on this avenue, at the foot of the hill, now contains the **Máximo Gómez Museum** (Dominican-born fighter for Cuban Independence). North, along Calle Universidad, on a hill which gives a good view, is the **University**.

Opened in May 1929, it has a large dome over a rotunda. This is a copy, on a smaller scale, of the US Capitol in Washington. At the centre of its floor is set a 24-carat diamond, zero for all distance measurements in Cuba. The interior has large halls and stately staircases, all most sumptuously decorated. ■ *Entrance for visitors is to the left of the stairway, US$3 to go in the halls, tours available, restaurant.*

The Capitol

Partagas, on Calle Industria behind the Capitolio, gives 30-min tours, every 15 mins 0930-1200, 1330-1500, US$10. The tour is very interesting but pricey. English, Spanish or French speaking guides available. You are taken through the factory and shown the whole production process from storage and sorting of leaves, to packaging and labelling (explanation in Spanish only). Four different brand names are made here; *Partagas*, *Cubana*, *Ramón Allones* and *Bolívar*. These and other famous cigars (and rum) can be bought at their shop here: open 0900-1700. Cigars are also made at many tourist locations.

Cigar factory

Cuba

A very pleasant park with a monument to **José Martí** in the centre. On its west side are the *Hotel Telégrafo* (being restored in 2001), the historic *Hotel Inglaterra* and the **Gran Teatro de la Habana**, a beautiful building with tours of the inside. The north side is entirely occupied by the *Golden Tulip Parque Central*, while the *Hotel Plaza* is in the northeast corner. Restoration of one of the sites of the Museo Nacional Palacio de Bellas Artes is taking place on the east side of the park.

Parque Central

The Jesuits built this church in 1672 on the slight elevation of **Peña Pobre** hill. The original church was largely destroyed by a hurricane in 1844 and rebuilt in its present neo-Gothic style in 1866-71. It has 10 tiny chapels, no more than kneeling places and some interesting stained glass depicting conquistadors.

Church of El Santo Angel Custodio

This is a beautiful Arab building housing shops and a restaurant/bar. It is now the **Palacio de la Artesanía**. ■ *0900-0200 Fri-Sun, with traditional dance at 2200.*

Palacio Pedroso

An 18th-century plaza, undergoing restoration since February 1996 as part of a joint project by UNESCO and Habaguanex, a state company responsible for the restoration and revival of old Havana. The former house of the Spanish Captain General, **Conde de Ricla**, who retook Havana from the English and restored power to Spain in 1763, can be seen on the corner of San Ignacio and Muralla. As restoration continues, 18th-century murals are being uncovered on the external walls of the buildings, many of which boast elegant balconies overlooking the plaza. The newly-restored Cuban Stock Exchange building, **La Lonja**, Oficios and Plaza San Francisco, is opposite the cruise ship terminal.

La Plaza Vieja

This huge, ornate building, topped by a dome, on Refugio entre Monserrate y Zulueta, facing Avenida de las Misiones, was once the Presidential Palace, but now contains the **Museo de la Revolución**. The history of Cuban political development is charted, from the slave uprisings to joint space missions with the ex-Soviet Union. The liveliest section displays the final battles against Batista's troops, with excellent photographs and some bizarre mementoes from the Sierra Maestra campaign. The yacht *Granma*, from which Dr Castro disembarked with his companions in 1956 to launch the Revolution, has been installed in the park facing the south entrance,

Museo de la Revolución
Look out for the bullet holes as you walk up the stairs to the stuffed mule & stuffed horse used by Che Guevara & Camilo Cienfuegos

surrounded by planes, tanks and other vehicles involved, as well as a Soviet-built tank used against the Bay of Pigs invasion and a fragment from a US spy plane shot down in the 1970s. ■ *T624091. Open Tue-Sun 1000-1700, US$4, guided tour 1030, US$10, cameras allowed, US$1 extra. Allow several hours to see it all, explanations mostly in Spanish.*

Museum tour For US$15 you can buy a one-day ticket from any of the museums, allowing you entrance to the Museo de la Ciudad, its Casa de la Plata and the following: **Casa de los Arabes** (with bar and restaurant, *Al Medina*), on Oficios between Obispo and Obrapía, a lovely building with vines trained over the courtyard for shade, includes a mosque, jewels and rugs. Open daily 0930-1830, US$1; **Casa de Africa**, on Obrapía 157 between San Ignacio and Mercaderes (Monday-Saturday 1030-1730, Sunday 0930-1230, US$2), small gallery of carved wooden artefacts and handmade costumes; **Vintage Car Museum**, Oficios y Jústiz (just off Plaza de Armas, open daily 0900-1900, US$1). There are a great many museum pieces, pre-Revolutionary US models, still on the road especially outside Havana, in among the Ladas, VWs and Nissans; **Casa de Guayasimín**, Obrapía 111 entre Mercaderes y San Ignacio, exhibition of works donated to Cuba by the late Ecuadorean artist Oswaldo Guayasimín (paintings, sculpture and silkscreens) occasionally other exhibitions. Guayasimín painted a famous portrait of Fidel Castro for his 70th birthday with his hands raised; **Casa de México**, opposite the above, also called La Casa de Benito Juárez, Obrapía entre Mercaderes y Oficios, a museum of Mexico in a pink building marked with the Mexican flag, open Tuesday-Saturday 1030-1730, Sunday 0930-1230, entrance US$1; **Casa de Simón Bolívar**, Mercaderes entre Obrapía y Lamparilla, contains exhibits about the life of the South American liberator and some Venezuelan art, open Monday-Saturday 1030-1030, Sunday 1030-1300, US$1; and **Casa de Asia**, Mercaderes entre Obrapía y Obispo, converted from a solar, a multi-family dwelling with a central courtyard, into an exhibition space of art, furniture and other artefacts donated from the Asian subcontinent.

Sights outside Old Havana

Plaza de la Revolución **Museo José Martí**, Plaza de la Revolución, in base of memorial. Beautifully restored and impressive museum, with lookout accessed by mirrored lift. ■ *Mon-Sat 0900-1600, US$3, lookout US$5 extra.* **Museo Postal Cubano**, Ministry of Communications, Plaza de la Revolución. History of the postal service and stamps and the story books of José Antonio de Armona (1765). ■ *Mon-Fri 0900-1600, US$1, T705193.*

Vedado
See map page 174

Museo Napoleónico, San Miguel 1159 esquina Ronda. Houses 7,000 pieces from the private collection of sugar baron, Julio Lobo: paintings and other works of art, a specialized library and a collection of weaponry. Check out the tiled fencing gallery. ■ *Mon-Sat 1000-1800, Sun 0900-1230, US$3, T791460.* The **Cuban pavilion** (Pabellón Cuba), a large building on Calle 23, is a combination of a tropical glade and a museum of social history. It tells the nation's story by a brilliant combination of objects, photography and the architectural manipulation of space. ■ *Closed Mon. Music and dancing from 2100 on Wed (reggae), Thu (son), Fri-Sun (disco).* **Casa de la Amistad**, Paseo 406, entre 17 y 19. A former mansion, a beautiful building with gardens, now operated by ICAP (Cuban Institute for Friendship among the Peoples) and housing the *Amistur* travel agency (see page 182). It has a reasonably priced bar, cafetería and tourist shop (0930-1800). Cuban music nights are US$5 for tourists; good traditional music in a nice setting. Lots of Cubans go there too, but there is no soliciting. You can eat in the garden, the food is consistently good with large portions. Two menus: one has lobster and shrimp, the other is a house menu. ■ *The bar and cafetería are open Mon-Fri 1100-2300 (with sextet), Sat 1100-0200 (with Cuban bands).* **Museo de la Danza**, G (Presidentes) esq Línea. Items from Alicia Alonso's personal collection and from the Ballet Nacional de Cuba. ■ *Tue-Sat 1100-1830, US$2*. **Galería Haydée Santamaría**, G esq 5, alongside Casa de las Américas. Work of Latin American artists, good representation of mostly 20th century styles. The gallery was renovated with the help of the city of Seville and reopened in 1999. ■ *Tue-Sat 1000-1700, Sun 0900-1300, US$2*. The **Cementerio Colón** should be visited to see the wealth of funerary sculpture, including Carrara Marbles; Cubans visit the sculpture of Amelia de Milagrosa and pray for miracles. ■ *US$1*. The Chinese cemetery is at Avenida 26 y 31.

Maqueta de la Ciudad (scale model of Havana) on Calle 28 113 entre 1 y 3. **Miramar** ■ *Tue-Sat 1000-1800, US$3*. Opened in 1995, this is fast becoming a great attraction. The model covers Havana and its suburbs as far out as Cojímar and the airport. Colonial buildings are in red, post-colonial pre-Revolution buildings in yellow and post-Revolution buildings in white. Good fun with every building represented and recommended for the end of your stay so that you can pick out the places you visited.

Excursions

The former seaside village, now a concrete jungle, featured in Hemingway's *The Old* **Cojímar** *Man and the Sea*, is an easy excursion (15 minutes by taxi) from central Havana. He celebrated his Nobel prize here in 1954 and there is a bust of him opposite a small fort. The coastline (no beach) is covered in sharp rocks and is dirty because of effluent from tankers.

Hemingway fans may wish to visit his house, 11 km from the centre of Havana, **San Francisco** where he lived from 1939 to 1960 (called the **Museo Ernest Hemingway**). The **de Paula** signpost is opposite the post office, leading up a short driveway. Visitors are not allowed inside the plain whitewashed house, which has been lovingly preserved with all Hemingway's furniture and books, just as he left it. But you can walk all around the outside and look in through the windows and open doors. The garden is beautiful and tropical, with many shady palms. Next to the swimming pool (empty) are the gravestones of Hemingway's pet dogs. ■ *0930-1600, US$5, T910809, closed Tue. Hemingway tours are offered by hotel tour desks for US$35. No toilets. Photos US$5*.

The **Jardín Botánico Nacional de Cuba** is well-maintained with excellent collec- **Parks & zoos** tions, including a Japanese garden with tropical adaptations. There are only a few signs and so not as informative as it might be. There is a good **organic vegetarian restaurant** (the only one in Cuba) using solar energy for cooking. There is only one sitting for lunch, but you can eat as much as you like from a selection of hot and cold vegetarian dishes and drinks for US$12. Water and waste food is recycled and the restaurant grows most of its own food. ■ *Wed-Sun 1000-1745, but in practice you may not be allowed in after 1530, US$5, T442516/18. Getting there: Km 3.5, Carretera Rocío, south of the city in Arroyo Naranjo, beyond Parque Lenín. Many hotel tour desks now organize day trips including lunch for US$25, better value than going independently and probably less effort. Taxi from Old Havana US$15-18 one-way*. **Parque Zoológico Nacional**, Km 3, Carretera de Capdevila. ■ *Wed-Sun, 0900-1515, T447613*. **Parque Zoológico de la Habana**, Avenida 26 y Santa Teresa, Nuevo Vedado. ■ *Tue-Sun 0930-1730, US$2, T818915*. **National Aquarium**, Calle 60 and Avenida 1, Miramar, specializes in salt water fish and dolphins. It was modernized in 1999 with a new section with interactive displays. ■ *Tue-Sun 1000-1745, T236401-6, F241242*. The **Parque Lenín aquarium** has freshwater fish on show.

Cuba

Essentials

Sleeping

■ on maps, page 166 and 174 We have not included many hotels at the lower end of the price range because they are generally not as good value as the private accommodation on offer. See page 173 for more budget accommodation. Payment for hotels used by tourists is in US$. Do not lose your 'guest card' which shows your name, meal plan and room number. Tourist hotels are a/c, with 'tourist' TV (US films, tourism promotion), restaurants with reasonable food, but standards are not comparable with Europe and plumbing is often faulty or affected by water shortages. Several important hotel renovation projects have been completed in Old Havana and these are now elegant places to stay.

Old Havana **LL-L**Golden Tulip Parque Central (Cubanacán), Neptuno entre Prado y Zulueta, T6066279, F606630, www.gtparquecentral.com, on north side of Parque Central. 281 rooms of international standard, excellent bathrooms, separate shower and bathtub, business centre, 2 restaurants, 2 bars, great view of Havana from pool on 9th floor, fitness centre, charming and helpful multilingual staff, efficient Dutch management, good breakfast but pricey, US$12.50. **LL-L** Santa Isabel (Habaguanex), Baratillo 9 entre Obispo y Narciso López, Plaza de Armas, T338201, F338391. Five-star, only 27 rooms, 10 of them suites, busy with groups, height of luxury, very well-equipped bathrooms, rooms on 3rd floor have balcony overlooking plaza, pool, restaurant, central patio with fountain and greenery and lobby bar, good view of the Palacio de los Capitanes Generales, El Templete and other local sights, great location. **L-A** Conde de Villanueva, Hostal del Habano (Habaguanex), Mercaderes 202 esq Lamparilla, T6292934, F629682, hconde@ ip.etecsa.cu 9 rooms and suites around peaceful courtyard, attractive red and green colour scheme, cigar theme with cigar shop, café, bar, good restaurant, highly regarded, friendly staff, named after Claudio Martínez del Pinillo, Conde de Villanueva (1789-1853), a notable personality who promoted tobacco abroad and helped to bring the railway to Cuba. **L-A** Florida (Habaguanex), Obispo 252 esq Cuba, T624127, F624117. Restored building dates from 1885, cool oasis, elegant restaurant, bar just off the street, serves great daiquirís, marble floors and pillars in courtyard, beautiful rooms with high ceilings, quiet a/c, TV, some balconies, some singles, small continental breakfast, parking. **AL-A** Sevilla (Gran Caribe), Trocadero 55 y Prado, T338560, F338582. Recently restored, 188 rooms of 1937 vintage on edge of Old Havana, most have no view, noisy a/c, pool, shops, sauna and massage, tourism bureau, elegant restaurant and bar on top floor with great night time views over Vedado and the Malecón, huge windows are flung open to let in the breeze. **AL-B** Inglaterra (Gran Caribe), Prado 416 entre San Rafael y San Miguel, T335937, F338254. 86 rooms, built in 1875 next to the Teatro Nacional, famous former foreign guests, regal atmosphere, but a bit drab, balconies overlook Parque Central, some single rooms have no windows but at least you won't get woken by the traffic, reasonable breakfast, lovely old mosaic tiled dining room, 1 of 4 cafés or restaurants with a variety of services and cuisines. **A-B** Ambos Mundos (Habaguanex), Obispo 153 esq Mercaderes, T66952931, F669532. Beautifully restored, Hemingway lived here for 10 years before moving to La Vigia in 1939, you can see his room on 5th floor where there is a nice terrace bar with jolly Cuban music, rooms small, some smell damp. **A-B** Plaza (Gran Caribe), Zulueta 267 esq Neptuno, or Ignacio Agramonte 267, T608583, F608591. 186 rooms, comfortable, high ceilings, noisy a/c, reasonable bathrooms, don't rely on toilet paper being provided, street front rooms very noisy, ask for one in the inner courtyard, good breakfast on 5th floor with fine view, poor dinner, service generally poor. **AL-B** Hostal del Tejadillo (Habaguanex), Tejadillo 12 esq San Ignacio. Great location, comfortable rooms, high ceilings, tall wooden shuttered windows, fridge, good breakfast inside or in the courtyard, lively bar with entertaining barmen and music in the afternoon/evening. **AL-B** Hostal Los Frailes (Habaguanex), Teniente Rey entre Mercaderes y Oficios, T629510, F629718, recepcion@habaguanexhlosfrailes.co.cu Very close to the Plaza Vieja and Basílica Menor de San Francisco de Asís, recently converted colonial building with interior patio and fountain, staff wear Franciscan habits, 22 rooms, including 4 suites with balconies on to the street, the others don't have windows, a/c, phone, satellite TV, minibar, all meals at *La Marina* restaurant, 10m from hotel. **C** *Hostal Valencia* (Habaguanex), Oficios 53 esquina Obrapía, T623201, F335628. Joint Spanish/Cuban venture modelled on the Spanish *paradores*, rooms named after Valencian towns, tastefully restored building, nicely furnished, pleasant courtyard with vines, music, good restaurant (see below), the *Comendador*, next door, opened in 1999, separate but using the facilities of the *Valencia*. **D-E** *Residencia Santa Clara*, in convent buildings, entrance on Sol y Cuba, T613335, F335696, see page 168. Lovely, can be noisy early morning, nice café, poor breakfast.

C *Caribbean* (Horizontes), Paseo Martí 164 esquina Colón, T338241/233. Remodelled, nice   **Central Havana** lobby, good security, convenient, 36 rooms, try and get one on 5th floor, fan and TV, popular with budget travellers, but avoid noisy rooms at front and lower floors at back over deafening water pump. **C-D** *La Casa del Científico*, Prado 212 esquina Trocadero, T624511. Beautiful colonial building, charmingly old-fashioned, shared or private bathroom, cheap breakfast, luxurious dining room and lounge in classic style, very pleasant atmosphere, friendly staff, reservations essential, often booked by groups, best budget option in old city, Asistur office on site.

LL-L *Meliá Cohiba* (Cubanacán), Paseo entre 1 y 3, T333636, F334555, www.solmelia.es   **Vedado** International grand luxury, high rise and dominating the neighbourhood, 342 rooms, 120 suites, shops, gym, healthclub, pool, gourmet restaurant, piano bar. **LL-AL** *Nacional de Cuba* (Gran Caribe), O esquina 21, T333564, F335054. 467 rooms, some renovated, good bathrooms with lots of bottles of goodies, some package tours use it at bargain rates, generally friendly and efficient service, faded grandeur, dates from 1930, superb reception hall, note the vintage Otis high speed lifts, steam room, 2 pools, restaurants, bars, shops, business desk in lobby for emails, faxes etc, exchange bureau, gardens with old cannons on hilltop overlooking the Malecón and harbour entrance, great place to watch people and vehicles. **AL** *Victoria* (Gran Caribe), 19 y M, T333510, F333109, reserva@gcvictoria.gca.cma.net 31 rooms, small, quiet and pleasant, tasteful if conservative, good bathrooms, small pool, parking, good cooking, in good order. **AL-B** *Presidente* (Gran Caribe), Calzada y G (Presidentes), T334394, F333753. Oldest hotel in Havana, refurbished, 160 rooms, 10 suites, pool. **A** *Habana Riviera* (Gran Caribe), Paseo y Malecón, T334051, F333154. 330 rooms, 1950s block, Mafia style, appearance suffers from being so close to the glitzy *Meliá Cohiba*, desolate square outside, which together with the hotel entrance is awash with prostitutes after dark, does a good breakfast, no need to eat again all day. **A** *Tryp Habana Libre* (Gran Caribe), L y 23, T334011, F333141, comer@rllibre.com.cu 606 rooms in huge block, prices depend on the floor number, most facilities are here, eg hotel reservations, excursions, Polynesian restaurant, buffet, 24-hr coffee shop, *Cabaret Turquino* 2200-0400, US$20 per couple, shopping mall, includes liquor store, cigar shop, jewellery and perfume, handicrafts, shoe shop, Air Jamaica, Photoservice, Banco Financiero Internacional, postal service.

There is a string of 4-star hotels west along the coast that are used by package tour operators;   **Miramar &** guests are often here for the first and last nights of their stay; not particularly convenient for   **further west** visiting the old city, but you do get a sea view.

Private accommodation

D *Jesús y María*, Aguacate 518 entre Sol y Muralla, T611378. Upstairs suite, a/c bedroom with   **Old Havana** twin beds, bathroom, living room and kitchenette with fan, fridge, also small outside sitting   *Only reports and* area, comfortable, clean, breakfast extra but enormous and delicious. More modest and   *recommendations* cheaper rooms off the courtyard downstairs. **E** *Orlando y Liset*, Aguacate 509 Apto 301 entre   *received in 2000-2001* Sol y Muralla, T675766/612705. Two rooms in a lovely clean apartment, great view over Old   *are included here* Havana from the terrace, garage, elevator, help with arranging buses, taxis or accommodation in other towns. **E** *Gustavo Enamorado Zamora*, Teniente Rey (Brasil) 115 entre Cuba y San Ignacio, T626287, meilin@cubaautrement.com Two spacious double rooms, shared bathroom, hot water, nice patio, warm atmosphere, kind and helpful, street noise, French spoken, breakfast available. **E** *Marta y Israel*, Compostela 359 entre Lamparilla y Obrapía,

Vedado

Gulf of Mexico

Monumento a
Calixto García

Casa de las
Américas o
Galería
Haydée
Santamaría

CVD
José
Martí

Malecón

Calzada

Boca de la Chorrera

Malecón

9

13

Paseo

14

18

1

Museo de
la Danza

Sagrado
Corazón de Jesús

Teatro
Mella

Linea

To Jardines 1830

1

3

5

7 (Calzada)

Maxim

Linea

3

Casa de la
Cultura
de Plaza

Museo de Artes
Decorativas

Iglesia del
Carmelo

11

Catedral
Episcopal

13

Av 2

21

Paseo

19

VEDADO

5

Av 4

Amistur

8

15

6

17

21

10

12

16

14

18

23

25

27

29

17

Italian
Embassy

Castillo del
Príncipe

10
20

Zapata

31

Museo
del Deporte

Teatro
Nacional o
& Café
Cantante

Museo
Postal
Cubano

35

Cementerio de Colón

37

Paseo

Plaza de la
Revolución

39

Monumento
José Martí

San Antonio Chiquito

NUEVO VEDADO

San Pedro

Av de Carlos M de Céspedes

Av de Rancho Boyeros

Independencia

Ermita

Calzada de Ayestarán

Panchit

To Zoo, Botanical Gardens & Airport

N

0 metres 200
0 yards 200

■ **Sleeping**
1 Adita
2 Armando Gutiérrez
3 Blue Building
4 Capri

5 Casa Blanca
6 Colina
7 Eduardo
8 Eduardo Cañete
9 Habana Riviera

10 Hostal Belkis
11 Jorge Coalla Potts
12 Luís y Alicia
13 Meliá Cohiba
14 Morro

Cuba

Cuba

T626862. Two rooms, one bathroom, fans, clean showers, breakfast included. **E** *Ronaldo Montano*, San Ignacio 205 Apto 304 entre Lamparilla y Obrapía, T620109. Room with a/c, king size bed, nice bathroom but not en suite, English spoken.

E *Marilys Herrera González*, Concordia 714 altos entre Soledad y Aramburo, T700608, www.casaparticular.tripod.com Bathroom with warm water, kitchen, fridge, kitchen, a/c, TV, all modern, clean and comfortable, breakfast available, laundry offered, Marylis is very kind and caring. **E** *Carlos Luis Valderrama Moré*, Neptuno 404 entre San Nicolás y Manrique, 2nd floor, T679842. Carlos and Vivian are former teachers, he speaks English, 1940s apartment, 2 rooms, front room has balcony overlooking street, good bathrooms, hot water, delicious breakfast US$3. **E** *Nilo y Cary*, Gervasio 216 entre Concordia y Virtudes, T627109. Only Spanish spoken, friendly and helpful, food available. **E-F** *Paula Montero*, San Rafael 313 entre Rayo y San Nicolás, T627452. Three rooms, shared bathroom, hot water, a/c, close to Old Havana. **E-F** *Ana María Rodríguez López*, San Lázaro 160 Apto 1 entre Aguila y Crespo, T637478. First floor apartment, 2 rooms, a/c, TV, fridge, hot water, 50m from Malecón and short walk to old city. **F** *Daisy y Jorge Castro Pérez*, Lealtad 308 entre Neptuno y San Miguel, T785038, daisycastro@yahoo.com Two rooms, a/c, hot showers, warm family atmosphere, good breakfast and dinner, low prices. **F** *Rosa Artiles Hernández*, Crespo 117 bajos entre Colón y Trocadero, T627574. Excellent place, very clean and friendly, 3 rooms, 1 has private bathroom, other 2 share, hot water, shared use of fridge, a/c, fan, radio, separate entrance, own key, sitting area, beautiful car on ground floor, structural adjustments made to building to accommodate it, no food, son speaks English, Rosa's sister in Santa Clara also rents rooms.

Central Havana

Vedado

E *Eduardo*, 25 359 Apto B entre L y K, T320956. Very nice, new, well-designed rooms, fridge, TV in room. **E** *Eduardo Cañete*, 27 202 esq L, Apto 34, T327026, almost opposite *Hotel Colina*, third floor apartment. Large a/c double bedroom and smaller single room with fan, balcony with great view, hot water in shower, small kitchen, living room, fridge, TV, Eduardo speaks a little English, he moves in with his mother when the apartment is rented, excellent location. **E** *Natalia Rodés León*, 19 376 p11B, entre G y H, T328909. Two rooms, one bathroom, fridge, TV, friendly lady, fought with Fidel in the Sierra Maestra.. **E** *Jorge Coalla Potts*, I 456 apto 11 entre 21 y 23, T329032. Friendly, helpful, contacts throughout the island, hot water, comfortable, no meals. **E** *Luís y Alicia*, Línea 53 Apto 9 entre M y N, T328439. Friendly couple, both doctors, Spanish speaking only, rooms cleaned daily, long stays possible, good view from 9th floor, popular so call in advance. **E** *Vedado Habana*, Paseo 313 Apto 43 esq 15, T34174, www.geocities.com/vedadohabana Run by Raúl and Magaly, English spoken, helpful, double bed, a/c, fridge. **E** *Hostal Belkis*, Calle 19 entre 20 y 22, T38628. Three bedrooms, 2 double and 1 triple, a/c, private bathroom, breakfast of eggs, juice and fruit included, friendly and helpful. **E** *Pedro Mesa López y Tobias López Márquez*, F 609 Apto 12 entre 25 y 27, T329057. Quiet area except for rooster, 3 rooms with attached bathrooms, fridge, a/c, excellent breakfast US$4, only Spanish spoken by friendly couple in their 60s. **E** *Blue Building*, 5 717 Apto 1 entre 8 y 10, T39769, www.geocities.com/bluebuilding Run by Octavio Fundora and Dr Moraima Arébalo, single or double rooms, a/c, hot water, TV, VCR, CD player, kitchen, English spoken. **F** *Casa Blanca*, C 13 917, entre 6 y 8, T35697. Run by Jorge Luis Duany and his mother, book through internet, www.caspar.net/casa/ English spoken, room with 2 double beds, private bathroom, a/c, parking, great breakfast. **F** *Tu Cuevita*, 11 1304 Apto 5 entre 22 y 24, T39807, www.greatrentals.com/Cuba/1308.html Run by César Duany (brother of Jorge Luis), his wife and daughter, room with 2 beds, private bathroom, hot water, a/c, TV, CD player, parking, English spoken, bicycle available. **F** *Armando Gutiérrez*, 21 62 entre M y N, Apto 7, 4th (top) floor, T/F321876. Large a/c room with 2 beds, bathroom, clean, hot water, Armando and his wife, Teresa, speak a little English and French. **F** *Adita*, 9 257 entre J y I, T320643, whole of the top floor. Large double rooms, bathroom, lots of antiques, breakfast included.

Playa **C-D** *Casa Miramar*, 30 3502 entre 35 y 37, T295579, www.casamiramar.com Three double rooms in typical early 20th-century house, all different, with bathroom, high quality, breakfast US$5 on the terrace, linen changed daily.

Eating

There are many **street stalls** and places where you can pick up snacks, pizza etc. Note that their prices are listed in pesos even though there is a $ sign posted. These can work out very cheap and are good for filling a hole at lunchtime, but don't expect a culinary masterpiece. Make sure you eat pizza fresh from the oven, 4 pesos a piece.

Paladares
Paladares are privately owned restaurants in Cuban houses

Old Havana *Doña Eutimia*, Callejón del Chorro, just off Plaza Catedral, by entrance to Taller Experimental de Gráfica, rather obscured by a vine. Tiny, no window, no menu, open daily 1200-2400. *Alhambra*, Virtudes esquina Consulado. Open 0800-2400, good meals for US$2-3. *Sevilla's*, Obispo 465, altos, entre Villegas y Aguacate. Open from 1130, good seafood but expensive. *La Julia*, O'Reilly 506A, T627438. Meals US$10, large portions, creole food. *Doña Blanquita*, Prado 158 entre Colón y Refugio. Run by English-speaking lawyer, simple but good food, pork, chicken or eggs, US$7-9, upstairs, inside with fan or on balcony if dry, neon sign. *La Moneda* at San Ignacio 77. Limited choice, good for fish with salad, beans and rice with fried banana, around US$8. *Don Lorenzo*, Acosta 260A, entre Habana y Compostela. Good, not far from *Santa Clara*.

Central Havana *La Guarida*, Concordia 418 entre Gervasio y Escobar, T624940. Film location for *Fresa y Chocolate*, good food, fish a speciality, slow service. *Bellomar*, Virtudes 169A esq Amistad. Good, US$6 for fish, salad, rice, friendly and obliging. *La Tasquita*, Jovellar (27 de Septiembre) entre Espada y San Francisco, T798647. Wonderful food, good for vegetarians with delicious sweet potato and Cuban fried eggs, served on mountains of rice and beans, plus good salads.

Chinese market At Zanja and Rayo, 1 block west of Galiano, there are several *paladares* in a small street. Tables inside or outside, menus on view, you will be pestered for your custom. Do not expect authentic Chinese cuisine. Chop suey or chow mein is about the most Oriental you can get. Meals around US$5. *El Flamboyán*; opposite is *Tien Tan*. Open 1200-2100, always full. *Tong Po Laug*, No 10. Cheap, pesos accepted. *El Pacífico*. Impressive, looks like a Chinese temple, food can be very good if it is open, if there is water, if there is cooking gas and if there is any food, problems which affect all the restaurants around here, all prices in pesos, therefore very cheap, around US$3-4 for 2, eg lobster chop suey for 13 pesos, lemonade 60 centavos etc.

Vedado *Marpoly*, K 154, T322471. Meat, poultry and very fresh seafood, large portions, lovely ambiance, house filled with antiques. *La Fuente*, 10 303, T292836. No menu but excellent food, international style, elegant dining room. *La Palma*, 27 de Noviembre 303 entre M y N, T783488. Courtyard dining, local cooking, large portions. *Le Chansonnier*, 15 entre H y I, T323788. Cheap and cheerful, good. *Doña Nieves*, 19, entre 2 y 4, T306282. Open Tue-Sun 1200-2400. *El Helecho*, 6 entre Línea y 11. *El Moro*, 25 1003, entre Paseo y 2. *Los Amigos*, M y 19, opposite *Victoria*. Good, US$12 including drinks. *El Escorpión*, nearby, even better. *Villa Babi*, 27 965 entre 6 y 8, T306373. Beautiful old home, near Cementerio Colón.

Near the university *La Reina*, San Lázaro 1214, apto 1, entre M y N. Open 1230-0100, T781260. A plate of food with salad and rice will cost US$5. Opposite is *Casa Karlita*, San Lázaro 1207, T783182. Both have small signs on street.

Nuevo Vedado *Acapulco*, 26 659 entre 35 y 37, T300197. *El Palenque*, Zoológico 110 entre 36 y 38, T811392. Cuban and Chinese. *Romeo y Julieta*, Ulloa 349, esquina Zoológico, T811170. Italian.

Miramar *La Cocina de Liliam*, 48 1311, entre 13 y 15. Open Sun-Fri 1200-1600, 1900-2300, good Cuban food in lovely garden, fish, crab, popular with locals. *La Fontana*, Av 3 305 esq 48, T228337. Open 1200-2400, good Cuban food, extremely popular, ask for *menu de la casa* for non-inflated prices, arrive early or make a reservation. *Mi Jardín*, 66 517 esq Av 5, T234627. Good Mexican and Italian food for under US$15. *El Palio*, Av 1 entre 24 y 26. Open air, Italian, wonderful fresh fish with choice of creative sauces. *La Esperanza*, 16 105 entre 1 y 3, T224361. Open 1200-1600, 1900-2330, closed Thu. Small sign, very popular, traditional Cuban food, reservations advisable, run by Hubert and Manolo in their living room surrounded by their paintings.

Old Havana *La Bodeguita del Medio*, Empedrado 207, near the Cathedral, open 1030-0100, T338857. Made famous by Hemingway and should be visited if only for a drink (*mojito* – rum, crushed ice, mint, sugar, lime juice and carbonated water – is a must, US$6), food poor, expensive at US$35-40 for 2 but very popular. *Floridita*, on the corner of Obispo and Monserrate, next to the Parque Central, T338856. Open 1200-0100, another favourite haunt of Hemingway. Recent face-lift and now a very elegant bar and restaurant reflected in the prices (US$6 for a daiquiri), but well worth a visit if only to see the sumptuous decor and 'Bogart atmosphere'. *La Zaragozana*, almost next door, Monserrate entre Obispo y Obrapía. Oldest restaurant in Havana, international cuisine, good seafood and wine, expensive, good service but generally food nothing special. *Castillo de Farnés*, Monserrate 361 y Obrapía, T631260. Tasty Spanish food, reasonable prices, good for garbanzos and shrimp, open 24 hrs, Castro came here at 0445, 9 Jan 1959, with Che and Raúl. *A Prado y Neptuno*, address of the same name, opposite *Hotel Parque Central*. Trendy, popular with ex-pats, overrated food but excellent tiramisu. *El Patio*, San Ignacio 54 esquina Empedrado, Plaza Catedral, T618504. Expensive, small portions, slow service, but has selection of national dishes, open 24 hrs, tables outside take up most of the square, lovely location. *La Mina*, on Obispo esquina Oficios, Plaza de Armas, T620216. Open 1200-2400, also expensive, traditional Cuban food, sandwiches, pasta, lots of liqueur coffees, tables and chairs outside with live Cuban music. *Dominica*, O' Reilly esq Mercaderes, T662917. Italian, very smart, set menus US$25-30, pasta

Restaurants
Restaurants are state-owned

Cuba

from US$6, pizza US$4.50-12 depending on size, vegetarian options, credit cards. *Café Literario* (Habaguanex), bar/café in the Palacio del Segundo Cabo, O'Reilly 4 esq Tacón. Open 1000-2000. *D'Giovanni*, Italian, Tacón entre Empedrado y O'Reilly, lovely old building with patio and terrace, interesting tree growing through the wall, overpriced pizza and spaghetti. Handicrafts shop in doorway specializes in miniature ornaments. *Gentiluomo*, Bernaza esq Obispo. Pasta, pizza, US$3-6, very tasty food, a/c. *Al Medina*, Oficios, entre Obrapía y Obispo, T630862. Arab food in lovely colonial mansion, dishes priced between US$4-11, try chicken in sesame, lovely fresh fruit juices US$1, good coffee, some seating on large cushions, show at 2130 Fri, Sat, also Mosque and Arab cultural centre off beautiful courtyard, open 1200-2300. *Torre de Marfil*, Mercaderes, entre Obispo y Obrapía. Good, inexpensive Cantonese menu, chop suey US$4, open 1200-2200, T623466, *Hostal Valencia* restaurant *La Paella* features the best paella in Havana, good food, charming, open 1200-2300. *Cabaña* (Habaguanex), Cuba 12 esq Peña Pobre, T335670, facing Av del Puerto. Bar and restaurant open 24 hrs. *Café del Oriente*, Oficios y Amargura. High class food, pleasant. Next door is *Café El Mercado*, more informal, pleasant terrace, open 24 hrs. *Café O'Reilly* (Habaguanex), O'Reilly 203 entre Cuba y San Ignacio. Coffee, snacks, pizza, spaghetti, sandwiches or the usual chicken and pork. *Café París*, Obispo y San Ignacio. Serves good and reasonably priced chicken for US$3.50, beer US$1, snacks and pizza around the clock, live music, lively in evenings. *Hanoi*, Av Brasil 507 y Bernaza, T631681. Open daily 1200-2300, Cuban food, 3 courses for US$5, plenty of food, live music sometimes, nice atmosphere. *Cafetería Torre La Vega*, Obrapía 114, next to the Casa de México. Open 0900-2100, does cheap breakfast, bland chicken and chips US$1.70, better value spaghetti US$0.65, beer US$1. *La Dichosa*, Obispo esq Compostela. Good place for breakfast or a snack, US$2-4.

Restaurants **Vedado** *El Conejito*, M esquina 17, T324671. Open 1800-2400, specializes in rabbit in several different sauces, quite expensive but worth it, nightclub attached used by sex tourists. *La Torre*, 17 y M, at top of Edif Fosca, T325650. Open 1200-2400, French chef, best French food in Havana, about US$40 per person but worth it. In the *Habana Libre Hotel*, try *El Barracón*, traditional Cuban with good fish and seafood at lobby level, open 1200-midnight, T305011, and *Sierra Maestra* restaurant and *Bar Turquino* on the 25th floor (spectacular views of Havana which makes the food acceptable, service bad). Cabaret 2230-0430. Along and near La Rampa there are some cheaper pizzerías and self-service restaurants. *Trattoria Markas*, O entre 23 y 25. Good Italian, even has mozzarella and olive oil. *La Azucena China* on Cienfuegos. Chinese food, charges US$1-2 for a main course. *Casa de la Amistad*, Paseo entre 17 y 19. 1100-2300, for chicken, snacks and pizza. *Centro de Prensa Internacional*, 23 2502 esq O. Basement bar open until 1900, good hamburgers for US$1.

Miramar *El Tocororo* (national bird of Cuba), 18 y Av 3, T242209. Excellent food at US$40-60 a head, open Mon-Sat 1230-2400, old colonial mansion with nice terrace, great house band, no menu, ostrich steak, prices fluctuate widely but one of the best restaurants in town. *La Cecilia*, 5 entre 110 y 112, T241562. Good international food, mostly in open air setting, good salsa from 2200, dancing outside until 0300, US$20 cover charge.

Casablanca *La Divina Pastora*, Fortaleza de la Cabaña, open 1230-2300, T338341. Expensive, fish restaurant, food praised. *Los XII Apostoles*, nearby on Vía Monumental. Fish and good criollo food, good views of the Malecón.

Parque Lenín *Las Ruinas*, 100 esquina Cortina Presa in Parque Lenín, open 1200-2400, T443336. One of the best restaurants in Havana, the ruined plantation house has been incorporated into a modern structure, mosquitoes at dusk, tours of Parque Lenín often include a meal here, otherwise take a taxi, US$15, try to persuade the driver to come back and fetch you, as otherwise it is difficult to get back.

Playa *La Ferminia*, Av 5, entre 182 y 184, T336555. International, elegant, lovely gardens, expensive. *El Rancho Palco* (Cubanacán), Av 19 y 140, Playa, T235838. Set in lovely jungle garden near the Palacio de las Convenciones, very popular with ex-pats for its Argentine steaks, good barbecued chicken, meats, typical *criolla* cuisine, expensive, good live music. *Palenque*, beside Expocuba pavillions 17 y 190, Siboney, T218167. Cheap, good food, speciality suckling pig US$6, open air, popular with locals and ex-pats.

Vegetarians

There is little choice – fill up at breakfast and top up with street snacks. Your best bet is the restaurant in the Jardín Botánico, *El Bambú*, see above, where lunch is served at around 1400. The cafetería at the *Hotel Nacional* serves a big bowl of spaghetti for US$4.50 and the *Golden Tulip Parque Central* has a vegetarian option, eg vegetable lasagne. Italian restaurants such as *Dominica*, in Old Havana, see above, offer meatless pizza and pasta. Some *paladares* will serve meatless meals with advance notice, but always ask for the *congris* to be cooked in vegetable oil.

A visit to the *Coppelia* open-air **ice cream parlour**, 23 y L, Vedado, is recommended, open 1000-midnight, payment in pesos, you might have to queue for an hour or so, not unpleasant in the shade, or pay in dollars to avoid the queue, US$2 for small portion. The parlour found movie fame in *Strawberry and Chocolate*. The building is a good example of the architectural creativity of the post-Revolutionary years, by Mario Girona, 1966. Alternatively, sample the Coppelia ice-cream in the tourist hotels and restaurants and some dollar food stores.

Cuba

Bars

The bar not to miss in Old Havana for Hemingway fans is *La Bodeguita* (see above, also for *La Floridita*), a favourite for tour parties. *Lluvia de Oro*, Obispo esq Habana. Good place to drink rum and listen to loud rock music or salsa, also food, open 24 hrs. Try a *mojito* in any bar. Tour groups are often taken to *O'Reilly*, on the street of the same name, for a *mojito*, pleasant upstairs, with balcony and musicians. *Bar Monserrate*, Av Bélgica y Obrapía. Beer US$1, *mojito* US$2, plenty of flavour but not very generous shot of rum, hot dogs US$2.50, filling meal featuring unidentifiable meat in breadcrumbs US$4, interesting to sit and watch comings and goings, high level of prostitutes/girls, though bar staff seem to have unwritten agreement whereby girls are allowed in with a foreigner, or if they buy a drink, but if girl to punters ratio gets too high, some of the girls have to leave, hustling is not excessive though. *Fundación Distilería Havana Club*, Av del Puerto 162 entre Sol y Muralla, has a rum museum, 0900-1700, a shop selling Havana Club souvenirs, a courtyard restaurant and two bars, one with nightly music. The trendy place to go is the *Habana Café* in the *Meliá Cohiba*, a 1950s theme place with old cars, small Cubana plane hanging from the ceiling, memorabilia on the walls, Benny Moré music and large screen showing brilliant film of old Cuban musicians and artistes, expensive and meals not recommended, turkey burger or veggie burger US$6, *limonada* US$2, beer US$1.75, entrance to the left of the main hotel entrance, open 1200-0100, live music at weekends 2230-0100, cover charge US$5-10 depending on the band. *Casa de la Amistad*, Paseo 406 (see above), bar with a beautiful garden extension, tasty cheap light meals optional, very peaceful surroundings. For Graham Greene *aficionados*, go to the *Hotel Sevilla*, have a drink and tapas in the courtyard by the fountain and fantasize about Wormold from *Our Man in Havana* being recruited into MI6 in the gents (which have unfortunately been modernized).

Visitors find that ordinary bars not on the tourist circuit will charge them in dollars, if they let foreigners in at all. If it is a local bar and the Cubans are all paying in pesos, you will have to pay in US dollars. Even so, the prices in most places are not high by Caribbean standards

Entertainment

Radio Taino FM 93.3, English & Spanish language tourist station, gives regular details of wide range of Cuban bands playing and venues, particularly in the programme at 1700-1900. The newspaper, *Opciones*, also has a listing of what's on.

Music & dance

Casa De La Trova, San Lázaro, entre Belascoán y Gervasio, where locals go to hear traditonal Cuban music, US$5, especially on Fri from 1800, thoroughly recommended. Both here and at the *Casa de la Amistad* (see 'Museums in Vedado'), you are very unlikely to be hustled. *Casa de la Cultura de Plaza*, Calzada y 8, Vedado. Concerts and shows, different artistes, different times. For bolero admirers, try *Dos Gardenias*, with popular Chinese restaurant and bar, Av 7, esquina 26, Miramar, Playa, T242353. Traditional boleros 2230-0300. *UNEAC*, 17 entre G y H, rumba Sat and other Cuban band performances. Events listed at entrance. At the *Teatro Nacional* there is a piano bar upstairs where you can hear quality music, nueva trova, bolero etc, beer US$2.50, downstairs in the theatre there are live concerts such as a Nueva Trova show for 10 pesos. You can find rumba on Wed at the *Teatro Mella*, Línea entre A y B. Also *Palmares*, Malecón y E, for rumba performances and disco dancing, 2100 until late. *Holá Ola*, Malecón, occasionally has big national groups, entry in pesos. The *Casa de la Música* in Miramar is a great place with a disco and stage in a beautiful old house, but expensive at US$20 and people have complained about the rampant sex trade, band comes on at 0200, so this is a real late night place. *Jardines 1830*, Malecón y 20, beside the road tunnel to Miramar, T334521, 553090. Top salsa bands play here, music daily 2200-0400, US$20, also a restaurant, you will be mobbed at the door by desperate Cubans. Comedy shows every night from 2300 at *Club Almendares*, Márgenes del Río Almendares, 49 C y 28. Cubans love slapstick and Benny Hill-style humour, minorities such as gays get hammered. *Café Gato Tuerto*, O entre 17 y 19, Vedado, T552696, 662224. Son, trova and boleros performed 2400-0500. Bohemian people and post-modern décor, funky, no cover charge, good restaurant on 1st floor, eat on balcony overlooking Malecón and *Hotel Nacional*.

Jazz *Coparrun*, *Hotel Riviera* (big names play there), jazz in the bar recommended. Fri nights at *Meliá Cohiba* from 2100. *La Zorra y el Cuervo*, 23 y O, Vedado, T662402. Entry US$5, opens 2130 for 1st set, 2nd set 2330, very popular with locals and tourists, great jazz and salsa every night, get there before 2300 if you want a table, gets packed later. UNEAC, H y 17, Thu nights, but check listings on gate. *Jazz Café*, Galería Primera y Paseo, Vedado, top floor of blue glass building. Live jazz bands from 2300 every night, including *Irakere*, US$5 cover charge, bar and restaurant, very popular, can be hard to get a table. During the annual Jazz Festival in Dec you can hear international as well as Cuban stars, free or US$5-10 per show, based at *Hotel Riviera* but in the 2 weeks before there are also events at the *Nacional* and the *Habana Libre*. Information from the Instituto de la Música, 15 entre D y E, Vedado, ask for schedule from Rita Rosa.

Nightclubs *Tropicana* (closed Mon, Línea del Ferrocarril y 72 No 4504, Marianao, 2200-0200) is internationally famous and open-air (entry refunded if it rains). It costs US$70 for the show and a 3-course meal, or US$60 for the show and a quarter bottle of rum and coke. Best to take a tour, which will include transport, as a taxi from Old Havana costs US$12. Reservations are recommended, T270110 between 1000 and 1600. If you fancy a cheap drink or snack go to *Rodneys*, a pseudo 1950s bar and restaurant designed by Cuban painter, Nelson Domínguez, just beyond the entrance to the show. All the main hotels have their own cabarets, eg *Parisien* at *Hotel Nacional*, excellent long show for US$30, make a reservation. *Capri* is recommended, at US$15 and longer show than *Tropicana* but the drinks are expensive at US$40 for a bottle of best rum. *Aché* in the *Meliá Cohiba*. The *Habana Libre* cabaret and disco is on the 25th floor, amazing views, the roof opens and you can dance under the stars, US$10, if you are in a group 1 person needs a passport, drinks expensive. Also *Havana Club*, the *Comodoro* disco (US$10), crowded, Western-style, US$5 for *Hotel Comodoro* guests. *Café Cantante*, Teatro Nacional, Paseo y 39, Plaza de la Revolución. Open nightly from 2200, 3 bands, US$10, sometimes it is US$15, although this place is well regarded, it is popular with *jinetero/as* and lone travellers have commented on feeling uncomfortable. *La Finca* at Playas del Este. The *Cabaret Nacional*, San Rafael y Prado, is a cheap version of the *Tropicana*, US$5 entry but expensive drinks. Shows at 2330 and 0030. Lots of prostitutes.

Cinemas The best are *Yara* (opposite *Habana Libre* hotel, T329430). *Acapulco*, 26 entre 35 y 37, Nuevo Vedado, T39573, from 1630. *Chaplin*, 23 entre 10 y 12, T311101. Arty films at 1700 and 2000, shop good for film memorabilia. *Payret*, Prado 503, esquina San José, T633163. Films shown continuously from 1230, and *La Rampa*, Rampa esquina O, T786146, from 1630. Many others, 2 pesos. Annual Film Festival in Dec (overlaps with Jazz Festival, above) in all cinemas. International films, no translations into English. Information in *Hotel Nacional*.

Teatro Mella, Línea entre A y B, Vedado, T38696. Specializes in modern dance; more tradi- **Theatres**
tional programmes at *Gran Teatro de la Habana* on Parque Central next to *Hotel Inglaterra*,
T6130769. Claims to be the oldest working theatre in the world, opened in 1837, wonderful
baroque building which seats 2,000. The Conjunto Folklórico Nacional and Danza
Contemporánea dance companies sometimes perform here. Highly recommended.
US$0.60. In Miramar, *Teatro Karl Marx*, Av 1 entre 8 y 10, T300720, 305521, renovated in
2000 and now famous for hosting the first rock concert by a Western band, *Manic Street
Preachers*, who played there in 2001 in the presence of Fidel Castro. *Amadeo Roldán*, Calzada
y D, Vedado. Newly renovated concert hall where you can hear the Orquesta Sinfonía
Nacional. Pay in pesos. *Opus* bar, open 1500-0300, serves light meals. Havana has some very
lively theatre companies. Fringe theatres include *Teatro El Sótano*, K entre 25 y 27, Vedado;
Sala Herbert de Blanck, Calzada entre A y B, Vedado; *Teatro Trianón*, Línea entre Paseo y A,
Vedado; *Teatro Fausto*, Prado y Colón, Habana Vieja. *Amistur* travel agency can help with
theatre and nightclub bookings.

Shopping

Original lithographs and other works of art can be purchased or commissioned directly from **Works of art**
the artists at the *Galería del Grabado*, at the back of the *Taller Experimental de Gráfica de la* **& handicrafts**
Habana, Callejón del Chorro 62, Plaza de la Catedral (open all day, closed Sun, T620979, *Shopaholics should*
F338121). You can watch the prints and engravings being made and specialist courses are *be aware that Cuba*
available, for 1 month, US$250, or 3 months, US$500. The *Taller Serigrafía* is another big *is not going to satisfy*
workshop, on Cuba 513, making screen prints; again, you can watch them being made and *your urges. There is*
buy things. *La Victoria*, Obispo 366 entre Compostela y Habana, T627914. Open 1000-1900, *little to spend your*
is an art gallery with a large choice of paintings at good prices, and books, owned by artist *money on without a*
Natividad Scull Marchena. Reproductions of works of art are sold at *La Exposición*, San Rafael *great deal of effort*
12, Manzana de Gómez, in front of Parque Central. Handicraft and tourist souvenir markets
have sprung up, especially the *feria de artesanías* (see below), on D and Av 1, Vedado, and on
the Rampa, open Tue-Sun 0900-1600; Che Guevara and religious *Santería* items lead the
sales charts. The *feria de artesanías* along Av del Puerto by Castillo de la Real Fuerza is a platform for many talented young artists to show off their skills, you may pick up a bargain, or
you may be asked to pay Miami-type prices. You need documentation to take works of art
out of the country or you may have them confiscated at the airport; galleries will provide the
necessary paperwork and even vendors in the market can give you the necessary stamp. Also
sold here are carvings, crochet, ceramics, boxes, jewellery, T-shirts, baseball bats and black
coral (illegal to bring in to many countries, so avoid). There is a special boutique, the *Palacio
de la Artesanía*, in the Palacio Pedroso (built 1780) at Cuba 64 (opposite Parque Anfiteatro),
where the largest selection of Cuban handicrafts is available; the artisans have their workshops in the back of the same building (open Mon-Sat 0900-1900).

In the Palacio del Segundo Cabo, O'Reilly 4 y Tacón, is the Instituto Cubano del Libro and 3 **Bookshops**
bookshops: *Librería Grijalba Mondadori*, excellent selection of novels, dictionaries, art
books, children's books from around the world, all in Spanish; *Librería Bella Habana*,
T628091-3, Cuban and international publications, and *Librería UNESCO Cultura*, which
stocks UNESCO publications, books on Cuba, a few thrillers in English and postcards. There
are second-hand bookstalls outside on the Plaza de Armas where you can pick up a treasure
if you know what to look for. *Casa Editorial Abril*, at end of El Prado, opposite Capitol. English,
French, German books, but selection poor, lots of scientific and cultural books on Cuba, in
Spanish. Other good bookshops near Parque Central: *Ediciones Cubanas* on Obispo 527
esquina Bernaza, T38942, 631989. Books on Cuba, also some stationery. *Fernando Ortíz*, 27
160 esq L, T329653. Quite a wide selection, mostly in Spanish, and some beautiful postcards.
El Siglo de las Luces, Neptuno esq Aguila, T635321, near Capitolio. Good place to buy *son*,
trova and jazz (rock) records. *Instituto Hidrográfico*, Mercaderes entre Oficios y Obispo,
T613625, F332869. Maps and charts, both national and regional, also prepaid phone cards.

Music & other souvenirs *Artex* shop on L esq 23 has excellent music section and tasteful T-shirts and postcards, T320632, open Mon-Sat 0900-2100, Sun 1000-1600. The *Caracol* chain, in tourist hotels (eg *Habana Libre*) and elsewhere, sell tourists' requisites and other luxury items such as chocolates, biscuits, wine, clothes, require payment in US$ (or credit cards: Mastercard, Visa).

Food For food shopping, there is the *Focsa Supermarket*, or the *Amistad*, on San Lázaro, just below Infanta. The *Isla de Cuba* supermarket on Máximo Gómez entre Factoría y Suárez has the best selection of food in Old Havana, with prices stamped on the goods to prevent overcharging. There are tourist mini-stores in most hotels, but they do not sell fresh food. The International Press Centre (open to the public) on La Rampa sells items like chocolate for dollars in a shop to the right of the entrance. Bread is available at the French bakery on 42 y 19 and in the Focsa shopping complex on 17 entre M y N.

Markets Farmers are allowed to sell their produce (root and green vegetables, fruit, grains and meat) in free-priced city *agromercados*. You should pay for food in pesos. There are markets in Vedado at 19 y B; in Nuevo Vedado, Tulipán opposite Hidalgo; in the Cerro district at the Monte and Belascoaín crossroads; and in Central Havana, the Chinese market at the junction of Zanja and Av Italia where you can eat at street food stalls (avoid Mon, not a good day).

Tour operators
See page 154
Bureaux in all the major hotels. Tours can be arranged all over Cuba by bus or air, with participants picked up from any hotel in Havana at no extra charge. Examples include a tour of the city's colonial sites (US$15, 4 hrs); a trip to the *Tropicana* cabaret (US$60, 4 hrs, US$70 with supper); Cayo Largo for the day by air with boat trip, snorkelling, optional diving, lunch (US$119, 12 hrs); Cayo Largo overnight (US$119); Guamá and the Península de Zapata with a stop en route at the *Finca Fiesta Campesina*, tour of crocodile farm, lunch (US$44, 9 hrs); Viñales and Pinar del Río, visiting *mogotes*, caves and tobacco factory, lunch (US$44, 9 hrs); a day on the beach at Varadero (US$35 or US$45 with lunch, 10 hrs); Trinidad and Cienfuegos overnight, visiting the colonial city and the Valle de los Ingenios (US$115); tour of Las Terrazas with walking and river bathing, lunch (US$44, 10 hrs). Prices vary between agencies and you can negotiate a reduction without meals. *Amistur*, Paseo 646, entre 19 y 17, T333544, F333515, is more geared towards independent travellers and can book you into good hotels in all the major cities at reduced rates. They are helpful with transport and tours and can also book excursions, restaurants, theatre and nightclubs, or help you find a guide.

Guides Many Cubans in Havana tout their services in their desperate quest for dollars, but in Old Havana this is now less of a problem since Castro's crackdown in 1999 which put police on every street corner. Elsewhere, they are a considerable nuisance and nearly all tourists complain of being hassled. If you feel you trust someone as a guide, make sure you state exactly what you want, eg private car, *paladar*, accommodation, and fix a price in advance to avoid shocks when it is too late. *Casas particulares* can often be a good source of information on reputable guides. You may find, however, that the police will assume your guide is a prostitute and prohibit him or her from accompanying you into a hotel.

Transport

Local
See also page 156
Bicycle hire Check the bicycle carefully (take your own lock, pump, even a bicycle spanner and puncture repair kit; petrol stations have often been converted into bicycle stations, providing air and tyre repairs). Cycling is a good way to see Havana, especially the suburbs; some roads in the Embassy area are closed to cyclists. The tunnel underneath the harbour mouth has a bus designed specifically to carry bicycles and their riders. Take care at night as there are few street lights and bikes are not fitted with lamps.

Buses The easiest way of getting around Havana is with *Vaivén*, a Rumbos service which covers many places of interest. For US$4 per day you can get on and off a 30-seater bus along the route; buses pass every 55 mins and there are 23 stops, several of which are hotels. There is a regular service on the *camellos*, long articulated buses on a truck bed, 20 centavos. They cover the main suburbs, M1 to Playa, M2 to the airport, M6 to Alamar, and mostly leave from Parque de la Fraternidad. Ask for the right queue. Other buses cost 40 centavos.

Car hire Hiring a car is not recommended for getting around Havana, roads are badly signed and there have been many accidents with tourists driving rental cars.

Taxis A fleet of white '*Turistaxis*' with meters has been introduced for tourists' use; payment in US$: sample fare, Ciudad Vieja to Vedado US$4. A cheaper way of getting around is via *Panataxi*, a call-out service, T555555, Panataxis also wait just outside the Plaza de la Catedral, the *Meliá Cohiba*, on 17 entre L y M, and at the airport, or ask your hotel to call one. They are navy and yellow Citröen cars, so they are the most comfortable, reliable and still the cheapest dollar service, at under US$15 from the airport to Vedado. *Habanataxi* is a call-out taxi service, T419600. Others include *Gaviota*, T331730, *Taxi OK*, T249518-9, 241226, *MiCar*, T242444, and *Fénix*, T639720/639580. The cheapest taxis are the very smallest. Ask for the '*oferta especial*' and you will be charged only US$0.45 per km, T335539-42. For longer trips some companies charge by the hour and some by the km, eg for an excursion including Cojímar, Santa María del Mar and Regla, Panataxi quoted US$25 while Habanataxi quoted US$35. Licensed *Cuban peso taxis* are mostly reserved for hospital runs, funerals etc, but after completing their quotas they can now freelance, see page 157. Beware of private moonlighters (yellow licence plates, often identifiable by their harassment); they could charge you over the odds, generally are not paying any taxes and you have no come-back in the case of mishaps. In Habana Vieja and Vedado, bicycle or tricycle taxis are cheap and readily available, a pleasant way to travel. A short journey will cost US$1, Old Havana to Vedado US$3, or pay around US$5 per hour, bargaining is acceptable.

Buses Terminal de Omnibus Interprovinciales, Av Rancho Boyeros (Independencia) by the Plaza de la Revolución. There are two ticket offices, the one painted blue is for foreigners and you pay in dollars. There is also a dollar tourist service, *Víazul*, which leaves from Av 26 entre Av Zoológico y Ulloa, Nuevo Vedado, T811413, 811108, 815652, F666092. See below under individual towns for details.

Long distance
See also page 156

Ferries There are ferries from Habana Vieja to Casablanca and Regla, which depart from San Pedro opposite Calle Santa Clara. If you are facing the water, the Casablanca ferry docks on the left side of the pier and goes out in a left curve towards that headland, and the Regla ferry docks on the right side and goes out in a right curve.

Trains Estación Central in Av Egido (de Bélgica), Havana, has what is claimed to be the oldest engine in Latin America, *La Junta*, built in Baltimore in 1842. Get your tickets in advance from LADIS office on Arsenal y Aponte, T614259, open 0800-2000 daily, pay in US$. The El Trece train leaves Estación Central daily at 1640, arrives Santiago de Cuba 0700, US$30.50, stopping at lots of places and cheaper than the Locura Azul train, which departs 1930 Mon, Wed, Thu, Sat and Sun, 11½ hrs theoretically. You can do the same journey by road in a fraction of the time, eg Havana-Pinar del Río, 2 hrs or less by taxi, 7-8 hrs by train. It is not unusual for the trains to break down, in fact Cubans refer to this as 'normal service'. It will be mended and carry on, but be prepared to spend a serious amount of time travelling.

Airlines Most are in Havana, at the seaward end of Calle 23 (La Rampa), Vedado. *Cubana*, www.cubana.cu, for international sales, 23 64, esq Infanta, T3344469/334950, for national sales, Infanta esq Humboldt, T706714 and phone numbers above; *Cubana Express* is at Av 5 entre 82 y 84, Miramar, just before the turning to the *Hotel Comodoro*, T242331/242833, open weekdays only. *Aerocaribbean*, 23 esq P, T334543, F335016, or at the airport, T453013, 451135, F335017. *Aeroflot*, 23 64, esq Infanta, T333200/333759, F333288, at the airport, T335432. *Air Jamaica*, Hotel Tryp Habana Libre, T334011. *ALM*, 23 64 entre Infanta y P, T333730, F333729. *AOM French Airlines*, 23 64, Interior, T334098, 333997, F333783, at the airport, F335464. *British Airways* flights should be confirmed with

Directory

Cuba

Cubana. *Copa*, 23 64, Interior, esq Infanta, T331758, 333657, F333951. *Iberia*, 23 74 esq P, T3350412, 335064, F335061, at the airport T335063. *LTU*, 23 64 esq Infanta, T333549/333525/333590, F332789, at the airport F335359. *Martinair Holland*, 23 esq P, T334364, 333730, F333729. *Mexicana de Aviación*, 23 esq P, T3335312, F333077, at the airport F335051.

Banks For dollar services, credit card withdrawals, TCs and exchange, *Banco Financiero Internacional*, Línea esq O, T333003/333148, F333006, open Mon-Fri 0800-1500, last day of the month until 1200, branch in *Habana Libre* complex, T333429, F333795, same times, and another branch in Miramar, 18 111 entre 1 y 3, T332058, F332458, charges 3% commission for foreign exchange deals. Exchange bureau in *Hotel Nacional*, open 0800-1200, 1230-1930, credit card cash advances. Buró de Turismo in *Tryp Habana Libre* also gives credit card cash advances. *Banco Metropolitano*, Línea 63 y O, T5531168, open Mon-Fri 0830-1500, cheapest (2%) for changing TCs, most hotels and airport cambios charge 4%. A Visa ATM in the lobby of the *Golden Tulip Parque Central* issues convertible pesos to a certain limit. Credit card advances from exchange houses, Cadecas, incur a standard 1.5% handling charge.

Communications Post: Oficios 102, opposite the Lonja, and in the *Hotel Nacional*, *Hotel Plaza* (5th floor, walk through dining area and turn right on to the terrace, open 0700-1900) and in the *Hotel Habana Libre* building. Also on Calle Ejido, next to central railway station and under the Gran Teatro de La Habana. Telephones: *The Empresa Telecomunicaciones de Cuba* (Etecsa) is on Av 33 1427 entre 18 y 14, Miramar, T332476, F332504. *Cubacel Telefonía Celular* is at 28 510 entre 5 y 7, Miramar, T332222, F331737. The large hotels of 4 or 5 stars such as the *Habana Libre*, *Plaza Central* and *Nacional* have international telephone, email and fax facilities. At the *Habana Libre* email is available 0700-1500. The *Parque Central* has an efficient business centre. At the *Hotel Plaza*, 5th floor, you can send faxes, US$5 to USA, US$7.50 to UK per min. **Email** is also available at the Post Office under the Ministerio de Comunicaciones on Plaza de la Revolución and the Bilblioteca de Ciencias in the Capitolio. There are 6 terminals, US$5 per hour, open Mon-Fri 0900-1700, you may have to wait up to 45 mins for one to be free. There is a separate queue for those wanting to use Hotmail or Yahoo, which don't work on all the computers because of the US embargo prohibiting the sale of strong encryption software to Cuba.

Embassies & consulates All in Miramar, unless stated otherwise: *Argentina*, 36 511 entre 5 y 7, T242972/2549, F242140. *Austria*, 4 101, esquina 1, T242852, F241235. *Belgium*, Av 5 7406 esquina 76, T242410, F241318. *Brazil*, Lamparilla, Habana Vieja, T6690512. *Canada*, 30 518, esquina 7, T2425167, F241069. *France*, 14 312 entre 3 y 5, T242132, 2422380, F241439. *Germany*, 13 652, F331586. *Greece*, Av 5, 7802, esquina 78, T242854, F241784. *Japan*, Office 501-512, Miramar Trade Centre, Av 3 esq 80, T333453, F248902. *Mexico*, 12 518 entre 5 y 7, T242498, F242294, open 0900-1200, Mon-Fri. *Netherlands*, 8 307 entre 3 y 5, T242511/2, F242059. *Peru*, 30 109 entre 1 y 3, T242477, F242636. *Sweden*, 34 510 entre 5 y 7, Miramar, T242831, F241194. *Switzerland*, Av 5, 2005, T242611, F241148. *UK*, 34, 702 y 704, T241771, F248104, 249214. embrit@ceniai.inf.cu. Commercial Section, open Mon-Fri 0800-1530. *Venezuela*, 36A 704 esquina 42, T242662, F242773. *The US Interests Section* of the Swiss Embassy, Calzada entre L y M, Vedado, T333551, 334401. *Spain*, Cárcel 51 esquina Zulueta, Habana Vieja, T3380256, F338006.

Medical facilities *The Cira García Clinic*, 20 4101 esquina 41, Miramar, T242811/14, F241633, payment in dollars, also the place to go for emergency dental treatment, the pharmacy (T24051, open 24 hrs) sells prescription and patent drugs and medical supplies that are often unavailable in other pharmacies, as does the *Farmacia Internacional*, Av 41, esq 20, Miramar (T245051, open Mon-Fri 0900-1700, Sat 0900-1200). *Camilo Cienfuegos Pharmacy*, L and 13, Vedado, T333599, open daily 0800-2000. *Optica Miramar*, 43 1803 entre 18 y 18A, T242590, ophthalmology consultants, contact lenses. *Servimed* (turismo de salud) 18 4304 entre 43 y 47, Playa, T332658, F332948, information on special treatments, spas and health facilities around the country. All hotels have a doctor on permanent duty, US$25 per consultation.

Useful addresses Police: T820116. Fire: T811115, 798561-69. Asistur: in the *Casa del Científico* hotel, Prado esq Trocadero, Old Havana, T625519, 638284, F338087, for medical and dental emergencies, repatriations, financial and legal problems, travel insurance claims, reservations.

Beaches around Havana

The beaches in Havana, at Miramar and Playa de Marianao are rocky, polluted and generally very crowded in summer. The beach clubs belong to trade unions and may not let non-members in. Those to the east, El Mégano, Santa María del Mar and Bacuranao, for example, are much better. To the west of Havana are Arena Blanca and Bahía Honda, which are good for diving and fishing but difficult to get to unless you have a car.

Off Avenida 5, 20 minutes by taxi from Havana, is the Marina Hemingway tourist complex, in the fishing village of **Santa Fe**. Fishing and scuba diving trips can be arranged here as well as other watersports and land-based sports. The Offshore Class 1 World Championship and the Great Island speedboat Grand Prix races have become an annual event in Havana, usually held during the last week in April, attracting power boat enthusiasts from all over the world. In May and June the marina hosts the annual Ernest Hemingway International Marlin Fishing Tournament, and in August and September the Blue Marlin Tournament. There are 140 slips with electricity and water and space for docking 400 recreational boats. The resort includes the hotel *El Viejo y El Mar* (Cubacán, 248 y Av 5, Santa Fe, T336336, F336823), restaurants, bungalows and villas for rent, shopping, watersports, facilities for yachts, sports and a tourist bureau.

Marina Hemingway

Cuba

Watersports *Club Náutico Internacional 'Hemingway'*, Residencial Turístico 'Marina Hemingway', Av 5 y 248 Playa, T/F241689, 246653. *Cubanacán Náutica 'Marina Hemingway'*, same address, T241150-57, F241149, VHF 16 and 72. Open Mon-Fri 0800-1700, boat trips, sport fishing, US$450 half day, motorized sports (waterskiing, banana boat), catamarans, sailing lessons in dinghies, windsurfing, diving and snorkelling. The dive centre, *Centro de Buceo La Aguja*, takes up to 8 divers on the boat.

Playas del Este

This is the all-encompassing name for a string of beaches within easy reach of Havana. East of the city is the pleasant little beach of **Bacuranao**, 15 km from Havana. At the far end of the beach is a villa complex with restaurant and bar. Then come **Tarará** (famous for its hospital where the Chernobyl victims have been treated), **El Mégano** and **Santa María del Mar**, with a long, open beach which continues eastwards to the intimate, pretty beach at **Boca Ciega** and **Guanabo** (four train departures daily in July and August from Estación Cristal, Havana, and buses from Havana), a pleasant, non-touristy beach 27 km from Havana, but packed with Habaneros at weekends. Cars roll in from Havana early on Saturday mornings, line up and deposit their cargo of sun worshippers at the sea's edge. The quietest spot is **Brisas del Mar**, at the east end. As a general rule, facilities for foreigners are at Santa María del Mar and for Cubans at Guanabo. The latter is therefore cheaper and livelier. Tourism bureaux offer day excursions (minimum six people) for about US$15 per person to the Playas del Este, but for two or more people its worth hiring a private car for the day for US$20-25.

LL-B *Villa Tarará*, T335510, F335499. 121 a/c units in villas with 2-5 rooms, TV, fridge, porch and parking, at the marina, restaurant, snack bar, grill, disco, watersports. **LL-L** *Villa Los Pinos* (Gran Caribe), Av de las Terrazas 21 entre 4 y 5, Santa María del Mar, T971361, F971524, informatica@pinos.gca.cma.net 26 houses, 2 rooms, sleep 4, most with pools or near the beach, grill restaurant, popular with Italians, Spanish and French in that order, lots of repeat guests, comfortable, private, good for entertaining friends, very flexible management, multilingual staff. **B-E** *Aparthotel Las Terrazas*, Av de las Terrazas entre 10 y Rotonda, T971344. 154, 1-3 bedroomed apartments, each with cooking facilities, fridge, radio and TV, in rather unattractive block opposite the beach, 2-tier swimming pool with children's area, restaurant,

Sleeping

Contact Horizontes for cheap all-inclusives, Islazul has hotels mainly for the cuban market, cheap and basic

bar, tourist bureau, disco in separate building, car and moped rental, great location but rather run down. **E** *Villa Playa Hermosa* (Islazul), 5 Av y 470, T962774, Guanabo. 33 rooms or chalets, good value, often used by party faithful and honeymooners. **E** *Gran Vía* (Islazul), 5 Av y 462, T962271, between Boca Ciega and Guanabo. Friendly service, better food than at the Horizontes hotels, US$3 for TV, US$5 key charge, live music. **Casas particulares** *Sra Eyda Iglesias Mora*, 494 A 5B10 entre 5B y 5C, T2903. **E-F** *Hugo Puig Roque*, 5 Av 47203 entre 472 y 474, T963426. Choice of rooms, bathrooms fair, good location, friendly. Prices negotiable, depending on season and length of stay. **E** *Aimé*, 472, Guanabo. Apartment with 2 double rooms, bathroom, living room, kitchen, porch. It may be possible to find privately rented apartments in Guanabo for US$15 a night with kitchen, ask around.

Eating *Restaurante Chino*, Via Blanco Km 19, one of the best Chinese restaurants in Cuba. There are many *paladares* in Guanabo and elsewhere along the coast, reasonable prices. If you are self-catering, there is a farmers' market in Guanabo selling fresh fruit and vegetables 6 days a week and a supermarket for bread and tinned goods. Hotels in Guanabo have cheap food, with live music. *Cafetería Pinomar*, Santa María del Mar, fried chicken, US$2.50 for a half, open 24 hrs, attractive. *Pizzería Al Mare*, 482, Guanabo, for pizza. *Café River Ristorante*, behind *Villa Playa Hermosa* entre 472 y 474. All dishes under US$3, beer US$0.85, open 1200-0200, cozy, funky.

Watersports The hotels provide some non-motorized watersports. *Marina Tarará*, run by Marinas Puertosol, Vía Blanca Km 19, T971462, F971333, VHF16, 19, 08, 72, has moorings for 50 boats, VHF communications and provisioning, yacht charters, deep sea fishing (US$250-450 per day depending on type of boat) and scuba diving, all of which can be arranged through the hotel tour desks. Note the advertising: the sea is funnier at Tarará.

Transport The 400 bus from near the Estación Central de Trenes can get you there, but getting back to Havana is problematic the longer you stay. The standard private taxi price is US$10, but getting a return taxi is more difficult. Cycling is a good way to get there. Use the *cyclobus* from the end of Zulueta to go through the tunnel under Havana Bay, or the ferry from the Aduanas building, and cycle through Regla and Guanabacoa.

Directory **Medical facilities** *Clínica Internacional Habana del Este*, Av de las Terrazas, between *Aparthotel Las Terrazas* and *Hotel Tropicoco* in Santa María del Mar, T06872689.

West from Havana

A dual carriage highway has been completed almost to **Pinar del Río**, the major city west of Havana. It takes two hours to get to Pinar del Río on the autopista, a rather surreal experience, with modern motorway junctions but virtually no traffic using them except horse-drawn buses to nearby villages. The autopista passes through flat or gently rolling countryside, with large stretches of sugar cane, tobacco fields and some rice fields, scattered royal palms and distant views of the Cordillera de Guaniguanico. An alternative route is to leave the autopista at **Candelaria** or **Santa Cruz de los Pinos** for the Carretera Central, quite a good road which adds only 20 minutes to the journey. It passes through more intensively farmed countryside, with citrus and other fruit trees. Villages straggle along the road, with colonnaded single storey traditional houses and newer post-Revolution concrete block structures.

Las Terrazas
Phone code: 8
Colour map 1, grid B2

On the autopista, 51 km west of Havana, the Sierra del Rosario appears on the right and a roadside billboard announces the turning to **Las Terrazas/Moka**, 4 km north of the autopista. However, after that there is little signposting; you will have to ask the way. The **Biosphere Reserve** covers 260 sq km of the eastern Sierra del Rosario. ■ *Admission to the Reserve, US$3, unless you have a reservation at the hotel.* Las Terrazas was built in 1971 as a forestry and soil conservation station, with nearby slopes terraced to prevent erosion. It is a pleasant settlement of white-painted houses overlooking the lake of San Juan. In Las Terrazas there is a *paladar* (US$7), craft workshops, a gym, a cinema and a museum which sometimes holds *canturías* or folk music sessions. The hills behind the hotel rise to the **Loma del Salón** (564m). There are several easy hiking trails of 3-8 km or more demanding whole-day hikes. The cost of a day hiking with a professional ecologist as guide is US$33-41 for one person, falling to US$14-18 with six people. Other activities include riding (US$6 per hour), mountain bikes (US$1 per hour), rowing on the lake (US$2 per hour) and fishing.

Sleeping Above the village is the 26-room **B** *Hotel Moka*, run in co-operation with the Cuban Academy of Sciences as an ecotourism centre, breakfast US$5, other meals US$15, transfer from Havana US$32, a/c, satellite TV, T852921, 802694, Havana marketing office, T333814/3900, F335516. The hotel complex is beautifully designed and laid out, in Spanish colonial style with tiled roofs, staff are friendly and knowledgeable, gardens behind the hillside site have a tennis court and a pleasant swimming pool where you can have food and drinks. This is an unusual opportunity to stay in a nature reserve with tropical evergreen forests, 850 plant species, 82 bird species, an endemic water lizard, the world's 2nd smallest frog and world-class experts on tap. Even the hotel receptionist is an ecology PhD.

If travelling by car, you can make a detour to Soroa, a spa and resort in the Sierra del Rosario, 81 km southwest of the capital, either by continuing 18 km west then southeast from Moka through the Sierra del Rosario, or directly from the autopista, driving northwest from Candelaria. As you drive into the area from the south, a sign on the right indicates the **Mirador de Venus** and **Baños Romanos**. Past the baths is the *Bar Edén* (open till 1800), where you can park before walking up to the Mirador (25 minutes, free on foot, US$3 on a horse). Fine views of the southern plains, the forest-covered Sierra and Soroa itself. Lots of birds, butterflies, dragonflies and lizards around the path; many flowers in season.

Soroa
Phone code: 8

Further north is an **Orchidarium** with over 700 species of which 250 are native to Cuba, as well as ferns and begonias (check if the orchids are in bloom before visiting). ■ *Guided tours between 0830-1140, 1340-1555 daily, US$3 and the Castillo de las Nubes restaurant (1200-1900, US$5-6).*

Sleeping **C-D** *Horizontes Villa Soroa*, T852122. 49 cabins and 10 self-catering houses, a/c, phone, radio, some have VCR and private pool, restaurant *El Centro* (quite good), lunch US$8, dinner US$10, disco, bar, Olympic-sized swimming pool, bike rental, riding nearby and handicrafts and dollar shop. A peaceful place. The hotel runs 1 day, gently paced hikes around the main sights of the area with picnic for US$10, to caves for US$12.

Pinar del Río

The capital of Pinar del Río province is lively and attractive, and it gives a good taste of provincial Cuba. The centre consists of single-storey neo-classical houses with columns, some with other interesting architectural detail.

Phone code: 82
Colour map 1, grid B1

There is a **cigar factory**, one of the town's main tourist attractions, which reputedly makes the best cigars in Cuba. ■ *Mon-Sat 0800-1700, US$5 for a short visit, avoid the youngsters selling cigars outside.* The **rum factory** (Fábrica de Guayabita) on Isabel Rubio makes a special rum flavoured with miniature wild guavas, *Guayabita del Pinar*, which comes in either dry or sweet varieties. Between the two is the pretty cream-coloured cathedral of **San Rosendo**. The **Museo Provincial de Historia** details the history of the town and displays objects from the wars of independence. ■ *Martí 58, Mon-Sat 0800-1700, US$0.25.* Further along Martí is the **Museo de Ciencias Naturales Sandalio de Noda**, with geological and natural history, not large, not much explanation, not much on typical Cuban animals. ■ *Mon-Sat 0800-1700, US$1.* The **Casa de la Cultura Tito Junco** on Martí esq

Rafael Morales is in a huge, recently-renovated colonial house and includes an art gallery, a hall for parties and 7 classrooms for teaching dancing, painting, singing, etc. ■ *Mon-Sat 0800-1800, evening activities according to scheduled programmes.* Another renovated building on Martí opposite the Wedding Palace, is the **Palacio de Computación**, inaugurated by Fidel Castro in January 2001. ■ *Mon-Sat 0800-2100, theatre, cafeteria and classrooms.*

Sleeping

A mafia of youths offer their assistance in taking you to the casa. They are after a commission and sometimes say that they are from Formatur, the tourism school

As you leave the autopista on the north side of José Martí, but in walking distance of the city centre, is the **C** *Hotel Pinar del Río*, José Martí final, T50707. Staff friendly and helpful, swimming pool, nightclub, car hire, in need of updating, beds too soft, sheets too short, hot water evenings only, poor lighting, no bedside light, poor TV reception, poor breakfast. **Casas particulares** **F** *Traveller's Rest*, 1 de Mayo 29 entre Isidro de Armas y Antonio Rubio, Apartment 16, T5681. Hot shower, a/c or fan, 2 rooms, good meals available, bicycle rental, excursions, parking US$1 a day. Run by Juan Carlos Otaño, also known as 'The Teacher', he speaks good English, some French and German, very friendly and helpful, he can arrange permits for the Guanahacabibes National Park. Do not buy cigars on the street from a young man calling himself 'Teacher', he is an imposter called Osmany dealing in fakes. **F** *Eloina*, on Isabel Rubio, no phone, is also good, central and not far from bus station. **F** *Villa Celeida*, Frank País (Sol), Pasaje A 4, entre Isabel Rubio y Gerardo Medina, T3633, 1 block from rum factory. Run by Sra Celeida Ramos Llano, a/c room.**F** *Don Cirilo*, Maceo 115, 50m from cigar factory. Run by retired doctor whose twin children are also doctors, 2 rooms, fan, hot water, colonial furniture in colonial house, breakfast US$3, dinner US$7, alcoholic and soft drinks US$1, garage US$1, some English spoken, terrace overlooks garden with birds from Africa, Australia and South America. **F** *Hospedaje Torres*, Adela Azcuy 7 entre Gerardo Medina y Isabel Rubio, no phone. Run by nice young lady, room with fan or a/c, clean and safe, excellent breakfast and dinner. **F** *José Antonio Mesa*, Gerardo Medina 67 entre Adela Azcuy y Isidro de Armas, T3173. Nice colonial building, 8 rooms, spacious, breakfast available, nice family but involved in paying commissions so unpopular with other renters. **F** *Noelia Pérez Blanco*, Gerardo Medina 175 entre Ceferino Fernández y Frank País, T3660. One room, two beds, fan or a/c, TV, hot water, garage US$2, roof with table and chairs, a little English spoken. **F** *Zunilda Rodríguez Hernández*, Acueducto 16 entre Méndez Capote y Primera Rpto Celso Maragota, T4639. Central, garage, 2 a/c rooms, private bath, hot water, breakfast and dinner available, her husband Julio fought with Che and Fidel, interesting. **F** *Sergio Serrat Picart*, Martí 255 altos, T5893. Nice, central and comfortable.

Eating

The state-run *Rumayor*, 2 km on Viñales road. Specializes in *pollo ahumado* (smoked chicken), overpriced at US$6.50, grim toilets, open 1200-2200, closed Thu, cabaret at night, see below. *La Casona*, Martí esq Colón. Charges in dollars, service slow but food good, a trio plays boleros, bar at the back, many *jineteros*. *Nuestra Casa* a *paladar* on Colón 161 entre Ceferino Fernández y Vandama. Pleasant, nicely decorated roof terrace, enormous meal for US$7, pork or chicken with 2 salads, yuca, masses of *papas fritas* and *congris*. *El Mesón*, Martí, opposite the Science Museum. A *paladar* run by Rafael, a former teacher, nice place, lunch or dinner US$6-7, open Mon-Sat 1100-2400. *Mar Init*, José Martí, opposite Parque de la Independencia, T4952. Open Tue-Sun 1930-2130, pay in pesos, fish is the speciality of the house. *Vueltabajo*, Martí y Rafael Morales. Open 0930-2000, food available, also bar selling rum, beer, soft drinks. *Coppelia*, Gerardo Medina. Open daily 0800-2330, ice cream can be bought in pesos, very cheap. *Terrazina*, Antonio Rubio y Primero de Mayo. Open 1130-1500, 1800-2200, pay in pesos, pizza, spaghetti, beer, you can eat for less than US$1. *Doña Yuya*, José Martí 68, entre Isabel Rubio y Colón. Open 1130-1430, 1830-2130, pay in pesos, beautiful architecture but terrible food. *Pinar Café*, Gerardo Medina, opposite *Coppelia*. Open daily 1800-0200, expensive restaurant, US$5 for soft drink, beers, bottle of rum and potato chips, also a show at 2130. *La India*, Martí, a shop with a quiet bar, terrace/balcony overlooks street, pleasant. *La Taberna*, Coro 103 opposite La Paquita amusement park for children. Open daily from 1800, pesos only, dinner around 50-60 pesos, beer 8-10 pesos, bar and patio.

The town is very lively on Sat nights, and to a lesser extent on Fri. There is live music every-where, salsa, son, Mexican music, international stuff. During the day in Parque Roberto Amarán you can hear traditional music (Mambo, Rumba, Cha, Cha, Cha, Danzón) Wed and Sat 1400-1520, Sun 0900. The *Casa de la Música* on Gerardo Medina next to *Coppelia* has live music daily except Mon, 1 peso, no drinks. *Disco Rita*, on González Coro, is an open-air venue popular with teenagers, where they play loud, US-style disco music, entry 2 pesos, the only drink on sale is rum at 25 pesos a bottle. *Bar La Esquinita*, on Isabel Rubio, 2000-0200, has live music, usually guitarist. *Rumayor* has a cabaret show at 2230-2400, followed by recorded music, US$5. The classy night life, is the disco in the *Hotel Pinar del Río*, US$1, 2000-0400, Thu-Sun, very popular, full every night, young crowd, nice atmosphere.

Entertainment

Local Car hire: Havanautos and Transautos both have offices in *Hotel Pinar del Río*.

Long distance Air: Alvaro Barba airport is northeast of the town, T63248. To Isla de la Juventud, 2 flights Mon and Fri, 1 flight Tue and Sat, US$22 1-way, rather like a flying bus. Reservations at the bus station at an office downstairs, only 2 seats for tourists. **Bus**: *Víazul*, T2571, 5255, daily from Havana to Viñales at 0900. It stops on request at Las Terrazas (US$6) and San Diego de los Banos (US$8), and gets to Pinar del Río (US$11) at around 1120 with no stops. The return bus leaves Viñales at 1330, stopping in Pinar del Río around 1400 and get-ting to Havana at 1645. There is also a daily *Astro* bus at around 1700, which is cheaper at US$7 but unreliable. The bus station is on Colón, north of José Martí, near Gómez. Pinar del Río to Viñales in a state taxi is US$10, although locals can hire a taxi for the same distance for about US$5. To Viñales by bus 1 peso on route for Bahía Honda, La Palma or Puerto Esperanza, but your name has to be on the list. **Train**: Overnight train from Havana at 2140. Take a torch, hang on to your luggage, don't sleep, noisy, train stops about 29 times, very slow, should get in about 0300 but often doesn't arrive until 0600. The line continues to Guane, 3 pesos or US$3. The railway station in Pinar del Río is on Av Comandante Pinares. Trains to Havana leave at 0900 on alternate days, and cost US$7.

Transport
Distances from Pinar del Río are 157 km to Havana, 159 km to María La Gorda, 103 km to Las Terrazas, 88 km to Soroa, 25 km to Viñales

Banks *Banco Financiero Internacional* (BFI), Gerardo Medina, opposite *Coppelia*, T78183, F78213. Open Mon-Fri 0800-1500. *Cadeca*, Gerardo Medina, next to *Coppelia*. Open 0830-1800. *Banco Popular de Ahorro*, Martí 113, opposite the chess academy. Mon-Fri 0800-1700, cash on credit cards. **Communications** Etecsa is at Av Alameda IIA, T4585-7, Parque de la Independencia. A 24-hr phone centre is at Gerardo Medina esq Juan Gualberto Gómez, domestic and calls abroad, phone cards for sale. Telecorreos in *Hotel Pinar del Río*. **Post Office:** Martí esq Isabel Rubio, Mon-Sat 0800-1700. Fax service abroad US$8 per page. At Telecorreos in *Hotel Pinar del Río* US$10.20 a page. **Medical facilities** Dentist, Martí 162, T3348. Open 0800-1700. **Pharmacy**, *Camacho*, Martí 62. Open daily 0800-2300. *Piloto*, under *El Globo Hotel*, open daily 0800-2400 with emergency service. Policlínico Turcios Lima, opposite Cathedral, Gerardo Medina 112, open Mon-Sat 0800-1700. **Tour agency** *Cubatur*, Martí 51, esq Ormani Arenado, T78405, open 0800-1700, tour guide Dora Pendas. *Rumbos*, Martí, next to *La Casona*, Mon-Fri 0800-1700, Sat 0800-1200, T771802, F771401, arumcupr@ip.etecsa.cu excursions to beaches, tobacco plantations etc, also maps and phone cards for sale, car rental.

Directory

Península de Guanahacabibes

The Península de Guanahacabibes, which forms the western tip of Cuba, is a Natural Biosphere Reserve and there is a scientific station at La Bajada. Guides can be hired here for walks into the Reserve. The reserve covers 1,175 sq km but has not yet been developed for ecotourism. The peninsula is formed of very recent limestone, with an irregular rocky surface and patchy soil cover. There are interesting fossil coastlines, caves and blue holes; but with dense woodland on the south coast and mangrove on the north, the peninsula is uninviting for the casual hiker. However, for keen natu-ralists there are 12 amphibian species, 29 reptiles including iguana species, 10 mam-mals (including *carabalí* and *jutia conga*) and 147 bird species, including nine of the 22 which are endemic to Cuba.

Phone code: 8
Colour map 1, grid B1

María La Gorda, in the middle of nowhere, and reputedly the best diving centre in Cuba, is an idyllic spot for relaxing or doing nothing but **diving**. *Cubamar* and *Puertosol* organize a package including accommodation, food, diving (US$100 per person a day, minimum 2 people) and transfers from Havana (US$70 each way, 4-5 hrs). The sea is very clear, very warm and calm, even when it is too rough to dive anywhere else in Cuba. There is good snorkelling with small coral heads close to the white sand beach, or you can go out on the dive boat.

Sleeping   **C-D** *María La Gorda*, T/F5382. Jul-Aug are most expensive, Nov-Easter high season, 3 meals US$31 per person, nowhere else to eat. Lovely location, rooms open onto the beach, hammocks between palm trees, excellent value, nicely decorated, simple but comfortable, a/c, hot water, minibar, TV, good service, friendly staff, buffet meals poor and dull, bar, shop, Telecorreos, dive shop on site with doctor specializing in hyperbaric medicine, US$30 per dive if not on a package.

Transport   A package tour or rented car are the only practical ways to visit by land. Private taxis charge around US$28 from Pinar del Río to La Bajada, where they have to leave you at the checkpoint. For visitors arriving by yacht, María La Gorda is a port of entry. There are 4 moorings, maximum draft 2m, VHF channels 16, 19, 68 and 72.

Viñales

Phone code: 8
Colour map 1, grid B1
As in so much of rural Cuba, horses, pigs, oxen, zebu cattle and chickens are everywhere, including on the main road

North of Pinar del Río, the road leads across pine-covered hills and valley for 25 km to Viñales, a delightful, small town in a dramatic valley in the **Sierra de los Organos**. The valley has a distinctive landscape, with steep-sided limestone mountains called *mogotes* rising dramatically from fertile flat-floored valleys, where farmers cultivate the red soil for tobacco, fruits and vegetables. An area of 132 sq km around Viñales has been declared a National Monument. Viñales itself is a pleasant town, with trees and wooden colonnades along the main street, red tiled roofs and a main square with a little-used church and a **Casa de Cultura** with an art gallery. Two km west is the **Mural de la Prehistoria**, painted by **Lovigildo González**, a disciple of the Mexican Diego Rivera, between 1959 and 1976, generally disliked as a monstrous piece of graffiti. 100 m before the Mural is *Restaurant Jurásico*, from where you can see the paintings and there is a swimming pool nearby. Bar open 0800-1630. 6 km north of Viñales is the **Cueva del Indio**, a cave which you enter on foot, then take a boat (US$3 for foreigners) with a guide who gives you a description, very beautiful. There is a restaurant nearby where tour parties are given a lunch of suckling pig (*lechón*).

Sleeping   **C** *Los Jazmines* (Horizontes), Carretera de Vinales Km 23.5, 3 km before the town, in a superb location with travel brochure view of the valley, T936205, F936215, book through Horizontes in Havana, T334042, F333722. 62 nice rooms and 16 *cabañas*, nightclub, breakfast buffet US$5 if not already included, lunch US$10, dinner US$12, unexciting restaurant, bar with snacks available, shops, swimming pool (US$5 including towels for day visitors and US$5 in vouchers for bar drinks), riding, easy transport. **C** *Horizontes La Ermita*, Carretera de la Ermita Km 2, 3 km from town with magnificent view, T893204. 62 rooms, a/c, phone, radio, shop, tennis court, wheelchair access, pool (not always usable), nicer public areas and food better than at *Los Jazmines*, breakfast included, lunch US$10, dinner US$12. **D** *Horizontes Rancho San Vicente*, Valle de San Vicente, near Cueva del Indio, T893200. 20 a/c *cabañas*, bar, restaurant, breakfast included, lunch US$8, dinner US$10, nightclub, shop, tourist information desk, nice pool, open to day visitors, good for lunch after visit to Caves, spa with warm sulphurous waters, mud baths, full-body massage etc.

Only reports and recommendations received in 2000-2001 are included here

Casas particulares   **F** *Doña Inesita*, Salvador Cisneros 40, T93297. Inés Núñez Rodríguez and her husband, both in their 80s, offer an upstairs apartment with own entrance, 2 bedrooms each sleep 3, sitting room, aged bathroom, cold water, balcony, terrace, a/c, but cheaper without, substantial breakfast US$5, vast dinner US$8, fruit, eggs and meat from their own garden, even coffee is home grown and roasted, the energetic couple are friendly and welcoming. **F** *Estévan Orama Ovalle*, Orlando Nodarse 13, T93305. Very knowledgeable and friendly hosts, big room, clean and safe, excellent breakfast and dinner, good *mojitos*. **F** *Villa Mirtha*, double room with 2 double beds, bathroom, hot water, good breakfast included, dinner US$6 for fish, beans, rice and salad, son David speaks French but no English. **F** *Yolanda y Pedro Somonte Pino*, Interior 7A (behind the Secundaria), no phone. Nice family, quiet, relaxing, little garden, 1 room with 2 beds, fan, bathroom, hot water, simple but clean, good breakfast with lots of fruit from the garden, dinner available. **F** *Marcelino y Yamile Arteaga González*, Salvador Cisneros 6, near the Cupet station, road to the cemetery, no phone. Welcoming and kind, great breakfast, US$3 and tasty dinner US$6. **F** *Villa Neyda*, Camilo Cienfuegos 41. Comfortable rooms, wonderful hospitality, good food with choice of meat or fish, Neyda's sister, at Camilo Cienfuegos 42, also rents rooms, same quality. **F** *Ricardo Suárez Correa*, Salvador Cisneros 46, T93269. Nice house, bathroom, yard. **F** *Villa Chicha*, Camilo Cienfuegos 22. Charming, typical single-storey house with rocking chairs outside, private bathroom, entertaining family. **F** *Casa Maura*, Salvador Cisneros 131, opposite *Don Tomás*. Big breakfast included, dinner US$5, hot water, bike rental US$3 per day. **F** *Villa Blanca*, Salvador Cisneros, Edif Colonial 2 Apto 12, T93319. Friendly couple, 2 bedrooms, fans, shared bathroom, balcony, breakfast and dinner.

Eating *Paladar Restaurant*, or *Valle Bar*, T93183, on the main street. Small, friendly, recommended, *pollo frito* US$4, spaghetti US$2.50, or just have a beer, US$1, and listen to the live music in the evening. Also licensed is *Casa Cocero*, which takes pesos. *Casa de Don Tomás* is the oldest house in Viñales (1879), state owned. Unexciting paella US$8 but cocktails a bargain at US$0.90. *Casa Dago*, popular restaurant/bar with good jazz salsa band, run by extraordinary character with impressive 1927 Ford Chevrolet, food indifferent, but once the music gets going and the rum starts flowing you could be dancing all night.

Transport **Bus** Bus terminal at Salvador Cisneros 63A. *Viazul* daily from Havana via Pinar del Río at 0900, US$12, arrives 1215, returns 1330, arrives in Havana at 1645 depending on the number of stops. *Astro* from Havana 0900 via Pinar del Río, returns 1430, arrives in Havana 1820, US$8, cheaper but less comfortable and unreliable. Local buses from Pinar del Río to Puerto Esperanza, La Palma and Bahía Honda all pass through Viñales. Tour buses from Havana will drop you off if you want to stay more than a day and collect you about 1600 on the day you want to return. Truck to Pinar del Río 2 pesos. **Car hire** *Transtur*, Ceferino Fernández 6 entre Salvador Cisneros y Final, T936060, cars from US$45 a day, fuel extra. Transtur also rents **bicycles**, US$2 per hour, US$0.75/hr for more than 5 hrs or US$10.10 per day, gears sometimes work, and **scooters**, US$23 per day plus fuel. Moped hire from *Casa de Don Tomás* US$20 per day. **Taxi** *Transtur* has a taxi service, US$0.40 per km, with waiting time of US$4 per hr. Viñales to Cayo Jutías US$40, Palma Rubia for Cayo Levisa US$22, Cuevas de Santo Tomás US$8. A tourist taxi to Havana is US$42, or US$12 each if there are four of you, 3 hrs.

Directory **Banks** *Bandec* does not do card transactions, but next door is *Banco Popular de Ahorro*, which does, open Mon-Fri 0800-1200, 1330-1630.

North coast The coast north of Viñales is worth a visit if you have transport. The best and closest, 50 km, beach is at **Cayo Jutías**, near Santa Lucía. A 6.7 km cay reached by a causeway, it is open to foreigners only, US$5 entrance, *Rumbos* bar/restaurant. Further east is **Cayo Levisa**, with a long, sandy beach and reef running parallel to the shore, with good snorkelling and scuba diving. Cayo Levisa is 15 minutes by boat from Palma Rubia. The jetty is on the south side and you follow a boardwalk through the mangroves to get to the hotel on the north side. Take insect repellent. Day trips or longer stays are organized by Horizontes; you can even visit by helicopter.

Sleeping **AL** *Cayo Levisa*, T335030 in Havana. Packages include transport from Havana, some or all meals and often watersports, book in Havana through any tour agency which deals with Horizontes or Cubamar. 20 cabins on beach, thatched, with verandahs, a/c, TV, comfortable but not luxurious, spacious, restaurant, bar, live music.

Cuba

East of Havana

The main road along the coast towards Matanzas and Varadero is called the **Vía Blanca**. There are some scenic parts, but you also drive through quite a lot of industry. The **Hershey Railway** runs inland from the Casablanca station in eastern Havana, more or less parallel to the Vía Blanca, and is an interesting way to get to Matanzas. This electric line was built by the Hershey chocolate family in 1917 to service their sugar mill, at what is now the Central Camilo Cienfuegos.

Some 60 km east of Havana is **Jibacoa** beach, which is good for snorkelling as the reefs are close to the beach and it is also a nice area for walking. It is pretty, with hills coming down to the sea, and a pleasant place to go for a weekend away from Havana.

Sleeping **B** *Superclubs Breezes (Jibacoa)*, Playa Arrojo Bermejo, Vía Blanca Km 60, T69285122, F69285150. Price per person, all-inclusive, no children under 16, 250 rooms and suites in 2-storey buildings, attractive setting with hilly backdrop and curved, sandy bay, well-equipped, comfortable, good food, vegetarian options, no motorized watersports to protect reef, excursions available, indoor games room, pool, lots of sports, wheelchair accessible, evening entertainment disappointing. **E-F** *Campismo El Abra*, further along rough track T83344, 83612. Cheaper if booked through Cubamar, 87, 2-3-bed cabins with fan or a/c, small rooms, very basic, hot, small shower, bicycles, small horses, badminton, pelota, bar, restaurant, Post Office and Cambio, enormous but murky pool, small, rocky beach, best to walk east or west, extensive grounds, lots of greenery and mosquitoes. 70% of guests are Cuban.

Matanzas

Phone code: 52
Population: 115,000
Colour map 1, grid A2

Matanzas is a sleepy town with old colonial buildings and a busy, ugly industrial zone. Both the rivers Yumurí and San Juan flow through the city. Most of the old buildings are between the two rivers, with another colonial district, Versalles, to the east of the Río Yumurí. This area was colonized in the 19th century by French refugees from Haiti after the revolution there. The newer district, Pueblo Nuevo, also has many colonial houses. The industrial zone runs along the north shore of the bay, with railways running inland and around the bay.

Although you will now find numbers written on the streets, locals still refer to names. Streets running N-S in the old town have even numbers, while streets running E-W have odd numbers

The town dates from 1693, but became prosperous with the advent of sugar mills in the 1820s, followed by the railway in 1843. Most of the buildings date from this time and by the 1860s it was the second largest town in Cuba after Havana. The **Galería de Arte Provincial** is on the **Plaza de la Vigía**. ■ *Mon 0900-1700, Tue-Sat 0900-1800, US$2.* Next door is **Ediciones Vigía**, where you can see books being produced. These are all handmade and in first editions of only 200 copies, so they are collectors' items, particularly if you get one signed. Also on Plaza de la Vigía is **Teatro Sauto**, a magnificent neo-classical building dating from 1862-63 and seating 775 people in three-tiered balconies. The floor can be raised to convert the auditorium into a ballroom. ■ *Tue-Sun, US$2.*

Museums Visit the **Museo Farmacéutico**, which contains the original equipment, porcelain jars, recipes and furnishings of the Botica La Francesa, opened in 1882 by the Triolet family. It was a working pharmacy until 1964, when it was converted into a fascinating museum, believed to be unique in Latin America. ■ *Milanés 4951 entre Santa Teresa y Ayuntamiento, on the south side of Parque Libertad, T23197. Mon-Sat 1000-1700, Sun 0800-1200, US$2.* The **Museo Provincial** is a large museum in the former **Palacio del Junco**, built by a wealthy plantation owner and dating from 1840. The historical exhibits include an archaeological display and the development of sugar and slavery in the province. ■ *Milanés entre Magdalena y Ayllón, T23195. Mon-Sat 1000-1700, Sun 0800-1200, US$1.*

Cuba

D-E *Hotel Canimao*, Km 4 Carretera Matanzas a Varadero, T668021. 120 rooms on hill above **Sleeping**
Río Canímar, pool (empty) with loud music all night, nightclub, good restaurant, excursions
offered on the river or to caves. **D-E** *El Valle*, T53300/53118, 7 km northwest of Matanzas, in
woodland in the Valle del Yumurí. Built 1985, 42 rooms, some with shared bath, pool, bowling alley, riding, good walking. **E-F** *Hotel Louvre*, 19th-century building on south side of
Parque Libertad, T4074. Variety of rooms and prices, opt for the a/c room with bathroom and
balcony overlooking the square, beautiful mahogany furniture, rather than the small, dark,
cupboard room in the bowels of the hotel, water shortages, no toilet paper, friendly, lush
garden in patio. Several **casas particulares** near the beach. Ask a tout in Parque Libertad, or
try **E** *Laurita*, T62333, hot water, TV, if she is booked she will know of somewhere else.

La Ruina. Very attractive *Rumbos* restaurant converted from sugar warehouse, open 24 hrs, **Eating**
dinner US$2.5-10, delicious pastries, great ice cream, pesos and dollars accepted, live music
at weekends. *Pekin*, 83 entre 292 y 294. Open daily 1200-1400, 1800-2100, foreigners pay in
dollars. *Año 30*, 272 entre 75 y 77. Open Mon-Sat 1200-1400. *Café Atenas*, 83 y 272 on Plaza
La Vigía. Open 24 hrs, snack food, modern design, strong lighting. *Paladar El Reloj*, 135 y 298.
Collection of old clocks, big criollo meal US$5. Cheap food at Mercado Central, complete
meal for less than US$2, pay in pesos, eg *Parillada Las Mariposas*, C 300 entre 95 y 97. Outdoor
tables. Around the corner, *Shanghai*, standard cheap Chinese. These and others serve whatever the market is selling, seasonal fruit and vegetables.

The Plaza Vigía is the place to go in the evenings; locals congregate here to chat, play domi- **Nightlife**
noes or draughts, or make music. The *Casa de la Trova* here, near the bridge, was where the
Muñequitas de Matanzas, a famous rumba band, was formed. The *Sala de Conciertos José
White de Matanzas*, on 79 entre 288 y 290, was formerly the *Lyceum Club* and is famous for
being the place where the *danzón* was danced for the first time in 1879; music is performed
here and all events are free. *Teatro Sauto* usually has live performances at the weekends.

Bus The long distance bus station is at 131 y 272, while the interprovincial terminal is at 298 **Transport**
y 127, both in Pueblo Nuevo. *Víazul*, Calzada Esteban esq Terry, T916445, passes through on
its Havana-Varadero route, leaves Havana 0800, 0830, 1600, 2 hrs, US$7, departs for Varadero
(and airport) 1010, 1035, 1810, 50 mins, US$6. Returns from Varadero 0800, 1600, 1800. *Astro*
from Havana at 0910 arrives around midday, US$4. **Train** The 3-4 hr journey via the Hershey
Railway, the only electric train in Cuba, is memorable and scenic if you are not in a hurry.
Those who wish to make it a day trip from Havana can do so, long queues for return tickets,
best to get one as soon as you arrive. Five trains daily, from the Casablanca station and two
from Havana Central Station to a station north of the Río Yumurí in Versalles. The station
south of the town at C 181, Miret receives regular and *especial* trains from Havana to
Santiago.

Banks *Banco Financiero Internacional* at 85 y 298 for exchange facilities and cash advances on credit **Directory**
cards. *Banco Nacional* at 83 (Milanés) y 282. **Communications** Post Office: at 85 y 290. **Telephone:**
office on 83 y 288, open 0630-2200 every day. **Medical facilities** Facilities for foreigners are available
in Varadero, but there is a pharmacy here, open 24 hrs, at 85 y 280.

Varadero

Cuba's chief beach resort, Varadero is built on the Península de Hicacos, a 20-km   Phone code: 5
sandspit, the length of which run two roads lined with dozens of large hotels. Develop-   Colour map 1, grid A2
*ment of the peninsula began in 1923 but the village area was not built until the 1950s.
The Du Pont family bought land, sold it for profit, then bought more, constructed roads
and built a large house, now the Xanadú clubhouse for the new golf course. Varadero is
still undergoing large-scale development with the aim of expanding capacity to 30,000
rooms. Despite the building in progress it is not over-exploited and is a good place for a
family beach holiday. The beaches are quite empty, if a bit exposed, and you can walk
for miles along the sand, totally isolated from the rest of Cuba.*

Sights **Museo Municipal**, with some Indian artefacts and paintings. ■ *57 y Av de la Playa. Tue-Sat 0900-1800, Sun 0900-1200, US$1.* The **Parque Josone**, Avenida 1 y Calle 59, is a large park with pool, bowling, other activities and a café. Towards the end of the peninsula, half way between Marina Chapelín and Marina Gaviota, is a cave, **Cueva de Ambrosio**, where dozens of Indian drawings were discovered in 1961. ■ *Tue-Sun 1000-1200, 1400-1600, US$2, but may be unattended unless a tour party is booked in to visit.* At the far end of the peninsula the land has been designated the **Parque Natural de Varadero**. It is an area of scrub and cactus, with a lagoon where salt was once made, and several km of sandy beach.

Beaches &
watersports
Beach vendors will
try to sell you T-shirts,
crochet work &
wooden trinkets.
Don't buy the black
coral, it is protected
internationally & you
may not be allowed
to take it into your
country

Varadero's sandy beach stretches the length of the peninsula, broken only occasionally by rocky outcrops which can be traversed by walking through a hotel's grounds. Some parts are wider than others and as a general rule the older hotels have the best bits of beach. However, the sand is all beautifully looked after and cleaned daily. The water is clean and nice for swimming but for good **snorkelling** take one of the many boat trips out to the cays. There are three **marinas** (see below), all full service with sailing tours, restaurants, fishing and diving. All their services can be booked through the tour desks in hotels. **Deep sea fishing** costs around US$250 for four people for half a day, but prices vary according to what exactly is on offer. The dive operators are *Barracuda* (Cubanacán), Av 1 entre 58 y 59, T667072, *Marina Gaviota* (Gaviota Group), T667755, and *Dársena de Varadero* (Puertosol), T668063. Average prices are US$35 for a single dive, US$70 for two tanks. A five-day ACUC certification course costs US$365. Varadero's **Dolphinarium** is at Autopista Km 12, beyond the Marina Chapelín, but the one on Cayo Macho (see 'Excursions' below) is a nicer location. You can indulge in almost any form of watersports, including windsurfing, parasailing, waterskiing, jet skiing and non-motorized pedalos and water bikes.

Other sports The large hotels all offer **tennis** courts, some have **squash** courts and **volleyball** is played on the beach, usually organized by the hotel entertainment staff. **Table tennis**, **billiards** and other indoor games are available if the weather deteriorates or you have had enough sun. There is a Canadian-designed **golf** course on Av Las Américas Km 8.5, upgraded in 1996-98 to 18 holes, par 72. The original nine holes were set out by the Du Ponts around their mansion, built in 1928-30, which is now the *Xanadú Club House*, and the new ones extend along the Sol Meliá resorts. Golf lessons are offered and there are two putting greens, and a driving range. Packages of 3-8 days are available with accommodation in the clubhouse. Pro-shop and equipment rental at Caddie House. International Amateur Golf Week will be held 1-8 April 2000. ■ *T667788, F668481/180. Bookings can be made through hotel tour desks or direct. Open daily, make reservations 24 hrs in advance.*

Varadero

■ **Sleeping**
1 Acuazul
2 Arenas Blancas
3 Beaches Varadero
4 Breezes

5 Brisas del Caribe
6 Caribe
7 Club Med
  Varadero1820
8 Cuatro Palmas Coralia

9 Gran Hotel
10 Herradura
11 Kawama
12 Los Delfines
13 LTI Bella Costa

There are many **sailing tours** to the offshore cays. The *Jolly Roger*, T667565, is a comfortable catamaran, US$70 including lunch and open bar, good food, several stops for snorkelling or beaches. They sometimes take you to the **dolphinarium** on Cayo Macho. It is isolated, apparently in the middle of nowhere, with large pens for the dolphins. Note that Cuba is in the habit of capturing dolphins from the wild (and selling them to other countries), a cruel practice causing considerable distress when they are separated from their pods/families and forced to perform to entertain tourists in return for dead fish. ■ *US$5 for a show, US$5 to swim with them.*

Cayo Mono lies five nautical miles north northeast of Punta de Morlas. During the nesting season in mid-year it becomes a seagull sanctuary for the 'Gaviota Negra' (*Anous stolidus*) and the 'Gaviota Monja' (*Sterna fuscata* and *Annaethetus*), during which time you can only pass by and watch them through binoculars.

Varasub 1, a Japanese semi-submersible carrying 48 passengers, has six daily departures, adults US$25, children US$20. Reservations can be made with Havanatur representatives or the Varasub offices: Avenida Playa 3606, entre 36 y 37, T667279, and others. The *Mundo Mágico* submarine goes down to a depth of 35m with 46 passengers for 55 minutes. It leaves from the Dársena Marina, T668060-5. You can also see underwater by taking a trip on the glass-bottomed boat, *Martín*, which does a three-hour tour over the reef, open bar and snorkelling equipment.

Excursions
All hotels, restaurants & excursions must be paid in US dollars. Don't bother to buy any pesos for your stay here. Book excursions at any hotel with a Tour Agency office

Cuba

Hotels can be booked in the tourist office. Many offer all- inclusive rates but they can be disappointing with a lack of variety in food and drink. The best all-inclusives are the international chains: *Breezes* (Superclubs/Cubanacán), Carretera Las Americas Km 3, T667030, F667005, clubvar@clubvar.var.cyt.cu; *Puntarena* (Superclubs/Gran Caribe), Av Kawama, T667120-9; *Beaches Varadero* (Sandals/Cubanacán), Carretera Las Morlas Km 14.5, T668470, F668335, varadero@beaches.var.cyt.cu; and *Club Med Varadero* (Gaviota), Autopista Sur Km 11, T668288, F668340. A Cuban-Spanish joint venture has a group of resort hotels managed by *Sol/Meliá Hotels* of Spain, www.solmelia.es **LL-L** *Meliá Las Américas* (Cubanacán), Autopista Sur Km 7, T667600, F667625. Plaza América shopping centre alongside. **LL-AL** *Sol Club Palmeras* (Cubanacán), T667009, F667008. **LL-L** *Meliá Varadero* (Cubanacán), T667013, F667012. *Sol Club Las Sirenas*, Av Las Americas y K, T668070, F668075, all-inclusive, and *Sol Club Coral*, Carretera Las Américas entre H y K, T667009, F667008. Shuttle service through the Sol/Meliá complex 0730-2300.

AL *Cuatro Palmas Coralia*, Av 1 entre 60 y 61, 166/640, F667583. 343 a/c rooms, also in bungalows and villas hacienda style, on beach, opposite Centro Comercial Caiman in heart of hotel strip, very pleasant, pool, tennis, bicycle and moped hire, tourism bureau, post office, lots of services. **L-AL** *Arenas Blancas* (Gran Caribe), 64 entre Av 1 y Autopista, T612299, 614492/99, F614490. 5-star, 354 standard rooms, facilities for disabled people, 76 more

Sleeping
■ *on maps*

There is no private accommodation in Varadero

rooms in smaller blocks, restaurants, snack bar, 2 pools, tennis, watersports, archery, mini golf, lots of facilities. **AL** *LTI Bella Costa Resort Hotel & Villas* (Cubanacán), Carretera Las Américas, Km 4.5, T667210/010, F667205. Good 4-star hotel at end of one section of sandy beach with rocky ironshore, landscaped gardens, attractive, well run, good service. Pool with swim up bar, watersports, tennis, lovely fish restaurant on small cliff overlooking sea. **AL** *LTI Tuxpán* (Cubanacán), Carretera Las Américas, Km 4, T667560, F667561. Also with very good facilities.

B *Acuazul*, Av 1 entre 13 y 14, T667132. 156 rooms, with pool, older style, not on beach, blue and white, lots of concrete. **B** *Villa Punta Blanca* (Gran Caribe), Reparto Kawama, T668050, F667004. All-inclusive, 4-star, 320 rooms, made up of a number of former private residences with some new complexes. **C** *Herradura*, Av Playa entre 35 y 36, T613725. Well-equipped suites, balcony, restaurant, bar, shop etc. **C** *Villa La Caleta* (Gaviota), 20 y Av 1, T667080, F3291. 46 a/c rooms with baths, phone, TV, minibar, restaurant, room service, pizzería, grill, bar, pool, scooter and bike hire, parking, convenient for nightlife. **C** *Villa La Mar*, Av 3 y 29. Convenient for Víazul but not the nicest beach, a/c, TV, hot water, smart and clean, pool, bar, excursions, buffet breakfast included but nothing special, cheap hotel for package deals booked from abroad. **D** *Caribe*, Av de la Playa y 30, T613310. 124 rooms, 2-star, not to be confused with the 4-star *Caribe* on K, T667280. **D** *Los Delfines*, Av Playa y 39, T667720, F667496. **D** *Varazul*, Av 1 entre C 14 y 15, T667132, F667229. Aparthotel, 69 rooms, quiet. **D** *Villa Sotavento*, dependency of *Acuazul*, 13 between Av 1 and Av Playa, T667132-4. 130 rooms, next to beach, clean, with bath, breakfast, US$5, buffet, very good.

Eating

All between US$9 & US$15 for a main dish

Mi Casita (book in advance), Camino del Mar entre 11 y 12, T63787. Meat and seafood, open 1800-2300. *La Cabañita* Camino del Mar esquina 9, T62215. Meat and seafood, open 1900-0100. *Oshin*, Chinese, in grounds of *Sol Palmeras*. Open 1200-1500, 1800-2300, popular, reservations essential. *Habana Café*, at *Club Las Sirenas*, T668070, copy of *Habana Café* at *Meliá Cohiba* in Havana. 1950s atmosphere, car, photos, music, open 1800-0200, snacks, cocktails, international food. *Halong*, Camino del Mar esquina 12, T63787. Chinese, open 1900-2300. *El Mesón del Quijote* at *Villa Cuba*, Carretera Las Américas, T63522. Spanish, open 1200-2300. *Albacora*, Av Playa y 59. Open 1200-2400, seafood, terrace with sea views, room available for changing if you've been on the beach, food described as disappointing, all dishes except *pescado*, US$12-18, but if you want fish you may be told '*no hay*'. *Lai-Lai* Av 1 y 18, T667793. Bar/restaurant, Oriental, Open 1200-0300. *Castelnuovo*, Av 1 y 11, T667794. Open 1200-2345, Italian. *La Fondue*, Av 1 y 64. Open 1200-2300, Swiss-French menu. *El Aljibe*, Av 1 y 36, T614019. Open 1200-2400, chicken and more chicken. *Las Américas*, Av Las Américas, T63856. Open 1200-2215, international food, beautiful setting, food good one night, inedible the next. *El Mirador*, at *LTI Bella Costa Resort*, on cliff overlooking the sea. Lovely fish restaurant, lobster US$18.50, shrimp US$14, open 1200-2300. *Bodegón Criollo*, Av Playa esquina 40, T667795. Open 1200-0100, pleasant atmosphere, copy of *Bodeguita del Medio* in Havana with graffiti on walls, popular, music, no vegetarian food. *Deportivo Kiki's Club*, Av 1 y 8. Open 1200-2345, sports theme, Italian food, sports shop and sporting exhibitions. *La Sangría*, snack bar on sea front, Av 1 entre C 8 y 9, T62025, open 24 hrs. In Parque Josone are: *El Retiro*, T667316, international; *Dante*, T667738, Italian; *La Campana*, T667224, criollo and *La Casa de las Antigüedades*, T667329, meat and seafood. *Coppelia*, Av 1 entre 44 y 46, T612866, open 1000-2245, in town centre, ice cream US$0.90.

Nightlife

Cinema *Cine Varadero*, Av Playa entre 42 y 43. **Discos** Most large hotels have one including: *La Patana*, Canal de Paso Malo, T667791, open 2200-0500, floating disco at entrance to the balneario; *La Bamba*, hottest in town at *LTI-Tuxpán*, biggest, most popular, T667560, open 2200-0400. **Nightclubs** *Cabaret Continental* at *Hotel Internacional*. US$40 with dinner, 2000, show and disco US$25, open Tue-Sun, 2100-0330, reservations T667038. *Cabaret Cueva del Pirata*, show in a cave, Autopista Sur Km 11, T613829. Open 2200-0300, closed Sun. *Mambo Club*, next to *Gran Hotel*. The Orquesta Tarafa plays here, they were famous in the 1950s. *Palacio de la Rumba*, Av Las Américas, Km 4, T668210. Open daily 2200-0500, US$10 entrance, includes bar, live salsa bands at weekends.

Most hotels have a tour agency on-site offering local and national excursions, boat trips, multilingual guides, transfers, booking and confirmation of air tickets, air charters, car rentals, reception and representation service. Flights to Trinidad can be booked through *Inter*, T614845, or *Cubatur*, T667401. Main offices of agencies: *Cubanacán*, T667061/834; *Gaviota*, T667684, 613465; *Rumbos*, T666666, 667630; *Cubatur*, T667269/217. **Tour operators**

Marina Chapelin is at Carretera Las Morlas, Km 12.5, T667550/565, VHF 16 and 72. Moorings for 20 boats, maximum draft 30m, boat rental, laundry, fishing. *Marina Dársena de Varadero*, is at Carretera de Vía Blanca Km 31, T63730, 63133, 62363, VHF, 16, 19, 68, 72. Moorings for 70 boats, maximum draft 5m, boat rental, showers, laundry, restaurants, bars, fishing, shops, day charters, diving, liveaboard for 20 people. *Marina Gaviota Varadero*, Peninsula de Hicacos Km 21, T667550/565, VHF 16. Ten moorings, 3m draft, showers, laundry, restaurant, bar, seafaris, yacht rental, fishing, dolphinarium, diving. **Marinas**

Local Car hire: *Havanautos*, agency in Varadero at Av 1 y 31, T63733, F667029, 163630 at airport, or through many hotels. *Cubacar* (Cubanacán) at: *Hotel Sol Palmeras*, T667359; *Hotel LTI-Tuxpan*, T667639; *Hotel Meliá Varadero*, T667013 ext 8191. *Transautos*, Av 2 y 64, T667336, or Av 1 entre 21 y 22. *Nacional* (Gaviota) at 13 entre Av 2 y Av 4, T63706, T/F667663. Hot tip: hire a car rather than jeep to avoid having your spare wheel stolen, insurance covers 4 wheels, not the spare (see page 157). **Moped rental**: US$9 per hr, US$15 for 3 hrs, extra hours US$5, a good way to see the peninsula but you will have no insurance and no helmet. **Bicycle hire**: from hotels, US$1 per hr. **Horse drawn vehicles** act as taxis, usually just for a tour around town. **Taxis** (cars) charge US$0.50 per km. The best place to hail a taxi is at any hotel as they usually wait there for fares. *Transagaviota*, T619761-2; *Turistaxi*, T613763/377; *Taxi OK*, T612827. **Transport**

Long distance Air The **Juan Gualberto Gómez airport** (VRA), T613016, 23 km from the beginning of the hotel strip, receives international scheduled and charter flights. *Cubana* or *Sansa* have domestic flights from Baracoa, Cayo Coco, Cayo Largo, Havana, Holguín, Santiago and Trinidad. Bus from airport to hotels US$10pp. Flights to Trinidad, 0900, 1630, leave from Kawama airstrip, just across the bridge on the mainland. **Bus** The interprovincial bus station is at Autopista Sur y 36, T63254, 62626. *Víazul*, T614886, has 3 daily buses Havana-Varadero via Matanzas and Varadero airport, 0800, 0830, 1600, 3 hrs, US$10 (returning 0800, 1600, 1800), and there is a regular Astro bus twice a day (0805 and 1600) from Havana to Varadero, via at Varadero airport, US$8, reserve 1-2 days in advance. *Víazul* Varadero-Trinidad 0730, 6 hrs, US$20, with stops in Cárdenas US$6, Coliseo US$6, Jovellanos US$6, Jagüey US$6, Santa Clara US$11 and Sancti Spíritus US$16, returns from Trinidad 1430.

Airlines All at the airport: *Aerocaribbean*, T53616; *Aerogaviota*, T63018, 62010; *Air Canada*, T612010; *Air Europa*, T613016; *AOM*, T613016; *Cubana*, T63612-14; *LTU*, T53611; *Martinair*, T53624. *Aerotaxi* is at 24 y Av 1, T62929. *Cubana* has an office at 9 esq 1, T667593. **Banks** *Banco Financiero Internacional*, Av Playa y 32, cash advance service with credit cards, open 0900-1900 daily. **Communications** Most hotels have post offices where you can buy stamps for use and in packets for collectors. Phone and fax services are also usually available but prices vary. The *Centro Internacional de Comunicaciones* is at 64 entre Av 1 y Av 3, T62103/, 62356, F667020. For cellular phones, *Cubacel* is at 25 y Av 1, Edif La Cancha, T667222/198, F667222. *Etecsa* is at 18 y Av 3, T667070, F667050. *DHL* is on 10 next to *Hotel Barlovento*, T/F667330. **Medical facilities** *Policlínico Internacional*, Av 1 y 61, T668611, 667710-1, F667226, clinica@clinica.var.cyt.cu International clinic, doctor on duty 24 hrs, a medical consultation in your hotel will cost US$25. The clinic has an excellent international pharmacy attached, T667226. Recompression chamber at the Centro Médico Sub Acuática at the *Hospital Julio M Arístegui*, just outside Cárdenas. **Useful addresses** Immigration and Police: 39 y Av 1, T116. Immigration is open Mon-Fri 0800-1130, 1300-1600, Sat 0800-1130 for visa extensions. **Directory**

Cuba

Cárdenas

Phone code: 5
Population: 75,000
Colour map 1, grid A2

Cárdenas is usually visited as a day trip from Varadero and is empty of tourists, friendly and a good place to meet Cubans. It was founded in 1828 and attractive, in the traditional 19th century Spanish colonial style of houses with tall windows, intricate lattices, high ceilings inside, ceramic tiled floors and interior gardens. Cárdenas was a wealthy sugar town in the 19th century. Its main claim to fame is that the Cuban flag was first raised here in 1850 by the revolutionary **General Narciso López**, a Venezuelan who tried unsuccessfully to invade Cuba by landing at Cárdenas with an army of 600 men (only six of whom were Cuban). There is a plaque at the *Hotel Dominica*, which Narciso López occupied with his men and is now a National Monument and a flagpole monument on Av Céspedes. **Plaza Molokoff** is worth a visit to see the decaying iron market building, put up in the 19th century on Av 3 oestey 12. It was built in the shape of a cross and the two-storey building is surmounted by a 15 m dome made in the USA. On Calle 2, overlooking the water, is the *Fábrica de Ron Arrechabala*, which makes both the Varadero and Bucanero label rums. The site has been a rum factory since 1878, when the Havana Club company was founded here.

Sleeping **E** *Dominica*, Av Céspedes y 9, T521502. 25 rooms in old sugar warehouse, converted to hotel in neo-classical style in 1919 and now a National Monument, big rooms and suites, some with balconies. *Dirección Municipal de Vivienda*, Laborde 18, T522852/414, Lanexys Abreu Guerra, has a list of legally registered **Casas particulares**, or just ask around. Most places have high ceilings, which are cool, but insect repellent is needed.

Eating *Café Espriú*, Rumbos, Plaza Echavarría, 2 blocks east of Céspedes. Popular, attractive, criollo food, great ice cream, reasonable prices, main course less than US$4, open 0800-2400, best place in town. *Café Cárdenas*, Av Céspedes. Club atmosphere, balcony overlooking street, terrace at the back or indoor tables, prices up to US$5.50, mainly criollo food, karaoke weekdays, live salsa or tríos at weekends. Cárdenas is not a great culinary experience; ask around for *paladares*. The public market has plenty of fresh fruit and vegetables.

Transport Bicycles or horses are the only carriers, 1 peso. Cárdenas is an easy bike ride from Varadero and a guard will watch your bike for 1 peso. The **bus** station is on Av Céspedes y 22, with services to Matanzas, Colón, Jagüey Grande, Havana and Santa Clara. To get to Varadero catch a bus from the corner of Av 13 oeste y 13, they should leave every hour, but as the principal demand is from hotel workers they are more likely to run according to shifts. *Víazul* will drop you here on request on their Trinidad-Varadero route, US$6 from Varadero, US$10 from Santa Clara, US$18 from Trinidad. Alternatively, *Astro* from Havana 0845, US$6, or *colectivo* taxi, US$15. Astro returns to Havana 1340 via Varadero and Matanzas. There are no facilities to charge in dollars and if you show your ticket stub from your arrival they will charge you only 6 pesos for your return. Get there early, the bus soon fills up, or buy a reserved seat ticket early in the morning.

Zapata Peninsula

Colour map 1, grid B2

The whole of the south coast of Matanzas province is taken up with the **Zapata Peninsula**, an area of swamps, mangroves and beaches. It is the largest ecosystem in the island and contains the **Laguna del Tesoro**, a 9.1 sq km lagoon over 10 m deep, an important winter home for flocks of migrating birds. There are 16 species of reptiles, including crocodiles. Mammals include the jutia and the manatee, while there are over 1,000 species of invertebrate, of which more than 100 are spiders.

There is a **crocodile farm** in **Boca de Guamá**, where they breed the native Rhombifer (*cocodrilo*). They also have tortoises, jutia and what they call a living fossil, the manjuari fish/alligator, on the farm. There are lots of shops, a bar and restaurant, occasional live bands and a ceramics factory. This is all a bit touristy; hotels and tourist agencies from Varadero, Havana and other places organize day excursions including lunch, a multilingual guide and a boat ride on the lagoon through the swamps to **Villa Guamá**, a replica Indian village. On one of the islets a series of life-size statues of Indians going through their daily routines has been carved by Cuban sculptor Rita Longa. Birdwatchers will see most at dawn before the tour buses arrive. Take insect repellent. ■ *Entrance to the crocodile farm 0900-1800, US$3; boat trip from Boca de Guamá to Villa Guamá US$10, 45 mins.*

The road south across the peninsula meets the coast at **Playa Larga**, at the head of the **Bahía de Cochinos**, commonly known as the **Bay of Pigs**. The US-backed invasion force landed here on 17 April 1961 but was successfully repelled. There is a small monument but most of the commemorative paraphernalia is at Playa Girón (see below). The beach is open and better than that at Playa Girón. The **Laguna de las Salinas**, 25 km southwest, is the temporary home of huge numbers of migratory birds from December-April. The rest of the year it is empty. ■ *Tours go from the Hotel Playa Larga, Mon and Wed mornings, US$15.*

West of Playa Larga, a track leads to **Santo Tomás** where, in addition to waterfowl, you can see the Zapata wren, the Zapata rail and the Zapata sparrow. The Park also runs a number of rare bird (Cuban parrots and Cuban parakeets), turtle and fish breeding programmes. Not far from the *Hotel Playa Larga* there is a good site for watching birds such as hummingbirds and the Cuban trogon. ■ *Park headquarters are near the Hotel Playa Larga, in the Empresa Municipal Agropecuaria, T7249. Here you can get permission to enter and pay the admission fee of US$10 per person as well as find a guide (obligatory), about US$50. Insect repellent essential.*

The resort at **Playa Girón** is isolated and small. The beach is walled in and therefore protected, but the sea is rocky. The **diving** and **snorkelling** is excellent and you can walk to the reef from the shore. There is a **museum** at the site of national pilgrimage where, in 1961 at the **Bay of Pigs**, the disastrous US-backed invasion of Cuba was attempted. ■ *The museum is open daily 0800-1700, US$2.*

D *Horizontes Villa Guamá*, Laguna del Tesoro, T592979. 59 a/c rooms in thatched cabañas on several little islands in the style of a Taino village, with bath, phone, TV, restaurant, bar, *cafetería*, nightclub, shop, tourist information desk, excursions, fishing for largemouth bass in the lake. **E** *Villa Horizontes Playa Larga*, at Playa Larga, T597219. Sometimes fully booked with tour groups, 59 a/c spacious rooms in fairly basic 1- or 2-bedroomed bungalows with bath, Russian fridges, some of which work, radio, TV, water goes off at night, restaurant, bar, nightclub, shop, tour desk open 0800-1300, birdwatching and watersports. Most people prefer to travel on to stay at Playa Girón. **C-E** *Villa Horizontes Playa Girón*, T594118. 292 rooms in bungalows or blocks of rooms, a/c with bath, buffet meals, bar, pool, diving, disco, tourist information desk, shop, car rental (no gas station nearby).

Casas particulares Playa Larga **E** *Roberto Mesa Pujol*, Caletón, Playa Larga, T7210. Double rooms, a/c, bathroom shared, hot water, garage, marvellous waterfront location, garden opens onto white sand beach where you can swim, palm trees, volleyball net. **E** *Ernesto Delgado Chirino*, Roberto's cousin, another waterfront property, same details. **F** *Mirta Navarro González*, T7286. Clean house, nice family with 3 children, 2 double rooms, 1 bathroom, a/c, US$3 for rather poor breakfast. **Playa Girón** There are 15 in houses and 2 blocks of apartments in Playa Girón. Coming from Cienfuegos, the 1st block is edif 2, the one behind, at an angle, is edif 1. Note that there are roosters behind the blocks for early morning wake up call. **E** *Hostal Luís*, Carretera a Cienfuegos esq Carretera a Playa Larga, www.cuba.tc/cuplayagiron.html Owned by Luís A García Padrón, 1 bedroom, a/c, hot water, parking, very clean and friendly. **E** *José García Mesa (Tito) y Yaquelín Ulloa Pérez*, Frente al edif 2. Room with bathroom, hot and cold water 24 hrs, parking, secure, very nice people. **E-F** *Mayra Ortega Mejías*, edif 1, Apto 19, neighbour's phone T4252. 2 rooms, 1 triple, a/c, TV, 1 with 2 double beds, no a/c, share family bathroom. **E-F** *Victoria Ugaldes y Roberto León*, T4186. Two rooms, shared bathroom, hot water, good cooking, nice people. **E** *Maritza López Flores*, edif 1, Apto 21, neighbour's phone T4266. Dinner, bed and breakfast, package

Sleeping

Cuba

deal, good food, double bed, clean, nice lady, share her bathroom. **F** *Miguel A Padrón y Odalys Figueredo*, behind edif 1, T4100. Brand new house, exceptionally clean, fan, helpful.

Eating   On the road to Playa Larga is *Rumbos' La Casa del Mar* bar and grill, open 1000-1800, near here is a place to swim. Ask at the *casas particulares*, about eating in private homes. Lobster and crocodile on the menu.

Transport   **Taxi**   An illegal taxi will charge about US$70 to Havana. Better to get a lift with a tour bus returning to Havana or Varadero, US$25-30. Alternatively, the Playa Larga hotel runs day trips to Havana on Mon and Thu, a 1-way ride will cost about US$25. **Bus**   Guagua to Playa Larga from edif 2, 0630, 30-40 mins, 1.45 pesos. To Havana, Fri, Sat, Sun, 10.50 pesos, passes through Playa Larga. Playa Girón and the Bay of Pigs can also be reached by truck or taxi from Cienfuegos (1½ hrs). If you do not want to stay overnight, ask the driver to wait while you visit the beach and tourist complex, and the site of national pilgrimage.

Cienfuegos

Phone code: 432   *Cienfuegos, on the south coast, is an attractive seaport and industrial city, sometimes*
Colour map 1, grid B3   *described as the pearl of the south, and there is a very Caribbean feel to the place. French immigrants at the beginning of the 19th century influenced the development and architecture of the city, which is a fascinating blend of styles.*

Sights   There are interesting colonial buildings around the Parque José Martí. On the east side on Calle 29 is **La Catedral Purísima Concepción**, built in 1868, which has a somewhat neo-gothic interior with silvered columns.   *Mass is at 0730 and the church is open until 1200.* On the north side, on Avenida 56, is the **Teatro Tomás Terry**, built in 1889 after the death of the Venezuelan Tomás Terry, with the proceeds of a donation by his family. It was inaugurated in 1890 with an audience of 1,200. The lobby has an Italian marble statue of Terry and is decorated with fine paintings and ornate gold work. The interior is largely original with wooden seats. Note the ceiling with exquisite paintings. ■ *Open daily 0900-1800, US$1 including guided tour.* On the west side is the **Palacio de Ferrer**, now the **Casa de Cultura Benjamín Duarte**, a beautiful building dating from 1894, with a magnificent tower on the corner designed to keep an eye on the port and shipping. Worth seeing for the marble floor, staircases and walls, carved in Italy and assembled at the palace. ■ *Mon-Sat 0830-1900, US$0.50 (including the tower, great views), guided tours in Spanish.*

Excursions   On the road to Trinidad between the villages of San Antón and Guaos, 23 km east of Cienfuegos, is the **Jardín Botánico de Cienfuegos**, a national monument founded in 1901 by Edwin F Atkins, the owner of a sugar plantation called Soledad, nowadays Pepito Tey. Atkins turned over 4.5 ha of his sugar estates to study sugar cane, later including other trees and shrubs which could be used as raw materials for industry. Different sections of the gardens are devoted to areas such as medicinal plants, orchids, fruit trees, bamboos and one of the world's most complete collections of palm trees. ■ *0800-1700 every day, US$2.50, children US$1, bar for drinks. Look out for 2 rows of palm trees leading to the garden from the entrance at the road. Bus from Cienfuegos stops outside, 20 centavos.* **Playa Rancho Luna** is about 18 km from Cienfuegos, near the *Hotel Rancho Luna*. The beach is quite nice but nothing special. The Centro de Buceo Faro Luna runs the diving here. If you continue along the road past the beach you get to the *Hotel Pasacaballo*. There is a jetty here and another further along a rough track to the left, from where you can get a little ferry (US$1) across the mouth of the Bahía de Cienfuegos to the village on the western side, site of the **Castillo de Jagua**. The castle was built at the entrance to the bay in 1733-45 by Joseph Tantete, of France. There is only one entrance via a still-working drawbridge across a dry moat. ■ *0800-1700 every day, entrance US$1 includes a tour. Ferries also from Av 46 in Cienfuegos harbour, US$0.50, several stops, 45 mins.*

A-D *Mercure Coralia Jagua* (Gran Caribe), Punta Gorda, C 37 No 1, T451003, F667454. 145 **Sleeping**
a/c rooms with view over bay, singles, doubles and triples available, 4-star, comfortable,
Palacio de Valle restaurant next door, gorgeous decor, live piano music, simple but good food
in snack bar, small pool, DHL office in hotel. **D-E** *Hotel Pasacaballo* (Islazul), Carretera a
Rancho Luna, Km 22, T96280/90. 150 rooms, not many foreign guests, seaside complex,
cafetería. **D-E** *Rancho Luna* (Horizontes), Km 16, T48120/3, F335057. 225 rooms with balcony, poor service, salt water pool, scuba diving, popular with Canadians in winter. **C** *Faro
Luna* (Cubanacán), Carretera Pasacaballo Km 18, Playa Faro Luna, T48162/65. 70 rooms,
4-star, nice, clean, hot water, TV, some staff friendly, aimed at individual travellers who want
to dive and sail. **D** *Villa Guajimico*, Carretera a Trinidad Km 42, Cumanayagua, T/F04328125,
best to book through Cubamar, in Havana, T662523-4, F333111, cubamar@
cubamar.mit.cma.net. Overlooks mouth of Río La Jutía, surrounded by cliffs, caves, coral reefs
and small beaches accessible only by boat. Three-star, 51 cabins, some triples, white with red
tiled roofs, a/c, bathroom, pool, restaurant, bar, parking, hobicats, good for excursions, a
great dive resort, 3 meals US$31, diving US$25, sailing US$10.

Casas particulares **E-F** *Delíz y Pedro Sierra*, C 37 3806 entre 38 y 40. 5 a/c rooms (avoid the *Numerous casas all*
first room on the ground floor, uncomfortable bed), private bathroom, TV, fridge, 24-hr hot *down C 37 to Punta*
and cold water, meals on request, parking, fantastic view of bay from balcony on first floor, *Gorda, too many to*
English spoken by well-educated health professionals who are very knowledgeable about *list here. We list only*
their country. **E-F** *Marta González González*, 39 6401 entre 64 y 66, 23268. Two a/c double *those reported or*
rooms, simple but clean, bathroom, hot water, nice family, cosy atmosphere, breakfast and *recommended in*
dinner available, Spanish only. **E-F** *Jerónimo García Escoriza*, 35 5806 entre 58 y 60, T6549. *2000-2001*
Kind and helpful, Spanish only, bathroom, food available. **F** *María Núñez Suárez*, Av 58 3705
Altos entre 37 y 39, T7867. A/c room with adjoining bathroom. Ask her husband and friends
to tell you stories about when they were young, fighting with Che in the Sierra Maestra, at
the Bay of Pigs or working in Ethiopia. **F** *Familia Puchi*, 39 5402 entre 54 y 56, T3802. Good,
clean, with breakfast. **F** *Maritza Guedes Brito*, 39 2202B entre 22 y 24, T3388. Two a/c rooms
independent of the rest of the house, shared bathroom, hot water, fridge, garage, owner is a
gynaecologist. **F** *Casa de Hospedaje Carlos*, Av 56 5104 entre 51 y 53, 1 min walk from bus
terminal. Big breakfast, dinner US$5, helpful, can arrange trips to Playa Girón. **F** *Leonor
Martínez*, 56 entre 29 y 31, T6143. Knowledgeable elderly couple, 3 rooms, colonial house
with tiled roof.

The place to go for its style, if not for the food, is *Palacio de Valle*, by *Hotel Jagua*, a building dat- **Eating**
ing from 1894 in a mixture of architectural styles but with Arab influences predominating,
incredibly ornate ceilings and other decorations. Open 1145-2300 for food, from 1000 for
drinks, meals US$10-22, speciality seafood, upstairs on the roof is a bar with good views and
another restaurant in the garden. On C 37, adjacent to the hotel, is *Los Laureles*, where meals
are cheaper. Also on 37, opposite the hotel, is *Cueva del Camarón*. Nice place to eat, clean,
open 1200-2300, meals around US$10-25. Nearby is *Covadonga*, on 37. Paella restaurant. *37 y
42*, 37 4204 entre 42 y 44, T6027. Open 1100-0100 or 0200, meals around US$6-10. *El Criollito*,
33 5603 entre 56 y 58, T5540. Open 24 hrs, meals US$7-8 include salad, chips, rice and coffee,
tasty fish, live music. *La Verja*, Boulevard (Av 54) entre 33 y 35. Open 1200-1800 daily, quite a
nice setting but food unappetizing, no fish or chicken, meals around US$6. *El Cochinto*, Prado y
4. Not a great choice but you pay in pesos, open 1900-2100. *1819*, Av Prado. Limited choice,
menu in dollars or pesos. Plenty of *paladares* on the Prado. *Coppelia* ice cream, on Prado y 53,
open Tue-Sun 1100-2300. *Helados Alondria*, known as *Terry Sodería*, between Terry Theatre
and Colegio San Lorenzo. Open 0900-2300, of ice cream delights.

Rumbos, Av 20 3905 entre 39 y 41, T1231, F1175. Trips to waterfalls and other local attractions. **Tour operators**

Local Coches: horse-drawn carriages operate in Cienfuegos. **Car hire**: *RentaCar* is in *Hotel* **Transport**
Jagua car park. *Havanautos* and *Servi Cupet Cimex* is at 37 entre 15 y 17. **Long distance Bus** Terminal at 49 esq Av 56. Tickets may be purchased 1 hr or so in advance from
the small office with a brown door, next to the Salón Reservaciones. To **Havana**, daily, 0600,

1000, 1230, 1500, 2350, 5 hrs, US$14. From Havana, 0630, 1220, 1630, 1945, 2130. To **Santiago de Cuba**, every other day, 1700, US$31. To **Camagüey**, every other day, 0800, 1400. To **Trinidad**, 0630, 1230, 5-6 hrs, US$3. To **Santa Clara**, 0700, 0900, 1¼ hrs, US$1.50. *Astro* has a daily 1430 service to **Matanzas**, US$14, via Cárdenas and Varadero, but check if it is running. Sun is a good day with people returning to work in Varadero. *Viazul, Gloria entre 56 y 58*, T8114/5720, passes through here on its Havana-Trinidad route. Leaves Havana 0815, 1300, 4 hrs to Cienfuegos, US$20, returns 0940, 1640. From Trinidad at 0800, 1500, 1 hr 35 mins, US$6, returns 1225, 1710. **Train** Terminal at 49 esq Av 58. To **Havana**, direct or via Santa Clara, on alternate days, 1030, 9 hrs, US$9.50, or 1430, arrive Santa Clara 1700, US$2.10, Havana 2300, US$9.50, all services generally slow and uncomfortable.

Directory **Banks** The *Banco Financiero Internacional* is on Av 54 esq 29, T/F335603, open 0800-1500 Mon-Fri, 3% commission on TCs. Cash advances on credit cards. **Medical facilities** *International Clinic*, Punta Gorda on C 37 202, opposite the *Hotel Jagua*, T/F8959, offering 24-hr emergency care, consultations, laboratory services, X-rays, pharmacy and other services. Pharmacy on Prado esq Av 60, open 24 hrs.

Santa Clara

Phone code: 422
Population: 200,000
Colour map 1, grid B3

Santa Clara is a pleasant university city in the centre of the island best known for being the site of the last and definitive battle of the Revolution and the last resting place of Che Guevara. It is 300 km from Havana and 196 km from Varadero.

History In December 1958, before Castro entered Havana, Batista sent an armoured train with military supplies including guns, ammunition and soldiers, to Santiago de Cuba to counter-attack the revolutionaries. However, **Che Guevara** and his troops were hiding in the outskirts of Santa Clara (on the Loma de Capiro and in the university), waiting for the train. On 28 December 1958 it was ambushed in the afternoon. The soldiers on the train surrendered quickly and the fighting for the train was soon over. However, the battle for the city lasted nearly four days, until 1 January 1959 when news spread that Batista had fled the country.

Sights Heading east on Calle Independencia towards Camajuaní, between Río Cubanicay and the railway line, is the **Monumento a la Toma del Tren Blindado**, where four of the carriages of Batista's troop train are preserved. There is a museum inside the wagons showing weapons and other things carried on the train. ■ *Tue-Sat 0900-1200, 1500-1900, Sun 0900-1200.* There is also a monument on top of **El Capiro**, the hill where Che and his troops waited to attack the train. You can get an excellent view of the city from here, just as Che did in 1958.

A monument to Che has been built in the **Plaza de la Revolución Ernesto Guevara**, with a huge bronze statue of Che on top of a large concrete plinth, a bas-relief scene depicting Che in battle and an inscription of a letter from Che to Fidel. The remains of Che and his comrades who fell in Bolivia have been interred here. It is on Prolongación Marta Abreu after the Carretera Central forks to the north; look out for La Victoria service station, entrance on Calle Rafael Tristá, which runs parallel. Under the monument is a museum, the **Museo Histórico de la Revolución**, with good displays in Spanish and a video about Che's life and role in the Revolution, as well as displays of the battle in Santa Clara. Recommended. ■ *Tue-Sun 0900-1200, 1400-1700, US$2. Bicitaxi US$1 per person from the centre.*

Sleeping **C** *Villa La Granjita* (Cubanacán), outside town at Km 2.5 on Maleza road, T26053, F28192. 75 rooms in thatched cabañas among fruit trees, cable TV, a/c, phone, pool, bar, shop, buffet restaurant, horses, night-time entertainment around the pool. **D** *Los Caneyes* (Horizontes), Av de los Eucaliptos y Circunvalación, T4512/5, F335009 (outside the city). Thatched public areas with 91 cabins, a/c, hot showers, TV, facilities for disabled people, pool, disco, evening entertainment by the pool, good buffet, supper US$12, breakfast US$4, excellent value, car rental, medical services, shop, tourism bureau, hairdresser, game shooting and fishing can be arranged, popular hotel for tour parties and hunters. **E** *Santa Clara Libre*, central, 1956 concrete building on Parque Vidal with bullet holes on the façade, preserved from the Dec 1958 battle when some of the police were using the building to defend the city from the revolutionaries, T27548, F5171. A/c and fans, phones, some rooms have TV, water shortages, lifts also erratic, noisy, car rental, observation deck with bar on top of the building, from where you get a great view of the city, cinema and disco, see entertainment.

Casas particulares E-F *Santiago Martínez y Lidia Viera*, Bonifacio Martínez 58A altos entre Síndico y Caridad, T26754. One nice room, hot shower, a/c, fridge, breakfast and dinner US$7 available. **E-F** *Martha Artiles Alemán*, Marta Abreu 56 (altos), entre Villuendas y Zayas, T5008, central but quiet, velo taxi outside. A/c, fan, shared bathroom, laundry, clean, breakfast US$3, dinner US$7-8, parking, own key to house. **E-F** *Noely González González*, Bonifacio Martínez 18, entre Serafín García (Nazareno) y EP Morales (Síndico), T216193. Large room with two big beds, fan, a/c, hot water, private bathroom, parking. **E-F** *María and Jorge García Rodriguez*, Cuba 209, Apdo 1, entre Serafín García (Nazareno) y E P Morales (Síndico), T22329. Two a/c rooms, clean, comfortable, owners very helpful and informative. **E-F** *Hostal Mauricio*, Martha Abreu 58 Altos entre Zayas y Villuendas. Owner is Belgian and speaks Spanish, English, French, German and Dutch, good location, 1 min from Parque Vidal. **F** *Ernesto y Mireya*, Cuba 227 altos entre Pastora y Síndico, opposite Iglesia La Pastora, T273501. Two double rooms with shared bathroom, big breakfast for US$3, Ernesto is funny and helpful, will arrange collection from bus station if you pay for taxi. **F** *Miriam Consuelo Ramos Rodríguez*, Independencia 265 Este Apto 1 entre Pedro Estévez y San Isidro, T202064. Ernesto's cousin, English spoken, huge room with 2 double beds and bathroom, US$3 for tasty breakfast, Miriam Consuelo is a one-person tourist office, she knows everything, large family and comedy dog. **F** *Mercedes*, Máximo Gómez 51 altos, entre Independencia y Martí,T20227. Central, 3 rooms, each with own bathroom, 2 with own terrace, the cheapest one at the top is the most private, friendly family, Mercedes practices Santería, high standard, good cooking. **F** *Yilian Ortiz Quijano*, Maceo 322 entre San Miguel y Nazareno, T26276. Friendly, breakfast US$5.

1878 Colonial, Máximo 8, near the Boulevard, T22428. Offers a variety of creole dishes, mainly pork in different styles, bar in the patio. *El Marino*, Paseo de la Paz y Carretera Central, T5594. Seafood, *paellas* a speciality. *La Carreta*, Carretera Central. Creole food in cosy environment. *Mandarín*, Chinese, Carretera Central beyond bus stations, reservations needed with Islazul on Calle Lorda, or T91010, open 1830-2230. *Florida Centre*, southeast of Parque. US$7 for a meal, huge plate of prawns. *Sol de Cuba* on Machado (Candelaria) entre Alemán y Carretera Central, up spiral staircase. Limited menu, US$6-8 for main dish, make sure rice and salad are included, not charged extra, slightly overpriced. *Rincón Criollo*, Cuba 410, entre Serafín Sánchez y Estrada Palma, T71309. Chicken and pork dishes US$2-3, others can be ordered, lunch 1200-1500 by reservation, dinner 1800-2400, food OK, nice surroundings, clean. *La Casona*, Carretera Central 6 entre Padre Chao y Marta Abreu, just by Río Bélico, T5027. Very tasty, nice old house with beautiful tiled floor but no tables or chairs, food served at standing counter to avoid *paladar* regulations, like a takeaway service, friendly hosts, open 1200-2400, very clean, proprietor Orlando Molina is a manager at *Los Caneyes* hotel restaurant. *La Terraza*, Serafín Sánchez 5 entre Cuba y Colón, T73117. Open 1200-2400, tables on upper storey terrace, main dishes US$10 including rice and salad. *El Rápido* café, on Lorda near Plaza, hot dogs, pizzas, sandwiches, beer, billiards table, only US$, also on Marta Abreu, opposite interprovincial bus station, if you have a wait. *Coppelia* ice cream, Colón just off Parque Vidal, corner of Mujica, 1000-2330. *La Marquesina*, 24-hr café next to theatre, pleasant place for a drink, popular with young people at night.

Eating

Begging can be persistent if you eat outside at a street café

Club Mejunje (mishmash), 2½ blocks west from Parque Vidal, Marta Abréu 107 entre Fabián y Juan Bruno Zayas, cultural centre and *Casa de la Trova* in a backyard full of artefacts and graffiti-covered walls, opens 1700, Wed-Sun, free, pay for rum in pesos, composers, singers, musicians and friends sing, play and drink together, friendly, welcoming, enjoyable. Larger events are staged in the courtyard, wide variety ranging from concerts to theatre, from shows for kids

Nightlife

Cuba

to shows for gays, 5 pesos for Cubans, US$1 for foreigners. Comedians, rock bands and other entertainers can be seen at Parque del Humor, Chaflán, off Parque Vidal, open Tue-Sun at 1500 and 2000, and on Sun also at 0900. There is a cinema on the ground floor of the *Hotel Santa Clara Libre* on Parque Vidal and the best local disco is in the basement, *Disco Basement*, opens Tue-Sun 2230-0400, US$5. The disco on the 10th floor has a reputation for prostitution; pimps entice tourists with underage prostitutes and then blackmail them.

Tour operators *Islazul* is at Lorda 6 entre Parque Vidal y Boulevard, just off Parque Vidal by the theatre, dealing mainly with Cubans, open Mon-Fri 0800-1130, 1300-1545, mostly hotel and restaurant reservations. *Rumbos Cuba* desk in *Café Europa* Independencia y Luís Estévez, tours arranged. Their main office is in *Hotel Los Caneyes*.

Transport **Local** Horse-drawn **coches**, or **taxi-buses**, go all over town and down Marta Abreu to the bus stations, 1 peso. There are also some **buses**, 40 centavos. Bicitaxi costs US$1 to most places in town, fix a price beforehand or they will overcharge you. For **taxi** service call T26856/956, or pick up a private car. **Cars** can be hired from the hotels.

Long distance **Bus** The municipal bus station for destinations within Villa Clara is on Marta Abreu, T26284, 1 km from centre, on corner with Calle Pichardo, white building. The intermunicipal bus station for long distances is on the same road with Oquendo, T92114, 1 km further out, in blue building. *Víazul* , Carretera Central Km 483 entre Independencia y Oquendo, T92113/91572. Buses on the Varadero-Trinidad route stop here, leave Varadero 0730, 3 hrs 15 mins, US$11, return 1710, leave Trinidad 1430, 2 ½ hrs, US$8, return 1050. Also buses Havana-Santiago, depart Havana 1500, 2000, arrive Santa Clara 1925, 2340, US$18, return 0335, 0720, depart Santiago 1500, 2000, arrive Santa Clara 0330, 0715, US$33, return 1930, 2345. There is no guarantee you'll get a seat as the buses are often full when they get here. Worth investigating the taxis outside the bus station if there are two or more of you, quicker, more convenient and possibly cheaper. *Astro* to **Havana** 2 daily, at 2350 (arrives 0430) and 1400 (1800), US$12; to **Santiago** alternate days 1900, 12 hrs, US$22.50; to **Cienfuegos** daily at 0710 (arrives 0900), US$2, 1120 (1230), US$2.50, and alternate days at 1440 (1600) US$2.50; to **Trinidad**, 1320, 3½ hrs, US$6; to **Varadero**, daily 0910 (arrives 1300), US$8; to **Camagüey**, alternate days, 1900, 5 hrs, US$10; to **Matanzas**, 1210, 4 hrs; to **Sancti Spíritus**, 0825, 2 hrs. Frequent delays, get numbered ticket then stay near departure gates until bus is ready and then join the scrum. **Train** The railway station, T22895, is north of Parque Vidal on Estévez and is much more central than either of the bus stations. There are 4 daily trains to Havana and 1 to Santiago; the *especial* stops here, heading east at 2048 (US$24, 10 hrs), and west at 0253 (US$12, 4 hrs). There is a train to Bayamo/Manzanillo at 0418 (US$18, 8 hrs), which on the return journey to Havana leaves Santa Clara at 0843. Similarly a train to Camagüey leaves at 2327 (US$9, 4 hrs), returning to Havana and passing through Santa Clara at 2338; a slow train, *lechero*, goes to Camagüey at 1415, 6 hrs or so; to Sancti Spíritus at 1319 (US$4, 2 hrs), returning to Havana at 0025. Two daily trains run Cienfuegos-Sancti Spíritus, passing through Santa Clara around 0700 and 1730. None of these times is reliable and the train may not even appear at any time.

Directory **Banks** The *Cadeca* office for changing currency and TCs (4% commission) is at Parque Vidal on the corner of Rafael Tristá and Cuba, T5690. *Bandec*, on the corner of Vidal and Tristá and Cuba, Visa and MC, open Mon-Fri 0800-1400, Sat 0800-1100. *Banco Financiero Internacional*, on Cuba just down from Parque Vidal, is open Mon-Fri 0800-1500, also Visa and MC. **Medical facilities** The best hospital for foreigners is the *Arnaldo Milián Castro Hospital*, at Circunvalación and Av Escambray in the Residencial Escambray area to the south of the town, T72016, 71234. If you need a taxi to take you there, T26956. Ambulance T22259, 23965. There is a 24-hr pharmacy at Luis Estévez 8 on the corner with Boulevard.

Trinidad

Trinidad, 133 km south of Santa Clara, is a perfect relic of the early days of the Spanish colony: beautifully preserved streets and buildings and hardly a trace of the 20th century anywhere. It was founded in 1514 by Diego Velázquez as a base for expeditions into the 'New World' and Cortés set out from here for Mexico in 1518. The five main squares and four churches date from the 18th and 19th centuries and the whole city, with its fine palaces, cobbled streets and tiled roofs, is a national monument and since 1988 has been a UNESCO World Heritage Site.

Phone code: 419
Population: 60,000
Colour map 1, grid B3

On the Plaza Mayor is the cathedral, **Iglesia Parroquial de la Santísima Trinidad**, built between 1817 and 1892. It is the largest church in Cuba and is renowned for its acoustics. On the left of the altar is a crucifix of the brown-skinned Christ of Veracruz, who is the patron of Trinidad. ■ *1130-1300, 1930-2000, mass daily at 2000-2100 when tourists are excluded.*

Sights

The **Museo Romántico** has an excellent collection of romantic-style porcelain, glass, paintings and ornate furniture, which belonged to the Conde de Brunet family and dates from 1830-60. ■ *Hernández 52, next to the church of Santísima Trinidad on the main square, T4363. Tue, Thu 0800-2200, Sat-Mon, Wed, Fri 0800- 1800, US$2, no cameras allowed.* **Museo Municipal de Historia**, an attractive building but rather dull displays in eight rooms of scientific, historical and cultural displays, walk up the tower for a good view of Trinidad. ■ *Simón Bolívar 423, T4460. Sun-Tue, Thu 0900- 1800, Wed, Fri 0900-2200, US$2.* Other museums worth visiting include: the **Museo de Arqueología Guamuhaya**, a general view of developments from precolumbian to post-conquest times, ■ *Simón Bolívar 457, esquina Villena, Plaza Mayor, T3420, Mon, Wed 0900- 2200, Sun, Tue, Thu, Fri 0900-1700, US$2.* **Museo de Arquitectura Colonial** exhibits specifically on the architecture of Trinidad, particularly aspects of the 18th and 19th centuries. ■ *Desengaño 83, T3208, Mon, Thu 0900-2200, Sat, Sun, Tue, Wed 0900 1700, US$2;* **Museo Nacional de Lucha Contra Bandidos**, housed in the old San Francisco convent, exhibits about the campaign in the Escambray mountains. ■ *Hernández esquina Piro Guinart, T4121, Tue, Fri 0900-2200, Wed, Thu, Sat, Sun 0900-1700, US$2.*

Begging has become persistent, mainly children and old women asking for dollars, soap, skin cream

Cuba

Inland from Trinidad are the beautiful, wooded Escambray mountains, whose highest point is **Pico San Juan**, also known as La Cuca, at 1,140m. Rivers have cut deep valleys, some of which, such as the Caburní and the Guanayara, have attractive waterfalls and pools where you can swim. The **Parque Natural Topes de Collantes** is a 110 sq km area of the mountains which contains many endemic species of fauna and flora. There are several paths in the area and walking is very rewarding with lovely views and lush forest. There is no public transport but day trips are organized to Topes de Collantes by *Cubatur* or *Rumbos* by jeep or truck, which take in swimming in a waterfall. You can see lots of wildlife, butterflies, hummingbirds and the tocororo. A great day out. Private tours do not go to the same places as jeep tours, whatever anybody tells you. ■ *Entrance US$6.50.*

Excursions

Rumbos will also take you to the **Torre de Manaca Iznaga** in the village of the same name about 15 km from Trinidad on the road to Sancti Spíritus, or you can hire a private car to take you for about US$10 or you can catch a train heading to Meyor or Condado, US$7 return, to Manaca Iznaga. The tower, built between 1835 and 1845 is 43.5m high, has seven floors and 136 steps to the top. It was built as a lookout to watch the slaves working in the valley at the sugar mills. It has UNESCO World Heritage status alongside Trinidad city, because of its historical importance. There is a great view of the surrounding countryside, including the **Valle de los Ingenios** (Valley of the Sugar Mills) and the Escambray Mountains as well as the roof tops of the village below. ■ *0900-1600 or 1700, US$2.*

Sleeping

■ *on maps*

C-D *Motel Las Cuevas* (Horizontes), Finca Santa Ana, T4194013/9. On a hill 10 mins' walk from town (good road), with caves in the grounds, view of the sea, 114 comfortable rooms in 60 chalets and apartments with a/c, phone, radio, hot water, and very clean, 2 swimming pools, bar, discotheque from 2200 in cave below reception, entrance US$5, dollar shop, post office, exchange facilities, car and motorbike rental, tour agencies (*Cubatur* and *Rumbos*), restaurant with buffet meals, breakfast US$4, evening meal US$12, not bad. **E** *Finca María Dolores*, Carretera Circuito Sur, T3581, also called *Casa de Campesino*, 3 km from Trinidad on the road to Cienfuegos. Garden setting near Río Guaurabo, 20 brick cabañas, 2 single beds, a/c, shower, clean, restaurant, shop, bar, quiet spot but noisy in the evening as it is an all-dancing, all-singing tour group destination, horse riding, cock fighting, milk the cows.

Look for the blue triangle symbol on the doors of the registered houses, there are dozens of them, 2000-2001 recommendations listed here

Casas particulares **E** *Hostal Casa Muñóz*, José Martí 401 entre Fidel Claro y Santiago Escobar, T3673. Very friendly, run by Julio César Muñóz Cocina and Rosa Orbea Cerrillo with their two children and Brandy the dog, English speaking, great house, built in 1800, 2 rooms with 2 double beds, private bathrooms, a/c and fans, parking, meals available. **E** *Carlos Gil Lemes*, José Martí 263 entre Colón y Fco J Zerquera, T3142, next to library. Beautiful late-19th century house with sumptuous tile decoration, English spoken, 2 rooms with shared bath, hot water, fans, garden courtyard, neighbour has a garage for rent, US$1 per night.

F *Gisela Borrell Bastida*, Frank País 486 (Carmen) entre Fidel Claro y Santiago Escobar, T4301, opposite *Gaviota*, about 200m from bus station. Bedroom with double and 2 single beds on ground floor, bathroom with hot shower, use of own dining room, sitting room, own entrance, breakfast US$2, dinner US$5, food excellent, lots of space, excellent value, family lives on other side of courtyard. **F** *Lazara Borrell Farías*, Colón 312 entre Maceo y Jesús Menéndez, T2454. 2 rooms each with bathroom, huge house in historic centre, friendly, good English. **F** *Martha Puig Jiménez*, Francisco Cadahía 236, entre Colón y Lino Pérez, T2361. Speaks fluent English, meals arranged, free coffee, house and courtyard spotlessly clean, fans, shared bathroom, hot water, friendly, informative, car parking arranged. **F** *Rafael Soler Valdés*, *Casa de Huéspedes El Rústico*, Juan M Martínez 54A entre Piro Guinart y Simón Bolívar, 1 block from Plaza Mayor, T3024. 5 rooms, a/c, bathroom shared , very clean. Rooms on top floor private, roof terrace, table for breakfast. Rafael was a professional chef and makes fantastic meals on request, US$8, ring doorbell if you come home late. Cousins in Santiago, Irma and Umberto, also rent rooms. **F** *Hostal Tatica*, Simón Bolívar (Desengaño) 502, entre Juan M Márquez y Fernando H Echerri, T2343. House is the first on the right as you leave the Plaza Mayor, built against the side of the church. Run by Margoles, long, thin room with double and single bed, no view, fan, bathroom, hot water erratic, large breakfast included, nice family, no English spoken, parking. **F** *Pedro Aliz Peña*, Gustavo Izquierdo 127 (Gloria) entre Piro Guinart y Simón Bolívar, T3776/3025, just by bus station where Víazul buses stop. Old house with high ceilings, patio, quiet, two spacious rooms, fans, simple but clean, new bathrooms, hot water, Pedro and Teresa are sociable and helpful, breakfast and dinner available, only Spanish spoken. **F** *Mercedes Padrón Jiménez*, Manuel Solano 7 (Pimpollo), T3068. Two rooms, one with own bathroom, more privacy than some, great cooking, vegetarians welcome, owner is former teacher and speaks the kind of Spanish that anyone can understand, phone ahead, popular. **F** *Mariela de Fernández*, Santiago Escobar 158 (Olvido) entre José Martí y Frand País, T3410. Spanish only, friendly and helpful, bathroom, food available. **F** *Dr Manuel Lagunilla Martínez*, a retired lawyer, he lives at Maceo 455 but rents rooms at José Martí 327. Colonial house, 3 rooms each with bathroom, hot water all day, breakfast US$2, English spoken. **F** *Carlos Hernández y Yait*, Independencia 35 entre Pablo Pichs y Conrado Benítez. Budget accommodation, 2 rooms, hot water, breakfast US$2, dinner US$5, use of kitchen, good location, friendly and helpful. **F** *Sara Sanjuan*, Simón Bolívar 266 entre José Martí y Frank País, T3997. Three rooms, sleep 3, a/c, colonial building, quiet courtyard with rocking chairs and roof terrace, excellent food, breakfast US$3, dinner US$8-9, pork and langostinos out of this world. **F** *María Esther Pérez*, Francisco Cadahía 224 (Gracia) entre Colón y Lino Pérez, T3258. Four bedrooms, 1 communal bathroom, a/c or fan, porch area, small kitchen, delicious meals US$5-6 including seafood with rice and vegetables, generous portions, breakfast US$2 with eggs and juice, bike hire US$3 per day, can arrange cheap taxi tours to Topes de Collantes.

Plaza Mayor, Villena 15, just off Plaza Mayor. Elegant setting, lobster US$19, steak and seafood, buffet dinner US$9, open 0830-2400. *El Jigüe*, Real 69 esq Guinart, T4316. Open 1100-1700 only unless a group comes in and then they open at night, live music, good food and atmosphere, most dishes US$7-8, chicken special US$12, lower prices for groups of over 10 people. A *Rumbos* restaurant is *El Mesón del Regidor*, Simón Bolívar 424, opposite Toro, T3756. Open 0900-1800 daily, US$7-8. *Santa Ana*, on Plaza Santa Ana. Open 0900-2200 every day, house special pork US$12, other dishes US$5-8. *Paladares* include *Daniel's*, Camilo

Eating
The price of beer in some restaurants drops from US$2 to US$0.60 after 1700 when the tours leave, but all the state-run places shut then too

Cuba

Trinidad

0 metres	100	
0 yards	100	

■ Sleeping
1 Carlos Gil Lemes
2 Hostal Casa Muñóz
3 Hostal Tatica
4 Lazara Borrell Farías

5 María Esther Pérez
6 Mariela de Fernández
7 Martha Puig Jiménez
8 Mercedes Padrón Jiménez
9 Pedro Aliz Peña
10 Rafael Soler Valdés
11 Sara Sanjuan

● Eating
1 Bar Daiquirí

2 Bar Las Ruinas de Segarta
3 Casa Fisher
4 Colonial
5 El Jazmín
6 El Jigue
7 El Mesón del Regidor
8 La Bodeguita
9 Plaza Mayor
10 Ruinas de Leonci
11 Santa Ana

12 Sol y Son

🏛 Museums
1 Museo de Arqueología
2 Museo de Arquitectura
3 Museo de Historia
4 Museo Nacional de Lucha Contra Bandidos
5 Museo Romántico

— Historical centre

Cienfuegos 20, T4395. Open 1100 until every one leaves, some courtyard tables, US$5-6 including side dishes, also rooms, a/c, but may be noisy from restaurant music downstairs. *Colonial*, Maceo 402, esquina Colón. Open daily 0900-2200, US$5-6, nice place, locally popular. *Sol y Son*, Simón Bolívar 283 entre Frank País y José Martí. Run by English-speaking ex-architect Lázaro, open 1200-2400, in 19th century house, courtyard, vegetarian special, excellent pork, tasty stuffed fish around US$10 with drinks, but all meals cost US$5 extra if you go with a guide. *Ruinas de Leonci*, Gustavo Izquierdo entre Simón Bolívar y Piro Guinart. Bar and restaurant, cosy small garden, wooden tables inside, live music every night. *Restaurante Don Antonio*, Izquierdo entre Piro Guinart y Simón Bolívar. Open 0800-late, in old colonial house with ornate columns and tiled floor, meals around US$6-8. Sit-down pizza restaurant where tourists can pay in pesos on Martí at Parque Céspedes. Lots of pizza stalls on Lino Pérez entre Martí y Maceo, but the best on Francisco Cadahía y Lino Pérez.

Bars *Casa Fisher*, Lino Pérez entre Cadahía y José Martí. In a nice old colonial house built in 1870, open 0900-0100. *Bar Daiquirí*, Lino Pérez entre Cadahía y José Martí. Open 24 hrs, also gallery of local art, kicks into life around 0200 when *Las Cuevas* nightclub closes. Unaccompanied Cuban women hanging around outside, beer US$1, mojito US$2, zombie US$4. *Bar Las Ruinas de Segarta*, Alameda entre Márquez y Galdós, in ruined courtyard. Open 24 hrs, also does fried chicken for US$1.50. *La Bodeguita de Trinidad*, Colón entre Martí y Maceo. Not as legendary as its Havana namesake, but a nice little music bar, open courtyard and with quaint sheltered booths for couples, trova group every night, entry free, beer US$1, cocktails US$2. Opposite is *El Jazmín*, bar in leafy courtyard, open late. The *Círculo Social de Obreros*, on Martí, serves rum in pesos, tourists welcome, an authentic drinking experience.

Nightlife **Music and dance** One block from the church is the *Casa de la Trova*, open weekend lunchtimes and daily in the evenings, 2200-0230, entry US$1 at night, but sometimes free. Excellent live Cuban music with a warm, lively atmosphere. There are mostly Cubans here, of all age groups, and it's a great place to join in with the locals having a good time. All drinks paid for in dollars, quite expensive. *La Canchanchara*, Villena 70, T4345. Open 0900-1900, cocktails, no food, serves a drink of the same name created out of rum, sugar, honey and lime. More touristy than Casa de La Trova (cigar and souvenir shop), but good live traditional music at lunchtimes. The disco at *Las Cuevas* (see 'Sleeping' above) is good, dance merengue and salsa with Cubans between the stalactites. *Casa de la Música*, up the steps past the church in Plaza Mayor, popular disco, full of tourists and Cubans, open 2300-0130 daily but not when it rains, live performers at weekends. A nice outdoor bar on the terrace leading up the steps, open till 0200. *Las Ruinas de Bruné*, Maceo entre Colón y Francisco Javier Zerquera. Nightly Afro-Cuban show for tourists in ruined colonial courtyard, very tacky and inauthentic, but worth seeing for the hilarious red teletubby running around the stage, who is supposed to be a devil. US$1, open 2100-2400. *La Parranda*, Villena, just off Plaza Mayor. An outdoor bar/music venue, very ad hoc farmyard atmosphere, but excellent live music every night, watched from semi-circle of seats, cocktails US$2, dancing, open from 2200 till late. *Coppelia*, still open after everything else is closed, music, pool, more Cubans.

Tour operators *Rumbos Cuba* office is on Simón Bolívar 430, T4414, 2264, open daily, can arrange tours and excursions and find out any information for travellers, will renew tourist cards, book flights from Trinidad and deal with *Cubana* enquiries. Staff speak French, English, German and Italian. *Cubatur*, Maceo esq Zerquera, open 0900-1200, 1300-1800, much the same tours and prices as *Rumbos,* Escambray US$25, Cayo Blanco US$25.

Transport **Local Car hire**: *Artex*, Lino Pérez y Martí, T2179, hires out microbuses. *Transtur*, Maceo esq Zerquera, T5314, cars and buses. *Transgaviota*, Frank País entre Escobar y Bolívar, T2282, buses, coaches and jeeps. *Nacional Rent A Car* is on José Martí 164 entre Cienfuegos y Lino Pérez, T4101, open 0800-2200 every day, but if all the cars are hired out then it closes, there is only a tiny sign on the door. There is also car hire at *Hotel Las Cuevas* and *Hotel Ancón*.

Long distance **Air** Daily flights to Havana 1355, US$60, with *Inter-Taca*, in Trinidad reservations can be made through *Rumbos* or *Cubatur*. In Havana, *Taca* is at *Hotel Habana Libre*,

T662702, F333728, lacsa@teleda.get.cma.net Flights to Cayo Largo de Sur, US$50. Two daily flights to Varadero. **Bus** Terminal on Piro Guinart entre Izquierdo y Maceo. *Víazul*, T2404/4448, from Havana 0815, 1300, arriving 1350, 1845, US$25, via Cienfuegos, returning 0800, 1500; from Varadero via Santa Clara and Sancti Spíritus at 0730, arriving 1325, US$20, returning 1430. *Víazul* also runs Trinidad-Santiago 1500, 2000, 12 hrs, via Sancti Spíritus, Jatibonico, Ciego de Avila, Florida, Camagüey, Sibanicú, Guáimaro, Las Tunas, Holguín, Bayamo and Palma Soriano. Astro bus for **Havana** leaves 1330 every other day, arrives 2230, US$21 a/c, US$17 without a/c.To **Sancti Spíritus**, daily, 0400, 1230, 2000, 2 hrs 40 mins, US$2.50. To **Cienfuegos**, daily, 0900, 1415, US$3. *Camión* (truck) leaves every other day, 0700, 1300, 2 hrs, 2.30 pesos. To **Santa Clara**, daily, 1715, arrive 2030, US$6. Ticket office open daily, 0800-1200, 1330-1700. **Train** The station is south of the town, walk south straight down Lino Pérez until you get to the railway line, turn left and you will see a shelter and an old building, beyond which is the 'office', T3348. Local services only. **Taxi** Tourist taxi to Playa Ancón, up to 5 people, from the bus terminal US$10 one way, 15 mins. To Topes de Collantes, up to 4 people, US$25 return with 3-hr wait there.

Banks *Bandec* is on José Martí 264 entre Zerquera y Colón, open Mon-Fri 0800-1700, Sat 0800-1600, will change TCs for dollars and cash advances on credit cards. Cadeca on Martí 164, half a block east of Parque Céspedes, open weekdays 0830-1800, Sun 0830-1200. There are *cambios* in *Hotel Las Cuevas*, *Hotel Ancón* and *Hotel Costa Sur*, where you can change TCs for dollars. **Medical facilities** The *Clínica Internacional*, run by Servimed, is on Lino Pérez 103 esq Anastasio Cárdenas, T3391, modern, with out-patient consultations, laboratory tests, X-rays, pharmacy, dentistry and 24-hr emergency care. A consultation fee is US$25, a call out fee US$40.

Directory

The best beach resort near Trinidad is Playa Ancón, not a town as such, just two resort hotels, with two more under construction. The beach is white sand and clean turquoise water, but sand flies appear after 1600. The best part of the beach is right in front of the *Hotel Ancón*, where there are straw sunshades and beach loungers. The rest of the beach has little shade. People are sometimes disappointed when they come here and expect something more spectacular. There is good **diving** less than 300m offshore.

Playa Ancón

Sleeping **B** *Ancón* (Gran Caribe), F6120/26. Price room only, though they encourage you to go all-inclusive, including 3 meals, drinks and such extras as snorkels, bicycles and horse riding, 279 rooms, hexagonal pool, good restaurant, snack bar by the pool does filling pizzas US$3-4, hot dogs US$2.50, disco and many facilities, including scuba diving and watersports, best beach here, popular with families. **B-C** *Costa Sur* (Horizontes), T6172. 131 rooms and chalets, run down and shabby, occasional hot water, a/c, bath, phone, balconies with mostly broken chairs, good value breakfast buffet for US$3.50, dinner buffet US$10, not bad, bar, nightclub, pool, shop, car rental and taxis, lovely beach if a bit narrow.

Sancti Spíritus

Sancti Spíritus, the provincial capital, is about 80 km northeast of Trinidad and 90 km southeast of Santa Clara. Like Trinidad, the town was founded by Diego Velázquez in 1514 and is one of Cuba's seven original Spanish towns and has a wealth of buildings from the colonial period.

Phone code: 41
Population: 80,000
Colour map 1, grid B4

The **Iglesia Parroquial Mayor del Espíritu Santo**, on Plaza Honorato, dates from 1522 when it was a wooden construction. Fray Bartolomé de las Casas gave his famous sermon here, marking the start of his campaign to help the indigenous people. The present building, of stone, replaced the earlier one in 1680, but it is acknowledged as the oldest church in Cuba because it still stands on its original foundations. The church is a National Monument, but it is not always open so you may not be able to look inside. The **Puente Yayabo** is considered a particular feature of Sancti Spíritus and is the only one of its type left on the island. The bridge was built in 1815 with five arches made of lime, sand and bricks. It is now also a National

Monument. The river itself has given its name to the *guayaba*, or guava, which grows along its banks, and also to the *guayabera*, a loose man's shirt without a tail worn outside the trousers and without a tie. The former **Teatro Principal** next to the bridge was built in 1839 and was the scene of all the major cultural, social and political events of the city. **Calle Llano** is a twisty street, with cobblestones right to the edge of the Yayabo River. **Parque Serafín Sánchez** is the centre of activity in the city where all major roads converge.

Embalse Zaza is a popular excursion for hiking, birdwatching, shooting and fishing, or just to go to the hotel (see below) and laze around the pool. The hotel can get busy at weekends.

Sleeping

There are 3 hotels in town around Parque Serafín Sánchez which are being refurbished to take foreigners. Otherwise, try the casa particulares listed

E *Plaza* (Islazul), T27102. 27 rooms in old colonial building, high-ceilings, refurbished in colonial style, some with balconies overlooking plaza, triples available, a/c, cold water, clean and comfortable, TV, bar, restaurant. **F** *Colonial*, Máximo Gómez Norte 23, T25123. 20 rooms, was being renovated 1999 so phone number may change. *Perla de Cuba* (Cubanacán). Beautiful colonial building takes up the whole of the north side of the Parque, under renovation. **D-E** *Zaza* (Horizontes), T26012, F668001, 10 km outside the town on the Zaza artificial lake, at Finca San José. 128 a/c rooms with bath, phone, restaurant, bar, nightclub, pool (check quality of water), games room, shop, car rental, medical services, tourism bureau, rather run down but pleasant and good value, shooting and fishing can be arranged. **Casas particulares** **F** *Sergio Orihuela Ruíz*, room in apartment, Agramonte 61, Apto 5 Altos entre Jesús Menéndez y Llano, CP 60 100, T23828. Opposite Iglesia Parroquial Mayor del Espíritu Santo, English spoken, meets most trains. **F** *Ricardo Rodríguez*, Independencia Norte 28. Local taxi driver, friendly, good price. **F** *Enrique Díaz Vázquez*, Martí 111 entre Sobral y San Cristóbal. Huge colonial house with lovely courtyard, private bathroom. **E** *Los Laureles*, T23913, 5 km north of town. 50 rooms, in semi-detached a/c chalets with solar power, large pool with bar, loud music day and night at weekends, almost exclusively Cuban guests, foreigners are stared at, extravagant Tropicana-style show Sat nights, overpriced, restaurant staff unwelcoming, occasional buses for workers going into town, taxis difficult to organize, private taxi US$10, reasonably convenient for Guayos railway station.

Eating

El Mesón, on Plaza Honorato del Castillo, in a building which was the first post office, closed Mon. *Rumbos* has the *Saratoga* café on the plaza, serving drinks and snacks, and a restaurant overlooking the river. *Shanghai*, Independencia, just off plaza. Chinese, mostly Cuban clientèle. Several *paladares* just across Puente Yayabo, then turn left or right. One of the best is *El Sótano*, Eduardo R Chivas 18 entre 26 de Julio y Jesús Menéndez. One of the tables is on a balcony overlooking river (mosquitoes), ask in advance for vegetarian food, large portions, good food, nice family. Street stalls also sell snacks including pizza, which are good value.

Nightlife

The *Casa de la Trova Miguel Companioni* is at Máximo Gómez Sur 26, for music. *Bar La Hermina*, over Puente Yayabo on the left, on a boat on the river with tables on the grass. *Bar La Quinta Helena*, on the left just before Puente Yayabo. Large, pleasant terrace, garden, patio, live music and concerts. There is a *Rumbos* Bar on Independencia Norte 32. Most night time activity happens around the Parque.

Transport

Bus The bus station is 2 km east of town on the Carretera Central, Km 388 entre Circunvalación y Carretera de Jíbaro. Walk out of town along Cervantes, follow signs to Ciego de Avila along Carretera Central, about 5 blocks past the zoo the bus station is on your right. *Víazul*, T24142/22162, stops here on both its Havana-Santiago and Varadero-Trinidad routes. Depart Havana 1500, 2000, arrive Sancti Spíritus 2045, 0100, return 0215, 0600, US$23; depart Santiago 1500, 2000, arrive 0210, 0555, return 2050, 0105, US$28; depart Varadero 0730, arrive 1210, return 1545, US$16; depart Trinidad 1430, arrive 1540, return 1215, US$6. Other buses to **Trinidad** several daily, 70 km, 2 hrs, trucks are often used, crowded and uncomfortable; **Ciego de Avila** 2 daily, 75 km, 2 hrs; **Santa Clara** several daily, 86 km, 2 hrs; also long distance buses to **Havana**, **Holguín** and **Santiago** daily. **Train** Station at Guayos, 15 km north. Taxi into town US$10. Touts offer transport and accommodation. Daily trains to Camagüey

0900, 1510, 1930, 2-3 hrs, US$6.50. The 'especial' to Havana at 2145, 9 hrs, US$14 and to Santiago at 2213, 8 hrs, US$22. **Taxi** You can negotiate a private taxi (*particular*) to take you to Trinidad for about US$25 or less, and to Santa Clara for around US$30, depending on the quality of your Spanish. Find a driver outside the bus station.

Banks *Banco de Crédito* on the plaza, cash advance on credit cards, open Mon-Fri 0800-1500. **Directory** *Cadeca*, Independencia 31, just off plaza, for TCs and currency exchange, open Mon-Sat 0830-1800, Sun 0830-1230, commission on TCs is 3% weekdays and 4% at weekends. **Medical facilities** Pharmacy on Independencia at the south western corner of Parque Maceo. **Tour companies & travel agents** On the square, at Cervantes 1, are *Havanatur*, T28308, for flights and tours, *Havanautos*, **T28403, for car hire, and *Islazul*,** T26390, for hotels and tours, but mostly for Cubans.

Ciego de Avila

Ciego de Avila was founded in 1849, and is an agricultural market town with a large thermal electricity plant. The main road from Havana to Camagüey passes straight through the middle of town; most people just keep going. The main square is the **Parque Martí**, with a church and the former town hall, **Ayuntamiento**, built in 1911, and now the provincial government headquarters.

Phone code: 33
Population: 85,000
Colour map 1, grid B4
Cuba

D *Hotel Ciego de Avila*, Carretera de Ceballos, T28013, 2 km out of town. 144 rooms in a **Sleeping** modern, 5-storey block, pool, taxis, Havanautos car hire, good food, breakfast included. E *Santiago-Habana*, Chicho Valdés y Honorato del Castillo, T25703. 76 rooms on the main road through town, run down but convenient.

Usual crop of low quality state run restaurants, including: *Mesón El Fuerte*, Av Las Palmas on **Eating** Plaza Camilo Cienfuegos; *Moscú*, Chicho Valdés 78, closed Wed; *Solaris*, on west side of Parque Martí, top floor of 12-storey building; *El Colonial*, Independencia 110, nice courtyard; *La Romagnola*, Chicho Valdés y Marcial Gómez, Italian; *Cafetería 12 Plantas*, Parque Martí, same building as *Solaris*, 24-hr *Rumbos* bar serving fried chicken and cold beer. *Paladares* are springing up and it would be best to investigate some of these. *Casa de la Trova*, at Libertad 130 y Simón Reyes.

Car hire *Havanautos* is at *Hotel Ciego de Avila*. **Air** There is an airport at **Ceballos**, 24 km **Transport** north of Ciego de Avila, Aeropuerto Máximo Gómez (AVI), which receives weekly scheduled flights from European cities, as well as twice weekly flights from Havana with *Cubana*. Charter flights also use this airport to get holiday-makers out to the resort hotels on Cayo Coco. **Bus** The bus station is on the Carretera Central just east of the zoo. *Víazul*, T2514/25109, stops here on its Havana-Santiago route. Departs Havana 1500, 2000, arrives Ciego de Avila 2205, 0220, returns 0100, 0440, US$27. Departs Santiago 1500, 2000, arrives 0055, 0435, returns 2210, 0225, US$24. There are other, cheaper buses to all the places on the main road from Havana to Santiago and a lot of others besides, such as Manzanillo, Holguín and Niquero. However, by the time the long distance buses get here they are nearly always full. **Train** Three trains daily to Havana. Most trains go through at night to **Holguín**, **Matanzas** and **Santiago**.

Airlines *Aerotaxi*, airport, T23937. *Cubana* Chicho Valdés 83 entre Maceo y Simón Reyes, T25316. **Directory**

Cayo Coco

Cayo Coco is a large island, 374 sq km, of mostly mangrove and bush, which shelter many migratory birds as well as permanent residents. The island is connected to the mainland just north of Morón by a 27 km causeway across the Bahía de Perros. The Atlantic side of the island has excellent beaches, particularly **Playa Los Flamencos**, with some 5 km of white sand and shallow, crystalline water. At certain times of the year you will see flamingos, after whom the beach is named. Cayo Coco is very

Phone code: 33
Colour map 1, grid B4

isolated and nearly all foreigners are here on an all-inclusive package of a week or so and do not go far. Marina Puertosol offers deep sea fishing and there is good diving. There are large, luxury resorts and plans to build an average of 1,000 hotel rooms a year, all four- or five-star, until Cayo Coco has 16,000 and the other cays have a further 6,000.

Cayo Guillermo, a 13 sq km cay with 5 km of beach, is connected to Cayo Coco by a causeway and there are plans to build a 35-km causeway to link it with Cayo Santa María to the west. Cayo Guillermo is protected by a long coral reef which is good for diving with plentiful fish and crustaceans, while on land there are lots of birds. Sand dunes, covered in palms and other vegetation, are believed to be in the highest in the Caribbean.

Sleeping **On Cayo Coco   AL-A** pp *Hotel Club Tryp Cayo Coco*, T301311 (locally), 333202, F333292 (in Havana), www.tryp.es Spanish and Cuban, the largest complex in Cuba, 1,000 rooms including a club, with a 250-room aparthotel and convention centre, like a village, shops, supermarket, pharmacy, disco, bowling alley, restaurants, bars, sports, beach a bit disappointing but facilities well planned. *Sol Club Cayo Coco* (Cubanacán), T301280, F301285. www.solmelia.es   270 rooms, lots of sports and entertainment for adults and children, several restaurants, disco, gym, pool. *Meliá Cayo Coco* 250 rooms, some round a lagoon, 5-star hotel. **On Cayo Guillermo**   *Venta Club Cayo Guillermo*, Italian run, 220 rooms, gourmet restaurant, *Bodeguita de Guillermo* overlooking beach. *Sol Club Cayo Guillermo* (Gran Caribe), T301760, F301748. 264 rooms in cabins with red tiled roofs. *Iberostar Daiquirí* (Gran Caribe), T301650. 312 rooms. *Meliá Cayo Guillermo*, 318 rooms.

Transport Only tour buses go to Cayo Coco, there are no public buses and a checkpoint at the beginning of the causeway effectively prevents Cubans without permission from visiting the cay. There is an airstrip for an air taxi service from Havana, but international flights and other large aircraft come in to the airport north of Ciego de Avila. A new, international airport is under construction.

Camagüey

Phone code: 322
Population: 772,000
Colour map 1, grid B4

Camagüey has been politically and historically important since the beginning of the 16th century and still has a lot of well-preserved colonial buildings, most dating from the 18th and 19th centuries. Many generations of revolutionaries have been associated with Camagüey and several key figures are commemorated, the most notable being Ignacio Agramonte, who was killed in action in 1873.

History
The town was originally called Puerto Príncipe, until 9 June 1903

The village of Santa María de Puerto del Príncipe was first founded in 1515 at Punta del Guincho in the Bahía de Nuevitas but moved several times until it was finally established between the Río Tínima and the Río Hatibonico. Moving inland was no protection against pirate attacks. It was the target of the Englishman Henry Morgan in 1668 and of French pirates led by François Granmont in 1679. Architects took the precaution of designing the layout to foil pirate attacks. No two streets run parallel, to create a maze effect, which is most unlike other colonial towns built on the grid system.

Sights **Nuestra Señora de la Merced**, a National Monument on Av Agramonte on the edge of the Plaza de los Trabajadores, was built in 1747 as a church and convent, the catacomb can still be seen. The original wooden cross on the bell tower was moved into the catacombs in 1999. On the walls are 17th and 18th-century paintings, but the most important treasure in the church is the Santo Sepulcro constructed in 1762 with the donation of 23,000 silver coins. **San Juan de Dios**, another National Monument, was built in 1728 as a church with a hospital attached, the first hospital in the village for men which also contained a home for the aged. Apparently this is the only church in Latin America which has the Holy Trinity as its central image.

Museo Provincial Ignacio Agramonte, first built as a cavalry barracks in 1848 was inaugurated on 23 December 1955 (the anniversary of Agramonte's birth).

There are exhibitions of history, natural history, paintings and furniture of the 17th and 18th centuries, but nothing special. ■ *Av de los Mártires 2 esquina Ignacio Sánchez. Tue-Sat 0900-1700, Sun 0800-1200, US$2.* At the **Museo Casa Natal Ignacio Agramonte** you have an obligatory guided tour in Spanish with exhaustive explanation of every single document on display. Only for serious students of revolutionary history. Ignacio Agramonte y Loynaz, a cattle rancher, one of the national heroes of the struggle against the Spanish, was born here on 23 December 1841. ■ *Av Ignacio Agramonte 49, T97116. Tue-Sat 1000-1800, US$2.*

C *Villa Maraguán* (Cubanacán), Circunvalación Este, on outskirts, T72017, 72170. Three-star, 32 rooms and 2 suites with terrace, 3 bars, restaurant, cafetería, car rental, pool, open air night time entertainment when tour parties are staying, video and games room, squash, billiards, table tennis, volleyball, children's playground, horse riding, medical services. **D** *Hotel Camagüey* (Horizontes), Av Ignacio Agramonte, T72015/82490. Good condition, modern, Soviet influenced architecture, pool, disco show, bar in the lobby and on 2nd floor, cafetería, buffet restaurant US$10, car hire. **D-E** *Gran Hotel* (Islazul), Maceo 67, entre Ignacio Agramonte y General Gómez, T92093/4, comazul@ teleda.get.cma.net. Colonial style, built 1939, renovated 1997, central, swimming pool, restaurant on top floor, good view, also cafetería and snack bar. **E** *Plaza* (Islazul), Van Horne 1, entre República y Avellaneda, T82413, 82457. 67 rooms with TV, fridge, colonial building right by railway station, the nicest, more expensive rooms face the front, with balcony, but rooms at the back are away from traffic noise, mediocre restaurant, bar, Altamira travel agency. **E-F** *Puerto Príncipe*, Av de los Mártires 60 y Andrés Sánchez, La Vigía (in town), T82469/82403, near museum and railway station. 77 rooms, a/c, bar, very slow restaurant, choose a room away from the nightclub on roof open until 0130 every night. **F** *Colón*, República 472 entre San José y San Martín, T83346, 83368. Old style built in 1920s, central, average restaurant, snack bar better, 2 grades of rooms, the better ones have a/c, ice , TV, friendly staff. **F** *Isla de Cuba*, República y San Estéban, T91515. In the heart of the city, 43 rooms, 2 grades.

Casas particulares **F** *Caridad García Valua*, Oscar Primeles 310 A entre Bartolomé Masó y Padre Olallo, T291554. Two rooms with private bathrooms, a/c or fan, fridge, garden, clean and nice, breakfast US$2-3, dinner US$5-7. **F** *Casa Rosello*, Carlos M de Céspedes 260 (Hospital) entre Hnos Agüeros y San Ramón, T92143/96879, ask for Pedro. Two beautiful rooms, bathroom, owner practices *Santería* and will show you some interesting things, garage opposite, US$1 per night. **F** *Tania Rent-a-Room*, San Ramón 285 entre San José y San Martín, 2 blocks from Av República. Big breakfast included, a/c, dinner US$5, very nice family, arrange trips to Santa Lucía for US$12. **F** *Migdalia Carmenates y Manolo Rodríguez*, Santa Rita 18 (El Solitario) entre República y Santa Rosa, T94403. Three rooms, a/c, fan, 2 share bathroom, 1 en suite, hot shower, garden, laundry US$2, garage US$2, nice house, positive atmosphere, good breakfast US$3, dinner US$6.

State-run restaurants, apart from those in hotels, include *Rancho Luna*, on Plaza Maceo, open 1200-1400, 1800-2200, and *La Volanta*, on Parque Agramonte, open 1200-2300, both of which offer Cuban food and you will be asked to pay in dollars. You can pay in pesos at *Pizzería La Piazza* on Agramonte on the corner with Maceo, but there may be a queue. On the Plaza de San Juan there are the *Parador de los Tres Reyes* and the *Campana de Toledo*, 2 small colonial-style restaurants serving Spanish food, pleasant, live music, meals from US$8. Near the railway station there is *El Paradero* cafetería and bar open 24 hrs and a bakery and cafetería also open 24 hrs. *Bar El Cambio* on Parque Agramonte is good.

Every Sat night a *Noche Camagueya* is held along República, when the street is closed to traffic and there is music everywhere and traditional food. The **Ballet de Camagüey**, ranked 2nd in the country after Havana's ballet company, often performs at the Teatro Principal, on Padre Valencia 64, T93048. Folk music is played at the *Casa de la Trova*, on the west side of Parque Agramonte between Martí and Cristo, closed Mon.

Sleeping

Eating

Nightlife

Cuba

Tour operators   *Rumbos*, López Recio 108, T94807, 97229, Mon-Fri 0800-1800. Many tours available, including to Cayo Sabinal and Santa Lucía.

Transport   **Local Car hire**: *Havanautos* is at *Hotel Camagüey*. There are Servi Cupet gas stations by the river on Carretera Central with Av de la Libertad, and a couple of blocks further south on the other side of the Carretera Central. **Taxi**: service T81247/98721. For a tourist taxi T72428. Bicitaxis charge about US$1 per person, fix price in advance.

Long distance Air Ignacio Agramonte International Airport (CMW) is 9 km from the centre on the road to Nuevitas, T61010. *Cubana* flies daily from Havana and once a week from London Gatwick. There are also charter flights from Toronto and Europe depending on the season. **Bus** Ticket agency, T71602. The Interprovincial bus station is southwest of the centre along the Carretera Central Oeste, esq Perú. *Víazul*, T72346/71646, stops here on its Havana-Santiago route. Depart Havana 1500, 2000, arrive Camagüey 2355, 0410, return 2305, 0250, US$33; depart Santiago 1500, 2000, arrive 2250, 0235, return 0010, 0425, US$18. Other cheaper buses also along this route, but they may be full when they arrive. **Train** Railway station, T92633/81525. Train ticket agency, T83214. Foreigners pay in dollars at Ladis office upstairs above the main ticket office opposite *Hotel Plaza*. Trains to **Havana** daily at 2219 and Mon, Wed and Fri at 1933, 10 hrs, US$21, stopping at **Guayos** (for Sancti Spíritus and Trinidad) at 2230, US$6.50. To **Bayamo** and **Manzanillo** at 0527. To **Holguín** at 2322. To **Morón** at 1208. The 'special' from Havana gets in to Camagüey at 0048 on its way to Santiago, 6 hours, US$12.50 and Guantánamo.

Directory   **Airlines** *Cubana* is at República 400 esq Correa, open Mon-Fri 0700-1500, Sat 0700-1100, T92156/91338. **Banks** The *Banco Financiero Internacional* is on Plaza Maceo. There is a *cadeca* on República entre Primelles y Santa Rita. **Medical facilities** 24-hr pharmacy on the corner of Avellaneda y Primelles.

Playa Santa Lucía

Phone code: 32
Colour map 1, grid B5

Santa Lucía is a beach resort 112 km northeast of Camagüey, where the sand stretches some 20 km along the northern coast near the **Bahía de Nuevitas**. This is a beautiful beach, protected by an offshore reef which contains over 50 species of coral and is much sought after by divers. The water is clear and warm, with an average temperature of 24°C. Diving is run by Marlin, which also has an underwater photo and video centre, T36404. There are 37 dive sites at depths of 5-40m in the area including a daily shark feeding site where up to 20 sharks congregate; some of them swim in between the divers. Contact Shark's Friends dive centre. It is a lovely place to come and relax but be aware that it is remote, there is no real town as such, and people who stay here are on all-inclusive package tours and see little of Cuba. 8 km from Santa Lucía is **Playa Los Cocos**, which is even better than Santa Lucía. The sand here is very white and the water crystal clear. There are some bars and seafood restaurants. Across the channel, west of Playa Los Cocos, is **Cayo Sabinal**, reached by road from Nuevitas or by boat, with *Seafaris*, from Santa Lucía. There are beautiful beaches of white sand which are practically deserted and the cay is a wildlife reserve housing the largest colony of pink flamingos in the Caribbean, plus many other birds which are rare or endangered elsewhere.

Sleeping   The resort is part of the Cubanacán group (www.cubanacan.cu), including joint venture hotels, restaurants, shopping centre, watersports, discos, tennis and other land sports and activities. All the hotels are all-inclusive and prices are per person sharing a double room. **A-C** *Cuatro Vientos*, T36160, F334533, aloja@cvientos.stl.cyt.cu 404 rooms and 8 suites, 4-star, marina, scuba diving. **B** *Club Mayanabo*, T36184-5, F365176, aloja@mayanabo.stl.cyt.cu Three-star, 212 rooms and 13 suites. **B-C** *Vita Club Caracol*, T365158-9. Three-star, sea front in large gardens, 150 2-storey cabañas with sea view. **B** *Gran Club Santa Lucía*, T365146-8, aloja@coral.stl.cyt.cu Joint venture with La Cascina of Italy,

3-star, 108 rooms on the beach, 144 garden rooms and 108 suites. **D** *Villa Tararaco*, T36262/36310. Two-star, 30 rooms.

State-run restaurants: *Las Brisas*, T36109, Creole; *Bonsai*, T36109, Chinese; and *Luna Mar*, **Eating**
T36284, Italian. There are also *paladares* where you can eat for a more reasonable price.

Air International flights use the airport near Camagüey, but there is a small airstrip, Joaquín **Transport**
de Agüero, for Aerotaxi services.

Medical services *Clínica Internacional*, T36203. **Tour operators** *Cubatur*, T36291. *Rumbos*, **Directory**
T36106.

Holguín

Holguín was founded in 1545. It is known as the 'city of the parks', four of which, *Phone code: 24*
Parque Infantil, **Parque Carlos Manuel de Céspedes**, the **Plaza Central** and *Population: 250,000*
Parque José Martí, lie between the two main streets: Antonio Maceo and Libertad *Colour map 1, grid B5*
(Manduley). There is a statue of **Carlos Manuel de Céspedes** in the park named
after him: he is remembered for having freed his slaves on 10 October 1868 and start-
ing the war of independence. The Plaza Central is named after **General Calixto
García Iñiguez** (statue in the centre), who was born in Holguín in 1837 and took
part in both wars of independence. He captured the town from the Spanish in 1872
and again occupied it in 1898 after helping the US forces defeat the colonial power in
Santiago de Cuba. His birthplace on Calle Miró 147, one block from the plaza, is now
a museum, **Casa Natal de Calixto García**. ■ *Mon-Fri 0800-1700, Sat 0800-1300,
US$1*. On the north side of the square is the **Museo Provincial**, built between
1860-1868 and now a National Monument. The most important item on display
here is the Hacha de Holguín, a precolumbian axe head carved with the head of a
man, found in 1860 on one of the hills around the city and believed to be about 500
years old. It has become the symbol of Holguín. ■ *Mon-Fri 0900-1700, Sat
0900-1300, US$1, US$3 with camera.*

Above the city is **La Loma de la Cruz**, a strategic hill which used to have a cross on
top until Hurricane Georges blew it down in 1998. On 3 May 1790, a Franciscan
priest, Antonio de Alegría, came with a group of religious people and put up the
cross. In 1929 stone steps were begun up the hill, which were finished 3 May 1950.
Every 3 May locals celebrate the Romerías de la Cruz de Mayo. They light candles
and offer coins.

D-E *Pernik* (Islazul), T481011. Near Plaza de la Revolución on Av Jorge Dimitrov y Av XX **Sleeping**
Aniversario. 202 rooms, mostly overnighters passing through, shops, bar, restaurant, empty
swimming pool, TV, a/c, nice view from top floor rooms, blue furniture, small bathrooms,
adequate. **D-E** *Villa El Bosque* (Islazul), T481012, just off Av Jorge Dimitrov. 69 rooms in
spread out villas, patio garden, fridge, basic shower room, TV, a/c, also 2 suites, **C**, good security, car rental, large pool, *El Pétalo* disco, popular. **D-E** *El Mirador de Mayabe* (Islazul),
T422160, T/F425347, outside the town, 24 rooms in cabins under the trees, tiled floors, a/c,
TV, wooden furniture, fridge, hot water, adequate bathroom, quiet, also a suite and **C** 4
rooms in a house at the top of the hill with a fantastic view.

Casas particulares **E** *Barbara Cuenca Sánchez*, Narciso López 48B entre Luz Caballero y
Aricochea, walking distance from town centre. **F** *Eddy G Osorio*, Frexes 166 entre Morales
Lemus y Narciso López. With bath, very good breakfast for US$1.50. **F** *Rolando Torres Cardet*,
José Antonio Cardet 202 entre Frexes y Aguilera, T425619. Very clean, a/c, small breakfast
included, free coffee, central. **F** *Rosalía Días V*, Frexes 176 entre Miró y Morales Lemus,
T423395. Excellent location, big room with bathroom, a/c, run by charming elderly lady, food
available. **F** *Evaristo Bofill and Mirtha Lago*, Luz Caballero 78 Altos entre Miró y Morales
Lemus. 2 large rooms, very clean, private bathroom, a/c, terrace, friendly and helpful family

Cuba

who make you feel at home and like a good laugh. **F** *Antonio Ochoa*, Morales Lemus 199 entre Martí y Frexes, T423659. Spanish-style house with courtyard, light and airy, two big rooms, discounts for long stays, a/c, fan, hot water, laundry, garage, breakfast US$2.50, dinner US$5. **F** *Isabel Sera Galvez*, Narciso López 142 entre Frexes y Aguilera, T422529. Two beautiful rooms in a lovely colonial house, bathroom, hot water, good food, US$4 dinner, US$1 garage with a neighbour.

Eating There are several *paladares*. *Aurora*, on Martí, has a good reputation and is popular. *Jelly Boom*, also on Martí, near the cemetery, is supposed to be the best in town; ask around for others as they change quickly. *José Pavón*, José A Cardet 180-F-1, T422687, family restaurant with apartment to rent. *Pizzería Roma* on Maceo with Agramonte at the corner of Parque Céspedes, is state-run. *La Begonia*, is a Rumbos *cafetería* on the Plaza Central. Outdoors under a flowering creeper, very pretty, good for a Mayabe beer, meeting place for *jineteras*. *El Tocororo*, across the square, also Rumbos but toasted sandwiches are cheaper here, open 24 hrs, wooden sculpture above door. *Cafetería Cristal*, corner of plaza with Libertad. Open 24 hrs, usual range of fastish food. For ice cream, *Coppelia* is on Parque Peralta. The 2 main hotels are rather far away from the restaurants and their own food is not recommended. *Taberna Pancho* is in the area, though, on Av Jorge Dimitrov, round the corner from the *Pernik* and serves beer and a reasonable burger.

Transport **Local** There is very little motorized public transport. The city is choked with *bicitaxis*, bicycles with an extra wheel and seat on the side, or cart behind, or horse drawn buses and taxis, charging 50-80 centavos. Out of town people wait at junctions for the *Amarillos* (traffic wardens dressed in yellow) to stop any truck or large vehicle and bundle on as many passengers as possible. **Long distance Bus**: The interurban bus terminal, notable for the number of horses, rather than vehicles, is on Av de los Libertadores after the coffee roasting plant and opposite the turning to Estadio Calixto García. The interprovincial bus terminal is west of the centre on the Carretera Central. *Víazul*, Carretera Central 19 entre 20 de Mayo e Independencia, T461036/422111, stops here on the Havana-Santiago route. Depart Havana 1500, 2000, arrive Holguín 0320, 0805, return 1855, 2325, US$44; depart Santiago 1500, 2000, arrive 1850, 2320, return 0325, 0810, US$11. A *colectivo* to Las Tunas costs 20 pesos.

Directory **Airlines** *Aerotaxi*, T462512. *Cubana* is in Edif Pico de Cristal, Libertad esquina Martí, Policentro, T425707, F46811. *LTU* at the airport, F335360. **Banks** *Bandec*, Arias 159, open Mon-Fri 0800-1500. **Medical facilities** The main hospital is west of the town centre on Av V I Lenin. There are medical services at the hotels *Pernik* and *El Bosque*.

Guardalavaca

Phone code: 24
Colour map 1, grid B6

Guardalavaca has been developed as a tourist resort along a beautiful stretch of coastline, indented with horseshoe bays and sandy beaches. The resort is in two sections: the older part is rather like a village, apartments for workers are here and there are a few shops, discos, bank, restaurant and bus stop, while newer hotels further west on the beach Estero Ciego (also referred to as Playa Esmeralda), are very isolated and there is nothing to do outside the hotels. There is a reef offshore for diving, which is very unspoilt and has a lot to offer.

Excursions The lagoon in the **Bahía de Naranjo** has a small marina, where sailing trips and fishing expeditions can be arranged. Near the mouth of the lagoon is an aquarium, 10 minutes by boat from the dock, with dolphins and a sea lion, and a restaurant.

West along the coast, **Playa Pesquero** is a lovely sandy beach, the east end is better for children as there are strong currents and deceptive sand bars to the west. There is a lifeguard on duty even out of season. The 309-room LTI *Costa Verde Beach Resort* (Gaviota), and the *Sol Club Playa Pesquero*, opened in 1999-2000.

A few km from Guardalavaca on a hill with a wonderful view, is the **Museo Aborigen Chorro de Maita** , a small but well-presented museum displaying a collection of 56 skeletons dating from 1490-1540, exactly as they were found. One is of a young Spaniard of about 22 years of age with his arms crossed for a Christian burial, but the rest are Amerindians, buried in the Central American style, lying flat with their arms folded across their stomachs. ■ *Tue-Sat 0900-1700, Sun 0900-1300, US$1 per photo, plus US$5 per film, small shop with souvenirs.*

The **Museo Indocubano Bani**, Gen Marrero 305 y Av José Martí, in **Banes** has a good collection of pre-columbian artifacts, probably the best in Cuba. The town of Banes was originally the site of the Bani chieftancy and the museum contains treasures discovered by the many archaeological digs in the area. ■ *Tue-Sat 0900-1700, Sun 0800-1200, US$1.*

L-B *Delta Las Brisas* (Cubanacán), T30218, F30018, reserva@deltsbsa,gvc.gyt.cu All-inclusive, 349 good sized sea view or inland rooms, 84 mini-suites, non-motorized watersports, small man-made beach, nice pool, organized entertainment, gym, tennis, bicycles, kids kamp, tour desk, car rental. **AL-C** *Atlántico* (Cubanacán), T30180/30280, F30200, recep@hatlant.gvc,cyt.cu Best position right on beach, 264 rooms with shower, long dark corridors, adequate but nothing special for the price, good food, set meal times, OK for vegetarians, bicycles, windsurfing, pedalos, sailing, diving, snorkelling, gym, entertainment, shops, pool, tennis. **A** *Villa Turey*, opposite bus stop. Not on beach, spread out villas and apartments around pool, 136 rooms, 3 suites (with 2 bedrooms, 2 bathrooms upstairs, sitting room, kitchenette and toilet downstairs), short walk to beach through other hotels. **AL-C** *Club Amigo Guardalavaca* (Cubanacán), T30121, F30221, recep@hguard.gvc.cyt.cu 234 smallish rooms, TV, basic bathroom, shower, outside a/c, run down, tennis courts but no balls.

Sleeping

Meliá Río de Oro, T30090-4. All-inclusive, 5-star, 292 junior suites, a/c. *Sol Club Río de Luna* (all-inclusive), T300304, F30035. Four-star and sister hotel next door, *Sol Río de Mares*, T337013, 30060-4 F30065. Four-star, half board only, most people on discounted packages, comfortable. All 3 hotels have lots of entertainment and sports, on land and in the water.

6 km along the coast at Estero Ciego are the best hotels in the area run by Sol Meliá, www.solmelia.es

El Cayuelo, short walk along coast from *Las Brisas*, good for lobster, open daily 0900-2300. Most hotel restaurants in the hotels offer buffet meals which get very dull after a few days. There are restaurants in the Centro Comercial but no *paladares* in the area.

Eating

There are dive shops on the beach near the *Atlántico* and the *Sol Río de Mares*, offering courses and fun dives, no jetty so you have to swim and carry tank and gear out to boat. Good, well-maintained equipment and safety record. Safety not so good with other watersports, where life-jackets are not always offered or worn.

Watersports

Santiago de Cuba

Santiago de Cuba is one of the oldest towns on the island, protected from the sea in an attractive bay surrounded by mountains. It is a lively city with plenty of music and other cultural activities. It is the place to come for carnival in July but there is lots going on at other times of the year too. It is easy to get out of the city for excursions to beaches, historical or interesting geological sites. Santiago, Cuba's second city, is not a colonial gem along the lines of Havana or Trinidad, but it does have an eclectic range of architectural styles from colonial to art deco. The city centre is cluttered, featuring many beautiful pastel coloured buildings in better condition than many of those in the capital.

*Phone code: 226
Colour map 1, grid B6*

Ins and outs

Santiago can be reached by air, train or bus. All major transport routes may be fully booked. International and domestic *Cubana* flights arrive at the **Antonio Maceo airport** (SCU), 8 km south of the city on the coast. Official and unofficial taxis around US$5-8, depending on the company and the distance. The long distance bus terminal is to the north of the city, by the

Getting there
See also page 226

Plaza de la Revolución. Outside are taxis, *colectivos*, trucks, buses and horse-drawn *coches*. The new railway station is more central, opposite the rum factory on Av Jesús Menéndez, and within walking distance of many **casas particulares** and some hotels in the centre.

Getting around Urban buses cost 20 centavos. There are also coches, 1 peso, motorbikes, US$1, and *bicitaxis*, US$0.50, for short journeys around town. Plaza Marte is a central hub for lots of local transport. For excursions there are buses and/or trucks on some routes out of town but it is easier to negotiate a day trip with a driver who can take you exactly where you want to go. Make sure everything is agreed and clear before you set off, as drivers have a reputation for moving the goalposts when you are a long way from base. Car hire is available if you want to drive yourself.

History Santiago de Cuba was one of the seven towns (*villas*) founded by Diego Velázquez. It was first built in 1515 on the mouth of the Río Paradas but moved in 1516 to its present location in a horseshoe valley surrounded by mountains. It was Cuba's capital city until replaced by Havana in 1553 and capital of Oriente province until 1976. During the 17th century Santiago was besieged by pirates from France and England, leading to the construction of the Castillo del Morro, still intact and now housing the piracy museum. Because of its location, Santiago has been the scene of many migratory exchanges with other countries; it was the first city in Cuba to receive African slaves, many French fled here from the slaves' insurrection in Haiti in the 18th century and Jamaicans have also migrated here. Santiago is more of a truly ethnic blend than many other towns in Cuba. It is known as the 'heroic city' (*Ciudad Héroe*) or '*capital moral de la Revolución Cubana*'. One of Cuba's foremost revolutionaries of the 19th century, **General Antonio Maceo**, is honoured in the **Plaza de la Revolución**, to the northeast of the centre, with a dramatic monument made of galvanized steel in searing, solid Soviet style, and a gargantuan bronze statue of the general on horseback surrounded by huge iron machetes.

Sights **Parque Céspedes** is in the centre of town and everything revolves around it. Most of the main museums are within easy walking distance. The *Hotel Casa Granda* flanks the entire east side of the small park. The **Cathedral**, Santa Iglesia Basílica Metropolitana, is on the south side, entrance on Félix Peña. The first building on the site was completed in 1524, but four subsequent disasters, including earthquakes and pirate attacks meant that the cathedral was rebuilt four times. ■ *0800-1200 daily, services Mon, Wed 1830, Sat 1700, Sun 0900, 1830.*

The **Cementerio Santa Ifigenia**, northwest of the city, features **José Martí's** mausoleum, a huge structure with a statue of Martí inside, designed to receive a shaft of sunlight all morning. Martí is surrounded by six statues of women, representing the six Cuban provinces of the 19th century. Also in the cemetery is the grave of **Frank País**, a prime mover in the revolutionary struggle and other notable figures such as Céspedes, the Bacardí family and the mother and widow of Maceo. There is a monument to the Moncada fallen and the tomb of Cuba's first president, Tomás Estrada Palma. Well worth a visit. ■ *Av Crombet, Reparto Juan G Gómez. US$1, extra US$1 to take pictures, price includes guided tour in Spanish and English.*

Museums Of the several museums, the best is the **Museo de Ambiente Histórico Cubano**, located in Diego Velázquez' house (the oldest in Cuba, started in 1516, completed 1530). Velázquez lived on the top floor, while the ground floor was used as a contracting house and a smelter for gold. Each room shows a particular period, featuring furniture, china, porcelain, crystal. ■ *At the northwest corner of Parque Céspedes, Félix Peña 612, T52652. Mon-Sun 0900-1700, US$2, with guided tour in English, French or German, camera fee US$1 per photo.*

The **Museo Emilio Bacardí**, was named after industrialist Emilio Bacardí Moreau, its main benefactor and collector of much of the museum's contents. This was the second museum founded in Cuba and has exhibits from prehistory to the

Revolution downstairs, one of the most important collections of Cuban colonial paintings and the archaeology hall has mummies from Egypt and South America. ■ *Two blocks east of the Parque, opposite the Palacio Provincial, entrance on Pío Rosado esquina Aguilera, T28402. Tue-Sat 1000-2000, Sun 1000-1800, Mon 1200-2000, guided tour in English. US$2.*

The **Museo Histórico 26 de Julio**, formerly the Moncada Garrison, was attacked (unsuccessfully) by Castro and his revolutionaries on 26 July 1953. When the revolution triumphed in 1959, the building was turned into a school. To mark the 14th anniversary of the attack, one of the buildings was converted to a museum, featuring photos, plans and drawings of the battle. Bullet holes, filled in by Batista, have been reconstructed on the outer walls. ■ *Av Moncada esquina General Portuondo, T20157. Tue-Fri 0900-2000, Sat, Mon 0900-1700, Sun 0900-1300, US$1. Guided tour in English, French, Italian. Camera fee US$1, video camera US$5.* The **Museo Casa Natal de Frank País**, is in the birthplace of the leader of the armed uprising in Santiago on 30 November 1956, who was shot in July 1957. ■ *General Banderas 226 y Los Maceos, T52710.* The **Museo de la Lucha Clandestina** highlights the support given by the local urban population during the battle in the Sierra Maestra. Exhibits revolve around Frank País, from his early moves to foment a revolutionary consciousness to his integration into the Movimiento 26 de Julio under Fidel Castro. ■ *At the top of picturesque Padre Pico (steps) and corner of Santa Rita and Jesús Rabí, T24689. 0900-1900 Tue-Sat, 0900-1700 Sun, US$2.* The **Casa Natal de Antonio Maceo**, built between 1800-1830, was the birthplace, on 14 June 1845, of Antonio Maceo y Grajales, one of the greatest military commanders of the 1868 and 1895 wars of independence. The museum houses his biography and details of his 32 years' devotion to the struggle for independence. ■ *Los Maceo 207 entre Corona y Rastro, T23750. Mon-Sat 0900-1700, US$1.*

The **Museo del Carnaval** exhibits a collection of instruments, drums and costumes from Santiago's famous July carnival. If you are not going to be there in July, this is the best way to get a flavour of the celebrations. ■ *On Heredia esquina Pío Rosado. Tue-Sat 0900-1800, Sun 0900-1200, US$2.* The **Casa del Caribe** is a world renowned cultural centre. If you are interested in *Santería*, there is a musical and religious ceremony at 0930 on Wednesdays. ■ *Off Av Manduley on 13 esquina 8.* The **Museo de la Religión** displays religious items particularly concerning *Santería*, but there are no written explanations of the exhibits, best to ask for a guide. ■ *13 206, esquina 10. Mon-Sat 0830-1700, free.*

South of Santiago

The Ruta Turística runs along the shore of the Bahía de Santiago to the **Castillo del Morro**, a clifftop fort with the **Museo de la Piratería**, a museum of the sea, piracy and local history, charting the pirate attacks made on Santiago during the 16th century. Pirates included the Frenchman Jacques de Sores and the Englishman Henry Morgan, and you can see many of the weapons used in both attack and defence of the city. From the roof you can admire the thrilling views over the Bay of Santiago and Cayo Granma and you can follow some 16th-century steps almost down to the waterline. ■ *T91569. US$3. Restaurant on a terrace with a great view, main dish US$6. Turistaxi to El Morro, US$10 round trip with wait.*

East of Santiago

Excellent excursions can be made to the **Gran Piedra** (26 km east) a viewpoint from which it is said you can see Haiti and Jamaica on a clear day, more likely their lights on a clear night. It is a giant rock weighing 75,000 tonnes, 1,234-m high, and reached by climbing 454 steps from the road (only for the fit). The view is tremendous and buzzards circle you. US$1 to climb. There are no buses but a private car will charge you about US$15 there and back (hotel tour desks will arrange a tour, good value).

Some 2 km before La Gran Piedra are the **Jardines de la Siberia**, on the site of a former coffee plantation, an extensive botanical garden; turn right and follow the track for about 1 km to reach the gardens. The **Museo La Isabelica** is at Carretera de la Gran Piedra Km 14, a ruined coffee plantation once owned by French emigrés from Haiti, the buildings of which are now turned into a museum housing the former kitchen and other facilities on the ground floor with farming tools and archaeological finds. Upstairs is the owners' house in authentic 19th-century style. ■ *Tue-Sat 0900-1700, Sun 0900-1300, US$2.*

On the Carretera Siboney at Km 13½ is **La Granjita Siboney**, the farmhouse used as the headquarters for the revolutionaries' attack on the Moncada barracks on 26

Santiago de Cuba

■ Sleeping
1 Aída Morales Valdés
2 Dinorah Rodríguez Bueno
3 Dr Javier Berdion Sevilla
4 Félix Corroso
5 Las Américas
6 Manrique Nistal Bello

July 1953. It now has a museum of uniforms, weapons and artefacts used by the 106 men who gathered here the night before, as well as extensive newspaper accounts of the attack. ■ *Tue-Sun 0900-1700, T9836, entry US$2.*

Siboney, 16 km east of the city, is the nearest beach to Santiago with a reef just offshore which is great for snorkelling. ■ *Take bus 214 from near bus terminal. Very crowded at weekends.* At Km 24 is the **Valle de la Prehistoria**, a huge park filled with

Cuba

life-size carved stone dinosaurs and stone age men. Great for the kids but due to the total absence of shade it is like walking around a desert. Take huge supplies of water and try to go early or late. ■ *Entrance US$2, extra US$1 to take photos.*

An **Aquarium and Dolphinarium** on this stretch of the coast has three sea-lion and dolphin shows daily, at 1000, 1130, 1445, however small the audience. The show is of a high standard and visitors are invited to dive in and play with the dolphins for an extra US$20, for about 10 minutes, but remember that Cuba captures dolphins from the wild, a cruel and unnecessary practice for the entertainment of tourists. The aquarium has many species of fish as well as turtle and sharks (feeding time is spectacular). There is a basic refreshment bar where you can get a sandwich for US$1 and a beach with trees for shade but no facilities. ■ *US$5.* **Laguna Baconao** is a large murky lake in a beautiful setting. Flanking the lake is a crocodile sanctuary, but they are kept in small enclosures with barely enough water to drink. ■ *US$1 to enter the Laguna Baconao area, which includes a boat ride to a floating bar in the middle of the lake.*

C *Club Coralia Santiago* (Gran Caribe), 3-star, Carretera Baconao Km 4, Arroyo La Costa, T54596, 28130, under renovation. **C** *Costa Morena* (Horizontes), Carretera Baconao, km 38.5, T56127/ 398113. Three-star, all-inclusive resort on both sides of the road (used to be two hotels), car hire, Visa accepted, scuba diving. **AL** *LTI Los Corales – Carisol* (Cubanacán), T86177, 28519, F335216, reserva@carisol.scu.cyt.cu. Three-star, 120 rooms and 46 junior suites, a/c, minibar, TV, all-inclusive, buffet and à la carte restaurant and cafetería, pool tennis, dive centre, beach volleyball, tennis, car and bicycle hire, child care, near **Playa Cazonal**, which is a very high quality beach for this area. Wear something on your feet when swimming and avoid standing on the coral reef.

West of Santiago Ten kilometres west of Santiago is **El Sanctuario de Nuestra Señora de la Caridad del Cobre ('El Cobre')** where the shrine of Cuba's patron saint, the Virgen de la Caridad del Cobre, is built over a working copper mine. The story goes that in the 17th century, three fishermen were about to capsize in Nipe Bay, when they found a wooden statue of the Virgin Mary floating in the sea. Their lives were saved and they brought the statue to its current resting place above the altar. Downstairs there are many tokens of gratitude left by Cubans who have been helped by the Virgin in some way. There is a pilgrimage here on 12 September. Watch out for the touts; probably best to take a bit of copper and offer 50 cents or some pesos, otherwise they will be waiting for you when you leave the church. ■ *There is no bus, so either hire a car and driver, about US$8, or get on a truck at the bus station for a few pesos.*

West from Santiago runs a coastal road along the Sierra Maestra with beautiful bays and beaches, completely deserted, some with black sand. It is only possible to visit by car. Many of the villages have connections with revolutionary events. **El Uvero**, about 60 km from Santiago, has a monument marking the attack by Castro and his men on the Batista troop HQ on 28 May 1957. The building which was attacked is now a small museum. About 20 km further west is a turning for **Pico Turquino** (1,974m), just before the village of Ocujal. You can drive a short distance and park and walk. This is the highest peak in the Sierra Maestra.

At **Pilón** (population 12,000) a small town with a harbour, the road turns inland towards the Golfo de Guacanayabo past **Ojo de Agua**. After the village there are three separate signs and plaques marking the spots where three groups of men who disembarked from *Granma* crossed the road in underground water conduits, before heading into the Sierra Maestra. The road follows the Río Sevilla to join up with the Manzanillo-Niquero road running down the other side of the peninsula to **Cabo Cruz** at the tip. Turn left to **Niquero** from where a dirt road leads to the spot where Castro's 82 revolutionaries disembarked from the yacht, *Granma*, on 2 December 1956 in a mangrove swamp just southwest of **Playa Las Coloradas**. By the road is a small park where a replica of *Granma* can be seen and a 2 km concrete path through the swamp takes you to a rather ugly concrete jetty and a plaque marking the occasion. The dirt road ends at **Cabo Cruz** at the tip of the peninsula.

Chivirico 2 all-inclusive *SuperClubs* hotels: **AL-B** per person *Sierra Mar* (*Cubanacán*), on **Sleeping**
Playa Sevilla, Carretera de Chivirico Km 60, T29110, F29007, sierrmar@smar.scu.cyt.cu 200
rooms, modern resort in terraced style, good sea view, many activities such as horse rental,
helicopter ride into the mountains, children are welcome; 12 km further west past Chivirico is
the smaller **Los Galeones** (Cubanacán), Carretera Chivirico, T29110, F26160,
galeones@smar.scu.cyt.cu For singles and couples over 16 only, marketed to honeymooners, weddings arranged free of charge, 32 rooms including 1 suite on a cliff overlooking the
Caribbean, 300 winding steps lead down to the sea, courtesy bus to *Sierra Mar*, a taxi from
the airport costs about US$50.

Marea del Portillo before you get to Pilón, there are 2 more resort hotels popular with
Canadian package tours: **C-D** per person *Marea del Portillo*, (Cubanacán), Carretera Granma
Km 12.5, T597102. All-inclusive, 3-star, 130 rooms, hot water, phone, tennis, beach volleyball,
watersports, car rental, shop. **A-B** per person *Farallón del Caribe*, (Cubanacán), Km 14,
T597081, F597080, dsk@hfarcar.ma.grm.cyt.cu All-inclusive, 4-star, 140 rooms, nice position. **D** *Villa Punta Piedra*, (Cubanacán), Carretera Pilón, T59442. Two-star, further west
along the coast. Watersports, scuba diving, snorkelling and sailing can be arranged at all the
resorts. Scuba diving is with *Centro de Buceo Albacora* who take up to 8 divers to 17 sites at
depths of 5-40m.

Essentials

L-A *Casa Granda* (Gran Caribe Accor, managed by Sofitel) Heredia 201 entre San Pedro y San **Sleeping**
Félix, near Parque Céspedes, T86600, F86035. Elegant building opened in 1914 and patron- *Phone code: 226*
ized by many famous people. 4-star, renovated and expanded in 2000, pool, a/c, fax service,
laundry, car hire, satellite TV, post office, 1 room for handicapped people, *Havanatur* and
Asistur offices. Excellent central location with terrace bar, poor service, overlooking park, 5th
floor bar with even better views over city (US$2 to go up if you are not staying at the hotel but
that buys your first cocktail), restaurant, snack bar, café, open 2000-0100, good. **AL** *Meliá
Santiago de Cuba* (Cubanacán), Av Las Américas entre 4 y M, Repto Sueño, T87070, F87170,
dircom@santiago.solmelia.cma.net Five-star, 302 rooms and suites, clean, good service,
excellent breakfast buffet US$9, lots of bars and restaurants, good view of city from roof top
bar, swimming pools open to day visitors for US$5, tennis, sauna, car hire, has business cen-
tre, post office and will change almost any currency into dollars.

B *Versalles* (Cubanacán), Carretera del Morro Km 1, T91014/91016/91504. 3-star, 61
rooms, very near airport, US$1 for visitors to use pool. **B-C** *Las Américas* (Horizontes),
T42011, F87075, Av de las Américas esquina Gen Cebreco, easy bus/truck access to centre,
private cars around bus stop in plaza opposite hotel.Rebuilt, 68 rooms, 2 mini-suites, lively,
high quality restaurant, variety of créole dishes, non-residents may use swimming pool
where they have cultural shows every night, helpful Rumbos agent, nice reception staff,
safety deposit, Havanautos and Transtur, Cadeca, shop, bicycle hire. **B-C** *Motel San Juan*
(Horizontes), Km 1 Carretera a Siboney, T87200/87116, F86137, hotel@sanjuan.scu.cyt.cu
out of town but nice location, turistaxi US$3.95, private car US$2. A complex with cabins,
110 very nice rooms, large and clean, intermittent hot water, large pool, bar and several
restaurants, good breakfast, high quality by Cuban standards, accepts pesos, queues at
weekends and during festivals. **D** *Balcón del Caribe* (Islazul), next to Castillo del Morro,
T91011. Three-star, 72 rooms overlooking the sea, quiet, pool, tourist office, simple Cuban
food, cold water in bungalows, pleasant but inconvenient for the town. **D** *Villa Santiago
de Cuba* (Gaviota), Av Manduley 502, entre 19 y 21, Reparto Vista Alegre, T41368/41346,
F87166. Three-star, car hire, tourist office, nearby pool for guests, quiet, no credit cards.
E *Rancho Club Motel* (Islazul), Carretera Central Km 4.5, Altos de Quintero, T33202/33280.
29 rooms.

Cuba

Only those reported or recommended in 2000-2001 are listed here

Touts around Parque Céspedes, also near all hotels

Casas particulares E-F *Marta Franco*, Corona 802 bajos entre San Carlos y Santa Rita, T51882, very central, about 100m west of Cathedral, apartment on ground floor of fairly modern block. Two rooms, one with a/c, bathroom between them, hot shower, breakfast US$3, dinner US$6, meals taken in family room, very good food, helpful and friendly family. E-F *Manrique Nistal Bello*, Princesa 565 entre Carnicería y Calvario, T51909, abarreda@abt.vo.edu.cu One room with one bed, another with two beds, bathroom, fridge, good food in large portions, some English spoken. F *Migdalia Gámez Rodríguez*, Corona 371 entre San Germán y Trinidad, T24569. Large, private room with shower, fan, quiet, friendly, great food. F *Margot's Inn*, San Fermín 207 entre Maceo y San Mateo. On the way from the railway station to the town centre very near the Antonio Maceo Museum, quiet neighbourhood. Margot is in her 70s and lives with her son, Tony, an English teacher, nice people, 1 room sleeps 3, shower, hot water, a/c, fridge. F *Dinorah Rodríguez Bueno*, Diego Palacios (Santa Rita) 504 entre Reloj y Clarín, T25834. Dinorah speaks a little English, independent room with ensuite bathroom, a/c, good food, patio, 10-min walk from Parque Céspedes. E-F *Félix Corroso*, San Germán 165 entre Rastro y Gallo, T53720. Known as Garden House, 2 rooms, a/c, fan, nice garden, breakfast US$3, dinner US$6-8. F *Nercy y Oscar Montoto*, San Gerónimo 560, T52192. Self-contained, luxurious 1-bedroom modern apartment. Opposite is F *Marisloe y Ernesto*, San Gerónimo 555, same phone number, T52192. Private 1-bedroom apartment with traditional features, beautiful tiled floor, stained glass windows, comfortable, friendly. F *Aderlaides Nunes*, San Gerónimo 558, T53939. Nice room in modern apartment block. F *Ana María González y César Falagón*, 12 308 entre 11 y 13, Rpto Vista Alegre, T42968. Two lovely rooms, independent of the rest of the house, shared bathroom, nice residential area, owner is a doctor, elderly Dobermann for security. F *Aída Morales Valdés*, Enramada 565 entre San Agustín y Barnada, T28612. Room with private bathroom, a/c, very good food, friendly family, central, only 1 block from Plaza Marte. F *Dr Javier Berdion Sevilla*, Corona 564 Apto B entre Enramadas y Aguilera, T22959. Two rooms, double bed, a/c, hot water in shared bathroom, radio, fridge, balcony, terrace, great view of the bay. F *Miriam Osorio Fonseca*, Aguilera 606 entre Barnarda y Plácido, T24723. Two rooms with en suite bathrooms, fan, hot water, terrace. F *Omar Frómeta*, Anacaona 194 entre Alfredo Zayas y Bravo Correoso, Santa Bárbara, close to *Hotel Meliá* and *Las Américas*. Nice apartment, a/c, hot water, terrace, balcony, dining room, private bathroom, stereo, fridge. F *Vicente Piñeiro González*, Bravo Correoso 407 ½ entre 11 y 12, Santa Bárbara. A/c bedroom, living room, private pathroom, hot water, use of kitchen, very nice couple.

Eating

Hotels have restaurants & mostly serve buffet meals

Three restaurants run by Rumbos (*Combinado* is the collective name) on Plaza Dolores (known as Búlevar locally), Italian, Chinese and creole food, quite expensive and low on local atmosphere; opposite them on Búlevar is *Matamoros*, which is better although prices are quite high with a system of US$1=1 peso; also *Las Enramadas*, Búlevar. Good atmosphere, cheap, basic food, nice setting. *La Taberna de Dolores*, Aguilera esquina Reloj, T23913. Spanish food, open 1900-2400, prices in pesos but tourists pay 1:1 in dollars. *Coppelia* ice cream on Félix Peña under the cathedral, open Mon-Fri 1000-2100, Sat-Sun 1100-2200, no queuing if you have dollars. *Isabelica*, Aguilera esquina Plaza Dolores. Open 24 hrs, serves only coffee, US$0.85, cigars rolled, bohemian hangout, watch out for hustlers, serious hassling by jineteros/as. *Casa del Té*, Aguilera esquina Lacret. Grow their own herbs, cheap herbal tea available. *Café Ajedrez*, Enramada y Santo Tomás. Open air café in cool architectural structure designed by Cuban architect, Walter A Betancourt Fernández.

Lots of good **paladares** (official ones have a sign outside) around Calles Heredia and Aguilera, and in Reparto Vista Alegre, near the hotels *Santiago*, *Las Américas* and *San Juan*. *Doña Cristina*, Padre Pico. Good reports. *El Balcón*, Independencia 253, Reparto Sueño, T27407. Good food, US$3, open 24 hrs, popular with locals. *Terrazas*, 5 50 entre M y Terraza, Ampliación de Terraza, T41491. *Paladar* on the upper floor open daily 1000-2400, tasty food, nicely presented, chicken US$6, pork US$5. If the gate is locked, whistle. Street stalls sell snacks in pesos, usually only open until early evening, some only at lunchtime. Most things cost 1 peso. Avoid *fritos*, they are just fried lumps of dough; most reliable thing is cheese, pork or egg sandwich; pizza is usually dry bit of dough with a few gratings of cheese. Lots of stalls along 'Ferreiro' or Av Victoriano Garzón, these are open later than others, especially up near

Hotel Las Américas. Also lots around bus station on Libertadores and a few along the bottom part of Aguilera, between Parque Céspedes and Plaza Dolores.

Club Tropicana Santiago, local show with emphasis on the sea and Santiaguerans, on Autopista Nacional Km 1.5, T43036/43610, open 2000-0300, closed Mon, also good restaurant and disco, *Disco Tropicana*, open 2200-0300, book direct or through a travel agent in any hotel, eg Rumbos US$50 including transport. *Cabaret San Pedro del Mar*, Carretera del Morro, Islazul-run, US$5 taxi, US$5 entrance, reasonable food. *Casa de la Trova*, Heredia 206 around the corner from *Casa Granda*. Two daily shows of music, morning and evening, traditional, acoustic Son music, open until 2400, US$1 and worth it, nice venue in beautiful building with patio where the bands play at night, also bar. *Grupo Folklórico del Oriente*, San Francisco y San Félix, folk groups play daytime till lunchtime, then again in the evening. *Ballet Folkórico Cutatumba*, Enramada, 2 blocks west of Plaza Céspedes. Superb show Sun 1030, US$3. *Casa de la Música*, Corona 564 entre Aguilera y Enramada, F86225. Live Cuban music every night 2000-0300, US$5 entrance, sale of CDs and tapes, worth trying. *Casa de los Estudiantes*, Heredia, near *Casa Granda*. Live music Sun 1330, US$1. *Sala de Dolores* on Plaza Dolores has classical and choral concerts. Lively nightly disco in *Santiago* and *Las Américas* hotels, to which Cubans are welcome, American disco music, hardly any salsa, *jinetera* pick-up places. *Disco Bar/Club 300*, Aguilera entre San Félix y San Pedro, close to Parque Céspedes, closed Wed, 1000-1800, 2200-0400, live and recorded music, snack bar. *Las Iris*, Aguilera entre Paraíso y Barnarda. Disco daily from 1000-1600, 22000400, snack bar open 24 hrs. *Buró de Información Cultural* on Plaza Marte has live music in its patio bar *Los Dos Abuelos*, every night, 2230-0200, also snack bar. *Casa del Caribe* on 13 154 esquina 8, T42285, live Afro-Cuban music and dance at weekends. *El Patio de Artex*, Heredia 304. Home of painters, Félix and José Joaquín Tejada Revilla, often live music with fantastic local bands, lots of dancing.

Nightlife

The **Festival del Caribe** begins in the 1st week in Jul with theatre, dancing and conferences, and continues later in Jul to coincide with the Moncada celebrations on 26 Jul. The **Carnival**, already in full swing by then (as it was in 1953, the date carefully chosen to catch Batista's militia drunk and off-guard and use the noise of the carnival to drown the sound of gunfire), traditionally stops for a day of more serious celebration, then continues on 27 Jul. Carnival is the third week of Jul, taking in Santiago's patron saint's day, 25 Jul. This carnival is regaining its former glory and is well worth seeing. Wear no jewelry, leave all valuables behind.

Festivals

On **New Year's Eve** you will find son bands playing in Plaza Marte and surrounding streets. Just before midnight everyone moves toward Parque Céspedes and sings the National Anthem. Then on the stroke of midnight the Cuban flag is raised on the Casa de Gobierno, commemorating the anniversary of the first time it was flown in 1902 when the Republic of Cuba was proclaimed.

Casa de la Artesanía, under the cathedral in Parque Céspedes, T23924. Open 0800-1730, also on Lacret 724 entre San Basilio y Heredia, T24027. *Cubartesana* on Félix Peña esquina Masó under the cathedral. *Salón Artexanda* on Heredia 304 entre Pío Rosado y Calvario. Handicrafts are sold on the street on Heredia entre Hartmann and Pío Rosado. **Music** *Casa de la Trova* sells CDs and tapes. *Artex* on Aguilera sells CDs, tapes and videos for dollars. *Enramadas* and *Siglo XX*, both on Enramada, are large stores with stalls inside selling records, books, clothes, jewellery, ornaments etc in pesos. On Enramada there is a second hand record shop. Several dollar stores can be found in the Parque Céspedes area, ask for 'shopping', especially on Saco. There is a good **bread** shop (dollars) called *Doña Neli* on Aguilera at Plaza Marte. *Panadería El Sol* is on Plaza Marte entre Saco y Aguilera. *Casa de Miel*, Gen Lacret, sells honey. *La Bombonera* is a dollar store selling **food** very near Parque Céspedes on Aguilera entre Gen Lacret y Hartmann, open Mon-Sat 0900-1800, Sun 0900-1200. Food market on Ferreiro opposite *Hotel Las Américas*.

Shopping

Rumbos Cuba is on Heredia opposite *Casa Granda* hotel, open 0800-1700 for tours and later for car hire. Organized city tours with guide, also day trips to all destinations around Santiago. Prices vary according to season and number of people; also flights and trips to Jamaica and

Tour operators

Cuba

Cuba

Santo Domingo. *Havanatur* main office is near La Maison on Av Manduley, T43603, with another office under the *Hotel Casa Granda*, offering the same as Rumbos but slightly more expensive. All the main hotels have tour agencies, usually outlets of Rumbos or Havanatur, and you can save time by using them rather than going to the main office. Islazul only deals with tourism for Cubans.

Transport   **Local Bus**: 20 centavos, run to the suburbs and outskirts. If there is no sign of a bus, catch a truck, ask driver the destination, pay flat rate 1 peso. Horse drawn coches are also 1 peso. **Car hire**: At the airport: *Transautos*, T92245; *Havanautos*, T91873, 86161; *Vía Rent a Car*, T91014. These and other agencies in main hotels. *Havanautos* also has an agency at La Punta service station, T39328. **Taxis**: there are 3 types: *Turistaxi* most expensive, eg US$8 from airport to town centre; *Taxis OK* also expensive; *Cubataxi*, T51038/9, cheapest (name on windscreen), eg airport to town US$5. You can also get a private taxi, lots of them hanging around Parque Céspedes and Plaza Marte, but they will charge about the same as a Cubataxi. For a longer journey, you can negotiate a price. However, get a written quote if possible as even Cubataxis have been known to renegue on their agreements and demand more and/or return to Santiago. You will be continually offered private taxis every time you go out. Motorbike transport can be arranged at Plaza Marte for about US$1. Bicitaxis cost US$0.50.

Long distance Bus: Terminal near Plaza de la Revolución at the top of Av de los Libertadores/Carretera Central. Buy ticket in advance at office on Yarayo (the 1st street on the left going north from the terminal), open daily 0600-1400. *Víazul*, T28484, is in an office to the left of the bus departure area, with a dark brown wooden door.For an overnight journey wear trousers and a fleece if you have one, as the a/c is very cold and even Víazul is not comfortable at night. To Havana, 1500, 2000, arrive 0720, 1130, US$51, from Havana 1500, 2000, arrive 0650, 1130, with intermediate stops in Jagüey, Santa Clara, Sancti Spíritus, Ciego de Avila, Camagüey, Las Tunas, Holguín and Bayamo. To Baracoa 0730, via El Cristo, La Maya, Guantánamo, San Antonio and Imías, arriving 1215, US$15, returning from Baracoa 1415, arriving Santiago 1900. Trucks are available outside terminal to most destinations, drivers shout destination prior to departure, pay in pesos. For a long journey avoid trucks without any kind of cover, or you will burn. **Train**: The new station is opposite the rum factory on Av Jesús Menéndez. Book tickets in advance from basement office in new terminal. Train travel is not as reliable or comfortable as bus travel. Take sweater for Havana journey, freezing a/c.

Directory   **Airlines** *Cubana* office on Félix Peña 673 entre Heredia y San Basilio, near the cathedral, open Mon-Fri 0900-1700, Sat 0900-1400, T24156/51579/22290. *Aerotaxi* at the airport, T91410 ext 2019. *Aerocaribbean* office under *Hotel Casa Granda*. Local and inter-Caribbean (some destinations) flights can also be booked in *Rumbos* or *Havanatur*. **Banks** *Banco Financiero Internacional*, Parque Céspedes at Santo Tomás y Aguilera, T22101, open Mon-Fri 0800-1600, dollar cash on Visa, change foreign currency and TCs. *BICSA*, Enramada opposite Plaza Dolores, for changing foreign currency and TCs. *Banco Popular de Ahorro*, Plaza Dolores, 0800-1500, Visa and Mastercard, prompt service. TCs can be changed in any hotel except those in the Islazul chain; commission is usually 2-3%. *Hotel Santiago* will change virtually any cash currency into dollars. TCs can be changed in the Havanatur office in *Casa Granda*. In the Asistur office under *Casa Granda* you can get cash advance on all major credit cards including American Express and Diners Club; they will also change American Express TCs, the only place who will do so in all Cuba. **Communications** DHL, opposite the bar, *El Baturro*, near Plaza Céspedes, has **email** facilities. **Medical facilities** *Clínica Internacional*, 13 y 14, Reparto Vista Alegre, T42589, along Av Raúl Pujol away from the city, opposite *Motel San Juan*, especially for tourists, has a dentist as well and pharmacy on site, everything payable in dollars, US$25 per consultation, the best clinic to visit to be sure of immediate treatment. There is a *pharmacy* next door to the *Casa de la Trova* on Heredia and another, open 24 hrs, on Victoriano Garzón y 10. **Useful addresses** Immigration: Inmigración y Extranjería on Av Raúl Pujol y 1, Reparto Santa Bárbara, open Mon, Fri 0900-1200, 1330-1630, Tue, Wed, Thu 0900-1200, in summer holiday mornings only. Go to Bandec on Parque Céspedes y Aguilera and buy special stamp (sello) for US$25, then return to Immigration for paper work (15 mins). **Police**: T116. The central police station is Unidad 2, Corona y San Gerónimo. Near to the hotels *Santiago* and *Las Américas* is Unidad 4, on Aguilera near the hospital and the market. **Fire**: Martí 517, T23242. **Asistur**: *Hotel Casa Granda*, Heredia esquina San Pedro, T86600, for all health, financial, legal and insurance problems for foreign tourists.

Bayamo

Bayamo is the capital of the province of Granma. It was the second town founded by Diego Velázquez in November 1513 and has been declared a Ciudad Monumento Nacional. However, it was burned to the ground by its own population in 1869 as an act of rebellion against the colonial Spanish; consequently the town has little to offer in the way of colonial architecture and is really rather uninteresting.

Phone code: 23
Colour map 1, grid B5

The **Iglesia de Santísimo Salvador** in the Plaza del Himno Nacional is a 16th-century church which was badly damaged by the 1869 fire, but is currently under restoration. **Casa Natal de Carlos Manuel de Céspedes**, is a museum dedicated to the life of the main campaigner of the 1868 independence movement, who was born here. ■ *On Maceo. Tue-Sat 0900-1700, Sun 0900-1200, US$1.*

Sleeping

C *Sierra Maestra* (Islazul), Carretera Central via Santiago de Cuba, T481013, 2 km from city centre. 204 rooms, delightful post-revolution 1960s building, thoroughly kitsch interior, avoid rooms overlooking noisy pool, plenty of nightlife, 3 bars, disco, mostly Cubans, helpful staff, car hire, credit cards accepted. Cheaper is *Villa Bayamo* (2-star) on the Carretera Manzanillo Km 5.5, T423102/423124. 34 rooms, 1 km from city centre. **E** *Royalton* (Islazul), on Maceo y Joaquín Palma, very central location, T422224/90/46/68. 33 rooms, a/c, private bathrooms, phones, restaurant, lobby bar and terrace bar open each night, toilets just beyond reception. *Hotel Central*, Av General García, is a basic, peso hotel, very central. **Casa particular F** *Ramón Enrique Alvarez Sánchez*, Pío Rosado 22 entre Ramírez y Av Fco Vte Aguilera, T423984. Enormous rooms, a/c, private bathroom, wife Carolina is a good cook.

Eating

Restaurante 1513, Gen García esquina General Lora, T425921. Open 1200-2200, small but recommended by many Bayameros. *La Casona*, Plaza del Himno Nacional, behind the church in a corner. Nice wooden bar, pizzas or spaghetti for 5 pesos, courtyard at the back completely covered at head height with flowering vine, lots of little green lizards, delightful, open 1300-2200. Lots of *paladares* and bars along Gen García, all charge in pesos, best every Sat night during *Noche Cubana*, some only open on Sat. *Sagitario*, Marmol 107, across the street is *Bartería*, on Av Francisco V Aguilera. Both recommended by locals. *Tropicrema*, Parque Céspedes. Cake and 2 scoops of ice cream, 1.80 pesos, very good and popular.

Nightlife

Casa de la Trova on the corner of Maspote and José Martí has shows during the afternoon and every night, quite touristy in high season. *Cabaret Bayamo* opposite *Hotel Sierra Maestra*, on Carretera Central, T421698. Open 2100-0200. Every Sat there is a *Noche Cubana*, when the whole of General García fills with stalls, ad hoc bars, pigs on spits, and the restaurants all put tables on the road. Everything is sold in pesos, even in the established bars.

Tour operators

Islazul office on Gen García 207. Open 0830-1700, also tourist information in *Hotel Sierra Maestra* and occasionally maps, but it is difficult to get information about day trips as they do not cater for many foreign visitors.

Transport

Local Horse and cart, 7 pesos from bus station to *Hotel Sierra Maestra*. **Car hire**: the *Havanautos* office is in Cupet Cimex gas station next to the bus station, on road to Jiguaní, T423223. **Long distance Air** Carlos Manuel de Céspedes airport is 4 km out of town; flight to Havana 3 times a week. **Bus** The terminal is on the corner of Carretera Central and Jesús Rabi, T424036. *Víazul*, T424036, stops here for 5 mins on its Havana-Santiago route, depart Havana 1500, 2000, arrive Bayamo 0440, 0930, US$44, depart Santiago 1500, 2000, arrive Bayamo 1730, 2200, US$7. There are also daytime buses to Santiago and to Guantánamo, occasionally there is a direct bus, otherwise change at Santiago. To **Manzanillo**, 2 daily, US$2.50, bus station 2 km outside Manzanillo. **Train** Station is at Saco y Línea. Daily trains to Santiago and Havana; 4 daily to Manzanillo, 2 hrs, 1.35 pesos.

Directory

Banks *Banco Nacional de Cuba*, Saco y Gen García. *Bandec*, Gen García 101. Visa and MC, open Mon-Fri 0800-1500. **Medical facilities** *Farmacia Principal Municipal*, 24-hr at Gen García 53.

Guantánamo

Phone code: 21
Population: 205,000
Colour map 1, grid B6

Guantánamo is the most easterly and most mountainous province on the island. The range of the Montañas de Nipe-Sagua-Baracoa runs through the province, ending in the Atlantic Ocean on the northern coast and the Caribbean Sea to the south. The area is notable for its many endemic species of fauna and flora, and also for the US naval base housing the rare species of US 'imperialists' in Cuba. Guantánamo, the provincial capital, had a large influx of Haitian, French and Jamaican immigrants in the 19th century. The architecture has much less of a Spanish colonial feel; the narrow, brightly coloured buildings with thin wooden balconies and wrought ironwork are more reminiscent of New Orleans than Madrid. This is also reflected in the local musical rhythms, notably the Tumba Francesa. The central square, **Plaza Martí**, has a church in the centre. The **Casa de la Cultura** is on the west side and the *Tumba Francesa* on the east. Two km north, the **Plaza de la Revolución** has a modernist carved stone monument to the heroes of all the wars of independence. The **Museo Municipal**, for local history is in a former prison. ■ *José Martí. Tue-Sat 0800-1800, Sun 0800-1200.*

The **US naval base** of Guantánamo (which cannot be easily visited from Cuba) was established at the beginning of the 20th century in the area known as Caimanera. The base is so little a part of the town that you will not, come across it unless you make a specific trip to Mirador de Malones to view it through binoculars.

The **Zoológico de Piedra** is an outdoor museum of stone animals, just outside of town, set in a beautiful hillside location with tropical vegetation. Many are bizarre, from tiny stone lizards to huge bison. All are carved directly from the rocks in their natural setting and you can buy miniature replicas from the sculptor on the way out.

Sleeping **E** *Guantánamo* (Islazul), Ahogados, esq 13 Norte, Plaza Mariana Grajales, Reparto Caribe, T381015, F382406, 15 mins' walk from the centre. Three-star, 112 rooms, 12 cabins, pool, clean, a/c, 2 bars and busy restaurant, food average, disco, mostly Cuban clientèle, staff pleasant and helpful. **E** *La Lupe* (Islazul), Carretera del Salvador Km 2, T326168/326180. Two-star but much nicer than *Guantánamo*, a bit far out of town, nice pool, peaceful atmosphere, 50 rooms, mostly cabins, sports area, a/c, restaurant, bar. **E** *Casa de Los Ensueños*, Ahogados esq 15 Norte, Reparto Caribe, T326304. Three rooms, a/c, TV, bar, 24-hr room service.

Eating *Restaurante Caribe*, on top of a tower block near *Hotel Guantánamo*. Local food, pay in pesos. Plenty of *paladares*, most of whom charge in pesos but will accept dollars. Price should be about 45 pesos per person, but some raise it for tourists. Two *paladares* on Av de los Estudiantes (Paseo) and a number of street stalls selling pork sandwiches for 5 pesos, some are there every day, all of them at weekends. Other *paladares* off Plaza Martí in the centre.

Tour operators Peter Hope, Public Relations Officer at the *Hotel Guantánamo* (Room 117, Mon-Sat), is the fount of all tourist information in the area and runs guided Islazul and Havanatur tours for foreigners, including to Mt Malones, to see the US base through Soviet binoculars. He speaks English, German and French. *Islazul* office is on Los Maceo entre Narciso López y Paseo.

Transport **Local Car hire**: *Havanautos* office is at Cupet Cimex gas station at the beginning of the Baracoa road. **Long distance Air** Aeropuerto Mariana Grajales (GAO) is 16 km from Guantánamo, off the Baracoa road. Daily (except Mon) scheduled flight at 0600 from Havana, returning 0855, plus a Sat flight at 0845 (1140). **Bus** The bus terminal, T326016, is 5 km southwest from the centre. Private cars and taxis run from the train and bus station to *Hotel Guantánamo*/town centre, US$1. Daily bus to **Havana**, 4 buses to **Santiago**, 1 bus to **Baracoa**. *Víazul* stops here on its Santiago-Baracoa route, depart Santiago 0730, 3 hrs 15 mins, US$6, depart Baracoa 1415, 6 hrs, US$10. **Camiones** to Baracoa leave from La Punta, 7 km from bus station (take a taxi) 4-5 hrs, 5 pesos. **Train** The station is in the centre on Calixto García. Daily trains to **Santiago**, **Havana** and **Holguín**.

Directory **Banks** *Banco de Crédito* at Calixto García esquina Carretera, changes TCs into dollars.

Baracoa

Phone code: 21
Colour map 1, grid B6

Close to the most easterly point of the island, Baracoa is an attractive place surrounded by rich, tropical vegetation and the perfect place to come and spend a few relaxing days on the beach. It was the first town founded in 1512 by Diego Velázquez, and for three years it was the capital of Cuba. Up until the 1960s it was really only accessible by sea until the viaduct, La Farola was built. This is a spectacular road, 30 km long, joined to the mountain on one side and supported by columns on the other. It is well worth the trip from Santiago (150 km, four hours' drive) for the scenery of this section of road, which winds through lush tropical mountains and then descends steeply to the coast.

The area is a UNESCO biosphere, with more than 10 rivers, including the **Río Toa**, **Sights** 120 km long and the widest river in Cuba. White water rafting is possible down the Río Toa, with different levels of difficulty. The **Río Yumurí** is 30 km east of Baracoa. This is the most spectacular of Baracoa's rivers, running through two deep canyons. You can take an organized tour (US$28), rent a private car (US$10) or take a *colectivo* taxi or truck to the Río Yumurí where the road ends. A canoe will ferry you across or you can hire one to take you upriver for US$1. You can continue walking upriver and swim, very quiet and peaceful.

Christopher Columbus arrived in Baracoa on 27 November 1492. He planted a cross, now housed in the church, **Iglesia de la Asunción**, and described a mountain in the shape of an anvil (*yunque*) which was thereafter used as a point of reference for sailors. The first maps of Cuba drawn by an Englishman showed the **Yunque de Baracoa** mountain, copies of which can be seen in the museum. Between 1639 and 1742, Baracoa's three forts were built. The oldest, **El Castillo**, was destroyed in 1652 by the French. The others were **Fuerte de la Punta**, now restaurant *La Punta*, and **Fuerte Matachín**, now the **Museo Municipal**. ■ *Daily 0800-1800, US$2.*

Baracoa has 56 archaeological sites, with many traces of the three Indian groups who lived there: the Siboney, the Taino and the Guanturabey. There is one surviving community of 300 Indians, called the **Yateras**, dating back to the Spaniards' arrival. They are integrated with the rest of society but only marry among themselves and maintain their traditions. They live in an isolated region along the shores of the Río Toa, but a visit can be organized through the Museo Municipal.

C-D *El Castillo* (Gaviota), Calixto García, Loma del Paraíso, T42147, F86074. 35 a/c rooms with **Sleeping** bath, phone, TV in lobby lounge, pool (US$2 for use by non-residents), parking, friendly staff, food OK, excellent views, very good breakfast. **A-D** *Porto Santo* (Gaviota), T43511, F86074. 53 rooms, 3 suites, a/c, bath, TV, restaurant, bar, shop, beautiful swimming pool, car hire, next to airport, beach, peaceful atmosphere, friendly. **E-F** *La Rusa* (Islazul), a bright yellow building on the Malecón, Máximo Gómez 13, T43011, islazul@gtmo.cu Named after the Russian lady, Magdalena Menasse, who used to run the hotel and whose photos adorn the walls, famous guests have included Fidel Castro, accommodation now basic, food average, nice location, good *paladar* opposite.

Casas particulares *Ikira Mahíquez Machado*, Maceo 168-A entre Céspedes y Ciro Frías, T42466. 2 rooms, also a separate part of the house with kitchen and garage, nice building, friendly family. **F** *Nelia y Yaquelín*, Mariana Grajales 11 entre Julio A Mella y Calixto García, T42652. Three generations of a delightful family offer a simple but comfortable place to stay, sea views, new private bathroom, small room, breakfast US$2, dinner US$5, both delicious and more than you can eat. **F** *Neida Cuenca Prada*, Flor Crombet 194 esq Céspedes, T43178. Upstairs rooms better than the one downstairs, kind and generous family, wonderful food and reasonably priced. **F** *Williams*, Martí 287, T42798. Very hospitable, car parking, US$1, available to non-guests. **F** *Daniel Pérez*, Coroneles Galano 6 entre Flor Crombet y Martí, T43274. Near the sea, private roof and room with new shower and a/c, nice family, good cooking. **F** *Sol E Gamboa Muguercia*, Emiliano Corrales 39 entre Libertad y Mariana Grajales. One room, a/c, double bed, good food, in quiet area a bit away from town centre, family

Cuba

atmosphere. **F** *Inés Morgado Terán*, Maceo 51 entre Peralejo y Coliseo, T43292. Room with private bathroom, a/c, no English spoken but Inés and her husband are warm and helpful. **F** *Lidia Cobas Leyva*, 10 de Octubre 161A entre Martí y Flor Crombet, T43464. **F** *Magalay Lafitr*, Maceo 161A entre Céspedes y Ciro Frías. **F** *Pedro Jiménez Martínez*, Flor Crombet 213 entre Coroneles y Reyes. Extremely nice family, great food, will cook anything you want, huge portions. **F** *Casa Ernesto*, Libertad 13 entre 1 Abril y M Grajales, 5 mins walk from Plaza Independencia towards *Hotel Porto Santo*. Room with a/c, big breakfast included, dinner US$3-4, traditional food from the region (fish in coconut milk), bike rental US$2 per day. **F** *Dr Sánchez Rosell*, Maceo 123 entre Frank País y Maraví, T43161. Friendly couple, private bathroom, fan, extremely clean, breakfast and dinner, on main road.

Eating   The isolation of Baracoa has led to an individual local cuisine, mostly featuring coconut milk and fish. 80% of Cuba's coconuts are grown here. Don't miss the *cucurucho*, a delicious mixture of coconut, fruit and sugar served in a cone of palm leaves and sold at roadsides for about 3 pesos. Lots of *paladares*, many of which are well-established, most offer pork, chicken, fish, turtle, some offer lobster. *La Colonial*, José Martí 123, T43161. Excellent subdued candlelit atmosphere, extensive menu. *Tropical*, José Martí 175. Good local specialities, calalú, vegetarian options, fish in coconut, book ahead for advance preparation of some dishes. The fort at La Punta, which juts out into the bay west of the town, has been converted to a pleasant, breezy, open air restaurant, *La Guama*, although everyone refers to it as La Punta. Nice setting, creole food, main courses (described on the menu as 'mean' plates) US$3-5.50. *Casa de Chocolate*, José Martí, near bus terminal. Local version of hot chocolate with water and salt.

Nightlife   *Casa de la Trova*, José Martí 149. Traditional music, Tue-Sun from 2100, US$1, good *son* and friendly atmosphere. *Casa de la Cultura*, Maceo 122. Live music in its patio. Nightly show of Afro-Cuban music by Yambú Akalé at *La Punta*, highly recommended, US$4, very interesting to see all the costumes and instruments. *Dancing Light* on Maceo just before Parque Central, disco for young Cubans although tourists will not feel out of place, drinks in dollars for tourists, small but lively, check out breakdancing show nightly by local youths. *Cuatro ochenta cinco (485)*, Félix Ruenes, bar with live band every night, US$1, great fun, everyone gets up to dance. Disco playing western music next door. Nightly dancing and live music at *Porto Santo* and *El Castillo*, the former is livelier. *Noche Cubana* on Sat, when Antonio Maceo fills up with food and drink stalls and there is dancing to street musicians.

Tour operators   All organized excursions are best arranged through Wilder Laffita, a very efficient Public Relations Officer at the *Hotel Porto Santo*, T43590, who works for Gaviota and is also the guide for all local ecotourism walks. Antonio (Tony) Mas at *Hotel El Castillo* also organizes local excursions, speaks perfect English and can sort out just about anything. A city tour, minimum six people, will cost US$8 per person. A day trip with lunch to **Playa Maguana**, a beautiful white sand beach 22 km from Baracoa is US$28.

Transport   **Local Car hire**: at the Servi Cupet station, Guantánamo road Km 4. **Long distance Air**: Airport 100m from *Hotel Porto Santo*. *Cubana* flight to Havana Tue, Sat 0950, to Havana via Santiago Sun, 1030, US$18 to Santiago. All times subject to frequent change. **Bus**: Main bus terminal at the end of Martí near Av de los Mártires, T42239, 43670, for buses to **Havana**, **Santiago**, **Camagüey**, **Guantánamo**. Make sure you reserve in advance at busy times and that your name is down on the list, *plano*, otherwise your reservation will not be valid. *Víazul* has a service to Santiago at 1415, arriving 1900, US$15, departing Santiago 0730, arriving Baracoa 1215, via El Cristo, La Maya, Guantánamo, San Antonio and Imías. Trucks to Guantánamo, Moa and other destinations from 2nd bus terminal on Coroneles Galana.

Directory   **Banks** *Banco Nacional de Cuba* is on Maceo but will change only TCs, you can not get cash advance on credit cards. *Porto Santo* and *El Castillo* hotels both change TCs. **Medical facilities** *Hospital Octavio de la Concepción y de la Pedraja*, on Carretera Guantánamo. Policlínica in the small barrio next to *Hotel Porto Santo*, where you pay in pesos, there is also a dentist here. *Clínica Dental* in Barrio de la Punta, near the fort. 24-hr pharmacy on Maceo 132.

Isla de la Juventud

There are three good reasons for visiting the Isla de la Juventud: diving, birdwatching   *Colour map 1, grid B2*
and checking out Cuban provincial life away from tourist resorts. The island is a good
place to go for a weekend out of Havana, although if you plan to see the whole island
you will need more time. In recent decades its population has been swelled by tens of
*thousands of Cuban and Third World students, giving rise to the modern name of **Isle***
***of Youth**. From the 19th century until the Revolution its main function was as a prison*
and both José Martí and Fidel Castro served time there.

The capital, Nueva Gerona, dates from the 19th century and remains the only sub- **Nueva Gerona**
stantial settlement. Surrounded by small rounded hills, it is a pleasantly laid-back   *Phone code: 61*
country town with a slow pace. As most development has taken place post-1959,
there are few historically interesting buildings. The **Río Las Casas** runs through the
town heading northwards out to sea, and this has traditionally been the main route
to the Cuban mainland. The boat which served as a ferry from the 1920s until 1974,
El Pinero, has been preserved by the river at the end of Calle 28.

The **Museo Municipal** building was once the Casa de Gobierno, built in 1853, one
of the oldest on the island. It is on the south side of the Parque Central and has a small
historical collection of items of local interest. ■ *Calle 30. Tue-Sat 0800-1700, Sun
0900-1300.* The **Museo de la Lucha Clandestina**, near *Coppelia*, has a collection of
photos and other material relating to the Revolution. ■ *Calle 37 y 30. Tue-Sat,
0900-1700, Sun 0800-1200.* The **Planetario y Museo de Historia Natural**, has exhibits relating to the natural history, geology and archaeology of the island, with a replica
of the cave painting. ■ *Calle 41 y 52. Tue-Thu 0800-1900, Fri 1400-2200, Sat
1300-1700, Sun 0900-1300, US$2.* Outside the town, 3 km west just off the road to La
Demajagua, is **Museo Finca El Abra**. This is where José Martí came on 17 October
1870, to spend nine weeks of exile and hard labour quarrying marble in the Sierra de
las Casas before being deported to Spain. You can see the contents of the house and
kitchen and some of Martí's belongings. ■ *Tue-Sun 0900-1700.*

The **Presidio Modelo** (the Model Prison), 4 km east of Nueva Gerona in Reparto   **Excursions**
Chacón, was built by the dictator Machado to a high-security 'panopticon' design
first developed by Jeremy Bentham in 1791 to give total surveillance and control of
the inmates. It is a sinister and impressive sight; wander around the guard towers
and circular cell blocks, and see the numbered, tiered cells. Inmates have included
many fighters in the independence struggle, Japanese Cuban internees in the Second
World War, and Fidel Castro and fellow Moncada rebels imprisoned 1953-55. He
closed the prison in 1967. ■ *Open Mon-Sat 0800-1700, Sun 0800-1300, US$2, cam-
eras US$1.*

The **Cueva del Punta del Este** contains paintings attributed to the original
Siboney inhabitants. They were discovered in 1910 by a shipwrecked French sailor
and contain 235 pictures on the walls and ceilings, painted long before the arrival of
the Spanish. They are considered the most important pictographs in the Caribbean
and have been declared a national monument. It is believed that they might represent a solar calendar. ■ *The only way to get there is by organized excursion. US$92 flat
rate divided between however many passengers there are.*

The **Cocodrilo** crocodile farm is a one-hour drive (any car) south and west from
Nueva Gerona, including several km of dirt road. Guided tour (in Spanish) of the
hatchery and the breeding pens where the crocodiles stay for 4-5 years until they are
released. ■*Entry US$3.*

Main tourist hotel is **C-E** *El Colony*, T98282. 40 mins by road from Nueva Gerona's small air-   **Sleeping**
port, very isolated, established as a diving hotel before Cuba reappeared on the world tourist   *Hotels can be booked*
map, diving centre with access to 56 buoyed diving locations. Swimming and snorkelling   *through Amistur*
not great because of shallow water and sea urchins, you have to wade a long way before it is

Cuba

deep enough to swim, but beach is white sand. 77 a/c rooms in main block and cabañas, in need of renovation, single and triple available, discounts for stays of over a week, TV. Lovely setting, pool, 3 restaurants, snack bar, store, basket ball, volleyball, tennis and squash courts, horse riding, disco Sat 2100-0600, excursions, busy with package tourists, so accommodation could be hard to find. **E** *Villa Gaviota* (3-star) on the outskirts of Nueva Gerona on the road to La Fe beside the river, T23290. 20 rooms, single and triple available, extra cots for children, a/c, fridge, TV, phone, pool where national swimming team trains, good service at poolside bar, restaurants, squash court and gymnasium, disco Thu-Sun 2130-0400, techno music, young crowd, dance and aerobics classes advertised, the nicest dollar place to stay if you are not diving or on a package. 1 km south of *Gaviota* is **F** *Rancho del Tesoro*, T24069, in woods close to the Río Las Casas. 60 rooms in blocks. In Nueva Gerona, **F** *La Cubana*, 39 y 16 above *Cubana*. 17 rooms with bath, but basic, formerly for Cubans only. Other peso places to stay include **F** *Los Codornices*, T24981, on the way to the airport. 40 rooms in a block or in cabañas, pool, own transport needed. **Casas particulares** *Roberto Figuerero Rodríguez*, 35 1809, entre 18 y 20, Apto 1, T4892. Friendly, help with cars and drivers and information in general. **F** *Andrés Corbello Pino*, 24 5305 entre 53 y 55. A/c, food available, US$7 dinner including drinks.

Eating If you are on a package you will probably take all your meals in hotels. Private restaurants are few and aimed mainly at locals. The best bet is to eat in people's homes, where you can get an excellent meal for US$5-6, with lobster, rice, beans, fried plantain etc, drinks extra. *El Tocororo*, opposite the park on Calles 39 y 16. Cuban dishes, pay in pesos, breakfast 0700-0900, lunch 1200-1400, dinner 1800-2000, but times seem flexible. *El Cochinito*, 39 y 24. State run, open 1400-2200, specializes in pork. *Cabaret El Dragón*, 39 y 26. Also state run but Chinese and Cuban food, restaurant and bar, open 1600-2200, Mon-Thu, 1600-0030 Fri-Sun, cabaret at weekends, deluxe atmosphere, upscale crowd; there is a *Mercado Agropecuario* at 41 y 40, fresh fruit and vegetables, and there are a few basic places to eat in this area where you can pay in pesos. For ice cream, *Coppelia* is at 37 y 32.

Bars *Casa de los Vinos*, 20 y 41. Open Mon-Wed 1400-2200, Fri-Sun 1400-2400, popular peso drinking spot with grapefruit, melon, tomato and grape wines in earthenware jugs, drink

Isla de la Juventud

orders finish at 2300, advisable to take glasses, avoid the snacks. *Taberna Gerona*, 39 y 22. Open daily 1100-2100, Cuban food and pub atmosphere, very friendly, strictly pesos.

El Patio, 24 entre 37 y 39. Open 2100-0300, cabaret, 2 shows nightly at weekends, at 2200 and 0100, entry US$3, lots of Cubans and popular. *La Movida* disco, 34 entre 18 y 20. Outdoors, US$3, Cubans pay in pesos, young student crowd, starts at 2200. *Villa Gaviota* disco, Thu-Sun, 2130-0400, entry US$1, cave-like atmosphere, picks up after midnight, young crowd, techno music. *Casa de la Cultura*, 37 y 24, check the schedule posted outside for dance events; beside the Servi Cupet petrol station on 39 y 30, no sign outside, café where you can dance, open 24 hrs, total mix of music, comfortable and friendly, best place. **Nightlife**

Local Travel can be difficult although nearly every car will turn into a taxi on request. Fares within Nueva Gerona are about US$2. The best way to see the island is to hire a private car with a driver/guide, which costs about US$40-60 a day. Motorbike hire from the hotels is US$7 per hour. Local transport is often by horse and cart. **Car hire**: *Havanautos* C 32 y 39, T24432, but the dollar hotels also have car hire desks. **Bus** Buses run to **La Fe**, the *Hotel Colony*, **Playa Bibijagua**, and bus marked 'Servicio Aereo', between the airport and the cinema, but don't rely on any of these to run on a regular basis. **Transport**

Long distance Air The Rafael Cabrera airport (GER) is nearly 5 km from town and there are 2 or 3 scheduled 40-min flights a day from Havana so you could do a day trip if you wanted. Fare US$22 1-way, book in advance. Aerotaxi to Pinar del Río US$22, like a flying bus. **Sea** An interesting way of getting to the island is by the 106-passenger *kometa* (a vintage Soviet hydrofoil), from Surgidero de Batabanó on the mainland south coast. There is a morning crossing and an evening crossing, which take 2 hrs, US$15. Connecting bus from **Havana** to Surgidero de Batabanó, 1 hr, from bus terminal on Boyeros at 0700 and 1300. Book a couple of days in advance at the terminal at the far end of the Boyeros entry, between 0600-1200, 2 pesos, at the office in the terminal. Snacks available at the terminal. On the *kometa* try for Salón A, the only one with a view. Those paying in dollars are usually directed to Salón C, with freezing air conditioning. Snacks available in pesos and beer at US$1. Customs entry both ways, remember 20-kilo weight limit. Alternatively, a ferry crosses on the same route Wed, Fri and Sun at 1930 from Havana train station and takes 6 hrs, US$10. In Havana tickets are sold at the station office. In Nueva Gerona the terminal is on the Río Las Casas at the end of Calle 22 and the ticket office is open daily 0600-1300. Fares in dollars, take your passport.

Airlines *Cubana* at 39 1415 entre 16 y 18, Nueva Gerona, T061-22531/24259. *Aerotaxi* at Siguanea airport, T98282, 98181. **Banks** *Banco Nacional*, 39 y 18, open Mon-Fri 0800-1400, Sat 1300-1500; Caja Popular de Ahorro, 39 y 26, open Mon-Fri 0800-1700. Best to bring enough cash from the mainland. **Medical services** Pharmacy at 39 y 24, open Mon-Fri 0800-2200, Sat 0800-1600. Take plenty of insect repellent, particularly for the Ciénaga or the *Hotel Colony*. **Directory**

Cayo Largo

Cayo Largo is at the eastern end of the Archipiélago de los Canarreos, 114 km east of Isla de la Juventud and 80 km south of the Península de Zapata. It is a long, thin, coral island, 26 km long and no more than 2 km wide. There are beautiful white sandy beaches protected by a reef, all along the southern coast which, together with the cristal clear, warm waters of the Caribbean, make it ideal for tourism. A string of hotels lines the southern tip of the island. The northern coast is mostly mangrove and swamp, housing hungry mosquitoes as well as numerous birds (pelicans being the most visible) and iguanas. Turtles lay their eggs at Playa Tortuga in the northeast, and there is a turtle farm at Combinado northwest of the airstrip. *Phone code: 5 Colour map1, grid B2*

The best beach on the island is the 2 km white sand **Playa Sirena**, which faces west and is spared any wind or currents which sometimes affect the southern beaches. Snorkelling and scuba diving can be done at Playa Sirena, 10 minutes' boat ride from **Beaches & watersports**

Cuba

the hotels and at **Playa Los Cocos**, which you can reach by bicycle. **Scuba diving** is good around the island. There is an extensive reef with gorgonians, sponges and lots of fish, while north of the island you will find large pelagics. **Sailing** is popular and there is a bareboat yacht charter fleet. The Marina Cayo Largo del Sur at Combinado has 50 moorings for visiting yachts, who don't have to buy a tourist card to come here if they are not going on to anywhere else in Cuba, because the island is a free port. To clear customs, call the marina on VHF 6, or maritime security (*seguridad marítima*) on VHF 16. There is **deep sea fishing** for marlin and other big fish, with international fishing tournaments held here. Other watersports include windsurfing, kayaking, jet skis, catamarans, and banana rides.

Sleeping   There are several hotels here at present, all in the Gran Caribe chain and grouped together under the name of the *Isla del Sur Hotel Resort*, T548111-8, F548201. All facilities shared and included in the package cost, which can be as low as US$185 per person for 2 day/1 night or US$400 per person for 4 nights, including air and ground transport from Havana, breakfast and dinner buffet. Prices include 3 meals and free use of all water sports and other activities such as tennis, horse riding and volleyball. Medical facilities, evening entertainment, disco, laundry, post office and fax services are all available. The hotels and the thatched *cabañas* are low-lying and pleasantly spread out in gardens by the beach, all rooms are a/c, with private bath, telephone and satellite TV. There is no private accommodation on the island and you will not need any pesos.

Eating   There are several buffet restaurants and thatched snack bars (*ranchones*) attached to the hotels, as well as a seafood restaurant at the *Pelícano* which has to be booked, a highly recommended Italian place at the *Villas* and a good pizzeria. Food is reported to be plentiful and fresh. You will not find any *paladares* here but there is lots of lobster.

Transport   **Local Car hire**: *Havanautos* and *Transautos* at the *Hotel Pelícano*. Motorcycles, bicycles, and jeeps are also available. **Long distance Air** There are several charters and scheduled international flights to Cayo Largo del Sur airport (CYO). *Aerogaviota* flies from Aeropuerto Playa Baracoa, **Havana**, a former military air base. There are also flights from **Varadero**, or by light plane or boat from **Isla de la Juventud**. *Aerotaxi* at the airport, T793255. If you come on a package tour from Havana you will probably fly on a 60-year-old Antonov bi-plane, at an altitude of 3,500 ft, scenic and quite an experience but perhaps not for the nervous.

Background

History

Spanish conquest   Cuba was visited by Cristóbal Colón (Christopher Columbus) during his first voyage to find a westerly route to the Orient on 27 October 1492, and he made another brief stop two years later on his way from Hispaniola to Jamaica. Columbus did not realize it was an island when he landed; he hoped it was Japan. He arrived on the north coast of 'Colba', but found little gold. He did, however, note the Indians' practice of puffing at a large, burning roll of leaves, which they called 'tobacos'. Cuba was first circumnavigated by Sebastián de Ocampo in 1508, but it was Diego de Velázquez who conquered it in 1511 and founded several towns, called *villas*, including Havana. The first African slaves were imported to Cuba in 1526. Sugar was introduced soon after. Tobacco was made a strict monopoly of Spain in 1717. The coffee plant was introduced in 1748. The British, under Lord Albemarle and Admiral Pocock, captured Havana and held the island in 1762-63, but it was returned to Spain in exchange for Florida.

Towards the end of the 18th century Cuba became a slave plantation society. By the 1860s Cuba was producing about a third of the world's sugar and was heavily dependent on slaves to do so, supplemented by indentured Chinese labourers in the 1850s and 1860s. An estimated 600,000 African slaves were imported by 1867.

Independence from Spain became a burning issue in Cuba as Spain refused to consider political reforms which would give the colony more autonomy. The first war of independence was in the eastern part of the island between 1868 and 1878, but it gained little save a modest move towards the abolition of slavery; and complete abolition was not achieved until 1886. Many national heroes were created during this period who have become revolutionary icons in the struggle against domination by a foreign power. One consequence of the war was the ruin of many sugar planters. US interests began to take over the sugar plantations and the sugar mills, and Cuba became more dependent on the US market.

From 1895 to 1898 rebellion flared up again in the second war of independence under the young poet and revolutionary, José Martí, together with the old guard of Antonio Maceo and Máximo Gómez. José Martí was tragically killed in May 1895 and Maceo in 1896. Despite fierce fighting throughout the island, neither the Nationalists nor the Spanish could gain the upper hand. However, the USA was now concerned for its investments and its strategic interests. When the US battleship *Maine* exploded in Havana harbour on 15 February 1898, killing 260 crew, the USA declared war on Spain. American forces were landed, a squadron blockaded Havana and defeated the Spanish fleet at Santiago de Cuba. In December peace was signed and US forces occupied the island for four years.

The Republic of Cuba was proclaimed in 1902 and the Government was handed over to its first president. However, the Platt Amendment to the constitution, passed by the US Congress, clearly made Cuba a protectorate of the USA. The USA retained naval bases and reserved the right of intervention in Cuban domestic affairs but, to quell growing unrest, repealed the Platt Amendment in 1934. The USA formally relinquished the right to intervene but retained its naval base at Guantánamo.

Around two thirds of sugar exports went to the USA under a quota system at prices set by Washington; two thirds of Cuba's imports came from the USA; foreign capital investment was largely from the USA and Cuba was effectively a client state. Yet its people suffered from grinding rural poverty, high unemployment, illiteracy and inadequate health care. Politics was a mixture of authoritarian rule and corrupt democracy. From 1924 to 1933 the 'strong man' Gerardo Machado ruled Cuba. He was elected in 1924 on a wave of popularity but a drastic fall in sugar prices in the late 1920s led to strikes; nationalist popular rebellion was harshly repressed. The USA tried to negotiate a deal but nationalists called a general strike in protest at US interference, and Machado finally went into exile. The violence did not abate, however, and there were more strikes, mob attacks and occupations of factories. In September 1933 a revolt of non-commissioned officers including Sergeant Fulgencio Batista, deposed the government. He then held power through presidential puppets until he was elected president himself in 1940. Batista pursued nationalist and populist policies, set against corruption and political violence. In 1940 a new Constitution was passed by a constituent assembly dominated by Batista, which included universal suffrage and benefits for workers such as a minimum wage, pensions, social insurance and an eight-hour day. In 1944 Batista lost the elections but corruption continued. Batista, by then a self-promoted general, staged a military coup in 1952. Constitutional and democratic government was at an end. His harshly repressive dictatorship was brought to a close by Fidel Castro in January 1959, after an extraordinary and heroic three-year campaign, mostly in the Sierra Maestra, with a guerrilla force reduced at one point to 12 men.

Fidel Castro, the son of immigrants from Galicia and born in Cuba in 1926 saw José Martí as his role model and aimed to follow his ideals. In 1953, the 100th anniversary of José Martí's birth, Castro and a committed band of about 160 revolutionaries attacked the Moncada barracks in Santiago de Cuba on 26 July. The attack failed and Castro and his brother Raúl were later captured and put on trial. Fidel used the occasion to make an impassioned speech denouncing corruption in the ruling class and

Independence movement

Cuba

Dictatorship

Revolution

the need for political freedom and economic independence. In 1955 the Castros were given an amnesty and went to Mexico. There Fidel continued to work on his essentially nationalist revolutionary programme, called the 26 July Movement, which called for radical social and economic reforms and a return to the democracy of Cuba's 1940 constitution. He met another man of ideas, an Argentine doctor called Ernesto (Che) Guevara, who sailed with him and his brother Raúl and a band of 82 like-minded revolutionaries, back to Cuba on 2 December 1956. Their campaign began in the Sierra Maestra in the east of Cuba and after years of fierce fighting Batista fled the country on 1 January 1959. Fidel Castro, to universal popular acclaim, entered Havana and assumed control of the island.

Communism & the 1960s From 1960 onwards, in the face of increasing hostility from the USA, Castro led Cuba into socialism and then communism. Officials of the Batista régime were put on trial in 'people's courts' and executed. The promised new elections were not held. The judiciary lost its independence when Castro assumed the right to appoint judges. The free press was closed or taken over. Trade unions lost their independence and became part of government. The University of Havana, a former focus of dissent, and professional associations all lost their autonomy. The democratic constitution of 1940 was never reinstated. In 1960 the sugar centrales, the oil refineries and the foreign banks were nationalized, all US property was expropriated and the Central Planning Board (Juceplan) was established. The professional and property-owning middle classes began a steady exodus which drained the country of much of its skilled workers. CIA-backed mercenaries and Cuban exiles kept up a relentless barrage of attacks, but failed to achieve their objective.

1961 was the year of the Bay of Pigs invasion, a fiasco which was to harden Castro's political persuasion. Some 1,400 CIA-trained Cuban emigrés landed in the Bahía de Cochinos (Bay of Pigs), but were stranded on the beaches when the Cuban air force attacked their supply ships. Two hundred were killed and the rest surrendered within three days. In his May Day speech, Fidel Castro confirmed that the Cuban Revolution was socialist. The US reaction was to isolate Cuba, with a full trade embargo. Cuba was expelled from the Organization of American States (OAS) and the OAS imposed economic sanctions. In March 1962 rationing had to be imposed.

In April 1962, President Kruschev of the USSR decided to send medium-range missiles to Cuba, which would be capable of striking anywhere in the USA. This episode, which became known as the 'Cuban Missile Crisis', brought the world to the brink of nuclear war, defused only by secret negotiations between John F Kennedy and Kruschev. Without consulting Castro and without his knowledge, Kruschev eventually agreed to have the missiles dismantled and withdrawn on condition that the west would guarantee a policy of non-aggression towards Cuba.

Economic policy during the 1960s was largely unsuccessful in achieving its aims. The government wanted to industrialize rapidly to reduce dependence on sugar. However, the crash programme, with help from the USSR, was a failure and had to be abandoned. The whole nation was called upon to achieve a target of 10 million tonnes of sugar by 1970 and everyone spent time in the fields helping towards this goal. It was never reached and never has been. Rationing is still fierce, and there are still shortages of consumer goods. However, the Revolution's social policies have largely been successful and it is principally these achievements which have ensured the people's support of Castro and kept him in power. Education, housing and health services have been greatly improved and the social inequalities of the 1940s and 1950s have been wiped out.

1970s Soviet domination During the second decade of the Revolution, Cuba became firmly entrenched as a member of the Soviet bloc, joining COMECON in 1972. The Revolution was institutionalized along Soviet lines and the Party gained control of the bureaucracy, the judiciary and the local and national assemblies. A new socialist constitution was adopted in 1976. Cuba's foreign policy changed from actively fomenting socialist revolutions abroad (such as Guevara's forays into the Congo and Bolivia in the 1960s) to supporting other left wing or third world countries with combat troops and technical advisers including Angola, Ethiopia, Nicaragua, Jamaica and Grenada. In September 1979, Castro hosted a summit conference of the non-aligned nations in Havana, a high point in his foreign policy initiatives.

By the 1980s, the heavy dependence on sugar and the USSR, coupled with the trade embargo, meant that the expected improvements in living standards were not being delivered as fast as hoped and the people were tiring of being asked for ever more sacrifices. In 1980, the Peruvian embassy was overrun by 11,000 people seeking political asylum. Castro let them go and he opened the port of Mariel for a mass departure of some 125,000 by sea in anything they could find which would float.

1980s dissatisfaction

This was the decade of the Latin American debt crisis, and Cuba was unable to escape. Development projects in the 1970s had been financed with loans from western banks, in addition to the aid from the USSR. When interest rates went up in 1982, Cuba was forced to renegotiate its US$3.5 bn debt to commercial banks, and in 1986 its debt to the USSR. The need to control public finances brought more austerity.

Before the collapse of the Soviet system, aid to Cuba from the USSR was traditionally estimated at about 25% of gnp. Cuba's debt with the USSR was a secret; estimates ranged from US$8.5 bn to US$34 bn. Apart from military aid, economic assistance took two forms: balance of payments support (about 85%), under which sugar and nickel exports were priced in excess of world levels, and assistance for development projects. About 13 million tonnes of oil were supplied a year by the USSR, allowing three million to be re-exported, providing a valuable source of foreign earnings. By the late 1980s up to 90% of Cuba's foreign trade was with centrally planned economies.

The collapse of the Communist system in Eastern Europe, followed by the demise of the USSR, very nearly brought the end of Castro's Cuba as well. There were signs that a power struggle was taking place at the top of the Communist Party. In 1989, Gen Arnaldo Ochoa, a hero of the Angolan campaign, was charged with drug trafficking and corruption. He was publicly tried and executed along with several other military officers allegedly involved.

In an effort to broaden the people's power system of government introduced in 1976, the central committee of the Cuban Communist Party adopted resolutions in 1990 designed to strengthen the municipal and provincial assemblies and transform the National Assembly into a genuine parliament. In February 1993, the first direct, secret elections for the National Assembly and for provincial assemblies were held.

1990s crisis & change

Economic difficulties in the 1990s brought on by the loss of markets in the former USSR and Eastern Europe, together with higher oil prices because of the Gulf crisis, forced the Government to impose emergency measures and declare a special period in peace time. Rationing was increased, petrol became scarce, the bureaucracy was slashed. In 1993, Cuba was hit by a storm which caused an estimated US$1bn in damage. In mid-1994, economic discontent boiled up and Cubans began to flee for Florida in a mass exodus similar to that of Mariel in 1980. It was estimated that between mid-August and mid-September 30,000 Cubans had left the country. Eventually the crisis forced President Clinton into an agreement whereby the USA was committed to accepting at least 20,000 Cubans a year, plus the next of kin of US citizens, while Cuba agreed to prevent further departures.

As the economic crisis persisted, the government adopted measures which opened up many sectors to private enterprise and recognized the dependence of much of the economy on dollars. The partial reforms did not eradicate the imbalances between the peso and the dollar economies, and shortages remained for those without access to hard currency. Cuba intensified its economic liberalization programme, allowing farmers to sell at uncontrolled prices once their commitments to the state procurement system were fulfilled. Importantly, the reforms also allowed middlemen to operate. Markets in manufactured goods and handicrafts also opened and efforts were made to increase the number of self-employed.

US pressure in the 1990s Before the Revolution of 1959 the USA had investments in Cuba worth about US$1,000mn, covering nearly every activity from agriculture and mining to oil installations. Today all American businesses have been nationalized; the USA has cut off all imports from Cuba, placed an embargo on exports to Cuba, and broken off diplomatic relations. Prior to the 1992 US presidential elections, President Bush approved the Cuban Democracy Act (Torricelli Bill) which forbade US subsidiaries from trading with Cuba. Many countries, including EC members and Canada, said they would not allow the US bill to affect their trade with Cuba and the UN General Assembly voted in favour of a resolution calling for an end to the embargo.

In 1996, US election year, Cuba faced another crackdown by the US administration. In February, Cuba shot down two light aircraft piloted by Miami exiles allegedly over Cuban air space and implicitly confirmed by the findings of the International Civil Aviation Organization (ICAO) report in June. The attack provoked President Clinton to tighten and internationalize the US embargo on Cuba and on 12 March he signed into law the (Helms-Burton) Cuban Freedom and Democratic Solidarity Act. The new legislation allows legal action against any company or individual benefiting from properties expropriated by the Cuban government after the Revolution. It brought universal condemnation: Canada and Mexico (Nafta partners), the EU, Russia, China, the Caribbean Community and the Río Group of Latin American countries all protested that it was unacceptable to extend sanctions outside the USA to foreign companies and their employees who do business with Cuba.

Recent events 1997 was the 30th anniversary of the death of Che Guevara in Bolivia, whose remains were returned to Cuba in July. During a week of official mourning for Che and his comrades in arms, vast numbers filed past their remains in Havana and Santa Clara, where they were laid to rest on 17 October. In December 1998 the remains of 10 more guerrillas killed in Bolivia in 1967 were also interred in the Che Guevara memorial in Santa Clara. They included Haydée Tamara Bunke, known as Tania.

In January 1998 the Pope visited Cuba for the first time and held open-air masses around the country. The Pope preached against Cuba's record on human rights and abortion while also condemning the US trade embargo preventing food and medicines reaching the needy. The visit was a public relations success for both Castro and the Pope. Shortly afterwards, 200 prisoners were pardoned and released.

In 1999 the UN Human Rights Commission expressed concern about 'continued repression' in Cuba, following the conviction of four Cubans for sedition. They were jailed for receiving funds and instructions from the USA aimed at obstructing foreign investment. Two Salvadoreans were sentenced to death for a bombing campaign in 1997 in which six Havana hotels and restaurants were attacked and an Italian killed. In 2000, Cuba requested the extradition from Panama of four Cuban exiles involved in a terrorist plot to kill Castro, but had to guarantee that they would not face the death penalty nor a jail sentence of more than 20 years, even though Cuba's penal code calls for death in cases of terrorism. In a crackdown against crime, the National Assembly approved increasing sentences and extending the death penalty. Police presence increased noticeably on the streets of Havana.

In November 1999 a six-year-old boy, Elián González, was rescued from the sea off Florida, the only survivor from a boatload of illegal migrants which included his mother and her boyfriend. He was looked after by distant relatives in Miami and quickly became the centrepiece of a new row between Cuban exiles, supported by right wing Republicans, and Cuba. The US Attorney General, Janet Reno, supported the decision by the US Immigration and and Naturalization Service (INS) on

5 January 2000, that the boy should be repatriated and reunited with his father in Cuba by 14 January, but she postponed the deadline to allow for legal challenges. Mass demonstrations were held in Havana in support of Elián's return but legal manoeuvres by US politicians stalled progress and caused further disputes. Amid enormous controversy, the US authorities siezed Elián on 22 April and reunited him with his father, who had travelled to the USA earlier in the month with his second wife and baby. The family finally took him home, amid celebrations in Cuba, where the boy had become a symbol of resistance to the USA.

Geography

The island of Cuba, 1,250 km long, 191 km at its widest point, is the largest of the Caribbean islands and only 145 km south of Florida. Gifted with a moderate climate, afflicted only occasionally by hurricanes, not cursed by frosts, blessed by an ample and well distributed rainfall and excellent soils, it has traditionally been one of the largest exporters of cane sugar in the world.

Old coral reefs have been brought to the surface, so that much of the northern coast consists of coral limestone cliffs and sandy beaches. By contrast the southern coastline is being gradually submerged, producing wetlands and mangroves. Limestones of various types cover about two-thirds of the island. In most areas, there is a flat or gently rolling landscape. There are three main mountain areas in the island. In the west, the Cordillera de Guaniguanico is divided into the Sierra del los Organos in the west, with thick deposits of limestone which have developed a distinctive landscape of steep-sided flat-topped mountains; and the Sierra del Rosario in the east, made up partly of limestones and partly of lavas and other igneous rocks. Another mountainous area in central Cuba includes the Escambray mountains north of Trinidad, a double dome structure made up of igneous and metamorphic rocks, including marble. The Sierra Maestra in east Cuba has Cuba's highest mountains, rising to Pico Turquino (1,974 m) and a rather different geological history, with some rocks formed in an arc of volcanic activity around 50 million years ago. Older rocks include marble, and other metamorphics. Important mineral deposits are in this area; nickel is mined near Moa.

Constitution and government

In 1976 a new constitution was approved by 97.7% of the voters, setting up municipal and provincial assemblies and a National Assembly of People's Power. The membership of the Assembly is now 595, candidates being nominated by the 169 municipal councils, and elected by direct secret ballot. Similarly elected are members of the 14 provincial assemblies, both for five-year terms. The number of Cuba's provinces was increased from six to 14 at the First Congress of the Communist Party of Cuba in December 1975. Dr Fidel Castro was elected President of the Council of State by the National Assembly and his brother, Major Raúl Castro, was elected First Vice-President. There are five other Vice-Presidents.

Economy

Following the 1959 revolution, Cuba adopted a Marxist-Leninist economic system. Almost all sectors of the economy were state controlled and centrally planned, the only significant exception being agriculture, where some 12% of arable land was still privately owned. The country became heavily dependent on trade and aid from other Communist countries, principally the USSR (through its participation in the Council of Mutual Economic Aid), encouraged by the US trade embargo. It relied on sugar, and to a lesser extent nickel, for nearly all its exports. While times were good, Cuba used the Soviet protection to build up an impressive, but costly, social welfare system, with better housing, education and health care than anywhere else in

Latin America and the Caribbean. The collapse of the Eastern European bloc, however, revealed the vulnerability of the island's economy and the desperate need for reform. A sharp fall in gdp of 35% in 1990-93, accompanied by a decline in exports from US$8.1bn (1989) to US$1.7bn (1993), forced the Government to take remedial action and the decision was made to change to a mixed economy.

Transformation of the heavily centralized state apparatus has progressed in fits and starts. The Government is keen to encourage self-employment to enable it to reduce the public sector workforce, but Cuban workers are cautious about relinquishing their job security. Some small businesses have sprung up, particularly in tourism. Free farm produce markets were permitted in 1994 and these were followed by similar markets at deregulated prices for manufacturers, including goods produced by state enterprises and handicrafts. Cubans are now allowed to hold US dollars and in 1995 a convertible peso at par with the US dollar was introduced.

The US trade embargo and the associated inability to secure finance from multilateral sources has led the Government to encourage foreign investment, principally in joint ventures. All sectors of the economy are now open to foreign investment and in some areas majority foreign shareholdings are allowed.

Structure of production **Sugar** is the major crop, and the second most important earner of foreign exchange after tourism. However, the industry has consistently failed to reach the targets set. Cuba's dream of a 10 mn tonne raw sugar harvest has never been reached and by 1998 output had fallen steadily to 3.2 mn tonnes, the lowest for 50 years. Poor weather and shortages of fertilizers, oil and spare parts cut output. The 1999/2000 harvest achieved its target of 4 mn tonnes, but world prices were low. **Tobacco** is a traditional crop with Cuban cigars world famous, but this too has suffered from lack of fuel, fertilizers and other inputs. Production is recovering with the help of Spanish credits and importers from France and Britain.

Diversification away from sugar is a major goal, with the emphasis on production of **food** for domestic use because of the shortage of foreign exchange for imports. The beef herd declined to four million in the first half of the 1990s because of the inability to pay for imports of grains, fertilizers and chemicals. Production is now less intensive and numbers are beginning to rise again. Similarly, milk production is also increasing.

The sudden withdrawal of **oil** supplies when trade agreements with Russia had to be renegotiated and denominated in convertible currencies, was a crucial factor in the collapse of the Cuban economy. Although trade agreements involving oil and sugar remain, Cuba has had to purchase oil from other suppliers with limited foreign exchange. As a result, Cuba has stepped up its own production: foreign companies explore for oil on and offshore and investment has borne fruit, but over 7 mn tonnes of hydrocarbons are imported annually, at a cost of US$1bn, and shortages of fuel remain.

Mining is attracting foreign interest and in 1994 a new mining law was passed. A Mining Authority was created and a tax system set up. Major foreign investors include Australian (nickel), Canadian (gold, silver and base metals) and South African (gold, copper, nickel) companies. Cuba has one small gold mine at Castellanos in Pinar del Río province. New, Canadian-backed projects in Pinar del Río at the Hierro Mantua site will produce gold and copper, and on Isla de la Juventud, gold and silver.

Tourism is now a major foreign exchange earner and has received massive investment from abroad with many joint ventures. New hotel projects are coming on stream and many more are planned. Most of the development has been along the Varadero coast, where large resort hotels attract package tourism, but Cayo Coco and Cayo Guillermo are now earmarked for major construction. Cuba has around 35,000 hotel rooms, of which two thirds are in beach resorts and a third in cities, although this is to rise to over 60,000 by 2006. Despite political crises, numbers of visitors have risen steadily from 546,000 in 1993 to over 2 mn now fifteen percent of visitors come from Canada, 13% from Italy, 11% from Germany and 10% from Spain. The target is for 7 mn tourists a year by 2010, bringing earnings of about US$11.8 bn.

Culture

The major characteristic of Cuban culture is its combination of the African and European. Black African traditions persist, inevitably mingled with Hispanic influence, in religion: for instance *santería*, a cult which blends popular Catholicism with the Yoruba belief in the spirits which inhabit all plant life. This now has a greater hold than orthodox Catholicism. Church and State were separated at the beginning of the 20th century. The domination of the USA after that time encouraged the spread of Protestantism, although Catholicism remained the religion of the majority. Nevertheless, Catholicism was not as well supported as in some other Latin American countries. After the Revolution relations between the Catholic Church and Castro were frosty. Most priests left the country. By the late 1970s the Vatican's condemnation of the US embargo helped towards a gradual reconciliation. A ban on religious believers joining the Communist Party has been lifted and Protestant, Catholic and other Church leaders have reported rising congregations. In 1996 Fidel visited Pope John Paul II at the Vatican and the Pope visited Cuba in January 1998. Castro has stated in the past that there is no conflict between Marxism and Christianity and has been sympathetic towards supporters of liberation theology in their quest for equality and a just distribution of social wealth.

Religion

From the mid-16th century to the late 19th, hundreds of thousands of African slaves were brought to Cuba. The most numerous and culturally most influential group were the Yoruba-speaking agriculturalists from of Southeast Nigeria, Dahomey and Togo, who became known collectively in Cuba as *lucumí*. It is their pantheon of deities or *orishas*, and the legends (*pwatakis*) and customs surrounding these, which form the basis of the syncretic **Regla de Ocha** cult, better known as **Santería**. Though slaves were ostensibly obliged to become Christians, their owners turned a blind eye to their rituals. The Catholic saints thus spontaneously merged or syncretised in the *lucumí* mind with the *orishas* whose imagined attributes they shared. Some two dozen regularly receive tribute at the rites known as *toques de santo*. Santería is non-sectarian and non-proselytizing, co-existing peacefully with both Christianity and the **Regla Conga** or **Palo Monte** cult brought to Cuba by *congos*, slaves from various Bantu-speaking regions of the Congo basin. Indeed many people are practising believers in both or all three. The **Abakuá Secret Society** is not a religion but a closed sect. Open to men only, and upholding traditional *macho* virtues, it has been described as an Afro-Cuban freemasonry, though it claims many non-black devotees. Also known as *ñañiguismo*, the sect originated among slaves brought from the Calabar region of southern Nigeria and Cameroon, whose Cuban descendants are called *carabalí*.

Afro Cuban religion

The Cuban Revolution had perhaps its widest cultural influence in the field of **literature**. Many now famous Latin American novelists (like Gabriel García Márquez, Mario Vargas Llosa and Julio Cortázar) visited Havana and worked with the Prensa Latina news agency or on the *Casa de las Américas* review. Not all have maintained their allegiance, just as some Cuban writers have deserted the Revolution. One such Cuban is Guillermo Cabrera Infante, whose most celebrated novel is *Tres tristes tigres* (1967). Other established writers remained in Cuba after the Revolution: Alejo Carpentier, who invented the phrase 'marvellous realism' (*lo real maravilloso*) to describe the different order of reality which he perceived in Latin America and the Caribbean and which influenced many other writers from the region (his novels include *El reino de este mundo, El siglo de las luces, Los pasos perdidos*, and many more); Jorge Lezama Lima (*Paradiso*, 1966); and Edmundo Desnoes (*Memorias del*

Literature

subdesarrollo). Of post-revolutionary writers, the poet and novelist Miguel Barnet is worth reading, especially for the use of black oral history and traditions in his work. After 1959, Nicolás Guillén, a black, was adopted as the national poet; his poems of the 1930s (*Motivos de son, Sóngoro cosongo, West Indies Ltd*) are steeped in popular speech and musical rhythms. In tone they are close to the work of the *négritude* writers (see under Martinique), but they look more towards Latin America than Africa. The other poet-hero of the Revolution is the 19th-century writer and fighter for freedom from Spain, José Martí. Even though a US radio and TV station beaming propaganda, pop music and North American culture usurped his name, Martí's importance to Cuba remains undimmed.

Music   Music is incredibly vibrant on the island. It is, again, a marriage of African rhythms, expressed in percussion instruments (batá drums, congas, claves, maracas, etc), and the Spanish guitar. Accompanying the music is an equally strong tradition of dance. A history of Cuban music is beyond the scope of this book, however there are certain styles which deserve mention. There are four basic elements out of which all others grow. The *rumba* (drumming, singing about social preoccupations and dancing) is one of the original black dance forms. By the turn of the century, it had been transferred from the plantations to the slums; now it is a collective expression, with Saturday evening competitions in which anyone can partake. Originating in eastern Cuba, *son* is the music out of which *salsa* was born. *Son* itself takes many different forms and it gained worldwide popularity after the 1920s when the National Septet of Ignacio Piñeiro made it fashionable. The more sophisticated *danzón*, ballroom dance music which was not accepted by the upper classes until the end of the last century, has also been very influential. It was the root for the *cha-cha-cha* (invented in 1948 by Enrique Jorrin). The fourth tradition is *trova*, the itinerant troubadour singing ballads, which has been transformed, post-Revolution, into the *nueva trova*, made famous by singers such as Pablo Milanés and Silvio Rodríguez. The new tradition adds politics and everyday concerns to the romantic themes. There are many other styles, such as the *guajira*, the most famous example of which is the song 'Guantanamera'; *tumba francesa* drumming and dancing; and Afro-Cuban jazz, performed by internationally renowned artists like Irakere and Arturo Sandoval. Apart from sampling the recordings of groups, put out by the state company Egrem, the National Folklore Company (Conjunto Folklórico Nacional) gives performances of the traditional music which it was set up to study and keep alive.

Cayman Islands

5

Cayman Islands

These three low lying little islands south of Cuba are green with pine and mangroves. Seven Mile Beach along the west side of Grand Cayman provides a welcome break for workers in the offshore financial centre. Nature conservation is top priority here, both on land and under water and there are a number of sanctuaries in the ponds and wetlands. The sister islands of Cayman Brac and Little Cayman are quiet, unhurried places where you can escape the crowds and relax without giving up your creature comforts. A dive destination ranked among the world's best, the islands offer a variety of thrilling dive sites. World-famous for their underwater scenery, there are tropical fish of all kinds in the waters surrounding the islands, especially in the coral reefs, and green turtles are now increasing in numbers, having been deliberately restocked by excess hatchings at the Cayman Turtle Farm.

A Foot in the door

- The **National Museum** gives an excellent introduction to the history of the islands and the way of life of the people.
- Feel the thrill of touching a **stingray** at Stingray City, rather like fondling a wet mushroom.
- Hike through the **Parrot Reserve** on Cayman Brac, one of the many Heritage Sites on the island.
- Kayak to **Owen Island** off Little Cayman for peace and tranquillity.
- Dive the wall, and then do it again, and again.

Essentials

Before you travel

Documents **Passports** or birth certificates and photo ID (but not voter registration card) but not visas are required for citizens of the USA, Canada, UK and British Dependent Territories. Passports are required for visitors of all other countries. Everyone also needs a return or onward airline ticket. Visas are not required for citizens of Great Britain or Commonwealth countries, Andorra, Argentina, Austria, Bahrain, Belgium, Brazil, Canada, Chile, Costa Rica, Denmark, Dominican Republic, Ecuador, El Salvador, Finland, France, Germany, Greece, Guatemala, Haiti, Iceland, Irish Republic, Israel, Italy, Japan, Kuwait, Liechtenstein, Luxembourg, Mexico, Norway, Oman, Panama, Peru, Portugal, San Merino, Saudi Arabia, South Africa, Spain, Sweden, Switzerland, the USA and Venezuela. If you are from any of these countries you may be admitted to the Cayman Islands for a period of up to six months. Resident aliens of the USA who show a valid US Alien Registration Card (Green Card) may enter and remain in the Cayman Islands for 30 days. **Visas** are required by all countries not included in the above list and should be applied for at the nearest British Consulate or High Commission Office. Temporary work permits are available for business people on a short visit, which can be obtained in advance from the Department of Immigration, PO Box 1098 GT, Grand Cayman, T9498344. If you want to work in the country you may not accept a job unless you have a government-issued work permit. No attempt should be made to take drugs into the country.

Money The legal **currency** is the Cayman Islands dollar (CI$). The **exchange rate** is fixed at CI$1 to US$1.20, or CI$0.80 to US$1, although officially the exchange rate is CI$0.84 to US$1. US currency is readily accepted throughout the Islands (although all change will be returned in CI$) and Canadian and British currencies can be exchanged at all banks. There is no exchange control. **Credit cards** are accepted nearly everywhere, but check that your hotel will accept them. Personal cheques are not generally welcome. Travellers' cheques are preferred. Most of the major international **banks** are represented in George Town, Grand Cayman but not all are licensed to offer normal banking facilities. Those which do include *Bank of Nova Scotia*, *Barclays Bank International*, *Canadian Imperial Bank of Commerce* and *Royal Bank of Canada*. Commercial banking hours are 0900 to 1600 Monday to Thursday, and 0900 to 1630 on Friday. The *Cayman National Bank* has a branch on Cayman Brac.

Climate
Average temperatures in winter are about 24°C & in summer are about 26°-29°C

The Cayman Islands lie in the trade-wind belt and the prevailing northeast winds moderate the temperatures, making the climate delightful all year round. Most rain falls between May and October, but even then it only takes the form of short showers. Hurricane season is June to October but the Cayman Islands have had little trouble since Hurricane Gilbert in 1988.

Tourist offices overseas

Canada *Travel Marketing Consultants, 234 Eglinton Ave East, Suite 306, Toronto, Ontario, M4P IK5 T416-4851550, F416-4857578.*
France/Benelux/Scandinavia *Horwath Axe Consultants, 12 Rue de Madrid, 75008, Paris, France, T53-424136, F43-873285.*
Germany/Austria/Switzerland *Marketing Services International, Walter Sthrer and Partner GmbH, Johanna-Melber-Weg 12, D-60599, Frankfurt, T69-6032094, F69-629264.*
Italy *G & A Martinengo, Via Fratelli Ruffini 9, 20123 Milano, T02-48012068, F02-463532.*
Spain *Sergat España SL, Pau Casals 4, 08021 Barcelona, T93-4140210, F93-2018657.*
UK *6 Arlington St, London SW1A 1RE, T020-74917771, F020-74097773, infouk@caymanislands.uk The Cayman Turtle newsletter is produced twice a year, primarily for travel agents, but also for anyone*

interested in visiting the islands. The London office is also the European headquarters for Cayman Airways, providing air reservations and tickets as well as a hotel reservations service (free). The Public Relations office for both organizations is McCluskey and Associates, 50 Sulivan Rd, London SW6 3DX, T020-73718900, F020-73718116.
USA *6100 Blue Lagoon Drive, Suite 150, Miami, Fl 33126-2085, T305-2662300, F305-2672932; 9525 W Bryn Mawr, Suite 160, Rosemont, Illinois 60018, T847-6786446, F847-6786675; Two Memorial City Plaza, 820 Gessner, Suite 170, Houston, Texas 77024, T713-4611317, F713-4617409; 420 Lexington Ave, Suite 2733, New York, NY 10170, T212-6825582, F212-9865123; 3440 Wilshire Blvd, Suite 1202, Los Angeles, California 90010, T213-7381968, F213-7381829.*

Getting there

From Europe *British Airways* has three scheduled flights a week from London Gatwick via Nassau, so two-centre visits are possible. There are also daily BA flights to Miami, which connect with Cayman Airways and only take an hour longer. **From North America** The national flag carrier, *Cayman Airways*, has regular services from Miami, Houston, Orlando and Tampa in the USA. *Northwest Airlines* flies from Detroit and Minneapolis. *American Airlines* flies from Dallas, Miami and Nashville. *US Air* flies from Boston, Charlotte, Kansas City, Philadelphia and Pittsburgh. *Continental* flies from New York (Newark). *Delta* flies from Atlanta and New York (JFK). *Air Canada* flies from Toronto. *Sunworld* from Cincinnati. **From the Caribbean** *Air Jamaica* and *Cayman Airways* share a service to Kingston; *Air Jamaica* also has services from Montego Bay. *Air Jamaica Express* is starting flights between Nassau, Santo Domingo and Grand Cayman. *Isleña* flies from La Ceiba, Honduras.

Air *All international flights land in Grand Cayman. Cayman Airways and Island Air connect the sister islands, Cayman Brac and Little Cayman*

No more than four cruise ships may be in port at any given time, or 6,500 passengers, whichever is greater. The islands are not served by any scheduled passenger ships but there are cargo services between the islands, Kingston in Jamaica, Honduras and Costa Rica and Miami and Tampa in the USA. The port at George Town comprises the south wharf, with a depth of 24 ft, and the west wharf, with a depth of 20 ft. The port at Creek, Cayman Brac, is equipped to handle the same class of vessels but Little Cayman has only a small facility.

Sea *30 major cruise lines visit Grand Cayman with 600 calls to port each year bringing over 1 million visitors*

Touching down

Air communications are good and there are two international airports, the **Owen Roberts International Airport** on Grand Cayman and the **Gerrard Smith Airport** on Cayman Brac. Owen Roberts International Airport is situated less than two miles from the centre of George Town and only 10 minutes' drive from most of the hotels on Seven Mile Beach. In a plaza outside the terminal there are car hire companies and a café, open from 0700.

Airport information

Airlines *Cayman Airways*, T9492311on Grand Cayman, T9481221 on Cayman Brac, www.camanairways.com *Island Air*, for flights to the sister islands, T9490241 (charters), T9495252 (reservations), F9497044, online reservations can be made on www.IslandAirCayman.com *Air*

Touching down

Official time Eastern Standard Time, 5 hours behind GMT, for the whole year.

Departure tax US$12.50 for all visitors aged 12 and over payable either in Cayman or US currency when you leave the Islands (includes US$2.50 environmental tax).

Safety The Cayman Islands are safe to visit and present no need for extra security precautions. However, drugs related offences have increased. The islands remain a major trans-shipment point. Care must be taken when walking on a road, especially at night; they are narrow and vehicles move fast.

Newspapers The Caymanian Compass is published Monday to Friday with a circulation of 25,000. Online you can get news and information with Cayman Net News at www.caymannetnews.com The television station CITN has its own website at www.caymanews.com.ky

Public holidays New Year's Day, Ash Wednesday, Good Friday, Easter Monday, Discovery Day (third Monday in May), the Monday following the Queen's official birthday (June), Constitution Day (first Monday in July), the Monday after Remembrance Sunday (November), Christmas Day and Boxing Day.

Jamaica, T9492300. **American Airlines**, T9498799. **Northwest Airlines**, T9492955/6. **United Airlines**, T9497724. **US Air**, T9497488. Charter companies: **Executive Air Services**, T9497766.

Tourist information Cable and Wireless, in conjunction with the Department of Tourism, provide a Tourist Hotline. By dialling 9498989 you can find out the week's events and local information. Further information may be obtained from the Cayman Islands Department of Tourism, The Pavilion, Cricket Square, Elgin Avenue, George Town, PO Box 67, George Town, Grand Cayman, BWI, T345-9490623, F9494053, toll free 1800-3463313, 0830-1700, www.caymanislands.ky The **Cayman Islands National Trust** has a lot of historical and environmental information about the islands, PO Box 31116 SMB, Grand Cayman, T9490121, F9497494, www.caymannationaltrust.org

Privilege Card From 15 April to 15 December, more than 90 tourist industry companies participate in a discount programme. With your Privilege Card you can get discounts on accommodation, restaurants (10% on food), watersports (20%), car rentals (20%), golf (10-25%), shopping (15%) and attractions on all three islands. Ask a travel agent for details.

Weddings There is no residency requirement, so you can get married on a day trip to the Cayman Islands, provided you obtain a special licence from the Administrative Secretary, Room 46, Government Administration Building, George Town, or from the District Commissioner's office at Stake Bay, Cayman Brac, for US$200. Contact the tourist office for more information.

Further reading The Cayman Islands Government Information Services (The Pavilion, Cricket Square, Grand Cayman, T9498092, F9498487) publishes a series of booklets including *Marine Parks Rules and Sea Code in The Cayman Islands* and several on banking, captive insurance, company registration, residential status, work permits, living in the Cayman Islands etc. The Department of Tourism publishes *The Rates & Facts Guide to the Cayman Islands* annually, giving hotel and transport prices as well as other useful information. The tourist office also has a list of books about the Cayman Islands which can be bought in the islands. The *Ordnance Survey* produces a 1:50,000 scale **map** of the Cayman Islands with an inset map of George Town in its World Map Series. For information contact Ordnance Survey, Romsey Rd, Maybush, Southampton SO9 4DH, T02380-792000, F02380-792404.

Where to stay

A government tax of 10% is added to the room charge and most hotels also add a 10-15% service charge to the bill in lieu of tipping. The winter season, running from 16 December to 15 April, is the peak tourist season. Visitors intending to come to the islands during this period are advised to make hotel and travel arrangements well in advance. There are substantial reductions during the rest of the year (see Privilege Card above), with cut rates or even free accommodation for children under 12. Most hotels offer watersports, scuba diving and snorkelling, and many have tennis courts, swimming pools and other facilities. Accommodation is plentiful and varied, ranging from resort hotels on the beach to small, out of the way, family-run guest houses. There is also a wide variety of cottages, apartments (condominiums) and villas available for daily, weekly or monthly rental. The Cayman Islands Hotel Reservations Service, T305-2666742, F305- 2672931, represents 67 properties in the Cayman Islands and can be contacted abroad direct or through the tourist office.

Getting around

Cayman Airways and *Island Air* provide inter-island services from Grand Cayman to Cayman **Air**
Brac and Little Cayman and return (see 'Airlines' above). There are four flights a day from Grand Cayman to Cayman Brac and Little Cayman with *Island Air*. You can have a full day on either sister island by booking flight 6131, departing Grand Cayman 0745, arriving Cayman Brac at 0825 and Little Cayman at 0845. The last return flight 6314 departs Cayman Brac at 1725, Little Cayman at 1745, arriving back in Grand Cayman at 1830. Fares are US$110 day trip Grand Cayman to Little Cayman or Cayman Brac (US$40 day trip Cayman Brac to Little Cayman); US$77 (US$20) one way; US$154 (US$40) ordinary return. A child's day trip fare is US$89, T9495252. A US$5 per passenger facility charge is added to fares from Grand Cayman.

Keeping in touch

The Philatelic Bureau releases six stamp issues a year. Stamps are sold separately or as a First **Post**
Day Cover from CI$0.10 to 2.00. Airmail postal rates are divided into three groups. **Group A**: the Caribbean, USA, Canada, Central America and Venezuela, first class 30 cents, second class, post cards, airletters 20 cents. **Group B**: Europe, Scandinavia, West Africa, South America, first class 40 cents, others 25 cents. **Group C**: East Africa, the Arabian sub-continent, Asia and the Far East, first class 55 cents, others 30 cents.

The Cayman Islands have a modern automatic telephone system operated by *Cable and* **Telephone**
Wireless, which links them with the rest of the world by satellite and by submarine cable. *IDD code: 1-345*
International telephone, email and facsimile facilities are available and about 108 countries can be dialled directly. There is also a telephone route to the UK via Mercury. Public international telephone booths and a telegram counter are at the Cable and Wireless offices at Anderson Square. ■ *0815-1700*. **Communication Station** is behind Colombian Emeralds Internation in George Town by the harbour. There are 32 telephones, 5 internet kiosks, a photocopier, fax machine and phone cards for sale. The international code is followed by a seven-digit local number. For overseas credit card calls (Visa and Mastercard) dial 110.

Food and drink

The range of restaurants is wide and all international styles are available from fast food to *Caymanian recipes*
gourmet. Check your bill, gratuities are sometimes added, sometimes not. Cayman-style fish *use seafood*
is sautéed with tomato, onion, pepper and piquant seasoning. Conch is available as chowder, *predominantly*
fritters, marinated etc. Try Caymanian Rum Cake for dessert. The *Tortuga Rum Company*, T9497701, has 17 retail outlets plus a 2,500 sq ft bakery (open to visitors) where up to 5,000 rum cakes are baked daily for shipment worldwide. While the recipe remains a family secret, a key component is the use of oak-aged private label Tortuga Gold Rum, which is not sold to the public. You can visit and sample the varieties of rum cake, purchase the 10 registered rum blends or other locally made items such as fudge, hot pepper sauce, steak sauce or flavoured coffee. The *Stingray Brewery*, Red Bay, east of George Town, T9476699, can also be visited. This microbrewery makes 1,500 barrels of beer annually for island consumption. ■ *The gift shop and brewery are open Mon-Sat 0900-1800*. Tours on request with free samples of dark and premium beer. *Icoa Chocolates*, Church Street, George Town, T9451915, is the only chocolate

Cayman Islands

shop, making handcrafted delicacies blended with local ingredients such as key limes, Caribbean spice, Cayman honey and coconut. ■ *Mon-Sat 0900-1800.*

Shopping

As a free port, there is duty-free shopping and a range of British glass, crystal, china, woollens, perfumes and spirits are available. US citizens are entitled to a US$400 exemption after being away from the USA for 48 hours

Black coral carvings and jewellery are widely available. Note that since the 1978 Cayman Islands Marine Conservation Law prohibited the removal of coral from local waters, manufacturers turned to Belize and Honduras for their supply. All the Central American countries are now members of CITES, so if you must buy it, check the source in case it has been procured illegally. Caymanite is a semi-precious gem stone with layers of various colours found only in the Cayman Islands. Local craftspeople use it to make jewellery.

At *Churchill's Cigar Store*, T9456141, you can buy Cuban seed tobacco, rolled and packaged in the Cayman Islands so it can be legally imported into the USA, look for Cayman Crown and Cayman Premium. The day's fish catch can be bought from the fishermen most afternoons opposite the Tower Building just outside central George Town. Otto Watler makes and sells honey in Savannah, sign on the right just after the speed limit notice.

Useful for arts and crafts is the *National Gallery of the Cayman Islands* (T9458111) comprehensive 'Art Trail' map which highlights the location of artists, studios, galleries, craftsmen's homes and retail outlets, related establishments and points of interest in the Cayman Islands. *Pure Art*, on South Church St (also at *Hyatt Regency*), sells the work of over 100 local artists and craftsmen and women; paintings, prints, sculptures, crafts, rugs, wallhangings etc. Open Monday-Saturday 1000-1600. *The National Gallery of the Cayman Islands* has a stall at Rum Point, Grand Cayman, selling work by local artists and craftsmen, run as a co-operative called *Native Done*. *The National Museum* on the waterfront in George Town has a popular, well-stocked gift shop for prints, posters, books and crafts. Open Monday-Saturday, 1000-1600, T9498368. The *National Trust House* headquarters on Courts Rd, T9490121, ntrust@candw.ky, open Monday-Friday 0900-1700, has a new gift shop featuring locally made gifts, Cayman-related books and Trust materials, including posters of the red-footed booby and the endangered blue iguana. *Caribbean Charlie's* in Northside, near Rum Point, offers a wide assortment of tropical crafts with handmade, custom designed and signed work, T9479452. The *Glassblowing Studio* on the waterfront in George Town is open Monday-Saturday 0830-2100, T9497020, and you can watch the artisans creating glassware and figurines for sale. Interesting if not to everyone's taste. They have two other stores: *Flameworks*, in the Anchorage Centre across from the Port Authority and in the Regency Court, next to the *Hyatt Hotel*. Caymanian artist Kara Julian has a gallery in Galleria Plaza, T9465272, where you can buy her art glass paintings in vivid colours and tropical designs, ranging from champagne flutes to soap dispensers. *Tropical L'Attitude Islands Gifts and Apparel*, T9451233, in Butterfield Square across from the main post office in George Town, sells gifts and clothing from around the world, batik, bags, baskets, jewellery, paintings, carvings and furniture. On Cayman Brac, *NIM Things* sells items made locally, including caymanite jewellery, straw bags and crochet. Open 0900-1800 at Spot Bay, east-end of the Main North Side Rd, but not always open. *Joe Tourist* is 'Made in Cayman' casual wear and accessory line. The children's range is decorated with stingrays, blue iguanas and green sea turtles. Adult clothing is in earth tones and Caribbean colours and uses natural fibres and textures in locally-made products such as straw hats, leather bags and burlap knapsacks made from recycled croaker sacks. Joe Tourist products are available only in the Cayman Islands, although you can order them on-line at www.joetourist.com. *The Book Nook* (which sells *Caribbean Islands Handbook* among other books, toys, gifts and games), is at Galleria Plaza, West Bay Rd, T9474686, and Anchorage Centre, T9497392, PO Box 1551, Grand Cayman, F9475053.

Flora and fauna

There are around 200 species of birds on the islands

Birds that inhabit the islands include the Antillean grackle, the smooth-billed ani, the green-backed heron, the yellow-crowned night heron and many other heron species, the snowy egret, the common ground dove, the bananaquit and the Cayman parrot. The endangered West Indian whistling duck can be seen on Grand Cayman and Little Cayman. If you are interested in birdwatching, go to the mosquito control dykes on the West Bay peninsula of Grand Cayman, or walk to the Cistern at East End. A former Governor was a keen birdwatcher and in 1993 he set up a fund to establish the **Governor Michael Gore Bird Sanctuary** on 3½ acres of wetland on Grand Cayman, where you can see 60 local species. There are nesting colonies of the red-footed booby and the magnificent frigate bird on Little Cayman. There is a parrot reserve on Cayman Brac on 197 acres of land donated to the National Trust by Donald Pennie. The **Brac Parrot Reserve** is the nesting ground for the endangered endemic Cayman Brac parrot, numbering about 400 birds. The reserve covers pristine ancient woodlands on a very rough and rocky terrain with a diversity of native trees, including species not present on Grand Cayman or Little Cayman. A 1-mile nature trail has been established through part of the reserve. The trail forms a loop which passes through several different types of terrain, from old farm land now under grass, past mango trees on red soil and through thickets and mature woodlands, a startling mixture of hardwoods and cacti. Signs and information boards are placed at strategic points along the trail and a brochure is available. *Birds of the Cayman Islands*, published by Bradley, is a photographic record; it costs £22. **Cardinal D's Park** on the outskirts of George Town, and the beginning of Seven Mile Beach, has four acres of natural lakes and woodlands. The bird sanctuary includes parrots, macaws, whistling duck and turtles. ■ *T9498855. Adults US$5, children US$2.50.*

Oncidium calochilum, a rare orchid, indigenous to Grand Cayman with a small yellow flower about ½in long, is found only in the rocky area off Frank Sound Drive. Several other orchid species have been recorded as endemic but are threatened by construction and orchid fanciers. There is protection under international and local laws for several indigenous species, including sea turtles, iguanas, Cayman parrots, orchids and marine life. For a full description of the islands' flora see George R Proctor, *Flora of the Cayman Islands*, Kew Bulletin Additional Series XI, HMSO (1984), 834 pp, which list 21 endemic plant taxa including some which are rare, endangered or possibly extinct.

The **Queen Elizabeth II Botanic Park** (officially opened by the Queen in 1994), is off Frank Sound Rd, Grand Cayman. A mile-long woodland trail has been cleared and an entrance garden created. In 1997 a second phase brought a Floral Colour Garden and a Heritage Garden, with endemic plants within the park. The gardens are very beautiful now that they have become well-established and are recommended for a day away from the beach even for those who know nothing about botany. Over 200 plants have been labelled so far, several of which are rare. Orchids bloom in May-June and there are breeding areas for the Grand Cayman Blue Iguana, the Grand Cayman parrot, the Cayman rabbit and the Cayman anole lizard. More gardens and sections are planned. Special events are sometimes held, such as an orchid show, in February, and a mango morning in August. There is a Visitor Centre, café and giftshop and a typical Caymanian cottage and garden has been built. ■ *T9473558 (information line), 9479462, F9477873, www.botanic-park.ky. Adults US$6.25, children 6-12 half price. Daily 0900-1830, last admission 1730.*

Indigenous animals on the islands are few. The most common are the agouti, non-poisonous snakes, iguana and other small lizards, freshwater turtle, the hickatee and two species of tree frog. Several animal sanctuaries have been established, most of which are RAMSAR sites where no hunting or collecting of any species is allowed. On Grand Cayman there are sanctuaries at Booby Cay, Meagre Bay Pond and Colliers Bay Pond; on Cayman Brac at the ponds near the airport and on Little Cayman at Booby Rd and Rookery, Tarpon Lake and the Wearis Bay Wetland, stretching east along the south coast to the Easterly Wetlands. The National Trust, T9490121, ntrust@candw.ky, has set up a Land Reserves Fund to buy environmentally sensitive land and protect natural resources. The first priority is the mountain area in North Side where the government donated 130 acres; another 200 acres need to be bought.

The Department of Tourism (T9490623) has produced a map of Cayman Brac depicting the location and full descriptions of 35 nature tourism sites as part of the Cayman Brac Development Project, funded by a grant from the European Union. The sites are either hiking trails, woodland walks, boardwalks out to wetlands, panoramic views including the Bluff and pristine beach sites, historic sites, swimming holes and areas, as well as the Brac Museum. All sites have proper signs so you do not have to hire a guide.

Cayman Islands

Diving and marine life

The best months for diving are Apr to Oct

Since 1986, a Marine Parks plan has been implemented to preserve the beauty and marine life of the islands. Even before then, however, a moorings project was in place. This has been highly successful in marine conservation and critical in protecting Cayman's fragile coral reefs and marine life from destruction by boat anchors. Permanent moorings have been installed along the west coast of Grand Cayman where there is concentrated diving, and also outside the marine parks in order to encourage diving boats to disperse and lessen anchor damage to the reefs. There are now 281 single and double-pin mooring sites around all three islands, 177 around Grand Cayman, 47 around Cayman Brac and 57 around Little Cayman. These parks and protected areas are clearly marked and strictly enforced by a full-time Marine Conservation Officer who has the power to arrest offenders. Make sure you check all rules and regulations as there have been several prosecutions and convictions for offences such as taking conch or lobsters. The import of spearguns or speargun parts and their use without a licence is banned. Divers and snorkellers must use a flag attached to a buoy when outside safe swimming areas. For further information call Natural Resources, T9498469.

Many of the better reefs & several wrecks are found in water shallow enough to require only mask, snorkel & fins; the swimming is easy & fish friendly

Although boats take snorkellers to many sites, you can snorkel quite happily from the shore. However, each island has a wall going down to extraordinary depths: the north wall of Cayman Brac drops from 60 to 14,000ft, while the south wall drops to 18,000ft. The deepest known point in the Caribbean is the Cayman Trench, 40 miles south of Cayman Brac, where soundings have indicated a depth of 24,724ft. *The Dive Sites of the Cayman Islands*, by Lawson Wood, published by New Holland (Publishers) Ltd in 1995 (ISBN 1 85368 767 7) describes 145 dive sites around Grand Cayman, 47 around Cayman Brac and 56 around Little Cayman, together with beautiful underwater photographs mostly taken by the author. One site it does not mention in this edition is the Russian frigate (a Brigadier Type II Class), brought from Cuba and deliberately sunk in 1996 to provide good wreck diving off Cayman Brac. The 95m relic of the Cold War was sunk on a sloping bed of sand 9-24m deep and only 30m from the shore, good for snorkellers as well as divers. It has been renamed the MV Captain Keith Tibbetts, after a popular resident of Cayman Brac, and its sinking was supervised by Jean Michel Cousteau, who stood on the bridge and 'went down with the ship.' Mounted underwater cameras will monitor the growth of coral etc.

The dive-tourism market is highly developed in the Cayman Islands and there is plenty of choice, but it has been often described as a cattle market with dive boats taking very large parties. Many companies offer full services to certified divers as well as courses designed to introduce scuba diving to novices; there are many highly qualified instructor-guides. There is a firm limit of a depth of 100ft for visiting divers, regardless of training and experience and the 69 member companies of the CIWOA will not allow you to exceed that. A complete selection of diving and fishing tackle, underwater cameras and video equipment is available for hire. The tourist office has a full price list for all operators. There is also the liveaboard *Cayman Aggressor IV* (US$1,695 per week all-inclusive), which accommodates 18 divers and cruises around Grand Cayman and Little Cayman. Contact **Aggressor Fleet Limited**, PO Drawer K, Morgan City, LA 70381, or PO Box 1882GT, Grand Cayman, T9495551, 1800-3482628, F504-3840817. A smaller liveaboard taking 10 divers maximum (US$1,295-1,595 per week all-inclusive) is the *Little Cayman Diver II*, which operates only around Little Cayman, T1800-458 BRAC, 813-9321993, F813-9352250, PO Box 280058, Tampa, FL33682.

Beaches and watersports

The beaches of the Cayman Islands are said to be among the best in the Caribbean

Various companies offer glass-bottomed boats, sailing, snorkelling, windsurfing, water skiing, water tours and a host of other activities. You can hire wave runners, aqua trikes and paddlecats, take banana rides and go parasailing. When waterskiing, there must be a minimum of two people in the boat so that one person can look out for hazards. There is year-round deep sea game fishing for blue marlin, white marlin, wahoo, yellow fin tuna and smaller varieties, and shorefishing in all three islands. Good fly fishing spots with local guides can be found on both Grand Cayman and Little Cayman.

Cayman Islands

Festivals

Pirates' Week is the islands' national festival and takes place in the last week of October. Parades, regattas, fishing tournaments, treasure hunts, historical and cultural 'district days' in Grand Cayman's five districts and on Little Cayman, are all part of the celebrations, which commemorate the days when the Cayman Islands were the haunt of pirates and buccaneers (T9495078). *Batabano* is Grand Cayman's costume carnival weekend, with street parades, music and dancing, which takes place in the last week of April or beginning of May. Cayman Brac has a similar celebration, known as *Brachanal*, which takes place in June. Everyone is invited to dress up and participate, and there are several competitions. *Cayfest*, the islands' national arts festival, takes place through most of April, with exhibitions, displays, dance and drama. The *Queen's Birthday* is celebrated in mid-June with a full-dress uniform parade, marching bands and a 21-gun salute. At the end of April is an eight-day *International Fishing Tournament* (replacing Million Dollar Month), with big prizes for catches of blue marlin, yellowfin tuna, wahoo and dolphin, contact the Cayman Islands Angling Club, T9497099, www.fishcayman.com for details. In mid-June, *International Aviation Week* attracts private pilots and flight demonstrations over Seven Mile Beach. The first weekend in July the Cayman Islands Restaurant Association holds an annual food festival: the *Taste of Cayman*, with lots of food and outdoor activities. Towards the end of October, baby turtles, bred at the Turtle Farm, are released into the wild. Christmas brings the Parade of Lights by boat on the waterfront, the Rotary Club's Annual Christmas Tree Lighting and Radio 3-99's 'Wacky House Light Tour'.

Health

Medical care on Grand Cayman is good and readily available. There is a 128-bed Cayman Islands Hospital in George Town, with accident and emergency unit, maternity, surgical and paediatric units, physiotherapy, radiology and laboratory services, dental clinic, eye clinic and pharmacy. For 24-hour ambulance and paramedic service on Grand Cayman, T911 or 555. The hospital is affiliated with the Baptist Hospital of Miami for patient referrals involving advanced care or treatment. All hospital beds are in single rooms. A two-person, double-lock recompression chamber is located by the hospital and supervised by a physician experienced in hyperbaric medicine. Out-patients pay a fixed charge per visit. Primary care is provided through four district health centres in Grand Cayman. There is a 12-bed hospital in Cayman Brac (T9482243/2245) and a clinic on Little Cayman staffed by a registered nurse. Open Mon-Fri 0900-1300, or on call 24 hours. A doctor visits Wed, T9480072.

See main health section page 47 for more information. Grand Cayman is sprayed frequently though it is advisable to bring insect repellent to combat mosquitoes & sandflies. Little Cayman is sprayed every 2 weeks

Grand Cayman

Grand Cayman is a prosperous island with a very British feel. The island is green with luxuriant vegetation, especially at the East End where there are pastures and grazing cows. North Sound is a 40-square mile lagoon with mangroves, although dredging schemes and urban growth threaten the mangrove habitat and the reefs. Some low-key but sophisticated development has taken place along the north coast around Cayman Kai, which has lovely beaches and good swimming and snorkelling. Most of the tourist development, however, is along Seven Mile Beach on West Bay, where there are hotels, condominiums, clubs, sports facilities, banks, restaurants and supermarkets.

Colour map 1, grid C2

Ins and outs

See page 247 for details of flights from London, Toronto and US cities as well as from neighbouring islands.

Getting there

Driving is on the left and the roads are in good order. See transport section page 263 for more details. The Public Transportation Board offers a recorded information service at T9455100, giving details on buses, taxis, limousines and tour buses, including routes and fares. There is

Getting around

an hourly bus service all over the island with marked stops, CI$1.50. If you stand by the road minibuses will toot their horns to see if you want a ride. Be careful of buses whose doors open into the centre of the road. Island tours can be arranged at about US$60 for a taxi, or US$10 per person on a bus with a minimum of 20 persons. Check with your hotel for full details. Taxi fares were expected to rise in 2001 for the first time since 1994, during which time the cost of living rose by 23%.

Diving and marine life

Dive sites Snorkelling and dive sites abound all round the island and include shallow dives for beginners as well as highly challenging and deeper dives for the experienced. Off the west coast there are three wrecks, arches, tunnels, caves, canyons and lots of reef sites close to shore which can be enjoyed by snorkellers and divers. Along the south coast the coral reefs are rich and varied with depths ranging from 15 ft to thousands of feet. The **East End wall** has pinnacles, tunnels and a coral formation known as **The Maze**, a 500-ft coral formation of caverns, chimneys, arches and crevices. There are several wrecks here also. Snorkelling is good near the *Morritts Tortuga Club* at the East End, also all along **Seven Mile Beach**, **North Sound**, **Smith Cove** in South Sound and off **Eden Rock**, near George Town. Along the north coast you can dive the **North Wall**. Near **Rum Point Channel** experienced divers can dive the Grand Canyon, where depths start at 70ft. The canyons, collapsed reefs, are 150ft wide in places. Other sites in this area towards **Palmetto Point** include the aptly-named **Eagle Ray Pass**, **Tarpon Alley** and **Stingray City**.

Dive centres The tourist office lists 32 dive operations on Grand Cayman, offering a wide range of courses and dive sites. Many are at more than one location, attached to hotels. All are of a high standard but you may want to make your choice according to the number of divers per boat. One of the newer operators, *Ocean Frontiers*, in the East End, has been highly praised in magazine surveys. The most popular and accessible dive sites are off South Sound or North West Point, where the wall or mini walls are close to shore and an easy swim. Boat dives go to the many sites along Seven Mile Beach or the North Wall, which is much more dramatic but generally a little rougher. Prices for a certification course start at US$300, rising to US$500; for qualified divers, a two-tank dive costs US$50-75 and a Stingray City dive US$40-60, depending on how far the boat has to come. Snorkelling trips are also available, US$20-40. The British Sub-Aqua Club is represented, T9490685.

Grand Cayman is host to a revolutionary product for youngsters under 12 who are too young to use standard scuba equipment. Children as young as four years old can now snorkel with a SASY (approved by PADI and NAUI). Supplied Air Snorkelling for Youth (SASY) is a scuba unit customised to fit children, but it is used only

Grand Cayman

Stingray City

Stingray City is a popular local phenomenon, where it is possible to swim with and observe large groups of extremely tame rays in only 12ft of water. Stingray City is better dived but half a mile away is the sandbar where sting rays also congregate, usually over 30 at a time, although there are thought to be around 250 in the area. The water here is only 1 to 3ft deep and crystal clear, so you hop out

of your boat and the rays brush past you waiting to be fed. Their mouths are beneath their head and the rays, 3ft across, swim into your arms to be fed on squid. They can give your arm quite a suck if they miss the food in your hand. A glass bottom boat leaves from the Rum Point Club to the sandbar and a nearby reef, 1100-1230, 1500-1630, US$28. From Morgan's Harbour boats charge US$35.

for snorkelling. The device consists of a small regulator attached to a pony tank and buoyancy vest which allows the child to float safely on the surface and view the marine world below without danger of being submerged. SASY units are available at all Red Sail Sports locations in Grand Cayman at the *Hyatt*, the *Westin, Holiday Inn* and the *Marriott* hotels (www.redsail.com). A non-profit foundation, Oceans for Youth, has been established to direct income from licensing and sales of SASY into an education programme about the marine environment.

An additional refinement, *Atlantis Research Submersibles Ltd*, PO Box 1043GT, Grand Cayman, T9497700, F9498574, operates a 20-ft research submarine, (two passengers, fare US$295 per person, five dives a day Monday to Saturday) to the 800ft deep Cayman Wall or to the wreck of the *Kirk Pride* at 780 ft. A larger submarine, with room for 48 passengers, is operated by *Atlantis Submarine*, PO Box 1043GT, Grand Cayman, T9497700; fares are US$55 for a one-hour day or night dive (children 4 to 12 half price), both to 100 ft along Cayman Wall. For US$29 you can take a one-hour ride in *Seaworld Explorer*, an underwater observatory which feels like a submarine but you are down only 4 ft. A diver will attract fish within view by feeding them (Don Foster's (Subsee) Ltd, T9498534, F9497538, PO Box 1544). The Nautilus Semi-Submersible is a 110-ft submarine which seats 80 people. Snorkelling trips to view the harbour at 30 ft are available, plus special cruises: sunset dinner cruise, comedy cruise and the island's only murder mystery cruise, US$29-35 including food and drinks, T9451355.

Fishing There are at least 14 companies on Grand Cayman offering fishing. The tourist office can give you a full list with prices, which depend on the type of boat you choose. Deep sea fishing boats can be chartered for a half day (US$350-700) or full day (US$500-1,500). Reef and bone fishing is about US$400-700 for a full day including all equipment, bait and lunch. There is an Angling Club, call Donna Sjostrom, T9497099, fishing@candw.ky

Beaches and watersports

West Bay Beach, now known as **Seven Mile Beach**, has dazzling white sand and is lined by hotels, tall Australian pines and silver thatch palms, the national tree. Beaches on the east and north coasts are equally good, and are protected by an off-shore barrier reef. On the north coast, at **Cayman Kai**, there is a superb public beach with changing facilities; from here you can snorkel along the reef to **Rum Point**. The beaches around Rum Point are recommended for peace and quiet, with shallow water safe for children. *Red Sail Sports* at Rum Point also ensure lots of entertainment, with wind surfers, sail boats, wave runners and water skiing as well as glass bottomed boat tours to see the sting-rays and scuba diving. There are hammocks, sunbeds, lockers, changing rooms, showers, restaurants, bar and Thomas the tabby cat. You can cross the North Sound by ferry from the *Hyatt Regency* to *Rum Point Club* (also under Hyatt management). ■ *T9499098. US$15 round trip, children 5 to*

Cayman Islands

12 yrs half price, under 5 yrs free. 120 passengers, 30 minutes, departs 1000, 1200, 1600 Mon-Thu, 1000, 1200, 1800 Fri-Sun, returns 1100, 1500, 1830 Mon-Thu, 1100, 1530, 2115 Fri-Sun. Around Rum Point at Water Cay and Finger Cay there are picnic sites on the lagoon. Take insect repellent. South of George Town there are good beaches for swimming and snorkelling at **Smith's Cove** and **Sand Cay**. In Frank Sound, **Heritage Beach**, just west of Cottage Point, is owned by the National Trust.

Sailing For information about sailing contact the *Cayman Islands Yacht Club*, PO Box 30 985 SMB, Grand Cayman, T9454322, F9454432, with docking facilities for 154 boats, 7ft maximum draft. *Aquanauts* at Morgan's Harbour, PO Box 30147SMB, T9451953, F9451954, also offers 15 slips accommodating boats of 6½ft draft and the usual facilities. For a social sailing club there is the *Grand Cayman Yacht Club*, Red Bay Estates, T9477913, PO Box 30513 SMB.

Windsurfing *Cayman Windsurf*, a BiC Centre, is at *Morritt's Tortuga Club*, East End, T9477492, F9476763, with a full range of BiC boards and UP sails and instruction available. *Sailboards Caribbean* (T/F9491068, windsurf@candw.ky) also offer rental and instruction, this is a Mistral certified school. Windsurfing at the East End is highly rated for people of all abilities. Beginners are safe within the reef, while outside the reef experienced sailors can try wave jumping or wave riding. Winds are brisk nearly all the year, with speeds of 15-25 knots. Lots of hotels' watersports operators offer windsurfing, sunfish, wave runners and other equipment.

Golf Jack Nicklaus has designed the Britannia golf course for the *Hyatt-Regency Grand Cayman Resort & Villas*. There is a nine-hole Championship course, an 18-hole executive course and an 18-hole Cayman course played with a special short-distance Cayman ball, but it can only be laid out for one course at a time; the executive has 14 par threes and four par fours, so it is short, while the short-distance ball with local winds is a tourist gimmick. ■ *T9498020 for starting times. To play the executive course with hire of clubs and compulsory buggie will cost you about US$70, the regulation course US$100 for 18 holes.* The Links, the 18-hole championship golf course is at Safehaven, with a par 71 course and a total yardage of 6,605 from the championship tees, although every hole has five separate tee areas to accommodate all levels of players. The club house is open daily with restaurant and bar open to golfers and non-golfers. Practice facilities include an aqua range, two putting greens, sand trap and pitching green (night lights). ■ *T9495988, F9495457, 0700-1800. 18 holes with cart/buggie costs US$110. You can hire clubs, US$1, take lessons or just practice, US$10 per 100 balls (you can buy balls at the bar if the clubhouse is closed).* Sunrise Golf Centre is a nine-hole par 3 layout ideally suited for junior and beginning golfers looking to sharpen their iron and short-game skills. Located at the end of Hirst Road in Savannah, the longest hole is 160yds while the shortest is 57yds. There is also a 300yd driving range, practice chipping and putting green. Rental clubs and PGA professional on site for lessons. ■ *Daily 0730-1800, US$15 for 9 holes, US$22 for 18 holes. Buckets for the driving range are US$4 small and US$6 large. T9474653.*

Other sports There are three **squash** courts at the *Cayman Islands Squash Racquets Association* at South Sound, also courts at *Downtowner Squash Club* in George Town. For information on matches contact John MacRury (T9492269). Most of the larger hotels have their own **tennis** courts but the *Cayman Islands Tennis Club* next door to the squash courts at South Sound has six floodlit tennis courts and a club pro. For match information contact Scott Smith (T9499464). For **soccer**, contact Tony Scott (T9497339) of the *Cayman Islands Football Association*. **Cricket** matches are played at the Smith Road Oval near the airport (although location may change with extension of runway); there are five teams in the *Cayman Islands Cricket Association's* league, details on matches from Jimmy Powell (T9493911) of the Cayman Islands Cricket Association. **Rugby** is played every Saturday between September and May at the *Cayman Rugby Football Club* at South Sound, for information phone Campbell Law (T9452387). **Horseriding** with *Nicki's Beach Rides*, T9455839, on trails and beaches in the northwest, or with *Pampered Ponies*, T9452262. *Eagles Nest Cycles* runs *The Harley Davidson Club*, T9494866, specializing in Harley Davidson **motorcycles** and souvenirs.

Motocross is popular in Grand Cayman and **stock car races** are held on the first Sunday of each month at the *Lakeview Raceway* (also known as Jay Bodden's Marl Pit) in George Town at 1300, CI$5 admission. The Cayman Motorsports Association's annual International Challenge Cup attracts racing drivers from Jamaica, Colombia, Canada and the USA. The association has built a new 30-acre racetrack, with a 20-acre family recreation area and 15-acre nature reserve, T9497135. No alcoholic beverages allowed.

You can go **bowling** at the *Stingray Bowling Centre and Arcade*, T9454444, at the Greenery on Seven Mile Beach, just north of the Strand Shopping Centre on West Bay Road. The centre has 10 lanes with Qubica automatic scoring, CI$4 per game with adult rental shoes for CI$3 and junior rental shoes for CI$2.50. Up to six people can play each lane and lanes can be rented by the hour for CI$24. There is also a pro-shop, you can have lessons, there is a snack bar, four satellite TVs and an arcade with video games. No alcohol, children under 12 must be accompanied by an adult.

If you want to entertain small children out of the sun (or rain), there are two indoor **play centres**: *O2B Kidz*, Merren's Shopping Centre on West Bay Road has 1,600 sq ft of play equipment, toddler area, ride-on games, small café, party room, height restrictions on play equipment. ■ *Daily from 0900 weekdays, 1000 on Sat and 1100 on Sun, US$6 per child, must be accompanied by an adult, T9465439. Smyles*, at the Islander complex just off the Harquail Bypass, more than 3,200 sq ft of tunnels, ball pit, snack bar, soft play area, arcade, games, event room, the largest indoor play centre. ■ *Daily, T9465800.*

George Town

The largest town and capital of the islands is George Town, which is principally a business centre dominated by modern office blocks. However, many of the older buildings are being restored and the government is trying to promote museums and societies to complement beach and watersports tourism.

Population: over 18,000

The **Cayman Islands National Museum**, in the restored Old Courts Building in George Town, opened in 1990 and is well worth a visit. There are exhibits portraying the nation's seafaring history, an audio visual presentation and a natural history display, as well as temporary exhibitions. The newest feature is a CD-ROM interactive exhibit, where you can touch the screen and access nearly 400 images of traditional sand yards, provision gardens and other features of typical Caymanian life as it used to be. Also audio segments where you can touch and hear accounts by older Caymanians about backing sand, caboose cooking, tending provision gardens, making grounds and sharing the harvest with neighbours. ■ *www.museum.ky T9498368. CI$4 adults, CI$2 children 6-18 years. Mon-Fri 0900-1700, Sat 1000-1400. There is a museum shop and* The Cool Caboose *for refreshments.*

Sights

Four of the older buildings which are being preserved are the work of a local boat-builder, Captain Rayal Brazley Bodden, MBE, JP (1885-1976). He was called upon to build the **Elmslie Memorial Church** (Presbyterian, on Harbour Drive, opposite the docks) in 1923. He put in a remarkable roof, with timbers largely salvaged from shipwrecks. Such was the general admiration that he was asked to design the **Town Hall**, a peace memorial for the First World War. It now looks tiny, but when it was opened in 1926 it was considered a grandiose folly, far too big for the island. Then came the **Public Library** nearby, with its beautiful hammer-beam roof and painted British university heraldic shields. Lastly the **General Post Office**,1939, which once housed all the colony's departments of government. Bodden surrounded the main façades of the building with art deco tapered columns. All his buildings have an inter-war flavour. They are one-storey, made of carefully shaped concrete blocks, poured to give a rustic, deep-grooved effect.

An archaeological dig on the waterfront on the site of **Fort George** has been sponsored by the Cayman National Trust. Unfortunately only a small part of the walls remain, much was demolished in 1972 by a developer who would have destroyed the lot if residents had not prevented him. The National Trust has designed a walking tour of George Town to include 28 sites of interest, such as Fort George, built around 1790, the Legislative Assembly, the war and peace memorials and traditional Caymanian architecture. A brochure and map (free) is available from the National Trust, PO Box 10, T9490121, F9497494, or the tourist office. Walking tours are also available for West Bay and Bodden Town.

Around the island

Some of the many things of interest to visit in Grand Cayman are included in a *Heritage One* passport, giving discounts of 25% off entry fees to the Museum, the Turtle Farm, Pedro St James and the Queen Elizabeth II Botanic Garden. The green and blue passports are stamped at each site but have no expiry date. They are available at each attraction, US$24 adults, US$13 children.

The **Cayman Turtle Farm**, at North West Point, houses over 17,000 green turtles and is the only commercial turtle farm in the world. Most of the turtles are used for meat locally since the USA banned the import of turtle meat, but in 1980-2000, some 30,000 turtles were released into the wild to replenish native stocks. They are released as yearlings weighing 3-6 lbs, usually during Pirates' Week in October. Those at the farm range in size from 2 oz hatchlings to breeding stock weighing an average of 38.5 lbs. You can also see loggerhead, hawksbill and ridley sea turtles, but the kemp's ridley are being transferred back to Cancún, Mexico. Polished turtle shells are sold here for about US$100, but their import into the USA is prohibited. A flora and fauna section of the farm includes the Cayman green parrot, a macaw called Crackers, a freshwater turtle, ground iguanas and agouti (known as the Cayman rabbit). ■ *PO Box 645GT, T9493893/4, F9491387, www.turtle.ky US$6 adults, US$3 children aged 6-12. Daily 0830-1700.*

West Bay is a colourful area with pretty old houses dating back to the seafaring days. The National Trust has a self-guided walkers' booklet of the area, directing you along lanes and paths and giving illustrated information about the district. The Pink House, built in 1912, is included in all tour itineraries as a typical Caymanian home. Originally home to the Bothwell family, it is now open to the public. Its traditional sand yard is raked every morning according to custom. The **Caymanian Heritage Museum** at the Four Way Shop on West Bay Road in West Bay is home to all sorts of artefacts. Next door is a cooking caboose where you can feast on Caymanian cooking of fish tea, fritters and fried fish. ■ *Fri 1200-2400, Sat 1000-2400, Sun 1200-1600.* **Hell**, situated near West Bay, is a bizarre rock formation worth visiting. Have your cards and letters postmarked at the sub-post office there. ■ *The post office is open Mon-Fri 0830-1300, 1400-1530, Sat 0830-1130.*

On the south coast at Savannah, just off the main coastal road, **Pedro St James** has been restored and developed into a national landmark. On 4 December 1831 an historic meeting was held here at which it was decided to split the island into districts with representation, and democracy was introduced. The site has the oldest known existing stone structure in the Cayman Islands. The original building is believed to have been built of quarried native rock around 1780 by William Eden, a plantation owner, and is the only known remains of a late 18th-century residence on the island. The upper floors are of mahogany with a fine balcony. There are a number of outbuildings and traditional activities which recreate plantation life. The Steadman Bodden house, a 100-year-old wattle and daub cottage was relocated in 1995 from the cruise ship landing at Spotts. An impressive Visitors' Centre has been built as a gateway to the Great House and grounds, offering the opportunity to learn about the history of the site before beginning the tour. The main attraction is a state-of-the-art multimedia theatre featuring a 20-minute show that brings to life the people, their dramas and the conditions in which they struggled, including a storm. ■ *T9473329. US$7.50 adults, US$3.75 children. Daily 0800-1700.*

There are caves in **Bodden Town**, believed to have been used by pirates, where you can see bones and stocks, and a line of unmarked graves in an old cemetery on the shore opposite, said to be those of buccaneers. Bodden Town was once the capital of the island and all shipping came here. Continuing east just after Half Moon Bay you will see blow-holes: waterspouts that rise above the coral rock in unusual patterns as a result of water being funnelled along passages in the rock as the waves come rolling in. At the east end of the island there is a good viewing point at the **Goring Bluff lighthouse**. A trip to **Gun Bay** at the east end of the island will show you the scene of the famous 'Wreck of the Ten Sails', which took place in 1788 (see page 268).

A drive along the north coast to **Rum Point** (see page 255) is picturesque, with views of the sea through the vegetation. There are lots of villas and plots of land for sale along the coast and all development is upmarket. The return journey can be made via the Botanic Park (see page 251) to make a circular trip.

The National Trust organizes guided village walks and has opened a nature trail, the **Mastic Trail**, a two-mile walk through farmlands, woodlands and mangroves. It starts near the south coast and ends near the north coast, from where a van will carry you back to the start. It takes about 2½ hours, moderate fitness recommended, US$30 per person. *Silver Thatch Excursions* is the only tour operator offering the National Trust escorted hikes along the trail and is highly recommended, T9456588.

For a pleasurable day's outing, arrange a boat trip to **North Sound** for US$35 or so. This will include snorkelling, fishing and a good look at marine life on a barrier reef. Your guide will cook fish, fresh marinated conch or lobster for you, delicious and highly recommended. You can also take a moonlit cruise aboard the *Jolly Roger* or the *Valhalla*, T9498988, with a sunset buffet dinner cruise. ■ *US$50; a cocktail cruise on Tue, US$30, or a happy hour cruise on Fri, US$15. Mon, Wed, Thu, Sat.*

Essentials

Seven Mile Beach LL *Grand Cayman Marriott Beach Resort*, PO Box 30371, T9490088, F9490288, marriott@candw.ky Right on the beach, 309 rooms, comfortable, pleasant, friendly service, 2 miles from George Town, watersports, tennis. **LL** *Westin Casuarina Resort*, PO Box 30620, T9453800, F9495825. 341 rooms, a/c, TV, phone, mini-bar, fan, marble bath, 2 pools, swim-up bar, tennis, dive shop, watersports, next to golf course. Nearby, **LL-L** *Hyatt Regency Grand Cayman*, PO Box 1588GT, T9497440, F9498032, britania@candw.ky 236 rooms, 55 villas, overlooking golf course and private waterway, lots of facilities, access for the disabled, an all-suite 5-storey tower is directly across the road from the main Hyatt complex, 53 one or two bedroom apartments, lots of amenities, all with seaviews and concierge. A villa complex, *Britannia Hyatt Villas*, extends between the golf course and the canal of North Sound, T9491234, F9498032, www.britanniavillas.com **LL-L** *Comfort Suites and Resort*, West Bay Road, just south of the *Marriott*, PO Box 30238 SMB, T9457300, F9457400, www.caymancomfort.com On the beach side of the road but not beachfront, about 300 ft from sea behind condos, 110 suites, studios and spacious 1-2 bedroom suites with full kitchens, some accessible for wheelchair guests, phones, restaurant, meeting room, fitness centre, child care facilities, pool, scuba and watersports rental on site, dive packages available. A new, 5-storey **LL-L** *Holiday Inn*, just south of *Indies Suites*, West Bay Road, T9464433, F9464434, www.holiday-inn.com opened in 2001 with 230 standard rooms and 1 penthouse suite, wheelchair accessible, non-smoking rooms available, a/c, TV, pool, dive and watersports operation, beach bar, lobby bar, massage, fitness centre, shops, restaurant and meeting room, access to beach.

Sleeping
There are about 50 hotels along Seven Mile Beach. All the major chains are represented, offering all types of luxury accommodation

Cayman Islands

There are lots of guest houses catering for divers in the suburbs south of George Town

Elsewhere Also new is **LL-L** *Cobalt Coast Resort & Suites*, north of Seven Mile Beach, past the Turtle Farm on Boatswains Bay, T9465656, F9465657, www.cobaltcoast.com Built in the style of a Great House, small and intimate, 18 rooms in 1-2 bedroom suites and villas sleeping up to 6, kitchens, *Duppies* restaurant, pool, jacuzzi, dock, dive shop on site. **At North Sound: LL-L** *Grand Caymanian Beach Club and Resort*, T9494403, www.grandcaymanian. com 5-star, full-service resort, studios, one to two bedroom suites, grand villas, all with lots of luxury facilities, kitchens, jacuzzis, pool, barbecues, children's playground, Kid's Club, fitness centre, gift shop, concierge, watersports. **At East End: LL-AL** *Morritt's Tortuga Club*, PO Box 496GT, T9477449, F9477669, reservations@morritt's.com Upmarket, suites and town houses, on beach, excellent windsurfing, pool with waterfalls and bar, full dive operation, packages available. **L-AL** *Cayman Diving Lodge*, PO Box 11, T9477555, F9477560, www.divelodge.com 10 rooms, including 2-tank boat dive and 3 meals, photo centre, great diving, snorkelling, bicycles, hammocks, internet access. **At West Bay: LL** *Breadfruit House*, Northwest Point Rd, T9491700. Same owner as *Divetech*, quaint Caymanian-style, opened 1999, apartments sleep 4, a/c, fans, kitchens, satellite TV, sound system, maid service, price includes 2-tank daily boat dive, night dive and unlimited shore diving. **At Bodden Town: LL-L** *Turtle Nest Inn*, T9478665, F9476379, www.turtlenestinn.com On a quiet, protected beach with excellent snorkelling, 8 one bedroom apartments with sofa beds, TV, phone, a/c, fans, laundry room, maid service, gas barbecue, pool, internet access. **South of George**

George Town

To Seven Mile Beach, Hell, West Bay & Cayman Turtle Farm

To Seven Mile Beach

Bodden Rd

ROCK HOLE

Eastern Av

Edward Avenue

Sports Field

School Rd

North Church St

Mary St

Fort St

9 10 11

2

Library

Panton Place

4

Edward St

Jennett St

North Sound Rd

Harbour Drive

Albert Panton

7

6

Docks

Cardinal Av

Hog Sty Bay

6

5

Shedden Rd

Crewe Rd

To Airport & East End

1

South Church St

3

To Seaview Hotel

Boiler's Rd

Goring Av

Pol

Government Administration Building

8

Elgin Av

Hospital Rd

Smith Rd

Pond Rd

To Coconut Walk Bay

N

0 metres   200
0 yards   200

▲ Others
1 Atlantis Submarine & Seaworld Explorer
2 Cayman Airways
3 Cayman Islands National Museum

4 Courthouse
5 Craft Market (public toilets)
6 Cruiseship docks (N and S terminals)
7 Customs

8 Dept of Tourism
9 Duty Free shops
10 Legislative Assembly
11 Town Hall

Town: **L-AL** *Coconut Harbour*, South Church St, ½ mile south of George Town, T9497468, F9497117, coccayman@aol.com 35 rooms, pool, a/c, fans, kitchenette, dive shop, unlimited shore diving, reef 20yds offshore, internet access. **L-AL** *Sunset House*, PO Box 479, T9497111, F9497101, www.sunsethouse.com 59 rooms, dedicated dive hotel on rocky shoreline, good shore diving, a bronze statue of a mermaid called Amphitrite (Poseidon's wife, queen of the sea) has been sunk in 50 ft of water for snorkellers and divers to enjoy. **AL** *Annie's Place*, 282 Andrew Drive, Snug Harbour, Seven Mile Beach, T9455505, F9454547, www. anniesplace.ky Two bedrooms, breakfast included, a/c, fan, TV, fridge, no smoking, 2 sitting rooms, one with TV and library, beach chairs and towels. **A-B** *Adam's Guest House*, PO Box 312, on Melmac Av, ½ mile south of George Town, T9492512, F9490919. Run by Tom and Olga Adams, excellent accommodation, US$10 additional person, a/c or fan, very helpful, about 300yds from *Parrots Landing* dive shop, travellers cheques or credit cards accepted. **A-B** *Wild Orchid Inn*, 120 Northward Rd, Bodden Town, T/F9472298, orchidinn@ candw.ky Breakfast included, a/c, kitchen, TV, jacuzzi, internet access. **AL-A** *Seaview Hotel and Dive Centre*, PO Box 260, T9450558, F9450559, seadive@candw.ky Pleasant small hotel, 15 rooms, a/c, fans, saltwater pool, hammocks, internet access, piano bar, award-winning restaurant, *Cayman Diving School* on site, T9464729, www.caymandivingschool.com excellent snorkelling and off-shore diving, credit cards accepted. **AL-B** *Eldemire's Guest House*, PO Box 482GT, South Church St, T9495387, F9496987. Room, studio or apartment, 1 mile from town, ½ mile from beach.

Self-catering Basic cottages may cost US$700-800 a week per house not per person. For those wishing to stay longer, two bedroom, furnished houses can be found away from the tourist areas in areas such as Breakers or Bodden Town for US$600-1,000 a month. Luxury villas and apartments, beachfront properties, can be rented through *Cayman Villas* (**L**), PO Box 681, George Town, T9454144, F9497471, www.ltravel.com/caymanvillas/, situated all round the island, along Seven Mile Beach and North Side, including the exclusive resort area of Cayman Kai.

There are dozens of restaurants on Grand Cayman ranging from gourmet standards, to smaller places serving native dishes. In George Town, there are many restaurants catering for the lunchtime trade of the office workers and a number of fast-food places, takeaways and delicatessens. Prices obviously vary according to the standard of restaurant, but for dinner, main courses start at about US$10 and range upward to US$60 or more for a full meal including wine. Lunch prices can be around US$7 to 10 and breakfast from about US$5. Excellent Sun brunch buffets, all you can eat, with orange juice and sparkling wine, at the *Hyatt* (recommended for meat, spit roasts) and the *Westin* (recommended for fish and sushi, but it also has pasta, spit roast, oyster and seafood bar, salads, fruit and cheese, you can stay there from 1100 to 1400 and visit the buffet as many times as you want) for about US$44 per person. During the high season it is advisable to reserve tables for dinner. People tend to eat early so if you reserve a table after 2000 you are likely to finish with the restaurant to yourself. There is a restaurant delivery service called Fine Dine-In, T9463463, ken@candw.ky which you can call daily 1730-2300 for all sorts of cuisines from 19 restaurants on the list (and growing). They also do video rental, drinks, etc for a real night in.

Eating
Fish, seafood & turtle meat are local specialities

George Town *The Bed Restaurant*, near Harquail Bypass, just opposite cinemas, T9497199, whimsically appointed like a lady's boudoir, popular, continental food with Thai and Mediterranean influences, the adjoining lounge is a favourite late night hang-out. *Breadfruit Tree Café*, Eastern Av and Coconut Place. Best spot for local delicacies, Mon-Sat, 1100-0300, only place open that late, no alcohol, busiest very late, serves cowfoot, fish tea, curry goat, jerk pork, jerk chicken etc, quaint, garden-like atmosphere in décor, best prices in town. *Casanova Restaurant*, old Fort Building, T9497633. Excellent, Italian, on the waterfront. *Champion House*, *I* and *II*, both on Eastern Av, George Town, T9492190 (*I*), T9497882 (*II*), cheap, local food. Recommended. *Grand Old House*, South Church St, T9499333, www. grandoldhouse.com Restored waterfront home, top notch service and seafood specialities. *Island Taste*, South Church St, T9494945. Upstairs outdoor patio overlooking harbour, excellent food. *Maxin's*, Fort St,

T9495447. French bistro, open breakfast onwards, moderately priced. *Paradise Bar & Grill* on waterfront, South Church St, T9451444. Good outdoor dining and regular drink specials. *The Almond Tree*, North Church St, on the waterfront, T9450155, www.almondtreehouse. com The thatched hut is a landmark, macaws and iguanas, opposite *Kirk's* supermarket, open air dining, 1100-2300, tarpon feeding 2030, the *Tree House Beach Bar* is here too. *Seymour's* has two 'stands', one in front of *The Planet*, off West Bay Rd, the other outside the Raquet Club near Cricket Square. Both open 2000-0100 for late crowds, sells Mannish Water, a local concoction of goats' parts rumoured to give a man extra potency, not sold to women, popular Fri, Sat night, couples line up to get a taste and eat great jerk pork and chicken. *The Brasserie*, Cricket Square, T9451815. Off the beaten path, undiscovered by many visitors, sophisticated menu, excellent wine selection, tapas bar daily, open for lunch and dinner, quite expensive. *Welly's Cool Spot*, North Sound Rd, T9492541. Native food at reasonable prices. *The Wharf*, on the outskirts of George Town on the way to Seven Mile Beach, T9492231. Bar open for happy hour 1700-1900, dinner daily 1800-2200, beautiful waterfront setting, quite a large restaurant, tarpon feeding nightly at 2100. *Pirate's Den*, Galleria Plaza, T9497144. Popular with ex-pats, breakfast, lunch and dinner, great Sun brunch buffet, open daily. *Benjamin's Roof*, Coconut Place, T9454080. Upstairs, continental and seafood specialities, live music downstairs, piano bar, moderately priced pastas, pizzas and entrées. For inexpensive fast food, *Chicken! Chicken!*, West Shore Centre, T9452290. Tasty spit-roasted chicken with assorted accompaniments, CI$20 for whole chicken plus 'fixin's', eat in or takeaway.

West Bay Road *Bamboo Lounge*, at the *Hyatt*, T9491234. Not your normal hotel restaurant, but great for sushi, shashimi, riqiri and specials, Japanese chef with flair, creative, generous portions, intimate and relaxing atmosphere, staff professional and friendly, popular with locals and visitors. *Coffee Grinder*, Seven Mile Shops, T9494833, a bakery. *Decker's 269*, T9456600. Built around a double decker bus, which serves as the bar, moderate prices, bistro style, nightly music, daily happy hours. *Eats Diner*, Cayman Falls, West Bay Road, T9475288. For breakfast. *Lantana's*, at the *Caribbean Club* on West Bay Rd. Fine, sophisticated dining, excellent food, featured by *Gourmet* magazine and *Bon Appetit*, who said the honey ginger salmon was the 'best of the year', also try the garlic soup, T9455595 for reservations. *Hook's Seafood Grotto*, next to *Treasure Island Resort*, T9458731. Looks like pirate's hideaway, breakfast, lunch and dinner, seafood and steak, cheerful. *Pirate's Buffet* at the *Marriott*, T9490088. Fri nights, all you can eat, music, fire eater, limbo dancer, reservations required. *Reef Grille*, at *Royal Palms Beach Club*, T9456358, www.reefgrill.com One of the hottest dining and entertainment spots, dinner daily 1730-2200, inside or out on the patio, wheelchair-accessible, American bistro, live bands Wed-Sat in May-Nov, Mon-Sat in Dec-Apr and special occasions at the *Royal Palms*, also watersports centre and beach facility open daily.

North *Calypso Grill* , Morgan's Harbour, T9493948. Lunch and dinner, 3-tiered dining area with panoramic view of North Sound, innovative menu, seafood and beef or salads and amazing desserts. *Cracked Conch*, Northwest Point Rd, T9455117. Near Turtle Farm, popular stopping place for excursions, very nice setting and atmosphere, lively, takeaways very popular. *Pappagallo*, Barkers, right in the north, see map, T9473479. Italian cuisine, expensive, on 14-acre bird sanctuary overlooking natural lagoon, eat inside the haphazardly thatched building or in outside screened patio, excellent food and extensive wine list, reservations essential, open daily 1800-2300.

South coast *Crow's Nest*, about 4 miles south of George Town, T9499366. Open lunch Mon-Sat, 1130-1430, dinner daily 1800-2200, a local's favourite, small, glorious position, dining on the patio overlooking the sea or inside, moderate prices, reservations essential. *The Lighthouse* at Breakers T9472047, www.lighthouse.ky 20 mins' drive east of George Town, good place to stop during island tour, light lunches, open air dining by sea, or smart dinners, moderately expensive.

North coast *Cecil's Restaurant*, *Kaibo Yacht Club* at Cayman Kai, T9479975. Cajun and New Orleans food, beach bar downstairs open daily 1100-1800, upstairs open Tue-Sat 1800-2230 for dinner and Sun for brunch featuring New Orleans classics like crawfish etouffe, jambalaya, red beans and rice, shrimp creole plus fresh Louisiana oysters, fresh local seafood always on the menu.

George Town: for local colour visit *Farmers*, off Eastern Av, near the school. *The Landmark* on **Bars**
Harbour Drive is fairly typical 'pub', popular with expatriates, food not recommended but great
for drinks. *Blue Parrot* on South Church St, T9499094, www.blueparrotcayman.com Open air
bar with outdoor TV sports screen, darts. In down town George Town, *Captain Bryan's Seaside
Patio*, T9496163. With a patio overlooking the harbour. *Rackham's Pub*, North Church St,
T9453860. Good rum based drinks, light meals, view of harbour, food good value. *The Tree
House Beach Bar* is an open-air bar right on the beach on North Church St. Thatched hut, pleasant tropical atmosphere. *West Bay Polo Club*, T9499892. Sports bar, speciality nights, eg sushi
on weekdays, always popular. *Lone Star Bar and Grill*, next to the *Hyatt Hotel*, West Bay Rd,
T9455175. Favourites with sports fans, showing international sporting events nightly, Tex-Mex
food, happy hour Mon-Fri 1700-1830.

Benjamin's Roof, Coconut Place, Tue-Sat 1930-2300, T9454080. Big screen TV in sports **Nightlife**
room, family dining room and Irish pub room. Paraguayan harpists play for dinner guests
Mon-Sat at *The Wharf*, T9492231. Hear jazz at *The Bed Restaurant*, Mon evenings,
T9497199. *Sharkey's* nightclub, Cayman Falls on West Bay Rd, T9475366, www.sharkeys.ky
Popular Mon nights, dancing to disco and reggae. *Apollo II Club*, North Side, T9479568,
local groups such as Cayman Edition, as well as rock, reggae and other Caribbean music.
McDoom's Club Inferno, Hell, West Bay, T9493263. *The Barefoot Man*, calypso and a dash
of country music is at Rum Point on Mon and Fri nights. *Coconuts Comedy Club*, is at
Sharkey's and *Hook's Seafood Grotto*. There is also a comedy cruise aboard the *Nautilus*, Tue,
1700-1930, US$18, cash bar. The Cayman National Cultural Foundation, T9495477, puts on
plays and musicals at the Harquail Theatre on West Bay Rd, T9495477. The Cayman Drama
Society uses the Prospect Play House, a small theatre on the road to Bodden Town. There is
a **cinema** on West Bay Rd with 2 screens, 2 showings a night Mon-Sat, CI$6 adults, CI$2.75
children, T9494011.

Car hire *Avis*, *National* and *Hertz* are represented and there are a number of good local **Transport**
companies as well, many of which are at the airport. Rental firms issue visitors with driving
permits on production of a valid driving licence from the visitor's country of residence. The
minimum driving age is 21 at some places, 25 at other companies, check. Most car hire firms
have boxes in the airport departure lounge where you can drop off your car keys prior to
departure, having left the car in the company's car park. *Ace Hertz*, PO Box 53GT, T9492280,
F9490572, standard jeep US$52 a day in winter, US$45 in summer, compact car US$27-34;
Andy's Rent A Car Ltd, PO Box 277 WB, West Bay, T9498111, F9498385, cheapest automatic
car US$35 in winter, US$25 in summer, weekly rates US$210 or US$150; *Just Jeeps*, PO Box
30497 SMB, West Bay Rd, T9497263, F9490216, US$45-65; *Cico Avis*, PO Box 400, T9492468,
F9497127, smallest standard car US$40 winter/summer, jeeps, automatics and mini vans
available, minimum 2 day rental, 1 day rental 25% extra, if paid in US dollars, add 25% for
conversion; *Coconut Car Rentals Ltd*, PO Box 1991 GT, T9494037, F9497786, from US$40/30
a day winter/summer or US$240/180 a week, jeeps US$52/47, US$312/282. Collision dam-
age waiver ranges from US$8-15 a day. **Bicycles** (cheapest US$10 per day), scooters
(US$20-25 per day) can also be rented, from *Bicycles Cayman*, North Church St, T9495572, or
Cayman Cycle Rentals, PO Box 31219 SMB, T9474021, at *Coconut Place*, *Hyatt Regency* and
Treasure Island. *Soto Scooters & Car Rentals*, PO Box 1081, Seven Mile Beach, T9454652,
F9454465, at Coconut Place, scooters US$25 per day, bicycles US$15 per day, mountain bikes
and tandems available. Bicycles are also available at Rum Point. **Taxi** taxis are readily obtain-
able at hotels and restaurants. In George Town there are always lots of taxis at the dock when
the cruise ships come in, otherwise hailing a taxi is most easily done in the vicinity of the post
office. Fares (expected to rise in 2001) are based on a fixed place-to-place tariff rather than a
meter charge and vary according to how many people there are and how much luggage
there is. For going a long distance (ie across the island) they are expensive. From the airport
to George Town is US$12, based on up to 4 passengers with 2 pieces of luggage each; to
West Bay US$23-29; to East End, US$49; to Rum Point US$60.

Cayman Islands

Cayman Brac

Colour map 1, grid C3 *Settlement on Cayman Brac has been determined by the Bluff, which rises from sea level at the west end to a sheer cliff at the east end. Most building first took place on the flatter land in the west, where the sea is a little calmer, and then spread along the north coast where the Bluff gives shelter. A number of Heritage Sites, linked by hiking trails, are being promoted, including bat caves, the old lighthouse and a place to watch the sunset. Cayman Brac is blessed with spectacular reef and wall diving with excellent visibility.*

Ins & outs **Getting there** *Cayman Airways* and *Island Air* fly from Grand Cayman and Little Cayman. There is no inter-island ferry service, you have to catch a small plane, used like a bus service. **Getting around** There are no buses, so taxis or car hire are the only options – or walk.

History The first three families of settlers arrived in 1833, followed by two more families in 1835. These five families, Ritch, Scott, Foster, Hunter and Ryan, are still well-represented on the island today. They made a living from growing coconuts and selling turtle shells and from the 1850s started building boats to facilitate trading. In 1886 a Baptist missionary arrived from Jamaica and introduced education and health care.

Diving & marine life Most of the sites are around the west end, with both shallow reef snorkelling, with beautiful coral gardens and lots of fish, and diving and deeper wall diving a bit further out. There are also a few wrecks among the 40 or so named dive sites including a newly-sunk Russian frigate (see page 252), which is within snorkelling distance of the beach and rises to about 10ft from the surface. On the north coast road, go west past the airport turning to Robert Foster Lane, which leads to the sea. You can locate the wreck by the buoys for dive boats.

    Reef Divers is at *Carib Sands*, offering diving at both Cayman Brac and Little Cayman sites, certification and resort courses, photo/video services and equipment rental. A two-tank dive costs US$50, snorkelling trips are US$20. *Brac Aquatics* is at the *Brac Caribbean Beach Resort*, T9481429, www.candw.ky/users/Cay3931, charging US$70 for a 2-tank dive.

Around the island The recently introduced Heritage Sites and Trails include 35 attractions and hikes to entice visitors away from the water and discover what is on land. It is not possible to drive all round the island because of the Bluff. The road linking the north and south coasts is roughly half way along the island. There are three roads running east-west, one along the north shore, one along the south coast and a third (unpaved) in the middle which runs along the top of the Bluff to the lighthouse. Although lots of roads

Cayman Brac

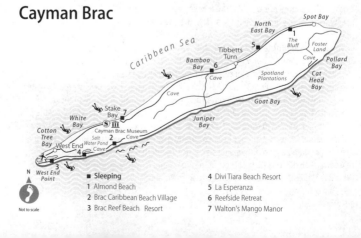

■ **Sleeping**
1 Almond Beach
2 Brac Caribbean Beach Village
3 Brac Reef Beach Resort

4 Divi Tiara Beach Resort
5 La Esperanza
6 Reefside Retreat
7 Walton's Mango Manor

have been built up on the Bluff, they are to service houses which have not yet been built, and do not lead anywhere. There are several, rather poor, farms and cows wander on the road. At the top of the Bluff it is sometimes possible to spot various orchids and there is a 197-acre **Parrot Reserve** (see page 251). A hiking trail has been cleared by the Cayman Brac National Trust, only for the able bodied as it is rocky, but there is a great view from the Bluff at the end of the path. You are only likely to see parrots at dawn or dusk, but it is a nice walk anyway through the bush.

From the airport the north shore road leads to **Cotton Tree Bay**, where in 1932 a hurricane flooded the area, killing more than 100 people and destroying virtually every house. The coconut groves were devastated and many people left the island at this time. Demand for turtle shell went into decline as the use of plastic increased and many men found that the only opportunities open to them were as sailors, travelling around the world on merchant ships.

Stake Bay is the main village on the north coast and it is well worthwhile visiting the small, but interesting **Cayman Brac Museum**. ■ *T9482622. Free. Mon-Fri 0900-1200, 1300-1600.* Further east at Creek, *La Esperanza* is a good place to stop for refreshment, in a glorious setting with good views and welcome sea breeze. At **Spot Bay** at the extreme east, follow a track up towards the lighthouse. Here you will find Peter's Cave and a good viewpoint. From the end of the north coast road you can walk through the almond trees to the beach, from where you get an excellent view of the Bluff from below.

Along the south coast, the best beaches are at the west end, where there are two dive resorts. There is a pleasant public beach with shade and toilets at **South East Bay**. Bat Cave and Rebecca's Cave are in this vicinity and can be visited. When you get to the end of the road, walk along the ironshore to the end of the island. There is a blow hole, lots of beachcombing opportunities and if you look for stripes in the cliff you may find caymanite, which is only found here and at the east end of Grand Cayman. Holiday homes have been built along this coast. Tourism is now the mainstay of the economy but construction of homes for foreigners has pushed up the price of land out of the reach of many local families. Most young adults leave the island for a career in financial services or government on Grand Cayman or other jobs further afield.

Rock climbing is popular along this coastline. There are 66 recognized climbing sites

LL-L *Brac Caribbean Beach Resort*, on the south coast, West End, PO Box 4 SPO, T9482265, F9482206, in USA 800-7917911. A condominium development, a/c, fans, on beach, reef protected, credit cards accepted, 10 units all 2-bedroomed, restaurant, pool, dive packages, laundry, maid service available, satellite TV, child and teenage discounts. *Cayman Villas*, T9474144, F9497471, have a cottage for rent, **LL-AL** *Reefside Retreat*, sleeps 4, ocean front, excellent snorkelling; other apartments and/or cottages at **L** *Almond Beach*, Spot Bay, T9480667, www.almondbeach.com On beach, good snorkelling. *Carib Sands*, T9481121, F9481122, www.caribsands.com Condos sleep 2-8, pool, *Reef Divers* on site. At West End Point: **AL** *Brac Reef Beach Resort*, PO Box 56 WE, T9481323, F9481207, www.bracreef.com 40 rooms, packages available, comfortable, nice beach, some sea grass, lovely dock with lookout tower, conference centre opened 2000 for large and small groups, internet access. **AL-B** *La Esperanza*, PO Box 28 SPO, Stake Bay, T9480531, F9480525, esperan@candw.ky Condos and house on north side, access to private beach on south side, restaurant, snorkelling, hammocks. **A-B** *Walton's Mango Manor*, PO Box 56 SPO, Stake Bay, T/F9480518, www.waltonsmangomanor.com CP, 5 rooms, antiques, verandah, hammocks, a/c, fans, TV, kitchenettes.

Sleeping

On Cayman Brac there are a few restaurants; *The Captain's Table*, at *Brac Caribbean Beach Village*. The best dining on the island, lobster, seafood and steaks. Recommended. *Blackie's*, at the Youth Centre, South Side, T9480232. Good ice cream. *La Esperanza*, T9480531, seafood, one of the nicest, tables at water's edge as well as a/c dining room, transport available, open Mon-Fri, 0900-0100, Sat 0900-2400, Sun 1200-2400 and *Lagoon*, T9487523, both at Stake Bay. *Sonia's*, White Bay, T9481214. Island food, open Mon-Sat 0900-1500, special diets

Eating

Cayman Islands

catered for, takeaway available. *Aunt Sha's Kitchen*, T9481581. Island style, local dishes, conch fritters, key lime pie, open breakfast, lunch, dinner, billiards, darts. For groceries, *Billy's Supermarket*, T9481321. At the Point, meat, fish, vegetables, etc.

Transport **Taxi** An island tour by taxi costs about CI$15, *Elo's Taxi and Tours*, T9480220, recommended, *Hill's Taxi and Tours*, T9480540, *Maple Edward's Taxi and Tours*, T9480448. **Bike** and **moped hire** *B&S Motor Ventures* for moped and bike hire, T9481546. **Car hire** *Brac Hertz*, T9481515, F9481380, *T & D*, T9482847, F9482329 and *Four D's*, T/F9481599, about US$35-40 per day for a car.

Little Cayman

Colour map 1, grid C3 *Little Cayman is small and low-lying with large areas of dense mangrove swamps, ponds, lagoons and lakes. The diving is excellent. Underwater visibility averages 100-150 ft all year. Bloody Bay wall, a mile-deep vertical drop, is one of the major dive sites worldwide and is highly rated by marine biologists and photographers.*

Ins & outs **Getting there** *Island Air* has small planes for island hopping from Grand Cayman and
There is no public Cayman Brac (see page 249). The airport consists of a wooden shack and a grass runway.
transport, a 25 mph **Getting around** Jeep hire (US$62-65 per day) is available here with *McLaughlin Rentals*,
speed limit & frequent T9481000, F9481001, daily and weekly rates, best to book in advance as last minute prices
signs for iguana or can be high. The office is 100yds away from airport. Roads are unpaved around the east half
duck crossings of the island but the main road goes all the way round the edge. You can not often see the
sea because of seagrape and other vegetation lining the shore.

History The first inhabitants of Little Cayman were turtlers who made camp on the southshore. After them, at the beginning of the 20th century, the population exploded to over 100 Caymanians living at Blossom on the southwest coast and farming coconuts. Attacks of blight killed off the palms and the farmers moved to the other two islands. In the 1950s, some US sport fishermen set up a small fishing camp on the south coast known as the *Southern Cross Club*, which is still in operation today as a diving/fishing lodge. A handful of similar small resorts and holiday villas have since been built but the resident population remains tiny.

Diving & There are dive sites all round the island, but the most popular spot is in the Marine
marine life Park in **Bloody Bay**, a two-mile stretch between Spot Bay and Jackson's Point off the north coast. Unlike the walls around the other islands, which begin at a depth of about 65 ft and drop down about a mile, the Bloody Bay wall begins at only 15-20 ft,

Little Cayman

Sleeping
1 Conch Club Condominiums
2 Little Cayman Beach Resort
3 Neptune's Berth
4 Paradise Villas
5 Pirate's Point Resort
6 Sam McCoy's Lodge
7 Sea View Villa
8 Southern Cross Club
9 The Cottage

Not to scale

which means you can snorkel over the drop-off. This is spectacular, with coral canyons and caves before you get to the outer reef. Shore diving from **Jackson's Point** is also spectacular, with coral heads rising from a 40-ft sandy bottom to about 10ft of the surface. Along the south coast you can snorkel or kayak out to **Owen Island**.

Sam McCoy's Dive Lodge is at the west end of Spot Bay. They have two dive boats of 28ft and 30ft. There is also a Marine Park off the south-coast opposite the airport, with *Pirate's Point Dive Resort* at one end. Diving can be arranged with *Pirate's Point*, *Sam McCoy's* or *Southern Cross Club* (voted second best dive resort in the world in 2000 by *Scuba Diving Magazine*, long-timers Terry and Jon are popular instructors with both novices and experienced divers). Newer dive operations are *Paradise Divers* (T9480001, F9480002), *Reef Divers Little Cayman Beach Resort*, South Sound (T3238727, F3238827) and *Blue Water Divers* (T9480032, F9480095). A two-tank dive costs US$50-73. There is also a liveaboard, *Little Cayman Diver II*, which takes 10 divers for US$1,690 per week all-inclusive (T813-932/1993, F813-9352250, PO Box 280058, Tampa, Fl 33682).

The bonefishing around Little Cayman is some of the best and just offshore. The 15-acre Tarpon Lake is home to the game fish from which the pond gets its name. Fishing is offered at *Sam McCoy's* (T9480026, F9480057), where bonefishing and tarpon is US$60 per half day and deep sea fishing is US$350 per half day and US$550 per full day on the 32-ft *Reel McCoy* fishing boat. At *Southern Cross Club* (T9481099) deep sea fishing is US$300 per half day and US$500 per day, while a half day of bonefishing for two people with guide is US$150. *Blue Water Divers* also offers bonefishing at US$180 per half day and deep sea fishing for US$500 per day.

Around the island

Little Cayman's swamps, ponds, lagoons and lakes make an ideal habitat for red-footed boobies and numerous iguanas. **Booby Pond Nature Reserve** attracts about 3,500 nesting pairs of red-footed boobies and 100 pairs of frigate birds. On the edge of the pond, the other side of the road from the museum, is the **National Trust House**, with an extensive veranda where you can look through a telescope or strong binoculars to watch the birds. ■ *The house is open Mon-Sat 1500-1800, but you can use the veranda any time.* Further east is **Tarpon Lake** (small sign on road), another good spot for seeing wildlife. A boardwalk has been built out into the lake and if you are lucky you might see some tarpon in the brown water.

The beaches by the hotels on the south coast are good, with fine sand, but the swimming is marred by huge swathes of sea grass in the shallow water. Many of the other beaches around the island are more gritty, but you will have them to yourself. The best beach for swimming and snorkelling is at **Sandy Point** at the east-tip of the island. Look for a red and white marker opposite a pond, a sandy path leads down to the beach. Other beaches are at **Jackson's Point** on the north-side and on **Owen Island** in South Hole Sound. This privately owned island 200yds offshore, is freely used by residents and visitors alike and is accessible by row boat or kayak. Snorkelling is good just to the west of *Pirate's Point Resort*, where the water is shallow just within the reef.

Blossom is by the airstrip, and there you will find the post office. ■ *Mon-Fri 0900-1100, 1300-1500, Sat 0900-1100.* Car hire, a grocery and hardware store, bank (open Wednesday) and the **Little Cayman Museum**. The museum is in a typical wooden house and has a small, but nicely presented, collection of local artefacts and antiques. ■ *T9481072. Free. Mon-Fri 1500-1700.* Little Cayman Baptist Church is the only church. Services Sun 1100, 1930, Wed 1930.

Sleeping
Accommodation consists of small hotels, diving lodges, a few private cottages & homes

LL *Southern Cross Club*, T9481099, F9481098, www.southerncrossclub.com Includes all meals, scuba, fishing, cabins on sandy beach, view of Owen Island, friendly, excellent staff, good food served family-style, indoor and outdoor bar, pool, internet access, one of the nicest places to stay. **LL** *Conch Club Condominiums*, PO Box 51, Blossom Village, T813-3238723, F813-3238827, www.conchclub.com. 8 units with 2 or 3 bedrooms, beachfront, pool, jacuzzi, diving, snorkelling, tennis, photo centre, restaurant. **LL-L** *Pirates Point*,

PO Box 43, Sefton Bay, T9481010, F9481011. Rooms in cabins, simple luxury, lovely big bathrooms, all inclusive with or without diving, 42-ft dive boat, 5 instructors, fishing, a/c, fan, TV, phone, small deep pool and 10-person jacuzzi, bar decorated with driftwood signs made by guests, owned by a cordon bleu chef, very relaxing, friendly. **LL-AL** *Little Cayman Beach Resort*, PO Box 51, Blossom Village, T9481033, F9481040, www.littlecayman.com. The only real hotel on the island and seems huge, 40 rooms, a/c, TV, on beach, dock facilities, spa, tennis, basketball, volleyball, pool, jacuzzi, diving, facilities for the handicapped, all-inclusive dive packages available. **L** *Sam McCoy's*, T9480026, F9490057, www.mccoyslodge. com.ky Includes transport, diving, 3 meals, fishing costs extra (see above), small scale, simple and low key, 8 rooms, tiny pool with jacuzzi jets, hammocks, not much of a beach, internet access. **L-AL** *Paradise Villas*, PO Box 30, T9480001, F9480002, iggy@ candw.ky Small, duplex, 1-2-bedroom cottages with kitchens, on the shore, restaurant *Hungry Iguana* next door **A-B** *The Cottage*, PO Box 35, Blossom Village, T/F9480095. Restored turn-of-the-century Caymanian house, now a CP, 2 bedrooms, beachfront, a/c, fans, diving and fishing arranged. Contact **Cayman Villlas**, T9474144, F9497471.

Eating *Hungry Iguana*, in the village at *Paradise Villas*, is the only independent restaurant, indoor or outdoor dining, good food, pizza on Sat, popular, shrimp, lobster often on menu, open breakfast (Sat, Sun only), lunch and dinner, takeaway available.

Background

History

The islands were first sighted by Columbus in May 1503 when he was blown off course on his way to Hispaniola. He found two small islands (Cayman Brac and Little Cayman) which were full of turtles, and he therefore named the islands Las Tortugas. A 1523 map of the islands referred to them as Lagartos, meaning alligators or large lizards, but by 1530 they were known as the Caymanas after the Carib word for the marine crocodile which also lived there. The first recorded English visitor to the Caymans was Sir Francis Drake in 1586, when he reported that the *caymanas* were edible. But it was the turtles which really attracted ships in search of fresh meat for their crews. The islands were ceded to the English Crown under the Treaty of Madrid in 1670, after the first settlers came from Jamaica in 1661-71 to Little Cayman and Cayman Brac. The first settlements were abandoned after attacks by Spanish privateers, but British privateers often used the Cayman Islands as a base and in the 18th century they became an increasingly popular hideout for pirates, even after the end of legitimate privateering in 1713. In November 1794, a convoy of 10 ships was wrecked on the reef in Gun Bay, on the East End of Grand Cayman, but with the help of the local residents there was no loss of life. Legend has it that there was a member of the Royal Family on board and that in gratitude for their bravery, King George III decreed that Caymanians should never be conscripted for war service and Parliament legislated that they should never be taxed.

From 1670, the Cayman Islands were dependencies of Jamaica, although there was considerable self-government. In 1832, a legislative assembly was established, consisting of eight magistrates appointed by the Governor of Jamaica and 10 (later increased to 27) elected representatives. In 1959 dependency ceased when Jamaica became a member of the Federation of the West Indies, although the Governor of Jamaica remained the Governor of the Cayman Islands. When Jamaica achieved independence in 1962 the islands opted to become a direct dependency of the British Crown.

In 1991 a review of the 1972 constitution recommended several constitutional changes to be debated by the Legislative Assembly (see Government). The post of Chief Secretary was reinstated in 1992 after having been abolished in 1986 and members of the executive committee are called ministers. There are three teams, or political groupings, the National Team, Team Cayman and the Democratic Alliance Group.

Sir Turtle

Turtles have always played a large part in the islands' folklore, dating back to 1503 when Columbus named them Las Tortugas. Generations of sailors stocked up on turtle meat while in the area and today there is a turtle farm, designed to replenish wild stocks and satisfy demand for the table.

In 1963 Suzy Soto designed the 'Sir Turtle' logo, of a peg-leg, swashbuckling, pirate turtle.

She sold it in the 1970s to the Department of Tourism for the grand sum of US$1, and it is now used intensively as a mascot and symbol for the Cayman Islands.

There was even a racehorse in the UK called 'Sir Turtle' (now sadly deceased), a hurdler sponsored by the Department of Tourism's British office and owned by Adrian Pratt, who had a good time on holiday in the islands.

A British Government White Paper on the future of its overseas territories, released in March 1998, caused a stir in financial circles and pricked the national conscience. The White Paper called for tighter regulations for tax havens which should be brought into line with EU standards. It also called for the country to reverse the law prohibiting homosexual activity in private between consenting adults, to conform with human rights legislation worldwide. There has been a debate in the islands about homosexuality ever since a cruise ship carrying gay passengers was turned away.

Geography

Grand Cayman, the largest of the three islands, lies 150 miles south of Havana, Cuba, about 180 miles northwest of Jamaica and 480 miles south of Miami. Grand Cayman is low-lying, 22 miles long and four miles wide, but of the total 76 square miles about half is swamp. A striking feature is the shallow, reef-protected lagoon, North Sound, 40 miles square and the largest area of inland mangrove in the Caribbean. None of the islands has any rivers, but vegetation is luxuriant, the main trees being coconut, thatch palm, seagrape and Australian pine. George Town, the capital of the islands, is located on the west side of Grand Cayman. Cayman Brac (Gaelic for 'bluff') gets its name from the high limestone bluff rising from sea level in the west to a height of 140ft in the east. The island lies about 89 miles east northeast of Grand Cayman. It is about 12 miles long and a little more than a mile wide. Little Cayman lies five miles west of Cayman Brac and is 10 miles long and just over a mile wide with its highest point being only 40 ft above sea level. Owen Island, an islet off the southwest coast of Little Cayman, is uninhabited but visited by picnickers.

People

The total population of mixed African and European descent is estimated at 40,000, of whom 10,000 are foreigners on work permits. Nearly everyone lives on Grand Cayman, most of them in George Town, or the smaller towns of West Bay, Bodden Town, North Side and East End. The population of Cayman Brac has fallen to 1,400. Little Cayman is largely undeveloped with only about 120 residents and frequented by sports fishermen. The Cayman Islands are very exclusive, with strict controls on who is allowed to settle. Consequently the cost of living is extremely high. On the other hand, petty crime is rare and the islands are well looked after (described as "a very clean sandbank"). Although Caymanians have considerable affection for Britain and do not seek independence, their way of life is Americanized. Higher education and advanced health care are usually sought in the USA and their geographical proximity influences travel choices. Many visitors to the islands never meet a Caymanian. To get to know local people you will have to get off the beach and drive into the districts. The high standard of living has deterred Caymanians from going into the hotel trade, regarding it as servitude, not service, and preferring the financial services industry.

District days during Cayfest in Apr & Pirates' Week in Oct are good times to meet local people

Cayman Islands

Government

A Governor appointed by the British Crown is the head of Government. The present Constitution came into effect in 1993 and provides for an Executive Council to advise the Governor on administration of the islands. The Council is made up of five Elected and three Official Members and is chaired by the Governor. The former, called Ministers from February 1994, are elected from the 15 elected representatives in the Legislative Assembly and have a range of responsibilities allocated by the Governor, while the latter are the Chief Secretary, the Financial Secretary, and the Attorney General. The Legislative Assembly may remove a minister from office by nine votes out of the 15. There is no Chief Minister. There have been no political parties since the mid-1960s but politicians organize themselves into teams. The Chief Secretary is the First Official Member of the Executive Council, and acts as Governor in the absence of the Governor.

Economy

Structure of production

The Cayman Islands is the largest offshore centre & the 5th largest financial centre in the world

The original settlers earned their living from the sea, either as turtle fishermen or as crew members on ships around the world. In 1906 more than a fifth of the population of 5,000 was estimated to be at sea, and even in the 1950s the government's annual report said that the main export was of seamen and their remittances the mainstay of the economy. Today the standard of living is high, with the highest per capita income in the Caribbean. The islands' economy is based largely on offshore finance and banking, tourism, real estate and construction, and a little local industry. Apart from a certain amount of meat, turtle, fish and a few local fruits and vegetables, almost all foodstuffs and other necessities are imported. The cost of living therefore rises in line with that of the main trading partners. The economy is highly dependent upon the fortunes of the US economy, with interest rates rising and falling according to those of US instruments.

At end-2000 there were 580 licensed banks and trust companies, 517 captive insurance companies and 3,014 registered mutual funds; the banking sector employs more than a tenth of the labour force and contributes 15.5% of gdp. The Cayman Islands Stock Exchange began operating in January 1997 at the same time as the establishment of a Monetary Authority, formed by the amalgamation of the government's financial services supervision department and currency board. As well as funds based in the Cayman Islands, the exchange hopes to attract overseas clients. The growth of mutual funds has been dramatic, helped by the growth of the internet and on-line brokerage services. In 1990 the Cayman Islands signed a mutual legal assistance treaty with the USA and in 1996 the Islands enacted the UK's 'proceeds of criminal conduct' law. There is now an exchange of information with the USA regarding the perpetrators of commercial crime, while banks now alert authorities to suspicious transactions by clients without breaching the confidentiality law. It is an offence for banks to conceal money laundering although tax crimes or tax evasion are excluded because of the Cayman's tax free status. There is also a large shipping registry, with 1,200 ships on the register in 1999.

Tourism revenues have risen sharply in recent years although income still fluctuates according to the strength of the US economy. In the 1990s cruise ship visitors soared with the introduction of calls by the cruise liner *Ecstasy* which carries 2,500 passengers. Cruise ship passengers outnumber stayover visitors by two to one, but the latter account for 90% of revenues. Nearly three quarters of all stayover visitors are from the USA.

Jamaica

6

Jamaica

Jamaica has been called the Island of Springs, and its Arawak name, Xaymaca, *meant 'land of wood and water'. It is indeed a beautiful island with rolling hills and steep gullies, and the spectacular Blue Mountains overlooking a coastline indented with bays and coves. Rain falls freely, water is abundant, the vegetation is luxuriant and colours are vibrant. The people have a culture to match, from reggae and rastafarianism to English plantation houses and cricket. The place lives and breathes rhythm: music is everywhere and Jamaica is a hub of creativity in the Caribbean.*

The advent of cruise ships and package tourism has led to overdevelopment of some coasts, but it is easy to escape the crowds. Every conceivable watersport is on offer in the resort areas on the north coast, where the beaches are safe for swimming. The south coast has fewer beaches but here there are important mangrove areas instead, which are home to crocodiles and the elusive manatee.

A Foot in the door

- Enjoy a sunset seafood dinner at **Fisherman's Inn** followed by a boat tour of the bioluminescent lagoon just east of the historic town of **Falmouth**, said to be the most active bioluminescent lake in the world.
- Catch the dawn with a **Blue Mountain sunrise**, not a cocktail, but still likely to give you a high as the mist surrenders quietly to the rising sun and the golden hue of dawn sweeps across the eastern sky, tinting cloud layers far below.
- Experience the culture of reggae and rastafarianism with a visit to the **Bob Marley Museum** in Kingston.
- Buy **jerk pork**, **chicken** or **fish** at the roadside, this delicious and tasty Jamaican speciality is excellent washed down with a cold Red Stripe beer.

Essentials

Before you travel

Documents Canadian and US citizens do not need passports or visas for a stay of up to six months, if they reside in their own countries and have some proof of citizenship (for example a birth certificate or certificate of citizenship with photo ID). Residents of Commonwealth countries (except Nigerians, who need a visa), Austria, Belgium, Denmark, Finland, France, Iceland, Eire, Israel, Italy, Luxembourg, Mexico, Netherlands, Norway, Spain, Sweden, Switzerland, Turkey and Germany, need a passport and an onward ticket for a stay not exceeding six months. Japanese visitors need a passport and a visa if staying more than 30 days. Citizens of all other countries must have a **visa**, **passport** and **onward ticket**. Immigration may insist on your having an address, prior to giving an entry stamp. Otherwise you will have to book a hotel room in the airport tourist office (friendly and helpful). For visa extensions, apply to Ministry of Social Security and Justice, Kingston Mall, 12 Ocean Boulevard, Kingston, T9220800. No

Jamaica

vaccinations are required unless you have visited Asia, Africa, Central and South America, Dominican Republic, Haiti, Trinidad and Tobago within six weeks of going to Jamaica.

Currency The Jamaican dollar (J$) is the local currency but foreign currency up to US$100 is legal tender for purchases of goods and services, with change given in J$.

Money

Exchange The Jamaican dollar floats on the foreign exchange market. The only legal exchange transactions are those carried out in commercial banks, or in official exchange bureaux in major hotels and the international airports. It is illegal to buy, sell or lend foreign currency without a licence. Banks pay slightly more for US$ travellers cheques than for cash. Retain your receipt so you can convert Jamaican dollars at the end of your stay. Most banks and exchange bureaux, including at the airport, will not accept US$100 bills because of forgeries. If using credit cards the transaction will be converted from the agreed J$ rate into US$ before you sign, be sure to verify exact rate that is being used, often a 5-10% downward adjustment can be instantly obtained by this enquiry.

Rates in Negril can be worse than in Montego Bay

In the mountains, the temperature can fall to as low as 7°C during the winter season. Temperatures on the coast average 27°C, rising occasionally to 32°C in July and August and never falling below 20°C. The humidity is fairly high. The best months are December to April. Rain falls intermittently from about May, with daily short tropical showers in September, with October and November being the rainy season.

Climate

Getting there

From Europe *British Airways* (Gatwick) and *Air Jamaica* (Heathrow) fly direct, between London and Kingston and Montego Bay with lots of connections from other European cities. *LTU International Airways* has a weekly flight to Montego Bay from Dusseldorf. *Air Europe* flies weekly from Milan. *Condor* flies weekly from Frankfurt to Montego Bay. There are many charter flights from Europe which change according to the season, check with travel agent. **From North America** *Air Jamaica* (www.airjamaica.com) has services to Kingston and/or

Air

Jamaica

Jamaica

 ## Touching down

Departure tax Airport departure tax of J$750, payable in Jamaican or US dollars by those who have stayed on the island for 24 hours or more. Cruise ship passengers pay a US$15 tax.

Hours of business **Offices:** usually open from 0830-1630 Monday to Friday. **Shop:** hours vary between 0830 and 0930 to 1600 and 1730, depending on area, Monday to Saturday; there is half-day closing (at 1200) on Wednesday in Down Town Kingston, on Thursday in uptown Kingston and Montego Bay, and on Friday in Ocho Rios. **Banks:** are 0900-1400 Monday to Thursday, 0900-1600 on Friday (there may be some local variations).

Official time Eastern Standard Time, five hours behind GMT and an hour behind the Eastern Caribbean.

Voltage 110 volts, 50 cycles AC; some hotels have 220 volts.

Weights and measures Metric.

Emergency numbers: Fire/Ambulance 110, Police 119.

Clothing Light summer clothing is needed all the year round, with a sweater for cooler evenings. Some hotels expect casual evening wear in their dining rooms and nightclubs, but for the most part dress is informal. Bathing costumes, though, are only appropriate by the pool or on the beach.

Tipping Hotel staff, waiters at restaurants, barmen, taxi drivers, cloakroom attendants, hairdressers get 10-15% of the bill. In places where the bill already includes a service charge, often personal tips are nonetheless expected. In some areas you may be expected to give a tip when asking for local information.

Drugs Marijuana (ganja) is widely grown in remote areas and frequently offered to tourists. Cocaine (not indigenous to Jamaica) is also peddled. Possession of either drug is a criminal offence. On average over 50 foreigners are serving prison sentences in Jamaica at any given moment for drug offences. The police stop taxis, cars etc in random road checks and search you and your luggage. Airport security is being continually tightened (sniffer dogs, etc).

Montego Bay from Atlanta, Baltimore, Boston, Fort Lauderdale, Los Angeles, Miami, New York, Orlando, Philadelphia, Phoenix. *Air Canada* flies from Toronto to Kingston and from Halifax, Montréal, Toronto and Winnipeg to Montego Bay. *American Airlines* flies to Kingston and/or Montego Bay from Houston, New Orleans, New York and Miami, with lots of connections from other cities through Miami. *TWA* flies from Boston and St Louis, Missouri to Montego Bay. *US Air* flies to Montego Bay from Baltimore, Buffalo, Charlotte, Philadelphia and Portland. *Northwest Airlines* from Detroit, Memphis and Tampa to Montego Bay. Enquire in Florida about cheap flights from Fort Lauderdale and Orlando. **From the Caribbean & Latin America** *Cayman Airways* and *Air Jamaica* connect the Caymans and Jamaica. *BWIA* flies to Kingston from Antigua, Barbados, Trinidad and Sint Maarten, while *ALM* flies to Kingston from Curaçao. There are *Cubana* and *Air Jamaica Express* flights from Havana to Kingston and Montego Bay. *Aerocaribbean* also flies from Holguín in Cuba to Montego Bay. *TCI SkyKing* flies from Providenciales to Montego Bay. *Copa* flies Panama City-Kingston and Montego Bay, while *Air Jamaica* also flies Panama City-Kingston. *Air Jamaica* uses Montego Bay as its regional hub, with flights from Barbados, Bonaire, Grand Cayman, Grenada, Havana (also to Kingston), Miami, Nassau, Providenciales, St Lucia and Trinidad. Flights are timed to connect with intercontinental arrivals and departures.

Boat It is extremely difficult to book a passage by ship to other Caribbean islands. About nine cruise lines call at Ocho Rios or Montego Bay weekly, mostly out of Miami, but some from Tampa, Ft Lauderdale or New Orleans.

Touching down

Airport information
See pages 284 & 304 for further details

There are two international airports: the **Norman Manley** in Kingston and **Sangster** in Montego Bay. Montego Bay airport is the only one really within walking distance of most hotels. The Kingston domestic airstrip is at **Tinson Pen** which is two miles from the centre of town on Marcus Garvey Drive, those at Ocho Rios and Port Antonio are a long way out of

Tourist offices overseas

Canada *1 Eglington Avenue East, Suite 616 Toronto, Ontario M4P 3A1, T416-4827850, F4821730.*
France *c/o Target International, 32 rue de Ponthieu, 75008 Paris, T331-45634201, F42256640.*
Germany *Postfach 900437, 60444 Frankfurt, T4961-84990044, F84990046.*
Italy *c/o Sergat Italia SRL, Piazza dei Cenci 7/A, 00186 Roma, T396-6875693, F6873644.*
Japan *3 Mori Building, 1-4-10 Nishi-Shinbashi Minato-ku, Tokyo 105, T813-35913841, F813-35913845.*

Taiwan *11F-8, No 200, Section 1, Tun Hwa S Road, Taipei, T8862-87738175, F877-35240.*
UK *1-2 Prince Consort Rd, London, SW7 2BZ, T020-72240505, F72240551, jtb_@compuserve.com*
USA *New York: 801 Second Ave, 20th Floor, New York, NY10017, T212-8569727, F8569730; Suite 1101, 1320 South Dixie Highway, Coral Gables, Miami, FL 33146, T305-6650557, F6667239; 3440 Wilshire Blvd, Suite 805, Los Angeles, CA 900010, T213-3841123, F3841780.*

town. At Kingston's Norman Manley airport you can change back excess Jamaican dollars into US$ at the bank in the departure lounge. There are also several reasonable shops there which will accept Jamaican currency (except for duty free goods). Allow plenty of time to check in for a flight; there are four separate security, baggage or documentation checks.

Airlines Air Jamaica, passenger information and reservations, Kingston office, 72 Harbour St, Kingston, or frequent flyer at 4 St Lucia Av, Kingston 5, ticket office and sales in Montego Bay at 9 Queens Drive, other offices in Negril, T9574210, Ocho Rios, T9742566. Montego Bay is its regional hub. *Air Jamaica Express*, reservations and information, 9 Queens Drive, T888-9524300. *British Airways* is in The Towers, Dominica Drive, Kingston 5, T9299020, 9400890 (Montego Bay). *BWIA*, 19 Dominica Drive, Kingston 5, T9293770, 9248364 (airport), 9524100 (Montego Bay). *American Airlines*, T9208887 (Kingston), 888-3592247 (Montego Bay).

Tourist information **Local tourist offices** I lelpline T0888-995-9999, www.jamaicatravel.com Head office at Pan Caribbean Building, 64 Knutsford Boulevard, Kingston 5, PO Box 360, T9299200, F9299375. Circulates detailed hotel lists and plenty of other information. Other offices in Jamaica: at the international airports; Cornwall Beach, Montego Bay, PO Box 67, T9524425 or T9522462, airport, nights, holidays, F9523587; Ocean Village Shopping Centre, Ocho Rios, PO Box 240, T9742582, F9742559; City Centre Plaza, Port Antonio, PO Box 151, T9933051, F9932117; Coral Seas Plaza, Negril PO, Westmoreland, T9574243, F9574489; Hendricks Building, 2 High Street, Black River PO, T9652074, F9652076. The 'Meet the People' programme can introduce you to Jamaicans with your interests and hobbies for different activities.

Local travel agents *UTAS Tours*, T9523820, F9793465. *Juta Jamaica*, T9520813, F9525355. *Caribic Vacations*, T9529874, F9533463. *Sun Venture Tours*, T9606685, F9208348, www.sunventuretours.com, a tour operator. Activities for nature lovers away from the beach, hiking, caving, safaris, bird watching and educational tours, run by Robert Kerr. For scheduled or charter flights to neighbouring islands, for example Cuba, Dominican Republic, try *Apollo Travel Services*, 14 Dominica Drive, New Kingston, T9298483, F9687214, also at 28 Main Street, May Pen, T9864270, and Shop No 3, Spanish Town Shopping Centre, T9845040, IATA members, recommended.

Maps The *Discover Jamaica* road map (American Map Corporation) costs US$1 but is widely available free from tourist offices. It has plans of Kingston, Montego Bay, Negril, Mandeville, Ocho Rios, Port Antonio and Spanish Town. The *ITM Road Map of Jamaica* (1:250,000, International Travel Maps, 345 West Broadway, Vancouver, BC, V5Y 1P8, Canada) also includes plans of Kingston, Montego Bay, Spanish Town, Mandeville, Port Antonio and Ocho Rios. Good clear series of 1:50,000 maps covering Jamaica in 20 sheets from Survey Department, 23½ Charles Street, PO Box 493, Kingston.

Security   The per capita crime rate is lower than in most North American cities, but there is much violent crime. This is particularly concentrated in downtown Kingston (90% of violent crime takes place in four Kingston police districts), but can be encountered anywhere on the island. Do not to walk any street in downtown Kingston after dark. The corporate area, which consists of the city of Kingston and the adjoining and much larger parish of St Andrew, is predominantly residential, but has a diverse mix of commercial and suburban and rural areas. While most areas are generally safe, advice should be sought on the most appropriate routes and means of travel. There are large areas of west Kingston where you should not go off the main roads even by day and even in a locked car. The motive is robbery so take sensible precautions with valuables. Gang warfare has been exacerbated by the US policy of deporting Jamaican criminals, who return to Kingston to shoot it out with local gangs.

Beware of pickpockets and be firm but polite with touts. Do not wear jewellery. Do not go into the downtown areas of any towns especially at night. Avoid arriving in a town at night. Take a taxi from bus stations to your hotel. Travellers have reported being threatened for refusing to buy drugs and incidents where Jamaicans have become aggressive over traffic accidents, however minor. Observe the obvious precautions and you should have no problem. The vast majority of Jamaicans welcome tourists and want to be helpful but the actions of the minority can leave you with the impression that tourists are not wanted. Crimes against tourists have fallen, but the hold up and robbery of two busloads of tourists led to the deployment of military patrols to reinforce the police in tourist areas. The disappearance of an American travel guide writer in Negril in 2000 was further cause for concern.

Where to stay

Larger hotels have introduced strict security to prevent guests being bothered by hustling   Because Jamaica is a major tourist destination there are a great many hotels and restaurants. Full and up to date information is available at all tourist information centres. We only mention those which have recently been recommended or in the news for whatever reason. All-inclusive resorts are extremely popular in Jamaica and development has been led by *SuperClubs* (www.superclubs.com) and *Sandals* (www.sandals.com), with hotels mainly along the north coast; some allow children but most are for couples. As a result of their popularity, other hotels have been forced to discount their rates, so bargains can be found.

Crime and tourism

The impact of tourism on a population of around two and a half million is massive, both economically and socially. Bad publicity abroad or a natural disaster, such as Hurricane Gilbert, can have a devastating effect. The crime rate is high but most of the serious crime is around Kingston, principally in West Kingston. Many country districts and north coast resorts are fairly safe and in fact less dangerous than US tourist cities such as Miami, Orlando and Washington DC. However, harassment of cruise ship passengers and other visitors by unsavoury vendors of drugs and services have contributed to the island's poor image abroad. Partly because of crime, all-inclusive resorts have become particularly important in Jamaica. A large proportion of tourists never leave these hotels except on an organized tour or to return to the airport.

Chris Blackwell's *Island Outpost* now has several small, luxury hideaways, popular with the rich and famous; in the UK at 421a Finchley Road, London NW3 6HJ, T0800-614790, in Jamaica 8 Worthington Av, Kingston 8, T968679214, F9686779.

Visitors on a low budget should aim to arrive at Montego Bay rather than Kingston because the former is the island's tourism capital with a greater variety of affordable accommodation. However, if you can arrange to fly out from Kingston you will have a chance to get the flavour of the Jamaican experience in both cities. Get hold of the tourist board's list of hotels and guest houses offering rates and addresses, and also a copy of *Jamaica Vacation Guide* (both free). Many small hotels and inns have grouped themselves as the 'Insider's Jamaica'. The tourist board has their brochure, or visit www.insidersjamaica.com

Accommodation is subject to a 15% value added tax called the General Consumption Tax, check whether it is included in a quoted room rate

Information/reservations for self-catering villas and apartments can be done through the *Jamaica Association of Villas and Apartments* (JAVA), Pineapple Place, Ocho Rios, Box 298, T9742508, F9742967, who represent over 300 private houses. Two websites for villas are www.villaconnections.co.uk and www.villasofjamaica.com Renting a villa may be an attractive option if you do not intend to do much travelling and there are 4/6 of you to share the costs (about US$1,000-1,500 per week for a nice villa with private swimming pool and fully staffed). You will, however, probably have to rent a car as you will have to take the cook shopping, etc. You can go ever more upmarket and pay US$2,000-14,000 a week for a fully staffed luxury villa through *Elegant Resorts Villas International*, T9932287.

Getting around

Air Jamaica Express (T9224661, www.airjamaica.com/express) flies to the two international airports, Boscobel Aerodrome at Ocho Rios, Negril, Tinson Pen in Kingston and Ken Jones Aerodrome at Port Antonio. Charges are reasonable but using this method of travel is not very satisfactory unless you can arrange to be met at your destination. Fares Kingston-Negril, US$75 one way, US$150 return, Kingston-Montego Bay, US$60 one way, US$120 return.

Air
All fares attract J$30 stamp duty

Public road transport is mostly by minibus. This is cheap but overcrowded and generally chaotic and only to be recommended for the young and fit. Be prepared also for a certain amount of physical abuse from the bus company front men as they compete for your custom. Country buses are slow and sometimes dangerous. There are also minibuses which ply all the main routes and operate on a 'colectivo' basis, leaving only when full.

Bus
"Step Up!" shouted by the conductors means please move down the bus, there is plenty of room at the back!

Driving times and distances of major routes: Kingston to Montego Bay 120 miles (3 ½ hrs), to Ocho Rios 55 miles (2 hrs), to Port Antonio 68 miles (2 hrs); Montego Bay to Negril 50 miles (1½ hrs), to Ocho Rios 67 miles (2 hrs); Ocho Rios to Port Antonio 67 miles (2½ hrs). A new road linking Kingston with Montego Bay and Ocho Rios is to be built by 2002, which may affect journey times. The speed limit is 30 mph in built up areas, 50 mph on highways. A North American driving licence is valid for up to three months per visit, a British licence 12 months and a Japanese licence 1 month. Drive on the left. Try to avoid driving outside towns at night. Roads, even on the coast, are twisty and in the mountains extremely so, add potholes and

Car
Petrol stations often close on Sun; note that fuel is paid for in cash

Jamaican drivers and you are an accident waiting to happen. Plan ahead because it gets dark early. Daylight driving isn't safety assured; the coastal road from Kingston to Port Antonio is in a particularly bad condition and the drivers awful. Breath tests from drunk driving are now in effect. Traffic jams, especially between Kingston and Spanish Town and in the centre of Montego Bay, have been exacerbated by an influx of cheap, Japanese, second-hand vehicles: 'deportees' in popular parlance.

Car hire Undoubtedly a rented car is the most satisfactory, and most expensive, way of getting about. All the major car rental firms are represented both at the airports and in the major resort areas. There are also numerous local car rental firms which are mostly just as good and tend to be cheaper. The tourist board has a list of members of the Jamaica U-Drive Association, Newlin Street, Ocho Rios, T9742852. Be prepared to pay considerably more than in North America or Europe (starting from about US$65 per day plus CDW of US$12 and tax of 12½%). Many companies operate a three-day minimum hire policy. *Island Car Rentals* is a well known firm, airport office T9248075, Montego Bay T9255771, Kingston T9268861. *Praise Tours & Auto Rentals Ltd*, 72 Half Way Tree Road, Kingston 10, T9293580, F9293555, good deals on longer rentals, no trouble with refunds, airport transfers, recommended. *Don's Car Rental*, headquarters 1 Worthington Avenue, New Kingston, Kingston 5, T9262181, F9260866, also offices at Negril Aerodrome, T9574366, *Trident Hotel*, Port Antonio, T9932241. In the resort areas of Montego Bay, Ocho Rios and Negril, jeeps are available for about US$90 a day, motorbikes and scooters from US$30 and bicycles from US$5. Watch out for sunburn.

Taxi There are taxis, with red PPV (Public Passenger Vehicle) licence plates, in all the major resort areas and at the airports. Some have meters, some do not. Only the JUTA taxis have officially authorized charges to all destinations, with others (Yellow Cab, Checker Cab etc), the important point is to ask the fare before you get in. It can be around US$3-4 for a short hop, US$5-6 from New Kingston to Down Town, US$7 from Down Town to Mona Campus. All taxis should charge the same to the airport, US$15-21 from New Kingston. The tourist information centres should also be able to help in this respect. Some 'non-tourist' taxis operate like minibuses, that is have a set route and can be flagged down. They will cram about six passengers into a small Nissan, Hyundai or Lada, but if you do not want to share you can hire it all to yourself. Negotiate the fare in advance. To take a taxi for long distance is expensive; a JUTA taxi from Kingston to Ocho Rios for example could cost US$100-120, rather more than a day's car hire, although you could negotiate a fare less than half that with a smaller taxi company.

Keeping in touch

Post There are post offices in all main towns. The sorting office on South Camp Road, Down Town Kingston, has a good and helpful philatelic bureau.

Telephone
IDD phone code: 876
Cable, telephone and fax services are operated by *Cable & Wireless Jamaica Ltd*. It has main offices in Kingston and Montego Bay, but calls can easily be made from hotels. 'Time and charge' phone calls overseas cost the same in hotels as at the phone company, but there is a 15% tax and a J$2 service charge. In fact, making an international call is often easier from a hotel. The only other method is a card phone, if you can find one which is working and you are prepared to queue. You can buy telephone cards at supermarkets J$50 but check that it is valid for the year you want to use it, several people have been sold out of date cards (particularly around January/February) and there is no refund. In 1999 the Government and Cable & Wireless signed an aggreement for a three-year transition to a fully competitive telecommunications sector. During that time, new lines will be installed and internet access will be provided at 60 post offices around the country.

Newspapers The daily paper with the largest circulation is *The Daily Gleaner*, which also publishes an evening paper, *The Star* and the *Sunday Gleaner*. *The Jamaica Herald* is a livelier daily than *The Gleaner*, also the *Sunday Herald*. The other daily is the *Observer*. *Money Index* is a financial weekly, in Montego Bay *The Western Mirror* is weekly. *Lifestyle* is a monthly glossy magazine, *Jamaica Journal* is a quarterly with interesting but academic articles.

Food and drink

There are many unusual and delicious vegetables and fruits such as sweetsop, soursop and **Food**
sapodilla. National specialities include codfish ('stamp-and-go' are crisp pancakes made with
salt cod) and ackee; curried goat; and jerked pork, highly spiced pork which has been cooked
in the earth covered by wood and burning coals. Chicken is cooked in the same way. Patties,
sold in specialist shops and bars, are seasoned meat or lobster in pastry; normally very good
value. Curried lobster is a delightful local speciality. Stew peas is chunks of beef stewed with
kidney beans and spices and served with rice. Along the coast, fish tea is a hotch potch of the
day's catch made into a soup, US$1 a cup.

Local rum (white or brown, overproof and underproof), and the cocktails which combine it with **Drink**
local fruit juices, or mixed with Ting, the carbonated grapefruit soft drink; Tia Maria, the coffee
liqueur and quite a lot of other liqueurs; Red Stripe lager, with which, the locals say, no other
Caribbean beer compares, about US$1.10 at road side bar, considerably more in a hotel. Try the
Irish Moss soft drink. All rums are very cheap duty free, typically US$13 for a three-pack.

Shopping

In the craft markets and stores you can find items of wood (by Rastafarians and Maroons),
straw, batik (from a number of good textile companies) and embroidery; the hand-knitted
woollen gold, red, green Rasta caps (with or without black dreadlocks affixed) are very cheap.
Jewellery from Blue Mountain Gems, near Rose Hall, Montego Bay area. For art and ceramics,
Devon House gallery, Chelsea Galleries on Chelsea Road, Gallery 14, Old Boulevard Gallery,
Grosvenor Gallery, Contemporary Art Centre in Liguanea. Blue Mountain coffee is excellent,
cheaper at airport duty free shop than in supermarkets or tourist shops.

Please remember to check with legislation (and your conscience) before buying articles
made from tortoiseshell, crocodile skin, and certain corals, shells and butterflies. Many such
animals are protected and should not be bought as souvenirs. It is illegal to take or possess
black or white coral in Jamaica; sea turtles are protected and you should refuse to buy
products made from their shells. The closed season for lobster fishing is April-June, so if
lobster is on the menu check where it has come from.

Some shopkeepers offer a 10-15% discount on all goods but in fact merely refrain from
adding the tax when payment is made. Street vendors never add tax.

Photographic film is reasonably easily obtained but take spares of essentials such as
Lithium batteries as they are difficult to find and expensive. Glare and UV light is constant,
take suitable filters. Do not photograph Jamaicans without their permission, the men,
particularly in Kingston, can get aggressive.

Flora and fauna

The 'land of wood and water' has resulted in a botanist's paradise. There are reported to be
about 3,000 species of flowering plants alone, 827 of which are not found anywhere else.
There are over 550 varieties of fern, 300 of which can be found in Fern Gully. The national
flower is the dark blue bloom of the lignum vitae. There are many orchids, bougainvillea,
hibiscus and other tropical flowers. Tropical hardwoods like cedar and mahogany, palms,
balsa and many other trees, besides those that are cultivated, can be seen. Cultivation,
however, is putting much of Jamaica's plant life at risk. Having been almost entirely forested,
now an estimated 6% of the land is virgin forest. A great many species are now endangered.

This is also a land of hummingbirds and butterflies (see page 296) sea cows and the Pedro
seal are found in the island's waters, although only about 50 sea cows, or manatee, survive.
There are crocodiles, but no large wild mammals apart from the hutia, or coney (a native of
the island and now an endangered species), the mongoose (considered a pest since it has
eliminated snakes and now eats chickens) and, in the mountains, wild boar. There are,
however, lots of bats, with 25 species recorded. Most live in caves or woods and eat fruit and
insects, but there is a fish-eating bat which can sometimes be seen swooping over the water

Jamaica

in Kingston Harbour. The Jamaican iguana (*Cyclura collei*) was thought to have died out in the 1960s, but in 1990 a small group was found to be surviving in the Hellshire Hills. There are five species of snakes, all harmless and rare, the largest of which is the yellow snake (the Jamaican boa), which can grow up to 3 m.

Good sites for bird watching are given in the text below; the three main areas are the Cockpit Country, the Blue Mountains and Marshall's Pen. The national bird is the red-billed streamertail hummingbird (*Trochilus polytmus*), also known as the doctor bird or swallow tail hummingbird. The male has a long, sweeping tail much longer than its body, and is one of Jamaica's endemic species. Other endemic birds are the yellow-billed parrot and the black-billed parrot, found in the Cockpit Country or Hope Zoo. There are 25 species and 21 subspecies of endemic land birds which are found nowhere else. A good place to see Jamaica's birds is the Rocklands Feeding Station, near Montego Bay. On weekday evenings you can watch the birds being fed and even offer a hummingbird a syrup and get really close. Many migratory birds stop on Jamaica on their journeys north or south. *Birds of Jamaica: a photographic field guide* by Audrey Downer and Robert Sutton with photos by Yves-Jacques Rey Millet, was published in 1990 by Cambridge University Press.

In 1989 the Government established two pilot national parks, the first in Jamaica, under the Protected Areas Resource Conservation (PARC) project. The Blue Mountain/John Crow Mountain National Park encompasses almost 200,000 acres of mountains, forests and rivers. Efforts are being made to develop the area for ecotourism and provide a livelihood for local people. The other national park is the Montego Bay Marine Park, which aims to protect the offshore reef from urban waste, over-fishing and hillside erosion leading to excessive soil deposition. Several initiatives on protected areas are under way, including the Negril Environmental Protection Area and the Negril Marine Park, Ocho Rios, Port Antonio Marine Park along the northern coast and the Portland Bight Protected Area and the Canoe Valley National Park along the south coast. All coral reefs are now protected and the sale of both black and white coral is banned. Also forbidden is the hunting of the American crocodile, the yellow and black-billed parrot and all species of sea turtle.

Diving and marine life

There are now marine parks in Montego Bay, Port Antonio and Negril. Management programmes have resulted in increased numbers of fish and other marine life. Although established in 1989, the Montego Bay Marine Park was officially opened in July 1992. It stretches from the east end of the airport to the Great River and contains three major ecosystems, seagrass bed, mangroves and coral reefs. Non-motorized watersports such as diving, snorkelling and glass bottom boat tours are permitted, but do not touch or remove anything.

There are several conservation groups involved in marine ecology. In St Ann, *Friends of the Sea* is a non-profit, non-governmental organization, formed in 1992, which concentrates on education and public awareness and draws attention to what is happening on land which might affect what happens underwater. The *Negril Coral Reef Preservation Society* was formed in 1990. It has installed permanent mooring buoys for recreational boats and works on educational programmes with schools. Together with the National Resource Conservation Authority and the Negril community, it has formed a marine park in conjunction with protected coastal and terrestrial habitats, aimed at protecting the coral reefs and improving fish stocks.

Around Negril there are many reef sites and a huge variety marine life: coral, sponges, invertebrates, sea turtles, octopus, starfish and lots of fish. Off Montego Bay and Ocho Rios there is wall diving quite close to shore and a few wrecks. Off Port Antonio fish are attracted to freshwater springs which provide good feeding grounds. The best wreck diving is off Port Royal and Kingston where, in addition to ships, you can explore the city which slid into the sea in the 1692 earthquake.

Dive centres   Nearly all dive operators are based along the north coast at hotels. They must be licensed by the Jamaica Tourist Board and most are members of the Jamaica Association of Dive Operators (JADO). They offer courses at all levels. Contact the tourist board for a full list of operators and map of dive sites. Diving can be included in a hotel package, but if you are doing it independently, a two-tank dive costs on average US$65. Dives are limited to 100 ft. There are hyperbaric chambers at Discovery Bay and Port Royal.

Deep sea fishing for white marlin, wahoo, tuna and dolphin (not the mammal) can be **Fishing** arranged at north coast hotels. A half-day charter costs US$400 for up to six people, plus a 10% tip for the crew, who will also expect to keep half the catch. There is a famous Blue Marlin tournament at Port Antonio and others at Montego Bay, Falmouth and Discovery Bay, as well as a James Bond Oracabessa Marlin Tournament. Contact the Montego Bay Yacht Club for details, T9798038, F9798262, mbyc@infochan.com

Golf is played at the *Constant Spring* (18 holes, green fee US$35, T9241610) and *Caymanas* **Other sports** *Clubs* (18 holes, green fee US$53, T9223386, c/o Liguanea Club) (Kingston), the *Manchester Country Club* (Mandeville, nine-hole, green fee US$14, T9622403), *Sandals Ocho Rios Resort & Golf Club*, formerly known as Upton (Ocho Rios, 18 holes, green fee US$70, golf and restaurant free for Sandals guests, T9750119/22), *Breezes Golf Beach Resort* (18 holes, green fee US$58, free for guests at *Breezes Runaway Bay*, the only golf school open to the public, T9732561), *Ironshore Golf and Country Club* (another Sandals course, free for guests, 18 holes, green fee US$45, T9532800), *Half Moon Golf Club* (advance booking necessary for this championship course, 18 holes, green fee US$95, T9532731, also **tennis** and **squash**) and *Wyndham Rose Hall Golf Club* (18 holes, green fee US$60, T9532650) (all east of Montego Bay) and Tryall Golf, Tennis and Beach Resort (Par 71, 6,920yds in 2,200-acre resort complex, green fee US$125, between Montego Bay and Negril, T9565681/3). The *Tryall* course is probably the best known and hosts the annual Johnny Walker World Championship. Advance bookings are essential. A new course near Negril is the *Negril Hills Golf Club* (T9574638), Par 72, 6,333yds, 18 holes in the hills, green fees US$58. The *Jamaica Golf Association* has information on tournaments, T9252325, jamaicagolf@cwjamaica.com

The island's main spectator sport is **cricket**, although overtaken by soccer in 1998 when Jamaica qualified for the World Cup. Test matches are played in Kingston. For details on matches ring *Jamaica Cricket Association*, T9670322, F9673976, www.greatvacations.com For **football** phone *Jamaica Football Federation*, T9290484. **Tennis** can be played at the *Eric Bell Tennis Centre*, Kingston. For **track and field** meets phone *Jam Amateur Athletics Association*. There are several **road races** during the year, including the High Mountain Coffee 10km and 5km races at Williamsfield, Manchester, which usually attract around 450 runners (contact John Minott, T9634211, F9634309, sanco@colis.com), and the Reggae marathon and half marathon starting at the Negril UDC playing field to Green Island and return (www. reggaemarathon.com). There is also the Treasure Beach Off-Road **Triathlon** in May, involving swimming, mountain biking and running (Jason Henzel, T9650636, F9650552, jakes@ cwjamaica.com). Horse **racing** at Caymanas Park, T9257780/9253312, every Wednesday and Saturday and most public holidays. **Polo** is played on Saturday afternoons at Drax Hall, near Ocho Rios, entrance free, and there are several polo clubs, for example Polo and Equestrian Club of Oakbrook, T9228581 for match details. International tournaments at Chukka Cove, Runaway Bay and Caymanas Polo Club, Kingston. For further information about clubs and matches, contact Shane Chin, T9525586, chilly@colis.com   **Riding** lessons and trail rides also available at Chukka Cove, which has probably the best facilities, T9722506. Hotels can arrange riding with local stables too and there are good facilities at the Equestrian Centre at *Half Moon Club*, Montego Bay, and *Good Hope*, where you can ride along the banks of the Martha Brae River. A three-hour beach ride costs about US$50, while a 2-3 day trek into the mountains costs US$285-500.

Holidays and festivals

Carnival (www.jamaicacarnival.com) has come only recently to Jamaica and is held around *Dancing for six hours* *Easter* time with floats, bands and mass dances, at various locations around the island, *a night for seven* attended by thousands. Byron Lee, the leading Jamaican calypsonian, spends a lot of time in *nights is the best way* Trinidad over Carnival period and then brings the Trinidad calypsoes back to Jamaica. Some *to get fit!* Trinidadian costumes, although not the really spectacular ones (logistically impossible), are

Jamaica

recycled for Jamaica's carnival. The annual reggae festival, **Reggae Sumfest**, is held in *August*, and last for five days with local and international musicians, contact the Summerfest office, T9520889, F9797437, info@reggaesumfest.com In August, the celebrations around **Independence Day** (*1 August*) last a week and are very colourful. The parade ends with a street dance at Half Way Tree, attended by thousands. The **Jamaica Film & Music Festival** is held at the Wyndham Rosehall, Montego Bay, in *November*. Film makers, musicians and artistes gather for discussions and a good time, culminating in an awards ceremony, www.jamericanfilmfest.com The tourist board publishes a twice-yearly calendar of events which covers the whole spectrum of arts and sports festivals, www.jamaicatravel.com/events Other cultural events are organized by the *Jamaica Cultural Development Commission* (JCDC) at theatres and elsewhere, T9265726, www.jcdc.org.jm

Kingston

Population: 750,000
Colour map 1, grid C5

The capital since 1870 and the island's commercial centre, Kingston has one of the largest and best natural harbours in the world. Following the earthquake of 1907 much of the lower part of the city (Down Town) was rebuilt in concrete. On the waterfront there are some notable modern buildings including the Bank of Jamaica and the Jamaica Conference Centre which also houses the National Gallery. Most of the new shops and offices are in the Parish of St Andrew, although visitors and even locals are often not aware of where one parish ends and the next begins. Crossroads and Halfway Tree (St Andrew) are referred to as midtown areas. Many shopping plazas are further north again along the Constant Spring Road and east along Old Hope Road to Liguanea. The old racecourse was redeveloped in the 1960s as the New Kingston district, which contains most of the big hotels and many banks and financial institutions. Kingston and St Andrew (Corporate Area) are busy urban areas with traffic congestion at major junctions. It is a place to work rather than holiday, although there are some important places of interest and several tour companies and car rental agencies are within easy reach. A city tour could extend as far as Devon House and the nearby Blue Mountains and beaches at Hellshire and Lime Key, followed by several night clubs. Reggae lovers should visit the Bob Marley Museum, but anywhere you may receive blasts of music from buses, bars and cars.

Ins and outs

Getting there
See transport, page 275, for further details

The international airport for Kingston is the **Norman Manley** (restaurant, good tourist office), 11 miles away, up to 30 mins' drive, on the peninsula opposite Kingston across the bay. An exchange desk in the arrivals lounge changes cash and travellers' cheques (at a slightly lower rate than banks). There is also an airstrip for domestic flights on Tinson Pen, 2 miles from the centre, 10 mins' drive. If you have flown in to Montego Bay on the north coast you can get to Kingston by air or overland by frequent bus.

Getting around
It is better to go into a hotel & order a taxi, rather than hailing one in the street

Bus travel in Kingston costs between US$0.23 and US$0.35. Travelling by bus is not safe after dark or even during daytime in certain areas. Take a taxi to/from the bus station although you will still get hassled and pestered during the short walk to the bus. Do not walk out of the bus station; the area is notorious. Crossroads, Pechon Street and Half Way Tree are the main bus stops, but buses coming from town are usually full by the time they reach Crossroads or Half Way Tree.

Sights

NB St Andrew is partitioned into zones numbered as Kingston. An address in the Parish of St Andrew will have a numbered zone, eg Kingston 10, while an address in the Parish of Kingston will have no zone number and the address will just be Kingston.

Among older buildings of note in the Down Town area are **Gordon House** (on Duke Street), which dates from the mid-18th century and houses the Jamaican legislature. Visitors are allowed into the Strangers' Gallery but must be suitably dressed (jackets for men and dresses for women). There is also the early 18th century parish church south of Parade, where Admiral Benbow is buried. **Parade** (Sir William Grant Park) is at the heart of the city centre; it is an open oasis amid the densely-packed surroundings. The name derives from the British soldiers' parades here during colonial rule. Now it is at the junction of the main east-west route through the Down Town area (Windward Road/East Queen Street-West Queen

Kingston orientation

Related maps:
A New Kingston, page 286
B Downtown, Kingston, page 288

■ **Sleeping**
1 Christar Villas
2 Crowne Plaza

● **Eating**
1 Fish Place
2 Gloria's Seafood

3 Guilt Trip
4 Susie's Bakery & Coffee Bar

Street/Spanish Town Road) and King Street/Orange Street which runs north to Cross Roads. At Cross Roads, the main route forks, left to Half Way Tree (recently renamed Nelson Mandela Park), straight on up Old Hope Road to Liguanea. These two roads encompass New Kingston.

The Parish Church at St Andrew at **Half Way Tree** dates from 1700. Half Way Tree, so called because it was a half-way stage on the road between the harbour and the hills, is a busy traffic junction which takes some negotiating in a car. This area is known as the Corporate Area (Kingston being that section of the Corporate Area south of the National Heroes Circle/Park) and most modern development is here. Hope Road, on the north edge of New Kingston, runs east from Half Way Tree. Just off it are **Devon House**, a former 'great house', built by Jamaica's first millionaire in the 1880s, at the corner of Trafalgar and Hope Roads, now renovated, complete with antique furniture, with craft shops and refreshment stalls. ■ *T9297029. Small admission fee to look inside the main house, US$3 for a guided tour, but the shops and restaurants in the grounds are open to all and well worth a visit. Tue-Sat, 1000-1700.* The **African Museum**, with exhibits on Jamaica's African heritage, is part of the

New Kingston

■ **Sleeping**		
1 Altamount Court	8 Terra Nova	4 Indies Pub
2 Four Seasons	9 The Indies	5 Island Grill
3 Hilton		6 Jam Rock Sports Bar & Grill
4 Johnson Holborn Manor	● **Eating**	7 Jerk Pork Restaurant
5 Mayfair	1 Akbar	8 Lyn's
6 Pegasus	2 Heather's	9 Red Bones
7 Sandhurst	3 Hot Pot	10 Trafalgar Restaurant & Bar

N
Not to scale

Jamaica

Devon House complex. Not far away is **King's House**, the official residence of the Governor-General and, nearby, **Jamaica House**, the Prime Minister's residence.

About 10 blocks east of Devon House, off Hope Road, is the **Bob Marley Museum**. The house where Marley used to live traces back to the time of his childhood and family, with paintings, newspaper cuttings, posters and other memorabilia. He died tragically of brain cancer in 1981 at the age of 36, having survived a controversial assassination attempt (the bullet-holes in the walls have been left as a reminder). There is an Ethiopian restaurant in the garden serving some of his favourite vegetarian dishes and a gift shop selling Jamaican and African artefacts. Marijuana plants grow profusely throughout the grounds and ganja is smoked openly in and around the restaurant and bar by staff. Photography is totally banned within the museum and grounds. ■ *0900-1700, Mon, Tue, Thu, Fri, 1230-1730, Wed, Sat. US$10 including obligatory guided tour, which takes 1 hr, including 20-min audio visual presentation. T9782991, 56 Hope Rd.*

Further east, along Old Hope Road, are the **Hope Botanical Gardens**. The land was first acquired by Major Richard Hope in 1671 and 200 years later the Governor of Jamaica, Sir John Peter Grant, bought 200 acres and created a botanical gardens. In 1961 a zoo was opened alongside the gardens (J$10, 1000-1700 daily). After extensive damage in 1988 by Hurricane Gilbert, plans have been made to transform the small, traditional zoo into a showcase for the different natural habitats of Jamaica and its indigenous animals. ■ *Free. 0830-1830.*

West of Downtown Kingston, near the May Pen Cemetery, is the **Bob Marley Culture Yard**, a project started by the *Trench Town Development Association* (TTDA), a community based NGO, to boost the inner city community of Trench Town, concentrating on the reggae heritage of Bob Marley and other great musicians who came from the area. Culture Yard is an attraction in the making, based on restoring the home and belongings of the reggae super star to be opened for visitors. ■ *Trench Town Development Association, 6 Lower First St, Trench Town, Kingston, T9484455, and 18 Collie Smith Drive, Kingston 12, T7576739.*

The swimming at Kingston is not very good. The sea at Gunboat beach, near the airport, is dirty. Better at Port Royal (see below). 'Hellshire', south of Port Henderson, is a locals' favourite, but is difficult to reach. Bammy and festival are prepared along the beach strip.

Beaches

Essentials

LL-L *Le Meridien Jamaica Pegasus*, 81 Knutsford Blvd, PO Box 333, T9263690, F9295855, www.meridienjamaica.com 300 rooms, pleasant service and atmosphere but nothing special. **LL-L** *Hilton Kingston*, 77 Knutsford Blvd, PO Box 112, Kingston 5, T9265430, F9297439. 303 rooms, usual Hilton facilities. **L** *Terra Nova*, 17 Waterloo Rd, T9269334, F9294933, www.cariboutpost.com/terra_nova 35 rooms, popular with business travellers, pool, bar, café and restaurant. **L-AL** *Crowne Plaza*, 211 Constant Spring Rd, Kingston 8, T9257674, F9054425. 132 rooms, high rise, business hotel with executive floor, gym, sauna, exercise facilities, tennis, squash, jogging trail, pool. **AL-A** *Christar Villas*, 99A Hope Rd, Kingston 6, T9787864, F9788068, christar@n5.com.jm 32 1-2 bedroom suites and studios with kitchenettes, pool, bar, restaurant, small gym. **AL-B** *The Gardens Liguanea*, 23 Liguanea Av, Kingston 6, T9275957, www.forrespark.com Town houses, with two rooms, private bathrooms and shared living and dining room downstairs, rent a room or the whole house, continental breakfast included, homely service, convenient location within walking distance of Sovereign Shopping Mall and the Bus Route, also close to the university. **A** *Altamont Court*, 1-5 Altamont Terr, T9294497, F9292118. 55 rooms, pool, restaurant. **A-B** *Four Seasons*, 18 Ruthven Rd, PO Box 190, T9297655, F9295964, www.hotelfourseasonsja.com Run by Mrs Stockhert, German, long-time knowledgeable resident, in a converted Edwardian house and gardens, 76 rooms, pool, bar, conference room, business centre, good cooking. **B-C** *Mayfair*, 4 West King's House Close, Kingston 10, PO Box 163, T9261610, F9297741. Beautiful setting

Sleeping
Morgan's Harbour is conveniently close to the airport and has complimentary transport there and back, 10 mins (see Port Royal); all the other main hotels are in or near New Kingston

Jamaica

(adjoining the Governor General's residence), balconies look towards mountains, 32 good rooms, also 8 houses, pool, food and service. Among the cheaper hotels is **B** *The Indies*, 5 Holborn Rd, T9262952, F9262879. 15 rooms, television US$6 extra, breakfast and lunch available, comfortable, pleasant patio, garden, helpful owners. Next door is the popular **D** *Johnson Holborn Manor*, 3 Holborn Rd, with breakfast and shower. Fan, clean, safe and quiet, very convenient for business in New Kingston, 3 good places to eat within 50 yds, luggage storage available, friendly, new annex. **B** *Sandhurst*, 70 Sandhurst Cres, Kingston 6, T9277239. 35 rooms, a/c or fan, restaurant. **D-E** *Retreat Guest House*, 8 Devon Rd, T9262565. 4 rooms, among the cheapest, safe area after dark. About 25 mins from Kingston is **AL-A** *Ivor Guest House* and restaurant, Jack's Hill, Kingston 6, T9271460, F9770033, www.cariboutpost/ivor High up in the hills overlooking Kingston and set in its own extensive grounds, 10 rooms, free transport to/from Kingston, charge for airport pickup, lunches US$12, dinners US$16 by reservation only. The *YMCA*, opposite Devon House on Hope Road, has a good swimming pool, many sports facilities and a cheaply priced restaurant. The tourist board can arrange B&B for you, which usually costs US$25-60 a night.

Up in the hills overlooking Kingston Bay is Island Outpost's *Strawberry Hill*, now a 12-villa luxury retreat but formerly a coffee and fruit plantation house, sadly destroyed by Hurricane Gilbert in 1988. Recommended weekend brunch of jerk meats, salt fish etc washed down with champagne and orange juice, US$25 per person, T9448400, F9448408, or contact Island Outpost in UK, 421a Finchley Rd, London NW3 6HJ, T0800 614790.

Downtown Kingston

Both Orange Street & Marescaux Rd converge at Cross Roads becoming respectively Old Hope Rd & Halfway Tree Rd

To Cross Roads

Orange St

Marescaux Rd

South Camp Rd

Jewish Cemetery

National Heroes Park

TRENCH TOWN/ JONES TOWN AREA

Sabina Park

To Spanish Town

North St

Spanish Town Rd

Orange St

King St

Gordon House

Ward Theatre

West Queen St

N Parade

Sir William Grant Park

East Queen St

S Parade

Parish Church

Pechon St

King St

Duke St

East St

Barry St

Harbour St

Crafts Market

National Gallery

Port Royal St

Conference Centre

RAE TOWN

Ocean Blvd

To Norman Manley Airport, Bath & Morant Bay

N

Not to scale

Jamaica

Over US$20 *Red Bones Blues Café*, 21 Braemar Av, Kingston 10, T9786091. 'Nouvelle Jamaican cuisine', quite expensive but lovely garden and blues music. At *Devon House* (see page 286), there is a plush expensive restaurant, a reasonably priced snack bar and delicious ice cream at *I Scream*. *Trafalgar Restaurant & Bar*, 38A Trafalgar Rd, Kingston 5, T7546989. Indoor and outdoor dining, set in garden, specializing in seafood, try the 'Trafalgar Steam', fish fillet in a cream sauce, other delights include lobster and shrimp in a variety of ways: thermidor, curried, deep fried, very tasty, great place for lunch or after work dining, open daily 1100-0100.

Eating
There are a great many places to eat in Downtown Kingston, New Kingston and the Half Way Tree area. There are plush establishments, inside and outside the hotels, and small places. Around the waterfront most places close at 1700

For the impecunious, meat patties may be had at US$0.25 each

US$10-20 On Holborn Rd, opposite the *Indies Hotel* is the *Indies Pub*, which is reasonable, and next door is the *Three Little Bears* with patisserie attached, cheap cakes and coffee, excellent lobster in the main restaurant and quite palatable Jamaican wine, main course for lunch under US$4, evening meal US$8-18, buffet Fri and Sun excellent value at US$8. *The Fish Place*, 136 Constant Spring Rd, Kingston 8, T9244063, or the Mall Plaza, 20 Constant Spring Rd, Kingston 10. Jamaican restaurant specializing in seafood, the best place in town for fish in all styles, prices around US$10-15, easy going, relaxed atmosphere, popular after-work dining and weekend stop for families and friends, live music sometimes. *Island Grill*, Shop 28, Twin Gates Plaza, 25 ½ Constant Spring Rd, Kingston 10, T9205016, and Sovereign Centre (Shopping Mall), Shop 16, 106 Hope Rd, Kingston 6, T9783535. 'Real Jamaican Jerk', Jamaican restaurant serving very tasty fast foods, affordable prices, several branches now appearing, jerk chicken and fish are popular, with a variety of side orders. *Racquel's 2000 Restaurant & Lounge*, 38A Trafalgar Rd, Kingston 10. T9201588. *Akbar*, 11 Holborn Rd. Very good Indian food, good service, nice atmosphere, US$20 for 3-course dinner and drinks for 2. On Chelsea Av is *Jerk Pork*, popular with locals. Nearby are Mexican and Indian restaurants, both very good but not cheap. *The Lychee Gardens*, shop 34 in the New Kingston Shopping Mall, on Dominica Drive, T9298619. Serves excellent Chinese food, moderately priced, several other eating places here, from takeaway pattie bakery to upmarket restaurant, popular lunch spot for office workers. *Heathers Garden Restaurant*, 9 Haining Rd, Kingston 5, T9607739. Very pleasant to sit outside, Middle Eastern and Jamaican dishes, US$3.25-9. *Lyn's Vegetarian Restaurant* and Performing Arts Auditorium, 7 Tangerine Pl, Kingston 10, T9293842, 9683487. *Guilt Trip*, 20 Barbican Rd, T9775130. Delicious pastries and desserts. *Susie's Bakery & Coffee Bar*, Southdale Plaza, T9685030. Recommended for light lunches and coffee.

Under US$10 *Hot Pot*, 2 Altamont Terr, Kingston 5, T9293906. Very cheap, serves good Jamaican food in a pleasant patio, also a take-out box for just over US$1, difficult to find it without asking for directions. On Knutsford Blvd there are lots of vans selling a satisfying lunch for US$1-1.50, often less, depending on what you eat. Many outlets of international takeaway chains all over the city, *Burger King* and *Kentucky Fried Chicken*, etc, as well as Jamaica's own variation, *Mothers*, also widespread. *Jamaican McDonald's*, 1 Cargill Av, corner of Cargill and Halfway Tree Rd, T9200411. Established since 1971, survived dispute with the mulitnational *McDonalds* on their entry into the market, provides a variety of fast food meals with a Jamaican flavour. *The Tastees*, chain serves good value takeaway patties and cakes, branches on Knutsford Blvd, Liguanea, Manor Park and Papine. In the grounds of the University of Technology at Papine is *Lillian's*, T9271615. Staffed by trainees, good cheap lunch for about US$3.

Tourists are strongly advised not to try, unless they have Jamaican friends, to probe deeply into real Jamaican nightlife, at least in towns. For genuine local dances and songs, see the advertisements in the local press. The *Jamaica Vacation Guide* (at hotels, tourist offices) has the latest information. Clubs and discos include *Asylum* 69 Knutsford Blvd), Kingston 5, T9061828, closed Mon, Ladies' night Tue (ladies free before 2300), Oldies' night Wed, Dance Hall night Thu, after work jam & disco Fri, international music Sat, disco night Sun. *Mirage*, Sovereign Shopping Centre, Liguanea, *Turntable*, Red Hills Rd, *Mingles* at *Courtleigh Hotel* (www.courtleigh.com), 85 Knutsford Blvd, Kingston 5, T9299000, a popular night club and disco, with food and drink, regular hangout for consultants and young

Nightlife
Most hotels have dancing at weekends

Jamaica

professionals, Latin night on Sat popular with cross-section of party goers. *Peppers* on Waterloo Rd, a good open air drinking spot, *the* place to go at night. *Half Time Sports Bar*, 61 Knutsford Blvd, T9061452, and *Jam Rock Sports Bar & Grill*, 69 Knutsford Blvd, T7544032. Young crowd, sports bars, music, TV, pool. *Devon House* is a good place for a quiet evening drink under the trees. *Centre Pole* at Mary Brown's Corner on Constant Spring Rd is rowdy and raunchy but fairly safe too. *Palais Royal*, 14 Ripon Rd, Kingston 5, T9061828. *Caesar's*, 5 Balmoral Av, Kingston 10. *Priscilla's*, 103 Constant Spring Rd, Kingston 5, T9699638. *Platinum Dance Club*, Dominica Drive, Kingston 5, T9081143, exotic dancers from Russia, closed Sun. **Rae Town**, just east of Downtown Kingston, is primarily a fishing community on the coast, but it is a very popular inner city hangout for locals and visitors, especially on Sun nights, offering a secure experience of street dance urban entertainment 'ghetto style', with typically heavy Dance Hall music from huge sound systems, and a variety of Jamaican food and drink from roadside bars and restaurants.

Entertainment There is a good School of Drama and several theatre and dance companies. Jamaica Dance Theatre is well known. Theatres include Ward Theatre (North Parade), Little Theatre (St Andrew, T9266129), The Barn, New Kingston Playhouse, Green Gables, Creative Arts Centre. Watch the press for details of performances.

Shopping In Down Town Kingston, the Jamaica Crafts Market at the corner of Ocean Blvd and Port
There are various
duty-free concessions Royal Street and many shops at west end of Port Royal Street have local crafts. The market is a
for visitors must for souvenir hunters, craft items are reasonably priced and there is a wide range of traditional Jamaican handicrafts. Off West Queen Street is an interesting local market, selling fish, fruit and general produce. Down Town is where Jamaicans shop for bargains, but be careful, particularly in the market, it can be dangerous and you need to be thick skinned to get through, even if you do not get robbed. Most shops are in the plazas along Constant Spring Road and in Liguanea. There is a smart little shopping centre in New Kingston. Reggae music shops can be found close together along Orange Street, just north of Parade. The best bookshop, particularly for Caribbean fiction, is *The Book Shop*, The Springs, 15-17 Constant Spring Rd, T9261800. Also very good is the *Kingston Bookshop* at 70B King Street, T9224056, and at the Pavilion Shopping Mall, Half Way Tree, T9684591. *Bookland* on Knutsford Blvd. Wide range of US magazines and newspapers and also *The Times*.

Transport **Bus** Fares from Kingston are: US$1.40 to Mandeville, US$2.75 to Montego Bay, US$1.50 to Negril, US$1.25 to Ocho Rios, US$2 to Port Antonio, 3 hrs, you are lucky if you get a seat. The buses are invaded by touts as they approach the bus station. **Local** The newly established government bus service, *Jamaica Urban Transit Company* (JUTC) has largely replaced the old bus franchise services with a fleet of newly acquired buses and a much more efficient service, significantly improving travel time and comfort around the corporate area. Tickets are US$0.23 for the first two stages and about US$0.50 for 3 stages. Buses and shared taxis to/from North Parade for the airport, US$0.35, but the service is infrequent, so allow for waiting time. To get to New Kingston by bus involves a change of bus (to No 27) Down Town. The recognized service to/from town from airport is JUTA, taxi/minibus, which charges US$17 to New Kingston (taxi dispatcher gives you a note of fare before you leave, can be shared). Alternatively, if you have not got much luggage, take taxi to Port Royal, US$9, ferry to Kingston (see below, Port Royal) and then taxi to New Kingston, US$5-6.

Directory **Banks** *National Commercial Bank of Jamaica*, 77 King St, Kingston and branches all over the island; the same applies to the *Bank of Nova Scotia Jamaica Ltd*, head office: Duke and Port Royal Sts, Kingston. *Citibank*, 63-67 Knutsford Blvd, Kingston; and other local banks. A string of **ATMs** has been installed in main centres from which you can withdraw cash from Visa and Mastercards. Immediate money transfers can be made via the Western Union Bank, behind the National Commercial Bank at the top of Knutsford Blvd. **Cultural centres** *The British Council* has an office in the First Life Building, 64 Knutsford Blvd, PO Box 575, Kingston 5, T9296915, F9297090. Information library, mainly on education, British newspapers available. **Embassies & consulates** British High Commission is at 26 Trafalgar Rd, Kingston 5, T9269050, F9297869, PO Box 575. 26 other countries represented. **Tourist office** Pan Caribbean Building, 64 Knutsford Blvd, T9299200.

Port Royal

Port Royal, the old naval base, lies across the harbour from Kingston. It was founded in 1650, captured by the English and turned into a strategic military and naval base. Merchant shipping developed under naval protection and the town soon became prosperous. It also attracted less reputable shipping and in 1660-92 became a haven for pirates such as Henry Morgan, with gambling and drinking dens and brothels protected by the six forts and 145 guns. The 'wickedest city in the world', with a population of 8,000, soon provoked what was thought to be divine retribution. On 7 June 1692 an earthquake hit east Jamaica, coursing along the Port Royal fault line and bringing with it massive tidal waves. The port, commercial area and harbour front were cut away and slid down the slope of the bay to rest on the sea bed, while much of the rest of the town was flooded for weeks. About 5,000 people died (of drowning, injuries or subsequent disease) and the naval, merchant and fishing fleets were wrecked. The town was gradually rebuilt as a naval and military post but has had to withstand 16 hurricanes, nine earthquakes, three fires and a storm (which in 1951 left only four buildings undamaged).

Population: 2,000

Nelson served here as a post-captain from 1779 to 1780 and commanded **Fort Charles**, built in 1655, key battery in the island's fortifications. The former British naval headquarters are now the **Fort Charles Maritime Museum**, with a scale model of the fort and ships. ■ *1000-1700 Mon-Thu, 1000-1600 Fri, US$1.* Part of the ramparts, known as Nelson's Quarterdeck, still stands. ■ *US$2.* The Giddy House was the Royal Artillery store, built in 1888 but damaged by the 1907 earthquake which caused it to tilt at an angle of 45°. The Victoria Albert battery complex was a boiler house and underground armoury with late 19th century guns to protect the harbour and tunnels. The old Naval Hospital was built in 1819 of prefabricated cast iron sections brought all the way from England, one of the earliest constructions of this type and built on a raft foundation. The old gaol can also be seen. This dates from the early 18th century and was used as a women's prison in the 19th century. **St Peter's Church**, though the restoration is unfortunate, is of historic interest, as is the **National Museum of Historical Archaeology**. The museum is little more than one room and the Fort Charles remains are more informative and substantive. ■ *US$0.30.* A US$60 mn tourist project for Port Royal was announced in 1998, to include renovation of the town, construction of a new museum, concert hall and shopping centre. ■ *Getting there: beyond the international airport, some 15 miles by excellent road. Can also be reached by boat from Victoria Pier; 7 daily, 20 mins, US$0.30.*

Boats may be hired for picnic bathing lunches on the numerous nearby cays or at Port Henderson. **Lime Cay** (about the size of a football field) is the most popular of the nearby islands, offering a white sand beach and crystal clear water. A seafood restaurant and bar operated by locals from Port Royal provides tasty fried fish and chicken meals. There is a full service marina at *Morgan's Harbour* with customs clearance, 24-hr security and fishing boats for hire.

Beaches and watersports

L *Morgan's Harbour* at Port Royal is a favourite holiday centre, T9678030, F9678073. 40 rooms, 5 suites, sea view, seminar rooms, scuba diving (packages available with Buccaneer Scuba Club at the marina, T9678061, F9678073), with waterskiing, fresh and saltwater swimming pools, beach cabins, a good seafood restaurant, and dancing, closest hotel to airport.

Sleeping

Spanish Town

Spanish Town, the former capital founded in 1534, some 14 miles west of Kingston (bus from Half Way Tree and from Orange Street), is historically the most interesting of Jamaica's towns and in desperate need of funds for renovation. Some funding has been secured and restoration has started on sections of the fine Georgian main square. Its English-style architecture dates from the 18th century. Well worth seeing

Jamaica

are the **Cathedral Church of St James**, the oldest in the anglophone West Indies dating back to 1714. The square houses the ruins of the **King's House** built in 1762 (Governor's residence until 1872 when Kingston became the capital) that burnt down in 1925. The façade has been rebuilt and within it is the **Archaeological Museum**, containing exhibits excavated here and a site history of 1534-1872. In the old stables is the **Jamaican People's Museum of Craft and Technology**. ■ *Mon-Fri, 1000-1700, US$0.20.* Also on the square are a colonnade (paint peeling off) and statue commemorating Rodney's victory at the Battle of the Saints (see under Guadeloupe and Dominica); the **House of Assembly** and the **Court House**. There is a museum with interesting relics of Jamaican history and accurate portrayal of life of the country people. The **park** in the centre is overgrown with weeds and the gates are padlocked. Outside town, on the road to Kingston is the **White Marl Taino Museum**. ■ *US$0.10. Mon-Fri, 1000-1600.* Restaurant: *Miami*, Cumberland Rd, near the market area; food is delicious, especially the pumpkin soup.

Eastern Jamaica and the mountains

North from Kingston Behind Kingston lie the Blue Mountains with Blue Mountain Peak rising to a height of 7,402 ft (2,256 m). This is undoubtedly one of the most spectacular and beautiful parts of Jamaica and an area which must be visited by keen bird watchers and botanists and also by those who like mountain walking. It is possible to explore some of the Blue Mountains by ordinary car from Kingston. Drive towards **Papine** and just before arriving there visit the **Botanical Gardens** at **Hope** (see above). After leaving Papine and just after passing the *Blue Mountain Inn* (good restaurant and nightclub), turn left to Irish Town and thence to **Newcastle**, a Jamaica Defence Force

Eastern Jamaica

1 Parade
2 New Kingston
3 Half Way Tree
4 King's House & Jamaica House
5 Hope Royal Botanical Gardens
6 University of the West Indies

training camp at 4,000 ft with magnificent views of Kingston and Port Royal. If energetic you may climb the road to **Catherine's Peak** directly behind the camp (about one hour for the moderately fit).

Beyond Newcastle lies **Hardwar Gap** and **Holywell National Park**. This is a recreational area within the Blue and John Crow Mountains National Park. ■ *The Park and the facilities are currently managed by an environmental non-governmental orgnization, the Jamaica Conservation and Development Trust (JCDT). The facility offers nature trails, camp sites, picnic areas, and three log cabins, **B**, two sleep 4 and one sleeps 6 people. There is an entry fee of US$10.00/adult and US$5.00/child for non-residents and US$1.00 for Jamaicans. Oately Mountain Trail is a commercial trail within the Hollywell Park for which there is a separate user fee of US$10.00/adult or US$5.00/child. This fee includes entry into the park and a guided tour. Bookings can be made through the JCDT, 1st floor, Workforce Development Building, 22b Old Hope Rd, Kingston 5, T9208278-82, F9206722, jcdt@kasnet.com* The Gap Café, at Hardwar, T9237078, has spectacular views and serves real Blue Mountain coffee. This whole area is full of mountain trails with innumerable birds, some unique to Jamaica. The picturesque little community of **Section** is at the junction of three roads and is a travel halt. There the road from Hollywell intersects with the Silver Hill to Buff Bay Road. A left turn from Hollywell takes you to Buff Bay and a turning off to the right to Silver Hill Gap. Section is the most popular spot on the north side of the Blue Mountains for purchasing genuine Blue Mountain Coffee. A coffee tour is offered which includes a demonstration of the traditional way of growing, preparing and roasting Blue Mountain Coffee, as done for the past 200 years. At **Silver Hill Gap**, the recently built **B** *Starlight Chalet,* T7989868 and office T9603070, www.jamaicamarketplace.com/starlight, boasts a spa, bar and guest house, with a growing clientele. The road from Silver Hill Gap to the left turn off to Clydesdale (about a 2 ½ mile drive) is badly in need of repairs and visitors should enquire whether the route is passable. A four-wheel drive jeep is advised to be safe. The road to Clydesdale and the **Cinchona botanical garden**, is unpaved and very steep between Clydesdale and Cinchona (4WD required, or walk, about an hour uphill but well worth it). The route from Silver Hill Gap continues past the turn off to Clydesdale to **Content Gap**, passing on route *Pine Grove Guest House.* Content is a three road junction, coming from Clydesdale the left turn goes to Gordon town and Kingston whereas the right goes to Mavis Bank and the Blue Mountain Peak.

Holywell National Park to Buff Bay

Jamaica

If you wish to go towards **Blue Mountain Peak** from Kingston (corporate area), you drive to the commercial township of Papine, continuing on the Gordon Town Road, you drive straight on at *Blue Mountain Inn* (instead of turning left), through Gordon Town and on through **Mavis Bank** four miles to **Hagley Gap**, if the Mahogany Vale

Around Blue Mountain

ford is passable. The community and the National Park have constructed a flat bridge which has made passage more secure even during the rainy season. However, as a precaution you should avoid all major rivers whenever flood warnings have been issued or during very heavy rains. Again, however, you will almost certainly not be able to get a car up to the starting point for the walk to the Peak. Public transport up the Blue Mountains is infrequent. There are some buses to Mavis Bank from the square in Papine on the outskirts of Kingston, US$0.60 but you will need to ask. To get to Papine, take a 70 or 75 bus along Hope Road. Taxis from Papine to Mavis Bank about US$7.50. Only four-wheel drive vehicles are advisable after Mavis Bank (no shortage of people offering to take you), and there are no petrol stations *en route*. There are two walking possibilities from Mavis Bank: either look for a four-wheel drive to Hagley Gap and walk from there to the starting point of the trail to the Peak (3½ miles uphill through villages), or walk the short cut (4 miles) from Mavis Bank. You may need to be guided for the first part (plenty of guides, Linford Morrison, lives near Police Station), across two small rivers and on to the path, which is then straight forward, a reasonably hard but lovely walk for two hours. Keep going when you eventually reach the village. Ask for *Whitfield Hall* or *Wildflower Lodge* (see below), the turning for which is just beyond Penlyne Castle School, by the Post Office. It is then a few minutes' walk. Four-wheel drive Land Rovers are available from *Whitfield Hall* (John Allgrove, T9270986) and *Wildflower Lodge* (Eric Leiba, T9295395). *Sun Venture Tours* provides complete tour services for the Blue Mountain Peak, with transfers from anywhere on the island to Penlyne Castle, meals, accommodation and interpretative guides.

Mountain lodges **B** *Pine Grove Hotel*, c/o 62 Duke Street, Kingston, T9228708, F9225895, about half an hour's drive beyond Gordon Town. This consists of a series of cottages with central feeding and the atmosphere of a ski lodge with double rooms, bathroom, kitchen area and couch. The proprietors, Barbara and Radwick, live there and are extremely welcoming and helpful. Apart from giving advice they will also provide four-wheel drive vehicles at very moderate cost to take guests to Cinchona and the start of the trail to Blue Mountain Peak, etc. They will also pick up guests from the airport (US$50) or from Kingston. A similar service is provided by **B-C** *Forest Park Guest House* on the main road near the Mavis Bank Coffee factory, T9275957/9278275, run by Jennifer Lyn.

E-F *Maya Lodge*, contact the *Jamaican Alternative Tourism, Camping and Hiking Association* (JATCHA) at Maya Lodge and Hiking Centre, Juba Spring, Peter's Rock Road, Jack's Hill, Kingston, T7020314. To get to Maya Lodge by public transport take the 76 or 76A bus from Duke Street (down town) or Knutsford Boulevard (New Kingston) to Barbican. From there take a shared taxi round the corner on Jack's Hill Road opposite the Texaco station, US$0.90, the taxis are sometimes very shared indeed. Alternatively, it is a 3½ mile walk uphill, not to be attempted after dark. Rooms or cabins, hostel style, camping in own tent or in hired tent (all plus 12½% to fund projects), restaurant, vegetarian options, menu repetitive, 15 acres of land in jungle setting, many paths for hikes around area. Highly recommended. A day's walk with a guide costs US$50. For a short tour of an organic farm ask for Willy, who will show you round his farm, interesting, reasonable rates, but only attempt it if you can walk up and down a steep hill and have old shoes. Willy is often used as a guide and will take you up into the forest on Mount Horeb giving you details of local lore and bush medicine as you go.

There are two lodges close to the point where the Blue Mount Peak trail begins. John Algrove (8 Almon Crescent, Kingston 6, T9270986) owns *Whitfield Hall Hostel*, a large wooden lodge with no electricity but gas for the kitchen and paraffin lamps, **F** per person, capacity 40, hostel or **D** private room accommodation, cold showers only. No meals unless you order them in advance, but kitchen with stoves and crockery, for guests' use. Very peaceful and homely with comfortable lounge, log fire and library (visitors' books dating back to the 1950s), staff friendly and helpful. If the hostel is full, camping is permitted. A couple of minutes' walk before *Whitfield Hall* is *Wildflower Lodge*, known locally as the White House T9295394/5 or write 10 Ellesmere Road, Kingston 10. It charges the same prices for dormitory or private room as *Whitfield Hall*, but is a bit more modern and the food is better, breakfast

US$3, evening meals US$5 but hard to tell the difference, substantial and excellent vegetables from the garden. Both lodges will arrange four-wheel drive transport from Kingston or Mavis Bank and offer guides and horses for walking or riding excursions.

The walk to **Blue Mountain Peak** (6½ miles from Whitfield Hall) takes three to four hours up and two to three hours down. The first part is the steepest. Some start very early in the morning in the hope of watching the sunrise from the Peak. The thrill of victory takes on new meaning once you've climbed Jacob's Ladder and posed atop the Trig Station on the highest point, Middle Peak (2,256 m), waiting anxiously … braving the bitter cold… to catch that first faint glow of sunlight. On clear mornings when the mist surrenders quietly to the rising sun, the of dawn sweeps across the eastern sky, tinting cloud layers far below. As often as not, though, the Peak is shrouded in cloud and rain in the early morning making it a depressing experience. You can leave in early daylight and almost certainly reach the top before it starts clouding over again (mid to late morning). In this case you do not need a guide as the path is straightforward. The trail winds through a fascinating variety of vegetation, coffee groves and banana plantations on the lower, south slopes, to tree ferns and dwarf forest near the summit (with some explanatory and mileage signposts). The doctor bird (national bird of Jamaica) is quite common, a beautiful swallow-tailed hummingbird. Quite hard to spot at first but recognizable by its loud buzz, especially near the many flowering bushes. You must take your own food and torch (spare set of batteries and bulb), sweater and rainproof if you set out in the darkness. There is one hut on the peak where you can stay overnight in some discomfort (empty concrete building with no door). The National Park authorities discourage overnighting at the Peak due to the absence of toilet facilities and inadequate waste disposal. There is a campsite with cabins (bunk beds and floor space rental), pit latrines, water and a shower at Portland Gap, about one hour up. Snacks and drinks are available at the ranger station; the rangers are very helpful. Another trail, to **Mossman Peak**, starts at Portland Gap, but is currently overgrown after 15 minutes, having not recovered from Hurricane Gilbert. In high season up to 500 people walk up Blue Mountain Peak every day, while in low season there will be only a handful. Considering the numbers, it is remarkably unspoiled and the views are spectacular.

The A4 road runs east out of Kingston, past the turn off to the airport and Port Royal, all along the south coast through Bull Bay, Yallahs, Morant Bay and Port Morant, before turning up onto the north coast to Port Antonio, Buff Bay and Annotto Bay, where it ends at the junction with the A3 running directly north from Kingston. Just beyond **Bull Bay** on the way to Yallahs, there is a plaque in memory of '**Three-Finger Jack**', one of Jamaica's legendary highway men and a folk hero-villain in the mould of Robin Hood. From the marker you get a magnificent view of Kingston harbour to the southwest, while to the north are the dry forested hills of the Port Royal Mountains, once the territory of Jack Mansong, or 'Three Finger Jack'. He had an apparently short career in 1780-81, when he fought a guerrilla war single-handedly against the British military and the plantocracy. It is not known whether he was born in Africa or Jamaica, but he is thought to have lost two fingers in a battle with a maroon called Quashee. This man later killed Jack in another fight, whereupon he cut off his head and three remaining fingers as trophies. Legends about Jack proliferated, books about him became popular, with one or two best sellers in Britain, and there was also a musical, or pantomime, about him. *Obi-* or *Three-Fingered Jack* had a run of some nine years at the Covent Garden, Haymarket and Victoria Theatres in London. (Further reading: L Alan Eyre, *Jack Mansong, 'Bloodshed or Brotherhood'*.)

About 300 yards from the junction of the A4 with the roads to Easington and Yallahs at Albion are the overgrown ruins of the **Albion Great House and Aqueduct**, often referred to as **Albion Castle**. Of the remaining structures the Great House and the waterwheel are the most impressive. It is also remarkable that

Climbing the peak
The Jamaican poet, Roger Mais (1905-1955), wrote a moving poem called 'All Men Come to the Hills' about men's desire to rest finally in the hills, wherever or however they have spent their lives and the Blue Mountains play a symbolic role for Jamaicans

Southeast coast

descendants of those who worked on the estate as slaves still occupy the 'slave house' today. In colonial times this was the leading producer of sugar in Jamaica and its crystal sugar was known as 'Albion Sugar'. On emancipation in 1838 there were about 450 slaves at Albion producing 400 hogsheads of sugar and more than double the quantity of rum produced at the end of the century. Its efficient waterwheels were supplied by a large aqueduct transporting water from the Yallahs River several miles away. One of the wheels had a diameter of 31½ ft and supported 88 buckets. These and other innovations in the milling and drying process made Albion Estate a leader in sugar production technology. Access to the property is through the estate gate just up the road. There is usually a caretaker in the old 'slave house' or someone to help you gain access.

Yallahs is one of the major towns in St Thomas and now very famous for jerk chicken (drum roasted). Its main street must have more jerk chicken stands than anywhere else. No one is quite sure where the town got its name, but it may have been named after a privateer, or buccaneer, called Captain Yhallahs, who operated in the area around 1671. On the other hand it may have been a corruption of Hato de Ayala, one of the large cattle ranches run by the Spanish when they occupied the island. Yallahs Salt Ponds stretch for about three miles, providing an outstanding landmark. Legend has it that two brothers argued over the sub-division of a piece of land and the argument became so fierce that the two plots of land sank, forming two of the three salt ponds. The hyper-saline ponds have created a unique ecosystem and several scientific discoveries have been made here. They are also a good birdwatching spot. A 4WD vehicle is recommended for visiting the beach side of the ponds, ask directions in town, best at *Miss Johnson's A&I Bar & Restaurant* in the centre, or contact the Yallahs Community Development Fund, T9825021. The first part of the journey is spoilt by the dumping of wrecked cars, but beyond that it is great going.

Morant Bay, the capital of St Thomas, is another town to have a colourful and legendary past. On 11 October 1865, it was the scene of the Morant Bay Rebellion, when a group of farmers and other disaffected citizens led by farmer and Baptist Deacon, Paul Bogle, marched to the Court House to complain about high taxes, the collapse of the sugar industry and the economic downturn, exacerbated by drought and outbreaks of smallpox and cholera. The Government was not sympathetic to the views of the people, the Court House was burned down and the uprising assumed dangerous proportions. The military rounded up the protestors and killed or sentenced to death hundreds of men and women who had allegedly taken part, while burning nearly 1,000 homes and flogging members of the surrounding communities. Today there is a statue to Paul Bogle at Morant Bay, and the monument is in remembrance of both him, George William Gordon and the 437 martyrs of those who fought and died for justice in 1865. The artist was Edna Manley, the wife of national hero, Norman Washington Manley, and mother of the late Hon Michael Manley, former Prime Minister of Jamaica.

John Crow mountains   North of Port Morant, **Bath** at the east end of the island is another place from which one can make attractive trips into the **John Crow Mountains** (named after the ubiquitous turkey buzzards). There is a modest but cheap hotel, *Bath Spa,* dating from 1727 whose main attraction is that it contains natural hot water spring baths which are most relaxing at the end of a long day. There are two passes above Bath, called the **Cuna Cuna Pass** and the **Cornpuss Gap**, which lead down to the source of the Rio Grande River on the north slopes of the mountain range. Both are tough going particularly the Cornpuss Gap. It is absolutely essential to take a local guide. The north slopes of the mountain range are the home of the unique and extremely rare Jamaican butterfly, *papilio homerus*, a large black and yellow swallowtail. It is the second largest butterfly in the world and the largest in the Americas, and is protected under international law (CITES) regulating the trade in endangered species. This butterfly is very spectacular in flight and easily recognisable because of its size. It can best be seen in May/June.

East of Port Morant, but not easily accessible, is the magnificent **Pera** beach between Port Morant and Morant Lighthouse. Near the lighthouse is another good beach but, like nearly all the beaches along the east coast round to Port Antonio, there is a dangerous undertow in certain spots. Just before reaching Manchioneal there is a road off to the left which leads to the **Reach Falls** or **Manchioneal Falls** (about three miles). Well worth a visit if you have a car or are prepared to walk (45 minutes with views of rolling forested hills) from the main road. No facilities at the falls, there may be an entry charge. Pretty tiers of smooth boulders, the highest fall about 15 ft, through a lush, green gorge. Buses from main road to Port Antonio infrequent, every 1-2 hours. Further northwest along the coast from Manchioneal to Long Bay cottages and guest houses have been built on the beach.

Port Antonio

Once the major banana port where many of the island's first tourists arrived on banana boats, Port Antonio dates back to the 16th century. Its prosperity has for many years been in gentle decline and it is now run down, but it has an atmosphere unlike any other town in Jamaica with some superb old public buildings. It is an excellent base from which to explore inland or along the coast. The rainfall in this part of the island is very high and in consequence the vegetation very lush. Boston Bay, Fairy Hill Beach (also known as Winnefred Beach), San San Beach, the Blue Lagoon (also known as the Blue Hole) and Frenchman's Cove Beach are notable beauty spots to the east of the town. **Boston Bay** is renowned for its local jerk food pits; several unnamed places by the roadside serving hot spicy chicken, pork or fish, chopped up and wrapped in paper, cooked on planks over a pit of hot coals, very good and tasty. Also worth visiting is **Nonsuch Cave**, a few miles to the southeast, where there are fossils and evidence of Taino occupation, **Somerset Falls** and **Folly Ruins**, an elaborate, turn of the century mansion built in the style of Roman and Greek architecture, now in ruins (partly because the millionaire American's wife took an instant dislike to it). It is a ghostly, crumbling old mansion in an open field with lovely views shared with grazing cows. ■ *Nonsuch Cave, 0900-1600 daily, US$5. Stalactites, gift shop and lunch area. Getting there: there is no public transport to Nonsuch Cave, return taxi fare US$10 including waiting time. For Somerset Falls, 0900-1700 daily, US$3. Getting there: take a bus to Buff Bay (any westbound Kingston bus) and walk 5 mins from there. The Folly is about half an hour's walk around the bay from the town. Take a right fork off the path before going into a clump of trees on the peninsula (leading towards lighthouse inside military camp).*

Population: 14,000

Jamaica

In the harbour it is possible to visit the 68-acre **Navy Island**, at one time owned by Errol Flynn, which has beaches (one nudist) and a moderately expensive restaurant. Return boat fare US$3, ferry operates 0700-2200 daily. Accommodation at the **AL** *Navy Island Marina Resort*, reservations, T9932667, F9932041. Rooms (14) or individual villas, restaurant, pool and bar open to non-guests, open view of bay. 'Errol Flynn Gallery' has display of movie stills and screenings of his golden oldies. The beaches on the island all belong to the resort but are open to non-guests. Snorkelling available (at the nudist beach), US$2 for half-day hire, but there are strong currents and not many fish. Many other sports and other activities on offer, including a complete wedding ceremony in the resort chapel.

Navy Island

Flynn also saw the potential as a tourist attraction for the bamboo rafts which used to bring bananas down the Rio Grande. Expert raftsmen now take tourists on these rafts down the river. One boatman is Keith Allen, with a registered licence, who can be contacted in Port Antonio at the Huntress Marina, but if you just turn up at Berrydale there are always rafters ready and willing to take you. Each raft (US$45 per raft from the ticket office, but if you arrive before it opens at 0830 or if you arrive by local bus, you can sometimes negotiate a fare of as little as US$25 with a rafter) takes

Rafting on the Rio Grande

two passengers and the trip takes 1½-2 hours (depending on the river flow) through magnificent scenery and with an opportunity to stop en route. Before you start make it clear who is buying the drinks. A driver will take your car down from the point of embarkation to the point of arrival. This is known as Rafter's Rest and is on the main coastal road. Recommended as a place to have a moderately priced lunch or drink in pleasant surroundings even if you are not proposing to raft. The return taxi fare is US$10, there are also buses, US$0.25, to Berrydale, the setting-off point, though infrequent. Returning from St Margaret's, downstream, is easier as there are plenty of buses passing between Annotto Bay and Port Antonio. Because of the frequent problems between raftsmen and the concessionaire it is advised that the local tourist office (Port Antonio) be contacted to find out whether the service is operational.

The Maroons   The Rio Grande valley is also well worth exploring, including a trip to the Maroons (descendants of escaped slaves) at **Moore Town**, but the roads are rough and public transport minimal. Ask for Colonel Harris there who is the leader of the Maroons and is recommended for guided tours. There is no telephone contact nor accommodation, return taxi fare US$15. To the west of the Rio Grande lie the north slopes of the Blue Mountains, many parts of which are still virtually unexplored. **Nanny Town**, the home of the Maroons, was destroyed by the British in 1734 and then 'lost' until the 1960s. There is recent archaeological evidence at Nanny Town to suggest that the Maroons originally took to the mountains and lived with (and possibly later absorbed) Taino peoples. There have been some dramatic discoveries of Taino wooden carvings which are now on display at the National Gallery.

Sleeping   **Port Antonio LL** *Trident Villas and Hotel*, PO Box 119, T9932602, F9932960, www.tridentjamaica.com 26 rooms/suites with sea view, MAP, antique furniture, private, tennis, croquet, pools, restaurants, afternoon tea. **L** *Jamaica Palace*, Williams Field, PO Box 277, T9932020, F9932459. 65 rooms, a/c, beach, pool, wheelchair accessible, watersports. On top of a hill overlooking both bays is **L-A** *Bonnie View*, set in its own working plantation, PO Box 82, T9932752, F9932862. Charming rooms, many with excellent views, bar and restaurant, horse riding and other activities also available. **Titchfield Hill**, 5 mins' walk from the town are **C-D** *De Montevin Lodge*, 21 Fort George St, PO Box 85, T9932604. Includes breakfast, shared bath, more expensive rooms have private bath, old Victorian house, restaurant serves set meals, US$8-10, very good value, and **C-E** *Ivanhoe* nearby. Some rooms with shared bath, patio with bay view. These are licensed but not recommended by the Tourist Board. Several nearby private houses also take guests. In the town centre **D** *Triff's Inn*, 1 Bridge St, T9932162, F9932062. Modern, clean, pleasant lounge area, 17 rooms, restaurant, bars.

Port Antonio has a Guest House Association offering good value lodging, excursions & transfers, www.go-jam.com   **Outside Port Antonio LL-L** *Goblin Hill Villas* at San San, reservations c/o 11 East Av, Kingston 10, T9258108, F9256248. 44 rooms in 1 or 2 bedroomed villas, kitchen, restaurant or housekeepers available for shopping and cooking, cheaper with no sea view, tennis, short walk to beach, pool, car hire, bar, TV room. **LL-AL** *Dragon Bay Beach Resort*, PO Box 176, T9938514, F9933284. Attractive resort, villas or rooms on secluded bay, diving, snorkelling, pool, beach volleyball, tennis, good restaurant. **L-B** *Fern Hill Club* at San San, T9937374, F9937373. 31 rooms and spa suites, cottages, all-inclusive available including tours, 4 pools, jacuzzi, restaurant, golf, tennis, windsurfing, sailing, diving, snorkelling, horse riding. At Frenchman's Cove, **LL-L** *Mocking Bird Hill*, PO Box 254, Port Antonio, T9937134, F9937133, www.hotelmockingbirdhill.com 15 mins from town, 5 mins' walk from beach, 10 rooms in Caribbean style villa in 7 acres of parkland, pool, gardens, nature trail, restaurant with Jamaican international and cuisine, Gallery Carriacou and gift shop exhibits owner's art, German, French, English and Spanish spoken. 12 miles west of Port Antonio just after Hope Bay at Rodney Hall, Black Hill, is **C-D** *I-tal Village*, T9130917, F9130987, www.italvillage.com 5 rooms with shared facilities, breakfast included, dinner, fruit and juices all day US$15-20, Jamaican and Italian organic vegetarian food, locally grown, weekly rates available.

Blue Lagoon, Fairy Hill, T9938491. Built over the water, great swimming in the deep blue water, Jamaican food, jerk specialities, fresh lobster, try the blue cocktail, live music and entertainment at weekends, open Mon-Wed 1100-1700, the blue cocktail, live music and *Marina* on a jetty in the harbour, T9933053. Mainly a bar popular with yachting fraternity, but good breakfast, evening meals also served, cold beer. *Coronation Bakery*, near Musgrave Market on West St. Good for cheap patties and spice buns. *Cream World*, good for ice cream, cakes and cheap snacks. *Stop Group Jerk Centre* on the bay out of town towards the Folly. Bar and jerk pork, chicken and fish, also music and dance until late.

Eating

Roof Club , 11 West St, T9933817 (may not work), disco and night spot where everything happens, with sign outside saying 'no drugs, no firecrackers, don't destroy furniture'. Popular with all social classes and types, melting pot of excitement, advisable for women to be escorted or in a group, weekends best nights. *Xtasy Disco*, on other side of road from *Roof Club* on West St, popular weekends, more locals than visitors here.

Nightlife

Tourist office Upstairs in City Centre Plaza on Harbour St, T9933051/2587, F9932117. Quite helpful, have timetables for local buses ("soon come"), which leave regularly when full, but at uncertain hours, from seafront behind Texaco station.

Directory

Between Port Antonio and the Buff Bay area there are several roads into the interior from such places as Hope Bay and Orange Bay. It is worth a detour if you have a car being well off the beaten track. Just to the east of Buff Bay is **Crystal Springs** with beautifully laid out gardens, a variety of fish in the clear waters of the streams, an aviary, a bird sanctuary and masses of orchids. There is a moderately priced restaurant, three cottages to rent (**L**) and camping sites, T9961400. Take any bus between Port Antonio and Kingston (US$0.40, about 45 minutes from Port Antonio), signposted at a turn-off between Orange Bay and Buff Bay (marked Spring Garden on Discover Jamaica road map). About 1½ miles along a flat paved road there is a small **swimming pool** surrounded by palms and flowering tropical plants. An idyllic spot, not busy during the week. Well worth a visit and a good base for exploring the foothills of the Blue Mountains. ■ *0900-1700 daily, US$3.*

Port Antonio to Buff Bay

From Crystal Springs the road goes on to Chepstow and thence to **Claverty Cottage** and **Thompson Gap**; spectacular scenery, waterfalls in the valleys and very remote. It is possible to walk from Thompson Gap over the Blue Mountains via Morces Gap and down to Clydesdale, but this is a full day's trip and only to be undertaken with an experienced local guide and there is a problem of getting transport to meet you at Clydesdale. It is also possible to take a bus for part of the way up the Buff Bay valley and then walk on either to Clydesdale or over the Hardwar Gap to Newcastle. Both very long trips and only for the really fit.

The north coast

The Kingston to Port Maria road (the Junction Road) passes through **Castleton Botanical Gardens** (in a very tranquil setting, well worth a visit, ask Roy Bennett to be your guide if available). The journey takes about two hours and there are plenty of minibuses. **Port Maria** itself is a sleepy and decaying old banana port but not without charm and lots of goats. East of Port Maria in **Robin's Bay** there is a camping and cottage resort on the beach, **AL-C** *Sonrise Beach Retreat* (formerly Strawberry Fields), standard or 'deluxe' cabins (sleep 5-6) with or without bath and tent sites, **F**, bath house, T/F9997169, two miles from village, transport essential or arrange pick-up with resort, meal plans and ecotour packages available, restaurant, nature trails, trampoline, volley ball, ping pong. A few miles to the west of Port Maria lies the attractive looking **D** *Casa Maria* hotel which has seen better days, PO Box 10, T9942323, F9942324, www.nwas.com/casamaria 20 rooms, beach, restaurants, bars.

Noel Coward's homes Close by the hotel is *Firefly*, Noel Coward's Jamaican home, now owned by the Jamaican National Trust. It is evocative of a stylish era and a highlight if you are interested in the theatre or film stars of that period and worth a visit if only for the magnificent view. ■ *0830-1700 daily except Fri, US$10, T9940920*. Noel Coward's other property, *Blue Harbour*, is half a mile from the hotel, and is where he used to entertain film stars, royalty etc. It is now a guest house with accommodation for up to 15 in the two-bedroomed Villa Grande, the one-bedroomed Villa Chica and the four-roomed Villa Rose, all much as Coward left it although there has been some hurricane damage and it is dilapidated. Prices range from **B-C** depending on season and number of guests, fans, saltwater pool, coral beach, good snorkelling and scuba, gardens, lovely views, PO Box 50, Port Maria, St Mary, T9942262.

Ian Fleming's home **Oracabessa** is another old banana port with a half completed marina and *Golden Eye*, the house where **Ian Fleming** wrote all the James Bond books. The house has been recently restored and is now a retreat owned by Chris Blackwell's Island Outpost. The James Bond beach lies in front of the house, small but highly recommended as safe and child friendly. Bars and fish meals available. **LL** *Goldeneye*, three bedroom villa with full time staff. *Goldeneye Village*, has a further six bedrooms, cottage-style, for rent as a whole or individually, all-inclusive. To the west of Oracabessa is Boscobel, where the air strip for Ocho Rios is located. Opposite the air strip are numerous houses for rent.

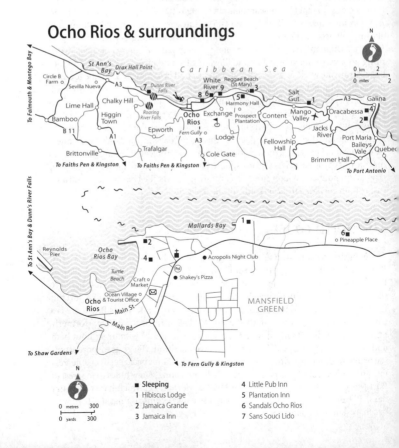

Ocho Rios & surroundings

	Sleeping		
■	1 Hibiscus Lodge	4	Little Pub Inn
	2 Jamaica Grande	5	Plantation Inn
	3 Jamaica Inn	6	Sandals Ocho Rios
		7	Sans Souci Lido

Jamaica

Ocho Rios

On a bay sheltered by reefs and surrounded by coconut groves, sugar cane and fruit plantations, is Ocho Rios. The town has become very popular, with many cruise ships making a stop here. It is 64 miles east of Montego Bay and claims some of the best beaches on the island. The beach in town is safe and well-organized with facilities, 200 yds from Main Street where most of the shops and vehicle hire companies can be found. **Shaw Park Gardens** are an easy walk from the town centre, up the hill on the edge of town. Nice gardens, recommended. ■ *0800-1700 daily, US$4, T9748888.*

Excursions The scenery of the surrounding area is an added attraction. Most spectacular are the beauty spots of **Fern Gully**, a marvel of unspoilt tropical vegetation, **Roaring River Falls**, which has been partially exploited for hydroelectric power, and **Dunn's River Falls**, tumbling into the Caribbean with invigorating salt and freshwater bathing at its foot. ■ *0900-1700 daily. US$6, locker US$1, bath shoes US$5 (rental) but not necessary if you move with care. Getting there: get there early before the coach parties arrive. Five-minute bus ride, US$0.20, from Ocho Rios, or 1-hr drive from Montego Bay (beware of pseudo guides who hang around and take you somewhere totally different, then try to sell you marijuana).* The minibus from Kingston to Ocho Rios costs US$2 and follows a spectacular route, up the gorge of the **Rio Cobre**, then across Mount Diablo. **Faith's Pen**, right on the top, is an enormous collection of huts selling food and drink, great for a stop but you may not get on another bus as they normally pass full. Near Moneague is *Café Aubergine*, T9730527, an upmarket and tasteful restaurant in an 18th-century house, about US$25 per person. The last section of road whizzes round a series of blind corners as you go through Fern Gully. Driving time is one hour 50 minutes once the bus has started. Alternatively, take a minibus from the Texaco petrol station on Da Costa Drive, Ocho Rios, for US$0.30 to Fern Gully. Lots of minibuses for return journey.

Historical attractions in the area include **Sevilla Nueva**, some nine miles to the west, which was where the Spanish first settled in 1509. The ruins of the fort still remain. The site is being investigated by the University of California at Los Angeles and the Spanish Government. Offshore, marine archaeologists, from the Institute of Nautical Archaeology at Texas A & M University, are investigating the **St Ann's Bay** area for sunken ships. Salvaged timbers are believed to have come from two disabled caravels, the *Capitana* and the *Santiago de Palos*, abandoned at Sevilla Nueva probably in 1503 during Columbus' last visit to Jamaica.

There are numerous **plantation tours** available to tourists all along the north coast. Details are widely publicized. Probably the most attractive, informative and certainly most

Jamaica

accessible, is the *Prospect Plantation Tour*, a short distance to the east of Ocho Rios nearly opposite the *Sans Souci Lido*. ■ *1030, 1400, and 1530 daily. US$12. T9742058*. Another, just southwest of St Ann's Bay, is *Circle B*, owned by former senator, Bob Miller. Very good tour of working plantation, recommended. ■ *Welcome drink and sample fruits of Jamaica, lunch can be included, T9722988*. **Harmony Hall** art gallery just east of Ocho Rios is worth a visit. There are frequent exhibitions of paintings and sculpture in a classic gingerbread house, as well as crafts, clothes and other gifts to buy. ■ *T9754222, www.harmonyhall.com, open 1000-1800. There is also an Italian restaurant*, Toscanini's, *open 1000-2200, closed Mon evenings, T9754785*. Wassi Art pottery workshop (Great Pond, T9745044) is delightful; there is a good selection in the salesroom and you can visit each artist. Ask your taxi driver to wait as it is several miles away. If you have your own transport you could combine a visit to Harmony Hall with spending time on **Reggae Beach**, 2km east of White River Bridge in a little cove between Little Bay and Frankfort Bay. A bright sign on the seaward side of the main road marks a somewhat inconspicuous entrance leading to a long, shaded driveway and then a beach hideaway bustling with activity. It is an easy going spot with clean water and a nice beach, but you also get jerk chicken, roasts at festivals, reggae music, dominoes and Red Stripe beer to complete the picture.

West of Ocho Rios is **Mammee beach**, which is beautiful and less crowded than Ocho Rios, though there is no shade.

Sleeping   **LL** *Jamaica Inn*, PO Box 1, T9742514, F9742449, www.jamaicainn.com 45 rooms, seaview, FAP, pool, private beach, elegant, men wear jackets and ties in the evenings, Winston Churchill used to stay here and Noel Coward drank here. **LL** *Plantation Inn*, PO Box 2, T9745601, F9745912. 63 rooms, 15 suites, 2 cottages, pool, beach, tennis, facilities for disabled, watersports, diving, fishing etc.

All-inclusives, usually booked from abroad: **LL-L** *Renaissance Jamaica Grande Resort*, PO Box 100, T9742201/9, F9742289, 720 rooms; **LL** *Sans Souci Lido*, PO Box 103, T9742353, F9941544, SuperClubs, couples only; **LL** *Sandals Ocho Rios Resort & Golf Club*, Main St, PO Box 771, T9745691, F9745700, and **LL** *Sandals Dunn's River Resort & Golf Club*, Mammee Bay, T9720563, F9721611. **LL** *Boscobel Beach*, PO Box 65, T9757330, F9757370, Superclubs, for families; **LL** *Couples*, T9754271, F9754439; **LL** *Club Jamaica Beach Resort* on Turtle Beach, PO Box 342, T97466329, F9746644, in USA T1-800-8182964.

AL-A *Hibiscus Lodge*, 83 Main St, PO Box 52, T9742676, F9741874. 26 rooms in gardens on cliff overlooking sea, manmade beach, pool, jacuzzi, tennis, *Almond Tree* restaurant. **B-C** *Little Pub Inn*, 59 Main St, T9742324, F9745825. Includes breakfast, small, nice rooms, a/c, nightly entertainment, games room, shopping arcade, restaurants and bars. **C** *La Penciano Guest House*, 3 Short Lane, T9745472, run by Lloyd Thomas. Rooms with shared or private bath, fan, TV, in town centre and therefore noisy, but clean and safe, friendly, helpful, bar open Fri and Sat night has nice view over Ocho Rios. About 1 mile from town centre, you can camp at Milford Falls, **F**, right by the waterfall, take Kingston road out of Ocho Rios, turn right at sign to Shaw Park Gardens then fork left up Milford Rd, stop at *George Barnes' shop* on right, he will take you there and provide you with information, food and drink, he has a tent or a rustic cabin with 1 bed to rent, good place to get away from city hustle.

Eating   On Main Street there are lots of restaurants offering Jamaican, international, seafood cuisine, including *The Almond Tree*, restaurant at the *Hibiscus Lodge*, T9742813. *The Lobsterpot*, Chinese, US$12-15 for lobster supper. *Jerk Pork*, same price for barbecued pork, fish or chicken. *Shakey's Pizza*, Main St. Nice bar and patio, fast, friendly service, smallest pizza from US$5.50. *Little Pub*, 59 Main St. Jamaican food and entertainment. *Bill's Place* on Main St.

Nightlife   The *Lion's Den* is a friendly club frequented by Rastafarians; rooms available, good food, clean. There is much fashionable nightlife in and around Ocho Rios. *Amnesia Night Club*, 70 Main St, T9742633. *The Acropolis* nightclub is lively and fairly safe.

Tourist office *Ocean Village*, Shopping Centre, T9742582/3. **Cycling:** *Blue Mountain Bicycle Tours*, Main St, T9747075, F9740635, bmtours@infochan.com, tours include an 18-mile downhill trip through the forest to a waterfall, no pedalling, food and drink and transfers included, don't expect much from the bikes.

Directory

Continuing west along the coast is **Runaway Bay**, an attractive and friendly resort. It is named for the Spanish governor Ysasi, who left quickly for Cuba in a canoe when he saw the English coming. Only five miles away is **Discovery Bay** where Columbus made his first landing. The **Columbus Park**, an outdoor museum, has exhibits and relics of Jamaican history. From Runaway Bay, the Runaway Caves can be visited where there is an underground lake in the Green Grotto. However, the place is littered with beer bottles; not recommended. ■ *0900-1700*. Among the hotels in this area is the **A** *Runaway Bay HEART Hotel*, PO Box 98, T9732671, F9732693, runaway.heart@cwjamaica.com, which has an adjoining hotel training centre and overlooks a golf course. The **LL** *Club Ambiance*, T9732066, F9732067, has been described as adequate for fine weather but lacking in indoor facilities when it rains. Golf is available at Runaway Bay Golf Club. There are several **LL** all-inclusive resorts here too, including *Breezes Runaway Bay* (SuperClubs, for couples and singles, PO Box 58, Runaway Bay, T9732436, F9732352).

West to Falmouth

Falmouth is a charming small town about 20 miles east of Montego Bay. It is the best example of a Georgian town and the Jamaica National Heritage Trust has declared the whole town a National Monument. It has a fine colonial court house, a church, some 18th-century houses with wrought iron balconies, and Antonio's, a famous place to buy beach shirts. There is good fishing (tarpon and kingfish) at the mouth of the Martha Brae, near Falmouth, and no licence is required. It is possible to go rafting from **Martha Brae** village. Expert rafters guide the craft very gently for the one-hour trip to the coast. ■ *US$36 from Montego Bay includes 2-person raft, lunch and transfers, 0900-1600, or take local bus from Montego Bay to Falmouth, US$0.50, hitchhike or walk 6 miles to upper station; end station is about 3 miles from Falmouth.* **Jamaica Swamp Safaris** is a crocodile farm where you can see lazy crocodiles with equally laid back guides. Bar and restaurant. Two James Bond films were made here. ■ *US$6 for adults.* Some 10 miles inland is the 18th-century plantation guest house of **Good Hope** amongst coconut palms. Deluxe accommodation in the superb setting of a working plantation, as well as day tours and horse riding – some of the best riding in Jamaica – and its own beach on the coast. ■ *Daily 1200-1600. US$10. T9543289.*

Falmouth

One and a half miles east of Falmouth is one of Jamaica's little known but exciting attractions, a bioluminescent lagoon, known locally as the **Luminous Lagoon**, where the water comes alive at night with sparkling blue-green lights from marine micro-organisms called dinaflagellates. The lagoon is said to be the most active bioluminescent lake in the world. Head for **AL-A** *Fisherman's Inn*, T9543427/ 9544078 (rooms with two single beds or two double beds), on the main road, heading to St Ann, where you can have an excellent seafood sunset dinner on the pool deck followed by a 25-minute tour on the lake. The dark, moonless night, a local guide with typical Jamaican sense of humour, and a small power launch, all of which can be booked through *Fisherman's Inn*, is all that is required. Less than five minutes out, the pitch-black water behind the boat begins to illuminate leaving a blue-green-white trail in its wake. The boat comes to a halt and streaks of light flash intermittently in every direction, like from darting fireflies, caused by small fry jumping out of the water. It's also possible to see larger fish tunnelling through the water carrying a wake of luminescence with them.

Collect some of the water from the lagoon in your hand and shake it to see it sparkle for several seconds

This is a strange and virtually uninhabited area to the south of Falmouth and to the southwest of Montego Bay. It consists of a seemingly endless succession of high bumps made of limestone rock. The tourist office and hotels in Montego Bay organize day trips (about US$50) to **Maroon Town** and **Accompong**, the headquarters

Cockpit Country

Jamaica

of the Maroons who live in the Cockpit Country area. An annual festival is held here, to commemorate the treaty with the British giving the Maroons lands and autonomy, at the beginning of January with traditional music and dance, T9524546, Kenneth Watson. Older locals can accurately describe what happened at the last battle between the Maroons and the British forces. Ask to see the **'Wondrous Caves'** at Elderslie near Accompong. If you have a car take the road on the east side of the Cockpit Country from Duncans (near Falmouth) to Clark's Town. From there the road deteriorates to a track, impassable after a few miles even for four-wheel drive vehicles, to **Barbecue Bottom** and on to Albert Town. The views from Barbecue Bottom are truly spectacular (the track is high above the Bottom) and this is wonderful birding country. If you wish to walk in the Cockpit Country make your way, either by car or on foot (no public transport), to the **Windsor Caves** due south of Falmouth. They are full of bats which make a spectacular mass exit from the caves at dusk. There are local guides to hand. The underground rivers in the caves (as elsewhere in much of Jamaica) run for miles, but are only for the experienced and properly equipped potholer. There is a locally published book called *Jamaica Underground*; many caves and good walks in the area. For caving, contact Mike Schwartz of *Windsor Great House*, T9973832, windsor@cwjamaica.com where there is rustic accommodation, T9973832, F9542566. It is possible to walk from the Windsor Caves across the middle of the Cockpit Country to Troy on the south side (about eight hours). It is essential to have a local guide and to make a preliminary trip to the Windsor Caves to engage him. Convince yourself that he really does know the way because these days this crossing is very rarely made even by the locals. It is also vastly preferable to be met with transport at Troy because you will still be in a pretty remote area. Sun Venture Tours offers tailor made tours of the Cockpit Country Crossing (Troy to Windsor the preferred route).

Montego Bay

Population: 92,000 *About 120 miles from Kingston, situated on the northwest coast, is Montego Bay, Jamaica's principal tourist centre with all possible watersport amenities. Known familiarly as Mo' Bay, it has superb natural features, sunshine most of the year round, a beautiful coastline with miles of white sand, deep blue water never too cold for bathing and gentle winds which make sailing a favourite sport. Doctor's Cave is the social centre of beach life. Gloucester Avenue, by Doctor's Cave, is one of the busiest streets for tourists, lined with duty-free shops, souvenir arcades, hotels and restaurants. In 2000, Montego Bay accepted an invitation to be twinned with another internationally famous, sprawling tourist resort: Varadero in Cuba.*

Ins & outs

Getting there The **Donald Sangster international airport** is only 2 miles from the town centre. Taxi from
See page 275 for airport to town US$7 or 20-min walk airport to Doctor's Cave. JUTA and JCAL are licensed
further details taxis.

Getting around The **Soon Come Shuttle** bus is operated on 2 routes: Central Route (every 15 mins) and Eastern Route (every 45 mins) stopping at hotels and some shops, tokens (US$1) purchased at hotels and special outlets, costs 2 tokens on Eastern Route, 1 on Central Route 1000-2400.

Sights

Forts & Of interest to the sightseer are the remaining battery, cannons and powder magazine
churches of an old British fort, **Fort Montego**, with landscaped gardens and crafts market, free, and the 18th-century church of **St James** in Montego Bay, built in 1778 and restored after earthquake damage in 1957. There are a few Georgian buildings, such

as the *Town House Restaurant*, 16 Church Street (good local art gallery next door), and the Georgian Court at the corner of Union and Orange Streets. The centre of town is **Sam Sharpe Square**, named after the slave who led a rebellion in 1831-2. The Burchell Memorial Church, established in 1824 by the Baptist missionary, Thomas Burchell, was where Samuel Sharpe served as a deacon.

Doctor's Cave for the underwater coral gardens, so clear that they can be seen with-   **Beaches**
out effort from glass-bottomed boats. ■ *US$1.70, children under 12 half price. 0900-1800 daily*. Doctor's Cave is the beach for relaxed sunbathing, while **Cornwall** is more sun 'n' fun, or beach 'n' boogie, with beach contests etc. ■ *US$1. 0900-1700 daily*. The **Walter Fletcher** beach has been converted to the **Aqua Sol** theme park, the latest addition to the list of attractions, offering rides and sports facilities. **Margueritaville** (see Nightlife, below) offers a mix of bar, restaurant, rides, slides and various forms of entertainment. Scuba diving can be arranged through about a dozen operators, several of which have outlets at more than one hotel. A single dive costs about US$45, a snorkelling trip US$25.

If you are staying in town, rather than at the hotel strip, there are beaches close by, either public ones with no services or private (US$0.50-2.00) with food, drinks, tennis, boat hire, snorkelling, shower, changing rooms etc. Walk from the traffic circle in the middle of town towards the hotels and the beach will be on your left. Mosquitoes can be a problem at certain times of the year or when the drains need cleaning out. Take repellent and coils.

Excursions

Out of town, to the east, are the great houses of **Rose Hall** and **Greenwood**. The latter was built by the forefathers of the poet, Elizabeth Barrett Browning, in 1780-1800. It has a colourful avenue of bougainvillea and mimosa and a panoramic view over the coast from the verandah. ■ *0900-1800 daily, US$10*. Rose Hall was started 10 years earlier, in 1770, by John Palmer. A lively legend of witchcraft surrounds the wife of one of his descendants, Anne Palmer. ■ *US$15 adults. 0900-1800 daily, Rose Hall Beach Club US$55 includes lunch, drinks, entertainment, watersports, 1000-1730 daily*.

Inland, seven miles from Montego Bay off the Maroon Town road (turn off east half a mile before the village of Johns Hall), is the recommended **C-F** *Orange River Lodge*, an old Great House overlooking the **Orange River Valley**, which has guest rooms, hostel accommodation in bunk beds, and camping, bring own tent, beautiful location, excellent food, friendly staff, excursions arranged, also shuttle service to Montego Bay. Good walking in the area, you can swim in the river or go canoeing and bird watching is good, T9792688 at Lodge or PO Box 822, 34 Fort Street, Montego Bay, T9527208, F9526241. Southeast of Montego Bay is the Taino rock carving at **Kempshot**, while to the southwest is the bird sanctuary at **Anchovy**: **Rocklands Feeding Station**, don't miss this, the doctor bird humming birds will even perch on your finger, knowledgeable guides. ■ *US$8.50, 1400-1700 daily, but members of bird watching societies will be admitted any time. Children under five are not admitted*. The road to Anchovy is too rough for ordinary cars. Three miles to the west of Anchovy is **Lethe**, the starting point for rafting down the Great River. Ten miles from Montego Bay on the Savanna-La-Mar road is the **Montpelier Great House**, on the site of the old Montpelier sugar factory which was destroyed during the 1831 rebellion, call Pat Ottey, T9524299, for bed and breakfast, **E-F**, children welcome. South of Anchovy, about 25 miles from Montego Bay, is **Seaford Town**, which was settled by Germans in the 1830s. Only about 200 of their descendants survive. Write to Francis Friesen, Lamb's River Post Office.

Lucea is a charming spot on the north coast where the *Tamarind Lodge* serves excellent Jamaican food. Visit the Rusea School, endowed by a refugee Frenchman in the 18th century, in a lovely location but badly damaged by Hurricane Gilbert.

Between here and Montego Bay (bus, US$0.88) is **Tryall**, with one of the best (and certainly the most expensive) golf courses on the island (see above, Sport). **LL** *Tryall Golf Tennis and Beach Club*, T9565600/5, F9565673, expensive, deluxe villas, one to two bedrooms. Continuing around the island's west end, the road passes through **Green Island** before reaching Negril (29 miles from Lucea). There are several pretty fishing villages between Lucea and Green Island, such as Cousins Cove, with small

Montego Bay

To Lucea & Negril

■ **Sleeping**
1 Breezes
2 Coral Cliff
3 El Greco
4 Ocean View Guest House
5 Sandals Inn

● **Eating**
1 Akbar
2 Greenhouse
3 Pelican Lounge
4 Marguerite's & Margueritavilla
5 Shakey's Pizza

6 Toby Inn
7 Town House

N

Not to scale

Jamaica

guest houses and seaside cottages for rent. On route to Negril from Montego Bay. beware of heavy construction work as the government has embarked on an ambitious road project, the Northern Jamaica Highway, which promises much-improved roadways and travel time along the north coast. In the meantime motorists will to put up with roads which are unpaved, poorly lit and marked detours, until the project's schedule completion in early 2002.

Essentials

In the super-luxury range are **LL** *Round Hill Hotel and Villas*, 10 mins west of Montego Bay on 98-acre peninsula, T9567050, www.roundhilljamaica.com Originally a coconut and pineapple plantation, it opened in the 1950s with the help of Noel Coward, popular with the rich and famous, celebrity owners include Paul McCartney, Ralph Lauren, Lord Rothermere. **LL** *Half Moon Golf, Tennis and Beach Club*, on 400 acres adjoining beach, T9532615, www. halfmoon.com.jm 340 rooms and 5-7 bedroomed villas with staff, golf, tennis, riding stables, squash, fitness centre, spa, theatre etc. **LL-L** *Coyaba Beach Resort and Club*, T9539150, F9532244, coyaba@n5.com.jm 50 rooms and suites, gardens, pool, jacuzzi, private dock, tennis, fitness room, watersports, hammocks on the shore, family-owned, 'elegantly relaxed'.

All-inclusives Several large, lavish resorts, including a 523-room **LL-L** *Holiday Inn Sunspree*, while Sandals have 3 all-inclusive resorts, **LL** *Sandals Inn*, **LL** *Sandals Montego Bay* and **LL** *Sandals Royal Caribbean*. SuperClubs have **LL** *Breezes Montego Bay* on Doctor's Cave Beach.

L-A *Cariblue* , Ironshore, T9532180, www.caribluehotel.com A dedicated dive resort, lots of packages, 20 a/c rooms, pool, deep sea fishing, sailing, snorkelling, windsurfing, glass bottom boats, day sails. **A-B** *Coral Cliff*, 365 Gloucester Av, T9524130, www.montegobay-jamaica.com/coralcliff Remodelled to allow slot machines, rooms variable, food reasonable, bar, pool and friendly service. **B** *The Guest House*, 29 Gloucester Av, T9523121, F9793176. Beautiful house with wide balcony overlooking sunset in the bay, get room at back to avoid traffic noise, includes huge nutritious breakfast, run by Irish and Canadian, very friendly. **AL-A** *Montego Bay Club*, Gloucester Av, T9524310, F9524639. Dominant 12-storey apartment hotel in centre of tourist area overlooking Doctor's Cave Beach, pool, tennis. There is a YMCA at Mount Salem with sports facilities available to members. **C-D** *Ocean View Guest House*, 26 Sunset Blvd, T9522662. 10 mins' easy walk from the airport, cheaper without a/c, many rooms overlook the bay, all clean, with bath, back-breaking mattresses, no advance bookings, but on arrival, ask tourist board to phone the hotel who will arrange free transport from the airport. **E** *Ridgeway Guest House*, 34 Queen's Drive, PO Box 1237, T9522709, F9791740. 5 mins' walk from airport, with bath and fan, friendly, clean, family atmosphere.

Self-catering Try **AL** *El Greco*, Queens Drive, PO Box 1624, T9406116, F9406115, www.montego-bay-jamaica.com/jhta/elgreco/ 64 1-bedroom and 32 2-bedroom suites on hillside overlooking bay, direct elevator access to Gloucester Av and Doctor's Cave Beach, grocery store, pool, beach towels, tennis, laundry, cook and nanny on request.

Service at restaurants can be begrudging but the food is excellent. On the way into town from the airport there are several reasonably-priced restaurants. Recommended is the *Pork Pit* next to *The Guest House*, 27 Gloucester Av, T9521046. Jerk chicken, pork and ribs sold by weight, service basic, and the *Toby Inn*, very good for cheap barbecued chicken and pork, cheap drinks, live band, romantic atmosphere. *Baba Joe's* (Barbara Joe's), Kent Av, near airport on way to Whitehouse Village, just past Sandals. Excellent fish, local style, about US$8 for meal with beer. *Orlan Caribe Vegetarian Restaurant*, 71 Barnett St. Tidy, comfortable, low prices, rather out of the way, open 1000-1600, vegetarian restaurant. The *Pelican*, Gloucester Av, T9523171. Excellent breakfasts, good value. *Akbar*, Gloucester Av, T9790113. *Patsy's Place*, 100 m from *The Guest House*. Small, good local dishes, excellent curried goat, cheap. *Walter's Bar and Grill*, 39 Gloucester Av, T9529391. Local food, nice garden, good value. *The Greenhouse*, T9527838, opposite St James Place shopping arcade. Good food, and inexpensive, Jamaican/American. *Marguerite's*, T9524777, on the seafront, 2 restaurants, one posh with a/c and *Margueritaville*

Sleeping
There are over 40 hotels, guest houses & apartment hotels listed by the tourist board & many more which are not

Eating
Most restaurants are happy for guests to bring wine & provide chillers & glasses. Rum is cheaper here than at airport duty free shops

Jamaica

Warnings

Security *Constant importuning is a major problem downtown and tourists are constantly hassled and hustled. Knife attacks and other muggings by thieves have been reported to us. Avoid the area northeast of Union Street. The unfortunate consequence of this is that tourists avoid the town centre and stay in the tourist strip, where the selling is not unpleasant, or, worse, stay confined to the all-inclusive resorts. If you do go into town, do not be fooled by those who 'just want to talk', nor by 'do you recognize me? Its Tony from the hotel'. Answer, 'which hotel?'*

Health *St James parish, which includes Montego Bay, has the highest incidence of AIDS in the country, with 198 cases per 100,000 population, compared with the national average of 83 per 100,000.*

next door on a patio sports bar and grill. *Le Chalet*, 32 Gloucester Av, T9525240. Clean, friendly, Chinese, Jamaican (good curried goat), European menu at a quarter of the price of neighbouring restaurants, free hotel transfers. *Town House*, 16 Church St (see above), T9522660. Mildly pungent, tasty stuffed lobster US$30, other dishes also good, US$12.50-27. *Natives Jerk Centre*, Market St. Garden, outside bar, jerk chicken or pork, fish dishes with rice 'n' peas, about US$7 for meal with beer. *Smokey Joe's*, St James St, just beyond Woolworths towards Courts. Good local restaurant, about US$6 for soup, main course, beer.

Nightlife *Margueritaville Caribbean Bar & Grill*, Gloucester Av, T9524777. Now quite an institution, very popular, 52 flavours of Margaritas and 32 oz 'bong of beer', sport on big TVs, Nintendo and kids' menu, waterslide from roof to sea, DJ at night, open daily from 1000, cover charge US$9 Fri-Sat. Disco on Cornwall Beach with volleyball on beach at night. Lots of hotels have discos and clubs.

Transport **Air** The **Donald Sangster international airport** is *Air Jamaica*'s regional hub and there are good connections with lots of airlines landing here. For those landing here who want to go to Kingston, there is a transfer service by Martins minibus which takes 5 hrs. It is also possible to get to the **Norman Manley airport**, Kingston, by taking the minibus from the town centre to Pechon Street, Kingston, from where the airport buses leave; US$4.50, 3 hrs. Do not buy at the airport duty free shop; everything is half the price at ordinary shops in town.

Road **Bicycle** rentals through *Montego Bike Rentals*, T9524984, and *Tropic Ride Car & Bike Rental*, T9527096.

Bus There is no need to take the expensive tourist buses, except that the regular buses get crowded. They depart when full. The regular buses are fast, very frequent and cheap, about US$2 from Montego Bay to Negril with a 30-second transfer in Lucea. There are more buses Montego Bay-Lucea than Lucea-Negril, which often causes a bottleneck. Buses from Kingston depart from Pechon Street, near the railway station, roughly every hour from 0600 to 1500, US$2.80. It is possible to get to Montego Bay from Port Antonio all along the north coast, a scenic journey involving changes in Annotto Bay (then shared taxi, US$1 per person, mad rush to squeeze into clapped-out Ladas, the locals give no quarter to slow tourists), Port Maria US$1, and Ocho Rios. Ochos Rios-Montego Bay by bus takes 2 hrs, US$1.50. The bus station for Kingston and Ocho Rios is behind Courts (Electrical). The bus station for Negril is off Barnett Street (beware pickpockets).

Taxi *JUTA* are usually found outside hotels. *JCAL*, T952-7574/8277, charges US$10 to Gloucester Av from *Sandals Montego Bay*, US$15 from *Wyndham*. A taxi Lucea-Negril costs about US$20. *UTAS Tours*, T9523820, F9793465, offer 12-hr day trip to Kingston via Dunns River Falls and Ocho Rios, US$60 for driver in a/c car; also 9-hr tour to Negril, US$21, with sunset drink at *Rick's Café*, Negril.

Directory **Tourist office** Cornwall Beach, T9524425.

Negril

Negril, on a seven-mile stretch of pure white sand on the west end of the island, is far less formal than other tourist spots but is still a one-industry town. The town is at the south end of Long Bay; at the north is the smaller Bloody Bay, where whalers used to carve up their catch. The Negril Area Environmental Protection Trust (NEPT) hopes to have the coastal area declared a national marine park and a grant has been awarded by the European Union (for information T9574473). The main part of the town has resorts and beaches but no snorkelling and you have to take a boat. In the West End of the village are beautiful cliffs and many fine caves, with great snorkelling but no beaches. In between is an area with neither beaches nor cliffs. Behind the bay is the Great Morass, which is being drained for development but remains a protected area as a natural wetland.

Watersports are a particular attraction and there are facilities for tennis and riding at *Babo's Horseback Riding Stable* and *Country Western Riding Stables*, ■ *US$30-35. 0800-1700 daily*. There is a dive shop at *Hedonism II*, T9574200, free for guests, and *Sundivers Negril*, a PADI five-star facility at *Poinciana Beach Resort*, diving lessons 0900 and 1200, resort course US$60, guided boat dives three times daily, US$30 single tank, US$45 for two tanks (also at *Rock Cliff Resort*). *Negril Scuba Centre* is at *Negril Beach Club* (T9574425, neg.scuba.centre@toj.com), while there are dive operations at *Swept Away* and *Sandals*.

Beaches & sports
There is clothes optional bathing at certain hotels, which is still quite rare in the Caribbean

By the *Poinciana Beach Resort* is the **Anancy Park** with boating lake, minigolf, go-karts, fishing pond, nature trail, video arcade and historical exhibitions. ■ *US$1-3. Tue-Sun 1300-2200*.

Hawkers ('higglers') are annoying and reported to be worse than at Montego Bay. They will interrupt whatever you are doing to push their drugs, hair braiding, aloe etc. Politely decline whatever they are offering (if you do not want it), they do not want to be shrugged off or ignored, but neither do they want to hold a long conversation with you. Fruit is readily available although not ready to eat; ask the vendor to cut it up and put it in a bag for you. To avoid the worst of the higglers go to the end of the beach near the crafts market where there are no stalls or bars. There are toilets and showers (US$0.30).

Inland, up in the hills, a golf course has been built: the *Negril Hills Golf Club* (T9574638, F9570222) is an 18-hole, Par 72, 6,333 yd course, with clubhouse, restaurant, pro shop and tennis.

All-inclusives **LL** *Hedonism II*, PO Box 25, T9575200, F9575289. 280-room all-inclusive adult resort. **LL** *Grand Lido Negril*, SuperClubs resort at south end of Bloody Bay, couples only, clothes optional. **LL** *Sandals Negril*. Sandals also has **LL** *Beaches Negril*. **LL** *Swept Away*, T9574061, F9574060. **LL-A** *Foote Prints on the Sands*, www.footeprintsjamaica.com **LL** *Poinciana Beach Resort*, T9575100, F9575229. Children's programmes, free pass to the Anancy Family Fun and Nature Park opposite.

Sleeping
A local rule is that no hotel should be taller than the tallest palm tree to minimize the visual & environmental impact of tourism

LL-E *Firefly Beach Cottages*, Norman Manley Blvd, on the beach and therefore not very private, T9574358, F9573447. From a basic cabin for 2, to studios, or 1-3 bedroomed cottages, or luxury villa, prices reduced in summer, gymnasium, minimum 1 week rental in winter, 3 nights in summer. **L-AL** *Negril Gardens Hotel*, T9574408, F9574374. 64 suites with balconies, gardenside or beach, a/c, TV, good for families. **L-AL** *Charela Inn*, on the beach, T957-4648, F9574414. 49 rooms, family owned and run, kayaks, sunfish, sailboards, restaurant, bar. **L-AL** *Negril Cabins*, Norman Manley Blvd, on Bloody Bay, across the road from the beach, T9575350, F9575381. 70 rooms in cabins on stilts, or more expensive rooms, pool, swim-up bar, private beach, restaurant, piano bar, beach parties, children's programme, security guards keep away 'higglers'.

Jamaica

Hotels to the west of centre, about 10-20 mins' walk, are better for mixing with locals

L-A *Rockhouse*, West End Road, T/F9574373, www.rockhousehotel.com On cliffs at Pristine Cove, just north of *Rick's Café*, 11 octagonal villas by the sea with fans, indoor bathrooms, outdoor showers, built of timber, stone and thatch, or 17 studios in thatched blocks in the garden, cliff-edge pool, restaurant above the water serving 'new Jamaican cuisine', open 0700-2300, no beach but steps down to sea, snorkelling and kayak rental, quiet, restful, Australian-owned, no children under 12 because of potentially dangerous cliffs. **AL-B** *Mariner's Inn and Diving Resort*, West End, T9570393, F9570391. On cliffs, 52 rooms, PADI and NAUI instructors for diving, kayaking, riding, volleyball. **A-C** *Ocean Edge Resort*, also on cliffs, T9574362, F9570086. 30 rooms. **A-C** *Heart Beat*, T9574329, heartbeat@cwjamaica.com, on West End cliffs. 9 rooms, 1, 2, or 3-bed cottages and efficiencies, run by Valerie Brewis, cafés and music nearby, great sunset watching from veranda. **C** *Emerald Hotel*, Westland Mountain Rd, T9574814, F9570708. Chalets, small pool, includes breakfast, TV, gardens with hammocks, short walk to beach. **C-E** *Tigress 1*, West End Rd. Cheaper rooms with fan, no hot water, shared bathrooms, higher priced rooms with a/c, hot water, private bath, all with kitchen facilities, good security, bar and pool in nice gardens, 20 mins' walk to beach and walking distance from town centre, friendly, clean, well-maintained, lots of repeat business. Accommodation **D** is available at the Yacht Club, West End Rd, T9995732. **D-F** *Lighthouse Park* on Negril's cliffs. Campsite, cabins, tent site.

The northern end is the more expensive part of town, but there are a few cheap cabins: **E** *Roots Bamboo* is very neat. **F** *Coconut International*, on the beach. Basic cabin, dirty, no fan. Next door is *Gloria's Sunset*, Jamaican family-run, clean, friendly, helpful, security guards at night, variety of accommodation, bar, restaurant. This whole beach is lined with clubs and is noisy. None of the cabins has any services, nor do they provide blankets, but they are right on the beach. When choosing a cabin check to see whether it has a fan, whether there is a mesh or screen to keep out mosquitoes (if not, buy 'Destroyers', 8-hr incense to keep bugs away) and whether it looks safe (many get broken into). Locals living along the beach will often let you camp on their property.

Eating *Rick's Café*, the 'trendy' place to watch the sunset, full ocean view from cliff top setting but pricey with it, Red Stripe beer or cocktail US$3, plastic bead money used, full restaurant next door, expensive, with even better view of sunset. *Cool Runnings*, with a chef/owner, is also recommended. *The Office*, on the beach. Open 24 hrs, provides a good choice of Jamaican food, reasonably priced and friendly service, a good place to meet the locals. *The Pickled Parrot* , West End Road, T9574864, on the cliffs, call for free pick-up. Serves Mexican, Jamaican and American food, large portions, also reached by snorkelling and catamaran cruises with dancing and limbo competitions en route, entertainment includes cliff diving, rope swing and waterslide over the rocks into the sea, US$1, unless you are on a tour. *Juicy J*, T9574213. Jamaican restaurant and bar. *Cosmo's*, Norman Manley Blvd, T9574784.

Jamaica

Negril

Eating cheaply is difficult but not impossible. The native restaurant-food stalls are good and relatively cheap; the local patties are delicious. Street hawkers will sell you jerk chicken for US$4-5, which is good but barely enough to whet your appetite. *The Bread Basket*, next to the banks at the mall in town is recommended, but even better is the *Fisherman's Club* supermarket, just off the beach in the main part of town near *Pete's Seafood*, which is a restaurant as well as a market and serves good local, filling meals for about US$4.

Nightlife Live reggae shows in outdoor venues most nights, featuring local and well known stars. Entrance is usually US$5-7, good fun, lively atmosphere, very popular. Nice bars are located along the beach, usually with music, unnamed bar next to *Coconut International* recommended, friendly service. For beautiful surroundings try the bar at the *Rock Cliff Hotel* on the West End Rd, friendly barman who mixes great fruit punches and cocktails. *Compulsion Disco*, Shop 24, Negril Plaza, T9574735.

Shopping Some of the all-inclusive hotels will take you on shopping trips, stopping at Times Square, for jewellery, perfume and gift shops. The mall in downtown Negril offers much the same but at slightly higher prices. The Craft Market is overwhelming, with 200 stalls of sarongs and wood carvings, not much in the way of variety, everyone wants your attention.

Transport Licensed, unmetered taxis have red license plates with the designation, PP before the numbers. Avoid unlicensed taxis. Local buses operate between Negril and Montego Bay stopping frequently. JUTA operated tour buses typically charge US$20 per person with a minimum charge US$60 per trip (1 passenger only) between Montego Bay and Negril. From the Donald Sangster airport minibuses run to Negril; you must bargain with the driver to get the fare to US$5-7. Lots of companies do bike rental. Gasoline is more than US$3 per gallon.

Directory **Banks** Two banks *National Commercial Bank* and *Nova Scotia* and several cambios in town including one at the *Hi-lo- Supermarket*. **Tourist office** In Coral Seas Plaza, T9574243.

The south coast

Savanna-La-Mar About 18 miles east of Negril, on the coast, is Savanna-la-Mar, a busy, commercial town with shopping, banks and so on, but no major attractions for tourists. It does not have a good beach, nor good quality restaurants and accommodation. Regular concerts are held at the remodelled St Joseph's Catholic Church, T9552648. Talented local musicians play under the auspices of Father Sean Lavery, formerly a professor of music at Dublin University, recommended. It can easily be reached by minibus from Negril and there are hourly buses from Montego Bay (US$2). The Frome sugar refinery, five miles north of Savanna-la-Mar, will often allow visitors to tour their facilities during sugar cane season (generally November-June). Another interesting and unusual outing in this part of Jamaica is to the six-mile long **Roaring River** and the **Ital Herbs and Spice Farm**, two miles north of Petersfield, from where it is remarkably well signposted. The farm, owned by an American, Ed Kritzler, employs organic methods. There is a cave at Roaring River and the farm is about half a mile further on. It is a very scenic area with interesting walks and tumbling streams suitable for bathing. A good restaurant serves fish and vegetable dishes at the Farm, best to order lunch before exploring. Totally basic accommodation in a hut available, popular but it is suggested you look before you book.

Bluefields Outside Savanna-la-Mar, the main south coast road (A2) passes by Paradise Plantation, a huge private estate with miles of frontage on **Bluefields Bay**, a wide protected anchorage with unspoiled reefs and wetlands teeming with birds. Just after Paradise, you come to Ferris Crossroads, where the A2 meets up with the B8 road, a well-maintained north-south connection and about 40 minutes' drive to Montego Bay via Whithorn and Anchovy. For the next four miles the A2 hugs the coast along a

Jamaica

beautiful stretch of road to Bluefields, where there is a lovely white sand beach mainly used by local Jamaicans and guests of the upmarket *Villas on Bluefields Bay*. There is no mass tourism either in Bluefields or in the adjacent village of **Belmont**, where plenty of reggae is always playing at the numerous fishermen's bars.

Sleeping In Belmont there are a few expatriate homes which might sometimes be available for rent: *Oristano*, the oldest home in west Jamaica, dating back to the 1700s, owned by the Hon William Fielding, an Englishman who does beautiful drawings of the Jamaican greathouses, PO Box 1, Bluefields, Westmoreland Parish. **A-D** *Ashton Great House*, higher up hillside, T/F9652036. Pool, restaurant, free ride from Bluefields, 24 rooms. **C-D** *Casa Marina*, in Cave, 2 miles from Bluefields. Friendly owner Manley Wallace, restaurant, small, private pier and gazebo.

East of Bluefields The south coast is known as the best part of Jamaica for deep sea fishing and boat trips go out from Belmont to the reefs or to off-shore banks. Snorkelling is also good because the sea is almost always very calm in the morning. The **Bluefields Great House**, now privately owned, was the place where Philip Gosse lived in the 1830s when he wrote his famous book, *Birds of Jamaica*, and reportedly contains the first breadfruit tree planted in Jamaica by Captain Bligh after his expedition to the South Pacific. The next six miles of coast southeast of Bluefields is one of the most beautiful, unspoiled coasts in Jamaica, but a 258-room *Sandals South Coast* resort is being built at **Auchindown**. However, much of the land is being left untouched on the resort's property. A bird sanctuary has been designated and a section of beach set aside as a turtle nesting area. Just beyond here, **B** *Natania's*, a guest house and seafood restaurant at Little Culloden, Whitehouse, has been praised. It is on the sea and has eight rooms (16 beds), food extra but good and at reasonable prices. The owner is Peter Probst. Transport from Montego Bay can be arranged, as also local tours, deep sea fishing and watersports.

The A2 road passes through Scotts Cove, where you leave Westmoreland and enter the parish of St Elizabeth. It proceeds to the town of Black River, travelling inland from there to Middle Quarters, YS Falls and Bamboo Avenue, after which it ascends to the old hill station of Mandeville.

Black River

Black River is one of the oldest towns in Jamaica. It had its heyday in the 18th century when it was the main exporting harbour for logwood dyes. The first car imported into Jamaica was landed here. Along the shore are some fine early 19th-century mansions, some of which are being restored.

At Black River, you can go by boat from across the bridge up the lower stretches of the Black River, the longest river in Jamaica. ■ *Daily 0900, 1100, 1230, 1400, 1600, US$15 per person, drinks included, 10 miles, 1½-2 hrs, 3 boats, 25 people per boat.* You should see crocodiles (called alligators in Jamaica, most likely at midday when they bask on the river banks) and plenty of birdlife in beautifully tranquil surroundings with a very knowledgeable guide. Contact *South Coast Safaris*, run by Charles Swaby in Black River, T9620220, F9652086. If you want to avoid large tour parties, go with a local, whose boats are through the fish market. The boats are smaller, open, slower, quieter and go further up river, which means you see more. They stop at a 'countryside bar' rather than the one the tour companies use. ■ *The trip takes about 2 hrs and costs US$27 for 2 including boatman and guide.*

Sleeping **D-E** *Waterloo Guest House*, in a Georgian building (the first house in Jamaica with electric light). Old rooms in the main house, or more expensive in the new annex, all with showers, very good restaurant (lobster in season). Two miles east of Black River is the **D** *Port of Call Hotel*, 136 Crane Rd, T9652360. A bit spartan but on the sea, a/c, pool. **D** *Bridge House Inn*, Crane Rd, T9652361, F2652081. 14 rooms, a/c, fan, kitchen facilities, shady garden with

Jamaica

hammocks leads down to beach, good Jamaican food, US$8-10 for a meal, staff friendly, bar, TV, lounge, ask for odd numbered room at front to avoid noise from club on the beach.

Bayside, near bridge. Excellent steamed fish with rice and peas for US$6, usually all gone by 1300. *Caribbe*, near bus station. Very good steamed fish and curried goat for US$6 with beer. *Superbus*, an old bus near bus station. Good cheap food, eg fried chicken with trimmings and beer for US$3. *Riverside Dock* restaurant and seafood bar is the most recent addition to the town's water's edge attractions, T9659486, 6343333, F6343388. Just up Black River from the coast, exquisite Japanese, Chinese and international seafood dishes, outside bar, pool tables, swings and slides for children, karaoke and local music. Safari rides up the Black River can be arranged through the restaurant with one of the local tour operators.

Eating

Road To get to Black River from Mandeville by bus involves a change in Santa Cruz.

Transport

Tourist office Hendricks Building, 2 High St, T9562074.

Directory

The road to Mandeville

On the south coast past Black River is **Treasure Beach**, a wide dark sand beach with body surfing waves, it is one of the most beautiful areas on the island. It is largely used by local fishermen as it is the closest point to the Pedro Banks. There is one small grocery shop and a bakery. A van comes to the village every day with fresh fruit and vegetables. This area is quite unlike any other part of Jamaica and still relatively unvisited by tourists. The local people are very friendly and you will be less hassled by higglers than elsewhere. You can take a daytime or moonlight tour to Sunny Island (Alligator Reef) from *Jake's*, T9652472.

Sleeping On the beach is **AL** *Treasure Beach Hotel*, T9650110, F9652544, 36 rooms. **A** *Jake's Place*, T9650635, F9650552, www.islandlife.com, part of Island Outpost chain, run by Jason Henzell. 14 rooms in small and exclusive, brightly painted cottages, arty, includes breakfast, good food, salt water pool, riding, cycling and hiking can be arranged, yoga and massage, music everywhere. **D** *Four M's Cottage*, Box 4, Mountainside PO, T/F9652472, T9650131. 4 rooms. Several houses can be rented: *Sparkling Waters*, *Folichon*, *Caprice*, and *Siwind* (PO Box 73, Black River), with its own cove.

To the east of Treasure Beach lies **Lovers' Leap**, a beauty spot named after the slave and his lover (his owner's daughter) who jumped off the cliff in despair ■ *US$3. 1000-1800 daily*, and Alligator Pond.

If you stay on the A2 instead of turning off at Black River, the road comes to **Middle Quarters**, on the edge of the Black River Morass (a large swamp); hot pepper shrimp are sold by the wayside, but insist that they are fresh (today's catch). Just after Middle Quarters is the left turn which takes you to the beautiful **YS Falls** (pronounced Why-Ess), an unspoiled spot in the middle of a large private plantation well worth visiting. ■ *US$9. 0930-1530, Tue-Sun, closed public holidays*. There is a 15-minute walk from where you park your car. You can bathe but there are no changing rooms or other facilities; plan a morning visit as there is no shelter in case of afternoon rain. Further along the main road is the impressive 2½-mile long **Bamboo Avenue**. North of Bamboo Avenue is **Maggotty**, on the (closed) railway line from Montego Bay to Kingston and close to the **Appleton Estate**, where tours of the rum factory are offered. ■ *For information contact Jamaica Estate Tours Ltd, T9976077, F9632243, or T9526606, Montego Bay. Regular tour parties come from Montego Bay and Negril hotels. US$12. 0900-1600, Mon-Fri*. Opposite the Maggotty train depot is the *Sweet Bakery*, run by Patrick and Lucille Lee, who can arrange accommodation in a Great House (**D**) or at a rustic campsite (**F**), very friendly and helpful, local trips organized, Mrs Lee is an excellent cook.

Jamaica

Mandeville

Population: 50,000   After Bamboo Avenue, the A2 road goes through Lacovia and Santa Cruz, an expanding town on the St Elizabeth Plain, and on up to Mandeville, a peaceful upland town with perhaps the best climate on the island. It is very spread out, with building on all the surrounding hills and no slums. In recent years, Mandeville has derived much of its prosperity from the bauxite/alumina industry (outside the town). There are lots of expensive homes and the town is congested.

The town's centre is the village green, now called **Cecil Charlton Park** (after the ex-mayor, whose opulent mansion, Huntingdon Summit, can be visited with prior arrangement). The green looks a bit like New England; at its northeast side stands a Georgian courthouse and, on the southeast, **St Mark's parish church** (both 1820). By St Mark's is the **market** area (busiest days are Monday, Wednesday and Friday – the market is supposed to be moved elsewhere) and the area where buses congregate. West of the green, at the corner of Ward Avenue and Caledonia Road, is the Manchester Club (T9622403), one of the oldest country clubs in the West Indies (1868) and the oldest in Jamaica. It has a nine-hole golf course (18 tee boxes, enabling you to play 18 holes) and tennis courts (you must be introduced by a member). Also, horse riding can be arranged, Ann Turner on T9622527.

Sleeping   **AL-C** *Astra Country Inn*, 62 Ward Av, PO Box 60, T9623265, F9621461. Reported for sale and run down, some way from the town centre, 22 rooms, pool, sauna, entertainment. In the centre is the **AL** *Mandeville Hotel*, 4 Hotel St, T9622138, F9620700. TV, spacious, pool, restaurant, excursions arranged, good. **C** *Kariba Kariba*, Atkinson's Drive, near New Green roundabout on Winston Jones highway, first right off New Green Rd, 45 mins' walk from centre, on bus route, T9623039. Bath, fan, 5 rooms or suites, including breakfast, TV lounge, bar, dining room. The owners, Derrick and Hazel O'Conner, are friendly, knowledgeable and hospitable, they can arrange for you to meet local people with similar interests and offer tours. Derrick is developing a 12-acre farm at Mile Gully (opportunity for work if you wish) and plans to develop a small campsite, bar, accommodation and other facilities.

Eating   *Bloomfield Great House*, 8 Perth Road, T9627130, bloomfield.g.h@cwjamaica.com Originally a coffee estate predating the town, part of its land was used to build the town, 600 ft above Mandeville, panoramic views. The Georgian Great House has also been used as a hotel, a dairy, a private home and more recently, *Bill Laurie's Steak House,* now owned by Ralph Pearce (Australian) and his wife Pamela Grant (Jamaican), who took 2 years to renovate, helped by a Croatian architect friend. Open for lunch and dinner, varied menu, fish 'n' chips, filet mignon, beer-batter shrimp, home made pasta, smoked marlin, cheesecakes are a speciality. *Pot Pourri*, on 2nd floor of the Caledonia Mall, just north of the Manchester Club. Clean and bright, good food and service. *International Chinese Restaurant*, Newport Rd. *Hungry Hut*, 45 Manchester Rd. Cheap, excellent food and service (owner, Fay, grew up in England and likes a chat).

Nightlife   The *Eclipse Disco*, Ward Av near the Manchester Club. The main disco, patronized by younger crowd, but good mix of music, closed Mon, Tue, after-work jam on Fri, Dance Hall night and live entertainment Sat, karaoke until 2200 and then oldies on Sun.

Shopping   *Westico Health Foods*, by the West Indies College, run by Seventh Day Adventists. They also run a vegetarian restaurant behind the church in the town centre, Mon-Fri. *Craft Centre*, sponsored by the Women's Club of Manchester, on Manchester Rd.

Excursions   Although some way inland, Mandeville is a good place from which to start exploring both the surrounding area and the south coast. In fact, by car you can get to most of Jamaica's resorts, except those east of Ocho Rios or Kingston, in two hours or less. Bird watchers and those interested in seeing a beautiful 'great house' in a cattle property should contact Robert Sutton at **Marshall's Pen**. Robert is the island's top ornithologist (23 of Jamaica's endemic bird species have been observed here).

■ *T9622260, US$10 for Great House tour by appointment only.* Also around the town you can visit the High Mountain Coffee. ■ *Free. Mon-Fri.* Also Pioneer Chocolate Factories, a factory making bammy (a delicacy from cassava root), the Alcan works, and local gardens.

There are interesting excursions north to **Christiana** (at about 2,800 ft, **B** *Hotel Villa Bella*, PO Box 473, Christiana, T9642243, F9642765, 18 rooms and suites, restaurant, in six acres with orchard of ortaniques and bananas, nature walks, riding, special interest groups catered for), southwest to the Santa Cruz mountains, and south to **Alligator Pond** on the coast. Eat on the beach at Blackie's *Little Ochie* , fish restaurant, everything freshly caught, six ways of cooking lobster, US$10. East of Alligator Pond is Gut River, where you can sometimes see alligators and manatees. Boat and fishing trips can be made to Pigeon Island, with a day on the island for swimming and snorkelling.

From Mandeville it is about 55 miles east to Kingston on the A2, bypassing May Pen, through Old Harbour then on to Spanish Town and Kingston. Before the May Pen bypass, a road branches south to **Milk River Bath**, the world's most radioactive spa. The baths are somewhat run down, but the medical properties of the water are among the best anywhere. ■ *T9024657, 0700-2100, daily, US$1.40, 15 mins, also restaurant and hotel.* About three miles from the baths is a marine conservation area, **Alligator Hole**, where manatees (sea cows) can sometimes be seen. Local boatmen will do their best to oblige.

Background

History

When Columbus landed on Jamaica in 1494 it was inhabited by peaceful Taino Indians. Under Spanish occupation, which began in 1509, the race died out and gradually African slaves were brought in to provide the labour force. In 1655 an English expeditionary force landed at Passage Fort and met with little resistance other than that offered by a small group of Spanish settlers and a larger number of African slaves who took refuge in the mountains. The Spaniards abandoned the island after about five years, but the slaves and their descendants, who became known as Maroons, waged war against the new colonists for 80 years until the 1730s although there was another brief rebellion in 1795. The Cockpit Country, or 'Look Behind Country,' where the Leeward Maroons hid and around Nanny Town where the Windward Maroons hid is still the home of some of their descendants.

The colony

After a short period of military rule, the colony was organized with an English-type constitution and a Legislative Council. The great sugar estates, which still today produce an important part of the island's wealth, were planted in the early days of English occupation when Jamaica also became the haunt of buccaneers and slave traders. In 1833 emancipation was declared for slaves (although a system of apprenticeship remained until 1838) and modern Jamaica was born. The framework for Jamaica's modern political system was laid in the 1930s with the foundation in 1938 of the People's National Party (PNP) by Norman W Manley, and the Jamaica Labour Party (JLP) by his cousin, Sir Alexander Bustamante in 1944. These two parties had their roots in rival trade unions and have dominated Jamaican politics since universal adult suffrage was introduced in 1944.

In 1958, Jamaica joined the West Indies Federation with nine other British territories but withdrew following a national referendum on the issue in 1961. On 6 August 1962, Jamaica became an independent member of the Commonwealth.

Independence

After 23 years as leader of the PNP, eight of them as Prime Minister in the 1970s and three as Prime Minister from 1989, Michael Manley, son of the party's founder,

The Manley Legacy

Jamaica

retired in March 1992 because of ill health. During Manley's first two terms in office between 1972 and 1980 he endorsed socialist policies at home and encouraged South-South relations abroad. He antagonized the USA by developing close economic and political links with Cuba. State control of the economy failed to produce the desired results and Mr Manley was rejected by the electorate. The conservative JLP led by Edward Seaga, held office for the next nine years. By 1989 however, Manley's political thinking had changed dramatically and he was re-elected with policies advocating the free market. He was succeeded by the Party Chairman, former deputy Prime Minister and Finance Minister P J Patterson. Mr Patterson promised to maintain Mr Manley's policies and deepen the restructuring of the economy.

The 1990s   General elections were held early on 30 March 1993 and the incumbent PNP was returned for a second term with a larger than expected majority, winning 55 of the 60 seats. Despite the landslide victory, the elections were marred by violence in which 11 people died, malpractices and a turnout of only 58%. The JLP boycotted parliament for four months while it demanded electoral reform and an inquiry into the election day events. It also refused to contest by-elections, two of which were held in the next 12 months and won by the PNP. Some concessions were made by the Government, such as reorganization of the police force to remove direct political control and the postponement of local government elections pending electoral reform. The reform drafted by the Electoral Advisory Committee was eventually completed in time for general elections in December 1997.

The 1997 elections gave the PNP a third consecutive term in office. The PNP won 50 seats while the JLP won 10 and the National Democratic Movement (NDM), a new party formed dy dissident JLP members in 1995, failed to win any. There was less violence than in previous campaigns, with only two deaths, but there were some electoral inefficiencies because of the new register and a few irregularities leading to re-run elections in a couple of constituencies. When he was sworn into office, Prime Minister P J Patterson promised that it would be the last time that the government would swear allegiance to the British monarchy. The PNP proposes an executive president but the JLP advocates a ceremonial president with a Prime Minister. The next general elections are due by end-2002. The three existing parties along with independents are likely to contest the elections when announced. Things were already hotting up in mid-2001 as violence between rival political gangs erupted in the run-up to these elections. Dozens of people were killed in clashes with the police and the army was called in to restore law and order in Kingston and other hot spots.

Geography

Jamaica lies some 90 miles south of Cuba and a little over 100 miles west of Haiti. With an area of 4,244 square miles, it is the third largest island in the Greater Antilles. It is 146 miles from east to west and 51 miles from north to south at its widest, bounded by the Caribbean. Jamaica has been called the Island of Springs, and its Taino name, Xaymaca, meant land of wood and water. The luxuriance of the vegetation is indeed striking. Like other West Indian islands, it is an outcrop of a submerged mountain range. It is crossed by a spectacular range of mountains reaching 7,402 ft at the Blue Mountain Peak in the east and descending towards the west, with a series of spurs and forested gullies running north and south. Tropical beaches surround the island, the best being on the north and west coasts, though there are some good bathing places on the south coast too.

People

The island is a fascinating blend of cultures from colonial Britain, African slavery and immigrants from China, India and the Middle East. Reggae and Rastafariansim have become synonymous with Jamaica; Bob Marley and Peter Tosh among the

Dreadlocks to reggae

Followers of the Rastafarian cult are easily recognizable by their long dreadlocks. They are non-violent, do not eat pork and believe in the divinity of the late Emperor of Ethiopia, Haile Selassie (Ras Tafari). Haile Selassie's call for the end of the superiority of one race over another has been incorporated into a faith which holds that God, Jah, will lead the blacks out of oppression (Babylon) back to Ethiopia (Zion, the Promised Land). The Rastas regard the ideologist, Marcus Garvey (born 1887, St Ann's Bay), as a prophet of the return to Africa (he is now a Jamaican national hero). In the early part of the 20th century, Garvey founded the idea of black nationalism, with Africa as the home for blacks, be they living on the continent or not.

The music most strongly associated with Rastafarianism is reggae. According to O R Dathorne, "it is evident that the sound and words of Jamaican reggae have altered the life of the English-speaking Caribbean. The extent of this alteration is still unknown, but this new sound has touched, more than any other single art medium, the consciousness of the people of this region" (Dark Ancestor, page 229, Louisiana State University Press, 1981). The sound is a mixture of African percussion and up-to-the-minute electronics; the lyrics a blend of praise of Jah, political comment and criticism and the mundane. The late Bob Marley, the late Peter Tosh, Dennis Brown and Jimmy Cliff are among the world-famous reggae artists, and many, many more can be heard on the island. Over the last few years, traditional reggae has been supplanted by Dance Hall, which has a much heavier beat, and instead of Marley's rather thoughtful lyrics, it is all about guns and sex, Shabba Ranks, Buju Banton and so on. Closely related to reggae is dub poetry, a chanted verse form which combines the musical tradition, folk traditions and popular speech. Its first practitioner was Louise Bennett, in the 1970s, who has been followed by poets such as Linton Kwesi Johnson, Michael Smith, Oku Onora and Mutabaruka. Many of these poets work in the UK, but their links with Jamaica are strong.

Two novels which give a fascinating insight into Rasta culture (and, in the latter, Revival and other social events) are Brother Man, by Roger Mais, and The Children of Sysiphus, by H Orlando Patterson. These writers have also published other books which are worth investigating, as are the works of Olive Senior (eg Summer Lightning), and the poets Mervyn Morris, the late Andrew Salkey and Dennis Scott (who is also involved in the theatre).

Jamaica

greats to have been born here. Over 90% of Jamaicans are of West African descent. Because of this, Ashanti words still figure very largely in the local dialect, which is known as Jamaica Talk. There are also Chinese, East Indians and Christian Arabs as well as those of British descent and other European minorities. The population is approximately 2.5 million. There is considerable poverty on the island, which has created social problems and some tension. Jamaicans are naturally friendly, easy going and international in their outlook (more people of Jamaican origin live outside Jamaica than inside). There is a 'Meet the People' programme which enables visitors to meet Jamaicans on a one-to-one basis.

The predominant religion is Protestantism, but there is also a Roman Catholic community. There are followers of the Church of God, Baptists, Anglicans, Seventh Day Adventists, Pentecostals and Methodists. The Jewish, Moslem, Hindu and Bahai religions are also practised. It is said that Jamaica has more churches per square mile than anywhere else in the world. To a small degree, early adaptations of the Christian faith, Revival and Pocomania, survive, but the most obvious local minority sect is Rastafarianism (see box above).

Economy

Once one of the more prosperous islands in the West Indies, Jamaica went into recession in 1973 and output declined steadily throughout the 1970s and 1980s. At the core of Jamaica's economic difficulties lay the collapse of the vital bauxite mining

Structure of production

and alumina refining industries. Jamaica is the world's third largest producer of bauxite after Australia and Guinea, but despite rising production of bauxite and alumina, earnings have slumped because of lower prices.

Manufacturing, which contributes over 18% to gdp, is mostly agricultural processing, such as rum, beer, cigarettes and foodstuffs. Garments exported to the USA and other miscellaneous manufactured articles have seen considerable expansion, but there is competition from Mexico for the US market and from imports as markets have been liberalized.

By comparison with manufacturing, agriculture is a less important sector in terms of contribution to gdp, though it generates far more employment. Sugar is the main crop, and most important export item after bauxite and alumina, but production costs are high and the industry is insolvent. Other export crops include bananas, coffee, cocoa and citrus fruits. Jamaica is famous for its Blue Mountain coffee, first produced in 1757, which commands a high premium in the world market.

Tourism is the second foreign exchange earner and contributes about 15% of gdp. Combined stopover and cruise arrivals passed the million mark in 1987 for the first time. In the early 1990s numbers continued to rise and hotel capacity increased but occupancy is only 60%, with many tourists put off by stories of crime and harassment. Nowadays, stopover visitors alone exceed 1 mn while cruise ship passengers continue to increase, with most ships calling at Ocho Rios.

Recent trends The Government turned to the IMF for support in 1976 and was a regular customer until 1995. In compliance with IMF agreements, the Government had to reduce domestic demand commensurate with the fall in export earnings, by devaluing the currency and reducing the size of its fiscal deficits. Jamaica has rescheduled its debt to creditor governments and also to foreign commercial banks. Some debt forgiveness has also been granted. The Jamaican dollar has been devalued, the foreign exchange market deregulated, and interest rates and credit ceilings kept high to reduce consumption, close the trade gap and rebuild foreign reserves.

Debt servicing remains a heavy burden, with amortization and interest payments accounting for 58% of budget expenditure. The economy went into decline again in 1996 and gdp fell every year in the rest of the decade. Some commentators forecast further unrest in the light of high unemployment (16%), low wages (16% of households are below the poverty line of J$700 income per adult per month), high interest rates and low economic activity.Emigration is high. Nevertheless, the Government forecasts better economic prospects for the new century, with positive gdp growth and lower interest rates.

Turks and Caicos Islands

7

Turks and Caicos Islands

Similar to the southern Bahamas islands, to which they are geographically linked, these flat, coral islands are a British Dependent Territory. Miles of sandy beaches attract sun-loving tourists to a water playground. Diving and snorkelling are superb among coral gardens, wrecks and walls which drop dramatically to the floor of the ocean. Most hotels are on the island of Providenciales, spread along Grace Bay on the north shore, and there are lots of facilities for sailing, diving and fishing. Grand Turk is the seat of government but is a quiet, unhurried place with a few small hotels and some pleasant colonial buildings. Other inhabited islands, North Caicos, Middle Caicos, South Caicos and Salt Cay have tiny populations – they are good places to escape the crowds.

A Foot in the door

- Explore the huge and beautiful **caves** on Middle Caicos, formerly home to Taíno Indians.
- See the **carvings in stone** dating back to the 17th century on the hill behind the old Mariner Inn on Provo.
- Go to the abandoned old **salt cellars** under the houses on Salt Cay.
- Don't miss the excellent **museum** on Grand Turk.
- Walk for miles along the deserted beach west of **Whitby**, North Caicos.

Essentials

Before you travel

Documents US and Canadian citizens need only a birth certificate or some other proof of identity to enter the Turks and Caicos. Other nationalities need a valid passport; a visa is not necessary except for nationals of communist countries. An onward ticket is officially required. Visitors are allowed to stay for 30 days, renewable once only.

Money The official **currency** is the US dollar. Most banks will advance cash on **credit cards.** Most hotels, restaurants and taxi drivers will accept travellers' cheques, but personal cheques are not widely accepted. Take lots of cash and small denomination US dollars when visiting an island without a bank, as it is often difficult to get change from big notes. There are **banks** on Grand Turk and Providenciales but not on the other islands. As well as domestic banking there is a growing offshore banking industry, regulated by the UK.

Turks & Caicos Islands

Temperatures average 75-85°F from November to May, reaching into the 90°s from June to October, but constant tradewinds keep life comfortable. Average annual rainfall is 21 ins on Grand Turk and South Caicos but increases to 40 ins as you travel westwards through the Caicos Islands where more lush vegetation is found. Hurricane Kate swept through the islands November 1985; Hugo and Andrew missed in 1992; there were several near misses in 1995 and Bertha passed through in 1996. El Niño upset the weather pattern in 1997/98 with more rainy days and rougher seas.

Climate
There is no recognized rainy season. Hurricane season is normally Jun-Oct

Getting there

Ports of entry for aircraft are Providenciales, South Caicos and Grand Turk, but the major international airport is on Providenciales. There are also airstrips on North Caicos, Middle Caicos, Pine Cay and Salt Cay. Flights from the USA come in to Providenciales and then, if you are not staying on Provo, you get a connecting flight to your destination on a small plane. See each island's Transport section for details.

Air
The first direct flight from Europe was started in June 2001, with a BA flight to Provo from London

There is no scheduled passenger service (cargo comes in regularly from Florida) and no port is deep enough to take cruise ships although some occasionally stop outside the reef and shuttle in passengers for half a day.

Boat
Evening weather radio report on VHF from Blue Water Divers on Grand Turk; Mystine on SSB

Ports of entry (British flag) Providenciales: Turtle Cove Marina, Caicos Shipyard, Leeward Marina, South Dock/Sapodilla Bay; Grand Turk; South Caicos; Salt Cay. Clear in and out with customs and immigration, VHF 16. On arrival, customs will grant seven days immigration clearance. Go to town to the Immigration Office (closed 1230-1430) to obtain a 30 day extension. Fuel and alcoholic drink may be purchased duty free with clearance to leave the country. The Customs Office is at South Dock, Provo, and there are Customs Officers at the airport all day too.

There are no bareboat charters

Marinas There are five marinas on Provo. **Leeward Marina** at Leeward Going Through, T9465553, F9465674, marina@tciway.tc, gas/diesel sales only, restaurant; **Turtle Cove Landing**, Sellar's Pond, T9464307, F9464771, long term dockage for boats up to 70 ft, 5 ft draft; **Turtle Cove Marina**, Sellar's Pond, T9464303, F9464326, turtlecovemarina@ provo.net, full service, all weather anchorage, 6 ft draft, 35 new slips (still under construction), RO, water and ice, premium prices; **South Side Marina**, T9464747, dockside T9464200, F9415776, hamilton&pratt@tciway.tc, diesel, gas, oil, water, 4½ft controlling depth, call for reservations; **Caicos Marina and Shipyard**, Long Bay, T9465600, F9465390, SSB 4143.6, (fuel, ice, dry storage, cabinet maker on the premises, Southwind Millworks, T9465700, and a machinist/diesel mechanic). South Caicos also has a marina.

Touching down

Scheduled service airlines are *TCA* (T9464255, F9462081, domestic emergency T9415353); *American Airlines* (T1-800-4337300, T9415700); *TCI Sky King* (T9461520 on Grand Turk, T9415461/4 on Provo, F9415127, King@tciway.tc); *Bahamasair* and

Airport information
It is worth checking in early when returning to Miami from Provo, to avoid long queues

*Map labels:*

Atlantic Ocean

Drum Point
EAST CAICOS
Columbus Passage
SOUTH CAICOS
GRAND TURK
Cockburn Town
Gibbs Cay
Long Cay
Long Cay
Martin Alonza Pinzon Cay (East Cay)
Penniston Cay
Cotton Cay
Balfour Town
Salt Cay
Big Sand Cay
Endymion Rock
South Rock

Touching down

Departure tax   *US$15.*
Voltage   *110 volts, 60 cycles, the same as in the USA.*
Useful addresses   *Chief Secretary (Grand Turk), T9462702 (Provo), T9464258, 9415123; Customs (Grand Turk), T9462993/4, (Provo), T9464214; Immigration (Grand Turk), T9462939, (Provo), T9464233; time/weather, T141.*
Clothing   *Dress is informal and shorts are worn in town as well as on the beach. Nudity is illegal although condoned by Club Med on Grace Bay. The islanders find it offensive and flaunting local protocol may elicit unwelcome stares and remarks. Islanders love to dress up in the evenings when they frequent live band nights at hotels or discos.*

Safety   *Providenciales is no longer as safe as it was before being discovered as a tourist and off-shore banking destination, but still safer than most Caribbean islands. It is not advisable to walk around alone at night or on deserted beaches. On Provo, take precautions about leaving valuables in your room or on the beach. Crime is on the increase. Traffic is fast and aggressive causing many accidents. Personal security is much better on Grand Turk and the other islands and a haven compared with most other Caribbean countries. Should you need it, the **police station** on Grand Turk is T9462299 and on Salt Cay, T9466929.*
*In an **emergency** anywhere T999.*

Lynx Air (to Grand Turk only from Provo). Charter airlines are **Global Airways** (T9413222 on Provo, T9467093 on North Caicos, F9467290, www.globalairways.com, run by the Gardiner family); **Inter Island Airways** (Provo T9465481, F9464040, after hours T9464466, Lyndon Gardiner); **Flamingo Air Services** (Grand Turk T9462109/8); **Provo Air Charter** (T9465578, F9465040).

Tourist information   **Local tourist office**   Turks and Caicos Islands Tourist Board, PO Box 128, Grand Turk, Turks & Caicos Islands, T9462321/2322, F9462733, www.turksandcaicostourism.com   On Provo the tourist office is at Diamond Stubbs Plaza, on the low road leading to what was once *Le Deck*, now called *Sibonné*, PO Box 174, T9464970, F9415494. Various maps and guidebooks have been published including *Where, When, How, Providenciales; Your Monthly Entertainment Guide*, placed in hotels and selected shops, free of charge; *Times of the Islands; International Magazine of the Turks and Caicos*, quarterly, US$4. Special Edition publishes a large, user-friendly road map of Providenciales each year, indicating the location of advertisers, pay/card phones, fuel stations and other information, contact Kathi Barrington, F9465122, brad@tciway.tc   Useful websites with lots of information on lodgings, particularly on the smaller islands are www.tcimall.tc and www.wherewhenhow.com

Local travel agents *Marco Travel Services*, Down Town, T9464393, F9464048, for reconfirmation of tickets, emergency check cashing, travel services, travellers' cheque sales, Amex representative. *Provo Travel Ltd*, run by Althea Ewing, at Central Square, Leeward Highway, T9464035, F9464081, helpful. On Grand Turk: *T & C Travel Ltd*, at *Hotel Osprey Beach*, Box 42, T9462592, F9462877, run by Daphne James, friendly, reliable.

Where to stay

There is a 10-15% service charge & 9% bed tax added to the bill   **Hotels** on Provo are aiming for North American standards and so they are expensive. Rack rates will not include tax and service, be sure to check what you are quoted. Most hotels on Provo are all-inclusive or condominium-style. Grand Turk, Salt Cay, South Caicos and North Caicos are better bets for inexpensive, charming, more 'islandy' lodgings. **Camping** is possible on beaches on most islands, but no water or sewage facilities and not encouraged. Contact the District Commissioner's office on each island for permission. If planning to stay on a deserted island take everything with you and leave nothing behind.

Tourist offices overseas

France *T01-42363660, F01-42364835,*
mkifr@easynet.fr
Germany *T06131-337929, F06131-99331,*
101514.3543@compuserve.com
Italy *T0296-451071, F0296-56487,*
elysian@login.it
UK *c/o Morris Kevan International Ltd,*
Mitre House, 66 Abbey Road, Bush Hill Park,
Enfield, Middlesex, EN1 2RQ, T020-83501017,

F020-83501000, www.mki.ltd.uk
USA *Trombone Associates Inc,*
420 Madison Avenue, New York NY 10017,
T212-2232323, F2230260, T1-800-2410824.
TCI Tourist Board, 11645 Biscayne Boulevard,
Suite 302, North Miami, FL 33181,
T305-8914117, F305-8917096,
T800-2410824,
tcitrsm@bellSouth.net

Getting around

Flight time from Grand Turk to the furthest island (Provo) is 35 minutes. *Turks & Caicos Airways* provides a twice daily service Provo to Grand Turk via the out-islands, US$120 round trip. *SkyKing, Global Airways* and *Inter Island Airways* also provide frequent flights between the islands. Private charters are readily available within the island group and can easily be arranged by asking around at Grand Turk or Provo airport, as charter pilots meet incoming international flights and wait to see if they can fill a plane in the mornings. They often hold up boards showing which island they are flying to. Do not pre-book as you may sit for 2-3 hours waiting for a particular plane; similarly if travelling to the out islands, do not buy a return ticket, whatever the airlines tell you, as you may have to pay twice if you come back with someone else. Your hotel or guest house can help you arrange your return flight when you are ready to leave (this does not include package tours). Private pilots fly seven days a week, *TCA* does not fly on Sunday.

Air
See page 341 for telephone numbers of charter companies

Bicycles and motor scooters can be rented from some hotels but can be relatively expensive compared with cars. Helmets are not mandatory but should be worn. Tourists invite trouble riding in bathing suits and bare feet and at night.

Bicycle

Rental cars are available on Grand Turk, North and South Caicos and Provo although demand often exceeds supply on Provo. Most roads are fairly basic, although those on Provo have been upgraded and paved, and all parts are easily accessible. Maximum speed in urban areas is 20 mph and outside villages 40 mph, but on Provo driving is erratic and no one (except visitors) pays heed to speed limits, not even the Traffic Department. There is no control. Local drivers do not dim their headlights at night. Pedestrians and cyclists should be careful on the roads because of speeding, dangerous drivers and heavy construction vehicles.

Car
Drive on the left. Watch out for donkeys on Grand Turk

On-island transport is restricted to expensive taxi service with a basic fare of US$2 per mile, although drivers are not always consistent. Complaints are frequent. Taxis can be hired for island tours, agree the price before hand.

Taxi
There are a few private buses

Keeping in touch

On Grand Turk the post office is on Front Street near Barclays Bank, T9462801. *Federal Express*, T9462542 (Grand Turk), T9464682 (Provo); *DHL*, T9464352 (Provo); *UPS* agent, T9462030, F9462995, incoming only package delivery, Cee's Building, Pond Street, Grand Turk and on Provo through *Provo Travel*, T9464080, F9464081. Postage for postcards US$0.50 to USA, US$0.60 Canada/UK, US$0.80 Europe, US$1.10 Africa. Letters each half an ounce US$0.60, US$0.80, US$1, US$1.25 respectively.

Post

Grand Turk, Provo and South Caicos have a modern local and international telephone service, with Cable and Wireless offices in Grand Turk and Provo. Telephone services on the North and Middle Caicos and Salt City are improving. There are three exchanges, 946 and 941 and 231

Telephone
IDD code: 649

Turks & Caicos Islands

for all cell phones. Local directory assistance T118, international operator T115; credit card calls T111, 1-800-8778000. The small volume of international calls means that costs are higher than in the USA. The local phone book has a list of charges to anywhere in the world. Phone cards are available from Cable and Wireless and from many outlets including Provo airport in US$5, US$10 and US$20 denominations plus 10%. The Cable and Wireless Public Sales Office in Grand Turk and Provo has a public fax service, F9462497/4210. Credit card calling, dial 111, three minutes minimum. Paging service is popular among businesses and cell phones are widely used. Many visitors bring their own cell phones, or you can rent one while on the islands. International calls from cell phones cost the same as from a regular phone. Internet service is also available. There is a telephone directory published by Olympia Publishing (saunders@tciway.tc) with lots of useful information about the TCI, more useful than the Cable & Wireless directory.

Food and drink

Seafood, lobster, conch with peas 'n' rice is standard island fare

Good, moderate to expensive meals in restaurants and bars are good quality. Watch out for specials with no posted prices. Wine by the glass is US$5. With over 50 restaurants and delis on Provo alone, prices are variable but local restaurants with native cuisine are reasonable. Many restaurants feature vegetarian meals and low fat cooking. All food is imported (except seafood) from Miami, occasionally from the Dominican Republic, and therefore not cheap. Many restaurants charge a 10% gratuity and/or 9% government tax. Restaurants owned and operated by belongers do not have to charge tax because they serve the local market. Some do not charge for service. Check your bill carefully and tip, or not, accordingly.

Entertainment

Local bands play mostly calypso, reggae and the traditional island music with its Haitian and African influences. On Provo, ask hoteliers and residents when and where live bands are playing. Latin influence in discos such as *Club Latino* (Downtown-Provo) and *Caribbean Macks* in Blue Hills, featuring soca, reggae and latino, loudly! Live entertainment, Friday nights, Ports of Call courtyard. *Club Med* has nightly dinner/show for guests and visitors who phone for reservations (T9465500). Nightlife does not start until 2200-2300. On Grand Turk, the *Salt Raker Inn* for music on Wednesday and Sunday nights.

Flora and fauna

A system of conservation has been set up: the islands boast 11 national parks, 4 sanctuaries, 10 nature reserves & 7 historical sites: entrance to sanctuaries by permit only

The islands support 175 resident and migrant species of birds, including flocks of greater flamingos, frigate birds, ospreys, brown pelicans, the ruby throated humming bird, the belted kingfisher, white billed tropic birds, black-necked stilts, snowy plovers, peregrine falcons, red-tailed hawks, northern harriers, Baltimore orioles and scarlet tanagers and many others. There are lizards, iguanas, two species of snake, including a pygmy boa, and two species of bat. The Turks and Caicos National Trust (in Providenciales, T9415710, Director, Mrs Ethlyn Gibbs-Williams) plans to develop and protect the Princess Alexandra National Park on Providenciales' north shore. The south parts of North, Middle and East Caicos have been designated an internationally important wetland under the Ramsar Convention for the protection of waterbirds, lobster, conch, flora and a fish nursery.

In 1998 the British Government approved an allocation of US$1.6mn for the Turks and Caicos to implement a Coastal Resource Management Programme. Its aim is to conserve the natural resources of the islands by more effective management of protected areas, revitalizing the National Parks Service, setting up a headquarters and a National Environment Centre on Provo. A public awareness programme will educate people about the benefits of national parks and a scientific monitoring programme will be initiated for the Marine Parks. The Government will work in collaboration with the National Trust to implement the programme and a 1% tax on food, drinks and accommodation goes into a special fund.

Diving and marine life

Marine life is varied and beautiful and can be enjoyed by snorkellers & sailors as well as scuba divers. Colourful fish and grouper can be seen on the coral and close to the shore there are green and loggerhead turtles and manta and spotted eagle rays. In January-March, humpback whales migrate through the deep Turks Island Passage on their way south to the Silver and Mouchoir Banks breeding grounds north of the Dominican Republic. Whale watching is co-ordinated by the Department of Environmental Heritage and Parks, who have drawn up rules to protect the whales. On Grand Turk contact Everette Freites of Oasis Divers, he has swum with the humpbacks. Beyond the reef are the game fish such as tuna, blue marlin, wahoo, snapper, bill fish and barracuda. Great care is being taken to conserve the reefs and the coral is in very good condition. The islands have become one of the most highly regarded diving locations in the region. Some of the best diving is off the wall at Northwest Point, West Caicos and French Cay. Do not take live coral, sea fans or other marine life. The use of spearguns is prohibited.

Because there is no soil run off from the islands, water visibility is excellent, although the sea is often rough in Feb-Mar. The best months for diving are Apr to Nov

On **Provo** there are nine land-based dive operations offering courses (resort course approximately US$130, full certification US$400) and dive packages. The standard cost of a two-tank dive is US$70. Several companies are based at **Turtle Cove**: *Flamingo Divers*, at *Turtle Cove Landing*, PO Box 322, Providenciales, T/F9464193, T800-2049282, www.Provo.net/flamingo, caters for small groups of experienced or novice divers, PADI and SSI instruction; *Provo Turtle Divers*, PO Box 219, T9464232, 1-800-3285285, F9415296, provoturtledivers@provo.net; *Turtle Cove Inn* at Turtle Cove marina and at *Ocean Club Resort*, and *Comfort Suites*, Grace Bay, run by Art Pickering, is also recommended for small groups of experienced divers at similar prices; *Ocean Vibes* at Turtle Cove Marina does small dive groups and other watersports, T9413141, oceanvibes@tciway.tc; *Caicos Adventures*, out of South Side Marina, T/F9413346, www.caicosadventures.tc, 36 ft custom boat trips to West Caicos, French Cay for small groups, full service, NAUI/CMAS.

Dive centres
There is a recompression chamber at Menzies Medical Practice on Provo, T9464242, DAN insurance is accepted

On **Grace Bay** there are: *Dive Provo*, located at the *Allegro Resort*, PO Box 350, T9465029/5040, F9465936, www.diveprovo.com, three boats, windsurfing, kayaks, shop in Ports of Call; *Big Blue Unlimited*, which specializes in eco-adventures, small groups, private charters, T9465034, F9465033, www.bigblue.tc

There are three live-aboard boats based in Provo for those who want to spend a week doing nothing else but diving. *Sea Dancer* (Peter Hughes Diving, T800-9-DANCER or 305-6699475, whatever@tciway.tc) operates from Sellar's Pond, Turtle Cove, has accommodation for 18 people and offers five dives a day around French Cay, West Caicos and Northwest Point. *Tao*, a 56 ft trimaran takes groups of nine for up to two weeks' sailing, diving and fishing in the Turks and Caicos and Bahamas, T9416767, F9415510, TAO@provo.net *The Turks and Caicos Aggressor*, contact the Aggressor Fleet Limited, PO Drawer K, Morgan City, LA 70381, T800-3482628, F504-3840817, www.aggressor.com

At **Leeward Marina** is *J & B Tours*, T9465047, F9465288, 24 ft dive boat, courses, one tank US$60, two tanks US$85 and *Silver Deep*, T9465612, F9464527, www.silverdeep.com, private dives, three divers US$280 including tanks, 4-6 divers US$85 per person including tanks.

On **Grand Turk** there are three very experienced dive organizers who have been diving these waters for decades. *Blue Water Divers Ltd* is on Front Street, next to the museum, PO Box 124, Grand Turk, T/F9462432, www.microplan.com Mitch Rolling offers a complete range of courses and special day trips with two small boats (bimini tops for shade). *Sea Eye Diving*, run by Cecil Ingham and Connie Rus, is a larger operation in a beautifully renovated building with underwater photography and a range of watersports on offer as well as a shop selling diving equipment and beach wear. They have three boats, maximum 12 divers per boat, NAUI and PADI instruction, US$55 per dive, frequent cay trips, dive packages with accommodation available, PO Box 67, T/F9461407, www.reefnet.on.ca /grandturk *Oasis Divers* is run by Everette Freites and Dale Barker, PO Box 137, Grand Turk, T9461128, www.oasisdivers.com, offering a complete range of courses to small groups aboard 28ft dive boats. They also have a small shop. The highlight of diving here is the wall off Cockburn Town,

The three dive shops on Grand Turk also offer whale watching in season, see Whale & dolphin watching, page 66

Turks & Caicos Islands

which drops suddenly from 40ft to 7,000ft only a quarter of a mile offshore. There are 25 moored sites along the wall where you can find coral arches, tunnels, canyons, caves and overhangs.

On **Salt Cay**, *Salt Cay Divers*, operated by Debbie Manos and Oliver Been is based at the *Mount Pleasant Guest House*, run by Tim Dunn, T9466906, www.saltcaydivers.com (see under Salt Cay). The dive boat is a 24ft Carolina skiff which takes you to the main dive site in five minutes. A two-tank dive is US$50, but most people stay at the guest house and take a five day package for US$914 which includes three meals, transfers and unlimited day and night diving. There are seven moored dive sites and off Great Sand Cay there is an 18th century British shipwreck, now a National Monument, the *Endymion*, still loaded with cannon. A wall chart telling her story is on sale at gift shops on the islands and at the Museum on Grand Turk. She was found in 1991 by Brian Sheedy with the help of a local historian, Josiah Marvel, and the only way to visit her is with Salt Cay Divers. It is thought that this is the only unsalvaged 18th century wreck in the world which the diving public can visit and explore. The wreck lies in about 25ft of water with the remains of two other ships nearby: a Civil War steamer and a ship dating from around 1900. The coral is prolific and the fish plentiful and huge. The best time for a visit is May-November.

On the west side of the Columbus Passage the wall along the east shores of **South Caicos** and **Long Cay** also drops gradually or steeply from a depth of about 50 ft, with many types of coral and a variety of fish of all sizes. Snorkelling is rewarding with several shallow reefs close to the shore. On South Caicos *Club Carib Dive and Watersports* offers excellent diving and snorkelling with eagle rays 5-10 minutes offshore, T9463444, F9463446, packages available. On **North Caicos** *Club Vacanze* will arrange diving and snorkelling, T9467119, F9467114.

Beaches and watersports

230 miles of white sand beaches & coral surround the islands

Grace Bay on Provo is the longest stretch of sand, at 12 miles, and despite the hotels it is possible to find plenty of empty space, but *no* shade. There is rarely any shade on the beaches. Most watersports can be arranged through the hotels or tour operators.

Day sails

Several tour operators represent all **day sails**, **scuba dives** or **snorkelling trips** or you can contact the captains direct or through your hotel. Sailing and beach cruising trips include: *Sail the Trade Winds Schooner*, *Atabeyra*, anchored at Leeward Marina, offering Pirates Cay full and a half day sails and ecology tours, cold drinks and snorkelling gear included, call *Sun Charters* T9415363 or the tour desk at your hotel; *Beluga*, Leeward Going Through, T/F9464396, VHF 68, 37ft catamaran, private full and half day sails; *Sand Dollar Cruises*, T946-5238/5407, F9465407, "cruise in comfort" to Little Water Cay, beach and snorkel half day trips, secluded island getaway with umbrella, snorkel, picnic and cold drinks. *Tao*, T9464783, F9415510, VHF 77, 56 ft trimaran, four double cabins, 1-2 week cruises in TCI and Bahamas, half day cruise, sunset or glow worm, Captain Dave Matthews has 20 years' sailing experience, half day cruise, sunset or glow worm; *Two Fingers*, T2316158, 36ft catamaran, *Phoenix*, 62ft catamaran and *Arielle*, 52ft catamaran, full and half day cruises, snorkelling, trips arranged by *Sail Provo*, T9464783, F9465527, sailprovo@tciway.tc Also at Leeward Marina, **Catch the Wave Charters**, T/F9413047, catchthewaveprovo@yahoo.com, 26 ft Bowrider, comfortable and roomy, specialize in private charters and offer bonefishing, waterskiing, beach cruising, reggae sunset cruises; *J & B Tours*, T9465067, F9465288, offers beach and snorkelling excursions, barbecues, waterskiing, island getaways, trips to Conch Farm, caves on Middle Caicos, glow worm cruises, fishing and scuba. *Silver Deep* (see page 327), offers similar beach cruises, glow worm charters, secluded getaways, trips to Middle and North Caicos. Exclusively at Sapodilla Bay, *Ocean Outback*'s 'Ultimate Getaway', all day adventure by 18 ft or 24 ft runabouts visiting settlers' ruins, pirate caves and rock carvings, snorkelling, beach BBQ, snacks, beers, round trip transportation included, T9410824, www.Provo.net/OceanOutback or contact tour desk at your hotel. *Ocean Obsession* offers day charters and sunset cruises aboard their 55-ft motor yacht, T9465011. **Windsurfing Provo** at *Ocean Club*, Grace Bay,

T9465649 and evenings T9465490, windpro@tciway.tc, offers hobie waves, hobie cats, small motor boats and kayaking as well as **windsurfing**.

Fishing is popular. Provo and Pine Cay have the best bonefishing though it is also possible at South Caicos, Middle Caicos, North Caicos and Salt Cay. May is the prime time. Fishermen have not organized themselves into offering packages, so you have to find your own accommodation and fishing guide. Shop around before committing US$250-300 per day because experienced visitor fishermen have reported a lack of skill, professionalism and simple amenities among local guides.

On **Providenciales**, the choices are: *Captain Barr Gardiner's Bonefish Unlimited* (Box 241, T9464874, F9464960), *Light Tackle and 'Black Diamond' Fishing and Boat Tours* (T9464451), Earl Musgrove. Leeward Going Through Marina is the best place to find and talk to fishermen, or try to reach them on the radio, VHF 16. *J & B Tours* (see above) will arrange full and half day fishing. *Gilley's* restaurant will cook your catch. *Silver Deep* (see above) includes bone, fly, light tackle and night fishing in his itinerary. The most experienced sports fishing operation on Provo is *Captain Bob Collins' Sakitumi Charters*, he has been fishing these waters on his 43ft Hatteras since 1989, T9464065, F9464141, www.provo.net/sakitumi US$650 per full day, US$350 per half day, VHF Channel 16 'Sakitumi'. There are four deep sea sport fishing operators in Turtle Cove Marina; *Sakitumi* (see above); *Gwod Phrienz* (Good Friends) contact Algie Dean, T9464342, F9415144, reservations@tciway.tc; *Gwendolyn*, 45ft Hatteras sportfisher, T9410412, 9465321, www.Provo.net/Gwendolyn/ Rates approximately US$400 half day, US$750 full day. On **Grand Turk** fishing can be arranged through Ossie (Oswald) Virgil, of Virgil's Taxis at the airport, or PO Box 78, T9462018. Ossie also arranges an annual Game Fishing Tournament in August. On **Middle Caicos** fishing and boating is arranged through the District Commissioner's Office, T9466100, with Dotis Arthur and her husband, Cardinal. On **South Caicos** a bonefish specialist is Julius 'Goo the Guide' Jennings, US$20 per hour, who can be contacted through the *Club Caribe*, T9463444, F9463446.

A US$10 sport fishing licence, for pole fishing only, is required from the Fisheries Department, Grand Turk, T9462970, or South Caicos, T9463306, or Provo, T9464017. Ask your guide whether the fishing licence is included in his package. Spear fishing is not allowed.

Parasailing with *Turtle Parasailing*, *Turtle Cove Inn*, costs US$60 a flight, T/F9415389, parasail@tciway.tc Exclusive **scooter** getaway to North Caicos with *Provo Fun Cycles*, T9465868. **Jetskis** are banned from any of the marine parks, although they may be used in parts of Leeward Channel and on the Banks and can be rented from *Sun and Fun Seasports* at Leeward Marina, T9465724.

An 18-hole championship **golf** course opened November 1992 (black tees 3,202yds, white tees 2,865yds). Owned by the water company, it is located within walking distance of the *Club Med*, *Allegro Resort*, *Grace Bay Club* and *Ocean Club*. Most hotels offer 3-5 day packages of green fees and mandatory carts, T9465991, F9465992, www.provogolfclub.com, licensed snackbar. An amateur open golf championship is held in October. The former Governor created a nine-hole golf course on Grand Turk in the grounds of his residence (see box on 333). There are **tennis** courts on Provo at *Club Med*, *Erebus Inn*, T9413527 and the *Allegro Resort*. There are also courts on Pine Cay and at the *Parrot Cay Resort* and on North Caicos at *Club Vacanze*. A small but active squash community welcomes visitors and can be contacted at *Johnston Apartments*, Kings Court, T9465683. *Island Network* sports and **fitness centre** with aqua/land aerobics is at Ports of Call across from *Allegro Resort*, contact Darlene, T9464240. *Fun & Fit Health Club*, at the *Erebus Inn*, offers weights and machines, aerobics, pool, tennis, personal training and nutrition advice. There is a certified fitness trainer, T9413527, ask for Lisa. On Grand Turk there is a small fitness centre next to South Primary School.

Fishing

Two international billfishing tournaments are held annually coinciding with the full moon in Jul, T9413781, F9464326. They are big events with lots of parties

Other activities

Other sports

Turks & Caicos Islands

Holidays and festivals

Public holidays New Year's Day, Commonwealth Day, Good Friday, Easter Monday, National Heroes Day (end May), the Queen's birthday (second week in June), Emancipation Day (beginning of August), National Youth Day (end-September), Columbus' Day and Human Rights Day (both in October), Christmas Day and Boxing Day.

Festivals Most events are linked to the sea and land-based activities are tacked on to regattas or fishing tournaments. In Providenciales the **billfishing tournament** (see above) is a big event with lots of parties every night. Provo Day festivities follow **Emancipation Day** in *August*. Festivities culminate in the choosing and inauguration of Miss Turks and Caicos Islands, who competes in international beauty pagents. On Grand Turk a fishing tournament and the **Cactus Fest** are held in *August*, with competitions for sports, costumes, bands and gospel; there is a float parade, dancing and an art exhibition. On North Caicos, **Festarama** is in *July*; on Middle Caicos, **Expo** is in *August*; on South Caicos the **Regatta** with associated activities is in *May*.

Health

There are no endemic tropical diseases & no malaria, no special vaccinations are required prior to arrival. Aids exists.

See main Health Section on page 47 of Essentials chapter

On Provo, *MBS Group Medical Practice*, Leeward Highway, Jon Delisser Building, open 0830-1700 Monday-Friday, 0830-1200 Saturday, recompression chamber. Dr Euan Menzies, T9464242. Dr Steve Bourne, T2311000. Optometrist, T9415842. Dentist, Dr Joe Pretorious and Dr Roxanne, T9464321. Chiropractor Dr Kathleen Simms. There is a new private clinic on Provo in the plaza on the road to the *Allegro* from Leeward Highway, Grace Bay Medical Clinic, Dr Sam Slattery, T9415252, cell T2310525. The government clinic on Provo is Myrtle Rigby Health Complex, Leeward Highway, near Down Town, T9413000. They have three doctors and 15 nurses and midwives, open daily. Ambulance services available and emergency medical air charter to USA or Nassau, full life support can be arranged, T999 or any doctor. There is no anaesthetist on Provo so surgery is done on Grand Turk, Nassau or Miami. On Grand Turk there is a small, understaffed hospital on the north side of town, T9462333, and a government clinic in town, T9462328, open 0800-1230, 1400-1630. Dr D O Astwood, T9462451, Dr L Astwood, T9463287. The other islands organize emergency air evacuation to Grand Turk hospital. There are two pharmacies on Provo: Island Pharmacy, T9464150, F9461942, and Super Value pharmacy, with pharmacist on call 7 days a week, T9413779.

Grand Turk

Population: 2,000
Colour map 3, grid A2

Grand Turk is not a resort island although there are a few struggling hotels and dive operations which concentrate mostly on the wall just off the west coast. The vegetation is mostly scrub and cactus, among which you will find wild donkeys and horses roaming. Behind the town are old salt pans, with crumbling walls and ruined windmills, where pelicans and other waterbirds fish. More abandoned salt pans can be seen around the island, particularly towards the south. The east coast is often littered with tree trunks and other debris which have drifted across from Africa, lending credence to the claim that Columbus could have been carried here, rather than further north in the Bahamas chain. Grand Turk is the seat of government and the second largest population centre, although it has an area of only seven square miles.

Ins and outs

Getting there
See transport, page 334, for further details

Airlines and schedules tend to change frequently. Most visitors to Grand Turk arrive with *American Airlines* to Provo and then shuttle over on a small aircraft, this works quite smoothly. *Bahamasair* began flying from Miami twice a week in 1999 but there was little confidence locally that it would last long. Alternatively, *Lynx Air* flies direct from Ft Lauderdale, comfortable, many advantages but lengthy flight. *TCA*, *Sky King* and *Inter Island*

Airways operate frequent inter-island flights and it is often possible to turn up on the day you want to travel and catch the next flight. Reservations are recommended, however, particularly when going to Provo.

Taxis are the only form of public transport (US$4 from the airport to the *Osprey Beach*, the nearest). Jeeps, cars and bicycles can be rented. **Getting around**

Around the island

Grand Turk

North
East Point

Lighthouse

Little Bluff Point

North Creek

The Ridge

North
Wells

Flamingo
Cove

North
Salina

Fitness
Centre

Island
House

Regal
Begal

Corry
Hill

Town Salina

Cockburn
Town

Red
Salina

St
Mary's

Colonel
Murray
Hill

Back / Salina

English Point

Barracks
Hill

Palm
Grove

Great
Salina

Aker's
Hill

The
Sound

Eves
Hill

South
Creek

Governor's
Beach

South
Wells

Hawkes
Nest
Plantation

Waterloo

Hawkes
Pond
Salina

Gun
Hill

South Pier

Fire
Hill

Matersons Point

Hawkes
Nest
Salina

Talbot Shoal

N

Hawkes Nest
Anchorage

White
Sands
Beach

Boaby
Rock Point

0 metres 500
0 yards 500

Cockburn Town, the capital and financial centre, has some very attractive colonial buildings, mostly along Duke Street, or Front Street, as it is usually known. The government offices are in a nicely restored, small square with cannons facing the sea. The town had a facelift in 1996-97: new stone planters were built along Front Street and trees planted; the post office and government buildings were painted in a combination of blues, ranging from deep turquoise to almost white, nicely matching the ocean; the Victoria Library was stripped and repainted and local landowners and householders were encouraged to clean up their property. Those who own old houses have been offered duty free import of materials for renovation and conservation work. New benches along Pond Street came complete with a litter bin beside them. However, in 1997/98 El Niño brought bad weather which caused damage to the sea walls. Holes opened up on Front Street and the sea started to fill them from the bottom. The trees on the west side lost all their leaves in the storms and the beaches were eroded. The rebuilding of the sea wall on Front Street started in 1999 to ensure that the old buildings will not suffer further sea damage and erosion. **Cockburn Town**

The oldest church on Grand Turk is **St Thomas' Anglican church** (inland, near the water catchment tanks), built by Bermudan settlers. After a while it was considered too far to walk to the centre of the island and **St Mary's Anglican church** was built in 1899 on Front Street overlooking the water. This is now a pro-Cathedral with the southern Bahamas and is the first cathedral in the islands. The **Victoria Library**, built to commemorate 50 years of Queen Victoria's reign, is also an interesting building, with shutters. Walking north along Front Street you come to **Odd Fellows**

Lodge, opposite the salt pier, which is thought to be one of the oldest buildings on the island and was probably the place where the abolition of slavery was proclaimed in 1832.

A new Tourist Board office was opened in 1999 in a renovated old town customs building and warehouse that sits right on the water at the north end of Cockburn Town. The work has been done sympathetically, in keeping with the old Bermudian architectural style and is a pleasant place to stop off during a walk round town.

Continue north to the **Turks and Caicos National Museum** opened in 1991 in the beautifully renovated Guinep Lodge. The exhibition on the ground floor is of the early 16th-century wreck of a Spanish caravel found on the Molasses Reef between West Caicos and French Cay in only 20ft of water. The ship is believed to have been on an illegal slaving mission in the islands, as evidenced by locked leg irons found on the site. A guided tour is highly recommended although not essential. Upstairs there is an exhibition of local artefacts, photos, stamps, coins, a few Taino beads, figures and potsherds. A local historian, the late Herbert Sadler, compiled many volumes on the theory of Columbus' landfall and local history, some of which are on sale at the museum. A **Science Building** has been completed beside the museum, which houses a conservation laboratory, the only one of its kind in the English-speaking Caribbean. It has a climate-controlled storage space and classroom and the aim is to demystify archaeology and introduce the islanders to their history. The most recent find was a Taino paddle buried in the peat bottom of North Creek, which has been carbon dated to 1100 AD. Also beside the museum is a new and delightful garden. All the plants are native to the islands and carry a code number so that you can identify them from a booklet. The original building on the site was destroyed by fire, but the oven from the old slave kitchen and the water catchment tank have been renovated and preserved as garden features. The museum is working on the reconstruction of a windmill to illustrate the impact of the salt industry on the islands. ■ *US$5 for non-residents, US$2 residents, US$0.50 students. Mon-Fri 1000-1600, Sat 1000-1300. For further information contact the curator, Brian Riggs, Box 188, Grand Turk, T9462160.*

There is now an attractive walkway beside the salinas behind the town. There is a shaded viewing spot for birdwatchers and trees have been planted all along Pond Street to improve the view. Elaine Huard runs an animal sanctuary (United Humanitarians) at her home on Duke Street, where she usually has up to 40 dogs and cats. She brings vets from Canada three times a year to provide free sterilizations, medicines and general care for the domestic and stray animals on the island. Her dedicated voluntary work has made her something of a national institution and she is always pleased to receive visitors. Donations welcome.

The Governor's residence, **Waterloo**, south of the airport, was built in 1815 by a Bermudian salt merchant as a private residence and acquired for the head of government in 1857. Successive governors and administrators have modified and extended it, prompted

Cockburn Town

- Poop Deck
- Blue Water Divers
- Odd Fellows Lodge
- Town Salina
- Victoria Library
- Red Salina
- Turks Island Passage
- Beachcomber
- Elaine's Animal Sanctuary
- Turks Head Inn
- Oasis Divers
- Salt Raker Inn
- Sea Eye Diving
- Courtyard Café
- Osprey Beach

The Battle of Waterloo

Governor John Kelly is a keen golfer and when he took over the Governor's residence, Waterloo, in 1996, he soon had designs on the 20 acres of wilderness surrounding his new home. The overgrown land was attacked by a battalion of volunteer kindred spirits to create a nine-hole, par three course. The acacia thorn bushes and vines fought back as trees not seen for years were exposed and park land appeared. The wilderness was finally dominated by a team

from Her Majesty's Prison and some heavy equipment operators who uprooted the big thorn trees. The opening of the golf club was planned for June 1997, the anniversary of the Battle of Waterloo, but actually took place in January 1998 with 43 players in the Governor's Trophy competition. Visitors may pay their green fee at the Governor's office – a slightly unusual arrangement. T9462308 and speak to the secretary, Cynara John.

partly by hurricane damage in 1866 and 1945, and by the Queen's visit in 1966. In 1993 the building was again renovated and remodelled; the works were so extensive they constituted a near rebuilding of the historic residence. Governor's Beach is one of the nicest beaches and excellent for snorkelling, with isolated coral heads rising out of the sand and a wide variety of fish and invertebrates.

Further south is an ex-USAF base, known as **South Base**, which is now used as government offices, and beyond there some pleasant beaches on the south coast, with good snorkelling at White Sands beach by the point. US Navy, NASA and Coast Guard bases were once important for the economy of Grand Turk; John Glenn, the first American to orbit the earth, splashed down off Grand Turk in the 1960s.

The cays southeast of Grand Turk are a land and sea national park, sheltering Turks Head cacti on **Martin Alonza Pinzon Cay**, frigate birds on **Penniston Cay** and breeding sooty terns, noddy terns and other seabirds on **Gibbs Quay**. The lagoons and red mangroves of South Creek are also a national park, serving as a nursery for fish, crabs and other sea life, as well as a reserve for birds.

North of Cockburn Town a paved road leads along The Ridge up the east side of the island to the 1852 lighthouse and another abandoned US base, from where there are good views out to sea. This is to be refurbished and converted into a Community College. A channel at the north point gives access to North Creek, an excellent hurricane shelter for boats.

Essentials

L *Osprey Beach*, PO Box 42, T9462232, F9462877. Under new ownership in 2001, rooms being renovated one at a time, those on ground floor open directly onto the sand, suites available with kitchenette. **L-AL** *Turks Head Inn* on Duke St, PO Box 58, T9462466, F9461716, tophotel@grand-turk.com, is recommended. Built in 1869 by Jonathon Glass first as a private house and later used as a doctor's dispensary, the American Consulate and a guest house for the British Government, it is set back from the beach surrounded by tall trees. Renovated and decorated in period style, 7 rooms, with wooden floors, beds and balconies, phone, minibar, two family rooms, outside dining and upstairs dining deck, pizza ovens, barbecue night with live local music, weekly dive slide show (Oasis Divers), dive packages. **L-A** *Salt Raker Inn*, PO Box 1, T9462260, F9462817, www.microplan.com/bluerake.htm/ is an old Bermuda-style building on Duke St, also built by Bermudan ship-wright Jonathon Glass in the 1840s, facing the beach. Run by Jenny Smith, it is very friendly, relaxed and unpretentious. 10 rooms, 3 suites, sea or garden view, balconies or patios, a/c, fan, fridge, TV, dive packages with *Bluewater Divers*.

North of town on Lighthouse Rd, **AL-A** *Island House*, PO Box 36, T9461519, F9462646. 8 different suites with kitchen and barbecue, spacious, fully equipped, TV, phone, a/c, fan, on edge of North Creek, pool, free laundry facilities, maid service, bicycles and golf carts available, diving, fishing etc can be arranged, popular with people who like to spend a month or

Sleeping
Several hotels have recently closed or are in receivership. Only those open in high season 2001 are listed here although some may reopen if sold

Turks & Caicos Islands

two on the island in the winter, attentive and welcoming management, contact Colin and Lucy Brooker, or their daughter, Donna. On Front St, Angela and Douglas Gordon have a large guest suite in **A** *Beachcomber House*, also referred to as 'The Gordons', behind the government buildings, close to beach and restaurants, PO Box 110, T9462470. Includes superb breakfast, with homemade bread and muffins, and huge afternoon tea, no tax or service charges, dive packages available, open Nov-Apr only, in UK T01507-608861 for bookings during summer months when the Gordons are off the island.

Eating

The best restaurants & bars are at the hotels

The outdoor *Salt Raker Inn* is recommended for good food and pleasant company. It is a popular meeting place and fills up on Wed and Sun barbecue nights when Mitch, from Blue Water Divers, plays the guitar and sings. The *Turks Head Inn* is a gathering place with a friendly bar and good food. *Water's Edge*, T9461680, offers a very cheerful, informal atmosphere for lunch and dinner with ample portions served and a reasonably-priced menu, lots of conch. Mitch entertains here on Saturday. Scooter rental available. *The Courtyard Café*, in the courtyard of the derelict part of *Osprey Beach* across the road from the beach, surrounded by trees. Phyllis Hayward serves breakfast from 0700 and lunches until 1500, excellent, freshly-prepared meals, pastas and salads and home made desserts, nothing fried. For local food and lunch specials try *Touch of Class* on the road south out of town, a/c, TV, bar, filling, tasty portions. *Regal Begal* serves local food, on the road north of town on the west side of North Creek, a favourite lunch place. The *Poop Deck* is a tiny bar. Set back from the road in the centre of town by the sea, local food and hamburgers at lunchtime, chicken and chips in the evenings. *Peanut's* snack bar at the airport. Hot snacks, peanuts and drinks.

Nightlife

Grand Turk is not an island where you will find lots of nightlife. Most of the evening activity takes place when people get together for meals and drinks at the small inns and restaurants. Do not expect a lot of action.

Shopping

The Shell Shack, at *Beachcomber House*, is where the artist Douglas Gordon creates jewellery from conch shell, shell and beach glass mirrors, clocks, lamps and candle covers, all different and collectable, made on the island, reasonable prices, commissions accepted. *X's Gallery*, on Duke St. Run by Xavier Tonneau, formerly proprietor of the *Turks Head Inn*, and his partner Sue Cottle, they sell their own paintings, hand drawn and painted maps of the islands, a selection of Haitian art work and some small antiques collected in the islands.

Transport

Air *Lynx Air* flies once a week, Saturday, from Fort Lauderdale, T305-7729808, 1995 West Commercial Boulevard, Ft Lauderdale. *TCA* flies from Cap Haitiën, Middle Caicos, North Caicos, Providenciales, Salt Cay and South Caicos. *Sky King* has scheduled flights from Provo and South Caicos. *Sky King* will also fly to Cuba, the Dominican Republic, Bahamas and Haiti on request.

Local Jeeps or cars can be rented from *Tropical Auto Leasing*, US$55 per day, everything included except fuel, T9461000; *Sunshine Auto Leasing*, by airport, T9461588, recommended, *Dutchie's Car Rental*, Airport Rd, T9462244, recommended, or *C J Car Rental*, T9462744. If you rent a bicycle, jeep or car, note that the islanders completely ignore the 20 mph speed limit in town (and 40 mph outside), particularly on Pond St, recommended to stay on Front St/Duke St route through town and exercise caution elsewhere. Fatal accidents have occurred. **Boat** For those arriving by sea, there is a safe harbour and marina at Flamingo Cove, North Creek, run by Leah and Kirk, T9462227.

Directory

Banks *Barclays Bank*, T9462831, F9462695; *Turks & Caicos Banking Co Ltd*, Box 123, Grand Turk, T9462368, F9462365; *Scotiabank* at Harbour House, PO Box 132, Grand Turk, T9462506, F9462667.

Salt Cay

Seven miles south of Grand Turk, Salt Cay is out of the past, with windmills, salt sheds and other remnants of the old salt industry and little else. The island was first visited by the Bermudans in 1645; they started making salt here in 1673 and maintained a thriving salt industry until its collapse in the 1960s. Production ceased all together in 1971. The main village is **Balfour Town**, divided into North Side and South Side, noted for its Bermudan buildings and pretty cottages with stone walls around the gardens. The **White House**, which dominates the skyline, was built in the 1830s of Bermudan stone brought in as ballast by the Harriott family during the height of the salt industry. The **Methodist Church** nearby, one of several churches on the island, is over 125 years old. Snorkelling is good and diving is excellent; there are 10 moored dive sites along the wall, with tunnels, caves and undercuts. In January-March you can often see the humpbacked whales migrating through the channel as they pass close to the west coast. The island has been designated a UNESCO World Heritage Site. On request dive operators on Grand Turk will take you to Salt Cay by boat, the dolphins will often accompany you on the trip. You will find several properties for sale on Salt Cay. Some settlers have recovered from a bout of 'paradise found' disease, having got tired of the weekly shopping trip by boat or plane to Grand Turk for all their groceries and basic supplies.

Population: 208
Plant life was curtailed during the salt raking days to prevent rainfall. Look into some of the ruined houses & you will find salt still stored in the cellars

Sleeping

The most expensive and exclusive hotel is the **LL** *Windmills Plantation* on a 2½ mile beach, although it was for sale in 2001 and had only a caretaker management. It appeals to people who want to do nothing undisturbed, 8 suites, including all food and drink, meals taken family style, local recipes, saltwater pool, no children, diving can be arranged with Salt Cay Divers, reservations (minimum 3 nights) *The Windmills Plantation*, 440 32nd St, West Palm Beach, FL 33407, T800-8227715, F407-8452982, on Salt Cay T9466962. **L-AL** *Castaways*, T9466921 or 315-5360737, www.vikingresort.com 6 1-bedroom villas along the beach north of *Windmills Plantation*, available for rent Nov-Apr, self-catering, take supplies with you or you will be forced to eat all your meals at the hotels. **AL** *Pirates Hideaway*, Victoria St, T/F9466909, www.windnet.com/pirate 4 rooms for B&B, or rent whole house for self-catering, sea views, balcony, fans, meals on request, bikes and kayaks for hire, boat trips, drive packages. **AL** *Sunset Reef*, in USA T410-8893662, F410-4675744, sunsetreef @aol.com 2 bedrooms with en suite bathrooms, all amenities. At the other end of the scale is the cheerful **A** *Mount Pleasant Guest House*, T9466927, mtpleasantinfo@yahoo. com In need of some renovation, a salt raker's house built in 1830, now owned by Tim Dunn, the grandson of the original salt raking family on the island, it can sleep 25 in 4 very simple rooms in the main house, 2 with shared bath, and in a separate annex/guest house which has 3 basic rooms downstairs with kitchen and living room and a dormitory with 7 beds upstairs, dive package including 3 excellent meals, transfers and unlimited diving (see Diving and marine life, above), processing facilities for dive photos, video/TV, library, outdoor restaurant/bar with the best food on the island. **B** *The Salt Cay Sunset House*, Victoria St, Balfour Town, T/F9466942, seaone@ tciway.tc Meal packages available, special

Salt Cay

■ **Sleeping**
1 Castaways
3 Mount Pleasant
Guesthouse
4 Pirates Hideaway
5 Sunset Reef
6 Windmills
Plantation

Not to scale

Turks & Caicos Islands

needs catered for, good food, former 1832 plantation home, high ceilings, 3 bedrooms with bath, fans, comfortable, verandah with *Blue Mermaid Sunset Café*.

Transport

There is a paved airstrip for small aircraft, around which a fence has been erected to keep out the donkeys

The island is served by *TCA*, with 2 5-min flights Mon, Wed, Fri from Grand Turk, one at 0645 and one at an indeterminate time (about 1530) in the afternoon, making a day trip possible. Alternatively, charter a flight, or get a seat on someone else's charter, which costs the same if you can fill the aircraft, or contact the District Commissioner's Office on Salt Cay (or *Mount Pleasant Guest House*, they cross regularly to do shopping) for details of ferries. The only public transport on the island is the taxi van run by Nathan Smith (T9466920), airport pickup and touring; there are very few vehicles of any sort.

South Caicos

Population: 1,198

The beaches going east & north are totally deserted. You can walk for miles beachcombing along the east shore

The nearest Caicos island, 22 miles west of Grand Turk, South Caicos was once the most populous and the largest producer of salt. It is now the main fishing port, having benefited from the most naturally protected harbour in the islands and is also known as East Harbour, or the 'rock'. As a result, yachts frequently call here and a popular annual regatta is held at the end of May. There is excellent diving along the drop off to the south and the best snorkelling is on the windward side going east and north. Boat trips can be organized with fishermen to the island reserves of **Six Hill Cays** and **Long Cay**. Further south are the two **Ambergris Cays**, Big and Little, where there are caves and the diving and fishing are good.

Cockburn Harbour is the only settlement and is an attractive, if rather run down, little place with lots of old buildings, a pleasant waterfront with old salt warehouses and boats of all kinds in the harbour. The District Commissioner's house, currently unoccupied, stands atop a hill southeast of the village and can be recognized by its green roof. The School For Field Studies is in the 19th-century *Admiral's Arm Inn*, and attracts undergraduate students from abroad to the island to study reef ecology and marine resources, but otherwise there are very few visitors. Wild donkeys, cows and horses roam the island and several have made their home in an abandoned hotel construction site along the coast from the Residency. The **salinas** dominate the central part of the island and there is a 'boiling hole', connected to the sea by a subterranean passage, which was used to supply the salt pans. It makes an interesting walk and you may see flamingos. Call Yolanda Mills, the helpful District Commissioner, for further information, T9463211.

Sleeping & eating

L-AL *South Caicos Ocean Haven*, in town, T9463444, F9463446, www.oceanhaven.tc 22 rooms, a/c, fishing can be arranged, also diving packages available, salt water pool, restaurant. **B** *Mae's Bed & Breakfast*, Forth Street, T9463207. 3 rooms, laundry service, no credit cards. A few people in the town rent out rooms. *Love's*, local dishes. *Muriel's*, Graham St, T9463535, native dishes. *Pond View*, T9463276, native dishes. *Dora's Lobster Pot* at the airport, T9463247.

Transport

TCA and *SkyKing* connect South Caicos with Providenciales and Grand Turk. *TCA* also flies to Middle and North Caicos. There are a few taxis on the island, US$4 from the airport to *South Caicos Ocean* Haven hotel.

East Caicos

Originally named Guana by the Lucayans

East Caicos has an area of 18 sq miles which makes it one of the largest islands. It also boasts the highest point in the Turks and Caicos, Flamingo Hill at 156 ft. A ridge runs along the north coast, but the rest of the island is swamp, creeks, mangrove and mudflats. Jacksonville, in the northwest, used to be the centre of a 50,000 acre sisal plantation and there was also a cattle farm at the beginning of the 20th century. The island is now uninhabited except for mosquitoes and wild donkeys. There is an abandoned railway left over from the plantation days and feral donkeys have worn paths through the scrub and sisal. Caves near Jacksonville, which were once mined for bat guano, contain petroglyphs carved on the walls and there is evidence of several Lucayan settlements. Splendid beaches include a 17-mile beach on the north coast. Off the north coast, opposite Jacksonville, is **Guana Cay**, home to the Caicos iguana. Yet another scheme to develop East Caicos is being proposed and hotly debated, a US$350mn cruise port and resort town, with a bridge to South Caicos. Conservationists are protesting against the potential damage to the Ramsar site and wildlife on the island, watch this space!

Middle Caicos

Also known as Grand Caicos, this is the largest of the islands, with an area of 48sq miles. Its coastline is more dramatic than some of the other islands, characterized by limestone cliffs along the north coast, interspersed with long sandy beaches shaded by casuarina pines or secluded coves. The south part of the island is swamp and tidal flats. There are three settlements linked by the paved King's Road, **Conch Bar**, where there is an airstrip, a primary school and guest houses, **Bambarra** and **Lorimers**. The caves between Bambarra and Lorimers, which were used by Amerindians as dwelling places, were later mined for guano. They are huge, complex and beautiful. There are now paths and some lights and guides to take you through them and they are well worth the time and expense. Day tours are available from Provo at around US$145 per person, including transport from Leeward, lunch, drinks, snorkelling and beachcombing, an all day affair. Archaeological excavations have uncovered a Lucayan ball court and a settlement near Armstrong Pond, due south of Bambarra, but these are not easily accessible. Evidence of the Lucayan civilization dates back to 750 AD. Loyalist plantation ruins can also be explored. Bambarra beach is an empty, curving sweep of white sand, fringed with casuarina trees. Middle Caicos regatta is held here and there are small thatched huts which serve as restaurants for the very popular end-August Expo (some litter remains), but otherwise there are no facilities. A sand bar stretches out to **Pelican Cay**, half a mile out, which you can walk to at low tide, popular with wading birds. The view from Conch Bar beach is marred by a rusting barge in shallow water, but there is afternoon shade at the west end under a cliff where the reef meets the land. A pretty cove, popular with day trippers, is **Mudjeon Harbour**, just west of Conch Bar, protected by a sand bar and with shade under a rocky overhang. The reef again juts out from the land here before branching out westwards along the rocky coastline. This can be spectacular in the winter months with the crashing waves. South of Middle Caicos is a nature reserve comprising a frigatebird breeding colony and a marine sinkhole with turtles, bonefish and shark. The blue hole is surrounded by sandy banks and is difficult to get to, but it shows up on the satellite photo of the islands on display in the museum in Grand Turk.

In December 1998 the Crossing Place Trail was reopened. This was formerly a path worn by Lucayan Indians and later by slaves travelling between plantations, and it runs for 12 dramatic and beautiful miles (seven miles can be cycled), along the north coast connecting Lorimers, Bambarra and Conch Bar. Developed by the National Trust to encourage ecotourism on the island, the trail takes in beaches, coastal cliffs, Conch Bar, Indian Caves and the Blowing Hole. It is well marked and there are plans to have shaded benches along the route. Tours from Provo and Grand Turk are available. Wear strong walking shoes.

Ask the District Commissioner's office, T9466100, for information and assistance, including boat tours and cave tours.

LL-L *Blue Horizon Resort* on Mudgeon Harbour beach, T9466141, F9466139, www.bhresort.com Offers 4 small and large studio cottages and a 2-bedroomed house, screened porches, on 50 acres (land for sale), weekly rental available, bicycles, fishing, tours arranged, bring own groceries or ask for accommodation to be stocked with your

Population: 272

Visit the huge caves in the national park at Conch Bar that link up with the sea. There are bats, stalactites, stalagmites & underwater salt lakes with pink shrimp

Sleeping

Turks & Caicos Islands

requirements. **LL** *Dreamscape Villa*, www.middlecaicos.com, Bambarra beach. 3 bedrooms, 2 bathrooms, outside shower, large veranda, 80 ft from water, hammock on deck. In the USA, 185 Highland Ave, White River Junction, VT 05001, Vermont, T802-2952652. In TCI, Ernest Forbes Jr, T9466175. **L** *Seascape Villa*, www.caicosvilla.com On 2 acres of beachfront, view of reef and gardens from screened veranda, only 6 houses on this 5-mile stretch of shore, 2 miles to town, sleeps 8, 2 bedrooms, a/c on first floor, 2 queen size beds in a/c loft, well-equipped kitchen, barbecue, games, books, caretakers. In Conch Bar: **L-AL** *Eagles Rest Villas*, T9466175, in USA T215-2554640, F813-7937157. 1 studio on 5 miles of beach, sometimes for rent, amenities offered are not always available. George and Martha Volz' **AL** *Villa*, contact 1255 Carolyn Drive, Southampton, PA, 18966, T215-3220505, F215-3220593 in the USA, or the District Commissioner's office, Dolphus Arthur, T9466100. A 3-bedroom house let for 3 day minimum, week or month, Dec-Apr. Stacia and Dolphus Arthur run **C** *Arthur's Guesthouse* next to Arthur's Store, T9466122. 1 double, 1 twin-bedded room, private bath, kitchen.

Eating Canned foods and sodas are available from the few small stores in Conch Bar and fresh food arrives weekly on the ferry from Provo. However, it is advisable to bring your own food. Annie Taylor is known for her cooking and runs a restaurant on demand in her house. *Johnson's Bar* is open in Conch Bar most afternoons and evenings for cold beer, dominoes and music. *T&J Boutique* in Conch Bar has ice creams, cold drinks and fried chicken on Fri.

Transport **Air** *TCA* fly from Grand Turk, South Caicos, North Caicos and Providenciales. After clearing customs upon arrival at Provo *SkyKing* and private pilots will also stop off if flying to North Caicos, or you can charter a plane. Reliable and recommended, *Global Airways*, run by Ferrington, Lindsey and Bennet Gardiner. Do not pre-book as you may sit 2-3 hours waiting for a particular plane. **Road** Carlton Forbes runs a taxi service and fares are based on US$2 per mile for 2 people, eg Conch Bar to Bambarra US$14, to Lorimers US$20. **Bicycle** *Sports Shack* in Conch Bar sells, rents and repairs bicycles. **Ferry** A ferry service for cargo and passengers runs between Provo, Middle and North Caicos, operated by owners of *Blue Horizons Development*, contact Dale Witt, T9466141, F9466139 for times and days (probably only Saturday) the *Dale Marie* runs. Hired bicycles (eg from Whitby Plaza, North Caicos, US$15 per person) may be taken on board for day trips and overnight stays on Middle Caicos.

North Caicos

Population: 1,275

The lushest of the islands, North Caicos has taller trees than the other islands and attracts more rain. Like Middle and East Caicos, the south part of the island comprises swamp and mangrove. The population has declined to 1,275 inhabitants living at the settlements of Bottle Creek, Whitby, Sandy Point and Kew.

You are advised to bring small denomination US dollar notes as there is no bank and it is difficult to cash US$50 or US$100, travellers' cheques or money orders around the island

There is one Nature Reserve at **Dick Hill Creek** and **Bellefield Landing Pond**, to protect the West Indian whistling duck and flamingos, and another at **Cottage Pond**, a fresh/salt water sinkhole, about 170 ft deep, where there are grebes and West Indian whistling duck. **Pumpkin Bluff Pond** is a sanctuary for flamingos, Bahamian pintail and various waders. **Three Mary's Cays** is a sanctuary for flamingos and is an osprey nesting site. Flocks of flamingos can also be seen on **Flamingo Pond**, but take binoculars. There is a viewing point at the side of the road, which is the only place from where you can see them and at low tide they can be a long way off. There is also good snorkelling at **Three Mary's Cays** and **Sandy Point beach** to the west is lovely. There is a rough road to Three Mary's Cays suitable for jeeps. The beaches are good along the north coast where the hotels are, although the best is a seven-mile strip west of Pumpkin Bluff, where there has been no development so far. It can be reached by walking along the beach or via a dirt road past the *Club Vacanze* car park. A cargo ship foundered on the reef in the 1980s, and is still stuck fast, making it of snorkelling interest. Construction of a new deep water harbour has begun and when finished it will extend from Pine Cay to Bellefield Landing and over Dick Hill Creek.

Kew, in the centre, is a pretty, scruffy little village with neat gardens and tall trees, many of them exotic fruit trees, to provide shade. There are three churches, a primary school, a shop and two bars. **Bottle Creek**, in the east, has a high school, clinic and churches. The paved road ends here and a rough road requiring four-wheel drive continues to Toby Rock. The backstreets of Bottle Creek run alongside the creek and here you can see the importance of water conservation, with people carrying buckets to and from the municipal water tap at the rain catchment area, while donkeys, goats and dogs roam around. The area is poor, but many people are building themselves bigger and better homes. **Whitby**, on the north coast, is rather spread out along the road, but this is where the few hotels are. Several expatriates have built their homes along Whitby Beach. Sandflies can be a problem in this area, particularly if there is not enough wind, take insect repellent. **Sandy Point**, in the west, is a fishing community. North Caicos is the centre of basket making in the islands and there are several women, including Clementine Mackintosh, Eliza Swan and Cassandra Gardiner, who are expert in their craft. Prices do not vary much from those in the shops in Providenciales or locally. Eliza Swan is based in Whitby and makes beautiful bags and baskets using many colours and designs. **Wades Green Plantation**, just to the west of Kew, is the best example of a Loyalist plantation in the islands, with many ruins, including a courtyard and a prison. Archaeologists from the University of California in Los Angeles carried out excavations in 1989. The boutique section of *Papa Grunt's* restaurant in the Whitby Plaza sells crafts, potions and insect repellent cheaper than on Provo.

Sleeping

All accommodation is in the Whitby beach area on the north coast

LL *Datai Villa*, www.datai-villa.com New in 1999, on beach, 2 separate buildings open on to patio with large deck, master bedroom in one, 2 further bedrooms in the other, sleep 2-6 people. **LL-L** *Club Vacanze* (formerly *The Prospect of Whitby*), T9467119, F9467114. A long-established hotel, nearly all guests are on an all-inclusive Italian package, luxury accommodation, very little English spoken by Italian staff, not recommended for non-Italians, pool, tennis. **LL-AL** *Ocean Beach*, T9467113, F9467386. 10 units in condominiums, room only or suites, with up to 3 bedrooms, dining room/lounge, freshwater swimming pool, diving on site and excursions with Beach Cruiser Charters. **LL-AL** *Pelican Beach Hotel*, T9467112, F9467139, www.tcimall.tc/pelicanbeach Friendly, relaxed, few facilities, 14 rooms, 2 suites, the older rooms face the beach, new packages available, run by Clifford and Susan Gardiner. **L-AL** *Bottle Creek Lodge*, T9467080, www.bottlecreeklodge.com Run by Howard and Cheryl Gibbs, members of Ecotourism Socety, lodge room or detached cabin, on top of small ridge on northeast side of Flamingo Pond, all rooms sea view, composting toilets, overhead banana leaf fans, special diets catered for, CP, kayaks, bicycles. **L-AL** *Oceanside Villa*, T/F9467301, joannesbnb@tciway.tc 3 bedrooms, 2 en suite bathrooms, large, bright, airy, comfortable, screened veranda, secluded, 300ft from beach, all rooms ocean view. Under same ownership is **AL-A** *Jo Anne's Whitby Plaza Bed & Breakfast*, T/F as for *Oceanside Villa*. Large, comfortable rooms or suites with bath, hot water, fans, king, queen or twin beds, private entrances and veranda, also 4-room housekeeping unit, short walk to Whitby beach, bicycle, kayak and canoe rental, *Papa Grunt's*, on premises. **A** *Hollywood Beach Condos*, Whitby, T9467185, F9464451. 4 1-bed units with kitchen on the beach, transportation, fishing, diving arranged, bring your own food. **A** *North Caicos Villas*, T/F9467308. One 1,200sq ft and one 800sq ft villa, all watersports, transportation arranged, bring your own food.

Eating

Simple local restaurants include *Club Titter's Restaurant and Bar*, near the airport, and *Marina View* on Kew Rd, very simple, not always open. Italian at the private *Club Vacanze*, reservations necessary. *Papa Grunt's Restaurant*, Whitby Plaza. Open 0830, credit cards accepted, indoor or screened veranda dining, native and American cuisine, fresh seafood, lots of conch, sandwiches with homemade bread US$5.75, pizza, salads, vegetarian platter, open Sun 1100-1400 for lunch. Phone, fax and email service offered in the office area. *Pelican Beach Hotel* serves good food but is only open if there are guests at the hotel.

Turks & Caicos Islands

Watersports   **Diving** *Beach Cruiser* at the *Ocean Beach Hotel*, T9467113, offers diving, US$50 for one-tank dive, US$80 for two-tank dive, minimum 4 people, packages and equipment hire available. Snorkelling trips also offered. **Fishing** US$200 a half day or US$375 a whole day, maximum four people, with *Beach Cruiser*. For unspoiled backwater bonefishing/flat bottom fishing, contact Whitby Plaza for trips on 27 ft launch boat. Lunch included with all day trips. **Sailing** There is a 20 ft pontoon 'flat top' boat for hire, from *Beach Cruiser*, offering trips of 1 hour, half day or full day, picnics, snorkelling etc, island hopping and visits to see iguanas on Salt Water Cay.

Transport   **Air** *Inter Island Airways* and *Global Airways*, run by the Gardiner family, popular private pilots, fly to North Caicos from Provo daily after your flight arrives. Cost is US$30 one way 12 mins. *TCA* has only one morning flight and one afternoon flight (never on Sun) from Provo but these are not reliable or leave to a set schedule (advise not to buy a return ticket despite what local airlines suggest as you may not return with same plane/pilot and you will have to pay again). If you wish to charter a plane the cost is US$125 (you have to pay for all the empty seats). **Road** For day trips or overnight stays you can rent a cruising bicycle at *Papa Grunts* restaurant at Whitby Plaza, island map supplied. Rates are US$15 per person per 24 hrs, for weekly rates seventh day free, credit card deposit required, T/F9467301. There are car hire facilities on North Caicos with *Saunders Rent A Car*, VHF Channel 16 'Sierra 7', or *Gardiners Auto Service*, US$35 for half day, US$70 for full day, plus US$10 tax. A taxi costs US$10 from the airport to Whitby for one person, US$12 for 2, US$15 for 3. Taxi from Sandy Point to Whitby is US$20. A tour of the island by taxi costs US$80-100, the drivers are friendly and knowledgeable but some tend to run their own errands while working.

Parrot Cay

The *Parrot Cay Resort*, a luxury, 56-room hotel, was built in 1992 on this 1,300-acre private island, but it only opened in December 1998. It has already attracted the rich and famous, with a guest list that includes Paul McCartney and Bruce Willis, and it is frequently featured in glossy magazines and TV travel shows. It has beautiful landscaping, the largest freshwater pool in the TCI, two restaurants, tennis courts, gym and offers all watersports. The furniture is Indonesian, some of the staff are Asian and the food is Asian-influenced. You can have a Thai, Balinese or Swedish massage. Cotton used to be grown here and there are the remains of a plantation house. The wetlands and mangroves are to be preserved to protect wildlife. Rates start at US$460 in low season. T9467788, F9467789, www.Provo.net/ParrotCay

Dellis Cay   Dellis Cay is uninhabited but frequently visited for its **shells**. You can be dropped off there for the day for shelling by a local charter boat out from Leeward Marina.

Pine Cay

Pine Cay is an 800-acre private resort owned by a group of homeowners who also own the exclusive 12 room **LL** *Meridian Club*. Children under six years are not allowed to stay in the hotel and there are lots of restrictions on where they are allowed if brought to a villa. The homes, which are very comfortable, with spectacular views, can be rented. A hurricane in 1969 left Pine Cay 5ft underwater for a while and since then the houses have been built slightly back from the beach and many of them are on stilts. There is a fairly well-stocked commissary or you can eat in the hotel; golf carts are used to get around the island. ■ *Nov-Jun. Reservations can be made through Resorts Management Inc, T800-3319154, 212-6964566, F212-6891598, locally T/F9465128.* Non-motorized watersports and tennis are available and excursions to other cays can be arranged. May is a popular time for bonefishing. Day trippers are not encouraged although visitors may come for lunch at the restaurant by prior reservation as long as they do not use the facilities; the homeowners value their privacy and put a ban on visitors if they feel there have been

The Turks and Caicos National Trust

The National Trust is a relatively new, non-profit, non-governmental conservation organization, working in co-operation with the Government, the World Wildlife Fund, The Nature Conservancy and local people to preserve the natural and historical heritage of the islands and develop sustainable tourism to keep the Turks and Caicos Islands 'beautiful by nature'. Projects in hand include: an exhibition on national parks, endangered animals and the islands' history in the departure terminal at Provo airport; a historically-oriented public park around the

Cheshire Hall plantation ruins near downtown Provo; public access to the 100-acre Bird Rock Point Natural Area on the northeast tip of Provo for walking and birdwatching; a fund-raising campaign and work with the Government on a financial framework for the long-term management of the national parks. For information on the National Trust, to become a member or volunteer, contact Ethlyn Gibbs-Williams, the National Trust of the Turks and Caicos Islands, Providenciales, T9415710.

too many. Pine Cay benefits from a few freshwater ponds and wells, so water is no problem here and the vegetation is more lush than on Provo. On the other hand mosquito control is a constant problem. Nature trails have been laid out around the ponds and through the trees. **Water Cay** is a nature reserve and although classified as a separate island, is joined to Pine Cay by sand dunes created during the 1969 hurricane. There is an airstrip, guests usually charter a flight, and a dock if they prefer to come in with the *Meridian Club's* exclusive shuttle boat.

Little Water Cay is the nearest island to Provo and inhabited by iguanas. The endangered Turks and Caicos rock iguana is now protected from threatening human presence by boardwalks which protect their burrows and nesting chambers, and there are strict rules against feeding them. A visitor's fee is charged to continue their protection. (Most tour operators have day trips, see page 328.)

Little Water Cay

Turks & Caicos Islands

Providenciales

'Provo' is 25 miles long and about three wide. Grace Bay stretching along the north shore has many hotels and condominiums but you can walk and snorkel without feeling crowded although a surge of building work has transformed the area beyond all recognition in the last ten years. Away from the smart hotels, condos and villas, however, the island is dry, scrubby and nothing like as pretty as the underwater world surrounding it. The reef is superb and attracts thousands of divers every year.

Population: over 10,000

Ins and outs

Scheduled internal flights with *TCA* and *SkyKing*. Charter companies are *TCA, Inter Island Airways, Flamingo Air Services, Provo Air Charter, TCI SkyKing* and *Global Air Charters*.

Getting there

Most roads are paved, contributing to fast, erratic driving by residents; speed limits (40 mph highway, 20 mph in town) are not observed, dangerous overtaking is common.Hired cars are not generally well serviced, exchanges are common. Taxis charge US$2 per mile, a ride for one person from the airport to the *Allegro* is US$12-15, and a round trip to a restaurant or Downtown can be US$40. Tours and shopping trips about US$25 per hour. Complaints have not lowered the rates. There are usually taxis at the large hotels, otherwise phone for one.

Getting around
See page 323 for international air services & transport for other details

Around the island

The **Princess Alexandra Marine Park** incorporates the reef offshore. Development of the island began in 1967 although it had been settled in the 18th century and there were three large plantations in the 19th century growing cotton and sisal. The three original settlements, **The Bight** (meaning Bay), **Five Cays** and **Blue Hills**, are fragmented and have not grown into towns as the population has increased. Instead shopping malls have been built along the Leeward Highway (Market Place, Plantation Hills, Central Square, Provo Plaza, retail stores, restaurants, lawyers and business offices). The Office of the Chief Secretary, banks, law firms, supermarkets, and travel agents are **Down Town**. **Turtle Cove** calls itself 'the heart of Provo', with a couple of hotels, a marina, dive operators, boat charters, deep sea fishing, restaurants, the tourist office, hairdressing and a few boutiques.

On the south side of the island, **South Dock** is the island's commercial port and here you will find the Customs Office and the Harbourmaster. **The Caicos Marina and Shipyard** on the south coast is many miles from shopping supplies.It changed hands in 1999 and the new management is still promising to upgrade the facilities. Also on the south side is a small marina: **South Side Marina**. To the west, **Sapodilla Bay** offers good protection for yachts in all winds west through southeast. It is open to the south through southwest. **Chalk Sound**, a national park inland from Sapodilla Bay, is a shallow lagoon of marvellous turquoise colours, dotted with rocky islets.

Providenciales

■ **Sleeping**
1 Airport Inn
2 Allegro Resort
3 Back of Beyond
4 Beaches Resort
5 Caribbean Paradise Inn
6 Coral Gardens
7 Club Mediteranée
8 Crystal Bay Resort Condominiums
9 Erebus Inn
10 Grace Bay Club
11 Island Princess
12 Ocean Club
13 Ocean Club West
14 Point Grace

Turks & Caicos Islands

At the northeast end, a deep channel known as **Leeward Going Through** is a natural harbour and a marina with fuel, water, ice and restaurant has been built here. There is a conch farm at the **Island Sea Centre** at Leeward. ■ *Hatchery tours 0900-1700, US$6 adults, US$3 children under 12, T9465330, F9465849, also gift shop.*

Northwest Point, a marine park offshore, has good beaches, diving and snorkelling. In 1993 a French television company shot a series of underwater game shows here and a treacherous road was bulldozed through to the beautiful beach. They left several tiki huts which offer much needed shade for a day on the beach. Two other good places to snorkel in the Grace Bay area are just to the east of Turtle Cove, where rays and turtles can be seen on Smith's reef near the entrance to the marina, just west of *Treasure Beach Villas*, and in front of *Coral Gardens Resort*, where there is a variety of life, including grouper; ask anybody for directions.

Inland, along Seasage Hill Road in Long Bay, is **The Hole**, a collapsed limestone, water-filled sinkhole next to a house called *By the Hole*. A tunnel to the right hand side gives access to the main pool. Do not attempt to descend. Ruins of Loyalist and Bermudian settlers' plantations and houses can be seen at **Cheshire Hall**, Richmond Hills and along the Bight road. On the hill overlooking the (closed) *Mariner Hotel* at Sapodilla Bay a pole marks the location of stones engraved with initials and dates in the 17th century possibly by shipwrecked sailors or wreckers. The view, even with the commercial dock in the foreground, is quite lovely, and it is free.

Essentials

There is still a lot of construction happening, with a *Yacht Club* being built at Turtle Cove. The newest development on Grace Bay Beach, the *Royal West Indies Resort*, rwi@tciway.tc, is yet another hotel/condominium with full service and restaurants. Three condominium/retail projects are being built in Grace Bay, behind the beachfront properties: *Trade Winds, Sea Side Condominiums* and *Weather Vanes at Grace Bay*, sales@wxvanes.com Expensive hotels and condos running from west to east along the north shore include: *Coral Gardens Resort, Beaches* (all-inclusive), *Sibonné, Alexandra Resort & Spa* (under construction), *The Sands, Point Grace, The Mansions, The Rennaisance* (under construction), *The Allegro Resort & Casino* (all-inclusive), *Grace Bay Club, Ocean Club West, The Grandview* (under construction), *Royal West Indies Resort, Club Med Turkoise* (all-inclusive), *Ocean Club.*

LL *Ocean Club West*, T9465880, F9465845, www.oceanclubresorts.com 7 buildings with 90 suites, all resort facilities available. **LL** *Point Grace*, T9465096, F9465097, www.pointgrace.tc 31 suites in 2 condos on the beach and 4 3-plex cottages directly behind them. **LL** *The Sands Resort*, T9465199, F9465198, www.thesandsresort. com On the beach, 105 suites and rooms in 5 buildings, 2 pools, extensive landscaping. **LL-L** *Allegro Resort & Casino* (known

Sleeping
When confirming rates & availability, check whether tax & service are included

Turks & Caicos Islands

Jo Jo

A bottle-nosed dolphin, known as Jo Jo, frequents the Princess Alexandra Marine Park along the north coast of Providenciales in the Grace Bay area, although he is also found occasionally in other locations. He is attracted by boats (particularly propeller noise and bubbles) and humans, apparently enjoying swimming and playing with people, while often coming in very close to the shore. If you are fortunate enough to see or swim with him, remember that he is a protected wild animal: do not touch him. He has been injured by propellers in the past, so take care if you are in a boat. Although there is a campaign for boats to fit a protective covering, very few watersports operators have agreed to do so. The Turks & Caicos Free Press of 27 March 1998 quoted one charter vessel captain as saying "We're not going to go crazy about one dolphin". The government has declared Jo Jo to be a National Treasure, but little is done to protect him. Dean Bernal, who runs public awareness campaigns on the island, has repeatedly called for special propeller guards to be fitted to Club Med waterski boats and has even offered to purchase them himself, to no avail. There is now a campaign to ban waterskiing in the marine park. For more information contact Jo Jo's warden at VHF 'Sea Base' channel 68 or 73 or T/F9415617, www.jojo.tc; the Jo Jo Dolphin Project is supported by the Bellerive Foundation. Dean Bernal can be contacted on jojo1@tciway.tc If you want to express your concern to the authorities, write to governoroffice@tciway.tc, with a copy to Dean.

formerly as *Turquoise Reef*, soon to become an Occidental hotel), newly renovated beach front all-inclusive, 222 rooms. **LL** *Grace Bay Club*, on beach, T9465757, F9465758, www.gracebay.com Luxury accommodation, 22 elegant condos, a/c, phone, TV, watersports, tennis, pool, jacuzzi, all amenities, French restaurant, beach bar. **LL-L** *Sibonné* (formerly *Le Deck*), T9465547, F9465770, www.sibonne.com 26 rooms and condos, golf packages, restaurant, lovely bougainvillea in the courtyard, pool. **LL-L** *Ocean Club Beach and Golf Resort*, PO Box 240, T9465880, F9465845, oceanclb@tciway.tc Condos on the beach, comfortable, well-equipped, balconies, some with good views the length of Grace Bay, spacious deck around pool with daytime snack bar, next to Provo Golf Club, packages available, free transport to airport, bike rentals. **LL-AL** *Coral Gardens Resort and White House Villa* on Grace Bay, T/F9413713, coralgardens@tciway.tc Best snorkelling site, now 30 'boutique residences' for sale or rental, 1-2 bedrooms or junior suite. **LL-AL** *Caribbean Paradise Inn*, T9465020, F9465022, www.paradise.tc 200yds from beach, by *Grace Bay Club*, 15 rooms, ocean or pool view, including breakfast buffet, snacks available, new, popular, dive gear storage, German-owned and managed. **LL-AL** *Back of Beyond*, Discovery Bay, T9414555, backofbeyond@tciway.tc 9-bedroom adobe style guest house with bar and restaurant. **LL-A** *Turtle Cove Inn*, T9464203, F9464141, tcinn@tciway.tc 3 rate schedules, special weekly 5 packages, recently renovated with new management, 30 rooms, poolside or ocean view, smallish rooms but comfortable, suite with kitchenette available, not on beach, all watersports, at the marina, cable TV, 2 restaurants.

L *Treasure Beach Villas*, T9464325, F9464108. Run down, 18 self-catering apartments, 1-2 bedrooms, no restaurant, swimming pool. **L-A** *Erebus Inn*, on hillside overlooking Turtle Cove, T9464240, F9464704, www.erebus.tc 26 rooms, larger than those in other hotels, and a few basic chalets with wonderful views liked by divers, dive packages available, all watersports at the marina, gym and fitness centre on site, pool, tennis, 2 rooms fully equipped for ham radio operators. **B** *Airport Inn*, T9464701/9413514, F9413281, airport@tciway.tc. 2 mins to airport, close to banks, groceries, restaurants, 25 rooms, 24-hr service, shops and restaurant on site, a/c, TV, special rates for pilots, 15% discount if you book room and rental car.

In the Sapodilla area there are self-catering villas: *Casuarina Cottages*, T9464474, F9464433. 3 units, US$800-1,000 a week. *Villa Bella Casa*, 3 bed villa on Leeward Beach, T/F9465037. US$2,500 per week, guest house US$1,500 per week. *The Cottage*, Grace Bay, call Kit T9465376, F9465792, southfleetwood@tciway.tc. Guest house with pool, sleeps 4, US$150 per night, US$1,000 per week. *Villa Camilla*, on Grace Bay, T617-7312194 for rates/availability. Accommodates 2-14 people, 3 bed/3 bath villa and guest house. Tojo Properties *Caribbean Ocean View Flats*, T9413101, F9413102. Villa with 4 large 2 bed apartments, pool, all amenities. **LL** *Crystal Bay Resort Condominiums*, T9464929, F9464825. 27 rooms, 5 miles from anywhere on the north shore, sales staff trying to sell condos.

There are plenty of self-catering condos & villas around the island

Turtle Cove Expensive places include *Sharkbite Bar and Grill*, Admiral's Club, on the water, 1100-2400, happy hour 1700-1900, nightly specials and events, T9415090. *Baci Ristorante*, T9413044. Fine Italian dining indoors and on the terrace overlooking the Pond. **Mid-range** restaurants where you can spend US$40-60 on a dinner for two with wine: *Sunset Restaurant & Bar*, at the Erebus overlooking Turtle Cove, T9464240, erebus@tciway.tc. Spectacular view, serving New Age Asian and Caribbean cuisine to popular acclaim. *Banana Boat*, T9415706. Dockside at Turtle Cove marina, Caribbean bar and grill, colourful, cheerful. The Terrace, T9464763. 'Creative' conch, seafood, lunch, dinner, closed Sun. *Tiki Hut*, at Turtle Cove Inn, T9465341. Breakfast, lunch and dinner, chicken or ribs every Wed night, US$10, extremely popular with ex-pats.

Eating

Dinner with wine at an expensive restaurant will easily cost US$100 for two

Down Town *Club Latino Bar & Grill*, open 24 hrs, slots, chicken 'n' ribs, nightclub and disco after 2000 behind Ward Construction building. *Lamont's*, T9416115. Pink building, native and absolutely-everything- American menu, to go, 0600-2300 Mon-Sat, 0900-2300 Sun. *Nyammings*, on Old Airport Rd, T9413709. New, native food with Jamaican twist. *Sweet T's Meals On Wheels*, next to Texaco service station. Native dishes, open 0600-2200, closed Sun, proprietor Mary Simmons. *Tasty Temptations*, next to the dry cleaners, T9464049. French breakfasts, sandwiches, fresh salads for lunch, good coffee, deli, open 0630-1500, closed Sat-Sun.

Down Town and on Airport Rd you will find the least expensive, but not necessarily cheap meals, catering to Islanders and office workers in town

Airport Road Within walking distance from the airport is *Fast Eddie's*, T9413176. Wed night buffet, open 0730-2300. Excellent native food, no alcohol on premises, reservations for groups. *Frances Place*, T9464472. Family dining 0600-2200, Jamaican touch, TV, slots, closed Sun. *Gilley's* is the only place to eat at the airport, a/c, noisy, local hangout, indifferent service and menu. 5 mins' walk from airport, *Rolling Pin Hotte Shoppe Restaurant*, T9415023. Immaculate indoor or outdoor seating, Trinidadian and native food, curry and roti, salads, 0900-2100, at Airport Plaza near *Airport Inn*. *Where Its At*, T9464185. Jamaican specialities by Yvette, curried goat and Presidente beer by the quart a must, generous portions, daily specials, 0630-2300, *Turn Table Disco* next door.

Leeward Highway *China Restaurant*, T9465377. Mandarin cuisine, Chinese chef, a/c, open daily, no lunch Sun. *Dora's Restaurant and Bar*, near PPC power station, T9464558. Open from 0730 until very late, local recipes, filling, eat in or takeaway. *Hey José Cantina*, near the Tourist Shoppe, Central Square Shopping Centre, T9464812. Great food, Mexican/American, tacos, huge pizza etc, mid-priced, 1200-2200, closed Sunday, takeaways. At Market Place, *Mackie's Café*, T9413640. Native style breakfast and lunch daily, stewed fish and Johnny cake, Sun morning, 0800-1900, fresh seafood. At Provo Plaza, east of WIV, TV satellite dishes, *Pizza Pizza*, T9413577, New York style pizza, 7 days a week, eat in or takeaway. Recommended. *Top O' The Cove Deli*, next to Napa auto at Suzie Turn. 'Little bit of New York-style deli', subs, bagels, order lunch by T/F9464694, beer, wine, picnic food, open 0630-1530 daily.

Grace Bay (west to east) *Coyaba* at *Coral Gardens*, T9465186. The name means 'heavenly' in Arawak and so is the food, expensive, closed Tue evening. *Jungle Hut Café*, in newly-opened Grace Bay Plaza, native cuisine, ladies' nights, closed Tue. *Bella Luna Ristorante*, in the *Glass House* west of *Allegro*, T9465214. Dinner 1800-2130 daily, nightly

Hotel restaurants are open to all, but visitors to all-inclusive beaches must have a day/evening pass

Turks & Caicos Islands

specials, reservations recommended. At the Ports of Call shopping centre across the street from *Allegro*, **Lattitudes**, Tex Mex, T9465832, F9464624. Seafood and more for lunch and dinner 6 days a week, mid-priced. **Barefoot Café**, in *Ports of Call*, T946-JAVA. 0630-late, daily bagels, subs, cappuccino, ice cream or dinners. Next to *Ports of Call*, **Caicos Café & Grill**, T9465278. Home made pasta with French flair, grilled fish and seafood, expensive, service personal but slow, go early or late to avoid crowds, open-air, open daily 1200-2400. *Coco Bistro*, past *Caicos Café*, east of *Allegro* near Club Med, behind Sunshine Nursery in mature palm trees, T9465369. Indoor dining/bar, or outdoors under the palms, Mediterranean cooking, specials every night, daily for dinner, reservations advised, expensive, congenial hosts and service. East of *Allegro Resort*, Anacaona restaurant and bar on the beach, T9465050. Thatched roof elegance, nouvelle cuisine with Caribbean flair, exclusive and also expensive, live music some evenings, guests only, reservations recommended. Adjacent to *Ocean Club*, **Gecko Grille**, Ocean Club Plaza, T9465885. Pretentious, expensive, opt for garden dining as indoor noise level unpleasant, bar opens 1630-2400, dining 1800-2200 daily. **Fairways Bar & Grill**, opposite *Ocean Club*, Provo Golf Course Clubhouse, T9465991. Breakfast, lunch and dinner, Wed lunch specials, Fri happy hour, popular with doctors, lawyers, business people and visiting golfers, same management as The Terrace in Turtle Cove.

Leeward going through At the east end of Providenciales is *Gilley's at Leeward*, T9465094. Open from 0800-2200, by the marina, breakfast, lunch specials, good food, friendly, superb service, meet local fishermen, arrange outings, boat trips, elegant, romantic dinners.

Blue Hills settlement *Conch House*, everything conch, 1100-late, Mon-Sat. *Caribbean Mack* (formerly *Roadrunner*). Soca, reggae, latino, nightly till late. *Smokey's On the Bay*, T9414453. Not to be missed, indoor or tiki hut dining on the beach, great native dishes, lobster, conch, buffets, sometimes live band. *Three Queens Bar & Restaurant*, T9415984. Excellent, reasonably-priced, local seafood lunches and dinners, by reservation only as the restaurant section is not always open.

Entertainment
Provo is not a party place, people come here for relaxation & to enjoy the water, not for the nightlife

Casino Small casino in the *Allegro Resort*. **Cinema** *Village Cinemas* is a new 2-screen movie theatre complex which will seat 370 people, T9414108. **Disco** *Casablanca Disco* immediately west of *Club Med*, open weekends, nothing ever happens until after midnight, loud music. *Where It's At Disco* on Leeward Highway, opened in 2000, loud 'island' music, DJ, drinks.

Transport **Air** **From North America**: *American Airlines* flies several times daily from Boston, Miami and New York. *TWA* flies from New York and Boston. *Delta* flies from Atlanta. **From Europe**: *British Airways* flies on Sun from Gatwick, other flights from Europe connect in Miami or New York. From **the Caribbean**: *Bahamasair* flies from Nassau; *TCI Sky King* from Cap Haitien (Haiti), Montego Bay (Jamaica), Puerto Plata, Punta Cana and Santo Domingo (Dominican Republic) and Santiago de Cuba; *Turks and Caicos Airways* from Cap Haitien. Within the Turks and Caicos Islands, there are scheduled flights to Grand Turk, Middle Caicos, North Caicos and South Caicos with TCI Sky King and Turks and Caicos Airways. For charters and other flights, see 'Getting around', page 325.

Be careful on the roads. Leeward Highway is specially risky

Bus *Stafford Morris' Blue Bus*, VHF16, pickup and delivery almost anywhere, including the airport, US$3 per person each way say Downtown to Grace Bay, T9413598 or flag him down. *Pelican Bus Service*, T9464092, VHF 67. **Car & bike hire** An economy car, quoted at US$39 per day will work out to US$61.50 with taxes and insurance. Deposits are at least US$400. A 'gold' credit card qualifies for an exemption of US$11.95 per day CDW. *Provo Rent A Car*, PO Box 137, T9464404, F9464993, rentacar@Provo.net, at the airport, T9465610, a/c vehicles, jeeps, vans, recommended. *Hertz*, PO Box 66, Central Leeward Highway, T9413910, F9415213. *Budget*, Down Town, Town Centre Mall, open Mon-Sat, 0800-1700, Sun 1000-1600, T9464709, worldwide reservations 800-5270700, Suzukis, Mitsubishis, 1 day free for weekly rental. *Tropical Auto Rental*, Tropicana Plaza and *Ocean Club Condos* at Grace Bay,

T9465300, F9465456, **Turks & Caicos National Car Rental**, Airport Rd, T/F9464701/ 9413514, F9413281, not always reliable vehicles delivery. **Rent-a-Buggy**, Leeward Highway, T9464158, Suzuki jeeps, VW Thing. **Provo Fun Cycles** at Ports of Call across from *Allegro*, single scooters US$25 per day, doubles US$39, packages, can take them to North Caicos on the ferry, Honda motorcycles, also bicycles and jeeps, T9465868, Provofuncycles@Provo.net; **Sunrise Auto Rental**, jeeps and scooters, Leeward Highway and *Club Med*, T9469730. **Avis** at airport and Bayview Motors, Leeward Highway, T9464705, F9464810, at *Club Med*, T9469730, Avis@provo.net, affiliated with Sunrise Auto Rental; **Scooter Bob's**, Turtle Cove Marina, T9464684, F9464283, vans, scooters and bicycles, Mon-Sat 0900-1700, Sun 0900-1200. **Taxi**: *Paradise Taxi Co*, T9413555. **Nell's Taxi**, T9413228, 9464971; **Island's Choice Taxi**, T9410409; **Provo Taxi Association** T9465481.

Banks *Barclays Bank Plc* at Butterfield Square, PO Box 236, Provo, T9464245, F9464573; *Scotiabank* is at the Town Centre Mall, PO Box 15, T9464750, F9464755.

Directory

Rugged and uninhabited but worth visiting for its beautiful beach on the northwest coast and excellent diving offshore. The east shore is a marine park. Inland there is a saltwater lake, Lake Catherine, which rises and falls with the tides and is a nature reserve, home to migrant nesting flamingos, ducks and waders. The ruins of Yankee Town, its sisal press and railroad are a surface interval destination for scuba divers and sailors.

West Caicos
Once frequented by pirates, there are many wrecks between here & Provo

An old pirate lair, now uninhabited, with exceptional marine life. It has been designated a sanctuary for frigate birds, osprey and nesting seabirds.

French Cay

Background

History

The islands' first dwellers were the peaceful Tainos, who left behind ancient utensils and little else. By the middle of the 16th century not one Lucayan, as Columbus named them, remained. Like the Lucayans in the Bahamas islands, they were kidnapped for use as slaves or pearl divers, while many others died of imported diseases. The discovery of the islands, whether by Columbus in 1492 or later by Ponce de León, is hotly disputed. There is a very convincing argument that Columbus' first landfall was on Grand Turk, not Watling Island in the Bahamas, now officially named San Salvador. The infamous Caicos Banks south of the Caicos group, where in the space of 1,000yds the water depth changes from 6,000 to 30ft, claimed many of the Spanish ships lost in the central Caribbean from the 16th to the 18th century.

The islands were named after the Turk's Head 'fez' cactus found growing on the islands. The name Caicos comes from the Lucayan, caya hico, meaning string of islands

The Bermudan traders who settled on the islands of Grand Turk, Salt Cay, and South Caicos in the 17th century used slaves to rake salt for sale to British colonies on the American mainland, and fought pirates and buccaneers for over 200 years. During the American Revolution, British loyalists found refuge on the islands, setting up cotton and sisal plantations with the labour of imported slaves. For a while, cotton and sisal from the islands were sold in New York and London, solar salt became the staple of the economy, and the Turks and Caicos thrived, but all these products encountered overwhelming competition from elsewhere. The thin soil was an added disadvantage and a hurricane in 1813 marked the demise of cotton plantations.

Following an alternation of Spanish, French and British control, the group became part of the Bahamas colony in 1766. Attempts to integrate the Turks and Caicos failed, rule from Nassau was unpopular and inefficient and abandoned in 1848. Links with Jamaica were more developed, partly because London-Kingston boats visited frequently. The Turks and Caicos were annexed to Jamaica in 1874.

Turks & Caicos Islands

After Jamaica's independence in 1962, they were loosely associated with the Bahamas for just over 10 years until the latter became independent. At that point, the Turks and Caicos became a British Crown Colony (now a Dependent Territory). The Anglican Church maintained its links with the Bahamas, which is where the Bishop resides.

The main political parties were established in 1976: the People's Democratic Movement (PDM) and the Progressive National Party (PNP). From time to time independence is raised as a political issue but does not have universal support.

The isolation of the Turks and Caicos and the benign neglect of the British government led to increasing use of the islands as refuelling posts by drug smugglers *en route* from South America to Florida. Constitutional government was suspended in 1986 after it was discovered that several Ministers were involved and direct rule from the UK was imposed while investigations continued into malpractice by other public officials. The Chief Minister and the Minister of Development were imprisoned for accepting bribes to allow drugs planes to refuel on South Caicos. The islands are still being used for trans-shipment of cocaine and other drugs.

In 1988, general elections restored constitutional government. These were won by the PDM, and Oswald Skippings took office as Chief Minister. The April 1991 elections brought the PNP, led by Washington Missick, back to power, but economic austerity measures and civil service job cuts cost the PNP its mandate and in 1995 the PDM was returned to office, holding eight seats over the PNP's four. The 13th seat was held by an independent. Continuity was assured when the PDM won the 1999 elections with a convincing mandate, taking nine seats while the PNP won four again. The Chief Minister is Derek Taylor, leader of the PDM since 1991.

Geography

Only 8 islands are inhabited

The Turks and Caicos islands comprise about 40 low-lying islands and cays covering 193 square miles, surrounded by one of the longest coral reefs in the world. They are separated by the Columbus Passage, a 22-mile channel over 7,000 ft deep which connects the Atlantic and the Caribbean, contributing to the area's profusion of marine life. Generally, the windward sides of the islands are made up of limestone cliffs and sand dunes, while the leeward sides have more lush vegetation. The south islands of Grand Turk, Salt Cay and South Caicos are very dry, having had their trees felled by salt rakers long ago to discourage rain. The other islands have slightly more rain but very little soil and most of the vegetation is scrub and cactus. The islands lie 575 miles southeast of Miami, Florida, directly east of Inagua at the south tip of the Bahamas and north of Hispaniola.

People

The main islands of the Turks group, Grand Turk and Salt Cay, shelter 20% of the colony's 7,901 'belongers', as the islanders call themselves, but only 15% of the total resident population of 19,000, which includes many Haitians, Dominicans and ex-pat North Americans. The rest of the population is scattered among the larger Caicos group to the west: South Caicos, Middle (or Grand) Caicos, North Caicos, and Providenciales, the most populous, known locally as 'Provo'; Pine Cay and Parrot Cay are privately owned resort islands; East and West Caicos, inhabited from 1797 to the mid-19th century, are now the private domain of wild animals. East Caicos is home to swarms of mosquitoes and wild cattle, while West Caicos harbours land crabs, nesting pairs of ospreys and flamingos. Most of the smaller cays are uninhabited. The people of the Turks and Caicos are welcoming and friendly. The development of tourism on Provo has changed attitudes there, however, and friendliness is not universal.

Government

The Turks and Caicos are a British Dependent Territory. The British monarch is Head of State, represented by a Governor, currently John Kelly. The Executive Council chaired by the Governor is formed by six ministers, the Financial Secretary, the Attorney General and the Chief Secretary, the last two being British government appointments. Mrs Cynthia Astwood, the first Turks Islander, took over as Chief Secretary when the British appointee left. The Legislative Council has 13 elected members and two party-appointed members.

Economy

The traditional economic activity, salt production, ceased in 1964, and for two decades there was little to generate legal income apart from fishing, government employment and some tourism. National resources are limited, even water has to be strictly conserved. Agriculture is almost non-existent. Practically all consumer goods and most foodstuffs are imported. The lack of major employment activities led in the 1960s and 1970s to thousands of local people emigrating to the nearby Bahamas or the USA to seek work. This trend has now been reversed as the economy has improved and the population is rising. Belongers have returned to work in the tourist industry and professionals trained abroad are returning to work as lawyers, accountants, etc. Poorly paid skilled and unskilled labour, much of it illegal, comes from Haiti and the Dominican Republic.

One area of growth has been that of offshore companies, over 14,000 of which were registered in the islands by 1997. There is no income tax, no company tax, no exchange control and no restriction on the nationality or residence of shareholders or directors. New legislation and the creation of the Offshore Finance Centre Unit (OFCU) were designed to regulate and promote the growth of offshore finance and encourage banking, insurance and trust companies. Five international banks have been granted offshore licences and some 2,000 offshore insurance companies have been licensed. Government revenue from offshore financial services was over US$6mn in 1997/98.

Budgetary aid from the UK for recurrent expenditure was eliminated in fiscal year 1986/87 and the islands are aiming to be self-financing. Capital aid from the UK remains, augmented by financial assistance from the European Community, the European Investment Bank and the Caribbean Development Bank.

One of the main areas of economic growth and revenue for the islands is tourism. Investment has taken place in infrastructure, particularly airfields, hotels and marinas, nearly all on Providenciales. The opening of a *Club Méditerranée* in 1984 doubled the number of visitors to the Turks and Caicos in two years. By 1991, the annual number of visitors reached 54,616, from 11,900 in 1980. The collapse of PanAm in 1992 threatened devastation of the local economy, only averted when American Airlines started flying from Miami to Provo. Numerous North American charters helped to push tourist numbers up to nearly 100,000 in 1997.

Turks & Caicos Islands

Haiti

8

Haiti

Haiti is famous for being the only country to have had a successful slave revolt: whites have not governed here for two centuries. As a result, African customs persist strongly, most noticeable in language, art, music, dance and religion, where voodoo is widely practised. Nevertheless, the influence of former French colonists and merchants is still evident, particularly in architecture, with many old buildings enhanced by the gingerbread style of elaborate fretwork, balconies and decorated gables. Language also reflects the French colonial past, with everybody speaking a French-based Créole. Haiti is the poorest country in the Western Hemisphere and the capital, Port-au-Prince, is a seething mass of humanity where everyone plies their trade in the streets to eke out a living. This is the most mountainous island in the Caribbean, but pressure for the land has led Haitians to cut down all their trees for fuel, leaving the hillsides bare. There is no mass tourism and exploring the country is a rewarding experience for the independent and adventurous of spirit. Fortifications and other historical landmarks dot the countryside, but the most impressive is the massive La Citadelle, built on top of a 900-metre peak to deter any French invasion.

A Foot in the door

- Spend Thursday evening at the charming and idiosyncratic **Oloffson Hotel** in Port-au-Prince, setting for Graham Greene's *The Comedians*. Live music performed by RAM, a 'voodoo beat' band with a large following.
- Catch the beat with the writhing, twirling, dancing **rara bands** each Sunday in Lent, a follow-up to Carnival but emanating from voodoo.
- Get a feel for the beauty of the countryside with a trek to **Bassin Bleu** and cool off in the pools at the foot of the green-blue waterfall.
- Head for the southwest to the tip of the peninsula for undisturbed beaches and the quiet life. **Anse du Clerc** has a small guesthouse on the beach with excellent food and buckets of tranquility.

Essentials

Before you travel

Documents All visitors need **passports** valid for at least six months after your departure date from Haiti. **Visas** are not needed for anyone staying 90 days or less, but everyone must have an onward ticket. All visitors, except cruise ship passengers, must complete an embarkation/disembarkation card on the plane; this is valid for 90 days, and may be extended. Don't lose the yellow card (exit visa) because you will need it when you leave. Keep your passport (or a copy) with you as identification to satisfy the many police controls when travelling in the interior. Baggage inspection is thorough and drug-enforcement laws are strict. There is no restriction on foreign currency. You may bring in 1 quart of spirits, and 200 cigarettes or 50 cigars. There are no export limitations.

Money
Try to break down large notes whenever possible

Currency The unit is the gourde (Cr: goud), divided into 100 centimes (Cr: kòb). Coins in circulation are for 5, 10, 20 and 50 centimes, notes for 1, 2, 5, 10, 25, 50, 100, 250 and 500 gourdes. Some 100 gourde notes are plastic, faded, smeared and look like forgeries; they are not. They have 'American Banknote Company' printed on them. Small denomination notes are in appalling condition and there is always a shortage of them. 500 gourde notes are next to useless unless you can break them down at a bank or spend them at expensive hotels: ask for smaller denominations. Coins are few and far between.

Exchange The gourde was tied at 5 to the US dollar during the US occupation. In the 1980s it began to trade at a slightly lower value on a parallel market, but the official rate was kept until 1991, when the Aristide government severed the tie and let the gourde float. From 7.5 to the dollar at the time of the September 1991 coup, it has fallen to 22 in 2001. So far, so good. Now it gets complicated. Haitians routinely refer to their own money as dollars, based on the old 5 to 1 rate. Thus, 5 gourdes is called a dollar, 10 gourdes is 2 dollars, 25 gourdes is 5 dollars, etc. Prices in shops are usually in Haitian dollars, therefore multiply by five to get the price in gourdes. Visitors must constantly clarify whether the price being quoted is in Haitian or American dollars, or gourdes, now increasingly used on bills.

The best exchange rate is obtained from money changers, whether those on the street or those working out of offices. It is perfectly legal (see section on Port-au-Prince) but not recommended for safety reasons. The rate in banks is not far behind and it is therefore better to trade with one of the many banks. It is foolish to come to Haiti with any currency other than US dollars or French francs. Currencies like sterling can be changed, but only at a massive loss. Travellers' cheques are difficult to change in some banks.

Credit cards Visa, Mastercard and American Express are widely accepted. Beware, card users will not get a good rate and are often charged a premium.

Travel hints

Haiti is especially fascinating for the tourist who is avid for off-the-beaten-track experience. In order that you may make the most of your visit, we offer the following hints.

Although it is one of the poorest countries in the world, most of whose citizens suffer from one kind of oppression or another, Haiti is proud of having been the only nation to have carried out successfully a slave rebellion.

Haitians at all levels are very sensitive to how they are treated by foreigners, commonly called 'blanc'. If you treat them with warmth and consideration, they will respond with enthusiasm and friendship. There is no hostility towards 'blanc'; if you feel threatened it is probably the result of a misunderstanding. For example if someone looks at you and draws one finger across his neck, it does not mean he wants to cut your throat. Rather, it means he is hungry and is asking for a dollar.

Eye contact is very important; it is not avoided as in some other countries.

Humour plays an important role in social interactions; Haitians survive by laughing at themselves and their situation.

Haitians are physical: touching and flirting a lot.

It is important to recognize the presence of each person in a social encounter, either with a handshake or a nod. When walking in the countryside, you usually wish bon jour *(before 1200) or* bon soir *to anyone you meet.* Salud *is another common greeting, at any time of day. Coffee or cola are often offered by richer peasants to visitors (Haitian coffee is among the best in the world).*

Do not expect straight answers to questions about a peasant's wealth, property or income.

It is assumed that each 'blanc' is wealthy and therefore it is legitimate to try to separate you from your riches. Treat such attempts with humour, indignation or consideration as you feel appropriate.

The climate is generally very warm but the cool on- and off-shore winds of morning and evening help to make it bearable. In coastal areas temperatures vary between 20° and 35°C, being slightly hotter in April-September. The driest, coolest months are December-March. In the hill resorts the temperature is cooler.

Climate
Haiti has 2 rainy seasons: Apr-May & Sep-Oct

Getting there

To Port-au-Prince From Europe: there are no direct flights, but *Air France* flies from Paris **Air** via Guadeloupe. **From North America**. *American Airlines* flies from New York, Orlando and Miami daily. Other airlines from Miami including *ALM*, *Air d'Ayiti* and *Air France*. *Air Canada* flies from Montréal. **From Central America**: *Copa* flies from Panama City. **From the Caribbean**: *ALM* from Curaçao; *Air France* from Guadeloupe and Martinique; *Aerolíneas Santo Domingo* from Santo Domingo; *AeroCaribbean* from Santiago de Cuba. **From South America**: *Air France* from Cayenne, French Guiane. **To Cap-Haïtien** *Turks and Caicos Airways* and *TCI SkyKing* from Providenciales. *TCA* also flies Monday and Friday from Grand Turk. There are also several unscheduled or charter flights, see the Turks and Caicos chapter.

Note that flights from Miami are frequently overbooked. You should be at the airport at least 2 hrs in advance. If you are not on a tight schedule, but have a confirmed seat, you may be asked to give your seat to a passenger with no confirmation in return for credit vouchers to be used on another flight within 12 months. Your original ticket will still be valid for the next flight, or for transfer to a different flight.

Cruise ships stopped calling at Port-au-Prince years ago, partly because of passenger **Sea** reaction to begging. Royal Caribbean and Crown cruise lines have leased private beaches near Cap-Haïtien for 1 day stopovers, and they have renewed their visits.

Road

See documents in Dominican Republic chapter & check with the Dominican Consulate to see if you need a visa

There is a 1-hr time difference between Haiti & the Dominican Republic

Travel to the Dominican Republic Taptaps and trucks ply the road to the border of the Dominican Republic at Malpasse/Jimaní, 1 hour. The Ouanaminthe/Dajabón crossing in the north is easily reached from Cap-Haïtien and is straightforward. You should not pay anything on leaving Haiti, but travellers have been asked for anything between US$10 and US$40 before their papers will be stamped. It is US$10 to re-enter Haiti. Visitors arriving in the Dominican Republic pay US$10. Mopeds ferry you between the Haitian and Dominican border posts for US$1. There are lots of money changers on both sides. The easiest way to get to Santo Domingo is with **Terra Bus** or **Caribe Tours**, both Dominican companies, who deal with all immigration and other formalities so all you have to do is get off the bus to take care of Dominican customs, excellent service, efficient, comfortable a/c buses which show at least two movies, snacks and drinks provided, recommended. **Terra Bus** (T2237882), is handled by Chatelain Tours (T2232400, 2225664) in Port-au-Prince. Fare US$50 one way, US$75 return or US$80 open return, child reductions, departs Monday 0800, arrives Santo Domingo 1530, other days except Saturday departs 1400, arrives 2000, leaves from Tabarre, between Pétion-Ville and the airport, US$20 by taxi from town centre. **Caribe Tours** is in Pétion-Ville, T2579379, and departs from the Angle (corner) of Rue Clerveaux and Gabart, daily at 0730, US$75 return, leaves Santo Domingo at 1100 for the return journey. **Tartan Tours** in Port-au-Prince; **Luz Tours**, T2231059, and **Kenya Express** (also T2231059) have weekly buses to Santo Domingo. Haitian travel agencies sometimes offer three or four day inclusive bus tours into the Dominican Republic. There are regular buses from the Dominican frontier town of Jimaní to Santo Domingo (six hours) and from Dajabón via Montecristi and Santiago de los Caballeros. Rental cars are not allowed to cross the border, but you could safely leave one at the border for a few hours during a quick excursion to Jimaní. Dominican buses leave Port-au-Prince most mornings for their return trip to Santo Domingo via Malpasse, but they have no fixed time or departure point (the trip can take up to 10 hours, with two hours at the border). Ask at the *Hotel Palace* on Rue Capois, where many Dominicans stay. Buses also leave from Rue du Centre, between *Auberge Port-au-Prince* and Rue des Miracles, around 3-4 per day, mostly 25-seater a/c Mitsubishis, US$20.

Touching down

Airport information

The information office at the airport is very helpful. The downstairs snackbar is cheap and friendly. Not so the upstairs restaurant at the west end of the terminal. The public area has a bookstore and a handicraft shop. Duty free goods and more crafts are on sale in the area reserved for departing passengers. Officials will allow camera film to be passed through outside the X-ray machinery.

Airlines *Air Canada* (T2460441/2); *Air France* (T2221700/1086, T2462085 at airport), 11 Rue Capois, corner Rue Ducoste, near *Le Plaza*; *ALM* (T2461090) 69 Rue Pavée, corner Rue du Peuple; *American Airlines* (T2231314, 2460100), Avenue Pie XII, near post office, always packed with people (also T2460110 at the airport); *Copa*, 35 Avenue Marie Jeanne, T2232366, or airport T2460946; *Haiti Trans Air* (T2234010/20/9258), Rue Capois near *Holiday Inn*. *Lynx Air* in Cap-Haïtien is 2621386; *TCA* T2320710.

Tourist information

Local tourist office The Tourism Secretariat, upstairs at 8 Rue Légitime (T2232143, F2235359) and half a block from the Musée d'Art Haïtien, has poor information and no maps or brochures. Supplementary information may be sought from the Haitian Association for the Tourism and Hotel Industry in Choucoune Plaza, Pétion-Ville, T2574647, at the *Hotel Montana*, or from travel agencies. ISPAN (Institute for the Protection of the Nation's Heritage) has information on forts and plantation houses, corner of Avenue Martin Luther King and Cheriez, Pont Morin (T2453220/3118). Also at Rue 15-B, Cap-Haïtien (T2622459).

Guides expect you to buy them food if you stop to eat

Guides Young men and boys offer their services as guides. In some places it's worthwhile, it is easier to get about, you can visit places off the beaten tourist track and avoid some of the frustrations of the public transport system though generally you can get by without one. Most guides speak English or pidgin English. **Chauffeurs-Guides** are cab drivers who cater to foreign visitors. Usually found outside the biggest hotels such as the *Le Plaza*, or at the airport,

Touching down

Departure tax *Visitors leaving by air must pay a US$25 departure tax in US currency and a 10-gourde security tax in Haitian currency. Do not buy international flight tickets in Haiti, especially not at the airport. Sales tax is very high and the application of exchange rates may be very arbitrary.*

Business hours *Government offices: 0700-1200, 1300-1600 (0800-1200, 1300-1800 October-April); banks: 0900-1300 Monday to Friday; shops and offices: 0700-1600 (an hour later October-April).*

Official time *Eastern standard time, five hours behind GMT; four hours behind early April to late October (dates vary each year).*

Voltage *110 volt, 60 cycle AC. Electricity supply is unpredictable as there are insufficient funds to maintain the service. Only if sufficient rain falls to operate the hydroelectric facility will the capital have power and water. Only the best hotels have sufficiently powerful generators to make up the deficiency (see Where to stay section). As the Oloffson is on the same circuit as the Presidential Palace, it is never blacked out.*

Weights & measures *Metric.*

Clothing *As in most other countries in the Caribbean beachwear should not be worn away from the beach and poolside. Dress is casual but never sloppy. Haitians appreciate good manners and style. Above-the-knee hems for women are considered risqué but acceptable. Men always wear a shirt, but a tie is not necessary in the evening.*

Tipping *Budget travellers, particularly outside Port-au-Prince, are a rarity. Expect to be the subject of much friendly curiosity, and keep a pocketful of small change to conform with the local custom of tipping on every conceivable occasion. Even cigarettes and sweets are accepted. Hotels generally add 10% service charge. Baggage porters at hotels usually get US$0.50 per bag. Do not fail to reward good service since hotel and restaurant staff rely on tips to boost their meagre salaries. Nobody tips taxi, publique, camionette or tap-tap drivers, unless exceptional service has been given.*

Safety *Despite all the political turmoil since 1986, security is not a major problem for the foreign visitor. In fact, Haiti has much less crime than most Caribbean countries. Take normal precautions. Carry handbags securely and do not leave belongings in sight in a parked car. During any political unrest it is advisable to limit your movements in the daytime and not to go out at night. Streets are usually deserted by 2300. Foreigners are not normally targeted at such times, but seek local advice.*

Haiti

their cars can be used like regular taxis or hired by the hour, half day, day or for a tour. The drivers usually speak French, plus a little English. They can be booked through the Association des Chauffeurs-Guides, T2220330, 18 blvd Harry Truman. A recommended private guide/driver is Lionel Elie, Rue St Surin 20 Bis, Pétion-Ville, T2572968, also an artist, used by visiting writers and film crews, speaks English, Spanish and a little German. Price negotiable depending on the job and whether you have your own transport. Max Church, a pastor who has been training English/French/Créole-speaking guides, can be called on 342622, Port-au-Prince. An English-speaking guide named Ed can be found on the corner of Rue José de San Martin and Av Panamericaine in Pétion-Ville. He is reassuringly protective and can help you do things like take a tap tap to Port-au-Prince and visit the Iron Market, excursions that you might not feel brave enough to do on your own. Guides cost about US$15-30 per day, depending where you go, and you should buy them food and drink. Prices have been hiked to make the most of the US dollars brought in by US, UN and NGO personnel. Bear in mind that most guides are 'on commission' with local shop and stall-keepers. So if you ask them to bargain for you, you will not necessarily be getting a good price, nor will they necessarily go where you want to go. If you don't want a guide a firm but polite *non, merci* gets the message across. It is best to ignore altogether hustlers outside guest houses, etc, as any contact makes them persist.

Travel agencies abroad In the UK, *Interchange*, 27 Stafford Road, Croydon, Surrey CR0 4NG, T0208-6813612, F7600031, interchange@interchange.uk.com, organize coach tours or independent packages of accommodation, transport and excursions.

Where to stay

Hotels   There are a few good hotels in Pétion-Ville, up the hillside from Port-au-Prince, mostly designed for businessmen, and a couple of international-standard beach hotels along the Côte des Arcadins, northwest of the capital. Elsewhere, however, lodgings can be idiosyncratic and variable in the quality of furnishings and service. See page 365. The *Association Hotelière et Touristique d'Haïti* is at Choucoune Plaza, Pétion-Ville, T2574647.

Camping   This is an adventure in Haiti. The dramatic scenery is very enticing but access to much of it is over rough terrain and there are no facilities. Campers have to take everything and create, or find their own shelter. Peasant homes dot the countryside and it is almost impossible to find a spot where you will be spared curious and suspicious onlookers. It is best to set up camp or lodging before dark. To prevent misunderstanding, it is important to explain to the locals your intentions, or better yet, talk to the local elder and ask assistance or protection. Offer to pay a small amount for use of the land.

Getting around

Air   *Mission Aviation Fellowship* (T2463993) and *Caribintair* (T2460737) have flights every day except Sunday to Cap-Haïtien (US$50 round trip). They also run 2 or 3 flights a week each to Jérémie (US$70 round trip). *MAF* additionally flies Tuesday, Thursday and Saturday to Hinche (US$40 round trip). Book and pay through travel agents. Flights leave from Aviation Générale, a small domestic airport 1 km east of the international airport. *Caribintair* also operates as a charter/air taxi company. *Marien Air* (T2620527), a Cap-based air taxi service run by Paul Takeo Hodges, flies anywhere in Haiti. It also offers flights to Port-au-Prince, the Dominican Republic, Turks and Caicos, Bahamas and Jamaica.

Haiti

Driving in Haiti is a hazardous free-for-all which some find exhilarating. The streets are narrow, with many sharp bends and one full of pedestrians in the towns. Outside towns you have to look out for animals, potholes, sleeping policemen and police roadblocks. In wet weather, city streets and main highways all get clogged with traffic and become impassable. Haitians use their horns constantly to warn pedestrians of their approach. There are few signs. Vehicles swerve unexpectedly to avoid potholes. Cars often don't stop in an accident, so, to avoid paying the high insurance excess, keep a pen and paper handy to take down a number if necessary. Fuel (leaded, unleaded or diesel) is usually available in the big provincial towns, but power cuts may prevent stations from pumping at certain times of the day. For driving to Cap-Haïtien, Les Cayes and Jacmel, an ordinary car is fine, but for Jérémie, Port-de-Paix or Hinche, a four-wheel drive is nessary. Foreigners may use an international driving licence for 3 months, then a local permit is required.

Road
*See also transport
under Port-au-Prince*

Car hire A small Japanese saloon car such as a Nissan Sunny, with a/c, rents for about US$45 per day, US$250 per week, unlimited mileage. A basic four-wheel drive starts at US$500 per week with US$500 deposit and excess of US$1,000 for damages. *Avis* (T2464161), *Hertz* (T2460700), *Dollar* (T2491800) and *Budget* (T2461366) all have bases near the airport; Avis is opposite the airport terminal, open 0800-1700, Hertz is in the Dynamic Entreprise Building and Dollar in the Firestone Building. Smaller companies include *Sunshine Jeep* (T2491155), *Secom* (564 Route de Delmas, T2571913) and *Sugar* (T2463413). Hertz is the only company with a base in Cap-Haïtien.

Hitchhiking Foreigners do not normally hitch, it is dangerous and not advisable. There are many young Haitian men who stick out a thumb asking for a 'roue libre', especially from foreigners. Use your discretion.

Keeping in touch

Always bad, the telephone system deteriorated even more during the 1991-94 embargo and now fewer than a third of calls get through. The Haitian international operator (dial 09) is hard to raise. However, *Teleco* offices in major cities are central and easy to use and the operators are helpful. Expect queues. The *Oloffson*, *Le Plaza*, *Montana* and *El Rancho* hotels have AT&T 'USA Direct' telephones for collect calls to the USA or calls anywhere in the world with an AT&T credit card, but even these connections can be problematic. Email service is very limited. The postal service is slow and poor.

Telephone
IDD phone code: 509

Newspapers *Le Nouvelliste* is the better of the two daily French-language newspapers. It is conservative, but tries to be impartial. Three weekly newspapers are published in French, all very one-sided, but on different sides. The pro-Aristide weekly *Libète* is the only Créole newspaper. **Radio** Radio stations use a mix of French and Créole. *Metropole* and *Tropic* are best for news. The satellite-beamed *Radio France Inter* is rebroadcast locally on FM 89.3. The *BBC World Service* can be heard on 15220 (early

Media

Haiti

Atlantic Ocean

Anse-à-Fouleur
Le Borgne
Limbé
Plage Labadie
Plage Cormier
Cap-Haïtien
Caracol
Fort Liberté
100
Limonade
121
Milot
Plaisance
Citadelle
Terrier Rouge
Ouanaminthe
Dajabon
Ennery
St Raphaël
St Michel de l'Attalaye
Pignon
Maïssade
300
Hinche
Thomassique
Chaîne Des Matheux
Montagnes Noires
109
Thomonde
Belladère
Arcahaie
Mirebalais
305
Lascahobas
cadins
Cabaret
100
300
Étang Saumâtre
Ibo
Croix-des-Bouquets
-au-Prince
Gressier Thor
Pétionville
Jimani
Lago Enriquillo
Malpasse
Kenscoff
Massif de la Selle
Mandàt
Jacmel
Marigot
Grand Gosier
Cayes
Jacmel
Belle Anse
Sea
Anse-à-Pitres

DOMINICAN REPUBLIC

morning) and 7325 (evenings). *Voice of America* is on 11915 (mornings) and 9455 evenings. **Television** A commercial TV station, *Télé-Haiti*, retransmits American, French, Canadian and Latin American stations (including CNN, CBS, NBC, ABC, HBO, etc) to cable subscribers, electricity permitting.

Food and drink

Food

Bakeries sell French croissants, baguettes, cakes and pastries, together with Créole bread & meat pasties

Most restaurants offer Créole or French cuisine, or a mixture of both. Haiti's Créole cuisine is like its Caribbean cousins, but more peppery. Specialities include *griot* (deep-fried pieces of pork), *lambi* (conch, considered an aphrodisiac), *tassot* (jerked beef) and rice with *djon-djon* (tiny, dark mushrooms). Fried plantains appear on every menu. As elsewhere in the Caribbean, lobster is widely available. Pétion-Ville has many good French restaurants. Some are French-managed or have French chefs. Haiti's wide range of micro-climates produces a large assortment of fruits and vegetables. It is popular to buy these in the regions where they grow and are freshest (prices can be bargained 40% below shop prices). The French influence is obvious in butcher shops where fine cuts of meat, cold cuts, paté and cheeses can be bought. American influence is felt in the supermarkets, where you can find almost everything. Most common are US-brand foods along with smaller amounts of Haitian, French and Middle Eastern brands. Vegetarians will find Haiti extremely difficult. Haitians cook nearly everything in pig fat, so even beans are to be avoided. One traveller survived on a diet of cornflakes, boiled eggs and fruit. Only the expensive restaurants and hotels will have a vegetarian option on the menu. There is one health/vegetarian shop on the corner of Rue Gregoire and Louverture, in Pétion-Ville, which stocks soya milk, a variety of different spices, grains and pulses and some organic products. It is quite pricey.

Drink

Haitian coffee is drunk strong & sweet, Rebo is the best brand

Haiti's Barbancourt rum is excellent. The 5-star is particularly recommended and a bottle sells for only US$7, although if you buy it at the airport on departure you can get a case of 5 bottles for about US$30. The distillery is in Damians and can be visited. Rum punch is popular but often over-sweet. The local beer, Prestige, may be too sweet for some palates but is an acceptable alternative to sweet, fizzy drinks. The Dominican beer, Presidente, is the best of the foreign beers sold in Haiti, but Beck's is more widely available. Heineken and Corona are also found, all selling at around US$0.75-1.50 depending on the brand. Soft drinks include Séjourne, Couronne and Sékola (banana), as well as the international brands of cola and lemonade.

Entertainment

Until the mid-1980s, Haiti used to be a very good place for nightspots. With the drop in tourism and Haitians hesitating to be out late in uneasy times, many places have had to close or curtail their level of entertainment. The few that survive offer a good night out. Following French custom, entertaining starts late in the evening, about 2030-2100. Nightclubbing starts around 2330 and continues into the small hours.

Flora and fauna

Haiti has no poisonous snakes or insects

Deforestation and soil erosion have destroyed habitats. Haiti is therefore poor in flora and fauna compared with its eastern neighbour. Three sites are worth visiting. One is **Lake Saumâtre**, 90 minutes east of the capital. Less brackish than Enriquillo, across the Dominican border, it is the habitat of more than 100 species of waterfowl (including migratory North American ducks), plus flamingoes and American crocodiles. The north side of the lake is better, reached via the town of Thomazeau (see page 374).

The other two are mountain parks. Relatively easy to reach is **Parc La Visite**, about five hours' hike from the hill resort of Kenscoff behind Port-au-Prince. On the high Massif de la Selle, with a mixture of pine forest and montane cloud forest, it has 80 bird species and two endemic mammals, the Hispaniolan hutia (*Plagiodontia aedium*) and the nez longue (*Solenodon paradoxus*). North American warblers winter there. It is also a nesting place for the black-capped petrel (*Pteradoma hasitata*). See page 374. Harder to reach is the **Macaya National Park**, at the tip of the southwest peninsula, site of Haiti's last virgin cloud forest. It has pines 45m high, 141 species of orchid, 102 species of fern, 99 species of moss and 49 species of liverwort. Its fauna include 11 species of butterfly, 57 species of snail, 28 species of amphibian, 34 species of reptile, 65 species of bird and 19 species of bat. In addition to the hutia, nez longue and black-capped petrel, its most exotic animals are the Grey-crowned Palm Tanager (*Phaenicophilus poliocephalus*) and the Hispaniolan trogan (*Temnotrogan roseigaster*). The endangered Peregrine falcon (*Falco pergrinus*) winters in the park. From Les Cayes, it takes half a day to get to a University of Florida base on the edge of the park which has basic camping facilities. Allow another 2 days each way for the 2,347m Pic de Macaya. See page 378. Paul Paryski (T2231400/1), a UN ecosystems expert, will give advice.

Leaf doctors, voodoo priests and sorcerers have a wealth of knowledge of natural remedies and poisons to be found in Haiti's surviving plant life. They do not share their knowledge readily. In his book *The Serpent and the Rainbow*, Harvard ethnobotanist Wade Davis gives a racy account of his attempts to discover which natural toxins sorcerers are thought to use to turn their victims into *zombis*. Almost any tree is liable to be chopped down for firewood or charcoal; a few very large species are not because they are believed to be the habitat of *loas* (spirit). Chief among them is the silkcotton tree, 'mapou' in Creole.

Shopping

The Iron Markets sell only food items, charcoal, knick knacks, etc and sometimes paintings if there is a tourist market. The Iron Market in Port-au-Prince would be a fascinating place to visit but for the hustlers who will latch on to you and make the experience hell. It is also extremely narrow and dirty; it is important to be careful, go with a group and do not carry valuables. Try out your bargaining skills at the Iron Markets in Jacmel and Cap-Haïtien. Haitians may tell you that many of the items for sale in the few tourist shops can be bought far cheaper in markets. That may be true for them, but market vendors jack up prices for the foreigner, who will have to haggle skilfully to bring them down. People always ask for a discount in shops, except at food shops. All handicrafts can be bought at a discount. See page 366 for best buys, and under towns for individual establishments.

Holidays and festivals

Public holidays New Year and Ancestors (1-2 January), Mardi Gras (the three days before Ash Wednesday), Americas Day (14 April), Good Friday (1 May), Flag and University Day (18 May), Assumption (15 August), Deaths of Henri Christophe and Dessalines (8 and 17 October), United Nations Day (24 October), All Saints (1 November), Armed Forces Day (18 November), Discovery of Haiti (5 December), 25 December. Corpus Christi and Ascension are also public holidays.

Festivals The standard of the **Port-au-Prince** *Carnival* has fallen since the Duvaliers left (see page 389). Nowadays few people wear costumes and the floats are poorly decorated. There is a cacophony of music blaring out from both stands and passing floats. Excitement is provided by the walking bands (*bandes-à-pied*), cousins of the Rara bands that appear after carnival (see below). Circulating on foot, drawing a large dancing, chanting crowd in their wake, they specialize in salacious lyrics and political satire. When crowds move in different directions there is boisterous pushing. Occasional knife fights do take place. Leave your money and valuables in the hotel safe, pick pockets are everywhere. The safest place to watch is from one of the stands near the *Hôtel Le Plaza*. Safer still and more peaceful are the Carnival celebrations in Pétion-Ville. Carnival climaxes on the three days before Ash Wednesday, but the government lays on free open-air concerts in different parts of the city during the three or four weekends of pre-carnival.

Many people prefer the *Carnival* a week earlier at Jacmel, 2-3 hours from the capital, where the tradition of elaborate, imaginative masked costumes still thrives. If you plan to stay in Jacmel you must book accommodation weeks, if not months, in advance, as it gets packed with people from Port-au-Prince and elsewhere.

Port-au-Prince carnival is immediately followed by *Rara*, dubbed the 'peasant carnival'. Every weekend during Lent, including Easter weekend, colourfully attired Rara bands emerge from voodoo societies and roam the countryside. They seek donations, so be ready with a few

Haiti

small notes. Beating drums, blowing home-made wind instruments, dancing and singing, some bands may have a thousand or more members. A good place to see it is the town of Leogane on Easter Sunday. Beware, the drinking is heavy and fights are common.

The Gede (pronounced gay-day) are *loas* who possess Voodooists on 1-2 November (*All Saints* and *Day of the Dead*). They can be seen in cemeteries or roaming the streets, dressed to look like corpses or undertakers. The lords of death and the cemetery, they mock human vanity and pretension, and remind people that sex is the source of life. They do this by dancing in a lewd fashion with strangers, causing much hilarity. For pilgrimages, see Saut d'Eau, Plaine du Nord and Limonade in the text below.

Health

See also main Health section in Essentials chapter, page 47

Prophylaxis against **malaria** is essential. Tap water is not to be trusted (drink only filtered or treated water) and take care when choosing food. The local herb tea can help stomach troubles; diarrhoea is often known as Haitian Happiness!. Hepatitis is common in some areas. Good professional advice is available for the more common ailments. Ask at the hotel desk for referrals to a doctor suited to your requirements. Office hours are usually 0730-1200, 1500-1800. A consultation costs about US$10-15. Hospital care and comfort varies. See page 369 for hospital listings in Port-au-Prince. Pharmacies/chemists can fill out prescriptions and many prescription drugs may be bought over the counter. A note on prostitution: there are no laws in Haiti to suppress it. Activity seems to be evident only at night with the commonly known areas being along the main roads in Carrefour and street corners in Pétion-Ville. After hours the prostitutes move into the dive-type joints, targeting foreigners. With regard to casual sex, there is a red alert in Haiti over Aids.

Further reading

History *The Black Jacobins*, by CLR James (about Toussaint); *Papa Doc and the Tontons Macoutes*, by Bernard Diederich and Al Burt. **Voodoo** *The Drum and the Hoe*, by Harold Courlander; *Divine Horsemen* by Maya Deren; *The Serpent and the Rainbow* by Wade Davis; *Mama Lola* by Karen McCarthy Brown. **Travelogue** *Bonjour Blanc: A Journey Through Haiti* by Ian Thomson, Hutchinson, 1992; *The Rainy Season: Haiti Since Duvalier*, by Amy Wilentz, Jonathan Cape, 1989. **Fiction** *The Comedians* by Graham Greene (set during Papa Doc's time); *The Kingdom of This World* by Alejo Carpentier (about Mackandal and Christophe); *Hadriana dans tous mes rêves*, by René Depestre, Gallimard 1988, Haiti's best known living writer who grew up in Jacmel where the story is set; *The farming of bones*, by Edwidge Danticat, Soho Press 1998, is a fictional account of the massacre of Haitians in the Dominican Republic in 1937. Two other novels of hers worth reading are *Krik! Krak!* and *Breath, Eyes, Memory*.

Port-au-Prince

Population: 846,247
Metropolitan area:
2,000,000
Colour map 3, grid B2

What Port-au-Prince lacks in architectural grace, it makes up for with a stunning setting. Steep mountains tower over the city to the south, La Gonâve island lies in a horseshoe bay to the west, and another wall of mountains beyond a rift valley plain rise to the north. Over the years the city has spilled out of its original waterfront location, climbing further into the mountains behind. A rural exodus has swollen the population from 150,000 in 1954 to over two million now. The worst bidonvilles *(shantytowns) are in a marshy waterfront area north of the centre, but most of the city is very poor. There are crowds of people everywhere, spilling off the sidewalks into the streets, moving to a cacophony of horns and engines.*

Ins and outs

The airport is on the northern edge of Delmas, 13 km outside Port-au-Prince, T2410516. Arrival can be pandemonium especially if more than 1 flight is being dealt with. Just get on with your affairs and try not to get distracted. Once through the squash inside you emerge into a squash outside, of taxi drivers and people awaiting friends. Knowledge of French is useful. Porters charge US$0.50 per bag. A taxi into town is US$20-25 depending on how hard you bargain, or take a seat in a taptap (open-backed truck), extra charged for large bag. To get to the airport cheaply take a shared taxi from the turning off Avenue Saint Martin (see map, formerly Avenue François Duvalier) for 3-4 km to Rue Haile Sellassie where taptaps marked 'Airport' gather; US$0.15 from here, 10 km. For those coming by bus from the Dominican Republic, see page 355.

Getting there
The so-called 'supervisors' at the airport are in fact taxi-drivers, touting for business

Shared taxis (called **publiques** or simply taxis) are flagged down.They charge a basic fare (Cr: kous) of US$0.20 that may double or treble (de kous, twa kous) depending on how far off the beaten track you go. A red ribbon tied to the inside rear-view mirror identifies them. French is needed. They stop work at about 1930. **Camionettes** (minibuses) and **Taptaps** (open-backed pickups with a brightly painted wooden superstructure) have fixed routes and fares (about US$0.15). They rarely circulate after 2030. They are difficult to manage with luggage. Camionettes to Pétion-Ville leave from Avenue John Brown, US$0.20.

Getting around
A regular taxi is hard to find. See transport for further details

Sights

The commercial quarter starts near the port and stretches inland to the east about ten blocks. It lacks charm or interest, except the area beside the port that was remodelled for the city's 1949 bicentennial. Known as the **Bicentenaire** (more formally, Cité de l'Exposition), it contains the post office, foreign ministry, parliament, American embassy and French Institute. It is now very run down. The central reference point for visitors is the large, irregularly shaped park called the **Champs de Mars** which begins to the east of the commercial quarter. The northwest corner is dominated by the white, triple-domed, presidential palace. It was built in 1918 on the site of a predecessor that was blown up in 1912 with its president inside. In the 1991 coup, President Aristide made a stand inside the present building. Just to the northeast is the colonnaded, white and gold army high command building, where soldiers nearly lynched Aristide after dragging him out of the palace. (He was saved by the French ambassador, the American ambassador, or General Cedras, depending on whose story you believe). Immediately behind the palace, to the south, is a large, mustard-yellow army garrison that was once the fief of the ill-famed Colonel Jean-Claude Paul, indicted in Miami in 1987 for drug smuggling and poisoned the following year.

Immediately to the east of the palace, on **Place des Héros de l'Independance**, the subterranean **Musée du Panthéon National (MUPANAH)**, T2228337, houses historical relics, including the rusted anchor of Columbus' flagship, the *Santa María*. It is not a very big museum, but worth the stop to learn a little about Haitian history and see some art displayed. Don't miss an 1818 oil painting of King Henri Christophe by Welshman Richard Evans, director of Christophe's Fine Arts Academy at Sans Souci. Two blocks north and two west, at the corner of Avenue Mgr Guilloux and the busy Rue Pavée, the **Sainte Trinité Episcopal Cathedral** has astounding biblical murals by the greatest naive artists, including Philomé Obin, Castera Bazile and Riguaud Benoit. Created in 1949, they are well worth seeing. The adjoining complex has a gift shop and a school whose students give excellent choral and classical music concerts (details from Sister Anne-Marie, T2225638). The pink and white stone Catholic Cathedral is four blocks to the north.

At the intersection of Rues Capois and Champ de Mars, the **Musée d'Art Haïtien** has Haiti's finest naive art collection, plus a craft shop and a small café in its garden. The collection is not large and there is no recent art, you will find that in the private

Haïti

galleries. ■ *T2222510. US$0.50. From 1000.* The **Maison Défly**, 7 Avenue John Paul II, built by an army commander in 1896, is in the Victorian 'gingerbread' style, characterized by steep roofs and gables, round turrets, high ceilings, balconies and rich fretwork embellishment. Not a distinguished example, it contains a museum with period furniture. ■ *T2224081. 0900-1300 Mon-Sat.* The Rue Capois has several hotels, restaurants and shops. At the southern end of Rue Capois, 1 km from the Champs de Mars, is the *Hotel Oloffson*, a much more imposing example of a gingerbread. West of Rue Capois are leafy neighbourhoods climbing into the foothills where the well-off built residences in the 19th century, and gingerbreads abound.

Watch out for pickpockets in markets, bus terminal areas & inside buses

Caution Shantytown dwellers don't welcome obvious sightseers and people with cameras. The area between the Champs de Mars and the waterfront is deserted after dark and should be avoided. It is safe to go to most places by car or taxi at night, but don't go about on foot. The political turmoil of the elections and the violent aftermath in 2001 meant that even in Pétion-Ville, generally considered safer than Port-au-Prince, it is not recommended that you go out after dark, or certainly not on the streets after 2100. Remember that frequent power cuts plunge entire neighbourhoods into darkness. Drivers must always carry a licence as police blocks are common at night. Be careful of traffic when walking around town. Street vendors crowd the pavements, forcing pedestrians into the path of vehicles. Many people have been knocked down and injured.

Street names Several major Port-au-Prince thoroughfares have two names, the official one used for maps and the telephone book, and the one commonly used in speech. Often the taxi drivers only know the second. Boulevard Jean-Jacques Dessalines is also known as Grand' Rue (Créole: Gran Ri); Avenue Lamartinière is Bois Verna (Cr: Bwa Vèna); Avenue Jean Paul II is Turgeau (Cr: Tijo); Avenue John

Haïti

Port-au-Prince orientation

Related maps:
A. Port-au-Prince centre, page 365
B. Pétion-Ville, page 370

N

Not to scale

Brown is Lalue (Cr: Lali); Avenue Paul VI is Rue des Casernes (Cr: Ridekazèn); Avenue Martin Luther King is Nazon (Cr: Nazon).

Essentials

Hotels **A** *Le Plaza* (formerly *Holiday Inn*), 10 Rue Capois, central location on Champs de Mars, T2239800/93. Jungly gardens, pool, tolerable restaurant, own generator, price includes taxes and electricity, children under 18 free if sharing room, all rooms a/c. **A-B** *Oloffson* (see above), Rue Cadet Jérémie at intersection with Rue Capois, PO Box 260, T2234000. Model for Hotel Trianon in Graham Greene's *The Comedians* and eccentrically managed by Haitian-American musician Richard Morse, this is Haiti's most charming hotel. However you pay for the atmosphere and carefully cultivated faded grandeur. The smaller rooms were built as a hospital and maternity wing by the US marines. Haunt of writers, journalists and film makers, Thu buffet and live music with RAM playing, well worth the money, pool, never lacks electricity, most rooms a/c, CP. **A** *Visa Lodge*, Rue des Nimes, Rte de l'Aéroport, T2491202/3/4, 2462662. Businessman's hotel in industrial zone near airport, pool, good restaurant, own generator, EP. **B** *Prince*, corner of Rue 3 and Ave N, Pacot, T2452764. Quiet hillside neighbourhood 15 mins' walk from taxis, own generator, all rooms a/c. **B** *Villa St-Louis*, 95 Bourdon, on the way to Pétion-Ville, T2456241, F2457949. CP, weekly rates, studio apartments. **B-C** *Park*, 25 Rue Capois, near *Le Plaza*, T2224406. Cheaper to pay in gourdes, safe, central, be prepared to wait an age for breakfast, no generator. **E-F** *Auberge Port-au-Prince*, 148 Rue du Centre. Buses from Dominican Republic disgorge their passengers amid hordes of vendors, very basic rooms with bath or inside room, fan, management surly, ground floor bar serves lunch but closes around 1900, good view from roof.

Guest houses **B** *La Griffonne*, 21 Rue Jean Baptiste, Canapé Vert, T2454095/3440. Quiet neighbourhood 5 mins' walk from Ave John Brown, own generator, rooms with private bath

and a/c, MAP. **B** *Sendral's*, Rue Mercier, Bourdon, near *Hotel Villa St-Louis*, T2456502. Own generator, rooms with private bath and fan, CP. **C** *May's Villa*, 28 Debussy, T2451208. Quiet neighbourhood at top of Ave John Paul II (Cr: Tijo), 10 mins' walk from nearest taxis, view, has a generator, but room lights come on with city power at about 2100, rooms with private bath and fan, CP.

NB Most of the best hotels are in Pétion-Ville, although just 15 mins away. Only the most expensive hotels and guest houses have air-conditioning plus sufficiently powerful in-house generators able to cope with the long electricity blackouts in the city. Some have a generator to give partial power to the bar but not to guest rooms. Water is also rationed, and many of the cheaper, central hotels lack both water and electricity much of the time. Check rooms in advance in the cheaper hotels, service may be deficient. Tax, service charge and energy surcharge are usually added to hotel bills. These extras have been included in the prices given here, which are very approximate because of exchange rate vagaries. While hotels are accommodating UN and NGO personnel, prices are usually quoted in US

Sleeping (margin note)

Haiti (margin note)

dollars and in consequence are high. Where possible, it is cheaper to pay in gourdes. Paying by credit card is more expensive.

Eating   Almost the only decent places to eat out at night in Port-au-Prince are the *Oloffson* or *Le Plaza*, or a row of terrace cafés selling barbecued chicken at the southeast corner of the Champs de Mars (starting near Rex theatre). Bars in this area will probably try and short change you. Well-off Port-au-Princiens go up to Pétion-Ville to dine out. The following restaurants are open during the day closing at about 1600: *Café Terrasse*, rear of Air France Bldg, 11 Rue Capois and Rue Ducoste, T2225468. Excellent lunch, favoured by international aid agency staffers. *Tiffany*, Blvd Harry Truman, Bicentenaire 12, north of Tele-Haiti, T2223506/ 0993. Haitian, French and American food. *Chez Yvane*, 19 Blvd Harry Truman, south of Tele-Haiti, T2220188. Créole lunch in new a/c premises. *La Perle*, 80 Rue Pavée, between Dessalines and Rue des Miracles. Pleasant, cool, enormous sandwiches, also spaghetti, omelettes. *Paradis de Amis*, 43 Rue Pavée, between Centre and Dessalines. Club sandwiches, omelettes, ice cream, a/c, popular with locals, cheap, large portions, spaghetti costs US$2. The restaurant at the *Museé d'Art Haïtien*, *Les Jardins du Musée*, T2228738, is a small oasis, but a bit pricey, popular with 'blancs', particularly French embassy staff, at lunchtime.

Drinks, such as cold beers, water, juice, rum, can be bought at the *Supermarket de la Bonne Foie*, 52 Rue Dr Marselly Seide. Open Mon-Sat 0730-1600, small, friendly, English spoken. Also at *Supermarket Express* up on the hill on John Brown. Cold beer and Guinness, UN customers.

Entertainment   RAM performs Thu at the *Oloffson*, the place to be. Otherwise, the best nightlife is to be found in Pétion-Ville (see separate section). There is a red-light district on the southwest Carrefour Road that has been badly eclipsed by AIDS and political turmoil. The central part of the establishments consist of spacious, breezy, outdoor discothèques. The Dominican beer on offer is excellent and cheap, but the Dominican prostitutes and loud Dominican merengue music may have scant appeal. The city's western limits, around Mariani, have several ill-lit waterfront nightclubs, such as *Le Lambi*, where couples dance groin-to-groin to live compas bands and the men eat plate after plate of spicy, fresh-caught lambi (conch) to boost their virility.

Cinemas   Cheap and interesting: the best are *Imperial* (a/c), Delmas; *Capitol* (a/c), 53, Rue Lamarre; *Paramount*, Champs de Mars. Popular foreign films (British, US, French) are shown; non-French films are dubbed into French.

Clubs   *Pétion-Ville Club*, near US ambassador's residence at the end of Rue Métreaux, a turning off Rue Panaméricaine, between Port-au-Prince and Pétion-Ville, T2577575. A social and sports club, with a nine-hole golf course. Other facilities include tennis courts, racketball, gym, pool, restaurant. A 1-year temporary membership costs US$125, otherwise you can only get in if you are with a full member. *Bellevue*, near Argentine Embassy on Panaméricaine, Bourdon, a social club with tennis courts. *Turgeau Tennis Club* on Ave Jean-Paul II (Cr: Tijo) near corner Martin Luther King (Cr: Nazon) has a few courts. *Jotac* near airport has tennis courts, gym and restaurant.

Shopping   **Art and craft**   Some galleries have a near monopoly on certain artists, so don't expect to see a cross-section of all the major artists in any one, good gallery. The paintings hung at the *Oloffson* are for sale. *Galerie Carlos Jara* (T2457164) has a fine collection at 28 Rue Armand Holly, Pacot, 10 mins' drive uphill from the *Oloffson*. *Le Centre d'Art*, 58 Rue Roy, Pacot, T2222018. In a beautiful but crumbling old house, 2 floors of artwork with stacks of paintings, upstairs, founded 1944, open Mon-Fri 0930-1300, 1430-1600, Sat 0930-1230. The *Nader* family has two galleries: one in Pétion-Ville (see page 372); the other at 18 Rue Bouvreuil (T2450565/4524) in the leafy Croix Desprez neighbourhood is now principally a museum; *Galerie Issa* (T2223287), 17 Ave du Chili (300m from *Oloffson*) is more like a wholesale warehouse, but cheap if you know what you are looking for. *Damballa Art Gallery*, 243 Rue Magasin de l'Etat. A hole-in-the-wall gallery, wonderful. Mass produced copies of the Haitian naïve masters are sold very cheaply around the Post Office, near the port. If you want to buy paintings, you are advised to take your time, look around, and be prepared for some serious bargaining. You will quickly learn which patterns are imitations or mass-produced just by seeing them repeatedly. Vendors sell 1st-class Voodoo flags outside the Musée d'Art Haïtien. Souvenir sellers also close to the *Holiday Inn*.

Comité Artisanal Haïtien, 29 Rue 3, Pacot (near *Oloffson*), T2228440. A co-operative selling handicrafts (no paintings) from all over Haiti at good prices 0900-1600 Mon-Fri, 1000-1200 Sat. *Ambiance*, 17 Ave M, Pacot, T2452494. Haitian jewellery and pottery. *The Rainbow*, 9 Rue Pierre Wiener, Bourdon, T2456655/6039. Sells handicraft and paintings. *Fanal*, 124 Ave Christophe, corner of Rue Waag, T2451948. Antiques, handicrafts, toys, open Mon-Fri 1000-1700, Sat 1000-1400.

Local Taxis *Nick's Taxis*, T2577777, based at 31 Rue Panaméricaine, in Pétion-Ville, is the only radio taxi company. It charges according to the meter. A new, reliable company in **Transport**

Port-au-Prince Centre

Haïti

Not to scale

Voodoo

Seeing a Voodoo ceremony or dance during a short visit is not easy. They are not announced in newspapers nor on the radio. Never go unless accompanied by a Haitian, or someone already known there. Most middle and upper-class Haitians do not attend ceremonies and won't know where or when they are happening. They may even be discomforted by your interest. Tell poor, working-class Haitians about your interest. You may strike lucky. To increase your chances, time your stay to coincide with 2 November (Day of the Dead), Christmas, New Year or Epiphany (6 Jan). There are many ceremonies around these dates. If invited, take a bottle or two of rum or whisky and be ready to give generously if there is a collection. Sometimes, on the contrary, a wealthy 'oungan' (priest) or 'mambo' (priestess) will insist on lavishing drinks and food on the visitor. Don't refuse. To take pictures with a still camera or video, ask permission. You may be asked to pay for the privilege. TV crews are usually asked to pay substantial amounts. An oungan may always be consulted in his 'ounphor' (temple) even if there is no ceremony. Be ready to plead poverty if the sum requested seems exhorbitant.

Max Beauvoir (T2342818/3723), an oungan intellectual with fluent English, has initiated foreigners. Purists questioned the authenticity of the regular voodoo dances he used to lay on for tourists, but he is unquestionably an authority and talks readily to visitors. Aboudja (T2458476, or through the Oloffson), an English-speaking TV news cameraman, has been initiated as an oungan although he does not practice regularly. He acts as voodoo consultant for visiting journalists and TV crews.

Pétion-Ville is **Sunny Taxi Services**, Rue Lambert between Rue Clervaux and Rue Rebecca, T5107000. A passing Publique that is empty can be persuaded to do a private job (Cr: flete). The driver removes the red ribbon. **Air** There are flights to Jérémie, Cap-Haïtien and Hinche. **Road** Fairly conventional-looking buses (Cr: bis) and/or colourfully converted trucks and pickups (Cr: taptap) provide inter-city transport. The place where buses and taptaps leave from is called a *station*. For example to get directions to the departure point for buses to Cap-Haïtien, ask for the *station Au Cap*. Most of the *stations* are somewhere on or between Boulevard Jean-Jacques Dessalines and the waterfront. There are no fixed departure times. Buses leave when they are packed. Roads are bad and journeys are long and uncomfortable. In trucks, it is worth paying more to sit up front with the driver.

Directory **Banks** *Promobank*, T2222461, corner of Lamarre and Ave John Brown, also a branch at Blvd du Quai and Rue Eden. *Scotiabank*, route de Delmas (beneath Canadian embassy) and branch on Rue des Miracles near corner of Blvd Dessalines. *Citibank*, T2462600, route de Delmas. Also several Haitian banks such as *Sogebank*, T2295000, and *Banque de L'Union Haïtienne*, T2230499. There are long queues in most banks for any kind of service. **Exchange:** banks offer a slightly higher rate of exchange than street changers and you are less likely to receive forged notes. Counterfeit 250-gourde notes are reported to be in circulation. Street money changers (Fr: *cambistes*) can be found on Rue Pavée, at the airport, or near the market in Pétion-Ville. It is perfectly legal but they will try and make as much as possible out of you. Check the rate on page 2 of the daily *Le Nouvelliste* newspaper. You may prefer to go in a car and do it through the window. The *cambiste* hands over the agreed sum in gourdes for you to count before you surrender the equivalent US dollar amount. They take only cash. If possible, use a *cambiste* you have seen regularly at a particular spot; never allow yourself to be steered to a *cambiste* by an informal guide. Currency dealers working out of offices give almost as good a rate. They also take TCs. Try Daniel Fouchard (T2231739) 14 Rue des Miracles, Banque de Boston Building. Many importers and big retailers give a good rate for cash, TCs and even personal cheques on US bank accounts. Try Didier Rossard (T2225163), upstairs at 115 Place Geffrard; M or Mme Handal at Express Market, Ave John Brown, 6 blocks down from *Villa St-Louis*. (See also page 354). **Communications** Internet access US$3 per hr at Centre de Formation JRC Software, Ave Magny 16, T2222632, jrcardozo@aol.com Open Mon-Sat 0800-1900, Sun 0800-1200. **Cultural Institutes** *Institut Haitiano-Americain* (T2223715) corner of Rue Capois and Rue St-Cyr, next to *Le Plaza*, 0800-1200, 1300-1700 Mon to Fri. The director is helpful to visiting travellers. *Institut Français*, corner of Blvd Harry Truman and Rue des Casernes, Bicentenaire, T2223720. 1000-1600 Tue-Fri, 0900-1700 Sat. Also has art exhibitions, concerts and plays. **Embassies** *Canada* (T2232358, F2238720), Bank of Nova Scotia Bldg, Delmas 18, BP 826; *Cuba* (T2576626), 18 Rue E Pierre Péguy-Ville, Pétion-Ville; *Dominican Republic* (T2571650, F2579215), 121 Rue Panaméricaine (50m down Rue José de San Martín), Pétion-Ville; *EC Delegation* (T2490141, F2490246), Delmas 60, Impasse Bravé 1, Rue Mercier Laham; *France* (T2220951, F2239858), 51 Place des Héros de l'Indépendance, on Rue Capois at the southwest corner of the Champs de Mars, near Hotel Palace, BP 1312; *Germany* (T2573128), 17 Rue Edmond Mangonès, Berthé, Pétion-Ville; *Japan* (T2455875, F2458834), Villa Besta Vista, Impasse Tulipe 2 Desprez, BP 2512; *Spain* (T2454410, F2453901), 54 Pacot, BP 386; *US* (T222-0200, F2231641), Boulevard Harry Truman, Bicentenaire, BP 1761 and consulate: (T2220200), 22 Rue Oswald Durand. **Hospitals & medical services** Hospitals: recommended hospitals (all in Port-au-Prince) are *Canapé Vert*, Rue Canapé Vert, T2451052/3/0984. *Adventiste de Diquini*, Carrefour Road, T2342000/0521. *Hospital Français de Haiti*, Rue du Centre, T2222323. *St Francois de Salles*, Rue de la Révolution, T2222110/0232. **Tour companies & travel agents** *Agence Citadelle*, 17 Rue des Miracles, Place du Marron Inconnu, T2235900, F2221792. Sightseeing tours in a/c buses, travel and tours to Dominican Republic and Cuba, as well as specializing in travel to South, Central America and the Caribbean islands (owner Bobby Chauvet is a leading Haitian ecologist). *Horizons Tours*, 192B Ave John Brown, T/F2458208. Tours to Cuba. *Agence Martine*, 18 angle Rues Ogé et Geffrard, Pétion-Ville, T2572740. Flights to Miami. *ABC Tours*, 156 Rue Pavée, near Sainte Trinité, T2220335, F2231855. Courteous, helpful. *Voyage Chatelain*, Rue Geffrard, T2232400, F2235065. Handles Terra Bus to Santo Domingo including immigration formalities. *Southerland Tours*, 30 Ave Marie Jeanne, T2231600, F2220580. Because of the collapse of tourism, sightseeing tours are set up only on request. For boat trips try Bernard, T2572399, who can arrange custom made excursions on a boat sleeping 4-6, although for day trips 8 are taken, price up to US$50 per person per day, sailing to Les Cayemites and Pestel is recommended, with good beaches.

Pétion-Ville

Pétion-Ville was once the capital's hill resort lying just 15 minutes from Port-au-Prince but 450 m above sea level and therefore cooler. Now it is considered a middle-class suburb with restaurants and boutiques. Three roads lead up from Port-au-Prince. The northernmost, the Route de Delmas, is ugly and dusty. Preferable to this is the Panaméricaine, an extension of Avenue John Brown (Cr: Lali), which is serviced by camionettes. The southernmost, Route du Canapé Vert, has the best views.

In Pétion-Ville, the main streets Lamarre and Grégoire are parallel to each other, one block apart, on the six blocks between the Panaméricaine and the Place St Pierre. Most of the shops, galleries and restaurants are on or between these two streets or within a couple of blocks of them.

Hotels LL-AL *El Rancho*, Rue José de San Martín, just off the Panaméricaine, T2574926, 2572080/4, F2574134, www.elrancho.inhaiti.com Elegant Resorts International, very pleasant, painted white with tiled roofs, balconies, beautiful view, 2 pools, fitness centre, tennis, 2 restaurants, bars, casino, nightclub, sauna, spa, EP, a/c. **L-A** *Montana*, Rue Cardozo, a turning off the Panaméricaine at the entrance to Pétion-Ville, T2574020, F2576137, htmontana@aol.com An oasis of luxury, best views over Port-au-Prince, especially from poolside restaurant, EP, a/c, phone, TV, airport transfers, conference facilities, built on hillside with lots of stairs, elevators, non-guests can use the pool for US$3. **A** *Villa Créole*, just beyond the *El Rancho* on José de San Martín, T2571570/1, F2574935. Tennis court, pool, good view, EP all a/c. **AL-B** *Kinam* at the corner of Rue Lamarre and Rue Moise, facing Place St-Pierre, T2570462. Mock Gingerbread house, 38 rooms, 3 suites, a/c, phone, TV, good restaurant, bar, small pool, handy location, under same ownership is *Le Ritz*, corner Rue Panaméricaine and Rue José San-Martin, T2576520/1, F2576508. Aparthotel, studios, good for business groups, conference facilities. **AL-B** *Ibo Lele*, at the upper side of Pétion-Ville, towards Montagne Noire, T2575668. Slightly cheaper than *Kinam*, with pool. **A-B** *Caraïbe*, central, 13 Rue Leon Nau, Nerette, PO Box 15423, T2572524. 12 rooms with large baths, a/c, restaurant, TV lounge, pool, built in 1920s, charming, friendly, helpful, family-run, French, English, Spanish spoken.

Sleeping
Most of the larger hotels with pools will let you use their facilities for the day for a small charge

Haiti

Guest houses *Doux Séjour*, 32 Rue Magny (quiet street five blocks from Place St Pierre), T2571560, F2576518. Weekly rates, apartments or rooms with fan and bathroom. *Marabou*, 72 Rue Stephen Archer, just behind St Pierre church, T2571934. Haggle for good rate for long stay. **C** *Ife*, 30 Rue Grégoire a busy street by the market, T2570737. Some a/c, CP. **C** *Villa Kalewes*, 99 Rue Grégoire (at the upper, quiet end of the street), T2570817. CP, pool. **D** *St Joseph's Home for Boys Guest House*, Delmas 91, T/F2574237, or write to Michael Geilenfeld, Lynx Air, PO Box 407139, Fort Lauderdale, FL 33340, USA. Rates include breakfast and dinner, vegetarian meals on request, laundry, bottled water, money exchange, security. For a fee the boys will escort you, give drum lessons, the home can also provide guides, translators, creole lessons, airport pickup, some of the boys perform in the Resurrection Dance Theatre, self-written dances based on their experiences when they lived on the street. Revenue from guests helps to pay for the boys, aged 8-18, who live and work as a family, running the guest house when not at classes. Founder Michael Geilenfeld was a brother with Mother Theresa before starting the home in 1985.

Eating   **Over US$10** *Hotel Kinam*, see above, French/Créole cuisine, very good, lovely ambiance, lambi in Créole sauce recommended, prices around US$9-23. *Chez Gérard*, 17 Rue Pinchinat, T2571949. Beautiful setting sith outside veranda and lush greenery growing everywhere, only items written on menu board are available, about 16/day, higher prices than some, appetizers US$4.50-16, entrées US$14-25, rum US$2.75-3.40, beer US$1.80. *Les Cascades*, 73 Rue Clerveaux, T2577589. Open Mon-Sat 1200-2300, long-established, beautiful décor, good French food, a place for lunch, dinner, brunch, cocktail, buffet, takeaway, wedding receptions etc. *Le Souvenance*, 8 Rue Gabart at the corner of Aubran, T2577688. Gourmet French cuisine. Recommended. Pricey. **US$5-10** *Cassagne*, at the corner of Louverture and Mettelus. Beautiful old home converted into a restaurant, outdoor and indoor seating, bar, stage, live DJ at weekends with dancing from 2300, very nice owner, Haitian/Créole cuisine, moderate prices, food on grill US$6-10, seafood a bit more expensive. *Fabrizio's*, 126 Rue Louverture, T2578433, fabrizio@haitiworld.com Really good Italian restaurant with some tasty dishes, meals from US$6-12, desserts, takeaway and delivery available, beer US$2.25, rum US$3.20-4.50 a glass. *Plantation*, Impasse Fouchard, turning off Rue Borno, T2570979. Excellent French chef, good wine. Recommended. *La Coquille*, 42 Rue Lamarre, T2572542. New in 2001, buffet place with good food, US$6.85 for mainly Créole food buffet, open 1200-1800, beer US$1.85-2.25, rum US$3. *Coin Des Artistes*, 59 Rue Panaméricaine, beneath Festival Arts Gallery, T2572400. Grilled fish and lobster, moderate prices. *Au Petit Louvre*, Rue Grégoire, north of Rue Darguin. Créole and Middle Eastern food, moderate prices, good but not everything on the menu is always available, try their *kibbis*. On the Kenscoff Road the *Altitude 1300*, 67 Laboule, T2559719. The place where the bourgeoisie go at weekends, with the best of créole cuisine. **Under US$5** *Ricky's Restaurant*, 34 Rue Faubert, T2578524. Mostly Créole dishes, US$4.50 buffet Mon-Sat 1200-1500 or 1600 depending on when they run out of food, beer US$1.60, rum US$1.80, also have great art work on display from the Gallery Valcin II. *Station 39*, 39 Rue Lamarre. Boasts the best Créole food, breakfast from US$1-2.75, sandwiches and pasta dishes for lunch US$1-3.50, meat and seafood for dinner US$4.50-9. *Chin Chin*, 49 Rue Geffrard, T2573155. Bar-pizzeria-restaurant, nor very clean, but prices low, beer US$1.40-2.25, rum US$1.60, coke US$0.90, pizza US$5-12.50, also some Middle Eastern dishes. *Harry's*, 97 Av Panamericaine, inside Bagatelle Plaza, T2571885. Bar, restaurant, pizzeria, small US$5.25, medium US$7.25, large US$9, ice cream, sandwiches, spaghetti, American and Haitian food, low to moderate prices. **Fast food** *Domino's Pizza*, 91 Av Panamericaine, T2575151. New in 2000, very clean and you can sit inside, also delivery, prices slightly higher than in North America, but if you have to have pizza…..! Small US$7.25, medium US$12, large US$17. *Mun Cheez*, Av Panamericaine on the corner of Rue Rebecca, T2562177. Open daily until 2200 except Sun 1400, mostly snack foods such as subs, burgers, pizza, salads, egg rolls, fries, also home delivery. *Food Planet*, 79 Rue Lambert. New in 2000, American type fast food with some Haitian dishes, open daily until 2100. *Les Délices Burger*, 97 Rue Grégoire, T2578468. Very good and large hamburgers, taste American, US$2.50-3.50, mini-pizza, nuggets and fries. *Star Mart/Tiger Mart*, are gas/petrol stations that also sell snack foods and usually very good pizza and sandwiches, found around the Av Panamericaine and also on

Rue Canapé Vert. **Cafés** *Presse Café*, 28 Rue Rigaud. Opened 2001, small, coffee and cake, US$1.15 for an expresso, sit and read, magazines and newspapers for sale, mostly in French. *Ice Cream*, 25 Rue Darguin. Quite good and tasty ice cream with 6-10 different flavours, also hot dogs, milkshakes and beer, cheap. **Bakeries** *Patisserie Marie Beliard*, on corner of Rue Lambert and Rue Faubert. Great bread, cakes, pâtés and French pastries. *Le Pouissaint d'Or*, 47 Rue Lamarre.

Café Des Arts, 19 Rue Lamarre (same house as Galerie Monnin), T2577979. Open 1900 until **Nightlife** late, dining and sometimes live music at weekends, large nice bar, beautiful setting, mostly French cuisine, grill US$9-14, pastas US$7.25-12, specialty entrées US$11-15. Upstairs is *Full Moon*. *Blues Blues Café*, Rue Borno between Rue Gregoire and Mettelus. Good setting, bar, live music, restaurant and small boutique, but the food is not great, mix of things and nothing spectacular, moderate prices. *Bash*, in the *Hotel El Rancho*, also Sat evening live jazz. *Harry's*, next to *Coin des Artistes*, see above, T2571885. Food OK, good value, 2 pool tables, often live music, latin and dance music, popular with families. *Ada Club*, 16 Rue Rigaud, '*Resto Dansant*', dancing club and eatery. *Sunset Bar*, 58 Rue Grégoire, T2576236. Run by Canadian Paul, good music, not too much compa, darts and table football, open late, relaxed atmosphere, mixed clientèle. *Guess Who*, Rue Grégoire. Pleasant terrace, often have

Pétion-Ville

N

Not to scale

Haïti

concerts. *Cheers*, 14 Rue Villatte. Great pina colada or food in a relaxed environment, ask in advance and you can rent videos and a room in which to watch them with friends.

Shopping   *La Promenade* at the intersection of Grégoire and Moïse (southeast corner of Place St-Pierre), a garden turned into small shopping promenade with an outdoor café, 1000-1800.

Art and handicrafts   *Galerie Nader*, 50 Rue Grégoire, PO Box 15410, T2575602, 2570855. The most expensive, but has an exceptional range of naïve and other modern Haitian artists, also exhibitions. *Expressions*, 55 Rue Mettelus, south of Rue Ogé, T2563471, expregal@haitiworld.com One of the Nader family galleries, English speaking owners, beautiful gallery, excellent and large selection of paintings. *La Galerie*, 37 Rue Clerveaux, T2570216. Great selection of paintings and cheaper than the two galleries above. *Galerie Bourbon-Lally*, 24 Rue Lamarre, corner of Rue Villate, T2576321/3397. Owned by Englishman Reynald Lally, good choice of naïve art. *Galerie Monnin*, 19 Rue Lamarre, in same house as Café des Arts, T2574430. *Galerie Marassa*, 11 Rue Lamarre, T2577712. Hand-painted boxes, trays. *The Red Carpet*, 86 Rue Panaméricaine, opposite turnings for *El Rancho* and *Villa Créole*, T2572048, F2573324. Large art collection, restaurant attached. *Festival Arts Gallery*, 1 Bis, Rue Gabart, T2577956. Haitian artists who have moved on from primitivism. *Galerie Valcin II*, corner of Rue Rigaud and Faubert. Paintings, crafts and souvenirs. *Galata*, Rue Faubert, T2571114. Mainly handicrafts, especially weavings, metalwork. *Fleur De Canne*, 34 bis, Rue Gabart, T2574266. Good quality craft in a charming store. Place St Pierre is a good place to find street vendors selling handicrafts, paintings, carpets, sculptures, plants, flowers etc, remember to bargain.

Books   *Asterix*, corner of Rue Ogé and Rue Grégoire, the place to get good French books, magazines (some in English), stationery. **Photography**   Lots of places for photo processing, including one on Rue Louverture between Lamarre and Grégoire, owned by Philippe, who speaks English and French, good quality, considerably cheaper than in the USA.

Food   *Foodmax*, corner of Rue Darguin and Rue Lamarre, is a supermarket which carries a lot of 'Western' items. *Royal Supermarket*, Rue Clerveaux, just north of Rue Louverture, also full of imported goods. *Appolo*, Rue Grégoire just north of Place St Pierre, small but best place to buy fresh meat. *Caribbean Supermarket*, Delmas 95, the biggest supermarket with the most varieties. **Dry Cleaning**   *National Dry Cleaning*, 74 Av Panamericaine opposite *Domino's Pizza*.

Tour operators   *Voyages Plus*, La Promenade St, T2573868. You can book *Caribe Tour* buses to the Dominican Republic here. *Multivision*, Angle Rue Lambert and Clerveaux, T2579771. English spoken.

Directory   **Banks** There are several banks for foreign exchange transactions: *BUH* and *Capital* are on Rue Lamarre. Open Mon-Fri 0900-1700, Sat 0900-1300, very slow and bureaucratic. *Sogébank*, on Rue Grégoire, on Rue Louverture and on Rue Lamarre gives faster service. *Promobank* is on the corner of Rue Rigaud and Faubert. *CitiBank* has an affiliate on Rue Louverture between Rue Faubert and Rue Clervaux. **Communications** *Teleco* is at the corner of Rue Magny and Rue Rigaud. All calls go through an operator, Faxes can be sent through *Speedy Fax* on Rue Louverture, between Rues Faubert and Clerveaux. *Mail 'n More*, 107 Rue Louverture, photocopying, email, fax, UPS, calling cards, new and clean building. DHL is at 21 Rue Gabart, T2576192, 2578446.

Excursions near Port-au-Prince

Beaches   The Gulf of La Gonâve beaches, the only ones that can be reached within an hours'
Haiti's best beaches   drive, are not particularly good compared with what you can find on the north coast
are far from the   of the island, but popular for a day trip out of the capital at weekends. Those west of
capital, on the   the capital are poor. The best of what's available is to the north. The first beaches you
Caribbean &   get to are rather gritty, but the sand improves as you go further north. The backdrop
Atlantic coasts   is of arid, deforested mountainside but the calm, clear, shallow water is excellent for
children. **The Côte Des Arcadins**, a 20-km stretch of beach hotels, begins 60 km
north of the capital. The hotels all have bars and restaurants, and charge admission
to day visitors. They may be crowded with wealthy Port-au-Princiens or aid agency
staff at weekends. There are also public beaches with no hotels. **The Arcadins** are

three uninhabited, sandy cays 3 km offshore which are surrounded by reef. The diving is excellent. **Isle La Gonâve** is also visible and dive boats visit the wall offshore.

Heading north along the Côte des Arcadins in geographical order: **C** *Kyona*, T257-6850/ 6863. Daily admission US$9 adults, US$$1.50 children, curved, gritty beach, loungers and tables in shade, lots of trees, locals sell paintings, turtle shells, black coral, basic rooms in bungalows or newer block, cold water, thatched open-air restaurant, volleyball, hotel dates from early 1960s. **AL** *Kaliko Beach Club*, at Km 61, PO Box 670, Port-au-prince, T2984607/8/9, F2984610, kaliko@haitiworld.com   All-inclusive, new in 1997, smart blue and white plantation style resort, popular with French Canadians, this is the noisiest of the resorts with music playing all the time, but it also has the most facilities to offer, 55 rooms (sleep 4) with fan or a/c, and growing, day pass US$40 with 2 meals, US$15 lunch only, pleasant beach but not spectacular, pool, tennis, gardens, entertainment, créole lessons, boat cruises, conference facilities, excursions. Just along the beach is *Pegasus Diving*, PO Box 15785, T2383140. For snorkelling trips at Les Arcadins, US$20, Anse à Pirogues, US$35, and La Gonâve US$50. Diving for certified divers only to Les Arcadins, US$70 including gear, and the wall at Isle La Gonâve, US$80, 30 mins on dive boat. Fishing also available, US$200 for two people, half day, including gear, Captain, drinks and boat rental. **A-B** *Wahoo Bay*, T2229653. Includes breakfast, day pass US$10, 20 large, clean rooms, a/c, upstairs rooms with balcony and good view of La Gonâve, good showers, delicious food with generous portions, pool, small but sandy beach, good swimming, loungers and tables with shade, windsurfing, horse riding, tennis, older resort but well maintained, building new rooms. **C** *Ouanga Bay*, at Km 65, PO Box 1605, Port-au-prince, T2983155-6, F2224422. Day pass US$3.50 until 1900, food and drinks cost extra, small sandy beach with man-made reef, quiet and private, wooden loungers, lovely new restaurant built over the water, 27 rooms and apartments right on beach, large beds, fan or a/c, TV and phones being added, bathrooms adequate, upstairs rooms reached by wobbly spiral staircases, English-speaking owner, friendly, watersports include snorkelling, windsurfing, pedalos and glass bottom boats with electric motors, diving arranged. After Montrouis, at Km 77 is **LL-L** *Moulin Sur Mer*, (Elegant Resorts International), T2221918, F2786720, moulinsm@haitiworld.com At the entrance is the **Musée Colonial Ogier-Fombrun**, in a stone 18th-century plantation building, open daily 1000-1700, adults US$2, students and children US$1, see the model of the original house and buildings, also museum pieces outside. The hotel is reached through the extensive gardens with Royal palms, peacocks, geese and ducks, beautiful setting on sandy beach, day pass US$10, 65 rooms FAP, Haitian furniture and art, a/c, hot water, tiled floors, phones, suites for families, also beach rooms for day use, two restaurants, vegetarian food available, tennis, volleyball, ping pong, pool, mini golf, playground, watersports including pedalos, kayaks, windriders, diving arranged, lots of languages spoken, golf carts for the less mobile.

Sleeping

Overnight stays at weekends are popular, you may need to book ahead, very calm at night, beautiful stars

The asphalt road to Kenscoff, in the mountains behind Port-au-Prince, starts just to the west of the Pétion-Ville police station, on the Place St-Pierre. After 10 minutes, there is a turnoff on the right at United Sculptors of Haiti, which sells good wood carvings. It skirts a huge quarry and climbs to **Boutilliers**, a peak topped by radio and television masts that dominates the city. Rewarded with a great view but promptly greeted by handicraft vendors and good-natured pestering. In about 20 minutes, the main Kenscoff Road reaches **Fermathe** where the large Baptist Mission has a restaurant selling sandwiches, hot dogs, fries, pizza, ice cream etc, with fine views south, and a store selling handicraft and souvenirs (taptaps and camionettes from near the market in Pétion-Ville). There is also a museum of the 'history of this land, of this people and of serving Satan'. Voodoo is seen by the Museum as the cause of all poverty in Haiti. A turnoff near the Mission leads to Fort Jacques and Fort Alexandre (10 minutes by car or an easy 45 minutes walk), two forts on adjoining summits built after the defeat of Napoleon. The views north over the Cul de Sac plain are breathtaking. Fort Jacques is restored.

Kenscoff is a hill resort where, 30 minutes (15 km) from Pétion-Ville, but 1,500m above sea level, members of the élite retire to their country homes in July and August

Other excursions

to escape the heat. A camionette from Pétion-Ville is US$0.30. **D** *Hotel Florville* is fairly basic and not especially friendly but provides refreshments and meals in a nice dining room. Marketday is on a Friday. You can drive just beyond **Furcy,** from where you can hike to the summit above Kenscoff that is topped by a radio mast (about one hour), or the summit just to the west, called Morne Zombi. The ridge just to the east of the radio mast can be reached by a surfaced road in poor condition. It offers views south over a rugged, dark massif that boasts Haiti's highest peak, the 2,674m La Selle. It can get cold at the top if its cloudy.

From the ridge, a four- or five-hour hike (at a comfortable pace) along a trail heading towards the village of **Seguin** brings you to **Parc La Visite**, a nature park covering part of the massif. It has pine woods, montane cloud forest at higher altitudes, dozens of big limestone caves (one 10 km long), and strange karst-formation rocks locals call 'broken teeth' (Cr: kase dan). See further page 360. A guide is required. Camp at a disused saw mill (Cr: siri) by the trail, where water is available from a fountain. Bring thick clothes and sleeping bags; temperatures can fall to freezing at night. A waterfall is a short hike away. For longer hikes and fine views, head east with a guide and climb the 2,282m Pic Cabaio or the 2,100m Pic La Visite (another camping site). The park keeper, Jean-Claude, rents horses. Seguin lies on a sloping plateau on the massif's southern face, about one hour beyond the park. **C** pp hostal/guest house, includes breakfast and dinner. Book in advance through the restaurant *Yaquimo* in Jacmel, they will send a guide with a mule/horse to carry your luggage and show you the way to the hostal. If you are very fit the walk can be done in less than three hours. From Seguin, a five-hour hike gets you to the south-coast village of Marigot, from where you can bus back to Port-au-Prince via Jacmel in 4 hours.

Wildlife enthusiasts should visit **Lake Saumâtre** (see page 360), at the eastern end of the Cul de Sac plain near the Dominican border. The newly improved road from Croix-des-Bouquets to the border crossing at Malpasse skirts the lake's southern side. The northern side offers more chance of seeing its wildlife. On Route Nationale 3 heading northeast from Port-au-Prince towards Mirebalais, fork right at the Thomazeau turnoff to the lakeside villages of Manneville and Fond Pite. It takes 90 minutes.

South of Port-au-Prince

Set off on the RN2, the highway heading west toward Les Cayes. The lush, densely populated coastal Léogâne Plain, 45 minutes west of the capital, offers a look at rural life. East and west of the town of Léogâne, the plain is dotted with small villages and criss-crossed by bumpy lanes. After Léogâne at the Dufort junction fork left. The road climbs steeply, winding through the mountains with good views.

Jacmel

The port of Jacmel is Haiti's prettiest, but also very run down, city. Its name derives from an Indian word meaning 'rich land'. A quiet place, Jacmel has changed little since the late 19th century when it was a booming coffee port and its wealthy merchants built New Orleans-style mansions using cast iron pillars and balconies imported from France or the United States. The charm of its Victorian architecture is matched by a setting at the head of a 3 km wide horseshoe bay, with streets winding down three small hills to a palm-fringed, black-sand beach. A hurricane swallowed up most of Jacmel's beach and what is left is dirty with pigs rooting around in the debris.

The best views can be had from the south-facing upper veranda of the *Manoir Alexandre*, a turn-of-the-century patrician home that is now a guest house. The main square is pleasant and busy with vendors; the *Hôtel de la Place* restaurant is a good place to have lunch and watch the world go by. One block to the east opposite the church is an iron market built in 1895. Saturday is market day. The street below the *Manoir Alexandre*, Rue Seymour Pradel, has another old residence, now an art gallery called *Salubria-Brictson Galleries*. Owner Bob Brictson is in residence only a few months of the year, but if you knock you will be shown his collection of world-wide art. Closer to the beach, on Rue Commerce, more 19th-century homes have been turned into galleries or handicraft stores. The Boucard family residence at the corner of Grand' Rue and Commerce, is especially fine. At the other end of Commerce, near the wharf, note the Vital family warehouse dating from 1865. The nearby prison was built in the 18th century. Jacmel's handicraft speciality is boxes, trays, place mats and other objects covered with parrots or flowers, hand-painted in bright colours.

Sleeping

B *La Jacmelienne*, T2883451. A modern, 2-storey hotel on the beach with pool, MAP, fans, no a/c, often no water either, all rooms with balcony and sea view, restaurant open-air and pleasant at night. **B-C** *Hotelflorida*, Rue du Commerce 29, near the Post Office, T2882805, F2883182. Breakfast available, homely, cosy living room, friendly staff, also **AL** suite with 4 beds. Next to the hotel is a French patisserie with lovely bread, pizza etc, where you can eat in the backyard. **C** *Hôtel de la Place*, 3 Rue de l'Eglise, T2882832, overlooks Place d'Armes. Good location, very central with lots to see and interesting people-watching, functional rooms with bathrooms, clean, pleasant restaurant, reasonable food. **D** *Manoir Alexandre*, Rue d'Orléans, T2882711. Large untended garden, faded grandeur, lots of character but shared bathroom has seen better days, lovely view from veranda, good sunset watching, breakfast included but no other meals available, appears to be run by school children. **F** *Guy's*, 52 Grand' Rue, T2883421. 10 rooms, includes breakfast, 2 with bathroom, clean, popular, good value.

Nightlife

Yaquimo Nightclub & Restaurant is 100m west of the wharf. Fairly good food, good atmosphere, live bands. Book here for the guest house in Seguin.

Shopping

There are lots of artists painting and selling their work along Portail Léogane. Most of the handicrafts are sold in the small shops by the entrance to *La Jacmelienne*.

Haiti

Transport

In Port-au-Prince, buses leave from the station Jacmel on Dessalines, a couple of blocks the other side of Chareron, 2½-3 hrs, US$1.50, lovely route, very crowded. In Jacmel buses leave from the gas station at the junction of Portail Léogane and Avenue de La Liberté.

Directory

Banks Exchange: *BMH*, 60 Grand' Rue, between bus station and *Guy's Guest House*, good rates, changes TCs. You can also change money at *La Jacmelienne*, but don't expect a good rate.

Beaches

Beaches on the south coast tend to have a slight undertow

A good dirt road leads east to fine white-sand beaches. The first is **Cyvadier**, a tiny cove down a side-road at Km 7. The cliffs and trees surrounding the beach prevent much sunbathing, but the water is clean and pleasant and it is very pretty. The surf can be rough at times. Fishermen cast their nets from the beach. A quiet hotel and restaurant, **L-A** *Cyvadier Plage*, T2883323, offers rooms with ceiling fans, balcony, private bath with constant water and electricity most of the time, price includes 3 meals (which at times take up to 2 hrs to be served, so order early), mostly seafood, fruit and vegetables, all fresh and local, swimming pool, secure, gates locked at night. At Km 15, just before Cayes Jacmel, is **Raymond-les-Bains**, a beach alongside the road. No facilities except showers. Beware of the slight undertow. Just after Cayes Jacmel, at **Ti Mouillage**, the road runs beside two beaches. The first has a basic restaurant. From Marigot, a pretty coastal village 10 km further on, a four-wheel drive can climb a rough trail to the village of Seguin and the Parc National La Visite (see under Excurions from Port-au-Prince).

Bassin Bleu

There are excellent views over Jacmel bay on the way

A 12 km track into the hills west of Jacmel leads to Bassin Bleu, a series of natural pools and waterfalls descending a limestone gorge in tiers. The biggest, deep, blue-green pool is framed by smooth rocks and draped with creeper and maidenhair fern. Jump in for a cool swim. It takes 1½-2 hours each way on foot or horseback (horses for hire in Jacmel or in the village up the hill on the other side of the river from Jacmel, about US$6-7, depending on the quality). Take a guide, fixing a price in advance, and water to drink. If it has not rained, the road is fine for a four-wheel drive three quarters of the way. The Jacmel guide hands over to a local guide for the last kilometre which is a rough path and, at one point, requires the aid of a rope. This means an additional small fee. Guides here can be a problem, only one with the rope is needed, but you will find that you may be accompanied by others who will later demand payment. Some are charming and helpful over the slippery rocks. Be prepared to pay for the diver from the uppermost rock into the pool. He expects to be paid for his 'show'. In sum, this is a very rewarding excursion and highly recommended, but you need deep pockets with lots of small change for tips.

West of Port-au-Prince

The southwestern peninsula is the greenest and most beautiful part of Haiti, its rugged western tip has forests, rivers, waterfalls and unspoilt beaches.

The Route Nationale 2 to Les Cayes is very scenic but is frequently almost non-existent and where there is any surface it is often seriously potholed. For the first 92 km it runs along the north coast of the peninsula. At Km 68 is the town of **Petit Goave** (Cr: Ti Gwav). Visit the *Relais de l'Empereur* (T2229557), once the residence of Emperor Faustin 1 (1849-56). The hotel is no longer operating, but the caretaker will show you around.

Just 2 km down a turn-off at Km 92 is the smugglers' port of **Miragoane**, a town of narrow streets that wind around a natural harbour or climb up a hill capped by a neo-gothic church. The town is dirty, dusty, crowded and poor, bars and restaurants no longer function and the hotel is for sale. Activity has moved up to the main road where there is a large market. In the centre of the market is a good café with parking space, medium prices. A four-wheel drive is needed for the dirt road that continues along the north coast, fording rivers and passing fishing villages, as far as

West of Port-au-Prince

Petit Trou de Nippes. At Petite Rivière de Nippes, 15 km along this road, a three hour trek inland on foot or horseback (take a guide) brings you to one of Haiti's four great waterfalls, **Saut De Baril**.

After Miragoane, the main road crosses the peninsula's spine and reaches the southern, Caribbean coast at Aquin (Km 138) where you can bathe in several rivers. At **Zanglais**, 6 km farther on, there are white sand beaches near the road. (Beware of slight undertow at any beach on the south coast.) Just beyond Zanglais a ruined English fort is visible on a small offshore island, with the remains of a battery emplacement opposite, on the mainland.

Les Cayes

On a wet, coastal plain 196 km west of Port-au-Prince, Haiti's fourth city, Les Cayes (Cr: Okay) sits. It is quiet but not without charm. The Fête de Notre Dame around 15 August is recommended. Spend the day swimming, eating, drinking and watching people, and at night the crowd moves to the *musique racine* until 0200 which is irresistible. Some people sleep on the beach because hotels are usually over-booked. Advance booking is necessary at this time. In Port-au-Prince, buses, or taptaps leave in the mornings from the same area as those for Jacmel on Blvd Dessalines, for the four hour trip (US$4). Visible from the waterfront is **Ile-à-Vache** (*Population*: 5,000), a 20 km-long island that was Henry Morgan's base for a 1670 raid against Panama. It has Indian remains and good beaches on the southern side near La Hatte, the biggest village. Visit it by renting a boat with outboard (about US$25 for the day) or take the daily ferry leaving at around 1600, and pay to sleep in someone's home. Or camp, after asking permission. A more regular service goes to **Port Morgan**, a wonderful, small resort/marina run by a French couple, Didier and Françoise Boulard, T2861600, F2861603, portmorgan@globelsud.net They have their own boat service to Les Cayes, US$10, and offer tours to local villages for market and other activities. There are some beautiful hikes in the area. Accommodation **B-C** per person in immaculate bungalows includes three meals, delicious French food, restaurant open for visitors, breakfast US$5, 0730-0930, lunch from US$9, 1200-1500, dinner from US$13.50, 1700-1800, reserve before noon. Very knowledgeable and helpful hosts, willing to help with travel arrangements on the mainland.

Excursions **Fortresse des Platons**, a huge ruined fortress on a 600m summit overlooking the coastal plain, can be visited in a one day excursion from Les Cayes. It was built in 1804 at Dessalines' behest. Take the coast road southwest out of the city. Just after Torbeck, a rough road heads inland up a river valley via Ducis to the village of Dubreuil (trucks from Les Cayes). From Dubreuil, the fortress is a two to three hour hike up a steep trail with great views. Carry on the same trail via Formond to enter the **Macaya National Park**, which has Haiti's last virgin cloud forest surrounding the 2,347 m Pic Macaya. See page 360 for the park's vegetation and wildlife. A University of Florida base at Plaine Durand (two hours beyond the fortress) has basic camping facilities. Hire guides for hikes into the lower montane rain forest. Only the very fit should attempt the hike to the top of the Pic Macaya. It entails climbing a 2,100 m ridge and then descending to 1,000m before tackling the peak itself. Allow at least two days each way and take a guide.

Beyond Torbeck, the coast road goes as far as **St Jean du Sud** where a small offshore cay is suitable for camping. Before St Jean du Sud, fork right at L'Acul for **Port Salut**, a 90-minute drive from Les Cayes (two buses a day, also some trucks). This small village (birthplace of President Aristide) has a wild, 800m-long, palm-lined beach with fine, white sand that is one of the most beautiful in Haiti. The town is a haven of paved roads and laid back people who do not hassle. The beaches are beautiful and totally empty. There is a pleasant waterfall, 10 minutes' drive, 30 minutes' walk, where you can swim. Ask locals for directions.

Sleeping **C** *La Cayenne*, T2860379, by the beach, on the main street. Price depends on whether you
& eating have a/c, pool, the only restaurant in town, poor service. **C** *La Concorde*, Rue Gabions de
Indigènes, T2860277. Rooms with bath, fan, EP, not always open, very comfortable. At the
end of the village is a **E** *Village Touristique*, BP 118, comfortable bungalows with shower, big
bed, mosquito screens, nice, quiet, right on beach, water but not always electricity, candles
supplied, contact Maurice, the caretaker; or rent rooms from locals. Two other hotels are
Impérial, in the town centre and *Meridien*, just before you enter Les Cayes, with a restaurant.
In Port Salut, *Village*, booking through the *P'tit Bistro* in Pétion-Ville, T2573042. A 20 mins'
walk beyond the former *Arada Inn*, now closed, leads to a good and noisy restaurant, US$3
for breakfast, US$6.25 for fish or lobster.

West coast The adventurous can take the coastal route from Les Cayes to **Jérémie**, around the
road peninsula's tip, a remote, rugged, lush region that has changed little in 200 years. It
has wild rivers, sand beaches, mountains falling steeply into the sea, and some of
Haiti's last rain forest. Allow four days. Les Cayes buses or taptaps may go as far as
Les Anglais, depending on the state of the road. A four-wheel drive may even get to
Tiburon. Thereafter, you must hike to **Anse d'Hainault** or even **Dame Marie**
before finding road good enough to be serviced by taptaps out of Jérémie. Alternatively, take your life in your hands and try getting a ride on sloops that carry merchandise and passengers along the coast. Residents in small villages all the way will
cook meals and rent beds for a few dollars. 'Pripri', rafts made of bamboo lashed
together and steered by a pole, ply the rivers. Anse d'Hainault and Abricots (25 km
west of Jérémie) have good beaches.

The scenic, hair-raising, 97 km mountain road from Les Cayes to Jérémie, across
the Massif de la Hotte, can be done in three hours, but it may be impassable after rain
and must be done in daylight. One hour's drive brings you to **Camp Perrin**, a hill
resort at the foot of the 2,347 m Pic de Macaya. Here there are several guest houses.
Rent horses for a two-hour ride to **Saut Mathurine**, Haiti's biggest waterfall. It has
good swimming in the deep, green pool at its base.

Fork right off the Jérémie Road at the Kafou Zaboka intersection for **Pestel**, a picturesque port dominated by a French fort. Worth seeing any time of the year, but
especially for the Easter weekend regatta, when many Rara bands come. The town is
pretty with old wooden houses, a hotel with nice rooms and a friendly owner. Five
minutes from Pestel there is the *Café de la Gare* restaurant run by a Frenchman and
his son (dancing in the evenings, happy hour Saturday evening), and a few bungalows for rent which are basic but OK, **C** for 2-4 people, by the sea. Charter a boat to
tour nearby fishing villages such as **Les Basses** (Cr: Obas) on the Baradères peninsula and **Anse-à-Maçon** on the offshore island of **Grande Cayemite** with its splendid view of the Massif de la Hotte and distant Pic Macaya. The beaches are very
beautiful and totally empty.

Jérémie With crumbling mansions overgrown by rampant vegetation, Jérémie is famed for
its poets, eccentrics and isolation. The road is bad. Some buses are still running from
Port-au-Prince, however, leaving from Jean-Jacques Dessalines near Rue Chareron
(US$8). The 12-hour overnight ferry ride is not recommended. At least 800 (maybe
as many as 1,500) Jérémie residents drowned when an overloaded ferry, the *Neptune*, sank on its way to Port-au-Prince in February 1993. The quickest and easiest
way of getting there is to fly. *Tropical Airlines* from Port-au-Prince, T2563626-8,
US$89. They may be booked up to 10 days ahead. Anse d'Azur, 4 km west of the
town, is a white-sand beach with a rocky headland at one end, home to a big cave
into which you can swim. The road west continues to the beaches of Anse du Clerc
and Abricots (see above).

Sleeping On a hill above the town, with a shady garden, is **D** *Hotel La Cabane* (MAP). Out of town,
20km west, about 1 ½ hrs drive from the airport, depending on the state of the road, is **D**
pp *Anse-du-Clerc Beach*, along the coast on the way to Abricots, T2463519 in Port-au-

Prince, ask for Jean Charles. The owners (Michel and Danielle Bonhomme, Haitian and Canadian) will collect you from Jérémie airstrip. There are seven rooms in small bungalows, shared bathroom, warm water, on a beach of polished pebbles. The seabed is sandy, so once you are in the water you can stand easily. It is a very peaceful spot. Dinner and breakfast are included in the per person rates, food excellent, local ingredients including lambi.

North of Port-au-Prince

The seaboard north of the capital is arid or semi-arid most of the way to Gonaïves, and all round the northwest peninsula as far as Port-de-Paix. This area was hit by drought and famine in 1997 and severe ecological damage has occurred. From Port-de-Paix to the Dominican border, it is quite lush and green. Route Nationale 1 hugs the coast for most of the first 85 km skirting the foot of the Chaine des Matheux mountains.

Cabaret (Km 35) is the former Duvalierville. Its ugly, modernistic buildings and pretensions of becoming Haiti's Brasilia were lampooned in *The Comedians*. **L'Arcahaie** (Km 47) is where Dessalines created the blue and red Haitian flag by tearing the white out of the French tricolor. Outside L'Arcahaie, a dirt road heads east high into the Chaine des Matheux to a region where coffee and indigo was grown in colonial times. A dozen ruined plantation houses survive. The turnoff is just before the point where the highway crosses the small Mi Temps River. Sailboats leave at mid-morning from Montrouis (Km 76) for the 22 km crossing to **Anse-à-Galets** (one guest house), the main town on barren **La Gonâve Island**. In 1997 a ferry capsized just off Montrouis as it was docking. At least 172 died when passengers all crowded to one side caused the boat to turn over only 50m from the shore. At Km 96, after the Côte des Arcadins beaches, the RN1 reaches the port of **St Marc** (**F** *Hotel Belfort*, 166 Rue Louverture, clean, basic). Several fine gingerbread houses are on streets to the east of the main street. A pretty valley runs inland southeast as far as Goavier.

RN 1 is asphalted to Cap-Haïtien, but is badly potholed for 65 km between Pont Sondé & Gonaïves

The highway crosses the river Artibonite at **Pont Sondé**, entering a region of rice paddies irrigated by canals. Fork right at the Kafou Peyi intersection, 2 km north of Pont Sondé, for **Petite Rivière de L'Artibonite** (Cr: Ti Rivyè), a picturesque town built by Christophe on a steep-sided ridge overlooking the river Artibonite. Its Palace of 365 Doors was Christophe's provincial headquarters. In 1802, there was a key battle at the Crète-à-Pierrot fort (five minutes walk above the town) in which Leclerc sacrificed 2,000 men to dislodge a force of 1,200 led by Dessalines.

About 8 km after **L'Estère**, a right turnoff runs southeast 25 km to **Marchand**, a town at the foot of the Cahos mountains that was briefly Dessalines' capital. Hike into the surrounding hills to visit seven big ruined forts built by Dessalines. Near the town is a spring with a natural swimming pool. Dessalines told his soldiers that bathing here made them immune to French bullets. The house of Dessalines' wife, Claire Heureuse, still survives in the town. You can also see the foundations of his own home. After the Marchand turnoff, the RN1 crosses a semi-desert called Savane Désolée.

Amid saltpans and arid lowlands, **Gonaïves** at Km 171 is an ugly, dusty town of 70,000 (Haiti's third largest). It is called the City of Independence because Dessalines proclaimed Haiti's independence here in 1804. The unrest that toppled Jean-Claude Duvalier in February 1986 also began here. **D** *Chez Elias* is a safe, clean guest house (T2740318), Rue Egalité opposite Teleco, rooms with fan and bathroom, MAP. At *Chez Frantz* (T2740348), Avenue des Dattes, the rooms are often taken by long-term residents, but the food is Gonaïves' best. *Rex Restaurant*, Rue Louverture, half a block from the market, has Créole food and hamburgers. Buses (US$3, four hours) leave Port-au-Prince mornings from the intersection of Boulevard La Saline and Jean-Jacques Dessalines. In Gonaïves, mopeds operate as taxis, charging US$0.20 a ride.

Haiti

After Ennery at Km 201, the RN1 climbs steeply up to the Chaine de Belance watershed and enters the green, northern region. **Limbé** at Km 245, has a museum, Musée de Guahaba, created by Dr William Hodges, a Baptist missionary doctor who runs the local hospital and supervises archaeological digs along the north coast (see La Navidad on page 384). The museum is not always open but you can ask for admission from his family who work at the Limbé hospital nearby. Fort Crète Rouge, above Limbé, is one of the many fortresses built by Christophe.

A rugged side-road from Limbé down to **Le Borgne** (Cr: Oboy) on the coast offers spectacular views. The 20 km either side of Le Borgne abound with white-sand beaches. The high, green mountains right behind add to their beauty, but the coast is densely inhabited and the beaches are often used as a public latrine. From Le Borgne to St Louis du Nord, the road is very bad but not impassable for four-wheel drive.

After Limbé, the main highway descends quickly, offering fine views over L'Acul Bay, where Columbus anchored on 23 December 1492, two days before his flagship sank.

Cap-Haïtien

Nowadays it usually referred to simply as Cap, or Okap in Créole

Cap-Haïtien, Haiti's second city, has a dramatic location on the sheltered, southeast side of an 824m high cape, from which it gets its name. It was the capital in colonial times, when it was called Cap-Français. Its wealth and sophistication earned it the title of 'Paris of the Antilles'. The colony's biggest port, it was also the commercial centre of the northern plain, the biggest sugar producing region. It was burned to the ground three times, in 1734, 1798 and 1802, the last time by Christophe to prevent it falling intact into the hands of the French. It was destroyed again by an 1842 earthquake that killed half the population. The historic centre's architecture is now Spanish influenced, with barrel-tile roofs, porches, arcades and interior courtyards.

Haiti

North of Port-au-Prince

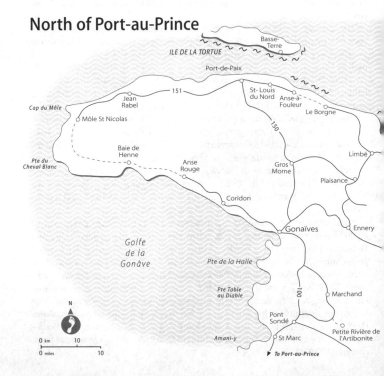

Vertières, an outlying district on the Port-au-Prince Road, is the site of the battle at which Dessalines's army definitively routed the French on 18 November 1803, forcing them to leave the island for good 12 days later. There is a roadside monument.

Cap appears to be more relaxed than Port-au-Prince and you will see people out on the streets at night. It is well worth visiting for its buildings and its surroundings but the people are not accustomed to tourists (*blancs*). The streets are filthy and streams of foul-smelling water run down them. The municipal government functions rarely and its services, such as street cleaning, are moribund. Do not drink the water, nor even use it to clean your teeth.

Sleeping

Cap-Haïtien gets electricity only 1900-2300

A-B *Beck*, on the mountainside, residential Bel-Air district, T2620001. Woodland setting, 2 pools, constant water, own generator, private beach at Cormier, German owner, rooms with private bath and fan, MAP. **A** *Mont-Joli*, on the hillside above town, T2620300/26, MontJoli@aol.com, has a pool, tennis court, good restaurant, own generator (runs 1000-1200 and 1730-0600), rooms with private bath and a/c, CP. Nearby is **C** *Les Jardins de l'Océan*, Boulevard de Mer, T2622277. Small hotel, nice terrace with seaview, good food à la carte, friendly atmosphere, cosy rooms all with bathroom, fan. **B** *Roi Christophe*, T2620414, corner of 24 and B. Central location in colonial house first built in 1724 as the French governor's palace (Pauline Bonaparte stayed here), lush gardens, pool, own generator (not big enough for a/c) runs 0600 until city power comes on, more expensive with a/c, cheaper with fan, CP. **F** *Brise De Mer*, 4 Carenage (on waterfront at northern edge of town), T2620821. Friendly but reportedly not very safe, own generator (but not on all the time), rooms with private bath and fan. **F** *Columbia*, Rue 5, 3-K. Fan, clean, safe, very helpful owner speaks English, they do their best to make you comfortable, even when there is no water or electricity, beer, soft drinks and home cooked spaghetti on request.

Eating

Cap 2000, Rue 5 and Blvd (not far from waterfront). Sandwiches, ice cream. A popular and cheap restaurant, good food but basic, is on Ave L just past the corner with Rue 1, near *Hotel Columbia*.

Shopping

Ateliers Taggart, T2621931, Rue 5 near Blvd (by *Cap 2000*). All kinds of handicrafts, especially weavings and metalwork, 1000-1700 Mon-Fri. Recommended. *Galerie Des Trois Visages*, excellent art gallery next to *Ateliers Taggart*. A tourist market by the port has handicrafts and naive paintings. Bargain hard. There is a supermarket, *Marina Market*, on the Blvd with Rue 13. Most shops close between 1700-1800.

Atlantic Ocean

Baie de l'Acul
Plage Labadie
Plage Cormier
Cap-Haïtien
Caracol
Plaine du Nord
Limonade
100
Citadelle Milot
Terrier Rouge
Fort Liberté
121
Grand Rivière du Nord
Ouanaminthe
Dondon
St Raphaël
St Michel de l'Attalaye
Pignon
300
Maïssade
Hinche
To the Dominican Republic
To Port-au-Prince

Haiti

Transport

Local Car rental: *Hertz*, T2620369. Check price quotes very carefully. Don't leave your passport as deposit. **Air** *MAF* and *Caribintair* both have six flights a week from Port-au-Prince. A Cap-based air taxi service, *Marien Air* (T2620527) offers flights to Port-au-Prince, the Dominican Republic, Turks and Caicos, Bahamas and Jamaica. **Buses** Buses leave Port-au-Prince from the station Au Cap opposite the big Texaco garage at the junction of Delmas Road and Boulevard La Saline between 0630 and 0830, when full. The 274-km trip usually takes 6-7 hrs. Fare US$5.80. It may be necessary to change in Gonaïves, 3½ hrs, US$2. There are two principal taptap stations in Cap: **Barrière Bouteille** at southern end of town for all destinations to Port-au-Prince, and **Port Metalique**, at A2, also south end of town, cross bridge for station for all destinations to Milot (outside *Hotel Bon Dieu Bon*), Hinche, Fort Liberté, Ounaminthe and the border.

Directory **Banks** *BNP*, good for changing TCs; also *Banque Union Haïtien* changes TCs, open until 1300. **Communications** Post Office: Ave B at Rue 17. **Tour companies & travel agents** *Cap Travel*, 84 Rue 23A, T2620517.

Excursions from Cap-Haïtien

Ruins The rich, alluvial plain to the south and east of Cap boasted a thousand plantation houses during the last years of the colonial period. ISPAN, T2622459, Rue 15 and Rue B in Cap, is a good source of information on these nearby colonial ruins, as well as Sans Souci and the Citadelle.

Beaches & hotels
The beaches in the town itself are dirty & lack charm

Excellent beaches on the north side of the cape can be reached in 20 minutes by car. The first is **Cormier Plage**, site of the recommended **A** *Hotel Cormier Plage* (T2621000). Simple chalets or rooms, including breakfast and dinner, excellent food, own generator turned on 0730-1100 and 1630-2330. Scuba diving with equipment for 10. Good wrecks and coral reefs. Run by a charming French couple, Jean-Claude and Kathy Dicqueman. If you call ahead, they will pick you up from the airport. Book ahead, because tour groups from Dominican Republic sometimes fill the place up. Take mosquito repellent.

Five minutes further west (30 minutes on foot), is **Labadie**, or **Coco beach**, a fenced-off sandy peninsula used by Royal Caribbean Lines as a private beach for its visiting cruise ships on Mondays and Tuesdays. The public may enter to use its facilities (pool, restaurants, watersports) for US$3.

Just beyond this beach, about 30 minutes walk, are steps down to **Belli Beach**, a small sandy cove with a hotel, **E**, nice rooms, WC, shower, fan, mosquito nets, they will cook good fish à la créole for US$4.50. Boats, some with outboards, can be rented here to visit nearby Labadie village, dramatically located at the foot of a cliff, and other beaches further along the coast, for example Paradise beach, 30 minutes, US$6, no facilities. Fix a price before boarding. Labadie village (about US$3 by boat, also reachable by scrambling over the rocks) has two guest houses, *Dessa Motel* and *Maison Amitié*, with basic rooms on the beach, both **F**. Employees will buy and cook food for a price to be negotiated. From the end of the road you can also take a boat round the cove (US$10 one way) to *Norm's Place*, an old French fortress, refurbished by an American who is very hospitable and runs it as a guest house, **E**, with excellent food and service.

Farther still, about 10 km west of Cap, is **AL** *Club Roche Sauvage*, T2622765, an all-inclusive, 144-bed resort with its own 300m beach. Spa and diving extra. Round trip air-and-sea transfer from Port-au-Prince another US$85 per person. Beyond Roche Sauvage is Labadie Shore, Crown Cruise Line's answer to Labadie Beach.

Transport Taptaps US$0.60 to Labadie from Cap leave frequently in the morning from Champs de Mars, away from the centre and the waterfront towards the mountains. Go up Rue 22 for about 10 mins' walk, ask if you get confused, it looks a bit rural. Taptaps will drop you at the gate to Coco Beach.

La Citadelle
Haitians call this the eighth wonder of the world

The massive, mountain-top fortress of La Citadelle was built by King Henri Christophe between 1805 and 1820 to deter any French reinvasion (see page 388). With walls up to 40 m high and 4 m thick, and covering 10,000 sq m, 20,000 people were pressed into its construction. It is dizzily perched atop the 900m high Pic La Ferrière, overlooking Cap and the entire northern plain, and controlling access to the Central Plateau. Its garrison of 5,000 soldiers (plus the royal family and its retinue) could have held out for a year. It is indeed impressive, and has breathtaking views. Restoration work has been under way for years and is well advanced. Behind the fortress, at the end of a 1.5 km level ridge with sheer drops on both sides, is the Site des Ramiers, a complex of four small forts which controlled the rear access. Worth visiting just for the views. ■ *Getting there: take the 25 km asphalt road south from Cap to the village of Milot in a publique (US$1) or taptap (US$0.30). Taptaps leave Cap in the morning. Hotels like the Mont Joli offer jeep tours for about US$60 per person, but don't count on the guide's information being correct. From Milot it is a steep 5 km hike through lush countryside up to the fortress (about 1½ hours, start early to avoid the heat; to find the road up to the Citadelle you need to walk through Sans Souci Palace). Wear stout shoes and be protected from the sun. Horses can be rented for about US$7 plus a tip for the man who leads the horse (dangerous in wet weather). Hire a guide even if you don't want one, just to stop others importuning and to make you feel safer (fix the fee in advance, US$10 for two, or more, for the walk). Several speak fluent French and English making the visit more interesting. Prices of refreshments at the Citadelle are higher than elsewhere (US$0.80 for a coke), but someone has had to carry them up there. Those with their own vehicle are able to drive to a carpark two thirds of the way up, reducing the walk to 1½ km. Horses available here too, US$3.50 plus tip (this last part is the hardest). Admission is US$5 to the Citadelle and Sans Souci but they will try and sell it to you for more including guide.*

Sans Souci

At Milot itself are the ruins of Christophe's royal palace, Sans Souci. More than a palace, it was an embryo administrative capital ranging over 8ha in the foothills beneath the Citadelle. Christophe sited his capital inland because of the difficulty of defending coastal cities against the overwhelming naval might of France and Britain. It included a printing shop, garment factory, distillery, schools, hospital, medical faculty, chapel and military barracks. Begun in 1810, inaugurated in 1813, ransacked after Christophe shot himself in the heart with a silver bullet in 1820, it was finally ruined by the 1842 earthquake that destroyed Cap. The admission to the Citadelle covers Sans Souci. If planning to visit both sites, arrive before 1300 to have enough time, as they close at 1700. There are no buses or taptaps back to Cap after 1700.

Morne Rouge

An uprising planned in this area directly led to Haiti's independence

Morne Rouge, 8 km southwest of Cap, is the site of Habitation Le Normand de Mezy, a sugar plantation that spawned several famous rebel slaves. Leave Cap by the RN1 and take a dirt road running north from a point about 75 m west of the turnoff to the town of Plaine du Nord. Its ruins include two aqueducts and bits of walls. Voodoo ceremonies are held under a giant tree in the village. Among its rebel progeny was Mackandal, an African chief's son who ran away, became a prophetic oungan and led a maroon band. After terrorizing the entire northern plain by poisoning food and water supplies, he was captured and burned alive in January 1758. **Bois Caiman** was the wood where slaves met secretly on the night of 14 August 1791 to hold a Voodoo ceremony and plan an uprising. (It is near the Plaine du Nord Road, about 3 km south of the RN1. Ask locals to guide you once you are in the area.) Their leader was an oungan and slave foreman from Le Normand de Mezy called Boukman. The uprising a week later was the Haitian equivalent of the storming of the Bastille. Slaves put plantation houses and cane fields to the torch and massacred hundreds of French settlers. It began the only successful slave revolt in history and led to Haiti's independence. Little is left of the wood now except a giant ficus tree overgrowing a colonial well credited with mystic properties.

Plaine du Nord

The town of Plaine du Nord, 12 km southwest of Cap, is a pilgrimage centre every year on 24-25 July due to the Catholic festival of St James, who is identified with the Voodoo spirit Ogou. Voodoo societies come from all over Haiti, camp in the streets and spend the two days in non-stop drumming and dancing. Many are possessed by Ogou and wallow in a much-photographed mud pool in one of its streets. On 26 July, the feast day of St Anne, most of the Voodoo societies at Plaine du Nord

Shiver me timbers

The buccaneers who settled on the north coast of Hispaniola were a mixed bunch of runaways and renegades. Some were escaped indentured labourers, who fled the gruelling life of the plantation; others were marooned sailors or deserters. Most were European, but there were a few blacks among them. Although some had a background in piracy, this was not their principal means of subsistence. What kept them alive and gave them their name were the wild cattle that roamed in the deserted northern plains of the island. These they rounded up and slaughtered, cooking the meat over wooden fires known as boucans. From these early barbecues came the English word buccaneer.

The disappearance of the indigenous population together with thriving herds of feral cattle and pigs, introduced by the Spanish in the early days of settlement, ensured a viable, if not comfortable, lifestyle. For several months each year, the buccaneers would hunt cattle in the interior, tanning hides for trade and curing meat on their boucans. Accompanied by dogs and armed with muskets, they collected enough of their bloody merchandise to return to the coast, where occasional trading exchanges took place with passing pirate or smuggling ships. So covered in blood were the buccaneers after their hunting expeditions that contemporary observers thought they were covered in ship's tar.

In return for meat and hides, the buccaneers wanted alcohol, tobacco and weaponry. These seem to have been among the few manufactured essentials in an otherwise rudimentary way of life. They lived in basic stilted shacks with palm roofs, modelled on the indigenous ajoupa, and wore home-made caps, belts and shoes of rawhide. Other clothes were rough cotton trousers and shirts.

The 'brethren of the coast', as they were called by the French historians Dutertre and Labat, inhabited a world without women. Even despite their reported lack of personal hygiene, they seem, however, to have entered into same-sex marriages, known as matelotage. These relationships probably had legal rather than emotional foundations, ensuring that the surviving member of a pair would inherit the other's assets on the death of the other. And death in the wilds of northern Hispaniola and nearby Tortuga Island was commonplace, through violence, malaria and other tropical hazards.

Although they were not first and foremost pirates, most buccaneers were not averse to a little casual predation. As their numbers grew, they occasionally set out to attack coastal traders, mostly Spanish, in long dugout canoes. After seizing whatever the unfortunate crews had on board, they would normally throw them into the sea before returning to their bases in the captured ship. Loot, it seems, was scrupulously shared out, with extra quotas going to those who had been injured in the adventure.

Over time, the buccaneers seem to have tired of piratical activity, and many began to farm smallholdings of coffee and sugarcane. As the French staked a claim to the western side of Hispaniola, so the forces of law and order arrived, discouraging brigandage and supporting more sustainable economic pursuits. The buccaneers eventually disappeared as a distinct community, some moving on to other pirate havens such as Port Royal, Jamaica, others remaining in Hispaniola as small farmers and hunters.

decamp to nearby **Limonade**, 15 km southeast of Cap, for another day and night of celebrations. A dirt road on the northwest side of Limonade leads to Bord De Mer De Limonade, a fishing village where Columbus' flagship, the *Santa María*, struck a reef and sank on Christmas Day, 1492. Columbus used wood from the wreck to build a settlement, **La Navidad**, which was wiped out by Taino Indians after he left. Its location was discovered by American archaeologist William Hodges while digging at the site of Puerto Real, a city founded years later on the same spot. The untrained eye will detect nothing of either settlement now, but the Hodges museum in Limbé, 20 km southwest of Cap, has relics.

Fort Liberté Fort Liberté, 56 km east of Cap, is a picturesque, French-designed town on a large bay with a narrow entrance. It is dotted with French forts that can be reached by boat. The best is Fort Dauphin, built in 1732. The bay was the site of the Caribbean's largest sisal plantation until nylon was invented. There are direct taptaps Cap-Fort Liberté, but it may be easier to return to Cap from the main road, which is 4 km from the centre of Fort Liberté. **D** *Bayaha*, Rue des Bourbons, by the sea, great view, terrace, quiet, good food, evening meal included in price, basic rooms, no a/c, cold water.

Ounaminthe is northern Haiti's chief border crossing. Accommodation is available at *Hotel Paradis* on the main street. The Dominican frontier town, Dajabón, is just 2 km from the Ounaminthe taptap station. Taptaps for US$2 from the Station Nordest in Cap; US$1.10 from Fort Liberté. The crossing is straightforward and the Haitain border office is very helpful. Buses leave Dajabón for many Dominican cities. The river Massacre, which forms the border, had this name long before the massacre of thousands of Haitians in the neighbouring part of the Dominican Republic under Trujillo in 1937, when the river was said to have been red with blood for days. The bridge across the river is packed with money changers and *motoconchos* (not necessary for transport to Haitian border post, which is about 1 km from Dominican side). The Dominican side of the border has been described as an armed camp, with heavy military presence controlling the flow of Haitian labour. The Haitian side, on the other hand, is more like a gypsy camp, with a thicket of tents, lean-tos and a crowd of money changers and 'guides'.

Frontier with Dominican Republic

For the rugged, the dirt road forking left 5 km before Milot could be an alternative route back to Port-au-Prince via Hinche and the Central Plateau (see page 387). A four-wheel drive is needed. It takes two to three hours. By public transport it takes much longer, up to two days to the capital. Vehicles tend to be old, it is very dusty and the worst stretch is from near Milot to Hinche. The first town is **Grand Rivière du Nord**, where another of Christophe's fortresses, Fort Rivière, sits atop a ridge to the east. It was used by the Cacos guerrillas who fought the US occupation from 1918 to 1920. The Americans captured the Cacos leader Charlemagne Peralte near here. **Dondon** has caves inhabited by bats. One is close to the town. The other, 90 minutes on foot or horseback up a river bed to the west of the village, has heads carved in relief on its walls, presumably by the original Indian inhabitants. In the rainy season, cars cannot ford the river near St Raphaël, but you can walk, with locals helping for a small fee.

South of Cap-Haïtien

The Northwest

Except for Tortuga island and a coastal strip running east from Port-de-Paix, the northwest peninsula is Haiti's driest, most barren region. In recent years, especially since the 1991 coup, it has teetered on the brink of famine and toppled over in 1997 when international agencies had to bring aid.

The 86-km mountain road from Gonaïves to Port-de-Paix via Gros Morne fords several rivers and takes four hours in a four-wheel drive, needed for travel anywhere in the northwest. (Minibuses from Gonaïves, big buses from Port-au-Prince, leaving from beside the station Au Cap.) **Port-de-Paix** once made an honest living exporting coffee and bananas. Now it specializes in importing contraband goods from Miami. Vendors tout the wares on all its unpaved streets. In 1992-93, its small freighters also ferried illegal immigrants into Miami. Despite the smuggling, it is safe.

D *Hotel Brise Marina*, about 10 minutes from the town centre northeast along the coast. The best in the area, clean, basic rooms with bathroom, pool, restaurant OK, nice view over the sea. **C** *Le Plaza*, a few hundred metres before *Brise Marina*, looks abandoned, not well maintained, missing light bulbs, no water in pool, possible to order lunch or dinner. *Holiday Beach*, in the town centre, basic.

Sleeping

A coast road runs west from Port-de-Paix along the north coast of the peninsula as far as Môle St Nicolas and then returns to Gonaïves via the south coast. **Jean Rabel** is a tense town which was the site of a peasant massacre in July 1987. At least 150 died in the clash, said to have been engineered by local Duvalierist landlords seeking to crush the attempts of Catholic priests to organize landless peasants. From Jean Rabel round to Baie de Henne, the landscape is arid, windy and dusty. Old people say they can remember when it was still green and forested.

Columbus first set foot on the island of Hispaniola at **Môle St Nicolas**. It has several ruined forts built by the English and French. General Maitland's surrender of Môle to Toussaint in 1798 marked the end of a five-year British bid to gain a toehold on this end of the island. Strategically located on the Windward Passage, just 120 km from Cuba, Môle was long coveted as a naval base by the USA. The hinterland has Haiti's lowest rainfall and little grows. The main occupation is making charcoal and shipping it to Port-au-Prince. Because few trees are left, charcoal makers now dig up roots. The peninsula's south side, especially from Baie de Henne to Anse Rouge, is a mixture of barren rock and desert, but the sea is crystal clear. There are few inhabitants. With salt pans on either side, Anse Rouge ships sacks of salt instead of charcoal.

Tortuga Island   A 30-minute drive to the east of Port-de-Paix by a good, dirt road takes you to **St Louis du Nord**, a pretty coastal town from where sailing boats cross the 10 km channel to Tortuga Island, the Caribbean's biggest pirate base in the 17th century. Nearly 40 km long, 7 km wide and 464m above the sea at its highest point, its smooth rounded shape reminded seafarers of the back of a turtle. (Tortuga in Spanish and La Tortue, its Haitian name, in French.)

Its present population of 30,000 is spread all over the island. The biggest south-coast villages, **Cayonne** and **Basse-Terre**, are less than 1 km apart. A ferryboat leaves Cayonne for St Louis du Nord at 0800 and returns at about 1000, charging locals US$0.50 each way. Foreigners may have to pay up to US$10, depending on their negotiating skills. Boats crossing at other times charge more. From Cayonne there is a narrow cement road up to Palmiste serviced by a single taptap, one of the four or five cars on the island. From Palmiste, the biggest village on the rounded spine, there are spectacular views of the corniche coastline stretching from Cap to Jean Rabel, and the towering mountains behind. The best view is from the home of French Canadian priest Bruno Blondeau (T268-5138/6709), the director of a Catholic Church mission who has effectively governed the island since 1977. He runs 35 schools and has built all 55 km of its road. His order also operates a small, basic hotel (**F**, EP).

The best beach, 2 km long, is at **Pointe Saline**, at the western tip (34 km from Palmiste, two hours by car). This is also the driest part of the island and there is little shade. **La Grotte au Bassin**, 6 km east of Palmiste, is a large cave with a 10 m high precolumbian rock carving of a goddess. There are two other big caves: **Trou d'Enfer**, near La Rochelle ravine, and **La Grotte de la Galerie**, 1 km east of Trou d'Enfer.

The largest historic ruin on the island is a 15m high lime kiln (four à chaux), built at the end of the 18th century. Fort de la Roche, 1639, was once Tortuga's biggest fortress (70m high). Its masonry foundations can be seen at a spring where women wash clothes on the hillside above Basse-Terre. Three cannon and a bit of wall remain from Fort d'Ogeron, built in 1667.

Northeast of Port-au-Prince

Grandly called the Route National 3, the 128-km dirt road northeast from Port-au-Prince to Hinche requires a four-wheel drive and takes at least five hours (much longer by public transport). It starts by crossing the Cul de Sac plain via Croix-des-Bouquets. Here, a newly improved road branches off southeast through a parched, barren region, skirting Lake Saumâtre (see page 360 and 374) before reaching the Dominican border at Malpasse (see page 356). On the north side of the plain, the RN3 zig-zags up a steep mountainside called Morne Tapion (great views back over Port-au-Prince) to reach Mirebalais, a crossroads at the head of the Artibonite valley. It is Haiti's wettest town. The road east leads to Lascahobas and the frontier town of Belladère, the least used of Haiti's three border crossings into the Dominican Republic. The road west heads down the Artibonite valley. Before it gets too bad, a left turnoff leads up into the hills to the charming village of **Ville-Bonheur** with its church built on the spot where locals reported an appearance of the Virgin in a palm tree in 1884. Thousands of pilgrims come every 15 July. The Voodooists among them hike 4 km to visit the much-filmed **Saut d'Eau** waterfall. Overhung by creepers, descending 30 m in a series of shallow pools separated by mossy limestone shelves, the fall seems enchanted. The Voodooists bathe in its waters to purify themselves and light candles to enlist the help of the ancient spirits believed to live there.

The RN3 heads north out of Mirebalais on to the Central Plateau, where the military crackdown was especially harsh after the 1991 coup because peasant movements had been pressing for change here for years. After skirting the Peligre hydroelectric dam, now silted up and almost useless, the road passes Thomonde and reaches the region's capital, **Hinche**. The F *Foyer d'Accueil* is an unmarked guest house above a school that is behind the blue and white church on the east side of the main square, basic rooms with fan, rarely any power, EP. The *Hotel Prestige*, also unmarked, at 2 Rue Cité du Peuple, near the market, has not so good rooms for the same price. In Port-au-Prince, buses leave from the station Au Cap at the intersection of Boulevard La Saline and route de Delmas. MAF operates about two flights a week. East of Hinche, **Bassin Zim** is a 20 m waterfall in a lush setting 30 minutes drive from town (head east on the Thomassique Road, then fork north at Papaye). The cascade fans out over a rounded, sloping, limestone rockface. At its foot is a 60 m wide natural pool with deep, milky-blue water that is perfect for swimming.

Background

History

Columbus visited the north coast of Hispaniola, modern Haiti, on his first visit to the West Indies, leaving a few men there to make a settlement before he moved on to Cuba. Columbus traded with the native Tainos for trinkets such as gold nose plugs, bracelets and other ornaments, which were to seal the Indians' fate when shown to the Spanish monarchs. A second voyage was ordered immediately. Columbus tried again to establish settlements, his first having been wiped out. His undisciplined men were soon at war with the native Tainos, who were hunted, taxed and enslaved. Hundreds were shipped to Spain, where they died. When Columbus had to return to Spain he left his brother, Bartolomé, in charge of the fever-ridden, starving colony. The latter sensibly moved the settlement to the healthier south coast and founded Santo Domingo, which became the capital of the Spanish Indies. The native inhabitants were gradually eliminated by European diseases, murder, suicide and slavery, while their crops were destroyed by newly introduced herds of cattle and pigs. Development was hindered by the labour shortage and the island became merely a base from which to provision further exploration, being a source of bacon, dried beef and cassava. Even the alluvial gold dwindled and could not compete with discoveries on the mainland. The population of some 400,000 Tainos in 1492 fell to about 60,000 by 1508. In 1512 the Indians were declared free subjects of Spain, and missionary zeal ensured their conversion to Christianity. A further 40,000 were brought from the Turks and Caicos, the Bahamas and Venezuela, but by 1525 the Indian population had practically disappeared. Sugar was introduced at the beginning of the 16th century and the need for labour soon brought African slaves.

Hispaniola

Haiti

Birth of a colony In the 17th century the French invaded from their base on Tortuga and colonized what became known as Saint Domingue, its borders later being determined by the Treaty of Ryswick in 1697. The area was occupied by cattle hunting buccaneers and pirates, but Governor de Cussy, appointed in 1684, introduced legal trading and planting. By the 18th century it was regarded as the most valuable tropical colony of its size in the world and was the largest sugar producer in the West Indies. However, that wealth was based on slavery and the planters were aware of the dangers of rebellion. After the French Revolution, slavery came under attack in France and the planters defensively called for more freedom to run their colony as they wished. In 1791 France decreed that persons of colour born of free parents should be entitled to vote; the white inhabitants of Saint Domingue refused to implement the decree and mulattoes were up in arms demanding their rights. However, while the whites and mulattoes were absorbed in their dispute, slave unrest erupted in the north in 1791. Thousands of white inhabitants were slaughtered and the northern plain was put to the torch. Soon whites, mulattoes and negroes were all fighting with shifting alliances and mutual hatred.

Toussaint Louverture Out of the chaos rose a new leader, an ex-slave called **François-Dominique Toussaint**, also known as Toussaint Louverture, who created his own roaming army after the 1791 uprising. When France and Spain went to war, he joined the Spanish forces as a mercenary and built up a troop of 4,000 negroes. However, when the English captured Port-au-Prince in 1794 he defected with his men to join the French against the English. After four years of war and disease, the English withdrew, by which time Toussaint was an unrivalled leader among the black population. He then turned against the mulattoes of the west and south, forcing their armies to surrender. Ordered to purge the mulatto troops, Toussaint's cruel lieutenant, **Jean-Jacques Dessalines**, an African-born ex-slave, slew at least 350. Mulatto historians later claimed that 10,000 were massacred. The same year, torrential rain broke the irrigation dams upon which the prosperity of the area depended. They were never repaired and the soil was gradually eroded to become a wilderness. By 1800 Toussaint was politically supreme. In 1801 he drew up a new constitution and proclaimed himself governor general for life. However, Napoleon had other plans, which included an alliance with Spain, complicated by Toussaint's successful invasion of Santo Domingo, and the reintroduction of the colonial system based on slavery. In 1802 a French army was sent to Saint Domingue which defeated Toussaint and shipped him to France where he died in prison. The news that slavery had been reintroduced in Guadeloupe, however, provoked another popular uprising which drove out the French, already weakened by fever.

19th-century revolution This new revolt was led by **Dessalines**, who had risen to power in Toussaint's entourage and was his natural successor. In 1804 he proclaimed himself Emperor of the independent Haiti, changing the country's name to the Indian word for 'high land'. Dessalines was assassinated in 1806 and the country divided between his rival successors: the negro **Christophe** in the north, and the mulatto **Pétion** in the south. The former's rule was based on forced labour and he managed to keep the estates running until his death in 1820. He called himself **Roi Henri Christophe** and built the Citadelle and Sans Souci near Milot. For a fictionalized account of these events, read Alejo Carpentier's *El reino de este mundo – The Kingdom of This World*, arguably the first Latin American novel to employ the technique of *lo real maravilloso*). Pétion divided the land into peasant plots, which in time became the pattern all over Haiti and led to economic ruin with virtually no sugar production and little coffee. Revolution succeeded revolution as hatred between the blacks and the ruling mulattoes intensified. Constitutional government rarely existed in the 19th century.

US intervention At the beginning of the 20th century, the USA became financially and politically involved for geopolitical and strategic reasons. Intervention in 1915 was provoked by the murder and mutilation of a president, but occupation brought order and the reorganization of public finances. Provision of health services, water supply, sewerage and education did not prevent opposition to occupation erupting in an uprising in 1918-20 which left 2,000 Haitians dead. By the 1930s the strategic need for occupation had receded and the expense was unpopular in the USA. In 1934 the USA withdrew, leaving Haiti poor and overpopulated with few natural resources. Migrants commonly sought work on the sugar estates of the neighbouring Dominican Republic, although there was hatred between the two nations. In 1937 about 10,000 Haitian immigrants were rounded up and massacred in the Dominican Republic (see Further reading).

In 1957 **François (Papa Doc) Duvalier**, a black nationalist, was elected president and unlike previous autocrats he succeeded in holding on to power. He managed to break the mulattoes' grip on political power, even if not on the economy. In 1964 he became President-for-Life, a title which was inherited by his 19-year-old son, **Jean-Claude (Baby Doc) Duvalier** in 1971. The Duvaliers' power rested on the use of an armed militia, the **Tontons Macoutes**, to dominate the people. Tens of thousands of Haitians were murdered and thousands more fled the country. However, repression eased under Jean-Claude though dissidence rose encouraged partly by US policies on human rights. Internecine rivalry continued and the mulatto elite began to regain power, highlighted by the President's marriage to Michèle Bennett, the daughter of a mulatto businessman, in 1980. Discontent began to grow with the May 1984 riots in Gonaïves and Cap-Haïtien, and resurfaced after the holding of a constitutional referendum on 22 July 1985 which gave the Government 99.98% of the vote. Several months of unrest and rioting gradually built up into a tide of popular insistence on the removal of Duvalier, during the course of which several hundred people were killed by his henchmen. The dictatorship of the Duvaliers (father and son) was brought to a swift and unexpected end when the President-for-Life fled to France on 7 February 1986.

Duvalier Dynasty

The removal of the Duvaliers left Haitians hungry for radical change. The leader of the interim military-civilian Government, **General Henri Namphy**, promised presidential elections for November 1987, but they were called off after Duvalierists massacred at least 34 voters early on polling day with apparent military connivance. New, rigged elections were held in January 1988, and **Professor Leslie Manigat** was handed the presidency only to be ousted in June when he tried to remove Namphy as army commander. Namphy took over as military president, but four months later he himself was ousted in a coup that brought **General Prosper Avril** to power. Dissatisfaction within the army resurfaced in April 1989, when several coup attempts were staged within quick succession and lawlessness increased as armed gangs, including disaffected soldiers, terrorized the population. Nevertheless, the USA renewed aid, for the first time since 1987, on the grounds that Haiti was moving towards democratic elections, promised for 1990, and was making efforts to combat drug smuggling. Under General Namphy, cocaine worth US$700mn passed through Haiti each month, with a 10% cut for senior army officers. However, Avril's position was insecure; he moved closer to hardline Duvalierists and arrests, beatings and murders of opposition activists increased. Foreign aid was again cut off in January 1990 when Avril imposed a state of siege and the holding of elections looked unlikely. Finally, in March, General Avril fled the country after a week of mass demonstrations and violence. Following his resignation, Haiti was governed by an interim President, Supreme Court judge, **Ertha Pascal-Trouillot**.

Democracy & the army

Despite poor relations between Mme Pascal-Trouillot and the 19-member Council of State appointed to assist her, successful elections were held on 16 December 1990. The presidential winner, by a landslide margin of 67% to 15%, was **Father Jean-Bertrand Aristide**; his nearest rival was the former finance minister Marc

1990 elections & coup

Haiti

Bazin. President Aristide ('Titide'), a Roman Catholic priest who was expelled from the Salesian order in 1988 for 'incitement to hatred, violence and class struggle', was sworn in on 7 February. His denunciations of corruption within the government, church and army over the previous decade had won him a vast following. Among his immediate steps on taking office were to start investigations into the conduct of Mme Pascal Trouillot and many other officials, to seek the resignation of six generals, to propose the separation of the army and police and to garner urgently-needed financial assistance from abroad for the new administration. Aristide's refusal to share power with other politicians, his attacks on the interests of the armed forces and the business elite and the actions of some of his militant supporters provoked his overthrow on 30 September 1991 by the army. Aristide fled into exile. Harsh repression was imposed after the deposition of Aristide; at least 2,000 people were said to have died in the first six months, almost 600 during the coup itself. People began fleeing in small boats to the United States' Guantánamo naval base on Cuba in an exodus that had reached 38,000 by May 1992. The USA brought it to an end by immediately repatriating everyone without screening political asylum claims.

International pressure International condemnation of the coup was swift, with the Organization of American States, led by the USA, imposing an embargo. While the EU and other nations did not join in the embargo, they did follow the OAS in suspending aid and freezing Haitian government assets. The sanctions hurt, but not sufficiently to promote a formula for Aristide's return; this was partly because of Washington's misgivings about his radical populism. The election of Bill Clinton to the US presidency in 1992 with the prospect of more decisive US action on restoring Aristide to power prompted United Nations involvement. Former Argentine foreign minister Dante Caputo was appointed UN special envoy for Haiti in December 1992. With Washington making it clear it was ready to step up sanctions, Caputo persuaded the army commander, **General Raoul Cedras**, to agree in February 1993 to the deployment of 250 civilian UN/OAS human rights monitors throughout Haiti. Further UN pressure was applied in June 1993 with the imposition of an oil embargo and a freeze on financial assets. As a result, an accord was reached in July whereby Aristide would return to office by 30 October, Cedras would retire and Aristide would appoint a new army chief and a prime minister.

As the 30 October deadline approached, it became clear that Aristide would not be allowed to return. In mid-October, the Haitian rulers humiliated the USA by refusing to allow a ship to dock carrying a 1,300-strong UN non-combat mission. Oil and arms sanctions were reimposed, yet Aristide supporters continued to be killed and harassed. Aristide's appointed cabinet resigned in mid-December as the régime showed no signs of weakening. In fact, as smuggled fuel from the Dominican Republic flowed in, Cedras and his collaborators set their sights on staying in power until the end of Aristide's term of office, February 1996.

Meanwhile, tensions between Aristide and the Clinton administration grew as the USA appeared unable, or unwilling, to break the impasse. Pressure from the US Black Caucus and from Florida politicians eventually persuaded Clinton to take more positive action. The policy of returning boat people was stopped. Tough worldwide sanctions, including a cessation of commercial flights, were initiated in May 1994 and the Dominican Republic was approached to control sanctions breaking. These measures led to a state of emergency in Haiti, but not an end to defiance.

Aristide's return Despite the lack of wholehearted support in the USA, an occupation of Haiti by 20,000 US troops, first proposed in June, began on 19 September 1994. Aristide returned to the presidency on 15 October to serve the remainder of his term, aided first by a 6,000 strong US force, then by 6,000 UN troops which replaced the Americans in March 1995.

General Cedras and his chief-of-staff, General Philippe Biamby, were talked into exile in Panama, while the third leader of the regime, police chief Michel François, fled to the Dominican Republic. In the months after the regime's demise, Aristide set about reducing the influence of the army and police and the USA began to train new recruits for a new police force. By April 1995, the absence of a fully-trained police force and of an adequate justice system contributed to a general breakdown of law and order. Many people suspected of robbery or murder were brutally punished by ordinary Haitians taking the law into their own hands. 'Zenglendo' thugs, often thought to be demobilized soldiers, were involved in the killing of political figures and others. The fear of violence disrupted preparations for legislative and local elections, held over two rounds in June and July 1995.

The elections gave overwhelming support to Aristide's Lavalas movement in the Senate (all but one of the seats up for election) and the Lower House (71 of the 83 seats) but the turn out was very low and the results were bitterly contested. Twenty three of the 27 competing parties denounced the election because of irregularities reported by international observers.

Economic reform under Aristide was slow and there was dissent within the Cabinet. Progress on judicial reform progressed but investigations into killings stalled. The US Senate consequently blocked disbursement of aid. Mob violence and extra-judicial killings continued, with the new police force unable to do anything about it.

Presidential elections were held on 17 December 1995 and for the first time power was transferred from one elected Haitian president to another. **René Préval**, a close aide of Aristide's, won a landslide victory with 87% of the vote, although only 25% of the electorate turned out and most opposition parties boycotted the event. He was inaugurated on 7 February 1996 and **Rosny Smarth** was later sworn in as Prime Minister. Agreement on a structural adjustment programme was reached with the IMF in May but was hampered by a hostile Congress and not approved until October. Haiti was treated as a political football in the US Senate, which was absorbed in its own presidential race. Aid only dribbled in, leaving civil servants and police unpaid and mounting violence in the streets. The UN Peacekeeping Force was repeatedly asked to stay for longer as the new police force was still unready to take over. Some arrests were made as the Government attempted to move against widespread corruption but nothing could be done about the nationwide violence which claimed hundreds of lives.

Rivalries within the ruling coalition, the Lavalas Political Organization, spilled into the open at the end of 1996 when Aristide launched a new group, the Lavalas Family (Fanmi Lavalas), which became a political party in time for the senatorial and local elections held in April 1997, at which less than 10% of the electorate voted. The major opposition parties boycotted the poll, claiming that the electoral council was controlled by Aristide, and later called for the results to be annulled. The second round of the senatorial elections was postponed indefinitely. It was feared that if the Lavalas Family gained control of the Senate, the reform package would be blocked.

In June, Prime Minister Rosny Smarth resigned. He blamed elements of Lavalas for stirring up political unrest and the electoral council for not annulling the April elections, which were marked by fraud. His departure increased concern in Washington that the faltering political and economic recovery programme would be brought down. Smarth remained in office until October pending the appointment of a successor, but he had still not been replaced a year later. The two opposing factions of the Lavalas movement were unable to resolve their quarrel over the April 1997 elections. Local elections were completed in mid-October, allowing the formation of a permanent electoral council which was dominated by Aristide supporters. At the end of November 1997, about 1,200 UN troops began to withdraw, leaving 300 police instructors in place for another year and 400 US troops who were engaged in construction and health care. Violence and murders continued. The Organization Politique Lavalas changed its name to Organization du Peuple en Lutte (OPL) to distance itself from Fanmi Lavalas, and in February 1998 it dropped its demands

René Préval

Haiti

to have the April 1997 elections annulled, but other parts of a political deal collapsed within a week. International donors were frustrated by the impasse, and it was claimed that millions of dollars of aid were being held up with a consequent brake on growth and poverty alleviation.

In July 1998, Education Minister Jacques Edouard Alexis was nominated as head of government. He had the support of the OPL but political infighting delayed his appointment. In January 1999, President Préval declared Alexis Prime Minister and announced he would no longer recognize parliament as its term had expired under the law governing the delayed 1995 elections. Nevertheless, amid violence and demonstrations, the Chamber of Deputies continued to meet, claiming it was entitled to sit for four years from October 1995. Confusion reigned and was intensified with the expiry of terms of office of municipal councils. A new government was finally sworn in on 26 March 1999 and a provisional electoral board two days later. The much-delayed legislative and municipal elections were held in May 2000 and were won overwhelmingly by the FL. Foreign observers described the elections as flawed but credible, but opposition parties denounced the results. Murder and harassment of candidates and their supporters before and during the vote did not prevent the USA and the UN praising the generally peaceful voting process, but certain results were disputed. However, the Government refused to reexamine the vote in the seats where the result was contested.

Opposition parties boycotted the presidential elections in November 2000 because of the flawed May elections and for the same reason the USA, Canada and the EU refused to send observers. Six candidates were found to stand against Aristide, but none of them campaigned because of pre-election violence. Aristide himself was rarely seen in the years he was out of office, preferring to stay at his walled compound in Tabarre in the north of Port-au-Prince. Official results gave Aristide 92% of the vote and he was inaugurated in February 2001. His party now holds 28 of the 29 Senate seats, over 80% of the seats in the Legislature and nearly all the mayoralties and municipalities. Violence has not stopped, however. Despite post-election declarations by Aristide for peace and democracy, his supporters have continued to carry out violent anti-opposition protests, while the opposition continues to question the legitimacy of the electoral process.

Geography

Haiti is an Indian word meaning 'high ground'. It is the Caribbean's most mountainous country. Except for a few small, mainly coastal plains and the central Artibonite River valley, the entire country is a mass of ranges. The highest peak is the 2,674m La Selle, southeast of the capital. Little remains of Haiti's once luxuriant forest cover, cut down for fuel or to make way for farming. With soil erosion and desertification far advanced, Haiti is an ecological disaster. The main regions still regularly receiving abundant rainfall are the southwest peninsula and the eastern two thirds of the northern seaboard.

People

About 95% are of virtually pure African descent. The rest are mostly mulattoes, the descendants of unions between French masters and African slaves, and some of Arabic descent, who tend to be merchants and shop owners. The Haitian culture is a unique mixture of African and French influences. Haiti was a French colony until 1804 when, fired by the example of the French Revolution, the black slaves revolted, massacred the French landowners and proclaimed the world's first black republic. Throughout the 19th century the Haitians reverted to a primitive way of life, indulging in a succession of bloody, almost tribal wars. Even today African cults, particularly voodoo, play a large part in everyday life like nowhere else in the Caribbean. The country is desperately poor and the standard of living is the lowest in the

Americas. According to UNICEF, only 20% of children reach secondary school. Illiteracy is believed to be about 80% of the population, with unemployment at around the same level. With per capita income running at US$400 a year, 62% are underfed, the third worst level in the world, exceeded only by Somalia and Afghanistan. The UN has highlighted the deteriorated state of infrastructure in urban areas, such as roads and lack of electricity and potable water, as well as the badly degraded environment, all attributed to political chaos and the resulting scarcity of international aid.

Government

Under the terms of the July 1993, UN-brokered agreement to restore democracy, Haiti has two legislative houses, a 27-seat Senate and an 83-seat Chamber of Deputies. The parliament in this form, with the elected president as chief of state, came into effect in October 1994.

Economy

Haiti is the Western Hemisphere's poorest country and among the 30 poorest in the world. Seventy five percent of the people fall below the World Bank's absolute poverty level. It is overpopulated. It lacks communications, cheap power and raw materials for industry. Its mountainous terrain cannot provide a living for its rural population.

Structure of production

Until the embargo, the main economic problem was chronic low agricultural productivity, compounded by low world commodity prices. Just 1% of the population controls 40% of the wealth. The average farm size is less than 1ha. Only a third of the land is arable, yet most of the people live in the country, using rudimentary tools to grow maize, rice, sorghum and coffee. Deforestation has played havoc with watersheds and agriculture. Only a fraction of the land is now forested, yet charcoal continues to supply 70% of fuel needs. Agriculture generates 32% of the gdp but employs more than half the workforce. Coffee is the main cash crop, providing 8% of exports. Sugar and sisal output has slumped as population pressure has forced farmers to switch to subsistence crops. A land reform programme was begun in 1997 in the Artibonite Valley to give land to families in an area where violent land disputes have been common. Agriculture was badly hit by a drought in the northwest in 1997, causing famine in that area, and Hurricane Georges in 1998, which brought flooding. Around 100 people are believed to have perished and many thousands were left homeless. The devastation was intensified because of the lack of trees and ground cover, which allowed flooding and erosion.

Industry and commerce is limited, and heavily concentrated in Port-au-Prince. Until the embargo, assembly operations turned out baseballs, garments and electronic parts for export to the USA. After the lifting of the embargo, factories were slow to reopen because of civil unrest and electricity shortages. In addition, a 40% increase in the minimum wage, to US$2.57 per day, made Haiti's pay level marginally higher than the Dominican Republic, to which many offshore companies had relocated. Vegetable oils, footwear and metal goods are still produced for domestic consumption. Manufactured goods make up two thirds of total exports. Tourism has all but disappeared, at first because of AIDS, then because of the political instability.

Culture

Although Haiti wiped out slavery in its 18th-century revolution, its society still suffers from the racial, cultural and linguistic divisions inherited from slavery. Toussaint's tolerant statesmanship was unable to resist Napoléon's push to reimpose slavery. It took the tyranny and despotism of Dessalines and Christophe. Haitian despots stepped into the shoes of the French despots. The new, mulatto ruling class considered its French language and culture superior to the blacks' Créole language and Voodoo religion, which it despised. The corruption and despotism of the black political class created by Duvalier suggest that, despite its profession of *noirisme*, it internalized the mulatto contempt for its own race.

Religion Voodoo (French: Vaudou) is a blend of religions from West Africa, above all from Dahomey (present-day Benin) and the Congo River basin. Like Cuba's Santería and Brazil's Candomblé, it uses drumming, singing and dance to induce possession by powerful African spirits with colourful personalities. These spirits, called *loas* in Haiti (pronounced *lwa*), help with life's daily problems. In return, they must be 'served' with ceremonies, offerings of food and drink, and occasional animal sacrifice in temples known as *ounphors*.

The essence of Voodoo is keeping in harmony with the *loas*, the dead and nature. Magic may be used in self-defence, but those in perfect harmony with the universe should not need it. Magic in the pursuit of personal ambitions is frowned on. The use of black magic and sorcery, or the use of attack magic against others without just cause, is considered evil. Sorcerers, called *bokors*, exist but they are not seen as part of Voodoo. The *loas* punish *oungans* (Voodoo priests) or *mambos* (priestesses) who betray their vocation by practising black magic. Many Haitians believe in the existence of *zombis*, the living dead victims of black magic who are supposedly disinterred by sorcerers and put to work as slaves.

Voodoo acquired an overlay of Catholicism in colonial times, when the slaves learned to disguise their *loas* as saints. Nowadays, major ceremonies coincide with Catholic celebrations such as Christmas, Epiphany and the Day of the Dead. Lithographs of Catholic saints are used to represent the *loas*.

The role of attack and defence magic in Haiti's religious culture expanded during the slave revolts and the independence war. Many rebel leaders were *oungans*, such as Mackandal, who terrorized the northern plain with his knowledge of poisons from 1748 to 1758, and Boukman, who plotted the 1791 uprising at a clandestine Voodoo ceremony. Belief in Voodoo's protective spells inspired a fearlessness in battle that amazed the French. As a result, many Haitian rulers saw Voodoo as a threat to their own authority and tried to stamp it out. They also thought its survival weakened Haiti's claim to membership of the family of 'civilized' nations. François Duvalier enlisted enough *oungans* to neutralize Voodoo as a potential threat. He also coopted the Catholic church hierarchy. He had less success with the Catholic grass roots which, inspired by Liberation Theology, played a key role in his son's 1986 fall and Aristide's election in 1990.

After several ruthless campaigns against Voodoo, most recently in the early 1940s, the Catholic church has settled into an attitude of tolerant coexistence. Now the militant hostility to Voodoo comes from fundamentalist Protestant sects of American origin which have exploited their relative wealth and ability to provide jobs to win converts.

Language

Haitian Créole is the only language of 85% of its inhabitants. It evolved from French into a distinct language. The other 15% speak Créole and French

Haitian Créole is the product of the transformation of French in Saint Domingue by African slaves who needed a common language, one the slave-owners were forced to learn in order to speak to their slaves.

More important is how Créole and French are used now. All Haitians understand Créole and speak it at least part of the time. Use of French is limited to the élite and middle class. The illiterate majority of the population understand no French at all. There is almost no teaching in Créole and no attempt is made to teach French as a foreign language to the few Créole-only speakers who enter the school system. Since mastery of French is still a condition for self-advancement, language perpetuates Haiti's deep class divisions. All those pushing for reform in Haiti are trying to change this. Radio stations have begun using Créole in the last 10 years. Musicians now increasingly sing in Créole. The 1987 constitution gave Créole equal official status alongside French. Even élite politicians have begun using Créole in speeches although some speak it poorly. Aristide's sway over the people is due in part to his poetic virtuosity in Créole. A phonetic transcription of Créole has evolved over the last 50 years, but little has been published except the Bible, some poetry and, nowadays, a weekly pro-Aristide newspaper, *Libète*. Créole is famed for its proverbs voicing popular philosophy and reflecting Haiti's enormous social divisions. The best teach yourself book is *Ann Pale Kreyòl*, published by the Créole Institute, Ballentine Hall 602, Indiana University, Bloomington IN 47405, USA. It is hard to find in Haitian bookshops. In the text above, 'Cr' means Créole version.

Haitian handicraft and naive art is the best in the Caribbean. Even such utilitarian articles as the woven straw shoulder bags and the tooled-leather scabbards of the peasant machete have great beauty. The *rada* (Voodoo drum) is an object of great aesthetic appeal. Haiti is famed for its wood carvings, but poverty has pushed craftsmen into producing art from such cheap material as papier maché and steel drums, flattened and turned into cut-out wall-hangings or sculpture. Haitian naive art on canvas emerged only in response to the demand of travellers and tourists in the 1930s and 40s, but it had always existed on the walls of Voodoo temples, where some of the best representations of the spirit world are to be found. Weddings, cock fights, market scenes or fantasy African jungles are other favoured themes. Good paintings can range from one hundred to several thousand dollars. Mass-produced but lively copies of the masters sell for as little as US$10. Negotiating with street vendors and artists can be an animated experience, offering insights into the nation's personality. **The arts**

Exposure to white racism during the US occupation shook some of the mulatto intellectuals out of their complacent Francophilia. Led by Jean Price Mars and his 1919 pioneering essay *Ainsi parla l'oncle* (Thus Spoke Uncle) they began to seek their identity in Haiti's African roots. Peasant life, Créole expressions and Voodoo started to appear together with a Marxist perspective in novels such as Jacques Romain's *Gouverneurs de la rosée* (Masters of the Dew). René Depestre, now resident in Paris after years in Cuba, is viewed as Haiti's greatest living novelist. Voodoo, politics and acerbic social comment are blended in the novels of Gary Victor, a deputy minister in the Aristide government before the coup.

Nigel Gallop writes: The poorest nation in the western hemisphere is among the richest when it comes to music. This is a people whose most popular religion worships the deities through singing, drumming and dancing. The prime musical influence is African, although European elements are to be found, but none that are Amerindian. The music and dance (and in Haiti music is almost inseparable from dance) can be divided into three main categories: Voodoo ritual, rural folk and urban popular. The Voodoo rituals, described above, are collective and are profoundly serious, even when the *loa* is humorous or mischievous. The hypnotic dance is accompanied by call-and-response singing and continuous drumming, the drums themselves (the large Manman, medium-sized Seconde and smaller Bula or Kata) being regarded as sacred. **Music & dance**

During Mardi Gras (Carnival) and Rara (see below), bands of masked dancers and revellers can be found on the roads and in the streets almost anywhere in the country, accompanied by musicians playing the Vaccines (bamboo trumpets). Haitians also give rein to their love of music and dance in the so-called Bambouches, social gatherings where the dancing is *pou' plaisi'* (for pleasure) and largely directed to the opposite sex. They may be doing the Congo, the Martinique or Juba, the Crabienne or the national dance, the Méringue. The first two are of African provenance, the Crabienne evolved from the European Quadrille, while the Méringue is cousin to the Dominican Merengue. Haitians claim it originated in their country and was taken to the Dominican Republic during the Haitian occupation of 1822 to 1844, but this is a matter of fierce debate between the two nations. In remote villages it may still be possible to come across such European dances as the Waltz, Polka, Mazurka and Contredanse, accompanied by violin, flute or accordion.

Haitian music has not remained impervious to outside influences during the 20th century, many of them introduced by Haitian migrant workers returning from Cuba, the Dominican Republic and elsewhere in the region (as well as exporting its own music to Cuba's Oriente province in the form of the Tumba Francesa). One very important external influence was that of the Cuban Son, which gave rise to the so-called 'Troubadour Groups', with their melodious voices and soft guitar accompaniment, still to be heard in some hotels. Jazz was another intruder, a result of the US marines' occupation between 1915 and 1934. Then in the 1950s two equally celebrated composers and band leaders, Nemours Jean-Baptiste and Weber Sicot, introduced a new style of recreational dance music, strongly influenced by the Dominican Merengue and known as Compact Directe ('compas') or Cadence Rampa. Compas (the 's' is not pronounced) dominated the music scene until the past few years, when it has become a much more open market, with Salsa, Reggae, Soca and Zouk all making big inroads. A number of Haitian groups have achieved international recognition, notably Tabou Combo and Coupé Cloué, while female singers Martha-Jean Claude and Toto Bissainthe have also made a name for themselves abroad. One excellent troubadour-style singer who has been well-recorded is Althiery Dorival. Also highly recommended is the set of six LPs titled 'Roots of Haiti', recorded in the country, but distributed by Mini Records of Brooklyn. Finally, no comment on Haitian music would be complete without reference to the well-known lullaby 'Choucounne' which, under the title 'Yellow Bird', is crooned to tourists every night on every English-speaking Antillean island.

Mike Tarr adds: A musical revolution came with the emergence of 'voodoo beat', a fusion of Voodoo drumming and melody with an international rock guitar and keyboard sound. Its lyrics call for political change and a return to peasant values. With albums out on the Island label, and US tours behind them, Boukman Eksperyans is the most successful of these bands. People who have ignored Voodoo all their lives are possessed at Boukman concerts. Other 'voodoo beat' bands of note are RAM, Boukan Ginen, Foula, Sanba-Yo and Koudjay. New bands are springing up all the time, RAM remains very popular, as are T-Vice, Sweet Micky, King Posse and Kompa Kreyol.

Haiti

Dominican Republic

9

Dominican Republic

The Dominican Republic, occupying the eastern two-thirds of Hispaniola, has some spectacularly beautiful scenery. The country is mountainous and has the highest peak in the Caribbean, Pico Duarte (3,175 m). It has many more forests than its neighbour, Haiti, and is green and fertile. Within a system of widespread food production are large sugar and fruit plantations and cattle ranches. The Republic has built up its tourist trade, and has much to offer in the way of natural beauty, old colonial architecture, attractive beaches, adventure sports, modern resorts and native friendliness. Public transport is good and it is easy and rewarding to explore by bus or hired car. Its population is mostly a mixture of black, white and mulatto, and is Spanish-speaking.

Essentials

Before you travel

Documents All visitors require a **passport** and most need a green **tourist card**, US$10, purchased from consulates, tourist offices, airlines on departure (eg American at Miami), or at the airport on arrival before lining up in the queue for immigration. Citizens of the following countries do not need a tourist card to enter: Argentina, Chile, Ecuador, Iceland, Israel, Japan, Peru, South Korea, Uruguay. The time limit on tourist cards is 90 days, but if necessary extensions are obtainable from Immigration, Huacal Building, Santo Domingo (T6852505/2535). The easiest method of extending a tourist card is simply to pay the fine (US$2 for each month over three months) at the airport when leaving. Check all entry requirements in advance if possible. You should have an outward ticket, although not always asked for.

Vaccinations You should be up to date with your typhoid, tetanus and polio inoculations. The vaccine against infectious hepatitis is a good idea. **Malaria** prevention is recommended, as it is present in the southwest and the west of the country. There is also dengue fever: the Aedes

Dominican Republic

♦ National parks	
1 Armando Bermúdez	8 José del Carmen Ramírez
2 Cabo Francés Viejo	9 Lagunas Redonda y Limón
3 Del Este	10 La Vega Vieja
4 El Choco	11 Loma Quita Espuela
5 Isabel de Torres	12 Los Haïtises
6 Isla Cabritos	13 Monte Cristi
7 Jaragua	14 Sierra Baoruco

mosquito breeds in urban areas and usually bites in the early morning and late afternoon. It is more prevalent when there has been lots of rain. There is no cure, so prevention is essential. There is rabies, so if you are at high risk get yourself vaccinated before you travel. In any case, if you are bitten seek medical help immediately.

Customs

Duty-free import permitted of 200 cigarettes or one box of cigars, plus two litres of alcoholic liquor and gift articles to the value of US$1,000. Military-type clothing and food products will be confiscated on arrival. Currency in excess of US$10,000 may not be taken out of the country without special permission. Airport police are on the lookout for illegal drugs. It is illegal to bring firearms into the country.

Money
In the countryside away from major centres, it can be difficult to change anything higher than a 100-peso note

Currency The Dominican peso (RD$) is the only legal tender. The peso is divided into 100 centavos. There are coins in circulation of 25 and 50 centavos, 1 peso and 5 pesos, and notes of 5, 10, 20, 50, 100, 500, 1,000 and 2,000 pesos. However, you will hardly ever see 25-centavo coins and people tend to round up or down to the nearest peso.

Exchange The exchange rate fluctuates against the dollar but is relatively stable. Banks and exchange houses *(casas de cambio)* are authorized to deal in foreign exchange. Cambios often give better rates than banks. You will be given a receipt and, with this, you can change remaining pesos back into dollars at the end of your visit (maximum 30% of dollars changed; cash obtained against a credit card does not count). There is sometimes a buyback charge. Do not rely on the airport bank being open. The US dollar is the best currency to bring. Most European currencies can be changed at the *Banco de Reservas* (and some other banks); Scandinavian currencies are very hard to change. If stuck at weekends, most hotels will change money; cash only. ATMs are an easy way to get cash and you will get close to the market rate, plus a commission of up to 5%. They are sometimes out of action at weekends and holidays and in small places they suffer from lack of maintenance and often do not work. If you bring **Travellers' cheques** they should be denominated in US dollars. In Santo Domingo and tourist places you will not have much trouble changing them, but in Santiago, only the *Banco Popular* on Calle del Sol is authorized to change travellers' cheques.

Credit cards Nearly all major hotels, restaurants and stores accept most credit cards. Several banks will give cash against Visa, Mastercard or American Express cards, usually with 5% commission. However, Amex is not much used on the north coast. It is advisable to inform your bank or credit card company before you use your card in

15 Submarino La Caleta
16 Valle Nuevo

♦ **Scientific reserves**
17 Del Ebano Verde
18 Samaná Bay Marine Sanctuary
19 Villa Elisa

Dominican Republic

A Foot in the door

- **Whale watching** in the **Bay of Samaná** is an absolute must in January-March, the ultimate thrill to see humpback whales breaching in front of your boat.
- Anyone who likes **windsurfing** should spend a few days at Cabarete, great winds, flat water and the beach bars to go with it.
- Indulge yourself by staying in one of the **restored colonial mansions** in the heart of old **Santo Domingo**, even the cheap hotels are elegant and atmospheric while the expensive ones are luxurious.
- **Hiking up Pico Duarte** must be a highlight for anyone fit enough to tackle the highest mountain in the Caribbean, the scenery is spectacular, forests, rivers, wildlife and, in the distance, the shining blue sea of the silver coast.
- The north coast beaches are among the best in the world, try the deserted **Playa Rincón** on the Samaná peninsula if you want to get away from hotels.

the Dominican Republic. **Some companies will put a stop on your card after you have used it twice. This is for your own protection as the Dominican Republic has a high rate of credit card fraud.**

Banks Among the commercial banks in the Republic are *Scotiabank* (Santo Domingo, Santiago, and Puerto Plata), *Chase Manhattan* (Santo Domingo and Santiago), *Citibank* (Santo Domingo and Santiago), *Banco de Reservas*, *Banco Popular*, *Banco Metropolitano*, *Banco Central*, *Bancrédito*, *Baninter*, *Banco Dominicano Hispano*, *Banco del Progreso* and others. The *Banco Popular* has CASH ATMs, which take ATH (A Todo Hora), Mastercard, Cirrus, Honor, Visa, Plus and Electron. The *Banco del Progreso* takes ATH, Mastercard, Visa, American Express, Honor, Plus, Cirrus, Maestro and Visa Electron. Money can be sent via *Western Union*, which operates through *Vimenca* but the exchange rate is, up to 20% worse than in banks.

Climate Rainfall is greatest on high ground, reaching more than 2,500 mm in parts of the Cordillera Septentrional, which faces directly into the northeast trade winds. The valleys between the mountain ranges are dry rain-shadow areas; some parts of the southwest are virtual semi-deserts. In winter, the northern parts of the island are affected by cold fronts which move down from the North American continent; these can bring heavy rain, grey skies, and squally northern winds. The average temperature is around 25°C. There is not much seasonal variation, although north coast winter temperatures can be cool during cold fronts. Altitude is an important influence, with an average fall of 6°C for each 1,000 m above sea level. There are reports of below-freezing temperatures on Pico Duarte. The Dominican Republic lies within the hurricane belt. Storms can strike at any time from June to November, but 60% of the hurricanes that have hit the Dominican Republic since 1871 have done so in September. Hurricane David devastated the country in 1979, killing 1,000 people and causing widespread disruption. The most recent direct hit was from Hurricane Georges in September 1998, which had maximum wind speeds of close to 200 kph.

Getting there

Air The main gateways are Santo Domingo, Puerto Plata and Punta Cana although there are
In addition to other international airports with limited services. Punta Cana is only worth flying to if you are
scheduled flights there staying at one of the all-inclusive hotels along the eastern coast. If you want to start your
are hundreds of travels on the south coast, including the capital, then fly to Santo Domingo. For the north
charter flights from coast use the airport outside Puerto Plata. It is possible to fly in to one and out of the other,
north America, Europe although that will obviously cost a little more. For details of airlines see Transport sections.
& south America

Boat Many passenger cruise lines from the USA, Canada and Europe call at the Dominican Republic on itineraries to various ports on Caribbean islands or the mainland. *Ferries del*

Caribe has a car and passenger ferry between the Dominican Republic and Puerto Rico, with a capacity for 250 vehicles and 550 passengers. The *Regal Voyager* (known as *El Ferry*) departs Mayagüez Monday, Wednesday, Friday, 2000, 10-12 hours, departs Santo Domingo Tuesday, Thursday, Sunday, 2000, prices from US$141 return, Mon-Fri, including port tax each way of US$11.50, US$161 at weekends, sleeper cabins available for up to four people, US$68 superior, US$58 standard and US$48 económica (without bathroom). Lots of discounts are available if you ask. In Santo Domingo, T809-6884400, F6884963, in Puerto Rico, T787-8324800, F8311810. You can also arrange onward transport by bus from Mayagüez to San Juan and from Santo Domingo to Terrabús destinations in the Dominican Republic and Haiti.

Ports of entry Santo Domingo, Luperón, Puerto Plata, Samaná, Punta Cana (with 24 hours' notice). **Boat documents** Customs fees US$10 per person. 30 days' immigration clearance. Declare weapons and check in with Customs officials ashore at each port of entry. Do not depart from anchorage before sunrise after picking up weapons. You have to clear Customs and Immigration at each port. The port captain will come on board with a group of officials, each of whom have been reported by yachties to ask for 'tips' of US$20-25 to expedite the paperwork.

Travel to Haiti **Air** *Air Santo Domingo* from Las Américas airport to Port-au-Prince Wednesday, Thursday, Friday, 1200, one hour, return 1230, prices from US$72 before tax, T6838020. *Caribair* has two flights daily Monday-Saturday at 0830 and 1330 and one flight Sun at 1000 from Herrera airport, returning from Port-au-Prince at 1130 and 1530 Monday-Saturday and 1530 Sunday, for US$180 return, T5426688. *Tropical Airways d'Haiti* fly daily from Herrera airport to Port-au-Prince at 0730, returning at 1730. **Bus** By far the easiest way is with *Terrabús*, which has a service between Santo Domingo and Pétion-Ville, US$50 one way, US$75 return, US$80 open return, T4721080, terminal at Av 27 de Febrero esq Anacaona, Plaza Criolla, Saturday-Monday departs 1200, arrives 0500, Wednesday-Friday departs 0600, arrives 1200, they deal with all border formalities for you (except customs). *Caribe Tours* also has a service to Haiti, departing daily at 1100, arriving in Port-au-Prince at 1400, US$75 return. The return bus leaves Port-au-Prince at 0700 (see Haiti chapter). There are cheaper options but they take longer and are less comfortable. A syndicate of Dominican operators runs 30-seat buses from outside the Haitian embassy, 33 Av Juan Sánchez Ramírez, just off Av Máximo Gómez between Independencia and Bolívar. Three or four leave every morning Mon-Fri 1100-1200 and take about seven hours or longer to Port-au-Prince, depending on the amount of merchandise to be inspected by Customs at the border. They return next day from Rue du Centre between Pavée and des Miracles at around the same time. Your passport must be processed in the embassy before boarding the bus. Be quick on arriving at the embassy, get through the gates, ignoring hangers on and cries of 'passport', unless you want to wait in the street and pay someone else US$10 to take your passport in. All the passports are processed together. Payments may be required. Do not wear shorts. Alternatively, take a minibus to Jimaní from near the bridge over the Río Seco in the centre of Santo Domingo, 6-8 hours; get a lift up to the Haitian border and then get overcharged by Haitian youths on mopeds who take you across 3 km of no-man's-land for US$3. From Haitian immigration take a lorry-bus to Port-au-Prince, 3-4 hours, very dusty. You can also take Dominican public transport to Dajabón, cross to Ouanaminthe and continue to Cap Haïtien. If driving to Haiti you must get a vehicle permit at the Foreign Ministry (T5331424). Hire cars are not allowed across the border. The drive from Santo Domingo to Port-au-Prince takes about six hours. Buy gourdes from money changers outside the embassy, or at the border, but no more than US$50-worth, rates are much better in Haiti. Also take US$25 for border taxes, which have to be paid in dollars cash.

Remember there is a 1 hr time difference between Haiti (GMT-5) & the Dominican Republic (GMT-4) in summer

Touching down

Airport information Details of airports are given in the text below. There are several: **Las Américas** (Santo Domingo, T5490450/80), **Herrera** (Santo Domingo, T5673900), **Gregorio Luperón** (Puerto Plata, T5860219), **Arroyo Barril** (Samaná), **Cibao** (Santiago, T5824894), **Punta Aguila** (La Romana, T5565565), **Punta Cana** (Higüey, T6868790) and **María Montéz** (Barahona,

Dominican Republic

Touching down

Departure tax US$10.

Hours of business Offices: 0830-1230, 1430-1830; some offices and shops work 0930-1730 Monday-Friday, 0800-1300 Saturday. **Banks:** 0830-1700 Monday-Friday. Government offices 0730-1430. **Shops:** normally 0800-1900, some open all day Saturday and mornings on Sunday and holidays. Most shops in tourist areas stay open through the siesta and on Sunday.

Official time Atlantic Standard Time, four hours behind GMT, one hour ahead of EST.

Voltage 110 volts, 60 cycles AC current. American-type, flat-pin plugs are used. There are frequent power cuts, often for several hours, so take a torch with you when you go out at night. Many establishments have their own (often noisy) generators.

Weights and measures Officially the metric system is used but business is often done on a pound per yard per US gallon basis. Land areas in cities are measured by square metres, but in the countryside by the tarea, one of which equals 624 sq m.

Clothing Light clothing, preferably cotton, is best all year round. It is recommended to take one formal outfit since some hotels and nightclubs do not permit casual dress.

Tipping In addition to the 10% service and 8% VAT charge in restaurants, it is customary in the nicer, sit down restaurants to give an extra tip of about 10%, depending on service. Porters receive US$0.50 per bag; taxi drivers, público drivers and garage attendants are not usually tipped.

T5247010). In 2001 a new domestic airport was being built to replace Herrera, 40 minutes north of the centre of Santo Domingo in the Higuero sector.

Dominican Republic

Tourist information The head office of the Secretaría de Estado de Turismo is in the Edificio de Oficinas Gubernamentales, Av México esq 30 de Marzo, Ala 'D', near the Palacio Nacional (PO Box 497, T2214660, F6823806, sectur@codetel.net.do There are no facilities for dealing with the general public. Although there are small tourist offices in most towns, the average traveller is more likely to notice private sector operators and get information from tour companies or guest houses. There are offices at **Las Américas International Airport**, in Santo Domingo in the colonial city on the first floor of the Palacio Borgella near the Cathedral (T6863858), **Gregorio Luperón Airport** at Puerto Plata, in Puerto Plata (Malecón 20, T5863676), in Santiago (Ayuntamiento, T5825885), Barahona (T5243650), Jimaní (T2483000), Samaná (T5382332), Boca Chica (T5235106), San Pedro de Macorís (T5293644), La Romana (T5506922), Baní (T5226018), San Cristóbal (T5283533), Pedernales (T5240409), Higüey (T5542672), El Seíbo (T5523402), Sosúa (T5712254), Cabarete (T5710962), Gaspar Hernández (T5872485), Río San Juan (T5892831), Nagua (T5843862), Las Terrenas (T2406363), Luperón (T5718303), Monte Cristi (T5792254), La Vega (T2421289), Bonao (T5253941), Constanza (T5392900). The Secretaría de Turismo website is www.dominicana. com.do, while the tourist magazine *La Cótica* can be found online at www.lacotica. com www.dr1.com has a daily news and weather service as well as features on most subjects of tourist interest, although many of them are rather out of date. www.hispaniola. com is a good site if you are likely to be spending most of your time on the north coast, while www.DRpure.com is a great site for adventure sports with background information too.

Local tour agents *Turinter*, Santo Domingo, T6864020, F6883890, www.turinter.com *Juan Perdomo Travel*, T5630744, *Emely Tours*, S F de Macorís 58, T6877114 (agent for Cubana and flights to Cuba), *Omni Tours*, T5656591, F5674710, or Punta Cana T6880977, F6880764, trips to Cuba, cruises and hotel special offers around the country. In Puerto Plata, *Connex Caribe*, Plaza Turisol, T5866879, F5866099, offers a wide variety of tours in town, to Santo Domingo and all over the Republic. *Iguana Mama* in Cabarete, T5710908, F5710734, www. iguanamama.com, run organized tours to climb Pico Duarte (see page 435), or hike, mountain bike, whitewater rafting or a number of other activities in the mountains or in the water, 1-8 day trips, also educational tours for students. *Espeleogrupo Santo Domingo*, T6821577, is an educational organization working to protect many anthropological and geological sites, to which they also

Dominican Republic

Tourist offices overseas

Argentina *Arenales 1942 1-B, Buenos Aires,*
T541-8137704, F8140824,
turismo_r.d@epsarg.com

Belgium *Avenida Louise 271, 8th floor, 1050*
Brussels, T322-6461300, F6493692,
repdom.benelux.info@skynet.be

Canada *2080 Rue Crescent, Montréal,*
Québec, H3G 2B8, T514-4991918, F4991393,
republiquedominicaine@op-plus.net; 35
Church Street, Unit 53 Market Square, Toronto,
Ontario M5E 1T3, T416-3612126, F3612130,
dominicantourism@globalserve.net

Colombia *Transversal 29 No 120-59, Barrio*
Santa Bárbara, Bogotá, T571-6291459,
F5207061, domreptu@multphone.net.co

France *11 Rue Boudreau, Paris 75009,*
T331-43129191, F44940880,
otrepdom@aol.com

Germany *Hochstrasse 17-2, D-60313*
Frankfurt am Main 1, T49-69-91397879,
F283430, domtur@aol.com

Italy *Piazza Castello 25, 20121 Milan,*
T3902-8057781, F865861,
repdom@opimaint.it

Puerto Rico *Avenida Ashford 1452, Suite*
307, Condado, San Juan, PR 00907,
T787-7220881, F7247293, ofiturdr@isla.net

Spain *Juan Hurtado de Mendoza 13, Apto*
305, 28036 Madrid 1, T3491-3509483,
F3506579, rep.domi@nauta.es

UK *For information contact the embassy at*
139 Inverness Terrace, London W2 6JF,
T020-77276232, F020-77273693; for tourist
brochures, call 0900-1600305.

USA *136E 57 Street Suite 803, New York, NY*
10022, T212-5881012/4, F5881015,
dr.info@ix.netcom.com; 561 West Diversey
Parkway Suite 214, Chicago, IL 60614-1643,
T773-5291336/7, F5291338,
domreptourism@msn.com; 2355 Salzedo
Street, Suite 307, Coral Gables, Miami, Florida
33134, T305-4444592/3, F4444845,
domrep@herald.infi.net

arrange technical and non-technical excursions, specifically Las Cuevas de Pomier in San Cristóbal and the Cuevas de las Maravillas in La Romana. The *Museo de Historia y Geografía* in Santo Domingo organizes archaeological and historical tours in the Republic, tours are announced in the newspapers. The co-ordinator is Vilma Benzo de Ferrer, T6886952.

Maps *Gaar*, on Arzobispo Nouel esq Espaillat, Santo Domingo, open Monday-Friday 0830-1900, Saturday 0930-1500. *Berndtson & Berndtson* publish a good road map, 1:600,000, with detail on Santo Domingo, Puerto Plata and Santiago, available locally for US$5. *Scheidig* publishes the *Mapa Geográfica de la República Dominicana*, which is approved by the Instituto Geográfico Universitario and available at Gaar for US$7. There are several other good maps of the country including *Hildebrand*, *Nelles* and *Texaco*.

Guides *The Asociación de Guías de Turismo de la República Dominicana* (Asoguiturd) can be contacted at Calle Vicente C Duarte 3, Apdo Postal 21360, Santo Domingo, T6820209. Nearly all their members speak English and other languages. However, outside the historic buildings in Santo Domingo, on the beaches and at other tourist attractions, visitors will be approached by unofficial English-speaking guides, sellers of rum, women or drugs. The only value in taking an unofficial guide is to deter others from pestering you (similarly, hiring a lounger chair on the beach). Beware of drug-pushers on the Malecón in Santo Domingo and near the Cathedral in Puerto Plata. Unofficial guides often refuse to give prices in advance, saying 'pay what you want' and then at the end, if they are not happy with the tip, they make a scene and threaten to tell the police that the customer had approached them to deal in drugs etc.

Rules, customs & etiquette Swim wear is for the beach only Although Dominicans dress to look sexy, they are also smart and well turned out. Prostitutes wear the skimpiest clothes so women should avoid association with that profession. It is advisable to take at least one smart outfit with you so that you can dress up in the evening. Shorts are not permitted in the cathedral in Santo Domingo. Keep away from anything to do with illegal drugs. You may be set up and find yourself facing an extended stay in a Dominican prison. It is polite to ask before taking photos of people. Normally they will agree cheerfully, but some may ask for a payment.

On no account change money on the streets. Banks and cambios offer the market rate and are safer. Be careful with 'helpers' at the airports, who speed your progress through the queues and then charge US$15-20 for their services. Single men have complained of the massive presence of pimps and prostitutes. Be prepared to say 'no' a lot. These problems do not occur in rural areas and small towns, where travellers have been impressed with the open and welcoming nature of the Dominicans. Violent crime against tourists is rare but, as anywhere, watch your money and valuables in cities late at night and on beaches. The streets of Santo Domingo are not considered safe after 2300. Purse snatchers on motorcycles operate in cities.

Politur, the Tourist Police, has a toll-free phone 1-200-3500, or at the office in Santo Domingo T6868639. There are also Politur offices in Puerto Plata, Luperón, Sosúa, Cabarete, Río San Juan, Las Terrenas, Samaná, Jarabacoa, Barahona, Boca Chica, Juan Dolio, La Romana, Bávaro, and Las Américas international airport. If you have anything stolen go to your local police station to report the crime and get a signed, stamped declaration for your insurance company.

Safety

Where to stay

There is a wide range of accommodation, from the 4-5 star, all-inclusive beach resorts run by international companies like Meliá, Barceló, Club Med and Occidental, to simple lodgings for local travelling salesmen. The cheaper all-inclusive hotels usually offer buffet food and local alcoholic drinks (rum and beer), which can get boring after a few days, you get what you pay for. In Santo Domingo the string of 4-5 star hotels along the Malecón are designed to cater for businessmen, diplomats and politicians and are of international standard, with business centres, elegant restaurants, casinos and conference centres. Note that five-star hotels charge an average of US$140 room only, plus 22% tax. In aparthotels, the average price is US$130 for two, but this can be negotiated down for long stays. There are plenty of nice places to stay in the **B-C** range, which offer peace and quiet, good food and comfortable rooms in pleasant locations. In more modest guest houses, a weekly or monthly rate, with discount, can be arranged. Hotels with rooms for US$10-15 per night will be basic with erratic plumbing and electricity; check the lock on the door.

All hotels charge the 22% tax; the VAT component is 12%

Getting around

Air Santo Domingo, Avenida 27 de Febrero 272, esq Seminario, T6838020, has regular flights between Santo Domingo (Herrera, T6836691, and Las Américas, T5491110) and Puerto Plata (US$56, daily, T5860385), Punta Cana (US$56, daily, T2211170) and El Portillo, Samaná (US$40, Monday-Saturday, T2406571); also flights from Puerto Plata to Punta Cana (US$66, daily). Fly drive available from around US$100. Several companies offer air taxi or charter services within the Republic, all based at Herrera airport. *Caribair*, T8426688, F5677033, caribair.sa@ codetel.net.do, has offices in all national airports and a fleet of charter aircraft including air ambulance and helicopters, with a daily service to Port-au-Prince for US$180 return. *Alas Nacionales*, T5426688; *Transporte Aéreo SA*, T5674549; *Coturisca*, T5677211. *Dorado Air* (T6861067) flies between Santo Domingo and Puerto Plata several times a day on Friday and Saturday. Air taxis charge around US$150 per plane to Samaná and US$220 to Punta Cana.

Air

Bus Long distance bus services are very good, with a wide network and several different companies. The three most comfortable and reliable are *Metro, Caribe Tours* and *Terrabus* Services from Santo Domingo: *Metro Expreso*, first class (T5667126, F5419454) operate from Calle Hatuey esq Av Winston Churchill, near 27 de Febrero and have buses to La Vega (US$3), Santiago (US$4.70), Puerto Plata (US$6), Nagua (US$5), Moca (US$4.50), San Francisco de Macorís (US$4), Sánchez/Samaná (US$5.60) and Castillo (US$4.50) daily. In Puerto Plata, T5866063, Santiago, T5839111, Nagua, T5842259. *Caribe Tours* (T2214422) operates from Av 27 de Febrero at Leopoldo Navarro; the bus terminal, with ticket office, café, information desk, cash machine (Visa, Electron, Plus), cambio and waiting area with TV; most of their services are in a/c buses, with video and toilet, punctual, good service, no smoking (US$3 to Bonao, US$3.30 to La Vega, US$4.70 to Jarabacoa, US$4 to Santiago, US$4.30 to Barahona, US$5.70 to

Road

Dominican Republic

Dajabón, Puerto Plata or Monte Cristi, US$6 to Sosúa, US$5.30 to Sánchez, Samaná or Río San Juan); they run to all parts except east of Santo Domingo. *Terrabús*, Plaza Criolla, Anacaona 15, T4721080, is an international company with services to Haiti and Puerto Rico (via the ferry, see above), but it also has linked domestic routes to Santiago (T5873000), Puerto Plata (T5861977) and Sosúa (T5711274). Their buses are very comfortable, offering television, snacks, pillows and blankets, while their terminals have food shops, toilets, television and children's play area. *Transporte del Cibao*, T6857210, opposite Parque Enriquillo in Santo Domingo, to Puerto Plata, cheaper at US$3.60, to Santiago US$3. *Transporte Espinal* (four blocks north of Parque Enriquillo) US$4 to Santiago, US$3 to La Vega, US$3 to Bonao. *La Covacha* buses leave from Parque Enriquillo (Av Duarte and Ravelo) for the east: La Romana, Higüey, Nagua, San Pedro de Macorís, Hato Mayor, Miches, etc. *Astrapu* does the same routes. *Expresos Moto Saad*, Av Independencia near Parque Independencia runs 12 daily buses to Bonao, La Vega and Santiago. *Línea Sur* (T6827682) runs to San Juan, Barahona, Azua and Haiti. *Guaguas* for Azua, two hours US$3, depart from Av Bolívar near Parque Independencia; easy connections in Azua for Barahona, San Juan and Padre las Casas. For bus offices in other towns, see text.

Bus services between most towns are efficient and inexpensive. In rural areas it can be easy to find a *guagua* (mini bus or pickup) but they are usually filled to the point where you can not move your legs and luggage is an uncomfortable inconvenience. There are also cars (*carros*) on some of these routes, which are equally dilapidated and crowded. It is possible to buy an extra seat in a *carro* or *guagua* to make yourself more comfortable.

Car A valid driving licence from your country of origin or an international licence is accepted for three months. Dominicans drive on the right. Many of them do not have licences. The Autopista Duarte is a good, four-lane highway between Santo Domingo and Santiago, but dangerous. It is used by bicycles and horse drawn carts as well as motorized vehicles, while drivers switch from one lane to the other without warning. Lots of shopping opportunities by the roadside contribute to the hazards, with vehicles swerving on and off the road. In 2000, the Autovía del Este was inaugurated, providing an excellent road from Santo Domingo out to the east, with good access roads to Higüey, Punta Cana airport, Hato Mayor and Sabana de la Mar. Minor roads and many city streets are in poor condition with lots of potholes. The speed limit for city driving is 40 kph, for suburban areas 60 kph and on main roads 80 kph. Service stations generally close at 1800, although there are now some offering 24-hour service. Gasoline prices are RD$38.80 for super unleaded (US$2.35), RD$35 (US$2.12) for unleaded and RD$22 (US$1.33) for diesel. Most police or military posts have 'sleeping policemen', speed humps, usually unmarked, outside them. In towns there are often 'ditches' at road junctions, which need as much care as humps. At night look out for poorly lighted, or lightless vehicles. Many *motoconchos* have no lights. There are tolls on all principal roads out of the capital: RD$5, exact change needed. Road signs are very poor: a detailed map is essential, plus a knowledge of Spanish for asking directions. Expect to be stopped by the police at the entrance to and exit from towns (normally brief and courteous), at junctions in towns, or any speed-restricted area.

Local drivers can be erratic; be alert. Hand signals mean only 'I am about to do something', nothing more specific than that

Car hire Avoid the cheapest companies because their vehicles are not usually trustworthy. Prices for small vehicles start at US$40 per day but can be as much as US$90. Weekly rates are better value. Credit cards are widely accepted; the cash deposit is normally twice the sum of the contract. The minimum age for hiring a car is 25; maximum period for driving is 90 days. **Mopeds** and **motorcycles** are everywhere and are very noisy. Most beach resorts hire motorcycles for between US$20 and US$35 a day. By law, the driver of a motorcycle must wear a crash helmet, but very few do; passengers are not required to wear one.

Taxi There are usually fixed *público* rates (see under Santo Domingo) between cities, so inquire first. Many drivers pack a truly incredible number of passengers in their cars, so the ride is often uncomfortable, but friendly. If travelling by private taxi, bargaining is very important. In Santo Domingo, *Apolo Taxi*, T5377771, is recommended if you need to call a taxi, cheap, friendly and efficient.

Motoconchos can be found on all the main streets and near the beaches

Motorcyclists (*motoconchos*) also offer a taxi service and take several passengers on pillion. In some towns, eg Samaná, *motoconchos* and cyclists pull four-seater covered rickshaws. During the day a short distance costs RD$10 for one passenger, although if it is less than 1 km they sometimes drop the fare to RD$5. For longer journeys negotiate fare first. During the night fares double.

Keeping in touch

Codetel offices in most towns have a computer for internet access, but don't expect it to work. **Internet** Cybercafés are now opening in tourist areas such as Cabarete and Las Terrenas, but, again, service is often down.

Don't use post boxes, they are unreliable. The postal system as a whole is very slow. For each **Post** 10 grams, or fraction thereof, the cost to Europe is RD$1; to North America, Venezuela, Central America and the Caribbean, RD$0.50; to elsewhere in the Americas and Spain, RD$0.70; to Africa, Australia, Asia and Oceania, RD$1.50. You can buy postal envelopes without stamps but with pictures of tourist sites, issued by the Instituto Postal Dominicano. It is recommended to use *entrega especial* (special delivery, with separate window at post offices), for RD$2 extra, on overseas mail, or better still a courier service (see under Santo Domingo).

Operated by the *Compañía Dominicana de Teléfonos* (Codetel, T2201111, www.codetel. **Telephone** net.do), or *Tricom* (T4766000 in Santo Domingo, T4718000 in Santiago). All local calls and *IDD phone code: 809* overseas calls and faxes to the Caribbean, European Community, US and Canada may be *Emergency number:* dialled directly from any Codetel or Tricom office (no collect calls to the UK, but they are *911* available to many other countries). Through Codetel you call abroad either person-to-person or through an operator (more expensive, but you only pay if connected). Calls and faxes may be paid for by credit card. For phone boxes you need 25-centavo coins. Phone calls to the USA cost RD$9.40 per minute, to Europe RD$23.80, to Australia RD$25.90, Puerto Rico RD$7.80, Haiti RD$10.90 and the rest of the Caribbean RD$12.90.

Newspapers There are eight daily papers in all, six in the morning, two in the afternoon. **Media** *Listín Diario* (www.listin.com.do) has the widest circulation; among the other morning papers are *La Nación, El Nuevo Diario, El Caribe, Hoy* (www.hoy.com.do), *El Siglo* (has good foreign coverage, www.elsiglord.com.do). In the afternoon, *Ultima Hora* (www.ultimahora. com.do) and *El Nacional* (www.elnacional.com.do) are published. *Primicias* is a Sunday paper. *Touring* is a multilingual tourist newspaper with articles and adverts in English, German, French, Spanish and Italian *La Información*, published in Santiago on weekdays, is a good regional paper carrying both national and international stories. www.dr1.com is a news and information service online. **Radio and television** There are over 170 local radio stations and seven television stations. Cable television is available. *Cadena de Noticias* transmits news programmes 24 hours a day and has a radio division. *Radio Mil, Radio Comercial, Radio Popular* broadcast news bulletins at 0530, 1200 and 1730. *Caribbean Travelling Network* (CTN) has news of tourist sites, good for visitors.

The official language is Spanish, although English, German, French and Italian are spoken in **Language** tourist resorts by guides and some hotel employees. English is the language most commonly taught to tourism workers. If you are planning to travel off the beaten track, a working knowledge of Spanish is essential.

Food and drink

Like most Caribbean cooking, local food tends to be calorific and spicy. The usual starches, **Food** rice, yams and plantains, underpin most meals, while chips/fries are usually also available. Dominicans like their food well seasoned, so sauces include a good deal of chilli, garlic, pepper and oregano. Strangely, the staple of *comida criolla* (Creole cooking) is the dish known as *bandera dominicana* (the Dominican flag), a colourful arrangement of stewed beef,

Dominican Republic

rice, plantains and red beans, which is actually rather unspicy. More exotic and challenging is the legendary *sancocho* or *salcocho prieto*, a hearty stew made of six or seven different types of meat as well as vegetables. Even traditional Dominican breakfasts can be a serious affair. The dish *mangú* is mashed plantain, drizzled with oil and accompanied by fried onions. Goat meat is a great favourite and usually comes either as roast (*chivo asado*) or stewed (*chivo guisado*). A *locrio* is a rice dish, accompanied by meat, chicken or sausages, and the formidable *mondongo* is a tripe stew. Another local speciality is the *asopao*, somewhere between a soup and a pilau-style rice dish (sometimes unappetizingly translated as soupy rice) that is served with fish or chicken. The ubiquitous street snacks such as *pastelitos* (pasties or turnovers filled with minced beef, chicken or cheese) are fried according to demand, as are *quipes* (cracked-wheat fritters with a meat filling) or *platanitos* (hot plantain crisps). *Tostones*, or twice-fried slices of plantain, are often served as a side dish. Most Dominican restaurants assume their customers to be carnivorous and the number of vegetarian restaurants is still limited. Fresh fruit is plentiful all year round and changes according to season. *Lechoza* (papaya) is commonly served at breakfast, as is *guineo* (sweet banana). More unusual are *jagua* (custard apple), *caimito* and *mamey*. Many *cafeterías* serve delicious fresh milk shakes (*batidas*), made out of any of these fruits, water and milk (optional, *con leche*).

Drink

Wine is imported and often indifferent and pricey, but locally produced drinks are extremely cheap

Statistics reveal that Dominicans account for one of the world's highest per capita consumptions of alcohol, and a look around any *colmado* (corner store) will confirm this fact. The Presidente brand of lager beer comes in two sizes (*pequeño* or *grande*) and seems to enjoy a near monopoly. Other beers such as Quisqueya and Bohemia are much less visible. *Mamajuana* is a home-made spiced rum mixed with honey and sweet wine, sold in markets and on street corners, frequently called the Dominican viagra. There are many rums (the most popular brands are Barceló, Brugal, Bermúdez, Macorix, Siboney and Carta Vieja). Light rum (*blanco*) is the driest and has the highest proof, usually mixed with fruit juice or other soft drink (*refresco*). Watch out for cocktails mixed with 151° proof rum. Amber (*amarillo*) or gold (*dorado*) is aged at least a year in an oak barrel and has a lower proof and more flavour, while dark rum (*añejo*) is aged for several years and is smooth enough, like a brandy, to be drunk neat or with ice and lime. Brugal allows visitors to tour its bottling plant in Puerto Plata, on Av Luis Genebra, just before the entrance to the town, and offers free daiquiris. In a discothèque, *un servicio* is a ½ litre bottle of rum with a bucket of ice and *refrescos*. In rural areas this costs US$3-4, but in cities rises to US$15. Despite being a major coffee-producer, the country does not always offer visitors good coffee, and much of what is served in hotels is either American-style watery instant or over-stewed and over-strong. Good coffee is available in small *comedores*, *cafeterías* and even from street vendors, who sell a small, dark shot for barely more than a peso.

Shopping

What to buy

The native amber is sold throughout the country. Do not buy amber on the street, it will as likely as not be plastic. Real amber fluoresces under ultra violet light (most reputable shops have a UV light); it floats in saltwater; if rubbed it produces static electricity; except for the very best pieces it is not absolutely pure, streaks, bits of dirt, etc, are common. Larimar, a sea-blue stone found only in the Dominican Republic, and red and black coral are also available (remember that coral is protected). Other souvenirs are leather goods, basketware, weavings and onyx jewellery. The ceramic *muñeca sin rostro* (faceless doll) has become a sort of symbol of the Dominican Republic. Paintings and other art work are on sale everywhere, but beware of the mass-produced Haitian-style naïve art. Thousands of these brightly-coloured, low-quality paintings are churned out for sale to tourists. Good Dominican art is for sale in the Santo Domingo galleries or you can buy direct from artists in Jarabacoa. There are excellent cigars, rum and coffee at very reasonable prices. Bargaining is acceptable in markets but rarely in shops. You will not get much of a discount but it is worth a try, particularly if you are buying in bulk. If you are taken into a shop by a guide you can expect to pay a premium so that he gets his commission.

Flora and fauna

The Dominican Republic offers luxuriant vegetation and exotic wildlife, combining a variety of habitats within a limited area. It is possible to move between the coastal reefs and beaches through thorn scrub and plantation into rainforest within a matter of miles. Increasingly the complexity and fragility of the ecosystem is being appreciated and the government has developed National Parks or Scientific Reserves.

Varied plant life is found within several tropical zones, from the arid tropical forest found in the west, where scrub and cactus predominate, to the subtropical forest on the slopes of the mountains and in the valleys and the mountain forests in the highlands where pine trees predominate. There is no primary rainforest left, but there are large areas of secondary forest which have suffered from only a limited amount of selective felling. There are many palm trees, including the royal palm (*Roystonea regia*) and the coconut palm (*Cocos nucifera*), as well as other tropical species such as Hispaniolan mahogany (*Swietenia mahogoni*), West Indian cedar (*Cedrela odorata*) and American muskwood (*Guarea guidonia*). The most common pine tree is the Creole pine (*Pinus occidentalis*). The national plant is the *caoba* (mahogany).

The **Jardín Botánico Nacional** and the **Museo de Historia Natural**, Santo Domingo, have a full classification of the Republic's flora. Of interest are the 67 types and 300 species of orchid found in this part of Hispaniola; there are a number of gardens which specialize in their cultivation. The Jardín Botánico holds an orchid show each year.

Along parts of the coast there are red (*Rhizophora mangle*), white (*Laguncularia racemosa*) and button (*Conocarpus erectus*) mangroves which provide a habitat for migrating birds and the manatee as well as fish, shrimp, mosquitoes and other biting insects. Other coastal habitats. These are home to large flocks of sea birds including the piratical frigate bird which chases smaller birds, forcing them to disgorge their catch. Another notable species is the tropic bird with its streamer-like tail feathers.

There is some confusion over which is the national bird. Some have it as the *sigua palmera* or palm chat (*Dulus dominicus*), an olive brown bird in the thrush family with bold streaks of white and brown on its underparts. It usually makes its nest high up in a palm tree in a communal structure with passages to the eggs in an inner chamber. Others name the *cotica* or Hispaniolan parrot (*Amazona ventralis*), which is green, very talkative and a popular pet although it is protected. Among other birds that can be seen are the *periquito* or Hispaniolan parakeet (*Aratinga chloroptera*), which is also green but with some red feathers, the *guaraguao* or red-tailed hawk (*Buteo jamaicensis*), and todies, known locally as *barrancolí*, which behave rather like fly catchers but nest in burrows. There are several hummingbirds (*zumbador*) throughout the country, including the Hispaniolan emerald (*Chlorostilbon swainsonii*), the Antillean mango (*Anthracothorax dominicus*) and the tiny Vervain hummingbird (*Mellisuga minima*). The Hispaniolan trogon (*Temnotrogon roseigaster*) is worth looking out for, with its green upper parts, grey breast, red underbelly and long tail streaked with white. It is known locally as a *papagayo*, or *cotorrita de sierra*, and although it is found chiefly in the mountains, it is also seen in mangroves. The Hispaniolan woodpecker, the *carpintero* (*Melanerpes striatus*) is found only on Hispaniola.

Indigenous mammals are few. There are two, rare and endangered species, however, which you are unlikely to see in the wild. They are both nocturnal. The *jutía*, or hutia (*Plagiodontia aedium*), is a small rodent which lives in caves and tree trunks. The *solenodonte*, or solenodon (*Solenodon pardoxus*), is an insectivore with a long nose, round ears and long tail, with the appearance of a large rat, which grows to about 30cm and can weigh 1 kg. Similarly in peril is the *manatí*, sea cow or manatee (*Trichechus manatus*), a sea mammal which lives in the mangroves and sea grass beds around parts of the island. The Taíno used to eat the manatee, who are slow moving and therefore easy prey, as did the pirates who hid in the waterways where they live. There are also lots of bats, many of which live in the plentiful caves found around the island.

There are two species of iguana found in the Dominican Republic, the rhinoceros iguana (*Cyclura cornuta*) and the Ricord iguana (*Cyclura ricordi*), both found in the hot, dry area in and around Lake Enriquillo where the terrain is rocky and cactus, scrub and thorn bushes such as acacia grow. Although of fearsome appearance, they are herbivorous and spend much of their time in the scrub feeding and trying to avoid man. They are best seen at the hottest time of the day as they disappear when it gets cool. In this area you can also find the American crocodile (*Crocodylus acutus*), one of the largest wild crocodile populations in the world.

National parks
The government has adopted six generic categories for environmental protection: areas for scientific research, national parks, natural monuments, sanctuaries, protected areas and wildernesses. The total number of protected areas (including panoramic routes, recreational areas and ecological corridors) is about 70. All are under the control of the Dirección Nacional de Parques (DNP). Armando Bermúdez and José del Carmen Ramírez National Parks, both containing pine forests and mountains in the Cordillera Central are the only remaining areas of extensive forest in the Republic; it is estimated that since the arrival of Columbus, two-thirds of the virgin forest has been destroyed. The reasons for the loss are fire and the establishment of smallholdings by landless peasants. The Reservas Científicas include lakes, patches of forest and the Banco de la Plata (Silver Banks), to which hump-backed whales migrate yearly from the Arctic for the birth of their young. Silver Banks lies some 140 km north of Puerto Plata but there is a proposal to include it in a Biosphere Reserve which would stretch as far as Los Haitises. The reserve protects fish, coral and several species of sea turtles as well as the whales. It is a rather dangerous area for shipping, with depths changing from 20 m to 1,800 m which gives the wildlife added protection.

Sport

Cycling

The scenery is breathtaking and the locals are so friendly that you may have a hard time making any great distance in one day, due to constant photo stops and invites for coffee

The Dominican Republic has miles of dirt roads and endless mule trails, making it a paradise for mountain bikers. There is also some good road biking if you don't mind sharing the roads with trucks, mules, motorbikes and *guaguas*. There are hundreds of great rides in the mountains and along coastal routes. These can change after hurricanes and rain storms. For example after Hurricane Georges in 1998, you could not drive a car over the road from Constanza to San José de Ocoa. It is now a great ride, but if they fix the road it will not be as good a mountain bike ride. The best time of year to mountain bike on the island is June - October. It tends to be dry and more single track is open, but you can bike all year round. It is hottest between 1200-1500, so if you want to cover large distances get an early start and take a long lunch break. In the mountains it is hot during the day, but gets cool at night, so dressing in layers and having warm clothing for after sunset is important. Good rain gear is also recommended. Carry at least two water bottles and make sure you drink more than you think you'll need.

Bike rental There are only a few places to rent mountain bikes. *Iguana Mama* based in Cabarete, www.iguanamama.com rents well maintained Specialized and Cannondale bikes, US$30 per day, US$140 per week. All have front suspension and some have full suspension. They include helmets, water bottles, repair kit and spare tubes and bike insurance with all bike rentals. They offer a 10-day Coast to Coast package tour for US$1,850, a five-day Dominican Alps trip for US$950, and a variety of whole-day and half-day tours ranging from US$40 to US$85. Highly recommended are the Cibao Downhill US$55 half-day or US$85 full day tours. The company is friendly and helpful and the multilingual staff know the country inside out. They pride themselves on giving something back to the country and 20% of income goes to local people and parks. The other place where you can rent a mountain bike is in Jarabacoa at *Rancho Baiguate* where they also do tours. Sometimes some of the local bike shops have bikes to rent. Equipment at hotels is often not well maintained; this doesn't mean that they are not great bikes for a coastal cruise, but anyone wanting a real mountain bike adventure should not be fooled into thinking that they have a suitable bike at their hotel.

Golf

Golf is big business here, with swathes of the coast east of Santo Domingo and along the north coast devoted to the sport

There are 23 golf courses with more being built or renovated, many more than any other country in the Caribbean. All the biggest and newest resorts have a golf course attached and golf is included in many package holidays. The three most famous golf courses are the **Teeth of the Dog**, at *Casa de Campo*, **Playa Grande**, near Río San Juan, and **Playa Dorada**, near Puerto Plata. The first is a Pete Dye designed masterpiece with eight holes right on the sea and judged one of the most beautiful courses in the world. (Golf shop T5232480, F5238800, green fee US$162 including cart, par 72 Championship course.) Next to it is **The Links**, par 71, green fee US$108, and the **Romana Country Club** (members only, par 72, green fee US$135 including cart, T5238600, F5238479) and a new par 72 course at **Altos de Chavón**, **Playa Grande** was designed by Robert Trent Jones Sr and has ten of its holes along the coast on top of cliffs but none is far from the sea. (Golf shop T5823302, F2485314, green fee US$81 including cart, par 72 course.) **Playa Dorada** was also designed by Robert Trent Jones Sr as part of a complex of all-inclusive hotels outside Puerto Plata. (Golf shop T3726020, F3202773, open 0730-1900, green fee US$28, cart US$22, par 72 Championship course.) There are many courses around Santo Domingo, of the country club variety, offering tennis and swimming and social activities for their members. Other 18-hole courses include **Las Aromas** in Santiago, which is hilly, with lovely views of the Cibao valley, wide fairways and lots of trees (golf shop T2765396, green fee US$13, par 70). In the Bávaro area there are four courses at the resort hotels and at **Punta Cana** a new Pete Dye course runs between the *Punta Cana Beach Resort* and the *Club Med* (T2212262, F6883951, www.puntacana.com).

The Dominican Golf Association organizes tournaments all year round, T4764898. For information about courses, tournaments, holidays, tours, pros, club membership etc, T2485263, F2482287. The tourist office distributes a *Golf Guide* in four languages with details and plans of each course. It is also on the internet at www.golfguide-do.com

Hiking

The Dominican Republic provides ideal conditions for medium-distance walking in the tropics. Distances and temperatures are manageable. Road transport, accommodation, restaurants and rum shops are all within convenient reach. Nevertheless, the illusion of remoteness can sometimes be complete. The two highest peaks in the Caribbean are here: Pico Duarte (3,087 m) and La Pelona (3,082 m), side by side in the Cordillera Central. Hiking up Pico Duarte is now a major attraction with 3,500 people making the ascent in 1999. Although most start from the Park entrance at La Ciénaga, there are other, longer routes you can take. There is a fee of RD$50 to enter any National Park in the Republic and you must always be accompanied by a guide, who will bring food and water and mules to carry your bags and the provisions. The guides are well-trained and highly experienced, but they only speak Spanish. Other areas for rewarding hiking are around Jarabacoa, Constanza and in the Valle Nuevo National Park, while easy climbs can be done up Pico Yaque, Mt Isabel de Torres outside Puerto Plata, or in the Sierra de Bahoruco in the southwest. Wherever you are in the country you will be able to find walking opportunities in the many ranges of hills and mountains, or even along the beach for a few kilometres. In rural areas farms and villages are reached by dirt tracks, rather than roads, which are proving popular with mountain bikers, horse riders and hikers. You may be greeted as a curiosity by local children but everyone will be pleased to see you and refreshments can usually be sought at a *colmado*, the village shop and bar. There are no large scale, reliable maps for walkers, although you can pick up regional maps from people like *Iguana Mama* in Cabarete (see above). If you are walking in the National Parks you will, in any case, have to have a guide. Walking sticks are advised, particularly if it has been raining and the tracks are slippery or muddy. You will need to carry plenty of water. Do not drink from the rivers unless you have a purification system with you.

Horse riding

Riding is available in several places, but like cycling, the mountains descending to the north coast are especially rewarding. No previous experience of riding is necessary as Dominican horses are unbelievably placid and well behaved. Complaints from tourists have led to improvements in their care and attention, but you still need to keep an eye out for a healthy horse and check there are no sores, particularly in the saddle area. You should also make sure that your saddle is well made and comfortable, for your own benefit as much as the horse's. If you are going to be in it for hours on end, you will suffer on a wooden saddle with no padding. Riding is western style, with neck reining, long stirrups and a raised pommel on the saddle to hang on to.

No one wears a hard hat, so check your insurance policy before setting out along mountain trails. It's not far to fall, but rocks are hard from any height

Spectator sports

The national sport is **baseball**. The Dominican Republic has produced a phenomenal number of great players and the game has become known as a way out of poverty, with thousands of small boys hoping to be plucked out of obscurity by team selectors and paid a

Dominican Republic

fortune to play their favourite game. The best players are recruited by US and Canadian teams who maintain feeder academies in the Republic; about half of the 300 professional Dominican players in the USA come from San Pedro de Macorís. The regular season starts on the last Friday in October and runs until the end of December, with national and big league players participating. At the beginning of January for three weeks, round robin semi-final matches are held, after which the two best teams compete in the Serie Final in the last week of January.

Basketball is the second sport, played on an amateur basis in the Olympic centre, the Palacio de los Deportes, and in sports clubs around the country, also matches at the Club San Lázaro and Club San Carlos. Every town has a good outdoor court where they play every evening and anyone can join in. The talent is good, there are a lot of Dominicans in the NBA. Be careful of slippery courts and keep your elbows out! In Santo Domingo **cockfights** take place at the Coliseo Gallístico de Santo Domingo, Av Luperón, near Herrera airport, T5653844, fights Sat, Sun, tickets from US$2, but the spectacle can equally well be seen at any rural town or village. Sunday is the big day for cockfighting, although you will often see them practising on other days. **Polo** matches are played at weekends at Sierra Prieta, 25 minutes from Santo Domingo, and at Casa de Campo, T5233333. **Horse racing** takes place at the Hipódromo V Centenario at Km 14.5 on the Autopista de las Américas, T6876060, grandstand ticket US$1. **Dog racing** at the Canodromo El Coco, off Autopista Duarte north of Santo Domingo, T5674461. **Boxing** matches take place frequently in Santo Domingo at the new Gimnasio-Coliseo de Boxeo (with a capacity to seat 7,000 but capable of holding 10,000 spectators) next to the baseball stadium, the Carlos Teo Cruz Coliseum, hotels and sports clubs, where you can also see **fencing, judo, karate** and **table tennis**. **Bowling** has now become a hugely popular pastime, with the opening in late 1996 of the Sebelén Bowling Centre (Bolera), Av Abraham Lincoln, esquina Roberto Pastoriza in a large commercial plaza in Santo Domingo. Built to host the 1997 Panamerican Bowling Games, it is said to be the world's most hi-tech bowling alley, with 24 lanes (more being built), computerized scoring and the usual bars, shops and video games on the periphery, also **billiards** and underground car park for 100 cars, open 1000-0200, T5400101.

Beaches and watersports

Beaches According to UNESCO, the Dominican Republic has some of the best beaches in the world: white sand, coconut palms and many with a profusion of green vegetation. They vary enormously in development, cleanliness, price of facilities, number of hawkers and so on. Boca Chica and Juan Dolio, for instance, are very touristy and not suitable for anyone seeking peace and quiet (except mid-week out of season). The best-known beaches are in the east of the Republic, including: Boca Chica, Juan Dolio, Guayacanes and Villas del Mar in San Pedro de Macorís; Minitas (Casa de Campo, La Romana), Bayahibe, Macao, Bávaro and Punta Cana in the far east, all taken up by resort hotels. Cayo Levantado, an islet with one hotel where the beach is used by day-trippers, Las Terrenas, Playa Bonita, Playa Rincón, Playa Portillo and Las Galeras, are all on the Samaná peninsula and hardly ever crowded. On the north coast, Playa Diamante at Cabrera, Playa Grande and Laguna Gri-Gri at Río San Juan, where you can also visit the lovely beaches of Puerto Escondido, Punta Preciosa in the Bahía Escocesa and Cabo Francés Viejo. East of Puerto Plata, recommended, although fully developed, beaches include Cabarete, Sosúa and Playa Dorada. West of Puerto Plata are Costambar, Cofresí, and several smaller beaches. Towards the northwest and the Haitian border there are uncluttered beaches at Bahía de Luperón, Playa El Morro, Punta Rucia, Cayos los Siete Hermanos and Estero Hondo. In the southwest the best beaches are Las Salinas, Monte Río, Palmar de Ocoa, Najayo, Nigua, Palenque, Nizao and those south and west of Barahona. The majority of beaches have hotels or lodgings but this area is rather neglected as far as tourism is concerned. The southwest is, however, popular with people from Santo Domingo and at weekends the beaches can get busy and noisy with those escaping the capital, many of whom have holiday homes along the coast. Watersports are available on most beaches east of Santo Domingo and along the north coast, but you are less likely to find facilities in the southwest except in certain places like Las Salinas, where windsurfing is popular.

Cabarete, near Sosúa, is one of the best windsurfing places in the world, attracting international competitors to tournaments there. Other centres are Playa Salinas (Baní), Boca Chica and Puerto Plata, while most beach hotels offer windsurfing facilities. Cabarete is the place to be in June, when the town is taken over by serious windsurfers. First there is the annual World Cup Windsurfing Competition and then Cabarete Race Week, www.cabareteraceweek.com The winds are at their best at this time of year attracting both professional and amateur racers. There are lots of competitions, fiestas and other events, contact Vela, T5710805, for information. Although the strength of the wind varies throughout the year, windsurfing is nearly always possible. Generally the mornings are calm, but by the afternoon the bay is full of sails flitting about like butterflies on a puddle. The windsurfing schools are all good, with excellent equipment. They do not all stock the same, so if you have a preference it is worth contacting them in advance to see what they can supply. Most of them stock other watersports equipment too, such as surf boards and kayaks.

Windsurfing
A useful website for windsurfing in Cabarete is www.hispaniola.com/Cabarete/windsurf.html, it has information on schools, events (a little out of date) and daily wind and wave reports

Guibia is a great surfing beach, but it is full of garbage and oil run off from the ships going to Ozama. Other surf beaches include Baoruco and Playa Pato in Barahona, La Preciosa, La Pasa and Playa Grande in Río San Juan, El Encuentro and El Canal in Cabarete, Sosúa Bay and La Boca in Sosúa, La Puntilla in Puerto Plata, Cofresí west of Puerto Plata, and El Macao near Bávaro in the east.

Surfing

For renting boats and **yachts**, contact the Secretaría de Turismo. There are no marinas with charter fleets at present but plans are being prepared. The *Punta Cana Resort* has a brand new marina and *Casa de Campo* is in the process of building one. Most beach resorts have small craft for rent by the hour or the half day. For independent yachtsmen the Dominican Republic is an excellent place to reprovision if cruising the islands.

Sailing

Several international **fishing** tournaments are held each year, the catch being blue marlin, bonito and dorado. There is an annual deep-sea fishing tournament at Boca de Yuma, east of La Romana, in June. For information about fishing contact Santo Domingo Club Náutico, Lope de Vega 55, T5661682, or the Clubes Náuticos at Boca Chica, T6854940, Cabeza de Toro, near Bávaro, and at Monte Cristi. However, these clubs are for members only, so you will need to know someone who is a member if you want to visit. For instruction contact Actividades Acuáticas at Boca Chica, T5234511.

Fishing

Jarabacoa is the centre for adventure sports, being blessed with three main rivers, the Río Yaque del Norte, the Jimenoa and the Baiguate, and their many tributaries. There are three companies active in watersports: *Aventuras del Caribe, Get Wet* and *Máxima Aventura*.
   Canyoning is done on the Río Jimenoa amidst beautiful scenery, unless the river is too full, as you can't do it at high water. Advanced level athletes can also go canyoning at La Damajagua near Imbert. **Cascading** is done at El Salto de Jimenoa and El Salto de Baiguate, elsewhere it can be done at the Cascada de Limón on the Samaná peninsula and Cascada Ojo de Agua near Gaspar Hernández. The Río Yaque del Norte is a level 3-4 river for **rafting**. There are several short rapids in gorges with lots of rocks and boulders to negotiate, followed by calmer sections of river. The rainy season (November and May) is more exciting than the dry season because the more water there is the faster it flows.
   The rainy season is also the favoured time of year for **tubing**, the best rivers being the Río Yaque del Norte, the Río Jamao and the Río Isabela. **Kayaking** is offered for beginners and advanced level by *Aventuras del Caribe*, which has all the equipment for class 5-6 rivers, found on the tributaries of the Río Yaque del Norte. Beginners are taken to the lower Yaque del Norte, the Río Yasica and the lower Río Bao, which are class 2.

River sports
Information on the internet can be found at www.DRpure.com, www.hispaniola.com/whitewater and www.ranchobaiguate.com

Diving and marine life

There is good diving all round the island despite there being relatively few underwater parks. The coral in most places is in good condition and the underwater landscape is varied and interesting. Offshore, the tropical reef provides a diversity of wildlife which you can see by scuba diving, snorkelling or taking a glass bottomed boat trip. There are over 50 species of hard coral (the form that builds reefs) with a variety of sizes and colours. Among the most dramatic are the staghorn and elkhorn corals which are found on the more exposed outer reefs. Brain coral forms massive round structures up to 2 m high, while pillar coral forms columns which reach a similar height. Soft corals, which include black corals (protected by CITES), sea fans and gorgonians, colonize the surface of the hard coral adding colour and variety. Associated with these structures is a host of animals and plants. Spiny lobsters may be seen lurking in holes and crevices along with other crustaceans and reef fish. The patches of sand between outcrops of coral provide suitable habitat for conch and other shellfish, although overfishing has affected their numbers. Among the most common fish are the grunts, butterfly, soldier, squirrel, angel and damsel fish. The quantity of fish varies from place to place, depending on the local fishing industry, as some areas have depleted stocks because of spearfishing. Nevertheless, in Dominican waters you can see whales, dolphins, grouper, barracuda and other large pelagics, as well as lots of colourful reef fish, turtles and invertebrates.

In the **Puerto Plata** area of the north coast, the diving is best around **Sosúa**. It is particularly good for first time divers, with sandy spots, reefs and interesting rock formations, while for more experienced divers there are tunnels, chimneys, overhangs and walls. Some sites are virgin, but many are fished out. In places the coral has been badly damaged and broken by overdiving. The best time of year is usually May-September, when the sea is calm and the visibility good. In high season, December-April, there can often be winds and rain which stir up the sand, reduce visibility and bring in a lot of rubbish which litters the dive sites. From Puerto Plata to Cabarete there are 16-17 dive operations, but you need to ask lots of questions to establish their safety record, standard of equipment and teaching ability. More conservation-minded divers should head further east to **Río San Juan**, where there are plans to make the area offshore of the **Laguna Grí Grí** an underwater park. There are varied dive sites for beginners or intermediate divers and the coral is in good condition. Lots of reef fish can be seen, and if you go over the wall you are likely to spot larger life such as barracuda. At the beginning of the year whales are sometimes seen, usually humpbacks during their migration and breeding season. The **Samaná peninsula** offers rewarding diving on its north side and there are several dive shops at Las Terrenas and one at Las Galeras. In season some of them offer whale watching as well as diving. There are dive sites all around the bays and headlands, including wrecks, caves, drop-offs and reefs. Snorkelling is also good here and many dive boats offer snorkelling excursions.

The all-inclusive resorts around **Bávaro** offer diving although this is not the best area in the country. Diving is also available at the *Punta Cana Resort*, where there is the longest reef on the island, stretching for about 30 km. For more interesting diving there are organized day-trips to Bayahibe and Catalina island on the southeast coast. **Bayahibe** is probably the best place for independent divers as there is reasonable, cheap accommodation and a good, German-run dive shop offering tailor-made programmes into the National Park. There are also several all-inclusive resorts with their own dive shops if you want to stay in more upmarket lodgings. The National Park offers some of the best diving in the country; the reef is in good condition, and although local fishermen are still going in and spearfishing, it is not overfished. There are nice dive sites all along the coast to **Saona island**, in the Park, with plentiful and colourful underwater life. **Catalina island**, with its wall and coral gardens, is a big attraction here but there is also **Catalinita**, north of Saona island, about one hour by boat from Bayahibe, where you can find sharks and rays, while dolphins will accompany you on your route. Nearer to Santo Domingo is **La Caleta** underwater park which has good reef and wreck diving, with two deliberately-sunk boats close to each other. There are no dive shops at La Caleta, most divers come on trips from nearby Boca Chica or from Santo Domingo.

Dive operators Most dive operations in the Dominican Republic make sure they can offer a variety of languages so that students can be taught in their own languages. PADI is the most widely offered instruction, although CMAS and others are available. A PADI Open Water certification can cost anything from US$290 to US$400, while a two-tank boat dive for qualified divers varies from US$50 to US$75, so it is worth shopping around. In case of emergencies, those with DAN insurance will be flown out to Miami. There is a recompression chamber in Santo Domingo, but there is no one to operate it, so the nearest is in Puerto Rico. A chamber is planned for the new hospital in the Punta Cana/Bávaro area.

Holidays and festivals

New Year's Day (1 January), Epiphany (6 January), Our Lady of Altagracia (21 January), Duarte Day (26 January), Independence Day (27 February), Good Friday (although all Semana Santa is treated as a holiday), Labour Day (1 May), Corpus Christi (60 days after Good Friday), Restoration Day (16 August), Our Lady of Las Mercedes (24 September), Christmas Day (25 December).

Public holidays

New Year is celebrated in the capital on Av Francisco Alberto Caamaño Deñó (formerly Av del Puerto) beside the river. The major bands and orchestras of the country give a free concert, which attracts thousands of people. The celebration ends with fireworks and the whole area becomes a huge disco. On *21 January* the day of the **Virgen de la Altagracia**, spiritual mother of the Dominicans, is celebrated with *'velaciones'*, or night-long vigils, and African-influenced singing and music, found in many towns. Higüey is the site of a mass pilgrimage and huge all-night party. **Carnival** (www.carnaval.com.do) is at the end of *February*, notable in Santo Domingo for the parade along the Malecón on 27 February. Carnival in Santiago de los Caballeros is very colourful; its central character is the piglet, which represents the devil. On the Sundays of February in Montecristi there are the festivals of the *toros* versus the *civiles*. La Vega also celebrates for several Sundays prior to Lent. There are other parades on **Restoration Day,** *16 August* .

Each town's saint's day is celebrated with several days of festivities known as *patronales*. Based in Catholicism, everyone gets involved and has a party. **Holy Week** is the most important holiday time for Dominicans, when there are processions and festivities such as the *guloyas* in San Pedro de Macorís, the mystical-religious *ga-ga* in sugar cane villages and the *cachúas* in Cabral in the southwest.

The **Festival Presidente de Música Latina** is held in *June* in the Olympic Stadium, featuring musicians from all over Latin America. The **merengue festival** in *July* (see Culture), includes festivals of gastronomy, cocktails, and exhibitions of handicrafts and fruit. Puerto Plata has a similar, annual **merengue festival** at the beginning of *October* on the Malecón La Puntilla, as does Sosúa, in the last week of *September* .

Dominican Republic

Santo Domingo

Travellers have been marvelling at this city since the beginning of the 16th century, when its streets, fortresses, palaces and churches were the wonder of the Caribbean and conquistadores set off from the port on the river to discover new territory for Spain in the Americas. Santo Domingo, the first European city in the Western Hemisphere, is now the capital and business centre of the Dominican Republic. It is busy and modern, sprawling along the Caribbean coast and inland along the banks of the Río Ozama. Restoration of the old city on the west bank of the river has made the area very attractive, with open air cafés and pleasant squares near the waterfront. Those who have wealth flaunt it by building ostentatious villas and driving German cars, but there is a distinctly uneven distribution of wealth and the slums are some of the worst in the Caribbean.

Population: 4,000,000
Colour map 3, grid B3

Ins and outs

Aeropuerto La Américas, east of Santo Domingo, is the international airport for the capital, receiving flights from North and South America and Europe. **Las Herreras**, on the western outskirts of town is for domestic and commercial flights, although many of these also go from Las Américas, so you should check. See Airport for details of taxis and buses. If you are

Getting there
See transport page 430 for flight details

arriving in the capital by bus, you will come in to that company's bus terminal. There is no central bus station. Taxis wait outside to take you to your hotel or other destination.

Getting around
*See Transport, page
430 for further details*

If you are limiting yourself to the colonial city, then you will be able to walk around all the places of interest. Further afield, however, distances are great. Public transport is varied: there are government-run buses on the arterial routes in and out of town for commuters; shared or privately-hired taxis called *públicos*, radio taxis and motorcycle taxis, known as *motoconchos*. Car hire is not recommended for the capital. **Tourist office** There is a tourist office in the colonial city in the Palacio Borgella, Isabel la Católica, near Plaza Colón, T6863858, and at Las Américas airport, T5420120.

History

The first wooden houses were built in 1496 by Christopher Columbus' (Cristóbal Colón) brother Bartolomé on the eastern bank of the Río Ozama after the failure of the settlement at La Isabela on the north coast. In 1498 the Governor, Nicolás de Ovando, moved the city to the other side of the river and started building with stone, a successful move which was continued by Diego Colón, Christopher's son, when he took charge in 1509. It then became the first capital city in Spanish America. For years the city was the base for the Spaniards' exploration and conquest of the continent. Santo Domingo holds the title 'first' for a variety of offices: first city, having the first Audiencia Real, cathedral, university, coinage, etc. In view of this, UNESCO has designated Santo Domingo a World Cultural Heritage site (Patrimonio Cultural Mundial). However, Santo Domingo's importance soon waned when Spain set up her colonies in Peru and Mexico with seemingly limitless amounts of silver and gold to finance the Crown. Hurricanes managed to sink 15 ships in 1508, 18 in 1509 and many more in later years. 1562 brought an earthquake which destroyed much of the town; 1586 brought Sir Francis Drake, who attacked from inland where defences were vulnerable, looted and pillaged and set the city alight. He was the first of many British and French pirates and privateers who attacked in the 16th and 17th centuries and rebuilding works were continually in progress.

In the 1930s, the dictator Rafael Leonidas Trujillo renamed the city Ciudad Trujillo and embarked on a series of public works. After his assassination in 1961 the city immediately reverted to the title of Santo Domingo, but his successor, Joaquín Balaguer, continued to build on a monumental scale. Prestigious projects such as the Faro a Colón took pride of place over social spending on education, health and housing for the poor. Governments since the 1960s have been criticized for concentrating on the capital and ignoring the provinces. As a result migration to the capital has surged and little has been done to prevent the growth of slums and poor barrios. However, the city is now more wealthy than ever before, tourism is booming and it is a lively and vibrant place to live or just spend a few days.

Sights

Colonial city

The colonial city (Zona Colonial, Ciudad Vieja) is now only about 1% of the total area of Santo Domingo but it is the first port of call for visitors, holding almost all the sights of historical interest. The Ciudad Vieja and adjacent Ciudad Nueva (new city - the area of middle-class housing of the 19th century, complete with *pulperías* – turn-of-the-century stores) are practically deserted on Sunday, a good time to stroll around and take in the architecture and atmosphere in peace. Calle Las Damas which runs alongside the Fortress, is the oldest paved (cobbled) street in the New World and is where the wife of Diego Colón and the ladies of the court would take their evening promenade. Plaza España lies at the end of Calle Las Damas and has lovely views over the river. At night time there are often cultural events laid on, such as music, folk dancing or theatre. Calle El Conde runs the length of the colonial city from the entrance gate, Puerta El Conde in the west, to the Fortaleza Ozama and the river in the east. It is a pleasant pedestrian boulevard with shops, bars and cafés.

Fortification of Santo Domingo began in 1503, with the construction of a tower to protect the entrance to the port. The city walls, only partially restored, were started in 1543 by the architect, Rodrigo de Liendo. All along the walls they built 20 defensive positions, six of them gates to the city and the others forts or bastions reserved for the military. The most important and largest fort was the **Fortaleza Ozama** or **Fortaleza de Santo Domingo**, overlooking the river and now bounded by the Av Francisco Alberto Camaaño Deñó, or Av del Puerto, running beneath it at the water's edge. It is the oldest fortress in America, constructed 1503-07 by Nicolás de Ovando.

Just to the west, is the **Catedral Basílica Menor de Santa María**, Primada de América, Isabel La Católica esquina Nouel, the first cathedral to be founded in the New World. Its first stone was laid by Diego Colón, son of Christopher Columbus, in 1514 (although there is some dispute and some people think it was after 1520); the first architect was Alonzo Rodríguez, but there were several who had a go at designing different bits of the church. It was finished in 1540 and inaugurated in 1542. Little remains of the original interior decoration, because when Drake sacked the city in 1586 his men removed everything of value, ransacking the place in the process. The alleged remains of Christopher Columbus were found in 1877 during restoration work. In 1892, the Government of Spain donated the tomb in which the remains lay, a neo-Gothic wedding cake of a monument, behind the high altar, until their removal to the Faro a Colón (see below). The cathedral was fully restored for 1992, the 500th anniversary of Columbus' first voyage, with new gargoyles and sculptures at the gates showing the indigenous people when Columbus arrived. The main doors, however, are original, and the 500-year-old key is still used to lock them at night. ■ *0900-1200, 1500-1630. No shorts allowed, women may be asked to wear skirts, not trousers.*

Parque Colón is outside the Cathedral, on its north side, next to Calle El Conde. A statue to Christopher Columbus (Cristóbal Colón) is in the middle, with a Taíno woman at his feet, a symbol now considered rather politically incorrect. The **Museo de Ambar**, El Conde 107 on Parque Colón, is upstairs, with a shop on the ground floor selling amber, larimar, black coral, local gold and pearls. Remember that black coral is protected by CITES and you may not be able to take it into your home country. ■ *T2211333, F6825101. US$1.*

A whole cluster of historical buildings lie either side of Las Damas running north from the Fortaleza Ozama. The first is the **Casa de Don Rodrigo de Bastidas**, built in to the city wall on Calle Las Damas in 1510. This was the house of the royal tax collector and mayor, who went on to colonize Colombia. It is large and built around an inner courtyard with arches around all four walls and enormous caucho trees. ■ *0930-1700, Mon-Fri. Free.* Beside it is the Casa de Ovando, the home of the man who did most to build the city at the beginning of the 16th century, but this is not currently open to the public as it is being developed into a hotel, the *Hostal Nicolás de Ovando*.

The **Casa de Francia**, opposite the *Hostal Nicolás de Ovando*, was built in the early 16th century. Next door is the **Convento de San Ignacio de Loyola**, Las Damas between Mercedes and El Conde, a Jesuit monastery and church. Finished in 1743, it has been the **National Pantheon** since 1958. The central nave forms a cross with the lateral chapels and a bronze lamp donated by the Spanish government (General Franco) hangs in the intersection. It was restored in 1955 by Trujillo with a generous amount of Italian marble and contains the tombs of, or memorials to, many of the country's heroes and patriots. The remains of Gen Pedro Santana, five times President, lie here, as do most of his successors. It also contains an ornate tomb built before his death for the dictator Trujillo, the 'Benefactor of the Fatherland', but after his assassination he was not given the honour of being buried here. ■ *Tue-Sun 0900-1700. T6820185. Free.* Cross the street again for the **Capilla de Nuestra Señora de Los Remedios**, built in the early 16th century as the private chapel of the Dávila family. By its side the **Reloj de Sol** (sundial) was built in 1753, near the end of Las Damas, so that court officials could tell the time by looking out of their windows.

One of the most significant historical buildings in this area is the **Museo de las Casas Reales**, on Calle Las Damas, in a reconstructed early 16th-century building which was in colonial days the Palace of the Governors and Captains-General, and of the Audiencia Real and Chancery of the Indies. The Audiencia Real was a supreme court made up of three judges, designed to check the power of the Governor, and its power extended to the rest of the Caribbean and the mainland coast around the Caribbean basin. It is an excellent colonial museum (often has special exhibits), with many items salvaged from ships sunk in local waters as well as furniture, art and military items. ■ *Tue-Sun 0900-1800. US$1. T6824202.*

The **Alcázar de Colón** at the end of Las Damas and Emilio Tejera, is a fortified house constructed without any nails by the first Viceroy, Diego Colón, in 1510-14 to house his court and his wife, María de Toledo. It was the seat of the Spanish Crown in the New World until the family left for Spain in 1577 and it was sacked by Drake in 1586. In 1770 the building was abandoned. Restoration began in 1957 and a second phase took place in 1965. Now completely restored, it houses the interesting **Museo Virreinal (Viceregal Museum),** with religious art and colonial artefacts. ■ *Daily*

Santo Domingo

0900-1700, US$0.75. **La(s) Atarazana(s)**, the Dockyards, near the Alcázar, are a cluster of 16th-century buildings which served as an arsenal, warehouses and taverns for the sailors in port, now restored to contain shops, bars and restaurants. The **Museo Naval de la(s) Atarazana(s)** at the end, contains recovered treasure from several shipwrecks, namely the *Concepción, Nuestra Señora de Guadalupe* and *Conde de Tolosa*. There are accounts of the many attempts to raise numerous 17th and 18th century ships which sank around the island and exhibits show what life was like on board ship at that time. ■ *Thu-Tue, 0900-1800. Free. T6825834.*

The **Casa del Cordón**, Isabel La Católica esquina Emiliano Tejera, was built in 1509 by Francisco de Garay, who accompanied Columbus on his first voyage to Hispaniola. It is now the offices and 'cultural centre' of the Banco Popular; free guided tours during working hours. Walk a block up Isabel la Católica and you get to the **Museo de Duarte**, Restauración esq Isabel la Católica, which contains items linked with the independence struggle and Juan Pablo Duarte, the national hero, whose home it was. ■ *Mon-Fri 0900-1700, US$0.75, T6890326, Isabel La Católica 308.*

The Casa was named for the cord of the Franciscan Order, sculpted above the entrance. It was initially used as a court house

Dominican Republic

N
Not to scale

Near the end of Isabel La Católica lies the only joint church and fort in Santo Domingo, the **Iglesia de Santa Bárbara**, just off Av Mella. Built in 1574 on the site of the city quarry in honour of the patron saint of the military, it was sacked by Drake in 1586, and destroyed by a hurricane in 1591. It was reconstructed at the beginning of the 17th century. Its design is rather lopsided and haphazard, its two towers being of completely different size and style and bearing little relation with the main entrance with its triple arches. Behind the church are the ruins of its fort, where there are good views and photo opportunities.

Don't miss the **Museo Mundo de Ambar**, Arzobispo Meriño 452, esq Restauración, in a restored 17th century building, which has a fascinating display of scorpions, butterflies and plants fossilized in amber, with microscopes and videos. A guided tour is recommended but not essential. The staff are very informative and will teach you how to tell real from fake amber. Craftsmen polish and shape raw amber for sale in an adjoining room. ■ *Daily 0900-1800. US$1. T6823309, F6881142.*

Round the corner and up the hill, the **Monasterio de San Francisco** (ruins), Hostos esquina E Tejera, was the first monastery in America, constructed in the first half of the 16th century, although dates vary. Sacked by Drake and destroyed by earthquakes in 1673 and 1751, it was repeatedly repaired or rebuilt. For about 50 years until the 1930s it was used as an asylum for the insane, and there are still metal brackets in places where patients were restrained with leg chains. A hurricane closed it down for good and the ruins are now used for cultural events.

Walk south down Hostos to the **Hospital-Iglesia de San Nicolás de Bari** (ruins), Hostos between Mercedes and Luperón, begun in 1509 by Nicolás de Ovando, completed 1552, was the first stone-built hospital in the Americas. In a Cruciform plan, the three-aisled Gothic-vaulted church was used for worship while two-storey wings were used for wards to cure the sick. Also plundered by Drake, it was probably one of the best constructed buildings of the period, it survived many earthquakes and hurricanes. In 1911 some of its walls were knocked down because they posed a hazard to passers-by; also the last of its valuable wood was taken. It is now full of pigeons.

South and west of the Cathedral there are several sights along Padre Billini. The **Museo de la Familia Dominicana** has a collection of furniture, antiques and memorabilia from the 19th century. It is housed in the **Casa de Tostada** (Calle Padre Billini esq Arzobispo Meriño), an early 16th-century mansion with a Gothic-Isabelline double window on its northern façade. The house was the home of the writer, Francisco de Tostado, the first native professor at the university, who was killed when Drake set about destroying the city in 1586. ■ *Mon-Fri, 0900-1700. US$0.80. T6895057.* One block further down Padre Billini is the **Convento de los Dominicos**, built in 1510. Here in 1538 the first university in the Americas was founded. The University itself has moved to a site in the suburbs.

The River At the mouth of the Río Ozama, the Avenida Francisco Alberto Caamaño Deñó (formerly Avenida del Puerto) gives access to the Antigua Ceiba, where Columbus moored his caravelles, the Plaza de Armas, the city's original drainage system and the old city wall. Steps lead up to the Alcázar de Colón where the Plaza de España has been created. The Avenida has become an open-air discothèque during fiesta time. The cruise ship terminal is here, at the foot of what will be the *Hostal de Nicolás de Ovando*, when it is fully restored. The eastern bank of the Ozama is being restored with a new footpath, the Vereda del Almirante, an amphitheatre and a new tourist harbour. The restaurants, *Bucanero, Remo Café* and *Café del Río* at the marina, have a lovely view of yachts and across the river to the colonial city. The **Monumento del Caña** is also on the eastern bank, a huge statue of a bullock cart laden with sugar cane. The **Capilla de La Virgen del Rosario**, also on the east side of the Río Ozama, near the Molinos Dominicanos at the end of Avenida Olegario Vargas, is on the site of the first church constructed in America, restored in 1943.

The mystery of Columbus' bones

After his death in 1506, Columbus was buried in Valladolid, Spain. In 1509 his body was apparently removed to Sevilla, thence together with that of his son Diego to Santo Domingo sometime in the 1540s. When France took control of Hispaniola in 1795, Cuba (still part of Spain) requested Columbus' remains. An urn bearing the name 'Colón' was disinterred from beneath the altar, sent to Havana and then back to the Cathedral in Sevilla in 1898, when Cuba became independent. In 1877, however, during alterations and repairs in Santo Domingo cathedral, the cache of urns beneath

the altar was reopened. One casket bore the inscription 'Almirante Cristóbal Colón', both outside and in. Experts confirmed that the remains were those of Columbus; the Spanish ambassador and two further experts from Spain were dismissed for concurring with the findings. A second pair of Spanish experts denied the discovery, hence the confusion over where the admiral's bones lay. The urn that was opened in 1877 is that which is now given pride of place in the Faro a Colón.

Joe Hollins

East of the Río Ozama

The **Faro a Colón (Columbus Lighthouse)**, built at great cost (and not without controversy) in the **Parque Mirador del Este**, is in the shape of a cross. Where the arms of the cross intersect is the mausoleum containing the supposed remains of Columbus. The navy mounts a permanent guard over the tomb. Spotlights project a crucifix of light into the night sky, spectacular on a cloudy night, Friday to Sunday 2000-2200 and on holidays. One of the rooms inside the lighthouse is a chapel, in others, different countries have mounted exhibitions (the British exhibit concentrates on the entries for the competition to design the lighthouse: the competition was won by a British design). The cost of building the lighthouse has been variously estimated between US$40 mn and US$250 mn. Slums were cleared and some of the 2,000 families evicted received a paltry sum of US$50 before losing their homes. Some 100,000 people are believed to have been adversely affected by the construction work, road building and slum clearance. There were demonstrations and some protesters were killed. In the light of the controversy the King and Queen of Spain declined an invitation to attend the 1992 celebrations and the Pope withdrew his acceptance to inaugurate the building. Two days before the ceremonies were to begin, President Balaguer's sister, Doña Emma, to whom he was devoted, inspected the Faro and hours later, she died, inspiring further belief that Columbus brings bad luck and that there was a curse, or *fukú* on the building. Balaguer, who had been held responsible for the whole enterprise and who was criticized for his megalomania, also stayed away from the inauguration, while he mourned his sister. ■ *Daily 0900-1700, US$1.50, US$0.30 for children, T5925217. Photography inside permitted, but no photos in the museums, no smoking, no eating, no drinking, no pets; guides are free, but give a tip; shorts above the knee not allowed.*

East of the Lighthouse in the Parque Mirador del Este are the *cenotes* (limestone sinkholes) **Tres Ojos** (Three Eyes), a popular tourist attraction. They used to be public bathing pools in the times of the Taínos, and Anacaona, the wife of Enriquillo, would bathe here, but now 'Tarzan' is the only person allowed to swim. A local man, he has been doing it since 1958 and is a tourist attraction in himself. ■ *Daily: US$1.30 adults, US$0.30 children and students. Ferry to the furthest lake US$0.30 adults, children US$0.20. Toilets. At the entrance vendors sell artesanías made from stalactites (light colour) and stalagmites (dark colour), an ecological horror. Guagua from Parque Enriquillo.*

West of the Río Ozama

Gazcue is a quiet, attractive residential area with expensive homes built in the 1930s and 1940s, stretching west of the Zona Colonial as far as Avenida Máximo Gómez. The coral pink **Palacio Presidencial** with a neo-classical central portico and cupola, built by Trujillo, is at the intersection of Doctor Delgado and Manuel María Castillo. It is used by the President, but guided tours of the richly decorated interior can be

Dominican Republic

arranged. ■ *T6864771 ext 340 or 360.* Opposite the Palacio's grounds, at Avenida México y 30 de Marzo, are the government offices. The 1955/56 World's Fair (Feria de Confraternidad) buildings now house the Senate and Congress.

The modern city to the west is very spread out because, until recently, there was no high-rise building. Av George Washington (also known as the Malecón) runs parallel to the sea; it often becomes an open-air discothèque, where locals and foreigners dance the merengue. The annual merengue festival is held here. The continuation (Prolongación) of Av México, which runs parallel to Avs Bolívar and 27 de Febrero, has many modern buildings, while Expreso Quinto Centenario, in the Villa Juana and Villa Francisca districts, is a new roadway which has rejuvenated these parts of the city.

The **Plaza de la Cultura**, founded by Pres Joaquín Balaguer on Av Máximo Gómez, contains the country's major museums alongside the national library and

Zona Colonial

Dominican Republic

■ Walls & fortresses
1 Fortaleza de Santo Domingo
2 Fuerte de San José
3 Fuerte de San Gil
4 Puerta de la Misericordia
5 Fuerte de Santiago
6 Puerta del Conde
7 Fuerte de la Concepción
8 Fuerte de la Caridad
9 Fuerte de San Lázaro
10 Fuerte de San Miguel
11 Fuerte de San Francisco
12 Fuerte de San Antón
13 Fuerte de Santa Bárbara
14 Fuerte del Angulo
15 Fuerte de la Carena
16 Puerta de las Atarazanas
17 Batería del Almirante
18 Puerta de San Diego
19 Fuerte de San Diego
20 Fuerte Invencible
21 Torre del Homenaje
22 Alcázar de Colón

✝ Religious buildings
1 Capilla de San Andrés
2 Iglesia del Carmen
3 Convento Regina Angelorum
4 Capilla de la Tercera Orden
5 Convento de los Dominicos
6 Iglesia Santa Clara
7 Catedral
8 Panteón Nacional
9 Capilla de los Remedios
10 Iglesia de Santa Bárbara (ruins)
11 Capilla de San Antón
12 Monasterio de San Francisco
13 Iglesia de la Altagracia
14 Hospital San Nicolás de Bari
15 Iglesia de las Mercedes
16 Iglesia de San Miguel
17 Iglesia de San Lázaro
18 Iglesia San Carlos
19 Capilla de la Virgen del Rosario

🏛 Museums
1 Casa de Tostado/Museo de la Familia Dominicana
2 Museo de las Casas Regles
3 Casa del Cordón
4 Museo Mundo de Ambar
5 Museo de Duarte

the ultra-modern, white marble **National Theatre** ■ *T6827255 (you will have to go to the ballet or opera to see the lavish interior)*. The **Museo del Hombre Dominicano** traces the development of the modern Dominican, from the Amerindians, in pre-Columbian times, who were hunters and gatherers, to the Spanish conquerors and the African slaves. There were about 400,000 Taínos on the island in 1492, but only 60,000 in 1508 and they had nearly all died by 1525. Despite their rapid annihilation their influences live on in Dominican life today, in agriculture, fishing, diet, housing, transport, *artesanía* and language, all explained here. There is a large display of Carnival costumes and a Dominican vodú altar. ■ *1000-1700, closed on Mon, US$0.60 foreigners, US$0.30 nationals, US$0.20 students, T6873622*. The **Museo de Arte Moderno** contains a huge amount of 20th-century Dominican art on four floors. ■ Tue-Sun 0900-1700, US$0.60, T6852153. The **Museo de Historia Natural** is of more use to Dominican schoolchildren learning about science, than to visitors wanting to find out about the natural history of the Republic, although there are some exhibits of interest. ■ *Tue-Sun 1000-1700, US$0.60, T6890106, café open 0700-1900*. The **Museo de Historia y Geografía** has a few Taíno exhibits, but most of the displays are from the 19th and 20th centuries, starting with the Haitian invasion and following on to the American occupation. A great deal of space is taken up by artefacts belonging to Trujillo, illustrating his wealth and vanity. The museum organizes ecological excursions to different parts of the country, see 'Local tour agents' page 404. ■ *Tue-Sun, 0930-1700, free, T6866668*.

Among the attractive parks are the Centro Olímpico, JF Kennedy and Máximo **Parks** Gómez, in the city centre, **Parque Mirador del Este** (Autopista de las Américas, a 7 km-long alameda) and Parque Mirador del Sur. The **Centro Olímpico** is a public park, but the sporting facilities are technically only for Dominicans. The Paseo de los Indios at **Parque Mirador del Sur** is a 7 km-long trail, popular for walking, jogging, cycling and picnics. Av Anacaona runs along the north side and many desirable residences overlook the park. On Av José Contreras are many caves, some with lakes, in the southern cliff of Parque Mirador del Sur. Along this cliff is the Av Cayetano Germosén, giving access to a number of caves used at one time by Taíno Indians. One such Lago Subterráneo has been opened as a tourist attraction. ■ *0900-1730. US$0.40*. Caves are also the setting for the *Mesón de la Cava* restaurant and the *Guacara Taíno* nightclub. The road, lined with gardens, links Avs Luperón and Italia. **Parque Mirador del Norte** has been constructed on the banks of the Río Isabela, near Guarícano and Villa Mella. There is a boating lake, picnic areas, restaurants, jogging and cycling trails. ■ *Tue-Sun, 0900-1800, US$0.40*.

The **Jardín Botánico Nacional**, Av de los Próceres, Urbanización Los Ríos, is named after a Dominican botanist, Dr Rafael M Moscoso, founder of the Botanical Institute at the University of Santo Domingo. Plants endemic to the island are showcased here. There are 300 types of orchid and a greenhouse for bromeliads and aquatic plants. The Botanical Gardens are highly recommended, especially the Japanese Garden, which is beautifully manicured; horse-drawn carriages and a small train tour the grounds (US$1, children US$0.55), which are extensive. ■ *Tue-Sun 0900-1800. US$0.75, children half price, T5676211, 5652860*.

Essentials

For cheap rooms in casas de pensión, or for apartments for rent for longer stays in or outside **Sleeping** the capital, look in the classified section of daily paper, *Listín Diario*. *Prices listed are high season rates & do not include taxes, normally 23%*

Zona Colonial AL-A *Francés* (Sofitel), Las Mercedes esq Arzobispo Meriño, T6859331, F6851289. Restored colonial mansion, 19 luxury rooms, lovely furnishings, restaurant in beautiful courtyard with fountain or indoors, superb French food, expensive but recommended. **B-C** *Mercure Comercial*, El Conde, T6885500. Newly renovated by the French group, Accor, to a high standard. **B-C** *Palacio*, Duarte 106 y Ureña, T6824730, F6875535, h.palacio@codetel.net.

Dominican Republic

do Colonial mansion, standard or superior rooms wi th fan. **B-C** *Hostal Nicolás Nader*, Duarte y General Luperón, T6876674. Includes taxes, colonial mansion, 9 rooms, best upstairs, beautifully furnished with lots of modern art for sale, friendly, personal service, pleasant. **D** pp *Plaza Toledo*, Isabel la Católica 163, T6887649, F2214167, www.dominican-rep.com/toledo. html Run by Bettye Marshall, restaurant, art gallery and rooms, clean and comfortable, breakfast included, 10% discount in restaurant and art gallery, all-inclusive packages available, airport transfers, no children, restored colonial house. **E** *Aída*, El Conde and Espaillat, T6857692, F6889350. A/c rooms have no windows, rooms with fan have balcony, some rooms sleep 3, family-run, very nice, no smoking, fairly quiet at night, but record shop below may be noisy in day, very central, popular, often full, Amex accepted. **E** *Montesino*, José Gabriel García III, T6883346, overlooking Malecón and Montesino's statue. 4 rooms, with bath, **F** with shared bath, fan, use of kitchen, will negotiate longer stays. **F** *Independencia*, Estrella casi esquina Arzobispo Nouel, near Parque Independencia. Price for single room, soap, towels etc provided, clean, convenient location, some rooms without windows, also has a club, bar (noisy all night), language school (across the street) and art exhibitions.

There are dozens of cheap hotels, especially around the Mercado Modelo; those on Av Duarte are usually used by prostitutes; have a good look before making any decision

North of the Zona Colonial D *Royal*, Av Duarte y 27 de Febrero, T6855400. Fully a/c, small pool, good restaurant, guaguas leaving to north and west across the street. **E** *Señorial*, Av Presidente Vicini Burgos 58 (Parque Eugenio María de Hostos), T6874367, F6870600. Swiss-run, a/c, good electricity and water supply, TV, friendly, clean and informal, good Italian food, popular with Swiss-Italian visitors, see the 1952 map on the wall. **F** *Ferdan*, Francisco Henríquez 107 y Carvajal, T2217710, just off Av Duarte. Buses to Boca Chica and to airport 2 blocks away, large clean rooms with bath, foreigners given rooms with windows, large discounts for long stays but you will be given room on top floors where generator does not reach and suffer power cuts.

Away from the old city along the Malecón are the modern international-style hotels

Along the Malecon Three 5-star hotels **LL-AL**, with business centres and sports facilities: **LL-AL** *Hotel V Centenario Intercontinental*, Av George Washington 218, T2210000, F2212020; **LL-AL** *Meliá Santo Domingo*, Av George Washington 365, T2216666, F6878150; **LL-AL** *Renaissance Jaragua Hotel & Casino*, Av George Washington 367, T2212222, F6860528. **B-C** *Cervantes*, Cervantes 202, T6868161, F6865754. 171 rooms, some suites, family-run, pool. **C-D** *La Casona Dorada*, Independencia y Báez, in Gazcue, near *Jaragua*. 25 rooms, patio for drinks, food or TV, laundry and dry cleaning, small pool, jacuzzi, 24-hr room service, courteous staff, secure parking. **E** *Alameda*, Calle Cervantes opposite *Cervantes*, T6855121. No frills but quite adequate, management amiable and helpful, English spoken, restaurant. Next door to *Napolitano* is **E** *Palmeras del Caribe*, Cambronal 1, T6893872. Nice rooms but small, pleasant garden, use of fridge, adjoining café.

Business travellers can often get cheaper rates than posted by requesting 'la tarifa comercial'

Near the university L-AL *Santo Domingo*, Av Independencia y Av Abraham Lincoln, T2211511, F5354050. Colonial style, plush and charming, main restaurant open 5 days a week for lunch, otherwise for receptions, *Café Tal*, less well-staffed. Opposite is its sister hotel **L-AL** *Hispaniola*, Av Independencia y Abraham Lincoln, T2217111, F5354050. Pleasant public areas, noisy, glitzy, casino off reception, bedrooms and corridors showing their age, bathroom adequate, very clean, good service, repairs carried out quickly, pool, disco. **B-C** *Continental*, Av Máximo Gómez 16, T6891151, F6878397. Includes taxes and breakfast, pleasant area, pool. **B-C** *Villa Italia*, Av Independencia 1107 casi esquina Alma Mater, T6823373, F2217461, hotel.villa@codetel.net.do 25 rooms, 3 suites, 1 apartment, a/c, phone, TV, jacuzzi on terrace, sea view, wooden furniture colour washed green, restaurant, fridge available for extra charge, attractive but service found lacking. **C-D** *Comodoro*, Av Bolívar 193, T6877141, T/F5412277. A/c, pool, reasonable, with fridges in rooms.

Near the Centro Olímpico L-B *Plaza*, Av Alma Mater, T5416226, F5417251. Suites with kitchenette, very comfortable, pool, gym, gourmet restaurant, coffee shop. **AL** *Barceló Gran Hotel Lina*, Av Máximo Gómez y 27 de Febrero, T5635000, F6865521, h.lina@codetel.net. do Good restaurant, well equipped, 200 rooms, casino, convenient for Caribe Tours terminal, painted orange and pink, computers with internet access.

Dominican Republic

Near Parque Mirador del Sur LL-AL *Dominican Fiesta Hotel y Casino*, Av Anacaona, T5628222, F5628938. 331 rooms and suites. **D** *Bellavista*, Dr F Defilló 43, Ens Bella Vista, T5320412, F5352988, hotelbellavista@codetel.net.do Good, clean, large rooms, popular with business travellers.

US$20+ Zona Colonial: *La Briciola*, Arzobispo Merino 152, T6885055. Recommended Italian cuisine in spectacular setting in courtyard of colonial house. *Caribbean Blue*, Hostos with El Conde, opposite *Mercure Comercial*, T5404931. Latin-Caribbean fusion dishes, great style. *Café Coco*, Padre Billini 53, T6879624. A small restaurant owned and run by 2 English-men, excellent food and service, menu changes daily, highly recommended, open 1200-1500, 1830-2230, closed Sun pm and all day Mon, reservations required, dinner for 2 with wine costs about US$75. In the Plaza España is *Museo de Jamón*, ceiling covered with hams, also delicious selection of tapas. **West of the Zona Colonial:** *Fellini*, Roberto Pastoriza 504, esq Winston Churchill, T5405330. Mediterranean cuisine, closed Tue.

Eating
Many hotels have 'bufet ejecutivos' at lunch time & gourmet restaurants for evening meals

US$15-20 Zona Colonial: *Ché Bandoneón*, on El Conde between Las Damas y Parque Colón. Argentine-owned, outdoor terrace, Argentine, criollo and French food, tangos, T6870023. *Retazos*, Calle Padre Billini at corner of Duarte, T6886196, specializing in Domini-can dishes, eg seafood such as crab stew or fish cooked in coconut milk, dinner for 2 about US$50. **West of the Zona Colonial:** *Mesón de la Cava*, Parque Mirador del Sur, in a natural cave. Good steaks, live music, dancing, great experience, very popular so reserve in advance, T5332818, F5338150, open daily 1200-1500, 1800-0100. *Asadero los Argentinos*, Av Independencia between Av Abraham Lincoln and Máximo Gómez. Excellent Argentine food. *Cappuccino*, Av Máximo Gómez 60, T6898600. Italian-owned restaurant and café, great Ital-ian food, suave, prices to match, Italian murals. *Les Fondues*, Av Winston Churchill, esq Paseo de los Locutores, T5620067. All types of fondue including chocolate, run by Swiss. *Río Miño*, Jardines del Embajador, Av Sarasota, Centro Comercial Embajador, T5345873. Creative con-temporary cuisine and good Spanish food, particularly the fish.

US$10-15 Zona Colonial: *Fonda La Atarazana*, La Atarazana 5, T6876287. Popular for créole and international cuisine, good seafood. **West of the Zona Colonial:** *Titanic*, in Parque Mirador del Sur, Chinese and international. *Sully*, Av Charles Summer 19 y Calle Caoba, T5623389. Excellent, lots of seafood in Dominican, French and Italian styles, full din-ner for 2 about US$50, closed Mon. *Restaurant Cantábrico*, Av Independencia 54, T6875101. Recommended fresh seafood, Spanish and criollo. *El Mesón de Castilla*, Dr Báez 8 esq Luisa O Pellerano, T6850453. Tapas and Spanish cuisine. *Sheherezade*, Roberto Pastoriza 226, T2272323. Arabian and Mediterranean food. *Café Berimbau*, Abraham Lincoln, esq Gustavo Mejía Ricart. Brazilian food. *Samurai*, Av Lincoln 902, T4723442. Very good Japanese, try the Sun brunch. *Chino de Mariscos*, Av Sarasota 38, T5335249, 5328350. Very good Chinese sea-food. *Aubergine*, Av Alma Mater y Av México. German food. *La Esquina de Tejas*, Av 27 de Febrero 343, T5606075. Spanish cuisine. *Boga Boga*, Plaza Florida, Av Bolívar 203, T5414150. Spanish, good jamón serrano and chorizo, US$15-20 for a meal. *Mario's*, Av 27 de Febrero 299, T5624441. Very popular, smart and formal, good Chinese food and also international dishes. *Seasons*, Roberto Pastoriza 14, T5652616. Spanish, hot and cold tapas. *Panchos Villa*, Abraham Lincoln 403, T5359429. Mexican, informal atmosphere, young crowd.

The Asociación Nacional de Hoteles y Restaurantes, Asonahores, T6874676, publishes a guide to the best restaurants in the capital, 'Guía de Restaurantes'

US$10 and under Zona Colonial: *Plaza Toledo*, Isabel la Católica 163, Plaza María de Toledo, T6887649, F2214167, solar.sa@codetel.net.do Combination café and art gallery owned by American Bettye Marshall, also guest house, see above, 3-course dinner for US$10. *Bariloche*, El Conde 203. Self-service food from about 1145, look at what is on offer then buy ticket at cash register, lasagne only US$1, *menú del día* US$3, huge portions. **West of the Zona Colonial:** *Lumi's Park*, Av Abraham Lincoln 809, T5404584. The place to be, outdoor seating under canvas, 'steak park', *churrasco*, excellent *mofongos*, full dinner for 2 with rum or beer US$30, open until dawn, also takeaway or local delivery. *Fogaraté*, Av George Washing-ton 517, T6860044. Typical Dominican specialities, excellent, buffet or à la carte. Recom-mended by Dominicans. *El Conuco*, Casimiro de Moya 152 y José Joaquín Pérez, road

There are numerous pizzerias, burger bars and American fast food chains. Cafeterias around the Mercado Modelo serve local lunches

Dominican Republic

running off behind Jaragua, T2213231. *Comida criolla, sancocho, chivo guisado, la bandera dominicana* and other typical dishes, home cooking, large portions, decorated like a thatched barn in the country, music in the evening. *Maniquí* Pedro Henríquez Ureña in the Plaza de la Cultura, T6882854. Busy at lunch time, try the crab in coconut, some vegetarian dishes such as vegetable lasagne. Good for the local dish *mofongo*, *Palacio del Mofongo*, Av George Washington 509, T6888121, or *Casa del Mofongo*, 27 de Febrero y Calle 7 Eva Mo, T5651778 (a long way from the centre). *Mandarín*, next to Palacio del Mofongo. Excellent Cantonese and Chinese food. *Spagghettíssimo*, Paseo de los Locutores 13, entre A Lincoln y W Churchill, T5653708. Italian, fish, seafood, meat, pasta, open air jazz on Wed, also home delivery.

Vegetarian   Two good vegetarian restaurants are *Ananda*, Casimiro de Moya 7, T6824465, and *Vegetariano*, Calle Luperón 9 (open 0800-1500). Also *Ojas*, Calle Jonas Salk 2, T6823940 and *El Terrenal*, Malecón y Estrelleta, T6893161, some vegetarian dishes.

Cafés   **Zona Colonial**   *La Cafetería Colonial*, El Conde 253. Good for coffee after meal at *Bariloche*, freshly ground. *The Village Pub*, in Calle Hostos 350, opposite the ruins of Hospital San Nicolás de Bari. A good place for snacks and drinks in a pub-type atmosphere; so is *La Taberna* (classical music) at Padre Billini with Las Damas. *Bachata Rosa*, La Atarazana 9, Plaza de España, T6160588, g.nader@codetel.net.do named after the popular album of Juan Luis Guerra, 2 huge screens with music videos. **West of the Zona Colonial** *France-Croissant*, Av Sarasota 82 y Dr Defilló, French bakery, tastiest pastries in the country, unsweetened wholemeal bread available, small café. **East of the Zona Colonial** *Café del Río*, Plaza la Marina, overlooking the Ozama River. Good place for a cold beer, near the Sugar Cane Monument on eastern side of river. Try a chimichurri (spiced sausage), throughout the city stalls sell sandwiches, chimichurris, hot dogs and hamburgers. Several small restaurants specialize in roast chicken, *pollo al carbón*, with a tasty wasa kaca sauce. The best of these is *Pollo Caribe* on Av Winston Churchill, just below Av Sarasota.

Discos & nightclubs
It is not a good idea to walk around town after about 2300, take a taxi, street lighting is not always good

The top hotels have the top dance floors, with admission prices of US$2-10, depending on whether there is a live band that night or recorded music. Things get going after midnight and they close around 0400. Dominicans dress up smartly to go dancing, so no jeans, T-shirts or trainers. Taxi drivers know all the best places. In the area west of the Colonial Zone along the **Malecón** where all the international hotels are you will find: *Salón La Fiesta* in the *Jaragua Hotel*, also *Jubilee*, T6888026, Dominican music. *Remington Palace*, Av Independencia, near the Malecón, live artists, upmarket ambience. *Maunaloa Night Club* in the Centro de los Héroes also has live music and comedians, dancing every night to Dominican music. *Club 60*, Máximo Gómez 60. Rock, merengue and ballads. *Neon* in *Hotel Hispaniola*. Upmarket, occasionally has live Latin jazz. Hotels *El Embajador, Meliá Santo Domingo, Jaragua* have orchestras every night playing Dominican music, free. Live music in many of these hotels coincides with happy hour, which is a pleasant way to get the evening's entertainment started. To hear *pericos ripiaos*, go on Fri or Sat night to the *colmados* near the Malecón in Ciudad Nueva; the groups move from place to place.

Further west *Guácara Taína*, Paseo de los Indios, Avenida Cayetano Germosén, T5330671, has shows of Taíno dancing in a deep natural cave with stalactites and indigenous pictographs, spectacular setting, huge, can fit over 2,000 guests, from 1700-0200, US$4-12 (also disco, all types of music, a/c, 2 dance floors, happy hours and fashion shows). For daytime tours of the cave T5302662 (0900-1700), or T5331051 (1700-2100), F5304632, reserve 24 hrs in advance. *Schizo Discotheque*, Plaza Andalucía, 3rd Floor, Gustavo Mejía Ricart, T6833982. *Trío Café*, Plaza Cataluña, Av Lope de Vega. *Il Grappolo Café*, Plaza Cataluña, Av Lope de Vega. *Beer House*, Gustavo Mejía Ricart esq Winston Churchill. *Tierra Luna Café*, Av Winston Churchill.

In the Zona Colonial *Sentimiento*, Hostos 99. Down market with lots of merengue.

In Villa Consuelo *El Rincón Habanero*, Sánchez Valverde y Baltazar de los Reyes. Working class enthusiasts of Cuban son dance between tables to old records of the 1940s and 1950s. *Secreto Musical Bar*, 1 block away, Baltazar de los Reyes and Pimentel, similar, headquarters of Club Nacional de los Soneros, rock, merengue, salsa and ballads.

There are two **gay** discos, *Disco Free*, Ortega y Gasset esq San Martín, mostly transvestite shows, open Thu-Sun, and *Penthouse*, Seibo y Marcos Ruíz, closed Tue, different shows every night with male strippers, transvestites, drag queens, etc. *Café Atlántico*, José A Aybar y A Lincoln, closed Sun, club for gays and straights, on several floors with several bars, large TV screens showing major sports events, popular with the young and affluent, has style. Sex tourism is rife in Santo Domingo and you will be taking a risk if you participate. Remember the age of consent is 18 and many foreigners end up being blackmailed for having sex with a minor. Pickpocketing is common. In any bar or disco, unattached men will be approached by girls (*chicas*), while unattached women are considered fair game. Girls in brothels are checked for sexually transmitted diseases, but those on the street are not.

Casinos Hotels *Dominican Fiesta*, *Santo Domingo*, *San Gerónimo*, *Meliá Santo Domingo*, *El Embajador* (recently remodelled, Las Vegas style), *Naco*, *Jaragua*, *Hispaniola*, remodelled in 2000, *Lina* and *Maunaloa Night Club*, Centro de los Héroes.

Theatres *Teatro Nacional*, Plaza de la Cultura, Av Máximo Gómez, T6879131, for tickets. *Palacio de Bellas Artes*, Av Independencia and Máximo Gómez, T6872494. *Casa de Teatro*, small drama workshop, Arzobispo Meriño 14, 16893430. **Cinemas** In the new Diamond Plaza mall, Av de Los Próceres, there are several cinema screens, also a cinema in the Plaza Central mall with food court. **Art galleries** There are many shops in the Zona Colonial selling Haitan and Dominican naïve art of dubious worth. The best gallery is the *Galería de Arte Nader*, Calle Rafael Augusto Sánchez 22, Torre Don Roberto, Ens Piantini T5440878, F5656204, www.naders.com The Nader family are hugely influential and stock collecters' items of Haitan, Dominican and other Latin American works of art, see also Sleeping above and Haiti chapter. *Ramírez Conde Centro de Arte y Antiguedades*, Av Roberto Pastoriza No. 704, Evaristo Morales, T5675613, F6836055, promovideo@codetel.net.do Works of art from the most famous Dominican painters.

Entertainment *(marginal heading)*

Mercado Modelo, Av Mella esquina Santomé, open Mon-Sat 0900-1230, 1430-1700, gift shops, handicrafts, paintings, foodstuffs, syncretic religious items; bargain to get a good price, most prices have been marked up to allow for this. Guides appointed to assist tourists get a 5-10% commission from the vendor. There are also 'speciality shops' at Plaza Criolla, 27 de Febrero y Máximo Gómez. Prices will be higher than in the Mercado Modelo, but you can bargain, or ask for discounts, if you are buying a large amount. The shop at the Museo del Hombre Dominicano sells ceramics, Taíno reproductions and works of anthropological interest. Calle El Conde, now reserved to pedestrians, is the oldest shopping sector in Santo Domingo; Av Mella at Duarte is a good spot for discount shopping and local colour. A flea market, *Mercado de las Pulgas*, operates on Sun in the Centro de los Héroes and at the Mercado de Oportunidades, 27 de Febrero. Cigars, including the premium Don Guillermo cigars, can be bought at *La Casa del Fumador*, near the Parque Colón, Fco Prats Ramírez 159, T5413390, F5414896, open Mon-Sat 1030-1400, 1500-2000, *Santo Domingo Cigar Club*, in the Hotel Jaragua and in the restaurant *Ambrosía*.

Shopping *(marginal heading)* Duty-free at Centro de los Héroes, La Atarazana, shops in large hotels; departure lounge at airport; all purchases must be in US dollars

Bookshops *Tienda Macalé*, Calle Arzobispo Nouel 3, T6822011, near cathedral. Open daily including Sun, has a wide selection of books, especially on the Republic's history. *The Book Shop*, Plaza Cataluña Gustavo Mejía Ricart 114, casi esq W Churchill, T4122777. *Centro Cuesta del Libro*, 27 de Febrero esq Lincoln. *Thesaurus*, Av Abraham Lincoln esquina Sarasota, sofas, reading areas, café, play area, cultural events with Dominican authors, some English language books, lots of educational books upstairs, wide choice and large by Dominican standards.

Music *Music Box*, Plaza Central. *Thiagos*, Calle El Conde. *Musicalia*, El Conde, T2218445, Tiradentes esquina Gustavo Mejía Ricart, T5622878. *Sonidium*, Proyecto José Contreras, Edificio 1, Local 110, Manzana 11, Av Independencia Km 10.5, T3284124. *CD Stop*, Plaza Central, T5495640. *Karen Records*, El Conde 251, T6860019.

Jewellery As well as the shops in the two Amber Museums (see above) there is *Ambar Nacional*, Calle Restauración 110, T6865700, which sells amber, coral and larimar, a sea-blue stone, at lower prices than the museums.

(marginal text, vertical) Dominican Republic

Tour operators A tour service covers the major sites of the city, in *merenguaguas parranderas*, buses without seats with names like La Gallera, La Monumental, La Criolla, La Bachatera, T5327154. There are several tours of the city, taking in the duty-free shops, nightlife, etc. Recommended travel agents in Santo Domingo for sightseeing tours include: *Metro Tours*, Av W Churchill, T5444580. *Domitur*, Av N de Cáceres 374, T5307313. *Prieto Tours*, Av Francia 125, T6850102. *Coco Tours*, T5861311, F5861237, www.cocotours.com *Turinter*, T6864020, F6883890, www.turinter.com

Transport **Air** From North America: Boston (*American Airlines*, *TWA* and *US Air*), Miami (*American Airlines*, *TWA* and *Aeromar*), New York (*Continental*, *TWA* and *American Airlines*), Philadelphia (*US Air*), other US cities, connections in Miami or San Juan, Puerto Rico. **From Europe**: Amsterdam (*Martinair*), Madrid (*Iberia* with connecting flights from most European and Spanish cities, *Air Europa*), Milan and Rome (*Lauda Air*), Paris (*Air France*),Dusseldorf, Frankfurt, Munich and Cologne/Bonn (*Condor*). **From the Caribbean**: Aruba (*American Eagle*, *Aeropostal* and *ALM*), Curaçao (*American Eagle*, *ALM* and *Aeropostal*),Havana (*Cubana*), Mayagüez, Puerto Rico (*American Eagle*), Providenciales, TCI (*TCI Sky King*), St Maarten and St Thomas (*American Eagle*) San Juan (*American Eagle*, *TWA*, *Iberia* and *Air Santo Domingo*), Santiago de Cuba (*Aerocaribbean*). **From Central America**: *Copa* from Panama City, San José, Guatemala City, Managua. **From South America**: from Caracas, *Aserca* and *Aeropostal*; other capital cities are connected through Miami or Panama City.

Airport **Aeropuerto La Américas**, 23 km out of town, T5490450/80, very clean and smart. Immediately on arrival there is a tourist office on your right (helpful, will make bus reservation if you want to go straight out of Santo Domingo), and just past that an office selling tourist cards, a blackboard indicates who needs a card. Check if you need a card, or else the long queue to get through immigration will be wasted. There is a cambio next to the booth where you buy your tourist card and a bank in the customs hall for exchanging dollars; it is open Sun and at night (good rates). Pesos can be changed back into dollars, at the bank in the departure hall, but only up to 30% of what you purchased on arrival, receipt required. Car hire is to the right as you come out of the customs hall. Remember you will need a 5-peso coin for the toll if you drive in to Santo Domingo. On departure, the queue for check-in can be long and slow for large aircraft (eg Iberia to Madrid), allow plenty of time. In the departure area are lots of duty-free shops, cafés, and limited seating. Upstairs there are good facilities with a burger restaurant which has plenty of seating and a good view of the airport.

Leaving the airport on the ground floor, the same floor as immigration and customs, you find the expensive, individual taxis. (Upstairs, outside the 2nd floor, *colectivo* taxis cram up to 6 passengers into the vehicle; much cheaper.) The drive from Las Américas International airport to Santo Domingo should take no more than 30 mins, but allow an hour, and cost no more than US$15 during the daytime although it varies between companies and US$20 is usual. From the capital to the airport for the return journey prices range from US$10 (*Alex Taxi*) to US$15 (*Apolo Taxi*). Most large hotels have a taxi or limousine service with set fares throughout the city and to the airport. Alternatively you can get from the airport to the colonial city for about US$1 if you walk, or take a motoconcho (motorcycle taxi), to the autopista (main road) and then catch a guagua (minibus) to Parque Enriquillo. On our return, catch any bus to Boca Chica or towns east and get a motoconcho from the junction. This is only really feasible if you are travelling light. If arriving late at night it may be better to go to Boca Chica (see page 459), about 10 km from the airport, taxi about US$15. Various tour agencies also run minibuses to the airport; check with your hotel.

Local Bus: *OMSA* buses run along the main corridors (corredores), Avs 27 de Febrero, Luperón, Bolívar, Independencia, John F Kennedy, Máximo Gómez and the west of the city, RD$3. **Car hire**: many places at the airport, on the road to the airport and on Malecón. There are more agencies, here are a selection: *MC Auto Rent-A-Car* (Av George Washington No 105, T6886518, F6864529, www.mccarrental.com), branches also at Las Américas Airport (T5490373) and Boca Chica (T5234414); *Nelly* (José Contreras 139, T5358800, from US$45 a day); *Dollar* (JF Kennedy y Lincoln, T5416801, from US$47 a day); *D-Rent* (T5451366),

German-run, cheap, good insurance; *Patsy*, cheap, daily rates from US$27 (T5498101). **Taxi**: *Carros públicos*, or *conchos*, are shared taxis normally operating on fixed routes, 24 hrs a day, basic fare RD$3. *Públicos* can be hired by one person, if they are empty, and are then called *carreras*. They can be expensive (US$3-4, more on longer routes); settle price before getting in. Fares are higher at Christmas time. *Públicos/conchos* also run on long-distance routes; ask around to find the cheapest. You can get to just about anywhere by bus or *público* from Parque Independencia, but you have to ask where to stand. *Conchos* running on a shared basis are becoming scarcer, being replaced by *carreras*. Radio taxis charge between US$3-5 on local journeys around Santo Domingo (US$10 per hour) and are safer than street taxis, call about 20-30 mins in advance: *Taxi Anacaona*, T5304800; *Apolo Taxi*, T5377771; *Taxi Express*, T5377777; *Taxi Oriental*, T5495555; *Alex Taxi*, T5403311; *Taxi Hogar*, T5682825; *Tecni Taxi*, T5672010; *Pronto Taxi*, T5414111. There are motorcyclists who offer a taxi service, known as *motoconchos*, RD$10, they sometimes take up to three passengers on pillion; they raise the noise level (in most towns) very considerably.

Long distance buses For bus information see Essentials page 407.

Airline offices In Santo Domingo: *Air Canada*, *ACES*, *Aeroméxico*, *Britannia*, *Lufthansa*, *LTU* and *Finnair* all at Gustavo Mejía Ricart 54, T5415151; *Air Europa*, 27 de Febrero; *TWA*, T6899151; *Aeromar*, T5334447; *Air France*, Avenida George Washington 101, T6868419; *ALM*, L Navarro 28, T6874567; *American Airlines*, Edif IN TEMPO, W Churchill, T5425151; *American Eagle*, Juan S Ramírez esq Mahatma Gandhi, T6820077; *Carnival Air*, T5635300; *Continental*, Av Winston Churchill, T5626688; *Copa*, Av 27 de Febrero, T4722223; *Lacsa*, T5667088; *Iberia*, Av Lope de Vega, T5080288; *Martinair*, M Gómez y Juan S Ramírez, T6886661; *Cubana*, Av Tiradentes, T2272040; at 27 de Febrero esq Tiradentes are *Varig*, T5659151; at George Washington 353 are *Hapag Lloyd*, T6828133 and *Condor*, T6828133. *Air Santo Domingo* information and reservations, T6838020, at Herrera airport T6836691, at Las Américas T5491110, at Punta Cana T2211170, at Puerto Plata T5860385.

Banks Many along Isabel La Católica, but check which banks accept which TCs, see page 401. *Casa de Cambio*, Quisqueya, Sánchez 205, off El Conde, gives a slightly better rate than banks.

Communications Internet Reserve in advance to use the internet service at the *Codetel* offices in Unicentro Plaza, T2204721, Cacique, T2207411 and Oficina Torre Cristal, T2205312. *Ciber Café*, La Lira 11, Av Roberto Pastoriza, near Abraham Lincoln, young crowd, friendly. *Dalitel*, Winston Churchill. **Post Office:** *Correo Central* is in La Feria, Calle Rafael Damirón, Centro de los Héroes, T5346218, F5346318. Open 0730-1700, Mon-Fri; 0730-1200, Sat. *Lista de correo* (poste restante) keeps mail for 2 months. There are post offices in *Hotel Embajador*, T2212131, AILA, T5420177, Ciudad Nueva, T6856970, and Sans Souci, T5931306. To ensure the delivery of documents worldwide, use a courier service: *American Airlines* (T5425151). *DHL Dominicana*, T5417988, *Servicio de Documentos y pequeños paquetes*, T5412119; *Emery Worldwide*, T6881855; *Federal Express*, T5679547; *Internacional Bonded Couriers*, T5425265. **Telephone:** international and long distance, also fax: *Codetel*, Av 30 de Marzo 12, near Parque Independencia, and 11 others throughout the city (open 0800-2200). **Internet** access also available but not always working, US$2 per hour, fax to Europe US$2 per page. Cheaper for phone calls is the *Tricom* office on Av Máximo Gómez between Bolívar and Independencia.

Embassies & consulates *Argentina*, Máximo Gómez 10, T6822977, F2212206; *Austria*, Las Amapolas 9, T7016637; *Belgium*, Abraham Lincoln 504, T5621661, F5623383; *Belize*, JF Kennedy, T5675023; *Bolivia*, Federico Geraldino 58, T5658573, F5659839; *Brazil*, Winston Churchill 32, T5320868, F5320917, brazil@mail.codetel.net.do; *Canada*, Máximo Gómez 30, T6851136, F6822691, canada@codetel.net.do; *Chile*, Anacaona 11, Mirador Sur, T5327800; *Colombia*, Abraham Lincoln y José A Soler, T5621670; *Costa Rica*, Malaquías Gil 11, Serrallés, T5656419, F5656467; *Denmark*, Abraham Lincoln 504, T5495100, F5623383; *Ecuador*, Rafael Augusto Sánchez 17, T5638363; *El Salvador*, José Brea Peña 12, T5654311; *Finland*, MH Ureña 77, T5494220; *France*, George Washington 353, T6892161; *Germany*, R Aug Sánchez, T5658811, F5675014; *Guatemala*, Santiago 359, Gazcue, T/F6895146; *Guyana*, JF Kennedy, T5673843; *Haiti*, Juan Sánchez Ramírez 33, T6865778, F6866096, Amb.haiti@codetel.net.do; *Honduras*, Salvador Sturla 12, T5655112; *Israel*, P Henríquez Ureña 80, T5421635; *Italy*, Manuel Rodríguez Objío 4, T6893684; *Jamaica*, Marginal 5, Aut 30 de Mayo, T5321079; *Japan*, Winston Churchill, Torre BHD, piso 8, T5673365; *Mexico*, Arzobispo Meriño 265 y Mercedes, T6876444, F6877872, mbamex@codetel.net.do; *Netherlands*, Mayor Enrique Valverde,

Directory

Dominican Republic

T5655240; *Panama*, Benito Monción 255, T6883789, F6853665; *Peru*, Pedro A Bobea y Anacaona, Edificio Curvo, Bella Vista, T5655851; *Philippines*, Independencia 201, T6896120; *Spain*, Independencia 1205, T5351615, F5351595; *Sweden*, Máximo Gómez 31, T6852131; *Switzerland*, Recodo 2, Edificio Monte Mirador, Bella Vista, T5333781, F5323781; *UK*, 27 de Febrero 233, Edificio Corominas Pepín, 7th floor, T4727111, F4727574; *Uruguay*, Calle Baltazar Brum 7, T6825565; *USA César Nicolás Penson, (embassy) T2212171, (consulate) 5412111, F6867437; Venezuela, Anacaona 7, Mirador Sur, T5378882, F5378780.*

Medical services *Clínica Abréu*, Av Independencia y Beller, and adjacent *Clínica Gómez Patiño* are recommended for foreigners needing treatment or hospitalization. Fees are high but care is good. 24-hr emergency department. For free consultation and prescription, *Padre Billini Hospital*, Calle Padre Billini y Santomé, Zona Colonial, efficient, friendly. **Pharmacies:** *Farmacia San Judas Tadeo*, Independencia 57 y Bernardo Pichardo, T6858165, open 24 hrs all year, home delivery, cosmetics, magazines, cafetería outside. Other 24-hr pharmacies are *Los Hidalgos*, 27 de Febrero 241, T5637103; *Farmacia Livia*, Arturo Logroño esq Ortega y Gasset, T5664811, *Farmacia Sara*, Av Duarte 305, T5366363, and *Dr Camilo* on Francisco Prats Ramírez. **Dentists:** Maritza Ortega and Fe María Ortega, 24-hr emergency service, T6884192/5323542.

North to Santiago

The Autopista Duarte, a four-lane highway, runs northwest from Santo Domingo, all the way to Santiago de los Caballeros, with the Cordillera Central on one side and the Cordillera Septentrional on the other. From there it reduces in size, becoming the Carretera Duarte, and follows the length of the Cibao Valley, running just north of the Río Yaque del Norte to its outlet on the coast at Monte Cristi. This is the main artery through the country, used by cars, trucks, *motoconchos*, cows, horse-drawn vehicles and others. The first town of any size just west of the *Autopista Duarte* is Bonao, 85 km from the centre of Santo Domingo and surrounded by rice paddies. To the east is the Falconbridge ferronickel mine, a large employer and major contributor to the region's economy. After Bonao on the Autopista Duarte, on the left, is the main road to Constanza.

Constanza

Population: 50,000, Altitude: 1,300 m

High up in the mountains, set in a circular valley formed by a meteor, is Constanza. Dubbed the Alps of Dominican Republic, the mountains provide a spectacular backdrop for what is a fairly ordinary town with no historical, religious or municipal buildings of note. The scenery is some of the best in the country, with rivers, forests and waterfalls and there are lots of good hikes in the area. In winter, temperatures can fall to zero or lower and there may be frosts at night, but during the day it is pleasant and fresh. In the 1950s, the dictator, Gen Trujillo brought in 200 Japanese families to farm the land and the valley is famous for food production, potatoes, garlic, strawberries, mushrooms and other vegetables, and for growing ornamental flowers. The main street is Calle Luperón, which runs east to west. Most of the cheap hotels and restaurants are here or nearby. La Isla gas station is at the east end, where taxis and *motoconchos* congregate. The Garlic Festival is held in the middle of June, with lots of dancing.

With a good, tough, four-wheel drive you can visit the **Parque Nacional Valle Nuevo**, through which passes the very poor but spectacular road from Constanza to San José de Ocoa, see below. Wonderful views and you pass the geographical centre of the island, marked by four small pyramids at the Alta Bandera military post about 30 km south of Constanza. There are also thermal springs, three Amerindian cemeteries and the Agua Blanca waterfall about 10 km south of the Colonia Japonesa, so you can walk it if you want. The waterfall is 150 m high, falling in three stages to a large pool at the bottom. The park's alpine plateau is at an altitude of about 2,640 m and has a large number of plants which are unique to the island in pine and broadleaf forests. It is also good birdwatching country.

B-C *Cabañas de la Montaña*, east of town towards Colonia Kennedy, T6822410 in Santo
Domingo, T3705626 in Constanza. Modern, rustic villas with kitchens, good for families,
lovely setting, tours arranged to waterfalls and hikes up into the mountains behind the hotel.
D-F *AltoCerro*, next door, T6960222, F5306193. Fairly new and also highly thought of, camping, hotel rooms and villas, excursions on horse back, bike rental, weekend barbecues. In
town there are several basic and not particularly comfortable hotels, check whether they
have hot water. **F** *Mi Casa*, Luperón y Sánchez, T5392472. Clean, bath, hot water, restaurant.

La Montaña, Ureña 40, Parque Anacaona. Open from breakfast to dinner, good food. **Eating**
Lorenzo's, Luperón 83. Excellent Dominican food, try the guinea fowl or rabbit cooked in *All the food here is*
wine, also sandwiches and pasta, noisy music or TV. *Cafetería El Rey*, on Parque Central. *wonderfully fresh,*
Good food, long menu, from pizzas to rabbit stew. *with local ingredients*

Road There are direct buses from Santo Domingo, Santiago, La Vega and Bonao, return **Transport**
from Constanza at 0600 or earlier (buses will often pick you up at your hotel if you inform
them in advance). The last direct bus back to Santo Domingo leaves at 1200. *Expreso*
Dominicano, Av Independencia, 100 m west of Parque Independencia, Santo Domingo, to
La Vega every hour 0700-1800, get off at junction for Constanza. You can get to/from the
Autopista Duarte by taking a *público* or *guagua* (US$1.50) to/from Constanza. Constanza can
also be reached from the south coast via San José de Ocoa (northwest of Baní, northeast of
Azua, **F** *Hotel Marien*, on the main square, without bath, clean, good value). If you are planning to drive this road yourself you must be in a very sturdy four-wheel drive vehicle, with
two spare tyres, food, drink and warm clothing in case you break down. Much of the road has
been washed away by Hurricane Georges and other storms, leaving huge holes and cracks. It
is popular with mountain bikers but not drivers. A four-wheel drive leaves Constanza (by the
crossroads at entrance to town) Mon, Wed, Sat 1200, US$4, 5 hrs. You can sit on the roof, but
beware weather changes. The front seat gets exhaust fumes.

Banks There is an ATM (Plus, Visa). **Tour guide** A recommended guide is Johny Tactuck, 18 Matilde **Directory**
Viña, T5392900.

La Vega

Further north up the *Autopista Duarte* is La Vega, a quiet place in the beautiful valley *Population: 200,000*
of **La Vega Real**. After the declaration of independence on 27 February 1844, La
Vega was the first place to raise the national flag, on 4 March. It was also the first
town to embrace the Restoration Movement in 1863. The town is nothing special
and most people only come here to change *guaguas* or buses or to visit the local
archaeological sites (see below), which can be reached by hiring a taxi in the Parque
Central or at the bus stations.

La Vega's **carnival** is one of the most colourful pre-lenten festivities in the country, with elaborate masks (*caretas*) of devils (*diablos cojuelos*), made mostly of *papier
maché*. Activities are held on six Sundays in February-March, in the afternoons from
1500-1800. *Comparsas*, sponsored music groups, compete and there are competitions for the best costumes. Materials are brightly coloured and hundreds of little
bells are sown into the costume. Watch out for the local custom of hitting people
with *vejigas*, balls on ropes, traditionally made from cows' bladders. There are currently over 90 'groups' of between 5-40 members, and it is estimated that some 1,500
people dress up every Sunday. It is a huge, noisy, rowdy affair. A collection of masks
can be seen in the **Casa de la Cultura**, on Calle Independencia, which also puts on
temporary art exhibitions. ■ *Mon-Fri 0930-1200, 1400-1700, free.*

About 5 km north is the turn for **Santo Cerro**, an old convent where the image of
Virgen de las Mercedes is venerated and pilgrims come every 24 September to pray
to Nuestra Señora de las Mercedes. Legend has it that Columbus raised a cross on the
summit of the hill in 1494. Inside the brick church on the hill is a hole in which the
cross is supposed to have stood. If you continue along the road to the other side of

Dominican Republic

the hill and into the valley the ruins of **La Vega Vieja** (Old La Vega) can be seen. It was founded by Columbus in 1494 but destroyed by an earthquake on 2 December 1562. Bartolomé de las Casas said the first Mass here and the first baptisms of Taínos took place here, on 21 September 1496. The first protest against the treatment of Indians was also made here in 1510, by Fray Pedro de Córdoba. La Vega Vieja is now a National Park and the foundations of the fortress, church and a few houses can be seen. ■ *Mon-Sat 0900-1200, 1400-1700. US$2.*

Essentials There are some basic hotels, **F**, in town on Calle Cáceres, but they are not recommended, and slightly better accommodation, **E**, along the highway. There is a *Codetel* office and an ATM on the Parque Central. *Caribe Tours* (T5733488), *Metro* (T5737099) and *Vegano Express* (T5737079) are on Carretera La Vega, the road coming in to town from the *autopista*, but *guaguas* can be found on the corner of 27 de Febrero y Restauración.

Jarabacoa

Jarabacoa is the place to come for adventure sports

The road from the Autopista Duarte to Jarabacoa winds through some beautiful pine forests. The climate is fresh, with warm days and cool nights. It is an important agricultural area, growing coffee, flowers, strawberries, watercress and other crops. Tourism is very important here, with visitors drawn to the mountains, rivers and waterfalls. The town itself is quite modern. Everything is in walking distance and most things can be found along the main street, Calle Mario Nelson Galán. Several notable artists and sculptors (marble and wood) live in the area and are willing to receive visitors to their studios or give classes.

Rivers & waterfalls are spectacular features in this area

The three main rivers are the Río Jimenoa, the Río Baiguate and the Río Yaque del Sur. The Baiguate flows into the Jimenoa and the Jimenoa then flows into the Yaque. There are several other tributaries which are being explored for new white water rafting locations. The **Jimenoa waterfalls** are worth seeing, 10 km from town, although they are often crowded with tour parties. Hurricane Georges wreaked havoc in 1998, washing away the power plant and bridge by the falls. A new walkway has been made, with wobbly suspension bridges (avoid too many people on them at any one time). The falls are large, with a tremendous volume of water and consequent noise. The last wall is used for canyoning. Mini-rafting is on offer at weekends, US$2. Entry US$0.60, which goes towards the upkeep of walkways. There is another waterfall dropping 75 m over a cliff on the Río Jimenoa, which is more difficult to get to and unsigned, off the road to Constanza, so you will have to ask for directions locally or go with a group. Closer to town, off the Constanza road, are the **Baiguate falls,** 3½-4 km, an easy walk, there is a signpost to the falls, fourth turn on the right after *Pinar Dorado*. A path leads from the road around the hillside, hugging the side of the gorge, until you get to some steps down to a sandy river beach and the rocks beneath the falls. There are usually lots of tours to the falls by jeep or horse (sometimes you can ride a horse back if the previous rider has opted for the jeep return).

Sleeping **B-C** per person, FAP, *Rancho Baiguate*, T5744940, F5861170, www.ranchobaiguate.com owned and managed by Omar and Estela Rodríguez. Lovely countryside setting beside river, extensive gardens, 27 rooms from standard to luxury, or small, medium and large, hot water, good bathrooms. Also 2 dormitories with 9 bunk beds in each with showers, toilets, lockers and shelves for students/groups (the hotel started out as a summer camp). Bracing unheated pool, soccer and basketball court, horse riding, helpful staff and management, friendly, English spoken, good place for buffet lunch, lots of tour parties come for the day. Free transport into town until 2200, if there are not many guests you eat supper at the *Rancho Restaurant*. Now under same ownership is **B-C** *Pinar Dorado*, T5742820, F6877012, on road towards Constanza before turnoff to *Rancho Baiguate*. About 20 mins' walk from centre, 43 rooms, remodelled for conferences and executive retreats for the US and local market. **F** *California*, on road to Constanza, Calle José Durán E 99, T5746255, F5744303, i.lupo@codetel.net.do Owned by Dutchman Jan Sheffers and his Dominican wife, new and growing slowly, 9 simple rooms, bathroom, hot water, fan, breakfast, bar, small pool, popular, friendly, best in season when the owners are there, standards go down in their absence. **D** *Brisas del Yaque*, Luperón esq Peregrina Herrera, T5744490. New, small rooms but good bathrooms, small balcony, TV, a/c, brick and wood décor, tiled floors. **F** *Hogar*, Mella 34, T5742739. Central, 5 mins' walk from *Caribe Tours* terminal, 8 rooms, twin beds, cold water, clean, huge old trees in patio.

Rancho Restaurant, opposite Esso station. Criollo and international, good food using locally **Eating** grown ingredients, belongs to *Rancho Baiguate*. The walls are lined with the work of several local artists (who often dine there with the owners) and a small gallery is planned off the dining area. *El Trebol*, small outdoor bar/restaurant under leafy canopy, sandwiches, hamburgers, tacos, *plato del día* US$2.50, specials on Sun US$3, vegetarian options. Several other *comedores* and *cafeterías*, including *D'lo Ultimos*, in town centre, best *batidas* (milk shakes) and *pastelitos* (stuffed pastries). *Salto Restaurant*, on road to Salto Jimenoa, T2239759, F5744940, vmg@codetel.net.do Pleasant setting by stream, pool, sauna, bar and excellent food, specialize in goat, guinea fowl, pigeon, duck, US$6-9, or for a snack ask for a plate of mixed *longaniza, carne salteada* and *tostones,* great with a cold beer. Buy strawberries beside the road, locally grown, but restaurants hardly ever have them.

There is a carnival in Feb, similar to that in La Vega, but on a smaller scale, rather chaotic with **Festivals** lots of music and rum all month.

White water rafting, canyoning, tubing, kayaking, rock climbing, horse riding, mountain bik- **Sport** ing, quad bikes, jeep safaris, paragliding and hiking are all on offer here. It is one of the starting points for climbing Pico Duarte. *Rancho Baiguate's* **Aventura Máxima** is the biggest adventure sports centre and has a small army of Dominican and international specialist guides and instructors for each activity. They have also taken over *Get Wet*, still run as a separate operation, which offers river activities. A third company, *Aventuras del Caribe*, T/F5742669, franz.lang@codetel.net.do is run by Franz Lang, an Austrian. He deals with small groups, is recommended for canyoning and kayaking and is very safety conscious.

Road *Conchos* in town US$0.60. *Motoconcho* to *Rancho Baiguate* US$1.20. To Santo **Transport** Domingo, *Caribe Tours*, T5744557, from its own terminal off the main street, 0700, 1000, *No transport* 1330, 1630, arrive 30 mins in advance (even earlier for the 0730 Mon bus), tickets sold only on *anywhere after 1800,* day of departure, US$4.66, 2½ hrs. To La Vega by *guagua*, US$1.20; if you want to go to the *very little after 1500* capital or Santiago, they will let you off at the right place to pick up the next *guagua*. To Constanza, you can get a 2-cabin pick-up truck via a very poor road over the mountains, but most people go back down to La Vega and up the Constanza road 10 km before Bonao. All transport can be found opposite the gas station.

Banks *Banco de Progreso* and tourist office by the Palacio Municipal near the bus stop. No ATMs in **Directory** town. 5 banks on Mario Galán. **Communications** *Codetel* about ½ km on the road to La Vega beyond the gas station. In town, *Tricom* is at Sánchez y Libertad. *Televimenca* and *Western Union* are at Herrera y Independencia, Mon-Sat, 0900-1200, 1400-1700. The *Centro de Copiado y Papelería*, a stationery shop on Calle Duarte 53, T5742902, has 6 computers for internet access, US$2.30 per hour, open 0800-1300, 1400-1900. **Medical services** *Clínica César Terrero*, at the junction, T5744397. *Farmacia San Miguel*, 16 de Agosto y Libertad, T5746536, Mon-Sat 0900-1200, 1400-1700. **Useful services** Market on M Galán. Police station at the road junction by the gas station where all the public transport congregates, T5742540.

Pico Duarte

In the Cordillera Central near Jarabacoa and Constanza is Pico Duarte, at 3,087 m *The driest time is* the highest peak in the Caribbean, but only just. Its neighbour, La Pelona, is only 5 m *Dec-Feb, but* lower at 3,082 m. During the Trujillo dictatorship, when Pico Duarte was inevitably *Mar-Nov is still good* named Pico Trujillo, one of his geographers erroneously added to the height of the mountain, allegedly to impress his *jefe* (boss). To this day, most maps have Pico Duarte at 3,175 m. There are several popular hiking routes, requiring differing degrees of stamina. Some of the routes take in other mountains as well. You will see a wide selection of native flora and birds, rainforest and pine forest, and several different eco-systems. It is very beautiful landscape and a great experience. If you are not shrouded in cloud there is a fantastic view looking down on clouds and other mountain peaks. The most popular routes are the 46 km trail from La Ciénaga near Jarabacoa, and the 90-km trail from Mata Grande near San José de las Matas. Whichever route you take you will have to pay a RD$50 national park fee (passport or copy required) and hire a guide. They speak only Spanish and you must pay them as well as feed them and tip them. You are not allowed to set off on your own. There are also other walks in the **Parque Nacional Armando Bermúdez** and the adjoining **Parque Nacional José del Carmen Ramírez**, but they all involve some steep climbing. Guides are available at the park entrance for any walks, not just to climb Pico Duarte.

La Ciénaga route At La Ciénaga the DNP has set up a nice little camp ground. You can sleep here and there is a tap in the yard for washing but facilities are very basic. Mules are definitely recommended for the average hiker, but it can be done without them if you are prepared to carry all your gear and water. The hike is moderate, for intermediate to advanced hikers, but very hard indeed for those who are not in regular training for hill climbing. Allow three days and two nights (or more if it rains, the paths turn to mud). ■ *Guagua from Jarabacoa to La Ciénaga or hitch (very little traffic). On your return, the last carro for Jarabacoa leaves at 1600.* Iguana Mama, *in Cabarete (see page 404) and* Rancho Baiguate *in Jarabacoa (see page 434) both offer tours of 3-9 days, or a custom-designed trek is possible if they have nothing else arranged. Walking sticks/hiking poles are highly recommended, particularly for the journey down, which can be hard on the knees and dangerous if wet and muddy. Take adequate clothing with you; it can be cold (below 0°C) and wet (it usually rains in the rainforest); also take a torch and matches.*

Santiago de Los Caballeros

Population: 690,000 Santiago de Los Caballeros is the second largest city in the Republic and chief town of the Cibao valley. The streets of the centre are busy, noisy, with lots of advertising signs; east of the centre it becomes greener, cleaner and quieter. The Río Yaque del Norte skirts the city with Av Circunvalación parallel to it. There are few sites of tourist interest, this is a modern, working city, although there are some old buildings. In the colonial part look out for tiles on the walls at street corners, with the old names of the streets, put there in 1995 to mark the 500th anniversary of the founding of the city.

Ins & outs
See transport, page 438, for further details

Getting there There are good links by road from Santo Domingo (four-lane highway all the way) and Puerto Plata on the coast. Several bus companies have services to the city. There is also an airport for domestic flights. **Getting around** The long distance bus terminals are scattered around the city and you will probably have to get a taxi to your destination. You can walk round the centre of the city but suburbs and outlying areas are best reached by bus or *carro público*. Calle del Sol is the main commercial street, with both vendors and the main shops. In the newer part of the town, Av Juan Pablo Duarte and Av 27 de Febrero have shopping plazas, banks and fast food restaurants, very much in the US style. **Tourist office** There is a tourist office in the basement of the Town Hall (Ayuntamiento), Av Juan Pablo Duarte; it has little information available, only Spanish spoken.

Sights On Parque Duarte are the **Catedral de Santiago Apóstol**, a neoclassical building (19th-century) containing the tombs of the tyrant Ulises Heureux (see History) and of heroes of the Restauración de la República; the **Museo del Tabaco**, a pink colonial building with large green rotting wooden doors ■ *Tue-Sat 0800-1200,*

1500-1800; the **Centro de Recreo** (one of the country's most exclusive private clubs) with Moorish-style arches and the **Palacio Consistorial** (1895-96). Also on Parque Duarte is the Plaza de la Cultura y Oficina Regional de Patrimonio Cultural, which is now the **Museo de la Villa de Santiago** and holds cultural and art exhibitions. ■ *Closes 1230 on Sat.* **Fortaleza San Luís**, overlooking the Río Yaque del Norte, is not open to the public as it is a military zone.

Other places worth visiting are the **Pontífica Universidad Católica Madre y Maestra** (founded 1962) and the **Monumento a los Héroes de la Restauración**, at the highest point in the city (panoramic views of the Cibao valley, commissioned by Trujillo in his own honour and remodelled in 1991 to include a *mirador*). You can climb up to the top of the monument for a panoramic view of the city, the valley and the mountains. Behind the monument is a theatre built by Balaguer in the 1980s, a rather impenetrable rectangular block with lots of Italian marble. This area is popular at weekends and fiestas and there are lots of bars and restaurants around the park. At carnival or any other outdoor celebration, this is the place to come. Rum shops sprout all over the open spaces and parades and parties occupy roads and squares.

Sleeping

A-C *Aloha Sol*, Calle del Sol 150, T5830090, F5830950. Rooms and suites, smart, upmarket, cool, restaurant *D'Manon* with local and international food. **B** *El Gran Almirante*, Av Estrella Sadhalá 10, Los Jardines, on road north, T5801992, F2411492. Popular with business visitors, quite good, casino, Spanish restaurant and tapas bar. **B-C** *Hodelpa Centro Plaza*, Calle Mella 54 esq del Sol, T5817000, F5824566, Apdo 459. Smart, modern, good restaurant, disco club *Tarari* next door, no parking facilities. **B-C** *Matum Hotel & Casino*, Las Carreras opposite Parque Monumento, T5813107, F5818415. 47 rooms, new ones with 2 beds, fridge, TV, phone, smart, old ones still a mess, pool. **C-D** *Don Diego*, Av Estrella Sadhalá, on road north, T5754186. Restaurant and nightclub. **C-E** *Ambar*, also on Av Estrella Sadhalá, T5751957. On Av Salvador Cucurullo in the centre there are four cheap hotels between 30 de Marzo and España: **F** *Dorado*, No 88, T5827563. With bath, basic, friendly. Opposite and better is **F** *Colonial*, No 115, T2473122. Small clean rooms with a/c and fan, good bathrooms, very hot water, fridge, TV, small cheap restaurant, friendly, luggage store. Also *Monterey*, No 92, I5824558 and *Lima*, on the corner, 30 de Marzo 57 esq Cucurullo, T5820620.

Eating

Pez Dorado, Calle del Sol 43 (Parque Colón), T5822518. Chinese and international, good quality food in generous portions, very popular for Sun lunch. At the upper end of the price range is *El Café*, Av Texas esq Calle 5, Jardines Metropolitanos. The favourite of businessmen and upper class society. Fresh homemade Italian food at *Ciao Ciao*, Av María R Sánchez, Los Jardines 13, T5831092. Run by an eccentric, entertaining Italian. Another Italian restaurant is *Il Pasticio*, behind the Supermercado Nacional. Eclectic place, great for late night drinks, a time when the owner, Paolo, is frequently there for conversation. There are several restaurants around the monument on Av Francia and Calle del Sol, popular on Sun. *La Brasa* has barbecued chicken. *Kukara Macara* has a rustic decor, cowboy style, lots of steak including Angus, prices up to US$20 for a huge, top class piece of meat, also seafood, tacos, sandwiches and burgers, open daily 1100-0300. *Los Tablones* on Calle del Sol has a good view of the monument, open air dining. Next door, *Puerto Sol* is cheaper and popular with a slightly younger crowd. *Maroma*, opposite *Mr Movies* on Calle Metropolitana. New, for elegant and trendy dining.*Olé* JP Duarte esq Independencia, restaurant and pizzería.

For the most spectacular view across the Cibao Valley, try *Camp David Ranch*. Drive (or take a taxi, fare about US$10) to Km 7 on Carretera Luperón, the turn-off is on the right, unsigned, before the *El Económico* supermarket; a 10-min climb up a winding, paved road to the ranch. The food quality is erratic, but the view is breathtaking. Next door is *El Generalísimo*, a piano bar decorated with classic cars from the Trujillo era. Some 10 bedrooms and suites reasonably priced in our **E** range. At the foot of the hill leading up to *Camp David Ranch* is **Rancho Luna Steak House**, Carretera Luperón Km 7.5, T5813136, F5813145, definitely not recommended for vegetarians. There is also **Cigar Ranch** on the way to *Rancho Luna* out of Santiago, a nice dining experience.

Dominican Republic

Entertainment Santiago is the home of *perico ripiao* (see Music and dance), a folk style of merengue, which can be heard in bars and clubs alongside more modern merengue, salsa, bachata and US disco music. The presence of a large university helps to generate a lively nightlife scene. Things start late and go on until dawn. The Monument is always a great place to hang out. *Metropolis Billards*, Estrella Sadhalá, in front of the PUCMM University in Plaza Alejo, has a cool bar and pool tables. *Dalí*, Av Juan Pablo Duarte, is also a good night spot. **Discos** *La Nuit*, in *Hotel Matum*; *El Alcázar*, in basement of *El Gran Almirante* hotel; *Ambis I* and *Ambis II*, Autopista Duarte Km 2, side by side, popular; *Antifas*, Don Pedro 50, gay club, live shows; *La Antorcha*, 27 Febrero 58; and *Las Vegas*, Autopista Navarrete Km 9. All modern. *Champion Palace* is a huge disco for 2,000 people, open daily. **Casino** The *Matum* and *Gran Almirante* hotels both have casinos open until around 0400. **Theatre** *The Gran Teatro del Cibao*, T5831150, seats 15,000 in its main auditorium, sometimes shows opera, while merengue concerts and plays are put on in the smaller concert hall.

Festivals Santiago's **carnival** is a pagan celebration surrounding Independence and Easter. Working class *barrios*, particularly La Joya and Los Pepines, have developed rival themes of Los Lechones and Los Pepines and there is much competition between them. The *lechones* have papier maché masks of stylized pigs, while the *pepines* have pointed horns on their masks, often hugely decorated. Parades start the weekend before Independence Day (27 Feb), moving off from Las Carreras and ending up at the Monumento a los Héroes de la Restauración after several hours.

Shopping The *Mercado Modelo Turístico* is at Calle del Sol and Av España. Cheap amber at Calle del Sol 60. Outside town, on Autopista Duarte, are many potteries where ceramics can be bought very cheaply.

Transport **Air** *American Eagle* fly from San Juan, Puerto Rico. See page 407, for domestic flights.

Bus Local OMSA buses on main routes, as in Santo Domingo. All *carros públicos* have a letter indicating which route they are on; *carros* cost US$0.25, *guaguas* US$0.25. Many congregate atLa Rotunda de las Pinas at the intersection of Estrella Sadalhá and Av 27 de Febrero. **Long distance** *Caribe Tours* (Av 27 de Febrero, Las Colinas, T5760790) bus to Puerto Plata US$2.66 every hour; it is easier to take *Caribe Tours* than *Metro* to Puerto Plata or the capital because *Metro* only takes passengers on standby on their Santo Domingo-Puerto Plata route. *Metro* terminal, Maimón y Duarte, T5829111, a block or so towards the centre on Duarte from the roundabout at Estrella Sadhalá (opposite direction from Codetel); 6 buses daily Santo Domingo-Santiago. *Terrabus* has its terminal at the junction of Calle del Sol and Av Francia by the Monument. Service to Santo Domingo with connections for the ferry to Puerto Rico or the bus to Haiti. Other companies from the capital with good, a/c buses include *Cibao* (from Parque Enriquillo) and *Transporte Espinal* (4 blocks north of Parque Enriquillo). To Samaná, go to Puerto Plata and take *Caribe Tours* from there. *Guaguas* to San José de las Matas leave from the Puente Hermanos Patiño, by the river not far from the centre. *Guaguas* for La Vega, US$1.20, go from the park at the corner of Restauración y Sabana Larga. Many other *guaguas* leave from 30 de Marzo with Salvador Cucurullo, average US$1.30, eg Puerto Plata 2 hrs, not recommended if you have lots of luggage. *Transporte del Cibao*, Restauración almost with the corner of J P Duarte, runs buses up to Dajabón in the northwest near the Haitian border, 2½ hrs.

Directory **Banks** *Scotiabank* on Parque Duarte, others on Calle del Sol between San Luís and Sánchez include *Banco Popular* (ATM), *Baninter*, *Citibank*, *Bancrédito* (ATM), *Banco del Progreso*, and *Banco de Reservas* (ATM). There are also a *Banco de Reservas*, *Bancrédito* and *Banco del Progreso* on Av 27 de Febrero. The only place you can change traveller's cheques is the *Banco Popular* on Calle del Sol esq Mella. **Communications** Post Office: on the corner of Calle del Sol and San Luís. **Telephone:** *Codetel* is at San Luís between Restauración and Independencia, and further out at the junction of Estrella Sadhalá and J P Duarte; take Carro A from the Parque. *Tricom* is on San Luís between Restauración and Beller, also on Av 27 de Febrero next to Bancrédito.

The north coast

The north coast boasts a stretch of shoreline of immense beauty, with sandy beaches, cliffs, coves and mangroves sandwiched between clear, blue sea and picturesque green mountains. It is home to the historic port of Puerto Plata, fishing villages, resorts and guest houses. To the west the climate is dry and the vegetation predominantly scrub and cactus, while to the east it is wetter and the vegetation lush, with the ubiquitous coconut palms towering above the beaches and greener than green golf courses.

Puerto Plata

Puerto Plata, sandwiched between Mt Isabel de Torres and the sea, is the main gateway on the northern coast, but the town itself is not much visited. The old town centre comprises dilapidated wooden houses and other colonial buildings behind warehouses and the power station alongside the docks. There is some renovation and some new building taking place. The seafront drive, the Malecón, sweeps along the beach for about 5 km, between the San Felipe fortress to the west on the point protecting the harbour and Long Beach to the east. Tourism is now concentrated in the all-inclusive beach resorts along the coast and many hotels have closed in town.

Population: 200,000

Getting there Domestic and international flights to the Gregorio Luperón international airport, 15 mins by road from town, there are many domestic flights from Santo Domingo and other airports with Air Santo Domingo and charter companies. Taxis are for hire at the terminal, or you can walk to the main road if you have not much luggage and hail a *guagua*. *Caribe Tours, Metro* and many other bus companies pass through or terminate at Puerto Plata and transport links are good. **Getting around** The old city and the fortress can be toured on foot as it is quite compact. For longer distances you can hop on a *motoconcho* or take a safer taxi. There are buses if you've got plenty of time and know where you are going. **Tourist office** There is a tourist office at the far east end of the Malecón in the little park in the same building as the Tourist Police, T5865000, F5863806.

Ins & outs

Puerto Plata, was founded by Nicolás de Ovando in 1502, although Columbus had sailed past the bay and named it the silver port because of the way the sun glistened on the sea. For many years it was used as a supply stop for the silver fleets on their way from Mexico to Spain, but it was prone to pirate attacks and it was eventually supplanted by Havana. In effect, this allowed buccaneers a free hand in the north and they roamed the hills hunting wild cattle and pigs and selling the hides and meat. After the War of Restoration in the 1860s, tobacco became the supreme commodity. The profitable trade attracted merchants, many of them from Germany, and they built luxury

History

Dominican Republic

Dominican Republic north coast

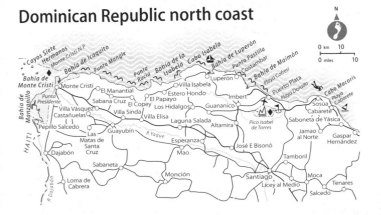

mansions, some of which still stand. Tobacco waned at the beginning of the 20th century, but by 1910 Puerto Plata was experiencing a boom in sugar prices and more building. Boom turned to bust with the Great Depression in the USA in the 1930s. In the 1960s investment in tourism and the construction of the Playa Dorada all-inclusive complex, provided thousands of jobs and is the mainstay of the region's economy.

Sights   The old city is contained within Av Colón, the Malecón and Calle José Ramón Torres. The hub of the old town is the **Parque Central**. In the centre is an early 20th century gazebo, or bandstand, and on the south side, the **San Felipe cathedral** is worth a visit. Also on the Parque Central is the **Patrimonio Cultural** in a majestic building dating from 1908 where there are interesting art exhibitions. The **Museo del Ambar**, Amber Museum, Duarte 61 esq Emilio Prud'home, houses a collection of rare amber. The museum is in a renovated house built by a German tobacco merchant, and there are a few relics of the family's occupation. The main museum is on the second floor containing amber from the Cordillera Septentrional, the mountains behind Puerto Plata, which contain the world's richest deposits of amber. ■ *Mon-Sat 0900-1700,US$2, T5862848. Amber Museum Shop at Playa Dorada Plaza, T3202215.*

A visit to the colonial fortress, **Fortaleza de San Felipe**, the oldest in the New World, on a promontory at the west end of the Malecón is recommended. Once the era of pirates and privateers was ended the fortress was long used as a prison. Juan Pablo Duarte was locked up here in 1844. The museum contains rusty armoury and photos of the excavation and renovation of the fortress, which was built in 1540. The museum is not especially interesting but if you climb the turrets you get a wonderful view of the coast and ships coming into the harbour. Outside there is a statue and monument to General Gregorio Luperón on a prancing horse. ■ *US$0.60. Guided tours available but not really necessary.* Nearby are the rusting remains of Puerto Plata's **lighthouse**, first lit on 9 September 1879, now in the top 100 list of the World Monuments Fund because it is so endangered.

Sleeping   **A-B** per person, *Ahmsa Puerto Plata Beach Resort & Casino*, at the east end of the Malecón
Cheap hotels can   on Long Beach, T5864243, F5874377. All-inclusive, 216 rooms in blocks, nice gardens, pool,
only be found in   well cared for, poor beach. **D** *Sofy's Bed & Breakfast*, Calle Las Rosas, T/F5866411, gillin.n@
the town centre   codetel.net.do Run by Canadian Noelle Gillin, look for sign of La Batera between the baseball stadium and the police station on Av Luis Ginebra, go down that street and the house is the third to last on the left, 3 rooms, great American breakfast on the terrace, popular with ex-pats, airport transfers are included if you stay a week. **D-E** *Sunshine Hotel*, Manolo Tavárez Justo 78, T5861771, on main road. Good for public transport, 20 rooms, a/c or fan, TV, balcony, hot water, bathrooms a bit dilapidated but adequate, lumpy pillows, sheets don't fit, parking, restaurant, open 0700-2400. At Plaza Anacaona, 30 de Marzo 94-98, are **E** *Hotel/Restaurant El Indio*, T/F5861201. With breakfast and fan, clean, restaurant serves good breakfast and fish, very good value, Mexican music on Sat, a patio with native plants, palm trees and hummingbirds. **E** *Portofino*, Hermanas Mirabal 12, T5862858. Long Beach area, small pool, 13 rooms, a/c, cable TV, hot water, own generator, parking, restaurant. **E-F** *Castillo*, José del Carmen Ariza 34, near Parque Central, look for the red awning of *Sam's Bar & Grill*, T5867267, sams.bar@codetel.net.do One-bedroom furnished apartment or rooms with private or shared bathroom, weekly and monthly rates available, own generator, hot water, TV, internet access, the first hotel in town, dating from 1890s. **E-F** *Aparta-Hotel Lomar*, Malecón 8, T3208555. Large rooms, warm water, cable TV, a/c or fan, some rooms with balcony overlooking sea, good value. **F** *Victoriano*, San Felipe 33, T5869752. Central, a/c, cable TV, fan or a/c, one or two beds, clean, friendly, own generator, hot water. **F** *Jimessón*, John F Kennedy 41, T5865131, close to Parque Central. Old colonial building, gingerbread, painted green and white, lobby furnished with antiques and old clocks, tiled floors, the rooms are in a newer building behind, but still old style, clean, a/c, cold water, pleasant, no restaurant.

Acuarela, Prof Certad 3 esq Pres Vásquez, T5865314. Open 1800-0200, garden café, in old **Eating** wooden house, excellent restaurant. *Aguaceros*, Malecón edif 32, near fire station, T5862796. Open from 1700, steaks, seafood, burgers, Mexican, tables on sidewalk, bar. *Anna's Bar and Grill*, Colón 59. Popular with ex-pats, satellite TV, dartboard. *Barco's*, Malecón 6, T3200388. Italian. *Café Cito*, San Felipe 23. Open Mon-Sat 1030-2400, garden café under mango tree, away from the hustle and bustle, jazz music, very good food, popular with the ex-pat crowd. *Comacho*, Circunvalación Norte (Malecón), T6856348. Good Dominican restaurant. *Jardín Suizo* , Malecón 32, T5869564. Run by Swiss James and his Dominican wife, excellent food. *Sam's Bar and Grill* on José del Carmen Ariza 34, near Plaza Central, T5867267, sams.bar@codetel.net.do American-run, good American food, satellite TV, meeting place, notice board, internet, rooms also available, see *Hotel Castillo*, above.

On Sun nights there is open air dancing on the Malecón, with huge sound systems on the **Bars &** road and street vendors selling drinks. Most of the nightlife is in Playa Dorada, see below. **nightclubs**

The Mercado Viejo is at Ureña and Separación and sells mostly hardware and furniture, **Shopping** although there is also a *botánica*, items relating to syncretist religion, witchcraft, vodú and folk healing. The Mercado Nuevo, at Isabela de Torres and Villanueva, sells handicrafts, rum, Cuban cigars, Haitian art and other souvenirs. *Macaluso's Jewelry Café*, Duarte 32 esq San Felipe, open Mon-Sat 0930-1800, is run by ex-pat Tony Macaluso, who has been here since the 1970s. He sells local jewellery, crafts and cold drinks and he doesn't pay commission to touts/guides, so his prices are slightly lower than elsewhere.

Air From North America: Boston (*TWA*), Miami (*American Airlines*), New Orleans (*American Airlines*), New York (*American Airlines*, *TWA* and *Continental*), Minneapolis (*Northwest Airlines*). **From Europe:** *Martinair* from Amsterdam; *Air Europa* flies from Madrid; *AOM* from Paris; *Condor* from Berlin, Dusseldorf, Frankfurt, Hamburg, Hanover, Leipzig, Munich and Stuttgart (some flights only in high season); *LTU* from Dusseldorf, Frankfurt, Munich and Munster; *Hapag Lloyd* from Frankfurt. **From the Caribbean:** *TCI Sky King* from Providenciales; *American Eagle* from San Juan.

Transport
For domestic flights, see Essentials, Getting around

Airport Gregorio Luperón international airport, T5860219/5860106, serves the entire north coast. It is 15-20 mins from Puerto Plata, 7 mins from Sosúa and 20 from Cabarete. Taxi from airport to Puerto Plata or Cabarete US$20, to Sosúa US$10 Small bank for exchange (closed weekends), car hire agencies and a few shops. Proper tipping for baggage handlers (in overalls) is about US$2 per bag and they will expect you to pay something even just for picking up a bag.

Local *Motoconchos*, US$0.60 almost anywhere in town, negotiate a fare for longer distances. *Guaguas*, leave Parque Central, more frequently, from the hospital on Circunvalación Sur to destinations along the north coast. Taxis charge US$5 from Puerto Plata to Puerto Dorado. They can be found around the Parque Central, at Long Beach near the *Ahmsa Puerto Plata Beach Resort*, or on Circunvalación Sur near *Caribe Tours*. **Long distance Bus** *Metrobus* (T5866062, Beller y 16 de Agosto), and *Caribe Tours* (T5864544, at Caribe Centro Plaza, Camino Real, just off the Circunvalación Sur) run a/c coaches to/from Santo Domingo, 4 hrs. To Santiago, *Caribe Tours*, every hour on the hour, 1000-1800, US$2.66. *Caribe Tours* run buses to Samaná via Sosúa (US$1.60) and Cabarete, 0700, 1600 daily, 3½ hrs. Alternatively you can use the *guagua* system, changing at each town, but this will take much longer, be more uncomfortable and more costly. **Car hire** Best arranged at the airport, more choice than in town. *Avis*, airport, T5860496. *Honda*, Carrera Luperón 2½ km, T5863136, at the airport, T5860233. *Puerto Plata Rent a Car*, Beller 7, Puerto Plata, T5863141. *Nelly Rent a Car*, Puerto Dorada, T3204888, at the airport, T5860505. **Motorcycle rental** US$20-30 a day, from any rental agency. Make sure to lock your motorcycle or scooter, as bike theft is big business in the area and there is no theft insurance on motorbikes.

Banks *Banco Popular* (24-hr ATM) on José del Carmen Ariza esq Duarte, opposite the cathedral, **Directory** *Banco Mercantil* (T5868977, F5868302) and *Banco del Progreso* (T3200504) are on the other side of

Dominican Republic

the square on Separación, either side of Beller. *Banco BHD* J F Kennedy, T3207919, F3207680; *Banco de Cambio Vimenca*, Av L Ginebra, T5864022; *Banco de Reservas*, J F Kennedy 16, T5862518, and at Playa Dorada, T3204830; *Banco Intercontinental*, Pte Castellanos, T5862350, F5864574; *Banco Metropolitano*, José del Carmen Ariza, T3200714, F3200841. **Communications** Internet: *Comp.Net*, Calle 12 de Julio 77, T5864104, US$3 per hour. *Hotel Castillo/Sam's Bar & Grill*, US$3 per hour, credit given for time not used. **Telephone**: *Codetel* is on Beller 48 esq Padre Castellanos, T5863803, and 27 de Febrero, T5863311, for domestic and international calls. *Tricom* long distance call centre is at 27 de Febrero 75, T4715005. Cheaper is *All American Cable & Radio* (AACR), on JF Kennedy 40, T5862660. **Post Office** On 12 de Julio 42 esq Separación, T5862377. **Medical services** Hospital *Ricardo Limardo*, J E Kunhardt, T5862210/5862237. There are several doctors with clinics. **Useful addresses** Immigration Dirección General de Migración, 12 de Julio 33, T5862364.

Excursions

Just 1 km past Puerto Plata, a *teleférico* (cable car) runs to the summit of **Loma Isabel de Torres**, an elevation of 779 m. A statue of Christ looks out over all of Puerto Plata, rather like the one in Rio de Janeiro; it also houses craft shops, a restaurant (quite pricey by Dominican standards) and there are beautifully manicured botanical gardens with a lovely view of the coast and mountains. ■ *US$6 round trip. Open daily except Wed with last trip about 1900 depending on the time of year. Entrance is south of the Circunvalación del Sur on a paved road marked teleférico. Hiking tours up the mountain can be arranged with Iguana Mama (see page 404). Hiking alone is not recommended. It is a moderate to hard hike, being quite steep in parts, and takes about three hours to get up to the top.*

Playa Dorada Just 6 km east of Puerto Plata, 4 km from the airport, is the beach resort of Playa Dorada with an exceptional golf course, and other sporting facilities. The *Playa Dorada Resort* is an umbrella name for a complex of 13 large all-inclusive hotels with over 4,000 rooms, offering similar services, eg pool, tennis, golf, best booked as part of a package from abroad. Not all of them are beachfront. There is a central shopping mall, the Playa Dorada Plaza, and lots of nightlife including discos and casinos. The beach is a glorious sweep of golden sand around the promontory on which stand most of the hotels, while the golf course weaves in and out of the hotels not on the beach.

Eating The food is good at all the main hotels; there is every variety of cuisine. In the Playa Dorada Shopping Mall is *Hemingway's Café*, T3202230. Good food and music, a/c, good service, open from 1100, fun at night and during the day, live bands at weekends, karaoke some nights.

Bars & nightclubs On the main road, 5 mins' walk from the entrance to Playa Dorada, is *Pat's Rum Runners Bar*, on the roadside. Makes a change from the hotel complex, pool table, sports TV, live music and karaoke at weekends. *Andromeda* in *Heavens Hotel* (the most popular club), *Charlie's* in *Jack Tar Village Casino* and *Crazy Moon* in *Paradise Beach Resort*; all three are popular and offer a mix of *merengue*, *salsa* and international pop music. All have cover charges, about US$2.

Entertainment There are 4 casinos on the north coast. *Jack Tar Village*, *Occidental Playa Dorada Hotel*, *Ahmsa Paradise Beach Club* and *Ahmsa Puerto Plata Beach Resort*. Only the last named is in Puerto Plata, the other three are in the Playa Dorada complex. The casinos feature slot machines, black jack, craps, roulette and poker.

Cinemas There are 3 cinemas in the Plaza Dorada which show foreign (mostly US) films with Spanish subtitles.

Shopping The Playa Dorada complex has the first real shopping mall on the north coast, called the *Playa Dorada Plaza*. Prices are slightly inflated, but the quality of all items, especially the locally-made ceramics, jewellery, and clothing, is superior to most sold by beach or street vendors. The mall includes a *Bennetton*, a selection of Tiffany lamps and some very original jewellery. Cigars, leather goods, amber, larimar, coffee and rum can all be found here.

Dominican Republic

Golf is the main attraction here at the *Robert Trent Jones Golf Course*, T3204262/3803, **Sport**
F3203773, www.playa-dorada-golf.com which is right in the middle of the resort, see Sport,
page 412. If you are staying at one of the resort hotels, green fees with caddy are about
US$33, outsiders pay about 10 % more. The hotels offer lots of sports for their all-inclusive
guests and activities away from Playa Dorada, like horse riding, are easily arranged. Most
watersports are also on offer through the hotels, but for scuba diving go to Sosúa.

Communications Internet: *Hot.com C@fé* in the Playa Dorada Plaza, T3425500, **Directory**
hot.com@codetel.net.do

West of Puerto Plata

To the west of Puerto Plata and within easy striking distance of the city, is
Costambar, which has a long stretch of sand with few waves, making it perfect for
children. There are restaurants beside the beach and supermarkets if you want to
cater for yourself. There is even a cybercafé for internet access, US$3 per hour. *Paul's
Pub & Cybercafé* is on the main street, T9707936, www.paulspub.com This is the
best place to look for self-catering accommodation, there are lots of villas and condos, some for as little as US$100 a week, excellent value if you are in a group.

    Cofresí beach has several hotels and cabins and is busy at weekends. There are *This is a good area to*
also comfortable, fully-staffed villas, contact Vacation Villa Referral Center (14 *stay in if you don't
want to get caught up*
Rolling Road, Wynnewood, Pennsylvania, USA 19096-3521, T610-8965815, *in the all-inclusive*
F610-6495422, www.puerto-plata.com *Chris & Mady's* is a thatched restaurant *style of holiday offered*
and bar overlooking the ocean, within walking distance of the *Hacienda* complex. *at Playa Dorada, but*
Good seafood at reasonable prices and you can watch sports on TV. *would rather be on the*

    Further west at **Bahía de Maimón**, 9 km from Puerto Plata, are two all-inclusive *beach than in the city*
hotels, Mambo and Merengue, T3204000, F3205555, www.riuhotels.com Nearly
1,000 rooms between them, on the beach, all the usual facilities on land and in the
water, shopping complex and *Pacha* disco.

Luperón is a typical Dominican village, with several markets selling fish, meat and **Luperón**
vegetables, basic restaurants and baseball field. It has fine beaches, suitable for
watersports and is popular with divers. Three kilometres from the village is Puerto
Blanco Marina, T2994096, surrounded by mangroves and providing good protection for yachts. *Motoconchos* charge less than US$1 from the village, and taxis
US$3. Watersports include snorkelling, fishing and scuba diving. The marina is
the place to be. The bar is popular, with a happy hour at 1700-1900. The restaurant
is known for its seafood and the food is cheap. Rooms are available, **E**, with a/c and
hot water. Catamaran tours are recommended as a great way to see the coast and
snorkel in some lovely secluded spots where the coral is alive and healthy. Frank
Guessard at the marina charges US$49 for day trips, US$19 for two hours, children
half price, T3225343 (cell), F5718052, tangomango@voila.fr He can also arrange
horse riding at *Mario's ranch*, which costs US$49 for a full day or US$29 for a
three-hour sunset ride.

A *Ciudad Marina Luperón Beach Resort*, T5718303. 3 restaurants, Italian, Brazilian and Mexi- **Sleeping**
can, bars, pools and jacuzzis, lots of watersports, tennis, riding, bicycles, ping pong, billiards,
gym and sauna, children's activities. **F** *Hotel Casa del Sol*, T5718403. Rooms clean, with bathroom. **F** *Dally*, 27 de Febrero 46, T5718034, F5718052. On the main road, popular, 8 rooms,
clean, fan, hot water, good restaurant (see below).

There are lots of Dominican restaurants which are best found by just walking around town. **Eating**
Always ask for bottled water and be careful with ice. *La Yola*, German-owned and well
known for its seafood. *Restaurante Dally*, 27 de Febrero 46, T5718034. Specializes in seafood. *Los Almendros*, T5718121. Good sea food. *Casa del Sol*, T5718403. Also with good
sea food.

Directory **Communications** Internet: *Punto Internet Café*, at *Farmacia Vanessa*, Independencia 7 esq Hugo Kunhart, US$2 per hour. **Medical services** There are 2 pharmacies, *Vanessa*, T5718201, see above, and *Alejandra*, Duarte 121, T5718135.

La Isabela West of Luperón by a new road is La Isabela, now a Parque Nacional Histórico.
Bring lots of mosquito Here, on his second voyage, on 29 May 1493, Columbus landed with 1,500 men on
repellent, 20 17 ships. He founded the first European town in the Americas, with the first
mosquitoes counted *ayuntamiento* and court, and here was said the first mass on 6 January 1494 by Fray
feasting on one leg! Bernardo Boil. Only the layout of the town is visible. The story goes that Trujillo
ordered the place cleaned up before an official visit, but his instructions were mis-
understood and workers bulldozed the whole site, pushing the ruins into the sea.
The restoration and archaeological excavation of La Isabela is being undertaken
by the Dirección Nacional de Parques. So far a variety of ruins have been found as
well as Taíno and Macorix pottery and the first Hispanic ceramics. For a good
guide call Celestino Torres, *el hombre mapa*, T2515220, who knows a lot about the
history of the area. He has been working for over 20 years giving tours. The
Guayacán tree on his property was there before Columbus landed. The wood is
very hard and the Guayacán is used to carve replicas of Taíno artifacts. ■ *Daily*
0800-1745. US$3. To get there either take a tour from Puerto Plata, or take a carro
público from Villanueva y Kundhard, Puerto Plata, to La Isabela village, US$3.50,
then a motoconcho to the ruins, US$7.25 return including wait at ruins, a lovely trip.
The reception area has a library and toilets. The guide speaks Spanish and some col-
loquialisms in other languages.

Sleeping & **D** *Aguaparque Miramar*, T3100633, T/F5718052. Studio apartment, beautiful view, quiet
eating atmosphere, nice facilities, Belgian-owned. Nearby is *Vista Mar*, T/F5718052, Belgian and
continental food.

Directory **Medical services** There is a municipal hospital, T5895266, a medical centre, T5895382, and a doctor,
Dr Aquino, T5895408. There are also 3 pharmacies, *Liranzo*, RM Rojas 28, T5895289; *Pardo*, Colón 16,
T5895231; *San José*, Rojas 8, T5895420.

Monte Cristi

Population: 22,000 At the far northwestern tip of the Dominican Republic is Monte Cristi, a 19th century town with a Victorian feel to it, while the sea around it is believed to hold the
treasures of 179 sunken galleons. The area around the town is arid, with cactus and
other desert plants, interspersed with rice paddies and tobacco plantations. A large
land and marine park stretches either side of the town along the coast, protecting the
mouth of the Río Yaque del Norte, with mangroves, a lagoon and lots of channels. Its
proximity to the Haitian border means that transport links are good. The town has
an interesting, big old clock on the Parque Central, made in France, but brought
here on the train *Lavonia* on 11 March 1895. Each of the four faces tells a different
time and they are all wrong, by at least half an hour. You can visit the house of
Máximo Gómez, the Dominican patriot who played an important role in the struggle for Cuban independence and in the Dominican Restoration. Inside there are pictures and mementoes of Máximo Gómez, an extensive library with a detailed atlas of
Cuba and a lot of books relating to Cuba, but very few about the Dominican Republic. ■ *0900-1200, 1500-1900. Av Mella, opposite Helados Bon.* Between the town and
Playa Juan de Bolaños there is a monument to José Martí (a rather lugubrious head
of Martí on a stick), the Cuban poet and independence fighter who came here in
September 1892 before sailing with Máximo Gómez to liberate Cuba.

Sleeping **E** *Chic Hotel Restaurant*, Benito Monción 44, T5792316. 50 rooms sleep 1-4, nice hotel, only
Spanish spoken, TV, hot water, phone, shag carpet or tiled, décor different in each room,
good food but slow service, avoid dodgy ice in water. **E-F** *Don Gaspar Restaurant & Hotel*,

Pte Jiménez 21 esq Rodríguez Camargo, T5792477, F5792206. Price depends on a/c, cable TV (with porn channel), hot water, Tony the receptionist is funny and informative, with exceptional English. **B** *Cayo Arena*, Playa Juan de Bolaños, T5793145, F5792096. Two-bedroomed apartments on the beach, great place to stay, pool, bar, security. **D** *Los Jardines*, beyond *Cayo Arena*, T5792091, hotel.jardines@codetel.net.do Small hotel run by Hervé and Dorca, 2 bungalows each with 2 rooms, fan or a/c, quiet, parking, beach chairs, boat excursions to the mangroves and Cayos Siete Hermanos, English and French spoken, jeep and bicycle hire, owner will collect you from *Caribe Tours* if you call, or a *motoconcho* costs US$0.30.

Don Gaspar Restaurant & Hotel, Pte Jiménez 21 esq Rodríguez Camargo, T5792477, F5792206. Also a hotel and disco with a variety of music and requests, good breakfast menu, eggs, *mangú*, juice and coffee for less than US$4, Dominican and Spanish dishes. *El Bistrot*, San Fernando 26, T5792091, the road to the beach. Same ownership as *Hotel Los Jardines*, local cuisine, seafood, goat etc, 3 blocks from the clock, open 1000-2400, prices from US$4 for spaghetti to US$15 for seafood. *Comedor Adela*, Juan de la Cruz Alvarez 41, T5792254. Family atmosphere, lots of choice, good food, parking available. *Cocomar,* by the monument to José Martí, T5793354. Good breakfast, if a little greasy, also lunch and dinner, meals range from US$3-50 per person, with the top price for the *Paella Marinera* or seafood platter, they will make what you want if they have the ingredients. *Club Náutico*, T5972530. You can get a typical Dominican lunch for about US$4 including bottle water, large beer US$1.75, small beer US$1, good view of Isla Cabrita and El Morro, gate on the guard at all times. *Helados Bon*, Av Mella, opposite the house of Máximo Gómez. Lots of ice cream varieties.

Eating
Chivo picante (spicy goat) is sold at roadside stands

Monte Cristi is famous for its pre-Lenten fiesta in Feb. On Sun the *toros* and the *civiles* compete against each other in the streets. The *toros*, just people dressed in costumes with elaborate bull masks, wielding whips with a ball be painful.

Festivals

Scuba diving is excellent in the area, with over 9 shipwrecks to explore, but there is no organized dive operation. **Fishing** is popular. Offshore there are barracuda, tuna, marlin, dorado and carite. If you are **sailing** in the lagoon or channels, be aware that when the tides change that water can rise or fall by about 1½ m. There is one channel in the lagoon, which apparently has some 50 different entrances but only one exit.

Watersports

Local Taxis and *motoconchos* congregate at the corner of Mella and Duarte. **Long distance** *Caribe Tours* is on Rodríguez Camargo esq Mella, services to Dajabón (34 km, border town opposite Ouanaminthe in Haiti) and Santiago, then on to Puerto Plata or Santo Domingo.

Transport

Banks *Banco de Reservas* is on Duarte 38, T5792392. **Casa de Cambio Frías** is on Duarte 40, T5792388. **Communications** Telephone: *Codetel* at Duarte 56, T5793021. **Medical services** *Hospital Padre Fantino* is on J Cabrera, T5792401. *The Red Cross* is on Mella 49, T5792894. There are two doctors: *Dra Suero*, Mella 3, T5792561, and *Dr Isidor*, Juan de la Cruz Alvarez, T5792317. Several pharmacies: *Sol*, on Mella 1a, T5792404, *San Juan Bosco*, on Benito Monción 49, T5792327, *Clara Nidia* on Duarte, T5791180, and *Pueblo* on Duarte 41, T5792394.

Directory

East of Puerto Plata

The coast east of Puerto Plata has some of the most beautiful beaches in the world, with a green backdrop of mountains descending to a narrow coastal plain, with palm trees, pale sand stretching for miles and sea of all shades of blue. Sosúa, Cabarete and Río San Juan are the main beach destinations, Cabarete being one of the best windsurfing locations in the Caribbean. From all these places you can get quickly up into the mountains for hiking, cycling, horse riding or whatever you fancy away from the beach.

Sosúa

28 km east of Puerto Plata

When you get tired of sitting on the beach you can roam up and down aimlessly looking at things you have no intention of buying, or sit and have a cold beer watching other people roaming up and down

Sosúa is a little town with a beautiful and lively 1-km beach. Vendors' stalls and snackbars line the path along the back of the beach and you will be offered anything from sunbeds to toilets. There is a smaller public beach on the east side of town, referred to as the 'playita', or Little Beach, where you will be less bothered by vendors. The beach is edged with rocks and only accessible from *Hotel Sosúa-by-the-Sea* on one side and a couple of other hotels behind it on the other side. Sosúa is unfortunately becoming increasingly busy and scruffy. The main street (correctly named Calle Pedro Clisante, but only ever referred to as Main Street, or Calle Principal in Spanish) is lined with a variety of shops, restaurants and bars. Little or no attention is paid to street names or numbers. The El Batey side of town (the side that houses most of the hotels and restaurants) was founded by German Jewish refugees who settled here in 1941. A synagogue and memorial building are open to the public. The western end of the town is referred to as Los Charamicos (the two ends are separated by the beach); this is the older side of town, where the Dominicans themselves generally live, shop and party. **Tourist Office** T5792254, F5792100, and at Pedro Clisante 12, T5713433.

Sleeping

There are several all-inclusives listed here

A *PierGiorgio Palace Hotel*, La Puntilla 1, T5712626, F5712786, www.piergiorgio.com On cliff-top, owned by Italian designer who fell in love with the property and built a 51-room hotel to fit with Victorian style building, now a restaurant. 28 rooms have sea view, all have balconies, 24-hr electricity, excursions, white stretch limo for airport transfers, boat or bus shuttle to beach 1000-1600, 2 pools and jacuzzi, all very smart, comfortable and great position, online reservation service. **B-C** *Coconut Palms Resort*, T5711625, F5711725, moru.invest@codetel.net.do 8 km outside Sosúa, 20 mins from Cabarete. Beautiful resort, scenic hilltop view, 1, 2, and 3 bedroom apartments, all units with kitchen facilities, shuttle bus to town and beach, variable rates, quiet garden, restaurant. **B** *Sosúa-by-the-Sea*, T5713222, F5713020, h.sosuabts@codetel.net.do Owned and operated by Austrian-Canadians, on cliff above Little Beach, immaculate, a/c rather inefficient in the rooms/studios, water pressure can be a problem, kitchenette, good restaurant, pool, beach loungers and towels, bar, price includes breakfast and dinner, good food and service, although you may get bored of the limited choice. **B-C** *One Ocean Place*, near Sosúa Sol, T5713131, F5713365, one.ocean@ codetel.net.do Aparthotel, 46 1-bedroomed apartments, a/c, TV, phone, hot water, fridge, restaurant, room only or all-inclusive, pool, 5-min walk to beach, volleyball court, children's playground. **C** (**AL** full board) *Playa Chiquita Beach Resort*, T5712800, slightly out of the way, located on own private beach. Good restaurant, accommodation and service, and casino, has shuttle to town and beach. **C** *On the Waterfront*, Dr Rosen 1, El Batey, T5712670. 27 cabins, clean but rather thin walls, extra charges for drinking water, fridge, on a cliff overlooking the sea, 5 mins to beach. **C** *Tropix*, T/F5712291 (address: EPS-D#274, Box 02-5548, Miami, FL 33103), 200 m uphill from Texaco station. Clean, 12 rooms, a/c or fan, minibar, some traffic noise, beautiful pool and landscaped garden, impeccable service, good food, use of kitchen facilities, attracts Peace Corps volunteers on their days off. **C-D** *Condos Dominicano*, T5712787, F5713430, www.condo4u.net Studios, 1 and 2 bedroom apartments, 20 units, daily, weekly or monthly rates, full kitchen, TV, garden, pool, generator, security guard, close to beach and shops. **C-D** *Margaritaville*, T/F5713553. On hilltop, clean, scenic, shuttle to town. **C-D** *JJ's Auberge*, Dr Rosen, El Batey, T5712569, F5712865, auberge.jj@ codetel.net.do 8 rooms around a pool, a few blocks from the beach, secluded, in trees, clean, a/c, friendly, informative service. **C-D** *Pensión Anneliese*, Dr Rosen, T5712208. Clean room with fridge, short walk to beach, right by *On the Waterfront* restaurant. **F** *Koch's Guest House*, El Batey, down a dirt side street, ocean front, no beach. Use of kitchen, breakfast extra. There are many other hotels, guest houses and villas for rent, ask around locally.

La Puntilla de PierGiorgio, Calle La Puntilla 1, T5712215. Right on cliff edge, part of hotel, see above, gourmet Italian restaurant, very pretty, lovely views, possibly the nicest place in town for a romantic meal, somewhere special. *On the Waterfront*, Calle Dr Rosen 1, El Batey, T5713024. Fish, seafood, snacks, happy hour 1600-1800, excellent food and a spectacular sunset overlooking the sea, all-you-can-eat barbecue on Fri night. Ask for one of the speciality coffees, the waiter puts on an excellent fire show with the rum and they taste amazing. Pleasant entertainment nightly, on the lookout point. For an equally good view over the water go the other side of the bay to Los Charamicos to *Atlántico*, T5712878, on the cliff road from the beach. Open 1200-1500, 1900-2300, closed Thu, seafood and steak interesting menu, main dishes US$8-15, seafood platter for two US$17.50, lobster US$15/lb. There are several restaurants on Main St serving international, French, Italian food, walk around and see what takes your fancy, they change frequently. Also several eating places along the beach, some with lobster tanks, OK for lunch. For Dominican food go to Los Charamicos where there are *comedores*. *Dundee's Burgers*, Calle Alejo Martínez, in-front-of-school yard, open 1900-0700, the place to go after a night of revelling, Dundee, the American-Dominican owner, is a local fixture. *Hotel Sosúa-by-the-Sea* serves the best value buffet breakfast in town. For delicious baked products go to the *German Bakery (Panadería Alemán)*, in Villas Ana María, residential area.

Eating

There fewer restaurants than there used to be, probably due to the increase in all-inclusive hotels

Merengue Club, huge open air club, open until 0300, no charge; next to it the *Hotel Central* has a pub, *Toff Toff*; *Tucan* disco is on the other side of the street. *La Roca*, last spot on Main St before the beach, Sosúa's oldest bar/disco/eatery, now a sports bar, big screen. *Moby Dick Disco*, by far the most popular disco, a/c, cover charge, beware of prostitutes/thieves hanging around. *Copacabana* also has girls working. Elsewhere, *High*, T5712129, disco by the casino at the east end of town, has a terrace and small indoor and outdoor swimming pool. Copacabana and High are international-style discos with a/c, modern disco lighting and sound systems, fairly smart, 80% tourists, the rest usually locals dancing with tourists and showing off their skills, best after 0100. *Eddie's Sports Bar* has 4 satellite dishes, can get anything, near *Super Super Supermarket*.

Bars & nightclubs

Lots going on in Main Street

Diving There are lots of dive operations, in town and on the beach, offering tuition and boat dives. There is no jetty and no large dive boats, so you must be prepared to wade out to a small boat, with probably no shade, and be capable of getting back into the boat without a ladder after your dive, which can be tricky if it is rough. A recommended and long-established dive shop is **Northern Coast Aquasports/Diving**, Pedro Clisante 8, T5711028, F5713883, www.northerncoastdiving.com Lots of courses, multilingual staff, several boats normally taking 4-6 divers, good with novice or experienced divers, probably the most professional operation on this stretch of coast. **Swimming** *Columbus Aqua Park* opened in 1997, 3 mins from the airport, Km 18, T5712642, F5712747. Open 1000-1800, US$10 adults, US$3 children, with water toboggans, 3 large pools, a lazy river, children's water play area, diving tower, restaurants, gift shops, bars, discos etc.

Watersports

Local In Sosúa, transport congregates by the *Texaco* station and the junction of Calle Dr Rosen and the Carretera. *Motoconcho* (motorcycle taxi), US$0.60 to anywhere in town. A taxi to/from Puerto Plata costs US$17, a *guagua* US$0.60 and a *carro público* US$7 if you take the whole car. Car and bike rentals are everywhere, shop around for prices. *Asociación de Renta Moto* Sosúa Cabarete, US$28-35 for 1-2 days, US$5-7.25 hourly, depending on type. *Pilar*, Pedro Clisante 1, T5713281. Friendly, Carretera Sosúa-Sabaneta, T5713575. **Bus** *Caribe Tours* from Santo Domingo, US$5.30. In Sosúa, T5713808.

Transport

Banks *Banco Popular* (ATM outside) on the small square at Calle Dr Martínez and Duarte. *Bancrédito* (ATM outside) T5711204 is further along on Duarte. *Banco de Reservas*, Urb Tavárez, T5713836, F5713181. *Banco del Progreso*, Pedro Clisante 12B, T5712815. *Vimenca*, Duarte 2, T5713800. **Communications** Internet On Duarte is an internet café, @, also *Tricom*, on the corner near *Bancrédito*. **Post Office** at E Kunhardt 8, T5712222. **Telephone** *Codetel*, Calle Dr Alejo Martínez, near corner with Dr Rosen, T2203697, F5712456 (also in Charamicos, T5712601, F5712900). **Medical services** The main hospital for the area is in Puerto Plata, but there are several clinics and pharmacies in Sosúa.

Directory

Dominican Republic

Cabarete

Cabarete, famous for world class **windsurfing**, is 14 km east of Sosúa. Although it has grown considerably since French Canadian windsurfers first staked their claim on this small fishing village it still maintains its small town character. It can't grow much more because of the lagoon just south of the main road. There is a wide range of places to stay, eat and dance the night away, and the centre is packed with activities for daytime and after dark. International windsurf competitions are held annually in June, www.CabareteRaceWeek.com Conditions vary according to season: in summer (mid-June to mid-September) there are constant trade winds but few waves, in winter there are days with less wind, but when it comes the waves can be tremendous. Winds are light in the mornings, when people sleep and sunbathe if they have been up late the night before, but get strong in the afternoon, when hundreds of sails flit about on the water like so many butterflies. Boards rent for US$50 per day, US$200 per week, with variations, make sure insurance is available. Highly recommended is the *Carib Bic Center*, T5710640, F5710649, www.caribwind.com It has excellent windsurfing gear for rent, with professional and experienced instructors, the nicest surf shop in town and a great bar and grill. They also rent kayaks, boogie boards, surfboards, hobiecats and snorkelling gear. Other windsurfing schools include *Vela/Spin Out*, T5710805; *Club Nathalie Simon* (French speaking), T5710848; *Happy* (German and English speaking), T5710784 and *Club Mistral*, T5710770.

There is no shortage of watersports for the adventurous

There is also **surfing** and **kitesurfing**. On the outskirts of town is El Encuentro, a surfing beach, with a consistent 'break' off the right and left. *Surf & Sport* surfing school, run by long time local surfer, Markus Bohm, offers daily lessons, US$25, for all ages and levels, T5710463. Several of the windsurf places also have surf boards for rent. *Fly High and Surf Kitesurf School*, www.flyhighandsurf.com (contact Stephan Ruther or Marcus Bohm, owner of *Surf & Sport*, both German), offers instruction in a bay about 1 km downwind of the windsurfers in Cabarete Bay, where there is flat water for the first 500 m and then a reef with waves. The first Kitesurfing World Cup was held in Cabarete in 2000. **Waterskiing** and **wakeboarding** (like waterskiing but with a surfboard) take place on the Río Yásica, 7 km from Cabarete, the only place in the Dominican Republic where you can do wakeboarding. Contact The Tropical Wakeboard Center, T7070048, F5710890, tropicwake@hotmail.com, they offer coaching for beginners or advanced in English, French or Spanish. **Scuba diving** is popular and there are many dive schools in the area. *Northern Coast Diving* in Sosúa covers the Cabarete area (see above); also *Dolphin Dive*, T5710842 and *Caribbean Divers*, T5710218.

Sleeping

Low rise hotels, condos & guest houses line the 2 km bay

There are 2 high seasons: Dec-Apr as usual and then mid-Jun to mid-Sep when the winds are strong and attract the windsurfing crowd. **L-A** *Nänny's Estate*, T5710744, F5710655, nanny.state@codetel.net.do A bit out of town and therefore quieter, a condo-hotel, 2 bedroom apartments built on two floors like town houses, with sun deck on the roof, spiral staircase might be a problem for the less able, on the beach, restaurant, pool, tennis. **L-B** *Palm Beach Condos*, T5710758, F5710752, CPBCondos@codetel,net.do Spacious, deluxe condos, 2 bedroom, 2 bathroom, hot water, fully equipped kitchens, patios with ocean views, on the beach, perfect for families and windsurfers, central but quiet, close to bakeries, restaurants and transport. **L-B** *El Magnífico*, T/F5710868, hotel.magnifico@codetel.net.do 10 luxury apartments, ocean view, a/c, classic Caribbean design and amazing art deco. **L-C** *Windsurf Apart Hotel*, T5710718, F5710710, www.windsurfcabarete.com Studio and 2-bedroom condos, satellite TV, phone, a/c, restaurant, all watersports, central, very good, across the street from Carib Bic centre, expanding with 140 new rooms by 2002. **A-C** *Cita del Sol*, T5710720, F5710795, cita.delsol@codetel.net.do French Canadian, restaurant, across the road from the beach, computers for internet access, pool.

B-C *Albatros*, T5710841, h.albatros@codetel.net.do 11 condos which can be divided, big airy apartments, coconut palms, tropical garden, 150 m from beach and centre of Cabarete.

B-C *Caracol Apart Hotel*, T5710788, F5710665, only steps from the beach, 5 mins from Cabarete centre. Terrace overlooking ocean, 2 pools, fully equipped kitchenettes. **B-C** *La Punta*, T5710897, lapunta@codetel.net.do 12 apartments on the beach, quiet, wonderful restaurant, *Otra Cosa*. **B-D** *Caribe Surf Hotel*, T/F5710788, at end of beach. Owned by Swiss, Teddy Muller, new, modern, clean, reasonably priced, 22 rooms, comfortable, clean, not fancy but quiet, on side street, nice grounds, small pool, restaurant, friendly staff. **B-E** *Wilson Beach House*, T5710616, F5713346, gaby_reiners@yahoo.com Big house with terrace, the nicest view of the bay, on the beach, rooms and apartments with kitchen. **B-F** *Casa Blanca*, T/F5710934. On main road, seaview, opposite *Rent-a-Moto*, 9 rooms, some singles, 7 apartments with kitchenette, clean, friendly, German owned and managed. **C-D** *Kaoba*, T5710837, F5710879, h.kaoba@codetel.net.do Fan, hot water, reductions for over 2 weeks, rooms, apartments, good value, separate restaurant for breakfast and evening meal, across the road from the beach, pool. **C-D** *Ali's Apartments*, T5710568, F5713346, apartahotel.ali@codetel.net.do Studios and apartments with kitchen, pool. **D-F** *Residencia Dominicana*, T/F5710890, resdom@hispaniola.com Excellent value, studios, some with kitchenettes, apartments, pool, tennis, bike rentals, watersports (kitesurfing, windsurfing, wakeboarding) movie screen, 4 films a week, TV/VCR rental, breakfast buffet US$3.25, evening restaurant, special price for long stays. **E-F** *Banana Boat*, T5710630. Finnish/Canadian owned, quiet, central, kitchen facilities, laundry.

Eating

Wide range of places to eat & drink, lots of beach restaurants & bars, varied cuisine. Restaurants change hands frequently

Blue Moon, T2230614, outside town near a village called Los Brazos. Excellent Indian food served on banana leaves, reservations required, make up a group for best results. *El Magnífico*, T5710968. Gourmet Dominican food, reservations required. *La Casa del Pescador*, T5710760. Excellent seafood. *Las Brisas*, T5710614. Buffet style dinners, affordable food. *Miros*, T5710888. Excellent dinners on the more expensive side. *New Wave*, T5710826. Serves one dish every night, Wed is popular for the excellent Indonesian satay. *Tropicoco*, T5710647. Fantastic Sat night buffet, a bit out of town. *Otra Cosa*, T5710897, at *La Punta*, see above. French Caribbean food. *Vento*, T5710977, on the beach. Italian food. *Ho La La*, T5710806. French, international food, good seafood, good pizza. *Chez León*, on the beach. Shady terrace, specialities of crèpes and waffles. *La Dolce Vita*, T5710718. Italian food, buffet Tue and Fri nights, Dominican buffet Thu night. *Bar Fly*, T5710529. International food, fish barbecue, Mexican specialities, Chinese fondue, reservations required. *The Castle Club*, T2230601, 20 mins from Cabarete in the mountains. Unique gourmet dining experience, private dinner parties for 4-10 guests, reservations need to be made at least two days in advance. *Onno's*, T3831448. Tapas bar in the centre of the beach, relaxed ambience. Cheap Dominican food is available at *Sandros*, opposite *Iguana Mama*, rough and ready but nice people, good fun and good food (US$3 for 'small' portion of stew, rice, salad, beans, more than enough, beer US$1) and also if you go just out of town on the same road that goes to the caves, in a small village they have recently opened 6 or 7 excellent, cheap, Dominican restaurants, *Mercedes* being one of the best. *El Tiguere* and *Gri Grí*, in Callejón de la Loma on the way to *Mercedes* are also cheap with great Dominican food. *Dick's* bakery serves you the best coffee in town.

Bars & nightclubs

Ask any local and they will point you in the direction of the party that night

The Green Room, small bar on the beach next to the Bic Centre, happy hour 1700-1900, great sangría. Two more bars on the beach are *Tribal* and *Pitu*, good atmosphere and music late into the night, also serving breakfast, lunch and dinner, don't miss the happy hour jugs of *caipirinha* at *Pitu*. Many of the beach restaurants double as bars and are open until after the sun comes up. You can dance the *merengue* or listen to rock bands. Live bands play certain nights of the week, with visiting artists from North America as well as Dominican bands.

Festivals

Cabarete hosts an international sand castle competition every Feb, when visitors construct fantastic mermaids, flowers, fruit and even the *Titanic*. There is also a Jazz Festival in the autumn which attracts lots of top performers.

Tour operators

Iguana Mama, T5710908, F5710734, www.iguanamama.com, is the only licensed biking tour operator on the north coast, on the main street heading towards Sosúa, but likely to move, so check. Guided daily tours, US$40-85, weekly trips including hiking up Pico Duarte,

Dominican Republic

whale watching in Samaná, bicycle rentals, Specialized Stump Jumpers and Rock Hoppers, all equipment, maps and insurance for US$30 per day. Also contact them for whitewater rafting, canyoning and cascading, they will put you in touch with the best companies. For kids, a jungle river tour, daily educational boat rides, daily and weekly family excursions (biking and cultural). *Iguana Mama* donates 20% of its profits to local schools. *Rancho Alcantara*, T5710816, F5710444, ranchoalcantara@yahoo.com offers horse riding trips through the mountains with swimming in waterfalls and a Dominican lunch, daily tours, 0930-1640, US$75, week long riding tours US$900, well-cared for native horses, a great day out for beginners or experienced riders.

Transport **Taxi** Cabarete-Sosúa US$8-9, airport US$20, Puerto Plata US$40. Always check price with driver before setting off. *Guagua* to Sosúa US$0.60. *Motoconcho* US$0.60 anywhere in town, negotiate price for anywhere further, price doubles at night.

Directory **Banks** *Banco del Progreso*, Carretera Luperón, T5710625. *Banco Fiduciario*, Carretera Cabarete, T5710662. **Communications** *Codetel* is on the left as you go out of town towards Sosúa. More central is *Telecabarete*, T5710260, F5710845, also cheaper at US$1 per min to Europe, US$0.60 to USA, fax US$1.30 per page, US$0.30 to receive, internet access US$1.30 per 15 mins, US$4 per hr, open 0900-2200 for phone calls, 0730-2200 for internet. *Tricom* long distance, Plaza Laguna Don Pepe 1, T4700846. **Medical services** *Servi-Med* medical centre, open 24 hrs, Carretera Cabarete 6, T5710413, close to *Iguana Mama*. **Tourist Office** T5710950, but the best place to go for tourism information is *Iguana Mama* (see Tour operators above). A website with extensive coverage of Cabarete is www.hispaniola.com. **Useful addresses** Police: T5710810.

Río San Juan Further east along the north coast, Río San Juan is a friendly town in an area now quite a tourist attraction. One major site of interest is a lagoon called **Laguna Gri-Grí**. Boats take visitors through the mangrove forests into the lagoon and to see caves and rocks, notably the **Cueva de las Golondrinas**, formed by an 1846 rockslide. It is several kilometres long and filled with swallows, from which it gets its name. Expect to pay about US$25 per person on a boat trip taking up to 20 people.

The main attraction here is the beach called **Playa Grande**, 5 km east of Río San Juan, one of the most beautiful beaches on the island, now being developed with large hotels, most of them all-inclusives. It is packed with people at weekends. There is public access to the beach, which is one of the longest white sand beaches on the north coast. When the swell is up in winter this is the place to be for good surfingn and has one of the best golf courses in the country (see sport, page 412), designed by Robert Trent Jones Sr with 10 of its tees at the edge of the ocean.

Playa La Preciosa was so named by surfers who come here to surf because of its beauty. It is a great place for photos and a lot more secluded than Playa Grande. *National Geographic* took one of their cover shots at this beach. It is the next left turn east after Playa Grande at the headland of the Parque Nacional Cabo Francés Viejo.

The **Tourist Office** can be reached at T5892831, F5892964.

Sleeping **C** *Club Costa Verde*, T2485555, F2485557. 94 rooms, a/c, pool, tennis, open bar, buffet restaurant, small disco, access to small beach in front of the hotel or free transfer to Playa Grande, 10 mins' drive, friendly service, lots of tours. **D-E** *Bahía Blanca*, T5892563, F5892528. Lovely location right on rocks above the sea, beach 75 m away, wonderful views, 3-floor, well-maintained, white building, lots of balconies, 30 rooms, hot water, good water pressure, no pool, no TV, no a/c, restaurant open for breakfast and dinner, no evening entertainment but near local bars and disco, mostly Dominican guests out from Santo Domingo, French Canadian run. Recommended. Also good is **E** *Coral Inn*, T2485435, F2485437. Italian-Canadian owned, cliff view, pool, breakfast included, food reflects owners' nationalities. Next best is **D-E** *Río San Juan*, on main street, Duarte, at brow of hill, T5892379. Many price variations, a/c, disco, pool, good restaurant and pizzeria, *Cachalotte*, opposite (the hotel offers boat trips on the lagoon). **E-F** *Santa Clara*, Padre Billini y Capotillo, opposite Mini Market. With or without bath and fan, electricity and water often off and then very hot.

Several large all-inclusives have been built in the area, offering lots of facilities

Dominican Republic

Scuba diving is offered by *Gri Grí Divers*, Gaston Deligne 4, next to the *Hotel Bahía Blanca*, **Watersports** T/F5892671, D.McEachron@codetel.net.do Staff at the dive centre speak English, Spanish, German and French and are helpful and friendly. PADI courses are offered, from a US$65 resort course to full certification at US$350 and advanced open water at US$265. A single dive is US$40, 2 dives on the same day US$70. There are about 20 dive sites ranging in depth from 8-40 m and some are spectacular, including caves, coral, and underwater mountains called the Seven Hills. Gri Grí Divers are trying to get the area declared an Underwater National Park.

Guagua from Sosúa, 1¼ hours, may have to change in Gáspar Hernández. Transport stops at **Transport** the junction of Duarte and the main road. *Caribe Tours* T5892633, to Puerto Plata US$6.30, to Samaná 0830 US$3.10, 3 hrs, to Santo Domingo 0730, 1500.

Banks *Agencia de Cambio e Inversiones Río San Juan*, Duarte 34, T5892455. *Banco Metropolitano*, **Directory** Duarte 38, T5892383, F5892493. *Banco Popular*, Bahía Príncipe, T2263234. **Medical services** There is a cardiology unit here, *Centro de Cardiología y Especialidades*, M Alejandro, T5892807, also two clinics. Also several pharmacies on Billini and Duarte. **Useful addresses** Police, T5892298.

The Samaná Peninsula

The Samaná Peninsula is in the far northeast of the country, geologically the oldest part of the island, a finger of land which used to be a separate island. In the 19th century the bay started to silt up to such an extent that the two parts became stuck together and the resulting land is now used to grow rice. Previously the narrow channel between the two was used as a handy escape route by pirates evading larger ships. A ridge of hills runs along the peninsula, green with fields and forests. There are several beautiful beaches, which have not been overdeveloped or 'improved'.

Samaná

The town of Santa Bárbara de Samaná, commonly known just as Samaná, is set in a protected harbour, within the Bahía de Samaná. Columbus arrived here on 12 January 1493, but was so fiercely repelled by the Ciguayo Indians that he called the bay the Golfo de las Flechas (the Gulf of Arrows). Nowadays two small islets offshore are linked by a causeway to the mainland, providing a picturesque focal point when looking out to sea and added protection for yachts. The town itself is not startling, there are no colonial buildings, no old town to wander around, but the location is most attractive and it is a lively place.

Dominican Republic

Samaná Peninsula

Dominican Republic

Humpback whales

A fully grown humpback whale (Megaptera novaeangliae) measures 12-15 m and weighs 30-40 tonnes. It is dark grey, or black, with a white belly and long white flippers. On its nose and flippers it has large nodules, not perhaps an attractive feature, but the hairs coming out of the lumps on its nose are used like a cat uses its whiskers. All humpbacks can be identified by the markings on their tails, or flukes, as no two are the same, and scientists have recorded thousands of them so that they can trace and monitor them. They even give them names. Humpbacks are famous for their singing. Only the males sing and they all sing the same song, repeating phrases over and over again, sometimes for hours, but each year they have a new refrain, a variation on the theme, which they develop during the journey. Maybe to keep the kids amused along the way, but more likely to attract a mate. The humpback is a baleen whale, which means that it scoops up huge gulps of water containing small fish or krill, then sieves it, squeezing the water out between the baleens, retaining the food. When they are in the Bahía de Samaná,

Banca Navidad (Navidad Bank) or the Banca de Plata (Silver Bank), they do not feed for the three months of their stay. The water is too warm to support their type of food, although a perfect temperature in which to give birth without harming the calf, which is born without any protective fat to ward off the cold. This fat is soon built up, however, in time for the return journey north to the western north Atlantic and Iceland, by drinking up to 200 litres a day of its mother's milk and putting on weight at a rate of 45 kg a day. Poor mum loses weight at an equivalent rate as she transfers her fat reserves to her baby.

The Dominican Republic has the most popular and well established whale watching in the Caribbean. The industry is centred on humpback whales, but pilot whales and spotted dolphins can also be seen in Samaná Bay, and bottlenose, spinner and spotted dolphins, Bryde's and other whales on Silver Bank. The season for both locales is January through March with whale watching tours in Samaná Bay 15 January-15 March. Whale watching started in 1991 and in 1999 32,000 people went on

Getting there Sánchez is the gateway town to the peninsula and all road transport passes through here. A good road runs along the southern side of the peninsula to Samaná with a spur over the hills from Sánchez to Las Terrenas on the north side. There are good bus services from Santo Domingo and from Puerto Plata and towns along the north coast. An airport outside Samaná at Arroyo Barril handles domestic flights. If coming from the east of the island you either have to fly, or go to Santo Domingo and get a bus from there, or head for Sabana de la Mar and get the ferry across the bay. There is no road connection through the Parque Nacional Los Haitises.

Getting around Samaná is a small town and it is easy to walk around most of the places of interest. For short excursions you can take a *motoconcho*, some of which have been fitted with tricycles like rickshaws. There are also *guaguas*, or minibuses, for a safer ride. There is no tourist office in Samaná. Samaná Tourist Service, T5382451, on the Malecón, sells tours but will also provide information; alternatively, T5382206 (Ayuntamiento), or 5382210 (Governor's office).

Sights The present town of Santa Bárbara de Samaná was founded in 1756 by families expressly brought from the Canary Islands. The city, reconstructed after being devastated by fire in 1946, shows no evidence of this past, with its modern Catholic church, broad streets, new restaurants and hotels, and noisy motorcycle taxis. Any remaining old buildings were torn down by Balaguer, a native of Samaná, in the 1970s as part of his grand design to make the Samaná peninsula into a huge tourist resort. When he was defeated in the 1978 elections his plans were discarded and Playa Dorada was developed instead. In contrast to the Catholic church, and overlooking it, is a more traditional Protestant church, white with red corrugated-iron roofing, nicknamed locally 'La Churcha'. It came originally from England, donated tours, most of them to Samaná Bay where the trips last 2-4 hours. The trips to Silver Bank are more educational and are usually arranged by specialist groups. There are currently about eight companies offering tours of up to a week.

The whole of Samaná Bay, Silver Bank and Navidad Bank is now a National Marine Sanctuary. The aim is to include the peninsula and Los Haitises National Park and have it all declared a Biosphere Reserve by UNESCO. During the season the Dirección Nacional de Parques monitors the whale watching and has four vigilantes, recognizable by their green caps, of which three are in Samaná and one at Silver Bank. They can be contacted at the offices of the Centre for the Conservation and Ecodevelopment of Samaná Bay (CEBSE), T5382042. A set of rules and guidelines has been drawn up by CEBSE, the DNP and the Association of Boat Owners in Samaná to regulate the activities of whale watching boats, including limits on how close they can get to whales and how long they can remain watching them. Data has been collected on the impact on breeding of whale watching, to

see if this new tourist attraction has been affecting the humpbacks. There has, however, been no change since 1987, with mothers and calves still in the same area and singers still in the same area, although more studies are to be undertaken on dive intervals, to see if they are being forced to stay down longer. For more information there is a general Samaná website www.samana.org.do Contact: Kim Beddall, Whale Samaná, Victoria Marine, PO Box 53-2, Samaná, T5382494, Kim.Beddall@usa.net Miguel Bezi, another operator, has five boats of different sizes. Contact: Transporte Marítimo Minadiel, Samaná, T5382556. For tours to see humpbacks on Silver Bank, north of Puerto Plata, contact: Bottom Time Adventures, PO Box 11919, Ft Lauderdale, FL 33339-1919, USA, T954-9217798, F954-9207798. For whale watching from land from January to March, but especially in February, try Cabo Francés Viejo, east along the coast from Puerto Plata, near Cabrera, as well as Punta Balandra and Cabo Samaná at the tip of the Samaná peninsula. At Cueva del Agua there is a land-based volunteer whale watching project.

by the Methodist Church. They started the custom of holding harvest festivals, which still take place today between the end of August and the end of October. The Malecón waterfront road is the main street in the town, lined with restaurants, bars and tour operators. The dock is here, for the ferry to Sabana de la Mar, some whalewatching tours and private yacht services. A causeway links two islands in the bay, which can be reached by taking the road to the *Hotel Cayacoa*.

Humpback whales return to Samaná Bay every year between December and March to mate and calve. Various half-day tours go whale watching, certainly worthwhile if you are in the area at that time of year. This is recognized as one of the ten best places in the world to see whales and very convenient for the average tourist as they are so close to the shore. *See box for more details*

L *Occidental Gran Bahía*, T5383111, F5382764, h.granb@codetel.net.do 110-room, charming luxury resort on coast road, 10 mins, 8 km east of town, also 8 villas with pool, all facilities available, less in low season, small beach, good food and service, compact 9-hole golf course, watersports, tennis, horseriding, heliport, shuttle service to Cayo Levantado. **L** *Cayacoa Beach*, T5383131, F5382985. On a hill overlooking the town, view of the bay, beautiful gardens, watersports. **LL-L** *Hotel Occidental Cayo Levantado*, on the island, 10 mins by boat from Samaná, T5383141, F5382998. White beaches, all-inclusive, 44 rooms in main building or bungalows, restaurant, beach bar. **C-D** *Tropical Lodge*, on Malecón heading east, T5382480, F5382068, caribecom.com/tropicalodge 17 rooms, own generator, continuous hot and cold water, fan, a/c, pool, pleasant, basic but clean and good restaurant. **E-F** *Nilka*, Santa Bárbara y Colón, T5382244. 11 rooms, with hot water, popular. **E** *Cotubanamá*, T5382557, go west along the Malecón to the roundabout and turn right, the hotel is one **Sleeping**

block up on the left. Clean, adequate, fan, bedside light, make sure you get a room with a door which locks properly, hot water sometimes, doesn't last long. **F** *Paraíso*, near *rotunda*, central but quiet, modern, good and clean, good cold shower. There are other **F** hotels, eg *King*, T5382404, *Casa de Huéspedes*, T5382475 and *Ursula*, T5382402.

Eating

The local cuisine is highly regarded, especially the fish & coconut dishes

Going east along the Malecón: *L'Hacienda*, T5382383. Grill and bar open from 1200, the best in town, excellent specials, main dishes US$8-10, about US$22 per person for 2 courses, drinks, tax and service. *Bar Le France*, T5382257. Café style. *Le Café de Paris*, brightly painted, pizzeria, good crêperie, ice cream, breakfast, cocktails, loud rock music, very slow service when busy, can take 45 mins to get the bill. *Café del Mar*, T5382021. Open for breakfast from 0800, then spaghettis, hamburgers and Dominican food, cocktails, good. *La Mata Rosada*, T5382388, opposite the harbour. French-run but lots of languages spoken, popular with ex-pats, not always open, seafood, about US$10 per person. *Camilo's*, T5382781. Local and not-so-local food, reasonable (takes credit cards).

Bars & nightclubs

There is a nightclub above *L'Hacienda* restaurant. Outdoor nightlife can be found along the Malecón, where several stalls are set up as bars at weekends and fiestas. There is usually music at one or other of the restaurants, whether live or recorded.

Festivals

Traditional dances, such as *bambulá* and the *chivo florete* can be seen at local festivals (4 Dec, the patron saint's day; 24 Oct, San Rafael).

Transport

Local *Concho* or *guagua* in town US$0.20; *carreras* US$3.50-4. *Guagua* to Sánchez from market place US$2. **Car hire** *Rentacar* is on the Malecón, next to *Mata Rosada* restaurant and opposite *Metro*. *Fabrizio y Daniele*, T2535727, have motorbikes and run moto tours. **Bus** From the capital either via San Francisco de Macorís (where *Caribe Tours* has a terminal, 5 hrs with ½ hr stop), Nagua and Sánchez, or via Cotui, Nagua and Sánchez (*Caribe Tours* and *Metro*, 4 hrs). Alternatively from the capital by bus or *público* to San Pedro de Macorís, then another to **Sabana de la Mar** and take the ferry across the bay. Return to Santo Domingo, *Caribe Tours*, T5382229, 5 daily. US$5.50. *Metro*, T5382851, at 0800, 1500, via Sánchez US$3, Nagua US$3, San Francisco de Macorís US$4.40, to Santo Domingo US$6. *Caribe Tours* from Samaná to Puerto Plata (US$5.50) via Sánchez, Nagua, Cabrera, Río San Juan, Gáspar Hernández, Cabarete (US$4) and Sosúa daily 1600, 4 hrs. *Línea Gladys* to Santiago, US$4.50, from traffic lights west of town. **Air** An airport for the peninsula is at Arroyo Barril (8 km from town, good road, only 25 minutes flying time from Santo Domingo), which is being upgraded to take international traffic. **Sea** There is a ferry across the bay from Sabana de la Mar to Samaná run by *Transporte Marítimo Tom Phipps*, T5382289. Morning crossings are usually calmer than the afternoon, when the sea can be choppy and rough. Many yachts anchor at Samaná. The Port Captain comes on board when you arrive, with a group of officials, each of whom may expect a tip to expedite the paperwork. It can be particularly bad at weekends and holidays.

Directory

Banks *Banco del Cambio*, behind *Samaná Tours*, changes TCs. *Baninter* has ATM inside, gives cash against Visa, 6% commission, open 0830-1500 Mon-Fri. Also *Banco de Reservas*, but no ATMs. **Communications** Internet: *Compucentro* in the same building as Codetel but round the corner on Calle Lavandier, has email facilities, T5383146, compucentro@hotmail.com, open 0900-1230, 1500-1800 Mon-Fri, US$2.75 per hour, minimum charge US$1. Post office: behind *Camilo's*, just off Parque. Telephone: *Codetel*, Calle Santa Bárbara, 0800-2200 daily for phone, fax and email. **Medical services** *The Clínica Vicente*, T5382535, is the most advanced in Samaná, with ultrasound and X-rays.

Excursions

Parque Nacional Los Haitises

Across the bay is the Los Haitises National Park, a fascinating area of 208 sq km of mangroves, humid sub-tropical forest, seagrass beds, cayes, *mogotes* and caves, which were used by the Taínos and later by pirates. The irregular topography of bumpy, green hills was caused by the uplifting of the limestone bedrock and subsequent erosion. There are anthropomorphic cave drawings and other pictures, best seen with a torch, and some carvings. Wooden walkways have been constructed through the caves and into the mangroves in a small area accessible to boats and tourists. The park is rich in wildlife and you can see lots of birds. Many of the caves have bats, but there are also manatee and turtles in the mangroves and inland the *solenodonte* (*Solenodon pardoxus*), a mammal and insectivore found only on Hispaniola. The endangered *solenodonte* is a bit like a shrew, very primitive with a long nose, round ears and a long tail, measuring 30 cm and weighing up to 1 kg. ■ *Visits to the Park can be arranged by launch for US$45 including lunch, with departures from Sánchez and Samaná on the north side of the bay, and Sabana de la Mar on the south side; various companies organize tours (eg Amilka Tours, T5527664, daily from Sánchez, takes large tour parties and is the most regular but does not always have the best guides). It takes longer to get there by boat from Samaná, so it is better to start from Sánchez. Sabana de la Mar is even closer, but excursions from there are very informal. The DNP, from whom permits must be obtained, also organizes tours, US$35 per person for 12 passengers (in Sabana de la Mar, T5567333).*

Cayo Levantado

The offshore island, Cayo Levantado, is a popular picnic place, especially at weekends when the beach is packed. The white sand beach is nice, though, and there are good views of the bay and the peninsulas on either side. Public boats go there from the dock in Samaná (US$6-8 return, buy ticket at Malecón No 3, not from the hustlers on the pier, lots of boats daily outward 0900-1100, return 1500-1700); alternatively, take a público or motoconcho 8 km out of town to Los Cacaos (US$3) to where, *Transportes José* and *Simi Báez* run boats to the island. Cayo Levantado is often included as a lunch and swim stop after a whale watching tour.

Las Galeras

At the eastern end of the peninsula is **Playa Galeras**. The 1-km beach is framed by the dark rock cliffs and forested mountains of Cape Samaná and Cape Cabrón. The village is popular with Europeans, several of whom have set up small hotels and restaurants, but it is still unspoilt. There is a fair amount of weed on the beach and some coral, so rubber shoes are a good idea, but it is 'unimproved', with trees for shade. If you walk east along the beach you come to the biggest hotel, *Casa Marina Bay*, set among masses of coconut palms. The beach here is sandy with no coral and very safe for children. There are very few vendors in Las Galeras and the beaches are hassle-free.

Twenty minutes away by boat, or 40 minutes by jeep (not suitable for cars) along a very rough 8-km track more suited to horses is the deserted **Playa Rincón**, dominated by the cliffs of 600-m high Cape Cabrón. The sand is soft, creamy golden and there are few corals in the water, which is beautifully clear. Many beaches are accessible only by boat. Others are reached by a dirt road, negotiable by ordinary cars. Check locally before swimming at deserted beaches where there can be strong surf and an undertow. Drownings have occurred frequently near El Valle.

Dominican Republic

Sleeping

AL-A *Villa Serena*, next to the shore, T5830000, F5380009, www.villaserena.com Croatian-owned, painted turquoise, pink and white, cool, plantation-style, 21 huge, stylish rooms, private terrace overlooking sea and little islet, rocky coast but small, sandy beach, gourmet restaurant, tours organized, free bicycles, snorkel gear for hire. **A** *Club Bonito*, T5380203, F6960082, club.bonito@codetel.net.do, the first hotel on the right along the beach track, orange building. Very central, Italian restaurant *Il Pirata*, with seafood specialities, bar, boutique, pool. **C** *Moorea Beach*, T5380007, T5380202. 12 rooms, seaview, 200 m from beach, in palm trees, painted white, in good order, pool, quiet but close to village centre, bar, restaurant, Dominican specialities, run by Bernard (German) and Eleni (Greek), breakfast included in price. **C** *El Marinique*, T5380262, www.elmarinique.com 5 cabañas and restaurant under palm trees, sea view from restaurant, excellent food, breakfast included, on water's edge but no beach, simple, clean, in nicely decorated cabins, mosquito screens and coils, small bathrooms with no door, water pressure poor, relaxed atmosphere, run by Andy and Nicole, the latter is a wonderful cook, papaya crepes with maple syrup recommended for breakfast, Andy has a country & western pizza bar and can take you fishing, tackle provided. Horses and boat trips also offered, meal and activity packages available. **E** *El Paradiso*, owned by Peter Traubel of Dive Samaná, T5380210. Cabins on main street, close to beach and dive shop. **F** *Villa Marina*, 800 m north of beach on road to Samaná. Italian-owned, 11 basic rooms with fan and bathroom, includes breakfast, excellent meals (fish platters or Italian food), served at reasonable prices under supervision of Vittorio Grillo, T/F5382545.

Eating Good food at the hotels. Behind the dive shop is *Jardín Tropical*, restaurant and bar, daily specials US$5. *L' Aventura*, good pizza for US$4.50. *Chez Denise*, T5380219. French food, crêpes, salads, from US$3.50. *El Marinique* (see above). Locals eat at the mini-*comedores* on the beach at the end of the road where the *guaguas* stop, not recommended for hygiene but plenty of local colour. You can find boatmen here for trips to other beaches.

Watersports **Diving** *Dive Samaná*, T/F5380001, at the end of the road on your left by the beach, run by Peter Traubel, boat *Highlander* takes 24 passengers or 12 divers, great diving, CMAS, no jetty, no service so load your own gear, no shade on board, good new rental equipment. Peter goes to 15 dive sites around the bay and the headland west to Puerto Escondido. Also coastal excursions, snorkelling trips, boat transfers and whale watching US$40 in season with underwater microphone.

Transport Las Galeras is 1 hr, US$1.75 by *guagua*, from either the market or the dock in Samaná, US$4.50 by *motoconcho*. All transport congregates where the road ends at the beach, by the *comedores* on the sand. *Guaguas* leave when more or less full but you won't have to wait long. Jeep and motorbike rental on the road to *Hotel Moorea Beach*.

Directory **Useful addresses** *Codetel* is on the main road next to *De Todo Un Poco*. *Tricom*, *Caribe Tours* and *Western Union Cambio* are by the Spanish restaurant *El Pescador*.

Las Terrenas
Insect repellent is necessary at dawn & dusk to combat the sandflies

On the north coast of the peninsula is Las Terrenas, with some of the finest beaches in the country, from which, at low tide, you can walk out to coral reefs to see abundant sea life. The beaches seem to go on for miles, fringed by palm trees under which are hidden a large number of small hotels and restaurants, often run by Europeans, attracted by the life style.It is a quiet, low key resort and never crowded, partly because it takes a while to get there; the beaches are mostly clean and remain beautiful. It is reachable by a 17-km road from Sánchez which zig-zags steeply up to a height of 450 m with wonderful views before dropping down to the north coast. The road Samaná-Las Terrenas via Limón is also a pretty route although perhaps not so spectacular from the top.

Where the road reaches the shore, at the cemetery in Las Terrenas village, a left turn takes you along a sandy track that winds between coconut palms alongside the white sand beach for about 5 km, past guest-houses and restaurants. At the end of the beach, walk behind a rocky promontory to reach **Playa Bonita**, with hotels, guest houses and restaurants. Beyond the western tip of this beach is the deserted **Playa Cosón**, a magnificent 6-km arc of white sand and coconut groves ending in steep wooded cliffs (1½ hour walk or US$1 on *motoconcho*).

A right turn at the waterfront in Las Terrenas takes you along a potholed road about 4 km to the largest hotel in the area, *El Portillo*, which looks rather out of place, being a large multistorey building. The airstrip is behind it on the other side of the road. 10 km further on is **El Limón**, a farming village on the road across the peninsula to Samaná. From El Limón you can ride or hike for an hour into the hills to a 40-m high waterfall on the Arroyo Chico and swim in a pool of green water at its foot. The **Cascada del Limón** (or El Salto de Limón) is a National Monument in 1996. Behind the falls is a small cave. There are four different access routes to the falls from the Samaná road, from the communities of Rancho Español, Arroyo Surdido, El Café and El Limón, from all of which you can hire horses, buy food and drinks and local produce or handicrafts. If taking a guide to the falls, fix the price in advance (the falls can be deserted, do not take valuables there). Access to the falls is regulated to prevent erosion and other ecological damage; it is prohibited to visit other than on foot or on horseback and only in daylight. *Motoconcho* from Las Terrenas to El Limón US$2.50, but they will try to charge US$5-10.

B-C *Las Cayenas*, T2406080, west end of Las Terrenas, beach front. Nice hotel run by Swiss-French lady, Marie Antoinette Piguet; all-inclusives are not listed here rooms with or without balcony including breakfast and taxes, also large room for 4, good value. **C** *Tropic Banana*, T2406110. 25 rooms, breakfast included, tennis, coaching available, pool, fans, screened windows, balconies, one of the larger guest houses, good value food, popular bar with live merengue nightly. **C-D** *Kanesh*, at end of west track to beach, T2406187, F2406233. Run by Tamil/Swiss, some rooms cheaper, clean, hot water, large rooms with balconies and sea view, good food, help with excursions. **E** *Aloha*, T2406287. Just off the beach road, quiet, hot water, clean, beautiful garden, run by Spanish, cheerful staff and friendly cats, breakfast included. **E-F** *L'Aubergine*, T2406167, F2406070. Price depends on room and number of people, run by French Canadians, near *Cacao* and beach, quieter than hotels on beach, very good, restaurant closed Sun. **C-E** *Villa Caracol*, along from *L'Aubergine*. Clean, friendly, quiet. **E** *Casa Robinson*, set back from beach, 200 m from village centre, T2406070. Rather noisy, double rooms with shower and terrace or small suites with kitchenettes and balconies. **E** *Los Pinos*, Swiss-run, family atmosphere, clean, excellent, large rooms with mosquito nets, shared bath, nice balcony, new restaurant, a steakhouse also serving meat fondues, helpful, transport to Sánchez can be arranged. **E** *La Louisiane*, T2406223, F2406070. French-run, 5 rooms, some with kitchen, good value, reduced rates for long stays. **E** *Casa Nina*, turn right for 800 m along the beach in Las Terrenas. French-run, renovated, cosy cabins. **F** *Casa de los Tres Locos*, on the way to Playa Bonita. Nice bungalows in huge garden, Austrian-run.

On **Playa Bonita** are **B-C** *Atlantis*, T2406111, F2406205, hotel.atlantis@codetel. net.do Breakfast included, French-run with excellent French cuisine, chef used to work for President Mittérand. **C-D** *Acaya*, Playa Bonita, T2406161, F2406166. Two buildings on the beach, 16 rooms, hot water, fan, terrace, dive shop, nice atmosphere, good breakfast and thatched restaurant, international menu with specialities like meat and fish fondue. **C-D** *Coyamar*, 1st hotel at Playa Bonita, German-run, 12 rooms, nice, cosy, beachfront, friendly, helpful. **E** *Casa Grande*, right on beach. Friendly, run by 2 German women, good kitchen, nice location. **E** *Papagayo*, T2406131, on beach road. Rather noisy beside disco, good, bath, clean, fans, screened windows, breakfast included, small bar and restaurant, dive shop on site. **E** *Casas del Mar*, run by French, Mme Guislaine, includes breakfast. **E** *El Rincón de Abi*, El Torcido 2, T2406639, F2406070, dtaza@hotmail.com, 100m inland, take turning by *Pizzería al Coco*. New in 2000, guest house in quiet neighbourhood, 6 rooms, buffet breakfast included, meals available US$6-10, local recipes, kitchen facilities for guests, run by Giselle and Jordi Taza, helpful and friendly, French and English spoken.

The restaurant in *Hotel Palo Coco* on main road is Spanish-run with daily menu for US$5.50 with glass of wine and dessert. *Pizzería al Coco*, Playa Bonita, next to *Mambo* disco. Good pizzas, Swiss-run, excellent Swiss food, nice atmosphere, also **C** bungalows to rent for 1-3 people. By the beach in the grounds of *Hotel Las Cayenas*, but independent, is *La Parrilla*, friendly, good food, open air or under thatched roof, also bar; *La Campanina*, next to *Hotel Aligio*. Good Italian food. *Aubergine*, next to *Hotel Cacao Beach*. Canadian-run, excellent seafood, fine French cuisine, also pizzas and some Chinese dishes. *Iñaki & Isabel*, between *Salsa* and *Casa Papón*. Pueblo de los Pescadores, best seafood in town, fresh daily, nice little restaurant right by the sea, friendly, owners are Basque. *Dinny*, beach front. Good Dominican food, serves excellent breakfast with *jugos* and lots of fresh fruit. *Bar Janine*, German-run, good food, good prices. *Indiana Café*, next to *Iñaki & Isabel*. Meeting point, nice seafront spot with good atmosphere, serves Mexican food. *Casa Azul*, Swiss/Dominican-run, sandwiches, salads, Spanish tortilla, hamburgers, good for breakfast, lunch or dinner, on beach by main junction. *Casa Papón*, right by the sea. Good food. *La Salsa*, thatched roof restaurant on the

Sleeping
Most hotels are small; those on beach have prices ranging up to 'B', but those in town or behind those on the beach can be very cheap

Eating

Dominican Republic

beach near *Trópico Banana*. French-owned, expensive. **Louisiana**, small bar, French-run, lovely spot. **Suni**, Dominican food, cheap and good on Calle Principal. Small places along main street may have only 1-2 items on menu but food is usually good and much cheaper than a restaurant. *Sucresale*, at the main road. French bakery, breakfast and pastries. *Le Saigon*, next to the Police station. Vietnamese-run, Vietnamese and Chinese food, very good. *Le Piaf*, a bar at the *pueblo de los pescadores* on the beach. Also **Pizza Playa**, very good pizzas, fish and other dishes.

Bars & nightclubs   Popular disco is **Mambo Bar**, next to *Papagayo*, open weekends only, also **Tibidabo** and **Nuevo Mundo**. There is often music at the bars and restaurants for less energetic entertainment. At weekends there is quite a lot going on, particularly along the beach road, with street sellers of food and drinks and impromptu drum music, but this is not Ibiza.

Sport   There are several dive shops, including one at *Tropic Banana*, T5899410, courses available, one of the best for watersports. Windsurfing and sailing are mostly only available at the all-inclusive resorts but equipment can be rented at the Pura Vida office, between the cemetery and *Paco Cabana*. Diving schools at the *Kanesh Hotel*, the *Castello Beach* (Alex Abbas) and the *Bahía Las Ballenas* hotel, Playa Bonita. Tennis lessons at *Tropic Banana*, 0900-1100, US$13.50 1 hr, US$20 2 hrs, sparring partner US$6.50 per hour. Horseriding can be arranged through *El Portillo* or *Tropic Banana* (stables run by Luc, who is Swiss) on healthy, well-schooled animals, for beach or mountain rides.

Tour operators   For tourist information and hotel booking service go to *Sunshine Services*, Calle del Carmen, T/F2406164, run by Swiss; Spanish, English, German, French and Italian spoken. Lots of information and help, also car and motorbike rental, excursions (about 25), fishing and boat trips. *La Casa de las Terrenas*, Calle Principal, T/F2406251, casater.resa@codetel.net.do, can also help with information, tours, bookings etc.

Transport   **Local** *Motoconchos* whizz up and down the road through the village and weave their way along the beach track, US$1, depending on how far you go. **Bus** *Caribe Tours* stops in Sánchez (T5382229) on the way to Samaná, from Santo Domingo or Puerto Plata. You will be met by *motoconchos*, US$3 to the *guagua* stop, up to US$4.50 to a hotel further along the beach. A taxi (minibus) Sánchez-Las Terrenas costs US$20, Samaná-Las Terrenas US$47. Note that *guaguas* which meet arriving *Caribe Tours* buses in Sánchez overcharge for the journey to Las Terrenas (US$4.75-9.50). Car hire Lots of car, jeep, *moto* hire. Motorbikes (US$15-25) and mountain bikes (no brakes) can be hired. Jeep rental US$60. There is a petrol/gasoline station.

Directory   **Banks** *Baninter* in *centro comercial* in the middle of the village. *Banco del Progreso* has an ATM but it is not always working. *Crediprogreso* in the centre Paseo down by the cemetery. *Agencia de Viajes Vimenca*, Remeses Vimenca, on the main road. *Western Union* for fast money transfers, exchanges money at the best rates in town. Another *casa de cambio* near *Tropic Banana*. **Communications** Telephone: *Codetel* has a phone and fax office, open daily 0800-2200, credit cards accepted. **Internet**: *CCL Comuni-Centro Las Terrenas*, at the junction where the road forks take the left fork heading for the beach, it is on your right, upstairs, US$0.60 per 5 mins, printout US$0.12, phone Europe US$1 per min, post cards, cambio downstairs.

East of Santo Domingo

The eastern end of the island is generally flatter and drier than the rest of the island, although the hills of the Cordillera Oriental are attractive and provide some great views. Cattle and sugar cane are the predominant agricultural products and this is definitely cowboy country. However, much of the sugar land has been turned over to more prosperous activities such as tourism, the Casa de Campo development being a prime example. The main beach resorts are Boca Chica, Juan Dolio, Casa de Campo, Punta Cana and Bávaro, but there are several other smaller and more intimate places to stay.

About 25 km east of Santo Domingo (RD$5 toll on *autopista*, past international airport) is the beach town of Boca Chica, the principal resort for the capital. Its days of being a quiet fishing village are long gone. It is set on a reef-protected shallow lagoon, with many kilometres of white sand. Tourist development has been intensive and, at weekends, the place is invaded by the citizens of Santo Domingo. There are many hotels, aparthotels and restaurants of different standards with lots of bars and nightlife. Vendors line the main road, selling mostly Haitian paintings of poor quality but they are colourful. The main street is closed to traffic at night and the restaurants move their tables on to the road.

Boca Chica
Do not visit at the weekend as it can be packed with people from the capital

There are three large all-inclusives, which are best booked as part of a package if you want a good deal. **LL-AL** *Coral Hamaca Beach Hotel & Casino*, T5234611, F5236767; **L** *Boca Chica Resort Beach Club*, T5632000, F5635236; and **L-A** *Don Juan*, T5234511, F6885271. **B-C** *Calypso Beach Hotel*, Caracol esquina 20 de Diciembre, T5234666, F5234829. Not on beach, but close, some rooms overlook small pool, new, well kept, pleasant, lots of plants, small bar, restaurant, higher price includes breakfast, billiards. On Calle Duarte at eastern end of town is **C-D** *Mesón Isabela*, T5234224, F5234136. Price for a room, more in apartment without tax, French-Canadian and Dominican owned, bar, pool, family atmosphere, quiet, personal service, breakfast, light lunches on request, across road to beach, cookers in some rooms. Next door is **C-D** *Neptuno's Club Guest House* (for restaurant, see below), with bath, free coffee, very satisfactory. **C-D** *Villa Sans Souci*, Juan Bautista Vicini 48, T5234461, F5234327. Includes tax, clean, beautiful, pool, restaurant, excellent French Canadian food, bar by pool, no a/c, airport transfers with advance notice. **C-D** and up *Las Kasistas del Sol*, Primera y 2 de Junio, away from beach, T5234386, F5236056. Pool, restaurant, clean, beautiful setting, good service, friendly. **D-E** *La Belle*, Calle Juan Bautista Vicini 9, T5235959, F5235077, on corner of highway. Very nice, a/c, pool, colour TV, permanent water and electricity (but may be turned off in low season when quiet). **C-D** *Mango*, near Calle Juan Bautista Vicini, T5235333. Fan, TV, pool, nice garden. **C-F** *Villa Don*, Calle Juan Bautista Vicini 11, T/F5234679. Variety of rooms, private or shared bathroom, hot water, apartment with kitchen, discounts for long stays, some with TV, a/c, fridge, one or two beds, clean, cheap rooms are basic but adequate, small pool, right by road, bar, credit cards accepted, price for longer stay negotiable. **D** *Costalunga*, Av del Sur, T/F5236883. Short walk to beach, Italian-run, spotlessly clean, a/c, TV, fridge, cooker, wall safe, bathroom, secure parking, pool, beauty salon, restaurant, travel agency and fax service, excellent value, security guard at night but no one to check you in if you've had a late flight. **F** *Don Paco*, Duarte 6, T5234816. Central, clean, friendly, own generator but not always on if few guests, ask for it to be turned on.

Sleeping
The cheapest guest houses are away from the beach up by the autopista

L'Horizon is excellent and *Buxeda* is recommended for seafood, especially *centolla* (crab). Also recommended is *Neptuno's Club*, T5234703, F5234251, east of *El Hamaca*. Built over water, with pier, good fish watching, swimming rafts, seafood, German-owned, menu is German and English, 0900-2230, closed Mon, reservations essential, now has replica of the *Santa María* for trips along the beach. Other good restaurants are *Casa Marina*, *Porto Fino*, *Pequeña Suiza*. On the beach *fritureras* sell typical dishes, among them the famous *yaniqueques* – Johnny cakes. There is a good all-night, palm-covered burger hut where people gather for late-night satellite TV entertainment.

Eating

There are numerous bars for couples on Calle Duarte. In the same area is plenty of variety for unattached males, female prostitutes are provocatively dressed, but beware of pickpockets and AIDS; otherwise mostly safe although poor street lighting can be alarming.

Nightlife

Road Taxi: Santo Domingo-Boca Chica US$25 (can be only US$15 from Boca Chica to Santo Domingo), US$15 from the airport. **Bus** *Guagua* US$1 from either Parque Enriquillo or Parque Independencia, or the corner of San Martín and Av París but not after dark; *Boca Chica Express*, US$1, 30-40 mins, stops running around 2100. **Car** If driving from the capital, look carefully for signposts to whichever part of Boca Chica you wish to go. Parking costs US$0.60 at the beach.

Transport

Dominican Republic

Directory **Banks** *Banco Popular* has an ATM and will change TCs at good rates. There are several exchange houses. **Communications** Phone calls can be made from *Televimenca/Western Union*, on main street, also Codetel, near *Coral Hamaca*.

Juan Dolio The Guayacanes, Embassy and Juan Dolio beaches, east of Boca Chica, are also popular, especially at weekends when they can be littered and plagued with hawkers (much cleaner and very quiet out of season). The whole area is being developed in a long ribbon of holiday homes, hotels and resorts, and a new highway is improving access. **Los Guayacanes** has a nice little beach and the village is less overcrowded than Boca Chica. Buses going along the south coast will drop you, and pick you up again, at the various turn-offs to the beaches. **Juan Dolio** village is low key, with hotels, apartments, a few small bars, a tour agency and dive shop. Tourist taxis from the Juan Dolio hotels charge US$44 for a return trip to Santo Domingo with a three-hour wait. Taxi to the airport US$20 one-way (T5262006).

Sleeping & **Los Guayacanes C** per person *Playa Esmeralda*, Paseo Vicini, T5263434, F5261744,
eating www.playa-esmeralda.com All-inclusive, thatched stone hotel on nice beach, shallow like Boca Chica and protected by reef, nice gardens, pool, quiet, low key, but beach can get busy at weekends with Dominicans from the capital, diving. **C-D** *Sol-y-Mar*, Calle Central 23, T5262514. Includes breakfast, very clean big rooms, own beach, helpful, French/Canadian-run, overpriced restaurant. **C-D** *Woody's Guesthouse & Deli*, Calle Central. Small beach, restaurant, Swiss owner, T5261226. Cheaper is **D-E** *Las Brisas*, family-run, also on Calle Central. Lots of apartments and hotels along the newly-paved beach road. *El Refugio de los Desperados*, near *Sol-y-Mar*. Basic but excellent cooking, try fresh lobster with pasta for US$4.50.

Juan Dolio All the large hotels are all-inclusive and offer pools, tennis, sports facilities, restaurants, bars and entertainment. The road between the beach and the highway is in poor condition; on it are **C-D** *Ramada Guesthouse*, T5263310, F5262512. Meals US$18.50 FAP, pool, disco bar, watersports; opposite is *Marco's* restaurant and bar, German. There is a good selection of modern, modestly-priced apartments for rent, by day, week, month or year, eg *Yamina*, T5261123 (operated by Villas del Mar Realty, reliable).

East of Juan Dolio is the resort of Villas del Mar and the beach area of Playa Real, with four all-inclusive Barceló hotels, www.barcelo.com Also **Metro Hotel & Marina**, T5262811, F5261808. at Km 11 on the road to San Pedro de Macorís, Villas del Mar, is **L** *Occidental Playa Real*, www.occidental-hoteles.com and *Meliá Juan Dolio*, T5261521, F5261409. There are also several apartment developments.

La Romana East of San Pedro de Macorís is La Romana. The town is dominated by its sugar fac-
Population: 101,350 tory, which belches smoke and can be seen all along the coast. There are still railways here which carry sugar to the **Central La Romana** and the trains' horns can be heard through the night. The town is very spread out, mostly on the west bank of the **Río Dulce**, which reaches the sea here.

Isla Catalina Off La Romana is Isla Catalina (also called Serena Cay). Although inland the southeast part of the island is dry, flat and monotonous, the beaches have fine white sand with some of the best bathing in waters protected by reefs and excellent diving. Travel agents run tours for US$30-68 including lunch, supper and drinks. Cruise ships also call at the island, disgorging some 98,000 passengers in a winter season. The island is under the permanent supervision of the Dominican Navy and the Ministry of Tourism. All works that may affect the vegetation have been prohibited. The Río Chavón area east of La Romana and Casa de Campo is a protected zone to safeguard a large area of red and black mangroves.

Casa de Campo Just east of La Romana on the road to Higüey you pass the entrance to Casa de Campo. This is the premier tourist centre in the Republic. The resort was built in 1974 by Charles Bluhdorn, the founder of Gulf & Western, which originally grew sugar cane on the land. After he died the Cuban-American family Fanjul bought it and opened it to paying guests in the 1980s. It is currently operated by Premier Resorts and is kept isolated from the rest of the country behind strict security. It has its own airport and is totally self-contained. Covering 7,000 acres, it is vast, exclusive, with miles of luxury villas surrounded by beautifully tended gardens full of bougainvillea and coleus of all colours. All sorts of famous people have stayed here, including Michael Jackson and Lisa Marie Presley when they got married in the Dominican Republic in 1994. It has won numerous awards and accolades from travel and specialist sporting magazines. A new Marina & Yacht Club with Customs on site is at the mouth of the Río Chavón, from where you can take boat trips up the river.

Sport is the key to the resort's success. There are lots of activities on offer and they are all done professionally and with no expense spared. The **tennis** club has 13 courts where you can have lessons with a pro or knock up with a ballboy, the club is busy from early in the morning to late at night. The **riding** school has some 150 horses for polo, showjumping, trail riding, or whatever you want to do. The **polo** is of a particularly high standard and international matches are held here. For those with a keen eye, there is a world-class **Sporting Clays** facility developed by the British marksman, Michael Rose, with trap, skeet and sporting clays. Above all, however, guests come here for the **golf**. There are two world class 18-hole courses designed by Pete Dye: 'The Links' and 'Teeth of the Dog'. The latter, ranked number one in the Caribbean and 29th in the world (Sep 1999, *Golf Magazine*'s top 100 courses of the world), has seven water holes which challenge even the greatest players. Another hazard is the resort's airport.

Sleeping **LL** *Casa de Campo*, 10 km to the east of La Romana, PO Box 140, La Romana, T5233333, F5238548, www.casadecampo.cc Operated by Premier Resorts & Hotels, Premier World Marketing, 2600 SW Third Avenue, 3rd floor, Miami, FL 33129, USA, T305-8567083, F305-8584677. Hotel, villas, bars, restaurants and country club. Lots of different packages for families, golf, tennis etc.

Transport The private international airport receives daily American Airlines flights from Washington DC via Miami, American Eagle and Dominair from San Juan. Air Santo Domingo has domestic flights to/from Puerto Plata and Punta Cana. Charter transfers can be arranged from Santo Domingo's international airport, Las Américas.

Altos de Chavón is an international artists' village in mock-Italian style built by an Italian cinematographer, in a spectacular hilltop setting above the gorge through which flows the Río Chavón. Students from all over the world come to the art school, but the village is now a major tourist attraction and is linked to *Casa de Campo*. There are several restaurants of a variety of nationalities, expensive shops and a disco. The Church of St Stanislaus, finished in 1979 and consecrated by Pope John Paul II, contains the ashes of Poland's patron saint and statue from Krakow. It is a perfect spot for a wedding with a lovely view of the river and great photo opportunities. An amphitheatre for open air concerts seating 5,500 was inaugurated with a show by Frank Sinatra (many international stars perform there, eg Julio Iglesias, Gloria Estefan, as well as the best Dominican performers). There is also an excellent little **Museo Arqueológico Regional**, with explanations in Spanish and English and lots of information about the Taínos. All the artefacts on display came from around this area.

Altos de Chavón

Transport Free bus every 15 minutes from *Casa de Campo*. *Carros públicos* from La Romana to *Casa de Campo* US$0.20. Taxi from La Romana US$15-20. Most people arrive on tour buses or hired car.

Dominican Republic

Bayahibe

About 25 km east of La Romana

Bayahibe is a fishing village on a small bay in a region of dry tropical forest and cactus on the edge of the Parque Nacional del Este, a great place to stay, with excursions, diving, budget lodgings and cafés. Its proximity to the park and offshore islands has made it popular with divers and many people consider it the best dive destination in the country. Small wooden houses and the green wooden church of the village are on a point between the little bay and an excellent, 1½ km curving white sand beach fringed with palms. There are lots of rooms and cabañas to rent and several bars and restaurants for low-budget travellers. Plenty of fishing and pleasure boats are moored in the bay and it is from here that boats depart for Isla Saona. At the end of the bay, however, is one of the all-inclusive resorts which have been built along the coast, east and west of the village, pushing at the boundaries of the national park to the east.

Isla Saona is a picture book tropical island with palm trees and white sandy beaches, set in a protected national park. However it is also an example of mass tourism, which conflicts with its protected status. Every day some 1,000 tourists are brought on catamarans, speed boats or smaller *lanchas*, for a swim, a buffet lunch with rum on the beach and departure around 1500 with a stop off at the 'swimming pool' a patch of waist-deep water on a sand bank, where more rum is served. The sea looks like rush hour when the boats come and go. If you arrange a trip independently on a *lancha*, a smaller, slower boat, the local association of boat owners assures uniform prices.

There are 5 all-inclusive hotels not listed here, mostly booked from abroad

Sleeping *Amhsa Casa del Mar*, T2218880, F2218881, amhsa@codetel.net.do, west of the **E** *Hotel Bayahibe*, T7073684, F5564513. New, best in village, rooms have 2 beds, bathroom, hot water, fan, balcony, restaurant, cafetería, right by the water and dive boats. *Cabañas* for rent, for as little as US$10, ask around, don't expect hot water; **E-F** Doña Olga's are good. Also **F** *Cabañas Trip Town*, T7073640. Clean, private bathroom, on main street, near beach.

Eating There are lots of small bars and restaurants, which frequently change hands. *Big Sur*, on the beach, Italian-owned, great food. *Restaurante La Punta*, seafood. *Café Caribe*, breakfasts and other meals. *Adrian café* and restaurant. *La Bahía*, fish dishes, international calls, main street, on the beach. *Cafetería Yulissa*, good breakfast, recommended. *El Oasis*, also recommended for breakfast.

Sport Diving The all-inclusive resorts have their own dive operations, but there is an independent dive shop in Bayahibe, *Scubafun*, run by Germans, Werner and Martina Marzilius, T3016999. Their clients range from *Casa de Campo* guests to backpackers, beginners to experienced divers. They are very flexible and will do almost anything on request. Wear shoes when you go in the water as there is broken glass. Some of the best diving in the country is in this area, in the National Park, and although local fishermen are still spearfishing, the reef is in good condition and there are plenty of fish, more in some areas than others. Dolphins are often seen from the boat, while underwater you find sharks and rays off Catalinita Island, east of Saona, reef sharks at La Parguera, west of Saona, the wreck of *St George* close to the *Dominicus* and fresh water caves inland for experienced divers. Two-tank dives with a beach stop cost US$56-75, depending on the distance, a trip to Saona, Catalina or Catalinita, including national park fees, drinks and snacks, costs US$75-100. A day trip to Saona Island costs US$44.

Transport Take the road which turns off the highway from La Romana to Higüey. A *carro público* La Romana-Bayahibe is US$2.50, or take a Higüey bus to the turnoff and take a *motoconcho*, US$1. A taxi from La Romana costs about US$10.

Higüey

The main town in the far east of the island is the modern, dusty and concrete Higüey. The **Basílica de Nuestra Señora de la Altagracia** (patroness of the Republic) can be seen for miles away. It is a very impressive modern building in a huge park surrounded by a wall, to which every year there is a pilgrimage on 21 January; the statue of the virgin and a silver crown are in a glass case on the altar and are paraded through the streets at the end of the fiesta. According to legend, the Virgin appeared in 1691 in an orange tree to a sick girl. Oranges are conveniently in season in January and huge piles of them are sold on the streets, while statues made of orange wood are also in demand. The Basilica was started by Trujillo in 1954, but finished by Balaguer in 1972. The architects were French, the stained glass is French, the bronze doors (1988) are Italian, portraying the history of the Dominican Republic.

Punta Cana

Punta Cana, on the coast due east from Higüey, has some beautiful beaches, good diving and an international airport. The area is not particularly pretty, the land is flat and the vegetation is mostly scrub and cactus, except for the palm trees along the beach. There are only two resorts and no small hotels. The *Club Med* opened in 1981 and was the first tourist resort, followed by the *Punta Cana Beach Resort* in 1988. Julio Iglesias and Oscar de la Renta have built villas in the exclusive Los Corales, a second home and hotel project, but it is all very private. Independent visitors find it difficult to find a public beach as the hotels will not allow non-residents through their property. The **Marina Punta Cana** has a capacity for 22 yachts and eight other sailing boats, immigration and customs services provided by officers at the Punta Cana airport (24 hours' notice required if arriving by sea). A golf course was built in 2000 between the *Club Med* and the *Punta Cana Beach Resort*.

Transport Air From North America: Detroit and Minneapolis (*North West Airlines*), Miami (*Lan Chile*, Aerolíneas Argentinas and *Aeromar*), New York (*TWA*). **From Europe:** Amsterdam (*Martinair*), Lisbon (*TAP*), Madrid (*Air Europa*), Paris (*AOM*), *Condor* from Berlin, Cologne/Bonn, Dusseldorf, Frankfurt, Hamburg, Hanover, Leipzig, Munich and Stuttgart. *LTU* from Dusseldorf, Frankfurt, Hamburg, Munich. *Hapag Lloyd* from Frankfurt, Hanover. **From the Caribbean:** San Juan (*American Eagle*, *Condor*), Providenciales (*TCI Sky King*). **From South America:** Bogotá (*Aces*), Santiago (*Lan Chile*), Caracas (*Aserca*).

Bávaro

Continuing round the coast, there are many other beaches with white sand and reef-sheltered water. The area now known as Bávaro was once a series of fishing villages, but they have disappeared under the weight of hotels which contrast with the shacks still hanging on in places. All the hotels are usually booked from abroad as package holidays and most of them are all-inclusive.

The **Manatí Park Bávaro** is a controversial tourist attraction with dolphins, sea lions, birds, a parrot show, turtles and dancing horses (pure bred Andalucian stallions like you see in Jérez de la Frontera or Vienna (shows Wednesday, Saturday 2145), as well as a replica Taíno village. The dolphins were caught in the wild and sold to the Park by Cuba, in a highly controversial deal. Conservation groups such as the Whale and Dolphin Conservation Society are keeping it under close scrutiny. ■ *0930-1800. US$21 adults, US$10 children. T5526100, F2219282, manatipark@ codetel.net.do*

The southwest

The far southwest of the Republic is a dry zone with typical dry-forest vegetation. It also contains some of the country's most spectacular coastline and several national parks. It is a mountainous area with great views and scary roads and the closer you get to the Haitian border the poorer and more deforested the country becomes. Tourism is not big business here yet, although there are some fascinating places to visit, such as Lago Enriquillo, a salt water lake below sea level and three times saltier than the sea, or the mines for larimar, a pale blue semi-precious stone used in jewellery. The towns and villages are unremarkable and unpretentious but give a fascinating insight into rural and provincial life in the Republic.

Dominican Republic

San Cristóbal To the west of Santo Domingo is **Haina**, the country's main port and an industrial zone, and then San Cristóbal, in the interior, 25 km from the capital. This was the birthplace of the dictator **Rafael Leonidas Trujillo** and most of the sites of interest are related to his involvement with the town. He was actually on his way to San Cristóbal to visit a mistress in his country home when he was gunned down on the road along the coast from Santo Domingo. A busy industrial and commercial centre, San Cristóbal does not have great charm, and it is possible to bypass it by taking the coast road via Nigua from Haina or Hatillo.

In the region of San Cristóbal are several sites of great natural and historical interest as well as some fine beaches. The caves at **El Pomier** are some 15 km north out of town (buses from Parque Central) on the same road as the Casa de Caoba, Trujillo's home, now disintegrating but open 0900-1700. It is a long, hot walk from the gate that marks the entrance to the **Reserva Antropológica**. An official guide leads a tour of the caves, pointing out the faint white pictograms in the first and most accessible cave, which is also inhabited by thousands of bats. Unfortunately, neglect has led to considerable damage to some of the images and there is evidence of graffiti. ■ *0930-1700 except Sun, US$3 for tour. Wear solid shoes or boots and bring a torch.* Two other caves, **Borbón** and **Santa María**, are not open to the public, but on public holidays, and on the local saint's day festival (6-10 June) religious ceremonies take place around the cave complex, featuring an eclectic mix of supposedly Taíno ritual and Aftican-influenced stick and drum festivals. Nearby are **La Toma** natural pools, for scenery and swimming. ■ *0900-1800 Mon-Fri, 0700-1930 Sat-Sun, US$1.30.*

South of San Cristóbal, the beaches at **Palenque**, **Nigua** and **Najayo** (*públicos* leave regularly from San Cristóbal's Parque Central) are mostly of grey sand. On a hill overlooking Najayo beach are the ruins of Trujillo's beach house. These beaches are popular as excursions from Santo Domingo and at weekends and holidays can be packed. There are lots of beach bars serving finger-licking fried fish and local food, washed down with ice cold beer. The music can be overbearing at times with many personal sound systems competing against each other on the beach or thumping bass coming from parked cars under the trees, but at Palenque the dark sand beach is deserted at the far end and you don't have to walk far to get away from the crowds. Good swimming at Palenque, rougher at Najayo but there is an artificial wave breaker.

Baní From San Cristóbal the road runs west through sugar cane country to Baní. Baní is the birthplace of Máximo Gómez, the 19th-century fighter for the liberation of Cuba (see also Monte Cristi). The **Casa de Máximo Gómez** is a modest museum with a mural in his memory, set in a shady plaza within walking distance of the main Parque Duarte, the centre of the town and a pleasant spot. ■ *0900-1700, closed Sun, free. Ask for directions from the main Parque.* Another attraction is the **Museo del Café Dominicano**, which is informative about the Dominican coffee industry and local peasant production. ■ *0900-1700, closed Sun, US$1.20. Opening times, however, are erratic.*

Of the two roads west out of Baní, take the one to **Las Calderas** naval base for Las Salinas. There is no problem in going through the base (photography is not allowed); after it, turn left onto an unmade road for 3 km to the fishing village of **Las Salinas**, passing the unique sand dunes of the **Bahía de Calderas**, now a national monument and an inlet on the **Bahía de Ocoa**, shallow, with some mangroves and good windsurfing and fishing. The dunes, the largest in the Caribbean, can be reached from the road, but there are no facilities and little shade. The views are spectacular, however. In the village is **C-D** *Las Salinas High Wind Center*, T3108141. Run by Jorge Domenech, 24-room hotel, clean, restaurant with Dominican cuisine and wonderful seafood including lobster caught locally, bar, pool, windsurf centre, great dock house where you can relax out of the sun. Also in the area on the coast is **C-D** *Boca Canasta Caribe Beach Club Hotel*, T2230664, F5225210. Run by Don Vito Rallo and Hans Dieter Riediger, 40-room hotel on the beach, a/c, hot water, café, bar, restaurant, massage room, diving, tennis, basket and volleyball, fishing, horse riding, windsurfing, sailing, waterski, jetski, car hire.

Barahona

Barahona is a comparatively young town, founded in 1802 by the Haitian leader, Toussaint Louverture, when he was briefly in control of the whole of Hispaniola. Its economy initially rested on the export of precious woods, for example mahogany, to Europe. In the 20th century the sugar industry took over. The large sugar mill at the northern end of town is surrounded by the shanty town district of Batey Central and is currently closed pending privatization negotiations. The main attractions of this rather rundown grid-system town revolve around the seafront Malecón, where most hotels and restaurants are to be found. The Parque Central, five blocks up, is the commercial hub of the town and a pleasant spot to sit (although tourists are liable to be pestered). The small, public beach at Barahona frequently has stinging jelly fish. It is also filthy, as is the sea, and theft is common. The best beach near town is called **El Cayo** and is reached by passing the sugar mill and surrounding slums and doubling back on to the sandy peninsula with palms (visible from the *Brisas del Caribe* restaurant).

Population: 100,000

Sleeping

LL-L *Amhsa Riviera Beach*, Av Enriquillo 56, T5245111, F5245798, www.amhsa.com Newly-built all-inclusive outside town with own beach. It is possible to negotiate a cheaper, room-only rate, especially out of season. **E** *Hotel Caribe* on same road, but closer to town, T5242185. Excellent open-air restaurant (*La Rocca*) next door. **E** *Hotel Guaracuyá*, T2330748, on its own beach nearer the town centre than the Amhsa. Rather gloomy and dilapidated, but good value, with a/c. In town, **E** *Micheluz*, Av 30 de Mayo 28, T5242358. A/c, cheaper with fan, cold water, restaurant. **F** *Gran Hotel Barahona*, Calle Jaime Mota 5, T5423442. Fan, restaurant, simple. **F** *Hotel Cacique*, Av Uruguay (behind Parque Infantil), T5244620. Basic, clean. In **Baoruco**, 16 km from Barahona, **L-AL** *Clarion Resort*, T5421111, F5426060, www. clarion-resort.com New all-inclusive opened in 2000 after many delays, 105 rooms, all facilities, private beach. **B-C** *Casa Bonita*, T6960215, F2230548, in hills. 12 rooms in bungalows with nice gardens, pool, spectacular view over forest and beaches, very clean rooms, excellent service, a/c available, expensive restaurant.

Eating

Brisas del Caribe seafood restaurant at northern end of Malecón, T5242794. Excellent food and service, reasonable prices, pleasant setting, popular at lunchtime. *El Curro Steak House*, Calle Luperón, opposite cinema, T5243645. Meat and fish specialities, good value, outside sitting area, owner speaks English. *La Rocca*, next to *Caribe Hotel* on Malecón. Great breakfast menu, inexpensive, but not as good as it was following change of ownership. *D'Lina Pizza* , Av 30 de Mayo. Cheap and very large portions. *Panadería del Sur*, Uruguay y Luperón. Recommended for fresh bread, breakfasts and snacks.

Nightlife

Three discos, *Imperio* next to *Riviera Beach*. *Costa Sur* with restaurant almost opposite *Riviera Beach*. *Mega Plus*, one block inland of *Riviera Beach*.

Watersports

Coral Sea Divers on site at *Riviera Beach*, excellent **diving** at nearby reefs and in the Bahía de Neiba, where experienced divers can see manatees. Run by German Michael Schroeder, US$35-45 per boat dive, depending on equipment rented.

Tour operators

The Barahona Ecological Society welcomes enquiries from Spanish-speaking visitors and offers ecotourism advice and possibly guides. Contact Roberto Dominici, T5245081, F5245131, r.dominici@codetel.net.do Julio Féliz is an English-speaking local guide who specializes in ecotourism and bird-watching, fees negotiable, T5246570, F5243929.

Transport

Air The international **María Montéz airport**, opened in 1996. In theory there are daily connections with Santo Domingo and Port-au-Prince with *Caribair*, T5472767, but in practice

Dominican Republic

there are very few flights. **Bus** Journey time from the capital is 3 hrs. Minibus fare is US$3, *público* US$4, *Caribe Tours* runs 2 buses a day (group transport also available with *Metro Tours*, *La Covacha* and *Taxi Raffi*). To Jimaní 2½ hrs, US$3.30. *Concho* or *guagua* in town RD$3/US$0.20; *carrera* US$3-4.

Directory   **Banks** *Banco Popular* on Parque Central has an ATM (Plus, Visa). **Communications** *Codetel* across the square from *Banco Popular*, open daily 0800-2200.

Excursions

Beaches south of Barahona   Those with a car can visit remote beaches from Barahona (public transport is limited to *públicos*). The road south of Barahona, runs down the coast through some of the most beautiful scenery in the Republic, mountains on one side, the sea on the other, leading to Pedernales on the Haitian border (146 km). All along the southern coast are many white sand beaches which offer some of the best snorkelling in the Republic. The first place is the pebble beach of **El Quemaito**, where the river comes out of the beach, the cold freshwater mixing with the warm sea; offshore is a reef. **B** *Hotel El Quemaito*, T/F2230999. Small Swiss-run beach resort, pleasant gardens, good restaurant.

After Quemaito is the village of **El Arroyo**. Inland about 15 km into the hills along a dirt track (4WD necessary, especially after rain, ask directions at the nearby *colmado*) are the open-cast mines where the semi-precious mineral, **larimar**, is dug. Larimar is mined only in the Dominican Republic and is mostly used for jewellery. The primitive mines are worth a visit if you have your own 4WD transport. Miners or local boys will sell you fragments of stone, usually in jars of water to enhance the colour, for US$5-10, depending on size and colour. When dry, larimar is a paler blue.

Back on the main road, you pass through **Baoruco** (see Sleeping above) and **La Ciénaga** (small stony beaches and rough tides). The road comes right down to the sea before **San Rafael** (about 40 minutes from Barahona) where a river runs out onto a stony beach. The forest grows to the edge of the beach. Where the road crosses the river is a *pensión* with a cold water swimming hole behind it (the swimming hole is safer than the sea as enormous waves surge onto the beach). Construction is under way here. At weekends it gets very crowded. The refreshing cold water *balneario* is free and there are normally a number of stalls selling drinks and fried fish. It is also possible to climb up the mountain alongside the river, which has small waterfalls and pools. At **El Paraíso**, 31 km from Barahona, are a Texaco station and **F** *Hotel Paraíso* (T2431080, big rooms with bath, clean, TV). *Paola* restaurant, on the main road, is recommended and cheap.

At **Los Patos** another river flows into the sea to form a cool bathing place; a great place to spend the day at a weekend to watch Dominicans at play, with excellent swimming and lots of family groups. Note that most of these beaches have domestic animals, so there are droppings on the sand. There are cool, freshwater lagoons behind several of the other beaches on this stretch of coast. **Laguna Limón** is a flamingo reserve. It is very dangerous to drive at night. Roads are impassable without four wheel drive after rain, long delays if a lorry gets stuck.

Enriquillo, 54 km south of Barahona (**F** *Hotel Dayira*, on main road, no phone, basic; **F** *Dormitorio Juan José*, even more primitive, no phone), is the last place for fuel until Pedernales, 80 km away, but no unleaded is available. After Enriquillo the road turns inland up to Oviedo and then skirts the Parque Nacional Jaragua as it runs a further 60 km to Pedernales. **Oviedo**, with the atmosphere of a desert settlement, has no hotels or decent restaurants and is one of the hottest places in the country.

Pedernales   Pedernales is the most westerly town of the Republic, on the Haitian border. This is a major crossing point for migrant Haitian workers who come over to work in the sugar cane plantations and in construction. There is no immigration office so in theory only Haitians may enter Haiti here. However, this prohibition is frequently flouted, as border guards are willing to turn a blind eye in return for a small sum (US$10 or so). It is advised, however, that you make yourself known at the Anse-à-Pitres police station on the Haitian side and that you return within a few hours. If there is a change of personnel at the border station, you may find yourself paying another 'tip'. There is no road link, but the crossing can be done on foot if the stream that divides the countries is not too high, or you can hire a *motoconcho*. Every Friday there is an informal market in the no-man's-land at the border crossing, where Haitians sell cheap counterfeit clothing brands, smuggled spirits and a vast array of plastic kitchenware. There are few decent hotels in Pedernales. The best is **C** *Caribe Sur*, on nearby Playa Pedernales, a/c, hot water. **F** *Rossy*, no phone, is extremely basic. Rudimentary *comedores* in town.

Parque Nacional Jaragua is the largest of the Dominican Republic's national parks. This area of subtropical dry forest and inhospitable prickly scrub also contains a marine zone, in which lie the uninhabited islands of **Beata** and **Alto Velo**. The vegetation is largely cactus and other desert plants, but there are also mahogany, frangipani and extensive mangroves. Of particular interest is the **Laguna Oviedo** at the eastern end of the Park, which is easily accessible from Oviedo. Here there are the country's largest population of flamingos as well as herons, terns, spoonbills and frigate birds. Animals include the Ricord iguana, the rhinoceros iguana and several species of bat. The lagoon is reached via the National Park office just outside Oviedo (0830-1630 daily) where a RD$50 entrance permit must be bought. Turn right on a rough track after the office to reach a hut, where *Blanco Tours* offers a highly recommended boat trip around the lake. An ex-soldier, Blanco is a knowledgeable guide (Spanish only), who will point out birds and iguanas and will take visitors to inspect a couple of Taíno cave sites with pictograms. A tour normally costs around US$50, but up to six people can take part for that price.

Parque Nacional Jaragua

Near the Haitian border, is the 200 sq km **Lago Enriquillo**, whose waters, 30 m below sea level, are three times saltier than the sea. Once linked to the bay of Port-au Prince and the Bahía de Neiba, the lake was cut off from the sea by tectonic movements some million years ago and the surrounding beaches and the islands are rich in ancient seashells and coral fragments. Wildlife includes some 500 American crocodiles, iguanas and flamingoes.Three islands in the lake, together with the lake and surrounding shoreline make up the **Parque Nacional Isla Cabritos.** You need to purchase a Dirección Nacional de Parques (DNP) permit (RD$50) at the ranger station east of La Descubierta (0700-1630) to visit the island and only groups with a guide are permitted to go there. The 30-minute boat trip to the island is offered by various local boatmen, who are recommended by the DNP staff at La Descubierta. It costs US$6 per person (maximum 18 people) to go with Elena Nunciatini, T5375831, cellular 2249525, F5668809. There are usually one or two boats waiting to take parties over, and they will wait for other passengers if you are on your own, since the price of about US$50 is payable by one or up to six passengers. **Isla Cabritos** is a flat expanse of parched sand, with cactus and other desert vegetation. It is extremely hot and oppressive around midday (temperatures have been known to rise to 50°C) and visitors are recommended to arrive as early as possible and to take precautions against sunburn. This barren island is home to the rhinoceros iguana and the Ricord iguana, both of which have become quite tame and approach boat parties in search of treats. The two smaller islands are **Barbarita** and **La Islita**. To visit the lake it is best to have one's own transport if short of time because, even though public transport runs both on the north and south shores, there is no guarantee of travelling on (or returning) the same day. Note that there is a filling station in Duvergé but no fuel elsewhere in this area.

Parque Nacional Isla Cabritos

There is no accommodation on the lake shore but basic lodging can be found at La Descubierta

Jimaní, at the western end of the lake (not on the shore), is about 2 km from the Haitian border. The space in between is a no man's land of rocky terrain crossed by an

Jimaní

Dominican Republic

extremely hot road, which fortunately has a constant coming and going of *guaguas* and *motoconchos*. Jimaní is an authorized crossing point for foreigners in general (as is Dajabón) and it is possible to leave the Dominican Republic here and cross into Haiti. You have to pay a US$10 departure tax, a US$10 entry tax and a further US$10 if you wish to return. Customs officers in Jimaní are not above taking items from your luggage. The immigration office closes at 1800 (or before). There is a semi-permanent market in the no man's land, in which Haitian merchants display vast quantities of mostly shoddy and/or counterfeit goods, Barbancourt rum and perfumes. Jimaní itself is a spread out town of single-storey housing which swelters in temperatures of up to 50°C. **E** *Hotel Jimaní*, T2483139, on road east out of town, appears to be converted military accommodation, no hot water, little service but nice pool, decent restaurant and ice cold beer. *Restaurant Los Lagos*, Duarte y Restauración, excellent *chivo y gandules* (goat and beans), stays open late as town's main meeting place, also has disco *Krystal*.

Background

History

The colony
See also the history section in the Haiti chapter, page 387 for more on Columbus' colonization of Hispaniola

Although the Spanish launched much of their westward expansion from Santo Domingo, their efforts at colonizing the rest of the island were desultory. Even Santo Domingo soon declined in importance, overwhelmed by the onslaught of hurricanes and pirate attacks. Drake sacked Santo Domingo in 1586 and the rebuilding costs were more than the fledgling colony could bear. The French invaded in the 17th century from their base on Tortuga and colonized what became known as Saint Domingue in the west. The French colony, the largest sugar producer in the West Indies, soon became the most valuable tropical colony of its size in the world, while the Spanish colony languished and was used mostly for cattle ranching and supplying ships on the route from the Old World to the New.

By the mid-18th century, the number of Spaniards in the eastern part of the island was only about one-third of a total population of 6,000. Since there was little commercial activity or population of the interior, it was easy prey for Haitian invaders fired with the fervour of their rebellion at the turn of the 19th century (see Haiti, page 387). Between 1801 and 1805, followers of Toussaint L'Ouverture and Dessalines plundered the Spanish territory. Sovereignty was disputed throughout the beginning of the 19th century with frequent incursions and occupations by Haitian forces. In 1822, Haiti's army took control for a further 22 years. This occupation lives on in the country's mythology as its lowest point, with the ruthless Haitians expropriating land and raising taxes. It was a very anti-Spanish and anti-white régime and many of the Spanish hierarchy left the island. Santo Domingo descended into poverty.

Independence

In February 1844 pro-independence forces led by three men, the writer **Juan Pablo Duarte**, the lawyer **Francisco del Rosario Sánchez** and the soldier **Ramón Mella**, defeated Haitian troops in Santo Domingo. The newly independent nation was called the Dominican Republic, supposedly free and independent of all foreign domination. However, the new leaders were not a cohesive group and once in power they soon succumbed to infighting. Duarte was sent into exile and the country underwent yet another period of instability, including more Haitian incursions. In November 1844, the strongman, **Pedro Santana**, assumed the presidency. He wanted to make the Republic a protectorate of France, Spain or Britain, but with no luck. The other leader, or *caudillo*, at this time, **Buenaventura Báez**, also favoured annexation and the USA was also approached.

A Spanish colony again

In 1861, Santana finally achieved re-annexation with Spain in the first and only recolonization in the Americas. It was a total failure. Spanish bureaucrats were incompetent, the clergy was once again dominated by reactionary Spaniards and military rule was repressive and contemptuous of the Dominicans. There was widespread hatred of Spain and an increasing number of guerrillas took to the hills to fight a war of attrition. Spain resented the money it had to spend on suppressing revolts and reinforcing its garrison, much depleted by yellow fever.

The resurrection in the countryside proved successful and became known as the War of Restoration (la Restauración), ending in 1865 when Queen Isabella II abrogated the treaty of annexation and evacuated Spanish officials and troops. The Restoration is remembered as a great moment in Dominican history, but governments still pursued the idea of annexation as the answer to their problems. They wooed the USA, but the US Senate could not muster enough support and a vote for the proposal was defeated. However, Germany became deeply involved in the economy, with its traders and bankers supporting the tobacco crop. German warships were sent on occasion to collect debts and the USA was becoming increasingly apprehensive about Germany's motives and sphere of influence. **The Restoration**

The USA intervened to prevent a European power gaining control of the country's customs on behalf of creditors. Roosevelt put the Dominican customs into receivership and under an agreement signed in 1905, the US authorities would collect import and export duties and distribute 55% to the country's creditors and 45% to the Dominican government. In 1907 a formal receivership treaty was signed, heralding the start of the USA's financial leverage in the region. Peace was not assured, however, and in 1916, when the presidency appeared to collapse in chaos, US marines were landed. During the US occupation the Dominican finances improved dramatically and the country became credit worthy again, but the American occupiers were deeply resented. Guerrilla fighters were suppressed by US troops. In 1920 the new Land Registration Act dispossessed peasant farmers who had held land communally in traditional holdings known as *terrenos comuneros*, in favour of private ownership, allowing Dominican and US investors to buy up land titles and purchase huge areas on the cheap. Some of these dispossessed small scale farmers formed armed bands, known as *gavilleros*, and waged intermittent guerrilla warfare against the Guardia Nacional and US forces. Eventually US troops were withdrawn in 1924, although the administration of the customs remained under US control. **US intervention**

In May 1930 elections were won by the armed forces commander, **Rafael Leonidas Trujillo Molina**, who became President. Thus began one of the most ruthless dictatorships ever seen in the Dominican Republic. With either himself or his surrogates at the helm (Héctor Trujillo, 1947-60, and Joaquín Balaguer, 1960-62), Trujillo embarked on the expansion of industry and public works and the liquidation of the country's debts. After a hurricane in 1930 seriously damaged Santo Domingo, he rebuilt it and renamed it Ciudad Trujillo in his own honour. Nevertheless, his methods of government denied any form of representation and included murder, torture, blackmail and corruption. For 30 years he ruled supreme, dispensing favours or punishment as he deemed appropriate. During his reign, in 1937, an estimated 10,000 Haitian immigrants were rounded up and slaughtered, prolonging the hatred between the two republics. The economy prospered with the expansion of the sugar industry and an influx of US capital, but much of the wealth ended up in the bank accounts of the Trujillo family, as the General appropriated companies and land. In 1961 Trujillo was assassinated and another power vacuum was created. **The Trujillo dictatorship**

Joaquín Balaguer had been part of Trujillo's government since 1930 and was nominally president at the time of the murder, although without any real power or legitimacy. He tried to hang on to the presidency, but there was violence and the military intervened. A Council of State was set up in 1962 which, with US approval and finance set the country on the path to some sort of representative democracy. The first free **The Balaguer presidencies**

Dominican Republic

elections for 40 years were held on 20 December 1962 in which Balaguer was defeated by **Professor Juan Bosch** of the Partido Revolucionario Dominicano (PRD). Bosch was a left-wing intellectual who had formed the social democratic PRD in exile. The party's policies for land reform with the redistribution of the vast estates held by the Trujillo family, together with an attack on unemployment and poverty, were over-whelmingly supported by the electorate. He took office in February 1963 but after seven months he was ousted by a military coup and sent into exile. A three-man civil-ian junta was installed with martial law and new elections were promised, but instabil-ity ruled, with several changes of government. With civil war raging in the capital and memories of Communist Cuba still fresh, the USA dispatched 23,000 troops on 28 April 1965 to control the country. The USA supported another provisional govern-ment, but there followed several months of fighting with the loss of some 3,000 lives. Finally, new elections were held in June 1966. They were won by Balaguer, returned from exile in New York. The economy was in tatters and US aid was crucial in rebuild-ing the country. The US peace keeping force returned home, calm descended for a while and Balaguer concentrated on imposing austerity and bolstering the country's finances. He retained power in the 1970 elections, again defeating Bosch, and remained in office with the help of a secret paramilitary force known as *La Banda*, the gang, until 1978, forging closer links with the USA, but not without facing coup attempts, right-wing terrorism and left-wing guerrilla incursions.

The PRD boycotted elections in 1970 and 1974, but the declining popularity of Balaguer led it to challenge him in 1978. A PRD President was returned: **Antonio Guzmán**, a wealthy landowner and former minister in Juan Bosch's brief govern-ment, whose chief aims were to reduce army power and eliminate corruption. His election was achieved after the intervention of President Carter of the USA, who pre-vented a military takeover when it became clear that the PRD was winning. Guzmán's successor, **Dr Salvador Jorge Blanco**, also of the PRD, presided over severe economic difficulties which led to rioting in 1984 in which 60 people died. The party split over the handling of the economy, helping Joaquín Balaguer to win a narrow majority in the 1986 elections giving him a fifth presidential term. The 1990 elections were contested by two octogenarians, Dr Balaguer (83) and Dr Juan Bosch (80), now of the Partido de la Liberación Dominicana (PLD). Dr Balaguer won a sixth term of office by a very narrow majority, which was subjected to a verification process after Dr Bosch alleged fraud had taken place in the capital. The May 1994 elections had the same outcome, after Balaguer had decided very late in the cam-paign to stand for re-election. His chief opponent was **José Francisco Peña Gómez** of the PRD, who was subjected to blatantly racist campaign abuse because of his dark skin and alleged Haitian ancestry. First results gave Balaguer the narrowest of victories. Peña Gómez, supported by many outside observers, claimed that fraud had taken place and the election was reviewed by a revision committee appointed by the Junta Central Electoral (JCE). The committee found numerous irregularities, but its findings were ignored by the Junta which awarded victory to Balaguer. To defuse the crisis, Balaguer signed a pact with Peña Gómez allowing for new elections in November 1995; Congress rejected this date, putting the new election back six months to 16 May 1996.

1996 election campaign

Almost at once campaigning began for the 1996 presidential election. The PRD selected Peña Gómez again while the PLD chose Leonel Fernández as its candidate, to replace Juan Bosch who had retired. Within the PRSC, jockeying for the candi-dacy was beset by scandals and power struggles, exacerbated by the absence of an appointment by Balaguer himself.

In the first round of the 1996 elections, Peña Gómez received 46% of the vote, compared with 39% for Leonel Fernández. However, in the second round, Balaguer gave his support to Fernández, in an effort to keep Peña from the presidency, and he won 51% of the vote. Balaguer continued to influence the new government's policies through Congress. The PLD was in a minority in both houses, holding only one

Senate seat, compared with 15 for the PRSC and 14 for the PRD, and 13 congressional seats, compared with 58 for the PRD and 48 for the PRSC, with one independent.

President **Leonel Fernández** was sworn in on 16 August 1996 and appointed a cabinet largely from his own party, after a cooling of relations with Dr Balaguer. His comparative youth signalled a breath of fresh air despite the continuing influence of the old *caudillos*. In his inauguration speech he pledged to fight poverty, while earlier promising to modernize the economy and fight corruption. In 1997 relations with the PRSC deteriorated rapidly because of investigations into land purchase scandals involving members of the previous administration. Land which was in national parks or in protected areas of special scientific interest, or expropriated under the agrarian reform programme for distribution to small farmers, was found to have been allocated to PRSC officials and sold on for profit, mostly for tourism development. There was also a shake up in the top ranks of the military and police, with some linked to drugs offences, others to unsolved murders and disappearances.

José Francisco Peña Gómez lost his fight with cancer and died in May 1998. Six days later, his party, the PRD, won a landslide victory in the congressional and municipal elections, winning 85 of the 149 seats in an expanded (from 120 seats) Chamber of Deputies and 24 of the 30 Senate seats. The governing PLD came second with 49 and four seats respectively, while the PRSC managed only 15 and two seats.

The Fernández administration

At the beginning of 1999 tension was eased among the three main political parties with the holding of talks to resolve issues concerning the Junta Central Electoral, which supervises elections, and the Liga Municipal Dominicana (LMD), which allocates finance to local authorities. Presidential elections in 2000 were keenly fought between the 93-year-old Balaguer for the PRSC, Danilo Medina for the ruling PLD and **Hipólito Mejía** for the PRD. The government was credited with achieving economic growth, but it was perceived that the benefits had not been widely enough distributed and corruption within the administration was alleged. Despite his age, blindness and other infirmities, Balaguer was seen as an influential power broker and a force to be reckoned with. Mejía won 49.87% of the vote, Balaguer 24.6% and Medina 24.9%. As no one achieved the 50% required for an outright win, a second round was technically necessary, but after both other candidates visited Balaguer, both he and Medina pulled out of the race, leaving Mejía the victor.

2000 elections

Government

The Dominican Republic is a representative democracy, with legislative power resting in a bicameral Congress: a 30-seat Senate and a 149-seat Chamber of Deputies. Senators and deputies are elected for a four-year term, as is the President, in whom is vested executive power.

Economy

The largest foreign exchange earner is tourism, with annual receipts exceeding US$2 bn. The industry generates 20% of gdp and employs about 5% of the labour force, 50,000 in direct jobs and 110,000 indirectly. New hotel projects brought the number of hotel rooms to 52,000 at end-2000, compared with 11,400 in 1987, and more than any other Caribbean country. More are being built and plans are to increase capacity by 50%. Nearly half of hotel rooms are sold on an all-inclusive basis.

There are six main agricultural regions: the north, the Cibao valley in the north central area, Constanza and Tiero, the east, the San Juan valley, and the south. Cibao is the most fertile and largest region, while the eastern region is the main sugar-producing area. **Sugar** was traditionally the main crop and times of prosperity have nearly always been related to high world sugar prices, but diversification out of sugar cane, the conversion of some cane lands into tourist resorts, the expulsion of Haitian

Structure of production

cutters and a slump in productivity led to lower volume and value of sugar production. Other traditional products grown for export include sugar, coffee, cocoa and tobacco, but they now account of only a third of total exports. Non-traditional products have been gaining in importance. These include fruit and vegetables, plants and cut flowers, marine products, processed foods, cigars and other agroindustrial products. Growth of the cigar industry has put the Dominican Republic in top place among the region's exporters, exceeding both Honduras and Cuba, with sales of around US$400 mn a year.

Since 1975 gold and silver mining has been of considerable importance. Large gold, silver and zinc deposits have been found near the Pueblo Viejo mine, where the oxide ores were running out, and a major gold and silver deposit has been discovered in the Haitian border area, which could mean a joint operation to establish an open cast mine. The country also produces ferronickel, which has overtaken sugar as the major commodity export earner. Reserves are estimated at 10% of total world deposits.

Despite the booming tourist economy roughly half the population lives in poverty, with a third lacking secure employment. Two thirds of the people are now in urban areas and many depend on the informal economy to survive. Remittances from relatives in the USA are the life blood of many families and even whole villages. Inequalities in income are glaring, with the poorest 20% receiving less than 5% of the national income. The rich live ostentatiously in luxury villas driving large cars and the oligarchy continues to dominate the economy as it has done since colonial times. From sugar cane and coffee, the powerful families (among them Bermúdez, Barceló and Jiménez) have moved into tourism and export manufacturing.

Culture

Art During the colonial era there was no national art to speak of. The only painters and sculptors were priests who were commissioned to copy religious themes, although occasionally they painted portraits of local dignitaries. The first major painting came the Restauración movement and the consolidation of independence from Haiti. The first important painter was **Alejandro Bonilla** (1820-1901), who was the first to paint in oils the portrait of Juan Pablo Duarte and later those of Francisco del Rosario Sánchez and Matías Ramón Mella. He also painted landscapes and local scenes, which are now of historical interest. The Spaniard **José Fernández Corredor** is credited with the foundation around 1883 of the first painting school in the country and trained **Arturo Grullón** (1869-1912) and **Abelardo Rodríguez Urdaneta** (1870-1933), a sculptor and painter who also turned his hand to photography. **Luis Desangles** (1861-1940), known affectionately as Sisito, whose paintings and portraits were popular at home and abroad, was notable for his delicate use of colour. From this period the artist **Leopoldo Navarro** (1862-1908), also stands out.

At the turn of the century **Enrique García Godoy** (1886-1947) specialized in oils and pastels. **Celeste Woss y Gil** (1890-1985) was the grande dame with a vocation for teaching and promoting women in culture and the arts. In 1939 at the World Painting Exhibition in New York, her oil painting *El Vendedor de Andullas* (The Tobacco Vendor) was awarded the Medal of Honor. In 1942 a milestone was reached with the creation of the Escuela Nacional de Bellas Artes (National School of Fine Arts). The first graduates from this highly-respected institution in the 1940s included Marianela Jiménez, Gilberto Hernández Ortega, Domingo Liz, Ada Valcárcel, Fernando Pena de Filló and Luichi Martínez Richez, who won the Biennial Sculpture Prize in Paris in 1955. **Jaime Colson** (1901-75) emerged on the scene as the leading Dominican artist. Colson was born in Puerto Plata but studied at the Real Academia de San Fernando in Madrid and the Escuela de la Lonja in Barcelona. He had a variety of styles and refined techniques which were versatile and universal and only considered himself 'Dominican because he was born Dominican'. His autobiography was entitled *Memoirs of a Nomadic Painter*. Jaime Colson, Yoryi

Morel and Darío Suro were precursors of *costumbrismo* (art of customs and manners). The 1960s heralded the end of Trujillo's tyranny and allowed freedom of expression not permitted before. However, it was the 1970s when contemporary art really developed and artists felt able to express themselves individually in an international context. Those who have gained an international reputation are Iván Tovar, Ramón Oviedo, Cándido Bidó, José Rincón Mora, José Ramírez Conde and Paul Giudicelli.

Exhibitions of Dominican art are held frequently in Santo Domingo galleries, for example the Voluntariado de las Casas Reales, Galería Nader, Museo de Arte Moderno, El Pincel, La Galería, and others. Street sellers of Haitian or Dominican copies of Haitian naïf art are not representative of what is going on in the Dominican art world and are merely gaudy paintings for tourist consumption. For details on contemporary Dominican painters, consult *Arte Contemporáneo Dominicano*, by Gary Nicolás Nader. The leading expert on all Dominican art is Cándido Gerón, who has written and produced some beautiful books, including *Antología de la Pintura Dominicana*, *Obras Maestras de la Pintura Dominicana* (two volumes, divided into generations, or decades, of important artists) and *Pintura Dominicana, Un Cuarto de Siglo (1970-96)*.

El Consejo Presidencial de Cultura and UNESCO have made an evaluation of murals painted in Santo Domingo, counting 187 as part of the national heritage. They can be found in the Centro de los Héroes, Universidad Autónoma de Santo Domingo, Palacio de Bellas Artes, buildings in the Plaza de la Cultura, the Ayuntamiento, Banco de Reservas and Instituto del Seguro Social. Murals have been painted by Jaime Colson, Jaime Vela Zanetti, Eligio Pichardo, José Ramírez Conde, Paul Giudicelli, Clara Ledesma and Amable Sterling.

Literature

Colonial Santo Domingo may have been the cradle of the New World, but it produced very little in the way of literature. What writing there was tended to be the work of Spanish functionaries or priests, such as the military commander and historian, **Gonzalo Fernández de Oviedo**, who wrote a thorough account of the colony in the 1550s. Much of the material in **Bartolomé de las Casas'** monumental *A Very Brief Account of the Destruction of the Indies* (1551) was based on the Friar's experiences in Santo Domingo. The first Dominicans to be published in the latter half of the 19th century, such as the poets **José Joaquín Pérez** (1845-1900) and **Salomé Ureña de Henríquez** (1850-96), followed the thematic and stylistic conventions of mainstream European romanticism, with the emphasis on stylized subjectivity and the celebration of nature. Indigenous themes also appeared, as Pérez in particular sought to romanticize the country's pre-Columbian past in a genre known as *indigenismo*. Although still read and appreciated in the Dominican Republic, neither poet enjoyed great success outside their own country. The first novel of any note was published in 1882. Entitled *Enriquillo*, **Manuel de Jesús Galván's** (1834-1910) epic account of the legendary *cacique* was both a romantic evocation of the 'noble savage' stereotype and an interesting meditation on Dominican cultural identity. For Galván, the figure of the insurgent Taíno leader was a heroic figure, symbolizing a mythical national resistance to foreign (in this case, Spanish) domination. But in presenting him as a precursor of the Dominican nation, Galván was also implicitly suggesting that contemporary Dominicans could trace their ancestry back to the original Taínos, contributing to the vogue among some coloured Dominicans of referring to themselves as *indios*.

The trend towards imitating European conventions continued into the 20th century. **Gastón Fernando Deligne** (1861-1912) was a poet whose darker, more introspective brand of lyricism testifies to the influence of Baudelaire and the French Symbolists. Dubbed the 'national poet', Deligne and his contemporary **Fabio Fiallo** (1866-1942) mirrored a preoccupation with aesthetic purity and verbal ingenuity. As with all facets of Dominican culture, the US occupation of 1916-24 proved a turning-point in the search for authentic forms of expression. But no sooner had a

Dominican Republic

radical generation of nationalist writers begun to find their voice to protest against the imposition of North American values than the long period of the Trujillo dictatorship was under way. For 30 years the régime tolerated no criticism whatsoever, stamping on any literary originality and encouraging only absurd paeans of praise to 'the Benefactor'. Two of the 20th century's most prominent Dominican writers chose exile. The opposition leader, **Juan Bosch**, wrote polemics against Trujillo, historical studies and, most readable, two collections of short stories that revealed a formidable grasp of narrative technique. Probably the greatest of the country's poets, **Pedro Mir**, also lived and wrote abroad until the late 1960s, producing *Hay un país en el mundo* (There's a Country in the World, 1949), an epic poem that tells of an imaginary but recognizable country's history of suffering and exploitation. In 1978, Mir published *Cuando amaban las tierras comuneras* (When They Loved the Communal Lands), a powerful fictional critique of the US occupation and its expropriation of traditional communal land. The conservative **Joaquín Balaguer** who remained on the island, wrote poetry, historical fiction and a biography of Juan Pablo Duarte. With the assassination of Trujillo in 1961, the exiles were able to return and politically committed writing was again allowed. Authors such as **Manuel del Cabral** wrote incisively about the social turmoil of the 1960s in books like *La Isla ofendida* (1965), while **Freddy Prestol Castillo**'s *El Masacre se pasa a pie* (1973) was a damning account of the 1937 massacre of Haitians ordered by Trujillo.

Curiously, the dictatorship itself, although stifling literary creativity for three decades, has inspired some of the country's most interesting recent writing. One of the country's most successful writers, **Julia Alvarez**, situates her *In the Time of the Butterflies* (1994) around the political assassination of the three Mirabal sisters by Trujillo's henchmen. The brutal methods and bizarre megalomania of the dictator have also caught the imagination of foreign writers, notably the Peruvian **Mario Vargas Llosa**, whose *La Fiesta del chivo* (The Goat's Feast) was published in 2000 to great critical acclaim. Dramatizing the worst excesses of the Trujillo period and the build-up to the dictator's assassination, the novel caused unease and controversy in Santo Domingo, where memories are long. Alvarez, together with **Junot Díaz**, typifies the new generation of Dominican writers, who have been as much shaped by their experience of life in the USA as in their parents' homeland. Both write in English as easily as in Spanish, and Díaz in particular has mastered the tough street-wise vernacular of young Dominicanyorks, the distinctive community of migrant Dominicans in New York and other US cities. His collection of short stories, *Drown* (1996) received rapturous reviews for its unsentimental and sometimes shocking portrayal of alienation and cultural displacement in the Dominican Diaspora. Julia Alvarez has also written perceptively about the tensions and contradictions experienced by those with double lives. In *How the García Girls Lost Their Accents* (1991), she looks at the trials and tribulations of a Dominican family in New York and their ambiguous relationship with *la isla*.

Music & dance   The most popular dance is the merengue, which dominates the musical life of the Dominican Republic and has spread across the water with migrants to colonize New York as well, giving it international status. **Merengue** is believed to have developed in the mid-19th century as a local version of European dances for couples, such as *contredanse*. An Afro-Caribbean flavour was added with lively rhythms and the lyrics began to reflect social commentary. It was the music of the people, from cane-cutters to dock workers, and frowned upon by the upper classes but, with regional variants it survived as a sort of folk music. Traditionally there would be four musicians, playing the *cuatro*, which is like a guitar, the *güira*, a cylindrical scaper of African origin but akin to the Indian gourd scraped with a forked stick, the *tambora*, a double-headed drum using male goatskin played with the hand on one head and female played with a stick on the other, and the *marimba*, a wooden box with plucked metal keys derived from an African instrument. Despite the regional variations, the merengue of the Cibao Valley around Santiago developed most strongly and gradually became known as the *merengue típico*. Here, in the 1920s, it was played with an accordion, introduced by the Germans in the previous century, a *güira*, *tambora* and *marimba*, with the accordion being the most important. Over the years, other instruments have been added, such as the saxophone, horn (trumpet or trombone) or electric bass guitar. A merengue would have a short introduction, *paseo*, then move into the song, or merengue, which would have the social or topical comment, followed by a call and response section, the *jaleo*. Although similar in many ways to some Cuban or other Latin music and dance, the steps of the merengue have always been simpler, with a basic two-step pattern, but at a fast tempo with much suggestive hip movement.

The other main music style you will find in the Dominican Republic is **bachata**, which also emerged from the peasant and shanty town dwellers. It was music for the soul, for the poor and downtrodden, the dispossessed farmers who were forced off the land in the 1960s and flooded into the urban slums with their guitar-based *canciones de amargue*, songs of bitterness. The traditional group had one or two guitars, maracas, bongo and marimba, with a solo male singer, who sang songs based on the Cuban *son*, Mexican *ranchera*, merengue and boleros. The songs expressed the frustrations of the newly-urban male, a *macho* without a cause, who was often unemployed and often dependent on a woman for his income. The sudden rise in popularity of bachata was principally due to **Juan Luis Guerra**, who experimented with the romantic, sentimental genre and sensitively created a poetry which appealed to everyone, particularly women. Most bachata songs are similar to boleros, with the guitar, the rhythm and the sentimentality, but faster than usual and with one singer rather than three.

There is a merengue festival in the last week of July and the first week of August, held on the Malecón in Santo Domingo. Puerto Plata holds its merengue festival in the first week of October and Sosúa has one last week of September. In addition to merengue, salsa is very popular in dance halls and discos (every town, however small, has a discothèque).

People

African slaves began to arrive in Santo Domingo from the 1530s. Although the proportion of slaves in the colony never came close to matching that in neighbouring Saint-Domingue, blacks nevertheless formed an important part of the colonial population. As the indigenous Taíno inhabitants were exterminated within half a century of European colonization, African slaves and their descendants became the largest non-European group. From the mixing of Africans and Europeans, emerged the coloured or mulato population to which the majority of Dominicans nowadays belong. Successive governments tried to attract non-African settlers, especially after independence, when fears of Haitian territorial ambitions were at their highest and the 'whitening' of the population was deemed desirable. Some Canarian and Italian migrants took up the offer of government-assisted relocation schemes, while an important community from the Middle East, mostly Syrians but known generically as *turcos*, arrived to establish businesses. Another group of immigrants, known as *cocolos*, left the English-speaking Caribbean islands of Tortola, Anguilla and St Kitts to work in the Republic's sugar plantations. Their descendants still live in and around San Pedro de Macorís. Under Trujillo, there was even an attempt to settle Japanese farmers near the border with Haiti, presumably as a deterrent to would-be smugglers and rustlers. This racial policy is no longer on the agenda, but it shows how the country's leaders have traditionally viewed the nation as white, Hispanic and Christian.

Conventional demographic surveys suggest that about 15% of Dominicans are white, 15% black and 65% mixed-race or mulato (the rest being of Middle Eastern or other origins). A whole vocabulary exists to describe skin colour and ethnic identity: most desirable, of course, is to be *blanco* (white), followed by *trigueño* (olive-skinned). Further down the hierarchy come *mulato* and *moreno* (meaning dark or swarthy), and at the bottom is the term *negro*, sometimes used affectionately but more normally a mark of disapproval or even an insult. Perhaps the most idiosyncratic racial category is that of the *indio*. It seems most unlikely that any contemporary Dominican could plausibly claim Taíno ancestry, since the island's indigenous Taíno population was effectively extinct only 50 years after the arrival of the first European colonists. Yet the term is widely used to describe non-white Dominicans, and many identity cards describe their bearers as Indians, colour-coded as *oscuro* (dark), *quemado* (burnt), *canelo* (cinnamon) or *lavado* (washed). An *indio oscuro* may therefore be a dark-skinned individual of mixed ethnic background. There is a certain aspiration towards the Indian; this can be seen not only in the use of the original name for the island, Quisqueya (and Quisqueyanos), but in place names (San Pedro de Macorís, from the Macorix tribe) and in given family names (Guainorex, Anacaona, etc).

Large-scale Dominican migration to the USA really began in the 1960s, after the death of Trujillo, but accelerated during the economically troubled 1980s. Officially, half a million Dominicans live in the USA, but some estimates suggest that as many more are permanently resident as illegal or undocumented migrants. Most migrants are based in New York or in other east coast urban areas, and perhaps the most conspicuous enclave is to be found in the north Manhattan neighbourhood of Washington Heights, nicknamed 'Quisqueya Heights'.

Afro-Caribbean religious beliefs have significant numbers of followers in the Dominican Republic. Mixing reconstructed Taíno rituals, Catholic saints and African divinities, believers worship archetypal lúas or gods, such as Anaísa, the goddess of love (based loosely on Santa Ana) or the Barón del Cementario (equivalent to the Christian San Elías), the guardian of the graveyard. Ceremonies involve music, dancing, trances and spirit possession, and often take place at what are thought to be holy Taíno sites or during rural village fiestas. Other well-known venues for *vodú dominicana* are the mostly black, inner-city barrios of Villa Mella and the western mountain town of San Juan de la Maguana. A connected phenomenon is the widespread Dominican interest in *brujería* or witchcraft. *Brujos* are thought to have supernatural powers, both benevolent and malevolent, and are consulted by a wide cross-section of people in search of cures for broken hearts, financial problems and the difficulties caused by *mal de ojo* (the evil eye). Market place stalls and so-called *botánicas* (shops selling religious paraphernalia of all sorts) testify to the country's fascination with spiritual and supernatural forces.

Geography

The western part of the Dominican Republic is dominated by four mountain ranges which run roughly NW-SE. Much the most impressive is the Cordillera Central, which rises to the twin peaks of La Pelona and Pico Duarte, which at 3,082 m and 3,087 m are the highest mountains in the Caribbean islands. The eastern half of the country is much flatter, except for the hills of the Cordillera Oriental which run roughly parallel to the northeast coast. There is a distinctive tropical limestone landscape in part of the Cordillera Oriental, to the south of Sabana de la Mar. The northern boundary of the Caribbean plate lies just north of Hispaniola. The whole island is an active seismic zone, and there have been eight major earthquakes since 1751, the most recent in 1953. The island is moving slowly east, while Cuba and the Bahamas are moving to the west; what is now Hispaniola was attached to southeastern Cuba around 20 million years ago. The mountain ranges of the western Dominican Republic are associated with strong faulting close to a slight irregularity in the plate boundary.

Puerto Rico

10

478

Puerto Rico may be part of the USA but its music and dance is a mixture of both Spanish and African rhythms. The country, as a result, is a mixture of the very new and the very old. It exhibits an open American way of life yet retains much of the more formal Spanish influences. This is reflected in the architecture, not just the contrast between the colonial and the modern in urban areas but also in the countryside, where older buildings sit side by side with concrete schools and dwellings; it is found in the cuisine, a plethora of fast food restaurants together with local cooking which has its roots in a hybrid Caribbean culture; and it is found in the music, where rock and salsa are played in beach resorts but where, in the hilly interior, rustic songs of Puerto Rican folklore can still be heard. However, be warned: if you do not stray beyond the tourist areas on the coast, you will have a very one-sided experience of this paradoxical dependent territory.

A Foot in the door

- Don't miss the **Tibes** and the **Caguana Indian Ceremonial Centers**, the best examples you'll see of Amerindian ball courts, ceremonial plazas and burial grounds.
- Get back to nature on **Mona Island** with huge iguanas and sea birds, once home to Taínos and then pirates.
- Head underground to explore the caves, sinkholes and underground **Río Camuy**, where you can find bats and pre-Columbian petroglyphs as you travel on a hot-line, rappel and body raft.
- For after dark-entertainment visit **Phosphorescent Bay** in Vieques Island.
- Chill out on beautiful **Flamenco Beach** on the island of Culebra, where the water is a clear turquoise and the sand pristine white.

Essentials

Before you travel

Documents   All non-US residents need a US visa, or a US visa waiver for participating countries. All requirements are the same as for the USA.

Money   **Currency**   United States dollar. Locally, a dollar may be called a *peso*, 25 cents a *peseta*, 5 cents a *bellón* (but in Ponce a *bellón* is 10 cents and a *ficha* is 5 cents). Most international and US credit cards are accepted. **Exchange**   Currency exchange at *Banco Popular*; *Caribbean Foreign Exchange*, 201B Tetuán, Old San Juan, T7228222, and at the airport; *Deak international* at the airport; *Scotia Bank* exchange only Canadian currency; *Western Union*

Puerto Rico

▲ Forests		
1 Aguirre	6 Ceiba	11 Guilarte
2 Boquerón	7 Cerrillos	12 Jobos
3 Cambalache	8 El Yunque	13 Maricao
4 Carite / Guavate	9 Guajataca	14 Piñones
5 Casa Pueblo	10 Guánica	15 Río Abajo

N

Not to scale

for cable money transfer, *Pueblo Supermarket*, Old San Juan. **Banks** *Banco Popular; Banco de San Juan; Banco Mercantil de Puerto Rico*; and branches of US and foreign banks. *Banco de Santander*, of Spain, is the second largest bank in Puerto Rico.

Tradewinds make the temperatures of 28-30°C bearable in the summer. Temperatures in the **Climate** winter drop to the range 21-26°C and the climate all the year round is very agreeable. Rain falls mainly from May to October, with most precipitation from July to October.

Getting there

From Europe *Martinair* from Amsterdam; *Avianca* and *Condor* from Frankfurt; *Iberia* from **Air** Barcelona and Madrid; *US Air* from London Gatwick. Lots of other flights with connections in JFK New York or Miami. **From Latin America** Most South and Central American countries are connected via Miami or Panama City but there are also direct flights from Caracas (*Lacsa, AA*), Bogotá (*Aces, Avianca*), Maracaibo and Valencia (*ALM*), most Central American capital cities via Panama City, (*Copa*) and San José (*Lacsa*). **From the Caribbean** Anguilla, Antigua, Aruba, Barbados, Casa de Campo (Dominican Republic), Curaçao, Dominica, Fort-de-France, Grenada, Pointe-à-Pitre, Port of Spain, Puerto Plata, Punta Cana, St Barts, St Croix, St Kitts, St Lucia, St Maarten, St Thomas, St Vincent, Santiago and Santo Domingo (Dominican Republic), Tortola and Virgin Gorda (BVI), with *LIAT, American Airlines, American Eagle, Air Caribienne, ALM, Air Santo Domingo* and others. **From the USA** A great many US cities are served by *American Airlines, Delta, American Trans Air, Northwest Airlines, Continental, Tower Air, TWA, US Air* and *United Airlines* .

Cruise ships call at San Juan and Ponce. *Ferries del Caribe* run a passenger and car (no hire **Boat** cars) ferry service to/from the Dominican Republic from Santo Domingo to Mayagüez (Tue, Thu, Sun, 2000, arrives 0800, returns Mon, Wed, Fri, same times) with a bus link across the

16 Susúa
17 Toro Negro
18 Vega

PR Panoramic Route

Puerto Rico

Touching down

Departure tax None is payable, although LIAT demands a 'security tax' of US$5.

Tourist Zone Police The Puerto Rico Tourist Zone Police are at Vieques Street, Condado (T7220738 and 7245210). They can help you settle problems with taxis. Emergency T911.

Tipping Service is usually included in the bill, but where no fixed service charge is included, it is recommended that 15-20% is given to waiters, taxi drivers, etc.

Language Spanish is the first language with less than 30% of the population speaking English fluently.

Safety We have received several warnings from travellers. Of all crimes 65% are related to drugs trafficking. La Perla is known as San Juan's most dangerous slum and the end of Calle Tanca should be avoided as it is a favourite drinking and drug dealing area for residents. Female tourists should avoid the Condado beach areas at night and all areas of San Juan can be dangerous after dark. Take precautions against theft from your person and your car, wherever you are on the island. Hiking on mainland beaches is not a good idea; never stay on a beach if you are alone, beautiful areas such as Carite or Route186 above El Verde look like great hiking spots but do not always attract people with good intentions. Safety in numbers. Take advice locally.

Water Drought has frequently forced the imposition of water rationing in greater San Juan and 10 other towns. Water remains in short supply despite emergency dredging of the Carraizo reservoir, which had lost 65% of its capacity because of silt.

island to San Juan (T8324800). There is a weekend passenger launch on the *Caribe Cay* between Fajardo and St Thomas, 1¾ hours, Saturday 0830, US$70 return, T8608809. **Ports of entry** Mayagüez, Ponce, Fajardo, San Juan (not Boquerón). **Boat documents** Clearance required from Customs, Immigration and Agriculture. Foreigners must meet same entry requirements as into USA (US$90 if you arrive without a visa). US vessels must pay a US$25 annual customs fee (a sticker). US citizens must clear into Puerto Rico when coming from USVI. Do not bring in fruit, vegetables or garbage into the USA/Puerto Rico. Boats and firearms must be registered after 60 days. **Marinas** There is a liveaboard community at Boquerón. Ponce is a good place to provision, with wholesale houses, Sears, Walmart, nearby. Fajardo is headquarters for marinas, boat supplies and haul-out. Puerto del Rey marina has 750 slips, transient rate US$1 per foot per day (includes water, electricity, cable TV); Palmas del Mar, 40 slips, also many houses on the water have space to rent with water and electricity. Small anchorage area has cleaner water than stagnant marina. Nothing nearby, car rental needed. **Anchorages**: Boquerón, La Parguera, Guánica, Ponce, Fajardo, Vieques, Culebra has many (see Bruce Van Sant's *Guide to the Spanish Virgin Islands*). Ponce Yacht Club (members) allows one night free to other Yacht Club members. Haul out: Isleta, Puerto del Rey, Palmas del Mar, Villa Marina. Get **weather** from VHF weather, VI Radio or local AM station.

Touching down

Airport information There are airport limousines to a number of hotels. Set rates for Taxi Turístico: Zone 1, Luis Muñoz Marín airport to Isla Verde, US$8; Zone 2, airport to Condado/Miramar, US$12; Zone 3, airport to Pier area in Old San Juan, US$16. Between and beyond the zones rates are metered (make sure the taxi meter is used; note that drivers prefer not to go to old San Juan, the beach areas are much more popular with them).

Airlines *ACES*, T800-8462237; *Air Canada*, T800-7763000; *Air France*, T800-2372747; *Air Jamaica*, T800-5235585; *Air St Thomas*, T800-5223084; *ALM*, T800-3277230; *American Airlines and American Eagle*, T800-4337300; *American Trans Air*, T800-2252995; *BWIA*, T800-5382942; *COPA*, T800-3592672; *Continental*, T800-5250280; *Delta*, T800-2211212; *Iberia*, T800-7724642; *Isla Nena*, T7416362; *Lacsa-Grupo Taca*, T800-2252272; *LIAT*, T7913838; *Northwest Airlines*, T800-3747747; *United Airlines*, T800-2416522; *Vieques Air Link*, T2533644, www.vieques-island.com/val

Tourist offices overseas

Argentina, T54-11-43144525.

Brazil, T55-11-8220533.

Canada, 2 Bloor Street West, Suite 700, Toronto, Ontario, M4W 3R1, T416-9699025, F9699478.

France, Express Conseil, 5 bis, rue du Louvre, 75001 Paris, T331-44778806, F42600545.

Germany, T49-69-350047.

Italy, T39-0266-714403.

Mexico, T525-2021844 ext 13.

Netherlands, T312-06427909.

Paraguay, T5952-1497264.

Spain, Calle Serrano, 1-2° izda, 28001, Madrid, T3491-4312128, 800-898920, F5775260.

UK, T0800-898920.

Uruguay, T5982-7104430.

USA, New York T800-2236530, F212-8181866, *Los Angeles* T213-8745991, F8747257, *Miami* T305-3818915, F3818917.

Venezuela, T582-7619930.

Local tourist offices The Puerto Rico Tourism Company, PO Box 902-3960, San Juan 00902-3960, www.prtourism.com, publishes lots of brochures and booklets including *Travel and Sports Planner*, www.travelandsports.com, and *Qué Pasa!* Which comes out every two months and has a useful Tourist directory. Information centres also at the international airport (T7911014, F7918033; next to the *Condado Plaza Hotel*, T7212400 (ext 2280); La Casita, near Pier One, Old San Juan, T7221709, F7225208; Rafael Hernández Airport, Aguadilla, T8903315, T8900220; Citibank Building, 53 McKinley East, facing plaza, Mayagüez, T8315220, F8313210; Casa Armstrong-Proventud, Plaza Las Delicias, Ponce, T8405695, F8435958. **Tourist information**

Regional tourist offices Adjuntas, T8292590; Añasco, T8263100 ext 272; Bayamón, T7988191; Cabo Rojo, T8511025; Camuy, T8982240; Culebra, T7423291; Dorado, T796-5740/1030; Fajardo, T8634013; Guanica, T8212777; Jayuya, T8285010; Luquillo, T8892851; Naguabo, T8740389; Rincón, T8235024; Vieques, T7415000. For details on museums, contact the Puerto Rico Institute of Culture, Museums and Parks Programs, T7245477. Out in the country, tourist information can be obtained from the town halls, usually found on the main plaza. Hours are usually Monday-Friday, 0800-1200, 1300-1430.

Local tour operators *Colonial Adventure*, T7290114, walking tour of San Juan's cultural and historical highlights Mon-Sat 0930 and 1400, US$20 including museum entry fees. *Countryside Tours*, T7239691, balbin@prtc.net Víctor Balbín takes you to the University of Puerto Rico, the first Governor's house in Trujillo Alto and a (hard to find) typical lunch, pointing out typical plants and trees along the way, US$30, delightful cultural experience, recommended to get to know Puerto Rico. *Hillbilly Tours*, day trips from San Juan into the hills, run by Edwin Betancourt, T7605618, helpful with information. *Tropix Wellness Outings*, Víctor López specializes in tailor-made tours, one day or many days, for example caves (vigorous, hiking, body rafting), kayaks (Culebra), hiking (rain forest), Guanica (dry forest), you stay in nice hotels and paradores, T2682173, F2681722, tropix@msn.com *Northwestern Land Tours*, T4477804, Andrés Alicea offers day trips to the Indian ceremonial centre, Guanica Forest, El Yunque, Ponce, Río Camuy Caves etc. *Copladet Nature & Adventure*, T7658595, copladet@coqui.net transport, custom day tours or longer. *Rico Suntours*, T7222080, riding, horseracing, nightlife. For caving (see page 488), *Aventuras Tierra Adentro*, T7660470, F7547543, aventuras@spiderlink.net 272B Avenida Pinero, University Gardens, Río Piedras, PR 00927, expert guides Rosario Boscarino and Francis Reyes will lead you through an exciting adventure. *Encantos Ecotours*, also known as *Piñones Ecotours*, T2720005, www.ecotourspuertorico.com, bikes and kayaks, tours and rentals, also surf rafting in Piñones.

Roman Catholic, Episcopal, Baptist, Seventh Day Adventist, Presbyterian, Lutheran, Christian Science and Union Church. There is also a Jewish community. At the Anglican-Episcopal cathedral in San Juan there are services in both Spanish and English. **Religion**

Puerto Rico

Where to stay

The summer season runs from 16 April to 14 December and is somewhat cheaper than the winter season, for which we give rates where possible. An 11% tax is charged on the room rate in hotels with casinos, 9% in those without casinos.

There are 18 *Paradores Puertorriqueños* to put you up while touring, some old, most new, some quiet and peaceful (for example *Coamo, Gripiñas, Juanita, Casa Grande*), some used by local families for boisterous entertainment, with prices at US$55-100d: the majority are to the west of San Juan; for reservations T7212884 or from the USA T1-800-4430266. Many *paradores* are not what the average traveller wants, so do some research first. They are based on the Spanish *parador*, convenient places to stay when on the road, but lack the old charm of their Spanish counterparts. The island is undergoing a 40% increase in the number of hotel rooms available by 2002, so expect construction work in some areas. The Sol Meliá hotel chain is building the first all-inclusive resort on the island, at Río Grande, which will consist of two hotels of 490 rooms each, while many existing hotels are renovating and expanding, offering conference and banqueting facilities to attract more custom.

Camping Camping is permitted in the forest reserves; you have to get a permit in advance (see below). Camping is also allowed on some of the public beaches. Beach campsites are generally not as safe except for large parties although Culebra, Mona Island and the private campgrounds of Cabo Rojo and Hatillo are all right. El Yunque rainforest, north side, is also not safe but the US Federal Forest Service is working on the problem and now lock the gates at 1800. The private campsite near the south entrance to the rainforest is much safer. Government agencies expect everyone to arrive or call before 1500. You can take *públicos* to some of the camping places, but with difficulty, car rental is advised.

The Government agency *Fomento Recreativo* (T722-1551 for reservations, PO Box 9022089, San Juan, PR 00904-2089) administers the following campgrounds and cabins: Luquillo Beach, Seven Seas (Fajardo), Punta Guilarte (Arroyo), Monte del Estado (Maricao), Boquerón, Tres Hermanos (Anasco), Rincón. Only Seven Seas is safe enough to recommend. Luquillo is a terrific campsite but you need to be in a large party to be safe. Two-bedroom cabins and villas are offered on five of their beaches, villas are newer and nicer.

The *Negociado del Servicio Forestal* (part of the Departamento de Recursos Naturales y Ambientales – DRNA) administers seven campgrounds and cabins and Mona Island, PO Box 9066600, Puerta de Tierra, San Juan, Puerto Rico 00906-6600, T7243724, F7215984. You need a permit and reservation, fee US$4 per person a night (cabins in Guilarte US$20), easiest to go to their office at Club Náutico by the marina at the Dos Hermanos bridges on the way to Old San Juan. They will also help you plan an itinerary. Permits and changes to reservations can be made at regional offices. Open reservations allowing flexibility within a certain time period can be made in advance by writing to Department of Natural Resources, Division of Forest Land Use Permits, PO Box 5887, Puerta de Tierra, San Juan, PR 00906. Their camp grounds are: Carite Forest, Toro Negro Forest Reserve, Guilarte Route 131 and 518, Coamo Hot Springs, Susua Dry Forest, Guanica Forest, Guajataca Forest, Rió Abajo Forest, Cambalache Beach. El Yunque rain forest is administered by the US Forest Service, T8881880 and ask for camping information, or get free permit at El Portal, Route 191, north side, before 1600. The *Autoridad de Conservación y Desarrollo de Culebra* (ACC) administers the Flamenco Beach campgrounds on Culebra, PO Box 217, Culebra, PR 00775, T7420700, US$10 per tent per night, they often accept walk-in reservations in winter but in summer, especially at weekends, it is like a zoo.

Getting around

Air Several local airlines operate services within Puerto Rico, including *American Eagle* and *Vieques Air Link*, and they have offices either at the **Luis Muñoz Marín International Airport**, or the **Isla Grande** Airport. There are three daily *American Eagle* flights between San Juan and Ponce and several to Mayagüez. Some charter or inter-island flights leave from the Isla Grande airport.

Bus stops are marked *Parada*, or *Parada de guaguas*. From the terminal near Plazoleta del Puerto in Old San Juan, **B21** goes along the upper road along the ocean (near *Caribe Hilton*) to Condado (Condado Plaza, El Canario) then up Avenida de Diego to stop 18 on Ponce de León, and then out to Plaza las Américas Shopping Mall. **A5** goes along the lower road to Ponce de León and then down Avenida de Diego to Isla Verde (*El San Juan, Ritz Carlton* etc) and to Iturregui terminal. To get to the airport by bus from Old San Juan is complicated. Take **A5** bus to Isla Verde terminal, then **C45** or **B40** to the airport. From Condado take **B21** to Avenida de Diego, then **A5**, then as above. **Metrobus 1** (US$0.50) goes from Old San Juan along the upper road along the ocean to Avenida Ponce de León and then to Rio Piedras. **Metrobus E** goes to Rio Piedras via the express way to Hato Rey.

Bus
City buses run to a 30 or 45 min schedule. Many don't operate after 2200

There are many car rental agencies, including at the airport, *Hertz* (T7910840, www.hertz.com), *Budget* (T7913685, www.budget.com), *AAA* (T7911465), *Leaseway* (T7915900, www.leaswaypr.com). *Target* (T7281447, www.targetrentacar.com), not at airport, among the cheapest, will negotiate rates. *Charlie's Rental* (T7282418, www.charliecars.com) in Condado and Isla Verde among the cheapest, 24-hour service. *L & M, Condado* (T7911160, www.imcarrental.com), free pick-up, make sure you get it even for day hire. For the less mobile, *Wheelchair Getaway Rent a Car* (T7264023, 800-8688028) has vehicles which can accommodate a wheelchair. A small car may be hired for as little as US$25 (not including collision damage waiver, US$12.50, insurance is sometimes covered by your credit card) for 24 hours, unlimited mileage (national driving licence preferred to international licence), but rates vary according to company and demand.

Car
The best and easiest form of transport if you want to see the island; public transport is not always easy and finishes early

Maps The *Rand McNally* road map is recommended (US$1.85); the *Gousha* road map costs US$2.95 at Texaco stations. The tourist office distributes an *Official Transportation Map* with town maps of San Juan, Caguas, Ponce, Mayagüez, Aguadilla and Arecibo, but a better road map of the whole island is the *ITM Traveller's Reference Map*, Scale 1:190,000, published by ITMB, 345 West Broadway, Vancouver BC Canada V5Y 1P8. A good map is essential because there are few signs to places, but frequent indications of Route numbers and intersections. Avoid driving in the San Juan metropolitan area as traffic can be very heavy. Car theft and burglar damage is a major problem in the San Juan area. Make sure you use all the security devices given you by the rental company. Many people actually recommend that you do not stop at red lights after 2200, because of hold-ups: just pause, look and go. Best not to drive at night; lock car doors.

All taxis are metered, charge US$1 for initial charge and US$0.10 for every additional half mile; US$0.50 for each suitcase; US$1 is charged for a taxi called from home or business. Minimum fee US$3. Taxi drivers sometimes try to ask more from tourists, so beware, insist that the meter is used, and avoid picking up a taxi anywhere near a cruise ship. If they refuse, tell them you will call Puerto Rico Tourist Zone Police, T7220738, or the Public Service Commission, T7515050, ext 253. They can revoke a taxi license. White tourist taxis with a logo on the side offer fixed rates to and from tourist sites, for example airport, San Juan Pier, but outside those areas they are metered. **Zone 4**, Piers to Old San Juan, US$6; **Zone 5**, Piers to Puerta de Tierra, US$6; **Zone 6**, Piers to Condado/Miramar, US$10; **Zone 7**, Piers to Isla Verde, US$16. When metered, tourist taxis charge US$1.30 per mile, ask for final price.

Taxi

There are also shared taxis, usually Ford minibuses (*carros públicos*) which have yellow number plates with the letters P or PD at the end and run to most parts of the island from one main plaza to the next. They usually carry about 10 people and are not particularly comfortable. The Río Piedras *terminal de públicos* handles all departures to the east. Many públicos for the west leave from *puntos* near parada 18 in Santurce. Also some leave from the main post office and others collect at the airport; elsewhere, ask around for the terminal. They do not usually operate after about 1600 and some connections do not operate after 1500, for example Río Piedras-Fajardo. They are also very scarce on Sunday and public holidays. *Público* to Caguas costs US$1.25; Río Piedras-Fajardo 1½ hours (US$3); to Ponce takes two hours (US$6-7). A service referred to as *línea* will pick up and drop off passengers where they wish. They operate between San Juan, and most towns and cities at a fixed rate. They can be found in the phone book under Líneas de Carros. *Públicos* are a good way of getting around, provided you are prepared to wait up to a couple of hours for the car to fill up. It is not recommended, however, if you want to get to out of the way places, such as the Arecibo Observatory, the Camuy Caves, or the Tibes Indian Ceremonial Centre, when a hired car is essential. If you hire a *público* for yourself it is expensive, for example San Juan airport to Ponce costs US$75.

Train An urban rail service is under construction in San Juan and trains are supposed to start running in 2001.

Keeping in touch

Post Inside the new post office building in Hato Rey, on Avenida Roosevelt, there is a separate counter for sales of special tourist stamps. In Old San Juan, the post office is in an attractive old rococo-style building, at the corner of San Justo and Recinto Sur. Stamps may be bought at hotels and the airport. *Poste restante* is called General Delivery, letters are held for nine days.

Telephone Operated by *Puerto Rico Telephone Co*, state-owned. Local calls from coin-operated booths
IDD phone code: 787 cost US$0.10, or US$0.25 from a private pay phone, but from one city to another on the island costs more (for example US$1.25 Ponce-San Juan). Local calls from hotel rooms cost US$2.60 and often a charge is made even if there is no connection. Payphones now charge a fee of US$0.25, either deducted from your prepaid card or with a coin. The cheapest way to phone abroad is from *Phone Home*, 257 Recinto Sur, Old San Juan, T7215431, F7215497, opposite the post office by Pier 1, US$0.36 per minute to the USA, discounts on all other calls abroad, no three-minute minimum charge, faxes also sent and received. Overseas calls can be made from the AT&T office at Parada 11, Avenida Ponce de León 850, Miramar (opposite *Hotel Excelsior*, bus T1 passes outside, a chaotic place), from an office next to the Museo del Mar on Pier One, and from the airport. Three minutes to New York, US$1.50 and to the UK, US$3. For Canada Direct, dial 1-800-4967123 to get through to a Canadian operator. The blue pages in the telephone book are a tourist section in English, divided by subject.

Media **Newspapers** *San Juan Star* is the only daily English paper. There are three Spanish daily papers of note, *El Mundo*, *El Vocero* and *El Nuevo Día*. **Radio** There are seven radio stations: WDAC-FM, 105.7FM Alfa Rock 106; WKAQ-FM, 104.7FM KQ105; WIOA-FM 99.9FM Cadena Estereotempo; WMEG-FM, 106.9FM La Mega Estación; WDOY-FM, 96.5FM Y-96; WOYE-FM, 94.7FM Cosmos 94; WOSO-AM, 1030AM Radio Woso.

Food and drink

Local food Good local dishes are the mixed stew *asopao*, (chicken, seafood, etc). *Mofongo*, mashed plantain with garlic served instead of rice, is very filling. *Mofongo relleno* is the *mofongo* used as a crust around a seafood stew. *Sancocho* is a beef stew with various root vegetables, starchy but tasty. *Empanadillas* are similar to South American *empanadas* but with a thinner dough and filled with fish or meat. *Pasteles* are yucca, peas, meat, usually pork, wrapped in a banana leaf and boiled. *Tostones* are fried banana slices. Rice is served with many dishes; *arroz con habichuelas* (rice with red kidney beans) is a standard side dish. Sometimes a local restaurant will ask if you want *provisiones*; these are root vegetables and are worth trying. *Comida criolla* means 'food of the island', *criollo* refers to anything 'native'. Some local fruit names: *china* is orange, *parcha* passionfruit, *guanábana* soursop, *toronja* grapefruit; juices are made of all these, as well as guava, tamarind and mixtures. *Papaya* in a restaurant may not be fresh fruit, but *dulce de papaya* (candied), served with cheese, a good combination. Guava is served in a similar manner.

Restaurants As most food is imported, you can eat as cheaply in a restaurant as you can by buying food in a grocery store. Outside San Juan a network of 42 restaurants, called **Mesones Gastronómicos**, has been set up. These places serve Puerto Rican dishes at reasonable prices. Most of the *Parador* restaurants are included; a full list is available from tourist offices.

Local beers are *Medalla* (a light beer), *Gold Label* (a premium beer, very good but hard to find) and *Indio* (a dark beer); a number of US brands and *Heineken* are brewed under licence. Rums include *Don Q*, the local favourite, *Palo Viejo*, *Ron Llave* and the world-famous *Bacardi* (not so highly regarded by puertorriqueños). *Ron Barrilito*, a small distillery, has a very good reputation. Many restaurants pride themselves on their *piñas coladas*. *Maví* is a drink fermented from the bark of a tree and sold in many snack-bars. Home-grown Puerto Rican coffee is very good.

Drink

Shopping

Puerto Rico is a large producer of rum, with many different types ranging from light rums for mixing with soft drinks to dark brandy-type rums (see above). Hand made cigars can be found in Old San Juan and Puerta de Tierra. There is a place in the bus station complex in San Juan where cigars are rolled using Dominican leaf, which is better than local leaf. Shopping malls inlcude *Plaza las Américas* in Hato Rey, others include *Plaza Carolina* in Carolina, *Río Hondo* in Levittown, *Plaza del Carmen* in Caguas and *Mayagüez Mall* in Mayagüez. There are many souvenir shops in Old San Juan. Imported goods from all over the world are available. Local artesanías include wooden carvings, musical instruments, lace, ceramics (especially model house fronts, for example from La Casa de Las Casitas, Cristo 250), hammocks, masks and basketwork. There are several shops in San Juan, but it is more interesting to visit the workshops around Puerto Rico. Contact the Centro de Artes Populares (T7246250) or the Tourism Company Artisan Office (T7212400 ext 2201) for details.

Many of the tourist shops in the old city sell Andean goods

Flora and fauna

Although less than 1% of the island is virgin forest, there are several forest reserves designed to protect plants and wildlife. At the highest altitude you find dwarf cloud forest, with palms, ferns and epiphytes. On exposed ridges it has a windswept appearance. Below the dwarf forest is the rainforest and below that the subtropical wet forest, with open-crowned trees and canopy trees such as *Cyrilla racemiflora*, which is large with reddish bark. Classifications below this include the lower wet forest (Tabanuco) and the subtropical moist forest zone, which covers most of Puerto Rico, and dry forest, found along the south coast and the eastern tip of the island. One of the most notable creatures on Puerto Rico is the inch-long tree frog called a *coquí*, after the two-tone noise it makes.

In **El Yunque Tropical Rain Forest** (called The Caribbean National Forest) there are an estimated 240 types of tree (26 indigenous), and many other plants, such as tiny wild orchids, bamboo trees and giant ferns. The total area is 11,270 ha and 75% of Puerto Rico's virgin forest is here. Several marked paths (quite easy, you could walk two to three in a day, no guide needed), recreational areas and information areas have been set up. It is also home to the Puerto Rican parrot, which has been saved from extinction but there are only 30 left. The whole forest is a bird sanctuary. (*Las aves de Puerto Rico*, by Virgilio Biaggi, University of Puerto Rico, 1983, US\$12.95, is available in San Juan, for example the bookshop in Fort San Cristóbal; Herbert Raffaele's *Guide to the Birds of Puerto Rico and the Virgin Islands* is also recommended.)

Mangroves are protected in **Aguirre Forest**, on the south coast near Salinas, at the Jobos Bay National Estuarine Research Reserve, at the west end of Jobos Bay from Aguirre, and at Piñones Forest, east of San Juan. Unlike the north coast mangroves, those on the south coast tend to die behind the outer fringe because not enough water is received to wash away the salt. This leaves areas of mud and skeletal trees which, at times of spring tide, flood and are home to many birds. In winter, many ducks stop on their migration routes at Jobos. Also at **Jobos Bay**, manatees and turtles can be seen. A short boardwalk runs into the mangroves at Jobos, while at Aguirre a man runs catamaran trips to the offshore cays, and there are some good fish restaurants; take Route 7710. For Jobos Bay take Route 703, to Las Mareas de Salinas (marked Mar Negro on some maps). Before going to Jobos, contact the office at Jobos, Box 1170, Guayama, Puerto Rico 00655, T8640105, or 7248774 in San Juan.

The largest number of bird species can be found at the 655-ha **Guánica Forest**, west of Ponce, which is home to 700 plant species of which 48 are endangered and 16 exist nowhere else. Guánica's dry forest vegetation is unique and the forest has been declared an International Biosphere Reserve by UNESCO. There are 10 marked trails through the forest, but it may be advisable to contact the wardens for directions before wandering off. It can be hot in the middle of the day so don't be too ambitious in which trail you choose. The Ballena Trail is quite short and you will see lizards, snakes, birds and a 700-year old guayacán tree, very gnarled and not as big as you might expect. If you want to head for the beach, Playa de Ventanas is within the Reserve. ■ *T7231770. Daily 0900-1700, no admission charge; wear protective clothing and take drinking water.* The **Punta Ballena Reserve** is next to the Guánica Forest and included in the Biosphere Reserve because of its coastal ecosystem. It contains mangrove forest, manatees, nesting sites for hawksbill turtles, and crested toads. Beach access off Route 333.

Puerto Rico has some of the most important caves in the western hemisphere

The Río Camuy runs underground for part of its course, forming the third largest subterranean river in the world. Near Lares, on Route 129, Km 9.8, the **Río Camuy Cave Park** has been established by the Administración de Terrenos (PO Box 3767, San Juan, T8983100), where visitors are guided through one cave and two sinkholes, open Tuesday to Sunday, and holidays 0800-1600, last trip 1545, US$10 for adults, US$7 for children, highly recommended, very easy, but entry is limited. The trip takes two hours and you may have to wait an hour beforehand, so allow plenty of time. There are fine examples of stalactites, stalagmites and, of course, plenty of bats. Keen photographers should bring a tripod for excellent photo opportunities. Several caving tour specialists can take you to a different and undeveloped part of the cave system. Offered in three degrees of difficulty, they explore underground caves, pre-Columbian petroglyphs, rivers and sinkholes. No prior knowledge needed but you need to be in good physical shape as you will have to travel on a hot-line, rappel and body raft, about US$85 for a day's adventure starting at dawn, returning to San Juan by 1800. See page 483 for tour agents. Also close is the privately-owned **Cueva de Camuy**, Route 486, Km 1.1; much smaller and less interesting, with guided tours, the area also has a swimming pool and waterslide, amusements, café, ponies, go-karts, entertainments. ■ *US$1, children US$0.50, daily 0900-1700 (till 2000 Sun).* Nearby is **Cueva del Infierno**, to which 2-3 hour tours can be arranged by phoning 8982723. About 2,000 caves have been discovered; in them live 13 species of bat (but not in every cave), the *coquí*, crickets, an arachnid called the *guavá*, and other species. Contact the Speleological Society of Puerto Rico (Sepri) for further details.

Other forest reserves, some of which are mentioned in the text below are Aguirre (T8640105), Boquerón (T8517260), Cambalache (T8811004), Carite (T7474545), Casa Pueblo Forest (T8524440), Ceiba (T8524440), Cerrillos (T7243724), Guánica (T8215706), Guajataca in the northeast (T8721045), Guilarte (T8295767), Maricao (T7243724), Mona Island (T7243724), Piñones (T7917750), Río Abajo (T8806557), Susúa (T7243724), Toro Negro (T8673040), Vega (T8332240), all of which can also be contacted through the Central Office in San Juan, T7243724, or at prforests@hotmail.com

Diving and marine life

The shallow waters are good for snorkelling and while a boat is needed to reach deeper water for most scuba diving, divers can walk in at Isabela. Visibility is not as good as in some other islands because of the large number of rivers flowing out to the sea, but is generally around 70 ft. However, an advantage is that the freshwater attracts a large number of fish. Manatees can occasionally be seen and humpback whales migrate through Puerto Rican waters in the autumn.

Dive centres   There are many companies all round the island offering boat dives, equipment rental and diving instruction, including *Caribbean School of Aquatics*, in Fajardo, T7286606, NAUI, PADI, sailing, Greg Korwek has 30 years' experience here, leader in safety standards, knows every reef; *Diving Center*, T8600183, Las Croabas, Edgar Espinosa, SSI, very knowledgeable, dives to suit your level of experience; *Coral Head Divers*, Marina de Palmas, Palmas del Mar Resort, Humacao (T8507208, F8504445, coralheaddivers@hotmail.com, US$50-75); *Caribe Aquatic Adventures*, San Juan Bay Marina, Miramar (T2818858, www.caribeaquaticadventure.com,

US$90-110). Diving also at some of the larger hotels. Companies in San Juan and to the east also dive Culebra and Vieques, but there are dive shops on those islands if you want to avoid long boat rides. Check how many divers are taken on the boats, some companies cater for small groups of 6-7 divers, but several of the larger operations take out parties of 40 or 80. Look for instructor's certificate, motor boat operator's licence and coast guard inspection sticker on the boat. If any are missing you will not be insured. The inspection sticker on the boat specifies how many paying passengers are allowed.

Luquillo Beach has two snorkelling spots: in town, off the point between the surfers' beach, **La Pared** and **Blue Beach** (the beach in front of the tallest condos), and at the point of the Balneario Luquillo, past the 'no swimming' signs (beware of current, and jet skis at weekends). **Seven Seas Beach** has some good snorkelling right off the beach and there are reefs to the east. *Caribe Kayak Tours & More*, near Fajardo, specialize in small groups for snorkelling and kayaking (ocean and Lagoon) starting from Seven Seas Beach, US$40, 4½ hours, includes lunch and equipment, T8897734. Many dive shops will also take you snorkelling.

Snorkelling
Always be aware of jet skis & other motorized craft: they will be oblivious of you

Beaches and watersports

Swimming from most beaches is safe; the best beaches near San Juan are those at **Isla Verde** in front of the main hotels; **Luquillo** to the east of San Juan is less crowded and has a fine-sand beach from where there are good views of El Yunque (controlled car parking, US$2 per car all day, if arriving by público from San Juan, ask to get off at Balneario Luquillo, which is 1 km west of the town). There are showers, toilets and lifeguards, food kiosks and souvenir shops, it is peaceful during the week but noisy at weekends. The north coast Atlantic sea is rougher than the east and south waters, particularly in winter; some beaches are semi-deserted. There are 13 *balneario* beaches round the island where lockers, showers and parking places are provided for a small fee. Some have cabins, tent sites or trailer sites. *Balnearios* are open Tuesday-Sunday 0900-1700 in winter and 0800-1700 in summer.

Swimming
Never leave anything unattended on the beaches in Puerto Rico. If you are alone it is probably best to leave

The most popular beaches for surfing are the **Pine Beach Grove** in Isla Verde (San Juan), **Jobos** (near Isabela in the northeast, not the south coast bay), **La Pared** in Luquillo, officially listed as dangerous for swimming but used for surfing tournaments, **Surfer** and **Wilderness** beaches in the former Ramey Field air base at Punta Borinquén, north of Aguadilla and **Punta Higuero**, Route 413 between Aguadilla and Rincón on the west coast. Several international surfing competitions have been held at Surfer and Wilderness.

    The **Condado lagoon** is calm with steady winds and is popular for windsurfing, as is **Boquerón Bay**, off Isla Verde beach, and **Ocean Park beach**. Only experts can cope with conditions on the northeast shore near Aguadilla: **Jobos**, **Wilderness** and **Surfer** beaches, where the winds are good and the waves break with excellent shape. **Rincón** is the same. **La Parguera** is great for slalom conditions, a great sail to Cayo Enrique on protected waters with lots of wind.

Surfing & windsurfing

Puerto Rico's coastline is protected in many places by coral reefs and cays which are fun to visit and explore. **La Cordillera** is a nature reserve of cays and rocks off the northeast tip of Puerto Rico, including Icacos, Diablo, Ratones and Las Cucarachas, which have a rich coral reef, clear water and sandy beaches. There is an abandoned limestone quarry on the south side of Icacos. The cays are easily accessible by boat from Las Croabas or Fajardo. You can also snorkel or scuba around the cays by seaplane from San Juan, Zoltan at *Seaplanes in Paradise,* knows all the best spots, US$150 per person for four people, T7250243, www.spiderlink.net/seaplanes. There are many sailboat excursions from Fajardo with snorkelling, lunch and drinks, usually US$55 per person on catamarans (also known as cattlemarans taking 49 people), more on the monohulls. Also sailboats from Marina del Rey, San Juan and **La Parguera**.

Day sails

There are four marinas at **Fajardo, Puerto del Rey**, the **Club Náutico** at Miramar and another at **Boca de Cangrejos** in Isla Verde (both in San Juan) and one at the *Palmas del Mar Resort* near Humacao. There is a marina for fishing boats at **Arecibo**. Sailing is popular, with

Sailing

winds of about 10-15 knots all year round. Craft of all sizes are available for hire. There are several racing tournaments; a major international regatta is the **Discover the Caribbean** series in September and October. Power boats appeal to the Puerto Rican spirit and there are a lot of races, held mostly off the west coast from Mayagüez Bay to Boquerón Bay. A huge crowd collects for the Caribbean Offshore Race, with professionals and celebrities participating.

Fishing   Deep-sea fishing is popular and more than 30 world records have been broken in Puerto Rican waters, where blue and white marlin, sailfish, wahoo, dolphin, mackerel and tarpon, to mention a few, are a challenge to the angler. An international bill fish competition is held in September at the Club Náutico de San Juan (T7220177), one of the biggest tournaments in the Caribbean. Fishing boat charters are available: for example *Mike Benítez Fishing Charters Inc*, at the Club Náutico de San Juan, PO Box 5141, Puerta de Tierra, San Juan, PR 00906, T7232292 (till 2100), 7246265 (till 1700), F7251336, www.mikebenitezfishing.com, prices from US$125-1,200. Others in San Juan include *Captain Mike's Sportfishing*, T7217335 and *Caribbean Outfitters*, T3968346, www.fishinginpuertorico.com Others around the island are mentioned in the text below. You can also fish in the many lakes inland where there are large-mouthed bass and peacock bass. Contact the Department of Natural Resources, T7248774, ext 445 for details. Marcos Hanke, T7631929, will take you fly fishing, US$200 half day, catch and release, knowledgeable about freshwater lakes.

Other sports   There are 18 **golf** courses around the island, many of which are professionally designed championship courses. The *Hyatt Cerromar* and *Hyatt Dorado* hotels in Dorado have four excellent 36-hole championship golf courses, T7961234, www.hyatt.com; among the 18-hole courses, *Berwind Country Club* (T8763056) accepts non-members on Tuesday, Thursday and Friday, *Palmas del Mar* (Humacao, T2852221, www.palmasdelmar.com), Westin Riomar (Río Grande, T8886000), and Punta Borinquén (Aguadilla, nine holes, T8902987) all have golf pros and are open to the public. Over 100 **tennis** courts are available, mostly in the larger hotels. There are also 17 lit public courts in San Juan's Central Park, open daily, with tennis pro, T7221646. The *Palmas del Mar* resort, at Humacao, has 20 courts. **Cockfighting** season is from 1 November to 31 August and is held at the new, a/c Coliseo Gallístico in Isla Verde, near the *Holiday Inn* (Route 37, Km 1.5) on Saturdays, 1300-1900, T7911557. Admission from US$4-10. **Horse racing** at El Comandante, Route 3, Km 15.3, T8762450, www.elcomandante.com Canóvanas is one of the hemisphere's most beautiful race courses. Races are held all the year round (Wednesday, Friday, Sunday and holidays, 1415-1730). Wednesday is ladies' day. Children under 12 not admitted at any time. On mountain trails or beaches, **riding** is a good way to see the island. Puerto Rico also prides itself on its paso fino horses. There are over 7,000 registered paso fino horses on the island and several horse shows are held throughout the year which are well worth attending. The two best known are the **Dulce Sueño Fair**, Guayama, the first weekend in March, and the **Fiesta La Candelaria**, Manatí, the first weekend in February. At Palmas del Mar, Humacao, there is an equestrian centre T8526000, ext 12721 which offers beach rides and riding and jumping lessons. Hacienda Carabalí, T8895820, reservations required, Luquillo, Route 992, Km 4, offers beach or hill riding and has paso fino horses, groups of up to 40 for trail rides. *Tropical Trails Rides*, Route 4466, Km 1.8, Isabela, beach, forest and cliff trails, Craig Barker has 20 beautiful paso fino horses, about 1½ hours west of San Juan, US$35 per two hours, T8729256. At the *El Conquistador Resort* complex, T8631000, ask for Richard and the ferry to the horses on Isla Palominos. **Polo** is becoming popular and the *Ingenio Polo Club* hosts the Rolex Polo Cup on its 25-acre grounds by the Loiza River in March.

Popular **spectator sports** are boxing and baseball (at professional level, also a winter league at San Juan stadium, US$4 for a general seat, US$5 box seat, Tuesday is Ladies' Night), basketball, volleyball and beach volleyball. Running is also popular. Puerto Rico is a member of the Olympic Committee. The island made a bid to host the 2004 Olympic Games.

Holidays and festivals

Public holidays

New Year's Day, Three Kings' Day (6 January), De Hostos' Birthday (11 January), Washington's Birthday (22 February), Emancipation Day (22 March), Good Friday, José de Diego's Birthday (16 April), Memorial Day (30 May), St John the Baptist (24 June), Independence Day (4 July), Muñoz Rivera's Birthday (17 July), Constitution Day (25 July), Dr José Celso Barbosa's Birthday (27 July), Labour Day (1 September), Columbus Day (12 October), Veterans' Day (11 November), Discovery of Puerto Rico (19 November), Thanksgiving Day (25 November), Christmas Day.

Festivals
There is a festival somewhere every week in Puerto Rico

Everything is usually (but not always) closed on **public holidays**. One of the most important is *24 June*, though in fact the capital grinds to a halt the previous afternoon and everyone heads for the beach. Here there is loud *salsa* music and barbecues until midnight when everyone walks backwards into the sea to greet the Baptist and ensure good fortune. **Día de la Constitución**, *25 July*, takes place at a weekend and it is almost impossible to get a hotel room. Reservations should be made in advance. Every town/city has local holidays for **crop-over festivals** (pineapple, tobacco, sugar cane, etc) and for celebration of the town's saint. These festivals can be great fun, especially the Carnival in Mayagüez late May. For lovers of classical music, there is the annual Casals Festival in June, which brings orchestras from all over the world for a couple of weeks of concerts. The festival was founded in 1957 by Pablo Casals, who created the Puerto Rican Symphony Orchestra and the Musical Conservatory. Tickets range from US$20-40, with a 50% discount for senior citizens, while children under 12 are free if accompanied by an adult, T7285744 for information. Another annual music festival in June is the Puerto Rico Heineken JazzFest, held in the open air at Sixto Escobar Park beside the sea. Founded in 1990, this also attracts international artists in Latin and contemporary jazz.

Health

See main Health section in Essentials chapter, page 24

'La monga' is a common, flu-like illness, nothing serious, it goes away after a few days. Avoid swimming in rivers: bilharzia may be present. There has been dengue fever, take care not to get bitten by mosquitoes. The northeast coast is particularly risky. Government and private hospitals. Ambulance, T3432500. Emergency T911.

San Juan

Puerto Rico

Population: about 1 mn
Colour map 3, grid B5

Founded in 1510, San Juan, the capital spreads several kilometres along the north coast and also inland. The nucleus is Old San Juan, the old walled city on a tongue of land between the Atlantic and San Juan bay. It has a great deal of charm and character, a living museum; the Institute of Culture restores and renovates old buildings, museums and places of particular beauty. The narrow streets of Old San Juan, some paved with small grey-blue cobblestones which were brought over as ships' ballast, are lined with colonial churches, houses and mansions, in a very good state of repair and all painted different pastel colours.

Ins and outs

Getting there

Getting a taxi from the airport is your best bet, buses from the airport to San Juan and back are complicated. There is a despatch desk for *públicos* at the airport. See further page 482.

Getting around

Small yellow buses, or trolleys, run around the old city all day 0600-2200, free, *paradas* (stops) are marked. They start from La Puntilla and Covadonga public car parks. There is also a trolley service in the Isla Verde beach area from Punta Las Marías. There is a city bus (*guagua*) service with a fixed charge of US$0.25 for standard route, US$0.50 for longer. (No change given; make sure you have right money.) They have special routes, sometimes against the normal direction of traffic, in which case the bus lanes are marked by yellow and white lines.

Bus stops are marked by white and orange signs or yellow and black notices on lampposts marked 'Parada'. Up until the 1950s tramcars ran between Río Piedras and Old San Juan along Avs Ponce de León and Fernández Juncos. To this day directions are given by Paradas, or tram stops, so you have to find out where each one is.

Sights

Some of the restored and interesting buildings to visit include **La Fortaleza**, the Governor's Palace, built between 1533 and 1540 as a fortress against Carib attacks but greatly expanded in the 19th century. It is believed to be the oldest executive residence in continuous use in the Western Hemisphere. Access to the official areas is not permitted. ■ *0900-1600 Mon-Fri, T7217000 ext 2211; guided tours in English on the hour, in Spanish every 30 mins.* The **Cathedral** was built in the 16th century but extensively restored in the 19th and 20th. The body of Juan Ponce de León rests in a marble tomb. ■ *Daily 0630-1700.* The tiny **Cristo Chapel** with its silver altar, was built after a young man competing in 1753 in a horse-race during the San Juan festival celebrations plunged with his horse over the precipice at that very spot. ■ *Tue 1000-1600.* Next to it is the aptly-named **Parque de las Palomas**, where the birds perch on your hand to be fed. This practice is best avoided, however, as we have heard of people contracting a lung virus and ending up in hospital. **San Felipe del Morro** was built in 1591 to defend the entrance to the harbour, and the 11ha **Fort San Cristóbal** was completed in 1772 to support El Morro and to defend the landward side of the city, with its five independent units connected by tunnels and dry moats, rising 46m above the ocean. Good views of the city. ■ *Both open daily 0900-1700. Free. T7296777, www.nps.gov/saju Tours of El Morro in English at 1100 and 1500, tours of San Cristóbal in English at 1000 and 1400.* The **Plaza del Quinto Centenario**, inaugurated on 12 October 1992 to commemorate the 500th anniversary of Columbus' landing, is a modernistic square on several

San Juan orientation

Puerto Rico

Related map:
A Old San Juan, page 494

N
Not to Scale

■ **Sleeping**
1 Aleli By the Sea
2 Beach Buoy Inn
3 Best Western Pierre

4 Caribe Hilton
5 Casa Mathiesen
6 Condado Plaza

7 Days Inn
8 El Canario Inn
9 El Canario By the Lagoon

levels with steps leading to a central fountain with hundreds of jets (good view of El Morro, the cemetery and sunsets). The restored **Cuartel de Ballajá**, once the barracks for Spanish troops and their families, was also inaugurated 12 October 1992 with the **Museum of the Americas** on the second floor tracing the cultural development of the history of the New World. ■ *Mon-Fri 1000-1600, Sat-Sun 1100-1700. Free. T7245052. Guided tours available weekdays 1030, 1130, 1230 and 1400.* The **Dominican Convent** built in the early 16th century, later used as a headquarters by the US Army, is now the office of the Institute of Culture, with a good art gallery. Cultural events are sometimes held in the patio, art exhibitions in the galleries. ■ *Open Wed-Sun, 0900-1200, 1300-1630. T7240700.* The 16th-century **San José** church, originally a Dominican chapel, is the second oldest church in the Western Hemisphere and once the family church of Ponce de León's descendants. Ponce was buried here until moved to the Cathedral in the 20th century. ■ *Mon-Sat 0830-1600, Sun mass at 1200.* The early 18th century **Casa de los Contrafuertes** believed to be the oldest private residence in the old city, now has periodic art exhibitions on the second floor and a small pharmacy museum with 19th-century exhibits on the ground floor. ■ *Wed-Sun, 0900-1630. T7245949.* The **Casa Blanca**, 1 Calle San Sebastián, was built in 1523 by the family of Ponce de León, who lived in it for 250 years until it became the residence of the Spanish and then the US military commander-in-chief. It is now a historical museum which is well worth a visit. ■ *Tue-Sun 0900-1200, 1300-1630. US$2 adults, US$1 children. T7244102. Guided tours Tue-Fri by appointment.* The **Alcaldía**, or City Hall, was built 1604-1789. ■ *Mon-Fri 0800-1600 except holidays. T7247171, ext 2391.* The **Intendencia**, formerly the Spanish colonial exchequer, a fine example of 19th-century Puerto Rican architecture, now houses Puerto Rico's State Department.■ *Mon-Fri 0800-1200, 1300-1630. T7222121.* The **naval arsenal** was the last place in Puerto Rico to be evacuated by the Spanish in 1898, exhibitions are held in three galleries. ■ *Wed-Sun, 0900-1200, 1300-1630. T7245949.* The **Casa**

Puerto Rico

10	El Canario By the Sea	13	Green Isle Inn	16	Radisson Ambassador
11	Embassy	14	Hostería del Mar	17	San Juan Marriott
12	Excelsior	15	No 1 On the Beach	18	Wyndham El San Juan

del Callejón is a restored 18th-century house containing two colonial museums, the architectural and the Puerto Rican Family. ■ *T7255250. Both closed for restoration.*

Museums Apart from those in historic buildings listed above, there are the **Pablo Casals Museum** in an 18th-century house beside San José church, with Casals' cello and other memorabilia. ■ *T7239185. US$1 adults, US$0.50 children. Tue-Sat 0930-1730.* The **San Juan Museum of Art and History**, Norzagaray y MacArthur, built in 1855 as a marketplace, now a cultural centre with exhibition galleries. ■ *Tue-Sun, 1000-1600. T7241875.* The **Casa del Libro** is an 18th-century house on Calle Cristo, has a collection of rare books, including some over 400 years old. ■ *Tue-Sat, except holidays, 1100-1630. T7230354.* And the **Museum of the Sea** on Pier One, with a collection of maritime instruments and models. ■ *Open when the pier is open for cruise ships. T7252532.* The **Indian Museum** at Calle San José 109 on the corner of Luna concentrates on Puerto Rican indigenous cultures, with exhibits, ceramics and archaeological digs. ■ *Tue-Sat 0900-1600. No admission charge. T7245477.* Another museum in the old city is a military museum at **Fort San Jerónimo**. ■ *Wed-Sun, 0930-1200, 1300-1630. T7245949.*

Metropolitan The metropolitan area of San Juan includes the more modern areas of Santurce,
San Juan Hato Rey, and Río Piedras. In **Santurce** a new museum opened in 2000, the **Museo de Arte de Puerto Rico**, showcasing 500 years of Puerto Rican sculpture, painting, drawing, photography and graphic arts. There are also temporary exhibitions, films

Puerto Rico

Old San Juan

and classes. The west wing contains the last remnant of the former Municipal Hospital and has a permanent collection in 18 exhibition halls. The east wing is a modern, 5-storey structure, designed by local architects, Otto Reyes and Luis Gutiérrez, containing an atrium, a conservation laboratory, an intereactive family gallery and ActivArte, a computer learning centre, as well as studios and workshops, museum shop, restaurant and café. *300 de Diego Av, Santurce, T9776277. Tue-Sun 1000-1700, the gallery is open Wed until 2000 for special interactive and educational programmes, US$5 adults, US$3 children, senior citizens and the physically challenged.* The **Sacred Heart University** with the **Museum of Contemporary Puerto Rican Art** is in Santurce. ■ *T2680049, Tue-Sat 0900-1600, Sun 1100-1700.* The modern **Centro Bellas Artes** (Fine Arts Center), opened in 1981, with theatres and halls at the corner of De Diego and Ponce de León. ■ *T7244751.*

Río Piedras was founded in 1714 but became incorporated into San Juan in 1951. On the edge of Río Piedras, the gardens and library of the former governor, Luis Muñoz Marín, are open to the public, with a museum showing his letters, photos and speeches. *T7557979. Tue-Sat 0900-1300.* The **University of Puerto Rico** at Río Piedras is in a lovely area. The **University Museum** has archaeological and historical exhibitions, and also monthly art exhibitions. ■ *T7640000, ext 2452. Open Mon-Fri, 0900-2100, weekends 0900-1500.* The **Botanical Garden** at the Agricultural Experiment Station has over 200 species of tropical and subtropical plants, a bamboo promenade (one variety can grow four feet in a day), an orchid garden (over 30,000 orchids), and an aquatic garden. ■ *T7634408, www.upr.clu.edu Daily 0800-1630.*

Hato Rey is the financial district of San Juan nicknamed 'the Golden Mile'. The **Luís Muñoz Marín Park** on Avenida Jesús T Piñero covers 35ha, which can be toured by a 1 km cable car. ■ *Open Tue-Sun 0900-1700.* The residential area **Miramar** has several moderately priced hotels as well as some expensive ones. Miramar is separated from the Atlantic coast by the **Condado lagoon** and the Condado beach area, where the luxury hotels, casinos, night clubs and restaurants are concentrated. From Condado the beach front is built up eastwards through Ocean Park, Santa Teresita, Punta Las Marías and Isla Verde. Building is expanding along the narrow strip beyond Isla Verde, between the sea and the airport. Along this road, Avenida Boca de Cangrejos, there are lots of food trucks selling barbequed specialities.

Excursions

A ferry, Old San Juan (Pier Two) – Hato Rey, Cataño, crosses every 30 minutes, 0600-2200, weather permitting, T7881155, US$0.50, to Cataño. In 1999 an enormous statue of Columbus made by a Georgian, Zurab Tsereteli, was assembled in sections here as a major tourist attraction. From Cataño waterfront, you can catch a *público* (US$1 per person), or bus C37 to about five blocks

Puerto Rico

from the **Bacardí rum distillery.** ■ *Route 888, Km 2.6, T7881500, www.bacardi.com There are free conducted tours around the plant Mon-Sat, every 30 mins 0830-1630, travelling from one building to the next by a little open motor train. Closed for Christmas holidays.*

On Route 2, shortly before Bayamón, is the island's earliest settlement, **Caparra**, established by Ponce de León in 1508. Ruins of the fort can still be seen and there is a **Museum of the Conquest and Colonization of Puerto Rico.** ■ *T7814795. Open daily 0900-1600.*

Essentials

Sleeping   Most of the large San Juan hotels are in **Condado** or **Isla Verde** and overlook the sea, with swimming pools, nightclubs, restaurants, shops and bars. To get value for money, it may be advisable to avoid the luxury hotels on the sea front. There is plenty of cheaper accommodation within walking distance of the beaches and lots of beachfront apartments at very reasonable prices for stays of a week or more, look in the local newspaper, *El Nuevo Día* for notices, usually quote monthly rates but available for shorter stays.

Condado LL with casinos, suites and all manner of luxury facilities are the following hotels: *Radisson Ambassador, San Juan Marriott Resort & Casino, Caribe Hilton*, and *Condado Plaza*. **LL-AL** *Days Inn Condado Lagoon*, 6 Clemenceau, T7210170, F7244356, www.daysinn.com 48 rooms, good, with good restaurant. **L** *Best Western Pierre*, 105 De Diego, T7211200, F7213118. Designed for business travellers or families. Good value are the three Canario hotels, B&B, www.canariohotels.com: **AL** *El Canario by the Sea*, 4 Condado Av, T7228640, F7254921. 25 rooms, close to beach, comfortable. **AL** *El Canario Inn*, 1317 Ashford, T7223861, F7220391. 1 block from the beach, good, clean, safe. **AL** *El Canario by the Lagoon*, 4 Clemenceau, T7228640, F7238590, 40 rooms with balcony, 1 block from beach. **AL-C** *Embassy*, 1125 Sea View, T7258284, F7252400, home.att.net/~embassyguesthouse 20 rooms, good bathroom, TV, a/c, pool on the beach. **A-B** *Aleli By The Sea*, 1125 Sea View St, T7255313, F7214744, on seafront. Kitchen facilities, good, no pool, parking.

Ocean Park L-B *Hostería del Mar*, 1 Tapia St, T7273302, F2680772, www.prhtasmallhotels. com, on the beach. 17 rooms, nice restaurant, nice place to stay. **AL** *Numero Uno on the Beach*, 1 Santa Ana, T7265010, F7275482. 12 rooms, safe behind barred doors and high walls, good beach but not safe after dark, with pool, gay friendly. **B-C** *Beach Buoy Inn*, 1853 McLeary, T7288119, F2680037. Also safe behind barred doors and high walls, but on busy road so some traffic noise, windows sealed in some rooms, no view but pleasant, complimentary breakfast with lots of coffee, Danish pastries and newspapers, no restaurant, helpful, parking, shopping close by, beach towels.

Isla Verde LL hotels with casinos, restaurants etc: *Ritz Carlton San Juan Hotel & Casino, San Juan Grand Beach*, www.sjgrand.com and *Wyndham El San Juan*, www.wyndham. com **A-C** *La Casa Mathieson*, Uno 14, T7268662, and *Green Isle*, Uno 36, T7264330, are jointly owned, greeninn@prt.net Both charge the same, both near airport, and have swimming pools, cooking facilities, friendly, free transport to and from airport. **B** *El Patio*, Tres Oeste 87, Bloque D-8, Villamar, T7266298. 14 rooms, swimming pool, use of kitchen, laundry.

Picturesque area, **Old San Juan LL** *El Convento Hotel & Casino*, a converted Carmelite nunnery at Cristo 100,
hilly cobbled streets, T7239020, F7212877, www.elconvento.com A charming hotel with a Spanish atmosphere
ocean views but no and the dining room is in the former chapel, exclusive, very good service, 58 rooms, swim-
beach swimming ming pool, nice garden in which to have a drink, unfortunately the plaza opposite is a nocturnal campsite for junkies/alcoholics and stray cats. **LL-A** *Galería San Juan*, Norzagaray 204, T7236515. 300-year-old rambling house with inner courtyards, artist's residence and studio, art, antiques, views everywhere, labyrinth, rooms and suites, breakfast included. **LL** *Wyndham Old San Juan*, T7215000, F2891950, www.wyndham.com New 240-room hotel by cruise ship dock, near the square, great view of bay from rooftop pool. **A-D** *Central*,

San José 202, T7222751. Good location on main plaza, but reportedly used by short stay visitors and drug dealers, very basic, no charm, ask for a room with fan away from a/c units, also ask for towels when checking in so you do not have to run up and downstairs again.
C-F *Enrique Castro Guest House*, Tanca 205, T7225436, at Relojería Suiza Mecánico Cuarzo, 2nd Floor (Box 947). Welcoming but rather old and dirty, run by Enrique and his son, Vincente, communal showers, some with hot water, rooms a/c, washbasin, fridge, kitchen available, rooms without a/c can be uncomfortably hot. **AL-B** *The Caleta*, 11 Caleta de las Monjas, T7255347, www.thecaleta.com Furnished studios and apartments, some with kitchens or kitchenettes, most have a/c, TV and phone, run by Michael Giessler, minimum 3-night stay, weekly, monthly and long term rates, coin laundry.

Miramar L-AL *Excelsior*, 801 Ponce de León, T7217400, F7230068, hotelexcelsior@ compuserve.com 140 rooms, studios and 2-room suites, popular gourmet restaurant, bar, pool, rooms overlooking freeway are noisy, business type hotel. Under same management is **B** *Olimpo Court*, 603 Av Miramar, T7240600. 45 rooms and studios with kitchenettes, restaurant, parking. **B** *Miramar*, 606 Av Ponce de León, T7226239, F7231180.'Not chic', but OK, business travellers on a budget, sea view from 5th floor front, dirty carpets, ask for room without carpet, longer stays possible.

Residential area, easy bus to old San Juan, not great at night

Old San Juan *Fortaleza*, Fortaleza 252. For Puerto Rican cuisine. *Bistro*, Cruz 152. A pleasant, small restaurant and bar with tasty local food at reasonable prices. *Chef Marisol*, Cristo. California cuisine with imported ingredients, including imported fish. *La Mallorquina*, San Justo 207, T7223261. The oldest restaurant in the Caribbean. Recommended. Also on San Justo: *Café de Paris*, No 256; *Szechuan*, Chinese, No 257, and other cafés and *Taco Maker*, No 255. There are several Mexican places in the city, eg *Parián* on Fortaleza; *Taza de Oro*, Luna 254, near San Justo. *Bodegón de La Fortaleza*, Fortaleza 312; *El Siglo XX*, Fortaleza 355, T7241849. Consistently good, great breakfast, lunch and dinner, not expensive, excellent service, spectacular paella. *La Danza*, corner of Cristo and Fortaleza, T7231642; *La Bombonera*, San Francisco 259. Restaurant and pastry shop, good value breakfast, 1960s atmosphere, antique coffee machine; *4 Seasons Café*, in *Hotel Central*, Plaza de Armas. For good value local lunches; *Tropical Blend*, juice bar in La Calle alley on Fortaleza; *El Batey* bar, Cristo 101, just behind El Convento. Recommended; *Cafetería Manolin*, San Justo 258. A/c, packed with locals at breakfast, Puerto Rican food, lunch specials daily. *Nono's*, San Sebastián y Cristo. Bar, burgers, salads, steaks, sandwiches, and nearby on San Sebastián (all on Plaza San José), *Patio de Sam* very good for local drinks (happy hour 1600-1900), and *Tasca El Boquerón*. On Av Ponce de León, *El Miramar*. Good, but not cheap. *La Buena Mesa*, 605 Ponce de León. Good, small, middle price range.

Eating

Condado There is a huge selection of restaurants in Condado, from the posh to all the fast food chain restaurants. Similarly, Isla Verde is well-served by the fast food fraternity; on the beach at Isla Verde is *The Hungry Sailor* bar and grill. Sandwiches, tapas, burgers, with a snack bar next door. *Cecilia's Place*, Rosa St, Isla Verde. *Frida's*, Av Domenech 128, Hato Rey, T7634827, www.letsdine.com/fridas. Mexican, around US$12, quite upscale, good.

Fondas For breakfast or lunch seek out the *fondas*, not advertised as restaurants but usually part of a private home, or a family-run eating place serving *criollo* meals which are filling and good value. Recommended in San Juan are: *Macumba*, 2000 Loíza. *Casa Juanita*, 242 Av Roosevelt, Hato Rey. Try chicken asopao or pork chops con mangú. *Cafetería del Parking*, 757 José de Diego. Interior, Cayey (specialities include *mondongo*, and *boronia de apio y bacalao* – cod and celery root). *D'Arcos*, 605 Miramar, Santurce. Speciality is roast veal with stuffed peppers and white bean sauce, also try *pega'o* (crunchy rice).

Jazz at The Place, Fortaleza 154 in old San Juan. No admission charge, drinks about US$2. *Shannons Irish Pub*, Condado. Bus from airport passes it, live music (rock and roll), beer US$2.50. Recommended. *Caribe Hilton* is a favourite nightspot, also the other 4-5 star hotels.

Nightlife

Puerto Rico

Shopping *The Bookstore*, in Old San Juan, 257 San José, T7241815, has an excellent selection of English and Spanish titles. *The Instituto de Cultura Puertorriqueña*, Plaza de San José, has a good book and record shop with stock of all the best known Puerto Rican writers (all in Spanish). Another record shop near here is *Saravá*, Cristo at the corner of Sol 101, local, Caribbean, jazz and 'world music'.

Directory See page 480 to 486 for listings of airline offices, bank, post, telephone services, hospitals, medical facilities and local tour agents.

El Yunque

El Yunque (see also page 487), or **Caribbean National Forest**, is a tropical forest and bird sanctuary, the largest rain forest in the US forest service system. The forest is divided into north side and south side, with no road connection. After a series of landslides everyone has given up and Route 191 is permanently closed in the middle; you have to drive all the way around to get to the south side or hike (a bit tricky to get past the landslides). Concrete trails to the various peaks: El Yunque (The Anvil) itself, Mount Britton, Los Picachos, as well as to waterfalls and look out towers giving excellent views. There are 13 trails in all, covering 37 km. The Baño Grande is the shortest, taking about 45 minutes and passing a large man-made pool built by the Civilian Conservation Corp in the 1930s. The Big Tree Trail is about the most strenuous, taking 1¾ hours and ending at La Mina waterfall. In view of the heavy rainfall, another name for the forest is Rain Forest. Visitors need not worry unduly, as storms are usually brief and plenty of shelter is provided. If you have worked up an appetite walking, on your way out, heading south on Route 191, there is a collection of food stalls on your left selling fish, plantain, yuca and fruit licuados, delicious. ■ *Caribbean National Forest, PO Box 490, Palmer, PR 00712, T8881810, F8885622, www.r8web.com/caribbean Getting there: via Route 3 from San Juan towards Fajardo, and then right on Route 191 at Palmer. The Palma de Sierra Picnic Grounds were due to reopen in summer 2001 after renovation. El Portal, Centro Forestal Tropical, at the entrance on Route 191, was reopened in May 2001 and has exhibitions, educational and conservation material, patios where you can relax and admire the view, 100-seat theatre showing a 30-min documentary film on El Yunque, in Spanish followed by an English version. US$3 adults, US$1.50 children and older people. Daily 0900-1700. The Park Service publishes a good map.*

The south side of the forest is approached from Naguabo up Route 191. No facilities have yet been developed but there are plans. The soil and weather here is different from the north. The north is red clay (and soggy) and the south is almost sandy (fine granite), while it is less humid and cooler. It is also quieter, with no tour buses or parking lots.

Sleeping **South side** *Robin Phillips* has several rustic cabins, **D**, and tent sites on his fruit farm. Robin and Sita will guide you through the forest or to the petroglyphs. Terrific views to the sea. Robin is full of information. T8742138 or write to Adventures with Nature, HC1, Box 4449, Naguabo, PR 00718 Also 2 excellent B&Bs on Route 191 through Naguabo, wonderful views of forest, rivers, waterfalls: *Casa Cabuy*, T8746221. *Casa Flamboyan*, T8746074. Pool, luxury. **Camping** is allowed with a free permit from El Portal before 1600, but there are no facilities and it is not recommended for security reasons.

Eastern tour

An interesting round trip through the east half of the island can be done by a series of públicos from San Juan – Río Grande – Luquillo – Fajardo – Humacao – Yabucoa – Guayama – Cayey – Aibonito – Barranquitas – Bayamón – San Juan. If travelling by car, a variant between San Juan and El Yunque takes you on Route 187 from Isla Verde, outside San Juan, to Loíza along a stretch of the north coast, which includes the **Piñones State Forest**, sand blown and palm-lined road. Some parts are unspoilt, some parts pass through apartment blocks on the outskirts of towns, and the road is a popular rush-hour route. The bay at Vacía Talega is beautifully calm. The section which joins the coast to Route 3 at Río Grande is also tree-lined and attractive. There is a big Westin resort and several golf clubs in the Río Grande area. A huge Sol Meliá resort is being built which will add nearly a thousand rooms to the hotel stock. In the hills above Rio Grande is **La Casa De Vida Natural Health Spa**, a holistic health retreat and vegetarian bed and breakfast, lots of therapies available, steam baths, jacuzzi, T8874359, www.lacasaspa.com

Luquillo was founded in 1797 when a group of colonizers led by Cristóbal de Guzmán moved from San Juan to escape frequent British naval attacks. The town was named after the Indian cacique Loquillo, who died a few years after the last Indian rebellion of Boriquén that took place following the seizure of the Spanish settlement of Santiago by the shores of the Río Daguao in 1513. In honour of the anniversary of its founding, in 1997 a new landscaped plaza municipal was inaugurated with a huge statue of the cacique Loquillo. There is a beach in town and a *balneario* west of town (see page 489); just by the latter is a row of restaurants on the slip road off the dual carriageway (Route 3). *Públicos* from San Juan to Luquillo are marked Fajardo, US$3, no return *públicos* after 1500.

Luquillo

Fajardo is a boating centre with several marinas and a public beach at Seven Seas; beyond Seven Seas is Las Croabas beach. Offshore is an uninhabited, but much visited, coral island, Icacos. **Las Cabezas de San Juan** is a nature reserve on the headlands (three promontories) north of Fajardo on Route 987, Km 6. A 19th-century lighthouse contains a nature centre and its observation deck has a great view of El Yunque and surrounding islands. There are trails and boardwalks, guides and explanatory signs of the different ecological habitats. ■ *T7225882, or T8602560 at weekends, www.fideicomiso.org US$5 adults, US$2 children. Fri-Sun, tours, reservations required.* Off Humacao Beach/*Balneario* is a tiny cay called **Cayo Santiago**, also known as **Monkey Island**. It is inhabited by over 500 tiny monkeys, which are protected. The island is closed to the public although there are sightseeing tours which get you close enough to see the monkeys through binoculars.

Fajardo

Sleeping West of Fajardo on the hill is **LL** *Wyndham El Conquistador Resort & Country Club*, 1000 Conquistador Av, T8631000, F8636500, www.wyndham.com A large complex with 918 rooms, 16 restaurants, casino, golf course for hotel guests only, lots of facilities, private ferry to nearby sandy cay, white beach. Further south is **LL-L** *Doral Resort at Palmas del Mar*, 170 Candelero Drive, near Humacao, T8526000, F8526320, www.palmas delmar.com, on long stretch of beach. Can be rough seas, condos, marina, 2 top golf courses, 20 tennis courts, horse riding, diving, marina, mega resort complex, many restaurants, pools etc. The only paradores on the east side are **B** *Martorell* at Luquillo, 6A Ocean Drive, T8892710, F8894520. Close to beach, includes breakfast, kitchen, shared bath. You pay for the location, advisable to reserve in advance here at any time. **AL-B** *La Familia*, on Route 987, Km 4, Las Croabas, Fajardo, T8631193, F8605345, www.hotellafamilia.com 35 rooms, rather small, a/c, bath, TV, breakfast included, pool. **A-B** *Las Delicias*, Fajardo Playa, T8631818. On the dock, across street from post office and customs building, convenient for ferry to Vieques and Culebra. Very good, nice staff, 21 rooms, a/c, restaurant, bar. **B** *Anchor's Inn*, Route 987 Km 27, Fajardo, T8637200. Nice rooms, a/c, TV, good facilities but no breakfast, bar/restaurant expensive, part of Mesones Gastronómicos programme. In Fajardo try **D** *Guez House de Express*, near ferry dock, 388 Union, T8631362, small.

   Camping on the beach, Seven Seas, Fajardo, T8638180. US$10 per tent, safer than some because of nearby trailer park but safety depends on numbers. Also on the beach (*balneario*) at Luquillo, T8895871. US$17 with electricity, US$13 without, take own tent, occasional security but best to pick a time when other campers are around, eg weekends and holidays, safety in numbers, not safe if less than 12 campers, shower, toilets, barbecue.

Puerto Rico

Eating   *Rosa's Seafood* in Fajardo, Route 195, Tablazo 536, T8630213. Puerto Rican food and steak. *Lighthouse*, near Roosevelt Roads. Inexpensive meals. *Plaza Caliente Seafood*, on the beach at Puerto del Rey Marina, T8609162.

Watersports   **Marinas** Isleta Marina, Playa Puerto Real, T6432180 (*Ventajero Sailing Charters*, T8631871, domingoj@coqui.net, day sails and overnight charters); Marina Puerto Chico, Route 987, Km 2.4, T8630834; Marina Puerto Real, Playa Puerto Real, T8632188; Puerto del Rey Marina, Route 33, Km 51.4, T8601000, www.puertodelrey.com (*Sea Ventures Pro Dive Center*, PADI 5-star, T800-7393483, www.divepuertorico.com, *East Wind* catamaran with underwater windows, 1000 departure to islands for beaches and snorkelling, T8603434, sailcats@hotmail.com); Sea Lovers Marina, Route 987, Km 2.3, T8633762; Villa Marina Yacht Harbour, Route 987, Km 1.3, T8635131 (*Club Nautico Powerboat Rentals*, T8602400, boatrent@coqui.net, *Caribbean School of Aquatics*, T7286606, catamaran for cruises and day sails, dive boat for snorkelling and diving); Wyndham El Conquistador Marina, 1000 El Conquistador Av, T8636594 (*Palomino Island Divers*, T8631000, Tropical Fishing & Tournaments, T2664524, deep sea sport fishing). Lots of other companies offering day sails, snorkelling, diving and fishing.

The southeast

One of the prettiest parts of Puerto Rico, lies south of Humacao, between Yabucoa and Guayama. Here are the villages of **Patillas** (*público* from Guayama) and **Maunabo** (*público* from Patillas, and from Yabucoa). There are a number of restaurants in this area, especially on the coast, which sell good, cheap food. **Yabucoa** is the east starting point of the Panoramic Route which runs the length of the island. There is an extension to the Route around the Cerro La Pandura and the Puntas Quebrada Honda, Yaguas and Toro; this affords lovely views of the Caribbean coast and Vieques island. **Guayama**, the cleanest town in Puerto Rico, it claims, has a delightful square, on which are the church and the **Casa Cautiño**, built in 1887, now a museum and cultural centre. Route 3, the coastal road around the east part continues from Guayama to Salinas (see below), where it joins Route 1 for Ponce.

Sleeping   Near Patillas is **AL-B** *Caribe Playa*, Route 3, Km 112, right on the Caribbean, T8396339, F8391817, www.caribeplaya.com 32 beachfront rooms, sleep 4, a/c, fan, TV, patio or balcony, comfortable, rather noisy road runs behind rooms, pool and whirlpool, children's pool, open air restaurant (order dinner in advance), library, sea bathing and snorkelling in a small, safe area, barbecue, hammocks, boat trips for fishing, diving, snorkelling, very friendly and helpful. Near Maunabo, is **C** *Playa Emajaguas Guest House*, off the Ruta Panorámica, Route 901, Km 2.5, T8616023. Lovely view, short walk down private path to empty beach (rough sea, currents), owned by Victor Morales and Edna Huertos, 7 apartments with kitchens, friendly, helpful, tennis court, pool table, horses. Good seafood restaurants nearby. At Yabucoa, **A-B** *Palmas de Lucía*, Route 901 at Route 9911, T8934423, F8930291, www.palmasdelucia.com New parador, 27 rooms, clean, pool, restaurant, waves can be rough at nearby beach. At Punta Guilarte, near Arroyo, there are cabins, **B**, on the beach, no camping, T8393565. Inland, north of Barranquitas is **C** *Residencia Margarita*, restaurant, useful for people following the Panoramic route.

Carite Forest   The Carite Forest lies west of Yabucoa on the Panoramic Route. Covering an area of 2,428 ha, its highest peak is Cerro La Santa at 903 m. The Forest Supervisor, Thomas Espinar (Km 20 Route 184), is very helpful and can tell you what there is to do including getting someone to bring you kayaks to rent on the lake. Bring permit from San Juan or Servicio Forestal regional office in Guayama, T8643262. Two camping areas: Charco Azul and Guavate (the latter closer to the forestry office, phone and supplies) with bathrooms. If you have a car you will be given a key to get it into the campsite. By *público*, from Rio Piedras terminal, San Juan, occasionally direct to Barrio Guavate, Carite, otherwise to Caguas and change. The *público* will drop you quite close to the office where you check in.

The south and west

A round trip through the west half of the island would take in Ponce, the second city (reached by motorway from San Juan via Caguas), Guánica, Parguera, San Germán, Boquerón, Mayagüez (the third city), Aguadilla, Quebradillas and Arecibo, with side trips to the Maricao State Forest and fish hatchery, the Río Abajo State Forest and Lake Dos Bocas, the precolumbian ceremonial ball-park near Utuado, and the **Arecibo observatory**, with the world's largest radio telescope. ■ *Route 625, T8782612, www.naic.edu, the Fundación Angel Ramos Visitor Center, open Wed-Fri 1200-1600, Sat and Sun 0900-1600.*

Off the motorway which runs from San Juan to Ponce is Baños de Coamo, which was the island's most fashionable resort from 1847 to 1958; legend has it that the spring was the fountain of youth which Juan Ponce de León was seeking. Take Route 153 from the motorway and then 546. It has been redeveloped by Paradores Puertorriqueños and still has a thermal bath (see under Sleeping). About 45 minutes southeast of Coamo is **Salinas**, a fishing and farming centre. There are several good seafood restaurants on the waterfront. The Marina de Salinas offers moorings and other services to yachties as well as boat transport to islands and accommodation, T7528484, F7687676, jarce@coqui.net

Baños de Coamo

Sleeping B *Baños de Coamo* at the end of Route 546, Coamo, Puerto Rico 00640, T8252186, F8254739, www.banoscoamo.com Thermal water springs (maximum 15 mins) and an ordinary pool (spend as long as you like), 48 rooms, bar, restaurant with limited hours.

Ponce

The city is now very pleasant to walk around. Much renovation has taken place in the heart of the city; the Casas Villaronga and Salazar-Zapater have been restored (the latter to accommodate the Museo de Historia de Ponce), other houses are being repainted in pastel shades, streets have been made into pedestrian areas, and the large, air-conditioned market on Vives and Atocho (north of the plaza) has been remodelled.

The cathedral is worth a look, and so is the black and red fire-station, built for a fair in 1883. Both buildings stand back to back in the main square, **Plaza Las Delicias**, which has fountains and many neatly-trimmed trees. Also on the plaza is the **Casa Armstrong-Poventud** (or Casa de las Cariatides), facing the Cathedral, with the Instituto de Cultura Puertorriqueño (Región Sur) and tourist information centre. ■ *Mon-Fri 0800-1200, 1300-1630; the Instituto is open 0900-1200, 1300-1600 Tue-Sun.* East of the plaza is the **Teatro La Perla**, painted cream, white and gold, the city's cultural centre (19th century), restored in 1990, as was the Alcaldía on the Plaza.

Sights

Ponce has a very fine **Museum of Art**, donated by a foundation established by Luis A Ferré (industrialist, art historian and Governor 1968-72) in a modern building designed by Edward Durrel Stone, with a beautiful staircase, now famous. It contains a representative collection of European and American art from the third century BC to the present day. As well as an extensive Baroque collection and fine examples of pre-Raphaelite painting, there is a small collection of precolumbian ceramics and two cases of beautiful Art Nouveau glass. Most of the best Latin American painters are exhibited and there are often special displays. ■ *Open daily 1000-1700. US$3 for adults, US$2 for children under 12. T8480511.*

There are 3 gardens here, 1 Spanish, 1 American & 1 Puerto Rican

The **Ponce History Museum** on Calle Isabela 51-53, near La Perla, opened in 1992 and has 10 exhibition halls with photographs, documents and memorabilia provided by locals, as well as models and other exhibits chronicling the city's history. Guided tours in English, Spanish or French. ■ *Weekdays 1000-1700, weekends 1000-1800, closed Tue. US$3 adults, US$1 children. T8447071.* The **Museo de la**

Puerto Rico

Música Puertorriqueña, Calle Cristina 70, T8449722. ■ *Tue-Sun 0900-1200 and 1300-1730, catalogue US$3.*

On **El Vigía** hill is the **Observation Tower**. ■ *Tue-Wed, 0900-1730, Thu-Sun 1000-2200. US$0.50.* The **Museo Castillo Serrallés** is also on El Vigía hill. This fine, 1930s mansion has been restored by the Municipio. ■ *US$3, children US$1.50, groups must reserve in advance. Tue-Sun 0900-1700. T2591774.*

Outside the town by the **Yacht and Fishing Club** is a good place to be at the weekend having a vibrant atmosphere. A wooden broadwalk, La Guancha, has been built along the edge of the harbour. There are kiosks selling pinchos and other local treats, simple meals, cold beer and drinks. At one end is an open-air stage for live music or DJs with big sound systems. The music is ear-splittingly loud, especially at weekends. A two-storey building houses a restaurant, small theatre, tourist office and police substation. There is also an observation tower you can climb up. The beach is being developed, with a large recreation area (tennis, basketball courts). ■ *Getting there: taxi or own car needed. Ponce Yacht & Fishing Club, T8429003, www.nautico.com*

Excursions

All the ball courts & plazas are said to line up with solstices or equinoxes

A short drive away on Route 503, Km 2.1, in the outskirts of the city, is the **Tibes Indian Ceremonial Center**. This is an Igneri (300 AD) and pre-Taino (700 AD) burial ground, with seven ball courts (*bateyes*) and two plazas, one in the form of a star, a replica of a Taino village and a good museum. The site was discovered in 1975 after heavy rain uncovered some of the stone margins of the ball courts. Under the Zemi Batey, the longest in the Caribbean (approximately 100 by 20 m), evidence of human sacrifice has been found. Underneath a stone in the Main Plaza, which is almost square (55 by 50 m), the bodies of children were found, buried ceremonially in earthenware pots. In all, 130 skeletons have been uncovered near the Main Plaza, out of a total on site of 187. The park is filled with trees (all named), the most predominant being the higuera, whose fruit is used, among other things, for making maracas (it's forbidden to pick them up though). ■ *Tue-Sun (and Mon holidays, when closed Tue), 0900-1600. T8402255, US$2; bilingual guides give an informative description of the site and a documentary is shown.*

Hacienda Buena Vista, at Km 16.8 on Route 123, north of the city, is another recommended excursion. Built in 1833, converted into a coffee plantation and corn mill in 1845 and in operation till 1937, this estate has been restored by Fideicomiso de Conservación de Puerto Rico. All the machinery works (the metal parts are original), operated by water channelled from the 360 m Vives waterfall; the hydraulic turbine which turns the corn mill is unique. ■ *Fri-Sun, tours at 0830, 1030, 1330 and 1530; groups of 20 or more admitted Wed and Thur. US$5 adults, US$1 children under 12. T7225882 (at weekends 8487020), www.fideicomiso.org. Reservations are necessary for the 2 hr tour (in Spanish or English).*

At weekends trips can be made to the beach at **Caja de Muerto**, Coffin Island, the ferry (if still running) leaves from La Guancha at 0900, returns 1600. There is a fishing pier, barbecue area, information office and beautiful beach with clear water. A trail to the 1880 lighthouse leads from White Beach where the dock is. Very good snorkelling. ■ *T8484575. US$5.50 return, children US$3.50.*

Sleeping

LL *Ponce Hilton & Casino*, 1150 Caribe Av, on the beach, T2597676, F2597674, www.ponce-hilton.com 153 rooms, convention centre for 1,500, all the business and sporting facilities you expect of a Hilton. **L-AL** *Ponce Holiday Inn & Tropical Casino*, Route 2, Km 221.2, west of the city on the bypass, T8441200, F8418683, www.holidayinn.com 116 refurbished rooms, tennis, pools, and golf arrangements made. **A-B** *Meliá*, 2 Cristina, just off main plaza, T8420260, F8413602, home.coqui.net/melia 77 rooms, a/c, TV, bath and breakfast, small stuffy rooms, not nice, roof top and garden terraces. **B** *Bélgica*, 122 Villa, in old centre, next to Plaza Delicias, on free trolley route for touring city, T8443255, F8446149.Refurbished, tasteful, clean, huge rooms with balcony overlooking city hall, some with 2 double beds, friendly. There are about 5 other guest houses. West of Ponce at **Guayanilla**, is **AL-B** *Pichi's* ,

Route 132, Km 204, T8353335, www.pichis.com, next to *McDonalds*. 58 big rooms, a/c, TV, phone, excellent service, pool, restaurant, bar, meeting rooms and banqueting facilities.

The restaurant of the *Meliá hotel*, **Mark's at the Meliá** is good and the award-winning **Eating** owner/chef is on the Puerto Rican National Team. There is a vegetarian restaurant in the Plaza del Mercado shopping centre, Calle Mayor, 4 blocks northeast from main plaza. Fast food places on main plaza.

There are several flights daily from San Juan. The *público* from San Juan takes 2 hrs. Públicos **Transport** serve outlying districts if you have not got a car. Most *carros públicos* leave from the intersection of Victoria and Unión, three blocks north of the plaza (fare to San Juan US$6-7; to Guayama, either direct or via Santa Isabel, US$3).

Tourist information The Puerto Rico Tourism Co is on the first floor inside the City Bank at the Plaza **Directory** Las Delicias in front of the Parque Bomberos, open Mon-Fri 0800-1700, T8430465, www.prtourism.com A tourist trolley bus makes a tour of the city, 1hr.

Guánica

Going west from Ponce is Guánica, the place where American troops first landed in the Spanish-American war. It has an old fort from which there are excellent views. Although Guánica has a history stretching back to Ponce de León's landing in 1508, the first of many colonist landings in the bay, the town was not actually founded here until 1914. For details on the Guánica Forest see page 503. A cabin site is being developed, rather primitive, with a visitor centre. The on-site forest supervisor is Miguel Canals. Outside Guánica is a *balneario* with a large hotel alongside, *Copamarina*. Scuba diving and other watersports are possible here with Dive Copamarina, T8210505, www.copamarina.com; the wall is close to the shore and there are drop-offs and canyons. You can get to **Gilligans Island** by 15-minute water taxi. Go past Balneario Caña Gorda on route 333, turn right towards Punta Jacinto and the pier. There is a fishing pier, barbecue area, information office and beautiful beach. ■ *0900-1700, closed Mon (or Tue if Mon is a holiday).*

LL-L *Copamarina Beach Resort*, Route 333, Km 6.5, T8210505, F8210070, www.copamarina. **Sleeping** com. Set in 6.5 ha tropical estate, 106 rooms, a/c, TV, balcony, 2 pools, tennis, watersports, PADI dive centre, tour desk, restaurants, on eelgrass beach but good swimming on Gilligans Island.

Further west is La Parguera, originally a fishing village and now a popular resort with **La Parguera** *paradores*, guest houses, fish restaurants, fast food outlets. Noisy on holiday weekends. Fishing, kayaking, mountain biking and other activities are offered. Parguera Divers are at *Posada Porlamar*, T8994171, for wall diving. *Parguera Fishing Charters*, T8994698, hometown.aol.com/mareja, will take you reef fishing or out to catch marlin, dorado, wahoo and tuna. Nearby is **Phosphorescent Bay**, an area of phosphorescent water, occurring through a permanent population of minescent dinoflagellates, a tiny form of marine life, which produce sparks of chemical light when disturbed. One hour boat trips round the bay depart between 1930 and 2230, every 30 minutes, US$12 per person, the experience is said to be rather disappointing, however, and it is best to go on a very dark night or even when it is raining. Mosquito Bay on Vieques is much better.

A-B *Villa Parguera*, Route 304, T8997777, F8996040, www.villaparguera.com 70 rooms, **Sleeping** sea view, by docks, rent boat to get to mangrove canals and cays for good swimming and snorkelling, restaurant, live music and dancing at weekends. **A-B** *Posada Porlamar*, Route 304, Km 303, T8994015, F8995558, netdial.caribe.net/~posada/. 24 rooms, TV, phone, on the canals, dock, watersports arranged, dive shop on site, dive packages available. **A-B** *Estancia La Jamaca* , Route 304, T/F8996162, inland. 8 rooms, quiet, country noises at night.

San Germán Inland from La Parguera, off the main Route 2, San Germán has much traditional charm; it was the second town to be founded on the island and has preserved its colonial atmosphere. It is an excellent base from which to explore the mountains and villages of southwest Puerto Rico. The beautiful little Porta Coeli chapel on the plaza contains a small, rather sparse museum of religious art. ■ *Wed-Sun, 0830-1200, 1300-1630.* A university town: it can be difficult to get cheap accommodation in term time. **B** *Oasis*, 72 Luna, T8921175, F8924546, has 52 rooms, not as close to the beach as it claims, but is ideal for the hills, getting old and shabby, water intermittent, restaurant, pool.

Boquerón

This is one of the cheapest spots on the island because it is a centre for the Compañía de Fomento Recreativo providing holiday accommodation for Puerto Rican families

On the south side of the west coast is Boquerón, in Cabo Rojo district, which has an excellent beach for swimming. It is very wide and long, admission US$1, camping, changing rooms, beach and first 30 m of sea packed with bodies on holiday weekends. About 1½ km away across the bay is a beautiful, deserted beach, but there is no road to it. The small village is pleasant, with typical bars, restaurants and street vendors serving the local speciality, oysters.

South of the town is **Boquerón Lagoon**, a wildfowl sanctuary; also the **Cabo Rojo Wildlife Refuge**, with a visitors' centre and birdwatching trails. The **Cabo Rojo lighthouse** (Faro), at the island's southwest tip is the most southerly point on the island with a breathtaking view; the exposed coral rocks have marine fossils and, closer inshore, shallow salt pools where crystals collect. The vegetation is dry scrub and you can find the slow growing hard wood, lignum vitae. Popular beaches in this area are **El Combate** (miles of white sand, undeveloped, but now a favourite with university students), south of Boquerón, and **Joyuda** (small island just offshore offers good snorkelling and swimming, but beach itself not spectacular) and **Buyé** (camping US$8 a night) to the north. At Joyuda you can go fishing, snorkelling or take a trip to Mona Island with Tour Marine Adventures, on the beach near *Perichi's*, T8519259, tourmarine@yahoo.com

Sleeping **C-D** *Canadian Jack's Guest House*, PO Box 990, Boquerón, PR 00622, T8512410. Private bathroom, colour TV, clean and comfortable but noisy on Fri, Sat nights when the streets are crowded with people partying, fantastic spot. Jack also rents hammocks overlooking the water. **A-B** *Boquemar*, end of Route 100, Int 101, Gil Bouye St, T8512158, F8517600. 75 rooms, a/c, bar, restaurant, pool, facilities for disabled, parking. At Cabo Rojo, **B** *Punta Aguila Villas*, T7254659, past the salt flats and *Agua El Cuello* restaurant. On shallow eelgrass beach but near 2 good swimming beaches, good hiking area, gazebos, jacuzzi, pool, 2 bedrooms. Next door is **AL-A** *Parador Bahía Salinas*, Route 301, Km 11.5, T2541212, F2541215, www.bahiasalinas.com Lovely setting, 24 rooms, most with porch for sunset watching, pool, kayaking, sailing, fishing, Caribbean Reef Divers on beach, T2544006, divingjm@coqui.net **AL-B** *Perichi's*, Route 102, Km 14.3, Playa Joyuda, T8513131, F8510560, perichi@tropicweb.net 41 rooms, well-run, with good award-winning restaurant. **B** *Centro Vacacional de Boquerón*, run by Fomento Recreativo, fully self-contained, with barbecues, beach cabins. Foreigners are welcomed, but it is so popular with Puerto Ricans that you may have to make an application up to 3 months in advance. There are other hotels and a *parador*, **A-B** *Joyuda Beach*, Route 102, Km 11.7, T8515650, F2553750, www.guiapr.com/joyudabeach 41 rooms, restaurant. **Camping** *Villa Plaza* (Denigno Ojeda Plaza) on the road to Cabo Rojo lighthouse, Route 301, Km 6.6, T8511340. Cabins, pool, electricity, security, US$25 per tent per night, US$20 for more than one day, take insect repellent.

Eating Joyuda is famous for seafood restaurants on the beach; inexpensive food, good quality, nice atmosphere, whole, grilled fish is a must, especially snapper (*chillo*).

Mayagüez Mayagüez is a crowded city with little of interest to the tourist. There are **botanical gardens**, at the Tropical Agricultural Research Station, near the University of

Puerto Rico. ■ *Mon-Fri, 0730-1630. Free.* The city also has a **zoo**. ■ *Tue-Sun, 0900-1630. Adults US$1, children US$0.50.* The tourist office is in the Municipalidad on Plaza Colón but has no tourist information available.

Sleeping L-AL *Mayagüez Resort & Casino*, Route 104, Km 3, T8317575, F2653020. 141 rooms in 20 acres, view of harbour, business hotel and resort of international standard. **A-C** *Embajador*, 111 Ramos Antonini, Este, T8333340, F8347664. 29 rooms, central, phones, TV, restaurant, facilities for wheelchair visitors, laundry room. **B** *El Sol*, 9 Santiago Riera Palmer St, East Mayagüez, T8340303, T/F2657567, home.coqui.net/bechara/hotel_e.htm 52 rooms, breakfast included, TV, fridge, phone, hair dryer, bar, restaurant, pool, in city centre. **E** *RUM Hotel*, hotel of the Recinto University of Mayagüez, T8324040. Safe, pool, library, similar prices at other branches of the University. North of Mayagüez at Tres Hermanos, Bahía de Añasco, at Route 115 Km 5, is a **campground** with beach and pool, **B** cabins sleep 6, camping with water and electricity US$10 per tent per night.

Eating *Vegetarian Restaurant*, José de Diego. Open 1100-1400. *Fuente Tropical*, same street. Run by Colombians, good fruit shakes and hamburgers. *Recomeni*, Vigo. Good inexpensive food, open all hours, eat in or takeaway.

Transport *Públicos* leave from a modern terminal in Calle Peral. Bus to San Juan US$10.

Mona Island
Colour map 3, grid B/C 5

Mona Island, 80 km west of Mayagüez, is fascinating for historians and nature lovers, with turquoise sea and white sand. Originally inhabited by Taino Indians and then by pirates and privateers, it is now deserted except for its wildlife. Here you can see 1m-long iguanas, colonies of sea birds and bats in the caves (possibly pirates too). Sixty-metre high cliffs are dotted with caves, ascending to a flat table top covered with dry forest. The island is managed by the Department of National Resources (T7221726), who have cabins to rent with prior permission. Camping is allowed at Sardinera Beach, where there are bathrooms. There are no restaurants or facilities. Take all your food and water with you and bring back all your rubbish.

Transport Boats from Boquerón or Cabo Rojo 4 hrs, US$1,200 for 20-person boat, less for 14-person boat, leave before dawn. Contact Captains Porfirio Andujar, T8517359, Ramón Peña, T2552031; Catalino Lallave, T2855129; David Rodríguez, T8511885; Luís Ortiz, T8516276. Planes to Mona are planned following work on the runway. Check with the PR Forestry Service or Vieques Air Link (Coptco Aviation T7290000 for private charter).

Directory Tour agencies *EcoAventuras*, PO Box 22768, San Juan, PR 00931-2768, T8665309. Karina Zuñiga has specialized trips about 5 times a year, providing meals, transport, tents, permits, information and planning, US$175 per person for 7 days with 20 people, US$135 per person for 4 days with 4 people. *Aventurisla*, PO Box 22242, San Juan PR 00931-22242, T7907816. Ricardo Otero offers much the same trip only you bring your own tent. *Tour Marine*, HC 1 Box 16346, Cabo Rojo, PR 00623-9719, T8519259, 3752625. Offers Mona Island charters for parties of 6-12, take your own tents.

Rincón
Humpback whales visit in winter & can be seen playing in the surf. Divers sometimes see them

Going north from Mayagüez, you come to Rincón, on the westernmost point of the island. Here the mountains run down to the sea, and the scenery is spectacular. For a great panoramic view visit the Punta Higuera Lighthouse, built on a cliff overlooking the surf where the Atlantic and Caribbean meet. The town itself is unremarkable, but the nearby beaches are beautiful and the surfing is a major attraction. The beaches are called Steps, Domes (named after the nearby nuclear storage dome) and the Public Beach, with lifeguard. Pools, Sandy Beach and Antonio's are north of Punta Higuera and popular with winter surfers. Domes and María's are further south and offer good, clean waves. *West Coast Surf Shop* (and tours) in Rincón, T8233935. PADI dive school, *Tanks-a-lot*, T8236301, also arrange excursions to the island of **Desecheo**, 19 km off the coast of Rincón. Desecheo is near Mona Island, but smaller, deserted, and has terrific diving offshore.

Puerto Rico

Sleeping and eating LL *Horned Dorset Primavera*, Route 429, Km 3, T8234030, F8235580, www.horneddorset.com No children under 12, no TV, no organized activities, 30 suites, Spanish colonial style, mahogany furniture, prides itself on offering privacy, good restaurant, beach not good for swimming, seafront rooms can be noisy if sea is rough with waves pounding on wall below, pool, nothing much to do. **AL-A** *Villa Cofresí*, Route 115, Km 12.3, T8232450, F8231770, www.villacofresi.com 51 rooms, on the beach, TV, kitchens, restaurant, bar, outdoor restaurant, watersports. **AL-A** *Villa Antonio*, alongside it, also at Route 115, Km 12.3, T8232645, www.villa-antonio.com. 55 rooms (1 or 2 bedrooms) on a good beach for swimming and near good surfing beaches, a/c, volleyball, tennis, pool, kitchen, TV, parking, bar and restaurant close by. **AL-A** *The Lazy Parrot Inn and Restaurant*, Route 413, Km 4.1, Barrio Puntas, T8235654, F8230224, www.lazyparrot.com In La Cadena hills overlooking coast, rooms sleep 4 in family room, also honeymoon suite, a/c, cable TV, fridge, restaurant closed Mon. At **Puntas** , Carmen's grocery store has rooms, basic, cooking facilities.

Transport Rincón can be reached by *público* from Mayagüez or (less frequent) from Aguadilla. Public transport is scarce at weekends.

Aguadilla North of Rincón the road leads to Aguadilla, another good spot for sunset watching. **Crash Boat Beach** is a popular surfing beach just to the north and lots of watersports are on offer. *Aquatica Underwater Adventures*, Route 110, Km 10, T8906071, www.aquatica.cjb.net, offers diving and fishing and trips to Desecheo. There is a golf course at the old Ramey base, originally designed for Eisenhower, Punta Borinquén Golf, Route 107, T8902987, with tuition, pro-shop and practice range.

Sleeping and eating L-B *La Cima*, Route 110, Km 9.2, Barrio Maleza Alta, T8902016, F8902017, www.lacima.com 40 rooms, a/c, TV, phone, pool, exercise room, within reach of 6 beaches and golf. **A-B** *Parador El Faro* , Route 107, Km 2.1, T8828000, F8913110, www.ihppr.com 50 rooms, built 1990, TV, phone, *Tres Amigos* restaurant for Puerto Rican and international food. Under same ownership is the 33-room **B-C** *Parador Borinquén* , Route 467, Km 2.1, T8910451, F8828008. **A-B** *Hacienda El Pedregal*, Route 111, Km 0.1, T8822865, F8822885, www.haciendaelpedregal.com 27 rooms, view of ocean and sunsets, attractive rooms, TV, phone, parking, restaurant, bar, pools.

North coast road

Route 2, the main road in the north, runs from Aguadilla through Quebradillas to Arecibo, then through urban areas to some extent from Arecibo and completely from Manatí to San Juan. South of Quebradillas in the Montañas Aymamón is the **Bosque Estatal de Guajataca**, a dry forest with a large number of bird species, on Route 446. There are over 40 walking trails with 40 km of maintained footpaths through the Karst region, three picnic areas and two camping areas with tent sites. The on-site supervisor is Edwin Avila. Get your permit in San Juan or the regional office in Aguadilla, T8904050 (see page 484). South of Arecibo in the Karst country is the **Bosque Río Abajo**, a 2,023-ha reserve off Route 10. It contains 70 trails and dirt roads, ideal for viewing plant and birdlife, 15 commercial plantations (teak, mahogany, maga trees), two new campsites, two natural springwater swimming pools and some amazing bamboo near the end of the road. The on-site forest supervisor is José Casanovas. There is also a private campsite at Dos Bocas: *T J Ranch*, a coffee farm run by Tony and Juanita, pool, toilets, no electricity, US$5 per person, breakfast on request, go over the dam on Route 146, first left straight up to the top, past phone booth, then at intersection turn left (small sign for T J Ranch), T8801217, HC02 Box 14926, Arecibo, PR 00612.

If you have the time it is much nicer to drive along the coast then along Route 2. Take Route 681 out of Arecibo, with an immediate detour to the Poza del Obispo beach, by Arecibo lighthouse. Here a pool has been formed inside some rocks, but the breakers on the rocks themselves send up magnificent jets of spray. The bay, with fine surf, stretches round to another headland, **Punta Caracoles**, on which is the **Cueva del Indio** (small car park on Route 681, US$1 charge if anyone is around). A short walk through private land leads to the cave, a sea-eroded hole and funnel in the cliff; watch out for holes in the ground when walking around. There are Taino/Arawak drawings in the cave. *Públicos* run along Route 681 from Arecibo. Rejoin Route 2 through Barceloneta. The State Forest of Cambalache is between Arecibo and Barceloneta. Cambalache Beach has two camping areas, La Boba and La Rusa, with water and showers. **Warning** Safety depends on numbers. There are eight trails and the beach. The on-site supervisor is Jorge Carnaval, T8787279.

The coast road is not continuous; where it does go beside the sea, there are beaches, seafood restaurants and some good views. Route 165, another coastal stretch which can be reached either through **Dorado** on the 693 (where there are three large Hyatt hotels and several golf courses, www.hyatt.com), or through Toa Baja, enters metropolitan San Juan at Cataño.

Near **Isabela** on the coast is **LL** *Villa Montana*, Route 4466, Km 1.2, T8729554, F8729553, www.villamontana.com Nice resort, tranquil spot, miles of sand dunes and surf, protected area for swimming, tennis, restaurant by pool bar, villas with kitchens, not much else, lots to do during the day but nothing at night. **AL-A** *Villas del Mar Hau*, T8722627, F8722045, www.indio.net/villashau Beachfront cabins, some with a/c, some with fans, a few tent sites, US$10, private farm on beach, horse riding nearby. At **Arecibo** there are several hotels and guest houses around the main square, **D** *Hotel Plaza*. Near **Quebradillas**, Route 2, Km 103.8, are **A** *El Guajataca*, T8953070, F8952204, gymguaja@caribe.net Beautifully located on a beach (dangerous swimming). 38 rooms, pool, entertainment, restaurant, bars. On the other side of the road, and higher up the hill at Km 7.9, Route 113, is **AL-A** *Vistamar*, T8952065, F8952294, www.paradorvistamar.com 55 rooms, also with pool, restaurant and bar with view down to ocean, live music Sat.

Sleeping & eating

Camping *Punta Maracayo Camping*, next to Sardinera beach, Km 84.6 on Ruta 2, T8200274. Owned by Hatillo Municipality, surreal with concrete dinosaurs, elephant etc next to campsite, small sheltered cove, calm water, good swimming, sand average, pool, cabins US$135 for 2 nights, US$25 additional nights, tent sites US$50 for 2 nights, US$20 additional nights, guard, fenced in, busy at weekends and in summer.

Panoramic Route

Heading east from Mayagüez is the Panoramic Route which runs the whole length of Puerto Rico, through some of the island's most stunning scenery. It passes through the Cordillera Central, with large areas of forest, and there are several excursions to various countryside resorts. Despite the fact that you are never far from buildings, schools or farms, the landscape is always fascinating. In the evening the panoramas are lovely and you can hear the song of the *coquí*. No trip to the interior should miss at least some part of the Panoramic Route, but if you want to travel all of it, allow three days. The roads which are used are narrow, with many bends, so take care at corners. The **Maricao State Forest** (Monte del Estado) is the most westerly forest on the Route; its visitors' areas are open from 0600 to 1800, T7243724. It is a beautiful forest with magnificent views, an observation tower and a fish hatchery.

Sleeping and eating AL *Parador Hacienda Juanita*, Route 105, Km 23.5, Maricao, T8382550, F8382551, www.haciendajuanita.com 21 modest rooms, breakfast and dinner included in price, part of an old coffee plantation, bar, restaurant, pool, volleyball, tennis, basketball, gardens, walking trails, parking, facilities for disabled, cool at night. **B** *Fomento Recreativo* cabins at Km 13.1, Maricao Rd 120, T8735632. Not a natural setting but cabins have a fireplace, sleep 6 and have cool mountain air up Monte del Estado. *Ginger Hill Vegetarian Guest House*, Las Marías, T8724079, gngrhill@prtc.net Remote, coffee plantation, paths, bed and breakfast meal plan in season. *The Yellow House*, east of Las Marías,

Puerto Rico

T8272758, Mr Birdsell. Very rustic guest house in the middle of nowhere. Recommended for budget travellers.

Susua & Guilarte South of the Panoramic Route between Sabana Grande and Yauco on Route 371 is the **Bosque Estatal de Susua**, a dry forest with recreational areas, a river, 40 tent sites and showers. Acquire permits in San Juan or the Ponce regional office, T8444051 (see page 484). As it approaches **Adjuntas** and the transinsular Route 10, the Panoramic Route goes through the **Bosque de Guilarte**, again with fine views, flowering trees, bougainvillaea, banks of impatiens (busy lizzie, *miramelinda* in Spanish), and bird song (if you stop to listen). Off Routes 131 and 518, south of Adjuntas, there is a trail through eucalyptus trees up to the peak with a nice view. It is cool, you are in the clouds. There are five basic cabins, **F**, with two sets of bunk beds, musty smell, bring permit, bedding, cooking things etc, shared bathroom, no electricity, barbecues, picnic tables. On site forest supervisor Rubén Padrón, get permit from San Juan or Ponce regional office, T8444051 (see Camping, page 484).

Sleeping and eating C *Hotel Monte Río*, 2 blocks from Plaza in Adjuntas, Calle H, T/F8293705. Pool, economical, convenient, restaurant and bar.

Toro Negro After Adjuntas, the road enters the **Toro Negro Forest Reserve**, which includes the highest point on the island, **Cerro de Punta** (1,338 m). This is a smaller area than El Yunque, with fewer rivers. There are many very tall eucalyptus trees along the road. Lago El Guineo and Lago de Matrullas are Puerto Rico's highest lakes. The reserve has five trails, one to an observation tower with views of the mountains and lakes. A camping area (14 tent sites), has showers and toilets. There is a natural springwater swimming pool further down the road open May-September. ■ *Permit needed from Servicio Forestal in San Juan or regional office in Ponce, T8444051. The on-site forest supervisor is René Román. The Recreation Areas in Toro Negro are open from 0800-1700.*

Jayuya Just north of the Panoramic Route is Jayuya, overlooked by Cerro de Punta and Tres Picachos in a beautiful mountain setting. It is known as the indigenous capital of Puerto Rico and is named after the Indian cacique Hayuya, the last to submit to the Spaniards. Two monuments commemorate the Taino heritage: a statue of Hayuya sculpted by Tomás Batista in 1969, and the Tumba del Indio Puertorriqueño, containing a Taino skeleton buried in the traditional foetal position. In November Jayuya celebrates an indigenous festival in honour of Hayuya. Sleep can be had at **AL-A** *Parador Hacienda Gripiñas*, Route 527 Km 2.7, T8281717, F8281719. 19 rooms in a coffee plantation house built in 1858, set in lovely gardens, friendly, pleasant, half-board available, bar, restaurant, pool, parking, facilities for disabled.

Cañon San Cristóbal After this high, lush forest with its marvellous vistas, the Panoramic Route continues to Aibonito, around which the views and scenery are more open, mainly as a result of
You can see the canyon from the top from a dirt road off Route 162, very impressive deforestation(**C-E** *Swiss Inn Guest House*, Route 14 Km 49.3, T7358500, run by Gregory Muñóz, 8 rooms with shower, fans, balcony, TV, microwave, fridge, price negotiable for longer stays, very friendly and helpful, up in the mountains). Thence to Cayey and, beyond, to another forest, Carite (also known as Guavate, see page 500). Finally the road descends into the rich, green valley which leads to Yabucoa. Between Aibonito and Barranquitas is the Cañón San Cristóbal, where you can climb down a mountain trail between steep walls to the bottom, where the temperature is considerably warmer, four-hour trip. ■ *Call Félix Rivera, T7355188, for a guide, you will need one to find the way. He usually meets people at La Piedra restaurant, on Route 7718, one of Puerto Rico's gastronomic delights.*

From various points on the Panoramic Route you can head north or south; for example Route 10 goes south from Adjuntas to Ponce, or north to Utuado and then on to **Río Abajo State Forest** where there are a swimming pool and various picnic spots. ■ *0600-1800*. It is approached through splendid views of the karst hills and the **Dos Bocas Lake**. Free launch trips are offered on this lake at 0700, 1000, 1400 and 1700; they last two hours and are provided by the Public Works Department. Route 10 reaches the north coast at Arecibo.

The Caguana Indian Ceremonial Park, west of Utuado, dates from about 1100 AD, and contains 10 Taino ball courts, each named after a Taino *cacique* (chieftain). The courts vary in size, the longest being about 85 m by 20 (Guarionex), the largest 65 by 50 (Agueybana). These two have monoliths in the stones that line the level 'pitch', and on those of Agueybana there are petroglyphs, some quite faint. None of the monoliths is taller than a man. A path leads down to the Río Tanamá. The setting, amid limestone hills, is very impressive. It is believed to be a site of some religious significance and has been restored with a small museum in the 13-acre landscaped botanical park containing royal palm, guava, cedar and ceiba. ■ *It is on Route 111 to Lares, Km 12.3. 0900-1700 (gate to the river closes at 1630). Free.*

Caguana Indian Ceremonial Park

Further west of Utuado, **Lares** is a hilltop town (*públicos* go from one block from church) from where you can either carry on to the west coast at Aguadilla, or head north on one of the many routes to the Atlantic coast. Route 453 passes **Lago de Guajataca**, continuing as Route 113 to Quebradillas. Route 455 branches west off the 453, leading via a short stretch of the 119 to the 457 and 446 (good view at the junction of these two). Route 446 traverses, as a single track, the **Bosque Estatal de Guajataca**. Route 129 goes to Arecibo, passing the **Río Camuy Cave Park**, with side trips to the Cueva de Camuy and the Arecibo Observatory (see page 488). Driving on the country roads in the area between the Panoramic Route and the north coast is twisty but pleasant, passing conical limestone hills (*mogotes*) and farms set among patches of lush forest.

Sleeping AL-C *Parador J B Hidden Village*, Route 416, Barrio Piedras Blancas, Aguada, T8688686, F8688701. 33 rooms built in 1990, a/c, bar, restaurant, pool, parking, facilities for disabled. **A-B** *Casa Grande*, Barrio Caonillas, Utuado, Route 612, Km 0.3, T8943939, F8943900, www.hotelcasagrande.com. 20 rooms in attractive mountain setting, former coffee plantation, balconies, hammocks, yoga, kayaking, bar, *Jungle Jane's* restaurant, pool.

Vieques

Vieques, a peaceful, relaxing, low-key island of rolling hills, is 11 km across the sea from Puerto Rico. It was catapulted into the limelight in 1999-2000 when locals campaigned for the removal of the US military from their bases at the east and west ends of the island. The island is about 34 km long by 6 km wide, the inhabitants mostly concentrated in the main town of Isabel Segunda. It was named Graciosa by Columbus, after a friend's mother, but was then better known as Crab Island by the pirates who frequented its waters.

Population: 9,400
Colour map 3, grid B6

Ins and outs

Fajardo is the closest sea and air port. Take the ferry from Fajardo or catch a plane from San Juan or Fajardo. *Vieques Air Link* (T7413266) have flights from Fajardo (10 mins, T8633020), San Juan International (30 mins, T7223736), as well as Isla Grande and St Croix (30 mins, T7789858) many times a day. *Isla Nena*, T7411577, and the charter airline, *Air Culebra*, T2686951, also fly to Vieques.

Getting there
See transport, page 512, for further details

Públicos meet you at the airport and ferry dock, posted rates (none higher than US$3.00), but some drivers will try to overcharge you, ask the price first, or let your hotel/guest house arrange transport for you. Car hire is widely available.

Getting around

Puerto Rico

Sights

*The biggest 'action'
is on Sat night in
Esperanza. Everyone
promenades along the
sea front dressed in
their finest, talking &
flirting, before going
to a nightclub or bar*

There is an excellent historical museum at the beautifully restored fort, **El Fortín Conde de Mirasol** which was the last fort begun by the Spanish in the Western Hemisphere. *Week days by appointment, T7411717, 7418651 evenings. Wed-Sun 1000-1600.* There is another interesting exhibit at the **Punta Mulas Lighthouse**. ■ *T7415000. Daily 0800-1630.*

The US Military owns two thirds of the island, the east third and west third, with the civilian population living on the middle strip. Both bases are theoretically open to the public upon presentation of any photo identification except on days when the red flag is up: when manoeuvers and/or bombing practice are underway. However, since December 1999 Naval security guards have prevented tourists gaining access to beaches even when no exercises have been taking place. The beaches can still be reached by boat. The Navy's reaction was as a result of the establishment of a protest camp at the gates. The US Navy is under pressure to leave and return the land to the people. In 1999 the Governor requested an immediate end of US weapons training on the island after a civilian was killed in a bombing error, see page 515. The military is heard but not much seen, planes and helicopters fly low but since only a handful of personnel are permanently stationed on the island, it is not a base town atmosphere. The land owned by the military is mostly untouched, creating a bird sanctuary and nature preserve.

**Beaches &
resorts** Vieques has over 52 beaches in secluded coves, the few developed beaches have people and exuberant groups of picnickers, the rest are deserted. Public **Sun Bay** has picnic and camping areas (no shade in camping area, but there is lots of petty theft so not many people camp there).

Tourism is an infant industry on this island, but is rapidly being promoted to provide employment and reduce poverty. Hotel construction includes the US$30 mn *Casa de Playa Beach Villages* a condo-hotel with 210 rooms and 70 villas. The port and airport are also being expanded and modernized. The small beach town of **Esperanza** is the main area of guest houses and tourist related restaurants, bars, dive companies (Blue Caribe Dive Center, SSI facility, full service, T7412522, PO Box 1574), etc. The **museum** in Esperanza has archaeological and natural history exhibits. ■ *Tue-Sun, 1100-1500, T7418850.*

Vieques

■ Sleeping
1 Casa del Francés
2 Crow's Nest
3 New Dawn
4 Ocean View
5 Posada Vistamar

Small, hardy, island horses, most with paso fino blood lines (that means smooth gaits with no bouncing) are still used as transport, and wild horses roam the island. Renting a horse is an exciting way to explore the beaches and coves.

Mosquito Bay, also known as **Phosphorescent Bay**, is a large, but very shallow bay, surrounded by mangrove trees and full of bioluminescent organisms. Sightseeing trips go at night (recommended are the tours that use non polluting electric boats or kayaks), US$15-18. The organisms glow when disturbed. The glow generated by a 13 cm fish is about a 39 cm circle of light brighter than a light bulb. Swimming in this glow is a wonderful experience. Clark, T7417600, has a small boat; Sharon Grasso at *Island Adventures*, T741-0717/0720, www.biobay.com, has an electric boat, naturalist; *Blue Caribe Divers*, T7412522, SSI, PADI, for kayak tours and night scuba dives.

Essentials

Esperanza LL-L *Inn on the Blue Horizon*, Route 996, Km 4.2, T7413318, F7410522, www.enchanted-isle.com/bluehorizon, on the beach west of Esperanza. Former pineapple plantation, run by Billy Knight and James Weis, from New York, 9 rooms with antique furniture, pool, popular bar and restaurant. **AL** *La Casa del Francés*, T7413751, F7412330, www.enchanted-isle.com/ lacasa, Route 996. 18 rooms, classical sugar plantation Great House, designated historical landmark, bar, restaurant, pool, 5-min walk out of Esperanza. **B** *Amapola*, Flamboyan 144, T7411382, F7413704, www.enchanted-isle.com/amapola A/c rooms with private baths. **C-D** *Bananas Guest House*, T7418700, facing the ocean. Popular, pleasant American restaurant, some rooms a/c. **D** *Tradewinds*, owned by Janet and Harry Washburn, PO Box 1012, T7418666. Bar, restaurant. Smaller and cheaper guest houses include: *La Central* (T7410106), *Posada Vistamar* (T741 8716); *La Concha* (T7412733). For apartments in Esperanza try *Acacia Apts*, 236 Acacia St, T/F7411856. Owned by Jürgen Meuser and Manfred Kissel, clean, cosy, friendly. Or *La Piña*, 222 Acacia St, T/F7412953. Owned by Elswith Petrakovic.

Isabel Segunda A-B *Ocean View*, Box 124, 751 Calle Plinio Peterson, T7413696, F7411793. Concrete block hotel right on water's edge next to ferry dock, 35 rooms with balconies, Chinese restaurant next door under same ownership, car rental for guests. **B-C** *Sea Gate Hotel*, near the fort, T7414661, F7412978. 16 rooms high up on hill, good views, pool, tennis. *Casa La Lanchita*, ocean front, T/7410023. *Vieques Inn*, downtown, T7411500. Inland is **L-AL** *Hacienda Tamarindo*, Box 1569, Vieques, PR 00765, Route 996, Km 4.5, T7418525, F7413215, www.enchanted-isle.com/tamarindo 16 rooms and suites, breakfast included, no children under 15, hotel built around a large tamarind tree, each room different, on hill with sea views, pool down the hill, run by Burr and Linda Vail. **L-B** *Crow's Nest*, Box 1521, Route 201, Km 1.6, T7410033, F7411294, www.enchanted-isle/crowsnest 15 rooms with kitchenettes or 2-bedroom suites with living areas, set in rolling hillside, pool, restaurant. Or **D** *New Dawn*, PO Box 1512, T7410495. An unusual guest house built on 2ha of land with horses grazing off the huge veranda, is 5 km from the beach, frequently booked by women's groups for retreats, 2-storey wooden house, large deck and hammocks, rooms, dorms **F** per person, and tentsites, all with shared bath and outdoor showers or you can rent the entire place (sleeps 20+) with or without a cook, for US$250 per day, US$3,000 per month. For villa rentals contact Connections (T7410023).

Eating   Almost all of the island's restaurants are part of a hotel or guest house listed above. There are numerous small places offering take out or eat in sandwiches, hamburgers, barbecue chicken, etc. **Esperanza** *Inn on the Blue Horizon* has *Café Blu* for fine dining, open Wed-Sun 1800-2200, lunchtimes Sat, Sun, reservations recommended, T7413318, and *Blu Bar* with happy hour 1600-1800 every day and lighter food 1200-2145, bar until 0030. *Bananas*, T7418700, Flamboyán St. Pub food and pizzas, beachfront, food until 2200-2300, bar open late, especially at weekends. *Crabwalk Café*, next to *Tradewinds*. Sandwiches, salads, open from 0800. *Trapper John's*, T7411325. Food until 2400, frozen drinks US$5. *La Central*, T7410106. For Puerto Rican food, *empanadas*. *Eddie's* for dancing, rum and beer, live music last weekend every month. **Isabel Segunda** *Café Mar Azul*, bar on ocean front, T7413400. Open 0900-0100, later at weekends, happy hour 1700-1800. *Taverna Española*, T7411175. Spanish food.

Transport   **Ferry**   From Fajardo, the car, cargo and passenger ferries leave Mon-Fri 0400 (cars), 0930 (passengers), 0930 (cars), 1300 (passengers), 1630 (passengers and cars), Sat, Sun 0930, 1500, 1800, no car ferries. Vieques-Fajardo Mon-Fri at 0600 (cars), 0700 (passengers), 1100 (passengers), 1330 (cars), 1500 (passengers), 1830 (cars), Sat, Sun 0700, 1300, 1630, in Fajardo call the Port Authority office to transport a car, T8630852, 900-4622005, in Vieques T7414761, open for reservations 0800-1100, 1300-1500, reservations needed for cars only, book 2-3 weeks in advance, US$26 average return, passenger fare is US$2.25 one way, crossing takes 1½ hrs. At weekends the ferries are often full and advance reservations are recommended. **Road**   Car rentals available at *Maritzas Car Rental* (T7410078), *Island Car Rentals* (T7411666), *Steve's* (T7418135), *Fonsin* (T7418163) or *Vieques Cars* (T7411212). Bicycle rental through *DYMC* (T3162617). Horse rentals can be arranged by your guest house.

Directory   **Tourist information**   Useful websites include www.vieques-island.com, www.enchanted-isle.com, www.viequespr.net and www.goto.com. **Useful numbers**   Police: T2020, Fire: T2111, Hospital: T2151.

Culebra

Population: 3,500
Colour map 3, grid B6

Culebra has a climate and landscape similar to that of the Virgin Islands, with tropical forest on the hills and palm groves near the beaches. It is even better than Vieques, with less petty theft, less heavy drinking, better accommodation, more peace and more beautiful beaches though the island is poor, with very high unemployment; most people who have jobs work for the municipality or in construction. It is about 11 km long and 5 km wide.

Ins & outs
See transport, page 514, for further details

Getting there   You can fly from San Juan International Airport, Isla Grande airport or Fajardo. Alternatively there are ferries from Fajardo, with or without cars. Ferries which take cars are slower and rougher and passengers tend to get seasick. **Getting around**   Public transport consists of vans. If they don't turn up at the airport you will have to walk into town. They also run from town to Flamenco Beach, but for access to other beaches, cars and bicycles can be hired and there is also a taxi service.

Sights   The main village, **Dewey** (called Pueblo by the locals) is attractively set between two lagoons. A visitor's information centre is in the City Hall. About 40% of the land is park or national reserve, including many beaches. The **Culebra National Wildlife Refuge** (T7420115), 600 ha, comprising 23 offshore islands and four parcels of land on Culebra, protects large colonies of sea birds, particularly terns, red-billed tropic birds and boobies, and nesting sea turtles: hawksbill, leatherback, loggerhead and green. Volunteers are welcomed to help Wildlife Refuge rangers count and protect nests and hatchlings. Contact Culebra Leatherback Project, PO Box 617, Culebra, PR 00775, T7420050, volunteers needed April-August.

There are good, sandy beaches, clear water and a coral reef. Flamenco Beach is 1½ km long with white sand and exquisitely beautiful clear turquoise water, a reef at one end and waves at the other. It is almost deserted except for a few guest houses at the far end selling a limited amount of drinks, but it becomes a zoo at summer weekends. **Culebrita** and **Luís Peña** are two small cays offshore with beaches. Both are wildlife sanctuaries.

Scuba diving is spectacular in the waters around Culebra, where the sea is clear and the pristine reefs provide lots to see. Dive shops are small and friendly, with flexible programmes and other watersports and boat trips on offer. *Culebra Divers* is opposite the ferry dock, run by Walter Rieder (Swiss) and Monika Frei (both instructors). You can get a week's dive package and guest house accommodation or just go out for the day, T7420803, www.culebradivers.com *Culebra Dive Shop*, T7420566. Kayak rental from *Ocean Safari*, Jim and Barbara Peterson (T3791973), US$25 half day, guided expeditions US$45 half day, US$70 full day, Jim will deliver to various places so you can kayak to nearby islands. Several people offer boat trips or water taxi, some of whom can also do fishing. *Pat's Water Taxi* and glass bottom boat trips, from the dock by *Dinghy Dock Restaurant*, T5010011, to Culebrita US$40, Luis Peña US$20, glass bottom tours US$15, snorkelling tours US$20-40. *Culebra Boat Rental*, T7873559, hires 6-person skiffs for exploring and transport. *Jack's*, T3977494, offers boat trips for snorkelling or water taxi service to the cays offshore, as do *Tanama Glass Bottom Boat*, T5010011, *Culebra Divers*, T7420803, *Guilins Water Taxi*, T7420575. Chris Goldmark, T5013119, does bonefishing, but was not operating in 2001. Contact him at 609-8843694.

Watersports

LL-AL *Villa Flamenco Beach*, on the beach, 2 miles from town, T7423275. Range of studios, 3-bedroom villas, nice place to stay, some with ocean view. **AL** *Rustic Eco-Cottages*, on the hill at Mosquito Bay, T7423136, PO Box 239, Culebra, PR 00775. One cottage sleeps 2, the other 4, includes breakfast, minimum 1 week rental, open Dec-Apr, solar power, composting toilets, no kitchens, no hot water, jeep rental needed, 2 mins down lovely trail to beach, good swimming and snorkelling, kayaks to rent, have to eat lunch and dinner out. **L-AL** *Club Seabourne Mini Resort*, Fulladoza Bay, T7423169, seabourne@gobeach.com Villas and rooms, breakfast included, good restaurant, bar, pool, view, 1 mile from town, car hire needed. **A** *Culebra Beach Resort*, T7420319. Run by Max and Esmeralda, next to *Villa Flamenco*, on the beach, nice, simple, clean rooms with kitchen, pleasant, helpful, lots of repeat business. **AL-A** *Villa Boheme*, Ensenada Honda, T/F7423508, on edge of town, harbour front. Family place, well-managed, clean, a/c, fans, 8 rooms with communal kitchen, 4 apartments with private kitchens, patio on the bay, lovely breeze. **AL-B** *Casa Ensenada*, T7423559. 3 self-contained units, each sleep 2-4, with kitchen, bathroom, private access, can be combined to sleep 10, a/c, fan, TV/VCR, patio, on bay, nice breeze. **B** *Arynar Villa*, T7423145, www.enchantedisle.com/villaarynar 2 rooms in lovely house on hill, less than a mile to town, bed & breakfast. **AL-B** *Posada La Hamaca*, 68 Castelar, T7423516, F7420181, www.posada.com Well kept, only 10 rooms, private bath, beach towels, book in advance, next to *Mamacitas* on the canal, can be smelly. **B-C** *Mamacitas Guest House*, T7420090. With or without kitchens, popular place to stay with popular restaurant, the most activity in Culebra, can be noisy at night. **B-C** *Villa Fulladoza Guest House*, T7423576, on the bay. Best value, kitchens, short walk to town, usually booked up. **C-D** *Kokomo*, PO Box 786, T7420719, opposite ferry dock. Warm side of town, some rooms a/c. *Casa Katrina*, T7423565, in town, view of bay. Weekly rates. **L-AL** *Tamarindo Estates*, T7423343, www.tamarindoestates.com Pool, dock, private bay, snorkelling, dirt access road with potholes, 2 miles to town, car hire needed, restaurant open occasionally, warm side of island. *Pelican Enterprise & Culebra Island Realty*, T7420052, www.culebraislandrealty.com do house rentals, island-wide.

Sleeping

Camping *Culebra Campgrounds* are government-run, US$10 per site, up to 6 people per tent, 2-night minimum, 140 tent sites, bathrooms and water provided but that's all. Not crowded during winter months, just turn up, office open 0700-1800, T7420700. To make a reservation (essential Jun-Sep) send US$20 cheque to Autoridad de Conservación y Desarrollo de Culebra, attn Playa Flamenco, Apartado 217, Culebra, PR 00775 USA.

Eating
Prices range from US$10-25 for a meal

There are several small restaurants in Dewey, offering local dishes and seafood. Takeaways available. *Dinghy Dock Restaurant* on the water in the lagoon, breakfast, lunch and dinner, American and Caribbean food. *El Pesquerito*, breakfast and lunch, Puerto Rican and seafood, US$3-8. *Wai-Nam*, Chinese, lunch and dinner, cheap. Also restaurants at the hotels, *Mamacitas*, *Seabourne*, *Tamarindo*. For those who are self catering, there are 7 grocery stores, *Culebra Deli*, a fish market and a liquor store. Everything is imported so prices are high.

Transport

Local Road Bicycle hire is US$12 per day from *Culebra Bike and Beach* (T7420434), Richard (T7420062) or Wille (T7420563); cars and jeeps from *Prestige* (7423242), *Richard and Kathy's Rentals* (T7420062), *Willy Solis* (T7423537), *R & W* (T7420563) and *Jerry's Jeeps* (T7420587). Taxi service with Marcelino (T7420292) or Cito (T7422787).

Air No direct flights Vieques-Culebra. Flights from San Juan International airport take 30 mins, from Isla Grande airport 30 mins and from Fajardo 15 mins. *Isla Nena*, at San Juan International airport, T(888)2636213, 7411577, in CulebraT7420972, flies 4 times a day San Juan-Culebra, US$60 one way, US$115 return, also 3 times a day Culebra-Fajardo, US$25 one way, and Culebra-St Thomas US$50 on the mail flight Tue and Thur. *Vieques Air Link*, T7420254 in Culebra, T8633020 in Fajardo, T7223736 in San Juan, San Juan Isla Grande-Culebra twice a day, US$50 one way, US$95 round trip, and 3 times a day Fajardo-Culebra, US$25. *Air Culebra* is a charter company, T2686951, 7420446, US$300 one way for up to 5 people.

At weekends the ferries are usually full, best to reserve a ticket

Sea The ferry from Fajardo to Culebra takes about 1½ hrs, and costs US$2.25 per person each way, cars about US$26 return. Fajardo-Culebra, Mon-Fri 0930, 1500, 1600 (cars), Wed, Fri 1000 (cars), Sat, Sun 0430 (cars, every other Sat), 0900, 1600. Return Culebra-Fajardo Mon-Fri 0700 (cars), 1100, 1630, Wed, Fri 1300 (cars), Sat, Sun 0700, 1400, 1730, 1800 (cars, every other Sat). Reservations 3-4 weeks in advance needed for cars. Fajardo ticket and information office is open 0800-1100, 1300-1500, T8630705, 1-800-9812005 (Culebra T7423161). (It is best to arrive in Fajardo in time for the last ferry if you are going to the islands; there is little to do in the town and it is not a cheap place).

Directory

Tourist Office Municipal tourist office, T7423291, F7420111, www.culebra.org

Background

History

Columbus, accompanied by a young nobleman, Juan Ponce de León, arrived in Puerto Rico on 19 November 1493. Attracted by tales of gold, Ponce obtained permission to colonize Boriquén (or Boriken), as it was called by the natives. Boriquén (later altered to Borinquén in poetry) meant 'land of the great lord' and was called that because of the belief that the god, Juracan, lived on the highest peak of the island and controlled the weather from there. The word 'hurricane' is derived from this god's name.

Because of Puerto Rico's excellent location at the gateway to Latin America, it played an important part in defending the Spanish Empire against attacks from French, English and Dutch invaders. After the Spanish-American war, Spain ceded the island to the United States in 1898. The inhabitants became US citizens in 1917, with their own Senate and House of Delegates, and in 1948, for the first time, they elected their own Governor, who is authorized to appoint his Cabinet and members of the island's Supreme Court. In 1952 Puerto Rico became a Commonwealth voluntarily associated with the United States.

The island's status is a matter of constant debate for both political and economic reasons as Puerto Rico is heavily dependent on US funding. The New Progressive

Party (NPP) favours Puerto Rico's full accession to the USA as the 51st state. The Popular Democratic Party (PDP) favours enhancement of the existing Commonwealth status. Pro-independence groups receive less support, the Puerto Rican Independence Party (PIP) struggles to gain seats in Congress. A referendum on Puerto Rico's future status was held in 1991, but voters rejected the PDP administration's proposals to guarantee that they remain citizens of the USA regardless of any change in Puerto Rico's political status. The 1991 vote was seen as a rejection of the policies of the governing party and Governor Rafael Hernández Colón subsequently decided not to seek re-election in the 1992 elections. The elections were convincingly won by the pro-statehood NPP, who secured 36 seats in the House of Representatives and 20 in the Senate. The new Governor, Pedro Rosselló, took office in January 1993.

In November 1993 another referendum was held on the future political status of the island. Voter turnout was high, at 73.6%, of whom 48.4% voted for Commonwealth Status, 46.2% for statehood and 4.4% for independence. Although the result was close, it was seen as a set-back for the pro-statehood government.

Governor Rosselló was re-elected and sworn in on 2 January 1997. The NPP won 19 seats in the Senate against seven for the PDP and one for the PIP. In the Lower House the NPP won 38, PDP 12 and PIP one. In both houses, extra seats were allocated to opposition parties as required by the constitution.

In December 1998 Puerto Ricans voted yet again in a referendum on the island's status. 46.5% of the vote was in favour of statehood, but 50.2% voted for 'none of the above' options, which were to continue the present Commonwealth status, enter the USA as a state of the union, free association, or become independent, with a 10-year transitional period for any change in status. 'None of the above' was included at the request of the opposition PDP, which supports the present Commonwealth status but objected to the wording on the ballot paper. Seventy-one percent of the electorate turned out to vote. Governor Rosselló was criticized for using US hurricane relief (US$1.5 bn) as an argument in favour of statehood and was widely accused of exploiting the emergency for political purposes. After the vote he argued that the statehood option had won, but with the majority against him it appeared unlikely that the US Congress would agree. In September 1999, 11 Puerto Ricans jailed for participation in Fuerzas Armadas de la Liberación Nacional (FALN) activities in 1974-83, were released early on the authority of President Clinton, on condition that they not take part in any armed operations nor associate with ex-prisoners. They were, however, allowed to participate in a pro-Independence rally.

The presence of the US Navy on Vieques became a source of much contention after a civilian was killed in April 1999 during bombing practice. Local people on Vieques and Puerto Rico protested and called for an end to the use of live ammunition and the return of military occupied land to the people of Vieques. There are also claims that bombing has damaged the environment, stunted economic growth and put at risk the health of residents. Exercises using live ammunition were suspended in May 1999 but demonstrators set up a protest camp at the base. Governor Rosselló rejected a US presidential panel's recommendation that exercises should continue for another five years. President Clinton offered to limit operations to 90 days a year instead of the previous 180, and then conceded that live ammunition would no longer be used, while offering US$40 mn in development aid for the island if residents accepted the five-year continuation. His proposals were rejected. A revised proposal from the Pentagon was also rejected and civil disobedience intensified during 2000. In May 2000 US Navy aircraft resumed bombing practice after removing and arresting 224 people from the military base. Dummy ammunition was used and those arrested were released without charge. In October 2000, thousands of NATO troops carried out an amphibious landing in a simulation of a UN peacekeeping mission. Fifty vessels took part in the beach 'invasion' in the largest exercise for four years. A referendum has been proposed to gauge local opinion, to be held sometime before February 2002.

Puerto Rico

In November 2000, Sila Calderón, of the PDP, a business executive and former Secretary of State in the previous PDP administration in the 1980s, was elected Governor on an anti-statehood platform. The PDP won the majority of seats in both houses, giving it a clear mandate not to become the 51st state of the union. The victory was also seen as a popular rejection of the agreement with the US administration to delay until 2003 the withdrawal of the Navy from its bombing range on Vieques despite whatever the islanders vote in the referendum. The Navy refused to transfer 8,000 acres of land on Vieques to the government, planned for 31 December, until Ms Calderón promised to stand by the agreement.

Geography

Puerto Rico is the smallest of the Greater Antilles. Old volcanic mountains, long inactive, occupy a large part of the interior, with the highest peak, Cerro de Punta, at 1,338 m in the Cordillera Central. North of the Cordillera is the karst country where the limestone has been acted upon by water to produce a series of small steep hills (mogotes) and deep holes, both conical in shape. There is an extensive cave system, much of which is open to the public or can be explored with expert guidance. The mountains are surrounded by a coastal plain with the Atlantic shore beaches cooled all the year round by trade winds. Offshore are the sister islands of Vieques, Culebra and the even smaller Mona Island, where facilities are limited to a camp site. Much of Vieques is a US military base, see above.

Government

Puerto Rico is a self-governing Commonwealth in association with the USA (Estado Libre Asociado de Puerto Rico). The chief of state is the President of the United States of America. The head of government is an elected Governor. There are two legislative chambers: the House of Representatives, 51 seats, and the Senate, 27 seats. Two extra seats are granted in each house to the opposition if necessary to limit any party's control to two thirds. Puerto Ricans do not vote in US federal elections, nor do they pay federal taxes, when resident on the island.

Economy

Structure of production

Great social and economic progress has been made in the past 30 years, as a result of the 'Operation Bootstrap' industrialization programme supported by the US and Puerto Rican governments, which was begun in 1948. Accordingly manufacturing for export has become the most important sector of the economy, in place of agriculture. Until 1976, US Corporations were given tax incentives to set up in Puerto Rico and their profits were taxed only if repatriated. Industrial parks were built based on labour intensive industries to take advantage of Puerto Rico's low wages. In the mid-1970s, however, the strategy changed to attract capital intensive companies with the aim of avoiding the low wage trap. Nowadays about 70% of manufacturing income is repatriated; manufacturing produces about 40% of total output, but only 20% if remittances are excluded, about the same as in the 1950s. Investment has also fallen recently to 17% of gdp, having risen from 15% in 1950 to 30% in 1970.

The principal manufactures are textiles, clothing, electrical and electronic equipment, chemicals and pharmaceuticals. Dairy and livestock production is one of the leading agricultural activities; others are the cultivation of sugar, tobacco, coffee, pineapples and coconut. Rum has been a major export since the 19th century and the island supplies 83% of all the rum drunk in mainland USA. Tourism is another key element in the economy although it contributes only about 7% to gdp. The industry is profitable and a large employer. Over four million people visit Puerto Rico each year (about one million are cruise ship passengers) and spend about US$1.9 bn.

Despite the progress made to industrialize the country, the economy has suffered from US budget cuts. Some 30% of all spending on gnp originates in Washington and high unemployment is possible because of food stamps and other US transfers. Migration is a safety valve, and there are more Puerto Ricans living in New York than San Juan. The economy depends heavily on tax incentives given to US mainland companies and on federal transfers.

The agreement between the USA, Canada and Mexico for the North American Free Trade Agreement (NAFTA) also has implications for Puerto Rico because of competition for jobs and investment. Although wage levels are lower in Mexico, Section 936 gives companies in Puerto Rico an advantage in pharmaceuticals and hi-tec industries. In low-skill labour-intensive manufacturing, such as clothing and footwear, Mexico has the advantage. Puerto Rico currently employs 30,000 in the clothing industry.

Culture

(Nigel Gallop writes:)The island was Spanish until 1898 and one of the oldest musical traditions is that of the 19th-century Danza, associated particularly with the name of Juan Morel Campos and his phenomenal output of 549 compositions. This is European-derived salon music for ballroom dancing, slow, romantic and sentimental. The Institute of Puerto Rican Culture sponsors an annual competition for writers of danzas for the piano during the Puerto Rican Danza Week in May. The peasants of the interior, the Jíbaros, sing and dance the Seis, of Spanish origin, in its many varied forms, such as the Seis Chorreao, Seis Zapateao, Seis Corrido and Seis Bombeao. Other variants are named after places, like the Seis Cagueño and Seis Fajardeño. Favoured instruments are the *cuatro* and other varieties of the guitar, the *bordonúa*, *tiple*, *tres* and *quintillo*, backed by *güiro* (scraper), *maracas*, *pandereta* (tambourine) and *bomba* (drum) to provide rhythm. One uniquely Puerto Rican phenomenon is the singer's 'La-Le-Lo-Lai' introduction to the verses, which are in Spanish 10-line *décimas*. The beautiful Aguinaldos are sung at Christmastime, while the words of the Mapeyé express the Jíbaro's somewhat tragic view of life. Many artists have recorded the mountain music, notably El Gallito de Manatí, Ramito, Chuito el de Bayamón, Baltazar Carrero and El Jíbarito de Lares. A popular singer is Andrés Jiménez, 'El Jíbaro', whose rustic songs of Puerto Rican folklore were honoured at Christmas 1993 by a concert with the Symphonic Orchestra of Puerto Rico and the Choir of the Conservatorio de Música de Puerto Rico, in which many traditional instruments were used.

Music & dance
There are several music festivals each year, celebrating different styles & forms, including a Jazzfest in May & the Casals Music Festival in Jun

Puerto Rico's best-known musical genre is the Plena, ironically developed by a black couple from Barbados, John Clark and Catherine George, known as 'Los Ingleses', who lived in the La Joya del Castillo neighbourhood of Ponce during the years of the First World War. With a four-line stanza and refrain in call-and-response between the 'Inspirador' (soloist) and chorus, the rhythm is distinctly African and the words embody calypso-style commentaries on social affairs and true-life incidents. Accompanying instruments were originally tambourines, then accordions and *güiros*, but nowadays include guitars, trumpets and clarinets. The Plena's most celebrated composer and performer was Manuel A Jiménez, known as 'Canario'.

There are relatively few pure black people in Puerto Rico, although the majority have some African blood, and the only specifically black music is the Bomba, sung by the 'Cantaor' and chorus, accompanied by the drums called *buleadores* and *subidores* and naturally also danced. The Bomba can be seen and heard at its best in the island's only black town of Loiza Aldea at the Feast of Santiago in late July. Rafael Cepeda and his family are the best known exponents.

The Jíbaro, mentioned above, is a common figure in Puerto Rican literature. The origin of the name is unknown, but it refers to the *campesino del interior*, a sort of Puerto Rican equivalent to the gaucho, native, but with predominantly hispanic

Literature

Puerto Rico

features. The Jíbaro, as a literary figure, first appeared in the 19th century, with Manuel Alonso Pacheco's *El gíbaro* emerging as a cornerstone of the island's literature. In 29 'scenes', Alonso attempted both to describe and to interpret Puerto Rican life; he showed a form of rural life about to disappear in the face of bourgeois progress. The book also appeared at a time (1849) when romanticism was gaining popularity. Prior to this period, there had been a definite gulf between the educated letters, chronicles and memoires of the 16th to 18th centuries and the oral traditions of the people. These included *coplas, décimas, aguinaldas* (see above) and folk tales. The Jíbaro has survived the various literary fashions, from 19th-century romanticism and *realismo costumbrista* (writing about manners and customs), through the change from Spanish to US influence, well into the 20th century.

One reason for this tenacity is the continual search for a Puerto Rican identity. When, in 1898, Spain relinquished power to the USA, many Puerto Ricans sought full independence. Among the writers of this time were José de Diego and Manuel Zeno Gandía. The latter's series of four novels, *Crónicas de un mundo enfermo* (*Garduña* – 1896, *La charca* – 1898, *El negocio* – 1922, *Redentores* – 1925), contain a strong element of social protest. As the series progresses, a new theme is added to that of local economic misery, emigration to New York, which booms after 1945. For a variety of domestic reasons, many fled the island to seek adventures, happiness, material wealth in the United States. While some writers and artists in the 1930s and 1940s, for example Luis Lloréns Torres, tried to build a kind of nationalism around a mythical, rural past, others still favoured a complete separation from the colonialism which had characterized Puerto Rico's history. For a while, the former trend dominated, but by the 1960s the emigré culture had created a different set of themes to set against the search for the Puerto Rican secure in his/her national identity. These included, on the one hand, the social problems of the islander in New York, shown, for example, in some of the novels of Enrique A Laguerre, *Trópico en Manhattan* by Guillermo Cotto Thorner, stories such as *Spiks* by Pedro Juan Soto, or plays like René Marqués' *La carreta*. On the other there is the Americanization of the island, the figure of the 'piti-yanqui' (the native Puerto Rican who admires and flatters his North American neighbour) and the subordination of the agricultural to a US-based, industrial economy. Writers after 1965 who have documented this change include Rosario Ferré and the novelist and playwright, Luis Rafael Sánchez. The latter's *La guaracha del Macho Camacho* (1976), an alliterative, humorous novel, revolves around a traffic jam in a San Juan taken over by a vastly popular song, *La vida es una cosa fenomenal*, a far cry from the Jíbaro's world.

US Virgin Islands

11

US VirginIslands

Dominican
Republic

**US VIRGIN
ISLANDS**

St John

St Thomas

Puerto
Rico

St Croix

Leeward Islands

*Caribbean
Sea*

Windward Islands

Barbados

Netherlands Antilles

*Isla de
Margarita*

Trinidad

VENEZUELA

The three US Virgin Islands may be very different from each other, but are all very American. St Thomas attracts cruise ships and when several are in port, the streets of town are heavily congested with shoppers. St John is dominated by the Virgin Islands National Park, which has been in existence since 1956 and has some excellent trails for walkers. St Croix is the poorest of the three but nevertheless still has a great deal to offer. All three have good hotels and are popular with the sailing fraternity.

US Virgin Islands

A Foot in the door

- Try a **coquito**, a local rum concoction of Cruzan rum, coconut and sugar, sold on the street.
- Dance to live music on the sand in the moonlight at **Miss Lucy's** restaurant on St John, where a pig roast is served every full moon.
- Avoid the crowds on St Thomas and take a boat to one of the **uninhabited islets** offshore.
- Take a tour of the restored **historic estates** on St Croix, sponsored by the St Croix Landmark Society several times a year.
- Find a **rock pool** on a beach on St Croix and soak in nature's own hot tub where tidal water is warmed by the sun.

Essentials

Before you travel

Documents US citizens do not, of course, require passports for visits to the US Virgin Islands but they do need proof of citizenship to return to the USA. Visitors of other nationalities will need passports, visas (or waiver for participating countries) and return/onward tickets, as they would for the mainland USA.

Money The US dollar is the currency. Credit cards are widely accepted in major tourist resorts and duty free shops, and most businesses.

Climate The climate in the Virgin Islands is very pleasant, with the trade winds keeping the humidity down. The average temperature varies little between winter (25°C or 77°F) and summer (28°C or 82°F). Average annual rainfall is 40ins. On 17 September 1989, Hurricane Hugo ripped across St Croix causing damage or destruction to 90% of the buildings and leaving 22,500 people homeless. In September 1995 the islands escaped the worst of Hurricane Luis but were hit by Hurricane Marilyn, causing damage estimated at US$3.5bn. St Thomas was the worst hit, with five deaths and a quarter of all homes destroyed. In 1999, President Bill Clinton declared St Croix a disaster area after it was hit by Hurricane Lenny, which killed three people and caused damage estimated at over US$32mn. The destruction caused is no longer evident.

Getting there

Air **From the USA** there are scheduled flights to St Croix and/or St Thomas with *American Airlines* (Boston, Miami, New York), *Delta* (Atlanta), *United Airlines* (Chicago, Washington DC), *Continental* (New York), *US Air* (Philadelphia, Charlotte). **From Europe** there are no direct flights, connections can be made via Miami or Puerto Rico, St Maarten and Antigua. Regional airlines link the USVI with **other Caribbean islands** and there are flights to Anguilla, Antigua, the Dominican Republic, St Barthélémy, Puerto Rico (San Juan, Vieques and Fajardo), St Kitts, Nevis, St Maarten and the BVI. *Air Sunshine*, a charter air line has flights to San Juan, St Thomas, St Croix, Tortola and Virgin Gorda, T888-8798900, 800-3278900. *Bohlke International Airways*, T7789177 has a charter service between St Thomas and St Croix and day trips to Virgin Gorda and Anegada in the BVI with lunch, swimming, sightseeing. *American Eagle*, *Gulfstream International*, *Cape Air* (www.flycapeair.com) and *Seaborne Aviation* (seaplane) all run services several times daily between Puerto Rico, St Thomas and St Croix.

During the winter season there are many charter flights from the USA (Midwest, Northeast), Canada, UK & Denmark

Boat Ocean going ships can be accommodated at **Charlotte Amalie** in St Thomas and Frederiksted and the **South Shore** cargo port in St Croix. There are regular services between the USVI and the BVI. *Native Son* (T7748685) and *Smith's Ferry* (T775292) alternate services from Charlotte Amalie to West End, Tortola (45 mins, US$35 return) and on to Road Town,

US Virgin Islands

Touching down

Departure tax *No departure tax at the airport (price of US$5 is included in the ticket).*

Hours of business *Banks open Monday-Friday, 0830-1500. Government offices open Monday-Thursday, 0900-1700. Banks, filling stations and government offices close for local holidays.*

Official time *Atlantic Standard Time, 4 hrs behind GMT, 1 hr ahead of EST.*

Useful addresses *Air Ambulance: Bohlke International Airways, T7789177 (day), 7721629 (night); recompression chamber 7762686. Ambulance: 911. Fire: 911. Police: 911.*

Voltage *120 volts 60 cycles.*

Clothing *Bathing suits are considered offensive when worn away from the beach, so cover up. There is even a law against it, you can get a fine for having your belly showing. It is illegal to go topless on Magens Beach.*

Tipping *As in mainland USA, tipping is 15%; hotels often add 10-15%.*

Safety *Take the usual precautions against crime: lock your car, leave valuable jewellery at home and be careful walking around at night. The tourist office recommends that you do not go to deserted beaches on your own but in a group. Couples have been held up at gunpoint and robbed and/or raped on the beach after dark. In 1996 the shooting on St Thomas of three tourists prompted the reinstatement of a 2200 curfew for youths under 16 and increased police patrols. However, eight tourists were later shot at in a restaurant car park. Other security problems, probably drugs related, have arisen on St John and St Croix. Youth unemployment is a problem.*

Tortola (90 mins, US$35 return), several daily, some stop in Red Hook. *Smith's Ferry* also to Virgin Gorda. **Inter Island Boat Services** (T7766597) several daily between Cruz Bay, St John and West End, Tortola; three times a week, Red Hook and Cruz Bay to Jost Van Dyke, BVI; twice a week Red Hook-Cruz-Virgin Gorda. **Nubian Express**, T284-4954999 between West End, Tortola, and St John and Red Hook, St Thomas, Sunday-Friday, three daily. **Caribe Cay** sails between St Thomas and Fajardo, Puerto Rico at weekends, US$70 return, T8608809 in Puerto Rico. **Ports of entry** Charlotte Amalie, St Thomas; Christiansted and Frederiksted, St Croix; Cruz Bay, St John. **Documents** The USVI are a territory of the USA but constitute a separate Customs district. US boats with US citizens have to clear in here when coming from Puerto Rico (can be done by phone on St Croix) and all other islands. To find out more about custom fees, call Mr Harrigan on T7742510, ext 223. St Croix customs T7731011. When arriving by boat it is essential to ensure that you have the correct visas for immigration purposes. All vessels must clear in upon arrival from a foreign port and all crew members aboard must go ashore with the captain to obtain entry into the USVI. Clearing customs and immigration on St John is a pain due to the crowded harbour. Anchor if you can find room, try northwest end of island or just outside harbour, you can walk from beaches at Hawksnest. On St Croix, foreign boats or boats with foreign passengers clear customs at Gallows Bay Dock.

Touching down

Local tourist office **On St Thomas**, the Tourist Information Centre at the airport is open daily 0900-1900. Offices at the town waterfront and at the West Indian Company dock are open 0800-1700 Monday-Friday (PO Box 6400, Charlotte Amalie, USVI 00804, T7748784, 800-3728784, F7744390). **On St Croix**, there is a Tourism Booth at the airport in the baggage claim area and next to it the First Stop Information Booth. In Christiansted there is a Visitor's Bureau on Queen Street on the corner with King Cross Street (open Monday-Friday 0800-1700, PO Box 4538, Christiansted, USVI 00822-4538, T7730495, F7735074), and in Frederiksted the Visitors' Centre is in the Old Custom House Building, Strand Street, USVI 00840 (T7720357). There is also an office next to the post office in Cruz Bay, St John (PO Box 200, Cruz Bay, USVI 00831, T7766450). www.usvitourism.com has a lot of tourist information. For a complete list of web sites check www.usvichamber.com

Tourist information
See individual islands for airport information

US Virgin Islands

Tourist offices overseas

Canada 3300 Bloor Street W, Suite 3120, Centre Tower, Toronto, Ontario, M8X 2X3, T416-2331414, F416-2339367.

Denmark Park Allé 5, DK-8000, Aarhus Center, T86-181933, F86-181934.

Italy Via Gherardini 2, 20145, Milan, T02-33105841, F33105827.

Puerto Rico 60 Washington St, Suite 1102, San Juan 00907, T787-7228023, F7246659, ncumpiano@usa.net

UK Molasses House, Clove Hitch Quay, Plantation Wharf, York Place, London SW11 3TN, T020-79785262, F020-79243171.

USA There are offices of the USVI Department of Tourism in the USA at: 500 North Michigan Av, Suite 2030, Chicago, IL 60611, T312-6708784, F6708788/9; 2655 Le Jeune Rd, Suite 907, Coral Gables, FL 33134, T305-4427200, F4459044; 1270 Av of the Americas, Suite 2108, New York, NY 10020, T212-3322222, F3322223; The Hall of States, 444 North Capital St, NW Suite 298, Washington DC, 20001, T202-6243590, F6243594; 245 Peachtree Center Av, Marquis One Tower, Suite MB-05 Atlanta, GA 30303, T404-6880906, F5251102; 3460 Wilshire Boulevard, Suite 412, Los Angeles, CA 90010, T213-7390138, F7392005, usvi_la@msn.com

Maps The Government offers a free road map, available at Tourist Information Offices and many other locations.

Finding out more The overload in brochures can be confusing. Some are published by the Tourist Board, some privately, and the information varies. The publications, *St Croix This Week*, *St John's Times*, *Virgin Island Playground*, *What To Do St Thomas and St John*, *St John Tradewinds* and *St Thomas This Week* have regularly updated tourist information, including shopping news, ferry schedules, taxi fares, restaurants, nightlife and other tourist news. *Island Trader* is published weekly, free, good source of events and activities.

Where to stay

See individual towns for further information There is an 8% tax on all forms of accommodation in the US Virgin Islands. Hotels may also charge 10-15% service, but most leave tipping to the individual. High season is mid-December to mid-April, but higher prices are sometimes into May despite lower hotel occupancy.

Getting around

Air There are lots of flights between St Croix and St Thomas. American Airlines offer several flights a day. Cape Air and other charter flights are available. Seaborne Aviation (seaplanes) (T7736442) has 9 flights a day between Christiansted Harbour and Charlotte Amalie, 18 minutes, US$75 one way for non-VI residents. Spectacular view arriving into St Croix and seeing the coral reef from the seaplanes. There is a strictly enforced 25-lb baggage weight (US$0.50/lb overweight but excess baggage may not travel until later). They offer a 2-night special from St Thomas at *Divi Carina* for gamblers and island tours on all the islands.

Car Driving in Charlotte Amalie during business hours is a slow business. It is best to park and walk (municipal car park beside Fort Christian). Country speed limits are 35 mph, in towns they are 20 mph, although the traffic is so heavy you will be lucky if you can go that fast. On St John the speed limit is 20 mph everywhere. Driving is on the left, even though the cars are lefthand drive. There is a seatbelt law for the driver and front seat passenger that the police enforce with a vengeance (US$50 fine).

Sea Ferry St Thomas-St John, 20 minutes from Red Hook (US$3 adult, US$1 child), 45 minutes from Charlotte Amalie (US$7 adult, US$3 child), Cruz Bay-Red Hook hourly, Cruz Bay-Charlotte Amalie seven a day. Can be a bit bumpy.

US Virgin Islands

Keeping in touch

Local telephone calls within the USVI from coin-operated phones are US$0.25 for each five minutes. Privately owned payphones charge for local calls, even 800 numbers. Vitelco and Vitelcellular do not make extra charges. Radio Shack offers pre-paid cellular service, T7775644, 7741314, so does Cellular One, bring your own phone or buy one of theirs, US$0.52 per minute in USVI and Puerto Rico.

Telephone
IDD code: 340

The Daily News is published daily, US$0.60, and on Thursday it includes the weekend section, a complete listing of restaurants, nightclubs, music and special events, for all three islands.

Media

Shopping

The USVI are a free port and tourist related items are duty-free. Shops are usually shut on Sunday unless there is a cruise ship in harbour. There are several local rums in white or gold, and some interesting flavoured rums such as coconut: Cruzan (guided tours of the distillery, on St Croix, Monday-Friday 0900-1130, 1300-1615, but phone in advance, T6922280; US$3 adults, US$1 children), Old St Croix and Brugal. Locally woven crafts (hats, baskets, brooms, fish traps, bookmarks, Christmas tree ornaments) are made from coconut palms, sabal and wild teyer palm. Baskets are made from wiss and hoop vines. Hand made moco jumbi dolls are works of art. Two shops in Christiansted specialize in local art: *Memories of St Croix* and *Kallaloo*, also the gift shop at the Whim Plantation. On St Croix mahogany trees that fall are recycled into works of art and furniture by LEAP (St Croix Life and Environmental Arts Project) In St Thomas the Native Arts Coop is a showcase for locally made goods (opposite the Vendors Plaza where a mixture of souvenirs are sold).

See individual towns for further information

Flora and fauna

The Virgin Islands' national bird is the yellow breast (*Coereba flaveola*); the national flower is the yellow cedar (*Tecoma Stans*). The mongoose was brought to the islands during the plantation days to kill rats that ate the crops. Unfortunately rats are nocturnal and mongooses are not and they succeeded only in eliminating most of the parrots and snakes. Now you see them all over the islands, especially near the rubbish dumps. There are many small lizards and some iguanas of up to 4ft long. The iguanas sleep in the trees and you can see them and feed them (favourite food hibiscus flowers) at the Limetree beach, at Coral World and Frenchmans Reef St John has a large population of wild donkeys which are pests; they bite, steal picnic lunches and ruin gardens.

Most of St John is a national park. Hassel Island, off Charlotte Amalie, is also a park. The National Parks Service headquarters is at Red Hook, St Thomas. Also in Red Hook is the Island Resources Foundation (T7756225; US office, 1718 P Street NW, Suite T4, Washington DC 20036, T2659712). This non-governmental office is also a non-profit-making consulting firm open to serious researchers and investigators seeking information on wildlife, tourism and the environment who may use the extensive library. It may also be used as a contact base for those seeking specialist information on other islands. The Audubon Society is represented on St John by Peg Fisher at the *At Your Service Travel Agency. Virgin Islands Birdlife*, published by the USVI Co-operative Extension Service, with the US National Park Service, is available for birdwatchers. The National Park Headquarters has an excellent, reasonably priced selection of reference books for marine life, flora, fauna and island history.

On St Croix, the National Parks Service office is in the Old Customs Building on the waterfront. Buck Island is listed as an underwater monument. In Christiansted, contact the Environmental Association, PO Box 3839, T7731989, office in Apothecary Hall Courtyard, Company Street. The Association runs hikes, boat trips and walks, and in March-May, in conjunction with Earthwatch and the US Fish and Wildlife Department, takes visitors to see the leatherback turtles at Sandy Point, one of 13 significant nesting sites worldwide (T7737545 for information). The association has made Salt River (see page 541) a natural park for wildlife, reef and mangroves. There are books, leaflets, etc, available at the association's

US Virgin Islands

office. On St John there is a Park Service Office (T7166201), with lots of information and interpretive programmes.

Holidays

Public holidays
For information on local festivals see individual island Essentials sections
New Year's Day, Three Kings Day (6 January), Martin Luther King Day (15 January), Presidents' Day (19 February), Holy Thursday, Good Friday, Easter Monday, Transfer Day (31 March), Memorial Day (28 May), Organic Act Day (18 June), Emancipation Day (3 July), Independence Day (4 July), Hurricane Supplication Day (23 July), Labour Day (beginning of September), Puerto Rico/Virgin Islands Friendship Day (mid-October), Hurricane Thanksgiving Day (mid-October), Liberty Day (1 November), Veterans' Day (11 November), Thanksgiving Day (mid-November), Christmas Day (25 December).

Health

See main Health section, page 47
St Thomas has a 250-bed hospital, T7768311, St John has a seven-bed clinic, T7766400, and St Croix has a 250-bed hospital, T7786311. All three have 24-hour emergency services. Mobile medical units provide health services to outlying areas. **Red Hook Family Practice** is open Monday-Friday 1000-1600, walk in.

St Thomas

Population: 51,000
Colour map 3, grid B6
St Thomas is on practically every cruise itinerary, and thousands of cruise ship passengers descend daily on Charlotte Amalie, the capital, for the ultimate shopping experience. Traffic grinds to a halt as congestion of roads and pavements becomes uncontrollable. Avoid the town when cruise ships are in port and explore the island. St Thomas rises out of the sea to a range of hills that runs down its spine. The highest peak, Crown Mountain, is 1,550ft. On St Peter Mountain, 1,500ft, is a viewpoint at Mountain Top. There are various scenic roads to drive along, such as Skyline Drive (Route 40), from which both sides of the island can be seen simultaneously, and Mafolie Road (Route 35) that leaves Charlotte Amalie, heading north to cross the Skyline Drive becoming Magens Bay Road, and descends to the beautiful bay.

Ins and outs

Getting there
See transport, page 535, for further details
The **Cyril E King** (STT) airport; the taxi stand is at the far left end of the terminal, a long way from the commuter flights from Puerto Rico and other islands. Taxi to town US$5 per person (US$5 for each additional passenger). There are public buses every 20 mins 0600-1900 from the terminal to the town, US$1. Boats come in to Charlotte Amalie or Red Hook in the east.

Getting around
There is a reasonable bus service running west from Charlotte Amalie to the university and east to Red Hook. If you wish to drive yourself, all types of wheels are available and rental firms are plentiful.

Diving and marine life

Dive sites
The waters around the islands are so clear that snorkelling is extremely popular
For divers, there are over 200 dive sites, caves, coral reefs, drop offs and lots of colourful fish to see, although be careful of short sighted barracuda if you swim into murky water. There are several wrecks of ships and even a wrecked plane to explore. *At-a-glance snorkeller's Guide to St Thomas* by Nick Aquilar describes 15 snorkel spots in detail. Spearfishing is not allowed and you may not remove any living things from underwater such as coral, live shells or sea fans.

Dive centres
Many of the resorts offer diving packages or courses and there are at least 15 dive companies. Complete lists are available for the Tourist Board. Some are listed below.

Equipment and instruction for underwater photography are available. A one-tank dive costs around US$50 while a two-tank dive starts from US$70. *Coki Beach Dive Centre*, T7754220, www.cokidive.com offers an introductory dive for US$40, cruise ships bring their guests here. *Chris Sawyer Diving Centre*, Red Hook, T7757804, www.sawyerdive.vi, specializes in quality service to small groups, great all-day wreck of the *Rhone* trip once a week (dives for locals on Sunday), certification classes every two weeks. There are many other operators around the island and at major hotels, including *Admiralty Dive Center*, www.admiraltydive.com *Divein*, www.diveinusvi.com St Thomas Diving Club, www.st-thomasdivingclub.com and *Underwater Safaris*, www.diveusvi.com There are also several liveaboard sail/dive charters, worth contacting if you want to spend more time on and under the water: *Regency Yacht Vacations* (T800-5247676), *VIP Yacht Charters* (T800-5242015), *Island Yachts* (T800-5242019), *Red Hook Charters* (T800-2334938). Some dive moorings have been placed around St Thomas but they are not particularly well maintained (check before using). There are plans to install more moorings to protect the reef from anchor damage.

The Atlantis **Submarine** dives to 90ft for those who can not scuba dive but want to see the exotic fish, coral, sponges and other underwater life. Building VI, Bay L, Havensight Mall, St Thomas, T7765650 for reservations, or 7760288 for information (also kiosk on waterfront, usually six dives daily), www.GoAtlantis.com You have to take a four-mile launch ride on the *Yukon III* to join the submarine at Buck Island. One hour day dives US$72, children 4-14 US$27, 15-17 US$36.

VI Ecotours, T7792155, offer **kayaking** and **snorkelling** in the marine sanctuary in the last mangrove lagoon left on the south side of St Thomas. No experience necessary. If there is enough demand they run a night trip, recommended. *New Horizons*, T7751171, www.newhorizons.daysails.com have day trips on a 65-ft sloop to deserted islands. *Caribbean Rafting Adventures*, T7759360, www.viwatersports.com will take you rafting.

The *Environmental Association of St Thomas-St John (EAST)* organizes whale watching during the migration season at the beginning of the year. Humpbacks are the most commonly sighted. Trips leave from the St Thomas' VI National Park dock in Red Hook on a 77-ft catamaran, US$55 for non-members, US$45 for EAST members, for information T7761976.

Whale watching

Beaches and watersports

There are 44 beaches on St Thomas. Few are deserted though out of season they are less crowded. The most inaccessible, and therefore more likely to be empty, are those along the northwest coast, which need four-wheel drive to get there. Otherwise, for solitude, take a boat to one of the uninhabited islets offshore. **Magens Bay** on the north coast is considered to be the finest on the island and wonderfully safe for small children. It has an entry fee of US$1 per person and a charge for cars. There are changing facilities and you can rent snorkelling equipment (but the snorkelling is not the best on the island) and loungers. Other good beaches are at **Lindbergh Bay** (southwest, close to the airport runway, good for plane spotters), **Morningstar Bay** (south coast near *Marriott Frenchman's Reef Beach Resort*, beach and watersports equipment for hire), **Bolongo Bay**, **Sapphire Bay** (east coast, beach gear for rent, good snorkelling) and **Brewer's Bay** (can be reached by bus from Charlotte Amalie, get off just beyond the airport). **Hull Bay** on the north coast is good for surfing and snorkelling. At **Coki Beach** (northeast, showers, lockers, water skiing, jet skiing) snorkelling equipment can be rented for US$6, snorkelling is good just off the beach. The **Coral World Marine Park and Undersea Observatory** is at Coki Beach, giving you a first hand view of a variety of marine life, from sharks to more docile creatures. ■ *T7751555, coralworldvi.com Open 0900-1700.* **Windsurfing** lessons and rentals at Morningstar, Magens Bay,

Sapphire Beach, Secret Harbour and the *Renaissance Grand. West Indies Windsurfing* will deliver rental equipment to wherever you are staying, T7756530, not only windsurfing boards but also sunfish and kayaks. Snorkelling gear can be rented at all major hotels and the dive shops. Sunfish sailboats for rent at Morningstar, Magens Bay and the *Renaissance Grand*. Parasailing at some hotels or call *Caribbean Parasail and Watersports*, T7759360, www.viwatersports.com who have a variety of jet skis etc to go fast and make a noise, or pedalos to go slowly and peacefully.

Day sails   Day sailing of all types and cruises are available. Half day sails from US$50, full day from US$100 and sunset cruises from US$40 are offered by many boats. Most expensive are those booked on a cruise ship, as lots of commissions have to be paid. Before taking a day trip on any boat, ask about size, any shade awning and the number of passengers. Many day sail boats limit their guests to six passengers, take a stop for snorkelling and provide drinks; however, it is often cheaper to take one that crowds the tourists on. You can explore on your own by renting a small power boat from *Nauti Nymph* (T7755066, www.st-thomas.com/nautinymph), 25-29ft Fountain Power Boats; *See An Ski* (T7756265), 22/24/28-ft makos single/double engines. *Virgin Islands Power* (VIP) Yacht Charters (bought end-1998 by the Winfair Group), T7761510, 800-5242015, F7763801, 6118 Frydenhoj, No 58, St Thomas, VI 00802-1402, has the largest power yacht charter fleet and sport fishing fleet in the Caribbean, bareboat or crewed, US$3,000-6,000 a week in summer, US$4,200-6,700 in winter. Charter yachts available in a wide variety of luxury and size, with or without crew, cost about the same as a good hotel.

St Thomas

■	**Sleeping**		
1	Best Western Carib Beach	5	Bolongo Beach Resort
2	Best Western Emerald Beach	6	Colony Point Pleasant
3	Blue Beard's Beach Club & Villas	7	Elysian Beach Resort
4	Blue Beard's Castle	8	Marriott Frenchman's Reef Resort
		9	Pavillions & Pools

N
Not to scale

US Virgin Islands

The annual Rolex Cup Regatta is held at St Thomas Yacht Club at Easter **Regattas**
(T7756320). Pigs in Winter is a two-day autumn regatta, with races from STYC to
Coral Bay and back. Other events include Caribbean Ocean Racing Triangle tune up
race in mid-February, Optimist regatta in mid-June, women's laser regatta in
November.

There is deep sea fishing with the next world record in every class lurking just under **Fishing**
the boat. The USVI Fishing Club Tournament is in June, contact the American Yacht
Harbour for details, F7765970. The Bastille Day Kingfish Tournament is in July and
the USVI Open Atlantic Blue Marlin tournament is held in August every year
(T7742752); other game fish include white marlin, kingfish, sailfish, tarpon, Alison
tuna and wahoo. No fishing licence is required for shoreline fishing; government
pamphlets list 100 good spots (T7756762). For sportfishing charters and information
contact Charterboat Centre (T800-8665714), also known as St Thomas Sports
Fishing, T7757990; Doubleheader Sportfishing, T7777317, www.dhsportfishing.
com; Marlin Prince, T6935929, www.marlinprince.com

There are a few public **tennis** courts (two at Long Bay and two at Sub Base), which **Other sports**
operate on a first come first served basis, but the hotel courts at the major resorts are
mostly lit for night time play and open for non-residents if you phone in advance to
book. There is an 18-hole, 6,022 yd **golf** course with lovely views at Mahogany Run,
green fee US$90 per person, cheaper after 1400 (T800-2537103). **Horse racing** is a
popular spectator sport. Bayside Spa and Fitness Centre, across from *Bolongo Bay*

US Virgin Islands

10 Magens Point Resort
11 Renaissance Grand Beach Resort
12 Ritz Carlton
13 Sapphire Beach
14 Secret Harbour Beach Resort

15 Secret Harbour Villas
16 Windward Passage Holiday Inn
17 Wyndham Sugar Bay

Resort, charges US$50 per month, no enrolment fee. Half Moon Stables offer trail rides and lessons, T7776088, www.halfmoonstables.com.

Charlotte Amalie

Harbour
Population: 12,331

The harbour at Charlotte Amalie, capital of St Thomas and also of the entire USVI, still bustles with colour and excitement, although the harbour area can be a startling contrast for the visitor arriving by sea from the British Virgin Islands. As the Fort Christian Museum puts it, "Oversized, architecturally inappropriate buildings have marred the scenic beauty of the harbour. Harbour congestion has become a major problem." One could add that by day the streets are congested too. At night visitors tend to stay within their resorts. But as the museum also says, there are still a number of historical buildings.

Danish influence

The town was built by the Danes, who named it after their King's consort, but to most visitors it remains 'St Thomas'. Beautiful old Danish houses painted in a variety of pastel colours are a reminder of the island's history. One recently opened to the public is **Haagensen House**, the home of a former Danish banker, with a courtyard, gardens and antique furniture. ■ *T7749605. US$6, free shuttle service from*

Charlotte Amalie

N

Not to scale

■ **Sleeping**
1 Bunker Hill
2 Galleon House
3 Lavalette House Hotel 1829
4 Miller Manor
5 Windward Passage Holiday Inn

Emancipation Garden. Daily 0900-1600. For a good view of the town and the surrounding area, take the **Paradise Point Tramway**, across the street from the cruise ship dock and Havensight Mall, actually a cable car which takes you on a seven-minute ride up 700ft to Paradise Point where there is an observation deck and a bar, a parrot show, nature walks and shopping. You can see the harbour and lots of neighbouring islands. Great photo opportunities. ■ *T7749809, F7749955, www.paradisepointtramway.com. Daily 0900-1700. US$12 round trip.*

There are over 14 historic churches in the USVI dating back to 1737. Some of them on St Thomas are picturesque and there is also one of the oldest synagogues in the Western Hemisphere (1833). Situated on Crystal Gade the synagogue is an airy, domed building, with a sand floor and hurricane-proof walls; it has books for sale in the office, iced springwater and visitors are given a 10 minute introduction for free. It is worth a visit. In 1996 the Hebrew Congregation of St Thomas celebrated the 200th anniversary of its founding with lots of services and commemorative events. The Dutch Reformed Church is the oldest established church, having had a congregation since 1660 although the present building dates from 1846. The Frederick Lutheran Church dates from 1820 and its parish hall was once the residence of Jacob H S Lind (1806-27).

Churches

● **Eating**
1 Bumpa's
2 Café Amici
3 Cuzzins Caribbean Restaurant & Bar
4 Gladys'
5 Hard Rock Café
6 The Green House
7 Planet Hollywood
8 Virgilio's

US Virgin Islands

Fortifications   There are several old fortifications within the town. **Bluebeard's Castle Tower** and **Blackbeard's Castle**, the latter allegedly built in 1679 and lived in by the pirate and his 14 wives (there is no proof of this), is now an inn and restaurant. The **Virgin Islands Museum** is in the former dungeon at Fort Christian (1666-80). There are historical and natural history sections and an art gallery.   *T7764566 to check times. Free, but donations welcome as much restoration work remains to be done. Mon-Fri, 0830-1630.* In contrast to the red-painted fort is the green **Legislative Building**, originally the Danish police barracks (1874), open Monday-Friday.

Other town sights   Government House, off Kongens Gade, was built in 1865-87. The Enid M Baa Library and Archive is on Main Street, it is another early 19th-century edifice. Two historical buildings which cannot be visited are the former Danish Consulate, on Denmark Hill and the house of the French painter, Camille Pissaro, on Main Street. The Dockside Bookshop in Havensight Mall (at the Cruise Ship Dock) has books and other publications on the Virgin Islands and the Caribbean in general. The Old Mill, up Crown Mountain Road from Sub Base traffic light is an old sugar mill open to the public. **Estate St Peter Greathouse and Botanical Gardens** has 500 varieties of plants, a stunning view and an art gallery for local artists.

Water Island   Water Island, at the west end of St Thomas' main harbour, is the smallest inhabited
Its name comes from   island. It is now known as the fourth USVI and is slowly being promoted along with
the freshwater ponds,   St Thomas, St Croix and St John. It was purchased from Denmark by the USA in
now salt ponds, that   1944 to use as a military base during the Second World War. **Fort Segarra** was built
were once plentiful   as an underground fort and later the island was used to test weapons. It was trans-
on the island   ferred to the Department of the Interior from Defense in 1952. A year later a 40-year lease of the entire island was given to a developer for construction of a hotel and homes. The hotel closed after Hurricane Hugo in 1989. The island's ownership was turned over to the VI Government and private island homeowners in December 1996. While the marina and hotel property is to be torn down, the local government has constructed open-air buildings on the beach available for public use. At weekends the beach is busy with local residents, charterboat guests and the anchorage is filled. During the week, the *Kontiki* floating booze cruise makes daily stops; other day-charter boats may also stop when weather is rough. The Water Island Ferry runs frequently from 0645-1800 Mon-Sat, US$7 round trip, with night runs Tue, Fri Sat, US$5 one way, and a reduced service Sun and holidays. Weekly and monthly passes are available and special runs can be arranged with the Captain. For details, see www.nerc.com/~vacation/ferry.html

Hassel Island   Hassel Island is part of US National Parks. There are ruins on the shore but no development has yet been carried out. Hire a boat or take your dinghy to the dilapidated dock; walk towards the ocean for a picnic and a great view of Frenchman's Reef and watch the ships entering the harbour; then hike on a trail to an old building; climb the wall at the back of the building to get an outstanding view of the area from Frenchman's Reef to Green Cay where you can see the surf breaking on three sets of rocks that are difficult to see from the water. Around the other end of the island is a small liveaboard boating community.

Essentials

There are many hotels, guest houses, apartments, villas and cottages on St Thomas, the cheaper places to stay are in town or up in the hills, while the newer, chain hotels on the beach are at the top of the range. Summer rates are about 20% cheaper than winter. There is a Hotel Association counter at the airport which can help you with reservations. Please note that non-inclusion does not imply non-recommendation. Unfortunately, because of the increase in crime, you should be cautious around downtown Charlotte Amalie at night. Also be careful if walking to the Crystal Gade Synagogue and never walk there at night.

Resorts, apartments and condominiums are clustered around the east end, such as the **LL** *Elysian Beach Resort* on Cowpet Bay, T7751000, F7760910. 180 rooms and suites, fitness centre, tennis, pool, jacuzzi, watersports centre offering diving, kayaking, parasailing, use of facilities at *Bluebeard's* (see below) and **LL-L** *Point Pleasant Resort*, 6600 Estate Smith Bay, T7757200, F7765694, www.pointpleasantresort.com Children sharing parents' room free under 21, 95 suites in 15 acres of tropical gardens, pool, tennis, watersports. Next door is **LL** *Renaissance Grand Beach Resort* on Water Bay, PO Box 8267, T7751510, F7752185, www.renaissancehotels.com 290 hill or beachside rooms and 36 suites, well-appointed, 2 pools, 6 lit tennis courts, fitness centre, restaurants, bars, children's programmes, complimentary watersports, sailing, fishing and diving can be arranged, conference facilities, lovely views over the resort's own beach to St John and the British Virgins. **LL** *Sapphire Beach Resort & Marina*, T7756100, F7772403, www.usvi.net/hotel/sapphire 171 rooms, pool, suites, villas, watersports, tennis, kitchens, restaurant, children under 19 free when sharing, children's activities. **LL** *Secret Harbour Beach Resort*, T7756550, F7751501, www.st-thomas.com/shb.vi. 64 suites, popular with honeymooners, watersports, tennis, kitchens, restaurant. On the south coast is **LL-L** *Bolongo Bay Beach Club & Villas*, 7150 Bolongo, T7751800, F7753208, www.bolongo.com EP, CP or all-inclusive family resort, kids' offers, pool, beach, tennis, kitchen facilities, 2 restaurants. Among others, and overlooking the entrance to Charlotte Amalie harbour and above Morningstar Beach, the huge **LL** *Marriott Frenchman's Reef Beach Resort*, PO Box 7100, T7768500, F7156191, www.marriott-fr.vi 408 rooms and suites, all facilities, and its 96-room sister property **LL** *Marriott Morning Star Beach Resort* alongside, www.marriott-ms.vi Lots of restaurants and bars, fitness centre, water ferry to town, watersports, pools, tennis, excursions, access for the disabled. West of Charlotte Amalie are **LL** *Best Western Emerald Beach Resort*, 8070 Lindbergh Bay, T7778800, F7763426, www.emeraldbeach.com 90 rooms, pool, bar, restaurant, 'The Palms' rooms have ocean and airport view, tennis, watersports. Its sister resort **L-AL** *Best Western Carib Beach Resort*, T7742525, F7744131, same website. Smaller at 60 rooms, pool, casual, both on Lindbergh Bay, sheltered beach at end of airport runway, only drawback is aircraft noise. On the same bay, **AL** *Island Beachcomber*, PO Box 302579, T7745250, F7745615, www.st-thomas.com/islandbeachcomber. 47 rooms, on beach, by airport, free shuttle to town. **LL** *Pavilions and Pools*, 6400 Estate Smith Bay, T/F7756110, www.pavilionsandpools.com. 25 rooms with salt pools, kitchens, restaurant, newly renovated, private. **LL** *The Ritz Carlton*, 6900 Great Bay, T7753333, F7754444. 152 rooms, very expensive and luxurious.

Small hotels and guest houses **L-AL** *Admiral's Inn*, T7741376, F7748010, www.admirals-inn.com 12 rooms, seaside on Frenchtown Point. **AL-A** *Danish Chalet Inn*, T7745764, F7774886, www.wininn.com Good value, 10 rooms, friendly owners. **A-B** *Island View Guest House*, T7744270, F7746167, www.st-thomas.com/islandviewguesthouse Great place to stay before or after a charter, near airport, great view. In Charlotte Amalie: **LL** *Bluebeard's Castle*, on hillside overlooking town, T7741600, F7745134. 183 rooms, sports, pool, free shuttle to Magens Bay Beach and to Veterans' Drive. Heading towards the airport, is **LL-L** *Windward Passage Holiday Inn*, PO Box 640, T7745200, F7741231. Pool, restaurant, 151 rooms, walking distance of shops and ferries, shuttle to beach. **AL** *Villa Blanca*, T7760749, F7792661, www.st-thomas.com/villablanca 14 rooms, large gardens, on hillside, view of town and harbour, pool, quiet, family run. **AL-A** *Bunker Hill Hotel*, 7A Commandant Gade, T7748056, F7743172, www.bunkerhillhotel.com 15 rooms, a/c, TV, pool, airport transfers. **AL-B** *Galleon House*, PO Box 6577, T/F7746952, www.st-thomas.com/galleonhouse Swimming pool, veranda, gourmet breakfast, snorkel gear provided, discounts for senior citizens. **B-C** *Miller Manor*, PO Box 1570, on the hill behind the Catholic Cathedral, T7741535, F7745988, millermanor-aida-leo@worldnet.attnet Clean, very friendly, a/c, 5 mins' walk to town, microwave and fridge in each room.

Water Island **L-AL** *Murray Villa* and **AL-A** *Limestone Reef Apartments*, T732-3296919, www.nerc.com/~vacation/ The 3-bedroom villa sleeps 6 and comes with a car, while the apartments are quite spacious and have a large patio with a good view out to sea and other islands. Long term rental is available.

Sleeping
The Department of Tourism website for hotel rates is very comprehensive and contains far more hotels than we have space for http://st-thomas.com/rates

US Virgin Islands

For luxury & peace rent your own island **Little St James**, a 72-acre island, off the southeast of St Thomas, has an antique-furnished villa, sleeps 8 and comes with 2 boats, captain and staff, all-inclusive. Contact *Caribbean Chapters* in the UK for rental information, T44-1244-341131, popular with the rich and famous, eg Kevin Costner.

Eating

The well lit waterfront is safe in the early evening hours, but in other areas you should take a taxi. There are many very good restaurants on the island, most of which are listed in Here's How and St Thomas This Week, or you can get details in your hotel

Award-winning ribs from *Bill's Texas Pit BBQ*, a mobile truck which shows up Tue-Sat in the Waterfront and Red Hook, also for lunch at Sub Base, the best on the island. The area west of the Market Square is more local, with restaurants and bars. *Bumpa's*, waterfront, T7765674. Upstairs, outdoors, small breakfast and lunch spot overlooking harbour, locally popular and inexpensive, no credit cards. *Café Amici*, in A H Riise's Mall, T7765670. Open Mon-Sat 1030-1530, Sun 1030-1500, Italian and Mediterranean food, moderate prices. Cuzzins Caribbean Restaurant & Bar, Back Street, T7774711. Open for lunch Mon-Sat, dinner Tue-Sat, good, large, local meals, lunch can be dinner! West Indian cuisine, conch, fish, also drinks such as sea moss and maubi, vegetarian plates available. *Glady's Café*, in Historic Royal Dane Mall, T7746604. Open 0700-1530, Mon-Sat, local dishes such as salt fish and dumplings, mutton stew. *Hard Rock Café*, T7775555, on waterfront at International Plaza, usual burgers and sandwiches, also vegetarian. *Hotel 1829*, on Government Hill, T7761829. Superb food and service, expensive, if you can't afford it go and have a look anyway, lovely old building and great view, happy hour 1700-2000, dinner daily. For great French cuisine, *The Banana Tree Grill* at Bluebeard's Castle, T7764050. Expensive, open for dinner Wed-Mon. *The Green House*, on harbour front, Veterans Drive, T7747998. Excellent restaurant at reasonable prices, attracts younger crowd, steak, ribs, burgers, open 0800-2200, serves drinks, bar open until 0200, happy hour 1630-1900. *Virgilio's*, between Main and Back Streets, up from Storetvaer Gade, T7764920. Italian, good food and service, not cheap, lunch 1130-1500, dinner 1700-2200 Mon-Sat. There are several places on Back Street, bars and bistros for breakfast, lunch or dinner.

Frenchtown *Alexander's Café*, T7744349. Grills, ribs, chilli and Italian, open Mon-Sat for lunch and dinner. *Craig and Sally's*, T7779949. International influences, new wave of American cuisine, very popular, open for lunch Tue-Sat, dinner Tue-Sun. *Hook, Line and Sinker*, T7769708. American, steak and seafood, vegetarian options, daily specials, open breakfast, lunch and dinner Mon-Sat. *The Point at Villa Olga*, at Villa Olga, T7744262. Not cheap, but excellent food.

Sub Base/Crown Bay *Tickle's Dockside Pub*, T7761595 at Crown Bay Marina, T7759425 at American Yacht Harbour. American, burgers, chicken and ribs, open daily for breakfast, lunch and dinner. *L'Escargot*, Sub Base, T7746565. Continental, inevitable snails in garlic butter, open Mon-Sat for lunch and dinner. *Molly Malone's*, above *Tickle's*, overlooking water, open Tue-Sun.

East End/Red Hook *Duffy's Love Shack*, Red Hook Plaza, T7792080. Good lunches, some unusual meals plus burgers, American, hotspot, very busy weekends, open daily. *Sopchoppy's*, waterfront, on upper level of American Yacht Harbour. *Latitude 18*, across the water from Red Hook Harbour, T7792495. Dinghy dock. Live entertainment occasionally, good food, varied, steak, seafood and pasta. *Romano's*, Smith Bay, T7750045. Italian and continental, lamb, seafood and pasta, open from 1800 Mon-Sat.

Nightlife

St Thomas offers the greatest variety of nightlife found in the Virgin Islands although many clubs have closed since the hurricanes

Bands and combos play nightly at most hotels. Several of the hotels offer limbo dancing three or four nights a week and the ubiquitous steel bands remain a great favourite with both visitors and inhabitants. At any time you will hear plenty of bass booming from the smart cars cruising the town's streets. *Coco Jo's*, at the *Marriott Beach Resorts*, T7768500, live entertainment and dancing, Crucian rum special 2000-2200, any rum-based drink US$2. *SIBS* on the mountain, Charlotte Amalie offers happy hour, bar, late night crowds, pool tables. *Room With A View* at *Bluebeard's Castle* offers free champagne to ladies 2200-0100. *Fat Tuesday*, downtown Charlotte Amalie, has happy hour all night and the famous Daiquiris. *Club Ryno*, Palm Passage, T7771059, has live jazz Fri nights. Frenchtown offers some

Beaches and watersports

North shore beaches can go from calm to a surfer's delight in winter when northerly swells roll in from the Atlantic, making the sea rough and dangerous. Go to the south for calm beaches and anchorages. In the national park there are snack bars at Cinnamon Bay and Trunk Bay only. Bring water and lunch if you are hiking or going to other beaches which will not be so crowded.

Day trippers off cruise ships head for Hawk's Nest, Cinnamon and Trunk Bays, avoid these areas if you want some space

Off **Trunk Bay**, the island's best beach, is an underwater snorkelling trail maintained by the National Parks Service. Not surprisingly, the beach tends to get rather crowded (especially when tour groups come in); lockers for hire, US$2 (deposit US$5), snorkelling equipment US$6 (deposit US$40) return by 1600. Other good beaches include **Hawk's Nest Bay**, **Caneel Bay**, **Cinnamon Bay** (there is a small museum of historical photographs and pictures here), **Salt Pond** (reached by Vitran bus, US$1 every two hours or so, when its running, excellent beach with good snorkelling and a spectacular hike to Ram's Head), **Lameshur Bay** (difficult road but worth it), **Maho Bay** (beach is 5 ft from the road, lots of turtles, sometimes tarpon, nice and calm) and **Solomon Bay** (unofficial nudist beach about 30 minutes' walk from the road). **Reef Bay** has excellent snorkelling. Frett's Maho Bay Shuttle goes around the north shore coast to any of the beaches, which is easier than trying to reach them by road. **Jumbie Bay** has very good snorkelling, as does the north shore of **Francis Bay**, but if it is choppy, try **Mary Creek** instead, where you can snorkel among the mangroves or out to the coral reef at Anna Point.

Windsurfers can be rented at Cinnamon Bay and Maho Camps, sunfishes at Maho Camp. *Coral Bay Watersports*, T7766850, next to *Serafina*, rents power boats, sport fishing and tackle, they also offer diving, snorkelling, kayaking and windsurfing. Half and full day sails and fishing trips can be arranged by *Connections*, T7766922, *Noah's Little Arks (Zodiacs)*, T6939030, *Proper Yachts*, T7766256. A recommended sailing and snorkelling trip is with Captain Phil on the *Wayward Sailor*, T6938555, US$85 for the day with a most knowledgeable host, who takes you out to the St James islands between St John and St Thomas. *Sadie Sea*, T7766421, is also good, offering a snorkelling tour around St John. You can rent a power boat with *Ocean Runner Powerboats*, T6938809. For one and two-tank **scuba dives**, wreck dives and night dives: *Low Key Watersports* at Wharfside Village, specializes in personal attention, also **kayaking**, T800-8357718, 6938999; *Cruz Bay Watersports*, three locations, T7766234, offers a free

St John

■ **Sleeping**

1 Caneel Bay Plantation	3 Concordia	5 Harmony Studios	7 The Westin Resort
2 Caribbean Villas	4 Gallows Point Resort	6 Inn at Tamarind Court	

Not to scale

snorkel map. Other dive operators are *Cinnamon Bay Watersports*, T7766330 (also kayaking and windsurfing), *East End Divers*, T7794994 or 6937519, Coral Bay. You can **snuba** (air in the boat, not on your back) at Trunk Bay, T6938063. *St John Snorkel Tours* have day and night tours, guided Reef Bay hikes, T7766922.

Regattas   Yacht races include St John Yacht Club Island Hopper Race (January); Coral Bay Yacht Club (meets at *Skinny Legs*) CATS (programme for children), ANTS (adults) and Thanksgiving Day Regatta.

Other sports   There is **tennis** at the large resorts and also two public courts available on a first come first served basis. You can go **rock climbing** with Adventures Unlimited, T6935763. **Horse riding**, Carolina Corral, T6935778, beach rides, sunset and full moon rides.

National park
There are 22 hikes in all, 14 on the north shore, 8 on the south shore

The population of St John fell to less than a thousand people in 1950 when 85% of the land had reverted to bush and second growth tropical forest. In the 1950s Laurance Rockefeller bought about half of the island but later donated his holdings to establish a national park which was to take up about two-thirds of the predominantly mountainous island. The **Virgin Islands National Park** was opened in 1956 and is covered by an extensive network of trails (some land in the park is still privately owned and not open to visitors). Several times a week a park ranger leads the Reef Bay hike, which passes through a variety of vegetation zones, visits an old sugar mill (Annaberg) and some unexplained petroglyphs and ends with a ferry ride back to Cruz Bay. The trail can be hiked without the ranger, but the national park trip provides a boat at the bottom of the trail so you do not need to walk back up the three-mile hill. You should reserve a place on the guided hike at the Park Service Visitors' Centre, Cruz Bay (on north side of harbour) open daily 0800-1630, T7766201; information on all aspects of the park can be obtained here, there are informative displays, topographical and hiking trail maps, books on shells, birds, fish, plants, flowers and local history, sign up here for activities. The trails are well maintained and clearly signed with interpretive information along the way. Insect repellent is essential. A seashore walk in shallow water, using a glass bottomed bucket to discover sea life, is recommended. There is a snorkel trip around St John in which the boat takes you to 5-6 reefs not accessible by land (and therefore less damaged), which is a good way to see the island even if you do not snorkel. An informative, historical bus tour goes to the remote East End. There are evening programmes at Cinnamon Bay and Maho Bay camps, where rangers show slides and movies and hold informal talks. For detailed information on what to do and where to find it, *Exploring St John* covers hiking trails, 39 beaches and snorkel spots, historic sites and jeep adventures. A fee of US$4 is charged to enter the park at Trunk Bay and to view the Annaberg ruins.

Essentials

Sleeping
Rates are published by the Department of Tourism, http://st-john.com /rates

LL *Caneel Bay Resort*, PO Box 720, T7766111, F6938280, www.caneelbay.com Lots of packages available in a variety of rooms or cottages, 166-room resort built in the late 1950s by Laurance Rockefeller, since 1993 managed by Rosewood Hotels and Resorts, several restaurants, bars, dress smartly after sunset, 11 all-weather tennis courts, complimentary watersports for guests including sunfish, windsurfers, also boat rentals, fishing and diving available, kids club and exercise club, ferry service between Caneel Bay and downtown St Thomas, also to sister resort of *Little Dix Bay* on Virgin Gorda, BVI. **LL** *Westin Resort*, PO Box 8310, T6938000, F6934500, www.westin.com 285 rooms and suites in 47 acres, huge pool, conference facilities, watersports, tennis etc. **LL-L** *Gallows Point Resort*, PO Box 58, T7766434, F 7766520, www.gallowspointresort.com 52 suites, fans, pool, watersports, kitchen facilities. **LL** *Suite St John* at Gallows Point, PO Box 567, T7766969, www. gallowspoint.com 8 1-bedroom condos, sleep 4, luxury, full kitchens, every convenience, pool, beach. Within walking distance of town are **LL** *Caribbean Villas*, PO Box 458, T7766152, www.caribbeanvilla.com 2-bedroom villas, pool, personal service, attentive management; and *Caribe Havens*, PO Box 455, T/F7766518, www.caribehavens.com Lovely views, 10 homes. **AL-C** *The Inn at Tamarind Court*, in Cruz Bay, PO Box 350, T7766378, F7766722, www.tamarindcourt.com Nothing special, adequate, motel style, inexpensive breakfast and dinner, bar, music and movies some nights.

At Cinnamon Bay (frequent taxibuses from Cruz Bay) there is a **AL-A** campground and chalet site run by the National Park Service, usually full so book in advance, maximum stay 2 weeks; bare site **E**, a few shared showers, food reasonably priced in both the cafetería and grocery store. Write to *Cinnamon Bay Campgrounds*, PO Box 720, St John, USVI, 00831, T776 6330, F7766458. At Maho Bay (8 miles from Cruz Bay, regular bus service) there is a privately run campground, **AL** *Maho Bay Camps Inc*, Box 310, Cruz Bay, St John, USVI 00831, T7766240, F7766504, www.maho.org **AL** 'tent cottages' are connected by a raised boardwalk to protect the environment, lots of steps, magnificent view from restaurant, lots of planned activities, attracts socially conscious, environmentally aware guests and staff, guests come back year after year, possible to work in return for your board. They also own **L** *Harmony Studios* (same address, phones, www.harmony-studios.com). Largely built from recycled materials, solar energy, 12 rooms, handicap access and **L-AL** *Estate Concordia Studios*, T6935855, F6935960, www.concordia-studios.com 9 luxury condos overlooking Salt Pond Bay and **AL** 5 eco-tents, multi-level tent cottages with kitchen and bathroom. Other apartments/condos include **LL-L** *Battery Hill*, T/F6938261, www.batteryhill.com 9 units, view, breezy, walk to beach or town. **LL** *Coconut Coast Villas*, T6939100, F7794157, www.coconutcoast.com 10 studios, 6m from water, kitchens, snorkelling. **LL** *Suite St John at Lavender Hill Estates*, T7766969, F7794486, www.lavenderhill.com 11 waterfront condos, private balconies, some have computers, pool. **LL-L** *Villa Bougainvilla*, T7766420, F7766920, www.DonaldSchnell.com Artist owned and maintained. **LL-L** *Villa Serenity*, T7766342, TerryRoberts@worldnet.att.net Owned and run by Terry Witham, lunch time cook at *Miss Lucy's*, price depends on occupancy level, 4 bedrooms, 3 bathrooms, large deck with hammock and lounge chairs, great view but very private, no clothes necessary, convenient location close to *Maho Bay Campground* and its transport and other facilities. To rent a villa through an agency, contact *Vacation Vistas*, PO Box 476, T7766462, www.vacationvistas. com 9 houses to rent all round the island, some with pools. *Catered to* has rental homes and luxury villas, PO Box 704, Cruz Bay, St John, USVI 00831, T7766641, F6938191, www.cateredto.com Others include *Vacation Homes*, PO Box 272, Cruz Bay, T7766094, F6938455 and *Windspree Vacation Homes*, T6935423, F6935623, www.windspree. com who have homes and villas in Coral Bay.

Eating

At the highest viewpoint on the island on Centerline Road, Bordeaux Mountain, is *Chateau Bordeaux*, T7766611. Fine dining, expensive, dinner only, reservations advised. **In Cruz Bay** *Asolare*, Northshore Rd, T7794747. Expensive, Euro-Asian cuisine, lovely setting, dinner only, reservations recommended. *Café Roma*, T7766524. Italian food and good pizza, open evenings, also vegetarian dishes. *Chilly Billy's* upstairs at the Lumber Yard, T6938708. Serves great Bloody Marys for breakfast or any time, open 0800-1400 daily, breakfast all day on Sat and Sun. *Ellington's* at Gallow's Point, T6938490. Continental and seafood, lunch and dinner, closed Mon. *Global Village Cuisine on Latitude 18*, in the middle of Mongoose Junction, T6938677. Open air garden restaurant, open 0830-2200, American and fish. *JJ's Tex Mex*, at the ferry dock in Cruz Bay. Great for breakfast or at any time. *Miss Lucy's*, on the way to Salt Pond, T6935244. Locally famous, worth the trip just for the conch chowder, full moon parties are a tradition, they roast whole pigs (1800-2100, US$10) and have a live band, closed Sep-Oct, ferries available from St Thomas. *Maho Bay Campground* run trips for the occasion, also Fri night steel band, Sat jazz night, Sun brunch with live jazz, closed Sep-Oct. *Morgan's Mango*, T6938141. Excellent seafood and steak, also vegetarian, open air dining, great sauces, open evenings only, 1730-2200, reservations recommended. *Paradiso*, at Mongoose Junction, T6938899. American food, has children's menu, eat indoors or on balcony, open Mon-Sat 1100-1500, quite expensive. *Café Wahoo*, overlooking Cruz Bay, T6938489. On three floors, Crow's Nest, Oyster Bar and Beach Bar, American influenced West Indian food, seafood, open 1100-2200. *Panini Beach*, T6937030. Pricey, seafood/Caribbean, dinner from 1800. *The Lime Inn*, T7766425. Seafood, steak, excellent lobster and pasta, all you can eat night on Wed, very popular with locals and visitors. *Uncle Joe's*, opposite the Post Office in Cruz Bay, no sign outside, just the barbecue grill. Great barbecued ribs. **At Coral Bay** *Skinny Legs* (named for owners), T7794982. Local hangout, soup, sandwiches, grills and fish, open daily 1100-2100. *Shipwreck Landing*, T6935640. American cuisine, conch fritters, frozen drinks, nightly specials, open air dining, live music every weekend.

Nightlife   Up to date information on events is posted on the trees around town or on the bulletin board in front of *Connections*. In Cruz Bay, the place to go and dance is *Fred's*, calypso and reggae Wed and Fri. Popular places to 'lime' (relax) are *Café Wahoo*, *JJ's*, and sitting in Cruz Bay Park, watching the world go by. See *Lucy's*, above for full moon hog roast and music.

Festivals   **Carnival**, St John's carnival is in the week of *4 July*, but there are lots of events in the two preceding weeks.

Shopping   Scattered around Cruz Bay and concentrated in Wharfside Village and Mongoose Junction are shops selling souvenirs, arts and crafts and jewellery. Right in the Park is Sparkey's, selling newspapers, paperbacks, film, cold drinks, gifts. The *St John Drug Center Inc*, open 7 days a week. For groceries: *Starfish Market* (the largest) and *Marina Market* in Cruz Bay, *Joe's Discount* near *Shipwreck Landing* in Coral Bay. *Maiden Apple*, health food store, 1st floor of Boulton Centre, T6938781. Liquor and drinks at *Cases by the Sea* near Coral Bay Watersports, grocery near *Shipwreck Tavern*, *Joe's Discount* and *Pickles Deli*. Food is expensive (rum is cheaper than water) and the selection is limited. If you are camping for a week, shopping at the big supermarkets on St Thomas is a good idea. Fish and produce is sold from boats a couple of times a week at the freight dock. *Love City Videos* at the Boulton Centre, rents videos. *Laundromat* next to *Raintree Inn*, Cruz Bay, Mon-Fri 0830-1730, Sat 0830-1200.

Transport   **Bus**   There are 2 Vitran buses, US$1 exact change only, from Cruz Bay to Coral Bay and Salt Pond about every hour. If one breaks down you have to wait for the next, a/c turned-off going up hill, turned on for descent. **Car**   Vehicles may be rented, but parking is very difficult and you may have to walk a long way from where you can leave your car. There are 3 fuel stations, open 0800-1900, in Cruz Bay and Coral Bay, may be closed on holidays. Rental agencies include: *Hertz*, T7766695; *Delbert Hill's Jeep Rental*, T7766637; *Budget*, T7767575; *Avis*, T7766374; *Cool Breeze*, T7766588, *St John Car Rental*, T7766103; rates start from US$50 per day. **Taxi**   Official taxi rates can be obtained from St John Police Department or by asking the taxi driver to show the official rate card (see page 535 for details). A 2-hr island tour costs US$30 for 1 or 2 passengers, or US$12 per person if there are 3 or more. Taxi from Cruz Bay to Trunk Bay, US$5; to Cinnamon Bay US$5.50. It is almost impossible to persuade a taxi to take you to Coral Bay, so hitchhike by waiting with everyone else at the intersection by the supermarket deli.

Ferry   Ferry to St Thomas: hourly 0700 to 2200 and 2315 to Red Hook, every 2 hrs 0715 to 1315, 1545 and 1715 to Charlotte Amalie (see page 536).

Anchorages   On St John, the US Park Service has placed moorings to protect the reefs and seagrass areas. A yacht is limited to anchoring in the US Park for no more than 14 days a year. Park moorings on north shore: Caneel Bay, Hawksnest, Cinnamon Bay, Maho, Francis Bay; on south shore: Salt Pond, Little Lameshur and Great Lameshur. Forbidden to anchor on south shore, moorings must be used. There are some private moorings for day charter boats in Maho Bay, Cruz Bay. Great Cruz Bay and Coral Bay are not within the park territory and have privately owned moorings.

Directory   **Banks** *Chase Manhattan* in Cruz Bay, T7757777. *Banco Popular de Puerto Rico*, T6932777. *Bank of Novia Scotia*, T6939932. St John's banking hours are 0830-1500 Mon-Fri. **Communications** Internet: *Cyber Celtic Café/Quiet Mon Pub*, Cruz Bay town above *La Tapa*, T7794799, www.quietmon.com

Connections West (Cruz Bay, T7766922), as well as arranging sailing trips and villa rentals, is the place for business services, local and international telephone calls, faxes, Western Union money transfers, photocopying, word-processing, notary, VHF radio calls and tourist information (they know everything that is happening). *Connections East*, T7794994. Does the same thing in Coral Bay. *Coral Bay Marine Services* for mail drop, message centre, if you have your own computer you can use their phone to access email. **Security** St John is not free of crime. There have been reports of attacks on Cinnamon Bay Beach, while crack cocaine is sold fairly openly on the streets in Cruz Bay. The island is generally safer than St Thomas, but do not be lulled into a sense of false security. Take the usual precautions. **Tour agencies** As well as the National Parks service in the text above, *Thunderhawk Trail Guides*, T7741112. Offer hikes through the national park. **Tourist information** The St John newspaper, *Tradewinds*, is published bi-weekly, US$0.50. The funny, informative, free, *St John Guidebook* and map is available in shops and also at the ticket booth at the ferry dock. **Tourist office** PO Box 200, Cruz Bay, T7766450.

St Croix

St Croix is perceived as the poor relation of the main group of islands, with a weaker economy and more youth unemployment, but its lack of development is part of its charm and there is more to see here than on St Thomas. Today agriculture has been surpassed by tourism and industry, including the huge Hovensa oil refinery on the south coast. The east of the island is rocky and arid terrain, the west is higher, wetter and forested. Columbus thought that St Croix looked like a lush garden when he first saw it during his second voyage in 1493. He landed at Salt River on the north coast, which has now been approved as a national park encompassing the landing site as well as the rich underwater Salt River drop off and canyon. It had been cultivated by the Carib Indians, who called it Ay-Ay, and the land still lies green and fertile between the rolling hills. St Croix is the largest of the group with 84 square miles, lying 40 miles south of St Thomas. The name is pronounced to rhyme with 'boy'. People born on the island are called Crucians, while North Americans who move there are known as Continentals.

Population: 63,000
Colour map 3, grid C6

St Croix has it all: swimming, sailing, fishing, excellent restaurants, good shopping & above all, great scuba diving

Ins and outs

See page 522 for details of flights to **Henry Rohlson** international airport. Taxis from the airport to Christiansted are US$5, to Frederiksted, US$4. A taxi dispatcher's booth is at the airport exit. Rates are listed in many publications. A bus service runs between the airport and Christiansted every 1½ hrs, change buses at La Reine terminal.

Getting there
See transport section for further details

A bus service runs between Christiansted and Frederiksted. The major car rental agencies are represented at the airport, hotels and both cities. A four-wheel drive car (US$50-60 a day) is ideal to drive along the scenic roads, for example to Ham's Bay or Point Udall. There is a distinct lack of road signs on St Croix, so if you use a car, take a good map.

Getting around

Diving and marine life

Scuba diving is good around St Croix, with forests of elkhorn coral, black coral, brain coral, sea fans, a multitude of tropical fish, sea horses under the Frederiksted pier (great day or night dive for novices, an easy shore dive and one of the best in the USVI), walls and drop offs, reefs and wrecks. The wrecks are varied, some 40 years old and some recent, with marine life slowly growing on the structures and schools of fish taking up residence. They range from 75-300 ft in length and 15-110 ft deep, providing something for everyone, from the beginner to the experienced. Butler Bay off Frederiksted is home for six shipwrecks. Nearby in Truck Lagoon there are the remains of around 25 old truck chassis that were sunk by Hess Oil to promote marine growth and create an artificial reef. The wrecks of the *North Wind*, *The Virgin Islander Barge* and *Suffolk Maid* are close together, but usually done as two separate leisurely dives otherwise you have to swim rather briskly to get round them all.

Dive sites

US Virgin Islands

There are also the *Rosaomaira*, the deepest of the wrecks, and the *Coakly Bay*, the newest, while in between them is the *Sondra*, a shallow dive which can even be snorkelled, although there is not a great deal remaining on the site. Just behind the *Sondra* is the wreck of a small sailing boat.

At **Buck Island** there are underwater snorkelling trails, the two main ones being Turtle Bay Trail and East End Trail. The fish are superb. The reef is an underwater national park covering over 850 acres, including the island. Hawksbill turtles nest on Buck Island and, during a 1993 Buck Island National Monument Sea Turtle Research Programme, Sandy Point Leatherbacks were also observed nesting there. Half day tours to Buck Island, including 1¼ hours snorkelling and 30 minutes at the beach can be arranged through hotels or boat owners on the waterfront at Christiansted. Anchorage is crowded 1000-1600 with day charters; watch the charter boat race for the best spots at 1000 and 1600. Only six operators are licensed to take day charters to the island, which means that they are often crowded, particularly when cruise ships are in town. Another attraction is the **Salt River coral canyon**.

Dive centres

During Feb, Mar & Apr you are likely to see humpbacked whales near the islands

Diving trips are arranged by several companies all round the island, many of which also charter boats out and offer sailing lessons. Dive companies include: *Dive Experience*, Christiansted, T7733307, 800-2359047, www.st-croix.com/diveexperience, who will dive even if only 2 people sign up, good offers on prices and good equipment, including masks with prescription lenses; *Anchor Dive Centre*, Salt River National Park, T/F7781522; *Cane Bay Dive Shop*, T7739913, F7785442, www.canebayscuba.com, great bay for snorkelling and wall diving, beach or boat dive; *Scubawest*, Frederiksted, T7723701, F7721852, www.divescubawest.com, specializes in pier night dives and wrecks; *St Croix Ultimate Blue Water Adventures* (SCUBA), T7735994, www.stcroixscuba.com. Dive packages can be arranged through your hotel. Boats sometimes go out to watch humpbacked whales during the months when they are often sighted around the islands.

St Croix

■ Sleeping	4 Carringtons Inn	8 Hibiscus
1 Buccaneer	5 Cormorant	9 Hilty House Inn
2 Cane Bay Reef Club	6 Cottages by the Sea	10 Hotel on the Cay
3 Carambola	7 Divi Carina	11 Innparadise

For those who don't want to get wet, there is the semi-submersible *Oceanique*, T7737060, with day and night excursions in Christiansted harbour and around Protestant Cay.

Beaches and watersports

Good beaches can be found at **Davis Bay**, **Protestant Cay**, **Buccaneer**, **the Reef**, **Cane Bay** (good snorkelling), **Grapetree Beach** and **Cormorant Beach**. Cramer Park on the east shore and Frederiksted beach to the north of the town, both have changing facilities and showers. Rainbow Beach Club, 1½ km north of Frederiksted, has a spectacular sandy beach, restaurant and beach bar. All beaches are open to the public, but on those where there is a hotel (*Buccaneer* – good snorkelling) which maintains the beach, you may have to pay for the use of facilities. Try the isolated beach to the east of the *Buccaneer Hotel* (walk across the golf course), at *The Waves* restaurant at Cane Bay, or explore and find your own. Generally the north coast is best for surfing because there are no reefs to protect the beaches. On the northwest coast, the stretch from Northside Beach to Ham's Bay is easily accessible for shell collecting (but watch out for sea urchins at Ham's Bay beach); the road is alongside the beach. The road ends at the General Offshore Sonorbuoy Area (a naval installation at Ham's Bluff), which is a good place to see booby birds and frigate birds leaving at dawn and coming home to roost at dusk. Shells can also be found on Sprat Hall beach (ask at *Sprat Hall Plantation* for details). There is an annual Coral Reef Swim towards the end of October, T7732100.

There are some nice rock pools on various beaches, where the sun warms tidal waters and creates nature's own hot tub, great for a soak

Water skiing, jet skiing, windsurfing and parasailing are all on offer (*St Croix Watersports*, T7737060). There are several companies offering day sails on crewed yachts. Annapolis International Sailing School has a dock with a few moorings, teaches sailing and may rent boats for day sailing to qualified individuals.

The **Mumm's Cup Regatta** is held in November, with three days of ocean racing off the east coast. Other races include the Hookanson Memorial Race in January and the John Stuart Jervis Memorial in December. Contact the St Croix Yacht Club for details, T7739531.

Other sports Most of the large hotels have **tennis** courts for residents, but you can also play at the *Buccaneer Hotel* (eight courts, US$5 per person for non-guests), the *Carambola* (four grass courts, two lit for night play and another five clay courts at the golf club, pro US$50 per hour, guests offered free 30 minute clinics Tuesday-Friday morning), Chenay Bay, Club St Croix, The Reef Club (two courts, US$5 per person, per hour), the *Tamarind Reef Hotel* (two cal grass courts, non-guests US$8 per person per hour, US$5 evenings) and others. There are four public courts at Canegata Park in Christiansted and 2 public courts near the fort in Frederiksted which can be used free of charge on a first come first served basis. Two 18-hole **golf** courses, one at the *Carambola* (T7785638), with pro shop, putting green and driving range, and the other at the *Buccaneer Hotel* (T7732100), also with putting

US Virgin Islands

BUCK ISLAND

Buck Island Channel
Green Cay
Teague Bay
ay Bay
Cramer Park
East End Bay
■13
82
Seven Hills
7
Grapetree Bay
Turner Hole
Grass Pt
Great Pond
62A
60
Robin Bay
Hill
Great Pond Bay
Spring Bay

12 On the Beach
13 Tamarind Reef
14 Waves at Cane Bay

green and pro shop. There is also a nine-hole course at The Reef (T7738844), green fee US$12.50. **Horse riding**: Paul and Jill's Equestrian Stables (T7722880 or 7722627), at Sprat Hall Plantation, one and a half miles north of Frederiksted, on Route 58, reserve three days in advance if possible for rides through the rain forest, past Danish ruins, for all levels of ability, English or Western styles, US$50 for two hours, no credit cards. You can play **croquet** at the *Tamarind Reef Hotel*. Rent a **mountain bike** and join St Croix Bikes & Tours for a tour of the rain forest or beach areas of west end of island, T7722343, www.stcroixbike.com. VI Cycling organize regular weekly rides and races for which there is a US$5 fee per participant, Mike Mcqueston T7730079.

In May a week of sports-related events culminate in the **St Croix International Triathlon** which attracts over 600 participants. Phone Tom Guthrie or Miles Sperber, T7734470, for details of running courses and tours. For the Virgin Islands Track and Field Federation, contact Wallace Williams (secretary), PO Box 2720, Christiansted, T7735715.

Christiansted

The old town square and waterfront area of Christiansted, the old Danish capital, still retain the colourful character of the early days. Overhanging second-floor balconies designed by the Danes to shade the streets serve as cool arcades for shoppers. Red-roofed pastel houses built by early settlers climb the hills overlooking Kings Wharf and there is an old outdoor market. Many of the buildings are being restored and the dock is being improved to take small cruise ships (the reef prevents large ships entering the harbour), but it is unlikely to be overrun with cruise ship tourism like St Thomas. Old Christiansted is compact and easy to stroll. The best place to

Christiansted

start is the Visitors' Bureau on the corner of King Cross Street and Queen Street. Here you can pick up brochures. Starting in February for six weeks the St Croix Landmarks Society runs house tours every Wednesday, T7720598.

Across the way is **Fort Christiansvaern**, which the Danes built in 1749 on the foundations of a French fort dating from 1645. ■ *US$2. 0800-1645.* See the punishment cells, dungeons, barracks room, officers' kitchen, powder magazine, an exhibit of how to fire a cannon, and the battery, the best vantage point for photographing the old town and harbour. The fort and the surrounding historic buildings are run by the National Parks Service. In front of the fort is the old customs house, now the National Parks Service office.

The **Steeple Building** is a minute's walk away. Built as a church by the Danes in 1734, then converted into a military bakery, storehouse and later a hospital, it is now a museum of the island's early history. ■ *US$2. 0930-1200, 1300-1500.* The area here is a treasury of old Danish architecture, and many of the original buildings are still in use. The West India and Guinea Co, which bought St Croix from the French and settled the island, built a warehouse on the corner of Church and Company Streets in 1749 which now serves as a post office, Customs House and public toilets.

Across the way from Government House on King Street is the building where the young Alexander Hamilton, who was to become one of the founding fathers of the USA, worked as a clerk in Nicolas Cruger's counting-house. Today the building houses the Little Switzerland shop.

Government House has all the hallmarks of the elegant and luxurious life of the merchants and planters in the days when 'sugar was king'. The centre section, built in 1742 as a merchant's residence, was bought by the Secret Council of St Croix in 1771 to serve as a government office. It was later joined to another merchant's town house on the corner of Queen Cross Street and a handsome ballroom was added. The Governor stays here when he works away from the political capital, Charlotte Amalie. Across Queen Cross Street from Government House is the Dutch Reformed Church.

Queen Cross Street leads into Strand and the fascinating maze of arcades and alleys lined with boutiques, handicrafts and jewellery shops. A boardwalk spans the entire waterfront of Christiansted, affording a wonderful stroll with lively restaurants, cafés and bars along the way. The boardwalk is well lit and security is tight with policemen on duty (however, beware the usual purse snatchers). The seaplane lands alongside the boardwalk and park benches provide vantage points to enjoy the view. There are plans to extend the boardwalk around Fort Chirstiansvaern all the way to Gallows Bay Marina. Along the waterfront there is also an aquarium. ■ *US$3. Wed-Sun, 1100-1600.* Just offshore is **Protestant Cay** (just called The Cay), reached by ferry for US$3 return for the pleasant beach, and the *Hotel on the Cay* with restaurants, pool, tennis, watersports.

Around the island

Agriculture was long the staple of the economy, cattle and sugar the main activities, and today there are the ruins of numerous sugar plantations with their Great Houses and windmills. **Estate Whim** is restored to the way it was under Danish rule in the 1700s and is well worth a visit; it is a beautiful oblong building housing a museum of the period, and in the grounds are many of the factory buildings and implements. ■ *T7720598, www.onepaper.com/landmarks. Adults US$5, children under 12 US$1. Mon-Sat 1000-1600.* There is a gift shop. Candlelight concerts and other parties and functions are held here, including an annual antiques auction, usually in March, www.stcroixlandmarks.com/auction **St George Botanical Garden**, just off Centreline Road (Queen Mary Highway), in an old estate, has gardens amid the ruined buildings. The 17-acre site was built on a Precolumbian settlement. ■ *US$5 for non-members. Mon-Sat 0800-1600.* Judith's Fancy, from the time of the French, is now surrounded by building developments and has less to see than the other two.

The **St Croix Heritage Trail** promotes culture, heritage and communities and was designated one of 50 Millennium Legacy Trails by the White House Millennium Council. There are many attractions to be toured, sites like churches are listed and points of interest are shown. A good guide is available covering all the highlights of the island in a space of 28 miles, www.millenniumtrails.org You can tour the restored historic estates sponsored by the St Croix Landmark Society several times a year. For information call the Whim Museum, T7720598, www.stcroixlandmarks.com

Frederiksted

Frederiksted, 17 miles from Christiansted, is the only other town on St Croix and although quiet, its gingerbread architecture has its own charm. Public taxis link the two towns and there are taxis from the airport to Frederiksted. Historic buildings such as **Victoria House**, 7-8 Strand Street, and the Customs House, have been repaired following hurricane damage. **Fort Frederik** (1752) is a museum; it was here that the first official foreign salute to the 13 US States was made in 1776 (see also **Sint Eustatius**). Also here was read the proclamation freeing all Danish slaves in 1848. An exhibition of old photos and newspaper articles and other display items show the destruction caused by hurricanes, including the one which hit Charlotte Amalie harbour. ■ *Free. Mon-Fri, 0830-1600.* A new **pier**, to accommodate at least two cruise ships, was built in 1993. On a non-cruise ship day Frederiksted seems like a ghost town, but every other Wednesday is **Harbour Night**, when cruise ships stay late and the town stays open with special entertainments.

The rain forest to the north of town is worth a visit. Two roads, the paved Mahogany Road (Route 76) and the unpaved Creque Dam Road (Road 58) traverse it.

Essentials

Best resorts **LL** *Buccaneer*, PO Box 25200, on Gallows Bay, north coast, T7732100, F7788215, www.thebuccaneer.com 132 luxury rooms, 340 acres, 3 beaches, sports including golf (see above), tennis, fitness centre, health spa, watersports centre, several restaurants, lots of packages available, and **LL-L** *Sunterra Resorts Carambola Beach*, on Davis Bay, PO Box 3031, north coast, T7783800, F7781682, www.sunterra.com 146 rooms in 25 2-storey villas, tennis with pro, golf packages available, pool, jacuzzis, snorkelling, scuba.

Christiansted **L** *Hotel on the Cay*, on Protestant Cay, see above, in Christiansted harbour, PO Box 4020, T7732035, F7737046. Free ferry service, 55 rooms, also timeshare with kitchenettes, excellent snorkelling, pool, beach, the only one in town, watersports, tennis, restaurants. **AL** *Caravelle*, 44A Queen Cross St, T7730687, F7787004, www.hotelcaravelle.com. 44 rooms, also good, with good restaurant, *Rumrunners*, pool, diving, transport to other sports facilities, diving packages available. **AL** *Danish Manor*, 2 Company St, T7731377, F7731913, www.danishmanor.com. Pool in old courtyard, renovated rooms. **AL** *King Christian*, 59 King's Wharf, PO Box 24467, T7736330, F7739411, www.kingchristian.com Basic, noisy with late night bands, a/c, fan, watersports, pool, convenient. **AL-B** *Pink Fancy*, 27 Prince St, 5 mins from shopping centre and waterfront, T7738460, F7736448, www.pinkfancy.com 18th-century townhouse, a National Historic Trust property, 13 rooms, tastefully furnished with antiques, all different, honeymoon packages, bar, pool. **AL** *Hilty House Inn*, T/F7732594 hiltyhouse@worldnet.att.net In a historic plantation house near town, house or cottage, breakfast included, pool. **C** *The Breakfast Club*, 18 Queen Cross St, T7737383, F7738642, www.the-breakfast-club.christiansted.vi.us 9 rooms with bath and kitchenette, gourmet breakfasts, hot tub on deck, nice view, manager is skilful golf player. **Near Christiansted:** **LL-L** *Cormorant Beach Club and Hotel*, T7788920, F7789218, www.cormorant-stcroix.com 1st class, beach, tennis, pool, deluxe, gay friendly. **West of Christiansted**, **L** *Hibiscus Beach Hotel*, T7734042, F7737668, www.1hibiscus.com 37 beach front rooms, hammocks on the beach, access for handicapped to beach, pool, restaurant, watersports in all-inclusive packages, lots of special deals offered. **L-AL** *Innparadise*, Estate Golden Rock on Little Princess Hill overlooking Christiansted, T7139803, F7138722, www.innparadisestcroix.com 5 rather small rooms, breakfast included, private or shared bath, minimum stay 3 days, no smoking, no pets, no children under 12, 10% discount if you're 50 or over. **L-A** *Carringtons Inn*, 4001 Estate Hermon Hill, T7130508, F7190841, www.carringtonsinn.com 5 decent-sized rooms, private bathrooms, breakfast included, pool with spectacular view.

Northeast coast **L** *Tamarind Reef Hotel*, T7734455, F7733989, www.usvi.net/hotel /tamarind 46 rooms, half have kitchenettes, a/c, fan, TV, balcony, all with seaview, two beaches, pool, snorkelling, boardsailing, kayaking at hotel, or diving, fishing, sailing from adjacent Green Cay Marina, croquet and tennis lawn, packages available.

Frederiksted Half a mile from town, **LL-A** *On The Beach*, T7721205, F7721757, www.gaytraveling.com/onthebeach Pool, 20 rooms, suites, villas, kitchenettes, restaurants, serves gay community. **A** *The Frederiksted*, 442 Strand St, T7720500, F ext 151. Modern, fridge, TV, phones, pool, restaurant, bar, good. **North of Frederiksted** **LL-L** *Cane Bay Reef Club*, PO Box 1407, Kingshill, T/F7782966, www.canebay.com 9 suites with balconies over the sea, pool, restaurant, bar, rough sea but short walk to beach, weekly rates cheaper. **LL-L** *Waves At Cane Bay*, PO Box 1749, Kingshill, T7781805, F7784945, www.thewavesatcanebay.com 12 oceanfront studios with balconies, cable TV, natural grotto pool, beach, good snorkelling and scuba from property. **South of Frederiksted** **AL-A** *Cottages by the Sea*, PO Box 1697, T7720495, F7721753, www.travelfacts.com/ Good beach, watersports, 6 day maid service, good.

There are several rental agents for villas and condominiums: *American Rentals*, 2001 Old Hospital St, Christiansted, T7738470, F7738472; *Island Villas*, 6 Company St, Christiansted, T7738821, F7738823, www.ecani.com/island.villas All with a wide price range; *Richards and Ayer Associates Realtors*, 340 Strand St, Frederiksted, T7720420, F7722958, www.ayervirgin islands.com

Sleeping

For hotel rates consult
http://st-croix.com/
rates

For small, intimate places to stay, often B&B, check the Small Inns of St Croix, www.smallinnsstcroix.com

US Virgin Islands

Eating
St Croix 'This Week' has a full listing of the very many places to eat, from low budget to elegant dining

Restaurant life on St Croix includes charcoal-broiled steaks and lobsters, West Indian Créole dishes and Danish and French specialities. Do not miss the open-air Crucian picnics. Local dishes include stewed or roast goat, red pea soup (a sweet soup of kidney beans and pork), callalou (dasheen soup); snacks, Johnny cakes (unleavened fried bread) and pate (pastry filled with spiced beef, chicken or salt fish); drinks, ginger beer, *mavi* (from the bark of a tree).

Christiansted *Top Hat*, Company St, between King Cross St and Queen Cross St, T7732346. Often mentioned in gourmet magazines, excellent and spotlessly clean but pricey at US$20-28 for entrées, Scandinavian food, Smorgaasbord, steaks and seafood, open Mon-Sat dinner only. *Lunchería*, on Company St, in the courtyard of Apothecary Hall, T7734247. Mexican food, cheap margaritas, live music, open Mon-Sat lunch and dinner. Also on Company St are *Harvey's Bar and Restaurant*, T7733433. Local cuisine, conch, callaloo, goat stew. *Margaritas*, Company St. Inexpensive Tex-Mex food, open Mon-Sat for lunch and dinner. *Tommy T's Paradise Café*, Queen Cross St, T7732985. Small local bar/restaurant, breakfast, lunch and dinner, sandwiches and daily specials, claustrophobic, no credit cards. *Indies*, Company St, T6929440. Seafood and West Indian restaurant, also Sushi on Wed and Fri nights at the bar. *Stixx on the Waterfront*, Pan Am Pavilion, T7735157. Informal, breakfast, lunch and dinner, pasta, pizza, seafood, daily specials, Sun brunch 1000-1400 includes champagne and mimosas, popular bar; watch the seaplanes from Kings Alley Yacht Club. *Rumrunners* on the waterfront at *Hotel Caravelle*, serves breakfast, lunch and dinner.

Frederiksted the *Blue Moon*, 17 Strand St, T7722222. Seafood and native dishes plus music, dinner Tue-Sat, daily specials, great Sun brunch with jazz. *Motown Bar and Restaurant*, T7729882, Strand St. Goat stew, conch, shrimp, open for breakfast, lunch and dinner daily, not expensive.

Out of town the restaurant at *Paradise Sunset Beach Hotel*, Ham's Bluff, has been recommended, great sunset too, seafood and local food, open Mon-Thu for lunch and dinner. *Baggy's Wrinkle* and *Baggy's Too* at St Croix Marina, Gallows Bay. Inexpensive daily specials, American food and barbecue, open Tue-Sun all day, no credit cards. *Cheeseburgers in Paradise*, on East End Rd, T7731119. Very popular, always crowded, open for lunch and dinner, inexpensive. *Columbus Cove*, Salt River National Park, near Columbus Landing. Open daily for breakfast, lunch and dinner, meat, fish and chicken platters, large portions, most dinners under US$15. *The Waves at Cane Bay*, T7781805. Romantic dining, expensive, good food and service, open for dinner Tue-Sat.

Nightlife
Most hotels provide evening entertainment on a rotating basis, the custom of many of the Caribbean islands, so it is sometimes best to stay put and let the world of West Indian music and dance come to you

The *Hibiscus Beach Hotel* hosts the Caribbean Dance Company on Fri at 2030, evocative, and a steel pan band on Wed at 1830, also electric mandolin on Thu and a jazz trio on Sat at 2000. Some restaurants also provide entertainment, eg *Tivoli Gardens* (Queen Cross and Strand Streets), *Lizards* (Strand St) and *The Galleon* (Green Cay Marina, piano bar). *The New Wreck Bar*, Hospital St. Crab races on Fri, folk guitar on Wed, Green Flash rock Thu-Sat. *The Blue Moon*, 17 Strand St. Live jazz every Fri and on full moons. *Kings Alley Yacht Club* has open-air bandstand with music afternoons and evenings. *Parrot's Perch* serves dinner, happy hour and evening entertainment. Every other Wed night in Frederiksted, Harbour Night, with arts, crafts, dancing, T7724242. Live music at *Deep End Bar* at Green Cay Marina. *Two plus Two Disco*, Northside Rd, west of Christiansted (closed Mon). Live entertainment Fri and Sat, US$5 cover charge; snack bar from 1200 till 1800. Most cultural events take place at the Island Centre, a 600-seat theatre with an open air amphitheatre seating another 1,600, where drama, dance and music are performed.

Festivals

St Croix's Festival lasts from early **December**, through Christmas to 6 January. There is another festival on the Saturday nearest to **17 March**, St Patrick's Day, when there is a splendid parade with floats and music (T7731139). *Mocko Jumbi* dancing (on stilts) takes place at festivals and on other occasions; for information on Mocko Jumbi, contact Willard S John, PO Box 3162, Frederiksted, St Croix, USVI 00840, T7738909 (day), 7720225 (evening). In **November** there is a Thanksgiving Jump-Up, T7138012.

St Croix Leap (Life and Environmental Arts Project, PO Box 245, Frederiksted, T7720421), on **Shopping** Route 76, the Paved Rain Forest Rd, is a non-profit woodworking centre, from which the artefacts may be bought direct. They take orders for custom made work and will ship finished work, anything from totem poles to salad servers in a variety of woods. *Many Hands*, Pan Am Pavilion, sells only arts and crafts from the Virgin Islands. For special jewellery go to *Sonya's*, in Christiansted, and see her hand-wrought gold and silver things. *The Natural Jewel*, King St, for pearl and larimar. St Croix Landmarks, museum store, teak, antique furniture, works by island artists, books and cards. The market in Christiansted is on Company Street, and has been on the site since 1735. *The Newstand* on Company St has US papers, magazines, other reading matter. *Quin House* on Company St has galleries, Caribbean maps and prints, museum replica jewellery, mahogany furniture. For groceries, *K-Mart*, *Cost U Less* at Sunshine Mall and *Extras*, and several *Pueblo* stores on the bus route. Gallows Bay has *Gallows Bay Market* (small, upscale, also US papers), PO, bank, bookstore, hardware store, marine store (another one at St Croix Marine). Laundry at Jonah's drop off at St Croix Marine.

Bus The bus service runs between Christiansted and Frederiksted, 0530-2130 every 30 mins **Transport** (every hour on Sun), US$1, timetable from airport or bus driver. **Taxi** A taxi tour costs US$25 per person, less for groups; contact St Croix Taxi and Tours Association, Henry E Rohlsen Airport, T7781088, PO Box 1106, Christiansted, F7786887; Combined Tours, T7722888. Taxi vans run between Christiansted and Frederiksted, US$2. If you want a limo service, try *Evans Limo Service*, T7734845. **Car hire** Rental agencies include *Avis*, at the airport, T7789355/9365. *Budget* at the airport, T7789636, or Christiansted (*King Christian Hotel* T7732285), also *Hertz*, T7781402, or *Buccaneer Hotel*, T7732100 Ext 737; *Caribbean Jeep and Car Rental*, 6 Hospital Street, Christiansted, T7734399; *Green Cay Jeep and Car Rental*, T7737227; *Berton*, one mile west of Christiansted, T7731516.

Anchorages St Croix divers have placed mooring buoys at wall dive locations to prevent damage to the reefs while anchoring. There are no restrictions to their use; they only ask that stays be limited to 4 hrs so that another boat might use reef for second dive of the day. In anchorages, all moorings are privately owned. Buck island has moorings placed within the snorkelling area for day use only. Overnight anchoring is not allowed and boats must anchor in sand at southwest end of island. Marinas at St Croix Marine, Anapolis Sailing School, St Croix Yachting Club, Green Cay Marina, Salt River Marina. Anchorages at Christiansted, Frederiksted (deep so very difficult), Green Cay, Teague Bay by St Croix Yacht Club (reciprocates with members of other yacht clubs).

Communications Internet at *A Better Copy*, on Company St between King Cross St and Queen Cross **Directory** St, open Mon-Fri 0900-1700, also fax and photocopying; at the Florence Williams Library; *Strand Street Station*, in the Pan Am Pavilion, Christiansted, internet café, mail boxes, photocopies, faxes, pay phones, film processing, open 0900-1900; at *St Croix Bike & Tours*, Custom St, near the pier in Frederiksted, cybercafé, *Ben & Jerry's* ice cream, bike rental and tours, www.stcroixbike.com The Post Office in Christiansted was moving in 2001 from near the wharf to the corner of Queen St with King Cross St. **Embassies & consulates** *Dutch*, T7737100. *Norwegian*, T7737100. **Tourist Office** PO Box 4538, Christiansted, T7730495, F7735074. In Fredriksted the Tourist Office and Visitor Centre was moving in 2001 to the Old Customs House. **Useful addresses People to people programme:** if you wish to contact someone in a similar profession to your own, contact Geri Simpson, PO Box 943, Kingshill, St Croix, USVI 00851, T7788007.

US Virgin Islands

Background

History

The islands were 'discovered' by Columbus on his second voyage in 1493 and, partly because of their number, he named them 'Las Once Mil Vírgenes' (the 11,000 virgins) in honour of the legend of St Ursula and her 11,000 martyred virgins. There were Indian settlements in all the major islands of the group and the first hostile action with the Caribs took place during Columbus' visit. Spain asserted its exclusive right to settle the islands but did not colonize them, being more interested in the larger and more lucrative Greater Antilles. European settlement did not begin until the 17th century, when few Indians were to be found. St Croix (Santa Cruz) was settled by the Dutch and the English around 1625, and later by the French. In 1645 the Dutch abandoned the island and went to St Eustatius and St Maarten. In 1650 the Spanish repossessed the island and drove off the English, but the French, under Philippe de Loinvilliers de Poincy of the Knights of Malta, persuaded the Spanish to sail for Puerto Rico. Three years later de Poincy formally deeded his islands to the Knights of Malta although the King of France retained sovereignty. St Croix prospered and planters gradually converted their coffee, ginger, indigo and tobacco plantations to the more profitable sugar, and African slavery was introduced. Wars, illegal trading, privateering, piracy and religious conflicts finally persuaded the French Crown that a colony on St Croix was not militarily or economically feasible and in 1695/96 the colony was evacuated to St Domingue.

A plan for colonizing St Thomas was approved by Frederik III of Denmark in 1665 but the first settlement failed. The Danes asserted authority over uninhabited St John in 1684, but the hostility of the English in Tortola prevented them from settling until 1717. In 1733 France sold St Croix to the Danish West India & Guinea Company and in 1754 the Danish West Indies became a royal colony. This was the most prosperous period for the Danish islands. After the end of Company rule and its trading monopoly, St Thomas turned increasingly toward commerce while in St Croix plantation agriculture flourished. St Thomas became an important shipping centre with heavy reliance on the slave trade. Denmark was the first European nation to end its participation in the slave trade in 1802. Illegal trade continued, however, and British occupation of the Virgin Islands between 1801 and 1802 and again between 1807 and 1815 prevented enforcement of the ban.

The Danish Virgin Islands reached a peak population of 43,178 in 1835, but thereafter fell to 27,086 by 1911. Sailing ships were replaced by steamships which found it less necessary to transship in St Thomas. Prosperity declined with a fall in sugar prices, a heavy debt burden, soil exhaustion, development of sugar beet in Europe, hurricanes and droughts and the abolition of slavery. In 1847 a Royal decree provided that all slaves would be free after 1859 but the slaves of St Croix were unwilling to wait and rebelled in July 1848. By the late 19th century economic decline became pronounced. The sugar factory on St Croix was inefficient and in the 20th century the First World War meant less shipping for St Thomas, more inflation, unemployment and labour unrest. The Virgin Islands became a liability for Denmark and the economic benefits of colonialism no longer existed. Negotiations with the USA had taken place intermittently ever since the 1860s for cession of the Virgin Islands to the USA. The USA wanted a Caribbean naval base for security reasons and after the 1914 opening of the Panama Canal was particularly concerned to guard against German acquisition of Caribbean territory. In 1917, the islands were sold for US$25mn but no political, social or economic progress was made for several years. The islands were under naval rule during and after the War and it was not until 1932 that US citizenship was granted to all natives of the Virgin Islands.

A devastating hurricane in 1928, followed by the stock market crash of 1929, brought US awareness of the need for economic and political modernization. Several years of drought, the financial collapse of the sugar refineries, high unemployment, low wages and very high infant mortality characterized these years. In 1931 naval rule was replaced by a civil government. In 1934, the Virgin Islands Company (VICO) was set up as a long term development 'partnership programme'. The sugar and rum industry benefited from increased demand in the Second World War. VICO improved housing, land and social conditions, particularly in rural areas, but the end of the wartime construction boom, wartime demand for rum and the closing of the submarine base, brought further economic recession. However, the severance of diplomatic relations between the USA and Cuba shifted tourism towards the islands. Construction boomed and there was even a labour shortage. With immigrant labour, the population increased and by 1970 per capita income reached US$2,400, five times that of the Caribbean region as a whole, with about half of the labour force engaged in tourist activities and tourism providing about 60% of the islands' revenues. With the shift from agriculture to tourism, VICO was officially disbanded in 1966, along with the production of sugarcane. Various tax incentives, however, promoted the arrival of heavy industry, and during the 1960s the Harvey Alumina Company and the Hess Oil Company began operating on St Croix. By 1970, the economy was dominated by mainland investment and marked by white-owned and managed enterprises based on cheap imported labour from other Caribbean islands.

In September 1989, St Croix was hit by Hurricane Hugo, which tore through 90% of all buildings and left 22,500 people homeless. The disaster was followed by civil unrest, with rioting and looting, and US army troops were sent in to restore order, The territorial government, located on St Thomas had been slow to react to the disaster on St Croix and was strongly criticized. After the hurricane, a referendum endorsed the establishment of some sort of municipal government on each island which would be more responsive to that island's needs and legislation to that effect was introduced into the Legislature in July 1993. St Croix's feeling of neglect led to attempts to balance the division of power between the islands, but calls for greater autonomy grew. After some delay, a referendum was held in October 1993, which presented voters with seven options on the island's status, grouped into three choices: continued or enhanced status, integration into the USA, or independence. However, the vote was inconclusive, with only 27% of the registered voters turning out, whereas 50% were needed for a binding decision. Of those who did, 90% preferred the first option, leaving the process of constitutional change in some disarray.

In 1993 the government of the USVI reached agreement with the Danish company, the East Asiatic Company Ltd, to buy the West Indian Company Ltd (WICO), whose major holdings on St Thomas included a cruise ship dock, the Havensight Shopping Mall, a 7.2-acre landfill, the former Danish consulate, Denmark Hill, and some undeveloped land. WICO had remained in Danish hands after the 1917 purchase of the islands by the USA and had retained the right to dredge, fill and develop submerged lands in the east part of St Thomas harbour, despite local opposition. The US$54mn sale was described locally as wiping out the last vestiges of Danish colonialism.

Geography and people

The US Virgin Islands, in which the legacies of Danish ownership are very apparent, contain four main islands: St Thomas, St John, St Croix and Water Island. There are 68 islands in all, that lie about 40 miles east of Puerto Rico, although most of them are uninhabited. They have long been developed as holiday centres for US citizens and because of that are distinct from the British Virgin Islands, which have only recently started to develop their tourist potential. The population, mainly black, has always been English-speaking, despite the long period of Danish control. Some Spanish is in use, particularly on St Croix. The West Indian dialect is mostly English, with inflections from Dutch, Danish, French, Spanish, African languages and Créole.

US Virgin Islands

Government

In 1936 the Organic Act of the Virgin Islands of the United States provided for two municipal councils and a Legislative Assembly in the islands. Suffrage was extended to all residents of twenty one and over who could read and write English. Discrimination on the grounds of race, colour, sex or religious belief was forbidden and a bill of rights was included. Real political parties now emerged, based on popular support. In 1946, the first black governor was appointed to the Virgin Islands and in 1950 the first native governor was appointed. In 1968 the Elective Governor Act was passed, to become effective in 1970 when, for the first time, Virgin Islanders would elect their own governor and lieutenant governor. The Act also abolished the presidential veto of territorial legislation and authorized the legislature to override the governor's veto by a two-thirds majority vote. The USVI is an unincorporated Territory under the US Department of Interior with a Delegate in the House of Representatives who (since January 1993) has a vote in sittings of the whole House. The Governor is elected every four years; there are 15 Senators; judicial power is vested in local courts. All persons born in the USVI are citizens of the United States, but do not vote in presidential elections while resident on the islands.

Economy

USVI residents enjoy a comparatively high standard of living (the cost of living is the highest in the USA), unemployment is low, at around 4% (mostly on St Croix), but the working population is young and there is constant pressure for new jobs. The islands used to rely on the alumina plant, and the Hess oil refinery, operating well below capacity, for employment and income, but nowadays the major economic activity is tourism. Over two million visitors come every year. The number of hotel rooms is now over 5,000, generating jobs for two-thirds of the labour force. There is a perennial conflict between the hotel industry, which provides employment, fixed investment and pays taxes, and the cruise ship industry, which contributes comparatively little to the islands and benefits St Thomas mostly.

Industry is better developed than in many Caribbean islands and exports of manufactured goods include watches, textiles, electronics, pharmaceuticals and rum. In 1998 Hess Oil Co and Petróleos de Venezuela signed a joint venture agreement to create a US$625mn company called Hovensa to operate the refinery on St Croix. Industrial incentives and tax concessions equivalent to those enjoyed by Puerto Rico, are designed to attract new investors with US markets to the islands. Over 30 large US corporations have set up manufacturing operations in the USVI and industrial parks are being built.

Agriculture has declined in importance since sugar production ended, and the poor soil prevents much commercial farming. Emphasis is placed on growing food crops for the domestic market and fruit, vegetables and sorghum for animal feed have been introduced. Fishing in the USVI waters is mostly for game rather than for commercial purposes. The islands' lack of natural resources makes them heavily dependent on imports, both for domestic consumption and for later re-exports, such as oil and manufactured goods.

British Virgin Islands

12

British Virgin Islands

BRITISH
VIRGIN ISLANDS

Tortola
Anegada
Virgin
Gorda

Leeward Islands

Dominican
Republic

Puerto
Rico

Caribbean
Sea

Windward Islands

Netherlands Antilles

VENEZUELA

The British Virgin Islands have a reputation for excellent sailing between the islands and there are many charter companies offering crewed or bareboat yachts. Windsurfing is also top quality and both sports organize races and regattas which attract competitors of international standard. Races are accompanied by lots of parties and related activities typical of the yachtie fraternity. There are plenty of hotels, and a few really special places in isolated spots – popular with newly weds or the seriously rich.

While there are some large resorts in the BVI, there are no high-rise hotels, casinos and very few nightclubs, as found in some of the other islands which depend heavily on tourism. In fact, there is very little to do at all on land and nearly everything happens in the beautiful water which surrounds the islands. If you are keen on watersports and sailing and have adequate finances (the Virgin Islands are not cheap), you will enjoy island hopping.

A Foot in the door

- Dive the wreck of **The Rhone** and introduce yourself to the local octopus in residence.
- A Painkiller is the local **rum**-based liquid anaesthetic, try it and see, preferably at sunset.
- Swim from your boat to the **Soggy Dollar Bar** on Jost Van Dyke, a yachtie favourite hangout.
- Walk for miles along the sandy beach or snorkel the reef off the north coast of Anegada, taking a break for a **lobster lunch** at Loblolly Bay.
- Sail to a deserted beach and just take it easy.

Essentials

Before you travel

Documents An authenticated birth or citizenship certificate or voter's registration may suffice for US or Canadian citizens. All other nationalities need a valid **passport** and a return or **onward ticket**. Visitors from some countries, such as Guyana, require a visa. The Chief Immigration Officer is in Road Town, T4943701.

Money **Currency** The US dollar is the legal tender. There are no exchange control restrictions. Try to avoid large denominated travellers' cheques. Cheques accepted rarely, cash is king. There is a 10% stamp duty on all cheques and travellers' cheques. **Credit cards** Credit cards are all right for most hotels and the larger restaurants, but not for the majority of the bar/restaurants. Credit cards are not accepted on Anegada except at the *Anegada Reef Hotel*. **Banks** *Bank of Nova Scotia*, Road Town, T4942526. *Barclays Bank*, Road Town, T4942173, F4944315, with agencies in The Valley, Virgin Gorda, T4955217, F4955163. *Chase Manhattan Bank*, Road Town, T4942662, F4945106. *Development Bank of the Virgin Islands*, T4943737. *Banco Popular de Puerto Rico*, Road Town, T4942117, F4945294. *VP Bank (BVI) Ltd*, 65 Main Street, Road Town, T4941100, F4941199.

Climate The temperature averages 84°F in summer and 80°F in winter. At night temperatures may drop about 50°F. Average annual rainfall is 40 ins.

Getting there

Air There are international airports on Beef Island for Tortola, on Virgin Gorda and on Anegada, but no direct flights from Europe or from the USA. The main airport is on Beef Island, with only local flights going to Virgin Gorda and no international scheduled services to Anegada. **From Europe** Same day connections can be made through Puerto Rico (*British Airways* from London, *Iberia* from Madrid) or Antigua (*BWIA* or *British Airways* from London). **From the USA** Connecting flights can be arranged through Puerto Rico or the USVI. *American Eagle* (T4952559), *Air Sunshine, Cape Air, Gulfstream* and *LIAT* fly several times a day from San Juan. **From the Caribbean** *LIAT* (T4951187) flies from Antigua, Grenada, St Kitts, St Maarten, St Vincent, Trinidad, Puerto Rico. *Caribbean Star Airlines* fly from Antigua, Barbados, Dominica, Grenada, Port of Spain, St Kitts, St Vincent. *American Eagle* flies from Anguilla, St Kitts, St Maarten, St Thomas, San Juan. *Winair* (T4942347) flies from St Maarten. *Air Sunshine* and *Cape Air* fly from St Thomas and San Juan. Virgin Gorda's air links are not especially good. *Air St Thomas* and *Air Sunshine* fly from St Thomas and San Juan, while *M & N Aviation* (T4955553) and *Air St Thomas* also fly from San Juan. *Seaborne Aviation* (T340-7736442) fly to West End, Tortola, from St Thomas with a seaplane three times a week. Charter flights with *Fly BVI* (T4951747), *Clair Aero Services* (T4952271), *Air St Thomas* (T4955935), *Caribbean Wings* (T4952309), *M & N Aviation* (T4955553) and *Air Sunshine* (T4958900).

Touching down

Departure tax *US$10, if you leave by air, and US$5 departure tax by sea. There is a cruise ship passenger tax of US$7.*
Emergency *Police, Fire or Ambulance, T999. The Virgin Islands Search and Rescue (VISAR) is a voluntary 24-hour marine service, T999 or Ch 16.*
Hours of business *Banks open Monday-Friday, 0900-1400, Barclays is open until 1500, Chase Manhattan until 1600, also Chase opens on Saturday 0900-1200. Shops*

open Monday-Friday, 0900-1700. Government offices open Monday-Friday, 0830-1630.
Official time *Atlantic Standard Time, four hours behind GMT, one ahead of EST.*
Voltage *110 volts, 60 cycles.*
Clothing *Island dress is casual and only the most exclusive restaurants require formal clothes. However, bathing suits are for the beach only, it is very offensive to locals to see bare chests and bellies, so cover up.*

There are frequent connections with the USVI and within the BVI, see the USVI chapter. **Boat** *Inter-Island Boat Services*, T4954166; also water taxi available, T7766501. *Native Son Inc*, T4954617, *Smiths Ferry Services*, T4942355, *Speedy's*, T4955240, *Nubian Princess*, T4954999. Fares between Tortola and St John are about US$40 round trip (US$28 children aged 3-11).

Ports of entry (British flag) Port Purcell at Road Town is the principal port of entry with an 800 ft, deep water berth and a 500 ft pier for cruise ships; Government Jetty, Road Town, is also used. There are others at West End (Soper's Hole), Tortola; St Thomas Bay, Virgin Gorda; and Great Harbour, Jost Van Dyke. Small cruise ships can be seen off many of the islands. Anegada is a port of entry, customs and immigration can be cleared 0715-1715 Monday-Friday, 0800-1530 Saturday-Sunday.

Boat documents Customs clearance fee US$0.75, harbour dues US$7, US$10.50 for a boat registered under the name of a corporation. The captain may clear the crew, taking passports and boat documentation ashore. You may clear in and out at the same time if staying less than 72 hours. Weekends incur overtime charges. *Jetskis must be declared on entry to the BVIs*

Anchorages The BVI National Parks Trust (T4943904) has placed moorings at many dive sites, available on a first come, first served basis. Purchase mooring use sticker from customs, fee US$2 per person per day or US$25 per week. Buoys are colour coded: yellow for commercial dive boats, white for a boat with divers, orange for snorkelling and day use, and blue for dinghy docks. Moorings have been placed and are maintained by Moor Seacure at *Cooper Island Beach Club*, Marina Cay, *Drake's Anchorage*, *Abe's* (Jost Van Dyke), Penn's Landing, Leverick Bay, *Rhymer's*, Cane Garden Bay, *Anegada Reef Hotel*, Soper's Hole Marina, *Harris' Place*, Vixen Point (Prickly Pear Island, Gorda Sound), *Last Resort* (Trellis Bay), at US$20 per night. In winter months, northerly swells and high surf can make northern anchorages (and landing at the Baths) untenable. Listen to ZBVI 780AM for weather reports. There are 12 marinas on Tortola, three on Virgin Gorda, one on Peter Island and one on Marina Cay.

Touching down

Local tourist office The BVI Tourist Board, 2nd floor, AKARA Building, Wickhams Cay 1, PO Box 134, Road Town, T4943134, F4943866, bvitourb@caribsurf.com; there is also an office at Virgin Gorda Yacht Harbour, T4955181, F4943866; some offices overseas can help with reservations. The *BVI Welcome* is a bimonthly colour tourist guide now on line as well, www.bviwelcome.com To find out what's on, weekly, monthly or annually, get the *Limin' Times*, T4942413, also on line, www.limin-times.com The *Tourism Directory* is published annually and is a detailed listing of services. The tourist board has these and many other brochures. **Tourist information**

British Virgin Islands

Maps The Ordnance Survey publishes a map of the BVI in its World Maps series, with inset maps of Road Town and East End, Tortola, tourist information and some text; Ordnance Survey, Romsey Road, Southampton, SO9 4DH, T01703-792792. The tourist office distributes a road map, updated annually with some tourist information on resorts, restaurants and what to do.

Where to stay

Hotels There is a 7% hotel tax and a 10% service charge in the BVI. Rates apply to double rooms, EP, winter-summer. **Camping** Allowed only on authorized sites. **Villas** There are some truly luxurious houses for rent if you can afford them, with the most famous, or infamous, being Richard Branson's house on Necker Island. A wide choice of stylish properties is on offer.

British Virgin Islands & national parks

Getting around

Clair Aero flies from Tortola to Anegada Monday, Wednesday, Friday and Sunday, US$27 **Air** one-way, or hire the whole plane, US$300, seats eight people, T4952271. *Fly BVI* is a small charter airline with 7 aircraft which is often cheaper and more convenient than a scheduled flight if there are a few of you, to Anegada US$125 one-way T4951747, 800-1-FLY BVI, F4951973,www.fly-bvi.com. Pack light, there is limited luggage space on the small aircraft. Alternatively take a day trip to Anegada, US$110 per person including taxi, air fare, lobster lunch at the *Big Bamboo*, contact Nikki and Barry Abrams, owners of Fly BVI.

♦ **National Parks**	6 Prickly Pear
1 Diamond Cay	7 Rhone's Anchor
2 Fallen Jerusalem	8 Rhone Marine Park
3 Gorda Peak Park	9 Spring Bay & The Crawl
4 Mt Healthy & Windmill Ruin	10 The Baths & Devil's Bay
5 Mt Sage	11 West Dog

N

Not to scale

British Virgin Islands

Tourist offices overseas

Germany *Wallstrasse 56, D-40878, Dusseldorf/Ratingin, T49-2102-711183, F49-2102-21177, rombergg@tonline.de* **Italy** *Piazza Castello 11, 2021 Milan, T392-72022329, F392-72022306, aigo@internetforce.com* **UK** *110 St Martin's Lane, London WC2N 4DY, T020-72404259, F020-72404270, christine.oliver@fcb.co.uk* **USA** *370 Lexington Avenue, Suite 1605, New York, NY 10017, T212-6960400, F212-9498254, bvitouristboard@ worldnet.att.net; 1804 Union Street, San Francisco, CA 94123, T415-7750344, F415-7752554, bvitbsfo@pacbell.net; 3390 Peachtree Road NE, Suite 1000, Lenox Towers, Atlanta, GA 30326, T404-2408018, F404-2332318; 3450 Wilshire Boulevard, Suite 108-17, Los Angeles, CA 90010, T310-2872200, F310-2872753.*

Road **Bicycle** All bicycles must be registered at the Traffic Licensing Office in Road Town and the licence plate must be fixed to the bicycle, cost US$5. *Last Stop Sports* in Nanny Cay rents and repairs mountain bikes, rental US$20 per day, T4940564, F4940593, lssbikes@surfbvi.com

Bus There is a local bus service on Tortola with cheap fares (US$2-4) but erratic timetable. Scheduled (but nowhere near actual) times are: Road Town to West End, 0700, 0835, 1000; West End to Carrot Bay, 0730, 0900, 1030. From Carrot Bay it goes to Road Town, East End and back to Road Town. In the afternoon it leaves West End at 1515 and 1645. Call **Scatos Bus Service** for information, T4945873.

Jeeps may be more useful for exploring secluded beach areas

Car There are only about 50 miles of roads suitable for cars. Drive on the left. Maximum speed limit 40 mph, in residential areas 20 mph. Minimokes and jeeps can be hired on Tortola, Virgin Gorda and Anegada. Car rental offices (or Police Headquarters) provide the necessary temporary BVI driving licence (US$10) but you must also have a valid licence from your home country. **Car hire** It is advisable to book in advance in the peak season. Rates range from US$40-45 per day for a small car, US$45-70 per day for jeeps. Credit card needed with US$500 deposit. **Tortola**: *Alphonso Car Rentals*, Fish Bay, T4948746, F4948735, cars US$40-45 per day, jeeps US$50-70 per day, 20% less in summer; *Avis Rent-a-Car*, opposite Botanic Gardens, Road Town, T4942193, or West End, T4954973, US$35-50 per day winter, US$25-40 summer, cheaper weekly rates; *Denzil Clyne Car Rentals*, West End, T4954900, jeeps US$45-85 per day in winter, US$40-60 in summer; *International Car Rentals*, Road Town, T4942516, F4944715, intercar@candwbvi.net, US$30-70 per day; *National Car Rental*, Duff's Bottom and Long Bay, T4943197, US$45-75 per day. **Virgin Gorda**: *Andy's Taxi and Jeep Rental*, The Valley, T4955511, F4955820, fischers@ candwbvi.net, VHF16, US$50-55 per day, guided tours US$30; *L & S Jeep Rentals*, South Valley, T4955297, F4955342, small or large jeeps, US$45-70 per day, US$280-455 per week, free pick up in Spanish Town; *Speedy's Car Rentals*, The Valley, T4955235 and Leverick Bay, T4955240 discount with return ferry ticket, US$40-80per day. **Anegada**: *Anegada Reef Hotel*, T4958002, F4959362, minibus and bicycle rentals; *DW Jeep Rentals*, The Settlement, T4959677, 2-door jeeps and Subaru vans, US$40-55 per day, US$240-300 per week, free drop off and pick up at airport.

Taxi *BVI Taxi Association*, T4942875, island tours arranged. **Taxi stands**: in Road Town, T4942322; on Beef Island, T4952378. Taxis are easy to come by on Tortola and fares are fixed, ask for a list or get one from the tourist office. The fare from Beef Island Airport to Road Town, Tortola is US$15 or US$8 if shared. On Virgin Gorda, *Mahogany Taxi Service*, The Valley, T4955469, F4955072, offers tours and day trips, as well as car and jeep rental.

Sea The ferry fares between Tortola and Virgin Gorda are about US$20 return and from Tortola to Jost Van Dyke US$15. Always check availability and departure times in advance. The *North Sound Express*, T4952138 has six daily crossings Beef Island-Spanish Town-Bitter End, 30 minutes, reservations essential. To Leverick Bay (for Mosquito Island), 25 minutes, US$20 one way, 1300, 1545, 1730. Return 0645, 0845, 1145, 1445, 1615. Bus service (not included in fare)

British Virgin Islands

to and from Road Town waterfront (Pussers) and Beef Island ferry dock. *Speedy's* , T4955240, has four crossings Monday, Wednesday, Friday and Saturday between Virgin Gorda and Road Town, six on Tuesday and Thursday, and two on Sunday, also a service continuing to St Thomas, Tuesday, Thursday and Saturday. *Smiths Ferry Services*, T4942355, 4954495, cross from Virgin Gorda to Road Town then West End on their way to St John and St Thomas four times a day Monday-Saturday, three times on Sunday. *Peter Island Ferry*, T4952000, has eight daily crossings from the Peter Island Ferry Dock, Road Town, to Peter Island, US$15 round trip. *Jost Van Dyke Ferry Service*, T4942997, four crossings a day between West End and Jost Van Dyke Monday-Saturday, three on Sunday. *Marina Cay Ferry*, T4942174, runs between Beef Island and *Pusser's Marina Cay* eight times a day.

Keeping in touch

There is a post office in Road Town, branches in Tortola and Virgin Gorda and sub-branches in other islands. Postal rates for postcards are US$0.30 to the USA, US$0.35 to Europe and US$0,45 to the rest of the world; for aerogrammes US$0.35; for letters to the USA US$0.45, to Europe US$0.50, to the rest of the world US$0.75.

Post

Direct dialling is available locally and worldwide. All telecommunications are operated by *Cable & Wireless*. Telephone, fax, data transmission, internet access and telegraph facilities are all available. Phone cards are available, US$5, US$10, US$15 and US$20, discount rates in evenings at weekends. To make a credit card call, dial 111 and quote your card number. Dial 119 for the operator or 110 for the international operator. *Cable & Wireless* is at the centre of Road Town at Wickhams Cay I, open 0700-1900 Monday-Friday, 0700-1600 Saturday, 0900-1400 Sunday and public holidays, T4944444, F4942506; also in The Valley, Virgin Gorda, T4955444, F4955702. They also operate Tortola Marine Radio, call on VHF Ch 16, talk on 27 or 84. The *CCT Boatphone* company in Road Town offers cellular telephone services throughout the Virgin Islands for yachts, US$5 per day for service, US$4 per minute; there is also a prepaid cellular service, *CCT Flexphone*, T4943825. To call VHF stations from a land phone, call Tortola Radio, T116. *Caribbean Connections* at *Village Cay Marina*, T4943623, has phone, fax, email, courier service. Moorings allows use of phone for collecting email. *Village Cay Marina* has a computer room. *Jolly Roger* has fax and email services.

Telephone
IDD phone code: 284

Newspapers *The Island Sun* is published on Friday, while the *BVI Beacon* comes out on Thursday. *The Limin' Times*, printed weekly, is a free magazine giving entertainment news: nightlife, sports, music etc. **Radio** *Radio ZBVI* broadcasts on 780AM. Weather reports for sailors are broadcast hourly from 0730 to 1830 every day. There are four FM stations: *Reggae* at 97.3, *Country* at 94.3, *Z Gold* at 91.7 and *ZROD* at 103.7.

Media

Food and drink

Most things are imported and will cost at least the same as in Florida. Try local produce which is cheaper, yams and sweet potatoes rather than potatoes, for example. Fish dishes are often excellent, try snapper, dolphin (fish, not the mammal), grouper, tuna and swordfish, and don't miss the lobster. Once the centre of rum production for the Royal Navy 'Pussers' (Pursers), rum is still available from *Pusser's* or supermarkets. Local rums of varying quality are also sold by hotels and restaurants.

There are lots of good restaurants across the islands

Shopping

There are gift shops and boutiques in Road Town, Tortola and in Spanish Town, Virgin Gorda. The BVI Philatelic Bureau or Post Offices sell stamps for collectors. You can also buy BVI coins, but they are not used as a currency. *Samarkand*, on Main Street, Tortola, sells gold and silver jewellery created by the local Bibby family with nautical themes; you can buy earings of yachts, pelicans, etc and they will make anything to order, samarkand@caribwave.com, also a branch at Soper's Hole Wharf, West End: *Caribbean Jewellers*. *Sunny Caribbee Herb and*

The BVI are not duty-free

British Virgin Islands

Spice Co (PO Box 286), is on Main Street with *Sunny Caribbee Gallery* next door, also at *Skyworld Restaurant* and *Long Bay Hotel*, selling spices, herbs, preserves and handicrafts, mail order and shipping services available. **Pusser's Co Store** in Road Town and West End, Tortola, and Leverick Bay, Virgin Gorda, sells nautical clothing, luggage and accessories as well as Pusser's Rum. **Turtle Dove Boutique**, in Road Town, has a good selection of gifts and home furnishings and is the only place selling a reasonable selection of books (other than romances and thrillers stocked by hotels). **Caribbean Handprints**, Main Street, has a silkscreen studio and shop with local designs and clothing made on site. An open air market close to the Tourist Office offers a selection of T-shirts and other souvenirs.

Diving and marine life

There is much to see around the Virgin Islands and considerable work is being done to establish marine parks and conserve the reefs. The Department of Conservation and Fisheries is in charge of the BVI's natural resources and a fisheries management plan aims to avoid over-fishing and help conserve the reefs. The 17½ km **Horseshoe Reef** off the south shore of Anegada is one of the largest reefs in the world and now a Protected Area, with an anchor and fishing ban in force. There are 80 visible wrecks around Anegada and many more covered by coral; about 300 ships are believed to have foundered on the reef.

Humpback whales migrate to the islands every year and the Department of Conservation and Fisheries is trying to estimate their numbers with the aim of designating the BVI waters as a marine mammal sanctuary. If you see any (mostly north of Tortola), let them know. Similarly, turtles are being counted with the help of volunteers in order to draw up environmental legislation to protect them. Leatherback turtles travel to north shore beaches to nest, but their numbers have been declining fast. Hawksbill and green turtles are more common but still endangered. For several months of the year the killing of turtles or taking their eggs is prohibited and the export of turtle products is illegal. If you see turtle on the menu, or a turtle shell product, please do not buy it. Despite the government's conservation policies, approval was granted for a captive dolphin programme, which started in 2001. Dolphins caught in the wild are now in the lagoon at Prospect Reef where tourists can swim with them. This controversial business is run by the same company as the new dolphinarium in Anguilla and the proposed one in Antigua.

There are over 60 charted dive sites, many of which are in underwater national parks. They include walls, pinnacles, coral reefs, caverns and wrecks. The most visited wreck is that of the *Rhone*, sunk in 1867 in a storm and broken in two. The bow section is in about 80 ft of water and you can swim through the hull. The stern is shallower and you can see the prop shaft and the propeller (and an octopus). Another wreck is the 246-ft *Chikuzen* sunk in 1981 about six miles north of Tortola, where you will see bigger fish such as barracuda and rays. Most Caribbean and Atlantic species of tropical fish and marine invertebrates can be found in BVI waters, with hard and soft corals, gorgonians and sea fans. Watch out for fire coral, sea urchins and the occasional bristle worm. Visibility ranges from 60-200 ft and the water temperature varies from 76°F in winter to 86°F in summer.

A moorings system has been set up to eliminate anchor damage to the coral and all users of the moorings must have a national parks permit. These are available through dive operators, charter companies, government offices and the National Parks Trust, T4943904. The revenue goes towards maintenance and new moorings. As yet, there is no legislation to prohibit anchoring in areas other than in the marine parks, but it is actively discouraged. National Parks Trust moorings (of which there are currently 180 with another 70 planned) are located at The Caves, The Indians, The Baths, Pelican Island, Carrot Shoal, dive sites at Peter Island, Cooper Island, Ginger Island and Norman Island, the *Rhone's* anchor, the wreck of the *Rhone*, the wreck of the *Fearless*, Deadchest Island, Blonde Rock, Guana Island, The Dogs and other popular diving and recreational sites.

Dive centres There are several dive shops around the islands which offer individual tours, package deals with hotels or rendezvous with charter boats. Rates depend on the distance to the dive site but are generally US$80-90 for two tanks, including equipment hire. A day's resort course and shallow dive costs aboutUS$95. **Baskin in the Sun**, established in 1969 and a PADI five-star dive centre, is at Prospect Reef, Peter Island and Soper's Hole. Packages can be arranged with all the major hotels and in fact they are often full with package business so book individual diving in good time. They win awards for excellence and readership surveys, T4942858, 800-6502084, F4944304, www.dive-baskin.com **Dive BVI**, another PADI five-star operation (also NAUI courses) is at Virgin Gorda Yacht Harbour, Leverick Bay and Marina Cay, Box 1040, Virgin Gorda, T4955513, 800-8487078, F4955347, www.divebvi.com **Blue Water Divers** has been at Nanny Cay since 1980 and is also at Hodges Creek Marina/Maya Cove, Box 846, Road Town, T4942847, F4940198, bwdbvi@surfbvi.com **Kilbride's Sunchaser Scuba** is at the *Bitter End Yacht Club*, North Sound, Box 46, Virgin Gorda, T4959638, 800-9324286, F4957549. **Underwater Safaris**, a PADI five-star, NAUI and SSI facility, is at *The Moorings*, Road Town (PO Box 139, T4943965, 800-5377032, F4945322), and has a small shop on Cooper Island which is used as a surface interval between dives in the area, for example the *Rhone*. Air refills are available here. *Underwater Safaris* (and most other companies) will take you anywhere you want to dive, even if there is only one passenger on the boat, and each dive tour location is determined by the first people to book, although they normally only go to sites within 30 minutes of Road Town. If you want your own dive boat for the day with your own instructor, contact **Underwater Boat Services**, T4940024, F4940623, www.scubabvi.com, VHF 16, minimum fee per boat US$250 or US$90 per person. Diving and watersports cruises can be booked with *Promenade Cruises* at *Village Cay Marina*, T4946020, F4960999, www.yacht promenade.com They take a maximum of 10 guests on a 65-ft trimaran with five crew including two dive instructors, with windsurfers, waterskiing and tubing for when you are not underwater. Another trimaran is the 105-ft *Cuan Law*, the world's largest, which has 10 state rooms, seven crew including dive instructors, kayaks, waterskis, hobie cats and underwater photography, T4942490, F4945774, www.diveguideint.com/cuanlaw Underwater photography, camera rental, and film processing is offered by **Rainbow Visions Photo Center**, Prospect Reef, Box 680, Road Town, T4942749. They often join dive boats and take video film of you underwater. Great fun and excellent quality but expensive.

Beaches and watersports

There are lovely sandy beaches on all the islands and many of them are remote, empty and accessible only from the sea. The clean, crystal-clear waters around the islands provide excellent snorkelling, diving, cruising and fishing. Most of the hotels offer a wide variety of watersports, including windsurfing, sunfish, scuba, snorkelling and small boats. *Jet skis are banned*

'Bareboating' (self-crew yacht chartering) is extremely popular and the way most visitors see the islands. The BVI are one of the most popular destinations in the world for bareboaters. If you do not feel confident in handling a yacht, there are various options from fully-crewed luxury yachts to hiring a skipper to take you and your bareboat out for as long as you need. You can also rent a cabin on a private charter yacht, several charter companies find this a useful way of filling a boat. Navigation is not difficult, the water and weather are generally clear and there are many excellent cruising guides and charts for reference. Most of the islands offer at least one beautiful bay and it is possible even at the height of the season to find deserted beaches and calm anchorages. Bareboaters are not supposed to sail to Anegada because of the hazardous, unmarked route through the reef and generally only crewed yachts go there. The exception is the fleet of Moorings, which organizes a special flotilla once a week from the *Bitter End Resort & Yacht Club* for its clients. If you are sailing independently, however, check the charts, ensure you approach in clear daylight when the sun is high, or call the *Anegada Reef Hotel* at Setting Point when you are within sight and they will direct you over the radio. Charter companies are too numerous to list here, there are many on Tortola and several more on Virgin Gorda. Contact the tourist office for a list of bareboats with prices. *Sunsail*, the largest charter in the Caribbean, moved in 2000 from Soper's Hole, West End, to a bigger facility at Maya Cove, half way between Road Town and Beef Island Airport, where it has some 150 yachts, restaurants, shops and provisioning. For crewed yachts, try **The Moorings**, T4942332, F4942226; **Yacht Connections**, T4945273, **Sailing**

F4944250, www.yacht-connections.com; *Sail Vacations* (operates the 72-ft luxury ketch *Endless Summer II*), T4943656, 800-3689905, F4944731, www.EndlessSummer.com; *Regency Yacht Vacations*, at the Inner Harbour Marina, Wickham's Cay I, T4951970, F4951415, www.regencyvacations.com (luxury 45-200 ft yachts for 2-20 people, gourmet cuisine, watersports); *BVI Yacht Charters*, T4944289, F4946552; *Catamaran Charters*, T4946661; *Wanderlust Yacht Vacations*, T/F4942405, www.wanderlustcharters.com, and several others, will be able to match your needs with the hundreds of charter yachts available. Marinas are plentiful with yard services, haul out, fuel docks, water and showers. You can even tour the islands on a hobie cat: the *Stickl Sportcamp* organizes special sailing trips around the BVI, called 'Island Hopping on Hobiecats', where you sail during the day in a group and stay overnight on different islands, www.stickl.com

Sailing and boardsailing schools offer three-hour to one week courses. The *Nick Trotter Sailing School* at the *Bitter End Resort & Yacht Club*, North Sound, T4942745, F4944756, has sailing and windsurfing courses for all ages with a wide variety of craft, very popular, principally for guests because of its isolated location. *Offshore Sailing School Ltd*, at *Prospect Reef*, T800-2214326, www.offshore-sailing.com, has courses on live-aboard cruising as well as learn-to-sail on dinghies. *Full Sail Sailing School* offers day sail and liveaboard courses with ASA certification at Seabreeze Marina, East End, T4940512, F4940588, fullsail@surfbvi.com For private instruction with ASA certification, call Linda Hall, Tortola Marine Management Bareboat Vacations, T800-6330155.

The annual spring Regatta is held in Sir Francis Drake's Channel, considered one of the best sailing venues in the world. It is one third of the Caribbean Ocean Racing Triangle (CORT) series of regattas, with the exact date each year revolving around the St Thomas Rolex Cup which is held over Easter. The Regatta may be held before or after Easter depending on whether Easter is early or late, www.bvispringregatta.org International yachtsmen and women compete alongside local islanders from Puerto Rico, the USVI and BVI as crew or hiring their own bareboats. The Regatta Village (and parties) is at the *Moorings Marina*, with several local restaurants serving low-priced meals. Contact the *Royal BVI Yacht Club*, T4943286, bviyc@surfbvi.com Ask for regatta discounts on rooms or slips. March 1988 was the first annual Dark and Stormy Race from Tortola to Anegada, started to celebrate the 25th anniversary that year of *Neptune's Treasure* restaurant run by Vernon Soares and family. Fireworks, dancing, food, drink and entertainment greet sailors on arrival in Anegada, where they take a day off before racing back to the West End Yacht Club (sponsored by the *Royal BVI Yacht Club*, T4943286 for information). The Annual Anegada Yacht Race is in August, with a route from Road Town to Anegada, and in November *Pusser's* sponsor a round-Tortola race. There are races of one sort or another going on all year round, check *The BVI Welcome*, or www.bviwelcome.com, for what is coming up, or contact the *Royal BVI Yacht Club*.

A cruising permit is required by everyone cruising in the BVI: 1 December-30 April, all recorded charter boats US$2 per person per day, all non-recorded charter boats US$4 per person per day; 1 May-30 November, US$0.75 and US$4 respectively. All privately-owned yachts cruising in the BVI are charged nominal cruising fees. Dive boats, sport fishing boats etc should contact the Customs Department for cruising permit regulations. Permits are required if you want to use any National Parks Trust moorings, call The Trust office at T4943904.

Several companies offer snorkelling tours and there are lots of yachts offering day-sails to all the little islands at around US$70-90 with snorkelling, beverages and sometimes lunch, but avoid them when the cruise ships are in town as they are often packed out. An interesting addition to day sail craft is the *Gli Gli* Carib canoe, which has been brought to the BVI following its original journey in 1997 from Dominica to Guyana as part of a celebration of Carib culture. Reservations with Aragorn Dick-Read, T4951849, dreadeye@surfbvi.com, tours include a BBC video of the canoe's construction, US$65 for a full day sail including traditional Carib lunch. All day sail boats should carry the symbol of the Daycharter Association of the British Virgin Islands (a circular badge with the name of the association surrounding an anchor and the flag) to prove they are properly licensed and have had safety checks.

Windsurfing is popular in the islands and there is an annual Bacardi Hi-Ho (hook in and hold **Windsurfing**
on) race which attracts windsurfers from all over the world, www.hiho-bvi.com The week
long event involves inter-island racing with accommodation on sailing yachts and lots of
watersports, fun and parties. *Boardsailing BVI* is at Trellis Bay, Beef Island, T4952447,
F4951626, and at Nanny Cay (a BiC Centre), T4940422, www.windsurfing.vi, with schools and
shops. As well as windsurfing they offer kayaks, surf boards and sail dinghies. *Hi Ho* at *Prospect
Reef*, T4948304, F4940003, has sales, rentals and instruction, also with kayaks and surfboards.
Both schools have good equipment for beginners and advanced sailors. *Last Stop Sports*, at
Nanny Cay, T4940564, F4940593, lssbikes@surfbvi.com, has rental windsurfers, single and
double kayaks, surfboards and bodyboards, lessons available. Many of the larger hotels have
watersports equipment for their guests.

Sport fishing is becoming more popular with many companies offering day trips aboard **Fishing**
sport fishing boats: *Anegada Reef Hotel*, Anegada, US$500-900, T4958002, F4959362, offers
sport fishing on a 46-ft Hatteras, inshore and bonefishing and has a tackle shop; *Pelican
Charters*, Prospect Reef, T4967386, has a 46-ft Chris craft sportfisherman, US$600-950 for
sportfishing, US$1,200 for marlin, full facilities. *Persistent Charters,* West End, T4954122,
charge US$350 half day, US$650 full day on a 31-ft Tiara, everything included. A local permit is
required for fishing, call the Fisheries Division for information, T4945682; spearfishing is not
allowed, hunting on land is also banned and no firearms are allowed. There are areas known
to house ciguatera (fish poisoning) around the reefs, so it is important to contact the Fisheries
Division before fishing of any kind is undertaken.

There is a **tennis** club on Tortola and many hotels have their own courts. **Golf** has not been **Other sports**
developed although a couple of the hotels have small practice courses. **Horse riding** can be
arranged through the hotels, or T4942262, Shadow's Stables, or T4940704, Ellis Thomas, for
riding through Mount Sage National Park or down to Cane Garden Bay, Tortola. Alex Parillon
has horses on Virgin Gorda. **Walking** and **birdwatching** are quite popular and trails have
been laid out in some places. Sage Mountain on Tortola and Gorda Peak on Virgin Gorda are
popular hikes. Spectator sports include cricket and soft ball. **Gyms** include *Bodyworks*,
T4942705, and *Cutting Edge,* T4959570. *Prospect Reef* has a healthclub called *Healthy
Prospects* where you can do aerobics (called *Body Images*, T4944713), yoga, tennis and
nine-hole pitch and putt, T4943311 ext 245.

Holidays and festivals

New Year's Day, Commonwealth Day (2nd Monday in March), Good Friday, Easter Monday, **Public**
Whit Monday in May, Queen's Birthday (2nd Monday in June), Territory Day (1 July), Festival **holidays**
beginning of August, St Ursula's Day (21 October), Prince Charles' Birthday (14 November),
Christmas Day, Boxing Day.

The **BVI Summer Festival** is held over two weeks at the end of *July* and beginning of *August*. **Festivals**
There is entertainment every night with steel bands, fungi and calypso music, a Prince and
Princess show and a calypso show. During the year there are many regattas, such as the
annual **BVI Spring Regatta** in *April*, **Foxy's Wooden Boat Regatta** in *September* and
windsurfing events, which attract many extracurricular activities and lots of parties.

Health

Peebles Hospital is a public hospital with X-ray and surgical facilities. Private X-ray and
laboratory facilities are offered by B&F Medical Complex and Medicure Ltd. There are 12
doctors on Tortola and one on Virgin Gorda, two dentists and a small private hospital, the
Bougainvillea Clinic which specializes in plastic surgery. Be careful in the sun, always use a
sunscreen.

British Virgin Islands

Tortola

Population: 16,000
Colour map 3, grid B6

Tortola, the main island, is where 81% of the total population live. Mount Sage, the highest point in the archipelago, rises to 1,780 ft, and traces of a primeval rain forest can still be found on its slopes. Walking trails have been marked through Mount Sage National Park. The south part of the island is mountainous and rocky, covered with scrub, frangipani and ginger thomas. The north has groves of bananas, mangoes and palm trees, and long sandy beaches.

Road Town

On the south shore, is the capital and business centre of the territory, dominated by marinas and financial companies, many of which line the harbour. Main Street houses many of the oldest buildings, churches and the colonial prison (replaced by a modern prison in 1997 for 120 inmates), and is the most picturesque street. Until the 1960s, Main Street was the waterfront road, but land infill has allowed another road, Waterfront Drive, to be built between it and the sea. A dual carriageway runs from Port Purcell to Fort Burt. Cruise ships call frequently at a dock in the Wickhams Cay area. There are many gift shops, hotels and restaurants catering for the tourist market. Very grand and imposing government offices have been built on the waterfront overlooking the harbour entrance. Banks, offices, Cable and Wireless, the tourist office and a small craft village are also in this area. All these buildings are built on infilled land, called Wickhams Cay; the restaurant *Spaghetti Junction* was once a bar overlooking the water but is now some way back, divided from the sea by roads and office buildings.

Tortola

The Governor resides in **Government House** above Waterfront Drive overlooking the harbour (T4942345). The house is in a classical style, painted white with green shutters and surrounded by beautifully tended gardens with a fine display of flamboyant trees in the front.

The four acre **Joseph Reynold O'Neal Botanic Gardens** near the Police Station in Road Town (free admission, donations welcomed) has a good selection of tropical and subtropical plants such as palm trees, succulents, ferns and orchids. There is a good booklet which gives a suggested route round the garden, pond, orchid house, fern house and medicinal herb garden. It is a peaceful place, luxuriant, with magnificent pergolas, recommended. The small **BVI Folk Museum** in a lovely old wooden building on Main Street behind *Pusser's Bar* is opened on request.

Around the island

There are also communities at East End and West End. **West End** has more facilities for visitors. *Sopers Hole* is a port of entry (ferries to St Thomas, St John and Jost Van Dyke leave from here) and popular meeting place for people on yachts. *Pussers* is alongside the moorings and there are several shops, including a dive shop and some boutiques. All the buildings are painted in bright pinks and blues. It is very relaxing to sip cocktails on the dock and watch the yachts come and go. The *Jolly Roger*, on the opposite side of the bay is a popular yachtie hangout. The area is famous for being the former home of Edward Teach (Blackbeard the pirate).

The best beaches are along the northwest and north coasts. **Smugglers Cove**, **Long Bay** and **Apple Bay**, West End, have fine sandy beaches. If you have no transport, Smugglers Cove is an hour's walk on a dirt road over a steep hill from West End. The beach is usually deserted. **Cane Garden Bay** is the best beach and yachts

Sir Francis Drake Channel

British Virgin Islands

■ Sleeping		● Eating
1 Cane Garden Bay & Callwood Distillery	5 Long Bay	1 Skyworld
2 Fort Recovery Estates	6 Prospect Reef Resort	▲ Other
3 Frenchman's Cay	7 Rudy's Mariner Inn	1 Bellamy Cay & Trellis Bay
4 Josiah's Bay Inn	8 Sandcastle	2 Marina Cay
	9 Sugar Mill	

can anchor there. There are two reefs with a marked gap in between. The Callwood Rum Distillery at Cane Garden Bay still produces rum with copper boiling vats and an old still and cane crusher in much the same way as it did in the 18th century. Apple Bay is popular with surfers from November for a few months, as is the east end of Cane Garden Bay and **Josiah's Bay**. **Brewers Bay** is a long curving bay with plenty of shade and a small campsite in the trees by the beach. Elizabeth Bay and Long Bay, East End, are also pleasant beaches. **Carrot Bay** is stony, there is no sand, but there are lots of pelicans and the village is pleasant, having a very Caribbean feel with several bars, palm trees and banana plants. Watch out for strong rip currents at some of the north shore beaches, and seek local advice before swimming, especially if the surfers are out.

Road Town

N

0 metres 200
0 yards 200

■ **Sleeping**
1 A & L Inn
2 Castle Maria
3 Fort Burt
4 Maria's by the Sea
5 Moorings - Mariner Inn
6 Treasure Isle
7 Village Cay

Tortola is superb, but the full flavour of the BVI can only be discovered by cruising round the other islands. You can also take day trips on the regular ferry to Virgin Gorda, with lunch and a visit to The Baths included if you wish.

Essentials

Road Town LL-AL *Treasure Isle*, on hillside overlooking the marina and Sir Francis Drake Channel, PO Box 68, T4942501, F4942507. 40 rooms and 3 suites, pool, tennis, restaurant, a/c, TV, convenient for business travellers, used by people on crewed yacht charters for first and last night, helpful staff at front desk. Under same ownership and used by *Treasure Isle* for all watersports is the **LL-A** *Moorings/Mariner Inn*, at the dockside for bareboat charters, PO Box 139, T4942332, F4942226. 36 standard rooms with kitchenette, 4 suites, fan, tennis, small pool by bar, briefing room for those setting out on yachts, informal and relaxed but well organized, *Underwater Safaris* dive shop on site. **L-AL** *Village Cay Resort and Marina*, PO Box 145, directly opposite on the other side of the harbour, T4942771, F4942773, www.villagecay.com. 18 clean, bright rooms, well-furnished although a bit sterile, TV, phone, cheaper rooms face inland, restaurant and bar overlooking yachts, good food, buffet with entertainment Fri 1800-2300, also showers, toilets and launderette for sailors. **LL-A** *Maria's By The Sea*, PO Box 206, T4942595, F4942420. By new government buildings, overlooks sea but no beach, older part is simple, all have kitchenette, a/c, TV, phone, double beds, new wing has bigger rooms, balconies, conference room, friendly, Maria's cooking recommended, specials include lobster, conch, steak, light and airy entrance with bar, pool. **L-C** *Sea View Hotel*, PO Box 59, T4942483, F4944952, jumukhal@surfbvi.com 22 rooms, 1 efficiency apartment, pool, quite noisy because of traffic but good value, 200 m further on is **LL-AL** *Fort Burt*, on hillside opposite Marina, PO Box 3380, T4942587, F4942002, fortburt@surfbvi.com Fort built by Dutch, first hotel on island built 1953, now part of the *Pussers* chain, 12 rooms, 6 suites, 2 of which have plunge pool, all have phone, fax and PC data ports, restaurant and bar, convenient location, good views. **AL-B** *Hotel Castle Maria*, up the hill overlooking Road Town, PO Box 206, T4942553, F4942111, hotelcastlemaria@surfbvi.com 30 rooms, some triple and quads, kitchenette, a/c, cable TV, pool, restaurant, bar, car rentals, popular with local business travellers. **B** *A & L Inn*, 3 Fleming St, PO Box 403, T4946343, F4946656. 14 rooms with 2 double beds, a/c, TV, phone, café. About the cheapest on the island is **C-D** *Wayside Inn Guest House*, Road Town, near library, PO Box 258, T4943606. 20 rooms, with fan, adequate but basic, shared bathrooms but not very clean.

South coast Heading west from Road Town you come to **LL-A** *Prospect Reef Resort*, PO Box 104, T4943311, F4945595, www.prospectreef.com A 15-acre resort specializing in package holidays, wide variety of rooms, studios, town houses and villas, some with sea view, some without, comfortable, welcoming, tennis, pitch and put, sea water pool, freshwater swimming lane pool, diving pool, health and fitness centre, *Baskin in the Sun* dive shop, marina, sailing, fishing, café and restaurant, conference centre for 150, car rental, complimentary sports equipment, boutiques, shuttle service. **LL-B** *Nanny Cay Resort and Marina*, PO Box 281, T4942512, F4943288. 42 rooms, a/c, TV, VCRs, kitchenette, phone, deluxe rooms have 2 queen-size beds, standard rooms are darker, smaller, restaurants, bars, boutiques, tennis, *Blue Water Divers* dive shop, car rental, windsurfing and sailing, used by short stay people going out on bareboat charters. **LL-L** *Villas at Fort Recovery Estate*, PO Box 239, T4954354, F4954036, www.fortrecovery.com 17 spacious and nicely furnished a/c villas of different sizes on small beach. Breakfast included, built around 17th-century Dutch fort, commissary, no restaurant, but à la carte room service available including complimentary dinner and snorkel trip for stays of over 7 nights, yoga, massage, good snorkelling offshore, pool, car essential. **LL-AL** *Frenchman's Cay Hotel*, PO Box 1054, West End, T4954844, F4954056, www.frenchmans.com Beautiful hillside location on the cay overlooking the south coast of Tortola, 9 villas, all with view, fans, phone, a quiet resort with lots of repeat business, small sandy beach with reef for snorkelling, hammocks, tennis (fee for non-guests), pool, library, games, short trail out to point, Sun beach barbecue, bar, restaurant, TV in clubhouse. **A-C** *Jolly Roger Inn*, T4954559, F4954184, www.jollyrogerbvi.com A small inn and

Sleeping (margin)

British Virgin Islands (margin)

bar on waterfront at Sopers Hole. Run by New Yorkers, live music at weekends so do not stay here if you want peace and quiet, convenient for ferries (see above), 6 brightly decorated, clean rooms, some with shared bathroom, fans, screens, singles, doubles, triples available, good breakfasts, busy restaurant and bar, meeting place, overnight mooring US$15/night for boats up to 60 ft, fax, email and ice services. *Little Thatch*, PO Box 8309, St John, USVI 00831, T4959227, F4959212, thatch@surfbvi.com A 54-acre private island off West End and Soper's Hole. Main house sleeps 10 and 5 cottages, pool, beach bar, watersports, volleyball, table tennis, badminton, US$9,250-10,550 all-inclusive island rental, 3 nights minimum.

Along this stretch of coast there are lots of rental villas, many of which are advertised simply with a notice outside, usually about US$100 per day

West coast Heading northeast, **LL-B** *Long Bay Beach Resort*, PO Box 433, T4954252, www.longbay.com 80rooms, studios and villas spread along the beach and up the hillside, a/c, TV, phone, fridge, 130-ft pool, the biggest in the BVI, tennis, pitch and put, spa and gym, car rental, 2 restaurants with vegetarian options, bars, surfboards, snorkelling equipment, nice beach, sandy with some rocks, level of sand can shift depending on season. **LL-B** *Sebastian's On The Beach*, PO Box 441, Apple Bay, T4954212, F4954466, www.sebastiansbvi.com Located either side of road, informal and popular surfers' hangout, 8 comfortable beachfront rooms with balcony, 4 rear rooms which connect, 12 more rooms across the road at rear of office around patio, 2 rooms above office, 10% service, fans, fridge, payphones, grocery 0800-2200, restaurant/bar overlooking sandy beach, happy hour 1600-1800, blend own rum, surfboards and boogieboards for rent. Expanded in 2000 with the construction of *Seaside Villas*, 9 luxury 2-bedroomed suites with huge balconies and views to Jost Van Dyke, fully equipped and every comfort. **LL-AL** *Sugar Mill Hotel*, PO Box 425, Little Apple Bay, T4954355, F4954696, www.sugarmillhotel.com 21 rooms, most with kitchenettes, prestigious restaurant, beach bar, pool, no children in season. **B-C** *Cane Garden Bay (Rhymer's) Beach Hotel*, Cane Garden Bay, PO Box 570, T4954639, F4954820. 27 basic but clean rooms, most with double bed and single bed, right on sandy beach, beach towels provided, store and shop, laundromat, restaurant/bar on beach, watersports companies on either side of hotel. **LL-B** *Ole Works Inn*, Cane Garden Bay, T4954837, F4959618, oleworks@candwbvi.net Built around 300-year-old sugar factory, on beach, 18 rooms, honeymoon tower, bar, restaurant, gift shop. **AL-B** *Sunset Vacation Apartments*, T4954751, F4959114. 8 1-bedroom and 2 2-bedroom apartments, close to beach, maid service. **AL-A** *ELM Beach Suites*, PO Box 96, T4942888, F4946455, elm@surfbvi.com 5 1-bedroom apartments, on the beach, beach bar serves lunch, cable TV, gift shop.

North coast **LL-B** *Lambert Beach Resort*, PO Box 534, East End, T4952877, F4952876, lambert@caribsurf.com On a beautiful cove, 38 rooms and suites in villas which can sleep 8, beach-front dining, pool, tennis, watersports, boat trips, diving and other excursions can be arranged, library, videos, Italian-owned, Italian décor. **LL** *Elizabeth Beach Resort*, now managed by *Lambert Beach Resort*. 2 and 3-bedroom villas, jeep included, on hillside with spectacular views from huge verandas across bay and down to sandy beach below. **LL** *Elizabeth Beach Villa*, Box 46, Virgin Gorda, T4959458, F4957034, trotter@surfbvi.com Run by Nick and Jenny Trotter, great view, huge doors onto 200 sq ft veranda with covered eating area, 3 bedrooms, a/c, beach, use of nearby resort's facilities. **A-B** *Josiah's Bay Inn*, PO Box 925, Josiah's Bay, T/F4951488, jbibvi@yahoo.com Short walk to beach, 1-4 bedroom apartments, kitchens, TV, balconies with sea view, weekly rates, maid service twice a week, popular with surfers, take insect repellent, close to 4 beaches. **LL-AL** *Josiah's Bay Cottages*, run by Best Vacations, Box 306, Road Town, T4946186, F4942000, bestvac @surfbvi.com 9 1-bedroom cottages in garden, 5-min walk to beach, pool.

East End **A-C** *Seabreeze Yacht Charters & Hotel*, PO Box 528, East End, T4951560, F4951561. 8 rooms for sailors, marina, yacht charters, pool, commissary. **LL-A** *Tropic Island Villas*, PO Box 3012, Road Town, Maya Cove, T4952002, F4952155, www.tropicisland.com Studios and 2 bedroom apartments.

Camping At *Brewer's Bay Campground* on north coast, PO Box 185, T4943463. Bare site US$10, tent hire US$35 for 2 people, babysitters available, beach bar and simple restaurant.

Self catering There is lots of self-catering accommodation in what are variously known as houses, villas, apartments, guest houses, 'efficiencies' or 'housekeeping units'. Prices are usually set on a weekly basis according to size and standard of luxury, and there is often a 30-40% discount in the summer. Contact the tourist office for a full list and individual brochures. Many are also listed on www.bviwelcome.com

Road Town Restaurants serving West Indian specialities include *C & F Restaurant*, Purcell **Eating** Estate, T4944941. Very popular with visitors and locals, excellent local food, slow but friendly service, dinner 1830-2300. *Mario's*, Palm Grove Shopping Centre, T4943883. West Indian specialities, clean, a/c, good service, generous portions, open daily 0700-2300, happy hour 1700-1900. *Happy Lion*, next to Botanic Gardens, T4942574. Mon-Sat from 0700, noted for fresh fish and local dishes, also apartments to rent. *Beach Club Terrace*, at Baughers Bay, T4942272. Open 0800-2200, fish, mutton, conch and other West Indian food. *Aries Club*, Baughers Bay, T4941537. 0700-2200, Mon-Sat, West Indian, seafood specialities. *Roti Palace*, Russel Hill, T4944196. East Indian specialities from Trinidad and Guyana, huge rotis. *The Fish Trap*, at the Columbus Centre, behind Village Cay Marina, T4943626. Open for lunch 1130-1500 Mon-Fri, 1130-1400 Sat and dinner daily 1830-2300, open-air, reservations recommended, good seafood, inside is a popular yachtie bar open 1630-late serving good lower-priced bar meals. *The Captain's Table*, on the waterfront by Village Cay Marina, T4946407. A French restaurant serving escargots, lobster, fish, lunch Mon-Fri, dinner daily from 1800. *Pusser's Co Store & Pub* on Main St, Road Town, T4942467. Yachties' meeting place, good pub atmosphere, open 1100-2200, on ground floor bar, store and restaurant for simple dishes such as English pies and New York deli sandwiches, nickel beer on Thu, really is US$0.05 but not recommended, Tue 'ladies night', 'pain killer' cocktails recommended, strongest is 'brain killer', *Pusser's* also at Sopers Hole, Marina Cay and Leverick Bay. Visit 3 and get *Pusser's* banner. *Tavern in the Town*, Road Town, next to *Pusser's*, T4942790. Traditional English pub food and atmosphere, sells Newcastle Brown Ale, garden looks out across harbour, open 1100-2300, closed Sat. *Mac's*, in the Clarence M Christian Building, T4946364. Local dishes, salads, pizza and pastries, open 0700-2000. *Midtown Restaurant*, Main St, T4942764. Curried conch, baked chicken, beef, whelk, saltfish, Mon-Sat 0700-2300. *Mr Fritz Oriental Restaurant*, in the Little Denmark building, T4945592. Classic Chinese dishes, lunch 1130-1530, dinner 1730 onwards. *Capriccio di Mare*, Waterfront Drive by ferry dock, overlooking water, T4945369. Italian café serving excellent coffee and delicious, if overpriced, snacks and continental lunches, open 0800-2100, Mon-Sat. *Spaghetti Junction*, Waterfront Drive opposite Palm Grove shopping centre upstairs in small blue building, T4944880. Italian, seafood and Caribbean dishes, open 1800-2200. *Café Sito*, in Romasco building, T4947413. West Indian and international food, daily specials, 1100-2300. *BVI Steak, Chop and Pasta House*, in *Hotel Castle Maria*, T4945433. Overlooking harbour, good food, congenial hosts Tom and Fran, open daily 0730-1000, 1130-1400, 1800-2200. *Virgin Queen*, Road Town, T4942310. Homemade pizza plus West Indian and European food, a popular watering hole for English and American residents, open 1100-2400, Sun-Fri, last orders for food 2200, 1800 until late on Sat. *Crandall's Pastry Plus*, T4945156. West Indian bakery across from Road Reef Marina, also rotis and main meals, 0800-1700. *Scato's Snack Bar*, T4942230. Above Sylvia's laundromat on Flemming Street, open daily 1200-2200, local dishes.

Nanny Cay *The Struggling Man*, Sea Cows Bay, between Road Town and Nanny Cay, T4944163. West Indian, breakfast, lunch and dinner. *Marina Plaza Café*, Nanny Cay Marina, T4944895. 0700-2100, Caribbean specials and international dishes. *Peg Leg Landing*, water's edge at Nanny Cay. Open from 1600, happy hour 1630-1830, bar meals from 1630, dinners from 1900.

West End *Pusser's Landing*, T4954554 and *Jolly Roger*, T4954559, fun, yachtie hangout, good pizza and burgers, good cheap breakfast, dinner US$7-15, open 0700-2300, and many more excellent restaurants in the hotels and yacht clubs. *Frenchman's Cay Hotel*, T4954844. Breakfast 0800-1030, lunch 1130-1430, dinner 1830-2100, closed Mon, West Indian and continental cuisine, pool and tennis court available for diners.

British Virgin Islands

Apple Bay *The Sugar Mill*, in an old mill in Apple Bay, T4954355, run by Californians, Jinx and Jefferson Morgan. Gourmet and elegant, 4-course dinner 1900, reservations, their cookbook is on-line, with some 250 recipes, hotel attached, breakfast and lunch at beach bar. *The Apple*, Little Apple Bay, T4954437. Specializes in local seafood dishes, happy hour 1700-1900 with coconut chips and conch fritters. *Sebastian's On The Beach*, T4954212. Breakfast, lunch, dinner, international, happy hour 1600-1800.

Carrot Bay *Mrs Scatliffe's*, T4954556. Upstairs in a yellow and white building opposite the Primary School, local cuisine, home grown fruit and vegetables, family fungi performance some evenings after dinner, lunch Mon-Fri 1200-1400, dinner daily 1900-2100, reservations essential. *Palm's Delight*, on the water, T4954863. Restaurant and snack bar, delicious barbecue and local cuisine, rotis and shrimp creole, open 1800-2200. **North Shore Shell Museum**, T4954714. Cracked conch, lobster, West Indian cooking, breakfast, lunch and dinner, happy hour 1600-1800. *Clem's By The Sea*, T4954350. West Indian specialities, goat stew, boiled fish and fungi, steel band, Mon, Sat, open 0900 until late.

Cane Garden Bay You can 'Jump Up' (Caribbean music), almost every night at *Rhymers*, T4954639. Serves breakfast, lunch and dinner, lobster special Thu night. Folk music and reggae at *Quito's Gazebo*, T4954837. Restaurant and beach bar at north end of Cane Garden Bay, lunch 1130-1500, rotis and burgers, dinner 1830-2130, fish fry Fri, closed Mon, local art work for sale. *Round Hill Catering*, T4959353. Open Mon, Tue, Thu, Fri, Sat, 1830-2130, reservations needed, home cooked local dishes served on balcony. There are a number of small restaurants serving excellent food along the road going towards the rum distillery ruins; check in the late afternoon to make reservations and find out what the menu will be.

Inland 10 mins' drive from Road Town or Cane Garden Bay is the *Skyworld Restaurant*, T4943567. With a panoramic view of all the Virgin Islands, food and prices reasonable, open from 1000, lunch 1130-1430, dinner 1700-1945, recommended for view. *Mario's Mountain View*, at the foot of Sage Mountain National Park, T4959536. Continental and local dishes, lunch 1100-1500, dinner 1830-2200.

East End *Brandywine Bay Restaurant*, run by Cele and Davide Pugliese, T4952301, F4951203, brandywn@surfbvi.com 10 mins' drive from Road Town, one of the most exclusive restaurants on Tortola, indoor and outdoor dining, grills and Florentine food, cocktails 1730, dinner 1830-2100, full meal without wine about US$35-40 per person, closed Sun, reservations, Channel 16, anchorage 15-ft draft. *De Cal*, T4951429, on Blackburn Highway at Fat Hog's Bay. Local style, rotis, pizza, breakfast, lunch, dinner, 0700-2200. *Pelican Roost*, at Tropic Island Yachts overlooking Maya Cove, T4951515. 0800-2200, conch, fritters, fresh fish. *Bing's Drop Inn Bar and Restaurant*, at Fat Hog's Bay, T4952627. Home cooked dinners, excellent conch fritters, also after hours dance spot.

If you are self-catering, you can get reasonably priced food from *K Mart's* and other supermarkets at Port Purcell or at the *Rite Way* supermarkets a little closer to town. At the entrance to the *Moorings*, Wickhams Cay II, is the *Bon Appetit Deli*, T4945199. Where you can get cheese and wine as well as regular provisions; they also do sandwiches and lunch specials and party services. In Road Town is *Fort Wines Gourmet Shop*, T4942388, a wine shop with a high class image but reasonable prices, you can also eat there, excellent light snacks (eg quiche) and wine by the glass.

Nightlife In Road Town, *The Pub*, at Fort Burt Marina, T4942608. Dancing Fri-Sat, they also serve lunches and dinners, happy hour 1700-1900 daily and all day Fri with free hot wings 1700-1900 and music 1800-2200. *Stone's Nest* is a weekend disco in Road Town, T4945182. The hotels organize live bands and movie nights. At East End is *Bing's Drop Inn Bar*, see above. *Pusser's Landing*, at Frenchman's Cay, T4954554. Bands on Fri and Sat. *Jolly Roger*, at West End, T4954559. Live music and Caribbean barbeque Tue, Fri, Sat in season, often has visiting bands. *The Bomba Shack*, on the beach in Apple Bay, T4954148. Music Wed and Sun, famous full moon party every month, sleep before you go, the party goes on all night. *Romeo's*, Apple Bay, T4954307. Thu barbecue and music, Sat fish fry and music. *Quito's Gazebo*, Cane Garden Bay, T4954837. Live music nightly and the beat is quickened at weekends and holidays, making it a popular beach front dance spot. *Calamaya*, Maya Cove, on the dock side at Hodge's Creek Marina, T4952126. Breakfast, lunch, dinner, Fri live music, happy hour with tapas 1600-1800, bar menu. For more classical music, concerts by visiting artistes and chamber orchestras are often held at the H Lavity Stoutt Community College, T4944994. See *The Limin' Times* for what's on.

Laundry *Sylvia's Laundromat*, next to Public Library on Flemming St, Road Town, T4942230. *Freeman's Laundromat*, beside Barclays Bank, Wickham's Cay, T4942285. Marinas usually have laundromats. See telephone listings for out of town laundries.   **Directory**

This island was famed as a hunting ground for beef cattle during the buccaneering   **Beef Island**
days. The island is linked to Tortola by the Queen Elizabeth bridge. The main airport of the BVI is here. (Taxi to Road Town, US$15.) Long Bay beach is on the north shore. Also Trellis Bay which has an excellent harbour and bars. *The Last Resort*, run by Englishman Tony Snell, based on Bellamy Cay, provides a lavish buffet menu plus one-man show cabaret, bar open all day, happy hour 1700-1900, dinner 1930, cabaret 2130, ferry service available, reservations required, T4952520 or channel 16. Also *Boardsailing* BVI, the *Conch Shell Point Restaurant* (T4952285, VHF Ch 16) and a painting and jewellery shop. **LL-A** *Beef Island Guest House* has four rooms on the beach, PO Box 494, East End, T4952303, F4951611, food available at its *De Loose Mongoose Bar*, VHF Ch 16, 0800-1600, 1800-2100, mostly burgers and sandwiches. *Airport Restaurant*, T4952323, West Indian, open from 0730, dinner by reservation.

This tiny private island of six acres just north of Beef Island was where Robb White   **Marina Cay**
wrote his book *Our Virgin Isle*, which was made into a film starring Sidney Poitier and John Cassavetes. A charming cottage hotel, **LL-AL** *Pusser's Marina Cay*, comprises most of the island, which is encircled by a reef, offering some of the best snorkelling in the BVI. Marina facilities (boats use mooring buoys and a dinghy dock), laundry, showers, diving, kayaking, sailing, snorkelling etc, there are four rooms and two villas available, MAP, T4942174, F4944775, marinacy@ surfbvi.com, or VHF ch 16, PO Box 626, Road Town. Bar, restaurant, beach barbecue on Friday, Pussers Co Store, selling clothes and travel accessories. Ferry service from Trellis Bay jetty, eight daily, ferries after 1900 on request for restaurant guests only. If sailing, enter from the north.

North of Tortola, Guana Island is an 850-acre private island and wildlife sanctuary   **Guana Island**
as well as having a very expensive hotel. **LL** *Guana Island*, PO Box 32, Road Town, T4942354, F4952900, www.guana.com 15 rooms in stone cottages, 1 secluded beach house, tennis, restaurant, watersports, US$35 for airport transfers, no credit cards. The island is available for rent for up to 30 guests. The owners discourage visitors apart from guests, in order to keep the island a sanctuary for wildlife. A few flamingos have been introduced to the island. They live in a small pond where the salinity fluctuates widely so their diets are supplemented with food and water if they need it. The birds used to live in a zoo, so they are fairly tame.

Northeast of Tortola are The Dogs, small uninhabited islands. West Dog is a   **The Dogs**
national park. On Great Dog you can see frigate birds nesting. The islands are often used as a stopping off point when sailing from North Sound to Jost Van Dyke, and are popular with divers coming from North Sound. The dive sites are not spectacular but there are some interesting rock formations, with canyons and bridges. The best anchorages are on George Dog to the west of Kitchen Point and on the south side of Great Dog.

British Virgin Islands

Virgin Gorda

Population: 5,000
Colour map 3, grid B6

Over a century ago, Virgin Gorda was the centre of population and commerce. It is now better known as the site of the geological curiosity called The Baths, where enormous boulders form a natural swimming pool and underwater caves. The island is seven miles long and the north half is mountainous, with a peak 1,370 ft high, while the south half is relatively flat.

Around the island

There are some 20 secluded beaches; the most frequented are **Devil's Bay**, **Spring Bay**, and **Trunk Bay** on the west coast. Between Devil's Bay and Spring Bay are **The Baths**. The snorkelling here is good, especially going left from the beach. Climbing over and around the boulders is fun for the adventurous and there is an easy trail with ladders and bridges for those who are not so agile. However, exploring in the water with a mask and snorkel is the best way to do it. Unfortunately the popularity of The Baths with tour companies and cruise ships has led to overcrowding. There are many day trips from Tortola and when a cruise ship is in port you cannot move on the beach. Choose carefully which day you visit. North of the island is **North Sound**, formed to the south and east by Virgin Gorda, to the north by Prickly Pear Island, and to the west by Mosquito Island. On the southeast tip is **Copper Mine Point**, where the Spaniards mined copper, gold and silver some 400 years ago; the remains of a mine built by Cornish miners in 1838 can be seen and work is being done, as funds permit, to stabilize the Engine House and other ruins. The rocky façade here is reminiscent of the Cornish coast of England. The amateur geologist will find stones such as malachite and crystals embedded in quartz. All land on Virgin Gorda over 1,000 ft high is now a national park, where trails have been blazed for walking. Just off the southwest tip of the island is **Fallen Jerusalem**, an islet which is now a National Park. There is a 3,000-ft airstrip near the main settlement, **Spanish Town**. The Virgin Gorda Yacht Harbour is here and besides the marina facilities with full yachting chandlery, there is a good supermarket, dive centre, bar/

Virgin Gorda

■ **Sleeping**
1 Biras Creek Estate
2 Bitter End Yacht Club
3 Drake's Anchorage
4 Fischer's Cove
5 Guavaberry Spring Bay
6 Leverick Bay
7 Little Dix Bay
8 Mango Bay Resort
9 Nail Bay Estate Villas
10 Ocean View
11 Olde Yard Inn
12 Paradise Beach Resort

British Virgin Islands

restaurant, a craft shop selling stamps, souvenir and clothes shops and phones, post box and taxis. **Bitter End** and **Biras Creek** are good anchorages and both have a hotel and restaurant. *Biras Creek* charges US$15 for moorings; yachtsmen may use Deep Bay beach but others are reserved for hotel guests. *Bitter End* charges US$20 including water taxi to shore in the evenings. There is no road to either resort, you have to get a hotel launch from Gun Creek or the North Sound Express from Beef Island to *Bitter End Resort & Yacht Club*. Saba Rock is just off *Bitter End*; formerly the home of the *Pirate's Pub and Grill*, now the *Saba Rock Resort*.

Essentials

South LL *Little Dix Bay*, PO Box 70, Virgin Gorda, T4955555, F4955661, Rosewood@ GTE.net Luxury 98-roomed chalet hotel, with four 1-bedroom suites, on ½-mile beach, watersports arranged, tennis, health and fitness centre, hiking trails in surrounding hills, quiet, lovely gardens in extensive grounds, no TV or pool, strict dress code after sunset, 70% repeat guests in winter, honeymooners in summer, children's programme isolated from rest of resort, lots of packages available, in USA T800-9283000, also owns and operates the airport and the Virgin Gorda Yacht Harbour, a large marina in St Thomas Bay offering most facilities. **LL-C** *Ocean View/The Wheelhouse*, PO Box 66, T4955230. 12 rooms, close to ferry and harbour, pink building, small rooms but adequately furnished, TV, fan, a/c, restaurant, bar. **AL-B** *Bay View Vacation Apartments*, The Valley, Box 1018, T4955224, F4955329. 2-bedroom apartments, kitchen, near town and beach, contact Nora Potter. **LL-AL** *Fischer's Cove Beach Hotel*, St Thomas Bay, PO Box 60, T4955252, F4955820, www.islandsonline.com/fischerscove 12 studio rooms, some with fan, some a/c, or 8 cottages with kitchenette, less space, some beachfront, balcony restaurant overlooking sea open 0730-2200, beach barbecue when calm. **LL-A** *Guavaberry Spring Bay*, run by Tina and Ludwig Goschler, PO Box 20, T4955227, F4955283, www.guavaberryspringbay.com Well-equipped wooden cottages, beautiful location, friendly, sandy beach with shade 5 mins' walk through grounds, to the south are The Baths, to the north The Crawl, a National Park enclosing a natural swimming pool and more boulders. They also manage **LL** *Island Time*, Little Trunk Bay, 5 bedrooms and bathrooms in separate units, tennis, pool, **LL** *On-The-Rocks*, Little Trunk Bay, 2 bedrooms, covered terrace, large garden, beach, **LL** *Las Brisas*, Top of the Baths, 2 bedrooms and **LL** *Casa Rocalta*, Spring Bay, 3 bedrooms. *Toad Hall*, contact Stephen and Marie Green, PO Box 7, T4955397, F4955708, www.toadhallvg.com Luxury rental home, 3 bedrooms with garden showers, private access to The Baths beach along spectacular wooden walkway, pool among the boulders, caves to explore, great for agile children, US$3,500-4,500 per week. **LL-A** *Olde Yard Inn*, owned by Carol Kaufman, PO Box 26, T4955544, 800-6539273, F4955986, oldeyard@ surfbvi.com Convenient for airport, 14 rooms, 1 suite, a/c available, downstairs rooms rather dark, pool, jacuzzi, health spa, poolside restaurant, St Lucian chef, good food, pleasant gardens, library with piano, games room, croquet, hammocks, small shop, complimentary shuttle or 10-15 mins on trail to beach, family-run. There are several villas to rent around The Valley and Spring Bay and a few agencies, eg Virgin Gorda Villa Rentals, Box 63, T800-8487081, 4957421, leverick@surfbvi.com

North Up the west coast, north of the Valley are two resorts which were built as one, so the villas are the same, **LL-A** *Mango Bay*, PO Box 1062, T4955672, F4955674, mangobay@ surfbvi.com 5 villas which can make 1-bedroomed units or the apartments can be connected to provide 2 or 3 bedrooms, very clean, light and airy, tiled floors, light colours, a/c, phone. **LL** *Katiche Point Greathouse*, www.katichepoint.com reservations through *Mango Bay*. Built recently, high up on a point looking over the bay to other islands in the distance, with its own horizon swimming pool, sunken bath made out of Virgin Gorda boulders in the master bedroom and hammocks in the Crow's Nest for great views, pretty shrubbery, narrow sandy beach, lovely sea view, jetty, kayaks, 4 suites or rent the whole place and include the master suite. **LL-AL** *Paradise Beach*, PO Box 1105, T4955871, F4955872, www.islandsonline. com/paradisebeach 7 units in 3 houses, snorkelling and fishing gear available, dinghy, quiet, rental car included. Further north at Nail Bay is a new development of villas,

Sleeping

British Virgin Islands

apartments and hotel, **LL-L** *Nail Bay Estate Villas*, T4948000, F4955875, www.nailbay. com They now manage *Diamond Beach Villas, Flame Trees, Sunset Watch* and *Turtle Bay Villa*, summer packages include car hire and you can also book dive packages. On the north coast is **L-AL** *Leverick Bay Hotel and Vacation Villas*, PO Box 63, T4957421, F4957367, leverick@surfbvi.com Offering a wide variety of spacious accommodation from hotel rooms to villas and condominiums built up a hillside with a great view of the jetty and the bay, *Pussers* is on site and all the buildings are painted the bright multi-colours which are *Pussers'* emblem, use *Pussers'* restaurant or cross the water to *Drake's Anchorage* on Mosquito Island opposite, tennis, pool, watersports, *Dive BVI* operates from here, food store, laundry, shops, beauty therapy and massage at *The Spa*, T4957375. Perhaps the most exclusive resort on the island is **LL** *Biras Creek*, PO Box 54, T4943555, F4943557, biras@surfbvi.com Member of the Relais et Chateaux group, reached by launch from Gun Creek, or on the North Sound Express from Beef Island, on a spit of land overlooking both North Sound and Berchers Bay, helipad added 2001 for transfers and daytrips. Luxury, beautifully decorated cottages and grand suites spread along the Atlantic coast, no children under 6, those under 8 are not allowed in the dining room but have early dinner and babysitter, no phones or a/c, 2 floodlit tennis courts with pro, sailing trips and other watersports arranged, free watersports instruction, small pool overlooking ocean, nice little beach in sheltered bay with mangroves, very private, beach barbecues, good menu and wonderful view from the split level restaurant, popular with honeymooners, sailing packages with some nights on board available. **LL** *The Bitter End Yacht Club and Resort*, North Sound, PO Box 46, T4942746, 800-8722392. Reached by launch from Gun Creek or the North Sound Express from Beef Island (US$18 one-way) or by yacht. Refurbished in 1999 in multi-million dollar project. Lively, popular, action-packed for water lovers with a marina, sailing in all sizes of boats for all ages, yacht charters, facilities for visiting yachts, fishing (reef and bone), windsurfing, diving, anything any water lover would want, plus instruction, stay on your boat, charter one of the 8 liveaboard yachts, or use the 100 rooms and chalets, comfortable big beds, very spread out along coastal hillside (used to be 2 resorts), can be a long walk from your room to the clubhouse but taxi service available, the older, cheaper rooms are closest, 3 restaurants, the *Clubhouse and Seafood Grill, the Carvery* and *the Emporium Pub*, shops, food stores, conference room, new telecommunications system, free room for children in summer, lots of packages or room only rates.

Eating For upmarket, elegant dining try *Biras Creek*, T4943555. 5-course fixed price dinner plus 15% service, 1930-2100, dress smartly. *Bitter End Yacht Club*, T4942746. For the sailing fraternity, champagne breakfast US$15, buffet lunch US$20, dinner US$30. *Giorgio's Table*, Mahoe Bay, T4955684. Next to *Mango Bay* resort at the foot of the point on which *Katiche Point* is built, authentic Italian food, 80% of ingredients imported from Italy, open 0900-2200. *Olde Yard Inn*, international food in a garden setting, small, intimate, classical music, lunch and dinner. Restaurants serving West Indian recipes include *Anything Goes*, The Valley, T4955062, VHF Ch16. Curries and seafood, 1100-2200, takeaway and delivery locally; *The Wheelhouse*, at *Ocean View Hotel* by Yacht Harbour, T4955230. Chicken or fresh fish served curried or with native sauce; *Spanish Town Café*, T4955555 ext 201. Gourmet food from the chefs at *Little Dix Bay Resort* at the commissary at the Yacht Harbour; *Fischers Cove*, T4955252. International and local food and beach barbecues. Also *Crab Hole*, South Valley, T4955307. Locals eat here, inexpensive West Indian food, curries, roti, callalou, conch, entertainment on Fri 0930-2400. *Lobster Pot*, at *Andy's Chateau de Pirate*, T4955252, VHF 16. Beach pig roast on Mon, seafood buffet on Thu, barbecue on Sat, all boat captains receive 'bliss pirate' cocktail and 30% off main course with ID. *The Bath and Turtle*, Virgin Gorda Yacht Harbour, T4955239. Standard pub fare, open 0730-2200 daily, live entertainment Wed, good place to wait for the ferry. *Mine Shaft Café & Pub*, Coppermine Rd, T4955260, www.islandsonline.com/mineshaft Bar open from 1000, restaurant from 1100, decorated as a mine shaft, lots of evening entertainment and miniature golf, adults US$5, kids US$3, West Indian barbeque Tue 1700-2200, try their special drink, 'cave-in'. *Pusser's* Leverick Bay, T4957369. Breakfast and lunch 0800-1800 at beach bar, dinner 1800-2200 on the veranda, steaks, seafood, pies. *Rock Café & Sports Bar*, T4945482. Open daily, mix of Italian and

Caribbean dishes, moonlight parties and round the world sports. *Mad Dog*, next to the parking lot at The Baths, T4955830. Drinks, sandwiches, T-shirts and friendly conversation, open 1000-1900. *Poor Man's Bar*, on the beach at The Baths. Also selling T-shirts, open 0930-1800, be sure to bring a bottle of water just in case it is shut, toilets round the back. *Top of the Baths*, T4955497. Indoor and outdoor dining, breakfast, lunch and dinner. *Saba Rock Resort*, opposite *Bitter End Yacht Club*, T4957711. Bar with deck over the water, pub grub at lunch time, buffet carvery and salad bar for dinner, also 5 rooms, water taxi service around North Sound.

Live music at *The Bath and Turtle* and *Little Dix Bay*, live music and/or DJ at *Pirate's Pub*, **Nightlife**
Pussers, *Bitter End*, *Andy's Chateau*, *Chez Bamboo* and *Copper Mine*. *Mine Shaft* (also a fun place to eat, see above), has sunset copper hour daily 1600-1800, monthly full moon parties, live band on Fri, Ladies' night. Check the bulletin board at the Virgin Gorda Yacht Harbour for special events and concerts.

Mosquito Island is privately owned by **LL** *Drake's Anchorage Resort* and enjoys **Mosquito**
beautiful views over North Sound to Virgin Gorda and Prickly Pear Island. This **Island**
125-acre island is just northwest of Leverick Bay and can only be reached by boat
(complimentary 5-min boat trip to hotel from Leverick Bay). There is a lovely beach
at South Bay, sandy with boulders, and there are trails leading from the hotel to this
and other quiet, sandy coves but they are for hotel guests only. The island can be
rented in its entirety, or you can just use the hotel, which has three villas, four suites
and four rooms, all ocean front, only 24 guests, very expensive, rates include three
meals and watersports, bars, restaurant open to outside diners, moorings, windsurfing, very quiet and relaxed atmosphere, PO Box 2510, Virgin Gorda, T4942254,
800-6246651, in the USA T617-9699913, F617-9691673, www.drakesanchorage.
com, restaurant open 0730-1000, 1200-1400, candlelit dinner seating time 1900,
French-style menu, reservations essential for dinner before 1500. Closed July,
August and September.

Prickly Pear Island forms the northeast edge of North Sound. It has a lovely beach at **Prickly Pear**
Vixen Point with a small beach bar and a watersports centre. This is a great spot for **Island**
volley ball, with a net permanently on the beach. Moorings near the *Sand Box* beach
bar, with showers and ice, T4959122, VHF 16. The only legal jetski rental operation
in the BVI is here. The island gets crowded when cruise ships come in.

This 74-acre, private island northeast of Virgin Gorda is owned by Richard Branson, **Necker Island**
who wanted a Virgin island to add to his Virgin enterprise. It is available for rent,
contact Necker Island (BVI) Ltd, 1 Uxbridge Street, London W8 7TQ, T020-
73136109, F77278343, toll free in USA 800-5574255, www.neckerisland.com The
house and two cottages, all in Balinese style, sleep 26, fully staffed and cost an arm
and a leg. New in 1999 was the Bali Cliff open-sided bedroom and bathroom, made
in Indonesia and re-assembled on the island. In 2000 a Balinese beach pool and dining pavilion were constructed. Lovely beaches, protected by a coral reef, tennis and
watersports provided, private. Powerboat from Beef Island, 40 minutes, expect to
get soaked, or go by helicopter, or boat from Virgin Gorda, much quicker.

In the chain of islands running southwest from Virgin Gorda is Cooper Island, **Cooper Island**
which has a beautiful beach and harbour at Manchioneel Bay with palm trees, coral
reefs and **L-A** *Cooper Island Beach Club* (PO Box 859, Road Town, T4943721,
F4943721, in USA Parlmes Enterprises Inc, Box 512, Turners Falls, MA 01376,
T413-8633162, 800-5424624, F413-8633662, info@Cooper-Island.com). British
owned and managed, there are 12 guest rooms with kitchen and bathroom, breakfast on request, lunch 1130-1430, dinner from 1830, reservations preferred, bar all
day from 1000, do your grocery shopping on Tortola, electricity generator evenings
only. **LL-AL** *Cooper Island Hideaways*, two beach front cottages, contact Ginny

Evans, 1920 Barg Lane, Cincinnati, OH 45230-1702, T513-2324126, ginnyevans@ aol.com The supply boat leaves Road Town Monday, Wednesday, Saturday, other days use *Underwater Safaris*' dive boat from *The Moorings*, Road Town; they have a small dive shop on the island and use the beach club for surface intervals or to pick up divers from yachts anchored in the bay, dive equipment for sale or rent, airfill station, photographic services.

Salt Island Very few people visit this lovely island, there are no ferries and access is only by private boat. There are two salt ponds from which salt is gathered by two ageing residents. A bag of salt is still sent to the British monarch every year as rent for the island, the remainder is sold to visitors and local restaurants. The two old men who live there welcome visitors and will show you the salt forming and packing process. They have a hut from which they sell conch shells and shell necklaces. There is a small settlement on the north side as well as a reef-protected lagoon on the east shore. The main reason people come here is for a rest stop between dives. The British mail ship *Rhone*, a 310-ft steamer, sank off Salt Island in a hurricane in 1867 and the site was used in the film *The Deep*. Those who perished were buried on Salt Island. The wreck is still almost intact in 20-80 ft of water and is very impressive. There are moorings provided at Lee Bay, just north of the *Rhone*, for those diving the wreck, to minimize anchor damage. The dive is usually divided between the bow section and the stern section; in the former you can swim through the hull at a depth of about 70 ft, be prepared for darkness. In calm weather it is possible to snorkel part of it.

Dead Chest A tiny island in Salt Island Passage, between Salt Island and Peter Island, this is reputedly the island where the pirate Blackbeard abandoned sailors: "15 men on a Dead Man's Chest – Yo Ho Ho and a bottle of rum!".

Peter Island This 1,000-acre island has a tiny population and offers isolated, palm-fringed beaches, good anchorage and picnic spots. The exclusive, luxury, **LL** *Peter Island Resort and Yacht Harbour* reopened 1999 after a complete facelift and hurricane repairs. It is built on reclaimed land jutting out into Sir Francis Drake Channel, forming a sheltered harbour with marine facilities. Built by Norwegians, there are chalet-type cottages, harbour rooms, or beach rooms, a pool, tennis, horseriding, watersports, fitness centre, massage room, dress formally in evening, T4952000, in USA 800-3464451, F4952500, www.peterisland.com. Eight daily ferry departures from Tortola, private guest launch from Tortola or St Thomas, helicopter from St Thomas or San Juan. The marina by the dive shop has a commissary selling basic foods, snacks and ice creams, and there are shower facilities for visiting sailors.

Norman Island The island is reputed to be the 'Treasure Island' of Robert Louis Stevenson fame.
Be careful with the wild cattle: their tempers are unpredictable The floating bar/restaurant *William Thornton II*, T4940183 or VHF Ch 16 is anchored in the Bight of Norman to the north of the island. The first *William Thornton*, a converted 1910 Baltic Trader sank in 1995. There is also the *Billy Bones* beach bar, open for lunch and dinner, but otherwise the island is uninhabited. Launch service from Fort Burt Marina, Road Town, daily at 1715. On its rocky west coast are caves where treasure is said to have been discovered many years ago. These can be reached by small boats and there are several day trips on offer. There is excellent snorkelling around the caves and the reef in front slopes downward to a depth of 40 ft. **The Indians** off the northwest of Norman Island are pinnacles of rock sticking out of the sea with their neighbour, the gently rounded **Pelican Island**. Together they offer the diver and snorkeller a labyrinth of underwater reefs and caves. There are moorings, US$20, and tie-up for dinghies.

Jost Van Dyke

Lying to the west of Tortola, the island was named after a Dutch pirate. It is mountainous, with beaches at White Bay and Great Harbour Bay on the south coast. Great Harbour looks like the fantasy tropical island, a long horseshoe shaped, white sandy beach, fringed with palm trees and dotted with beach bar/restaurants. The local people are very friendly with lots of stories to tell. Jost Van Dyke is a point of entry and has a Customs House at the end of the dock at Great Harbour. In January 1991, the island was provided with electricity for the first time and a paved road. There are moorings in Little Harbour where a marina is slowly being built and anchorages at Great Harbour, Sandy Cay and Green Cay. It is surrounded by some smaller islands, one of which is **Little Jost Van Dyke**, the birthplace of Dr John Lettsome, the founder of the British Medical Society.

Population: 300

Sleeping **LL-AL** *Sandcastle*, at White Bay, T4959888, F4959999, www.sandcastle-bvi.com Owned by Debby Pearse and Bruce Donath, 4 wooden cottages, basic amenities but great for total relaxation, hammocks between palm trees on the beach, snorkelling, windsurfing. *The Soggy Dollar Bar* is popular at weekends, most people arrive by boat and swim or wade ashore, aspires to be the birthplace of the infamous 'painkiller'. **LL-B** *Rudy's Mariner Inn*, Great Harbour. T4959282. 5 rooms, beach bar and restaurant, kitchenettes, grocery, water taxi. Also *Rudy's Villa*, 2 rooms, bathroom. **LL-AL** *Sandy Ground Estates*, PO Box 594, West End, Tortola, T4943391, F4959379, sandygroundjvd@candwbvi.net 8 luxury villas, provisioning, free water taxi from/to Tortola. **LL** *White Bay Villas*, T410-6267722, F6267222, jkwhitebay@aol.com 1, 2 and 3 bedroomed villas, luxury, cheaper in summer. *White Bay Campground*, T4959312. Nice site, right on beautiful, sandy, White Bay, tents US$35, or bare sites US$15 (3 people).

Eating **Little Harbour** *Harris' Place*, T4959302. Open daily, bar, restaurant, grocery, water taxi, live music, Harris calls his place the friendliest spot in the BVIs, breakfast, lunch and dinner, happy hour 1100-1500, live music, all you can eat lobster night on Mon, ferries from Tortola and St Thomas/St John arranged for these feasts. *Sidney's Peace and Love*, T4959271 or VHF Ch 16. Open from 0900, happy hour 1700-1830, pig roast Mon and Sat 1900, US$20, or all you can eat pig and ribs, US$20, barbecue rib and chicken Sun, Tue and Thu, US$15, otherwise lunch and dinner usual steak, fish, shrimp or lobster. *Abe's By The Sea*, T4959329, F4959529, abes@bvimail.com Breakfast, lunch and dinner, grocery store, happy hour 1700-1800, pig roast on Wed, US$18, call VHF Ch 16 for reservations, also has 3 rooms overlooking harbour, can be 1 apartment, **B**, friendly family.

Great Harbour *Sandcastle* (see above), White Bay. For breakfast, lunch and gourmet, candle-lit dinner (must reserve dinner and order in advance to your specifications). *Ali Baba's*, T4959280. Run by Baba Hatchett, west of the Customs House. Breakfast, lunch and dinner, happy hour 1600-1800. *Rudy's Mariner's Rendezvous*, reservations T4959282 or VHF Ch 16. Open for dinner until 0100, US$12.50-22.50. *Club Paradise*, T4959267, F4959633 or VHF Ch 16. Open daily, Mon lobster special US$20, Wed pig roast US$15, live entertainment regularly, lunch 1030-1600, dinner 1800-2100. *Foxy's Bar*, T4959258. Friendly and cheap, lunch Mon-Fri rotis and burgers, dinner daily, reservations by 1700, spontaneous calypso by Foxy, master story-teller and musician, in afternoon until end of happy hour, big parties on New Year's Eve and other holidays, hundreds of yachts arrive, wooden boat regatta on Labour Day draws hundreds of boats from all over the Caribbean for a 3-day beach party, very easy to get invited on board to watch or race, special ferry service to USVI and Tortola. *Happy Laury*, T4959259. Very good value for breakfast, happy hour is 1500-1700, try the Happy Laury Pain Killer. Restaurants take turns in sponsoring a pig roast nightly in season.

Sandy Cay This small uninhabited islet just east of Jost Van Dyke is owned by Laurance Rockefeller. It is covered with scrub but there is a pleasant trail set out around the whole island, which makes a good walk. Bright white beaches surround the island and provide excellent swimming. Offshore is a coral reef.

British Virgin Islands

Anegada

Population: 153

Unique among this group of islands because of its coral and limestone formation, the highest point is only 28 ft above sea level. There are still a few large iguanas, which are indigenous to the island. The Anegada Rock Iguana is part of a national parks trust breeding programme after numbers declined to only 100, largely because juveniles fell prey to wild cats. Contact Rondel Smith, the national parks trust warden on Anegada (also a taxi driver), who can take you to see their burrows in the wild and the hatchlings in pens outside the Administration Building in the Settlement. Flamingos also used to be numerous on the island but were decimated by hunters. Twenty flamingos were released in 1992 in the ponds and four wild ones joined them two years later. In 1995 they bred five chicks, something of a record with flamingos reintroduced into the wild and now there are 41 birds. They are best seen from the little bridge over The Creek on the road from the *Anegada Reef Hotel* to the airport turn off. Hawksbill and Green Turtles nest all along the north shore; the Government VHF has drawn up a conservation policy and the waters around the island are protected. The waters abound with fish and lobster, and the extensive reefs are popular with snorkellers and scuba divers who also explore wrecks of ships which foundered in years past. Some were said to hold treasure, but to date only a few doubloons have been discovered. Anegada has excellent fishing and is one of the top bone fishing spots in the world. From the wharf on the south shore, all the way round to the west end, across the entire north shore (about 11 miles) is perfect, uninterrupted, white sandy beach. Any fences on the beach are to keep out cattle, not people. Loblolly Bay is popular with day trippers, partly because it has a beach bar at either end (*The Big Bamboo* at the west end is busier and more accessible than *Flash of Beauty* at the east end), the only places where there is shade, but also for the reef just off shore where snorkellers can explore caverns and ledges and see coral, nurse sharks, rays, turtles, barracuda and shoals of colourful fish. The beach is generally deserted. Bring water and sun screen.

The Settlement is a collection of wooden homes and some newer houses, a smart new government building, a few bars, little shops, a bakery, jeep hire and church.

Sleeping **LL-L** *Anegada Reef Hotel*, T4958002, F4959362 or by VHF Ch 16. 18 rooms, where there is an anchorage, fishing packages, dive equipment, beach bar, restaurant, great service, famous lobster barbecue, if arriving by yacht radio in advance for directions through the reef, minibus and bicycle hire, taxi service, boutique, closed Sep-Oct. Also under same management, **AL-B** *Anegada Reef Cottages & Villa*, at Setting Point. 2-bedrooms, 2 bathrooms. **A-B** *Ocean Range*, in the Settlement, T4959023. Single and adjoining rooms, kitchenettes available, sea view. *Anegada Beach Cottages*, Box 2710, Anegada, Pomato Point, T4959466, F916-6833304, www.anegadabeachcottages.com Rates on request, snorkelling, fishing.

Anegada

■ Sleeping
1 Anegada Reef Hotel

L *Bonefish Villa*, Nutmeg Point on beach, close to restaurant, T4958045, smgeorge@ worldnet.att.net Includes service and taxes.

Camping *Anegada Beach Campground*, T4959466. US$20-36 prepared site, bare site US$7 per day, plus 10% service, no credit cards, beach bar, restaurant, snorkelling. *Neptune's Treasure*, T4959439. Campsite and tents available US$15-25 per night, US$90-150 per week, US$7 bare site, no cooking, restaurant on site. *Mac's Place* campsite, T4958020. 8 ft by 10 ft tent US$38, prepared sites US$15-35, showers, toilets, grills, eating area.

Pomato Point Beach Restaurant, T4959466, VHF Ch 16, barbecue dinners, reserve by 1600. **Eating** *Neptune's Treasure*, T4959439. Breakfast, lunch, dinner, camping available, delicious breads and chutneys, make sure you take some home. *Big Bamboo*, T4952019. See above, Aubrey and his wife serve delicious lobster and conch on the beach at Loblolly Bay, VHF Ch 16. *Anegada Beach Club*, T4959466, VHF 16. Garden setting, on waterfront, breakfast, lunch and dinner (reservations required for dinner), barbecue lobster. *Anegada Reef Hotel*, T4958002. Breakfast, lunch and dinner but reserve by 1600 for dinner. *Cow Wreck Bar and Grill*, T4959461, on the beach. Open for lunch and dinner, lobster, conch and ribs. *Dotsy's Bakery and Sandwich Shop*, in The Settlement, T4959667. Open 0900-1900 for breakfast, lunch and dinner, fish and chips, burgers, pizza as well as breads and desserts. *Flash of Beauty*, at east end of Loblolly Bay, T4958104, VHF 16. Drinks, snacks and seafood, including lobster, open 1000-2100. Ask around in The Settlement for restaurants serving native dishes. Recommended to make dinner reservations before 1600 at all restaurants.

The island is very quiet and relaxed. A short stretch of concrete road leads from The Settlement **Transport** to the airport turn off; all other roads on the island are sand. There is no public transport except taxis and the best way to get around is to hire a jeep, bicycle or walk (take an umbrella for the sun or walk in the early evening). There is an airstrip 2,500 ft long and 60 ft wide, which can handle light aircraft. Day trips by boat from Tortola are available. There is no regular ferry service.

Background

History

Although discovered by the Spanish in 1493, the islands were first settled by Dutch planters before falling into British hands in 1666. In 1672 the Governor of the Leeward Islands annexed Tortola and in 1680 planters from Anguilla moved into Anegada and Virgin Gorda. Civil government was introduced in 1773 with an elected House of Assembly and a part-elected and part-nominated Legislative Council. Between 1872 and 1956 the islands were part of the Leeward Islands Federation (a British Colony), but then became a separately administered entity, building up economic links with the US Virgin Islands rather than joining the West Indies Federation of British territories. In 1960 direct responsibility was assumed by an appointed Administrator, later to become Governor. The Constitution became effective in 1967 but was later amended in 1977 to allow the islands greater autonomy in domestic affairs. In 1994, the British Government accepted a proposal from a constitutional review commission for the Legislative Council to be enlarged from nine to 13 seats. The four new members represent the territory as a single constituency. This plan created the first mixed electoral system in the UK, in which voters have one vote for their constituency member as usual, plus four votes for the new territory-wide representatives. The British government pushed it into effect before 6 December 1994, the last date for the dissolution of the legislature. There was considerable disquiet in the BVI and in the UK at the way in which it was rushed through without prior consultation and without the support of Mr Stoutt's government.

Mr H Lavity Stoutt, of the Virgin Islands Party (VIP), became Chief Minister in 1967-71 and again in 1979-83 and in 1986. At the elections in February 1995 the

British Virgin Islands

Virgin Islands Party, still led by Mr Lavity Stoutt, won a third consecutive term in office with six seats. The Concerned Citizens' Movement (CCM) and the United Party (UP) each won two seats. Three independents were elected and one formed an alliance with the VIP. However, Mr Stoutt died in May 1995 and the Deputy Chief Minister Ralph O'Neal took over as Chief Minister. The VIP won the by-election after Mr Stoutt's death.

In the May 1999 elections the VIP retained power, winning seven seats, but it faced a less divided opposition. The newly-formed National Democratic Party (NDP), led by Orlando Smith, attracted support from young professionals, winning five seats, while the CCM won one and the UP failed to win any.

Geography The British Virgin Islands (BVI), grouped around Sir Francis Drake Channel, are less developed than the US group, and number some 60 islands, islets, rocks, and cays, of which only 16 or so are inhabited. They are all of volcanic origin except one, Anegada, which is coral and limestone. Most of the land was cleared years ago for its timber or to grow crops, and it is now largely covered by secondary forest and scrub. In the areas with greatest rainfall there are mangoes and palm trees, but generally the islands can look brown and parched, green and lush only just after rain. Mangrove and sea grape can be found in some areas along the shore.

People The two major islands, Tortola and Virgin Gorda, along with the groups of Anegada and Jost Van Dyke, contain most of the total population of about 20,000, which is mainly of African descent. The resident population was only 10,985 in 1980 and most of the increase has come from inward migration of workers for the construction and tourist industries. About half the present population is of foreign origin. There has recently been a return flow of people from the Dominican Republic, whose parents and grandparents were originally from Tortola, seeking a higher standard of living. Everyone speaks English.

Government A nearly self-contained community, the islands are a Crown Colony with a Governor appointed by London, although to a large extent they are internally self-governing. The Governor (Frank Savage, appointed 1998) presides over the Executive Council, made up of the Chief Minister, the Attorney-General and three other ministers. A Legislative Council comprises 13 members elected by universal adult suffrage (of which nine represent district constituencies and four represent the whole territory), one member appointed by the Governor, a Speaker elected from outside by members of the Council, and the Attorney-General as an ex-officio member.

Economy

The economy is based predominantly on tourism; the islands offer up-market tourism in quiet, unspoiled surroundings and earnings are around US$150 mn a year. There are approximately 1,300 hotel rooms, half of which are on Tortola and a third on Virgin Gorda, the rest being scattered around the other islands, but nearly half of those visitors who stay on the islands charter yachts and only sleep on land for their arrival and departure nights.

Tourism in the BVI was hit badly by the recession in 1991. A new charter yacht strategy was announced in 1992, removing import duty and introducing licences to encourage more business. The Government aimed to attract quality operators in a more highly structured environment with streamlined entry regulations. Crewed yachts have been pushed rather than increasing bare boat charters. In another development to promote the islands, the British Virgin Islands Film Commission was set up to encourage film production in the islands and the previous permit fee was lifted. Film crews bring considerable economic benefit through their use of local services and labour.

Since 1991 the tourism industry has shown improvement, particularly in the numbers of cruise ships calling. A new US$6.9 mn, 550-ft cruise ship pier was inaugurated at Road Town, Tortola, which can accommodate two medium-size cruise liners. The Government is aiming to attract the upper end of the cruise market and not to encourage the very large ships. Tourist arrivals and earnings are now growing steadily at about 4-5% a year.

A growth industry of the last decade is the offshore company business and shipping, which benefited from uncertainty in Hong Kong and Panama. International Business Company legislation passed in 1984 allows locally registered foreign companies tax exemptions with little currency risk as the US dollar is the national currency. By the end of 1997 over 250,000 companies had been registered as IBCs (of which about 35,000 had transferred from Hong Kong when it was returned to China) and fees from new licences generated substantial revenues. In 1997 licence fees for banks and trust companies were doubled to US$20,000 a year. Diversification of the offshore financial centre is being sought; currently over one third of government revenue comes from this sector. In 1994 the Legislative Council passed an insurance law, designed to regulate all insurance business in the BVI including captive insurance and reinsurance. New legislation to cover mutual funds was approved in 1996. The Act came into force at the beginning of 1998 and during its first year 1,700 licence applications were processed.

Industry on the islands is limited to small scale operations such as rum, sand or gravel, and desalination plants are being built. Farming is limited to fruit, vegetables and some livestock, some of which are shipped to the USVI. Fishing is expanding both for export, sport and domestic consumption. However, nearly all the islands' needs are imported.

Although the budget is in surplus, the Government is still receiving British capital assistance, as well as funding from the EC, the Caribbean Development Bank and the Commonwealth Development Corporation. Loans have also been raised from commercial banks. The British government is now curtailing its capital funding and other sources of foreign finance are being explored.

British Virgin Islands

Leeward Islands

13

Leeward Islands

The Leeward Islands are a geographical grouping of small, mostly volcanic islands in the northeastern Caribbean. The islands are a mixture of French, Dutch and British colonies and ex-colonies and combine within a small area very varied and rich cultures. Whereas in colonial times they were nearly all sugar producers, today they rely on tourism for a large part of their foreign exchange earnings and jobs. From luxury resorts to intimate guesthouses, gourmet restaurants to barefoot beach bars, there is a wide range of attractions on offer. Sailing, diving and other watersports are also well developed and highly rewarding.

Antigua

Population: 65,000
Colour map 4,
grid B/C3

*A family holiday destination with great beaches, watersports and safe swimming.
Direct, non-stop flights from Europe and North America make this island ideal for
introducing children to the Caribbean. Good transport links with other islands facilitate two-centre holidays or more extensive island hopping. English Harbour is particularly picturesque, with yachts filling a historic bay that has been a popular staging post
for centuries. Nelson's Dockyard and ruined forts are overlooked by the old battery on
Shirley Heights, now better known for Sunday jump-ups and reggae bands.*

Ins and outs

Getting there
*See transport
page 603, for
further information*

Antigua has excellent communications by air with Europe and North America as well as with
neighbouring islands, making it ideal for a two-centre holiday or the starting point for more
protracted island hopping. It is not so easy to get there by sea, other than on a cruise ship or
cargo boat, as there are no formal ferry links except to Montserrat.

Getting around
*Drive on the left,
watch out for pot
holes, narrow streets
& animals straying
across the street in
the dark*

Renting a **car** or **motorcycle** is probably the best way to see the islands' sights if you have only
a short time to spend, as the bus service is inadequate, but be aware that roads are very bumpy
and narrow, so motorcycles are dangerous. **Cycling** is not very interesting, the roads are generally flat and traffic is moderate. There are car hire rental companies are in St John's and some at
airport, most will pick you up. Be careful with one way streets in St John's. At night people do
not always dim their headlights. **Minivans** (shared taxis) go to some parts of the island (for
example Old Road) from the West End bus terminal by the market in St John's. **Buses** serve the
southern part of the island but not the north, so there are no buses to the airport.

Antigua

Leeward Islands

A Foot in the door

- Visit **Nelson's Dockyard** and the forts of **English Harbour** and **Shirley Heights**, for a reminder of colonial maritime history.
- See local crafts being made at the **Blind Workshop**.
- Get a group together for a moonlight bonfire in the **cave on Windward Beach**, English Harbour.
- Watch the sunrise on beautiful **Half Moon Bay Beach**.

Climate

Antigua is a dry island with average rainfall of about 45ins a year and although September-November is considered the rainy season, the showers are usually short. Temperatures range from 73°F to 85°F between winter and summer and the trade winds blow constantly. Antigua has been in the path of several hurricanes since 1995, which was a particularly devastating year. In 1999 Hurricane Lenny brought floods and mud slides and caused damage estimated at EC$136 mn.

Flora and fauna

Around 150 different birds have been observed in Antigua and Barbuda, of which a third are year-round residents and the rest seasonal or migrants. Good spots for birdwatching include **McKinnons salt pond**, north of St John's, where thousands of sandpipers and other water birds can be seen and where yellow crowned night-herons breed. **Potworks Dam** is noted for the great blue heron in spring and

Barbuda

Essentials

Documents *A valid onward ticket is necessary. American, Canadian and British nationals need only photo ID and proof of citizenship.* **Passports** *but not* **visas** *are required by nationals of other Commonwealth countries and British Dependent Territories, if their stay does not exceed six months. The following countries need valid passports but not visas: Argentina, Austria, Belgium, Brazil, Chile, Denmark, Finland, France, Germany, Greece, Ireland, Italy, Japan, Liechtenstein, Luxembourg, Malta, Mexico, Monaco, Netherlands, Norway, Peru, Portugal, Spain, Suriname, Sweden, Switzerland, Turkey and Venezuela. Nationals of all other countries require visas, unless they are in transit for less than 24 hours. Visitors must satisfy immigration officials that they have enough money for their stay. You will not be allowed through Immigration without somewhere to stay. The Tourist Office can help you and you can always change your mind later.*

Money **Currency** *Eastern Caribbean dollars are used, at a rate of EC$2.65 = US$1. It is advisable to change some currency at the airport on arrival.* **Exchange** *US dollars are accepted in most places, but no one will know the exchange rate of other currencies. The conventional rate of exchange if you want to pay in US dollars is EC$2.50=US$1, so it is worth changing money in a bank.* **Credit cards** *are accepted, especially Visa and American Express, but small restaurants will take only cash or Travellers' cheques. Always verify whether hotels, taxis etc are quoting*

you US or EC dollars, you can be cheated. Take care not to get left with excess EC$ on departure, you will not be able to exchange them for another currency except at a very poor rate with a taxi driver. The airport **bank** *is open 0900-1500, Monday-Thursday, closes at 1330 on Friday just as American Airlines come in from New York, closed when BWIA flight comes in from Europe.*

Departure tax *Airport departure charges amount to US$30 per person. Children under 12 pay half. Cash only.*

Communications *The IDD code for Antigua and Barbuda is 268.*

Ports of entry *(Own flag). All yachts must clear in and obtain a cruising permit in Antigua but may clear out of either Antigua or at the C & I office in Barbuda. Customs and Immigration offices are at English Harbour (no overtime charges), Crabbs Marina, St John's and Jolly Harbour (boats must be brought inside the marina for exit clearance).*

Boat documents *Entry fees are US$2 for boats up to 20ft, US$4 for 21-40ft, US$6 for 41-80 ft. Monthly cruising permits are US$8 for boats up to 40 ft, US$10 for 41-80 ft. There are additional fees for anchoring or stern to dockage in English Harbour and Falmouth, an EC$5 charge per person plus electricity and water used. Dinghies must show lights at night and barbecues are prohibited in the harbour. The Antigua and Barbuda Marine Guide is distributed free by the Department of Tourism and contains lots of information on anchorages and marine supplies, www.antiguamarineguide.com*

many water fowl. **Great Bird Island** is home to the red-billed tropic bird and on **Man of War Island**, Barbuda, frigate birds breed.

Diving and marine life

Dive sites
There are barrier reefs around most of Antigua which are host to lots of colourful fish and underwater plant life

Diving is mostly shallow, up to 60 ft, except below **Shirley Heights**, where dives are up to 110 ft, or **Sunken Rock**, with a depth of 122 ft where the cleft rock formation gives the impression of a cave dive. Popular sites are **Cades Reef**, which runs for 2½ miles along the leeward side of the island and is an underwater park; **Sandy Island Reef**, covered with several types of coral and only 30-50 ft deep; **Horseshoe Reef**, **Barracuda Alley** and **Little Bird Island**. There are also some wrecks to explore, including the *Andes*, in 20 ft of water in Deep Bay, but others have disappeared in the recent hurricanes. Diving off Barbuda is more difficult unless you are on a boat with full gear and a compressor, as no one offers diving there. The water is fairly shallow, so snorkelling can be enjoyable. At **Pasture Bay**, on Long Island, the hawksbill turtle lays its eggs from late May to December. The Wide Caribbean Sea Turtle Conservation Network

Marinas There are marinas at English Harbour, Falmouth Harbour (Antigua Slipway, Falmouth Harbour Marina, Catamaran Marina, Antigua Yacht Club), Parham Harbour (Crabbs Slipway), Jolly Harbour, St James's Club, and anchorages at Cades Reef, Carlisle Bay, Morris Bay (Curtain Bluff), Ffryes Bay, Crab Hill Bay, Five Islands Bay, Deep Bay, Morris Bay (Jolly Beach), Dickenson Bay, Parham Harbour and at several of the small islands if you can negotiate the reefs, for example Long Island, Guiana Bay, Green Island and Nonsuch Bay

Business hours Banks: 0800-1400 Monday-Thursday; 0800-1200 and 1400-1600 Friday. Bank of Antigua opens Saturday 0800-1200. **Shops:** 0800-1200, 1300-1600 Monday-Friday. Thursday and Saturday are early closing day for most non-tourist shops. On Sunday everything closes except churches and Kings Casino, although Kentucky Fried Chicken and Epicurean opens in the afternoon.

Official time Atlantic standard time, four hours behind GMT, one ahead of EST.

Voltage 220 volts usually, but 110v in some areas, check before using your own appliances. Many hotels have transformers.

Tourist offices overseas Canada: 60 St Clair Avenue East, Suite 304, Toronto, Ontario, M4T IN5, T416-9613085, F9617218. **France:** 43 Avenue de Friedland, 75008 Paris, T33-1-53751571, F33-1-53751569. **Germany:** Thomas Str 11, D-61348, Bad Homburg, T49-617221504, F49-617221513. **Italy:** Via Santa Maria alla Porta 9, I-20123 Milan,

T/F39-2877983. **UK:** Antigua House, 15 Thayer Street, London W1M 5LD, T020-74867073/5, F020-74869970, antbar@msn.com **USA:** 610 Fifth Avenue, Suite 311, New York, NY 10020, T212-5414117, F5414789; 25 SE 2nd Avenue, Suite 300, Miami, FL 33131, T305-3816762, F305-3817908.

Safety Normal precautions against theft should be taken. There have been some serious incidents on isolated beaches, so caution should be taken in these areas. Generally, however, despite the poverty, Antigua is free from hassle for the traveller.

Health Tiny sandflies, known locally as 'Noseeums' often appear on the beaches in the late afternoon and can give nasty stings. Keep a good supply of repellent and make sure you wash off all sand to avoid taking them with you from the beach. Do not eat the little green apples of the manchineel tree, as they are poisonous, and don't sit under the tree in the rain as the dripping oil from the leaves causes blisters. Some beaches, particularly those on the west coast, get jelly fish at certain times of the year, for example July/August.

Public holidays New Year's Day, Good Friday, Easter Monday, Labour Day (first Monday in May), Whit Monday (end-May), Queen's Birthday (second Saturday in June), Caricom Day, beginning of July (whole island closes down), Carnival (first Monday and Tuesday in August), Independence Day (1 November), Christmas Day and Boxing Day.

(Widecast) organizes turtle watches. Huge controversy in 2001 surrounded the Government's approval of a captive dolphin programme by the same company which opened dolphinariums in Anguilla and the BVI the same year. Dolphins are being caught in the wild and taught to perform tricks and swim with tourists, in the name of education and conservation (but in reality for profit), in return for frozen fish and antibiotics. The Prime Minister stated that Antigua's tourist industry had to keep up with the competition in the attractions it offered to cruise ship visitors.

Dive centres Dive shops are located nearly all round the island and include: Aquanaut Diving Centre, at *St James's Club*, T4605000; Dive Antigua, *Rex Halcyon Hotel*, T4623483, F4627787, www.diveantigua.com; Curtain Bluff Dive Shop, *Curtain Bluff Hotel*, T4628400 (certified hotel guests only); *Deep Bay Divers* in St John's at Redcliff Quay, T4638000, www.deepbaydivers.com; *Dockyard Divers* at Nelson's Dockyard, T4601178, F4601179; www.dockyarddivers.com; *Octopus Divers* at English Harbour, T4606286, F4638528, octopusdivers@candw.ag; *Jolly Dive* at *Jolly Beach Resort*, T4628305, www.kokomocat. com/jollyd.htm; *Long Bay Hotel*, T4602005 (certified hotel guests only).

Leeward Islands

Beaches and watersports

The nearest beach to St John's is **Fort James** which can be pleasant, with its palm trees and a few boulders. However it gets crowded at weekends and at times it becomes rough and so has a milky appearance, lots of weed and is not good for swimming. It is also rather secluded and confrontations with drug-users have been recorded there, so do not go alone. Further away, but better, is **Dickenson Bay** but there are hotels all along the beach which fence off their property and some pump sewage into the sea which can be smelly. **Soldier's Bay**, next to the *Blue Waters Hotel*, is shallow and picturesque. Instead of following the sign, park your car in the hotel car park, which has shade, walk left across the property, climb through the hole in the fence and in about three minutes you are there. Also good is **Deep Bay** which, like most beaches, can only be reached by taxi or car. There are several nice beaches on the peninsula west of St John's, past the *Royal Antiguan Hotel*. On **Trafalgar Beach** condominiums have been built on the rocks overlooking the small, sheltered bay. If you go through Five Islands village you come to **Galley Bay**, a secluded and unspoilt hotel beach which is popular with locals and joggers at sunset. The four **Hawksbill** beaches at the end of the peninsula, one of which is a nudist beach (free public entry, very secluded, security guard on duty, pleasant atmosphere), are crescent shaped, very scenic and unspoilt. Take drinks to the furthest one as there are no facilities and you may have the place to yourself. At **Half Moon Bay**, in the east there is plenty of room; the waves can be rough in the centre of the bay, but the water is calm at the north end. This lovely long, white sand beach faces east and is a great place to watch the sun popping right out of the ocean. Alternatively organize a barbecue on the beach when there is a full moon. Near English Harbour is **Galleon Beach**, which is splendid, but again can only be reached by taxi or car or water taxi from English Harbour, EC$2. It has an excellent restaurant. There is a cave on Windward Beach, near English Harbour, which is good for a moonlight bonfire (go in a group, not just as a couple). Follow the road past the Antigua Yacht Club leading to Pigeon Beach and turn left to Windward Beach on a bumpy track, best with a four-wheel drive. Also excellent is **Pigeon Point**, reached by turning left at the *Last Lemming* restaurant and following the path up and over the hill. **Dark Wood Beach**, on the road from St John's to Old Road round the southwest coast, is very nice, quiet, with a bar and restaurant at the south end.

Day sails Antigua offers sailing, waterskiing, windsurfing, parasailing, snorkelling and deep-sea fishing. Cocktail and barbecue cruises are reasonably priced. *Shorty's Glass Bottom Boat* at Dickenson Bay, takes people out to the coral reefs; there are also excursions to Bird Island, food and drink provided. Trips round the island with stops at smaller islands such as Bird Island, Prickly Pear Island, or even Barbuda or Montserrat, can be arranged for US$60-90 on the catamarans run by *Kokomo Cat* (T4627245, www.kokomocat.com) and *Wadadli Cats* (T4624792, www.wadadlicats.com). *Sentio* is a luxury 50ft sailing yacht for small groups, honeymooners, families, for special trips, beach exploring, overnight to Barbuda or sailing instruction (T4647127). The *Caribbean Queen* is a 69 ft catamaran which sails the Antiguan waters with a live steel band, barbecue, snorkelling and more (T4618675, www.ticruises.com). There is also, of course, the *Jolly Roger* (T4622064), a wooden sailing ship used for entertaining would-be pirates, with Wednesday and Friday lunchtime cruises from Jolly Beach, Thursday cocktail cruises from the *Royal Antiguan*, and Saturday night barbecue and dancing cruise, helped along with rum punch.

Sailing The *Antigua Yacht Club* holds races every Thursday and anyone wishing to crew should listen to English Harbour Radio at 0900 on VHF 68/06 that morning. *Jolly Harbour Yacht Club* holds Saturday races as well as the **Red Stripe Regatta** in February and **Jolly Harbour Regatta** in September. The **Classic Regatta** in the second half of April is spectacular, with yawls, ketches, schooners and square-masted

Races are held throughout the year

vessels displaying their sails. During Classic Week you can ride on a Classic yacht in the regatta by donating US$100 to charity (*The Hourglass Foundation*), contact Nancy and Hans Smit at the *Gold Smitty* in Redcliff Quay, T4622601. **Antigua Sailing Week** begins at the end of April with five days of races and noisy parties, attracting hundreds of boats, www.sailingweek.com The first Carib Cup Regatta was held in July 1995 with five teams of three boats competing.

A marina was built at Jolly Harbour in 1992, just south of Ffryes Point. Several day charter boats have moved there. For cruisers or bareboat charters Antigua offers good provisioning and marine supplies abound, with facilities to haul out boats as well. Haulout can be done at Antigua Slipway or Jolly Harbour; there are several other marinas as well. Charter fleets include *Sun Yacht Charter Services* (T5622893, charterservices@candw.ag) and *Nicholson's Yacht Charters*, T4601093, nicholsoncy@candw.ag. There are too many anchorages to list.

For fishing charters, *Nightwing, a 35-ft Bertrum* leaves from Falmouth Harbour, US$350 for 4 hours, US$500 for 6 hours, US$650 for 8 hours, plus tip, T4605337, F4638779, www.fishantigua.com*Overdraft*, a 40-ft fibreglass deep-sea fishing boat also leaves from Falmouth Harbour, US$400 for 4 hours, US$500 for 6 hours, or US$600 for 8 hours, T4644954, F4623119, www.antiguafishing.com *Obsession* is a 45-ft Hatteras which again leaves from Falmouth Harbour, T4623174, www.charternet.com/charters/obsession

Fishing

There is a sport fishing tournament over the Whit weekend at the end of May

Dickenson Bay is the only beach with public hire of watersports equipment but some hotels will hire to the public especially out of season, for example the *Jolly Beach Resort* near Bolan's Village (bus from West End bus station). *Halcyon Cove Watersports* at the *Rex Halcyon Cove* has waterskiing, windsurfing (lessons for beginners) and small sailing craft for rent, T4620256. The *Sandals* all-inclusive resort on Dickenson Bay will admit outsiders, at US$150 per couple 1000-1800 or US$130 for the evening, giving you the use of all sports facilities, meals, bar etc. *Patrick's Windsurfing School* (T4619463, windsurfingantigua@hotmail.com) at Dutchman's Bay north of the airport, offers instruction to beginners (guarantee to achieve in 2 hours or no charge), intermediate and advanced windsurfers. Patrick will travel to any hotel requested. *Pineapple Beach Allegro Resorts* has a variety of watersports (T4632006). *Destination Antigua* offers kayaking, T5603982.

Watersports

There are two **golf** courses: a professional (but rather dried out) 18-hole one at Cedar Valley, near St John's, T4620161 and an 18-hole course at Jolly Beach. The Antigua Open is played at Cedar Valley in November. Rental equipment available at both courses, but not very good at Cedar Valley. Miniature golf can be played at *Putters Bar & Grill*, Dickenson Bay, T4634653, where there is a challenging, 18-hole, floodlit course.

Many of the large hotels have **tennis** courts: *Royal Antiguan Hotel*, T4623733, Deep Bay; *Hodges Bay Club*, T4622300; Temo Sports, a tennis and squash club open to the public in English Harbour (sports complex with floodlit tennis courts, glass-backed squash courts, bar/bistro, equipment rental, open Monday-Saturday 0700-2200, no credit cards, T4601781, VHF 68). The Jolly Harbour development includes BBR Sportive, with lit tennis and squash courts (US$20 per 30 minutes) and a 25 m swimming pool, open 0800-2100, food and drink available, T4626260, VHF Channel 68.

Riding is available for beginners through the hotels. *St James's Club* arranges horseriding, T4605000. *Spring Hill Riding Club*, on the road to Rendezvous Bay, offers tuition from BHS qualified instructors, English style, show jumping, cross country course, horses and ponies, beach rides, forest rides, open daily from 0730, contact Sarah Scott, T4638041. **Horse racing** takes place on public holidays at Cassada Garden Race Track.

Other sports

Leeward Islands

Cricket is the national sport and test matches are played at the Recreation Ground. There are matches between Antiguan teams and against teams from neighbouring islands. The cricket season runs from January to July. Seasons for other spectator sports are: netball January-July, basketball September-December, volleyball December-July, football August-February.

Organized **hikes** are arranged frequently to historical and natural attractions and can be a good way of seeing the island. Once a month the Historical and Archaeological Society organize hikes free of charge, PO Box 103, St John's, T4621469. Hash House Harriers arrange hikes off the beaten track every other Saturday at 1600, free of charge, contact Bunnie Butler T461 0643 or David Crump T461 0686. For other walking and exploring, see Tour operators in Essentials.

St John's

Population: 30,000

Most activity now takes place around the 2 quay developments

Built around the largest of the natural harbours is St John's, the capital. It is rather quiet and run-down and are rather tatty but parts have been developed for tourism and the town is a mixture of the old and the new. New boutiques, duty-free shops and restaurants are vying for custom. **Redcliffe Quay** is a picturesque area of restored historical buildings now full of souvenir shops and the only toy shop in town. **Heritage Quay**, opened in 1988, is a duty free shopping complex strategically placed to catch cruise ship visitors. It has a casino and a big screen satellite TV and is

St John's

● Eating
1 Hemingway's
2 Redcliffe Tavern
3 The Hub

🚌 Buses
1 East Bus Stand
2 West Bus Stand

Leeward Islands

a cool, pleasant place to have a drink. When a cruise ship is in dock hundreds of passengers come ashore and it becomes very crowded.

However, St John's does have interesting historical associations. Nelson served in Antigua as a young man for almost three years, and visited it again in 1805, during his long chase of Villeneuve which was to end with the Battle of Trafalgar. Some of the old buildings in St John's, including the Anglican Cathedral, have been damaged several times by earthquakes, the last one in 1974. A cathedral in St John's was first built in 1683, but replaced in 1745 and then again in 1843 after an earthquake, at which time it was built of stone. Its twin towers can be seen from all over St John's. It has a wonderfully cool interior lined with pitchpine timber. Donations requested.

The **Museum of Antigua and Barbuda** at the former Court House in Long Street is worth a visit, both to see the exhibition of precolumbian and colonial archaeology and anthropology of Antigua and for the Court House building itself, first built in 1747, damaged by earthquakes in 1843 and 1974 but now restored. There is also Viv Richards' cricket bat, with which he scored the fastest century, various 'hands on' items and games. The *Historical and Archaeological Society (HAS)* based at the museum publishes a useful and interesting newsletter, full of stories about the islands and research developments. They also organize field trips. You can also visit Viv Richards' childhood home on Viv Richards' Street. ■ *T/F4624930/1469, museum@candw.ag Free, although donations requested; gift shop. Mon-Fri 1000-1500, Sat 1000-1300.* The **Museum of Marine and Living Art**, Gambles Terrace, opposite Princess Margaret School, T4621228, F4621187, exhibits of seashells, shipwrecks and precolumbian history. Recommended weekly lectures by appointment, Thursday 1000, on the evolution of the earth and the formation of the continents and civilizations.

Museums

A short drive west of St John's are the ruins of **Fort Barrington** on a promontory at Goat Hill overlooking Deep Bay and the entrance to St John's Harbour. These fortifications were erected by Governor Burt, who gave up active duty in 1780 suffering from psychiatric disorders; a stone he placed in one of the walls at the Fort describes him grandly as 'Imperator and Gubernator' of the Carib Islands. The previous fortifications saw the most action in Antigua's history with the French and English battling for possession in the 17th century. At the other side of the harbour are the ruins of **Fort James**, from where you can get a good view of St John's. There was originally a fort on this site dating from 1675, but most of what can now be seen dates from 1749. To get there, head north out of St John's, turn west by *Barrymore Hotel* to the sea, then follow the road parallel to the beach to the end.

Fortifications

Around the island

Antigua, with about 108 square miles, is the largest of the Leewards, and also the most popular and the most developed. Its dependencies are nearby Barbuda and Redonda. The island is low-lying and composed of volcanic rock, coral and limestone. Boggy Peak, its highest elevation, rises to 1,330 ft. There is nothing spectacular about its landscape, although its rolling hills and flowering trees are picturesque. Its coastline however, curving into coves and graceful harbours with 365 soft white sand beaches fringed with palm trees, is among the most attractive in the West Indies.

On the other side of the island from St John's, is **English Harbour**, which has become one of the world's most attractive yachting centres and is now a 'Hot Spot' at night for tourists. Here 'Nelson's Dockyard' has been restored and is one of the most interesting historical monuments in the West Indies. It was designated a national park in 1985 (Parks Commissioner, T4601379). ■ *US$1.60, children under 12 free. Souvenirs and T-shirts are on sale at the entrance.* The **Nelson's Dockyard Museum** has recently been renovated to give the complete history of this famous Georgian Naval Yard and the story of famous English Harbour. See *Admiral's Inn*, with its

Finding your way around is not easy and street names are rarely in evidence. The Ordnance Survey map, US$7.50, is recommended if you are exploring the island. A map hand drawn by Brian Dyde is also available

Leeward Islands

boat and mast yard, slipway and pillars still standing but which suffered earthquake damage in the 19th century. The *Copper and Lumber Store* is now a hotel, bar and restaurant. *HQ's* is a popular new dining spot in the dockyard. The Ralph A Aldridge shell collection in a wall case is fascinating, all the shells were found in Antiguan waters. On the quay are three large capstans, showing signs of wear and tear. Boat charters can be arranged from here; also a 20-30 minute cruise round the historic Dockyard for US$6 on *Horatio*, from outside the *Copper and Lumber Store*, depending on seasonal demand. A footpath leads round the bay to **Fort Berkeley** at the harbour mouth, well grazed by goats, wonderful views. Near the Dockyard, Clarence House still stands where the future King, William IV stayed when he served as a midshipman in the 1780s.

On the left of the road from English Harbour to Shirley Heights are the remains of the British Navy's magazines and a small branch road to the Dow Hill Interpretation Centre. There is a gift shop, restaurant, small museum with shell display and an audio visual room which puts on a display about every 30 minutes on Antigua's history, highly recommended. Local guides also available.

Watch the sun set over the west coast with a sundowner and maybe you'll see the green flash

At **Shirley Heights**, overlooking English Harbour, are the ruins of fortifications built in the 18th century with a wonderful view. Some buildings, like officers' quarters, are still standing, restored but roofless, which give an idea of their former grandeur. At the lookout point, or Battery, at the south end is a bar and restaurant. On Sunday a steel band plays 1500-1800, followed by reggae 1800-2200, very loud and popular, can be heard at the dockyard below. Barbecued burgers, chicken, ribs and salad. There is often some activity on Thursday too. It is rather touristy and very crowded, the crowd is often drunk and drugs are sold.

Great George Fort, on Monk's Hill, above Falmouth Harbour (a 30 minute walk from the village of Liberta, and from Cobb's Cross near English Harbour) has been less well preserved. There is a museum of precolumbian artefacts in the Dow Hill tracking station building (formerly used in connection with the US Apollo space programme). It can be visited by prior arrangement, or on Thursday afternoons there are tours, starting from Nelson's Dockyard and taking in Dow Hill (check the details at Nicholson's travel agency). If advance notice is given, the Antigua Rum Distillery welcomes visitors.

Fig Tree Drive between Old Road and the Catholic church on the road going north from Liberta, is a steep, winding, bumpy road, through mountainous rainforest. It is greener and more scenic than most of the island, but the rainforest is

English Harbour & Shirley Heights

Related map:
A Nelson's Dockyard, page 597

scanty and incomparable with islands like Dominica. If travelling by bicycle make sure you go *down* Fig Tree Drive from the All Saints to Liberta road, heading towards Old Road, the hill is very steep.

Boggy Peak, in the southwest, is the highest point on the island and from the top you can get wonderful views over to Guadelupe, St Kitts, Nevis and Montserrat. It is a good walk up, or you can take a car. From Urlings walk (or take minibus) about ½-¾ mile in the direction of Old Town. There is a clear track on the left (ask the bus driver to drop you off there) which is very straight then ascends quite steeply. When you get to the top, walk round the fence surrounding the Cable and Wireless buildings to get a good view in all directions. It takes over an hour to walk up (signs say it is a private road) and you are advised not to wander around alone.

If you have a car, try taking the road out to the airport from St John's. Do not enter the airport but take the right fork which runs alongside it. After about 1½ miles take a right turn down a small road to St George's Church, on Fitches Creek Bay, built in 1687 in a beautiful location, interesting gravestones. From there, follow the rough road round the coast to **Parham**, which is interesting for being the first British settlement on the island and having an unusual octagonal church, St Peter's, which dates from the 1840s, is lovely and flamboyant, trees surround the church and enhance its attractiveness. From Parham go due south and then east at the petrol station through Pares to Willikies. On this road, just past Pares Village, is a sign to **Betty's Hope**, a ruined sugar estate built in 1650 and owned by the Codrington family from 1674-1944. Restoration was carried out by the Antigua Museum in St John's and it was officially opened in 1995. One of the twin windmills can sometimes be seen working, making it the only operational 18th-century windmill in the Caribbean.■ *There is a visitors' centre (open Tue-Sat 1000-1600) which tells the story of life on a sugar plantation. Well worth a visit. For a guided tour contact the Antigua Museum, T4624930.*

After Willikies the road is signed to the *Pineapple Beach Club* at Long Bay, but before you get there, take a right turn down a small road, which deteriorates to a bumpy track, to **Devil's Bridge** at Indian Town Point. The area on the Atlantic coast is a national park where rough waves have carved out the bridge and made blowholes, not easily visible at first, but quite impressive when the spray breaks through. Good view of Long Bay and the headland.

Returning through Willikies to Glanvilles, take a left turn shortly after St Stephen's Church down a small road south past Collins Dam. When you meet up with

Nelson's Dockyard

N

Not to scale

1 Admiral's Inn, with Pitch & Tar Store, Provision Store
2 Boat House & Sail Loft
3 Copper & Lumber Store (Hotel)
4 Market building; (Cable & Wireless, Bank & shops)
5 Naval Officers' House museum & shops
6 Officers' Quarters (Art studios, shops & toilets)

Leeward Islands

the main road (petrol station) turn left and then right towards St Phillips. The scenery after this village is quite attractive, there are several ruined sugar mills dotting the landscape. The road continues on to Half Moon Bay and to Mill Reef(a private, gated club, no entry).

Essentials

Sleeping

There is a 10% service charge & 8.5% government tax at all hotels. Porters expect a tip of EC$1-2 per bag

There are hotels, resorts and apartments all round the island and more are being built all the time. We have not space to mention them all, this is a selection. Various websites mentioned give up to date information. The greatest concentration of developments is in the area around St John's, along the coast to the west and also to the north in a clockwise direction to the airport. A second cluster of places to stay is around English Harbour and Falmouth Harbour in the southeast of the island. Many may be closed Sep-Oct. Full lists of hotels, apartments, villas and guesthouses should be available from the tourist office booth at the airport, although it is not always easy to get hold of, and they will book you a hotel room on arrival if you have not already done so. There are lots of self-catering apartments available all round the island but a common complaint is that sufficient provisions are not available locally and you have to go into St John's for shopping. **Camping** is illegal.

St John's L-A *Heritage Hotel*, Heritage Quay, PO Box 1532, St John's, T4621247/8, F4621179, heritagehotel@candw.ag   Right by cruise ships, caters for business travellers, discounts available. In same management group is **AL** *City View*, Newgate Street, PO Box 2692, T5620256-9, F5620242, cityviewhotel@candw.ag   38 rooms with patios, a/c, kitchen, fridge, cable TV, phone, restaurant and room service, conference room. **A-B** *Courtsland*, Upper Gambles, PO Box 403, T4621395, F4621699. **C** *Joe Mike's Hotel*, in Corn Alley and Nevis St, PO Box 136, T4621142, F4626056, joemikes@candw.ag   Special rates can be negotiated but not by phone, rooms OK, no balconies, weak a/c, no food but downstairs are fast food, restaurant and bar, casino, ice cream parlour, cocktail lounge, beauty salon and mini-mart. **C** *Roslyn's Guest House*, Upper Gambles, very near cricket ground, PO Box 161, T4620762. 2 double rooms, friendly lady owner. **C** *Murphy's Apartments*, PO Box 491, All Saints Road, T4611183. Run by Elaine Murphy, apartments modernized, every amenity, breakfast US$5, also longer term lets, lovely garden. **E** *Pigottsville Guest House*, at Clare Hall, PO Box 521, T4620592. No signs, about 2 miles from the airport and within easy walking distance of St John's, 20 rooms.**E-F** *Montgomery Hotel*, Tindale Road, T4621164. Usually plenty of room except during carnival and cricket matches, central but not a very nice part of town, noisy roosters across the street, scruffy and basic, 24 small rooms, 8 with private bath, rest with shared bath, rats in downstairs rooms, no water after midnight, cable TV, the owner also has some apartments north of St John's.

West of St John's LL *Hawksbill Beach Resort*, 4 miles from St John's (a US$12 taxi ride), PO Box 108, T4620301, F4621515, www.hawksbill.com   39 acres and four lovely beaches, good food, pleasant rooms with ceiling fans, friendly staff, tennis, table tennis, pool, watersports, rooms in two-storey blocks or cottages.

Runaway Bay LL-AL *Barrymore Beach Club*, PO Box 1774, on Runaway Bay, 2 miles from St John's, T4624101, F4624140. Rooms and apartments, clean, comfortable, on 1½ miles of white sand beach. Recommended. **LL-B** *Runaway Beach Club*, on Runaway Bay, PO Box 874, T4621318, F4624172. Friendly, beachfront cabins, 24 rooms or villas, 110V electricity, excellent beach restaurant, *The Beach*. **AL-A** *Sand Haven Hotel*, PO Box 246, T4624491. On clean, sandy beach with shade from palm trees and sea grape, 16 double or family rooms includes breakfast, special deals for visiting cricket teams, 5-10 min beach walk from *Barrymore Beach Apartments*, vehicle hire needed.

Dickenson Bay LL-A *Antigua Village*, PO Box 649, St John's, T4622930, F4620375. Studio or beach front 1-2 bedroomed villa, there is a small store for provisions, nothing exciting, watersports. **LL** *Sandals Antigua*, PO Box 147, T4620267, F4624135, sandals@candw.ag

ANTIGUA **599**

Couples only, all-inclusive, 191 comfortable rooms, lots of sports and other facilities. **LL-AL** *Rex Halcyon Cove Beach Resort*, PO Box 251, T46202568, F4620271. 210 rooms, on the beach with full watersports facilities and fishing, pool and tennis. The Warri Pier is a great place to watch the sunset with a sunset cocktail. **LL-AL** *Siboney Beach Club*, PO Box 222, T4620806, F4623356, siboney@candw.ag 12 a/c suites in gardens by beach, restaurant, watersports available nearby, good except that the condos on one side are an eyesore and whatever was on the other side is now abandoned and crumbling into the sea.

North coast LL-AL *Blue Waters*, PO Box 256, T4620290, F4620293, www.blue waters.net 77 rooms and villas on beach, room only or all inclusive, pool, watersports.

Southwest AL *Jolly Harbour Beach Resort, Marina and Golf Club*, PO Box 1793, T4626166, F4626167, www.jollyharbour-marina.com A/c, rooms, suites, villas on waterfront, plenty of activities, watersports, pool, tennis, squash, golf, shopping centre and restaurants. **AL** *Jolly Beach Resort*, Jolly Beach, PO Box 744, T4620061, F4629000 (formerly *Club Antigua*). All-inclusive including watersports, adjacent to marina. **LL-AL** *Coco's Antigua*, PO Box 2024, T4602626, F4629423, cocos@candw.ag 20 rooms in chattel style cottages, view of Jolly Beach, built on a bluff, fan, fridge, restaurant. **LL** *Curtain Bluff*, PO Box 288, T4628400, F4628409, www.curtainbluff.com On small peninsula, beaches either side, 63 rooms with seaview, suites, refurbished in 2001 and luxurious, restaurant, tennis with shop, croquet, putting green, all-inclusive.

Falmouth Harbour AL-A *Falmouth Beach Apartments* (same management as *Admiral's Inn*), PO Box 713, St John's, T460-1027/1094, F4601534. Good value, 23 hillside or beach front studio apartments on or near private beach but somewhat spoilt by massive yachts anchored just offshore and noisy at night, very clean, friendly staff, boats and other watersports equipment, all apartments have lovely view of harbour. **AL-B** *Catamaran Hotel and Marina*, on narrow beach, friendly, PO Box 958, T4601036, F4601506.

English Harbour AL-A *Admiral's Inn*, PO Box 713, T4601027, F4601534. 14 rooms of varying sizes in restored 17th-century building, very pleasant, transport to the beach, complimentary sunfish and snorkelling equipment, excellent location, good food. **LL-A** *Copper and Lumber Store* (restored dockyard building), PO Box 184, T4601058, F4629215. Studios and suites available, boat transport to nearby beaches. **LL-AL** *Galleon Beach*, PO Box 1003, T4601024, F4601450, galleonbeach@candw.ag 1 or 2 bedroom villas with additional sofa bed, on beach at Freemans Bay, *Colombo's* Italian Restaurant on site, fully equipped, tennis, sunfish, windsurfing, ferry to Nelson's Dockyard. Recommended. **LL-AL** *The Inn at English Harbour*, PO Box 187, St John's, T4601014, F4601603. Set in 10 acres with lovely white sand beach, 6 hillside rooms with view of bay, 22 beach front rooms, beach bar or terrace restaurant, watersports provided, tennis and golf nearby.

Southeast LL *St James's Club*, PO Box 63, T4605000, F4603015, reservations@antigua-resorts.com On peninsula in Momora Bay, all-inclusive, 253 rooms and villas, lots of facilities, casino, marina, 3 restaurants, three pools, championship tennis.

East LL *Long Bay Hotel*, PO Box 442, T4632005, F4632439, www.longbay-anti gua.com Open Oct-May, MAP, 18 rooms, 5 cottages, 1 villa, sandy beach, tennis, diving, watersports, family-run. **LL** *Mango Bay*, PO Box W1400, on the water in St Phillips parish, T4606646, F4608400, www.u-c.com/MangoBay-Antigua Sister hotel in Barbados, all-inclusive, 64 rooms, all watersports and nightly entertainment provided, French chef. **AL** *Harmony Hall*, T4604120, F4604406, www.harmonyhall.com Includes breakfast and use of boat, meal plans available, excellent restaurant, pool, dock for visiting yachts, beach, very popular. *Browns Bay Villas*, T4604176, www.brownsbayvilla.com Six comfortable 2-bedroom, 2-bathroom villas with kitchen near *Harmony Hall* on Browns Bay.

Long Island **LL** *Jumby Bay*, was purchased by Halfmoon Jamaica and reopened Dec 1999 but refurbishment and expansion continue at the 300-acre property, which will have 68 rooms, 12 2-3 bedroom villas and private cottage, with an infinity swimming pool, spa and tennis.

Near airport If you are changing planes and have to stop over, **A-D** *Amarylis*, on Airport Road, PO Box 2624, T4628690, F5620375. 22 rooms, comfortable, with *Calypso Café*, good West Indian and seafood in a nice atmosphere. **B** *The Airport Hotel*, T4621191, F4621534. Where some airlines dump you if a missed connection is their fault, is rather basic but adequate for a night stop, friendly staff, restaurant and bar with outdoor patio, reasonably priced food, happy hour drinks Mon-Fri.

Eating

Oranges are green, while the native pineapple is black

In addition to a wide selection of imported delicacies served in the larger hotels, local specialities, found in smaller restaurants in St John's, often very reasonable, should never be missed: saltfish (traditionally eaten at breakfast in a tomato and onion sauce), pepper-pot with fungi (a kind of cornmeal dumpling), goat water (hot goat stew), shellfish (the local name for trunk fish), conch stew and the local staple, chicken and rice. Ducana is made from grated sweet potato and coconut, mixed with pumpkin, sugar and spices and boiled in a banana leaf. Tropical fruits and vegetables found on other Caribbean islands are also found here: breadfruit, cristophine, dasheen, eddo, mango, guava and pawpaw (papaya). Locally made Sunshine ice cream, American style, is available in most supermarkets. Imported wines and spirits are reasonably priced but local drinks (fruit and sugar cane juice, coconut milk, and Antiguan rum punches and swizzles, ice cold) must be experienced. The local Cavalier rum is a light golden colour, usually used for mixes. Beer costs US$2-2.50 in bars, although street bars in the market are cheaper. cases of beer can be bought at good prices from Wadadli Brewery on Crabbs peninsula. There are no licensing restrictions. Tap water is safe all over the island. Most luxury hotels provide rainwater. If you are planning to eat out in hotels, you need to allow at least US$300 per person per week, but it is possible to eat much more cheaply in the local restaurants in St John's.

A 7¾% tax on all meals and drinks is added to your bill. Restaurants tend to move, close down or change names frequently

St John's *Chutneys* on Fort Rd, T4622977. Serves good Indian food (Indian chef), US$18-28 per person. *Hemingway's*, T4622763. Drink, lunch or dinner West Indian style upstairs on cool veranda overlooking Lower St Mary's Street at entrance to Heritage Quay, open Mon-Sat from 0830, main course US$9-22. *Home*, Gambles Terrace, T4617651, 20-min walk from tourist area but worth it. Caribbean haute cuisine, Italian pasta dishes, exotic desserts, about US$30-37 per person, very elegant but no stiff formality, friendly atmosphere, service excellent, welcoming to families, run by Antiguan Carl Thomas and his German wife Rita, open from 1800-2300. *O'Grady's*, Nevis St. Good for pub grub, US$9-10, darts and pool, packed on Wed when Laurie Stevens sings. *Mama Lolly's*, in Redcliffe Quay, T5621552, mamalol@candw.ag Best vegetarian food, average US$9-10. *Pizzas in Paradise*, at Redcliffe Quay, T4622621. Very popular at lunch time, salads and sandwiches as well as pizzas, around US$9-10, open Mon-Sat 0830-2300. *The Redcliffe Tavern*, T4614557. Good lunch, EC$17-35, evening main course EC$25-40, open Mon-Sat 0800-2330. *Smoking Joe's*, opposite the cricket ground. For barbecued ribs, chicken, etc, Joe is a local calypsonian. *The Hub*, Long St and Soul Alley, opposite the Museum, T4620616. Open daily from 0730 until 2200 (or later for drinks), good meals, live jazz on Sat night, local cuisine, friendly, pleasant atmosphere. For fast food lovers there is *Kentucky Fried Chicken* on High and Thames Sts, and a 2nd branch on Fort Rd, T4621973. *Charlie's Outdoor Café*, at Jasmine Court Mall on Friars Hill Rd, T5622233. Open for breakfast, lunch and afternoon tea, in tropical garden setting in West Indian colonial style mini shopping mall, salads, soups and sandwiches, around US$9.

In Hodges Bay area, near the airport, *Le Bistro*, T4623881. Excellent French food, dinner only, closed Mon. At airport, *Big Banana*, is surprisingly good, clean and efficient, closed Sun.

Runaway Bay Cricketing friends Richie Richardson and David Folb (Chairman of Lashings Cricket Club in Maidstone, Kent), took over *Lashings Beach Café* at *Sandhaven* in 1999, bar and restaurant, from chilli to lobster, special deals at hotel for visiting cricket teams, if you beat the Lashings team you get free food and drinks. Late night hot spot with loud music and dancing. *The Beach*, formerly *Spinkers*, T4624158. Same owners as the *Big Banana*, open daily for breakfast, lunch and dinner, East meets West theme, with smoked sushi, Middle Eastern dishes and salads, pastas and seafoods, main dishes around US$18-20, credit cards accepted, reservations suggested. On Wed and Fri nights, 1630-2100, except when raining, an English family serves fish and chips (and shrimp and Pot Pies) for around US$5-10 from a truck on the road outside *Buccaneer Cove* at Dickenson Bay, T5602334, just past the *Siboney* driveway, very busy, lots of locals, not to be missed.

Galley Bay *Chez Pascal*, overlooking Galley Bay, T4623232. Gourmet, authentic French food from French chef Pascal, expect to pay over US$55 per person.

Jolly Harbour At Jolly Harbour marine complex there is an Italian *trattoria*, *Al Porto*, T4627695. Pasta, pizzas, seafood in al fresco setting, poor service, meals from US$10, open daily lunch and dinner, closed 1500-1900. *Peter's* next door. Excellent, barbecued fresh fish and lobster, prices from EC$15. Recommended. *OJ's Beach Bar & Restaurant*, Crab Hill, T4600184, on beach. Excellent setting, simple menu but good food and service, economical prices, no credit cards.

English Harbour There is a restaurant and bar on Shirley Heights, steel band and barbecue every Sun afternoon (see page 596). *Abracadabra* just outside Nelson's Dockyard, T4602701. Lively video bar, live music some evenings, Italian and Continental dishes, open every evening, closed Sep-Oct. *Eden Café* is next to *Abracadabra*, in a 300-year-old building. Breakfast specials are 100% fruit smoothies and fresh French pastry, Mediterranean salad specialities at lunch, around US$9-10, Fri-Sat open midnight till 0400 for late night sandwiches and coffee for the dancing crowd, credit cards accepted. *Admiral's Inn*, Nelson's Dockyard, T4601027. Breakfast (slow but good value, recommended), lunch and dinner (limited selection but good, slightly overpriced), yachtsman's dinner EC$40, closed Sep. *HQ*, upstairs in the historic Headquarters Building inside English Harbour, T5622562. Open daily for all three meals, dinner reservations suggested, credit cards accepted. *The Dry Dock*, at the entrance to the Antigua Yacht Club Marina. Open every day, restaurant and bar, prices around US$15, with big screen TVs for sport and Antigua Race Week events.Near St James' Club, *Alberto's*, T4603007. Choice dining spot frequented by ex-pat 'locals' plus celebrities like Eric Clapton, Timothy Dalton, Italian run, open air tropical setting, fresh seafood and pasta always available, expect to pay over US$55, reservations essential. Recommended. *Catherine's Café* at the Antigua Slipway in Nelson's Dockyard, T4605050. French chef, divine crêpes, quiches, assorted salads, lovely setting right on water, open daily, breakfast and lunch only, average price US$18-20. Highly recommended. At *Galleon Beach Club*, English Harbour, *Colombo's* T4601452. Italian restaurant, recommended for good food but expensive, open 1200-1500, 1900-2230, reggae band Wed. *Grace Before Meals*, between English Harbour and Falmouth Harbour. A cheaper alternative to the many expensive restaurants, rotis, pizzas and other good value meals to eat in or take away. Between English and Falmouth Harbours, *Le Cap Horn*, T4601194. Pizzeria, Argentine Churrasco steak, lobster, some French dishes, great food, open 1830-2300. *Mario's Pizzeria*, T4601318. Delicious pizza baked in stone ovens, around US$7-8, also famous for fresh bread. *Southern Cross*, expensive Italian restaurant, over US$55 per person, upstairs on newly constructed jetty off Antigua Yacht Club, delicious food, wonderful setting, closed in summer. *The Copper and Lumber Store* is overpriced, you pay for the 'atmosphere', which is not to everybody's taste and the portions are small, but excellent.

East *Eastern Parkway*, also known as *Harry's Bar* is at Half Moon Bay Beach, T4604402. Open-air covered beach bar, snacks, cold drinks, burgers and local specialities like bread and saltfish, goat curry, very casual dining on premises or takeaway, good value at around US$5-6, open daily. *Harmony Hall*, T4604120, www.harmonyhall.com Excellent Italian restaurant written up in many gourmet magazines, lunch daily, from US$22, dinner Fri-Sat, reservations essential, art gallery, panoramic view of Green Island, to where you can have a complimentary boat trip.

Festivals **Antigua** Carnival is at the end of *July* and lasts until the 1st Tuesday in *August*. The main event is 'J'ouvert', or 'Juvé' morning when from 0400 people come into town dancing behind steel and brass bands. Hotels and airlines tend to be booked up well in advance. For information contact the Carnival Committee, High St, St John's, T4620194. **Barbuda** has a smaller carnival in *May*, known as '*Caribana* '. An annual **jazz festival** is held, usually in late *May*, with concerts at Fort James, the *Sandpiper Reef Hotel*, King's Casino and on the *Jolly Roger*. Contact the Tourist Office for a programme. A **hot air balloon festival** is held at the end of *October*.

Nightlife The largest hotels provide dancing, calypso, steel bands, limbo dancers and moonlight bar-
English Harbour area becues. There is a cinema (very old movies), nightclubs, discothèques and casinos. English
has become the 'hot Harbour is safer for evenings out, especially for women alone. At the entrance to the Dock-
spot' for tourists yard, **Hype-Bar**, owned by two former London DJs, its all music.In the Dockyard, Fri night **Copper and Lumber** have 2 for the price of 1, Wed Jazz, Thur karaoke. **Galley Bar** is popular with occasional entertainment. **Mad Mongoose**, **The Dry Dock** and **Abracadabra** nearly always lively, with dancing at **The Dry Dock Abracadabra**. In St John's, **Julian's** upstairs bar has jazz nights. **Ribbit Club**, near Deep Water Harbour, very local; **Putters**, Dickenson Bay, has mini golf course. The **Kings Casino** in Heritage Quay awaits cruise ship passengers. Be warned that casino employees entice you off the street with the lure of winning easy money. After an initial spell of amazing luck, one reader (not a gambler) lost US$3,500 in 20 mins. Casinos at *Royal Antiguan* (only slot machines) and *St James's Club*. The newest is **Casino Riviera**, Runaway Bay, opened 1999 with gaming tables, bar, restaurant serving lunch and dinner and live evening entertainment. At **Dubarry's** bar there is jazz on Sun night, rum punch party on Tue, barbecue on Thur, take swimsuit, parties tend to end up in, not just by, the pool. **Miller's**, at Fort James. Serves lunch, dinner, or just drinks, often has live music, for example reggae bands, especially on Sun after Shirley Heights, owned by a local jazz hero. Laurie Stevens, British, provides nightly, musical entertainment around the island: Mon, **Tradewinds**; Tue **Halcyon Hotel**; Wed, **O'Grady's Irish Pub** on Nevis Street; Fri, **Columbos** in English Harbour; enquire about other evenings. His wife, Lisette, is a palmist, so ask about a reading if you want to see into the future. A free newspaper, *It's Happening, You're Welcome*, contains lots of information on forthcoming events.

Shopping The market building is at the south end of Market Street but there are goods on sale all
Market day in around. In season, there is a good supply of fruit and vegetables, which are easy to obtain on
St John's is Sat the island. The main supermarket in St John's is **Bryson's**, on Long Street. **Woods Center** is a new, modern shopping mall with a wide variety of shops including **The Epicurean Supermarket**, the most modern, well stocked supermarket on the island, a drugstore, post office, dental clinic, dry cleaners and numerous other shops. **Gourmet Basket** on Airport Rd in the Island Provision Compound, near **Best Cellars Wines**, has gourmet items and a deli.Most grocery stores open 0800-2200, although many close at 1300 on Thu. You can buy fish from the fishing boats at the back of the Casino or from **Caribbean Seafoods** in Cassada Gardens near the horse racetrack (T4626113), large selection of cleaned and ready to cook seafood, freshly caught (by their own fishing boat), vacuum packed and quick frozen. Heritage Quay (public toilets) and Redcliffe Quay are shopping complexes with expensive duty-free shops in the former, and boutiques. The latter has bars and restaurants and a parking lot, free if you are shopping there. There are several shops on St Mary Street and others nearby, which stock clothing, crafts and other items from neighbouring islands, for example **Caribelle Batik**, T4622972. There are two grocery and liquor stores at *Antigua Yacht Club* dock. Some tourist shops offer 10% reductions to locals: they compensate by overcharging tourists. Duty free shops at the airport are more expensive than normal shops in town. **The Map Shop** (St Mary Street) carries a good selection of Caribbean literature plus reference books and guides to history, culture, fauna and flora of the Caribbean. **PC Book Revue**, further up the road has lots of old issues of magazines. The public library on Market St has a good Caribbean section, particularly non-fiction, for those who want to read but not buy. **Harmony Hall**, Brown's Bay Mill, near Freetown, T4604120. An art gallery and gift shop, open daily 1000-1800, exhibiting and selling paintings, sculpture and crafts from leading Caribbean artists, popular for a lunch stop at the restaurant while touring by car or yacht.

Air V C Bird airport, some 4½ miles from St John's, is the centre for air traffic in the area. *British Airways* (T4620876, from London Gatwick, connections with Barbados, Port of Spain and St Lucia), *BWIA* (from London Heathrow) and *Virgin Atlantic* (from Gatwick), *Condor* (direct from Frankfurt), *Air France* (from Paris). *American Airlines* (from Orlando, Miami), *Continental* (from Newark, NJ), *BWIA* (from New York, Miami), *BWIA* and *Air Canada*, T4621147 (from Toronto). There are frequent air services to neighbouring islands (Anguilla, Barbados, Barbuda, Dominica, Martinique, Grenada, Guyana, Jamaica, Nevis, Guadeloupe, Trinidad, St Barts, St Croix, St Kitts, St Lucia, St Maarten, St Thomas, St Vincent, Puerto Rico, Tortola) operated by *LIAT* (T4620700), *Caribbean Star* (T4802550), *BWIA* (T4620260), *Continental*, *American Eagle*, *Air Guadeloupe*, *Air St Kitts/Nevis* (T4658571). *Carib Aviation* (T4623147) arranges charters to neighbouring islands in planes carrying 5, 6 or 9 passengers and can often work out cheaper and more convenient than using *LIAT*. The office is at the airport, T4623147, 0800-1700, after office hours T4611650. They will meet incoming flights if you are transferring to another island, and make sure you make your return connection. Also day tours. **Helicopter** *Caribbean Helicopters*, helitours, custom charters and day trips, daily, 15-min island tour, US$75 per person, 30-min tour US$130, 45-min Montserrat Volcano tour, US$190, T4605900, F4605901, www.caribbeanhighlights.com/helicopter/default.htm **Ferry** to Montserrat leaves Heritage Quay 0630, 1600, returning from Little Bay 0800, 1730, US$55.50/EC$150 return. Be at the dock at least an hour beforehand to clear immigration, which stops 30 mins before departure (time limit strictly enforced). At weekends and holiday times get there even earlier. French boat, previously used between French Antilles, good condition, efficient. There are occasional boat services to St Kitts and Dominica; see boat captains at Fisherman's Wharf. There is a cargo boat to Dominica once a week and you can arrange a passage through Vernon Edwards Shipping Company on Thames Street; very basic facilities.

Local Bicycle Bicycle hire from *Cycle Krazy* on St Mary's St, T4629253. *Bikes Plus*, T4622453. **Bus** Buses are banned from the tourist area (north of the line from the airport to St John's), but run frequently between St John's and English Harbour, EC$2.50. There are also buses from the east terminal by the war memorial to Willikies, whence a 20-min walk to Long Bay beach and to Parham. There are no buses to the airport and very few to beaches though two good swimming beaches on the way to Old Road can be reached by bus. Bus frequency can be variable, and there are very few after dark or on Sun. Buses usually go when they are full, ask the driver where he is going. They are numbered and destinations are on display boards at the West Bus Station. Buses to Old Road are half hourly on average, though more frequent around 0800 and 1600. **Car hire** A local driving licence, US$20, valid for three months, must be purchased on presentation of a foreign licence. There is a 24-hr petrol station on Old Parham Road outside St John's. Petrol costs US$2.25 per gallon everywhere. A complete list of car hire companies is available on the Board of Tourism web site. *Hertz*, T4624114/5; *Avis*, T4622840, *Dollar Rental*, T4620362 (Factory Road); *National*, T4622113; at *Oakland Rent-A-Car* you can negotiate good rates, contact Ann Edwards, T4623021. Rates are from US$58 per day, US$225 a week (no mileage charge), including insurance charges, in summer, more in winter. **Hitchhiking** is easy in daylight but at night you might fall prey to a taxi driver. **Taxi** Taxis have TX registration plates. In St John's there is a taxi rank on St Mary Street, or outside Bryson's supermarket. They are not metered and frequently try to overcharge, or else have no change, so agree a price first, they should have a EC$ price list so ask to see it. There is a list of government approved taxi rates posted in EC$ and US$ at the airport just after customs. From St John's to Runaway Bay, 10 mins, is US$6. From the airport to *Admiral's Inn*, *St James's Club*, *Falmouth Beach Apartments*, *Curtain Bluff*, *Harmony Hall*, Darkwood Beach etc is US$24/EC$64; to *Sandals*, *Antigua Village* and Dickenson Bay area US$13/EC$34; to *Blue Waters* US$10/EC$27; *Hawksbill* and Five Islands US$16/EC$42. From the airport to town EC$21 per person. If going to the airport early in the morning, book a taxi the night before as there are not many around. A day tour normally costs about US$70 for 1-4 people, US$76 for 5-7 people. Taxi excursions advertised in the hotels are generally overpriced. Tips for taxi drivers are usually 10% of the fare.

Directory **Banks** *Scotia Bank, Barclays Bank, Royal Bank of Canada, Canadian Imperial Bank of Commerce, Antigua and Barbuda Investment Bank, Antigua Commercial Bank*, all in the centre of St John's. Mosts banks take Mastercard and Visa. The *Swiss American Bank of Antigua* is open on Sat morning (also a branch in St John's). A tax of 1% is levied on all foreign exchange transactions but there may be additional charges on TCs. Casinos will change TCs without a fee. *American Express* is at Antours near Heritage Quay, staff helpful and friendly. **Communications** Post: Post office at the end of Long Street, St John's, opposite the supermarket. Open Mon-Thu, 0815-1200, 1300-1600, until 1700 on Fri; also a Post office at the airportand at English Harbour. A postcard to the USA costs EC$0.45. *Federal Express* is on Church Street. *DHL* is in the Vernon Edwards building on Thames Street. **Telephone:** *Cable and Wireless Ltd*, Long Street, St John's, the Woods Mall and at English Harbour. **Internet** Cable and Wireless Cybercafé at Antigua Yacht Club (bring your own computer, or use theirs). Also email, messages, etc, at *International Connections* at AYC dock and at the Internet Café on Upper Church Street in St John's. **Embassies and consulates** The *British High Commission* is at the Price Waterhouse Centre (PO Box 483), 11 Old Parham Road, St Johns, T4620008/9, F4622806. **Tourist information** Local tourist office: *Antigua Tourist Office*, corner of Nevis St and Friendly Alley. T4620480, F4622483,www.antigua-barbuda.org deptourism@candw.ag Open 0830-1600 (Mon-Fri) and 0830-1200 (Sat). Gives list of official taxi charges and hotel information. Also has an office at airport, will help book accommodation principally at the more expensive resorts. The Antigua Hotels and Tourist Association, PO Box 454, Island House, New Gates St, St John's, T4620374, F4623702, www.antiguahotels.org **Tour operators:** *Mac's Tracks*, run by Brian MacMillan, PO Box 107, St John's (home T4627376), F4611187, 2-4 hr hikes on special request, from US$10 per person, exploring the countryside, lunch and transport to start of hike can be arranged, to Boggy Peak, Mt McNish, Monterose Hill, Signal Hill and Green Castle Hill. *Tropikelly Trails*, PO Box W1920, St John's, T4610382, US$65 per person, Mon-Fri tours includes drinks, lunch, hotel pick-up, 5-6 hrs to Body Pond, Monks Hill, the pineapple farm at Claremont Estate, Boggy Peak and the silk cotton tree at Cades Bay, where 10 people can stand inside the hollow trunk.

Barbuda

Population: 1,500
Colour map 4, grid B3

The people of Barbuda are unusually tall, descendants of the Corramante tribe in Africa and used by Codrington in his experiments in slave breeding, see page 606

Some 30 miles to the north is Barbuda, a flat coral island some 68 miles square, one of the two island dependencies of Antigua. Most of the population live in the only village on the island, **Codrington**, which stands on the edge of the lagoon.

Barbuda has some excellent beaches and its seas are rich with all types of crustaceans and tropical fish. **Palaster Reef** is a marine reserve to protect the reef and the shipwrecks (there are around 60 ships documented). You can swim from the beach to the reef. This is one of the few islands in the area where there is still much wildlife, although much of it introduced by man: duck, guinea fowl, plover, pigeon, wild deer, pigs, horses and donkeys.

There is an impressive **frigate bird colony** in the mangroves in Codrington Lagoon, particularly on Man of War Island where hundreds of birds mate and breed in August-December. Local fishermen will take you out there; you can get quite close for photography or just to watch. Popular with ornithologists working nine months of the year in Antarctica, who spend their holidays coming to see 'their' frigate birds in Codrington Lagoon. Ask the guide to drop you at Palm Bay on the west side of the lagoon and pick you up 4-5 hours later.

Meanwhile walk the 17 miles of beaches, up north or down south, but bring a hat and sunscreen. The caves near Two Foot Bay are interesting to explore. There are no beach bars or vendors, you will probably be the only person for miles. There is no shade except around Palm Beach where there is a lot of litter. The island has a Martello Tower and fort. The tower is 56ft high and once had nine guns to defend the southwest approach. It now has a swarm of killer bees in the cellar – take care. From Codrington, River Road runs three miles to **Palmetto Point** (with beautiful pink sand beaches), past Cocoa Point and on to Spanish Point, a half-mile finger of land that divides the Atlantic from the Caribbean Sea. There is a small ruin of a lookout post here and the most important Arawak settlements found in Barbuda.

One of Barbuda's main sources of income is the mining of sand. In 1993 a High Court injunction against the mining led to a severe cash crisis and public employees were not paid for several months. The injunction was imposed pending the resolution of a dispute between the Government and the island council over who has authority for sand mining. Mining of sand at Palmetto Point allegedly damaged a pure water supply. The Minister of Agriculture and two businessmen were convicted of breaching the injunction, but the Minister was subsequently pardoned by the Governor General.

Barbuda is being developed as a tourist resort with attractions for **snorkellers** and **divers** such as exploring old wrecks. The elkhorn coral and staghorn coral formations are very impressive. Take your own scuba equipment or hire it from Byron Askie (certified divers only, single tank dive with equipment and boat US$165 each). Snorkelling equipment is available but is more expensive than on Antigua.

Sleeping

LL *Coco Point Lodge*, T4623816, F4625340, in the USA T212-9861416. Charges US$750 double per night including all meals and drinks and airfare from Antigua, is quiet and exclusive, islanders and non-guests are not admitted. **LL** *K-Club*, T4600300, F4600305, or through Elegant Resorts or Unique Hotels, T01453-835801, F01453-835525. Owned and designed by Italians, 34 rooms, from US$1,200 a night (US$950 off season) plus US$200 air fare, with its own 9-hole golf course (the grass was laid on soil cleared from the mangrove swamp so there are problems now with salt) as well as watersports, welcomes islanders and non-residents, open mid-Nov to end-Aug, no children under 12. **LL** *Palmetto Beach Hotel*, T4600442, F4600440, www. CaribComInc.com, beach front on 11-mile beach at Palmetto Point. 22 junior suites and a villa with two more suites, FAP, tennis, pool, water sports, bikes, volleyball, library. **A** *Nedd's Guest House* in Codrington, T4600059. Clean and airy rooms upstairs, call prior to arrival and fix room rate with Mr McArthur Nedd, use of kitchen, mini-mart downstairs, bakery just behind the guesthouse in the next street, no road name signs. Houses are also available for rent at about US$35-70, phone Evans at the car rental for help. *Bus Stop Guest House*, T4600081. Bed and breakfast. **A** *Byron Askie's Guest House*, T4600065. 4-bedroomed house. *The Island Chalet Guest House*, in the heart of Codrington, T7730066/4600065, Mrs Myra Askia. 4 rooms with double bed and rollaway can sleep 3, shared kitchen and living room facilities, car rental and tours arranged. Several private homes offer accommodation, although these change if a long-term rental is taken. **C** *Ileene Nedd*, T4600419, has a 1-bedroom house or a 3-bedroom house for rent. **B-C** *Francis Guest House*, T4600346, offers a single room, double room or suite with kitchen. **C** *Dennis Harris*, has a 3-bedroom house.

Eating

The Lime, at the jetty where you embark for boat trips is a nightspot. Do not expect many 'mod cons' on Barbuda. Several small snack bars, ask locally. The *Palm Tree* and *Park Terrace*, at the airport, are both restaurants for local food.

Shopping

Excellent 1:25,000 **maps** should be available from the Codrington post office or the map shop in Jardine Court, St Mary's, St John's (also good 1:50,000 maps of Antigua). It is safer to get one before you arrive in Barbuda, you can not rely on anything being in stock.

Transport

Easily reached by air (taking 10 mins), or (with some difficulty and at a high price, US$150) by boat from St John's. **Air** There are two airports. The main one is just south of Codrington. *Carib Aviation* will arrange charters and day trips. Return ticket costs US$63, or US$67 if you buy it less than 3 days before departure. The 2nd airport is near Cocoa Point and only serves *Coco Point*. Day tours from Antigua include the Bird Sanctuary, Highland House, the Caves and the Martello Tower, contact Barbara Japal, Caribrep, T4632070, F5601824. **Boat** Charter boats do day trips but you will not see much of Barbuda. **Road** It is possible to hire jeeps:US$54 per day or US$60 overnight including insurance, from Junie Walker, T4600159. Mr Linton Thomas has a pick up truck for US$50 per day or US$65 overnight. **Horses** can be hired in Codrington, otherwise everywhere is a long hot walk, so take drinks with you. The *Barbuda Taxi Association* will do tours, T7279957, so will Mrs Elenora Thomas at the Barbuda Tourist Office, T4600077. The US$65 day tour includes collection and return to the airport, a boat trip to the bird sanctuary, lunch at the *Palm Tree Terrace*, a visit to the caves, martello tower and other points of interest.

Leeward Islands

Directory Barbuda has a newly established Tourism Department located in Antigua at the Department of Tourism on lower Nevis Street. Director is Ms. Claudia Richards (T461-1208). There will soon be a Web site dedicated only to Barbuda. Efforts are being made to standardize and regulate the services provided on Barbuda in order to upgrade the tourism market.

Redonda

Colour map 4, grid C2 Antigua's second dependency, 35 miles to the southwest and at half a mile square, is little more than a rocky volcanic islet and is uninhabited. Columbus sighted the island on 12 November 1493 and named it after a church in Cadiz called Santa María la Redonda. He did not land, however, and thus did not formally claim the island. Neither did anyone else until 1865 when Matthew Dowdy Shiell, an Irish sea-trader from Montserrat, celebrated the birth of a long-awaited son by leading an expedition of friends to Redonda and claiming it as his kingdom. In 1872, the island was annexed by Britain and came under the jurisdiction of the colony of Antigua, despite protests from the Shiells. The Title of King was not disputed, however, and has survived to this day. The island was never inhabited although for some years guano was extracted by the Redonda Phosphate Company until the works were blown away by a hurricane.

In 1880 MD Shiell abdicated in favour of his son, Matthew Phipps Shiell, who became King Felipe of Redonda but emigrated to the UK where he was educated and became a prolific and popular novelist. His most well known novel was *The Purple Cloud* (1901), which was later made into a film, *The World, the Flesh and the Devil*, starring Harry Belafonte. On his death in 1947 he appointed as his literary executor and successor to the throne, his friend John Gawsworth, the poet, who became Juan, the third King of Redonda, but continued to live in London. His reign was notable for his idea of an 'intellectual aristocracy' of the realm of Redonda and he conferred titles on his literary friends, including Victor Gollancz, the publisher, JB Priestley, Dorothy L Sayers and Lawrence Durrell. This eccentric pastime hit a crisis when declining fortunes and increasing time spent in the pub sparked a rash of new titles to all and sundry, a number of abdications in different pubs, and the succession was, and still is, disputed.

The *Redondan Cultural Foundation* is an independent association of people interested in Redonda, its history and its monarchs, which tries to steer through the minefield of Redonda politics. It was established in 1988 by the late Reverend Paul de Fortis and exists to promote the writings of MP Shiell, John Gawsworth and other authors of the realm's 'intellectual aristocracy'. It celebrates Redonda as 'the last outpost of Bohemia'. The foundation published *The Kingdom of Redonda 1865-1990* in association with the Aylesford Press (1991), and also publishes a regular newsletter.

Meanwhile, on Redonda, all is much the same for the goats, lizards and sea birds, who live an undisturbed life apart from the occasional bird watcher who might come to find the burrowing owl, now extinct on Antigua.

Background

History Antigua (pronounced Anteega) was first inhabited by the Siboney (stone people), whose settlements date back to at least 2400 BC. The Arawaks lived on the island between about AD 35 and 1100. Columbus landed on his second voyage in 1493 and named the island Santa María de la Antigua. Spanish and French colonists attempted to settle there but were discouraged by the absence of freshwater springs and attacks by the Caribs. In 1632 the English successfully colonized the island and, apart from a brief interlude in 1666 when held by the French, the island and its dependencies, Barbuda and uninhabited Redonda, remained British. Sir Christopher Codrington established the first large sugar estate in Antigua in 1674 and leased Barbuda to raise provisions for his plantations. Barbuda's only village is named after him. Forests were cleared for sugarcane production and African slave labour was imported. Today, many Antiguans blame frequent droughts on the island's lack of trees to attract rainfall, and ruined towers of sugar plantations stand as testament to the destruction and consequent barrenness of the landscape. In the 17th and 18th centuries, Antigua was important for its natural harbours where British ships could be refitted safe from hurricanes and from attack. The Dockyard and the many fortifications date from this period. *Shirley Heights, The Story of the Red Coats in Antigua*, by Charles W E Jane, published by the Reference Library of Nelson's Dockyard National Park Foundation at English Harbour, Antigua, in 1982, gives a detailed account of the military history of the island and the building of the fortifications.

The slaves were emancipated in 1834 but economic opportunities for the freed labourers were limited by a lack of surplus farming land, no access to credit, and an economy built on agriculture rather than manufacturing. Conditions for black people were little better than under slavery and in many cases the planters treated them worse. Poor labour conditions persisted and violence erupted in the first part of the 20th century as workers protested against low wages, food shortages and poor living conditions. In 1939, to alleviate the seething discontent, the first labour movement was formed: the Antigua Trades and Labour Union. Vere Cornwall Bird became the union's president in 1943 and with other trade unionists formed the Antigua Labour Party (ALP). In 1946 the ALP won the first of a long series of electoral victories, being voted out of office only in 1971-76 when the Progressive Labour Movement won the general election. For a graphic account of the terrible conditions in which black people lived and worked during slavery and its aftermath, read *To Shoot Hard Labour (The Life and Times of Samuel Smith, an Antiguan Workingman 1877-1982)*, by Keithlyn B Smith and Fernando C Smith, published by Karia Press, London, and Edan's Publishers, Toronto.

Antigua was administered as part of the Leeward Islands until 1959 and attained associated status, with full internal self-government in 1967. Antigua and Barbuda, as a single territory, became independent in November 1981, despite a strong campaign for separate independence by Barbuda. Vere C Bird became the first Prime Minister and in 1989, at the age of 79, he took office for the fourth consecutive time. The general elections were marked by some irregularities and allegations of bribery, but the ALP won 15 of the 16 seats for Antigua in the 17 seat House of Representatives, the remaining seats being taken by the United National Democratic Party and the Barbuda People's Movement, for Barbuda. Mr Bird appointed a largely unchanged cabinet which included several members of his family.

In 1990 the Government was rocked by an arms smuggling scandal which exposed corruption at an international level when allegations were made that Antigua had been used as a transit point for shipments of arms from Israel to the Medellín cocaine cartel in Colombia. Communications and Works Minister, Vere Bird Jr, the Prime Minister's son, became the subject of a judicial inquiry, following a complaint from the Colombian Government, for having signed authorization documents. His Cabinet appointment was revoked although he remained an MP. The Blom-Cooper report recommended no prosecutions although it undermined the credibility of the Government and highlighted the rivalry between the two sons, Vere Jr and Lester Bird. The report also recommended that Vere Bird Jr be banned for life from holding public office.

Repeated calls for the resignation of Prime Minister Vere Bird were ignored although several ministers resigned from his Government. Demonstrations were organized in 1992 by the newly-formed three-party United Opposition Front, seeking the resignation of the Prime Minister amid allegations of his theft and corruption. Fresh allegations of corruption were published in 1993 by the weekly opposition newspaper, *Outlet*, concerning property development contracts and misuse of public funds, resulting in a libel action issued by Lester Bird. *Outlet*, edited by Tim Hector, has for many years been the most outspoken critic of the Bird administration, frequently exposing corruption and fraud.

Leeward Islands

Tourism versus conservation – more controversy

*In 1997 the government signed an agreement with Johan Holdings Berhad, of Malaysia, for the construction by Asian Village Holdings of a tourist resort on **Guiana Island** off the northeast coast of Antigua, together with Crump Island, Hawes Island and the mainland area of Coconut Hall. This massive development will cover 1,500 acres and comprise 2,000 hotel rooms (6 hotels), villas and condominiums, two golf courses and a casino. Guiana Island is an ecologically sensitive area and the Antiguan government has been criticized for not demanding a full environmental impact study. A debate in the House of Representatives on the development was boycotted by the opposition UPP, resulting in the approval of a government motion to authorize the project. The UPP complained that there had been no public discussion of the issue, while Prime Minister Bird promised 4,000 jobs, US$100mn in foreign exchange earnings, tax income, business opportunities and more besides. The group of islands is surrounded by reefs, with*

mangroves providing important nesting sites and nursery grounds. Guiana Island, 352 acres, is home to the fallow deer (Dama dama), the endangered West Indian tree duck (Dendrocygna arborea) and the tropical mocking bird (Mimus gilvus). Most of the islands are covered with xerophytic trees and scrub. Remains of Indian habitation have been found on Guiana Island, dating from around 3,000 BC. In the mid 18th century it was owned by Charles Tudway of Parham Hill estate. In 1812, Sir William Codrington III bought the island and farmed it until it was sold out of the family in 1929. A British couple who lived on the island for 30 years and cared for the deer, were removed in 1997 and their house demolished; 300 fallow deer are also to be removed. The old Great House is uninhabited but there was a proposal to restore it, creating a lodge and interpretation centre for a nature reserve. Archaeologists appealed for the chance to study the island before it went under the bulldozer. Development began in 1998.

Vere Bird finally retired as Prime Minister in February 1994 at the age of 84. He was succeeded by his son, Lester, who led the ALP into the general elections held in March, winning its ninth out of 10 elections held since 1951. The Government's unpopularity was reflected in the vote and the ALP saw its representation cut from 15 to 11 seats in the House of Representatives. The Barbuda People's Movement retained its seat, while the United Progressive Party (formerly the United Opposition Front), led by Baldwin Spencer, won five seats, the largest number for any opposition party in the country's history. Tim Hector was appointed an opposition senator, having stood against Vere Jr in the election and lost. Vere Bird Jr, who is the chairman of the ALP, was not appointed to the new cabinet. In 1995, Hugh Marshall, a former trade minister launched a new party, the People's Democratic Movement.

The new government was not free of allegations of corruption scandals (Ivor Bird, a younger Bird brother and general manager of the ZDK radio station was arrested and fined for taking possession of 12kg of cocaine at the airport) although Prime Minister Bird made efforts to portray a more professional administration. Economic adjustment was given priority and new tax policies sparked protest demonstrations and strikes. Efforts were made to clean up Antigua's poor reputation with the appointment in 1996 of a special advisor on control of illicit drugs and money laundering. Eleven offshore banks were closed by end 1997 and new legislation was approved in 1998 to close loopholes taken advantage of by international criminal organizations. However, this did not go far enough to satisfy US and UK regulators, who believed money laundering was still taking place. The Government bowed to the criticism and set up a committee in 1999 to study the areas of concern in its offshore financial services legislation.

In March 1999 the ALP won its sixth successive general election, increasing its representation in parliament to 12 seats, while the UPP won four and the BPM retained the Barbuda seat. The new cabinet was notable for the appointment of Vere Bird Jr as Minister of Agriculture, Lands and Fisheries.

Antigua and Barbuda is a constitutional monarchy within the Commonwealth and the British Crown is represented by a Governor General. The head of government is the Prime Minister. There are two legislative houses: a directly elected 17-member House of Representatives and a 17-member Upper House, or Senate, appointed by the Governor General, mainly on the advice of the Prime Minister and the Leader of the Opposition. Antigua is divided into six parishes: St George, St John's, St Mary, St Paul, St Peter and St Phillip. Community councils on Antigua and the local government council on Barbuda are the organs of local government. The Barbuda Council has nine seats, with partial elections held every two years.

The economy was long dominated by the cultivation of sugar, the major export earner until 1960 when prices fell dramatically and crippled the industry. By 1972 sugar had largely disappeared and farming had shifted towards fruit, vegetables, cotton and livestock. The economy is now based on services, principally tourism and offshore banking where improvements in legislation were made in 1999-2000 to prevent money laundering. Hotels and restaurants contribute about 25% of gross domestic product and employ about one third of the work force. Tourism receipts make up about 60% of total foreign exchange earnings and there are about 5,000 hotel rooms. Tourist numbers have often been hit by hurricane damage but the start of Virgin Atlantic air services from London helped tourist arrival statistics.

There is some light industry which has been encouraged by tax and other incentives, but manufacturing for export is hampered by high wages and energy costs. A major expansion of tourist infrastructure has taken place, with development of harbour, airport, road and hotel facilities. This investment has not yet touched the bulk of the population and in rural areas small wooden shacks still constitute the most common form of dwelling, often alongside resorts and villa developments. Economic growth slowed in the early 1990s; political instability and corruption discouraged private sector investment, while government finances were weakened by high levels of debt, wages and tax evasion. Since the 1995 hurricane, however, gdp has picked up and strong growth rates recorded.

St Kitts and Nevis

The islands of St Kitts (officially named St Christopher) and Nevis are in the north part of the Leeward Islands in the Eastern Caribbean. Slightly off the beaten track, neither island is overrun with tourists. St Kitts is developing its southern peninsula where there are sandy beaches, but most of the island is untouched by tourism. Rugged volcanic peaks, forests and old fortresses produce spectacular views and hiking is very rewarding. Two miles away, the conical island of Nevis is smaller, quieter and very desirable. Here, plantation houses have been converted into some of the most romantic hotels in the Caribbean, very popular with honeymooners. While one federation, the sister islands are quite different. St Kitts, the larger, is more cosmopolitan and livelier, while Nevis is quieter and more sedate. Wherever you go on these two small islands there are breathtaking, panoramic views of the sea, mountains, cultivated fields and small villages.

Colour map 4, grid B2

Ins and outs

Getting there
See transport,
page 630, for
further details

There are charter flights, which tend to be seasonal, but no direct scheduled flights to St Kitts and Nevis from Europe or North America, you have to fly to a neighbouring island and change planes. Cruise ships call at St Kitts, but otherwise there are few links by boat with other islands and they tend to be informal.

Getting around
Driving is on the left

Buses on both islands are cheap and speedy. Drivers are generally very obliging and, if asked, may even divert their route to accommodate you. They run from very early in the morning until 2300 on St Kitts, but on Nevis there is a reduced service after 1600 and very few

Leeward Islands

★ A Foot in the door

- Join a **salsa class** on Wednesday night at the *Bayembi Café Dance Floor* (conveniently next to *Mango's Bar*), where the music is spicy and the atmosphere is lively and friendly.
- Take a **donkey ride** on Nevis, the island where they joke that there are more donkeys than people.
- St Kitts is Sugar City; visit the **sugar factory** while this way of life still exists, try some cane juice and watch the whole production process.
- Ask about **politics** for a lively debate; every Kittitian and Nevisian has a view on secession and their political parties and will fill you in on the intrigue .
- **Catch a bus** and take a ride around St Kitts, the best way to experience the island, the villages, the people and their culture.

after 1800. Buses are identified by their green H registration plate, flag them down with a wave. **Cars**, jeeps, mini mokes can be hired from a variety of agencies on both islands. The main road on St Kitts is, for the most part, very good and motorists, especially bus drivers, can be very fast. Watch out for corners and be alert at all times. The main road is not as good on Nevis, where storm ditches frequently cross the paved road; drive slowly and carefully. Traffic has increased and parking in both Basseterre and Charlestown is difficult. Several passenger **ferries** including the *Caribe Queen, Carib Breeze* and *MV Sea Hustler* operate on a regular schedule between St Kitts and Nevis.

Climate The weather is pleasant all year round but the best time to visit is during the dry months from Nov-May. The temperature varies between 17°C and 33°C, tempered by sea winds and with an average annual rainfall of 55 ins on St Kitts and 48 ins on Nevis.

Flora and fauna

St Kitts & Nevis have the earliest documented evidence of honey bees in the Caribbean

Both islands are home to the green vervet monkey, introduced by the French some 300 years ago, now dwelling on the forested areas in the mountains. They can be seen in many areas including Brimstone Hill. Scientists have been studying these attractive little creatures and many have been exported; being relatively free of disease they are used for medical research. The monkey is the same animal as on Barbados but the Kittitians used to eat them. Another animal, the mongoose, imported by colonists to kill rats in the sugar estates and snakes never achieved its original purpose (rats being nocturnal whereas the mongoose is active by day) and survives in considerable numbers. It has contributed to the extinction of many species of lizard, ground nesting birds, green iguanas, brown snakes and red-legged tortoises. There are also some wild deer on the southeast peninsula, imported originally from Puerto Rico by Philip Todd in the 1930s. In common with other West Indian islands, there are highly vocal frogs, lots of lizards (the anole is the most common), fruit bats, insect bats and butterflies, although nothing particularly rare. Birds are typical of the region, with lots of sea fowl like brown pelicans and frigate birds to be seen, as well as three species of hummingbirds. Fish abound in local waters (rays, barracuda, king fish and brilliantly coloured smaller species) and the increasingly rare black coral tree can be sighted in the reef of the same name.

St Kitts and Nevis are small islands, yet have a wide variety of habitats, with rainforest, dry woodland, wetland, grassland and salt ponds. The forests (of which a small percentage are rain forests) on the sister islands are restricted in scale but St Kitts is one of the few areas of the world where the forest is expanding. It provides a habitat for wild orchids, candlewoods and exotic vines. Fruits and flowers, both wild and cultivated, are in abundance, particularly in the gorgeous gardens of Nevis. Trees include several varieties of the stately royal palm, the spiny-trunked sandbox tree, silk cotton, and the turpentine or gum tree. Visitors can explore the rainforests

Secession - a hot political potato

When in St Kitts and Nevis don't miss the opportunity to speak to residents about politics. Don't take sides, just ask a leading question. You are sure to get an earful and be exposed to all the intrigue and intensity that is St Kitts/Nevis politics. When in Nevis ask them about secession then ask the average Kittitian about secession. You will get largely differing views. Ask about the Labour Party (SKNLP) and the PAM. You will be amazed at how willing people are to tell you about "politics", but not before looking around to see who is listening, so you feel as though you are getting real inside information. Don't take everything you hear verbatim, just listen and get a feel for the political climate. Red clothing is worn by Labour supporters and yellow clothing by PAM supporters, but only the real stalwarts on either side continue the clothing colour coding for long after the election takes place. As a tourist you can wear whatever colour you like.

on foot with guides and gentle hikes through trails and estates also reap many rewards in terms of plant-gazing. Several trails are clear and do not need a guide, although it should be noted that there are no marked trails; care should be taken and advice sought. Comparatively clear trails include Old Road to Philips, the old British military road, which connected the British settlements on the northeast and south-west coasts of St Kitts without going through French territory when the island was partitioned. There are also trails from Belmont to the crater of Mount Liamuiga, from Saddlers to the Peak, from Lamberts or the top of Wingfield Heights to Dos d'Ane lake (known locally as Dos d'Ane pond).

Diving and marine life

Dive sites

There is very good snorkelling and scuba diving. Most dive sites are on the Caribbean side of the islands, where the reef starts in shallow water and falls off to 100 ft or more. Between the two islands there is a shelf in only 25 ft of water which attracts lots of fish, including angelfish, to the corals, sea fans and sponges. There is black coral off the southeast peninsula, coral caves, reefs and wrecks with abundant fish and other sea creatures of all sizes and colours. Off St Kitts good reefs to dive include **Turtle Reef** (off Shitten Bay) which is good for beginners and snorkelling, **Coconut Reef** in Basseterre Bay and **Pump Bay** by Sandy Point. Much of the diving is suitable for novices and few of the major sites are deeper than 70 ft. Several wrecks and some other sites are actually shallow enough for very rewarding snorkelling although the very best snorkelling around St Kitts is only accessible by boat.

Dive centres

Kenneth's Dive Centre based in Basseterre (Bay Road, and also at Timothy Beach, T4657043, F4656472); Kenneth Samuel (friendly, helpful) is a PADI-certified Dive Master offering courses, dive packages (single tank dive US$50, US$75 two-tank dive, four day package US$245) and all equipment. There are facilities for people with disabilities. He uses catamarans, *Lady Peggy* and *Lady Madonna,* or a 32ft motor launch, *Lady Majesta. Pro-Divers* gives PADI instruction, T4653223, F4650265, prodiver@caribsurf.com, dive gear available for rent, dive packages available, single-tank dive US$45, two-tank dive US$70, resort course US$75, three-day PADI Open Water certification US$300, three-hour snorkelling US$35. Ocean kayaks available for hire. *St Kitts Scuba* is at *Birdrock Beach Hotel,* offering PADI instruction, T4651189, F4653696, two-tank dive US$65, resort course US$65, PADI Open Water certification US$350.

Snorkelling off **Oualie Beach**, Nevis, is excellent and also good at Nisbett Beach and Tamarind Bay. Good dive sites include Monkey Shoal, where you can find angel fish, black durgons, octopus, flying gunnard and maybe nurse sharks in the overhangs, crevices and grottos of this densely covered reef. Devil's Caves are another series of grottos, where you can see lobster and squirrel fish and often turtles riding

Leeward Islands

Essentials

Documents US and Canadian visitors do not require passports but need only produce proof of citizenship to stay up to six months. Other nationalities need passports and a return ticket but for up to six months visas are not required for Commonwealth and EU countries, Finland, Iceland, Liechtenstein, Norway, San Marino, Sweden, Switzerland, Turkey, Uruguay, Venezuela and nationals of other member countries of the OAS, with the exception of the Dominican Republic and Haiti who do require visas. Visas can be extended for US$20 per month for the first three months and then US$30 for the following three months up to a maximum of six months.

Currency East Caribbean dollar: EC2.70=US$1. US dollars accepted. When prices are quoted in both currencies, for example for departure tax, taxi fares, a notional rate of EC$2.50 = US$1 is used. There are no restrictions on the amount of foreign currency that can be imported or exported, but the amount of local currency exported is limited to the amount you imported and declared. Visa is the most widely used, Access/Mastercard and Diners Club are not so popular.

Departure tax There is an airport departure tax of US$17 per person, not payable for stays of less than 24 hours (or when you leave on the same flight number as you arrived the previous day, that is slightly more than 24 hours), and an environmental levy of US$1.50.

Ports of entry (Own flag). List all anchorage stops on cruising permit at the Port Authority in Basseterre and clear with immigration in Nevis. Charges are EC$20 up to 20 tons, EC$35 up to 30 tons, EC$38 up to 50 tons. Port dues EC$6-25 based on size. There is no additional charge in Nevis once you have cleared in St Kitts.

Anchorages Port Zante Marina in Basseterre, White House and Ballast Bay are the best on St Kitts, Oualie Beach on Nevis is beautiful. Good groceries, alcoholic drinks, laundry, propane. Can have fuel delivered to dock and buy water by the cubic ton. Marina charges including water: under 40ft, US$0.40 per foot; 40-70ft, US$0.60; over 70ft, US$1.20. For information, Port Authority, T4658121, Port Zante, T4665021.

Official time Atlantic Standard Time, four hours ahead GMT, one ahead of EST.

Voltage 230 volts AC/60 cycles (some hotels have 110V).

Media *Newspapers* The Observer, The

the surge. Nag's Head, just off Oualie Beach, is a schooling ground for big fish such as king mackerel, barracuda, jacks and yellowtail snappers. *Scuba Safaris*, a 5-star operation run by Ellis Chaderton, is based at Oualie Beach, T4699518, F4699619: diving (US$45 for a single-tank dive, US$80 for two tanks), PADI and NAUI instruction and equipment rental. Trips to see bottlenose dolphins and sometimes humpback whales can be arranged.

Beaches and watersports

St Kitts Most of the beaches are of black, volcanic sand but several of the beaches fringing the southeast peninsula have lighter coloured sand. Swimming is very good in the Frigate Bay area where all watersports are available. The southeast peninsula itself has white sand beaches. **Banana Bay, Cockleshell Bay** and **Mosquito Bay** all have sandy beaches, calm water and picturesque views of Nevis just across the straits. There has been little development here so far, but there is the *Turtle Beach Bar and Grill* at Mosquito Bay with a complete range of watersports on offer. Villas are planned here and hotels on other peninsular beaches. Swimming is not safe on the Atlantic side of the island because of strong currents.

Leeward Island Charters' *Caona II*, a 47-ft catamaran, 67-ft *Eagle*, or *Spirit of St Kitts*, a 70-ft catamaran, T4657474, F4657070, office next to the *Ballahoo* restaurant above the Circus for bookings and private charters, take visitors on a sail, snorkel and beach barbecue. Sailing is becoming increasingly popular. The *St Kitts-Nevis Boating Club* (T4658766) organizes sunfish races which are fun, check the bulletin board for details at *PJ's Pizza Bar* (T4658373), Frigate Bay, the *Ballahoo* (T4654197)

Democrat, *the* Leeward Times (weekly) or The Labour Spokesman *(twice weekly). Other useful publications are* The St Kitts and Nevis Visitor *(annual), the official publication of the Hotel and Tourism Association, available at hotels and the tourist offices. Check the range of* **books** *at St Christopher Heritage Society, Basseterre, and Museum of Nevis History, Charlestown.* St Kitts, Cradle of the Caribbean *by Brian Dyde and* Nevis, Queen of the Caribees *by Joyce Gordon are both published by MacMillan.* **Radio and TV** *AM/FM ZIZ Radio medium wave 555 kHz and 96 FM; Choice 105 FM. VON Radio in Nevis 895 kHz medium wave and Radio Paradise 825 kHz. Two TV stations: the state run ZIZ and Nevis-based Christian station Trinity Broadcasting.*
Tourist offices overseas Canada *365 Bay St, Suite 806, Toronto, T416-3686707, F3683934, skbnevcan@sympatico.ca*
Germany: *Walter Kolbstrasse 9-11, 60594 Frankfurt, T49-699621640, F49-69610637.* **UK**: *10 Kensington Court, London W8 5DL, T020-73760881, F020-79376742, StKitts.Nevis@btinternet.com* **USA** *414 East 75th St, New York NY 10021, T212-5351234, F212-7346511 and Benford Assoc, 1464*

Whippoorwill Way, Mountainside, NJ 07092, T908-2326701, F908-2330485.
Laundry *Warners, Bird Rock Road, Basseterre, T4658630, including dry cleaning (allow a week). Others include Dr Cleaners, T4668075/6; the People's Store, T4652056; Elite Laundry Enterprise, T4656508. In Nevis, Clean Wash Laundrette, T469-0681/1188.*
Safety *Note that the penalties for possession of narcotics are very severe and no mercy is shown towards tourists. Theft has increased, do not leave your things unattended in a car or on the beach.* **Health** *Mains water is chlorinated, but bottled water is available if preferred for drinking, particularly outside the main towns. Dairy produce, meat, poultry, seafood, fruit and vegetables are generally considered safe. A yellow fever or cholera vaccination certificate is required if you are arriving from an infected area.*
Public holidays *New Year's Day (1 Jan), Carnival Day/Las' Lap (2 Jan), Good Friday, Easter Monday, May Day (1st Mon in May), Whit Monday (end of May), the Queen's birthday (June), Aug Mon/Emancipation Day (beginning of the month), National Heroes Day (16 Sep), Independence Day (19 Sep), Christmas Day (25 Dec), Boxing Day (26 Dec).*

in Basseterre, or Dougie Brookes who manages the boatyard *Caribee Yachts*, T4658411. *Blue Water Safaris* has one boat, *Caretaker* (38 ft) and two catamarans, *Falcon* (55 ft) and *Irie Lime* (65 ft), offering fishing (US$60 per person), moonlight cruises (US$25), party cruises (US$25), Nevis day tours (US$60), sunset cruises (US$35) and snorkelling trips (US$35), private snorkelling, sailing and fishing charters (US$360 half day), T4664933, F4666740, waterfun@caribsurf.com *Mr X Watersports*, located next to *Monkey Bar* in Frigate Bay, T4654995, rents windsurfing and snorkelling equipment, fishing trips and weekly all-inclusive packages.

There is a wide range of other water-based activities, such as jet-skis, waterskiing, windsurfing etc. *Fantasy Parasailing* takes up to six up in the air with optional dips in the sea, T4668930, F4651802, bentels@caribsurf.com Deep sea fishing can be arranged; Oliver Spencer, a fisherman based in Old Road is happy to take visitors, T4656314. In summer there is a race for windsurfers and sunfish to Nevis.

Nevis had superb white sandy beaches, particularly on the leeward and north coasts although these were struck by Hurricane Lenny in 1999 and much of the sand was washed away. The beautiful four mile **Pinney's Beach** is only a few minutes' walk from Charlestown and is never crowded. The entire middle stretch of Pinney's Beach has been given over to a 196-room *Four Seasons Hotel*. The sun loungers are for guests only but the public has access to the beach. Huge amounts of sand were imported after Lenny and breakwaters were built to protect the beach by the hotel. Watersports facilities are available at *Oualie Beach Club. Nevis Watersports*, at Oualie Beach, T4699060, offers waterskiing, US$20 per pull, US$60 for 30 minutes;

Leeward Islands

deep sea fishing US$80 per hour (minimum three hours); snorkelling US$30 per half day. Watersports also at *Newcastle Bay Marina*, T4699395 or information from *Mount Nevis Hotel and Beach Club*, T4699373, F4699375. On the Atlantic side of Nevis, the beaches tend to be rocky and the swimming treacherous; there is, though, an excellent beach at White Bay in the southwest. *Turtle Tours Nevis Kayaking and Snorkelling Adventures* in Cotton Ground, Nevis, offer a 3-hr tour along the coastline, including snorkelling and a light picnic lunch of local fruits, pastries and drinks, T4698503, www.beach-works.com/turtletours/turtletours.html

Other sports   **Horse riding**   On St Kitts there are *Trinity Stables* (beach tours US$25 per hour, rainforest tour US$40), T465-3226/9603, and *Royal Stables* at West Farm, T4652222, F4654444, on Nevis at the *Hermitage Plantation*, T4693477, F4692481, where they also have horse-drawn carriage tours, US$50 per 30 minutes and horse riding US$45 for 1½ hours. There is also the *Nevis Equestrian Centre*, Main Rd, Clifton Estate, Cotton Ground, T4698118, guilbert@caribsurf.com, run by John and Erika Guilbert. They offer 10 different rides with a combination of trail and beach, English or Western saddles, for novice or experienced riders. They even have a 6-hr cross island ride, but don't try that if you're not used to sitting in a saddle. Nevis horses are Thoroughbred/Creole crosses, mostly retired from racing on Nevis (see below). **Cycling** *Blue Water Safaris* (see above) now offer mountain biking tours (US$15), island biking tours and beach outings. *Fun Bikes St Kitts*, T4663202/6622088, have all-terrain quad bikes, fully guided tours, riding through cane fields, rain forest, villages and plantations with spectacular views of St Kitts, three excursions daily at 0830, 1130 and 1400, for about three-four hours. **Golf** Royal St Kitts Golf Course is an 18-hole international championship golf course at Frigate Bay (T4658339, 4654463 – use and hire of buggies compulsory) and there is a nine-hole golf course at Golden Rock, St Kitts (T4658103), where a fun day is held on the last Sunday of the month. On Nevis, the *Four Seasons* has an 18-hole golf course (T4691111, F4691112). **Triathlon** The St Kitts Triathlon is held on the second Sunday in May. Professional triathletes compete to gain official points to qualify for the Olympic games; this is preceded by an amateur race. The grandstand is at *Timothy Beach Hotel*. On Nevis **horse racing** is the second most popular sport after cricket. The *Nevis Turf and Jockey Club* meets six times a year to race island thoroughbreds: New Year's Day, Tourism Week (February), Easter, August during Culturama, Independence Day and Boxing Day. Facilities past Market Shop and down Hanley's Road include a new grandstand seating 200, washrooms, a parimutual booth, good food and dancing well into the night, T4698442. There is a minimum of five races and horses sometimes come from neighbouring islands. Contact Richard Lupinacci at the *Hermitage Inn* for details, T4693477, F4692481. Look out for the more amusing donkey races. Nevis is known for the number of donkeys there. A donkey ride is an unusual and exciting way to see the sights. Make sure you have on jeans. There are some organised donkey rides through hotels and tour agents.

St Kitts

Population: 35,340

St Kitts has an area of 68 square miles, made up of three groups of rugged volcano peaks split by deep ravines and a low lying peninsula in the southeast where there are salt ponds and fine beaches. The dormant volcano, Mount Liamuiga (3,792ft, pronounced Lie-a-mee-ga) occupies the central part of the island. The mountain was previously named Mount Misery by the British, but has now reverted to its Carib name, meaning 'fertile land'. The foothills of the mountains, particularly in the north, are covered with sugar cane plantations and grassland, while the uncultivated lowland slopes are covered with forest and fruit trees.

Basseterre

The small port of Basseterre is the capital and largest town. By West Indian stand-ards, it is quite big and as such has a quite different feel from its close neighbour, Charlestown. It was founded some 70 years later in 1727. Earthquakes, hurricanes and finally a disastrous fire destroyed the town in 1867 and consequently its build-ings are comparatively modern. There is a complete mishmash of architectural styles from elegant Georgian buildings with arcades, verandas and jalousies, mostly in good condition, to hideous 20th-century concrete block houses. In recent years, the development of tourism has meant a certain amount of redevelopment in the centre. An old warehouse on the waterfront has been converted into the Pelican Mall, a duty-free shopping and recreational complex. It also houses the Ministry of Tourism and a lounge for guests of the *Four Seasons Hotel* in Nevis awaiting trans-port. A new deep water cruise ship berth has been built on the waterfront on 25 acres of reclaimed land between Bramble Street and College Street in the heart of Basseterre, capable of accommodating the largest ships afloat, together with a sailing and power boat marina, and berthing facilities for the inter-island ferry, the *Caribe Queen*. An expanded shopping area with space for craft vendors and small shops is under construction.

At the south end of Fort Street on Bay Road is the imposing façade of the Old Trea-sury Building, with a dome covering an arched gateway. It is being converted into a museum of national culture and arts to be completed by 2002. The first phase was completed in time for Carifesta in 2000 and the building now houses the **St Christo-pher Heritage Society**, which has a small, interesting display of old photographs and artefacts. They work on conservation projects and are grateful for donations.

Population: 15,000

St Kitts

■ **Sleeping**
1 Bird Rock Beach
2 Fairview Inn
3 Forr Thomas
4 Golden Lemon
5 Inner Circle Guest House
6 Morgan Heights Condos
7 Ocean Terrace
8 Ottleys Plantation Inn

Leeward Islands

■ *T4655584. Mon-Tue, Thu-Fri 0830-1300, 1400-1600, Wed, Sat, 0830-1300.* Next door is the post office. ■ *Weekdays 0800-1500, 0800-1100 on Thu, 0800-1200 on Sat.*

The Circus, styled after London's Piccadilly Circus (but looking nothing like it), is the centre of the town. It is busiest on Friday afternoon and comes alive with locals 'liming' (relaxing). The clock tower is a memorial to Thomas Berkely, former president of the General Legislative Council. Head north up Fort Street, turn left at the main thoroughfare (Cayon Street) and you will come to **St George's church**, set in its own large garden, with a massive, square buttressed tower. The site was originally a Jesuit church, Notre Dame, which was raised to the ground by the English in 1706. Rebuilt four years later and renamed St George's, it suffered damage from hurricanes and earthquakes on several occasions. It too was a victim of the 1867 fire. It was rebuilt in 1856-69 and contains some nice stained glass windows. There is a fine view of the town from the tower.

Independence Square was built in 1790 and is surrounded now by a low white fence; eight gates let paths converge on a fountain in the middle of the square (it looks like the Union Jack when seen from the air). There are gaily painted muses on top of the fountain. Originally designed for slave auctions and council meetings, it now contains many plants, spacious lawns and lovely old trees. It is surrounded by 18th-century houses and at its east end, the Roman Catholic cathedral with its twin towers. Built in 1927, the Immaculate Conception is surprisingly plain inside. At 10

Basseterre

■ Sleeping	● Eating	
1 Central Guest House	1 Artecchino	8 Pizza Lovers
2 Earle's Vacation Home	2 Ballahoo	9 Ribs & Rolls
3 Glimbaro Guest House	3 Bayembi Café	10 Star of India
4 Palms Hotel	4 Burger World	11 Vegetarian Plus
5 Park View Inn	5 Charlie's Jazz Bar	
6 Seaview Inn	6 Circus Grill	
7 Wellington's Haven	7 Mango's	

N   Not to scale

North Square Street you can visit the very attractive building housing The **Spencer Cameron Art Gallery**. See Rosey Cameron-Smith's paintings and prints of local views and customs as well as an impressive selection of the work of other artists too, T/F4651617. On West Independence Square, the courthouse reflects the old one which burnt down in 1867. It is an impressive building in the colonial style. The Bank of Nova Scotia houses some interesting paintings of Brimstone Hill by Lt Lees of the Royal Engineers, circa 1783.

The **International House Museum** on Central Street is a must see for visitors. It was designed by Winston Zack Nisbett, a cultural preservationist who happened to be close to the previous owner of the property, Edgar Challenger, a well-known trade unionist and historian, who died in January 2001. Challenger's residence was a gold mine of traditional utensils and equipment used in 1920-40, as well as books on the history of the Federation. ■ *1000-1700 Mon-Fri, 1000-1300 Sat, 1300-1700 Sun, US$5 for visitors, EC$5 for locals, T4650542.*

Basseterre is very quiet on Sunday and most of the restaurants are closed, but with the increase in tourism more places are opening, especially if a cruise ship is in.

Around the island

A clockwise route around the island will enable you to see most of the historical sites. A cheap way of touring the island is to take a minibus from Basseterre (Bay Road) to Dieppe Bay Town, then walk to Saddlers (there might be a minibus if you are lucky, but it is only ½ mile up the road) where you can get another minibus back to Basseterre along the Atlantic coast. There are several good island tours, including excellent hiking tours to the volcano and through the rain forest with *Kriss Tours* (US$50 per full day, overnight camping US$90, T4654042) and *Greg's Safaris*, pleasant and informative, (US$40-80, T4654121, F4650707, www.skbee.com/safaris). **Periwinkle Tours** offers guided walks (US$30-35, T4656314, F4657210).

Evidence of sugar cane is everywhere on the comparatively flat, fertile coastal plain. You will drive through large fields of cane and glimpse the narrow gauge railway which is now used to transport it from the fields. Disused sugar mills are also often seen. Around the island are the **Great Houses**: Fairview, Romney Manor (destroyed by fire in 1995), Golden Lemon, the White House, Rawlins and perhaps most famous for its colonial splendour, Ottley's. They have nearly all been converted into hotels and have excellent restaurants.

Mountain treks The island is dominated by the southeast range of mountains (1,159ft) and the higher northwest range which contains **Mount Verchilds** (2,931 ft) and the crater of **Mount Liamuiga** (3,792ft). To climb **Mount Liamuiga** independently, get a bus to St Paul's. Just after the village entrance sign there is a track leading through farm buildings which you follow through the canefields. After 20 minutes take a left fork, ask people working in the fields if you are unsure. At the edge of the forest, the track becomes a path, which is easy to follow and leads through wonderful trees. If you hear something crashing through the upper branches, look up quickly before the monkeys disappear. At 2,600ft is the crater into which you can climb, holding on to vines and roots; on the steady climb from the end of the road note the wild orchids in the forest. A full day is required for this climb which is really only for experienced hikers. To get beyond the crater to the summit you need a guide. You can reach the attractive, but secluded, Dos D'Ane pond near **Mount Verchilds** from the Wingfield estate, a guide is recommended.

The west coast The west coast particularly is historically important. It is guarded by no less than nine **forts** and the magnificent Brimstone Hill Fortress. Taking the road out of Basseterre, you will pass the sites of seven of them: Fort Thomas, Palmetto Point Fort, Stone Fort, Fort Charles, Charles Fort, Sandy Point Fort and Fig Tree Fort. The remaining two are to the south of Basseterre: Fort Smith and Fort Tyson. Little

See the island with Mr Cool

Adventure seekers must see St Kitts by minibus. This is no sanitized island tour in air conditioned comfort, but you will get the experience of a lifetime and get a taste of Kittitian culture. The bus terminal in Basseterre is filled with buses that would be glad to take you to villages around the island. You will be asked to "dress over" to make space for one more person. Locals hustle to get their favourite bus, which is known not by the sign that says where it is going to but its given name such as Ninja, Big Blue, West, Mr Humble, Roughest and Mr Cool. They are all well decorated (painted) in accordance with their names. Avoid the rush hour unless you are really hard core but it is fascinating to get on the bus when there is a really hot debatable issue. The older passengers will be sure to make a comment as they climb aboard the bus, saying something like, "Lord and Saviour of mankind forgive my foolish ways," or "Lord have mercy," or "Oh my saviour help us." If for some reason you step into a quiet bus, just enjoy the ride, try to get a window seat and see the villages of St Kitts. To get back to town simply catch a bus that is going back in the opposite direction. It won't be long before a bus comes along – it may even be the same bus. The bus driver will be happy to show you.

remains of any of them. A peaceful spot to admire some of Stone Fort's ruins is a swing for two built by local Rastaman, Jahbalo. At Trinity Church, turn right, up the dirt path. At the well preserved sugar mill there are some ruins to your right. Climb the small mound to find the swing with a view towards cane fields and the Caribbean (sunset recommended).

The first point of historic interest is situated just before Old Road Town. Sir Thomas Warner landed at Old Road Bay in 1623 and was joined in 1625 by the crew of a French ship badly mauled by the Spanish. Initially befriended by the local Carib chief Tegreman, as many as 3,000 Caribs, alarmed at the rapid colonization of the island, tried to mount an attack in 1626. 2,000 of them were massacred by the combined French and English forces in the deep ravine at **Bloody Point** (the site of Stone Fort). An amicable settlement meant that the English held the central portion of the island roughly in line from Sandy Point to Saddlers in the north to Bloody Point across to Cayon in the south. French names can be traced in both of their areas of influence (Dieppe Bay Town in the north, the Parishes are called Capisterre and Basseterre in the south). The southeast peninsula was neutral. This rapprochement did not last many years as following the colonization of Martinique and Guadeloupe, the French wished to increase their sphere of influence. St Kitts became an obvious target and in 1664 they squeezed the English from the island. For nearly 200 years the coast was defended by troops from one nation or another.

At Old Road Town you turn right to visit **Wingfield Estate**. You drive through a deserted sugar mill and the edge of rain forest. Unfortunately Romney Manor was destroyed by fire in 1995 but the beautiful gardens remain with pleasant views over the coast and a giant 350-year old saman tree. ■ *The estate is home to Caribelle Batik, open Mon-Fri, 0830-1600, T4656253, F4653629.* Apart from a well stocked shop you can watch the artists producing the highly colourful and attractive material. A guide will explain the process. Also near here the remains of the island's Amerindian civilization can be seen on large stones with drawings and petroglyphs. If you keep driving to the left of Romney Manor and Caribelle Batik, you will find one of the highest paved roads on the island. It is a tough climb so be sure to have a sturdy car or legs. Follow the road up until it ends. A large flat rock at the top is perfect to admire the spectacular view of the mountains in solitude. To the right hand side is a smaller path that leads to an incredible overview of Bat Hole Ghaut. Magnificent views of tropical rainforest in myriad greens. A very secluded spot.

At the village of **Middle Island**, you will see on your right and slightly up the hill, the church of St Thomas at the head of an avenue of dead or dying royal palms. Here is buried Sir Thomas Warner who died on 10 March 1648. The raised tomb under a canopy is inscribed "General of y Caribee". There is also a bronze plaque with a copy of the inscription inside the church. Other early tombs are of Captain John Pogson (1656) and Sir Charles Payne, "Major General of Leeward Carribee Islands" who was buried in 1744. The tower, built in 1880, fell during earth tremors in 1974.

Turn right off the coastal road just before *J's Place* (drink and local food, open from 1100, T4656264, watch the caged green vervet monkeys, they are very aggressive) for the **Brimstone Hill Fortress National Park**, one of the 'Gibraltars of the West Indies' (a title it shares with Les Saintes, off Guadeloupe). Sprawled over 38 acres on the slopes of a hill 800ft above the sea, it commands an incredible view of St Kitts and Nevis and on clear days, Anguilla (67 miles), Montserrat (40 miles), Saba (20 miles), St Eustatius (5 miles), St-Barts (40 miles) and St-Martin (45 miles) can be seen. The English mounted the first cannon on Brimstone Hill in 1690 in an attempt to force the French from Fort Charles below. It has been constructed mainly out of local volcanic stones and was designed along classic defensive lines. The five bastions overlook each other and also guard the only road as it zig zags up to the parade ground. The entrance is at the Barrier Redan where payment is made. Pass the Magazine Bastion but stop at the Orillon Bastion which contains the massive ordnance store (165ft long with walls at least 6ft thick). The hospital was located here and under the south wall is a small cemetery. You then arrive at the Prince of Wales Bastion (note the name of J Sutherland, 93rd Highlanders 24 October 1822 carved in the wall next to one of the cannons) from where there are good views over to the parade ground. Park at the parade ground, there is a small snack bar and good gift shop near the warrant officer's quarters with barrels of pork outside it. Stop for a good video introduction at the DL Matheson Visitor Centre. A narrow and quite steep path leads to Fort George, the Citadel and the highest defensive position. Restoration is continuing and several areas have been converted to form a most interesting museum. Barrack rooms now hold well-presented and informative displays (pre-columbian, American, English, French and Garrison). Guides are on hand to give more detailed explanations of the fortifications. The fortress was eventually abandoned in 1852 but was inaugurated as a national park by the Queen in October 1985. Brimstone Hill Fortress National Park was made a UNESCO World Heritage Site on 4 October 2000. ■ *0930-1730 daily, entrance EC$13 or US$5 for foreigners, EC$2 for nationals, it is highly recommended both for adults and children (half price). Allow up to two hours. The local minibus to Brimstone Hill is EC$2.25, then walk up to the fortress, less than 30 minutes but extremely steep. For fit climbers only.*

Brimstone Hill

To continue the island tour, drive on, looking out for the **Plantation Picture House** at *Rawlins Plantation Inn* on the right, up a long drive through canefields. Here there is a lovely art gallery with stunning views, housing paintings and prints by Kate Spencer. ■ *T4657740. 1100-1700.* Keep driving up the road to Rawlins Plantation. Tour the magnificent gardens full of tropical plants and flowers. Back on the main road, continue north. There is a a black sand beach at **Dieppe Bay** which is a good place to stop for lunch, at the upmarket and excellent *Golden Lemon*. Pass through Saddlers and stop at the **Black Rocks**. Here lava has flowed into the sea providing interesting rock formations. Continue on to **Ottley's Plantation** which is also worth a visit. The grounds are not as magnificent as at Rawlins but there are easy, well-marked short walks through the rainforest. Continue on the main road through Cayon (turn right uphill to Spooners for a look at the abandoned cotton ginnery) back to Basseterre via the RL Bradshaw Airport. With advance notice, you can tour the sugar factory near the airport, very interesting and informative. ■ *Tours are only during harvest season, Feb-Aug, T4658157.*

The north coast

   In the hills of St Peter's, just north of Basseterre, is **Nature's Kingdom**, a miniature, island-style wildlife observatory which features animals, fruit trees and plants from around the world. Meet Tom and Jerry, the friendly monkeys. ■ *T4657038. Tours are available. Bar and barbecue.*

The southeast To visit the southeast peninsula, turn off the roundabout at the end of Wellington
peninsula Road (opposite turning to the airport) and at the end of this new road turn left. This
leads to the narrow spit of land sandwiched between North and South Frigate Bays.
This area is being heavily developed, the natural lagoons providing an additional
attraction. A number of establishments have been built, including the *Royal St Kitts
Beach Resort and Casino*, with tennis courts and an 18-hole golf course. A Hyatt
hotel is planned for Friars Bay, with 200 rooms and 75 villas, and the Golf View
Estates development at Frigate Bay adds another 37 condominiums. Other hotels
are expanding or renovating. The six-mile Dr Kennedy A Simmonds Highway runs
from Frigate Bay to Major's Bay. After Frigate Bay the peninsula is almost deserted
and quite different from the rest of the island. The road climbs along the backbone of
the peninsula and overlooks North and South Friars Bays where you may see green
vervet monkeys before descending to White House Bay. Skirt the Great Salt Pond.
Half way round turn left to reach Sandbank Bay, a lovely secluded bay (unmarked
left turn down dirt road opposite Great Salt Pond). Continue on the main highway
and turn left for Cockleshell Bay and Turtle Beach (good for watersports and stunning views across to Nevis). The main road leads to Major's Bay. At the moment
most of the peninsula is isolated and extremely attractive, although tourist development is planned. There are roads to the beaches, which you can walk or drive. If you
are on foot you should be fit, as the peninsula road is largely an uphill climb.

Nevis

Population: 9,000 *Across the two-mile Narrows Channel from St Kitts is the beautiful little island of
Nevis. The islands covers an area of 36 square miles and the central peak, 3,232 ft, is
usually shrouded in white clouds and mist. It reminded Columbus of Spanish
snow-capped mountains and so he called the island "Las Nieves". (It reminds others, in
the wet, of the English Lake District, as does St Kitts.) For the Caribs, it was Oualie, the
land of beautiful water. Smaller than St Kitts it is also quieter. The atmosphere is civilized, but low-key and easy-going; all the same, it is an expensive island. Less fertile
than St Kitts, the principal crop used to be cotton but only 32 acres were planted in
1995. Agricultural workers have left their smallholdings for jobs in hotels or driving
taxis as numbers of tourists, particularly from North America, have risen.*

Charlestown

The main town is Charlestown, one of the best preserved old towns in the Caribbean. Situated on Gallows Bay and guarded by Fort Charles to the south and the long
sweep of Pinney's Beach to the north, it is a small town with a compact centre. At first
sight it would be easy to be disappointed. However there are several interesting
buildings dating from the 18th century and the excellent Museum of Nevis History.

    D R Walwyn's Plaza is dominated by the balconied Customs House built in 1837
on a much older site and housing the Customs and Agricultural Ministry. Immediately to the north is the post office. Opposite it on the other side of the square is the
tourist office. **Memorial Square** is larger and more impressive than D R Walwyn's
Plaza, the War Memorial is in a small garden. Explore the courthouse and library. It
was built in 1825 and used as the Nevis Government Headquarters but largely
destroyed by fire in 1873. The curious little square tower was erected in 1909-10. It
contains a clock which keeps accurate time with an elaborate pulley and chain system. Visit the library and you can see them together with the weights among the
elaborate roof trusses. ■ *Mon-Fri 0900-1800, Sat 0900-1700. The courthouse is not
open to the public, look in through the open windows.*

    Along Government Road is the well-preserved **Jewish Cemetery** dating back to
1679, it is locked although entrance is allowed. The key is just above the cemetery at
Hunkins shop. At the small market a wide range of island produce, including

avocados, ginger root, yams and sweet potatoes, is on sale but go early if you want to catch the bustle. **Markets** are held on Tuesday, Thursday and Saturday mornings, best on Saturday. Market Street to the right houses the philatelic bureau. ■ *0800-1600 Mon-Fri, air conditioned*. The **Cotton Ginnery** was, until 1994, in use during the cotton picking season (February-July). In 1995 it was moved out to the New River Estate, Gingerland, where it is in a renovated building next to the sugar mill ruins there. As part of the Nevis Port upgrade, another Cotton Ginnery building now houses 10 gift shops and a restaurant. On Chapel Street the **Wesleyan Holiness Manse** built in 1812 is one of the oldest stone buildings surviving on the island while the Methodist Manse (next to the prominent Church) has the oldest wooden structure, the second floor being built in 1802.

The **Museum of Nevis History** at the Birthplace of Alexander Hamilton is next to the sea and set in an attractive garden which contains a representative collection of Nevis plants and trees. The original house was built around 1680 but destroyed in the 1840s probably by an earthquake. This attractive two storey house was rebuilt in 1983 and dedicated during the Islands' Independence celebration in September of that year. The Nevis House of Assembly meets in the rooms upstairs (again restored after being damaged by Hurricane Hugo), while the museum occupies the ground floor. Alexander Hamilton, Nevis' most famous son, was born in Charlestown on 11 January 1757. He lived on Nevis for only five years before leaving for St Croix with his family. About half of the display is given over to various memorabilia and pictures of his life. The Museum of Nevis History contains examples of Amerindian pottery, African culture imported by the slaves, cooking implements and recipes, a rum still, and a model of a Nevis lighter. There are also the ceremonial clothes of the Warden which were worn on the Queen's birthday and Remembrance Day. A section is devoted to the conservation of reefs, conch and the rain forest. There is a small shop which sells local produce and some interesting books. All proceeds go to the upkeep of the museum. ■ *T4695786, Mon-Fri 0900-1600, Sat 0900-1200, US$2.*

Charlestown

To Pinney's Beach & Newcastle

Old Hospital Rd
Craddock Rd
Low St
Museum of Nevis
St Paul's
Wesleyan Holiness Manse
Methodist Manse
Chapel St
Methodist
To St Kitts
TDC Travel
Main St
Prince Charles St
Pier
Cotton Ginnery
D R Walwyn's Plaza
Customs
Happy Hill Alley
Mall
Market St
Philatelic Bureau
Memorial Square
Prince William St
Jewish Cemetery
Court House & Library
Carib World Travel Agency
Island Rd
Government Rd

To Grove Park Cricket Ground, Bath & Fig Tree

N
Not to scale

● Eating
1 Cotton House Restaurant
2 Eddy's
3 Muriel's Cuisine
4 Saints & Sinners Restaurant
5 Unella's Restaurant & Bar

Around the island

Taking the road south out of Charlestown, you can visit the rather unkempt **Fort Charles**. Fork right at the Shell station and again at the mini roundabout, keep right along the sea shore (rough track), past the wine company building and through gates at the end of the track. The fort was built before 1690 and altered many times before being completed in 1783-90. Nothing much remains apart from the circular well and a small building (possibly the magazine). The gun emplacements looking across to St Kitts are being badly eroded by the sea, eight cannon point haphazardly to sea. The Nevis Council surrendered to the French here in 1782 during the siege of Brimstone Hill on St Kitts.

Back on the main road and only about half a mile outside Charlestown lies the largely ruined **Bath Hotel** and **Spring House**. Built by the Huggins family in 1778, it is reputed to be one of the oldest hotels in the Caribbean. The Spring House lies over a fault which supplies constant hot water at 108°F. ■ *Mon-Fri 0800-1700, Sat 0800-1200, EC$5 to bathe, EC$1.50 towel rental. Most locals bathe further downstream for free.* A new building has been erected here to house the **Horatio Nelson Museum** dedicated in 1992 to commemorate the 205th anniversary of the wedding of Admiral Nelson to Fanny Nisbet. Based on a collection donated by Mr Robert Abrahams, an American, the collection contains memorabilia including letters, china, pictures, furniture and books (request to see the excellent collection of historical documents and display of 17th century clay pipes). A replica of Nelson's military uniform was unveiled at the Museum and presented to the local government by the British High Commissioner in January 2001. It is well worth a visit as it contains an interesting insight into the life of Nelson and his connection with Nevis. He was not always popular having come to the island to enforce the Navigation Acts which forbade the newly independent

Nevis

0 km 1
0 miles 1

■ **Sleeping**
1 Airport View Apartments
2 Al's Guest House
3 Donna's Guest House
4 Fort Ashby Beach Cottages
5 Four Season's Resort
6 Golden Rock Plantation Inn
7 Hermitage Plantation Inn
8 Hill Top Vacation Apartments
9 Hurricane Cove Bungalows
10 Inn at Cades Bay
11 Johnathan's Villa
12 Meadville Apartments
13 Montpelier Plantation Inn
14 Mount Nevis
15 Oualie Beach
16 Pemo's Guest House
17 Philsha's Guest House
18 Sea Spawn Guest House
19 Sunset View Apartments
20 Tranquility Annexe
21 Yamseed Inn

● **Eating**
1 Bananas
2 Beachcomer Bar & Grill
3 Cla Cha Del & Bar
4 Jade Garden
5 Julian's at Cliffdwellers
6 Martha's Tea House
7 Miss June's
8 Newcastle Bay Marina
9 Sand Dollar Bar & Grill
10 Seafood Madness
11 Sunshines by the Sea
12 Tequila Sheila's

American states trading with British Colonies. Nelson in his ship *HMS Boreas* impounded four American ships and their cargoes. The Nevis merchants immediately claimed £40,000 losses against Nelson who had to remain on board his ship for eight weeks to escape being put into gaol. It was only after Prince William, captain of *HMS Pegasus*, arrived in Antigua that Nelson gained social acceptability and married the widow Fanny Woodward Nisbet (reputedly for her uncle's money: this proved a disappointment as her uncle left the island and spent his wealth in London). ■ *Mon-Fri, 0900-1600, Sat 0900-1200, US$2, gift shop.*

At Stoney Grove is the new **Caribbean Cove** amusement park, with Disneyland-style miniature golf, bumper boats, video arcade and a restaurant. ■ *T4691286, F4691354. Sun-Thur 1000-2200, Fri-Sat 1000-2400, adults EC$17.50, children EC$7.50.*

More evidence of the Nelson connection is found at the **St John's Fig Tree Anglican Church** about two miles on from the Bath House. Originally built in 1680, the church was rebuilt in 1838 and again in 1895. The marriage certificate of Nelson and Fanny Nisbet is displayed here. There are interesting memorials to Fanny's father William Woodward and also to her first husband Dr Josiah Nisbet. Many died of the fever during this period and taxi drivers will delight in lifting the red carpet in the central aisles for you to see old tomb stones, many connected with the then leading family, the Herberts. The graveyard has many examples of tombstones in family groups dating from the 1780s.

Slightly off the main road to the south lies **Montpelier Great House** where the marriage of Nelson and Nesbit actually took place; a plaque is set in the gatepost. The plantation is now a hotel with pleasant gardens. Enormous toads live in the lily ponds formed out of old sugar pans. A very pleasant place for lunch or a drink. Beyond the house lies **Saddle Hill** (1,250 ft). It has the remains of a small fort and it is reputedly where Nelson would look out for illegal shipping. You can follow several goat trails on the hill, giant aloes abound, a track starts at Clay Ghaut, but most trails beyond the fort are dense and overgrown. The *Hermitage* (another of the Great Houses) is signposted left just after the sign for the Montpelier. Near Montpelier is the **Botanical Garden**, seven acres of cactus, bamboo, orchids, flowering trees and shrubs, heliconias and rose gardens, a mermaid fountain, a greenhouse with bridges, ponds, waterfall and tea house with English high tea and gift shop. The landscaping is beautiful and it is the perfect spot for relaxation, picnics, small gatherings, weddings and wedding receptions (be sure to plan ahead though). ■ *Gardens open 0800-1700, EC$20, children half price, tea house 1000-1700, T4693399, F4692875.*

The small parish of **Gingerland** is reached after about three miles. Its rich soils made it the centre of the island's ginger root production (also cinnamon and nutmeg) but it is noteworthy for the very unusual octagon Methodist Church built in 1830. You turn right here along Hanleys Road to reach **White Bay Beach**. Go all the way down to the bottom and turn left at the Indian Castle experimental farm, past the race course (on Black Bay) and Red Cliff. There is a small shelter but no general shade. Beware, this is the Atlantic coast, the sea can be very rough and dangerous. On quieter days, the surf is fun and provides a welcome change from the quiet Leeward coast at Pinney's. There is a reef further out which is good for fishing (several fishing boats in the bay, one may take you out). There are good views across to Montserrat. On the way back beware of the deep (and hidden) storm drain crossing the road near the church. At Clay Gaut, Gingerland, is the **Eva Wilkin Gallery** in an old windmill. Started by Howard and Marlene Paine, it has a permanent exhibition of paintings and drawings by Nevisian Eva Wilkin (whose studio it was until her death), prints of which are available, also antique maps, etc.

After Gingerland the land becomes more barren. Several sugar mills were built here because of the wind, notably **Coconut Walk Estate**, **New River Estate** (fairly intact) and the **Eden Brown Estate**, built around 1740. A duel took place between the groom and best man at the wedding of Julia Huggins. Both men were killed, Julia became a recluse and the great house was abandoned. It has the reputation of being haunted. Although government owned and open to the public, the ruins are in a poor condition and care should be taken.

The island road continues north through Butlers and Brick Kiln (known locally as Brick Lyn), past St James church (Hick's village), Long Haul and Newcastle Bays (with the *Nisbet Plantation Inn*) to the small fishing community of **Newcastle**. You can visit the Newcastle Pottery where distinctive red clay is used to make among other things the traditional Nevis cooking pot. The Newcastle **Redoubt** can be seen from the road. Built in the early 17th century, it was used as a refuge from Carib attack and may have been the site of a Carib attack in 1656. The airport is situated here.

The road continues through an increasingly fertile landscape and there are fine views across the Narrows to the southeast peninsula of St Kitts, looking for all the world like the west coast of Scotland. Note **Booby Island** in the middle of the channel, it is mostly inhabited by pelicans (all birds are referred to as boobies by the local population). It offers good diving. The road between here and Charlestown often passes gardens which are a riot of colour. The small hill on your left is **Round Hill** (1,014ft). It can be reached on the road between Cades Bay and Camps Village (there is supposed to be a soufrière along this road). Turn off the road at Fountain Village by the methodist church. There are good views from the radio station at the top over Charlestown, across to St Kitts and beyond to Antigua. Do not expect to see much wildlife however. There is a small beach at **Mosquito Bay** and some good snorkelling can be had under the cliffs of Hurricane Hill. The *Oualie Beach Hotel* offers a range of watersport facilities including scuba diving and snorkelling equipment. On Sunday afternoons there is often live music and a barbecue at Mosquito Bay. Sailing trips can be negotiated with locals.

Under Round Hill lies **Cottle Chapel** (1824). It was the first Anglican place on Nevis where slaves could be taught and worship with their master. Ruined now, its beautiful little font can be seen in the Museum of Nevis History. Nearby, just off the island road, lies **Fort Ashby**. Nothing remains of the Fort (it is now a restaurant on Cades Bay although the cannons are in their original positions). It protected Jamestown, the original settlement and former capital, which was supposedly destroyed by an earthquake and tidal wave in 1690, and was originally called St James' Fort. Drive past the Nelson springs (where the barrels from *HMS Boreas* were filled) and **St Thomas' Church** (built in 1643, one of the oldest surviving in the Caribbean) to Pinney's Beach. There are many tracks leading down to the beach often with a small hut or beach bar at the end of them. The *Four Seasons Hotel* lies in the middle of the beach. The sun loungers are reserved for guests only but the beach is public. Behind the resort is the Robert Trent Jones II golf course which straddles the island road. The manicured fairways and greens are in marked contrast with the quiet beauty of the rest of the island but the hotel's considerable efforts at landscaping have lessened its impact.

There are many interesting walks over old sugar plantations and through the rain forest on **Mount Nevis**. *Sunrise Tours* (T4692758) arranges trips to Nevis Peak (four hours round trip, US$35 per person), Saddle Hill (1½ hours, US$30) or the Water Source (3 hours, US$40). *Heb's Nature Tours* is run by Michael Herbert, Rawlins Village, Gingerland, T4692501, offering similar tours: Mount Nevis (5 hours, US$35-40), Rainforest hike (4 hours, US$25-30), Saddle Hill hike (3 hours, US$20-25), medicinal plants (2 hours, US$15) and Camp Spring (2½ hours, US$15-20), price depends on numbers. *Top to Bottom* is run by biologists Jim and Nikki Johnson, who are very flexible and organize walks to suit you, also a night-time, star-gazing walk, mostly 2-3 hours, US$20 per person, children half price, snacks of fruit and coconut included (T4699080). David Rollinson of *Eco-Tours* (T4692091, droll@caribsurf.com) is very knowledgeable; he offers 'eco rambles' over the 18th century Coconut Walk and New River Estates and a 'Sugar trail' Mountravers hike over the old Pinney Estate (US$20 per person) as well as Sunday morning strolls round historic Charlestown (US$10 per person). *All Seasons Streamline Tours*, T4691138, F4691139, at Bath Estate, offer a/c mini-bus tours around the island.

Essentials

There is a wide variety of accommodation ranging from first class hotels to rented cottages, but it is advisable to book well in advance. Large reductions are available in summer. The St Kitts/Nevis Hotel Association can be reached at PO Box 438, Basseterre, St Kitts, T4655304, F4657746.

Basseterre LL-AL *Ocean Terrace Inn* (*OTI*), T4652754, F4651057, tdcoti@caribsurf. com Apartments and suites, 3 pools, wedding gazebo, fitness centre, beach shuttle, *OTI* also organizes tours and other activities such as scuba diving, evening shows and has a fairly expensive but nice restaurant with views over Basseterre harbour, good service throughout. **L-A** *Palms Hotel*, PO Box 64, T4650800, F4655889, www.palmshotel.com, central, on the Circus. 12 pleasant junior, 1 and 2-bedroom suites, mini bar, tea and coffee machine. **C-E** *Central Guest House and Apartments*, T465-2278/4062, ideally located in the heart of town. Rooms with or without kitchenette. **C-E** *Glimbaro Guest House*, Cayon St and Market St, T4651786, F4659832. A/c, cable TV, some rooms with bath and patio, cheaper rooms with shared bathrooms, 10% off weekly rates, fans, phone, *Pisces* restaurant with good local food, especially fish. **C-E** *Parkview Inn*, Victoria Rd, next to Parkview Amusements, Box 64, T4652100. Very basic. **C-E** *Sea View Inn*, Bay Rd, T4652278/4654062, opposite buses. 10 double rooms, 6 suites, a/c, good restaurant, convenient for central Basseterre.

Outside Basseterre The highly recommended **LL** *Rawlins Plantation*, 16 miles from Basseterre in the northwest of the island, T4656221, F4654954, Rawplant@caribsurf. com Pricey, but beautiful, tranquil and offers grass tennis, swimming pool, horse riding and croquet, no credit cards accepted, 10 cottages, laundry service and afternoon tea included. **LL-L** *The Golden Lemon Hotel and Villas*, Dieppe Bay, T4657260, F4654019, in the USA T1-800-6337411, www.goldenlemon.com, on black sand beach about 15 miles from Basseterre. 34 rooms, having built some 1-2 bedroom beachfront cottages with pools next to the original great house building dating from 1610, pool, tennis, watersports, restaurant, each room is tastefully furnished with West Indian antiques, lovely atmosphere, no children under 18. Highly recommended. 520ft above sea level in 35 acres, is the **LL** *Ottleys Plantation Inn*, PO Box 345, T4657234, F4654760, www.ottleys.com Rooms in the 1832 great house or cottages, a/c, fans, restaurant, pool, nice walks, beach shuttle, tennis/golf shuttle, packages including some meals available. **LL-A** *Bird Rock Beach Hotel*, owned/managed by former Director of Tourism, Larkland Richards, PO Box 227, T4658914, F4651675, brbh@ caribsurf.com 38 rooms/suites, a/c, TV, up on the cliffs overlooking the tiny black sand beach and industrial estate, inconvenient suburban location, taxi to Basseterre US$8, pool, tennis, volleyball, watersports, 2 restaurants, 3 bars. **AL-B** *Morgan Heights Condominiums*, PO Box 735, T4658633, F4659272. Beautiful views of Atlantic Coast and southeast peninsula, breezy, friendly management, excellent restaurant. The **AL-B** *Fairview Inn*, close to Basseterre is a cottage complex situated around an 18th century great house, Box 212, T4652472, F4657050, wall@caribsurf.com **B-C** *Earle's Vacation Home*, PO Box 604, T4657546, F4667868. Family-style furnished, self-contained 1-2 bedroom apartments. **B-D** *Vacation Inn*, corner of Cayon and College St, T465-4628/0363. Convenient for town, noisy but clean. Reductions for children under 8, a/c, fans, restaurant, pool. West of Basseterre, **C** *Trinity Inn Apartments*, Palmetto Point, T4653226, F4659460, www.islandimages.com-trinity A/c, pool, restaurant, riding stables, very friendly, excellent value. **C-D** *Inner Circle Guest House*, in the village of St Paul's, 14 miles from Basseterre, reached by minibus, T4665857. Newly built, clean and comfortable, friendly hosts, village experience.

Frigate Bay area Dominating Frigate Bay with its rooms, condos, golf course and casino is the all-inclusive **LL-L** *Royal St Kitts Beach Resort & Casino*, T4651290, F4651031, on 26 acres with convention and banqueting centre, nightclub and disco. Others in the **LL-AL** price range offering rooms, suites, cottages and condos with all the usual sports and night time entertainment, include *Island Paradise Beach Village*, PO Box 444, T4658035, F4658236, Islandparadise@caribsurf.com; *Papillon St Kitts*, PO Box 341, T4658037/8, F4656745 (newly

Leeward Islands

refurbished and managed by Rex Resorts); *Coconut Beach Club (Timothy Beach Resort)*, PO Box 81, T4658597, F4657723; *Frigate Bay Resort*, PO Box 137, T4658935, F4657050, www.frigatebay.com; *Leeward Cove Condominium*, PO Box 123, T4658030, F4653476;, *Paradise Beach Resort & Casino*, T4668063; *Sea Lofts on the Beach*, PO Box 813, T/F4651075. **B** *Gateway Inn*, PO Box 64, T4657155, F4659322, gateway@caribsurf.com 10 self-catering apartments, a/c, phone, TV, laundry, 10 mins from beach or golf course. **C** *Rock Haven Bed & Breakfast*, PO Box 821, T/F4655503. Suite with kitchen facilities, TV, laundry facilities, views of both coasts, great breakfasts.

Sleeping: Nevis Accommodation on Nevis tends to be up-market, in reconstructions of old plantation Great Houses, tastefully decorated in an English style (collectively called The Inns of Nevis). Some have reciprocal arrangements whereby you can stay at one and use the facilities of the others. They are well worth a visit. After the 1998 hurricane season the hotels made a tremendous effort to repair damage in time for the winter season. *The Four Seasons* employed 700 workers to restore the gardens and buildings, and planted 7.5 acres of grass turf and hundreds of mature palms. The other plantation inns suffered less damage and lost only a few of their trees. *The Four Seasons* was badly hit again by Hurricane Lenny in 1999 and remained closed for a year.

LL *Four Seasons Resort*, on Pinney's Beach, PO Box 565, T4691111, F4691112, www .fourseasons.com 196 rooms including 17 suites, villas for rent or purchase, Robert Trent Jones II 18-hole golf course, pro-shop, Peter Burwash tennis complex, pools, watersports, fitness centre, conference centre, 24-hr business services, restaurant and all entertainment including children's activity programme and live music, particularly in high season, transport by boat from St Kitts US$65 per person return. The **LL** *Nisbet Plantation Beach Club*, St James, built on site of 18th-century plantation on ½ mile beach unfortunately close to airport, T4699325, F4699864, www.nisbetplantation.com 38 comfortable rooms in cottages/suites with ceiling fans, tennis, swimming pool, croquet, a beach bar and pavilion, huge breakfasts, delicious afternoon tea and excellent dinner, all included in rates, laundry, local phone calls and postage complimentary. Highly recommended. **LL** *Tamarind Bay Cliffdwellers Villas*, PO Box 311, T4698262. A distinctive new villa resort on Tamarind/Jones Bay with private home atmosphere and luxury hotel facilities offering beachfront and hillside locations.

LL-L *Hermitage Plantation*, St John's Parish, T4693477, F4692481, www.hermitagenevis. com Run by Richard and Maureen Lupinacci, very friendly, beautiful cottages, 4-poster beds, tennis, pool, massage, reflexology etc, stunning setting, many guests extend their stay, romance/equestrian/adventure/diving packages offered. Highly recommended. **LL-L** *Montpelier Plantation Inn and Beach Club*, also St John's, PO Box 474, T4693462, F4692932, www.montpeliernevis.com 750ft above sea level but with private landscaped beach as well, a favourite with British tourists, delightful, friendly and helpful, pool, tennis, beach shuttle, child reductions, 17 rooms. The **LL-L** *Mount Nevis Hotel and Beach Club*, PO Box 494, T4699373, F4699375, www.mountnevishotel.com Built 1989, family-owned, 32 rooms and studios, a/c, TV, VCR, phone, breakfast included, pool, fitness centre, massage.

LL-AL *Golden Rock Plantation Inn*, St George's Parish, T4693346, F4692113, www.golden-rock.com 7 cottages, 15 rooms in 18th-century plantation house, 2-storey suite in old windmill for honeymooners/families, antique furniture, 4-poster beds, ocean view all the way to Montserrat, family plan available, pool, tennis, beach shuttle, specialist interest tours, principally of ecological content, excellent hiking excursions, enjoy afternoon tea and watch the monkeys. **LL-AL** *Hurricane Cove Bungalows*, T/F4699462, www. hurricanecove.com, on hillside with wonderful seaview. 11 1-3 bedroomed, well-equipped wooden bungalows of Finnish design, some with private pools, swimming pool, above Oualie beach, path down to beach, good snorkelling. Sports facilities nearby, 3 night minimum stay in winter, long term discounts. Highly recommended. **LL-AL** *Old Manor Estate and Hotel*, PO Box 70, T4693445, F4693388, reservations 0800-8927093, www.cpscaribnet. com/oldmanor In restored 1690 sugar plantation has 14 rooms including a cottage 800ft above sea level, tropical gardens, beach shuttle, pool, beach restaurant. **LL-AL** *Oualie Beach Hotel*, on the beach, T4699735, F4699176, www.oualie.com Safe for children, friendly, informal, comfortable, mountain bikes, diving and other watersports, 32 well equipped rooms, studios, all with view of bay, deluxe rooms on beach, email access for guests. **LL-AL** *Pinney's Beach Hotel*, in Charlestown, PO Box 61, T4695207, F4691088. 48 rooms, 7 cottages, pool, watersports, horse riding, on the beach, dining room has no view, food and service reported poor off season, rooms in need of redecoration.

There are also many guesthouses, apartments and cottages: **AL-B** *Philsha's Guest House*, T4695253. **A** *Fort Ashby Beach Cottages*, T4695648. **A** *Yamseed Inn*, T4699361. 4 rooms including delicious breakfast, lovely view of St Kitts, beautiful gardens, excellent value. Friendly, helpful owner Sybil Siegfried can arrange crossings from St Kitts and car hire. **A-B** *Airport View Apartments*, Newcastle, T4691102, aptsnevis@islands.vi. **A-B** *Tranquility Annexe*, Zetlands, T4692304. **A-D** *Hilltop Vacations Apartments*, T4693635. **B-C** *Johnathon's Villa*, Mount Lily, T4699148. **B-D** *Al's Guest House, Apartments and Cottages*, PO Box 447, T469-0378/5256, in Farms Estate. **C** *Sunset View Apartments*, Church Ground, T4695648. **C** *Sea Spawn Guest House*, PO Box 233, T4695239, 5 min walk north of Charlestown, 2 from Pinney's Beach. 6 fishing boats, car rental and kitchen and dining facilities, quiet. **C** *Pemo's Guest House*, Camps Rd, T4699188. **C-D** *Donna's Guest House*, Charlestown, T4695648.

Food on the whole is good. Apart from almost every kind of imported food and drink, there is a wide variety of fresh seafood (red snapper, lobster, king fish, blue parrot), and local vegetables. There are certain dishes that you certainly must try. Some of them are: conkey (usually available during Easter), ital which the local rastas make (food seasoned with all natural spices, no salt but very delicious), also try black pudding, goat water, saltfish and johnny cakes and souse. They are all foods which Kittitians love to eat, especially on Saturdays when no one wants to eat at home. The excellent local spirit is CSR – Cane Spirit Rothschild – produced in St Kitts by Baron de Rothschild (now in a joint venture with Demerara Distillers Ltd of Guyana). It is drunk neat, with ice or water, or with 'Ting', the local grapefruit soft drink (also highly recommended). Tours of the CSR factory are possible. The hotels have restaurants, usually serving local specialities. Most of the Plantation Inns on both islands offer Sunday brunch, usually a three course meal and excellent value at around US$25 per person.

Eating: St Kitts

Basseterre From US$40 pp including tax but not drinks: *Georgian House*, South Independence Square, T4654049. Open Wed-Sat 1830-2130, reservations only. From US$25: In the *Georgian House's* walled garden is *Mango's Bar and Bistro*, T4654049, complete with mango and banana trees, good food and a favourite hangout for visitors and locals alike, open Mon-Sat 1130-1600, dinner 1830-2130, Fri dancing until late. *Fisherman's Wharf*, T4652754, beside OTI offers tasty fresh fish, barbecue chicken etc and help yourself to vegetables for US$25-35, conch chowder recommended. *Star of India*, Victoria Rd, T4661537. Chef from Bombay, authentic Indian food. *Arlecchino*, Amory Mall, Cayon St. Italian restaurant, friendly owner, Jasmine makes a delicious coffee shake, T4659927, open 0900-1500, 1800-2230. *Bayembi Cultural Café*, Bank St, T466280. Good snacks, occasional Fri night street parties. **From US$15:** *Ballahoo* on the corner of Bank St and Fort St, T4654197, F4657070. Great meeting place, lovely view of the Circus, excellent local food at reasonable prices, open Mon-Sat 0800-2200. Also *Circus Grill*, T4650143. Good well-presented food, a bit more expensive than *Ballahoo*, open Mon-Sat 1130-2200. *Stone Walls*, Princess St, T4655248. Excellent food, special theme nights, open Mon-Sat 1700-2300, in pleasant garden. *Vegetarian Plus* in TDC Mall, T4650709. Open Mon-Sat 0800-2300, one of the few places open on Sun 1000-2200. Good, predictable Chinese food is at *Kim Sha*, Bay Rd, T4660022, and *Kim Xing*, Cayon St, T4666692. Generous portions, fast service, reasonable prices. *Rank's Eat Rite Specialities*, corner St Johnson Av and Union St, T4658190. Fresh, low fat meals, quaint, clean, friendly, veggie/fish burgers, tuna melt, fish meals, local drinks. *Leyton Internet Café*, Amory Mall, T4667873. Sending emails home is a bit expensive (see below), but good freshly baked cakes, pastries, sandwiches, coffee and tea. *Oasis Café*, TDC

There are many places offering snacks, light meals, ice creams and drinks in Basseterre and in the Frigate Bay area. Look out for places selling excellent local patties and fruit juices

Leeward Islands

Mall, Basseterre, T4657065. Open Mon-Sat. **Under US$15**: *Cisco's Place*, Church St, T4659009. Inexpensive lunches and delicious Chinese food on weekend nights. *Royal Ethiopian*, Cayon St, T4657741, vegetarian. *Jakki's*, T4656043, on Cayon St across from *Uncle T's* (for fast food, greasy, cheap). Great local snacks and baked goods, relax on *Jakki's* open air balcony. *Victor's Hideaway*, Stainforth St, New Town, Basseterre, T4652518. Open 0900-1500, 1830-late. *Chef's Place*, Church St, T465176. Good breakfasts and West Indian food at reasonable price, 0900-2100 Mon-Sat, no credit cards. *Pizza Lovers*, George St, New Town, T4656870. Filling, tasty, cheap. For a very local experience try *Razba's Veggie Pizza Parlour*, on St Johnston's Av, T4656738. Most of the clientele are Rastafarian vegetarians who come for a good 'lime' and are friendly to new faces. Similar atmosphere 2 blocks away at *Rasco-Tec*, look for the Bob Marley mural, T4668843. *The Family Snackette*, Liverpool Row, T4652601. Quaint setting, local food and drinks. *Central Delight Refreshment Bar*, Central St, T4651142. A place to relax, ice cream, hamburgers, hot dogs, sandwiches. *Ribs and Rolls*, Princess St, T4663474. Ribs and pastries. *Burger World*, Fiennes Av, T4665576. All kinds of burgers for all tastes, open 1000-midnight.

The only international fast food chain is the rather expensive *Kentucky Fried Chicken* on Bay Rd, T4667751. The popular and cheaper local equivalent is *Redi-Fried Chicken*, on the ground floor of the cinema on Bay Rd, T4651301. Tasty chicken and chips, moderate prices. Local bakeries have a variety of savoury and sweet baked goods at affordable prices. Most now have small dining sections as the competitive bakery business heats up. The main bakeries are *Fancy Loaf*, T4655415, *American Bakery*, T4652136, *Island Bakeries Ltd*, T4658034, *Browne & Sons*, T4652776, *Fraites & Sons*, T4654629 and *Fulton's*, T4659538.

Frigate Bay From US$40 *The Patio*, T4658666. Open Dec-May, local and international cuisine, complimentary white wine and open bar with dinner, run by Peter and Joan Mallalieu like a private dinner party so reservations essential, entrées US$25-30, dress smartly. *Marshall's*, at *Horizons Villa Resort*, T4668245. Romantic poolside dining with ocean view, exquisite food, not to be missed. *Breezes*, at *Papillon St Kitts*, T4658037. Breezy with excellent ocean view, pricy menu with tasty, but small, portions. From US$25 *Sunset Café*, *Timothy Beach Resort*, T4653020. Serves local seafood, burgers, open daily, 0700-2300, good. *Cisco's Atlantic Bistro*, T4667007. Big portions, open daily, kitchen hours 1900-2200, bar 1730-2230, reservations before opening time T4669009, ask for Shanta. *Doo Wop Days*, an Italian Café and Bar, T4651960, F4658506. Owned by Joe and Linda Pozzolo who have 50's, 60's and 70's entertainment and karaoki on weekends. From US$15 *PJ's Pizza*, T4658373. Open from 1000 Tue-Sat. At the end of the peninsula, out at *Turtle Beach Bar and Grill*, T4699086, F4667771. Excellent barbecue, vegetarian options, friendly, open daily 0945-1800 and Thu-Sat 1900-2100, live steel band on Sun and lunch time.

Around the island From US$40 For elegant dining in a cool, natural environment, try the *Royal Palm* at *Ottley's Plantation Inn*, away from the hustle and bustle. From US$15 Small restaurants around the island serving West Indian food, include *Manhattan Gardens*, Old Road Town, T4659121. Across the street, try *Sprat Net*, by the sea, T4656314. Run by Spencer family, serves fresh fish and goat water, busy at weekends. Highly recommended for good atmosphere and reasonably priced food, one of the places to be at weekends, open Thu-Sun. Under US$15: In Cayon in the east, *Penny's*, and *Off Limit Bar*, T4669821. Cater mostly for locals, local food, burgers, drinks, spacious and clean in village setting.

Eating: Nevis
Most restaurants only open in the evenings in the off season or even shut completely

The best restaurants are in the hotels and it is usually necessary to reserve a table; exceptional cuisine as well as barbecues and entertainment on certain nights of the week. **Charlestown:** There are very few eating places and none of them is expensive. *The Rainbow Café*, behind Barclays Bank. Open daily 0700 until late, warm smiles, great service, soothing music, cold drinks, expresso cappuccino, bagels, sandwiches, roti, croissants. *Callaloo* on Main St, T4695389. Serves lunch from US$4 and dinner from US$6, local food, hamburgers, sandwiches, pizzas from 1800, open Mon-Thu 0700-2200, Fri, Sat 0700-2400, no smoking, bring your own wine, friendly service. *Eddy's* on same street is a tourist favourite for local food, T4695958. Drinks and music with string bands, bush bands or steel bands Sat 2000-2300, Happy Hour Wed 1700-2000. *Cotton House*, T4690305, at the Cotton Ginnery

Mall. Local food with sea view, specializes in goat water and souse. *Calypso Bistro*, Heritage Plaza, T4695110. Courtyard garden bar and grill. *Saints and Sinners*, T4690445, Lower Craddock Rd. Local dishes and seafood.

Around the island From US$25: The *Oualie Beach Club* does local lunches and dinners, T4699735, 0700-2100. *Oualie Beach* has a Caribbean buffet on Sat with live music and masquerade dance, and surf and turf beach barbecue on Tue. *Sunshines by the Sea*, T4695817. Seafood and Sun bonfire on Pinney's Beach.*Beachcomber Bar and Grill*, T4691192, F4693388, on Pinney's Beach. A great place to meet people. *Seafood Madness*, T4690558. Great for takeaway orders, at the *Sea Spawn Guest House*. *Bananas*, Cotton Ground, T4691891. Creative bistro menu with a romantic setting, weekly specials. *Jamestown Beach Café*, T4699224. Open daily from 1000. *Jade Garden*, T4699762, Newcastle. Healthy cuisine, salads, pizza, deli. *Newcastle Bay Marina*, T4699395. Italian and Spanish dinners. *Unella's By the Sea*, T4695574, on the Waterfront offers great views although the service is slow. *Julian's at Cliff dwellers*, T4698262, F4655195, on Tamarind Bay offers spectacular views of St Kitts. *What's New Under the Sea*, Tamarind Bay, T4691291. Dine on an aquarium table, try 'wings and stings', open daily for lunch 1200-1600, Fri happy hour 1730-1830. At *Caribbean Cove*, there is an American-style restaurant, T4691286. At the Botanical Gardens *Martha's Tea House* serves sandwiches, scones with Devonshire cream and tapas, panoramic views, T4693680. **From US$15**: *Miss June's*, Jones Bay, T4695330. Open three times a week, Caribbean dinner party, preceded by cocktails and *hors d'oeuvres*, wine, dessert, coffee and liqueurs included in price, numbers strictly limited so reservations essential. *Mem's Pizzeria*, Prospect Garden, T4691390. Excellent lobster pizza, seafood recommended. *Sand Dollar Bar and Grill*, T4695319, F4690614, next to the *Four Seasons Hotel*. Offers entertainment and happy hour Tue-Fri, closed Mon, party night is Fri, very popular. For excellent local food try *Cla Cha Del Restaurant and Bar*, T4691841, completely out of the way in Newcastle (close to the airport) with good atmosphere at weekends. *Tequila Sheilas*, T4698633, F4690129, on Cades Bay. *The* place to be at weekends with dancing until late. For a more local, relaxed atmosphere try *Muriel's Cuisine*, T4695920 on Happy Hill. *Hill Top Bar and Restaurant*, T4693635, on Pond Hill. **Under US$15**: *Culturama Bar*, Jessups, T4695206. Seafood specialities.

Nightlife

Steel pan on Fri nights at *OTI*. A good place for a drink in Basseterre is *TOTTs*, opposite Post Office on the Bay Rd. *Malloy's Irish Pub*, next to Bird Rock Beach and a second location at Baker's Corner, Basseterre, close to the bus stop for buses going up the west side, not as picturesque, but easy to find. One-of-a-kind alternative to other forms of nightlife on St Kitts, friendly Irish atmosphere with reasonably priced Irish snacks. *Charlie's Jazz Bar and Grill*, upper end of Cayon St, T4666393. Newest entertainment spot, very cool, cozy and classy atmosphere, popular with the 'upper crust' as well as more budget minded locals and visitors, live artistes (local and international) and recorded jazz, open Tue-Thu 1700-2400, Fri-Sun 1700-0200, salsa night on Thu, talent night on Fri, with instruments at the bar if you haven't got your own. *Flamingo Restaurant and Bar*, T4650898, on Monkey Hill. Pool tables and a small dance floor. Most dance floors provide a wide variety of music to suit anyone's taste and entrance costs US$3.50-18.50, depending on the occasion, with overseas performers commanding the upper limit. *Sprat Net*, *Manhattan Gardens*, *BCA* and the *Inner Circle* are more likely to feature local bands playing local music. *Mango's* and night clubs have a great mix of calypso, soca, salsa, hip-hop, reggae, dance hall, R&B, house, techno and other types of music. *Mango's*, T4654049, is the only dance venue known to cater more for tourists (however locals frequent the place on Fri nights, when it is *the* place to be) by offering the type of music they are familiar with. Recommended is the salsa class on Wed night at the *Bayembi Café Dance Floor*, next to *Mango's*, taught by Shelagh James. You will leave after your first class well on the way to salsa greatness. There are many residents of Latin American origin and their influence has generated a great deal of interest in salsa. Friendly and lively atmosphere and you can move on to *Mango's* afterwards. Latin night on Sat is increasingly popular with locals as well as the Latin American community. Don't expect to sit down all night, no dance rules, just enjoy yourself. The *Lighthouse Disco* is very popular with locals on Sat and Sun nights, a club scene, gets going after midnight. For the real local experience you may want to visit another of the dance clubs or dance spots out in the country area: *BCA*, T4657606/7, at Saddlers; *Manhattan Gardens*, T4659121, and *Sprat Net*, in Old Road Town, *Off Limit*, in Cayon, T4669821, and the new *Inner Circle Club*, at St Paul's, where action takes place by announcement. These venues are frequented by some of the region's top DJs. Nightclubs include *Lions Den Club*, T4652582, in Bird Rock, and *Eclipse* at Canada Estate, T4668188. Fairly smart, open Fri and Sat 2200-0530. On Sun *Turtle Beach* at the end of the southeast peninsula usually has sunset dancing until midnight. Dance spots on **Nevis** include *Under the Sea* at Tamarind Bay, T4691291, where anything goes; *Tequila Sheilas* at the end of Pinney's Beach, T4698633; *Sand Dollar Bar & Grill*, next to *Four Seasons*, T4695319.

Festivals

St Kitts & Nevis are very proud of their masquerade traditions

The liveliest time to visit **St Kitts** is for the **carnival** held over *Christmas* and the *New Year*. It gets bigger and better every year with parades, calypso competitions and street dancing. For details, contact the Department of Tourism. St Kitts also holds a music festival at the end of *June*; 4 nights of calypso, reggae, R&B, jazz, street style, gospel, country and western and rap, with local and famous overseas artists. On **Nevis**, the annual equivalent of carnival is **Culturama**, held in end-*July* and *August*, finishing on the first Monday in August. There is a Queen show, calypso competition, local bands and guest bands and many 'street jams'. The Nevis Tourist Office has full details or contact the Department of Culture, T4695521, Mon-Fri 0800-1600.

Shopping

Shop opening hours 0800-1600, Mon-Sat. Early closing on Thu & also Sat for some shops

The shopper has plenty of choice and is not swamped by US or British merchandise. Shops are well stocked. Local Sea Island cotton wear and cane and basketwork are attractive and reasonable. There are three vendors' markets: at the Craft House on the Bay Road, at Port Zante and on Lower College St Ghaut and Liverpool Row. *Walls Deluxe Record and Bookshop* on Fort Street has a good selection of music and Caribbean books, open Mon-Thur 0800-1700, Fri 0800-1800, Sat 0800-1630. *Brown Sugar* clothing line, Upper Central St, T4664664, is owned by Judith Rawlins, a young local designer. Her clothing is very attractive, Caribbean style without the bright colours, all designed and sewn by Judith herself. *The Island Hopper Boutique* at the Circus, underneath the *Ballahoo* restaurant, stocks the Caribelle Batik range of cotton fashions and also carries clothes from Trinidad, St Lucia, Barbados and Haiti; open 0800-1600 Mon-Fri, 0800-1300 Sat, T4652905; also at The Arcade, Charlestown, Nevis, T469-1491/5426. The Stonewall Boutique on Princes Street sells quality local crafts and imports. *The Plantation Picture House*, at Rawlins Plantation is Kate Spencer's studio and gallery of portraits, still life and landscapes in oils and watercolours, her designs are also on silk, open 1100-1700. She also has a shop in Basseterre, on Bank Street, just off the Circus, called Kate, with paintings, prints, silk sarongs, hats by Dale Isaac, and another shop in Main Street, Charlestown. *Glass Island*, 4 Princes St, T/F4666771, www.glassisland.com, is a working glass shop which produces glass tiles, platters, jewellery and gifts. There are several local craft shops in Charlestown. Next to the tourist office is *Nevis Handicraft Co-operative*. On the road to the *Four Seasons Hotel* is an industrial estate with shops selling crafts and a toy shop. In Newcastle there is a pottery with red clay artefacts including bowls and candleholders. You can watch potters at work. The kilns are fired by burning coconut husks.

The public **markets** in Basseterre and Charleston are busiest Sat morning, good for fruit and vegetables, also fish stalls and butchers. Supermarkets in Basseterre include *B & K Superfood* on the south side of Independence Square and George Street, *Horsfords Valumart* on Wellington Road, and *Rams* on Bay Road and at Bird Rock. On Nevis, there are well-stocked supermarkets: *Nisbets* in Newcastle and Superfood, Parkville Plaza, Charlestown.

There are philatelic bureaux on both St Kitts and Nevis which are famous (the latter more so) for their first day covers of the islands' fauna and flora, undersea life, history and carnival. The St Kitts bureau is in *Pelican Shopping Mall*, open Mon-Wed, Fri-Sat 0800-1200, 1300-1500, Thu, 0800-1100. The Nevis bureau is open Mon-Fri, 0800-1600.

Transport

Air *JMC Airways* offers a weekly charter flight directly into St Kitts from London and is the most convenient way to get there from the UK. Connections to North America and Europe can be made through San Juan (*American Eagle* and *LIAT*), St Maarten (*LIAT* and *Winair*), Barbados (*LIAT*) and Antigua (*LIAT*). There are good connections with other Caribbean Islands (Anguilla, Grenada, St Croix, St Eustatius, St Lucia, St Thomas and Tortola) with *LIAT*, *Caribbean Star* and Windward Islands Airways (*Winair*). Weekly charters include *Royal* from Toronto throughout the year and seasonal weekly charters from Detroit, Chicago, Dallas and Boston. Flights to Nevis from Anguilla *Coastal Air Transport*, Antigua (*LIAT*), St-Barths *Coastal Air Transport*, St Croix *Coastal Air Transport*, St Kitts (*LIAT*) and St Maarten (*LIAT* and *Winair*). *Nevis Express* has up to 10 daily flights between St Kitts and Nevis, US$20, 6 mins, also charter service. The grander hotels on Nevis will arrange chartered air transfers from Antigua or St Kitts for their guests (for instance, Carib Aviation from Antigua), highly recommended to avoid the crush.

Airport RL Bradshaw International, St Kitts' main airport, is two miles from Basseterre. It is possible to get a bus from Basseterre (bus stop at the roundabout northeast of Independence Square, EC$1.25) to the airport and walk the last 5 mins from the main road; some buses might go up to the terminal. If you have not much luggage, it is easy to walk from Basseterre to the airport. There is no currency exchange at the airport. There are duty free and gift shops and a café. There is also an airport on Nevis, at Newcastle airfield, seven miles from Charlestown (on the main road, bus to Charlestown EC$3.50). A runway extension is being built to enable jets to land. There is a small snack shop at the airport. Expect to have your baggage searched on your way in to either island. Departure delays have been minimized by improved facilities on both islands.

Sea The new port in Basseterre is Port Zante, which can accommodate 2 of the largest cruise ships and will eventually boast a huge hotel, casino and many shops. **Ferry** The crossing between St Kitts and Nevis takes about 45 mins and costs EC$20 round trip. Departs Basseterre, Mon 0800, 1600; Tue 1300; Wed 0700, 1600, 1900 (good day for day trip); Fri 0830, 1600; Sat 0830, 1600. Departs Charlestown, Mon 0700, 1500; Tue 0730, 1800; Wed 0800, 1800; Fri 0730, 1500; Sat 0730, 1500. Confirm sailing times with Ministry of Communications, T4652521, Mon-Fri 0800-1600. Tickets can only be purchased from the quay just prior to departure, so turn up about 1 hr in advance to avoid disappointment. Island tours operate from St Kitts and there is also a water taxi service between the 2 islands: US$25 return, minimum 4 passengers, 20 mins, operated by Kenneth's Dive Centre, T4652670 in advance, or ProDivers, US$20, 10 mins, T4653223, 4699086. The *Four Seasons Hotel* has ferry boats running exclusively for guests' flights.

Local Bus Minibuses do not run on a scheduled basis but follow a set route (more or less), EC$1-3 on most routes, EC$3 from Basseterre to the north of the island, frequent service from the bus terminal close to the market area on the Bay Road from where buses go west to Sandy Point. To catch a bus east, wait off Bakers Corner at the east end of Cayon Street, not obvious, ask someone. There are no minibuses to Frigate Bay and the southeast peninsula. On Nevis buses start outside Foodworld Cash & Carry supermarket and go to all points, but not on a regular basis, EC$1-3, an island tour is possible, if time consuming.

Car hire Fuel is US$2 per gallon. Most rental companies will help you obtain the obligatory temporary driving licence, EC$100, valid for a year, from the Fire Station, Ponds Road, Police Station, Cayon Street, or Inland Revenue Dept, Bay Road, above Post Office. If you rent for 3 day minimum you can arrange for a car on the sister island if you do a day trip to St Kitts or Nevis. Hire companies include: *TDC Rentals*, West Independence Square, Basseterre, T4652991, F4651099, or Bay Road, Charlestown, T4695960, F4691329, also at *Four Seasons*, T4691111; *Caines Rent-A-Car*, Princes Street, Basseterre, T4652366, F4656172; *Sunshine Car Rental*, Cayon Street, Basseterre, T4652193, Hondas and Korando jeeps. Others include *A & T Car*, T4654030; *Delisle Walwyn*, T4658449; *Huggins*, T4658080; *Courtesy Car Rentals*, T4657804; *G & L*, T4668040/1. If you are arriving in St Kitts from Nevis, there are several car hire companies on Independence Square, some 3 mins' walk from the ferry pier. One of the most convenient is *Avis Car Rental*, South Independence Square St, T4656507, F4666846

If visiting at carnival time you should book car hire a long time in advance

Leeward Islands

(Suzuki jeeps, Nissan automatics, efficient). *Nisbett Rentals Ltd*, 100yds from Newcastle airport, Minimoke US$40 per day, collision damage waiver US$8 per day, recommended, particularly if you are flying in/out of Nevis, T4699211, open 0700-1900. *Avis*, T4691240, and *Discount*, T4690343. Also on Nevis through Striker's (Hermitage), T4692654, Carlton Meade; **bicycle rental** on Craddock Road, T4695235. Companies insist on you having collision damage waiver, which adds another US$5-10 to quoted rates. There is a 5% tax on car rentals.

The Visitor magazine & airports have a list of recommended fares. There is no need to tip

Taxi Taxis have a yellow T registration plate. Maximum taxi fares are set, for example: **On St Kitts**, from Airport to Basseterre EC$18, to Frigate Bay, EC$29, to Sandy Point EC$40. From Basseterre to Old Road, EC$27, to Frigate Bay, EC$20, to Middle Island, EC$27 to Sandy Point, EC$32, to Romney Manor (return) EC$68, to Brimstone Hill (return) EC$86.40. Taxis within Basseterre cost EC$10, with additional charges for waiting or for more than two pieces of luggage. Between 2300-0600 prices rise by 25%. A southeast peninsula tour is EC$106, an island tour EC$159. **On Nevis** a taxi from the airport to Charlestown costs EC$37, to *Oualie Beach*, EC$24, to the *Montpelier Inn*, EC$55, to *Hermitage Inn*, EC$45 and to *Nisbet Plantation Inn*, EC$21. Fares from Charlestown to *Pinneys Beach Hotel*, EC$13, to *Four Seasons* EC$18, to *Cliffdwellers* EC$26.50, to *Oualie Beach* EC$29, to *Mount Nevis Hotel* EC$42. A 50% extra charge is made on Nevis between 2200 and 0600. An island tour of Nevis costs US$50 for about 3 hrs, but you can bargain it down if no cruise ship is in port. The number of taxis on Nevis quadrupled to some 130 in the five years to 1999 to meet the demand from tourists.

Directory **Airlines** *Caribbean Star Airlines*, at the airport, T4655929. *LIAT*, *TDC Airline Services*, PO Box 142, Basseterre, T465-2511/2286, and *Evelyn's Travel*, on Main Street, Charlestown, general sales agent for *BWIA*, *LIAT*, *American Airlines* and *British Airways*, PO Box 211, Charlestown, T469-5302/5238; *BWIA*, T4652286 on St Kitts, T4695238 on Nevis; *American Eagle*, T4658490 (St Kitts); Winair, Sprott Street, Basseterre, T4652186 on St Kitts, 4695583 on Nevis; *Carib Aviation*, T4653055 (the Circus, Basseterre and R L Bradshaw airport, St Kitts), F4653168, T4699295 (Newcastle Airport, Nevis). *Nevis Express*, T4699755/6, F4699751, www.nevisexpress.com *Air St Kitts Nevis*, PO Box 529, Basseterre, T4658571, F4699018, a charter company specializing in day excursions and other services to neighbouring islands for example Saba, St Maarten, Antigua, Guadeloupe, Barbados, USVI. Also air ambulance with medical staff. **Banks** *The Eastern Caribbean Central Bank (ECCB)* is based in Basseterre, and is responsible for the issue of currency in Antigua and Barbuda, Dominica, Grenada, Montserrat, St Kitts and Nevis, St Lucia and St Vincent and the Grenadines. There is a local bank on St Kitts: *St Kitts-Nevis-Anguilla National Bank* (5 branches: on the corner of Central Street and West Independence Square Street; Pelican Mall; Sandy Point, T465-2204/6331/2701 open 0830-1500 except Thu 0830-1200, Sat 0830-1100, a branch at Saddlers Village, T4657362, opens 0830-1300 except Thu 0830-1200 and Sat 0830-1100) and on Nevis, West Square St, Charlestown, T4695244, same hours. In addition, on Nevis, there is the *Nevis Co-operative Banking Co Ltd* and the *Bank of Nevis*. Foreign banks on St Kitts: *Barclays Bank Plc* (on the Circus, Basseterre, T4652519, open Mon-Thu 0800-1500, Fri 0800-1700, the other at Frigate Bay, open Mon-Thu 0800-1300, Fri 0800-1300, 1500-1700, T465-2264/2510), *Royal Bank of Canada* (on the Circus, Basseterre, T4652519, open Mon-Thu 0800-1500, Fri 0800-1700, T465-2259/2389), *Bank of Nova Scotia* (Fort Street, open Mon-Thu 0800-1500, Fri 0800-1700, T4654141); on Nevis, *Barclays* (T469-5467/5309) and *Bank of Nova Scotia* (T4695411). Open 0800-1500 Mon-Thu, Fri until 1700. Avoid lunchtimes (1200-1300) and after 1500 on Fri as banks are busy with local workers. If you are in a hurry, choose a foreign bank as their queues are often shorter. Visa and MasterCard accepted by all 3. ATMs are available at all banks but dispense local currency only. **Communications Post:** Post office in Basseterre is on Bay Road, open Mon-Sat 0800-1500 except Thu when it closes at 1100 and Sat at 1200; in Charlestown on Main St, open from 0800-1500 except Thu, closes at 1100, and Sat at 1130. Airmail letters to the UK take up to 2 weeks. Courier services including *DHL, Fed Ex*, on both islands. **Telephone:** the telephone company, *Cable & Wireless*, has digital telecommunications systems for the two islands and international direct dialling is available. Telemessages and faxes can be sent from the main office on Cayon Street, Basseterre. Credit card calls T1-800-8778000. USA direct public phones available at C & W office. Phone cards are sold in denominations of EC$10, 20 and 40. Coin boxes take EC quarters minimum and EC dollars. Codes: 869-465/6 (St Kitts), 869-469 (Nevis). Call charges are from US$5 for 3 mins to the USA, Canada or the UK. *The Boat Phone Company* on the Victoria Road, T/F4663003, F4653033, offers cellular phone service for yachts. **Internet** There is an internet station at the Pelican Mall on the Bay Road in Basseterre, also *Leyton's Internet Café* at the Amory Mall, T4667873, EC$0.25/minute or EC$15 per hour.

Embassies and consulates Venezuelan Embassy and an Embassy of the **Republic of China** on St Kitts. There are also Honorary Consuls of **Spain**, **Germany**, **Trinidad and Tobago**, **France** and the **Netherlands**. The acting **British High Commissioner** is in Antigua. **Tourist information** Local tourist office: The St Kitts Department of Tourism (Pelican Mall, PO Box 132, Basseterre, T465-2620/4040, F4658794, mintc&e@caribsurf.com) and the Nevis Tourist Office (Main Street, Charlestown, T4691042, F4691066, nevtour@caribsurf.com) are both extremely helpful, with plenty of information available, open Mon-Fri 0800-1600, with the Nevis office also open Sat 0900-1200.

Background

Before Columbus's arrival in 1493, there were Amerindians living on both islands, **History** whose relics can still be seen in some areas. As in most of the other islands, however, they were slaughtered by European immigrants, although the Caribs fought off the British and the French for many years and their battle scenes are celebrated locally. St Kitts became the first British settlement in the West Indies in 1623 and soon became an important colony for its sugar industry, with the importation of large numbers of African slaves. In April 1690 a severe earthquake struck, causing heavy damage to St Kitts, Nevis and Redonda. It was followed by a tidal wave which compounded the damage and, it is believed, destroyed Nevis' first capital, Jamestown.

For a time St Kitts was shared by France and England; partition was ended by the Peace of Utrecht in 1713 and it finally became a British colony in 1783. From 1816, St Christopher, Nevis, Anguilla and the British Virgin Islands were administered as a single colony until the Leeward Islands Federation was formed in 1871. (For a detailed history of Nevis during this period, read *Swords, Ships and Sugar–A History of Nevis to 1900*, by Vincent Hubbard, available in St Kitts and Nevis bookshops.)

From 1958, St Kitts-Nevis and Anguilla belonged to the West Indies Federation until its dissolution in 1962. In 1967 their constitutional status was changed from Crown Colony to a state in voluntary association with Britain, in a first step towards self-government. Robert L Bradshaw was the first Premier of the Associated States. Local councils were set up in Anguilla and Nevis to give those islands more authority over local affairs. Anguilla broke away from the group and was re-established as a Crown Colony in 1971. During the 1970s independence was a burning issue but Nevis' local council was keen to follow Anguilla's lead rather than become independent with St Kitts. Negotiations were stalled because of British opposition to Nevis becoming a Crown Colony. Eventually, on 19 September 1983, St Kitts and Nevis became independent as a single nation.

The main political parties are the People's Action Movement (PAM), the St Kitts and Nevis Labour Party (SKNLP), the Nevis Reformation Party (NRP) and the Concerned Citizens Movement (CCM). Dr Kennedy Simmonds (PAM) was elected Prime Minister in 1980 and held office until July 1995. Elections in November 1993 were highly controversial when the PAM and the SKNLP each won four seats, the CCM two and the NRP one. The CCM declined to join in a coalition government to form a majority with either major party. The Governor then asked Dr Kennedy Simmonds to form a minority government with the support of the NRP, the PAM's previous coalition partner. This move was highly unpopular, given that the Labour Party had won 54.4 % of votes cast in St Kitts compared with 41.7 % for the PAM. A state of emergency was declared for 10 days in December because of rioting and other disturbances, a curfew was imposed for five days and a detachment of soldiers from the Regional Security System joined the local police force for a week. Negotiations between Dr Denzil Douglas, the SKNLP leader, and Dr Simmonds, for a caretaker government for six months followed by fresh elections, failed. More clashes greeted the budget presentation in February 1994 with the SKNLP boycotting parliament (except to take the oath of allegiance in May) in support of fresh elections.

Also during 1994, St Kitts was rocked by a corruption scandal linked to senior political officials involving drugs trafficking, murder and prison riots. It was alleged that traffickers were exploiting St Kitts and Nevis and avoiding the better monitored, traditional routes. The crisis pushed the Government into calling a forum for national unity, at which it was decided that a general election should be held, three years ahead of schedule. In the meantime, all parties in the National Assembly participated in decisions on matters such as foreign investment and a code of conduct to regulate political activity. A Commonwealth observer team monitored the elections to prevent a recurrence of the 1993 disturbances.

In the months leading up to the 3 July elections, British police officers were brought in to assist the local police force. The campaign itself was marred by political party rivalry which was often violent, but the result was an overwhelming victory for the SKNLP, which won seven seats. The PAM was reduced to one, while the CCM and the NRP continued to hold two seats and one seat respectively. Dr Denzil Douglas became Prime Minister. In 1998 the police force was returned to local command.

In 1992 Mr Simeon Daniel, the Premier of Nevis for 21 years, lost his assembly seat in elections which saw Mr Vance Amory (CCM) become the new leader. Mr Amory is in favour of the secession of Nevis from the federal state and legislation was prepared in 1996. However he failed to get it debated in the House of Assembly in November because of a boycott of the session by the NRP. Caricom proposed the establishment of a commission to examine the future relations of St Kitts and Nevis in an attempt to avoid a hasty and messy secession. A three-member commission was sworn in at end-1997 to review the constitution.

Elections for the Nevis Island Assembly were held in February 1997 and Mr Amory was returned to power. The CCM retained its three seats and the NRP held its two seats. Nevis' assembly voted unanimously for secession in 1997. However, a referendum on succession in July 1998 was unsuccessful when it failed to gain the approval of two-thirds of the electorate. Talks on constitutional reform were held in 1999 between the Federal Government and the Nevis Island Administration.

In September 1998 Hurricane Georges devastated the island of St Kitts. About 75 percent of homes were extensively damaged. A record clean up brought the island back to normal by the end of the year and most tourist facilities were open for business by the winter high season. In November 1999 the leeward side of both islands was hit by Hurricane Lenny, which brought high seas and flooding, wiping out many beaches and damaging hotels. *The Four Seasons Hotel* in Nevis remained closed for a year for repairs which included importing sand and constructing a breakwater to protect the beach by the hotel. St Kitts and Nevis was spared any natural disasters in 2000, giving it a much-needed break and an opportunity to ease the burden on its economy.

General elections were held in March 2000 and the SKNLP was returned to power, winning all eight seats in St Kitts. There was no change in Nevis, the CCM winning two seats and the NRP one. Dr Kennedy Simmonds, leader of the PAM since 1976, announced his resignation in 2000. The new leader of the opposition is Mr Lindsey Grant, a lawyer. The PAM had claimed massive fraud in the elections, in which it lost its single seat although the party won 35.5% of the vote in St Kitts.

Government St Christopher and Nevis is a constitutional monarchy within the Commonwealth. The British monarch is Head of State and is represented locally by a Governor General. The National Assembly has 11 seats, of which three are from Nevis constituencies and eight from St Kitts. There are also four nominated Senators. Under the Federal system, Nevis also has a separate legislature and may secede from the Government of the Federation.

Economy Sugar, the traditional base of economic production, nowadays accounts for only about 2% of gdp, although it still occupies a dominant role within the agricultural sector and generates about a third of export revenues. Low prices for sugar in the world markets, hurricane damage, droughts, cane fires and the falling value of the euro, mean the industry runs at a loss. The Government has been encouraged to diversify away from sugar dependence and reduce food imports. More vegetables, sweet potatoes and yams are now being grown, while on Nevis, Sea Island cotton and coconuts are more common on smallholdings. Livestock farming and manufacturing are developing industries. There are enclave industries, such as electronic assembly, data processing and garment manufacturing (now over a quarter of total exports), which export to the USA and Caricom trading partners, while sales of sugar-based products such as pure cane spirit go mainly outside the region.

Tourism has become an important foreign exchange earner, and now contributes about 10% of gdp. The construction industry has benefited from the expansion of tourist infrastructure. The Government is increasing cruise ship arrivals with a port improvement project now enabling two cruise liners to berth at the same time, while stopover arrivals will be encouraged by the large resort development projects on the southeast peninsula of St Kitts, and airport improvements.

Anguilla

Anguilla is known for its luxury hotels and extensive sandy beaches. Its high standard of living makes it one of the safest islands and consequently one of the most relaxing. Visitors amuse themselves in the water during the day and eat at excellent restaurants and bars at night, taking in a weekend beach party with live music. There's not much else to do on this low-lying coral island, but that's why people come here.

Population: 8,960
1992 census

Ins and outs

International access points for Anguilla are Antigua, St Maarten or San Juan, Puerto Rico. From there you get a small plane, or boat from St-Martin, to Wallblake Airport or Blowing Point ferry terminal. Hotel transfers are not allowed, so you have to take a taxi on arrival.

Getting there
See transport, page 644, for further details

There are several **car hire** companies on the island. Hired cars can not be picked up from the airport because of local regulations, they have to be delivered to your hotel, but they can be dropped off at the airport. Watch out for loose goats on the roads. **Hitchhiking** is very easy and it is also possible to hire **bicycles**.

Getting around
Driving is on the left. Speed limit 30 mph

The climate is subtropical with an average temperature of 80°F and a mean annual rainfall of 36 ins, falling mostly between Sep and Dec. Any cloud and rain early in the day has usually cleared by mid-morning.

Climate

Flora and fauna

Although you will see colourful gardens with flowering hibiscus, bougainvillea and other tropical plants, the island is mostly covered with scrub. The **north coast** has the most unspoilt open areas which have not been cultivated or built on. There are steep cliffs of over 100ft high, with caves and sink holes, and inland are areas of dense vegetation. The most common plants are the white cedar, pigeonwood, manchineel, frangipani, five-finger trees, bromeliads and cacti. In this area you can find lizards, iguanas, snakes, bats and birds. **Katouche Valley** has a beach, a mangrove pond and a forest where you can find orchids and bromeliads and some patches of bamboo among the pepper cinnamon, mawby, sherry and turpentine trees. The valley ends at Cavannagh Cave, which was mined for phosphorous in the 19th century, but now is home to bats, birds, crabs and lizards. Birdwatching is good at **Little Bay**, Crocus Bay's north point and at the many ponds and coves, T4972759 for information. It is intended that the wetlands will eventually become sanctuaries. Ninety three species of birds have been recorded on Anguilla, including the blue faced booby, kingfisher and the great blue heron. The national bird is the turtle dove, which is protected.

A tree planting programme has been organized by the Anguilla Beautification Club (ABC); donations are welcome and you can 'adopt a tree'. Contact ABC Trees, PO Box 274, Anguilla

Leeward Islands

A Foot in the door

- Take a **lobster lunch** at Island Harbour followed by some gentle snorkelling.
- **Sail** to one of the cays and spend a leisurely few hours exploring, snorkelling and relaxing.
- Do a spot of **birdwatching** in the ponds and wetlands.

Diving and marine life

Dive sites   The Government is introducing a marine parks system, installing permanent moorings in certain areas to eliminate anchor damage. Designated marine parks include Dog Island, Island Harbour, Little Bay, Prickly Pear, Sandy Island, Seal Island and Shoal Bay. Mooring permits are required. Do not remove any marine life such as coral or shells from underwater. Spear fishing is prohibited. *Stoney Bay Marine Park Underwater Archaeological Preserve* was opened in March 1999 for limited public diving, although surveying, mapping and historical research was not complete. The park is protecting the wreck of a Spanish ship, *El Buen Consejo*, which ran aground on 8 July 1772 off the northern tip of Anguilla while on its way to Mexico with 50 Franciscan missionaries bound for the Philippines. It now lies about 100 yd offshore at a depth of 30 ft, with cannons, anchors and historical artefacts. Dives are fully guided and can only be done with *Shoal Bay Scuba and Watersports*. You are shown a video and given an overview of the ship's history before you go down. Eventually dive trails with plaques will be installed.

There are good dives just off the coast, particularly for novices or for night dives, while the others are generally in a line due west of Sandy Island, northwest of Sandy Ground, and along the reef formed by **Prickly Pear Cays** and Sail Island. Off **Sandy Island**, there are lots of soft corals and sea-fans, while at Sandy Deep there is a wall which falls from 15-60ft. There are also several wrecks, nine of which have been deliberately sunk as dive sites around the island, the most recent in 1993.

Further west, **Paintcan Reef** at a depth of 80ft contains several acres of coral and you can sometimes find large turtles there. Nearby, **Authors Deep**, at 110 ft has black coral, turtles and a host of small fish, but this dive is more for the experienced diver. On the north side of the Prickly Pear Cays you can find a beautiful underwater canyon with ledges and caves where nurse sharks often go to rest. Most of the reefs around Anguilla have some red coral; be careful not to touch it as it burns.

Dive centres   *Anguilla Divers*, based at *La Sirena*, Meads Bay and Island Harbour, dive the east end of the island and offer PADI courses, in English, French, German or Spanish, T4974750, F4974632, axadiver@anguillanet.com *Shoal Bay Scuba & Watersports*, T4974371. Dive master, Douglas Carty, has his own boat, *Desha*, and offers diving, boat trips and charters, US$50 for a single tank, US$90 for two-tank dives and packages available, T4974567, dcarty@anguillanet.com

Beaches and watersports

The beaches are clean, and many of them are relatively unpopulated, but nude (or topless for women) swimming or sunbathing is not allowed

There are 12 miles, 45 beaches, of fine white coral sand and crystal clear water. Most of them are protected by a ring of coral reefs and offshore islands. **Shoal Bay** is the most popular beach and claims to be one of the most beautiful in the Eastern Caribbean. There are hotels, snack bars for lunch, although only one has a toilet. The snorkelling is good, with the closest of two reefs only 10 yards from the shore and you can rent snorkelling equipment. You can also rent lockers, beach umbrellas, loungers, rafts and towels. **Mead's Bay** is also popular with more expensive bars, hotels and watersports. A controversial dolphin lagoon has been built here, stocked with dolphins from Cuba, allegedly caught in the wild, which have been trained and are giving performances. Conservationists have protested against keeping the dolphins in captivity for the amusement of tourists. For further information, contact the *Whale and Dolphin Conservation Society*, see page 68. The same company, *Dolphin Fantaseas*, has recently opened a dolphinarium on the British Virgin Isalnds and another has been approved for Antigua, all in the name of 'conservation and education'. **Road Bay/Sandy Ground** has most nightlife and restaurants and is the starting point for most day trips, dive tours and a popular anchorage for visiting yachts. Watersports equipment rentals can be organized here. **Scilly Cay** is a small cay off Island Harbour with good snorkelling. A free ferry takes you to the bar on a palm-clad beach where walls are made from conch shells. Live music on Wednesday, Friday and Sunday. *Smitty's Bar*, across the water at **Island Harbour** is less sophisticated, tables made from old cable barrels, TV, pool room, popular with the locals. The restaurant was rebuilt after Hurricane Luis flattened the first one in 1995. Smitty gets his fish, crayfish (US$20) and lobster (US$25) straight off the boats. Beach chairs and umbrellas are complimentary and snorkelling is good just off the beach. **Captain's Bay** is rougher but the scenery is dramatic and not many people go there. The dirt road is full of potholes and goats and may be impassable with a low car. At **Crocus Bay** the rocks on both sides have nice coral and underwater scenery. There is a bar/restaurant and toilets. At the end of **Limestone Bay** is a small beach with excellent snorkelling, but be careful, the sea can be rough here. **Little Bay** is more difficult to reach but eagle rays and turtles can be seen and as well as excellent snorkelling it is a birdwatcher's and photographer's dream; turn right in front of the old cottage hospital in the Valley, after about half a mile there are some trails leading down to the water, fishermen have put up a net for the last bit. Glass bottom boats and cruise boats also come here or you can get a boat ride from Crocus Bay.

   Windsurfing and **sailing** are readily available and some of the hotels offer water skiing, paddle boats, snorkelling, fishing and sunfish sailing. Parasailing can be arranged at Shoal Bay. Anguilla Watersports offer waterskiing, T4975821. Jet skiing is prohibited. There are glass bottom boats which can be hired for one or two people to operate themselves or crewed for groups. Sport fishing is available, contact *Gotcha*, T4972956; *Johnno's*, T4972728; *Rampoosin*, T4978868; *Sandy Island Enterprises*, T4975643; *No Mercy*, T4976383. Yacht or motorboat charters are offered with beach and snorkelling cruises around the island or trips to St Phillipsburg, St Maarten, charters to Saba, Statia, St Barts on request. Operators change frequently

Anguilla

Essentials

Documents All visitors need an onward ticket. All must also have a valid **passport**, except US citizens who need only show proof of identity with a photograph. **Visas** are not required by anyone. Proof of adequate funds is required if the Immigration Officer feels so inclined.

Currency The East Caribbean dollar. US dollars always accepted.

Departure tax There is a departure tax of US$10 at the airport and US$2 at the ferry.

Boat documents (Own flag). In Road Bay get a cruising permit for other anchorages. Customs and Immigration at Blowing Point ferry port and Road Bay at Sandy Ground (at Police Station next to Johnno's on north side, near small pier). Free **anchorage** in Road Bay and Blowing Point. Fees are based on official tonnage. Charter boats pay additional anchoring fees. Bring your crew lists. There is a **departure tax** of EC$5 per person. Little Bay,

Sandy Island and Prickly Pear have permanent moorings, other places have designated anchoring sites. Boats may not anchor in Rendezvous Bay or Little Bay. Every boat visiting a marine park must get a permit to tie up or anchor, fee US$15 for private vessels, US$23 for charter boats. If you want to scuba dive you pay a fee of US$4 per tank.

Business hours Government offices 0800-1600 Monday-Friday; **banks** 0800-1500 Monday-Thursday, 0800-1700 Friday. **Shops** open 0800-1700 or 1800, some grocery stores are open until 2100, a few on Sunday. **Gas stations** are open in The Valley, Monday to Saturday 0700-2100, Sunday 0900-1300, and at Blowing Point, Monday to Sunday 0700-2400.

Official time GMT minus four hours; EST plus one hour.

Weights and measures Metric, but some imperial weights and measures are still used.

but in 2000 the following were in Anguillian waters: Captain Kasha Brooks of Island Yacht Charter Co, T4973743, F4973738, has *Pyrat*, a 35-ft power boat and a 30-ft Beneteau sailboat, *Eros; Adventure Star*, a 32-ft motorboat, T4974750; *El Tigre*, Sail Anguilla catamaran, T4973304; *Chocolate* catamaran, T4973394; Sandy Island Enterprises has a motorboat, T4975643; *Gotcha*, 30-ft motorboat, T4972956; *Sail My Way*, 30-ft sailboat, T4976655; *No Mercy*, motorboat, T4976383; *Its Fun Time*, 32-ft power boat for day trips and fishing, T/F4976511, funtimecharters@ yahoo.com **Boat racing** is the national sport, the boats being a special class of wooden sloop made in Anguilla. There are frequent races, but the most important are on Anguilla Day (30 May) and during Carnival Week in August.

Other sports There are public **tennis** courts at Ronald Webster Park. Several hotels have tennis courts. The *Malliouhana* has four championship courts for guests only; *Cinnamon Reef* has two at a cost of US$25 per hour for non-residents, free for guests; *Cap Juluca, Sonesta* and *Cove Castles* all have courts for guests' use only, others make a charge for non-guests: *Carimar Beach Club*, US$20 per hour; *The Mariners*, US$20 per hour; *Masara Resort*, US$10 per hour; *Rendezvous Bay*, US$5 per hour; *Spindrift Apartments*, US$5-10 per hour. For spectator sports, call the Sports Officer, T4972317, for information on fixtures. There is **cricket, basketball, soccer, volley ball, soft ball, cycling** and **track and field**. Cricket is played at the Ronald Webster Park, including international matches. **Horse riding**, with trail rides or riding lessons, is offered by El Rancho del Blues, T6164. *Body & Soul Health and Fitness Club*, Sandy Ground, T/F4978364, offers aerobics, reebok step and soca dance classes. The Optimist Triathlon is held at the beginning of October, with teams of three competing in fun or serious categories: bicycle, road run and swimming.

Voltage *110 volts AC, 60 cycles.*
Communications *The international code is 264-497, followed by a four-digit number. See page 645 for further details.*
Media Newspapers Chronicle *daily,* The Daily Herald, The Light, *a local weekly.* What We Do In Anguilla *is an annual tourist magazine and a monthly tourism newspaper updates it, www.anguillatourguide.com* Anguilla Life *is a quarterly magazine.*
Radio *Radio Anguilla (T2218) is on medium wave 1505 kHz and ZJF on FM 105 MHz.*
Tourist offices overseas *Germany, c/o Sergat Deutschland, IM Guldenen Wingert 8-C, D-64342, Seeheim, T49-6257-962920, F49-6257-962919, r.morozow@t-online-de*
Italy, *Piazza Bertarelli 1, 20122 Milan, T39-02-72022466, F39-02-72020162, Bdp-comunicazione@iol.it*
UK, *3 Epirus Road, London, SW6 7UJ, T020-79377725, F020-79384793,*
windotel@BTInternet.com
USA, *c/o Westcott Group, 39 Monaton Drive, Huntington Station, NY 11746, T516-4250900, F516-4250903, info@westcott-group.com*
Puerto Rico, *Amarylis Davila, RSVP Travel Service, PO Box 16328, San Juan, T/F787-7250882, atbpr@hotmail.com*
Clothing *Bathing costumes are not worn in public places. Nude bathing or nude sunbathing is not allowed.*
Public holidays *New Year's Day, Good Friday, Easter Monday, Labour Day, Whit Monday, end of May (Anguilla Day, commemorates the Anguilla Revolution which began 30 May 1977), the Queen's official birthday in June, the first Monday (August Monday) and the first Thursday (August Thursday) and Friday (Constitution Day) in August, 19 December (Separation Day), Christmas Day, Boxing Day.*

Around the island

Anguilla is a small island, about 35 miles square, and the most northerly of the Leeward Islands. It is arid, covered with low scrub and has few natural resources. However, it has excellent beaches and superb diving and snorkelling, protected by the coral reefs. The island's name is the Spanish word for 'eel', a reference to its long, narrow shape. Its Carib name was Malliouhana. The people of Anguilla, predominantly of African descent but with some traces of Irish blood, are very friendly and helpful and it is one of the safest islands in the Caribbean.

The island is low lying and, unlike its larger sisters, it is not volcanic but of coral formation

Near **The Valley**, the island's administrative centre, with a population of 500, **Wallblake House** is a restored, 18th-century plantation house where the priest from **St Gerard's Roman Catholic Church** lives. The Church itself is worth a visit to see the unusual ventilation. Several resident artists exhibit their work on Saturday mornings during the winter season in the grounds of Wallblake House. In February there is an annual garden party on the lawn for St Gerard's Church, with music, dinner and a bar, US$20. The Archaeological and Historical Society has tours in season on Tuesday from 1000, T4972759. **Anguilla National Museum** is in a restored Anguillian cottage just west of the Public Library, T4975297. It holds cultural and environmental exhibitions and there is information on hiking trails and historical sites.

Local deposits of clay have been found and pottery is now made on the island. The work of Barbadian potter and sculptor, Courtney Devonish, and his students, is on display at the **Devonish Cotton Gin Art Gallery** in the Old Factory Plaza opposite the Catholic Church, T4972949. There are sometimes pottery demonstrations on Saturday. At **Sandy Ground Village**, you can see the salt pond, around Great Road Pond, although it is not currently in operation. There is a mini museum at the *Pumphouse* bar, Sandy Ground. The building was once part of the salt factory and equipment used in the salt making process is on display, T4975154.

A local historian, Mr Colville Petty OBE, collects traditional household artefacts, displayed in what is known as the **Heritage Collection Museum**. ■ *South Hill Plaza on the main road, T4978737, F4974067, petty@anguillanet.com US$5, children under 12 US$3. Mon-Sat 1000-1700, Sun1300-1800.*

Leeward Islands

Northeast of The Valley, by Shoal Village, is **The Fountain** national park. Its focus is in fact a cave which has a source of constant fresh water and a series of Amerindian petroglyphs. Artefacts have been found and it is hoped they will be housed in a museum at the site, but the national park is still closed. Anguilla awaits detailed archaeological investigation, but it is thought that the island had several settlements and a social structure of some importance, judging by the ceremonial items which have been found. Contact the National Trust at the Museum Building in The Valley, or the Anguilla Archaeological and Historical Society for more information. Both are involved in several publications including a Review (PO Box 252). There is a very small museum of artefacts found on site at the *Arawak Beach Resort*, together with replicas of furnishings, pottery and baskets, T4974888, F4974498.

Big Spring Cave is an old Amerindian ceremonial centre where you can see petroglyphs. It is near **Island Harbour**, a fishing village with Irish ancestory. The National Trust has a map of archaeological and historical sites of Anguilla, worth getting if you want to explore caves, Amerindian sites or sugar mill rounds, T4973041, PO Box 1234.

Islands off shore Day trips can be arranged to some of the neighbouring islands or to the offshore islands and cays. **Sandy Island** is only 15 minutes from Sandy Ground harbour and is a pleasant desert island-type place to swim, snorkel and spend half a day or so. ■ *Motorboats or sailboats cross over hourly 1000-1500, US$8 per person. Lunch or drinks available from a beach bar under coconut palms, T4976395/4975643.* There are trips to **Prickly Pear**, six miles from Road Bay, which is well worth a visit, where you can snorkel if you are not a scuba diver, or to some of the other cays where you can fish or just have a picnic. **Scrub Island**, two miles long and one mile wide, off the northeast tip of Anguilla, is an interesting mix of coral, scrub and other vegetation and is worth a visit. It is uninhabited, except by goats, and can only be reached by boat. There is a lovely sandy beach on the west side and ruins of an abandoned tourist resort and airstrip. There can be quite a swell in the anchorage, so anchor well. Boats go from Road Bay, Shoal Bay or Island Harbour. Chartered yachts and motorboats leave from Road Bay or from Island Harbour for Scilly Cay, privately owned by Eudoxie and Sandra Wallace and also named **Gorgeous Scilly Cay**. They also have their own boat with a free ferry service. ■ *1000-1700, lunch only, live music Wed, Fri, Sun, closed.*

Essentials

Sleeping
A 10% tax & 10-15% service charge will be added to the bill

Anguilla has the reputation of catering for upmarket, independent travellers. This is reflected in the number of relatively small, but expensive hotels and beach clubs. Bargains can be found in the summer months, with discounts of up to 50%. The Anguilla Department of Tourism has a list of all types of accommodation. Inns of Anguilla is an association of over 20 villas or small hotels at moderate prices.

The following have flexible accommodation in rooms, suites, studios or villas, winter- summer prices quoted. **Anti-clockwise from Road Bay LL-L** *The Mariners Cliffside Beach Resort*, Sandy Ground, T4972671, F4972901, www.mariners.com 66 rooms, suites and cottages, gingerbread style, very cute, 8½ acres, on beach, watersports, pool, tennis. **LL** *Malliouhana Hotel*, Mead's Bay, PO Box 173, T4976011, F4976011, UK T0117-9241003. 55 rooms, no credit cards, suites up to US$2,175, every luxury, 'sprawlingly sybaritic public areas', very posh, attentive service, award-winning restaurant on beach, watersports (most complimentary), tennis, two pools, children welcome, playground and pool by the beach (hotel is closed Sep and Oct each year for refurbishment). **LL-AL** *Carimar Beach Club*, Mead's Bay, PO Box 327, T4976881, F4976071, www.carimar.com 24 comfortable 1-3 bedroom apartments, beach, tennis, dive package available. **LL** *Frangipani Beach Club*, luxury resort on Mead's Bay beach, T4976442, F4976440. 15 units, Spanish style tiled roofs, multilevel, tiled floors, fans, cool, comfortable. **LL-AL** *La Sirena*, Meads Bay, T4976827, F4976829, www.la-sirena.com 20 individually designed rooms, 5 villas, short walk to beach through gardens, 2 pools, restaurant, dive centre, 10% discount for repeat visitors. **LL-L** *Coccoloba Valtur*, Barnes Bay, T4978800, F4978126. 100 rooms, suites, villas all-inclusive, Italian-run, emphasis on health with fitness centre and cardio-aerobics instruction, day pass available for spa, beautiful beach, 2 pools, colourful gardens, gingerbread verandahs round the villas. **LL** *Cove Castles Villa Resort*, Shoal Bay West, T4976801, F4976051, T800-3484716, PO Box 248, futuristic architecture, 4 3-bedroom villas, 8 2-bedroom beach houses, very expensive, housekeeper, phone, TV, beach, tennis, sunfish, bicycles included, watersports available. **LL** *Cap Juluca* at Maundays Bay, T4976666, F4976617, www.capjuluca.com Moorish design, bright white, luxury resort, 98 rooms, every facility here, with 2 beaches, pool, watersports, tennis, also suites and 3-5 bedroom villas, CP, full children's activity programmes with watersports and tennis, 179-acre estate. **LL** *Sonesta Beach Resort Anguilla*, on Merrywing Bay, T4976999, F4976899, sonesta@anguillanet.com Opulent Moorish style, 100 rooms and suites, large pool, 2 tennis courts, fitness centre, conference centre, 2 restaurants, complimentary afternoon tea. **LL** *Anguilla Great House*, Rendezvous Bay, T4976061, F4976019. 27 simple rooms, open-air restaurant and bar on beach, pool, kayaks, windsurfers, sunfish, snorkelling and fishing gear. **LL-AL** *Rendezvous Bay Hotel*, PO Box 31, T4976549, F4976026, www.rendezvousbay.com 30 rooms, villas up to US$425, beach, tennis, family run, helpful, rooms with veranda only a few metres from the sea, moderately good snorkelling, lovely beach, run by the Gumbs family. **LL-L** *Cinnamon Reef*, Little Harbour, T4972727, F4973727, in the USA and Canada T800-3467084, F914-7635362, in the UK, T01453-835801, F01453-835525. 22 villa rooms, beach sheltered, no surf but good snorkelling and sunfish sailing, pool, tennis, library, spectacular dining room, good food, friendly service, no children under 12 in winter. **LL-L** *Arawak Beach Resort*, PO Box 433, T4974888, F4974898. Octagonal villas on the northeast coast near Big Spring ceremonial centre, overlooking Scilly Cay, mini museum, health bar and restaurant. **LL-AL** *Fountain Beach*, Shoal Bay, T4973491, F4973493. 14 rooms, studio, or 2 bedroom suite, a/c, fans, kitchen facilities, restaurant, pool, beach. **LL-A** *Masara Resort*, Katouche Bay, T4973200, F4973223. 10 units, 1 or 2 bedrooms, beach nearby.

For something a bit different, *Hotel de Health* near Sandy Hill Bay, T4974199, F4974194. Combines medical services with your holiday, 17 self-contained units, wheelchair access, cardiopulmonary clinic, caters for guests with special medical needs including renal dialysis, team of Canadian doctors may perform minor elective surgery.

Villas and apartments Among the cheapest to rent are **A-B** *Syd Ans Apartments*, Sandy Ground, T4973180, F4975381, www.inns.ai/sydans 1 bedroom apartments, Mexican restaurant, close to Tamariain Watersports. **A-C** *Sea View*, Sandy Ground, T4972427. 1-3 bedrooms, ceiling fans, kitchen facilities, beach nearby, clean, comfortable, enquire at the house next door for a room. **B** *La Palma*, Sandy Ground, T4973260, F4975381. 3 studios, on beach, restaurant, ceiling fans.

At Lower South Hill, **AL** *Inter Island*, T4976259, F4978207. 14 rooms, apartments, fans, kitchen facilities, restaurant. **LL-L** *Paradise Cove*, T4976603, F4976927, para-cove@anguillanet.com 14 1-2 bedroomed units with kitchen, jacuzzis, Olympic size pool, children's pool, café, a/c, fans, maid service, near beach. **LL-AL** *Blue Waters Beach Apartments*, Shoal Bay West, T4976292, F4976982. 9 1-2 bedroomed, self-catering apartments on the beach, fans, restaurant, baby sitting and maid service. **LL-A** *Ferry Boat Inn*, Blowing Point, T4976613, F4976713. 8 1-2 bedroomed apartments with view of sea and St Martin, a/c, fans, restaurant, daily maid service. **LL-L** *Shoal Bay Villas*, T4972051, F4973631, sbvillas@anguillanet.com 13 spacious 1-2 bedroomed suites and studios with kitchen, near *Le Beach* restaurant, open 0700-2200, pool, watersports. **LL-A** *Harbour Villas*, T4974393, F4974196, hvillas@anguillanet.com. Overlooking Gorgeous Scilly Cay, 7 apartments, 1-3 bedrooms, kitchens, laundry facilities, balcony, gardens lead down to beach.

Anguilla Connection Ltd at Island Harbour, T4974403, F4974402, www.luxuryvillas.com. Selection of 1-4 bedroom villas and apartments for rent, with several services on offer, US$170-500. *Select Villas of Anguilla*, Innovation Center, George Hill Road, T4975810, F4975811. 10 villas of different sizes around the island, cheapest US$650 per week in summer, most expensive US$1,100 per week in winter, daily rates available.

Guest houses Travellers on a lower budget or those wanting to avoid hotels can find accommodation in one of about 10 guest houses. These include **E** *Casa Nadine*, The Valley, T4972358. 11 clean rooms, EP, with shower, kitchen facilities, basic, but very friendly and helpful, price reductions for longer stays, good views over The Valley from the roof. **A** *Lloyd's Guesthouse*, Crocus Hill, T4972351, F4973028, www.lloyds.ai Run by Vida, David, and Christine Lloyd, CP, 12 rooms, all with bathroom, TV, fan, old-fashioned charm, public rooms show signs of wear, optional meal plan, family-style dining with other guests, mostly from other Caribbean islands, local dishes, drinks served but no bar.

Anguilla under US$100 is a package including some meals, accommodation, ground transfers, car rental, tax and gratuities. For details contact *Innovative Marketing Consultants*, same company as *Select Villas of Anguilla*, above.

Eating
Gourmet restaurants in hotels are expensive

There are many excellent places to eat on the island for all palates and all budgets, from the elegant to beach barbecues. Beach bars and casual waterfront places provide a good lunch, for example *Smitty's*, see page 637. The tourist guide *What We Do In Anguilla* has a listing. Most of the restaurants are small and reservations are needed, particularly in high season. There is now a smooth Anguillian Rum, a blend from other islands matured in oak barrels designed to be drunk on the rocks rather than in a punch. Visit the rum tasting room at PYRAT Rums' factory on Sandy Ground road, open Mon-Fri 0800-1700, T4975003.

Ship's Galley, Sandy Ground, T4972040. Breakfast, lunch and dinner, West Indian cooking, closed Wed. *Barrel Stay*, Sandy Ground, T4972831. Overpriced because of all the charter boat tourists, French/Creole, fish soup, lobster, steak, open for lunch and dinner. *Arlo's Place*, South Hill, T4976810. Italian American, homemade pasta, open 1900-2200, closed Sun. *KoalKeel*, The Valley, T4972930, F4975379. Also expensive, in a restored 18th-century home of the island's administrator, known as Warden's Place, with 100-year-old rock oven, Euro-Caribbean style, chef Leonard 'Smoke' Sharplis prepares 5 or 7 course menus, open Tue-Sat dinner only, pastry shop open daily. *Old House*, George Hill, T4972228. Overlooking airport, watch flights from an old concrete home, happy hour 1700-1900, hot appetizers, open daily for breakfast, lunch and dinner, local food, seafood and grills. *The Ferry Boat Inn*, Blowing Point, on beach near ferry terminal, T6613, www.ai/ferryboatinn View of St Maarten, European and West Indian food, lunch and dinner except Sun, also rental apartments, well-equipped, airy, maid service. *Le Saint Clair*, T4972833, F4973663, VHF 16. French/Caribbean restaurant on beach front in Sandy Ground, some Japanese dishes, open lunch and dinner, Sun brunch with live music 1000-1600, US$15, live jazz Mon, Thu, Sat, closed Sun night. *Ripples*, Sandy Ground, T4973380. Award-winning chef, try his lobster fritters, varied menu including vegetarian, open daily 1830-2300. *Leduc's*, Barne's Bay, near *Coccoloba*, T4976393. In an old Anguillian house, French cuisine, lunch and dinner, 3-course prix-fixe 1830-1930. *Blanchard's*, Meads Bay, run by Bob and Melinda Blanchard, elegant wine list and fine dining with Oriental influences. Two doors west, on the beach, is *Cocoplums*, T4976072. Good fish and seafood with local dishes such as plantains, rice & peas, vegetarian options, main dishes US$14-30. *Roy's Place*, Crocus Bay, beach front, T4972470. Draught beer, fresh seafood, happy hour 1700-1900, Sun brunch of roast beef and Yorkshire pudding, open 1200-1400, 1800-2100, closed Mon. For Chinese breakfast, lunch and dinner, *The Landing Strip*, T4972268. View of airport, eat in or takeaway, Clarita Mason Mall on George Hill Road, open daily. *Flight Deck*, on hill next to airport, T4972835. Bar and restaurant, local cuisine, breakfast, lunch and dinner, live music Fri, Sat nights. *Zara's Seafood Restaurant*, Shoal Bay, in gardens of *Alamanda Beach Club*, T4973229. Local chef, Rotary Club meets here Thu 1800 for dinner. *Le Beach Bar & Restaurant*, oldest restaurant on Shoal Bay East, T4975598. Steakhouse, surf'n'turf, salad bar, pizza, open daily for breakfast, lunch and dinner, happy hour 1700-1830, near *Shoal Bay Villas*. *Trattoria Tramonto & Oasis Beach Bar*, Shoal Bay West, next to *Blue Waters*, T4978819, northern Italian chef, serious Italian cuisine, lunch casual 1200-1500, sunset champagne cocktails 1700-1800, dinner 1900-2130, only 10 tables so reservations essential, closed Mon. *Madeiriman Reef*, Shoal Bay, T4973833, breakfast, lunch and dinner, barefoot or elegant. *Hibernia*, Island Harbour, T4974290. Run by

French and Irish couple, international menu with influences from their travelling experiences, closed low season. *Pepperpot*, The Valley, opposite high school, T4972328. Open 0700-2200, local food, local customers, especially after work, rotis, salt fish, curried goat, patties, takeaway available.

For those who are self-catering, *Fat Cat*, Main Road, George Hill, T4972307. Meals to go from the freezer, picnic meals, pies and cakes, open 1000-1800, closed Sun. *Gee Wee's Bakery & Catering*, on West End main road, between Shell station and *La Sirena* hotel, T4976462. Breads, cakes, pastries, sandwiches, Jamaican jerk chicken and pork, parties catered for, eat in, takeaway or delivery service. *Shalack's Café*, opposite *Albert's Supermarket*, T4973272. Cafeteria-style restaurant has variety of ready prepared meals, come in or order. *Vista Food Market*, South Hill Roundabout, T4972804. Good selection, cheeses, meats, pâtés, wines, beer, Cuban cigars etc, open Mon-Sat 0800-1800. *Ashleys Supermarket*, South Valley. Open Mon-Fri 0700-2030, Sat 0700-2200, has a good range including produce from other islands.

Nightlife

Out of season there is not much to do during the week. On Fri the whole island changes, several bars have live music, check the local papers

On Fri go to *Johnno's Place*, Sandy Ground; on Sun to brunch at *Roy's Place*, Crocus Bay, draught beer, then around 1500 at *Johnno's Place* for a beach party. When the music dies people go to the neighbouring bar, *Ship's Galley*, for the night shift. *Uncle Ernie beach bar* on Shoal Bay has a live band playing all day on Sun. *Madeariman Reef Restaurant*, Shoal Bay, soca, calypso, reggae on Fri, Sat, Caribbean night with Spraka Wed. *Gorgeous Scilly Cay* has live daytime music on Wed, Fri and Sun, T4975123. At the weekend the *Dragon Disco* opens around midnight. *Mirrors Night Club and Bar*, at Swing High, above Vista Food Market, juke box with music from 1960s to now, happy hour nightly at 1900-2000, live entertainment at weekends. *The Dunes*, reggae and folk music from the Caribbean during March at the full moon at Rendezvous Bay. *The Pumphouse*, in the historic Anguilla road Salt Co Factory, Mon-Sat 1900-0200, eat, drink, dance or relax, T4975154.

In high season the resort hotels have live music, steel bands etc, check in the tourist *What We Do in Anguilla* monthly magazine. Look for shows with North Sound, Missington Brothers the most popular bands. Dumpa and the Anvibes is led by Pan Man Michael (Dumpa) Martin, who has recorded a CD/cassette with a blend of local music. There is no theatre but plays are sometimes put on at the Ruthwill Auditorium. The Anguilla National Creative Arts Association (ANCAA) has a performing arts section, the National Theatre Group, which has training workshops and performs at hotels during high season. Visitors with theatre expertise are welcome to participate. Contact the theatre co-ordinator, Ray Tabor, T6685, rbtabor@anguillanet.com. The Mayoumba Folkloric Theatre puts on a song, dance and drama show at *La Sirena*, Meads Bay, on Thu nights, T4976827.

Festivals

Carnival is at the beginning of **Aug** (the Fri before the first Mon), when the island comes to life with street dancing, Calypso competitions, the *Carnival Queen Coronation*, the *Prince and Princess Show*, nightly entertainment in The Valley and beach barbecues. The annual *Moonsplash Music Festival* is a 3-day event held in March at *Dune Preserve* on Rendezvous Bay, organized principally by Bankie Banx. There are international and local artists, including *Bankie Banx and the Dune People*, www.dunepreserve.com The *Anguilla International Arts Festival* is held every other year (next in 2003, dates to be announced) and includes workshops and an arts contest. For details T4972949, F4972735, www.artfestival.ai

Shopping

General *Ellie's Record Shop* sells Caribbean and international music, T4975073, F4975317 .Open 1000-1800 at Fairplay Commercial Complex. There are lots of places selling T-shirts, beachwear and gifts. *Caribbean Fancy* boutique and gift shop is at George Hill at the traffic light, T4973133, F4973513.

Art galleries *Devonish Art Gallery*, George Hill Landing, T4972949, F4972735, http://devonish.ai, with works by Courtney Devonish and other local and international sculptors, painters, potters etc. *Loblolly Gallery*, South Hill Plaza, West End, T4972263. Open Tue-Sat 0900-1700, features 4 local artists working in oil and acrylic. *L'Atelier* , Michèle Lavalette, a French artist and photographer who specializes in flowers, in oil, acrylic and

Leeward Islands

pastels, has her studio in North Hill, T4975668. Open daily 1000-1730, she has designed post-age stamps. Mother Weme (Weme Caster) sells originals and limited edition prints of her paintings of local scenes from her home on the Sea Rocks, near Island Harbour, T4974504 for an appointment, prices for prints start from US$75 and for her acrylic and oil paintings from US$300. *Savannah Gallery*, on the road to Crocus Bay, The Valley, T4972263, F4974017. Paintings, prints and crafts from all over the Caribbean, a lot of Haitian art, several local artists too. *The Arts and Craft Centre*, next to the Public Library, T4972949. Pottery, lace, locally made dolls, shell art, paintings and prints. *Cheddie's Carving Studio*, on the main road west, T4976027. Cheddie Richardson is a wood sculptor who uses the rose berry roots found among the rocks on the shore, some of his pieces have been cast in bronze. Jo-Anne Mason has produced a map of all the art galleries with a brief description of each, available in hotels and galleries, www.anguillaart.com

Bookshop *National Bookstore*, in the Social Security Complex next to Cable and Wireless, The Valley. Open Mon-Sat 0800-1700, wide selection of novels, magazines, non-fiction, children's books, tourist guides, Caribbean history and literature, managed by Mrs Kelly. A *Dictionary of Anguillian Language* has been published in a 34 page booklet, edited by Ijahnia Christian of the Adult and Continuing Education Unit following the Cultural Educational Fest.

Tour operators *Malliouhana Travel and Tours*, The Quarter, T4972431/4972348, F4973166, mtt@anguillanet.com *Bennie's Travel and Tours*, Caribbean Commercial Centre, transfers, car rental, island tours, day trips, T4972788/4972360, F4975052, bennies@anguillanet.com *J N Gumbs' Travel Agency* is the local LIAT and Winair agent, T4972238/9, F4973351.

Transport **Air** **Wallblake airport** is just outside The Valley, T2514. *LIAT* has daily flights from Antigua; (T268-4620700), or *Caribaviation* (T268-4623147) charter flights will meet any incoming flight and fly you to Anguilla without you having to clear customs in Antigua. *LIAT* also connects Anguilla with St Thomas (the LIAT office is at Gumbs Travel Agency, T4972238 and also at T4972748). *American Eagle* (T4973131/4973500) has a daily air link with Puerto Rico which connects with their other US flights and they also fly daily from St Croix. *Winair* (T4972238/4972748, F4973351) provides several daily flights from St Maarten (10 mins). *Coastal Air Transport* (T4972431) flies from St Croix, USVI. *Tyden Air* (T4972719, F4973079, The Valley) operate charters and air taxi services to the British and US Virgin Islands, St Maarten and St Kitts. In St Maarten, you can get bookings for Anguilla on the spot. *Transanguilla*, another air taxi service, offers the 5 min flight for US$35 each way.

Boat The principal port is **Sandy Ground**, T4976403. The service for the 20-min ferry between Blowing Point and Marigot starts at about 0730 and continues every 30-40 mins until 1900, US$10 daytime, US$12 night-time, one way (pay on board). You pay the US$2 departure tax after putting your name and passport number on the manifest (at booth at head of pier in Marigot or find the ferry clerk in the waiting area near Immigration Office) and before boarding at Marigot but you pay the fare on the boat. The same applies when leaving from Anguilla. *Link Ferries* run a high speed catamaran service from Blowing Point to Marigot, 0840, 1240, 1730, return 1120, 1430, 1800 and from Blowing Point to Juliana airport 1210, return 1400, complimentary drinks on board, help with luggage at airport, also private charters anytime, T4972231/4973290, F4973290, www.ai/link/ On Tue, the *MV Deluxe* does a day trip to St Barths, T4976289, F4976322, leaves 0915, returns 1700, US$65 return.

Car hire A local driving permit is issued on presentation of a valid driver's licence from your home country and can be bought at car rental offices; US$10 for three months. There are several car hire companies, including *Apex (Avis)*, The Quarter, T4972642, F4975032; *H and R*, The Valley, T4972656/4972606; *Island Car Rentals*, T4972723, F4973723, islandcar@anguillanet.com *Summer Set Car Rental*, T4975278/4975778, F4975444, summerset@anguillanet.com *Highway Rent-a-Car*, George Hill, by the traffic lights, T4972183, F4972306, www.rental cars.ai, *Rodco*, www.mrat.com/rodco. Rates are from US$25 per day off season, US$40 per day high season, plus insurance, jeeps from US$45. You can normally bargain for a good rate if you rent for more than 3 days, seventh day is usually free, some offer discounts on internet bookings. Fuel costs US$1.84 per gallon for regular, US$1.86 unleaded. **Bicycle hire** Rented from *Happy Trails Mountain Bike Rentals*, PO Box 354, George Hill Rd, T4975810, F4975811.

Taxi Expensive and the driver usually quotes in US dollars, not EC dollars; rates are set by the government: from Wallblake airport to The Valley costs about US$6; from The Valley to Blowing Point (ferry) US$12. To hire a taxi for a tour of the island works out at about US$40 for two people, US$5 for additional passengers. Dispatchers are at the airport (T4975054) and ferry (T4976089), there is no central office.

Banks In The Valley, *Barclays Bank International*, T4972301/4972304, F4972980, Box 140. **Directory**
National Bank of Anguilla, T4972101, F4973310, www.nba.ai *Scotiabank*, Fairplay Commercial Centre, The Valley, T4973333, F4973344, ATM linked to Plus, Visa and Mastercard accepted, maximum withdrawal US$600. **Communications Post:** The main post office is in The Valley, T4972528, F4975455. Open Mon-Fri 0800-1530. Commemorative stamps and other collections sold. **Telephone:** *Cable and Wireless*, T4973100. Operates internal and external telephone links (IDD available), cellular, internet and fax services, open Mon-Fri 0800-1700, Sat, Sun, holidays 0900-1300. Caribbean phone cards are available throughout the islands. There are 2 AT&T USA direct telephones by Cable and Wireless office in The Valley and by the airport. For credit card calls overseas T1800-8778000. *Bits & Bites*, Sandy Ground, next to *Johnno's*, is a breakfast and internet café, also rooms to rent. **Medical facilities** The *Princess Alexandra Hospital*, T4972551/2. **Emergency:** T911/999. **Pharmacy:** T4972366/4972738. **Optometrist:** T4973700. Most people drink bottled water but there is also rainwater or desalinated water for household use. **Tourist offices** *Anguilla Department of Tourism*, PO Box 1388, Old Factory Plaza, The Valley, T4972759, F4972710, www.anguilla-vacation.com,net.ai atbtour@anguillanet.com Open weekdays 0800-1700. The office at the airport is closed at lunchtime, but the customs officers will often phone for a hotel reservation for you. TV Cable Channel 32 shows a 30-min programme called Touring Anguilla, which goes out continuously, giving information on the island. The Hotel Association can be contacted at ahta@anguillanet.com The *Anguilla National Trust* welcomes members, office in the Museum Building, The Valley, T4975297, F5571, axanat@anguillanet.com

Background

The earliest known Amerindian site on Anguilla is at the northeast tip of the island, **History** where tools and artefacts made from conch shells have been recovered and dated at around 1300 BC. Saladoid Amerindians settled on the island in the fourth century AD and brought their knowledge of agriculture, ceramics and their religious culture based on the god of cassava. By the sixth century large villages had been built at Rendezvous Bay and Sandy Ground, with smaller ones at Shoal Bay and Island Harbour. Post Saladoid Amerindians from the Greater Antilles arrived in the tenth century, building villages and setting up a chiefdom with a religious hierarchy. Several ceremonial items have been found and debris related to the manufacture of the three-pointed zemis, or spirit stones, associated with fertility rites. By the 17th century, Amerindians had disappeared from Anguilla: wiped out by enslavement and European diseases.

Anguilla was first mentioned in 1564 when a French expedition passed en route from Dominica to Florida, but it was not until 1650 that it was first colonized by the British. Despite several attempted invasions, by Caribs in 1656 and by the French in 1745 and 1796, it remained a British colony. From 1825 it became more closely associated with St Kitts for administrative purposes and ultimately incorporated in the colony. In 1967 St Kitts-Nevis-Anguilla became a State in Association with the UK and gained internal independence. However, Anguilla opposed this development and almost immediately repudiated government from St Kitts. A breakaway movement was led by Ronald Webster of the People's Progressive Party (PPP). In 1969 British forces invaded the island to install a British Commissioner after negotiations had broken down. The episode is remembered locally for the unusual presence of

Leeward Islands

the London Metropolitan Police, who remained on the island until 1972 when the Anguilla Police Force was established.

The post of Chief Minister alternated for two decades between the rival politicians, Ronald Webster and Emile Gumbs, leader of the Anguilla National Alliance (ANA), the latter holding office in 1977-80 and 1984-94. Mr Gumbs (now Sir Emile) retired from politics at the general elections held in March 1994. These elections proved inconclusive, with the ANA, the Anguilla United Party (AUP) and the Anguilla Democratic Party (ADP) each winning two seats and an Independent, Osbourne Fleming (who was Finance Minister in the ANA government) winning the seventh. A coalition was formed by Hubert Hughes, leader of the AUP, and Victor Banks, ADP, and the former was sworn in as Chief Minister. Mr Hughes had been a Minister in the 1984 ANA government, but had been dismissed in 1985, subsequently joining the opposition AUP, then led by Ronald Webster.

The March 1999 general elections were won by the governing coalition: the AUP and the ADP won two seats each while the ANA won three. Hubert Hughes (AUM) was sworn in as Chief Minister. His period of office was short-lived, however. The House of Assembly was paralysed after Mr Hughes lost a legal case against the Speaker and the ruling coalition fell apart when the ADP leader, Victor Banks, resigned from the administration and allied his party with the ANA. New elections were held in March 2000. The ANA again won three seats, the AUP two, ADP one and an independent one. Osbourne Fleming, leader of the ANA, became Chief Minister on 6 March, in coalition with the ADP.

Anguilla was another island to be badly hit by Hurricane Lenny in November 1999. Flooding reached depths of 14 ft and livestock perished. Most hotels managed to clean up for the winter season, only one remaining closed until well into 2000.

Government

In 1980, Anguilla became a British Dependent Territory with a Governor to represent the Crown. A new constitution was introduced in 1982, providing for a Governor, an Executive Council comprising four elected Ministers and two ex-officio members, and an 11-member legislative House of Assembly presided over by a Speaker. In 1990 the constitution was amended to give the Governor responsibility for international financial affairs. A new post of Deputy Governor was created, to replace the Permanent Secretary for Finance as a member of the Executive Council and House of Assembly.

Economy

The main economic activities used to be livestock raising, lobster fishing, salt production and boat building, but tourism is now the major generator of foreign exchange and employment. There are some 800 rooms available in guest houses, villas and apartments and hotels, although the number is steadily rising. Growth has been led by tourism, construction, communications and financial services.

There is some offshore banking and the Government aims to establish a reputable offshore financial services industry. Thirty out of the 43 offshore banks, who pay an annual licence fee to the Government, had their licences cancelled in 1990 following a review of the sector. At end-1991 the House of Assembly approved legislation to tighten control of offshore finance, giving the Governor complete and final authority over the granting of licences. New financial services legislation enacted in late 1994 led to an increase in the number of registered offshore financial companies.

Previously, high levels of unemployment led to migration to other Caribbean islands and further afield, but the unemployment rate has fallen from 26% in 1985 to almost nil and shortages of labour have delayed expansion programmes, as well as putting pressure on prices and wages. Work permits have been granted to more than 1,000 non-Anguillans, but many people have two jobs. Workers' remittances are crucial, particularly since the 1984 suspension of budgetary support in the form of UK grants-in-aid, although the British Government does still provide aid for the development programme, along with other donors such as the EU and the

Caribbean Development Bank. There is no income tax and the Government gets its revenues from customs duties, bank licences, property and stamps.

Montserrat

The 'Emerald Isle', with its Irish influences, is currently developing tourist activities in the north of the island as the southern part of the island has been evacuated. The capital, Plymouth and several villages have been destroyed by volcanic action but new communities, mountain walks, beaches and historical sites in the safe north are being discovered by tourists, who numbered over 15,000 in 2000. As an illustration of the volatility of the region's geology, Montserrat is incomparable, but evacuees have returned from abroad, while the still-active volcano is now attracting tourists.

Colour map 4, grid C2

Ins and outs

William H Bramble Airport, on the east coast is closed because of falling ash or other volcanic activity. Air service is now provided by helicopter to **Gerald's Heliport** from Antigua. You get a good view of the island and the volcano on the 20-min flight from Antigua. Alternatively there is a **ferry** from Antigua which takes an hour.

Getting there
See transport, page 652, for further details

Roads are paved and fairly good, but narrow and twisty. There are many pebbles on the roads and you must be careful, especially when walking on inclines. Drivers travel fast, passing on blind corners with much use of their horns. There are several **car hire** companies (the cars are mostly Japanese). **Hitching** is safe and easy because people are so friendly. Similarly, don't be afraid to pick them up when you are driving. The standard fare in mini-buses is EC$2. Outside the fixed times and routes they operate as taxis and journeys can be arranged with drivers for an extra fee. **Taxis** are usually small buses, which can be shared. Fares are set and listed by the Tourist Board.

Getting around
Driving is on the left

Although tropical, the humidity in Montserrat is low and there is often rain overnight which clears the atmosphere. The average temperature is 26-27°C with little variation from one season to another. The wettest months are November, December and January.

Climate

Flora and fauna

Studies of the effect of the volcanic eruptions on flora and fauna have not yet, to our knowledge, been undertaken. Natural vegetation is confined mostly to the summits of hills, where elfin woodlands occur. At lower levels, fern groves are plentiful and lower still, cacti, sage bush and acacias. Flowers and fruit are typical of the Caribbean with many bay trees, from which bay oil (or rum) is distilled, the national tree, the mango and the national flower, *Heliconia caribaea* (a wild banana known locally as 'lobster claw'). There are 34 species of birds resident on the island and many more migrants. Unique to Montserrat is the Montserrat oriole, *Icterus oberi*, a black and gold oriole named the national bird. There are also the rare forest thrush, the bridled quail dove, mangrove cuckoo, trembler and purple throated carib. Many of these can be seen along the Centre Hills trail in the middle of the island between the ash-covered Soufriere Hills and the Silver Hills. The vegetation here is biologically diverse and supports a variety of wildlife. Montserrat cannot boast many wild animals, although it shares the terrestrial frog, known as the mountain chicken, only with Dominica. Agoutis, bats and lizards, including iguanas which can grow to over 4 ft in length (they used to take the balls on the golf course, mistaking them for eggs), can all be found and tree frogs contribute to the island's 'night-music'. A walk around the Silver Hills in the extreme north reveals a dramatic coastline where you can find lots of seabirds.

Leeward Islands

A Foot in the door

- Visit the **Volcano Visitor's Centre** for all you ever wanted to know or see about the volcanic eruptions.
- Go beachcombing on **Old Road Bay** for pumice and other debris deposited by the volcano.
- Celebrate **St Patrick's Day** in the sun with Irish Montserratians. Go dancing in **Little Bay** where nightlife is on the beach.

The Montserrat National Trust has been relocated to Olveston, on the North Main Road, T4913086, F4913046. A new Natural History Centre and a Botanical Garden are now open. There will be a volcanic interpretative centre created with the help of the Montserrat Volcanic Observatory and the reference library on the island's fauna and flora will be accessible for visitors.

Beaches and watersports

Montserrat's beaches are volcanic 'black' sand, which in reality means the sand may be a silvery grey or dark golden brown colour. The single white coral beach is at Rendezvous Bay in the north of the island. It is a stiff hike from Little Bay along a very steep mountainous trail (not suitable for small children). Take food and water, it is a long hot walk until you reach your refreshing swim. There is no shade on the beach, avoid the poisonous manchineel trees and the spiney sea urchins among the rocks at the north end. You can also take a boat and it is quite a good idea to walk there and arrange for a boat to come and pick you up at an agreed time. The best of the rest of the beaches, all on the west of the island and black sand, are Woodlands (National Trust, beach house, washrooms), where you can safely swim through caves, Lime Kiln Bay, tiny Bunkum Bay, Carr's Bay and Little Bay in the north. Iles Bay and Old Road Bay (by the *Vue Pointe Hotel*) are subject to volcanic mud flows and are not recommended. However, Old Road can be interesting for picking up pieces of pumice and wood swept down from the volcano. Sports fishing can be arranged with Danny Sweeney, Olveston, T4915645, mwilson@candw.ag

Diving and marine life

Before the volcano disrupted normal life, Montserrat was gaining a modest reputation as an undiscovered destination with much virgin diving. The National Trust is planning to set up a National Marine Park which will include a reef building project. The best sites are along the northwest coast and have not been harmed at all by the volcano. Shore diving is good from Lime Kiln Bay, where there are ledges with coral, sponges and lots of fish; Woodlands Bay, where there is a shallow reef at 25 to 30 ft; and at Little Bay. There are some shallow dives from boats, suitable for novices or a second dive, but also deep dives for experienced divers. Pinnacle is a deep dive, dropping from 65 to 300 ft, where you can see brain coral, sponges and lots of fish. Diving and kayaking are offered by *Sea Wolf Diving School*, Woodlands, T4917807, F4913599, krebs@candw.ag A shore dive costs US$40, a single tank boat dive US$50, two tanks US$70, scuba equipment hire US$30, snorkel gear rental US$10, PADI Open Water certification course US$375. Wolf and Inge Krebs started the dive operation in the early 1990s and there is little they don't know about Montserrat underwater, www.swiftsite.com/seawolfdivingschool

Around the island

The **volcano** is now a tourist attraction spectacular views of the volcano and its damage can be viewed in safety from the top of Garibaldi Hill in the west and Jack Boy Hill in the east. Both these vantage spots are in the safe northern zone. From here you can see the grey, ash-covered flanks of what was Chances Peak, in stark contrast with the Centre Hills, which are still green, forested and fertile. Plymouth, the former capital, was flooded with ash up to the first floor of the colonial buildings and completely destroyed. Even if you don't see the volcano in action, you can watch videos at the *Montserrat Volcano Visitor's Centre* and the *Montserrat Volcano Observatory (MVO)*, Mongo Hill, T4915647, F4912423, www.mvomrat.com The scientists at the Observatory monitor eruptions and issue warnings when necessary. An expert guide will give you a tour of the Observatory and explain the work of the scientists, showing the seismographs and explaining the chronology of events. Visiting time for the public to the MVO is 1530-1600 Mon-Fri. If the volcano is dangerously active visitors are excluded, of course. Staff at the Observatory are to move in mid-2001 from the existing premises, five miles north of the volcano, to a new building three miles northwest of the volcano.

Montserrat

Essentials

Documents A valid **passport** is required except for US, Canadian and British visitors, who must only show proof of citizenship for stays of up to six months. Citizens of Caricom countries may travel with their official ID card. **Visas** may be required for visitors from Haiti, Cuba and Eastern bloc countries, which can be obtained from British consulate offices. An onward or return ticket is required.

Currency The currency is the East Caribbean dollar (EC$). The exchange rate is fixed at EC$2.67 = US$1, but there are variations depending on where you change your money. US and Canadian dollars are widely accepted. All major credit cards are accepted, as are traveller's cheques.

Customs 200 cigarettes, 50 cigars, 40 ozs of alcoholic beverages, six ozs perfume. Little Bay (Main Office, Bredes), open 0800-1600 Monday-Friday, for yachts and small craft, T4913816, 4912456, F4916909, customms@candw.ag

Departure tax US$8 for Caricom residents and US$13 for visitors.

Hours of business Government offices: 0800-1600, Monday-Friday. Shops: the same as government but early closing Wednesday and Saturday afternoons.

Communications The international code for Montserrat is 664, followed by a seven-digit number. See page 653 for further details.

Official time Atlantic Standard Time, four hours behind GMT, one ahead of EST.

Essentials

Sleeping

With the re-occupation of the area on the west coast, south to the Belham River Valley, hotels are now reopening. There are a few guest houses open in the north. Hotel tax is 10%

Hotels **L-A** *Tropical Mansions*, Sweeneys, T4918273, F4918275, hotel@candw.ag. New in 1999, 18 rooms, some with kitchenette, honeymoon suite, pool, restaurant. **L-AL** *Vue Pointe*, Old Road Bay, PO Box 65, T4915210, F4914813, vuepointe@candw.ag Reopened in 2000 after extensive renovations, family-run, traditionally the premier hotel on the island. Lunch sandwich menu daily at bar, lunch and evening meal from *Jumping Jack's* beach bar, *Etcetera* dress shop serves coffee and pastries/sandwich lunch, can all be signed for.

Guest houses (offering B&B) **B** *Grand View*, Baker Hill, T4912284, F4916876, grand@candw.ag Twin beds, private or shared bathroom, or double bed, kitchenette and private bathroom, TV, parking, dinner by reservation only, transfers on request. **B** *Rita's*, Mahogany Drive, Woodlands, T4914006. Two double rooms with bathroom, 1 downstairs large and comfortable with own kitchen, 1 upstairs with use of kitchen, TV, fan, local phone calls. **C** *Erindell*, Woodlands, T4913655, erindell@candw.ag Run by Shirley and Lou Spycalla, private entrance, twin beds, private bathroom, TV, phone, fans, cooking facilities, pool, free laundry, discounts for Caricom residents. **B** *Montserrat Moments Inn*, PO Box 196, Manjack Heights, T4917707, flogriff@candw.ag Four rooms with fridge, a/c or fan, continental breakfast included, other meals by reservation, shared kitchenette, email, laundry facilities.

Rooms and apartments **C** *Egret House*, Woodlands, T/F4915316. Apartment overlooks Woodlands Beach, sleeps 2, no children, bedroom with large bed, sitting room, kitchen, bathroom, shower, stairs to sundeck and pool, TV, phones, fans. **A** *David and Maureen Hodd*, Olveston, T4915248, F4915016. Weekly and monthly rates, discounts for Caricom residents, apartment sleeps 2, views of sea and mountains, quiet, TV, phone, washing machine, kitchen, meals can be arranged. **C** *David and Clover Lea*, St Peter's, T4915812, lead@candw.ag 2-bedroom guest house with 2 bathrooms, veranda, or 1 bedroom with bath and veranda, or room adjoining main house with 2 beds which can be pushed together or bunked, bathroom, deck, fridge, TV, phone, email, tent and camping equipment available, family atmosphere, the Leas have 3 sons to enliven your stay. **C** *Richard Aspin*, Olveston, T4916346, F4918867, monmedia@candw.ag. In residential area, 2-bedroom, 1 bathroom apartment, large kitchen, sitting room with veranda, bedroom patio opens onto gardens. **C** *Levons and Camilla Watts*, Olveston, T4913179, amswt@email.com Self-contained 1-bedroom apartment, phone, TV, kitchenette, laundry facilities.

Port of entry *Little Bay, 55m jetty with a depth of 1.7m-4.6m. Contact the Montserrat Port Authority, channel 16, for mooring details.*
Voltage *Electric current is 220/110 volts, 60 cycles.*
Media **Newspapers** *There are two weekly newspapers, the Montserrat News and the Montserrat Reporter.* **Radio** *Radio Montserrat ZJB relays the BBC World Service news at 0700 daily and the Voice of America news at 0800. Gem Radio is an exclusive outlet for the Associated Press.*
Television *Satellite TV Cable is operational in most areas, and stations broadcasting from nearby islands can be received.*
Diplomatic representation *All embassies and consulates are based in Antigua.*

Tourist offices overseas *Germany, Montserrat Tourist Board/West India Committee, Lomer Strasse 28, D-22047 Hamburg 70, T4940-6958846, F4940-3800051.* **UK**, *c/o CTO, 42 Westminster Palace Gardens, Artillery Row, London SW1P 1RR, T020-72224325, F020-72224325, cto@carib-tourism.com* **USA**, *c/o CTO, 80 Broad St, 32nd floor, New York, NY 10004, T212-6359530, F212-6359511, get2cto@dorsai.org*
Public holidays *New Year's Day, St Patrick's Day (17 March), Good Friday, Easter Monday, Labour Day (first Monday in May), Whit Monday (7th Monday after Easter), first Monday in August, Christmas Day, Boxing Day (26 December) and Festival Day (31 December).*

Villa rental Montserrat has a large number of comfortable villas built by ex-pats, many of them Canadians, as holiday or retirement homes. Although a lot of them were built close to Plymouth and are now in the exclusion zone, many were around Old Towne, Olveston and Woodlands, and apart from a coating of ash from time to time, escaped any damage. Most have their own pools, terraces with lovely views, gardens and maid service. Rental agencies include: *Kirwan's Secluded Hideaway*, Olveston, T4913405, F4912546; *Montserrat Enterprises Ltd*, Old Towne, T4912431, F4914660; *Neville Bradshaw Agencies*, Old Towne, T4915270, F4915069; *Jacquie Ryan Enterprises Ltd*, Olveston, T4912055, F4913257; *Tradewinds Real Estate*, Old Towne, T4912004, F4916229, www.tradewindsmontserrat. com; *West Indies Real Estate*, Olveston, T4918666, F4918668, www.wirealest.com

A large frog called mountain chicken, indigenous here and in Dominica, is the local delicacy. Goat water stew is another local dish commonly found on the menu. Most other foods, like steak and fish, are imported.

Eating
Several places do takeaway meals. A lot of the eating places are not open all the time, others only open if you make a reservation in advance, so it is best to check

Working in a roughly south-north direction, **Old Road** *Jumping Jack's Beach Bar*, next to the tennis courts, run by Danny and Margaret, T4915645. As well as sport fishing and boat rental, Danny offers great lunches, snacks and evening dinners, a beach barbecue on Sun and Thu, fish, chicken and side dishes. **Salem** *Monica's Bar*, T4914182, Takeaway lunches. *Village Place*, for Jamaican jerk pork and chicken. *Wilson's Place*, T4913048. Open Mon-Sat, the place for jerk. **Runaway Point** *Etcetera Shoppe*, 540 Runaway Point Circle, T4915146. Call for reservations, only open for Wed lunch, Fri night dinner and Sun brunch. **Olveston** *The Attic*, T4912008. Open for breakfast and lunch. **Woodlands** *Ziggy's Restaurant*, T4918282, Mahogany Loop, second turning on the right from the main road. Dinner by reservation only, the island's leading restaurant, international cuisine, Ziggy has been serving great food since the early 1990s, lobster quadrille, jerk pork, chocolate sludge. **Fogarty Hill** *The People's Place*, T4917528. Lunches and takeaway meals, local food, great roti. **Cudjoe Head** *Fins & Wings*, T4918219. Lunch or takeaway, fish, chicken, local drinks. **Baker Hill** *Grand View*, a guest house with restaurant and bar open to non residents for breakfast, lunch and dinner (by appointment). **Brades Main Road** *Tina's Restaurant*, T4913538. Local food, chicken and fish and local vegetables, prices from US$16.50-24 for a meal. *Tuitt's Pizzeria*, T4914606. Open Mon-Sat for pizza. *Economy Bakery*, T4916678. Fresh bread, sandwiches and snacks. **Carrs Bay** *Root's Man Beach Bar*, T4915957. Vegetarian meal in rustic setting, orders only. **Little Bay** *Good Life Night Club & Restaurant*, T4914576. Newly built on a hillside overlooking the beach, great disco for weekend dancing, check for meal hours,

Leeward Islands

prices from about US$16.50. *Bitter End Beach Bar*, T4913146. Seafood and snacks on the beach, lunch from US$5.50-9.50, dinner from US$7.50. **Davy Hill Main Road** *Di's Snackette*, T4915450. Lunches and snacks. *Annie's Snackette*, T4915380. Snacks and takeaway. **Sweeney's** *Richard Samuel's*, T4912475. Fresh bread and snacks. *La Colage Bar & Restaurant*, T4914136. Creole cuisine, lunch from US$5.50, dinner from US$7.50, boutique for clothes and accessories attached. *Morgan's Spotlight Bar & Restaurant*, T4915419. Local food, large portions, goat water. *Peter's Bakery*, a whole range of tasty, freshly baked snacks. **Gerald's** *Cockpit Bar & Restaurant*, at Gerald's Heliport, T4914478. Montserrat version of the airport café, serves breakfast and lunch, popular for 'liming'. **St John's** *JJ's Cuisine*, Main Road, T4919024. Breakfast, lunch and dinner, international cuisine, call ahead. *Howe's Flamboyant Bar*, T4913008. Pool table for entertainment after a meal. *Tropical Mansions*, hotel restaurant is open to non-residents, international food.

Entertainment Regular entertainment and nightlife is not a feature of Montserrat. Most things happen at the restaurants, such as the *Good Life Night Club & Restaurant* and *Bitter End Beach Bar*, see above. Bands come over from Antigua from time to time and perform calypso and other shows which are very popular, see Culture, below.

Festivals Not surprisingly in the 'Emerald Isle', **St Patrick's Day** (a national holiday) is celebrated on *17 March* with concerts, masquerades and other festivities. The **Queen's Birthday** is celebrated on the 2nd Sat in *June* with parades, salutes and the raising of flags. Another national knees-up is **August Monday Weekend**, connected to **Emancipation Day** on *1 August*, commemorating the abolition of slavery in 1834. There are beach barbecues and picnics all weekend. Cudjoe Head Day on the Sat starts with a big breakfast and carries on late into the night, while St Peter's Anglican Fete is held in the village rectory grounds on the Mon. The island's main festival is the **Christmas** season, which starts around *12 December* and continues through New Year's Day. There are shows, concerts, calypso competitions, jump ups and masquerades and of course lots of festivities and parties on **New Year's Eve**, helped down with lots of goat water.

Shopping Montserrat is not the place to come for shopping, but there are places where you can find locally printed T-shirts, local Sea Island goods, crafts, jams, jellies and tropical drinks. For music, T-shirts and other clothing go to *Arrow Manshop*, Salem, T4913852, or *Sweeneys*, T4916355. Photos of Montserrat and the volcano are sold at *Kevin's Photo Shop*, Cudjoe Head, T4916177, and at *Woolcock's Craft & Photo Gallery*, Davy Hill, T4912025, while *Sea Wolf*, Woodlands, T4917807, have postcards of underwater Montserrat and other crafts and gifts. Art and crafts and other souvenirs at *Oriole Gift Shop*, Salem, T4913086, next to the National Trust. *Kiernon's Products*, Cudjoe Head, T4916385, sells local pepper sauce, guava cheese, jellies, liqueurs and other local goodies. Leslie and Cynthia Williams sell honey in Brades, T4914014. *Howe's Enterprises*, in St John's makes a wide range of rums, jellies, jams, sauces and seasonings, all in attractive packaging, good gifts.

Tour operators Sightseeing tours can be arranged with *Carib World Travel*, Sweeneys, T4912714, F4912713; *Double X Tours*, Olveston, T4915470, meader@candw.ag; *Grant Enterprises & Trading*, Olveston, T4919654, casselj@candw.ag; *Jenny's Tours*, St John's, Antigua, T268-4619361, burkeb@candw.ag; *Runaway Travel*, Sweeneys, T4912776, runaway@candw.ag

Transport **Air** Helicopter seats available, several daily except Wed from Antigua, US$66 return. Check
You can take only with agent for times, which are always changing and make sure you book well in advance
one piece of luggage otherwise it can be hard to get on. Agents in Antigua are *Carib Aviation*, VC Bird Interna-
on the helicopter, tional Airport, T268-4623147, F268-4623125, caribav@candw.ag Agents in Montserrat are
but unlimited **Montserrat Aviation Services**, Nixons, T4912533, F4917186. Charter helicopter service is
amounts on the boat offered by *Caribbean Helicopters*, Jolly Harbour, Antigua, T268-4605900, F268-4605901, helicopters@candw.ag They also do a 45-min aerial Montserrat Volcano Tour from Jolly Harbour, Antigua, for US$190 per person, around and over the cone. **Boat** *Opal Express* ferry from Heritage Quay, St John's, Antigua, to Little Bay, Montserrat, seats 300, a/c, leaves

Antigua 0630, 1600, returns from Little Bay 0800, 1730, 1 hr, EC$150 return Mon afternoon to Fri morning. Agents in Antigua, *Carib World Travel*, Lower Redcliffe St, St John's, T268-4802980, F268-4802985; in Montserrat, *Montserrat Aviation Services* (see above). **Car hire** With a valid driving licence, you can obtain a local 3 month licence (EC$30/US$12) at the Police Station in Salem, open 24 hrs Mon-Fri, T4912555. *Be-Peep's Car Rentals*, Olveston, T4913787, for cars and jeeps; *Equipment & Supplies Ltd*, Olveston, T4912402, for cars and vans; *Ethelyne's Car Rental*, Olveston, T4912855; *Grant Enterprises & Trading*, Olveston, T4919654; *KC's Car Rentals*, Olveston, T4915756; *Montserrat Company Ltd*, Old Towne, T4912431; *Neville Bradshaw Agencies*, Olveston, T4915270; *Joe Oliver*, Barzey's, T4914276, for jeeps; *MS Osborne Ltd*, Brades, T4912494; *Pickett Van Rentals*, Salem, T4915470, for vans; *Zeekies Rentals*, Baker Hill, T4914515. **Taxi** A recommended taxi driver for tours and taxi service is Joe Phillip, T4913432, phillipj@candw.ag

Banks *Bank of Montserrat*, St Peters, T4913843, F4913163, open Mon, Tue Thu 0800-1400, Wed **Directory** 0800-1300, Fri 0800-1500; *Royal Bank of Canada*, Olveston, T4912426-8, F4913391, open Mon Thu 0800-1400, Fri 0800-1500. The American Express agent is *Carib World Travel*, at Davy Hill, T4912714, F4912713. **Communications Post**: Post Office open Mon-Fri 0815-1555, T4912457. The Philatelic Bureau is in Salem, T4912996, F4912042. It has 6 issues a year and a definitive issue every 4-5 years, having issued its own stamps since 1876. The volcanic eruption is featured, as is the eclipse of the sun. **Telephone**: *Cable and Wireless* (West Indies) Ltd, at Sweeneys, T4912112, F4913599 (open Mon-Fri 0800-1600), operates the telecommunications system with a digital telephone system, international dialling, telegraph, fax and data facilities. Phone cards are available, as are credit card service, toll free 800 service and cellular phones. **Internet**: *CompuGET* is a cybercafé in Brades, T4912654, granten@candw.ag **Media** The only local radio station, *ZJB* posts a daily, local, 10-min audio news broadcast on the internet at www.mratgov.com/newsradio.htm *The Montserrat Reporter*, the country's only (weekly) newspaper, is informative and can be found on www.montserratreporter.org **Medical facilities** There is a government health service. The hospital is in St John's, for most routine and surgical emergencies, T4912802. Private doctors and a dentist are also available. Serious medical cases are taken by helicopter to Antigua or Guadeloupe. During the rainy season there are mosquitoes and 'no-see-ums', but a good anti-bug repellent should suffice. Rooms that lack a/c often provide mosquito nets for beds. No poisonous snakes or insects. **Tourist Information** Local tourist office: *Miss Ernestine assell*, Director of Tourism, Salem, T4912230, F4917430, www. visitmontserrat.com

Background

Columbus sighted Montserrat on 11 November 1493, naming it after an abbey of the **History** same name in Spain, where the founder of the Jesuits, Ignacio de Loyola, experienced the vision which led to his forming that famous order of monks. At that time, a few Carib Indians lived on the island but by the middle of the 17th century they had disappeared. The Caribs named the island Alliouagana, which means "land of the prickly bush". Montserrat was eventually settled by the British Thomas Warner, who brought English and Irish Catholics from their uneasy base in the Protestant island of St Kitts. Once established as an Irish-Catholic colony, the only one in the Caribbean, Catholic refugees fled there from persecution in Virginia and, following his victory at Drogheda in 1649, Cromwell sent some of his Irish political prisoners to Montserrat. By 1648 there were 1,000 Irish families on the island. An Irishman brought some of the first slaves to the island in 1651 and the economy became based on sugar. Slaves quickly outnumbered the original British indentured servants. A slave rebellion in 1768, appropriately enough on St Patrick's Day, led to all the rebels being executed and today they are celebrated as freedom fighters. Montserrat was invaded several times by the French during the 17th and 18th centuries, sometimes with assistance from the resident Irish, but the island returned to British control under the Treaty of Versailles (1783) and has remained a colony to this day.

There are several small political parties, including the New People's Liberation Movement (PLM), the National Development Party (NDP), the National Progressive Party (NPP), the Movement for National Reconstruction (MNR) and the People's Progressive Alliance (PPA). On 2 April 2001 General Elections saw the

Leeward Islands

Hurricanes and volcanoes

In 1989, Montserrat was devastated by Hurricane Hugo, the first hurricane to strike the island for 61 years. No part of the island was untouched by the 150mph winds as 400-year-old trees were uprooted, 95% of the housing stock was damaged or destroyed, agriculture was reduced to below subsistence level and even the 180 ft jetty at Plymouth harbour completely disappeared, causing problems for relief supplies. However, within a few months, all public utilities were restored and the remaining standing or injured trees were in leaf again.

In 1995 the lives of Montserratians were again disrupted, this time by volcanic activity. The residents of Plymouth and villages in the south were evacuated to the north as lava, rocks and ash belched from the Soufrière Hills for the first time since the 1930s. Activity increased in 1997; during March and April pyroclastic flows reached two miles down the south side of the volcano, the former tourist attractions of the Great Alps Waterfall and Galways Soufrière were covered, there was a partial collapse of Galways Wall and lava flowed down the Tar River Valley. In May the volcanic dome was growing at 3.7 cubic metres per second and in June a huge explosion occurred when a sudden pyroclastic flow of hot rock, gas and ash poured down

the volcano at 200mph. It engulfed 19 people, destroyed seven villages and some 200 homes including Farm's and Trants to the north of the volcano. The flow, which resulted from a partial collapse of the lava dome, came to within 50 yds of the sea, close to the airport runway, which had to be closed. The eruption sent an ash cloud six miles into the air and people were forced to wear ash masks. In August another bout of activity destroyed Plymouth, which caught fire under a shower of red hot lava. It now looks like a lunar landscape, completely covered by grey ash. In December 1997 there was a huge dome collapse which created a 600 m amphitheatre around Galways Soufriére. The lava flows destroyed the deserted communities of St Patrick's, Gingoes and Morris and severely damaged Trials, Fairfield and Kinsale, south of Plymouth. The White River delta was increased to about 1½ km and the water level rose by about 1 m. During 1998-99 dome collapses continued, with ash clouds at times up to eight miles high, but scientists reported that the dome, while still hot, was gradually cooling and entering a quieter phase. In 2000, however, there was further activity. For daily scientific updates about the volcanic activity: www.geo.mtu.edu/volcanoes /west.indies/soufriere/govt

New PLM Party of John Osborne (a former Chief Minister) win seven of the nine seats in the Legislative Council. The NPP, led by Reuben T Meade, won the remaining two seats.

The main concern of the government since the eruption of the volcano in 1995 and thereafter is to replace the destroyed infrastructure of the south. With British funding there have been new schools, housing, hospital, fuel terminal, power station, factory shells, offices, roads, water systems, port and heliport all built. There are still 150 people living in evacuation shelters out of a total population of 5,000, and it is hoped to re-house these by the end of 2001. In all, close to £200 mn has been spent by the British Government to rebuild Montserrat. A few Montserratians are beginning to return home from overseas and there has been a big influx of workers from other Caricom countries to help the rebuilding process.

Geography   Montserrat, known as 'the Emerald Isle', is dominated by three mountain ranges. Mount Chance, in the Soufrière Hills, rises to 3,000 ft above sea level. This active volcano had been erupting for two years before it exploded in August 1997 destroying some villages and the capital, Plymouth. As a result, the south, which like the rest of the island used to be all lushly green, is now grey with ash. Montserrat was off-limits for tourism for a few years but the still-active volcano is now attracting visitors and facilities are being restored. It is about 11 miles long and seven miles wide, although the volcano's eruptions have increased the land surface in the south. Its nearest neighbours are Nevis, Guadeloupe and Antigua.

A British dependent territory, Montserrat has a representative government with a **Government** ministerial system. Queen Elizabeth II is Head of State and is represented by a resident Governor (Mr Tony Longfellow was appointed Governor in 2001). The Government consists of a Legislative and an Executive Council, with elections being held every five years for membership in the former. The head of Government is called the Chief Minister; a Speaker presides over the nine-member Legislative Council. As executive authority and head of the civil service, the Governor is responsible for defence, internal security and external affairs. A constitutional reform in 1989 added financial services to the Governor's powers and recognized Montserrat's right to self-determination. Montserratians have frequently discussed the pros and cons of opting for independence, but the official position is that economic independence must precede political independence, so with the current volcanic uncertainties colonial status may remain for many years to come.

Tourism used to contribute about 30% of gdp, it was the largest supplier of foreign **Economy** exchange and the Government actively encouraged investment in tourism projects. The influx of foreign residents in the 1980s saw a sharp rise in real estate deals and building construction with a parallel dependence on imports of capital and consumer goods. Gross domestic product grew rapidly at the end of the 1980s, expanding by 12.8% in 1988, although a slower rate was recorded in 1989 because of the devastation wreaked by Hurricane Hugo. Ninety-five percent of the housing stock was totally or partially destroyed; production and exports were disrupted, infrastructure was severely damaged; public sector finances were hit by reduced income and greater expenditure demands; tourism slumped. Similar economic disruption occurred as a result of the volcanic eruption in 1995-1997 (see box) when the south had to be evacuated to the north. Most ex-pats left the island and tourists stayed away. The island now depends on aid from the UK but is beginning to recover, with new construction and hotels opening up again.

The vast majority of the people are of African descent. Before the volcano erupted **People** there was an influx of white Americans, Canadians and Britons who purchased retirement homes on the island. Montserratians are notable for their easy friendliness to visitors, speaking English flavoured by dialect and the odd Irish expression. There is virtually no crime and everyone leaves their doors unlocked. The population used to hover around 11,000, but emigration since the volcano started erupting in 1995 has reduced numbers. Some Montserratians are living in temporary accommodation in Antigua and others have relocated elsewhere in the Caribbean or in the UK. Evacuees are returning, however, with the British government paying their travel costs (subject to certain restrictions).

The Irish influence can still be seen in national emblems. On arrival your passport is **Culture** stamped with a green shamrock, the island's flag and crest show a woman, Erin of Irish legend, complete with her harp, and a carved shamrock adorns the gable of Government House. There are many Irish names, of both people and places, and the national dish, goat water stew, is supposedly based on a traditional Irish recipe, although some historians claim it is of African origin. A popular local folk dance, the Bam-chick-a-lay resembles Irish step dances and musical bands may include a fife and a drum similar to the Irish bodhran.

The African heritage dominates, however, whether it be in Caribbean musical forms like calypso (the veteran Arrow is now an international superstar and can still be found on the island, having moved his operation north out of the volcano evacuation zone), steel bands or the costumed masqueraders who parade during the Christmas season. Another element in the African cultural heritage are the Jumbie Dancers, who combine dancing and healing. Only those who are intimate with the island and its inhabitants will be able to witness their ceremonies, though. Local choirs, like the long-established Emerald Community Singers, mix calypso with

Leeward Islands

traditional folk songs and spirituals in their repertoire, and the String Bands of the island play the African shak-shak, made from a calabash gourd, as well as the imported Hawaiian ukelele.

There are drama and dance groups in Montserrat, which perform occasionally. Sir George Martin's famed recording studios, the Air Studios, on the edge of Belham Valley, used to attract rock megastars such as Elton John, the Rolling Stones and Sting to the island, but the studios were closed after Hurricane Hugo. Natural disasters, such as the volcanic eruption, have left a legacy on the cultural output of the island, generating art, songs, poems, photography, stories, etc. In 1997, Sir George Martin organized a gala fundraising concert for Montserrat at the Royal Albert Hall in London, which included (Sir) Paul McCartney, (Sir) Elton John, Eric Clapton, Sting, Mark Knopfler, Jimmy Buffet and Arrow, who had used Air Studios in the past. At the same time a show was put on at Gerald's Bottom on Montserrat by other musicians who had used the recording studios. *The Climax Blues Band* reformed for the occasion and Bankie Banks appeared, along with 18 local acts in what was optimistically called 'Many Happy Returns'. A second 'Many Happy Returns' concert was held in 1999 to coincide with St Patrick's Day festivities, after a previous attempt in 1998 was postponed because of Hurricane Georges. Local and London-based bands, choirs and acts attracted a crowd of 3,000, or 75% of the population at that time, and the finale was provided by the king of soca, Arrow and his band. Lately, some of the touring calypso shows such as Shadow and Sparrow, that have played Antigua, have taken the ferry over to Montserrat and put on memorable shows at the *Bitter End Beach Bar* in Little Bay.

NB On Montserrat a Maroon is not a runaway slave but the local equivalent of 'barn-raising', when everyone helps to build a house, lay a garden, etc.

Further reading In the Macmillan series, *Montserrat: Emerald Isle of the Caribbean*, by **Howard A Fergus**, has been recommended, his *History of Montserrat* was published by Macmillan in 1994 and is an interesting and informative work; also *Alliouagana Folk*, by **J A George Irish** (Jagpi 1985), as an introduction to Montserratian language, proverbs and traditions. There are a number of local poetry anthologies, available locally. *Fire from the Mountain*, by **Polly Pattullo** (Constable 2000) is an account of the explosion in 1997 of the Soufrière Hills volcano. *Volcano!* By **Cathy Buffonge** (3 editions), a chronicle of Montserrat's volcanic experience from day one in 1995 until 1998, is privately published by the author and available at several gift shops and other outlets on Montserrat and in several bookshops in Antigua.

Netherlands Antilles, the 3 S's

14

The '3 S's', Saba, Sint Eustatius (Statia) and Sint Maarten are 880 km north of the rest of the Netherlands Antilles group, the ABC islands (Aruba, Bonaire and Curaçao), which lie off the coast of Venezuela. Each has a distinct character and flavour, St Eustatius being the poorest, Saba the smallest and despite some development still deserving of its official title, 'the unspoiled Queen', and Sint Maarten the most developed and wealthy.

Lacking in natural resources, they all depend to a greater or lesser degree on tourism for their foreign exchange revenues, but are developing their potential in different ways. Saba's strength is the richness of the underwater world surrounding the island and is noted for its pristine diving locations. Sint Maarten has the best beaches and resorts, while St Eustatius promotes its historical associations and is known as 'the historic gem'.

A Foot in the door

- When 2-3 m **tarpon** and **barracuda** are just around that rock and colourful fish and coral abound, what else should you do but dive, dive, dive?
- When you've done with diving try walking the 1,064 irregular steps up **Mount Scenery** to get your heart and lungs pumping and enjoy the view of neighbouring islands across the sea.
- Don't miss the highest hotel in the Kingdom of the Netherlands! **Willards of Saba** offers peace and quiet with glorious views, but its quite a hike to get up there.

Saba

Population: 1,200
Colour map 4, grid B1

This tiny Dutch island Saba, pronounced 'Say-bah', rises out of the sea, green and lush. An extinct volcano, its peak is aptly named Mount Scenery. Underwater, the landscape is equally spectacular and divers treasure the marine park, noted for its 'virginity'. When not under water, visitors find walking challenging and rewarding. Ancient trails weave their way around the island, the most stunning being the 1,064 irregular steps up Mount Scenery through different types of tropical vegetation according to altitude. Lodging is in small, friendly hotels, guest houses and cottages, where you won't need a key – there is no crime.

Ins and outs

Getting there By air (20 mins) or by sea (1 ½ hrs) from Sint Maarten. Saba claims to have the world's shortest airport runway although there are plans to build a longer one. Large aircraft cannot be accommodated. Planes do not land in bad weather in case they skid off the end. Sit up front behind the pilots for an excellent view of Saba when landing. On windy days the boat crossing can be very rough.

Getting around There are no buses on the island but you can hire a jeep or car. Hitchhiking is safe, very easy and a common means of getting about. It is about 1½ hrs hike from the airport to Windwardside, through different scenery, vegetation and climate. There are taxis at the airport and a few others around the island. They can be hired for tours (US$40) and the drivers are knowledgeable guides. Some are also fishermen or hotel owners, so they can be valuable contacts.

Climate The average temperature is 25-28°C, 78-82°F during the day but at night it can fall to 16-18°C, the low 60°Fs. The higher up you get, the cooler it will be; so take a jersey, if hiking up the mountain. Average annual rainfall is 42 inches

Flora and fauna

In September 1998, Hurricane Georges passed just a few kilometres south of Saba, with wind speeds of 180 mph high up in the hills. Many of the bigger trees were blown down, but the island quickly recovered and the lower mountain slopes became green and lush after the rain. The Elfin Forest took longer to recover. Underwater, there was some damage to shallow reefs, but deeper sites were untouched. However, in 1999 Hurricane Lenny attacked from the west, the Caribbean side of the island, and almost totally destroyed the rainforest. Most of the trees were blown down or snapped off so that the mosses and rainforest undergrowth did not grow. Other plants grew very fast but did not renew the forest. Since the hurricane local people have worked very hard to restore the forest and it is getting back to its old shape.

Vegetation on Saba changes according to altitude and a walk up Mount Scenery used to be a sightseeing highlight for the many different types of tropical vegetation.

At an altitude of 490-610 m there is secondary rain forest with trees of between 5 and 10 m high. Further up there are tree ferns of 4-5 m, then palm trees, then at 825 m the cloud forest begins (known as Elfin Forest), where you find the mountain mahogany tree (*freziera undulata*). Since Hurricane Lenny, however, the forest remains only in protected pockets. Wildlife on the island is limited to the endemic anole lizard (*anolis sabanus*, widespread), iguanas (the green iguana, *iguana iguana,* the island's largest, can be seen on Old Booby Hill in the afternoon, sunbathing), a harmless red-bellied racer snake (*alsophis rufiventris*, can be seen on the Sandy Cruz and Mary's Point trails if you are quiet), and over 60 species of birds have been recorded, with many migratory birds coming to nest here. The trembler and the purple-throated hummingbird can be seen in the Elfin forest and the Sandy Cruz rain forest, where you can also find the wood hen (bridled quail dove).

The Saba Conservation Foundation (SCF) preserves the environment on land and underwater, developing protected areas, maintaining trails and promoting nature conservation. The Foundation can be contacted through the tourist office or write to Saba Conservation Foundation, The Bottom, Saba. Janine leSueur is the executive director of the SCF (janini@hotmail.com) and can be contacted for information on hiking and rates. The trail manager and hiking guide of the SCF is James Johnson, appointments are made through the Saba Trail Shop, T4162630. In the USA the Friends of the Saba Conservation Foundation (FSCF) raises money for conservation, 506 Tiffany Trails, Richardson, Texas 75081.

Saba

Nature trails

1 Crispeen Track
2 Flat Point
3 Maskehorne Hill Trail
4 Mount Scenery Stairwell
5 Sandy Cruz Track
6 Sulphur Mine Track
7 The Ladder

0 metres 500
0 yards 500

Essentials

Documents See page 1013. Saba is a free port so there are no customs formalities.

Currency The florin or guilder is the local currency, but US dollars are accepted everywhere. Visa and Mastercard are the only widely accepted credit cards. Hotels and dive shops accept credit cards, but no one else does. You may be charged extra for using credit cards because of the slow processing arrangements.

Departure tax Airport departure tax is US$5 to Netherlands Antilles, US$10 elsewhere.

Ports of entry (Dutch flag). Go ashore to clear immigration with the Harbourmaster at Fort Bay or with the Police in The Bottom.

Anchorages Fort Bay has three free moorings but it is rolly with southeast winds. The Ladder and Well's Bay moorings (yellow buoys) are available for use by yachts for US$2 per person for anchoring and snorkelling, and US$3 per person for each dive you take on your own. Use a strong line and plenty of scope. Marine patrol will collect fees and explain the rules and regulations. The

Marine Park has a leaflet with map of anchorages and dive sites.

Tourist office overseas Antillenhius, Badhiusweg 173-175, 2597JP Den Haag, The Netherlands, T31-70-3512811, F31-70-3512722. Dutch Caribbean Travel Center, Karlstrasse 12, 60329 Frankfurt/Main, Germany, T49-69-24001830, F49-69-24271521, dutch.caribbean-tc@t-online.de. The Tourist Board's website is: www.turq.com/saba

Official time Atlantic Standard Time, four hours behind GMT, one ahead of EST.

Police T4163237.

Voltage 110 volts AC, 60 cycles.

Communications The international phone code is 599 followed by 7 digits beginning with 416.

Public holidays New Year's Day, Good Friday, Easter Sunday and Monday, Queen's Coronation Day (30 April), Labour Day (1 May), Ascension Day (Thursday), Saba Days (beginning of December), Christmas Day, Boxing Day.

Diving and marine life

Diving tourism is popular in the marine park, which is noted for its 'virginity'

There are many dive sites of 27-30 m and if you are doing three dives a day you must follow your dive tables and stay within your limit. It is recommended that you take every fourth day off and rest or go hiking. All dive operations offer à la carte diving and arrange taxi pick-ups from hotels. The waters around Saba became a marine park in 1987 and 30 permanent mooring buoys have been provided for dive boats (less than half of which are for big boats). The park includes waters from the highwater mark down to 60 m all the way around the island. Spearfishing is prohibited (except by Sabans, free diving in certain areas), as is the removal of coral or shells (Sabans are limited to 20 conch per person a year without the use of scuba). Saba has no permanent beaches so diving and snorkelling is from boats, mostly along the calmer south and west coasts.

Saba's rugged, volcanic terrain is replicated underwater where there are mountains, swim throughs, lava flows, overhangs, reefs, walls, pinnacles and elkhorn coral forests

The west coast from **Tent Bay** to **Ladder Bay**, together with **Man of War shoals**, **Diamond Rock** and the sea offshore comprise the main dive sites, where anchoring and fishing are prohibited. From Ladder Bay to Torrens Point is an all-purpose recreational zone which includes Saba's only beach at **Well's Bay**, a pebbly stretch of coast with shallow water for swimming and areas for diving, fishing, and boat anchorage. The beach comes and goes with the seasons and ocean currents but when it is there it is scenic and good for snorkelling. The concrete road ends here but there are no facilities so take your own refreshments and arrange for a taxi to pick you up later. Another anchorage is west of Fort Bay. East of Fort Bay along the south, east and north coast to Torrens Point is a multiple use zone where fishing and diving are permitted. Some of the most visited dive sites are **Third Encounter**, **Outer Limits**, Diamond Rock and Man of War. **Tent Reef** is also a favourite. **Ladder Labyrinth** is a dive site which is good for snorkelling.

Dive operators have been granted permits and they collect the mandatory visitor fees to help maintain the park which is now self-financing. The marine park office is at Fort Bay, PO Box 18, The Bottom, T/F63295, www.sabapark.com It is managed by a Dutchman, David Kooistra, and a Saban, Percy Tenholt, who are very helpful and keen to talk about conservation. Percy gives an illustrated lecture at 1830 on Tuesday at *Juliana's*, or on demand for groups. The guide to the dive sites, *Guide to the Saba Marine Park*, by Tom Van't Hof, published by the Saba Conservation Foundation, is highly recommended, available at dive shops, the museum and souvenir shops, US$15. Saba now has a four person recompression chamber at Fort Bay, donated by the Royal Netherlands Navy, which is administered through the Marine Park but operated by medical school people. Summer visibility is 23-30 m with water temperatures of about 30°C, while winter visibility increases to 38 m and water temperatures fall to 24°C.

Not much fishing is done in these waters, so there is a wide range of sizes and varieties of fish to be seen. Tarpon and barracuda of up to 2½ m are common, as are giant sea turtles. From January to April humpback whales pass by on their migration south and can be encountered by divers, while in the winter dive boats are often accompanied by schools of porpoises. Smaller, tropical fish are not in short supply and together with bright red, orange, yellow and purple giant tube sponges and different coloured coral, are a photographer's delight. Divers are not allowed to feed the fish as it has been proved to alter fish behaviour and encourage the aggressive species.

There are three dive shops on Saba. *Saba Deep* in the Fort Bay harbour, T4163347, F4163397, www.sabadeep.com has NAUI, PADI, SSI, TDI and IANTD instructors and is a full service dive centre with Nitrox and Drager Rebreathers. They have two 25-ft and one 30-ft fibreglass boats for small groups. Three dives daily and return to the harbour between dives for the surface interval. All your gear is washed and taken care of during your stay and loaded on the boat for you, or there is well-maintained rental equipment (shortie wet suit US$10). Dive rates are US$56 single dive, US$101 double, US$141 triple, US$82 night, all including equipment, marine park fees and taxes. Dive packages, also including accommodation and transfers, are available.

Dive centres

The Marine Park fee is US$3 per person per dive, collected by the dive shops

Sea Saba Dive Centre has two locations: office and extensive retail shop at Lambee's Place, Windwardside, T4162246, F4162362, www.seasaba.com, close to hotels, shops and restaurants; Fort Bay harbour depot for all rental equipment and compressors as well as a fabrication shop (useful for yachties). They offer PADI and NAUI courses from beginner to Divemaster and also Nitrox diving at US$59 a week, unlimited. Sea Saba has two large, 40-ft boats, with shade and sun deck, but limit groups to 10 divers. Two morning dives between 0930 and 1330 with the surface interval spent at Well's Bay for sunbathing, snorkelling or ocean kayaking, so it can be enjoyed by non-divers as well. Drinks are available on board, some people take snacks for the 60-90 minute interval. The atmosphere is relaxed and unrushed. A la carte diving at US$90 for two dives, including tax and equipment. Night dives on request.

Saba Divers at *Scout's Place*, Windwardside, T4162740, F4162741, www.sabadivers.com Run by Wolfgang Tooten and Barbara Schäfer, of Germany. PADI, SSI, DAN, CMAS courses offered in several languages, diving and accommodation packages available. The dive shop is at *Scout's Place* and is under the same management. You don't have to stay there to dive with them, but if you do you will get a 10% discount on diving. They normally do a two-tank dive in the morning, 0930-1330 and afternoon and night dives are available on request, US$41 per dive. Equipment, tanks and weights US$10 a day. Special prices for yachties, who can be picked up from their boat, contact the office or the boat, *Big Blue*, on VHF Ch 16.

Walking

Before the road was built people got about Saba by donkey or on foot and there are still numerous steep trails and stone steps linking villages which make strenuous, yet satisfying, walking. The *Saba Conservation Foundation* (see Fauna and flora above) preserves and marks trails for those who like a challenge and for those who prefer a gentle stroll. All of them are accessible from the road and many can be done without a guide. However they are all on private land and you are requested not to stray off the tracks. Named trails include: The Ladder, Crispeen Track, Maskehorne Hill Trail, Mt Scenery Stairwell, Sandy Cruz Track, Sulphur Mine Track and Flat Point.

The most spectacular hike is probably the one from Windwardside up 1,064 steps of varying sizes and intervals to the crest of **Mount Scenery**, best done on a clear day otherwise you end up in the clouds. It is a hard slog, 1½ hours each way, but a road goes part of the way up. The summit has now been cleared (Cable & Wireless have built a telecommunications tower there by helicopter drops) and there is a spectacular view down to Windwardside and the surrounding isles if it is not cloudy. Take a sweater and waterproof jacket, it can be very rough and slippery after rain. There are lots of birds, lizards, snakes and land crabs, and the botanical changes are noticeable as you climb. There is also a five-hour walk through a variety of ecosystems circling Mount Scenery. Starting from Windwardside, walk up the road to Upper Hell's Gate, then take the Sandy Cruz trail to the banana plantation. Proceed on the Sandy Cruz trail extension to Troy Hill, where you meet the road which takes you to The Bottom. A short walk up the road out of The Bottom towards Windwardside brings you to the start of the Crispeen trail, which is followed back to Windwardside.

There is a picnic place overlooking Ladder Bay

The Ladder is a long path of stone steps from the shore up to The Bottom, up which all provisions used to be hauled from boats before the road was built. For the **Sulphur Mine** take the turning at **Hell's Gate** (church has a big sign saying Hell's Gate outside it!), past the (temporarily closed) *Gate House Hotel* and keep on to the end of the houses. After some steps the trail begins. Walk for about 20 minutes until you get to a sign for a turning to the right leading down to the remains of the old mines and the cliffs of the north coast, with splendid scenery. It is also possible to carry on along the island, through forests less damaged by the hurricanes, towards **Mary's Point**. However, the Conservation Foundation does not recommend you go far along this old path as several people have got lost. Best to take a guide. There are

Windwardside

To Hell's Gate

● Saba Chinese

Brigadoon
■

Roman Catholic
Church of St Paul's
Conversion
✝

Y2K Grill   Carmel
& Bakery   Shop
            ○
Breadfruit   El Momo
Gallery   Folk Art
         ○   ○   Lambee's Place
Sea Saba
Dive Shop   ○
         ⓢ   Barclays
Holy Trinity ✝
Anglican ■

Harry L Johnson Museum 🏛

Juliana's/Tropics Café/
Johnson's Rent a Car ■

Captain's Quarters
(temporarily closed) ■

The Level

■ The Cottage Club

Antilles
ⓢ
✉ Library
Scout's Place &
Saba Divers
         ○ Guido's   El Momo Cottages

Booby Hill

N

0 metres   50
0 yards   50

magnificent views of the northern coastal cliffs but there is a danger of rock falls set off by feral goats which may be above you. A very nice lookout point is from **Booby Hill**, up the 66 terraced steps to the Booby Hill Peak.

The tourist office has leaflets on the nature trails and hiking on Saba, but in many places a guide is recommended. Interpretative and directional signs are variable because of weather damage. *Saban Trails… A Walking & Hiking Guide* published by the *Saba Conservation Foundation*, gives information on 11 trails and the flora, fauna and historical remains. However it was published in 1998 before Hurricane Lenny. James Johnson, T4163281 work, T4163307 home, a local man and the trails manager, does guided tours after 1500 weekdays and all day at weekends, US$40-50 per group, maximum eight people. He knows the island intimately and carries a bush knife to hack away obstacles. Although he only knows local plant and animal names, he makes up for his lack of scientific knowledge in stories about past inhabitants (his relatives).

There is a **tennis** court (concrete) at the Sunny Valley Youth Centre in The Bottom **Other sports** which is open to the public. **Basket ball** and **volley ball** matches are held, contact the tourist office for a schedule.

Around the island

There are four picture book villages on Saba, connected by a single spectacular 10½ km road which begins at the airport and ends at the pier. The road itself is a feat of engineering, designed and built by Josephus Lambert Hassell (1906-83) in the 1940s, who studied road construction by correspondence course after Dutch engineers said it was impossible to build a road on Saba. From the airport, the road rises to **Hell's Gate** and then on through banana plantations to **Windwardside**, where most of the hotels and shops are situated. There is a small museum, a bank and post office. **Lambee's Place**, originally the home of Josephus Lambert Hassell, now houses the tourist office, Sea Saba Dive Shop, Breadfruit Gallery, El Momo Folk Art and *Y2K Café* (bakery, bar and grill). The **Harry L Johnson Museum** was once a sea captain's house, built in 1840 and a typical, tiny, four-room Saban house on one floor. It is filled with antique furniture and family memorabilia. The kitchen is in its original state. ■ *US$2, 1000-1200, 1400-1600, Mon-Fri.*

The road goes on past Kate's Hill, Peter Simon's Hill and Big Rendezvous to **St John's**, where the schools are, and which has a wonderful view of St Eustatius, then climbs over the mountain and drops sharply down to **The Bottom**, the island's seat of government, with a population of 350. The Bottom is on a plateau, 245 m above the sea, and gets its name from the Dutch words *de botte*, meaning 'the bowl'. It can be hot, as there is little breeze. Leaving The Bottom, the road makes its final descent to Fort Bay, where small cruise ships, yachts and the ferry from St Maarten arrive at the 85 m pier. Most of the houses on the island are painted white with red roofs and some have green shutters. Heleen Cornet's book, *Saban Cottages*, gives background information on some interesting houses. There are watercolour workshops.

Essentials

There are no resort hotels yet on Saba and even the most expensive are small and friendly. **Sleeping** Dec-Apr is the busiest and most expensive season, although divers come throughout the *Hotels do not usually* year. July is also busy because of Carnival and students return from foreign universities. All *give you a room key;* the hotels offer dive packages with the three dive shops. There is a 5% room tax, sometimes a *there is no crime.* 3% turnover tax (TOT) and usually a 10-15% service charge. *The four policemen on the island boast that the cells are only*

Windwardside AL-A *Captain's Quarters,* T4162201/4162522, F4162377. Closed for *used as overspill when* repairs in 2001, sea captain's house, sea view, restaurant, bar, pool. **AL** *The Cottage Club,* *the hotels are full!* outside Windwardside, on hill with wonderful views of Mount Scenery, English Quarter and the sea, T4162486/4162386, F4162476, cottageclub@unspoiledqueen.com Owned by Johnson family who also own supermarket, 10 white cottages with red roofs in local style, kitchen, TV, phone, natural stone swimming pool. **AL-A** *Juliana's*, further up the hill, T4162269, F4162389, www.julianas-hotel.com Owned by Juliana and Franklin Johnson, descendants of original settlers, 9 rooms, smaller than at *Captain's Quarters* but each has bathroom, cable TV, balcony or patio, also 1 bedroomed apartment and 2 renovated Saban cottages with 2 bedrooms, mountain and ocean views, pool, café, bar. **A-B** *Ecolodge Rendez-Vous*, 20 mins' walk from Windwardside, T4163348, F4163299, www.ecolodge-saba.com Due to open Jan 2002, 12 Saba style simple cabins sleeping 2-4 (2 downstairs, 2 in the loft), restaurant, sun deck, solar-powered hot tub, solar showers, composting toilets, home grown fruit and vegetables, 5-min hike from nearest road but donkey, Eco, will carry your bags, family-run by artist Heleen Cornet, conservationist Tom van't Hof, their son, Bernt, who is a chef, his partner Angelique and his cousin JJ. **A-B** *Scout's Place*, T4162205, F4162388, sabadivers@unspoiled queen.com Being redeveloped by a German couple in 2001 as a dive resort, packages available, beautiful views, 4 basic but comfortable rooms in former government guesthouse, 10 rooms in new wing, each with bathroom and balcony, most with cable TV, fan and fridge, simple, relaxed, slow service, pool, restaurant, bar.

On Booby Hill LL *Willard's of Saba*, T4162498, F4162482, willard@sint maarten.net The highest hotel in the Kingdom of the Netherlands! Seven luxury or VIP suites in main building or bungalows further up the hill, all with incredible views, tennis, jacuzzi, solar heated pool, restaurant with fireplace, long walk out of town up a slope so steep some taxi drivers refuse to go up it, jeep therefore recommended, good for those who want peace and quiet and are prepared to pay for it, no children under 14. **C** *El Momo Cottages*, half way up Jimmy's Hill, 5 mins from Windwardside, T/F4162265, www.elmomo.com Up 60 steps, superb view, beautiful garden, 5 rooms, built in gingerbread style, separate bathroom building, simple but clean, friendly, great breakfast US$5.95, snacks available, pool, the only place for budget travellers, so essential to book.

The Bottom AL *Cranston's Antique Inn*, T4163203, F4163469. 130-year old inn, 5 rooms, 4-poster beds, pool. **LL-L** *Queen's Gardens Resort*, PO Box 2, T4163494, F4163495, www.queen saba.com Troy Hill, overlooking The Bottom. 12 1-2 bedroom apartments, fully equipped, spectacular view, garden, discounts for weekly rates, *Mango Royale* restaurant.

The tourist office has a list of 1-3 bedroom **cottages** and **apartments** for rent from US$50 a night, which can be let on a weekly or monthly basis, and can also provide hotel rates. **Windwardside** contact David Johnson, T4162254, for **B** *Effie's Cottage*, 1 bedroom, **B** *The Look Out Cottage*, 2 bedrooms, 5-min walk from Windwardside at **the Level** are: **C** *Renz Apartment*, T4162316 (Mr and Mrs Renz), sleeps 2, pool. **B** *Carpenter's Cottage*, T4162224 (Mrs Pape), toddpape@wwa.com 1 double and 1 single bedroom. **AL** *Daphne Cottage*, T4163361 (Chuck and Ed Vaughn). 2 bedrooms. **Booby Hill AL** *Hall 'n Judy's Cottage*. Three bedrooms, pool, terrace, patio and gardens, terrific view, minimum stay 7 nights.

Eating **Windwardside** At *Scout's Place*, T4162205. Breakfast 0700-1000, lunch, sandwiches and salads. *Saba Chinese Restaurant*, T4162353. Cantonese food, salads, steaks, good food, great view, open Tue-Sun 1730-2300, also lunch on Sun 1100-1500, from US$8, best bet for a late meal, no reservations. *Tropics Café* at *Juliana's*, Windwardside, T4162469. Does daily breakfast, burgers and snacks at lunchtime, sandwiches with homemade bread, full dinner daily except Mon US$9-16, go early, poolside with sea view, takeaway available. *Brigadoon*, T4162380. In old Saban house close to centre, good reputation with locals, open daily 1800-2100, dinner from US$10, lunch for groups by reservation only, international, creole and Caribbean food, fresh seafood, lobster tank. *Y2K Café*, Lambee's Place. Bakery, bar and grill, pastries and pizzas, kids' menu, great restaurant, lunch and dinner, closed Sun.

Many restaurants close by 2130. Eat early

Rest of the island *Mango Royale*, at *Queen's Garden Resort*, The Bottom (see above). Run by French chef and his wife, French cuisine with Caribbean flair using local fresh ingredients, excellent pastries, interesting wines, check for theme nights, poolside barbecues, dinner and dance, Sunday brunches, etc. *Lollipop*, T4163330. A small restaurant on the mountainside overlooking The Bottom on the way to St John's, free taxi pick-up (waiter is also the driver), excellent 3-course meal for about US$20, fresh lobster, conch melts in the mouth, local cuisine including goat and land crab, open breakfast, lunch or dinner, recommended for lunch, walk it off afterwards. *Midway Bar & Restaurant*, St John's, T4163367. Local food, goat, chicken, special barbecues, good view, dinner only, reservations required, no credit cards, free transport offered. *In Two Deep*, Fort Bay, T4163438. Used by divers, open 0800-1600, New England style food, overlooks water, lunch US$10-12.

Most of the nightlife takes place at the restaurants. At weekends there are sometimes barbecues, steel bands and dances. Generally, though, the island is quiet at night. In Windwardside, *Guido's* on Fri, Sat, pool room makes way to a disco, popular with all sections of the community, soca, reggae, rap and disco, loud.

Nightlife

Coronation Day & **Queen's Birthday** is *30 April*, when there are ceremonies commemorating the coronation of Queen Beatrix and the Queen's birthday. **Carnival** (Saba Summer Festival) is a week near the end of *July* and is celebrated with jump-ups, music and costumed dancing, shows, food, games and contests including the Saba Hill Climb. There are parades on the last weekend and Carnival Monday at the end is a public holiday. **Saba Days** are a mini-carnival at the first weekend in *December*, when donkey races are held, with dancing, steel bands, barbecues and other festivities.

Festivals

Local crafts have been developed by the *Saba Artisan Foundation* in The Bottom and include dolls, books and silk-screened textiles and clothing. The typical local, drawn-thread work 'Saba Lace' (also known as 'Spanish Work' because it was learned by a Saban woman in a Spanish convent in Venezuela at the end of the last century) is sold at several shops on the island. Taxi drivers may make unofficial stops at the houses where Saba lace, dolls, pillows etc are made. Boutiques in Windwardside sell a variety of gifts. There are several **art galleries** in Windwardside where local artists have their studios and sell their watercolours, oil paintings, prints and sculptures. Ask the tourist office for a leaflet. **Saba Spice** is the local rum, very strong (150° proof) and mixed with spices, particularly cloves, and sugar.

Shopping
Shops open 0900-1200, 1400-1800

Air   *Winair*, the only scheduled airline, has 5-6 daily 20-seater flights from St Maarten (15 mins, US$119 return) some of which come via St Eustatius. It is essential to reconfirm your return flight. **Sea**   If sailing, *The Voyager*, a monohull boat carrying 150 passengers, leaves the main pier, Marigot, St-Martin, Tue 0830, returns 1615, leaves **Bobby's Marina**, Philipsburg, Sint Maarten, Thur 0900, returns 1615, one way US$40 (children half price), return US$60. Island tour of Saba with lunch, US$30, reservations recommended. Dockside Management, Sint Maarten, T5424096, F5422888, voyager.sxm@wanadoo.fr *The Edge* sails Wed, Fri, Sun at 0900, 1 hr, from Simpson Bay/Pelican Marina, St Maarten, T5444505, US$40 one way, US$60 return, but be sure to check, often not running. A deep water pier at Fort Bay allows cruise ships to call. **Local Car hire**   Drive on the right. *Caja's Enterprises NV*, at The Bottom, T4163460, F4163463; *Mike's and Son Car Rental*, The Bottom, T/F4163259. Doing it through a hotel can cost you US$10 more. **Taxi**   *Eddie*, T/F4162640; *Wilfred*, T4162238; *Garvis*, T4162358; *Billy*, T4162262; *Evelyn*, T4163292; *Anthony*, T4162378; *Manny*, T4163328; *Wayne*, T4162277.

Transport

Banks *Barclays Bank*, Windwardside, T4162216. Open 0830-1530, Mon-Fri, currency exchange, advances, transfers, TCs. *Antilles Banking*, Windwardside. Open Mon-Wed 0830-1500, Thu-Fri 0830-1600. **Communications** **Post**: airmail takes about 2 weeks to the USA or Europe. Federal Express is available. The post office in Windwardside is open 0800-1200, 1300-1700. **Telephones**: most hotels have direct dialling worldwide, otherwise overseas calls can be made from Landsradio phone booths in Windwardside or The Bottom. **Medical services** Hospital: T4163288. **Tourist office** *The Saba Tourist Board* (Glenn Holm, Zuleyka and Angelique) is at Lambee's Place in Windwardside, open Mon-Fri, 0800-1200, 1300-1700, PO Box 527, T4162231-2, F4162350, www. turq.com/saba Plenty of leaflets and maps and the staff are friendly and helpful.

Directory

Background

History
See also background
to the Netherlands
Antilles, the ABC
chapter, page 1045

History Saba was first discovered by Columbus on his second voyage in 1493 but not colonized. Sir Francis Drake sighted it in 1595, as did the Dutchmen Pieter Schouten in 1624 and Piet Heyn in 1626. Some shipwrecked Englishmen landed in 1632, finding it uninhabited. In 1635 the French claimed it but in the 1640s the Dutch settled it, building communities at Tent Bay and The Bottom. However, it was not until 1816 that the island became definitively Dutch, the interregnum being marked by 12 changes in sovereignty, with the English, Dutch, French and Spanish all claiming possession.

Geography The island is an extinct volcano which shoots out of the sea, green with lush vegetation but without beaches. In fact there is only one inlet amidst the sheer cliffs where boats can come in to dock. The highest peak of this rugged island is Mount Scenery (887 m), also known as 'the Mountain', and the highest point in all the Netherlands. Because of the difficult terrain there were no roads on Saba until 1943, only hand-carved steps in the volcanic rock. The main road has concrete barriers, partly to prevent cars driving over the edge and partly because of landslides, which can be frequent after rain. Saba, pronounced 'Say-bah', only 13 sq km, lays claim to the world's shortest runway (400 m). It lies 45 km south of St Maarten and 27 km northwest of Sint Eustatius.

People Although the island was once inhabited by Caribs, relics of whom have been found, there is no trace of their ancestry in the local inhabitants. The population is half white (descendants of Dutch, English and Scots settlers) and half black. Their physical isolation and the difficult terrain has enabled them to develop their ingenuity for self sufficiency and to live in harmony with their environment. Originally farmers and seafarers, the construction in 1963 of the Juancho E Yrausquin Airport on the only flat part of the island, and the serpentine road which connects it tenuously to the rest of the island, brought a new and more lucrative source of income: tourism.

　The island's geographical limitations have meant that tourism has evolved in a small, intimate way. About 24,000 tourists visit each year, most of whom are day trippers. There are only 100 beds available in the hotels and guest houses, as well as a few cottages to rent. Those who stay are few enough to get to know the friendliness and hospitality of their hosts, who all speak English, even though Dutch is the official language. In 1993 the Dutch Government stopped 'driver licence tourism'. Previously, driving tests taken in Saba were valid in Holland, where it is more difficult to secure a licence. The system brought Saba an income of about US$300,000 a year. Currently, the major source of income is the US Medical School, opened in 1993, which attracts over 250 (mainly US) students from overseas, who spend about US$1,000 a month. Development is small scale; the island still merits its unofficial title, 'the Unspoiled Queen'. There is no unemployment among the workforce of 600. The island is spotlessly clean; the streets are swept by hand every day.

Sint Eustatius

Colour map 4, grid B1

Only 2,100 people live on this Dutch outpost and very few tourists make the effort to visit. It has a rich colonial history and a prosperous past, but having made its fortune in the 18th century out of the slave trade and commerce in plantation crops, it lost it in the 19th century with the abolition of slavery and has never really recovered. The main town, Oranjestad, still has the fortifications and remains of warehouses from its heyday, parts of which are being restored as hotels and restaurants. A lot of renovation has already taken place, tourism is picking up and this is an off-the-beaten-track destination worthy of investigation, particularly by divers. There are walking trails up into the rainforest of the extinct volcano, the Quill, and diving is good in the marine park. The name 'Statia' comes from St Anastasia, as it was named by Columbus, but the Dutch later changed it to Sint Eustatius.

A Foot in the door

★

- **Hike up the Quill**, a dormant volcano with lush rainforest in its crater: tree ferns, bromeliads, mahogany and begonias, where locals hunt for land crabs by flashlight at night.
- Dive the wrecks and reefs in the **marine park** where there are lots of big fish to bump into but very few other divers.
- Visit the ruins of the 18th-century **synagogue** and the Jewish **cemetery** to get an idea of Statia's colonial and prosperous past.
- Go beachcombing at **Zeelandia Beach** a 3 km stretch on the windward side of the island. Great after a storm to see what has been washed up from Africa.

Ins and outs

It is possible to get to Statia in a day from many US cities, but you will have to change planes in Sint Maarten. All flights are in small planes, although the airport has been extended to 1,600m to allow larger jets to land. There are currently no ferries.

Getting there
You get an impressive view of The Quill when you come in to land

There is no public transport on the island but cars and taxis can be hired. Driving is on the right, but some roads are so narrow you have to pass where you can. Watch out for cows, donkeys, goats and sheep roaming around freely. They are a traffic hazard. Taxi drivers are well-informed guides and can arrange excursions, although most places are within walking distance if you are energetic (less than 30 mins' walk airport to town).

Getting around
See transport, page 676, for further details

Average temperature is around 31°C in the daytime and 27°C at night. Average rainfall is 45in a year. Water temperature in the sea is 26-29°C depending on the time of year.

Climate

Flora and fauna

Despite the small size of the island, in the 17th and 18th centuries there were more than 70 plantations, worked intensively by slaves. As a result, most of the original forest has disappeared except in the most inhospitable parts of the volcano. Nevertheless there are 17 different kinds of orchid and 58 species of birds, of which 25 are resident and breeding, 21 migrants from North America and 12 seabirds. The harmless racer snake is found here, as on Saba, and there are iguanas, land crabs, tree frogs and lots of butterflies. Unfortunately there are lots of goats too, which eat everything in sight.

STENAPA, the St Eustatius National Parks Foundation, was founded in 1996. This organization is responsible for the marine park, The Quill, Boven, Gilboa Hill, Signal Hill and Little Mountain. These areas and portions of The Quill, above 250 m, are now protected. In 1998 The Quill was declared a national park, consisting of the volcano and the limestone White Wall to its south. The Quill is protected from the 250 m line, but the White Wall is protected down to the high water line. STENAPA has developed the 14-acre Miriam C Schmidt Botanical Garden on the southeast side of The Quill in the area called 'Behind the Mountain'. There is a picnic pavilion, barbecue areas, marked trails, a bee yard and orchid gardens.

At the crater of **The Quill** there are many species usually found in tropical rain forest: huge tree ferns; mahogany; giant elephant ears; begonias; figs; plantains; bromeliads; the balsam tree and many more. The southern slope of the mountain has not been fully explored by botanists. In the future STENAPA hopes to attract scientists to study plants, animals and marine life. Recently experts have been on the island to study the endangered iguanas and the rare racer snake. The Antilles Iguana (*Iguana delicatissima*) is rare and threatened. The young and females vary from bright green to dull grey, while the large males can be nearly black. The population is stronger here than on neighbouring islands because the mongoose was never introduced here. Neither was the Green Iguana, with which it has interbred on some islands. They are now protected by law and human consumption is no longer allowed. The Red-bellied Racer (*Alsophis rufiventris*) is a small snake found only on Statia and Saba. It is brown with black markings on its back and a pink belly. It is not poisonous and kills its prey (small reptiles, baby rats) by strangulation.

Diving and marine life

Water visibility can be over 30 m and diving and snorkelling are very good

Statia's waters offer a wonderful combination of coral reefs, marine life and historic shipwrecks. Diving is excellent, with plenty of corals, sea fans, hydroids and big fish such as groupers and barracudas, as well as rays, turtles and the occasional dolphin but unlike some other Caribbean diving destinations, you will not bump into any other divers underwater. St Eustatius Marine Park was established in 1996 and became operational in 1998. STENAPA has identified four protected areas: the

Sint Eustatius

N

Not to scale

Nature trails

1 Around the mountain	**5** Soldier Gut	**9** The Quill
2 Corre Corre Bay	**6** The Crater	**10** Venus Bay
3 Gilboa Hill	**7** The Mazinga	**11** White Bird
4 Jenkins Bay	**8** The Panorama	

Essentials

Documents *See page 1013. There are no customs regulations as Statia is a free port.*
Currency *The currency is the Netherlands Antilles florin or guilder, but US dollars are accepted everywhere.* **Credit cards** *are not widely used (Amex hardly ever accepted, Visa and Mastercard better). Check at hotels and restaurants. US$100 bills often not accepted.*
Departure tax *Airport departure tax is US$5 for Antilles, US$10 international. If you visit for the day and pay departure tax on St Maarten, you do not have to pay the tax when you leave Statia. If you pay the tax on Statia and are in-transit on St Maarten you do not have to pay tax on St Maarten. You will need to show your tickets and boarding pass for your next flight at the tax window.*
Airlines *Windward Islands Airways (Winair) T82362/82381, F82485.*
Ports of entry *The Harbour Office is open 0800-1700, after hours sailors should see guard at the gate who will give directions to the local police station. If not leaving before 0800 clear customs in the morning, T82205, F82888, VHF Channel 14. The Harbour Master, Murvin Gittens, works Monday-Friday, 0800-1600. Fly an Antillean flag.*
Anchorages *Oranje Baii is the only anchorage, prices are based on tonnage, 0-5 tons US$5; 6-15 tons US$10; +16 tons US$15.*

These rates are valid for three days. After three days, sailors pay an extra fee of US$5 per day. The long pier accommodates ships with draft not exceeding 14ft, the short pier has vessels with draft of up to 10ft. Marine weather is on VHF 1 or 162.550 MHz continual broadcast. Blue Bead Restaurant sells ice.
Official time *Atlantic Standard Time, four hours behind GMT, one ahead of EST, all year.*
Voltage *110 volts A/C 60 cycles.*
Tourist office overseas *In* **USA/Canada***: Gail Knopfler, Classic Communications International, PO Box 6322, Boca Raton, FL 33427, T561-3948580, F4884294, statiatourism@juno.com In* **Europe***: Antillen Huis, Badhuisweg 173-175 Postbus 90706, 2509 LS 's-Gravenhage,* **Holland***, T70-3066111, F3066110;* **Germany***, T0692400 183, F069-24271521, Dutch.Caribbean-TC@t-online.de*
Communications *The international phone code is 599-1, followed by 5 digits.*
Clothing *No topless bathing anywhere on the island and men are not allowed to walk without shirts on in public streets.*
Public holidays *New Year's Day (fireworks at midnight), Good Friday, Easter Sunday, Easter Monday, Queensday (30 April), Labour Day (1 May), Ascension Day, Statia Day (16 November), Christmas Day, Boxing Day.*

southern part from Crooks Castle to White Wall is a restricted fishing zone; the wreck sites in Oranje Bay, STENAPA Reef (a modern wreck site) and the northern marine park are open for fishing and diving. Marine park fees are US$3 per dive, US$3 per snorkelling trip when using the park buoys, US$35 for a non-resident annual pass. You may not anchor anywhere in the park, spear guns and spear fishing are prohibited in all waters around Statia, nothing may be removed, whether animals, plants or historical artefacts, you may not touch or feed marine life. The marine park office is at Lower Town, close to the harbour.

Dive Statia is run by Rudy and Rinda Hees T3182435, F3182539, www.divestatia. com They have a comfortable, purpose-built, 26ft catamaran for diving, on which they take up to 10 divers and two dive masters/instructors. They also have a 14-ft rigid boat for training or special dives. A full range of courses is offered at this Gold Palm 5-star PADI operation, including nitrox certification, and families with children of 12 and above are welcome. They do three dives a day with night dives on request. All dives are fully guided, although photographers are allowed plenty of freedom to get the right shot. Most people take a package of dives, which is the best value, but if you just turn up a single tank dive will cost you US$35. Equipment rental is available, PADI Open Water four-day course US$350, snorkel trips US$25 with equipment, accommodation and diving packages available with most hotels.

Dive centres
You must by law dive with a local company

Netherlands Antilles

Morning glory

In 1884, a Dutch botanist, Willem Suringar, visited Statia, and collected a morning glory in fruit on Signal Hill which was described as new to science. Named Ipomoea sphenophylla *(wedge shaped leafed Ipomoea), it was not found by subsequent visiting botanists so the species was put first on the endangered list and then declared extinct. However, in 1994, a vine in the tree tops was found by Edwin Gawlik on the property of Statia Terminals which is believed* *to be the same pink-flowered morning glory. The area has been closed off and the plant will be protected. The same habitat is also home to a rare iguana and several orchids. Specimens of the plant are being studied in the USA, where it has been noted that the flowers are unusual in having many with free petals, a character not known in* Ipomoea, *while the insects that have been seen to visit and pollinate the flowers on Statia are not those usually associated with tubular flowers.*

On leaving Statia Customs officials may give you and your luggage a rigorous search if they discover you are a diver. They are looking for treasure, or artefacts – beware

Golden Rock Dive Centre, is opposite the *Blue Bead Restaurant*. Owned by Glen Fairs, T/F3182964, www.goldenrockdive.com One dive US$45, hotel/dive packages, PADI open water course US$350. *Golden Rock* also offers charter fishing and boat trips to Saba. *Scubaqua* (PADI, SSI, CMAS) is at the *Golden Era Hotel*, T/F3182160, scubaqua@megatropic.com with their own pier. They have one boat, taking 12 divers, and an inflatable for dive courses. Groups per instructor are no more than six and the captain stays on board the boat. Drift diving for whale watching is organized between end-January and April and they also offer waterskiing, wakeboards and fishing trips. A single dive costs US$29, equipment rental US$20, snorkelling trips with lunch on the beach US$25, full Open Water certification course with equipment is US$350. The *MV Caribbean Explorer*, 16-passenger, 100ft liveaboard, includes Statia in its week-long tour of the northeast Caribbean, with five dives in the Marine park. Contact Explorer Ventures Ltd, www.caribexplorer.com, see page 687.

Beaches and watersports

Oranje Beach stretches for 1½ km along the coast away from Lower Town. The length and width of the beach varies according to the season and the weather, but being on the Leeward side it is safe for swimming and other watersports. On the Windward side are two fine beaches but there is a strong undertow and they are not considered safe for swimming. **Zeelandia Beach** is 3 km of off-white sand with heavy surf and interesting beachcombing, particularly after a storm. It is safe to wade and splash about in the surf but not to swim. There is a short dirt road down to the beach; do not drive too close to the beach or you will get stuck in the sand. Avoid the rocks at the end of the beach as they are very dangerous. **Lynch Beach**, also on the Atlantic side, is small and safer for children in parts, but ask local advice. Stay near the shore. There is no lifeguard at any of the beaches.

Other sports   There is little to offer on Statia for the sporting enthusiast. At the Community Centre on Rosemary Laan: **tennis** (US$5), **basketball**, **softball** and **volleyball**; changing rooms are available. Tennis, volleyball and basketball also at Gene's Sports Complex, T3182711, as well as **table tennis**, **dominoes**, **checkers**, open Monday-Saturday 1430-2230, Sunday 0800-1800. There is also a children's playground.

Walking

The tourist office has a guide leaflet describing 11 trails. **Quill** hikes with local guides are available with a voucher system from the tourist office or participating hotels. Hikers should be aware that some of these trails are in bad condition, overgrown and sometimes difficult to follow. STENAPA is in the process of restoring and extending

Statia's trail system. They plan to make a trail from town to the botanical garden which will wind around the south side of The Quill. STENAPA also plans to restore the path around the rim of The Quill (damaged in 1989 by Hurricane Hugo). The foundation has built a new, clearly marked, trail from Rosemary Lane to the rainforest crater at the top of The Quill, which is remarkable for its contrast with the dry scrub of the rest of the island. After about 20 minutes' walk there is a left turn to The Quill. Carry on if you want to overlook the White Wall. The walk up to the lip of the crater is easy. You will see butterflies, all sizes of lizards, hundreds of land crabs and, if you go quietly, some snakes (for example the red-bellied racer snake). At the top in one direction is the panorama trail. The other direction leads to the highest point, called **Mazinga**, which affords a magnificent view. The first 10 minutes of the walk to the Mazinga is easy, then there is a turn to the left marked. From here it becomes a scramble because of hurricane damage. The last 20 m up to the summit itself is for the very experienced only. The plant life includes mahogany and bread fruit trees, arums, bromeliads, lianas and orchids. Although it is still quite a hike (approximately 45 minutes), the new path is in much better shape and it is not nearly as steep as the old trail. From the rim, hikers can walk down a path to the centre. The vegetation in the crater is very dense and a local guide is recommended. The crater is the breeding ground for land crabs, which Statians catch at night by blinding them with a flashlight. Charley (brother of Roland Lopes at the tourist office) works as a professional hiking guide. He arrives at dawn in full combat uniform and beret like Rambo and tends to go quickly without much explanation, fine for the walk round The Quill crater but better to go alone if birdwatching.

A road, and then a track, leads round the lower slopes of The Quill to the **White Wall**, a massive slab of limestone which was once pushed out of the sea by volcanic forces and is now clearly visible from miles away across the sea. You can also see it from **Fort de Windt**, built in 1753, the ruins of which are open to the public, at the end of the road south from Lower Town. St Kitts can also be seen clearly from here. About 14 forts or batteries were built around the island by the end of the 18th century but the ruins of few of them are accessible or even visible nowadays. STENAPA has made a new trail to the **Boven**, the highest peak on the north side of the island. This is a strenuous hike (four hour round trip and steep at times) but well worth it for the view, for dedicated hikers.

Oranjestad

Oranjestad is the capital, set on a cliff overlooking the long beach below and divided between Upper Town and Lower Town. The town used to be defended by **Fort Oranje** (pronounced Orahn'ya) perched on a rocky bluff. Built in 1636 on the site of a 1629 French fortification, the ruins of the fort have been preserved and large black cannons still point out to sea. The administrative buildings of the island's Government are here. The fort was partly destroyed by a fire in 1990, but has been restored since then. Other places of historical interest include the ruins of the **Honen Dalim Synagogue** built in 1739 (being restored in 2001) and the nearby cemetery. Statia once had a flourishing Jewish community and was a refuge for Sephardic and Ashkenazic Jews, but with the economic decline after the sacking of Oranjestad by Admiral Rodney, most of the Jewish congregation left. The **Dutch Reformed Church**, consecrated in 1755, suffered a similar fate when its congregation joined the exodus. The square tower has been restored but the walls are open to the elements. The surrounding graveyard has some interesting tombs. Legend has it that it was here that Admiral Rodney found most of his booty after noticing that there were a surprising number of funerals for such a small population. A coffin, which he ordered to be opened, was found to be full of valuables and further digging revealed much more.

On Wilhelminaweg in the centre, the 18th-century Doncker/De Graaff House, once a private merchant's house and also where Admiral Rodney lived, has been restored and is now the **Museum of the St Eustatius Historical Foundation**. There is a pre-columbian section which includes an Amerindian skeleton and a reconstruction of 18th-century rooms at the height of Statia's posperity. It is worth a visit for the graphic descriptions of the slave trade. Archaeological excavations at Golden Rock near the airport have uncovered a large Amerindian village with the only complete floor plan of Indian houses found in the Caribbean. All the houses are round or slightly oval, ranging in size and accommodating anything up to 30 people. Large timbers up to 8 m high were set in deep holes for the framework of the biggest houses. The museum contains some pottery buried in the ceremonial area of the village next to a grave. ■ *T82288, US$2 or US$1 for children, 0900-1700 Mon-Fri, 0900-1200 Sat, Sun and holidays, the curator normally shows you around, explaining the history of the exhibits.*

It is possible to walk round the village and see the sights in a morning. The museum or tourist office will provide you with a Walking Tour brochure listing the historical sites and other walking tours. In its heyday Lower Town stretched for 3 km along the bay, with warehouses, taverns and slave markets attracting commercial traffic. Parts are now being restored as hotels or restaurants. Seven privately-owned houses have been renovated as part of the Historic Core Development Plan. If you like beach combing, blue, five-sided slave beads over 200 years old can be found along the shore at Oranjestad.

Berkels family museum is on the Lynch Plantation, a domestic museum with a collection of household utensils and antiques on the northeast side of the island, T3182338.

Oranjestad (St Eustatius)

Essentials

The *Talk of the Town*, one of the longest established hotels, has been leased to the new medical school on Statia and is not seeking other guests for a few years. **LL-AL** *Old Gin House*, T3182319, F3182135, www.oldginhouse.com Now owned by *Holland House Hotel* on Sint Maarten and upgraded into a luxury place to stay. Built with old bricks of 18th-century cotton gin house, 2 fancy suites, 14 rooms, large beds, a/c, TV, phones, CP, the nicest place to stay, English manager, William, will ensure you have a wonderful time, credit cards accepted. **AL-B** *Kings Well*, between Upper and Lower Town in Kings Well, north end of beach by Smoke Alley, T/F3182538. Run by Win and Laura, popular with divers and sailors, rooms sparsely furnished but large, CP, ceiling fans, not always very clean, some rooms overlook bar, more expensive have superb sea view, accepts Visa/Mastercard. **A** *Golden Era Hotel*, Lower Town, T3182345, F3182445, goldera@sintmaarten.net On the beach, modern, 20 rooms, not much charm but convenient and dive shop on premises, manager Roy Hooker is also the cook, friendly but extremely slow service, snack bar/restaurant good, credit cards. **C** *Country Inn*, at Concordia near airport, Biesheuvelweg, owned by Mrs Iris Pompier, T/F3182484. 6 guest house rooms, noisy a/c but essential, TV, fridge, CP, other meals on request, hot and cold water, travellers' cheques but no credit cards. **C** *Henriquez Guesthouse* at Prinseweg, T3182424. On road to airport, 3 mins' walk, 9 apartments, 1 or 2 bedrooms, a/c, TV, mini-fridge, bar and restaurant, barbecue, weekly and monthly rates negotiable. Off the road towards The Quill, **D** *Daniel's Guest House*, on Rosemary Laan, T3182358. Unmarked, ask in Brown's supermarket at bottom of road, Miz Brown is very helpful, no hot water but use of kitchen, taxi available.

Sleeping
Expect a 7% government tax, 15% service charge on top of quoted rates & sometimes a 5% surcharge.

The tourist office has a list of home rentals

The Old Gin House, recently renovated, gourmet dining, Belgian chef used to have a Michelin star in Belgium. Creole and international food at the *Golden Era Hotel*, service can be slow. *The King's Well*, good lobster, steak, German food, Jaeger and Wiener Schnitzels, cocktails, friendly atmosphere, owners like to chat and play cards with guests, lunch is served 1200-1400, dinner from 1800-2100, reservations requested. *Smoke Alley*, Austrian-owned, open air restaurant overlooking the water, varied menu, Mexican, burgers, etc, a fun place to be, very popular, occasional live music, lovely place to watch the sunset, closed Tue. Cheaper meals at *Chinese Restaurant*, Prinseweg 9, T3182389. Shut Sun, tell cook not to put in monosodium glutamate, no credit cards. *Happy City Chinese Restaurant*, around the corner from Duggins Supermarket, T3182540. Open 1130-2300, a/c, no smoking, closed Wed. *Ocean View Terrace*, just by tourist office and Governor's House, T3182733. A nice place to take a break while touring town or to have a drink and watch the sunset, Chef Percyvan Putten has improved the menu considerably, seafood specials and shrimp creole highly recommended, daily specials are reasonably priced, sometimes have live music, happy hour and BBQ on Fri, good place to meet locals, although service could be friendlier, closed Tue. *Blue Bead Bar and Restaurant*, right on beach, T3182873. West Indian, American, Indonesian and international food, reasonably priced daily specials, lunch Mon-Sat 1130-1430, Sun brunch 1100-1430, dinner 1800-2100, bar hours 1000-2200, occasionally stays open later. *Cool Corner*, on the square opposite museum, T3182523. Currently the most popular bar on the island, run by Chucky, a friendly Chinese who manages to serve drinks, talk to customers and prepare decent Chinese food. *Sonny's Place*, next to *Mazinga Gift Shop*, T3182609. Popular hangout for locals and terminal employees, pool and football tables, music is good, if sometimes too loud, Sonny serves good creole and Chinese food at reasonable prices, lunch and dinner, chicken, fish and daily specials recommended, service can be slow.

Eating
Tap water is usually rainwater & not for drinking

Self-catering For fresh **fish**, go to the fish processing plant (Statia Fish Handling) at Lower Town opposite short pier, Mon-Fri, usually 0800-1300 depending on the catch, they will clean the fish for you. If it is not available at the fish plant approach the local fishermen at the harbour. Grocers sell frozen fish. Lobster is available fresh Nov-Mar. Fresh **bread** is baked daily in outdoor charcoal-fired stone ovens and best bought straight from the oven at "fresh bread time", which varies according to who makes it. Bake sales are announced by the town crier: open air **takeaway** meals of local dishes some Fri and Sat, from 1100, usually at *Charlie's Place* just

Netherlands Antilles

below *Mazinga Gift Shop* and Africa Crossroads Park opposite museum. Hotels serve purified water. Bottled water is sold at groceries.

Nightlife Statians like partying and every weekend something is always going on. Quite often you will hear a 'road block' from far away: cars stopped with huge stereos blaring and everyone jumping up in the street. Ask anybody what is going on next weekend, or just wait for the music to start in the evening. The only nightclub is *Largo Height Disco* by the cable TV station at Chapel Piece, closed Wed, busy mainly Fri and Sat, run by Pamela Hook, good zouk music and local food.

Shopping Lots of shops or businesses are in people's homes with no visible sign of the trade from the outside, but if you ask for help it will be willingly given and you will find the right place. Offices and stores are usually open 0800-1800, although supermarkets stay open until 1900. *Mazinga Gift Shop* sells local books and a wide range of gifts and duty free liquor, T3182245, F3182230. Some local crafts, mostly woodworking, are sold at *Paper Corner, Dive Statia* and *Under the Tree* next to *Allrun Supermarket*. Arts and crafts also sold at the *Little House on the Bay*, run by the St Eustatius Historical Foundation.

Festivals There are several occasions for celebrations during the year. On **Easter Monday** there are beach picnics with music and drinking. Former **Queen Juliana's birthday** is celebrated on *30 April* with cultural events, sports, food and music. **Emancipation Day** on *1 July* has ceremonies and celebrations of the abolition of slavery. The **Antillian Games** are held in the 2nd week of *July* with sporting competitions between all the islands of the Netherlands Antilles. **Carnival**, the main event of the year is held over ten days in *July-August*, is celebrated with steel bands, picnics, sports and contests and also including a Grand Parade on the last Sunday of the month. Just about everybody who can walk on the island shows up in costume and marches through town. **Antillian Day** is on *21 October*, with flag ceremonies, games and fetes. **Statia/America Day** is on *16 November*, with lots of cultural festivities and activities commemorating the First Salute to the American Flag by a foreign government in 1776. On **Boxing Day** actors parade through the streets depicting the social, cultural or political group of the year, stopping at various homes for food and drink.

Transport **Air** *Winair* has several daily 20-min flights from St Maarten (US$110 return) connecting with flights from the USA, Europe and other islands. There are other connecting Winair flights from Saba (10 mins). *Golden Rock Airways* can arrange charters. **Local** **Car hire** To hire a **car** you need a driving licence from your own country or an international driver's licence. The speed limit is 50 km (31 miles) per hour and in residential areas it is 30 km (19 miles) per hour. Companies include *Brown's*, T3182266, F3182454, US$45 per day including tax and insurance, weekend deals; *Rainbow*, T3182811, F3182586, US$35 plus US$5 CDW; *Walters*, T3182719, US$35 plus tax and insurance; *ARC*, T3182595, F3182594, US$35 plus tax and insurance, near airport; *Lady Ama's Services*, T3182712, F3182572, US$30-45, 5% surcharge on day rates; *Avis*, T3182421/3182303, F3182285, US$40 per day, US$35 second day (CDW is US$7.50 per day, US$50 per week); *Co-Rentals*, T3182941, F3182940, US$35 per day, 5% surcharge insurance and gasoline; *R/DSON Jeep Rental*, T3182149, US$30 per day, US$180 per week. Try *Lopes Car Rental*, T3182291, for **cars**, **motor bikes** and **donkey carts**. **Taxi** Airport to town is US$4, most other trips US$2-4 per person. An island tour costs US$40 for 4 people, US$7 for every additional passenger.

Directory **Banks** *Barclays Bank*, Emmaweg, T3182392, F3182734. Open Mon-Fri 0830-1530. The Post Office Bank, *Post Spaarbank*, is open Mon-Fri 0730-1600. The *Windward Islands Bank* is by *Mazinga Gift Shop*, open Mon-Fri 0830-1200, 1330-1530, T3182846, F3182850. **Communications** Post: the post office is at Fiscal Rd, T3182207, F3182457. Open Mon-Fri 0730-1600. Airmail letters to the USA, Canada, Holland, US$1.25 1st 10 gm, to the Caribbean US$1, postcards US$0.62 and US$0.51, aerograms US$0.71. Express mail is available. Limited banking services also available. There are special stamp issues and First Day Covers for collectors. *DHL* agent is Peggy van der Horde-Jacobson, Lampeweg 33, T/F3182401, packages to the USA US$22-30 1st 90 gm. Lady Ama's Services is agent for *Federal*

Express. **Telephone:** Fax and cablegrams at Landsradio, Van Tonningenweg. Open Mon-Fri, 0730-1930, Sat, Sun 1200-1800, pay phone on the wall for local calls, accepts only US quarters (US$0.25). For operator assisted overseas prepaid and collect calls, telegrams, telex and fax pay at counter when you place your call. Telephone cards of US$10 and US$17 can be used at phone booth outside near Police Station and at the corner of Korthalsweg, at the airport, at the harbour and the road to the airport, for local or international calls. **Medical facilities** The *Queen Beatrix Medical Centre* is on Prinsesweg, T3182371 for an ambulance, or T3182211 for a doctor. 2 doctors are on 24-hr call. Outpatient hours are 0800-1200, Mon-Fri, or by appointment, from 1400, Sat-Sun from 1000 for emergencies only. The resident dentist is Dr JM Tjien A Fat, at the Medical Centre Mon-Fri 0800-1700, T3182371/3182211 or at home T/F3182750. **Tourist offices** *The St Eustatius Tourism Development Foundation*, Fort Oranjestraat, Mon-Fri 0800-1700, T/F3182433, T3182213, www.turq.com/statia Tourism Information booth at the airport, T3182620; at the Harbour Office, T3182205. *The St Eustatius Historical Foundation*, Wilhelminaweg 3, PO Box 71, Oranjestad A255, T3182288, F3182202 c/o Eutel. The Foundation publishes a newsletter 4 times a year and runs the Museum (see above) and the Tourist Information Center and Gallery, 'Little House on the Bay', a replica gingerbread house, open Mon-Sat 0930-1200, Sun 1500-1700, but staffed seasonally by volunteers so opening times are approximate. Local artists and artisans sell their work here. *STENAPA*, Jan Faber, President, White Wall Road, St Eustatius, Netherlands Antilles, T/F3182661. Good information on walks, trails and conservation at the office by the dock.

Background

Sint Eustatius, or Statia, was originally settled by Caribs and evidence of their occupation dates back to AD 300. The island was sighted by Columbus on his second voyage but never settled by the Spanish. The Dutch first colonized it in 1636 and built Fort Oranje, but the island changed flag 22 times before finally remaining Dutch in 1816. The island reached a peak of prosperity in the 18th century, when the development of commerce brought about 8,000 people to the tiny island, over half of whom were slaves, and the number of ships visiting the port was around 3,500 a year. Trading in sugar, tobacco and cotton proved more profitable than trying to grow them and the slave trade was particularly lucrative, gaining the Island the nickname of 'The Golden Rock'.

The island still celebrates 16 November 1776 when the cannons of Fort Oranje unknowingly fired the first official salute by a foreign nation to the American colours. At that time, Statia was a major trans-shipment point for arms and supplies to George Washington's troops, which were stored in the yellow ballast brick warehouses built all along the Bay and then taken by blockade runners to Boston, New York and Charleston. However, the salute brought retaliatory action from the English and in 1781 the port was taken without a shot being fired by troops under Admiral George Brydges Rodney, who captured 150 merchant ships and £5mn of booty before being expelled by the French the following year.

With continuing transfers of power, the economy never recovered, many merchants were banished and the population began a steady decline. The emancipation of slaves in 1863 brought an end to any surviving plantation agriculture and the remaining inhabitants were reduced to subsistence farming and dependency upon remittances from relatives abroad. Prosperity has returned only recently with the advent of tourism and the island is still relatively underdeveloped.

History

See also background to the Netherlands Antilles, the ABC chapter, page 1045

56 km south of St Maarten and 27 km southeast of Saba, the island is dominated by the long-extinct volcano called 'The Quill' at the south end, inside which is a lush rainforest where the locals hunt land crabs at night. Visitors are advised, however, to go there only during the day. The north part of the island is hilly and uninhabited except for Statia Terminals, a fuel depot; most people live in the central plain which surrounds the airport.

Geography

Statia is quiet and friendly and the poorest of the three Windward Islands, with only 2,100 people living on the 30.6 sq km island. A variety of nationalities are

People

Netherlands Antilles

represented, the island having changed hands 22 times in the past, but the majority are of black African descent. Everybody speaks English, although Dutch is the official language and is taught in schools.

Economy   The traditional economic activities of fishing, farming and trading have been augmented by an oil storage and refuelling facility, but the major hope for prosperity, tourism, has had a slow start. Stayover visitors fell from 10,000 in 1994 to an average of 8,500 in 1995-97. Hotel capacity fell and the general quality also declined. However, in 1998-99 there was a small resurgence in the hotel business, with the opening of the renovated 14-room *Old Gin House* in town and the island is now popular with divers looking for something a bit different and off the beaten track. It remains the sort of place where you will be greeted by passers by and there is no crime.

Sint Maarten

Colour map 4, grid B1   *Shared amicably between Holland and France, this island offers you two cultures within easy reach of each other. Good international air transport links have encouraged the construction of large resort hotels with casinos and duty free shopping in the Dutch part. The French part is considered more 'chic' and crowded with restaurants is dedicated to the serious business of eating well. There are no border formalities, only a modest monument erected in 1948, which commemorates the division of the island three centuries earlier. Both sides have good harbours and marinas and are popular with the sailing crowd. Heavily populated, there are not many places on the island where houses have not been built, so this is not a place to come to get away from it all, but it is ideal for a fun beach holiday perhaps in combination with another quieter island nearby.*

Sint Maartin

■ **Sleeping**

1 Club Orient	5 Belair
2 La Samanna	6 Cupecoy
3 Pavillon Beach	7 Maho Beach
4 Royal Beach	8 Radisson
	Vacation Villas

N

Not to scale

Netherlands Antilles

★

A Foot in the door

- If you get a kick out of **shopping**, then this is the place to indulge yourself, with bargains galore, particularly just before hurricane season when many of the shops board themselves up and try and get rid of their stock.
- Visit the **French side for lunch**, where the food is, well, French and delicious.
- Have a day on the water, book yourself a **day-sail** on a yacht or catamaran to visit other islands, laze around and do some snorkelling – relax.
- If you are not bothered about staying on the beach, book a room in the delightful **Pasanggrahan Royal Inn**, the oldest hotel where the Dutch Royal Family used to stay and once the Governor's home.

Ins and outs

Sint Maarten has good long distance air connections, with charter and scheduled flights from Europe, the USA and the Caribbean. It is used as a jumping off point for many of the less developed or smaller islands in the area which do not have the capacity to receive large aircraft, such as Saba or Anguilla. The international airport is on the Dutch side of the island, but is used by both the French and the Dutch parts.

Getting there
See transport, page 686, for further information

There can be a shortage of **cars** or jeeps for hire in high season. It is advisable to request one from your hotel when you book the room. Out of season car rental is inexpensive. The roads on both sides of the island are very busy and full of pot holes, making them rather unsafe for mopeds or walking, particularly at night. There is a fairly regular **bus** service during the day between Philipsburg and Marigot but no regular bus service between Philipsburg and the airport. However, occasional buses run from Philipsburg to Mullet Bay, past the airport, US$1.50. Mini-vans or tour buses offer **tours** and are generally cheaper than **taxis**. Island tours from US$15; for more information ask at the **tourist office** on Captain Hodge Square or at the airport. The main tourist administration building is at the Vineyard Building, 33 WG Buncamper Road, Philipsburg. Free posters of Sint Maarten.

Getting around

Average temperature is 26.5° C, 80° F and average annual rainfall is 45in.

Climate

Flora and fauna

In 1997 the *Nature Foundation Sint Maarten* (T5420267, F5420268) was set up, with assistance from the WWF, to protect and manage natural parks and educate the general population and students on their significance. Two parks form the initial programme, a marine park covering the coastal waters and some adjacent coastline from Oyster Bay to Cupecoy Beach, and a hillside park in the Cul-De-Sac area. A nature conservation newsletter is published, which will give details of progress.

Diving and marine life

Water visibility is usually 23-38m and the water temperature averages over 21° C, which makes good snorkelling and scuba diving, from beaches or boats. **Wreck Alley** on Proselyte Reef, has several wrecks which can be explored on one dive. *HMS Proselyte* is a 200 year-old British frigate (mostly broken up and covered in coral, although cannons and anchors are visible), while *The Minnow* and *SS Lucy* are modern ships deliberately sunk as dive sites. Diving the east side of the island is recommended in good weather, either from the shore or drift diving from a boat. The coral barrier reef is undamaged by silt run off and there are lots of fish, fed by Atlantic currents.

Dive sites

Essentials

Documents *See page 1013. In addition, under a 1994 Franco-Dutch immigration accord, visitors to Dutch Sint Maarten have to meet French immigration criteria, even if not visiting the French side. Therefore, many nationalities now have to obtain a French visa before embarking on a shopping trip to Philipsburg. The local immigration officials are particularly concerned that you fill in your tourist card with a hotel address, even if you do not know whether you'll be staying there.*

Currency *Netherlands Antilles guilders or florins are the official currency, but the most common currency is the US dollar, which you need never change at all. You will get a poor exchange rate for French francs. It is often difficult to get change from payments in any currency other than US dollars.* **Credit cards** *widely accepted.*

Departure tax *US$6 when leaving for the Netherlands Antilles, US$20 for other destinations at Juliana Airport except for French visitors returning to Guadeloupe or France. Passengers staying less than 24 hours are exempt. Travel agents ask for US$3 to confirm flights. Airport flight information T52161.*

Boat documents *Yacht clearance is done at the port, both in and out. Off season hours 0900-1200, 1300-1600 Monday-Friday, 0900-1200 Saturday, longer hours in season, page port Authority for Sunday clearance.*

Ports of entry *(Dutch/French flag) Philipsburg and Marigot.*

Anchorages *Great Bay, Orient Beach, Oyster Bay, Marigot, Simpson Bay, Simpson Bay Lagoon Marinas: Great Bay Marina, Bobby's Marina, in Simpson Bay Lagoon: Simpson Bay Yacht Club, Island Water World, Port de Plaisance Marina, Palapa Marina. Mail/fax/phone: Dockside Management and The Mailbox. Charter fleets: include Jet Sea,*

Moorings, Nautor Swan, Sunsail, Stardust ATM, Sun Yachts.

Marinas *No fee yet for Simpson Lagoon bridge. Dutch bridge openings 0600, 1100, and 1730, outbound boats first. The French side opens Monday-Saturday 0900, 1400, 1730, Sunday 0900, 1730. Good groceries and laundry in Lagoon. Radio net VHF 78 at 0730. Send mail with someone flying out or Federal Express. Duty free Caribbean headquarters for boat parts, outboard motors, beer.*

Tourist offices overseas *Holland Minister Plenipotentiary of the Netherlands Antilles, Antillenhuis, Badhuisweg 173-175, Postbus 90706, 2509 LS's-Gravenhage, T070-3066111, F070-3066110.* **Canada** *3300 Bloor Street West, Suite 3120-Centre Tower, Toronto, Ontario M8X 2X3, T416-2334348, F416-2339376.* **USA** *St Maarten Tourist Bureau, 675 Third Avenue, Suite 1806, New York, NY 10017, T1-800-7862278, 212-9532084, F212-9532145; Yesawich, Pepperdine and Brown, Public Relations Division, 1900 Summit Tower Boulevard, Suite 600, Orlando, FL32810, T407-8751111, F407-8751115.* **Brazil:** *Av Ipiranga 318, Bloco A, CEP 01046-010, São Paulo, T55-11-2145588, F55-11-2583575; Av Rio Branco 181-c, 3303, CEP 20040-007, Rio de Janeiro, T55-21-2201484, F55-21-2203212.*

Communications *The international phone code is 599-54 followed by 5 digits.*

Official time *Atlantic Standard Time, four hours behind GMT, one ahead of EST.*

Voltage *110 volts AC. Note that it is 220 volts on the French side.*

Public holidays *New Year's Day, Carnival Monday (April), Good Friday, Easter Monday, 30 April, Labour Day (1 May), Ascension Day, St Maarten Day (11 November), Christmas Day, Boxing Day.*

Dive centres Training with NAUI instructors or just equipment rental is offered by *Leeward Island Divers*, 6 Wellington Rd, Cole Bay, T5442262-3, F5442274, *Ocean Explorers* at Simpson Bay, T5445252, *Trade Winds Dive Center* at Great Bay Marina, T5475176, PADI and SSI certification also offered, US$45 single tank 15m dives 0900, 1100, 1300 Monday-Friday, 1000, 1300 Saturday, Sunday.

Beaches and watersports

Every conceivable form of watersport is usually available Surfing is possible all year round from different beaches depending on the time of the year. The bays on the south and west shores are excellent for swimming, diving and fishing, and the beaches are of fine white sand. The most popular beach is

Hurricanes Luis and Lenny

St Maarten was one of the islands worst hit by Hurricane Luis in September 1995. Six people were killed, damage of US$1bn was reported and at least 2,000 people lost their jobs in the tourist industry when hotels and about 300 yachts were smashed. The shanty towns housing Haitians and Dominicans (many of them illegal immigrants) were flattened and the Government moved quickly to bulldoze the remains, offering jobs and a tent camp for those with papers and deportation for those without. Rebuilding of public buildings, including the hospital, started quickly; cruise ships returned in October but the airport was closed to commercial traffic until November. Only a third of all the private homes were insured, while others (including the Dawn Beach Resort) were victims of a crooked insurance broker who
disappeared with their premiums. Only half the island's hotel rooms were open for the winter season and several resorts remained closed. The hurricane highlighted low building standards and dodgy construction practices, particularly with newer houses. As soon as Phillipsburg got back to normal, it was hit by another hurricane, and then another, until it had been hit by a total of six in 1996-99. In November 1999, Lenny struck from the Caribbean side, bringing winds and floods and more death and damage. Most hotels closed for repairs, flights were cancelled and cruise ships stayed away until December. Many insurance companies have decided to cease providing cover for Sint Maarten. Many businesses nowshut at the beginning of the hurricane season in June, boarding up their property until the coast is clear again.

Mullet Bay, where you can rent umbrellas, beach chairs et cetera. It can get crowded in season and all weekends. On the east side is **Oyster Pond**, a land-locked harbour which is difficult to enter because of the outlying reefs, but which is now home to a yacht club and is a centre for bare boat charter. **Dawn Beach** nearby is popular with body surfers and snorkelling is good because of the reefs just offshore; **Guana Bay**, next to Dawn Beach, is the bodysurfers' best beach. **Maho Beach**, by the airport, has regular Sunday beach parties with live music competitions; don't forget to duck when planes arrive. The most westerly beach on the Dutch side of the island is **Cupecoy**, where rugged sandstone cliffs lead down to a narrow sandy beach, providing morning shade and a natural wind-break. This is the only beach where nudity is more or less accepted.

There are **boat charter companies** with sailing boats and motor boats, with or without a crew. You find most of them around Bobby's Marina, Philipsburg, from US$200 a day for bare boat. There are around 40 boats offering different trips around the islands, some just going out for snorkelling on the reefs or taking cruise ship passengers around. The *Swaliga*, a motor catamaran (US$50 per person plus US$7 port charge) sails daily to St Barts from Philipsburg. Also the 70-ft motor cata-maran, *Quicksilver*. There are several other sailings from Philipsburg which can be booked through Dockside Management (T5423436-7, F5422858) or hotels. On cer-tain days there are sailings from Pelican Marina at Simpson Bay, or from Marigot. The trip to St Barts is normally quite rough and unpleasant on the way there but more pleasant on the return journey. Check the weather, the swell and the waves can be up to 3½ m even on a nice day. The *Golden Eagle*, a new wing mast 76-ft catama-ran sails to Tintamarre from Great Bay Marina, four hours, US$45 per person, breakfast on board, snorkelling gear, T575828/5430068. Most boats offer some snacks, sodas and rum punch. Trips cost from US$50-75, plus departure tax. Check what is available from Marigot too. Some of the time share resorts offer free boat trips with snorkelling, lunch, taxis, (you pay departure tax), if you participate in a sales drives. For **fishing** there are numerous boats available for a whole (US$500-750) or half (US$280-375) day from Bobby's Marina, Pelican Marina or Great Bay Marina. Arrangements can be made through the hotels or contact *Lee-ward Islands Divers*, see above, or *Rudy's Fishing*, Beacon Hill, T5452177. Marlin, barracuda, dolphin (not the mammal) and tuna are the best catches. Game fishing tournaments are held all year round.

Netherlands Antilles

The largest annual regatta, the **Heineken Regatta**, takes place each February or March and lasts for three days with a round the island race on the Sunday. It is well attended with nearly 300 boats in nine classes. A race to Nevis and back is held in mid-June with a day for resting/parties. Other regattas held are for catamarans, match racing with charter boats, windsurfing et cetera. For more information check with St Martin Yacht Club, Simpson Bay (La Palapa Marina) or ask Robbie Ferron at Budget Marina in Philipsburg. A popular half day excursion is match racing on *Canada II, True North, True North IV* or *Stars and Stripes*, boats from the Americas Cup, US$60, races Wednesday 1315, three hours (T5443354, Bobby's Marina).

Other sports   All the large hotels have **tennis** courts, many of which are lit for night play, but check availability. There is an 18-hole championship **golf** course at *Mullet Bay Resort*, which stretches along the shores of Mullet Pond and Simpson Bay Lagoon. Running is organized by the *Road Runners Club*, St Maarten, with a fun run of 5-10 km every Wednesday at 1730 and Sunday at 1830, starting from the *Pelican Resort & Casino* car park. On Sunday at 0700 there are two 20 km runs. There are monthly races with prizes and an annual relay race around the island to relive the legendary race between the Dutch and the French when they divided the island. Contact Dr Fritz Bus at the *Back Street Clinic* or Malcolm Maidwell of *El Tigre*, T5444309/5422167. *Crazy Acres* Riding Centre takes groups **horseriding** every weekday morning at 0900 from the Wathey Estate, Cole Bay, to Cay Bay, where horses and riders can swim, T5442793. Make reservations two days in advance. *Lucky Stables* in Cape Bay, T5445255, F5442371, takes groups on a 2-hour trail and beach ride, daily, three rides a day at 0930, 1500 and 2030, US$50 per person, children under 12 US$30.

Philipsburg

Philipsburg, the capital of Dutch St Maarten, is built on a narrow strip of sandy land between the sea and a shallow lake which was once a salt pond. It has two main streets, Front and Back, and a ringroad built on land reclaimed from the salt pond, which all run parallel to Great Bay Beach, perhaps the safest and cleanest city beach anywhere. A lot of sand was lost during Hurricane Lenny, but it was replenished in April 2000 and is now a beautiful 20-m wide beach. Front Street is full of shops offering duty-free goods. Back Street contains low cost clothes shops and low budget Chinese restaurants.

The **St Maarten Museum** at Museum Arcade on 7 Front Street, is a restored 19th-century house, exhibiting the history and culture of the island. There is a museum shop. ■ *1000-1600 Mon-Fri, 0900-1200 Sat, closed Sun.* The historic **Courthouse** dating from 1793, on De Ruyterplein, better known as Wathey Square, faces the pier. In the past it has been used as a Council Hall, a weigh station, jail and until 1992, a Post Office. Now renovated, it is used exclusively as a courthouse.

The **harbour** is frequented by cruise ships and a host of smaller craft and the town gets very crowded when cruise ships are in port. Captain Hodge's Wharf can handle 1,800 passengers per hour and has a tourist information desk, telephones, toilets, taxis and live entertainment, but in January 2001 a new cruise ship harbour was opened outside Philipsburg where cruise ships now dock. For information on outdoor concerts, choirs, theatre and art exhibitions, ask at the Cultural Center of Philipsburg on Back Street (T5422056).

There is a **zoo** on Arch Road in Madam Estate, close to New Amsterdam shopping centre (difficult to find, ask for directions), with a small exhibition of the fauna and flora from the islands. ■ *T5432030, US$5, children 2-12 years US$2, weekdays 0900-1700, weekends 1000-1800.*

There are several ruined fortresses, but not a lot remains of them. **Fort Amsterdam** was the first Dutch fort in the Caribbean, built in 1631 but captured by the Spanish in 1633 and partly pulled down before they left the island in 1648. It was still used for military purposes until the 19th century and as a signalling and communications station until the 1950s. Fort Amsterdam can be reached through the grounds of a private timeshare development. The guard allows visitors to park outside and walk to the fort. **Fort Willem** has a television transmitting tower and there is a good view from the top. Construction was started by the British, who called it Fort Trigge, at the beginning of the 19th century, but the Dutch renamed it in 1816. Fort Bel-Air and Sint Peter's Battery gave way to modern development although a few ruins are still visible near Great Bay Marina.

You can take a day trip round the island, visiting the ruined Fort Amsterdam overlooking Philipsburg and the French part of the island. It is well worth having lunch in one of the many French restaurants in Grand Case or the other French villages. Generally, however, there is not much of either historical or natural interest to see on the island, and most excursions are day trips to neighbouring islands: Anguilla, St Barthélémy, Saba, St Eustatius, St Kitts or Nevis, either by boat (see Beaches and watersports) or by plane. Timeshare resorts such as *Pelican* and *Divi Little Bay* offer trips to other islands and excursions in return for listening to their sales pitch.

Around the island

Essentials

There is a 5-8% Government tax on all hotel bills and a 10-15% service charge. Some add an energy surcharge. Prices are high but package deals in summer can be good value if you are prepared to shop around.

Sleeping
Camping is safe but seek permission from landowner

Large resort hotels **LL-L** *The Towers At Mullet Bay*, close to airport, 8 km from Philipsburg, T5453069, F5452147. Casino, watersports, golf, tennis, pool, 81 units, a/c, kitchenettes, TV, VCR etc. **LL-L** *Cupecoy Beach Club*, perched on a cliff above Cupecoy beach, T5452086 T/F5452243, kbtsales@up.net   Condo/villa resort, pool, tennis, casino. **LL-L** *Maho Beach Resort & Casino*, T5452115, F5453180. 615 rooms/suites, casino, pool, tennis, 20% service charge, right by airport. **LL-A** *Pelican Resort & Casino*, on Simpson Bay, T/F5442503, F5442133, info@pelicanresort.com   5 pools, tennis etc, 342 1-2 bedroom suites, lots of facilities. **LL-AL** *Divi Little Bay Beach Resort*, Fort Amsterdam, T5422333, F5425410. 159 rooms, tennis, 2 pools, watersports. **LL-AL** *Great Bay Beach Hotel & Casino*, T5422446, F5423859, greatbay@mail.com   Convenient for Philipsburg, all resort facilities, all-inclusive packages available, activities organized, games around the pool, barbecue buffet Mon, 285 rooms-suites.

Mid-sized hotels and resorts **LL** *Belair Hotel*, at Little Bay, T5423362, F5425295, belair@sintmaarten.net   67 1-2 bedroomed suites, tennis, pool, open air restaurant. **LL-AL** *Holland House Hotel*, T5422572, F5424673, hollandhousehotel@megatropic.com   54 rooms downtown, most with kitchenettes, open air restaurant, on the beach, convenient, see 'Nightlife'. **LL-AL** *La Vista*, near *Pelican*, T5443005, F5443010, lavista@megatropic.com   24 suites and cottages, tennis, pool, horse riding. **A-C** *Seaview Hotel*, on Great Bay Beach, Philipsburg, T5422323, F5424356. 45 rooms, some with showers, casino, a/c, TV, children under 12 free. **LL-L** *Atrium Resort*, Kim Sha Beach in Simpson Bay, T5422126, F5442128, atrium@sintmaarten.net   87 1-2 bedroom suites, beach front restaurant, wheelchair facilities, watersports etc at the *Pelican*. **LL-L** *Caravanserai*, Beacon Hill Road 2, on Burgeux Bay, close to airport, T5454000, F5454001. Shopping mall, casino etc, 118 deluxe suites and bungalows, coffee shop, pool, tennis, whirlpool. Also on Simpson Bay, **LL-C** *White Sands Beach Club*, T5454370, F5452245. 11 rooms, private retreat, couples only, special deals for cash customers, all beach front units, no restaurant but several nearby. Airport runway runs parallel to this part of Simpson Bay. **LL-AL** *Radisson Vacation Villas at Oyster Bay*, on peninsula, T5436040, F5436695, oyster@sintmaarten.net   Formerly known as *Oyster Bay Beach Resort*, 40 rooms, next to Dawn Beach in large grounds, pool, watersports, boat rental. **LL-L** *Princess Heights*, 156 Oyster Pond Road, Dawn Beach, T5436906, F5436007, emillee@megatropic.com   15 luxury villas with full kitchens, pool.

Netherlands Antilles

Small hotels **L-A** *Pasanggrahan Royal Inn*, in Philipsburg, T5423588, F5422885. Formerly the Governor's home, the oldest inn and where the Dutch royal family would stay when visiting Sint Maarten, 30 rooms, pool, no children under 12, nice atmosphere. **LL-A** *Summit Resort Hotel*, on hill overlooking lagoon with view of Marigot, T5452150, F5452615, info@thesummitresort.com   A/c suites with king size bed and queen size sofa bed, balconies, kitchenettes, pool with view from sundeck, tennis, beach shuttle, outdoor café. **LL-A** *Mary's Boon Beach Plantation*, on Simpson Bay beach, T5454235, F5453403, info@marysboon.com   14 studios with kitchenettes, pets welcome but no children under 14. **B-C** *Sea Breeze*, 8 Welgelegen Rd, Cay Hill, T5426054, F5426057, seabreeze@sintmaarten.net   5 mins from Little Bay Beach, 30 rooms, most with kitchenette, pool, quaint residential area. **B** *Midtown Motel*, 42 Back St, T5426838. Built end 1995, clean, modern, very friendly, near shops, casinos etc, now also a *Midtown Motel II* in Philipsburg, T5420590.

Apartments The Tourist Office has a list of apartments, villas and houses to rent weekly or monthly. The best way of finding an apartment is to look in the newspaper. There are several apartments for rent on Back St. A studio will cost about US$400-500 per week in a good location. Apartments at Simpson Bay Beach cost US$350-500 per week.

Front Street (guest houses) **C-E** *Marcus*, 7 rooms, T5422419, **E** *Seaside*, 5 rooms. On **Back St**: **B-C** *Lucy's*, T5422995. 9 rooms, clean and adequate, friendly and helpful, but overpriced, no children under 6; **C-E** *Jose's*, T5422231. Prepay for 6 nights, get 7th free, 11 rooms, very basic, mosquitoes and cock roaches. **AL-C** *Joshua Rose*, 17 Back St, T5424317, F5430080, joshrose@sintmaarten.net. Slightly better, a/c but still mosquitoes, 14 rooms, walk to beach, Chinese Restaurant.

Simpson Bay **AL-B** *Morning Glory*, 6 Roberts Drive, T/F5445288, lucybaker@megatropic.com. 14 apartments on beach, no credit cards. **L-AL** *The Horny Toad*, 2 Vlaun Drive, T5454323, F5453316, hornytoad@sintmaarten.net   8 studios, no children under 7,

Philipsburg

right on beach, not seriously troubled by aircraft noise, well cared for, pretty patio gardens. **A-B** *Calypso*, PO Box 65, Simpson Bay, T5454233, F5452881. 8 efficiency apartments.

Pointe Blanche A-B *Great Bay Marina*, T5422167. 10 rooms, fridge, a/c, TV, grocery, pier facilities. **AL-B** *Tamarind*, Goldfinch Rd, Point Blanche, near Philipsburg, T5422246, tamarind@sintmaarten.net   48 apartments with kitchenettes, swimming pool, deli.

Cole Bay A-B *Carl's Unique Inn*, Orange Grove, T5442812, F5445376, carlsinn@ sintmaarten.net. 16 a/c studios and rooms including breakfast, meeting facilities, bakery and grocery downstairs. **C** *Ernest*, Bush Road 36, T5422003. Swimming pool, 16 rooms, a/c, TV. **B-C** *George's Guesthouse I & II*, T5422126, T/F5445363. 10 rooms in Cole Bay, 10 rooms in Philipsburg, a/c, kitchen.

All the major hotels have restaurants with international cuisine. The traditional local liqueur is *guavaberry*, made from rum and the local berries, whose botanical name is *Eugenia Floribunda*. They are not related to guavas. The berries are found on the hills and ripen just before Christmas. Used nowadays mostly in cocktails.   **Eating**

Philipsburg Expensive*Le Bec Fin*, Front St 119, T5422976. French, elegant, favoured by the Dutch Royal Family and winner of awards, allow US$60 per person. Highly recommended. *Le Bec Fin Café* serves American and seafood. Front St is full of good restaurants. Americanized French at *L'Escargot*, Front St 84, T5422483. Prices around US$50 per person. *Da Livio*, west end, T5422690. High class Italian restaurant on waterfront, run by Livio Bergamasco and his British wife, excellent seafood and pasta, not cheapat around US$60 per person for a full meal, excellent service, best waiters. *San Marco*, Front St, is an Italian restaurant, nice location overlooking sea, good for a break from shopping, T5422166. **Moderate** *Shiv Sagar*, Front St 3, T5422299. Indian food, large portions, Tandoori specialities. Indonesian rijsttafel at for US$30-40 per person at *Old Captain*, Front St 121. *Mark's Place*, at Bush

Rd 70, next to the Food Center supermarket, has European food for US$20-30 per person. On the waterfront you can find a Japanese Sushi Bar and a Chinese restaurant. **Cheap** *Kan Kantrie*, Front St 5, right on the beach. Authentic Surinamese and local cuisine, wonderful food for less than US$10. *The Jerk Grill and Bar*, EC Richardson St 29, opposite the police station. Local and Jamaican food, very popular with tourists and locals, US$10 per person. *Anand*, Hotelsteeg 5, T5425706, in the alley next to *L'Escargot*. Indian restaurant, cheap, popular with tourists and locals alike, US$20 per person. *Harbour View*, Front St 89, T5425200, right by the sea. Very popular, European and local food at about US$15 per person. *The Big Cheese Bar and Pizzeria*, beachside terrace on Front St, The best pizza in Philipsburg, US$10-15 per person, also darts and snooker. For the budget minded try Back St where you mostly find Chinese and *roti* places. *Grill and Ribs*, Simpson Bay Rd, T5454498. The best ribs on the island, all you can eat for US$12.95, reservations essential.

Simpson Bay area *Turtle Pier Bar and Restaurant*, Airport Rd 114, T5452562. Reason-

Map labels:
N
Not to scale
Walter Nisbeth Rd
Government Building
Taxis
E Camille Richardson St
Vogestreet
To North Shore
Pharmacy
Cultural Centre
CA Cannegieter St
Terpentin
Library
Wilhelmina
Hendrik
Catholic
Wathey Square
Pastoristeeg
Old St
Dc Steeg
Front St
Secretarissesteeg
Joshua Rose Guesthouse
Pasanggrahan
St Maarten Museum
Bobby's Marina
Great Bay Marina
To Point Blanche

ably priced at US$10 maximum per dish with an interesting setting in a mini zoo with parrots, monkeys, turtles etc, live music 2 or 3 times a week; *Lynette's*, Airport Rd, T5452865. Local restaurant with good seafood and steak quite close to airport US$40 per person including wine and tip, weekly calypso revue with *King Beau Beau*, and upstairs is *Clayton's* sport bar, where you can see most major sporting events on a big screen TV. *Don Carlos*, T5453112. Tasty Mexican food, US$10-15 per person for dinner, open daily 0730-2230, Mexican buffet Thu, US$12.95, all you can eat. *Boat House*, T5445409. For drinks and food, live music several times a week, reservations essential. *Tokyo* Atlantis Casino. Cupecoy, sushi bar and restaurant. *The Greenhouse Bar and Restaurant*, next to Bobby's Marina at Great Bay, T5422941. View over yachts, menu includes hamburgers, steak and local fish, appetizers of chicken legs, potatoes, are highly recommended, the burgers are a disappointment, disc jockey, dancing, every night between 1700 and 1900, 2 drinks for the price of 1. *Vermeer Café* at New Amsterdam shopping centre. A Dutch coffee shop/café, very popular for late drinks. *Subway* is the place to find a healthy sandwich for under US$10, at Front St, T5420690, WJA Nisbeth Road, T5420679, and Airport Rd, T5453355. *Kangaroo Court Café* next to the Court House is popular with tourists, nice inner porch, sandwiches, all kinds of coffee and tea and freshly baked bread and cakes every morning. The most popular bars with nice sunsets are *Greenhouse* and *Chesterfield*, Great Bay, T5423484. Where you can find yachtsmen if you want to hitchhike by boat. On the French-Dutch border, *Captain Oliver's* has wonderful food in a perfect atmosphere with fish swimming under your table, live music and buffet on Sat nights.

Nightlife There are 9 casinos and they are a major attraction, most opening from noon to 0200. The largest is *Casino Royale* at the *Maho Beach Hotel*, open 1300-0400 daily. *Lightning* is across from Simpson Bay Yacht Club Marina on Airport road, also sport via satellite. The *Studio 7* discothèque at Grand Casino, Mullet Bay, is the most visited, entrance US$10 including one drink, can be higher if they have a special show, all drinks US$6, the disco starts late, recommended to pass the time in *Cheri's* bar, a 5-min walk away, when people leave there most head for the disco. *Comedy Club* (Maho) have stand up comedians Tue-Sun, 2130 and 2330, US$10 cover charge, most comedians from HBO or Carsons, well worth the price. Most resorts have live entertainment, such as limbo dancing, fire eating or live music, both local and international. *Holland House* hotel is popular with locals and tourists on Fri evenings when the best DJ in Philipsburg performs there. In Philipsburg, *The Movies*, on Pondfill, has newly released films, US$6. *The News* is good for dancing, with live music every other night, extremely popular. Look out for *Jack* (Irish folk songs etc), *G-Strings* (pop-rock 1950s-70s), *King Beau Beau*, the most popular bands of the last few years, whose music fills all the bars. Opposite the New Amsterdam shopping centre there is a bowling centre, with bowling allies, a cyberpub, restaurants and play areas for the kids.

Festivals Carnival starts in *mid-April* and lasts for 3 weeks, culminating in the burning of King Mouí-Mouí. It is one of the biggest in the area, with up to 100,000 people taking part. Most events are held at the Carnival Village, next to the University.

Shopping **Duty-free** shopping is a tourist attraction, but it helps if you have an idea of prices at home to compare, and shop around as prices vary. In the electronics and camera shops many outdated models are on display. European visitors planning to take home hi-fi or domestic appliances should make sure that they can be switched to 220 volts. Check your duty-free allowance when returning home. Most of the shops are along Front St. Open 0800-1200, 1400-1800. The large **food** stores have imported foods from Holland, France and the USA (good wine, beer and spirits prices). *Barrel Liquor*, 114 Old St (a mini mall), sells the cheapest **liquor** in town. Many liquor stores will deliver to your hotel or boat.

Transport **Air** **From Europe** *KLM* from Amsterdam in a joint operation with ALM, *Air France* and *AOM French Airlines* from Paris. **From North America** Charlotte (*US Air*), Fort Lauderdale (*American Airlines*), Hartford (*US Air*), Los Angeles (*American Airlines*), Miami (*American Airlines*), New York (*American Airlines*, *Continental*, *TWA*), Philadelphia and Pittsburgh

(*US Air*). **From the Caribbean** There are many from: Anguilla, Antigua, Aruba, Barbados, Curaçao, Dominica, Jamaica, Nevis, Pointe-à-Pitre, Port of Spain, Saba, St Barthélémy, USVI (St Croix and St Thomas), St Eustatius, St Kitts, Puerto Rico, Santo Domingo and the British Virgin Islands (Tortola), with a variety of regional and international carriers. The international airport is **Juliana**, at Simpson Bay. A taxi into Philipsburg costs US$10-12. If you need to eat while waiting for a plane, the best place is a bar/restaurant across the street with a supermarket. **Sea** There are no long distance sea communications except cruise ships which usually stay 5-9 hrs. *The Voyager*, a high speed motorboat leaves 0830 Thu from **Bobby's Marina** for Saba, return same day 1615, US$40 one way, US$60 return; *Voyager* also to St Barths, Mon, Tue, Wed, Fri, US$50 return, plus US$7 port surcharge, T5424096. Boats to Anguilla leave from the French side. See page 681 for boats to St Barths. The *MV Caribbean Explorer*, a 100ft, 16 passenger liveaboard dive boat leaves Philipsburg every Sat for a week-long tour of the northeast Caribbean including Saba, Statia, St Kitts. Contact Explorer Ventures Ltd, PO Box 488, Mabank, Texas 75147-0488, T903-8878521, F903-8878526, www.caribexplorer.com

Local Bicycle 2-wheeled transport hire from *Super Honda*, Bush Rd Cul-de-Sac, T5425712; *Moped Cruising*, Front St, T5422330; *OK Scooter Rental*, at *Maho Beach Hotel* and *Cupecoy Resort*, T5442115, 5444334. Mountain bike hire from *Tri-Sport Rent a Bike*, Airport Rd, T5454384, US$20 per day, delivery and pickup available, guided tours. **Bus** There is a fairly regular bus service from 0700 until 2400 to Marigot (US$1.50 Philipsburg-Marigot), French Quarters and St Peters, and from Marigot to Grand Case on the French side. After 2000 there are few buses. The best place to catch a bus is on Back Street. Buses run along Back St and Pondfill and only stop at bus stops. Outside towns, however, just wave to stop a bus. Fare is usually US$1 in town, US$1 for short trips, US$2 for long trips. There is no regular bus service between Philipsburg and the airport although the route to *Mullet Bay Resort* passes the airport. Buses on this route run mostly at the beginning and the end of the working day (although there are a few during the day) and drivers may refuse to take you, or charge extra, if you have a lot of luggage. **Car hire** Foreign and international driver's licences are accepted. Drive on the right. The speed limit is 40 kph in urban areas, 60 km per hour outside town, unless there are other signs. Many car hire companies have offices at the airport or in the hotels; free pick up and delivery are standard and you can leave the car at the airport on departure. Prices range from US$25-55 per day. Car hire companies include: *Risdon's Car Rentals*, J Irausquin Blvd 20, T5423578, and at Airport Rd, T5454239, F5425269; *Avis*, Airport Rd, T5452847 and at the airport, T5453959; *Hertz*, Airport Rd, T5454541; *Budget*, Airport Rd, T5454030, *Cannegie Car Rental*, Front St, T5422397, airport, T5454329 and at Simpson Bay, T/F5453465; *Empress Rent-a-Car* T5443637 and at hotels; *Thrifty Car Rental*, at the airport, T5454231, 5452373. **Taxi** There are plenty of taxis, which are not metered so check the fare first, which is fixed according to your destination. Trips to other beaches or tours of the island can be arranged with taxi drivers: island tour US$35 plus US$2 for each additional passenger; hourly rate US$10 plus US$2.50 each additional 15 mins. From Philipsburg to Juliana airport US$10-12, Dawn Beach US$18, Marigot US$15, Mullet Bay US$5, Pelican Resort US$8, all for 2 passengers, additional passengers US$2 each. Night tariffs are an extra 25% 2200-2400, an extra 50% 0001-0600. Pick up taxi at the square next to the Court House in Philipsburg (T5422359) or Juliana airport (T5454317). **Hitchhiking** is possible but allow 30 mins waiting time; it is definitely not recommended for women.

Airlines Airline offices at the airport: *ALM*, T5454240/5454210. *Air Guadeloupe*, T5454212. *KLM*, **Directory** T5454747. *LIAT*, T5454203. *American Airlines*, T5452040. *Air France*, T5454212. *Air St Barthélemy*, T5453651. *BWIA*, T5454646. *Continental*, T5452788. *Winair*, T5454230/5454237, F5454229/5452002. **Banks** *Scotiabank*, Back St, T5422262/5423317, 1% commission on TCs. *Windward Islands Bank*, T5422313. Charges US$5 per TCs cashed. *Barclays Bank*, 29 Front St, T5423511. *ABN-AMRO Bank*, Emmaplein, T5423505. *Antilles Banking Corporation*, CA Cannegieter St 24, Philipsburg, T5425908, other branches at Airport Rd and *Mullet Bay Resort*. *SFT Bank*, Airport Rd, T5452070. **Communications** Post: 2 safe places for holding mail are *Bobby's Marina*, PO Box 383, Philipsburg and *Island Water World*, PO Box 234, Cole Bay. It is not possible to send a parcel by sea, only airmail which is expensive. **Telephone:** telephone codes for the Dutch side of the island can be bought at

Netherlands Antilles

Landsradio telecommunications office in Cannegieter St, open 0700 until midnight, or at Landsradio's offices at Simpson Bay, Cole Bay and St Peter's. Note that card phones at Juliana airport, although marked as 'téléphone' and displaying instructions in French, do not work with French phone cards. **Internet:** *Notions*, cybercafé on the airport road near Simpson Bay. *St Maarten Yacht Club Marina Business Centre* and *Simpson Bay Marina Business Centre* have computers and email service. *Holland House Hotel* offers free internet service on two computers. **Medical facilities** There is a new hospital on Cay Hill with 60 beds, all basic specialism, a haemodialyse department and 24-hr emergency services, T140. **Ambulance:** T911. A helicopter airlift to Puerto Rico is available for extreme medical emergencies. **Media** **Newspapers:** *The Daily Herald* and *The Today* come out six times a week. After 1500 in the shops on Front Street or at the airport you can find US newspapers (*New York Times*, *Miami Herald* and *San Juan Star*). American magazines (30-40% more expensive than the USA) are especially good at Paiper Garden, Front Street. **Radio:** PJD2 Radio is on medium wave 1300 kHz and FM 102.7 mHz. **Tourist offices** Vineyard building, 23 Walter Nisbeth Rd, 1st floor, T5422337, F5422734, www.st-maarten.com. Well supplied with brochures and guides to St Maarten, and the monthly *St Maarten Holiday*. Sightseeing tours available by bus or by car. **Useful numbers** Police: T5422222. Fire: T5454222/5426001.

Background

History

See also background to the Netherlands Antilles, the ABC chapter, page 1045

The Amerindians who originally settled on the island named it Sualouiga, meaning land of salt. The belief that Columbus discovered the island on his second voyage in 1493 is disputed, with historians now claiming it was Nevis he named St Martin of Tours, and that later Spanish explorers misinterpreted his maps. Nevertheless, the Spanish were not interested in settling the island and it was not until 1629 that some French colonists arrived in the north, and then in 1631 the Dutch were attracted to the south part by the salt ponds. By this time, there were no Caribs left on the island and the two nationalities lived amicably enough together. Spain then reconsidered and occupied Sint Maarten from 1633 to 1648, fending off an attack by Peter Stuyvesant in 1644 which cost him his leg.

When the Spanish left, the Dutch and French settlers returned and after a few territorial skirmishes, they divided the island between them with the signing of the 23 March 1648 Treaty of Mount Concordia. Popular legend has it that the division was settled with a race starting from Oyster Pond. The Frenchman went north and the Dutchman went south, but the Frenchman walked faster because he drank only wine while the Dutchman's penchant for Genever (a drink similar to gin) slowed him down. Since 1648, however, St Maarten has changed hands 16 times, including brief occupations by the British, but the Dutch-French accord has been peaceably honoured at least since it was last revised in 1839.

At the height of its colonial period, sugar cane and livestock were the main agricultural activities, although the poor soil and lack of rain meant they were not very profitable. The abolition of slavery in 1863 broke up the plantation system and the population began to decline as ex-slaves left to look for work elsewhere. Most of the salt produced from the Great Salt Pond behind Philipsburg was exported to the USA and neighbouring islands, but by 1949 this industry had also ended and a further exodus to other islands took place. The remaining population survived on subsistence farming, fishing and remittances from relatives abroad.

However, in 50 years the island has become unrecognizable, hotels and resorts, villas and guest houses now line the shore and there is no bay untouched by tourism. In 1997, 885,956 cruise ship passengers spent a day in St Maarten (not including yachties), while 647,721 people landed at Princess Juliana International Airport to visit St Maarten (and French St-Martin), attracted by the duty-free shopping, casinos and a wide range of accommodation, as well as the beaches and watersports. Little of historical interest remains, except the walls of Fort Amsterdam overlooking Philipsburg, and a few other ruined fortifications, but this has not hindered the tourist industry, which is among the most successful in the region. For those who want more than sun, sand and sea, St Maarten's well-developed transport links make it an excellent jumping-off place for visiting other islands. Nearly 250,000 people are usually classified as in transit, making their way to other destinations with only a brief stop over in St Maarten.

Controversy arose in 1992 over the Dutch Government's decision in July to introduce 'higher supervision' of the St Maarten Island Council following an inquiry into its administration. The change meant that expenditure decisions by the island government had to be approved by the Lieutenant-Governor. In February 1993 supervision was tightened further with all major decisions requiring approval. There had been many reports of crime, corruption and financial maladministration and the USA was particularly concerned about suspected widespread drug smuggling through Juliana airport, where there were no customs controls. During 1993 several prominent members of government, including the hugely influential Dr Claude Wathey, leader of the St Maarten Democratic Party and former Prime Minister, his son Al Wathey, formerly the airport board chairman, Ralph Richardson, the former Lieutenant Governor, and Frank Arnell, the airport manager as well as other influential colleagues, came under judicial investigation in connection with irregularities in the airport and Great Bay harbour expansion projects. Investigations were also carried out in France, Italy and other countries. In 1994, the four men were jailed for forgery and perjury, while two Italians were jailed for drugs trafficking (Dr Wathey died in January 1998). The St Maarten executive council agreed to introduce customs checks at seaports and Juliana airport from January 1994 in an effort to control trafficking in arms, drugs and illegal immigration. The higher supervision order was extended until 1 June 1994 and France and the Netherlands agreed jointly to monitor air and sea traffic around the island.

In 1994 the electorate were asked whether they wished to remain part of the Netherlands Antilles, have separate status within the kingdom (like Aruba), have complete integration with the Netherlands, or be independent. At the referendum in October, 59.8% voted for the status quo, while about 30% wanted separate status. This was the lowest vote in favour of remaining in the Federation, compared with 90.6% in St Eustatius, 86.3% in Saba, 88% in Bonaire and 73.6% (in 1993) in Curaçao.

The island's council election in April 1995 gave five seats each to the Democratic Party (DP) and the St Maarten Patriotic Alliance (SPA). The latter had governed since June 1994 in alliance with the Progressive Democratic Party. The Serious Alternative People's Party (SAPP) won the remaining seat on the 11-member council and agreed with the DP to form an alliance which took office in July. The DP won 4,323 of the 9,536 votes cast against 4,177 for the SPA, while the DP's leader, Sarah Westcott-Williams won the highest individual vote with 2,204. However, the coalition government collapsed in October 1995 following the resignation of one DP commissioner and two from the SAPP.

In May 1999 new island council elections were held which produced a majority government and marked the end of unstable coalitions. The DP won seven seats, the SPA three and the National Progressive Party (NPP) one. In April 2000 the electorate once again was asked whether they wished to remain part of the Netherlands Antilles or become independent. A majority of approximately 60% voted for 'status aparte' like Aruba. However, so far the Netherlands have not agreed to this.

Geography The island is shared amicably by the Dutch, who have the southern 37 sq km of the island, and the French, calling their half Saint-Martin, who own the northern 52 sq km, an arrangement settled by the 1648 Treaty of Mount Concordia. The salt ponds in the south of the island attracted the Dutch and during the early 19th century the island enjoyed modest prosperity. With the abolition of slavery however, the population declined, as did the salt exporting industry. In the last 20 or so years the island has flourished once again, this time as a beach holiday destination. The Dutch side of the island has the main airport and seaport and the majority of tourists. The west part of the island is low-lying and mostly taken up by the Simpson Bay Lagoon, which provides a safe anchorage for small craft. The lagoon is separated from the sea by a narrow strip of land on which the airport has been built. The rest of the Dutch part is hilly and dry and covered with scrub, although it can quickly turn green after rain. The French side is noticeably Gallic and few speak English.

People The population of at least 62,000 (33,459 in St-Maarten and 28,518 in St Martin) has mushroomed with the tourist boom: the 1950 St Maarten census gave the total population at 1,484. While many of the residents were formerly ex-patriates who returned to their island, there is a large proportion who have come from other Caribbean islands to seek work. Few people speak Dutch, the official language, although Papiamento has increased with the migration of people from the ABC Dutch islands. Nearly everybody speaks English and there is a large Spanish-speaking contingent of guest workers from the Dominican Republic.

French Antilles

15

French Antilles

The French Caribbean Islands form two Départements d'Outremer: one comprises Martinique, and the other Guadeloupe with its offshore group, Marie-Galante, Les Saintes, La Désirade, and two more distant islands, Saint-Barthélémy and the French part of Saint-Martin (shared with the Dutch). Geographically, the main islands form the north group of the Windward Islands, with the ex-British island of Dominica in the centre of them. Saint-Barthélémy and Saint-Martin are in the Leeward group.

The larger islands of Guadeloupe and Martinique both have an area of mountains and forests where you can find rushing streams, waterfalls and pools for bathing in. The best beaches, however, are in the more arid parts, which are flatter. The smaller islands are fairly hilly but dry, particularly those in the Leeward group. Some beautiful French colonial architecture remains, sometimes with iron balconies and intricate fretwork, but many modern buildings are concrete blocks and lack charm, looking as though they have been picked up in France and dropped on the islands by mistake.

The islands have the same status as any Département in European France. The inhabitants are French citizens. The currency is the French franc. The people speak French. Visitors are often surprised by how French the islands are. The connection with France confers many benefits on the islands, which enjoy French standards of social legislation etc, but it also drives up the cost of living, which is rather higher than some other parts of the Caribbean. The African connection is also strong, dating back to slavery on the plantations. Most people speak Créole, a mix of African grammatical forms from a number of languages and much-adapted French vocabulary. There are African rhythms and instruments in the music and African influences in art and literature.

Essentials

Before you travel

Documents The regulations are the same as for France. In most cases the only document required for entry is a **passport**, the exceptions being citizens of Australia, South Africa, Bolivia, Dominica, St Lucia, Barbados, Jamaica, Trinidad, Haiti, Honduras, El Salvador, Dominican Republic, Turkey, when a **visa** is required. In 2000, for a trial period of three months, St Lucians were allowed to enter without visas for visits of up to 15 days. If successful, the scheme may be extended to other countries in the Organization of Eastern Caribbean States (OECS). Any non-EU citizen staying longer than three months needs an extended visa. Citizens of the United States and Canada staying less than three weeks do not need a passport, although some form of identification with a photo is required. An onward ticket is necessary but not always asked for.

Customs With the abolition of EU frontiers, Europeans are able to bring back the same entitlements as from mainland France. However you could run into problems if returning via Antigua, with a long, uncomfortable wait in transit. Take a direct flight to France if buying in bulk.

Money Banking hours are given under the various islands, as are the names of banks. There are money-changing offices in the big hotels and at airports. The French franc is the legal tender, but US$ are preferred in Saint-Martin and are widely accepted elsewhere. There is no limit to travellers' cheques and letters of credit being imported, but a declaration of foreign bank notes in excess of 3,500F must be made.

Vaccination Vaccination certificates are not required if you are French, an EU citizen, American or Canadian, but if you come from South America or some of the Caribbean Islands an international certificate for small pox and yellow fever vaccinations is compulsory.

Food and drink

Restaurants Restaurants divide fairly neatly into expensive French cuisine or more moderate créole. There is sometimes a *plat du jour* as there would be in France and, particularly in Guadeloupe, very reasonable three course *menu touristique* meals. Children may find créole food rather spicy.

Local cuisine A delightful blend of French, African, and Indian influences is found in Créole dishes, and the cuisine is quite distinctive. Basic traditional French and African recipes using fresh local ingredients; seafood, tropical fruits and vegetables are combined with exotic seasonings to give original results rich in colour and flavour. Here are local specialities not to be missed.

Ti-boudin, a soft well seasoned sausage; *court bouillon de poisson* or *blaff* is *lambis* (conch), red snapper or sea urchin cooked with lime, white wine and onions; *ragout*, a spicy stew often made with *chatrous* (squid), or conch, or with meat; *colombo*, a recipe introduced by Hindu immigrants in the last century, is goat, chicken, pork or lamb in a thick curry sauce; *poulet au coco*, chicken prepared with onions, *piment* (hot peppers) and coconut; chunks of steakfish (usually tuna, salmon, or red snapper) marinaded and grilled; *morue* (salt cod) made into sauces and *accras* (hot fishy fritters from Africa) or *chiquetaille* (grilled), or used in *feroce d'avocat*, a pulp of avocados, peppers and manioc flour; *langouste* (lobster), *crabe* (crab), *écrevisses, ouassous, z'habitants* (crayfish), *gambas* (prawns) and *vivaneau* (snapper) are often fricaséed, grilled or barbecued with hot pepper sauce. Also popular are *crabe farci* (stuffed crab) and *oursin farci* (stuffed urchin).

Main dishes are usually accompanied by white rice, breadfruit, yams or *patate douce* (sweet potatoes) with plantains and red beans or lentils. *Christophine au gratin*; a large knobbly pear-shaped vegetable grilled with grated cheese and breadcrumbs, or a plate of fresh *crudités* are delicious, lighter side dishes.

French Antilles

Tourist offices overseas

Belgium *Service Official Français du Tourisme: 21 Avenue de la Toison d'Or, 1060 Brussels, T25130762, F25143375.*

Canada *French Government Tourist Office, 1981 Avenue MacGill College, Suite 490, Montréal, Quebec, H 3A 2W9, T514-2884264, F8448901; 30 St Patrick Street, Suite 700, Toronto, T416-5934723, F9797587; Office du Tourisme de la Martinique au Canada, 2159 Rue Mackay, Montréal PQH 3G 2JZ, T514-8448566, F8448901.*

France *Office Inter-Régional du Tourisme des Antilles Françaises, 2 Rue des Moulins, 75001 Paris, T44778600, F49260363; Gîtes de France, 35 Rue Godot de Mauroy, 75009 Paris, T47422543. Guadeloupe Tourist Office, 43 rue des Tilleuls, 92100 Boulogne, T33-01-46040088, F46047403. Saint-Martin Tourist Office, 12, rue de Madrid, 75008 Paris, T3301-53424100, F43873285.*

Germany *Bureau du Tourisme de la Guadeloupe, Bethmannstrasse 58, 6000 Frankfurt AM Main 1, T0049-69283293, F69287544, guadeloupe@karibik.org; Fremdenverkehsamt Martinique, Westendstrasse 47-D, 60325 Frankfurt am Main, T49-6997-590497, F6997-590499.*

Italy *Via Larga, 7, 20122 Milan, T392-58486655, F58486222.*

Spain *Administration: Gran Via, 59-28013 Madrid, T5418808, F5412412.*

Sweden/Denmark *Ny Ostergade 33, DK 1101 Copenhagen, T45-33114912, F45-33142048; The Commercial Representative Office Nordic Countries, PO Box 4031 Fregativägen 14, South 181 04 Lidingo, T468-7655865, F7659360.*

Switzerland *Löwenstrasse 59, Postfach 7226, 8023 Zurich, T12213578, F12121644.*

UK *178 Piccadilly, London, T020-76292869, F020-74936594.*

USA *French West Indies Tourist Office, 444 Madison Av, 16th floor, New York, NY 10020, T212-7571125, F212-8387855; The Martinique Promotion Bureau, 444 Madison Av, 16th floor, New York, NY10022, T212-8387800, F8387855, Martinique@nyo.com; French Government Tourist Office, 645 North Michigan Avenue, Suite 3360, Chicago, Illinois 60611, T312-7517800; French Government Tourist Office, 9454 Wilshire Blvd, Beverley Hills, CA 90212, T310-2716665; Guadeloupe Tourist Office, 161 Washington Valley Road, Warren, NJ 07059, T88-4-GUADELOUPE, F732-3020809. French Government Tourist Office, Suite 205, 2305 Cedar Spring Road, Dallas, TX 75201, F214-7204010.*

Exotic fresh fruit often ends the meal; pineapples, papayas, soursops and bananas can be found all year round and mangoes, mandarin oranges, guavas and sugar apples in season. Ice cream (*glace*) is also a favourite dessert.

As in other Caribbean islands the main alcoholic drink is rum. Martiniquan rum has a distinctive flavour and is famous for its strength, but rum from Guadeloupe and Marie Galante has been equally praised. It is nearly all made from the juice of the cane, unlike elsewhere in the Caribbean where it is made from molasses. *Ti punch* is rum mixed with a little cane syrup or sugar syrup and a slice of lime and is a popular drink at any time of the day. *Shrub* is a delicious Christmas liqueur made from macerated rum and orange peel. *Planteur* is a rum and fruit juice punch. There is a huge choice of Martiniquan rum, recommended brands being Trois Rivières, Mauny, St James, Neisson and St Clément. There are different brands on Guadeloupe. Try Damoiseau and especially on Marie Galante, Père Labat. French wines are everywhere and are not expensive in supermarkets or even small village shops. The local beer is *Lorraine*, a clean-tasting beer which claims to be 'brewed for the tropics'. *Corsaire*, made in Guadeloupe, is bitter tasting and insipid. Locally-brewed Guinness, at 7% alcohol by volume, stronger than its Irish counterpart, is thick and rich. *Malta*, a non-alcoholic beverage similar to malt beer, is produced by most breweries and said to be full of minerals and vitamins. Thirst quenching non-alcoholic drinks to look out for are the fresh fruit juices served in most snackbars and cafés. Guava, soursop, passion fruit, mandarin, and sugar cane juice are commonly seen.

Drink
Tap water is drinkable

Background

History

Both the main islands were sighted by Columbus on his second voyage in 1493, but no colonies were established by the Spanish because the islands were inhabited by the Caribs (who are now virtually extinct); it was not until 1635 that French settlers arrived. Because of their wealth from sugar, the islands became a bone of contention between Britain and France; other French islands, Dominica, St Lucia, Tobago, were lost by France in the Napoleonic wars. The important dates in the later history of the islands are 1848, when the slaves were freed under the influence of the French 'Wilberforce', Victor Schoelcher; 1946, when the islands ceased to be colonies and became Departments (Départements d'Outre Mer - DOM); and 1974, when they each also became economic Regions.

Culture

Language   The cultural, social and educational systems of France are used and the official language is French. However, Créole is widely spoken on Guadeloupe and Martinique; it has West African grammatical structures and uses a mainly French-derived vocabulary. Although still not officially recognized, it is the everyday language of the Guadeloupean and Martiniquan people and can be heard on the radio, where some stations use it almost exclusively. English is not widely spoken, although it is becoming more common in hotels and particularly on St-Barts, where it is understood nearly everywhere and on St-Martin, where it is the common language. A knowledge of French is therefore a great advantage.

Carnival   Another feature common to the two main islands is the pre-Lenten Carnival, said to be more spontaneous and less touristy than most. There are also picturesque Ash Wednesday ceremonies (especially in Martinique), when the population dresses in black and white, and processions take place that combine the seriousness of the first day of the Christian Lent with the funeral of the Carnival King (Vaval).

Music & dance   Also shared are the African dances: the *calinda*, *laghia*, *bel-air*, *haut-taille*, *gragé* and others, still performed in remote villages. The famous biguine is a more sophisticated dance from these islands, and the mazurka can also be heard. French Antillean music is, like most other Caribbean styles, hybrid, a mixture of African (particularly percussion), European, Latin and, latterly, US and other Caribbean musical forms. Currently very popular, on the islands and in mainland France, is zouk, a hi-tech music which overlays electronics on more traditional rhythms. Guadeloupe has a more overt African culture than Martinique, and here, the *gros-ka*, now written as spoken in Créole, *gwo-ka* (Big Drum), has seven distinct rhythms, some, like the *Mendé*, directly attributable to African origins. Musicians such as Robert Oumaou work within this framework, outreaching via such styles as jazz to create new and vibrant music.

Customs   Traditional costume is commonly seen in the form of brightly-coloured, chequered Madras cotton made into a variety of elegant outfits. It is the mixture of French and Créole language and culture that gives Martinique and Guadeloupe an ambience quite different from that of the rest of the Caribbean. An extra dimension is added by the Hindu traditions and festivals celebrated by the descendants of the 19th century indentured labourers.

A Foot in the door ★

- Indulge in some noisy spectator sport at the raucous **bullock cart racing** on Grande-Terre.
- Tour the **rum** distilleries, taste the goods and, if you are still standing, visit the rum museum.
- Visit the beautiful gardens of **Le Domaine de Valombreuse** and treat yourself to some tropical flowers which will be packed for export to take home.
- Take a day trip to **Les Saintes**, or better still, stay overnight to really unwind into a traditional way of life.
- Hike through the forests, climb the mountains and cool off in the streams and waterfalls of the **national park on Basse-Terre**.

Sports The spectacles of cockfighting and mongoose versus snake are popular throughout the French Islands. Betting shops are full of atmosphere (they are usually attached to a bar). Horseracing is held on Martinique, but not Guadeloupe, but on both islands gambling on all types of mainland France track events is very keen.

Literature The dominance of French educational and social regimes on its colonial possessions led, in the 1930s and 1940s, to a literary movement which had a profound influence on black writing the world over. This was *négritude*, which grew up in Paris among black students from the Caribbean and Africa. Drawing particularly on Haitian nationalism (1915-30), the *négritude* writers sought to restore black pride which had been completely denied by French education. The leaders in the field were Aimé Césaire of Martinique, Léopold Senghor of Senegal and Léon Damas of Guyane. Césaire's first affirmation of this ideology was *Cahier d'un retour au pays natal* (1939); in subsequent works and in political life (he was mayor of Fort-de-France) he maintained his attack on the "white man's superiority complex" and worked, in common with another Martiniquan writer, Frantz Fanon, towards "the creation of a new system of essentially humane values" (Mazisi Kunene in his introduction to the Penguin edition of *Return to My Native Land*, 1969).

Guadeloupe

This is France in the tropics, the islands having the same status as any French département on the mainland. They have many of the same smells too: coffee, croissants, baguettes and other French foods, which you can wash down with French wines. Guadeloupe is really two islands: the western Basse-Terre, which is mountainous and forested, 'green Guadeloupe', with a huge national park on and offshore, and Grand-Terre, to the east, which is smaller, flatter and more densely populated. Large areas of the island are used for growing sugar cane, particularly on Grand-Terre and bananas and other fruits and flowers thrive on the rich volcanic soil of Basse-Terre. The best beaches are of golden sand from the coral limestone of Grand-Terre. Tourists come mostly from France. The outer islands of Les Saintes, La Désirade and Marie Galante are easily reached from Guadeloupe but are quiet and untouched by mass tourism.

Population: 422,000
Colour map 5, grid A4

Ins and outs

Getting there
See transport, page 714, for further details

All European connections are with France and there are several daily flights with *Air France* and other airlines from Paris, while *Aerolyon* has a scheduled service from a few other French cities. Apart from *Air Canada*, which flies from Montréal, the only other scheduled services from North America are Air France's daily flights from Miami, although connections can be made with *American Eagle's* flight from San Juan, Puerto Rico. Connections are good with neighbouring islands if you want to island hop. This is also possible by sea, as there are lots of ferries between Guadeloupe, Les Saintes, Martinique, St Lucia and Dominica. Cruise ships call frequently and are increasingly using the French Antilles as a useful stopover on their way back to the Mediterranean.

Guadeloupe & outer islands

Bus There are three main bus terminals in Pointe-à-Pitre, see page 714 for specific running times. It is possible to cover the whole island by bus in a day – cheap, interesting and easy, but exhausting. You can just stop the bus at the side of the road or wait at the bus stations in the villages. Buses are crowded at peak times; have your money ready when you get off.

Car Car hire is available mainly at the airport, but can also be arranged through the major hotels. A small, old Peugeot will cost about US$50 per day. International and local agencies

Getting around

Buses play zouk music at top volume – exhilarating or deafening, depending on your mood

French Antilles

Essentials

Exchange *Hotels give the worst rates, then banks, but their rates vary so shop around. Post offices change dollars but not all makes of travellers' cheque, slow service. The best rates can be found in Edouard Saingolet, Bureau de Change, rues Nozières et Barbès, Pointe-à-Pitre (T903463), open daily (morning only Saturday and Sunday). There is one exchange facility at the airport and it is closed all day Monday. There is a 24-hour automatic teller at Bas-du-Fort marina which accepts most European currencies, US, EC and Canadian dollars and yen. It can be difficult to change EC dollars.*

Departure tax *No departure tax. It is included in fares.*

Ports of entry *(French flag) Deshaies, Basse-Terre and Pointe-à-Pitre are ports of entry but Iles des Saintes is not. No charge for EU or US citizens. French forms to fill in.*

Anchorages *Pointe-à-Pitre has good groceries, marine supplies, fuel, water, free 220 electricity, bus to town from marina.*

Free dinghy dock in marina. Duty free fuel when you clear out of the country. Charter companies include Moorings, Jet Sea, Stardust ATM.

Voltage *220 volts AC, 50 cycles.*

Hours of business *Shops: 0800-1200, 1430-1700 weekdays, morning only on Saturday; **government offices**: open 0730-1300, 1500-1630 Monday and Friday, 0730-1300 Tuesday-Thursday. **Banks:** 0800-1200, 1400-1600 Monday to Friday.*

Useful addresses *Gendarmerie: T820059, **Police**: T821317 in Pointe-à-Pitre, 811155 in Basse-Terre; **Nautical assistance**: T829108.*

Public holidays *New Year's Day; Easter Sunday and Easter Monday; Labour Day on 1 May; Ascension Day; Whit Monday; 8 May VE Day; 27 May Slavery Abolition Day; National/Bastille Day on 14 July; Schoelcher Day on 21 July; Assumption Day in August; All Saints Day on 1 November; All Souls Day on 2 November Armistice Day on 11 November and Christmas Day.*

are represented. Pointe-à-Pitre has a dual carriage ring road which runs from Gosier across the Rivière Salée to the industrial centre at Baie-Mahault and south towards Petit-Bourg. **Taxis** are rather expensive; they are metered and some now accept credit cards. All fares increase at night. They are mainly found at the airports and outside the main hotels, although you can also phone for one. From the airport to Place de la Victoire, US$11-14, more at weekends. **Bicycles** can be rented.

Climate The temperature on the coasts varies between 22°C and 30°C, but is about 3°C lower in the interior. January to April is the dry season (called *carême*), July to November the wet season (*l'hivernage*), with most rain falling from September to November. Trade winds moderate temperatures the year round.

Flora and fauna

The comparatively low-lying Grande-Terre is mainly given over to sugar cane and livestock raising. Mostly a limestone plateau, it does have a hilly region, Les Grands-Fonds, and a marshy, mangrove coast extending as far north as Port-Louis.

The island's **national park**, known as the **Parc Naturel** (Habitation Beausoleil, BP 13 Montéran, 97120 Saint-Claude, T802425, F800546), the seventh largest in France, includes 30,000 ha of forest land in the centre of Basse-Terre, which is by far the more scenic part. As the island is volcanic there are a number of related places to visit. The park has no gates, no opening hours and no admission fee. Do not pick flowers, fish, hunt, drop litter, play music or wash anything in the rivers. Dogs are banned. Trails have been marked out all over the park, including to the dome of Soufrière volcano with its fumaroles, cauldrons and sulphur fields (see below). The national park includes three protected land and sea reserves, open to the public: **Les Réserves Naturelles des Pitons du Nord et de Beaugendre, La Réserve Naturelle du Grand Cul-de-Sac Marin** and **La Réserve Naturelle de Pigeon**, or **Réserve Cousteau** (see below). The waters after which the Caribs named the island come hot (as at the Ravine Chaude springs on the Rivière à Goyaves), tumbling (the waterfalls of the Carbet River and the Cascade aux Écrevisses on the Corossol), and tranquil (the lakes of Grand Étang, As de Pique and Étang Zombi).

A **Maison du Volcan** at Saint-Claude (open 1000-1800) and a **Maison de la Fôret** (1000-1700) on the Route de la Traversée give information on the volcano and its surrounding forest. From the Maison de la Forêt there are 10, 20 and 60-minute forest walks which will take you deep among the towering trees. The **Cascade aux Ecrevisses**, a waterfall and small pool, is about 2 km from the Maison (clearly marked) and is a good place to swim and spend the day; popular with the locals. Also on the Route de la Traversée is the **Parc Zoologique et Botanique** above Mahaut, which allows you to see many of the species which exist in the Natural Park, such as mongoose, racoon, iguana and land turtle, unfortunately in very small cages. ■ *Open 0900-1700. Entrance 25F, children 15F. T988352. It is worth a visit for the fine panoramic views from the café (free drink included in entrance ticket) and the Ti-Racoon restaurant is simple but excellent, serves lunch daily except Mon.*

The national park's emblem is the *raton laveur* (racoon) which, although protected, is very rare. You are much more likely to see birds and insects in the park. On La Désirade a few agoutis survive, as well as iguana, which can also be found on Les Saintes. Much of the island's indigenous wildlife has vanished.

The vegetation of Basse-Terre ranges from tropical forest (40% of the land is forested: trees such as the mahogany and gommier, climbing plants, wild orchids) to the cultivated coasts: sugar cane on the windward side, bananas in the south and coffee and vanilla on the leeward. As well as sugar cane on Grande-Terre, there is an abundance of fruit trees (mango, coconut, papaya, guava, etc). On both parts the flowers are a delight, especially the anthuriums and hibiscus.

Diving and marine life

On the Leeward Coast (Côte-Sous-le-Vent, or the Golden Corniche), is the **Underwater Reserve** developed by Jacques Cousteau. *Nautilus*, from Malendure beach, south of Mahaut, black sand, T988908, F988566, is a glass-bottom boat which takes you round the marine park, departs 1030, 1200, 1430 and 1600, US$11.50 adults, half price children 5-12 years. The boat anchors for about 15 minutes off **Ilet Pigeon** for snorkelling, but it is rather deep to see much. In wet weather the water becomes too murky to see anything. The boat is often booked solid by cruise ship visitors. Diving trips can be arranged at *Les Heures Saines*, T988663, at Rocher de Malendure, or *Chez Guy et Christian*, Plaisir Plongée Caraïbe, T988243, F988284, friendly, recommended for beginners' confidence, well equipped, packages with accommodation provided, at Pigeon, Bouillante. There are lots of other companies along this coast and on Grand-Terre, with no shortage of dive sites.

King Papyrus is a glass-bottom boat which runs excursions through the Rivière Salée and the mangroves of Grand Cul de Sac Marin, to l'Îlet Caret and coral reef off the northeast coast of Basse-Terre, see 'Day sails' below.

Beaches and watersports

Petit Havre is popular with its small coves and reefs offshore. Here are mostly fishermen and locals and a small shed selling fish meals and beer. The best is at **Ste-Anne** where the fine white sand and crystal clear water of a constant depth of 1.5 m far from shore make idyllic bathing; the **Plage du Bourg** in town is ideal for young children, the **Plage de la Caravelle** west of town, is excellent; part is public and part with access only through the *Club Med*. About 2 km from the town is the **Plage de Bois Jolan**, reached down a track, where the water is shallow enough to walk to the protecting reef. Further east are good beaches at St-François and the 11-km road to Pointe des Colibris skirts the Anse Kahouanne with lots of tracks going down to the sea; sand is limited but there are snorkelling possibilities.

Guadeloupe has excellent beaches for swimming, mostly between Gosier and St-François on Grande-Terre. More deserted beaches can be found on the northeast of Grande-Terre

French Antilles

On the north coast of the peninsula is **Plage Tarare**, where there is a good restaurant by the car park. This used to be a nudist beach, but nudism is now illegal. **Plage de l'Anse à la Gourde** has good sand and is popular with campers at weekends.

On the leeward coast of Basse-Terre are some good beaches. South of Pointe Noire on the west coast is **Plage Caraïbe**, which is clean, calm and beautiful, with restaurant *Le Reflet* (helpful owners), picnic facilities, toilets and a shower. A small, black sand beach, **La Grand Anse**, just west of Trois Rivières, has a barbecue and drinks (expensive) on the beach and a shower and toilets (which do not always work). In the northwest, **La Grande Anse**, 30 minutes' walk north of Deshaies, is superb and undeveloped with no hotels, golden sand but no snorkelling except round a large rock where the current is quite strong. Body surfing is good when the waves are big. Beach restaurant at the south end with charcoal-grilled chicken and rice. On Sunday local people sell hot créole food quite cheaply. The beaches on the north coast of Basse-Terre can be very dangerous and at **Plage de Clugny** there are warning signs not to swim as there have been several drownings.

Most of the hotels on the seaboard offer **windsurfing** for guests and visitors, and some arrange **waterskiing** and **diving** courses. Windsurfers gather at the *UCPA Hotel Club* in Saint François. The tradewinds are best December-May and the best places are St-François, Ste-Anne and Gosier. Courses and board rental are available at *Sport Away Ecole Nathalie Simon*, St-François, T/F887204, *LCS*, Ste-Anne, T881517, F881521, and *UCPA*, St-François, T886480, F884350. Surfing is also now popular at Le Moule, Port-Louis, La Pointe des Châteaux, Sainte-Anne and St-François. The *Comité Guadeloupéen de Surf* is at the *Karukera Surf Club*, Le Moule, T231093. There is also the *Arawak Surf Club*, T236068, F237589.

Sailing

Sailing boats can be chartered for any length of time from Captain Lemaire, Carénage A, Route du Gosier, 97110 Pointe-à-Pitre. With a crew of three the cost works out at about US$75-100 per person per day, excluding food, or US$250-300 per boat. There are two marinas between Pointe-à-Pitre and Gosier, and good, shallow-draught anchorage at Gosier. The **Route du Rhum** boat race is held every four years, with multi-hull boats racing between Saint-Malo and Pointe-à-Pitre. The record is 14 days, 10 hours and 8 minutes.

Day sails

There are several excursions offered, ranging from the booze cruise or sunset cruise variety to more scientific and educational trips

King Papyrus at Marina Bas du Fort, Gosier, T909298, F907171, takes you on an all day cruise to Ilet Caret with a visit to the mangroves. The mangroves can also be visited on water scooters, T887193 in St-François, or T850277 for excursions starting from Morne-à-l'Eau. *La Compagnie des Bateaux Verts, the Green Boat Company,* Marina Bas-du-Fort, T907717, F907920, starts with the Aquarium and then takes you to the marine park on the 48-passenger glass-bottomed *Kio*, with scientists on board to explain the oceanographic ecosystems. *Falling Star*, a 46-ft catamaran, offers all-day sails to the island of Petite-Terre, T885396, F887794. *Awak,* a 46-ft vedette with a glass bottom, also goes to Petite-Terre, T885353, F886043. From Pigeon Buillante there are several glass bottomed boat excursions: *Aquarius* has three 2-hour trips, at 1000, 1230 and 1500, T988730, F901185. *Nautilus* has two glass-bottomed boats and a submarine for visits to the ocean floor, see above.

Fishing

Deep sea fishing is best off the Côte-sous-le-vent, where the fishing area is about 20 minutes from Ilet Pigeon

Blue marlin, kingfish, barracuda, bonita can be fished all year round, but there are seasons for other species. There are lots of fishing contests organized throughout the year. Well equipped boats go out for full or half day excursions from Bouillante: *Fishing Club Antilles*, T987010, Francis Ricard, T987377; and from Le Rocher de Malendure: Franck Nouy, T987084, who also offers 5 and 8-day trips. Fishing boats also go out from Marina Bas du Fort and Gosier.

Hiking in the Parc Naturel, contact the *Organisation des Guides de Montagne de la Caraïbe (OGMC)*, Maison Forestière, 97120 Matouba, T800579. Approximate hiking times, mileage and description of terrain and flora are included in the booklet *Promenades et Randonnées*. **Horseriding** at *Le Criolo*, Saint-Félix, T97190 Gosier, T840486, La Martingale, La Jaille, T262839 and *Ranch Caraïbes*, T821154. Also *Horse Farm*, St-Claude, T815221, F819073, for groups of 6-12 people riding in the forest. In August a keenly watched **cycling** race takes place over 10 days, going to all parts of the island. Le Tour Cycliste de la Guadeloupe draws competitors from Guadeloupe and internationally and is an excuse for festivities and parties. The *Association Guadeloupéenne de VTT* (mountain biking association) can be contacted at Pointe-à-Pitre, T828267. For cycling tours of Guadeloupe, *Karucyclo*, T822139, 284659. There is one 18-hole, international **golf course** at Saint-François (T884187, F884220), designed by Robert Trent Jones on the edge of the lagoon.

Other sports
A guided hike to La Soufrière will cost around US$45, make sure the guide speaks a language you understand

French Antilles

Bullock cart racing is popular on the west coast of Grande-Terre and draws large crowds. They race along the flat, then turn sharply and charge up a steep hill. The wheels are then chocked and they have to see how far they can get, zig-zag fashion, with about 10 minutes of very hard work. Much shouting, plenty of beer, food tents and an overloud PA system. **Cockfighting** is very popular and there are pits all over the place. The season runs from November to July and involves serious gambling. The only pit open all year is Bélair, Morne-à-l'Eau, Tuesday, Thursday, Friday and Sunday, T242370. Visitors are welcome.

Pointe-à-Pitre

On Grande-Terre at the south end of the Rivière Salée, Pointe-à-Pitre is the chief commercial centre of Guadeloupe. The ports for commercial and cruise shipping are at its heart while the airport, Pole Caraïbes, is nearby. The inhabitants call themselves 'Les Pointus'. The city lies to the south of the Route National N1 to Basse-Terre and any of the intercepts will take you to the old city centre. It is quite compact, a functional city, variously described as characterless, or colourful and bustling. Its early colonial buildings were largely destroyed by an earthquake in 1843; nowadays it is an odd mixture of parts which could have been transplanted from provincial France and parts which are Caribbean, surrounded by low-cost housing blocks.

*Population: 141,000
Colour map 5, grid A4*

The central **Place de la Victoire** is where the French Revolutionary troops defeated the British invaders in 1794. Robespierre had sent his fellow Jacobin, Victor Hugues off from Paris with two aims: throw out the British and bring the Terror to the island. He brought a portable guillotine in his luggage, set it up here, and guillotined or shot over 700 whites, and even a few men of colour, for bearing arms on the British side. Most were from the plantocracy. Their estates were confiscated, and all slaves freed. The streets adjacent to the square contain the oldest buildings, mostly from the 19th and early 20th centuries. Note the Sous-Préfecture, once a barracks, which is now being restored. There are some flame trees at the north end and pleasant gardens. In the middle is a bust of Félix Eboue (1884-1944), the only black Governor in colonial times, 1936-38. There is a bandstand and lots of cafés surrounding the park with tables outside, very pleasant, but crowded with office workers at lunch time. At its south end is **La Darse**, where the inter-island ferries tie up. When the boats arrive/depart there is plenty of activity and chaotic scenes with buses and taxis fighting for space. At the southwest corner of the Place is a war memorial dedicated to *La Guadeloupe et ses enfants, morts pour La France 1914-18*, flanked by two First World War guns. Behind it is the **tourist office** in an old building. On the east side of the Square is the late art deco Renaissance Cinema.

Sights

The **Place de l'Eglise** lies northwest of the Place de la Victoire behind the *Hotel Normandie* and contains the ochre-coloured **Basilique de St Pierre et St Paul**, an 1840s structure held up by unusual metal columns supporting a gallery running around the top of the church with some elaborate gingerbread-style metal work.

Outside there is a bubbling fountain and a bust of Admiral Gourbeyre, the Governor who helped the people of Pointe-à-Pitre after the huge 1843 earthquake in which 5,000 lost their lives and most buildings were partially or completely destroyed (see also Fort Louis Delgrès, Basse-Terre). The square is flanked by the 1930s art deco Palais de Justice and looks colourful with stalls selling flowers on the street.

The red-roofed central **market** place (between rues Peynier, Fréboult, St-John Perse and Schoelcher) is indeed bustling, with the nearest thing to local hustlers, women (some wearing the traditional Madras cottonhead ties) who try to sell you spices, fruit, vegetables or hats. There are other markets on the dockside in Place de la Victoire, between Boulevard Chanzy and the docks and between Boulevard

Pointe-à-Pitre : centre

To Airport, Morne-à-l'Eau & Le Moule

To Trois Rivières & Basse-Terre

Rt Nat 1

R des Abymes

Rue Martin Luther King

Blvd Legitimus

R Félix Eboué

To Les Abymes

Cemetery

R Youry Gaganne

Sacre Coeur

R Paul Lacave

Rue Hincelin

Rue du Cimetière

Cultural Centre

Faubourg Fréboult

R des Citées Unies

Mairie

Arts Centre

To Gosier

Blvd Chanzy

Blvd Hanne

R Abbé Grégoire

R d'Ennery

Rue Bébian

Quai 4

Rue Nassau

R Lamartine

R Nozières

Basilique de St-Pierre et St-Paul

Rue F Arago

R Barbès

R Henri IV / Jean Jaurès

R Schoelcher

R Frėboult

R de l'Église

R Gal Ruillier

R Alsace Lorraine

Quai Lefebvre

R Sadi Carnot

Flower

R Alexandre Isaac

Rd de Champ-Bertrand

R Dugommier

R Vatable

R Peynier

Schoelcher Museum

RV Hugues

R Gambetta

R Cdt Mortenol

Fg V Hugo

To Martinique

R Achille René-Boisneuf

R St-John Perse

R Povence

Place de la Victoire

R Lethière

Massabielle

Quai Foulon

R Delgrès

St-John Perse Museum

Q Layrle

Sous-prefecture

R Massabielle

Quai 3

Quai Lesseps

Q Lardenay

La Darse

R Duplessis

Boats to Les Saintes & Marie Galante

R Denfert

Customs

R Dubouchage

Quai 2

Tender Pier

La Canne 'a Sucre (Creole)

R Raspail

Quai 1

To Bas du Fort, Gosier & Ste-Anne

N

Not to scale

■ **Sleeping**
1 Bougainvillée
2 Normandie
3 Schoelcher

🚌 **Buses**
1 To Basse-Terre & Trois Rivières
2 To Gosier, Ste-Anne & St-François
3 To Airport
4 To Abymes, le Moule & Anse Bertrand

Victor Hugues: Opportunist Revolutionary

A baker's son, from Marseille, Victor Hugues was determined to make his way in the world, and went to Saint-Domingue, then a French colony, now Haiti, where he found prosperity as the baker to the French army. However, the Haitians started their own revolution: ruined, Hugues returned to France, and saw his chance by throwing himself in with the most extreme revolutionaries. Though he had seen his brother and uncle killed in Haiti, he posed as a friend of the blacks, and was rewarded by being sent as Commissioner for the National Convention to the Antilles, to free the slaves, use them as the instrument to force out the British (he started revolts in St Lucia, St Vincent and Grenada with his agents), and seize royalists' property. He became the master of Guadeloupe, digging

up the body of the former British commander and exhibiting it. He seemed pitiless. He was also greedy: he soon married a rich planter's daughter, and put the 'freed' slaves to forced labour in the cane fields, at which they were made to sing revolutionary songs in praise of the Republic. The US government put pressure on Paris to remove him (he was interfering with US trade). French government officials invited him to a banquet on board a warship: at its end, he was arrested, and the vessel weighed anchor immediately for France. Later, he was sent as Governor to French Guiane, where slavery was again established, He returned to France and, after some years, went back to Guiane to run a plantation, of course with slave labour.

Légitimus and the cemetery. Local handicrafts, particularly Madras cotton (from which the traditional costumes of the local women, are made), are good buys.

Musée Schoelcher celebrates the liberator of the slaves. He gave some of his personal art collection in 1883 to Guadeloupe. Though damaged by hurricanes, the collection survives in its original, elaborately decorated, specially built, 'Belle Epoque' home. Other exhibits on his life and on the slave trade. ■ *0900-1230, 1400-1730, closed Wed, Sat afternoon and Sun, entry 10 F. 24 rue Peynier, T821804.* **Musée Saint-John Perse**, in a lovely colonial-style house, is dedicated to the poet and diplomat. His real name was Alexis Saint-Léger, but he was born in Guadeloupe of planter stock. The collection gives a picture of the lifestyle of island whites, the 'bekes'. ■ *0830-1230, 1430-1730, closed Sat afternoon and Sun, entry 10F, children half price. 9 rue Nozières et A R Boisneuf, T900192.*

Grande-Terre

Just outside Pointe-à-Pitre on the N4 towards Gosier is **Bas du Fort**, the site of the large new marina, said to be the biggest in the Caribbean. The aquarium is also here, at Place Créole. It has about 30 ponds with species only from the Caribbean Sea, including fish, turtles and nurse sharks. ■ *Daily 0900-1900, 35F, children under 12, 20F. T909238.* At the next turning off the main road to Gosier (follow the signs to the CORA hypermarket) are the ruins of the 18th-century fortress, **Fort Fleur d'Epée** which once guarded the east approaches to Pointe-à-Pitre. There are now pleasant, shady gardens within the ramparts. Art exhibitions are regularly held either in the officers' quarters or in the underground rooms. Also note the graffiti with pictures of old sailing ships. Excellent views of Pointe-à-Pitre and across Petit Cul-de-Sac Marin towards the mountains of Basse-Terre. ■ *Daily 0800-1800, free.*

Gosier itself is the original holiday centre of Guadeloupe, with hotels, restaurants, nightclubs. The corridor leading to it from Pointe-à-Pitre is built up, extending up into the hills above the coast road. Nevertheless, Gosier is a pleasant place with plenty of atmosphere. There is a marvellous picnic spot overlooking a small beach (Plage de l'Anse Canot). Don't miss the little island about 100 m offshore (Ilet du Gosier) and lighthouse. You could swim to it, there is a channel marked by buoys, but watch out for speed boats. Fishermen provide a regular ferry service and locals

Gosier

picnic here at weekends. Old Gosier has one of the finest hotels in the island, the *Auberge de la Vieille Tour*, built around an 18th century windmill tower. Great views from its bar terrace. The room rates drop dramatically in low season. Old Gosier has a great selection of restaurants, ranging from high cuisine at the *Auberge* and *La Mandarine* to takeaways on the main street, Blvd Charles-de-Gaulle. The modern part of the resort with three-star beach hotels is at the western side, between Pointe de la Verdure and under Fort Fleur de l'Epée. Built on reclaimed mangrove marshes, the beaches are quite acceptable with the usual watersports facilities.

South coast east of Gosier The south coast between Gosier and **Sainte-Anne** is hilly with cliffs, making it particularly suited to development and on most headlands there are huge condominium developments looking across the sea to Marie-Galante as well as to the south tip of Basse-Terre. Sainte-Anne is a small, pleasant town and has a small church with a slightly crooked spire overlooking the square. Here you will find the **Plage de la Caravelle**, rated by some as the best on the island. The land gradually subsides towards **St-François**, originally a fishing village but now home to *Méridien, Hamak, La Cocoteraie* and *Plantation Sainte-Marthe* which are all luxury hotels. There is a light aircraft landing strip and 18-hole par 71 golf course designed by Robert Trent Jones. You can catch the ferry to La Désirade from here. Watersports equipment can be hired from several companies at the marina.

The rugged **Pointe des Châteaux** at the easternmost tip of the island is part of the national park. From the car park, there is a small, self-guided walk to the cross (**Pointe des Colibris**) erected in 1951, on the point where there are two 'compass' tables showing distances to various landmarks. The limestone outcrop is quite steep in places but the view over the inshore island of **La Roche** (housing a colony of sooty terns, *sterna fuscata*) to La Désirade in the distance, is spectacular especially on a windy day when the sea whips over the rocks. It is worth taking the slightly longer return path around the headland as you get good views of the completely flat **Petite Terre** with its lighthouse and on clear days Marie-Galante (30 km), Les Saintes (60 km) and Dominica (75 km). Note the **Grandes Salines** (salt lagoons) where flamingoes were once common. There are stalls selling handicrafts, spices and a local aphrodisiac, *Bois Bande*. A tree bark, this is also available as a liqueur ('gives strength to men, pleasure to women') and as an infusion in rum. Note that the beach between the two points is dangerous.

East coast
Take a good map as it is easy to get lost on the little roads in the sugar cane fields

Between Saint-François and **Le Moule**, a colonial mansion at **Zévallos** can be visited. Le Moule was the original capital of Guadeloupe and there are still some cannon from the fortifications against English attack. A precolumbian Arawak village, called Morel, has recently been uncovered on the beautiful sandy beaches north of the town. The **Musée d'Archéologie Précolombienne Edgar Clerc** is at La Rosette. It houses the collection of the researcher, Edgar Clerc, of artefacts found on Guadeloupe and also puts on temporary exhibitions. ■ *0900-1230, 1400-1730, free.* On the Abymes road (D101) from Le Moule is the **Distillerie Bellevue**, makers of Rhum Damoiseau. ■ *Tours Mon-Fri 0800-1400.* From Le Moule you can either return to Point-à-Pitre through **Les Grands Fonds**, or continue up the rugged, rough Atlantic coast to **Pointe de la Grande Vigie** in the extreme north. After travelling through the small towns of La Rosette, Gros Cap and Campèche (small restaurant/bar), the countryside becomes more barren. At **Porte d'Enfer** (Hell's Gate) there are a number of barbecue places and little huts at the mouth of an inlet. You can camp here. There is not much sand and the sea can be dangerous, do not go too far out. The coastline from here is very rocky with cliffs and spectacular views.

Leeward coast Grande-Terre's leeward coast has beaches at Port-Louis and Petit-Canal which are the usual concrete towns with restaurant and filling station. North of Anse Bertrand there is a fine clean, sandy beach, Anse Laborde, which has plenty of shade, a restaurant, and a reef close to the beach, good for snorkelling. Inland, at **Morne-à-l'Eau**,

Louis Delgrès

Born in Martinique, Louis Delgrès, a mulatto, enlisted in the French colonial forces at 17 to fight against the English in the last year of the American War of Independence. As a professional soldier he was captured by the British in 1794, sent to England as a prisoner, exchanged by the revolutionary government for a British soldier, and sent to Guadeloupe as a lieutenant. He first fought against black rebels but then, recognizing the justice of their cause, he changed sides and took command. Entrenched in the fort at Basse-Terre (then called Fort Saint-Charles) he defied General

Richepance, who had been ordered by Napoléon to disarm the black troops and re-impose slavery. Faced with overwhelming force, Delgrès issued a moving letter to French public opinion and to "the entire universe, a last cry of innocence and despair". He claimed that because of racial prejudice, in spite of their loyalty, they were to be hounded to death. This declaration, on 10 May 1802, is now to be seen in bronze on the walls of the fort. Eighteen days later, at Matouba, on the slopes of La Soufrière, they were all killed or executed.

French Antilles

there is a remarkable terraced cemetery built around a natural amphitheatre, very attractive on All Saints Day when lit by thousands of candles.

Basse-Terre

On the other wing of the island, Basse-Terre is the administrative capital of Guadeloupe and the entire Department. There are some very pretty and authentic old buildings of the colonial period in the city. It is a charming port town of narrow streets and well laid-out squares with palm and tamarind trees in a lovely setting between the sea and the great volcano La Soufrière.

There is an interesting 17th-century cathedral and the ruins of **Fort Louis Delgrès**, well preserved and full of interesting ramparts and bastions (original building 1667, considerably enlarged in the 18th century. The British occupied the fort in 1759-1763 and again in 1810-1816. It was fought over and renamed many times, being given its present name in 1989 in memory of the man who resisted the re-imposition of slavery to the death. ■ *T813748, daily 0700-1700, free.* The **Grande Caverne**, formerly the billet of the non-commissioned officers, is now a cultural museum, with an exhibition of clothes and photographs of the area. In the cemetery is the commemorative monument to Admiral Gourbeyre. The date is not that of his death (he disappeared at sea in 1845) but of 8 February 1843 when there was a huge earthquake; the Admiral worked tirelessly to help its victims.

Sights
Market day is Sat

Saint-Claude, a wealthy suburb and summer resort 6 km into the hills, is surrounded by coffee trees and tropical gardens. **Matouba**, above Saint-Claude, is an East Indian village in lovely surroundings (waterfall and springs) with a good restaurant. On the outskirts of the village is a monument to Louis Delgrès on the spot where he and his companions were caught and killed by Napoléon's troops. There are **hot springs** a good walk above the village (1,281 m) and the bottling plant for the local mineral water.

On Basse-Terre island one of the main sights is the volcano La Soufrière, reached through a primeval rain forest. A narrow, twisty road leads up from Basse-Terre town to a car park at **Savane à Mulets** (1,142 m) from where the crater, 300 m higher, is a 1½ hour climb up the Chemin des Dames, a fascinating trail with changing flora, but becoming eroded through overuse. Buses go to Saint-Claude from where it is a 6-km walk to Savane à Mulets. From the top there is a spectacular view, if you are not enveloped in clouds, which is usually the case, observe the mountain for a few days to see whether early morning or midday is clearest, above the lush jungle foliage on the east slopes and sulphurous fumes spurting over yellow and orange

La Soufrière
The best clothing for the climb is the least; jackets worn against the dampness merely compound the problem; but take a sweater, it can get quite chilly. Leave some spare clothes in the car

rock. The summit is quite flat; the main vent is to the south and there are discs in the ground to help you find it in the fog. It is possible to come down on the Trace Micael, along a forest path, to the **Chutes de Carbet** waterfalls where the water becomes cool and clear. Carry on down, past more waterfalls, until you get to a car park (often full, parking can be a problem).

If starting from the bottom, take a bus from Capesterre to Routhiers, US$1.50, then walk along the D3 road until it ends. Follow a trail and within 50 minutes you will reach the third waterfall of 20 m. Go back 100 m and follow the trail upwards again until you reach the 110 m, second waterfall, 711 m above sea level. The path is stony, rough going and often very muddy. You have to cross the Carbet on a rope bridge (*passerelle*), but this had disappeared in 2000, so you may have to do without. You can swim in the warm, sulphuric pool below the fall but if you visit when there is rain higher up, beware of flash floods. From here you can continue climbing to the first waterfall, at 125 m, or turn southeast to the picnic place, Aire d'Arrivée, 15 minutes, where there are barbecue stalls (good chicken). The D4 road starts here and

Basse-Terre

descends to St-Sauveur. Along the road to the Chutes du Carbet are **Les Jardins de Saint-Eloi**, flower gardens open to the public. You can buy flowers here or have them packed for export.

La Citerne, a neighbouring volcano, has a completely round crater. There is a trail but part requires climbing ladders straight up the wall. Also on this side are **Grand Etang** and **Etang Zombi**. You can drive, hitchhike or walk down the D4 road from the Chutes de Carbet to the edge of Grand Etang and walk around it, about one hour through lush vegetation. Do not swim in the lake because of bilharzia. There are also marked trails to **Etang de l'As de Pique**, high above Grand Etang to the south on the slope of la Madeleine (two hours) and the Trace de Moscou which leads southwest to the Plateau du Palmiste (2½ hours), from where a road leads down to Gourbeyre. Walk down to St-Sauveur for fine views over banana plantations, the coast and Les Saintes. Allow at least five hours to walk from Capesterre to St-Sauveur via the waterfalls and Grand Etang and wear good hiking shoes.

Parc Naturel

You can walk the Trace Victor Hugues, along the main ridge of Basse-Terre (a 29-km hike), and a number of other Traces. A parallel route follows the River Moreau from Goyave up to the Chutes du Moreau. Turn off the N1 opposite the turning to Goyave and signposted to the falls. The made up road turns to gravel and then ends. From here the trail will take you about two hours with five river crossings, so take appropriate footwear. After the fifth crossing the trail rises steeply and there are steel ropes to help you up the slope. From here it is another 10 minutes to the falls. Also recommended is the River Quiock trail, but take the Serie Bleu map; despite being well marked originally, storm damage has made it difficult to find all the markers. It can be very muddy, wear good boots. You can start from the car park at the Cascade aux Ecrevisses (see above) on the D23. Walk 300 m along the road and take a path to the right (follow the sign to the Pathfinders camp) to Piolet, near the entrance to the Bras-David-Tropical-Parc on the other side of the road. The trail leads down to where the River Quiock meets the larger river Bras-David, carefully cross the river, then the trail heads west along the Quiock until returning to the D23. Hitchhike back to your car (if you have one). The walk will take you 3-4 hours depending on the state of the trail.

Other features of the Natural Park are described under Flora and fauna, above. For hiking guides, contact the Bureau des Guides, Basse-Terre, T991873. The Association of Mountain Climbing Guides is at St-Claude, T802425

East coast

With a population of 18,000, **Capesterre-Belle-Eau** is Guadeloupe's third largest town and is an important agricultural centre with lots of shops, restaurants and a market. Above the town is the garden of Paul Lacavé. To the north is the **Allée de Flamboyants**, a spectacular avenue of flame trees which flower May-September. South of the town is the **Allée Dumanoir**, a magnificent 1 km avenue of royal palms.

At **Sainte-Marie**, a statue erected in 1916 commemorates the site of Columbus' landing in 1493. It has now been defaced by nationalists. South of Sainte-Marie, near Carangaise, there is a Hindu temple, built in 1974 by René Komla, richly decorated with statues of Vishnu and Ganesh outside.

The most northern town on this side of Basse-Terre is **Petit-Bourg**, on the opposite side of the bay from Pointe-à-Pitre and overlooking the little islands in the Petit Cul-de-Sac Marin. Inland from here, at Cabout, is **Le Domaine de Valombreuse, Parc Floral**, where over 1,000 species of flowers can be found and masses of birds enjoying the plant life. Flowers are for sale and can be packed for export and collected at the airport. ■ *0900-1700, T955050, F955090, valomb@outremer.com Guided tours available for groups, restaurant by a river in the forest open for lunch, and for dinner for groups of 10 or more by reservation.*

Southern Basse-Terre

Besides the Maisons du Volcan and de la Fôret (see above), there are **Maisons du Café** at La Grivelière, Vieux Habitants (T984842) and a **Centre de Broderie**, Fort l'Olive, Vieux-Fort (daily 0830-1800, T920414), showcasing the work of some 40 lacemakers and embroiderers. Vieux-Fort is on the island's southwest tip, the other side of the Monts Caraïbes from the main Basse-Terre to Pointe-à-Pitre road. There are

French Antilles

attractive gardens surrounding the lighthouse, with good views. Good créole restaurant with dance hall attached.

Amerindian rock carvings dating from around 300-400 AD, are at the **Parc Archéologique des Roches Gravées**, near Trois Rivières, on Basse-Terre's south coast; the most important is a drawing of the head of a Carib chief inside a cave. The archipelago of Guadeloupe has a large concentration of inscribed stones. The site is now in a garden setting, with wardens (it's a good idea to consult the leaflet because some of the engravings on the stones are hard to decipher; many are badly eroded; the pamphlet also explains the garden's trees). ■ *T929188, 0830-1700, US$0.60 entry, children free, The park is a 10-min walk down from the church in Trois Rivières where the buses stop.* Five minutes further down the hill is the boat dock for Les Saintes (paying car park).

West coast Between Basse-Terre town and the Route de la Traversée on the west coast are **Vieux-Habitants**, with a restored 17th-century church, and the underwater reserve (see page 701). Contact the Syndicat d'Initiative de Bouillante, T987348, for information on the Bouillante area, which considers itself the capital of diving, including gîtes, restaurants and dive operators.

A good hike is the Trace des Contrebandiers, three hours, from the Maison du Bois, Pointe Noire. A long but beautiful road takes you to the Trace. When you leave the trail on the other side you need to hitchhike because there are no buses.

North of the Traversée, on the N2, is **Pointe Noire**, a small fishing town. Just south of the town is the **Maison du Bois** at Bourg, a cabinet-making and woodworking centre with a permanent exhibition of furniture and other things made of wood. ■ *Daily, 0915-1700, US$0.70.* Also near here at Grand Plaine is the **Maison du Cacao**, with displays on the origin of cocoa, its cultivation and processing and you can taste it. ■ *Daily 0900-1700 except Sun 0900-1300, T982523, F982123.* On the Côte-Sous-Le-Vent are the calm, clean beaches at Ferry and Grand-Anse and the rougher ones at Deshaies. **Deshaies** is attractive, strung out along the beach with cliffs at each end; there are hotels, restaurants (*Le Madras* and the more expensive *Le Mouillage*, offering local food such as fish, créole chicken), basketball and tennis courts.

Northern Round the north of Basse-Terre is the town of **Sainte-Rose** where you can visit the **Basse-Terre** rum museum, **Musée du Rhum**, at the **Distillerie Reimonencq**, Bellevue Ste-Rose. In addition to the exhibitions on sugar and rum making, there is a display of butterflies and other insects in the **Galerie des Plus Beaux Insectes du Monde** and 30 model sailing ships from the earliest to the present day. ■ *T287004, F288255, open 0900-1700 Mon-Sat, adults US$6, children half price.* The road continues south to Lamentin and the hot springs at Ravine Chaude (Thermal Station T257829). Near Lamentin you can visit the **Domaine de Séverin** distillery at La Boucan, still using a paddle wheel. Guided tours are available twice a day on a miniature train. You can taste and buy both white and aged rums and fruit punches and special air packages can be ordered. ■ *Open 0800-1300, 1400-1800, Sun 0900-1200, tours in the morning except Sun. T289196, F283666. Restaurant open for lunch Tue-Sun, and dinner Thu, Fri, Sat, local specialities, accommodation available, recommended.* There is also the **Grosse-Montagne** distillery for guided tours and tastings.

Essentials

Sleeping: **Pointe-à-Pitre A** *Anchorage Hôtel Saint John*, rue Quai Lesseps, T825157, F825261. A/c, TV, **Grande-Terre** balcony, comfortable, very good. **B-C** *Normandie*, 14 Place de la Victoire, T823715. With shower *The tourist board has* and a/c, cheaper without bath, popular, best to book in advance, restaurant good. **C-D** *current hotel price lists* *Schoelcher*, rue Schoelcher. Not very clean, reasonably-priced restaurant. **C-D** *Relais des Antilles*, *(they run an* corner of rue Massabielle and rue Vatable, just off the Place de la Victoire. Basic, noisy but friendly, *information desk at* cheap, with toilet. **C-D** *Karukera*, 15 rue Alsace-Lorraine. With bath, no fan, not good. **C-D** *Pen-* *the airport but do not* *sion Mme Rilsy*, T918171, 34 Bis Rue Peynier. CP, very friendly. Reported to take students only. *make reservations)*

Bas du Fort Bay/Gosier (tourist area). **LL** *Auberge de la Vieille Tour*, Montauban, 97190 Gosier, T842323, F843343. Named after an 18th-century sugar tower incorporated into the main building, it is the flagship of the Accor Group, a Sofitel Coralia hotel. On a bluff over the sea, beach, pool, tennis, 182 rooms, 3 2-room bungalows and 8 rooms in French colonial style, gourmet restaurant, with the only Maître Cuisinier in the French Antilles. **LL-L** *Coralia Marissol Bas-du-Fort*, 15 mins from Pointe-à-Pitre, T908444, F908332, 195 rooms and bungalows, restaurants, discothèque, tennis, beach with watersports and a spa/gym with instructors and physiotherapist. Its neighbour the **LL-L** *Novotel Coralia Fleur d'Epee* has absolutely identical facilities, though in differently styled accommodation. **LL-A** *Canella Beach*, Pointe de la Verdure,T904400, F904444. 146 studios and suites on waterfront, kitchens, balconies, pool, children's pool, tennis, beach, multilingual staff, excursions and watersports arranged, 11 km from airport, restaurant overlooks man-made beach. **LL-AL** *La Créole Beach*, Pointe de la Verdure, T904646, F904666. 156 rooms, good sized rooms, pool, bar and restaurant, watersports arranged, tennis, volley ball and putting green available. Also under same management are **LL-A** *Les Résidences Yucca*, 100 studios and LL-AL Hôtel Mahogany, 64 rooms and suites, which share facilities of La Créole Beach. **C** *Serge's Guest House*, on seafront, T841025, F843949. Very basic, not very clean, convenient for buses and beach, has nice garden and swimming pool. In the same area, **B** *Les Flamboyants*, T841411, F845356. Pool, seaview, some kitchenettes, friendly, is clean, a/c. A smaller establishment is the **E-F** *Hotel Corossol*, Mathurin, T843989. 8 rooms, friendly, good meals, 20 mins' walk to Gosier. Many places advertise rooms to let.

Sainte-Anne *Club Méditerranée* has a hotel-village: *La Caravelle*, on a spectacular white sand beach, perhaps the best on Guadeloupe, surrounded by a 13 ha reserve, T854950, F854970. Near Sainte-Anne: **AL** *Relais du Moulin*, T882396, F880392. 40 a/c bungalows, recommended restaurant, pool. **AL** *Auberge le Grand Large*, T854828, F881669. Neither grand nor large, but friendly and with good restaurant on the beach. **AL** *Mini Beach*, T882113, F881929. 1 km from town, also on the beach, relaxed, good location, many restaurants nearby, can fall to half price in summer, good restaurant, excellent fish soup, a meal in itself. Between Gosier and Ste-Anne, at **La Marie-Gaillarde**, is **B-C** *La Marie-Gaillarde*, T858429, overlooking Les Grands Fonds, 2 km from Petit Havre beach. 9 rooms can fit 3-4 people, with restaurant and bar. **LL-AL** *La Toubana*, T882578, F883890, toubana@leaderhotels.gp 32 cottages, a/c, kitchenettes, phones, terraces, pool, private beach, tennis, pocket billiards, views of nearby Caravelle beach, *Club Med* and islands, *Toubana* is Arawak for 'little house', restaurant serves French and Créole cuisine.

Saint-François **LL** *Méridien*, T885100, F884071. Modern conventional seaside complex, 265 rooms, beach, of watersports, pool, golf, tennis, flying school, dock, discothèque, casino. **LL** *La Cocoteraie*, Av de l'Europe, T887981, F887833, cocoteraie@wanadoo.fr 50 deluxe suites, beach front, pool side, garden view or marina view, between lagoon and golf course, spectacular pool, tennis, beautiful architecture. **LL-L** *Plantation Ste-Marthe* (Euro Dom Hotels), T931111, F887247, psm@netguacom.fr Former sugar plantation on hill away from sea, new colonial-style buildings, 120 magnificent rooms with large terrace, a/c, restaurant, bars, 900 sq m swimming pool, close to golf course, fully equipped conference centre. **LL-AL** *Anse des Rochers Anchorage*, BP 215, 97118 St François, T939000, F939100, www.hôtels-anchorage.com 228 spacious rooms in 3 buildings plus 32 villas with 4 rooms each, a/c, kitchenettes, beautiful seaside resort, Créole architecture, in 25 acres of gardens, fine restaurants, huge pool, tennis, volleyball, excursions, watersports, golf nearby. **LL** *Hamak*, T885999, F884192, hotel.hamak@wanadoo.fr 54 bungalows, private beach, marina, landing strip, sports. **AL-A** *Hôtel Kaye'la*, T887777, F887467, on the marina. Built 1990, 75 rooms for up to 4 people, a/c, pool, bar, restaurant, walking distance to Saint-François restaurants, convenient for boat trips from marina. **C** *Chez Honoré*, Place du Marché, T884061, F886073. Clean, simple, friendly, noisy because of the disco next door. Good seafood.

Pointe des Châteaux **LL** *Iguana Bay Villas*, T884880, F886719. 17 villas, 2-3 bedrooms, private pools, overlooking La Désirade, pretty beach, private. **Le Moule** **LL-AL** *Tropical*

Club Hotel, Le Moule, T939797, F939700, Plage des Alizés. 100 rooms, 1-4 people, kitchenette, phone, terrace, fan, pool, volley ball, ping-pong, restaurant, snack bar, in coconut grove on beach, watersports, tennis and golf available nearby.

Sleeping:
Basse-Terre
Accommodation is neither plentiful nor high class in Basse-Terre city

Basse-Terre E *Hotel Basse-Terre-Charlery*, 56 rue Maurice Marie Claire, T811978. Central, basic, clean and cheap, good oriental restaurant next door. Also central is **D** *Le Drouant*, 26 rue Dr Cabre. At **Saint-Claude AL-A** *St Georges*, Rue Gratien Parize, T801010, F803050. 40 rooms including 2 suites, fitness room, squash, pool, billiards, meeting rooms, bar, restaurant *Le Lamasure*, snack bar. **A-B** *Relais de la Grand Soufrière*, T800127, F801840, regular bus service to Basse-Terre, including Sun, an elegant but rather poorly converted old plantation mansion, a/c, attractive surroundings, old wooden furniture, friendly staff. **Bouillante LL-A** *Domaine de Malendure*, T989212, F989210. 50 loft suites with views of Ilet Pigeon, on hillside, 400 m from sea, good location for diving or walking, pool, restaurant, car rental, shuttle to Malendure beach or Grand Anse beach, car rental in advance recommended. **Deshaies L** *Fort Royal*, T255000, F255001. Dramatically set on a promontory between 2 beautiful but rather rough beaches. **LL-AL** *Pointe Batterie Villas*, T285703, F2805728. 24 1-2 bedroom villas, a/c, decks, pool, new, on the water, charming, some have private pools, excellent restaurant. **B** *La Vigie*, overlooking Deshaies bay, T284252. Small studios with kitchenette, bathroom, terrace, fan, cleaned daily. **D** *Chez M Eric Bernier*, T284004 or 284270. Rooms on waterfront, opposite *Le Mouillage* restaurant more rooms are available. **E** *Chez Jean Memorin*, T284090, just outside town on hill in direction of Grand Anse beach. 1 bedroom, TV. **AL-B** *Auberge de la Distillerie*, Route de Versailles, Tabanon, T942591, F941191. 16 rooms, pool, jacuzzi, pocket billiards, country inn at entrance to Parc Naturel surrounded by pineapple fields, créole restaurant, *Le Bitaco* and small pizza café, the owner also designed **AL-A** *Créol'Inn*, Bel'Air Desrozières, T942256, F941928. 20 cabins in wooded area, kitchenette, hammocks, pool, barbecue, snack bar. **Trois Rivières C** *Le Joyeux*, a US$0.50 bus ride from the centre of the town (bus stop right outside) or short walk, in Le Faubourg, 100 m above the sea, T927478, F927707. Six simple rooms, kitchenettes, Créole restaurant, bar, disco, closed Mon except for reservations, good views to Les Saintes, very friendly, Monsieur will drive you to the boat dock for nothing. **LL-AL** *Le Jardin Malanga*, T926757, F926758. Beautifully renovated 1927 Créole house and bungalows, hillside setting in banana plantation, lovely views, terraces, mini-bar, bath tubs, huge beds, pool, car rental in advance recommended. **AL** *Grand'Anse*, T929047, F929369. Bungalows, also has Créole restaurant and views. *Les Gîtes de l'Habitation Cardonnet*, T927055. Five self-contained cottages.

Gîtes
Throughout the island there are a large number of gîtes for rent on a daily, weekly or monthly basis. Weekly rates range from US$100 to US$450, but most are in the US$150-225 bracket. The tourist offices in both Pointe-à-Pitre and Basse-Terre have lists of the properties available and should be consulted in the first instance, or you can contact the Association Guadeloupéenne des Gîtes Ruraux et du Tourisme Vert (Relais Guadeloupe des Gîtes de France), BP 759, 97171 Point-à-Pitre, Cedex, T916433, F914540, www.gites-2-france.fr, who have an office next to the Tourist Office on rue Provence. Gîtes are arranged by the local Syndicats d'Initiative. For example, the Syndicat d'Initiative de Deshaies, T284970, lists 14 local people who let gîtes. Some gîtes are quite isolated, so choose one that is conveniently located. The Syndicats charge a 5% rental fee. One recommended gîte in Trois Rivières is **E** *Chez Dampierre*, T989869, a bungalow for two in a beautiful garden, convenient location.

Camping
Compared with metropolitan France, camping is not well organized and the tourist office does not therefore have much information. *Camping Traversée* is the only camp site at present, near Mahaut on Basse-Terre, not suitable for tents after heavy rain, they float away. Otherwise ask mayors if you may camp on municipal land, or owners on private property. Camper vans can be arranged through Découverts et Loisirs Créoles in Abymes, T205565.

French Antilles

There is an excellent guide *Ti Gourmet Guadeloupe,*. Get it from the tourist board, from hotels and restaurants. Menus start (3-course lunch) at US$8. Also available, free, the booklet *Delices de la Guadeloupe* has a descriptive list of local dishes, some recipes, and selected Créole restaurants.

Eating: Grande-Terre
Apart from the hotel restaurants, there are a large number of restaurants, cafés & pâtisseries on Guadeloupe. Many are closed in the evening

Pointe-à-Pitre *La Canne a Sucre*, Quai No 1, Port Autonome. Faces the sea, mixes créole and French, menu US$10, créole buffet Sat 1200, also does teas, ice-creams. *Oasis*, rues Nozières et A R Boisneuf, T820270. French food. *Relais des Antilles*, near the *Auberge Henri IV*, in a private house, good Créole cooking, cheap meals (ask Valentin at the *Auberge* for directions). *Krishna*, 47 rue A R Boisneuf, Indian. **Grande-Terre holiday coast** *La Case Créole*, Route de la Rivière. *Chez Rosette*, Av Général de Gaulle, both Créole at Gosier. *Le Boukarou*, rue Montauban, T841037. Good Italian, pizza made on charcoal grill, moderately priced. Lots of small restaurants in **Gosier**: pizzas, Vietnamese, Chinese and of course French. The local pizza house is near the park, good for takeaways. The *pâtisserie* is good for an early morning coffee while collecting the *baguettes*; *La Mandarine*, highly rated, funny staff, worth a stop; *Chez Gina*, in a little village cafétière, 2½ km inland, up the hill, excellent food, order in advance in the morning for an evening meal, 4 courses and apéritif, served in a sort of garage with flowers, friendly, don't be put off by the untidy surroundings. *Côté Jardin*, at Bas du Fort marina. French. *La Plantation*, same location, same cuisine. **Sainte-Anne** *Chez Yvette* is budget-priced. *La Toubana*, T882557, perched high above village overlooking *Club Med*. Nice but expensive French cuisine, lobster specialities, pool and sun deck, take swimming gear. **Saint-François** *Le Vieux Port*, T 884660. Menu 70F, sea-side, in typical Créole house, wonderful lobster, fish. *Madame Jerco* has good food in a small creaking house. Close to the old harbour of St-François, *Kotesit*, T884084, fresh langouste and other seafood, don't miss the 'marquise au chocolat'. On the way to Pointe des Chateaux, *Iguane Café* uses local fresh ingredients, good service. At **Campêche** there is a small restaurant in the middle of the village, cheap and welcome relief if travelling in this area.

Chez Paul in **Matouba**, T802920, has been recommended for Créole and East Indian cuisine. At **Bouillante**, *Chez Loulouse*, Plage de Malendure, T987034, beach restaurant, créole fair. *Restaurant de la Phare*, **Vieux Fort**, good créole cooking, excellent fresh fish, reasonable prices, dance hall attached. **Deshaies** *Karacoli*, beside Grand Anse Beach. Authentic Créole cooking at its best, the local Salcede brother and sister who run it have won many awards, fish and shellfish superb, menu US$11. Other reasonably priced restaurants include *Le Madras* and *Le Mouillage*, serving créole food. For breakfast try the *boulangerie* opposite *Le Mouillage* for croissants, pain au chocolat, coffee, juice. The *Relais de la Grande Soufrière*, at **Saint-Claude**. Very good créole meals at reasonable prices, T800127. At **Petit Bourg,** *Domaine de Valombreuse*, Cabout. in the heart of the forest, T955050. Watch the many-coloured birds while you eat, crayfish special, menus begin at US$8.50. For a description of local cuisine, see page 694.

Eating: Basse-Terre

Around the Marina Bas-du-Fort there are several bars with live music, such as *Velvet*, *Le Jardin Brésilien*, *Zoo Rock* and *La Mexicana*. There is also a disco, *La Citée Perdue*. Other discos can be found in Gosier: *Le 116* (the favourite of the younger crowd), *Le Caraïbe II*, *New Land,* and the most exclusive, *Le Zenith*. Salsa fans have fun at the *Lolapalooza* in the heart of Gosier. At Le Moule, there is *Shiva*. In the Basse-Terre area the *Plantation* is the most exclusive disco. There is a casino, Cinéma L'Image, restaurant and cabaret in Gosier, route des hotels, Pointe de la Verdure, casino open from 2100, closed Sun, bring identification, T841833, local and international artistes at the cabaret. Another casino at St-François, open from 2100, closed Mon, bring identification, Av de l'Europe, T884131. Two cinemas in Pointe-à-Pitre, Renaissance, with 2 screens, T820194, and Rex, with 4 screens, T822020. Basse-Terre also has the D'Arbaud cinema, 2 screens, T811835.

Nightlife

Carnival warm-up starts on Epiphany with different events each Sun, until the climax on the last weekend, with the frenetic parading of *les jours gras* Sun, Mon, and *Mardi Gras*. On Ash Wednesday (*Mercredi des Cendres*) devils and she-devils dance and sing to tam-tams as the

Festivals

effigy of Valval, the spirit of Carnival, is taken off to be burned and thrown into the sea. The **Fish and Sea Festival** is in *mid-April* with beach parties, boat races, crab races, etc. **La Fête des Cuisinières** (Cooks' Festival) in the middle of *August* is a lot of fun with parades in créole costumes and music as well as food and cooking. It is held on the feast of St Lawrence, the patron saint of women cooks, and the event starts with a Mass. Some 250 cordon bleu cooks from the Women's Cooking Association wear their typical colourful dresses with madras scarves and lots of jewellery for the parade through Pointe-à-Pitre. Other festivals include the **Fête du Gwo Ka** (Festival of the Big Drums) in *July*, the **Old Creole Songs Festival** in *October*, **St Cecilia's Day** in *November* .

Shopping *Good Mamouth Supermarket* near the airport US$0.50 by bus from Pointe-à-Pitre. There are lots of hypermarkets just like in France, stocked with excellent cheese counters and massive wine departments. They also sell chemist sundries, toys, electrical equipment, film, cameras etc. Most have film processing facilities where prints will be ready in 24 hours or less. Generally open Mon to Sat 0800-2030. Most things are imported from France. In Gosier there is a supermarket on the road to Plage de l'Anse Canot, open on Sunday, otherwise hypermarkets are better value and cleaner. Small minimarts, local corner shops, can also be found.

Tour operators The *Organization des Guides de Montagne de la Caraïbe* has its Guadeloupe branch at St-Claude, T802425. Guides certified by the French government are available for hikes of 1-5 days. *Emeraude Guadeloupe*, St-Claude, T819828, F819812, also offers hiking in forests and mountains, with cultural visits and contact with local families, also lodging in small hotels, mountain bike excursions and other activities. *Parfum d'Aventures*, St-François, T884762, F884791, has canoes and kayaks, 4WD excursions, hiking and water scooters. *Guadeloupe Découverte*, Jarry, T252087, F266665, similar trips with canoes and kayaks, hiking, mountain biking and 4WD excursions. Also *Sports d'Av*, Jarry, T325841, F266665.

Transport **Air From Europe** Like Martinique, Guadeloupe is on *Air France*'s direct route from Paris (about 8 hours). Other French airlines with services to Guadeloupe include *AOM French Airlines* (from Paris), *Air Liberté* (Paris), *Aerolyon* (Lyon, Marseille, Nantes, Toulouse). *Condor* flies from Frankfurt. **From North America** *Air Canada* has direct flights from Montréal. *Air France* and *Air Guadeloupe* fly from Miami. *American Eagle* has flights from San Juan, with connections from the USA. **From the Caribbean** *LIAT* offers inter-Caribbean connections to Antigua, Barbados, Dominica, Fort-de-France and St Lucia. *Air Guadeloupe* connects Pointe-à-Pitre with Antigua, Dominica, Fort-de-France (lots of flights every day), La Désirade, Marie-Galante, Port-au-Prince, St Barts, Sint-Maarten, St Martin, San Juan, Santo Domingo and Terre-de-Haut. Other services include *Air France* from Antigua, Caracas, Cayenne, Fort-de-France and Port-au-Prince; *Cubana* from Havana. **Airport** Le Raizet airport was replaced in 1996 by the new, modern **Pole Caraïbes airport**. The former is still used for regional flights, while the latter is for international ones. Information, T211472, arrivals, T903232, departures, T903434. They are quite far apart, a taxi ride, and if you have a rental car (kept on the old airport side of the airfield) you will have to get the shuttle to the new terminal. There is no bus service to the new airport, but take the shuttle bus to Le Raizet and then bus into town from the other side of the car park, over roundabout and outside Cora (Mamouth) supermarket, US$0.80 to Place de la Victoire. No buses Sat afternoon or Sun. Taxi fares (T207474) from the airport are approximately US$20 to Gosier, US$40 to Sainte-Anne, US$60 to Saint-François and US$16 to Bas-du-Fort. Prices go up by 40% 2100-0700, all day Sun and on holidays.

Sea Numerous cruise lines sail from US and French ports. Pointe-à-Pitre has berths for four cruise ships and marinas for yachts. There are fast, scheduled ferry services between Pointe-à-Pitre, Marie-Galante, Les Saintes, Dominica, St Lucia and Martinique. *L'Express des Iles* has a car ferry daily from Pointe-à-Pitre to Fort-de-France at 0800 Mon-Sat, 1400 Sun and an additional service at 1200 on Fri, 3 hrs 45 mins. See St Lucia and Dominica chapters for details of services to those islands. *ATE/Trans Antilles Express* (*L'Express des Iles*) offers excursions with accommodation, day trips with lunch, or transport only, T831245, F911105, La

Darse, Pointe-à-Pitre. Agents include *T-Maritimes Brudey Frères*, Centre St-John Perse, 97110 Pointe-à-Pitre, T916087. You can get a small motor-sail vessel to Dominica from Pointe-à-Pitre for not much less than the flight. The boat leaves at 1300, 3 days a week, takes 2 hrs.

Road Bus: in Pointe-à-Pitre there are 3 main bus terminals: from rue Dubouchage, La Darse (by Place de la Victoire), buses run to Gosier (US$0.70), Sainte-Anne (US$2), Saint-François (US$2); for north Grande-Terre destinations, buses leave from the Morne Ferret and Mortenol station, off Blvd Légitimus. From Bergevin station, Blvd Chanzy (near the cemetery) they go to Trois Rivières (US$4) and Basse-Terre (US$4.25, 2 hrs). Pointe-à-Pitre to La Grande Anse, US$3, 1¾ hrs. Buses from Pointe-à-Pitre to Deshaies leave from Gare Routière, 1¼ hrs, US$3.50. Basse-Terre to Trois Rivières, 20 mins. The terminal in Basse-Terre is on Boulevard Général de Gaulle, between the market and the sea. Buses run between 0530 and 1800, leaving for the main destinations every 15 mins or so, or when full. After 1800 and after 1300 on Sat and Sun it is often impossible to get anywhere. The airport bus leaves from 0800 from outside Renaissance Cinema, Place de la Victoire, Pointe-à-Pitre, US$0.80.

Car There can be major traffic holdups in the rush hour in and around Pointe-à-Pitre; expect to find slow moving traffic on the major routes for up to 20 km out of the capital. Bottlenecks include the roundabout at the university at Bas-du-Fort, the turning to Le Raizet and beyond to Abymes and the turnoff to Baie-Mahault. In the city, parking is a nightmare in the daytime. There are no car parks, just meters. There are 2 zones, green (about US$0.70 for maximum 8 hours) and orange (cheaper). The system does not operate 1230-1400. Most traffic is one way.

Car hire *Avis*, T211354, F211355; *Budget*, T827250, F917208; *Europcar*, T266064, F268373; *Hertz*, T938945, F916959, and there are offices at the airport. At Trois Rivières, Rosan Martin, *Location de Voitures*, is close to the dock, T929424, 262F per day, unlimited mileage, for a Renault B571, deposit US$430 or credit card. *Tropic-Car*, 25 rue Schoelcher, T918437, F913194, evenings and weekends T840725, has a variety of models for hire. Fully equipped camper vans can be hired from several agencies: *Antilles Local Soleil*, Gosier, T957200; *Vert'Bleu Location*, T285125, F285295. There are also **mopeds** for hire in Pointe-à-Pitre, Gosier, Saint-François, or through hotels. **Motorbikes** from *Equateur Motos*, T845994, F845977. *Dom Location*, Rue Saint-Aude Ferly, Saint-François, T/F888481, hires scooters, motorbikes and cars half day to 1 week, scooters US$25 per day. Mokes and scooters can be rented at Sainte-Anne. If you don't have a credit card you normally have to deposit up to US$700 for a car; US$430 for a scooter; and US$145 for moped or bicycle. **Bicycle** rental from *Velo-Vert*, Pointe-à-Pitre, T831574, *Le Relais du Moulin*, near Sainte-Anne, T882396, *Rent-a-Bike*, *Meridien Hotel*, Saint-François, T845100, *Atlantic*, Saint-François, around US$10 per day.

Airline offices *Air France*, Boulevard Légitimus, Pointe-à-Pitre, T825000/823000/826161; *Air Canada*, T836249/211277/211334; *LIAT*, T211393; *Air Liberté*, T930858/211468/266131; *AOM*, T211484; *American Airlines*, T211366; *Nouvelles Frontières* for charter flights, T903636, Pointe-à-Pitre. *Air Guadeloupe*, T211290/824700, 10 rue Sadi Carnot, Pointe-à-Pitre, T901225. **Banks** *Banque Nationale de Paris* (good for Visa cash advances), *Banque Populaire*, *Banque des Antilles Françaises*, *Crédit Maritime* , *Crédit Agricole* and *Société Générale de Banque aux Antilles*, all have branches throughout the island. Banks charge 1% commission and 4% *dessier* (filing fee). No commission charged on French traveller's cheques. Exchange is handled up to midday so go early to avoid the late morning pandemonium. *American Express* is at Petreluzzi Travel, 2 rue Henri IV, English spoken, helpful. Credit cards are widely accepted, including at the hypermarkets. **Communications** Post : Post office and telephone building in Pointe-à-Pitre is on Boulevard Hanne, crowded, sweltering. Post and phones in Basse-Terre is on rue Dr Pitat, between Dumanoir and Ciceron, smaller but a bit more comfortable than the Pointe-à-Pitre office. Parcel post is a problem and you can usually send parcels of up to 2 kg only. In Pointe-à-Pitre there is an office near the stadium where you can mail parcels of up to 7 kg by air but it is unreliable; one correspondent sent a tent but received a cake wrapped in the same paper. Unlike in France, stamps are not sold in bars and tobacconists, go to post offices in small towns to avoid the crush of the main offices. **Telephone**: For local calls you must buy phone cards (*télécartes*, US$6 or US$14, from a *tabac*), fairly essential when phoning ahead to book accommodation; to call

Directory

abroad, you must hand over identification at the desk (calls to the USA US$1.85 per minute, Europe US$2.65 per minute, Australia US$3.30 per minute; hotels charge twice as much). You can not make a credit card or collect call abroad from a pay phone. You can not have a call returned to a pay phone either. **Embassies & consulates** Belgium, T268477, F268612. **Denmark**, Blvd Pte Jarry, 97122 Baie Mahault, T266610, F266618. **Ecuador**, T942172, F820813. **Germany**, T823737, F830429. **Netherlands**, 5 rue de Nozières, Pointe-à-Pitre, T820116, F913508. **Sweden**, Impasses Georges Claude, 97122 Jarry, T952957, F950199. Diplomatic representation also in Martinique. **Hospital** T891010/891120 in Pointe-à-Pitre. There are 9 hospitals and 15 clinics. There are also 3 health spas for alternative treatments: René Toribio-Ravine Chaude, T257592, F257628, with water coming directly from the Soufrière volcano; Manioukani Spa, Marina de Rivière-Sens, T990202, F816523, for thalassotherapy; the Harry Hamousin Centre, T805353, F800608, with hot sulphurous water coming from the Matouba springs at a temperature of 49.6°C. **Tourist information** Local tourist offices: Tourist offices in Guadeloupe, www.antilles-info-tourism.com/guadeloupe: 5 Square de la Banque, BP 422-97163, Pointe-à-Pitre, T820930, F838922 (the Gîtes office next door is helpful); Maison du Port, Cours Nolivos, Basse-Terre, T812483; Av de l'Europe, Saint-François, T884874, and at airport. **Maps** The Serie Bleu maps (1:25,000, seven maps of Guadeloupe, No 4601G-4607G) issued by the Institut Géographique National, Paris, which include all hiking trails, are available at the bigger book stores in the rue Frébault in Pointe-à-Pitre, and at *Le Joyeux* hotel in Trois Rivières/Le Faubourg for US$7.50. Also available from MapLink in the USA, T805-6926777. National Park: Parc Naturel de la Guadeloupe, Habitation Beausoleil, Montéran, BP 13-97120, Saint-Claude, T802425, F800546.

Les Saintes

Population: 2,036
Colour map 5, grid A4

On Les Saintes, a string of small islands named Los Santos by Columbus, only Terre-de-Haut and Terre-de-Bas are inhabited. The people are mostly descendants of poor Breton colonists who until recently survived with little intermarriage with the majority West Indian races. Sugar cane was never introduced here as a plantation crop and so large numbers of black slaves never came either. The population is predominantly

Terre-de-Haut & Les Saintes

light-skinned and many people have blue eyes. Some still wear the round bamboo and linen hat, the salako, which the locals call a chapeau annamite. A Saintois sailor brought one back from Indo-China (Annan) over a century ago, and everybody took to it. Fishing is still the main occupation on the islands, but tourism is increasingly important. The islands are a popular excursion from Guadeloupe now, but are not too spoilt, and with a good, natural harbour, many small cruise ships spend the day here. Nevertheless, to get a better idea of the islanders' traditional way of life, staying overnight is recommended so that you can appreciate it once the day trippers leave at 1600. Public holidays are particularly heavy days with hundreds of day trippers.

Terre-de-Haut is the main island visited by tourists. Irregularly shaped and surprisingly barren, it is about 6 km long and 2 km wide at its widest point. Most of the 1,500 inhabitants live around the Anse Mire, looking across the **Ilet à Cabrit** where there are the ruins of Fort Joséphine. There are some excellent beaches including that of Pont Pierre, also known as Pompierre, where snorkelling is good and camping is possible, Marigot, L'Anse du Figuier (good diving, no shade), L'Anse Crawen (nudist) and Grand'Anse (white sand, rougher waters, swimming not allowed). The UCPA sailing school at Petit Anse offers half or full day sailing or windsurfing courses. Walking on the islands is good, either from the town to the beaches, or to the top of **Le Chameau** (TV mast on top) on Terre-de-Haut's west end (spectacular views of Les Saintes, Marie-Galante, Guadeloupe and Dominica). Killer climb. It may be only 350 m or so, but it is steep going up.

An easy trail, Trace des Crétes, starts at Terre-de-Haut. Turn right at the pier, follow the main street about 100 m, turn left at the chapel and follow the road up to Le Marigot (look out for the *sentier du morne morel* sign behind the restaurant on the south side of the bay) and on to the beach of Baie de Pont Pierre, a lovely golden beach with rocks, Roches Percées, in the bay. Boats and diving equipment can be rented at

Les Saintes

the landing stage. Goats can be a nuisance if you decide to picnic here. At the end of the beach the trail leads up the hill where you have a good view of the islands, if you keep left, one branch of the trail leads to Grand'Anse beach. The 'white' cemetery, **La Cimétière Rose**, worth visiting, pretty, with paths bordered by shells, is close to the beach and from here you can walk back to Terre-de-Haut, about 1½ hours in total. Alternatively, you can walk along Grand'Anse and on to Pointe Rodriguez and the small cove Anse Rodriguez below it.

There are beautiful views also from **Fort Napoléon**, high up above the town on Pointe à l'Eau, and the museum in the fort gives the French view of the decisive sea battle of Les Saintes (1782 – the English Admiral Rodney defeated and scattered the fleet of France's commander the Comte de Grasse, who was sailing to attack Jamaica). The fort itself dates only from the 1840s. The exhibitions are good with interesting models of the ships and battles. A guide will give you a 30-minute tour (in French) of the main building. If not historically-minded, just sit and watch the weather. There are exhibits also of local fishing (including a *saintois*, a local fishing boat, originally with blue and white striped sail, but now diesel-powered) and crafts, a bookshop and drinks on sale. Around the ramparts is the **Jardin Exotique** which specializes in growing succulents and includes a wild area where plants native to Les Saintes are grown. ■ *0900-1230 except 1 Jan, 1 May, 15-16 Aug and 25 Dec. US$3 to enter, students with identity cards and children 6-12 half price.*

Terre-de-Bas Terre-de-Bas is home to about 1,500 people, mostly fishermen. There is a pottery which also gives some employment, but many have left for work in France. Boats land at **Grande Baie** which is a small inlet guarded by a fort and two small statues. You get good views of La Coche and Grand Ilet (two of the uninhabited islands) on the way across. There is a good little information centre at the dock. Buses will meet the ferry and you can go to the main settlement at Petite Anse where there is a new fishing port as well as the secondary school for the islands and a pretty little church with a red roof (tour approximately 40 minutes US$4.25). The beach at Grand Anse is very pleasant and there are a few bars and restaurants nearby (*A La Belle Etoile* is actually on the beach). There is a track which runs from Petite Anse to Grand Anse which is a good walk. It is very quiet compared with Terre-de-Haut. Salakos and wood carvings are made by local inhabitants.

Sleeping
There is a shortage of water on the island

Terre-de-Haut **LL-A** *Bois Joli*, reached by 10-min boat ride or 5-min scooter ride from town, at the west end of the island on hillside, T995038, F995505, gorgeous setting, hotel van transport to town or airport, 22 rooms, 8 bungalows, MAP, pool, bar, restaurant, 2 beaches, watersports. **AL** *Kanaoa*, Anse Mire, T995136, F995194. 8 rooms, 2 studios, 6 bungalows, a/c, but rather basic, fair restaurant used by tour groups, evening entertainment in season, English spoken, beautiful waterfront setting 10 mins' walk from landing jetty, very quiet.**B** *La Saintoise*, T995250, in town. 10 rooms, CP, a/c, restaurant. *Auberge Les Petits Saints aux Anacardiers*, La Savane, T995099, F995451. Former mayor's house overlooking town and bay, furnished with French antiques, attractive, intimate, 10 rooms, 2 bungalows, 1 suite, a/c, clean, pool, sauna, art gallery, good restaurant. **B** *Jeanne d'Arc*, T995041, at Fond de Curé village on south coast, good, 10 rooms. **Terre-de-Bas** There is one hotel, *Le Poisson Volant*, 9 rooms, T998147.

On both Terre-de-Haut and Terre-de-Bas there are rooms and houses to rent; tourist office has list of phone numbers. Recommended are Mme Bonbon, T905052, on the road to the airfield, who has several rooms; Mme Bernadette Cassin, T995422, clean studio under her house on road to cemetery, cheaper without kitchen facilities, if she is full she has family and friends who offer rooms; and Mme Maisonneuve, T995338, on the same road as the *Mairie*. Reservations are generally recommended in peak season, especially Christmas and New Year. The telephone at the jetty only takes phone cards.

Eating
Plenty of restaurants, specialize in seafood and offer menus for about 60F

Terre-de-Haut Home made coconut rum punches are recommended, particularly in the little bar on the right hand side of the *gendarmerie* in front of the jetty. Check beer prices before ordering, cheapest US$2. *Le Mouillage* restaurant, T995057, recommended. *Le Genois*, T995301, excellent and cheap pizza house on water's edge by harbour square, also does takeaways. *La Saladerie*, at top of steps on road to Fort Napoléon, T995343, popular, not always open out of season. *Galerie de la Baie*, first floor overlooking harbour, snacks and very expensive ice cream. The *boulangerie* next to the *Mairie* is open from 0530, good. The supermarkets are expensive, double French prices. There are a couple of markets every morning on the road towards the post office, good for fresh produce. **Terre-de-Bas** There are 2 or 3 restaurants serving créole food and snacks.

Transport **Air** Three daily flights from Pointe-à-Pitre, some via Marie-Galante, 15 mins, *Air Guadeloupe*, US$26 one way, US$52 return, children US$40return. **Ferry** Deher CTM (T995068, F995683) have 6 daily boats from Trois Rivières (Guadeloupe) to Terre-de-Haut, US$13.50 round trip. *Trans Antilles Express* from Pointe-à-Pitre to Terre-de-Haut daily 0800 all year, returning 1600; also from Marina Saint-François, Tue, Wed, Thu, 0800, Dec-May, returning 1600 same days, all US$23 round trip, children US$12. *Transport Maritimes Brudey Frères*, T900448, from Marina Saint-François to Les Saintes Mon, Fri, 0800 Dec-May, and from Darse, Pointe-à-Pitre to Les Saintes and Marie Galante daily 0800, returning 1545, same prices as Trans Antilles Express. There are also day charters from Pointe-à-Pitre and Saint-François Marina in high season. The crossing takes about 45 mins, but it can be rough, not suitable for those prone to seasickness. The ferry between Terre-de-Haut and Terre-de-Bas, *Navette L'Inter*, runs about 5 times a day (0645, 0930, 1130, 1500 and 1545 from Terr-de-Haut, 0800, 1045, 1145, 1520, 1615 from Terre-de-Bas, some departures cancelled at weekends, holidays etc), US$3.50, US$2 for children, return) passing the Pain de Sucre. **Road Bus**: mini-buses take day trippers all over Terre-de-Haut; tour of the island US$7.50, bus up to Fort Napoléon, US$1.50 (or 25 mins' walk). No transport after dark. **Bike**: there are few cars, unlike on Guadeloupe. Scooter rental, US$30 per day, also bicycles, several central locations, US$11.50 per day. It is not necessary to hire a scooter for the whole day, as you can walk to most places, but it may be nice to have one in the afternoon to go to the beach at Pompierre or Figuier. Scooters are banned from the town 0900-1200, 1400-1600 and have to be pushed. At the Mairie you can get some very basic information and a poor map.

Marie-Galante

Marie-Galante, a small pancake-round, mostly flat island of 158 sq km, 22km south *Population: 13,463* of Grande-Terre, is simple and old-fashioned but surprisingly sophisticated when it *Colour map 5, grid A5* comes to food and drink. It was named by Christopher Columbus after his own ship, the *Santa María La Galante*, and has three settlements. The largest is **Grand-Bourg** (rather run down) in the southwest with a population of around 8,000; **Capesterre** is in the southeast and **Saint-Louis** (sugar factory, see the bullock carts delivering cane during the cutting season) in the northwest. By Grand-Bourg plage try the *batterie de sirop*, selling a treacle-like sugar cane syrup mixed with rum and lime or with water.

If you want an authentic (and proud of it) island, friendly, but determined to preserve its own way of life, this is it. There is only one medium-sized hotel. The islanders are resisting further hotel developments. Stay instead, they say, in our own gîtes, or in our guesthouses. No fast food or tatty tourist traps here. It's a traditional rural way of life, based on sugar cane. Peasant proprietors still take canes to the mill by ox-cart. This makes a good photo, which they don't mind a bit. It needs more than a day trip if you are to unwind and fully appreciate its atmosphere. The beaches, so far almost completely untouched by the tourist flood, are superb. By Capesterre, the Plage de la Feuillère has fine sand beaches and is protected by the coral reef offshore. Follow the path north to Les Galeries, which are large cliffs eroded by the sea to make a covered walkway over 15 m above sea level. There is a pleasant beach at **Anse de Vieux Fort**, the site of the first settlement on the island in 1648 and of a series of fierce skirmishes between the French and the Amerindians.

The **Trou à Diable** (off the D202) is a massive cave which runs deep into the earth. To visit it, it is essential to have strong shoes, a torch with extra batteries, and a guide. The descent requires ropes and should not be attempted unassisted.

The D202 road meets the D201 at La Grande Barre, from where there are good views of the north end of the island and to Guadeloupe. On the coast there are limestone cliffs over 30 m high which have been eroded in places to form spectacular arches with the sea splashing through them. One is at Gueule Grand Gouffre and another, less good example, further east at Caye Plate.

In the 19th century the island boasted over 100 sugar mills; a few have been restored and may be visited: Basses, Grand-Pierre, Agapy and Murat. Only at Bézard, (around 7km due north of Capesterre, can you appreciate the glory of a great windmill in full sail. The former plantation houses of **Château Murat** and **Brille** are interesting. Murat gives a good impression of the great 18th-century sugar plantations; below the sweeping lawn lies the old sugar mill with cane crushing

French Antilles

machinery still intact. Behind the house is a walled herb garden. ■ *Museum open Mon-Thu 0900-1300, 1500-1800, Sat and Sun 0900-1200, free.*

The **Bellevue** rum distillery on the D202 is a cottage industry. The rum (*'agricole'*, made from sugar cane) is very powerful and you will be invited to taste and buy. You may also be offered bags of brown sugar and dessicated coconut, a surprisingly nice combination. At the **Distillerie Bielle** you can taste and buy rum as well as ceramic rum flasks made at the pottery *atelier*. ■ *1000-1200, Mon-Sat, T979362.* The **Distillerie Poisson** in the west on the N9 makes the Père Labat rum and is open for visits (also small museum) with tastings of rum and liqueurs. Fascinating old 19th century machinery, still in use. ■ *0700-1100, Mon-Sat, free, T970379.*On the road to **Duclos**, going north, is the *mare au Punch*, the 'sea of Punch'. The story is, that when the revolution came, the slaves gathered together all the rum they could find and, in this pond, made the biggest bowl of punch the Caribbean had ever seen to celebrate. Alas, as the display boards (in French and English) honestly indicate, this attractive tale is unlikely, but it's a good story, with underlying truth of the fight against oppression.

Sleeping **St-Louis** *Le Salut* is in the town centre south of the pier, T970267. 15 rooms, a/c, restaurant and bar. North of St-Louis, 2km from Vieux-Fort beach on a cliff, is *Au Village de Menard* , T970945. 7 bungalows, pool, mountain bikes, English spoken. Near St Louis is **L-AL** *Cohoba*, at Folle Anse, T805-9679850 in Europe. 100 rather small rooms, 30 with kitchenettes, some have sitting room with sofa bed sleeping one, a/c, TV, 2 restaurants, generous portions of Créole food, charming staff, dramatic pool, large conference room, bar, superb white sand beach, windsurfing. Other hotels are in **C-D** range. There is a family *pension*, **E** *La Coquillage*,

Marie Galante

room only or half-board available. **Grand-Bourg** *L'Auberge de l'Arbre à Pain*, Rue Jeanne d'Arc, T977369. 7 rooms, CP, a/c, restaurant and bar. **Capesterre**, *Hotel Hajo*, Beaurenom, T973276. 6 rooms, fan, restaurant and bar. *Le Soleil Levant*, 42 rue de la Marine, on hill overlooking Capesterre and sea, T973155, F974165. 10 rooms and studios, tiny pool, kitchenettes, restaurant for breakfast and dinner, evening entertainment, car rental. *Le Touloulou*, T973263, F973359. On the Grand Bourg road, 2 km from Capesterre. Clean, well equipped bungalows backing directly on to the sea, discothèque and restaurant nearby. *Le Belvedere*, 4 km from Capesterre, 5km from Grand-Bourg, 2 mins from the beach, T/F973295. 7 rooms, 12 beds, terrace restaurant in the trees open for lunch and dinner, creole seafood, crayfish, bouillabaisse, evening entertainment, welcome cocktail. There are rooms to let (inquire at the tourist board), and gîtes, contact Gîtes de France Guadeloupe, BP 759, 97110 Pointe-à-Pitre, T916433, F914540. For accommodation, 24-hr advance booking is necessary.

There is a cinema in Grand-Bourg, *El Rancho*. **Entertainment**

Air To get to the island there are regular flights (20 mins) from Pointe-à-Pitre, which is only **Transport** 43 km away (*Air Guadeloupe*, as above, US$52 round trip, children US$39). *Marie-Galante Aviation*, T977702, offers charters and air taxi service. **Sea** There are ferries between Pointe-à-Pitre and Grand-Bourg and it is possible to do a day trip (US$12 one way, US$23 return, children US$12, 1-1½ hrs, times are posted on the booth at the dockside): The *Maria* and *Trident* (Brudy Frères, Centre St-John Perse, Point-à-Pitre, T916087) have daily crossings to Grand Bourg via Saint-Louis, 0545, 0800, 1500 Mon-Fri, 0800, 1300 Sat, 0800, 1645 Sun, returning 1300, 1630 Mon-Fri, 0930, 1630 Sat, 1530, 1800, 1900 Sun. *Trans Antilles Express*, T831245, Quai Gatine Gare Maritime, Pointe-à-Pitre, has fast catamarans taking 300-450 passengers. To Grand-Bourg departing 0800, 1230, 1700 Mon-Sat, 0800, 1700, 1900 Sun, returning from Grand-Bourg 0600, 0900, 1545 Mon-Sat, 0600, 1545 1800 Sun. To Saint-Louis 1230 Mon, Sat, returning 0700 Mon and 1800 Fri. Saint-François to Saint-Louis departing Tue and Thu 0800, returning same days 1645. *Amanda Galante*, a car ferry, T831989, crosses from Pointe-à-Pitre to Saint-Louis in 1½ hrs, US$80 car and driver return, US$7 for each passenger, takes 22 cars and 156 passengers. *Trans Antilles Express* offer full and half-day tours to Marie-Galante from Pointe-à-Pitre, includes boat trip, visits to beaches, the towns, sugar factories, rum distillery (plus tasting) and other sites (0800-1630 daily, except 0730 weekends, US$33, or US$26 for half day, meals US$10.50 extra). Generally you are better off hiring a car or scooter and doing it independently. You can also get a ferry Les Saintes-Marie Galante-Saint-Louis on Tue and Thu in high season. **Road Bus**: on the island there are buses and taxis. **Car hire**: self-drive cars can be hired from the airport or in the towns. Rates for a full day US$36, for part of a day US$27 (US$285 deposit); scooters US$21 (US$145 deposit).

Tourist information Passage des Braves, 97112 Grand-Bourg, T978197, F978190. The very friendly **Directory** Marie-Galante Bureau du Tourisme is at Rue du Fort, BP15, 97112 Grand-Bourg, T975652, F975654.

La Désirade

La Désirade is an attractive but rather arid island, 10km east of the Pointe du Chateau *Population: 1,700* on Grande-Terre, whose inhabitants make a living in fishing, sheep-rearing and culti- *Colour map 5, grid A5* vating cotton and maize. A road 10 km long runs from the airport along the south coast to the east end of the island, where a giant cactus plantation can be seen. At the northeast end of the island is Pointe du Mombin where there is an outstanding view of the coastline. There are excellent beaches, such as at Grande Anse and Souffleur. Perhaps the nicest is in the east at a village called Baie-Mahault, enhanced by a good restaurant/bar, *Chez Céce*, where you can sample dozens of different rum punches. The northern part of the island is rugged, with cliffs against which the Atlantic waves crash, and ravines, savagely beautiful but inhospitable, no one lives here.

Columbus named the island La Desiderada as it was the first land he saw on his second voyage in 1493. Archaeological research has shown evidence of Amerindian settlement but it was uninhabited when Columbus passed by. La Désirade was occupied by the French for the first time in 1725, when all the lepers on Guadeloupe were deported there during an epidemic. In 1930 a leper hospital was built, but it was closed in 1954.

Rainfall is very low here and the dry season lasts from January to August. The lack of freshwater has always hampered economic activity. In 1991, however, La Désirade was linked to Grande-Terre underwater with a freshwater supply. A plaque at l'Anse des Galets commemorates this. The dryness and few people have helped wild life to survive: rare birds, the agouti (a large and very edible rodent, the size of a small rabbit), and the iguana (also edible).

Sleeping & eating D *L'Oasis du Désert*, Quartier Désert Saline, T200212, 8 rooms, restaurant, reservations advisable. *Le Mirage*, T200108, F200745, 7 rooms, restaurant. *Le Kilibibi*, T200097, local specialities. *La Payotte*, seafood, T200194. *Chez Marraine*, T200093, créole.

Transport **Air** There are daily 10-min air services from Guadeloupe 0700, 1545 Mon, Thu, Fri, return 0730, 1615 (*Air Guadeloupe*), US$51 round trip, children US$39. **Sea** Boat services from St-François, Guadeloupe, by Vedette Impériale, a rapid motorboat, T885806, journey time 45 mins. Departs Mon-Fri and Sun 0800 and 1700, Sat 0800, 1400, 1700, return Mon-Fri 0615 and 1600, Sat 0615, 1100, 1600, Sun 0600, 1600, US$17 return, children half price. Some companies offer day trips with tours and meals for US$43. **Road** Taxi/minibuses normally meet incoming flights and boats. There are bicycles and scooters for hire.

Background

History Christopher Columbus discovered Guadeloupe in 1493 and named it after the Virgin of Guadalupe, of Extremadura, Spain. The Caribs, who had inhabited the island, called it *Karukera*, meaning 'island of beautiful waters'. As in most of the Lesser Antilles, the Spanish never settled, and Guadeloupe's history closely resembles that of Martinique, beginning with French colonization in 1635. The first slaves had been brought to the island by 1650. In the first half of the 17th century, Guadeloupe did not enjoy the same levels of prosperity, defence or peace as Martinique. After four years of English occupation, Louis XV in 1763 handed over Canada to Britain to secure his hold on these West Indian islands with the Treaty of Paris. The French Revolution brought a period of uncertainty, including a reign of terror under Victor Hugues. Those landowners who were not guillotined fled; slavery was abolished, only to be restored in 1802 by Napoléon. The slaves were finally freed in 1848, largely because of the work by Victor Schoelcher. After 1848, the sugar plantations suffered from a lack of manpower, although indentured labour was brought in from East India.

Despite having equal status with Martinique, first as a Department then as a Region, Guadeloupe's image as the less sophisticated, poor relation persists. In common with Martinique, though, its main political voice is radical (unlike the more conservative Saint-Barthélémy and Saint-Martin), often in the past marked by a more violent pro-independence movement.

Geography Guadeloupe is really two islands, Basse-Terre and Grande-Terre, separated by the narrow bridged strait of the Rivière Salée. To the west is mountainous Basse-Terre, with the volcano Grande Soufrière (1,484 m) at its centre. It has an area of 848 sq km, a total of 150,000 inhabitants, and the administrative capital of the same name on its southwest coast. The commercial capital is Pointe-à-Pitre, situated in the flat half of the island, Grande-Terre. On the cliff-edged Caribbean coast, there was only one low-lying and hospitable shore (*terre* means shore in French, as well as land, hence, Basse-Terre). This was settled first, substantially from the 1640s, and became the capital. At that time, only the mountainous western island was called Guadeloupe. On its east coast was another settlement, Capesterre (which means that part of an island first sighted on the voyage from Europe). Grande-Terre came into its own around two or three decades later, when sugar cane cultivation took off. Grande also means wide in French, which it is. As it assumed the greater commercial importance the name 'Guadeloupe' came to mean both islands.

Economy Agriculture and, increasingly since the 1970s, tourism are the principal activities. Bananas have displaced sugar as the single most important export earner accounting for a quarter of all exports. Sugar and its by-products (rum and molasses) generate about 15% of exports. Melons and tropical flowers have been promoted for sale abroad, while many other fruits, vegetables and coffee are grown mainly for the domestic market.

Wages and conditions similar to those in metropolitan France force the price of local products to levels viable only on the parent market; 66% of all exports go to France and 11% to Martinique (most exports are agricultural products). At the same time, the high rate of imports raises local prices above those of the island's non-French neighbours. Consequently there has been little move towards industrialization to satisfy a wider market and unemployment is high.

Saint-Martin

Saint-Martin, the largest of Guadeloupe's outer islands, at 52 sq km, is the smallest island in the world to be divided between two nations: France and the Netherlands. See Netherlands Antilles section for general description and information. The French part used to be a sleepy place, but has become very Americanized since the building of the yacht marina and lots of luxury hotels. There is no restriction on travel between the two halves of the island. The French side is a sub-prefecture of Guadeloupe, with the sub-prefect appointed in Paris. There is an elected town council, led by a mayor. The economy is entirely dependent upon tourism, with the twin attractions of duty-free shopping and the sea.

Population: 28,518
Colour map 4, grid B1

Saint-Martin

■ **Sleeping**
1 Club Orient
2 La Samanna
3 Pavillon Beach
4 Royal Beach
5 Belair
6 Cupecoy
7 Maho Beach
8 Radisson Vacation Villas

French Antilles

★ A Foot in the door

- You'll be spoilt for choice when it comes to dining, lots of open air **waterfront bistros** and bars offering French gourmet food in the tropics.
- Celebrate **Bastille Day** the Caribbean way with boat races and jump-ups.
- For a morning away from the beach visit the **butterfly farm** where there is a lovely collection of colourful specimens.
- Visit the Dutch side of the island for a **shopping** spree and pick up some bargains to take home.

Ins and outs

Getting there

See also Sint Maarten, for connections with neighbouring islands

Air International flights arrive at the Juliana airport on the Dutch side. On the French side is the **Espèrance airport** which can only take 20-seater light planes. Airport information, T875303. *Air Caribienne* has scheduled services to Espérance from Fort-de-France, Pointe-à-Pitre, Saint- Barthélémy and San Juan, Puerto Rico. *St Barth Commuter* flies from St-Barts. A 5-seater helicopter run by *Héli-inter Caraïbes*, T873588, runs day tours to St-Barts, US$700, and Anguilla, US$645, from Anse Marcel every day. Charters also available. *Trans Helico Caraïbes* offers helicopter tours of St-Martin; US$170 for 10 mins for 4 people, US$370 for 25 mins, T290541, 872187. **Ferry** Besides the ferry to Anguilla, connections can be made with Saint-Barthélémy; St Barts Express, T879903, twice daily except Sun and holidays, departs Gustavia 0715, 1530, departs Marigot market place 0900, 1715 (see page 731 for further details). *Voyager* high speed ferries linking St-Martin with St-Barts depart Marigot waterfront 0845 Mon-Sat, 1½ hrs, depart Gustavia 1600, US$50 return plus US$6 port fees, T871068. Can be an unpleasant trip. If rough, take the plane. Try putting a notice up at the Capiteneri Marina Port La Royale for hitching a lift to other islands.

Getting around

It is easy to hitchhike

Buses run from Marigot to Grand Case (terminal at Star Market gas station) (US$1) and from Marigot, French Quarters and St Peters to Philipsburg, normally from 0600-2200, every 15 mins approximately, US$1.50. Traffic jams on Sat evening cause serious delays. **Car hire** from several agencies, for example *L C Fleming*, Les Portes de St Martin, Bellevue, T875001 (also travel agency). *Avis Bellevue*, T875060. Many others. Scooter rental from US$20 per day including helmets and insurance from *Concordia*, T871424. Plenty of **taxis**, with controlled fares depending on the distance and number of people, no meters. You find them next to the tourist office in Marigot, T875654, in Grand-Case, T877579. From Juliana airport to Marigot about US$15, Marigot to Grand Case US$10, Marigot to Oyster Pond, US$26, 2½-hr island tour US$50, add 25% 2200-2400 and 50% 2400-0600.

Marigot

The capital of French Saint-Martin, lies between Simpson Bay Lagoon and the Caribbean sea. ('Marigot' is a French West Indian word meaning a spot from which rain water does not drain off, and forms marshy pools.) Shopping is good. Boutiques offer French prêt-à-porter fashions and St-Barts batiks, and gift shops sell liqueurs, perfumes, and cosmetics at better duty-free prices than the Dutch side.

Sights

At the *Marina Port La Royale* complex there are chic shops, cafés and bistros where you can sit and watch the boats. Rue de la République and rue de la Liberté also have good shopping with fashion names at prices below those of Europe or the USA. Marigot has a large crop of art galleries, including *Camaïeu* on rue Kennedy, Espace Expo Marina Royale, *Galerie Valentin* at 117 Les Amandiers, *Galeries Gingerbread* and *Mahogany* at the Marina Royale, *Graffiti's* at Les Amandiers and *Roland Richardson* at Front de Mer. A fruit market is held every morning in the market place

Essentials

See also Essentials, page 694

French Antilles

Exchange *The US dollar is as widely used as the franc, but watch the rate.* **Credit card** *transactions are usually in US$. It is sometimes difficult to get change from payments in francs. Dollars are preferred. The best place for exchange is the post office in Marigot where they will change all currencies and travellers' cheques, but normally only into francs. There are several exchange houses for changing from francs to dollars, one in rue du Kennedy and one in the Marina Royale complex. Two* **banks***, both on rue de la République, Marigot, Banque des Antilles Françaises and Banque Française Commerciale.*

Departure tax *See page 680 for departure tax from Juliana airport. There is a 15F departure tax from Espèrance airport.*

Ports of entry *(French flag) Marigot. See page 36 for further details.*

Marinas *Captain Oliver's Marina, Oyster Pond, T873347; Marina Port La Royale, Marigot, T872043; Port de Lonvilliers, Anse Marcel, T873194; Régie du Port de Marigot, T875906.*

Hours of business *Shops open around 0900 and close between 1800-1900 with normally a 2-hour lunch break between 1200-1500, depending on the shop.* **Banks** *open 0830-1530 Monday-Thursday, till 1630 on Friday; both slightly different from the Dutch side.*

Voltage *220 volts, 60 cycles (compared with 110 volts on the Dutch side).*

Useful addresses Gendarmerie: *T875010.* **Police**: *T878833.* **Fire**: *T875008.*

Communications *The international code for St-Martin is 590. See page 728 for further details.*

Media *Newspapers* Le Monde, France Soir *and* Le Figaro *from France are available 1-3 days after publication.* France Antilles, *same day. A few German and Italian magazines are sold at Maison de la Presse (opposite post office) and other locations.*

Public holidays *See page 700.*

next to Marigot harbour. It is best on Wednesday and Saturday. On the right hand side of the market place is the tourist office and taxi rank; also the only public toilet on the French side. From here it is a 10-minute walk to **Fort St Louis** (restored 1994) overlooking Marigot Bay and Marigot. Follow the signs from the tourist office.

On the waterfront the historical and archaeological **Museum** 'On the trail of the Arawaks', has a well-presented exhibition from the first settlers of Saint-Martin around 3500 BC to 1960. ■ *0900-1300, 1500-1830, Mon-Sat, T292284, may open longer during high season. US$5 (US$2 children).*

Around the island

Grand Case, 13 km from the capital, is anything but grand. It is a quaint town between an old salt pond (which has been partially filled in to provide the Espérance airstrip) with a long sandy and secluded beach. At the far northeast end is another beach, Petite Plage, delightfully *petite* in a calm bay. Every other Saturday all year round there are sailing races of old fishing boats between Anguilla and St-Martin, mostly to Grand Case. Ask for information at the *Ranch Bar* at the beach (live music every Sunday).

Anse Marcel, north of Grand Case, is a shallow beach, ideal for small children. South of Grand Case is **Friar's Bay**, a sheltered bay with a couple of restaurants, from where you can walk along a path to **Happy Bay**. Inland, **Pic Paradise** (424 m) is a good lookout point from where, on a fine day, you can see Anguilla, Saba, St Eustatius, St Kitts, Nevis and St-Barts. However, the 20-minute trail is poorly marked and the view becoming obscured by thick vegetation at the summit. By four-wheel drive you can reach the top on the track used for access to the radio-television transmitting tower at the top, take a turn off at Rambaud on the Marigot-Grand Case road. There are also footpaths from **Colombier** (1½ km) and **Orléans** (1 km). Colombier is a small, sleepy village with some wonderful gardens, well worth a visit. In Orléans you can visit Roland Richardson, the only well-known native artist on St-Martin, whose home is open 1000-1800 on Thursday, T873224.

On the Atlantic, **Cul-de-Sac**, is a traditional village, and departure point for boats to the **Île de Tintamarre** and **Pinel Island** (US$5 per person return) just offshore. The sea is calm and fishing boats come in here. **Baie Orientale** (Orient Bay) is beautiful but rough (beware of its undertow). There are several new developments along the beach and the area is often overrun with day visitors and shrinking. Windsurfers and catamarans can be hired from the south end of the beach, friendly staff, good protected area for beginners and more open waters. For the intrepid, or foolhardy, depending on your point of view and courage, there is bungee jumping from a parasail at 100 m, US$85, not done on very windy days. From here you can find boats to Caye Verte, just offshore.

There is a **butterfly farm** on Le Galion Beach Road next to the Bayside Riding Stables, Baie L'Embouchure, run by John Coward (claims family ties to the more famous Noel). ■ *Admission US$2-5 per person, depending on the owner's mood, open 0900-1630, daily, T873121.*

Further south, snorkelling is good at Coconut Grove. Topless bathing is accepted at all beaches on the French side, but not on the Dutch.

From Marigot to Anguilla by ferry boat (20 minutes). Sailing trips with lunch and snorkelling to beaches on St-Martin or smaller islands such as Tintamarre, Sandy Island or Prickly Pear (see Anguilla), cost about US$70 per person. Boat charter companies, with or without crew, are around *Marina Port La Royale*, about US$360 per day for four people on a yacht with crew, or US$200- 1,500 for a motor boat. A full range of diving services is offered by several companies: *Blue Ocean* at Baie Nettlé, T878973, *Octoplus* at Grand-Case, T872062, *Scuba Fun* at Anse Marcel, T873613, *Sea Dolphin* at the *Flamboyant*, Baie Nettlé, T876072, and Sea Horse Diving at the *Marine Hotel*, T878415. Sport fishing can be arranged at the Marina Port Royale, Marina Anse Marcel or Marina Oyster Pond.

Horse riding at *Caïd* and *Isa*, Anse Marcel, T874570, daily rides at 0900 and 1500 if there is enough demand, US$45, 2½ hours. Beach rides also with *OK-Corral*, Oyster Pond, up to Orient Bay, US$50 per person, 2½ hours, T874072. For nature hikes, contact Serge L'homme if you can get hold of him. He runs a spice stall in Marigot market and on hikes he makes fruit punch while his wife cooks lunch. You can also contact the *Association of Hiking Guides*, T292020.

Essentials

Sleeping

The tourist office lists only those in the upper range, guest houses in Grand Case are rented from US$350-450 per week, but for low budget accommodation you would be better in the Dutch half

Hotels LL *La Samanna*, Baie Longue, T876400, F878786. One of the most exclusive resorts in the Caribbean, 80 rooms, suites and villas, mediterranean-style hotel overlooks spectacular beaches, set in 55 acres with lush gardens, excellent dining, fitness centre, pool, all watersports, tennis. **Baie Nettlé: LL-L** *Anse Margot*, T879201, F879213, on beach in gardens between lagoon and sea. 96 rooms and suites in eight buildings, Créole-inspired architecture, spacious rooms, lots of luxuries, two pools, two jacuzzis, good restaurant. **LL-AL** *Marine Hotel Simson Beach*, T875454, F879211, a Mercure Coralia hotel. 175 rooms and loft suites, lagoon, pool or garden views, kitchenettes, on beach, popular, pool, children's pool, tennis, beach volleyball, indoor games, aquagym, windsurfing, restaurant, bar, evening entertainment. **AL-A** *Royal Beach*, T/F878989. Modern, beachfront but not all rooms have seaview, pool, bar, restaurant, watersports nearby. **Grand Case: AL-B** *Hévèa*, 163 Boulevard de Grand Case, T875685, F878388. Small colonial-style hotel, 4 rooms, 3 studios, 3 apartments with kitchenettes, gourmet restaurant, beach across the street. **AL-A** *Grand Case Beach Club*, 23 Route de Petite Plage, T875187, F875993. 76 rooms and apartments, watersports, on the beach, orchestra plays in the evening in high season. **AL** *Chez Martine*, T875159, F878730. Five rooms, 1 suite, excellent restaurant, overlooks Grand Case Bay. **LL-A** *Le Pavillon Beach*, Plage de Grand Case, T879646, F877104. New, elegant hotel on lagoon, walking distance from Grand Case, 6 studios, 17 suites and one honeymoon suite, kitchenettes, phones, beach, watersports and land sports can be arranged. **Anse Marcel: LL-AL** *Le Meridien*, BP 581, T876700, F873038. In two parts: *L'Habitation*, 266 rooms and *Le Domaine*, 145 rooms, the latter more expensive but both 4-star, marina alongside for boat trips, surrounded by 150-acre nature reserve, two pools, jacuzzis, health club, tennis, squash, racquet ball courts, archery, shuttle to towns and casino, 4 restaurants, bars. **Baie Orientale: LL** *Club Orient* (naturist), T873385, F873376. Tennis, volleyball, watersports, massage, 80 rooms or chalets for 3-4 people, restaurant. **L-AL** *Mont Vernon*, T876200, F873727, MontVernon @aol.com 370 suites, large swimming pool, facilities for children, land sports and watersports. **Oyster Pond: LL** *Captain Oliver's*, T874026, F874084. Right on the border, 50 bungalows with kitchenette and balcony, pool, boat shuttle to Dawn Beach, 2 restaurants, evening entertainment, lots going on here at Captain Oliver's Marina, Moorings-Sun Yacht on site for yacht charters and other watersports on offer. **Marigot: B** *Rosely's*, T877017, F877020, 39 studios, 7 duplex, Concordia. Pool and jacuzzi in garden, kitchenette, restaurant, English spoken. **C** *Malibu*, also in Concordia, a few blocks from the centre of Marigot, T879898, F879234. 43 rooms, modern, kitchens, fridge.

Guest houses **Grand Case, A-B** *Les Alizés*, T877109, F877351. 8 rooms, kitchenette, TV, beach. **A-B** *Morning Star*, T879385, F877208. 12 rooms, a/c. **C** *Grand Case Beach Motel*, T878775, F872655. 7 rooms, kitchenette, garden, a/c, beach. **Galisbay, C** *Le Cigalon*, Rue Fichot, T870819, F877984. 10 rooms, garden, a/c. **St James, C** *Fantastic*, Rue Low Town, T877109, F877351. 20 rooms, kitchenette, TV, a/c. **Orléans, B-C** *Rising Sun Inn*, T873352. 12 rooms, a/c. **Baie Orientale, AL** *Maison de Récréation*, T874398, F874397. Two rooms, a/c, garden, TV, breakfast, pool, beach.

Apartments and villas There are several agencies listed by the tourist office which can arrange short or long term lets: *Carimo*, T875758. *C Coudart*, T872013. *IMAGE*, T877804. *IMMO-DOM*, T870038. *Immobilier St-Martin Caraïbe*, T878761. *Immobilière Antillaise*, T870095. *Impact*, T872061. *Investimmo*, T877520. *Sprimbarth*, T875865. For luxury villas contact *French Caribbean International in the USA*, T800-3222223, www.frenchcaribbean.com

Eating

Picturesque gourmet dining places on the seashore are the islanders' favourites

French cuisine in all hotel restaurants on the French side is quite good but expensive. The likelihood of finding a cheap meal is rare but the absence of tax on alcohol makes retail purchases inexpensive. Many restaurants close in Sep-Oct.

Marigot The *Claude Mini-Club*, T875069, with its bar and dining arbour, French and créole, serves a Caribbean buffet Wed and Sat, closed Aug and Sep. *La Maison sur le Port*, T875638, offers excellent French cuisine and seafood. *Le Bar de la Mer*, Boulevard de France, T878179, serves lunch and dinner, good place to go before a disco. Many bars on the water front next to the tourist office serving barbecue lunch and dinner. For travellers on a small budget try the snackbars and cafés on Rue de Hollande. There are also lots of restaurants overlooking the boats at Marina Port la Royale, many with open air dining. *Brasserie de la Gare*, a brasserie and pizzeria, open daily 1130-2230, T872064. More upmarket and expensive is *Jean Dupont*, T877113. French gourmet with some Vietnamese and Thai specialities, open 1130-1530 (except Sun in low season), 1730-2300. *La Belle Epoque*, French gourmet, Italian and Créole. *L'Arhawak*, international, music, US$10-25. Browse around, see what takes your fancy. Food at these restaurants is usually around US$20-30 per person.

Grand Case has a reputation of having more restaurants than inhabitants. Most are on the street next to the beach but these are generally more expensive than those on the other side of the boulevard and not recommendable on a windy night. *Fish Pot*, 82 Boulevard de Grand Case. Overlooking the sea, sea food, excellent food and formal service but at a price, T875088, F872037, open 1130-1500 in high season, dinner 1800-2230. *Rainbow* 176 Boulevard de Grand Case, T875580. Traditional French cuisine, good service. *L'Alabama*, 93 Boulevard de Grand Case, T878166. Owners Pascal and Kristin are most welcoming, traditional French food in garden away from traffic noise, US$30-50 per person. *L'Amandier*, French cuisine, bar, pool, sea view, US$25-40 per person. At the small snackbars near the little pier you can find barbecue fish, ribs and lobster as well as other local snacks, very popular at weekends and holidays, recommended. At weekends there is usually live music in one of the bars/restaurants along the beach. *Chez Yvette*, Quartier d'Orléans, T873203. No sign, simple interior, authentic créole cooking. **Baie Orientale** *Bikini Beach* for Spanish *tapas, paella* and *sangria*, helped along with Brazilian music some nights, T874325.

Festivals Carnival is held pre-Lent in February and most of the events are on the waterfront in Marigot. It is not as big and grandiose as on the Dutch side, where carnival is held a few weeks later, but there are calypso and beauty contests and a Grand Parade. **Bastille Day** (*14 July*) has live music, jump-ups and boat races; the celebrations move to Grand Case the weekend after (more fun) for **Schoelcher Day** on *21 July*. In Grand Case on **New Year's Day** there is a small parade with live music, while at **Easter** another parade is held with a lot of dancing.

Nightlife *L'Atmosphere* is a disco for 'chic' French people, at Marina Port La Royale, very little English spoken, drinks US$6. *Le Bar de la Mer*, T878179, at the waterfront is a popular meeting place for French-speaking young travellers, with live music once a week. *La Fiesta*, Marigot waterfront. South American music, Brazilian house band, popular bar for locals. *Pasha*, popular with youngsters, lots of European music. Grand Case normally has live music Fri-Sun in high season with beach party style entertainment in one of the many bars. *Surf Club South*, Cul-de-Sac, T295040. Run by Andy Susko, a New Jersey-type bar, has beach parties every other Sun, all food and drinks US$1, with mainly 60s and 70s music, great fun. *Circus* bar, T877864, in Baie Nettlé in the newly built resort area, a popular night bar, live music once in a while. *Le Privilège Disco* at Anse Marcel, T874617. US$10 entrance, one drink included, one of the best but taxis expensive to get there, open from 2300, closed Mon, in Sep only opens Thu, Fri, Sat. Every full moon there is a beach party at Friar's Bay starting around 2100-2200, barbecues on the beach every Fri and Sat. Fri evenings and Sun afternoons (popular with all the family) everybody goes to *Booboo jam*, at Baie Orientale, where there is lots of merengue, salsa and zouk.

Directory **Airline offices** Marigot: *Air Caraïbes*, T292525. *Air France*, T510202. *Air Guadeloupe*, T510303. *Nouvelle Frontières*, T872779. *Tropical Helicopter Services*, T879481. **Grand Case**: *Air Caraïbes*, T878480. *Air Guadeloupe*, T877659. *Air St-Barthélémy*, T871036. *Air Saint-Martin*, T871036. *Trans-Helico-Caraïbes*, T290541/872187. Bellevue: *AOM*, T292525. Anse Marcel: *Heli-Inter Caraïbes*, T873588. Many others at Juliana airport on the Dutch side. **Banks** Banks with ATMs include *Banque des Antilles Françaises (BDAF)*, Rue de la République, Marigot, T291330. *Banque Française Commerciale (BFC)*, Bellevue, T875380. *Banque Inchauspe & Cie*, Les Portes de St-Martin, T872121. **Communications** Post: The post office will hold mail, but only for two weeks. Letters sent c/o Capiteneri Marina Port La Royale, Marigot, will be kept 4-6 weeks. Telephone: There are several telephone booths on the French side but they only take telephone cards. 120 units for 90F, sold at the post office and at the bookshop opposite. There are 8 telephones on the square in Marigot and 2 in Grand Case in front of the little pier. To call the Dutch side use the international code and vice versa. Calls from one side of the island to the other are expensive. **Cultural Associations** *L'Association Archéologique Hope Estate*, Rtd de Fort St-Louis, BP 38, T873941, set up in 1989 to protect the island's heritage, Docteur François Petit, T292284. *La Fondation Historique et Culturelle de Saint Martin*, an umbrella organization for all the artistic movements on the island, under the leadership of Roland Richardson, T873224. **Medical facilities** Hospital: T875007 **Ambulance**: T878625 (day), 877200 (night). **Tourist information** Local tourist office: Port de Marigot, 97150 Saint-Martin, T875721, F875643, www.st-martin.org

Saint-Barthélémy

Population: 5,038
Colour map 4, grid B1

Saint-Barthélémy (also known as St-Barts or St-Barth's), in the Leewards, has lush volcanic hillsides and 32 splendid white sandy beaches, most of which are protected by both cliff and reef. It has gained a reputation as the place to go for the rich and famous. It is chic, expensive and its many beautiful beaches are dotted with luxury hotels and villas, designed for those who appreciate privacy. Gourmet French restaurants and créole bistros can be found all over the island. This is a place to indulge yourself and be a part of the jet set.

French Antilles

A Foot in the door

- Stir yourself and hike to **Colombier beach**, the most beautiful on the island. You'll appreciate it far more after a walk than if you take a boat ride.
- Treat yourself to some very **fine dining**, from coffee and croissants for breakfast at a harbour front café, to a gourmet evening meal with fine French wine, St-Barts is not short of skilful French chefs.
- **See and be seen.** Spot the celebrities, identify the designer labels. St-Barts is chic and the in-crowd holidays here.

Ins and outs

St-Barts is only a short hop from St Maarten/Martin and there are dozens of daily flights from both the French and Dutch sides from 0700-1700 in small planes. There are also good links with other neighbouring islands. It is difficult to get there in a day from Europe, although it is possible from Paris via St Maarten. From the USA the best connections are via San Juan, from where the last flight leaves at 1515. You can also get there by boat from St-Martin.

Getting there
Only small planes carrying a maximum of 20 passengers can land on the short runway

Taxi tours are available for a quick tour of the island, but if you are renting a villa you will need car or mini moke hire for visiting different beaches or for shopping.

Getting around
See page 734 for further details

Diving and marine life

There is excellent diving all round St Barts, especially out round the offshore rocks, like the Groupers, and islands like Ile Fourche. Sometimes in May the migrating sperm whales pass close by. From April to August female sea turtles come to Colombier, Flamands and Corossol to lay their eggs. There are four **dive shops** in Gustavia: *La Bulle*, T276225; *St Barth Plongée*, T275444; *Marine Service*, T277034, *West Indies Dive*, T279179 and *Odysée Caraïbe*, T275594. A single dive costs about US$50, or there are packages of five or 10 dives for US$220 or US$400. PADI open water certification costs US$480.

Deep sea fishing for marlin, tuna, wahoo and dolphin can be arranged with *Océan Must Marina* at La Pointe, Gustavia, T276225, F279517, VHF 10, who also charter boats for cruising, diving, waterskiing and offer a full service marina. *Marine Service* at Quai du Yacht Club, Gustavia, T277034, F277036, VHF 74, also do deep sea fishing trips and the same watersports and boat rentals. The price depends on the type of boat (4-8 people) and ranges from US$470-640 for a half day to US$780-1,100 for a full day with open bar and picnic lunch. The catch is the property of the boat.

Beaches and watersports

The main resort area is **Baie de Saint-Jean**, which is two beaches divided by Eden Rock, the most visited beach with several bars and restaurants open for lunch or a snack, watersports, but no waterskiing, small boats, snorkelling rentals, ideal for families, good windsurfing, safe swimming, some snorkelling. Motorized watersports are only allowed 150 m off the beach. Others are **Lorient**, **Marigot**, **Grand Cul de Sac** on the north coast, **Grande Saline**, **Gouverneur** on the south, and **Colombier** and **Flamands** at the northwest tip, to name but a few.

Some beaches are more accessible than others, most are uncrowded

To get to **Gouverneur** from Gustavia take the road to Lurin. A sign will direct you to the dirt road leading down to the beach, lovely panoramic view over to the neighbouring islands, where there is white sand with palm trees for shade. A legend says that the 17th-century pirate, Montbars the Exterminator, hid his treasures in a cove here and they have never been found. Also a very good spot for snorkelling. **Colombier** beach is the most beautiful on St Barts. It cannot be reached by car but is well worth the 20-30 minutes' walk for the majestic views of the island. Park the car at Colombier, there are several trails going down to the beach. There are also several day tours by boat from Gustavia. **Flamands** beach is of very clean white sand, bordered with Latania palm trees. The surf can be rough, watersports available. In **Corossol** is the **Inter Oceans Museum**, a private collection of 9,000 seashells, corals and stuffed fish from all around the world. ■ *T276297. Tue-Sun 0900-1230, 1400-1700 (Mon groups only). 20F.* **Petite Anse de Galet**, in Gustavia, 3-5 minutes' walk from Fort Karl, is also known as Shell beach because it is covered in shells, not sand. Trees give shade and swimming is safe, shelling is of course extremely good.

St Barts is a popular mid-way staging post on the yachting route between Antigua and the Virgin Islands. Boat charters are available, also courses in, or facilities for, windsurfing (**Toiny** is the windsurfers' favourite beach), snorkelling (very good, particularly at Marigot), waterskiing and sailing. *Windsurfing Paradise*, Baie de Saint-Jean, T277122, is a BiC Centre, offering lessons and equipment rental. *Eden Rock Beach Club Gleveau Henri*, also at Baie de Saint-Jean, T277477, has Fanatic equipment for rent, while at the *Saint-Barth Beach Hotel*, Grand Cul-de-Sac, *Wind Wave Power* has Mistral gear at their windsurf school. Surfboard rental (not windsurfing) at Hookipa, T277131. Sailing and snorkelling cruises are offered by several catamarans. They go to Colombier beach, Fourchue Island, Tintamarre, Anguilla or St-Martin. Half day cruises cost US$55-60, whole day with lunch US$90-95, sunset cruises US$46, or with dinner, US$70-80.

Other sports **Tennis** at several hotels, guests take priority: *St-Barth Beach Hotel, Manapany, Flamboyant Restaurant, Isle de France, Guanahani*. Also at ASCCO in Colombier, 2 lit courts, T276107, AJOE in Lorient, two courts, one lit court, T276763. Some opportunities for **hiking**. **Horse riding** at Flamands, Laure Nicolas, T278072.

Saint-Barthélémy

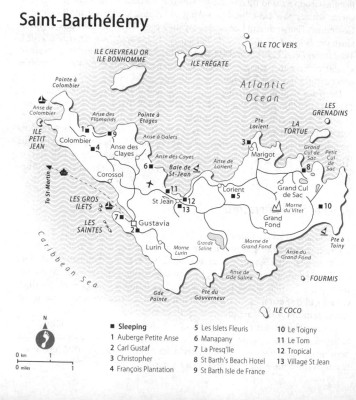

■ Sleeping		
1 Auberge Petite Anse	5 Les Islets Fleuris	10 Le Toigny
2 Carl Gustaf	6 Manapany	11 Le Tom
3 Christopher	7 La Presq'ile	12 Tropical
4 François Plantation	8 St Barth's Beach Hotel	13 Village St Jean
	9 St Barth Isle de France	

Essentials

Currency As on Saint-Martin, dollars are widely accepted but shops and restaurants will give a bad rate of exchange.
Anchorages (French flag) Outside the inner harbour of Gustavia, daily anchorage fee of US$2.50-5, depending on location. Inside the main harbour, stern to or on double moorings, fees are based on length of boat. Water, waste disposal, showers and toilets are available at the dock. Other anchorages around the island are free. Provisioning and some marine supplies.
Hours of business 0800-1200, 1430-1700, morning only on Wednesday and Saturday.
Useful addresses Gendarmerie:T276012. **Police**: T276666. **Fire**: T276231. **Sub Prefect**: T276328. **Radio** St Barts: T277474, broadcasting on FM 98 mHz.
Public holidays See Guadeloupe, page 700. See below for festivals.

See also page 694

Gustavia

In Gustavia, the capital, there are branches of several well known French shops (such as Cartier). The small crowd of habitués is mostly young, chic, and French. The food, wine, and aromas are equally Gallic. The harbour or Carénage was renamed Gustavia after the 18th-century Swedish king, Gustavus III, and became a free port, marking the beginning of the island's greatest prosperity.

Sights

In 1852 a fire severely damaged the capital, although the Swedish influence is still evidenced in the city hall, the belfries, the Forts (Karl, Oscar and Gustave), the street names and the trim stone houses which line the harbour. In the southeast inner corner in front of the Anglican church, is a truly massive anchor. Probably from a British Royal Navy Frigate, and dating from the late 18th Century, it weighs 10 tons. Marked "Liverpool...Wood...London", it came to Gustavia by curious means in 1981. The cable of a tug towing a barge across from St Thomas fouled on something at the entrance of the harbour. A local man dived down to have a look and found the anchor. It is thought that the cable dragged it up as the tug left St Thomas. Suspended below water, unseen, it got carried across. **St Barts Municipal Museum** with an exhibition of the history, traditions and local crafts of the island, is at La Pointe, near the *Wall House*. ■ *Mon-Thu 0830-1230, 1430-1800, Fri 1500-1800, Sat 0830-1200, entrance 10F, T278907.*

From Gustavia, you can head north to the fishing village of **Corossol** (see above), continuing to Colombier and the northwest beaches; south over Les Castelets and the hills of Morne Lurin to Anse du Gouverneur; or to Saint-Jean and beaches and settlements on the east end. A hired car can manage all the roads.

Essentials

Sleeping

Gustavia LL *Carl Gustaf*, rue des Normands, Gustavia 97133, T277900, F278237, carlgustaf@compuserve.com, overlooking harbour, 14 1 or 2-bedroom suites, luxury, with high prices to match, breakfast and airport transfers, kitchenette, private mini pool and sun deck, fax, stereos, gym-sauna, pool side restaurant, short walk to beach. **C** *La Presqu'île*, T276460, F277230. 10 rooms. Restaurant specializes in French and Créole cooking.

North coast L-AL *Auberge de la Petite Anse*, T276489, F278309. 16 bungalows, pool, no restaurant, only Amex credit card accepted, receptionist only there when you check in or out, picturesque but difficult path to Colombiers Beach starts here. At Colombier, overlooking Flamands beach is **LL** *François Plantation*, T298022, F276126, info@francois-plantation.com Elegant plantation style hotel with 12 bungalows, pool, good restaurant, breakfast in room. **LL** *St Barth Isle de France*, BP 612, Baie de Flamands 97098, T276181, F278683, isledefr@saint-barths.com Luxury hotel, 31 rooms, bungalows and suites, tennis, 2 pools, squash, fitness centre, open air restaurant, marble bathrooms, can arrange watersports and horse riding, closed Sep-Oct. The luxury, 4-star **LL** *Manapany Cottages*, T276655, F277528. Cottages, suites, apartments and rooms on hillside, descending to beach, 56 beds in all, largest pool on the island, tennis, jacuzzi, some villas have private pools, 2 gourmet restaurants. **LL-L** *Emeraude Plage*, T276478, F278308, emeraudeplage@wanadoo.fr 24 bungalows, 3 suites, 1 villa, terrace, kitchen, beach. **LL** *Filao Beach*, T276484, F276224, Iain filao@compuserve.com On beach, 3-star hotel, poolside bar and restaurant. **LL** *Le Tom Beach Hotel*, Plage de St-Jean, T275313, F275315. 12 rooms on beach, luxury 4-poster beds, a/c, fans, private terraces, popular restaurant with good view and fresh lobster specialities, multilingual staff. **LL-AL** *Village St-Jean*, T276139, F277796, vsjhotel@compuserve. com on hillside overlooking Baie de Saint-Jean. 20 1-2 bedroom cottages with kitchenettes, 4 rooms with mini-fridge, special packages available, pool, jacuzzi, Italian restaurant, short walk to beach, managed by Charneau family, watersports facilities. **LL** *Eden Rock*, T277294, F278837, info@edenrockhotel.com On a promontory in St-Jean bay. Clear waters all around you, 2 beaches, watersports centre and 27-ft boat for fishing, short walk along beach to airstrip, 2 fine restaurants, lobster tank, exceptional wine cellar, 12 rooms, all luxuries,

Gustavia

multilingual staff. **LL-AL** *Le Tropical*, St-Jean beach, T276487, F278174, tropicalhotel@ compuserve.com 20 seaview and gardenview rooms with cool white bedlinen and drapes, overlooking beach, in lush garden, pool with panoramic sea view, short walk to beach, excursions arranged, closed 1 Jun-15 Jul. Five mins from Baie de St-Jean is **LL-L** *Yuana*, Anse des Cayes, T278084, F277845, www.yuana.com On hillside in gardens overlooking coastline, 12 rooms, kitchenette, balcony, TV video, all quite new and light and airy, pool, breakfast, laundry, own boat, *Le Yuana*, for deep sea fishing and excursions. A few hundred yards from Lorient beach is **LL** *La Banane*, T276825, F276844, labanane@wanadoo.fr Pastel painted bungalows, all different, 9 rooms, beautifully furnished and decorated, 2 pools, lots of bananas, fine dining,breakfast, airport transfers and tax and service included in rate. In the hills above Lorient, **LL-L** *Les Islets Fleuris*, Hauts de Lorient 97133, T276422, F276972, caraibes@saint-barths.com Seven studios, pool, kitchenettes, lovely views over coastline, maid service, car rental available with room package. **LL** *The Christopher Hotel*, Pointe Milou, T276363, F279292, christopherhotel@compuserve.com A Sofitel Coralia hotel with 4 stars. 41 rooms, a/c with sitting room and bathroom, terrace, balcony or patio, 3 rooms with facilities for the disabled, shuttle service to beaches, large pool, Total Fitness Club, watersports arranged, closed in Sep.**LL-L** *El Sereno*, T276480, F277547, serenohotel@ wanadoo.fr 18 rooms, 9 villas, 14 suites, fridge, large pool, superb restaurant, gardens, hammocks, private beach, the hotel also manages **LL-L** *El Sereno Beach Villas*, 9 villas on hillside, kitchen, use of hotel facilities. **LL** *St Bart's Beach Hotel*, T276070, F277557, www. saintbarthbeachhotel.com 36 rooms and 8 luxury villas, pool, gym, tennis, windsurfing school, built on strip of land between sea and lagoon, conference facilities. In the east, at Anse de Toiny, **LL** *Le Toiny*, T278888, F278930, www.letoiny.com 4-star hotel, includes breakfast, service, tax and airport transfers, 13 villa suites, plunge pools, restaurant, bar, room service, high luxury, closed Sep-Oct. **B-C** *La Normandie*, Lorient, T276166, F279883, www.st-barts.net/lanormandie 8 large or small a/c rooms, fridge, breakfast US$6.50.

Apartments and villas In the USA contact *French Caribbean International*, T800-3222223, www.frenchcaribbean.com On St-Barts contact the following agencies: *Sibarth Real Estate*, BP 55, Gustavia, 97133 St-Barts, T276238, F276052, 105062.1516@compuserve.com *New Agency*, Quai de la République, Gustavia, T278114, F278767. *Claudine Mora Immobilier* (CMI), Galeries du Commerce, Saint-Jean, T278088, F278085. *Immo-Antilles*, Gustavia, T279046, F276795. *Ici et Là*, Quai de la République, T277878, F277828.

There are many excellent restaurants all over the island, mostly French but some Créole and Italian. Very few vegetarian options but nearly all restaurants serve seafood. Several good ones on Saint-Jean beach; the hotel restaurants are generally good.

Eating
Food in St-Barts is expensive. Expect to pay minimum US$25 for dinner

Gustavia *Wall House*, T277183 for reservations, for good French cuisine on the waterfront with harbour view but overpriced wine; *Au Port* also offers fine dining overlooking the harbour, better value for money. T276236 for reservations, one of the most expensive restaurants on the island; *Le Repaire* is a good restaurant at the *Yacht Club*, overlooking the harbour open 0600-0100, closed Sun, on rue de la République, offers few but well-prepared French dishes (also has a few rooms to let, T277248); *Bar Le Select* is a central meeting spot, an informal bar for lunch with hamburger menu, but also one of the most popular night-time bars and sort of general store, with a few tables in a small garden. *L'Escale*, across the harbour, a pizza, pasta place with low prices for St Bart's but still expensive, closed Oct, T278106. A local place serving Créole food is *Eddy's*, T275417, closed Sun. For early starters try the bakery on rue du Roi Oscar II, they open 0600, closed Mon. *La Crêperie* on the same street is open 0700-2300, closed Sun, and does American and Continental breakfast as well as sweet and savoury *crêpes*, salads and ice creams. Not to be missed is *La Gloriette*, on the beach at Grand Cul de Sac, T277566, serving superb, authentic Créole cuisine.

Carnival is held before Lent, on Mardi Gras and Ash Wed. The **Festival of Gustavia** is *20 August*, with dragnet fishing contests, dances and parties, while *24 August* is the day of the island's patron saint, St-Barthélémy, when the church bells ring, boats are blessed and there

Festivals

French Antilles

are regattas, fireworks and a public ball. On *25 August* the **Feast of St Louis** is celebrated in the village of Corossol, with a fishing festival, *petanque, belote,* dancing and fireworks. In the last week of *July* the northern villages hold special events. **Fête du Vent** is held in Lorient on *26-27 August* with dragnet fishing contests, dancing, lottery and fireworks.

The **St Barts regatta** in *February* is the main event for sailors. Other regattas should be checked at *Lou Lou's Marine Shop,* Gustavia, because none is fixed annually. Every other year in *May* there is a transatlantic sailboat race from Brittany in France to St-Barts. The local traditional sailboats participate on all public events with their own regattas like **Bastille Day, Gustavia Day** and one regatta a month.

A **music festival** is held annually in *January* with 2 weeks of classical, folk, jazz music and ballet performed by both local school children and guest artistes and musicians from abroad in Gustavia and Lorient churches. A **gourmet festival** is held in *April,* and an **International Art exhibition** in *December.* On the last weekend in *April* is the **St-Barth Festival of Caribbean Cinema,** a small, informal festival for filmmakers throughout the Caribbean. All films are shown in their original language (with French subtitles).

Nightlife
Most of the nightlife starts around the bars at Bay Saint Jean

In Gustavia at *Bar Le Select* (closed Sun). In Lurin try *Why Not?* (open from 2100, disco, billiards, T278867), *La Banane* Cabaret Show now plays at *El Sereno Beach Hotel.* There are discos at *Le Petit Club* in Gustavia, T276633, lepetitclub@saint-barths.com open from 2200 and *Le Feeling,* Lurin, T278867. Contact the tourist office for details of concerts and ballets held in the Jan music festival, see above.

Shopping
Wide range of goods are available from T-shirts to duty-free luxury goods and fine wines. There are 5 small shopping centres in Saint-Jean: La Savane, Les Galeries du Commerce, La Villa Créole, Centre Commercial de Sain-Jean and Centre Commercial de Neptune. St-Barths is the place to find designer labels such as Gianni Versace, Hermès and Ralph Lauren.

Transport
Air Scheduled flights from Anguilla (*Coastal Air Transport*), Fort-de-France (*Air Caribienne*), Pointe-à-Pitre (*Air Caribienne*), St Croix (*Coastal Air Transport*), Sint Maarten (*Winair, Air Caribienne, Saint Barth Commuter*), St Martin (*Saint Barth Commuter, Air Caribienne*), St Thomas (*Air St Thomas, Air Caribienne*). Charters available locally with *St Barth Commuter,* T275454, *Air St Martin,* T276190 and *Air Caraïbes,* T279941, *Winair* T276101, *Air St-Barthélémy* T277190, *Air St Thomas* T277176. **Sea** *Gustavia Express* goes to St Martin, Mon-Sat, departs Gustavia 0715, 1530, departs Marigot market place 0900, 1715, adults one way US$36 including US$6 tax, round trip US$56, children up to 12 US$26 and US$31, cheaper for residents, ID required, T275410, 277724, F277723 in Gustavia, T879903, F877303 in St-Martin. *Voyager* have scheduled services between St Maarten/St Martin, St-Barts and Saba, contact St-Barth Ship Service for details, Quai de la République, T277738, F276795. Several catamarans go to St-Barts from Sint Maarten, leaving in the morning and returning in the afternoon so you can do a day trip. There are no other regular boats to other islands. **Car hire** Many agencies at the airport. *Hertz* T277114, *Avis* T277143, *Budget* T276630, *Turbe* T277142, *Gumbs Rental* T277532, *Questel* T277322, *Aubin* T277303, *Europcar* T277333, *Soleil Caraïbes* T276718, *Island Car Rental* T277001. It is not easy to hire a car for only one day, except out of season, mini mokes from 210F per day: ask your hotel to obtain a car if required. Scooters can be rented from *Rent Some Fun* T277059, *Chez Beranger* T278900, *Saint Barth Moto Bike* T276789. *Denis Dufau,* Saint-Jean, T275483, is a Harley Davidson shop. There are two gas stations, one near the airport terminal, open Mon-Sat 0730-1700, the other in Lorient open Mon-Wed, Fri 0730-1700, Sat morning. There is self-service with payment to the cashier, or automatic service machine open 24 hrs using Visa card, maximum allowance F600. There is a **taxi** stand at the airport T277581, and in Gustavia T276631. **Minibuses** (and ordinary taxis) do island tours, 21/2-3 hrs, US$45 for two people, dropping you off at Baie de Saint-Jean and collecting you later for the boat if you are on a day trip.

Banks *Banque Nationale de Paris* (0745-1200, 1405-1530) with an ATM that is supposed to work 24 **Directory**
hrs with US and European credit cards, Visa, Mastercard and Eurocard, but is reported to work only with
the French 'carte bleue', T276370, F278570. *Banque Française Commerciale* (0745-1215, 1400-1630,
Mon, Tue, Thu, Fri), withdrawals at counter with Visa, Mastercard and Eurocard, T276262, F278775,
both in Gustavia. BFC head office is at Saint-Jean, Galeries du Commerce (open Tue-Fri 0815-1215,
1400-1700, Sat 0800-1300) where there is an ATM open 24 hrs for withdrawals in US$ or F, T276588,
F278148. Crédit Martiniquais, at Le Carré d'Or in the centre of Gustavia (open Mon-Fri 0815-1215,
1400-1615), T278657, F278279. *Crédit Agricole*, rue Bord de Mer, Gustavia, ATM accepts nearly all
cards including eurocheque cards (cheaper than cash advance with credit card), also automatic bank
note exchange machine (open Tue-Fri 0800-1300, 1430-1700, Sat 0800-1300), T278990, F276461.
Crédit Lyonnais West Indies, rue Auguste Nyman, Gustavia (open Mon-Fri 0900-1200, 1400-1700),
T279200, F279191. **Communications Post:** In Gustavia there are 3: open 0800-1500 Mon, Tue, Thu,
Fri, 0800-1200 Wed, Sat, T276200, F278203; in Saint-Jean: open 0800-1400 Mon, Tue, Thu, Fri,
0730-1100 Wed, Sat, T276402. In Lorient: open 0700-1100 Mon-Fri, 0800-1000 Sat, T276135.
Telephone: The SiBarth agency on General de Gaulle in Gustavia, T276238, F276052, has a fax service
and a mail holding service. There are phone booths on the Quai de Gaulle, at the airport, Galeries du
Commerce and Flamands, among other places. There are some phones which take coins but most take
phone cards. There is a USA Direct phone at the airport; you can phone the USA using a phone card and
have the recipient return the call to the payphone. **Medical facilities** T276035. **Doctor** on call:
T277304. **Tourist information** Local office Quai de Gaulle, Gustavia, T278727, F277447. Open
Mon-Thu 0830-1230, 1430-1800, Fri 0930-1230, 1430-1600. St Barths Online: www.st.barths.com

Background

Although called Ouanalao by the Caribs, the island was renamed after Christopher **History**
Columbus' brother, Saint-Barthélémy when discovered in November 1496. It was
first settled by French colonists from Dieppe in 1645. After a brief possession by the
Order of the Knights of Malta, and ravaging by the Caribs, it was bought by the
Compagnie des Iles and added to the French royal domain in 1672. In 1784, France
ceded the island to Sweden in exchange for trading rights in the port of Göteborg. In
1801, St Barts was attacked by the British, but for most of this period it was peaceful
and commercially successful. The island was handed back to France after a referendum in 1878.

St Barts is administered by the sub-prefect in Saint-Martin and is a dependency of **Government**
Guadeloupe. The island has its own elected mayor, who holds office for seven years. **& economy**
Much the same as Saint-Martin, St-Barts relies on its free port status and its anchor-
ages and beaches for the bulk of its revenue. It is only 21 sq km, 230 km north of
Guadeloupe, 240 km east of the Virgin Islands, and 35 km southeast of
Saint-Martin.

St-Barts is inhabited mostly by people of Breton, Norman, and Poitevin descent **People**
who live in quiet harmony with the small percentage of blacks. Norman dialect is still
widely spoken while many islanders also speak English, but French is the dominant
language. A few elderly women still wear traditional costumes (with their characteristic starched white bonnets called *kichnottes*); they cultivate sweet potato patches
and weave palm fronds into hats and purses which they sell in the village of Corossol.
The men traditionally smuggled rum among neighbouring islands and now import
liqueurs and perfumes, raise cattle, and fish for lobsters offshore. Immigrants from
mainland France have taken the best jobs in hotels and restaurants though and relations there are sometimes strained. St-Barts has become a very 'chic' and expensive
holiday destination; the Rockefellers, Fords, and Rothschilds own property on the
island, while the rich, royal and famous stay in the luxury villas dotted around the
island. It is popular with both French and North American visitors and, despite the
limitations of its airstrip, it is claimed that twice as many tourists as the island's population pass through each month.

★ **A Foot in the door**

- Make the most of the delicious créole food, **eat out** as much as you can and, after a night on the town, head for the mobile eateries on Blvd Chevalier de Ste-Marthe next to the Savane.
- Don't miss the atmospheric ruins of **St-Pierre**, the 'Petit Paris' which was crushed and burned in 1902 when the volcano exploded and killed 30,000 people.
- Lie on the 4-km beach at **Le Diamant**, admire Diamond Rock offshore and imagine the lives of the 20 British sailors stationed there in 1804 for over a year.
- Treat yourself to a night at the elegant **Plantation Leyritz**, a former plantation house in the extreme north.

Martinique

Population: 399,000
Colour map 5, grid B5

Like Guadeloupe, Martinique at first glance is a piece of France transported to the tropics, where language and customs have adapted to the climate. There is something for everybody here: a variety of hotels; good beaches; watersports; historical attractions; beautiful scenery; hiking; birdwatching and countless other activities. Tourism is well developed in the south, but a large part of the more mountainous north is taken up by protected rainforest. The scenery is dramatic and very beautiful, with lush rainforest coating the slopes of the mountains and swathes of sugar cane grown on the plain. The volcano, Pelée, last erupted in 1902, when it destroyed the former capital, St-Pierre, killing all but one of its 26,000 inhabitants. The ruins and vulcanology museum are a fascinating insight into island life before 1902. It was on Martinique at the end of the 17th century that the Dominican friar, Père Labat, perfected the process of making rum, an enterprise that continues today, with great success.

Ins and outs

Getting there
See page 750 for further details

There are several daily flights from Paris and weekly flights from some other French cities, but no direct flights from any other European countries. The only direct flights to the USA are with *Air France* to Miami, so North American connections are best done there or go via San Juan, Puerto Rico. Links with neighbouring islands are good, both by air and by sea, so island hopping is easily done.

Getting around

There are no buses to the airport (though the Ste-Anne buses go close), a metered taxi is the only way of getting into town, costing US$10-17. Buses are best for short journeys while collective taxis, known as Taxicos, run all over the island. If you want to drive yourself, there are numerous car hire firms at the airport and around town, see page 750 for details.

Climate

The lushness of Martinique's vegetation is evidence that it has a far higher rainfall than many of the islands, due to its mountainous relief. The wet season lasts from June to late November and the frequency of sudden heavy showers make an umbrella or raincoat an essential piece of equipment. The cooler dry season lasts from December to May and the year round average temperature is 26°C although the highlands and Montagne Pelée are quite cool.

Watersports

Sailing and **windsurfing** at *Club de la Voile de Fort-de-France*, Pointe de la Vièrge, T614969, and Pointe des Carrières, T633137; *Club Nautique de Marin*, Bassin la Tortue, Pointe du Marin, T749248; *Club Nautique du François*, Route de la Jetée, T543100; *Club Nautique du Vauclin*, Pointe Faula, T745058; *Yacht Club de la Martinique*, Fort de France, T702360; *Base de Plein Air et de Loisirs*, Anse Spoutourne, Tartane, T582432. There are glass bottom boats, motor boats, sailing boats for excursions and lots of craft for hire. Windsurfing is available on hotel beaches where there are board rentals. Jet skiing, sea scooters and waterskiing at Pointe du Bout hotel beaches, *Marouba Club* (Carbet) and Pointe Marin beach in Ste-Anne. Many hotels like Bambou, La Dunette, Diamant-les-Bains organize **fishing** trips with local fishermen for their guests. Deep sea fishing can be arranged at *Bathy's Club* (*Meridien*), T660000 or *Rayon Vert*, T788056, around US$575 per boat.

Yole (yawl) races (large sailing boats with coloured sails and teams of oarsmen) are an amazing sight at festivals all over the island from July to January. In Fort-de-France races take place in November and December from the little beach next to Desnambuc quay. Other major sailing occasions include the Schoelcher International Nautical Week in February, with sailing and windsurfing competitions;

Martinique

N

Not to scale

Essentials

See also page 694

Documents See page 694.

Customs In Fort-de-France open 0800-1100, 1300-1700 daily, including holidays, no overtime fees charged; at Le Marin from 0730 until lunchtime, at St Pierre on Wednesday morning.

Money *Cost of living* Remember that the standard of living is high and expect to pay French prices or higher, which means expensive. Small beers or cokes cost around 15F in a tourist bar, 10F in a local bar, 6F in a supermarket, petrol 5F per litre, a nice meal at a good restaurant including wine will be at least 350F for two. A 2-3 course set lunch will cost 60-70F per person, with house wine at around 7F a glass.

Ports of entry (French Flag) Fort-de-France, St-Pierre, Le Marin. No fees or visas for EU or US citizens. French forms to clear in and out.

Anchorages The facilities are among the best in the Caribbean. Anchorages at St-Pierre, Fort-de-France, Anse Mitan, Les Trois-Ilets, Anse Noir, Grand and Petit Anse d'Arlets, Ste-Anne, Cul-de-Sac Marin. Marinas at Fort-de-France, Les Trois-Ilets, Le Marin. The marina at Pointe du Bout is reported safe, but congested and hot. Major charter companies include Moorings Antilles at Club Nautique du Marin (T747539, F747644), Sun Sail (Soleil et Voile,

Capitainerie Marina Pointo du Bout, T660914), and Stardust (Port de Plaisance du Marin, T749817, F749812). Many other smaller companies. Excellent provisioning, stock up on French wines.

For those looking to hitch on a boat, consult the noticeboards at the Yacht Clubs, especially the bar at the Public Jetty and refuelling at the west end of Boulevard Alfassa on the Baie des Flamands.

Hours of business *Shops* are open from 0900-1800 (**banks** from around 0730) and until 1300 on Saturday. Nearly everything closes from 1200-1500 and on Sunday.

Laundry There are several launderettes in Fort-de-France; Lavexpress, 61 rue Jules-Monnerot; Laverie Self-Service, Lavematic, 85 rue Jules-Monnerot, Terres Sainville, T637043. Laundry service behind Pointe du Bout marina, also at Bakoua Marina dock.

Useful addresses *Fire department*: T18. **Police**: T17. Gendarmerie, rue Victor Sévère, 97200 Fort-de-France, T635151. **Hôtel de Police**: T553000. **Sea rescue**: T639205, 632088. radio phone (international), T10. **Radio taxi**: T636362.

Voltage The electric current is 220 volts AC. **Weights and measures** The metric system. **Public holidays** See page 700.

International Sailing Week in March (Yacht Club of Fort-de-France); the Aqua Festival, the Great Nautical Celebration at Robert in April; the Yawl Regatta Tour of Martinique in July or August, when over a period of eight days about 20 yawls set off for a colourful race.

Diving is especially good along the coral reef between St-Pierre and Le Prêcheur, over the wrecks off St-Pierre and along the south coast. A medical certificate is required unless you are a qualified diver, in which case you need your certification card. There are lots of dive operators, most of which are based at the large hotels.

For those who do not dive, there are the *Kelennea* glass-bottomed boat at Marina Pointe du Bout, Trois Ilets, T660550, F660552 and the *Aquabulle* at Marin, T746969, which has a glass hull. To get even further under the water, there are two semi-submersibles: *Aquascope Seadom Explorer*, Marina Pointe du Bout, T683609 and *Zemis Aquascope*, Rue de Caritan, Ponton de la Mairie, T748741.

Other sports **Tennis** courts are at many large hotels; *Bakoua*; *Club Méditerranée*; *Plantation Leyritz*; *Novotel*; *Meridien, Framissima, Hôtel Casino la Batelière* and others where visitors can play at night as well as during the day. There are also about 40 clubs round the island where you can play by obtaining temporary membership. For more information contact *La Ligue Regional de Tennis*, Petit Manoir, Lamentin, T510800.

Golf At Trois-Ilets is a magnificent, 18-hole championship golf course designed by Henry Trent Jones, with various facilities including two tennis courts, shops, snackbar, lessons and equipment hire. Green fees in high season are US$46 and in low season US$39, or you can book for a week (US$285, US$227) or a month (US$960, US$900). Electric carts and other equipment are available for rent. Contact *Golf Country Club de la Martinique*, 97229 Trois-Ilets, T683281, F683897. Two mini-golf courses are at Madiana Plage à Schoelcher and Anse l'Etang à Tartane.

Riding is a good way to see Martinique's superb countryside; Ranch Jack, Morne Habitue-Quartier Espérance, T683769; Black Horse, La Pagerie, Trois-Ilets, T683780; La Cavale, Diamant, T762294; and others offering schooling, hacking and other facilities. At *Plantation Leyritz* there are two horses for guests' use.

Cycling Touring the island by bike is one of the activities offered by the Parc Naturel Régional. For information T731930. VT Tilt, Anse Mitan, Trois-Ilets, offers excursions by bike and cycle groups, T660101, F511400.

Spectator sports Mongoose and snake fights and cockfights are widespread from December to the beginning of August at Pitt Quartier Bac, Ducos, T560560; Pitt Marceny (the most popular), Le Lamentin, T512847, Pitt Cléry, Rivière-Pilote, T626169 and many others. Horse racing is at the Carrère racetrack at Lamentin, T512509.

Fort-de-France

Fort-de-France was originally built around the Fort St-Louis in the 17th century. The settlement's first name was Fort-Royal and its inhabitants are still called Foyalais. The city of today consists of a bustling, crowded centre bordered by the waterfront and the sprawling suburbs which extend into the surrounding hills and plateaux. The bars, restaurants, and shops give a French atmosphere quite unlike that of other Caribbean cities. Traffic is very dense and street parking is almost impossible. Park near la Savane (US$0.40 per hour). Most people live in the suburbs and even the discos are out of the old town centre, which is deserted at weekends after Saturday midday. The port is to the east of the town centre, where the Baie du Carenage houses the naval base, yacht club, cargo ships and sometimes luxury cruise liners.

The impressive **Fort St-Louis** still functions as a military base. Built in Vauban style, it dominates the waterfront. Once inside beware the low ceiling arches. Wonderful views from the top. At the Gate there is a visual display and gift shop. Identification is required when you buy the ticket. Parts of the fort are off-limits as it is an active military base. ■ *Excellent, informative guided tours (English, Spanish, French), every half hour, 0900-1530 Mon-Fri, 1000-1500 Sat, 1 hr, US$3.50, by Les Amis du Fort-St- Louis. T605459*. Adjacent to the fort is **La Savane**, the old parade ground, now a park of 5 ha planted with palms, tamarinds, and other tropical trees and shrubs. The park contains statues of two famous figures from the island's past: Pierre Belain d'Esnambuc, the leader of the first French settlers on Martinique; and Empress Josephine (now beheaded), first wife of Napoléon Bonaparte, who was born on the island.

The **Bibliothèque Schoelcher** is situated on the corner of Rue Victor Sévère and Rue de la Liberté, just across the road from the Savane. Schoelcher (1804-1893) devoted his life to the abolition of slavery. He gave his library to Martinique but most was burned in the fire. The building to house the collection was commissioned, but not built, before the fire. It was designed by Henry Picq, a French architect married to a woman from Martinique. The Eiffel engineering company constructed it in iron, shipped it to the island and it opened in 1893. On the exterior you can see the names of freedom campaigners, including John Brown, of the USA, William Wilberforce, of the UK and Toussaint Louverture, of Haiti. Today it still functions as a library and regularly holds exhibitions. ■ *0830-1730, Mon-Thu, 0830-1200, Fri-Sat. T702667.*

Just along the Rue de la Liberté towards the seafront is the **Musée Départemental d'Archéologie Précolombienne**. It contains relics of the Arawak and Carib Indians: pottery, statuettes, bones, reconstructions of villages, maps, etc. Worth a visit. ■ *0900-1300, 1430-1700 Mon-Fri, 0900-1200 Sat. US$1.50. T715705.* In the centre

Sights

of town, in the Square of Père Labat, Rue Schoelcher, there is a second chance to see the architecture of Henri Picq with the **Cathedral of St-Louis** which towers above the Fort-de-France skyline. This, too, is mainly of iron, in a romanesque-byzantine style. The arms of past bishops, in stained glass, give colour to the choir. In a beautiful creole villa dating back to 1887, is the **Musée Régional d'Histoire et d'Ethnographie de la Martinique** on Boulevard Générale de Gaulle, opposite the Atrium Theatre. It is a modern museum, opened in 1999, and strong on the origins, customs and traditions of the people of Martinique. ■ *US$3, T728187, F637411.*

The **Parc Floral et Culturel** (also called **Galerie de Géologie et de Botanie** or **Exotarium**) is a shady park containing two galleries, one of which concentrates on the geology of the island, the other on the flora, and mid-19th century wooden barracks now housing 11 workshops for local artisans. Almost 2,800 species of plants have been identified in Martinique and the Parc Floral has a very good selection. ■ *0900-1230 Mon-Fri, 1430-1730, closed Sat, Sun. US$1.75 adults, US$0.50 children. T706841.* Next

Central Fort-de-France

Bus Stations
1 Bus Terminal
2 Taxi Collectif Terminal

N
Not to scale

to the Parc Floral are a feature of Fort-de-France not to be missed, the **markets**. The fishmarket is by the Madame River, facing the Place José Martí, where fishermen unload from their small boats or *gommiers*. Close by is one of several markets selling fruit, vegetables and flowers as well as exotic spices. The markets hum with activity from 0500 to sunset, but are best on Friday and Saturday. A fresh green coconut hacked open with a machete, makes a refreshing drink for about US$1.

The northwest coast

The coastal road heading north through Schoelcher from Fort-de-France hugs the coast, zigzagging north through **Case-Pilote** (named after a friendly Carib chief) where there is a 17th-century church. It then passes through several fishing villages and is flanked by beaches that gradually become blacker with volcanic sand. **Le Carbet** is where Columbus is presumed to have landed (monument). A *carbet* was the great meeting house of the Caribs. There are several good restaurants, mostly fish, on the beach. **Habitation Anse Latouche** is at the end of Carbet village on the coast. The ruins of a 17th-century sugar plantation are surrounded by a beautiful garden focusing on local flowers and shrubs and an exhibition of butterflies. There is not much left of the main house, having been destroyed by the 1902 volcanic eruption (see below), but there is a beautiful viaduct at the back of the gardens which leads from a dam to a big waterwheel which used to drive the sugar mill. ■ *Mon-Sat 1000-1600. Entry US$2, children 7-12 US$1.50, or US$5.80 and US$2 for joint entry to Balata Gardens. T781919.* At the popular beach of **Anse Turin** just north of Le Carbet, is the small **Gauguin Museum**. The artist stayed at Anse Turin during 1887 before he went to Tahiti. The museum has copies (mostly photographic) of letters, sketches and some reproductions of his work. Nothing is original. Local artists' paintings and ceramics are sometimes on sale. There is an interesting section on the local traditional women's costume and its elements, *la grande robe, le madras*, and *le foulard*, the head-tie which was knotted to indicate how engaged the wearer's affections were. ■ *0900-1730 daily. US$3. T782266.*

To the north of Carbet is the famous **St-Pierre**. The town is well worth a visit and is an eerie reminder of destructive natural forces that dominate life in the Caribbean. The modern village is built on the ruins of the former capital of Martinique, which was destroyed by a cloud of molten volcanic ash when Montagne Pelée erupted on 8 May 1902. As the cultural and economic capital, the town was known as the 'Petit Paris' of the West Indies. Out of 30,000 inhabitants (St-Pierrotains) there was only one survivor, named Auguste Cyparis (also known as Sylbaris), an illiterate casual labourer who had been thrown drunk into a cell for the night. Today his small cell is one of the ruins that visitors can still see. The prison is beside the remains of the once splendid and celebrated theatre of St-Pierre on Rue Victor Hugo. You can see the broad sweep of steps up to the entrance, the huge stage area, the first floor boxes and the rusting remains of the electric stage lighting. In the **Musée Volcanologique Franck-Perret, Museum of Vulcanology** is an interesting collection of objects (mostly by Perret, an American) and documents evoking life before 1902 and remains from the disaster: household metal and glass objects charred and deformed by the extreme heat, photographs and volcanology displays. ■ *0900-1700 daily. US$1.50. T781516.* The bridge over the Rivière Roxelane, built in 1766, leads to the oldest part of the town, the **Quartier du Fort**. The ruins of the church are among the most moving.

St-Pierre

The next village on the coastal road is the picturesque fishing village of **Le Prêcheur**. Madame de Maintenon, who married Louis XIV lived here. The three bells outside the church date from that time. The road then continues towards the spectacular beach of **Anse Céron** where the sand seems to be at its blackest. A rock called the Pearl juts out from the sea which is roughish but swimming is possible. It is a wild and beautiful beach, a pleasant change from the calm, white sand tourist beaches in the south. Turn inland to **Habitation Céron**, a plantation where the early sugar buildings are largely intact and there is an attractive botanic walk. There are huge ponds where succulent crayfish are raised. These, with homegrown fruit and vegetables make an excellent three-course lunch for US$25 including a rum punch. ■ *0930-1700 daily. T529453.* The coastal road ends a kilometre or two further on at another beach, Anse Couleuvre.

Watch out for fer-de-lance snakes & bilharzia in the streams

It is possible to follow a track 18 km through the rainforest around the northern coast, but a guide is essential (see directory, page 752). The first 20 minutes on a concrete road are discouraging, but once in the forest the path is cooler and the views beautiful. At the extreme north of the island is another small fishing village, **Grande Rivière** set in breathtaking scenery characteristic of this part of the island; plunging cliffs covered with the lush vegetation of the rainforest. The island of Dominica faces the village from across the sea. Winding roads lead through the mountains to the next village, Macouba, perched on top of a cliff.

The tropical rainforest and La Montagne Pelée

Route de la Trace

La Route de la Trace winds through the tropical rainforest on the slopes of the Pitons du Carbet from Fort-de-France to **Morne Rouge** on the southern slope of Montagne Pelée. The town was hit by a second eruption of Pelée on 20 August 1902. A new park has been opened, called **Le Jardin de la Pelée**, on the hill above the town, where there is a fine display of local flora, well labelled, and information on the volcano (T524251). From Morne Rouge there is a road to St-Pierre on the coast, so a circuit is possible. The forest itself is truly magnificent, covering the sides of the steep, inland mountains (Les Pitons de Carbet and Pelée) with a bewildering array of lush, green vegetation that stretches for miles. Giant bamboo, mountain palms, chestnut and mahogany trees, over a thousand species of fern and many climbing and hanging parasitic plants and orchids are examples of rainforest vegetation. The forest is protected as part of Martinique's Parc Naturel and makes interesting walking country (see directory, page 752).

At **Balata**, not far from the capital along the Route de la Trace is the bizarre sight of the **Sacré Coeur**, a smaller version of Paris's votive Sacré-Coeur de Montmartre, perched high up in the forest. A little further along the road is the **Le Jardin de Balata** with superb views across the Baie de Fort-de-France to Trois-Ilets. The gardens feature a collection of 3,000 species with magnificent anthuriums, ranging from dark maroon, crimson and pink to white. Look out for the numerous hummingbirds and brilliant green lizards. ■ *0900-1700 daily. US$5.80, children aged 7-12, US$2, includes entry to Habitation Anse Latouche. T644873, F647340. Signs are in French.*

As the Route de la Trace winds its way through the rainforest, the flanks of the surrounding mountains are clearly visible, covered with cultivated tropical flowers such as anthuriums and ginger lilies. **La Montagne Pelée** is reached via a track branching off the Route de la Trace, between Morne Rouge and **Ajoupa-Bouillon**, where there is a delightful garden-park, **Les Ombrages Botaniques**. ■ *0900-1700. US$3, children US$1.50.* From the car park at the foot of the volcano there is a view of the Atlantic Coast, Morne Rouge and the bay of St-Pierre. The mountain air is deliciously fresh and cool even at the foot of the volcano. Not far away are **Les Gorges de la Falaise**, a series of small gorges along 3 km of the Falaise River, wonderful for swimming in, accessible only by following the course of the river on foot. Much of the walk is actually wading in the water and you clamber over waterfalls, making the carrying of cameras impractical unless waterproofed. ■ *The local Syndicat d'Initiative in Ajoupa-Bouillon organizes guided tours up the river, T533287. US$6.50 including waterproof pack and fruit juice.*

North coast

The area of **Basse-Pointe** is the pineapple cultivation area of the island, where huge fields of spikey pineapple tops can be seen. Basse-Pointe is an old settlement with a late 17th-century church and a good view of the cliffs from the cemetery. Inland from here is **Plantation Leyritz**, a former plantation complex, complete with slave houses and machinery. The restored 18th-century owner's house is now an elegant hotel where the French government has entertained the presidents of the USA and Senegal. You can walk round the gardens and eat in what was once the sugar boiling house. There is an exhibition of tiny tableaux featuring dolls made from plants and vegetables, exploiting the colours and textures of tropical leaves. ■ *1000-1830 daily, T785392*. The coast road continues from Basse-Pointe to Macouba (see above) and Père Labat's church.

From the N1 road along the northeast coast of the island tempting beaches with crashing waves are visible, but the Atlantic Coast is too dangerous for swimming. However, there is a safe beach at Anse Azérot, just south of **Ste-Marie**. To the north is **Fond St-Jacques**, a cultural centre which used to be a Dominican monastery and sugar plantation. Buildings date from 1689 and at its height the Dominicans utilized 1,000 slaves. It was here that Père Labat perfected the distilling of rum. His memoirs are a prime source of information on plantation life. Modern exhibitions are also held at the centre. ■ *Mon-Fri 0800-1700, adults US$2, children US$0.75. T691012.* Nearby, **Musée du Rhum Saint-James** in the St James Distillery, includes an explanation of the process of rum production and its history, and rum tasting. ■ *Mon-Fri, 0900-1700 and Sat, Sun 0900-1200, admission and tour free. T693002.*

The seafront at **La Trinité** is a grand promenade with modern and 19th-century buildings and monuments, which looks out onto the **Presqu'île de la Caravelle**, where the vegetation is scrubby but the scenery is gently interesting. The peninsula has beaches at **Tartane** (the only village on the Caravelle), **Anse l'Etang** (the best, surfing possible) and **Anse du Bout**. It is an area protected by the **Parc Naturel** of Martinique; several well-marked paths criss-cross the peninsula so that visitors can enjoy the varied flora and fauna. It is also possible to visit the historic ruins of the **Château Dubuc** and various buildings that belonged to the Dubuc family, including slave smugglers and privateers. ■ *0830-1730 daily. US$2, children US$1. T474548.*

Southeast coast From the Caravelle peninsula the Atlantic coast is characterized by deep, protected, shallow, sandy bays, good for swimming, surfing and sailing. The road runs southeast through Le Robert and Le François to the more mountainous area around **Le Vauclin** where the main activity is fishing. There are some interesting art-deco buildings from the 1920s on its steep streets. There are innumerable islets offshore. The **Baignoire de Josephine** has sand-banks and is featured on local boat trips. **Pointe Faula** is a very safe beach here, with dazzling white sand and shallow water. To the south of Vauclin a road leads to **Anse Macabou**, a group of impressive white sand beaches.

South Martinique

The small village of **Les Trois-Ilets**, across the bay from Fort-de-France, has a charming main square and is surrounded by tourist attractions. Empress Josephine, born Marie Josèph Rose Tascher de la Pagerie, was baptized in the church on the square. Her mother is buried here and the church, restored with money from Napoléon III, is rather a shrine to the Napoleonic legend. Even more so is **Le domaine de la Pagerie**, the family's sugar plantation, about 4 km from the village. Josephine was probably born here in 1763, and lived here until she was 16. In 1766 a hurricane blew away the graceful plantation house and the family lived above the sugar boiling house. Now an attractive evocation of that time, the ruins can be seen and, in the renovated kitchen, a stone building, there is an excellent collection of

French Antilles

Islands of three queens

Martinique was historically the aristocrat of the French Antilles, looking down on the more bourgeois Guadeloupais. Josephine, the first wife of Napoléon I was born at Trois Ilets. Her cousin, Aimée Dubuc de Rivery, was kidnapped on the high seas, and sold to the Sultan of Turkey, becoming one of his favourite wives, and mother of his successor. Madame de Maintenon spent much of her youth in the island: later she secretly married Louis XIV. Thus, as is sometimes said,

Martinique became known as 'the island of three queens'. Delgrès, who fought Napoleon's troops seeking to re-impose slavery, was a mulatto from Martinique. The island has been the birthplace of many black writers, including Aimé Césaire (b 1913), the doyen of négritude and of black cultural awareness. The blood of Africa also flowed, via Martinique, through the veins of Colette, one of whose ancestors came from the island.

furniture, documents and portraits. *Tue-Fri 0900-1730, Sat-Sun 0900-1300, 1430-1730, US$3, children US$0.75. T683455, F683841.* At Pointe Vatable, 2 km east of Trois-Ilets, is the sugar cane museum (**La Maison de la Canne**) which uses documents, machinery and superb models of sugar processing plant to illustrate the history of the Martiniquan sugar industry. Recommended. Guided tours are available. ■ *0900-1700 daily except Mon, US$2, children US$0.75. T683204.*

A short bus ride from Trois-Ilets is the tourist complex of **Pointe du Bout**, directly opposite Fort-de-France, and linked by *vedettes* (regular ferries) every 15 minutes. Three companies operate the service. Return tickets cost US$5 and are valid on all ferries (bicycles at no extra charge). There is a marina, a créole village, where some of the shops, cafés, bars, restaurants and souvenir stands can be found, discothèques, sport facilities and a conglomeration of luxury hotels. There is plenty of evening entertainment. The first beach after stepping off the ferry is a crowded strip of sand in front of the *Hotel Meridien*, almost completely covered with deckchairs for hire. Perhaps preferable is the beach at **Anse Mitan**, a five-minute walk away, where there are numerous reasonably priced restaurants and bars. There is a direct ferry from the capital every 15 minutes. **Anse à l'Ane**, a little way along the coast to the west is quieter than Anse Mitan and Pointe du Bout and has a pleasant atmosphere. At **Grande Anse** is a magnificent beach, less frequented by tourists than the beaches at Pointe du Bout, although it does get more crowded at weekends. The pretty village of **Anse d'Arlets** is nearby. Direct ferry from Fort-de-France. Just south of Anse d'Arlets and around the **Pointe du Diamant** is **Le Diamant**. This is an idyllic golden sand beach stretching for 4 km along the south coast and dominated by the famous **Rocher du Diamant** (Diamond Rock). This huge 176 m rock, of volcanic origin, is about 4 km out to sea and was occupied by the English during the Napoleonic Wars. They stationed four cannons and about 20 sailors there in 1804 before the French reconquered it a year and a half later. Negotiate with a fisherman if you want to visit.

Inland and to the east of Diamant is the town of **Rivière-Pilote**, the largest settlement in the south of the island. The **Mauny Rum distillery** is located here, where free guided tours are available. ■ *Mon-Fri 0930-1730, Sat 0900-1300. T626208.* The famous **Cléry cock-fighting pit** stages regular mongoose-snake fights. ■ *Sun afternoon, T626169.* From the town of **Le Marin**, southwards are long white sand beaches lined with palm groves, and calm clear sea which epitomize the classic image of the Caribbean. Marin itself boasts a very fine 18th-century Jesuit church. The largest marina on the island is here.

At **Ste-Anne** an extensive *Club Méditerranée* complex has its own section of beach adjacent to the long public beach, T767272 for an all-inclusive day pass. From Ste-Anne there is a spectacular view along the southwest coast, including Rocher du Diamant. Ste-Anne beach is picturesque and shady with trees that overhang the sea in some places. The water is calm, ideal for toddlers. There is a wide selection of lively bars and restaurants, some selling snacks or *menu du jour*, others more expensive. You can rent all types of watersports equipment: windsurfers, catamarans, seedoos, kayaks, sunfish, or take a sea plane ride. The swimming area is marked off with yellow buoys. Irregular ferries sail from Fort-de-France, 2½-3½ hours. There is a fine Jesuit church of 1766 opposite the jetty.

The road heading east from Marin leads to the beach at **Cap Chevalier**, a popular family beach at weekends, but choppy, as it faces the Atlantic. Among others along the barrier reef, the **Ilet Chevalier**, a bird sanctuary, is visible from here.

At the southernmost tip of the island is the famous Grande Anse des Salines and the beaches of Dunkerque, Baham and Anse Trabaud, all of which are remarkably attractive. Inland from Anse Trabaud lies the salt marsh and the forest petrified by former lava flow. Birdwatching is good at the Etang des Salines and in the sandy marshes around the Baie des Anglais.

Essentials

Information and reservations can be made through Centrale de Réservation, BP 823-97200 Fort-de- France Cédex, T715611, F736693. The tourist office at the airport is helpful and will telephone round the hotels to get you a room for your first night if you have not booked beforehand. Alternatively, for *gîtes* and country guest houses, contact the *Fédération Martiniquaise des Offices de Tourisme et Syndicat D'Initiative*, Maison du Tourisme Vert, 9 Boulevard du Géneral de Gaulle, BP 1122, 97248 Fort-de-France Cédex, T631854, F701716. Generally, prices are high, but there are some surprising out-of-season bargains at the best resort hotels which can work out cheaper than at inferior hotels nearer Fort-de-France. Some hotels add 10% service charge and/or 5% government tax to the bill.

Sleeping *Two useful websites are www.club-hoteliers-martinique.asso.fr & www.martinique-hotel.com*

Pointe du Bout and **Les Trois-Ilets** These are the main tourist centres, and are well equipped with shops, nightclubs, casinos, a marina, facilities for golf, watersports and tennis as well as several beaches. Trois-Ilets benefits from the facilities of Pointe du Bout and the pleasant beaches of Anse Mitan and Anse à l'Ane, a 20-min ferry ride from Fort-de-France. The main hotels are **LL-AL** *Meridien*, 97229 Trois-Ilets, T660000, F660074. Recently renovated huge modern complex with 295 rooms and traditional bungalows dating from the 1960s in splendid, mature landscaped grounds. The marina village is fun to walk through (you could take a picnic lunch, food and drink is expensive). Excellent evening entertainment, sometimes the national ballet company. **LL** *Bakoua* (named after traditional Martiniquan straw hats), T660202, F660041, a *Sofitel Coralia* hotel. Créole ambience with touch of sophistication, 139 apartments and rooms, 2 restaurants, excellent buffet of local dishes, tennis, fitness centre, pool, on beach, evening entertainment includes the ballet, Martinique-style cabaret in English and French. **LL-L** *Novotel Coralia Carayou*, Pointe du Bout, 97229 Trois Ilets, T660404, F660057. 201 spacious rooms in 7 acres of gardens overlooking Fort de France bay, right on beach, walking distance to shops, restaurants at marina, 2 restaurants, watersports. **A-B** *Auberge de l'Anse Mitan*, T660112, F660105. A friendly, family-run hotel with apartments and rooms. **B-C** *Le Nid Tropical*, rents studios and has a lively beach bar and restaurant, T683130, F684743. Also camping, see below. **B** *La Bonne Auberge*, T660155, F660450. Again basic but clean, offering underwater fishing and watersports.

Fort-de-France **AL-B** *Squash Hotel*, 3 Boulevard de Verdun, T630001, F630074. 108 modern rooms, pool, 3 squash courts, gym, dancing room, saunas, jacuzzi, billards, conference facilities, impersonal, concrete ambience, but friendly staff. **A-B** *Impératrice*, T630682, F726630, rue de la Liberté. 1950s décor and architecture, apparently unchanged since it was built in 1957. **B** *La Malmaison*, rue de la Liberté, opposite the Savane, T639085, F600393. Good and clean, spacious, recommended for price range. Both these hotels have lively bars and restaurants frequented by a young crowd. **B-C** *Le Gommier*, 3 rue Jacques Cazotte, T718855, F730696. One of the oldest buildings in town. Has clean spacious rooms and good continental breakfasts, friendly management. In the elegant suburbs of Didier is the **B-C** *Victoria*, Route de Didier, 97200 Fort-de-France, T605678, F600024, on hillside overlooking bay.

Popular with businessmen as well as holiday makers, 37 rooms, good restaurant, a/c, TV, phone, fridge, buses into town every few minutes, pool. The **C** *Balisier* on 21 rue Victor Hugo is also very centrally located with a view over the port, T/F714654. Good value. **C** *Carib*, 9 rue du Matouba, T601985. Newly renovated, a/c, wrought iron beds, hardwood floors, very clean and appealing, good location. Recommended. On rue Lazare Carnot is **C** *Un Coin de Paris*, T700852, F630951. Small, friendly and cheap. **Schoelcher**, on the outskirts of Fort-de-France, is **LL-L** *Framissima* , T614949, F617057. Pool, tennis courts, gym, disco, conference facilities, restaurant, bars, casino, very fine hotel. Recommended.

Diamant Miles of superb, uncrowded beach with magnificent views of coastal mountains and, of course, Diamant Rock. **LL-L** *Novotel Coralia Diamant*, at Pointe de la Chery Diamant, T764242, F762287, H046@accor-hotels.com Recently extended, in garden setting, 181 a/c rooms, 4 rooms for wheelchair guests, beach or pool views, 4 restaurants, including creole, tennis, archery, pedal boats etc, **AL** *Mercure Inn Coralia Diamant* , at Pointe de la Chery Diamant, T764600, F762599. On hillside in tropical garden, 149 rooms with kitchenette, 2 rooms for wheelchair guests, panoramic views of Rocher du Diamant, 3 restaurants, creole, Italian and international. **AL** *Calypso*, Les Hauts du Diamant, 97223 Diamant, T764081, F764084, 500 m from beach, walking distance to village. 60 rooms and suites in 11 buildings, superb views of Diamant Rock, pool, bar, restaurant, car rental. **AL-B** *Diamant les Bains*, T764014, F762700. Fine views over swimming pool and sea. **AL** *Le Village du Diamant*, T764189, F635332. 59 basic, beachside bungalows, rooms or apartments for rent.

Ste-Luce AL-B *Pierre et Vacances*, at Pointe Philippeaux, T621262, villagesteluce@ martinique-hotels.com Holiday village familiarly called *Village de Sainte-Luce*, with 334 nicely decorated apartments, ranging from studios for 2-3 people to apartments with 3 rooms for 6 people, 10 apartments for wheelchair guests, near the beach, views to Rocher du Diamant and on clear days to St Lucia, diving and watersports. **AL** *Mercure Inn Coralia Les Amandiers*, by Fonds Larion beach at Désert, a district of Ste-Luce village, T623232, F623340, les.amandiers@martinique-hotels.com Along the beach, close to the fishing village, nice 3-star hotel, 117 rooms, all with terrace or loggia, 4 rooms for wheelchair guests. **A** *Amyris*, by the beach of Pointe Philippeau, T621200, F621210, amyris@cgit.com Three-star, in Karibéa chain, 110 rooms of which are wheelchair-accessible, all amenities, very nice. In the same hotel chain, 2km from Ste-Luce and 300 m from the beach is *Caribia* aparthotel, T622062, F625952, in the Désert area. 76 apartments. **B** *Aux Délices de la Mer*, T625012. Offers fishing amongst other activities, only 5 rooms, créole restaurant.

Outside Ste-Anne To the north, is the *Club Med Village Les Boucaniers*, T767452, F767202. Lots of tennis and land based sports, waterskiing, windsurfing, sailing, diving and golf at extra cost, no children under 12, 313 rooms. Just south of Ste-Anne on sandy beach is **LL-AL** *Hôtel Anse Caritan*, BP 24, 97227 Sainte-Anne, T767412, F767259. 96 rooms with views across to Diamond Rock, a/c, terraces, kitchenettes, phone, pool, restaurant, watersports and excursions arranged. **L-AL** *Domaine de Belleford*, 97227 Sainte-Anne, T769232, F769140. Recently renovated, 186 rooms and suites in 5 sections, 500 m from beach, popular with Europeans, terraces, kitchenettes, four pools, two restaurants, bar, boutiques, car rental.

Atlantic coast LL-B *La Frégate Bleu*, T545466, F547848. Seven spacious, elegant seaview rooms, kitchenettes, terraces, charming hilltop site, gingerbread trimmings, rooms decorated with antiques, Persian rugs, four-poster beds, helpful, English-speaking staff. **B-C** *Chez Julot*, rue Gabriel Peri, **Vauclin**, T744093. A modest but pleasant hotel, one street back from foreshore road, a/c. Restaurant, bar. **A-B** *Les Brisants*, T543257, F546913, at **François** provides good Créole cuisine. On the old NI, near **Trinité**, within easy reach of the Caravelle peninsula, **A-B** *St Aubin*, T693477, F694114. A magnificent colonial-style hotel, once a plantation house, splendid location, views and exterior, but interior badly damaged by 1960s refurbishment, 15 a/c rooms. **AL** *Le Village de Tartane* is near the pretty fishing village of **Tartane**, T580633, F635332. Bungalows with kitchenette around pool. In Tartane, **B-C** *Madras*, hotel and restaurant, on the beach, spotless rooms, seaview or road view, T583395, F583363. **A-C** *Hôtel Primerêve*, Anse Azérot, just south of Sainte Marie, T694040, F690937. 20 rooms, 80 suites, new hotel on hillside, elegant, 5-min walk to superb beach, secluded cove, pool, good restaurant, tennis, snorkelling, easy access to rainforest. **LL** *Habitation Lagrange*, Le Marigot, T536060, F535058. 16 rooms, one suite, 4 poster beds, terraces, luxury, in tropical gardens, 18th century buildings, decorated in colonial style, private, romantic, beautiful pool, tennis, superb restaurant, in the rainforest, 20 mins from beach.

Basse Pointe **AL-A** *Plantation de Leyritz*, T785392, F789244. A former plantation house set in beautiful grounds with a lot of insects because of all the fruit trees and water, glamorous accommodation, excellent restaurant serving local specialities, efficient and friendly service, pool, tennis courts, health spa, discothèque. In the remote, northern-most commune, **Grand-Rivière**, a small fishing village surrounded by rainforest and close to several idyllic black sand coves, **D** *Chanteur Vacances* simple, clean hotel with 7 rooms, shared facilities, restaurant, T557373.

West coast One of the few hotels within easy reach of the ruined town of **St-Pierre**: is **C** *La Nouvelle Vague*, T781434. Five rooms over bar, overlooks beach. On **Carbet's** enormous black sand beach are **C** *Le Cristophe Colomb*, T780538, F780642, good value, and the more upmarket **LL-AL** *Marouba Club*, T780021, F780565, which has apartments and bungalows, pool, disco, CP or MAP rates.

Finally, convenient for the airport, at **Ducos**: in the plain of Lamentin, **C** *Airport*, six rooms, basic a/c, hot water, no restaurant, T560183.

Youth hostels Fédération des Oeuvres Laiques (FOL) has a hostel, along the Route de Didier, Rue de Prof Raymond Garcia, T640410, 640017, head office at 31 Rue Perrinon, Fort de France, T635022, F638367. It is several km from the town centre and difficult to find. No public transport in evenings, taxis can make staying here expensive. Rooms, **C**, sleep 2 or 4 with shower and toilet, basic.

Camping The most convenient campsite for Fort-de-France is at Anse à l'Ane, *Le Nid Tropical* campsite, US$10 for 2 people if you have your own tent, US$14, if you rent one, also cabins and apartments with kitchenette, T683130, F684743. A small bakery/restaurant on the beach serves cheap meals, bread and pastries. On the south coast, Ste-Luce has a good campsite with adequate facilities in the *VVF Hotel*, but the beach is not nice. There are no tents for hire. T625284. *Camping Municipal* at Ste-Anne is a popular campsite with a pleasant situation in a shady grove right on the beach, US$7, cheap food available. Next to the *Club Med*, it is on the cleanest and nicest beach. You can rent tents from *Chanteur Vacances*, 65 Rue Perrinon, Fort-de-France, T716619, around US$5 per day.

Sampling the French and Créole cuisine is one of the great pleasures of visiting Martinique. Snack bar or fast food, including burgers and chips are at the lower end of that range. A meal at a decent restaurant without wine would range from US$7-15, depending on the venue and the menu. Here are some worth seeking out. For a description of local food, see page 694.

Eating
The small booklet, Ti Gourmet Martinique, gives many restaurants, with details and prices.

Fort-de-France *Le Blenac*, 3 rue Blenac, T701841. Closed Sun evening. *King Creole*, 56 Av des Caraïbes, T701917. Closed Sat midday and Sun. For crêpes and salads try *La Crêperie*, 4 rue Garnier Pagès, T606209. Closed Sat midday, Sun. *Espace Créole*, 8 rue Voltaire, T700595. Open Mon-Sat 1100-2200. *Le Victor Hugo*, 69 rue V Hugo, T636108. Closed Sun midday. *Marie Sainte*, 160 rue V Hugo, T700030. Open daily except Sun. In the market at Fort-de-France are small kiosks selling créole *menu du jour* for US$7 including dessert and drink, other meals also served, with tablecloths and flowers on table, Miriam enthusiastically greets customers at *Chez Louise* and explains menu in English. For an Italian atmosphere try *Le Vieux Milan*, 60 Av des Caraïbes, T603531. Excellent pizza for US$7-11, closed Sat, Sun.

French Antilles

There are several restaurants serving Vietnamese and Chinese food, including *Le Cantonnais*, Marina Pointe du Bout, T660233. Open daily. *Le Chinatown*, 20 rue Victor Hugo, T718262. Mon-Fri lunch. *Indo*, 105 route de la Folie, T716325. Vietnamese, closed Sun evening and Mon. *Le Jardin de Jade*, Anse Colas, T611550. Closed Sun evening. *Le Kiwany's*, 2 rue Kernay, Trinité, T584244. Closed Sun evening, Mon. *Le Xuandre*, Vietnamese, Voie No 2 Pointe des Nègres, T615470. Evenings only, closed Mon. Other nationalities are also well represented: *Le Couscousser*, 1 rue Perrinon, looking out on to Bibliothèque Schoelcher. Excellent with choice of sauces and meats to accompany *couscous*, reasonably priced, interesting, rather young Algerian red wine goes well with the food, open Mon-Fri 1200-1500, 1900-2300, Sat 1900-2300, T600642. *Les Cèdres*, Lebanese, in rue Redoute de Matouba. Excellent humous, kebabs and other Lebanese meze, owner speaks English, all major credit cards accepted. *Le Salambo*, Tunisian, Patio de Cluny, T704778. Closed Sun, Mon, Tue. *Le Beyrouth*, Lebanese, 9 rue Redoute de Matouba, T606745. Lunch menu from US$11.50. *Le Méchoui*, Moroccan, Pte Simon, behind Bricogite. Reservations preferred, takeaway service, T715812, open 1200-1600, 1900-2400, closed Sun. *Las Tapas de Sevillas*, Spanish, 7 rue Garnier Pagès, T637123.

For travellers on a smaller budget wishing to eat out in the capital there are plenty of good snackbars and cafés serving various substantial sandwiches and *menus du jour*. The area around Place Clemenceau has lots of scope; *Le Clemenceau* is very good value and extremely friendly, try the *accras* or a fresh *crudité* salad. *Le Lem* on Boulevard Général-de-Gaulle has superior fast food at low prices and a young crowd. It also stays open later than many restaurants that close in the evenings and on Sun. Behind the Parc Floral on rue de Royan is the *Kowossol*, a tiny vegetarian café which serves a cheap and healthy *menu du jour*. The pizzas are recommended and the fruit juice is especially delicious – try *gingembre* (ginger) or *ananas* (pineapple). On François Arago *Los Amigos* and *Le Coq d'Or* are particularly good for substantial sandwiches for around US$2. Try *poisson* (steak fish) or *poulet* (chicken). *Le Renouveau* on Boulevard Allègre offers delicious, filling *menus du jour* for US$6, again with a warm welcome. As in France, there are *Traiteurs* opening up, offering stylish takeaway meals which you select at the shop, helpful to vegetarians. Ask for the latest list at the tourist office.

The place to head for in the evening when these eateries close (except *Le Lem* which stays open until 2100), is the **Boulevard Chevalier de Ste-Marthe** next to the Savane. Here, every evening until late, vans and caravans serve delicious meals to take away, or to eat at tables under canvas awnings accompanied by loud Zouk music. The scene is bustling and lively, in contrast to the rest of the city at night-time and the air is filled with wonderful aromas. Try *lambis* (conch) in a sandwich (US$2) or on a *brochette* (like a kebab) with rice and salad (US$4). Paella and *Colombo* are good buys (US$6) and the crêpes whether sweet or savoury are delicious.

Anse Mitan Amongst the many restaurants across the Baie des Flamands is the charming *L'Amphore* where the fresh lobster is delicious, T660309, closed Mon-Tue, lunchtime, open every evening 1900-0300. *Bambou* is a little further along the beach, specializes in fresh fish and offers an excellent *menu du jour*. *Chez Jojo* on the beach at Anse à l'Ane, T683743, has a varied seafood menu. Two-star restaurants include *Auberge de l'Anse Mitan*, T660112. Open every evening, reservations required. *Hemingway's* off Anse Mitan beach. Flat fee for créole buffet, small or large plate, opens 1900, arrive early for first sitting, soon fills up. *La Bonne Auberge*, Chez André, T660155. *La Langouste*, T660499. Open daily. *La Villa Créole*, T660553. Closed Sun-Mon lunch. At Diamant, *La Case Créole*, Place de l'Église, T660000. French and Créole, seafood and other specialities, open daily 1100-1600, 1900-2330. *Hôtel Diamant Les Bains* has a reasonable and well-situated restaurant specializing in seafood, T764014. Shut Wed. There are several other restaurants in the town which front directly on to the beach, mostly offering créole cooking and seafood. In Pointe du Bout marina, *La Marine Bar and Restaurant*, good pizza, drink wine, not beer, good seafood platter. *l'Embarquerie* snack bar by ferry dock has happy hour 3 times a day, 1030-1130, 1430-1530, 1700-1800, buy a local Corsaire beer, get one free. *Pizzeria* and snack bar at innermost corner of Pointe du Bout marina sells beer for 10F. Reasonably priced salads and   *menu du jour* at *Hibiscus*

Restaurant with use of hotel pool for the afternoon. *Bakou Hotel* dock bar is a great place to meet yachties and watch the sunset.

West coast At Carbet the *Grain d'Or*, a spacious airy restaurant, is another good spot to sample Martinique's seafood specialities, T780691, open daily. *Le Trou Crabe*, at Le Coin, at beginning of village, T780434, F780514. Open daily except Sun evenings, beach restaurant, rather smart, French and créole cuisine, offers Lyonnais specialities. Directly on the beach, *L'Imprévu*, T780102, F780866. Open daily except Sun and Mon evenings, créole musical entertainment Fri evening except during Lent, very local, créole specialities including shark, lobster, three courses and house wine from US$22. On the coast, north of St-Pierre is *Chez Ginette*, good food but overpriced, T529028, closed Thu.

North coast The restaurant at *Plantation Leyritz* near Basse Pointe is in the restored plantation house and has waterfalls trickling down the walls giving a cool, peaceful feel to the place, elegant dining, good food and service, open daily, T785392. At Grand' Rivière, *Chez Tante Arlette* serves excellent créole food in cool, pleasant surroundings, finished off with home made liqueurs, rue Louis de Lucy de Fossarieu, T557575.

South coast At Ste-Anne, dine in style at the *Manoir de Beauregard* or at *Les Filets Bleus*, on the beach and lighter on the pocket, T767342, closed Sun evening, Mon. *Anthor* on front street and *L'Ouire Mer* serve reasonable créole meals and pizza. *Les Tamariniers* chef decorates expensive dishes with flowers, closed Tue evenings, Wed. *Poi et Virginie*, overlooks bay with good seafood, closed Mon. At Cap Chevalier, *Chez Gracieuse* is a good, moderate-price créole restaurant, choose the terrace and order the catch of the day, T767231, open daily.

Entertainment

For those whose visit does not coincide with any festivals, there is plenty of other entertainment

The *Ballet Martiniquais* (T634388) is one of the world's most prestigious folk ballet companies. Representing everyday scenes in their dance, they wear colourful local costume and are accompanied by traditional rhythms. Information about performances and venues, usually one of the large hotels (*Novotel, Caritan, Méridien, Bakoua*) can be obtained from the tourist office. Every year in July, SERMAC (Parc Floral et Culturel and at the Théâtre Municipal) organizes a two-week arts festival in Fort-de-France with local and foreign artistes performing plays and dance, T716625. CMAC (Centre Martiniquais d'Action Culturelle, Av Franz Fanon, Fort-de-France, T617676) organizes plays, concerts, the showing of films and documentaries all year round and an annual festival in December.

Cinemas There are several comfortable, a/c cinemas in Fort-de-France and the various communes. No film is in English; tickets cost US$4.25. A state-of-the-art multiscreen complex is in the Palais de Congres de Madiana, T721515, northwest of the centre of Fort-de-France at Schoelcher. Turn off the main highway just before Anse Madame, taking the road right, leading to the university. The road to the Palais is the first on the right.

Theatres The main theatres are the *Théâtre Municipal* in the fine old Hôtel de Ville building and *Théâtre de la Soif Nouvelle* in the Place Clemenceau. The *Théâtre Atrium*, on the corner of rue de la Redoute du Marouba, opened in 1998, state of the art hall, shows every evening, operas, plays, concerts, dance etc, T607878, F608820, atrium-info@cgste.mq

Festivals

The main pre-lenten carnival, **Mardi Gras**, takes place in *February or March* when the whole of Martinique takes to the streets in fantastic costume. On **Ash Wednesday**, black and white clad 'devils' parade the streets lamenting loudly over the death of Vaval. At **Eastertime**, the children fly coloured kites which once had razors attached to their tails for kite fights in the wind. At **Toussaint** in *November*, the towns are lit by candlelight processions making their way to the cemeteries to sit with the dead. Every village celebrates its **Saint's Day** with games, shows and folk dancing, usually over the nearest weekend. The town of Saint-Marie holds a **cultural festival** in *July*, and Ajoupa-Bouillon has a **festival of the crayfish**, while in *August* the town of Marin holds its **cultural festival**. Among the many other festivities there is the **Martinique Food Show**, in *April*, a culinary fair with lots of competitions; **the May of**

St-Pierre, in *May*, which commemorates the eruption of the volcano La Montagne Pelée; the biennial International **Jazz Festival**, or **World Crossroads** of the Guitar, in *December*.

Nightlife

Choubouloute, the local entertainments guide, is found in most bars and hotels

Nightclubs abound and tend to be expensive (US$10 to get in and the same price for a drink, whether orange juice or a large whisky). At *Le Coco Loco*, rue Ernest Deproge in Fort-de-France, a bar and restaurant with dinner shows, regular jazz sessions are held, T636377. Along Blvd Allègre in Fort-de-France: *Bella Vitta* at No 4, *L'Exclusif* and *L'Extase* at No 20. *Le Cheyenne*, rue Joseph Compère, down town Fort-de-France. *Waïkiki* is a bar with entertainment at Pointe Simon, down town Fort-de-France. *La Feuille de Tôle*, is an entertainment bar in Schoelcher town centre. There are several **bars** (*piano bar* or *café théâtre*) where you can listen to various types of music, some have karaoke or cabaret some nights. On rue E Deproge 28, is *Le Mayflower*, a bar and restaurant, pub style with karaoke, and at No 104 is *Le Terminal*, a bar/nightclub. *Latin's Club* is a piano bar at rue Lamartine, Fort-de-France. *Le Pub*, is a bar and restaurant open late down town at Pointe Simon, Fort-de-France. *Le Tribal*, 14 François Arago, Fort-de-France, has a bar and restaurant and a disco. Others around the island include *L'Amphore*, a bar and restaurant with karaoke, on the beach of Anse Mitan at Trois Ilets; *Boule de Neige* is a bar and ice cream shop at the marina at Trois Ilets; *L'Endroit*, bar and restaurant at Pointe Marin, Ste Anne, T767674. **Discos** are plentiful and you can here a wide range of music. In **Fort-de-France**: *Manhattan*, rue François Arago, also *Le Tribal*, see above, *Cheyenne*, at Parking Pilo, *Le Negresco*, at Pointe Simon, *Xénakis Club*, 6 rue Paul Nardal. **Out of town**, *L'Alibi*, on the outskirts at Morne Tartenson; *L'As*, at Quartier Lementin, Soudon; *La Baraka*, Pointe du Bout, Trois Ilets; *Chalet*, Quartier Rivière Salée, Laugier; *Crazy Night*, at Sainte-Luce on the road to Diamant; *H' Club*, Quartier Ducos, Beauville; *L'Etoile de Choco*, Saint-Joseph; *Palatio*, on the outskirts of Fort-de-France at Village de Rivière Roche; *Starion*, also on the outskirts at 180 Av Maurice Bishop; *Top Night Club*, at Trinité in the northeast at Zone Artisanale Bac; *Zipp's Club*, Dumaine, François, T546545. Most large hotels lay on Caribbean-style evening entertainment for tourists; limbo dancers, steelbands; etc. The new, main **casino** is at Schoelcher, the *Casino Batelière Plaza*, with tables and slot machines, open 1000-0300, at the entrance to the *Hôtel Framissima*. *Hôtel Meridien* at Pointe du Bout, Trois-Ilets, has a casino 2100-0300, proof of identity is required for entry. Casinos charge 60F entrance fee if you are not staying at the hotel, take passport or identification card.

Shopping

Fort-de-France has ample scope for shoppers, with an abundance of boutiques selling the latest Paris fashions, as well as items by local designers, and numerous street markets where local handicrafts are on sale. Seekers of clothing and perfume should head for rue Victor Hugo and its two *galleries* (malls). Jewellery shops are mostly in rue Isambert and rue Lamartine, selling crystal, china and silverware, and unique gold jewellery. At markets in the Savane and near the cathedral bamboo goods, wickerwork, shells, leather goods, T-shirts, silk scarves and the like are sold. Wines and spirits imported from France and local liqueurs made from exotic fruits are readily available, and Martiniquan rum is an excellent buy. There are large shopping centres at Cluny, Dillon, and Bellevue and the big La Galléria on the airport road. Annette supermarket at Le Marin has a free shuttle service from the Marina. St Anne has several small groceries open daily, catering to the tourist trade. American and Canadian dollars are accepted nearly everywhere and many tourist shops offer a 20% discount on goods bought with a credit card or foreign travellers' cheques.

Transport

Air Scheduled direct flights from Europe, from France only, are with *Air France*, *Air Liberté* *AOM French Airlines* and *Corsair International* which have flights from Paris. *Aerolyon* from Lyon, Nantes, Toulouse. *Air France* also has direct flights from Cayenne, Caracas, Miami, Pointe-à-Pitre, Port-au-Prince. Ask *Air France* for youth fares if under 26, or for seasonal prices. *Nouvelles Frontières* has charter flights from France. *Air Caraïbe* has afternoon flights from San Juan, so same-day connections are possible from the USA. Local airlines include *Air Caraïbe* and *LIAT* which between them fly from Antigua, Dominica, Guadeloupe, St Barts, St Lucia, St-Martin, Port-au-Prince, San Juan, Santo Domingo. *Cubana* from Havana. **Airport** Lamentin Airport, T421600. A new, modern airport. There is a tourist office for hotel reservations and information, T421805, *Crédit Agricole* and *Change Caraïbes* for foreign currency exchange (see below), car rental offices and ground tour operators. To get to the airport at Lamentin, either take a taxi, or take a bus marked 'Ducos' and ask to be set down on the highway near the airport. The fare is US$1.25 and the buses take reasonable-sized luggage. Do not attempt to cycle to or from the airport, and Fort-de-France or Trois-Ilets, as the highway is 4 lanes each way, traffic is heavy and fast, and the shoulder is almost non-existent.

Sea *L'Express des Iles* hydrofoil ferry service to St Lucia, Dominica and Pointe-à-Pitre, Guadeloupe. Fares and schedules are published in the daily newspaper, *France-Antilles* or contact Terminal Inter Iles 97200 Fort-de-France, T631211, F633447. Overnight packages available with several hotels, also car hire Agents are Brudey Frères, 108 rue Victor Hugo, 97200 Fort-de-France, T700850 for timetable information. Martinique is on the route of most Caribbean cruises. Information on travelling by cargo boat can be obtained from the travel agency next door to the CGM office at the harbour, but if going to South America it is cheaper to fly.

Local Bus: There are plenty of buses running between Fort-de-France and the suburbs which can be caught at Boulevard Général-de-Gaulle. The buses are all privately owned and leave when they're full and not before. Short journeys cost around US$0.85 if paid for in advance more if paid on the bus, and the buses run from 0500-2000 approximately. To request a stop shout *"arrêt"*! To go further afield the *taxi collectif* (estate cars or minibuses) are the best bet. 'Taxicos', or TCs, run until about 1800 and leave Pointe Simon for all the communes; Ste-Anne US$5.60, Diamant US$2.70, St-Pierre US$2.60. **Car hire**: *Europcar Interent*, Aéroport Lamentin, T421688, F518115, Fort-de-France T733313 and several hotels; *Hertz*, kiosk at the airport, T421690, F514626; *Avis* at the airport, T421692. Prices start from US$30 a day for a Citroën AX or Renault 5. It will normally be cheaper to have unlimited mileage. You can get a discount if you book your car from abroad at least 48 hrs in advance. An international driver's licence is required for those staying over 20 days. Car hire companies in Fort de France close at weekends. If you want to return a car you have to go to the airport, you can't even drop off the key in town. One look at Fort-de-France's congested streets will tell you it's well worth avoiding driving in the city centre. Parking in central Fort-de-France is only legal with a season ticket and the capital's traffic wardens are very efficient; cars may be towed away. **Motorcycle**: Mopeds can be hired at *Funny*, in Fort-de-France, T633305; *Discount*, Trois-Ilets, T660534; and *Grabin's Car Rental*, Morne Calebasse, T715161. Motorcycles of 125cc and over need a licence, those of 50cc do not. Rental for all is about US$25 per day. A bicycle can be hired for US$7 per day, US$36 per week, US$50 per fortnight, from *Funny*, T633305; *Discount*, T660437; *TS Location Sarl*, 1634282, all in Fort-de-France. **Taxi**. There is a 40% surcharge on taxi fares between 1900 and 0600 and on Sun. Taxi stands are at the Savane, along Boulevard Général-de-Gaulle and Place Clemenceau.

Ferry There are ferries running between Desnambuc quay on the seafront and Pointe du Bout, Anse Mitan and Anse à l'Ane. These run until about 2300 to Pointe du Bout and 1830 to Anse Mitan and Anse à l'Ane and apart from a few taxis are about the only form of transport on a Sun or after 2000. Make sure you get on the right one. The 20-min ferry from Fort de France to Trois-Ilets costs US$4 return, is punctual, pleasurable and saves a 45-min drive by road. To the *Méridien* there is only 1 boat each hour (don't believe boatmen who say they go near, they drop you at Anse à l'Ane which is a long hot walk away). There are also irregular ferries from Fort-de-France to Ste-Anne, 2 ½ -3 ½ hrs. For information about ferry timetables call 730553 for Somatour and 630646 for Madinina.

Airline offices *Air France*, T553300; *Air Liberté*, T425051, 421837; *AOM French Airlines*, T700916, **Directory** 590560; *Air Martinique*, T421660, 511111; *Nouvelles Frontières-Corsair*, T705970; *American Airlines*, T421919, 511229; *LIAT*, T421602, 512111. Charter companies include *Air Foyal*, T511154; *Air Caraïbe*, T511727; *Air St-Martin*, T515703; *Jet Aviation Service*, T515703; *Antilles Aero Service*, T516688; *Envol*, T684549 (sight seeing trips round the island). **Banks** *Change Caraïbes*, Airport, open 0730-2130 Mon-Sat, 0800-1200, 1400-2100 Sun, T421711, rue Ernest Deproge, 97200, Fort-de-France, open 0730-1800 Mon-Fri, 0800-1300 Sat, T602840; *Crédit Agricole* also has an office at the airport for currency exchange, open 0730-1230, 1430-1800 Tue-Fri, 0800-1130 Sat, T512599, also at rue Ernest

Deproge, T731706, closed Mon, open Sat morning. *Banque Française Commerciale*, 6/10 rue Ernest Deproge, T638257. *Banque des Antilles Françaises*, 34 rue Lamartine, T607272, *Société Générale de Banque aux Antilles*, 19 rue de la Liberté, T597070. *Crédit Martiniquais*, 17 rue de la Liberté, T599300. *BRED*, Place Monseigneur Romero, T632267. *Martinique Change*, 137 rue Victor Hugo, T638033 and in Trois-Ilets T660444. *Banque National de Paris*, 72 Av des Caraïbes, T594600 (the best for cash advances on Visa, no commission). Banks and exchange houses charge 5% commission on travellers' cheques. Not all banks accept US dollar travellers' cheques. Some banks charge US$2-4 for any size transaction, so change as much as you think you're going to need. Always go to the bank early; by mid-morning they are very crowded. Do not change US dollars at the Post Office in Fort-de-France, nor at restaurants, supermarkets and shops because you lose about 30% because of the poor exchange rate and commission. Check the rate when you pay for anything with US dollars cash, credit card purchases are better. *American Express* at Roger Albert Voyages, 10 rue Victor Hugo, upstairs, efficient. **Communications** Post: Post offices are open from 0700-1800 and Sat mornings. The main post office is on rue de la Liberté and always has long queues. Post card to USA US$0.50. **Telephone**: Nearly all public telephones are cardphones except a few in bars and hotels which take coins. At the PTT office in rue Antoine Siger, just off the Savane, there are numerous card and coin phones and *Télécartes* (phone cards) are sold. These can also be bought in most newsagents, cafés, and some shops for US$5 upwards. A 50-unit card (about US$8) lasts nearly 4 mins when phoning North America; a 120-unit card costs about US$16. Don't get caught out on arrival at the airport where there are only cardphones. Try the tourist office where they are very helpful and will phone round endless hotels to find the unprepared new arrival a room. You can not have a call returned to a payphone. Directory enquiries, T12. To make a long distance credit card or collect phone call from a pay phone: buy the smallest card possible and insert in phone, dial 0800-990011 to get USA direct English speaking operator for credit card or collect or dial USA DIRECT calls. Other lines available for Sprint and MCI. Check in the phone book for other numbers. To dial non-French islands in Caribbean dial 00 plus three-figure code and local number. **Embassies & consulates** See also Guadeloupe directory. Germany Acajou, BP 423,97292, Le Lamentin, T503839. **Mexico** 31 Rue Moreau de Jonnes, 97200, Fort-de-France, T605024. **Spain** Route de Chateauboeuf, 97200, Fort-de-France, T750312. **Switzerland** CA Californie, 97232, Le Lamentin. **UK** Honorary Consul Mme Jane-Alison Ernoult, T615630. **Hospitals** There are 18 hospitals and clinics which are well equipped and well staffed. EU citizens have reciprocal state health rights and hospitals are up to metropolitan France standards. In an emergency: *SAMU*, Pierre Zobda Quitman Hospital, 97232 Le Lamentin, T751515. Ambulance service T715948. *The Sea Water Therapy Centre* is at Grand Anse, 97221 Carbet, T780878. **Tourist information** Local tourist office Lamentin Airport, T421805; Bord de la Mer, Fort-de-France, T637960, F736693, www.martinique.org www.touristmartinique.com www.martinique.cci.fr Office Départemental du Tourisme de la Martinique, BP 520, 97206 Fort-de-France Cédex. There are local information bureaux (Syndicat d'initiative) all round the island, many of which can be found through the town hall (mairie). **Local travel agents**: Guided tour: of the island by bus, trips on sailing boats and cruise ships around Martinique and to neighbouring islands, and excursions on glass-bottom boats are organized by the following companies: *STT Voyages*, 23 rue Blénac, Fort-de-France, T716812; *Carib Jet*, Lamentin Airport, T519000; *Madinina Tours*, 89 rue Blénac, 97200 Fort-de-France, T706525, F730953; *Caribtours*, Marina Pointe du Bout, 97229 Trois-Ilets, T660448, F660706; *Colibri Tours*, Immeuble Laouchez-ZI, Cocotte 97224, Ducos, T771300, F771289; *AVS* Angle des rues F Arago et E Deproge, Fort-de-France, T635555; *M Vacances*, 97290 Marin, T748561, F747107; *Biguine Voyages*, 51 rue Victor Hugo, Fort-de-France, T718787, F605596. Ms Mylene Richard, *Caribbean Spirit*, 23 rue Simón Bolívar, 97200 Fort-de-France, T274651, F724651, arranges tours and accommodation for the physically disadvantaged. Touring on foot: contact the *Parc Naturel Régional*, Boulevard Général-de-Gaulle, T731930, for well-organized walks in the island's beauty spots such as the rainforest and the Caravelle Peninsula. The charge is 60-80F per person and includes the coach fare to the walk's starting point. Guides can be found through the tourist office, or at Morne Rouge for climbing Montagne Pelée and at Ajoupa-Bouillon for the Gorge de la Falaise walk.

Background

History   When Christopher Columbus sighted Martinique in 1493, it was inhabited by the Carib Indians who had killed or absorbed the Arawaks, the previous settlers of the Lesser Antilles some 200-300 years previously. He did not land until 15 June 1502, when he put in at Le Carbet. Columbus named the island Martinica in honour of St Martin; the Caribs called it Madinina, or island of flowers.

The Spanish never settled. In 1635 Martinique was colonized by the French under the leadership of Pierre Belain d'Esnambuc. His nephew, Jacques du Parquet, governed in 1637-58 and started to develop the island; when he died, his widow took over. The cultivation of sugar cane and the importation of slaves from West Africa commenced. Fierce battles took place between the Caribs and the French until 1660 when a treaty was signed under which the Caribs agreed to occupy only the Atlantic side of the island. Peace was shortlived, however, and the Indians were soon completely exterminated. Louis XIV bought many of the du Parquet land rights and appointed an administrating company, making Martinique the capital of France's Caribbean possessions.

During the 17th and 18th centuries England and France fought over their colonial possessions and in 1762 England occupied Martinique for nine months, only to return it with Guadeloupe to the French in exchange for Canada, Senegal, the Grenadines, St Vincent, and Tobago. France was content to retain Martinique and Guadeloupe because of the importance of the sugar trade at the time.

More unrest followed in the French Caribbean colonies when in 1789 the French Revolution inspired slaves to fight for their emancipation. White artisans, soldiers, small merchants and free people of mixed race also embraced its principles. In 1792 a royalist governor re-established control but he was expelled by a revolutionary force sent from France. The capital, Fort-Royal became République-Ville and Paris abolished slavery. Martinique was occupied by the English again from 1794 to 1815 (with one interruption), at the request of the plantation owners of the island who wanted to preserve the status quo and put down slave revolts.

Slavery was finally abolished in 1848 in the French colonies and in the following years 25,000 immigrant workers from India and a few from Indo-China came to Martinique to supplement the remaining workforce on the plantations.

In 1946 Martinique became an overseas Département (DOM), with all the rights of any department in metropolitan France. The bill was steered through the National Assembly by Martinique's Deputy, Aimé Césaire (1913-), poet, mayor of Fort-de-France and a pioneer of *négritude* (see page 697). In 1974 Martinique also became a Région, giving it more economic advantages and investment and funding opportunities.

Political parties include the Progressive Party of Martinique, Socialists, Communists, Union for French Democracy, Rally for the Republic and several small left-wing parties. A small independence movement exists but most people prefer greater autonomy without total independence from France.

In 1988 Martinique voted for the Socialist François Mittérand for president and in the 1995 elections the island remained socialist. In the second round the socialist candidate, Lionel Jospin received 58.9% of the vote compared with 41.1% for the present incumbent, Jacques Chirac. However, the turnout was low at only 48.9% of the electorate, lower than the 79.2% turnout in France as a whole. In the National Assembly elections in 1997 the right wing Rassemblement pour la République (RPR) held two seats in Martinique but lost a third to a supporter of independence from France. The fourth Martinique seat was retained by the left wing Parti Progressiste Martiniquais.

Geography

The island is 65 km long and 31 km wide with mountains in the north and south and a low-lying 'waist' where most people live. The coastline is irregular in the southern half, with peninsulas and promontories protecting islets and sandy bays. The Caribbean Sea is to the west, the Atlantic Ocean to the east. Martinique's neighbouring islands are Dominica to the north and St Lucia to the south. Martinique is volcanic in origin and one active volcano still exists, La Montagne Pelée (1,397 m), situated to the northwest, which had its last major eruption in 1902. The rest of the island is also very mountainous; the Pitons de Carbet (maximum 1,196 m) are in the centre of the island and La Montagne du Vauclin (504 m) is in the south. Small hills or *mornes* link these mountains and there is a central plain, Le Lamentin, where sugar cane is planted. An extensive tropical rainforest covers parts of the north of the island, as well as pineapple and banana plantations. The coastline is varied: steep cliffs and volcanic, black and grey sand coves in the north and on the rugged Atlantic coast, and calmer seas with large white or gold sand beaches in the south and on the Caribbean coast.

Government Martiniquans are French citizens and Martinique, a Département, is officially and administratively part of France. The President of the French Republic is Head of State. Local government is run by a Prefect (appointed by the French Minister for the Interior), the General Council (locally elected) and the Regional Council (elected). There are two different legislative bodies: the General Council (45 seats, elected for six years) and the Regional Council (41 seats). The Département is represented by four directly elected Deputies to the National Assembly in Paris, by two indirectly elected Senators in the Senate and by one representative on the Economic and Social Council. The General Council votes on matters of interest to the department, administers and manages local services and allocates funds to the local councils: *communes*. Martinique has 34 *communes*, each with a mayor and elected municipal council.

Economy Martinique is dependent upon France for government spending equivalent to about 70% of gnp, without which there would be no public services or social welfare. Even so, unemployment is high at over a quarter of the labour force, the economy is stagnant and the balance of payments deficit expands continuously. The economy is primarily agricultural, about 5% of the economically active population is engaged in farming and fishing, and the main export crops are bananas, rum and melons, while aubergines and flowers are being developed. Crops grown mainly for domestic consumption include yams, sweet potatoes, Caribbean cabbages, manioc, breadfruit, plantains, tomatoes and green beans. Fishing contributes to the local food supply but much of the domestic market is met by imports. Most manufactured goods are imported, adding to the cost of living. There is some light industry and the major industrial plants are an oil refinery, rum distilleries and a cement works, while there is also fruit canning, soft drinks manufacturing and polyethylene and fertilizer plants.

Tourism is the greatest area of economic expansion. Of the total stopover visitors, 80% come from France and 3% from the USA, while of the total cruise ship visitors, 72% come from the USA, 14% from the whole of Europe and 9% from Canada. Tourism income is now around US$300 mn a year; cruise ship passengers spend an average of US$22 per person.

Windward Islands

16

Windward Islands

The Windward Islands include four independent nations: Dominica, St Lucia, St Vincent and the Grenadines and Grenada as well as the French Antilles which are departments of France. They form a series of volcanic peaks jutting out and forming a barrier between the Atlantic Ocean and the Caribbean Sea. Sulphur fumaroles and hot springs can be found on some islands where the volcanoes are dormant but not dead. There are large areas of rainforest with national parks protecting places of biodiversity or natural beauty, and the islands are a haven for birds and other wildlife. Hikers and birdwatchers are spoilt for choice in the larger islands of the Windwards, while yachtsmen are similarly blessed when navigating among the smaller Grenadines, one of the world's most popular sailing destinations. Bananas are still an important source of income on the Windward Islands, but agriculture is diversifying with other tropical fruits and flowers now being exported. Tourism is the leading foreign exchange earner, providing the jobs which have been lost in traditional activities.

A Foot in the door

- Dive at **Champagne** and swim through the bubbles of hot underwater springs.
- For adventurous hiking try **Morne Diablotin**, the highest peak, found in the Northern Forest Reserve.
- Spend time in **Calibishie**, a fishing village overlooking Guadeloupe.
- The **World Creole Music Festival** in October is worth risking hurricane season for.

Dominica

Colour map 5, grid A5

Known as the 'Nature Island' of the Caribbean, Dominica (pronounced Domineeca) is the place to come for dense forests, volcanic hills, rivers, waterfalls and the Boiling Lake. It is also a highly regarded diving destination, with a good marine park system, and for much of the year you can see whales and dolphins offshore. Hotels around the island are small, intimate and low-key, greater development being deterred by the lack of beaches. It is the only island where Caribs have survived and they still retain many of their traditions such as canoe carving. The island's culture and language are an amalgam of the native and immigrant peoples; Carib, French, English, African.

Ins and outs

Getting there

See transport, page 775, for further details

There are no direct flights **from Europe** or **North America** to Dominica. Connections must be made in Puerto Rico, St Maarten, Antigua, St Lucia or the French Antilles. There is a reliable ferry service from St Lucia and the French Antilles, but if you are prone to seasickness you might prefer to fly as it can be rough in the channel.

Getting around

There are few road signs, but with a good map finding your way is not difficult

Road It is a good idea to rent a car or jeep as buses take a lot of planning but Dominicans drive fast in the middle of the road so you may want to take a taxi so you can enjoy the views. Main roads are fairly good; the Portsmouth-Marigot road built in 1987 is excellent, but in towns and south of Roseau, roads are very narrow and in poor condition. The tourism office in the Old Market, Roseau, sells Ordnance Survey maps. **Hitching** rides in the back of the ubiquitous pick-up trucks is possible although often difficult at weekends. You have nothing to fear if you offer local people a lift, all are unfailingly courteous. Apart from the Soufrière/ Scotts Head route, it is difficult to get anywhere on the island by **public transport**, and return to Roseau, in one day because buses leave Marigot, or wherever, to arrive in Roseau around 0700, then return at about 1300. It is just possible to get to Portsmouth and return in one day, the first bus is at 1000, returning at 1600.

Climate

Daytime temperatures average between 70° F and 85° F, though the nights are much cooler, especially in the mountains. The rainy season is from July to October though showers occur all through the year. Note that the mountains are much wetter and cooler than the coast, Roseau receives about 85 in of rain a year, while the mountains get over 340 in.

Flora and fauna

There are several national parks, including the **Morne Trois Pitons** (17,000 acres) in the south, the **Central Forest Reserve** and the **Northern Forest Reserve**, which together protect rainforest covering much of the island's mountainous interior. At the highest levels on the island is elfin woodland, characterized by dense vegetation and low-growing plants. Elfin woodland and high montane thicket give way to rainforest at altitudes between 1,000 and 2,500 ft, extending over about 60% of the island. Despite the large area of forest, protection is essential against cutting for farmland and other economic pressures, as a water source and as a unique facility for

Dominica

Sleeping
1 Anchorage
2 Anse-à-Liane Lodge
3 Castaways

4 Castille Apartment/
   Ocean View
   Apartments & Roger's
   Fish Shack & Bar
5 Castle Comfort Lodge
6 Carib Territory
7 Coconut Beach
8 Evergreen
9 Floral Gardens
10 Herche's &
   Sundowner Restaurant

11 Lauro Club
12 Ocean View Cottage
13 Olive's
14 Picard Beach
15 Pointe Baptiste
16 Reigate
17 Sea Cliff Cottages
18 Sister Sea Lodge
19 Sunset Bay Club
20 Veranda View
21 Windblow Estate

22 Windswept
23 Zandoli Inn

● **Eating**
1 Dom Can Café
2 Old Mill
3 Purple Turtle
4 Tiawanese Delicacies
   & Spiders, All One Bar
   & Zam Zam's Bars

Windward Islands

Essentials

Documents *All visitors entering Dominica must be in possession of an* **outward ticket** *and a valid* **passport**. *Proof of citizenship with photo only is acceptable for US and Canadian citizens. A Carte identité allows French nationals to visit for up to two weeks. Visas are required by nationals of communist countries: they can be obtained from the Ministry of Home Affairs, Government Headquarters, Roseau. Immigration will normally grant you a stay of 21 days on arrival; extensions can be applied for but you will need a return or onward ticket.*

Currency *East Caribbean dollar.*

Departure tax *EC$50/US$18.50. Day trippers pay EC$5; under 12s are free.*

Ports of entry *(Own flag) Roseau, Portsmouth and Anse du Mai in the east. Obtain coast-wide permit. EC$1 to clear in. Customs main office is at the deep water harbour at Woodbridge Bay where all the large ships come in (T4484462) but you can also clear at the Bayfront. Other offices are at Roseau, Anse de Mai, Portsmouth and at both airports.*

Anchorages *Salisbury, Castaways Beach Hotel, Layou River. A marina is being built at the Coconut Beach Hotel near Portsmouth, with slips for 40 boats, full service. Do not anchor in Scotts Head/Soufrière Bay (marine reserve) or Douglas Bay or where fishing activities are underway. Waste disposal at the commercial docks in Portsmouth and Roseau.*

Hours of business *Government offices: Monday, 0800-1300, 1400-1700, Tuesday to Friday, close one hour earlier in the afternoon; the only government offices open on Saturday are the tourist kiosk in Old Market Plaza, and the tourist office at Canefield airport (open daily 0615-1115, 1415-1730 – or last flight); the Melville Hall tourist office is only open at flight arrival times.* **Shops:** *0800-1300, 1400-1600, Monday-Friday, 0800-1300 Saturday. Some of the larger supermarkets in Roseau stay open until 2000 and tiny, local shops may still be open at 2200 even on Sunday.* **Banks:** *0800-1500 Monday-Thursday, 0800-1700 Friday.*

Communications *The official title,* **Commonwealth of Dominica**, *should always be used in addresses to avoid confusion with the Dominican Republic. The International phone code is 767. See page 777 for further details.*

Official time *Atlantic Standard Time, four hours behind GMT, one ahead of EST.*

Useful numbers *T999 for Police, Fire and Ambulance.*

---

scientific research. It is hoped that tourism can coexist with conservation, since any losses, for whatever reason, would be irreversible.

The **Cabrits Peninsula** in the northwest was declared a national park in 1986. Covering 1,313 acres, its twin hills covered by dry forest, is separated from the island by marshland (a pier and cruise ship reception centre have been built) which is a nesting place for herons and doves and hosts a variety of migrant bird species. A walk through the woods and around the buildings of **Fort Shirley** (abandoned in 1854) will reveal much flora and wildlife. The scuttling hermit (or soldier) and black crabs, ground lizard (abòlò) and tree lizard are most visible.

Dominica is a botanist's & a birdwatcher's paradise

In addition to the huge variety of trees, many of which flower in March and April, there are orchids and wild gardens of strange plant life in the valleys. Bwa Kwaib or Carib wood (*Sabinea carinalis*) was declared the national flower in 1978 which can be found mostly growing along parts of the west coast.

Indigenous birds to the island are the Imperial parrot, or Sisserou (*amazona imperialis*), which is critically endangered, and its marginally less threatened relative, the Red-necked parrot, or Jacquot (*amazona arausiaca*). The Sisserou has been declared the national bird. They can be seen in the Syndicate area in the northwest which is now a protected reserve and the site of a future information and research centre for visitors and scientists (accessible by four-wheel drive only). There is a nature trail but signs are difficult to spot. The parrots are most evident during their courting season, in April and early May. To get the best from a parrot-watching trip, it is worth taking a guide. Bertrand Jno Baptiste, of the Forestry Division (T4482401) is highly recommended and charges EC$80 a group. While there are other rare species, such as

Voltage *220/240 volts AC, 50 cycles.*

Language *English is the official language but **patois** is spoken widely. It is very similar to that spoken on St Lucia and to the créole of Martinique and Haiti but people tend to speak more slowly (see page 780).*

Radio *DBS broadcasts on AM 595 kHz and FM 88.1, 88.6. 89.5, 103.2 and 103.6 MHz. Kairi Fm is the most listened to radio station with a more lively presentation style than the state-owned DBS. It is on FM 93.1, 107.9 MHz. Vol is on AM 1060 KHz, FM 102.1, 90.6 MHz. There are two religious radio stations (one Protestant and one Catholic) as well as a repeater for St Lucian Radio Caribbean International on FM 98.1 Mhz.*

Tourist offices overseas France *KPMG Axe Consultants, 12 Rue de Madrid, 75008 Paris, France, T53-424100, F43-873285.*

UK *Dominica High Commission, 1 Collingham Gardens, Earls Court, London SW5 0HW, T020-78351937, F020-73738743, or the Caribbean Tourism Organization, Suite 3.15, Vigilant House, 120 Wilton Road, Victoria, London SW1V 1JZ, T020-72338382, F020-78738551.* **USA** *Dominica Tourist Office, 10 East 21st Street, New York, NY 10010, T212-4757542, F4759728, Dominicany@msn.com*

Clothing *informal, though swimsuits are not worn on the streets. A sweater is recommended for the evenings. When hiking take a raincoat and/or a pullover; a dry T-shirt is also a good idea. Take good walking shoes.*

Safety *Crime is rising and there have been mugging cases on beaches at Castle Bruce in the east and Hampstead on the northeast coast. There are often robberies around Calibishie and you must never leave valuables unattended on the beaches in that area, even if you can see them. Grand Bay is an area to avoid at carnival time, which is celebrated with much 'enthusiasm', including guns and machetes. Theft is normally non violent and is of cash and easily sellable items (for example jewellery) rather than credit cards. Always report theft to the police, they generally have a shrewd idea of where to look for stolen goods and jewellery is often recovered.*

Public holidays *1 January; Carnival; Good Friday and Easter Monday; first Monday in May; Whit Monday; first Monday in August; 3/4 November (Independence); Christmas Day and Boxing Day. 2 January is a merchant's holiday, when all shops and restaurants are closed, although banks and hotels remain open; Government offices will in most cases not be open.*

---

the Forest Thrush and the Blue-headed hummingbird, there are a great many others which are easily spotted (the Purple-throated Carib and Antillean-crested humming-birds, for instance), or heard (the Siffleur Montagne). Waterfowl can be seen on the lakes, waders on the coastal wetlands (many are migrants). There are various bat caves, most particularly at Thiband on the northeast coast.

There are fewer species of mammal (agouti, manicou-opossum, wild pig and bats), but there is a wealth of insect life (for example, over 55 species of butterfly) and reptiles. Besides those mentioned above, there is the rare iguana, the crapaud (a large frog, eaten under the name of mountain chicken) and five snakes, none poisonous (includes the boa constrictor, or tête-chien). Certain parts of the coast are used as nesting grounds by sea turtles (hawksbill, leatherback and green). As a result of over-hunting, the Forestry Division has extended the close season for hunting wildlife like crapaud. Visitors should be mindful of this when thinking about ordering such foods in restaurants.

The Forestry Division in the Botanical Gardens, Roseau, has a wide range of publications, trail maps, park guides, posters and leaflets (some free) on Dominica's wildlife and National Parks, T4482401, F4487999.

Diving and marine life

Many drop-offs are close to the beaches but access is poor and boats are essential. Dominica is highly regarded as a diving destination and has been featured in most diving magazines as 'undiscovered'. Features include wall dives, drop-offs, reefs, hot, freshwater springs under the sea, sponges, black coral, pinnacles and wrecks, all in unpolluted water. Due to steep drops the sediment falls away and visibility is excellent, at up to 30 m depending on the weather.

Dive sites There is a marine park conservation area in **Toucari Bay** and part of **Douglas Bay**, north of the Cabrits, but the most popular scuba sites are south of Roseau, at **Pointe Guignard**, **Soufrière Bay** and **Scotts Head**. An unusual site is **Champagne**, with underwater hot springs where you swim through bubbles, fascinating for a night dive, also good for snorkelling, lots of life here. This area in the southeast, **Soufrière-Scotts Head**, is now a marine park without moorings so that all diving is drift diving and boats pick up divers where they surface. Areas may be designated for diving and other areas for fishing. Along the south and southeast coast there are more dive sites but because of the Atlantic currents these are for experienced, adventurous divers only. Note that the taking of conch, coral, lobster, sponge, turtle eggs et cetera is forbidden and you may not put down anchor in coral and on reefs; use the designated moorings. Snorkelling is good in the same general areas as diving, including Douglas Bay and the Scott's Head/Soufrière Bay Marine Reserve.

Whale watching is extremely popular, although the success rate is relatively low. The World Wildlife Fund and many marine conservation groups have used Dominica as a base for documentaries and conferences, so much is known about the local population. It appears that female whales and their calves are in the Caribbean waters for much of the year, with only the mature males leaving the area to feed for any length of time. If your trip is successful, you could be treated to the sight of mothers and their young swimming close to the boat, or young males making enormous jumps before diving below the waves. Dolphin are abundant too, particularly in the Soufrière Bay area and even if you miss the whales your boat is accompanied by a school of playful dolphin. Several different types of whales have been spotted not far from the west shore where the deep, calm waters are ideal for these mammals. Sperm whales are regularly seen, especially during the winter months, as are large numbers of spinner and spotted dolphins. You can also sometimes see pilot whales, pseudorcas, pygmy sperm whales, bottlenose dolphins, Risso's dolphins and melon-headed whales. Whale watching trips can be arranged with the *Anchorage Hotel* (Thursday, Sunday 1400-1800), *Dive Dominica* (Wednesday, Sunday 1400), *Rainbow Sportfishing* or *Game Fishing Dominica* and cost US$40-50 per person.

Dive centres Scuba diving is permitted only through one of the island's registered dive operators

Snorkelling trips are or with written permission from the Fisheries Division. Single-tank dives are from
around US$26, US$42 and two-tank dives are from US$63. *Dive Dominica Ltd*, at the *Castle Com-*
particularly *fort Lodge* T4482188, F4486088, www.divedominica.com, offers full diving and
recommended for the accommodation packages, courses, single or multiple day dives, night dives and
Champagne area equipment rental. Owned by Derek Perryman, this company is one of the most friendly and experienced operations, recommended for its professional service. *Anchorage Dive Centre*, T4482638, F4485680, anchorage@cwdom.dm, US$65 two-tank dive is based at the *Anchorage Hotel*, Castle Comfort, with a sister operation at the *Portsmouth Beach Hotel*. This is another long established operation with a good reputation, owned by Andrew Armour. *Dive Castaways* at the *Castaways Beach Hotel*, T4496244, F4496246, www. castaways.dm, US$65 one dive, US$65 for two-tank dive, covers the northern dive sites. *Cabrits Dive Centre*, operate from Picard Estate, Portsmouth, T4453010, F4453011, cabritsdive@cwdom.dm A PADI five-star dive centre diving and snorkelling in the less-visited north of the island; *East Carib Dive* at Salisbury T4996575, F4496603, www.eastcaribdive.dm is based at the *Lauro Club*, contact Gunther Glatz; and *Nature Island Dive* at Soufrière T4498181, F4498182, www.natureislanddive.dm, also kayaking and mountain biking, is run by a team of divers from around the world. A two-tank dive is US$70, snorkelling trip US$26, equipment rental US$16. Ask them about accommodation and dive packages, they have a bayside wooden cottage on stilts with porch for up to

four divers, *Gallette. Anse-à-Liane Lodge & Dive Centre* is at Colihaut, T4466652, F4466651, www.ansealianedive.com, offering PADI and BSAC courses, accommodation, restaurant and excursions.

Beaches and watersports

The Caribbean side of Dominica gains or loses sand according to swells and storms but the black coral sandy areas are few and far between. A small one exists just off Scotts Head (favoured as a teaching ground for divers, snorkellers and canoeists, so sometimes crowded), but further north you must travel to Mero beach or *Castaways Beach Hotel*. **Macousheri Bay** and **Coconut Beach** near Portsmouth are probably the best areas for Caribbean bathing. Don't be tempted to swim anywhere near Roseau or the larger villages because of effluent. For some really beautiful, unspoilt, white sandy beaches, hire a four-wheel drive and investigate the bays of the northeast coast. **Turtle Beach, Pointe Baptiste, Hampstead** and **Woodford Hill** are all beautiful but on the Atlantic coast terrific underswells and freak waves make swimming dangerous. Look at the sea and swim in the rivers is the safest advice. Very strong swimmers may be exhilarated by **Titou Gorge**, near Laudat, where the water flows powerfully through a narrow canyon and emerges by a hot mineral cascade.

Compared with other Caribbean islands, Dominica has few good beaches, but does have excellent river bathing

    Game Fishing Dominica is a new operation at the *Castaways Beach Hotel* (T4496638) with charters at US$400 half day or US$600 full day. *Rainbow Sportfishing/Charters* can take you **fishing** in the Martinique channel, which is a migratory route, or take you on a cruise to Martinique or Les Saintes, T/F4488650, rollei@cwdom.dm The first Dominica International Sportfishing Tournament was held in 1996 and annually since then in May. **Sea kayaks** can be hired from Nature Island Dive, rates are US$11 per hour, US$26 per half day and US$42 per full day, lifejackets and instruction in Soufrière Bay provided. Guided tours are available.

Very few watersports are on offer

    Gusty winds coming down from the hills make **sailing** difficult and unreliable; conditions are rarely suitable for the beginner. The best harbour for yachts is Portsmouth (Prince Rupert Bay), but you should guard your possessions. Stealing from yachts is quite common. The new jetty in Roseau (see below) is designed for small craft, such as yachts, clearing for port entry. Both the *Reigate Waterfront* and *Anchorage Hotels* have moorings and a pier, and yachtsmen and women are invited to use the hotels' facilities.

Football and **cricket** are among the most popular national sports; watch cricket in the beautiful setting of the Botanical Gardens or at the dramatic pitch at Petit Savanne where two sides of the boundary line run along a cliff overlooking the Atlantic. Hitting a six will mean the loss of a ball into the ocean. The next best pitch is at Macoucherie, close to the rum distillery. **Basketball** and **netball** are also enthusiastically played. There are hard **tennis** courts at the privately-owned Dominica Club (T4482995), *Reigate Hall* and *Castaways*, rental for minimal fee, bring your own racket. **Cycling** is growing in popularity and the island's roads, although twisty, are good. Mountain bikes can be hired from *Nature Island Dive* at Soufrière, see Transport page 776, where there are marked off-road trails. **Hiking** in the mountains is excellent, and hotels and tour companies arrange this type of excursion. **Mountain climbing** can be organized through the Forestry Division in the Botanical Gardens, Roseau, T4482401. Guides are necessary for any forays into the mountains or forests, some areas of which are still uncharted. **Horse riding** can be arranged through *Evergreen Hotel*, T4483288. Dave Winston at High Ride Stables operates from Bellevie Chopin on the road to Grand Bay (T4486296, highridestables@yahoo. com), US$25 per person per hour.

Other sports

Windward Islands

Roseau

The town is in chaos on the days cruise ships come in

Roseau (pronounced *Rose-oh*), the main town, is small, ramshackle and friendly, with a surprising number of pretty old buildings still intact. The houses look a bit tatty with rusting tin roofs and a general lack of paint, but there is still some attractive gingerbread fretwork in the traditional style on streets like Castle Street. Quite a lot of redevelopment has taken place over the last few years, improving access and making the waterfront more attractive. The Old Market Plaza has been made into a pedestrian area, with shops in the middle. The old, red market cross has been retained, with 'keep the pavement dry' picked out in white paint. Between the Plaza and the sea is the old post office, now housing the **Dominican Museum**, which is well worth a visit. The post office is on the Bay Front at the bottom of Hillsborough Street. It has a colourful mural depicting the development of Dominica's postal service, and a Philately Counter. The **market**, at the north end of Bay Street, is a fascinating sight on Saturday mornings from about 0600-1000; it is also lively on Friday

Roseau

■ Sleeping
1 Bon Marché Guest House
2 Cherry Lodge
3 Continental Inn
4 Fort Young
5 The Garraway
6 Kent Anthony's Guesthouse
7 Sutton Place
8 Syme Zees Guesthouse & Restaurant
9 Vena's Guesthouse, Ma Bass Central Guesthouse & The World of Food

● Eating
1 Cartwheel
2 Guiyave
3 La Robe Créole
4 Laughing Lobster
5 Mousehole Too
6 Orchard
7 Paiho
8 Pearl's Cuisine
9 Port of Call
10 Ti-Caz (Coco Rico)
11 Torino's

🚌 Buses
1 Northbound Buses
2 Southbound Buses
3 Buses to Trafalgar & Laudat

N — Not to scale

morning, closed Sunday. The sea wall was completed in late 1993, which has greatly improved the waterfront area of town, known as the **Bay Front** or **Dame Eugenia Charles Boulevard**, after the Prime Minister who promoted the development. The Roseau jetty, destroyed by Hurricane David in 1979, was rebuilt in the Seawall and Bay Front Development Project for the use of yachts and other small craft. A promenade with trees and benches, a road from the Old Jetty to Victoria Street, and parking bays take up most of the space. A new T-shaped cruise ship jetty was completed in 1995 and for several weeks in the winter season ships tower above the town pouring forth tourists into 16-seater taxis for tours around the island. Although small, you may need to ask for directions around Roseau. Streets have been given signs but it is still tricky to find your way around.

The 40-acre **Botanical Gardens** dating from 1890 are principally an arboretum; they have a collection of plant species, including an orchid house. Several Jacquot and Sisserou parrots can be seen in the bird sanctuary in the park, thanks in part to the Jersey Wildlife Preservation Trust. Breeding programmes are underway and it is hoped that some of the offspring will be released to the wild.

The town has no deep-water harbour; this is at **Woodbridge Bay** over a mile away, where most of the island's commercial shipping is handled, and some tourist vessels are accommodated.

Around the island

The Trafalgar waterfalls in the Roseau Valley, 8 km from the capital, have been the most popular tourist site for many years. Hot and cold water flowed in two spectacular cascades in the forest, but unfortunately the volume of the hot fall was sharply diminished by a hydroelectric scheme higher up and a landslide after the September 1995 hurricanes covered both the hot and cold water pools. The path to the falls is easy to follow, but if you want to go further than the viewing point, take a guide because there is a lot of scrambling over rocks and it can be difficult at times. Trying to cross over the falls at the top is very hazardous. Bathing is possible in pools in the river beneath the falls. There are always lots of guides, you will probably be approached well before reaching the start of the trail. Some guides can be abusive if you insist on going alone. Agree the price before setting out, around EC$10 for two or more people in a group. The Trafalgar Falls are crowded because they are close to the road (bus EC$5 from outside the Astaphan supermarket in Roseau or two-hour walk). A natural sulphur pool has been set up at *Papillote* restaurant by the falls, in lovely gardens. Its a great place to relax by moonlight with a rum punch. There is also a one hour trail from the sulphur springs of the tiny settlement of Wotten Waven through forest and banana plantations across the Trois Pitons River up to the Trafalgar Falls.

Trafalgar waterfalls
Entrance to this and other 'ecological' sites in Dominica is US$2; tickets should be bought in advance from agencies

Much of the south part of the island (17,000 acres) has since 1975 been designated the Morne Trois Pitons National Park and in 1998 it became a World Heritage Site. Evidence of volcanic activity is manifested in hot springs, sulphur emissions and the occasional small eruption. Its attractions include the **Boiling Lake** (92°C), which may be the largest of its kind in the world (the other contender is in New Zealand) and reached after a six-mile climb from Laudat. You have to return on the same path as an alternative trail is no longer maintained. An experienced guide is recommended as the trail can be treacherous, particularly if the mist descends, but it is easy to follow once you are on it (guides charge about EC$100 per couple, EC$180 for two couples; Lambert Charles, T4483365, strong and knowledgeable; Kenrich Johnson, friendly, informative; Edison and Loftus Joseph, Wotten Waven, T4489192 at a telephone box, cheaper than organized tours, the brothers are shoe makers).

In the valley below the Boiling Lake is a spectacular region known as the **Valley of Desolation**, where the forest has been destroyed by sulphuric emissions. A small volcanic eruption in 1997, not considered cause for alarm, caused ash to scatter over an area of about 50 ft sq. At the beginning of the trail to the Boiling Lake is the Titou

Morne Trois Pitons National Park
In 1999 a guide fell in the lake while trying to recover a dropped camera. He was burned up to his waist and spent three months in hospital in Martinique recovering

Gorge, now considerably damaged by rock fall from the hydroelectric development in the area, where a hot and a cold stream mingle. However, there is nothing more refreshing or soothing after hiking to and from the Boiling Lake than swimming through the Titou Gorge. A new track, the Kent Gilbert Trail, has been cut; it starts in La Plaine and is about 4½ miles long. It affords views of the Sari Sari and Bolive Falls, but avoids the Valley of Desolation. While this makes it a less strenuous route, it also renders it less impressive.

Also in the park is the **Freshwater Lake**; it is to the east of **Morne Macaque** at 2,500 ft above sea level, and can be reached by road (two miles from Laudat). Do not swim here, it is the drinking water reservoir for Roseau. A trail leads in 45 minutes on foot (follow the road where the river joins the lake about half a mile to the pipeline, take the path to the left through the dense forest) to the highest lake in the island, Boeri, situated between Morne Macaque and **Morne Trois Pitons**. Work on a hydroelectric project in this area was completed in 1991. There have been lasting consequences for both the Trafalgar Falls (a diminished flow of water) and the Freshwater Lake (a lower water level).

The National Park Service has built a series of paths, the Middleham Trails, through the rain forest on the northwest border of the park. The trails are accessible from Sylvania on the Transinsular Road, or Cochrane, although the signs from Sylvania are not clear. The road to Cochrane is by the Old Mill Cultural Centre in Canefield, once through the village the trail is marked. About 1½-2 hours' walk from Cochrane are the **Middleham Falls**, about 250 ft high, falling into a beautiful blue pool in the middle of the forest. Once past the Middleham Falls the trail emerges on the Laudat road. Turn inland at *Sisserou Hotel* and then immediately right behind the Texaco garage (30 minutes' walk from Roseau) a steep road leads 2½ miles up to Giraudel (50 minutes' walk). From behind the school here a trail goes up through a succession of smallholdings to **Morne Anglais** (3,683 ft) (2 hours' walk from Giraudel). This is the easiest of the high mountains to climb and you get some lovely views of the whole island. The trail is fairly easy to follow but someone will need to show you the first part through the smallholdings. Ask in the village or go with *Dominica Tours*.

South of Roseau In the far south are the villages of **Soufrière** and **Scotts Head**. Both are worth visiting for their stunning setting on the sea with the mountain backdrop and brightly painted fishing boats pulled up on the shore. There are plenty of buses (EC$3) to Scotts Head, over the mountain with excellent views all the way to Martinique. Ask around the fishing huts if you are hungry, and you will be directed to various buildings without signs where you can eat chicken pilau for EC$6 and watch dominoes being played. There is a friendly café, *Sundowner*, on the main road just across from the most active fishing area (this boasts the only lavatories for the use of visitors).

On the south coast is **Grand Bay**, where there is a large beach (dangerous for swimming), the 10 ft high Belle Croix and the **Geneva Estate**, founded in the 18th century by the Martinican Jesuit, Father Antoine La Valette, and at one time the home of the novelist Jean Rhys. From Grand Bay, it is a two hour walk over the hill, past Sulphur Spring to Soufrière. Grand Bay should be avoided during Carnival, which is celebrated over-enthusiastically and aggressively. Tourists were attacked in 1997 with guns and machetes wielded by a group of men in costumes. The area has a reputation for violence related to the growing of marijuana.

Leeward coast The Leeward coastal road, north from Roseau, comes first to **Canefield**, passing the turning for the twisting Imperial Road to the centre of the island, and then the small airport. The coast road passes through **Massacre**, reputed to be the settlement where 80 Caribs were killed by British troops in 1674. Among those who died was Indian Warner, Deputy Governor of Dominica, illegitimate son of Sir Thomas Warner (Governor of St Kitts) and half-brother of the commander of the British troops, Colonel Philip Warner. From the church perched above the village there are good views of the coast. The next village is **Mahaut** and just north of here near DCP a newly paved road, called Warner Road, climbs steeply up towards Morne Couroune. It then levels out and joins the main Layou Valley road at the Layou Valley Plaza, a few kilometres west of the Pont Cassé roundabout. The views are stunning and are best when coming down hill.

North of the Transinsular road are the **Central Forest Reserve** and **Northern Forest Reserve**. In the latter is **Morne Diablotin**. Take a bus from Roseau to Dublanc, walk 1½ hours on a minor road and you will see a sign. The trail to the summit is very rough, about three hours steep walking and climbing up and 2½ hours down, not for the faint hearted, you are advised to take a guide.

Portsmouth The coastal road continues to Portsmouth, the second town. An excellent market is held here twice a week with all local fruits, vegetables and spices for sale. Nearby are the ruins of the 18th-century **Fort Shirley** on the Cabrits, which has a museum in one of the restored buildings (site pass required, US$2 at the gate). It is very run down but there is an excellent plan of how the fort once was. Clearly marked paths lead to the Commander's Quarters, Douglas Battery and other outlying areas. The colonial fortifications, apart from the main buildings which have been cleared, are strangled by ficus roots, and cannon which used to point out to sea now aim at the forest. A new visitors' centre has been built at the cruise ship jetty (small ships only). Prince Rupert Bay has been much visited: Columbus landed here in 1504 and in 1535 the Spanish Council of the Indies declared the bay a station for its treasure ships. Sir Francis Drake, Prince Rupert and John Hawkins all visited the bay to trade with the Caribs. Construction of Fort Shirley began in 1774. It was abandoned by the army in 1854 and its restoration began in 1982.

Indian River From the bridge just south of Portsmouth, boats make regular, one-hourly trips up the **Indian River** (EC$25 per person), a peaceful trip (40 minutes) through a tunnel of vegetation as long as you are not accompanied by boatloads of other tourists. Competition for passengers is keen. Negotiate with the local boatmen about price and insist they use oars rather than a motor. There is a bar open at the final landing place on this lovely river which accommodates large numbers of cruise ship passengers and serves them the very potent spiced rum, aptly named *Dynamite*. You can then continue on foot through fields and forest to the edge of a marsh where migrating birds come in the winter months. The river and the swamps and marshes are being considered for inclusion in the national parks system.

Portsmouth

The north From Portsmouth, one road carries on to the **Cabrits National Park** and the island's north tip at **Cape Melville**. An unpaved road leads off this at Savanne Paille; impassable except on foot, it is a beautiful route over the mountain, through a valley with sulphur springs, to Penville on the north coast, from where you can pick up the road heading south. Allow several hours.

Another road from Portsmouth heads east, following the Indian River for much of the way, winding up and down to the bays and extensive coconut palm plantations of the northwest coast, Calibishie, Melville Hall airport and Marigot. There are some beautiful sandy beaches at Hampstead and Larieu. **Calibishie** is a charming fishing village looking out towards Guadeloupe. There are hiking trails to the forest and wide, sandy beaches nearby; local guides are available. Transport to most areas in the northern part of the island is good, as is accommodation in and around the village. There are some small grocery stores, restaurants, post office, petrol station and a health clinic. Fishing boats come in at around 1630 and sell their catch at the bayside.

Transinsular road The shortest route from Roseau to Marigot and Melville Hall is via the Transinsular Road. It climbs steeply with many bends from Canefield. Along this road you will see coconut and cocoa groves; look out for the land crabs' holes, the orange juveniles come out in the daytime, the white adults at night. There are banana plants all along the gorge, together with dasheen, tannia, oranges and grapefruit. At Pont Cassé, the road divides three ways at one of the island's few roundabouts. One branch turns left, down the Layou Valley, to join the Leeward coast at Layou; the Transinsular Road goes straight on, through Bells, to Marigot; the third branch goes east (the path up the Trois Pitons is signed on the right just after the roundabout, three hours to the summit), either to Rosalie and La Plaine on the southeast Windward coast, or to Castle Bruce and the Carib Territory. The northern road, to Marigot, follows the Pagua River as it descends from the Central Forest Reserve to Pagua Bay on the Atlantic Ocean. At Hatton Garden, on the Bay, just south of Marigot, is **Habitation Chabert**, a restored 19th-century lime and sugar factory, now a museum of French and Créole furniture, artefacts, weapons and maps. ■ *US$4. Daily 0900-1600.*

Heading west from Pont Cassé the road affords some spectacular views. Layou River has some good spots for bathing, one of which is particularly good. Just over five miles from the roundabout there is a narrow foot path on the right, immediately before a sizeable road bridge. It passes through a banana field to the riverside. On the opposite bank a concrete bath has been built around a hot spring to create an open-air hot tub (Glo Cho) with room for four or five good friends.

Heading north from Pont Casse, a 20-minute walk from *Spanny's Bar* on the main road leads you to Penrice Falls, two small waterfalls. There is great, but cold, swimming in the pool at the second fall.

At Bells there is a fascinating and beautiful walk to **Jacko Flats**. Here a group of maroons (escaped slaves) led by Jacko had their encampment in the late 17th and early 18th centuries. Carved into the cliffs of the Layou River gorge, a flight of giant steps rises 300 ft up to a plateau on which the maroons had their camp. Ask at the *Paradise Bar* in Bells for a guide and dress for river walking since much of the trail is in the river itself.

Heading east from Pont Casse, the **Emerald Pool** is a small, but pretty waterfall in a grotto in the forest, 15 minutes by path from the Pont Cassé-Castle Bruce road. Avoid the area on days when cruise ships have docked, as hundreds of passengers are taken to visit the Pool, with resulting damage to its delicate ecology. There is a picnic area, and toilet facilities are being built. There are no buses from Roseau but you can catch a minibus to Canefield and wait at the junction for a bus going to Castle Bruce.

The Atlantic coast This coast is much more rugged than the Caribbean, with smaller trees, sandy or pebbly bays, palms and dramatic cliffs. Castle Bruce is a lovely bay and there are good views all around. After Castle Bruce the road enters the **Carib Territory**, although there is only a very small sign to indicate this. At the north end there is another sign, but it would still be easy to drive through the territory without seeing anything of note except a few small souvenir shops selling basket work. In fact, there is much to see; to appreciate it fully, a guide is essential. **Horseback Ridge** affords views of the sea, mountains, the Concord Valley and Bataka village. At **Crayfish River**, a waterfall tumbles directly into the sea by a beach of large stones. A visitors' centre is under construction.

The Save the Children Fund has assisted the Waitikubuli Karifuna Development Committee to construct two traditional buildings near **Salybia**: a large oval *carbet* (the nucleus of the extended Carib family group), and an A-frame *mouina*. The former is a community centre, the latter a library and office of the elected chief. The Carib chief is elected for five years and his main tasks are to organize the distribution of land and the preservation of Carib culture. In 1999, Garnet Joseph was elected chief of the Carib community and chairman of the Carib Council, replacing Hilary Frederick (1979-84, 1994-99). The dilapidated Church of the Immaculate Conception at Salybia is being restored as a Carib Museum (opening date uncertain; it has been replaced by the new church of St Marie of the Caribs, which opened in May 1991), its design is based on the traditional *mouina* and has a canoe for its altar, murals about Carib history both inside and out. Outside is a cemetery and a three-stone monument to the first three Carib chiefs after colonization: Jolly John, Auguiste and Corriett.

Traditional methods of making canoes from tree trunks can be seen in the Carib Territory. In May 1997 a group of 11 Caribs paddled a 35 ft canoe, carved from a gommier tree, to Guyana via Martinique, St Lucia, St Vincent, Grenada and Trinidad and Tobago, reversing the migratory journey of their ancestors.

L'Escalier Tête-Chien, at Jenny Point in Sineku is a line of rock climbing out of the sea and up the headland. It is most obvious in the sea and shore, but on the point each rock bears the imprint of a scale, circle or line, like the markings on a snake. It is said that the Caribs used to follow the snake staircase (which was made by the Master Tête-Chien) up to its head in the mountains, thus gaining special powers. There are more prosaic, geological explanations.

Taking the road from Pont Cassé to the southeast part of the island, you come to Rosalie. Cross the River Rosalie and go south to Pointe Daniel and Délices, passing through La Plaine. At La Plaine a fairly easy trail can be followed to the **Sari Sari Falls** (about 150 ft high). At Délices, you can see the **Victoria Falls** from the road. The Forestry Division plans to improve the rugged trail to the Falls. Be sure to take an experienced guide if you attempt the steep hike to these Falls (or the Sari Sari Falls) and avoid it in the rainy season. The White River falls in to the Atlantic at **Savane Mahaut**, reached by a steep road from Victoria Laroche down to the sea. There are delightful places to picnic, rest or swim in the river. At the weekend local families picnic and wash their cars here. If it has not rained much the previous day you can follow the river up, jumping from one to another of the big stones in the river bed. Be wary of flash floods and do not attempt to cross the river if there has been heavy rainfall as you might not be able to get back. Sea bathing here is very dangerous.

A road has been cut between the village of **Petite Savanne** and the **White River** linking the south and east coasts. It is extremely steep but offers spectacular views including of both the Victoria Falls and the steam rising from the Boiling Lake.

Essentials

Hotels LL-A *Fort Young Hotel*, within the old fort, T4485000, F4488065, www.fortyounghotel.com Ocean front rooms and suites of an excellent standard and full conference facilities for the business traveller, lots of facilities, service brusque, food adequate, pool, exercise room, jetty, waterfront restaurant, the atmosphere is more relaxed on weekends, special events like concerts and barbecues and a popular Happy Hour every Fri, 1800-1900. **L-AL** *Garraway*, Place Heritage, 1 Bay Front (Dame Eugenia Charles Boulevard), T4498800, F4498807, www.delphis.dm/garraway.htm 31 rooms and suites, again of a good standard, conference facilities, restaurant, cocktail bar, senior citizen discounts and weekend deals available to encourage tourists. **AL-B** *Sutton Place Hotel*, 25 Old St, T4498700, F4483045, www.delphis.dm/sutton.htm One of the newest hotels on the island, 8 rooms, beautiful décor, excellent service, self-catering suites available.

Sleeping Roseau
There are some small, informal hotels, guest houses & apartment facilities here.

Do verify whether tax (5%) is included in the quoted rate

Windward Islands

Guest houses C *Honychurch Apartment*, 5 Cross St, T4483346. Very central, discounts for a week, even nicer to stay at their *D'Auchamps Apartments* up in the Trafalgar Valley and hire a car, see below. **D-E** *Cherry Lodge*, 20 Kennedy Av, T4482366. Historic and quaint, some rooms with bath, rooms can be noisy and mosquitoes abundant, coils provided but no fans, good value meals available to order. **D-E** *Ma Bass Central Guest House*, 44 Fields Lane, T4482999. 7 rooms, fans, food available. **E** *Vena's Guesthouse*, 48 Cork St, T4483286. 15 rooms, prices higher during carnival, Jean Rhys' birth place, interesting, rather inefficient, rooms small and grim, rooms without bath more spacious and comfortable but noisy, *The World of Food* restaurant is next door.

Apartments are available to rent in & around Roseau, check at the Tourist Office, look in the New Chronicle, Tropical Star or ask a taxi driver

Sleeping: South of Roseau

Outside Roseau, up a steep and windy hill (King's Hill), is **L-C** *Reigate Hall*, T4484031, F4484034. A splendid location but laid back management, recommended for sunset rum punch to watch the Green Flash. 15 rooms and suites, a/c, service in restaurant sloppy and slow, bar, swimming pool, tennis courts, dive packages with Dive Dominica. Further up the Roseau Valley are **A-E** *Chez Ophelia Cottage Apartments*, T4483438, F4483433, mariem@mail.cwdom.dm Your host is the famous singer Ophelia, Dominica's 'First Lady of Song', close to Trafalgar Falls. **C** *Cocoa Cottage*, T4480412. A neat, clean and homely B&B in the middle of Trafalgar Valley.

Castle Comfort

L-A *Evergreen*, T4483288, F4486800, www.delphis.dm/evergreen.htm 16 rooms, with breakfast, a/c, TV, bar, good restaurant overlooking the sea. **AL** *Exotica*, T4488839, F4488829, www.exotica-cottages.com Nestled under the peaks of Morne Anglais close to Giraudel, new ecotourism centre, run by Athie Martin, president of the Dominica Conservation Society, 8 wooden cottages, sympathetic design, good base for hiking, self-catering, with advance the *Sugar Apple Café* will prepare meals. **AL-A** *Castle Comfort Lodge*, T4482188, F4486088, www.castlecomfortdivelodge.com Very friendly, professional, 15 rooms, excellent local food, good service. A 7-night 10-dive package available includes transfers, 1-night dive, unlimited shore diving, tax and service, US$990 (see page 762). **AL-B** *Anchorage*, on seafront, T4482638, F4485680, www.anchoragehotel.dm Waterfront restaurant, rooms rather tatty and run down, bar, friendly but slow service, food nothing special although Thu buffet very good and popular with locals, swimming pool and diving facilities, a 7-night, 10-dive package available, squash court with rather low ceiling. A friendly and delightful place to stay, family-run, with good restaurant and excellent service is **AL-C** *Reigate Waterfront*, T4483111, F4484034. Restaurant with well-known barbecue Wed night, 24 rooms, host to weekly shows in the month before carnival and noisy.

Near Canefield

LL-A *The Wesleeann Hotel and Suites*, T4490419, F4492473, towers over 8th Street in Canefield. Tastefully decorated apartments with kitchen, bathroom, balcony and daily maid service, for daily or longer rental. **AL-C** *The Hummingbird Inn*, Morne Daniel, Roseau, T/F4491042. Rooms (small, luggage a problem) or a suite, run by Mrs Finucane who is knowledgeable on Dominica, peaceful, simple, comfortable, good food, slow service, stunning views down the hill over the sea, 5 minutes north of Roseau, on bus route. **A** *Crescent Moon Cabins*, T/F4493449, www.delphis.dm/ crescentmooncabins/, high above Mahaut but reached from the main Transinsular Road, about 30 mins from Roseau. Well-furnished wooden cabins in a delightful, secluded setting, double and single bed, run by Ron and Jean Viveralli, good home cooking, local style, fresh fruit and vegetables from on-site greenhouse and gardens, own roasted coffee, fresh spring water, breakfast US$8, lunch US$10, can be packed for picnic, dinner US$15, car hire recommended, *Island Car Rentals* will give a discount for guests. **B-C** *Sunset Guest House*, T4491339, near Canefield airport. Friendly, clean, near bus route to Roseau.

Near Trafalgar Falls

AL-A *Papillote Wilderness Retreat*, T4482287, F4482285, www.papillote.dm 10 suites or cottage in beautiful botanical gardens landscaped by owner Anne Jean Baptiste, with hot mineral pool and geese, birdwatching house, food good but slightly limited for long stay; restaurant for non-residents near road, lunch and dinner, food well prepared and nicely presented, closed Sun (avoid days when cruise ship passengers invade, reservations required), arts and crafts boutique, take torch and umbrella, good road from the nearby village of Trafalgar all the way to the falls car park, spectacular setting. On the road to Trafalgar and Papillote, the Honychurch family rents self-contained cottages on their lovely estate, **C** *D'Auchamps*, T4483346, honychurchs@cwdom.dm The beautiful botanical gardens are closed to the public now but the cottages are still available and guests can enjoy the lush gardens, the *Garden Cabin* sleeps maximum 3, no hot water, outside shower, the *Small Cottage* sleeps 4, hot water, fully equipped. **B-C** *Roxy's Mountain Lodge* in Laudat, T/F4484845, bruneyr@cwdom.dm 2,000 ft above sea level, established 1960, good breakfast and hearty supper, friendly owners, 17 basic rooms, good beds, hot showers, also apartment, 4-6 people, convenient for visiting Boiling Lake, Boeri Lake, Middleham Falls, Trafalgar Falls and Freshwater Lake, all within walking distance, guides arranged if required, transport into Roseau 0700 except Sun, returning 1615, EC$3. **C-D** *Falls View Guest House*, within sight of the falls, T/F4480064.10 rooms, good walking, Dominican cuisine, bar.

South coast In Scotts Head is **B-D** *Herche's Place*, Bay Street, T4487749, F4498000, herches@cwdom.dm 10 rooms, fans, a/c, TV, *Sundowner Café*, watersports, diving, fishing arranged. *Ocean View Apartments*, T4498266. Owned by the very hospitable Frank and Caroline Charles, 1 or 2-bedroom apartment, large secluded garden with fruit trees, mosquito nets, also 2 rooms in main house, maid and laundry service offered and transport to airport. **AL** *Zandoli Inn*, T4463161, F4463344, www.zandoli.com, south coast at Roche Cassee near fishing village of Stowe. New, well laid out, secluded, superb mountain and seaviews to Martinique, 5 rooms with balconies, includes continental breakfast, plunge pool, 6 acres of seaside tropical forest.

Leeward coast **AL-A** *Castaways*, Mero, PO Box 5, T4496244, F4496246, just north of St Joseph. Convenient with hired car for visiting all parts of the island, on black sand beach, restaurant, beach barbecue on Sunday, popular, watch out for beach cricket balls, staff slow but friendly, reasonable rooms all with balcony and seaview but in need of redecoration, ask for fan and mosquito net, good tennis court, sailing sometimes available, dive shop attached, German spoken, dive package available. **AL-A** *Sunset Bay Club*, Batalie Beach in the middle of the west coast, T4466522. Run by Belgian family, all-inclusive or room only, bungalows, suites, pool, sauna. *Anse-à-Liane Lodge*, north of Colihaut, T4466652, F4466651, www.ansealianedive.com Friendly owners, 10 rooms, 5 mins from sea with diving on beach below, a/c, restaurant, decent food, pool, tours planned.

Portsmouth **AL-B** *Picard Beach Cottage Resort*, T4455131, F4455599, pbh@cwdom.dm An attractive open-sided restaurant and bar, self-catering cottages which, at a pinch, can sleep 4, good sea bathing with coral reef, 7-night, 10-dive, package available. Further apartments are being built on the beach. On Picard Beach, **B** *Coconut Beach*, T4455393, F4455693. Beachfront bungalows, apartments, snorkelling, diving, windsurfing, volleyball, excursions, restaurant, marina planned. **C** *Sister Sea Lodge*, Prince Rupert's Bay. Beach bar, T/F4455211, sangow@cwdom.dm Fresh fish and 6 apartments set in lovely gardens, spacious, self-contained, insect nets, 2 double beds, bathroom, run by Elka and Harta (German) Sango, yachts can moor in the bay, sandy outside beach bar. **D** *Casa Ropa*, on Bay Street, T4455492, F4455277. Rooms or apartments with bath, single downstairs, friendly, clean. **E** *Douglas Guest House*, Bay Street, T4455253. Single, double or triple rooms, ask for fan, clean, next to noisy disco and cinema.

North coast **Calibishie** **LL-B** *Pointe Baptiste* estate rents out the Main House, sleeping 8, includes cook and maid, weekly rates available, spectacular view from the airy verandah, house built in 1932, wooden, perfect for children, cot, also smaller house sleeping 2, self-catering, book locally through the housekeeper Geraldine Edwards, T4457322. **L-A** *Eden Estate House* is also available for rent, T4482638, F4485680. 3 bedrooms, in middle of coconut and fruit plantation, only 3 miles from Melville Hall airport, maid service can be provided. **AL** *Wind Blow Estate*, Calibishie, www.delphis.dm/windblow/ or in the USA Lewis Watkins, 18875 Cortez Blvd, Brooksville, Florida, T352-7997353. Apartments, 1 or 2 bedrooms, fans, sun deck, great view of Guadeloupe and Marie Galante, parking, security guard, sisserou parrot nests on the estate. In Calibishie, **AL-C** *Veranda View*, T4458900, lawrence@cwdom.dm Run by Mrs Teddy Lawrence, facing beach, beautiful view of Guadeloupe, clean, 3 bright and large rooms, includes breakfast, light cooking facilities, hot showers. **A-B** *Sea Cliff Cottages*, 15 mins' walk from Calibishie, T/F4458998 Dec-May, T/F6137563116 Jun-Nov, sherwood@ mv.igs.net 3 cottages, 1-3 bedrooms, kitchens, veranda, fruit trees in the garden for seasonal use, path to beach, snorkelling good, river good for children to play in, small island within swimming distance. **C** *Windswept Guest House*, T4458982/7236, between Calibishie and airport. Quiet, secluded, clean, close to excellent beach. In **Marigot D** *Thomas Guest House*, west end of main street, T4455591. Clean, basic, near Melville Hall airport (check in advance if it is open).

Inland   **A** *Layou Valley Inn*, T4496203, F4485212. 5 rooms, very comfortable, excellent cuisine, high in the hills with superb views, need a car to get there. **A-B** *Floral Gardens*, Concord Village, at the edge of the Carib Territory, T/F4457636. Comfortable rooms, CP, apartments, 10% discount for stays of 5 days and over, dinner, excellent food but expensive and service very slow, lovely gardens by the Pagua River where you can swim, 15 mins away from beaches of Woodford Hill, electrics basic, ask for a mosquito coil for your room, many minibuses in the morning, easy to get a pick-up, bus to Roseau EC$9, 1 hr, bus to airport and Woodford Hill Beach, lovely walks in the area, either into the Carib territory or around Atkinson further north. Charles Williams and his wife, Margaret, run the **C-E** *Carib Territory Guest House*, Crayfish River, on the main road, T4457256, www.delphis.dm/ ctgh.htm She cooks if meals are ordered in advance but there are no restaurants nearby as an alternative and you may go hungry, water intermittent, good base for exploring, he also does island-wide tours but is better on his own patch. About a mile away, **F** *Olive's Guest House* at Atkinson, T4457521. Slightly set back off the road, bamboo huts, comfortable, friendly, meals extra.

Camping is not encouraged and, in the national parks, it is forbidden. Designated sites may be introduced in the future.

Eating:
Roseau
5% sales tax is added to meal charges

On weekdays in the capital the lunch hour begins at 1300 and places fill up quickly. Dominicans eat their main meal at lunch time and it is often hard to get anything other than takeaways after 1600 or on Sun except at hotels. If you have a car, try different hotel restaurants on different nights and check when the barbecue specials etc are being held. Generally, Dominicans eating out do so in restaurants at lunchtime and in hotels at night.

US$17 and above At the *Fort Young Hotel* there are two restaurants: *Marquis de Bouille*, at the front of the hotel, serves international and créole food with themed buffet lunches, barbecue with steel band Mon night, while *The Waterfront* has a charming, wooden balconied seafront location with a more romantic and elegant style. *La Robe Créole*, 3 Victoria St, T4482896. Créole and European, vegetarian available, good but expensive, service inattentive, open Mon-Sat 1100-1500, 1830-2130. **US$13-17** *Restaurant Paiho*, 10 Church St, T4488999. Good Chinese food, delicious fruit punch, uncrowded, slightly pricey, open Mon-Sat 1100-1500, 1730-2230, Sun 1800-2200. **US$9-13** *Torino's*, above Prevo Cinemall on corner of Old St, Kennedy Av. Excellent home made pasta, evenings only, great pizzas on Sat from 2000, and the best cappuccino on the island, open 0800-2200 Mon-Sat. *The World of Food*, next to *Vena's Guesthouse*. Local dishes but unexciting, good breakfast about EC$10, lunch and dinners EC$20-30, drink your beer under a huge mango tree which belonged to writer Jean Rhys's family garden. *Taiwanese Delicacies*, between Newtown and Castle Comfort. New Chinese restaurant with a good atmosphere, good food and friendly hosts, see Nightlife, below for karaoke. **US$5-9** *Ti-Caz (Coco-Rico) Café*, Bayfront. French restaurant, bar, wine store and grocery, excellent range, good service, pleasant environment, sidewalk café. *Guiyave*, 15 Cork St. For midday snacks and juices, patisserie and salad bar, popular, crowded after 1300. *Syme Zees*, two locations, guest house in Laudat, and a bar/restaurant on King George St. Famous for Thu night jazz, also a good lunchtime spot for generous helpings, fried fish recommended. *Cornerhouse*, 6 King George V St, T4499000. Opposite Old Market, open Mon-Thu 0730-2200, Fri-Sat 0730-2400, soups, salads, sandwiches, excellent bagels, music, books, magazines, newspapers, internet access, popular pub quiz night Wed 2000. *Continental Inn*, 37 Queen Mary St, Roseau, T4482214/5. Open 0700-2130, créole cuisine, mountain chicken, seafood, rotis, delivery in Roseau area, credit cards accepted. **US$2-5** *Laughing Lobster*, Great George St, between Woodstone Mall and *Orchard Restaurant*, T4499372. Basic décor but great food, including vegetarian, real value for money, fish dinner for US$2.25, open 0900-1700. *Pearl's Cuisine*, 50 King George V St. Good local food and slowish service, with nice balcony. Under the same ownership as *La Robe Créole* is the *Mousehole Café*, underneath. Excellent for little pies and local pasties. *Mousehole Too*, 10 Kennedy Av, near Whitchurch Centre, T4482896. Has seating, open 0800-1500.; *Creole Kitchen Ltd*, in Woodstone Shopping Mall on corner of George St and Cork St. Fried or barbecued chicken, sandwiches, burgers, cold drinks, open Mon-Thu 0800-2300, Fri-Sat 0800-1200, Sun 1500-2300. *Cottage Restaurant*, Hillsborough St. Friendly, fish, rice, salad and provisions for EC$10. For vegetarian food try *Back-A-Yard*, on Castle St, just up the hill from the *Garraway Hotel*. Lots of 'snackettes', for example *Hope Café*, 17 Steber Street. Good local dishes and snacks, lively, open till late; *Celia's Snack*, on Great Marlborough St, EC$1.50 for delicious bread and codfish, good local ice cream, fruit juice. *Erick's Bakery* has a small patisserie on Old St for 'tasty island treats'.

Evergreen Hotel, at Castle Comfort, see above. Good reputation, pleasant seafront location, meals from US$13 per person. On Thu night the *Ocean Terrace Restaurant* at the *Anchorage* has a good value barbecue buffet and reggae band. If staying in town there are 2 places worth taking a taxi to eat: *Papillote* (see page 770), T4482287. Book before 1600, take swimming costume and towel for bathe in sulphur pool under the stars; *Reigate Hall Hotel* (also see above), book ahead, slow service but ask to eat out on balcony overlooking valley of Roseau, catch the sunset for spectacular view. *George Chicken Shack* , on roadside between Emerald Pool and Pont Cassé. Small bar, cold beer and great fried chicken. *La Flambeau Restaurant* at Picard Cottage, near Portsmouth. Comfortable, has an attractive beachside setting and a varied menu. *Purple Turtle*, Lagoon, Portsmouth, T4455296. On beach, open Mon-Fri 1000-2300, Sat-Sun 1000-0200, snacks and full meals, local and international food, karaoke at weekends. *Mango's Bar & Restaurant*, Bay Street, Portsmouth, T4453099. Yellow and white house with tin roof, mural inside of island life, varied menu, open daily 0800-2300, credit cards accepted. The *DomCan's Café* is pleasantly located right on the beach at Calibishie, T4458769. Good service, open 0900-2200, lunch of sandwiches and burgers, dinner fish, chicken, mountain chicken. *New Stop Café and Bar*, close to Trafalgar Falls. Overlooking river, just down the road from *Papillotte*, tiny, outdoors, seats 10-15 people, delicious food, contact the proprietors in the morning (c/o Mayfield Denis) to arrange menu, also good for beer, conversation and reggae. *The Sundowner Café*, *Herche's Place Hotel*, T4487749. Open Tue-Sun, jazz nightly, extensive menu, specializes in fish and seafood, meals around US$9-15, great view of Scott's Head. *Chez Wen*, Scott's Head, T4486668. Overlooking the bay serving shellfish and drinks, popular with divers. *Marilyn's*, by the Rosalie River in the east, about 1 mile from boxing plant, run by Americans Marilyn and Tony, lovely setting on covered patio with river gushing over large rocks amid lush foliage, limited menu of local and American food, rooms to rent planned.

**Eating:
around
the island**

Fried chicken, bakes (a fried dough patty filled with tuna, codfish or corned beef) and rotis (pancake-like parcel of curried chicken and veg) are the most popular snacks available in most bakeries. There is plenty of local fruit and vegetables, fish and 'mountain chicken' (crapaud, or frog) in season. Try the seedless golden grapefruit, US$1 for 6 in the market. The term 'provisions' on a menu refers to root vegetables: dasheen, yams, sweet potatoes, tannia, pumpkins, etc. To buy fresh fish listen for the fishermen blowing their conch shells in the street; there is no fish shop but fish can be bought in the market on Fri and Sat, get there early, usually EC$7 per pound. Try the sea-moss drink, rather like a vanilla milk shake (with a reputation as an aphrodisiac), also drunk on Grenada, see page 866. There is little in the way of international or fast food on the island except, *Kentucky Fried Chicken*, corner of Great George Street and Great Marlborough Street and *Perky's Pizza*, corner of Queen Mary Street and Cork Street. Good range, tasty, not too expensive.

Local food

Windward Islands

Nightlife Friday is *the* night out, with people (locals and tourists alike) moving from *Fort Young*'s Happy Hour across to *La Robe*'s Happy Hour or to *Garraway*'s, into town and *Cornerhouse*, then on to *Cellar's Bar* for karaoke night with a distinct Caribbean flavour. If you've still got energy, its on to *Ashma's Bar* or to one of the discos such as *Magic, Scorpio's* or *Warehouse* (see below), which never get going until after midnight. However, there are a growing number of places to eat and hang out south of Roseau, in the 2-mile stretch from the city centre to the village of Loubiere. They represent a good cross section of bars, places to eat and nightspots, ranging from down-to-earth to up-market. There is no place that only tourists go. Heading from Roseau, **Taiwanese Delicacies**, between Newtown and Castle Comfort, start your evening with brazed shrimp or sweet & sour. If its happening, partake of some karaoke. **Zam Zam's** in Castle Comfort, lively mix of locals, tourists and ex-pats at this seaside bamboo hut. The place really gets going as it fills up when people pop in for 'one for the road'. **All One Bar**, also known as **Duncan's**, a similarly nice casual spot with tables by the sea and a good range of drinks. **The Old Mill Restaurant/Magic Disco**, near Loubiere, 2 miles south of Roseau, T4487778, restaurant, bar and beer garden are open every night except Mon 1900-2400, Wed is cocktail night, grill open all day every day, mixed reviews on food, the disco, *Magic Nightclub,* is open till late Thu-Sun, very popular on Fri, starts at 2200 finishes around 0400, regular live performances from popular local bands like *Swinging Stars, WCK, First Serenade.* **Spiders**, Loubiere, is guaranteed to be open when everywhere else has closed, it is a hole in the wall with great Caribbean music, some of the cheapest beers, fried chicken and the famous Spider Pies (they are actually fish and cost just EC$1.25.

For lovers of zouk music, look out for live performances by **WCK, Midnight Groovers** or **First Serenade**. Mid-week entertainment at **Anchorage** and **Reigate Waterfront** hotels. Weekends at **Fort Young Hotel**, Fri night happy hour 1800-1900, live music, popular with ex-pats, tourists and locals alike, nightclub open Fri and Sat. **Symes-Zee** on King George V Street is the spot to be on Thu night with live jazz and friendly atmosphere. **Cellars Bar**, downstairs at *Sutton Place Hotel*, Old Street. Lively after-work bar, big screen TV, karaoke, jazz, a/c. Discos at Canefield: **Warehouse** on Sat, in converted sugar mill by the airport, gets going after 2400. Recommended. The disco at the **Q-Club** on Friday gets going after 2400. **Scorpio's Disco**, Morne Daniel, upmarket, a/c, gets going after 2400. In Portsmouth, **Rivers International Nightclub and Bar**, opposite Ross University. Open Fri-Sun from 2200, a/c, local and international music T4454777.The Arawak House of Culture, Hillsborough Street in Roseau, next to Government Headquarters, can seat 540 for plays, concerts, dance shows and recitals. Performances are also held at the Old Mill Cultural Centre in Canefield. **Carib Cinema**, Old Street and Kennedy Av. A/c, 2 bars, 4 shows at weekends, 1 nightly on weekdays, T4481819, F4499523.

Festivals

During Carnival, laws of libel & slander are suspended

The main one is **Carnival**, on the Mon and Tue before **Ash Wednesday**; it is not as commercialized as many in the Americas as it lacks the sponsorship of a carnival like Trinidad's, but it is one of the most spontaneous and friendly. Sensay costume has returned to the streets: layer upon layer of banana or cloth is used for the costume, a scary mask is worn over the face, usually with horns, and large platform clog boots finish the effect. Large quantities of beer are required for anyone who can wear this costume and dance the streets for several hours in the midday sun. The **Independence Folk Festival** starts in late **September** running up to **Independence Day** in **November**. Independence celebrations (3/4 Nov) feature local folk dances, competitions, storytelling, music and crafts. On **Créole Day**, the last Fri in *October*, the vast majority of girls and women wear the national dress, 'la wobe douillete', to work and school and most shop, bank clerks etc speak only Créole to the public. **Domfesta**, The Festival of the Arts, takes place during *June* and includes exhibitions by local artists (notably Kelo Royer, Earl Etienne, Arnold Toulon), concerts and theatre performances (see local papers, *The Chronicle, The Independent* or *The Tropical Star*, for details or ask at hotel.) In *October* Dominica hosts the **World Creole Music Festival**, with Cadence, Zouk, Compas, Bouyou and Soukous. Artists come from other islands such as Haiti, Martinique and Cuba, or further afield from Africa, the UK and Louisiana, as well as those from Dominica. In 2000, the local bands playing were *Midnight Groovers*, led by Phillip 'Chubby' Mark, known as the 'King of Cadence-Lypso', and Anthony Gussie with his band *Black Affairs Plus*, who sings in French,

English, Créole and Kokoy. A season ticket costs US$46, or you can pay US$22 on the gate. For information about any festivals contact the Dominica Festivals Commission, 23 Great Marlborough St, Roseau, T4484833, F4480229, dfc@cwdom.dm An annual **Divefest** is held in **July**, with lots of activities, races, underwater treasure hunts, cruises etc. Funds are being raised for a recompression chamber, contact the Watersports Association, T4482188, F4486088, dive@cwdom.dm

  Around the island villages hold their own festivals: Isidore in Grand Bay at Pentecost; Fête Marin (St Peter's) in Portsmouth in Jun-Jul, as well as in Soufrière/Scott's Head, Colihaut/Dublanc and Anse de Mai; St Theresa in Salisbury in Oct; St Anne in Mahaut on 26 Jul; St Géraud in St Joseph in Oct and Feast of La Salette in Point Michel in Sep.

Shopping

Straw goods are among the best & cheapest in the Caribbean; they can be bought in the Carib Territory & Roseau

The *Craft Market*, at the Old Market, is a good place to start and get an idea of what is available. Best shops for crafts in Roseau are the *Caribana*, 31 Cork St, T/F4487340, which also has an art gallery for Dominican artists and, for the famous vetiver-grass mats, *Tropicrafts*, Queen Mary St, where you can see the women making the mats. It takes 4 weeks to complete a 10 ft mat. Note 4% extra charged on VISA. *Rainforest*, 17 Old St, T4488834, well produced local and other Dominican goods, US$1 given towards protection of Dominica's eco-system, owner Helen Rolle runs *Rainbow Art School*, which was responsible for the mural in Bay Street. Portsmouth has a sizeable craft shop at the Cruise Ship Berth on the Cabrits but prices are much higher than in Roseau, for example a bar of coconut soap was 4 times the price. Other good buys are local Bay Rum (aftershave and body rub), soap, tea, coffee, marmalade, hand cream, shampoo, spices, chocolate and candles. Bello 'Special' or 'Classic' pepper sauce is a good souvenir. The public market is lively and friendly. Try a jelly coconut. *Cee-Bee's Bookshop*, 20 Cork St and *Paperbacks* at 6 King George V St. For Caribbean and other English books and magazines. *Front Line Co-operative Services Ltd*, 78 Queen Mary St, T4488664. Books, CDs, cassettes, stationery, photography etc. *Dominica Pottery* has a showroom on corner of Bayfront and Kennedy Av with plenty of original pieces made by inmates of the prison. Batiks are made locally and available from *Cotton House Batik*, 8 Kings Lane. Many local crafts available at the *NDFD Small Business Complex*, 9 Great Marlborough St. *Whitchurch Supermarket*, Old St. A good range at reasonable prices, open Mon-Thu 0800-1900, Fri-Sat 0800-2000. The largest supermarket is *Brizee's Mart*, 5 mins from Roseau centre, T4482087, Canefield. Open Mon-Thu 0900-2000, Fri-Sat 0900-2100.

  If you are in a self-catering cottage anywhere on the island, local farmers may visit with their fresh produce for sale. At Portsmouth there is an excellent market twice a week where you can find fresh fruit, vegetables and spices locally grown. Fishing villages such as Calibishie are good sources of fresh fish; go down to the bay side around 1630 when the boats come in and get some kingfish or snapper for your evening meal.

Transport

Air From Antigua, *LIAT*, *Caribbean Star*; Barbados, *Eastern Caribbean Express*, *Caribbean Star*, *Air Jamaica*; Grenada, *Caribbean Star*; Pointe-à-Pitre, *LIAT*, *Air Caraibes*; Port of Spain, *Caribbean Star*; St Lucia, *Eastern Caribbean Express*, *Air Jamaica*, *LIAT*; Sint Maarten, *Air Caraibes*; St Vincent, *Caribbean Star*; San Juan, *American Eagle*. **Airport** Dominica has 2 airports, the older **Melville Hall** (DOM) in the northeast, which handles most planes (including **Liat**), and **Canefield** (DCF) near Roseau, which takes only very small aircraft. Check which your flight will be using. Variable winds and short landing strips mean that planes do not land before 0600 or after 1800 in the dark. Melville Hall has no currency exchange facilities, so if you are arriving from Europe it is best to have US dollars to hand. Melville Hall is 36 miles from Roseau; shuttle taxis cost US$18 per person, whichever route the driver takes. From Melville Hall to Portsmouth by taxi is EC$30. These rates are per seat; find someone to share with, or it will be assumed you want the vehicle to yourself, which is much more expensive. Canefield is only a 10 mins drive from Roseau; taxi fare to town is US$8 per person for up to 4 passengers. Minibus (public transport) fare from Canefield to Roseau is EC$1.50. (You must flag one down on the highway passing the airport, frequent service weekdays, very few on Sun.)

Sea A ferry service operates between Dominica and the French islands and on to St Lucia. It leaves Roseau for Fort-de-France Mon, Wed, Sat 1015, Fri 1415 and Sun 1615, 2 ½ hrs,

Port tax on departure from Roseau is EC$7

Windward Islands

US$102 return, for Pointe-à-Pitre Mon 1600, Wed, Fri 1700, Sat 1100, Sun 1730, 1 ¾ hrs, US$89 return, for Castries Fri 1415, Sun 1615, around 3-3 ¾ hrs, US$116 return. Day trips are only possible to Fort-de-France on Mon and Wed, all other routes require an overnight stay. The L'Express des Iles agency office is upstairs in the Whitchurch Centre, T4482181, F4485787. The channel where the Atlantic meets the Caribbean can be very rough sometimes so this crossing is not for the faint-hearted.

Local Bicycle: Mountain bikes can be rented from *Nature Island Dive*, T4498181, F4498182, US$11 per hour, US$21 half day, US$32 per day. Biking excursions also arranged, US$84 per person with guide. Roads are good for cycling, traffic is generally light with the exception of the stretch from Roseau to Layou. Between Canefield and Pont Casse it is very steep, twisty and challenging.

Bus Minibuses run from point to point. Those from Roseau to the northwest and northeast leave from between the east and west bridges near the modern market; to Trafalgar and Laudat from Valley Road, near the Police Headquarters; for the south and Petite Savane from Old Market Plaza. They are difficult to get on in the early morning unless you can get on a 0630 bus out to the villages to pick up schoolchildren and return in similar fashion. Many buses pass the hotels south of Roseau (for example *Anchorage*). Fares are fixed by the Government. Roseau to Salisbury is EC$3.50, to Portsmouth EC$7.50, to Woodford Hill EC$9, to Marigot EC$9, to Castle Bruce EC$7, Canefield EC$1.50, Laudat EC$3, Trafalgar EC$2.25, Soufrière/ScottsHead EC$3.

Driving is on the left. The steering wheel may be on either side. The speed limit is 10 mph near schools, 20 mph in Roseau & villages. No limit elsewhere

Car You must purchase a local driving permit, valid for 1 month, for US$11, for which a valid international or home driving licence is required. The permit may be bought from the police at airports, rental agencies, or at the Traffic Dept, High Street, Roseau or Bay Street, Portsmouth (Mon to Fri). **Car hire** Rates are about US$60 per day for a car, including collision damage waiver and 5% tax, and US$70 for a jeep; unlimited mileage for hiring for three days or more. A car rental phone can be found at the airport and several of the companies will pick you up from there and help to arrange the licence. *Island Car Rentals*, Goodwill Road, Roseau, T448-2886/3425, F4480737, www.delphis.dm/flydrive.htm Offers packages with choice of accommodation at 23 hotels island-wide, for example 7 nights US$499 per person, 2 nights US$245, free delivery and pick up anywhere, 24-hr emergency service. *Garraway Rent-a-Car*, 17 Old St, Roseau, T4482891, a/c car US$50 per day; *Best Deal*, T4499204, www.delphis.dm/bestdeal/index.htm Popular and reliable; *Anselm's*, 3 Great Marlborough St, T4482730, F4487559. *Budget*, Canefield Industrial Estate, opposite airport, T4492080, F4492694, recommended as cheaper, more reliable and informative than some other companies, courteous and efficient, cars in good condition.Also recommended for service (friendly, no hassle with replacing vehicle after accident) is *Courtesy Car Rental*, 10 Winston Lane, Goodwill, Roseau, T4487763, F4487733, www.delphis.dm/courtesycarrental Cars from US$39/day, and jeeps up to US$66/day, cheaper for longer, plus tax and CDW, free pick up and drop off from Canefield, ferry and hotels within 5 miles of office, but not from Melville Hall, which incurs extra charges. *Wide Range Car Rentals*, 79 Bath Rd, T4483181, F4483600. Rents out old Lada cars for US$30 per day, not recommended for smaller roads, also Suzuki jeeps, US$60 per day including 80 miles and collision protection free; Valley, T4483233, F4486009, www.valleycarrentals.com On Goodwill Road, next to Dominican Banana Marketing Corporation, or in Portsmouth, T4455252, free delivery to Canefield and within 5 miles of Roseau or Portsmouth offices, cars in need of maintenance but in the cheaper category; also on Goodwill Road, *S T L*, US$387 per 10 days including EC$20 licence and insurance, T4482340, free deliveries as for Valley, but only in Roseau area. It is extremely difficult to hire a vehicle between Christmas and New Year without prior reservation.

Taxis and minivans have HA or H on the license plate

Taxi A sightseeing tour by taxi will cost US$18 per hour per car (4 people), but it is wise to use experienced local tour operators for sightseeing, particularly if hiking is involved. Fares on set routes are fixed by the Government. Ask at your hotel for a taxi and if you want one after 1800 you should arrange it in advance. In Roseau, *Mally's Tour & Taxi Service*, 64 Cork

St, T448-3360/3114, F4483689 (if planning a day trip out of town on public transport, you can sometimes arrange to be picked up and returned to Roseau by their airport taxi service), *Eddie*, 8 Hillsborough St, T4486003, and others.

Airline offices *LIAT*, King George V St, Roseau, T4482421/2, Canefield airport T4491421, Melville Hall T4457242. Agent for *Air Guadeloupe* and *Helenair* is **Whitchurch Travel**, Old St, Roseau, T4482181, or Canefield Airport, T4491060. **Cardinal Airlines**, T4487432, F4498923. **American Eagle**, T4457204. **Mussons Travel**, also for flight bookings, T4482550.

Banks *Royal Bank of Canada*, Bay St, Roseau, T4482771. **Barclays Bank Plc**, 2 Old St, T4482571 (branch in Portsmouth, T4455271). **National Commercial Bank of Dominica**, 64 Hillsborough St, T4484401. Opens lunchtime, branch at Portsmouth, T4455430. **Banque Française Commerciale**, Queen Mary St, T4484040. **Scotia Bank**, 28 Hillsborough St, T4485800. American Express agent is Whitchurch Travel, T4482181, efficient and helpful for emergency cheque cashing. Visa and Mastercard well accepted with cash advances from all banks.

Communications Post: Hillsborough St and Bay St, Roseau, 0800-1600 Mon-Fri. A mural depicts the development of the postal service in Dominica. It has a list of other stamp sellers around the island. *Paperbacks* on Cork St and other stationers or gift shops.A postcard to the USA or Europe costs EC$0.55, letters EC$0.90. Parcels go airmail only. Post your mail at the main post office if possible, post boxes around the country are not all in operation and there is no indication of which ones have been taken out of service. DHL is in the Whitchurch Centre, represented by Whitchurch Travel Agency, T4482181, F4485787. **Telephone:** telephone and fax services at **Cable & Wireless (Dominica))**, Mercury House, Hanover St, Roseau. Open 0700-2000, Mon-Sat. Phone cards are available for EC$10, 20 and 40. *Cable & Wireless* has cellular service, credit card calling and a cybercafé on Kennedy Av, Roseau, T4481000, F4481111, www.cwdom.dm *Cornerhouse*, 6 King George St, T4499000. 3 computers for internet access, cornerhoused@hotmail.com, with salads, snacks and juices.

Embassies and Consulates *Venezuelan Embassy*, T4483348. *Embassy of the Republic of China*, T4491385. Honorary Consuls include *Belgium*, T4482168. *France*, T4482033. *Guyana*, T4482594. *Netherlands*, T4483841. *Spain*, T4482063. *Sweden*, T4482181. *UK*, T4481000.

Medical services Hillborough St clinic is quite large with pharmacy attached. *Princess Margaret Hospital*, T4482231. New casualty department built with French money, good and efficient, but note that you have to pay in advance for everything (for example EC$80 for consultation, EC$160 for X-ray). Outside Roseau there are also hospitals in Grand Bay, T4463706; Marigot, T4457091 and Portsmouth, T4455237. *The New Charles Pharmacy*, T4483198, F4485285. Open 0830-1630, offers free prescription delivery in Roseau.

Tourist information Local tourist offices: the Dominica Division of Tourism has its headquarters in the National Development Corporation, in a converted Rose's Lime Juice factory, Valley Road, Roseau (T4482045, F4485840, www.dominica.dm). There is a Dominica Information Desk in the arrival section of VC Bird International Airport, Antigua, open daily. A useful brochure is *Discover Dominica* available free from the tourist offices at both airports or in the Old Market Square (open Mon-Fri 0800-1600, Sat 0900-1300). Other useful guides and booklets are produced by the Forestry Division and are available from their offices in the Botanical Gardens, priced from EC$0.25-EC$15. **Tour operators**: island tours can be arranged through many of the hotels. The most knowledgeable operators are **Ken's Hinterland Adventure Tours and Taxi Service (Khatts Ltd)**, Ken and Clem recommended, lots of languages spoken, 62 Hillsborough Street, Roseau, T4484850, F4488486, khatts@cwdom.dm *Lambert Charles*, strong on conservation and hiking, no office but T4483365. Bobby Frederick of *Ras Tours*, T4480412 is featured in *National Geographic Traveller Magazine*, tours can be tailored to visitors needs and a half day tour costs US$40; *Alfred Rolle's Unique Tour Services*, Trafalgar Village, T448-7198, or through *Papillote*, Alfred is recommended. *Escape*, T4485240, www.delphis.dm/escape, open Nov-Apr, offers river rafting, river hiking, tubing and other adventure activities, from US$70 per person (minimum US$140), includes equipment, transport, guide, insurance, canyoning and cascading offered. Check beforehand which tours are offered on a daily basis or once or twice a week. You may have to wait for the tour you want or be offered an alternative. German, French, Spanish and English are offered at different agencies. The *Whitchurch Travel Agency*, Old Street, Roseau, T4482181, F4485787, www.whitchurch.com, handles local tours as well as foreign travel and represents American Express

Travel Related Services, several airlines and L'Express des Iles. *Fun, Sun Inc* at 21 Hanover St, T4486371, F4481606. **Maps:** The Ordnance Survey, Romsey Road, Southampton, SO9 49H, UK, T01703-792792, publishes a 1:50,000 colourful map of Dominica, with a 1:10,000 street map insert of Roseau, includes roads, footpaths, contours, forests, reserves and National Parks. This can be bought at the Old Market tourist office in Roseau.

Background

History The Caribs, who supplanted the Arawaks on Dominica, called the island Waitikubuli ("tall is her body"). Columbus sighted it on 3 November 1493, a Sunday (hence the modern name), but the Spanish took no interest in the island. It was not until 1805 that possession was finally settled. Until then it had been fought over by the French, British and Caribs. In 1660, the two European powers agreed to leave Dominica to the Caribs, but the arrangement lasted very few years; in 1686, the island was declared neutral, again with little success. As France and England renewed hostilities, the Caribs were divided between the opposed forces and suffered the heaviest losses in consequence. In 1763, Dominica was ceded to Britain, and between then and 1805, it remained British. Nevertheless, its position between the French colonies of Guadeloupe and Martinique, and the strong French presence over the years, ensured that despite English institutions and language the French influence was never eliminated.

During the 19th century, Dominica was largely neglected and underdevelopment provoked social unrest. Henry Hesketh Bell, the colonial administrator from 1899 to 1905, made great improvements to infrastructure and the economy, but by the late 1930s the British Government's Moyne Commission discovered a return to a high level of poverty on the island. Assistance to the island was increased with some emphasis put on road building to open up the interior. This, together with agricultural expansion, house building and use of the abundant hydro resources for power, contributed to development in the 1950s and 1960s.

In 1939, Dominica was transferred from the Leeward to the Windward Islands Federation; it gained separate status and a new constitution in 1960, and full internal autonomy in 1967. The Commonwealth of Dominica became an independent republic within the Commonwealth in 1978. The Dominica Labour Party dominated island politics after 1961, ushering in all the constitutional changes. Following independence, however, internal divisions and public dissatisfaction with the administration led to its defeat by the Dominica Freedom Party in the 1980 elections. The DFP Prime Minister, Miss (now Dame) Mary Eugenia Charles, adopted a pro-business, pro-United States line to lessen the island's dependence on limited crops and markets. She was re-elected in 1985 and again in 1990, having survived an earlier attempted invasion by supporters of former DLP premier, Patrick John. (For a thorough history of the island, see *The Dominica Story*, by Lennox Honychurch, The Dominica Institute, 1984, revised and republished 1995, ISBN 0-333-62776-8.)

In the general election of 1990 the Dominica Freedom Party (DFP) retained its majority by a single seat, winning 11 of the 21 seats. The official opposition was the recently-formed (1988) United Workers Party (UWP) led by Edison James with six seats, while the former official opposition party, the Dominica Labour Party (DLP) won four seats. A by-election in 1993 increased the UWP's representation to seven seats while the DLP lost one.

In 1995 Dame Eugenia retired at age 76, having led her party since 1968, and the DFP campaigned for the June general elections under the leadership of Brian Alleyne, External Affairs minister in her government. However, the contest was won by the UWP, with 11 seats, while the DFP and the DLP won five each. Mr Edison James was sworn in as Prime Minister. Mr Alleyne and Mr Rosie Douglas, leader of the DLP, were to share the position of Leader of the Opposition, taking the post a year at a time. In 1996, Mr Alleyne resigned and was replaced as leader of the DFP by Charles Savarin, who was elected unopposed.

General elections were held in January 2000, at which the DLP won 42.9%, the UWP 43.4% and the DFP 13.6% of the vote, while the turnout was 60.2% of the electorate. The DLP and DFP formed a coalition and on 3 February Rosie Douglas was sworn in as Prime Minister. One of the new government's first decisions was to shelve plans for a new airport and related hotel development in the northeast, a project which the DFP and DLP had criticized when in opposition on the grounds of cost and inappropriate location. However, the country was stunned by the death of Rosie Douglas, aged 58, in October 2000. He was replaced by his deputy, Pierre Charles.

Geography

Dominica is one of the largest and most mountainous of the anglophone Windward Islands. The highest peak, Morne Diablotin, rises to 4,747ft and is often shrouded in mist. It is known as the Nature Island of the Caribbean with parks and reserves protecting vast areas of forest that cover most of the interior. In addition, the frequent rainfall and many rivers have led to some very dramatic seascapes with beautiful hard and soft coral. It is 29 miles long and 16 miles wide, with an area of 290 square miles.

People

Materially, it is one of the poorest islands in the Caribbean, but the people are some of the friendliest. Many of them are small farmers, the island's mountainous terrain discourages the creation of large estates. In Dominica, over 2,000 descendants of the original inhabitants of the Caribbean, the once warlike Caribs, live in the Carib Territory, a 3,700-acre 'reservation' established in 1903 in the northeast, near Melville Hall airport. There are no surviving speakers of the Carib language on the island. The total population, which is otherwise almost entirely of African descent, is around 74,400, of whom about 29% live in the parish of St George, around Roseau, the capital, on the Caribbean coast. Other parishes are much more sparsely populated. The parish of St John, in which Portsmouth (the second largest town) is situated contains only about 5,000 people, or seven percent of the population.

Like St Lucia, Dominica was once a French possession and although English is the official tongue, most of the inhabitants also speak créole French (French-based patois). In the Marigot/Wesley area a type of English called 'cocoy' is used; the original settlers of the area, freed slaves, came from Antigua and are mostly Methodists. Catholicism predominates, though there are some Protestant denominations and an increasing number of fundamentalist sects, imported from the USA.

Government

Dominica is a fully independent member of the British Commonwealth. The single chamber House of Assembly has 31 members, 21 elected by the constituencies, nine Senators appointed by the President on the advice of the Prime Minister and Leader of the Opposition, and the Attorney-General. The Prime Minister and Leader of the Opposition also nominate the President, currently Vernon Shaw, who holds office for five years.

Economy

Owing to the difficulty of the terrain, only about a quarter of the island is cultivated. Nevertheless, it is self-sufficient in fruit and vegetables and agriculture contributes about 20% to gross domestic product. The main products are bananas (the principal export), coconuts (most of which are used in soap and cooking oil production), grapefruit, limes and other citrus fruits. Bananas were badly hit by Hurricane Hugo in 1989 when over 70% of the crop was damaged and by Hurricane Luis in 1995 when 95% of the crop was lost. The opening up of the European market in 1992 affected Dominica's banana industry. Together with the other Windward Islands producers it has to compete with the large exporters from the US dollar areas, mainly in Latin America. Other crops are under development, such as coffee, cocoa, mango, citrus and root crops such as dasheen, which are being promoted to diversify away from bananas. There is a very successful aqua culture project, prawn farming.

Manufacturing industry is small but takes advantage of locally-generated hydro-electricity. Under pressure to purchase Caribbean products for their cruise ships, Royal Caribbean Cruise Lines buys 3 mn bars of soap a year from Dominica

Coconut Products (DCP), Dominica's largest business. In 1995, Colgate Palmolive, the US transnational company, acquired a controlling interest in DCP. Labour intensive electronic assembly plants and clothing manufacturing are being encouraged for their foreign exchange earnings potential, while data processing is also growing. There is a large pool of labour for garment production which attracts manufacturers, but they often move on to other areas when their duty-free concessions expire, usually after 10 years. Tourism is being promoted with the emphasis officially on nature tourism. Total stayover visitor arrivals are around 74,000 a year. The aim is for the development of sustainable long-term tourism projects. Several new hotels and expansions of existing facilities are planned.

There is controversy over the Government's decision in 1992 to grant economic citizenship to investors; the first to be granted passports all came from Taiwan. By the end of 1994 615 people had been granted economic citizenship; they paid US$7.1 mn into an escrow account, of which US$5.4 mn was withdrawn to buy shares in a linked hotel company. Since then there has been a surge of interest from Eastern Europe, and in 1999 it was reported that 300 Russians had bought passports, for US$50,000 each. The US State Department expressed concern about money laundering and Canada arrested a group of Chinese-Dominicans on suspicion of running a smuggling operation.

In 1997 the first offshore banks were registered in a bid to increase fee income from abroad. Legislation was prepared for international shipping registration, offshore trust companies and exempt insurance companies. Six internet gambling companies were also granted operating licences. International Business Companies (IBC) can be formed over the internet and the Government has chosen to follow the British Virgin Islands model for registration because it does not require such demanding regulatory work or supervision as the Barbados model, which needs a double taxation treaty.

Culture   Popular culture reflects the mixture of native and immigrant peoples. While most places on Dominica have a Carib, a French or an English name, the indigenous Carib traditions and way of life have been localized in the northeast, giving way to a dominant amalgam of Créole (French and African) tradition. Dominicans are proud of their local language, which is increasingly being used in print. A dictionary was published in 1991 by the Konmité pou Etid Kwéyol (Committee for Créole Studies). You can get hold of this at the Cultural Division, 30 Queen Mary Street on the corner of King George V Street in Roseau. There has recently been a great increase in the awareness of the arts and crafts. Both at Caribana, the craft and art gallery (see page 775), the Alliance Française French cultural centre, and in the media, the poets, writers and artists of Dominica have been reading or exhibiting their work. Ask at Caribana, T4487340, when the next poetry workshop or exhibition, is to be held, or wander the side streets of Roseau to find small shops and galleries. Gallery Number 4, at 4 Hanover St near the Old Market, is home to a number of artists, including Ellingsworth Moses and Earle Etienne.

There is a thriving music scene, helped by the establishment recently of the WICE recording studio in Dominica. Popular local bands include *WCK*, *First Serenade* and *Midnight Groovers*, who you can often catch at discos and nightclubs. The Créole Music Festival in October is a great time to find out what is going on in regional music trends, whether it is Cadence, Soukous, Compas, Zouk or Bouyou (see Festivals above). Dance and choral artists are active mostly around Christmas, when there are diverse concerts given by church choirs and Dominica's National Chorale.

Literature   The best known of Dominica's writers are the novelists Jean Rhys and Phyllis Shand Allfrey. Rhys (1894-1979), who spent much of her life in Europe, wrote mainly about that continent; only flashback scenes in *Voyage in the Dark* (1934), her superb last novel, *Wide Sargasso Sea* (1966), which was made into a film in 1991, her uncompleted autobiography, *Smile Please* and resonances in some of her short stories draw on her West Indian experiences. Allfrey published only one novel, *The Orchid House* (1953); *In the Cabinet* was left unfinished at her death in 1986. Allfrey was one of the founder members of the Dominica Labour Party, became a cabinet minister in the short-lived West Indian Federation, and was later editor of the *Dominica Herald* and *Dominica Star* newspapers. *The Orchid House* was filmed by Channel 4 (UK) in 1990 for international transmission as a four-part series.

St Lucia

Very popular as both a family holiday destination and a romantic paradise for honeymooners, St Lucia (pronounced 'Loosha') offers something for everyone. Its beaches are golden or black sand, some with the spectacular setting of the Pitons as a backdrop, and many are favoured by turtles as a nesting site. Offshore there is good diving and snorkelling along the west coast, with a marine park along part of it. Rodney Bay is one of the best harbours in the West Indies, with a marina for 1,000 yachts, and windsurfing and other watersports are available. The mountainous interior is outstandingly beautiful and there are several forest reserves to protect the St Lucian parrot and other wildlife. Sightseeing opportunities include sulphur springs, colonial fortifications and plantation tours. St Lucia has a rich cultural heritage, having alternated between the French and English colonial powers, both of whom used African slaves, and has produced some of the finest writers and artists in the region, including two Nobel prize winners. The films Dr Doolittle, Water and Superman II were shot here.

Colour map 5, grid B5

Windward Islands

Ins and outs

St Lucia is well served with scheduled and charter flights from Europe and North America and you can often pick up quite cheap deals on package holidays. Connections with other islands are good and it is easy to arrange a multi-centre trip. Some flights from Europe come via Antigua, and some from the USA via Barbados. You can also get to St Lucia by sea from neighbouring islands, either with the ***Windward Lines*** from Venezuela, Trinidad, St Vincent and Barbados (temporarily suspended in 2001), or ***Express Des Iles*** from the French Antilles. Cruise ships also call.

Getting there
See transport, page 808, for more details

Bus is the cheapest means of getting around St Lucia. The service has been described as tiresome by some, but as reliable by others. St Lucia's buses are usually privately-owned minibuses and have no fixed timetable. The north is better served than the south and buses around Castries and Gros Islet run until 2200, or later for the Friday night Jump-up at Gros Islet. There are several **car hire** companies on the island, some of which are open to negotiation, but it is cheaper and more reliable to hire in advance. Signposting has been greatly improved so that renting a car and exploring by yourself is now much easier. Castries roads are very congested and there are more one-way streets than ever. If **cycling**, the best way to get round the island is anti-clockwise, thus ensuring long but gradual uphills and steep, fast downhills.

Getting around
Driving on the left

The dry season is roughly from Jan-Apr. The rainy season starts in May lasting almost to the end of the year. The island lies in lattitudes where the northeast trade winds are an almost constant, cooling influence. Rainfall varies (according to altitude) in different parts of the island from 60 to 138 in. Tropical storms in the 1990s caused flooding and mudslides as the rain poured off the hills, taking banana plantations in its path. In November 1999 Hurricane Lenny hit from the west. High waves caused severe damage to beaches and property on the west coast, many small houses and the new craft market, among other businesses, were washed away at Soufrière.

Climate
The mean annual temperature is about 26°C

A Foot in the door

- Take a walk on the wild side and explore the **Atlantic beaches** where the **turtles** lay their eggs.
- Visit the luxuriant **Mamiku Botanical Gardens** for a slice of colonial history on a working plantation.
- Treat yourself to a meal at the **Ladera Resort** overlooking the majestic Pitons.
- Snorkel or shore dive at the marine park at **Anse Chastenet**.
- The **Jazz Festival** gets better and better every year, great concerts and fringe events.

Flora and fauna

Some of these areas are very isolated and you are recommended to get in touch with the relevant organizations before attempting to visit them. The fauna and flora of St Lucia is very similar to that of Dominica, the Windwards chain of islands having been colonized by plants and animals originally from South and Central America, with some endemic species such as sisserou and jacquot. Rainforest would have covered most of the island prior to European colonization but the most dramatic loss has been in the last 20 years. Much of the remaining forest is protected, mainly for water supply, but also specifically for wildlife in places. There are many orchids and anthurium growing wild in the rain forests, while tropical flowers and flowering trees are found everywhere. To date, more than 1,500 different species of flowering plants have been documented, including imported exotica like the hibiscus and flamboyant, with nine endemic species. Roger Graveson (at *La Panache Guesthouse*, Gros Islet) is working with the Forestry and Lands Department on a complete listing of the plants of St Lucia. He has created a computerised data base complete with photographs. There are several endemic reptile species including St Lucia tree lizard, pygmy gecko, Maria Islands ground lizard and Maria Islands grass snake. The only snake which is dangerous is the fer de lance which is restricted to dry scrub woodland on the east coast near Grande Anse and Louvet and also near Anse La Raye and Canaries in the west. The forest dwelling agouti is rarely seen, but the manicou is present throughout the island, and is frequently seen on the road, a victim of the night time traffic. The mongoose, first introduced into Jamaica in 1872 to control the rats in the cane fields, is also present. Several species of bats have been recorded.

The national bird is the colourful St Lucian parrot *(Amazona versicolor)*, which can be seen in the dense rain forest around Quillesse and Barre de l'Isle. Other endemic birds are the St Lucia oriole (endangered), Semper's warbler (believed extinct) and the St Lucia black finch (endangered). In the north of the island birdwatching is good at Bois d'Orange swamp, Piton Flor Reserve and Grand Anse; in the west at Edmond Forest Reserve and in the south Eau Piquant Pond, also called Boriel's Pond.

The **transinsular rainforest walk** from Mahaut to Soufrière via Fond St Jacques (about two to 2½ hours Mahaut to Fond St Jacques) is good for birdwatching. You need a permit from the Forestry Department, US$10 (US$5 for children). Tours are franchised to tour operators and a guide is certainly useful but organized tours are often noisy and scare the parrots higher into the mountains. Get your own permit from the Forestry Department at Union if you feel confident about finding your own way. There is a good chance of seeing the St Lucian parrot on the Barre de l'Isle rainforest walk, for which a permit is also needed. The ten-mile trail from Barre de l'Isle to Quillesse includes the climb all the way up to Mount La Combe (about two hours from the road). There is now an eco-lodge at the Quilless end, where hikers can stay overnight (extra fee for this). Bird watchers are advised to get a permit and organize a private trip in a small party.

In the north of the island Union is the site of the Forestry Department headquarters, where there is a nature trail, open to the public, a medicinal garden and a small, well organized zoo. The Forestry Department also organizes hiking across the island through rainforest and mature mahogany, Caribbean pine and blue mahoe plantations which will give you the best chance of seeing the St Lucia parrot, as well as other rainforest birds: thrashers, vireos, hummingbirds, flycatchers etc. Contact Adams

St Lucia

Sleeping

1 Anse Chastanet
2 Caribbees Hotel
3 Fox Grove Inn
4 Friendship Inn
5 Green Parrot Inn
6 Hummingbird Beach Resort
7 Jalousie Hilton Plantation
8 Ladera Resort
9 Mago Estate
10 Marigot Bay Hotel
11 Marigot Beach Club
12 Mordern Inn
13 Rendezvous
14 Sandals Halcyon Beach
15 Sandals St Lucia
16 Seahorse Inn
17 Skyway Inn
18 Still Plantation & Beach Resort
19 The Inn on the Bay
20 Top of the Morne Apartments
21 Villa Beach Cottages
22 Wyndham Morgan Bay

N

0 km 3
0 miles 3

Essentials

Documents *Citizens of the UK, USA and Canada may enter with adequate proof of identity, as long as they do not intend to stay longer than six months. Citizens of the Organization of Eastern Caribbean States (OECS) may enter with only a driving licence or identity card. **Visas** are not required by nationals of all Commonwealth countries, all EC countries except Eire and Portugal, all Scandinavian countries, Switzerland, Liechtenstein, Turkey, Tunisia, Uruguay and Venezuela. Anyone else needs a visa, check requirements etc at an embassy or high commission. Without exception, visitors need a **return ticket**. You also need an **address** for where you are staying.*

*On **arrival** you will be given a 42-day stamp in your passport. The immigration office at the central police station in Castries is very bureaucratic about extensions; they cost EC$40 per period and it is worth getting one up to the date of your return ticket.*

__Work permits__ are very difficult to get and cost EC$5,000, plus EC$100 for the application form. If you work for a volunteer, educational or international organization you can obtain an exemption of work permit which is free. This is the responsibility of your employer.

Currency *East Caribbean dollar. Change currency at a bank where you can get 5-10% less on the exchange than at hotels. There is no rate quoted for many currencies, such as Deutsch Marks; if you insist, Canadian banks will convert them first into Canadian dollars and then into EC dollars, but you get a poor rate. The Thomas Cook representative is on Brazil Street.*

Departure tax *At both airports there is a departure tax of EC$54, US$20, except for St Lucian nationals going anywhere and Caricom nationals travelling within Caricom, for whom it is EC$35, US$13.*

Ports of entry *(Own flag) Rodney Bay (Customs open 0800-1800 but overtime charges from 1600), Marigot, Castries, Soufrière (clear in at police station) and Vieux Fort. Pratique EC$10 up to 100 tons. Clearance EC$5 for under 40 ft, EC$15 for over 40 ft. Navigational aids EC$15. EC$25 for a 24-hour permit to visit the Pitons at Soufrière. Charter boats pay additional fees. Permission is granted to stay up to two months, extensions cost extra.*

Anchorages *There are anchorages at Rodney Bay, Castries, Marigot Bay (managed by Moorings), Soufrière (see page 787) and Vieux Fort. Marinas at Rodney Bay, Marigot and Castries Yacht Centre.*

Hours of business *Shops: 0800-1230, 1330-1700 Monday-Friday (shops close at 1200 on Saturday); Banks: 0800-1300 Monday-Thursday, plus 0800-1700 on Friday; Government offices: 0830-1230, 1330-1600 Monday-Friday.*

Official time *Atlantic Standard Time, four hours behind GMT, one ahead of EST.*

Voltage *220v, 50 cycles.*

Weights and measures *Imperial, though metric measurements are gradually being introduced.*

Toussaint, T4502231 ext 306 or 4502078, who is in charge of all Forestry Department tours. Wear good shoes and expect to get wet and muddy. Camping in the rainforest is now possible. Hike the nearly 10-mile forest trail from Barre de l'Isle to Quillesse; overnight in a forest house or camp in a tent. Recommended only for the physically fit and experienced hikers. A new trail has been opened up in the Edmond Forest Reserve: the Enbas Saut Falls trail (below the Falls), moderate to strenuous, at the foot of Mount Gimie, with a combination of rainforest, cloud forest and elfin woodlands.

The isolated east coast beaches are rarely visited and have exceptional wildlife. Leatherbacks and other **turtles** nest at Grand Anse and Anse Louvet. This area is also the main stronghold of the white-breasted thrasher and St Lucia wren; there are also iguanas (although you will be lucky to see one) and unfortunately the fer de lance snake, although attacks are extremely rare. The bite is not always fatal but requires hospitalization (it is extremely painful). Avoid walking through the bush, especially at night, and wear shoes or boots and long trousers.

La Sorcière and Piton Flore are densely forested mountains in the north with excellent rainforest vegetation. Piton Flore can be walked up in 40 minutes although it is a strenuous climb and you will need to ask how to get to the top, from where

Communications *The International code for St Lucia is 758. See page 810 for further details.*
Media Newspapers *The Voice comes out three times a week, and* The Mirror, The Weekend Voice, One Caribbean, The Crusader *and* The Star *appear weekly.*
Radio *There is a commercial radio station, Radio Caribbean International (RCI), which broadcasts daily in Kweyol and English, and a government-owned station, Radio St Lucia (RSL), which also broadcasts in Kweyol and English. It has some fine programmes such as* Sports Zone *and if you want to hear the concerns of St Lucians listen to Constitution Park at 1400 (only the Thursday broadcast is in Kweyol). RCI and RSL have 2 FM and an AM station each. A third station, the Wave (formerly GEM), has 2 FM, and broadcasts rhythm and soul.*
Television *Two local stations: HTS on Channel 4 and DBS on Channel 10. HTS has an occasional programme in Kweyol and speeches by government officials. There is much cable TV.*
Tourist offices overseas France *ANI, 53 Rue François Ler, 7th floor, Paris 75008, T47-203966, F47-230965.*
Germany *Postfach 2304, D-61293 Bad Homberg 1, T06172-304431, F06172-305072.*
UK *421a Finchley Road, London NW3 6HJ, T0171-4313675, F0171-4317920, stlucia@pwaxis.co.uk* **USA and Canada** *9th Floor, 820 2nd Avenue, New York, NY 10017, T800-4563984.*
Clothing *Lightweight clothing all year; a summer sweater may be needed on cooler evenings. Short shorts and swimming costumes are not worn in town. An umbrella or light mac may be handy in the wet season.*
Safety *When visiting the waterfalls and sulphur springs on Soufrière note that 'guides' might expect large payments for their services. Be prepared to say no firmly, they are persistent and bothersome. Children may try to squeeze money out of tourists offering to dive for a dollar in the harbour. Visiting with a hired car (H reg) can be a hassle and beach bums will even follow you into the church. The signs to Sulphur Springs are sometimes removed so you have to ask the way and are expected to give a tip. Readers' letters have spoken of harassment and hostility towards tourists and there is drug abuse and crime. However, the problem is not on the scale of Jamaica. People staying at well-protected resorts and using organized tours generally have no problem. Be careful taking photographs, although everybody seems to be accustomed to cameras in the market. The use and sale of narcotics is illegal and penalties are severe. Most readily available is marijuana, which is frequently offered to tourists, but hard drugs can also be a problem.*
Public holidays *New Year's Day, Independence Day on 22 Feb, Good Friday, Easter Monday, Labour Day on 1 May, Whit Monday, Corpus Christi, Carnival, Emancipation Day in Aug, Thanksgiving Day, National Day on 13 Dec, Christmas Day and Boxing Day.*

there are spectacular views. It is the last recorded location of Semper's warbler, an endemic bird now probably extinct.

In the south, Cap Moule à Chique has spectacular views and good bird populations. The **Maria Islands**, just offshore, are home to two endemic reptiles, a colourful lizard and small, rare, harmless snake, the Kouwes snake (see page 63). The lizard, *Cnemidophorus vanzoi*, is known as *zandoli te* in kweyol. The males, about 18 cm long, sport the colours of the national flag. The National Trust (T4525005, natrust@candw.lc) and *Eastern Caribbean Natural Areas Management Programme (ECNAMP)* run day trips with a licensed guide. All participants must be capable swimmers. Interpretive facilities are on the mainland at Anse de Sables, where you can arrange boat transport. Unauthorized access is not allowed. Good beach, excellent snorkelling. From 15 May to 31 July public access is not permitted while the birds are nesting in their hundreds on the cliffs and on the ground. However, you can visit the **Fregate Islands Nature Reserve**, handed over to the National Trust by the Government in 1989. Frigate birds nest here and the dry forest also harbours the trembler, the St Lucian oriole and the ramier. The reserve includes a section of mangrove and is the natural habitat of the boa constrictor (tête chien). **Praslin Island** is

Turtles at Grand Anse

A 1,000-pound amphibian slips from the ocean waves and pauses on the edge of the surf. All is quiet. In the light of the moon, rain or not, she hauls her heavy body further up the beach. A cluster of people stand motionless and nearly breathless, fearful that the giant sea turtle will sense them and return to the ocean without laying her eggs. The leatherback turtle (Demochelys coricea) roams the open oceans, feeding on a diet of giant jellyfish. Only a mature female comes ashore and then only to make a nest and lay 60-120 eggs, perhaps several times in one season but only every two to three years.

All sea turtles are endangered. Sand mining, construction close to the water, human and other animal and bird predators, destroy habitats. The eggs are a popular aphrodisiac, considered particularly effective if taken from the female before they are laid, killing the proverbial goose that laid the golden egg. Grand Anse beach in St Lucia is one of the most important beaches in the Caribbean for the nesting leatherbacks. From honeymooners to retirees, tourists and St Lucians, all hope for a memorable experience when the sea turtle comes ashore, counting the leathery eggs as they drop, perhaps being able to touch her as she lays, oblivious to all.

Annette Blackburn

one of only two islands where the St Lucian whiptail lives. They used to live only on Maria Major Island until being successfully introduced here to prevent annihilation by hurricanes or any other natural disaster. ■ *Entrance to Fregate Islands Nature Reserve US$5 (no tour guide), children 5-12 US$0.75, residents US$1.85. Eastern Nature Trail min 4 people US$12 per person, tour guide US$16. With transport, guide and lunch US$45, including boat ride to Praslin Island US$55. The same package for only two people is US$60 and US$65. For the Maria Islands, US$35 for one person, US$30 for two people and a group rate (min 8 people) is US$25 per person. The package of transport, tour, lunch for min 4 people is US$75 per person.*

In 1997 the Tourist Board announced the development of a series of nature trails as part of a nature/heritage tourism programme. There are gentle hikes and strenuous climbs, including a two and a half mile Morne Tabac climb, a ridge hike beginning at Malmaison; the Anse Galet Nature Walk and the eight mile Morne Gimie Climb over four mountain peaks. New nature interpretation centres and national parks are being developed. One new trail is the Millet trail, which meanders around the catchment area of the Roseau Dam and offers the chance to see quite a few birds. You can also hike from one side of the island to the other, from Micoud to Soufriere, a five-mile, five-hour trek.

The St Lucia National Trust (T4525005) has fairly regular field trips, usually the last Sunday of the month, popular with locals and tourists of all ages. The cost varies (cheaper for members) according to transport costs, membership US$10 a year. Turtle watching is organized during March to July when green, hawksbill and leatherback turtles come ashore on Grand Anse to lay eggs (set off at 1600, return around 0700, take food, drink, torch, insect repellent, good walking shoes, warm clothing, tents supplied, be prepared for wind, rain or perfect nights, children welcome, contact Jim Sparks for information, T4528100 work, T4501915 home).

Diving and marine life

Dive sites
Visitors must dive with a local company

There is some very good diving off the west coast, although this is somewhat dependent on the weather, as heavy rain tends to create high sediment loads in the rivers and sea. Diving on the east coast is not so good and can be risky unless you are a competent diver. Several companies offer scuba diving with professional instructors, catering for the experienced or the novice diver. One of the best beach entry dives in the Caribbean is directly off **Anse Chastanet**, where an underwater shelf drops off from about 10 ft down to about 60 ft and there is a good dive over **Turtle Reef** in the bay, where there are over 25 different types of coral. Below the **Petit Piton** are impressive sponge and coral communities on a drop to 200 ft of spectacular wall. There are gorgonians, black coral trees, huge barrel sponges and plenty of other beautiful reef life. The area in front of the *Anse Chastanet Hotel* is a Marine Reserve, stretching from the west point at **Grand Caille North** to **Chamin Cove**. The area is buoyed off and only the hotel boats and local fishermen's canoes are allowed in. Just by the jetty, a roped-off area is used by snorkellers and beginner divers and is an exceptionally rewarding spot. Other popular dive sites include **Anse L'Ivrogne**, **Anse La Raye Point** (good snorkelling also at **Anse La Raye**) and the **Pinnacles** (an impressive site where four pinnacles rise to within 10 ft of the surface), not forgetting the **wrecks**, such as the *Volga* (in 20 ft of water north of Castries harbour, well broken up, subject to swell, requires caution), the *Waiwinette* (several miles south of Vieux Fort, strong currents, competent divers only), and the 165-ft *Lesleen M* (deliberately sunk in 1986 off Anse Cochon Bay in 60 ft of water).

Divers should not take any coral or undersized shellfish. It is illegal. Corals and sponges should not even be touched. It is also illegal to buy or sell coral products on St Lucia. The *Soufrière Marine Management Association* coordinates problems between local fishing boats, divers and yachts and preserves the environment between Anse Chastanet and Anse L'Ivrogne to the south. They have placed moorings from Anse Chastenet along the coast just past The Pitons. Yachts are required to take moorings. Collection of marine mammals (dead or alive) is prohibited, spearguns are illegal and anchoring is prohibited. Yacht moorings are US$15 for 1-2 nights and US$21 for up to a week. Rangers come by at night to collect the fee and explain the programme. Dive moorings have been installed and are being financed with Marine Reserve Fees, US$4 daily, US$12 a year.

The Fisheries Department is pursuing an active marine protection programme

Scuba St Lucia (PADI five-star, SSI and DAN) operates from Anse Chastanet, www.scubastlucia.com or contact them through the hotel, three dive boats with oxygen on each one, photographic hire and film processing, video filming and courses, day and night dives, resort courses and full PADI certification, multilingual staff, pick up service Monday to Saturday from hotels north of Castries, day packages for divers, snorkellers, beginners and others include lunch and equipment. *Buddies Scuba* (PADI, BSAC) at Rodney Bay Marina, T/F4529086, two-tank day dives, one-tank night dives, camera rental, open water certification or resort course, dive packages available. *Moorings Scuba Centre* at Marigot Bay, T4514357, and *Frog's Diving* at the *Windjammer Resort* on Labrellotte Bay, T4520913, both offer PADI courses. A single-tank dive costs around US$35-55, introductory resort courses are about US$65-90, a 6-dive package US$175 and open water certification courses US$380-495, plus 10% service charge.

Dive centres

Whale and dolphin watching is now becoming popular. Sightings have been good and interest is high. Nov-June is best when sperm whales and sometimes humpbacks are seen (see Whale and dolphin watching, page 65) *Douglas Sailing Tours*, run by Douglas Rapier, T4577777, charges US$95 for a full day sailing tour to Martinique with whale watching on the way. Two branches of the Hackshaw family also offer tours. *Captain Mike's* has just added two more boats to their fleet (sport fishing and pleasure cruises, T4527044, www.captmikes.com), while David Hackshaw and son Christopher operate other boats (hackshawc@candw.lc). The Soufrière Water Taxi Association, T4597239, will also arrange trips.

Beaches and watersports

The Atlantic east coast has heavy surf and is dangerous but with very spectacular and isolated beaches and is difficult to get to without local knowledge or the Ordnance Survey map and four-wheel drive) which make a pleasant change from the west coast. Many are important habitats and nesting places for the island's wildlife. **Cas en Bas** Beach can be reached from Gros Islet (45 minutes' walk, or arrange taxi), it is sheltered, shady and a bit dirty but challenging for experienced windsurfers. **Donkey Beach** can be reached from there by taking a track to the north (20 minutes'

All the west coast beaches have good swimming but many are dominated by resort hotels. Many lost sand during Hurricane Lenny in 1999 (see page 62) walk), the scenery is wild and open and it is windy. To the south of Cas en Bas Beach are **Anse Louvet**, **Anse Comerette** and **Anse Lapins**, follow the rocks, it is a 30-minute walk to the first and an hour to the last. Access is also possible from Monchy. They are deserted, wind-swept beaches and headlands. There are Indian stone carvings on **Dauphin Beach**, which can be reached from Monchy (reasonable with jeep). Once on the beach, wade across the river and walk back in the flat, clear area below the bush land, after about 50 m you'll find long stones with regular depressions. Another 20 m and you'll find a stone pillar about which Robert Devaux wrote: "The carving appears to be a family of three – male, female and child. It is finely executed and must have taken some prehistoric 'Michelangelo' a considerable time to complete the carving" (*St Lucia Historic Sites*, St Lucia National Trust, 1975, highly recommended, in the library at the Folk Research Centre). It is now used as the St Lucia National Trust's logo. Unfortunately the stone pillar has been badly tampered with. A few metres further inland is the ruin of a colonial church tower, destroyed in 1795 during the French Revolution of St Lucia together with the rest of the settlement. **Grande Anse**, further south, is a long windy beach, currently not open to the general public although turtle watching is organized. Sand miners were destroying the beach but they have now been banned. Development is rumoured, with two hotels and 1,000 houses. It is not safe to swim here, there is a strong undertow.

Louvet has a special, spooky atmosphere

Anse Louvet is a sheltered beach in a stunning setting, reached from Desbarra (three hours' walk but no longer drivable) or Aux Leon (two hours' walk or drive if possible, but track is steep, washed out and impassable on a wet day). Ask locally about the state of the roads, which change frequently. Walking takes as long as driving; if you walk take lots of water. La Sorcière mountain forms a long wall which seems to separate Louvet from the rest of the world. Rugged cliffs are beaten by waves and there is a blow hole. A high waterfall in the forest can be reached by following the river from the ford in the main valley (little water flow). Vanilla grows wild in the sheltered valley.

The beaches on the west coast north of Castries can be reached by bus with a short walk down to the sea. **Vigie** (1½ miles from Castries) is a lovely strip of sand with plenty of shade, popular and cleaned regularly. Its only drawback is that it runs parallel to the airport runway but that is compensated by the lack of hotels (except *Rendezvous* at one end) and low levels of pollution. Used by locals and no hassling. **Choc Bay** has good sand, shade and chairs next to the restaurant, *Wharf* (get off the bus after *Sandals Halcyon*). Used mainly by cruise ship passengers and locals, there are kayaks, sea cycles and sunfish for hire. **Marisule** is a small beach, but popular with the locals. **Labrellotte Bay** is also popular and you can get lunch at *East Winds* or *Windjammer Landing*. **Trouya** is a small, usually deserted bay (except on public holidays), best reached on foot or four-wheel drive. **Rodney Bay** has another excellent beach at Reduit, dominated by the *Papillon, Rex St Lucian* (parasailing) and *Royal St Lucian* hotels, where you can use their bars and sports hire facilities but it is crowded with their guests. The northern part of the bay is cut off by the marina and it is now a 45-minute walk or five to 10 minute bus ride into Gros Islet. There are more beaches on the way to **Pigeon Island**, with ample shade and two small beaches on Pigeon Island itself. Further north by *Odyssey St Lucia* **Smugglers' Cove** is another good snorkelling spot.

Heading south from Castries there are beaches at all the small towns but they are not generally used by tourists and lack of proper sanitation means they are often polluted. Beaches away from habitation are always a better bet. **Marigot Bay** is a popular tourist spot. **Anse Chastanet** is well used and claims to have the best snorkelling on the island (see page 786). **Anse Cochon** is also popular, visited by boats doing day trips, being accessible only by sea with no facilities. The smell of motor boats can be unpleasant. The trade winds blow in to the south shore and the sandy beach of **Anse de Sables** near Vieux Fort offers ideal **windsurfing**. The sea here is wild and invigorating and comes straight across the Atlantic.

At **Marigot Bay** and **Rodney Bay** you can hire any size of craft, the larger ones coming **Sailing** complete with crew if you want. Many of these yachts sail down to the Grenadines. Rodney Bay has been developed to accommodate 1,000 yachts (with 232 berths in a full-service boatyard and additional moorings in the lagoon) and hosts the annual Atlantic Rally for Cruisers race, with about 250 yachts arriving there in December 2000. Charters can be arranged to sail to neighbouring islands. At Rodney Bay Marina is: *Destination St Lucia (DSL)*, T4528531, yachts from 38-52 ft, bareboat charters, multilingual staff. At Marigot Bay: *The Moorings*, T4514357, bareboat fleet of 38-50 ft Beneteaus and crewed fleet of 50-60 ft yachts, 45-room hotel for accommodation prior to departure or on return, watersports, diving, windsurfing. Soufrière has a good anchorage, but as the water is deep it is necessary to anchor close in. There is a pier for short term tie-ups. **Fishing** trips for barracuda, mackerel, king fish and other varieties can also be arranged. Several sport fishing boats sail from Rodney Bay Marina. There is an annual billfish tournament, at which a Martiniquan recently landed a 707-lb blue marlin, putting the earlier record of 549lbs in the shade.

As some of the best views are from the sea, it is recommended to take at least one **Day sails** boat trip. There are several boats which sail down the west coast to Soufrière, where you stop to visit the volcano, Diamond Falls and the Botanical Gardens, followed by lunch and return sail with a stop somewhere for swimming and snorkelling. The price usually includes all transport, lunch, drinks and snorkelling gear; the *Unicorn*, a 140-ft replica of a 19th-century brig which started life in 1947 as a Baltic trader (used in the filming of *Roots*) sails 0930 Monday to Friday in high season, and has been recommended, US$85 per person, children under 12 years US$40 except on Friday, when they only have to pay US$25, including lunch and the inevitable rum punch. Champagne and sunset cruises on Monday, Wednesday, Thursday and Friday, 1700-1900, adults, US$40, children US$20. Can be booked through hotel tour desks (*Unicorn* is based at Vigie Marina, T4526811). Other excursions on catamarans (*Endless Summer I, Endless Summer II, Sun Kiss, Mango Tango, Tango II*) and private yachts can be booked with tour operators in Castries or through the hotels. At the swimming stop on the return journey local divers may try to sell you coral. It is illegal and if you buy it a reef dies as a result. The catamarans are usually very over-crowded and devoid of character but cost the same as the *Unicorn*. An alternative to the brig is to charter a yacht with skipper and mate; a 40-ft Beneteau for up to six people (eight if some children) costs around US$350 per day and will take you wherever you want including drinks and meals. Motor boats can also be chartered for customized trips including fishing and snorkelling. Only local companies are allowed to operate day charters. Recommended is *Dinask*, a 40-ft sailing boat at Rodney Bay, contact Capt Christian Bonnaudeau (Capt Moustache), T4847060, F4520183, www.perso.wanadoo.fr/ourneso/dinask/htm A day charter costs US$400 for 1-4 people, with a capacity for up to eight more at US$5 per person. A week's trip to the Grenadines costs around US$2,700, low season, for up to four passengers, skippered by Christian (who bakes bread) and Lysiane (who does most of the cooking), both are licensed with many years' experience in the area.

There is a 6,815-yd, par 71, 18-hole **golf** course and driving range at Cap Estate, the **Other sports** St Lucia Golf & Country Club (green fee US$65 for 9 holes, US$85 for 18 holes, golf carts mandatory, T4508522, www.stluciagolf.com) and a private course for guests at La Toc. **Cycling** has become very popular, mostly in groups with a guide. Several operators offer tours: *Carib Travel*, T4522151, have 15 Rockhoppers and offer a trip starting at Paix Bouche through mountain villages down to Gros Islet. *Bike St Lucia*, T4597755, www.bikestlucia.com are on a small beach just north of *Anse Chastenet* (linked to *Scuba St Lucia*) and offer off-road riding on trails through the forest (jungle biking). They have a fleet of Cannondale F800 CAAD-3 bikes, which are not for use away from their dedicated trails. Accessible only by boat, they organize transfers from your hotel, lunch, snorkelling, etc.

Horses for hire at *Trim's Stables*, Cas-en-Bas, T4508273, riding for beginners or advanced; also offers lessons, one-hour rides US$40, 2hrs US$50 and picnic trips to the Atlantic, US$75. *Country Saddles*, T4500197, highly recommended for a ride through the countryside and the seashore, US$55 good horses, guides are encouraging with beginners but still manage to give the more experienced lots of fun. The *International Riding Stables* in Gros Ilet also does trail rides and caters for all levels of rides, T4528139, choice of English or Western style, US$35 for 1 hour, US$50 for 2, US$70 for half-day picnic trip. *North Point Riding Stables*, Cap Estate, takes groups to Cas-en-Bas Beach, Donkey Beach, Pigeon Point or Gros Islet, US$35 for one and a half hours, minimum age 12, T4508853. *Fayolle Stables & Riding School* has a large number of mounts and offers similar sessions, US$40 1hr, US$50 2 hrs, US$75 half-day trip with beach barbecue. Prices quoted usually include transport to and from your hotel. Ask at Trim's Stables for information on horse racing, which is usually held on public holidays at Cas-en-Bas and in Vieux Fort.

Cricket and **football** are the main spectator sports, also basketball, netball and volleyball are increasingly popular. Every village has a cricket game at weekends or after work in the season, using makeshift equipment such as sticks or palm frond bases as bats. **Combat** is a new game played 0900-1200 at weekends, T4529634, you are provided with fatigues and compressed gas cylinder guns which fire orange paint balls. Two teams battle to capture the flag.

Castries

Population: 60,000

The capital, Castries, is splendidly set on a natural harbour against a background of mountains. It used to be guarded by the great fortress of Morne Fortune (Fort Charlotte and Derrière Fort). There is a spectacular view from the road just below Morne Fortune where the town appears as a kaleidoscope of red, blues, white and green and it promises much. However, it can be a disappointment as close to the town is thoroughly modern but the bustle of its safe streets more than compensates. The city centre is very crowded when cruise ships come in.

Sights

Castries used to be twinned with Taipei but now it has close relations with mainland China and there are plans to build a sports stadium, a four-lane highway from Vieux Fort to Castries and other projects with Chinese investment

Largely rebuilt after being destroyed by four major fires, the last in 1948, the commercial centre and government offices are built of concrete. Only the buildings to the south of Derek Walcott Square and behind Brazil Street were saved. Here you will see late 19th and early 20th century wooden buildings built in French style with three storeys, their gingerbread fretwork balconies overhanging the pavement. The other area which survived was the market on the north side of Jeremie Street. Built entirely of iron in 1894, it was conceived by Mr Augier, member of the Town Board, to enhance the appearance of the town and also provide a sheltered place where fruit and produce could be sold hygienically. A new market has been built next door to house the many fruit sellers on the ground floor, while on the first floor and in an arcade opposite are vendors of T-shirts, crafts, spices, basket work, leeches and hot pepper sauce. On the eastern side of the old market there is a little arcade with small booths where vendors provide good vegetarian food, créole meals and local juices. Further along Jeremie Street on the waterfront is a new shopping centre with duty-free shops: La Place Carenage, almost opposite Pointe Seraphine. There is a regular ferry service between the two every 10 mins, US$1. Good restaurant upstairs at Carenage. The tallest building in the city is the seven-storey Financial Centre at the corner of Jeremie and Bridge Streets, with a joyous sculpture by local artist, Ricky George.

Derek Walcott Square was the site of the Place D'Armes in 1768 when the town transferred from Vigie. Renamed Promenade Square, it then became Columbus Square in 1893. In 1993 it was renamed in honour of Derek Walcott, the poet (see page 813). It was the original site of the courthouse and the market. The library is on its west side. The giant Saman tree is about 400 years old. On its east side lies the **Cathedral** which bursts into colour inside. Suffused with yellow light, the side altars are often covered with flowers while votive candles placed in red, green and yellow jars give a fairy tale effect. The ceiling, supported by delicate iron arches and braces is decorated with large panelled portraits of the apostles. Above the central altar with its four carved screens, the apse ceiling has paintings of five female saints with St Lucy in the centre. The walls have murals by Dunstan St Omer, one of St Lucia's better known artists (see page 813). They are of the stations of the cross and are unusual in that the people in the paintings are black. The figures in his murals in rural churches are of local people.

As you wander around the town, note the **Place Jean Bapiste Bideau** (a sea captain who dedicated his life to freedom and heroically saved the life of Simón Bolívar) and the mural on Manoel Street by the St Lucia Banana Growers Association building. It was painted in 1991 by Dunstan St Omer and two of his sons and depicts scenes of St Lucian life: banana boats, tourism, 18th-century sea battles, the king and queen of the flower festivals and Carib Indians.

Castries

■ Sleeping	● Eating		
1 Auberge Seraphine	1 Aft Deck	4 Chung's	7 Froggie Jack's
	2 Café au Lait	5 Coal Pot	8 Kimlans
	3 Café Panache	6 Flamingo	9 Royal Castle

Most Ministries have moved into new Government Buildings on John Compton Highway on the waterfront. Some offices are still scattered all over town, but a fourth building is under construction for them.

On the outskirts of Castries is **Pointe Seraphine**, a duty-free complex, near the port. From Castries take the John Compton Highway north towards Vigie airport and branch off just past the new fish market. All of the goods are priced in US dollars and it consists largely of chic boutiques. A tourist board information desk serves the cruise ship passengers. ■ *0800-1630 Mon-Fri. There are plenty of people who will 'mind your car' here. Ignore them.* The rather curious pyramid-shaped building is the Alliance Française, the French cultural centre built in conjunction with the St Lucia Ministry of Education.

Excursions If you continue on the John Compton Highway past the sports complex, turn left at the roundabout to go to the airport, you are sandwiched between the runway on your left and the beautiful Vigie beach on your right. There is a small war cemetery here commemorating those from the British West Indies regiment who lost their lives and a new monument and resting place dedicated to the St Lucian women who also served. You can drive around Vigie point. After the airport, go straight ahead past the French Embassy. Continue around the peninsula and on the descent, there is a turn to the lighthouse for lovely views. There is much evidence of the military past with some of the decrepit buildings still in use at the highly rated secondary school for boys, St Mary's College.

Just south of Castries you can walk (unfortunately only on the main road, allow about one hour each way) or drive to the Governor's Mansion with its curious metalwork crown, at the top of Morne Fortune. From here carry on to **Fort Charlotte**, the old Morne Fortune fortress (now Sir Arthur Lewis Community College). You will pass the Apostles' battery (1888) and Provost's redoubt (1782). Each has spectacular views, but the best is from the Inniskilling Monument at the far side of the college (just beyond the old Combermere barracks) where you get an excellent view of the town, coast, mountains and Martinique. It was here in 1796 that General Moore launched an attack on the French. The steep slopes give some idea of how fierce the two days of fighting must have been. As a rare honour, the 27th Inniskillings Regiment were allowed to fly their regimental flag for one hour after they took the fortress before the Union Jack was raised. The college is in good condition having been carefully restored in 1968. Sir Arthur Lewis, Nobel Laureate in Economics, is buried in the grounds of the Community College which bears his name. The site is just in front of the steps leading to the Inniskilling Monument.

On returning to Castries, branch left at the Governor's mansion to visit **La Toc** point with its luxury *Sandals* hotel. Take the road to the hotel through its beautiful gardens and take the path to the right of the security gate if you want to visit the beach. Further on is the road leading to Bagshaws studio. Down a long leafy drive, you can buy attractive silkscreen clothes and household linens and visit the printshop to watch the screen printing process. ■ *Mon-Fri 0830-1600, Sat 0830-1200. Carry your return ticket for a discount.* Close to Bagshaws is La Toc Battery, the best restored military fort, visited mostly by cruise ship visitors. For information call Alice Bagshaw, T4526039, or inquire at the shop.

North to Pointe Du Cap

The part of the island to the north of Castries is the principal resort area, it contains the best beaches and the hotels are largely self contained. It is the driest part of the island. The John Compton highway leaves Castries past Vigie airport and follows the curves of Vigie Beach and Choc Bay. Where the road leaves the bay and just before it crosses the Choc River, a right turn to Babonneau will take you past the **Union Agricultural station** (about one mile) where there is a nature trail and interpretive centre (see Flora and fauna above).

Back on the main highway, the road passes the turning to Labrellotte Bay (dominated by the *Windjammer Hotel*) before reaching Rodney Bay and the town of Gros Islet. Here is the site of the **US Naval Air Station of Reduit**. Built in February 1941, the Americans made an attempt to reclaim the swamps and the bay was dredged. It was the first of a chain of bases established to protect the Panama Canal. Acting as a communications centre (code name 'Peter Item'), it supported a squadron of sea planes. The base was eventually closed in 1947. It was not until much later when a causeway and marina were built that the wetlands vanished. The whole area now supports a mass of tourist facilities including the *Papillon, Rex St Lucian* and *Royal St Lucian* hotels on the beach, restaurants and sport facilities. On the hillside at the south end of the bay the *Caribbean Jewel Beach Resort* opened in 2001 and there are plans for a new 200-room hotel at beach level. You can pass through the entrance gates of the old Naval Air Station or take the next left turn off the main road at the junction leading to *JQ's Mall*, to reach the hotels and restaurants. If you drive past them all to the end of the road there is good access to the beach. Rodney Bay is an excellent base for watersports; it is ideal for windsurfing. At the back of the development is a 1,000-boat marina. Development is still taking place and at Rodney Heights a huge area has been set aside for condominiums. The normally sleepy fishing village of **Gros Islet** holds a popular jump-up in the street each Friday night, from 2200, music, dancing, bars, cheap food, rather touristy but enjoyed by night owls. Try the grilled conch from one of the booths selling local dishes but stay away from anyone offering drugs.

Rodney Bay

About three quarters of a mile after Elliot's Shell filling station on the outskirts of Gros Islet, turn left to Pigeon Island National Landmark, once an island, now joined

Pigeon Island

Rodney Bay

to the mainland by a causeway on which a 300-room *Hyatt Regency* hotel has been built with a bright blue roof. The park was opened by Princess Alexandra on 23 February 1979 as part of St Lucia's Independence celebrations (entrance EC$5). It has two peaks which are joined by a saddle. The higher rises to a height of about 360 ft. Owned and managed by the National Trust, the island is of considerable archaeological and historical interest. Amerindian remains have been found, the French pirate François Leclerc (known as Jamb de Bois for his wooden leg) used the large cave on the north shore and the Duke of Montagu tried to colonize it in 1722 (but abandoned it after one afternoon). From here, Admiral Rodney set sail in 1782 to meet the French navy at the Battle of Les Saintes (see under Guadeloupe). It was captured by the Brigands (French slaves freed by the leaders of the French revolution) in 1795 but retaken in 1798 by the English. Used as a quarantine centre from 1842 it was abandoned in 1904 but became a US observation post during World War II. The island finally became the home of Josset Agnes Huchinson, a member of the D'Oyly Carte Theatre who leased the island from 1937 to 1976. The bay became a busy yacht haven and 'Joss' held large parties to entertain the crews. Her abandoned house can still be seen on the south shore of the island. On the lower of the two peaks lies **Fort Rodney**. The museum (located in the Officers' Mess and recently rebuilt to the original design) contains an interesting display of the work of the National Trust.

■ *Entry to park and museum, EC$10 for visitors, EC$5 for residents, open every day 0900-1700; museum closed Sun. The park also contains Jambe de Bois restaurant, open from breakfast until 2130, which is recommended for snacks and a cool drink and the Captain's Cellar, under the museum, with an old pub atmosphere and small lawn overlooking Burgot Rocks and Le Sport, with invigorating breezes coming off the sea. Entry to the park after 1700 is free but you are restricted to the restaurants.* You can swim off either of the two small beaches to the left of the gate. The park is a good place for watching sea birds. There used to be a colony of pelicans, and Josset used to refer to Burgot Rocks as Pelican Island, but it is believed that DDT used by the American forces to exterminate sandflies was responsible for their disappearance.

North coast The road north passes through the Cap estate (golf course and the *Club St Lucia*) to **Pointe du Cap**, a viewpoint some 470 ft high with a splendid panorama along the coast. A good circular walk from Gros Islet can be done to Cas-en-Bas taking the road past *La Panache Guesthouse* (ask the owner, Henry Augustin for directions if necessary, he is always willing to help) down to the beach (sheltered, shady, a bit dirty), then following tracks north until you reach the golf course, from where you return along the west coast to Gros Islet. You will see cacti, wild scenery, Martinique and no tourists. The sea is too rough to swim. If exploring the Atlantic beaches by vehicle, make sure it is four-wheel drive, check your spare tyre and tools, take OS map and water, be prepared to park and walk, and if possible

Rodney Bay centre

St Lucia Yacht Club

Customs/ Immigration

Peppers

JQ Mall

■ **Sleeping**
1 Bay Gardens
2 Candyo Inn
3 Harmony
4 Islander
5 Marlin Quay
6 Palm Tree
7 Papillon
8 Rainbow
9 Rex St Lucian
10 Royal St Lucian

4 Eagles Inn
5 Elena's
6 Le Nouveau Bistro
7 Memories of Hong Kong
8 Mortar & Pestle
9 Razmataz
10 Shamrock's Pub
11 Spinnakers
12 Thai Royal
13 The Cat's Whiskers
14 The French Restaurant
15 The Lime
16 Three Amigos
17 Triangle Pub

● **Eating**
1 Burger Park
2 Buzz
3 Charthouse

N
Not to scale

take a local person with you. Always take local advice on the state of the roads, which change quickly. For more details, see above, Beaches and watersports.

The road to Monchy from Gros Islet is a pleasant drive inland through several small villages. You gradually leave the dry north part of the island and climb into forest. The ridge between Mount Monier and Mount Chaubourg gives particularly impressive views over the east coast. You will also pass through Paix Bouche where it is thought that Napoleon's empress Josephine was born. There are no road signs. Watch out for the names on schools and if in doubt at junctions bear west. At the larger village of Babonneau, you can turn right to follow the river down to the coast at Choc Bay or go straight on to Fond Cacao where a west turn will take you back to Castries. The road to Forestière is the access point for the climb to Piton Flor (1,871 ft).

East coast to Vieux Fort

The new road from Castries to Cul de Sac, known as the Millennium Highway, was immediately popular with cars and trucks. It is quite a straight road running along the sea and is a welcome relief from the hairpin curves of the old Morne Road. The Castries end starts at the roundabout on La Toc Road, goes through two short tunnels and comes out in the Cul de Sac valley, where a right turn takes you towards the beautiful Marigot Bay and the West Coast Road to Vieux Fort. A jog to the left and then a quick right takes the East Coast Road to the southern end of the island. The West Coast Road is full of mountain curves but has less traffic than the East Coast. Together they present a very scenic drive round the island.

The transinsular road goes through extensive banana plantations with the occasional packaging plant, through the village of Ravine Poisson before climbing steeply over the **Barre de l'Isle**, the mountain barrier that divides the island. There is a short, self-guided trail at the high point on the road between Castries and Dennery, which takes about 10 minutes and affords good views of the rainforest and down the Roseau valley. There is a small picnic shelter. It can be slippery after rain. The experience is rather spoilt by the noise of traffic. A longer walk to **Mount La Combe** can also be undertaken from this point. Be careful in this area as it is known as the drug growing region. Cyclists and hikers have reported that the locals are not particularly friendly and their stares can make you feel uncomfortable.

The road descends through Grande Rivière to Dennery where the vegetation is **Dennery** mostly xerophytic scrub. Dennery is set in a sheltered bay with Dennery Island guarding its entrance and dominated by the Roman Catholic church. Here you can see the distinctive St Lucia fishing boats pulled up on the beach. Carved out of single tree trunks, the bows are straight and pointed rather than curved and are all named with phrases such as 'God help me'. A US$6 mn fishing port has been built with improved moorings, cold storage and other facilities, with Japanese assistance. There are lots of small bars but no other facilities. You can follow the Dennery River inland towards Mount Beaujolais. At Errard there is a photogenic waterfall. Permission should be obtained from the estate office before attempting this trip. ■ *Plantation tour with lunch and hotel transfers costs US$50. Book through tour company.*

Fregate Island Nature Reserve, on the north side of Praslin Bay has a small but **Fregate Island** interesting visitor centre. The two small islands provide nesting sites for the frigate bird and the north promentory of Praslin bay gives a good vantage point. Birds nest on the offshore rocks and a trail runs down to the shore and back up by another route. Call the National Trust, T4525005 for a guide. The area is also of some historical interest as there was an Amerindian lookout point in the reserve. It was also the site of a battle between the English and the Brigands. It used to be known as Trois Islet and the nearby Praslin River is still marked as Trois Islet River on maps today.

Praslin is noted as a fishing community with traditional boat building. The road leaves the coast here and goes through banana plantations and the villages of **Mon**

Repos and Patience. Mon Repos is a good place to see the flower festivals of La Rose and La Marguerite. Between Praslin and Mon Repos are the **Mamiku Gardens**: Botanical Gardens and Woodland Walks on an estate owned by Baron de Micoud when he was Governor of the island for France in the 18th century but later a British military post and site of a battle with brigands. There is an on-going excavation at Mamiku which is producing interesting finds from the ruins of the house where the British soldiers were surprised by the brigands. ■ *T4528236/4553729, F4529023, www.mamiku.com Daily 0900-1700, EC$15 for foreigners, EC$10 for locals, there is a snack bar and souvenir shop.* The coast is regained at **Micoud**. There are one or two restaurants (including *Palm*, simple and clean), a department store, post office and a branch of Barclays bank. They make wine here: banana, guava, pineapple and sugar cane brewed and bottled under 'Helen Brand' and available in some supermarkets. Their ginger wine is recommended, light, not too sweet, with just the right amount of 'bite'. One mile west of Micoud is Latille Gardens with fruit, flowers, trees and waterfalls. From Mahaut Road follow signs to the south. Tours can also be arranged through hotels and include a walk through the Descartes Rainforest Trail, T4540202.

Mangrove swamps can be seen at **Savannes Bay Nature Reserve**. The bay is protected by a living reef and is a very active fishing area. The shallow bay is excellent for the cultivation of sea moss, an ideal breeding ground for conch and sea eggs. Scorpion island lies in the bay and to the north are more archaeological sites on Saltibus Point and Pointe de Caille (the latter excavated by the University of Vienna in 1983 and 1988).

Vieux Fort
Population: 14,000

After about three miles you reach Vieux Fort, the island's industrial centre, where the Hewanorra international airport is situated. It is an active town with a good Saturday market and a lot of traditional housing. Traditional gaily-painted trucks were used for transport and are still used on special occasions, although they have been replaced by the ubiquitous Toyota vans and minibuses. The area is markedly less sophisticated than the north of the island. The town boasts two new supermarkets in malls, *JQs* and *Julian's*. The latter has a cinema. The post office is on Theodore Street which with the police station is right in the middle of the town. Fishing boats are pulled up on the small beach but there is no proper beach here. On Clarke Street you will pass the square with a war memorial and band stand. The bus terminal is at the end of Clarke Street near the airport. Vieux Fort makes a good base for exploring the south of the island.

The perimeter road skirts Anse de Sables beach (no shade, good windsurfing), the base for *Club Med* watersports and looks across to the **Maria Islands**. The interpretive centre on the beach is not always open. If you want to visit **Cap Moule à Chique,** turn left at the T junction and follow the road to the banana loading jetty (on Wednesday you will pass truck after truck waiting to be weighed). Bear left and go up a badly maintained track. Finally go left again through the Cable and Wireless site up to the lighthouse. The duty officer will be glad to point out the views including the Pitons, Morne Gomier (1,028 ft) with Morne Grand Magazin (2,022 ft) behind it. Unfortunately Morne Gimie (3,118 ft) is largely obscured. Further to the east is Piton St Esprit (1,919 ft) and Morne Durocher (1,055 ft) near Praslin. The lighthouse itself is 730 ft above sea level and also has good views over the Maria islands and southwest to St Vincent.

West coast to Soufrière and the Pitons

The West Coast Road is in excellent condition with good signposting and many viewpoints. It is a very curvy, but spectacular, drive down to Soufrière. Take the transinsular highway out of Castries and instead of branching left at Cul de Sac bay carry straight on. The road quickly rises to La Croix Maingot where you get good views of the Roseau banana plantation.

On reaching the Roseau valley, one of the main banana growing areas, take the sign-posted road to Marigot Bay (plenty of 'guides' waiting to pounce). A good place to stop for a drink, the *Marigot Bay Resort* dominates both sides of the valley. In between is a beautiful inlet which is a natural harbour and provided the setting for *Dr Doolittle*. It supports a large marina and not surprisingly a large number of yachts in transit berth here to restock with supplies from the supermarket and chandler. You will notice a small strip of land jutting out into the bay. This has a small beach (not particularly good for swimming) and can be reached by the *gingerbread express* (a small water taxi, EC$2 return, refundable at *Doolittle's* if you eat or drink there) either from the hotel or the customs post. It is a good place for arranging watersports and the staff of the resort are most helpful. There is a police station and immigration post here. High above the bay are *Albert's* bar, popular alternatives to Gros Islet on Friday nights, and *Club Maygo*, a disco which attracts late night business. Right in the bay, straddling the mangroves at the eastern end, is *JJ's Paradise*, a bar and res-taurant, noisy but fun. There are also rooms.

Marigot Bay

At the bottom of the Roseau Valley, the road to Vanard and Millet branches off to the left (signposted). Millet is high up in the mountains and offers a good view of the rainforest. The road ends there. An interesting detour is **Jacmel** (take first right hand turn off Vanard road). If you take the first left turn in the village you reach the church, the altarpiece of which was painted by Dunstan St Omer (see page 813). Father Cecil Goodman can be asked to open the church if it is not already open. Donations welcome to maintain the church.

The main road continues to Soufrière and passes through the fishing villages of **Anse La Raye** and Canaries (no facilities). To the south of Anse La Raye, taking the last road to the left before you reach the bridge, a well-restored sugar mill, La Sikwi, can be visited, EC$5 or EC$15 with guide. It is near the river on the way to a waterfall, in a garden containing many regional crop species. Boa constrictor come here to be fed and with luck you will see one. The bar and restaurant open on demand. A narrow, steep, bad road branches off to the right just before Canaries and leads to a former restaurant at Anse Jambette run by Chef Harry from the *Green Parrot* (no regular service, used for private functions). Half way along this road, before it gets really steep, you can park and climb down the hill towards Canaries. There is a man-made cave and oven used by escaped slaves. Difficult to find (as intended), you need a knowledgeable local to show you where it is. There are also many waterfalls in the vicinity of Canaries, some of which are visited by organized tours. If you go inde-pendently you need a four-wheel drive and a guide. The closest is right at the end of the road into the rainforest, others are 30 minutes to 2½ hours walk away. It is safe to swim. South of Canaries is Anse La Liberté, a National Trust site which should be open soon as a hiking and camping site. It can be reached by water taxi from Canaries, EC$2, or on foot from Belvedere along a trail (10 minutes down, 15 min-utes up) which will become a nature trail. There are many brigand holes in the area.

Canaries

After Canaries the road goes inland and skirts Mount Tabac (2,224 ft) before descending into Soufrière. This is the most picturesque and interesting part of the island, with marvellous old wooden buildings at the foot of the spectacular Pitons, surrounded by thick vegetation and towering rock formations looming out of the sea. Note that Petit Piton is dangerous to climb (several people have fallen off in recent years) and also that it is restricted Crown Lands, so you need permission. This does not stop local guides offering to show visitors up, though, for about US$50. Because of its location, the town is a must for tourists although it is not geared for people wanting to stay there. It can help to have a hotel guide or dayboat skipper with you. In any event it is not cheap. Indeed, it is essential if you have no transport of your own and want to see the volcano and the Pitons, as there are no buses back to Castries after midday unless you make a roundabout journey via Vieux Fort. To do this, leave Castries at 0800, the ride can take two hours. After visiting Soufrière, wait

Soufrière
Population: 9,000

Soufrière was severely damaged in Nov 1999 by Hurricane Lenny, which brought 20-ft waves & destroyed about 70 houses & infrastructure

Windward Islands

at the corner opposite the church and ask as many people as possible if they know of anyone going to Vieux Fort; you will get a lift before you get a bus. It is important to get off at Vieux Fort 'crossroads', where there are many buses returning to Castries by another route, 1¼ hours. Buses to Castries leave from the market area. If you arrive by boat head for the north end of the bay, you will find plenty of help to tie up your yacht (EC$5) and taxis will appear from nowhere. It is a much cheaper alternative to tying up at the jetty. ■ *Organized tours are available from the hotels further north, by sea or road, from around US$65-80 including lunch, drinks, transfers and a trip to Soufrière, Diamond Gardens and the Sulphur Springs (see below).*

Soufrière is a charming old West Indian town dating back to 1713 when Louis XIV of France granted the lands around Soufrière to the Devaux family. The estate subsequently produced cotton, tobacco, coffee and cocoa. During the French Revolution, the guillotine was raised in the square by the Brigands but the Devaux family were protected by loyal slaves and escaped. It is on a very picturesque bay totally dominated by the Pitons. The water here is extremely deep and reaches 200 ft only a few yards from the shore, which is why boats moor close in. To reach Anse Chastanet from here take the rough track at the north end of the beach (past the yacht club) about one mile. This is an absolute must if you enjoy snorkelling (the south end near the jetty is superb but keep within the roped off area, the north end is also good with some rocks to explore, but avoid the middle where boats come in). The hotel has a good and inexpensive restaurant (although if you are on a budget you may prefer to take a picnic) and the dive shop is extremely helpful, they will hire out equipment by the hour. The *Unicorn, Endless Summer* and day boats stop here for snorkelling and a swim in the afternoon on their return to Castries.

Diamond Gardens

Most visitors come to the town to see the Diamond Gardens and Waterfall and the Sulphur Springs. There are no road signs in Soufrière and locating these two places can be difficult (or expensive if forced to ask). From the square take the road east past the church (Sir Arthur Lewis Street) and look for a right hand turning to reach the Diamond Gardens. These were developed in 1784 after Baron de Laborie sent samples taken from sulphur springs near the Diamond River to Paris for analysis. They found minerals present which were equivalent to those found in the spa town of Aix-la-Chapelle and were said to be effective against rheumatism and other complaints. The French King ordered baths to be built. Despite being destroyed in the French Revolution, they were eventually rebuilt and can be used by members of the public. The gardens are better than ever; well maintained and many native plants can be seen. ■ *T4524759. Entrance EC$7 (children EC$3), daily 1000-1700, EC$7 to use the outdoor hot baths, EC$10 for private bath. Only official guides are allowed in, do not accept offers from those at the gates. All the car parks are free, no matter what some people may tell you.*

Sulphur Springs

It is extremely dangerous to stray onto the grey area. The most famous 'crater' was formed a few years ago when a local person fell into a mud pocket. He received third degree burns

To get to the Sulphur Springs take the Vieux Fort road between wooden houses about half way along the south side of Soufrière square. Follow the road for about two miles (you can stop off on the way to visit the **Morne Coubaril Estate**, an open-air farm museum, guided tour EC$15, working family plantation, processes cocoa, copra, cassava, T4597340) and you will see a sign on the left. You will also be able to smell the springs. Originally a huge volcano about 5 km in diameter, it collapsed some 40,000 years ago leaving the west part of the rim empty (where you drive in). The sign welcomes you to the world's only drive-in volcano, although actually you have to stop at a car park. The sulphur spring is the only one still active, although there are seven cones within the old crater as well as the pitons which are thought to be volcanic plugs. Tradition has it that the Arawak deity *Yokahu* slept here and it was therefore the site of human sacrifices. The Caribs were less superstitious but still named it *Qualibou*, the place of death. There is a small village of about 40 inhabitants located inside the rim of the volcano. Water is heated to 180°F and in some springs to 275°F. It quickly cools to about 87°F below the bridge at the entrance. There has been much geothermal research here since 1974. From the main viewing platform, you can see over a moonscape of bubbling, mineral rich, grey mud. ■ *EC$3, every day 0900-1700. There are good, informative guides (apparently compulsory) on the site but you must be prepared to walk over uneven ground. Allow approximately 30 mins.*

In the valley between Petit Piton and Gros Piton, a luxury all-inclusive resort, *Jalousie Hilton Resort & Spa*, has been built despite complaints from ecological groups and evidence from archaeologists that it is located on a major Amerindian site. An important burial ground is believed to be under the tennis courts and there have been many finds of petroglyphs and pottery. A rather fine petroglyph is at the back of the beach in front of Lord Glenconner's *Bang Between the Pitons*. Lord Glenconner used to own much of the land here. Take the turning opposite the Morne Coubaril Estate on the unsigned concrete road. Half way along the drive to *Jalousie* you will see a little sign to a small, warm waterfall on your left. Someone will collect about US$2 for access. You can relax in the warm waters after the hassle of visiting Soufrière.

South of Soufrière

South of Soufrière, near Union Vale estate, is the new two-hour Gros Piton trail. The village of Fond Gens Libre is at the base of the mountain, accessible by jeep or high-clearance car although you will have to ford a couple of streams. Enquire at Forestry, T4502231. Call Charmaine Desir, Fond Gens Libre Tour Guides Association, T4593833, to arrange a guide. The trip up and back is about six hours. A guide costs about EC$20, but if you have your own transport you can do it on your own. It is strenuous, so you must be in good physical condition. It should not be attempted in wet weather.

The road from Soufrière to Vieux Fort takes about 40 minutes by car. The branch of the road through **Fond St Jacques** (another church painted by Dunstan St Omer) runs through lush rain forest and a track takes you to the west end of the rain forest trail. In a few miles the road rapidly descends from Victoria Junction (1,200 ft) to the coastal plain at **Choiseul**. Choiseul is a quaint old West Indian village, there is a fish market and church on the beach. Caraibe Point is the last place on St Lucia where Caribs still survive, a small community of potters living in simple thatched houses. North of Choiseul is a petroglyph, visible from the road, although you must park and then walk a little way. Outlined in white, under a protective roof, it is just down the cliff toward the sea. On the south side of Choiseul is the Art and Craft development centre teaching skills in bamboo handicrafts and you can buy pottery and carvings, as well as baskets.

Southeast of Choiseul, there are Arawak petroglyphs on rocks in the Balenbouche River. You will probably need somebody to show you the way from Balenbouche or Saltibus. Balenbouche Estate is an old sugar plantation where you can stay in the estate home or in a cottage, good local food. A team from the University of Bristol did an archaeological dig here in January 2001 and an exploratory trip along the River Doree, where there are a number of petroglyphs. There is also an ancient aqueduct connected in some way to the irrigation system at Balenbouche and the canal that carried water to the wheel at the sugar mill. Stonefield Estate also has very fine petroglyphs, but you will need to ask if someone will show you them in the bush. This is a working cocoa plantation, also with luxurious accommodation, T4530777. The village of Labourie also has accommodation available if you ask around.

Essentials

Many of the hotels are resorts, providing everything their guests need. Apart from those around Rodney Bay, they are remote and you will have to arrange car hire or expensive taxis to get around the island or go to restaurants. All-inclusive resorts (namely the two *Sandals* resorts, *Club St Lucia, Club Med, Le SPORT, Wyndham Morgan Bay* and *Rendezvous*) are usually, but not always booked from abroad. Many smaller hotels have grouped themselves as The Inns of St Lucia, representing a third of the total number of rooms on the island.

Sleeping
There is a 10-15% service charge & a 8% government tax on all hotel bills

Windward Islands

Service isn't always added to the bill, check. Tipping of 10-15% is customary: porters (US$1 a bag); taxi drivers & others in service expect tips

Larger hotels Working roughly north to south down the west coast: **Far north LL** *CAPri*, Smugglers Cove, T4500009, F4500002, www.capristlucia.com 10 a/c rooms in a villa which used to be the Chinese embassy, British-run, peaceful location, 4-poster beds, fans, small pool, walking distance to Smugglers Beach (used by *Club St Lucia*), guests can use the facilities of *Le Sport*.

Gros Islet L-C *Tropical Breeze*, 38 Massie St, Massade, Gros Islet, T/F4500589. Guesthouse and 1-4 bedroomed apartments, fully equipped, TV, phone, kitchens, group rates on request, backs on to police station. **B** *Glencastle Resort*, Massade, on hillside overlooking Rodney Bay, T4500833, F4500857. New, luxurious, good value for money, a/c, pool, 17 rooms, restaurant. **B-D** *B&B Hotel*, on Gros Islet highway, Massade, PO Box 497, T4508689, F4508134, within walking distance of Marina, beaches and Pigeon Island causeway. A/c, fans, kitchenettes in some rooms, noisy at night with loud music. **C-E** *Alexander's Guesthouse*, T4508610, F4508014, a new building on Mary Thérèse St, 1 min from beach. Clean, safe, friendly, helpful, kitchen, credit cards accepted. **D** *Bay Mini Guest House*, Bay St, painted bright orange, the only guesthouse on beach, T4508956. Minimum stay 2 nights, spacious rooms, fan, bathroom, 2 studios with kitchenettes, run by Klaus Kretz, speaks German and English. **D** *La Panache*, T4500765, F4500453, augustinh@candw.lc, on Cas-en-Bas Rd. Run by Henry Augustin, helpful and friendly, also Roger Graveson, who is working with the Forestry Department to complete a listing of the plants of St Lucia, can give information on Atlantic beaches and coastal walking, bird watching tours (whether staying there or not), includes tax and service, 7 rooms, 2-bedroom apartment, own bathroom, fridge, some with cooking facilities, hot water, insect screens, clean, fans, pleasant hillside gardens with plants labelled, good meals, breakfast daily US$3-8, tasty créole dinners (Henry's grandmother's recipes) some evenings US$11 by reservation only, snacks during day, bar with excellent alcoholic and non-alcoholic cocktails, laundry US$4 per load, no food Friday nights when everyone goes to *Jump-up*. Highly recommended.

Rodney Bay is the place to stay if you want the beach, restaurants and nightlife on your doorstep

Rodney Bay The *Hyatt Regency* opened in 2000 on Pigeon Point, a landmark because of its bright blue roof and offering the first casino on St Lucia. **LL-L** *Rex St Lucian*, T4528351, F4528331, rexstlucian@ candw.lc Right on the beach, 120 a/c rooms, restaurants, pool, entertainment, good facilities, conveniently located, with *Papillon* all-inclusive section, 140 rooms and butterfly-shaped pool, watersports, tennis, discotheque, restaurants and the **LL** *Royal St Lucian*, its sister property, next door, T4529999, F4529639. 98 luxury suites, interconnecting pools, swim up bar and waterfalls, restaurants, use of sports facilities at *Rex*, bit inconvenient. Facilities for wheelchair users at both hotels. **LL-A** *Islander Hotel*, T4528757, F4520958, short walk to Reduit beach, but close to all Rodney Bay facilities. Under new ownership in 2001, with plans to replace it with a 300-room, 7-storey *Radisson Resort & Casino*, not locally popular. **AL-B** *Rainbow*, T4520148. F4520158, rainbow@candw.lc Further down same road as *Rex* and *Royal*, across the road from the beach, next to *Gazebo* restaurant where local bands play at weekends, tennis, fitness centre, pool, snack bar, very colourful, pleasant. **AL** *Harmony Marina Suites*, on lagoon, close to beach, T4528756, F4528677. Recently modernized studios and apartments, restaurant, bar, pool, mini-mart, watersports including canoeing. **A-B** *Candyo Inn*, T4520712, F4520774. 8 suites, 4 rooms, a/c, pool, snack bar, good value, lovely inner patio, has won awards, used as overflow by overbooked hotels. **AL-A** *Bay Gardens Hotel*, T4528060, F4528059, baygardens@candw.lc 71 rooms, 2 pools, restaurant, a/c, TV, conference facilities. **A-C** *Sunny Isles Hotel*, T4580800. 18 rooms, a/c, cable TV, pool, some rooms have kitchenette and veranda. **D** *Villa Zandoli*, just down the road from the Thai restaurant, T4528898. Small, inexpensive.

Labrellotte Bay LL *East Winds Inn*, T4528212, F4529941, eastwinds@candw.lc 26 hexagonal bungalow rooms, in tropical gardens close to the beach, all-inclusive. **LL-L** *Windjammer Landing*, T4520913, F4520907, www.wlv-resort.com A beautiful resort in a lovely hillside setting, but isolated, probably the best villa complex with hotel facilities, 1-bedroomed suites clustered together, 2/4-bedroomed villas more spread out with own plunge pool, luxury resort, tennis and all watersports available, on a much-improved beach with new jetties, honeymoon, family, diving packages available, 30 min walk to a bus route or EC$20 taxi to Rodney Bay.

Choc Bay A-B *Orange Grove Hotel*, T4528213, F4528094, in the hills of Bois d 'Orange, by a new shopping centre. All-inclusive, 51 rooms, 11 suites, pleasant staff, very comfortable, rectangular pool, complimentary bus to beach or town, fairly cheap packages but other places are better situated.

Gablewoods Mall B *Friendship Inn*, T4524201, F4532635. Rooms with kitchenette and baby sitting services, small pool, restaurant. Nearby the **D-E** *Sundale Guest House*, T4524120. Very popular, includes breakfast, own bathroom, fan, TV in lobby, check availability. Further north, on highway to Gros Islet, **D-E** *The Golden Arrow*, T4501832, F4502329. 15 clean, pleasant rooms, all with private bathroom, no single rooms, walking distance from beach and bus, friendly host, breakfast and dinner available. **D** *Parrots Hideaway*, T/F4520726. 4 rooms with private bathroom, 5 rooms share 2 toilets, discounts for long stays, bar, restaurant, creole menu, charming hostess.

Castries AL-B *Auberge Seraphine*, Vigie Marina, T4532073, F4517001. 22 rooms, pool, restaurant, a/c, TV. **B** *Caribees*, La Pansée, overlooking Castries, T4524767, F4531999, Caribbees@candw.lc New, 60 rooms, pool, tennis, a/c, TV, good restaurant, courtesy bus to town. **C** *Harbour Light Inn*, City Gate, T4523506, F4519455. 3 min walk to Vigie Beach, parking, 16 rooms, a/c or fan, private bath, hot water, cable TV, balcony all round building, panoramic view, restaurant, bar. **C** *Chesterfield*, southern end of Bridge Street, T/F4521295. Central, 16 rooms, tropical garden, some rooms with balcony, great view, a/c, kitchen, excellent value. **E** *Chateau Blanc*, on Morne du Don Road, 7 rooms with fan and bathroom, basic but good central location, food available, T4521851, F4527967; **E** *Thelma's Guesthouse*, Waterworks Rd, T4527313. No sign, white building, green awnings, above (closed) *Rising Sun* restaurant, shared bathroom, lounge, kitchen, clean, central, owner Theresa Debique is warm and caring.

Morne Fortune (above Castries) **AL-A** *Green Parrot*, PO Box 648, Castries, T4523399, F4532272. 62 rooms, a/c, balconies, adjacent to excellent restaurant of same name, MAP supplement US$45. **AL-A** *Top of the Morne Apartments*, Morne Fortune, T4523603, F4590936. 1-2 bedrooms for 1-5 people, very friendly, spectacular view, car rental, pool. **C** *Bon Appetit*, near *Dubois Guesthouse*, T4522757, F4527967. Beautiful view, clean, friendly, cable TV, restaurant, 3 rooms with bathroom includes breakfast, book early for evening meal, popular. Recommended.**E** *Morne Fortune Guest House*, T4521742. Single rooms are big enough for 2, shared bathrooms, spacious, well equipped kitchen for self-catering, very clean, restaurant, bakery close by, when coming from town turn left at Shell station on the Morne and right at the T-junction, guest house on right after 100 m, across the road from the Sir Arthur Lewis Community College campus, where there are 2 restaurants. Run by Mrs Regina Willie, helpful, informative, monthly rates available, good access to public transport.

Marigot Bay LL-AL *Marigot Bay*, T4514357, F4514353. A Club Mariner resort, dive shop, sailing, yacht chartering and watersports, there is a pleasant beach 300 yds away by ferry. Across the bay is **LL-A** *Marigot Beach Club*, T4514974, F4514973, www.marigotbeach. com Waterfront restaurant and bar, *Café Paradis* open from 0800, sailing, kayaking, PADI dive shop run by Rosemond Clery, pool, sundeck, beach, studios with kitchenette, fans, bathrooms and patio or villas with 1-3 bedrooms on hillside. **AL** *Seahorse Inn*, north side of Marigot Bay, Castries, T4514436, F4514872, www.seahorse-inn.com 8 bedrooms, more planned, waterside cottage with own dock US$600-950 per week, beach short walk, pool, restaurants including *Doolittle's* within walking distance, watersports arranged. **AL** *The Inn On the Bay*, T4514260, F4514264, www.saint-lucia.com Only 4 rooms, spacious, overlooking Marigot Bay, great view from pool and balcony, CP, tours and car hire arranged, run by friendly Normand Viau and Louise Boucher. Next door and just before you fall off the cliff, is **AL-C** *Cliff House*, T4514241, www.cliff-house.com Owned by Alice Bagshaw of silk screen

Windward Islands

factory, 2 rooms, CP, spectacular view, can rent whole house, car hire and airport transfers arranged, both properties along half mile unpaved road, away from Marigot Bay activities, secluded, beautiful views.

Several hotels in this area enjoy fabulous views of the Pitons and the coast; perched on hillsides in beautiful tropical gardens and forests, truly peaceful

Soufrière LL-L *Anse Chastanet*, T4597000, F4597700, www.ansechastenet.com Hillside and beachside suites, really special, romantic, luxurious, stunning views in all directions, open balconies, airy, only drawback is the walk uphill after overindulging at dinner, the best scuba diving on the island, consistently highly rated dive operation, diving packages available, watersports, tennis, spa, lovely beach setting, restaurant on the beach and halfway up the hill, live music in the evenings, walks and excursions available, isolated. Highly recommended. **LL** *Jalousie Hilton Resort and Spa*, T4597666, F4597667, www.hilton. com 115-room luxury resort built amid much controversy over its location at the foot of the Pitons, interesting snorkelling further along the shore, but swimming and snorkelling at the resort disappointing. **LL** *Ladera Resort*, T4597323, F4595156, www.ladera-stlucia. com Spectacular setting between Gros Piton and Petit Piton, 1,000 ft up, 24 rooms, each lacking a west wall over a drop that only Superman could climb, providing an uninterrupted view of the Pitons, 1-3 bedroomed villas and suites, every luxury, very cold plunge pools, sixties style swimming pools, used to film *Superman II*, good restaurant, lots of birds and mosquitoes. **LL-L** *Stonefield Estate*, T4597037, F4595550, www.stonefieldvillas.com 15 villas sleeping 1-8 on 26-acre estate, 2 pools, Japanese garden, petroglyphs, cook and staff, beach shuttle, view of Pitons, beautifully furnished. **LL-AL** *Mago Estate Hotel*, T4595880, F4597352, www.mago-hotel.com Originally a private home, built by an architect into the cliff and incorporating all the natural and geological features, now a small, luxury hotel with 6 beautiful open fronted rooms framed by bougainvillea overlooking bay, Pitons and mountains, four-poster beds, roomy, open bathrooms, breakfast included, MAP available, pool bar in the roots of a huge mango tree, tree house above, lounge bar built into rock formation and mango trees, Yin & Yang healthfarm if you need a detox. **AL-B** *Humming Bird Beach Resort*, T4597232, F4597033, hbr@candw.lc Only 10 rooms and a hillside cottage, nice gardens, pool, beach, near Soufrière. **AL-B** *The Still Plantation and Beach Resort*, T4597261, F4597301, duboulayd@candw.lc 400-acre plantation, apartments, studios on the plantation or beachfront rooms, popular, pool, beach restaurant, spectacular view of Pitons. **B** *Chez Camille*, 7 Bridge St, T4595379, clean and friendly, family room available, kitchen, good restaurant attached (does takeaways). **D-E** *Home Guesthouse*, T4597318, on the main square. Clean, pay cash, TC's not accepted. **E** Peter Jackson rents a double room in his house on the edge of Soufrière, T4597269. Basic but good, full cooking facilities, Peter is friendly and helpful. **D** *La Mirage Guesthouse*, T4597010. English owner of Jamaican descent, Gilroy Lamontaigne, 4 rooms sleep 3, with bathroom, fan and fridge, lounge with cable TV, restaurant.

Coubaril B-C (per person) The Benedictine nuns have 22 rooms with private bathrooms, a/c, fans, dinner and breakfast included, in a lovely wooded setting, tranquil, secluded, 15 min easy walk along wooded road to frequent public transport. To get there, head south to the Morne junction at the Shell station, then right turn down hill, take second right to the nunnery, T4521282, the chapel is packed for Christmas Eve mass.

East coast B-C *Foxgrove Inn*, T4553271, F4553271. 12-bedroomed hotel, on hillside with view of Praslin Bay and Fregate Islands, beach 2 km, pool, nature trails, riding stables, good food, breakfast included, half board available, discounts for long stay, owned by Mr and Mrs Louis-Fernand, new conference room for 100 has view to Atlantic. **C** *Manje Domí*, 5 km south of Micoud, T4550729. Guesthouse with restaurant and bar, turn at Anse Ger junction, 1½ km to guesthouse on top of hill. 4 rooms, each with patio, screens, fans, very low-key, countryside setting, excellent breakfast included, meals are seafood, fresh local vegetables, fruits, pleasant, the name means 'good eating, good sleeping' in Kweyol, and it lives up to its name.

Vieux Fort A-B *Sky Way Inn*, T4547111, F4547116. Restaurant, nightclub, pool, shuttle service to airport and beach. **B** *Juliette's Lodge*, Beanfield, PO Box 482, Vieux Fort, T4545300, F4545305. 16 rooms, a/c, TV, bathroom, all with ocean view, restaurant, bar, 10 min to beach, close to airport, run by Juliette and Andrew Paul, friendly, helpful. **D-F** *St Martin*, T/F4546674, on main street. Clean, friendly, cooking and washing facilities. There is also a *Club Méditerranée* at Vieux Fort, reservations through Paris Office, T331-55262627, or locally T4546546, F4549641, pool, lots of windsurfing, sailing, tennis.

L-AL *Villa Beach Cottages*, Choc Beach, T4502884/4522691, F4525416, www. villabeachcottages.com Beachfront cottages with gingerbread fretwork, wooden shutters and jalousies, 1 or 2 bedrooms with 4-poster beds, a/c, fans, TV, phone, data ports, kitchen, living room, balcony with hammocks, Derek Walcott used to spend his holidays in what is now called the 'Nobel Cottage', lovely honeymoon villa, 9 new villa suites, *Coconuts* restaurant with bar and grill, car rental, tours desk. Alternatively, or in combination, under same ownership is **LL-AL** *La Dauphine Estate*, a 4-bedroom G*reat House* and 2-bedroom *Chateau Laffitte* on a 200-acre plantation 5 miles from Soufrière. Built in 1890 in gingerbread style, surrounded by lush gardens and hills, recently refurbished to modern standards, housekeeper/cook provided, good hiking along nature trails and through fruit plantation. *Marlin Quay*, Gros Islet, T4520393, F4520383. On the waterfront in Rodney Bay, a villa resort offering a variety of rooms, studios and 1-2 bedroomed terraced villas, very comfortable and spacious, well equipped, views over lagoon, some with jacuzzi on roof, decks, verandas. Highly recommended for families or couples, restaurants attached, 2 pools, one small, one 40 ft long for exercise swimming.

Apartment hotels & villas
There are several apartment hotels & villas for rent. Full details from tourist offices

Windward Islands

Camping

Not recommended, not encouraged, particularly on beaches, no facilities, lots of sandflies and very strong land crabs which could break into your tent! The National Trust is planning to open Anse La Liberté (see above) for camping in 2001, www.natrust.com natrust@candw.lc

Eating

All the large hotels have a selection of restaurants and there are snack bars and restaurants all along the west coast. Most places add on a 10% service charge, the menu usually specifies and it is rarely left to your discretion

Street vendors Mr Emilio by the bus stop on Peynier St, across from the Courthouse, Castries, for ice cream, EC$2.50 for a cup. Snokone ice cream vendors roam the beach and streets, a cup of ice cream should cost EC$2.50, but the hygiene standards of the vendors leave a lot to be desired. In Castries cold drinks are sold on street corners, EC$1 for a coke, drink it and return the bottle. Coconut water sold by vendors is always refreshingly cool and sterile. Drink from the coconut. Vendors outside *Julian's* at Gablewoods Mall sometimes sell home made cassava bread and a local delicacy called permi made of cornmeal and coconut wrapped up in a banana leaf. For other foods such as bakes, floats, fish, chicken, dal rotis (split pea), be sure that they are freshly cooked for the best flavour.

Castries *Kimlans*, Derek Walcott Square, T4521136. Upstairs café and bar with verandah, cheap, serves local food, open 0700-2300 Mon-Sat. *Café Panache*, on Derek Walcott Square, next door to the Central Library on Bourbon St, in the 100-year old former home of Nobel Laureate Sir Arthur Lewis. Downstairs is the cocktail lounge and buffet breakfast and lunch, popular with locals, upstairs is the high class dining room, more expensive, for evening meals, looking out over the square, good food, amiable service, moderate prices. *Chung's*, on the corner of Coral and Brazil Street, upstairs above Starlite, T4521499. Open 1100-2000 or so, pleasant and airy, good food, inexpensive, for EC$16.50 you get soup, 3 choices from the menu and coffee, MSG used in a few dishes, if you don't want it, say so, will also cater for allergies, such as wheat, just ask, everything delicious. Recommended. *Flamingo*, William Peter Blvd. Favourite local place for a cheeseburger (EC$6.50) or roti, open until about 1600, closes about 1200 on Sat, not pretty but that's OK, for a chicken roti specify you want it without skin and bones, which the St Lucians eat. *Quick Bite*, on Mongiraud, adjacent to the S&S building, T4523063. Vegetarian salad bar and takeaway, specializes in soya meals. There are about 10 good value local eateries in the street adjoining the central market, tables outside, heaped plates of local food, lunchtime only.

South of Castries On the Top of the Morne, *Bon Appetit* is recommended for its daily specials and spectacular views, but is not cheap, meals from EC$35, T4522757. Also on the Morne, *San Antoine*, T4524660. A plantation great house, lovely gardens, elegant dining room, closed until mid-2001. In the same area *The Green Parrot*, T4523399. 4-course dinner

EC$95, serves excellent lunches daily, lots of Caribbean specialities and good selection of tropical vegetables, have a cocktail in the lounge before dinner, the chairs are worth it alone, shows Wed, Sat, ladies' night Mon.

North of Castries *D's Restaurant*, *Edgewater Beach Hotel*, T4537931. Indoor or on patio, relaxing setting on beach, good selection on menu, mainly lunch time, creole special EC$20. Recommended. *Froggie Jack's*, tucked away at Vigie Cove, T4581900, riouxj@candw. lc Great views of harbour at sunset, open for lunch and dinner, try their home-smoked local fish, run by former executives at *Anse Chastenet* and *Jalousie*. *Coal Pot*, outstanding, at Vigie Marina, T4525566. French chef, *the* place to eat at the moment, reservations essential, lunch and dinner except Saturday when dinner only, closed Sunday. Next to it is the little *Café au Lait*, which does takeaway, T4530959. *Vigie Beach Bar*, beside *Rendezvous Hotel* serves good rotis and inexpensive cold beers; in Gablewoods Mall there are three food outlets open from 0800-2100 daily: Southeast Asian, pizza, ice cream. *Tiggis*, T4524815, a/c, very good food and service, popular for lunch but dinner looks like leftovers, open Mon-Sat 0830-2200, soups, meals, baguettes, sandwiches, desserts, free salad bar with all dinners, choose your own fresh sauce. *Miss Saigon* next door, T4517309. Serves full English breakfast, EC$18, Chinese and Oriental lunch and dinner, open daily. *Friends* at Casa Vigie, first floor, just below the Venezuelan embassy. Patisserie and café, very good sandwiches, attractive, open Mon-Thu, Fri 1000-2400, Sat 1000-1800, lovely walk from here to the Vigie lighthouse. *The Wharf* restaurant, bar and dancing at Choc Bay, short distance past Gablewoods Mall. Beach setting, very pleasant, waiter service to your sunbed, varied menu, reasonable prices, beer EC$5-6, house wine EC$6, BLT EC$12, hamburger EC$15, happy hour 1800-1900 daily, open 0900-2400. *En Bas Bwapen Creole Kitchen*, behind a galvanized fence at the bend in the Castries to Gros Islet road as it runs by the airport runway, T4521971. Breakfast and lunch, very local, most expensive meal EC$10 with local juice. *BJ's Pepper Pot*, along the main road in Marisule, about halfway between Castries and Rodney Bay, T4501030. Speciality is Jamaican cooking, prices up to EC$18, open Tue-Sat, from 1100.

Rodney Bay *Memories of Hong Kong*, opposite *Royal St Lucian* hotel, T/F4528218. Chinese chef from Hong Kong, expensive but excellent, you can inspect the kitchens, open Mon-Sat 1700-2230. Same owners also run *Thai Royal*, opposite Scotia Bank, T4529249. Open Mon-Sat 1700-2230, private dining room available. *The Lime* serves good meals and snacks at moderate prices, T4520761. Friendly, open from 1100 till late, closed Tue. *Triangle Pub*, across from *the Lime*, T4520334. Open daily 1100-late, local food and barbecue, eat in or take out, live bands, pan, jazz. *Razmataz*, opposite *Royal St Lucian*, T/F4529800. Indian, good, friendly, open from 1600, happy hour 1700-1900, if you're still around after that, John plays guitar and sings romantic songs from the 60s and 70s, or on Sat a belly dancer weaves her way around the diners, closed Thu. *Shamrock's Pub*, T4528725. 6 TVs, pool tables, darts, pub grub, open daily. *Capone's*, is a restaurant in the speakeasy style of the 1920s, open for dinner only and quite expensive, but attached to a *pizzeria*, open from 1100, both closed Sun-Mon, with prices starting at EC$12, T4520284. *Charthouse*, T4528115. Closed Sun, known for its steak, seafood and spare ribs, excellent rib steak. *Café des Arts*, a French restaurant and wine bar, serving items such as barracuda with *herbes de Provence*, French onion soup, beef tenderloin with pepper sauce, downstairs is the *Boutique de Café des Arts*, selling hand painted china and an impressive range of hand crafted silver jewelry. *Elena's* ice cream parlour, underneath *Café des Arts* (the old *Snooty Agouti*), has tables under umbrellas outside in a small courtyard, home made ice cream and local fruit sorbets, good cappuccino. Further along the road and directly on the beach at Reduit is *Spinnakers*, T4528491. Breakfast, lunch and dinner daily, with full English breakfast EC$26, happy hour 1800-1900, excellent location, though food and service suffer when it is busy, good too for coffee and desserts, they also hire out loungers for EC$5 per day. Just by *Spinnakers* is *The Cat's Whiskers*, T4528880. Traditional English pub food, Sunday roast beef and Yorkshire pudding, steak and kidney pie, Cornish pasties, etc, closed Mon, open 0800-2300. *Eagles Inn*, at the entrance to Rodney Bay Marina. You can sit and watch the boats go by and enjoy good and not too expensive cuisine. Great fish. *The French Restaurant*, at the marina, waterfront, T4500022. French Créole cuisine, seafood a speciality, open daily 1600-2400, reservations advisable, free entrance to *Le Chalet* night club with dinner receipt. *Three Amigos*, also at the marina, T4520351. Mexican restaurant and bar, daily poolside Mexican barbecues, open from 0700. *Le Nouveau Bistro*, close to marina, T4529494. Seafood a speciality, also English pub grub and daily specials, happy hour drinks, nice setting on waterfront, outside deck nice for sitting out in the evenings, open daily all year round. At Pigeon Island, *Jambe de Bois*, serves full breakfast and reasonably priced meals until 2130, run by the former owners of *Snouti Agouti*, offering gooey cakes, salads, art gallery, book swap, internet access at EC$20/hr.

Cap Estate *The Great House Restaurant*, T4500450. Traditional tea from 1630-1730 and watch the sunset, happy hour 1730-1830, dinner expensive, 1900-2200, closed Mon.

Marigot Bay Several hotels for lunch and dinner, but *JJ's Restaurant and Bar* on the bay is a cheaper alternative, T4514076. Specializes in fresh local dishes and seafood, open from 1000 till late, reasonably priced crayfish, crab and lobster (in season), Wed night crabs and a live band, Fri salsa, Sat live band. *Chateau Mygo*, T4524772. St Lucian-Indian cuisine, open daily 0700-1100, serves traditional hot bakes and cocoa tea for breakfast, credit cards accepted, reservations advised. *Shack Bar & Grill*, T4514145. Built over the water, tie up for dinghies, burgers, steaks, seafood, open Mon-Fri from 1500, Sat-Sun from 1200, happy hour 1700-1900, reservations recommended for dinner 1830-2200.

Soufrière *The Still* specializes in authentic St Lucian dishes, T4597224. Open daily 0800-1700 it is not cheap but serves local vegetables grown on site. *Spotlight* near *Home Guesthouse* and Barclays Bank. Good local food, tuna and kingfish recommended, lunches and dinners EC$16-25. *Jacquot*, on Church Street, try the Jacquot Special cocktail. *The Humming Bird*, T4597232, is a good place to eat and take a swim. French, Créole and seafood, daily specials, good but expensive, barman is a great fund of information on horoscopes, good views, open from 0700. *Dasheene*, at *Ladera Resort*, T4597323. Good food, award-winning Austrian chef cooks with local produce, wonderful views, worth coming here even if only for a drink just for the views. Recommended. The *Purity Bakery* near the church in the main square serves breakfast with good coffee, rolls and cakes. *Le Haut Plantation* on the west coast road 1 km north of Soufrière. Huge TV in sports bar, open 1000-2100, also 6 rooms, small. At Étangs Soufrière, on the road to Vieux Fort, is *The Barbican* restaurant and bar, T4597888. Run by the very welcoming Mr and Mrs Smith, local food at local prices, good home cooking, not sophisticated, but clean, popular. *The Old Courthouse*, T4595002. Bar, restaurant, batik gallery, French Créole and Southeast Asian dishes, waterfront dining, open daily, credit cards. On Market St there is a pleasant rasta eating place run by *Jalam*, in a wooden house up a couple of steps from street level, small, clean, he cooks in the yard behind, cheap, EC$10 for a dal, a roti and 2 fresh juices.

Vieux Fort *Il Pirata*, T4546610, Italian restaurant on the beach, prices from EC$25, attached to a motel, open Tue-Sun 0700-2130. Close to Hewanorra airport and near *Club Aquarius* by sign for beach cottages to rent is the *Annex*, T4546200. Open from 0900 to midnight weekdays, 1000-0200 weekends, good food. At Anse de Sables beach is *Reef*, next door to the *Club Med* windsurfing facility, owned by Cecile Wiltshire, pleasant bar, local drinks and delicacies, reasonable prices, tables out by the beach as well as inside the building. A bit further down is *Sandy Beach* restaurant and bar on the beach and on the highway .Excellent location, delightful stopping place, good food, a bit overpriced but not dreadful, have a swim and lunch. *Sapphire*, near bus station, opposite football pitch. Good local food at low prices, run by Frenchman who brought his mother from France to cook, she speaks no English or Patois.

Festivals

There is lots of music, dancing & drinking. Everything goes on for hours, great stamina is required to keep going

Carnival is a high point in the island's cultural activities, when colourful bands and costumed revellers make up processions through the streets. After some debate it was decided to move Carnival in 1999 from **Febuary to July**, partly so as not to conflict with Trinidad's Carnival. On the Saturday are the calypso finals, on Sunday the King and Queen of the band followed by J'ouvert at 0400 until 0800 or 0900. On Monday and Tuesday the official parades of the bands take place. Most official activities take place at Marchand Ground but warming-up parties and concerts are held all over the place. Tuesday night there is another street party.

Independence Day is **22 February** and is celebrated quite extensively. There is a large exhibition lasting several days from the various ministries, business and industry, and NGOs, such as the National Trust, and various sporting events, serious discussions and musical programmes. On the Sunday preceeding **1 May**, the *Festival of Comedy* is held at Pigeon Point (Cultural Centre if it is raining), organized by the National Trust. The annual *St Lucia Jazz Festival* in **May** is now an internationally recognized event, drawing large crowds every year. Most concerts are open-air and take place in the evening, although fringe events are held anywhere, anytime, with local bands playing in Castries at lunchtime. As well as jazz, played by international stars, you can hear Latin, salsa, soca and zouk, steel drums or Bob Marley. For more details www.stluciajazz.com Tickets from US$35 or a season pass US$230. On 29 June St Peter's Day is celebrated as the Fisherman's Feast, in which all the fishing boats are decorated. The *Feast of the Rose of Lima* (Fét La Wòz), on **30 August**, and the *Feast of St Margaret Mary Alacoque* (La Marguerite), on **17 October**, are big rival flower festivals. Members of the societies gather in various public places around the island to dance and sing in costume. The first Monday in **October** is *Thanksgiving*, held either to give thanks for no hurricane or for survival of a hurricane.

Another very interesting festival is *Jounen Kweyol* (Creole Day), on the last Sunday in **October**, although activities are held throughout the month.Four or five rural communities are selected for the celebration. There is local food, craft, music and different cultural shows. Expect traffic jams everywhere that day because people like to visit all the venues across the island. A lot is in kweyol/patois, but even without basic language skills you will have a good time and a chance to sample mouth-watering local food.

St Cecilia's Day, held on **22 November**, is also known as *Musician's Day* (St Cecilia is the patron saint of music). *St Lucy's Day*, **13 December**, used to be called Discovery Day, but as Columbus' log shows he was not in the area at that time, it was renamed. It is now known as the National Festival of Lights and Renewal. St Lucy, the patron saint of light, is honoured by a procession of lanterns. For details contact Castries City Council, T4522611 ext 7071.

Nightlife

In May, nightlife is dominated by the annual jazz festival with lots of outdoor concerts

Most of St Lucia's nightlife revolves around the hotels, while some restaurants host live bands. The choice varies from steel bands, jazz groups, folk dancing, crab racing, fire eating and limbo dancers. The hotels welcome guests from outside.

Around Rodney Bay, venues like *The Lime* are popular places for those who just want to hang out. *Indies* is a nightclub and disco (over 21s) next to the *Bay Gardens Hotel*, Rodney Bay, and *Le Chalet*, near the Rodney Bay Marina are the hot spots. *Back Door@Indies* is also good, a good selection of Caribbean and international music can be heard, depending on the night, look out for specials, Wed package for US$15 includes admission, free drinks and round trip taxi to nearby hotels, EC$20 cover charge Fri and Sat, free shuttle bus from major hotels, late night happy hour 2200-2400. *Café Panache*, on the square in Castries and *Annex* in Vieux Fort have live music regularly, the former also encourages local poets. *JJ's*, Marigot, casual, good mixture of locals and tourists, Caribbean music in simple disco, Fri can be very busy, Sat pleasantly so, frequent shows, live bands, karaoke, taxi service can be arranged, T4514076. The highlight of the week, for locals and visitors however, is Fri night's jump up at Gros Islet, where it is hard to resist getting involved. For a more cultural evening, tours are available to La Sikwi, patois for sugar mill, at Anse La Raye. There is a visit to the 150 year-old mill, followed by a full costume play reliving life in the village on a stage set into the hills with jazz bands and local acts.

There are (irregular) **shows**: concerts, drama, dance, comedy, at the National Cultural Centre (Castries), the *Light House Theatre* (Tapion) and the *Great House Theatre* (Cap Estate). They can give you a better taste of St Lucian culture than hotel shows which are adapted to international taste. A new theatre and banqueting facility, *Gaiety*, was due to open in 2001 for the Jazz Festival, just north of Gros Islet, with seating for 3,000 under cover and another 5,000 outside. Contact the Department of Culture for programmes as shows are often poorly advertised. Tickets available at the Department of Culture and *Sunshine Bookstore* (Gablewoods Mall). International stars also give performances, eg Seamus Heaney, Vladimir Ashkenazy and Lesley Garrett gave readings/concerts in 1999-2000.

Pointe Seraphine, next to the main port in Castries, is a designer-built, **duty-free** shopping **Shopping** centre (same opening hours as other shops, so closed Sat afternoon), with many tourist-oriented outlets, restaurants, entertainment and tour operators.In the centre Llewellyn Xavier has an art gallery selling his own work as well as an interesting range by other artists including Derek Walcott and Canute Caliste (see page 813). Goods bought here can be delivered directly to the airport. Cruise ships can tie up at the complex's own berths.

Batik fabrics and cotton clothing from *Caribelle Batik* on Old Victoria Road, The Morne and Bridge Street; Bagshaw's silk screening workshops at La Toc, T4522139, are very popular, studio open Mon-Fri 0830-1630, Sat 0830-1200, also shops at *Marigot* and *Windjammer*; souvenirs from Pointe Seraphine, Hewanorra duty-free and Soufrière; high quality local crafts and paintings from *Artsibit*, corner of Brazil and Mongiraud Streets, open Mon-Fri 0900-1700, Sat 0930-1300. *Eudovics Art Studio*, T4522747, in Goodlands, coming down from the Morne heading south, sells local handicraft and beautiful large wood carvings. Daniel Jean-Baptiste makes hand-painted, limited edition, silk artwork, call T4508000 for a private studio visit.

Bookshops *Sunshine Bookshop*, Gablewoods Mall (open Mon-Fri 0900-1745, Sat 0900-1630) and JQ Mall (open Mon-Sat 0900-1800, Sun 1000-1300), books, foreign newspapers and magazines, open Mon-Fri 0830-1630, Sat half day; *Book Salon*, Jeremie Street on corner of Laborie Street, good selection of paperbacks, several books on St Lucia, also stationery. *Rodney Bay Shipping Services* runs a book exchange, 2 for 1, mostly spy thrillers and light novels, not a huge selection, but useful.

Market day in Castries is Sat, very picturesque (much quieter on other days, speakers of Patois pay less than those who do not). A new public market has been built on the Castries waterfront, with the old market building renovated and turned into a craft market. *Wire World*, booth 3, charming figures by the award-winning Paulinus Clifford, T4538727, also at Pointe Seraphine, he and the next artisan, Augustus Simon, a potter, T4521507, will craft to order. Buy a coal-pot (native barbecue) for EC$12 and bring it home on your lap. Buy a cocoa stick or 10 for US$5. To make hot chocolate, put two tablespoons of grated cocoa in a pan with half a pint of water and boil for 15 min, strain, then add dry milk, sugar, cinnamon and nutmeg to taste. There is a *Fisherman's Co-operative Market* on the John Compton Highway at the entrance to Pointe Seraphine. Fish is also sold by a Martiniquan woman inside the public market, good variety, hygienically displayed, and at an outlet outside the supermarket at JQ's Mall, Rodney Bay. Many fishermen still sell their catch wherever they can. Fish is cheap and fresh. *JQ's* supermarket at the traffic lights at the end of the Vigie runway, open Mon-Fri 0800-1900, Sat 0800-1600, bank next door, fair range of goods, also supermarket on the William Peter Boulevard. *Gablewoods shopping Mall*, between Rodney Bay and Castries, has a selection of boutiques, gift shops, book shop, post office, pharmacy, deli, open air eating places and *Julian's Supermarket*, open Mon-Thu 0800-2000, Fri, Sat until 2100, Sun 0800-1300. Next door is a delicatessen with a choice of frozen and defrosted foods. A few doors away is the *Sea Island Cotton Shop*, the main outlet for Caribelle Batik clothes. *Garden Gate Flowers* has takeaway boxes (cargo transport) and bouquets (hand luggage) of pink and red ginger, heliconia, anthuriums, 48 hrs notice required for export, US$12-30, at Bois D'Orange T4529176, at Hewanorra T4547651, F4529023. At *Rodney Bay Shopping Centre*, is *Vibes Music Store*, T4580056, www.vibesmusicstore.com with all the latest releases in a variety of styles. On the way to Gros Islet from Castries turn left just after the Texaco station for the studio *Zaka's*, where masks and totems are carved from driftwood collected along the Atlantic coast or discarded lumber off-cuts found in the forest. Prices from EC$140, open Mon-Fri 1000-1500, T4520946, also available from *Jambe de Bois* at Pigeon Island. Rodney Bay Marina has a variety of shops: Llewellyn Xavier has opened a gallery here, *Caribbean Art*

Gallery, with inexpensive beautifully framed prints as well as his own work and that of local artists, T4528071. *Le Marché de France* Supermarket is one of the few to open on Sun morning; the *Bread Basket* sells excellent fresh loaves, sandwiches and cakes. Soufrière has a market on the waterfront.

Transport

If leaving the country temporarily with electronic equipment such as computers, register the goods at the airport to avoid problems on return

Air   **From Europe**   The only direct scheduled services are with *BWIA, Virgin Atlantic* or *British Airways* (via Antigua) from London, *Condor* from Frankfurt and *Air Liberté* from Paris. **From North America**   *BWIA* has flights, via Barbados from New York, and Miami. *Air Jamaica* from New York and Philadelphia, other cities planned. **From Canada**   *Air Canada* flies from Toronto. Charter flights include *Apple Charters, Signature, Air 2000, Canada 3000* and *JMC.* **From the Caribbean**   Lots of flights from Antigua (*LIAT*), Barbados (*LIAT, Eastern Caribbean Express, Air Jamaica*), Dominica (*LIAT, Air Jamaica*), Grenada (*LIAT, Air Jamaica, Eastern Caribbean Express*), Guadeloupe (*LIAT, Air Guadeloupe*), Montego Bay (*Air Jamaica*), Martinique (*LIAT, Air Guadeloupe*), San Juan (*American Eagle*), St Vincent (*LIAT, Eastern Caribbean Express*), Trinidad and Tobago (*BWIA, LIAT*).

Airports   St Lucia has two airports: **George F Charles Airport** (formely Vigie) (T4521156), for inter-island flights (*EC Express, Liat, BWIA, American Airlines* from San Juan) only (2 miles from Castries, taxi for US$7.50, no exchange facilities), and **Hewanorra International Airport** (T4546355) in the Vieux Fort district, where international flights land; there is an air shuttle to Vigie by helicopter, 12 mins, US$90. Alternatively a taxi to Castries costs US$56 (though, out of season, you can negotiate a cheaper rate) and it will take you 1½-2 hrs to reach the resorts north of Castries. A new service is the St Lucia Air Shuttle, run by *Paradise Tourist Services*, Rodney Bay, behind *Julian's supermarket*, by reservation only, US$17.50 one way, US$33 round trip, per person, credit cards accepted, T4529329, F4580979, www. stluciatip.com   If you are travelling light you can walk to the main road and catch the minibus or route taxi to Castries, or if you are staying in Vieux Fort you can walk there, but be careful of the fast traffic. No baggage storage yet available at Hewanorra. Try to arrange it with one of the Vieux Fort hotels.

Boat   *Windward Lines Ltd* operate a weekly passenger and cargo ferry service (suspended 2001) linking Venezuela (Güiria or Pampatar, Margarita), Trinidad, St Vincent, Barbados and St Lucia. *Express Des Iles*, links St Lucia with the French Antilles and Dominica, reservations Cox & Co Ltd, William Peter Boulevard, T4522211/3, F4531868, or travel agents. You can not buy a ticket at the dock, so remember to buy weekend tickets in advance as the office is shut then. Departs Castries for Fort-de-France Mon 0700, Tue 1700, Wed 1300, Sat 0700, Sun 1300, 1hr 20 mins, return Tue 0800, Wed 0800, Fri 1630, Sat 1700, Sun 1830, EC$256 return, Sat is the only day a day trip is possible. On Wed, Sat and Sun, the boat continues to Roseau (3 ½ -4 hrs) and Pointe-à-Pitre (5 ¾-6 ¼ hrs), returning from Pointe-à-Pitre Fri 1200 and Sun 1400, and Roseau Fri 1415 and Sun 1615. Alternatively you can take a day sail to Martinique for US$95, departing at 0730 returning 2030, you can help sail the yacht, watch for dolphins and enjoy the sunset. Many cruise lines call. Captain Artes of the S/H *Krios*, Rodney Bay Harbour, runs a boat taxi (sailing) service: to Martinique, 3 days, US$315 plus customs charges, Customs officers will contact his boat for you. Highly recommended, even for the seasick.

Local   Bus   There are several bus stands in Castries, at the bottom of Darling Rd on the west side of the gardens and extending back to the multi-storey car park on Peynier St. Route 1 is Castries to Gros Islet, Route 2 Castries to Vieux Fort, Route 3 Castries to Soufrière, Route 4 Vieux Fort environs, Route 5 Castries central zone. Each route then has sub-routes, eg Route 1a is Castries-Gros Islet-Massade-Cap Estate, Route 1b is Castries-Union-Balata-Babonneau-Garrand, etc. Short journeys are only EC$1-1.25, rising to EC$2 Castries to Gros Islet, or to Soufrière, EC$7; from Gros Islet to Rodney Bay EC$1; from Soufrière to Vieux Fort EC$4; children half price. Ask the driver to tell you when your stop comes up, they are usually co-operative.

Car Car hire starts at about US$45 per day for a small car, jeep rental is US$70 per day, US$295-390 a week; if you hire for 8 days you will be charged for one week and one day. Some car hire companies are open to negotiation. Insurance is another US$15-20 per day. A 5% tax is added to everything. A temporary licence costs US$11. If arriving at George F L Charles (formerly Vigie) airport, get your international licence endorsed at the immigration desk (closed 1300-1500) after going through Customs. Car hire companies can usually arrange a licence. Car rental agencies include *Avis*, Vide Bouteille (T4522700, F4531536) and lots of other locations; *Hertz* headquarters at Rodney Bay (T4520680, F4528980), rates from US$55; *Budget*, in Castries, airport and Marisule T4520233, F4529362; *Gibin* at Rodney Bay Marina, T4529528, has Suzuki jeeps US$70 and cars US$45-70, manual or automatic, a/c or not. Most have offices at the hotels, airports and in Castries. Check for charges for pick-up and delivery. If dropping off a car at George F L Charles airport you can sometimes leave the keys with the tourist desk if there is no office for your car hire company. *Wayne's Motorcycle Centre*, Vide Bouteille, T4520680, rents **bikes**; make sure you wear a helmet and have adequate insurance. Filling stations are open Mon-Sat 0630-2000, selected garages open Sun and holidays 1400-1800. Leaded fuel costs US$2.25, unleaded US$2.40.

It is often cheaper to organize car hire from abroad. You can only hire a car if aged 25 or over

    Ferries around the island include: *Rodney Bay Ferry* shuttles between the marina shops, *Marlin Quay, St Lucian Hotel, Mortar and Pestle* and *Pigeon Island*, fares within the marina US$4 return, children under 12 half price, T4520087, F4528816, also half day trips to Pigeon Island including lunch, US$40, bookings at the Yellow Hut by the entrance to the *Lime Restaurant*'s car park. The *Gingerbread* express in Marigot Bay costs US$1 return, but is refunded by *Doolittle's Restaurant* if you eat or drink there and present your tickets. **Water taxis** and **speedboats** can be rented.

Taxi Fares are supposedly set by the Government, but the US$60 Castries-Soufrière fare doubles as unlucky tourists discover that there are no buses for the return journey. *Club St Lucia*, in the extreme north, to Castries, about 10 miles away, costs US$15-18 one way for 1-4 people, US$3.75 per additional passenger. Fare from Castries to Gros Islet (for Fri evening street party), US$12; to Pigeon Island National Park, US$15.50 one way; to Vigie airport, US$5; to Hewanorra airport, US$56; Vigie airport to Rodney Bay US$16; Marigot Bay to Hewanorra airport US$45; to Vigie airport US$22, to Castries US$20 (30 mins). If in doubt about the amount charged, check with the tourist office or hotel reception. You can see a copy of the fixed fares at the airport. At rush hour it is almost impossible to get a taxi so allow plenty of time, the traffic jams are amazing for such a small place. A trip round the island by taxi, about US$20 per hour for 1-4 people, can be arranged with an additional US$5 per hour for a/c. Recommended taxi drivers are Kenneth James, T4536844, 4519778, Barnard Henry, T4501951, Samson Louis, T4500516 (or through the *Rex St Lucian* taxi stand) and Raymond Cepal, pager T4843583.

Registered taxis have red number plates with the TX prefix. Minibuses have the T prefix

Airlines The following airlines have offices on Brazil St, Castries: *LIAT* (T4523051, or at Hewanorra airport T4546341, or George F Charles (Vigie) airport T4522348, F4536584); *Air Canada* (T4523051, at Hewanorra T4546249); *Air Jamaica* at Hewanorra, T4548869, reconfirmations only; *British Airways* is at Cox and Co Building, William Peter Boulevard (T4523951, F4522900 and at Hewanorra T4546172); *Air Martinique*, George F Charles Airport (T4522463); *American Eagle* at George F Charles airport, T4521820/1840; *American Airlines* ticket office on Micoud near Bridge St, no phone; *Helenair*, at George F Charles airport, T4527196, F4527112. *St Lucia Helicopters* at Pointe Seraphine, T4536950; *Paradise Helicopters*, T4509203, information@paradisehelicopters.com *Eastern Caribbean Helicopters*, T4536952.

Directory

Banks *Bank of Nova Scotia* (T4522292), *Royal Bank of Canada* (T4522245), *Canadian Imperial Bank of Commerce* (T4523751), all on William Peter Blvd, Castries; *Barclays Bank* (T4523306), and the *St Lucia Co-operative Bank* (T4522881), on Bridge St, *National Commercial Bank*, Waterfront (T4522103), Castries. *Barclays, CBC, National Commercial Bank* and *St Lucia Co-operative Bank* have branches in Vieux Fort, and Barclays and National Commercial Bank in Soufrière; *Barclays* and *Royal Bank of Canada* (T4529921) at Rodney Bay marina. Banks opening hours vary, but most are open 0800-1500 Mon-Thu, 0800-1700 Fri. *Barclays Bank, Bank of Nova Scotia, Co-operative Bank* and *Royal Bank of Canada* at Rodney Bay open Sat until 1200, as do the *National Commercial Bank* in Castries and in Gros Islet.

Windward Islands

Communications Post: Main post office is on Bridge St, Castries, open Mon-Fri, 0830-1630, Sat, 0800-1200, poste restante at the rear.Fax and photocopying facilities upstairs. Postcards to Europe EC$0.50, to the USA EC$0.40; letters to Europe EC$1.10, to the USA and UK EC$0.95. The DHL office is on Bridge St. **Telephone:** the island has an adequate telephone system, with international direct dialling, operated by Cable and Wireless, Bridge St, Castries. There is a sub-office on New Dock Rd, Vieux Fort. Fax facilities at both offices. Hotels do not generally allow direct dialling, you will have to go through the operator, which can be slow and costly. Intra-island calls are EC$0.27 in the Castries zone, EC$0.45-0.75 to other zones, depending on time of day and day of week. Pay phones use EC$0.25 and EC$1 coins. Cable and Wireless phone cards are sold for EC$10, EC$20, EC$40 or EC$53; with these you can phone abroad. There is a credit card phone at Vigie airport operated via the boat phone network, open daily 0800-2200. The International code for St Lucia is 758. Call USA T1-800-6747000; Sprint Express T1-800-2777468; BT Direct T1-800-3425284; Canada Direct T1-800-7442580; USA Direct phone at Rodney Bay Marina, or T1-800-8722881. If you want to dial a toll-free US number, replace the 800 with 400. You will be charged a local call. **Internet** There are internet services at the *Gablewoods Mall* office of Cable & Wireless, where there are several terminals, EC$5 for 30 mins, at *Jambe de Bois* on Pigeon Island, EC$10 per hour, and also in the University Centre.

Embassies & consulates *Danish* Consulate, Cap Estate Golf Club, PO Box 328, Castries, T4508522/3, F4508317. *French* Embassy, Clarke Avenue, Vigie, T452-2462/5877, F4527899. *Italian* Vice Consul, Reduit, PO Box GM 848, T4520865, F4520869. *Netherlands* Consulate, M & C Building, Bridge St, PO Box 1020, Castries, T4522811, F4523592. *Organization of American States*, Vigie, T4524330. *Organization of Eastern Caribbean States*, Morne Fortune, T4522537. *UK*, British High Commission, NIS Building, Waterfront, PO Box 227, Castries, T4522484, F4531543, open Mon-Fri 0830-1230. *Venezuelan* Embassy, Casa Vigie, PO Box 494, Castries, T4524033, F4536747, open Mon-Fri 0900-1430.

Language schools *Alliance Française de Sainte Lucie*, in the pyramid at Pointe Seraphine, T4526602, courses and cultural events, art exhibitions, library etc. Spanish lessons at all levels at the *Venezuelan Institute*, Sans Souci, T4522555. Patois lessons at the Folk Research Centre, T4522279.

Medical facilities Most villages have health centres. The new Tapion hospital has 12-14 doctors' offices, laboratory, but no casualty department. For emergency T999; Aerojet Ambulance for air evacuation, T4521600, F4532229; Victoria Hospital, Castries, T4522421/4537059; St Jude's, Vieux Fort, T4546041, Soufrière Casualty, T4597258, Dennery, T4533310. Larger hotels have resident doctors or doctors 'on call', visits cost about EC$50. If given a prescription, ask at the Pharmacy whether the medication is available 'over the counter', as this may be cheaper. The AIDS hotline is T4527170. As on most Caribbean islands, there is dengue fever (see page 53), carried by the mosquito, Aedes egyptii so take anti-mosquito repellent.

Tour companies & travel agents Most hotels will arrange tours (US$40-80) to the island's principal attractions around Soufrière either by road, boat or helicopter. Coach tours are cheaper and are usually daily in high season, falling to once or twice a week off season. Alternatives are to go by boat (easy between Castries and Soufrière, some hotels have their own boats: *Anse Chastanet, Jalousie Plantation, Windjammer Landing* and *Sandals*) or by helicopter (recommended for a spectacular view of the sulphur springs). From Pointe Seraphine a north island helicopter tour costs US$45, 10 mins; south island US$80, 20 mins; a heli-hike with tour of Atlantic beaches and Cactus Valley US$65, T4500806; helicopters can also be hired for airport transfers, US$100 from Pointe Seraphine to Hewanorra, also pick-up from some hotels. Local tour operators offer highly recommended plantation tours; Errard, Marquis and Balenbouche offer fascinating insights into colonial history and local environments. A tour of a working banana plantation, US$50, is recommended, you see a lot of the country and see and taste a lot of native fruit and vegetables. There are now ten sites which comprise the St Lucia Heritage Tours, T4516058, F4516940, heritagetours@candw.lc, including Latille Falls (20-ft waterfall and pools where you can swim), Fond d'Or Nature and Historical Park (hiking trails to plantation house ruins, Amerindian remains and the beach), Fond Latisab Creole Park (demonstrations of traditional methods of making cassava bread, catching cray fish etc) and the Folk Research Centre (19th century building on Mount Pleasant documenting kweyol culture and history). Costs vary from US$2-12, depending on the activities offered, a full day tour booked through a tour agency will be around US$60. More are being developed. St Lucia Distillers has an excellent rum factory tour with tasting, shop for purchases, south towards Marigot, T4514258. The National Trust (PO Box 595, Castries, T4525005, F4532791, natrust@candw.lc) runs excursions to Maria Island and Fregate Island Reserve, see Fauna and flora, above, US$75 to Maria Island if booked through a tour agency, You can take a carriage ride through the north of the island, or spend an evening cruising into the sunset with as much champagne as you can drink. There are also day trips to neighbouring islands: day sail to Martinique US$95, Dominica US$215, Grenadines including sail, US$199-245, Barbados US$230 and others. The main tour agencies are *St Lucia Reps/Sunlink Tours*, T4528232, F4520459, www.stluciareps.com. *Spice Travel*, T4520866, www. casalucia.com; *Solar Tours*, T4519041; *Barnards Travel*, T4522214; *Barefoot Holidays*, T4500507, F4500661, www.travelfile.com/get/baredays.html In Vieux Fort *is Rainbow Option Tours & Services*, run by Nadine Edwards (T4548202), Paula Edwards (T4549156) and Julius James (T4545014). *ATV Adventures* have guided ATV rides, T4526441, F4522810, mctours@candw.lc. **Maps** of the island may be obtained from the Land Survey in the last government building. At 1:50,000 they are the best but not 100% accurate. Ordnance Survey, Romsey Rd, Southampton, UK (T01703-792792), produce a map of St Lucia in their World Maps series which includes tourist information such as hotels, beaches, climbing and climate. The Tourist Board map is free.

Tourist offices *St Lucia Tourist Board*, Sure Line Building, almost opposite *D's Restaurant* at *Edgewater Beach Hotel*, north of Castries, PO Box 221, Castries, St Lucia, T4524094, F4531121, www.stlucia.org, slutour@candw.lc There are Tourist Board information centres at the Pointe Seraphine Duty-Free Complex; Jeremie St, opposite the Fire Dept; George F Charles Airport (most helpful but closed for lunch 1300-1500), T4522596; Hewanorra Airport (very helpful, particularly with hotel reservations, only open when flights are due or leave), T4546644 and Soufrière (very helpful, local phone calls free), T4597419. *The Tropical Traveller* is distributed free to hotels, shops, restaurants etc every month and contains some extremely useful information, www.tropicaltravellers.com The St Lucia Hotel and Tourism Association publishes a tourist guide, *Visions of St Lucia*, PO Box 545, Castries, T4525978, F4527967, www.stluciatravel.com.lc also of a high standard and widely available.

Background

Even though some St Lucians have claimed that their island was discovered by **History** Columbus on St Lucy's day (13 December, the national holiday) in 1502, neither the date of discovery nor the discoverer are in fact known, for according to the evidence of Columbus' log, he appears to have missed the island and was not even in the area on St Lucy's Day. A Vatican globe of 1520 marks the island as Santa Lucía, suggesting that it was at least claimed by Spain. In 1605, 67 Englishmen en route to Guiana made an unsuccessful effort to settle though a Dutch expedition may have discovered the island first. At this time the island was inhabited by Caribs. There are Amerindian sites and artefacts on the island, some of which are of Arawak origin, suggesting that the Caribs had already driven them out or absorbed them by the time the Europeans arrived, as no trace of the Arawaks was found by them. The Indians called their island Iouanalao, which may have meant: where the iguana is found. The name was later changed to Hiwanarau and then evolved to Hewanorra. In 1638 the first recorded settlement was made by English from Bermuda and St Kitts, but the colonists were killed by the Caribs about three years later.

In 1642 the King of France, claiming sovereignty over the island, ceded it to the French West India Company, who in 1650 sold it to MM Houel and Du Parquet. There were repeated attempts by the Caribs to expel the French, several governors were murdered. From 1660, the British began to renew their claim to the island and fighting for possession began in earnest. The settlers were mostly French, who developed a plantation economy based on slave labour. In all, St Lucia changed hands 14 times before it became a British Crown Colony in 1814 by the Treaty of Paris.

From 1838, the island was included in a Windward Islands Government, with a Governor resident first in Barbados and then Grenada. Universal adult suffrage was introduced in 1951. The St Lucia Labour Party (SLP) won the elections in that year and retained power until 1964. The United Workers' Party (UWP) then governed from 1964-79 and from 1982 onwards. In 1958 St Lucia joined the West Indies Federation, but it was short-lived following the withdrawal of Jamaica in 1961-62 (see page 315). In 1967, St Lucia gained full internal self-government, becoming a State in voluntary association with Britain, and in 1979 it gained full independence.

Windward Islands

From 1964 until 1996 the UWP was led by Mr John Compton, who held power in 1964-79 and subsequently won elections in 1982, 1987 and 1992. In 1996 Mr Compton retired as leader of the UWP (subsequently receiving a knighthood in the 1997 UK's New Year's Honours List) and was replaced as Prime Minister and leader of the party by Dr Vaughan Lewis, former Director General of the Organization of Eastern Caribbean States (OECS), who led the party into the 1997 elections. The leader of the SLP, Julian Hunte, resigned after his party's poor performance in the by-election which brought Dr Lewis into parliament. He later announced his intention of standing as an independent in the 1997 general elections. He was replaced by Dr Kenny Anthony.

The May 1997 elections were a triumph for the SLP, who had been in opposition for 25 years apart from a brief period in 1979-82. They won 16 of the 17 seats, with the UWP gaining the single remaining seat, a result which took even the SLP by surprise. The new government's priorities were to diversify the economy, create employment, conduct an audit of public spending and investigate corruption claims. In 1998, the UWP unanimously elected Sir John Compton (73) as its leader again after Dr Vaughan Lewis declined the nomination, but Sir John later resigned and Dr Vaughan Lewis is now the leader.

Geography

St Lucia is the second largest of the Windwards, lying between St Vincent and Martinique with an area of 238 square miles. The scenery is of outstanding beauty, and in the neighbourhood of the Pitons, it has an element of grandeur. The highest peak is Morne Gimie, 3,118 ft, but the most spectacular are Gros Piton, 2,619 ft, and Petit Piton, 2,461 ft, which are old volcanic forest-clad plugs rising sheer out of the sea near the town of Soufrière on the west coast. A few miles away is one of the world's most accessible volcanoes. Here you can see soufrières: vents in the volcano which exude hydrogen sulphide, steam and other gases and deposit sulphur and other compounds in pools of boiling water. The mountains are intersected by numerous short rivers which in places debouch into broad, fertile and well-cultivated valleys.

Government

St Lucia is an independent member of the Commonwealth and the British monarch is the Head of State, represented by a Governor General (Dame Pearlette Louisy, the first woman to hold the post). The 17-member House of Assembly is elected every five years, while the 11 members of the Senate are appointed by the Governor General, six on the advice of the Prime Minister, three on the advice of the Leader of the Opposition and two of his own choice. The Constituency Boundaries Commission has recommended that the number of constituencies is increased from 17 to 19 in time for the general elections to be held by 2002.

Economy

St Lucia's economy has historically been based on agriculture, originally sugar, but since the 1920s particularly on bananas and also cocoa and coconuts. It has the largest banana crop in the Windward Islands, but production has slumped and the industry is in turmoil. Farmers have suffered because of low prices, storm damage and labour disputes. Greater competition in the European banana market, particularly after EC unification in 1992, is leading to diversification away from bananas; dairy farming, flowers and fisheries are being encouraged.

There is also some industry, with data processing and a diversified manufacturing sector producing clothing, toys, sportswear and diving gear, and 14% of the workforce is now engaged in manufacturing. However, unemployment in the manufacturing sector rose sharply in 1996 with the closure of three foreign-owned garment factories, which had been operating for nearly 10 years, the period during which tax-free concessions are granted. Since then, more companies have closed (garments, informatics) and jobs lost. Tourism is now the major foreign exchange earner, and some 250,000 visitors stay on the island each year.

Patois for beginners

Until recently, Kweyol was not a written language but it has been developed to facilitate teaching.

For people interested in learning a few phrases of Créole, or Kweyol, there is a booklet, Visitors Guide to St Lucia Patois, available for EC$14 in bookshops, Valmont's Book Salon on the corner of Jeremie and Laborie Streets by the Tourist Office, and Sunshine Books in Gablewoods Mall and Rodney Bay.

For the more ambitious reader there are traditional story booklets which explain a lot about country life. Short stories are written in a style a child can understand with an English translation at the back. Examples are Mwen Vin Wakonte Sa Ba'w (I am going to explain it to you), which has a tale for every letter of the alphabet about an animal starting with the same letter, or Se'kon Sa I Fèt (know how it is done), a book about farm life. These books, part of a series of eight aimed at a St Lucian readership, are not available in shops. Contact the Summer Institute of Linguistics, Box 321, Vieux Fort, price around EC$5 each.

The Folk Research Centre (PO Box 514, Mount Pleasant, Castries, T4522279, F4517444, open Monday-Friday 0830-1630) preserves and documents the local culture and folklore and has published several books, a cassette (EC$30) and CD (EC$60): Musical Traditions of St Lucia. A Handbook for Writing Creole gives the main points and features, while a Dictionary of St Lucian Creole and Annou Di-Y an Kweyol, a collection of folk tales and expressions in Creole and English, accompany it well.

In 1999 the New Testament was published in Kweyol.

With thanks to Ulrike Krauss.

Culture

There is a good deal of French cultural influence. Most of the islanders, who are predominantly of African descent (though a few black Caribs are still to be found in certain areas), speak Creole/Kweyol, a similar language to French, and in rural areas many people, particularly the older generation, have great difficulty with English. There is a French provincial style of architecture; most place names are French; about 79% of the population are Roman Catholics. The French Caribbean also has an influence on music, you can hear zouk and cadance played as much as calypso and reggae. The Folk Research Centre (see box) has recorded local music. *Musical Traditions of St Lucia* has 32 selections representing all the musical genres, with information on the background of the various styles. *Lucian Kaiso* is an annual publication giving pictures and information on each season of St Lucian calypso. In the pre-Christmas period, small drum groups play in rural bars. Traditionally, singers improvise a few lines about people and events in the community and the public joins in. The singing is exclusively in Kweyol, wicked and full of sexual allusions.

One of the Caribbean's most renowned poets and playwrights in the English language, **Derek Walcott**, was born in St Lucia in 1930. He has published many collections of poems, an autobiography in verse, *Another Life*, critical works, and plays such as *Dream on Monkey Mountain*. Walcott uses English poetic traditions, with a close understanding of the inner magic of the language (Robert Graves), to expose the historical and cultural facets of the Caribbean. His books are highly recommended, including his narrative poem *Omeros*, which contributed to his winning the 1992 Nobel Prize for Literature. Other St Lucian writers worth reading are the novelists **Garth St Omer** (for instance *The Lights on the Hill*) and Earl Long (an MD in the USA), and the poets Jane King-Hippolyte, Kendal Hippolyte, John Robert Lee and Jacintha Lee, who has a book of local legends. New authors to emerge in the 21st century include Anderson Reynolds, with his novel *Death By Fire*, and Michael Aubertin (head of the Dept of Culture) with his period romance *Neg Maron*. John Robert Lee has also published a book of poetry, *Artefacts*.

St Lucia has also produced painters of international renown. **Dunstan St Omer** was born in St Lucia in 1927 into a Catholic family and is best known for his religious paintings. He created the altarpiece for the Jacmel church near Marigot Bay, where he painted his first black Christ, and reworked Castries Cathedral in 11 weeks in

1985 prior to the Pope's visit. St Omer and his four sons have also painted other countryside churches (Monchy and Fond St Jacques) and a quarter of a mile of sea wall in Anse La Raye. **Llewellyn Xavier** was born in Choiseul in 1945 but moved to Barbados in 1961, where he discovered painting. Galleries in North America and Europe have exhibited his work and his paintings are in many permanent collections. Xavier returned to St Lucia in 1987, where he was shocked by the environmental damage. He has since campaigned vigorously for the environment through his art. *The Global Council for Restoration of the Earth's Environment* is a work created from recycled materials including prints, postage stamps and seals and logos of preservation societies. It is on permanent display at the artist's studio, T4509155 for an appointment, but he also has a gallery at the Rodney Bay Marina.

Other outstanding artists include **Ron Savory**, Ron's Atelier and Framing Co, Vide Bouteille Industrial Park, just past the roundabout at the end of the airport runway (called La Clery junction), T4524412. His rich rainforest scenes and his dancing figures are impressive and he sells collectables, souvenir art, paintings from originals to limited prints to prints, expensive to inexpensive. **Sean Bonnett St Remy** paints wonderful local scenes, village scenes with nostalgic charm and accuracy, he can be contacted at Photographic Images, 42 Brazil Street. **Winston Branch** is splashy, modern abstract, and shows internationally from London to Brazil. A recent display of his at the Alliance Française was painted directly on the walls. He is currently teaching in the USA. **Chris Cox** paints St Lucian birds, such as the parrot and the nightjar. He won an award at the Arts Award ceremony in January 2000 and can be contacted at Forestry. **Arnold Toulon**'s Modern Art Gallery in Bois d'Orange, T4529079, also exhibits local artists including **Cedric George** and **Nancy Cole,** along with his own works. **Alcina Nolley**, an artist and teacher of art, can refer you to many artists and artisans, particularly of the Arts and Crafts Association, T4532338, nolleym@candw.lc

The last week in January is Nobel Laureate Week, with lectures celebrating the two Nobel prize winners produced by the island (Sir Arthur Lewis and Derek Walcott). They were both born on 23 January. Other events include the annual Arts Awards, during which the Cultural Centre is packed.www.stlucia-arts.com

St Vincent and the Grenadines

Colour map 5, grid C5

St Vincent is green and fertile and very pretty, with its fishing villages, coconut groves, banana plantations and volcanic interior. It is widely known for the superb sailing conditions provided by its 32 sister islands and cays and most visitors spend some time on a yacht, even if only for a day. Bareboat and crewed yachts are available for as long as you require, wherever you want to go. There are also very competitive regattas and yacht races held throughout the year, accompanied by a lot of parties and social events. The Grenadines have a certain exclusivity, some of the smaller islands are privately owned and Mustique is known for its villas owned by the rich, royal and famous. There are some fabulously expensive and luxurious places to stay, but there are also more moderate hotels, guest houses and rental homes for those who don't want to spend all their time afloat.

Ins and outs

Getting there
See transport, page 829, for further details

Air There are no direct services from Europe or North America but same day connecting flights are available through Antigua, Barbados, Puerto Rico and Trinidad. Light aircraft connect some of the Grenadine islands with Barbados and provide an air taxi service. **Sea** Many people arrive on yachts, having sailed across the Atlantic or through the Caribbean. Limited ferries and cargo boats link St Vincent with most of the southern Caribbean islands. There is also an informal international ferry on a wooden fishing boat between Union Island and Carriacou (Grenada). See page 830.

A Foot in the door ★

- **Hiking up the volcano** is great: demanding but rewarding exercise and visually spectacular, highly recommended for a day away from the sea.
- The sea, the sea…. That's what its all about. No trip to St Vincent and the Grenadines is complete without, at the very least, one day under sail, whether you're the skipper or the sunbather.
- The **Tobago Cays** are a **snorkeller's** paradise, but don't touch, just enjoy the underwater scenery as you float on the surface.
- **Canouan's beaches** go on for ever, soft pale sand, clear blue sea, empty, perfect.
- For total indulgence when you win the lottery, book yourself in to **Petit St Vincent**. This small, luxury resort on a tiny island in the southern Grenadines, is only accessible by boat but it's within striking distance of a dozen other islands – beautiful views across the sea from your hammock.
- **Bequia** is the best place for restaurants and bars and great as part of a two-centre holiday: a villa here and then a yacht to see the rest of the islands, or take the ferry and see how the other half lives.

Air Flights within the Grenadines are cheap and reliable. *SVG Air* and *Mustique Airways* fly daily from St Vincent to Bequia, Canouan and Union Island (20 mins), and also to Mustique. **Sea** There are several ferries carrying cargo and passengers between St Vincent and Bequia, while the mail boat, the *Barracouda*, links St Vincent with Bequia, Canouan, Mayreau and Union Island with a twice weekly service. **Road** Most, but not all, of the islands have a cheap bus service, which can be a minibus or a pick-up truck with seats in the back. Car hire is available on St Vincent and Bequia, but is hardly worth it on the smaller islands, which can be seen by bus, taxi, bicycle and on foot.

Getting around
Air taxi services connect the islands with short hop flights lasting only a few minutes

Temperatures the year round average between 77°F and 81°F (25-27°C), moderated by the trade winds; average rainfall is 60 inches on the coast, 150 inches in the interior, with the wettest months May to Nov. Best months to visit are therefore Dec to May. You can expect a shower most days in the hills of St Vincent, but the Grenadines are less forested and therefore much drier. Low season is Jun to mid-Dec.

Climate

Flora and fauna

St Vincent has a wide variety of tropical plants, most of which can be seen in the **Botanical Gardens**, where conservation of rare species has been practised since they were founded in 1765. There you can see the mangosteen fruit tree and one of the few examples of *spachea perforata*, a tree once thought to be found only in St Vincent but now found in other parts of the world, as well as the famous third generation sucker of the original breadfruit tree brought by Captain Bligh of the *Bounty* in 1793 from Tahiti. Other conservation work taking place in the gardens involves the endangered St Vincent parrot, *Amazona guildingii*, which has been adopted as the national bird. An aviary, originally containing birds confiscated from illegal captors, now holds 12 parrots. The main colonies are around Buccament, Cumberland-Wallilabou, Linley-Richmond and Locust Valley-Colonarie Valley. They are protected now by the Wildlife Protection Act, which covers the majority of the island's birds, animals and reptiles and carries stiff penalties for infringements. A parrot reserve is being established in the upper Buccament Valley.

Another protected bird unique to St Vincent is the whistling warbler, and this, as well as the black hawk, the cocoa thrush, the crested hummingbird, the red-capped green tanager, green heron and other species can be seen, or at least heard, in the Buccament Valley. There are nature trails starting near the top of the Valley, passing through tropical forest, and it is possible to picnic. The **Vermont Nature Trail** can

Essentials

Documents All visitors must have a passport and an onward, or return, ticket. Nationals of the UK, USA and Canada may enter for up to six months on proof of citizenship only. As well as the three countries already mentioned, citizens of the following countries do not need a visa: all Commonwealth countries, all the EU countries (except Eire and Portugal), Chile, Finland, Iceland, Liechtenstein, Norway, Switzerland, Sweden, Turkey, Uruguay, Venezuela. You will be asked where you will be staying on the island and will need a reservation, which can be done through the Tourist Office at the airport, before going through immigration (or you can make one up). You will usually be given entry until the day of departure on your ticket. If you are only given entry of a few days and want to stay longer, extensions are easily obtained for EC$20.

Customs 200 cigarettes, or 50 cigars, or 250 grams of tobacco, and 40 fluid ounces of alcoholic beverage may be imported duty free.

Currency The East Caribbean dollar, EC$.

Departure tax There is a departure tax of EC$30, or US$12.50.

Ports of entry (Own flag) Wallilabou, on the northwest coast, Kingstown, Bequia (police station), Mustique and Union Island (airport, EC$10 weekdays during working hours, EC$25 overtime, holidays and weekends). Yachtsmen often anchor at Blue Lagoon or Young island and bus/taxi to Kingstown to complete customs and immigration formalities. Fees are EC$10/US$4 per person (EC$25 on Saturday on Union Island) and charter yachts are charged US$2 per foot per month. For an exit stamp, go to the airport customs and immigration one day before departure.

Anchorages On Bequia the local businesses cater to the boating community, delivering water, fuel, laundry, beer and groceries. Men and boys meet yachts in the northern St Vincent anchorages and ask to assist in tying stern line to a tree or offer other services. EC$7 is the current fee for tying up; other services negotiable. Others meet boats in Bequia, Union and the Tobago Cays, offering to supply bread, ice, vegetables, fruit, lobster, or conch (lambi) as well as selling T shirts and jewellery. They can take 'no' for an answer, but will return if you say 'maybe tomorrow'. Anchorages at Wallilabou, Young Island, Petit Byahaut, Blue Lagoon, Bequia, Palm (Prune) Island, Mustique, Canouan, Mayreau (Salt Whistle Bay and two others), Tobago Cays, Union Island (Clifton, Frigate Island, Chatham Bay), Petit St Vincent. **Marinas** at Caribbean

---

be reached by bus, from the market square in Kingstown to the road junction in Peniston near the *Emerald Valley Casino*; the sign for the trail is not clearly marked. It is a long walk through the village to the trail, but rewarding in the views of village and rural life. If travelling by car, look for the Vermont Nature Trail sign about one mile past Questelles. The car park, at 975 ft, is close to the Vermont Nature Centre. Get a trail map from the information hut on the right. A guide is not necessary unless you want scientific information as you walk along this marvellous trail. There is a rest stop on the trail, at 1,350 ft, and a Parrot Lookout Platform at 1,450 ft. It is a beautiful trail, through thick forest and is probably the best place to see the St Vincent parrot. Be prepared for rain, mosquitoes and chiggars, use insect repellent. Anyone interested in nature trails should visit the Forestry Department (in the same building as the Land and Survey Department), who have prepared official trail plans, published in conjunction with the Tourism Department. A pamphlet details the Vermont Nature Trails, Wallilabou Falls, Richmond Beach, Trinity Falls, Falls of Baleine, Owia Salt Pond and La Soufrière Volcano Trails. The tourist office may also have a supply of pamphlets.

Diving and marine life

The underwater wildlife around St Vincent and the Grenadines is varied and beautiful, with a riot of fish of all shapes and sizes. There are many types and colours of coral, including black coral at a depth of only 30 ft in places. On the New Guinea Reef (Petit Byahaut) you can find three types of black coral in six different colours. The

Charter Yacht Yard, Lagoon Marina, Bequia Slipway, Anchorage Yacht Club on Union Island. **Moorings** at Young Island, Blue Lagoon, Friendship Bay, Union Island, Palm Island, Petit Byahaut (US$10 fee is deducted if you have dinner), Mustique. For possibilities of crewing on yachts, check the notice board at the Frangipani Yacht Services, Bequia.

Hours of business Shops: 0800-1200, 1300-1600 Monday-Friday (0800-1200 only, Saturday); **government offices**: 0800-1200, 1300-1615 Monday-Friday; **banks**: 0800-1200 or 1300 Monday-Friday, plus 1400/1500-1700 on Thursday or Friday. The bank at the Airport is open Monday-Friday 0830-1230, 1530-1730.

Official time Atlantic Standard Time, four hours behind GMT, one hour ahead of EST.

Voltage 220/240 v, 50 cycles, except Petit St Vincent and Palm Island, which have 110 v, 60 cycles.

Media Newspapers The Herald is daily and contains news from wire services, including pages in French, Italian, Spanish etc. Three newspapers, The Vincentian, Searchlight and The News, are published weekly. The News is editorially independent and by far the best.

Radio Four radio stations: AM 705kHz, Nice FM 96.3, Hitz FM 107.3, WE FM 99.9. Weather can be heard on SSB weather net 4001 at 0800, 8104 at 0830. **TV** Two TV stations and Krib cable (26 channels).

Tourist offices overseas UK 10 Kensington Court, London W8 5DL, T020-79376570, F020-79373611, svgtourismeurope@aol.com **USA**: 801 2nd Avenue, 21st floor, New York, NY 10017, T212-6874981, 800-7291726, F212-9495946, svgtony@aol.com and 6505 Cove Creek Place, Dallas, Texas, 75240, T214-2396451, 800-2353029, F214-2391002, scubasvg@aol.com

Canada: 32 Park Road, Toronto, Ontario M4W 2N4, T416-9245796, F416-9245844, svgcan@home.com

Clothing Wear light, informal clothes, but do not wear bathing costumes or short shorts in shops or on Kingstown's streets.

Laundry Call on VHF, or phone, for companies to come and pick up. Laundrymat is available on St Vincent with several washers and dryers if you wish to do it yourself.

Public holidays 1 January, Discovery and National Heroes Day (22 January), Good Friday and Easter Monday, Labour Day in May, Whit Monday, Caricom Day and Carnival Tuesday (in July), August Bank Holiday first Monday in August, Independence Day (27 October), Christmas Day and Boxing Day.

coral is protected so do not remove any. There are 10 marine protected areas including the northeast coast and the **Devil's Table** in Bequia, **Isle de Quatre**, all **Mustique**, the **east coast of Canouan**, all of **Mayreau**, the **Tobago Cays**, the whole of **Palm Island**, **Petit St Vincent** and the surrounding reefs. However, the protected areas are very poorly policed and there are no marine park fees. The Tobago Cays receive around 150 yachts a day in high season. Even if the yachts anchor on sand, their dinghies can be seen anchored on the coral reef taking snorkellers to view the treasures they are destroying. Spearfishing is strictly forbidden to visitors and no one is allowed to spear a lobster. Buying lobster out of season (1 May-30 September) is illegal as is buying a female lobster with eggs. Fishing for your own consumption is allowed outside the protected areas. Contact the Fisheries Department for more information on rules and regulations, T4562738.

There are facilities for **scuba diving, snorkelling, deep sea fishing, windsurfing** and **waterskiing**, with instructors for novices. There is reef diving, wall diving, drift diving and wrecks to explore. The St Vincent reefs are fairly deep, at between 55 to 90 ft, so scuba diving is more rewarding than snorkelling. Dive sites include **Bottle Reef, the Forest, the Garden, New Guinea Reef** and **the Wall**. In Kingstown Harbour there are three wrecks at one site, the Semistrand, another cargo freighter and an ancient wreck stirred up by Hurricane Hugo, as well as two cannons, a large anchor and several bathtubs from the old wreck. **Bequia** is also considered excellent, with a leeward wall and 30 dive sites around the island and nearby, reached by boat within 15 minutes. The **Devil's Table** is good for snorkelling as well as diving. Other dive sites are M/S Lirero, the Wall off West Cay, the

Bullet, the Boulders and Manhole. The best snorkelling is found in the Tobago Cays and Palm Island. There is snorkelling and diving around most of the other islands with at least one dive shop on each inhabited island. As well as the specialist companies, many of the hotels offer equipment and services for their guests and others.

Dive centres On St Vincent: *Dive St Vincent* (Bill Tewes) at Young Island Dock, T4574928, F4574948, www.divestvincent.com, NAUI, PADI certification courses, camera rental, trips to Bequia and the Falls of Baleine; *Dive Fantasea*, at Villa Beach, offering dives around St Vincent and tours to the Grenadines, also snorkelling, T4574477, F4575577, www.divefantasea.com; *Wallilabou Dive Experience*, at Wallilabou, convenient for yachties anchored in the bay, T/F4560355, walldivexp@caribsurf. com *Petit Byahaut*, mostly for guests, but visitors may use the facilities if they are not too busy, T/F4577008, VHF68. There are other dive shops on Bequia, Canouan and Union, see below for details. Some operations offer 'yachties' discounts. A

St Vincent

two-tank dive costs around US$70-90, snorkellers US$20, full scuba equipment rental US$45, open water certification US$435-500.

St Vincent is a whaling nation and each year two whales, usually humpbacks, are killed off Bequia (see below and Whale and dolphin watching, page 68). In addition, short-finned pilot whales, known as 'black fish' are caught in Vincentian waters for the local market. For those who would rather watch than eat these mammals, Hal Daize runs coastal boat tours of St Vincent visiting the Falls of Baleine as well as whale and dolphin watching. *Sea Breeze Nature Tours*, T4584969, www.vincy.com/seabreeze

Beaches and watersports

St Vincent has splendid, safe beaches on the leeward side, most of which have volcanic black sand and are undeveloped by hotels. The lightest coloured sand can be found on the south coast in the Villa area, where there are several hotels, watersports and marinas. Just offshore is Young Island (see below), which has a small, golden sand, 'improved' beach. The windward coast is more rocky with rolling surf and strong currents. All beaches are public. Some are difficult to reach by road, but boat trips can be arranged to the inaccessible beauty spots. Sea urchins are a hazard, as in many other islands, especially among rocks on the less frequented beaches. Nearly all the inhabited islands of the Grenadines have at least one golden sand beach, and often many more, some fringed with palm trees, others without any sun protection. *Paradise Windsurfing* has five different locations and offers different levels of instruction, call Basil Cumberbatch, T4583222.

Sailing Sailing is excellent, indeed it was yachtsmen who first popularized the Grenadines and it is one of the best ways to see the islands. You can take day charter boats, easily arranged through hotels, or charter your own boat. There is a variety of boats for skippered day charters. Talk to the operators about size and predicted wind conditions if you are inclined towards seasickness. The large catamarans are usually quite stable so that you will hardly know you are on a boat, but they take quite large groups. If you hire a local yacht or motor boat for a day, make sure that the captain has life jackets and other safety equipment (eg a radio) on board and that he is properly insured. This may seem obvious, but do not take anything for granted and be prepared to ask lots of questions. A tourist and his son taking a short hop boat ride between islands recently found themselves drifting hopelessly off course when the boat's engine failed. The captain had no radio and they were eventually found several days later at death's door off the Venezuelan coast.

Bareboat and crewed yachts are available through *Sunsail*, the largest sailing company in the world, at Blue Lagoon, T4584308, www.lagoonmarina.com *Barefoot Yacht Charters* (Blue Lagoon), an American Sailing Association (ASA) sailing school and the longest established charter company, T4569526, F4569238, www.barefootyachts.com; *Blue Water Charters* at the *Aquatic Club*, Villa, T4561232, F4562382; *Nicholson Yacht Charters*. over 70 crewed yachts, in USA T800-6626066, F617-6610554. On Union Island at Clifton, there are *Moorings*, T4588777, *VPM DuFour Antilles*, T4588894, and *Star Voyage, Bambou Yachting and Overseas Sailing. Kathryn B*, a spectacular 105-ft, three-masted, gaff-rigged topsail schooner, is in the Grenadines Jan-Apr, offering 6-night cruises from St Vincent to the southern Grenadines and back, T800-500 6077, Kathrynb@midcoast. com There are also a few local, independent yacht charters, such as *Grenadine Escape*, who have a yacht and a speed boat available for sunset, one-day or longer trips, very flexible, land tours and villa rental also arranged if you want a few days on dry land, crewed and run by Guy (St Vincentian captain) and Lara (British and an excellent cook) Hadley, T4574028, F4586326, www.grenadine-escape.com

Yacht races include the **Bequia Easter Regatta**, in which there are races for all sizes and types of craft, even coconut boats chased by their swimming child owners

Cricket Grenadine style

Cricket is played throughout the Grenadines on any scrap of ground or on the beach. In Bequia, instead of the usual three stumps at the crease, there are four, and furthermore, bowlers are permitted to bend their elbows and hurl fearsome deliveries at the batsmen. This clearly favours the fielding side but batsmen are brought up to face this pace attack from an early age and cope with the bowling with complete nonchalance. Matches are held regularly, usually on Sundays, and sometimes internationals are staged. In Lower Bay v England, which Lower Bay usually wins, the visitors' team is recruited from cricket lovers staying in the area. Ask at De Reef; it is best to bat at number 10 or 11.

or model sailing yachts chased by rowing boats. Everyone is welcome and there are crewing opportunities. There are other contests on shore and the nights are filled with events such as dancing, beauty shows and fashion shows. The centre of activities is the *Frangipani Hotel*, which fronts directly on to Admiralty Bay. The Canouan Yacht Race is in August.

Other sports Many of the more expensive hotels have **tennis** courts but there are others at the Kingstown Tennis Club and the Prospect Racquet Club. **Squash** courts can be found at the *Cecil Cyrus Squash Complex* (St James Place, Kingston, reservations T4561805), the *Grand View Beach Hotel* and the *Prospect Racquet Club*. Spectator sports include **cricket** (Test Match cricket ground at Arnos Vale, near the airport), **soccer**, **netball**, **volleyball** and **basketball**. Pick up games of basketball are played on St Vincent after 1700, or after the heat has subsided, at the Sports Complex behind the airport. Everyone is welcome, although it can get very crowded and there is only one court, arrive early. There is also a court in Calliaqua (same times), but it is right on the street. Players beware, fouls are rarely called, although travelling violations are. No one is deliberately rough but overall the game is unpolished, unschooled but spirited. For fun **running**, the Hash House Harriers meet on Sunday afternoon, contact Joe Sheridan, T4571310 (day) or 4584119 (night).

Kingstown

The capital, Kingstown, stands on a sheltered bay and is surrounded on all sides by steep, green hills, with houses perched all the way up. However, it is a generally unattractive port city with the waterfront dominated by the container port, cruise ship terminal, fish market and bus station. There is no promenade along the seafront and buildings along the reclaimed land look inland rather than out to sea. The overall effect is noisy, busy and untidy, rather than being a tourist attraction in itself. The most attractive and historical buildings are inland along the three main parallel streets, Bay Street, Long Lane and Grenville/Halifax Street, also known as Front Street, Middle Street and Back Street. The town is always busy as there are few shops in the rest of the island, but Friday is the busiest day.

The Centre Kingstown is known as the 'city of arcades' and it is possible to walk around most of the centre under cover. There are even building regulations to encourage the practice in new construction. The shopping and business area is no more than two blocks wide, running between Bay Street and Halifax Street Grenville Street, also called Front Street and Back Street. There are quite a lot of new buildings, none of them tall. The government financial services building in front of the police station is large, modern, concrete and not particularly pretty. The New Kingstown Fish Market, built with Japanese aid, was opened in 1990 near the Police Headquarters. This complex, known as Little Tokyo, has car parking facilities and is the point of departure for minibuses to all parts of the island. It has a strange little turret which looks like a guard tower. The War Memorial, flanked by two small cannon, is being preserved.

On Halifax Street at the junction with South River Road is the Old Public Library, an old stone building with a pillared portico. It was supposed to be renovated with French aid and made into the Museum of St Vincent, but the project has been dormant for several years. Alliance Française is on the first floor. There are public toilets to the rear.

The Market Square in front of the Court House is the hub of activity. A new covered market with cream and brown horizontal stripes has been built from Upper Bay to Halifax Street to replace the outdoor affair and make it more hygienic. Fruit and vegetables are downstairs and clothing is upstairs, but the vendors upstairs are not doing any business and are moving back on to the streets where they came from, selling from the backs of cars. In the middle of the market building is a circular area where farmers sell their produce direct to the consumer on Fridays.

The jetty

At the jetty where the boats for the Grenadines berth, you can see island schooners loading and unloading, all of which is done by hand. The men throw crates from one to the other in a human chain; the whole business is accompanied by much shouting and laughter. When the banana boat is in dock, the farmers queue in their pick-ups

Windward Islands

Kingstown

■ Sleeping	● Eating	
1 Cara Lodge	1 Attic	5 KFC
2 Cobblestone Inn	2 Basil's	6 Rainbow Palace
3 Kingstown Park	3 Bounty	7 Royal Castle
Guest House	4 Chung Wua	8 Vee Jay's

to unload their boxes of bananas, and the food and drink stalls on the road to the Reception Depot do good business. A new cruise ship terminal has been built alongside the container port, which provides a rather unattractive introduction to the city for passengers who have to pass by dilapidated warehouses. However, the Government which took office in 2001 has plans to clean up and beautify the area.

Cathedrals Kingstown has two cathedrals, St George's (Anglican) and St Mary's (Roman Catholic). **St George's**, which was consecrated in 1820, has an airy nave and a pale blue gallery running around the north, west and south sides. It became a cathedral in 1877 when the Diocese of the Windward Islands was constituted and the chancel and transepts date from 1880-87. The cupula was blown down by a hurricane in 1898 and after that battlements were added to the tower. There is an interesting floor plaque in the nave, now covered by carpet, commemorating a general who died fighting the Caribs. Other interesting features include a memorial to Sir Charles Brisbane (1772-1829) who captured Curaçao and a miniature of the action. Plaques to the rich, the good and the innocent line the walls, nearly all of which were carved in London. A lovely stained glass window in the south transept was reputedly commissioned by Queen Victoria on the death of her grandson. She took exception to angels in red rather than the traditional white and it was put into storage in St Paul's Cathedral. It was brought to St Vincent in the 1930s. **St Mary's** is of far less sober construction, with different styles, Flemish, Moorish, Byzantine and Romanesque, all in dark grey stone, crowded together on the church, presbytery and school. Building was carried out throughout the 19th century, with renovation in the 1940s. The exterior of the church is highly decorated but dark and grim, while the interior is dull in comparison but quite light and pretty. The Methodist church, dating from 1841, also has a fine interior, with a circular balcony. Its construction was financed largely through the efforts of freed slaves. There is a little bell tower at the south end, erected in 1907.

Botanical Gardens
Established in 1765, they are the oldest in the Western Hemisphere

In Kingstown the Botanical Gardens just below Government House and the Prime Minister's residence are well worth a visit (for a description see above under Fauna and flora). In the Gardens, there is a very interesting **Archaeological Museum** of Amerindian artefacts, some of which date from about 4,000 BC. The most spectacular exhibit is the bat effigy. Outside is a collection of shrubs which may have been planted in a Carib garden. Anyone interested in St Vincent history, flora or fauna should talk to the curator, Dr Earle Kirby (Doc); he is very knowledgeable and friendly. Unfortunately, the museum is badly neglected and only open Wednesday morning 0900-1200 and Saturday afternoon 1500-1800. Dr Kirby is elderly and not always at the museum. Occasionally he will open the museum and give a personal tour for especially interested visitors. The **Nicholas Wildlife Complex** has parrots, agouti, Barbados Green Monkey and St Vincent Parrot, but not very well housed. The Gardens themselves are open 0600-1800 daily. They are about a 20-minute walk from the market square: go along Grenville Street, past the cathedrals, turn right into Bentinck Square, right again and continue uphill to the gate. Or take a bus, EC$1 from the terminal.

Fort Charlotte
The views of Kingstown & surroundings are spectacular. On a clear day the Grenadines & even Grenada are visible

Fort Charlotte (completed 1805) is on the promontory on the north side of Kingstown Bay, 636 ft above sea level, 15 minutes' drive out of town (EC$1.50 from bus terminal to village below, if you ask the driver he might take you into the fort for EC$1-2, worth it if it is hot). Although the fort was designed to fend off attacks from the sea, the main threat was the Black Caribs and many of its 34 guns (some of which are still in place) therefore faced inland. The gatehouse, 1806, was where Major Champion of the Royal Scots Fusiliers was killed on 13 October 1824 (see plaque in St George's Cathedral) by Private Ballasty. The murderer was executed at the scene of the crime. In the old barrack rooms, a series of paintings shows the early history of St Vincent. Painted by William Linzest Prescott in 1972, they suffer from poor lighting and their condition is deteriorating. There is also a coast guard lookout which controls the comings and goings of ships entering the port. Ask the guard to point out landmarks to you. Below, the ruins of a military hospital can be seen, as well as a bathing pool at sea level on the end of the point, used when the fort housed people suffering from yaws. The National Trust and the Caribbean Conservation Association (CCA) are proposing to develop Fort Charlotte as part of an Eastern Caribbean plan for historic military sites, with an Interpretive Centre, gift shop and museum. The National Trust of St Vincent and the Grenadines, PO Box 752, T4562591, has further information.

Around the island

The highest peak on the island, La Soufrière volcano, rises to about 4,000 ft. In 1970 an island reared itself up out of the lake in the crater: it smokes and the water round it is very warm. Hiking to the volcano is very popular, but you must leave very early in the morning and allow a full day for the trip. About two miles north of Georgetown (van from Kingstown to Georgetown EC$4, you can ask the driver to make a detour to the start of the trail for an extra charge) on the Windward side you cross the Dry River, then take a left fork and walk/drive through banana plantations to where the trail begins. It takes about three hours to reach the crater edge and it is a strenuous hike along a marked trail, the first three miles are through the Rabacca plantation, then up, along Bamboo Ridge and all the way to the crater's magnificent edge; the top can be cloudy, windy, cold and rainy, take adequate clothing and footwear. A walking stick is recommended. There is an alternative, unmarked and even more challenging route from the Leeward side starting from the end of the road after Richmond, but you will need a guide. After crossing a river delta, turn right into a ravine and climb; it will take about four hours. There are guided tours which start on the Windward side and end on the Leeward side, about 6-7 hours, around US$30 if there are about ten of you, with the advantage that you are met at your destination by the driver and do not have to worry about finding scarce public transport. Leave an extra set of clothes in the van in case you get wet through. Take water and insect repellent.

An easier climb is up **Mount St Andrew**, near Kingstown. A tarmac track runs up to the radio mast on the summit of the peak, at 2,413 ft, passing first through banana and vegetable gardens and then through forest. There are no parrots but otherwise virtually all the species of birds which can be found on the Vermont Nature Trail. It is particularly good for the Antillean crested hummingbird and black hawks. The view from the summit covers the Grenadines and the Vermont and Mesopotamia valleys. To reach the track either take a van running along the Leeward Highway and ask to be put down at the junction with the Mount St Andrew road, or start your walk in Kingstown.

Works are being undertaken to improve the surface of the roads and most of the beauty spots are accessible by road. The Leeward Highway is a dramatic drive, passing through Questelles and Layou. Much of this road has been improved to **Barrouallie** (pronounced Barrelly), a small whaling village. This drive along the west coast towards La Soufrière should not be missed; it has been described as a 'tropical corniche'. There are lush valleys and magnificent seaviews. It is a very crumpled landscape and the road is steep and twisty. Minibuses race along at great speed and some passengers complain of queasiness.

The road leaves Kingstown and initially heads inland. There are views down into Campden Park Bay, where the East Caribbean Group of Companies has a deep water port complex and flour mill. The road passes through the small village of Questelles before rejoining the coast briefly at Buccament Bay and down into Layou where there are a few excellent examples of gingerbread houses. Up the Buccament Valley at Peniston is the *Emerald Valley Casino*, which has villa accommodation, but you should check before going there as it is not always open and the resort is in financial difficulties, T4567824, www.emeraldvalleycasino.com

La Soufrière & Mount St Andrew

The Leeward coast
The drive from Kingstown to the end of the road at Richmond takes about 2 hrs

There are some interesting **petroglyphs** and **rock carvings** dating back to the Siboney, Arawak and Carib eras. The best known are just north of Layou, carved on a huge boulder next to a stream. They can only be visited on payment of US$2 for the owner, Mr Victor Hendrickson to open the gate to the fenced off area. Ask the local children to show you his house and then the petroglyphs (for a tip), well worth a visit.

Passing Mount Wynne and Peter's Hope, **Barrouallie** is the next village of any size. It is a fishing village and on the beach are fishing boats and nets while pigs and chickens scratch about. The local speciality catch is 'black fish', in reality a short finned pilot whale, which grows to about 6 m. Here there is a petroglyph known as the Ogham Stone, dated at 800 BC in the playground of the Anglican secondary school. There is a theory that it is in Celtic script. If the children are not in class they will highlight the picture in white chalk for you. The road also passes through the remains of a sugar mill (the furnace chimney is still standing) and then heads inland from the popular anchorage and restaurant at Wallilabou Bay. A stone gateway marks the entrance to the **Wallilabou Falls** (Wally-la-boo). You can swim here but the falls are not much more than a spurt (2 m at the most). There are no changing rooms here. On the opposite side of the road is a nutmeg plantation. You can get there by car or by bus from Little Tokyo Fish Market to Barrouallie and walk from there.

The road goes inland along the Wallilabou valley before quickly rising over the ridge into the North Leeward district. From here onwards all the villages are clearly marked with good road signs. The wooden pipeline from the hydroelectric scheme follows the road and is most visible at the aptly named Spring Village. Another pretty beach is reached at Cumberland and the road climbs quickly to Coulls Hill with perhaps the best view on the coast. The road through *Chateaubelair* (restaurant, use their facilities to change for a swim and have a snack), skirting Petit Bordel (drugs financed speed boats on the beach) with small islands offshore to **Richmond** and Wallibou beach is most attractive. There are some beach facilities at Wallibou.

Another set of falls, also on the Leeward side, is 20 miles north of Kingstown; **Petit Wallibou Falls** are a double waterfall in a very remote region and you can bathe at the bottom of the second waterfall. To get there, go through Richmond and turn right up the side road beside the (closed) Richmond Vale Academy; follow this road for one mile, it then turns into a track for two miles. At the river the top of the waterfall is on your left. There is a steep climb on the left hand side of the waterfall to reach the pool where you can swim. **Trinity Falls** are 45 minutes' walk from Richmond in the Wallibou Valley, set deep in a canyon in the rainforest. The only known hot springs are in the canyon, having appeared since the last volcanic eruption. The road has been badly eroded and it is best to park about 40 minutes' walk from the car park, except that there is a lot of loose gravel and you may fall. From the car park it is another 45 minutes' walk to the Falls (reasonable physical fitness required), through lovely rainforest. There is a sign down the river warning about undertow, but note that this also applies to the pool by the Falls. The current is very strong, swimmers have been sucked under and the sides are steep, with nothing to hold on to. In addition, the wind erosion has loosened boulders which are now potentially dangerous.

A boat trip to the falls of **Baleine** (on the northwest coast) is recommended. A few minutes up a river which originates on Soufrière, you come to the falls. At the base is a natural swimming pool. You can climb up the side behind the falls and then jump off into the pool. It is possible to reach the falls on foot, but the easiest way is to take an excursion by motor boat, which includes a stop for snorkelling, and a picnic lunch, for US$35-40. A new walkway was to be built by end-2001, allowing boats to tie up at a jetty and passengers to walk easily to the falls, thereby encouraging cruise ship tourism. Previously you had to anchor offshore, swim to the mouth of the river and then clamber over rocks to get to the pool.

The Windward coast   The Queens Drive takes you into the hills south of Kingstown and gives splendid views all around. The Marriaqua Valley with its numerous streams is particularly beautiful. In the Valley, beyond Mesopotamia (commonly known as Mespo), the lush, tropical gardens of **Montreal** are worth a visit; anthuriums are grown commercially there, but only for the domestic market. The owner, Timothy Vaughn, is a well-known landscape gardener in Europe and this is his first tropical garden, full of organic flowers and colourful foliage, with glorious views of Argyll and Mesopotamia Valley. It is designed in three sections, one of which includes a wild garden leading down to a river and a pool where you can swim. ■ *Open Dec-Aug, 0900-1600, closed Sun and holidays, EC$5.* A commercial flower farm run by the Hadley family on the Windward coast can be visited by prior arrangement. Here they grow heliconias, anthuriums and orchids, acres of different coloured flowers are grown to exacting standards.

The road meets the **Windward Highway** at Peruvian Vale. It gets progressively drier as the road goes north hugging yellow sandstone cliffs which contrast with the white waves surging in towards the black volcanic beaches. A number of banana packaging stations are passed especially around Colonarie. There is a particularly impressive view of the coast just after the **Black Point tunnel**. The tunnel is 350 ft long and was constructed by Colonel Thomas Browne using Carib and African slaves in 1815. It was blasted through volcanic rock from one bay to the other and the drill holes are still visible, as are storage rooms and recesses for candles. It is very atmospheric and there are a few bats as well as local people washing in the water which pours out of the rock. It provided an important link with the sugar estates in the north and sugar was hauled through the tunnel to be loaded on to boats in Byera Bay. Black sand Byera Beach is the longest in St Vincent and the sea is rough, but in the days of the sugar plantations the coast curved round more giving greater protection to shipping and there was a jetty. You can not see the tunnel from the road, which goes over the top of the headland above it. Turn down towards the sea between the gas station and the river down a dirt road which leads to Black Point Recreation Site where cricket is played and hundreds of people gather for Easter Monday celebrations.

Little waterfalls and pools, such as Kiss Me and Cheyne Spout, can be found on river walks from the Windward Highway, contact Grenadine Escape

Georgetown is almost like a ghost town, with one or two quite well maintained houses, the rest haven't been painted for years. It is an economically depressed area since the sugar mill closed a few years ago. The economy has also suffered from the loss of sea cotton and arrow root as well as sugar and now there are problems with bananas. A number of houses have been abandoned. There are lots of churches. The Anglican church is a miniature of St George's Cathedral in Kingstown. There is, however, a restaurant and guest house, which does good business from visitors to the volcano, see above.

The road to **Sandy Bay** (beyond Georgetown), where St Vincent's remaining Black Caribs live, is now good, however you have to cross the Dry River, a jumble of rocks, grit, rubbish and dead wood swept down from the mountains above, which sometimes is not dry and therefore not passable. Rocks and sand are extracted for the building industry. Sandy Bay is poor but beyond it is an even poorer village along a rough dirt road, **Owia**. Here is **Salt Pond**, a natural area of tidal pools filled with small marine life. The rough Atlantic crashes around the huge boulders and lava formations and is very picturesque. The villagers have planted flowers and made steps down to the Salt Pond area. There is also an arrowroot processing factory which can be visited. Past Owia is **Fancy**, the poorest village on the island, also Black Carib and very isolated, reached by a rough jeep track which makes a pleasant walk. Baleine Falls (see above) are a two mile hike from here around the tip of the island, rugged and not recommended for the unadventurous. Fishing boats can be hired in Fancy to collect you (do not pay in advance).

The airport is just southeast of Kingstown at **Arnos Vale**, a residential area where there is also a sports complex. The road runs round the runway and down towards the coast at Indian Bay. There are several hotels in this area, stretching along the seafront to Calliaqua Bay. It is very pleasant, with light sand beaches, Young Island just offshore, Bequia in the distance and dozens of yachts moored offshore. Many people

The south

Windward Islands

stay here rather than in the capital, as it is an easy commute into Kingstown if you need to go in, while there are marinas, dive shops, the best restaurants and watersports facilities here. The southeast of the island is drier and has different vegetation and birdlife. Take a van running to Stubbs and alight at the post office by the Brighton road junction. Walk into Brighton village and find a guide who can lead you to see, among others, the mangrove cuckoo, smooth-billed ani, broad-winged hawk and green heron. When tidal conditions are right it is possible to cross to Milligan Cay. To see seabirds in the bay visit early morning or late afternoon. The beaches north of here on the Atlantic coast are dramatic, with crashing waves, but do not swim here. The currents are dangerous and even strong swimmers have drowned so do not take risks.

Young Island

Pick up the phone at the crossing to see if you will be allowed over

A tiny, privately-owned islet, 200 yds off the coast at Villa, with the only resort hotel on St Vincent. **Fort Duvernette**, on a 195-ft high rock just off Young Island, was built at the beginning of the 19th century to defend Calliaqua Bay. The 100 steps up to the fort have been partially washed away by hurricanes and rock falls have left it unsafe so you can no longer visit the fort. **LL** *Young Island Resort*, T4584826, F4574567, www.youngisland.com; all accommodation in 30 cottages (MAP), yachts are US$500-650 per day, part sailing and honeymoon packages available. There is a lovely lagoon swimming pool, surrounded by tropical flowers and a golden sand beach overlooking Indian Bay, helped along with imported sand after Hurricane Lenny removed what was there before.

Essentials

Sleeping

Government tax of 7% on hotel rooms; most add a 10% service charge. Camping is not encouraged. There are no organized campsites

Kingstown **LL-L** *Camelot Inn*, T4562100, F4562233, caminn@caribsurf.com Originally the governor's residence and the oldest guest house on the island, but refurbished 1996 with 22 luxury rooms and 2 honeymoon suites, Camelot theme rigorously carried through with *King Arthur's Restaurant*, the Knight's room, etc, very upmarket but for sale in 2001, pool, tennis, gym, beauty salon, free transport to beach, quite a walk into town through an unsavoury area. **L-A** *Cara Lodge*, T4561897, F4562027, www.carahotels.com The best place to stay in town, good for business travellers, within walking distance of the centre but up a hill away from the bustle, large rooms or excellent suites in a separate building across the road, email and other business facilities, good restaurant and bar, friendly and efficient service. On Upper Bay St, **A-B** *Cobblestone Inn*, T4561937, F4561938, cobblestone@caribsurf.com Upstairs in a charming building which used to be a sugar and arrowroot warehouse, violet and white décor, mostly quiet but avoid room 22, noisy from street below, rooms good, breakfast extra, restaurant and bar.**C** *Kingstown Park Inn*, T4572964, F4572505. 7 rooms, fans, a/c in 1 room,TV. **D** *Bella Vista Inn*, behind *Camelot*, Kingstown Park, T/F4572757. 7 rooms, 3 with private bath, fans, run by Nzinga Miguel and her daughter Cleopatra, friendly, homely atmosphere, breakfast EC$10, dinner on request EC$15. **D-E** *Leslie's Guest House*, Kingstown Park, T4562863, 1 min from *Camelot*. 10-min walk downhill to town, shared bathroom, clean, cool, nice garden, large veranda, Leslie Waldron very friendly and helpful. **Close to Kingstown: AL-A** *Tropic Breeze Hotel*, Queen's Drive, T4584618, F4564592, www.tropicbreezesvg.com 17 rooms with balconies, 6 a/c, restaurant, bar, pool. **B** *New Montrose Hotel*, T4570172, F4570213, www.newmontrosehotel.com 25 modern rooms, some with kitchenettes, balcony, TV, phone, view of Kingstown and Grenadines, walking distance from Botanical Gardens.

There are lots of apartments close to the sea, contact the Tourist Office for a list

Villa and Indian Bay (3 miles from town, close to airport) **LL-AL** *Grand View Beach*, Villa Point, T4584811, F4574174, www.grandviewhotel.com A former cotton plantation house, 19 rooms, 1st class, pool, tennis, squash, fully-equipped gym, excursions arranged, restaurant, room service. **LL-AL** *Sunset Shores*, T4584411, F4574800, www.sunsetshores.com 32 rooms, a/c, TV, on the beach, sunfish, windsurfers, snorkelling gear, pool, dining room, bar. **AL** *Villa Lodge Hotel* and the adjacent *Breezeville Apartments*, Villa Point, T4584641, F4574468, www.villalodge.com 10 rooms and 10 1-2 bedroom apartments overlooking Indian Bay, discounts for longer stay, a/c, fans, TV, internet access, pool with lovely view, restaurant, bar. **AL-A** *The Lagoon Marina and Hotel*, Blue Lagoon, Ratho Mill, T/F4584308, www.lagoonmarina.com 19 rooms with lovely view, Sunsail yacht charter, full service marina, bar, restaurant, nice pool with slide, scuba diving, windsurfing. **AL-B** *Casa de Columbus*, T4584001, F4574777, www.casadecolumbus.com Hotel on beach, nice verandah, good snorkelling just outside the hotel, daily or weekly rates, 2 bedroomed apartments available, sleep 3-4, a/c, kitchenettes, restaurant, watersports nearby. **A-B** *Beachcombers Hotel*, T4584283, F4584385, www.beachcombershotel.com Small, family-run, includes breakfast, laundry service, restaurant and bar, also sauna and steam room. **A-B** *Coconut Beach Inn*, T/F4574900. Nice, clean, comfortable rooms, beautiful seaview, good restaurant (see below). **B-C** *Umbrella Beach*, T4584651, F4574930. 9 double rooms with kitchen, bath, balcony, restaurant, pool, tennis, nice, simple, opposite Young Island. **C** *TranQuillity Beach Apartment Hotel*, Indian Bay, T4584021, F4574792. Excellent view, kitchen facilities, fans, TV, laundry service, restaurant, clean, friendly, very helpful owners, Mr and Mrs Providence. **D** *Sea Breeze Guest House*, Arnos Vale, near airport, T4584969. Cooking facilities, 6 rooms with bath, no credit cards, noisy, friendly, helpful, bus to town or airport from the door.

Leeward coast **LL** *Petit Byahaut*, T/F4577008, VHF68, www.outahere.com/petitbyahaut, set in a 50-acre valley in a lovely secluded bay with a nice beach, very pretty. No road, TV or phones, luxury 10 ft x 13 ft tents with floors, queen-sized bed, shower, toilet, sink, sitting area and hammock in each tent, includes all meals, great snorkelling, sail and row boats, kayaks, hiking, airport and water taxi transfer, 3 night minimum stay, scuba diving from beach or kayaks included but diver certification and first dive checkout (US$50) required, guided dives US$40 per person, you can hire the whole resort for 8-14 people, access only by boat, ecological and conservation emphasis, solar powered.

Windward coast **D** *Ferdie's Footsteps*, on the main street in Georgetown, red pillars and blue walls, shop downstairs, entrance at the side on Cambridge St, T4586433. Food and accommodation, also 3-bedroom house for monthly rental.

Kingstown *Vee-Jay's* restaurant on Lower Bay St is friendly and offers good local food, open Mon-Sat 1000-1900, Fri until late, also *Vee-Jay's Rooftop Diner & Pub* on Upper Bay St, T457-2845/1395, above Roger's Photo Studios. Open Mon-Sat 0900-2200, sandwiches, rotis etc for lunch, good local juices, cocktail bar, entrées EC$12-45, great steel band. *The Attic*, West Indian/European, multi-screen sports broadcasts, a/c, open 1100 until late. *Bounty Restaurant and Art Gallery*, Egmont St, upstairs, T4561776. The oldest restaurant in town, windows open to catch the breeze, breakfast and lunch, patties, rotis, cakes and pastries, iced coffee/tea, Mon-Fri 0730-1700, Sat 0730-1330. *Rainbow Palace*, West Indian fast food, Grenville St, T4561763. Open Mon-Fri 0800-1630, Sat 0800-1400. For genuine West Indian food and local company *Basil's Bar and Restaurant* (see below) has a branch underneath the *Cobblestone Inn*, in Upper Bay St, T4572713. Buffet 1200-1400 Mon-Fri for hungry people,

Eating
Kingstown has several restaurants in the centre serving local food or fast food, but the better restaurants are in the Villa beach area several miles east

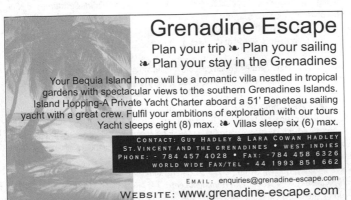

EC$32, acceptable but not startling, also à la carte lunch and dinner, open 0800-2200, pleasant for an evening drink and a chat. *Cobblestone Roof Top Restaurant*, belonging to the *Cobblestone Inn*, T4561937. West Indian lunches and hamburgers, open Mon-Sat 0700-1500, good place for breakfast. *Sweetie Pie Bakery and Café*, between the Grenadines dock and the shops.

Fast food At the bus station (Little Tokyo) you can buy freshly grilled chicken and corn cobs, good value and tasty. Cafés on the jetty by ferry boats serve excellent, cheap, local food, eg salt cod rolls with hot pepper sauce. On market days fruit is plentiful and cheap, great bananas. Takeaway food from *Pizza Party*, T4564932, in Arnos Vale by the airport. Delivery and takeaway of pizza, chicken, ice cream, snacks, until 2300, no credit cards. *Chung Wua*, Upper Bay St, T4572566. Open Mon-Sat 1100-2230, Sun 1700-2200, Chinese eat in or takeaway, no credit cards, from EC$10. *Royal Castle*, is on Grenville St. Chicken meal EC$8.10, veggie burger EC$5.25, veggie platter EC$8.75.

Villa area *The French Restaurant*, T4584972. VHF Channel 68, open Mon-Sat 0900-2130, Sun 1700-2130 (in high season), prices EC$40-85 for main course, lobster from the tank, lovely beach view. The *Lime Restaurant & Pub* on the waterfront at Villa, T4584227. A casual menu and a dinner menu, reasonable prices, credit cards accepted, open 0930-2400. *Beachcombers* on Villa Beach, T4584283. Light fare and drinks, very casual, pizzas, samosas, burgers, popular with children, good value, or à la carte menu, open air, food 0700-2200, bar open later, happy hour 1700-1830. *Slicks*, T4575783. VHF68, moderate prices, building decorated with artwork of owner and other local artists, light meals or full dinners, lobster, steak, Italian, French, US and West Indian cuisine. *The Aquatic Club*, T4584205. West Indian and international, lunch 1100-1400, dinner 1800. The adventurous should try *Papa Spoon's Rasta Ranch* on the Callaquia playing field for inexpensive local, all natural food served in calabash bowls. *Villa Lodge Hotel* is a good place to eat, not cheap but wonderful piña colada. *Sunset Shores Restaurant*, overlooking Young Island, T4584411 for reservations. International, full English, West Indian or continental breakfast, open 0700-2130, buffet with live entertainment Wed, barbecue Sat, Sun brunch 1200-1500, credit cards. *Surfside Beachbar/Restaurant*, T4575362. Informal Continental/West Indian, pizza and seafood, 1000-2200, closed Mon. *Barefoot Bistro*, T4569880. International, waterfront pub-style restaurant with yachtsmen's specials and light meals available on the verandah, open 0800-2300 daily, dinghy dock. *Triangle Pub*, Villa Flat, Calliaqua, T4574270. Callaloo soup, curried conch, conch souse and other fishy features, barbeque and live music Fri night, open daily from 1100.

Leeward Coast *Stephens Hideout*, T4582325. West Indian and seafood, restaurant on Leeward Highway, Cumberland Bay, Beach Bar on the bay, call ahead for made to order meals or picnic on beach, open 0900-2230, no credit cards, tours arranged. *Wallilabou Anchorage*, T4587270. Caters mainly for yachties, mooring facilities, West Indian specialities, chicken, fish or veg lunch, juices, email access EC$5/15 mins. *Beach Front Restaurant & Bar*, Chateaubelair, T4582853. Eat inside or outdoors, roof terrace with shade, good view of bay, rotis and fish meals for lunch, happy hour Fri, there can be a swell here so if you are on a yacht it is sometimes better to stop at Wallilabou.

Windward Coast *Ferdie's Footsteps*, see Sleeping above, Georgetown. Local food, useful stop for lunch if you have climbed the volcano, inexpensive.

Nightlife

Several hotels and restaurants have live music some evenings, especially in high season. There is always something going on in the Villa area

Emerald Valley Casino, T4567824. Call for transport, closed Tue. *Basils Too*, T4584205. Offers lunch, dinner and dancing on Villa Beach by Young Island. Check for happy hours at bars for lower-priced drinks, snacks and often entertainment. *Aquatic*, in Villa (see restaurants). Is one of the main nightspots on the island, admission EC$20, more if there is a live band, which there sometimes is at weekends. *Calliaqua Culture Pot*, is a form of street party in the beach area, where you can find music and food, singing and dancing, arts and crafts, every Fri from 2000. In Kingstown, *Touch Entertainment Centre*, T4571825. Opened its dance hall in 1993, run by the Vincentian band, *Touch*. *The Attic*, see Eating above. Nightly live entertainment, jazz, karaoke, dancing, large screen video, music bar open 1200 till late. Other nighttime places are *Veejays* on Upper Bay St and *Dano's* on Grenville St. *Russell's Cinema*; *Cinerama*, T4856364. 3 screens, every night.

St Vincent's carnival, called **Vincy Mas** , is held in the last week of *June* and the 1st week of **Festivals**
July for 10 days. Mas is short for masquerade, and the 3 main elements of the carnival are the costume bands, the steel bands and the calypso. During the day there is J'Ouverte, ole mas, children's carnival and steel bands through Kingstown's streets. At night calypsonians perform in 'tents', there is the King and Queen of the bands show, the steel bands competition and Miss Carival, a beauty competition with contestants from other Caribbean countries (a talent contest, a beauty contest and local historical dress). Thousands of visitors come to take part, many from Trinidad. From *16-24 December*, there is a **Carolling Competition** and **Nine Mornings Festival**, during which, for 9 mornings, people parade through Kingstown and dances are held from 0100. There is also an art and craft exhibition.

Kingstown market (do not take photos of the vendors) for excellent fresh fruit and vegeta-   **Shopping**
bles and supermarkets. Grocery and wine availability is improving, with several gourmet provisioning spots catering to yachts and guests staying on the island; *Standard Grocery*, Lower Middle Street, Kingstown, T4561553; *CK Greaves Co Ltd*, Upper Bay Street, Kingstown and Arnos Vale; *Sunrise Supermarket*, opposite airport at Arnos Vale, T4571074. One of the best in the Caribbean, very well stocked. *Midway*, near cricket field in Arnos Vale, T4565430. Open Mon-Sat 0730-2100, Sun 0730-1200, wide selection and delivery service, provisions for yachts. The local rum is Sunset, at around US$4-5, except for the very strong rum which will set you back about US$5-6 a bottle and blow your head off.

The St Vincent Philatelic Society on Bay Street, between Higginson Street and River Road, sells stamps in every colour, size and amount for the novice and collector alike. Service is helpful but slow in this second floor warehouse, complete with guard. *The Artisans Art & Craft Centre*, Bay Street, T4562306. Upstairs in the Bonadie Building, sells handicrafts from about 70 artisans around the country, open Mon-Fri 0830-1600, Sat 0830-1200. For handicrafts, resort wear and books, *Noah's Arkade*, Blue Caribbean Building, Bay Street, Kingstown (T4571513, F4569305, lmg@caribsurf.com), and at the *Frangipani* on Bequia (T4583424). *Nzimbu Arts & Craft*, McKies Hill, T4571677, www.gligli.com Goat skin drums, batik and banana leaf artwork, Nzimbu can often be found on Bay St on Fri, selling his crafts on the roadside.

SVG Tours, T4584534, F4564721, svgtours@caribsurf.com Run by Dominique David, an   **Tour operators**
agronomist by training and very interesting on farming and botany. Hikes up the volcano, tours of the rainforest, waterfalls, gardens and nature trails, also arranges day trips to other islands and sailing. *HazECO Tours*, T4578634, F4578105, www.begos.com/hazecotour Similar tours, also with emphasis on nature. See Beaches and watersports for tours by sea.

Air *LIAT* flies from Antigua, Barbados, Beef Island (BVI), Dominica, Grenada, Guadeloupe,   **Transport**
Martinique, Port of Spain (Trinidad), St Lucia and San Juan (Puerto Rico). *BWIA* flies from Barbados and Port of Spain. Inter island charters are also operated by *SVGAir* and *Mustique Airways*. *SVGAir* has daily scheduled flights Barbados-Bequia as well as to/from Grenada and internal Grenadines flights. Their air taxi service will only fly for two or more passengers, but you may buy two seats. Not only do they weigh your luggage, but small planes also need to know the weight of their passengers, so be prepared to divulge this information. **Airport** ET Joshua airport, small and rather chaotic, is two miles from Kingstown. The taxi fare to town is EC$20 (with other fares ranging from EC$15-40 for nearer or more distant hotels set by government); minibus to Kingstown EC$1.50, 10 mins. Frequent and easy minibuses also run east if you need to get to Young Island or Calliaqua. The airport currency exchange desk is open Mon-Fri 0830-1230, 1530-1730, often more convenient than a bank and with shorter queues, Visa/Mastercard accepted. If your luggage is lost en route to St Vincent, obtain a Property Irregularity Report (PIR) from the airline otherwise you will have to keep coming back to the airport to check if it has arrived. **Sea** *Windward Lines Ltd* operates a passenger and cargo ferry service on the *MV Windward* from Trinidad (suspended 2001). In Kingston,

the offices of Windward Lines are up a steep flight of steps from the ferry. See below for inter-island ferries.

Local   Road Minibuses from Kingstown leave from the Little Tokyo Fish Market terminal to all parts of St Vincent island, including a frequent service to Villa and Indian Bay, the main hotel area; they stop on demand rather than at bus stops. At the terminal they crowd round the entrance competing for customers rather than park in the bays provided. They are a popular means of transport because they are inexpensive and give an opportunity to see local life. No service on Sun or holidays. Fares start at EC$1, rising to EC$2 (Layou), EC$4 (Georgetown on the Windward coast), to EC$5 to the Black Carib settlement at Sandy Bay in the northeast (this is a difficult route, though, because buses leave Sandy Bay early in the morning for Kingstown, and return in the afternoon). The number of vans starting in Kingstown and running to Owia or Fancy in the north is limited. The best way is to take the early bus to Georgetown and try to catch one of the two vans running between Georgetown and Fancy (EC$10). To get to Richmond in the northwest take a bus to Barrouallie and seek onward transport from there. It is worthwhile to make a day trip to Mesopotamia (Mespo) by bus (EC$2.50).

Car Driving is on the left. A local driving licence, costing EC$40, must be purchased at the airport, the police station in Bay Street, or the Licensing Authority on Halifax Street, on presentation of your home licence. However, there is no need to pay if you have an International Driving Permit and get it stamped at the central police station. There are limited road signs on St Vincent. **Car hire** Note that the use of cars on the island is limited, so that only jeeps may be used to go beyond Georgetown on the east coast. Charges at *Kim's* (T4561884, F4561681, mail@kimsrentals.com) for example are: EC$100 per day for a car, with restrictions on where you drive in the north, EC$125 for a jeep, 60 miles free per day, EC$1 per mile thereafter, weekly rental gives one day free, EC$1,000 excess deposit in advance, delivery or collection anywhere on the island, phone from airport for collection to save taxi hassle, credit cards accepted. Among other agencies (all offering similar rates and terms) are *Ben's* T/F4562907, *David's* T/F4564026, *Star Garage* T4561743, F4562726, *UNICO* T4565744, F4565745.

Bicycles Cycling is rewarding but be careful in the north, which is a drug producing area. The ride between Layou and Richmond is a strenuous four hours one way, but absolutely spectacular. Expect long, steep hills and lots of them. *Sailors Cycle Centre*, T4571712, http:\Vincy.com/ Sailor's.htm Middle St, owned by Trevor 'Sailor' Bailey, who also operates Sailor's Wilderness Tours for escorted hiking and biking.

Taxi Taxi fares are fixed by the Government but you must check with the driver first to avoid overcharging. Late at night and early morning fares are raised. Kingstown to Airport EC$20, Indian Bay EC$25, Mesopotamia EC$40, Layou EC$40, Orange Hill EC$80, Blue Lagoon EC$35, airport to Young Island EC$20, airport to Blue Lagoon EC$25. Hourly hire EC$40 per hour. *Vibie Taxi* recommended, T4565288, 4565781, helpful. *Young Island Taxi Association* can be reached through Young Island on VHF 68.

Directory   Airlines LIAT, Halifax Street, Kingstown, T4571821 for reservations, airport office T4584841, F4572000, on Union Island T4588230; *Mustique Airways*, T458-3183/4380, F4564586; *SVGAIR*, Blue Lagoon, St Vincent, T4575124, 4583713, F4575077, www.svgair.com, air taxi service to Barbados, Martinique, St Lucia, Grenada and within the Grenadines; *Trans Island Air (TIA)*, T246-4181654, F246-4280916. **Banks** *Barclays Bank Plc, Scotia Bank, National Commercial Bank* of St Vincent, all on Halifax Street. The NCB, opposite the market, is open Mon-Thu 0800-1300, Fri 0800-1700, Visa and Mastercard, exchange, but no ATM. Another NCB branch on Lower Bay St is open Mon-Fri 0900-1500 (Visa, MC) Caribbean Banking Corporation, 81 South River Road on the corner with Middle St opposite the Old Library, Kingstown (open Mon-Thu 0800-1300, Fri 0800-1700, exchange and ATM facilities), and at Port Elizabeth, Bequia. *National Commercial Bank* has branches at ET Joshua airport, Georgetown, Barrouallie and agencies at Layou and Chateaubelair. When you cash TCs you can take half in US dollars and half in EC dollars if you wish. Some banks have 24-hr ATMs, but they will not necessarily accept your card. **Embassies & consulates** *UK*, British High Commission, Grenville Street, Box 132, Kingstown, T4571701 (after hours T4584381), F4562750; *Netherlands* Consulate, in the East

Caribbean Group of Companies building in Campden Park, T4571918; *China*, Murray Road, T4562431; *Venezuela*, Granby Street, T4561374; *France*, Middle Street, Box 364, Kingstown, T4561615; *Italy*, Queen's Drive, T4564774. **Communications Internet** Some hotels, such as *Cara Lodge*, offer email and internet service for guests, while marinas (eg *The Lagoon* and *Mariners Hotel*) and other places frequented by yachties are good places to try. **Post:** Halifax Street. Open 0830-1500 (0830-1130 on Sat, closed Sun). *St Vincent Philatelic Services Ltd*, General Post Office, T4571911, F4562383; for old and new issues, World of Stamps, Bay 43 Building, Lower Bay Street, Kingstown. **Telephone:** operated by Cable and Wireless, on Halifax Street; there is a 5% tax on international phone calls. Phone cards and fax available. Portable phones can be rented through *Boatphone* or you can register your own cellular phone with them upon arrival, T4562800. The international code for St Vincent is 784, followed by a seven-digit local number. From many cardphones you can reach USA Direct by dialling 1-800-8722881. **Medical facilities** *Kingston General Hospital*, T4561185. Emergency T999. **Tourist information** Local tourist office: *St Vincent and the Grenadines Department of Tourism*, 3rd floor, Finance Complex, Bay Street, PO Box 834, Kingstown, T4571502, F4562610, www.svgtourism.com, open Mon-Fri 0800-1200, 1300-1615; helpful desk at ET Joshua airport, T4584379, hotel reservation EC$1; on Bequia (by the jetty), T4583286, open Sun-Fri 0900-1230, 1330-1600, Sat morning only; on Union Island, between the dock and the *Clifton Beach Hotel*, T4588350, open daily 0800-1200, 1300-1600. There is a desk in the arrivals hall at the Grantley Adams airport on Barbados, open daily from 1300 until 2000 or the last flight to St Vincent (T4280961). This is useful for transfers to LIAT after an international flight. The Tourist Office and the Hotel Association (www.svghotels.com) publish *Escape*, a good magazine on the islands giving details of accommodation, restaurants and shopping as well as articles of interest. Bequia publishes its own brochure, *Holiday Bequia*, and Mustique Airways also has a magazine. **Maps:** a map of St Vincent, 1:50,000 (and Kingstown, 1:10,000), EC$15, is available from the Ministry of Agriculture, Lands and Survey Department, Murray Road. In 1992 the Ordnance Survey (Southampton, UK) brought out a tourist map of St Vincent, 1:50,000, with insert of Kingstown, 1:10,000, double sided with Grenadines on the reverse, with text panels giving information, walks etc, but it is not available in St Vincent.

The Grenadines

The Grenadines, divided politically between St Vincent and Grenada, are a string of 100 tiny, rocky islands and cays stretching across some 35 miles of sea between the two. They are still very much off the beaten track as far as tourists are concerned, but are popular with yachtsmen. The southern Grenadines are particularly beautiful, a cluster of picturesque, hilly islands with glorious white sand beaches and rocky coves, excellent harbours and lots of opportunities for snorkelling, diving and other watersports.

Getting there
Island hopping by boat is easy and cheap, but be flexible in your schedule. Be prepared to get wet from the spray as the crossings are often rough

Sea All the ferries are old and look as though they are held together with many layers of paint. However, they are cheap and cheerful and an excellent way of getting around if the sea is not too rough. Admiralty Transport Co Ltd, T4583348 for information, admiraltrans@caribsurf.com run 2 ferries: MV *Admiral 1* and MV *Admiral II*, with interchangeable schedules from Kingstown to Bequia, 1hr, EC$15 one way, EC$28 return on the same boat. They start in Bequia, leaving there at 0630, 0730, 1400 and 1700 Mon-Fri, departing Kingstown at 0900, 1030, 1630 and 1900. On Sat the ferry departs Bequia 0630, 1015 and 1700, departing Kingstown 0900, 1230 and 1900, on Sun and holidays it leaves Bequia at 0730 and 1700, departs Kingstown at 0900 and 1900. The MV *Bequia Express*, T4583472, bequiaexpress@caribsurf.com also runs on the same route, from Bequia 0630 and 0930 Mon-Fri, returning from Kingstown 0800 and 1300, with additional services on Mon, Wed and Fri at 1630 from Bequia and 1800 from St Vincent; on Sat it leaves Bequia at 0630 and returns from Kingstown at 1130; on Sun and holidays it departs Bequia at 0700 and 1630, returning at 0930 and 1800.

MV *Barracouda* sails on south on Mon and Thu from Kingstown at around 1030 to Bequia, Canouan, Mayreau and Union Island, arriving at around 1530-1600; on Tue and Fri she returns to St Vincent via Mayreau, Canouan and Bequia, leaving Union Island at 0630, arriving St Vincent 1200. On Sat she sails Kingstown-Union-Kingstown with no intermediate stops. All times are approximate, depending on the amount of goods to be loaded and schedules change frequently. Cargo takes priority and passengers are allowed on board once all the goods are stowed.

On holidays day trips are often arranged, eg from Kingstown to the beach on Canouan. There are 3-4 cabins, two of which are used by the crew but you can negotiate for one quite cheaply if you need it. The *Barracouda* is the islands' main regular transport and carries everything, families and their goods, goats and generators; she rolls through the sea and the trip can be highly entertaining but note that the timetable is very unreliable. Fares: one stop EC$15, two stops EC$20, three stops EC$25 etc, eg Kingstown to Bequia EC$15, to Canouan EC$20, to Mayreau EC$25, to Union EC$30; Bequia to Canouan EC$15, to Mayreau EC$20, to Union EC$25; Canouan to Mayreau EC$15, Union EC$20; Mayreau to Union EC$15.

For other services, check at the Grenadines dock in Kingstown. There are often excursions from Kingstown to Bequia and Mustique on Sun. From Bequia you can take a boat trip to Mustique for US$40 per person by speedboat from Friendship Bay or by catamaran from Port Elizabeth, ask at Sunsports at *Gingerbread*. Throughout the Grenadines local power boats can be arranged to take small groups of passengers almost any distance. If possible try to ensure that the boat is operated by someone known to you or your hotel to ensure reliability. Prices are flexible. Do not expect a dry or comfortable ride if the sea is rough.

To travel further south to Carriacou (Grenada), you can catch a fishing boat ferry, the *Jasper*, from Ashton, Union Island to Carriacou 0700, 1 hr, Mon and Thu, although days vary according to demand and weather, returning Carriacou-Union Island from Hillsborough Pier, 1500, EC$15. You will probably have to sit on deck and hang on to whatever you can, as the hold is usually full of luggage and crates of soft drinks for sale in Carriacou. Although not absolutely essential, you should check out with immigration at the airport in Clifton the day before you travel. The boat captain will take you through Grenadian formalities on arrival at Hillsborough. In high season more frequent boat trips are organized, ask at hotels, take your passport and expect thorough searches of you luggage at Customs and Immigration.

Bequia

Population: 6,000

Named the island of the clouds by the Caribs (pronounced Bek-*way*), this is the largest of the St Vincent dependencies. Nine miles south of St Vincent and about seven miles square, Bequia attracts quite a number of tourists, chiefly yachtsmen but also the smaller cruise ships and, increasingly, land-based tourists. Tourism is becoming much more important as more cruise ships stop and the number of yachts increases. More hotel rooms, villas and apartments are being added. The island is quite hilly and well forested with a great variety of fruit and nut trees. Its main village is **Port Elizabeth** and here Admiralty Bay offers a safe anchorage. Boat building and repair work are the main industry. Experienced sailors can sometimes get a job crewing on boats sailing on from here to Panama and other destinations. When you get off the ferry you will find to your left the fruit and veg market, with some clothes stalls and souvenirs. Straight in front of you is the green-roofed tourist kiosk run by the Bequia Tourism Association, and across

St Vincent & the Grenadines

the road the administration and finance building. Next to it is the Bayshore Mall, a new blue and white building which contains a bank, a few shops and airline offices. The Anglican St Mary's Church was built of local limestone and ballast bricks in 1829, replacing an earlier church which was destroyed by a hurricane in 1798. It is open and airy and has some interesting memorial stones. The southern part of the bay is known as Belmont, where a pleasant waterfront walkway runs past hotels, restaurants, bars and dive shops on the narrow strip of sand. Above Port Elizabeth a paved road runs to the late 18th century **Hamilton Battery**, which used to guard the bay.

The nearest beach to Port Elizabeth is the pleasant Princess Margaret beach which shelves quickly into the clear sea. It was named after the princess in 1958 when she swam there while visiting the island by yacht. However, access is deliberately made difficult and there are no beach bars to spoil this tree-lined stretch of soft sand. At its south end there is a small headland, around which you can snorkel from **Lower Bay**, where swimming is excellent and the beach is one of the best on the island. Hurricane Lenny washed up extra sand in 1999 and the shore now shelves quite steeply into the sea.Damaged trees are further evidence of the swell but there are still plenty of trees for shade. Local boys race their homemade, finely finished sailing yachts round the bay. In the village there are several places to stay as well as good restaurants and bars on the beach and up the hillside. Lower Bay gets very busy at holiday times and there is always lots going on.

Away from the west side of the island the beaches are empty. Take a taxi over the hills to the east coast and the wild beaches on that side of the island. There are bigger trees on the Windward side, including hard woods such as white cedar, used for making boats. Drive through coconut groves to **Spring Bay**, where there is a hotel and a beach bar (may be closed) and a pottery in a partially renovated sugar mill. Spring Pottery and artist's studio produces domestic pottery and gardenware as well as local paintings, open daily 0730-1630, The Old Sugar Mill, Spring, T4573757.

Bequia

N

| 0 km | 1 |
| 0 miles | 1 |

■ **Sleeping**
1 Bequia Beach Club
2 Blue Tropic
3 De Reef Apartments
4 Frangipani
5 Friendship Bay

6 Friendship Garden
 Apartments
 & Island Inn Apartments
7 Gingerbread & L'Auberge
 des Grenadines
8 Julie's Guesthouse

9 Kings Ville Apartments
10 Old Fort
11 Plantation House
12 Spring on Bequia
13 The Village Apartments

Windward Islands

Industry Bay is another nice beach surrounded by palms with a brilliant view across to Bullet Island, Battowia and Balliceaux where the Black Caribs were held before being deported to Roatán. Some luxury homes have been built at the north end of the bay. Food and drink available at the *Industry Beach Bar*.. Both beaches are narrow with shallow bays and a lot of weed, making them less good for swimming and snorkelling. In the wet season there can also be a lot of runoff from the hills. The road was paved in 2001 as far as Industry, but very rough after that. North of Industry at Park Beach, is **Old Hegg Turtle Sanctuary** in the northeast corner of the island. Not to be missed, an extremely worthwhile conservation project founded and maintained by a Bequian, a former fisherman, Orton 'Brother' King, to save the hawksbill turtle (*Eretmochelys imbricata*). Local people contact him if they see turtles hatching and he goes to the beaches to collect them, releasing them into the wild when they are about 2 ½ years old. There is only about a 50% success rate and a lot of injuries from the turtles biting each other, but it is still better than the natural survival rate. A few green (*chelonia mydas*) and leatherback (*dermochelys coriacea*) turtles can also be seen in the tanks. EC$10/US$5 entrance fee, but donations warmly welcomed to maintain the facilities and feed the turtles. Larger tanks are needed if the enterprise is to improve its success rate. ■ *T4583245, F4573322, oldhegg@vincysurf.com*

The walk up **Mount Pleasant** from Port Elizabeth is worthwhile (go by taxi if it is too hot), the shady road is overhung with fruit trees and the view of Admiralty Bay is ever more spectacular. There is a settlement of airy homes at the top, from where you can see most of the Grenadines. By following the road downhill and south of the viewpoint you can get to **Hope Bay**, an isolated and usually deserted sweep of white sand and one of the best beaches. At the last house (where you can arrange for a taxi to meet you afterwards), the road becomes a rough track, after half mile turn off right down an ill-defined path through cedar trees to an open field, cross the fence on the left, go through a coconut grove and you reach the beach. The sea is usually gentle but sometimes there is powerful surf, a strong undertow and offshore current, take care. **Friendship Bay** on the south coast is particularly pleasant, with a long sandy beach; there is some coral but also quite a lot of weed. It takes about 30 mins to walk from Port Elizabeth to the *Friendship Bay Hotel*, at the east end of the bay, or a taxi costs EC$15. Alternatively, you can take a dollar bus (infrequent) in the direction of Paget Farm, get out at the junction (EC$1.50) and walk down to the west end of the bay via the hotels (*Blue Tropic Hotel* and *Bay View Apartments*) and *Friendship Divers*. It is a much shorter distance to walk along the sand than along the road behind the beach, which is steep in places. Lots of villas have been built at this end of the island and although it is a nice, quiet place to stay you should consider car hire for shopping and trips to restaurants and other beaches.

At **Paget Farm**, whale harpooning is still practised from February to May (the breeding season) by a few fishermen who use three 26-ft long cedar boats, powered by oars and sails. If you can arrange a trip to **Petit Nevis**, to the south, you can see the whaling station and find out more about Bequia's whaling tradition. Despite pleas from conservationists, a humpback mother and calf have been harpooned off Bequia each year for the last few years. Bequia has an annual quota of two whales and with limited technology and power it is easier to kill a calf and then its mother rather than an adult male. There is a small whaling museum on the way to Paget Farm, Athneal's petite museum, which has a collection of whale bones beside the path to the house and old photos and tools of the trade in one room, US$2.

The tourist office can help you arrange a visit to the cliffside dwellings of **Moon Hole** at the southwest end of the island, where a rocky arch frames the stone dwelling and the water comes up the front yard. People live here without any electricity or running water.

Sleeping   **Port Elizabeth**   **LL** *Plantation House Hotel*, T4583425, F4583612, www.hotel-plantation. com Rebuilt after 1988 fire, on beach at Admiralty Bay at the far end of the Belmont walkway, 27 rooms in pink and turquoise cottages with verandas, gingerbread style, all MAP, honeymoon packages etc, restaurant in replica plantation house, tennis, swimming pool, watersports, jetty, Dive Bequia dive shop alongside, entertainment at weekends. **L-C** *Frangipani*, T4583255, F4583824, www.frangipani.net Cheaper rooms share bathroom, Bequia suites have kitchen, good facilities and sea view, on beach along Belmont walkway, pleasant, bar, mosquito net provided, Noah's Arcade on site. **L-B** *Gingerbread*, T4583800, F4583907, www.begos.com/gingerbread Added new luxury apartments with kitchens overlooking Admiralty Bay, old apartments at lower rates. 1-bedroomed with kitchen and bathroom, restaurant and bar upstairs, café downstairs, dive shop, tennis, waterskiing, Surf'n'Send internet/email access on site, on Belmont walkway by the beach, friendly. **A-C** *L'Auberge des Grenadines*, on Belmont Walkway, T/F4583201, frenchella@caribsurf.com French restaurant with 6 rooms to let, fans, TV, some but not all with ensuite bathrooms. **C-D** *Julie's Guest House*, T4583304, F4583812. 19 rooms with bath and shower, close to ferry dock, mosquito nets in rooms, good local food, good cocktails in noisy bar downstairs, meeting place for travellers to form boat charter groups. **Mount Pleasant L-AL** *The Old Fort*, T4583440, F4573340, www.oldfortbequia.com A 17th-century French built fortified farmhouse, probably oldest building on Bequia, magnificent views with a good breeze on top of the hill, quiet and peacefull, idyllic restaurant (must book), pool with view of 25 islands, beach within walking distance, 5/6 rooms, also available as a rental villa to sleep 10-14, excursions, diving, boat trips arranged. Highly recommended. Call Otmar Schaedle, multilingual. **Friendship Bay LL-AL** *Friendship Bay*, T4583222, F4583840, www.friendship.com Lovely location, but in need of renovation, 27 rooms, ocean front or ocean view, plumbing temperamental, boat excursions, water and other sports facilities, friendly, *Spicy'n Herby* beach bar, food OK but expensive, children can play on the beach while you eat, happy hour Sat, Sun 1700-1800, live music after that. **L-A** *Bequia Beach Club*, Friendship Bay, T4583248, F4583689, www.bequiabeachclub.com 10 rooms, fans, mosquito nets, restaurant, bar, on the beach with trees for shade, casual and unsophisticated, diving, windsurfing, tennis nearby, day sails, weekly barbecues. **A** *Blue Tropic*, T4583573, F4573074. Popular with Germans, 10 rooms, view of bay, restaurant, bar, free bikes, 100m to the beach where there are mats and sun chairs, dive packages with *Friendship Divers*. **Spring Bay LL-AL** *Spring on Bequia*, T4583414, F4583305, springonbequia@caribsurf.com Part of a 200-year-old working plantation, set among coconut palms, 10 rooms, pool, tennis, bar, restaurant, beach bar on unspoiled beach. **Lower Bay AL-A** *KingsVille Apartments*, Lower Bay, T4583404, F4583000, kingsville@caribsurf.com Run by Bert and Kay King, 1-2 bedroom apartments in cottages, right by the beach, a/c, modern, convenient for restaurants. **A-B** *Keegan's Guesthouse*, T4583254, F4573313. Lovely position on the beach, 11 rooms, fan, mosquito nets, includes breakfast and evening meal, will cater for vegetarians, also 1-2 bedroom apartments US$300-425 per week, table tennis, volley ball, no credit cards. **A-B** *Creole Garden Hotel*, T4583154, F4573696, www.creolegardens.com above Corner Bay and Lower Bay beach, MAP, studios with bath, porch, refrigerator. **A-D** *De Reef Apartments*, Lower Bay, T4583484, F4573103. 1-2 bedrooms in gardens by the beach, fans, kitchens, good location, restaurant and bar on the beach.

Villas There are several villas for rent around the island, most of which are handled by letting agencies. The main agency is *Bequia Villa Rentals*, PO Box 23, Bequia, T4583393, F4583417, beqvilla@caribsurf.com There is also *Friendship Bay Villa and Apartment Rentals*, PO Box 9, Bequia, T4583222, F4583840, labambas@caribsurf.com

In Port Elizabeth *Le Petit Jardin*, Back St, T4583318, VHF 16 and 68. French and international, open daily 1130-1400, 1830-2130, reservations preferred, EC$30-85 for entrées. *Porthole*, T4583458. Local creole dishes, rotis, Mexican, fish. *Tantie Pearl's Café & Restaurant*, T4573160, VHF 68. West Indian cooking, lobster and conch sandwiches and light lunches from 1130, dinner from 1830, up on Cemetery Hill 2 mins by taxi above Port Elizabeth, nice breeze. *Daphne's*, just off the main street, T4583271. Cooks excellent créole meals to eat in or takeaway, no credit cards. *Fernando's Hideaway*, T4583758. Local style fresh food, dinner Mon-Sat, special goat water soup. **Along Belmont walkway** *L'Auberge de Grenadines*, T4583201. French with emphasis on lobster, large tank of live specimens, lobster lunch

Eating
Of the hotel restaurants, The Old Fort, see above, is one of the nicest and most romantic for a gourmet dinner up on Mount Pleasant

Windward Islands

EC$28, lobster burgers very filling, entrées around EC$45, 3-course set dinner for EC$70, closed Thu, happy hour 1730-1830.*Mac's Pizzeria*, T4583474. Very popular, open 1100-2200, closed Mon, get there early or reserve in advance, even in low season, also take-aways, try the lobster pizza, pricey at EC$60 for a small one, but covered with lobster, don't add other ingredients. *Green Boley*, T4583247. Local bar with fast food, rotis EC$5-10, burger and chips EC$12, fish and chips EC$18. The *Gingerbread Café* has sandwiches and snacks all day, open 0700-1800, also *Gingerbread BBQ*, outdoors on bayside 1200-1500, and *Gingerbread Restaurant & Bar*, T4583800, upper floor of *Gingerbread* complex, overlooking Admiralty Bay. Open 0800-2130, reservations recommended in season for dinner, West Indian and international, live music 3 nights a week. *Whaleboner*, T4583233. Food fresh from their own farm, EC$5-65, pizza and roti EC$8, open Mon-Sat 0800-2200, Sun 1400-2200. The *Frangipani* has sandwiches and snacks all day, slow service but friendly and you have a good view to look at, Thu night barbecue, buffet, steel band.

At Lower Bay *De Reef*. Lovely position on the beach, popular with yachties and locals, set meals and bar snacks, the place for Sun lunch. *Coco's Place*, T4583463, VHF 68. Fabulous view over harbour, up on hill at end of bay, lovely balcony, friendly pub and local kitchen, lunch and dinner daily, Fri lobster special EC$60, live music Tue, Fri. *Dawn's Créole Garden*, at the far end, T4583154. Open from 0800, breakfast, lunch and dinner, good home cooked food, fairly expensive, must book for dinner. *Keegan's*, T4583304, right on the beach. Local meals, open for breakfast, lunch and dinner, inexpensive 3-course meals and bar snacks all day. reservations advised in high season for dinner.

Nightlife Jump ups and live music can be heard on different nights in the hotels, including *Plantation House*, *Frangipani*, *Friendship Bay*, and *Gingerbread*. Check bars for happy hours. There is something going on most nights either at Admiralty Bay or Friendship Bay. Look in *Bequia this week* which has daily listings. Bands play reggae music in the gardens of several hotels, popular with residents and tourists.

Shopping
There are several marine stores & fishing tackle shops here

There is a market for fruit and veg by the jetty and there are small supermarkets in Port Elizabeth, including *S & W*, *Knights*, *Bequia Food Store* and *Doris fresh foods*, with improving selection of groceries and beverages but at higher prices than in St Vincent; for cash and carry purchases of items like soft drinks or beer (good for yacht provisioning), go to Euro shopper up the hill in Belmont on the road to Paget, open Mon-Sat 0800-1800, T4573932, VHF 68; fish is sometimes on sale in the centre by the jetty. Overlooking Admiralty Bay on Belmont walkway, *Crab Hole*, T4583290 is a boutique where silk screened fabrics are made downstairs and sewn into clothes upstairs, open 0800-1700 Mon-Sat in season, closing earlier out of season. *Noah's Arcade*, at the *Frangipani* on Belmont walkway, T4583424, is a branch of the enterprise on St Vincent, stocking gifts, books, handicrafts and T-shirts, and also showcasing the artwork of resident artists, whatever their origin, open Mon-Fri 0900-1700, Sat-Sun 0900-1300. Also don't miss *Mauvin's* and *Sargeant Brothers'* model boat shops (the latter up the hill going out of town), where craftsmen turn out replicas of traditional craft and visiting yachts. *Bequia Bookshop* in Port Elizabeth, T4583905, is run by Iain Gale, who keeps an excellent stock of books, particularly of Caribbean literature, maps and charts. Many of these shops stock Scrimshaw knives, intricately designed and engraved by Sam McDowell, whose studio is at the Banana Patch, Paget Farm. See also under St Vincent page 829.

Sports Tennis can be played at the *Gingerbread, Friendship Bay, Plantation House* and *Spring* hotels. Scuba diving with *Bequia Dive Adventures*, Belmont walkway, next to *Mac's Pizzeria*, T4583826, VHF68 and 16, www.BequiaDiveAdventures.com full-service PADI dive centre, three trips daily, 0900, 1130, 1430; *Dive Bequia*, Belmont, T4583504, VHF16 or 68, www.dive-bequia.com run by Bob Sachs, who opened the dive shop in 1984, this company has the biggest boats, with shade and more room to move around and manoeuvre tanks and gear; *Dive Paradise*, Friendship Bay, T4583563, harald@paradisebequia.com; and *Friendship Divers*, Friendship Bay, T4583422, bequia@friendshipdivers.de SSI/CMAS, German-speaking, 1-5 dives for US$39 each not including equipment, no shade on boat. Diving is good around Pigeon Island, where there is lots of coral and fish, afternoon and night dives are usually on the leeward side of the southwest peninsula, there are a few sites around Isle à Quatre and shallow dives for training can be done around Petit Nevis. Sport fishing can be arranged on the *Ocean Catcher*, a power boat, T4583093, or *Passion*, a 60-ft catamaran, T4583884, passion@caribsurf.com; SY *Puka* is a 51 ft Benneteau, privately chartered to small parties, call Lara Hadley, T4574028, www.grenadine-escape.com

Most tours of Bequia are little more than taxi tours taking around 3 hours. For travel arrangements try CITS, in the Bayshore Mall, T4583062, cits@caribsurf.com or Grenadine Travel at the *Gingerbread*, Belmont, T4583795. For tours by yacht to neighbouring islands and for snorkelling: the *Friendship Rose* is an 80-ft auxiliary schooner, which used to be one of the ferries for the island, T4583373; *Meteor* is a 51-ft yacht, T4583222; *Passion* is a 60-ft catamaran, offering day trips to Mustique, US$60, the Tobago Cays, US$75, or St Vincent and the Falls of Baleine, US$75, contact Heidi Pritchard, Belmont, T4583884, passion@caribsurf.com; *Quest* is a 44-ft centre cockpit yacht based at Paget, T4583917, owned by Johnny Ollivierre, who also has *Petrel*, a 47-ft Swan for day trips to Mustique; SY *Pelangi* is a 44-ft cutter, based at the *Frangipani Hotel*, T4583255. frangi@caribsurf.com; SY *Puka* is a 5 ft Benneteau, privately chartered to small parties, call Lara Hadley, T4574028, www.grenadine-escape.co

Tour operators & travel agents

Air J F Mitchell Airport, named after the former Prime Minister, has been built on reclaimed land with a 3,200-ft runway, a terminal and night landing facilities, at the island's southwest tip. **Road** Buses (minivans and open pick-up trucks called dollar vans) leave from the jetty at Port Elizabeth and will stop anywhere to pick you up but do not cover the whole island, a cheap and reliable service. For about US$60, you can take a taxi tour around the island, lasting about 3 hrs.Car hire is available at around EC$140/day, cheaper if you rent for a week, try Phil's Car Rental, T4583304, Lubin's Car Rental, T4583349, Handy Andy Rentals, T4583722, or B & G Jeep Rentals, T4583760. Ryan & Gus's Rentals have mokes, T4573238, short and long term rental, price negotiable. If you are staying in an apartment, your landlord may already have an agreement with a supplier and can offer you a good deal. Cycling is really enjoyable, lots of hills but not too steep and not a lot of traffic, great views and beaches scattered all over the island. Walking is also rewarding, but take water and sunscreen. **Taxi**: on Bequia, taxis (when they are not operating as buses) are pick-up trucks with benches in the back, brightly coloured with names like 'Messenjah', call them by phone or VHF 68. **Sea** Water taxis scoot about in Admiralty Bay, Princess Margaret Beach and Lower Bay for the benefit of the many yachts and people on the beach, whistle or wave to attract their attention, fare EC$10 per trip. There are day charters to other islands (see above, Beaches and watersports). For those arriving on yachts, there are anchorages all round either side of the channel in Admiralty Bay, Princess Margaret Beach, Lower Bay, Friendship Bay and off Petit Nevis by the old whaling station. Bequia Slipway has dockage, some moorings are available.

Transport

Banks *National Commercial Bank*, T4583700, has an ATM for Visa and Mastercard. *Caribbean Banking Corp*, T4583845, does not. **Communications** Internet: plenty of places due to the number of yachties. Surf'n Send, downstairs at the *Gingerbread* complex, email, photocopying, computer accessories, open Mon-Fri 0800-1730, Sat 0800-1430, T4583577; Sam Taxi & Tours Ltd, behind the new Revenue Building, internet access EC$20/hr, also printing, scanning, yacht clearance, brokerage and numerous other services for yachties, T4583686; Icon, in Port Elizabeth, T4573727; RMS, Port Elizabeth, T4583556; Sailor Cyber Café, Ocar Reform, T4573105. The Post Office is on Back St behind CBC, open Mon-Fri 0830-1500, Sat 0830-1200. **Customs & immigration** On the main road by the dock, open Mon-Fri 0830-1600, Sat 0830-1200, Sun 0900-1200, 1500-1800. Overtime fee may be charged outside office hours and on holidays. **Laundry** Papa Mitch, next to Bequia Bookshop, T4583722, VHF68, EC$8 per 10lb load or service wash and dry for EC$17 a load, free pick up and delivery, showers EC$5. Also Sam Taxi & Tours, see Communications, above, Handy Andy, see car hire above, Daffodil Marine Services, T4583942, VHF69, and Light House Laundry, T4573187. **Medical facilities** *Bequia Casualty Hospital*, Port Elizabeth, T4583294. See also under St Vincent, page 830. **Police** Turn up the road by the banks, past the hospital and the police station is on your right before you get to the Clive Tannis Playing Field, T4583350, VHF16. **Tourist information** Information booth at the dock, run by the Bequia Tourism Association, 0830-1800 Mon-Fri, 0830-1400 Sat, 0830-1200 Sun, T4583286, F4583954, www.bequiasweet.com They publish *Bequia this week*, which has daily listings of what's on.

Directory

Windward Islands

Mustique

Lying 18 miles south of St Vincent, Mustique is three miles long and less than two miles wide. In the 1960s, Mustique was acquired by a single proprietor who developed the island as his private resort where he could entertain the rich and famous. It is a beautiful island, with fertile valleys, steep hills and 12 miles of white sandy beach, but described by some as 'manicured'. The whole of the island, its beaches and surrounding waters for 1,000 m are a conservation area. It is no longer owned by one person and is more accessible to tourists, although privacy and quiet is prized by those who can afford to live there. Most visitors are day-trippers from Bequia or other neighbouring islands on private or chartered yachts, who stay on the beach and eat at *Basil's*. There is no intention to commercialize the island; it has only one petrol pump for the few cars (people use mopeds or golf carts to get around). Apart from the private homes, there are two hotels, one beach bar, a few boutiques, shops, a small village and a fishing camp. All house rentals are handled by the Mustique Company, which organizes activities such as picnics and sports, especially at Easter and Christmas.

There is sailing, diving, snorkelling and good swimming (very little waterskiing). Riding can also be arranged or you can walk or hire a moped to tour the island. The main anchorage is Brittania Bay, where there are 18 moorings for medium sized yachts with waste disposal and phones. Take a picnic lunch to Macaroni Beach on the Atlantic side. This gorgeous, white sand beach is lined with small palm-thatched pavilions and a well kept park/picnic area. It is isolated and wonderful. Swimming and snorkelling is also good at Lagoon Bay, Gallicaux Bay, Britannia Bay and Endeavour Bay, all on the leeward side. L'Ansecoy Bay in the north is a wide beach, notable for the wreck of the French liner the *Antilles*, which went aground offshore in 1971. Jet skis and spear guns are banned.

Basil's Bar and Restaurant is *the* congregating spot for yachtsmen and the jet set. Snorkelling is good here too. From it there is a well beaten path to the *Cotton House Hotel*, which is the other congregating point. There is an honour system to pay for moorings at *Basil's Bar*, EC$50 a night, EC$20 second night.

Mustique

0 metres 500
0 yards 500

■ **Sleeping**
1 Cotton House   2 Firefly

LL *Cotton House*, T4564777, F4565887, www.cottonhouse.com A 20-room refurbished (by **Sleeping**
Oliver Messel) 18th-century cotton plantation house built of rock and coral, very expensive,
pool, tennis, windsurfers, sailfish, snorkelling, all complimentary, horseriding and scuba diving available, sailing packages tailor made. Smaller, slightly less expensive **LL** *Firefly*,
T4563414, F4563514, www.mustiquefirefly.com All 4 rooms with view overlooking the bay,
bed and breakfast, two-tiered pool with a view, bar with sunset view. 50 of the 82 private residences are available for rent, with staff, from US$3,500 per week in summer for a
2-bedroomed villa to US$30,000 per week in winter for a villa sleeping 14. Contact The
Mustique Company Ltd, T4584621, F4564565, www.mustique-island.com

Basil's Bar , T4584621 for reservations. For seafood and nightlife, open from 0800, entrées **Eating**
EC$10-75. Locals' night on Mon with buffet for EC$35, Wed is good with barbeque and
jump-up. On Sat go to the *Cotton House*. Reservations required at the *Cotton House* and
Firefly. Up the hill from *Basil's* is the local *Piccadilly* pub, where rotis and beer are sold, and
pool is played; foreigners are welcome, but it is best to go in a group and girls should not
go on their own.

Air International connections are best through Barbados, a 50-min flight with Mustique Air- **Transport**
ways, although other connections are possible via Grenada and the neighbouring islands of
St Vincent, Bequia, Canouan and Union with either Mustique Airways or SVG Air. The airstrip,
being in the centre of the island is clearly visible, so check-in time is five minutes before take
off (that is after you've seen your plane land). **Sea** Since the island has no freshwater, it is
shipped in on Mustique Boats *Robert Junior* (T4571918) and the *Geronimo*. Both take passengers and excursions on Sunday (EC$20, two hour trip). Many people arrive on private or char-
tered yachts for a day trip or longer stay.

Canouan

A quiet, peaceful, crescent-shaped island, Canouan lies 25 miles south of St Vincent,
with excellent reef-protected beaches. Evidence of human occupation has been
found dating back to 200BC, pendants and pottery shards having been found during
construction work on the airport and hotels. The island was valuable for plantation
crops during the colonial period, namely sugar then cotton, which was grown until
1924. The Snagg family who owned the land were unable to keep the plantation
going and the north reverted to acacia scrub and thicket. The estate was sold to the
government in 1946. Other local family names include the Comptons and the Mit-
chells, shipwrights who arrived in the 19th century. At that time there was plenty of
cedar (for the hull), mahogany (for planking) and bamboo (for masts) for ship
building and a successful industry was born. In 1939 Reginald Mitchell built the
largest schooner ever in the Lesser Antilles. The three-masted *Gloria Colita* was 165
ft long, 39 ft wide and weighed 178 tons. Unfortunately only two years later it was
found abandoned and awash in the Gulf of Mexico and no one knows what happened to Capt Mitchell and his crew.

The village, on the leeward side in Grand Bay, is **Charlestown**, founded after a
devastating hurricane destroyed the settlement at Carenage Bay in 1921. It is architecturally uninteresting, untidy and scruffy. The main anchorage is here and the
white sand beach is superb, running the length of the bay and broken only by the
jetty. On holidays, day trips are organized from St Vincent on the *Barracouda*, and
then the beach is full of people. Dozens of cricket matches are held on the sand, ranging from little boys to family groups to serious young men who carefully measure
their wicket and dispute calls. Balls constantly go in the water and stumps are made
of any sticks found on the beach. The north end of the beach, in front of the *Tamarind Beach Hotel*, is cleaned daily and enjoyed by guests, locals and friendly dogs.
The beach at the *Canouan Beach Hotel* in the southwest is splendid with white sand
and views of numerous islands to the south. You can anchor here, with Corbec and
Rameau Bays as other possibilities. In settled weather, South Glossy and Friendship

Bays make possible anchorages, with excellent snorkelling. Diving and snorkelling are good at all these anchorages and on the reefs on the windward side. Mahault Bay on the north coast is beautiful, isolated, with steep hills all around, and great for a picnic. Turtles come here to nest. Dive trips can be arranged through Blueway Diving at the *Tamarind Beach Hotel*. Both the *Canouan Beach Hotel* and the *Carenage Bay Resort* organize boat trips to the Tobago Cays and non-hotel guests are permitted to make up numbers if the boat is not fully booked.

Much of the north of the island, 800 of the island's 1,866 acres, is now taken up by the new, exclusive development, *Carenage Bay Resort*, built with Italian investment and since 2000 managed by Rosewood Hotels. The 155 hotel villas take up the whole of Carenage Bay, stretching up the hillsides, and are so spread out that guests have golf carts to get around. There are two nice beaches, but being on the windward side the sea is often choppy and has a fair amount of weed. The centre of the bay is taken up with an 18-hole, par 72 golf course designed by Roy Case, being extended up and over the hill in 2001. The only old building left from the original settlement is a church, just outside reception, in which you can still get married, although normal services are no longer held. The development has not been without controversy. Although most residents appreciate the job opportunities, a vocal minority has occasionally mounted road blocks in protest at being denied access to beaches in the north, previously open to the public via public roads. The beaches are still technically open to the public, up to the high water mark, but access has to be from the sea, making a visit problematic. The resort is protected by security guards and barriers and few guests venture out.

Sleeping **LL** *Carenage Bay Resort & Golf Club*, T4588000, F4588885, www.carenagebay.com 155 rooms/suites in villas, rather strange modernistic design in a variety of pastels, with main building painted a ragged terracotta, every conceivable luxury, art work by Italian Costanzo Rovati, casino and nightclub, golf, gym, health club, sailing, windsurfing, good pool, tennis, yacht and speed boat charters, fishing. Shuttle between here and the *Tamarind* every 30 mins. Car and cart rental. The sort of place where your beach umbrella is adjusted for you every 15 mins and waiters greet you with rum punches on the beach on your return from a

Canouan

0 metres 500
0 yards 500

■ **Sleeping**
1 Canouan Beach
2 Carenage Bay Resort
3 Tamarind Beach

sailing excursion, you will either enjoy being pampered or find it pretentious, popular with honeymooners. **LL** *Canouan Beach Hotel*, South Glossy Bay, T4588888, F4588875, www.grenadines.net/canouan/canouanbeachhotelhomepage.htm 32 deluxe bungalows and main building, in the south close to the airport, all-inclusive, French speaking, fabulous beach, very relaxing, daily excursions on their catamaran. **LL-L** *Tamarind Beach Hotel*, T4588044, F4588851, cantbh@caribsurf.com Set in lovely mature gardens, green and lush, 42 comfortable rooms, all with sea view and right on beach, everything wood and wicker, no phones or TV, internet access US$7, popular restaurant, humming with yachties and staff from the *Carenage Bay Resort* at night, watersports, PADI dive shop on site, long dock for dinghies, moorings rather rolly, more comfortable sleeping to anchor in north corner of bay. They also provide water, ice, bread, showers, to yachties. You are recommended to phone in advance to book rooms. There are rooms to rent in the village if you ask around; also possible to rent houses.

Italian food is a feature of the expensive *Carenage Bay Resort* and you can get great stone baked pizzas there and at the *Tamarind Beach Hotel*. A few local restaurants have opened in the village and are much cheaper than the hotels. *R&C Restaurant and Bar*, up the hill opposite the entrance to the *Tamarind Beach Hotel*, T4588264, VHF16. Run by Catherine and Roland Williams, open from 0730, seafood and local dishes such as roti, EC$8, good and filling, nice and breezy with good view over the harbour. There is a new bar by the ferry dock but it is not always serving food. *Pompey*, on the main street, and *Honeycomb*, up the hill heading east out of town, also serve local food.

Eating
The hotel restaurants serve international food with local specialities

Air There is a new runway and terminal building built partly with finance from the *Carenage Bay Resort*, which has persuaded *American Eagle* to fly in from San Juan, Puerto Rico. This will be the best way of getting here from the USA; from Europe there is a good service from Barbados (55 mins) or Grenada (20 mins) with *SVGAir*, *TIA* or *Air Mustique*. These small planes also link Canouan with other islands nearby, Martinique (1hr), St Lucia (40 mins), St Vincent (15 mins). **Sea** The *Barracouda* calls here on its way from St Vincent to Union Island and back twice a week, with occasional day trips at holiday times. **Road** There is no public transport. Walking is rewarding and distances are not great although the island is hilly. There are trails in the north, ask at the *Carenage Bay* for directions. Jeep rental at the hotels.

Transport

Banks *National Commercial Bank*, in centre of village at the road junction, T4588595, open Mon-Wed, Fri 0800-1300, Thu 0800-1300, 1430-1700, always busy with slow queues, not enough motivated staff, no ATM. **Communications** Internet: at the *Tamarind Beach Hotel*, US$7/hr. *The Carenage Bay Resort* has facilities for computer connections in every room. Post office: on the main street on the left heading south, no sign outside, the building used to be a bar and still looks like one.

Directory

Mayreau

A small privately-owned island with deserted beaches and only one hotel and one guest house. The village is tightly packed on the hillside above the harbour. You can reach it only by boat and the *Barracouda* calls on its way from St Vincent to Union. There is no deep water dock, though, so goods and passengers are offloaded into little boats and dinghies which then struggle to the jetty in great danger of being swamped by a wave. The beaches are glorious and Mayreau is a popular stop-off point for yachties, particularly in Salt Whistle Bay, a perfect horse shoe shaped bay in the northwest, on a spit of land with a long, wild beach on the other side, which is to windward. Several day charters include the bay as a useful lunch stop when visiting the Tobago Cays. The only disadvantage to its popularity is that it can be noisy at night in season with revellers enjoying entertainment at the restaurant and on board their yachts. Parts of Mayreau are within the Tobago Cays Marine Park and a marine environment interpretation centre is planned as a tourist attraction and to aid conservation by the Mayreau Environmental Development Organization (MEDO), T4588458. This is one of the EC-funded pilot projects for sustainable development and community-based initiatives being carried out in the Eastern Caribbean, to encourage economic diversification through nature tourism.

Sleeping & eating **LL** *Salt Whistle Bay Club*, T4588444, F4588944, VHF16. 10 rooms in rather gloomy cottages, MAP, yacht charters and picnics on nearby islands. The restaurant is open to non-guests, entrées around EC$45-65, seafood and imported meat. **B-C** *Dennis' Hideaway*, T4588944. 5 rooms, bar, restaurant, good food and drinks at reasonable prices, yacht charter. *J & C Bar and Restaurant*, has the best view of the harbour with soft music, boutique, room for a large group, good lobster, fish and lambi, for parties of four and over the captain's dinner is free; *Island Paradise*, everything is prepared fresh, good lobster, fish and curried conch, half price happy hour 1800-1900, barbecue Fri with local band, free ride up the hill, skipper's meal free with more than three for dinner. There is a payphone in the village with an overseas operator for credit card calls.

Union Island

The most southerly of the islands belonging to St Vincent, Union Island is 40 miles from St Vincent and only three miles long by one mile wide. It has two settlements, **Clifton** and **Ashton**. 75% of the population live in Ashton, but 95% of the action takes place in Clifton. Union is distinguished by some dramatic peaks. Mount Olympus (637 ft) is in the northwest, while Mount Parnassus (920 ft) and Mount Taboi (1,002 ft) stand side by side in the centre-west and in the centre-east are the jagged Pinnacles (925 ft). The landscape around Ashton is more rugged and mountainous than around Clifton, where the airport is situated, partly on reclaimed land. Arrival by air is spectacular as the planes fly over the hills and descend steeply to the landing strip. Parnassus, or 'Big Hill', is a good hike. Take the upper level road in Ashton. In front of a clearing are some steps leading to a path. After 2-3 minutes, fork to the left. The path winds round the hill to the top, from where the views are as fine as one would imagine. North of the airport is Fort Hill (450ft), where the site of a 17th century French fort gives a panoramic view of dozens of islands. A walk around the interior of the island (about two hours Clifton-Ashton-Richmond Bay-Clifton) is worth the effort, with fine views of the sea, half a dozen neighbouring islands, pelicans and Union itself. The Union Island Ecotourism Movement (UIEM) was

Mayreau & the Tobago Cays

created in 1996 with the aim of coordinating efforts with community groups to encourage land-based tourism. Five guides have been trained with EC finance to maintain trails and escort visitors, although not a lot of progress has been seen so far. Contact Matthew Harvey, T4858317, F4858467, or Ynolde Hutchinson, T4858486, for more information about the nature trails.

The beach at **Chatham Bay** is beautiful and deserted, but not particularly good for swimming as there is a coral ledge just off the beach. Snorkelling and diving are good though. It is one of the last undeveloped anchorages in the Grenadines. There is no road and you have to walk 30 minutes along a footpath through the bush from the end of the road just above Ashton down to the bay. Women should not go there alone, there have been reports of attacks. **Bloody Bay** has a long, sandy beach, best reached from the sea, although there is some surf. **Richmond Bay** is also pleasant, good for swimming and easily reached as the road runs alongside it. However, it is dirty and there is broken glass on the sand, so take care. Round the point, **Belmont Bay**, or Big Sands, is another sandy beach, with villas for rent.

Clifton serves as the south point of entry clearance for yachts The immigration office and customs are at the airport, so if you arrive by boat you check in at the *Yacht Club* and the airport. Similarly on departure, check out at the airport, even if you are leaving by ferry from Ashton to Carriacou (although it is not the end of the world if you don't). For visiting yachts there are anchorages at Clifton, Frigate Island and Chatham Bay, while the *Anchorage Yacht Club* marina has some moorings. There is also a 20-berth marina at Bougainvilla, T4588678, bougainvilla@caribsurf.com, a smart new complex of businesses next to the *Anchorage,* offering apartment accommodation, a restaurant, a boutique, a wine shop, internet access and laundry at *Erika's Marine Services* (see below), the offices of Moorings, VPM Dufour Yachting, Bamboo Yachting, Oversea Sailing, Star Voyage, Wind and Sea Ltd (cruise ship agent and charter), and Unitech Marine supply and repair.

A good reason to visit Union Island is to arrange day trips to other islands or to find a ride on a yacht to Venezuela towards the end of the season (May-June). Day trip boats to other islands leave from Clifton around 1000 and are all about the same price, EC$120, including lunch. Yannis Tours, moored at the *Clifton Beach Hotel* arranges tours to the nearby Tobago Cays (see below), Palm Island, Petit St Vincent and other small islands. They have a comfortable catamaran, which is recommended if the sea is a bit rough, and provide breakfast, lunch, rum punch and soft drinks, T4588513. Alternatively, you can hire a local skipper to take you in a smaller

Windward Islands

Union Island

■ **Sleeping**	2 Clifton Beach	4 St Joseph's
1 Anchorage Yacht Club	3 Palm Island Resort	5 Sunny Grenadines

0 metres 700
0 yards 700

boat wherever you want to go. This is recommended if the sea is calm so that you can spend the maximum time snorkelling at the Tobago Cays. The SVG Water Taxi Association sets prices, so don't be fooled into a 'good rate'. Check at the tourist booth, in 2001 a water taxi to the Tobago Cays for 3-4 people was US$80 one way.

Sleeping

Apartments and villas are opening up and if you ask around you should find reasonable self-catering accommodation

L-B *Anchorage Yacht Club*, Clifton, T4588221, F4588365, www.ayc-hotel-grenadines.com. Beside the runway, full marina service, French restaurant, terrace bar, steel band or piano music, 15 rooms, special rates for yachties, small beach, boutique, very sad shark pool with very bored nurse sharks in very little water. **A-D** *Clifton Beach Hotel and Guest House*, T/F4588235, www.cliftonbeachhotel.com. Rooms on the waterfront, cottages, guest house and apartment at other locations including Big Sands. Rather dilapidated and run down but comfortable, clean and friendly nonetheless, MAP available, restaurant overlooking water by Capt Yannis catamaran, a/c, dodgy electric showers, laundry, friendly service, water and ice for boats, bike, car and jeep rental. **A-D** *St Joseph's Guest House*, Clifton, T4588405, www.unionisland.com The nicest place to stay, new guest house built just above the new RC church, run by Father Andrew Roach, stupendous views of Palm Is, PSV, Petit Martinique and Carriacou, delightfully breezy and peaceful on the spacious balconies, 2 rooms share kitchen on balcony, 2-bedroomed cottage, 1-bedroom annex apartment on church, 2 dormitories for youth groups sleep up to 15 each at a squeeze, meeting facilities with computer room, access to beach at the bottom of the hill, good snorkelling, jeep rental. Father Andrew organizes classes in screen printing and computers for local youngsters and volunteer labour from guests is always welcome. You don't have to be religious to stay here, all are made to feel at home. **E** *Lambi's Guest House*, Clifton, T/F4588349/4588359. A/c, restaurant, bar, lively steel band every night. There is not much in Ashton, except the new *BBB Marine View Apartments*, which might be worth a try if you want to stay in that area.

Eating

In Clifton, *The West Indies*, at the Bougainvilla complex overlooking the sea, T4588311, VHF16. Probably the best restaurant for breakfast, EC$20-30, lunch (panini, burgers, chicken nuggets) or dinner, entrées EC$35-55, international style, local ingredients and imported meat, open air, pleasant, interesting tropical fish tank with more than just fish. The *Anchorage* restaurant has been criticized for serving bland, overpriced food, the occupants of the shark pool are given food rejected by customers. *Lambi's Restaurant*, next to the *Clifton Beach Hotel*, reached by alley from main street or from the sea, casual, barn-like dining room with long tables for parties, excellent steel band every night, get there by 1800 for the happy hour, EC$45 buffet starts around 1900, free water taxi service or free moorings if you eat there, also rooms to rent. *Sydney's Bar & Restaurant*, T/F4588320, VHF 16, Clifton, towards the airport. Owned by Sydney, who handpaints T-shirts for sale in Tobago Cays, and run by Marin from Munich, local meals, snacks, seafood crêpes, pasta, happy hour 1800-1900, two for one, also guest house. *Jennifer's Restaurant*, West Indian food at reasonable prices, music at weekends. Several other local places which come and go, sometimes seasonally. In Ashton, *Janti's*, T4588343, VHF16. Small restaurant and bar on the left as you go into Ashton from Clifton, snacks available but dinner reservations required, good food and lots of it, specializes in local fish, lobster in season, lots of vegetables, vegetarian meals available, excellent fruit juices and punches, free taxi if there are enough of you, Janti is often to be found in Clifton in the mornings touting for business. Most places have a happy hour 1800-1900, with half price drinks, good value.

Festivals

At Easter there are sports, cultural shows and a calypso competition. In **May**, is the *Big Drum Festival*, an event which marks the end of the dry season, culminating in the Big Drum Dance, derived from African and French traditions. It is also performed on other occasions, for weddings or launching boats and even in times of disaster.

Shopping

Fruit and veg stalls line the road by the ferry dock, with the best of what's in season. There are a few supermarkets in Clifton, *Lambi's*, next to the *Clifton Beach Hotel*, T4588022, VHF68, and *Grand Union* (also a guest house), to your right as you come off the main dock, T4588178, will deliver to the dock, and 4-5 smaller groceries sell fresh produce and hardware. For luxury foodstuffs and the best steaks, *Captain Gourmet*, on the main street, T4588918, full of French yachties buying baguettes, croissants, cheese and other delicacies, good but expensive wine. Wine also sold at the *Grenadines Vine Shop*, in the Bougainvilla complex, T4588289, VHF16. There is also a nice boutique in the Bougainvilla, which sells gifts, cruising guides, cook books and fish guides etc. More gift shops can be found all along the main street.

Grenadines Dive, T4588138, gdive@caribsurf.com and *The Dive Shack*, T4588508, offer scuba diving, mostly around the Tobago Cays. **Sports**

Eagle's Travel Agency, opposite NCB just past Grand Union supermarket, T4588179, F4588095, eagtrav@caribsurf.com for reservations and ticketing for local airlines. *James Travel*, on the main street next to Captain Gourmet, T4858306, offers similar services. **Travel agents**

Air Scheduled and charter services from St Vincent, Grenada, Barbados and St Lucia with *SVG Air*, *Air Mustique* and *TIA*. The road from the airport to Clifton passes a mangrove swamp being used as a dump prior to filling it in to get rid of mosquitoes and enable building to take place. **Sea** There is an international ferry service between Ashton and Hillsborough on Carriacou. The *Jasper* is a wooden fishing boat which makes the one-hour trip to Hillsborough at 0730, Mon and Thu, EC$15, returning same day around 1500. The captain takes you through immigration procedures, but you should check out at Immigration at Clifton airport the night before. Expect to have your bags thoroughly searched on arrival at Customs and Immigration at Hillsborough. The *Barracouda* is the main link with the other islands in the St Vincent Grenadines, see above. The SVG Water Taxi Association sets rates for water taxis. From a yacht in harbour to land is US$2pp during the day and US$3pp at night. Clifton to Ashton or Palm Island is US$30 for 3-4 people one way, Chatham Bay, Mayreau, PSV or Petite Martinique US$60. **Land** Minibuses run between Clifton and Ashton, EC$2. They convert to a taxi on request. Bicycles can be hired from *Erika's Marine Services*, T4858335, US$18/day, US$64/week. **Transport**

See under St Vincent, page 830. **Banks** The NCB is to your right as you come off the dock, open Mon-Thu 0800-1300, Fri 0800-1300, 1500-1700, T4588347. There is an ATM, but if it is broken try *Erika's*, see below. **Communications** Internet: *Erika's Marine Services* at the Bougainvilla complex, run by Heather Grant (Canadian), T4858335, F4858336, VHF68, erika@caribsurf.com, fast machines, EC$10/15 mins, open Mon-Sat 0900-1730, also Sun 0900-1400 in season. Additional services include bicycle hire, laundry, book exchange, telephone, fax, computer rental, DHL, cash advances on Visa, Mastercard and Eurocard with 10% commission, currency exchange at EC$2.50=US$1. Internet access at *Western Union*, upstairs on main street, Clifton, 4 terminals, some keyboards work better than others, EC$5/15 mins, open Mon-Fri 0800-1630, Sun 0800-1700, or later if you are already on the machine, also phone calls, EC$7/min to Europe, EC$5 to North and South America, EC$3 to the Caribbean and EC$10 elsewhere. *Union Island Communications Centre (Unicom)*, is opposite the main gates to the *Anchorage* by the airport, T4588660, F4588665, internet access EC$0.50/min or EC$25/hr. Phone calls can be made via cardphone at *Anchorage Hotel*, the airport or in town. USA direct operator can also be reached by dialling 1-800-8722881 and credit card calls or operator assisted calls can be made. Post Office: on the main street in Clifton, on the right as you walk to Ashton. Stamps for postcards/letters to the Caribbean EC$0.60/0.70, Australia EC$0.75/1.40, to Canada/USA EC$0.65/0.90, to Europe EC$0.70/1.10. Federal Express, T4588843; DHL, T4858335. **Tourist office** On your left as you come off the ferry, before you get to the *Clifton Beach Hotel*, T4588350, open daily 0900-1600, limited information. **Useful numbers** Fire, T999; Hospital, T4588339; Police, T4588229; *Harvey's Pharmacy*, T4588596; Doctor, T4588547/4588339; Customs, T4588360 (airport), T4588294 (seaport), open Mon-Fri 0-900-1800. **Directory**

Tobago Cays

The Tobago Cays are a small collection of islets just off Mayreau, protected by a horseshoe reef and surrounded by beautifully clear water. The beaches are some of the most beautiful in the Caribbean and there is diving and snorkelling on Horseshoe reef and wall. There are day charters out of St Vincent, Bequia, Canouan and Union Island. Anchor damage, together with over-fishing and removal of black coral has led to the death of some of the reef; hard coral lies broken on the bottom, but overall it is in remarkably good condition considering the volume of visitors it receives. The cays have now been declared a marine reserve, although nothing is done to police it. Do not touch anything underwater, coral dies if you do. The Tobago Cays are crowded with unlimited charter boats, liveaboard boats or day charter catamarans, which can number over 150 in high season.. Mooring buoys have been put in to prevent anchoring on the reef, but there are not enough. Although the yachts anchor on sand, their dinghies do not and they are damaging the coral by putting down anchor wherever they want to snorkel. The flat, calm water within the reef has become popular as a place to kitesurf. Although exciting to watch and exhilarating to do, it is extremely dangerous with so many snorkellers on the surface of the water and is an accident waiting to happen. There are also anchorages west of Petit Rameau in the cut between Petit Rameau and Petit Bateau, or to the south of Baradel. You can shop at your boat or on the beach. Ice, fresh fish, lambi, lobster, T-shirts, even French designer clothes.

Petit St Vincent

Locally referred to as PSV, this is a beautiful, privately-owned, 113-acre island with one of the Caribbean's best resorts, the *Petit St Vincent*. Here you will find laid-back luxury, casual and stylish, with an excellent standard of service. If relaxation is what you want, you can get it here in spades. There are lots of trees and flowers providing a peaceful atmosphere and you can see most of the southern Grenadines from one view or another, even Mustique on a really clear day. The island is owned and managed by Hazen Richardson, with help from his wife, Lynn, a staff of 80 (for 44 guests) and seven rather elderly labradors. Accommodation is in 22 secluded cottages mostly on the northeast side of the island, which have the most glorious views of the reef and the changing colours of the sea, encompassing all the blues and turquoises imaginable. Steps lead down the cliffs to the beach below, where you can snorkel. There is a tennis court, fitness track and water toys: sunfish, hobie cats, windsurfers, glass-bottom kayaks. You can have room service (especially nice for breakfast) or eat in the central building. Communication with the administration is done with coloured flags hoisted outside your cottage, staff come round in golf carts to pick up your requests. Picnics can be arranged on the south-facing beach (hammocks and shade thoughtfully provided) or on the tiny islet Petit St Richardson. You can snorkel and dive off the Mopion and Punaise sandbar islands to the northwest. The island can be reached by the resort's launch from Union Island. The resort will charter a flight from Barbados to Union Island for US$160 per person one way, children half price. The one anchorage is on the south side opposite Petite Martinique, protected by a reef, where there is also a jetty. Beaches are public, so don't be surprised to see local children from Petite Martinique swimming or playing cricket near the anchorage.

Sleeping **LL** *Petit St Vincent Resort*, T4588801, F4588428, www.psvresort.com One of the Leading Hotels of the World. FAP, includes room service and all facilities, closed Sep/Oct.

Palm Island

Also known as Prune Island, is another privately-owned, luxury resort, about a mile from Union Island, with coral reefs on three sides. The island was developed by John and Mary Caldwell, after they had made several ocean voyages. John is the author of *Desperate Voyage*, a book describing his first ocean crossing; he sailed from the USA to Australia to meet Mary, with virtually no experience. The boat was demasted, wrecked on a reef and John was stranded on an island and forced to eat slime off the bottom of the boat until he was rescued. The Caldwells later arranged to lease this low-lying, swampy island from the St Vincent government and their family still runs the resort.

There are four beaches, of which the one on the west coast, Casuarina, is the most beautiful, helped along with copious amounts of sand washed up by Hurricane Lenny in 1999. A casual bar and restaurant facing Union Island is open to yachties and passengers of small cruise ships, but the rest of the island is reserved for guests. Even access to the beach from the jetty is prevented by ropes and notices. Water purchase is possible for yachts, moorings available. Sailing, windsurfing, scuba diving, snorkelling, fishing, tennis, health club all available for guests; a dive master is also available to accompany yacht visitors, snorkelling and diving is usually on the Mopion and Punaise sandbar islands. Shared charter flights can be arranged on *Mustique Airways* from Barbados to Union Island, where you will be met and brought over by the resort's launch, 10 mins.

Sleeping

LL *Palm Island Resort*, T4588824, F4588804, www.palmislandresort.com Apartments and individual bungalows, FAP.

Background

History

By the time Columbus discovered St Vincent on his third voyage in 1498, the Caribs were occupying the island, which they called Hairoun. They had overpowered the Arawaks, killing the men but interbreeding with the women. The Caribs aggressively prevented European settlement until the 18th century but were more welcoming to Africans. In 1675 a passing Dutch ship laden with settlers and their slaves was shipwrecked between St Vincent and Bequia. Only the slaves survived and these settled and mixed with the native population and their descendants still live in Sandy Bay and a few places in the northwest. Escaped slaves from St Lucia and Grenada later also sought refuge on St Vincent and interbred with the Caribs. As they multiplied they became known as 'Black Caribs'. There was tension between the Caribs and the Black Caribs and in 1700 there was civil war.

In 1722 the British attempted to colonize St Vincent but French settlers had already arrived and were living peaceably with the Caribs growing tobacco, indigo, cotton and sugar. Possession was hotly disputed until 1763 when it was ceded to Britain. It was lost to the French again in 1778 but regained under the Treaty of Versailles in 1783. However, this did not bring peace with the Black Caribs, who repeatedly tried to oust the British in what became known as the Carib Wars. A treaty with them in 1773 was soon violated by both sides. Peace came only at the end of the century when in 1796 General Abercrombie crushed a revolt fomented the previous year by the French radical Victor Hugues. In 1797, over 5,000 Black Caribs were deported to Roatán, an island at that time in British hands off the coast of Honduras. The violence ceased although racial tension took much longer to eradicate. In the late 19th century, a St Vincentian poet, Horatio Nelson Huggins wrote an epic poem about the 1795 Carib revolt and deportation to Roatán, called *Hiroona*, which was published in the 1930s.

In the 19th-century labour shortages on the plantations brought Portuguese immigrants in the 1840s and East Indians in the 1860s, and the population today is largely a mixture of these and the African slaves. Slavery was abolished in 1832 but social and economic conditions remained harsh for the majority non-white population. In 1902, La Soufrière erupted, killing 2,000 people, just two days before Mont Pelée erupted on Martinique, killing 30,000. Much of the farming land was seriously damaged and economic conditions deteriorated further. In 1925 a Legislative Council was inaugurated but universal adult suffrage was not introduced until 1951.

St Vincent and the Grenadines belonged to the Windward Islands Federation until 1959 and the West Indies Federation between 1958 and 1962. In 1969 the country became a British Associated State with complete internal self-government. Government during the 1970s was mostly coalition government between the St Vincent Labour Party (SVLP) and the People's Political Party. In 1979 St Vincent and the Grenadines gained full independence, but the year was also remembered for the eruption of La Soufrière on Good Friday, 13 April. Fortunately no one was killed as thousands were evacuated, but there was considerable agricultural damage. In 1980 Hurricane Allen caused further devastation to the plantations and it took years for production of crops such as coconuts and bananas to recover. Hurricane Emily destroyed an estimated 70% of the banana crop in 1987.

The National Democratic party (NDP), held power under Prime Minister James Mitchell (Sir James after receiving a knighthood in the 1995 New Year Honours list) from 1984 until 2001. In the 1998 elections, the NDP won eight of the 15 seats in the House of Assembly, compared with 12 previously, and its share of the vote fell. The remaining seats were won by the United Labour Party (ULP), which called for new elections within nine months because the ULP won 54.6% of the vote compared with only 45.3% for the winning NDP. The Government was often criticized for its handling of the economy and for failing to deal with drug trafficking and health and education issues. US officials believed that offshore banks in St Vincent were being used to launder drugs money and that the southern Grenadines are a transshipment point for cocaine. Marijuana is grown in the hills of St Vincent and the USA regularly carries out eradication exercises. Farmers complain that have no alternative crop to grow, particularly since the collapse in banana exports, brought on by US trade policies.

Political tensions in 2000 were defused by the mediation of the Caribbean Community (Caricom). Conflict arose when the government introduced a bill to increase pension and gratuities for members of parliament which was passed by the House of Assembly in April. The ULP, trade unions and other organizations organized strikes and called for the government's resignation. The Caricom agreement, signed in May, called for general elections to be bought forward by two years and held no later than end-March 2001. Sir James Mitchell (69) resigned the leadership of the NDP in August 2000. The 2001 elections resulted in a landslide victory for the ULP, which won all the seats in the House of Assembly. The party was led by Ralph Gonsalves, who became Prime Minister.

Geography St Vincent, and its 32 sister islands and cays which make up the Grenadines, were until fairly recently, almost unknown to tourists except yachtsmen and divers. They remain uncrowded. St Vincent is very picturesque, with fishing villages, coconut groves, banana plantations and fields of arrowroot, of which the island is the world's largest producer. It is a green and fertile volcanic island, with lush valleys, rugged cliffs on the leeward and windward coasts and beaches of dark or black volcanic sand. The highest peak on the island is La Soufrière, an active volcano in the north rising to about 4,000 ft. It last erupted in 1979 but careful monitoring enabled successful evacuation before it blew. The steep mountain range of Morne Garu rises to 3,500 ft and runs southward with spurs to the east and west coasts. Most of the central mountain range and the steep hills are forested. St Vincent is roughly 18 miles long and 11 miles wide and has an area of 133 square miles, while the Grenadines contribute another 17 square miles all together.

People About a quarter of the people live in the capital, Kingstown and its suburbs. 8% live on the Grenadines. Sixty-six percent of the population is classed as black and 19% as mixed, while 2% are Amerindian/black, 6% East Indian, 4% white and the remainder are 'others'. In the north of the island there are people of Carib descent, see History above. Nelcia Robinson, above Cyrus Tailor shop on Grenville Street, is an authority on Black Caribs/Garifuna and is the co-ordinator of the Caribbean Organization of Indigenous People on St Vincent.

Government St Vincent and the Grenadines is a constitutional monarchy within the Commonwealth. The Queen is represented by a Governor General. There is a House of Assembly with 15 elected representatives and six senators.

Economy The St Vincent economy is largely based on agriculture and tourism, with a small manufacturing industry which is mostly for export. The main export is bananas, the

Milton Cato 1915-1997

Milton Cato was a key figure in the development of democracy and independence in St Vincent and the Grenadines. From a poor family, he pulled himself up through a scholarship to grammar school, and after serving in the Canadian Volunteer Army in the War, was called to the bar in 1949. He returned from London to set up business in Kingstown and became involved in politics, then in its infancy, with plantation workers only recently having won the vote. In 1955 he founded the St Vincent Labour Party (SVLP), and when St Vincent became part of the West Indian Federation, he went in 1958 to Trinidad as one of his island's representatives. After the collapse of the Federation he entered St Vincent's parliament in 1961 and led the

SVLP to victory in the 1967 elections, becoming Chief Minister. In 1969 he participated in the negotiations which gave the island the status of Associated Statehood. He remained in power, with a brief interlude in 1972-74, and led St Vincent into independence in 1979. In the general elections of that year the SVLP won 11 of the 13 seats in the newly independent House of Assembly. However, economic stagnation and natural disasters, together with allegations of corruption, hit the popularity of Cato's government and the SVLP was defeated in the elections of 1984 which brought James Mitchell to power. Milton Cato retired a year later, shunning honours or public recognition of his service to his country, and died on 10 February 1997.

fortunes of which used to fluctuate according to the severity of the hurricane season, but the fall in prices brought about by the new European banana policy has hit hard. The Banana Growers Association is in debt and has been attempting to cut costs, but investment has place in improving land, irrigation and packing sheds. Quality, prices, planting and production have all recovered strongly. Nevertheless, the Government is encouraging farmers to diversify and reduce dependence on bananas with incentives and land reform. Arrowroot starch is the second largest export crop, St Vincent is the world's largest producer, although it is still very small scale. Arrowroot is now used as a fine dressing for computer paper as well as the traditional use as a thickening agent in cooking. Other exports include coconuts and coconut oil, copra, anthurium lilies, orchids, sweet potatoes, tannias and eddoes. Over half of all exports are sold to the UK.

Fishing has received government promotion and substantial aid from Japan. In 1998 Japan gave the island a grant of 776 mn yen (about EC$4.5 mn) for the construction of fishery centres in Kingstown and elsewhere, having previously granted EC$12 mn in 1996 for construction of jetties and fish refrigeration facilities in St Vincent, Canouan and Bequia, 72 mn yen (about US$7 mn) for a coastal fisheries development project and 916 mn yen for the national fisheries development plan. In return, St Vincent supports Japan on whaling issues.

St Vincent emerged as the largest flag of convenience in the Caribbean, with 521 ships on its register in 1990. In 1991 about 100 more were added as a direct result of the Yugoslav conflict, most of which came from Croatia and Slovenia. However, ships carrying the Vincentian flag have a poor record for safety, second only to Romania and have often been detained by European port officials for unseaworthiness.

Tourism in St Vincent and the Grenadines is important as a major employer and source of foreign exchange. The Government has encouraged upmarket, often yacht-based tourism, principally in the Grenadines. Expansion is limited by the size of the airport and the willingness of international airlines to fly into the islands. In 2001 the news that American Eagle was pulling out of St Vincent was a blow to the economy, unlikely to be fully compensated by the later announcement that it would start flying into Canouan. A plan to extend the airport runway to take jumbo jets has long been under discussion with possible finance from Taiwan, France and Kuwait. Stopover tourist arrivals are around 60,000 a year. Visitor expenditure is about US$50 mn a year.

A Foot in the door

- A rum punch with **nutmeg** is essential at sunset; nutmeg jelly for breakfast.
- For unsurpassed beauty, experience the rainforest with a **hike in the mountains**, cooling off in waterfalls and pools.
- Stroll around the harbour in **St George's**, watching the boats and the bustle.
- Take a day trip on the hovercraft to **Carriacou**.
- Make the most of the **local food**, try callaloo, curry goat or oildown.

Grenada

Colour map 5, grid C4

Known as the spice island because of the nutmeg, mace and other spices it produces, Grenada (pronounced 'Grenayda'), the most southerly of the Windward Islands, is volcanic in origin, has a beautiful mountainous interior and is well endowed with lush forests and cascading rivers. Hikers and nature lovers enjoy the trails in the national parks, where many different ecosystems are found, from dry tropical forest and mangroves on the coast, through lush rainforest on the hillsides, to elfin woodland on the peaks. St George's, the capital, is widely acknowledged as the prettiest harbour city in the West Indies, blending the architectural styles of the French and English with a picturesque setting on steep hills overlooking the bay. The southern coast, with its sandy beaches, protected bays and rocky promontories, is being developed for tourism and there is a wide range of places to stay.

Ins and outs

Getting there
See transport, page 869, for further details

Air links with Europe and North America are not good and usually involve a change of plane in San Juan, Trinidad or Barbados. Direct flights from London are being discontinued, although it is hoped that BWIA will step in to fill the gap. There are scheduled services but these are seasonal. Unless you are on a yacht or a cruise ship it is not easy to get there by sea either, although there is a ferry between Union Island (St Vincent) and Carriacou, allowing island hopping from the north.

Getting around
Driving is on the left. Be prepared for no road signs, no indication which way the traffic flow goes (just watch the other cars) & few street names

There is a good and colourful bus service connecting St George's with most parts of the island. It is cheap, but driving is fast and roads are twisty, so if you have a tendency to car sickness this may not be for you. One alternative is car hire, if you are good at finding your way around and are not intimidated by local drivers. Maps are often not accurate, so navigation becomes particularly difficult. Also be careful of the deep storm drains along the edges of the narrow roads. Cycling is good around Grenada, with accommodation conveniently spaced. The ride between Sauteurs and Victoria is peaceful with spectacular views. From Gouyave to St George's via Grand Etang is difficult but rewarding with some steep hills in the beautiful forest reserve and small, friendly communities. Allow 5-6 hrs. There are plenty of tours offered if you would prefer someone else to do the driving, usually by minibus and reasonably priced and informative.

Climate
The average temperature is 26°C. December and January are the coolest months. The rainy season runs from June to November. In November 1999, the west coast of Grenada was hit badly by Hurricane Lenny and was declared a disaster area, as was the west coast of Carriacou and the whole of Petit Martinique. There was no storm and in fact the sun shone brightly as the hurricane passed much further north, but a tremendous swell, with the sea rising many feet above normal, caused flooding. Sea walls collapsed, taking coastal roads with them, cutting off some villages, while floods hit harbour front restaurants in St George's and beach hotels at Grand Anse. Most of the damage has now been repaired although work on rebuilding the Leeward coastal road continued in 2001. Winter (high) season prices come into effect from 16 December to 15 April. The tourist season is at its height between December and March, although visitor numbers also pick up in July and August.

Flora and fauna

A system of national parks and protected areas is being developed. Information is available from the Forestry Department, Ministry of Agriculture, Archibald Avenue, St George's. The focal point of Grenada's nature tourism is the **Grand Étang National Park**, eight miles from the capital in the central mountain range. It is on the transinsular road from St George's to Grenville. The Grand Étang is a crater lake surrounded by lush tropical forest. At times of volcanic activity in the region, the water level in the lake has risen sharply, as it has in other crater lakes and lagoons on the island. A series of trails has been blazed which are well worth the effort for the beautiful forest and views, but can be muddy and slippery after rain. The **Morne**

Grenada

Essentials

Documents *Citizens of the UK, USA and Canada need only provide proof of identity (with photograph) and an onward ticket (but note that if you go to Grenada via Trinidad, a passport has to be presented in Trinidad). For all others a passport and onward ticket are essential, though a ticket from Barbados to the USA (for example) is accepted. Departure by boat is not accepted by the immigration authorities. Citizens of certain other countries (not the Commonwealth, Caribbean – except Cuba, South Korea, Japan and most European countries) must obtain a visa to visit Grenada. Check before leaving home. When you arrive in Grenada expect to have your luggage examined very thoroughly. It may take you at least 45 minutes to get through passport control and customs. You must be able to give an accommodation address when you arrive.*

Currency *East Caribbean dollar: EC$2.70 = US$1.*

Departure tax *For stays of over 24 hours, departure tax is EC$50, (EC$25 for children 2-12). EC$10 airport tax is charged on departure from Lauriston Airport, Carriacou.*

Ports of entry *(Own flag) Hillsborough on Carriacou, the site of the former Grenada Yacht Services at St George's, Grenada Marine, St David's Harbour and Spice Island Marina at Prickly Bay. No port fees for clearing in or out of Prickly Bay or St George's during normal working hours, Monday-Friday 0800-1600, overtime charges will apply outside those hours. On Carriacou, moor in Tyrrel Bay and take bus to Hillsborough. Three crew and/or passenger lists, immigration cards for anyone going ashore, ships stores and health declaration, port clearance from the last country and valid passports. Monday-Thursday 0800-1145, 1300-1600, Friday until 1700. To clear out of the country take the boat to Prickly Bay (where they can see the boat), and four copies of the crew list.*

Firearms must be declared. Seal in a proper locker on board or take to an official locker on shore to be returned on departure. Yachting fees on Grenada are: less than 50 feet US$10, 50-100 feet US$12.

Anchorages *Halifax Harbour (may have smoke from garbage burning), St George's Lagoon (security problems noted), True Blue Bay, Prickly Bay, Mount Hartman Bay, Clark's Court Bay, Port Egmont, Calivigny Harbour, Westerhall Bay. Hog Island can be used as a day anchorage; government and coast guard uncertain about overnight use; occasionally clear out all boats but then don't come back for a while. Can dinghy to Lower Woburn from Mount Hartman or Hog Island to catch bus to St George's, otherwise taxi from Secret Harbour. Prohibited anchorages: Grand Anse Bay, Prickly Bay (Lance aux Epines), Pingouin (Pink Gin) Beach, Point Salines, Tyrrel Bay (Carriacou), Mangrove Lagoon, the entire inner Lagoon. The outer Lagoon is prohibited to yachts and other liveaboard vessels. The Mangrove Lagoon may only be entered to shelter from a hurricane. Marine weather for Grenada and the Windward Islands on VHF Ch 6 at 1000.*

Marinas *Spice Island Marine Services in Prickly Bay (Lance aux Épines), T444-4257/4342, F4442816, has a small boatyard with bar, restaurant, ship's store, laundry and mini-market, where boats can be stored or repaired on land as well as stern-to-dock, fuel and water.* **Grenada Marine** *at St David's harbour, east of Little Bacolet Bay, T4431667, F4431668, www.grenadamarine.com has haulout facility with 70-ton, 30-ft wide lift, customs and immigration, repair services, storage, restaurant and bar, beach, internet café, laundry, showers/ The* **Moorings Secret Harbour** *base in Mount Hartman has stern-to-docks, fuel and water, a mini-mart*

Labaye nature trail is only 15 minutes' long, return same route; the shoreline trail around the lake takes 1½ hours and is moderately easy; much further, 1½ hours' walk, is **Mount Qua Qua**. The trail then continues for an arduous three hours to **Concord Falls**, with an extra 30-minute spur to **Fedon's Camp** (see page 860). From Concord Falls it is 25 minutes' walk to the road to get a bus to St George's. These are hard walks (Mount Qua Qua, Fedon's Camp, Concord): wet, muddy, it rains a lot and you will get dirty. Take food and water. A guide is not essential, but useful. Three new trails were opened in 2000, two in the Grand Etang area and one at Annandale. All hikes are graded for difficulty.

with basic food and drink, **Rum Squall** bar, will hold message/fax and mail for yachties, T4444548, F4444819. Day charter services, bareboat or with captain, from the marina. Carriacou Yacht Services in Tyrrel Bay provide mail, phone, fax and message service to yachts.

Hours of business Banks: 0800-1300 or 1400 Monday-Thursday; 0800-1200 or 1300, 1430-1700 Friday. **Shops**: 0800-1600 Monday-Friday, 0800-1300 Saturday. Government offices: Monday-Friday 0800-1145, 1300-1600, closed Saturday.

Official time Atlantic Standard Time, 4 hours behind GMT, 1 ahead of EST.

Voltage 220/240 volts, 50 cycles AC.

Media Newspapers There are no daily papers, only weeklies, including Grenadian Voice, Indies Times, Grenada Guardian, The National, and The Informer.

Radio There are nine radio stations, on AM 535, AM 1440, FM 89.5, 90.1, 96.3, 98.5, 101.7, 105.5 and 106.3 kHz. The Voice of Grenada is on 95.7 and 103 FM.

Television There are four television stations but many hotels have satellite or cable reception.

Tourist offices overseas Austria c/o Discover the World Marketing, Stephans Platz 6/3/7, 1010 Vienna, T512-868640, F512-868660, discover_vie@compuserve.com **Canada** 439 University Av, Suite 920, Toronto, Ontario M5G 1Y8, T416-5951339, F416-5958279, tourism@grenadaconsulate.com **Germany** Uhlandstrasse 30, D-53340 Mechenheim, T02225-947507, F02225-947508, RMTours87@aol.com **UK** 1 Battersea Church Road, London SW11 3LY, T020-77717016, F020-77717181, grenada@cibgroup.co.uk **USA** 317 Madison Avenue, Suite 1522, New York, NY 10017, T212-6879554, 800-9279554,

F212-5739731, noel@rfcp.com

Clothing Casual, lightweight summer clothes suitable all year. Bathing costumes not accepted off the beach.

Laundry Tangie's Laundry & Dry Cleaning Service, Sugar Mill Roundabout, St George's, T4444747, next to the Sugar Mill Night Club, pick up and delivery service. Also Super Kleen, T4408499, Henry's Safari Tours, T4445313, and Spice Island Marina, T4444257.

Safety On the Carenage in St George's, you may be pestered for money, particularly after dark, but it is no more than a nuisance. Unemployment and drug abuse are problems; more than three quarters of the prison population have been sentenced for drug related crimes. Night police patrols have been introduced in hotels and beach areas. In the countryside people are extremely helpful and friendly and there is no need anywhere for anything other than normal precautions against theft. If visiting St George's it is best to pick a day when there are no cruise ships in port, to avoid hassle from vendors and touts. Carriacou is generally safe, despite smuggling, but avoid deserted beaches. Two Swedish tourists were murdered on the beach in 2000 in the middle of the day, which just proves you can never be too careful. Locals were (and still are) shocked and a man was quickly apprehended.

Public holidays New Year's Day (1 January), Independence Day (7 February), Good Friday and Easter Monday, Labour Day (1 May), Whit Monday (in May/June), Corpus Christi (June), August holidays (first Monday and Tuesday in August) and Carnival (second weekend in August), Thanksgiving (25 October), 25 and 26 December.

Communications The international code for Grenada is 473. See page 870 for further details.

An interpretation centre overlooking the lake has videos, exhibitions and explanations of the medicinal plants in the forest, T4406160. Leaflets about the trails can be bought here for EC$2-3 each. There is a bar, a shop and some amusing monkeys and parrots. The Park is open 0800-1600, entrance US$2, closed Saturday but there are some stalls open selling spices and souvenirs. There is overnight accommodation at Lake House, T4427425 or enquire at forest centre, also for camping.

The high forest receives over 160 inches of rain a year. Epiphytes and mosses cling to the tree trunks and many species of fern and grasses provide a thick undergrowth. The trees include the gommier, bois canot, Caribbean pine and blue mahoe. At the summit, the vegetation is an example of elfin woodland, the trees stunted by the wind, the leaves adapted with drip tips to cope with the excess moisture.

Apart from the highest areas, the island is heavily cultivated. On tours around the country look for nutmeg trees and the secondary product, mace, cloves, cinnamon, allspice, bay, turmeric and ginger. In addition there are calabash gourds, cocoa, coffee, breadfruit, mango, paw paw (papaya), avocado, and more common crops, bananas and coconuts. Sugar cane is used to make rum at three distilleries. Many of the spices can be seen at the Douglaston Estate or the Nutmeg Co-operatives in Gouyave or Grenville. Laura's Spice and Herb Garden, near Perdmontemps in St David's, has samples of herbs and spices grown in their natural habitat (EC$5, closed Sat).

Leatherback turtles come ashore here in Apr, May & Jun

In the northeast, 450 acres around **Levera Pond** was opened as a National Park in 1994 (US$1 entrance). As well as having a bird sanctuary and sites of historic interest, Levera is one of the island's largest mangrove swamps; the coastal region has coconut palms, cactus and scrub, providing habitat for iguana and land crabs. There are white beaches where turtles lay their eggs and, offshore, coral reefs and the Sugar Loaf, Green and Sandy islands (boat trip to the last named on Sunday, see Ferries). You can swim at Bathway but currents are strong at other beaches. The coast between Levera Beach and Bedford Point is eroding rapidly, at a rate of several feet a year. South of Levera is **Lake Antoine**, another crater lake, but sunken to only about 20 ft above sea level; it has been designated a Natural Landmark.

On the south coast is **La Sagesse Protected Seascape**, a peaceful refuge which includes beaches, a mangrove estuary, a salt pond and coral reefs. In the coastal woodland are remains of sugar milling and rum distilleries. To get there turn south off the main road opposite an old sugar mill, then take the left fork of a dirt road through a banana plantation. Close to the pink plantation house (accommodation available), a few feet from a superb sandy beach, is *La Sagesse* bar and restaurant, good food, nutmeg shells on the ground outside. Walk to the other end of the beach to where a path leads around a mangrove pond to another beach, usually deserted apart from the occasional angler, fringed with palms, good snorkelling and swimming, reef just offshore.

Marquis Island, off the east coast, can be visited; at one time it was part of the mainland and now has eel grass marine environments and coral reefs. Nearby is **La Baye Rock**, which is a nesting ground for brown boobies, habitat for large iguanas and has dry thorn scrub forest. It too is surrounded by coral reefs.

Grenada is quite good for birdwatching. The only endemic bird is the Grenada Dove, which inhabits scrubby woodland in some west areas. In the rainforest you can see the emerald-throated hummingbird, yellow-billed cuckoo, red-necked pigeon, ruddy quail-dove, cocoa thrush and other species, while wading and shore birds can be spotted at both Levera and in the south and southwest. The endangered hookbilled kite (a large hawk) is found in the Levera National Park and nowhere else in the world. It uses its beak to pluck tree snails (its only food) out of their shells. A pile of shells with holes in them is evidence that a kite ate there. Watch also for the chicken hawk. Yellow-breasted bananaquits are very common.

There is little remarkable animal life: frogs and lizards, of course, and iguana, armadillo (tatoo) and manicou (possum), all of these are hunted for the pot. The tree boa (*Corallus enydris*) is known locally as a 'sarpint' and eats rodents. It grows to about six feet and sleeps during the day 50-70 feet above the ground in the tree tops. The higher they live the darker colour they become. They are quite common, but rarely seen, being nocturnal. One oddity, though, is a troop of Mona monkeys, imported from Africa over 300 years ago, which lives in the treetops in the vicinity of the Grand Étang. Having also been hunted for the pot (a male can weigh 50lbs) they are now endangered. Another import is the mongoose.

Windward Islands

Diving and marine life

The reefs around Grenada provide excellent sites for diving. A popular dive is to the wreck of the Italian cruise liner, *Bianca C* which went down in 1961. Other dive sites include **Boss Reef**, **the Hole**, **Valley of Whales**, **Forests of Dean**, **Grand Mal Point** (wall dive), **Dragon Bay** (wall dive) ends at Molinière, **Happy Valley** (drift with current to Dragon Bay). Three wrecks from cargo ships off Quarantine Point, St George's, are in strong currents. Molinière reef for beginners to advanced has a sunken sailboat, the *Buccaneer*; Whibble Reef is a slopey sand wall (advanced drift dive); Channel reef is a shallow reef at the entrance to St George's with many rusted ships' anchors; Spice Island reef is for resort dives and beginners as well as the wrecks *Red Buoy*, *Veronica L* and *Quarter Wreck*. Dive sites around Carriacou include **Kick Em Jenny** (a submarine volcano), **Isle de Ronde**, **Sandy Island**, **Sister Rocks** (to 100 ft, strong currents), **Twin Sisters** (walls to 180 ft and strong currents), **Mabouya Island**, **Saline Island** (drift dive). The reef suffered some damage in 1999 from Hurricane Lenny, but the diving here is still good.

The best **snorkelling** is around Molinière Point and up to Dragon Bay and Flamingo Bay. Flamingo Bay is named after a snail, not a bird. Snorkelling trips by boat will usually bring you to this area, often in the afternoons so that divers on board can do a shallow dive as well. You can see a wide variety of fish and invertebrates on the rocks and coral, even moray eels in holes if you look carefully.

Dive sites

Dive companies change locations and resort affiliations rapidly, but there is usually one at any of the larger resorts. *Dive Grenada* is at *Allamanda Beach Resort*, T4441092, F4445875, www.divegrenada.com, PADI courses, wreck dives for experienced divers, night dives, snorkelling. *Eco Dive and Trek* at *Coyaba Beach Resort*, in Grand Anse, and at *True Blue Bay Resort*, offers PADI courses, underwater video and photography, snorkelling, kayak and sunfish instruction, also home of Grenada's Turtle Conservation Project, which links turtle and reef monitoring with conservation programmes at local schools, T4442133, F4442245, www.scubadivegrenada.com   *Sanvics Watersports*, *Grand Beach Resort*, is an all-inclusive operation with trips to islands, T4444371, F4445227, sanvics@caribsurf.com *Scuba World* at the *Rex Grenadian*, T/F4443864, scubaworld@caribsurf.com *1st Spice Divers Grenada*, at *Secret Harbour* and *the Moorings*, Lance aux Epines, T4441126, F4441127, www.spicedivers.com, operate from a pier at Mount Hartmann Bay with a 30 ft boat, courses offered in English, Dutch, German, French and Spanish, run by Peter and Gerlinde Seupel, quality personal attention. *Spice Island Diving* is at the *Spice Island Beach Resort*, T4443483, F4445319, www.spicebeachresort.com On Carriacou both dive operations are German speaking: *Tanki's Watersport Paradise*, at L'Esterre Bay, Carriacou, T4438406, F4438391, www.cacounet.com/paradise, and *Carriacou Silver Diving* at Main Street, Hillsborough, T/F4437882, www.scubamax.com, run by Max and Claudia Nagel, an enthusiastic German couple who have been on the island since 1993, two boats, very professional.

Dive centres
5% tax is added to all diving and snorkelling rates

A basic scuba dive costs about US$40 per person, a two-tank dive is US$65-75, equipment rental US$10, resort course US$75, snorkelling trips US$20-25; dive packages and open water certification are available. Several charter boats doing day trip sailing excursions also offer scuba equipment. The nearest recompression chamber is in Barbados or Trinidad, both 30 minutes by air ambulance. Members of the Grenada Scuba Diving Association all carry oxygen on board their boats. Snorkelling equipment hire costs about US$12 for three hours, sometimes for a day; again, there are plenty of opportunities for this. Glass-bottomed boats make tours of the reefs. The *Carriacou Islander* is a 35-ft motor catamaran with an observation window which can be raised or lowered as required and cruises around Carriacou and Petit Martinique.

Humpback whales can be seen off Grenada and Carriacou during their migrations in December-April. Pilot whales and dolphins are also found in Grenadian waters (see *Whale and Dolphin Watching*, page 68). Contact Mosden Cumberbatch (see below) for whale watching tours, he has a power catamaran especially designed for whale watching, US$60 including sandwiches and drinks for lunch, five-hour trip.

Beaches and watersports

There are 45 beaches on Grenada. The best are in the southwest, particularly **Grand Anse**, a lovely stretch of white sand which looks north to St George's. It can get crowded with cruise passengers, but there's usually plenty of room for everyone. Beach vendors have a proper market with 78 booths, washroom facilities, a tourist desk and a jetty for water taxis, to prevent hassling on the beach, but it is not working very well as not enough customers visit it.**Morne Rouge**, the next beach going southwest, is more private, has good snorkelling and no vendors. There are other nice, smaller beaches around **Lance aux Épines**. The beaches at **Levera** and **Bathway** in the northeast are also good, wild and unimproved.

Windsurfing, waterskiing and **parasailing** all take place off Grand Anse beach. Windsurf board rental about US$7 for 30 minutes, waterskiing, US$15 per run, parasailing US$25. The *Moorings' Club Mariner* Watersports Centre at *Secret Harbour*, T4444439, F4444819, has small sail boats, sunfish, windsurfing, waterskiing, speedboat trips to Hog Island including snorkelling. Inshore sailing on sunfish, sailfish and hobiecats is offered by Grand Anse and Lance aux Épines hotels and operators. Rates are about US$10 for 30 minutes for sunfish rental.

Day sails
See Carriacou, Tour operators, for day sails on that island

Sailing in the waters around Grenada and through the Grenadines, via Carriacou, is very good. Sheltered harbours, such as Halifax Bay on the Leeward coast, can be found and there are marinas on the south coast. *First Impressions* has two catamarans accommodating 35 people for all types of charters, day, overnight, sunset, call Mosden Cumberbatch, T4403678, www.catamaranchartering.com US$60 per person day sail, snorkelling included, US$30 sunset cruise. *Carib Cats*, T4443222, offer full-day, snorkelling or sunset cruises. *Catch the Spirit*, T4444753, sanvics@ caribsurf.com, offer customized trips for snorkellers, divers or fishermen. *Island Dreams* is a 45-ft yacht for private charter for up to 10 people, US$60 per person with lunch, Bob and Judi, T4433603. *Firefly* is a 38-ft sloop available for day sails or charters, T4438625, studio@caribsurf.net The *Moorings Secret Harbour* Watersports Centre has skippered charters at US$25 per person half day, US$50 per person whole day, minimum four people, T4444439. Trips go to Carriacou, Sandy Island, Calivigny Island and Hog Island, or up the coast, stopping at beaches for barbecues or reefs for snorkelling. There are lots of other companies offering day sails, no shortage of choice.

On the first weekend in August the **Carriacou Regatta** is held, which has developed into a full-scale festival, with land as well as watersports and jump-ups at night (T4437930). **La Source Grenada Sailing Festival** is held annually in January-February with several races and regattas, organized by the Grenada Yacht Club, T4402500, www.grenadasailingfestival.com. Other races include the Bank of Nova Scotia Yacht Race in March, the Venezuela Independence Day Regatta in July, the Grand Anse Yacht Race in September (T4403050) and Grand Anse Match-Yacht Racing in October (T4403050). In November an end-of-hurricane-season yacht regatta sponsored by Carib Beer is timed to coincide with Beach Fest, a weekend of beach parties and watersports (T4403050).

Fishing

Deep-sea fishing can be arranged through *Grenada Yacht Services, Bezo Charters*, call Graham or Ian (T443-5477, westrum@caribsurf.com), *Evans Chartering Services*, call Bob or Jill (T4444422, bevans@caribsurf.com) and Tropix (T4404961). At the end of January each year, Grenada hosts **The Spice Island Game Fishing Tournament**, T4402198 for information.

Other sports

Cricket, the island's main land sport, is played from January to June. The locals play on any piece of fairly flat ground or on the beaches. **Soccer** is also played. Hotels have **tennis** courts and public courts are found at Grand Anse and Tanteen, St George's. There is a nine-hole **golf** course at the Grenada Golf and Country Club, Woodlands, above Grand Anse; the club is open daily 0800 to sunset, but only till 1200 on Sunday (T4444128). **Volleyball** can be played at the Aquarium Beach Club after snorkelling on the reef. It is a fun spot on a secluded beach just below Point Salines off the airport road, T4441410. An annual international **triathlon** is held in January, with a 1 km swim along the Grand Anse beach, a 25 km bicycle race to the airport, St George's and back to the hotel, then a 5 km run to the Carib brewery and back in individual and relay style. For information, contact Paul Slinger, T4403343.

A National Stadium has recently been built at Queens Park, to the north of St George's, which will be used for cultural events and exhibitions as well as sports, and have shops, offices, restaurants and bars. Sports facilities will include an international football and athletics stadium with a capacity for 15,000, a test match cricket ground and a cycle track.

St George's

St George's is one of the Caribbean's most beautiful harbour cities. The town stands on an almost landlocked sparkling blue harbour against a background of green and hazy blue hills, with its terraces of pale, colour-washed houses and cheerful red roofs. The capital was established in 1705 by French settlers, and much of its present-day charm comes from the blend of two colonial cultures: typical 18th-century French provincial houses intermingle with fine examples of English Georgian architecture. Unlike many Caribbean ports, which are built around bays on coastal plains, St George's straddles a promontory. It therefore has steep hills with long flights of steps and sharp bends, with police on point duty to prevent chaos at the blind junctions. At every turn is a different view or angle of the town, the harbour or the coast.

> *The tourist board publishes a pamphlet, Historic Walking Tour of St George's, which is recommended*

The Carenage runs around the inner harbour, connected with the Esplanade on the seaward side of Fort George Point by the **Sendall Tunnel**, built in 1895. There is always plenty of dockside activity on the Carenage, with food, drinks and other goods being loaded and unloaded from wooden schooners. Cruise ships come in on the south side of the bay and the ferries and hovercraft from Carriacou and Petite Martinique dock in the middle. Restaurants, bars and shops line the Carenage and it is pleasant to sit and watch all the bustle. The harbour is in fact the crater of an old volcano. In 1867 the water in the lagoon started to boil and the air stank of sulphur. The water level in the harbour has on three occasions risen about five feet above sea level, causing flood damage on the Carenage.

The small **National Museum**, in the centre of town (corner of Young and Monckton Streets) is worth a visit. It used to be the *Antilles Hotel*, part of the former French barracks built in 1704. From 1767-1880, the British used parts as a prison, then the ground floor became a warehouse and upstairs a hotel. Note the cast iron balcony, not many of which are left in St George's. Displays are rather dusty and old-fashioned, but cover a wide range of historical topics, pre-columbian, natural history, colonial, military, independence, the Cuban crisis, some items from West Africa, exhibits from the sugar and spice industries and of local shells and fauna. ■ *US$2, open Mon-Fri 0900-1630, Sat 1030-1300, T4403725.*

Fort George (1706) on the headland is now the police headquarters, but public viewpoints have been erected from which to see the coast and harbour. Photographs are not allowed everywhere. Some old cannons are still in their positions; tremendous views all round. The French called it Fort Royale but the British named it Fort George. After the overthrow of Eric Gairy's government in 1979 it was briefly renamed Fort Rupert, but reverted to George after the return of democratic rule in 1983. Just down from the Fort is St Andrew's Presbyterian Kirk (1830) also known as Scot's Kirk. On Church Street are a number of important buildings: St George's Anglican Church (1825), the Roman Catholic Cathedral (tower 1818, church 1884) and the Supreme Court and Parliament buildings (late 18th, early 19th century). St George's oldest religious building is the Methodist Church (1820) on Green Street.

The **Public Library** is an old government building on the Carenage which has been renovated and stocked with foreign assistance. In this part of the city are many brick and stone warehouses, roofed with red, fish tail tiles brought from Europe as ballast. A serious fire on 27 April 1990 damaged six government buildings on the Carenage, including the Treasury, the Government Printery, the Storeroom and the Post Office. Restoration work has been carried out. Also on the Carenage is a monument to the Christi Degli Abbissi, or Christ of the Deep, moved from the entrance to the harbour, which commemorates "the hospitality extended to the crew and passengers of the ill-fated liner", *Bianca C*. It stands on the walkway beside Wharf Road.

St George's

● **Eating**
1 Carenage Café	3 Rudolf's
2 Nutmeg	4 Tout Bagay

The Market Square, off Halifax Street (one of the main streets, one steep block from the Esplanade), is always busy. It is the terminus for many minibus routes and on Saturday holds the weekly market.

Just north of the city is **Queen's Park**, which is used for all the main sporting activities, carnival shows and political events. It is surrounded by a turquoise palisade. From **Richmond Hill** there are good views (and photo opportunities) of both St George's and the mountains of the interior. On the hill are Forts Matthew (built by the French, 1779), Frederick (1791) and Adolphus (built in a higher position than Fort George to house new batteries of more powerful, longer range cannon), and the prison in which are held those convicted of murdering Maurice Bishop.

Around the island

The Eastern Main Road heads east from Richmond Hill through numerous villages, twisting and turning, and there are a few places of interest for short excursions from St George's. To see a good selection of Grenada's flowers and trees, visit the **Bay Gardens** at Morne Delice (turn off the Eastern Main Road at St Paul's police station, the gardens are on your left as you go down). It's a pleasant place with a friendly owner; the paths are made of nutmeg shells. They will show you around if you want and explain the uses of all the fruits, herbs and spices. EC$5. If you take the next turning off the Eastern Main Road, just before the Texaco station, you reach the **Morne Gazo Nature Trails** on your right. Morne Gazo (or Delice Hill) rises to 1,140 ft and the Forestry Department has created trails covered with nutmeg shells in the forest. At the summit a lookout platform has been built around a tree, giving a panoramic view of the island, down to the airport in the south, across to La Sagesse and up to the hills around Grand Etang. Information leaflets are available in several languages. ■ *Open Mon-Sat 0900-1600, Sun 1000-1500, closed public holidays, EC$5, car park.* Just a bit further along the Eastern Main Road near Perdmontemps, is the turning for **Laura Spice and Herb Gardens**, where you can see nutmeg, cloves and all the other spices and herbs grown on the island, see Flora and fauna above. ■ *EC$5, closed Sat.*

East of St George's

From the Carenage, you can take a road which goes round the Lagoon, another sunken volcanic crater, now a yacht anchorage. It is overlooked by the ruins of the *Islander Hotel*, which was taken over by the revolutionary government and subsequently destroyed in the intervention.

Carrying on to the southwest tip you come to **Grand Anse**, Grenada's most famous beach. Along its length are many hotels, but none dominates the scene since, by law, no development may be taller than a coconut palm. Rather surprisingly, the St George's University School of Arts and Sciences has a campus here, right on the beach. Access to the beach and parking is at Camerhogue Park at the north end by the Spiceland shopping mall. From Grand Anse the road crosses the peninsula to a roundabout, from where roads lead off to the Point Salines airport or the Lance aux Épines headland. The road to Portici and Parc à Boeuf beaches leads to the right, off the airport road; follow the signs to *Groomes* beach bar on Parc à Boeuf (food and drink available). Portici beach is virtually deserted, with good swimming despite a steeply shelving beach and excellent snorkelling around Petit Cabrits point at its northeast end. The next road to the right leads to Magazine Beach and the *Rex Grenadian Hotel*, then comes Pink Gin Beach and, practically as far as you can go, is the all-inclusive *La Source*, all very close to the airport. On the south side of the peninsula, at **Prickly Bay** (the west side of Lance aux Épines) are hotels, the Spice Island Marina and other yachting and watersports facilities. Luxury homes take up much of Lance aux Épines down to Prickly Point. There is a glorious stretch of fine white sand, the lawns of the *Calabash Hotel* run down to the beach, very nice bar and restaurant open to non-residents, steel bands often play there. The next bay west, True Blue Bay, is smaller and quieter, but also has a hotel and yachting facilities as well as the university's School of Medicine on one headland.

The southwest

From the Point Salines/Lance aux Épines roundabout you can head east along a road which snakes around the south coast. At **Lower Woburn**, a small fishing community (which can be reached by bus from St George's), you can see vast piles of conch shells in the sea, forming jetties and islets where they have been discarded by generations of lambi divers. Stop at *Island View Restaurant* or a local establishment, *Nimrod and Sons Rum Shop*. Yachtsmen visit this spot to sign the infamous guest register and to be initiated with a shot of Jack Iron rum (beware, it is potent!). Past Lower Woburn is the **Clarks Court Rum Distillery** (tours available with rum sales, tip the guide). It is a steam driven operation, unlike the river Antoine water wheel system. Any number of turn-offs, tracks and paths, go inland to join the Eastern Main Road, or run along the rias and headlands, such as Calivigny, Fort Jeudy, Westerhall Point or La Sagesse with its nature reserve (see above). Many of Grenada's most interesting and isolated bays are in the southeast, accessible only by jeep or on foot; taxi drivers can drop you off at the start of a path and you can arrange to be picked up later.

The west coast The west coast road from St George's suffered damage from the swell caused by Hurricane Lenny in 1999 and repair work was still being carried out in 2001, although this was not causing serious delays. It is a beautiful seafront road, hugging the shore all the way to Duquesne Bay in the north with lovely views.

Heading north out of St George's, past Queen's Park stadium and Grand Mal Bay, you can turn inland to see petroglyphs, or rock carvings, near **Hermitage** (look for a sign on the road). On the coast, there is good snorkelling at Molinière Point and north at Dragon Bay, Flamingo Bay and up to Beausejour Bay. Beauséjour Estate, once the island's largest, is now in ruins (except for the estate Great House). It is owned by the Neckles family and is private, but from the road you can see the remains of the sugar mill and distillery on the opposite side of the road from the sports ground. Beyond Beauséjour is Halifax Bay, a beautiful, sheltered harbour, and the second most protected harbour in Grenada, but onland it is marred by a rubbish dump with smoke rising from it. Looking back over Halifax harbour is another old plantation house, Woodford Estate, a wooden building with pretty tiles, which is unfortunately falling apart.

At Concord, a road runs up the valley through nutmeg, cocoa, cashew, guava and clove trees to the First **Concord Falls** (45 minutes hot walk from the main road or go by car, driving slowly, children and vendors everywhere). It is very busy at the end of the road with tour buses and spice stalls everywhere. There are toilets and changing facilities (small fee) if you want to bathe in the small cascade, but there is not much water in the dry season. The Second Concord Falls are a 30-40-minutes' walk (each way), with a river to cross seven times; there is no need for a guide but it is advisable. The path is reasonable, but it is slippery when wet. Three hours further uphill is **Fedon's Camp**, at 2,509 ft, where Julian Fedon (see page 878) fortified a hilltop in 1795 to await reinforcements from Martinique to assist his rebellion against the British. After bloody fighting, the camp was captured; today it is a Historical Landmark. It is possible to hike from Concord to Grand Étang in five hours, a hard walk, wet and muddy but rewarding. The trail is hard to spot where it leaves the path to the upper falls about two thirds of the way up on the left across the river. There is no problem following the trails in the opposite direction.

North of Concord, just before Gouyave (pronounced *gwarve*), is a turn-off to **Dougaldston Estate**. Before the revolution 200 people were employed here in cultivating spices and other crops. Now there are only about 20 workers, the place is run down, the buildings in disrepair, the vehicles wrecked. Still, you can go into a shed where bats fly overhead and someone will explain all the spices to you. They still dry spices in the traditional way on racks which are wheeled under the building if it rains. Samples cost EC$5 for a bag of cinnamon, cloves or nutmeg, or there are mixed bags; give the guide a tip.

Gouyave, 'the town that never sleeps', is a fishing port, nutmeg collecting point and capital of St John's parish. There are a few interesting old buildings; the Post Office, just past the shiny red fire engine, has an iron balcony. At the Nutmeg Processing Station, you can see all the stages of drying, grading, separating the nutmeg and mace and packing (give a tip here too). On the top floor mace is dried for four months in Canadian pine boxes before being graded. There are three grades, used for culinary spice, corned beef or cosmetics, and only Grenada produces grade one mace for cooking. On the first floor, nutmeg is dried on racks for two months, turned occasionally with a rake. After testing they are graded, with the lighter ones used in medicine and the heavier ones for culinary spices. The husks are used for fuel or mulch and the fruit is made into nutmeg jelly (a good alternative to breakfast marmalade), syrup or liquor. The Station is a great wooden building by the sea, with a very powerful smell. A tour for US$1 is highly recommended. No photos. A little shop sells nutmeg products. There are two other processing plants, at Victoria and Grenville, but this is the largest. There is also a nutmeg oil distillery at Sauteurs. All are open to the public. Gouyave is the principal place to go to for the Fisherman's Birthday festival. On the last Friday in every month from May-December, Gouyave is open to tourists on a grand scale, with tours and walks during the day. In the evening the main street is closed to traffic, there is food, drink and music and dancing.

The north

Just outside Victoria, another fishing port and capital of St Mark's Parish, is a rock in the sea with Amerindian petroglyphs on it (best to know where to look over the parapet). The road continues around the northwest coast, turning inland at Duquesne (pronounced *Duquaine*) where there is a beautiful grey sand beach (not particularly clean because of fishing), before returning to the sea at **Sauteurs**, the capital of St Patrick's parish, on the north coast. The town is renowned as the site of the mass suicide of Grenada's last 40 Caribs, who jumped off a cliff rather than surrender to the French (see page 877). Leapers Hill is appropriately in the cemetery by the church. There has been some sea erosion and the protective rail has disappeared, so make sure you are not next to go over the edge. There are some interesting grave stones to look at while you are there, some of the local population have lived to a ripe old age. Behind Sauteurs is McDonald College from whose gate there are marvellous views out to sea, with the Grenadines beyond the town's two church towers, and inland to cloud-covered mountains. In March Sauteurs celebrates St Patrick's Day with a week of events, exhibits of arts and crafts and a mini-street festival.

Morne Fendue plantation house is just south of Sauteurs and a popular place for tour groups to stop for lunch. The house was built in 1912 and still has all the old mouldings, cornices and light fittings of that time. Once owned by Betty Mascoll MBE, it is now run by Dr Jean Thompson, who has built a new accommodation wing with splendid views of the north from Sauteurs on the coast to Mt Catherine inland. The buffet lunch features local specialities and is served in the large dining room of the old colonial house or on the veranda. Reservations essential. Accommodation is available in the new rooms or in the atmospheric old house, where guests have said it is like sleeping in a museum, see Sleeping below.

The east coast

From Sauteurs a road approaches **Levera Bay** (see above) from its west side. Turn left at *Chez Norah's* bar, a two-storey, green, corrugated iron building (snacks available); the track rapidly becomes quite rough and the final descent to Levera is very steep, suitable only for four-wheel drive. A better way to Levera approaches from the south. The road forks left about two miles south of Morne Fendue, passes through river Sallee and past Bathway Beach. The river Sallee Boiling Springs are an area of spiritual importance; visitors are inspired to throw coins into the fountain while they make a wish. **Bathway Beach** is a popular weekend spot when it can get busy. It is a huge dark golden stretch of sand, with cliffs at either end, trees for shade, a beach bar, picnic tables, and the Levera National Park visitors' centre. The word Bathway comes from a fish called the batwey. There is a ridge of rocks just offshore, parallel with the beach, which provides protection for swimming, almost like a swimming pool, but you must not swim beyond the rocks or you will be drowned. From here a dirt road leads past Levera Pond, where a wooden walkway allows you to walk out onto the water and a trail (1 ½ hrs) runs round the pond. Birds are best seen early morning or late evening. Swimming is good at the beautiful and wild Levera Beach where leatherback turtles come to nest in April-June, and there is surf in certain conditions. It is not as busy as Bathway because not many people want to subject their vehicles to the dusty/muddy, potholed, dirt road. Do not swim far out as there is a current in the narrows between the beach and the privately-owned Sugar Loaf Island. Further out are Green and Sandy Islands; you may be able to arrange a trip there with a fisherman, a few of whom keep their boats on Levera Beach.

On the east side of the island, the coastal road runs south past the circular crater lake, Lake Antoine (see above) where, like St George's and Grand Etang, the water has risen at times of volcanic activity, notably in 1902. Nearby is the **River Antoine Rum Distillery**, driven by a water mill, the oldest in the Caribbean (guided tours, T4427109). The only modern equipment is the lock for government control. Try the 151° proof rum, they sell all by the bottle. People in the south are rather snooty about the smell and taste of the rum distilled here, saying that they can smell it on your breath next day. The **Dunfermline Rum Distillery** can also be visited. There are no organized tours but the staff will show you around and explain the process.

Amerindian remains can be seen at an archaeological dig near the old **Pearls airport**. Apparently it's so unprotected that lots of artefacts have been stolen. The airport is worth a quick visit to see the two old Cuban and Russian planes and the duty-free shop, a ghost town, although the runway is well used for driving lessons, cricket, biking and social encounter in general.

Grenville is the main town on the east coast and capital of St Andrew's Parish, the largest parish in Grenada with a population of about 25,000. It is a collection point for bananas, nutmeg and cocoa, and also a fishing port. You can tour the Nutmeg Cooperative Processing Station, US$1, with samples of nutmeg and mace (tip the guide). There are some well-preserved old buildings, including the Court House, Anglican Church, police station and Post Office. Saturday is market day, worth seeing. Weavers turn palm fronds into hats, baskets and place mats.

The Rainbow City Festival is held here at the beginning of August, with arts and crafts displays, street fairs, cultural shows and a 10-km road race. Funds are being raised to restore and convert the old Roman Catholic church into a library, museum, art gallery and cultural centre. Construction of the church began in 1841 and was used as a church until 1915, when mosquitoes finally triumphed over worshippers. From 1923-1972 it was used as a school, but then abandoned.

Two miles south of Grenville are the **Marquis Falls**, also called Mount Carmel Falls, the highest in Grenada. Trails are being improved, with signposts and picnic areas. Marquis village was the capital of St Andrew's in the 17th and 18th centuries. Nowadays it is the centre of the wild pine handicraft industry. Historical sites nearby are Battle Hill and Fort Royal. From here boats go to Marquis Island (see above).

The interior

Mount St Catherine can be climbed quite easily, contrary to popular opinion, although in places it is a climb rather than a walk

There are several routes up Mount St Catherine, perhaps easiest from Grenville. Take a minibus to the Mount Hope road, this is a four-wheel drive track which becomes the path up the mountain. It takes about two hours from leaving the minibus. A guide is not necessary. Do not go alone, however, and do not go if you suffer from vertigo. Do not take chances with daylight. For information on this and anything else, contact Mr and Mrs Benjamin at Benjamin's Variety Store, Victoria Street, Grenville. If they do not know the answer they will know someone who does. Mrs Benjamin is on the Tourist Board. Telfer Bedeau, from Soubise, is the hiking expert, and can be contacted on T4426200.

The transinsular, or hill road, from Grenville to St George's used to be the route from the Pearls airport to the capital, which all new arrivals had to take. Now it is well-surfaced, but twisty and narrow. The minibus drivers on it are generally regarded as 'maniacs'. To give an idea of the conditions, one bend is called 'Hit Me Easy'. The road rises up to the rain forest, often entering the clouds. If driving yourself, allow up to 1½ hours from Levera to St George's and avoid the mountain roads around Grand Étang in the dark, although the night-time sounds of the dense jungle are fascinating. Shortly before reaching the Grand Étang (full details above), there is a side road to the St Margaret, or **Seven Sisters Falls**. They are only a 30-minute walk from the main road, but a guide is essential, or else get very good directions. A guide will show you a circular route, which is steep but more interesting than returning on the same path and takes two hours. The trail runs over private land, so a small fee is payable to the owners who keep the paths clear, at their place by the main road. After Grand Étang, there is a viewpoint at 1,910 ft overlooking St George's. A bit further down the hill is a detour to the **Annandale Falls** which plunge about 40 ft into a pool where the locals dive and swim. Tourists are pestered for money here, for diving, singing, information, whether requested or not. If coming from St George's on Grenville Road, fork left at the Methodist Church about half way to Grand Étang.

The peaks in the southeast part of the Grand Étang Forest Reserve can be walked as day trips from St George's. **Mount Maitland** (1,712 ft), for instance, is a pleasant morning out. Take a bus from the Market Place to Mardigras, or if there is none, get off at the junction at St Paul's and walk up. At the Pentecostal (IPA) church, turn left and immediately right. The paths are reasonably clear and not too muddy, but shorts are not recommended and long sleeves are preferable. The walk takes less than an hour each way and there are good views from the top over both sides, with some hummingbirds.

Mount Sinai (2,306 ft) is not as spectacular as Mount St Catherine, nor as beautiful as Mount Qua Qua, but is not as muddy either. Take a bus from St George's to Providence, then walk up (two hours) the particularly lovely (and friendly) road to Petit Étang and beyond, where the road turns into a track in the banana fields. The path up the mountain is hard to spot; it begins behind a banana storage shed and must be closely watched. The terrain is a bit tricky near the top. There is a path down the other side to Grand Étang. Local opinions differ over how badly you would get lost without a guide as the paths are no longer maintained.

The highest point in the southeast is known on the Ordnance Survey map as **South East Mountain** (2,348 ft), but to locals as Mount Plima (Plymouth?). You can get up to the ridge, from where there are fine views, but both this summit and the nearby Mount Lebanon are inaccessible without a guide and machete. Here too it used to be possible to descend to Grand Étang but it is difficult now. For this area take a bus from St George's to the junction for Pomme Rose and walk up through the village. Mayhe Hazard lives near the top of the village and is the local expert on the trails (traces). He is good company and may be prepared to guide in the area; he will certainly show you the trail to the ridge, which you could never find alone.

Windward Islands

Essentials

Sleeping
Hotel rooms are subject to a 10% service charge & 8% tax on accommodation, food & beverages

Grenada is particularly well served with good, mid-range, small hotels and guest houses. Although large-scale tourism is starting to be developed, most of the hotels are still small enough to be comfortable and friendly even if they do cater for package tours. The majority of hotels are in the Grand Anse area. In St George's there are more guest houses than hotels

St George's C *Tropicana Inn*, Lagoon Road, T4401586, F4409797, tropicana@cpscarib net.com 20 double rooms, bath, a/c, some with patio, cater to business as well as vacation traveller, family run, overlooks marina, on bus route.

Grand Anse LL-AL *Allamanda Beach Resort and Spa*, T4440095, F4440126, siesta@caribsurf.com 46 rooms, pool, fishing, boating, bar, café, restaurant, games room, scuba diving and watersports, tennis, massage, gym. **L-AL** *Coyaba*, T4444129, F4444808, coyaba@caribsurf.com Popular with package tours, but very comfortable, lots of facilities, 70 rooms on 5½ acres, 3 are wheelchair accessible, large pool with swim-up bar. **LL-AL** *Grenada Grand Beach Resort & Convention Centre*, T4444371, F4444800, higda@caribsurf. com Garden view, or beachfront, suites or rooms, many facilities, restaurant pricey, open 0700-2300, golf course, swimming pool and 800-seat conference centre. **LL** *Spice Island Beach Resort*, T4444258, F4444807, spiceisl@caribsurf.com Ocean front suites, garden view, or pool suite, no children under 12 in pool suites, no children under 5 in winter, all inclusive available on request, lots of sports and other facilities on offer, fitness centre, health spa. Shared facilities with sister property, **L-AL** *Blue Horizons Cottage Hotel*, T4444316, F4442815, blue@caribsurf.com 32 rooms, games room, parking, pool, its *La Belle Créole* restaurant is one of the island's best. **LL-A** *The Flamboyant*, T4444247, F4441234, www.flamboyant.com 61 units in rooms, suites and cottages, pool, free snorkelling equipment, at the south end of Grand Anse, lovely views, steep walk down to beach but transport for people with mobility problems to restaurant and beach, quite a walk to bus stop. **B-C** *South Winds Holiday Cottages and Apartments*, T4444310, F4444404, cdavid@ caribsurf.com Monthly rates on request, 1-2 bedrooms, electric mosquito killer, large kitchen, terrace or balcony, simple but clean, good restaurant, friendly staff and dogs, 5-10-min walk from beach, good view, also car hire.

Morne Rouge AL-B *Gem Holiday Beach Resort*, T4444224, F4441189, gem@caribsurf. com Rooms vary in quality, 1- or 2-bedroomed apartments, lovely beach, good position but hot, a/c nice and cool, enjoyable beachside lounge also popular with locals, restaurant limited.

Point Salines LL Laluna, T4390001, F4390600, www.laluna.com The newest and most expensive on the island, 16 1-2 bedroom cottages, height of luxury, open Italian/Indonesian style, computer outlets, private plunge pools as well as main pool, dining room on beach, children under 10 not welcome in high season. **LL-L** *Rex Grenadian*, T4443333, F4441111, grenrex@caribsurf.com 212 rooms, gym, pool, tennis, 2 beaches, watersports, scuba diving, 6 restaurants and bars, conference facilities, 5 rooms for handicapped guests. **LL** *La Source*, T4442556, F4442561, lasource@caribsurf.com At the extreme south of the island, 100 rooms, all-inclusive, steep hike to some rooms, pool, nine-hole golf course, health and leisure facilities, beaches not as good as Grand Anse, limited availability, popular.

True Blue L-A *True Blue Bay Resort & Marina*, T4438783, F4445929, www.truebluebay. com, close to airport and medical school on pleasant south coast bay, quite remote, 25-min walk to nearest bus stop. Small, intimate, helpful and friendly, British-Mexican owners, large rooms, cottages and apartments, kitchenettes, a/c, fan, sea view, balconies with hammocks, child friendly, high chairs and play equipment, car hire, dock facilities, boat charter available, dive shop on site, small beach, sea rather murky, restaurant over water, good food, Mexican specialities and separate bar, *Stuart's Waterfront Bar*, see below.

Lance aux Épines LL *Calabash*, T4444334, F4445050, calabash@caribsurf.com Winner of a prestigious Golden Fork award for quality of food and hospitality, posh, 30 suites, 8 with private pool, 22 with whirlpool, expensive, MAP on beach, nice grounds, tennis, games room, health and beauty facility. **LL-AL** *Secret Harbour*, T4444439, F4444819, secret@caribsurf. com. 20 luxury rooms, chalets built into the rock face overlooking the harbour, private, wonderful views, pool, friendly, steel band at times, no children under 12 accepted, this is a Club Mariner Resort and bareboat or crewed yacht charters are available from the marina. **L-AL** *Coral Cove Cottages*, T4444422, F4444718, coralcv@caribsurf.com Several, lovely, well-equipped cottages, beautiful view of Atlantic, 15 mins walk to Lance aux Epines, own beach and jetty, good snorkelling, pool, very private, great for children.

South coast AL *Petit Bacaye Cottage Hotel*, on bay of same name, T/F4432902, www.petit.bacaye.com Very desirable place to stay, romantic hideaway on beach, only 5 thatched self-catering cottages with kitchenettes, 1-2 bedrooms, mosquito nets over mahogany beds, no TV or radio, includes tax and service, restaurant on beach for breakfast, lunch and dinner, fisherman call daily, catch can be cooked to order, reef and own islet 200 m offshore, jeep and guide hire arranged, sandy beach round the bluff. **AL-C** *La Sagesse Nature Centre* (see page 854), T/F4446458, isnature@caribsurf.com 9rooms, small, excellent, perfect setting, an old plantation house on a secluded, sandy bay (the sea may be polluted in the rainy season, seek the hotel's advice), child-friendly, good restaurant, excursions.

Guest houses St George's C *Mamma's Lodge*, Lagoon Rd, T4401623. Double and single rooms, pleasant, friendly, very clean, nice view, includes breakfast, no credit cards, not listed by the Tourist Office. **D** *Mitchell's Guest House*, H A Blaize Street, T4402803. Central, 9 double and 2 single rooms with fan, breakfast on request, downstairs rooms dark and not very private, no towels, town noises, ability to sleep through cock crowing essential. **C-D** *St Ann's Guest House*, Paddock, beyond Botanic Gardens (some distance from centre), T4402717, pfrank@caribsurf.comIncludes excellent breakfast, friendly, entrance forbidden to 'prostitutes and natty dreds', meals (communal) good value, a bit difficult to sleep because of dogs and roosters, take ear plugs. **Grand Anse C** *Roydon's*, on busy Lagoon Rd, T/F4444476, roydons@caribsurf.com. EP or MAP, helpful staff, fans, private bathroom, very nice even if a bit overpriced, credit cards accepted, good restaurant, good for buses into town but 10 mins' walk from beach, run by Roy and Donnet De Freitas. **Grenville C** *Grenada Rainbow Inn*, St Andrew's, T4427714, F4425332, drainbow@caribsurf.com Award-winning small hotel, run by Neitha Williams (Aunty Nits) and her daughter Yvonne Williams, 12 rooms or apartments, buses stop outside, organic food, earthen oven for barbecue, credit cards accepted. A few miles north at **Dunfermline** is **E** *Sam's Inn*, T4427313, F4427853. 16 a/c rooms, restaurant and bar, use of kitchen, hot water, balconies, country setting, view of Pearl's airport, small store close by, Mrs Ellen Sam is very friendly owner. **Morne Fendue C-D** *Morne Fendue Plantation House*, see page 861, T4429330, F4429888, caribbean@caribsurf.com Good base for exploring the north, including Bathway beach and the Carib jump at Sauteurs. 8 rooms in new block with wonderful views and in old house, real period pieces with old furniture and a cast iron roll-top bath with eccentric plumbing. Evening meals on request and entertainment planned for high season. **Victoria C** *Hotel Victoria*, Queen St, on the waterfront, T4449367, F4448104. Basic rooms but nice location. **Gouyave E** *Patino's*, at the end of the town on the waterfront above a small bar. Does not look like a guest house so you may have to ask for directions, but worth the effort. 2-bedroom apartments with kitchens, Patino is very friendly, lived in Canada. Good base for nutmeg factory and Concord Falls.

Villas and apartments There are many furnished villas and apartments for rent from various agents, daily or weekly rental. *Villas of Grenada*, T4441896, F4444529, gpm&vog@ caribsurf.com Luxury villas, some with pool, some with beach, up to 5 bedrooms, maid service, other staff available. **D** *RSR Apartments* on Lagoon Road, St George's, T4403381, F4408384, bastjo@hotmail.com Recommended for good value, 1 or 3 bedroom apartment, kitchen, living room, bathroom, veranda, guard at night, also cockroaches, bus into town.

Windward Islands

Camping Camping is not encouraged as there are no facilities, but it is permitted in the Grand Etang National Park and in schools and church grounds on Carriacou.

Eating

Rum punches are excellent. Be sure to try the local sea-moss drink (a mixture of vanilla, algae & milk)

Grenada's cooking is generally very good. Lambi (conch) is very popular, as is callaloo soup (made with dasheen leaves), souse (a sauce made from pig's feet), pepper pot and pumpkin pie. There is a wide choice of seafood, and of vegetables. Goat and wild meat (armadillo, iguana, manicou) can be sampled. Nutmeg features in many local dishes, try nutmeg jelly for breakfast, ground nutmeg comes on top of rum punches. Of the many fruits and fruit dishes, try stewed golden apple, or soursop ice cream. There are three makes of rum, whose superiority is disputed by the islanders, *Clark's Court, River Antoine* and *Westerhall Plantation Rum*, made by Westerhall Distilleries. All three can be visited for a tour and sampling of rum and products for sale. Several readers have endorsed Westerhall Plantation Rum for its distinct flavour and aroma. The term 'grog', for rum, is supposed to originate in Grenada: taking the first letters of 'Georgius Rex Old Grenada', which was stamped on the casks of rum sent back to England. Grenada Breweries brew *Carib Lager, Guinness* and non-alcoholic malt beers.

There is quite a wide choice of restaurants, apart from the hotels mentioned above, and you are recommended to eat the local dishes, which are very good. Tax of 8% and service of 10% is usually added to the bill. Unless stated otherwise, restaurants below are in **St George's**. *Tout Bagay*, on the Carenage near the Library, T4401500. Excellent location, upstairs and over the water, good view of all the boats in harbour, delicious food, not expensive but quite classy and currently the best place to eat in the city. *Nutmeg*, on the Carenage above the Sea Change Book Store, T4402539. Delicious local dishes and its own famous rum punch, very popular, but avoid if you do not want to see turtle on the menu, open Mon-Sat 0800-2300, Sun 1600-2300. *Rudolf's*, also on the Carenage, T4409946. Entrées EC$18-50, but good, local and international food, steak, lamb chops, seafood, pity about the manicou stew, in friendly pub atmosphere, excellent rum punch, open Mon-Sat 1000-2400. *Carenage Café*, in the Otway building on the Carenage. Open 0800-1500 for breakfast, snacks and lunch, two computers for internet access make this the only cybercafé on the island – when they work – very popular, long queues for the terminals, EC$5/15 mins, sofas, book swap. *Tropicana*, on the Lagoon, T4401586. Popular, Chinese and local food, good, entrées from EC$10-45, excellent egg rolls and rotis, vast portions. Seating inside or out on covered patio, barbecues, open 0730-2400, reservations recommended in high season, also takeaway. *New Mamma's*, Lagoon Road, T4401459. Multifarious local foods which the conservation-minded may not want to try (famous for wild meat dishes when in season but you don't always know what you are getting, you may not be told until you've finished that there is no wild game that night), need to book, full dinner EC$45, 1930-2100, bar open until 2400. *Patrick's*, T4400364, also on Lagoon Rd, is even better, with a greater variety and interesting combinations of local foods, breadfruit salad and green papaya salad are outstanding while Patrick is very entertaining, high camp. Very popular. On Melville Street, near waterfront taxi stand, *Deyna's*, T4406795. New, modern, good local food at local prices, and lots of it, rotis, open Mon-Sat 0800-2100, Sun 1000-1600, crowded at lunch. *Pitch Pine Bar*, Esplanade, T4401976. Fun place on the waterfront for a drink or meal, curry mutton, fish broth.

At the St George's end of Grand Anse is *Coconut Beach Restaurant*, T4444644. French creole food and fruit juices and punches, barbecues and live music Wed, Sun evenings in high season, open 1230-2200, closed Tue. *Fish 'n' Chick*, at Sugar Mill roundabout, T4444132. Barbecue and grilled fish and chicken, local fast food and takeaway. *Brown Sugar Restaurant*, above *South Winds Holiday Cottages* in Grande Anse, T4442374. Panoramic view of Grand Anse Bay and St George's Harbour, complementary transport, thought by many to be the best place for callaloo, new ways of presenting traditional Grenadian cuisine, vegetarian and children's meal available, steel band on Tue, Fri, good musicians on Sun, open 1800-2300. *Aquarium Restaurant*, T4441410, Point Salines Beach. Open 1000-2300 except Mon, Wed specials, Sun barbeque, showers, toilets, snorkelling offshore, good food, lobster, fish, steak, sandwiches, live music and buffet from 1900 first Sat in month, dinner reservations requested. *Red Crab*, Lance aux Épines, T4444424. Excellent local seafood and international, entrées from EC$25, fabulous steak dinner EC$60, live music Mon, Fri in season, darts

Wed nights, closed Sun. *Island View Restaurant and Nightclub*, Clark's Court Bay, Woburn, T4441878, VHF 16. Open 1000-2300, casual games room with pub food, pool tables, pinball machine etc, disco from 2200 Fri and Sat, dinghy dock, boat outings arranged with food and drinks. *La Sagesse* (see page 854 and 865) fresh lobster, grilled tuna, outdoor restaurant, beautiful location, walk it off afterwards, good hiking over the mountain, T4446458 for reservations which are recommended, especially for dinner, US$30 for return transport, lunch, guided nature walk with exotic fruit tasting, dinner packages available, entrées EC$15-50.

Bars Happy hours at marinas: *Boatyard Bar* at Prickly Bay Marina. 1730-1830, TV and live music several times a week in season, also good food at the Yacht Club. *Rum Squall Bar* at Secret Harbour Marina. Inexpensive weekly barbecue and daily happy hour 1600-1700. *Grenada Yacht Club* in St George's. Happy hour Wed, Fri, Sat 1800-1900, yachtsmen and others welcome, great place to sit and watch the boats entering the lagoon (and see if they are paying attention to the channel markers or run aground). *Stuart's Waterfront Bar*, at True Blue Bay, T4391377, moorings available. British-run, open Mon-Sat, 1500-2300, Sun 1200-2300, happy hour 1700-1900, good cocktails and bar snacks or move on to the restaurant at the *True Blue Bay*, very popular Fri night when students come over from the medical school on the other side of the bay, but can be busy any time. *Casablanca Sportsbar*, Grand Anse, above the banks, T4441631. Games, pool, snooker, large TV, open until 0300.

Festivals *Easter* is a time for lots of events, both religious and otherwise. There are dinghy races from Grand Anse to the Yacht Club, a kite flying competition at the old Pearls airport, with music, food and drink, and other activities.

Carnival takes place over the 2nd weekend in *August*, although some preliminary events and competitions are held from the last week in July, with calypsos, steelbands, dancing, competitions, shows and plenty of drink. The Sun night celebrations, Dimanche Gras, continue into Mon, J'Ouvert; Djab Djab Molassi, who represent devils, smear themselves and anyone else (especially the smartly dressed) with black grease. On Mon a carnival pageant is held on the stage at Queen's Park and on Tue the bands parade through the streets of St George's to the Market Square and a giant party ensues. For information on playing Mas with a band contact Derrick Clouden (T4402551) or Wilbur Thomas (T4403545) of the Grenada Band Leaders Association. During Carnival it is difficult to find anywhere to stay and impossible to hire a car unless booked well in advance.

Also in *August*, over the first weekend, are the **Carriacou Regatta** (see above) and the **Rainbow City cultural festival** in Grenville which goes on for about a week.

Throughout the island, but especially at Gouyave, the **Fisherman's Birthday** is celebrated at the end of *June* (the feast of Saints Peter and Paul); it involves the blessing of nets and boats, followed by dancing, feasting and boat races. **Independence Day** is *7 February*.

Grenada holds a **Spice Jazz Festival** in *May or June*, with lots of music, cooking, sports. Concerts are mostly held in the big hotels, such as the *Rex*, or at the stadium, and tickets are quite expensive although a season ticket is better value. In 2001 there was also a street party in Gouyave. It doesn't yet have the reputation and popularity of St Lucia's jazz festival, but it is growing.

Nightlife

The Boatyard at the marina on L'Anse Aux Epines Beach has bands playing Wed and Fri nights with open air dancing until 0300, soca, dance music; *Castaways*, L'Anse Aux Epines, T4441250, restaurant from 1700-2200 and disco from 2200; *Fantazia Disco* on Morne Rouge Beach, T4444224, in a big shed, full of Grenadians, funky, soca, fast calypso, reggae, hot and steamy, starts midnight, until dawn, best night is Wed when they have old soul and reggae – 'oldies for goldies'; *Le Sucrier*, in the Sugar Mill at Grand Anse roundabout, behind the *Fish & Chick*, from midnight, Fri and Sat best nights, edgy feel, heavy dudes hang out outside the *Fish & Chick*, DJs or live music. The *Regal Cinema* is off Lagoon Road, next to *Tropicana*, movies nightly at 2030, EC$5 for double feature. The *Marryshow Folk Theatre* in the University of the West Indies building on Tyrrel Street, has concerts, plays and special events.

The resort hotels provide evening entertainment, including dancing, steelband and calypso music, limbo, etc. There are not a great many discothèques and nightclubs outside the hotels and low season can be very quiet

Windward Islands

Shopping Grenada prides itself on its spices, which are ideal souvenirs. They are cheaper in the supermarket than on the street or in the market. They can be seen in preparation on tours to the Nutmeg Processing Station, the Dougaldston Estate, or visit Laura's Spice & Herb Garden near Perdmontemps to see them growing. *Arawak Islands Ltd* make a range of spices, sauces, herbal teas, candied nutmeg pods, perfumes, soap, bath goodies and massage oils, scented candles and incense sticks; factory and retail outlet on the Upper Belmont Road between Grand Anse and St George's, open Mon-Fri 0830-1630, mail order also available, PO Box 432, T/F4443577, www.arawak-islands.com *De la Grenade Industries* make nutmeg jams, jellies, syrups, sauces and drinks, available in supermarkets and groceries, PO Box 788, St George's, T4403241, F4407626, www.delagrenade.com Their nutmeg syrup is an essential ingredient for a Grenadian rum punch, also delicious on pancakes. *The Grenada Co-operative Nutmeg Association* purchases nutmeg from its membership of 7,000 farmers and markets it worldwide. It sells nutmeg oil in 15 ml and 30 ml bottles, PO Box 160, St George's, T4402117, F4406602, gcnanutmeg@caribsurf.com *Spice Island Perfumes* on the Carenage sells perfumes and pots pourris made from the island's spices, as well as batiks, T-shirts, etc. *Grenada Craft Centre* on Lagoon Road, next to the *Tropicana Inn* houses Grenadian craftspersons selling jewellery, pottery, batik, wood, basketry and T-shirts. *Art Fabrik* 9 Young Street, T/F4400568, batikart@caribsurf.com Batik clothing and gift shop, expensive, artisan demonstrating batik at table by door, 0830-1630 Mon-Fri, 0900-1300 Sat. *White Cane Industries* on the Carenage adjacent to the Ministry of Health, featuring a wide variety of arts and crafts made by skillful blind Grenadians. You can purchase straw and palm wares, and items in wood. There is duty-free shopping at the airport and on the Carenage for cruise ships.

There are several places where you can buy art by resident, if not local, artists. *The Yellow Poui Art Gallery*, T4403001, sells Grenadian paintings, sculpture, photography, antique prints and engravings, and is worth a visit, above *Gifts Remembered* souvenir shop on Cross Street, open Mon-Fri 0900-1600, Sat 0915-1215. *Art in Grenada*, on second floor Grand Anse Shopping Complex, T4442317, designco@caribsurf.com open Mon-Sat 1000-1700, fine art gallery, showcasing the work of Richard Buchanan, Susan Mains and others, artists resident temporarily or permanently on the island.

St George's Bookshop is on Halifax Street, T4402309, reasonable selection of Caribbean and international literature as well as school texts; *Sea Change* , T4403402, is on the Carenage, beneath the *Nutmeg* bar, it has *USA Today* when cruise ships come in. *Fedon Books*, side entrance on Herbert Blaize St, open Mon-Fri 0900-1700, Sat 0900-1300, Caribbean novels, geography, cooking and children's books.

Tour operators
There is a 5% tax on all tours Lots of companies offer day tours of the island, stopping to visit waterfalls, nutmeg processing plants, and have lunch at Morne Fendue or a picnic on Bathway beach. These are usually in minibuses or small buses and are primarily designed to give cruise ship passengers a taste of the island, so they can seem a bit rushed. Those offering something a bit different include *Ecotrek* (part of *Ecodive*), T4447777, for coastal and rainforest walks and island safaris, tailor made tours for small groups or even a single person, US$45. *Mandoo Tours*, T/F4401428, www.grenadatours.com island tours US$40-55 and trekking, Concord Falls US$90pp full day, Mt Qua Qua US$40 half day, Seven Sisters Falls US$40. For guided hikes contact Telfer Bedeau in the village of Soubise on the east coast; you must ask around for him (or T4426200 or see if the Tourism Department can put you in touch). *Spice Island Trekking*, T4445985, www.spiceislandtrekking.com hiking half or full day, moderate to difficult, US$35-45, children half price, student reductions, also cycling tours and bike rental, US$15/day, US$65/week. Dennis Henry, of *Henry's Safari Tours* (T4445313, F4444460, VHF channel 68, safari@caribsurf.com) conducts tours of the island and is very well informed on all aspects of Grenada. Henry's also services yachts, dealing with laundry, gas, shopping etc. *Arnold's Tours*, Archibald Avenue, T4400531, F4404118, offers similar services to Henry's, also recommended, but in German as well.

Transport **Air** **From Europe** Both *British Airways* (scheduled) and *JMC* (charter) announced they were pulling out in 2001, leaving *Condor* the only European airline flying from Munich once a week via St Lucia. *BWIA* was expected to fill the gap with a service from London, but this was unconfirmed as we went to print.**From the USA** *BWIA* flies from Miami and New York via Port of Spain, Trinidad. *Air Jamaica* from New York and Philadelphia via Montego Bay. **From the Caribbean** *BWIA* connects Grenada with Trinidad and Tobago. *LIAT* flies to Grenada from Antigua, Barbados, BVI, Dominica, Martinique, St Lucia, St Vincent, San Juan, Trinidad and Tobago. Charter or air taxi services such as *SVGAir* and *TIA* connect Grenada with Carriacou and neighbouring islands in the Grenadines. **Airport** The **Point Salines airport** is five miles from St George's: taxis only, fixed rates as advertized to St George's, EC$30 (US$14), 15 mins; EC$25 (US$10) to Grand Anse and Lance aux Épines. Journeys within a one-mile radius of the airport EC$7 (US$2.75). Add EC$10 (US$3.75) to fares between 1800 and 0600. However, if you start walking down the road towards St George's, you will find that the taxi changes into a bus and will pick you up for much less (only feasible with light luggage). If you are energetic, it takes an hour to walk to Grand Anse, longer to St George's. **Sea** Apart from cruise ships there are no international services. Grenada and Carriacou are linked by ferries, of which the best and quickest is a hovercraft, the *Osprey*.

Local Buses run to all parts of the island from the Market Square and the Esplanade in St George's; on the Esplanade look for the signs in the square, ask around. Fares are EC$1 within St George's, EC$3 to Grand Étang, and EC$5 to Grenville. There is also a regular bus service between Grenville and Sauteurs. It can be difficult to get a bus away from Grand Etang in either direction as most of them are full. The last buses tend to be in mid-afternoon and there are very few on Sun. **Taxi** Fares are set by the tourist board. On Grenada, taxis charge EC$4 for the first 10 miles outside St George's, then EC$3 per mile thereafter (an additional EC$10 charge is made after 1800 and before 0600). From the airport it is EC$25 to Grand Anse, Lance aux Epines or True Blue Bay, EC$30 to St George's. A taxi tour of Grenada costs about US$40-55 per person for a full day or US$15 per person per hour. Island tours of Carriacou cost the same as on Grenada. Taxis and buses are heavily 'personalized' by the drivers with brightly coloured decorations and names like 'Rusher with Love' or 'Danny Boy', while large speakers blast out steel bands or reggae music; taxi drivers will adjust the volume on request. A **water taxi** service runs from in front of the *Nutmeg* restaurant, St George's to the Grand Anse beach. **Hitchhiking** is quite easy though the roads are not very good.

Car hire Cars can be rented from a number of companies for about US$55 or EC$150 a day, plus US$2,500 excess liability and 5% tax (payable by credit card). You must purchase a local permit, on presentation of your national driving licence, for EC$30/US$12; a local permit is not required if you hold an international driving licence. Companies in St George's include *Spice Island Rentals* (Avis), Paddock and Lagoon Road, T4403936; *Dollar Rent-a-Car*, airport, T4444786, F4444788; *David's*, at the airport and several hotels, T4443399; *McIntyre Bros*, cars and jeeps, T4443944, F4442899, macford@caribsurf.com; *Maitland's* (who also rent motorcycles), Market Hill, T4444022, also an office at the airport which is often open for late arrivals when others are closed; *C Thomas and Sons,* cars, minibuses, jeeps, T4444384, mixed reports. We have received reports that daily rates quoted over the phone are not always honoured when you pick up the car; check that the company does not operate a three-day minimum hire if you want a rate for one day only, this often applies in high season. **Bike** rentals can be arranged with Ride Grenada, T4441157. Bike parts, but no repairs, at Ace Hardware, Lagoon Rd, south end.

Airlines *LIAT*, The Carenage, St George's, T4402796/7 (4444121/2 Point Salines, 4437362 Carriacou); **Directory** *British Airways*, T4402796; *BWIA*, The Carenage, St George's, T4403818/9 (T4444134 at airport); *Air Europe*, T4445678; *JMC*, T4402796; *Martin Air*, T4444732.

Banks *Barclays Bank* (branches in St George's-Halifax Street, Grand Anse, Grenville and Carriacou), T4403232; *National Commercial Bank of Grenada* (Halifax Street and Hillsborough Street, St George's, Grand Anse, Grenville, Gouyave, St David's, Carriacou), T4403566; *Scotiabank* (Halifax Street, St George's), T4403274, branch at Grand Anse; *Grenada Bank of Commerce* (Halifax and Cross Street, St George's, and Grand Anse), T4404919; *Grenada Co-operative Bank* (Church Street, St George's, Grenville and Sauteurs), T4402111.

Communications Internet *Carenage Café*, in the Otway building on the Carenage. Open 0800-1500 for breakfast, snacks and lunch, two computers for internet access make this the only cybercafé on the island – when they work – very popular, long queues for the terminals, EC$5/15 mins, sofas, book swap. *James Computer Service*, T4401600, Scott St at top of alley going up from Daihatsu on Carenage, side entrance to first floor for computers and internet access, pay downstairs at main entrance, EC$20/hr, a/c, functional, good and fast machines, no queues. **Post:** the General Post Office in St George's is at Burns Point near the pier, south of the Carenage, open 0800-1600 Mon-Fri, only postage stamps are sold during the lunch hour, 1200-1300. Villages have sub-post offices.**Telephone:** *Cable & Wireless Grenada Ltd*, T4401000, gndinfo@caribsurf.com, with offices on the Carenage, St George's, operates telephone services, including USA Direct and calls to USA on Visa card, etc, fax and cellular phones. Payphones take coins or phone cards, available at outlets near payphones. Home Direct Service can be made from any phone, if you have a credit or telephone charge card, and is available to the UK through BT Direct and to Canada through Teleglobe. Credit card holders and Visaphone card holders' access number is 1-800-8778000 for domestic and international calls. If you dial 1-800-8722881 at any public phone (no coin required), you get through to AT and T. A call to the UK costs approximately EC$37.50 for 5 mins. Grentel Boatphone provides mobile cellular phone service.

Embassies & consulates *The British High Commission* is at Grand Anse Shopping Centre on the main road in a new building by Barclays Bank, on the other side from the *Grand Hotel* with its bright blue-roofed conference centre, T440-3222/3536, F4404939. *The Venezuelan Embassy* is at Archibald Avenue, St George's, T4401721/2. *USA*, Lance Aux Epines Stretch, St George's, T4441173, F4444820, usemb_gd@ caribsurf.com; *Republic of China*, Archibald Avenue, T4403054; *Netherlands*, Grand Etang Road, St George's, T4402031; *Guyana*, Gore Street, St George's, T4402189; *France*, T4402547; *European Community*, Archibald Avenue, T4403561;

Medical facilities St George's General Hospital is at Fort George's Point. There is also Princess Alice Hospital in Grenville, Princess Royal Hospital in Carriacou and the private St Augustine Medical Centre. Black Rock Medical Clinic in Grand Anse Shopping Centre has 24-hr emergency service. For an ambulance, T434 in St George's, T724 in St Andrew's and T774 on Carriacou. SunSmile Dental Care Clinic at Grand Anse offers dental treatment Mon-Sat and emergency care.

Tourist information Local tourist office: Grenada Board of Tourism, Box 293, Burn's Point, St George's, T440-2279/2001/1346, F440-6637, www.grenadagrenadines.com www.grenada.org gbt@caribsurf.com0800-1600, very helpful, lots of leaflets. There is also a cruise ship office, T4402872, and tourist office at the airport, helpful, hotel reservation service, T4444140. On Carriacou the Board of Tourism is on Patterson St, Hillsborough, beside the Osprey office, T4437948, F4436127, carrgbt@caribsurf.com The Grenada Hotel Association is at Ross Point Inn, Lagoon Road, PO Box 440, St George's, T4441353, F4444847, www.grenadahotelsinfo.com. **Maps** Grenada National Parks publishes maps and trail guides, worth having for the Grand Étang National Park and related walks. The Overseas Surveys Directorate, Ordnance Survey map of Grenada, published for the Grenada Government in 1985, scale 1:50,000, is available from the Tourist Office, from the Lands and Surveys Department in the Ministry of Agriculture (at the Botanic Gardens) and from shops for EC$10.50-15 (it is not wholly accurate). Also available from Ordnance Survey, Southampton, are two separate sheets, North (1979) and South (1988) at 1:25,000 scale.

Carriacou

Population: 6,800   *Carriacou (pronounced Carr-ycoo) is an attractive island of green hills descending to sandy beaches. It is much less mountainous than Grenada, which means that any cloudy or rainy weather clears much quicker. Efforts are being made by the Government to curb contraband and drug smuggling in Carriacou, but a lot comes in around Anse la Roche, where there are picturesque smugglers' coves. Hurricane Lenny caused severe damage in 1999 because of the tidal surges it brought to the west side of the island. The waves undermined a small part of the seafront road in Hillsborough and part of the road to Tyrell Bay was washed away. Repairs have been carried out, but evidence of the swell can still be seen.*

There are flights from Barbados and Grenada in small planes, or you can get there by sea on a hovercraft, large ferries for cargo and passengers or yacht. It is a lovely route, following the length of Grenada's western coastline before crossing the channel to Carriacou and seeing the Grenadines coming into view. Look out for dolphins on the crossing, which follow the boats. The *Osprey* hovercraft is recommended for the most reliable service and the boat is in good condition. In heavy seas you may be better opting for a schooner, which despite being smaller, ride the waves better than the larger boats which may make you seasick, said to be worse going to Carriacou than coming back. Times of all services are subject to change and you must check.

Getting there

See transport, page 876, for further details

Minibuses run to most parts of the island and will convert to a taxi to take you off route. Car hire is available, which is useful if you are staying in self-catering accommodation away from Hillsborough and need to shop. Cycling is recommended, the traffic is very light. Many of the roads are in very poor repair, giving the semblance of off-road cycling, although some of the main roads have recently been repaved. Potential for lots of flat tyres in the dry season as there is an abundance of cacti. Walking is equally rewarding, the heat being the main problem. There is good walking on the back roads and the woods are teeming with wildlife such as iguanas. Some beaches can only be reached on foot or by boat. Water taxis are on hand to take you to beaches in remote parts of the island, or to the islets offshore for picnics and snorkelling.

Getting around

Carriacou's capital is **Hillsborough** and has a population of about 1,000. It dates from a colonial settlement towards the end of the 18th century and was used by Admiral Ralph Abercrombie who came with 150 ships to launch an attack on the Spanish in 1796 and capture Trinidad. Main Street runs parallel to the sea and the hub of activity is the dock area where you find Customs, Immigration, Police, taxis, buses and fruit and vegetable stalls. Also along Main Street there are guest houses, a few restaurants, bars, a supermarket, shops, internet access, banks and a dive shop. The town is also blessed with a lovely beach, a huge curve of white sand with good

Sights

Carriacou

Windward Islands (vertical text, right margin)

swimming, despite the presence of the jetty and large cargo ships. One of the streets running inland from Main Street is Paterson Street, at the junction of which is the ticket office for the *Osprey* hovercraft. Along Paterson Street are the telephone office, the tourist office and the small museum. The **Carriacou Historical Society Museum** has exhibits from Amerindian settlements in the island and from later periods in its history. ■ *Mon-Fri, 0930-1600, Sat 1000-1600. Small shop for gifts, cards, books and local music.*

On the one hand, the islanders display a strong adherence to their African origins in that the annual Big Drum Dances, which take place around Easter, are almost purely West African. The Tombstone Feasts are unique. On the other hand, French traditions are still evident at L'Esterre and there is a vigorous Scottish heritage, especially at **Windward**, where the people are much lighter skinned than elsewhere on the island as a result of their Scottish forebears. Windward used to be the centre for the craft of hand-built schooners but in recent years the boat builders have expanded to Tyrrel Bay. Begun by a shipbuilder from Glasgow, the techniques are unchanged, but the white cedar used for the vessels now has to be imported from Grenada or elsewhere. The sturdy sailing vessels are built and repaired without the use of power tools in the shade of the mangroves at the edge of the sea. To demonstrate the qualities of these local boats, the Carriacou Regatta was initiated in 1965. It has grown into the major festival described above. You can still see the boats being built and repaired along the beach at Windward overlooking Petite Martinique and Petit St Vincent, follow the paths through the mangroves, avoiding the huge crab holes.

The remains of several plantations and their sugar mills can be seen around the island. Just north of Hillsborough, the Anglican Rectory is in what remains of the Beausejour Great House, on a slight hill so that the master could watch his slaves in the sugar and cotton fields below. The house is now single storey, having lost the second floor in Hurricane Janet in 1955. At Belair Park by a nature centre and a forest reserve, you can see the ruins of the old government house, set in parkland at 800 feet above sea level with lovely old trees. The house was stripped bare during the US

Hillsborough

N

0 metres 50
0 yards 50

■ **Sleeping**	4 Millies Guest House	● **Eating**
1 Ade's Dream	5 Patty's Villa	1 Anchor Bar
2 Gramma's Apartments	6 Peace Havea	2 Callaloo By the Sea
3 John's Unique Resort	7 Silver Beach	3 Sand Island Café

invasion of Grenada but the park is now used to hold the annual Maroon Festival. On Hospital Hill, Belair, northeast of Hillsborough, there is an old sugar mill, stunning views. The tower is well preserved, but not much else is left. The slaves had to carry the sugar cane all the way up the hill. The best views, however, are from the Princess Royal Hospital itself, built on top of the hill in 1907-09 because of an outbreak of malaria. The wind up on the hill is too strong for mosquitoes and it was also considered a nice, quiet spot for patients to recuperate. From here you get a fabulous view of Hillsborough, and most of the southern part of the island. A few old cannons were put here in 1948. Under the flamboyant tree in the courtyard there are some large tortoises (*morrocoy*) living a rather bored existence.

South of Hillsborough the road runs along the coast through Coconut Grove (missing the palms on the beach since Hurricane Lenny washed them away in 1999) and across the airport runway to Paradise Beach and **L'Esterre**. Paradise Beach is one of the nicest beaches on the island, with calm sea and good swimming. The local painter, Canute Calliste, has his studio at L'Esterre. His naive style captures the scenes of Carriacou (kite flying, launching schooners, festivals). He is also an accomplished violinist and performs the quadrille, a dance which is part of the island's cultural heritage. The road then cuts across the peninsula to **Harvey Vale**, at Tyrrel Bay. Visitors should see the oyster beds at **Tyrrel Bay** where 'tree-oysters' grow on mangrove roots. Tyrrel Bay is a favourite anchorage for the many yachts which visit the island and the mangroves are a hurricane hole.

There are interesting underwater reefs and sandy islets with a few palms on them, ideal for snorkelling and picnicking. **Sandy Island** is a tiny, low-lying atoll in Hillsborough Bay off Lauriston Point, a sand spit with a few palm trees for shade and a bit of scrub, often used for television commercials. Safe and excellent swimming and snorkelling, take food, drink and plenty of suntan lotion. Boat from Paradise Beach, five minutes, or from Hillsborough EC$60, 30 mins each way, pick a day when the islet is not swamped with boat loads of cruise ship visitors. These small cruise ships offload 200 tourists to trample all round the islet and their anchor chains do untold damage to the coral. Yachts also anchor here and there are no mooring buoys in place yet. Alternatively try **White Island**, a similar islet in Manchineel Bay off the south coast, ask for boats at *Cassada Bay Hotel*.

North of Hillsborough, Bogles is the most northerly village on the west side of the island and the end of the concrete road. From here four-wheel drive or at least high clearance is necessary in the wet season. The Bogles emporium is an old building at the junction of the road to Windward, built in the mid-19th century by a merchant. Although desperately in need of renovation, the top floor overhang still has the original iron supports, denoting prosperity at the time of construction. A beautiful beach is **Anse La Roche**, which faces west and has a spectacular view across the strait to the mountains of rugged Union Island. Snorkelling is good, particularly among the rocks at the side. Walk from Bogles along the dirt road heading northwards, past the *Caribbee Inn* and forking right at Honey Hill House; after about 30 mins the road starts to rise, turn left at the large tree which overhangs the track and follow a narrow path through the woods to a ruined farmhouse. The path leads to the right, through bushes; keep to the downhill side of the open slope, bear right down a steep slope leading through more trees to the beach. Take food and drink and no valuables of any sort, there are no facilities and few people, about 45-min walk each way. We have received reports that it is very easy to get lost finding Anse La Roche beach and it might be easier to take a water taxi there. Very peaceful, watch the yachts rounding the headland on their way to anchorage; at night turtles swim ashore to lay their eggs.

This end of the island has the highest elevation, High North Peak, which rises to 955 feet and is part of a protected area. The **Kido Ecological Research Station** is near Anse La Roche and High North Park, where you can go birdwatching, hiking, cycling, whale watching and even volunteering for one of the conservation projects. However, you should contact them in advance as their pack of dogs deters uninvited

Windward Islands

visitors. There has been local opposition to their plans to convert the whole of the north of the island (including privately owned land) into a national reserve, T/F4437936, kido-ywf@caribsurf.com

Instead of turning off the track to Anse La Roche, carry on walking northwards; the well-shaded, grassy road rounds Gun Point with lovely views of the Grenadines. The British placed a cannon here in the 1780s. A path leads down (opposite a mauve-painted house) to the beach at **Petit Carenage Bay**, which has coarse, coral sand, good swimming and modest surf in some conditions. Returning to the road, Windward is a few minutes walk further on, a few shops and local bars. The Caribbean coast is spectacular in places and a walk from Windward to Dover, then following the coast road until it becomes a dirt road leading to Dumfries, is very pleasant and secluded.

Sleeping
Out of season the island is quiet. Not all the hotels are open

Hotels **LL-AL** *Caribbee Inn*, Prospect, T4437380, F4438142. Run by Robert and Wendy Cooper, a British couple and fount of all knowledge about what's happening on the island, as well as being known for their macaws, rescued from the illegal pet trade. Lovely but isolated setting on promontory above the sea, north of Bogles, spacious rooms, all different, 4-poster beds with mosquito nets, hammocks on balcony or veranda, louvre windows propped open to catch the breeze, fans, thick gardens all around, lizards and biting insects, take repellent, good but expensive food, path down to rocky bay for swimming and snorkeling, 40 mins' walk to Anse la Roche. **B-D** *Grand Vue*, Belair Rd, overlooking Hillsborough, T4436348. 14-room apartment hotel opening 2001, fans, TV, restaurant, bar, good views.

Guest houses **Hillsborough**: **A-C** *Green Roof Inn*, on hillside overlooking sea, 10 mins north of town, just past the desalination plant, T/F4436399, greenroof@caribsurf.com Swedish owned, 3 double rooms with private bathroom, 1 single and 1 double with shared bathroom, adjoining rooms for family suite, extra beds available, mosquito nets, fans, sea view or garden view, airport/jetty transfers and breakfast at 0800 included, restaurant (see below), sandy area in front of hotel for swimming, day trips arranged. **C** *Patty's Villa*, Main St, Hillsborough, T4438412. Run by Hilda and Kervin Stiell, the nicest place to stay in town, on the beach, close to the dock, beautifully restored West Indian house with fretwork, green and white, 2 apartments, sleep 2, mosquito net, fan, kitchen, bathroom, garden with chairs overlooking harbour and beach. **C-D** *Peace Haven Guest House*, south of pier, Main St, Hillsborough, T4437475. Basic, small but good rooms, share small kitchen and bathroom, contact Lucille Atkins, very friendly and helpful, on the seafront a few hundred yards south of the jetty, also apartments. **C-E** *John's Unique Resort*, Main St, heading north, T4438346, F4438345, junique@caribsurf.com Unmissable for its bright blue roof, good location and new, but standard of accommodation could have been better. **C-F** *Ade's Dream*, T4437317, F4438435, adesdea@caribsurf.com, Main St, Hillsborough. 23 rooms or apartments, close to dock, well-equipped, own kitchenette or share large kitchen, very clean and popular, run by hard working and friendly Mrs Mills (good reports), supermarket downstairs open daily, restaurant across the road with sea frontage. **D** *Grammas Apartments*, Main and Patterson Streets, Hillsborough, above the bakery, T4437255, F4437256. 7 rooms, well-equipped, good. **D** *Millies Guest House*, Main St, Hillsborough, T4437310, F4438107. Room or 1-, 2-, or 3-bedroomed apartments with kitchen, bathroom/shower, fans, a/c, ocean view. **E** *Sand's Guest House*, T4437100, between Hillsborough and the airport. Quiet, basic but clean, across the road is a nice beach, 11 rooms, with or without shared kitchen and bathroom, or apartment. **L'Esterre**: **B-D** *Paradise Inn*, on Paradise Beach, T4438406, F4438391, paradiseinn@caribsurf.com Owned by Tanki, who also runs the dive shop on site, popular with divers, 7 rooms. **D-E** *Hope's Inn*, T4437457. On bayfront close to Paradise Beach, quiet, basic, 6 rooms and an apartment, self-catering. **Harvey Vale/Tyrrel Bay**: **C** *Scraper's*, T/F4437403, scrapers@caribsurf.com Local restaurant and 6 rooms in cottages, across the road from the sea, with or without a/c. **C** *Carriacou Yacht Club*, T4436123, F4436292. Designed for yachties to spend time on land, 4 rooms with self-catering facilities, nothing fancy. **Bogles**: **A-C** *Bogles Round House*, T/F4437841. Run by Kate Strobel, 3 cottages built around a round house, self-contained, sleep 2-3, comfortable, located away from the main tourist areas, path down to sea, excellent restaurant. **Windward**: **A-D** *Bayaleau Point Cottages*, T/F4437984, goldhill@caribsurf.com. 4 lovely, well-equipped wooden, painted cottages, very clean, beautiful view, own little beach, good snorkelling, owners Ulla and Dave Goldhill are helpful, friendly, food and drink on request, good for children.

Villa and apartment rental LL-C *Down Island Ltd*, villa rental agents, T4438182, F4438290, www.islandvillas.com

The **market** near the pier in Hillsborough comes alive on Mon when the produce is brought in. 'Jack Iron' rum (180° proof) is a local hazard, it is so strong that ice sinks in it. It is distilled in Barbados but bottled in Carriacou; it costs around EC$10 per bottle and is liberally dispensed on all high days and holidays (fairly liberally on other days too). There are some basic local bar/restaurants but they often run out of food quite early or close in the evenings, check during the day if they will be open for dinner; finding cheap meals can be difficult at weekends.

   In Hillsborough *Anchor Bar*, Main St. Owned by Bill Paterson, at the junction with Patterson St, rum shop facing the street but if you go round the side passage you find a café on a balcony overlooking the sea, cheap and cheerful, chicken, conch and fish meals, chicken wings and a cold beer make a good lunch/snack. *Callaloo by the Sea*, Main St, on the beach, T4438004. Probably the best restaurant in town, good drinks, nice veranda overlooking sea with view of dock, breezy, good for a swim before lunch, popular, entrées EC$16-50, plenty of choice, good value despite upmarket appearance, open daily. *E & A's*, very close to the pier. Good local cooking, ask for a large plate of vegetables. *Sand Island Café*, opposite *Gramma's Bakery*, T4436189. Set over the water, Grenadian chef, Jenson, seafood and pizzas, very local, closed Sun.

   North of Hillsborough *The Green Roof Inn*, on hillside overlooking the sea, 10 mins' walk north of Hillsborough, T4436399. On second floor veranda with spectacular views of Hillsborough bay and sunset, roof, but no walls, Swedish owned, mainly seafood, lobster, barracuda, swordfish, Caribbean ingredients with European preparation, open Tue-Sun for dinner, lunch on request. *Bogles Round House*, in Bogles, T/F4437841. Kate Strobel, a New Yorker, cooks and serves excellent, tasty meals in the round house, evening reservations must be made in the morning and you have to choose your main course in advance, 3-course meal about EC$60, vegetarians welcome. *The Caribbee Inn* , at Prospect north of Bogles, T4437380. Candlelit dining in country house hotel, see Sleeping, above, creole gourmet cooking, homemade bakeries, expensive meals priced in US$, reservations only.

   Several small bars and restaurants in **Tyrrel Bay** which do takeaways and other services such as emails and faxes for visiting yachts. *Scraper's*, Tyrrel Bay, T4437403, scrapers@caribsurf.comVery good lunch but not much atmosphere, Mr Scraper and his family are very hospitable. The ice cream parlour just round Tyrrel Bay after *Scrapers* is recommended. *Poivre et Sel*, above Alexis Supermarket, difficult to find, T4438390, VHF 16. Excellent French food, French chef, try the lobster crêpe, a nice change from West Indian, casual but lively meeting place for the local French community. *Turtle Dove*, T4438322, VHF16. Pizzeria, bar, internet, fax, Italian food, lunch 1200-11400, dinner from 1900 by reservation, run by Luciana, Daniela and Scarlett.

Carriacou celebrates its **carnival** at the traditional Lenten time, unlike Grenada. It is not spectacular but it is fun and there is a good atmosphere. An interesting feature of Carriacou's carnival is the Shakespeare Mas, when participants, or 'pierrots' (*paywos*) dress up and recite from Shakespeare's plays. If they forget their lines or get something wrong, they are thumped by the others with a bull whip, so their costumes require a lot of padding and they wear a special cape which covers the back of the head. It is very competitive and carnival has traditionally been very violent, with battles between villages or between north and south of the island, led by their carnival 'kings'. The police have in the past frequently had to restore peace. At the end of *April* is the 3-day **Maroon Music Festival**, a recent revival of traditional customs held in the historic Belair Park. You can see a display of the Big Drum Nation Dance, string band music and quadrille dancing, as well as more modern entertainment such as reggae late into the night. There are also stalls selling local food, cultural and art exhibitions,

Eating
Food is limited in variety, especially fresh vegetables, but according to season you can get onions, tomatoes, potatoes, cucumbers etc from Grenada

Festivals

Windward Islands

www.grenadines.net/carriacou/maroonmusicfestival.html In *August* is the **Carriacou Regatta** (see above), with races for work boats, yachts, model boats, donkeys and rowing boats, as well as the greasy pole, tug-o-war and cultural shows, contact the Carriacou Regatta Committee, T4437930, www.grenadaexplorer.com/events/carriacou_regatta.htm. The **Parang** takes place in *mid-December* and runs over 3 evenings (Fri-Sun) from about 2100-0200 at the Tennis Club in Hillsborough (entrance EC$20 per night). It is a musical celebration: local groups perform on Fri, Sat is the most lively night with visiting Calypsonians and performers from Grenada and other islands judged by visiting dignitaries, and Sun is comedy day, with in-jokes likely to be lost on visitors.

Tour operators Taxi drivers will offer to take you on a tour of the island, the Tourist Office will give you a recommendation if you want or contact the Carriacou Owners and Drivers Association, T4437386, VHF16. A full tour of the island is set at EC$150 for 2 ½ hrs, and a half tour for half that. Several captains offer tours of nearby islands by boat. Be sure to check safety equipment, they are not licensed by the government and do not have to conform to safety regulations. If the engine fails has he got oars or sails as an alternative? Is there a radio? Life jackets? A motor boat on its way to White Island for a picnic broke down and drifted for 3 days, eventually being found off the Venezuelan coast. Brian Fletcher has a 40-ft Morgan sloop, *Cinderella*, for day or overnight tours of the Grenadines, T4437277, F4437165. Reggie Haemer or Captain Bubb, T4438468, 4437752, has a 41-ft Morgan ketch, *Chaika*. Captain Carl McLawrence, T4437505, has a West Indies sloop, *Good Expectation III*. Water taxis will also take you on trips to the little islands offshore or to other Grenadines close by: Snaggs water taxi, T4438293, VHF16; Scooby water taxi, T4336622, speed boat.

Transport **Air** Carriacou's airport is **Lauriston**, a EC$10 taxi ride from Hillsborough, EC$20 from Mount Pleasant. Disconcertingly, the main road goes straight across the runway, traffic is halted when aircraft are due. A fire engine drives out from Hillsborough to meet incoming flights, bringing the Immigration Officer, who clings to a platform at the back in Keystone Cops fashion. There are now lights for emergency night flights, but not so long ago all the taxis would be called out to light the runway with their headlights. Every day *TIA* fly from Barbados and *SVG Air* from Grenada, linking with North American and European flights. **Sea** *Osprey Lines*, T4408126 (Grenada), T4438126 (Carriacou), F4439041, osprey@caribsurf.com operate a punctual and efficient hovercraft service, the *Osprey Express*, from Grenada to Carriacou and Petite Martinique. Their office in Hillsborough is on the corner of Main St and Paterson St, worth getting your ticket in advance if you want to catch the early morning boat, then you can just walk straight on with your luggage. On Mon-Fri the twice daily service starts in Petite Martinique 0530 and 1500, leaving Carriacou 0600 and 1530, arriving in St George's harbour opposite the fire station 1¼ hrs later. It returns from Grenada at 0900 and 1730, leaving Carriacou for Petite Martinique at 1030 and 1900. On Sat the two services to Grenada are the same but there is only one crossing back from Grenada, at 0900, then on Sun it starts in Grenada at 0800 and 1730, leaving Carriacou for Petite Martinique at 0930 and 1900, returning from Petite Martinique and Carriacou at 1500 and 1530 respectively. Fares are EC$10 Petite Martinique to Carriacou, EC$20 return, EC$50 Grenada to Carriacou, EC$90 return. A second hovercraft service, the *Lexiana Jet Express*, is part of the Alexis franchise, T4436930, F4437179. An older and less reliable vessel, it leaves Carriacou Mon-Sun at 0615 and 1515, returning from Grenada at 0915 and 1730 Mon-Sat and 0800 and 1730 on Sun, EC$40 one way, EC$75 return. A ferry (*Alexia II, Alexia III, Adelaide B)* also sails from the Carenage, St George's to Hillsborough, Carriacou, Tue 0930, Wed 1000, Fri 1100, Sat 0800, Sun 0700, returning Mon 1000, Wed 0930, Thu 1000, Sat 0900, Sun 1200, EC$20 one way, EC$ 30 return, weekends EC$35, 3-4 hrs. Cargo boats leave from the other side of the Carenage from the *Osprey Express*, normally EC$20, bicycles EC$10 or free, usually daily but enquire locally for days and times. There are also unscheduled services between these islands; by asking around you might be able to get a passage on one. Carriacou is 1 hr by boat from Union Island; fishing boats leave irregularly, enquire locally, fare about EC$15 between Hillsborough and Ashton. The ferry, *Jaspar,* twice a week (see above, Union Island).

Water taxis to beaches cost EC$60-100 depending on the length of the journey. Fishing and sailing trips from Hillsborough pier or ask at hotels. **Yachts** can be hired by the day from Tanki's diving base near the airport; ask for Captain Dennis. **Road** Buses go from Hillsborough to Bogles, Windward (EC$2.50) and to Tyrrel Bay. To get from Tyrrel Bay to Windward you would have to change buses in Hillsborough. Buses cost EC$1.50 for one mile, EC$2.50 for more than that. The same van may be a taxi and cost US$10, ask for "bus" and be prepared to wait. The normally excellent service goes to pieces if it is wet. There are also plenty of **taxis**, which cost EC$15 from the airport to Hillsborough, up to a maximum fare of EC$30 to Petit Carenage. Other fares are EC$20-25. You can hire a **car** or jeep. *Desmond's*, T4437271; *Quality Jeep Rental*, T?F4438307; *Sunkey's Auto Rentals*, T4438382.

Airline offices See page 869. **Banks** *Barclays Bank* is on Main St on the left as you head south. The *National Commercial Bank* is on Main St on the left as you head north, both open Mon-Thu 0800-1400, Fri 0800-1730. Currency exchange is quicker and easier at *Barclays*. **Communications** Internet: *John's Print Shop*, on the main street in Hillsborough, next to Barclays Bank, upstairs by a side entrance, T4438207, www.grenadines.net EC$10/30 mins including drink, also sells inter-island air tickets. *The Studio*, next to *Alexis supermarket* on Tyrrel Bay, T/F4438625, VHF 16, has email and internet access, mail drop, bookswap, bar, coffee shop, music, closed Sun, small and pleasant. **Useful numbers** Police and Immigration, Hillsborough, T4437482; Princess Royal Hospital, Belair, T4437400; Hillsborough Health Centre, T4437280; Charles Pharmacy, T4437933.

Directory

Petite Martinique

Petite Martinique is the only offshore island from Carriacou on which people live, about 900-1,000 of them, descended from French fishermen, Glaswegian ship-wrights, pirates and slaves. Its area is 486 acres, rising to a small, volcanic peak, and only a very small channel separates it from Petit St Vincent, where many people work at the resort. The principal legal occupations are boatbuilding and fishing, but for generations the islanders have been involved in smuggling and they are notice-ably more prosperous than their neighbours on other islands. There was excitement in 1997 when the government proposed to build a house for 12 Coast Guard person-nel in the campaign against drug smuggling. Hundreds of people, about half the population, turned out to demonstrate against the arrival of government surveyors and clashed with armed police and the Special Services Unit.

Population: 1,000

There is a dock with fuel, water, ice and other yachting supplies. Water taxis are available from Windward on Carriacou. The *Osprey Express* and the other ferries call here after Hillsborough coming from St George's, and the mail boat from Carriacou calls on Monday, Wednesday and Friday.

Sleeping and eating D *Sea Side View Holiday Cottages*, T4439007, F4439210, 1 2-bedroomed and 2 1-bedroomed, self-contained cottages near beach, supermarket and boutique. **D-E** *Melodie's Guest House*, T4439052, F4439093, melodies@caribsurf.com 9 rooms, some with balconies, ceiling fans, beach front, dining room or outdoor dining under gazebo, entertainment in season, tours and watersports offered. **E** *Miracle Mart Guest House*, T4439065, F4439022, jhingram@caribsurf.com 3 rooms, 4 beds, fan, kitchen, restau-rant. *Palm Beach Restaurant and Bar*, on the beach, menu emphasizes seafood, good roti, free water taxi service for those anchored in Petit St Vincent, Mon-Sat 1000-2200, Sun 1400-2200, T4439103, VHF 16.

Background

When Columbus discovered the island on his third voyage in 1498, it was inhabited by Caribs, who had migrated from the South American mainland, killing or enslav-ing the peaceful Arawaks who were already living there. The Amerindians called their island Camerhogue, but Columbus renamed it Concepción, a name which was not to last long, for shortly afterwards it was referred to as Mayo on maps and later

History

Spaniards called it Granada, after the Spanish city. The French then called it La Grenade and by the 18th century it was known as Grenada. Aggressive defence of the island by the Caribs prevented settlement by Europeans until the 17th century. In 1609 some Englishmen tried and failed, followed by a group of Frenchmen in 1638, but it was not until 1650 that a French expedition from Martinique landed and made initial friendly contact with the inhabitants. When relations soured, the French brought reinforcements and exterminated the Amerindian population. Sauteurs, or Morne des Sauteurs, on the north coast, is named after this episode when numerous Caribs apparently jumped to their death in the sea rather than surrender to the French.

The island remained French for about 100 years, although possession was disputed by Britain, and it was a period of economic expansion and population growth, as colonists and slaves arrived to grow tobacco and sugar at first, followed by cotton, cocoa and coffee. It was during the Seven Years' War in the 18th century that Grenada fell into British hands and was ceded by France to Britain as part of a land settlement in the 1763 Treaty of Paris. Although the French regained control in 1779, their occupation was brief and the island was returned to Britain in 1783 under the Treaty of Versailles. The British introduced nutmeg in the 1780s, after natural disasters wiped out the sugar industry. Nutmeg and cocoa became the main crops and encouraged the development of smaller land holdings. A major slave revolt took place in 1795, led by a free coloured Grenadian called Julian Fedon (see page 860), but slavery was not abolished until 1834, as in the rest of the British Empire.

In 1833, Grenada was incorporated into the Windward Islands Administration which survived until 1958 when it was dissolved and Grenada joined the Federation of the West Indies. The Federation collapsed in 1962 and in 1967 Grenada became an associated state, with full autonomy over internal affairs, but with Britain retaining responsibility for defence and foreign relations. Grenada was the first of the associated states to seek full independence, which was granted in 1974.

Political leadership since the 1950s had alternated between Eric (later Sir Eric) Gairy's Grenada United Labour Party (GULP) and Herbert Blaize's Grenada National Party. At the time of independence, Sir Eric Gairy was Prime Minister, but his style of government was widely viewed as authoritarian and corrupt, becoming increasingly resented by a large proportion of the population. In 1979 he was ousted in a bloodless coup by the Marxist-Leninist New Jewel (Joint Endeavour for Welfare, Education and Liberation) Movement, founded in 1973, which formed a government headed by Prime Minister Maurice Bishop. Reforms were introduced and the country moved closer to Cuba and other Communist countries, who provided aid and technical assistance. In 1983, a power struggle within the government led to Bishop being deposed and he and many of his followers were murdered by a rival faction shortly afterwards. In the chaos that followed a joint US-Caribbean force invaded the island to restore order. They imprisoned Bishop's murderers and expelled Cubans and other socialist nationalities who had been engaged in building a new airport and other development projects. An interim government was set up until elections could be held in 1984, which were won by the coalition New National Party (NNP), headed by Herbert Blaize, with 14 seats to GULP's one in the legislature. After the intervention, Grenada moved closer to the USA which maintains a large embassy near the airport, but on 1 December 1999 diplomatic relations with Cuba were restored and embassies were opened in St George's and Havana.

Further reading on this era of Grenada's history includes: *Grenada: Whose Freedom?* by Fitzroy Ambursley and James Dunkerley, Latin America Bureau, London, 1984; *Grenada Revolution in Reverse* by James Ferguson, Latin America Bureau, London, 1990; *Grenada: Revolution, Invasion and Aftermath* by Hugh O'Shaughnessy, Sphere Books, London, 1984; *Grenada: Revolution and Invasion* by Anthony Payne, Paul Sutton and Tony Thorndike, London, Croom Helm, 1984; *Grenada: Politics, Economics and Society*, by Tony Thorndike, Frances Pinter, London 1984, and many others.

In 1987, the formation of a new opposition party, the National Democratic Congress (NDC), led to parliamentary changes. Further divisions within the NNP preceded Mr Blaize's death in December 1989; his faction, led by Ben Jones, became the National Party, while the New National Party name was retained by Keith Mitchell's faction. In general elections held in 1990, each of these parties won two seats while the NDC, led by Nicholas Brathwaite (formerly head of the interim administration), won seven. The GULP gained four seats.

In 1991 the Government decided to commute to life imprisonment the death sentences on 14 people convicted of murdering Maurice Bishop after world wide appeals for clemency. Amnesty International and other organizations have appealed for the release of Mrs Phyllis Coard, one of the 14 convicted, on grounds of ill-health following years of solitary confinement. She was allowed to go to Jamaica for cancer treatment in 2000, but was not pardoned.

In February 1995 Mr Brathwaite retired and was succeeded by George Brizan. General elections were held in June 1995. The NDC campaigned on its economic stabilization policies, but faced keen opposition from the NNP, led by Keith Mitchell, and GULP, led by Sir Eric Gairy. The NNP (32.7% of the vote) won eight seats, the NDC five (31.1%) and GULP two (26.8%), so Keith Mitchell became Prime Minister. Sir Eric Gairy failed to win a seat. In December 1995, Grenada's eighth political party, the Democratic Labour Party (DLP), was launched by Francis Alexis, former deputy leader of the NDC, thereby reducing the NDC to four seats. In June 1997, Prescott Williams launched the Grenada Progressive Party, aimed to appeal to women and young people. Sir Eric Gairy died in August 1997 and GULP split into two factions. In a much postponed election in April 1998, Herbert Preudhomme was elected leader, after many accusations of fraud and recounts.

The most recent general elections, in January 1999, were an unparalleled victory for the NNP, which won all 15 seats with 62% of the vote. The opposition parties were too numerous and weak to provide an effective challenge, although the NDC received 24% of the vote. Keith Mitchell was sworn in for a second term as Prime Minister. The Government is considering the resumption of executions for murder (last carried out in 1978). The announcement was criticized by the regional human rights movement, Caribbean Rights.

In 2000, a Truth and Reconciliation Commission was established to investigate events in 1976-91. The inquiry was expected to take six months and cover the last three years of Gairy's authoritarian rule, the New Jewel Movement revolution in 1979, the establishment of the People's Revolutionary Government, the bloodshed of October 1983, the US invasion, the trial and subsequent reprieve from execution in 1991.

Geography

Grenada, the most southerly of the Windwards, has two dependencies in the Grenadines chain, Carriacou and Petit (often spelt Petite) Martinique. They, and a number of smaller islets, lie north of the main island. The group's total area is 133 square miles. Grenada itself is 21 miles long and 12 miles wide. The highest point is Mount St Catherine, at 2,757 ft. The island seems to tilt on a northeast-southwest axis: if a line is drawn through ancient craters of Lake Antoine in the Northeast, the Grand Étang in the central mountains and the Lagoon at St George's, it will be straight. Northwest of that line, the land rises and the coast is high; southeast it descends to a low coastline of rias (drowned valleys). The island is green, well forested and cultivated and is blessed with plenty of rain in the wet season. Grenada is described as a spice island, for it produces large quantities of cloves and mace and about a third of the world's nutmeg. It also grows cacao, sugar, bananas and a wide variety of other fruit and vegetables. Some of its beaches, specially Grand Anse, a dazzling two-mile stretch of white sand, are very fine. The majority of the tourist facilities are on the island's dry southwest tip, but the rest of the island is beautiful, rising from a generally rugged coast to a spectacular mountainous interior. With an area of 13 sq miles, Carriacou is the largest of the Grenadines. It lies 23 miles northeast of Grenada; 2½ miles further northeast is Petit Martinique, which is separated by a narrow channel from Petit St Vincent, the southernmost of St Vincent's Grenadine dependencies.

Government Grenada is an independent state within the Commonwealth, with the British monarch as Head of State represented by a Governor General (Daniel Williams since 1996). There are two legislative houses, the House of Representatives with 15 members. and the Senate with 13 members. The Government is elected for a five-year term.

People The population of some 98,400 (of which 7,000 live on Carriacou and Petit Martinique) is largely of African (85%) or mixed (11%) descent. In contrast to other Windward Islands which have had a similar history of disputed ownership between the French and English, the French cultural influence in Grenada has died out. Nevertheless, it is a predominantly Catholic island, though there are Protestant churches of various denominations, and a Baha'i Centre. Many people who emigrated from Grenada to the UK are returning to the island and are building smart houses for their retirement which are in stark contrast to the tiny, corrugated iron shacks which are home to many of their countrymen. The population is very young; 38% are under 15 years old and nearly 26% are in the 15-29 years' age bracket. Youth unemployment is a problem.

Economy In the last decade, Grenada has seen a huge expansion of its tourism industry and the economy has been driven by the construction sector meeting demand for new hotels, villas and infrastructure projects. Stopover visitors and cruise ship passengers have risen steadily and the yacht charter business has also expanded considerably. However, the rise in the numbers of tourists was checked in 2000 when Carnival announced in November 1999 that it was ending calls to Grenada. It claimed that the landing fee of US$3 per person and environmental levy of US$1.50 were excessive. Carnival previously accounted for about half of the annual income of EC$9 mn from cruise passengers. In 2001 the airlines, British Airways and JMC, announced that they, too, would be pulling out of Grenada, hitting the British and European markets.

Agriculture accounts for about 12% of gdp but is falling. The number of farmers has fallen by 25% since 1961, with the area of prime farming land falling by 50% to about 30,000 acres in the same period. The major export crops are nutmeg, bananas and cocoa; nutmeg and mace together account for about 14% of all exports and Grenada is a leading world producer of this spice. There is also a nutmeg oil distillation plant which produces oil from defective nutmeg.

Barbados

17

Barbados

Barbados has a long-established tourist industry and is highly experienced in providing efficient service to a wide clientele. Tourists who come here looking for the 'untouched' Caribbean are in for a disappointment. It hasn't got the best beaches in the Caribbean, there are no volcanoes, no rainforest, no virgin coral reef, but it has pleasantly rolling countryside with fields of sugar cane, brightly painted villages, flowering trees and open pastures and visitors come back time and time again. You can pay hundreds or thousands of dollars for a hotel room and be truly cosseted or rent a moderate apartment and look after yourself. You can play golf (the courses are very highly rated), tennis, squash and any number of other sports, or you can watch cricket, horseracing or polo. There is lovely walking along the rugged north and east coasts on the Atlantic side, while watersports are offered along the more protected west and south coasts on the Caribbean. For sightseeing, there are fortifications, plantation houses, museums, rum distilleries and gardens. Barbados' history as a British colony is evident in its political system and place names, but times are changing. You can no longer stand in Trafalgar Square and look at Nelson's statue; the Lord High Admiral has been moved and the square now honours National Heroes.

A Foot in the door

- Don't miss a plate of **flying fish and chips**.
- **Explore** the east coast, where the Atlantic crashes against the cliffs.
- Tour a **rum** plant, taste, buy and enjoy.
- Experience British colonial military history at the **Garrison** and see the memorials around the race course.
- Take in a Sunday village **cricket** match or an international at the Kensington Oval.

Essentials

Before you travel

Documents

Work permits are very difficult to obtain; regulations are strictly enforced

Visitors from North America, Western Europe, Commonwealth African countries, Argentina, Venezuela, Colombia, and Brazil need a **passport** but no **visas**. US visitors may get in on a driving licence, but the immigration officers are not keen on this. Visitors from most other countries are usually granted a short stay on arrival, and tourist visas are not necessary. Officially, you must have a ticket back to your country of origin as well as an **onward ticket** to be allowed in. Immigration officers do check. You will also need an accommodation address on arrival, they do not check your reservation but if you say you do not know where you will be staying, you will be sent to the back of the queue.

State the maximum period you intend to stay on arrival. Overstaying is not recommended if you wish to re-enter Barbados at a later date. Extending your stay is possible at the Immigration Office, Careenage House on the Wharf in Bridgetown (T4269912), costs US$12.50 and is fairly time consuming. When visiting the Immigration Office, which is open from 0830-1630, take your passport and return ticket. Tickets are inspected quite carefully.

Money

Currency The currency unit is the Barbados dollar, which is pegged at B$2.00 for US$1.00. Many tourist establishments quote prices in US dollars, if you are not careful a hotel room may end up costing twice as much as you bargained for. Banks will only change the US dollar, Canadian dollar, EC dollar, sterling, Deutschmark and Euro. Other currencies they will not exchange. **Credit cards** are accepted in the large resorts, their use is now widespread.

Banks *Barclays Bank*, the *Royal Bank of Canada*, *CIBC Caribbean Ltd*, *Scotiabank*, *Caribbean Commercial Bank*, *Barbados Mutual Bank* and *Barbados National Bank* all have offices in Bridgetown. The first five also have branches in the main south and west coast tourist centres. Opening hours for banks are 0800-1500 Mon to Thu, and 0800-1300 and 1500-1700 on Fri. *Caribbean Commercial Bank* in Hastings and Sunset Crest is also open on Sat from 0900 to 1200. The *Barbados National Bank* has a branch and a bureau de change at the airport; the latter is open from 0800-2400, but inaccessible unless you are actually arriving or departing. All banks now have cash machines at most branches which you can use with a credit card after hours. Banking facilities in *JB's* and *Big B Supermarkets* are open 1000-1900 Mon-Thu, 1000-2000 Fri, 1000-1500 Sat. Banks are thin on the ground on the east coast, but the supermarket at Belleplaine has a Royal Bank counter.

Getting there

Flights to Barbados are heavily booked at Christmas & for Crop Over

Barbados' popularity as a tourist destination has resulted in good transport connections with many flights from Europe and North and South America. Until the grounding of Concorde in 2000, this high-speed service from London was very popular with wealthy visitors to the island, and it is hoped that it will fly again in 2001. Barbados can also be reached by sea, either by cruise ship through the Caribbean, or with Windward Lines (suspended 2001) from Venezuela and neighbouring islands. The Grantley Adams International Airport is 16 km from Bridgetown, near the resorts on the south coast and connected to the west coast beaches by the ABC Highway which bypasses the capital.

Touching down

The airport is modern and well equipped. Clearing Immigration can be a problem and it can take an hour to clear a 747. If three 747s arrive together expect delays. There is a *Liat* connection desk before Immigration. There is a helpful Tourism Authority office, *Barbados National Bank* (very slow), (bureau de change in the arrivals and departure areas is open from 0800-2400), a post office, car hire agencies and quite a wide range of shops (good for stocking up on film or alcohol even if just going on a day trip) including an Inbound Duty Free Shop (very useful, saves carrying heavy bottles on the plane).

Barbados

■ **Sleeping**
1 Sam Lord's Castle
2 Villa Nova

▲ **Other**
1 Andromeda Gardens
2 Animal Flower Cave
3 Banks Brewery
4 Barbados Zoo Park
5 Barclays Park
6 Clapham, Harry Bailey Observatory
7 Codrington College

8 Cotton Tower
9 Drax Hall
10 East Point Lighthouse
11 Farley Hill House & Wildlife Reserve
12 Flower Forest
13 Folkestone Marine Museum, Underwater Park & St James Church
14 Four Square Rum Factory
15 Garrison
16 Graeme Hall Swamp

17 Gun Hill Signal Station
18 Harrisons Caves
19 Morgan Lewis Mill
20 Mount Gay Distillery
21 Portvale Sugar Factory
22 St John's Church
23 St Nicholas Abbey
24 Sunbury Plantation House
25 The Aquatic Centre
26 Turners Hall Woods
27 Tyrol Cot
28 Welchman Hall Gully

0 km   2
0 miles   2

Barbados

Touching down

Departure tax There is a departure tax of B$25, not payable for stays of than 24 hours.

Embassies Australian High Commission, Bishop's Court Hill, T4352843. **Belgian** Consulate, Rockley Resort, T4357704. **Brazilian** Embassy, 3rd Floor, Sunjet House, Fairchild St, T4271735. **British** High Commission, Lower Collymore Rock, St Michael, PO Box 676, T4366694, F4365398. **Canadian** High Commission, Bishop's Court Hill, St Michael, T4283550. **Colombian** Embassy, Dayrells Rd, T4296821. **Cuban** Embassy, Collymore Rock, T4352769. **Danish** Consul, c/o Yankee Garments, T4244995. **Dutch** Consul, c/o Chickmont Foods, T4188000. **French**, Hastings, Christ Church, T4356847. **German**, Banyan Court, Bay St, St Michael, T4271876. **Guatemalan Embassy**, 2nd Floor, Trident House, Broad St, T4353542, F4352638. **Israeli** Consul, T4264764. **Italy**, T4371228. **Norwegian** Consul, T4297286. **People's Rep of China**, Golf View, Rockley, T4356890. **Swedish** Embassy, Branckers Complex, Fontabelle, St Michael, T4274358. **US** Consular Section, Alico Building, Cheapside, Bridgetown, T4364950. **Venezuelan** Embassy, El Sueño, Hastings, Christ Church, T4357619.

Official time Atlantic Standard Time, 4 hours behind GMT, 1 ahead of EST.

Voltage 120 volts (American standard) and 50 cycles per second (British standard). Some houses and hotels also have 240-volt sockets for use with British equipment.

Safety Bridgetown is still much safer than some other Caribbean cities but crime rates have increased. Local people are now more cautious about where they go after dark and many no longer go to Nelson St or some other run-down areas. Baxters Rd, however, is generally quite safe although the former attracts prostitutes while the latter attracts cocaine addicts (paros). Take care when walking along deserted beaches and watch out for pickpockets and bag snatchers in tourist areas. Families with small children to care for at night rarely notice any crime and have commented on how secure they felt on Barbados. If hiring a car, watch out for people who wash the vehicle unasked and then demand US$5. Police have patrols on beaches and plain clothes officers around some rural tourist attractions.

Notice board on left, as you come out of arrivals, lists taxi fares

Across the car park there are two lively rum shops, one of which, *Frankie's*, does good meals and snacks; the shop in the gas station is open when terminal shops are closed, selling food, papers etc. Taxis stop just outside customs. Check the notice board on the left as you come out of arrivals, as it gives the official taxi fares. Talk to the dispatcher if necessary. Drivers may attempt to charge more if you haven't checked. There is a bus stop just across the car park, with buses running along the south coast to Bridgetown, or (over the road) to the *Crane* and *Sam Lord's Castle*.

Airline offices The *Liat* office is at St Michael's Plaza, St Michael's Row (T4366224). *BWIA* (T4262111), *British Airways* (T4366413), are all on Fairchild St. *American Airlines* (T4284170) has offices at the airport. *Virgin Atlantic* is in Hastings, T7447477.

Tourist information **Local tourist office** The Barbados Tourism Authority has its main office in Harbour Rd, Bridgetown (T4272623, F4264080, www.barbados.org). There are also offices at the deepwater harbour (T4261718) and the airport (T4280937). Two good sources of information are *Visitor* and the *Sun Seeker*, published fortnightly and distributed free by Barbados's two daily newspapers. *Sun Seeker* has an amazing listing of every possible club and society, down to Progressive Ballroom Dance and Clay Pigeon Shooting. If you want to meet fellow Soroptimists, Rehabilitation Therapists, Astronomers or Girl Guides...there you go. Also lists where to worship, entertainment and daily events. *Signature* is a free glossy magazine with articles on culture, profiles, environment, business etc. *Sporting Barbados* (www.sportingbarbados.com) is another free glossy, plenty of useful information. *Ins and Outs of Barbados*, www.insandouts-barbados.com also free, is published annually, a glossy with lots of historical articles as well as advertising and distributed by the Barbados Hotel & Tourism Association, 4th Av Belleville, St Michael, T4265041, F4292845, bhta@inaccs.com.bb *Exploring Historical Barbados*, by Maurice Bateman Hutt, is quite good but it was published in 1981.

Tourist offices overseas

Benelux, Weekenstroo Public Relations, Breiterlaan 298, 2596 Den Haag, T3170-3280824, F3170-3280838, benelux@barbados.org
Canada, 105 Adelaide St W, Suite 1010, Toronto, Ontario, M5H 1P9, T416-2149880, toll-free 1-800-268 9122, F416-2149882, canada@barbados.org/canada
France, c/o Tropic Travel, 8-10 Rue St Marc, 75002 Paris, T33-0142365118, F42365119, france@barbados.org
Germany, Staatliches Fremdenverkehrsant Barbados, Neue Mainzer Strasse 22, D-60311 Frankfurt/Main, T069-24269630, F069-230077, germany@barbados.org
Italy, 20145 Milano, Via Gherardini 2, T0233105841, F0233105827, italy@barbados.org

Sweden, Skeppsbron 22, 1130 Stockholm, T460-84115066, F84115067, sweden@barbados.org
UK, 263 Tottenham Court Rd, London W1P 0LA, T020-76369448/9, F6371496, btauk@barbados.org
USA, 800 Second Ave, New York, NY 10017, T212-9866516/8 or toll-free 800-2219831, F212-5739850, btany@barbados.org; 150 Alhambra Circle, 10th Flr, Coral Gables, FL 33134, T305-4427471, F305-5672844, bt@miami@barbados.org; 3440 Wilshire Blvd, Suite 1215, Los Angeles, CA 90010, T213380 2198/9, toll free 800-2219831, F213-3842763, btla@barbados.org
The Barbados Embassy in **Caracas** (Quinta Chapaleta, 9a Transversal, Entre 2 y 3 Avenidas, Altamira, T582-391471, F323393) can also provide tourist information.

Barbados

Local tour agencies Bus tours **L E Williams** (T4271043, US$50-65 day tour, has a sign up in the bus: 'no 10 % service charge is paid with the tour price', heavy pressure selling of tapes, limited drinks from bar), **Bartic tours** (T4285980), **Sunflower Tours** (T4298941), **International Tour Services** (T4284803), **Bajan Tours** (T/F4372389, cheaper and better value than some, no pressure on tipping, US$32.50 per half day, US$50 full day including lunch), **Island Safari** (T4325337, tour is with 4WD Landrovers so can get to some less accessible beaches, US$40 per half day, US$57.50 full day with lunch, US$90 land and sea tour, kayaking also on offer), **Adventureland** (T4293687, also 4WD and same price), **Ultimate Outback Tours** (T4205418, limbolady@sunbeach.net, also 4WD) and **Blue Line** (T4239268, tours for US$25-55, including entrance fees to sites visited). Longer tours generally include lunch at the Atlantis Hotel in Bathsheba. A criticism of the tours with some companies is that it can take 1½ hours to pick up everyone from hotels and those further north do not get the full tour through Bridgetown and Holetown. If there are 4 of you, it is more flexible to take VIP tours in a limousine with Sally Shearn, T4294617, US$40 per hour, minimum 4 hours, a variety of tours or design your own, admission charges not included. The Transport Board, T4366820, also does a round the island tour by bus on Sunday, aimed mainly at locals and costing only US$5, to the fury of the higher priced competition; book ahead and take your own picnic. **Grenadine Tours**, T4358451, http://Barbados.org/tours/gttours and **Caribbean Safari Tours**, T4275100, do day tours to Grenadines and other islands, with yacht charter if you want. The latter is at the Ship Inn, St Lawrence.

Newspapers The Advocate, also publishes The Sunday Advocate and Sun Seeker (fortnightly) **Media** tourist magazine, see above. The Nation (publisher also of Sunday on Saturday, Sunday Sun, The Visitor tourist fortnightly and Barbados Business Authority, Monday, US$0.50). Broad Street Journal is a free business weekly. **Radio** CBC Radio, medium wave 900 kHz; Starcom Gospel, medium wave 790 kHz; BBS, FM 90.7 MHz; Love FM, FM 104.1 MHz; Radio Liberty, FM 98.1 MHz, FAITH 102 FM. **Television** One terrestrial channel, CBC, mostly US imports. Also multi-choice TV with 30 channels and satellite-based Directv with 70 channels. **Maps** Ordnance Survey Tourist Maps including Barbados in the series, 1:50,000 scale with inset of Bridgetown 1:10,000.

Barbadians are a religious people and although the main church is Anglican, there are over **Religion** 140 different faiths and sects, including Baptists, Christian Scientists, Jews, Methodists, Moravians and Roman Catholics. Times of services can be found in the Visitor and Sunseeker.

Getting around

Road

Petrol costs US$1 per litre. The speed limit is 55 mph. Drive on the left

The island is fairly small but it can take a surprisingly long time to travel as the rural roads are narrow and winding. The Adams Barrow Cummins highway runs from the airport to a point between Brighton and Prospect, north of Bridgetown. This road (called the ABC, or industrial access highway) skirts the east edge of the capital, giving access by various roads into the city. Roads into Bridgetown get jammed morning and afternoon. Drivers need a visitor's driving permit (Visitor Registration Certificate) from Hastings, Worthing, or Holetown police stations (cost US$5). You will need this even if you have an International Driving Licence. Car hire companies usually sort it out for you.

Mini-mokes are fun but not recommended in the rainy season

Car hire This is efficient and generally reliable. A medium sized car will cost on average US$105 per day, US$400 per week. *Sunny Isle Motors*, Dayton, Worthing, T4357979; *Stoutes Car Rentals* (T4354456/7, F4354435) are particularly helpful, and will arrange to meet you at the airport if you telephone in advance; *L E Williams* (T4271043) has slightly lower rates for some vehicles; *Regency Rent-a-Car*, 77 Regency Park, Christ Church, T4275663, F4297735, free pick up and delivery. *Wander Auto Rentals & Taxi Services Inc*, T4354813, T2304817 (mobile). There are often discounts available (including free driver's permit) and tourist magazines frequently contain 10% vouchers.

It is also possible to hire a light **motorcycle** or a **bicycle**: motor scooters about US$45 per day, US$205 per week, bicycles US$12.50 per day, US$50 per week, although there will also be a deposit to pay. Fun Seekers, Rockley Main Rd, T4358206. **Cycling** is best on the east coast, but traffic is heavy everywhere and rush hour from 1600 makes cycling unpleasant almost anywhere on the island.

See also 'Transport', page 910

Buses are cheap and frequent, but also crowded. There is a flat fare of B$1.50 (B$1 for schoolchildren in uniform) which will take you anywhere on the island. Almost all the routes radiate in and out of Bridgetown, so cross-country journeys are time-consuming if you are staying outside the city centre. However, travelling by bus can be fun. There are some circuits which work quite well; for example: 1. Any south coast bus to Oistins, then cross country College Savannah bus to the east coast, then direct bus back to Bridgetown; 2. Any west coast bus to Speightstown, then bus back to Bathsheba on the east coast, then direct bus back to Bridgetown. Out of town bus stops are marked simply 'To City' or 'Out of City'. For the south coast ask for Silver Sands route.

Taxis are expensive. There are plenty at the airport, the main hotels, and in Bridgetown. There are standard fares, displayed just outside "arrivals" at the airport, and are also listed in the *Visitor* and the *Sunseeker*. You may have to bargain hard for tours by taxi but always agree a fare in advance. They will sometimes try to exceed the official rate per hour of US$16.

Keeping in touch

Post

The General Post Office Headquarters is in Cheapside, Bridgetown and there are District Post Offices in every parish. Collections from red post boxes on roadsides. Local postal rates are US$0.25 for priority, US$0.20 non-priority. Airmail rates to North America US$0.60 or US$0.25, to Europe US$0.70 or US$0.35, to the Caribbean US$0.45 or US$0.25. There is an express delivery service of 48 hours worldwide: to the Caribbean US$14-18, USA US$23, Europe US$28. A Philatelic Bureau issues first-day covers four times a year.

Telephone

IDD phone code: 246

Calls from a pay phone cost 25 cents for three minutes. Otherwise local calls are free. Many business places will allow you to use their telephone for local calls. International calls can be made from most hotels or (more cheaply) from Barbados External Telecommunications (Wildey). Faxes can also be sent from and received at BET's office by members of the public. BET has a public office on the Wharf in Bridgetown for international calls and fax. Phone cards are available for US$5, 10, 20, 30 from phone company offices, *Cave Shepherd* or *Super Centre* supermarkets; a cheaper way of making overseas calls than using hotel services, and can be used on most English-speaking islands except Trinidad, Jamaica, Guyana, Bahamas. **Internet**:

Business services and internet access on the west coast at *Global Business Centre*, West Coast Mall, Sunset Crest, T4326508, F4326519, open Mon-Fri 0900-1700, Sat 0900-1300. In Bridgetown, *Promotech*, unlimited access US$35 a month, *Netcafé*, Sogo Plaza, 20 Broad St, T4354736. Also in Broad St Mall, Bridgetown, US$0.13 per minute, 8 minute minimum, Mon-Thu 0900-1700, Fri 0900-1800, Sat 0900-1400, opposite CIBC. *Connect*, just off Broad St, upstairs from Windjammer on Lancaster Lane opposite *Cave Shepherd*, from US$2.50, Mon-Thu 0900-1700, Fri 0900-1800, Sat 0930-1430, T2288648. In St Lawrence Gap, *Bean 'n Bagel Café*, 'gourmet coffee' and free beer when you spend US$10 or more, light meals all day, open 0700-1730.

Food and drink

Food

Fresh fish is excellent. The main fish season is Dec-May, when there is less risk of stormy weather at sea. Flying fish are the national emblem and a speciality with two or three to a plate. Dolphin (dorado, not a mammal in spite of its name and now usually called Mahi Mahi on restaurant menus as in the USA) and kingfish are larger *steak-fish*. Snapper is excellent. *Sea eggs* are the roe of the white sea urchin, and are delicious but not often available. Fresh fish is sold at the fish markets in Oistins, Bridgetown and elsewhere in the late afternoon and evening, when the fishermen come in with their catch. *Cou-cou* is a filling starchy dish made from breadfruit or corn meal. *Jug-jug* is a Christmas speciality made from guinea corn and supposedly descended from the haggis of the poor white settlers. Pudding and *souse* is a huge dish of pickled breadfruit, black pudding and pork.

Drink

Malibu, the rum & coconut drink, now also in a lime flavour, comes from Barbados

Barbados rum is probably the best in the English-speaking Caribbean, unless of course you come from Jamaica, or Guyana or … It is worth paying a bit extra for a good brand such as VSOP or Old Gold, or for Sugar Cane Brandy, unless you are going to drink it with Coca Cola, in which case anything will do. A rum and cream liqueur, *Crisma*, has now been introduced, popular in cocktails or on the rocks. The *Malibu Visitor's Centre*, T4259393, runs a tour, US$7.50, luncheon tour, US$27.50 and a special day pass, including lunch and transport from your hotel, US$37.50. *Falernum* is sweet, slightly alcoholic, with a hint of vanilla. *Corn and oil* is rum and falernum. *Mauby* is bitter, and made from tree bark. It can be refreshing. *Sorrel* is a bright red Christmas drink made with hibiscus sepals and spices; it is very good with white rum. Banks beer has Bajan Light and other beers; they do brewery tours Tue, Thu 1000-1300, call in advance T4292113. Water is of excellent quality, it comes mostly from deep wells sunk into the coral limestone.

Shopping

Prices are generally high, but the range of goods available is excellent. Travellers who are going on to other islands may find it useful to do some shopping here. If coming from another Caribbean island there are strict controls on bringing in fresh fruit and vegetables, because of the mealy bug infestation.

Street vendors are very persistent but generally friendly even when you refuse their wares

Barbados

The best stocked **supermarket** is *JB's Mastermart* in Wildey. *Big B* in Worthing and Supercentre in Oistins and Holetown are also good, and are easier to reach by public transport. Also in Holetown is the *Gourmet Shop* selling a lot of luxuries. *Patisserie Flindt*, Holetown, also Quayside Centre, Worthing, *Savoy*-trained chef makes delicious (expensive) French pasties, cakes and chocolates (US$5 for a chocolate mousse, US$1.50 for one chocolate), very good coffee, good for a light meal. Food is not cheap but generally most things are available and good quality. Supermarkets are now open on Sun 0900-1300. *Big B* in Worthing is open 0800-1900 Mon-Tue, 0800-2000 Wed-Sat, 0900-1300 Sun, photocopying available. *Julie'N* on the corner of Rendezvous and Highway 7, satisfactory. Large new Julie'N hypermarket on St Barnabas Highway, corner of Highway 5, and in Rendezvous, typically American with wide range of surrounding shops, usually provides free transport back home with shopping within 3 mile radius, which include some south coast hotels. Julie'N also has the biggest supermarket in central Bridgetown, north side of bridge opposite Treasury Building.

Duty-free shopping is well advertised. Visitors who produce passport and air ticket can take most duty-free goods away from the store for use in the island before they leave, but not camera film or alcohol. Clothing is significantly cheaper duty-free, so don't go shopping without ticket and passport. Cameras and electrical goods may be much cheaper in an ordinary discount store in the USA or Europe than duty free in Barbados. A duty-free shopping centre for cruise ship passengers in Bridgetown inside the deep water harbour: the *Bridgetown Cruise Terminal* has 21 shops, hand carts selling crafts, 13 chattel houses selling T shirts etc, car hire, bicycle hire, dive shop, agency to arrange horse riding, outlet for tours off the beaten track, two fast food restaurants, steel band twice a day plus other entertainment.

Broad Street is dominated by enormous **jewellers**: *Colombian Emeralds*, *Diamonds International*, *Diamonds in Paradise*, *Jewelers Warehouse* and *Little Switzerland*. *The Art Foundry* (Heritage Park, Foursquare, St Philip, Mon-Fri, 0900-1700, T4180714), have paintings, sculpture, prints, photographs, installation art and craft for sale. The *Verandah Art Gallery* (Bridgetown, Mon-Fri 0900-1630, Sat 0900-1300, T4262605) has a reasonable selection with some Haitian art and temporary exhibitions. The *Barbados Gallery of Art*, Bush Hill, The Garrison, St Michael, T2280149, sells prints and has exhibitions. *Medford Craft World*, Whitehall Main Road, T4251919, and *Medford Craft Shop*, Barbarees Hill, T4273179, have wooden carvings etc. Other good displays of craft items are at *Pelican Craft Village*, rebuilt in 2001 on the Princess Alice Highway near the harbour, where you can watch artisans at work. *Red Clay Potter y* and *Fairfield Gallery* just outside Bridgetown sells very good ceramics, T4243800. *Earthworks & Potters House*, Edgehill Heights No 2, St Thomas, T4250223, for ceramics, also has small restaurant/café. *Potter's House Gallery*, has crafts on sale and also a lunch club restaurant/café, open Mon-Fri 0900-1700, Sat 0900-1300, for lunch club T4252890. There is also a street market in Temple Yard where Rastafarians sell leather and other goods.

Bookshops are much better stocked than on other islands. *The Cloister* on Hincks St, T4262662, probably has the largest stock with a good range of Caribbean material and sells Footprint Handbooks. *The Book Place* on Probyn St specializes in Caribbean material and has a good secondhand section. *The Pages* Bookshop at Cave Shepherd also has a good selection. Also *Roberts Stationery*, *The Book Shop*, *The Bookstop* .

Camera repairs Louis Bailey in Da Costa Mall in Broad St is well-equipped, expensive. Professional Camera Repair, Room 1, Collins Building, Broad St, Bridgetown, T4267174.

Holidays and festivals

Public holidays New Year's Day, Errol Barrow Day (21 January), Good Friday, Easter Monday, National Heroes Day (28 April), Labour Day (1 May), Whit Monday (7 weeks after Easter), Emancipation Day (1 August), Kadooment Day (first Monday in August), Independence Day (30 November), Christmas Day and Boxing Day.

Festivals For a diary of events and festivals see http://barbados.org/eventcd.htm *Crop Over* is the main festival (**1 July** to **7 August 2000**), with parades and calypso competitions over the weekend leading up to Kadooment Day (the first Monday in August), and calypso 'tents' (mostly indoors though) for several weeks beforehand. The celebrations begin with the ceremonial delivery of the last canes on a brightly-coloured dray cart pulled by mules, which are blessed. There is a toast to the sugar workers and the crowning of the King and Queen of the crop (the champion cutter-pilers). The bands and costumes have improved but are a pale imitation of what Trinidad has to offer. However, even Trinidadians now take Barbadian soca and calypso seriously and talk of the Bajan invasion. The big crowd is on the Spring Garden Highway outside Bridgetown Monday afternoon, which has roadside music and places selling drinks for two weeks before Kadooment. Next to the Highway there is Festival village, an area for open-air parties with live music, small entry fee. Baxters Road Mall runs for a couple of weekends beforehand; the road is closed off for fried fish, music and beer. Some related activities take place in July. For more information contact the National Cultural Foundation, T4240909, http://barbados.org/cropover.htm.

The Holetown Festival (February, contact Alfred Pragnell, T4356264), commemorating the first settlers' landing in February 1627, and the *Oistins Fish Festival* at Easter(contact Dan Carter, T4273272), celebrating the signing of the Charter of Barbados and the history of this fishing town, are much less elaborate. There are competitions and a big street party with music goes on until late at night. Many villages will also hold a 'street fair' from time to time.

NIFCA, the *National Independence Festival of Creative Arts* is a more serious affair, with plays, concerts and exhibitions in the four weeks before Independence on **30 November**. The *Holders Season* (**end March**), is a popular, festival started in 1992 with a season of opera, Shakespeare, cabaret and sporting events such as cricket, golf and polo. Performances are staged outdoors at Holders, an old plantation house. Contact Carol Walcott, T4326385, F4326461 for details.

Congaline Carnival is held in late **April**, finishing with a Mayday jump up in the streets from Garrison Savanna to Spring Garden. Bajan and other Caribbean music. Contact the National Cultural Foundation, T4240909.

There is a **jazz** festival held usually the second week of **January**, contact Gilbert Rowe, T4374537, www.barbadosjazzfestival.com and for lovers of Gospel music the Gospel Fest is held in **May**, contact Adrian Agard, T4307300.

Diving and marine life

Scuba diving to the reefs or the wrecks around the coast can be arranged with *Underwater Barbados*, Coconut Court Hotel, Hastings, or Carlisle Bay Centre, Bay St, St Michael, T/F4260655; *West Side Scuba Centre* at *Sunset Crest Beach Club*, Holetown, T/F4322558, putnam@sunbeach.net *Hightide Watersports*, T/F4320931, hightide@sunbeach.net, at the *Boatyard* and *Sandy Lane Hotel*. *Exploresub*, St Lawrence Gap T4356542, F4284674, x-sub@caribsurf.com *Carib Ocean Divers* at *Royal Pavilion* and *Glitter Bay*, T4224414. *Blue Reef Water Sports* at *Glitter Bay* T4223133. *Reefers and Wreckers* at *Kings Beach* T4225450; *Roger's Scuba Shack*, *Boatyard*, Bay Street, T2463483, and several others. These companies also offer PADI diving courses, equipment rental and other facilities such as snorkelling. The only BSAC accredited school (also PADI and NAUI courses) is *Coral Isle Divers* on the Careenage in Bridgetown, T/F4319068, coralis@caribnet.net, who use a 40-ft catamaran dive boat. The *Barbados Sub Aqua Club*, a branch of the British Sub Aqua Club (BSAC) meets at 0800 on Sunday at the *Boatyard Pub* on the waterfront on Bay St, Bridgetown. They do not hire out equipment but if you have your own they are most welcoming to members from other branches, T4216020, Rob Bates. One of their groups dives for old bottles on a reef just offshore where ships have anchored for some 350 years. There is a recompression chamber at St Anne's Fort, T4278819, or tell the operator if there is an emergency. A new offering is Snuba, when you have a mask and air tube and can go deeper than snorkelling without the hassle of scuba, US$35, T4359037.

For those who want to see the underwater world without getting wet, the *Atlantis Submarine* is at Shallow Draft Harbour, T4368929, day and night dives at US$80, children aged four to 12 half price. The tour starts with a short video and then you go by bus to the deep water port or join the launch at the Careenage. The boat takes about 10 minutes to get to the submarine, sit at the front to be first on the sub, an advantage as then you can see out of the driver's window as well as out of your own porthole. Two divers on underwater

Barbados

scooters join the submarine for the last 15 minutes, putting on a dive show. Booking is necessary, check in 30 minutes before dive time, whole tour takes 1½ hours.

Beaches and watersports

Beaches
Beach vendors now have a licence and stalls. Unscrupulous cocaine and sex vendors still operate but are more subtle in their approach than in the past

There are beaches along most of the south and west coasts. Although some hotels make it hard to cross their property to reach the sand, there are no private beaches in Barbados. For example, just north of Speightstown there is a narrow road between *Almond Beach* and the *Port St Charles Marina*, which ends in a small car park giving access to the good beaches which front these properties. The west coast beaches are very calm, and quite narrow, beach erosion is a serious worry and the Government's Coastal Conservation Unit is trying to sort it out. A swell can wash up lots of broken coral making it unpleasant underfoot. The south coast can be quite choppy. The southeast, between the airport and East Point, has steep limestone cliffs with a series of small sandy coves with coconut trees, and waves which are big enough for surfing. **Bottom Bay** is currently *the* place to go. Be careful on the east side of the island, currents and undertow are strong in places. Don't swim where there are warning signs, or where there are no other bathers, even on a calm day. **Bathsheba**, on the east coast, is quite spectacular, with wonderful views. Some hotels sell day passes for the use of their facilities: pool, showers, deck chairs, etc. Work on the new *Sandals Resort* at **Paradise Beach** has been shelved and the site is for sale. Meanwhile, with no hotel, the beach is beautifully deserted and the hotel has thoughtfully left its sun loungers behind. Go to north end of Spring Gardens Highway, then up west coast road Highway 1 for about half a mile, then turn sharp left. Drive down to Batts Rock Beach, walk south to get to Paradise Beach. You can keep going along the shoreline as far as Deepwater Harbour, a nice walk, mostly beach. Near the south end of this stretch at **Brandon's Beach** and accessible also from Spring Gardens Highway, is *Weiser's Beach Bar*, T4256450, which has beach volleyball and an afternoon happy hour, but it can be crowded if there's a cruise ship in.

Sailing
There are a large number of **motor and sailing boats** available for charter by the day or for shorter periods. *Tall Ships Incorporated*, T4300900, tallships@sunbeach.net, runs *Excellence I* and *II*, *Irish Mist*, *Tiami* and *Spirit of Barbados* catamarans, *Harbour Master* and *Jolly Roger* (the last two being boozy fun cruises), US$61.50, except *Jolly Roger*, US$55. *Ocean Mist*, 60-ft power catamaran, also 4-day trip to Grenadines, or eco-marine heritage cruise with hotel transfers, lunch, snorkelling, Sun-Thu 0930-1530, T4367639. *Stiletto* catamarans, T2313829, *Cool Runnings* catamarans, T4360911, *Small Cats*, T4216419, *Kool Kat*, T4209507, *Why Not*, T2303792, *Ocean Rebel*, T4287192, *Heat wave*, US$62 for lunch/snorkel/cruise, T4237871, *Gallivanter* (sports fishing), T4374044, *Calypso Charters*, T4267166, *Secret Love*, T4321972, lunch and snorkelling US$49 per person, sunset snorkelling cruise US$37.50. *Limbo Lady*, Patrick and Yvonne Gonsalves take no more than eight people on their 48-ft yacht and give you a really good day/evening out, with snorkelling, fishing, sunset cruise with delicious canapés, Cava and singing by Yvonne, who plays the guitar, T4205418, F4203254. Others are moored in the Careenage in Bridgetown, with a telephone number displayed. Most are equipped for fishing and snorkelling, and will serve a good meal on board. Rates and services offered vary widely. The big sailing event is the Mount Gay/Boatyard Regatta, held in late May, contact the Barbados Yachting Association, T4356494. The *Barbados Sailing and Cruising Club* has its clubhouse and facilities at Aquatic Gap, St Michael, T4264434, and welcomes visitors. A second Atlantic Rowing Race starts in Tenerife in Oct 2001, finishing in Barbados. **Glass-bottomed boats** can be hired from several private operators along the west coast.

Fishing
Deep sea fishing can be arranged with *Blue Jay Charters*, T4222098 (competitive prices, discounts offered), *Blue Marlin*, *Idyll Time*, T4364322, 4356669, *Barracuda Too*, T4267252, *Canon II*, T4246107, *Billfisher II*, T4310741 or *Honey Bea III*, T4285344. The Barbados Game Fishing Association (230 Atlantic Shores, Christ Church, T4222016, Julie Packer, Secretary) runs an international tournament in Apr.

Windsurfing
The south coast is good for windsurfing and the International Funboard Challenge is held in Mar. The Barbados Windsurfing World Cup is in Jan. The best surfing is on the east coast and

the Barbados International Surfing Championship is held at the Soup Bowl, Bathsheba, in late Nov. Contact the *Barbados Windsurfing Association* at Silver Sands, T4287277, or the *Barbados Surfing Association*, Roger Miller, T4265837

Skyrider Parasail, T4350570 and *Ultimate High*, T2314386 for **parasailing**. **Jetskis** are allowed only on certain beaches: Brown's and Brandon's near Bridgetown, Dover on south coast, Mullins on west.

Other sports

Athletics A multi-purpose gymnasium is part of the Sir Garfield Sobers Sports Complex at Wildey, St Michael, T4376016. Badminton, bodybuilding, boxing, basketball, gymnastics, handball, judo, karate, netball, table tennis, volleyball and weightlifting, plenty of changing rooms and showers and also sauna and massage rooms, a medical room and warm-up/practice area. Adjacent is the Aquatic Centre, with an Olympic-size **swimming** pool, tennis courts, hockey, football and cricket pitches outside. Badminton is also played at the Community College, St Michael, Tue 1930, Sat 1300, equipment available.

Contact the National Sports Council, Blenheim, St Michael, T4366127, for information on any sport not mentioned here

Bridge The Sun, Sea and Slams International Bridge Festival is held in Oct and ordinary players get a chance to play against people like Zia Mahmood of the *Guardian*'s bridge column plus other big stars. Call Barbados Bridge League or Lady Burton, T4293724. They have a duplicate game Mon, Wed, 0900 (T4357441), Thu 1930, Fri 0900, Sat 1430 (T4293189).

Cricket Lots of village cricket all over the island at weekends. A match here is nothing if not a social occasion. For information about the bigger matches at Kensington Oval phone the Barbados Cricket Association, T4361397. If you and your local team want to tour Barbados, contact *Sporting Barbados*, T2289122, F2280243, www.sportingbarbados.com for help with discounts and keeping the costs down.

Cycling Contact the Mountain Bike Association, Wayne Robinson, T4310419, or Robert Quintyne, T4293367.

Draughts and **dominoes** are played to a high standard. Join a rum shop match at your peril. Barbados has the current world champion draughts player, Suki King.

Football Contact the Barbados Football Association, T2281707.

Golf There are five courses, the best and most prestigious of which has traditionally been Sandy Lane, which now has a new 18-hole course, a 9-hole course and a second 18-hole course under construction, all on 600 acres of former sugar cane land next to the hotel, T4322946/4321311/4321145. However, a new 18-hole, par 72, course at Royal Westmoreland Golf and Country Club, St James, T4224653, has opened with 27 holes spread over 480 acres on a hilly site in St James with views over the west coast. To play here you must be staying in one of the villas or at a hotel with an access agreement. Members can use the hotel's beach club facilities 5 mins drive away. Construction of 350 villas around one of the 9-hole loops has now started, 3 club houses, a swimming pool and 5 tennis courts. The *Almond Beach Village* was built next to the 9-hole Heywoods course in the northwest, T4224900, there is also an 18-hole course at Belair, near *Sam Lords. Rockley* has no clubhouse and is not highly rated, 9 holes, T4357880. The Barbados Academy of Golf is at Balls in Christ Church, T4207405, open 0600-2200, with happy hour and a half 1600-1730. There are a putting green, driving range, 18-hole mini course (fun for families, not serious golfers), lessons and balls (US$6 per bucket). Durants course has reopened as Barbados Golf Club, with 18 holes, T4208205. Green fee US$115 in high season, US$79 in low season, also tuition, 3- and 7-day passes, etc. The Barbados Open Golf Championship is held in Dec.

Gym The World Gym near Bussa roundabout on ABC Highway is not easy to reach, except by car. Others include GSM Fitness Consultants at Needham's Point, T4361024 and West One at *Sunset Crest* near Holetown on west coast.

Hockey is played on an astroturf hockey pitch at Wildey, near Sir Garfield Sobers Gymnasium. The Banks International Hockey Festival is the largest event of its type in the Americas and is held in Aug (19-25 Aug 2001) with 37 local teams and 26 from overseas. Hockey Federation T4299430, or Will Alleyne, T4267347.

Horseracing At the Garrison on Saturday for most of the year. Again, this is something of a social occasion. The Sandy Lane Gold Cup Race, held in Mar, sometimes features horses from neighbouring islands. For information on race meetings phone Barbados Turf Club, T4263980.

Barbados

The National Trust

The National Trust runs an Open House programme of visits to interesting private houses on Wednesday afternoons from January to April every year (B$15, children 5-12 half price, B$6 for members of foreign National Trusts, see below, Boyces Garage do a tour plus entrance for B$35, T4251103. A National Trust Heritage passport is available: pick up a free booklet and get it stamped at Andromeda Gardens (B$12), Welchman Hall Gully (B$11.50), Sir Frank Hutson Sugar Museum (B$15), Tyrol Cot (B$11.50) and then you get free admission to Gun Hill, Bridgetown Synagogue, Arbib Nature trail and Morgan Lewis. The National Trust Headquarters is at Wildey House, Wildey, open 0800-1600, T4369033,

4262421, natrust@sunbeach.net, which houses the Trust's collection of antique furniture and the Euchard Fitzpatrick and Edward Stoute photography collections. The Duke of Edinburgh Award Scheme (Bridge House, Cavans Lane, Bridgetown, T4369763) and National Trust joint scheme also arrange early Sunday morning walks to places of historical and natural interest. There is a reciprocal free entry to National Trust Properties for members of the National Trust in the UK, Australia, New Zealand, Fiji and Zimbabwe. The same arrangement applies to members of the National Trust for Historic Preservation in the USA and the Heritage Canada Foundation.

Motor racing on the circuit in St Philip. There is off-road karting at Bushy Park Race Circuit, St Philip, Mon-Sat 1030-1700. The Barbados Rally Club, T4387068.

Polo Barbados Polo Club near Holetown, St James, T4321802. National and international matches are played at Holders Hill between Sep and Mar, every Sat at 1400.

Riding There are 8 riding schools offering beach and/or country rides. Some do not give instruction and cater for pleasure riding only. *Congo Road Riding Stables*, T4236180, 1-hour ride including lift to and from hotel is US$25, beginners or advanced; also Brighton Stables on west coast, T4259381; Beau Geste Stables, St George, T4290139; Tony's Riding School, St Peter, T4221549; Caribbean International Riding Stables, St Joseph, T4331453; Highland Adventure Centre, Canefield, St Thomas, US$60 for 1 ¼ hrs; Trevena Riding Stables, St James, T4326404 and Big C Riding Stables, Christ Church, T4374056. The Barbados Equestrian Association, Sandra Sampson, T4288857.

Road tennis is also a local game with defined rules, played with a low wooden 'net' on some minor (and some main) roads. The World Road Tennis Series is held at the end of Nov.

Running The Run Barbados Series is held in early Dec and is comprised of a 10 km race and a marathon. Contact Morris Greenidge at the Barbados Tourism Authority, T4272623, or Carl Bailey, Runners Choice Promotions, T4294199, www.runnerschoice.com

Squash *Rockley Resort* has 2 courts, T4357880, Barbados Squash Club, Hastings, 3 courts, T4277193, *Casuarina Hotel*, T4283600. Squash Racquets Association, Craig Archer, T4242612.

Tennis There are good courts at *Royal Pavilion* and *Glitter Bay* (Peter Burwash Tennis Centre at Royal Westmoreland Golf Course). *Paragon*, T4272054, *Rockley Resort*, T4357880, *Sam Lord's*, T4237350, *Crane Hotel*, T4326220.

Walking The most beautiful part of the islands is the Scotland District on the east coast. There is also some fine country along the St Lucy coast in the north and on the southeast coast. Walking is straightforward. The *Ordnance Survey*, Southampton, UK, produces a map of Barbados in its tourist map series, 1:50,000 scale with 1:10,000 inset of Bridgetown available from the Public Buildings in Bridgetown, from the museum, in the airport and from some bookstores in town. There is a particularly good route along the old railway track, from Bath to Bathsheba and on to Cattlewash. The National Trust, together with the Duke of Edinburgh Award Scheme, T4369033, and the Future Centre and Heart Foundation, organizes walks at 0600 Sun and at 1530 (depending on season). Details are usually printed in the *Visitor* and *Sunseeker* magazines. Their walk to Chalky Mount in the Scotland District has been recommended. The Highland Adventure Centre will also organize a 2-hr hike for US$32.50, including transport from the hotel and one drink. They also offer mountain biking at US$45 for 1 ½ hrs.

Barbados

Water Polo is played at the Barbados Aquatic Centre, where visitors are welcome to join in practice sessions with the team, which is sponsored by the local beer company, Banks. Training is every Mon and Wed at 1830, while matches are played every Saturday at 1400. Call Stephen Lewis, T4296767 (work), 4286042 (home).

Bridgetown

The capital, Bridgetown, is on the southwest corner of the island. The city itself covers a fairly small area. It is busy and full of life. There are no really large buildings except Tom Adams Financial Centre, which houses the central bank. The suburbs sprawl most of the way along the south and west coasts, and quite a long way inland. Many of the suburban areas are very pleasant, full of flowering trees and 19th-century coral stone gingerbread villas. There are two interesting areas, downtown Bridgetown with National Heroes Square on the north side of the Careenage and the historic area at Garrison.

Colour map 5, grid C6

Barbados

Ins and outs

You can get a bus or taxi from the airport to Bridgetown. Minibuses and route taxis run around the capital, cheaply and efficiently, but terribly slow in rush hour. See page 888 for details. The Tourism Authority does a useful free leaflet with map for a self-guided walking tour of Bridgetown.

Getting there

Sights

National Heroes Square was until 1999 called Trafalgar Square, with a statue of Lord Nelson, sculpted by Sir Richard Westmacott and predating its London equivalent by 36 years. It has recently been the subject of some controversy as it was thought to link Barbados too closely with its colonial past. First Nelson was turned through 180° so that he no longer looked down Broad Street, the main shopping area, but now he is to be removed, when a suitable home can be found. The square is now celebrating 10 official national heroes, including Sir Grantley Adams. There is a memorial to the Barbadian war dead and the fountain commemorates the piping of water to Bridgetown in 1861. To the north is the Parliament Building. Built in 1872, the legislature is an imposing grey building with red roof and green shutters. Built in gothic style, the clock tower is more reminiscent of a church. You can walk between the buildings (providing you are correctly dressed).

Take the northeast exit out of National Heroes Square along St Michael's Row to reach the 18th-century **St Michael's Cathedral**. It has a fine set of inscriptions and a single-hand clock. The first building was consecrated in 1665 but destroyed by a hurricane in 1780. The present cathedral is long and broad with a balcony. It has a fine vaulted ceiling and some tombs (1675) have been built into the porch. Completed in 1789, it suffered hurricane damage in 1831. If you continue east, you reach **Queen's Park**, a pleasant, restful park just outside the city centre. **Queen's Park House** is now a small theatre (Daphne Joseph Hackett Theatre) and art gallery. There is a small restaurant and bar, which does a good lunch and a buffet on Friday.

The **synagogue** is an early 19th-century building on the site of a 17th-century one, one of the two earliest in the Western hemisphere. The original synagogue, was built in the late 1660s by Jews fleeing Recife, Brazil, who heard that Oliver Cromwell had granted freedom of worship for Jews and gained permission to settle in Barbados. The tomb of Benjamin Massiah, the famous circumciser of 1782 lies on the left hand side of the graveyard, just inside the entrance. The synagogue was out of religious use for 60 years, and in the 1950s was the office of the Barbados Turf Club. Recently painstakingly restored, it is now used for religious services again and is open to visitors. It is supported by only 16 families now. ■ *Mon-Fri, 0900-1200, 1300-1600.*

Swan St is now a lively pedestrian street where Barbadians do their shopping. Street music is sometimes performed. This is in marked contrast to the large shopping malls and department stores on Broad St. Here you will find a whole range of sophisticated shops catering for tourists. The Government plans eventually to ban traffic from Broad St as part of a plan to regenerate the city centre. More developments are planned along by the Careenage where old warehouses are being converted into restaurants, discos, smart shops. Multi-storey car parks, a marina and port expansion are also part of the US$25mn project.

The **Harry Bayley Observatory** in Clapham is not far from Banks Brewery. A chance for northern visitors to look at the Southern Hemisphere stars. ■ *T4261317. Fri nights 2030-2330.*

The **Mount Gay Visitor Centre** at Brandons, St Michael, does a very good 45-minute tour of the blending and bottling plant, with an exhibition of rum, rum tasting and shop near the deep water port in Bridgetown on the Spring Garden Highway. For their distillery tour, see page 900. ■ *T4258757. B$12, or a special luncheon tour B$50. 0900-1600 Mon-Fri.* The **Malibu Visitors' Centre**, Brighton, St Michael, is near the West India Rum Refinery. The adjacent beach has watersports. ■ *T4259393. US$6 for tour, US$27.50 tour with lunch, also day pass. Mon-Fri 0900 with the last tour at 1545, free shuttle from hotel.* **Banks Brewery** has a tour and also do a 'beer trail', whereby you get your card stamped in participating bars and restaurants around the island. With five stamps you get a free brewery tour, 15 get you a T-shirt. ■ *T4292113. US$5 adults, US$2.50 children 10-15, no children under 10, proceeds to charity. Tour on Tue and Thu 1000 and 1300.*

Bridgetown

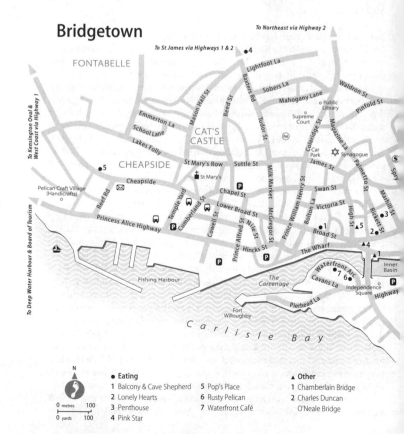

● Eating
1 Balcony & Cave Shepherd
2 Lonely Hearts
3 Penthouse
4 Pink Star
5 Pop's Place
6 Rusty Pelican
7 Waterfront Café

▲ Other
1 Chamberlain Bridge
2 Charles Duncan
O'Neale Bridge

A short bus ride from town is **Tyrol Cot**, built in 1850, home of Sir Grantley Adams. There is a Heritage Village with craftwork on sale, plus chattel-house museum, gardens and restaurant in the old stables. Run by the National Trust.■ *T4242074. US$5.75, children US$2.90. Mon-Fri 0900-1700.*

Cross the Careenage by the Charles Duncan O'Neale Bridge (one of the bus terminals and market area are just to the west) and follow Bay St around the curve of Carlisle Bay. You will pass St Patrick's Cathedral (Roman Catholic), the main government offices with St Michael's Hospital behind it before reaching the historic Garrison area. From here you can visit **Fort Charles** on Needham Point (turn right at the Pepsi plant). The fort was the largest of the many which guarded the south and west coasts, but is currently part of a building site because it forms part of the gardens of the *Hilton Hotel* which is being rebuilt. Only the ramparts remain but there are a number of 24 pounder cannons dating from 1824. There is a military cemetery here and the Mobil oil refinery was the site of the naval dockyard. Built in 1805, it was subsequently moved to English Harbour, Antigua. The buildings were then used as barracks before being destroyed in the 1831 hurricane.

The Garrison Area

Carry on up the hill to the **Garrison Historical Area**, which contains many interesting 19th-century military buildings, grouped around the Garrison Savannah. There are numerous buildings surrounding the parade ground, now the six furlong race course. These were built out of brick brought as ballast on ships from England. They are built on traditional colonial lines, the design can be seen throughout the Caribbean but also in India. Painted bright colours, some now contain government offices. There are several memorials around the oval shaped race course, for instance in the southwest corner, the 'awful' hurricane which killed 14 men and one married woman and caused the destruction of the barracks and hospital on 18 August 1831 and outside the Barbados Museum in the northeast corner to the men of the Royal York Rangers who fell in action against the French in Martinique, Les Saintes and Guadeloupe in the 1809-10 campaign.

Across the road is **St Anne's Fort** which is still used by the Barbados defence force. You cannot enter but look for the crenellated signal tower with its flag pole on top. It formed the high command of a chain of signal posts, the most complete of which is at Gun Hill (see below). The long, thin building is the old drill hall. **The Main Guard**, overlooking the savannah, has a nice old clock tower and a fine wide verandah. It has been turned into an information centre and houses exhibits about the West Indian Regiment. The Garrison Secretary of the Regiment, Major Michael Hartland, T4260982, is here. Outside is the **National Cannon Collection** which he created, an impressive array of about 30 cannon, some are mounted on metal 'garrison' gun carriages (replaced with wooden ones during action as they were prone to shatter). There are also a

To East Coast via Highways 3, 4 & 5

Roebuck St
Crumpton St
Harrison College
Queen's Park
Garnet St
Queen's Park
Church St
St Michael's Cathedral
Constitution Rd
St Michael's Row
LIAT
Constitution River
Footbridge
River Rd
Bridge St
Bus Terminus
Fairchild St
Nelson St
King William St
Queen St
Beckwith St
Spruce St
Jordan La
Probyn St
Wellington St
Bay St

To Hospital, Wildey & Southeast via Highway 6

To Garrison, Rockley, Oistins & Airport via Highway 7

4 National Heroes Square
5 Parliament Buildings

Barbados

number of newer howitzers, dating from 1878. Major Hartland welcomes visitors but he is still creating a Regimental museum, so make an appointment first.

The **Barbados Museum** is housed in the old military prison on the northeast corner of the savannah. Based on a collection left by Rev N B Watson (late rector of St Lucy Parish), it is well set out through a series of 10 galleries. It displays natural history, local history (in search of *Bim*), a fine map gallery including the earliest map of Barbados by Richard Ligon (1657), colonial furniture (Plantation House Rooms), military history (including a reconstruction of a prisoner's cell), prints and paintings which depict social life in the West Indies, decorative and domestic arts (17-19th century glass, china and silver), African artefacts, a children's gallery and one to house temporary exhibits. The museum shop has a good selection of craft items, books, prints, and cards. The *Museum Café* under the trees in the museum courtyard is a delightful place for a drink or for lunch. ■ *T4270201/4361956. US$5 for adults, US$2.50 for children. Mon-Sat 0900-1700, Sun 1400-1800.* Library available for research purposes. ■ *US$10 for visitors, US$5 for locals, plus VAT. Mon-Fri 0900-1300.*

The **Barbados Gallery of Art**, at the top of Bush Hill, across the savanna from the museum, has a collection of paintings and visual arts from Barbados and the Caribbean. ■ *T2280149. US$2.50 adults, US$1 children, Tue-Fri, Sat US$1 adults, children free. 1000-1700.* **George Washington House**, close by, is where he stayed in 1751. The National Trust has launched an appeal for restoration funds. Re-opening is planned for 2003, information from Penelope Hynam, T2289033, gwbarbados@caribsurf.com

Nearby there are stables for the race course. The Barbados Turf Club holds meetings on Saturday during three seasons (January-March, May-October and November-December). The biggest one being the Sandy Lane Gold cup held in March. Races go clockwise. A good place to watch is from the Main Guard. At other times, it is used as a jogging course for people in the mornings, when you can see the horses being exercised, or on weekday evenings. There is also rugby, basketball, etc, played informally in the Savannah, go and see what is going on on Sunday afternoons. There is a small children's playground in one corner. Later, at night, prostitutes parade here.

Also near Garrison is **Mallalieu Motor Collection**, with a Vanden Plas Princess, Wolseley and Lanchester. ■ *T4264640, US$5, by appointment.*

Around the island

Being the most easterly island and extremely difficult to attack, there are few defensive forts on Barbados. Instead the great houses of the sugar growing plantocracy give the island its historic perspective and most of its tourist attractions. Many parish churches are also impressive buildings. The island is not large but it is easy to get lost when driving. Deep gullies cut in the coral limestone which is the surface rock over most of the island. These are often full of wildlife and plants but make travelling around very confusing. It sometimes helps to remember that the island is divided into 11 parishes named after 10 saints, Christ Church being the eleventh. A good map is essential. The bus service is cheap and efficient and recommended even for families with small children.

The west coast

The mass development of the west coast was carried out only recently. The beaches are easily eroded and can be covered with broken coral after storms. The road north of Bridgetown on Highway 1 is wall to wall hotels. Highway 2a runs parallel inland and goes through the sugar cane heartland, with small villages and pleasant views.

Holetown Holetown today is a thoroughly modern town but was the place where the earliest settlers landed on 17 February 1627. The Holetown monument commemorates Captain John Powell claiming the island for England. Initially named Jamestown, it was renamed Holetown because of a tidal hole near the beach. It was quite heavily defended until after the Napoleonic Wars. Little trace of the forts can be seen now. Well worth visiting is **St James Church**. Originally built of wood in 1628, it was replaced by a stone structure in 1680. This building was extended 20 ft west in 1874 when columns and arches were added and the nave roof raised. You can see the original baptismal font (1684) under the belfry and in the north porch is the original bell of 1696. Many of the original settlers are buried here (although the oldest tombstone of William Balston who died in 1659 is in the Barbados Museum). Church documents dating to 1693 have been removed to the Department of Archives. It was beautifully restored between 1983-86.

On the beach at the back of the church is the post office and also the **Folkestone Park and Marine Reserve**. Here you can snorkel in a large area enclosed by buoys. The reef is not in very good condition but there are some fish. Snorkelling equipment for hire as are glass bottomed boats which will take you over the reef to two small wrecks further down the coast. A diving platform about 100 yds offshore allows you to snorkel over the wrecks. There are toilets and a shower here. ■ *The small museum is open Mon-Fri 1000-1700. Slide shows are held about every hour. US$1.*

The **Portvale Sugar Factory** (best in the crop season, February to May) and **Sir Frank Hutson Sugar Machinery Museum** inland has an exhibition on the story of sugar and its products. ■ *T4320100 to check. US$7.50 when factory is running Feb-May, US$4 the rest of the time, children half price. 0900-1700, Mon-Sat.*

Follow the coast road and glimpse the sea at Gibbes and Mullins Bays to reach Speightstown where William Speight once owned the land. An important trading port in the early days, when it was known as Little Bristol. Speightstown is now the main shopping centre for the north of the island. There are several interesting old buildings and many two-storey shops with Georgian balconies and overhanging galleries (sadly many have been knocked down by passing lorries). The Lions Club building (Arlington) is 17th-century, built very much on the lines of an English late medieval town house.

Speightstown
Pronounced Spitestown or Spikestong in broad dialect

The National Trust runs the **Arbib Nature & Heritage Trail**, starting in Speightstown. There are routes of 5½ kms and 7½ kms, starting from St Peter's church. ■ *US$7.50, reservations T4262421. Walks are not daily, so call ahead to find out when they are scheduled.*

In 1996 construction started on a marina at Heywoods Beach just north of Speightstown, known as Port St Charles. The US$60mn project will include 145 residential units, a restaurant, a yacht club, heliport and watersports as well as have a capacity for nine mega-yachts and 140 yachts on completion of the final phase in 2002. Most units have already been sold, with prices ranging from US$0.6mn to US$3mn; some are available for short term holiday rental, **LL-L**.

St Lucy

The road north of Speightstown is mercifully free of buildings and there is a good sandy beach on **Six Men's Bay**. Go through Littlegood Harbour and notice the boat building on the beach. The jetty you can see is at Harrison Point. You are now entering the unspoilt (apart from Arawak Cement Plant) parish of St Lucy. Almost any of the roads off Highway 1b will take you to the north coast, at first green and lush around Stroud Point but becoming more desolate as you approach North Point. The northwest coast, being slightly sheltered from the Atlantic swells, has many sandy coves (Archers Bay). The cliffs are quiet and easy to walk. You may spot turtles swimming in the sea.

The **Animal Flower Cave** at **North Point** is a series of caverns at sea level which have been eroded by the sea. The animals are sea anemones. There are various 'shapes' in the rock which are pointed out to you. ■ *The main cave can be closed due to dangerous seas, so T4398797 around 0930 to enquire. US$1.50 (US$1 if you cannot see full cave). The floor of the cave is very stony and can be slippery.*

Barbados

Following the rocky coast, turn into the semi-abandoned *North Point Surf Resort* (park outside the wall to avoid being charged for parking, the buildings are half ruined now, and there is an enormous empty swimming pool) where you can walk around the Spout, which has lots of blow holes and a small, rather dangerous beach.

Good walks along the cliffs can be enjoyed, for instance from River Bay to Little Bay along the Antilles Flat, but beware as there is no shade and there are shooting parties during the season. If driving, several back roads go through the attractive communities of Spring Garden and St Clements. At Pie Corner you can rejoin the coast and visit **Little Bay**. This is particularly impressive during the winter months with the swell breaking over the coral outcrops and lots of blowholes. Note the completely circular hole on the north edge of the Bay. If you climb through this natural archway in the cliff, there is a big, calm pool, just deep enough to swim between the cliffs and a line of rock on which the enormous waves break and send up a wall of spray. Wear shoes to stop your feet getting cut to pieces on the sharp rock.

At **Paul's Point** is a popular picnic area. If the ground looks wet park at the millwall by the Cove Stud Farm as it is easy to get bogged down. You will get a good view of **Gay's Cove** with its shingle beach (safe to swim in the pools at low tide) and beyond it the 240-ft high **Pico Teneriffe**, a large rock (named by sailors who thought it looked like the mountain on Teneriffe in the Canaries) on top of a steeply sloping cliff. The white cliffs are oceanic rocks consisting of myriad tiny white shells or microscopic sea creatures. The whole of the coast to Bathsheba is visible and it is easy to see the erosion taking place in Corben's Bay. Indeed you get an excellent impression of the Scotland District, where the coral limestone has been eroded. The whole of this coast between North and Ragged Points has been zoned, no further development will be allowed along the seafront.

The **Mount Gay Rum Distillery** is reached off the road between the St Lucy church junction and Alexandra. ■ *Tours Mon-Fri at 1100 and 1400, must be arranged in advance. They also have a visitor's centre in St Michael (see page 896).*

The Scotland District

Just to the northwest is **St Nicholas Abbey** which is approached down a long and impressive avenue of mahogany trees. Dating from around 1660, it is one of the oldest domestic buildings in the English-speaking Americas (**Drax Hall**, St George, open occasionally under the National Trust Open House programme, is probably even older). Three storied, it has a façade with three ogee-shaped gables. It was never an abbey, some have supposed that the 'St' and 'Abbey' were added to impress, there being lots of 'Halls' in the south of the island. Visitors are given an interesting tour of the ground floor and a fascinating film show in the stables behind the 400-year-old sand box tree. Narrated by Stephen Cave, the present owner and son of the film maker, its shows life on a sugar plantation in the 1930s. You will see the millwall in action and the many skilled workers from wheel wrights to coopers who made the plantation work. The importance of wind is emphasized. If the windmill stopped the whole harvest came to a halt as the cane which had been cut would quickly dry out if it was not crushed straight away. The waste was used to fuel the boilers just as it is today in sugar factories. There is a collection of toy buses and lorries in the stables.

Going back down the steep Cherry Tree Hill you come to the National Trust-owned **Morgan Lewis Mill**, a millwall with original machinery which the National Trust is attempting to restore to working condition. More funds are needed to finish the job. You can climb to the top of it. Note the 100-ft tail, this enabled the operators to position the mill to maximize the effect of the wind. It is on a working farm. ■ *T4227429. US$5. Mon-Sat, 0900-1700.* On the flat savannah at the bottom of the hill is a cricket pitch, a pleasant place to watch the game at weekends.

The **Barbados Wildlife Reserve**, established with Canadian help in 1985, is set in four acres of mature mahogany off Highway 2. It is an excellent place to see lots of Barbados green monkeys close up. They have a collection of the large red-footed Barbados tortoise. Also (non-Barbadian) toucans, parrots and tropical birds, hares, otters, opossums, agoutis, wallabies, porcupines, and iguanas. You can observe pelicans and there is a spectacled caiman (alligator) in the pond. The primate research centre helps to provide farmers with advice on how to control the green monkeys who are regarded as a pest. The animals are fed near it at about 1600. The centre has also developed a nature trail in the neighbouring Grenade Hall Forest, ask for further details. An early 19th-century signal station next to Grenade Hall Forest has been restored. The wonderful panoramic view gives you a good idea of its original role in the communications network. ■ *T4228826. US$11.50, children half price. Daily 1000-1700. Café and shop. Getting there: bus from Bridgetown, Holetown, Speightstown or Bathsheba.*

Most of the animals are not caged, you are warned to be careful as you wander around the shady paths as the monkeys can bite

Farley Hill House, St Peter, is a 19th-century fire-damaged plantation house; a spectacular ruin on the other side of the road from the Wildlife Reserve, set in a pleasant park with views over the Scotland District. There is a large number of imported and native tree species planted over 30 acres of woodland. ■ *T4223555. US$1.75 per vehicle. Daily 0830-1800.*

From Farley Hill it is possible to walk more or less along the top of the island as far as **Mount Hillaby**, through woods and then canefields. However, it helps to know where you are going as the paths have a mind of their own and losing them can be uncomfortable. You will see plenty of monkeys on the way and good views.

The Atlantic Parishes

The five-mile East Coast Rd, opened by Queen Elizabeth on 15 February 1966 affords fine views. From Belleplaine (local pottery for sale), where the railway ended, it skirts Walker's Savannah to the coast at Long Pond and heads southeast to **Benab**, where there is **Barclays Park**, a good place to stop for a picnic under the shady casuarina trees, or there is a good beach bar with meals. A walk up **Chalky Mount** has been recommended for the magnificent views of the east coast, easily reached at the end of the bus line from Bridgetown. If you ask locally for the exact path you are likely to be given several different routes. Walk down through the meadows to Barclays Park for a drink when you come down. There is no paved road. Staff in the café will know times of buses to either Bathsheba or Speightstown. The East Coast Rd continues through **Cattlewash**, so named because Bajans brought their animals here to wash them in the sea, to Bathsheba.

The tiny hamlet of **Bathsheba** has an excellent surfing beach (see page 892). Guarded by two rows of giant boulders, the bay seems to be almost white as the surf trails out behind the Atlantic rollers. Surfing championships are often held here. A railway was built in 1883 (but closed in 1937) between Bridgetown and Bathsheba. Originally conceived as going to Speightstown, it actually went up the east coast to a terminus at Belleplaine, St Andrew. The cutting at My Lady's Hole, near Conset Bay in St John is spectacular, with a gradient of 1:31, which is supposed to have been the steepest in the world except for rack and pinion and other special types of line. The railway here suffered from landslides, wave erosion, mismanagment and underfunding so that the 37-mile track was in places in very bad condition. The crew would sprinkle sand on the track, the first class passengers remained seated, the second class walked and the third class pushed. There is good walking along the old railway track, through Bath to Conset Bay, although you have to scramble on some bits.

Above the bay at Hillcrest (excellent view) are the **Andromeda Gardens**. Owned by the Barbados National Trust, the gardens contain plants from all over Barbados as well as species from other parts of the world. There are many varieties of orchid, hibiscus and flowering trees. ■ *T4339261. US$6, children US$3. Every day, 0900-1700. The Hibiscus Café at the entrance is a useful place to stop for refreshment.*

Barbados

The Atlantis Hotel has traditionally been a good place for lunch especially on Sunday (1300 sharp) when an excellent buffet meal containing several Bajan dishes is served. Almost an institution and extremely popular with Bajans, so book ahead. However, Enid Maxwell, who ran it from 1945-2001, has now relinquished the reins, and it is not known if the new owners will change its character.

From Bathsheba you can head inland to **Cotton Tower signal station** (National Trust owned. Not as interesting as Gun Hill). Then head south to Wilson Hill where you find Mount Tabor Church and **Villa Nova**, another plantation Great House (1834), which has furniture made of Barbadian mahogany and beautiful gardens. It was owned by the former British Prime Minister, Sir Anthony Eden, and until 1994 was part of the National Trust's heritage trail. It has now been bought by Swiss investors who have been promising for some years to open it as a five-star country resort hotel, T4361710, F4361715. You can continue from here via Malvern along the scenic **Hackleton's Cliff** (allegedly named after Hackleton who committed suicide by riding his horse over the cliff) or via Sherbourne (F *Coconut Inn*, two-room guest house run by Geoff and Terry Browne, who also do excellent Bajan lunches) to Pothouse, where **St John's Church** stands with views over the Scotland District. Built in 1660 it was a victim of the great hurricane of 1835. There is an interesting pulpit made from six different kinds of wood. You will also find the grave of Fernando Paleologus "descendant of ye imperial line of ye last Christian emperors of Greece". The full story is in Leigh Fermor's *The Traveller's Tree*.

Turn left after a few miles for the downhill road to **Bath**. Here you will find a safe beach, popular with Barbadians and a recreation park for children. It makes a good spot for a beach barbecue and a swim and a beach bar does a good lunch.

Codrington College is one of the most famous landmarks on the island and can be seen from Highway 4b down an avenue of Cabbage Palm trees. It is steeped in history as the first Codrington landed in Barbados in 1628. His son acted as Governor for three years but was dismissed for liberal views. Instead he stood for parliament and was elected speaker for nine years. He was involved in several wars against the French and became probably the wealthiest man in the West Indies. The third Codrington succeeded his father as Governor-General of the Leeward islands, attempted to stamp out the considerable corruption of the time and distinguished himself in campaigns (especially in taking St Kitts). He died in 1710, a bachelor aged 42, and left his Barbadian properties to the Society for the Propagation of the Gospel in Foreign Parts. It was not until 1830 that Codrington College, where candidates could study for the Anglican priesthood, was established. From 1875 to 1955 it was associated with Durham University, England. Apart from its beautiful grounds with a fine avenue of Royal Palms, a huge lily pond (flowers close up in the middle of the day) and impressive façade, there is a chapel containing a plaque to Sir Christopher Codrington and a library. There are plans to develop it as a conference centre. You can follow the track which drops down 360 feet to the sea at the beautiful Conset Bay. ■ US$2.50. *Getting there: you can take the Sargeant St bus as far as Codrington College, then walk 7 miles back along the Atlantic Coast to Bathsheba.*

At **Ragged Point** is the automatic **East Point lighthouse** standing among the ruined houses of the former lighthouse keepers. There are good views north towards Conset Point, the small Culpepper island, and the south coast. Note the erosion to the 80-ft cliffs caused by the Atlantic sweeping into the coves. An atmospheric station close to the shoreline measures air quality; this is the first landfall after blowing across the Atlantic from the coast of Africa.

The centre

Northeast of Holetown and reached from St Simon's Church are **Turners Hall Woods**, a good vantage point. It is thought that the wood has changed little to that which covered the island before the English arrived. The 50-acre patch of tropical mesophytic forest has never been clear-felled (although individual trees were often

The Easter Rebellion

The 1816 Easter Rebellion was an uprising by slaves who thought (incorrectly) that William Wilberforce had introduced a bill in the English parliament granting slaves their freedom. It was thought by the slaves that the Barbados plantation owners were denying them this freedom. Despite destroying a large acreage of cane fields, no owners or their families were killed and

the uprising was quickly crushed by the West Indian Regiment. Several hundred slaves were killed in battle or hanged afterwards, including the best-known leader, an African called Bussa, and Washington Francklyn, a free man of mixed race who was thought, probably erroneously, to have planned the rebellion. 123 slaves were exiled to Sierra Leone.

taken out). You can walk over the steep paths here and see many species, ranging from the sandbox tree to Jack-in-the-box and the 100-ft locust trees supported by massive buttresses. The island's first natural gas field was here and the main path through the wood is the remains of the old road.

On Highway 2, take the Melvin Hill road just after the agricultural station and follow the signs to the **Flower Forest**, a 50-acre, landscaped plantation, opened in 1983 with beautifully laid out gardens. Dropping downhill, the well-maintained paths afford excellent views over the valley to the east coast. To the west you can see **Mount Hillaby**, at 1,116 feet the island's highest point (see above for walking from Farley Hill). It too contains species not only from Barbados but also from all over the world, they are beautifully arranged with plenty of colour all year round. There is a *Best of Barbados* shop, cafeteria and toilets. Good information sheet. ■ *T4338152. US$7, children 5-16 half price. Daily 0900-1700.*

Close by and to the south on Highway 2 is **Welchman Hall Gully**, a fascinating walk through one of the deep ravines so characteristic of this part of Barbados. You are at the edge of the limestone cap which covers most of the island to a depth of about 300 feet. There is a small car park opposite the entrance (despite the sign to the contrary). Maintained by the National Trust, a good path leads for about half a mile through six sections, each with a slightly different theme. The first section has a devil tree, a stand of bamboo and a judas tree. Next you will go through jungle, lots of creepers, the 'pop-a-gun' tree and bearded fig clinging to the cliff (note the stalactites and stalagmites); a section devoted to palms and ferns: golden, silver, macarthur and cohune palms, nutmegs and wild chestnuts; to open areas with tall leafy mahogany trees, rock balsam and mango trees. At the end of the walk are ponds with lots of frogs and toads. Best of all though is the wonderful view to the coast. On the left are some steps leading to a gazebo, at the same level as the tops of the cabbage palms. ■ *T4386671. US$6, children B$6. Daily, 0900-1700.*

Roads in this area are often closed by landslides & circuitous routing may be necessary

Harrison's Cave nearby has an impressive visitors' centre which has a restaurant (fair), shop and a small display of local geology and Amerindian artefacts. You are taken into the cave on an electric 'train'. The visit takes about 20 minutes and you will see some superbly-lit stalactites and stalagmites, waterfalls and large underground lakes. There is a guide to point out the interesting formations and two stops for photo-opportunities. Interesting as it is, it is all rather overdone, you have to wear hard hats (to prevent complaints of bumped heads) and serviettes (to catch the drips) on your head despite the fact that the caves are totally stable. ■ *T4386640. Daily 0900-1600. US$12.50, children US$5. Getting there: the bus from Bridgetown to Chalky Mount stops near Harrison's Cave and the Flower Forest.*

If you take Highway 2 heading to Bridgetown you will pass **Jack-in-the-Box gully**, part of the same complex of Welchman Hall Gully and Harrison's Cave. **Coles Cave** (an 'undeveloped' cave nearby, which can easily be explored with a waterproof torch or flashlight) lies at its north end.

At **Gun Hill** is a fully restored signal tower. The approach is by Fusilier road and you will pass the Lion carved by British soldiers in 1868. The road was built by Royal

Scot Fusiliers between September 1862 and February 1863 when they were stationed at Gun Hill to avoid yellow fever. The signal station itself had its origins in the slave uprising of 1816. It was decided that a military presence would be maintained outside Bridgetown in case of further slave uprisings. It was also intended for advance warning of attack from the sea. The chain of six signal stations was intended to give very rapid communications with the rest of the island. The hexagonal tower had two small barrack rooms attached and would have been surrounded by a pallisade. They quickly lost importance as military installations but provided useful information about shipping movements. Informative guides will explain the workings of the signal station and point out interesting features of the surrounding countryside. You will not necessarily get the same story from all the guides. ■ *T4291358. US$5 (children half price), guide book US$1. Mon-Sat 0900-1700.*

Near Gun Hill is the **Francia Plantation**, house and gardens are open to the public, with old furniture, maps and prints, although the house is currently for sale and its future is open to doubt. ■ *T4290474. US$5 including a drink. Mon-Fri 1000-1600.*

Orchid World, at Groves, St George, is a 6½-acre orchid garden under the same management as the Flower Forest. ■ *T4330306. US$7. 0900-1700.*

The southeast coast

The area around Six Cross Roads was where the Easter Rebellion of 1816 took place (see box). You can visit one of the great houses (Oughterson Plantation House is no longer in operation). Turn north at Six Cross Roads for **Sunbury Plantation**. Some 300 years old, the house is elegantly furnished in Georgian style, much of it with mahogany furniture, and you can roam all over it as, unusually, there is access to the upstairs private rooms. In the cellars, you can see the domestic quarters. There is a good collection of carriages. The house and museum were damaged by fire in 1995 but have been restored and opened again. ■ *T4236270. US$6. 1000-1630 every day. There is a restaurant in the courtyard. A 5-course plantation house dinner with all the trimmings costs US$75 per person for groups of 15 or more.*

Sam Lord's Castle on the southeast coast is the site of an all-inclusive hotel. It is high on the list of tourist attractions because of the reputation of Sam Lord who reputedly lured ships onto Cobbler's Reef where they were shipwrecked. There is supposed to be a tunnel from the beach to the castle's cellars to facilitate his operation. The proceeds made him a wealthy man although the castle was supposed to have been financed from his marriage to a wealthy heiress. The castle is not particularly old or castle-like, being in fact a regency building. Unfortunately the rooms are poorly lit making it difficult to appreciate the fine mahogany furniture or the paintings. Note the superb staircase, you are not allowed upstairs. Wander down to the cove where there is a good example of a turtlecrawl, a salt water pond enclosed by a wall. Here turtles were kept alive until wanted for the kitchen. Today the hotel, in conjunction with the Barbados Wildlife park, keeps a few hawksbill turtles, a shark and a congor eel. ■ *US$5 entrance charge (children US$2.50) even though the hotel reception forms part of the 2 rooms open to the public.*

Foursquare Rum Factory and **Heritage Park**, in an old sugar factory, with sugar machinery, craft market, pottery, bottling plant, folk museum, pet farm, pony stables and Foundry Art Gallery. ■ *T4201977. US$6 adults, children half price. Rum punch and miniature included. Mon-Fri, 0900-1700, Fri-Sat 1000-2100, Sun 1200-1800.*

Crane Bay, southwest of Sam Lord's Castle, is worth a detour. It is a pleasant cove overlooked by 80-ft cliffs. *Crane Hotel* often charges for admission, but it is worth it for a drink and the spectacular view over the bay from the cliff top restaurant.

The south coast

Oistins, the main town in the parish of Christ Church, was named after Edward Oistine, a plantation owner in the area. It was important in colonial times as the place where the 'Charter of Barbados' was signed in 1652, giving the island to the Commonwealth Parliament. It is now the main fishing port. Christ Church parish church overlooks the town and is notable for its cemetery containing the Chase Vault. When the vault was opened in 1812 for the burial of Colonel Thomas Chase, the lead coffins were found scattered around inside. It happened again in 1816, 1817, 1819 and 1820, whereupon the coffins were removed and buried separately in the churchyard.

Graeme Hall Swamp, Worthing, near St Lawrence Gap, has 80 acres of wetland and mangroves around a lake. It is a natural habitat for birds and there are 18 resident species and 150 migrants. A boardwalk is open to the public but the rest is to be a bird sanctuary for scientific research only. Three endangered Caribbean duck species are found here.

The largest expanse of inland water in Barbados

Essentials

Super luxury Most of these are on the west coast and cost over US$300 a night. *Sandy Lane*, www.sandylane.com has recently been rebuilt and rates vary from US$1,200 to US$6,000 a night depending on season and category. Golf, tennis, state-of-the-art spa with everything from detox to pedicures. If you can't afford to stay here, it is worth going to the restaurant just to see the place (good food and not all that expensive), but you have to book ahead to get past the gate. The 330-room all-inclusive *Almond Beach Village*, T4224900, F4220617, www.almondresorts.com on the old *Heywoods Resort* site, with its 161-room sister resort, *Almond Beach Club*, T4327840, F4322115, 4 miles away. *Almond Beach Village*, . On 30 acres of land with a 9-hole golf course, 1 mile of beach, 9 pools, 4 restaurants, shops, watersports centre, nightclub and children's play areas, families or couples welcome. *Glitter Bay*, T4224555, F4221367, and *Royal Pavilion*, T4225555, F4223940, are very smart, next to each other in 30-acre grounds, www.c photels.ca One is 'Spanish Colonial Style', the other a pink palace. Perhaps better value to stay elsewhere and visit for a drink or afternoon tea, but well worth looking at, the guests as spectacular in some cases as the (faultless) interior design and landscaping, tennis, fitness centre, swimming pools, beauty salon, watersports and boutiques also on offer at one or other of the sister hotels. *Little Good Harbour*, T4393000, F4392020, www.littlegoodharbourbarbados.com Small wooden villas around pool, some accommodation in 18th century Fort Rupert, very nicely laid out and furnished, good restaurant. Elegant Resorts, www.eleganthotels.com has 4 beachfront properties within 5 miles, guests may use the facilities of all 4 and there is a free water taxi between them: *Colony Club*, T4222335, F4220667. 97 colonial-style rooms and suites, in 7 acres of palms, ponds and free form pool with swim up bar. *Crystal Cove*, T4322683, F4328290. 88 rooms and suites, also with pools and gardens, swim up bar through waterfall. *Tamarind Cove*, T4321332, F4326317. 165 rooms each with 2 beds. *Coconut Creek*, T4320803, F4320272. 53 rooms with 2 beds, pool, tennis. Elegant Resorts also run *Turtle Beach Hotel*, a new resort on the south coast, St Lawrence Gap, T4287131, F4286089. All-inclusive, 167 rooms, sometimes used by airlines if there is a delay for passengers, amazing breakfast, stock up before you head back to the airport. *Lone Star Motel*, next to restaurant of same name, T4190599, F4190597, www.thelonestar.com 4 huge rooms, uncluttered, simple mahogany furniture building was originally a garage built in 1940s by Romy Reid, who ran a bus company and called himself the Lone Star of the west coast, then it was a nightclub and then a house, owned by Mrs Robertson, of the jam company, who waterskied offshore until her late 80s. *Cobblers Cove*, St Peter, T4222291, F4221460, www.barbados.org 40 rooms, small and exclusive, run by Hamish Watson, wins lots of awards, high proportion of repeat business. *Coral Reef Club*, Holetown, St James, T4222372, F4221776, www.barbados.org Member of Elegant Resorts of Barbados and Prestige Hotels, London, lovely landscaped gardens, lawn running down to sea, cottage style, very highly regarded; also in Holetown, under same management, *Sandpiper Inn*, T4222251, F4221776, www.barbados.org Family-run, with award-winning restaurant, delicious but expensive food, both have large grounds and are on long beach.

Also on the west and south coasts, good but not as luxurious, **LL-AL** *Casuarina Beach Club*, St Lawrence Gap, T4283600, F4281970, www.casuarina.com On beach, 180 rooms, pool, tennis, well-managed and good reports. **LL-AL** *The Savannah*, between Garrison Savannah and beach, T2283800, F2284385, www.gemsbarbados.com/savannah 21 rooms in recently

Sleeping

Most accommodation offered is very pleasant, if not particularly cheap. 15% VAT is levied on hotel services

Barbados

renovated historic building, antique furniture, each room different, earth-friendly bathroom goodies, special Caricom rate, recommended for business visitors.

Near the airport LL-A *Crane Beach*, T4236220, F4235343, www.thecrane.com Fairly near the airport, but definitely a taxi ride away, spectacular cliff top setting, good beach, and good pool, tennis, luxury prices and usually fairly quiet with only 18 rooms, but they are building an extra 250 units as a time share, totally changing the character of the hotel. **L-B** *Silver Sands Resort*, Christ Church, T4286001, F4283758, www.barbados.org 20 minutes' drive from airport, on the sea at South Point, rooms spacious and well-equipped, good service, food dull, good beach but take care swimming, waves strong and high, good for surfing but children and weak swimmers should use the pool.

Good value LL-A *Sandy Beach Island Resort*, Worthing, T4358000, F4358053, sandbar@ caribsurf.com 128 rooms, wide beach, enough sand for volleyball etc, calm water with reef just offshore, 2-bedroom suites with kitchen and living room perfect for families. **L-A** *Sandridge*, 1 mile from Speightstown, T4222361, F4221965, sandridge@caribsurf.com Good-sized rooms or family apartments with cooking facilities, north-facing balconies overlook pool, friendly staff and management, watersports free for guests, good value barbecue evenings, excellent for families. **AL-A** *Time Out at the Gap*, St Lawrence Gap, T4205021, F4205034, www. gemsbarbados.com 76 rooms, aimed at sports and nightlife age group, pool.

Apartments and guest houses L-C *Chateau Blanc Apartments*, First Av, Worthing, T4357518, F4357414, www.barbados.org Good value studios, well-equipped but old kitchen facilities, friendly management, also has 1-2 bedroomed apartments on beach front. **A-C** *Angler Apartments*, Derricks, T/F4320817, www.barbadosahoy.com/angler. Owners live on premises, priority given to service, friendly, informal, family orientated, restaurant, freshly made Caribbean dishes, will prepare special meals on request, some home-grown vegetables. **A-C** *Fred La Rose/Bonanza/Venice Gardens*, Dover, T4289097, F4283924, bonanza@sunbeach.net Studio, 1 or 2 bedrooms, helpful, quite convenient but not too clean. There are several other cheap places to stay in this area, all within walking distance of each other. **A-C** *Little Paradise* in Paradise Village, Black Rock, north of Bridgetown on Princess Alice Highway, T4243256, F4248614. 1-2 bedroom apartments, a/c, fridge, very pleasant. **A-C** *The Nook Apartments*, Dayrells Rd in Rockley, T/F4276502, nookbdos@sunbeach.net. Apartments with pool, maid service, clean, secure, convenient for shops and restaurants, discounts for airline staff and Caricom residents. **B-C** *Meridian Inn*, Dover, T4284051, F4206495, www.meridianinn.com Studios, kitchenettes, balconies, daily maid service, beach, credit cards. All these are well served by the south coast bus routes. **B-C** *Roman Beach Apartments*, Enterprise, T4287635, F4300406, francesroman@sunbeach.net Friendly, comfortable studios, on beautiful beach. **C** *Melrose Beach Apartments*, Worthing, T4357985, F4357984, melroseba@sunbeach.net Good location, 14 units, a/c available. **C** *Tree Haven*, Rockley, T4356673, F4366673, arturoolaya@caribsurf.com A short bus ride from the centre of town, excellent studio apartments opposite the beach, very clean, helpful and friendly owner. **D-E** *Cleverdale*, Fourth Av, Worthing, T4281035, F4283172, karibik@sunbeach.net 4 rooms, with shared or private bathroom, close to beach, breakfast room, living room, kitchen, veranda and barbecue for guests to share, clean and good value, also internet access and help with finding alternative accommodation, run by Europeans, Brigitte Taylor and Heidrun Rice. **E** *Shells Guest House*, First Av, Worthing, T4357253, F4357131, www.shelguest.com With breakfast, good value, well run, good location, 6 rooms with fan, 5 bathrooms, TV room, excellent food in restaurant. **E** *Angle House*, Upper Bay St, Bridgetown, T4279010, near *Grand Barbados*. Clean, central, convenient, nothing special.

"Getaways" B *Atlantis*, Bathsheba, T4339445. On the east coast, with a spectacular setting, changed hands in 2001, check what is happening. **AL-A** *Edgewater Inn*, Bathsheba, T4339900, F4339900, www.edgewaterinn.com Pool overlooking sea, quiet, popular with Venezuelans. Also at Bathsheba, the *Round House Restaurant* has 4 rooms. **AL-A** *Sea-U*, guest house, T4339450, F4339210, http://axses.com/ency/bta/hotels/seau.ctm 4 spacious rooms, run by nice German lady, evening meal US$15, breakfast US$5, lots of hammocks, ask the owner to arrange car hire for you at the airport.

Villa rental Agents and property managers including *Alleyne, Aguillar and Altman*, the most upmarket and a Christie's affiliate, T4320840. *Realtors Limited*, Riverside House, River Rd, St Michael, T4264900, F4266419. *Bajan Services Ltd*, Seascape Cottage, Gibbs, St Peter, T4222618, F4225366. *Rival Enterprises Ltd*, Flamboyant Av, Sunset Crest, St James, T4326457, F4322422, rival@caribsurf.com 1-bedroom apartments to 3-bedroom villas in gardens, **LL-B** in season, cheaper in summer, well located, near restaurants, shops and beach. Weekly rates for a small villa on the beach start at US$1,000 in the summer but can be twice the price in the winter, plus tax.

YMCA One **F** hostel at Pinfold Street, Bridgetown, T4263910/1240 which can accommodate 24 people, dormitory beds or single rooms, breakfast B$3.50, lunch B$4.

Barbados has a very wide range of places to eat, many of them in an interesting setting and an open air water front or garden terrace. The price range in a restaurant for a main course is US$12-40, but in cheap places you can get a filling meal for US$6.

Eating

There is a good listing in the Visitor

From US$20 The two smartest places are now: *Lone Star*, T4190599, with caviar bar on west coast, lunch US$15-3,000, wonderful setting, beach level, plenty of space, not ruinous if you choose carefully; and *Emerald Palm*, also on west coast, T4224116. **The Fish Pot**, at *Little Good Harbour Hotel*, north of Speightstown, in 18th century Fort Rupert. Imaginative menu, nice setting, main course lunch from US$13, dinner from US$20. *Le Mer*, at Port St Charles Marina. German master chef, Tue-Fri lunch US$15, dinner main course from US$25, Sun brunch. *Mango's*, Speightstown, T4220704. Nice waterfront setting, dinner only, US$20-30 main course. *Mullins Beach Bar*, just south of Speightstown, T4221878, has gone very posh, with lunch from US$15, dinner from US$32.50, set menu US$77.50 excluding booze, running battle with locals over attempted enclosure of beach, worth a visit to see the *trompe l'oeil* monkey murals. *La Maison*, Holetown, T4321156, award winning restaurant in beautiful setting on beach, gourmet but rather pretentious, US$20-40 main course for dinner. **The Mews**, 2nd St, Holetown, T4321122. Quite expensive but superb food, mix of local and French dishes, dinner main course from US$27.50, very pretty house, tables on balcony or interior patio. Recommended. *Sakura*, T4325187. Japanese, dinner main course from US$25. **The Fathoms**, Paynes Bay, St James, T4322568. Always good, especially the oriental lobster stirfry, good value, beautiful at night in gardens overlooking beach under shade of large mahogany tree, also delightful at lunchtime, open all day every day, recommended for service as well as food. *Nico's Champagne Wine Bar*, T4326386, on the west coast, closed Sun. Paul Owen's **The Cliff**, Derricks, St James, T4321922. Dinner main course from US$27.50, worth the prices for a glimpse of the décor, stunning desserts, attractive and delightful meal, another recommended as the best food on the island, sushi bar and separate grill planned, innovative food. *Lobster Alive Bistro & Beach Bar*, Carlisle Bay on beach, T4350305. Mostly lobster flown in from the Grenadines, but also other seafood and delivery. *Josef's*, T4356541/4283379. On St Lawrence Gap, small, delightful, is well used by Barbadians, you need to book well ahead, arrive early and have pre-dinner drinks on the lawn with the sea lapping the wall a few feet below you.

US$10-20 At Holetown, on 1st Street are *Angry Annie's* (T4322119, dinner main course from US$20). *Baku Brasseries*, T4322258, same building, different owners. *Bellini's*, T4357246. Italian menu, not just spaghetti and pizza. *Café Sol*, grill and Margarita bar at the *Ship Inn*, T4359531, dinner only, very popular, Mexican American. *Carib Beach Bar* at Worthing, near former *Rydal Waters Guest House*, T4358540, has inexpensive meals and drinks, barbecue and music twice a week, excellent rum punches, happy hour 1700-1800 Mon-Fri, great fun even if you are not eating. *Cocomos*, Holetown, T4320134, right on beach, service and food recommended, nice atmosphere. *David's Place*, on waterfront, in Worthing, T4359755. Very good food and service and friendly, reasonable prices. *Fronds Vegetarian* at Edgehill St Thomas, T4252020. Linked to the Future Centre, which promotes organic farming and sustainable development, closed Mon, reservations only. In Bridgetown, On the west coast,

Jambalayas, St Lawrence Gap, T4356581. Lively, range of dishes from wider Caribbean including Hispanic, dinner only. *La Terra*, T4321099. Same owners as *Olives* and better than *Waterfront Café* on the Careenage, T4270093, interesting food, plenty to look at and a good social centre in the evenings, closed Sun. *Olives*, T4322112. Mediterranean/Caribbean, dinner main course from US$15. Recommended. *Sitar*, 2nd Street, Holetown, T4322248. Indian, dinner main course from US$15, veg lunch buffet US$15. *Pisces*, T4356564. Much larger, also on St Lawrence Gap, good fish dishes, an excellent vegetarian platter and a perfect waterfront setting, but deals with tour reps have increased their custom at the cost of quality and comfort. *Raffles*, (T4326557, African atmosphere), and *Roundhouse* on cliff, good, lovely restored location, overlooks sea, ask for breadfruit chips. *Sitar*, 2nd St, Holetown, T432 2248. Indian, dinner main course from US$15, veg lunch buffet. *Tam's Wok* (T4328000, cheaper than most Holetown places with dinner main course from US$12.50). *The Boatyard* in Bay Street, full of divers and friends at weekends, food unimportant. *The Lamplighter* at junction of Rendezvous and Highway 7, next to *Palm Garden Court Hotel*, same management, owned by British woman and her Bajan husband, new, small, attractive gardens, enjoyable. *Whistling Frog*, T4205021, in *Time Out in the Gap* hotel, pub sports bar with Bajan flavour, lively. Near Bathsheba on east coast. On the south coast, *39 Steps*, T4270715, on the coast road near the Garrison is well run and lively, lunchtimes and evenings, closed Sun, imaginative blackboard menu and choice of indoors or balcony, opened by Josef, previously of restaurant of that name, see below, popular, so book at weekends.

US$10 Island wide fast food from *Chefette* chain with 10 branches and increasing variety, salad bars at Holetown, Rockley and Warrens (ABC Highway) branches only, good value steak, fish meals, etc, pizza delivery T4366000. *Pizza Man Doc* has 6 branches and does deliveries. *Chicken Barn*, Bay Street and Worthing (big portions if you're hungry). For those who like that sort of thing there are several *Kentucky Fried Chickens*, although for vegetarians the salad bars here and at the *Chefettes* (see above) have been recommended. West Coast places include *Fisherman's Pub* in Speightstown, good meal for US$7 and right on seafront. In Bridgetown you have *Balcony Upstairs*, in Cave Shepherd on Broad St, lunch Mon-Fri 1100-1500. *Pop's Place*, on Cheapside Rd, T4305979. Nice setting, very clean, only US$6 for good, filling lunch. *Port Hole*, Fontabelle, friendly bar near Board of Tourism Office, good solid lunch for US$5.50. *The Food Court* in the Imperial Plaza, Bridgetown, has veggie and salad bar sections as well as Chinese, creole, etc. *Pink Star*, in Baxter's Road, open late. On the south coast, *Christie's Canteen*, at Light and Power Company, on Bay St and at Spring Gardens which are open to the public and do a huge traditional lunch; in Worthing on the main road opposite the Plantation supermarket, the *Roti Hut* is cheap but nasty, nothing like rotis on Trinidad. In the east, the *Pot and Barrel*, no name board, good inexpensive meals, just outside *Sam Lord's Castle*, much cheaper and worth a try. *Barclays Park Beach Bar* on the east coast does rum punch and light meals (closed after 1830). Good reports about *Sand Dunes* at Belleplaine, Beach Bar at Bath and *Lighthouse Restaurant & Bar*, at Ragged Point, T4339450, light lunch US$7,50, dinner US$15-20.

Entertainment **Cinemas** One cinema in Bridgetown (Globe); Vista cinema on south coast, US$4-5, Olympia Multiplex at Sheraton Centre, plus a drive-in not far from the south coast.

Dances and fêtes For something less glossy and more Bajan, it might be worth trying one of the dances which are advertized in the *Nation* newspaper on Fri: ballroom dancing to slows and 'back in times'. People hire a dance hall, charge admission (usually US$5), provide a disco, and keep the profits. There are very few foreigners, but the atmosphere is friendly, and the drinks a lot cheaper than in the smarter nightclubs. A more permanent home for this sort of thing is the beautifully named *Lonely Hearts*, upstairs opposite the Treasury Building Close, just off Heroes Sq in Bridgetown. There are also fêtes, younger crowd and Jamaican-style dub music, advertised by poster and sometimes on the radio. Venues include *Penthouse*, close to Parliament buildings in Bridgetown, *Cactus* in Silver Sands, *Liberty* in Black Rock, *De Base* on Bay St in Bridgetown, etc. Unfortunately, there have been a few fights at 'Dub' fêtes and they are no longer as relaxed as they were.

Rumshops **Baxters Rd** in Bridgetown used to be the place to try but fewer people go there now. The one roomed, ramshackle, rumshops are open all night (literally), and there's a lot of street life after midnight, although you might get pestered by cocaine addicts. Some of the rumshops sell fried chicken (the **Pink Star** is recommended, it has a large indoor area where you can eat in peace and the place also has clean lavatories) and there are women in the street selling fish, seasoned and fried in coconut oil over an open fire. Especially recommended if you are hungry after midnight. The Government plans to upgrade Baxters Rd as a tourist attraction. **Nelson St** rumshops are really houses of ill repute but have amazing larger-than-life naif paintings on the outside. Interior upstairs bar décor is a curious mix of girlie pix, fluorescent pointilliste and lifesize portraits of politicians. **Oistins** on a Fri night is a major event for both Bajans and tourists. Lots of small shops selling fish meals and other food, dub music one end and at the other a small club where they play oldies for ballroom dancing. It continues on Sat and Sun, though a bit quieter, some food places also stay open through the week. Also recommended is **Fisherman's Pub** on the waterfront in **Speightstown**, lots of music on Wed and Fri (no entry charge) otherwise fairly good all week. They also serve good cheap meals, lunchtime and evenings.

If you drink in a rumshop, rum and other drinks are bought by the bottle. The smallest size is a mini, then a flask, then a full bottle. The shop will supply ice and glasses, you buy a mixer, and serve yourself. The same system operates in dances, though prices are higher; night clubs, of course, serve drinks by the glass like anywhere else. Wine, in a rumshop, usually means sweet British sherry. If you are not careful, it is drunk with ice and beer.

Nightclubs

Look in Visitor and Sun Seeker for information about what's on each night

There are quite a selection. Most charge US$12.50 or more for entry on 'free drinks' night, less when you are paying for the drinks. It's worth phoning in advance to find out what is on offer. There are live bands on certain nights in some clubs. Most do not get lively until almost midnight, and close around 0400. Some have a complicated set of dress codes or admission rules, which is another reason for phoning ahead.

After Dark, St Lawrence Gap, recently redecorated, huge selection at the bar, very lively, live music quite often, more Bajans than tourists. Others are *Harbour Lights*, T4367225, lots of tourists and expats, open-air on the beach, local and disco music, crowded on Wed, US$12,50 entry covers drinks Wed, Fri, no cover charge Sun or Thu, beach party on Mon. *The Boatyard*, T4362622, is the sailor's pub in front of the anchorage at Carlisle Bay, Bay St, free drinks on Tue, US$12.50 with live band, very lively all week, popular with landlubbers too. *The Ship Inn* in St Lawrence has a big outdoor area and is often packed, especially at weekends, live music every night, happy hours 1600-1800 and 2200-2300.. Also *Reggae Lounge* in St Lawrence Gap, a bit sleezy but can be fun. *Chiller's*, in Worthing, north side of main road opposite *Sandy Beach*, is a lively pub with music and dancing, no entry charge. The *Waterfront Café*, T427093, is really a bar/restaurant, not a dance place, but has live entertainment Mon-Sat, most nights are jazz or steel pan. The beach bars can be lively (see listings above), but pick your night. *McBride's Irish Pub*, St Lawrence Gap, T4356352, has DJ, live music every night except Fri, which is karaoke. *Bubba's Bar* in Rockley has 10-ft video screen plus 10 other TVs for watching sports while you drink. *Coach House*, Paynes Bay, St James, T4321163, lively pub. *Adriana's Entertainment Centre*, Queen St, Speightstown, T4190126. *Casbah*, in Holetown, same building as *La Terra* and *Baku* restaurants, is billed as 'European style' and 'Moroccan themed', free drinks Thu, Latin beat Wed, quieter than the other clubs and fewer locals.

Party cruises The *Jolly Roger* run 4-hr daytime and evening cruises along the west coast to Holetown, near the Folkestone Underwater Park (where the fun and games take place) from the deepwater harbour. The drinks are unlimited (very). There is also a meal, music, dancing, etc, US$55 for the dinner cruise. On daytime cruises, there is swimming and snorkelling. The *Harbour Master*, which unlike the other cruises pulls up on the beach, 100 ft long, 40 ft wide with four decks, see above, Sailing.

Shows Some of the better ones are: Tropical Spectacular Dinner Show at the *Plantation Restaurant* US$67.50 with buffet dinner and transport from hotel, Wed and Fri, starts 1830, show and drinks US$37.50, T4285048. *1627 And All That*, Tyroll Cot, Thu, 1830, US$57.50, colourful show, bar, hors d'oeuvres, buffet dinner, tour of 17th century market place and cultural village, steel band, complimentary transport, T4281627, 4296016 to book.

Theatres There are several good semi-professional theatre companies. Performances are advertized in the press. It is usually wise to buy tickets in advance. Most people dress quite formally for these performances. The *Daphne Joseph Hackett Theatre* in Queen's Park or the *Frank Collymore Hall* in the Central Bank are common venues.

Transport **Air   From North America** Atlanta (*BWIA*), Miami (*American Airlines* and *BWIA*), New York (*American Airlines*, *Air Jamaica*, *BWIA*), Philadelphia (*Air Jamaica*), Washington DC (*BWIA*); *Air Canada* flies from Montréal and Toronto. *BWIA* also flies from Toronto. **From Europe** *British Airways*, *Virgin Atlantic* and *BWIA* have several flights a week from London. *Concorde* hopes to renew its scheduled service in winter 2001. There are also lots of charter flights which are usually cheaper and recommended if you are staying only on Barbados. **From South America** *Liat*, and *BWIA* from Georgetown, Guyana; *Aeropostal* from Caracas and Porlamar; *Tropical International Airways* stops in St Kitts and Barbados between London and Natal, Brazil. **From Caribbean Islands** Connections with Caribbean islands are good, from Antigua (*Liat*, *Caribbean Star*, *BWIA*), Dominica (*Liat*, *Caribbean Star*, *Air Jamaica*), Fort-de-France, Martinique (*Liat*), Grenada (*Liat*, *BWIA*), Kingston, Jamaica (*BWIA*), Montego Bay (*Air Jamaica*), Pointe-à-Pitre, Guadeloupe (*Liat*), Port of Spain, Trinidad (*BWIA*, *Liat*), St Kitts (*Caribbean Star*, *Tropical International Airways*), St Lucia (*Liat*, *BWIA*, *Air Jamaica*), St Maarten (*BWIA*), St Vincent (*Liat*, *BWIA*), San Juan, Puerto Rico (*American Eagle*), Tobago (*Liat*) and Tortola, BVI (*Caribbean Star*).

Check different airlines for inter-island travel, the Trinidad route is particularly competitive, *British Airways* often has good offers between Barbados, Antigua and St Lucia and a comfortable plane. It is usually worth organizing ticketing at the start of your journey so that Barbados appears as a stopover rather than as the origin for any side trips you make.

Helicopters For those who want to make a lot of noise buzzing around the island, *Bajan Helicopters* do tours from US$75 per 20 minutes, US$125 per 30 minutes right round the coastline. The heliport is near the deep water harbour at Bridgetown, T4310069.

Several companies run mini-cruises based on Barbados. The cruise ship passenger tax is US$8.50

Sea *Windward Lines Limited* run a weekly passenger/car/cargo ferry service (suspended 2001): Trinidad – St Vincent – Barbados – St Lucia – Barbados – St Vincent – Trinidad – Güiria (or every other week to Pampatar, Margarita). **To Venezuela** is especially good value as you see several islands and have somewhere to sleep on the way. Restaurant on board. Seasickness pills available, payable in almost any currency. There are a few sunbeds on the upper deck, so you could sleep under the stars or bring a hammock. Barbados is not well served by small inter-island schooners. You may be able to get a passage to another island on a yacht, ask at the harbour or at the *Boatyard* on Carlisle Bay. Mooring facilities are available at the Shallow Draft next to the Deep Water Harbour, or there are calm anchorages in Carlisle Bay.

Bus Around Bridgetown, there are plenty of small yellow privately-owned minibuses and route taxis with ZR numberplates; elsewhere, the big blue and white Mercedes buses (exact fare required or tokens sold at the bus terminal) belong to the Transport Board, T4366820. Private companies tend to stick to urban areas while the public buses run half empty in rural areas. There is a City Circle route, clockwise and anti-clockwise round the inner suburbs of Bridgetown which starts in Lower Green. Terminals for the south: Fairchild St for public buses, clean, modern; Probyn St, or just across Constitution River from Fairchild St for minibuses; further east by Constitution River for ZR vans. Terminals for the west: Lower Green for public buses; west of Post Office for minibuses; Princess Alice Highway for ZR vans. During the rush hour, all these terminals are chaotic, particularly during school term. On most routes, the last bus leaves at midnight and the first bus at 0500. There are two routes from the airport: Yorkshire buses go straight to Bridgetown, others go along the south coast past the hotels to Bridgetown. Make sure you get the right one.

Taxi Between the airport and any point north of Speightstown, US$27.50, to Holetown, US$19, to Bridgetown Harbour US$15, to Garrison US$12, to Oistins US$8; between the city centre and *Sam Lord's Castle* US$19, to Oistins US$10, Dover US$9; between *Sandy Lane* and Oistins US$18. Fares are quoted also by mile (US$1.25) or kilometre (US$0.75) but there are no taxi meters. Vehicles which look like route taxis but with ZM numberplates, are taxis plying for individual hire, and will charge accordingly. **VIP limo services** (T4294617) hire a vehicle with driver for a whole-day tour at a cost of US$150 for up to four persons.

Background

History

There were Amerindians on Barbados for upwards of a thousand years. The first Europeans to find the island were the Portuguese, who named it 'Os Barbados' after the Bearded Fig trees which grew on the beaches, and left behind some wild pigs. These bred successfully and provided meat for the first English settlers, who arrived in 1627 and found an island which was otherwise uninhabited. It is not clear why the Amerindians abandoned the island, although several theories exist. King Charles I gave the Earl of Carlisle permission to colonize the island and it was his appointed Governor, Henry Hawley, who in 1639 founded the House of Assembly. Within a few years, there were upwards of 40,000 white settlers, mostly small farmers, and equivalent in number to about 1% of the total population of England at this period. After the 'sugar revolution' of the 1650s most of the white population left. For the rest of the colonial period sugar was king, and the island was dominated by a small group of whites who owned the estates, the 'plantocracy'. The majority of the population today is descended from African slaves who were brought in to work on the plantations; but there is a substantial mixed-race population, and there has always been a small number of poor whites, particularly in the east part of the island. Many of these are descended from 100 prisoners transported in 1686 after the failed Monmouth rebellion and Judge Jeffrey's 'Bloody Assizes'.

The two principal political parties are the Barbados Labour Party (BLP) and the Democratic Labour Party (DLP). A third party is the National Democratic Party (NDP), but it is no longer very active. The DLP held office in 1986-94. Economic difficulties in the 1990s eroded support for the government. The Prime Minister Erskine Sandiford narrowly lost a vote of confidence in June 1994, and stood aside for his Finance Minister David Thompson, who led the party into a general election on 6 September. The BLP won the elections with 19 seats, compared with eight for the DLP and one for the NDP. Mr Owen Arthur, then 44, an economist, became Prime Minister and took on the portfolios of Finance and Economic Affairs. In the January 1999 general elections, the BLP was returned with an overwhelming vote of confidence. It won 26 of the 28 seats, while the DLP won the other two. The NDP did not contest the elections.

Geography

Barbados is 21 miles long and 14 miles wide, lying east of the main chain of the Leeward and Windward islands. Most of the island is covered by a cap of coral limestone, up to 600,000 years old. Several steep inland cliffs or ridges run parallel to the coast. These are the remains of old shorelines, which formed as the island gradually emerged from the sea. There are no rivers in this part of the island, although there are steep-sided gullies down which water runs in wet weather. Rainwater runs through caves in the limestone, one of which, Harrison's Cave, has been developed as a tourist attraction. The island's water supply is pumped up from the limestone. In the Scotland District in the northeast, the coral limestone has been eroded and older, softer rocks are exposed. There are rivers here, which have cut deep, steep-sided valleys. Landslides make agriculture and construction hazardous and often destroy roads.

Government

Barbados has been an independent member of the Commonwealth since November 1966. The British Monarch is the Head of State, represented by a Governor General. There is a strong parliamentary and democratic tradition. The House of Assembly is the third oldest parliament in the Western Hemisphere and celebrated its 350th anniversary in 1989, although voting was limited to property owners until 1950. There are 21 senators appointed by the Governor General, of whom 12 are on the advice of the Prime Minister, two on the advice of the Leader of the Opposition and seven at his own discretion to reflect religious, economic and social interests. 28 single-member constituencies elect the House of Assembly.

A 1998 Commission on the constitution chaired by a former BLP leader and Attorney General, Sir Henry Forde QC, recommended abolition of the monarchy, with the Governor General replaced by a ceremonial president, changes in the composition of the Senate, and replacement of the London-based Privy Council as final appeal court by a Caribbean Court of Justice.

Economy **Structure of production** There are few natural resources and sugar is still the main crop but many producers have abandoned the land, while trying to get planning permission for golf courses or housing developments. The factories and most estates are under the management of the Barbados Agricultural Management Co.

There is some export-oriented manufacturing and an expanding offshore financial sector with a good reputation. There is a well-established service sector, and a wide range of light industries which produce mainly for the local, regional, and North American markets. Manufacturing is the second largest foreign exchange earner. Informatics is a growing business, employing around 2,000 people. There is a small oil industry. Barbados National Oil Company's onshore field in St Philip produces enough for local requirements (although it is refined overseas). There is also enough natural gas for piped domestic supply to urban and suburban areas. Conoco has an offshore exploration programme which has yielded promising preliminary results.

By far the main foreign exchange earner is now tourism, which accounts for 15% of gdp and employs 10,300 people. In 2000, 545,027 stopover tourists and 533,278 cruise ship passengers visited the island, the highest totals on record. In contrast with most Caribbean islands, the UK is the main tourist market, accounting for 41% of arrivals in 2000 compared with 21% from the USA. Total tourist expenditure was US$750.5mn in 1997. In that year there were 12,138 beds on the island, of which 10,008 were in hotels, 168 in guest houses and 1,962 in apartments. Tourism projects planned or in progress include a complete rebuilding of the *Barbados Hilton*. Plans are also being developed for the site of the former oil refinery, between the *Barbados Hilton* and *Grand Barbados* hotels on the south coast. A beachfront site which was to be a Sandals resort has been empty since 1993 and is now for sale. Barbados currently has no hotels with more than 330 rooms, and the only major hotel chain represented is Hilton International. The emphasis on small scale tourism may be an advantage in the British market, but has held back sales in North America. The redevelopment of the former refinery site and the long-delayed Sandals project are expected to address this problem.

Culture **People** Barbados has a population of 268,000. This is more than any of the Windwards or Leewards, and is considered enough to make the island one of the 'big four' in the Caribbean Community. With population density of 1,614 per square mile in 2000, Barbados is one of the most crowded countries in the world.

Because Barbados lies upwind from the main island arc, it was hard to attack from the sea, so it never changed hands in the colonial wars of the 17th and 18th centuries. There is no French, Dutch, or Spanish influence to speak of in the language, cooking or culture. People from other islands have often referred to Barbados as Little England, and have not always intended a compliment. Today, the more obvious outside influences on the Barbadian way of life are North American. Most contemporary Barbadians stress their Afro-Caribbean heritage and aspects of the culture which are distinctively 'Bajan'. There are extremes of poverty and wealth, but these are not nearly so noticeable as elsewhere in the Caribbean. This makes the social atmosphere relatively relaxed. However, there is a history of deep racial division. Although there is a very substantial black middle class and the social situation has changed radically since the 1940s and 50s, there is still more racial intolerance on all sides than is apparent at first glance.

Literature Two Barbadian writers whose work has had great influence throughout the Caribbean are the novelist George Lamming and the poet Edward Kamau Brathwaite. Lamming's first novel, *In The Castle Of My Skin* (1953), a part-autobiographical story of growing up in colonial Barbados, deals with one of the major concerns of anglophone writers: how to define one's values within a system and ideology imposed by someone else. Lamming's treatment of the boy's changing awareness in a time of change in the West Indies is both poetic and highly imaginative. His other books include *Natives Of My Person*, *Season Of Adventure* and *The Pleasures Of Exile*.

Brathwaite is also sensitive to the colonial influence on black West Indian culture. Like Derek Walcott (see under St Lucia) and others he is also keenly aware of the African traditions at the heart of that culture. The questions addressed by all these writers are: who is Caribbean man, and what are his faiths, his language, his ancestors? The experience of teaching in Ghana for some time helped to clarify Brathwaite's response. African religions, motifs and songs mix with West Indian speech rhythms in a style which is often strident, frequently using very short verses. His collections include *Islands*, *Masks* and *Rights Of Passage*.

Heinemann Caribbean publish the *A to Z of Barbadian Heritage* which is worth reading (new edition in preparation). Macmillan publish *Treasures of Barbados*, an attractive guide to Barbadian architecture. *Hell or Barbados - Irish Slavery in Barbados* by O'Callaghan, Bantry. *Barbados - Photos from Within*, Miller Publications, good photo book. *Geology of Barbados*, Hans Machel, Barbados Museum publication. *Art in Barbados*, Alessandra Cummins et al, Ian Randle Publishers. Several books of old photos edited by Ann Watson Yates, of which the best is probably *Bygone Barbados*. *History of Barbados*, Schomburgk, 1848, has been reprinted, a natural history and geography of the island in early Victorian times.

Barbados

Barbados

Trinidad and Tobago

18

Trinidad and Tobago

Trinidad and Tobago are only just off the coast of Venezuela, yet they share little of the culture of South America. The people are a cosmopolitan mix of African, East Indian, Chinese, white and Syrian and their music, cuisine, culture, society and politics reflect the amalgamation of those races through conflict and harmony. Trinidad's ebullient carnival is world famous and attracts thousands of visitors but its wealth comes from oil, gas and manufacturing rather than tourism and so its beaches remain empty and unspoilt. Beach tourism has been developed on the smaller, sister island of Tobago, where hotels are spreading around the coastline, but there are still glorious bas and coves and resorts are low key. Both islands have a large area of rainforest, home to a huge array of flora and fauna, and birdwatching is a major attraction.

Essentials

Before you travel

Documents **Passports** are required by all visitors. **Visas** are not required for visits of under three months by nationals of most Commonwealth countries, West European countries, Argentina, Brazil, Colombia, Israel, Iceland and Turkey; holders of OAS passports; for US citizens for visits up to three months; and for Venezuelans for stays of up to 14 days. Some Commonwealth citizens do need visas, however; these include Australia, New Zealand, India, Sri Lanka, Nigeria, South Africa, Uganda, Tanzania, and Papua New Guinea. A visa normally requires 48 hours' notice. A waiver for those with no visa can be obtained at the airport, but it costs TT$50. Entry permits for one to three months are given on arrival; a one month permit can be extended at the immigration office in Port of Spain (at 67 Frederick St). This is a time-consuming process, so try and get a three-month entry permit if planning a long stay. Business visitors are allowed to work without a work permit for one month in each calendar year.

Only those coming from an infected area need a yellow fever inoculation certificate

Even though you may not get asked for it all travellers need a **return ticket** to their country of origin, dated, not open-ended, proof that they can support themselves during their stay, an address at which they will be staying in Trinidad (the tourist office at the airport can help in this respect). A ferry ticket to Venezuela has often satisfied immigration officials instead of a full return ticket to your own country. People going to Venezuela can obtain a

Trinidad

tourist card (free of charge) at the BWIA office; this means buying a return ticket but this can be refunded or changed if an alternative ticket out of Venezuela is later purchased.

Duty-free imports: 200 cigarettes or 50 cigars or 250g tobacco, one litre wine or spirits, and TT$1,200 worth of gifts. Perfume may not be imported free of duty, but may be deposited with customs until departure. Passengers in transit, or on short visits, can deposit goods such as liquor with customs at the airport and retrieve it later free of charge. Duty free prices at the airport are low. **Customs**

The **currency** is the Trinidad and Tobago dollar, TT$. Notes are for TT$1, 5, 10, 20 and 100. Coins are for 1, 5, 10, 25 and 50 cents. **Money**

Exchange The Trinidad and Tobago dollar was floated in April 1993, but the float is tightly managed and the exchange rate has remained around TT$6.30 = US$1 since 1996. Banks generally will change only certain currencies: Eastern Caribbean, US and Canadian dollars, and sterling. The Royal Bank will change Swiss and French francs, Deutsch marks and Dutch guilders. Republic Bank's Independence Square branch changes a much wider range of currencies by not Jamaican or most South American currencies. On departure you can change TT$ back into US$ at *First Citizens Bank* at Piarco, open until 2200, but they charge US$10 minimum fee. Better to use small amounts of TT$ in the duty free shops.

Travellers' cheques and major **credit cards** are accepted almost everywhere on Trinidad. On Tobago there are no **banks** outside Scarborough; travellers' cheques are changed by large hotels but if you are travelling to the northern end of the island make sure you have enough TT$ as not everyone accepts US$. All banks charge a fee for cashing travellers' cheques, some more than others, so check first. ATMs are widely distributed and accept credit and debit cards with the Cirrus symbol. Royal Bank ATMs in West Mall, Park St, Maraval and the airport will give US$ as well as TT$.

The climate on the islands is tropical, but, thanks to the trade winds, rarely excessively hot. Temperatures vary between 21° and 37°C, the coolest time being from December to April. There is a dry-ish season from January to mid-May and a wet season from June to November. Rain usually falls in heavy showers. **Climate**
Humidity is fairly high. Trinidad & Tobago are outside the hurricane belt

Getting there

BWIA and other airlines have scheduled flights from Toronto, Washington DC, New York and Miami in North America and from London, but there are several charter flights from those and other cities such as Frankfurt, many of them straight to Tobago. Connections are good with the north of South America, with flights to Caracas, Paramaribo and Georgetown. There are many flights to other Caribbean islands if you want to island hop (see Transport, below). **Air**

Trinidad & Tobago

Tourist offices overseas

TIDCO's website is www.tidco.co.tt, tourism-info@ tidco.co.tt Another website is www.visittnt.com

Canada *RMR Group, Taurus House, 512 Duplex Ave, Toronto, M4R 2E3, T416-4858724, F416-4858256.*
Germany *Basic Service Group, Am Schleifweg 16, D-55128, Mainz, T49-06131-73337, F06131-73307.*
Italy *Ian Rocks, Via Sant Allessandro 688, Caronno Pertusella, 21042 VA, T392-96451070, F96564870.*

UK *Mitre House, 66 Abbey Rd, Bush Hill Park, Enfield, Middlesex, EN1 2RQ, T020-83501009, F020-83501011, anna@ttg.co.uk*
USA *Keating Communications, 350 Fifth Ave, New York, NY10018, T1-888-595-4TNT, 212-7602400, F212-7606402. Press information, 331 Almeria Av, Coral Gables, F1-33134, T305-4444033, F305-4470415.*

Trinidad & Tobago

Sea

See Essentials, page 949 for the Windward Lines ferry schedule

There is a weekly ferry service (suspended 2001) connecting Trinidad with Venezuela, St Vincent, Barbados and St Lucia, which is a good way of visiting several islands if you have the time. There are also less formal services offered by captains, mainly between Venezuela and Trinidad. The ferry service between Trinidad and Tobago is not cheap, quick or comfortable.

Crew will be admitted for 90 days; a 90-day extension costs US$30 per person

Yachts **Chaguaramas, Trinidad**, and **Scarborough, Tobago** are the ports of entry. In Chaguaramas, take the boat to the customs dock (open 24 hours, overtime 1600-0800 and weekends and holidays) to clear on arrival in Trinidad and fill in combined Customs and Immigration form. Overtime for after hours, weekends and holidays is high, so it pays to arrive during normal working hours.

Departure by sea Clear out with Customs and Immigration. Pay port fees of US$8 for each month that the boat was in Trinidad and Tobago waters. To go from one island to the other clear out with Immigration and in on the new island. Clear Customs only when making final departure from the country. New arrivals must be signed aboard the vessel as crew by Immigration in Chaguaramas.

Departure by air Boats can be left in storage; yacht yards will help with paperwork, present it to Customs and clear with Immigration within 24 hours of departure for exemption from departure tax. When returning to Trinidad by air, go to third party line at airport to get paperwork to take with baggage to Chaguaramas Customs to clear. Arriving outside office hours leave boat parts for weekday review. Arriving guests should have return ticket and letter to Trinidad Immigration stating vessel name and official number.

There has been a huge increase in facilities in the 1990s, principally to take advantage of Trinidad's location outside the hurricane belt

Marinas The Trinidad marinas are all west of Port of Spain along the coast to Chaguaramas. *Trinidad and Tobago Yacht Club* (TTYC), Bayshore, T/F6374260, a private club, leases members' slips to visiting yachts when available, 60 in-water berths, security, restaurant, bar, laundry. *Point Gourde Yachting Centre*, T6275680, F6254083, 65 in-water berths, full service marina. *Trinidad and Tobago Yachting Association* (TTYA), Chaguaramas, T/F6344376, a private members' association with moorings and anchorage available to visiting yachts, full service haul out yard, 15-ton marine hoist, moorings, repair shed, bar, laundry. *Power Boats Mutual Facilities*, Chaguaramas, T6344303, F6344327, haul-out and storage, 50-ton marine hoist, 23 in-water berths, boat storage, marine supplies, fibreglass repairs, welding, woodworking, apartments, grocery, restaurant, laundry. *Peake Yacht Services*, Chaguaramas, T6344423, F6344387, full service marina, 150-ton marine hoist, capable of beams to 31ft, 21 in-water berths, boat storage, 10-room hotel, restaurant, Mini-Mart, laundry, skilled maintenance, recommended. *Industrial Marine Services* (IMS), Chaguaramas, T6344328, F6344437, full service haul-out and storage yard, 70-ton marine hoist, paint shop, chandlery, sail maker, fibreglass repair, welding, woodworking, sandblasting, restaurant, laundry. *Crews Inn Yachting Centre*, Chaguaramas, T6344384, is best-equipped with on-shore facilities, including a 46-room hotel with pool and gym, *Lighthouse* restaurant, *Republic Bank* with ATM, *Econocar* car rental agency, T6342134, hair salon, *Travelsure* travel agency, T6344000, and duty free liquor

Touching down

Departure tax *There is a TT$75 exit tax payable in local currency, or US$15, plus a TT$25 security fee. Passengers in transit do not have to pay, but are required to obtain an 'exempt' ticket from the departure tax window before being allowed through to the immigration officers on the way to the departure lounge. Visitors leaving by sea pay the departure tax to the shipping agent. Your immigration card must be presented on departure. See also page 920.*

Business hours *Government offices: 0800-1600, Monday-Friday. **Banks:** 0800-1400, Monday-Thursday, 0800-1200, 1500-1700, Friday. Some banks have extended hours until 1800. **Businesses and shops:** 0800-1600/1630, Monday-Friday (shops 0800-1200 on Saturday). Shopping malls usually stay open*

until about 2000, Monday-Saturday.

Communications *The international phone code is 868. See pages 950 and 963 for further details.*

Official time *Atlantic Standard Time, 4 hours behind GMT, 1 hour ahead of EST.*

Voltage *110 or 220 volts, 60 cycles AC.*

Weights & measures *Trinidad and Tobago have gone metric, so road signs are given in kilometres, but people still refer to miles.*

Clothing *Beachwear is for the beach. In the evening people dress more smartly but are less formal than, for example, the Bahamians.*

Tipping *If no service charge on bill, 10% for hotel staff and restaurant waiters; taxi drivers, 10% of fare, minimum of 25 cents (but no tip in route taxis); dock-side and airport porters, say 25 cents for each piece carried;*

---

store. Tardieu Marine nearby will lift and dry storage. **Humming-bird Marina**, also nearby, has a restaurant. All locations charge a fee to anchored boats for use of shoreside facilities.

Touching down

Trinidad Piarco International is 16 miles southeast of Port of Spain. Try to avoid overnight connections here. Airline schedules ensure that it is possible to arrive at Piarco after the check-in counters have closed until next morning, so you cannot go through to the departure lounge. *Sky cap* has 24-hour left luggage service. There is seating under three covered areas but it is not comfortable for an overnight wait. If you are in transit always check that your bags have not been off-loaded at Piarco, most are not checked through despite assurances. To eat at the airport, there is the *Pizza Boys* 24-hour restaurant upstairs in the terminal building and a variety of fast food outlets downstairs, including *KFC*. Indian delicacies, like 'doubles' or roti, can be had at informal food stalls to the right as you exit the terminal. If intending to take the bus to Piarco airport, allow plenty of time to ensure arriving in time for checking in. Note that a new terminal was due to open by mid-2001 (as we went to print), which is expected to improve service and increase user costs in all areas.

Tobago Crown Point airport is within walking distance of the hotels in the southwest. Crown Point airport is also uncomfortable for a long wait, often with no food available after you have been through immigration control. There are a few shops, snack bars and a bank with an ATM outside the terminal building but only a small duty free inside.

Airport information (margin)

Airlines offices *BWIA* is at 30 Edward St (T6252470, 6255866/8, F6252139), opens for reservations at 0800; be prepared for a long wait, particularly for international tickets. Internet booking through www.bwee.com is hassle-free but does not include special deals so it can be more expensive. BWIA at Piarco airport, T6693000 (open later than Edward St office); also at Carlton Centre, San Fernando, T6579712/6485, and at Crown Point airport, Tobago, T6398741/2. *American Airlines*, 90 Independence Square (T6235008, F6690261, Piarco, T6644838/47312). *Air Canada* is at 88 Independence Square (T6252195, F627304, at Piarco T6644065). *LIAT*, 30 Edward St, T6252470, at Piarco airport T6645458, on Tobago at Crown Point airport, T6390484. *Surinam Airways*, Cruise Ship Complex, Wrightson Rd, T6274747. *ALM*, 13 Pembroke St, Port of Spain, T 6238243, or Piarco, T6694770. *Guyana Airways 2000*, 13 Pembroke St, Port of Spain, T6272753.

There is a 15% VAT on airline tickets purchased in Trinidad & Tobago (margin)

Tourist information

Local tourist office *The Tourism and Industrial Development Company of Trinidad and Tobago Ltd (TIDCO)*, 10-14 Phillips St, 3rd Floor, Port of Spain, T6231932, 623-INFO, F6233848 is the sole tourism agency. Lists of hotels, restaurants, tour operators, monthly schedule of events, maps for sale etc. TIDCO also has an office at the airport, T6695196, helpful with hotel or guest house reservations for your first night. You can also buy maps of Trinidad and Port of Spain here. In Tobago the *Division of Tourism* is in Scarborough, NIB Mall, there is a kiosk, and the head office is on the third level, next to *Buddy's Restaurant* (T6392125, F6393566), or at Crown Point airport, T6390509. *TIDCO Tobago* is at Unit 12, TIDCO Mall, Sangster's Hill, Scarborough, T6394333, F6394514. *The National Carnival Commission* is at 82-84 Frederick St, Port of Spain, T6238867.

Maps Large-scale and island-wide maps of both Trinidad and Tobago can be bought from the Lands and Survey Division, 118 Frederick St, T6279204.

Safety

Care must be taken everywhere at night and walking on the beach is not safe. Stick to main roads and look as if you know where you are going. The incidence of theft has risen sharply

The people of both islands are, as a rule, very friendly but several areas are no longer safe at night, especially for women. To the east of Charlotte St, Port of Spain becomes increasingly unsafe. You should avoid Laventille, Morvant and East Dry River at night. Central Port of Spain is fairly safe, even at night, as there are plenty of police patrols. Avoid the area around the port or bus terminal except when making a journey. A favourite local saying is 'Tobago is Paradise, Trinidad is New York', at least half of which is accurate. Take care accordingly but do not underestimate crime in Tobago. We have received reports of theft and muggings on the Pigeon Point road and parts of Scarborough are known to have crack houses. Do not walk in the Turtle Beach area after dark. There have also been attacks on tourists near waterfalls and in other beauty spots. Soft top jeeps are at risk of theft. Leave nothing in them. If there is no safe where you are staying take your valuables (passport, tickets etc) to a bank in Scarborough; the *Royal Bank* charges US$12 for two weeks. Women alone report feeling 'uncomfortable', particularly if they look like a tourist. Male and female prostitution has become a problem in Store Bay and elsewhere. HIV infection rates are high on both islands. Do not be tempted to dabble in narcotics. Penalties are severe and foreigners and their vehicles may be searched. One or two tourists have been killed as a result of suspected drug deals.

Where to stay

See pages 941 & 957 for further details

Hotels There are many hotels on the islands and the better known ones are expensive, but there are very good guest houses and smaller hotels which are reasonable. Information about accommodation can be obtained from TIDCO, see Tourist information above. VAT (15%) is charged by all hotels and in most a 10% service charge is added to the bill. Some, like the *Hilton*, add a 2% surcharge. **Camping** On Trinidad it is unsafe and is not recommended. Try the Boca Islands to the west. On Tobago, it is possible near the Mt Irvine beach. Ask the taxi drivers for advice on where to camp.

Getting around

Air *BWIA* flies the Trinidad to Tobago route offering at least eight daily flights; the crossing takes 20 minutes and costs US$48 return. Departures, however, are often heavily booked at weekends and holidays, particularly Christmas and afterwards (at other times tickets can often be bought the same day).

Road

Driving is on the left and the roads are narrow and winding

On Trinidad there are good dual carriageways from Port of Spain south to San Fernando, west to Diego Martin and east to Arima, but other roads are not of a high standard. Neither is the driving. Taxis are apt to stop suddenly (eg just before a green light, or blocking a junction). No entry signs are misleadingly placed: some have a little notice underneath saying they apply only to public transport (private cars can enter). The rush hour on Trinidad starts early and ends late. Traffic is very heavy. Allow an hour or more to leave Port of Spain in the late afternoon. There are lots of pot holes almost everywhere and traffic weaves about all over the place at high speed to avoid them. Allow a full day if going from Port of Spain to Toco in the

Trinidad & Tobago

northeast or to the far southwest, if you want to have time to see anything or relax before returning. On rural roads there are prominent km posts. The older mile posts are still often there too and are used in some postal addresses (eg 21 mile post, Toco Road). In some of the more chaotic suburbs, light poles have a similar role (eg M Smith, opposite Light Pole 12, Smith Trace, Morvant). On Tobago the roads are fairly good in the south but badly maintained further north. The road between Charlotteville and Bloody Bay is for four-wheel drive vehicles only and then only in the dry season. Speeds are such on this road that the butterflies overtake you; you are better off walking. Mountain bikes are fine if you can stand the hills and the heat. International and most foreign driving licences are accepted for up to 90 days, after that the visitor must apply for a Trinidad and Tobago licence and take a written test. Visitors must always carry their licence and insurance with them. Documents are inspected at police road blocks, which are frequent at night on many main roads. Do not leave anything in your car, theft is frequent. Be careful where you park in Port of Spain, police are diligent and will tow the car away. It costs US$17 to retrieve it. There are several car parks (eg Independence Square and Pembroke St), mostly charging US$0.50 an hour.

Car hire

Some companies only rent for a minimum of 3 days

Rental can be difficult on **Trinidad**, particularly at weekends, because of heavy demand. Best to make reservations in advance. Several companies do not accept credit cards, but require a considerable cash deposit. Small cars can be rented from US$30 a day upwards, unlimited mileage, check tyres before driving off. Deposit varies from company to company, as does method of payment, book in advance. Insurance costs US$1. Many companies have offices at the airport.

Bus

On all routes, purchase your ticket at the kiosk before boarding the bus; you may have to tender the exact fare

In **Trinidad**, the word 'taxi' includes most forms of public transport. The word 'travelling' means going by bus or taxi rather than by private car. Buses are run by the *PTSC*. Air-conditioned buses, Express Commuter Service (ECS), with a/c lounge for waiting passengers, run on main routes from City Gate Terminal to Arima, Chaguanas, Five Rivers and San Fernando, also from Arima to Sangre Grande. Rural buses are extremely infrequent. The PTSC office (T6237872) is located at the remodelled South Quay railway station, called City Gate, and is the main terminal for both buses and maxi taxis. You can get information showing how to reach the various sights by bus.

On **Tobago** all buses originate in Scarborough. Schedules are changed or cancelled frequently. The route taxi system is difficult for the foreigner, being based on everyone knowing every car and therefore where it is going, but official route taxis have an H (for hire) at the start of the licence plate. Ask for directions for where to assemble for a particular route.

Taxi

Look for cars with first letter H on licence plates (no other markings)

Taxis are expensive. St Christopher's taxis or airport taxis operate from the main hotels, Ice House taxis (T6276984) and Independence Square Taxi Service (T6253032) from Independence Square. Helpful drivers approach all stray white people on Independence Square, but this can be confusing if you are really looking for a route taxi (or a beer). There are fixed fares (eg US$20 to the airport during the day, US$30 after 2200), but agree on a price

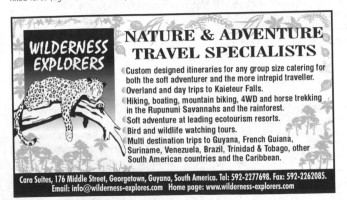

before the journey and determine whether the price is in TT$ or US$. Take a taxi if you have a complicated journey, or you have heavy baggage, or it is raining. At night it can be a lot cheaper than getting robbed. **Route taxis** (similar to colectivos) are very cheap but not as comfortable. These cannot be distinguished from ordinary taxis, so ask the driver. They travel along fixed routes, like buses, but have no set stops, so you can hail them and be dropped anywhere along the route. During rush hour it is not easy to hail them, however, and in general it takes time to master how they work. Be warned that route taxis are not covered by insurance so you cannot claim against the driver if you are involved in an accident. They are the only means of transport on some suburban routes, such as to St Ann's, and in rural areas away from main roads. Travelling to remote areas may involve three or more taxis, not really a problem, just ask where the next one stops. Major routes run all night and are amazingly frequent during the day, others become infrequent or stop late at night. There are also 'pirate' taxis with the P registration of a private car, which cost the same as the ordinary taxis, although you can sometimes bargain with the drivers. 'Ghost' taxis accept fares and drive off with your luggage as well – be warned. Be careful if hitching on Tobago as the cars that stop often prove to be pirate taxis. **Maxi-taxis** are minibuses which cover longer distances than route taxis; they are frequent and go as fast as the traffic will allow, often a bit faster (see Transport, page 208).

Sea | **Boats** From Port of Spain to Tobago once a day at 1400 Monday-Friday and 1100 on Sunday
Taking the ferry is | and public holidays, no crossings on Saturday; return crossings from Scarborough at 2300
very time consuming; | Monday-Friday and Sunday. The crossing is supposedly five hours. Hammocks can be slung at
it is a lot less hassle | night; the a/c is very cold, locals take a blanket. The trip can be rough. Tickets are sold at the
to fly | Port Authority (T6392417 in Tobago or T6232901 in Trinidad, also at the Royal Bank in San Fernando) on the docks, US$8 or US$10 return, cabin for two US$25 when available, children under 12 half price, under three free, office hours Monday-Friday 0700-1500, 1600-1800, 1900-2200. Buy passage in advance, everyone will recommend you to queue at 0800, but 1000 is usually early enough. At peak times such as Christmas it is best to book several days ahead. You need a boarding pass and not just a ticket before you can board.

Keeping in touch

Media | **Newspapers and books** The main daily papers are the *Daily Express*, the *Trinidad Guardian* and *Newsday*. The *Mirror* on Friday and Sunday has interesting investigative journalism. The *Independent* is a weekly, on Wednesday. *Trinidad and Tobago Review* is a serious paper, published occasionally. *Tobago News* is weekly. There are several racier weekly papers which appear on Friday or Saturday. *Punch*, *Bomb*, *Heat* and *Blast* are sensational tabloids, not to be missed by the visitor who wants the gossip. There is a local "yachtie" newspaper *The Boca*. The official visitor's guide, *Discover Trinidad and Tobago* is published twice a year and distributed free to all visitors by TIDCO and through hotels. **Radio** ICN Radio (610 AM), Radio Trinidad (730 AM), Music Radio (97 FM), 98.9 Yes FM, WABC (103 FM), ICN Radio (100 FM), Radio 95 FM, Radio Tempo (105 FM), Radio 96.1 FM, Rhythm (Radio 95.1 FM), Radio 1CN (91.1 FM), Sangeet (106.1 FM), Love Radio (94.1 FM), Gem Radio (93 FM), Central Radio (90.5 FM), Power (102 FM). **Television** Three local TV stations: CCN TV is independent, TTT and The Information Channel are government-owned. There are 62 cable channels, mostly US, but also the BBC and Indian channels. Tobago has its own menu of 56 channels, including Deutsche Welle TV.

Food and drink

Food | A wide variety of European, American and traditional West Indian (or creole) dishes (these
The variety of juices | include pork souse, black pudding, roast sucking pig, sancoche and callaloo stews, and
and ice creams made | many others) is served at hotels and guest houses. There is also, of course, a strong East
from the fruit is | Indian influence in the local cuisine and also lots of Chinese restaurants. Seafood,
endless. Try the street | particularly crab and shrimp (very large), is excellent. Local oysters, which grow on
vendors in St James | mangrove roots, are cooked and sold around the Savannah (delicious, but possibly a health risk). There is a local fish called salmon, which is a white fish, no relation to the

Scottish/Canadian variety. Smoked herring and salt cod are often eaten with a fried bake, especially for breakfast. The many tropical fruits and vegetables grown locally include the usual tropical fruits: pineapples large and juicy, pawpaws, very good sapodillas, and starchy eddoes and yam tanias. Citrus season is Jan-Mar, mangoes and avocados (locally called zaboca) come later in the year. Coconut water from a fresh nut (scoop out the soft jelly afterwards) is refreshing, usually sold around the Savannah, Port of Spain and on Independence Square after dark, TT$2 per nut. A distinctive local herb is chadon beni (from the French for blessed cauldron), a bit like coriander leaves in taste if not in appearance.

For those economizing, the *roti*, a chapatti pancake which comes in various forms, filled with peppery stew, shrimp or vegetable curries, is very good, US$1.30 or so for vegetable, up to US$2.60 for shrimp. *Buss up shut* (bust-up shirt) is a torn up paratha, or Indian bread accompaniment to curries. *Pelau*, savoury peas and rice and meat cooked with coconut and pepper, is also good, but when offered pepper sauce, use in moderation unless you are accustomed to fairly hot curries or *chili* dishes. Try also *saheena*, deep-fried patties of spinach, dasheen, split peas and mango sauce. *Pholouri* are fritters made with split peas. *Buljol* is a salt fish with onions, tomatoes, avocado and pepper. *Callaloo* is a thick soup based on dasheen leaves. *Doubles* are curried chick peas (channa) in two pieces of fried barra (mini pancakes). *Pastelles*, eaten at Christmas, are maize flour parcels stuffed with minced meat, olives, capers and raisins, steamed in a banana leaf (known as *hallacas* in Venezuela). A *hops* is a crusty bread roll. If you go to Maracas Bay, have *shark-and-bake*, a spicy fried bread sandwich of fried shark with a variety of sauces such as tamarind, garlic, *chadon beni*; also sugar cakes, made with grated coconut. Dumplings are a must on Tobago, particularly good with crab. A local sweet in Tobago is *benny balls*, made from sesame seeds.

Drink
There are lots of rums to try, many of which deserve better than to be swamped with punch or coke

A local drink is *mauby*, slightly bitter and made from the bark of a tree. There is also ginger beer, and of course rum punch. Sorrel is a bright red Christmas drink made from hibiscus flowers and you can get sorrel and ginger beer shandy or a sugary sorrel-flavoured soft drink. Fresh lime juice is also recommended; it is sometimes served with a dash of Angostura bitters (another local product). Local beers are *Carib* and *Stag*, both owned by the same company which also brews *Heineken, Mackeson, Royal Stout* and *Guinness*. The place to drink Guinness is the *Cricket Wicket*, in Tragarete Rd, opposite the Queen's Park Oval.

Holidays and festivals

Public holidays

New Year's Day, **Carnival** Monday and Tuesday, before *Ash Wednesday* (not officially holidays but everyone regards them as such), **Spiritual Shouter Baptist Liberation Day** (*30 March*), **Good Friday**, **Easter Monday**, **Indian Arrival Day** (*30 May*) celebrating the arrival of Indian labourers in 1845, **Corpus Christi**, **Eid ul-Fitr** (changes according to religious calendar, will be towards the end of the calendar year in 2001 and 2002), **Labour Day** (*19 June*), **Emancipation Day** (*1 August*), **Independence Day** (*31 August*), Divali (depends on religious calendar, usually Nov), **Christmas Day**, **Boxing Day** .

Special events

All Souls' Day (*2 November*) is not a holiday, but is celebrated. The Hindu festival of **Divali** is a holiday, but **Puagwa** (*February/March*) is not. Similarly, of the Moslem festivals, **Eid ul-Fitr** is a public holiday, but **Eid ul-Azha** and **Yaum um-Nabi** are not (all fall 10 to 11 days earlier each year).

Carnival
Fair-skinned visitors should avoid the skimpy costumes at carnival tramps. You will be 2 full days in the hot sun and sun block lasts about 5 mins

Trinidad Carnival culminates each year on the two days before Ash Wednesday which marks the beginning of the Christian season of Lent (11-12 Feb 2002). In practice, the festivities start months ahead, with the Mas' camps abustle, the calypsonians performing most nights of the week and the impressive Panorama taking place with the competing steelbands at the Queen's Park Savannah stadium: preliminaries, then the semi-finals, then the finals, which are held on Carnival Saturday before Mas' proper. **Band launching parties**, where band leaders show off their costume designs, start before Christmas. **Calypso 'tents'**, where calypsoes are played, start in Jan. Try *SWWUT* Hall on Wrighton Rd, De Luxe Cinema on Keate St and Spektakula on Henry St. Panyards start practising every

Trinidad & Tobago

night even earlier; visiting one is usually no problem. *Amoco Renegades* are at 17a Oxford St, Port of Spain; *Exodus* is at St John's Village on Eastern Main Rd, St Augustine; *Witco Desperadoes* are at Laventille Rd, Port of Spain; *BWIA Invaders* are opposite the Oval in Tragarete Rd. There are parties most of the time from then on. The biggest public fetes on successive weekends from Jan, then also midweek, at the Fire Service, flour mill, licensing authority, water authority (WASA), army, customs, etc, may have a crowd of 20,000 or more. There is lots of crowd participation and flag-waving, a bit like a big football match. The largest is usually the *PSA Caribbean Brass* Festival in a sports field near Long Circular Rd. Getting a ticket in advance (slightly cheaper) from somewhere like *Rhyners Records* in Port of Spain or *Crosby's* in St James, or arriving early (eg 2130) saves a struggle at the gate; most go on until 0400-0500.

Panorama steel band finals are held a Carnival Saturday before Dimanche Gras. Parties on Sunday start early. The Dimanche Gras show at the Savannah that night has a little bit of everything. There are two main carnival shows for children: the *Red Cross Kiddies* Carnival one week before carnival proper, and the school-based children's carnival the following Saturday. On Carnival Monday, the festivities start with '*J'Ouvert*' at 0200, which involves dressing up in the cheapest and most outlandish disguises available ('old mas'), including 'mud' (watered-down red, brown, blue or black paint), which will inevitably be transferred to the spectators and is murder to wash out of your clothes. In the afternoon is the *Parade of Bands* at the Savannah, featuring the very large and colourful bands, portraying a wide sweep of historical and cultural events. Though the Savannah is the main venue, on both Carnival Monday and Tuesday the bands march right round Port of Spain and are required to appear before the judges at other locations, including Independence Square and Victoria Square.

Tickets for all National Carnival Commission shows (about US$10 for most events) are sold at the Queen's Park Savannah, where the shows are held. You can join one of the Mas' camps by looking in the newspaper for the times and locations of the camps. If you are early enough you can get a costume which will allow you to participate in one of the 'tramps' through town. The Tourist Office has a list of names and addresses of the bands to whom you can write in advance to organize a costume (US$120 and more). There is a lot of alcohol consumed during the road marches but there are no drunken brawls. Police are much in evidence on the streets. Note that it is illegal to sell tapes of carnival artists but 'bootleg' tapes and CDs are inevitably sold on the streets. If you have the strength, don't forget *Last Lap*, which means jumping up with a steel band around Port of Spain to squeeze the last ounce out of the festival, prior to its official end at midnight on Tuesday. On Ash Wednesday there are huge beach parties at Manzanilla on the east coast and elsewhere, with traffic to match.

Some useful contact details: the **National Carnival Commission**, www.carnivalncc.com T6271350; the **National Carnival Bands Association**, T6271422; *Pan Trinbago*, www.pantrinbago.com T6234486; *Trinbago Unified Calypsonians Association*, T6275912, truekaiso@hotmail.com

Other festivals There is a festival or special event of some kind just about every week of the year. **Point Fortin Borough Week** is in late April, early May, with steel bands and street parties. **La Divina Pastora** in the southern town of Siparia is in May, celebrated by Catholics and Hindus. **St Peter's day** in Carenage is the first weekend in July; **The Hosay**, or Hosein Festival, commemorating the murder of Mohammed's sons-in-law, Hussein and Hassan, starts 10 days after the first appearance of the new moon in the Moharrun month of the Moslem calendar (March 2002). These are Shia festivals, commemorating a defeat by the Sunni. Most Trinidad Muslims are Sunni and disapprove of the event. Although lots of beer and rum is consumed, try not to flaunt it immediately around the *tajjas*. Also celebrated is the Moslem festival of **Eid-ul-Fitr**, to mark the end of Ramadan. Two principal Hindu festivals are **Phagwa**, or Holi, the colour, or spring, festival on the day of the full moon in the month of Phagun (February/March), and **Divali**, the festival of lights, usually in the last quarter of the year. At Phagwa everyone gets squirted with brightly coloured dyes (abeer); strict Hindus have their doubts about some of the dancing styles. Divali is more of a family affair and involves a lot of rather good food in Indian homes, with pretty oil lamps or deyas burning outside. The display at Felicity in central Trinidad is well known. On 29 August in Arima the

Feast of St Rose of Lima is celebrated; the parish church is dedicated to her. Descendants of the original Amerindians come from all over the island to walk in solemn procession round the church (see below, *Arima*).

Tobago There is a carnival but it is very quiet compared with Trinidad's. On Easter Monday and Tuesday, there are crab, goat and donkey races at Buccoo Village (see box page 955). The Tobago Heritage Festival lasts for the second fortnight of July, with historical re-enactments, variety shows and parades.

Flora and fauna

The rainforests of the Northern Range running along the north coast and the wetlands on the east and west coast are more extensive, more dense and display a greater diversity of fauna and flora than any other ecosystems in the Caribbean. The Forestry Division of the Ministry of Agriculture, Land and Marine Resources (Long Circular Rd, St James, Port of Spain, T6227476, contact them for information on guided tours and hikes) has designated many parts of Trinidad and Tobago as national parks, wildlife reserves and protected areas. On Trinidad, the national parks are the Caroni and Nariva Swamps, Chaguaramas, and Madamas, Maracas and Matura in the north range of hills.

Trinidad combines the species of the Caribbean chain from Jamaica to Grenada with the species of the continental rainforests of South America

The variety of fauna on Tobago is larger than on other similar sized islands because of once being attached to South America. It is home to 210 different bird species, 123 different butterfly species, 16 types of lizards, 14 kinds of frogs, two dozen species of snakes (all of them harmless), and it has some spectacled caymans at Hillsborough Dam. The best place to see one of the world's most beautiful birds, the blue crowned Mot Mot, is in the Grafton Wildlife Sanctuary, where they are fed daily at 1600 at the abandoned Copra House.

Wetlands

Trinidad has mangrove swamps, fresh swamps, grassy fresh water marshes, palm marshes and water-logged savannah land, covering 7,000 acres of the Central Plain. A permit from the Forestry Division is necessary for trips into restricted areas such as the Nariva Swamp and Bush Bush Island in the Aripo Scientific Reserve; 72 hours' notice is required, visit with a guide who can arrange it for you.

The **Nariva Swamp**, the largest freshwater swamp in Trinidad is a Wetland of International Importance under the Ramsar Convention. It contains hardwood forest and is home to red howler monkeys and the weeping capuchin as well as 55 other species of mammal of which 32 are bats. Birds include the savannah hawk and the red-breasted blackbird. A tour by kayak is recommended (T6247281 or 6292680) you will see more than you would on a motor boat. You paddle silently across fields of giant water lilies, through channels in thick forest of mangroves and towering silk cotton trees with monkeys and parrots chattering overhead and exotic butterflies fluttering around you. The **Caroni Swamp** is usually visited in the late afternoon as it is the roosting place of scarlet ibis and egrets. You go out through mangroves into a lagoon where the boat's engine is turned off so that you can quietly watch the birds. No permit is necessary, see below, 'Around the island'.

Rainforests

The slopes of the Northern Range are covered with forest giants like the silk cotton trees, which carry creepers and vines and the thick forest canopy of mahogany, balata, palms and flowering trees like the poui and immortelle which provide cover and maintain a cool, damp environment no matter the heat of the day.

The **Northern Range Sanctuary**, Maracas, or El Tucuche Reserve, is a forest on the second highest peak, at 3,072 feet, covering 2,313 acres. It contains some interesting flora, such as giant bromeliad and orchids, as well as fauna, including the golden tree frog and the orange-billed nightingale-thrush. There are several hiking trails, the most popular of which is from Ortinola estate; guides can be hired. The 7-mile trek to the peak takes five hours through dense forest; the views from the top are spectacular; for information contact the *Field Naturalists' Club* (see below). Walking alone is not recommended in the northern hills, join a group or at least walk with someone who knows the (often badly defined) trails well.

The **Trinity Hills Wildlife Sanctuary** lies west of Guayaguayare and was founded in 1934. Its forests are home to a large variety of birds, monkeys, armadillos (tatoos) and opossums (manicou). Permission to visit must be obtained from the Petroleum Company of Trinidad and Tobago (Petrotrin) in Pointe-a-Pierre.

The **Valencia Wildlife Sanctuary** contains at least 50 species of birds including antbirds and tanagers. Several mammals live here: deer, quenk, agouti, tatoo. Near Valencia is the Arena Forest, one of ten recreation parks, while five areas have been designated scenic landscapes (Blanchisseuse, Maracas and Toco-Matelot on the north coast, Cocos Bay on the Atlantic, and Mount Harris on the Southern Rd, south of Sangre Grande). Permission to visit certain forests and watershed areas must be obtained from the Water and Sewerage Authority (WASA), Farm Rd, Valsayn, St Joseph. Their ponds often serve as home to caymans and a variety of waterbirds and are easily accessible off the main highway east of Port of Spain. Permits for Hollis Reservoir have been suspended until further notice. Although about 46% of the island remains forested, there is much concern about the loss of wildlife habitats, with damage from hunting, illegal logging and clearing of wetland for rice cultivation.

It is possible to do voluntary work with Environment Tobago, Robinson St, Rollocks Building, Scarborough, T6607462

On Tobago, apart from two national parks (Buccoo Reef and the virgin and secondary forests of east Tobago), there are the Goldsborough natural landmark, the Kilgwyn scientific reserve, the Grafton nature conservation area, the Parlatuvier-Roxborough scenic landscape, and three recreation parks (including Mount Irvine). At the **Grafton Bird Sanctuary** the blue crowned mot mots are fed at 0800 and 1600 at the Old Copra House. They are not tame enough to be hand fed but it is still a spectacular sight. Many of the small islands off the coasts of the two larger ones are reserves for wildlife and are important breeding grounds for red-billed tropic birds, frigate birds, man-o-war and other sea birds (for instance Saut d'Eau, Kronstadt Island and Soldado Rock off Trinidad, and Little Tobago, see below, St Giles and Marble Islands off Tobago). Many flowering trees can be seen: pink and yellow poui, frangipani, cassia, pride of India, immortelle, flamboyant, jacaranda. Among the many types of flower are hibiscus, poinsettia, chaconia (wild poinsettia – the national flower), ixora, bougainvillea, orchid, ginger lily and heliconia. The *Horticultural Society of Trinidad and Tobago* (PO Box 252) has its office on Lady Chancellor Rd, Port of Spain, T6226423.

The islands boast 60 types of bat, and other mammals include the Trinidad capuchin and red howler monkeys, brown forest brocket (deer), collared peccary (quenk), manicou (opossum), agouti, rare ocelot and armadillo. A small group of manatee is being protected in a reserve in the Nariva Swamp. Other reptiles include iguanas and 47 species of snakes, of which few are poisonous: the fer-de-lance, bushmaster and two coral snakes.

Birdlife

The aboriginal name for the island of Trinidad was Ieri, which just means island

Trinidad and Tobago together have more species of birds than any other Caribbean island, although the variety is South American, not West Indian. No species is endemic, but Tobago has 13 species of breeding birds not found on Trinidad. Most estimates say that there are 433 species of bird, including 41 hummingbirds, parrots, macaws, the rare red-breasted blackbird, the nightingale thrush and the mot mot. There are also 622 recorded species of butterfly. The most accessible bird-watching sites are the **Caroni Bird Sanctuary**, the **Asa Wright Centre**, the Caurita Plantation and the **Wild Fowl Trust**.

Recommended is *A Guide to the Birds of Trinidad and Tobago*, by Richard ffrench (Macmillan Caribbean), with introductory information on rainfall, the environment and vegetation as well as birds. *Birds of Trinidad and Tobago*, also by Richard ffrench (M Caribbean Pocket Natural History Series) is a shorter guide with colour photos of 83 of the more common species. *Birds of Trinidad and Tobago – A Photographic Atlas*, by Russell Barrow (MEP Trinidad, 1994) is the most recent bird book, with clear and striking pictures.

You can also contact the **Trinidad Field Naturalists Club**, PO Box 642, Port of Spain (T6248017 evenings only, walks on Sunday). *The Trinidad and Tobago Field Naturalists' Club Trail Guide*, by Paul Comeau, Louis Guy, Ewoud Heesterman and Clayton Hull, was published in 1992, 288 pages on 48 trails, difficult to obtain. ffrench and Bacon's *Nature Trails of Trinidad*, first published in 1982 has been revised by Dr Victor Quesnel and reissued by SM Publications Ltd under the auspices of the Asa Wright Nature Centre. Each October Trinidad and Tobago hold **Natural History Festivals** to foster understanding of the islands' flora and fauna.

Diving and marine life

The waters around Tobago are becoming known as an unspoilt diving destination and several dive shops have started operations. Every known species of hard coral and lots of soft corals can be found, and there is a huge brain coral, believed to be one of the world's largest, off Little Tobago which you can see on a glass bottom boat tour. The Guyana current flows round the south and east shores of Tobago and supports a large variety of marine life. Dive sites are numerous and varied, there are walls, caves, canyons, coral gardens and lots of fish. There is exciting drift diving but it is not recommended for novices. The only thing better than racing past dancing sea fans at three knots is to do it again at five knots. You are swept along the coral reef while, high above, manta rays flap lazily to remain stationary in the current as they sieve out the plankton. Snorkelling is also excellent almost everywhere, with good visibility. Some of the most popular sites are **Arnos Vale**, **Pirate's Bay**, **Store Bay**, **Man O'War Bay** and **Batteaux Bay**. In 1997 a new site was added, with the sinking of the *Scarlet Ibis*, renamed the *Maverick*, a 350ft roll-on/roll-off ship. This artificial reef lies 100ft deep on a sandy bed and already coral is growing and schools of fish are being attracted to the wreck.

Coral reefs flourish almost all round Tobago

The most varied marine wildlife off Trinidad is in the channels called the **Bocas**, between the islands off the northwest peninsula (The Dragon's Mouth). However, the currents are cold, so protective gear is essential. Safer, if less spectacular diving and snorkelling at many north coast beaches, particularly **Maqueripe** on the west peninsula, a few miles north of the marinas. The waters flowing from the Orinoco around Trinidad reduce visibility, but the sea is full of nutrients. There is lots to see but you may not be able to see it, especially in the rainy season.

The leatherback **turtle** nests March to September on several beaches on Trinidad (Matura, Fishing Pond on east coast, Paria, Tacaribe and Grand Riviere on north coast) and Tobago (Great Courland Bay known as Turtle Beach, Stonehaven Bay, Bloody Bay and Parlatuvier), up to eight times a season, laying 75 to 120 eggs each time about 10 days apart. Incubation is 60 days.

Turtle-watching tours are organized by the Asa Wright Nature Centre

There is a full list in *Discover Trinidad and Tobago*. **Tobago Dive Experience**, at *Manta Lodge*, T6604888, and the *Turtle Beach*, T6397034, is the only company of offer both NAUI and PADI certification, www.tobagodiveexperience.com **Aquamarine Dive Ltd** (Keith and Alice Darwent) is at *Blue Waters Inn*, Speyside, T6604341, F6394416, amdtobago@trinidad.net *(Blue Waters Inn tends to be full throughout the year so book early.)* This is a five-star PADI facility, dives are around Little Tobago and all escorted by at least two dive masters because of the currents. Full range of courses available. **Man Friday Diving,** Charlotteville, T/F6604676, mfdiving@tstt.tt, covers the area from Charlotteville to Speyside. Other dive operators include **Pro Scuba**, *Rovanel's Resort*, Store Bay, T6397424, proscuba@tstt.net.tt and several more people involved in diving, fishing and other watersports, who are not listed here. A single tank dive costs on average US$35, night dives US$45, PADI Open Water course US$300, rental of BCD and regulator US$6-7, mask, fins and snorkel US$8-10.

Dive centres
The Association of Dive Operators in Tobago, T639703/6391279 keeps a list of operators who meet their safety standards

Beaches and watersports

Maracas Bay, 10 miles/16 km from the capital, has a sheltered sandy beach fringed with coconut palms; despite small waves there can be a dangerous undertow here and at other beaches and drownings have occurred, do not swim far out and watch the markers. Crowded on Sundays but fairly quiet otherwise. Lifeguards are on duty until 1800; there are changing rooms, showers etc, car parking and cabanas for beach vendors. Try 'shark-and-bake', shark meat in a heavy fried dough, a Maracas speciality, or the 'shark and bread', a roll with shark meat in it, very tasty, especially after a drinking session at 0300, sold all along the beach. There are buses to Maracas Bay running every four hours from the bus terminal, or route taxis from Park St, but all transport is irregular and infrequent. Easy at weekends but less frequent during the week. Difficulties in catching the bus have led travellers to recommend car hire or taxis: from Port of Spain a hotel or Ice House taxi costs US$25.

Beaches
The best beaches on Trinidad are on the north coast and the views from the coastal road are spectacular as you drive through forest and look down on sandy bays and rocky promontories

Trinidad & Tobago

Next to Maracas Bay is **Tyrico Bay** (surfing, lifeguard, another horseshoe-shaped beach with a dangerous undertow and sandflies). **Las Cuevas**, also on the north coast (like Maracas Bay there are changing rooms, showers, lifeguards, surfing is good here but beware of the sandflies in the wet season), is a picturesque bay with fishing boats moored at one end. Even at weekends most of the beach is empty, but a large hotel development is planned. There are smaller beaches at **La Fillette** and at **Blanchisseuse** where one beach has a sweet water lagoon where the river runs into the sea and the place is kept clean by the owners of *Cocos Hut* restaurant who are establishing a 28-acre nature reserve on the banks of the river. There are lots of birds but also mosquitoes and sandflies. Leatherback turtles come on to Blanchisseuse beach in the nesting season but most of the eggs are eaten by dogs. The coast road ends at Blanchisseuse. At the northeast end of the island, near Toco, are a number of bays, including **Balandra** for good bathing.

The Atlantic coast from Matura to Mayaro is divided into three huge sweeping bays, with huge palm trees in some places. Of these bays **Mayaro** and **Manzanilla** both have beautiful sandy beaches, but be careful of the Atlantic currents, swimming can be dangerous. There are several beach houses to rent at Mayaro, heavily booked in peak holiday periods, some are poor, check beforehand. Manzanilla has new public facilities and one hotel. From nearby Brigand Hill Lighthouse, a TSTT signal station, you can get a wonderful view of the east coast, the Nariva Swamp and much of Trinidad. Light patches of green are rice fields encroaching on the swamp. In the southwest, near La Brea and the Pitch Lake is the resort of Vessigny. The southwest, or Cedros, peninsula is a three-hour car trip from Port of Spain to the unspoilt beaches and miles of coconut palm plantations. Generally, the beaches are difficult to get to except by taxi or car.

Tobago is noted for its beaches, two of the best being only minutes from the airport: **Store Bay**, popular with locals, lots of vendors, food stalls and glass bottom boats; and **Pigeon Point**, a picture postcard beach fringed with palms with calm, shallow water protected by **Buccoo Reef**. You have to pay to use the facilities at the beach (US$2), but you get changing facilities, umbrellas and beach bars. Here also there are lots of glass bottom boats going out to Buccoo Reef and a catamaran for coastal tours and swimming in the **Nylon Pool**, a shallow area offshore. Other good beaches on the leeward side of the island are **Stone Haven Bay, Mount Irvine Bay** and **Courland Bay**, one of the longest. All have resort hotels and watersports. **Englishman's Bay** is another lovely bay, with the forest coming down to the beach and a river running into the sea. The east coast is more rugged and windswept, with cliffs and coves carved out by the Atlantic Ocean. **Hillsborough Bay**, just outside Scarborough, has a glorious long beach with overhanging palms, but the sea is dangerous because of rip tides. Do not swim there. **Big Bacolet Bay**, also known as Minister Bay, is great for surfing, body surfing and boogie boarding, but watch out for the currents. In the northeast, **King's Bay** has a beach bar, toilets and huts for shade. There is a signpost to the beach, almost opposite the track to King's Bay Waterfall. **Speyside** and **Charlotteville** both have protected bays, from the former you can take glass bottom boat trips to **Little Tobago** with bird-watching, walking and snorkelling included (about US$12.50) and from the latter you can walk to Pirate's Bay through the forest. Snorkelling is good on the reef here.

Sailing   Yachting has become big business in Trinidad and there are now several marinas attracting custom from other islands more at risk from hurricanes. Provisioning is excellent and there are boat repair and maintenance facilities; local teak costs a fraction of US prices, workmen are highly skilled, services are tax free and spare parts can be imported duty free. Marinas have both dry storage and stern-to docks. Facilities have been built at Courland Bay, Tobago, to attract the yachting crowd.

Every July/August, there is a power boat race from the Trinidad and Tobago Yacht Club (TTYC), Trinidad to Store Bay, Tobago. The Trinidad and Tobago Yachting Association (TTYA) (www.ttya.org/ayw/index.html) sponsors Carnival Fun Race and a weekly racing programme in winter and spring. Each year Tobago has a sailing week in May, sponsored by Angostura and Yachting World Magazine; many crewing possibilities, lots of parties.

For **surfing** or **windsurfing**, contact the *Surfing Association of Trinidad and Tobago*, T6374533, and the *Windsurfing Association of Trinidad and Tobago*, T6592457.

Kayaking (including tuition) is available at many hotels on Tobago or at the *Chaguaramas Kayak Centre* run by Merryl See Tai, 500m after the Alcoa dock, just before Pier

One, T6337871. You can hire kayaks for use in the bay or go on excursions along the coast, up rivers or to the Bush Bush Sanctuary in the Nariva Swamp. Walking tours and overnight expeditions also arranged.

Charters can be arranged, for deep sea fish or bonefish and tarpon in the mangroves and flats. Prices for deep sea fishing are around US$250 per four hours, US$400 per eight hours, maximum six people and for bonefishing US$150 per four hours, maximum three people. On Tobago contact Capt Gerard 'Frothy' De Silva, Friendship Estate, Canaan, T6397108. He has a custom built, 38ft sports fishing boat, *Hard Play*, and two 23ft skiffs for flats fishing. The annual International Game Fishing Classic is held in February/March, the Kingfish Tournament is in June and a Funfish Tournament is in November. Contact the Trinidad and Tobago Game Fishing Association, T6245304, for information.
Fishing

Cricket is very popular. Test matches are played at Queen's Park Oval, west of Queen's Park Savannah, Port of Spain; take a cushion, sunhat/umbrella, whistle (!) and drinks if sitting in the cheap seats. It is a private club but a friendly gate guard might let you in for a look around. For information, ring Queen's Park Cricket Club, T6222295/3787. There are smaller grounds for club cricket throughout both islands. Hockey and soccer are also played at the Oval (Football Association T6245183/7661) or at the Jean Pierre stadium. Also played are rugby, basketball, cycling and marathon running. There is **horse-racing** at Santa Rosa Park, Arima, about 15 km outside Port of Spain. Horse-hire near Fort George.

Other sports
Dwight Yorke is the best known of the dozen Trinidadian and Tobagonian footballers playing for top clubs internationally

  Swimming at the *Hilton Hotel*, US$4 (US$2 children), *Cascadia Hotel* (chutes and waterslides, very busy at weekends and holidays) or *La Joya* at St Joseph, check first for availability, T6621184; see below for swimming and **golf** at St Andrews (Moka) Golf Club (T6292314); there are five other golf clubs on Trinidad, including a nine-hole public course at Chaguaramas (T6344349); squash, Long Circular Mall, T6221245, 0600-2200 (0900-1700 Saturday), US$3 for 40 mins, advance booking essential.

  Tennis: Trinidad Country Club Maraval, T6223470/2111/2113, temporary membership, advance booking necessary, also at *Hilton Hotel*, Tranquility Square Lawn Tennis Club (T6254182) and public tennis courts at Princes Building Grounds, Upper Frederick St (T6231121). The *Cascadia Hotel*, Ariapita Rd, St Ann's has two **squash** courts with seating for 100 spectators per court, tennis courts, sauna and **gym** with lots of equipment and facilities, open for non-members, 0600-2100 Monday-Friday, 0900-1700 Saturday, T6233511. Squash also at Pelican Squash Club, *Pelican Inn*, Cascade, T6374888, equipment for hire, and at Body Works Squash Courts, Long Circular Mall, T6221215.

  On Tobago, **golf** and **lawn tennis** at Mount Irvine Bay, T6398871: green fee US$20 per day, tennis US$3 in day, US$6 at night. Squash at *Grafton Beach Resort*, 0800-2200, US$9.50 for 45 mins including court, ball and racket rental. Black Rock has a basketball league in late August, early September; you can play before or after the games. At the *Turtle Beach Hotel* it is possible to play **volleyball**.

Port of Spain

Port of Spain lies on a gently sloping plain between the Gulf of Paria and the foothills of the Northern Range. It is full of life and an exciting city to spend time in. The streets are mostly at right-angles to one another; the buildings are a mixture of fretwork wooden architecture and modern concrete, interspersed with office towers. Within easy reach of the port are many of the main buildings of interest.

Population: 51,000 (350,000 including suburbs) Colour map 6, grid C6

Ins and outs

The taxi fare from **Piarco airport** to Arouca is US$7 and to the centre of Port of Spain is US$20, to Maraval US$24, Diego Martin US$27, San Fernando US$31 (50% more after 2200). Taxi despatchers find taxis for new arrivals, ask to see the rate card for taxi fares. Unlicensed taxis outside the main parking area charge less, depending on the volume of business. Public
Getting there
See page 922 for further details

Trinidad & Tobago

Trinidad: a foot in the door

- Drive along the coast to **Blanchisseuse**; swim in the river and walk through the forest.
- See the winding roads of the **Central Range**. Get lost. Lunch off fresh oranges and stop at a bar.
- Stroll round the **Savannah** at sunset. Drink the water from a fresh coconut and eat oysters.
- Lime on the Brian Lara promenade on a Friday evening or lime all day at a cricket match in the Oval.
- Get ready for Carnival - band launchings, big fetes, Panorama, J'Ouvert.

transport is much cheaper. To get to Port of Spain walk out of the airport and cross the road to catch a route taxi, to Highway or to Arouca (US$0.30). Then take a route taxi or maxi taxi from the junction into Port of Spain (US$0.90). People are very helpful if you need to ask. There are also a few buses, see Transport page 949. Tickets not available at the airport. From City Gate terminal you will have to walk to Independence or Woodford Square for a route taxi. This is not advisable at night, especially if carrying luggage. Take a taxi.

Getting around You can see most of the sights of Port of Spain by walking around the town centre. For further afield, however, there are taxis, buses, route taxis and maxi taxis.

Sights

On the south side of **Woodford Square**, named after the former governor, Sir Ralph Woodford, is the fine **Anglican Cathedral Church of the Holy Trinity** (consecrated 1823), with an elaborate hammer-beam roof festooned with carvings. It was built during Woodford's governorship (1813-28) and contains a very fine monument to him. **The Red House** (completed 1907) contains the House of Representatives, the Senate and various government departments. It was the scene of an attempted overthrow of the Robinson Government by armed black Muslim rebels in July 1990. The rebels held the Prime Minister and several of his Cabinet captive for five days before surrendering to the Army. On the west side of the Red House, at the corner of St Vincent and Sackville Streets, can still be seen the skeletal remains of the former Police Headquarters, which the rebels firebombed before launching their assault on the Red House. The first Red House on this site was, ironically, destroyed by fire in 1903 during riots over an increase in water rates. On the opposite side of the Square to the Cathedral are the modern Hall of Justice (completed 1985), the old Central Library and City Hall (1961), with a fine relief sculpture on the front. A new National Library is under construction nearby. The 'University of Woodford Square' is Trinidad's equivalent to Speaker's Corner in London's Hyde Park.

On **Independence Square** (two blocks south of Woodford Square) are the **Roman Catholic Cathedral of the Immaculate Conception**, built on the shore-line in 1832 but since pushed back by land reclamation. The central area of Independence Square, from the cruise ship complex to the Cathedral, has been made into an attractive pedestrian area, known as the **Brian Lara Promenade** in honour of the Trinidadian cricketer and former West Indies captain, Brian Lara. This is lively in the evening, especially on Fridays, with people liming, drinking beer or playing chess. Behind the Cathedral is **Columbus Square**, with a small, brightly-painted statue of the island's European discoverer. South of Independence Square, between Edward and St Vincent Streets is the financial complex, two tall towers and **Eric Williams Plaza**, housing the Central Bank and Ministry of Finance. Also, a little to the south of the square is the old neo-classical railway station, now known as **City Gate**, a transport hub for taxis and buses travelling between Port of Spain and eastern Trinidad. Close to the waterfront is the **San Andres fort**, built about 1785 to protect the harbour, and a small lighthouse which has settled into the soft ground with a rakish tilt.

To the north of the city is **Queen's Park Savannah**, a large open space with many playing fields and a favourite haunt of joggers. Fresh coconuts, oysters and Indian snacks are on sale in the afternoons and a craft market at Carnival time. It was the site of Trinidad's main racecourse for decades, until racing was centralized in Arima. In the middle of the Savannah is the Peschier cemetery, still owned and used by the family who used to own the Savannah. Below the level of the Savannah are the Rock Gardens, with lily ponds and flowers. Opposite are the **Botanic Gardens**, founded in 1818 by Sir Ralph Woodford. There is an amazing variety of tropical and sub-tropical plants from Southeast Asia and South America, as well as indigenous trees and shrubs.

Adjoining the Gardens is the small **Emperor Valley Zoo**, dating from 1952, which specializes in animals living wild on the island. It has a number of reptiles, including iguanas, four species of boas and the spectacled caiman. ■ *0930-1800, no tickets after 1730, adults TT$4, children 3-12, TT$2.* Also next to the gardens is the presidential residence: a colonial style building in an 'L' shape in honour of Governor James Robert Longden (1870-74). Just off the Savannah (on St Ann's Rd) is Queen's Hall, where concerts and other entertainments are given.

There are several other Edwardian-colonial mansions along the west side of Queen's Park Savannah, built in 1904-10 and known as the **Magnificent Seven** (after the film of the same name). From south to north, they are Queen's Royal College; Hayes Court, the residence of the Anglican Bishop; Prada's House, or Mille Fleurs; Ambard's House, or Roomor; the Roman Catholic Archbishop's residence; White Hall, which has regained its status as the Prime Minister's office; and Killarney, also known as Stollmeyer's Castle (now owned by the Government). Apart from Hayes Court, which was built in 1910, all were built in 1904. A walk along the north and west sides of the Savannah can be made in the early morning (before it gets too hot), arriving outside Queen's Royal College as the students are arriving and the coconut sellers are turning up outside. The Anglican Church of All Saints at 13 Queen's Park West is also worth a visit; its stained glass windows are recently restored. Knowsley, another 1904 building, and the ugly new headquarters of the BP Amoco Oil Company, formerly the historic *Queen's Park Hotel* (1895), both on the south side of the Savannah, are interesting buildings too. For a history of Port of Spain buildings, with illustrations, read *Voices In The Street*, by Olga J Marrogordato (Inprint Caribbean Ltd 1977, but out of print).

Just off the Savannah, at the corner of Frederick and Keate Streets, is the small **National Museum**, in the former Royal Victoria Institute. It has sections on petroleum and other industries, Trinidad and Tobago's natural history, geology, archaeology and history, carnival costumes and photographs of kings and queens, and art exhibitions (including a permanent exhibition of the work of the 19th-century landscape artist, M J Cazabon, see further page 967). ■ *Tue-Sat 1000-1800, free. T6235941.*

Suburbs The suburbs around Port of Spain vary considerably, some are desirable places to live, others are to be avoided (see 'Safety', page 922). To the east is Sea Lots, a rough squatter area on the shoreline. Beetham Estate is even rougher public housing along the highway. Laventille is a working class hillside suburb, breezy with good views, two big water tanks, Our Lady of Laventille and the Desperadoes panyard (see Festivals, page 925). For a pleasant drive in the hills with attractive views of city, sea, and mountains, go up Lady Young Rd, about two miles from Savannah, to a lookout 563 ft above sea level (not on a taxi route, but some cars take this route from the airport), by Lady Chancellor Rd (not always safe, even by car) and to the Laventille Hills to see the view from the tower of the shrine of Our Lady of Laventille. In the northeast, Belmont is an area of older housing, rather run down. Cascade is a pretty valley with houses stretching up the hillsides. St Ann's is another pretty valley with the Prime Minister's residence and the mental hospital. To the northwest, Newtown is crowded, commercial and run down, while St Clair is spacious, expensive and quiet. Maraval is in the next valley with the road running through it to Maracas on the

Trinidad & Tobago

Port of Spain

Trinidad & Tobago

N

Not to scale

coast. Away from the city centre, to the west of Port of Spain, is the suburb of Woodbrook, containing Ariapita Av, which is full of restaurants and pubs, while St James is known as the city that never sleeps. In Ethel St there is a large new Hindu temple, the Port of Spain Mandir, and on Nepaul St is the childhood home of VS Naipaul. From **Fort George**, a former signal station at 1,100ft, there are also excellent views. The fort was built around 1804 and formerly called La Vigie. Although it was never used to defend the island, in times of danger people from Port of Spain brought their valuables up here for safe keeping. To reach it take the St James route taxi from Woodford Square and ask to get off at Fort George Rd. From there it is about one hour's walk uphill passing through some fairly tough residential territory. You can get a taxi from Bournes Rd, St James, if you don't fancy the walk, or take a taxi up and walk down.

Around the island

Midway along the Western Main Rd to Chaguaramas a road runs off to the north, through the residential area of Diego Martin. At the north end of the Diego Martin Valley, the **Blue Basin** waterfall and natural landmark, is about a five-minute walk along a path from the road. (If you do leave your car to visit the fall, leave nothing of value in it. You are also advised to visit the falls in a group of five or six people if possible to avoid being robbed.) At the nearby River Estate is a waterwheel which was once the source of power for a sugar plantation.

The Western Main Rd, with many pretty views, especially of the Five Islands and the nearby Carrera island prison, runs on past West Mall in Westmoorings, a featureless modern suburb where there is a large new residential development and the Chamber of Commerce. From here the road continues along the coast past the *Trinidad and Tobago Yacht Club (TTYC)* (opposite Goodwood Park where the rich live) and to **Carenage**, where there is a fish market and a remarkable little church, St Peter's Chapel, on the waterside. **St Peter's Day festival**, the first weekend in July, is a mini-Carnival with street parties running late into the night, music and steel pan, but no costumes. On the Sunday there is a religious service, the original core of the celebration, but now barely visible. The Alcoa transhipment facility for Guyanese bauxite is next and then the Kayak Centre, T6337871, which also has mountain bikes, before you are into **Chaguaramas**, on the bay of the same name. On your left is Pier One, a small marina with restaurant and entertainment facilities, popular at weekends, and further along is Chagville, a dirty public beach opposite the Chaguaramas Convention Centre. This area used to belong to the US navy 1945-64 but is now under the control of the Chaguaramas Development Authority (CDA), T6344364. Most of the old military buildings are still there, with new uses, including a rather under-used hotel.

Just after the police post which marks the start of the old military base, turn right for the **Tucker Valley**. The old village on the right was emptied to make way for US forces; a half-ruined church and a cemetery can still be seen. The main road leads to a car park with steps down to the Maqueripe beach. On a clear day you can see the Güiria peninsula of Venezuela. Turnings to the left from the main road lead to the Chaguaramas public golf course; the club house is a good place for a drink. Cliff top paths from the car park run to the headland to the east and a longer one to the west leading eventually to the golf club. Also from the golf course is the short trail to **Edith Falls**, a nice walk, but there is barely a trickle of water in the falls except after heavy rain. Just south of the beach an asphalted road to the east is usually barred to vehicles. On foot, it leads to the cliff tops and eventually to the North Post at the head of the **Diego Martin Valley**. A good walk, but getting back is a problem unless you arrange for a car at the other end.

Further along the coast road, the **Chaguaramas Military History and Aviation Museum** has exhibitions of VE Day and Trinidad's role in both world wars with intricate models as well as relics. ■ *Entry through military checkpoint, TT$10 adults,*

Chaguaramas
Chaguaramas was the focus of international attention in May 1999, when the Miss Universe pageant was held there

Trinidad & Tobago

TT$5 children, PO Box 3126, Carenage, T6344391, knowledgeable staff. Next you come to the Yachting Association, Power Boats, Peake's and Industrial Marine Services (IMS), all offering services to the yachting clientele and the area is packed with boats stacked on land or in the water. ■ *Buses from Port of Spain to Chaguaramas run about every 30 mins, TT$2.*

From Chaguaramas you can sometimes get a launch (known locally as a *pirogue*, expect to pay US$25 round trip although locals pay about TT$15) to **Gaspar Grande**, one of the islands offshore, on which are the **Gasparee Caves**. ■ *TT$5*. Try to get a *pirogue* with a canvas shade as these are used to dealing with tourists and are likely to be more reliable. The Gasparee Caves are certainly worth a visit. It is about a 20-minute boat ride from the Crews Inn marina. The landing stage is at the west end of Gaspar Grande which has many weekend homes. The caves are about 15 mins from the landing stage up a good path through woods, quite steep in places and hot. The caves are locked and it is necessary to have a guide from the house at the end of the path (drinks available). The complex of caves is large but you are only shown one, with good steps leading down and naturally lit from a blow hole. There is a beautiful lake (tidal) at the bottom with stalactites which the guide will light. Some of the path around the cave is quite slippery. Despite what the boatman may tell you, there is now no swimming allowed in the cave. Be prepared for a wait at the landing stage as despite all assurances, a number of boatmen will not wait for you, preferring to return to the island and then come back to pick you up (which they usually do). Don't be afraid to ask another boatman to take you back, you will of course have to pay again though. As well as going to the caves, ask the boatman to take you across to **Scotland Bay**. There are excellent views of the other islands making up the Dragon's Mouth. This is much frequented by boats and yachts at the weekend but is virtually deserted during the week. **Monos Island**, at the west tip of Trinidad, has many deep caves and white sandy beaches, popular with more affluent Trinidadians.

The north coast

It is possible to walk to Maracas from Port of Spain in about three hours, take a maxi or route taxi to Maraval and then hike from there

North of Port of Spain is **Maraval**, just beyond which is the 18-hole St Andrews golf course at **Moka** (there is also a swimming pool, US$3 for non-members). The North Coast Rd branches left off Saddle Rd (which runs through Maraval back over the hills to meet the Eastern Main Rd at San Juan), leading to Maracas Bay, Las Cuevas and Blanchisseuse (see page 929). There is a lookout point on the road to Maracas Bay at the *Hot Bamboo Hut*, where a track goes steeply down to a secluded beach. The stall-holder can call the toucans in the forest, take binoculars to see them fly close and answer him. There is an attractive hiking route across the Northern Range

Trinidad northwest

from the Maracas Valley near St Joseph, but you will need a local guide. The Northern Range locations for hiking are best reached from the coastal villages, where there are small hotels, guest houses and restaurants.

East of Port of Spain

The east-west corridor from Port of Spain is a line of industrial and residential suburbs linked by the Eastern Main Road and more quickly by a dual carriageway. Although the flat bits are mostly unattractive, you are never more than a mile or two from the hills and both high and low income neighburhoods extend up the hillsides, with wonderful views of Central Trinidad and across to the Gulf of Paria. The older centres along the Eastern Main Road (San Juan, Curepe, Tunapuna, Arouca) are lively, with shops, small bars, Chinese restaurants and fruit and vegetable markets, the latter jamming up the traffic even on Sunday morning. Just east of Port of Spain is the **Angostura rum distillery**, which has tours Tuesday and Thursday, 0830 and 1300, T6231841. An old warehouse is now CCA7: artists' studio space, with occasional exhibitions, T6251889. At Champs Fleurs is the **Carib brewery**, then the Mount Hope teaching hospital. Further on is **St Joseph**, which was once the seat of government, as San José de Oruña. Here you can find the imposing Jinnah Memorial Mosque. North of St Joseph is the Maracas Valley (not directly linked with Maracas Bay, although there is a footpath from here to the bay), which has a 300 ft waterfall about two miles from the road.

Further east, high on a hill, is **Mount St Benedict** monastery, reached through St Johns Rd in St Augustine. Although the monastery was founded by a Belgian, the first Benedictine monks came from Bahia, Brazil, in 1912. It started with a tapia hut but construction of the main building on Mt Tabor began in 1918. The monastery has a retreat, lots of educational facilities, a drug rehabilitation centre, a farm and a guest house and is popular with birdwatchers and walkers. There are marvellous views over the Caroni Plain to the sea. A priority maxi taxi from Port of Spain to St Augustine to Tunapuna takes 20 minutes, TT$3, then a route taxi up St John's road and then St Michael's Road will take you close to the monastery, but unless you pay to go off route it is still a stiff walk uphill. Otherwise take a private taxi all the way. From Caura Road, a little further east, a route taxi will take you up the valley of the Caura River, where the pools are popular spots for weekend picnics (river limes).

This is the oldest Benedictine complex in the Caribbean

A little further along the Eastern Main Rd at Arouca, the Golden Grove Rd branches south to Piarco international airport. If you turn north at this point a road winds 10 km up into the forested mountains to the **Lopinot Complex**, an estate built by the Comte de Lopinot (see page 963) at the turn of the 19th century. Originally called La Reconnaissance, it is now a popular picnic spot and destination for school trips; there is a small museum. There is a bar across the road, open 'anyday, anytime'.

High on a ridge in the Maracas Valley are the only known Amerindian petroglyphs (rock drawings) in Trinidad, known as the **Caurita** drawings. They are probably Arawak and show a series of faces with curving lines indicating limbs. To get there it is a stiff climb of one to 1½ hrs in the valley, with access from the main cross roads between San Juan and Tunapuna.

Arima, is 25 km east of Port of Spain, reached by bus or route taxi. The landmark at the centre is the Dial, an old public clock. In 2001 it was being

Arima
Population: 26,000

repaired after an argument with a heavy truck, but should be replaced soon. A few miles west of Arima is a small but interesting Amerindian museum at the Cleaver Woods Recreation Centre, housed in a reproduction Amerindian long house, entrance free but donations welcome. In Arima there is a group of people who regard themselves as descendants of the original Amerindians of the area, although there are none left of pure blood. They have a figure head Carib queen and call themselves the **Santa Rosa Carib Community**. West of the church in the centre of town is the Santa Rosa Carib Community Crafts Centre selling traditional crafts: cassava squeezers, serving trays, carvings etc.

North of Arima

About 8 miles north of Arima, off the Blanchisseuse Rd, you can get (by car or taxi from Arima, US$7, the driver should wait for you, or a warm 2½ hour walk up hill through lovely forests) to the **Asa Wright Nature Centre**, an old plantation house overlooking a wooded valley and a must for bird-lovers. The Nature Centre now owns 700 acres of forest (not all of which are at the centre) and the annual Christmas bird count usually numbers 161-186 (1990-94) species. There is a beautiful man-made pool where you can swim, a network of trails and guided tours. Sit on the verandah and watch the hummingbirds. Take binoculars. The rangers are very knowledgeable and can tell you about the plants and insects (easier to see) as well as the birds. The rare oil-birds in Dunstan Cave (also called Diablotin Cave) can only be seen if you stay more than three nights; their numbers had dwindled but 138 were counted on 1994 bird count day. Field trips for guests are also organized to the Caroni Swamp, Nariva Swamp, Aripo Savannah, Arena Forest and Blanchisseuse, while turtle watching tours are also offered to the east and west coasts during leatherback nesting season March-September. ■ *The centre is open daily 0900-1700. US$10 entrance and tour, plus US$9 or TT$50 for a good buffet lunch, or you can just have sandwiches, see below for accommodation. Give 48 hrs notice of your visit.*

Do not enter the caves without a flashlight, rope and other equipment. A knowledgeable guide is recommended

This road carries on to Blanchisseuse. A 9-mile (14 km) walk from the road are the **Aripo Caves** (the longest system in Trinidad) with spectacular stalagmites and stalactites (in the wet season, June to December, a river runs through the caves). Oilbirds can be seen at the entrance. Only fully equipped spelunkers should venture beyond the entrance. To get there, turn at Aripo Rd off the Eastern Main Rd, turn right at the four-mile post, over the bridge into Aripo village. Keep left, continuing uphill to a wide bend to the left where you may park off the road and begin the walk uphill. After a couple of minutes turn left at the small house. After a further 10 minutes take the trail to the right of the junction and to the left at the next junction, continuing uphill along the river. At a shelf of rock there is a well cleared trail away from the river. Keep to this trail heading north until the top of the hill. Go downhill five minutes to the stream which leads into the cave.

This town was named after the washerwomen who did their laundry in the Marianne River

Blanchisseuse has a population of about 3,000 and is divided between the Upper Village and Lower Village, with the Arima road being the dividing line. There is a post office, health centre, RC Church, government offices and police station in Lower Village, while Upper Village has the school, recreation field and several wood and leather artisans. All this part of the coast is very beautiful with the forest coming down to the sea. You can hike east all along the coast from here to Matelot and on to Grand Riviere, starting at the 100-year-old Silver Bridge just outside the village. It can be done in a day, or two if overnighting in Paria and a guide is useful, ask Fred (at *Laguna Mar*) or Barbara Zollna (at *Zollna House*) to arrange it.

From Arima you can drive, taxi or hitchhike, to Brasso Seco and Paria. From here the trail runs to **Paria Bay**, which is possibly the best beach on the island, about 8 miles/13 km, ask directions, or see the Tourism and Industrial Development Co (TIDCO) *Sites (trail guide)* book for the route. There is a primitive shelter on the beach but no other facilities so take provisions with you. At the beach, turn right to get to the bridge over the Paria River, from where it is a five-minute walk inland to the spectacular Paria waterfall. Another path from the beach leads west to Blanchisseuse (7 miles/11 km), where the track forks.

The northeast coast is one of the most remote and unspoiled parts of the island, partly because the tarmac road does not extend along the whole of the north coast from Blanchisseuse. Grand Riviere lies in the middle of this area. It has a long and lovely beach, with accommodation and eco-tourism. Guest houses can organize tours into the forest and along the path to Blanchisseuse, and in season you can watch the protected turtles laying their eggs in the sand. **Northeast coast**

Grande Riviere is easy to reach by private car but not easy by public transport. From Port of Spain take a bus (faster than a maxi) to Arima, TT$4. From Arima to Sangre Grande there are buses and maxis (ask around) but a route taxi may be easiest; turn left just past Scotia Bank and the third lot of route taxis is for Sangre Grande. At Sangre Grande buses, maxis and route taxis all stop in the same place. It is relatively easy to get a maxi to Toco and possibly on to Sans Souci, but this is still a 10-km walk (very pleasant, no traffic) through the woods to Grande Riviere. There are buses in the morning from Grande Riviere to Sangre Grande at 0600 and 1000, returning at about 1600, and there will be maxis and route taxis at these times for people going shopping. As a last resort a route taxi in Sangre Grande would very soon become a private taxi. Whichever way you go, its worth it.

If you are driving yourself, from Arima the road runs either to Toco at Trinidad's northeast tip (which is well worth a visit with a few small beaches nearby for bathing) or, branching off at Valencia, to the east coast. Left fork at Valencia, then left again at Honey Corner (bottles of locally made honey on sale), through small villages, woods and after Salybia, beaches a short distance off the road to the right. The **Salybia Waterfall** is is close to the 21-km post, cross the bridge and turn left immediately after the old 14¼-mile post into the Salibea/Matura Trace. Follow a 20-minute, rather rough drive and park in front of two houses. Walk 15 minutes along the trail, turn left at the junction, continue about 10 minutes to a second junction where the path narrows on the right going slightly uphill into Mora Forest. Keep on the trail, crossing first a small stream and then a larger river. Ten minutes later at another junction you may bear right over a small hill or walk upstream. Either will get you to Salibea Waterfall and pool in 10 minutes. The pool is 6m deep and recommended for good swimmers. There is a picnic area.

At **Galera Point**, reached off the road which goes to Toco, over a rickety wooden bridge, there is a small, pretty lighthouse. If you arrive before 1530 it is often open and you can climb to the top for a breathtaking view from the ramp. You can continue by car (quite a long drive) to **Grande Riviere** and the *Mount Plaisir Estate* and *Grand Almandier* hotels on a wide, sandy beach. There is a wide river, also good for bathing and hiking trails in the hills behind. Staff at the hotels are very knowledgeable about the area and can help you arrange tours along the coast or hiking and camping in the forest.

Driving south from Port of Spain along the highway (turn right at the Grand Bazaar shopping mall) or the old Southern Main Road (turn right opposite the big *KFC/Pizza Hut*) you see sugar, citrus and rice fields, and maybe a few buffalypso (buffaloes which have been selectively bred for meat), Hindu temples and mosques. There are boat trips to the **Caroni Bird Sanctuary** (signposted from the Highway), the home of scarlet ibis, whose numbers are dwindling as the swamp in which they live is encroached upon. The boats leave around 1600 from near the Visitor's Centre in order to see the ibis returning to their roost at sunset. It is a spectacular sight and you will also see egrets, herons and plovers. ■ *Bus or route taxi from Port of Spain or San Fernando to Bamboo Grove Settlement no 1, on the Uriah Butler Highway, from where the boats leave, TT$2.50 or TT$5 respectively. Maxi taxi (green bands) from Independence Square. Ask to be dropped off at the Caroni Bird Sanctuary. There are two boat operators in the swamp:* Moodoo Tours *and* Winston Nanan *(T6451305), US$10, group rates available. Nanan rarely guides now and not all his boatmen are informative; enquire at the Asa Wright Centre for more detailed tours. Take mosquito repellent and if possible a cold bag with drinks, although Nanan sells drinks on board, repellent is essential when you get off the boat at the end of your trip.* **South of Port of Spain**

On the left before you get to Chaguanas, a large blue statue of the Hindu God, Lord Shiva and a large white statue of Viveka Nanda, a Hindu philospher, mark the site of the annual Divali Nagar exhibition in October/November. **Chaguanas** is a busy place, not an architectural must, but full of bargains for the shopper. At the centre is the imaginatively named junction: Busy Corner. The Lion House (leaving the town centre on the main road to the east, close to the police station) is the original for VS Naipaul's *A House for Mr Biswas*. Continuing south on the Southern Main Road parallel to the Highway, **Carlsen Field** has several small potteries, using open wood-fired kilns. Most of the pots are a bit unwieldy, but wind chimes etc are easily portable, as are the tiny lamps, or *deyas*, which are made for Divali. Take the turning right for **Brechin Castle** sugar factory, quite a landmark, although not open to the public. Turn off the Main Road at **Chase Village**, and 5 km to the west is **Waterloo**, where a small Hindu temple has been built in the sea. It is reached by a short causeway and it is the successor of a structure built by Siewdass Sadhu, a sugar worker who built on a site in the shallow waters of the Gulf of Paria when he was unable to find a place to build on land. Continuing south on the Southern Main Road is the **Point Lisas** industrial estate.

Alternatively, turning left off the Highway at **Freeport,** or points south, takes you into the Central Range through sugar and citrus fields, then forests, with cocoa trees. There are cocoa houses with a sliding roof so that the beans can dry in the sun but go under cover when it rains. Pretty little villages with wooden houses and well kept gardens overflow with hibiscus and bougainvillea. The roads are narrow and winding, so unless you are a map reading wizard, you are bound to get lost. At **Chickland Village** near Freeport is the **Ajoupa Pottery**, T6730604 (see Shopping, page 949), with a wooden 19th century estate house, well worth a visit. The turning to Gran Couva continues to the **La Vega** garden centre, a pleasant place to stroll, with a small lake, birds and flowers.

San Fernando
Population: 60,000

San Fernando on the southwest coast is a busy, hot city, as yet not spoilt by tourism but spoilt by just about everything else. A highway connects Port of Spain with San Fernando, making it a 30-minute drive (90 minutes in the afternoon rush hour, one hour by taxi at most other times). The waterfront area is a mess in spite of continual talk of restoration. However, Harris Promenade is pleasant; the city's answer to the Brian Lara Promenade in Port of Spain. City Hall, the Our Lady of Perpetual Help church and the old railway engine are worth a look. Library Corner has the old Carnegie public library and is the main centre for maxis and route taxis. Coffee Street is also lively. Above the city is San Fernando Hill, oddly shaped as a result of quarrying and easily picked out from Northern Range viewpoints or from Chaguaramas. Recently landscaped, you can either walk or drive to the top for a spectacular view.

North of San Fernando are the principal industrial area of **Point Lisas** and the **Pointe-a-Pierre** oil refinery. Within the oil refinery is the 26-hectare **Wild Fowl Trust**, a conservation area with two lakes and breeding grounds for many endangered species. Many birds bred in captivity are later released into the wild. ■ *1000-1700, Sat 1200-1600, Sun 1030-1800, T6375145, Ms Molly Gaskin or Mrs K Shepard on T6624040, call 48 hrs in advance to get permission to enter the compound (there are many entrances, it can be confusing).*

The lake has been described by disappointed tourists, as looking like a parking lot, although others have pointed out that it is parking lots that look like the Pitch Lake

A famous phenomenon to visit on the southwest coast just after La Brea is **Pitch Lake**, about 47 ha of smooth surface of black tar; it is 41 m deep. If care is taken it is possible to walk on it, watching out for air holes bubbling up from the pressure under the ooze. In the wet season, however, most of the area is covered with shallow fresh water. The legend is that long ago the gods interred an entire tribe of Chaima Indians for daring to eat sacred hummingbirds containing the souls of their ancestors. In the place where the entire village sank into the ground there erupted a sluggish flow of black pitch gradually becoming an ever-refilling large pool. The lake can be reached by taking a bus from Port of Spain to San Fernando (US$1 by air-conditioned express, by route taxi it costs US$1.75) and then route taxi from there to La

Brea (US$0.75). Insist on a professional guide, who should report to the security guard before taking you around, as locals who pose as guides harass tourists for large tips. Agree on a price in advance as there are no fixed rates. Sometimes there are crowds of guides who are difficult to avoid, but on the other hand it is difficult to understand the lake without explanation. Pompei, trained by the Tourist Board, is recommended, he is tall and stout.

Beyond La Brea the road continues to **Point Fortin**, a small but busy town with a new Liquefied Natural Gas plant and a small beach. The road carries on down the southwest peninsula, deteriorating as it goes, through **Cedros** (fishing village, beach) to **Icacos**, from where the mangroves of the Orinoco delta are clearly visible a few miles across the water. From the Point Fortin-Icacos road there are side roads leading to beaches such as Erin or Columbus Bay.

East of San Fernando

East of San Fernando the main road runs through rolling hills with sugar cane fields, past the Usine Ste Madeleine sugar mill to **Princes Town**, then continues to Rio Claro and Mayaro on the east coast. It runs parallel to the south coast, most of which is fairly inaccessible. Near Princes Town is the **Devil's Woodyard**, one of 18 mud volcanoes on Trinidad. This one is considered a holy site by some Hindus (it is also a natural landmark). It last erupted in 1852 and the bubbling mud is cool.

The south coast

From St Julien, east of Princes Town, a road leads 30km (slow driving) to the fishing village of **Moruga**. Every year around the middle of July they have an unusual celebration of Columbus' 1498 landing on the beach. Fishing boats are decked out as caravels, complete with the red Maltese cross. Columbus, a priest and soldiers are met by Amerindians (local boys, mostly of East Indian and African extraction); after the meeting everyone retires to the church compound where the revelry continues late into the night.

The **Karamat Mud Volcano**, Moruga, erupted in 1997. Thick mud spurted 50 m high, killing one man, burying animals alive and engulfing houses, leaving 100 homeless. Seek local advice before visiting. From Penal Rock Rd proceed west to the 8-mile post. On the right head down Haggard Trace driving south until the Moruga West oil field gate. Enter on the road and continue left for 1 mile. Pass a series of tank batteries, No 7, on the left, and continue to an oil pump on the right. Take the side road for 400 yds. Park near the oil pump at a well-head. Do not take the side track into the forest road. Continue up hill. There is another mud volcano at **Piparo**, which erupted suddenly in 1994, destroying a section of the village and cutting off the approach by road from the northeast. What remains is a big expanse of dry mud. Nearby is a large and tasteless house, with adjoining Hindu temple. Now a drug rehabilitation centre, it was once the home of the notorious drug dealer and murderer, Dole Chadee, who was hanged in 1999 along with his associates. The original eruption of the volcano was seen by some villagers as divine retribution for Chadee's activities.

It is quite difficult to get beyond Arima and San Fernando by bus, but there are route taxis, privately-operated maxi taxis, or you can hire a car. A full-day circuit of the island can be driven from Port of Spain south to San Fernando, east to Mayaro then north to Sangre Grande and Arima. An alternative route back from Mayaro runs through Biche and the eastern fringe of the Central Range to Sangre Grande. This road is very beautiful and slow.

Essentials

Sleeping
VAT of 15% will be added to your bill

If you intend to stay in Trinidad for carnival you must book a hotel well in advance. Most hotels raise their prices steeply and make you stay for the full period. Some are booked a year ahead. If arriving without accommodation arranged at Carnival time, the tourist office at the airport may help to find you a room in a hotel or with a local family, though this like hotels will be expensive. However, there are cancellations and hotels which have not sold their full package may make rooms available at the last minute. You will probably find something, but not necessarily of the price or quality you would prefer. For most of the year, hotels in Port of Spain cater almost exclusively for business visitors and conferences and bookings can be hard to find if you coincide with a big meeting.

Port of Spain area LL-L *Hilton*, on a rise at the corner of Lady Young and St Ann's Rds, Northeast Queen's Park Savannah, T6243211, F6244485, hiltonpos@wow.net Public areas and pool deck are on top and 394 rooms and 25 suites on lower levels, facilities for the disabled, view and breeze from pool level excellent, all facilities, restaurants, bars, eating by the pool is not expensive, non-residents can eat/swim there, tennis, badminton, gym, conference centre, ballroom, executive suite, frequent entertainment. **LL-B** *Cascadia*, 67 Ariapita Rd, St Ann's, T6240940, F6278046, up in the hills. 68 rooms, children under 12 free, rooms and suites vary, nice pool, chutes and waterslide (TT$25 for non-guests to use pool), sports and conference facilities, *Coconuts Club* disco, restaurant, bar, busy at weekends. **L** *Crowne Plaza*, Wrightson Rd, T6253366, F6254166, in the business centre. Recently renovated (was *Holiday Inn*), all facilities very nice, friendly, small pool. **AL-A** *Kapok*, 16-18 Cotton Hill, St Clair, Northwest Queen's Park Savannah, T6226441, F6229677, stay@kapok.co.tt 95 rooms, friendly, comfortable, light, big windows, some studios with kitchenette, try to get room on upper floors for good view and away from traffic noise, excellent *Tiki Village* restaurant with Chinese and Polynesian cuisine, small pool, shopping arcade. Recommended. **AL-B** *Normandie*, off St Ann's Rd, at the end of Nook Av (No 10), T6241181, F6240108, normandie@wow.net 53 standard, superior and loft rooms, a/c, reduced rates for businessmen, swimming pool, in a complex with craft and fashion shops, art gallery and restaurants, comfortable, nice furnishings, wooden floors, good restaurant, outdoor theatre 'Under the Trees',and *Breakfast Shed* for lunch. Recommended.

Below US$20 a **Central Port of Spain C** *Par-May-La's Inn*, 53 Picton St, T6282008, T/F6284707,
night are few & far parmaylas@trinidad.net Specially convenient for carnival and cricket, double or triple
between in the rooms with bathroom, a/c, TV, phone, some cheap singles, facilities for the disabled, family
capital & some are run by Bob and Pamela Gopee, friendly, helpful, parking, local cuisine with roti, evening
not recommended meals on request, credit cards accepted. Nearby the same family has 15 apartments,
by TIDCO **C** *Sun Deck Suites*, 42-44 Picton Street, T6229560. A/c, with cooking facilities, sleep 2/3.
D-E *Copper Kettle Hotel*, 66-68 Edward St, T6254381. Central, good value, clean, safe, hot and dingy rooms with shower, price depends on whether you have a/c, friendly and helpful staff, good restaurant. **E** *The Abercromby Inn*, 101 Abercromby St, T6235259, F6276658, aberinn@carib-link.net 17 rooms, a/c, TV, phone, laundry facilities, some large and some very small economy rooms, clean, no food, have to order from outside, 5 mins' walk to Queen's Park Savannah, karaoke lounge. **E** *Mardi Gras Guest House*, 134A Frederick St, T6272319. Price rises in carnival week, with private bath, dining room, bar. **E** *Pearl's Guest House*, 3-4 Victoria Square East, T6252158. Access to kitchen, can prepare own meals, laundry room, very friendly, family home from home, excellent location for Carnival. **F** *Royal Guest House*, 109 Charlotte St, T6231042, in front of gas station. Coffee shop next door owned by same family, shared bathroom, good beds, friendly, safe.

Woodbrook   C-D *Kitty Peters*, 26 Warren St, breakfast extra, immaculately clean, hot water showers, fans, quiet area, friendly. **D** *ML's Gingerbread House*, 25 Stone Street, T6253663, F6224415, mark@wow.net Run by Mona Lyndersay, Victorian house with turrets, fretwork and jalousies, antique furnishings, fruit and flower garden, featured on 1994 postage stamp, 3 double rooms with bathrooms, CP, other meals on request, varied cuisine, excursions arranged. **D** *La Calypso Guest House*, 46 French St, T6224077, F6286895. Ask for room at back or high up for less noise, clean, safe, efficient, kitchen, helpful, jacuzzi, car hire available, breakfast US$3, pool at their other guest house. **E** *Schultzi's Guest House and Pub*, 35 Fitt St, T/F6227521. CP, kitchen, hot shower, mixed reports, helpful owner, Lisa Nichol-Yeates, transport available to airport or dock.

St James   C *Trini House*, 5A Lucknow St, T/F6287550. 3 rooms, CP, English, German, Italian and French spoken by owner Michael Figuera, pan tuition.

St Ann's   C *Alicia's Guest House*, 7 Coblentz Gardens, T6232802, F6238560. 17 rooms, all different, some dark, some cheap, all a/c, fan, TV, phone, fridge, family rooms, suites, small pool, jacuzzi, exercise machine, meals available, excursions organized.

Cascade   C *Pelican Inn*, 2-4 Coblentz Av, T/F6276271. 14 rooms, squash court, pub, very lively with music on Wed, Fri, Sun, great entertainment but not good for an early night. **E** *Scott's Guest House*, 5 Pomme Rose Av, Cascade, T6244105. Friendly, safe area, can be booked from airport.

Maraval   The best guest houses are in this area, only 10 mins by maxi taxi from the Savannah.   **B-C** *Zollna House*, 12 Ramlogan Terrace, La Seiva, Maraval, T6283731, F6283737. Owned by Gottfried (Fred) and Barbara Zollna, small guest house, food varied with local flavour, special diets catered for, breakfast and dinner US$6 and US$12 per person respectively, Barbara is very knowledgeable about Trinidad and knows all about B&B places. **C** *Carnetta's House*, 28 Scotland Terrace, Andalusia, Maraval, just off Saddle Rd, T6282732, F6287717, carnetta@trinidad.net. Children under 12 free, prices double during carnival, a/c, all rooms different sizes, some fridges, some kitchenettes, TV, phone, ironing board, carpets, family room, laundry, nice gardens, grow some produce, meals on request, parking, family atmosphere, videos for TV, lots of repeat business, maxi taxi will drop you at gate for extra US$0.50, run by Carnetta and Winston Borrell, the same couple own **C** *Carnetta's Inn*, 99 Saddle Rd, Maraval, T6225165/2884. 14 rooms in 2 adjacent properties, all rooms with mini-fridge, most with kitchenette, single, double, triple and connecting rooms, TV, a/c, phone, internet access, *Bamboo Terrace* restaurant serves local cooking, Shipwreck Bar for special cocktails. **C** *Monique's Guest House*, 114-116 Saddle Rd, Maraval, T6283334, F6223232, Moniques@carib-link.net, on way to golf course and north coast beaches. Easy access from city, maxi taxi US$0.50, 10 rooms in main house, 10 more over the hill, large rooms, different sizes sleep 4/5, a/c, TV, phone, some kitchenettes, good food in restaurant, clean, attractive, facilities for the disabled, Monica and Michael Charbonné are helpful and hospitable. **C** *Tropical Hotel*, 6 Rookery Nook Rd, Maraval, T6225815, F6224249. A/c, pool, maid service, bar and restaurant attached, short walk from the Savannah, friendly, helpful.

Chaguaramas   AL *Crew's Inn*, T6444384, www.crewsinnltd.com   46 rooms, clean and well run, pool, gym, shops, bank and *Lighthouse* restaurant on same marina site. **C** *The Bight*, Lot 5, Western Main Rd, T6344389, F6344387. 10 rooms, sports bar, marina. **C-D** *The Cove*, T6344319. Rather run down, pool, seaside bathing in dirty water, maid and laundry, kitchenette, one 3-bedroom apartment **B**, breakfast US$6, lunch/dinner US$10.

Near the airport   A *Bel Air International*, Piarco, by the airport, close to old terminal, T6644771/3, F add ext 15, belair@tstt.net.tt Small room, overpriced, typical airport hotel, swimming pool, good bar and restaurant (expensive breakfast) but noise from planes. **B** *Pax Guesthouse*, Mt St Benedict, Tunapuna, T/F6624084, stay@paxguesthouse.com   Built 1932, original furniture made by monks, 18 rooms, popular with birdwatchers, 147 species of

Trinidad & Tobago

bird on estate, donkey trails into forest, rooms have high ceilings, no a/c necessary, one family room, most share showers, simple but wholesome food, lovely view of central Trinidad as well as of occasional monk. **B** *LeSportel Inn and Nature Tours*, Centre of Excellence, Macoya Rd, Tunapuna, T6633902-4. Part of massive football complex sponsored by FIFA, 34 a/c rooms, pool, transport into Port of Spain nearby. **C** *Sadila House*, run by Savitri and Dinesh Bhola, Waterpipe Rd, Five Rivers, Arouca, T6403659, F6401376, close to airport. 3 rooms, CP, credit cards accepted, weekly and group rates available, a/c, TV. **C-D** *Valsayn Villa*, 34 Gilwell Rd, Valsayn North, T/F6451193. Very large, modern, private house with beautifully furnished rooms and lovely garden, or fully furnished villas **B** and up, in one of the safest residential areas, close to university, 15 mins from airport, 20 mins by bus from down town Port of Spain, excellent home-cooked Indian meals available. **D** *Airport View Guesthouse*, St Helena Junction, Piarco airport 1.5 km, T6643186. Convenient, a/c, hot water, double rooms have 2 double beds, breakfast US$5, restaurant nearby serving American style food. **D-E** *The Caribbean Lodge*, 32 St Augustine Circular Rd, Tunapuna, T6452937, (15-30 mins to Port of Spain by bus on the priority route). Shared or private shower, a/c, single rooms available, comfortable, laundry facilities, breakfast room.

Northern Range **LL-L** *Asa Wright Nature Centre*, 7½ mile mark, Blanchisseuse Rd, Arima, PO Box 4710, Arima, T6674655, F6670493. Price includes all meals, rum punch, tax and service, 2 main house rooms colonial style, high ceilings, wooden furniture and floors, fan, bathroom, 24 standard rooms and bungalow in gardens, all designed to be private and secluded, facilities for the disabled, verandahs for birdwatching, 80% of guests in high season are birdwatching groups. **E** *Alta Vista*, up the road from *Asa Wright*, no phone on premises but T6298030, F6293262 for reservations. 6 self-contained wooden cabins, meals with advance notice, attractive swimming pool made by damming a stream, verandah overlooking forest, nice waterfall along a trail, TT$10.

Arima **C** *Chateau Guillaumme*, 3 Rawle Circular, T6676670, joanwilliam@yahoo.com Run by Matthew and Joan William, 2 double and 2 triple rooms, bathroom, very clean, lower price for long stay, airport transfers, very helpful.

It can be hard to get a hotel room on the north coast in the low season when many places shut; self-catering may be difficult with few shops, no bank, no car rental

North coast Maracas **L-AL** *Maracas Bay Hotel*, T6691914, F6691643, west of beach. Includes breakfast and dinner, 36 a/c rooms with shower, each with porch overlooking bay, clean but rather characterless and spartan, nature trails, watersports.

Blanchisseuse **B-C** *Laguna Mar Nature Lodge*, at milepost 65½ just before suspension bridge over Marianne River. *Cocos Hut* restaurant attached, owned by Fred Zollna, close to beach and lagoon, see Beaches and watersports, 10 rooms with 2 double beds, bathroom, jogging trail, write c/o Zollna House, 12 Ramlogan Terrace, La Seiva, Maraval, or T6283731, F6283737. **C** *Second Spring*, 13 Damier Village, T6643909, F6234328. Cottage or 3 studios including breakfast and service, at milepost 67¾, rustic, comfortable, in gardens on clifftop with wooden walkway, spectacular views of coast, beaches in walking distance, restaurant 5 mins' walk, owned by Ginette Holder who is friendly and hospitable, excellent value. **C** *Surf's Country Inn*, Lower Village, T6692475. Good restaurant on hill above coast road, 3 rooms, CP, owners plan 6 cabanas to sleep 4, nice furnishings, picturesque, small beach below. **C** *The Almond Brook*, Upper Village, Paria Main Rd, Blanchisseuse, T6420476. 2-bedroomed cottage on beach and 'couples retreat' up the hill, both same price but latter CP. **Grand Riviere B** *Mount Plaisir Estate Hotel & Spa*, Hosang St, on bay of same name at eastern end of north coast, T6708381, F6804553, www.mtplaisir.com 10 beachfront rooms right by where the leatherback turtles nest, breakfast, nature trails, birdwatching, with excursions organized for really keen twitchers, overnight camping tours with local guide, restaurant, long drive through Toco. Recommended. **B** *Le Grand Almandier*, 2 Hosang St, T/F6701013, www.legrandalmandier.com Also on the beach, cheaper, but no single rates, good standard of accommodation, CP, excellent food, cater to individual tastes including vegetarian, ask for the corn soup, meal plans available, a few suites sleep 4-5, knowledgeable and accessible proprietor.

Balandra Bay At milepost 23 on the Toco Main Rd, north of Balandra Bay is Mr Hugh Lee Pow's **E** *Green Acres Guest House*, on a farm backed by the ocean. 3 good meals a day included, very kind and restful. *Manzanilla Calypso Inn*, ¼ mile off main road where road joins beach, on Calypso Rd at south end of Manzanilla, T6685113, T6685116. The only hotel, run by Meena Singh and her daughter Arisa, 10 motel-style rooms, large dining room overlooking scenic part of the beach, meals on request, nice place.

Mayaro on the southeast coast has beach houses to rent but check their condition, some are unacceptable. **C** *Azee's*, at 3½ mile mark Guayaguayare Rd, Grand Lagoon, Mayaro, T6309140, F6304619. 5 rooms, restaurant, not quite respectable. **C-E** *Harry's*, Grand Lagoon, south end of Mayaro. Right on beach (plastic litter), nice grounds, rather peculiar building, apartments range in size from tiny room with double bunk bed, kitchenette, bathroom, a/c, TV, to larger units, some with verandahs, watch out for TT$50 service charge. **C** *Mrs Paria's*, guest house, just beyond the BP/Amoco compound. Self-contained room, TV, breakfast, beautiful modern home.

San Fernando There is not a lot of choice, **B** *Royal Hotel*, 46-54 Royal Rd, T6524881, F6523924, royal@tstt.net.tt A/c, kitchenette, lovely hilltop garden. **AL-B** *Tradewinds*, 38 London St, St Joseph Village, San Fernando, T6529463, F6538733. 13 rooms, kitchenette, bar, restaurant. **B-C** *TJ's By The Sea*, South Trunk Rd, La Romaine, T6579278, tjsea@tstt.net.tt. Restaurant and pool, south of the city on road to La Brea, by the sea is really just the muddy Gulf of Paria. **D** *Mikanne Hotel and Restaurant*, 15 Railway Av, Plaisance Village, Pointe-a-Pierre, T/F6592584. 13 rooms, a/c, private bath, meal plans, TV on request, pleasant, convenient for oil refinery and Wild Fowl Trust.

Port of Spain *Solimar*, 6 Nook Av, close to the *Normandie*, T6246267. International, prices US$25-40, very good service, outdoor dining, excellent food, reservations advisable and essential at weekends. *Veni Mangé*, 67A Ariapita Av, T6244597. Small, friendly, good food, imaginative menu includes vegetarian dishes, around US$20. Open Mon-Fri 1130-1430, dinner Wed only 1930-2230. *Il Colosseo*, 47 Ariapita Av, T6233654. Good Italian food. *Tamnak Thai*, 13 Queens Park East, T6250647. Excellent Thai restaurant, beautiful setting, with chefs imported from Bangkok. In same building is *Apsara*, very good food, Indian rather than Indo-Trini, prices US$25-40. *Roxan's*, Corner Ariapita Av and O'Connor St, Woodbrook, T6224425. A new Arabic restaurant, very good, especially for lunch. *Little Lisbon*, Long Circular Rd. Brought Portuguese food to Trinidad. *Woodford Café*, 62 Tragarete Rd. Open 1100-2200, Mon-Sat, Creole fare, around US$20 for a meal, 16222233. *Ali Baba*, T6225557, on first floor level in Royal Palm Plaza shopping mall on Saddle Rd, Maraval. Open-air dining with a roof, Arabic and other dishes, US$10 and upwards, excellent service, popular, run by a Lebanese, Joe. *Gourmet Club*, upstairs at Ellerslie Plaza, Maraval, T6285113. Italian, expensive but good, prices US$25-40, nice decor, open 1100-2300 weekdays, Sat 1800-2300. *Chutney Rose*, Fitt St and Ariapita Av, T6288541. Good, authentic Indian food, meals US$25-40. Nearby is *Flavours on the Avenue*, Cornelio St and Ariapita Av, T6288687. Creative international menu, good. *Verandah*, 10 Rust St, St Clair, T6226287. Caribbean ingredients but not just the standard dishes, Mon-Fri lunch, Thu and Sat dinner. *Café Gordon*, 39A Gordon St, T6275514. Breakfast 0730-1100, lunch 1100-1500, small, pleasant, Indian-owned, different lunch menu every day with choice of 2 dishes,meals around US$10. *Tasca Latina*, 16 Phillips St, T6253497. Good Venezuelan style food, meals around US$10 sometimes Latin music. *Uptop Bar and Restaurant*, 46 Ariapita Av, T6285300. Breezy rooftop setting in old cocoa house, good food, around US$10.

Eating

Plenty of choice west of city centre: Ariapita Av for smarter restaurants, Cipriani Blvd for mid-price and Maraval Rd for cheap and cheerful

Chinese If you've a yen for the best pepper shrimps in the Caribbean, the Chinese restaurants in Trinidad are generally good, with chefs often direct from China. However, the standard can drop abruptly when the chef gets his US visa. There are plenty, the menus are fairly 'authentic', even in some cheap places, although others can be greasy and nasty. Some of the good ones are: *Tiki Village*, see above, *Kapok*. *Kam Wah*, 74-76 Maraval Rd. Developing a reputation as not just another Chinese restaurant. *The Swan Chinese Restaurant*, Maraval

Trinidad & Tobago

Rd. Unprepossessing interior but very good food, around US$10. *Hong Kong City Restaurant*, 86A Tragarete Rd, is the place, good food around US$10 but rather snooty service. *Jenny's* on the Boulevard, 6 Cipriani Blvd. Wide variety of mainly Chinese dishes in elaborate setting, US$25-40, lively bar downstairs also Chinese, around US$10. *Davises*, 100 Oxford St, T6250144. Specializes in 'new island cuisine', combining classical gourmet cooking with fresh local ingredients.. *De Backyard*, 84 Picton St. Local dishes, also Chinese, US$10.

Fast food outlets where you can get a meal for around US$5: *Joe's Pizza*, St James. Good, also other Italian dishes. *Pizza Burger Boys*, Frederick St, and Ellerslie Plaza, Boissiere Village, Maraval (for takeaway T6282697, best of its type, will deliver to boatyards and marinas). The first *Pizza Hut* opened in Curepe but the largest one in the world is *Pizza Hut Roxy*, which used to be a cinema, Tragarete Rd roundabout. *Royal Castle*, 49 Frederick St and other locations throughout Trinidad. Chicken and chips with a local flavour, also does fish and veggie burgers.

All along Western Main Rd in St James there are lots of cafés, snack bars and restaurants, all reasonably priced around US$5-10, lots of choice. The *Pelican Inn*, Coblenz Av, Cascade. Serves food, but is mainly a pub, hugely popular (late arrivals at the weekend have to park 600m away). At the cruise ship harbour, *Coconut Village*, good food, cheap. *Breakfast Shed*, opposite *Crowne Plaza*, a big hall with several kitchens where locals eat, US$3.50 for very substantial lunch with juice. The best places for *roti* are *Patraj* at 159 Tragarete Rd, Port of Spain (if you are watching cricket at the Oval come here and queue for food rather than buying anything other than nuts inside the ground), *Hot Shoppe*, in Maraval Rd and Mucurapo Rd, which are of a slightly heavier texture, *Dawn's*, at Crystal Stream in Petit Valley, and the lady in the street opposite *Smokey and Bunty* in St James. Next to the Maraval Rd branch of *Hot Shoppe*, the jerk chicken/jerk pork places have good, spicey Jamaican-style food. The **Excellent City Mall** upstairs, **Town Centre Mall** and **Voyager Mall** on Frederick St have indoor halls with a varied and good selection of stands selling cheap food of different nationalities during the day, seating in the middle. **People's Mall**, between Frederick and Henry Streets has small booths selling fish broth and similar. *The Bocas*, on Queen St is good for fish dishes. *Willie's Ice Cream*, branches in Arima, Montrose, Mid Centre Mall, Coffee St, Marabella and Tunapuna, and franchises in other places, tropical fruit flavours. If you like good bagels and speciality breads, try *Adam's Bagels*, 15A Saddle Rd, Maraval, or 34 Henry St, Port of Spain, T62-BAGEL. Salads, sandwiches, soup and bagel.

Chaguaramas *Pier One*, T6344472, F6344556. Like country club, restaurant, conference facilities, family club, marina, seafood, live entertainment at weekends, open 1100-2300, popular at weekends, pool, kayaks, dinghies, fishing area. *Anchorage*, Point Gourde Rd, T6344334. For seafood, open 1100-2400 Mon-Sat, dancing, live entertainment some evenings, popular with yachties, meals around US$20. *Pisces*, TTYC. Moderately priced local food and special nights, call for reservations. *Windjammers*, TTYA. Fast food and inexpensive local dishes around US$10 after sailing with TTYA members. *The Bight*, Peake's, bar and restaurant with outdoor dining overlooking the Chaguaramas anchorage. *Sail's*, at Power Boats East. Meals around US$10.

East of Port of Spain *Botticelli*, at the City of Brand Bazaar, Valsayn, T6458733. Italian, pricey at US$25-40, good. *Valpark Chinese Restaurant*, Valpark Shopping Plaza, Churchill Roosevelt Highway, Curepe, T6624520, meals for US$10. Also in the shopping plaza is *Chelsea's Under the Dome*, steak and seafood, around US$20. Going further east there are very few classy places., but plenty of Chinese restaurants. *Chinese Wok*, in Trincity Mall, T6403542, is good and also has branches in Tunapuna, T6625296, Chaguanas, T6656637 and Arima T6672250. Very different and slow paced is *Pax Guesthouse* on Mt St Benedict, above Tunapuna, T6624084. Where tea is a tradition and all the bread, cakes, jam, honey etc are handmade by the monks, wholesome and tasty, lovely views of Trinidad from patio. Also lunches and dinners, book 24 hrs ahead, excellent value at TT$45.

Chaguanas A good Chinese restaurant is *Kam-Po*, 53 Ramsaran Park, T6654558, opposite Centre Pointe Mall. Also has high quality imported US steaks and seafood, meals around US$10. *Buffet King*, Centre Pointe Mall, T6718795. Mid-price, mix of Chinese and non-Chinese dishes, with salad bar and dessert bar. *Bougainvillea*, 85 Rivulet Road, Brechin Castle, Couva, T6364837. Chef claims to specialise in 'American, Italian, Spanish, Creole, Chinese and seafood delights'.

San Fernando Not a lot of choice. For Chinese food try try *Soongs Great Wall*, 97 Circular Rd, T6522583, round the corner from the *Royal Hotel*. Very good reputation, but not as good as it used to be, meals around US$20, the distinctive, Trinidadian version of Chinese food. Also *Canton Palace*, Cross Crossing shopping mall, prices around US$20. *Pagoda*, Independence Av, cheaper at about US$10. *Jenny's Wok*, Cipero Road. Around US$20 for US steak as well as Chinese food. More basic are *Charlie's Black Pudding*, on Ruth Av, and *Ali's Rotis*, on Hubert Rance St, both around US$5.

North coast At Blanchisseuse, *Surf's Country Inn*, North Coast Rd, T6692475. Good value, delicious meals, beautiful setting, changing rooms available. *Cocos Hut*, also on coast road at Mile 65½ by Marianne River. Small, friendly, no menu, but usually a choice of fish or meat dishes, slow service but all food freshly cooked; both these restaurants offer rooms. Don't forget the shark-and-bake at Maracas, see 'Food', page 925.

Bars and clubs Trinidad abounds in evening entertainment. For those wishing to visit the places where the local, rather than tourist population go, anyone in the street will give directions. The atmosphere will be natural and hospitality generous; it will not be luxurious but the local rum is likely to flow. Mon local song and dance at the *Hilton* is less authentic in atmosphere than the steel band concerts on Fri at the same venue. Entrance US$2. Outside the hotels places run late, starting to get lively around 2300-midnight and closing 0400-ish. Fri has a bigger crowd than Sat but no night is completely quiet.

Nightlife
St James is normally livelier at night than Port of Spain

Most of the smarter places are in Chaguaramas. For those not staying at a marina that means car or private taxi. The main places are *Pier One*, *MOBS Two*, *The Anchorage*, and *The Base*, all but the last are partly open air, lively most weekends, sometimes big fetes, live music etc. All inclusives are 'free drinks' once you have paid the cover charge, or else free drinks up to a certain time. Less expensive are the 'cooler fetes', where you take a cooler with ice and your own frinks. Car parking can be a problem, also traffic jams in and out on the road through Carinage. Other hazards include drivers who have been overenthusiastic with the free drinks.

Closer to Port of Spain, at West Mall is *Upper Level*, Wed-Sun, with a good after-work lime early on Fri and Caribbean night on Thu. Unlike Chaguaramas, it is walking distance from the yellow band maxi route going west, so attracts non-car owners. St James is famously the City That Never Sleeps. *Smokey and Bunty* is a lively rum shop, usually open until dawn or after at weekends. Most expats and tourists go at least once. However, it can irritatingly beset by crack addicts, prostitutes etc. *Jazzy's*, just down the road, is lively on Fri and has karaoke some week nights. On Cipriani Blvd, close to the Savnnah, *Jenny's* has a lively downstairs pub-style bar, with snacks, Fri lime starts after work around 1700. Across the road are *Martin's* and *Syps*, not so smart but just as much fun. A block or two away is *Rafters*, 6a Warner St, smart and better bar meals than *Jenny's*. *Mas Camp Pub*, Ariapita Av, Woodbrook. Nightly entertainment including calypso and steel band, best place to see live calypso out of season (cover charge usually US$4). The Silver Stars Steel Orchestra (formed in the 1950s) can occasionally be seen in rehearsal (check beforehand) at the Panyard, 56 Tragarete Rd, Newtown, Woodbrook, Port of Spain. Silver Stars plays at local parties, cruise ships or on the beach, workshops for individuals or groups can be arranged, contact Michael Figuera, T/F6287550. More central, *The Pickle House*, Abercromby St, orange building, different types of music on different nights, New Orleans jazz, rhythm and blues, local music, Latin American and panang in the run up to Christmas. In St Ann's/Cascade, the main spot is *The Pelican* (down hill from *Hilton*), 2-4 Coblentz Av, Cascade, T6247486. Cover charge on Wed, Fri, Sun, when biggest crowd goes and there is often live music. Car parking problems, try the Scouts car park on St Ann's main road if *Pelican* car park is full. *Club Coconuts* in *Cascadia Hotel*, St Ann's, lively and crowded.

Trinidad & Tobago

Different styles of music on different nights, with noticeable effect on ethnicity of patrons attracted, eg more Afro-Trinis on Thu for dub and soca night.

In central Port of Spain clubs and bars tend to me more rough and ready, but can be quite fun. Several lively bars on and close to Brian Lara Promenade, though some are very dirty. *Two Plus*, on Henry St is busy on Fri with Laventille people and opens late. In Barataria, the poshest place is *Club Liquid*, Roundabout Plaza, politically well connected, glitzy, water running down the walls for decorative effect. On the other side of Barataria is *The Lair*, younger crowd and not nearly so posh. In Grand Bazaar is *The Beer Garden*, with open air and indoor sections, very busy. Also *The Parrot*, Grand Bazaar, Uria Butler Highway, Valsayn, older and richer crowd and extremely crowded. Further east in Tunapuna, several small and lively bars, such as *The Sanctuary* and *The Palace*, lively at weekends. All along the Eastern Main Road there are bars and restaurants with a good crowd, especially on Fri, take your pick. The best panyard in the east is *Exodus*, at Tunapuna. The centre of Arima is full of life in the evenings, especially Fri after work. Lots of little bars, cheap Chinese restaurants, some of which open late. *Sylvester's*, on Hollis St is informal, open air, lively on Fri. Also *Hero's Sports Bar*, on Malabar Rd, pool tables etc. In Chaguanas, *The Tunnel*, Ramsaran St, also busy at weekends. South of Chaguanas at Edinburgh and Chase Village are some fairly raunchy strip clubs which are frequently raided by the police. Risky and best avoided. In San Fernando, Coffee St is lively, with plenty of unpretentious bars, etc. The best Panyard pre-Carnival is *Skiffle Bunch*, on Coffee St, or *Vat 19 Fonclaire*, on Dottin St.

For night clubs, *Club Celebs*, Gulf City Mall, La Romaine, T6527641, or *HiRPM*, same mall, T6523760. If you want karaoke, *The Lounge*, Carlton Centre, St James St, T6522749. There are several casinos, some of which run through the night. They are small and seedy by Bahamian or Aruban standards, but you can lose money just as effectively: slot machines, blackjack, roulette etc, with 'free' sandwiches to keep you at it and 'free' drinks if you lose heavily. Best known are *Ma Pau*, in Ariapita Av and *Island Club*, at Grand Bazaar shopping mall. Alternatively you can lose money in smaller amounts in most bars and neighbourhood shops through government-run gambling: Play Whe, which is based on traditional Chinese gambling and the weekly Lotto draw.

Theatres *Queen's Hall*, 1-3 St Ann's Rd; *Little Carib*, White and Roberts Streets; *Central Bank Auditorium*, Eric Williams Plaza, Edward St. In San Fernando, *Naparima Bowl* reopened after a lengthy period of renovation; the folk theatre of the South National Institute of Performing Arts (T6535355). See press for details of performances. See Culture section in Background, page 968.

Cinemas Two cinemas: **Globe** and **Strand**, at Park Plaza on Park St and Tragarete Rd. Another cinema, **De Luxe,** at north end of Frederick St is worth visiting for glorious if run down art deco design. Houses a calypso tent in Carnival season and also (free) embassy-sponsored European film festival in Oct-Nov. Cinemas are very cheap and occasionally show something good. Beer, snacks etc on sale. Audiences are audibly enthusiastic, particularly for sex and violence.

Shopping
Bargains can be found in fabrics, carvings, leather & ceramics

Most shops take US dollars but at a poor exchange rate. The main Port of Spain shopping areas are Frederick St, Queen St, Henry St and Charlotte St (fruit and vegetables), less exciting but pleasanter are Long Circular Mall at the junction of Long Circular Rd and Patna St, St James, West Mall, Cocorite, Port of Spain, Ellerslie Plaza on the way to Maraval, close to Savannah. There are also good but pricier local designers such as Meiling or Richard Young of *The Cloth*. Try shops in *Kapok* and *Normandie* hotels, also *Ilda's* boutique in Long Circular Mall (Italian run). Purchases can be made at in-bond shops in Port of Spain and at the airport. There is a huge selection of duty-free shops, accessible to both arriving and departing passengers, selling everything, including computers; alcohol and cigarettes are generally very good value. *T-Wee* shop is recommended for booze and has the best aged rums, eg Guyanese El Dorado. There is a flower shop at the airport which packs orchids, ginger lilies, anthuriums etc in boxes who they won't get crushed on the flight.

Markets offer wide varieties of fruit. Handicrafts can also be purchased at markets. In Port of Spain there are street vendors on Frederick St, Independence Sq and elsewhere selling hand painted T-shirts etc. The People's Mall between Frederick st and Henry St is a maze of booths selling clothes, shoes, etc along with bars and barbers' shops, lively in the afternoon, especially Fri. Crafts also at East Mall on Charlotte St and at the cruise ship complex. There are several kilns in the Freeport area, turn off the Uriah Butler Highway before the Hindu temple for Chase Village where most of the pottery is unpainted; the potters sell it on to others for decoration and glazing. Good quality local pottery in a variety of designs is available from Ajoupa Pottery, owned by Rory and Bunty O'Connor. You can get it in Port of Spain but a wider selection can be viewed at their kiln at Freeport, central Trinidad; T6225597 at Port of Spain shop at Ellerslie Plaza, or T6730604 at kiln/factory. Batik can be bought at many places including the Ajoupa pottery shop at Ellerslie Plaza. The Central Market is on the Beetham Highway, big, cheap fruit and veg, opens very early. Fresh fish by Western Main Road in Carenage or on the Highway near Valsayn.

For **music**, try *Crosby's Music Centre*, 54 Western Main Rd, St James, or *Rhyner's*, 54 Prince St, Port of Spain. Production costs are a problem so prices of local CDs are high, and despite being the main music outlets in this island of music they frequently have no stock. If you are going to Tobago, *Arcade Record Store*, Castries Rd, Scarborough, will make tape compilations to your specification.

For **bookshops** *Metropolitan Books*, Colsort Mall, has a good selection; *R I K Services Ltd*, Queen St, Port of Spain, and 104 High St, San Fernando, mostly school books; *Ishmael M Khan and Sons*, 20 Henry St, Port of Spain. Black literature at *Afrikan World Books* and *Kultural Items*, Park Plaza on Park St and St Vincent St, T/F6272128, good selection, history, contemporary issues. *Paper Chase* is a small shop with a good selection in the *Normandie* hotel. There are second hand bookshops in Town Centre Mall and various side streets. Generally the selection is poor, particularly for Caribbean novels which is disappointing in a country with such a long literary tradition and most bookshops make their money on school texts.

Air From North America *Air Canada* and *BWIA* from Toronto to Port of Spain. *BWIA* and *American Airlines* from Miami and New York to Port of Spain. *BWIA* also from Washington DC. *North American Airlines* has charters from New York to Tobago and on to Trinidad. **From Europe** *BWIA* from London to Port of Spain. *British Airways* from London Gatwick to Tobago. Several charters, including *JMC* (was *Air Caledonian*) from London Gatwick to Tobago and *Condor* from Frankfurt and Munich. **From South America** To Port of Spain, *Aeropostal* from Caracas via Porlamar, *BWIA* from Caracas daily; *BWIA* and *Surinam Airways* from Georgetown, Guyana; *Surinam Airways* from Paramaribo. **From the Caribbean** *BWIA*, *Liat*, *ALM* and *Caribbean Star* connect Trinidad and Tobago with other Caribbean islands including Antigua, Barbados, Curaçao, Grenada, Jamaica (Kingston), St Lucia, St Maarten, St Vincent, San Juan, Puerto Rico. *BWIA* operates the domestic shuttle Trinidad-Tobago, with a new airline, *Tobago Express*, planning to start operations in 2001. *BWIA* launched a new regional service in 1999, *BWee Express*, with new 50-seat Havilland Dash-8 aircraft, with flights from Trinidad to Tobago, Barbados, Grenada, St Lucia and St Vincent.

Transport

Sea See 'Getting around', page 924 for the ferry between Trinidad and Tobago. A weekly 250-passenger and cargo ferry service (suspended 2001) run by *Windward Lines Limited* sails from Trinidad. For information and tickets contact Global Steamship Agencies Ltd, Mariner's Club, Wrightson Rd, PO Box 966, Port of Spain, T6242279, 6252547, F6275091. Every Fri morning a boat carrying racing pigeons leaves for **Güiria, Venezuela.** Contact Francis Sagones, T6320040; or talk to Siciliano Bottini in the Agencia Naviera in Güiria for sea transport in the other direction. Fishing boats and trading vessels ply this route frequently and can often be persuaded to take passengers. A Trinidadian, Adrian Winter Roach, travels at least once a week with his boat *El Cuchillo*, and charges US$60 one way, US$100 return, he can be contacted in Venezuela through the Distribuidora Beirut, Calle Valdez 37, Güiria, T/F81677. From Cedros in southern Trinidad it is sometimes possible to travel by small boat to Tucupita in Venezuela. Lots of shipping lines have a service going north, go to Queen's Wharf and ask to speak to the captains. For **Guyana**, try *Abraham Shipping Company Ltd*, 10 Abercromby St, T6241138/1131, they handle 90% of the Guyana and Suriname trade. Be careful to get your passport stamped at both ends of the journey. Remember that drug dealers operate in these waters and behave with extreme caution. Small boats are likely to be intercepted by Venezuelan or Trinidad coastguards, or both.

Bus *Express Commuter Service (ECS)* every 15-20 mins, 0600-2100 Mon-Sat, every 30 mins 0700-1900 Sun, from City Gate Terminal, Port of Spain, to San Fernando, US$1, or US$0.60 to other destinations: Arima, Chaguanas, Five Rivers. *PTSC* (T6237872) bus from City Gate to Chaguaramas every 60-90 mins, 0500-2200, US$0.30. Bus to airport from City Gate, 4 times daily, 0630, 0700, 1515, 1545, 45 mins, return 0715, 0745, 1600, 1630.

Car hire Car rental firms are numerous and include: *Auto Rentals Ltd*, Uptown Mall, Edward St, Port of Spain (623-7368), Piarco airport (T6692277), and at Cruise Ship Complex, 1 D Wrightson Rd (T6248687). *Bacchus Taxi and Car Rental*, 37 Tragarete Rd (T6225588). *Lord Calloo*, 100 la Paille Village, Caroni (T/F6695673), helpful, check tyres. *Singh's*, 7-9 Wrightson Rd (6254247) and at airport (T6455417, F6643860). *Southern Sales and Service Co Ltd*, El Socorro Extension Road, San Juan, T6275623-4 (24-hr service), recommended. *Autocenter Ltd*, 6 Ariapita Av, T6284400. *Econo Car Rentals*, 191-193 Western Main Rd, T6228072, one of the cheapest. If you prefer an executive limousine, contact *Executive Limousine Service*, 70 Sackville St, Port of Spain, T6252624. **Bicycles** Excellent bike shop, *Geronimo's Cycle and Sport Ltd*, 15 Pole Carew St, Woodbrook, Port of Spain, T6222453, owned and managed by former professional cyclist, Gene 'Geronimo' Samuel.

Maxi-taxi These are colour coded: yellow for Diego Martin and west, red for east, green for San Fernando, brown or black for maxis which start in San Fernando and travel south from there. The green and red ones set off mostly from the City Gate Terminal; the yellow band from further west on South Quay; most Carenage and Chaguaramas maxis start from Green corner on St Vincent and Park Streets (Globe cinema); Maraval maxis start from Oxford and Charlotte Streets. Check exact route before starting, eg east taxis are either 'San Juan' or 'all the way up' the Eastern Main Rd to Arima, or 'highway', which is faster and runs closer to the airport but misses places like Tunapuna and Curepe. Fares start at US$0.30 and run to Arima, US$1; to Chaguanas, US$1; to San Fernando, US$1.75. If you are worried about being overcharged, pay with TT$10 and look as though you know how much change to expect, but drivers are usually very helpful and friendly.

Route taxi In Port of Spain most sedan taxis (saloon cars, often rather beat up) set off from close to Independence Square and use fast food restaurants as markers. They leave to the west from Chacon St close to *MacDonalds*, for Chaguanas and San Fernando from near *KFC*, close to *Royal Castle* for Arima. Those for St Ann's and St James leave from Woodford Square, for Carenage from Green Corner (St Vincent and Park Streets), and for Maraval, Belmont and Morvant from Duke and Charlotte Streets (also from here infrequently on to Maracas and the north coast). Fares in town US$0.50, further out US$0.75. If you are in a hurry you can pay for any remaining empty seats and ask the driver to go. They will also go off-route for a little extra but going off route to the *Hilton* costs US$7.

Directory **Banks** In Port of Spain: *Republic Bank Ltd*), 11-17 Park St, T6254411, F6230371, also at airport, very slow, open 0800-1100, 1200-1400, on Fri 0800-1200, 1500-1700. *Royal Bank of Trinidad and Tobago*, 3B Chancery Lane, T6234291. *Bank of Nova Scotia*, Park and Richmond Sts, T6253566. *Citibank*, Queens Park East, T6251040. *Citicorp Merchant Bank*, same address, T6233344. *Western Union Money Transfer*, Uptown Mall, Edward St, Port of Spain, T6236000, and 10 other locations in Trinidad and Tobago. Bank branches in all major centres. Many suburban or shopping mall branches open 1000-1800. Republic Bank branch and ATM at Crew's Inn Marina. Peake's Yacht Yard has a branch with a 24-hour cash machine and a teller from 0900-1400.

Communications **Post**: TT Post, now a corporation being run by New Zealanders, has its Port of Spain office inside the Excellent City Mall on corner of Frederick st and Independence Sq. Post Offices elsewhere are being revamped and sell stationery etc, though good quality cards are almost impossible to find, there or anywhere (try *Card Loft* in West Mall and look also for the informative historical cards by a local artist, Adrian Camps-Campins). Stamps for Europe TT$4.50 upwards, USA

TT\$3.75. **Telephone:** The main *Telecommunications Services of Trinidad and Tobago Ltd* (TSTT) offices on Frederick St and Independence Sq operate international telephone and fax. The service for international calls has improved greatly, with direct dialling to all countries, but charges remain high. The fax number for the public is F6270856; they phone the recipient to say a fax is waiting. The fax service shuts outside working hours except for 'life or death' messages. This means no faxes for 3 days over Carnival, so get it sent to your hotel. Phone cards are available for TT\$20, 30, 60, or 100 plus 15% VAT, from TSTT offices, banks, airport, cruise ship complex etc. Can be used for local calls but most pay phones don't work. There is also a 'Companion Card', giving prepaid international calls from any phone, with per minute rates even higher than a normal call. Home Direct Service for AT&T, Sprint and MCI available from TSTT, Cruise Ship Complex in Port of Spain, TTYC, TTYA and Peake's Yacht Yard, also at Penitence St, San Fernando. In Tobago, at airport and TSTT offices. To activate an overseas TDMA compatible cellphone, visit TSTT office in Frederick St, Port of Spain (Mon-Fri 0800-1600), West Mall or Trincity Mall (Mon-Sat 1100-1800), DSM Plaza, Chaguanas (Mon-Fri 0800-1600), St James St, San Fernando (Mon-Fri 0800-1600), Wilson Rd, Tobago (Mon-Fri 0800-1600), with credit card and ID. Allow 1 hr for service. Initial charge TT\$200, then TT\$15/day plus TT\$2.50/minute airtime and any international costs. Most UK and European cellphones are not TDMA compatible and can't be activated. The telephone directory seems deliberately designed to confuse. Quite a lot of places, eg University of the West Indies, are listed under 'T' for 'The'. Government departments are all on blue pages in the front, but not in alphabetical order. **Internet** Cyber cafés: several, including *Interserve* (Chamber of Commerce building, near West Mall), *Mariner's Office* (Crews Inn Marina). *Photo King*, at City Gate, Port of Spain, has computer access for email, TT\$20 per hour.

Embassies and consulates (Port of Spain, all listed on blue pages at beginning of phone book), **Argentina**, Tatil Building, Maraval Rd, T628557. **Brazil**, 18 Sweet Briar Rd, St Clair, T6225779, F6224323. **Canada** High Commission, 3-3A Sweet Briar Rd, St Clair (T6226232). **China**, 39 Alexandra St St Clair, T6226976. **Colombia**, 16 Queen's Park West, T6228614. **Costa Rica**, Mutual Bds, Queen's Park West, T6280652. **Denmark**, 20-22 Tragarete Rd, T6251156, F6238693. **Dutch**, Life of Barbados Building, 69 Edward St, PO Box 870, T6251210/1722, F6251704. **France** Embassy, 6th floor, Tatil Bldg, Maraval Rd, T6227446, F6282632. **Germany**, 7-9 Marli St, PO Box 828 (T6281630/2, F6285278). **Guyana**, 3rd floor, Park Plaza, Corner of Park and St Vincent Streets, T6271692, F6233881. **India**, 6 Victoria Av, T6277480. **Jamaica** High Commission, 2 Newbold St, St Clair, T6224995/7, F6289180. **Japan**, 5 Hayes St, St Clair, T6226105/5838, F6220858. **Mexico**, Algico Plaza, St Vincent St, T6276988. **Nigeria**, 3 Maxwell Phillip St, T6226834. **Panama**, 1A Dere St, T6233435. **Suriname**, Tatil Building, Maraval Rd, T6280704. **UK** High Commission, 19 St Clair Av, St Clair, T6222748, F6224555, a very smart, modern building, its upper floors have an excellent view over Queen's Park Oval. **USA**, 15 Queen's Park West, T6226371/6, F6285462, 0700-1700. **Venezuela**, 16 Victoria Av, Embassy, T6279823/4, 0900-1300, 1400-1600, Consulate at same address, T6279773/4, visa section only open mornings. Changes of address, and other representatives, can be checked at the Ministry of External Affairs, T6234116/60.

Hospitals There are run down and overcrowded public hospitals in Port of Spain, San Fernando and Scarborough in Tobago, as well as several district hospitals and community health centres. The Port of Spain General Hospital is at 169 Charlotte St, T6232951. Mount Hope, T6454673, is a teaching hospital and its facilities are a bit better. The St Clair Medical Centre, T6281451, is private, TT\$3,500 for admittance to ward, credit card or cash in advance, overseas insurance not accepted.

Tourist information Local tour operators *Trinidad and Tobago Sightseeing Tours*, run by Gunda Busch-Harewood, 12 Western Rd, St James, T6281051, F6229205. Pleasant and quite reliable, speaks German, will arrange accommodation and car hire and has a representative on Tobago (Margaret Hinkson, T6397422, F6229205). Gunda also offers evening tours and is a good contact for liming, parties etc. She uses *in Joy Tours* who run sightseeing tours, deep sea fishing, panyard visits etc, T6337733, F6228974. *The Travel Centre Limited*, Level 2, Uptown Mall, Edward St, Port of Spain, T6235096, F6235101 (PO Box 1254) is an American Express Travel Service Representative. Walking tours, cave exploration, horse riding in the Northern Range, kayaking expeditions and other trips off the beaten track can be arranged with *Caribbean Discovery Tours Ltd*, 9B Fondes Amandes Rd, St Ann's, T6247281 run by Stephen Broadbridge together with Merryl See Tai of the Kayak Centre, T6292680 (see page 930), camping (in basic-luxury tents or cabins) or lodging in guest houses arranged for longer trips, tailor-made tours. Roger Neckles, a local bird photographer, runs specialist minibus tours for birdwatchers. *Banwari Experience Ltd*, 64 Prince St, Port of Spain, T624-TOUR, F6751619, banwari@tstt.net.tt, run by Andrew Welch, offers cultural and nature tours, hiking, history, birdwatching, carnival.

Trinidad & Tobago

A foot in the door

- Walk from **Anse Fourmi to Charlotteville** for spectacular scenery and birdwatching.
- Take a glass bottom boat to **Little Tobago**, snorkel over the massive brain coral and see the nesting red-billed tropic birds.
- Try **crab and dumplings** at a local restaurant.
- Attend Sunday School on **Buccoo Beach** and party the night away.

Tobago

Colour map 6, grid C6 *Tobago is not as bustling as Trinidad but tourism is booming. Nevertheless, it is ideal for those in search of relaxation. The tourist area is concentrated on the southwest end and about six miles from the capital, Scarborough. There are small hotels and guest houses scattered all around the island, however, offering peace and quiet in beautiful surroundings. The forest on the central hills provides a spectacular backdrop for the many horseshoe bays around the coast and there is good walking, sailing and diving. Tobago is 26 miles long and only nine miles wide, shaped like a cigar with a central 18-mile ridge of hills in the north (the Main Ridge, highest point 1,890 ft) running parallel with the coast. These northeast hills are of volcanic origin and the southwest is flat or undulating and coralline. The population is concentrated in the west part of the island around Scarborough. There are small farms but*

Tobago

■ Sleeping	3 Coco Reef	7 Manta Lodge
1 Blue Waters Inn	4 Grafton Beach Resort	8 Ocean Point
2 Bougainvillea	5 Hilton Hotel	9 Old Donkey Cart
GuestHouse	6 Kariwak Village	Guest House

the main ridge is forested and quite wild. The climate is generally cooler and drier, particularly in the southwest, than most parts of Trinidad.

Scarborough

Although there is a ferry from Trinidad, Tobago is best reached by air. Scarborough is only 15-25 minutes' drive from Crown Point Airport and many beach hotels are within walking distance of the airport. Scarborough is small enough to walk around, but for trips to the suburbs or further afield take a route taxi or hire a car.

Ins & outs
See page 962 for further transport details

In Scarborough itself the **Botanic Gardens** on the hill behind the Mall are worth a visit. There are also some interesting buildings, such as the House of Assembly on James Park (built in 1825), and Gun bridge, with its rifle-barrel railings. New development has included a new deep water harbour and cruise ship terminal. Scarborough Mall is modern, concrete and rather tatty but most activity is around here: the tourist office, post office, library and bus station as well as the market, where you can find local varieties of fruit and vegetables, clothing, meat and fresh coconut water. There are banks on Main St. Just off Main St, George Leacock has turned his home into a museum, quite interesting.

Sights
The town is pleasant but perhaps not worth an extended visit

Above the town is **Fort King George**, which is well maintained and has good views along the coast. This fort reflects the turbulent history of the Caribbean. Building commenced in 1777, continued under the French in 1786 (Fort Castries), renamed Fort Liberté in 1790 after the garrison revolted, recaptured by the British in 1793, returned to France in 1801 and when the island was ceded to Britain in 1802, it was named Fort King George in 1804. It was decommissioned in 1854. There are two of artist Luise Kimme's huge wooden figures in the middle of the parade ground which are very attractive. You can visit her workshop on Sunday but its best to ring first, T6390257.

At the Barrack Guard House is the **Tobago museum**, with an excellent display of early Tobago history including Amerindian pottery, shells, military relics, maps and documents from the slave era. ■ *Mon-Fri, 0900-1700, doors close 1630, adults US$0.50, children US$0.15.* The gardens are attractive and well kept and there are excellent views over Scarborough. There are a number of historic buildings here which can be seen apart from the museum. Buildings include the Officers' Mess, the Magazine (almost hidden under an enormous silk cotton tree), the Bell Tank (still with water in it and an amazing echo), a fine arts centre which has displays by local artists as well as a permanent exhibition. A number of cannon mounted on metal garrison gun carriages can also be seen. At the same location is a hospital through which you have to drive to get to the fort.

10 Richmond Guest House
11 Tropikist

Trinidad & Tobago

Around the island

If you are driving around Tobago, the 1:50,000 map, usually available from the tourist office in Scarborough, at US$3.50, is adequate, although note that many of the minor roads are only suitable for four-wheel drive. If you are hiking, get the three 1:25,000 sheets, not currently available in Tobago but obtainable from the Lands and Survey Division, Richmond St, Port of Spain, or a good map shop abroad. It is possible to walk anywhere. There is book of trails.

East from Scarborough Off the coastal road you can go to the Forest Reserve by taking a bus from Scarborough to **Mount St George** and then walking or hitching to **Hillsborough Dam**. The lake is the drinking water supply for the island so no swimming, you may find a man to take you on the lake in a rowing boat. It is a lovely forest setting. A four-wheel drive vehicle is necessary if you want to drive but walking there is recommended. From there continue northeast through the forest to **Castara** or **Mason Hall** on an unpaved, rough road. A guide is not necessary, there is only one path. Birdwatching is excellent (oropendulas, mot-mots, jacamans, herons) and there are cayman in the lake, but look out for snakes (none of them poisonous). Alternatively, take a taxi to Mason Hall (ask the taxi to drop you at the road for the Hillsborough dam) and walk to Mount St George via Hillsborough Dam, which is easier walking as the track is on the level or downhill, about nine miles. By Mount St George (Tobago's first, short-lived principal town, then called George Town) is **Studley Park House** and **Fort Granby** which guards Barbados Bay.

The road continues through **Pembroke** and **Belle Garden** and nearby is **Richmond Great House**, now a hotel. It has a lovely view but is not as 'great' a house as some of the plantation houses on other islands. **Roxborough**, the island's second town, also on the Windward coast, is worth a visit. The **Argyll River** waterfalls near Roxborough comprise four beautiful falls with a big green pool at the bottom, a 10-minute walk upstream from the road which can be very muddy. You can't miss them because of all the rather overpriced and pushy guides standing in the road.

A good walk is the road from Roxborough to Parlatuvier and Bloody Bay through the Main Ridge Forest Reserve. There is hardly any traffic and you go through singing forests with masses of birds (early morning or late afternoon is the best for

Scarborough

Buccoo: Goat-racing centre of the world

Think of famous sports arenas around the world: Lords and cricket, Twickenham and rugby, Henley and rowing and the name of Buccoo doesn't loom large. But Buccoo is the goat-racing centre of the world. The Buccoo Goat Race Festival was started in 1925 by Samuel Callendar and has had several venues around the village before the current purpose built track behind the beach facilities at Buccoo was constructed in 1985. Easter Tuesday was chosen because Good Friday and Easter Saturday were already taken for marble pitching, Easter Sunday for the Moravian Love Feast and Easter Monday for horse racing.

The course is about 100 metres long and there is a maximum of 10 goats per race. Each jockey has to wear the silk of the goat's owner, white shorts and bare feet. Jockey and goat proudly walk around the ring with Mr Patterson giving the crowd helpful guidance on the form before walking down to the start. There is betting but it is all rather discreet. The goats are then loaded into the starting stall (accompanied by much banter from the commentators perched precariously in the judges' box). A yellow flashing light signifies

that they are under starters orders, the gates flip open and the race is on. Goats lead with the jockey running behind holding the goat on a short length of rope. This is no gentle jog, the goats are very fast and the jockeys give Linford Christie a good run for his money. Of course the jockey has little control over his goat and the best fun is had when the goat suddenly veers across the other runners. The finish is often chaotic with all 10 runners nearly ending in the grandstand at the end of the course. This may be one reason why the race was moved from the Battery. The closeness of the cliffs overhanging the sea made it unpopular. The races are often very close and the judges may be called on to study video evidence before declaring the winner.

The afternoon is interspersed with various cultural events and the occasional crab race. Huge sound rigs on the street above the course compete with each other and sometimes drown the commentators. If you are lucky the Prime Minister will attend. Rum and beer flow and the whole day is topped off by an enormous jump up until late into the night.

Patrick Dawson

spotting great numbers) including cocricos, collared trogon, mot-mots, jacamans, humming birds. After the five-mile marker is a semi-circular trail in the forest called Gilpin's Trace. There are great views from the hut at the top of the road. If you walk Gilpin's Trace and want to try other, lesser known trails, Kelton Thomas is a recommended guide, contact him through the airport information centre. Wordsworth Frank is also good, he runs glass bottom boat tours too. Beyond Roxborough is **King's Bay**, with waterfalls near the road in which you can swim. These are sometimes dry, however, so a refreshing swim cannot be guaranteed.

From the fishing village of Speyside you can visit Little Tobago, a forested islet off the northeast coast, and sanctuary for birds. There are wild fowl and 58 species of other birds, including the red-billed tropic bird found here in the largest nesting colony in the north Atlantic. Boats across cost US$12.50 (includes a guided tour of the islet and snorkelling). There are lots of glass bottomed boats and fish and coral to see, boatmen will find you (see page 930). Go early in the morning to see the birds. If you want to camp, you are supposed to have prior permission from the Forestry Division at Studley Park, T6394468. They also have a rudimentary camp on the main ridge by the Roxborough-Parlatuvier road, which can be used by arrangement. At Speyside, you can sling a hammock near the government centre on the beachfront. It is well lit but it may be windy. A night-guard might keep your belongings under lock.

Speyside & Little Tobago

From Speyside you can climb **Pigeon Peak**, at about 1,900 ft the highest point on the island. There are two routes up the hill through the forest, the shorter one is steeper than the longer, so both take about three hours. There is also a track on the Speyside Road from Charlotteville, 100m on the right before the turning to Flagstaff Hill. This is suitable for a four-wheel drive to begin with. After about 30 mins' walk you clamber down into a stream bed and up again, from where it becomes a rough, steep path through old banana plantations and then woodland. There is no trouble following the path here, there are even markers cut into or painted on to trees, and there are many birds. However when the ground becomes flatter it becomes confusing. A guide therefore is essential and Lebeque Jack has been recommended. Remember there are lurid, yet true, tales of tourists being lost up here for days. The actual summit is above the woodland, through grass and small shrubs, and has a trig point. From the top you can see the north and south coasts and offshore islets.

Charlotteville A trip to Charlotteville in the northeast is recommended. The easiest way to get there is by one of the seven buses a day from Scarborough, TT$8. There are maxi taxis from Scarborough (TT$10, three a day but not on Saturday, when the Adventist drivers do not work, for the return journey you can arrange to be picked up). There are magnificent views on the way and the village itself is on a fine horse-shoe bay with a good beach, lifeguard, good swimming and snorkelling and two dive shops. The Americans erected a radio tracking station in the Second World War on Flag Staff Hill overlooking Charlotteville (take the rough track off the main Speyside-Charlotteville road about one kilometre). There are several seats and a bandstand here. Half way along the rough road to Flagstaff Hill there is a cattle path to the right. Follow this as it descends and curves to the left. Near the bottom it meets another, wider trace (trail). Turn left and this will eventually bring you back to Charlotteville. It is a pleasant, shaded walk. From Charlotteville, it is a 15-minute walk to **Pirate's Bay**, which is magnificent and unspoilt and good for snorkelling. Also adjacent is **Man O'War Bay**. **Campbellton Bay** is a 30 to 40-minute walk from Charlotteville (ask locally for directions) through dense forest to a secluded beach, mostly used only by fishermen. It is fairly easy to hitch a ride from Charlotteville to Speyside.

The north coast The road between Charlotteville and Plymouth along the Caribbean coast is very poor; four-wheel drive is needed for part of the way and then only in dry weather, or in summer, maybe. Best on a mountain bike or on foot. The stretch between L'Anse Fourmi and Charlotteville is usually impassable and a notice says you travel at your own risk (work has been abandoned on road improvements, supposed to be completed sometime). You are much better off on foot and it is a wonderful hike. In fact hikers are opposed to any paving of the road. The views are worth the trouble with lots of lovely bays beneath you. Get a taxi to L'Anse Fourmi and walk (a comfortable four hours) along the track to Corvo Point, Hermitage (bush rum for sale), Man O'War Bay and Charlotteville. The terrain is undulating. Bird life is plentiful, including parrots, and you may see iguanas. The stretch of road between L'Anse Fourmi and Moriah is smooth, traffic is light and it is very picturesque. Take water with you.

At the southwest end of the island there are many hotels and resorts. The Crown Point area is developing rapidly and parts feel like a building site, with associated litter. At **Store Bay** are the ruins of small **Milford Fort**, and brown pelicans frequent the beautiful but crowded beach, which is a good place to watch the sunset. The fort was once Dutch (Bella Vista) but was overrun by the Indians. The British maintained a small battery here but it is now no more than a nice garden. **Pigeon Point** has the island's most beautiful beach, clean and with calm water, though US$2 is charged for adults and US$0.50 for children for use of the facilities. There are huts, tables and benches, lockers, bars, shopping, boat hire and watersports. It is another good place to watch the sunset.

From **Mount Irvine Bay**, where there is an attractive, palm-fringed championship golf course (the hotel of the same name has a good beach – surfing) you can walk up to **Bethel** (about two miles), the island's highest village, for excellent views across the island. Another beach which is well worth a visit is **Turtle Bay**.

The main town on this coast is **Plymouth**, with **Fort James** overlooking **Great Courland Bay** (site of the Courlander settlement in the 17th century). Destroyed several times, the present fort was erected in 1800. Also here is the Latvian Monument, designed by a local artist, it was erected in 1976 and represents "Freedom". A much-quoted attraction in Plymouth is the enigmatic tombstone of Betty Stevens (25 November 1783), which reads: "She was a mother without knowing it, and a wife, without letting her husband know, except by her kind indulgences to him."

Hidden in the forest some miles from **Arnos Vale** is the **Arnos Vale Sugarmill**, dating from 1880; a recommended excursion, it is possible to hitchhike. The Arnos Vale Waterwheel Park has a small museum, gift shop, restaurant and stage where shows are put on. It is difficult to continue along this coast by public transport, Plymouth to Parlatuvier (no accommodation)is not a recognized route. You have to go instead via Roxborough, with a lovely journey from there through the forest.

The small village of **Castara** on the coast can be seen in 10 minutes but is a pleasant place to visit. There is a small bay with a sandy beach and a snorkelling reef, or a 10-minute walk inland will take you to an easily accessible waterfall. Eating places are readily available and there is accommodation.

Glass-bottomed boats for visiting this undersea garden leave from Pigeon Point, Store Bay andBuccoo Bay. The charge is about US$15 for 2 to 2½ hrs, with shoes and snorkel provided; wear a hat. Longer trips with barbecue cost around US$50-60, worth it if you eat and drink plenty. The dragging of anchors and greed of divers have tarnished the glory of this once marvellous reef, though, and you may prefer to make the trip to Speyside where there are also glass bottomed boat trips over a pristine reef. Elkhorn and other corals have been badly damaged by snorkellers and divers walking on them. Boat trips also include the **Nylon Pool**, an emerald-green pool in the Caribbean. Boats leave between 0900 and 1430, depending on the tide. Be selective in choosing which boat – and captain – you take for the trip; some are less than satisfactory (Selwyn's *Pleasure Girl* has been recommended, so has Archie and Mala's *Come to Starcheck*, others include Hew's Tours, Hewlett Hazel, T6399058, F6397984, Kenneth Christmas, Buccoo Reef Cooperative, Buccoo Point, T6398582, or after 1900, T6398746). From Scarborough to Buccoo by bus is TT$2. Taxis also go to Buccoo.

Buccoo Reef
The reef is now protected by law; it is forbidden to remove or destroy the corals or other marine life

Essentials

Tobago Plantations, T6371025, www.tobagoplantations.com is a new 750-acre development around Petit Trou Lagoon which, when completed will have a hotel, villas, condominiums bungalows, 18-hole championship Jack Nicklaus golf course (opening June 2001), marina, shopping centre, wildlife refuge and tropical fruit plantation. In 2000 the 200-room *Tobago Hilton* opened as part of the development, all rooms with seaview and no more than 30m from white, sandy beach.

Sleeping
There are many cheap guest houses & many people take in visitors; ask at any village store

Near Crown Point LL-AL *Coco Reef*, T6398571, F639-8574, cocoreef-tobago@trinidad.net, in North America T800-2211294. Modelled on a Bermudan hotel, peach and white walls, red roof, 96 rooms, suites and villas on man-made beach, pretty view of Pigeon Point, height of luxury but no character, close to airport and in main hotel area. Beyond Pigeon Point is **AL** *Lagoon Lodge*, Bon Accord, T6398555, F6390957. Approached down poor track, isolated, split level cabins sleep 2 adults and 2 children, fully equipped, TV, music, phone, fan, a/c, airy, comfortable, ideal for self-catering, owner provides fruit, eggs, milk, maid/cook available, set in 4 acres of gardens with chickens, peacocks, rhea, boardwalk through mangroves to sea lagoon, jetty with hammock, kayak and sailboat, very private, tranquil. Mosquitoes in wet season. Turn right out of the airport and take the first right for **AL-A** *Kariwak Village*, T6398545/8442, F6398441, kariwak@tstt.net.tt Very nice, compact rooms in cabins, restaurant with excellent food, no beach, small pool, no radios or TV, meeting facilities, owners involved in the arts, exhibitions held here, yoga and therapy, retreats. **AL-B** *Tropikist*, T6398512, F6390341. 53 good-sized a/c rooms with balcony, pool, loungers, large lawn, swings, restaurant overlooks sea, indifferent food, small beach but not suitable for swimming, painted white with lots of bougainvillea, right by airport.

A-C *Belleviste Apartments*, Sandy Point, T/F6399351, bellevis@tstt.net.tt 20 self-contained apartments, kitchenette, pool, near airport.

B-C *Arthur's By The Sea*, Crown Point, T6390196, F6394122, arthurs@trinidad.net Kind and helpful, a/c, pool, 4 min walk from safe beach. **B-C** *Conrado Beach Resort*, Milford Extension Rd, between Store Bay and Pigeon Point, T6390145. CP, beach front, standard or superior rooms, some small, some with balconies, TV, phone, some roadside view, priced accordingly, restaurant on beach for breakfast, inside for night-time, good snorkelling offshore on small reef, fishing boats moored outside, family owned, excellent service. **B-C** *Crown Point Beach Hotel*, T6398781/3, F6398731, crownpoint@trinidad.net Studios and cabins, pool, *Best of Thymes* restaurant, excellent food. **B-C** *Sandy Point Village*, T6398533, F6398534. 44 large rooms and suites, some split level, TV, kitchenette, balcony, quiet a/c, in pleasant gardens, pool, beach rooms under restaurant open on to sea, poor beach, most people go to Store Bay, airless disco in basement, *The Deep*, music goes on until early hours. If you turn right out of the airport, and take the first right, you come to **D-E** *Store Bay Holiday Resort*, T6398810, F6399733. 5 min walk, do not be fooled by taxi drivers who will charge US$5 for the ride, about the cheapest in this area, but self-catering only, 16 apartments, clean, well-furnished, kitchen, gardens, night time security guard, small pool, friendly, good value. Close by is **B-C** *Toucan Inn*, T6397173, F6398933. Includes tax and service, African style huts, good food and entertainment.

C-D *Jetway Holiday Resort*, 100m from airport terminal, T/F6398504. Can be noisy until after 2200, 9 pleasant self-contained units with cooking facilities, friendly, helpful, a few min walk to Pigeon Point and Store Bay. **C-D** *James Holiday Resort*, Crown Point, T/F6398084. Standard room. **L** 3-bedroom apartment maximum 12 people, car and jeep rental, credit cards accepted, 2 min walk from airport, TV, patio or balcony, restaurant. **C-D** *Surf Side Holiday Homes*, Milford Rd Extension, Store Bay, T6393521, F6284707, www.trinidad.net/surfside 30 self-contained apartments, a/c, walking distance to beaches. **D** *Serenity Apartments*, 14 Centre St, Canaan, T639-0753/2370, F6390753, serenapt@tstt.net.tt Run by Miss Selma Alfred, 5 double and triple rooms, kitchenette, a/c, balcony, daily cleaning, 2 min walk to buses, evening meals by arrangement, airport pick-up, tours arranged. **E** *Spence's Terrace*, Crown Point, T6398082. Room, kitchenette, bathroom, balcony, new and fresh. Recommended. **F** *Balgobin & Dorris Guest House*, and taxi service, John Gorman Trace, Milford Rd, Crown Point, T6397328. 15 min walk from airport and beach, nice, clean rooms with bathroom and cooking facilities, mosquito nets on windows, fan, quiet and safe, friendly owners. There are lots of guest houses and small hotels along the road between the airport and Pigeon Point. **F** *Lewis Villa*, T6398022. Small units with kitchen, good value. **F** *Classic Resort Guest House*, walk straight out of airport turn left at junction and follow road round, past Milford Fort, following signs for Sandy Point, T6390742. Double room with kitchen and lounge with TV, friendly. Near beach, car rental available.

Lowlands area AL-C *Ocean Point*, Milford Rd, Lowlands, T/F6390973, www.ocean point.com Studios sleep 3, suites fit 5, dive packages available, a/c, TV, pool, sundeck, 2 min walk from sea, transport needed, family-run, friendly. Recommended. In USA T800-6924094, UK T020-87414894. On the same road, **B-C** *Hampden Inn Guest House*, Lowlands Post Office, Milford Rd LP 171, T/F6397522. CP, German spoken, standard or superior rooms all on ground floor, hammocks, large bathrooms, restaurant/bar, pool, bike hire, TV, dive packages, no pool. **B** *Coral Reef*, T6392536, F6390770, 17 rooms, 18 apartments, 30 years old and showing it, basic, dark corridor, no view, hard beds, old carpets, pool, a/c. **C** *Viola's Place*, Birchwood Triangle, Hampden, T/F6399441, violasplace@hews-tours.com 14 self-contained rooms, kitchenette, pool, airport pick-up.

Mostly guest houses or bed & breakfast **Scarborough** About ½ mile south of Scarborough is the **B-C** *Old Donkey Cart House Resort*, 73 Bacolet St, T6393551, F6396124. Run by Gloria Jones-Knapp, 2 min from beach on hillside with seaview. CP, tax and service, charming rooms in old house or apartments in new building, restaurant, good food, pool. **B** *Horizons Tobago Apartments*, 89 Bacolet Point,

T/F7091648, www.toben.com 1 and 2-bedroomed apartments, a/c, large private pool, good amenities. 10 min drive from Scarborough is **C** *Ocean View*, John Dial, T6396796. Recommended. Under same management is **C** *Windy Edge*, Concordia, 12 min drive from the harbour. 600 ft above sea level overlooking the Atlantic and the Caribbean, spacious grounds, quiet, highly recommended, CP, evening meals by arrangement US$25-30, route taxis pass by, T6395062.**D** *Miriam's Bed and Breakfast*, or *Federal Villa*, Crooks River, T6393926. 3 rooms, shared bath, fan, modest but clean and comfortable, 7-min walk to harbour, run by friendly and helpful Miriam Edwards, secretary of the Bed and Breakfast Association. **E** *Sea Breeze Motel*, Milford Rd, Scarborough, T6396404. Spotlessly clean, bathroom, TV, on seafront west of the port, recommended as base for touring. **E** *Old Plantation House*, Bacolet Garden, T6392431. Three double rooms, private, peaceful, 5 mins' walk to beach. **E-F** *Hope Cottage*, Calder Hall Rd, corner of Ottley St, not far from hospital, T6392179, F6397550. 15 rooms, 3 with private bathroom, fan, pleasant, kitchen can be used, mini-market nearby, spacious public rooms, bar, restaurant, verandah, homely, peaceful, popular with students, entrance between 2 tamarind trees, brought from India and planted when original house was built in early 19th century. **E-F** *Earl Kitaka Gordon*, Bagatelle 2, T6350211. Hand built beautiful wooden house in large garden right in middle of town, no electricity yet, price depends on whether you want to eat food from the garden, goat for fresh milk.

Contact the *Association* c/o *Federal Villa*, 1-3 Crooks River, Scarborough, T6393926, F6393566, or the Tourism Development Authority on Tobago; the brochure lists 14 properties, mostly in the southwest or near Scarborough, about US$25d.

Windward coast   L-A *Blue Waters Inn*, Batteaux Bay, Speyside, T6604341, F6605195, bwi@bluewatersinn.com   An isolated and delightfully unsophisticated hotel, 38 rooms, 1-2 bedroom bungalows and self-catering units, caters for people who want to sit on the beach, bird watchers and divers, includes tax and service, dive packages with Aquamarine Dive on site, tennis, very pretty bay, no other development, view of Little Tobago. **L-B** *Manta Lodge*, Windward Rd, Speyside, T6605268, F6605030, info@mantalodge.com. 22 standard, superior or loft rooms, rather sterile, loft has no view, a/c essential as hot under roof, superior rooms, though cheaper are better, with balcony, view and more air, small pool, bar, restaurant, caters mainly to divers, packages available with Tobago Dive Experience. **A-B** *The Speyside Inn*, Windward Rd, Speyside, T/F6604852, speysideinn@trinidad.net 6 rooms, 2 cabins, lovely airy rooms, nicely furnished, excellent value, tax included, CP with home made breads, dinner by reservation only, small beach across road, view of Little Tobago, close to *Jemma's* restaurant.**C-E** *Bougainvillea Guest House*, by Fort Granby, Studley Park, T6602075, F6602133. Includes CP, and airport transfer, owned by Hilton McFarlane who also lectures in medicine at UWI, beautiful location on hillside overlooking bay, lots of birds, fruit trees, stress free, all rooms different, some small, some family rooms, some shared bathrooms, some new rooms, beach 3 min walk, small pool. One **F** guest house in Roxborough, ask for Mrs Carter, Police Station Rd, 2 rooms, kitchen, shower, quiet, friendly.

Charlotteville   Accommodation here is expanding all the time, particularly at the cheaper end, and you will not be short of offers. **B** *Man O'War Bay Cottages*, T6604327, F6604328, pturpin@tstt.net.tt 10 cottages, sleep 4, minmum 2 nights, spacious, well-equipped kitchen, right on beach with tropical gardens behind, barbecue facilities, expensive shop with limited range, check your bill carefully.**B-C** *Charlottevilla*, opposite, T6605919. High quality 1-bedroom apartments, kitchenette. **C-E** *Cholson's Chalet* has rooms or 1-3 bedroomed apartments separated from the beach by the road, contact Hewitt Nicholson (T6392847) or Pat Nicholson (T/F6398553), the price sometimes rises after you have moved in. This place is very popular indeed and you may need to book in advance even in low season; in high season advance bookings of less than a week are not accepted. **D** *Morre's*, Bellaire Rd, Charlotteville, T6604799, contact Susan Simon. 4 double rooms, 1 2-bedroom self-contained apartment, all with kitchen facilities. **E** Mrs May Williams has ground floor apartment, 2 rooms sleep 6, communal kitchen, bathroom, house faces jetty, between 2 shops painted blue, quite pleasant. **E** Marshall and Michelle Jack (twins), 13A Pirates Bay Rd, T6605923, 6604419. Shared bathroom, no soap or towels but very clean, use of good kitchen, so close to sea that you could jump in from window, so don't stay there if the noise of the sea keeps you awake. **F** *Alyne*, very friendly, clean, comfortable.

CastaraD-E *The Naturalist Beach Resort*, Castara Village, T6395901, F6605357, natural@ trinidad.net 5 rooms, beach nearby, snorkelling. **E** *Blue Mango*, T6392060. Owned by friendly Colin Ramdeholl, simple but charming, good walking and swimming nearby, eating places in the village.

Culloden Bay **LL** *Footprints Eco Resort*, T6600118, F6600027, www.footprint secoresort.com Set in 62 acres of nature reserve, 2 villas, 4 studio apartments and honeymoon retreat, more planned, all on stilts, well-equipped, palm roofs, wooden, solar powered with a/c, jacuzzi, great views over sea, good fixed menu, salt water pools at low tide, good snorkelling on reef, guests encouraged to plant a tree, very noisy cocrico birds at dawn calling across the valley, Mia Persad and staff willing to take you around if you have no transport. You get to it from Golden Lane which passes the enormous silk cotton tree that is supposed to be the grave of Gan' Gan' Sarah.

Arnos Vale **L-AL** *Arnos Vale Hotel*, T6392881, F6393251. 38 rooms, beautiful surroundings in tropical forest, great birdwatching, Mot Mots and other birds come to be fed at 1600, afternoon tea-time, hospitable, dive shop, new 30-room complex being built at site of old water wheel. **D** *Arnos Vale Vacation Apartments*, Arnos Vale Road, Plymouth, T/F6391362, trade-info@tidco.co.tt Run by Victor Forde, 1-2 bedroom apartments, kitchen, large living room area, fully furnished, beautiful garden with fruit trees and tropical birds, transport to airport, car hire available.

Plymouth **LL-L** *Mount Irvine Bay Hotel and Golf Course*, T6398871, F6398800. Rooms, suites or garden cottage, luxury furnishings, TV, phone, pool, beach, sauna, gym, mediocre food at *Sugar Mill* restaurant, tennis, gardens of 16 acres. **LL-L** *Grafton Beach Resort*, Stonehaven Bay, Black Rock, T6390191, F6390030, grafton@trinidad.net 108 rooms, luxury. Highly recommended. A/c, pool, TV, friendly and efficient service, good food, excellent beach front location, facilities for the disabled. **LL** *Le Grand Courlan* is its sister resort next door, T6399667, F6399292, legrand@trinidad.net 78 luxury rooms, 10 1-bedroom suites, 8 garden rooms with jacuzzis, all have phone, fan, a/c, hairdryers, minibar, handsome furnishings, shops, pools, restaurants, business centre, health spa, fully equipped gym, very upmarket compared with other hotels on Tobago. **LL** *Sanctuary Villa Resort*, Grafton Estate, T6399556, F6390019, www.sanctuaryvillas.com, just inland. Luxury villa development, fantastic views across island to Pigeon Point and Buccoo Reef from hill, bordered by 260-acre bird sanctuary. **AL** *Rex Turtle Beach Hotel*, PO Box 201, Plymouth, T6392851, F6391495. 125 rooms, overlooking garden, railings on upper floor balconies unsafe for children, pool, on beach, tennis, a/c, service and management good, Sun West Indian buffet highly recommended, especially the curried crab. **AL-D** *Cocrico Inn* and *Courland Bay Villa*, T6392961, F6396565, cocrico@ tstt.net.tt 16 rooms, kitchenette or 4-room villa and apartment, restaurant, swimming pool, friendly, clean, excellent meals, laundry service. **C-E** *King Solomon's Mine Holiday Resort*, T6392545. Owned by Leroy Solomon, at the end of George St off Shelbourne St where buses run, rooms or apartments, kitchen, beautifully furnished, good view from upstairs balcony, popular with Germans. **B** *La Belle Creole*, Mt Irvine, T6390908. Run by Mrs Gerhild Oliver, English, German, French and Italian spoken, right by golf course, 5 min walk from beach, bed and breakfast, dinner on request, queen sized beds. **B-C** *Old Grange Inn*, Buccoo Junction, Mt Irvine, T6390275, F6399395, grangeinn@trinidad.net 18 rooms, pool, restaurant, bar, a/c. **B-D** *Blue Horizon*, Jacamar Drive, Mt Irvine, T6390432/3, F6395006. 14 self-contained rooms, kitchenette, pool. **E** *Green Acres*, Daniel Trace, Carnbee, T6398287. Clean rooms with shower, safe, some with kitchens, CP, delicious local food, friendly family, US$4-5 taxi service. Highly recommended. **E** *Michael Baker's* apartments, Daniel Trace, Carnbee, T6398243. Owner is chief of lifeguards and singer. **E-F** *Rolita Tea Hut*, Old Grange Rd, Mt Irvine, opposite *Blue Horizon*. Small guest house run by Roy and Pat Cousins, rooms with shower and WC, pool, meals available 0700-2100 daily, also lunch boxes, 20 min walk from beach. T6397970.

In Buccoo on Battery St, **F** *Aunty Flo's*, T6399192. Nice, friendly, run by Mrs Flora Howie, very little maintenance, plumbing erratic. **F** *Tante Loo*, Plymouth. Basic but friendly guest house.

Around Store Bay and Crown Point There are a number of restaurants, many have tables outside near the beach. *Blue Notes*, 2 mins walk from airport. Small bar and restaurant run by a jazz lover. Excellent local food.The *Beach Bar* has music all day on Sat, and a barbecue from 2000-2400, for US$17 per head for drinks and small portions of fish and chicken, poor value unless you drink a lot. *Miss Jean's*, US$2 and less for all kind of 'ting', a full meal with drinks for 2 costs less than US$10, crab and dumplings are a speciality but the crabs are woefully small because of overfishing. *Miss Esme*, T6388323. Flying fish and bake. *Golden Star*, Crown Point, T6390873. Restaurant and bar, lobster thermidor and grilled king fish in creole sauce. *Copratray*, Store Bay Local Rd, Bon Accord. Fri night barbecue a speciality. *Taj Terrace*, corner Pigeon Point Rd and Store Bay Rd, T6399020. One of the few Indian restaurants on Tobago. *Dillon's Seafood Restaurant*, Crown Point, T6398765. Open daily from 1800 except Mon, good food and service, though a little expensive. *Bonkers*, at Store Bay Local Rd, Crown Point, T6397173. Serves creole food, live music, popular. *Joy's*, in Buccoo. Small, friendly, good local food for US$3.50, barbecue on Wed for US$2.50. *La Tartaruga*, Buccoo Bay, T6390940. Italian restaurant café-bar, excellent Italian food, limited menu, expensive, reservations essential.

Patinos, Shirvan Rd, T6399481. Run by Kenneth and Marcia Patino with their son as chef, excellent food, delicious West Indian platter at lunchtime, evening steel band once a week, reservations needed. Good accommodation also. *The Lush*, Shirvan Rd. Good food, pool and table football, a bit sleazy. *Shirvan Mill* on Shirvan Rd. Specializes in seafood and steaks, expensive and romantic, T6390000.

The *Black Rock Café* on Black Rock main road, T6397625. Recommended for very good food, slow service, very busy. *Under the Mango Tree*, Black Rock. Very tasty local food, US$17 for full meal. *The Seahorse Inn*, next to *Grafton Beach Resort*. Excellent dinners, extensive menu. *Peacock Mill*, Friendship Estate, Canaan, T6390503. Restaurant and bar in old sugar mill with lots of peacocks wandering around and coming to be fed at around 1700, their squawks accompany the jazz sometimes featured outdoors under the trees. *Indigo*, 2 Horse-shoe Ridge, Pleasant Prospect, Grafton, T6399635, indigo2@tstt.net.tt Local and foreign dishes, very good food, garden setting, also accommodation. On Plymouth Rd, *Amadeus*, T6396734. European style bistro and bar, owner-run, imaginative light menu, excellent desserts, Sat-Thu.

Charlotteville *Phebe's Ville View* , Charlotteville. Nice view of the bay, very good and cheap meals, try the prawns if available, dumplings and curried crab also recommended, very friendly, rooms and apartments for rent at reasonable prices, Phebe also has a laundry and special prices for people on yachts. *Gail's*, Charlotteville, on seafront as you walk to Pirate's Bay. Breakfast and dinner, no lunch, all fresh, very tasty, delicious vegetables and salad, Gail is a genius with fish, very friendly.

Speyside *Jemma's Sea View*, Speyside, T6604066, on a tree top platform by the beach. Good, filling lunch or dinner, fixed menu but 2 choices, TT$40, slow service, nice atmosphere, no alcohol and closed Sat (Adventists), you can get hassled here for boat trips.

Scarborough The *Blue Crab*, at the corner of Main St with Fort St, Scarborough, T6392737. Specializes in local food, very good lunch but slow service, reasonable prices, nice view over harbour. *Kings Well Inn*, corner Burnette and Carrington Streets, T6393883. Run by Kim and Cheryl Cleveland, famous for bake and buljol and homemade ginger beer. *Rouselles*, Bacolet St, T6394738. One of the best, seafood, short but excellent menu, very busy Sat. *La Laconda*, 73 Bacolet St, T6393551. Local and international cuisine in tropical garden atmosphere. *Old Donkey Cart*, Bacolet, T6393551. Good food, European wines, nice shady garden setting or in old house if it is raining, closed Wed except Dec-Apr. *De Bamboo Bar & Restaurant*, Milford Rd, Scarborough, next to *Sea Breeze Motel*. Recommended, lobster good value, 3-course meal US$20.

Eating
Most of the food from the huts on the beach is reheated

Trinidad & Tobago

Nightlife   Though not as lively as Trinidad, Tobago offers dancing in its hotels. The Buccoo Folk Theatre gives an attractive show of dancing and calypso every Thu at 2100. There is a *Tobago Folk Performing Company*. In Scarborough, *Golden Star Entertainment Centre*, nightly. *Michael's Bar*, Black Rock, recommended for friendly evening entertainment. The *Lush Pub*, Shirvan Rd, Store Bay, is recommended. Look in on the entertainment spots in the Crown Point area – *The Deep*, Sandy Point Village and *Toucan Inn* and *Bonkers*, Store Bay Local Rd. There is also the *Golden Star*, Milford Rd, Store Bay. Don't miss Sunday School on Buccoo Beach, a big party starting early every Sunday evening with live music, followed at about 2300 by a DJ playing until early in the morning. Entertainment is available every night of Tobago Race Week, mostly at Crown Point but also at *Grafton Beach* or *Grand Courlan* hotels.

The **cinema** in Scarborough is good value, US$1.10 for two films, but the audience can be a bit noisy. On a quieter level, the Public Library in Charlotteville is stocked with all the literature in the English language you ever wanted to read and some German books too.

Shopping   On Tobago, you can get excellent handicrafts at the *Cotton House*, Bacolet St, just outside Scarborough (taxi US$2.50), batik studio, high standard, pictures and clothes at reasonable prices. They also have an outlet at Sandy Point. Local batiks also at the *Backyard*, Milford Rd, Crown Point and locally produced artefacts at *Shore Things*, Pigeon Point Rd. *Arcade Record Store*, Castries Rd, Scarborough, will make tape compilations to your specification. *Francis Supermarket* at Crown Point is not particularly well stocked but is open Monday-Saturday 0800-1800, Sunday and holidays 1000-1400. The main supermarket is *Penny Savers* on main road at Milford, good range including pharmaceuticals, open long hours and holidays, has ATM (blue machine).

Transport   **Air**   There are many seasonal and regular charters to Tobago in addition to the following scheduled flights: from Antigua (*BWIA*), Barbados (*BWIA, Liat*), Frankfurt (*Condor*), Grenada (*BWIA, Liat*), Kingston (*BWIA*), London (*British Airways*), Miami (*BWIA*), Port of Spain (*BWIA, Liat*), St Lucia (*BWIA*), St Maarten (*BWIA*). Other flights connect through Port of Spain.

Car hire   *Auto Rentals Ltd*, Crown Point Airport (T6390644, F6390313). *Peter Gremli Car Rental*, Crown Point, T6398400. *Rodriguez Travel*, Clark Trace, Bethany, T6398507. *Banana Rentals* at *Kariwak Village*, cars and jeeps, US$21 per day, scooters US$10 per day (deposit US$60), bicycles US$4 per day (T6398441/8545). *Suzuki Jeep Rental* (and small cars), and *Cherry Scooter Rental* at *Sandy Point Beach Club* (scooters and deposit cheaper than Banana). *Tobago Travel*, Store Bay Rd, Crown Point (T6398778/8105, F6398786), *Baird's*, Lower Sangster Hill Rd (T6392528). *Rollock's Car Rental Service*, Lowlands (T6390328, after hours T6397369), US$48 per day, recommended. *Hill Crest Car Rental Service*, 47 Mt Pelier Trace, Scarborough, T/F6395208. *Thrifty Car Rental*, *Turtle Beach Hotel*, T6398111 and other agencies. **Bicycles**   Bike repairs and parts at *Numeral Uno* hardware store in Carnbee, a good contact for joining local riders for some fun road riding.

Bus and route taxi   Buses originate in Scarborough. Every hour on the hour between Scarborough and Crown Point (airport), TT$2, 25 mins. Bus Scarborough-Plymouth hourly on the hour, return on the half hour, half-hourly in busy times, via Carnbee, Buccoo junction, Mt Irvine and Black Rock. To Charlotteville 7 buses a day, TT$8, first one at 0430, 1½ hrs and then return. Also some maxis on this route. On Tobago, route taxis charge TT$4 and leave from Republic Bank in Scarborough. The Crown Point Airport route is the best, every 15-30 mins, 0530-1830; Black Rock route is fair, every 30 mins Mon-Fri 0530-2030, every 60-75 mins Sat and Sun until 2000. Route taxis to Charlotteville start from Burnett Square, TT$9-10 depending on whether vehicle is minibus or car, 1-1½ hrs.

Taxi   Taxi fares are clearly displayed as you leave the airport: to Crown Point US$6, Pigeon Point US$7, Scarborough US$10, Mt Irvine, Roxborough US$33, Speyside US$40, Charlotteville US$45.

Banks On Tobago, there are no banks or ATMs in the north of the island. ATMs can be found at the airport, *Penny Savers Supermarket* on Milford Rd and in Scarborough. Known locally as 'blue machines', they accept Visa, Plus, Mastercard and Cirrus. **Communications** Telephone There is a TSTT telephone office in Scarborough. Home direct service for AT&T, Sprint and MCI available from TSTT office and at the airport. **Hospital** Scarborough (T6392551). **Tourist information** Local travel agents *AJM Tours* at the airport, T6390610, F6398918, day trips on Tobago and to Margarita, Angel Falls, Grenada and the Grenadines. Peter Gremli is a recommended tour guide, friendly, knowledgeable and popular. Taxi drivers have set rates for sightseeing tours and can be more flexible than an organized tour. A day tour on Trinidad can include the Asa Wright Centre and the Caroni Swamp with sightseeing along the way. See also page 950.

Background

History

Trinidad was discovered by Columbus and he claimed it for Spain on his third voyage in 1498. Whether he named the island after the day of the Holy Trinity, or after a group of three hills that he spied from the sea is in dispute. At that time there were at least seven tribes of Indians living on the island: the Arawaks, Chaimas, Tamanaques, Salives, Chaguanes, Quaquas and Caribs, the last being divided into four sub-groupings, the Nepoios, Yaios, Carinepagotos and Cumanagotos. The peaceful Arawaks were the majority and lived in the south part of the island, having originally come from the upper regions of the Orinoco river. The north part was populated by Indians of the Carib strain from the Amazon area who were aggressive and warlike. It was their hostility which prevented successful colonization until the end of the 17th century when Catalan Capuchin missionaries arrived. However, European diseases and the rigours of slavery took their toll on the Indian population and by 1824 there were only 893 Indians left on Trinidad.

The first Spanish governor was Don Antonio Sedeño who arrived in 1530 but who failed to establish a permanent settlement because of Indian attacks. In 1592 the governor, Don Antonio de Berrio y Oruna, founded the town of San José de Oruna (now St Joseph). It was destroyed by Sir Walter Raleigh in 1595 and not rebuilt until 1606. In 1783 a deliberate policy to encourage immigration of Roman Catholics was introduced, known as the Royal Cedula of Population, and it was from this date that organized settlement began with an influx of mostly French-speaking immigrants, particularly after the French Revolution. Many also came from St Lucia and Dominica when these islands were ceded to Britain in 1784, others came with their slaves from the French Caribbean when slavery was abolished and from Saint Domingue after the war of independence there (eg the Compte de Lopinot, whose house in Lopinot has been restored, see page 937).

British rule in Trinidad began in 1797 when an expedition led by Sir Ralph Abercromby captured the island. It was formally ceded to Britain by Spain in 1802 under the Treaty of Amiens. (VS Naipaul's *The Loss of El Dorado* is a fascinating, if pessimistic, account of the early Spanish settlement, Sir Walter Raleigh's raid, and the early years of British rule). African slaves were imported to work in the sugar fields introduced by the French until the slave trade was abolished in 1807. After the abolition of slavery in 1834, labour became scarce and the colonists looked for alternative sources of workers. Several thousands of immigrants from neighbouring islands came in 1834–48, many Americans from Baltimore and Pennsylvania came in 1841, Madeirans came seeking employment and religious freedom and were joined by small numbers of European immigrants, British, Scots, Irish, French, Germans and Swiss. There was also immigration of free West Africans in the 1840s. In 1844 the British Government gave approval for the import of East Indian labour and

Columbus' arrival

Spanish rule

British rule

Trinidad & Tobago

the first indentured labourers arrived in 1845 (Indian Arrival Day, 30 May, is now a public holiday). By 1917, when Indian immigration ceased, 141,615 Indians had arrived for an indentured period of five years, and although many returned to India afterwards, the majority settled. The first Chinese arrived in 1849 during a lull in Indian immigration. Initially these were men only and this naturally encouraged intermarriage, but later arrivals included women. In 1866 the Chinese Government insisted on a return passage being paid, and this put an end to Chinese immigration. Persistent labour shortages led to higher wages in Trinidad than in many other islands and from emancipation until the 1960s there was also migration from Barbados, Grenada and St Vincent. More recently, in the 1980s and 1990s there has been immigration from Guyana.

Colonial Tobago **Tobago** is thought to have been discovered by Columbus in 1498, when it was occupied by Caribs. He is said to have called the island 'Bella Forma'; the present name is a corruption of tobacco, which the Caribs used to grow there. In 1641 James, Duke of Courland (in the Baltic), obtained a grant of the island from Charles I and in 1642 a number of Courlanders settled on the north side. In 1658 the Courlanders were overpowered by the Dutch, who remained in possession of the island until 1662. In this year Cornelius Lampsius procured Letters Patent from Louis XIV creating him the Baron of Tobago under the Crown of France. After being occupied for short periods by the Dutch and the French, Tobago was ceded by France to Britain in 1763 under the Treaty of Paris. But it was not until 1802, after further invasions by the French and subsequent recapture by the British, that it was finally ceded to Britain, becoming a Crown Colony in 1877 and in 1888 being amalgamated politically with Trinidad. By some reckonings Tobago changed hands as many as 29 times because of its strategic importance and for this reason there are a large number of forts.

Dr Eric Williams The first political organizations in Trinidad and Tobago developed in the 1880s, but in the 1930s economic depression spurred the formation of labour movements. Full adult suffrage was introduced in 1946 and political parties began to develop. In 1956, the People's National Movement (PNM) was founded by the hugely influential Dr Eric Williams, who dominated local politics until his death in 1981. The party won control of the new Legislative Council, under the new constitutional arrangements which provided for self-government, and Dr Williams became the first Chief Minister. In 1958, Trinidad and Tobago became a member of the new Federation of the West Indies, but after the withdrawal of Jamaica in 1961 the colony, unwilling to support the poorer members of the Federation, sought the same independence rights for Trinidad and Tobago. The country became an independent member of the Commonwealth on 31 August 1962, and became a republic within the Commonwealth on 1 August 1976. Dr Williams remained Prime Minister until his death in 1981, his party drawing on the support of the majority African elements of the population, while the opposition parties were supported mainly by the Indian minority.

Contemporary politics In 1986, the National Alliance for Reconstruction (NAR) ended 30 years' rule by the PNM which had been hit by corruption scandals and the end of the oil boom of the 1970s, winning 33 of the 36 parliamentary seats in the general election.

The 1991 elections brought another about turn in political loyalties, with Patrick Manning, of the PNM, leading his party to victory, winning 21 seats. By mid-term the Government was suffering from unpopularity and lack of confidence. Its economic policies were blamed for higher unemployment, lack of growth and rising crime. However, the opposition was not strengthened by the formation of three new parties, which were likely to split any anti-Government vote. In 1995 the economy began to improve and the Prime Minister took a gamble in calling early general elections to increase his majority. His tactic failed, however, when the United National Congress (UNC), led by Basdeo Panday, and the PNM both won 17 seats. Although the PNM received 48.8% of the vote compared with 45.8% for the UNC, Basdeo

Jamaat-Al-Muslimeen

On 27 July 1990 Trinidad was shaken by an attempted overthrow of the Government by a Muslim fundamentalist group, the Jamaat-al-Muslimeen, led by the Imam Yasin Abu Bakr. Imam Yasin Abu Bakr. The rebels held the Prime Minister, A N R Robinson, eight of his Cabinet and other hostages, until their unconditional surrender on 1 August. A total of 23 people were killed in the disturbances and about 500 were injured (including the Prime Minister) during the bombing of the police headquarters, the takeover of the parliament building and TV station and subsequent rioting. Despite a promise of an amnesty, 114 Jamaat members were arrested and charged with offences including murder and treason. After taking their case to the courts their appeal was heard in 1992 and the amnesty was reinstated, leading to the release of prisoners. The Government's appeal against the decision was turned down by the High Court in 1993. It then turned to the Privy Council, which heard its case in 1994. The Judicial Committee of the Privy Council ruled that the amnesty was not valid, because the Muslimeen breached its conditions when they continued to hold hostages and make demands for four days after the amnesty was granted instead of ending their insurrection immediately. The Muslimeen will therefore receive no compensation for wrongful imprisonment but neither can they be rearrested and charged for offences committed during their rebellion.

Panday formed an alliance with the NAR, who again won the two Tobago seats, and he was sworn in as Prime Minister on 9 November 1995. A lawyer and trade union leader, he was the first head of government of Indian descent.

Elections were held in December 2000, after a bad-tempered campaign. The opposition PNM accused the Government of large-scale corruption. With high energy prices and continuing economic growth, the UNC claimed a record of strong 'performance' and attacked the personality of Patrick Manning (PNM leader). The UNC won 52% of the popular vote and 19 of the 36 seats. However, the PNM disputed this result in a number of court cases, alleging electoral malpractice. The refusal of the President, Arthur Robinson, to appoint seven defeated UNC election candidates as ministers provoked a further constitutional crisis and more court cases. However, in spite of racially based party loyalties, there appeared to be no danger of political violence. Elections for the Tobago House of Assembly were held on 29 January 2001 and were won by the PNM, with the NAR second and the UNC a poor third.

People

Trinidad has one of the world's most cosmopolitan populations. The emancipation of the slaves in 1834 and the adoption of free trade by Britain in 1846 resulted in far-reaching social and economic changes. To meet labour shortages over 150,000 immigrants were encouraged to settle from India, China and Madeira. Of today's population of approximately 1,276,000, about 40% are black and 40% East Indian. The rest are mixed race, white, Syrian or Chinese. French and Spanish influences dominated for a long time (Catholicism is still strong) but gradually the English language and institutions prevailed and today the great variety of peoples has become a fairly harmonious entity, despite some political tension between blacks and those of East Indian descent. French patois is still spoken here and there, eg in the village of Paramin, just north of Port of Spain. Tourism plays a very small role in Trinidad's economy. In the 1960s and 1970s the official policy was to discourage tourism, and although this has now changed, with increasing numbers of cruise ship passengers and yachties, visitors are still a rarity in most parts of the island, big hotels are set up for business visitors and some tourist services may be lacking. Arrival statistics have grown, mainly business visitors, visiting friends and relatives, yachties and holiday makers in Tobago. Probably because of the lack of commercial tourism, many Trinidadians are genuinely welcoming to strangers.

Tobago's population, mainly black, numbers about 51,000. The crime rate is catching up with Trinidad's but the people are still noticeably helpful and friendly. Tourism is a major source of income here and considerable investment has gone into hotels and infrastructure in the last few years.

Religion Catholics are still the largest religious group but Hindus are not far behind. The Anglican Church and Methodists are also influential, as are many evangelical groups. Spiritual Baptists blend African and Christian beliefs; the women wear white robes and head ties on religious occasions. They can be seen performing baptisms in the sea on the coast to the west of Port of Spain on Sunday nights. Orishas follow a more purely African tradition. Most East Indians are Hindu, some are Muslim, others have converted to Christianity, particularly Presbyterianism (Canadian Presbyterian missionaries were the first to try converting the Indian population).

Government Trinidad and Tobago became a republic within the Commonwealth on 1 August 1976 under a constitution which provides for a President and a bicameral Parliament comprising a 31-seat Senate and a 36-seat House of Representatives. Tobago has its own 12-seat House of Assembly, which runs many local services. In February 1997 the first contested presidential election was won by Arthur NR Robinson, the former prime minister and leader of the NAR. He was sworn in for a five-year term, succeeding Noor Hassanali, who retired after serving two terms. The electoral college which votes for the president is made up of the House of Representatives and the Senate.

Economy

Structure of production Petroleum, natural gas and their products dominate the economy, providing about a quarter of gdp, one fifth of government current revenue and three quarters of foreign exchange earnings. Three quarters of oil production comes from marine fields. Production is around 123,000 barrels a day but proven reserves are enough to last only 11 years. There is one refinery, at Pointe-a-Pierre, the other at Point Fortin having been mothballed. The island has substantial proven reserves of natural gas of 21.30 trillion cu ft, producing about 1.4 billion cu ft daily in 2000. These are used as a basic raw material for the production of petrochemicals such as methanol and ammonia, to provide liquefied natural gas for export and to provide electric power throughout the country. New plants will raise annual methanol capacity to 2.97 million tonnes by 2001 and ammonia capacity to 3.45 million tonnes, making Trinidad and Tobago the world's largest exporter of both. Trinidad's mineral deposits include asphalt from the pitch lake at La Brea on the southwest coast, gypsum, limestone, sand and gravel, which are mainly used for construction.

The first settlers had no difficulty in raising a variety of crops, with coffee, sugar and cocoa being the major exports. Today, however, agriculture contributes 2.1% of gross domestic product and employs only 8.8% of the labour force. Coffee and cocoa production has declined and the sugar industry makes heavy losses. However, smaller, private farmers produce fruits and vegetables successfully for the local market.

An attempt is being made to diversify the economy and lessen the dependence on oil and natural gas. Tourism is an important source of foreign exchange, but only really in Tobago. Stayover arrivals were 358,800 in 2000, but many of those to Trinidad were business visitors or Trinidadians living overseas, with some yachties and eco-tourists. Tobago now has 2,174 hotel rooms available, following an expansion in construction, notably a 200-room Hilton hotel, while Trinidad has 2,062 rooms. There has been some increase in cruise traffic. Port of Spain attracted 66,000 cruise passengers in 2000, with another 16,500 in Tobago.

Culture

The most exciting introduction to the vivid, cosmopolitan culture of this Republic is, of course, **Carnival**, or 'De Mas', as locals refer to the annual 'celebration of the senses'. Alongside a strong oral/literary tradition goes a highly developed visual culture, reflecting the islands' racial melange. The most obvious examples are the inventive designs for the carnival bands, which often draw on craft skills like wire bending, copper beating, and the expressive use of fibreglass moulds. A fabled, controversial Mas' designer is Peter Minshall, who designed the opening ceremony for the 1992 Barcelona Olympic Games (thousands twirled silk squares in one sequence) and the Atlanta Games in 1996. Fine painters and sculptors abound, too, and there are some good commercial galleries in Port of Spain. Michel Jean Cazabon, born 1813, was the first great local artist (an illustrated biography by Aquarela Gallery owner Geoffrey MacLean is out of print, but there is an illustrated book on the Lord Harris Collection with plenty of information). Contemporary work to look out for includes paintings and other artwork by Christopher Cozier, Irenée Shaw, Che Lovelace, Mario Lewis, Wendy Nanan, Emheyo Bahabba (Embah), Francisco Cabral, also Anna Serrao and Johnny Stollmeyer, known for their crafts as well as artwork. Established artists include Pat Bishop, Isaiah Boodhoo, LeRoy Clarke, Kenwyn Crichlow and Boscoe Holder. A space with contemporary work on show and a good contact point for local artists is *CCA7* on Fernandes-Angostura distillery compound, T6251889, www.cca7.org Commercial galleris include 101 Tragarete Road, or *1234* in the *Hotel Normandie*, or *Art Creators* in de Lima Apts, St Anns, also close to the *Normandie*.

The extraordinary spectacle of carnival (see page 925) is considered by many to be safer, more welcoming to visitors and artistically more stimulating than its nearest rival in Rio de Janeiro. Commercialization is undermining many of the greatest Mas' traditions, but some of the historical characters like the Midnight Robber and the Moko Jumbies can be glimpsed at the Viey La Cou old time Carnival street theatre at Queens Hall a week before Carnival and often at J'Ouvert (pronounced joo-vay) on Carnival Monday morning and in small, independent bands of players. But it's a great party, enlivened by hundreds of thousands of costumed masqueraders and the homegrown music, calypso and steelband (usually referred to as 'pan').

Calypsonians (or kaisonians, as the more historically minded call them) are the commentators, champions and sometime conscience of the people. This unique musical form, a mixture of African, French and, eventually, British, Spanish and even East Indian influences dates back to Trinidad's first 'shantwell', Gros Jean, late in the 18th century. Since then it has evolved into a popular, potent force, with both men and women (also children, of late) battling for the Calypso Monarch's crown. This fierce competition takes place at the Sunday night Dimanche Gras show at the Queens Park Savannah, which in turn immediately precedes the official start of J'Ouvert at 0400 on the Monday morning, marking the beginning of Carnival proper. Calypsonians band together to perform in 'tents' (performing halls) in the weeks leading up to the competition and are judged in semi-finals, which hones down the list to six final contenders. The season's calypso songs blast from radio stations and sound systems all over the islands and visitors should ask locals to interpret the sometimes witty and often scurrilous lyrics, for they are a fascinating introduction to the state of the nation. Currently, party soca tunes dominate although some of the commentary calypsonians, like Sugar Aloes, are still heard on the radio. There is also a new breed of 'Rapso' artists, fusing calypso and rap music. Chutney, an Indian version of calypso, is also becoming increasingly popular, especially since the advent of radio stations devoted only to Indian music. Chutney is also being fused with soca, to create 'chutney soca'.

Pan music has a shorter history, developing this century from the tamboo- bamboo bands which made creative use of tins, dustbins and pans plus lengths of bamboo for

Trinidad & Tobago

percussion instruments. By the end of the Second World War (during which Carnival was banned) some ingenious souls discovered that huge oil drums could be converted into expressive instruments, their top surfaces tuned to all ranges and depths (eg the ping pong, or soprano pan embraces 28 to 32 notes, including both the diatonic and chromatic scales). Aside from the varied pans, steelbands also include a rhythm section dominated by the steel, or iron men. For Carnival, the steelbands compete in the grand Panorama, playing calypsoes which are also voted on for the Road March of the Year. Biennally, the World Steelband Festival highlights the versatility of this music, for each of the major bands must play a work by a classical composer as well as a calypso of choice. On alternate years the National Schools Steelband Festival is held, similarly in late October/early November. A pan jazz festival is held annually in November, with solos, ensembles and orchestras all emphasizing the versatility of the steel drum.

Other musical forms in this music-mad nation include **parang** (pre-Christmas). Part of the islands' Spanish heritage, parang is sung in Spanish and accompanied by guitar, cuatro, mandoline and tambourine. The big annual parang competitions are at Paramin, in a natural hillside amphitheatre to the north of Port of Spain, and at Lopinot, in the east, towards Arima. For the Hindu and Muslim festivals, there are East Indian drumming and vocal styles like chowtal, which is particularly associated with Phagwa in early March.

Throughout the year, there are regular performances of plays and musicals, often by Caribbean dramatists, and concerts by fine choirs like the Marionettes Chorale and the Lydian Singers, sometimes accompanied by steelbands. There is a lot of comedy but some serious plays too, see press for details. Theatres include the Little Carib Theatre (T6224644), Space Theatre (T6230732), the Central Bank Auditorium (T6230845) and Queen's Hall (6241284).

Background reading is a help for a visit at any time of the year. Some authors to investigate are CLR James, Samuel Selvon, Shiva Naipaul, all now deceased, as well as Shiva's more famous brother, VS Naipaul. Also, the historian and past prime minister Dr Eric Williams, Earl Lovelace and newcomer Valerie Belgrave (whose *Ti Marie* has been described as the Caribbean *Gone with the Wind*). Although the tradition of performance poetry is not as strong here as in, say, Jamaica (calypso fulfils some of its role), the monologues of Paul Keens-Douglas, some of which are on album or cassette, are richly entertaining and a great introduction to the local dialect or patois.

The Venezuelan Islands

19

The Venezuelan Islands

Isla de Margarita is the largest of Venezuela's 72 islands in the Caribbean. It first became popular with Venezuelan tourists taking advantage of its duty free status to go on a shopping spree but, following a property boom, foreign tourists are now also attracted by low prices as hotels struggle to fill their rooms. The beaches are long, sandy and varied, those facing east having excellent surfing and windsurfing. More difficult to get to, Islas Los Roques are a national park, treasured for long stretches of white beaches, snorkelling and diving on the reef and many nesting sites for sea birds. Other islands are even more remote and are best visited by yacht, giving you the freedom to explore without worrying where you are going to sleep.

A Foot in the door

- **Margarita** is a beach lover's mecca. There are rough ones for surfing, calmer ones for windsurfing and quiet ones for swimming and sunbathing. Take bucket loads of sunscreen.
- Watch the sunset at the little fort of La Galera on a promontory overlooking the fishing town of **Juan Griego**, where you can go for dinner afterwards at one of the many seafront restaurants.
- The best way to get to the other Venezuelan islands is by **yacht**, this gives you the flexibility to explore all those deserted cays and empty beaches without worrying about where you're going to spend the night.
- Birdwatchers can overdose on birds on **Isla de Aves**, home to sooty and brown noddy terns, frigate birds and other gulls, as well as being a nesting site for green turtles.

Essentials

Before you travel

Documents Entry is by **passport** and **visa**, or by passport and **tourist card**. Tourist cards (*tarjetas de ingreso*) are valid only for those entering by air and are issued by most airlines to visitors from: Andorra, Antigua and Barbuda, Argentina, Australia, Austria, Barbados, Belgium, Brazil, Canada, Chile, Costa Rica, Dominica, Denmark, Finland, France, Germany, Ireland, Italy, Iceland, Japan, Liechtenstein, Luxembourg, Lithuania, Malaysia, Mexico, Monaco, Norway, Netherlands, New Zealand, Paraguay, Portugal, St Kitts/Nevis, St Lucia, San Marino, St Vincent, South Africa, Spain, Sweden, Switzerland, Taiwan, Trinidad and Tobago, UK, Uruguay and USA. Valid for 60 days, tourist cards are not extendable. Overstaying without an extension can lead to arrest and a fine when you try to depart.

To enter the country overland or by sea, you must obtain a tourist visa in advance. Apply to a Venezuela consulate prior to arrival. For a tourist visa, you need one passport photo, passport valid for six months, references from bank and employer, onward or return ticket, completed and signed application form. The fee in the UK is £22 (costs vary from country to country). For extensions go to DIEX, Av Baralt on Plaza Miranda in Caracas, T483 2744, take passport, tourist visa, photograph and return ticket; opens 0800, passport with extension returned at end of day. DIEX offices in many cities do not offer extensions. Transit visas, valid for 72 hours are also available, mostly the same requirements and cost (inward and onward tickets needed). *DIEX* in Caracas will not exchange a transit for a tourist visa. It appears that you cannot get a visa in advance in the USA or Canada, so to apply for an overland visa in Colombia or Brazil you need: passport, one photo and an onward ticket. In Manaus you also need a yellow fever inoculation certificate. Consuls may give a one-year visa if a valid reason can be given. To change a tourist visa to a business visa, to obtain or to extend the latter, costs £42 in UK. Visas to work in Venezuela also cost £42 and require authorization from the Dirección General Sectorial de Identificación y Control de Extranjeros in Caracas. Student visas require a letter of acceptance from the Venezuelan institution, proof of means of support, medical certificate, passport photo, passport and £42. It generally takes two days to issue any visa. Tourist visas are multiple entry within their specified period.

Nationals of countries not listed above must obtain a consular visa in advance. All travellers to Venezuela are advised to check with the consulate before leaving home as regulations are subject to change.

NB Carry your passport with you at all the times when you are in Venezuela as the police mount frequent spot checks and anyone found without identification is immediately detained (carrying a certified copy for greater safety is permissible, though not always accepted by officials). Border searches are very thorough and there are many military checkpoints in military areas, at which all transport is stopped. Have your documents ready and make sure you know what entry permits you need; soldiers may be unfamiliar with regulations for foreigners. Do not lose the carbon copy of your visa as this has to be surrendered when leaving the country.

You may bring into Venezuela, free of duty, 25 cigars and 200 cigarettes, two litres of alcoholic drinks, four small bottles of perfume, and gifts at the inspector's discretion. New items to the value of US$1,000 may be brought in.

Customs

Currency The unit of currency is the bolívar, which is divided into 100 céntimos (owing to devaluation, céntimos not in use). There are coins for 5, 10, 20, 50, 100 and 500 bolívares, and notes for 5, 10, 20, 50, 100, 500, 1,000, 2,000, 5,000 and 10,000 bolívares. There is a shortage of small coins and notes: many shops round up prices unless you have small change or notes.

Money
People are reluctant to take 5,000 & 10,000 bolívar notes because these denominations are frequently forged. Beware of forged Amex TCs & US$ notes

Exchange To convert unused bolívares back into dollars upon leaving, you must present the original exchange receipt (up to 30% of original amount charged); only banks and authorized *casas de cambio* can legally sell bolívares. *Casas de cambio* may change travellers' cheques more readily than banks, but they always insist on seeing a passport and may also insist on proof of purchase. *Ital Cambio* seems to be the most fastidious; they may even take your photo. Commission charges vary but several institutions change Thomas Cook travellers' cheques without commission, eg *Ital Cambio*, *ABN Amro Bank* and *Banco Provincial*. You should be wary of using cash machines throughout the country as machines are often old or tampered with. Visa and Mastercard transactions inside banks offer good rates and, although slower, are much safer. *Corp Banca* is affiliated with American Express, no commission, some branches cash personal cheques from abroad on an Amex card. *Unibanca*, *Banco de Venezuela* and *Banco Mercantil* (not all branches) handle Visa and ATM transactions, including cash advances and Banco Mercantil handles Mastercard. *American Express* assistance T0212-2084922; *Mastercard* T8001-2902; *Visa* T8001-2169. It is quite common for tour companies not to accept credit cards, other than for flights, so you will need cash or travellers' cheques for buying tours.

Since 1997, it has become very difficult to change dollars cash or travellers' cheques in Venezuela. Visitors are strongly advised to use Visa or Mastercard. If changing money in hotels, do not take sterling or any other European currencies. Rates of exchange in hotels are generally poor.

Tropical, with little change between season.

Climate

Getting there

From Europe There are regular flights from London, Paris, Amsterdam, Frankfurt, Madrid, Rome, Milan and Lisbon. **From North America** Cities which have direct flights to Caracas are New York, Miami, Orlando, New Orleans, Chicago, Atlanta, Dallas and Houston. **From Latin America and the Caribbean** South American cities from which there are direct flights to Caracas are Bogotá, Medellín, Buenos Aires, Santa Cruz (Bolivia), Rio de Janeiro, São Paulo, Manaus, Santiago de Chile, Lima, Quito and Guayaquil. From Central America there are flights from Mexico City (daily), San José and Panama City (Lacsa). Caribbean cities with flights to Venezuela are Santo Domingo (Dominican Republic), San Juan (Puerto Rico), Curaçao, Aruba, Bonaire, Port of Spain, Barbados, Fort-de-France (Martinique – Air France twice a week), and Havana.

Air

Ports of entry Do not try to clear Customs and Immigration without an agent in commercial port, well worth the fee. Get your tourist card at a Venezuelan embassy before arriving, although if you arrive during a major storm officials may make an exception. **Security** During the busy hurricane season security problems increase; thieves arrive by night in boats with bolt cutters and fast engines and steal dinghies, motors and other items left on deck. Best security is in marinas. Porlamar even has trouble with swimmers during the day. Fewer problems in the outer islands of La Blanquilla, La Tortuga, Los Roques, Los Aves and Los Testigos, but trouble reported in coastal anchorages eg Cumaná, Mochima, Morrocoy, Puerto La Cruz. Take all precautions possible.

Sea
See pages & 985 for details of Windward Lines & other ferries

The Venezuelan Islands

Touching down

Departure tax *Passengers on international flights pay an exit tax of approximately US$30 payable in bolívares or dollars. Minors under 12 years of age do not pay the exit tax. There is a 1% tax on the cost of all domestic flights, plus an airport tax which varies according to the airport.*

Business hours *Banks: open from 0830 to 1530, Monday to Friday only.* **Government** *offices: hours vary, but 0800-1200 are usual morning hours. Government officials have fixed hours, usually 0900-1000 or 1500-1600, for receiving visitors. Business firms generally start work about 0800, and some continue until about 1800 with a midday break.* **Shops:** *0900-1300, 1500-1900, Monday to Saturday. Generally speaking, Venezuelans start work early, and by 0700 everything is in full swing. Most firms and offices close on Saturday.*

Official time *Atlantic Standard Time, four hours behind GMT, one hour ahead of EST.*

Voltage *110 volts, 60 cycles, throughout the country.*

Weights & measures *Metric.*

Hotel price grades *LL over US$150; L US$100-150; AL US$ 66-99; A US$46-65; B US$31-45; C US$21-30; D US$12-20; E US$7-11; F US$6 and under.*

Tourist offices overseas

Germany Im Rheingarten 7, D-53225 Bonn, T0049228-400920, F0049228-400922, www.botschaft-venezuela.de UK 56 Grafton Way, London W1P 5LB, T020-73876726, F020-73833253, www.venezlon.demon.co.uk USA 1099 30th St, NW, Washington DC 20007, T1-202-3422214, F3426820, www.embavenez-us.org

Tipping *Taxi drivers are tipped if the taxi has a meter (hardly anywhere), but not if you have agreed the fare in advance. Usherettes are not tipped. Hotel porters, US$0.50; airport porters US$0.50 per piece of baggage. Restaurants, between 5% and 10% of bill.*

Safety *Cameras and other valuables should not be exposed prominently. In Caracas, carry handbags, cameras etc on the side away from the street as motor-cycle purse-snatchers are notorious. Hotel thefts are becoming more frequent.*

Touching down

Airport information To avoid overbooking the Government obliges airlines to post a passenger list, but it is important to obtain clear instructions from the travel agent regarding confirmation of your flight and checking-in time. Passengers leaving Caracas on international flights must reconfirm their reservations not less than 72 hours in advance, it is safer to do so in person than by telephone; not less than 24 hours for national flights (if you fail to do this, you lose all rights to free accommodation, food, transport, etc if your flight is cancelled and you may lose your seat if the plane is fully booked). Beware of counterfeit tickets; buy only from agencies. If told by an agent that a flight is fully booked, try at the airport anyway. International passengers must check in two hours before departure or they may lose their seat to someone on a waiting list. Handling charge for your luggage US$0.50.

Airport facilities 28 km from Caracas, near the port of La Guaira: **Maiquetía**, for national flights, **Simón Bolívar** for international flights, adjacent to each other (5 min walk – taxis take a circular route, fare US$2.25; airport authorities run a shuttle bus between the two every 10 minutes from 0700). Many facilities close on 1 January, including duty and money exchangers. Several *casas de cambio* open 24 hours (*Italcambio*, good rates, outside duty-free area; also *Banco Industrial*, branch in international terminal and another, less crowded, in baggage reclaim area). If changing TCs, you may be asked for your purchase receipt; commission 2½%. There are cash machines for Visa, Amex and Mastercard. Pharmacy, bookshops, basement café (good value meals and snacks, open 0600-2400, hard to find; cafés and bars on 1st floor viewing terrace also good value), tourist office (see below). No official left luggage; ask for Paulo at the mini bar on the 1st floor of international terminal. Look after your belongings in both terminals. Direct dial phone calls to USA only, from AT&T booth in international departure lounge. CANTV at gates 15 and 24, open 0700-2100, long-distance, international and fax services. When several flights arrive close together there are long queues for immigration.

From airport to Caracas Taxi fares from airport to Caracas cost US$18 minimum, depending on the quality of the taxi, the part of city, or on the number of stars of your hotel, regardless of distance. Overcharging is rife and taxi drivers can be aggressive in seeking passengers. Fares are supposedly controlled, but it is essential to negotiate with the drivers; find out what the official fare is first. After 2200 and at weekends a surcharge of 20% may be added, you may get charged up to US$40. Drivers may only surcharge you for luggage (US$0.50 per large bag). If you think the licensed taxi driver is overcharging you, make a complaint to Corpoturismo or tell him you will report him to the Departamento de Protección del Consumidor. The airport shuttle bus (blue and white with "Aeropuerto Internacional" on the side) leaves from east end of terminal, left out of exit (in the city, under the flyover at Bolívar and Av Sur 17, 250 m from Bellas Artes metro, poorly lit at night, not recommended to wait here in the dark), regular service from 0700 to 2300, bus leaves when there are enough passengers; fare to international terminal US$3.50. The bus is usually crowded so first time visitors may find a taxi advisable.

Always allow plenty of time when going to the airport, whatever means of transport you are using: the route can be very congested (two hours in daytime, but only 30 minutes at 0430). Allow at least two hours checking-in time before your flight. Airport bus or *por puesto* to airport can be caught at Gato Negro metro station.

Tourist information

Local tourist office *Corpoturismo*, Apartado 50.200, Caracas, main office for information is floor 37, Torre Oeste, Parque Central, T5765696. The tourist office at the international airport has good maps, helpful; some English spoken, open 0700-2400; tourist office at national terminal open 0700-2100. When manned both offices will book hotels and reconfirm flights. Websites with useful information and links are www.auyantepuy.com www.terra.com.ve www.infoguia.net www.cyberven.com and www.venezuelaonline.com For the latest national news www.el-universal.com and http://el-nacional.terra.com.ve are two of the best Venezuelan dailies on the web (Spanish).

The Venezuelan Islands

Where to stay

Hotels *Fairmont International*, Torre Capriles, Planta Baja, Plaza Venezuela, Caracas, T7828433, F7824407, will book hotel rooms both in Caracas and in other towns, no booking fee, recommended as helpful. All, except luxury class hotels charge officially controlled prices.
Camping In Venezuela camping is a popular recreation, spending a weekend at the beach, on the islands, in the *llanos* and in the mountains. It is not, however, possible at the roadside. If camping on the beach, for the sake of security, pitch your tent close to others, even if they play their radios loud.

See box on page 974 for details of hotel price grades

Getting around

Air
Beware of overbooking during holiday time, especially at Caracas airport

Most important places are served by *Aeropostal*, *Aereotuy*, *Air Venezuela*, *Aserca*, *Avensa*, *Avior*, *LAI*, *Laser*, *Santa Bárbara* and *Servivensa* which fly to a variety of destinations. None is perfect. Internal airlines offer special family discounts and student discounts, but this practice is variable (photocopies of ISIC card are useful as this allows officials to staple one to the ticket). Sometimes there is little difference between 1st class and tourist class fares.

Car

All visitors to Venezuela can drive if they are over 18 and have a valid driving licence from their own country; an international driving licence is preferred. If you have an accident and someone is injured, you will be detained as a matter of routine, even if you are not at fault. Do not drive at night if you can help it (if you do have to, do not drive fast). Carry insect spray if you do; if you stop and get out, the car will fill with biting insects. Self-drive tours, and fly-drive are available, the latter through *National Car Rental*, which has a wide network of offices. Basic rates for a car are from US$20-50 per day depending on make; government tax of 16.5% is also added. Rates tend to be the same in all cities, except on Margarita, which is more expensive. Car and personal insurance (US$10-17.50 per day) is strongly recommended.

Bus   Buses are relatively cheap, but the quality of long-distance travel varies a lot. There are numerous services between the major cities. The colectivo taxis and minibuses, known in Venezuela as *por puesto*, seem to monopolize transport to and from smaller towns and villages. Outside Caracas, town taxis are relatively expensive.

Sea   You can also charter a yacht and visit the Venezuelan islands. A Venezuelan captain must be

See page 26 for arriving by yacht in your own vessel   on board, even on a bareboat charter. He knows the rules, regulations and places to go, which makes it easier. A recommended yacht is *El Gato*, Captain Pinky can be contacted through Cumanagoto Marina. A typical 12-day cruise starts from the mainland with a downwind sail to Los Testigos for a few days of relaxation, snorkelling or diving, then to Juan Griego, on north coast of Margarita with a night in a hotel, on to La Blanquilla to visit two beautiful, white sand beaches, spending the night ashore in tents, and back to Margarita. Charters can be designed to suit your needs, day sails or longer.

Keeping in touch

Post   *Ipostel*, the national postal service, offers an international express mail service (EMS), which guarantees delivery in 2-3 days depending on destination. It costs from US$20 for up to 1 kg. Normal airmail letters cost US$0.90 for up to 10 grams and usually take 2-3 days to the USA. *Ipostel* also offer EEE, which is a domestic express service, guaranteeing delivery next day. An alternative to *DHL* and other courier companies is *Grupo Zoom*, who sell A5 or A4 envelopes for international postage, guaranteed delivery in 3-4 days, cost US$10-15.

Telephone   All international and long distance calls are operated by *CANTV* and can be dialled direct.

IDD code: 58   Major cities are linked by direct dialling (*Discado Directo*), with a three-figure prefix for each town in Venezuela. In 2001 all phone codes in the country were being changed. City codes were changed on a rolling programme throughout the year and all should have taken place by the time this volume is in print. The new codes are given in the text below. Mobile phone codes were due to change in late 2001, the number 4 being prefixed to existing codes. There are *CANTV* offices for long-distance and international calls. Collect calls are possible to some countries, at least from Caracas, though staff in offices may not be sure of this. Most public phones on prepaid *CANTV* cards (*tarjetas*) in denominations of 3,000 and 5,000 bolívares. Buy them from *CANTV* or numerous small shops bearing the *CANTV* logo, or a scrap of card reading "*Si! hay tarjetas!*" They are also sold by street vendors. Make sure they are still in their clear plastic wrapper with an unbroken red seal. Many small shops impose a 25% handling charge and *tarjetas* may be out of stock. When making international calls from a public booth, ensure that it has a globe symbol on the side. International calls are cheaper with a *tarjeta*, minimum needed Bs5,000, but you get little more than a minute to Europe. To make an international call, dial 00 plus country code, etc. Canada direct: 800-11100. For UK, BT Direct, 800-11440 (BT chargecard works from any phone). For collect calls to Germany T800-11490. International calls are charged by a series of bands, ranging from about US$1 per minute to USA and Canada, to US$2 to UK, to US$2.15. There are various reduced and economy rates according to band. **Fax** rates are as for phones. **Email** is becoming more common and public access to the internet is fairly widespread with cybercafés opening in both large and small towns. The best places for cybercafés are Caracas and Mérida.

Food and drink

Food   There is excellent local fish (*pargo* or red snapper), crayfish, small oysters and prawns. Of true

Venezuelans dine late   Venezuelan food there is *sancocho* (a stew of vegetables, especially yuca, with meat, chicken or fish); *arepas*, a kind of white maize bread, very bland in flavour; toasted *arepas* served with a wide selection of relishes, fillings or the local somewhat salty white cheese are cheap, filling and nutritious; *cachapas*, a maize pancake (soft, not hard like Mexican *tortillas*) wrapped around white cheese; *pabellón*, made of shredded meat, beans, rice and fried plantains (vegetarian versions available); and *empanadas*, maize-flour pies containing cheese, meat or fish. At Christmas only there are *hallacas*, maize pancakes stuffed with chicken, pork, olives, etc boiled in a plantain leaf (but don't eat the leaf). A *muchacho* (boy) on the menu is a cut of beef. *Ganso* is also not goose but beef. *Solomo* and *lomito* are other cuts of beef. *Hervido* is chicken or beef with vegetables. *Contorno* with a meat or fish dish is a choice of chips, boiled potatoes, rice or yuca. *Caraotas* are beans; *cachitos* are *croissants* of bread. *Pasticho* is what the Venezuelans call Italian *lasagne*. The main fruits are bananas, oranges, grapefruit, mangoes, pineapple and papaya. Some Venezuelan variants of names for fruit: *lechosa* is papaya, *patilla* is water melon, *parchita* passion fruit, and *cambur* a small banana. A delicious sweet is *huevos chimbos* – egg yolk boiled and bottled in sugar syrup.

Drink

Venezuelan rum is very good; recommended brands are *Cacique*, *Pampero* and *Santa Teresa*. There are four good local beers: *Polar* (the most popular), *Regional* (with a strong flavour of hops), *Cardenal* and *Nacional* (a *lisa* is a glass of keg beer; for a bottle of beer ask for a *tercio*); *Brahma* beer (lighter than *Polar*), is imported from Brazil. There are also mineral waters, gin and good, local wine. The Polar brewery has joined with Martell (France) and built a winery in Carora. Wines produced are 'Viña Altagracia' and 'Bodegas Pomar.' 'Bodegas Pomar' also produces a sparkling wine in the traditional champagne style. Liqueurs are cheap, try the local *ponche crema*. The coffee is very good (*café con leche* has a lot of milk, *café marrón* much less, *cafe negro* for black coffee, which, though obvious, is not common usage in the rest of Latin America). Visitors should also try a *merengada*, a delicious drink made from fruit pulp, ice, milk and sugar; a *batido* is the same but with water and a little milk; *jugo* is the same but with water.

Holidays and festivals

Public holidays

There are two sorts of holidays, those enjoyed by everybody and those taken by employees of banks and insurance companies. Holidays applying to all businesses include: 1 January, **Carnival** on the Monday and Tuesday before Ash Wednesday (everything shuts down Saturday-Tuesday; make sure accommodation is booked in advance), Thursday-Saturday of **Holy Week**, 19 April, 1 May, 24 June (the **feast day of San Juan Bautista**, a particularly popular festival celebrated along the central coast where there were once large concentrations of plantation slaves who considered San Juan their special Saint; some of the best-known events are in villages between Puerto Cabello and Chuspa, to the east, such as Chuao, Cata and Ocumane de la Costa), 5 July, 24 July, 12 October, 25 December. Holidays for banks and insurance companies include all the above and also: 19 March and the nearest Monday to 6 January, Ascension Day, 29 June, 15 August, 1 November and 8 December. There are also holidays applying to certain occupations such as Doctor's Day or Traffic Policeman's Day. From 24 December-1 January, most restaurants are closed and there is no long-distance public transport. On **New Year's Eve**, everything closes and does not open for a least a day. Queues for tickets, and traffic jams, are long. Business travellers should not visit during Holy week or Carnival.

Health

See Health section in Essentials chapter

Water in all main towns is heavily chlorinated, so safe to drink, although most people drink bottled water. Medical attention is good. State health care is free and said to be good (the Clínica Metropolitana in Caracas has been recommended). A doctor's consultation costs about US$10. On the coast from Cumaná east precautions against vampire bat bite are warranted since they can be rabies-carriers. Lights over hatches and windows are used by local fishermen to deter bats from entering boats and shore cabins. If bitten seek medical advice. Some rivers are infected with bilharzia and in some areas there are warning signs; check before bathing. Protection against mosquito bites is advised as dengue fever has been present since 1995.

Further reading

Venezuela Handbook, by Alan Murphy & Mick Day (Footprint Handbooks, £10.99). *GAM*, the monthly *Guía Aérea y Marítima de Venezuela*, gives details of all flights into and within the country, but also of hotels, travel agents, car hire, etc. The *Guide to Venezuela* (925 pages), by Janice Bauman, Leni Young and others, in English (available in Caracas) is a mine of information and maps, US$11. *Elizabeth Kline's Guide to Camps, Posadas and Cabins/Guía de campamentos, posadas y cabañas in/en Venezuela* is published every other year and gives a comprehensive survey of these establishments. (Apartado 63089, Caracas 1067-A, Venezuela, T0212-9451543, ekline@cantv.net).

For information on the **national parks** system, and to obtain necessary permits to stay in the parks, go to Instituto Nacional de Parques (Inparques), Museo de Transporte, Edificio Sur, Avenida Rómulo Gallegos, Parque del Este (exit Parque del Este metro opposite park, turn left, office is a few hundred metres further on up a slight incline), T2841956, F2344238, Caracas, or to the local office of the *guardaparques* for each park (www.marnr.gov.ve/).

Isla de Margarita

Margarita is the country's main Caribbean holiday destination. Some parts are crowded but there are undeveloped beaches and colonial villages. Despite the property boom and frenetic building on much of the coast and in Porlamar, much of the island has been given over to natural parks. Of these the most striking is the Laguna La Restinga Isla de Margarita is in fact one island whose two sections are tenuously linked by the 18 km sandspit which separates the sea from the Restinga lagoon. At its largest, Margarita is about 32 km from north to south and 67 km from east to west. Most of its people live in the developed eastern part, which has some wooded areas and fertile valleys. The western part, the Peninsula de Macanao, is hotter and more barren, with scrub, sand dunes and marshes. Wild deer, goats and hares roam the interior, but four-wheel drive vehicles are needed to penetrate it. The entrance to the Peninsula de Macanao is a pair of hills known as Las Tetas de María Guevara, a national monument covering 1,670 ha.

Isla de Margarita

Ins and outs

There are many flights from Caracas and other Venezuelan cities, as well as international scheduled services, some from neighbouring Caribbean islands, but also from further afield. It is worth investigating charter flights from Europe and North America. There are also ferries from Puerto La Cruz and Cumaná in Venezuela, and the *Windward Lines* service (suspended 2001) from Trinidad, Barbados, St Lucia and St Vincent, see Essentials, which is an excellent way of touring the southern Caribbean.

Getting there
See transport, page 985, for further details

The roads are generally good and most are paved. A bridge connects the two parts. Sign posts are often poorly-positioned. It is best not to drive outside Porlamar after dark. Beware of robbery of hired vehicles. Check conditions and terms of hire very carefully for your liability. Public transport is available if you don't want to drive.

Getting around
Car hire is a cheap way of getting around

The climate is exceptionally good, but rain is scant. Water is piped from the mainland but water trucks also deliver to resorts to keep up with demand.

Climate

Flora and fauna

Despite the property boom and frenetic building on much of the coast and in Porlamar, much of the island has been given over to natural parks. Of these the most striking is the **Laguna La Restinga**. Launches provide lengthy runs around the mangrove swamps, but they create a lot of wash and noise. The mangroves are fascinating, with shellfish clinging to the roots. The launch will leave you on a shingle and shell beach (don't forget to arrange with your boatman to collect you), and you can rummage for shellfish in the shallows (protection against the sun essential). Flamingoes live in the lagoon. There are mangroves also in the Laguna de las Marites Natural Monument, west of Porlamar. Other parks are Las Tetas de María Guevara, Cerro el Copey, 7,130 ha, and Cerro Matasiete y Guayamurí, 1,672 ha (both reached from La Asunción). Details of Inparques, the national parks office, are given on page 978. By boat from Porlamar you can go to the Isla de los Pájaros, or Morro Blanco, for both bird-spotting and underwater fishing. In Boca del Río there is a Museum of the Sea.

Diving and marine life

The Venezuelan Islands are fast becoming new dive destinations with sites found off Margarita, La Blanquilla, Los Testigos, Las Frailes and Los Roques. There is good snorkelling and diving off **Cubagua** on a sunken barge and a ferry with cars still inside. At **Farallón**, near Pampatar, there is an underwater religious statue, large brain coral, large sea fans and large fish, including barracuda, in about 12 m of water. **La Macura** is a rock patch where holes in boulders are home to large, colourful parrotfish. **Los Frailes**, eight small islands northeast of Margarita are ideal for current dives and rich underwater life including moray eels, barracudas and oysters.

The Venezuelan Islands

Beaches and watersports

Nude sunbathing is forbidden. Topless bathing is not seen, except at some resort pools and beaches, but the tanga (hilo dental – dental floss) is fairly common

Apart from the shopping, what attracts the holidaymakers from Venezuela and abroad are the beaches: long white stretches of sand bordered by palms. In Porlamar, the main beach suffers from its popularity: calm shallow water, pedalos for hire, windsurf classes; but that by the *Bella Vista*, although crowded with foreign tourists, is kept clean. For a more Venezuelan atmosphere go northeast to Pampatar, which is set around a bay favoured by foreign yachtsmen as a summer anchorage; jet skis for hire on a clean and pretty beach. A scale model of Columbus' *Santa María* is used for taking tourists on trips. A fishing boat can be hired for US$20 for 2½ hours, four to six passengers; shop around for best price, good fun and fishing. The beaches on the eastern side are divided into ocean and calm beaches, according to their location in relation to the open sea. The former tend to be rougher (good surfing and windsurfing) and colder. Windsurfing instruction and equipment rentals can be found. Water is uniformly clear and unpolluted. It is still possible, even in high season, to find practically deserted beaches. Restaurants, *churuatas* (bars built like Indian huts), sunshades and deckchairs are becoming widespread. (Hire charges are about US$1.50 per item.)

Other sports **Golf** can be played at the *Isla Bonita Golf and Beach Hotel*, where there is an 18-hole, par 72 course in the Valle Pedro González, T657111, open to all. **Horse riding** is organized through the desert, mountains and beaches of the Peninsula de Macanao and the wilderness area of Cabatucán, beginners welcome, T819348.

Porlamar

Phone code: 0295
Population: 85,000

Most of the hotels are at Porlamar, 20 km from the airport and about 28 km from **Punta de Piedra**, where most of the ferries dock. It has a magnificent cathedral. At Igualdad y Díaz is the **Museo de Arte Francisco Narváez**. The main, and most expensive, shopping area is Avenida Santiago Mariño; better bargains and a wider range of shops are to be found on Gómez and Guevara. The centre of the city is crowded with cars and shoppers, while to the east there is continuing, apparently chaotic development of big holiday hotels and condominiums, separated by vast

Porlamar

N
Not to scale

■ Sleeping	3 Palermo	● Eating
1 Bella Vista	4 Porlamar	1 Los 3 Delfines
2 Imperial & Tamá	5 San Miguel	

The Venezuelan Islands

areas of waste ground and construction sites. Costa Azul is the main *urbanización*, served by a long strip of featureless sand known as Playa Moreno. At night everything closes by 2300; women alone should avoid the centre after dark. Porlamar has many casinos, all of which lack legal status. Note that in Porlamar there is a Calle Mariño and an Avenida Santiago Mariño in the centre.

Ferries go to the **Isla de Coche** (11 km by 6 km), which has over 4,500 inhabitants and one of the richest salt mines in the country. They also go, on hire only, to **Isla de Cubagua**, which is totally deserted, but you can visit the ruins of Nueva Cádiz (which have been excavated).Large catamarans take tourists on day sails to Coche.

Around the island

The capital, La Asunción, is a few kilometres inland from Porlamar. It has several colonial buildings, a cathedral, and the fort of **Santa Rosa**, with a famous bottle dungeon. ■ *Mon 0800-1500, other days 0800-1800.* There is a museum in the Casa Capitular, and a local market, good for handicrafts. Nearby are the Cerro Matasiete historical site, where the defeat of the Spanish on 31 July 1817 led to their evacuation of the island, and the Félix Gómez look out in the Sierra Copuy.

La Asunción
Population: 30,000

Between La Asunción and Porlamar are the Parque Francisco Fajardo, beside the Universidad de Oriente, and **El Valle del Espíritu Santo**. Here is the church of the **Virgen del Valle**, a picturesque building with twin towers, painted white and pink. The Madonna is richly dressed (one dress has pearls, the other diamonds); the adjoining museum opens at 1400, it displays costumes and presents for the Virgin, including the "milagro de la pierna de perla", a leg-shaped pearl. A pilgrimage is held in early September. Proper dress is requested to enter the church. Throughout the island, the churches are attractive: fairly small, with baroque towers and adornments and, in many cases, painted pink.

Pampatar has the island's largest fort, **San Carlos Borromeo** (built 1662 after the Dutch destroyed the original fort), and the smaller **La Caranta**, where the cannon show signs of having been spiked. Visit also the church of Cristo del Buen Viaje, the Library/Museum and the customs house. There is an amusement park to the southwest of Pampatar, called **Isla Aventura**, with ferris wheel, roller coaster, water slide, dodgems etc. ■ *Fri and Sat, 1800-2400, Sun, 1700-2400, and more frequently in peak holiday season. Entrance in peak season is US$5 adults, US$3.35 children, includes all rides; in low season entrance is US$0.50 and each ride US$0.30-0.60.* The beach at Pampatar is picturesquely circled with palm trees and kiosks selling local fresh fish from the fishing fleet anchored in the bay. Limited local services and watersports. A scale model of Columbus' Santa María is used for taking tourists on trips. A fishing boat can be hired for US$20 for 2½ hours, 4-6 passengers; shop around for best price, good fun and fishing. Restaurants and services crowded at weekends. La Caracola beach has an ultralight airport, kiosks, beachchairs. Bella Vista, near town, is calm, with restaurants and services.

Pampatar
Population: 25,000

On the eastern coast is **Playa Guacuco**, reached from La Asunción by a road through the Guayamurí reserve: a lot of surf, fairly shallow, palm trees, restaurant and parking lot; excellent horseriding here or up into the hills, US$30 for two hours, contact Harry Padrón at the ranch in Agua de Vaca, or phone travel agent on 611311. Before Punta Cabo Blanco are **El Cardón** and **Puerto Fermín**/El Tirano (Lope de Aguirre, the infamous conquistador, landed here in 1561 on his flight from Peru), El Caserío handicrafts museum is nearby. Beyond the point is **Parguito**: long and open, strong waves, best for surfing, full public services.

East coast

Playa El Agua, 45 minutes by bus from Porlamar is 4 km of stone-free white sand with many *kioskos*, which have palm-leaf shade areas. The sea is very rough for children, but fairly shallow (beware the strong cross current when you are at waist deep). This is the most popular beach on the island and at Venezuelan holiday times it is overcrowded. At other times it is ideal for sunbathing and walking; the fashionable part is at the southern end; the northern end is popular with younger people, is less touristy, has fewer facilities, and less shade. It is possible to see the island by Ultralight from here at weekends. Contact Omar Contreras, T0295-617632 or José-Antonio Fernández T0295-623519, English spoken. There is bungee jumping, parasailing and most watersports. Activities abound at weekends in peak season. **El Humo** is less crowded and well known, with deeper water and stronger currents, but it is a nice beach.

Manzanillo is a picturesque bay between the mountains. The water gets deep rather suddenly, fishing huts, fish sold on beach, apartments, expensive restaurant, **Playa Escondida** at the far end.

North coast   The coast road is interesting, with glimpses of the sea and beaches to one side, inland vistas on the other. There are a number of clifftop look-out points. The road improves radically beyond Manzanillo, winding from one beach to the next. **Playa Puerto la Cruz** (the widest and windiest beach) adjoins **Pedro González** (population: 3,700), with a broad sweeping beach, running from a promontory (easy to climb) to scrub and brush that reach down almost to the water's edge (ask for Antonietta Luciani at *Restaurant Pedrogonzález*, she has an apartment to rent, US$40 per day, sleeps six, well-equipped, and recommended, as is her restaurant).

Further west is **Juan Griego**, a small, sleepy town whose picturesque bay is full of fishing boats, drawn up on the narrow beach or moored offshore. The little fort of **La Galera** is on a promontory at the northern side, beyond which is a bay of the same name with a narrow strip of beach, more fishing boats and many seafront restaurants. La Galera is a good place to watch the famous Juan Griego sunset. **Playas Caribe**, north of La Galera, has beach restaurants, palm trees, some deserted caverns at the south end and the water is usually rough.

Inland from Juan Griego   South of Juan Griego, the road goes inland to **San Juan Bautista** (a pleasant colonial town ringed by hills; *por puesto* from Juan Griego), then to Punta de Piedra, the ferry dock, see below (a pleasant stretch through cultivated land and farms at regular intervals; *por puesto* Juan Griego to ferry). Due south of San Juan is **El Yaque**, near the airport and the mouth of the Laguna de las Marites. This is an international windsurfers' hangout. It has flat water and windy conditions. Surf boards can be hired at the *Club El Mistral*, good service, very helpful and friendly, half day costs US$30. It is being rapidly developed with small hotels, but it suffers from aircraft noise and lacks public transport (taxi from Porlamar, US$8). The hinterland around El Yaque is very bleak.

Near San Juan is Fuentedueño park which has special walks. A branch goes northwest to La Guardia at the eastern end of La Restinga. The dyke of broken seashells stretches to the Península de Macanao: on its right a spotlessly clean beach, on its left the lagoon. At the far end are many little restaurants and a cluster of fishermen's huts with landing stages from which the launches make trips into the labyrinth of canals and mangroves in the lagoon (US$14 per boat taking five passengers; bus from Porlamar harbourfront US$1, ask driver to drop you off).

Peninsula de Macanao   This western part of the island is quite underdeveloped, although it is hardly an untouched paradise. Some of the beaches are highly regarded: Manzanilla, Guayaconcito, Boca de Pozo, Macanao, Punta Arenas (many fishermen live here, have a lunch of fresh fish after your watersports) and Manglanillo. Harbour at Chacachacare. El Tunal is a shadeless, isolated beach near a small fishing village. La Pared has one fish restaurant with an excellent setting to watch the sunsets.

Essentials

La Asunción B *Ciudad Colonial*, La Margarita, T423086. Upmarket, pleasant. **D** *de la Asunción*, Unión, 2 blocks from Plaza Bolívar, T420902. With bath, a/c, fridge (rooms with balcony cost more but face noisy road, rooms without window cost less). Frequent *por puesto* service stops in front of hotel.

Sleeping
See page 974 for
hotel price grades

Pampatar AL *Flamingo Beach*, T624822, F620271. 5-star, all-inclusive, food, drinks, entertainment, service, taxes, casino, good value. **C** *Residencial Don Juan*, with bath and fan, apartments sleeping 6 are available.

Porlamar The following are all recommended. **L** *Hilton*, Costa Azul, T624111, F620810. Sailing dinghies for hire (ask for special rates when booking). **AL** *Bella Vista*, Av Santiago, T617222, F612557. Swimming pool, beach. **AL** *Dynasty*, T621411, F625101. Opposite *Hilton*, nice restaurant, pool. **A** *Stauffer*, T612911, F618708. Large rooms, excellent service and restaurant, bar on roof, casino. **A** *Marbella Mar*, Av Principal y Calle Chipichipi, T624022, F624488. Free bus service to the beach. **A** *Colibrí*, Av Santiago Mariño, T616346. New rooms, **C** in older rooms, a/c. **A** *Imperial*, Av Raúl Leoni, Vía El Morro, T616420, F615056. Best rooms in front have balcony, comfortable, safe, a/c, good showers, triple rooms available, English spoken. **C** *Porlamar*, Igualdad y Fajardo, T630271. Good restaurant and video bar *La Punta*, a/c or fan, hot water. **D** *Brasilia*, San Nicolás. Quiet, nice new rooms at back. **D** *Malecón*, Marina y Arismendi, T635723 .Seaview from front rooms, very helpful and generous. Dangerous area at night, best to take a taxi. **D** *Palermo*, Calle Igualdad, opposite cathedral. Best rooms on top floor with views of plaza. **D** *Robaldar*, Igualdad, near Libertad. Shower, a/c **E** *Tamá*, next to *Imperial*. Popular, basic, OK, excellent restaurant and atmosphere, bar is German-run, lots of languages spoken. Many others near Plaza Bolívar (eg **E** *San Miguel*, good value).

Playa El Agua AL *Lagunamar*, a few km north of Pampatar, T620711, F621445. Occupies a vast spread of flat coastland, 9 pools and 6 restaurants. **A** *Casa Trudel*, Dan and Trudy O'Brien (Dutch/Canadian owners), Apdo 106, Isla Margarita, 6301, Porlamar, Venezuela T/F490558, www.islamargarita.com/trudel.htm 4 rooms, CP, homely atmosphere, no young children, evening food service, barbecue once a week, 5 mins' walk from beach. Under same ownership, **A** *Trudel's Garden Vacation Home*, Calle Miragua. 6 large, 2-bedroom houses set in a beautiful garden, 200 m from beach, fresh towels daily, fully-equiped kitchens. **A** *Pelican Village*, at north end. Small group of bungalows, satellite TV, pool, restaurant, bar, German-run, quiet. **B** *Residencias Miramar*, Av 31 de Julio-Carretera Manzanillo, esq Calle Miragua, 3 mins from beach, 1 min from supermarket. Family-run, self-catering apartments, comfortable, barbecue. **C** *Hostería El Agua*, Av 31 de Julio Vía Manzanillo, T48935. Contact Sarah Studer, English, French, German and Italian spoken, good beds, fan, fridge, laundry facilities, 4 mins' walk from beach. **C** *Chalets de Belén*, Calle Miragua next to *Trudel's Garden*. 2 chalets, kitchen facilities, cold showers, no towels provided.

Manzanillo A *Hotel Karibek*, overlooks the sea. Wonderful view, quiet rooms, CP, extremely clean, balcony, bath, fan, swimming pool, bar and restaurant adjacent, easy taxi ride to other beaches. **B** *Pahayda Vilas*, sign at main road, nice apartments, large rooms, 2 baths for 4 people. 100 m further on towards Playa Azul, beach house with rooms to let and German-owned restaurant, good food.

Juan Griego B *El Yare*, El Fuerte, T530835, 1 block from beach. Some suites with kitchen, owner speaks English. **D** *Nuevo Juan Griego*, next to beach. English spoken, very popular, expensive restaurant. **D** *Aparthotel y Residencia El Apurano*, Calle La Marina y El Fuerte, T530901. Friendly, English speaking manager, 2-bedroom apartments with bath, hot water, a/c, but no utensils or towels (because of theft). **D** *Hospedaje El Caney*, Guevara 17, T514-3875345, F514-6823774 in Montréal. With bath, patio, kitchen facilities, small rooms, pleasant. **D** *Patrick's*, El Fuerte, next to *Hotel Fortín*, T/F534089. French-run, a/c rooms with fine sunset views, excellent restaurant and bar. **E** *Residencia Carmencita*, Calle Guevara 20,

T55561. A/c, private bath. **E** *Fortín*, opposite beach, a/c, cold water, most rooms have good views, good restaurant and tables on the beach. **E** *La Posada de Clary*, Los Mártires, T530037. Restaurant, also apartments for 4, **D**, a/c, kitchen, parking.

El Yaque   **B** *California*, T0414-951907, F950908. 46 rooms, small pool.

Isla del Coche   *Coche Speed Paradise*, Playa da Punta, T0149-9527226. 48 rooms, more under construction, windsurfing, sandsurfing, swimming, weekend buffet recommended, beautifully landscaped with desert paths, shells, rocks and driftwood, pool can be used by yachties during the week, see the macaws being 'watered' in the afternoon. *Isla de Coche*, T991431. 23 rooms, older resort, pool, windsurfing.

Eating   **Porlamar**   *Doña Martha*, Velázquez near Hernández. Colombian food, good, inexpensive. *El Punto Criollo*, Igualdad near *Hotel Porlamar*. Excellent value, good. *Rancho Grande*, Guevara, near Playa El Agua bus stop. Colombian, good value. Recommended. *El Pollo de Carlitos*, Marcano y Martínez. Nice location, live music most nights, good food and value. *Bahía* bar-restaurant, Av Raúl Leoni y Vía El Morro. Excellent value, live music. *Los 3 Delfines*, Cedeño 26-9. Seafood. Recommended. *La Isla*, Mariño y Cedeño. 8 fast food counters ranging from hamburgers to sausages from around the world. *Dino's Grill*, Igualdad y Martínez, T642366. Open 0700-1400, buffet lunch, indoor/outdoor seating, grill, homemade sausages, wood-fired pizza oven, cheap, friendly, good service. Recommended. On 4 de Mayo: *El Picadilly*, good cheap lunch, and *Dragón Chino*, great Chinese food.

Pampatar   *El Farallón*, excellent seafood restaurant beside Castillo. Seafood soup recommended, bowl of shellfish and meal on its own. Also beach restaurant *Antonio's* and *Trimar*, seafood.

Playa El Agua   *Restaurant El Paradiso*, southern end. Rents out cabins, small but comfortable. *Kiosko El Agua*, helpful, English spoken. *Posada Shangri-Lá* is recommended, *Casa Vieja*, seafood, *La Dorada*, French owned by Gérard and Hilda, with good beach view, good value. *Mini Golf Café*, from the corner of *Miramar* turn left after 300m. Run by Matthias, ask for special dishes cooked by Yvonne, internet access (good rates). Many beach restaurants stay open till 2200. Don't hang around after then.

Juan Griego   *Restaurant Mi Isla* is recommended. *Viña del Mar*, opposite *Hotel Fortín*. A/c, attractive, excellent food. *Juan Griego Steak House*, same building as *Hotel El Yare*. Good value. Recommended. Also *El Buho*. French-owned pub. *Viejo Muelle*, next door. Good restaurant, live music, outside beach bar.

Festivals   Many on the island, including 16-26 March at Paraguachí (Feria de San José); 27 July at Punta de Piedra; 31 July (Batalla de Matasiete) and 14-15 August (Asunción de la Virgen) at La Asunción; 8-15 September at El Valle; 4-11 November at Boca del Río, 4-30 November at Boca del Pozo; 5-6 December at Porlamar; 27 December-3 January at Juan Griego.

Nightlife   **Porlamar**   *Mosquito Coast Club*, behind *Hotel Bella Vista*. Good *merengue* and rock music, bar outside. Also does excellent Mexican meals (beware of overcharging on simple items like water). *Village Club*, Av Santiago Mariño. Recommended disco for good music with a variety of styles but expensive drinks, cover charge. *Doce 34*, Av 4 de Mayo. 2 dance floors. Highly recommended.

Shopping   **Porlamar**   Besides all duty-free shops, *Del Bellorín*, Cedeño, near Santiago Mariño. Good for handicrafts. Good selection of jewellery at *Sonia Gems*, on Cedeño. Many other places on the main street are overpriced. When purchasing jewellery, bargain hard, don't pay by credit card (surcharges are imposed), get a detailed guarantee of the item. Designer clothes are cheap in many places, especially on Blvd Guevara, Blvd Gómez, Calles Igualdad and Velázquez; cosmetics and perfumes also good value.

Supertours, Calle Larez, Quinta Thaid, T618781, F617061. Tours of the island and elsewhere. **Tour operators**
Zuluoga Tours, San Nicolás entre Arismendi y Mariño No 16-40. Helpful. Ask travel agents
about excursions on the sailing catamaran, *Catatumbo*, recommended.

Air Airport del Caribe General Santiago Mariño (PMV), between Porlamar and Punta de **Transport**
Piedra is comfortable and modern and has the international and national terminals at either *Aug & Sep are*
end. Bus from Plaza Bolívar, US$1, taxi US$10. There are many flights a day from Caracas, with *vacation months:*
Avensa, *Aeropostal*, *Laser* and *Air Venezuela*, 45 mins flight; tickets are much cheaper if pur- *flights & hotels are*
chased in Venezuela in local currency. Reservations made from outside Venezuela are not *fully booked*
always honoured. *Aeropostal* (office in *Hotel Bella Vista* shopping complex) also flies to Barbados and Port of Spain. *Avensa* on Calle Fajardo, Porlamar, T617111, airport 691021, has 4
flights a week from Madrid via Caracas and there are scheduled German flights from Munich
and Dusseldorf. Charter flights to Trinidad US$95 return. *Aerotuy* (LTA) has a fleet of small
planes for trips to national parks, eg Canaima, Los Roques, Delta del Orinoco and Isla La
Blanquilla. It operates *posadas* on Los Roques as well as 3 large charter catamarans.
T095-632211 (Porlamar), F617746, or in Caracas T02-7638043, F7625254.

Road Bus: several bus companies in Caracas sell through tickets from Caracas to Porlamar,
arriving about midday. Buses return from Porlamar from terminal at Centro Comercial Bella
Vista, at bottom end of Calle San Rafael (it takes about 4 hrs). *Por Puestos* serve most of the
island, leaving mainly from the corners of Plaza Bolívar in Porlamar. Fares: to Punta de Piedra
(from 4 blocks from Plaza Bolívar, towards sea-front), US$0.75, to the ferry terminal US$0.85;
to La Asunción, US$0.35, from Calle Fajardo, half a block from Igualdad; to Pampatar,
US$0.25; to La Restinga (from La Marina y Mariño), US$1, El Agua (from corner of Guevara
and Marcano), US$0.65; Juan Griego, US$0.65. Several offices at the airport. **Car hire**:
Ramcar, at airport and *Hotel Bella Vista*, recommended as cheap and reliable, non-deduct-
ible insurance (as do *Hertz* and *Avis*); others on Av Santiago Mariño. In all cases check the
brakes. Scooters can also be hired from, among others, *Maruba Motor Rentals*, La Mariña
(English spoken, good maps, US$16 bike for 2, US$13 bike for 1). Motor cycles may not be rid-
den between 2000 and 0500. There are service stations in towns, but check the gauge on the
fuel pump carefully: overcharging is common. **Taxi**: taxi fares are published by the magazine
Mira but are not uniformly applied by drivers. If you want to hire a taxi for a day you will be
charged US$10-15 per hour. Always establish the fare before you get in the car. There is a
30% surcharge after 2100.

Sea Ferry (very busy at weekends and Mon) **From Puerto La Cruz**, to Margarita (**Punta de**
Piedra): Conferries, Los Cocos terminal, T677221, and *Hotel Hesperia*, Puerto La Cruz,
T653001, to Margarita, 4 a day between 0800 and 0100 each way (extras at 0400 and 1600 at
busy times), 5 hrs, passengers US$12.50 one way 1st class, US$8.50 2nd (in enclosed middle
deck with limited views), children and pensioners half price, cars, US$25. A fast ferry,
Margarita Express, takes 2 hrs, US$20. Ferries not always punctual. **From Cumaná** , Conferry
Terminal, Cumaná Puerto Sucre, T311462, ferries at 0700 and 1600 to Margarita, returning
1000 and 2000, US$7.50 one way for passengers. A ferry from Punta de Piedra to Coche sails
Mon-Fri, 1600, returns 1730, Sat and Sun, 0800 and 1730, returns 0530 and 1730.

Windward Lines (suspended 2001) sails to Pampatar, Isla Margarita every other week
from Trinidad, continuing to St Vincent, Barbados and St Lucia. Contact Windward Lines
agent, Julio César Acosta, Acosta Asociados, T0281-657393, 0294-820058, or mobile
04149-9948115, grupoacosta@cantv.net efficient, speaks English, ensures immigra-
tion/customs goes smoothly. He sells tickets under a canopy on the quay some hours before
the ferry sails. Immigration and customs sit next to him. **Yacht**: on arrival, take your dinghy to
Vemesca (Venezuelan Marine Supply) in Porlamar which is the main anchorage. Clear in and
out at the Port Captain's office. It can be very crowded in hurricane season and rolly with
southeast winds. Lock up the boat, dinghy and motor as thefts are common. A few boats
stop in Pampatar, and Juan Griego makes a good stopping point when coming from La
Blanquilla. On Isla de Coche by *Paradise Speed* (move close to ferry dock at night and stay out
of way of fishermen), El Saco, Cubagua. Dinghy thefts and other security problems at

The Venezuelan Islands

Porlamar, Coche and Cubagua. Fuel and water at Porlamar dock, fuel but no water at Juan Griego. Occasionally possible to get a slip at Concorde marina. Supplies at Vemesca and several local marine stores.

Directory **Banks** *Casa de cambio* at Igualdad y Av Santiago Mariño. Also *Cambio La Precisa*, Maneiro entre Mariño y Blvd Guevara. Good rates. Banks are open 0830-1130, 1400-1630. There are often long queues. Don't change money with street people, you will be short changed. **Communications** Email: *News Café*, 4 de Mayo, open 0800-2400. **Post Office:** Calle Arismendi. **Telephones:** *CANTV*, Bolívar, entre Fajardo y Fraternidad. **Tourist office** A tourist information booth on 4 de Mayo has map, coupon booklet, *La Vista* tourist magazine. Travel agencies can also provide a tourist guide to Margarita. A good English-language newspaper, *Mira*, is published on the island; the editor/publisher acts also as an inexpensive tour guide; Av Santiago Mariño, Ed Carcaleo Suites, Apdo 2-A, Porlamar (T613351). The best map is available from Corpoven. Websites: www.islamargarita.com and www.margaritaonline.com

Islas Los Roques

Prices are higher than the mainland & infrastructure is limited but the islands are beautiful & unspoiled

Islas Los Roques lie 166 km north of La Guaira; the atoll, of about 340 islets and reefs, constitutes one of Venezuela's loveliest national parks (225,153 ha). There are long stretches of white beaches and almost 20 km of coral reef with crystal-clear water ideal for snorkelling (best at the southern part of the archipelago) and diving. There is also rewarding birdwatching, with 92 species recorded. There are many bird nesting sites (eg the huge gull colonies on Francisqui and the pelicans, boobies and frigates on Selesqui); May is nesting time at the gull colonies. For more information write to La Fundación Científica Los Roques, Apdo No 1, Av Carmelitas, Caracas 1010, T0212-326771. The islands are best visited midweek as Venezuelans swarm here on long weekends and at school holidays (low season is Easter to July). Average temperature 29°C with coolish nights. You will need strong sunblock as there is no shade. Park entry US$15 from the Park Headquarters on Gran Roque.

Many of the islands' names are contractions of earlier names: eg Northeast Cay is Nordisqui, 'Sarky' comes from Sister Key, 'Selesqui' from Sailors Cay, 'Francisqui' from Frances Cay, 'Dos Mosquices' from Domus Key, where there are sea turtles and a Marine Biology Centre researching the coral reef and its ecology.

Gran Roque
Phone code: 0212

Gran Roque is the main and only permanently inhabited island. The airport is here, as is the national guard, three grocery stores, public phones, medical facilities, a few restaurants and accommodation. There is nowhere to change travellers' cheques. Park Headquarters are in the scattered fishing village (*Population*: 900). You can negotiate with local fishermen for transport to other islands: you will need to take your own tent, food and (especially) water. **Madrisqui** has nine summer houses. **Francisqui** is three islands joined by sandspits, with calm lagoon waters to the south and rolling surf to the north. For windsurfing, *Happy Surf*, Francisqui.

Diving & marine life

This is one of the least visited diving spots in the Caribbean. You can arrange packages to stay ashore in a lodge and/or on board a sailing yacht and dive daily. *Eola* is a yacht, fully equipped, with cabins, chartered for US$120 per day, all inclusive, highly recommended as a worthwhile way of getting some shade on the treeless beaches. Run by Italians Gianni and Jaqueline. *Guaicamar* is a 75-ft yacht with 3 cabins, a/c, bathroom, hot water, dining room, kitchen, all-inclusive, use of equipment, contact Inversiones Navales, T0212-352295, F343279. The *Pelícano Club* has accommodation, excursions, boat trips and diving. **Boca del Medio** is an easy dive east of the island chain in clear, shallow water of about 10-15 m, with a great variety of coral, fauna and flora. **Piedra de la Guasa** is a 10-25 m underwater cliff where you can see grouper, snapper, barracuda, horse-eye jack etc. **Olapa de Bavusqui** are caves where you can observe sharks and a variety of crustaceans. At **Boca de Cote** there are spectacular cliffs dropping to 55 m with lots of different fish and coral. **Cayo Sal** is an impressive site with cliffs and caves filled with multicoloured sponges and black coral. At **Noronoqui** there is a labyrinth of antler coral and at Nordesqui there are a few shipwrecks and many lobsters.

Gran Roque AL *Canto de la Ballena*, on the seafront, T518225. Full board, excellent food, relaxed, fans, can pay with travellers' cheques. **AL** per person *Posada Bora La Mar*, T2843891. 4 basic rooms, with bathroom and ceiling fan, run by María Agustín, good food. **B** per person *Posada de Judith*, 3 comfortable rooms with bathroom; and *La Mecha*, 2 rooms with bathroom; both are run by Judith Campagna de Puig, T2713660, who also runs *Campamento Lilo*, where lodging is what nature provides and you eat what you catch, also organizes activities. **B** per person *Gremary*, T/F3372765. 11 basic rooms, the oldest *posada* on the island, some with bathroom, lunch and transport extra, run by Gregorio Romero. There are many other posadas, ranging from **D** per person to **LL**. These include: *Las Palmeras* and *Natura Viva*, both have 15 double or triple rooms with bathroom and fans, and are bookable through Aerotuy.

Sleeping & eating
See page 974 for details of hotel price grades

Cayo Francés One *posada*, **A-B**, T02-7930694, F7939579. Full board including drinks, good food, friendly staff, nice beach, snorkelling gear, water and light 24 hrs, fan, bargaining possible if you stay for several days; also hammock sites and camping. *Crasqui*, on Cayo Crasqui, contact *Sun Chichi* hotels, T02-9935866, F916549. 25 double and triple cabin-style tents, with primitive communal bathrooms, interesting construction, water from desalination plant, all-inclusive, meals, beach activities, drinks.

Camping is permitted in certain areas only. You need a permit from Inparques, T0212-2347331, F2344238 in Caracas, or the office in Gran Roque. Tiny but irritating biting insects in the calmer months can make camping miserable. Leave nothing on the ground, the crabs eat everything!

Air Flights from Maiquetía or Porlamar. *Chapi Air* from Maiquetía at 0800, returning at 1600, US$110. *Aerotuy* (T0212-7638043, F7625254) fly from Maiquetía daily. 2-day package (return flight, accommodation, meals, drinks, catamaran excursion with snorkelling and diving equipment), from US$300 per person (1-day from Margarita US$150). **Sea** If you arrive by yacht, Los Roques are not a port of entry, although you may stay 14 days if exit clearance from the previous country lists Los Roques on the way to an official port. If you have not got your own yacht, you will have to negotiate with local fishermen for boats from Gran Roque to the other islands and take a tent and all your provisions and water.

Transport

Other Venezuelan Islands

Islas Los Testigos are the first islands approached by yachts coming from Grenada or Trinidad. This is a protected area where spearfishing and scuba diving are forbidden. You can fish with a hand-line from a yacht or buy fish and lobster in season from any of the 150 fishermen who live on the islands. There is a vast colony of frigate birds and large sand dunes can be found on the windward side of the major island. There is no airport or ferry. No official clearance is given, the coastguard officer stands by VHF16 and can give temporary clearance, usually up to 48 hours. Also worth mentioning are the **Archipelago of Las Aves**, west of Los Roques, where fishing and diving are good. There are no commercial enterprises and the islands are visited mostly by yachts travelling between Venezuela and Bonaire.

Much closer to the mainland are two areas of reefs and islands which have been designated national parks. There is no way to get to them other than by spending time in Venezuela itself

La Tortuga is Venezuela's second largest island, lying west of Margarita. It is a low, dry island with wonderful beaches, good snorkelling, gorgeous water and a week's worth of anchorages. Visit **Los Palaquemos** by dinghy, an offshore reef with a few visible rocks. The small airstrip is used by small planes from Caracas at weekends. Further out are **La Blanquilla** and **La Orchila** (a military installation, do not land), both with coral reefs. La Blanquilla can be reached as a day trip from

Margarita with Línea Turística Aerotuy (LTA). It has a secluded white sand beach with crystal clear water and excellent snorkelling. While it lacks palm trees, shade can be found in caves along the shore. You can swim into underwater caverns while snorkelling. Most yachts anchor at Playa Yaque. Americano Bay is just north of Playa Yaque and has white sand beaches, clear water, good snorkelling and is a lovely spot to watch the sunset from the deck of a yacht. About 500 km north of Margarita, at the same latitude as Dominica, is **Isla de Aves**, 65 sq km of seabirds (sooty and brown noddy tern, frigate birds, gulls) surrounded by crystal clear water. The island is also a nesting site of the endangered green turtle. There is a Venezuelan coast guard station.

Parque Nacional Morrocoy

The national park of Morrocoy comprises hundreds of coral reefs, palm-studded islets, small cosy beaches and calm water for water-skiing, snorkelling, and skin-diving. The park is reached from Tucacas in the south and Chichiriviche in the north. With appropriate footwear it is possible to walk between some of the islands. The largest, cleanest and most popular of the islands is **Cayo Sombrero** (busy at weekends); even so it has some deserted beaches, with trees to sling a hammock. **Playuela** is beautiful and better for snorkelling (beware of mosquitoes in the mangrove swamps), while **Playa del Sol** has no good beach and no palm trees. **Bocaseca** is more exposed to the open sea than other islands and thus has fewer mosquitoes. **Cayo Borracho** is one of the nicest islands. Much of the coral in the park was destroyed in 1996 and the potential for scuba diving has fallen greatly. Beginners will still get good value for money but there isn't much to interest advanced divers.

Adjoining the park to the north is a vast nesting area for scarlet ibis, flamingoes and herons, the **Cuare Wildlife Sanctuary**. Most of the flamingoes are in and around the estuary next to Chichiriviche, which is too shallow for boats but you can walk there or take a taxi. Birds are best watched early morning or late afternoon.

Sleeping You may **camp** on the islands but must first make a reservation with Inparques (national parks), T8008487, 0800-2000 Mon-Sun; reserve at least 8 working days in advance giving all details; US$2.50 per person per night, 7 nights maximum, pay in full in advance (very complicated procedure). Very few facilities and no fresh water; Cayo Sombrero and Paiclas have restaurants, Boca Seca has a small café (closed Mon); Sombrero, Playa Azul and Paiclas have ecological toilets. At weekends and holidays it is very crowded and litter-strewn (beware rats).

Transport **Chichiriviche** is gaining a reputation for rip-offs and robberies. The islands are beautiful, but attitudes to tourists are not good (early 2001). Playa Sur and other areas are not safe; muggings reported.

From Tucacas Prices per boat range from US$20 return to Paiclas to US$40 return to Cayo Sombrero (maximum 7 per boat). Ticket office is to the left of the car entrance to the park. Recommended boatmen are Orlando and Pepe. **From Chichiriviche** Prices per boat vary according to distance; eg, US$15 to Cayo Muerto, US$50 to Cayo Sombrero. A 3-4 hr trip is US$50 per boat; 5-6 hr trip US$70 (maximum 8 per boat); bargaining essential. There are two ports; one close to the centre and Playa Sur. The latter has a ticket system which is supposed to guarantee that you will not be cheated and that you will be picked up on time for return trip.

Tucacas

Phone code: 0259
Population: 15,100

Tucacas is a hot, busy, dirty and expensive town, with lots of new building in progress, where bananas and other fruit are loaded for Curaçao and Aruba.

The only accommodation within the park is **AL** per person *Villa Mangrovia* on the Lizardo Spit between Tucacas and Chichiriviche. 3 rooms, good service, reservations through *Last Frontiers*, UK (01296-658650) or *Journey Latin America*, UK (T020-8747 8315/0161-832 1441). **B** *Hotel Manaure*, Av Silva, T831683. A/c, hot water, clean, good restaurant. **D** *La Suerte* on main street. Very clean, a/c, **E** with fan, with small shop. Next door is **E** *Las Palmas*, with shower, fan, kitchen and laundry facilities, helpful, cheap boat trips to islands. Opposite is **E** *La Esperanza*. Fan, with bath, fridge, clean, German owner arranges trips to islands. Cheap accommodation is difficult to find, especially in high season and at weekends, hotels are generally more expensive than elsewhere in Venezuela. *La Entrada*, good, cheap meals for US$2, open weekday lunchtime only. **Camping** Gas available in Tucacas or Puerto Cabello for camping in the Park.

Sleeping & eating *See page 974 for details of hotel price grades*

Diving equipment can be hired from near the harbour. *Submatur*, Ayacucho 6, T830082, F831051, owner Mike Osborn, 4 day PADI course US$330, 1 day trip 2 dives US$65 (US$45 with own equipment); also rents rooms, fan and cooking facilities.

Sport

Guilica, 2 blocks up from *Hotel La Esperanza* on Av Principal, T/F830939. Tours to islands, also bird watching. *Valadero Tours*, round corner from *Hotel La Esperanza*. Tours to islands and mainland destinations, fax service, will reconfirm flights.

Tour operators

Frequent *por puesto* from Valencia, US$5, bus US$2.50. Coro, US$5. Bicycles can be hired in town.

Transport

Banks *Unibanca*, cash advance on credit cards only. Hotels and travel agents will change money but at very low rates, if they have enough cash.

Directory

The Venezuelan Islands

Chichiriviche

A few kilometres beyond, towards Coro, is the favourite, and hence expensive, beach resort of Chichiriviche, which gets very crowded at holidays and weekends.

Population: 7,000

Hotels A *La Garza*, Av Principal, T86711. Attractive, pool, restaurant, full board, cheaper without, comfortable, popular, post box in lobby, daily collections, changes cash. **A** *Náutico*, T86024. Friendly, clean, MAP and trip to islands, fans, popular. **A** *Parador Manaure*, Mariño T86121, F86569. Sharing apartments for 5, clean, small pool, fully-equipped kitchen. **B** *Villa Marina*, T86503. Aparthotel, good, clean, safe, pool. **B** *La Puerta*, out of town, next to the port, T86621. Very clean, nice bar and restaurant, helpful owners. **C** *Capri*, Zamora, T86026, near docks. Shower, fan or a/c, clean, pleasant Italian owned, good restaurant and supermarket. **D** *Residencial Linda*, 1 block from docks. Italian owners, friendly, helpful, use of kitchen. **D** *Posada La Perrera*, Riera, near centre, 150 km from bus stop. Quiet, fan, clean, laundry facilities, patio, hammocks, luggage stored, Italian owner, tours arranged, very good. **D** *Residencial Delia*, Mariño 30, 1 block from *Gregoria*, T86089. 4 double rooms, CP, shared bath, clean, organizes tours, very friendly. **E** *Posada Alemania*, Cementos Coro, T850912. German-run, runs tours, rents snorkel gear, 200 m from Playa Sur, nice garden. **E** pp *Morena's Place*, Sector Playa Norte, 10 mins' walk from the bus stop, T/F850936, cvanmarcke@vln1186.ve.mbr.com Beautifully decorated house, fan, hammocks, helpful hosts, English spoken.

Sleeping & eating *See page 974 for details of hotel price grades*

Diving *Centro de Buceo Caribe*, Playa Sur. Runs PADI courses for US$360, 1 day diving trip US$65, rents equipment, rooms for rent, **D**, with cooking facilities.

Sports

Valadero Tours, 2 blocks from Banco Industrial on opposite side. Tours to islands US$16-19 per person, and to other parts of the country. Cheaper tours available with *Morrocoy Tours*, behind gas station near *Hotel La Garza*, or from *Ulrich's Lodge* restaurant on main street towards port.

Tour operators

Transport	**Buses** To Puerto Cabello, frequent *por puestos*, 2 hrs, US$3.50. Direct buses from Valencia or take bus from Morón to Coro and get out at turnoff, 1½ hrs, US$1.75.

Directory	**Banks** *Banco Industrial*, opposite bus terminal on main street. The only bank in the state of Falcón which changes dollars cash, open 0930-1530. *Valadero Tours* (see above) may change cash and TCs at very poor rates.

Mochima National Park

Puerto La Cruz	Venezuela's second Caribbean coastal national park is Mochima, 55 km from the port of Puerto La Cruz. This city is 320 km, five hours east of Caracas. It is the main commercial centre in this part of the country, especially for oil, but is also a popular holiday centre with good watersports and yachting facilities. The park itself also includes the mainland coast between Los Altos and Cumaná. The beaches and vistas of this stretch of the coast are beautiful. Since both Puerto La Cruz and Cumaná are ferry terminals for Margarita, Mochima can easily be incorporated into a visit to this part of Venezuela.

Isla de la Plata	The easiest island to reach is Isla de la Plata, yet another supposed lair of the pirate Henry Morgan. It has a white sand beach, and clear waters which are ideal for snorkelling. There are food and drink stalls, but take drinking water as there is none on the island. Also take a hat and sunscreen. It's about 10 minutes by boat to the island. Further away, and larger, are the **Chimana islands** with beautiful beaches (Grande, Sur, del Oeste), in the waters around which there is snorkelling and good scuba diving. The islands are very popular and consequently are badly littered. All have restaurants, snack-bars and thatched shelters for hire.

Other islands	Other islands in the vicinity are Monos (also good for scuba diving), **La Borracha**, **El Borracho** and **Los Borrachitos**, and **Caracas de Oeste** and **Caracas del Este**. All are in sheltered waters and are easy to explore by boat.

Mochima National Park

Three companies offer trips to the islands: *Transtupuerto*, on Paseo Colón entre Buenos Aires y Sucre, T667138, trips to closest islands (Islas Chimanas and Las Borrachas) for US$8, day tour around several islands with stops US$30-40, includes snorkelling equipment and soft drinks; *Transporte Turístico Virgen del Valle*, offers similar deals (food extra); *Transtupaco*, next to *HotelHesperia*, no tours, they act as a taxi to the islands.

Transport
Boat trips to the islands are cheaper from Santa Fe or Mochima (see below)

Alternatively, you can reach the islands with the *Embarcadero de Peñeros*, on Paseo Colón, behind the *Tejas Restaurant*. Departures from 0900-1000, return at 1600-1630; US$6 per person. Tourist office in Puerto La Cruz, *Coranztur* (Paseo Colón entre Buenos Aires y Sucre, T688170, open Mon-Fri 0800-1200-2100, French, English, Italian and Dutch spoken) provides tour operators for day trips to various islands for swimming or snorkelling; 6-hr trip to four islands costs US$25 per person, including drinks. The islands to the east (Isla de Plata, Monos, Picuda Grande and Chica and the beaches of Conoma and Conomita) are best reached from the port at **Guanta** (taxi from town, or *por puesto* from Freites between Av 5 de Julio and Democracia, and ask to be dropped off at the Urb Pamatacualito).

Santa Fe

Further east from Puerto La Cruz is Santa Fe, larger and noisier than Mochima, but a good place to relax. The attractive beach is cleaned daily. It has a market on Saturday.

Phone code: 093

B *Playa Santa Fe Resort and Dive Center*, T0414-7733777, Santafe@telcel.net.ve Renovated *posada* with various rooms and suites, laundry service, restaurant, owner Jerry Canaday speaks English, diving trips US$65, transport to beaches, mountain bike rental. **C** *Café del Mar*, T210009. 1st hotel on beach, fan, very clean, good restaurant, tours to islands US$5-10 per person, also to Gran Sabana, Orinoco Delta, owner Matthias Sauter, German spoken. **C** *Siete Delfines*, on beach, T/F0293-314166, **D** without breakfast, safe, fan, terrace where you can cook, bar, laundry service, ask here for information, watersports, beach games, owner speaks German, English, Italian and some French. **D** *Bahía del Mar*, T210073. Pleasant rooms with fan, upstairs rooms have a cool breeze, French and English spoken. **D** *Las Palmeras*, T0414-7736152. Behind *Cochaima*, fan, room for 5 with fridge and cooker, French spoken. **D** *Posada Los Angeles*, T0414-7755445. With fan, room for 4 with fridge and cooker, Italian restaurant. **D** *La Sierra Inn*, near *Café del Mar*, T0414-933116, comfortable rooms with fans, self-contained garden suite with fridge and cooker, run by Sr José Vivas, English spoken, helpful, tours to islands from US$10 per person. **E** *Cochaima*, on beach. Run by Margot, noisy, popular, fan, next to restaurant of same name(slow service), safe. **E** *El Portugués, Sr Julio César*, last *posada* on beach, cooking facilities, very helpful. **F** *Posada Lodging*, opposite *Club Naútico*, basic, shared bath. Other places to eat: *Club Naútico*, fish and Venezuelan dishes, open for lunch and dinner. *Los Molinos (Julios)*, open all day from 0800, beach bar serves sandwiches, hamburgers, beer and cocktails.

Sleeping & eating
See page 974 for details of hotel price grades

Playa Blanca
Playa Marita
Las Playuelas
ISLA CARACAS DEL ESTE
Península de Manare
Bahía Mochima
ISLA LOS VENADOS
Ensenada Tigrillo
Mochima
To Cumaná (approx 20 km)
Cerro Aceite Castillo
Punta Gorda
Golfo de Santa Fe
Playa Santa Cruz
Santa Fe
Playa Los Hicacos

N

0 km   3
0 miles 3

The Venezuelan Islands

Sports   **Diving** In Puerto La Cruz: *Explosub*, *Hotel Hesperia*, Puerto La Cruz, T653611, T/F673256. Efficient, helpful, will dive with 1 person, US$75 per 2 dives. *Lolo's Dive Centre*, Guanta Marina, Bahía de Guanta, T683052, F682885, or contact Eddy Revelant, cellnet 04149-801543. Experienced, English spoken, collect you from hotel and provide lunch, US$60 per 2 dives, 2-3 person minimum, 4-day PADI course US$300. Hotels and travel agents organize trips. The nearest recompression chamber is on Isla Margarita. In Mochima: *Rodolfo Plaza* runs a diving school for beginners and hires equipment, also walking and canoeing trips around Mochima; contact him in Caracas (Los Palos Grandes, Av Andrés Bello entre 3a y 4a transversal, T0212-9612531). *Francisco García* (2 doors down from Rodolfo), also runs a diving school (PADI courses) and shop, T0293-932991. *Fantasea Dive Center*, T/F210073, scuba24@ hotmail.com, PADI courses all levels, including 4-day PADI certification course US$300, also basic **D** accommodation.

Transport   *Por puesto* at 0600 and bus to Cumaná (US$1.75), and Puerto La Cruz (US$1.40). It is sometimes difficult to get the bus from Puerto La Cruz to stop at Santa Fe, *por puesto* may be a better bet, US$2, 1 hr, or taxi, US$23 including wait. Jeep, boat or diving tours available. Fishermen offer trips but their prices are extortionate. Boat trips to Playas Colorada or Blanca cost US$15 per person; better to hire your own boat for half the price, or hitch down the road to Colorada. Ask for Thomas, he has a boat and will take you wherever.

Mochima town

The small, colourful weekend resort of Mochima, beyond Santa Fe, is 4 km off the main road, hitching difficult. The sea is dirty near the town. Boats to nearby beaches, such as Playa Marita and Playa Blanca, and around the islands, US$12-15, depending on the distance (up to six people). Arrange with the boatman what time he will collect you.

Sleeping   **C** *Posada Gaby*, at end of road with its own pier next to sea, T0414-7731104, F0293-330462. A/c or fan, breakfast available, lovely place, take guests to islands for US$6-7 per person. **D** *Posada Mochimero*, on main street in front of *Restaurant Mochimero*. A/c or fan. **D** *Villa Vicenta*, Av Principal, T0414-9935877. Basic rooms with cold water, owner Otilio is helpful. **E** *Posada Beatriz*, T0414-7732262. Run by Sr Juan Remez, fan, use of kitchen. Sr César Bareto rents rooms for 2 and house for 4 or more, **D**. Also ask Sra Milagros Cova, whose properties all have bed linen and kitchen utensils, Doña Cruz, or Mama Inés.

Eating   A highly recommended restaurant is *El Mochimero*, on waterfront 5 mins from jetty, lunch and dinner.*Brisas de Mochima*, at the end of the main road behind the statue, fish dishes, lunch and dinner. *Dulce y Salado*, next to jetty, delicious *pastelitos* and *empanadas*, homemade cakes and juices. *Mi Compay*, close to jetty, hearty breakfasts, *arepas*, juices and coffee.

Transport   From Puerto La Cruz, the trip can be organized by taxi, US$40 including the journey home. Buses do not travel between Santa Fe and Mochima, *por puestos* can be taken, bargain hard on the price, US$15-21 is reasonable. Once in Mochima it is very difficult to find a taxi, you should arrange to be picked up again by the same driver if just staying for 1 day. Bus to Cumaná, 1400, US$1.40. At Christmas, Carnaval and Easter this part of the coast becomes extremely congested, so patience is needed as long queues of traffic can develop. Robbery may be a problem, but if you take care and use common sense, the risk is minimal. It can also become littered and polluted, especially on the islands. Camping on the islands in Mochima National Park is not advisable.

Background

History

Christopher Columbus made landfall on the nearby Paria Peninsula in August 1498. Two years later, a settlement had been established at Santiago de Cubagua (later called Nueva Cádiz) to exploit the pearls which grew in its waters. Cubagua became a centre for pearling and for slavery, as the local Indians were used, under appalling duress, to dive into the oyster beds. By 1541, when Santiago was destroyed by an earthquake and tidal wave, the pearl beds had been almost exhausted, but the Greek word for pearl, *margarita*, was retained for the main island of the group.

Margarita, and the nearest town on the mainland, Cumaná, were strongholds of the forces for the independence of South America from Spain. Between 1810 and 1817, the island was the scene of revolts and harsh Spanish reprisals. The liberator Simón Bolívar declared the Third Republic, and was himself declared Commander in Chief of the Liberating Army, at Villa del Norte (now Santa Ana) in 1816. After the war, the name of Nueva Esparta (maintaining the Greek allusion) was conferred in recognition of the bravery of Margarita in the struggle. Subsequent events have been nothing like so heroic, with life revolving around fishing and small agriculture. After a regeneration of the the pearl industry at the end of the 19th century, it has gone into decline, the oyster beds having all but disappeared through disease.

Geography

When the Spaniards landed in East Venezuela in 1498, in the course of Columbus' third voyage, they found a poor country sparsely populated by Indians who had created no distinctive culture. Four hundred years later it was still poor, almost exclusively agrarian, exporting little, importing less. The miracle year which changed all that was 1914, when oil was discovered near Maracaibo. Today, Venezuela is one of the richest countries in Latin America and is one of the largest producers and exporters of oil in the world.

Venezuela has 72 island possessions in the Caribbean, of which the largest and the most visited is Isla de Margarita. This island, and two close neighbours, Coche and Cubagua, form the state of Nueva Esparta. Most of the other islands are Federal Dependencies (whose capital is Los Roques) stretching in small groups of keys to the east of Bonaire. Two other sets of islands are incorporated in the national parks of Morrocoy (west of the country's capital, Caracas) and Mochima, east of Caracas.

Economy

The island's tourism boom began in 1983, largely as a result of the fall in the value of the bolívar and the consequent tendency of Venezuelans to spend their holidays at home. Margarita's status as a duty-free zone has also helped. Venezuelan shoppers go in droves for clothing, electronic goods and other consumer items. Gold and gems are good value, but many things are not. There has been extensive building in Porlamar, with new shopping areas and Miami-style hotels going up. A number of beaches have also been developed. All-inclusive resorts and timeshare have expanded on the northeast corner of the island and there is a glut of hotel rooms and apartments. The island's popularity means that various packages are on offer, sometimes at good value, especially off-season.

Local industries are fishing and fibre work, such as hammocks and straw hats. Weaving, pottery and sweets are being pushed as handicraft items for the tourists.

Netherlands Antilles, the ABC Islands

20

Netherlands Antilles, the ABC Islands

Dominican Republic

Virgin Islands

Leeward Islands

Puerto Rico

Windward Islands

Caribbean Sea

NETHERLANDS ANTILLES

Aruba Curaçao Bonaire

Isla de Margarita

Trinidad

VENEZUELA

The Netherlands Antilles consist of the islands of Aruba, Bonaire and Curaçao, popularly known as the 'ABCs' (60-80 km off the coast of Venezuela south of the hurricane belt), and the '3 S's': Sint Eustatius (Statia), Saba, and the south part of Sint Maarten (St-Martin) in what are generally known as the Leeward Islands (880 km further north in the hurricane belt). Because of the distance separating the north islands from the other Dutch possessions, the 3 S's are described in a separate section earlier in the Handbook.

There is some confusion regarding which islands are Leeward and which are Windward: locals refer to the ABCs as 'Leeward Islands', and the other 3 S's 'Windward', a distinction adopted from the Spaniards, who still speak of the Islas de Sotavento and de Barlovento with reference to the trade winds.

Each island is different from the others in size, physical features, the structure of the economy and the level of development and prosperity.

A Foot in the door

- **Diving** and more diving, in pristine conditions and with excellent facilities.
- Some 11,000 **flamingoes** also think this is a top spot; see their conical nests on the salt pans and watch them taking off at sunset in a huge pink cloud to overnight in Venezuela.
- In this arid climate the springs at **Fontein** are a surprising sight, with fresh water pouring through the walls of a cave into pools where you can plunge and soak.
- You'll find cool jazz on warm Bonaire when the **Bonaire Jazz Club** meets.

Bonaire

Population: 11,000
Colour map 6, grid B2

The diving here is among the best in the Caribbean, with pristine reefs and wonderful visibility as there are no rivers to muddy the waters and it is out of the hurricane belt. The climate is dry and the vegetation little more than scrub and cactus but it is prized by birdwatchers. Once important as a salt producer, this Dutch island now makes its living out of tourism. Bonaire is the least densely populated of the ABC islands and the inhabitants are mostly of mixed Arawak, European and African descent. They are a very friendly and hospitable people. The island is clean, quiet, peaceful and very safe. As in Curaçao and Aruba, Dutch is the official language, Papiamentu the colloquial tongue, and Spanish and English are both widely spoken.

Ins and outs

Getting there   **Air**   Flamingo airport (BON) can accommodate 747 jumbo jets with a runway of over 4km. Long distance direct flights are limited; you can fly from Amsterdam and Brussels in Europe and Chicago and Miami in the USA, although there are lots of connecting flights via Curaçao, Montego Bay and San Juan, see Transport, page 1009.

Getting around
See transport, page 1009, for further details

There is no regular bus, but a so-called 'autobus' (AB on the licence plate) passes at certain places in town and takes you to the street or place you want to go for a few guilders. There are taxis at the airport but they are difficult to find around the island. Taxis do not 'cruise' so you must telephone for one, T7178100. The best way of getting about is to hire a car, scooter or mountain bike. Distances are not great but the heat is. Some hotels have a shuttle service to town. Hitching is fairly easy.

Flora and fauna

An environmental awareness for preservation of the reefs and the island's natural state pervades society here like no other Caribbean destination. Nature and the environment is even a subject for study in the primary school system thanks to a grant given in 1996 by the World Wildlife Fund. All of the water to 60 m deep and much of the countryside, fauna and flora of Bonaire is protected.

Bonaire has one of the largest (between 3,500 and 11,000 depending on the season) Caribbean flamingo colonies in the Western Hemisphere, and these birds build their conical mud nests in the salt pans. Pleas from wildlife conservationists convinced the Salt Company that it should set aside an area of 56 ha for a flamingo sanctuary, with access strictly prohibited. The birds, initially rather startled by the sudden activity, have settled into a peaceful co-existence, so peaceful in fact that they have actually doubled their output and are now laying two eggs a year instead of their previous one. They can be seen from the roads in the south and in Goto Meer Bay in the northwest, in the salt lake near Playa Grandi, and in Lac Bay on the southeast coast of Bonaire, feeding on algae and crustaceans which give them their striking rose-pink colour.

There are also two smaller bird sanctuaries at the Solar Salt Works and Goto Meer. At Pos'i Mangel, in the Washington Park, thousands of birds gather in the late afternoon. Bronswinkel Well, also in the Park, is another good place to see hundreds of birds and giant cacti. The indigenous Bonaire Green Parrot and the endangered Yellow Shouldered Amazon (*Amazona barbarebdis rothschildi*) can be seen in the Park and at Onima. About 190 species of birds have been found on Bonaire as well as the flamingoes.

An annual Birdwatching Olympics and Nature Week is held in September, with prizes for those who spot the greatest number of species

There are lots of iguanas and lizards of all shapes and sizes. The big blue lizards are endemic to Bonaire, while the Anolis, a tree lizard with a yellow dewlap, is related to the Windward Islands Anolis species rather than to the neighbouring Venezuelan species. The most common mammals you are likely to see are goats and donkeys, herds of which roam the island eating everything in sight except the cacti. Bonaire's only native mammal is the bat, of which eight species have been identified, all fish, fruit and insect eaters.

Diving and marine life

Bonaire's combination of low rainfall, little runoff, fringing reef and gin clear water with visibility of 30 m or more makes for diving that is unsurpassed in the Caribbean. Bonaire's reefs have been protected since 1971, the Marine Park celebrated its

Bonaire

Netherlands Antilles, the ABC islands

■ **Sleeping**
1 Bayside Resort
2 Black Durgon Inn
3 Bonaire Caribbean Club
4 Buddy Dive Resort
5 Captain Don's Habitat
6 Caribbean Court
7 Carib Inn
8 Divi Flamingo
9 Eden Beach
10 Harbour Village
11 Lac Bay Resort
12 Lion's Dive
13 Plaza Resort Bonaire
14 Sand Dollar Condominium
15 Sorobon Beach Resort

Essentials

Documents See page 1013.

Departure tax There is a departure tax of US$6 (NAf 10) on local flights and US$20 (NAf 36) on international flights.

Hours of business Shops are open 0800-1200 and 1400-1800, Monday-Saturday, or until 2100 on Friday, and for a few hours on Sunday if cruise ships are in port. Supermarkets are open 0800-2000 and some on Sunday 1100-1400.

Voltage 127 volts, 50 cycles. 220 volts available at some resorts.

Tipping 10-15% in restaurants, which is often added automatically to the bill. Tax is 10%. Dive shops 10%.

Radio The news is broadcast in Dutch on Voz di Bonaire, FM 94.7 MHz, Monday-Saturday on the hour 0700-1800. Transworld Radio broadcasts in English on 800 KHz MW daily 0700-0830, 2200-2400, news 0700 Monday-Friday, 0800 and 2200 daily, 2300 Saturday and Sunday; Caribbean weather forecast 0730 Monday-Friday, 0800 Saturday and Sunday. Radio Nederland, 6020 KHz at 0630, 6165 and 15315 KHz at 2030, 9590 and 11720 KHz at 2330. The Papiamento broadcast is on 97.1 FM.

Tourist offices overseas

Canada RMR Group Inc, Taurus House, 512 Duplex Avenue, Toronto, Ontario, M4R 2E3, T416-4844864, 800-8266247, F416-4858256.

Europe Interreps BV, Visseringlaan 24, 2288 ER Rijswijk, The Netherlands, T31070-3954444, F31070-3368333, interrep@interrep.demon.nl

USA Adams Unlimited, 10 Rockefeller Plaza, Suite 900, New York, NY 10020, T212-9565912, 800-2662473, F212-9565913, lisa@adams-pr.com

Venezuela Flamingo Representaciones, Yazmín Pérez de Ramírez, Av Humboldt, Edif Humboldt, Piso 1 Apt 5, urb Bello Monte, Caracas, T9534653, F9511625.

Bonhata, the Bonaire Hotel and Tourist Association, also promotes the island, T7175134, F7178240, PO Box 358.

Public holidays New Year's Day, Good Friday, Easter Monday, Queen's Birthday and Rincon Day (30 April), Labour Day (1 May), Ascension Day, Bonaire Day (6 September), Christmas Day and Boxing Day. **Carnival** takes place over about six weeks from the end of January to the beginning of March, with parades, jump-ups and the election of King and Queen of the Carnival and 'Prince and Pancho'. Several days are devoted to the Tumba festival, a Tumba being a winning song. Carnival is organized by the Fundashon Karnival Boneiru (Fukabo). Dates for the main adult parade are 25 February 2001, 10 February 2002, 2 March 2003, 22 February 2004, 6 February 2005.

25th anniversary in 2001 and was designated a National Park in 1999. Surrounding the island are corals harbouring over a thousand different species of marine creatures. Ranked as one of the three top dive spots in the world, and number one in the Caribbean (followed by Grand Cayman Island and Cozumel), Bonaire led the movement for preservation of underwater resources. Surrounding the whole island is a protected marine park from the high water mark down to 60 m. Two areas have been designated marine reserves, with no diving allowed; along Playa Frans, north to Boca Slogbaai, and west of Karpata. Lac Bay, a natural nursery for fish, is also part of the Marine Park because of its extensive mangroves and seagrass beds. Stringent laws passed in 1971 ban spearfishing and the removal of any marine life from Bonaire's waters. It is a serious offence to disturb the natural life of the coral reefs. Permanent anchors have been placed in all dive spots to avoid doing any unwarranted damage. Do not touch the coral or other underwater life, such as sea horses; move anything to create a better photo, feed the fish, as it is not natural and encourages more aggressive species; drop litter, particularly plastic which does not decompose and can be harmful to sea creatures; or kick up sand with your fins as it can choke and kill the coral. All qualified divers are required to do a check out dive before they can do any diving, whether from the shore or a boat. Advanced buoyancy courses are available free of charge and are highly recommended for training you to keep horizontal along the reef and so limit fin damage to coral. Sea turtles can be seen at several sites around Bonaire and Klein Bonaire. Turtle spotters can report sightings to the *Sea Turtle Conservation Bonaire (STCB)* via a form available in all

Bonaire Sky Park

Bonaire's skies are usually clear and always free of pollution. Residents like to call the heavens at night the Sky Park; a place where there's no admission fee and nature holds sway. One of the best features of the Sky Park is the fact that it holds both northern and southern hemisphere stars. During the winter peak tourist season, just after dark, you'll see two bright stars winking emerald and white light at you. The brighter, although not by much, is Sirius, the Dog Star,

the eye of Canis Major, familiar to those who live in the north. But the other is a true southern star, the wonderful Canopus, that bright star that most northerners have never seen. In fact it's the second brightest star visible from Earth. If you wait until midnight you'll easily spot the Southern Cross low in the southern sky. And if you can stay awake for a couple more hours you can spot Alpha Centauri, the star closest to Earth, rising just as Canopus sets.

dive schools, or contact the Bonaire Marine Park, T7178444, www.bmp.org The STCB has a twice-yearly newsletter, for information stcb@bonairelive.com Every month an underwater clean up is organized by *Green Submarine*, Kaya Playa Lechi, T7172929, to clear all the rubbish washed up by the sea. Vacationers are welcome on these dives. Divers are usually asked to bring their own tanks and air, but dive shops may provide complimentary tanks. Snorkellers are also welcome.

On the east side of the island there is a shelf and a drop-off about 12 m from the shore down to a 30 m coral shelf and then another drop down to the ocean floor. The sea is rather rough on that side for most of the year although it sometimes calms down in October or November. Along the west side of the island the sea is calm and there are numerous dive sites of varying depths with wrecks as well as reefs. The most frequently dived sites include, **Rappel**, **Pink Beach**, **Small Wall**, **Angel City** and the **Town Pier**. There are also dozens of sites for boat dives off Klein Bonaire, just 1½ km from Kralendijk. *Bonaire Diving Made Easy* is recommended and can be obtained from dive shops for US$10, or online from the *Bonaire Reporter*, the local English language newspaper, www.bonairereporter.com/divingguide.htm

Snorkelling is excellent at **Andreas, Oil Slick Leap, Tori's Reef, Windsock Steep** and along the east side of **Klein Bonaire**. Dive boats usually take snorkellers along for about US$12. The Sea and Discover marine education service, T7175322, deaandis@bonairelive.com offers snorkelling excursions with a marine biologist guide for US$30 per person. The *Skiffy* water taxi provides round trips to Klein Bonaire for US$10. While some think it's a crime to visit Bonaire and not get wet, you can spy on the underwater world through the windows of the glass bottom boat, *Bonaire Dream*. The 8.5-m boat motors in protected water to show its passengers some of Bonaire's prettiest reefs and fish. The boat leaves from the *Harbour Village* marina at 1600 on Wednesday and Friday. It can take up to 15 people on the 1½ hour tour, US$22.50, T7807838 or 5666061. Tickets available at local hotels.

According to the Year 2001 Reader Survey carried out by *Rodale's Scuba Diving Magazine*, three of Bonaire's dive operators received A ratings from its readers: *Captain Don's Habitat, Great Adventures Bonaire* (at the *Harbour Village*) and *Toucan Diving* (at the *Plaza Resort Bonaire*). The main schools are *Dive Bonaire* (T7178285, F7178238, at the *Divi Flamingo*), *Buddy Dive* (T7175080, F7178647, www.buddydive.com), *Habitat Dive Center* (T7178290, F7177346), *Dive Inn Bonaire* (T7178761, F7178513, next to the *Sunset Inn*), *Sand Dollar Dive and Photo* at the *Sand Dollar Condominium Resort* next to *Den Laman* restaurant (T7175433, F7175252, sand$dive@bonairenet.com), *Great Adventures Bonaire* and *Great Photo Adventures* (T7177500, F7177507) at the *Harbour Village Beach Resort*, with instruction in several languages, *Bon Bini Divers* at the *Coral Regency Resort* (T7175425, F7174425, www.bonbinidivers.com), *Green Submarine* (T/F7172929, dive@greensubmarine.com), *Blue Divers* (T7176860, F7176865, www.bluedivers.com), *Photo Tours Divers* at the *Caribbean Courts Resort* (T7175353,

Dive centres
For underwater images of the reef, see www.BonaireWeb-Cams.com updated every two minutes

La Dania's Leap

Divers and snorkelers can have a thrilling, yet safe, experience by doing a drift dive from shore. First drive north to the La Dania's leap dive site. Unload your gear. Have the driver continue another 2 km and park the car at the Karpata dive site. After he/she walks back to the group, proceed to the edge of the cliff. Don your gear and jump into the sea. It's less than a 2 m drop. Turn right and head north.

The coral here is especially beautiful and massive. Swim slowly because the slight current will push you along. You will know you are coming to your exit point when you pass an huge old ship's anchor. The exit at Karpata has an old concrete pier and steps carved in the cliff that will return you to the place where you parked your car. This adventure should take about 45 minutes.

ext 328, www.bonairephototours.com), and the newest dive school, *WannaDive*, at the *Eden Park Resort* (T7908111). Prices are competitive, ranging from US$25-50 for a two-tank dive if you have your own equipment. Add a 10% service charge on most diving and 5% sales tax on all training courses and rentals. All packages include tank, air, weights and belt; equipment rental varies, US$6-11 for a BC jacket, US$6-11 for a regulator, US$6-10 for mask, snorkel and fins. Camera and other equipment rental widely available (*Sand Dollar Dive & Photo Shop*, T7175433, *Photo Tours*, T7175353 ext 328, F7175363).

All dive operations are well equipped and well staffed with a good safety record. If booking a package deal check whether their week-long dive packages include nightly night dives, or only one a week. For less experienced divers it is worth choosing a dive boat which keeps staff on board while the leader is underwater, in case you get into difficulties. In the case of reasonably experienced divers, some dive masters do not always get into the water but stay on board. Shore diving is available nearly everywhere, weather and sea conditions permitting. The guide book, *Bonaire Diving Made Easy* details the entry and dive site conditions.

There is a US$10 per person levy for maintenance of the marine park which has to be paid only once every calendar year. You will be given a marine park tag to wear on your gear when scuba diving. There is a **recompression chamber** at the San Francisco Hospital Emergency Room and doctors trained in hyperbaric medicine. An Annual Dive Festival is held in June.

Beaches and watersports

Be careful at Playa Chiquitu, or Chikitu, there is a memorial plaque there for good reason. The surf is strong and it is dangerous to swim but it is pleasant for sunbathing

Bonaire is not noted for its beaches; the sand is usually full of coral and rather hard on the feet, and those on the leeward coast are narrow, although beaches in front of some hotels have been helped with extra sand. They do offer peace and quiet, though, and you will not get pestered by people trying to sell you things. **Pink Beach**, at the southern tip of the island is popular, the water is shallow and good for swimming, but there is no shade and the sand is gritty. Recommended are **Sorobon** (a private, nudist resort where non-guests pay US$10 for admission), Kai at **Lac Bay** which has an area of mangroves at the north end of the bay, and in the northeast **Playa Chiquitu**. In the Washington-Slagbaai National Park are two attractive bays: **Playa Funchi**, which is good for snorkelling, but has no sand and no facilities so the area is very smelly, and **Boca Slagbaai**, where the ruins of colonial buildings are scheduled to be restored in 2002 and you can see flamingoes wading in the salinja behind the beach. Nineteenth-century houses and a salt barn were damaged by a sea swell in 1999, but will soon be rebuilt.

Fishing You can charter a fishing boat through your hotel and arrange half or full day trips with tackle and food included. Bonaire has good bonefishing and also deep sea fishing. Two independent charter companies are *Piscatur*, run by Captain Chris Morkos, T7178774, F7174784, half day US$275 for four people, US$425 full day in

38-ft diesel boat, or US$125 half day for two people, US$225 full day in 15-ft skiff; and *Big Game*, a 30-ft Bertram sport fisherman run by Captain Cees and his son Thomas, US$325 half day, US$450 full day for up to five people, T7176500, F7176500, www.bonairenet.com.biggame/indexbgs.htm Fishing boats with diving gear can be chartered from *Nautico Bonaire*, Kaya Jan NE Craane 24, T7175800, F7175850. There is an annual **Bonaire International Fishing Tournament**, held at the end of March, which attracts participants from throughout the Americas.

The annual **Bonaire Sailing Regatta** is held in early-October. This has grown into a world class event with races for seagoing yachts, catamarans, sunfishes, windsurfers and local fishing boats. The smaller craft compete in Kralendijk Bay, while the larger boats race round Bonaire and Klein Bonaire. The windsurfers race in Lac Bay. Held over five days, the event attracts crowds and hotel reservations need to be made well in advance. For information call the Regatta office, T7177425, F7175576. There are also monthly regattas for several classes of small boats. In December *Aquaspeed Sailing Club* organizes the **End-Of-Year Regatta**, with competitions for windsurfing, sunfish, yachts and fishing boats, starting from in front of the Regatta House in Playa, contact Elvis Martinus, T7172288. The Marina at *Harbour Village* is the only full-service marina in Bonaire. There are 60 slips for boats up to 110 ft with showers, laundry, fuel, water, chandlery etc, and has a shop for repairs.

Sailing

Sailing trips with snorkelling and beach barbecue, often on Klein Bonaire, or sunset booze cruises, from US$38 per person plus 10% service, are offered on *Samur* (PO Box 287, T7175592, F7176677, samur@bonairelive.com), a 56-ft Siamese junk built in Bangkok in 1968, based at *Captain Don's Habitat*, with pick up service from most resorts. Others include *Oscarina*, a 42-ft cutter, T7907674, F7178240. The 56-ft ketch, *Sea Witch*, offers trips to the nearby Venezuelan Las Aves islands as well as day sailing around Bonaire cell phone 5607449, F7177359, kroon@bonairenet.com, PO Box 348, dive gear on board, maximum of four guests; *Woodwind* is a 37-ft trimaran offering sailing and guided snorkelling around Bonaire and Klein Bonaire, cell phone 5607055, F7178238. *Bonaire Boating*, T7175353 ext 505, F7175622, www.abc-yachting.com, have charter boats and offer day sails, motorboats and a 3-day package to Islas las Aves with diving equipment. They can also take you big game fishing, snorkelling, kayaking and sunset sailing. Their Watersports & Adventure Centre is at the *Caribbean Court Resort*. *Skiffy Water Taxi*, run by the amiable Henk Ram, offers a watertaxi service to Klein Bonaire from Nautico Bonaire and most hotels, T5607254. The Baka de Laman water taxi runs from *Karel's Beach Bar*, T5607126, F7172568.

Day sails

On the leeward side offshore winds allow you to sail in protected water. At Lac Bay on the windward side of the island where the water is calm and shallow, there is a constant onshore wind. The bay is about 8 sq km but a coral reef just outside the bay breaks up the waves. However, the adventurous can get out of the bay at one end where long, high waves enable you to wave ride, jump or loop. *Jibe City* (closed September, T7175233, F7174455, www.jibecity.com) run by Ernst Van Vliet, is a BIC/TIGA Centre and has the latest models and Gaastra sails with retail shop and *Hangout Bar*. Lessons from US$45 per hour, rentals from US$55 per day, US$265 per week. *The Place*, managed by Elvis Martinus and Bonaire's first Olympian, Paun Sargosa, is also on Lac Bay, featuring top notch gear, T7172288, F7175279. Windsurfing rentals and instruction are available along with kayak, sunfish, mini speed boats, water skiing, sea sausage rides, small hobie cat, waterskiing, hydrosliding and paddle boats. *Parasail*, T7174998, 5670940, has waterskiing and banana boat rides in addition to parasailing. A few dive shops rent kayaks, quite a good way of getting to Klein Bonaire without a boatload of other people. *Jibe City* rents kayaks in Lac Bay for a whole (US$30 single kayak, US$35 double) or half day (US$20/25) or a couple of hours (US$10/15). *Discover Bonaire* at *Sand Dollar Dive & Photo* offers courses, guided trips and rentals of

Windsurfing
Conditions are ideal for windsurfing with winds of 15-25 knots in December-August and 12-18 knots in September-November

various models of sit-in or sit-on-top kayaks. A full-day guided trip is US$90, half day US$50, sunset excursion US$35. Rental is US$10 per hour, US$45 per day for a single kayak, US$15 and US$50 for a double kayak.

Other sports There are **tennis** courts at the *Divi Flamingo Beach Resort*, open 0800-2200, T7178285 and the *Harbour Village Beach Resort*; *Sand Dollar Condominium Resort*, open 0900-2100, T7178738. There is also **horse riding**. Kunuku Warahama has horses and playgrounds for the children as well as lots of other animals. Lunch and dinner also available, T7175558, not always open, so phone ahead. **Walking** and **birdwatching** are popular in the Washington/Slagbaai National Park, particularly climbing up Mount Brandaris, the highest point on the island. **Cycling** is popular and tours are organized or there is a cycling trails map if you want to go it alone. Bikes can be rented at several hotels and mountain bikes from *Cycle Bonaire*, T7177558, *de Freewiler* at Kaya Brion 1, downtown, T7178545, or *Bonaire Boating*, T7175353. In May a Mountain Bike Challenge Race is held and in October a Mountain Bike speed challenge race.

Kralendijk

Population: 1,690
Most people who work in the town live within walking distance in the suburbs of Antriol, Hato, Niki Boko and North Saliña

Kralendijk, meaning coral dike, the capital of Bonaire, is a small, sleepy town with colourful buildings one or two storeys high. It is often referred to locally as simply 'Playa', because of its historic position as the main landing place. The town is just a few blocks long with several streets projecting inland. In 1999 a seaside promenade project was completed along the Playa section of Kralendijk, which will eventually be extended south to the *Divi Flamingo* hotel. Most of the shops are in the small Harbourside Shopping Mall and on the main street, the name of which changes from J A Abraham Boulevard to Kaya Grandi to Kaya Gob Debrot. The **Museum** (Department of Culture), tucked away on a side street near the big Catholic church with the clock tower, houses snippets of folklore, art, archaeology, old photographs and a shell collection. Small enough for you to get personal attention if you want it. ■ *Weekdays 0800-1200, 1300-1700, Kaya J van der Ree 7, or Kaya Sabana 14, T7178868, small donation requested.* The small **Fort Oranje** has been renovated and now houses the Bonairean court of justice as well as a permanent archaeological collection with items found during the renovation. The shorefront plaza, **Wilhelminaplein**, has a monument to the Bonaireans who were killed in the Merchant Marine in the Second World War, and a **vegetable market** built like a Greek temple

Around the island

The island can be toured in a day if you start early but it is more pleasant to do a north tour on one day and a south tour another. Take food and drinks, there are rarely any available along the way, and aim to picnic somewhere you can swim to cool off. Dominating the skyline outside Kralendijk is a long hill or **Seru Largu**. A good paved road leads to the top for spectacular views of the town, Klein Bonaire, the salt hills and the surrounding sea and farmland. It's quiet and undeveloped except for a few benches, and is a favorite spot for a picnic.

The north
The road is new and smooth but narrow; watch out for iguanas and lizards sunbathing

North of Kralendijk the road passes most of the hotels, past the Power and Water Distillation Plant along the 'scenic' road, which offers several descents to the sea and some excellent spots for snorkelling along the rocky coastline. The first landmark is the Radio Netherlands station which has masses of aerials. Note that the road becomes one-way after the radio station, do not turn round. At the abandoned Karpata Landhuis, if you turn right you go directly to Rincon, climbing to the top of the hill for a steep descent and a good view of Rincon and the Windward coast. Alternatively, continue along to the Bonaire Petroleum Company (BOPEC) where the road turns inland to Goto Meer Bay, the best place to see flamingos close up, on another road to Rincon.

On the first Saturday of the month the sleepy village of **Rincon**, Bonaire's oldest settlement where the slaves' families lived, comes alive with a street market, the *Marshe Rincon*. It wasn't intended as a tourist attraction but has become one for the visitors lucky enough to find out about it. Dozens of stands are set up to sell fresh produce, plants, handicrafts, pastries, local foods, clothing and assorted goods. It is the only scheduled time for the *Soldachi* (hermit crab) tours. Founded by two Rincon ladies, the tours leave from the Marshe centre and are either on foot, with a guide who explains the architecture, history and culture of Rincon, or by bus, around Rincon, the Lourdes Grotto, the Altamira overlook, Ita's Garden and the museum at Washington Park. ■ *Walking tour 0900-1000, US$5.60, bus tour 1030-1200, US$8.50, T7172670 or 7176435, wilmari@bonairelive.com*

East of Rincon is a side road to the **Boca Onima** caves with their Arawak Indian inscriptions. Indian inscriptions in several caves around the island can still be seen, but they have not been deciphered. In the same area there's a special spot that few people, even locals, have ever visited. The springs of **Fontein** opened in 2000 after being off limits for a decade. On Bonaire it's very unusual to see fresh water pouring through the walls of a cave and flowing freely down the hill. The water has nurtured

Kralendijk

Netherlands Antilles, the ABC islands

■ **Sleeping**	**3** Rochaline	● **Eating**	**4** Rendez-Vous
1 Club Nautico	**4** Sunset Inn & Dive Inn	**1** Beefeater	**5** Zeezicht
2 Divi Flamingo		**2** Cozzoli's Pizzeria	
Beach Resort		**3** Mona Lisa	

huge trees and tropical fruit groves along its path. You can tour the area, picnic and cool off in one of three pools fed by the spring water. ■ *Usually open on Sun or by appointment, free, call Alejander Werner, T7905363 for information.*

Washington/
Slagbaai
National Park

The road leading north from Rincon takes you to Washington/Slagbaai National Park, which occupies the north portion of the island, about 5,460 ha, and contains more than 190 species of birds. The park was set up in 1969. ■ *Daily 0800 to 1700 (no entry after 1500). NAf17.50, US$10, children up to 15 NAf 5, US$3. Bicycles only on guided tours as per park rules, arrangements must be made in advance for bike entry. Toilet at the entrance. Bring food and water.* There is a small store selling food, drinks and souvenirs at the entrance. Behind the shop there are displays of traditional crafts of lime and charcoal making and a museum of local historical items plus a room with geological explanations, bird pictures and a shell collection opposite the office. No hunting, fishing or camping is permitted. You can choose to drive a 34-km or a 24-km tour, the roads being marked by yellow or green arrows. You will get a route map when you pay to get in. The road is dirt, rough in parts, and the long route, which passes lovely beaches (including Playa Cocolishi, almost paved in tiny shells), can be very hot and tiring unless you make several stops to swim and cool off. It is possible to drive round in an ordinary car but many car rental agencies discourage the use of their normal cars, especially after rain, and four-wheel drive is preferable. Allow plenty of time: once you have chosen your route you have to stick to it. Even the short route takes a minimum of two hours. Check your spare tyre before you start. *Cycle Bonaire* is now permitted to take cycling tours into the park but other two-wheeled transport is not allowed. There are guided hiking excursions up Mount Brandaris (260 m, the island's highest point), or you can do it on your own; hiking trails have been marked. An area has been set aside for rappelling. Do not expect much variation in vegetation, the overall impression is of miles of scrub and cactus, broken only by rocks or saliñas. However, it is truly unspoiled and uncommercialized. You can drive to view Goto Meer on the longer route but you can get a better view from the observation point outside the Park. The return to Kralendijk inland through the villages of **Noord Salinja** and **Antriol**.

The south
Remember the flamingos are easily frightened, so move quietly if near them

The tour south passes the airport and Trans World Radio's towering 213 m antenna which transmits 50,000 watts. The salt pier dominates the view along the coastal road and the salt pans are a stunning pink/purple colour. Further on are the snow-white salt piles and the three obelisks which guided the sailing ships coming to load salt: blue, white, and orange, dating from 1838, with the tiny huts that sheltered the slaves who worked the saltpans. The roofs of the slave huts reach only to waist level and it is startling to think of men sharing one of these structures.

At the south tip of the island is **Willemstoren**, one of Bonaire's three main lighthouses, which dates from 1837. Pass Sorobon Beach and the mangrove swamps to **Boca Cai** at landlocked **Lac Bay**, with its clear water excellent for underwater exploration. The extensive seagrass beds and surrounding mangroves are an important nursery for marine creatures. What seem to be snow-capped hills from a distance are great piles of empty conch shells left by the local fishermen at Boca Cai. Near the Sorobon Resort is the Sea Hatch Bonaire shrimp farming project. Take the road back to Kralendijk through the village of **Nikiboko**, or a straight route west to the airport area. There is a **Donkey Sanctuary** just south of the airport, founded in the mid-1990s by a Dutch woman, Marina Melis. At any one time she is likely to have 20 or more donkeys which are sick or disabled, although some stick around even after they are healed. It is a well-organized facility and visitors are welcome. ■ *Tue-Sun 1000-1600, T5607607, donkeyshelp@bonairelive.com free entry but donations welcome.*

Essentials

High season rates (16 Dec to 2 weeks after Easter) are roughly double low-season rates in the more expensive hotels; the cheaper ones tend to charge the same all year round. Aug is 'family month' with lots of good deals. All the hotels with on site dive shops, and some others besides, offer dive packages which give better value than the rack rates listed here. In addition there are lots of apartments and condos for rent, not mentioned here. Ask the tourist office for details.

Sleeping
A US$5.50 or US$6.50 per person per night government tax and 10-15% service charge must be added

South of Kralendijk A-C *Sunset Inn*, Kaya L D Gerharts 22, T7178291, F7178118. Only 7 rooms, some rooms with kitchenettes, bicycle rental, across the road from the sea, within easy walking distance of town, next to Dive Inn dive shop. **LL-AL** *Divi Flamingo Beach Resort & Casino*, J A Abraham Blvd 40, T7178285, F7178238, in USA 800-3673484, F919-4192075, www.divibonaire.com Totally renovated in 2000, 145 units, standard rooms or more luxurious, is on a small artificial beach, snorkelling or diving just off the beach is excellent, tennis, pools, jacuzzi, dining is outdoors. Next door is **L-A** *Bruce Bowker's Carib Inn*, J A Ahraham Blvd 46, T7178819, F7175295, bruce@caribinn.com Rooms, apartments and 3-bedroom house, a/c, cable TV, pool, dive shop. **LL-AL** *Plaza Resort Bonaire*, J A Abraham Blvd 80, T7172500, F7177133, info@plazaresortbonaire.com 200 rooms, suites and villas, diving, tennis, racquet ball, watersports, casino, pool, beach, striving to be 5-star resort. Using all the same facilities is **LL-L** *Port Bonaire Resort*, part of the *Plaza Resort*, a condo-resort, villas and apartments, on waterfront, no beach, pool. **LL-AL** *Caribbean Court Bonaire*, J A Abraham Blvd, T7175353, F7175363, www.caribbeancourt.com 21 apartments, 1-3 bedrooms, overlooking canal, close to airport, Dutch colonial style, fully equipped.

Kralendijk B-C *Hotel Rochaline*, Kaya Grandi 7, T7178286, F7178258. 10 rooms, a/c, functional, bar facing sea, restaurant. Popular and often full is the **B-C** *Palm Studios* attached to Blue Divers Diveshop on Kaya den Tera 2, T7176860, F7176865, www.bluedivers.com 10 rooms, a/c, common shower and kitchen, big garden, clean, cosy, pool, recommended for budget travellers/divers.

North of Kralendijk LL *Bayside Resort*, Kaya Jan NE Craane 24, T7175800, F7175850. Short walk to town, 1-bedroom suites sleep 4, 2-bedroom penthouses sleep 6, fully equipped, balconies overlooking charter boats; **LL** *Harbour Village Beach Resort and Marina* on Playa Lechi, Kaya Gob N Debrot 72, T7177500, F7177507, www.harbourvillage.com Renovated in 2001, rooms, suites and villas, restaurants, bars, fitness centre, tennis centre, pool, spa, private beach, 64-slip and mega-yacht marina and dock, dive shop, and non-motorized watersports, upmarket resort, look out for promotional packages but make sure you get what is on offer, and check your bill carefully. **AL-A** *Eden Beach Apartment Resort*, Kaya Gobernador N Debrot 74, T7176720. Good value, new property, well - equipped, *WannaDive* dive shop and *Bongos Restaurant* on the premises. **LL-L** *Sand Dollar Condominium Resort*, Kaya   Gobernador   N   Debrot   79,   T7178738,   F7178760,   T1800-2884773, sanddollar@bonairenet.com, 76 apartments, a/c, rocky shoreline, tennis, pool, sailing, sport fishing, bicycle and kayak rental next door at *Sand Dollar Dive and Photo*. **L-AL** *Buddy Beach and Dive Resort*, Kaya Gob N Debrot 85, T7175080, F7178647, www.buddydive.com, 68 rooms and apartments all with sea views, a/c, kitchen, pool, Buddy Watersports Center. **LL-AL** *Lions Dive Hotel Bonaire*, Kaya Gob N Debrot 91, T7175580, F7175680, www.bonairenet.com Suites and apartments some sleep 6, diving with Bon Bini Divers, pool, sundeck. **LL-AL** *Captain Don's Habitat*, Kaya Gob N Debrot 103, T7178290, F7178240, in USA T800-3276709, F305-3712337, 93 rooms, cottages and nice villas of differing standards, well laid out seafront bar and restaurant, dive packages, family packages, special excursions for children during their family month every Aug, pool, dive shop with world's youngest snorkelling instructor, mountain bike rental. A little further along the coast is **AL-C** *Black Durgon Inn/Pilot Fish Apartments*, Kaya Gobernador N Debrot 145, T7175736, F7178846, 8-room inn, 1-bedroom apartments, 2/3-bedroom villa, with view of Klein Bonaire, relaxing, non-commercial, dive shop. About 5km north of Kralendijk is

B-C *Bonaire Caribbean Club*, T7177901, F7177900, www.bonairecaribbeanclub.com New owners were renovating the *Club* in 2001, 18 rooms, good view from *Hill Top Bar and Restaurant*, dive gear for rent, caves nearby, good walking.

Windward coast **LL-L** *Sorobon Beach Resort*, at Lac Bay, T7178080, F7176080, sorobon@bonairenet.com Clothes optional, 30 chalets on the beach, restaurant for hotel guests, small shop for self-catering, free trips to town for shopping daily, snorkelling, kayaks, windsurfing. **LL-AL** *Lac Bay Resort*, Kaminda Sorobon 64, T7178198, F7175686. In protected nature area, studios, apartments and 3-bedroom villa, good view from *Kon Tiki* restaurant and bar.

Eating

All food is imported, so fruit and vegetables in the market are not cheap. Try local dishes such as salt fish or goat stew but maybe not iguana soup, which is sometimes on the menu

International food at the major hotels varies on different nights of the week with barbecues or Indonesian nights, etc. Main courses in the upper-priced restaurants are about US$12-20, but several restaurants do bar snacks, 'Bar Hop', if you want to economize. **Water** Comes from a desalination plant, has an excellent taste and is safe to drink. Take water with you on excursions. Do not, however, wash in or drink water from outside taps. This is *sushi* (dirty) water, treated sufficiently for watering plants but nothing more.

There are over 80 restaurants on this small island. The **hotels** mostly offer good restaurants with fine views over the sea. *The Lion's Den*, at the *Lion's Dive Hotel*, T7173400, has one of the most spectacular views and a stylish menu.*Rum Runners at the Reef* at *Captain Don's Habitat*, T7177303. Breakfast, lunch and dinner with theme nights, eg Bonairean food, Mexican or barbecue, with live music some nights. *Captain Wook's Marina Bar & Compadres Restaurant*, T7177500, one of the restaurants at the *Harbour Village* marina. Tex-Mex specialities and you can use the cascade pool and outdoor pool table. *It Rains Fishes*, at the *Bayside Resort*, T7178780. Dinner only.

In Kralendijk, *Rendez-Vous*, Kaya L D Gerharts 3, T7178454. Award-winning chef, dinner, seafood specials, vegetarian choice, good vegetables, small and friendly, closed Sun. *Mona Lisa*, on Kaya Grandi, T7178718. Closed Sun, bar and restaurant, interesting, imaginative food, Dutch chef enjoys discussing the menu, expect to pay NAf 25-35 for main course, friendly service, popular with Europeans. *Mi Poron*, Kaya Caracas 1, a block from Roman Catholic Church, T7175199. Many antiques, welcoming patio, daily specials, authentic *krijollo* restaurant, open 1200-1400, 1800-2200. *Croccantino*, Kaya Grandi 48, T7175025. Italian, in historic town house, a/c dining room or garden dining, open daily for lunch and dinner. *Capriccio*, Kaya Isla Riba I, T7177230. Closed Tue, Italian, homemade pasta, pizza, lunch and dinner. *The Dome*, in the town centre. Sports bar and restaurant with sandwiches, cakes, coffee and juices, satellite TV with sport and results from Europe and the USA, not open for dinner. *Beefeater*, Kaya Grandi 12, T7177776. Open from 1600 daily, steak and seafood, local specialities, good vegetarian selection, small. *Zeezicht*, Kaya JNE Craane 12, T7178434. On the waterfront, Bonaire's oldest restaurant, does breakfast, lunch and dinner, sandwiches and omelettes as well as fish, steak, pasta and some Indonesian, open daily. In The Harbourside shopping mall there is, *Cozzoli's Pizzeria*, T7175195. For fast food, breakfast, lunch and dinner, *The Garden Café*, behind the Tourist Office on Kaya Simon Bolivar 1, T7173410, features Middle Eastern meals. *The Swiss Chalet*, Kaya Simon Bolivar 21, T7173366. International food and Swiss specialities, very friendly owners. *De Islander*, Kaya Caracas 326, T7173420. West Indian cuisine and American favourites in a spotless atmosphere. South of town, just past *Carib Inn* is *Richard's Waterfront Dining*, J A Abraham Boulevard 60, T7175263. American owner, happy hour 1700-1900, dinner 1830-2230, closed Mon, seafood and steak specialities. *Blue Moon*, Kaya CEB Hellmund 5, T7178617. On waterfront, set menu or à la carte, French and international, open for food 1800-2200, happy hour 1700-1830, closed Wed. *Den Laman Seafood Restaurant*, at the roundabout near the northern hotels, T7178955. Open for lunch and dinner, lots of fresh fish and lobster. *Maiky Snack Kaminda*, New Amsterdam 30, T09-5670078. An out-in-the-country spot to get home-made local food, soup, main dish and drink US$8.50, dinner only.

There are lots of Chinese restaurants. *Mentor's*, Kaya Korona 140, T7174999. Lunch and dinner, cheap, large portions of Chinese food. *Great China* , Kaya Grandi 39, T7178886; *Shanghai Bar Restaurant*, Kaya L D Gerharts 17, T7178838, all open for lunch and dinner. As in the other Dutch Antilles, Indonesian food is good and popular. *Old Inn*, on J A Abraham Blvd opposite *Plaza Resort*, T7176666. Indonesian Rijsttafel a speciality, also steak, fish and children's menu, dinner only, closed Wed. There are also a couple of Surinamese restaurants: *Surinaamse Bar Restaurant*, Kaya A Cecillia 31, T7172127 and *Spanhoek*, Kaya L D Gerharts, T7176686. For pizza, try *Pasa Bon Pizza and Bar*, Kaya Gob Debrot 42, T7901111. Most restaurants can prepare food for takeaway.

On the windward side of the island, *Beachclub Kontiki* next to the *Lac Bay Resort*, T7175369, kontiki@bonairelive.net Seafood, steaks, salads and wide variety of international cuisine, friendly, casual, beautiful view, Caribbean décor, open 1200-1500, 1830-2200, closed Mon. Home of the *Bonaire Jazz Club*. The beach bar, *Hang Out*, at Jibe City is recommended for terrific sandwiches, drink, shade, rest and regaining energy for windsurfing.

Check schedule of Bonaire's *Weekly Happenings* update at tourist office, or in the free English language weekly, *The Bonaire Reporter*. *Paradise Disco* is at Kaya LD Gerharts 11, T7177345, open weekends from 2300. *Karel's Beach Bar* has a live band, Kaya K Craane 12, from 2200 Fri and Sat. *Harbour Village Beach Resort* has a mariachi band on Sat night at its *Compadres Mexican Grill* restaurant. The Bonaire Jazz Club meets on the first Sun of the month at the *Kon Tiki* and the *Sorobon Resort*, 3 hrs of music, US$5.60, informal, outdoors, visiting musicians from Europe and the USA join the regular musicians (Bonairean, Dutch and Venezuelan) and music ranges from standard jazz to selections from Broadway with a Latin beat, call *Kon Tiki*, T7175369, for details. There are casinos at the *Divi Flamingo Beach Resort* (open 2000 except Sun, T7178285) and *Plaza Resort* (T7172450). There is a **cinema** on Kaya Prinses Marie, *The Movies Bonaire*, T7172400, www.InfoBonaire.com/cinema, for what's on, usually closed Mon and Tue. Slide and video shows include: Mon, sea turtle slide show, presented by Sea Turtle Conservation Bonaire at *Buddy Dive Resort*, 1900, T7175080; Tue, *When the Sun Goes Down*, marine nightlife while night diving and snorkelling by Sipke Stapert, in front of *Sand Dollar Dive and Photo*, 2000, T7175433; Tue, *Sage of the Deep*, stories and slides, a 'show and tell' by Captain Don himself, Conference Room at *Capt Don's Habitat*, 2000, T7172925; Thu, *Week in Review*, slide show by *Exposures* photo shop, *Rum Runners Restaurant* at *Capt Don's Habitat*, 1900, T7178290; Fri, *Week in Review*, video presentation by *Toucan Dive Shop*, at *Coconut Crash Bar*, *Plaza Resort*, 1700, T7172500.

The Bridge Club of Bonaire, 'Ups and Downs',welcomes players Wed for a friendly night of duplicate bridge, at *Mi Poron Restaurant*, 1930, T7175199. Call before 1400 to reserve. *Lions Club* meets every 2nd and 4th Thu of the month at 2000 at Kaya Sabana 1. All visiting Lions are welcome, T7175330, ext 632 or 7174944. *Rotary* lunch meetings are held every Wed, 1200-1400 at *Rendez-Vous Restaurant*, Kaya L.D. Gerharts 3. All visiting Rotarians are welcome, T7178454.

Nightlife
Some contrived typically Caribbean night time entertainment and gambling, but Bonaire's real nightlife revolves around free slide and video shows at hotels and dive shops

The *Harbourside Shopping Mall* contains small boutiques and a 1 hr photo processing shop, *Kodalux*, T7178123. *Photo Tours* at *Plaza Resort Bonaire*, also offers full underwater facilities and equipment rental. Local arts and crafts are largely sea-based and fabrics. The *Fundashon Arte Industri Bonairano* and the privately owned *Caribbean Arts and Crafts shop* are both in Kralendijk for souvenirs. *Palu Wiri*, which plays local, native instruments, has recorded 2 CDs, available locally, of Bonairean and Antillean songs. The largest supermarket is *Cultimara*, T7178278, with groceries and some household goods, or there are several minimarkets. *Sand Dollar Grocery*, open daily, is located in a small plaza in front of the *Sand Dollar Beach Club* along with *Lovers Ice Cream Parlour*. Near the *Divi Flamingo* a turning opposite leads to *Joke's* grocery and mini-market.

Shopping
Bonaire is not a major shopping centre, though some shops do stock high quality low duty goods. Sales tax is 5%

Air *KLM*, *Air Holland* and *Martinair* fly non-stop from Amsterdam on different days of the week. *Sobelair* flies twice a week from Brussels. If you are a diver and it is specified on your airline ticket, *KLM* will allow you an extra 10 kg baggage allowance for diving equipment (regular allowance 20 kg tourist class, 30 kg business class) without incurring overweight charges. *ALM* flies from Aruba, Curaçao and Miami and several other places via Curaçao (eg Caracas, Kingston, Maracaibo, Port-au-Prince, Port of Spain, St Maarten, San Juan, Santo Domingo and Valencia in Venezuela). Several other international airlines fly to Curaçao,

Transport

48km away, from where frequent daily flights are available to Bonaire. *Air Jamaica* flies from Chicago and other American cities via Montego Bay. *American Eagle* flies 3 times a week from San Juan, Puerto Rico, where you can make connections with US cities.

Sea There is no regular ferry service from Venezuela or the other islands but a coaster, *Don Andrés*, makes a weekly run from Muaco, La Vela in Venezuela, and several round trips to Curaçao each week as well. You have to contact the captains direct, ask at the *capitanía* or the maritime agency 2 blocks from the Plaza Bolívar in Muaco, or the Port Captain's office in the waterfront Fort Amsterdam on Bonaire. It can be a rough journey with heavy seas.

Road Bicycle Available to rent from most hotels' front desks. *De Freeweiler*, on Kaya AEP Brion, just off Kaya Grandi downtown, T7178545, sells, rents and repairs touring and mountain bikes. Bike hire from US$7 per day, US$40 per week. *Cycle Bonaire/Discover Bonaire,* has Trek mountain bikes and offers rentals, repairs and guided tours. Bike rental is US$15 per day or US$75 per week, while guided excursions are US$40 half day including drinks and US$65 whole day including lunch but not including bike rental. Also *Hot Shot*, see above, and *Bonaire Boating*, with an office in the *Divi Flamingo Hotel*, T7175353, ext 505, F7175622, and some hotels. *Discover Bonaire* has tours through the kunuku and Washington/Slagbaai National Park. The roads in the south are flat and in good condition but there is no shade and you would need lots of water and sun screen. In the north it is more hilly and the roads are not as good. For mountain bikers there are lots of unpaved trails and goat paths.

You must have a valid driver's licence. Minimum age for car rental varies between agencies from 21-26

Car hire *A B Car Rental* at the airport, PO Box 339, T7178980, F7175034. *Budget*, T7174700, F7173325. *Sunray Car Rental*, at the airport, T7175230. *Trupial Car Rental*, Kaya Grandi No 96, T7178487. *Avis*, J A Abraham Blvd 4, Kralendijk, T7175795, F7175793. There are nearly a dozen other companies not listed here, plenty of choice, many have offices in the hotels. At the busiest times of the year, it is best to reserve a car in advance. Four-wheel drive vehicles are not easy to find, and it is best to order one well in advance. Most cars are manual, not automatic. There are lots of pickups and minivans for divers wanting to carry gear around for shore diving. Some companies prohibit the use of ordinary cars on unpaved roads and in Washington/Slagbaai Park. There is a government tax of US$4 per day plus 2% on the rental fee. The speed limit in built-up areas is 40 kph, outside towns it is 60 kph unless otherwise marked. Several of the roads in Kralendijk and the tourist road north of the Radio Netherlands towers are one-way. There are 4 filling stations, open Mon-Sat 0700-2100. The Kralendijk station is also open Sun 0900-1530.

Motorcycle Small motorcycles can be rented from US$18 a day; shop around as there are several new scooter shops and rates are competitive: *Hot Shot Scooter and Cycle Rental,* Kaya Bonaire 4, T/F7177166; *De Freeweiler*, T7178545; *Macho Scooter Rentals*, T7172500; *Orlando's Bonaire Motorcycle Shop*, Kaminda Djabou 10, T7178429, 7904409, rent big twins or other interesting motorcycles for US$50 a day.

Taxi Drivers carry list of officially approved rates, including touring and waiting time, but be sure to agree a price beforehand. The short trip from the airport to the *Divi Flamingo Beach Resort* is US$8.50; fares increase by 50% from midnight-0600. Taxis have TX on their licence plates. Taxis are available at the airport but do not cruise for business elsewhere. Any hotel will call a taxi for you. To call a taxi yourself, T7178100 for the taxi stand at the airport.

Directory **Airlines** *ALM*, T7178500. *KLM, Air Jamaica, American Eagle*, T7178300. **Banks** Open 0800 or 0830-1530 or 1600, Mon-Fri. All have ATMs. TCs and credit cards are widely accepted. *Royal Bank of Trinidad & Tobago (ABN-AMRO)*, T7178417, F7178469; *Maduro & Curiel's Bank (Bonaire) NV*, T7177249, F7172645, is a full service Antillean bank with a branch in Rincon, T7176266; *Antilles Banking Corporation Bonaire*, T7174500, F7174510; *Banco di Caribe NV*, T7178295, F7175153. **Communications** **Telephone** Direct dialling to the USA with a credit card is available at the airport and at Telbo in town. The international code for Bonaire is 599, followed by a 7-digit number. For information on services, contact Telbo, T7177000, F7175007. To rent a cellular phone,

Netherlands Antilles, the ABC islands

T09-5692244/6999. **Internet**: *De Tuin eetcafe* is a cybercafe on Kaya L D Gerharts 9, T7172999, for internet access, lunch and dinner. Internet service providers are BonaireLive!, T7175180, F7175181 and BonaireNet, T/F7177160, **Post**: J A Abraham Blvd, Kralendijk, on the corner of Plaza Reina Wilhelmina opposite the ABN bank, open 0730-1200, 1330-1700 for stamps and postage, 1330-1600 for money orders etc. Airmail to the USA and Canada is NAfl.75 for letters, NAf0.90 for postcards. There is also Express Mail and Federal Express. Rocargo Services, T7178922, F7175791, is the FedEx and cargo agent. **Medical facilities** The Hospitaal San Francisco in Kralendijk has 60 beds, T7178900. There is an air ambulance for emergency evacuation and a recompression chamber for scuba diving accidents. The emergency phone number is T191. There is a dentist at Chirino Dental Clinic, T7178106. Opticians at *Optica Antillana*, T7178815, and *Ram's Optica*, T7175612. **Tourist information** Local tourist office Kaya Simón Bolívar 12, Kralendijk, T7178322, F7178408, www.InfoBonaire.com The Bonaire Hotel and Tourism Association (Bonhata) is at T7175134, F7178534, info@bonhata.org The Bonaire tourist map shows all the dive and snorkelling sites around the island as well as the best bird watching places. *The Official Roadmap with Dive Sites* is available in some shops and adequate for most purposes. It gives a good street plan of Kralendijk, dive sites and points of interest on Bonaire and Klein Bonaire, but tends to indicate as 'beach' areas which are rocky cliffs. The *Bonaire Reporter* is the island's weekly English language newspaper and is available free on Bonaire or on the internet at www.bonairereporter.com It contains up to date information for island visitors. **Local travel** agents *Bonaire Tours*, T7178778, F7174890, head office Kaya L D Gerharts 22, for large or small groups, 2 hr north or south tour, half or full day Washington Park tour, day trip to Curaçao. *Bonaire Nature Tours* for small groups, maximum 7 people, 0900-1800, led by Dutch biologist/dive instructor, Klaus Bakker, tours can be tailor-made, T/F7177714. Taxis have fixed prices for sightseeing tours. *Discover Bonaire*, Kaya Gob N Debrot 79, T7175252, F7177690, www.discover bonaire.com, for kayaking, nature tours, guided snorkelling and mountain biking, tours plus 10% service. *SkiffyWatertaxi*, T/F5607254, trips to Klein Bonaire Mon-Sat, US$10 per person, on Sun by appointment. Sunset and evening cruises Tue, Fri, Sat, and snorkel trips. *Bonaire Travel & Tours*, at the corner of the Lourdes Mall. Useful addresses Immigration, T7178000. Government main number, T7175300. Police, T7178000. Stinapa (Park Authority) and Bonaire Marine Park, T7178444.

Curaçao

Curaçao is the largest of the Netherlands Antilles and its capital, Willemstad, has some very fine Dutch colonial architecture painted in a variety of pastel colours, while in the countryside there are several beautiful plantation houses, called landhuisen. *It also has one of the most important historical sites in the Caribbean: a synagogue dating back to 1732, which is the oldest in continuous use in the Western Hemisphere. For most of the 20th century the island's fortunes, like Aruba, depended on its oil refinery, which pro-cesses Venezuelan crude oil, but more recently tourism also has become more impor-tant. Diving has grown very popular since the establishment of an underwater park to preserve the reef and there are dive sites all along the leeward side of the island.*

Population: 170,000
Colour map 6, grid B1

Ins and outs

Flights from Europe originate in Amsterdam, while flights from North America connect in Miami or San Juan. Curaçao has traditionally had good links with South America and it is easy to get to from Venezuela, Colombia and Ecuador, making it a good stopping off place on your way to or from that continent. **Hato airport** is about 12 km from Willemstad and if you don't want to pay for a taxi there are buses in to Punda and Otrabanda.

Getting there
Airlines & their routes change frequently so check the latest flight guide

Willemstad is a great place to walk around and there are tours if you want a guide who can explain all the architecture and history to you. The two halves of the city are connected with a pontoon bridge, the Queen Emma Bridge, which you can walk across when it is not open for shipping. Collective taxis and buses will take you further afield to most parts of the island, alternatively rent a car and explore on your own. There are about 4 car rental agencies at the airport, all the offices are together so it is easy to pick up price lists for comparison. One or two companies usually have desks in each of the major hotels. Look in local tourist literature or newspapers for news of special deals on offer, there is lots of choice. There have been

Getting around
See transport, page 1027, for further details

A Foot in the door

- Take in the **underwater world**, diving, snorkelling or by visiting the Seaquarium.
- Trace the **Jewish heritage** and visit the 1732 synagogue, museum and cemetery.
- Walk around historical **Punda** and **Otrabanda**, the two sides of the capital, Willemstad, and cross over the swing bridge for a spectacular view of the two halves.
- Join local office staff for a typical, filling lunch of **goat stew and funchi** at the Old Market, where numerous cooks prepare tasty Curaçaoan meals in huge pots on charcoal fires.
- Stock up on the original **Curaçao liqueur** and tour the distillery.

problems with unsafe cars, inadequate insurance and licensing. Those listed in the transport section are considered reputable. Taxis are easily identified by the signs on the roof and TX before the licence number. There are taxi stands at all hotels and at the airport, as well as in principal locations in Willemstad.

Diving and marine life

The waters around Curaçao contain a wide variety of colourful fish and plant life and several wrecks (*Superior Producer*, near the water distillation plant, and a tugboat in Caracas Bay) which have foundered on the coral reef just offshore. The reef surrounds the island and consists generally of a gently sloping terrace to a depth of about 10 m, then a drop off and a reef slope with an angle of about 45°. The coral formations are spectacular in places and there are many huge sponges; one in Boca Sta Martha is so big it is known as 'the double bed'. There are lots of fish and you are likely to see barracuda, moray eels, spiny lobsters, turtles, manta rays and maybe sharks. Underwater visibility averages 24 m and water temperature varies between 24-27°C. There are lots of opportunities for successful underwater photography.

Many of the large resort hotels have dive shops on site. They have been encouraged by the establishment in 1983 of the Curaçao Underwater Park managed by the Netherlands Antilles National Parks Foundation (Stinapa), which stretches from the *Princess Beach Hotel* to East Point. The park extends out from the shore to a depth of 60 m and covers 600 ha of reef and 436 ha of inner bays.

Over 40 permanent mooring buoys for boats have been placed at dive sites along the south coast as part of Stinapa's programme for sustained utilization of the reef. A few of the sites can be dived from the shore (West Point, Blauwbaa, Port Marie, Daaibooi, Vaersen Bay, San Juan, Playa Kalki), but most of the coastal strip is private property and boat dives are necessary. The *Guide to the Curaçao Underwater Park*, by Jeffrey Sybesma & Tom van't Hof, published in 1989 by Stinapa and available locally, describes the sites and discusses conservation. For independent divers and snorkellers without a boat there is the *Complete Guide to Landside Diving and Snorkelling Locations in Curaçao*, by Jeffrey Sybesma and Suzanne Koelega, including a map with the sites and roads to them. No harpoons or spear guns are allowed and make sure you do not damage or remove coral or any other sea creatures.

Dive centres There are many dive operators, not all of which are mentioned here, and it is worth shopping around before booking a package deal. The *Curaçao Diving Operators Association (CDOA)* standardizes safety regulations and should be contacted if you have any complaints or suggestions. Most operators offer a single boat dive for around US$30-35, a two-tank dive for US$55-60 and snorkelling trips including equipment for about US$15-20, but check when booking whether 10% service is included in the quoted price. *Underwater Curaçao* (T4618131, F4657826) at the *Lions Dive Hotel* next to the Seaquarium is one of the larger operations with two dive boats for 20 divers each and two scheduled dives a day. It has a large air station, equipment rental, a retail shop and offers several courses. *Curaçao Seascape* at the

Essentials

Documents Most nationalities (including US and Canadian citizens) need a passport and onward/return ticket. Visas are needed by citizens of Albania, Bulgaria, China, Cuba, Dominican Republic, Democratic Kampuchea, Former Yugoslavia (except Slovenia), Former USSR, Haiti, Libyan Arab Jamahiriya, North Korea, Romania and Vietnam. Transit visitors and cruise ship passengers must have proof of identity for a 24-hour, or less, stay on the island. Immigration procedures at the airport are quick and easy.

Money The currency is the guilder, divided into 100 cents. There are coins of 1, 2½, 5, 10, 25, 50 cents and 1 and 2½ guilders, and notes of 10, 25, 50, 100, 250 and 500 guilders. Old and new coins are in circulation. **Exchange** The exchange rate is US$1=NAf1.77 for bank notes, NAf1.79 for cheques, although the rate of exchange offered by shops and hotels ranges from NAf1.75-1.80. Credit cards and US dollars are widely accepted.

Departure tax There is an airport tax of US$6 on departure to the Netherlands Antilles or US$20 to Aruba or other destinations. This must be paid at a separate kiosk after you check in.

Official time Atlantic Standard Time, 4 hours behind GMT, 1 hour ahead of EST.

Voltage 127/220 volts AC, 50 cycles.

Tourist offices overseas Argentina: Paraguay 880, 1st floor of 7 (1057), Buenos Aires, T541-3115965/2488, F541-3128849. **Germany:** Arnulfstrasse 44, D-80335 Munich 2, T4989-598490, F4989-5504045. **Holland:** Vasteland 82-84, 3001 BP Rotterdam, PO Box 23227, T3110-4142639, F3110-4136834, ctbenl@wirehub.nl **UK:** Axis Sales and Marketing, 421a Finchley Road, London NW3 6HJ, T0171-4314045, F0171-4317920. **USA:** 475 Park Avenue South, Suite 2000, New York, NY10016, T212-6837660, 1800-2703350, F212-6839337, curacao@ix.netcom.com; 330 Biscayne Blvd, Suite 808, Miami, FL33132, T305-3745811, 800-4458266, F305-3746741. **Venezuela:** Torre la Previsora, Local No 3, Planta Baja, Av las Acacias con Bolívar, Urb las Caobos, PO Box 63345, Caracas, T602-7814622, F602-7826582.

Safety There is a drugs problem in Willemstad and you are advised to be careful in Otrabanda at night and avoid the outer stretches of Pietermaai even by day (crack houses). If strangers stop you on the street asking 'alles goed?' (everything OK?) be assured that they are not enquiring after your mood.

Health The climate is healthy and non-malarial; epidemic incidence is slight. Rooms without air-conditioning or window and door screens may need mosquito nets during the wetter months of November and December and sometimes May and June, and, although some spraying is done in tourist areas, mosquitoes are a problem. Some anti-mosquito protection is recommended if you are outdoors any evening. Beware of a tree with small, poisonous green apples that borders some beaches. This is the manchineel (manzanilla) and its sap causes burns on exposed skin.

Public holidays New Year's Day, Carnival Monday (February), Good Friday, Easter Monday, Queen's Birthday (30 April), Labour Day (1 May), Ascension Day, Flag Day (2 July), Christmas on 25 and 26 December.

Netherlands Antilles, the ABC islands

Curaçao Sheraton Resort, T4625000, is also good. Eden Roc Dive Centre is at the Holiday Beach Hotel, and is a PADI five-star facility, T4628878. Marlies' Coral Cliff Diving at Santa Martha Bay (T8642822, F8642237) has a deliberately sunk airplane in shallow water just offshore for divers and also offers introductory or certification courses and package deals, also windsurfing US$10 per hour, with sunfish, hobiecats and pedalboats available, prices not including 10% service. Habitat Curaçao is an offshoot of Captain Don's Habitat in Bonaire, at Rif St Marie, offering PADI, NAUI and SSI courses, boat dives, shore dives, snorkelling, photography, all equipment available for rent, lots of package deals, T8648800, F8648464. Sami Scuba Centre Dive School Wederfoort has been in operation since 1966, very friendly, reputable, mostly shore dives, the drop starts 25 m from dive centre; a six-day package including air, weights and no tank limit, costs US$120, a PADI open water course is US$257, accommodation and restaurant available, contact Eric and Yolanda Wederfoort, Marine Beach Club, St Michielsbaai, T8884414, F8692062, www.divewederfoort.com. Out at Westpoint and Playa Kalki are All West Diving *and Adventures*, T8640102, offering courses, boat dives, introductory dives (US$30) and equipment for rent. Students are given preferential rates.

Seaquarium   The Seaquarium, southeast of Willemstad, just beyond the *Lions Dive Hotel*, has a collection of undersea creatures and plants found around the island, which live in channelled sea water to keep them as close as possible to their natural environment. The Seaquarium was built in 1984, the lagoons and marina being excavated so as to leave the original coastline untouched and do minimal damage to the reef offshore. A new attraction is the shark (lemon and nurse) and animal (turtles, stingrays) encounter programme, where you get in the water with them to feed them, good for photography, US$55 for diving (no previous experience necessary), US$30 snorkelling. Good quality photos of visitors feeding the sharks are offered at US$25 for 12. ■ *0830-1700. US$13.25, children under 15 US$7.50, after 1600 US$3 and US$1.50 respectively. T4616666. There is a restaurant, snack bar and shops selling shells and coral in marked contrast to the conservation efforts of the Underwater Park administration. The Seaquarium can be reached by bus marked Dominguito from the post office at 35 minutes past the hour (except for 1335), which passes the Avila Beach Hotel.*

The *Seaworld Explorer* is a cruising underwater observatory, not a submarine, you sit in the hull and look out of the windows as the vessel moves along the wall. ■ *Several daily departures, one-hour trip, US$29, children US$19, T4610011.*

Beaches and watersports

Topless sunbathing is not recommended on public beaches but is tolerated on private beaches

There are several good beaches on Curaçao. The northwest coast is rugged and rough for swimming, but the southwest coast has some sheltered bays and beaches with excellent swimming and snorkelling. Windsurfing, waterskiing, yachting and fishing are available at resorts. Many of the beaches are private and make a charge per car (amount depends on day of the week and popularity, US$3-6) but in return

Curaçao

you usually get some changing facilities, toilets and refreshments. Public beaches are free but most have no facilities and some are rather dirty and smelly.

Heading south out of Willemstad are the two small, artificial beaches at the *Avila Beach Hotel*, where non-residents pay an entrance fee. The sand is imported and the sea is not calm enough to see much if you snorkel but the breakwaters make it pleasant for swimming. You can get to the beach at **Piscadera Bay** near the *Sheraton* hotel by catching one of their shuttle buses from beside the Rif Fort in Otrabanda. Southeast of Willemstad, by the *Princess Beach Hotel*, the *Lions Dive Hotel* and the Seaquarium (see above), is a 450 m, man-made beach and marina with all watersports available. It can be crowded and noisy with music; motorized watersports are all down one end. ■ *0830-1800. Entrance to the beach is US$2.25. Showers and toilets. Mambo Beach Club for night-time entertainment.* Past the Seaquarium is a residential area and private beach on **Jan Thiel Bay**, good swimming and snorkelling, entrance NAf6 per car, changing facilities, drinks and snacks. **Santa Barbara** located at the mouth of Spanish Water Bay on the Mining Company property, is a favourite with locals. Behind Spanish Water Bay rises **Mount Tafelberg**, where phosphate mining used to take place. ■ *Open 0800-1800. Entrance US$2.25 per person. Changing rooms, toilets and snack bars. You can take a bus from the post office, get off at the Mining Company gate and hitchhike down to the beach, or take a taxi, it is too far to walk.* Across the bay, which is one of the island's beauty spots, is the Curaçao Yacht Club, with a pleasant bar. There are four yacht clubs in Spanish Water. **Caracas Bay Island** has recently been developed as an attraction for day-trippers, offering biking, horse riding, a tour of the fort and watersports such as kayaking, canoeing, guided snorkelling tours, windsurfing and jet skis. The *Baya Restaurant on the Beach*, open 1200-2300, has French Oriental cuisine, while there is also the *Baya Beach Club*, for a day time drinking spot or night time entertainment, particularly busy Saturday nights when the disco is action packed for visiting DJs. The new *Curaçao Howard Johnson* hotel in Willemstad has an agreement for its guests to be shuttled to *Baya Beach Club* for beach activities, so it is always likely to be busy. ■ *T7470777, www.caracasbayisland.com*

Travelling northwest from Willemstad heading towards Westpoint, there are lots of coves and beaches worth exploring. A left turn soon after leaving town will take you to **Blauw Bay**, good for snorkelling but a Curasol development is under construction and the beach is now closed, or to **St Michiel's Bay**, a fishing village and tanker clearing harbour (free). **Daaibooibaai**, south of St Willibrordus is a public beach and gets very crowded on a Sunday. Further up the coast, **Port Marie** (private, charge per car) is sandy but there is no shade. There is a little restaurant and dive area to change, rinse off equipment etc. **Cas Abao beach** has pretty with good snorkelling and diving from shore in beautiful clear water. ■ *Changing facilities, showers, shade huts, lounge chairs cost US$3, US$3 per car per day, US$5 at weekends and holidays, snacks and beverages.* **San Juan**, a private beach with lots of coral is off to the left of the main Westpoint road down a poor track, entrance fee charged. **Boca Sta Martha**, where the *Coral Cliff Resort* is located, is quiet with nice sea. ■ *Beach entrance US$4.50 for non-residents, no pets or food allowed on the beach, some shade provided.* **Lagun** is a lovely secluded beach in a small cove with cliffs surrounding it and small fishing boats pulled up on the sand. It is safe for children and good for snorkelling. ■ *There are facilities and some shade from trees. Some buses pass only 50 m from the beach.* **Jeremi**, a public beach with no charge, is of the same design, slightly larger sandy beach with a steep drop to deep water and boats moored here, protected by the cliffs. Further up the coast, **Knip** is a more open, larger, sandy beach again with cliffs at either end. Many people rate this the best beach on the island, but the stairway down to the beach was destroyed by the storms of 1999. There are some facilities here and it is very popular at weekends when there is loud music and it gets crowded and noisy. **Playa Abau** is big, sandy, with beautiful clear water, surrounded by cliffs. ■ *Some shade provided, toilets, well organized, popular at weekends and busy.* Nearing the west tip, **Playa Forti** has dark sand and good swimming. There is a restaurant on the cliff top overlooking the sea which gets very busy at weekend lunchtimes. The beach at **Westpoint** below the church is stoney and littered, the only shade comes from the poisonous manchineel trees. Fishing boats tie up at the pier but bathers prefer to go to Playa Forti. Beyond Westpoint is **Kalki beach** which is good for snorkelling and diving as well as bathing. *Westpoint is the end of the road, about 45 mins by car or 1 hr by bus from Otrabanda, US$1.*

Day sails   Many charter boats and diving operators go to **Klein Curaçao**, a small, uninhabited island off East Point which has sandy beaches and is good for snorkelling and scuba diving, a nice day trip with lunch provided. The most popular charter boat is *Waterworld* which leaves at 0900 from the Seaquarium Marina for Klein Curaçao day trips (US$18) and to Banda Abou, sunset, snorkelling or party trips on request; motor boat takes 100 passengers and departures sometimes depend on whether there is a cruise ship in port, T4656042. Other companies include *Mermaid*, T5601530, *Miss Ann*, T7671579 and *Bounty*, T5601887. There are snorkel, snorkel-picnic and sunset trips; also day sailing trips from Willemstad up the coast with barbecue lunches at, for example, Port Marie, for about US$55, to the East End with lunch at Santa Barbara, and weekend sailing trips to Bonaire, accommodation on board, for about US$225. One such sailing ship is the 120 ft *Insulinde*, T5601340, shore T8688710, F4616633, www.insulinde.com, beautiful trip, including lunch but not drinks. You can also go on hovercraft excursions to various beaches for snorkelling or for sunset tours, with *Neptune Hovercraft Tours*, T8641500. Deep sea fishing charters can be booked with several companies including Boca Sami, Hemingway Fishing Charters, T5630365.

Sailing   The **Curaçao International Sailing Regatta** is held in January with competitions in three categories, short distance (windsurfers, hobie cats, sunfish etc), long distance (yachts race 112 km to Klein Curaçao and back) and open boat (trimarans, catamarans etc race 32 km to Spanish Water and back), all starting from the *Santa Barbara Beach Resort*. For details, contact the *Lion's Dive Hotel*, T4618100. The **Sami Sail Regatta** in April is organized by the fishing village of Boca St Michiel. The **International Blue Marlin tournament** is held in March. The Yacht Club is at Brakkeput Ariba, z/n, T7673038 or contact Mr B van Eerten, T7675275. *Sail Curaçao* has sailing courses, rentals and boat trips, also surfing lessons, T7676003.

Other sports   *Rancho Alegre*, T8681181, does **horse riding** for US$20 per hour, including transport. *Ashari's Ranch* offers horses for hire by the hour inland (US$20), or 1½ hours including a swim at the beach (US$30), open 1000-1900, Groot Piscadera Kaya A-23, T8690533, beginners as well as experienced riders, playground for children. *Rancho Alfin*, T8640535, has guided rides through the Christoffel Park, no experience necessary or, alternatively they offer **mountain biking**, guided or alone. Biking is also available at Caracas Bay Island, see above. There is **bowling** on the island,

Curaçao Bowling Club, Chuchubiweg 10, T7379275, six lanes, US$11 per hour, reservations advised. The Curaçao Golf and Squash Club at Wilhelminalaan, Emmastad, has a 10-hole sand **golf** course open 0800-1230, green fee US$15 for 18-hole round, and two **squash** courts, US$7, open 0800-1800, T7373590. The 18-hole *Blue Bay Golf & Beach Resort* opened in 2000. *Santa Catharina Sport and Country Club*, T7677028, F7677026, has six hard **tennis** courts, a **swimming** pool, bar and restaurant. The large hotels have tennis courts: the *Holiday Beach*, *Marriott* and the *Princess Beach* have a pro. For information about **running**, contact *Road Runners Club Korsou*, Barbara Beach, T7678126/4617304. **Triathlons** are sometimes organized, with sea swimming, mountain biking and trail running, contact *Vista Bike and Body Beach*, Boca Sint Michiel, T8682576/4625620.

Willemstad

Willemstad, capital of the Netherlands Antilles and of the island of Curaçao, is full of charm and colour. The architecture is a joyous tropical adaptation of 17th-century Dutch, painted in storybook colours. Pastel shades are used for homes, shops and government buildings alike. Fanciful gables, arcades, and bulging columns evoke the spirit of the Dutch colonial burghers.

Population: 140,000

The earliest buildings in Willemstad were exact copies of Dutch buildings of the mid-17th century, high-rise and close together to save money and space. Not until the first quarter of the 18th century did the Dutch adapt their northern ways to the tropical climate and begin building galleries on to the façades of their houses, to give shade and more living space. The chromatic explosion is attributed to a Governor-General of the islands, the eccentric Vice-Admiral Albert Kikkert ('Froggie' to his friends), who blamed his headaches on the glare of white houses and decreed in 1817 that pastel colours be used. Almost every point of interest in the city is in or within walking distance of the shopping centre in **Punda**, which covers about five blocks. Some of the streets here are only 5 m wide, but attract many tourists with their myriad shops offering international goods at near duty-free prices. The numerous jewellery shops in Willemstad have some of the finest stones to be found anywhere. There is a red and white trolley train which takes 60 passengers around the streets of Punda several times a day.

The **Floating Market**, a picturesque string of visiting Venezuelan, Colombian and other island schooners, lines the small canal leading to the Waaigat, a small yacht basin. Fresh fish, tropical fruit, vegetables and a limited selection of handicrafts are sold with much haggling. Visit early in the morning. In the circular, concrete, public market building nearby there are straw hats and bags, spices, butcheries, fruit and vegetables for sale, while in the old market building behind, local food is cooked over charcoal and sold to office workers at lunchtime.

Markets

Nearby on Hanchi Snoa, is one of the most important historical sites in the Caribbean, the **Mikvé Israel-Emanuel synagogue**, which dates back to 1732, making it the oldest in continuous use in the Western Hemisphere. In the 1860s, several families broke away from the Mikvé Israel congregation to found a Sephardi Reform congregation which was housed in the Temple Emanuel (1867-1964) on the Wilhelminaplein. In 1964, however, they reunited to form the Mikvé Israel-Emanuel congregation, which is affiliated with both the Reconstructionist Foundation and the World Union for Progressive Judaism. The big brass chandeliers are believed to be 300 years older than their synagogue, originating in Spain and Portugal, their candles are lit for Yom Kippur and special occasions. The names of the four mothers, Sara, Rebecca, Leah and Rachel are carved on the four pillars and there are furnishings of richly carved mahogany with silver ornamentation, blue stained glass windows and stark white walls. The traditional sand on the floor is sprinkled there

Synagogue

daily, some say, to symbolize the wandering of the Israelites in the Egyptian desert during the Exodus. Others say it was meant to muffle the sound of the feet of those who had to worship secretly during the Inquisition period. ■ *Services are held Fri 1830 and Sat 1000. Dress code for men is coat and tie and ladies equally conventional. Normally open 0900-1145 and 1430-1645, free.*

In the courtyard is the **Jewish Cultural Historical Museum**, occupying two restored 18th-century houses, which harbours an excellent permanent exhibition of religious objects, most of which have been donated by local Jewish families. There are scrolls, silver, books, bibles, furniture, clothing and household items, many 18th-century pieces and family bequeathments. Two circumcision chairs are still in use. Outside are some tombstones and a ritual bath excavated during restoration work. A small shop sells souvenirs, the Synagogue Guide Book and *Our Snoa*, papiamento for Synagogue, produced for the 250th anniversary in 1982. *Sephardim: The Spirit That Has Withstood The Times*, by Piet Huisman (Huisman Editions, The Netherlands, 1986) is an interesting illustrated account of the Sephardic communities of the Caribbean and the Americas, setting them in their historical context. Available in the synagogue shop and bookshops in town. Unfortunately, for those who want deeper research of the Jewish families, the *History of the Jews of the Netherlands Antilles*, by Isaac south and Suzanne A Emmanuel, two volumes, is no longer in print. ■ *Museum T4611633, F4611214. Open the same hours as the Synagogue, closed Jewish and public holidays. US$2, children US$1.*

Jewish cemetery West of the city, on the Schottegatweg Nord, is one of the two Jewish cemeteries, Bet Chayim (or Beth Haim), consecrated in 1659 and still in use. There are more than 1,700 tombstones from the 17th and 18th centuries, with bas-relief sculpture and inscriptions, many still legible. It is a little out of the way but well worth a visit. It is also a fine example of what atmospheric pollution can do, as the tombstones have suffered from the fumes from the surrounding oil refinery.

Willemstad orientation

Related map:
A *Willemstad centre, page 1010*

Not to scale

■ **Sleeping**
1 Avila Beach
2 Holiday Beach
3 Trupial Inn

Fortkerk

This 18th-century Protestant church, at the back of the square behind **Fort Amsterdam**, the Governor's palace, still has a British cannonball embedded in its walls. It is not as large as the synagogue museum, but is well laid out, with some interesting items, eg original church silver and reproductions of old maps and paintings of Curaçao. Note the clock in the ceiling of the church and make sure you are shown the still-functioning rain water cistern inside the church. It was once the main source of fresh water for the garrison. ■ *Mon-Fri 0900-1200, 1400-1700. US$2/NAf3, children US$1, you get a guided tour of the church and the associated museum.T4611139, F4657181.*

Forts

Two forts, **Rif Fort** and **Water Fort** were built at the beginning of the 19th century to protect the harbour entrance and replace two older batteries. All that is left of Rif Fort is a guard house dating from about 1840 but you can walk on the walls and eat at the restaurants in the vaults. The Water Fort Arches have been converted to house shops, bars and restaurants.

Museums

The **Maritime Museum** opened in 1998 in a 1729 colonial mansion on the Waaigat inlet near the Floating Market. It has permanent and temporary exhibitions of marine history relating to Curaçao and the Caribbean, with video presentations and multimedia displays. The museum has its own boat for tours of the harbour and ferrying cruise ship passengers and a harbourside café and gift shop. *van Brandenburg, T4652327. Mon-Sat 1000-1700, admission US$8.50 for adults, US$4.50 for students and children under 12, call for reservations for the daily tour of the museum, the harbour through the Annabaai, the Brionwerf and the refinery.* Another good museum in this area relating to Willemstad's maritime and trading history is the **Kura Hulanda**, with exhibits of the slave trade, tracing it back to the capture of slaves in Africa, their trans-Atlantic crossing and eventual sale as commercial goods. ■ *Klipstraat 9, T4621400, F4621401, www.kuruhulanda.com*

The **Philatelic Museum** is on the corner of Keukenstraat and Kuiperstraat in a recently restored building which is the oldest in Punda (1693). There is a comprehensive permanent display of Dutch Caribbean stamps, plus temporary exhibitions. ■ *Mon-Fri, 0900-1200, 1330-1700, Sat 1000-1500, admission US$2 or NAf3.50 for adults, NAf1.75 for children. T4658010, F4617851.*

The Central Bank of the Netherlands Antilles owns and operates a **Numismatic Museum**, Breedestraat 1, Punda, with a collection of coins and notes from the Netherlands Antilles and some from other countries, as well as a display of precious and semi-precious gemstones on loan from a local collector. ■ *Mon-Fri 0830-1130, 1330-1630. Free. T4613600, F4615004.*

The Octagon, Simón Bolívar's sisters' house where Simón Bolívar stayed during his exile in Curaçao in 1812, is near the Avila Beach Hotel reached down a small road off Penstraat just before you get to the hotel. The building is in need of some repair work and looks neglected although there is an attendant (make sure his dogs are chained). There

Netherlands Antilles, the ABC islands

is one octagonal room downstairs, with some manuscripts, pictures and books, and a similar one upstairs, with a bed and some furniture; not much to see unless you are a Bolívar aficionado. ■ *Closed lunchtimes.*

There are often special exhibitions in the World Trade Centre which are worth looking out for. These may include collections from museums in Holland or elsewhere. ■ *T4636105.*

Bridges The swinging **Queen Emma bridge** spans St Anna Bay, linking the two parts of the city, Punda and Otrabanda (the latter means 'the other side' in Papiamento, and people tend to refer to 'Punda' and 'Otrabanda' rather than 'Willemstad'). Built on 16 great pontoons, it is swung aside some thirty times a day to let ships pass in and out of the harbour. The present bridge, the third on the site, was built in 1939. While the bridge is open, pedestrians are shuttled across for free by small ferry boats. The bridge is closed to vehicular traffic.

The new **Queen Juliana** fixed bridge vaults about 50 m over the bay and connects Punda and Otrabanda by a four-lane highway. Taxis will often offer to stop at the bridge so you can get a panoramic view and photo of Willemstad on one side and the oil refinery on the other. Although you can reach it on foot it is not open for pedestrians; the wind and the way it shakes will explain why.

Otrabanda Parts of **Otrabanda** are gradually being restored and there are many old houses here, both small, tucked away down alleys, and large mansions or town houses. The Belvedere, an Otrabanda landmark, was restored in 1992-93. Breedestraat is the main shopping street, the **Basilica Santa Ana**, founded in 1752 and made a Basilica in 1975 by Pope Paul VI, is just off here. The houses fronting on to the Pater Euwensweg, the highway heading west along the coast, once overlooked the Rifwater lagoon, now reclaimed land. Along St Anna Bay, past the ferry landing, is **Porto Paseo**, a restored area with bars and restaurants, popular on Friday evenings when there is music and dancing, or you can just sit and admire the view. The old hospital has been restored and is now the *Hotel and Casino Porto Paseo*. A new cruise ship pier has been built at Otrabanda for liners too big to reach the existing terminal in Willemstad harbour.

On the outskirts of Otrabanda, on van Leeuwenhoekstraat, is the **Curaçao Museum**, founded in 1946 (housed in an old quarantine station built in 1853) with a small collection of artefacts of the Caiquetio Indian culture, as well as 19th and 20th century paintings, antique locally-made furniture, and other items from the colonial era. Labels are inadequate and the hand-out leaflets only partly make up for this. In the basement there is a children's museum of science, but it is limited and rather outdated, almost a museum piece in itself. On the roof is a 47-bell carillon, named The Four Royal Children after the four daughters of Queen Juliana of the Netherlands, which was brought from Holland and installed in 1951. Lots of explanatory leaflets are given out at the museum, with a suggested route map. ■ *Daily, except Sat, Mon-Fri 0900-1200 and 1400-1700, Sun 1000-1600. US$2.25/NAf5.30, US$1.25/NAf2.60 for children under 14. T4623873, F4623777.*

Scharloo Another area within walking distance of Punda and worth exploring, is **Scharloo**, across the Wilhelmina bridge from the floating market. A former Jewish merchant housing area, now under renovation, there are many substantial properties with all the typical architectural attributes; note the green house with white trimmings known as the Wedding Cake House at Scharlooweg 77. Under a five to 10 year plan to restore the buildings, companies or government departments take them over for use as offices in many cases. Reading matter of architectural enthusiasts includes the expensive but magnificently illustrated *Scharloo – a 19th-century quarter of Willemstad, Curaçao: historical architecture and its background*, by Pauline Pruneti-Winkel (Edizioni Poligrafico Fiorentino, Florence 1987), and a more general collection of essays with illustrations, *Building up the Future from the Past: Studies on the Architecture and*

Historic Monuments of the Dutch Caribbean, edited by Henry E Coomans and others (De Walburg Pers, Zutphen, the Netherlands, 1990).

The **S E L Maduro Library** is at the **Landhuis Rooi Catootje**, the site, in 1954, of the Round Table Conferences which led to the Statuut between the Dutch Kingdom and its Caribbean territories. The library, in the beautifully restored landhuis, contains all manner of things Caribbean and the conference table still stands in the dining room. ■ *Open by appointment but well worth the effort, T7375119. Take the Rond minibus from Punda and ask to be let off next to the chicken factory, a site better known to most drivers than the house itself.*

Around the island

Set in 503 ha in the east part of the island is **Brievengat**. Its exact date of construction is unknown, but it is believed to date from the early 18th century. It was used in the 19th century to produce cattle, cochineal and aloe, but a hurricane in 1877 devastated the plantation and the house which were gradually abandoned. Shell later took over the property to extract water from the subsoil, but in 1954 when it was in a state of ruin Shell donated it to the Government who restored it to its former grandeur. The windows and the roof are typical of the local style but unusual are the arches extending the length of the house and the two towers at either side, which were once used to incarcerate slaves. ■ *Daily 0915-1215, 1500-1800, entrance US$2, children half price, bar and snacks, live music on Wed and Fri and often on Sun, check beforehand, open house on Sun 1000-1500 with folklore show at 1700 on last Sun of the month. T5652156. Take the bus marked Punda-Hato from Punda at 15 mins past the hour and get off at the Sentro Deportivo Korsou.*

Chobolobo, at Salinja, came into the Senior family in 1948 and Senior & Co make the Curaçao liqueur here, using a copper still dating from 1896 and the original Valencia orange known locally as Laraha. The clear, orange, amber, red, green and blue are for cocktails and all taste the same; others are chocolate, coffee, rum raisin. Chobolobo is worth visiting, but if you resist the temptation to buy Senior & Co's products you will find them cheaper in the duty free lounge at Hato Airport although they occasionally run out of some brands. The original Curaçao Liqueur can only be purchased on the island. Copy cats are exported from Holland etc. ■ *Mon-Fri 0800-1200, 1300-1700. Free and visitors may taste the liqueur. T4613526.*

Near the Hato international airport on Rooseveltweg, are the **Hato Caves** which contain stalactites and stalagmites, a colony of long nose bats and pools among spectacular limestone formations. There are also some **Caquetio rock drawings** believed to be 1,500 years old. ■ *Guided tours every hour, the last one at 1600, 1000-1700, adults US$4, children US$2.75. T8680379, F8688114.*

Jan Kok is the oldest landhouse on the island, dating from 1654 and overlooking the salt flats where flamingoes gather. *1100-2100 high season and 1100-1900 on Sun low season. Bar and restaurant, guided tour Tue, Thu 0900-1300 through the salt pans and the landhouse. T8648087. Take the bus marked Lagun and Knip from the Riffort, Otrabanda, at half past the even hour in the morning or half past the odd hour in the afternoon.* **Santa Martha**, built in 1700 and restored in 1979, is used as a day care centre for the physically and mentally handicapped but is open to visitors. ■ *Mon-Thu, 0900-1200, 1300-1500, Fri 0900-1200, if you call in advance, T8641559.* **Ascension**, built in 1672 and restored in 1963, is used by Dutch marines stationed on the island. ■ *First Sun of the month 1000-1400 only. T8641950. Local music, handicrafts and snacks. Take bus marked Westpunt from Otrabanda (see below).* **Landhuis Kenepa** or **Knip**, near the beach of the same name, is a restored 17th-century landhouse where there was a slave rebellion in 1795. It has a collection of antique furniture and an exhibition about the Kenepa people. ■ *T8640244, F640385. On the same bus route as Jan Kok.*

The Christoffel Park covers an area of 1,860 ha in the west of the island, including Mount Christoffel at 375 m, which was formerly three plantations. These plantations,

The restored country estate houses, or landhuizen, emerge here and there in the parched countryside. Not all of them are open to the public but it is worth visiting some of those that are

Netherlands Antilles, the ABC islands

Savonet, Zorgvlied and Zevenbergen, are the basis for a system of well marked trails, blue (9 km), green (7½ km or 12 km) and yellow (11 km), and there is a red walking trail up Mount Christoffel which takes about four to five hours there and back. You can see a wide range of fauna and flora, including orchids, the indigenous *wayacá* (*lignum vitae*) plant, acacias, aloe, many cacti, calabash and the tiny Curaçao deer. The ruins of the Zorgvlied landhouse can be seen off the green route. The Savonet route takes you to the coast and along to Amerindian rock drawings, painted between 500 and 2,000 years ago in terracotta, black and white. In this area there are also two caves (take a strong torch), one of which is about 125 m long and you have to crawl in before you can stand up (lots of bats and lots of guano on the ground) and walk to the 'white chamber'(stalactites and stalagmites) and the 'cathedral'.

The 17th-century **Savonet Plantation House** is at the entrance to the park on the Westpoint road, but it is not open to the public. However, several outbuildings are used. There is a small museum with archaeological exhibits, Guided tours are available, special walks at dawn or dusk are organized at random, check in the newspapers, evening walking tours to see the Curaçao deer, maximum eight people, reservations essential. Stinapa publishes an excellent *Excursion Guide to the Christoffel Park, Curaçao,* by Peer Reijns, 1984, which is available at the Park administration. A basic map of the trails is also provided. The bus Otrabanda-Westpunt passes the entrance to the park. Rancho Alfin at the park also does tours, walking, mountain biking or horse riding, including night trips, sunrise trips and a romantic package for honeymooners, T8640535. ■ *Museum. Mon-Sat 0800-1600, Sun 0600-1500. T8640363. Park. From 0800 Mon-Sat, NAf35 per person, admission to the mountain side closes at 1400 and to the ocean side at 1500, although you can stay in until later. On Sun the park opens at 0600 and closes at 1500, no admittance after 1300 and 1400 for inland or sea routes.*

Essentials

Sleeping New hotel, villa or timeshare developments are springing up all over Curaçao. Several huge resorts are planned around Knip beach, Lagun, Cas Abao, Piscadera, Parasasa, Cornelis Bay and Jan Thiel, but there is also work going on in Willemstad, with a new *Curaçao Howard Johnson* and the all-suites resort *Hotel Floris* opposite the World Trade Center, both opening in 2001. Be prepared for construction work. Several small hotels have organized themselves into the *Curaçao Apartments and Small Hotel Association (CASHA)*, www.curacaoweb.com/casha Many hotels have no hot water taps, only cold because the water pipes are laid overground, so the water in them is warmed by the sun during the day and is cold at night. Time your shower accordingly.

There is a 7% government tax & 10% (sometimes 12-15%) service charge to be added to any quoted room rate & many hotels add an extra US$3 per day energy surcharge

Willemstad (hotels) **LL-A** *Plaza Hotel and Casino* in the *Van der Valk* chain, on Punda seafront, T4612500, F4616543, www.plazahotelcuracao.com Very central, huge tower dominates the skyline by the fortress walls, 224 rooms and 19 suites, most with sea or harbour view, price per room includes service, tax, bargain for a cheaper rate for several nights, popular with the Dutch, good food, shops, restaurants, diving, boat excursions, pool, child care. Also very central is **LL-AL** *Hotel and Casino Porto Paseo*, de Rouvilleweg 47, T4627878, F4627969. Room or 2-bedroom suite, CP, swimming pool, dive shop, in attractive restored old hospital, under new ownership and being renovated and expanded in 2001. 15 mins' walk east of the centre is the family-owned **L-AL** *Avila Beach*, Penstraat 130, T4614377, F4611493, http://avilahotel.com Built in 1811 as Governor's residence but most rooms in an old hospital wing, small and with no sea view, very popular, always full, cool reception area, service friendly but slow, no pool, lovely bar shaped like a ship's prow on the beach, great for evening cocktails, pleasant outdoor dining, live music Wed. A new extension has been built in an attractive colonial style, **LL-L** *La Belle Alliance*, the other side of the pier (bar and restaurant, *Blues*, excellent fish, meat not so good, live jazz Thu, Sat, closed Mon) on another man-made beach, 40 hotel rooms, and some apartments, all rooms and suites with sea view, conference facilities and ballroom, tennis, both the beaches are protected by breakwaters and have imported sand for pleasant swimming. **A-B** *Trupial Inn*, Groot Davelaarweg 5, T7378200, F7371545. In residential area, 74 rooms, a/c, newly decorated, nice, pool, restaurant, tennis, open air bar, entertainment, shuttle bus to downtown, suites available. **C** *Hotel San Marco*, Columbusstraat 5, Punda, T4612988, F4616570. 89 rooms, completely renovated, a/c, TV, safe, clean, excellent value. **C-D** *Pelikaan Hotel*, Lange Straat 78, T4623555, F4626063. In the heart of Otrabanda, newly rebuilt, small, comfortable, clean, 40 rooms, a/c, restaurant.

Willemstad (guest houses and apartments) **C** *Bon Auberge*, Hoogstraat 63-65, T4627902, F4627579. Dutch owned, friendly, clean, conveniently located in Otrabanda close to shops and transport, 23 rooms, hot water, some have a/c, others fans, not all have bath, 4 good apartments for US$200 per week. **C** *El Conde Hotel*, Roodeweg 75, near hospital, T/F4627611. Some rooms noisy, basic, 7 rooms, a/c. **C** *Bramendie Apartments*, Bramendieweg 103, in Dominguito, T4655337. 10 apartments with kitchenette, porch, TV, a/c, phone with deposit, car rental, good discount for long stay. **C** *Douglas Apartments*, Salinja 174, T4614549, F4614467. A/c, cots available, towels and linen provided, kitchenettes, a/c, phone, fax facilities, on 1st floor of shopping gallery, bus stop outside. Outside town, **C** *Wayaca Apartments and Bungalows*, Gosieweg 153, T7375589, F7369797. A/c, TV, phone, supermarket, launderette, tennis, minimum 1 week, car rental can be included; houses also available usually on weekly basis or longer. **C** *Art and Nature Inn*, 17 Valkensweg, T8682259. 10 mins' drive from Willemstad, bungalow with kitchenette and bathroom, each of 12 studios is decorated with murals, mosaics and paintings by the proprietor, Geerdine Kuypers, an internationally known artist, speaks 6 languages, great hostess, 5-min drive to supermarket. A good small hotel is **D** *Buona Sera (Bonacera) Inn*, Pietermaai 104, T4618286. On the road to the Bolívar museum, not a very safe area, 16 rooms, sleeps 1-4, a/c, private bathroom, recently built seaview restaurant and bar, plans to create small beach, family-run, friendly, English, Dutch, Spanish, French and Papiamento spoken. **E** *Estoril*, Breedestraat 181, Otrabanda, T4625244. In Scharloo, **D-E** *Park*, on Frederikstraat 84, T4623112. Bath and fan, not nice, noise from road, fleas, not clean enough, both *Estoril* and *Park* cater to 'short stay' visitors, not recommended.

The tourist board's main office at Pietermaai 19 has a very large list of guest houses and apartments (not all of which it recommends)

Willemstad centre

Sleeping
1 Otrabanda
2 Porto Paseo
3 Van der Valk Plaza

Not to scale

E *Mira Punda*, Van de Brandhofstraat 12. Near floating market, fan, cold water, clean, private bath, in restored mansion, bar downstairs has lots of local colour.

East of Willemstad On Dr Martin Luther King Boulevard is the **LL-AL** *Princess Beach Resort and Casino*, 600 m from the Seaquarium on a narrow beach, T7367888, F4614131, www.princessbeach.com Pools, restaurants, bars, shops, 341 rooms and suites make this the biggest resort on the island, popular, lots of packages, including diving, and all-inclusive available, food good at all 3 restaurants, conference centre, fitness centre with massage, good entertainment. Next door is the **AL** *Lion's Dive*, T4618100, F4618200, http://lionsdive.com Attractive, not high rise, wooden balconies give it style but needs renovating, poor plumbing, 72 rooms, TV, small pool, unlimited use of Seaquarium, dive shop on site, dive packages available, fitness centre, windsurfing, restaurant, nice atmosphere, friendly staff, helpful service, caters for hard-core diving fraternity, courtesy bus to town. **LL-A** *Seru Coral*, Koral Partier 10, T7678499, F7678256. A new resort in the east part of the island, in the middle of nowhere but great restaurant, nice pool, nice studios, apartments and villas, 3 miles from beach, 18 from airport, 9 miles from town. *Santa Catharina Sport & Country Club*, same ownership, T7677028, F7677026. Tennis, fitness centre, football pitch, pool, restaurant, bar, with studios, suites and bungalows all with kitchenettes, phone, TV, terrace overlooking northeast coast.

West of Willemstad Along the coast are **LL-L** *Curaçao Marriott Beach Resort & Emerald Casino* , next to the International Trade Centre, Piscadera Bay, T7368800, F4627502. 248 luxury rooms and 34 suites, very comfortable, excellent service, upmarket resort, Dutch colonial style, on a private beach, freeform pool, whirlpools, tennis, fitness centre, kids programme, watersports, casino, conference facilities. **LL-L** *Curaçao Sheraton Resort & Casino*, T4625000, F4625846. 194 rooms and suites, private beach, pool, scuba, watersports, fitness centre, casino. **AL** *Piscadera Bay Resort*, T4626303, F4625962. 94 semi-detached bungalows for 2-4 people, beach with dive shop and bar/restaurant, monthly rental can be arranged. Two minutes from the airport is **B** *Holland*, T8688044, F8888114. 45 rooms, a/c, TV, phone, business services, restaurant, pool, car rental, casino, diving. **B** *Bulado Inn*, in Boca St Michiel fishing village, Red A'Weg, T8695731, F8695487. Family run, very nice, good value, call and check for deals, 17 a/c rooms, all ocean view, restaurant, bar, pool, nicely landscaped, tennis, meeting rooms, car rental, parking, 10 mins walk from beach. **LL-B** *Habitat Curaçao*, linked to *Captain Don's Habitat* in Bonaire, at Rif Baai, T8648800, F8648464, www.habitatdiveresorts.com. 76 suites and cottages, expanded in 2001 with another 14 2-bedroom cottages around sea water pond, with meeting rooms, pool, restaurant, bar, beach, free town shuttle bus, dive centre, lots of packages available. **C** *Landhuis Cas Abao*, T8603525, F8649460. Dates from 1751, rebuilt 1993, stylish, rooms vary but have good views, secluded beach, minimum stay 4 days, no credit cards, beautiful area, restaurant closed in evenings and owners leave premises after 1900, long drive to find a decent evening meal. **B-C** *Landhuis Daniel*, weg naar Westpunt, T/F8648400. Another landhuis guest house, built by Daniel Ellis in 1711 on extensive property leading to sea, used as an inn for travellers on the east-west route for centuries, renovated 1997, 4 rooms in plantation house, 4 more in small row house by pool, breezy French Caribbean restaurant, dive packages available. **LL-B** *Coral Cliff*, resort and casino on Santa Marta Bay, T8642666, F8641781. Quiet beach, nice sea, some shade provided, entrance US$4.50 for non-residents, sprawling, concrete block hotel, rooms or suites, good sea view from restaurant on hill, dive shop on premises, excellent diving from beach, watersports, mini golf, horse riding arranged, free airport pickup, shuttle service to town. **B-C** *Bahia Inn*, near Lagun beach, T8684417. Small, basic, adequate, several beds in each room, building work all along this coastal road. At Westpoint, **A-C** *All West Apartments*, T4612310, F4612315, dive shop attached, T8640102, F8640107, allwest@cura.net A/c studios and apartments, caters to individuals, adventure diving, PADI courses, boat and shore diving, small scale. **C-D** *Jaanchie Christian's*, T8640126. Popular restaurant with 4 rooms to let, a/c, bathroom, CP, double beds, can fit extras in, usually full, phone for reservation.

Camping *Brakkeput*, adjoining Spanish Waters, Arowakenweg 41A, PO Box 3291, T674428. School parties catered for, sports fields, showers and toilets, tents available, US$1.25 per person overnight with minimum charge US$18.75, cheaper for youth organizations. Camping is allowed on some beaches, but there are no facilities and you have to bring your own fresh water supplies.

Native food is filling and the meat dish is usually accompanied by several different forms of carbohydrate, one of which may be *funchi*, a corn meal bread in varying thickness but usually looking like a fat pancake (the same as *cou-cou* in the Eastern Caribbean). Goat stew (*stoba di kabritu*) is popular, slow cooked and mildly spicey (milder and tastier than Jamaican curry goat), recommended. Soups (*sopi*) are very nourishing and can be a meal on their own, grilled fish or meat (*la paria*) is good although the fish may always be grouper, red snapper or conch (*karkó*), depending on the latest catch; meat, chicken, cheese or fish filled pastries (*pastechi*) are rather like the *empanadas* of South America or Cornish pasties. While in the Netherlands Antilles, most visitors enjoy trying a *rijsttafel* (rice table), a sort of Asian smørgasbørd adopted from Indonesia, and delicious. Because *rijsttafel* consists of anywhere from 15 to 40 separate dishes, it is usually prepared for groups of diners, although some Curaçao restaurants will do a modified version of 10 or 15 dishes.

A selection of European, South American (mostly Chilean) and Californian wines is usually available in restaurants. Curaçao's gold-medal-winning Amstel beer, the only beer in the world brewed from desalinated sea water, is very good indeed and available throughout the Netherlands Antilles. Amstel brewery tours are held on Tue and Thu at 1000, T4612944 for information. Some Dutch and other European beers can also be found. Fresh milk is difficult to get hold of and you are nearly always given evaporated milk with your tea or coffee. Curaçao's tap water is excellent; also distilled from the sea.

Eating

10% service is added to the bill in restaurants but an extra 5% is appreciated

Willemstad One of the most highly regarded restaurants in Willemstad is *The Wine Cellar* on Concordiastraat, T4612178. Owned by chef Nico Cornelisie, a master rotisseur, in small old house, only 8 tables, chilly a/c, very good food but unexciting wine list, local fish and meat (ostrich) particularly good, reservations recommended, closed Sun. *Alouette*, in a restored house, Orionweg 12, T4618222. Very popular, reservations recommended, French-style food, low-calorie or vegetarian meals available, comparatively small menu but changed frequently, except for the goat cheese crêpe which is such a favourite it is a permanent fixture, excellent food and service, attractive decor, open 1200-1430, 1900-2200, later at weekends. *Mi Kalbas* , de Ruyterkade, opposite post office, T4621010. Very good food, local specialities and international menu, full bar, run by former food and beverage manager at *Princess Beach*. *Larousse*, also in an old house on Penstraat 5, almost opposite the *Avila Beach*, T4655418. French menu with local and imported North Sea fish, quiet, open 1800-2400, closed Mon. *Fort Nassau*, reservations T4613450. Spectacular location with a panoramic view from the 200-year old fort, American-style menu using local ingredients, open Mon-Fri 1200-1400, Mon-Sun 1830-2300. *De Taveerne*, in an octagonal mansion, Landhuis Groot Davelaar, T7370669. Beef and seafood, à la carte menu, antique furnishings, closed Sun. *Bistro Le Clochard*, in the Rif Fort walls overlooking the harbour, T4625666/4625667, www.bistroleclochard.com. French and Swiss cuisine, choose fresh local fish rather than imported, open Mon-Fri 1200-1400, 1830 onwards, Sat evenings only, open Sun in Dec-Mar. *La Pergola*, in the Waterfort Arches, T4613482. Serves Italian food, fish, pizza, terrace or a/c dining, open 1200-1400 Mon-Sat, 1830-2230 daily. *Grill King*, in the Waterfort Arches, T4616870. Friendly and has good international food, open Mon-Sat 1100-2300, Sun 1700-2300. There are several restaurants in the Arches, nice variety, pleasant location, good for a meal or just drinks. Some other moderately priced yet good restaurants include *Fort Waakzaamheid* , T4621044. Lovely sunset views from the terrace on top of the fort, which is on a hill above Otrabanda, medieval atmosphere, restaurant and tavern, good food and menu, open daily 1200-1400, 1800-1030, reservations suggested, dinner US$15-20. *Tasca Restaurant Don Quijote*, Gosieweg 148, T7369835. Spanish, seafood and daily specials, good paella, takeaway, happy hour 1700-2000, open weekdays 1700-0100, closed Tue. *Green Mill*, Salinja Galleries, T4658821. Lunches or dinners, happy hour Mon-Thu 1800-1900,

Fri 1700-1830, menu with good variety. *Café con Leche*, behind cinema. Cuban-Curaçaoan, daily specials, moderately priced, fish, chicken, good desserts. *Cactus Club I*, Van Staverenweg 6, T7371600, in the Mahaai area. Tex Mex food, fun atmosphere, blended and frozen cocktails, local dishes also available, service with a smile. *Cactus Club II* on the beach at the Seaquarium, T4651265. *Hook's Hut*, between *Marriott* and *Sheraton* hotels Thatched tiki hut bar and restaurant next to the sea, good drinks and ambience, food OK.

For an **Indonesian** meal it is best to make up a party to get the maximum number of dishes but this is not essential. The *Indonesia*, Mercuriusstraat 13, T4612606. Wonderful Javanese food specializing in 16 or 25-dish rijstaffel, essential to book, often several days ahead, open 1200-1400, 1800-2130 daily, dinner only on Sun. *Mambo Beach* , at the Seaquarium, T4618999. Wed Indonesian buffets. *Surabaya* in the Waterfort Arches, T4617388. Has good food but overpriced and no hot plates to keep it warm, vegetarian menu too, open Tue-Fri 1200-1400, Tue-Sun 1800-2300.

The best place to try **local food** in Willemstad is the old market building beyond the round concrete market tower by the floating market, here many cooks offer huge portions of good, filling local food cooked in huge pots on charcoal fires, at reasonable prices, choose what you want to eat and sit down at the closest bench or one of the nearby tables having first ordered, takeaway available, very busy at lunchtimes, the best dishes often run out, make sure you have the right money available. The best restaurant for local food is *The Golden Star*, Socratesstraat 2, T4618741. Informal, friendly, plastic table cloths, fun, TV showing American sport, home cooking, very filling, goat stew washed down by a couple of Amstels recommended, popular with locals and tourists, open daily 1200-2300, live music Sat 1900-2300, takeaway available.

On the **Westpoint** road, opposite the entrance to the Christoffel Park, is *Oasis*, T8640085. Seafood and creole dishes but also offering chicken and ribs, open 1200-2400, weekends 1030-0300, dinner served until 2100, dancing afterwards. *Playa Forti*, atop a cliff overlooking beach of same name, wonderful view, very popular lunchtime at weekends, Colombian and local dishes. Further along the road in Westpoint is *Jaanchie's*, T8640126. Another weekend lunchtime favourite with local families although no sea view, huge, filling portions, see the bananaquits eating sugar, parties catered for, takeaway service, bus stops outside for return to Willemstad,.

A good fish restaurant is *Pisces*, at the end of Caracasbaaiweg, T7672181. Reservations recommended. Also darts, karaoke and internet. *El Marinero*, Schottegatweg Noord 87B, T7379833. Moderately priced seafood dishes, lunch 1200-1500, dinner 1830-2330. *Fisherman's Wharf*, Dr Martin Luther King Blvd, close to *Princess Beach*, T4657558. Very good seafood, lunch and dinner. *Seaside Terrace*, T4618361. Little beachside restaurant near *Princess Beach Hotel*, more like a snack stand but great fresh, huge, lobster for US$28, as well as seafood of all kinds as well as chicken, pork etc, and a US$7 barbecue on Sun with live entertainment, a few tables to watch sunset, open 1000-2200 Tue-Sun. *Octopus*, Marinebadplaats, St Michielsbay, T8881244. Fresh fish, local food, bar, restaurant and terrace by the sea, run by Eric and Yolanda Wederfoort, see Diving and marine life. Chinese food at *Ho Wah*, Saturnusstraat 93, T4615745. *Ham Yuen*, Fokkerweg 25, T4613462. Locals' favourite Chinese food. *Sawasdee*, Van Eyck V Voorthuyzenweg 5, near Curaçao Museum, T4626361. Thai restaurant, takeaway available, open 1830-2200.

For drinks, snacks or cheap lunches, *Downtown Terrace*, also in Gomezplein, T4616722. You can hear the chimes from the Spritzer and Fuhrmann bells, great selection of Belgian beers. There is plenty of fast food to cater for most tastes, including pancake houses, and *Pizza Hut* at Pietermaiplein prides itself on having won awards. *Domino's Pizza*, on Schotlegatweg Oost 48, T7366555. 12 in pizzas from US$9.60, delivery service. *Denny's*, attached to side of *Holiday Beach Hotel*, T4625232. Good food at good prices, some local dishes, takeaway available, is open 24 hrs. Late night fast food, local fashion, can be found at truk'i pans, bread trucks which stay open until 0400-0500 and sell sandwiches filled with conch, goat stew, salt fish and other Antillean specialities. Great fruit shakes at *Trax's*, a van at the Otrabanda side of the Queen Emma bridge. Wonderful home made ice cream, large variety, at *Vienna Ice Café*, on Handelskade in Punda.

For 'night-owls', there are **casinos**. All the large hotels have them, with many gaming tables and rows and rows of fruit machines, open virtually all hours. There are many nightclubs and disco, several of which are in the **Salinja area**: *Façade* (Lindberghweg 32-34, T4614640, open 2200-0400 except Mon and Thu, happy hour on Fri from 1800) and *Club 99* (Lindbergweg) are favoured by wealthy locals of all ages, you will not be let in wearing jeans or trainers and they have airport-style metal detectors at the door; *Infinity* is at Fort Nassau, open Fri and Sat, 2100-0200, T4613450; *Havana Club* (formerly *the Pub*) is at Salinja 144; for all-night music and dancing, *La Paix* and *De Fles* (the *Flask*) have been recommended for salsa and merengue, you may be the only foreigner there, take local currency; other places for Latin music are *Salsipuedes*, at De Ruyterkade 55, Punda, T461090, salsa dancing, classes, concerts, and *Tututango*, at Plaza Mundo, Merced, T4654633. (If you want to improve your salsa or merengue, you can take lessons at *Salsa City*, T5610782, or at the *Danzarte Academy*, T6674616. In Otrabanda, *Rum Runners* is recommended for cocktails and harbour view. *The Music Factory*, Salinja 131, T4610631. Open Mon-Sat 1700-0300, Fri live music, Sat DJ, special drinks nights with half-price brand names 2200-2400. On the Seaquarium beach is the *Mambo Beach Club*, a good nightspot with happy hour and dancing Sun, restaurant during the week, T4618999. At Caracas Bay Island is the *Baya Beach Club*, best on Sat night, several DJs on different nights, disco and drinking spot. The Centro Pro Arte presents concerts, ballets and plays. *Mirage*, a 'gentleman's club', has a show for men only Wed 2300 and Sat midnight, T8681170. *Classy Lady*, adults only, T4625250. **Cinema** *The Movies Curaçao*, T4651000, www.themoviescuracao.com shows recent releases. While on the subject of entertainment, one of the most bizarre sights of Curaçao, not dealt with in the tourist brochures, is the government-operated red-light area. Close to the airport, it resembles a prison camp and is even guarded by a policeman.

Nightlife
K-Pasa is a weekly dining and entertainment guide, widely available, www.k-pasa.com

Curaçao, Aruba and Bonaire all hold the traditional pre-Lent **carnival**. On the *Sunday*, a week before, is the children's parade. Curaçao's main parade is on the Sunday at 1000 and takes 3 hs to pass, starting at Otrabanda. The following Mon most shops are closed. On the Mon at 1500 there is a children's farewell parade and there is a **Farewell Grand Parade** on the Tuesday evening when the Rey Momo is burned.

Festivals

    Several **music festivals** are held throughout the year. You can hear *tumba* around carnival time. Contact the Curaçao Jazz Foundation, T4658043, for details of the May and November jazz festivals and the Festival Center, T7376343, for details of *salsa* (August) and *merengue* (May) festivals. For the **Golden Artists Music Festival** in *October*, T4655777.

Shops open on Sun morning and lunchtimes if cruise ships are in port. Weekday opening is 0830-1200 and 1400-1800. The main tourist shopping is in Punda (see above) where you can pick up all sorts of duty-free bargains in fashion, china etc. *Arawak Craft Products*, Mattheywerf 1, Otrabanda, T4627249, F4628394, near cruise ship dock and ferry, tiles, reliefs of Dutch style houses and other ceramics, you can watch the potters and artists and even make your own, *Arawak Art Gallery* upstairs, open 0900-1800, on Sun also if cruise ship in dock.

Shopping
Willemstad's jewellery shops are noted for the quality of their stones

Bookshops *Boekhandel Mensing* in Punda has a limited selection of guide books and maps. Larger and more well stocked bookshops are out of the centre of Willemstad. *Mensings' Caminada* and *Schottegatweg and Van Dorp* in the *Promenade Shopping Centre*, good maps and guide book section. *Van Dorp* shops are also located in most large hotels; they stock *Footprint Handbooks*. The public library is a modern building in Scharloo, cross the bridge by the floating market, turn right along the water and it is on your left. *The Reading Room* has books in Dutch, English, Spanish, French and Papiamento, T4617055.

Air From Europe *KLM* and *ALM* fly direct from Amsterdam several times a week and KLM has connecting flights to Guayaquil and Quito. *Sobelair* flies from Brussels. **From North America** There are flights from Miami with *American Airlines* and *ALM*; connecting flights from other US cities generally go through Miami. **From South America** *Avianca* flies from Bogotá; *ALM* and *Aeropostal* fly from Caracas; *ALM* also flies from Valencia and Maracaibo. *Surinam Airways* and *ALM* fly from Paramaribo. **From the Caribbean** from Aruba (*ALM*,

Transport

American Eagle), Bonaire (*ALM, Sobelair*), Havana (*Cubana, Aeropostal*), Kingston (*ALM*), Port au Prince (*ALM*), Port of Spain (*ALM*), Sint Maarten (*ALM*), San Juan (*ALM, American Eagle*) and Santo Domingo in the Dominican Republic (*ALM* and *Aeropostal*).

Road Bus There are collective taxis, called buses, and identified by an AC prefix on their licence plates, which charge about US$1 anywhere. *Konvoois* are big buses which run to a schedule and serve outlying areas of Curaçao. There is a terminal at the post office by the circular market in Punda and another near the Rif Fort in Otrabanda. To the airport get a bus marked Hato from Punda at 15 mins past the hour from 0615 to 2315, or from Otrabanda at 15 mins past the hour from 0615 to 2320, returning on the hour, usually full. Buses to Westpunt leave from Otrabanda on the odd hour, last bus 2300, return on the even hour. Buses and minibuses to Dominguito (the Seaquarium) and Caracas Bay run from Punda. A bus marked Schottegat runs from Punda via the Octagon Bolívar Museum, the *Trupial Inn Hotel*, the Curaçao Golf and Squash Club, the Jewish cemetery and the Curaçao Museum to Otrabanda. The Lagun and Knip bus route leaves Otrabanda at half past the even hour in the mornings and on the odd hour in the afternoons via the Curaçao Museum, the University, Landhuis Jan Kok, Santa Cruz beach, Jeremi beach, Lagun Beach and Bahia beach, returning from Knip on the alternate hour. While the service in and around Willemstad is efficient, the service to Westpunt is erratic and planning is needed to avoid getting stranded. The standard city bus fare is NAf1 with no apparent timetables or bus stops, very passenger-friendly and recommended. Outside town you may get charged a variety of fares, particularly on minibuses. Check beforehand or ask what others are paying.

Car hire Companies include *Budget* (best rates, ask for specials or coupons), *Europcar/ National*, *Avis*, *Caribe Rentals*, *Dollar Rent a Car*, *Star Rent a Car*, *Vista Car Rental*. Prices start at about US$35 daily, unlimited mileage, includes insurance, deposits from US$250; jeeps, minimokes, buggies, scooters and bikes also available. Foreign and international driving licences are accepted. Traffic moves on the right.

Taxi It is not always possible to get a taxi to the airport early in the morning or late at night so if you are going to a night club arrange your taxi in advance (sometimes the driver will turn up a little early and join you on the dance floor). Taxis do not have meters but fares are fixed. Fares from the airport to *Holiday Beach*, US$15, *Van der Valk Plaza* or *Avila Beach* US$18, *Lions Dive* US$20, *Coral Cliff* US$27. Airport displays taxi fares to main hotels. Try and pay in guilders as taxi drivers do not always have the right change for dollars. Fares for sightseeing trips should be established at beginning of trip, the usual price is US$20 for the 1st hour and US$5 for each subsequent 15 mins. Tipping is not strictly obligatory. The high price of taxis is a common complaint. Taxis do not always go looking for business and it can be difficult to hail one. Best to telephone from a hotel lobby or restaurant/bar, one will arrive in a couple of mins. For taxi fares or complaints T8690747, or go to a taxi stand and just get into an empty car, the driver will then turn up. Drivers do not always know the area as well as they should, even restaurants can sometimes be tricky for them to find. The rear windows of many taxis do not work, which makes the car uncomfortable in the hot climate. Courtesy vans operated by the hotels can be more comfortable.

Sea It is possible for the adventurous and persistent to get a boat from Muaco at La Vela. You have to contact the captains direct as the practice of taking passengers is discouraged. Try Nelson García (T6522533) of *Carmen Reynely* or Douglas Zavala (T378268) of *Trinidad II* (neither speaks English). The *capitanía* is not much help, try the maritime agency 2 blocks from Plaza Bolívar for help in contacting captains. The journey takes 9 hrs, head seas all the way, not for the seasick.

Directory **Airlines** *ALM* (T8695533) has an office in Gomezplein in Punda where you can pay your departure tax and avoid the queues at Hato Airport. There is also an ALM office in the International Trade Centre and at the airport. *ALM* often has flights at rather unsociable hours, tends to lose luggage and is jokingly known in Dutch as 'Altijd Laat Maatschappij', the Always Late Company. *KLM* (T4652737) offices are also at Gomezplein. *American Airlines* at the airport; *Avianca*, T8683659. *Aeropostal*, T8882818. *Pelican Air*,

T4628155, does helicopter tours of the island. **Banks** *ABN-AMRO Bank, Antilles Banking Corp* , *Maduro & Curiel Bank* on Plaza Jojo Correa, T4611100, *Banco di Caribe* on Schottegatweg Oost, T4616588. Banking hours are 0800-1530 Mon-Fri. At the airport the bank is open 0800-2000 Mon-Sat, 0800-1600 Sun. ATMs at *ABN-AMRO Bank* and *Maduro & Curiel Bank* (Visa, Mastercard and Cirrus, issuing either US$ or NAf). **Communications** Telephone: All American Cables & Radio Inc, Keukenstraat; Kuyperstraat; Radio Holland NV, De Ruytergade 51; Sita, Curaçao Airport. Prepaid phone cards are available for international calls from Antelecom, Belvédère House, T124. Telephone rates abroad are published in the telephone book, but beware if phoning from a hotel, you can expect a huge mark up, check their rates before you call. To Europe, US$3.05 per minute, to the USA US$1.60, to Australia and Africa US$5.55, to the Netherlands Antilles US$0.55, Central America US$3.90, Venezuela US$1.10, Leeward and Windward Islands US$1.75. There are other companies offering lower rates, so shop around, eg TSI charges US$0.70 per minute to the Netherlands, US$0.50 to the USA (T8696590, 5601988) and Amtel charges US$0.61 and US$0.49 respectively (T7375327, 4610304). You can rent a mobile phone from the Post Office, already programmed for the local system with a prepaid card, no roaming or excess charges. There is a booth in the airport arrivals hall and you can return the phone at the PO opposite the entrance to the departure hall. For **internet access**, there is a cybercafé in the Salinja Galleries. The public library has 2 public internet terminals. **Medical facilities** The 550-bed **St Elisabeth Hospital** is a well-equipped and modern hospital with good facilities including a coronary unit and a recompression chamber (T462-4900). For emergencies, T110 (hospital), 112 (ambulance). The **Sentro Mediko Santa Rosa**, at Santa Rosaweg 329, is open 7 days a week, 0700-0000, laboratory on the premises. **Tourist information** Local tourist office The main office of the *Curaçao Tourism Development Bureau* is at Pietermaai 19, Willemstad, PO Box 3266, T4616000, F4612305. There is an information office on Breedestraat, east of Hendrikplein, and at the airport. There are several websites with information on the large hotels, restaurants and other tourist details: www.curacao.com/tourism www.curacao-tourism.com *The Curaçao Hotel and Tourism Association (CHATA)* is at Kaya Junior Salas 1, T4651005, in down town Punda, offering helpful information, assistance in finding a hotel, brochures, maps, etc. There are also several Visitor Information Centres dotted round Willemstad and some booths sponsored by resort hotels, which have irregular hours. *Members of Curaçao Hospitality Services* look after the parking lots and are trained in first aid and how to give directions. **Local travel agents** One of the best island tours available is with *Casper Tours*, T5610721/4653010, informative, fun, covers east to west, 0900-1600 including lunch at a local restaurant for US$35 (cruise ships' tours from US$15) in a/c mini buses, English, Dutch and Spanish spoken. *Taber Tours*, http://curacao.com/tabertours (branch at airport and at many hotels) do a variety of tours, usually in large Greyhound type buses. *Old City Tours* do a walking tour of Otrabanda, 1715-1900, US$5.55 including a drink, T4613554. *Dornasol Tours*, T8682735, highly recommended local guide with minibus, full or half day eco-tours by biologist and historian Lies van de Kar, English, Dutch, German and Spanish spoken, also tours of Jewish sites. **Maps** Curoil nv publishes a good road map with a satellite photo of the island with superimposed information, town street plans and an excellent index, available in Mensing and other bookshops. **Useful addresses** Police and fire: T114.

Aruba

Aruba is the smallest of the 'ABC' group of islands, only 25 km north of Venezuela. It has been closely linked with the Venezuelan oil industry for most of the 20th century, but when times were hard, a decision was made to diversify into mass tourism. The coastal strip on the leeward side of the island with the best beaches is now wall-to-wall hotels, with all those of more than 300 rooms allowed to have a casino. A wide range of watersports are on offer, including excellent windsurfing, which is world class. On land there is a golf course among the sand dunes in the north and efforts are being made to tempt visitors away from the beach and develop ecotourism.

Colour map 6, grid B1

Ins and outs

Like the other Dutch islands, there is a scheduled flight from Amsterdam with *KLM*, but otherwise poor connections with Europe. Many more flights bringing sun-worshippers, honeymooners and gamblers come from North America, including several US cities, and also from South America, with flights from Venezuela, Colombia and Peru.

Getting there

A Foot in the door

- Blow your mind away **windsurfing** in the shallow waters off the northeast coast.
- Pay for your next holiday indulging your urges in the many **casinos**.
- Explore the bat-filled but spacious **caves** of the east coast where there are huge chambers, long tunnels and Amerindian drawings.
- Lie on the beach - an antidote to stress and adrenalin rushes - but don't just stay by your hotel, explore some of the less frequented **beaches in the south**.

Getting around

See transport, page 1043, for further details

There are buses and taxis, otherwise you can hire a car, motorcycle or bicycle. Most people don't bother and simply book a seat on a tour bus if they want to get away from the beach and hotel for a while. The airport is only 3.5km south of Oranjestad, the capital, but nearly all the hotels hug the coast north of town; there are buses on the route from Oranjestad to San Nicolas in the extreme southeast, and taxis, which have a set charge for each hotel based on distance.

Climate

Aruba is out of the hurricane belt and the climate is dry. The hottest months are Aug-Oct and the coolest are Dec-Feb, but the temperature rarely goes over 32°C or below 26°C. A cooling trade wind can make the temperature deceptive. Average rainfall is 51 cm a year, falling in short showers during Oct-Dec.

Flora and fauna

As well as various kinds of lizards, Aruba has large iguanas, that are hunted to prepare a typical Arubian soup

Aruba has 48 different types of native trees, 11 of which are now very scarce and in some cases have only 5 examples left. The loss of native trees is due to wood cutting, changing weather and marauding goats. A tree planting programme is under way and negotiations with goat owners are in progress to keep them out of protected areas. About 170 species of birds can be found on Aruba, and about 50 species breed on the island but if you include the migratory birds which come in November-January the total rises to around 300 species. The most common birds are the trupiaal (with its bright orange colours), the chuchubi, the prikichi (a little parrot) and the barika geel (the little yellow-bellied bird you will find eating the sugar on the table in your hotel). The shoco, a burrowing owl, is endangered. An interesting place to see waterfowl is the **Bubali Plassen**, opposite the Olde Molen. Here you can often find cormorants, herons and fish eagle. Brown pelicans can be found along the south shore. Two kinds of snakes can be found on Aruba: the Santanero, a harmless little snake (however, be careful when you pick it up, because it defecates in your hand) and the not-so-harmless rattle snake. Aruba's rattle snake, the cascabel, is a nearly extinct unique subspecies and does not use its rattle. Rattle snakes live in the triangular area between the Jamanota, Fontein and San Nicolas. The best place to go looking for rattle snakes, if you really want to, is the area south of the Jamanota mountain. In the unlikely event that you get bitten, go immediately to the hospital. They have anti-serum.

The **Arikok National Park** covers a triangle of land between Boca Prins and San Fuego and bounded on the east by the sea as far as Boca Keto. After decades of discussion the plan converts 17% of the island into a protected park area. Work is continuing to provide trails, clean up and upgrade the park, clearing litter and reconstructing benches and a stairway built at Fuerte Prins in the 1960s. The three centres will be linked by trails for cars and walkers. Arikok Centre contains the 184.5 m Arikok hill, the second highest point in Aruba. Prins Centre in the northeast includes the former Prins Plantation, the functioning Fontein Plantation and the Fontein Cave. The Jamanota Centre in the south includes the 189 m Jamanota hill, the highest point the island, and the old gold mining operation at Miralamas. The Spanish Lagoon area is also included. www.arubanationalparks.com

Diving and marine life

Visibility in Aruban waters is about 30 m in favourable conditions and snorkelling and scuba diving are very good, although not as spectacular as in the waters around Bonaire. A coral reef extends along the west side of the island from California reef in the north to Baby Beach reef in the south, with dives varying in depth from five to 45 m. There are lots of dive sites suitable for beginners where you can see morays, grouper, eagle rays, manta rays and sting rays, as well as lobsters, parrot fish, angel fish and others. The coral is in good condition and varied. The northwest of the island has fields of seagrass which attract leatherback turtles during the nesting season and are home to hawksbill, green and loggerhead turtles all year. The other side of the island is only for experienced divers as there are strong currents and it is often rough. Organized boat trips regularly visit two wrecks worth exploring, although they can get a bit crowded. One is a German freighter, the *Antilla*, which was scuttled just after the Second World War was declared and is found in 20 m of water off Malmok beach on the west coast. You can see quite a lot just snorkelling here as parts of the wreck stick up above the water. Snorkelling boat trips usually combine Malmok beach and the wreck. The other wreck is nearby in 10 m of water, the *Pedernales*, a flat-bottomed oil tanker which was hit in a submarine attack in May 1941, while ferrying crude oil from Venezuela to Aruba. Only the central part of the tanker remains, the US military took away the two end pieces, welded them together and made a new ship which was used in the Normandy invasion. The *Aruba Watersports Association* recently sunk a DC-3 aeroplane near the *Pedernales*, to be another wreck dive site only 10 m deep, and the *Star Gerren* tanker was sunk in 2000 at a similar depth for snorkellers and divers opposite the high rise hotel strip by Hadicurari. Be very careful not to touch anything underwater; not all the dive

Netherlands Antilles, the ABC islands

Aruba

Essentials

Documents US and Canadian citizens only require **proof of identity**, such as passport, birth certificate, certificate of naturalization, with photo ID if not using a passport. Other nationalities need a **passport**. Those who need a **visa** include citizens of Afghanistan, China, Cuba, Dominican Republic, Iraq, Iran, Cambodia, Korea, Libya, Mauritania, Mongolia, Burma, Syria, Vietnam, Peru, Haiti, Albania, Croatia, Serbia and Bosnia, unless they are legally residing in a country whose citizens do not need a visa. A return or onward ticket and proof of adequate funds are also required for all visitors. Dogs and cats are permitted entry if they have a valid rabies and health certificate but, no pets are allowed from South or Central America. Check with your hotel to see if they are allowed to stay.

Customs People over 18 are allowed to bring in one fifth of liquor, 200 cigarettes, 50 cigars and 250 grammes of tobacco.

Currency Aruba has its own currency, the Aruban florin, not to be confused with the Antillean guilder, which is not accepted in shops and can only be exchanged at banks. The **exchange rate** is Afl1.77=US$1, but shops' exchange rate is Afl1.80. US dollars and credit cards are widely accepted, even on buses, and the Venezuelan bolívar is also used. ATMs dispense only Aruban currency.

Voltage 110 volts 60 cycle AC same as USA.

Departure tax Aruba Passenger Facility Charge is US$20, or Afl36. If flying out to the USA, you will clear US customs and immigration in Aruba, which saves you time at the other end (US Immigration, T831316). There are two terminals for international and US-bound flights, with restaurants, duty-free shops and other services.

Tourist offices overseas Argentina, Av Córdoba 859 Piso 8, Buenos Aires 1054, T/F54-11-3118053, 3152015. **Brazil**, Rua Cel Joaquim Ferreira Lobo, 314-04544-150, São Paulo, T5511-8227033, F8299916. **Canada**, 86 Bloor Street West, Suite 204, Toronto, Ontario M5S 1M5, T416-9751950, F416-9751947, toll free 800-268 3042, ata.canada@toaruba.com **Colombia**, Calle 114, No 9-45, Oficina 701, Torre B, Teleport Business Park, Bogotá, T571-6292879, F6292902.

The Netherlands, Schimmelpenninncklaan 1, 2517 JN, Den Haag, T70-3566220, F3604877, ata.holland@visitaruba.com

USA, 199 Fourteenth Street, NE, Suite 2008, Atlanta, GA 30309-3688, T404-8927822, F404-8732193, ata.atlanta@toaruba.com; I Financial Plaza, Suite 136, Fort Lauderdale, FL 33394, T954-7676477, F7670432, ata.florida@toaruba.com; 401 Wilmette Av, Westmont, IL 60559, T603-6631363, F6631362, ata.chicago@toaruba.com; 12707 North Freeway, Suite 138, Houston, TX 77060, T281-87-ARUBA, F281-8727872S, ata.houston@toaruba.com; 1000 Harbor Blvd, Ground level, Weehawken, NJ 07087, T201-3300800, F3308757, toll free (800) TO ARUBA, ata.newjersey@visitaruba.com **Venezuela**, Centro Ciudad Comercial Tamanaco, Torre C, Piso 8, Oficina C-805, Chuao, Caracas, T582-9591256, F9596346, ata.venezuela@visitaruba.com

Clothing Swim suits are not permitted in the shopping area. Most casinos require men to wear jackets and smart clothes are expected at expensive restaurants, otherwise casual summer clothes worn all year. Public nudity of any kind is illegal although topless sunbathing is tolerated on most resort beaches.

Public holidays New Year's Day, GF Betico Croes Day (25 January), Carnival Monday (beginning of February), Flag Day (18 March), Good Friday, Easter Sunday and Easter Monday, Queen's Birthday (30 April), Labour Day (1 May), Ascension Day (May), Christmas Day, Boxing Day.

masters bother to warn you of the dangers of fire coral and hydroids. An annual Aruba Perrier Reef Care Project takes place over a weekend in June or July when everyone gets together to preserve the underwater environment and clean up debris and pollution from the main dive sites and beaches. Local dive operators help out and local hotels provide refreshments.

Netherlands Antilles, the ABC islands

There are several scuba diving operations and prices start from about US$35 for a single tank dive. Snorkelling from a dive boat varies from US$10-22. *Aruba Pro Dive* is at about five resorts, T825520, F877722, but tries to keep groups small at an average of six divers. *Red Sail Sports*, L G Smith Blvd 83, PO Box 218, T861603, F866657, and at hotels, sailing, snorkelling, diving with PADI, SSI, IDEA, HSA certification courses, windsurfing, waterskiing, hobie cats etc, accommodation packages available, this is a large, reputable international operation and an expensive one. Others include *Pelican* (PADI, NAUI, SSI, T872302, F872315), *Unique Sports of Aruba* (PADI, T/F860096, uniquesports@visitaruba.com), *SEAruba* (T/F838759), who offer diving in the southeast and to Venezuela, *Native Divers* (IDD, PADI, T/F864763), *Dax Divers* (PDIC, T/F851270) and *Dive Aruba* (PADI, T827337, F821817).

Dive centres
For further information on dive sites, dive operators and marine news contact the Aruba Tourism Authority or visit the website, www.scuba. aruba.com

Atlantis Submarines, T836090, operate a two-hour trip, including the boat ride to the Atlantis VI, which descends to 30 m and explores the *MI Dushi I* and *Morgenster* shipwrecks or the *Sonesta* aeroplane wreck. A semi-submersible, *Seaworld Explorer*, T862416, offers a tour along the Arashi Reef and the *Antilla* wreck, at 1130, 1330 and 1630 daily.

Beaches and watersports

There are good, sandy beaches on both sides of the island although fewer on the east side which is rough and not so good for swimming. Travelling north along the west coast from Oranjestad an excellent road takes you to the main resort areas where nearly all the hotels are gathered. **Druif Beach** starts at the *Tamarijn Aruba Beach Resort*, extending and widening along the coast to the sister hotel, the *Divi Aruba*, with good windsurfing. At the *Manchebo* there is a huge expanse of sand, often seen in advertisements. North of here is **Eagle Beach** where the 'low rise' hotels are separated from the beach by the road, and then **Palm Beach** where the 'high rise' hotels front directly on to the beach. These three sandy beaches extend for several kilometres, the water is calm, clear and safe for children, although watch out for watersports and keep within markers where provided.

Of the 3 ABC islands, Aruba stands out as having the best beaches, all of which are public & free

A residential area and the new golf course stretches up from Arashi to the lighthouse and the coast is indented with tiny rocky bays and sandy coves, the water is beautiful and good for snorkelling, while shallow and safe for children. It is also a fishing ground for the brown pelicans. At night they normally sleep in the shallow water close to the lighthouse. A little way after the lighthouse there is a very spectacular place where high waves smash against the rocks at a small inlet. There is a blow hole, where water sometimes spouts up more than 5 m.

At the other end of the island is **Seroe Colorado**, known as 'the colony', which used to be a residential area for Exxon staff but is currently used as temporary housing. You have to enter the zone through a guard post, but there is no entrance fee and no hindrance. There are two west facing beaches here worth visiting. **Rodgers Beach** has a snack bar, showers, yachts and is protected by a reef but is in full view of the refinery. **Baby Beach**, on the other hand, is round the corner, out of sight of the refinery, in a lovely sandy bay, protected by the reef, nice swimming and snorkelling, very busy on Sunday, with toilets but little shade. **Sea Grape Grove** and **Boca Grandi**, on the east coast of the south tip has good snorkelling and swimming, being protected by a reef, and is popular with tours who come to see the largest elkhorn coral. Experienced windsurfers come here to wave jump. The prison is near here, remarkable for the pleasant sea view from the cells. Other beaches on the east side of the island are **Boca Prins**, where there are sand dunes, and further north from there, reached by a poor road, is **Dos Playa** where there is good surf for body surfing. The beach here is closed to vehicles because of nesting turtles. The landscape is hilly and barren because of serious overgrazing by herds of goats. **Andicouri** is also popular with surfers, note that you may not approach it through the coconut grove which is private property, there are signs to direct you the right way.

Netherlands Antilles, the ABC islands

Virtually every type of watersport is available and most hotels provide extensive facilities. Activities which are not offered on site can be arranged through several tour agencies such as *De Palm Watersports*, T824545, *Pelican Watersports*, T831228 and *Red Sail Sports*, T824500. You can hire jetskis, waterskis, wave runners, banana boats, snorkelling equipment and other toys. Parasailing can be done from the high-rise hotels. Glass bottomed boat trips from various locations are around US$20-25, but can be more for a sunset cruise.

Windsurfing North of Palm Beach is an area of very shallow water with no hotels to break the wind, known as Fisherman's Huts, which is excellent for very fast windsurfing. Surfers from all over the world come here to enjoy their sport and professionals often come here for photo sessions. Although speeds are high and there is a strong offshore wind, surfing is quite safe and there are several rescue boats to get you back if the wind blows you to Panama. This beach is called **Malmok** (south end) or **Arashi** (north end) and there are many villas and guest houses across the road which cater for windsurfers. There are several operators of high quality: *Roger's Windsurf Place*, L G Smith Blvd 472, T/F861918, www.rogerswindsurf.com, windsurf packages available, boards and accommodation; *Sailboard Vacation Windsurf Village*, L G Smith Blvd 462, T862527, boards of different brands for rent. *Aruba Boardsailing* offer windsurf courses for kids and teenagers, T860989. For information about the Aruba Hi-Winds Pro/Am boardsailing competitions, contact *ATA Special Events*, T823777 ext 239, www.hiwinds.aruba.com They usually take place in June. At the same time a Windsurfing Festival combines a consumer trade show, with all the latest gear, and music and food on the beach.

Day sails Several yachts and catamarans offer cruises along the coast with stops for snorkelling and swimming. A morning cruise often includes lunch (about US$40-50), an afternoon trip will be drinks only – and then there are the sunset booze cruises (about US$20-30). The largest catamaran is Red Sail Sports' *Fiesta*, which carries 90 passengers, while its sister ship, *Balia*, a 53-ft racing catamaran, does all the usual cruises and is available for private charter at US$450 an hour, minimum two hours, T864500/861603; *Pelican I* is a 50-ft catamaran running along the west coast from Pelican pier, T872302; *Wave Dancer*, another catamaran, departs from *Holiday Inn* beach, T825520; *Octopus* is a 40-ft trimaran, departing from *Holiday Inn* pier, also available for private charter, snorkelling and sailing cruises, US$20-35, T833081; *Mi Dushi* is an old sailing ship built in 1925 which starts cruises from the *Aruba Grand Beach Resort* pier, morning and lunch US$45, snorkelling and sunset US$27.50, sunset booze cruise US$25, pirate sails and beach party US$40, T823513/828919.

Sailing Near Spanish Lagoon is the Aruba Nautical Club complex, with pier facilities offering safe, all-weather mooring for almost any size of yacht, plus gasoline, diesel fuel, electricity and water. For information, write to PO Box 161, T853022. They also organize an annual 'catch and release' deep sea fishing tournament every October. A short sail downwind from there is the Bucuti Yacht Club with clubhouse and storm-proofed pier providing docking, electricity, water and other facilities. Write to PO Box 743. A Catamaran Regatta is held annually in November in front of the Palm Beach hotels, with competitors from the USA, Europe and Venezuela. For information contact the *Aruba Tourism Authority*, T823777. Also in November is the Seaport Yacht Race with races from Havana to Seaport Marina, around the island and from Punto Fijo in Venezuela. For details contact Mr Henk Grim at the Seaport Marina, T839190, F839197.

Fishing Over a dozen charter boats are available for deep sea fishing. You can fish for red snapper, grouper and triggerfish with *Rainbow Runner*, T831689, or there is deep sea fishing with *Driftwood Fishing Charters* from Seaport Marina, T832515, and others. The tourist office has a list so you can contact the captain direct, or else go through *De Palm Tours*. Whole day trips including food and drinks range from

US$350-480, depending on the number of people on board. A deep sea fishing tournament is held in October at the *Aruba Nautical Club*, T853022 for information.

Golf In 1995 the 18-hole, par 71, Tierra del Sol Golf Course opened near the light-house, designed to fit in with the natural landscape and with the sea on two sides. A community of homes and villas has also been designed to blend in with the surrounding vegetation with a full-service clubhouse, swimming pool, golf practice range and tennis and fitness complex. It took over 30 years to get the golf course built because of difficulties with the barren landscape and the lack of water, but in 2000 it was voted the fourth best golf course in the Caribbean. Many hotels are signing up for preferential rates for their guests, otherwise contact Tierra del Sol on T860978, F860671. There is a nine-hole golf course with oiled sand greens and goats near San Nicolas, golf clubs for rent US$6, green fee US$10 for 18 holes, US$7.50 for nine holes, T842006, Saturday and Sunday members only, open daily 0800-1700. At the *Holiday Inn* is an 18-hole mini-golf course. A mini golf course called Adventure Golf has been built opposite *La Cabana*, close to Bubali, in a nice garden.

Other sports

There are **tennis** courts at most major hotels. The *Aruba Racquet Club* is at Rooi Santo 21 in the Palm Beach area and has eight lit courts, an exhibition centre court, pro shop, pool, aerobics classes, fitness centre, bar and restaurant. Open 0800-2300, for reservations, T860215. There is usually an international tennis tournament in September. **Horseriding** at *Rancho El Paso*, Washington 44, near Santa Ana Church, T873310, daily rides except Sunday, one hour through countryside, US$15, or two hours part beach, part *cunucu*, US$30, special trips on Paso Fino horses for experienced riders. The National Horse Fair, a three-day international competition for Paso Fino horses is held here in April. *Rancho Daimari* also has Paso Fino horses and offers 2½ hours rides with snorkelling, daily at 0900 and 1500, a/c transport from your hotel included, T860239. *Rancho del Campo* takes riders into the national park or to the natural bridge, 2½ hours, 0930 or 1530, US$45 including transport and snorkelling, T850290. *Rancho Notorious*, T860508, has a choice of three trails, to the Alto Vista chapel, the California Lighthouse or a sunset beach ride.

Bowling The *Eagle Bowling Palace* at Pos Abou has 16 lanes, of which six are for reservation, open 1000-0200, US$9 from 1000-1500, US$10.50 from 1500-0200, US$1.20 shoe rental, T835038; also three racquetball courts available. There is an international bowling tournament in April, T826443 for details, and an international youth tournament in July. *Wings Over Aruba*, at the airport, T837104, F837124, has a pilot school, with sightseeing **flights**, aerial photography, aircraft rental; sightseeing in a seaplane US$130 per 30 minutes, trial flying lesson US$120 per 90 minutes. **Sailcarts** available at a special rink not on the beach, *Aruba Sailcart N V*, Bushiri 213, T836005, open 0900-sunset, US$15 per 30 minutes for a single cart, US$20 per 30 minutes for a double cart. **Drag races** are held several times a year at the Palo Marga circuit near San Nicolas, call the *Aruba Racing Association*, T841315. **Triathlons** and **marathons** are held periodically, contact the tourist office for details or IDEFRE, JG Emanstraat, Oranjestad, T824987, F836478.

Sky diving is now available in Aruba with *Sky Dive Aruba*, T937151. Beginners can do a tandem jump from 10,000 ft with a 5-min parachute ride to a drop zone near the Fisherman's Huts on the salt pans on the northwest coast. An early morning jump is US$195 and afternoon US$215. There are plans to cater for certified jumpers and those who want to get their TAFF certification.

Oranjestad

Oranjestad, the capital of Aruba, is a busy little freeport town where 'duty-free' generally implies a discount rather than a bargain. The main shopping area is on Caya G F (Betico) Croes, formerly named Nassaustraat, and streets off it. Many of the buildings in the colourful Antillean style are actually modern and do not date from colonial times as in Willemstad, Curaçao.

Population: 21,000

Netherlands Antilles, the ABC islands

There is a small museum in the restored 17th-century Fort Zoutman/Willem III Tower, Zoutmanstraat. ■ *Mon-Fri, 0900-1200, 1330-1630, entrance US$1.15. T826099.* Named the **Museo Arubano**, it contains items showing the island's history and geology, with fossils, shells, tools, furniture and products. It is not particularly well laid out, the displays are unimaginative and old-fashioned but it is still worth going if only to see the building. The fort, next to the Parliament buildings, opposite the police station, dates from 1796 and marks the beginning of Oranjestad as a settlement. Built with four guns to protect commercial traffic, in 1810-1911 it sheltered the government offices. The tower was added around 1868 with the first public clock and a petrol lamp in the spire, which was first lit on King Willem III's birthday in 1869 and served as a lighthouse. The Fort was restored in 1974 and the tower in 1980-83. The **Archaeological Museum** on J E Irausquin 2-A, is small, but cleverly laid out in three parts, Preceramic, Ceramic (from 500 AD) and Historic (from 1500-1800 AD when the Indians used European tools). The two main sites excavated are Canashitu and Malmok and most objects come from these. The descriptions are in English and

Oranjestad

Papiamento, easy to read and educational. There are some interesting publications available in English. Recommended, the best museum in the ABCs. ■ *Mon-Fri 0900-1630. T828979.* A numismatic museum, **Mario's Worldwide Coin Collection**, also known as the **Museo Numismatico**, Zuidstraat 27, not far from Fort Zoutman and the Central Bank of Aruba (where it is possible to buy specimen sets of Aruba's extremely attractive coins) has a large collection of coins from over 400 countries and coins from ancient Greece, Rome, Syria and Egypt. A bit cramped, but with a lot of fascinating material, the museum is run by the daughter of the collector, Mario Odor; donations welcomed. ■ *Mon-Fri, 0730-1200, 1300-1600.* There is an extensive collection of shells at **De Man's Shell Collection**, Morgenster 18, T824246 for an appointment. The **Cas di Cultura**, Vondellaan 2, has concerts, ballet, folklore shows and art exhibitions, T821010. *Gasparito Restaurant/Art Gallery* has an exhibition of Aruban art for sale and display, Gasparito 3. ■ *0900-2300 daily. T867044.* Galeria Eterno, Emenstraat 92. Also exhibits local artists. ■ *Mon-Fri 1000-1700 or by appointment. T839484, F839575.*

Around the island

Aruba is the smallest and most westerly of the ABC group lying 25 km north of Venezuela and 68 km west of Curaçao. Like Curaçao and Bonaire, Aruba has scant vegetation, its interior or *cunucu* is a dramatic landscape of scruffy bits of foliage, mostly cacti, the weird, wind-bent divi divi (*watapana*) trees and tiny bright red flowers called *fioritas*, plus huge boulders, caves and lots of dust. Flashes of colour are provided by bougainvillea, oleanders, flamboyant, hibiscus and other tropical plants. You will need a couple of days to see everything on offer inland without rushing. The Esso Road Map marks all the sites worth seeing and it is best to hire a car (four-wheel drive if possible, but not essential) as you have to go on dirt roads to many of them and there is no public transport. Tour agencies do excursions, about US$20-28 for a half day tour of the island, see page 1045.

Traditional Aruban houses are often protected from evil spirits by 'hex' signs molded in cement around doorways & surrounded by cactus fences

The village of **Noord** is known for the **Santa Anna Church**, founded in 1766, rebuilt in 1831 and 1886, the present stone structure was erected in 1916 by Father Thomas V Sadelhoff, whose portrait is on the twelfth station of the Cross. It has heavily carved neo-Gothic oak altar, pulpit and communion rails made by the Dutchman, Hendrik van der Geld, which were the prize work shown at the Vatican Council exhibition in 1870. They were then housed in St Anthony's Church at Scheveningen in Holland, before being given to Aruba in 1928. The church is popular for weddings, being light and airy with a high vaulted ceiling and stained glass windows. ■ *Services are held Mon, Wed and Fri at 1830, Sat at 1900 and Sun at 0730 and 1800.* Not far from Noord on the north coast is the tiny **Chapel of Alto Vista**, dating from 1952 but on the site of the chapel built by the Spanish missionary, Domingo Antonio Silvester in 1750. It is in a spectacular location overlooking the sea and is so small that stone pews have been built in semi circles outside the Chapel.

Also on the north coast are the ruins of a gold mine at **Seroe Gerard** and a refinery at **Bushiribana** in a particularly bleak and sparsely vegetated area. The machinery at the mill, right on the coast, was damaged by sea spray and moved to Frenchman's Pass in 1824. A partly paved road leads to the natural bridge where long ago the roof of a cave collapsed, leaving only the entrance standing. It is actually fairly low and not as spectacular as tourist brochures would have you believe. There is a souvenir shop and you can get snacks here.

Inland, extraordinary rock formations can be seen at **Casibari** and **Ayó**, where huge, diorite boulders have been carved into weird shapes by the wind. At Casibari steps have been made so that you can climb to the top, from where you get a good view of the island and the Haystack. There is a snack bar and souvenir shop. Ayó does not have steps, you have to clamber up, but a wall is being built up around the rocks to keep out the goats. There are some Indian inscriptions. Toilets, a snack bar and souvenir shop are planned. The 541 ft **Hooiberg**, or Haystack, has steps all the way up. Very safe, even with children, the view is worth the effort.

At the village of **Santa Cruz**, just southeast of the Haystack, a cross on top of a boulder marks the first mission on the island. Travelling east from here you pass the **Arikok National Park**, where there are some well laid out trails for easy, but hot, walking. There are some interesting rock formations, indigenous fauna and flora and Amerindian art. See 'Flora and fauna' above. The road leads to Boca Prins (dune sliding) and the **Fontein** cave. Work has been completed to restore the Amerindian drawings in the cave, clean up the more recent graffiti and install a car park and picnic benches. The cave is open to visitors during daylight hours only. There is a large chamber at the entrance, with natural pillars, and a 100 m tunnel leading off, halfway down which are Indian paintings. Despite the desolation of the area, there is a well near the caves with brackish water, which a Japanese man uses to cultivate vegetables for the Chinese restaurants on the island. Further along the coast are the **Guadirikiri** caves, two large chambers lit by sunlight, connected by passages and pillars, with a 100 m tunnel, for which you need a torch. Bats live in this cave system. The road around the coast here is very bumpy and dusty, being used by quarry trucks. A third cave, **Huliba**, is known as the Tunnel of Love. Again, no entry fee but helmets (US$7) and torches available. The walk through the tunnel takes 20-30 minutes with a 10-minute return walk overground. Be prepared for a certain amount of scrambling and rock climbing in the dark, you are told to follow the arrows.

The road then takes you to **San Nicolas** where there is a strong smell of oil. The Lago Oil Refinery (Exxon) was built in 1928 and was the largest refining plant in the world during the Second World War, when it supplied the allies. The effect on San Nicolas was dramatic. It drew immigrant workers from 56 countries and the community thrived. However, after the war a steady decline set in. After the closure of the oil refinery in 1985, San Nicolas was a ghost town, but now that Coastal Oil has taken over the refinery, activity is beginning to pick up. Old wooden houses are being demolished and new concrete houses built instead. A landmark is *Charlie's Bar*, which has been in operation since 1941; a good place to stop for refreshment to see the souvenirs hanging everywhere. Efforts are being made to rejuvenate the town and attract tourism.

Returning northwest towards Oranjestad you pass through Savaneta, where the Dutch marines have a camp. Turn off to the left to *Brisas del Mar*, a good seafood restaurant open to the sea, very popular. At Pos Chiquito, a walkway leads through mangroves to *Isla di Oro*, a restaurant built like a ship where there is dancing at weekends and pedalos and watersports. A little further on a bay with shallow water and mangroves is ideal for snorkelling beginners. The view is not spectacular but you can see many colourful fish. **Spanish Lagoon**, once a pirates' hideout, is a seawater channel, at the mouth of which is the Aruba Nautical Club and the water desalination plant. At the other end is a bird sanctuary where parakeets breed and the ruins of the Balashi gold mill dating from 1899, where the machinery is better preserved than at Bushiribana. There is quicksand in the area around the bird sanctuary, so it is not advisable to walk there. Nearby is **Frenchman's Pass** where the French attacked the Indians in 1700. From here you can turn east again to drive up **Jamanota**, at 189 m the highest elevation on the island.

Essentials

Sleeping

A 17.66% tax/ service charge must be added; some hotels also add a US$1.50-5.75 per day energy surcharge

Glittering luxury hotels jostle for space along Druif Bay, and Eagle and Palm beaches. At the end of the 1990s nearly all the resorts along this hotel strip added rooms or upgraded existing facilities. Decent, cheap accommodation is now very difficult to find. The *Aruba Apartment Resort and Small Hotel Association (ARASA)* members offer accommodation at less than US$100 but to get a double room at that price at one of the large hotels you will have to negotiate a package deal in advance. Summer rates are substantially less than high season winter rates (16 Dec-15 Apr).

Around Oranjestad Closest to the airport, but only a 10-15 min walk into town, is the **LL-AL** *Caribbean Town Beach Resort*, L G Smith Blvd 2, T823380, F832446. Convenient for business travellers, 63 rooms and suites built round a pool, children under 18 sharing free, large rooms, most with kitchenette, oceanside rooms are cheaper than pool side as they overlook the road but a/c reduces traffic noise, Surfside beach club and watersports centre across the road. In Oranjestad on the waterfront is the **LL-AL** *Aruba Marriott Resort*, at Seaport Village, L G Smith Blvd 9, T836000, F825317, www.arubasonesta.com Deluxe highrise, 300 rooms, Seaport Village shops and Crystal casino on the premises. Also **LL-L** *Aruba Marriott Suites*, at Seaport Village, at L G Smith Blvd 82, by Seaport Market place. 250 1-bedroom suites, pools and small beach, no beach at the hotel but guests may use a private island reached by motor launch from the hotel lobby which has watersports and all facilities, even a private honeymooners' beach, the only drawback being that the island is right at the end of the airport runway. Just outside town to the west in a rather unattractive industrial area immediately after the free zone, is the **L-AL** *Bushiri Beach Resort*, L G Smith Blvd 35, T825216, F826789, www.bushiri.com A 150-room all-inclusive, often booked solid, reserve in advance, price per person, child discounts, indoor and outdoor kids activities, on man-made beach, gym, table tennis, lots of activities, good reputation for food.

Punta Brabo Beach The low-rise resort hotel development starts on Punta Brabo Beach, Druif Bay, all hotels are on the beach and offer swimming pools, tennis, watersports, shops, restaurants etc: **LL** *Tamarijn Aruba Beach Resort*, J E Irausquin Boulevard 41, T824150, F834002, www.tamarijnaruba.com One of the Divi hotels, all-inclusive, rates fluctuate monthly, highest at Christmas, 236 rooms, beachfront, but not much beach, watersports, land sports, resort is next to Alhambra Bazaar and Casino, shares facilities with **LL** *Divi Aruba Beach Resort Mega All-inclusive*, next along the beach at J E Irausquin Blvd 45, T823300, F834002, www.diviaruba.com 203 rooms and suites, honeymoon packages, all-inclusive, windsurfing, tennis, pool. *Divi Village*, at J E Irausquin Blvd 47, T835000, F820501. 132 apartments and free form pool. Next is the **L-AL** *Manchebo Beach Resort*, J E Irausquin Blvd 55, Manchebo, T823444, F832446, www.manchebo.com Run by Best Western, 71 rooms with balcony or terrace, dive shop and windsurfing on huge expanse of beach. **LL-AL** *Bucuti Beach Resort*, J E Irausquin Blvd 55-B, T831100, F825271, www.bucuti.com Attractive design, pleasant resort, 63 rooms, some with kitchenette, some suites, balconies, sea view, fitness centre, business centre. **LL-AL** *Casa del Mar*, J E Irausquin Blvd 51-53, Punta Brabo Beach, T827000, F826557, www.casadelmar-aruba.com 147 luxury 2-bedroom (time- share) apartments on the beach and 1-bedroom suites not on the beach, rather boring architecture, children's playground, gamesroom, tennis, pool, minimarket, laundromats.

Northwest coast

N

Not to scale

Netherlands Antilles, the ABC islands

■ **Sleeping**
1 Allegro Resort Aruba
2 Amsterdam Manor
3 Aruba Beach Club
4 Aruba Grand Beach
  Resort & Casino
5 Aruba Marriott Resort
  & Stellaris Casino
6 Aruba Phoenix Beach
  Resort
7 Bucuti Beach Resort
8 Bushiri Beach Resort
9 Casa del Mar
10 Divi Aruba Beach
  Resort Mega
  All-Inclusive

11 Divi Village
12 Holiday Inn Aruba
  Beach Resort & Casino
13 Hyatt Regency Aruba
  Beach Resort & Casino
14 La Cabana
15 La Quinta
16 Manchebo Beach
  Resort
17 Mill Condominium
  Resort & De Olde
  Molen Restaurant
18 Playa Linda Beach
  Resort
19 Radisson Aruba
20 Tamarijn Aruba Beach
  Resort
21 Wyndham Aruba
  Beach Resort & Casino

LL-AL *The Aruba Beach Club*, same address, T823000, F834871, mshipabccdm@setarnet.aw shared facilities, 131 rooms with kitchenette, for up to 4 people, family orientated.

Eagle Beach LL-AL *La Cabana*, J E Irausquin Blvd 250, T879000, F875474, www.lacabana.com Massive resort, 803 studios and suites, tennis, squash, fitness centre, waterslide, children's pool and playground, casino and condominiums. **LL-AL** *Amsterdam Manor*, J E Irausquin Blvd 252, T871492, F871463, www.amsterdammanor.com Low-rise, pleasant, 72 painted Dutch colonial style studios and apartments with sea view, kitchen, pool, bar and restaurant.**LL-AL** *La Quinta*, J E Irausquin Blvd 228, T875010, F876263. Timeshare with rentals, 54 apartments with kitchenette, pools, tennis.

Hotels with over 300 rooms have casinos **Palm Beach** After the sewage treatment plant and Pos Chiquito the road curves round Palm Beach where all the high rise luxury hotels are. All have at least 1 smart restaurant and another informal bar/restaurant, some have about 5, all have shops, swimming pools, watersports, tennis and other sports facilities on the premises and can arrange anything else. The first one is **LL-AL** *Aruba Phoenix Beach Resort*, J E Irausquin Blvd 75, T861170, F861165, www.diviphoenix.com The name reflects the fact that this hotel was once the *Aruba Royal*, abandoned but resurrected by Divi, 101 a/c studios and apartments, fitness centre, 2 pools, jacuzzi, watersports. **LL-L** *Wyndham Aruba Beach Resort and Casino*, J E Irausquin Blvd 77, T864466, F863403. 444 rooms, behind it is the restaurant *De Olde Molen*, an imported windmill around which **LL-A** *The Mill Condominium Resort* has been built, J E Irausquin Blvd 330, T867700, F867271. 200 rooms and suites with kitchens, sauna, excercise room, tennis, 2 pools, beach club membership across the road. **LL-L** *Aruba Grand Beach Resort & Casino*, T863900, F861941. 200 rooms and suites, Olympic size swimming pool. The oldest hotel along here is the renewed and extended **LL-L** *Radisson Aruba* , J E Irausquin Blvd 81, T866555, F863260, arubasales@ radisson.com Covers 14 acres, 372 rooms and suites, not all with sea view, new pool area with 2 freeform pools, tennis, fitness centre, games room, watersports, conference centre, resort spa, golf putting, usual luxury facilities. **LL-L** *Allegro Resort Aruba*, J E Irausquin Blvd 83, T864500, F863191. 421 rooms and suites with sea view and balcony, full service, deluxe, Red Sail diving and watersports on site. The next hotel along is the **LL** *Hyatt Regency Aruba Beach Resort & Casino*, J E Irausquin Blvd 85, T861234, F865478. 360 rooms and suites, designed for a luxury holiday or for business meetings and incentive trips, built around a huge 3-level pool complex with waterfalls, slides and salt water lagoon, in beautiful gardens, health and fitness centre, Red Sail diving and watersports, very popular, great for children or business travellers, always full. **LL** *Playa Linda Beach Resort*, J E Irausquin Blvd 87, T861000, F863479, www.playalinda.com A timeshare resort of suites and efficiencies, health club, games room. **LL-AL** *Holiday Inn Aruba Beach Resort & Casino*, J E Irausquin Blvd 230, T863600, F865165, www.holidayinn-aruba.com 600 rooms with balcony, dated concrete block style, pools, tennis, diving, casino, lots of other facilities. **LL** *Aruba Marriott Resort and Stellaris Casino*, L G Smith Blvd 101, T869000, F860649. 413-room hotel next to the *Holiday Inn*, lots of facilities and luxuries, *Vela Windsurf Centre*, *Red Sail Watersports*.

Apartments and guest houses The Aruba Tourism Authority publishes a list of apartments and guest houses. Weekly or monthly rates are more advantageous. If you arrive at a weekend the tourist office in town will be shut and you cannot get any help except at the airport. In the district of Noord, **C** *Cactus Apartments*, Matadera 5, Noord, T822903, F820433. **C** *Coconut Inn*, Noord 31, T866288, F865433. 40 a/c studios and 1-bedroom apartments, TV, balcony, kitchenette, pool, near beach. **B-C** *Turibana Plaza Apartments*, Noord 124, T867292, F862658, turibana@setarnet.aw *Roger's Apartments*, windsurfing packages only, L G Smith Blvd 472, Malmok, T861918, F869045. **LL-A** *Boardwalk Vacation Retreat*, Bakval 20, Noord, T866654, F861836, www.theboardwalk-aruba.com Right by the *Marriott*, 150 m to the beach, 1 or 2-bedroom casitas with living room and kitchen, hammocks, fans, a/c, well equipped, nice furnishings, mini market, pool with jacuzzi, gardens with flowering plants, palm trees and hummingbirds. *Windsurf Village*, L G Smith Blvd 462, *The Boulevards*, L G

Smith 486, and *The Edges Guesthouse*, L G Smith Blvd 458, all run by *Sailboard Vacations Windsurf Villages*, windsurfing packages only, T862527, F861870. **A-C** *Vistalmar*, Bucutiweg 28, T828579 daytime, T847737 evenings, F822200. One-bedroom apartments with car run by Alby and Katy Yarzagaray, friendly, wooden jetty for swimming and sunbathing, near airport, laundry facilities. Also Mr and Mrs Kemp, **C** *A1 Apartments*, Pagaaistraat 5, T828963, F834447, a1apts@visitaruba.com Fully furnished a/c rooms with kitchenette, 10-15 mins walk from main shopping centre and public beach at *Bushiri Beach Hotel*.

Camping Permit needed from police station, on Arnold Schuttrstraat, Oranjestad, who will advise on locations. It can take 10 days to get a permit and you must have a local address (ie hotel room). The permit costs one Afl4 stamp and it appears you can camp anywhere.

Service charge on food and drinks is 15% at the hotels but at other places varies from 10% to 15%. Most tourists are on MAP at the hotels, many of which have a choice of formal or informal restaurants. The Aruba Gastronomic Association (AGA) has a dine around programme at 27 restaurants.

Eating

With few exceptions, meals on Aruba are expensive and generally of the beef-and-seafood variety, but you can get some excellent food

For Aruban specialities, *Gasparito*, Gasparito 3, T867044. Aruban and seafood, wins awards for cuisine, average price US$25, open daily except Wed 1730-2200, art gallery attached exhibiting Aruban works. *The Old Cunucu House*, Palm Beach 150, T861666. In a typical, low Aruban house, serving Aruban and international food, average price US$20, open 1800-2300. *Brisas del Mar*, Savaneta 222A, T847718. Seafood specialities, right on the sea, cool and airy, recommended, reasonable prices, open 1200-1430, 1830-2200, closed Mon. *La Nueva Marina Pirata*, at Spanish Lagoon, T857150. Seafood and Aruban dishes, around US$20, open 1800-2300, Sun 1200-2300, closed Tue, follow the main road to San Nicolas, turn right at *Drive Inn*. If you are in San Nicolas and want to try a local Aruban establishment serving creole food, try *Freddy's Snack*, Mauritsstraat 4A, T847888, open 0730-2330, main dishes around US$6, nothing fancy, no credit cards. The hotels have some very good gourmet restaurants, but outside the hotels the best French restaurant is *Chez Mathilde*, Havenstraat 23, T834968. Open for lunch and dinner, expect to pay around US$30 per person. *Boonoonoonoos*, Wilhelminastraat 18A, T831888. Open Mon-Sat 1100-2230, Sun 1700-2230, has French and Caribbean specialities and the average price is around US$15, menu is posted on www.visitaruba.com. *Villa Germania*, Seaport Market Place, T836161. German food for breakfast, lunch and dinner, around US$13, open 0800-2200. *Twinkle Bone's*, Turibana Plaza, Noord 124, T869806. Open 1600-2400, prices around US$18, prime rib, great lobster and shrimp, singing chefs and waiters. Several Argentine restaurants serving steak, seafood and Argentine specialities, *El Gaucho*, Wilhelminastraat 80, T823677. Open 1130-1430, 1800-2300, menu and reservations online at www.visitaruba.com Have an aperitif beforehand at the *Garufa Cigar & Cocktail Lounge* across the street and they will page you when your table is ready. One of the most recent places to open is the Brazilian restaurant, *Texas de Brazil*, JE Irausquin Blvd 374, Palm Beach, T864444. Meat and more meat, waiters bring it round all the tables as they do in Brazil, huge salad bar, open Tue-Sun, 1800-2300. There is also now a Cuban restaurant, *Cuba's Cookin'*, Wilhelminstraat 27, T880627. Cuban cuisine, accompanied by a live trio playing Cuban music, a cigar salon where you can enjoy a *cohiba*, open Mon-Sat 1130-2230, Sun 1700-2200, meals around US$20-25. *The Buccaneer*, Gasparito 11 C, T866172. Decorated as a sunken pirate's ship with aquariums, seafood, around US$20-25, open Mon-Sat from 1730-2230, no reservations. *Qué Pasa?*, Schelpstraat 20, T833872. A good, intimate restaurant in the centre of Oranjestad, with prices around US$15, open 1800-0100, Italian/international.

Several Oriental restaurants, *Warung Djawa*, Wilhelminastraat 2, T834888. Serves Indonesian and Surinamese food, open Mon-Fri, 1130-1400 for weekday rijstafel buffet lunch, and Wed-Mon 1800-2300, all you can eat, many recommendations. For Japanese food try *Sakura* , Wilhelminastraat, 4, T824088, also Thai, quite cheap at around US$15, open 1200-2300 Mon-Sat, *Sake House* , Caya Betico Croes 9, T830405, the most expensive at an average US$25, open 1200-2300, or *Benihana* , Sasakiweg, T826788, around US$20, open 1200-2300. Most restaurants have vegetarian options on the menu, but the only vegetarian restaurant is *The Green House*, Palm Beach 29, T865241, fairly cheap at around US$15 but only open for lunch 1100-1400.

Charlie's Bar, Zeppenfeldtstraat 56, San Nicolas, T871517, international, Aruban and seafood, has become more expensive at around US$20-25, open 1200-2130, bar until 2200. *Eetcafé The Paddock* on L G Smith Blvd 13, T832334. Outside or indoor seating, sea view, very good, great saté, inexpensive for Aruba, Amstel on draught and the *daghap* (dish of the day) forUS$7, live music on Sun. *Café The Plaza* at the Seaport Market Place, T838826, has a nice terrace and you can get a good, reasonably priced meal there, daily specials, food 1000-2400, but open until 0200. For night owls in need of food the white trucks (mobile restaurants) serve local food and snacks from 2100- 0500 at around US$5, located at Wilhelmina Park, the post office and the courthouse.

Nightlife The major attraction is gambling and there are 11 casinos on the island. Hotels must have
The legal age for 300 rooms before they can build one; those that do usually start at 1100 and operate 2 shifts.
consumption of A few are open 24 hrs. Arubans are allowed in to casinos only 4 times a month. Some hotels
alcohol and entry to and casinos offer Cuban-style shows, dancing and live bands playing Latin or jazz as well as
nightclubs is 18 piano bar-type entertainment. These change regularly, but there is usually something on at the major hotels even if it is only limbo or karaoke. Dancing spots include *Bahia*, Weststraat, Oranjestad, *Club City One*, Sasakiweg, Eagle Beach, *E-Zone*, Weststraat, Oranjestad, *La Fiesta*, Aventura Mall, Oranjestad, and plenty of others in hotels or elsewhere. *Garufa Cigar & Cocktail Lounge*, Wilhelminastraat 63, Oranjestad, T823677, catches the clientele of *El Gaucho* before and after their meal for aperitifs or coffee and cigars, as well as after-work office staff unwinding. Party animals who want to be driven around bar hopping book a seat on *Kukoo Kunuku*, an open sided painted wooden bus, which takes you to 5 stops including an Aruban dinner and a champagne beach halt, US$55, Aruba Adventures, Turibana Plaza 124, T862010. Places open late for drinking and passing the time include *Café The Plaza*, in Seaport Market Place, and *Eetcafé The Paddock*, LG Smith Blvd 13, see restaurants, above, both open until 0200. The *Seaport Cinema* in Oranjestad has 6 screens showing US films. The *Drive-In Theatre* in Balashi occasionally shows European or Latin American films.

Festivals The most important festival of the year is **Carnival**, held from the Sun 2 weeks preceding Lent, starting with Children's Carnival. There are colourful parades and competitions for best musician, best dancer, best costume etc. The culmination is the Grand Parade on the Sun preceding Lent. Other festive occasions during the year include **New Year**, when fireworks are let off at midnight and musicians and singers go round from house to house (and hotel to hotel); **National Anthem and Flag Day** on *18 March*, when there are displays of national dancing and other folklore, and **St John's Day** on *24 June*, which is another folklore day: 'Derramento di Gai'. For visitors who do not coincide their trip with one of the annual festivals, there is a weekly Bonbini show in the courtyard of the Fort Zoutman museum on Tue 1830-2030, US$3, music, singing and dancing, interesting but overenthusiastic MC, bartenders from hotels mix cocktails and special drinks. The programme is altered every week, so those on a 2-week holiday do not sit through the same thing twice. Local dance music, such as the fast, lively *tumba* is very influenced by Latin America. Arubans are fond of *merengue*. Throughout the year there are several different music and dance festivals. The **International Theatre Festival** takes place every other year; for information contact CCA, Vondellaan 2, T821758. There is also a **Dance Festival** in *October* at the Cas de Cultura, for information T/F830223.

Shopping In addition to Caya G F (Betico) Croes shopping areas include the Port of Call Market Place, Seaport Village Mall, Harbour Town, The Galleries, Strada I and II and the Holland Aruba Mall. A wide range of luxury items are imported from all over the world for resale to visitors at cut rate prices. Liquor rates are good, but prices for jewellery, silverware and crystal are only slightly lower than US or UK prices. There is no sales tax. There are also local handicrafts such as pottery and artwork, try *Artesanía Arubiano*, on L G Smith Blvd 178, opposite *Tamarijn Hotel*, T837494, or ask the Institute of Culture, T821010, or the Aruba Tourism Authority, T823777, for more information. *Galeria Harmonia*, Main St, St Nicolas, exhibits and sells local artists' work, T842969. Bookshops include *Van Dorp* in Caya G F (Betico) Croes is the main town centre bookshop. The light and airy *Captains Log* in the new Harbour Town development has a few books and reading material but is mostly souvenirs. Many bookshops in the hotels have some paperbacks.

Air **From Europe** *KLM* has direct flights from Amsterdam, going on to Lima. *Martinair* has a charter flight from Amsterdam. **From North America** Atlanta (*Delta*), Boston (*TWA* and *American Airlines*), Chicago (*US Air*), Fort Lauderdale (*TWA*), Houston (*Continental*), Miami (*American Airlines*, *ALM*, *Martinair* and *Surinam Airways*), Minneapolis (*Sun Country Airlines*), New York (*American Airlines*, *Continental*, *US Air* and *Delta*), Philadelphia (*American Airlines* and *US Air*), St Louis (*Sun Country Airlines*), San Francisco (*American Airlines*), Tampa (*American Airlines*) and Washington DC (*Continental*). There are also many charter services from Boston, Chicago, Cleveland, Detroit, Hartford, Los Angeles, Philadelphia, Minneapolis, Pittsburgh and Toronto, mostly in the winter season. Scheduled services from Canada involve a change of plane in Miami. Charter service from Canada is available through *Air Canada*, *Royal Air*, *Canada 3000* and *Skyservice* on a seasonal basis. **From South America** Lots of flights from Venezuela: Barcelona, Caracas, Las Piedras, Maracaibo, Porlamar and Valencia with *ALM*, *Servivensa*, *Aeropostal*, *Aserca* and *Santa Barbara Airlines*. From Colombia, *Avianca* fly from Bogotá and Medellín. *KLM* from Lima. **From the Caribbean** From Sint Maarten with *ALM*, San Juan with *American Airlines*, *TWA* and *ALM*, from Santo Domingo with *Aeropostal*, as well as frequent flights from Bonaire and Curaçao with *ALM* .

Transport

Road **Bus** The bus station is behind Parliament on Zoutmanstraat. Route 1 starts in San Nicolas and runs through Oranjestad via the hospital to Malmok, Mon-Sat, 0455-2255 hourly, returning from Malmok on the hour, journey time 55 mins. Route 2 also runs from San Nicolas on a slightly different route to Oranjestad and Palm Beach, more or less hourly, 0525-2200. Route 3 runs between Oranjestad and San Nicolas, 0550-2030 and Route 4 runs from Oranjestad through Noord to Palm Beach almost hourly on the half hour. There are also extra buses running between Oranjestad and the *Holiday Inn* (schedules available at the hotels and the tourist office). One-way fare is US$1. Otherwise there are 'jitney cars' which operate like colectivos; the fare is US$1.25. A jitney or bus from Oranjestad to San Nicolas will drop you at the airport.

Car hire There are some 23 car hire companies. *Airways* (Sabana Blanco 35, T821845, airport T829112), *Hertz* (L G Smith Blvd 142, T824545, airport T824886), *Avis* (Kolibristraat 14, T828787, airport T825496), *Budget* (Kolibristraat 1, T828600, airport T825423), *Dollar* (Grenedaweg 15, T822783, airport T825651) and *Toyota* (L G Smith Blvd 114, T834832, airport T834902) have offices in Oranjestad and at the airport. Many companies also have desks in the hotels. Prices begin at US$35 daily, US$215 weekly, with unlimited mileage. Often when you rent a 4WD vehicle (recommended for getting to beaches like Dos Playa) you cannot take out all risks insurance. You must have a valid foreign (held for at least 2 years) or international driver's licence and be at least 21 to rent a car. Requirements vary between companies with a minimum age of 21-25 and a maximum of 65-70. Beware of aggressive local drivers. Driving is on the right and all traffic, except bicycles, coming from the right should be given right of way, except at T junctions. Good maps are available at petrol stations.

Motorcycle A rental 50cc moped or scooter costs around US$30 a day, a 250cc motorcycle US$40, a Harley Davidson SP1100 US$90 and insurance is US$8-15 a day, depending on the size of engine. *Big Twin* rents Harley Davidson, T839322, F828660. *Pablito's Bikes Rental*, L G Smith Blvd 228, T878300, F870042, at *La Quinta Beach Resort*, Eagle Beach, men's, ladies, children's **bicycles**, US$3 per hour, US$8 half day, US$12 per 24 hrs. Other companies include *Donata*, T878300, F870707, *Dream Cycles*, T824329, F838199, *George*, T825975, *Nelson*, T866801, *New York*, T863885, *Semver*, T866851 and *Ron's* T862090.

Taxi Telephone the dispatcher at Pos Abao 41 behind the Eagle Bowling Palace on the Sasaki road, T822116. Drivers speak English, and individual tours can be arranged. Ask for flat *Taxis do not have meters* rate tariffs. From the airport to Oranjestad is US$9, to the low rise hotels US$12 and to the high rise hotels US$14 per taxi, not per person, maximum 4 passengers.

Sea Boat The harbour is 5 mins walk from the town, there are a tourist information centre and some souvenir shops which open if a cruise ship is in. A fruit boat leaves once a week for Punto Fijo, Venezuela; check with Agencia Marítima La Confianza, Braziliëstraat 6 (T823814), Oranjestad. There used to be a ferry to Venezuela, check with Rufo U Winterdaal, Eman Trading Co, L G Smith Blvd 108, Oranjestad (PO Box 384), T821533/821156, F822135.

Directory **Airline offices** Airline offices for all airport lines T824800. *American Airlines*, T822700. *ALM*, T838080. *Avianca/SAM*, T826277. *KLM*, T823546/7. *Viasa*, T836526. *Servivensa*, T827779. *Aeropostal*, T837799. *Vasp*, T825995. **Banks** *ABN/AMRO Bank*, Caya G F (Betico) Croes 89, T821515, F821856, at the Port of Call shopping centre (close to the harbour where the cruise ships come in) on L G Smith Blvd; ATMs at these offices and at Sun Plaza Building, L G Smith Blvd 160 and Dr Horacio Oduber Hospital, for Cirrus or Mastercard. *Aruba Bank NV*, Caya G F (Betico) Croes 41, T821550, F829152, and at L G Smith Blvd 108, T831318. *Banco di Caribe NV*, Caya G F Croes 90-92, T832168, F834222. *Caribbean Mercantile Bank NV*, Caya G F (Betico) Croes 51, T823118, F824373, ATM for Cirrus or Mastercard here and also at Palm Beach 48 (Noord), Zeppenfeldstraat 35 (San Nicolas), Santa Cruz 41 (Santa Cruz), L G Smith Blvd 17, Seaport Village Mall. *Interbank*, Caya G F (Betico) Croes 38, T831080, F837152. *First National Bank*, Caya G F (Betico) Croes 67, T833221, F821756. *Western Union Money Transfer Service*, T824400. *American Express* representative for refunds, exchange or replacement of cheques or cards is *SEL Maduro & Sons*, Rockefellerstraat 1, T823888, open Mon-Fri 0800-1200, 1300-1700. *Aruba Bank*, *Caribbean Mercantile Bank* and *Interbank* are Visa/Mastercard representatives with cash advance. Aruba Bank at the airport is open daily 0800-1600 except on official holidays. **Communications** Post: The Post Office at J E Irausquinplein is open 0730-1200, 1300-1630. Postal rates to the USA, Canada and the Netherlands are Afl 1.40 for letters and Afl0.60 for postcards. Letters to Europe Afl 1.50, postcards Afl 0.70. Collectors can subscribe for new issues by contacting the Philatelic Service, T821900, F827930. **Telephone:** Modern telephone services with direct dialling are available. Aruba's country and area code is 297. Hotels add a service charge on to international calls. The ITT office is on Boecoetiweg 33, T821458. Phone and fax calls, email and mariphone calls at Servicio di Telecommunicacion di Aruba (Setar), at Palm Beach opposite *Hyatt Regency Aruba Beach Resort*, in Oranjestad just off the Plaza and next to the Post Office Building at Irausquinplein, Oranjestad. **Internet:** There is an internet café with access for US$7 per 30 mins. Email services at some hotels are complimentary for guests: *Bucuti, Casa del Mar/Aruba Beach Club, Hyatt*. The local television station is Tele-Aruba, but US programmes are also received. **Embassies & consulates** Brazil, E Pory Ierlandstraat 19, T821994. **Chile**, H de Grootstraat 1, T821085. **Costa Rica**, Savaneta 235-B, T847193. **Denmark**, L G Smith Blvd 82, T824622. **Dominican Republic**, J G Emanstraat 79, T836928. **Germany** , Scopetstraat 13, T821767. **Honduras**, Bilderdijkstraat 13, T821187. **Italy**, Caya G F Betico Croes 7, T822621. **Liberia**, Windstraat 20, T821171. **Panama** , Weststraat 15, T822908. **Peru**, Waterweg 3, T825355. **Portugal**, Seroe Colorado 73, T846178. **El Salvador**, H de Grootstraat 1, T821085. **Spain**, Madurostraat 9, T823163. **Sweden** , Havenstraat 33, T821821. **Venezuela**, Adriane Lacle Blvd 8, T821078. **Laundry** *Wash 'n' Dry Laundromat*, Turibana Plaza, Noord. *Hop Long Laundromat*, Grensweg 7, San Nicolas. *Dakota Laundry*, Amandelstraat 3, Oranjestad. *Aruba Laundromat*, Hendrikstraat 30, Oranjestad. **Medical facilities** All the major hotels have a doctor on call. There is a well-equipped, 280-bed hospital (Dr Horacio Oduber Hospital, LG Smith Blvd, T874300, F873348) near the main hotel area with modern facilities and well-qualified surgeons and dentists. Posada Clinic Aruba, L G Smith Blvd 14, T820840, F835664, offers haemodialysis service, multilingual staff, reservations 3 months in advance, modern equipment. Labco Medical and Homecare Service, Cabuyastraat 6A, Ponton, PO Box, 1147, T825541, F826567, 24-hr service, free delivery, rents items such as wheelchairs, crutches, bedpans etc to visitors. The emergency telephone number for the Ambulance and Fire Department is 115. Also for ambulance in Oranjestad, T821234 and in San Nicolas, T845050. Air Ambulance, Mr Rupert Richards, T829197, F835664. Drinking water is distilled from sea water and consequently is safe. The main health hazard for the visitor is over-exposure to the sun. Be very careful from 1100-1430, and use plenty of high factor suntan lotion. **Tourist information** Local tourist offices *Aruba Tourism Authority*, L G Smith Boulevard 172, Oranjestad, PO Box 1019, near the harbour, T823777, F834702, www.aruba.com Also at airport (open daily until about 1900, helpful for accommodation) and cruise dock. Staff are friendly and efficient. The *Aruba Hotel and Tourism Association*, LG Smith Boulevard 174, PO Box 542, Oranjestad, T822607, F824202. They have a hotline for complaints and compliments, T839000, Mon-Fri 0900-1700, answering machine at other times.

Their official guide is the annual *Aruba Experience*, which is also on the internet, www.aruba-experience.com Another very good site on Aruba is www.visitaruba.com **Local travel agents** *De Palm Tours*, L G Smith Blvd 142, T824400, F823012, www.depalm.com, also with offices in many hotels, sightseeing tours of the island and excursions to nearby islands or Venezuela. Their Mar-Lab Biological Tour, US$25 including a visit to Seroe Colorado, and snorkelling at Boca Grandi. *Aruba Transfer Tours and Taxi*, Pos Abou z/n, T822116. Julio Maduro, *Corvalou Tours*, T821149, specializes in archaeological, geological, architectural, botanical and wildlife tours, a mine of information on anything to do with Aruba, strongly recommended. For a combination 6-hr tour with lunch, US$35, call archaeologist Egbert Boerstra, T841513, or Julio Maduro, or Private Safaris educational tour, T834869. Mr Boerstra has been involved in excavation work at Ser'l Noka, Malmok, Savaneta, Tanki Flip and Canashito and has worked with the project to establish the Arikok National Park. There are lots of companies offering tours of the island by minibus with a swimming and snorkelling stop at Baby Beach, about US$30.

Background

History

The first known settlers of the islands were the Caiquetios, a tribe of peaceful Arawak Indians, who lived in small communities under a chieftain or a priest. They survived principally on fish and shellfish and collected salt from the Charoma saltpan to barter with their mainland neighbours for supplements to their diet. There are remains of Indian villages on Curaçao at Westpunt, San Juan, de Savaan and Santa Barbara, and on Aruba near Hooiberg. On each of the ABC islands there are cave and rock drawings. The Arawaks in this area had escaped attack by the Caribs but soon after the arrival of the Spaniards most were forcibly transported from Curaçao to work on Hispaniola. Although some were later repatriated, more fled when the Dutch arrived. The remainder were absorbed into the black or white population, so that by 1795, only five full-blooded Indians were to be found on Curaçao. On Aruba and Bonaire the Indians maintained their identity until about the end of the 19th century, but there were no full-blooded Indians left by the 20th century.

The islands were encountered in 1499 by a Spaniard, Alonso de Ojeda, accompanied by the Italian, Amerigo Vespucci and the Spanish cartographer Juan de la Cosa. The Spanish retained control over the islands throughout the 16th century, but because there was no gold, they were declared 'useless islands'. After 1621, the Dutch became frequent visitors looking for wood and salt and later for a military foothold. Curaçao's strategic position between Pernambuco and New Amsterdam within the Caribbean setting made it a prime target. In 1634, a Dutch fleet took Curaçao, then in 1636 they took Bonaire, which was inhabited by a few cattle and six Indians, and Aruba which the Spanish and Indians evacuated. Curaçao became important as a trading post and as a base for excursions against the Spanish. After 1654, Dutch refugees from Brazil brought sugar technology, but the crop was abandoned by 1688 because of the very dry climate. About this time citrus fruits were introduced, and salt remained a valuable commodity. Much of Curaçao's wealth came from the slave trade. From 1639-1778 thousands of slaves were brought to Willemstad, fed with funchi and sold to the mainland and other colonies. The Dutch brought nearly half a million slaves to the Caribbean, most of which went through Curaçao.

Wars between England and the Netherlands in the second half of the 17th century led to skirmishes and conquests in the Caribbean. The Peace of Nijmegen in 1678 gave the Dutch Aruba, Curaçao, Bonaire and the three smaller islands in the Leeward group, St Eustatius, Saba and half of St Martin. Further conflicts in Europe and the Americas in the 18th century led to Curaçao becoming a commercial meeting place for pirates, American rebels, Dutch merchants, Spaniards and créoles from the mainland. In 1800 the English took Curaçao but withdrew in 1803. They occupied it again from 1807 until 1816, when Dutch rule was restored, during when it was declared a free port. From 1828 to 1845, all Dutch West Indian colonies were governed from Surinam. In 1845 the Dutch Leeward Islands were joined to Willemstad in one colonial unit called Curaçao and Dependencies. The economy was still largely based on commerce, much of it with Venezuela, and there was a ship building industry, some phosphate mining and the salt pans, although the latter declined after the abolition of slavery in 1863.

In the 20th century the economy prospered with the discovery of oil in Venezuela and the subsequent decision by the Dutch-British Shell Oil Company to set up a refinery on Curaçao because of its political stability, its good port facilities and its better climate than around Lake Maracaibo. In 1924 another refinery was built on Aruba, which brought unprecedented wealth to that island and the population rose. The Second World War was another turning point as demand for oil soared and British, French and later US forces were stationed on the islands. The German invasion of Holland encouraged Dutch companies to transfer their assets to the Netherlands Antilles leading to the birth of the offshore financial centre. After the War, demands for autonomy from Holland began to grow.

Government

The organization of political parties began in 1936 and by 1948 there were four parties on Curaçao and others on Aruba and the other islands, most of whom endorsed autonomy. In 1948, the Dutch constitution was revised to allow for the transition to complete autonomy of the islands. In 1954 they were granted full autonomy in domestic affairs and became an integral part of the Kingdom of the Netherlands. The Crown continued to appoint the Governor, although since the 1960s this has gone to a native-born Antillian. Nevertheless, a strong separatist movement developed on Aruba and the island finally withdrew from the Netherlands Antilles in 1986, becoming an autonomous member of the Kingdom of the Netherlands, the same status as the whole of the Netherlands Antilles.

The Netherlands Antilles now form two autonomous parts of the Kingdom of the Netherlands. The main part, comprising all the islands except Aruba, is a parliamentary federal democracy, the seat of which is in Willemstad, Curaçao, and each island has its own Legislative and Executive Council. Parliament (Staten) is elected in principle every four years, with 14 members from Curaçao, three from Bonaire, three from Sint Maarten and one each from Saba and St Eustatius.

A new Government of the five-island federation was sworn in in June 1998. Suzanne Römer, of the Partido Nashonal di Pueblo (PNP) is the Prime Minister, at the head of a six-party coalition cabinet, with 13 of the 22 seats, Within the coalition, the PNP has three seats, the Partido Laboral Krusado Populat (Curaçao) three seats, the Frente Obrero de Liberashon (Curaçao) two seats, the Democratic Party (Sint Maarten) two seats, the Partido Democratico Bonairiano (Bonaire) two seats, and the Windward Islands People's Movement (Saba) one seat.

Separate status for some or all of the islands has been a political issue with a breakaway movement in Curaçao and St Maarten. The Netherlands Government's previous policy of encouraging independence has been reversed. The Hague has been trying to draw up a new constitution governing relations between the Netherlands, the Antilles Federation and Aruba. A round-table conference was held in 1993 to establish the basis for future relations including financial support but ended without any decision on Aruba's desire to cancel proposals for independence in 1996, Curaçao's demand for *status aparte* and future relations of the islands with the Netherlands if the Federation collapses.

In November 1993 a referendum was held in Curaçao on its future status within the Federation. The Government was soundly defeated when the electorate unexpectedly voted to continue the island's present status as a member of the Antillean federation (73.6%), rejecting the other options of separate status (11.9%), incorporation in the Netherlands (8.0%) and independence (0.5%).

Referenda were also held on the other islands, Saba, Statia, St Maarten and Bonaire with the aim of restructuring the Antilles. The vote in October 1994 was overwhelmingly in favour of the status quo, with 90.6% support in Statia, 86.3% in Saba, 88.0% in Bonaire and 59.8% in Sint Maarten.

Economy

Bonaire's economy is heavily dependent on tourism, with small operations for solar salt mining, oil trans-shipment, a rice mill and radio communications industry. Cargill Corporation, the world's largest private company, operates the salt industry, which benefits so greatly from the constant sunshine (with air temperatures averaging 27°C and water 26°C), scant rainfall (less than 560 mm a year), and refreshing trade winds. A shrimp farm started operations in 1999. Sea Hatch Bonaire is near Sorobon and offers tours.

Bonaire

Tourism is specialized and most visitors are divers. The USA is the largest single market, followed by the Netherlands, Venezuela and Germany. Accommodation for tourists is split fairly evenly between hotels and condominiums or villas, amounting to about 1,100 rooms and still growing. Financial assistance for the development of tourism has been provided by the EU and Holland, which have financed the expansion of the airport and development of other infrastructure.

Curaçao has a more diversified economy than the other islands, yet even so, it suffered severe recession in the 1980s and unemployment is around 13% of the labour force. The major industry is the oil refinery dating back to 1917, now one of the largest in the world, to which the island's fortunes and prosperity are tied. Imports of crude oil and petroleum products make up two thirds of total imports, while exports of the same are 95% of total exports. That prosperity was placed under threat when Shell pulled out of the refinery in 1985, but the operation was saved when the island government purchased the plant, and leased it to Venezuela for US$11 mn a year. Despite the need for a US$270 mn reconstruction, principally to reduce pollution, the Venezuelan company, PDVSA, signed a 20-year lease agreement which came into effect in 1995, ending its previous system of short term operating leases. Bunkering has also become an important segment of the economy, and the terminal at Bullenbaai is one of the largest bunkering ports in the world. The island's extensive trade makes it a port of call for a great many shipping lines.

Curaçao

Coral reefs surrounding the island, constant sunshine, a mean temperature of 27°C (81°F), and refreshing trade winds lure visitors the year round, making tourism the second industry. Curaçao used to be a destination for tourists from Venezuela, but a devaluation of the bolívar in 1983 caused numbers to drop by 70% in just one year and several hotels had to be temporarily taken over by the Government to protect employment. A restructuring of the industry has led to a change of emphasis towards attracting US and European tourists, as well as South Americans, and numbers have now increased. Cruise visitor numbers have been boosted by the arrival of the megaship *Rhapsody of the Seas*, which carries 2,000 and calls 26 times a year. The single largest market for visitors to Curaçao is Holland, with 30% of stayover arrivals, followed by the USA with 15% and Venezuela with 14%. There are about 2,500 hotel rooms, with more planned to be built. Diving has been promoted and Curaçao now registers about 10,000 visiting divers a year.

A third major foreign currency earner, the offshore financial sector, is actively seeking new areas of business, including captive insurance and mutual funds, in a highly competitive market. There are 61 banks, of which only 14 are licenced to carry out domestic business, the rest are offshore.

Gold was discovered in 1825, but the mine ceased to be economic in 1916. In 1929, black gold brought real prosperity to Aruba when Lago Oil and Transport Co, a subsidiary of Exxon, built a refinery at San Nicolas at the east end of the island. At that

Aruba

Netherlands Antilles, the ABC islands

time it was the largest refinery in the world, employing over 8,000 people. In March 1985 Exxon closed the refinery, a serious shock for the Aruban economy, and one which the Government has striven to overcome. In 1989, Coastal Oil of Texas signed an agreement with the Government to reopen part of the refinery by 1991, with an initial capacity of 150,000 barrels a day, but despite plans to increase it, present capacity is only about 140,000 b/d.

The economic crisis of 1985 forced the Government to turn to the IMF for help. The fund recommended that Aruba promote tourism and increase the number of hotel rooms by 50%. The Government decided, however, to triple hotel capacity to 6,000 rooms, which it was estimated would provide employment for 20% of the population. Hotel construction has expanded rapidly and marketing efforts have attracted investors and visitors from as far afield as Japan. By 1990 tourist accommodation in 15 major high rise and low rise hotels reached 3,326 rooms, with many more available in small hotels, guest houses and apartments. Nevertheless, by 1992 the Government was facing a financial crisis because of state guarantees totalling NG516 mn for three hotel projects which had run into financial difficulties and on which work had ceased: the 466-room *Beta Hotel* (NG170 mn), the 376-room *Eagle Beach Hotel* (NG186 mn) and the 411-room *Plantation Bay Hotel* (NG160 mn). Although the Dutch government provided a loan for the hotels' completion in 1992, the Aruban government now faces heavy interest and principal repayments for 15 years to banks. These will be funded by unpopular higher excise duties, petrol prices and import duties. In mid-1993, the *Plantation Bay Hotel* was sold to the Marriott chain. In 1995 its opening raised the total to 6,626 rooms in hotels, a figure which rose to 7,103 by 1996. By 2000 nearly all the hotels had undergone alterations, adding rooms or upgrading existing facilities. Total employment in tourism absorbs 35% of the workforce. The economy is now overwhelmingly dependent on tourism for income and in 2000 combined stayover and cruise ship passengers exceeded the 1 million mark for the first time with more than 25 cruise lines visiting each month and even more airlines adding Aruba to their routes from the USA.

Efforts are being made to diversify away from a single source of revenues into areas such as re-exporting through the free trade zone, and offshore finance. Aruba is still dependent on the Netherlands for budget support and the aim is to reduce the level of financial assistance. New legislation has been approved to encourage companies to register on the island by granting tax and other benefits. Regulations are generally flexible and unrestricting on offshore business, although efforts are being made to ensure an efficient level of supervision.

There is no unemployment on Aruba and labour is imported for large projects such as the refinery and construction work. Turkish guest workers came to help get Coastal started and Philippinos work in the high rise hotels. The Government is encouraging skilled Arubans to return from Holland but is hampered by a housing shortage and a consequent boom in real estate prices.

Footnotes

21

Footnotes

Index

A

B

N

O

P

Map index

Footnotes

Shorts index

Footnotes

Advertisers index

Will you help us?

We try as hard as we can to make each Footprint Handbook as up-to-date and accurate as possible but, of course, things always change. Many people email or write to us – with corrections, new information, or simply comments. If you want to let us know about your experiences and adventures – be they good, bad or ugly – then don't delay; we're dying to hear from you. And please try to include all the relevant details and juicy bits. Your help will be greatly appreciated, especially by other travellers. In return we will send you details about our special guidebook offer.

email Footprint at:
cih2002_online@footprintbooks.com

or write to:

Elizabeth Taylor
Footprint Handbooks
6 Riverside Court
Lower Bristol Road
Bath
BA2 3DZ
UK

Sales & distribution

Footprint Handbooks
6 Riverside Court
Lower Bristol Road
Bath BA2 3DZ England
T 01225 469141
F 01225 469461
discover
@footprintbooks.com

Australia
Peribo Pty
58 Beaumont Road
Mt Kuring-Gai
NSW 2080
T 02 9457 0011
F 02 9457 0022

Austria
Freytag-Berndt Artaria
Kohlmarkt 9
A-1010 Wien
T 01533 2094
F 01533 8685

Freytag-Berndt
Sporgasse 29
A-8010 Graz
T 0316 818230
F 3016 818230-30

Belgium
Craenen BVBA
Mechelsesteenweg 633
B-3020 Herent
T 016 23 90 90
F 016 23 97 11

Waterstones
The English Bookshop
Blvd Adolphe Max 71-75
B-1000 Brussels
T 02 219 5034

Canada
Ulysses Travel Publications
4176 rue Saint-Denis
Montréal
Québec H2W 2M5
T 514 843 9882
F 514 843 9448

Europe
Bill Bailey
16 Devon Square
Newton Abbott
Devon TQ12 2HR. UK
T 01626 331079
F 01626 331080

Denmark
Nordisk Korthandel
Studiestraede 26-30 B
DK-1455 Copenhagen K
T 3338 2638
F 3338 2648

Scanvik Books
Esplanaden 8B
DK-1263 Copenhagen K
T 3312 7766
F 3391 2882

Finland
Akateeminen Kirjakauppa
Keskuskatu 1
FIN-00100 Helsinki
T 09 121 4151
F 09 121 4441

Suomalainen Kirjakauppa
Koivuvaarankuja 2
01640 Vantaa 64
F 09 852751

France
FNAC – major branches

L'Astrolabe
46 rue de Provence
F-75009 Paris 9e
T 01 42 85 42 95
F 01 45 75 92 51

VILO Diffusion
25 rue Ginoux
F-75015 Paris
T 01 45 77 08 05
F 01 45 79 97 15

Germany
GeoCenter ILH
Schockenriedstrasse 44
D-70565 Stuttgart
T 0711 781 94610
F 0711 781 94654

Brettschneider
Feldkirchnerstrasse 2
D-85551 Heimstetten
T 089 990 20330
F 089 990 20331

Geobuch
Rosental 6
D-80331 München
T 089 265030
F 089 263713

Gleumes
Hohenstaufenring 47-51
D-50674 Köln
T 0221 215650

Globetrotter Ausrustungen
Wiesendamm 1
D-22305 Hamburg
T040 679 66190
F 040 679 66183

Dr Götze
Bleichenbrücke 9
D-2000 Hamburg 1
T 040 3031 1009-0

Hugendubel Buchhandlung
Nymphenburgerstrasse 25
D-80335 München
T 089 238 9412
F 089 550 1853

Kiepert Buchhandlung
Hardenbergstrasse 4-5
D-10623 Berlin 12
T 030 311 880
F 030 311 88120

Greece
GC Eleftheroudakis
17 Panepistimiou
Athens 105 64
T 01 331 4180-83
F 01 323 9821

India
India Book Distributors
1007/1008 Arcadia
195 Nariman Point
Mumbai 400 021
T 91 22 282 5220
F 91 22 287 2531

Israel
Eco Trips
8 Tverya Street
Tel Aviv 63144
T 03 528 4113
F 03 528 8269

For a fuller list, see www.footprintbooks.com

Italy
Librimport
Via Biondelli 9
I-20141 Milano
T 02 8950 1422
F 02 8950 2811

Libreria del Viaggiatore
Via dell Pelegrino 78
I-00186 Roma
T/F 06 688 01048

Netherlands
Nilsson & Lamm bv
Postbus 195
Pampuslaan 212
N-1380 AD Weesp
T 0294 494949
F 0294 494455

Waterstones
Kalverstraat 152
1012 XE Amsterdam
T 020 638 3821

New Zealand
Auckland Map Centre
Dymocks

Norway
Schibsteds Forlag A/S
Akersgata 32 - 5th Floor
Postboks 1178 Sentrum
N-0107 Oslo
T 22 86 30 00
F 22 42 54 92

Tanum
Karl Johansgate 37-41
PO Box 1177 Sentrum
N-0107 Oslo 1
T 22 41 11 00
F 22 33 32 75

Olaf Norlis
Universitetsgt 24
N-1062 Oslo
T 22 00 43 00

Pakistan
Pak-American Commercial
Hamid Chambers
Zaib-un Nisa Street
Saddar, PO Box 7359
Karachi
T 21 566 0418
F 21 568 3611

South Africa
Faradawn CC
PO Box 1903
Saxonwold 2132
T 011 885 1787
F 011 885 1829

South America
Humphrys Roberts
Associates
Caixa Postal 801-0
Ag. Jardim da Gloria
06700-970 Cotia SP
Brazil
T 011 492 4496
F 011 492 6896

Southeast Asia
APA Publications
38 Joo Koon Road
Singapore 628990
T 865 1600
F 861 6438

In Hong Kong, Malaysia,
Singapore and Thailand:
MPH, Kinokuniya, Times

Spain
Altaïr
C/Balmes 69
08007 Barcelona
T 933 233062
F 934 512559

Altaïr
Gaztambide 31
28015 Madrid
T 0915 435300
F 0915 443498

Libros de Viaje
C/Serrano no 41
28001 Madrid
T 01 91 577 9899
F 01 91 577 5756

Il Corte Inglés – major
branches

Sweden
Hedengrens Bokhandel
PO Box 5509
S-11485 Stockholm
T 08 611 5132

Kart Centrum
Vasagatan 16
S-11120 Stockholm
T 08 411 1697

Kartforlaget
Skolgangen 10
S-80183 Gavle
T 026 633000
F 026 124204

Lantmateriet Kartbutiken
Kungsgatan 74
S-11122 Stockholm
T 08 202 303
F 08 202 711

Switzerland
Office du Livre OLF
ZI3, Corminboeuf
CH-1701 Fribourg
T 026 467 5111
F 026 467 5666

Schweizer Buchzentrum
Postfach
CH-4601 Olten
T 062 209 2525
F 062 209 2627

Travel Bookshop
Rindermarkt 20
Postfach 216
CH-8001 Zürich
T 01 252 3883
F 01 252 3832

Tanzania
A Novel Idea
The Slipway
PO Box 76513
Dar es Salaam
T/F 051 601088

USA
Publishers Group West
1700 Fourth Street
Berkeley
CA 94710
T 510 528 1444
F 510 528 9555

Barnes & Noble, Borders,
specialist travel bookstores

Footnotes

Footnotes

Footnotes

Footprint travel list

Footprint publish travel guides to over 120 countries worldwide. Each guide is packed with practical, concise and colourful information for everybody from first-time travellers to travel aficionados . The list is growing fast and current titles are noted below. For further information check out the website **www.footprintbooks.com**

Andalucía Handbook
Argentina Handbook
Bali & the Eastern Isles Hbk
Bangkok & the Beaches Hbk
Barcelona Handbook
Bolivia Handbook
Brazil Handbook
Cambodia Handbook
Caribbean Islands Handbook
Central America & Mexico Hbk
Chile Handbook
Colombia Handbook
Costa Rica Handbook
Cuba Handbook
Cusco & the Sacred Valley Hbk
Dominican Republic Handbook
Dublin Handbook
East Africa Handbook
Ecuador & Galápagos Handbook
Edinburgh Handbook
Egypt Handbook
Goa Handbook
Guatemala Handbook
India Handbook
Indian Himalaya Handbook
Indonesia Handbook
Ireland Handbook
Israel Handbook
Jordan Handbook
Laos Handbook
Libya Handbook
London Handbook
Malaysia Handbook
Marrakech & the High Atlas Hbk
Myanmar Handbook
Mexico Handbook
Morocco Handbook

Namibia Handbook
Nepal Handbook
New Zealand Handbook
Nicaragua Handbook
Pakistan Handbook
Peru Handbook
Rajasthan & Gujarat Handbook
Rio de Janeiro Handbook
Scotland Handbook
Scotland Highlands & Islands Hbk
Singapore Handbook
South Africa Handbook
South American Handbook
South India Handbook
Sri Lanka Handbook
Sumatra Handbook
Syria & Lebanon Handbook
Thailand Handbook
Tibet Handbook
Tunisia Handbook
Turkey Handbook
Venezuela Handbook
Vietnam Handbook

Also available from Footprint
Traveller's Handbook
Traveller's Healthbook

Available at all good bookshops

ANGUILLA (U.K.)
ST. MARTIN (FR.)
ST. BARTHELEMY (FR.)

ST. MAARTEN
(NETH.)
SABA (NETH.) Barbuda
Spanish Point Codrington

ST. EUSTATIUS (NETH.) St. John's ANTIGUA AND
T. KITTS Charlestown Nevis English Harbour Antigua BARBUDA
(St. Christopher) Redonda
NEVIS Plymouth
MONTSERRAT (U.K.) GUADELOUPE (FR.)
Le Moule La Désirade
Saint-Louis Pointe-à-Pitre
Basse Terre Grand-Bourg Marie Galante
Îles des Saintes Capesterre
Portsmouth Marigot
DOMINICA
Roseau
MARTINIQUE (FR.)
Saint-Pierre Sainte-Marie
Fort-de-France Le François
Sainte-Anne
Castries Gros Îslet
ST. LUCIA Dennery
Soufrière Vieux Fort

Château belair Georgetown
ST. VINCENT Kingstown St. Vincent
AND THE Port Elizabeth Bequia
GRENADINES Mustique The
Canouan Grenadines
Union
Hillsborough Carriacou
GRENADA Ronde
St. George's Grenville

Tobago
Plymouth Cha
Canaan Scarbor

Toco
Blanchisseuse
Port Sangre Grande
of Trinidad
Spain Pierreville
San Fernando
Guayaguayare
Bonasse Moruga

ANTIGUA · BARBADOS · CARACAS · GRENADA · GUYANA · JAMAICA
LONDON · MIAMI · NEW YORK · ST. LUCIA · ST. MAARTEN · ST. VINCENT
TORONTO · TRINIDAD & TOBAGO · WASHINGTON DC

One truly West Indies Airline has the Caribbean covered

BWIA, the airline that truly reflects the heart and soul of the West Indies, offers you a daily schedule of flights from Heathrow to a host of Caribbean destinations.

Our wide-bodied jets, with a new livery that reflects the spirit of the West Indies, offer an in-flight comfort, service and style that comes with a typical Caribbean smile. To further whet your appetite, the finest Caribbean food and drink provide a true taste of the West Indies from the moment you board the plane.

For more information about the one truly West Indian airline that has the Caribbean covered, telephone, visit our website at www.bwee.com or see your Travel Agent.

BWIA
West Indies
A I R W A Y S

SHARING OUR WARMTH WITH THE WORLD

www.footprintbooks.com
A new place to visit

Caribbean Islands

Map 2 The Bahamas

Map 3 Hispaniola, Puerto Rico, Turks & Caicos Islands & the Virgin Islands

Map 4 Leeward Islands

Anegada Passage

Sombrero

A

Atlantic Ocean

Dog Island

Scrub Island

Anguilla

Island Harbour

The Valley

Blowing Point

Marigot

Saint-Martin

Sint Maarten

Philipsburg

Gustavia *St Barthélémy*

Barbuda

Codrington Lagoon

Codrington

Saba

B

Sint Eustatius

Oranjestad

·Mt Liamuiga▲

Mt Verchilds▲ *St Christopher (St Kitts)*

Basseterre

Newcastle

Charlestown *Nevis*

Long Island *Guiana Island*

St John's *Parham*

Antigua

English Harbour

Caribbean Sea

Redonda

N

0 km   20

0 miles   20

C

L e e w a r d   I s l a n d s

Montserrat

▲Chances Peak (Volcano)

Guadeloupe Passage

Guadeloupe *Basse-Terre*

1   **2**   **3**

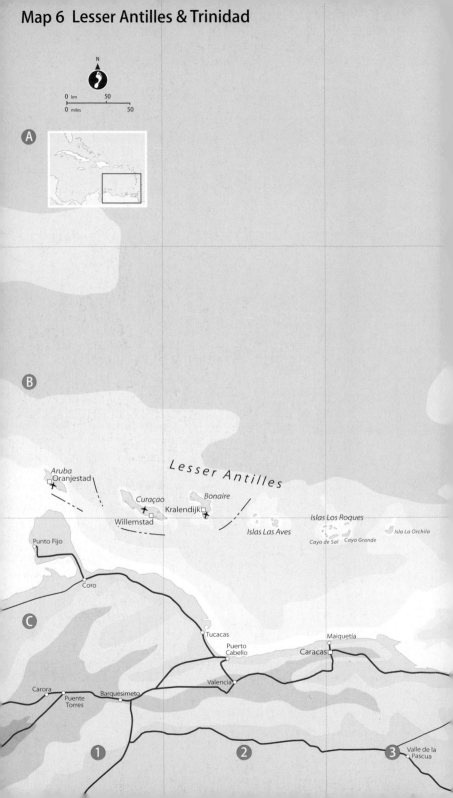

Map 6 Lesser Antilles & Trinidad

N

0 km 50
0 miles 50

A

B

Lesser Antilles

Aruba
Oranjestad

Curaçao
Willemstad

Kralendijk *Bonaire*

Islas Los Roques

Islas Las Aves

Cayo de Sal *Cayo Grande*

Isla La Orchila

Punto Fijo

Coro

C

Tucacas

Maiquetía

Puerto
Cabello

Caracas

Carora

Puente
Torres

Barquesimeto

Valencia

1

2

3 Valle de la
Pascua